University Casebook Series

May, 1984

ACCOUNTING AND THE LAW, Fourth Edition (1978), with Problems Pamphlet (Successor to Dohr, Phillips, Thompson & Warren)

George C. Thompson, Professor, Columbia University Graduate School of Business.
Robert Whitman, Professor of Law, University of Connecticut.
Ellis L. Phillips, Jr., Member of the New York Bar.
William C. Warren, Professor of Law Emeritus, Columbia University.

ACCOUNTING FOR LAWYERS, MATERIALS ON (1980)

David R. Herwitz, Professor of Law, Harvard University.

ADMINISTRATIVE LAW, Seventh Edition (1979), with 1983 Problems Supplement (Supplement edited in association with Paul R. Verkuil, Dean and Professor of Law, Tulane University)

Walter Gellhorn, University Professor Emeritus, Columbia University.
Clark Byse, Professor of Law, Harvard University.
Peter L. Strauss, Professor of Law, Columbia University.

ADMIRALTY, Second Edition (1978), with Statute and Rule Supplement

Jo Desha Lucas, Professor of Law, University of Chicago.

ADVOCACY, see also Lawyering Process

AGENCY, see also Enterprise Organization

AGENCY—PARTNERSHIPS, Third Edition (1982)

Abridgement from Conard, Knauss & Siegel's Enterprise Organization, Third Edition.

ANTITRUST: FREE ENTERPRISE AND ECONOMIC ORGANIZATION, Sixth Edition (1983), with Problems in Antitrust Supplement

Louis B. Schwartz, Professor of Law, University of Pennsylvania.
John J. Flynn, Professor of Law, University of Utah.
Harry First, Professor of Law, New York University.

ANTITRUST SUPPLEMENT—SELECTED STATUTES AND RELATED MATERIALS (1977)

John J. Flynn, Professor of Law, University of Utah.

BUSINESS ORGANIZATION, see also Enterprise Organization

BUSINESS PLANNING (1966), with 1983 Supplement

David R. Herwitz, Professor of Law, Harvard University.

BUSINESS TORTS (1972)

Milton Handler, Professor of Law Emeritus, Columbia University.

CHILDREN IN THE LEGAL SYSTEM (1983)

Walter Wadlington, Professor of Law, University of Virginia.
Charles H. Whitebread, Professor of Law, University of Southern California.
Samuel Davis, Professor of Law, University of Georgia.

CIVIL PROCEDURE, see Procedure

CLINIC, see also Lawyering Process

COMMERCIAL LAW (1983)

Robert L. Jordan, Professor of Law, University of California, Los Angeles.
William D. Warren, Professor of Law, University of California, Los Angeles.

COMMERCIAL LAW, CASES & MATERIALS ON, Third Edition (1976), with 1982 Bankruptcy Supplement

E. Allan Farnsworth, Professor of Law, Columbia University.
John Honnold, Professor of Law, University of Pennsylvania.

COMMERCIAL PAPER, Third Edition (1984)

E. Allan Farnsworth, Professor of Law, Columbia University.

COMMERCIAL PAPER (1983) (Reprinted from COMMERCIAL LAW)

Robert L. Jordan, Professor of Law, University of California, Los Angeles.
William D. Warren, Professor of Law, University of California, Los Angeles.

COMMERCIAL PAPER AND BANK DEPOSITS AND COLLECTIONS (1967), with Statutory Supplement

William D. Hawkland, Professor of Law, University of Illinois.

COMMERCIAL TRANSACTIONS—Principles and Policies (1982)

Alan Schwartz, Professor of Law, University of Southern California.
Robert E. Scott, Professor of Law, University of Virginia.

COMPARATIVE LAW, Fourth Edition (1980)

Rudolf B. Schlesinger, Professor of Law, Hastings College of the Law.

COMPETITIVE PROCESS, LEGAL REGULATION OF THE, Second Edition (1979), with Statutory Supplement and 1982 Case Supplement

Edmund W. Kitch, Professor of Law, University of Chicago.
Harvey S. Perlman, Professor of Law, University of Virginia.

CONFLICT OF LAWS, Eighth Edition (1984)

Willis L. M. Reese, Professor of Law, Columbia University,
Maurice Rosenberg, Professor of Law, Columbia University.

CONSTITUTIONAL LAW, Sixth Edition (1981), with 1983 Supplement

Edward L. Barrett, Jr., Professor of Law, University of California, Davis.
William Cohen, Professor of Law, Stanford University.

CONSTITUTIONAL LAW: THE STRUCTURE OF GOVERNMENT (Reprinted from CONSTITUTIONAL LAW, Sixth Edition), with 1983 Supplement

Edward L. Barrett, Jr., Professor of Law, University of California, Davis.
William Cohen, Professor of Law, Stanford University.

CONSTITUTIONAL LAW, CIVIL LIBERTY AND INDIVIDUAL RIGHTS, Second Edition (1982), with 1983 Supplement

William Cohen, Professor of Law, Stanford University.
John Kaplan, Professor of Law, Stanford University.

CONSTITUTIONAL LAW, Tenth Edition (1980), with 1983 Supplement (Supplement edited in association with Frederick F. Schauer, Professor of Law, College of William and Mary)

Gerald Gunther, Professor of Law, Stanford University.

CONSTITUTIONAL LAW, INDIVIDUAL RIGHTS IN, Third Edition (1981) (Reprinted from CONSTITUTIONAL LAW, Tenth Edition), with 1983 Supplement (Supplement edited in association with Frederick F. Schauer, Professor of Law, College of William and Mary)

Gerald Gunther, Professor of Law, Stanford University.

CONSUMER TRANSACTIONS (1983), with Selected Statutes and Regulations Supplement

Michael M. Greenfield, Professor of Law, Washington University.

CONTRACT LAW AND ITS APPLICATION, Third Edition (1983)

The late Addison Mueller, Professor of Law, University of California, Los Angeles.
Arthur I. Rosett, Professor of Law, University of California, Los Angeles.
Gerald P. Lopez, Professor of Law, University of California, Los Angeles.

CONTRACT LAW, STUDIES IN, Third Edition (1984)

Edward J. Murphy, Professor of Law, University of Notre Dame.
Richard E. Speidel, Professor of Law, Northwestern University.

CONTRACTS, Fourth Edition (1982)

John P. Dawson, Professor of Law Emeritus, Harvard University.
William Burnett Harvey, Professor of Law and Political Science, Boston University.
Stanley D. Henderson, Professor of Law, University of Virginia.

CONTRACTS, Third Edition (1980), with Statutory Supplement

E. Allan Farnsworth, Professor of Law, Columbia University.
William F. Young, Professor of Law, Columbia University.

CONTRACTS, Second Edition (1978), with Statutory and Administrative Law Supplement (1978)

Ian R. Macneil, Professor of Law, Cornell University.

COPYRIGHT, PATENTS AND TRADEMARKS, see also Competitive Process

COPYRIGHT, PATENT, TRADEMARK AND RELATED STATE DOCTRINES, Second Edition (1981), with Problem Supplement and Statutory Supplement

Paul Goldstein, Professor of Law, Stanford University.

COPYRIGHT, Unfair Competition, and Other Topics Bearing on the Protection of Literary, Musical, and Artistic Works, Third Edition (1978)

Benjamin Kaplan, Professor of Law Emeritus, Harvard University,
Ralph S. Brown, Jr., Professor of Law, Yale University.

CORPORATE FINANCE, Second Edition (1979), with 1982 New Developments Supplement

Victor Brudney, Professor of Law, Harvard University.
Marvin A. Chirelstein, Professor of Law, Yale University.

CORPORATE READJUSTMENTS AND REORGANIZATIONS (1976)

Walter J. Blum, Professor of Law, University of Chicago.
Stanley A. Kaplan, Professor of Law, University of Chicago.

CORPORATION LAW, BASIC, Second Edition (1979), with 1983 Case and Documentary Supplement

Detlev F. Vagts, Professor of Law, Harvard University.

CORPORATIONS, see also Enterprise Organization

CORPORATIONS, Fifth Edition—Unabridged (1980), with 1983 Supplement

The late William L. Cary, Professor of Law, Columbia University.
Melvin Aron Eisenberg, Professor of Law, University of California, Berkeley.

CORPORATIONS, Fifth Edition—Abridged (1980), with 1983 Supplement

The late William L. Cary, Professor of Law, Columbia University.
Melvin Aron Eisenberg, Professor of Law, University of California, Berkeley.

CORPORATIONS, Second Edition (1982), with 1982 Corporation and Partnership Statutes, Rules and Forms

Alfred F. Conard, Professor of Law, University of Michigan.
Robert N. Knauss, Dean of the Law School, University of Houston.
Stanley Siegel, Professor of Law, University of California, Los Angeles.

CORPORATIONS, THE LAW OF: WHAT CORPORATE LAWYERS DO (1976)

Jan G. Deutsch, Professor of Law, Yale University.
Joseph J. Bianco, Professor of Law, Yeshiva University.

CORPORATIONS COURSE GAME PLAN (1975)

David R. Herwitz, Professor of Law, Harvard University.

CORRECTIONS, SEE SENTENCING

CREDIT TRANSACTIONS AND CONSUMER PROTECTION (1976)

John Honnold, Professor of Law, University of Pennsylvania.

CREDITORS' RIGHTS, see also Debtor-Creditor Law

CRIMINAL JUSTICE, THE ADMINISTRATION OF, Second Edition (1969)

Francis C. Sullivan, Professor of Law, Louisiana State University.
Paul Hardin III, Professor of Law, Duke University.
John Huston, Professor of Law, University of Washington.
Frank R. Lacy, Professor of Law, University of Oregon.
Daniel E. Murray, Professor of Law, University of Miami.
George W. Pugh, Professor of Law, Louisiana State University.

CRIMINAL JUSTICE ADMINISTRATION, Second Edition (1982), with 1983 Supplement

Frank W. Miller, Professor of Law, Washington University.
Robert O. Dawson, Professor of Law, University of Texas.
George E. Dix, Professor of Law, University of Texas.
Raymond I. Parnas, Professor of Law, University of California, Davis.

CRIMINAL LAW, Third Edition (1983)

Fred E. Inbau, Professor of Law Emeritus, Northwestern University.
James R. Thompson, Professor of Law Emeritus, Northwestern University.
Andre A. Moenssens, Professor of Law, University of Richmond.

CRIMINAL LAW (1982), with 1983 Supplement

Peter W. Low, Professor of Law, University of Virginia.
John C. Jeffries, Jr., Professor of Law, University of Virginia.
Richard C. Bonnie, Professor of Law, University of Virginia.

CRIMINAL LAW, Third Edition (1980)

Lloyd L. Weinreb, Professor of Law, Harvard University.

CRIMINAL LAW AND PROCEDURE, Sixth Edition (1984)

Rollin M. Perkins, Professor of Law Emeritus, University of California, Hastings College of the Law.
Ronald N. Boyce, Professor of Law, University of Utah.

CRIMINAL PROCEDURE, Second Edition (1980), with 1983 Supplement

Fred E. Inbau, Professor of Law Emeritus, Northwestern University.
James R. Thompson, Professor of Law Emeritus, Northwestern University.
James B. Haddad, Professor of Law, Northwestern University.
James B. Zagel, Chief, Criminal Justice Division, Office of Attorney General of Illinois.
Gary L. Starkman, Assistant U. S. Attorney, Northern District of Illinois.

CRIMINAL PROCEDURE, CONSTITUTIONAL (1977), with 1980 Supplement

James E. Scarboro, Professor of Law, University of Colorado.
James B. White, Professor of Law, University of Chicago.

CRIMINAL PROCESS, Third Edition (1978), with 1983 Supplement

Lloyd L. Weinreb, Professor of Law, Harvard University.

DAMAGES, Second Edition (1952)

Charles T. McCormick, late Professor of Law, University of Texas.
William F. Fritz, late Professor of Law, University of Texas.

DEBTOR–CREDITOR LAW (1984)

Theodore Eisenberg, Professor of Law, Cornell University.

DEBTOR–CREDITOR LAW, Second Edition (1981), with Statutory Supplement

William D. Warren, Dean of the School of Law, University of California, Los Angeles.
William E. Hogan, Professor of Law, New York University.

DECEDENTS' ESTATES (1971)

Max Rheinstein, late Professor of Law Emeritus, University of Chicago.
Mary Ann Glendon, Professor of Law, Boston College.

DECEDENTS' ESTATES AND TRUSTS, Sixth Edition (1982)

John Ritchie, Emeritus Dean and Wigmore Professor of Law, Northwestern University.
Neill H. Alford, Jr., Professor of Law, University of Virginia.
Richard W. Effland, Professor of Law, Arizona State University.

DECEDENTS' ESTATES AND TRUSTS (1968)

Howard R. Williams, Professor of Law, Stanford University.

DOMESTIC RELATIONS, see also Family Law

DOMESTIC RELATIONS, Successor Edition (1984)

Walter Wadlington, Professor of Law, University of Virginia.

ELECTRONIC MASS MEDIA, Second Edition (1979)

William K. Jones, Professor of Law, Columbia University.

EMPLOYMENT DISCRIMINATION (1983)

Joel W. Friedman, Professor of Law, Tulane University.
George M. Strickler, Professor of Law, Tulane University.

ENERGY LAW (1983)

Donald N. Zillman, Professor of Law, University of Utah.
Laurence Lattman, Dean of Mines and Engineering, University of Utah.

ENTERPRISE ORGANIZATION, Third Edition (1982), with 1982 Corporation and Partnership Statutes, Rules and Forms Supplement

Alfred F. Conard, Professor of Law, University of Michigan.
Robert L. Knauss, Dean of the Law School, University of Houston.
Stanley Siegel, Professor of Law, University of California, Los Angeles.

ENVIRONMENTAL POLICY LAW (1982)

Thomas J. Schoenbaum, Professor of Law, Tulane University.

EQUITY, see also Remedies

EQUITY, RESTITUTION AND DAMAGES, Second Edition (1974)

Robert Childres, late Professor of Law, Northwestern University.
William F. Johnson, Jr., Professor of Law, New York University.

ESTATE PLANNING, Second Edition (1982), with Documentary Supplement

David Westfall, Professor of Law, Harvard University.

ETHICS, see Legal Profession, and Professional Responsibility

ETHICS AND PROFESSIONAL RESPONSIBILITY (1981) (Reprinted from THE LAWYERING PROCESS)

Gary Bellow, Professor of Law, Harvard University.
Bea Moulton, Legal Services Corporation.

EVIDENCE, Fifth Edition (1984)

John Kaplan, Professor of Law, Stanford University.
Jon R. Waltz, Professor of Law, Northwestern University.

EVIDENCE (1968)

Francis C. Sullivan, Professor of Law, Louisiana State University.
Paul Hardin, III, Professor of Law, Duke University.

EVIDENCE, Seventh Edition (1983), with Rules and Statute Supplement (1984)

Jack B. Weinstein, Chief Judge, United States District Court.
John H. Mansfield, Professor of Law, Harvard University.
Norman Abrams, Professor of Law, University of California, Los Angeles.
Margaret Berger, Professor of Law, Brooklyn Law School.

FAMILY LAW, see also Domestic Relations

FAMILY LAW (1978), with 1983 Supplement

Judith C. Areen, Professor of Law, Georgetown University.

FAMILY LAW AND CHILDREN IN THE LEGAL SYSTEM, STATUTORY MATERIALS (1981)

Walter Wadlington, Professor of Law, University of Virginia.

FEDERAL COURTS, Seventh Edition (1982), with 1983 Supplement

Charles T. McCormick, late Professor of Law, University of Texas.
James H. Chadbourn, late Professor of Law, Harvard University.
Charles Alan Wright, Professor of Law, University of Texas.

FEDERAL COURTS AND THE FEDERAL SYSTEM, Hart and Wechsler's Second Edition (1973), with 1981 Supplement

Paul M. Bator, Professor of Law, Harvard University.
Paul J. Mishkin, Professor of Law, University of California, Berkeley.
David L. Shapiro, Professor of Law, Harvard University.
Herbert Wechsler, Professor of Law, Columbia University.

FEDERAL PUBLIC LAND AND RESOURCES LAW (1981), with 1983 Supplement

George C. Coggins, Professor of Law, University of Kansas.
Charles F. Wilkinson, Professor of Law, University of Oregon.

FEDERAL RULES OF CIVIL PROCEDURE, 1984 Edition

FEDERAL TAXATION, see Taxation

FOOD AND DRUG LAW (1980), with Statutory Supplement

Richard A. Merrill, Dean of the School of Law, University of Virginia.
Peter Barton Hutt, Esq.

FUTURE INTERESTS (1958)

Philip Mechem, late Professor of Law Emeritus, University of Pennsylvania.

FUTURE INTERESTS (1970)

Howard R. Williams, Professor of Law, Stanford University.

FUTURE INTERESTS AND ESTATE PLANNING (1961), with 1962 Supplement

W. Barton Leach, late Professor of Law, Harvard University.
James K. Logan, formerly Dean of the Law School, University of Kansas.

GOVERNMENT CONTRACTS, FEDERAL (1975), with 1980 Supplement

John W. Whelan, Professor of Law, Hastings College of the Law.
Robert S. Pasley, Professor of Law Emeritus, Cornell University.

INJUNCTIONS, Second Edition (1984)

Owen M. Fiss, Professor of Law, Yale University.
Doug Rendleman, Professor of Law, College of William and Mary.

INSTITUTIONAL INVESTORS, 1978

David L. Ratner, Professor of Law, Cornell University.

INSURANCE (1971)

William F. Young, Professor of Law, Columbia University.

INTERNATIONAL LAW, see also Transnational Legal Problems and United Nations Law

INTERNATIONAL LAW IN CONTEMPORARY PERSPECTIVE (1981), with Essay Supplement

Myres S. McDougal, Professor of Law, Yale University.
W. Michael Reisman, Professor of Law, Yale University.

LAW, SCIENCE AND MEDICINE (1984)

Judith C. Areen, Professor of Law, Georgetown University.
Patricia A. King, Professor of Law, Georgetown University.
Steven P. Goldberg, Professor of Law, Georgetown University.
Alexander M. Capron, Professor of Law, Georgetown University.

LAWYERING PROCESS (1978), with Civil Problem Supplement and Criminal Problem Supplement

Gary Bellow, Professor of Law, Harvard University.
Bea Moulton, Professor of Law, Arizona State University.

LEGAL METHOD (1980)

Harry W. Jones, Professor of Law Emeritus, Columbia University.
John M. Kernochan, Professor of Law, Columbia University.
Arthur W. Murphy, Professor of Law, Columbia University.

LEGAL METHODS (1969)

Robert N. Covington, Professor of Law, Vanderbilt University.
E. Blythe Stason, late Professor of Law, Vanderbilt University.
John W. Wade, Professor of Law, Vanderbilt University.
Elliott E. Cheatham, late Professor of Law, Vanderbilt University.
Theodore A. Smedley, Professor of Law, Vanderbilt University.

LEGAL PROFESSION (1970)

Samuel D. Thurman, Dean of the College of Law, University of Utah.
Ellis L. Phillips, Jr., Professor of Law, Columbia University.
Elliott E. Cheatham, late Professor of Law, Vanderbilt University.

LEGISLATION, Fourth Edition (1982) (by Fordham)

Horace E. Read, late Vice President, Dalhousie University.
John W. MacDonald, Professor of Law Emeritus, Cornell Law School.
Jefferson B. Fordham, Professor of Law, University of Utah.
William J. Pierce, Professor of Law, University of Michigan.

LEGISLATIVE AND ADMINISTRATIVE PROCESSES, Second Edition (1981)

Hans A. Linde, Judge, Supreme Court of Oregon.
George Bunn, Professor of Law, University of Wisconsin.
Fredericka Paff, Professor of Law, University of Wisconsin.
W. Lawrence Church, Professor of Law, University of Wisconsin.

LOCAL GOVERNMENT LAW, Revised Edition (1975)

Jefferson B. Fordham, Professor of Law, University of Utah.

MASS MEDIA LAW, Second Edition (1982)

Marc A. Franklin, Professor of Law, Stanford University.

MENTAL HEALTH PROCESS, Second Edition (1976), with 1981 Supplement

Frank W. Miller, Professor of Law, Washington University.
Robert O. Dawson, Professor of Law, University of Texas.
George E. Dix, Professor of Law, University of Texas.
Raymond I. Parnas, Professor of Law, University of California, Davis.

MUNICIPAL CORPORATIONS, see Local Government Law

NEGOTIABLE INSTRUMENTS, see Commercial Paper

NEGOTIATION (1981) (Reprinted from THE LAWYERING PROCESS)

Gary Bellow, Professor of Law, Harvard Law School.
Bea Moulton, Legal Services Corporation.

NEW YORK PRACTICE, Fourth Edition (1978)

Herbert Peterfreund, Professor of Law, New York University.
Joseph M. McLaughlin, Dean of the Law School, Fordham University.

OIL AND GAS, Fourth Edition (1979)

Howard R. Williams, Professor of Law, Stanford University.
Richard C. Maxwell, Professor of Law, University of California, Los Angeles.
Charles J. Meyers, Dean of the Law School, Stanford University.

ON LAW IN COURTS (1965)

Paul J. Mishkin, Professor of Law, University of California, Berkeley.
Clarence Morris, Professor of Law Emeritus, University of Pennsylvania.

PATENTS AND ANTITRUST (Pamphlet) (1983)

Milton Handler, Professor of Law Emeritus, Columbia University.
Harlan M. Blake, Professor of Law, Columbia University.
Robert Pitofsky, Professor of Law, Georgetown University.
Harvey J. Goldschmid, Professor of Law, Columbia University.

PERSPECTIVES ON THE LAWYER AS PLANNER (Reprint of Chapters One through Five of Planning by Lawyers) (1978)

Louis M. Brown, Professor of Law, University of Southern California.
Edward A. Dauer, Professor of Law, Yale University.

PLANNING BY LAWYERS, MATERIALS ON A NONADVERSARIAL LEGAL PROCESS (1978)

Louis M. Brown, Professor of Law, University of Southern California.
Edward A. Dauer, Professor of Law, Yale University.

PLEADING AND PROCEDURE, see Procedure, Civil

POLICE FUNCTION, Third Edition (1982), with 1983 Supplement

Reprint of Chapters 1–10 of Miller, Dawson, Dix and Parnas's CRIMINAL JUSTICE ADMINISTRATION, Second Edition.

PREPARING AND PRESENTING THE CASE (1981) (Reprinted from THE LAWYERING PROCESS)

Gary Bellow, Professor of Law, Harvard Law School.
Bea Moulton, Legal Services Corporation.

PREVENTIVE LAW, see also Planning by Lawyers

PROCEDURE—CIVIL PROCEDURE, Second Edition (1974), with 1979 Supplement

The late James H. Chadbourn, Professor of Law, Harvard University.
A. Leo Levin, Professor of Law, University of Pennsylvania.
Philip Shuchman, Professor of Law, Cornell University.

PROCEDURE—CIVIL PROCEDURE, Fifth Edition (1984)

Richard H. Field, late Professor of Law, Harvard University.
Benjamin Kaplan, Professor of Law Emeritus, Harvard University.
Kevin M. Clermont, Professor of Law, Cornell University.

PROCEDURE—CIVIL PROCEDURE, Third Edition (1976), with 1982 Supplement

Maurice Rosenberg, Professor of Law, Columbia University.
Jack B. Weinstein, Professor of Law, Columbia University.
Hans Smit, Professor of Law, Columbia University.
Harold L. Korn, Professor of Law, Columbia University.

UNIVERSITY CASEBOOK SERIES—Continued

PROCEDURE—PLEADING AND PROCEDURE: State and Federal, Fifth Edition (1983)

David W. Louisell, late Professor of Law, University of California, Berkeley.
Geoffrey C. Hazard, Jr., Professor of Law, Yale University.
Colin C. Tait, Professor of Law, University of Connecticut.

PROCEDURE—FEDERAL RULES OF CIVIL PROCEDURE, 1983 Edition

PRODUCTS LIABILITY (1980)

Marshall S. Shapo, Professor of Law, Northwestern University.

PRODUCTS LIABILITY AND SAFETY (1980), with 1983 Case and Documentary Supplement

W. Page Keeton, Professor of Law, University of Texas.
David G. Owen, Professor of Law, University of South Carolina.
John E. Montgomery, Professor of Law, University of South Carolina.

PROFESSIONAL RESPONSIBILITY, Third Edition (1984), with 1984 Selected National Standards Supplement

Thomas D. Morgan, Dean of the Law School, Emory University.
Ronald D. Rotunda, Professor of Law, University of Illinois.

PROPERTY, Fifth Edition (1984)

John E. Cribbet, Dean of the Law School, University of Illinois.
Corwin W. Johnson, Professor of Law, University of Texas.

PROPERTY—PERSONAL (1953)

S. Kenneth Skolfield, late Professor of Law Emeritus, Boston University.

PROPERTY—PERSONAL, Third Edition (1954)

Everett Fraser, late Dean of the Law School Emeritus, University of Minnesota.
Third Edition by Charles W. Taintor, late Professor of Law, University of Pittsburgh.

PROPERTY—INTRODUCTION, TO REAL PROPERTY, Third Edition (1954)

Everett Fraser, late Dean of the Law School Emeritus, University of Minnesota.

PROPERTY—REAL AND PERSONAL, Combined Edition (1954)

Everett Fraser, late Dean of the Law School Emeritus, University of Minnesota.
Third Edition of Personal Property by Charles W. Taintor, late Professor of Law, University of Pittsburgh.

PROPERTY—FUNDAMENTALS OF MODERN REAL PROPERTY, Second Edition (1982)

Edward H. Rabin, Professor of Law, University of California, Davis.

PROPERTY—PROBLEMS IN REAL PROPERTY (Pamphlet) (1969)

Edward H. Rabin, Professor of Law, University of California, Davis.

PROPERTY, REAL (1984)

Paul Goldstein, Professor of Law, Stanford University.

PROSECUTION AND ADJUDICATION, Second Edition (1982), with 1983 Supplement

Reprint of Chapters 11–26 of Miller, Dawson, Dix and Parnas's CRIMINAL JUSTICE ADMINISTRATION, Second Edition.

PUBLIC REGULATION OF DANGEROUS PRODUCTS (paperback) (1980)

Marshall S. Shapo, Professor of Law, Northwestern University.

PUBLIC UTILITY LAW, see Free Enterprise, also Regulated Industries

REAL ESTATE PLANNING (1980), with 1980 Problems, Statutes and New Materials Supplement

Norton L. Steuben, Professor of Law, University of Colorado.

REAL ESTATE TRANSACTIONS (1980), with Statute, Form and Problem Supplement

Paul Goldstein, Professor of Law, Stanford University.

RECEIVERSHIP AND CORPORATE REORGANIZATION, see Creditors' Rights

REGULATED INDUSTRIES, Second Edition, 1976

William K. Jones, Professor of Law, Columbia University.

REMEDIES (1982)

Edward D. Re, Chief Judge, U. S. Court of International Trade.

RESTITUTION, Second Edition (1966)

John W. Wade, Professor of Law, Vanderbilt University.

SALES (1980)

Marion W. Benfield, Jr., Professor of Law, University of Illinois.
William D. Hawkland, Chancellor, Louisiana State University Law Center.

SALES AND SALES FINANCING, Fourth Edition (1976), with 1982 Bankruptcy Supplement

John Honnold, Professor of Law, University of Pennsylvania.

SALES LAW AND THE CONTRACTING PROCESS (1982)

Reprint of Chapters 1–10 of Schwartz and Scott's Commercial Transactions.

SECURED INTERESTS IN PERSONAL PROPERTY (1984)

Douglas G. Baird, Professor of Law, University of Chicago.
Thomas H. Jackson, Professor of Law, Stanford University.

SECURED TRANSACTIONS IN PERSONAL PROPERTY (1983) (Reprinted from COMMERCIAL LAW)

Robert L. Jordan, Professor of Law, University of California, Los Angeles.
William D. Warren, Professor of Law, University of California, Los Angeles.

SECURITIES REGULATION, Fifth Edition (1982), with 1983 Cases and Releases Supplement and 1983 Selected Statutes, Rules and Forms Supplement

Richard W. Jennings, Professor of Law, University of California, Berkeley.
Harold Marsh, Jr., Member of the California Bar.

SECURITIES REGULATION (1982), with 1983 Supplement

Larry D. Soderquist, Professor of Law, Vanderbilt University.

SENTENCING AND THE CORRECTIONAL PROCESS, Second Edition (1976)

Frank W. Miller, Professor of Law, Washington University.
Robert O. Dawson, Professor of Law, University of Texas.
George E. Dix, Professor of Law, University of Texas.
Raymond I. Parnas, Professor of Law, University of California, Davis.

UNIVERSITY CASEBOOK SERIES—Continued

SOCIAL WELFARE AND THE INDIVIDUAL (1971)

Robert J. Levy, Professor of Law, University of Minnesota.
Thomas P. Lewis, Dean of the College of Law, University of Kentucky.
Peter W. Martin, Professor of Law, Cornell University.

TAX, POLICY ANALYSIS OF THE FEDERAL INCOME (1976)

William A. Klein, Professor of Law, University of California, Los Angeles.

TAXATION, FEDERAL INCOME (1976), with 1983 Supplement

Erwin N. Griswold, Dean Emeritus, Harvard Law School.
Michael J. Graetz, Professor of Law, University of Virginia.

TAXATION, FEDERAL INCOME, Fourth Edition (1982)

James J. Freeland, Professor of Law, University of Florida.
Stephen A. Lind, Professor of Law, University of Florida.
Richard B. Stephens, Professor of Law Emeritus, University of Florida.

TAXATION, FEDERAL INCOME, Volume I, Personal Income Taxation (1972), with 1983 Case Supplement; Volume II, Taxation of Partnerships and Corporations, Second Edition (1980), with 1983 Legislative Supplement

Stanley S. Surrey, Professor of Law, Harvard University.
William C. Warren, Professor of Law Emeritus, Columbia University.
Paul R. McDaniel, Professor of Law, Boston College Law School.
Hugh J. Ault, Professor of Law, Boston College Law School.

TAXATION, FEDERAL WEALTH TRANSFER, Second Edition (1982)

Stanley S. Surrey, Professor of Law, Harvard University.
William C. Warren, Professor of Law Emeritus, Columbia University.
Paul R. McDaniel, Professor of Law, Boston College Law School.
Harry L. Gutman, Instructor, Harvard Law School and Boston College Law School.

TAXATION OF INDIVIDUALS, PARTNERSHIPS AND CORPORATIONS, PROBLEMS in the (1978)

Norton L. Steuben, Professor of Law, University of Colorado.
William J. Turnier, Professor of Law, University of North Carolina.

TAXES AND FINANCE—STATE AND LOCAL (1974)

Oliver Oldman, Professor of Law, Harvard University.
Ferdinand P. Schoettle, Professor of Law, University of Minnesota.

TORT LAW AND ALTERNATIVES, Third Edition (1983)

Marc A. Franklin, Professor of Law, Stanford University.
Robert L. Rabin, Professor of Law, Stanford University.

TORTS, Seventh Edition (1982)

William L. Prosser, late Professor of Law, University of California, Hastings College.
John W. Wade, Professor of Law, Vanderbilt University.
Victor E. Schwartz, Professor of Law, American University.

TORTS, Third Edition (1976)

Harry Shulman, late Dean of the Law School, Yale University.
Fleming James, Jr., Professor of Law Emeritus, Yale University.
Oscar S. Gray, Professor of Law, University of Maryland.

*

University Casebook Series

EDITORIAL BOARD

DAVID L. SHAPIRO
DIRECTING EDITOR
Professor of Law, Harvard University

EDWARD L. BARRETT, Jr.
Professor of Law, University of California, Davis

ROBERT C. CLARK
Professor of Law, Harvard University

OWEN M. FISS
Professor of Law, Yale Law School

JEFFERSON B. FORDHAM
Professor of Law, University of Utah

GERALD GUNTHER
Professor of Law, Stanford University

HARRY W. JONES
Professor of Law, Columbia University

HERMA HILL KAY
Professor of Law, University of California at Berkeley

PAGE KEETON
Professor of Law, University of Texas

ROBERT L. RABIN
Professor of Law, Stanford University

JOHN RITCHIE
Professor of Law, University of Virginia

SAMUEL D. THURMAN
Professor of Law, University of Utah

LAW, SCIENCE

AND

MEDICINE

By

JUDITH AREEN

Professor of Law,
Professor of Community and Family Medicine,
Georgetown University

PATRICIA A. KING

Associate Professor of Law,
Georgetown University

STEVEN GOLDBERG

Associate Professor of Law,
Georgetown University

ALEXANDER MORGAN CAPRON

Topping Professor of Law, Medicine and Public Policy
University of Southern California

KF 3821
A7
L 39
1984

Mineola, New York

THE FOUNDATION PRESS, INC.

1984

COPYRIGHT © 1984 By THE FOUNDATION PRESS, INC.

All rights reserved

Printed in the United States of America

Library of Congress Cataloging in Publication Data

Main entry under title:

Law, science, and medicine.

  (University casebook series)

  Includes index.

  1. Medical laws and legislation—United States—
Cases. 2. Medicine—Research—Law and legislation—
United States—Cases. 3. Science and law—Cases.
I. Areen, Judith C. II. Series.

KF3821.A7L39 1984   344.73'041   84–8181

ISBN 0–88277–179–5   347.0441

J.A.

To Rich, Alexander, Stephanie,
Benjamin and Jonathan.

P.A.K.

To Roger, Elizabeth and Grayce.

S.G.

To Missy, Joe and Becky.

A.M.C.

To Jay Katz, David L. Bazelon
and Morris B. Abram.

*

PREFACE

As we complete this manuscript, there are daily reminders of the currency and importance of the issues addressed here, from the control of nuclear energy to governmental intervention in neonatal intensive care units, from developments in genetic engineering to the allocation of artificial organs. Although such issues arise with increasing frequency—in courtrooms, legislative chambers and executive agencies as well as in the popular and professional press—our society often seems perplexed about how to deal with them.

A major source of this problem is the lack of exposure that most people in the fields of law, science and medicine have to each others' values, methods and assumptions. This has led to a gulf of misunderstanding between scientists and nonscientists. This gulf may widen as more complex issues are presented by the growing sophistication and powers of the physical and life sciences (from their theoretical underpinnings to their technological applications) and as a few well-publicized incidents make the public apprehensive about progress in science and medicine.

To be able to work across traditional boundaries, students of law, medicine and science need exposure to materials from one another's discipline—as well as from the humanities and the social sciences—presented within a structure that allows the students to unravel the issues, analyze their content, and construct a framework for their own future roles as informed practitioners in a society seeking new relationships at the interface of law, science and medicine. Such are the objectives we attempt to fulfill in this book.

The book begins by examining, in Part One, two scientific developments that present enormous challenges to our society: genetic engineering and nuclear energy. The overarching issue is how ought society to learn about and respond to science and medicine. Specifically, five themes are explored in these two introductory chapters:

- *The use and misuse of scientific or medical expertise in making public policy.* What factors determine when an expert's views are invaluable and when they are irrelevant, and what weight should such views be given by the public and its representatives?

- *Who decides: the need to find appropriate institutions to promote, to direct, and even to curtail science and medicine.* What are the strengths and weaknesses of agencies, legislatures, courts, the executive, private groups, and individual scientists and lay people when the question is who shall control science or medicine at the various stages of their development and use?

- *The application of risk assessment or cost-benefit analysis to scientific and medical issues.* How if at all should these techniques guide those making public policy in the face of scientific and medical uncertainty?

● *The contrasting value systems of law, science and medicine.* How can one reconcile science's ethic of progress toward verifiable truth, the law's preference for individual rights and interests and its obligation to provide for the orderly resolution of disputes even when information is imperfect, and medicine's commitment to patients' well-being?

● *The ethical and religious implications of developments in science and medicine.* When science and medicine arguably alter the very nature of humanity, what are the consequences from an ethical or religious viewpoint?

These themes are pursued in a variety of contexts throughout the remaining chapters. Part Two explores alternative means for controlling science and medicine, with chapters on both public and private controls, including control by the individual consumer, and self regulation by the professionals. Part Three examines the problem of reducing risks to life and health by public regulation on the one hand and by the distribution of public benefits on the other. The proper role for risk assessment and cost benefit analyses is explored as is the problem of achieving a fair distribution of risks or burdens in our society. Part Four presents, for more detailed study, a series of issues on the frontiers of law's intersection with science and medicine.

This book looks to the future at least as much as to the present and the past. We hope the materials will inspire readers to rethink traditional professional roles, both by the examples provided here and by the absence of other exemplars at present. Scientists and physicians who become aware of the legitimate scope and times for public involvement in their fields can move beyond the narrow role of "expert witness." Likewise, lawyers and other architects of public policy can—indeed, must—create new means for handling a myriad of difficult problems, from individual decisionmaking about gravely ill, incompetent patients to societal decisionmaking about nuclear fission. To achieve such goals, law students cannot limit their study to appellate opinions, for they will have to be more than litigators, and science and medical students must look beyond technical papers if they wish to be effective participants in the world outside the laboratory and examining room.

The book is designed as a basic text in a course on law, science and medicine, although it can also serve for more specialized courses and seminars on either law and medicine or law and science by tailoring the materials to areas of interest. A law and science course might cover Chapters 1–5, 9 and 10. A law and medicine course might center on Chapters 1, 3 and 6–8. In either case, the basic subject matter of the course can be enriched by assigning materials from a related area; for example, a law and medicine seminar could add Chapter 2 on nuclear energy to allow students to explore the many points of comparison between the physical and the life sciences.

In order to respect the complexity of the subjects presented without producing a work of encyclopedic length, we have chosen merely to describe in a few brief notes certain subjects traditionally grouped under headings such as forensic science, medical malpractice or the legal aspects of health care administration. These are not unimportant subjects, although we suspect that they are or should be treated in courses on evidence, torts or advanced administrative law. Those wishing to supplement their knowledge on these subjects will find citations to the leading cases, statutes and secondary sources.

There are many friends and colleagues who have assisted us in this project. We are particularly indebted for suggestions from James Childress, Richard Cooper, Richard Delgado, Harold Edgar, Peter Hutt, Robert Levine, Richard Lonsdorf, Richard Merrill, Larry Palmer, Steven Salop, William Schultz, Leo Slaggie, Alan Weisbard, Edith Weiss, and Roger Wilkins. We have also benefitted from discussions with our colleagues at the Kennedy Institute of Ethics, especially Tom Beauchamp, Ruth Faden, William May and Warren Reich.

We are grateful as well to the many students of law, medicine and disparate other fields at Georgetown, Pennsylvania and Yale whose questions and ideas over the years have shaped much of what is presented. Special mention must be made of the research and drafting performed on this book by Joy Archer, Jon Brick, Robert Conflitti, Donald Davis, Diana Engel, David Feller, Martha Foley, Dierdre Golash, Harvey Hyman, John Kastelic, John Mandler, Susan McHugh, Jennifer Milson, David Novak, Dawn Sunday, Stephen Vajtay, and of the assistance provided by David Balton, Peter Cinquegrani, Denise-Marie Di Lello, James Hammond, Jan Montgomery, and Jenelle C. Prins-Stairs in processing and organizing the final manuscript. Dean David J. McCarthy, Jr., encouraged our interest in the field and provided research assistance. The staff of the law center's secretariat patiently typed and retyped the evolving manuscript. Finally, our special thanks go to our families for sustaining us and understanding our absences during the work.

JUDY AREEN
PATRICIA KING
STEVEN GOLDBERG
ALEX CAPRON

Washington, D.C.
June 1984

NOTE ON EDITING

Deletions from materials are indicated by ellipses except when the omitted material consists only of citations or footnotes. All footnotes are numbered according to the original source except when noted. For the sake of brevity, the term President's Commission is used in referring to the works of the President's Commission for the Study of Ethical Problems in Medicine and Biomedical and Behavioral Research.

ACKNOWLEDGMENTS

The editors gratefully acknowledge permission to reprint the following materials:

Altimore, The Social Construction of a Scientific Controversy: Comments on Press Coverage of the Recombinant DNA Debate, 7 Science, Technology & Human Values 24, 27, 29–30 (1982). Reprinted with permission of the MIT Press.

American Medical Association, Current Principles of the Judicial Council of the American Medical Association, 1982. Reprinted with permission of the American Medical Association.

American Medical Association, Principles of Medical Ethics, 1980. Reprinted with permission of the American Medical Association.

American Psychiatric Association, Statement on the Insanity Defense, The American Journal of Psychiatry, vol. 140:6, pp. 681–688, 1983. Copyright © 1983, the American Psychiatric Association. Reprinted by permission of the American Psychiatric Association.

Asimov, Isaac, I., Robot 6–8 (1950). Copyright © 1950 by Isaac Asimov. Reprinted by permission of Doubleday & Company, Inc.

Association of American Medical Colleges, The Maintenance of High Ethical Standards in the Conduct of Research (1982). Reprinted by permission of the Association of American Medical Colleges.

Babbage, Charles, Reflections on the Decline of Science in England, and Some of its Causes 174–179 (1830). Reprinted with the permission of Augustus M. Kelley, Publishers.

Bazelon, David L., Coping With Technology Through the Legal Process, 62 Cornell L.Rev. 817, 818–824, 828–829 (June 1977). Copyright © by Cornell University. All rights reserved. Reprinted with permission of Cornell Law Review and Fred B. Rothman and Company.

Beauchamp, Tom L., Ethical Theory and Bioethics, in Contemporary Issues in Bioethics 4–11, 13–24, 26–31 (T. Beauchamp and L. Walters, eds. 1982). Reprinted with permission of Wadsworth Publishing Company and Thomas Beauchamp.

Beauchamp, Tom L., A Reply to Rachels on Active and Passive Euthanasia, in Ethical Issues in Death and Dying, 246, 249–253 (T. Beauchamp & S. Perlin, eds. 1978). Copyright © 1975, 1977 by Tom. L. Beauchamp. Reprinted by permission.

Beecher, Henry, Ethics and Clinical Research, 274 New England Journal of Medicine 1354–1360 (1966). Reprinted with permission of the New England Journal of Medicine.

Beres, Louis, Apocalypse 123–126 (1980). Copyright © 1980. Reprinted by permission of the University of Chicago Press and Louis Beres.

Berg, Baltimore, Brenner, Robin and Singer, Asilomar Conference on Recombinant DNA Molecules, *Science* 188: 991–994 (1975). Copyright © 1975 by the American Association for the Advancement of Science. Reprinted with permission of AAAS and Paul Berg.

Berlin, Isaiah, Two Concepts of Liberty, in Four Essays on Liberty 118 (1969). Copyright © 1969 by Oxford University Press. Reprinted with permission of Oxford University Press.

Blaiberg, Philip, Looking at My Heart 56–57, 65–66, 69, 70 (1968). Copyright © 1968 by Dr. Philip Blaiberg. Reprinted with permission of Stein and Day Publishers.

Boden, Margaret A., The Social Implications of Intelligent Machines, in The Microelectronics Revolution 439, 440–441 (T. Forester ed. 1981). Reprinted with permission of The MIT Press and the Institute of Electronic and Radio Engineers.

Bok, Sissela, Lying: Moral Choice in Public and Private Life, 221–231, 234–240 (1978). Reprinted with permission of Pantheon Books.

Brandt, Allan, Racism and Research: The Case of the Tuskegee Syphilis Study, Hastings Center Report 21–29 (Dec. 1978). Reproduced by permission of The Hastings Center. Copyright © 1978 by the Institute of Society, Ethics and Life Sciences, 360 Broadway, Hastings-on-Hudson, N.Y. 10706.

Burger, Edward J., Jr., Science at the White House. Baltimore, The Johns Hopkins University Press, 1980, pp. 114–115.

Burt, Robert A., Taking Care of Strangers: The Role of Law in Doctor-Patient Relations 155–158. Reprinted with permission of The Free Press, a division of MacMillan, Inc. Copyright © 1979 by Robert A. Burt.

Calabresi, G., and Bobbitt, P., Tragic Choices 181–191 (1978). Reprinted by permission of W.W. Norton & Company, Inc. Copyright © 1978 by the Fels Center of Government.

Caplan, Arthur, The Artificial Heart, 12 Hastings Center Report 22–24 (Feb. 1982). Reproduced with permission of The Hastings Center. Copyright © 1982 by the Institute of Society, Ethics and Life Sciences, 360 Broadway, Hastings-on-Hudson, N.Y. 10706.

Capron, Alexander, The Law of Genetic Therapy, in The New Genetics and The Future of Man, 150–152 (Hamilton, ed. 1972). Copyright © 1972 by Capron. Reprinted by permission.

Capron, Alexander, Legal Considerations Affecting Clinical Pharmacological Studies in Children, 21 Clinical Research 141–150 (February 1973). Reprinted by permission of the American Federation for Clinical Research.

Capron, Alexander, Tort Liability in Genetic Counseling. Copyright © 1979 by the Directors of the Columbia Law Review Association, Inc. All rights reserved. This article originally appeared at 79 Colum.L. Rev. 618, 668–670 (1970). Reprinted by permission.

Capron, Alexander, and Kass, Leon, A Statutory Definition of the Standards for Determining Human Death: An Appraisal and a Proposal, 121 U.Pa.L.Rev. 87, 93–95, 97, 100–101, 104–106, 108 (1972). Reprinted by permission of the University of Pennsylvania Law Review.

Cardozo, Benjamin N., The Paradoxes of Legal Science 1–4 (1956). Copyright © 1956 by Columbia University Press. Reprinted with permission of Columbia University Press.

Casper, Barry M., Is the Proposed Science Court What We Need? *Science* 194: 29–30 (1976). Copyright 1976 by the American Association for the Advancement of Science. Reprinted with permission of AAAS and Barry Casper.

Casper, Barry M., The Rhetoric and Reality of Congressional Technology Assessment. Reprinted by permission of THE BULLETIN OF ATOMIC SCIENTISTS, a magazine of science and public affairs. Copyright © 1978 by the Educational Foundation for Nuclear Science, Chicago, Ill. 60637.

Cassel, Eric, The Nature of Suffering and the Goals of Medicine, 306 New England Journal of Medicine 639 (1982). Reprinted with permission of the New England Journal of Medicine.

Childress, James F., Who Shall Live When Not All Can Live? 53 Soundings 339–362 (Winter 1970). Reprinted with the permission of Soundings and Professor Childress.

Cooper, Richard M., Freedom of Choice in the Real World, 34 Food, Drug and Cosmetic Law Journal 612–624 (December 1979). Reprinted with the permission of the Food, Drug and Cosmetic Law Journal.

Cooper, Richard M., The Role of Regulating Agencies in Risk/Benefit Decision Making, 33 Food, Drug and Cosmetic Law Journal 755, 766–773 (December 1978). Reprinted with the permission of the Food, Drug and Cosmetic Law Journal.

Cowart, Dax S., and Robert B. White, "Please Let Me Die," Transcript of Videotaped Interview Between Donald Cowart and Robert B. White, M.D., May 8, 1974. Reprinted with the permission of Dax Cowart and Dr. White, Professor of Psychiatry, The University of Texas Medical Branch, Galveston, Texas, and Training and Supervising Analyst, Houston/Galveston Psychoanalytic Inst., Houston, Texas.

Crouch and Wilson, Risk-Benefit Analysis 9–11, 12–16, 19–21, 48–49 (1982). Reprinted with permission from Crouch and Wilson's *Risk-Benefit Analysis*. Copyright 1982, Ballinger Publishing Company.

Curie-Cohen et al., Current Practice of Artificial Insemination by Donor, 300 New England Journal of Medicine 585 (1979). Reprinted with permission of the New England Journal of Medicine.

Curran, William, J., Reasonableness and Randomization in Clinical Trials, 300 New England Journal of Medicine 1273–1275 (1979). Reprinted with permission of the New England Journal of Medicine.

Dalkey and Helmer, An Experimental Application of the Delphi Method to the Use of Experts. Reprinted by permission of Dalkey and

Helmer, Management Science, Volume 9, Number 3 (April 1963) pp. 458–460, The Institute of Management Sciences.

Davis, B.D., Evolution, Epidemiology and Recombinant DNA, *Science* 193: 442 (1976) (letter). Copyright © 1976 by the American Association for the Advancement of Science. Reprinted with permission of AAAS and Professor Davis.

Davis, Bernard, Profit Sharing Between Professors and the University? 304 New England Journal of Medicine 1232 (1981). Reprinted with permission of the New England Journal of Medicine.

Delgado, Richard, and David R. Millen, God, Galileo and Government: Toward Constitutional Protection for Scientific Inquiry, 53 Wash.L. Rev. 349, 354–355, 358–361 (1978). Reprinted with the permission of Washington Law Review, Professors Delgado and Millen, and Fred B. Rothman and Company.

Delong, Solow, Butters, Calfee and Ippolito, Defending Cost-Benefit Analysis: Replies to Steven Kelman, 5 *Regulation* 39–42 (March–April 1981). Reprinted by permission of the American Enterprise Institute for Public Policy Research and Gerard Butters.

Derbyshire, Robert C., Medical Licensure and Discipline in the United States (1969). Copyright © 1969 by The Johns Hopkins University Press. Reprinted by permission.

Diamond, Sondra and Roy Bonisteel, "I Am Not What You See," A Canadian Broadcasting Corporation Film Dialogue, from C. Swinyard, ed., Decision Making and the Defective Newborn 465, 466–476 (1978). Courtesy of Charles C. Thomas, Publisher, Springfield, Illinois.

Donahue, Phil, Interview, Transcript #08033. "Donahue" transcript segments courtesy of Multimedia Entertainment.

Duff and Campbell, Moral and Ethical Dilemmas in the Special Care Nursery, 289 New England Journal of Medicine 890 (1973). Reprinted with permission of the New England Journal of Medicine.

Duffy, P., Jr., Drug Testing in Prisons: The View From Inside. In Basson, M.D. Lipson, R.F. Ganos, D.L. (eds. 1981): "Troubling Problems in Medical Ethics," New York: Alan R. Liss, Inc.

Dworkin, Gerald, Paternalism. Copyright © 1972, THE MONIST, La Salle, Illinois. Reprinted from vol. 56, no. 1, Jan. 1972 by permission.

Dworkin, Roger B., Death in Context, 48 Ind.L.J. 623, 628–631, 636–639 (1973). Reprinted with permission from the Indiana Law Journal and Fred B. Rothman and Company.

Electric Power Research Institute, A Feasibility Study for Enhancing the Development of Fusion Energy. EPRI report ER–778–SR–124–128. Copyright © 1979 Electric Power Research Institute. Reprinted with permission.

Englehardt, H. Tristram, Medicine and the Concept of Person, in Contemporary Issues in Bioethics 94–99 (T. Beauchamp and L. Walters, eds.

1982). Reprinted with permission of Wadsworth Publishing Company and H. Tristram Englehardt.

Englehardt, H. Tristram, Rights and Responsibilities of Patients and Physicians, in Medical Treatment of the Dying: Moral Issues 9, 24–26 (M. Bayles and D. High, eds. 1978). Copyright © by Schenkman Publishing Company, Cambridge, MA 02138. Reprinted with permission of Schenkman Publishing Company.

Fellner and Marshall, Kidney Donors: The Myth of Informed Consent, The American Journal of Psychiatry, vol. 126:9, pp. 1245–1251, 1970. Copyright © 1970. Reprinted by permission of the American Psychiatric Association and Dr. Fellner.

Fletcher, Ethics and Amniocentesis for Fetal Sex Identification, 301 New England Journal of Medicine 550 (1979). Reprinted with permission of the New England Journal of Medicine.

Forsberg, Randall, A Bilateral Nuclear-Weapon Freeze, 247 Scientific American 2 (November 1982). Reprinted with permission of W.H. Freeman and Company. Copyright © 1982 by Scientific American, Inc. All rights reserved.

Fost, Consent as a Barrier to Research, 300 New England Journal of Medicine 1272–1273 (1979). Reprinted with permission of the New England Journal of Medicine.

Freidson, Eliot, Profession of Medicine 71–74, 77 (1973). Copyright © 1970 by Harper & Row, Publishers, Inc. Reprinted with permission.

Fried, Charles, Children as Subjects for Medical Experimentation, in Research on Children 107, 111–115 (J. van Eys, ed. 1978). Copyright © 1978 by University Park Press, Baltimore, Md. Reprinted with permission.

Fried, Charles, Equality and Rights in Medical Care, 6 Hastings Center Report 29–34 (Feb. 1976). Reproduced with permission of The Hastings Center. Copyright © 1976 by the Institute of Society, Ethics and Life Sciences, 360 Broadway, Hastings-on-Hudson, N.Y. 10706.

Fried, Charles, Medical Experimentation: Personal Integrity and Social Policy 25–26 (1974). Reprinted with permission of Elsevier Science Publishers B.V.

Friedman, Milton, Capitalism and Freedom 149–160 (1962). Reprinted with permission of the University of Chicago Press.

Gass, Ronald P., Codes of Health Care Professions, Volume 4, pages 1725–1726. Reprinted with permission from The Free Press, a division of MacMillan, Inc., and the Kennedy Institute of Ethics, Georgetown University. From Encyclopedia of Bioethics, Warren T. Reich, Editor-in-Chief. Copyright © 1978 by Georgetown University, Washington, D.C.

Gerjuoy, H., A New Perspective on Forecasting Methodology, in The Study of the Future: An Agenda for Research 14, 22–23 (W. Boucher ed. 1977). Reprinted with permission of the Futures Group and Dr. Gerjuoy.

Gilinsky, Victor, The Need for Nuclear Safeguards, 17 Atomic Energy Law Journal 143–144, 150–151 (Summer 1975). Reprinted with permission of Invictus Publishing Company.

Goldberg, Steven, Controlling Basic Science: The Case of Nuclear Fusion, 68 Geo.L.J. 683, 694–696, 724 (1980). Reprinted with the permission of the publisher. Copyright © 1980, The Georgetown Law Journal Association.

Goldberg, Steven, The Constitutional Status of American Science, 1979 U.Ill.L.F. 1, 7–10 (1979). Reprinted with the permission of the Board of Trustees of the University of Illinois.

Golding, Martin, P., Obligations to Future Generations, in Responsibilities to Future Generations, ed. by E. Partridge (Prometheus Books, Buffalo, N.Y. 1980). Reprinted with permission of Prometheus Books.

Green, Harold, The Role of Law in Determining Acceptability of Risk, in Societal Risk Assessment 256–258 (Schwing and Albers, eds. 1980). Reprinted with permission of Plenum Press Publishing Corporation.

Grobstein, Clifford, Recombinant DNA Research: Beyond the NIH Guidelines, *Science* 194: 1134–1135 (1976). Copyright © 1976 by the American Association for the Advancement of Science. Reprinted with permission of AAAS and Clifford Grobstein.

Hellawell, Robert, CHOOSE: A Computer Program for Legal Planning and Analysis, 19 Colum.J.Transnatl.L. 339, 340–346, 356–357 (1981). Reprinted with permission of Columbia Journal of Transnational Law.

Hightower, Jim, Hard Tomatoes, Hard Times 43, 47–49 (1973). Copyright © Schenkman Publishing Company. Reprinted with permission of Schenkman Publishing Company.

The Hippocratic Oath, in Ludwig Edelstein, Ancient Medicine (O. Temkin and C. Temkin eds. 1967). Reprinted with permission of The Johns Hopkins University Press.

Hoffman, Banesh, Albert Einstein 69–82 (1972). Reprinted with the permission of Viking Press, Inc.

Hofstadter, Douglas: Godel, Escher, Bach 677–679 (1979). Reprinted with permission of Basic Books, Inc., Publishers.

Imbus and Zawacki, Autonomy for Burned Patients When Survival Is Unprecedented, 297 New England Journal of Medicine 308–309 (1977). Reprinted with permission of the New England Journal of Medicine.

Ingelfinger, Franz, J., Informed (But Uneducated) Consent, 287 New England Journal of Medicine 465–466 (1972). Reprinted with permission of the New England Journal of Medicine.

Jackson and Younger, Patient Autonomy and Death With Dignity, 299 New England Journal of Medicine 404 (1979). Reprinted with permission of the New England Journal of Medicine.

Jenson and Fantle, Soldiers Grove: Moving Into the Solar Age. This article originally appeared in Alternative Sources of Energy Magazine, Issue # 43. For subscription information, write to them at 107 S. Central Avenue, Milaca, Minnesota 56353.

Jonas, Hans, Philosophical Reflections on Experimenting With Human Subjects, in Experimentation With Human Subjects 1–4, 9–14, 18–21, 24–26 (P. Freund, ed. 1970). Copyright © 1970 by The American Academy of Arts and Sciences. Permission to reprint granted by George Braziller, Inc., New York City.

Jonsen, Albert R., Ethics, the Law, and the Treatment of Seriously Ill Newborns. Reprinted with permission from Legal and Ethical Aspects of Treating Critically and Terminally Ill Patients 236, 237–241, edited by A. Edward Doudera and J.B. Silvers (Ann Arbor: AUPHA Press, 1982).

Jungk, Robert, Brighter Than a Thousand Suns 131–132 (1958). Reprinted with permission of Harcourt Brace Jovanovich, Inc.

Kahn, Herman, Thinking About the Unthinkable, 18–19, 22–24, (1962). Copyright © 1962 by permission of the publisher, Horizon Press, New York.

Kass, Leon, The New Biology: What Price Relieving Man's Estate, *Science* 174: 782 (1971). Copyright © 1971 by the American Association for the Advancement of Science. Reprinted with permission of AAAS and Leon Kass.

Katz, Jay, Informed Consent—A Fairy Tale?, 39 U.Pitt.L.Rev. 137 (1977). Reprinted with the permission of the University of Pittsburgh Law Review.

Katz and Capron, Catastrophic Diseases: Who Decides What? 185–196 (1978). Reprinted with permission of the publisher. Copyright © 1975 by Russell Sage Foundation.

Kelman, Steven, Cost-Benefit Analysis: An Ethical Critique, 33–34 *Regulation* (January–February 1981). Reprinted by permission of the American Enterprise Institute for Public Policy Research.

Kelman, Steven, Letter to the Editor, 5 *Regulation* 2–3 (May–June 1981). Reprinted by permission of the American Enterprise Institute for Public Policy Research.

Kidder, Tracy, The Future of the Photovoltaic Cell, 245 Atlantic 68, 74 (June 1980). Copyright © 1980 by Tracy Kidder. Reprinted with permission of The Atlantic Monthly and Tracy Kidder.

Kluge, Eike-Henner, The Ethics of Deliberate Death, 15–18 (1981). Reprinted from The Ethics of Deliberate Death by Eike-Henner Kluge by permission of the Associate Faculty Press, Inc., Port Washington, N.Y.

Krauthammer, Charles, Science ex Machina, The New Republic, June 6, 1981, pp. 19–20. Reprinted by permission of THE NEW REPUBLIC. Copyright © 1981 by The New Republic, Inc.

ACKNOWLEDGMENTS

Kuhn, T.S., The Structure of Scientific Revolutions 10–11, 52, 84–85, 165–167, 172 (1962). Reprinted with permission of the University of Chicago Press.

Lambright, W. Henry, Governing Science and Technology 3–7 (1976). Copyright © 1976 by Oxford University Press, Inc. Reprinted by permission of Oxford University Press.

Leaf, Alexander, The MGH Trustees Say No to Heart Transplants, 302 New England Journal of Medicine 1087–1088 (1980). Reprinted with permission of the New England Journal of Medicine.

Letters to the Editor, 303 New England Journal of Medicine 1967 (1980). Reprinted with permission of the New England Journal of Medicine.

Levi, Edward H., Introduction to Legal Reasoning 1, 3–5, (1949). Reprinted with the permission of the University of Chicago Press.

Lorber, John, Early Results of Selective Treatment of Spina Bifida Cystica, 4 British Medical Journal 201, 202–204 (1973). Reprinted with permission of the British Medical Journal and John Lorber.

Lovins, Amory, Energy Strategy: The Road Not Taken? 55 Foreign Affairs 55, 71–81 (October 1976). Excerpted by permission of Foreign Affairs, October 1976. Copyright © 1976 by the Council on Foreign Relations, Inc.

Lovins, Amory, Prepared Testimony, in The Energy Controversy 28–31 (H. Nash ed. 1979). Reprinted with permission of Friends of the Earth and Amory Lovins.

Lowrance, William, The Nature of Risk, in Societal Risk Assessment 5–8 (Schwing and Albers, eds. 1980). Reprinted with permission of Plenum Press Publishing Corporation.

Martin, James A., The Proposed Science Court, 75 Mich.L.Rev. 1058, 1069–1076 (1977). Reprinted with permission of The Michigan Law Review and Professor Martin.

Marx, Karl, The Grundrisse 152 (McClellan ed. 1971). Copyright © 1971 by David McClellan. Reprinted with permission of Harper & Row, Publishers, Inc.

Mazlish, Bruce, The Fourth Discontinuity, Technology and Culture Vol. 8, pp. 1–8 (January 1967). Copyright © 1967 by Bruce Mazlish. Reprinted with the permission of the University of Chicago Press and Bruce Mazlish.

McCalla, Alex F., Politics of the Agricultural Research Establishment. Reprinted by permission from The New Politics of Food, edited by Don F. Hadwiger and William P. Browne (Lexington, Mass.: Lexington Books, D.C. Heath and Company. Copyright © 1978, D.C. Heath and Company).

Meinel and Meinel, Soft Path Leads to a New Dark Age, in The Energy Controversy 225, 226–228, 232–233 (H. Nash ed. 1979). Reprinted with permission of Friends of the Earth and the Meinels. This article also appears in Soft v. Hard Energy Paths 70–71, 75–76 (C.B. Yulish ed. 1977).

Mendelsohn, Everett, The Emergence of Science as a Profession in Nineteenth Century Europe, in The Management of Scientists 3, 40–43 (Hill ed. 1964). Copyright © 1964 by Northeastern University. Reprinted by permission of Beacon Press.

Merton, Robert K., Social Theory and Social Structure 607, 610–612, 612–613, 614. Reprinted with permission of The Free Press, a division of MacMillan, Inc. Copyright © 1967, 1968 by Robert K. Merton.

Merton, Robert K., The Sociology of Science 276–277 (N. Stover ed. 1973). Reprinted with the permission of the University of Chicago Press.

Metz, William D., Report of Fusion Breakthrough Proves to be a Media Event, *Science* 201: 192–194 (1978). Copyright © 1978 by the American Association for the Advancement of Science. Reproduced with permission of AAAS.

Milunsky, Aubrey, The Prevention of Genetic Disease and Mental Retardation 64–71 (1975). Reprinted by permission of W.B. Saunders Co., Philadelphia, and Aubrey Milunsky.

Morison, Robert, Bioethics After Two Decades, 11 Hastings Center Report 8–9, 12 (April 1981). Reproduced with permission of The Hastings Center. Copyright © 1981 by the Institute of Society, Ethics and Life Sciences, 360 Broadway, Hastings-on-Hudson, N.Y. 10706.

NAS–NRC, Committee on Recombinant DNA Molecules, Potential Biohazards of Recombinant DNA Molecules, *Science* 185: 303 (1974). Copyright © 1974 by the American Association for the Advancement of Science. Reprinted with permission of AAAS.

National Academy of Sciences, Food Safety Policy: Scientific and Societal Considerations S1–S7, 9.12–9.21, MS2–MS4 (February 28, 1979). Reproduced with the permission of the National Academy of Sciences, Washington, D.C.

National Academy of Sciences, Risk and Decision-Making: Perspectives and Research 2–5, 11–13, 14–17, 20–24, 27–33, 36–38 (1982). Reproduced with the permission of the National Academy of Sciences, Washington, D.C.

National Council of Churches, Message from Three General Secretaries (June 20, 1980). Reprinted with permission of the National Council of Churches of Christ in the USA.

Noonan, John T., An Almost Absolute Value in History, in The Morality of Abortion: Legal and Historical Perspectives 1, 51–58 (J.T. Noonan ed. 1970). Copyright © 1970 by the President and Fellows of Harvard College. Reprinted by permission.

ACKNOWLEDGMENTS

Note, The California Natural Death Act: An Empirical Study of Physicians' Practices, 31 Stan.L.Rev. 913 (1979). Reprinted with permission of Stanford Law Review.

Panel on Scientific Communication and National Security, Scientific Communication and National Security 2–3, 5–6 (1982). Reproduced with the permission of the National Academy of Sciences, Washington, D.C.

Pattulo, E.L., Institutional Review Boards and the Freedom to Take Risks, 307 New England Journal of Medicine 1156–1158 (1982). Reprinted with permission of the New England Journal of Medicine.

Pauling, Linus, Reflections on the New Biology. Originally published in 15 UCLA L.Rev. 267, 268–272. Copyright © 1968, The Regents of the University of California. All rights reserved. Reprinted with permission of UCLA Law Review and Linus Pauling.

Pellegrino, Edmund, Humanism and the Physician 147–150 (1979). Copyright © 1979 by The University of Tennessee Press. Reprinted with permission of The University of Tennessee Press.

Pennock, Oyer et al., Cardiac Transplantation in Perspective for the Future, Journal of Thoracic and Cardiovascular Surgery, vol. 83, p. 168 (February 1982). Reprinted with permission of the C.V. Mosby Company.

Perle, Richard, A Freeze Means Thin Ice, The New York Times, September 7, 1982, at 23. Copyright © 1982 by the New York Times Company. Reprinted by permission.

Pigman and Carmichael, An Ethical Code for Scientists, *Science* 111: 643–644 (1950). Copyright © 1950 by the American Association for the Advancement of Science. Reprinted with permission of AAAS.

Polanyi, Michael, Science, Faith and Society 63–65 (1946). Reprinted with the permission of the University of Chicago Press.

Price, Don K., Government and Science 164–167 (1962). Reprinted by permission of the New York University Press. Copyright © 1954 by New York University.

Primack and von Hipple, Advice and Dissent 40. Copyright © 1970 by Basic Books. Reprinted with permission of Basic Books, Inc., Publishers.

Quirk, Paul J., Food and Drug Administration, in The Politics of Regulation 191, 211–217 (James Q. Wilson ed. 1980). Reprinted with permission of Basic Books, Inc., Publishers.

Rabkin, Gillerman and Rice, Orders Not to Resuscitate, 295 New England Journal of Medicine 364 (1976). Reprinted with permission of the New England Journal of Medicine.

Rachels, James, Active and Passive Euthanasia, 292 New England Journal of Medicine 78, 79–80 (1975). Reprinted with permission of the New England Journal of Medicine.

Ramsey, Paul, Ethics at the Edges of Life: Medical and Legal Intersections 189, 191–195, 200–203, 212–215, 218–219 (1978). Copyright © 1978. Reprinted with the permission of Yale University Press.

Ramsey, Paul, Fabricated Man 139–140, 148–151 (1970). Copyright © 1970. Reprinted with the permission of Yale University Press.

Ramsey, Paul, The Patient as Person: Exploration in Medical Ethics 120–123 (1970). Copyright © 1970. Reprinted with the permission of Yale University Press.

Raphael, Bertram, The Thinking Computer: Mind Inside Matter 1–6, 159–164, 309–316 (1976). Reprinted with permission of W.H. Freeman and Company. Copyright © 1976.

Reiser, David E., and Andrea K. Schroeder, Patient Interviewing 90–93, 96 (1980). Copyright © 1980 by the Williams & Wilkins Co., Baltimore, Md. Reprinted with the permission of the authors and the Williams & Wilkins Co.

Rennie, Drummond, Consensus Statements, 304 New England Journal of Medicine 665–666 (1981). Reprinted with permission of the New England Journal of Medicine.

Rhoads, Steven E., How Much Should We Spend to Save a Life?, in Valuing Life 285, 287–295, 301–303, 306–309 (Rhoads ed. 1978). Reprinted with the permission of Westview Press.

Rogers, Michael, Biohazard 48–57, 60–72, 74–89, 92–93, 99–100, 183–184 (1977). Copyright © 1973, 1975, 1976, 1977, by Michael Rogers. Reprinted with permission of Alfred A. Knopf, Inc.

Russo, Paul et al., Microprocessors in Consumer Products, in The Microelectronics Revolution 130, 134–135 (T. Forester ed. 1981). Reprinted with permission of The MIT Press.

Rutstein, David D., The Ethical Design of Human Experiments, in Experimentation With Human Subjects 383–385, 387–389 (P. Freund, ed. 1970). Copyright © 1970 by The American Academy of Arts and Sciences. Permission to reprint granted by George Braziller, Inc., New York City.

Samet, Hanan, Computers and Communication: The FCC Dilemma in Determining What to Regulate, 28 DePaul L.Rev. 71, 72–73, 75–76, 80–83 (1978). Reprinted with permission of DePaul Law Review and Professor Samet.

Schell, Jonathan, The Fate of the Earth 181–182 (1982). Copyright © 1982, by Jonathan Schell. Reprinted with permission of Alfred A. Knopf, Inc. Originally appeared in *The New Yorker*.

Schumacher, E.F., Small is Beautiful: Economics as if People Mattered. Copyright © 1973 by E.F. Schumacher. Reprinted with permission of Harper & Row, Publishers, Inc.

Shenkin and Warner, Giving the Patient His Medical Record: A Proposal to Improve the System, 289 New England Journal of Medicine 688–

691 (1973). Reprinted with permission of the New England Journal of Medicine.

Sieghart, P., et al., The Social Obligations of the Scientist, 1 Hastings Center Studies 7–16 (No. 2, 1973). Copyright © 1973 by the Institute for Society, Ethics and the Life Sciences, 360 Broadway, Hastings-on-Hudson, N.Y. 10706. Reproduced with permission of The Hastings Center.

Sinclair, Molly, How Does Society Put a Price Tag on Human Life?, The Washington Post, Sunday, March 22, 1981, at B1, col. 1. Reprinted with the permission of the Washington Post.

Singer, Peter, Animal Experimentation: Philosophical Perspectives, Volume 1, pp. 79–83. Reprinted with permission of The Free Press, a division of MacMillan, Inc., and the Kennedy Institute of Ethics, Georgetown University. From Encyclopedia of Bioethics, Warren T. Reich, Editor-in-Chief. Copyright © 1978 by Georgetown University, Washington, D.C.

Singer and Soll, Guidelines for DNA Hybrid Molecules, Science 181: 1114 (1973) (letter). Copyright © 1973 by the American Association for the Advancement of Science. Reprinted with permission of AAAS and Dr. Singer.

Slovic, Fischhoff and Lichtenstein, Facts and Fears: Understanding Perceived Risk, in Societal Risk Assessment 190–194, 205–212 (Schwing and Albers, eds. 1980). Reprinted with permission of Plenum Press Publishing Corporation.

Slovic, Fischhoff and Lichtenstein, Informing People About Risk. Reprinted from Banbury Report 6, Product Labeling and Health Risks. Louis Morris, Michael Mazis and Ivan Barofsky eds. 1983, with permission from Cold Spring Harbor Laboratory, Cold Spring Harbor, N.Y., and Paul Slovic.

Smith, R. Jeffrey, Hawaiian Milk Contamination Creates Alarm, Science 217: 137–139 (1982). Copyright © 1972 by the American Association for the Advancement of Science. Reprinted with permission of AAAS.

Snow, C.P., The Two Cultures and a Second Look 4–7, 10–11 (1964). Reprinted by permission of Cambridge University Press.

Stanford University, License Agreement. Reprinted with permission of Stanford University, Office of Technology Licensing.

Stern, Philip M., with Green, Harold P., The Oppenheimer Case: Security on Trial 179–180, 239–241, 270–279, 371, 495–496. Copyright © 1969 by Harper & Row, Publishers, Inc. Reprinted with their permission.

Stich, Stephen P., "The Recombinant DNA Debate," Philosophy and Public Affairs, Vol. 7, No. 3 (Spring 1978). Copyright © 1978 by Princeton University Press. Excerpts, pp. 193–4, 196–8, reprinted with permission of Princeton University Press.

Stinson, Robert and Peggy, On the Death of a Baby, 244 Atlantic 64 (July 1979). Copyright © 1979 by Robert and Peggy Stinson. Reprinted by permission of the Stinsons. See also *The Long Dying of Baby Andrew* (Atlantic—Little, Brown 1983) by the same authors.

Swazey, Sorenson and Wong, Risks and Benefits, Rights and Responsibilities: A History of the Recombinant DNA Research Controversy, 51 S.Cal.L.Rev. 1019, 1021–1022, 1024–1029, 1068–1074 (1978). Reprinted with the permission of the Southern California Law Review.

Talbott, Richard E., Science Court: A Possible Way to Obtain Scientific Certainty for Decisions Based on Scientific "Fact"?, 8 Environmental Law 827–833. Reprinted with permission of Environmental Law and the author.

Thomas, Lewis, Dying as Failure. Reprinted from volume no. 447 of THE ANNALS of the American Academy of Political and Social Science. Copyright © 1980 by The American Academy of Political and Social Science. All rights reserved.

Tribe, Laurence, Technology Assessment and the Fourth Discontinuity: The Limits of Instrumental Rationality, 46 S.Cal.L.Rev. 617, 648–650 (1973). Reprinted with permission of the Southern California Law Review and Laurence Tribe.

Tribe, Laurence, Ways Not to Think About Plastic Trees: New Foundations for Environmental Law. Reprinted by permission of Prof. Tribe, the Yale Law Journal Company and Fred B. Rothman & Company from The Yale Law Journal, Vol. 83, pp. 1315, 1317–1322.

Trulik, John A., The Courtroom Status of the Polygraph, 14 Akron L.Rev. 133, 134–141, 144–145 (1980). Reprinted by permission of Akron Law Review.

U.S. Bishops, Pastoral Letter on War and Peace, excerpts from The Challenge of Peace: God's Promise and Our Response, reprinted in 13 Origins 1, 9–10, 13–14, 18, 19 (May 19, 1983). Copyright © 1913 by the United States Catholic Conference, Washington, D.C. All rights reserved. Reprinted with permission.

Veatch, Robert M., A Theory of Medical Ethics 21–25 (1981). Copyright © 1981 by Robert M. Veatch. Reprinted by permission of Basic Books, Inc., Publishers.

Veatch, Robert M., What is a "Just" Health Care Delivery? Reprinted with permission from Robert M. Veatch and Roy Branson's *Ethics and Health Policy*, copyright 1976, Ballinger Publishing Company.

Wade, Nicholas, Madness in Their Method, 188 The New Republic 13 (1983). Reprinted by permission of THE NEW REPUBLIC. Copyright © 1983 by The New Republic.

Wald, George, The Case Against Genetic Engineering, The Sciences 7–8, 10–11 (September/October 1976). Reprinted with permission of the New York Academy of Sciences.

Walsh and Culliton, Office of Management and Budget: Skeptical View of Scientific Advice, edited from John Walsh, Office of Management and Budget: The View from the Executive Office, 183 *Science* 180–184 (1974); John Walsh, Office of Management and Budget: New Accent on the "M" in OMB, 183 *Science* 286–290 (1974); and Barbara J. Culliton, Office of Management and Budget: Skeptical View of Scientific Advice, 183 *Science* 392–396 (1974). Copyright © 1974 by the American Association for the Advancement of Science. Reprinted with permission of AAAS and the authors.

Walters, LeRoy, Research Involving Animals, in Contemporary Issues in Bioethics 569–570 (T. Beauchamp and L. Walters, eds. 1982). Reprinted with permission of Wadsworth Publishing Company and LeRoy Walters.

Wanzer, Sidney H., et al., The Physician's Responsibility Toward Hopelessly Ill Patients, 310 New England Journal of Medicine 955, 958–959 (1984). Reprinted with permission of the New England Journal of Medicine.

Watson, James D., Moving Toward the Clonal Man, 266 Atlantic 50 (May 1971). Copyright © 1971 by James D. Watson. Reprinted with permission of the Atlantic Monthly and James D. Watson.

Watson, James D., The Double Helix 197, 205, 217–218, 220, 222 (1968). Excerpted from *The Double Helix* by James D. Watson with the permission of Atheneum Publishers, Inc. Copyright © 1968 by James D. Watson.

Weizenbaum, Joseph, Computer Power and Human Reason: From Judgment to Calculation 207–210, 226–227 (1976). Reprinted with permission of W.H. Freeman and Company. Copyright © 1976.

Wiley and Neustadt, "Videotex" Calls For New Legal, Regulatory Thinking, Legal Times, July 6, 1981, at 11. Reprinted with permission of Legal Times.

Willrich and Taylor, Nuclear Theft: Risks and Safeguards, 20–21, 171 (1974). Reprinted with permission from Willrich and Taylor's *Nuclear Theft: Risks and Safeguards.* Copyright 1974, Ballinger Publishing Company.

World Medical Assembly, Declaration of Helsinki, 1964 (Revised 1975). Reprinted with the permission of the World Medical Assembly.

Zachary, R.B., Life With Spina Bifida, 2 British Medical Journal 1460–1462 (1977). Reprinted with permission of the British Medical Journal and R.B. Zachary.

Zelen, Marvin, A New Design for Randomized Clinical Trials, 300 New England Journal of Medicine 1242–1245 (1979). Reprinted with permission of the New England Journal of Medicine.

*

SUMMARY OF CONTENTS

*

TABLE OF CONTENTS

PART TWO. CONTROLLING SCIENCE AND MEDICINE: THE ROLES OF INDIVIDUALS, GROUPS AND THE STATE

PART THREE. ACHIEVING THE GOALS OF PUBLIC POLICY: AVOIDING HARM AND PROMOTING FAIRNESS

TABLE OF CONTENTS

PART FOUR. EXPLORING PROBLEMS AT THE FRONTIER

TABLE OF CONTENTS

TABLE OF CONTENTS

TABLE OF CASES

The principal cases are in italic type. Cases cited or discussed are in roman.
References are to Pages.

TABLE OF AUTHORITIES

Principal authorities are in italic type, others are in roman, arranged alphabetically by author or by title when no author is named. References are to Pages.

TABLE OF STATUTES AND REGULATIONS

Materials quoted are in italic type; those cited or discussed are in roman.
References are to Pages.

LAW, SCIENCE AND MEDICINE

*

Part One

THE EVOLVING RELATIONSHIP OF SCIENCE AND MEDICINE TO THE LAW

Chapter One

THE DEVELOPMENT AND IMPACT OF GENETIC ENGINEERING

In 1965 Rollin Hotchkiss coined the term "genetic engineering" to describe what has now come to encompass a wide range of techniques by which scientists can alter the genetic properties of cells. The rapidity with which this field has developed is startling; the past several decades have witnessed breathtaking developments not only in basic knowledge about genetics but also in its application.

Without understanding the scientific principles at work, human beings have used selective breeding and the like to cause genetic changes in plants and animals for many millenia. Additionally, many alterations have occurred inadvertently, including through the ordinary practice of medicine; people whose genetic disorders would in an earlier era have caused death at a young age have been helped to live to adulthood, thereby allowing genes for their disorders to be passed on. But these earlier effects on the genes of plants and animals seem slow and imprecise when compared with those being achieved today by "gene splicers."

This field thus provides a good starting point for the study of law, science and medicine. It is a field in ferment and one that draws some of the brightest minds—not only those with an interest in biology but others from physics, chemistry and mathematics—who are interested in the building blocks of life at the molecular level. The process of discovery presents concerns about immediate safety as well as the long-term effects of knowledge. And the discoveries being made are swiftly translated into practical applications, in agriculture, industry and medicine—which in turn raise issues for officials in a wide range of agencies from the local to the federal—and even international—levels.

A. DECODING THE STRUCTURE OF LIFE— AND CHANGING IT

---

1. BUILDING BLOCKS OF LIFE

The materials below trace scientific developments from Mendel's work on heredity through modern ideas in genetic engineering. These materials are not designed as a comprehensive historical report, but rather to provide an introduction to the technical aspects of recombinant DNA while demonstrating the cumulative nature of scientific progress and the excitement of the scientific endeavor.

2

CONGRESS OF THE UNITED STATES, OFFICE OF TECHNOLOGY ASSESSMENT, IMPACTS OF APPLIED GENETICS

29–35 (1981).

The major conceptual boost for the science of genetics required a shift in perspective, from the simple observation that characteristics passed from parents to offspring, to a study of the underlying agent by which this transmission is accomplished. That shift began in the garden of Gregor Mendel, an obscure monk in mid-19th century Austria. By analyzing generations of controlled crosses between sweet pea plants, Mendel was able to identify the rudimentary characteristics of what was later termed the gene.

Mendel reasoned that genes were the vehicle and repository of the hereditary mechanism, and that each inherited trait or function of an organism had a specific gene directing its development and appearance. An organism's observable characteristics, functions, and measurable properties taken together had to be based somehow on the total assemblage of its genes.

Mendel's analysis showed that the genes of his pea plants remained constant from one generation to the next, but more importantly, he found that genes and observable traits were not simply matched one-for-one. There were, in fact, two genes involved in each trait, with a single gene contributed by each parent. When the genes controlling a particular trait are identical, the organism is homozygous for that trait; if they are not, it is heterozygous.

. . .

Genes were real—Mendel's work made that clear. But where were they located and what were they? The answer, lay within the nucleus of the cell. Unfortunately, most of the contents of the nucleus were unobtainable by biologists in Mendel's time, so his published findings were ignored. Only during the last decades of the 19th century did improved microscopes and new dyes permit cells to be observed with an acuity never before possible. And only by the beginning of the 20th century did scientists *rediscover* Mendel's work and begin to appreciate fully the significance of the cell nucleus and its contents.

Even in the earliest microscopic studies, however, certain cellular components stood out; they were deeply stained by added dye. As a result, they were dubbed "colored bodies," or chromosomes. Chromosomes were seen relatively rarely in cells, with most cells showing just a central dark nucleus surrounded by an extensive light grainy cytoplasm. But periodically the nucleus seemed to disappear, leaving in its place long thready material that consolidated to form the chromosomal bodies. Once formed, the chromosomes assembled along the middle of the cell, copied themselves, and then moved apart while the cell pinched itself in half, trapping one set of chromosomes in each of the two halves. Then the chromosomes themselves seemed to dissolve as two new nuclei appeared, one in each of the two newly formed cells.

Thus, the same number of chromosomes appeared in precisely the same form in every cell of an organism except the germ, or sex, cells. Furthermore, the chromosomes not only remained constant in form and number from one generation to the next, but were inherited in pairs.

They were, in short, manifesting all the traits that Mendel had prescribed
for genes almost three decades earlier. By the beginning of the 20th century, it was clear that chromosomes were of central importance to the life
history of the cell, acting in some unspecified manner as the vehicle for
the Mendelian gene.

. . .

With all this research, nobody yet knew what the gene was made of.
The first evidence that it consisted of deoxyribonucleic acid (DNA)
emerged from the work of Oswald Avery, Colin MacLeod, and Maclyn
McCarty at the Rockefeller Institute in New York in the early 1940's.
. . .

. . .

It had been in 1868, just 3 years after Mendel had published his findings, that DNA was discovered by Friedrich Miescher. It is an extremely
simple molecule composed of a small sugar molecule, a phosphate group
(a phosphorous atom surrounded by four oxygen atoms), and four kinds
of simple organic chemicals known as nitrogenous (nitrogen-containing)
bases. Together, one sugar, one phosphate, and one base form a nucleotide—the basic structural unit of the large DNA molecule. Because it is
so simple, DNA had appeared to be little more than a monotonous con-
glomeration of simple nucleotides to scientists in the early 20th century.
It seemed unlikely that such a prosaic molecule could direct the appearance of genetic traits while faithfully reproducing itself so that information could be transferred between generations. Although Avery's results
seemed clear enough, many were reluctant to accept them.

Those doubts were finally laid to rest in a brief report published in
1953 by James Watson and Francis Crick. By using X-ray crystallograph-
ic techniques and building complex models—and without ever having actually seen the molecule itself—Watson and Crick reported that they had
discovered a consistent scientifically sound structure for DNA.

The structure that Crick and Watson uncovered solved part of the genetic puzzle. According to them, the phosphates and sugars formed two
long chains, or backbones, with one nitrogenous base attached to each
sugar. The two backbones were held together like the supports of a ladder by weak attractions between the bases protruding from the sugar molecules. Of the four different nitrogenous bases—adenine, thymine, guanine, and cytosine—attractions existed only between adenine(A) and
thymine(T), and between guanine(G) and cytosine(C). Thus, if a stretch
of nucleotides on one backbone ran:

A–T–G–C–T–T–A–A. . . .

the other backbone had to contain the directly opposite complementary
sequence:

T–A–C–G–A–A–T–T . . .

The complementary pairing between bases running down the center of
the long molecule was responsible for holding together the two otherwise
independent chains. Thus, the DNA molecule was rather like a zipper,
with the bases as the teeth and the sugar-phosphate chains as the strands
of cloth to which each zipper half was sewn. Crick and Watson also
found that in the presence of water, the two polynucleotide chains did not
stretch out to full length, but twisted around each other, forming what
has undoubtedly become the most glorified structure in the history of biology—the double helix.

Figure 9.—Replication of DNA

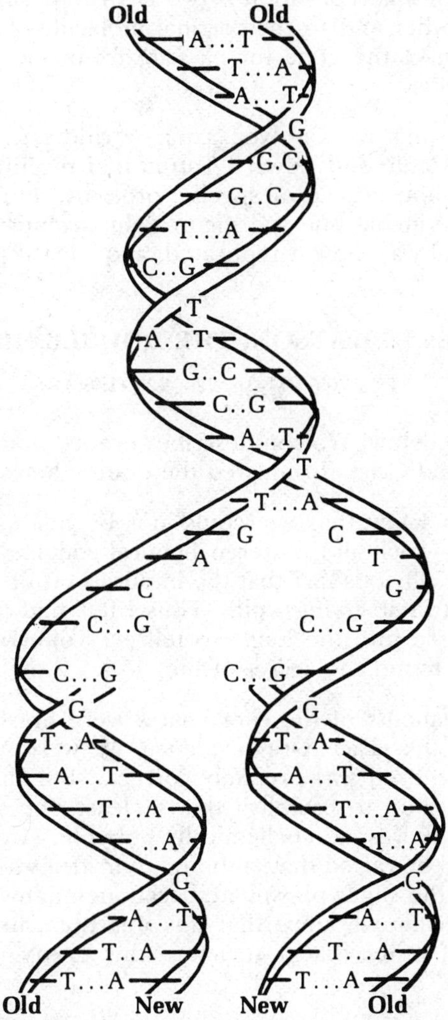

Old   Old

A...T
T...A
A...T
G
G.C
G..C
T...A
C..G
T
A...T
G..C
C..G
A..T
T
T...A
G   C
A   T
C   G
C...G C...G
C...G C...G
G   G
T..A   T..A
A...T A...T
T...A T...A
..A   T..A
G   G
A...T A...T
T..A   T...A
T...A T...A

Old   New   New   Old

When DNA replicates, the original strands unwind and serve as templates for the building of new complementary strands. The daughter molecules are exact copies of the parent, with each having one of the parent strands.

Source: Office of Technology Assessment.

The structure was scientifically elegant. But it was received enthusiastically also because it implied how DNA worked. As Crick and Watson themselves noted:

If the actual order of the bases on one of the pair of chains were given, one could write down the exact order of the bases on the other one, because of the specific pairing. Thus one chain is, as it were, the complement of the other, and it is this feature which suggests how the deoxyribonucleic acid molecule might duplicate itself.

When a double-stranded DNA molecule is unzipped, it consists of two separate nucleotide chains, each with a long stretch of unpaired bases. In the presence of a mixture of nucleotides, each base attracts its complementary match in accordance with the inherent affinities of adenine for thymine, thymine for adenine, guanine for cytosine, and cytosine for guanine. The result of this replication is two DNA molecules, both precisely identical to each other and to the original molecule—which explains the faithful duplication of the gene for passage from one generation to the next. (See figure 9.)

Crick and Watson's work solved a major riddle in genetic research. Because George Beadle and Edward Tatum had recently discovered that genes control the appearance of specific proteins, and that one gene is responsible for producing one specific protein, scientists now knew what the genetic material was, how it replicated, and what it produced.   .   .   .

JAMES D. WATSON, THE DOUBLE HELIX

197, 205, 217–18, 220, 222 (1968).

[In the passage below, Watson describes events immediately following the day when he and Crick formulated the double helix model for DNA.]

However, we both knew that we would not be home until a complete model was built in which all the stereochemical contacts were satisfactory. There was also the obvious fact that the implications of its existence were far too important to risk crying wolf. Thus I felt slightly queasy when at lunch Francis winged into the Eagle to tell everyone within hearing distance that we had found the secret of life.   .   .   .

The final refinements of the coordinates were finished the following evening. Lacking the exact X-ray evidence, we were not confident that the configuration chosen was precisely correct. But this did not bother us, for we only wished to establish that at least one specific two-chain complementary helix was stereochemically possible. Until this was clear, the objection could be raised that, although our idea was aesthetically elegant, the shape of the sugar-phosphate backbone might not permit its existence. Happily, now we knew that this was not true, and so we had lunch, telling each other that a structure this pretty just had to exist. .   .   .

[Watson and Crick were well aware that while they had been at work, Linus Pauling had also been attempting to determine the structure of DNA.]

Pauling first heard about the double helix from Delbrück. At the bottom of the letter that broke the news of the complementary chains, I had asked that he not tell Linus. I was still slightly afraid something would go wrong and did not want Pauling to think about hydrogen-bonded base pairs until we had a few more days to digest our position. My request, however, was ignored. Delbrück wanted to tell everyone in his lab and knew that within hours the gossip would travel from his lab in biology to their friends working under Linus. Also, Pauling had made him promise to let him know the minute he heard from me. Then there was the even more important consideration that Delbrück hated any form of secrecy in scientific matters and did not want to keep Pauling in suspense any longer.

Pauling's reaction was one of genuine thrill, as was Delbrück's. In almost any other situation Pauling would have fought for the good points of his idea. The overwhelming biological merits of a self-complementary DNA molecule made him effectively concede the race. . . .

The final version was ready to be typed on the last weekend of March. Our Cavendish typist was not on hand, and the brief job was given to my sister. There was no problem persuading her to spend a Saturday afternoon this way, for we told her that she was participating in perhaps the most famous event in biology since Darwin's book. . . .

NOTE

The editor of the journal Nature had the following observations on the thirtieth anniversary of the publication of Watson and Crick's discovery:

> . . . Rarely can there have been an occasion when the effect of a discovery has been to provide so quickly a persuasive answer to a question in the forefront of many people's minds: what is the genetic material, and how does it work?

> Newton's theory of gravitation was a welcome surprise to some of his contemporaries, but a matter of indifference to most of them. Darwin's evolution, widely recognized as important, had to be rammed down the throats of many of his contemporaries. The significance of Planck's quantum went unrecognized (even by Planck). Einstein's special relativity, even with its echoes of earlier work by Lorentz and Poincaré, made sense to some people but nonsense to others. Even the development of the quantum theory in 1925 and 1926, which predicated the most radical revision of the conception of physical reality (not yet complete) but which also made possible what now passes for physical science (not to mention the electronics industry), was blunted, at the time, by confusion—Schrödinger's sneaking hope that wave mechanics would reconcile the inconsistencies of classical mechanics, the lack of a language (whose grammar Dirac provided), conceptual disputes (which persist) and sheer complexity.

> The effect of the publication of the correct structure for DNA was much more immediate. If major discoveries are keys to locked doors, this key has been quickly fitted to its lock and the door has swung open on well-lubricated hinges. Much of the pleasureable excitement of the past thirty years has been the way in which simple expectations of nature have been repeatedly confirmed. . . .

Maddox, Good Cause for Celebration, 305 Nature 177 (1983). To place the discovery of the structure of DNA into the context of scientific development, see the excerpts from Thomas Kuhn's Structure of Scientific Revolutions, in Sec. C.2, infra.

PRESIDENT'S COMMISSION FOR THE STUDY OF ETHICAL PROBLEMS IN MEDICINE AND BIOMEDICAL AND BEHAVIORAL RESEARCH, SPLICING LIFE

29–36 (1982).

Not all the DNA in chromosomes seems to have a function. The portions with the coded instructions to the cell to perform a particular function (usually to manufacture one particular protein) are called genes. Within the gene are the actual coding regions (called exons), between which are DNA sequences called introns. Genetic information is transferred from the DNA in the nucleus to the cytoplasm by RNA (ribonucleic acid), which is a copy of one strand of the DNA. During this transfer, the introns are spliced out of the RNA. The resulting RNA messengers pass through the cell's protein-synthesizing machinery (called ribosomes), like a punched tape running through a computer to direct a machine's operation.

Proteins—the hormones, enzymes, connecting material, and so forth that give cells and organisms their characteristics—are made up of amino acids. The information carried by the RNA determines how the amino acids combine to make specific proteins. There are 20 amino acids, each one determined by a specific combination of three of the nucleotide "letters" into a "codon." On average, each gene contains slightly more than 300 codons.

Although all cells in an organism carry basically the same genetic material in their nuclei, the specialized nature of each cell derives from the fact that only a small portion of this genetic material (about 5–10%) is active in any cell. In the process of developing from a fertilized egg, each type of cell switches on certain genes and switches off all the others. When "liver genes" are active, for example, a cell behaves as a liver cell because the genes are directing the cytoplasm to make the products that allow the cell to perform a liver's functions, which would not be possible unless all the genes irrelevant to a liver cell, such as "muscle genes," were turned off.

Accidents and Diseases. Occasionally—perhaps because of an error that occurs for some unexplained reason when the cell replicates or because of an outside influence such as a virus or radiation—the specific sequence in a DNA molecule is altered by a change of one or more nucleotides. Such a change is called a mutation. If a mutation occurs in a gene that is active in that cell, the cell will produce a variant protein, as will its daughter cells since they will inherit the same mutation. If other cells of the same type continue to perform their functions properly, the existence of a small amount of variant protein will usually have no adverse effects on the individual. Some mutations, however, are very harmful; for example, a defective protein can be lethal, or a malignant tumor can result from a mutation that alters a gene in a single somatic cell.

Mutations that occur in somatic cells only affect the progeny of that mutant cell, so that the effects of such mutations are restricted to the individual in whom they occur. In the germ cells, however, mutations result in the altered DNA being transmitted to all cells—somatic and germinal—of an offspring. Inherited mutations that result in deleterious effects are termed genetic diseases. Even though an inherited mutation is present in the DNA sequence of all the body cells, it only affects the function of those specialized cells that manufacture the defective product. For example, a mutation in the gene for rhodopsin (a protein necessary for vision) may result in color blindness, but since the gene is only active in cells in the eye it has no other known effects on a color-blind individual.

THE TECHNOLOGY OF GENE SPLICING

Gene splicing techniques have been understood by scientists for only a decade. During that time, they have been used primarily in microorganisms. Though experiments with higher animals indicated the possibility of using gene splicing for human therapy and diagnosis, numerous hurdles had to be crossed before such steps could be taken. . . .

Recombinant DNA Techniques. It was once thought that genetic material was very fixed in its location. Recent findings demonstrate that genetic recombination (the breaking and relinking of different pieces of DNA) is more common between and within organisms—from viruses and bacteria to human beings—than scientists realized. In fact, genetic exchange is a mechanism that may, in evolutionary terms, account for the appearance of marked variations among individuals in a given species.

If DNA replication were the only mechanism for the transfer of genetic information, except for rare instances of mutation each bacterium would always produce an exact copy. In fact, three general mechanisms of genetic exchange occur commonly in bacteria. The first, termed transduction, occurs when the genetic material of a bacteriophage (a virus that infects bacteria) enters a bacterium and replicates; during this process some of the host cell's DNA may be incorporated into the virus, which carries this DNA along when it infects the next bacterium, into whose DNA the new material is sometimes then incorporated.

In a second process, called conjugation, bacterial DNA is transferred directly from one microorganism to another. Some bacteria possess plasmids, small loops of DNA separate from their own chromosome, that give the bacteria the ability to inject some of their DNA directly into another bacterium. And third, bacterial cells can also pick up bits of DNA from the surrounding environment; this is called transformation.

These mechanisms—naturally occurring forms of gene splicing—permit the exchange of genetic material among bacteria, which can have marked effects on the bacteria's survival. The rapid spreading of resistance to antibiotics, such as the penicillin-resistance in gonorrhea bacteria and in *Hemophilus influenzae* (the most frequent cause of children's bacterial meningitis), documents the occurrence of genetic transfers as well as their benefit, from a bacterial standpoint.

The basic processes underlying genetic engineering are thus "natural" and not revolutionary. Indeed, it was the discovery that these processes were occurring that suggested to scientists the great possibilities and basic methods of gene splicing. What is new, however, is the ability of scientists to control the processes. Before the advent of this new technology, genetic exchanges were more or less random and occurred usually within the same species; now it is possible to hook together DNA from different species in a fashion designed by human beings.

The key to human manipulation of DNA came with the discovery, in the early 1970s, of restriction enzymes.[7] Each restriction enzyme, of which about 150 have so far been identified, makes it possible to cut DNA at the point where a particular nucleotide sequence occurs. The breaks, which are termed "nicks," occur in a staggered fashion on the two DNA strands rather than directly opposite each other. Once cut in this fashion, a DNA strand has "sticky ends"; the exposed ends are ready to "stick" to another fragment that has been cut by the same restriction enzyme (see Figure 5). Once the pieces are "annealed" and any remaining gaps are ligated, the "recombinant DNA" strand will be reproduced when the DNA replicates.

---

7. These enzymes, which make it possible to cut DNA at predetermined places, exist as part of the defense system that bacteria use to respond to foreign DNA (from a virus, for example). Restriction enzymes cut the DNA of the invader into small pieces, while another substance protects the bacteria's own DNA from getting sliced.

Figure 5: Creation of "Sticky Ends" by a Restriction Enzyme

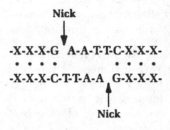

One restriction enzyme produced by *E. coli*, named Eco RI, recognizes the DNA sequence -G-A-A-T-T-C- on one strand and -C-T-T-A-A-G- on the other. It does not cut clearly across the two strands, however, but between the G and A on both strands, leaving each with exposed bases that can stick to another DNA strand that has been cut in the same fashion and also has an exposed -A-A-T-T- sequence.

Recombinant DNA studies have been performed primarily in laboratory strains of the bacterium *Escherichia coli*, which is normally present in the human intestine. This bacterium possesses only one small chromosome, but it may also contain several ring-shaped plasmids. Plasmids turn out to be useful vehicles (or vectors) by which a foreign gene can be introduced into the bacterium. A plasmid can be broken open with restriction enzymes, and DNA from another organism (for example, the gene for human insulin) can then be spliced into the plasmid (see Figure 6). After being resealed into a circle, the hybrid plasmid can then be transferred back into the bacterium, which will carry out the instructions of the inserted DNA (in this case, to produce human insulin) as if it were the cell's own DNA. In addition, since plasmids contain genes for their own replication independent of bacterial DNA replication, many copies of the hybrid plasmid will be present in each *E. coli* cell. The end result is a culture of *E. coli* containing many copies of the original insulin gene and capable of producing large amounts of insulin.

The process of isolating or selecting for a particular gene is commonly called cloning a gene. A clone is a group all of whose members are identical. Theoretically, this technology allows any gene from any species to be cloned, but at least two major steps must be taken to make use of this technology. First, it is quite easy to break apart the DNA of higher organisms and insert fragments randomly into plasmids—a so-called shotgun experiment—but identifying the genes on these randomly cloned pieces or selecting only those recombinant molecules containing a specific gene is much more difficult. Because scientists do not yet fully understand what controls gene regulation, inducing expression of the inserted genes has been a second major hurdle. Recently, scientists have been successful in getting a recombinant gene to function in multicell animals and, with the discovery of what are termed transposable elements, even in correcting a defect in some fruit flies' genes. This development serves as a reminder that many technical barriers that loom large are rapidly overcome. Of course, new knowledge sometimes also reveals further, unanticipated technical difficulties to be overcome.

Figure 6: Splicing Human Gene into Plasmid

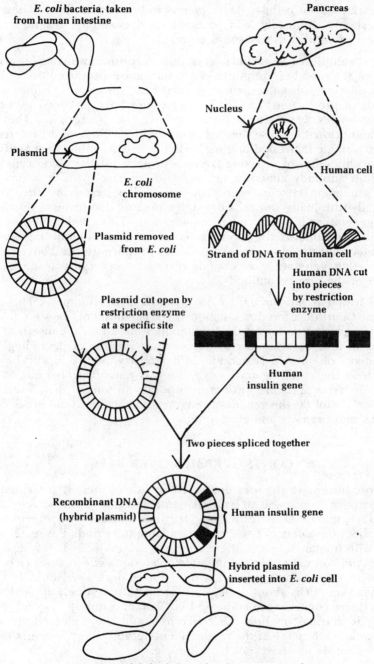

E. coli bacteria, taken
from human intestine

Pancreas

Nucleus

Plasmid →

Human cell

E. coli
chromosome

Plasmid removed
from *E. coli*

Strand of DNA from human cell

Human DNA cut
into pieces
by restriction
enzyme

Plasmid cut open by
restriction enzyme
at a specific site

Human
insulin gene

Two pieces spliced together

Recombinant DNA
(hybrid plasmid)

Human insulin gene

Hybrid plasmid
inserted into *E. coli* cell

Bacteria with hybrid plasmid replicate, creating clone
capable of producing insulin

Source: President's Commission.

Cell Fusion. Cutting apart DNA chains is not the only way that scientists can transfer genetic material from one cell to another. Cell fusion, which involves the breaking down of cell membranes and the merging of two different types of cells, can also be regarded as a form of genetic engineering although it does not involve direct manipulation of DNA segments. It is being vigorously explored by biomedical scientists who are attempting to map the specific location of human genes on chromosomes and to learn about cellular development and differentiation. These advances should ultimately lead to better understanding, diagnosis, and treatment of various diseases and cancers.

For example, researchers can now produce what are termed monoclonal antibodies. Antibodies are substances produced by the body to fight foreign substances, such as microbial "invaders." Unlike other methods of production, cell fusion techniques have provided especially pure antibodies against a particular invader (or "antigen"). They are called monoclonal because they are produced by a clone of cells descended from a single fabricated original. First, scientists stimulate a mouse to produce antibodies by injecting it with a protein. White blood cells containing an antibody aimed at fighting the "disease" (which is how the mouse's immune system regards the injected proteins) are then fused chemically with malignant cells through a process that involves dissolving and regenerating the cells' outer membranes. This combination—called a hybridoma—inherits the cancer cells' ability to proliferate rapidly and indefinitely and the blood cells' capacity to produce the antibody. Scientists can thus generate a huge clone of cells, which can provide a large amount of the desired antibody.

Cell fusion is not limited to the creation of hybridomas. The 1980 Supreme Court decision that sanctioned the patenting of "new life forms" did not involve recombinant DNA techniques but rather the insertion into bacteria of four naturally occurring plasmids capable of degrading four components of oil [see Diamond v. Chakrabarty, Sec. B.5, infra]. The Court held the resulting microorganism was patentable because it was new (as bacteria in nature did not incorporate all four of the plasmids at once) and useful (as the genetically engineered bacteria could break down oil spills more rapidly and efficiently).

2. CONTROVERSIES OVER SAFETY

Before turning to the uses that may be made of these new techniques, it is necessary to examine an issue that emerged early in the development of the recombinant DNA technique. It is not unusual for concerns to be raised about the safety of research once a laboratory finding is ready to be tested with human subjects (these concerns are addressed in Chapter 6, infra). And concerns over the possibly deleterious effects on society and particularly on the environment are often raised once a scientific development has been, or is about to be, transformed into a widely applied technology (these concerns are addressed in Chapter 5, infra). Genetic engineering is unusual because the concerns about the wider effects were voiced at an early stage of the research and because they were first raised by the scientists involved, not by laypeople.

The public expression of the scientists' doubts about the "biosafety" of some gene splicing led both to a temporary moratorium on certain research and to means (an international meeting, official and unofficial committees, etc.) of replacing the moratorium with rules and procedures for safety. The materials that follow raise several questions: Why did "whistleblowers" appear, and what motivated them? Was the method used the best one at society's disposal to control a possibly dangerous area of scientific exploration, and if not, what means would have been preferable?

JUDITH P. SWAZEY, JAMES R. SORENSON AND CYNTHIA B. WONG, RISKS AND BENEFITS, RIGHTS AND RESPONSIBILITIES: A HISTORY OF THE RE-COMBINANT DNA RESEARCH CONTROVERSY

51 S.Cal.L.Rev. 1019, 1021–22 (1978).

The chain of events that led to the rDNA moratorium in 1974 begins in 1971, when Stanford researcher Paul Berg develops a prototype recombinant method by which he plans to join DNA from SV40 tumor virus with DNA from phage lambda bacterial virus and insert the combination into *Escherichia coli (E. coli)*. At a Cold Spring Harbor course on tumor viruses in the summer of 1971, Berg's proposed experiment is described by one of his graduate students, Janet Mertz, to cancer researcher Robert Pollack who later describes his reaction on hearing about Berg's plan:

> I had a fit. SV40 is a small animal tumor virus; in tissue cultures in the lab, SV40 also transforms individual *human* cells, making them look very like tumor cells. And bacteriophage lambda just naturally lives in *E. coli*, and *E. coli* just naturally lives in people. [Mertz] seemed to see it as a neat academic exercise. And I said, of all stupid things, at least put it into a phage, then, that doesn't grow in a bug that grows in your gut! Because what if the combination escapes from the lab: then you have SV40 replicating in step with the *E. coli* and a constant exposure of the cells in your gut to the DNA of SV40. Which is a route in for the virus that never occurs in nature and therefore something you might not be prepared to fend off.

Pollack acts on his concerns by calling Paul Berg who, in turn, begins to consider the possible implications of his proposed experiment and learns that his Stanford colleagues are also uneasy about the SV40 recombination. Berg also shares his growing doubts about the possible risks of the experiment, and what he sees as attendant ethical issues, with other associates who will figure prominently in the rDNA controversy. These include a young Massachusetts Institute of Technology (MIT) specialist in rDNA viruses, David Baltimore, NIH nucleic acid researcher Maxine Singer, and her husband Daniel, a Washington lawyer and active member of the Institute for Society, Ethics and the Life Sciences. After several months of personal soul searching and discussion, Berg decides to defer his experiment: in effect, the first moratorium on rDNA research has quietly taken place.

When Berg tells Robert Pollack of his decision, some 6 months after Pollack's call to Berg, the Stanford scientist asks Pollack to help him organize a small meeting on biohazards in tumor virus research. Pollack readily agrees because he feels that the risks of the research and the often lax safety standards in laboratories pose a " 'pre-Hiroshima condition—It would be a real disaster if one of the agents now being handled in research should in fact be a real human cancer agent.' " Subsequently, and prophetically, some 100 researchers meet at the Asilomar Conference Center in January 1973 to discuss biohazards in biological research.

By the time of "Asilomar I," the complex techniques that Berg had planned to use in 1971 to form the SV40-phage lambda hybrid have been superseded by a rapid series of independent discoveries that, in concert, yield an elegantly simple method of producing DNA recombinants. Two of the critical developments are the discovery of restriction enzymes by H.W. Boyer and his colleagues at the University of California, San Francisco, and the discovery by Stanley Cohen, of Stanford, that the bits of extrachromosomal DNA called plasmids are ideal vehicles for carrying an rDNA molecule into a functional bacterial cell.

The first experiments by the Stanford and San Francisco researchers involve the use of an *E. coli* plasmid, pSC101. At the outset of these experiments, Cohen and his colleagues recognize the potential risks of their new technique, as had Pollack and then Berg with the proposed SV40 experiment.

Cohen and his Stanford associate, A.C.Y. Chang, are concerned enough to decide to exercise some control over the use of pSC101 by asking researchers who request the plasmid to confine its use to certain types of presumptively low-risk experiments. As Cohen and Chang know, their decision is one that violates a major norm of scientific research. "Investigators normally facilitate the free exchange of bacteria and other experimental strains they have isolated or developed," Cohen later writes, "but Chang and I were concerned that manipulation of certain genes could give rise to novel organisms whose infectious properties and ecological effects could not be predicted."

MAXINE SINGER AND DIETER SÖLL, GUIDELINES FOR DNA HYBRID MOLECULES

181 Science 1114 (1973) (letter).

Those in attendance at the 1973 Gordon Conference on Nucleic Acids voted to send the following letter to Philip Handler, president of the National Academy of Sciences, and to John R. Hogness, president of the National Institute of Medicine. A majority also desired to publicize the letter more widely.

We are writing to you, on behalf of a number of scientists, to communicate a matter of deep concern. Several of the scientific reports presented at this year's Gordon Research Conference on Nucleic Acids (June 11–15, 1973, New Hampton, New Hampshire) indicated that we presently have the technical ability to join together, covalently, DNA molecules from diverse sources. Scientific developments over the past two years make it both reasonable and convenient to generate overlapping sequence homologies at the termini of different DNA molecules. The sequence homologies can then be used to combine the molecules by Watson-Crick hydrogen bonding. Application of existing methods permits subsequent covalent linkage of such molecules. This technique could be used, for example, to combine DNA from animal viruses with bacterial DNA, or DNA's of different viral origin might be so joined. In this way new kinds of hybrid plasmids or viruses, with biological activity of unpredictable nature, may eventually be created. These experiments offer exciting and interesting potential both for advancing knowledge of fundamental biological processes and for alleviation of human health problems.

Certain such hybrid molecules may prove hazardous to laboratory workers and to the public. Although no hazard has yet been established, prudence suggests that the potential hazard be seriously considered.

A majority of those attending the Conference voted to communicate their concern in this matter to you and to the President of the Institute of

Medicine (to whom this letter is also being sent). The conferees suggested that the Academies establish a study committee to consider this problem and to recommend specific actions or guidelines, should that seem appropriate. Related problems such as the risks involved in current large-scale preparation of animal viruses might also be considered.

NATIONAL ACADEMY OF SCIENCES—NATIONAL RESEARCH COUNCIL, COMMITTEE ON RECOMBINANT DNA MOLE-CULES,* POTENTIAL BIOHAZARDS OF RECOMBINANT DNA MOLECULES

185 Science 303 (1974) (letter).

Recent advances in techniques for the isolation and rejoining of segments of DNA now permit construction of biologically active recombinant DNA molecules in vitro. . . .

Several groups of scientists are now planning to use this technology to create recombinant DNA's from a variety of other viral, animal, and bacterial sources. Although such experiments are likely to facilitate the solution of important theoretical and practical biological problems, they would also result in the creation of novel types of infectious DNA elements whose biological properties cannot be completely predicted in advance.

There is serious concern that some of these artificial recombinant DNA molecules could prove biologically hazardous. One potential hazard in current experients derives from the need to use a bacterium like *E. coli* to clone the recombinant DNA molecules and to amplify their number. Strains of *E. coli* commonly reside in the human intestinal tract, and they are capable of exchanging genetic information with other types of bacteria, some of which are pathogenic to man. Thus, new DNA elements introduced into *E. coli* might possibly become widely disseminated among human, bacterial, plant, or animal populations with unpredictable effects.

Concern for these emerging capabilities was raised by scientists attending the 1973 Gordon Research Conference on Nucleic Acids, who requested that the National Academy of Sciences give consideration to these matters. The undersigned members of a committee, acting on behalf of and with the endorsement of the Assembly of Life Sciences of the National Research Council on this matter, propose the following recommendations.

First, and most important, that until the potential hazards of such recombinant DNA molecules have been better evaluated or until adequate methods are developed for preventing their spread, scientists throughout the world join with the members of this committe in voluntarily deferring the following types of experiments.

• *Type 1:* Construction of new, autonomously replicating bacterial plasmids that might result in the introduction of genetic determinants for antibiotic resistance or bacterial toxin formation into bacterial strains that

---

* The signatories of this letter included Paul Berg, *chairman,* and David Baltimore, Daniel Nathans, Richard Roblin, James D. Watson, Sherman Weissman, and Norton Zinder, who met at the request of the NAS in April 1974 to formulate a response, and four other scientists active in recombinant research, Herbert W. Boyer, Stanley N. Cohen, Ronald W. Davis, and David S. Hogness, who were asked to join in the appeal for the moratorium and international meeting. [Eds.]

do not at present carry such determinants; or construction of new bacterial plasmids containing combinations of resistance to clinically useful antibiotics unless plasmids containing such combinations of antibiotic resistance determinants already exist in nature.

• *Type 2:* Linkage of all or segments of the DNA's from oncogenic or other animal viruses to autonomously replicating DNA elements such as bacterial plasmids or other viral DNA's. Such recombinant DNA molecules might be more easily disseminated to bacterial populations in humans and other species, and thus possibly increase the incidence of cancer or other diseases.

Second, plans to link fragments of animal DNA's to bacterial plasmid DNA or bacteriophage DNA should be carefully weighed in light of the fact that many types of animal cell DNA's contain sequences common to RNA tumor viruses. Since joining of any foreign DNA to a DNA replication system creates new recombinant DNA molecules whose biological properties cannot be predicted with certainty, such experiments should not be undertaken lightly.

Third, the director of the National Institutes of Health is requested to give immediate consideration to establishing an advisory committee charged with (i) overseeing an experimental program to evaluate the potential biological and ecological hazards of the above types of recombinant DNA molecules; (ii) developing procedures which will minimize the spread of such molecules within human and other populations; and (iii) devising guidelines to be followed by investigators working with potentially hazardous recombinant DNA molecules.

Fourth, an international meeting of involved scientists from all over the world should be convened early in the coming year to review scientific progress in this area and to further discuss appropriate ways to deal with the potential biohazards of recombinant DNA molecules.

The above recommendations are made with the realization (i) that our concern is based on judgments of potential rather than demonstrated risk since there are few available experimental data on the hazards of such DNA molecules and (ii) that adherence to our major recommendations will entail postponement or possibly abandonment of certain types of scientifically worthwhile experiments. Moreover, we are aware of many theoretical and practical difficulties involved in evaluating the human hazards of such recombinant DNA molecules. Nonetheless, our concern for the possible unfortunate consequences of indiscriminate application of these techniques motivates us to urge all scientists working in this area to join us in agreeing not to initiate experiments of types 1 and 2 above until attempts have been made to evaluate the hazards and some resolution of the outstanding questions has been achieved.

JUDITH P. SWAZEY, JAMES R. SORENSON AND CYNTHIA B. WONG, RISKS AND BENEFITS, RIGHTS AND RESPONSIBILITIES: A HISTORY OF THE RECOMBINANT DNA RESEARCH CONTROVERSY

51 S.Cal.L.Rev. 1019, 1024–29 (1978).

Berg, Baltimore, and Roblin hold a press conference [on July 18, 1974] at the NAS headquarters in Washington prior to the publication of their committee's unprecedented call for the rDNA research moratorium.

Explaining to the press why his committee has decided on a moratorium, Berg states:

> We've taken this route because we feel that the scientific community should be given a chance to regulate itself in its movement in the future. . . . I think most scientists agree very readily that the hazard is there and would like to see the hazard removed in some way, either by showing that . . . it's just a potential . . . or that we change the technology [for this kind of research] in a way that avoids it.

Asked whether the concern about biohazards is like that faced by atomic scientists during World War II, Roblin replies, "In a way, though this situation has been somewhat harder to deal with than that because . . . many of the biohazards . . . are still only potential." Adds David Baltimore:

> [A]lthough our dilemma . . . may differ from that of the atomic scientists in many details . . ., we all grew up with a question of the correctness of using the atomic bomb as one of the great moral dilemmas of the second part of the twentieth century. And I don't think that any of us are untouched by that . . . . I think you can see . . . a direct line of thinking.

. . .

The word moratorium is derived from the Latin *moratorius,* "serving to delay," and is defined in the *Oxford English Dictionary* as "a legal authorization to a debtor to postpone payment for a certain time." As it applies to research, and as the Berg letter made clear, a moratorium is the temporary cessation, or, in some cases, marked slowdown, in the use of a technique, procedure, or experiment, rather than a permanent abandonment.

To our knowledge, the 1974 moratorium on certain types of DNA experiments was a rare, perhaps unique, event in the history of basic science research. One somewhat comparable action was contemplated in 1939 by a group of atomic scientists, who discussed keeping a veil of secrecy around research pertaining to nuclear chain reactions, an action that would have dramatically slowed progress in that area of basic research. The scientists, however, recognized that such secrecy and implied moratorium ran counter to strongly held norms and traditions of scientific research, and the plan was abandoned fairly quickly. Those norms and traditions include the interrelated beliefs that the ability to carry out basic research in an unrestricted manner is one basis of successful science, that scientists have a societally given right to free inquiry, and that the goals and conduct of basic research are and ought to be developed almost wholly within the scientific community.

. . .

. . . The first moratorium, called by Paul Berg in 1971 on his proposed SV40 experiment, was generated initially by external pressures—the concerns of Pollack's and Berg's colleagues about the possible short- and long-term biohazards of the research. While Berg's moratorium was informally declared and pertained only to his own work, it had a wider effect. Both because of Berg's status and because of the complex experimental techniques involved, " 'the people who had initially opposed it, said, good, great, nobody else is going to do it if you're not going to do it.' "

A second, partial moratorium was effected in 1973 by the decision of Cohen and Chang to control informally distribution of their pSC101 plasmid to any researcher who requested it, and to exercise informal controls based on their assessment of the potential hazards of proposed experiments.

. . . The subsequent decision of Berg's NAS committee at their April 1974 MIT meeting to call for a worldwide moratorium on certain types of rDNA research was a decision initiated and developed by the scientists themselves, out of concern for the as-yet-unassessed but potentially hazardous consequences of their research. The moratorium itself was formally sanctioned by the NAS and announced publicly via a press conference and a letter in two of the world's major science journals, *Science* and *Nature.*

As far as is known, the moratorium was observed internationally during the 7 months between July 1974 and the February 1975 conference scheduled by the Berg committee. Given the strong counterpressures to halting a given line of scientific research, particularly one with the newness, excitement, and promise of high yields represented by rDNA techniques, the moratorium was indeed a rare event. The moratorium's observance owed much to the Berg letter signatories' high prestige within the international scientific community of rDNA researchers and to the real and symbolic institutional authority of the NAS in the United States and of the Medical Research Council [MRC] in Great Britain, which formally instructed its scientists to comply with the moratorium recommendations. . . .

NOTES

1. The action of the MRC in Great Britain, in virtually declaring illegal all the experiments covered by the Berg letter, may have occurred because British scientists were just then recovering from the shock of the first civilian biohazard casualties in the West: a young technician who worked across the hall from a laboratory at the London School of Hygiene and Tropical Medicine where research was conducted on the smallpox virus became infected and was hospitalized; before the technician's disease was correctly diagnosed, the virus had spread to her hospital roommate's son and daughter-in-law, who died of virulent forms of the disease.

2. Although much concern was expressed with how liability would be determined if something went wrong, the law's other (and perhaps more important concern) is prevention of harm. The question whenever risky human behavior is involved, as Professor Roger B. Dworkin of Indiana University School of Law has observed, is "how can we prevent things from going wrong in the first place, and how great a set of risks are we willing to run in exchange for what and how certain a group of benefits?"

Recombinant DNA research poses liability and compensation issues that differ from conventional ones only in magnitude. Standard theories can easily be applied to assign liability for injuries caused by accidents arising out of recombinant DNA work. The size of the potentially injured populace is so great, however, that adequate compensation becomes a major problem, perhaps so major it transforms a difference in size into a difference in kind. . . .

Conduct control may be attempted in a variety of ways, each of which will reflect both substantive and institutional choices. Substantive choices include decisions about whether some or all recombinant DNA procedures ought to be prohibited, discouraged, treated neutrally, encouraged, or required; which activities to place into each category; and in the middle ranges of the continuum how vigorous the encouragement or discouragement should be. Other substantive choices include decisions about the degree of safety to require (risk to tolerate); uses of recombinant DNA procedures to be prohibited, required, etc. (e.g., production of insulin, "gene therapy"); and who is to receive the benefits of the technique (only "the public," private developers, etc.). . . .

Dworkin, Biocatastrophe and the Law, in The Recombinant DNA Debate 225–226 (Jackson & Stitch, eds. 1979).

3. How ought a moratorium to be enforced? Suppose that an attorney who represents a leading scientific journal is informed that the editors plan to refuse to publish the results of any research carried out in violation of the recombinant DNA moratorium. What advice should the attorney give to the editors? Does it make any difference if the editors are acting pursuant to an agreement among the editors of all the reputable scientific journals in the field? By what procedures would the editors ensure that their sanction was being applied fairly? What good or bad results are likely to flow from such an editorial decision?

GEORGE WALD,*
THE CASE AGAINST GENETIC ENGINEERING

16 The Sciences 7–8, 10–11 (Sept./Oct. 1976).

Recombinant DNA technology faces our society with problems unprecedented not only in the history of science, but of life on the Earth. It places in human hands the capacity to redesign living organisms, the products of some three billion years of evolution.

Such intervention must not be confused with previous intrusions upon the natural order of living organisms; animal and plant breeding, for example; or the artificial induction of mutations, as with X-rays. All such earlier procedures worked within single or closely related species. The nub of the new technology is to move genes back and forth, not only across species lines, but across any boundaries that now divide living organisms, particularly the most fundamental such boundary, that which divides prokaryotes (bacteria and bluegreen algae) from eukaryotes (those cells with a distinct nucleus in higher plants and animals). The results will be essentially new organisms, self-perpetuating and hence permanent. Once created, they cannot be recalled.

This is the transcendent issue, so basic, so vast in its implications and possible consequences that no one is as yet ready to deal with it. We can't deal with it until we know a lot more; and to learn those things we would have to venture out into this no-man's land. It is nothing like making new transuranic elements. New elements only add to the simple series of integral atomic numbers that underlie the Periodic System. Their numbers are limited and their properties highly predictable. Not so new organisms. They can be as boundless and unpredictable as life itself.

Up to now living organisms have evolved very slowly, and new forms have had plenty of time to settle in. It has taken from four to 20 million years for a single mutation, for example the change of one amino acid in the sequence of hemoglobin or cytochrome c, to establish itself as the species norm. Now whole proteins will be transposed overnight into wholly new associations, with consequences no one can foretell, either for the host organisms or their neighbors.

It is all too big, and is happening too fast. So this, the cental problem, remains almost unconsidered. It presents probably the largest ethical problem that science has ever had to face. Our morality up to now

* Wald won the Nobel Prize in medicine or physiology in 1967 for his work on the chemistry of vision. [Eds.]

has been to go ahead without restriction to learn all that we can about nature. Restructuring nature was not part of the bargain; nor was telling scientists not to venture further in certain directions. That comes hard. With some relief, most biologists turn away from so vast and uncomfortable an issue and take refuge in the still knotty but infinitely easier technical questions: not *whether* to proceed, but *how*. For going ahead in this direction may be not only unwise but dangerous. Potentially, it could breed new animal and plant diseases, new sources of cancer, novel epidemics.

We must never forget that the first intimation of these potential hazards came from workers in this field. All honor to them. . . . I have up to now said almost nothing of the potential benefits of this technology. I think that the most certain benefits to come out of it would be scientific: increased understanding of important biological phenomena, such as the mechanisms that turn specific gene activities on and off, that trigger cell multiplication and differentiation, that regulate cell metabolism. We are also offered the prospect of large practical benefits: teaching cereal plants to fix their own nitrogen from the air, new bacterial syntheses of drugs and hormones, the hope that increased understanding of cancer may lead to its cure. I cannot think of a single instance of such developments, scientific or practical, that does not also involve large potential risks. . . .

First, I think it essential to open a wide ranging and broadly representative discussion of the central issue: whether artificial exchanges of genetic material among widely different living organisms should be permitted.

Second, in consideration of the potential hazards and our present state of ignorance, I would confine all recombinant DNA experimentation that transcended species boundaries to one or a few national or regional laboratories where they can be adequately confined and supervised. There, every attempt should be made to define the hazards that are now only guessed at. If trouble should arise, I would expect it to involve first the workers in such laboratories and their families, whose health should be carefully monitored. Until such trials have told us better what to expect, this kind of investigation should have no place in crowded cities or educational institutions.

Third, industrial research and development in this area need most of all to be brought under control. The usual secrecy that surrounds industrial research is intolerable in a province that can involve such serious consequences and hazards. The need for licensing, inspection and supervision will probably require national legislation. Hearings in the Congress should begin at once to consider these issues. . . .

BERNARD D. DAVIS,*
EVOLUTION, EPIDEMIOLOGY, AND RECOMBINANT DNA

193 Science 442 (1976) (letter).

In attempting to assess the hazards of incorporating eukaryotic DNA into bacteria it is not enough simply to set up hypothetical scenarios: we must also try to judge critically the underlying assumptions. The first

* Davis is Adele Lehman Professor of Bacterial Physiology at Harvard Medical School, and a member of the National Academy of Sciences. [Eds.]

assumption is that these experiments will breach an ancient barrier between eukaryotes and prokaryotes and will thereby produce a radically novel class of organisms.

Principles from evolution and bacterial ecology offer our best guides for judgment. Bacteria in nature have long been exposed to DNA from lysed mammalian cells—for example, in the gut and in decomposing corpses. *Escherichia coli* can take up DNA after damage to the cell envelope, and one would expect random phenotypic variation to produce such damage occasionally (perhaps at frequencies of 10^{-5} to 10^{-10}). Homologous DNA is efficiently incorporated after entry, because its potential pairing with long regions of host cell DNA facilitates enzymatic crossover. Indeed genetic recombination between bacteria (transformation) has even been observed in the human host. Incorporation of non-homologous DNA is much less efficient but nevertheless can occur, presumably by transient pairing between adventitious short regions of complementarity. For example, deletions based on such "illegitimate recombination" occur at frequencies of about 10^{-9}.

With such low frequencies of both entry and incorporation, one could not expect to demonstrate natural hybridization between bacteria and man. Nevertheless, its scale almost certainly compensates for its inefficiency. Every person's gut is a huge chemostat, and the total population excretes about 10^{22} bacteria per day. Hence over the past 10^6 years human-bacterial hybrids are exceedingly likely to have already appeared and been tested in the crucible of natural selection. If so, experimental DNA recombination will not be yielding a totally novel class of organisms.

A second assumption is that some of the recombinant strains are likely to spread and cause epidemics. Evolutionary principles are again pertinent. Nature selects for genetic balance: the contribution of a gene to Darwinian fitness depends on the rest of the genome. In bacteria, specifically, the introduction of a substantial block of foreign DNA would almost always lower the growth rate. With the short generation time of bacteria such a difference would lead to rapid outgrowth by competitors (unless the introduced genes promoted adaptation to alterations in the environment, such as the wide use of an antibiotic).

This argument is reinforced by a large body of epidemiological and experimental evidence. . . .

While bacteria carrying mammalian genes are . . . unlikely to menace the public health, the risk of laboratory infection is much larger, since a heavy infecting dose of even a poorly communicable organism can cause disease in an individual. But this danger resembles that encountered with known pathogens, and it can be minimized by similar means. . . .

I conclude that the risks in research on recombinant DNA require reasonable precautions but do not warrant public anxiety: A greater danger may be that the presumed analogy to nuclear weapons will lead to demands for virtually absolute freedom from risk. Yet the analogy to our mastery over infectious diseases is more apt. And if this field had faced similar demands, from its start, we might still be losing one-quarter of our children to communicable diseases. Is the balance of risk and benefit in research on recombinant DNA so much more unfavorable?

NOTES ON PRESUMPTIONS, ARGUMENTS AND THE LAW

1. Is it just a matter of personal style—or a matter of professional attitude—that leads Watson, a prize-winning scientist, to write about finding "the secret of life" and "the most famous event in biology since Darwin's book," while Harold Green, a law professor and practicing attorney, writes that he is "happy to say" there is nothing "unique or novel" in recombinant DNA research that should insulate it from regulation? Green, A Legal Perspective on Recombinant DNA Research, in Recombinant DNA: Science, Ethics, and Politics 200 (J. Richards ed. 1976). Science often appears to make progress in a way that the law does not. Scientists look forward as they seek a form of ever-improving truth; lawyers often look back to precedent as they seek to resolve disputes where the ultimate truth of the matter may be unknowable. What are the consequences of this disparity when law regulates science?

2. Carl Cohen, a professor of philosophy at the University of Michigan, analyzed the use of what he terms "heavy question arguments" by opponents of recombinant DNA research, such as Erwin Chargaff, professor emeritus of biochemistry at Columbia University, who in a famous letter to Science in 1976 posed a whole series of heavy questions, including "the principal question to be answered is whether we have the right to put an additional fearful load on generations that are not yet born," and "Have we the right to counteract, irreversibly, the evolutionary wisdom of millions of years, in order to satisfy the ambition and the curiosity of a few scientists?" Professor Cohen points out: "Whatever may be suggested by a question, or implied by the terms used in it, or inferred by the hearer from the attitude of the person doing the asking, the interrogative does not express any proposition whatever. It cannot, therefore, be true or false." Cohen, Restriction of Research with Recombinant DNA: The Dangers of Inquiry and the Burden of Proof, 51 S.Cal.L.Rev. 1081, 1088 (1978).

3. Professor Green notes that in recent years the government has reversed its tendency to adopt health and safety regulations "too late after many people have been hurt." Green, supra. In most fields (food additives, toxic chemicals, etc.), however, a developed technology rather than an infant science is at issue. Is the experience with atomic energy comparable (see Chs. 2 and 9 infra)?

It is generally true that scientific researchers need not demonstrate the safety of their investigations as a condition of proceeding. But can review be triggered by the expression of genuine concern about risks by knowledgeable parties? In the case of recombinant DNA, do the initial warnings by scientists of possible disasters from research mishaps have continuing force once the same scientists suggest that subsequent experience has led them to doubt that any unusual risk exists? In other words, once triggered can a process of decision be called off by anything short of a judgment on the merits? If the cost of bringing to public attention the potential problems arising from a line of work includes the risk that a process of review will irreversibly be set in motion, "whistle blowers" will be disinclined to draw attention to problems in any field they would not want to see stifled. On the other hand, a certain amount of lawyerly skepticism ought to greet any sudden reversal of views by people with a self-interest, so that the parade of scientific "expert witnesses" testifying to their newly found comfort with recombinant DNA research may not in and of itself eliminate all the earlier concerns.

To suggest that the "burden of proof" issue lies at the heart of the recombinant DNA debate is not to suggest that it is a single issue or, indeed, that one determination of *who* bears *what* burden of going forward with *what* evidence and persuading *whom* will be satisfactory for all aspects of public policy regarding recombinant DNA. One ground for suggesting different burdens might be that the risks motivating concern in the first place are of different sorts. Tristram Engelhardt, for instance, distinguishes *physical* risks (which are self-explanatory) from social risks (those that flow from the disruptive effects of new theories and data on existing values and beliefs). Another way of slicing the conceptual pie is according to the stage of the research process, between the risks of *means* (e.g., will a lab worker, or a member of the public, contract a grave or even untreatable infection because of inadequate rules and precautions in a research setting or because of a failure to carry out those that do exist?) and the risks of *ends* (e.g., is there information about human beings that ought simply not be known to anyone or might the techniques developed be misused for evil ends, such as biological warfare?).

Capron, Prologue: Why Recombinant DNA?, 51 S.Cal.L.Rev. 973, 977 (1978).

4. Looking at the history of recombinant DNA in this chapter, one naturally thinks of science as something subject to regulation. Often, however, science is the source of regulation, as researchers establish the risks involved in various products and activities. See Ullmann, Science and the "Regulation" Bogey, 403 Ann.N.Y.Acad.Scis. 69, 70–76 (1983). These issues are explored more fully in Ch. 5, infra.

5. Although the initial concerns of the DNA researchers, and the scientists and nonscientist onlookers who soon joined in the debate, were framed in terms of biosafety, other deeper concerns soon became apparent and may help to explain why this type of research gained much more public attention than other work on pathogens of at least equal hazard that had been going on in laboratories for years.

PRESIDENT'S COMMISSION FOR THE STUDY OF ETHICAL PROBLEMS IN MEDICINE AND BIOMEDICAL AND BEHAVIORAL RESEARCH, SPLICING LIFE

14–17 (1982).

In announcing hearings in Cambridge on Harvard's proposed recombinant DNA laboratory in 1976, Mayor Alfred E. Vellucci gave voice to the general disquiet about genetic engineering: "They may come up with a disease that can't be cured—even a monster. Is this the answer to Dr. Frankenstein's dream?"

This "Frankenstein factor" conveys the public uneasiness about the notion that gene splicing might change the nature of human beings, compounded by the heightened anxiety people often feel about interventions involving high technology that rests in the hands of only a few. Indeed, the frequent repetition of the Frankenstein theme by scientists as well as members of the public is quite apt.

Dr. Frankenstein was a creator of new life; gene splicing has raised questions about humanity assuming a role as creator. As [Lewis Thomas] notes:

> The recombinant DNA line of research is already upsetting, not because of the dangers now being argued about but because it is disturbing in a fundamental way, to face the fact that the genetic machinery in control of the planet's life can be fooled around with so easily. We do not like the idea that anything so fixed and stable as a species line can be changed. The notion that genes can be taken out of one genome and inserted in another is unnerving.

Some scientists were quite unsettled by the prospect. One leading scientist [Robert L. Sinsheimer]—who had been an articulate proponent in the

1960s of the hope for improvement that science offered to the "losers" in nature's "genetic lottery"—came to have grave reservations:

> Do we want to assume the basic responsibility for life on this planet— to develop new living forms for our own purposes? Shall we take into our hands our own future evolution? . . . Perverse as it may, initially, seem to the scientist, we must face the fact that there can be unwanted knowledge.

Dr. Frankenstein's creation was a frightening monster; gene splicing has raised fears about strange new life forms. Some of these—particularly in the popular press—were farfetched:

> Simply put, you take a cell from some plant or animal and extract the chemical (DNA) that governs all the physical and mental characteristics of the whole being. Do the same with another, totally different, plant or animal. Graft the two together, Presto! Shake hands with an orange that quacks, with a flower that can eat you for breakfast—or even with the Flying Nun.

Other concerns with new genetic combinations were more immediate. Some biologists pointed to what they believed are the rigid natural barriers against transfer of genetic material between lower life forms that lack a defined nucleus (such as bacteria) and higher forms (such as plants and animals). Particularly in so-called shotgun experiments, in which the genetic information in an animal cell is broken into many pieces and each is inserted into bacteria so that it will multiply and can be studied, these scientists voiced concern that some of the genetic material might prove very harmful in its new setting even though a risk is not shown, or perhaps does not even exist, when it is part of the total package of genetic material in the original cell.

The Frankenstein story also seems appropriate because the scientist there sought to control his monster, calling to mind the concerns raised about the distribution of power and control associated with gene splicing: "Each new power won *by* man is a power *over* man as well." Of equal or greater concern was the view, expressed by some scientists, that even the scientists could not control the "monster." . . .

Finally, the Frankenstein analogy comes to mind because of people's concern that something was being done to them and their world by individuals pursuing their own goals but not necessarily the goal of human betterment. . . . Mayor Vellucci of Cambridge voiced what may be a widely held skepticism about researchers when he declared: "I don't think these scientists are thinking about mankind at all. I think that they're getting the thrills and the excitement and the passion to dig in and keep digging to see what the hell they can do." The fear was that for researchers, creating a new life form—even a monster—would be a matter of curiosity; for the public, it would be an assault on traditional values.

Thus, as the laboratory hazards of gene splicing were being contained, concerns about the hazards this technology could pose to human and social values began to bubble to the surface of public awareness. . . . New ideas can change the world in psychological and philosophical terms just as radically as new techniques can change it materially. Many examples exist of such changes being wrought by the discoveries of science. In the sixteenth century Copernicus showed that the earth revolved around the sun, not the sun around the earth, and thus upset the notion that humanity was at the center of the universe. Similarly, in the last century, the theory of evolution propounded by Charles Darwin challenged the belief that human beings were uniquely created by claiming that they are the biological kin to other living things and that species have slowly differentiated through the undirected agency of natural selection among randomly occurring changes.

The recent work in molecular genetics may again unseat some widely held—if only dimly perceived—views about humanity's place in nature and even about the meaning of being human. Old concepts are already being revised by some scientists, and it cannot be long before the new knowledge and new scientific powers begin to have an impact on general thinking. As a biochemical researcher [Maxine Singer] observed:

> Once we thought the DNA of complex organisms was inscrutable. Now we cope with it readily. We thought of DNA as immovable, a fixed component of cells. Now we know that some modules of DNA are peripatetic; their function depends on their ability to move about. . . . We thought genes were continuous stretches of DNA. Now we know . . . (they) . . . may be interrupted dozens of times, and spliced together . . . when needed. We have learned that genes are fungible; animal genes function perfectly well within bacteria and bacterial genes within animal cells, confirming the unity of nature. We need no longer depend on chance events to generate the mutations essential for unraveling intricate genetic phenomena.

3. THE ROLE OF EXPERTISE IN CONTROLLING SCIENCE

The scientific expert is a familiar figure in American political debate. Wald and Davis are not the first famous scientists to disagree sharply, nor will they be the last. The task, of course, is to determine on which issues expertise is relevant and why. It seems appropriate to be wary of what one commentator has termed "the generalization of expertise." * On the other hand, is it feasible to draw a sharp line between the scientific and non-scientific components of a decision? Moreover, are certain people "expert" about social norms or values the ones to be looked to for decisions about the social control of science?

DON K. PRICE, GOVERNMENT AND SCIENCE

164–67 (1962).

In the lower levels of the pyramid of policy the problem may be mainly scientific—that is to say, it may be a problem that can be solved by the precise research methods of one of the sciences. How can an explosive be made more powerful? What kind of testing process will identify the man with the fastest reaction time? What can be done to make an airplane fly faster? These are questions that science can take hold of. To get an airplane that will fly faster you put to work an aeronautical engineer, or rather a propulsion engineer and an aerodynamic engineer, supported by a number of more specialized colleagues. Their purposes and their skills correspond to the purposes of certain very specialized subdivisions of several government agencies.

Just a little higher on the pyramid of government policy the sciences begin to give less precise answers, and usually in terms of statistical probability rather than absolutes, because the questions themselves are of

---

* Veatch, Generalization of Expertise, 1
Hastings Cntr. Studies 29 (No. 2, 1973).

a different nature: What combination of bomb load and fuel load should a bomber of a certain type have in order to get the maximum speed, with acceptable armor protection, at which pilots may be expected to fly with reasonable safety? At this level a number of different types of scientists need to work together on operations research, which in turn must be guided by a number of policy assumptions supplied by operating officials.

Finally, when you go still farther toward the top of the organization, the problems begin to frustrate science completely: What proportion of our resources shall be put into bombing planes by comparison with land forces or naval vessels or air defense? How much shall we rely on building up supplies of weapons, and how much on encouraging a stable economy? How do we appraise the intentions of any potential enemy?

Much more often than not, the controlling elements in the vast web of government decisions (even though they may well be questions on which it is important to have the advice of scientists, or on which men with scientific background ought to make the decisions with full executive authority) are least likely to be the questions that can readily be answered precisely by scientific research. Aerodynamics has been one of the more dynamic of the sciences in its social consequences. Yet the way in which it will make its contribution is often prescribed by the answer to the questions being considered at the next higher level of the pyramid. Whether applied research in that field will receive support and what problems it will be asked to consider will depend (in the hypothetical example we have been using) on decisions about the bombing system as a whole and about the relative demands of speed and range and armament and maneuverability. And as we look at still higher levels on the pyramid of government it is clear that whether we develop more long-range bombers or more battleships or interceptor planes will depend mainly on the military strategists and that whether we develop any of them (and how many) will depend on the still less scientific judgments of the diplomats and the politicians about our views of other nations and on our decision concerning how much national armament is required for national security.

Scientific methods are the most useful in determining *how* a specific thing is to be done; the more specific the thing, the more precise the determination. They are less often and less immediately useful in determining *whether* or *when* such things are to be done and *how much* effort or money is to be spent on them. But these are the controlling decisions, the decisions that must be made in the upper levels of the hierarchy if a government is to have any unity of purpose and action. This necessity, too, leads the higher officials to deal with the less scientific aspects of their major problems.

A final reason is one that has to do with the way in which responsibilities are delegated in any organization. Any issue that can be reduced to precise and objective terms is one that a superior can delegate with confidence to a subordinate. . . .

But then we come to questions that, step by step, become less objective in their nature. How many bacteria can the water system tolerate? How much should the city spend on reducing infant mortality by public health measures? How much salary should it pay the public health officer? These questions become progressively more difficult to anwer in precise numerical or objective terms; more difficult to answer in ways that others can readily check by methods on which there is a professional consensus; more dependent on factors on which research does not give a conclusive and verifiable answer and on which the scientist's opinion may be as prejudiced as any layman's.

For the sake of simplicity I have been talking as if each problem in government were either precise and scientific or the opposite. This alternative, of course, is not so. Most problems of any importance are made up of a mixture of factors, some of which can be stated in quite precise terms and tested by objective research, while others are much more vague and general and more dependent on interests, values, and ideals. Any system of staff work for an executive then becomes a sort of sieve, screening out those aspects of the problems that can more nearly be solved by science (as well as the quite different category of problems that are not important enough) and bringing to the executive for decision only those aspects of the problem that he is not willing to delegate. . . .

JOEL PRIMACK AND FRANK von HIPPEL, ADVICE AND DISSENT

40 (1974).

Should science advisors answer only purely technical questions and seek merely to identify but not address issues requiring political choice? In practice, it has been found impossible to make such a clean separation between the functions of science advisor and policy maker. At the higher levels of government, science advisors have been repeatedly called upon to help make policy as well as render technical judgments.

One reason why the roles of advisor and decision maker cannot be clearly separated is that decisions on questions like the safety of a new drug or the environmental impact of the SST are never in practice based on adequate information. The various benefits and costs are usually largely a matter of guesswork. And postponing a decision until better information becomes available in itself constitutes a decision. Obviously, only a person familiar with the technical information is in a good position to estimate the risks arising from uncertainty. And an advisor who understands the technical issues may also be helpful in judging how heavily to weigh these issues against other, nontechnical considerations.

Because public officials must often rely upon the combined political and scientific judgment of their technical advisors, they tend to choose as advisors scientists whose political views are similar to their own. Presidential science advisors were routinely selected on this basis. But while shared assumptions may improve communication, they may also effectively result in political views determining technological policies without sufficient regard for technical considerations. In some cases balance has been achieved within the executive branch when opposing factions have established their own advisory groups, each having different political biases. . . .

CHARLES KRAUTHAMMER, SCIENCE EX MACHINA

The New Republic 19–20 (June 6, 1981).

For a generation scientists have been taking political sta⌐ plicitly in their capacity as scientists. Physicists working fo⌐ armament, for example, have claimed special attention by vi⌐ special knowledge. Theirs is a worthy cause but an empty clai⌐

son who makes the Bomb knows no more about how to prevent its use than a historian or a diplomat or any informed citizen. Nuclear physicists do have a *moral* claim to special attention on this issue because, like all workers, they feel a particular responsibility to see to it that the product of their labor is not used for harm. (Similarly, the farmer shares a citizen's responsibility to see that children do not get poisoned milk; but as a farmer, he feels a particular responsibility that no one be harmed by *his* milk.) Logically, the moral authority that the nuclear physicist possesses should extend equally to the person who digs the silos. But, of course, no one would read the Bulletin of the Atomic Silo Diggers.

Doctors have hopped on the bandwagon too. The New England Journal of Medicine recently published a manifesto by the leaders of International Physicians for the Prevention of Nuclear War. They soberly outline the consequences of nuclear war and ask other physicians to join them in a crusade against nuclear weapons. Another worthy endeavor, but why are they speaking as physicians? "It may be argued," they concede, "that nuclear war is an issue in the political and social domain and that physicians need confront it only as concerned citizens." They raise this objection only to deny it. They reason that since nuclear war is a threat to health, physicians have something special to say about it. Really? Hospital orderlies and meat inspectors also are concerned with health. Would anyone pay them particular attention on this issue? And nuclear war is a threat to everything: flowers, animals, steel mills, amusement parks. Should their custodians claim special attention as well? Would anyone listen to Florists Against Nuclear War? But for some reason people will listen to doctors. And that brings us to the doctors' final—and real—reason: "Physicians bring excellent credentials to the task of public education on this topic. They are widely respected as teachers and accustomed to interpreting scientific findings for their patients and for the public at large." In other words, people are in the habit of deferring to someone in a white coat. When it comes to nuclear weapons, physicians have no special knowledge, nor do they have the moral burden of the nuclear physicists. They have something better: simple, undifferentiated, multipurpose authority. For a good cause, why not exploit it?
. . .

NOTE

Experts can identify and explain new scientific developments. They also can often foresee the implications of such developments more easily than non-experts. But should experts ever play a special role in legal and social decisions involving science? Price suggests that science *per se* has little importance in most ultimate policy decisions. Why then are scientific experts so prominent in public debate on issues like recombinant DNA? Is it because, as Primack and von Hippel contend, that experts are needed to estimate risks, or is it, as Krauthammer argues, that we are "in the habit of deferring to someone in a white coat"?

If scientists have no special role to play in ultimate social choices because those choices amount in the end to value decisions, that argument can perhaps be extended. Many believe Supreme Court decisions on the meaning of the Constitution amount in the end to the application of one's values. Does that mean here is no particular reason to have attorneys on the Supreme Court?

B. DECIDING WHETHER—AND HOW—
TO REGULATE

Policies, unlike Greek gods, seldom spring full blown from the brow of a single creator; indeed, their development is usually more disorderly and rocky than contemplated in the Administrative Procedure Act, especially when the "policy" in question is actually a set of informal practices, an agreement among colleagues, or some other form of self-regulation. Thus, in order to understand the development of the rules that have been adopted for the field of science being examined in this Chapter, one needs to see how arguments were advanced, positions tried out, and policies eventually adopted.

The events surrounding the first collective responses—by the scientific community and then by governmental bodies—to the concern about recombinant DNA research are colorful (even dramatic), but they are unusual in the annals of science only for the extent of attention they attracted at the time from outsiders (journalists, social scientists, and lawyers). The passions, the personal idiosyncracies, and the political inclinations of the biomedical scientists involved—as displayed in their willingness to enter into a group process, their readiness to acknowledge their own self-interests, their comfort (or discomfort) in engaging in the politics of compromise and consensus, and so forth—do not set them off from nuclear physicists, inorganic chemists, engineers, or any other scientific specialists. Thus, besides their inherent interest as history, the details presented here about the unfolding of policies to control genetic engineering are of interest for the light they shed on the strength and weaknesses of several alternative means of policymaking, particularly the contrast between self-regulation and various forms of governmental regulation and oversight. The question for each participant along the way might have been: should there be further regulation of this field, and if so, how much and by what means?

1. SELF–REGULATION

MICHAEL ROGERS, BIOHAZARD

48–57, 60–72, 74–89, 92–93, 99–100 (1977).

By January 1975, one month before the conference, pressure was intense. Yet the moratorium was almost universally observed in the eight months between publication of the letter and the first sunny Sunday at Asilomar. . . .

During the months between the publication of the letter and the conference itself, now set for the last week in February 1975, Berg concentrated on details of organization. At a second MIT meeting, an organizing committee had been established consisting of Berg, Baltimore, Singer, Roblin, and two Europeans—Niels K. Jerne of Switzerland, then head of the European Molecular Biology Organization, and Sydney Brenner, a central figure in molecular genetics on the Medical Research Council staff in Cambridge, England. . . .

The rest of the second MIT meeting was devoted to selecting chairmen for the individual committees, which by then had been narrowed to three interest groups: animal virus DNA; animal and plant cell DNA; and bacterial plasmids and phages.

Each committee would submit suggestions for participants. . . .

Already the Asilomar attendance list was growing rapidly. The organizing committee felt that it was incumbent upon them to create a representative group and yet one that was also small enough to operate effectively. Inevitably, dark mutterings about "intellectual lockouts" and the like were heard.

. . .

The molecular biologists invited by Berg and company descended upon California's Monterey peninsula on very nearly the same day as did the monarch butterflies. The Asilomar Conference Center is a scatter of rustic dormitories and meeting halls hidden in a seaside forest of redwood and Monterey pine, just outside the tiny town of Pacific Grove. . . .

. . . The weather that Sunday was crisp and the sky bright blue—the finest February climate that the Monterey peninsula can offer—and it seemed an auspicious start for the conference which by the late evening had drawn nearly 150 scientists from every corner of the planet.

Early the following morning, the full moon still bright over the blue-black Pacific, the breakfast bell tolled in the center of the conference compound, and soon the molecular biologists filed through the dawn light and into the redwood chapel that served as center for the next four days. Inside, the chapel was dim and gloomy, with theater-type seats, exposed beams, and an elevated stage that, even stripped of ecclesiastical accouterments, was still unmistakably reminiscent of an altar. The implicit metaphor did not go unobserved. "Here we are," a young scientist from the East Coast told me later that night, "sitting in a chapel next to the ocean, huddled around a forbidden tree, trying to create some new commandments—and there's no goddamn Moses in sight."

. . .

"We can outdo evolution," was how David Baltimore, trimly bearded and clad in an embroidered Levi shirt, put it. At the outset, he labeled as peripheral the ethical issues of genetic engineering itself, as well as the potential use of the new techniques in biological warfare. While those questions are real ones, he said, they were not the specific charge of the Asilomar conference—a charge which the next four days would reveal to be plenty all by itself. "If we come out of here split and unhappy," Baltimore concluded, "we will have failed the mission before us."

And with that the mission began. . . .

The question, vociferously argued, regarded a variety of *E. coli* known as K–12, isolated decades earlier from the stool of a diphtheria sufferer at Stanford, and by now the bacterium of choice for much laboratory work—including, of course, recombinant DNA. While *E. coli* may well be the best-studied cellular organism on the planet, there was one critical area about which no one, clearly, knew much at all: How likely was it that this *E. coli* K–12, so long laboratory-pampered, could survive in the human gut, should it escape its test tube carrying some newly implanted and potentially unpleasant genetic information?

A series of British researchers proceeded that morning to demonstrate an experimental penchant for mixing cultures of millions of K–12 into half-pints of milk, swallowing same, and then monitoring their subsequent stool for evidence of bacterial survival. . . .

While the English minimized the odds of the K–12 strain surviving in human beings, two American researchers, who had helped draft the plasmid group report and who became central figures in the guideline-writing process, were not so certain.   Stanley Falkow, a cheerful, unassuming microbiologist from Seattle, pointed out that the *E. coli* K–12 is occasionally capable of transmitting its plasmids, which would be carrying the new genetic information, to other, related bacteria.   And that might be all it would take for the new information to survive, in the gut, past the death of the K–12 strain itself.   And Roy Curtiss, an imposing, long-haired researcher from Alabama, suggested that thought should also be given to the survival of *E. coli* in sewer systems, where it might well have the opportunity to swap new genetic information with literally billions of its fellows. . . .

These two speakers gave the first hints of what would begin to look like an inescapable fact: Before the advent of recombinant DNA techniques, human beings apparently knew more about *E. coli* than almost anyone would ever care to learn; but once we started manipulating that organism in ways not possible in nature, it grew distressingly clear that we really knew very little at all.

. . .

"This is what we know how to do," one East Coast microbiologist plaintively told a reporter, midway in the proceedings.   "This is what we're used to doing.   I mean, we all get together, we want to know what everybody else is doing."

During the first two days of sessions, it was apparent that the conference attendees would really rather talk about almost anything but the issue at hand.   "I felt," Maxine Singer said later, "that there was too much traditional science at the beginning." . . .

Yet the field was sufficiently new and diverse that such traditional briefing was both welcome and necessary for many of the conferees.   The talk was at least sufficiently original that after hearing certain papers, researchers queued up at Asilomar's two pay telephones to relay word back to their laboratories.   The discussion helped define, moreover, just what was at stake in the experimenter's right to investigate the new technology. A major portion of it was in the realm of pure research—specifically, a process of cloning DNA fragments.

. . .

[W]hen, early Tuesday morning, the floor was opened for discussion on the first real matter of business—the lengthy recommendations of the plasmid group—there was utter silence in the redwood chapel.

The proposal was hardly uncontroversial.   In thirty-five single-spaced pages, it established an elaborate six-stage classification of experiments by the degree of risk they implied, along with the safeguards required for performing each class of experiment, and even included one class of experiments that would be altogether forbidden.   At first, there was not a single comment from the assembly.   One of the five plasmid group members gave a brief pep talk, encouraging participation.   Still nothing.   Berg stared out at the audience briefly and then moved for the adoption of the report as it stood—and only then, with almost audible creaking, did the wheel of discussion begin to turn.   And it proceeded to run right downhill into chaos.   Odd, I thought at the time, that a roomful of the leading minds on the leading edge of science can't agree on how to run a meeting.   But the proceedings that bright morning began to resemble some obscure primitive tribe, eons ago, accidentally stumbling by trial and error onto the secrets of parliamentary procedure.

There was, in fact, a great deal to talk about in the plasmid group report, which would provide the model upon which the next ten months of guideline formulation would be based. . . .

Each class of experiment would require a higher degree of physical containment, increasing the laboratory precautions against the culture being manipulated escaping—through exhaust fan, drain, or researcher's body—into the outside world. . . .

The containment levels, numbered also in the plasmid group's report, added up to a different kind of figure: the expense that each researcher would have to pay in order to upgrade his laboratory containment facilities sufficiently to allow the work he was interested in doing. . . .

The first solid criticism that morning came from Joshua Lederberg, one of the two Nobel laureates in attendance. Lederberg expressed sympathy with the effort as a whole and then proceeded to voice an objection that, months later, would prove rather telling. "If we can't communicate the tentativeness of this document," he said, "then we are in trouble." With five minutes' consideration, he suggested, the plasmid group's paper appeared decent enough. But what final interpretation would it find? "There is a graver likelihood," he intoned ominously, "of this paper crystallizing into legislation than any of us would like to think."

Lederberg, a large, bearded, well-nourished man, wore loose, brightly patterned sports shirts at Asilomar, giving him the look of a senior California academic who spends his weekends in hot baths at Esalen or perhaps gardening. He had, however, two very different connections to the Asilomar proceedings. It had been his research into plasmids in the early 1950s, in the course of which he named those tiny rings of DNA, that earned him his Nobel prize. And a decade after that, Lederberg had been involved in what may yet turn out to be an extremely farsighted bit of scientific caution: convincing NASA that the biological isolation and decontamination of returning space vehicles was an absolute necessity, on the off chance that they might carry extraterrestrial infective agents against which life on earth would be defenseless. Lederberg's campaign resulted in containment facilities for spacecraft (and in several terrifying novels as well). It had, moreover, a curious parallel with the new issue of recombinant DNA: In both, the fear was speculative, the precautions costly, but the consequences of inaction were potentially disastrous.

. . .

. . . After Lederberg's observation, [British antibiotic resistance expert Ephraim] Anderson rose immediately to ask the plasmid group a single question: "Which members have had experience with the handling and disposal of pathogenic microoganisms capable of causing epidemic *disease?*"

There was embarrassed silence, some laughter.

"It's no joking matter," Anderson persisted.

The entire panel finally sheepishly admitted that all of them had probably had a little.

Anderson—a portly, imposing gentleman—glared coldly. "If you're going to set down guidelines," he said, "you should *know* something of the matter. That's not a terribly profound principle; it doesn't take a great deal of cerebration to arrive at."

Anderson picked up the elaborate plasmid group report and read a selected sentence: " 'For our purposes, pathogenicity and virulence are defined similarly as "the ability to cause disease." ' " The Englishman closed the paper slowly. "This," he said, "must stand as the greatest oversimplification of all time."

He continued. The chairman of the group finally cut him off, thanked him for the "input," and asked for a written critique. "This is, after all," he apologized, "a rather terse document."

Anderson continued to stand. "You could have fooled me."

Alterations, the leader assured him, would be made; the working document was assembled, after all, in six days.

"And why couldn't you do it in six days?" the Englishman wanted to know. "After all, the Lord created the world in only seven."

. . .

Before long . . . the discussion was rather forcefully brought back to fundamentals by the only other Nobel laureate in attendance, James Watson, then both Harvard professor and director of the Cold Spring Harbor laboratory. Watson, unlike Lederberg, seemed almost to cultivate the persona of the absent-minded academic: tall, pale, thin, shirt collar turned up, wispy brown hair tugged so constantly that it stood out from his head in total disarray. He spoke with a regular punctuation of grimaces, and in the midst of any given sentence, his gaze could wander off into space, a consummate 2000-yard stare.

Watson, of course, had been involved with the recombinant DNA question since the outset; his signature was on the moratorium letter. Thus it came as rather a surprise when, Tuesday morning, he rose to say that he thought the moratorium should end, and that it should end, moreover, without the complex kind of categorical restrictions that the plasmid paper represented. "Common sense," was Watson's prescription. "We can just suffer the possibility that someone will sue us for a million dollars if things don't work out." The proper response to the problem, Watson felt, was simply education.

Maxine Singer was on her feet immediately to ask precisely what had changed during the past six months to justify lifting the moratorium. Since, by definition, nothing *had* happened—at least experimentally— there was little Watson could say. "Some things are gross stupidity," he said, "but I don't know how we can legislate against it. We'll end up with situations in our labs where we know people are cheating a bit and ultimately we'll end up with massive dishonesty." Watson shrugged, looked around, sat down.

. . .

Finally Sydney Brenner stood up to speak. . . .

"Does anyone in the audience believe," he asked . . . "that this work—prokaryotes at least—can be done with absolutely no hazard?" He waited through a long silence. "This is not a conference to decide what's to be done in America next week," he continued finally. "If anyone thinks so, then this conference has not served its purpose."

There are two separate elements to the problem, Brenner explained. "Objective scientific things, which we can reach agreement on, and then an extraneous set of elements which might be called political. In some countries, this might be done by the government, and once the guidelines were set, and you broke them, there'd be no question about the censure of one's peers—the police would simply come out and arrest you." This is an opportunity, Brenner concluded, for scientists to demonstrate their ability for self-regulation—"to reject the attitude that we'll go along and pretend there's no biohazard and hope we can arrive at a compromise that won't affect my own small area, and I can get my tenure and grants and be appointed to the National Academy and all the other things that scientists seem to be interested in."

It was the first time Brenner had spoken out at the conference, and the effect was undeniably tonic. Equally tonic, in an altogether different way, were Brenner's activities following the noon lunch break. During the long hiatus between lunch and the next scheduled session . . . Brenner held an informal chapel meeting aimed at what in the months after developed into a curious new fillip in biological research: "disarming the bug," as Brenner referred to it—the deliberate creation of "ecologically disabled organisms."

. . .

Brenner, much earlier, had jokingly suggested that the bacterial host for recombinant DNA work should be, rather than *E. coli, Pasteurella pestis*—the plague germ. It would be so dangerous, Brenner said, that everyone would be petrified to use it. "Either that, or we design the bug so that essentially nothing can go wrong."

. . .

[T]he session itself was a considerable success and marked, in fact, the first of two major turning points in the Asilomar proceedings: By the end of that afternoon the odds on fairly rapid construction of the new, crippled strains looked so good that onlookers had renamed Brenner's "Mark One" safe vectors "Mach One."

That confidence was, to say the least, excessive, and one can only wonder whether Asilomar might have ended differently, had the real difficulties—and the long dry season before the return to the proscribed work—been fully known.

. . .

The discussion [late Tuesday] afternoon involved the guidelines suggested by the group assigned to study the manipulation of DNA from animal viruses. The fear that oncogenic—tumor-producing—bits of DNA from such viruses might manage to propagate and then somehow operate in *E. coli* had been a major concern of the moratorium letter. The possibility was only theoretical, but it yielded perhaps the most terrifying scenario of all: a contagious form of cancer-causing bacteria.

The response of the virus group, thus, seemed oddly muted; it was a single terse page that brushed aside the question of safer vectors and prescribed containment procedures not very different from those already in use. The paper was odd in another way as well: Of the three working groups at Asilomar, the virus group was the only report to include a minority opinion. "Given the limited amount of information available at this time," wrote the dissenter, "I believe that the risks associated with the widespread, semicontained use of the procedure exceed the rewards from the information to be gained."

The lone voice belonged to Andrew M. Lewis, Jr., from the National Institute of Allergy and Infectious Disease (NIAID), who took the podium late Tuesday to describe his experience with an obscure class of viruses known as "non-defective adenovirus 2-SV 40 [Simian virus] hybrids."

The viruses themselves may have been arcane, but the implications of his talk were far less so. Lewis—in his thirties, conservatively dressed, with an unmistakably serious mien—was the first person in the United States to be burdened with the distribution of a brand-new, laboratory-created— and potentially hazardous—tumor virus.

. . .

"The question we faced," Lewis described it at Asilomar, "was whether one individual had the right to decide to distribute potentially hazardous laboratory-created recombinants."   The decision was forced rather quickly, when the provocative new hybrids were described at the Cold Spring Harbor Tumor Virus Workshop in August 1971.   The reaction to Lewis's reluctance was immediate: threats of congressional action, administrative pressure from NIH, even a group letter to *Science* should Lewis try to withhold the new hybrids.   And on the other hand, concerned researchers warned that if Lewis went ahead with the distribution, they would file for a federal environmental impact statement.

"I felt," said Lewis, "that voluntary compliance by interested investigators was the most satisfactory method," and so he decided to require a formal document—felicitously dubbed a Memorandum of Understanding and Agreement—from each laboratory that requested the viruses, stipulating that the researchers themselves would assume full moral and legal responsibility for the novel viral agents.

About two years after that, Lewis stopped growing the virus altogether.   And by the time of the conference at Asilomar, he was no longer so certain about the notion of voluntary compliance.   "Several major laboratories," he said, "have thus far not supported the memorandum.   In addition, our original request to restrict the distribution of the first hybrid seems to have been ignored by one or more of these same laboratories."

. . .

. . . Lewis's implications, clearly, were not popular ones.   The chapel audience remained quiet and cold, and midway through his presentation Lewis began to lean intently over the big wooden podium, grasping his pointer, straight up, like a spear carrier in an Italian opera. The source of the hostility seemed no mystery: Asilomar was, after all, *about* self-regulation—and Lewis's first-hand testimony was not exactly in the spirit of things.

. . .

Tuesday night, the virus group report had developed into a vigorous, sprawling debate that managed to make the plasmid group discussion seem rather mild.   And the virus argument was in turn soon to be dwarfed by the disagreements over the third and final working group report, presented Wednesday afternoon, on the little-examined prospect of cloning segments of DNA from the higher organisms.

The technical name for this subject was "cloned eukaryotic DNA"— referring to genes from all organisms higher on the scale of things than bacteria, from yeast through plants to human beings.   The area was likely to be the most promising of all recombinant DNA technology and also the least understood.

. . .

The working group on eukaryotic DNA had produced a paper midway in scope between the plasmid and virus group efforts.   To head the group, Berg had selected a Carnegie Institute researcher named Don

Brown—a rangy, crewcut, mildly abrasive man who had been one of the first to use the new recombinant DNA technique. His object of study had been the African frog *Xenopus,* a small green amphibian whose agreeable fecundity has long made it a laboratory favorite. Brown's views on the safety of cloning eukaryotic DNA were thus, by familiarity, rather liberal, but Berg considered Brown open-minded, and thought that if Brown himself could be persuaded on the matter, then the recommendation itself would carry that much more weight.

The notion, would, however, once more underscore the unavoidable conflicts of interest in even the most benign use of insiders, when, late Wednesday afternoon, the eukaryote group members took their seats on the chapel stage, and presented the eukaryote paper to the assembled.

Their recommendations followed the plasmid group's lead of numbered categories of risk, and that, right away, launched disagreement.

Joshua Lederberg, still worried about keeping things tentative, but giving a bit of ground, suggested that the specific categories might be reduced to something like high-medium-low.

"But shouldn't we benefit," someone asked, "from the experience we have?"

James Watson, slumped low in the middle of the audience, muttered to his neighbor: "But there *is* no experience."

"I have to emphasize," said Brown, on stage, "that there was a great deal of consensus among the members of our panel."

"So is there in the State Department!" Watson exclaimed softly. He sat for a moment and then whispered quietly to his seatmate, "These people have made up guidelines that don't apply to their own experiments."

"Stand up and say it," his companion urged softly. "You can say it; I can't."

Finally, with sufficient prompting, Watson rose to ask, "Why, according to the panel, is *Xenopus* DNA safer to work with than, say, cow DNA?"

Chairman Brown frowned, and looked slightly embarrassed. "It wouldn't be fair for me to answer that question," he said, and turned to the panel. "Anybody like to defend *Xenopus?*"

While there were, in fact, some defenses to be made, no one at that point felt like doing it. Finally Watson sat, shaking his head. "He refused to anwer the question," Watson announced softly to anyone within range.

Paul Berg stood to get the session back on course. "We have to make a decision," he said. "Can we measure the risks numerically?"

Watson, *sotto voce,* exploded, "We can't even *measure* the fucking risks!"

. . .

Berg stood again. "If our recommendations," he said, "look self-serving, then we run the risk of having standards imposed. We must start high and work down. We can't say that a hundred and fifty scientists spent four days at Asilomar and all of them agreed that there was a hazard—and they still couldn't come up with a single suggestion. That's telling the government to do it for us."

At this, Watson, inspired, was up like a shot. "We can tell them they couldn't do it either!"

Barely audible beneath the laughter was Berg, again. "But we can't just let this thing drift . . . ."

But drifting, however, was precisely what the conference seemed to be doing. By early Wednesday evening there was hardly a sense of anything approaching unanimity, and it was difficult, moreover, to see how one might develop. But something was already happening beneath the surface of the conference and, by chance, a new impetus was just about to arrive.

The Wednesday night program looked fairly innocuous: the presentations by the lawyers recruited by Daniel Singer regarding ethics and legal liability. It seemed a relief—lawyers are at least supposed to have some knack for public speaking and the evening promised, if nothing else, a bit of diversion.

And so, at first, it seemed. Daniel Singer . . . concluded with a thorough three-part breakdown of risk-benefit analysis that neatly subsumed the major issues of the previous three days. "We should not pretend," Singer concluded, "that we are not making ethical judgments."

. . .

The second speaker was Alex Capron [who] . . . launched into a merciless "outsider's analysis" that within moments had jaws dropping all over the chapel. Much of the previous discussion, he suggested, had been altogether irrelevant to the central issue.

The Asilomar audience grew suddenly very quiet. Many of the arguments advanced against establishing guidelines, Capron said, had been equally inapplicable. "Academic freedom," he noted acidly, "does not include the freedom to do physical harm." And "prior restraint"—a notion that Lederberg had briefly floated on Tuesday—makes perfect sense and is justified when it involves restraint from doing physical damage.

"This group," Capron suggested flatly, "is not competent to assign overall risk."

The question of earlier that day instantly came to mind: If *we* can't do it, who can?

"It is the right of the public," Capron continued confidently, "to act through the legislature and to make erroneous decisions."

That was hardly reassuring to hear from a lawyer, and it was clear that the audience in the redwood chapel was growing a bit uncomfortable.

Capron then made it worse, by suggesting a hypothetical situation wherein Congress itself might insert its grubby political fingers into the delicate process. . . .

But then again, the lawyer continued, legislation might not be all that bad: The law might provide, say, liability insurance for biohazard accidents.

. . .

But the best—or perhaps worst—was yet to come. The final speaker was a lawyer named Roger Dworkin. . . [on] "Conventional aspects of the law," as he put it, "and how they may sneak up on you—in the form, say, of a multimillion dollar lawsuit."

Abruptly, the audience grew very quiet. The subject of legal responsibility had not yet been dealt with in the fundamental terms of precisely who gets sued should something go dreadfully wrong.

Dworkin's job was to do just that, and having himself just squirmed through three days of the scientists' abstruse technical jargon, he took some relish in trotting out some of his own profession's—torts, liability, proximate cause, OSHA—to illustrate just how finely, if not fairly, the wheels of law can grind.

. . .

[T]here may already be laws on the books that could apply to recombinant DNA engineering, he suggested. OSHA, for example—the Occupational Safety and Health Act—could conceivably be invoked to protect laboratory workers. According to OSHA, the lawyer explained, "the workplace must be free of hazard. Not relatively free," he emphasized. "The statute says *free.*" And the person who sets those standards is the Secretary of Labor.

. . .

Moments after Dworkin concluded his presentation and the lawyers took their seats on stage, the molecular geneticists rallied to the defense.
. . .

Joshua Lederberg finally took the lead and with some eloquence elaborated an intricate analogy involving the risks and responsibilities of accidentally importing a deadly African virus.

"That argument," said Dworkin, "with all due respect, is almost entirely beside the point. If we are remiss about our international travel regulations, we should move to correct that situation, rather than taking it as reason for being equally remiss about our approach to the biohazard question."

Lederberg returned to his seat, big tan arms folded across his chest like a wounded Buddha.

"This body," Dworkin continued, "probably doesn't even know its power. The law has a tradition of listening to and respecting expert groups that regulate themselves. On the other hand, there is precedent for ruining groups that don't—physicians, for example. Malpractice law has always been skewed in the direction of the physician, physicians have refused to testify against each other, and as a result they are now being massacred in court."

. . .

Thursday provided the grayest dawn of all for the International Conference on Recombinant DNA Molecules. And most of the organizing committee were still awake to see it. The night before, commencing just after the evening session with the lawyers, had been devoted to a nonstop round of manic writing and rewriting to draft some sort of coherent statement that the conference, as a body, might adopt.

. . .

"Even if they voted our statement down," Maxine Singer said later, "we'd agreed to send it in ourselves." The statement materialized early Thursday morning as a freshly duplicated five page handout titled, "Statement of the Conference Proceedings."

The first paragraph set the tone: "The new techniques combining genetic information from very different organisms place us in an area of biology with many unknowns. It is this ignorance that has compelled us to conclude that it would be wise to exercise the utmost caution. Nevertheless, the work should proceed but with appropriate safeguards."

The Statement was, clearly, a compromise: The six-category classification of risk was now uniformly condensed to high-moderate-low. The virus group recommendations had been tightened. But there was still no flat proscription of the experiments some had earlier called unreasonably hazardous.

Yet it was nonetheless a strong statement: If adopted, many researchers would have to go home and spend thousands of dollars on new laboratory containment equipment in order to do the experiments they could have done at no extra expense eight months earlier. The notion of comprehensive new safety regulations could hardly have been comforting. "Already," one researcher told me that morning, "we spend two months a year applying for grants; now we're afraid we'll spend another month filling out more forms. And the forms don't protect anybody; they just take more time."

The statement was handed out as the scientists walked into the chapel. At nine, Berg stood briefly to announce a half-hour reading period while the organizing committee rather fitfully occupied their chairs on the stage. Their uncertainty became clearly manifest at the end of the reading period, in a short-lived but valiant effort to keep anything from actually coming to a vote.

The attempt started briskly enough. Berg concluded the reading period with a crisp observation: "I would like," he said, "to terminate this meeting at noon, and I hope that by then we will have reached the point at which that is possible." Because of that deadline, Berg suggested, it would be best to reach consensus by means other than voting. "This is not a statement of the conference," he reassured the audience, "it is a statement from the organizing committee, an attempt to pull together the views as we see them."

The statement was, however, not *signed* by the committee, and while Berg hastened to add that the omission was an oversight, it didn't exactly get the proceedings off on the very best foot.

The trouble began with the first paragraph. A minor quibble over wording arose and Berg reassured the researcher that all of the material discussed that morning would be included in the final report. "I take your comment to heart," Berg said, "and I'm sure we intended it, but somehow it got left out."

. . .

The word "Provisional" was quickly added to the title of the statement. But even that was not enough. David Botstein of MIT stood to say, rather plaintively, "Somehow—maybe we can tell the press to go away—we should get some feeling of whether eighty percent of the people in this place like it, or hate it, or *something*. Because I don't want to shuffle off my responsibility on you. I think maybe an overwhelming majority of the people here are willing to commit themselves to something of this sort."

Botstein had a more accurate sense of the feeling than did the organizing committee at that point. . . .

By then, however, Sydney Brenner was signaling for attention, and it was Brenner, finally, who faced what was clearly inevitable. "I think," he said slowly, "that the first paragraph contains an extremely important statement of principle, and I would in fact be quite willing to see how that is received by showing hands." And after a brief summation—work should go forward but with significant controls—Brenner called for a vote: "And so who is in favor of it?"

The vote was virtually unanimous. Berg, looking slightly puzzled, resumed his chairman's duties. "And are there any opposed?" No hands appeared at all.

"After that first vote," Maxine Singer said later, "I relaxed, because the vote was so overwhelmingly different than what I expected that I realized then that I was a lousy politician."

"It was then," Berg agreed, "that we realized that we'd been listening to the wrong people. A few people were doing all the talking, and a lot of people had been quiet. And the quiet ones were in favor of coming out with something just as we had, and it was the Lederbergs and the Watsons and a few others who were doing all the talking and confusing us. We thought they were reflecting what everybody wanted and felt."

Apparently not. The 150 scientists at Asilomar were almost unanimously in favor of regulating the exotic new technology. Precisely how to regulate it, however, was another matter altogether.

. . .

[T]here was no real mention of excessively dangerous work in the final report, and one long-haired California researcher, in baggy sweater and thick eyeglasses, suggested rather vociferously that there should be. "What I would like to see," he said, "is the statement that *some* of the work should go ahead."

"It's not spelled out," Berg agreed.

"We could insert," Brenner suggested, "that there were some members of the meeting who felt that there are experiments so dangerous that they cannot be safely executed with any currently available containment procedures. I believe that is a statement of fact."

There was a brief silence. "Is that 'some members,'" asked someone, "or the majority?"

The question was hardly an idle one. If there was any element of philosophical discomfort in the noble self-regulation attempt, it was in the notion of the right of free inquiry. The history of science records myriad abridgments of that right, involving individuals like Copernicus as well as whole generations of scientists like the Soviet biologists trained under the eccentric genetic doctrine of Trofim Lysenko. There are sufficient examples, certainly, to make most modern researchers a bit paranoid about even the most apparently benign and humanitarian efforts to control the boundaries of their own curiosity. And while the whole notion of the moratorium may have been interpreted by some as a similar abridgment of that right, nowhere was it more sharply reflected than in the idea of flatly proscribed experiments.

. . .

Berg did his best to prod things past this sticky juncture, but the morass of disagreement was deep indeed. At the outset of the quibbling, Sydney Brenner interrupted from his stage-left seat once again: "I would just like to say," he said wearily, in almost a half-speed caricature of his previously animated delivery, "that we have no legal power here to compel *anybody* to do *anything,* and this has been so since the first letter.

"The letter asked people to take this into consideration. It asked people to defer. On the whole, it was widely accepted. Now—what we are trying to do *here* is decide whether we should further slow up, make further considerations, before we rush pell-mell into the field. I don't want, and I've said this over and over again, to carry the can for *anybody* here. If we make a definition such that by some rewording it is thought by some people that this allows them to try certain things—and let us just say something *happens*—then I don't want those people to say, well, I did it because the Berg committee said I could. I don't want to carry the can for *any* of you."

. . .

Joshua Lederberg, who had earlier railed at the excessive specificity of the six-level classification of risk, had by now changed his mind. "The gap," he said, "between 'low' and 'moderate' is an enormous one from an operational standpoint. The plasmid report suggested a number of intervening stages which were entirely reasonable. But the difference between low and moderate is considerable reconstruction of a laboratory facility. I do not accept it as a reasonable statement of procedure, because it is too severely step-functioned."

Someone else followed up immediately, suggesting that it looked, upon close reading, as if certain kinds of research allowed under the moratorium letter were now to be deferred until a safer vector was developed. And thus the Asilomar conference would not in fact end the moratorium, but *extend* it. Was that the intention of the committee?

It was quite true. No safe vectors then existed, and much of the research depended upon their availability. Richard Novick hemmed and hawed, but finally admitted, "It was the judgment of the committee that when one reaches the level of the warm-blooded animals, the risk of encountering tumor viruses was great enough that one didn't want to fool around without built-in containment, both physical and biological."

. . .

"Might I ask your committee how they propose to deal with the question of type-VI experiments?" inquired a middle-aged Englishman. "It has been put to me by people in the U.K. that at this time they can see no possible experiment, with our current state of knowledge, involving, say, smallpox DNA virus and these types of vectors. It's not that they couldn't *design* such experiments—it's just that the combination of risks and benefits leads them to put them in a type-VI category."

"But that's like doing a *head* transplant." another English researcher muttered softly to a colleague. "It's simply something one wouldn't *do.*"

"I thought," said Berg, "that we'd agreed to indicate that there was a split, a difference of opinion among people at the conference as to whether certain experiments should be judged not permissible at the present time."

The English researcher continued to stand. "Could we, perhaps, for my benefit as much as anyone, test that feeling? Perhaps there *isn't* a split. Could we test?"

"There have been three groups that have avoided this issue," someone agreed. "It's really a matter of principle." An amendment to the early portion of the statement was read, emphasizing that "there are organisms that could be created with current methodology that comprise risks of such intensity that such organisms ought not to be created at the present time."

"Can I talk to this, please?" Ephraim Anderson asked. "While I disagree with a good deal of the plasmid group's pronouncements, the one thing I did *not* disagree with was that there are certain organisms with which we should not *start* experimental work of this sort." Anyone, he said, could sensibly compose a list of those organisms. "They are hot, and should not be worked with."

"Okay," Berg said finally. "One view says that there are experiments that should be performed only in the highest containment facilities available today. And the second point of view says that there is a class of experiments that should not be done at all with present methods."

Berg didn't even need to count hands. "Well," he said, "it's quite clear that the majority supports the latter. If we have time, perhaps we can come back to this section." He paused for a moment, then moved on. "Please keep your comments brief."

. . .

It looked for just a moment as if the whole effort might tip over into sprawling chaos. Half a dozen people started to speak simultaneously. Lederberg fumed silently; Don Brown, standing, looked incredulous; Berg looked exhausted; and then suddenly Sydney Brenner quietly interrupted.

"Could I ask whether," he inquired slowly, "we might jump to section 6? In the paragraph that states, 'This document represents our best assessment of the potential biohazards . . . ,' I would like to change the word 'best' to 'first.' "

There was a brief silence, and then, for the first time in two hours, sustained laughter.

"I think," Brenner continued finally, "that we should emphasize that these are extremely complex issues and that we may be wrong. I am very sympathetic to the minority points of view and I am not prepared to say that this is absolutely the right way to do it. Perhaps that would satisfy Professor Lederberg—that at least one member of this committee is demonstrably in favor of the view that there are, in fact, uncertainties."

. . .

The remainder of the provisional statement was, in contrast, almost totally uncontroversial. It dealt with implementation—education, review boards, and the like—and once the discussion moved off the territory of specific work, the level of controversy dropped and the organizing committee once more found themselves the major contributors.

In the midst of section 4, the noon lunch bell rang. Berg moved immediately to the last section—a brief paragraph that expressed some of the gaping questions that remained in the initial risk assessment, from the basic question about eukaryotic programming in prokaryotic organisms, to the provocative notion that perhaps free DNA molecules themselves, outside of their biological containers, could infect plant or animal cells.

. . .

Very quickly, the second lunch bell rang in the courtyard outside the chapel. "If I'm correct, then," Berg said, "we've proceeded through the whole document, by the second lunch bell if not the first. And so I would like, in a sense, to formalize our actions here, by asking for a show of hands of those people who support the entire document, including the amendments we've discussed individually. All those in favor of this as a provisional statement, please raise your hands."

. . .

Somewhere around four hands rose in opposition. "Okay," said Berg. "Again I would say that there is substantial agreement here on that point."

Daniel Singer stood then to "express a view of these proceedings from the outside." Regardless of the ultimate outcome, he said, he was uplifted by the way the community of scientists had organized for social responsibility. "I think you have embarked on a continuing obligation," he concluded, "with respect to this particular problem of recombinant DNA molecules, and you have set a very high standard indeed. You are a tough act to follow for other groups of scientists who must necessarily embark on this same kind of exercise in the future. It's been nice being here."

. . .

PAUL BERG, DAVID BALTIMORE, SYDNEY BRENNER, RICH ARD O. ROBIN III AND MAXINE F. SINGER, ASILOMAR CONFERENCE ON RECOMBINANT DNA MOLECULES *

188 Science 991–94 (1975).

I. Introduction and General Conclusions

This meeting was organized to review scientific progress in research on recombinant DNA molecules and to discuss appropriate ways to deal with the potential biohazards of this work. . . .

. . .

The new techniques, which permit combination of genetic information from very different organisms, place us in an area of biology with many unknowns. Even in the present, more limited conduct of research in this field, the evaluation of potential biohazards has proved to be extremely difficult. It is this ignorance that has compelled us to conclude that it would be wise to exercise considerable caution in performing this research. Nevertheless, the participants at the Conference agreed that most of the work on construction of recombinant DNA molecules should proceed, provided that appropriate safeguards, principally biological and physical barriers adequate to contain the newly created organisms, are employed. Moreover, the standards of protection should be greater at the beginning and modified as improvements in the methodology occur and assessments of the risks change. Furthermore, it was agreed that there are certain experiments in which the potential risks are of such a serious nature that they ought not to be done with presently available containment facilities. . . .

II. Principles Guiding the Recommendations and Conclusions

Although our assessments of the risks involved with each of the various lines of research on recombinant DNA molecules may differ, few, if any, believe that this methodology is free from any risk. Reasonable

* Summary statement of the report submitted to the Assembly of Life Sciences of the National Academy of Sciences and approved by its Executive Committee on May 20, 1975.

principles for dealing with these potential risks are: (i) that containment be made an essential consideration in the experimental design and (ii) that the effectiveness of the containment should match, as closely as possible, the estimated risk. Consequently, whatever scale of risks is agreed upon, there should be a commensurate scale of containment. Estimating the risks will be difficult and intuitive at first, but this will improve as we acquire additional knowledge; at each stage we shall have to match the potential risk with an appropriate level of containment. Experiments requiring large-scale operations would seem to be riskier than equivalent experiments done on a small scale and therefore require more stringent containment procedures. The use of cloning vehicles or vectors (plasmids, phages) and bacterial hosts with a restricted capacity to multiply outside of the laboratory would reduce the potential biohazard of a particular experiment. Thus, the ways in which potential biohazards and different levels of containment are matched may vary from time to time, particularly as the containment technology is improved. . . .

. . .

IV. Implementation

In many countries steps are already being taken by national bodies to formulate codes of practice for the conduct of experiments with known or potential biohazard. Until these are established, we urge individual scientists to use the proposals in this document as a guide. In addition, there are some recommendations which could be immediately and directly implemented by the scientific community.

. . .

V. New Knowledge

. . .

Nothing is known about the potential infectivity in higher organisms of phages or bacteria containing segments of eukaryotic DNA, and very little is known about the infectivity of the DNA molecules themselves. Genetic transformation of bacteria does occur in animals, suggesting that recombinant DNA molecules can retain their biological potency in this environment. There are many questions in this area, the answers to which are essential for our assessment of the biohazards of experiments with recombinant DNA molecules. It will be necessary to ensure that this work will be planned and carried out; and it will be particularly important to have this information before large-scale applications of the use of recombinant DNA molecules are attempted.

NOTES ON ASILOMAR

1. What seems to have been the underlying premise of the conference? Could the conferees' conclusions be based on new knowledge about risks (unavailable when the moratorium was called), in the absence of an organized effort to discover it? Would the few reports of some small, recently conducted experiments be enough? If not, would the basis for acting one way or the other—to continue, modify or lift the limitations set forth in the 1974 letter—be simply the opinions of the people at Asilomar that they wanted to get on with the work?

2. To a lay person, all the scientists gathered at Asilomar might seem to have been expert biologists; the scientists, however, saw themselves as subspecialists in different disciplines who were ignorant of the details of the other subspecialties involved. To what extent does the report of the deliberations show that the par-

ticipants wanted (or could have used) the advice of particular "experts"? Again, is such deference to expertise appropriate under the circumstances?

3. To what extent do the organizers seem to have tried to assemble a "representative" group? If that were an objective, what interests should have been represented? On such wide-ranging issues, can a group be representative both of the interests involved and of the knowledge necessary to discuss the issues and still be kept small enough so that useful interchange is feasible during the meeting?

4. A statement of rules can become an apparent sanction to perform any act that comes within the rules, as one member of the organizing committee commented. Is this undesirable? Unavoidable?

5. At one point, a researcher suggested that there are experiments one simply would not carry out. How does a scientist come to know what experiments fall into this class? Is it self-evident? Universally agreed upon? Officially set forth?

6. What is the role of the press in formulating science policy? In the case of Asilomar, the organizers allowed the press in (after some initial reluctance) to what was otherwise a closed meeting of scientists (and the four invited lawyers). The meeting participants seem to have been reasonably happy with the press coverage of the conference, although the scientists certainly had moments of doubt. Michael Rogers recounts the dismay of some when, at the conclusion of the meeting, they were asked questions by a few of the top reporters in attendance "that suggested they had spent the previous days locked in a very dark closet." M. Rogers, Biohazard 55 (1977).

On the journalists' side, certain compromises were also made, such as agreeing not to file any stories until after the full four-day meeting was completed. Is it reasonable to restrict public access to information in this way? On the other hand, would the scientists have been correct in refusing to discuss the subject with the journalists at all, unless the latter showed themselves to be knowledgeable about the science and hence less likely to make mistakes that could distort what the scientists said?

7. In the months after the meeting, some of its leading participants began to express qualms about the possible public reaction to the questions the scientists were raising.

Viewed as a rather public soul-searching and self-education, these discussions are invaluable. The main danger is that some political imperative may forge these tentative questions into iron-clad regulations which will be with us long after their origins have been forgotten. After all, similar questions can be raised about the widest range of human activities: should it be lawful to keep domestic cats when we suspect that they harbor toxoplasmosis, and possibly leukemia as well? . . . [S]hould we forbid international travel simply because our quarantine procedures do not guarantee that exotic diseases will be kept out?

For each of these cases, and many more, the apparently innocuous doctrine, "As long as there is any risk, don't do it!" can only bring a loss to human welfare. We must instead make every feasible effort to assess both the risks and the benefits of a given course of action—only then will we be able to find the optimal balance. . . .

. . . Those who consider themselves guardians of the public safety must count the costs to the public health of *impeding* research, as well as the speculative *hazards* of research.

Lederberg, DNA Splicing: Will Fear Rob Us of Its Benefits?, Prism 37–38 (Nov. 1975). Drawing on a statement by Senator Edward Kennedy that society must give its "informed consent" to technological innovation, Dr. Lederberg also argued that this "surely includes knowing the hazards of saying no to the prospects of significant medical advances." Cf. Truman v. Thomas, Ch. 3, Sec. B.1, infra.

8. Picking up on the religious theme that Rogers had noticed at the meeting, molecular biologist Erwin Chargaff criticized the "Bishops of Asilomar":

At this Council of Asilomar there congregated the molecular bishops and church fathers from all over the world, in order to condemn the heresies of which they themselves had been the first and the principal perpetrators. This was probably the first time in history that the incendiaries formed their own fire brigade. The edict published in due course, which lists the various forbidden items, reads like a combined curriculum vitae of the conveners of the conference.

Chargaff, A Slap at the Bishops of Asilomar, 190 Science 135 (1975). What other arguments about self-interest could be raised, and which way do they cut?

9. In January 1982, the American Association for the Advancement of Science awarded its first Scientific Freedom and Responsibility Award to four scientists. Among the four were Maxine Singer, organizer of the Asilomar conference; Paul Berg, leader of the 1974 moratorium on research; and Norton Zinder, a leader in developing gene-splicing techniques and in bringing the issues to public attention. The AAAS cited the three for their "leadership in the recombinant DNA debate."

2. ADMINISTRATIVE SUPERVISION

The meeting at Asilomar did not mark the end of self-regulation; indeed, while the rules and regulations have become more elaborate, they continue to rest on the bedrock of self-policing and of personal and group responsibility that has characterized the field since the 1973 Gordon conference. Yet the Asilomar meeting can probably be described as the high-water mark for self-regulation—at the very least, thereafter the questions would no longer be debated solely by scientists at secluded locales like the conference grounds in Pacific Grove but would instead be taken up in more open forums where other, nonscientific participants would play important, even dominant, roles.

The transition was very gradual because the initial review by the government, on February 28, 1975, the day after the Asilomar conference ended, came in a meeting in San Francisco of a special committee that had been appointed the previous October to advise the Director of the National Institutes of Health (NIH), the principal sponsor of recombinant DNA research. The committee, chaired by DeWitt Stetten, Jr., M.D., Ph. D., NIH's deputy director for science, was made up entirely of biomedical scientists and was more of a "kitchen cabinet" for NIH Director Donald S. Fredrickson than a group of outsiders to the field; in fact, included among the members were scientists actively involved on the leading edge of the research. At the next meeting of the committee (termed the RAC, for Recombinant DNA Advisory Committee), one such scientist, David Hogness of Stanford, was appointed chairman of a subcommittee to draft guidelines.

Meeting again in mid-July 1975 at Woods Hole, Massachusetts, the committee produced a substantially revised set of guidelines which weakened the containment measures proposed by the Hogness subcommittee.

Following this meeting, many letters were received [by NIH] which were critical of the guidelines. The majority of critics felt that they were too lax, others that they were too strict. All letters were reviewed by the committee, and a new subcommittee, chaired by Dr. Elizabeth Kutter was appointed to revise the guidelines.*

At its fourth meeting, on December 4–5, 1975, in La Jolla, California, the committee adopted "proposed guidelines" by comparing the three draft versions (Hogness, Woods Hole, and Kutter) line-by-line and adding new material as needed. These guidelines were somewhat stricter than those that emerged from the Asilomar meeting; they were accepted by Paul Berg as being in the spirit of Asilomar, but were criticized by others as "tailored to fit particular experiments that are already on the drawing boards." †

Although all meetings of the committee were public, the primary non-members in attendance had been researchers—including some like Berg and Maxine Singer who had originally been members of the committee but had resigned. To broaden the range of advice, Dr. Fredrickson decided to have a special meeting of the Director's Advisory Committee in February 1976 at NIH. This group included "a chief judge in the U.S. Court of Appeals, the provost of MIT, the chairman of a west coast medical school, the president of the National Consumers League, the president of the National Academy of Sciences, and the chairman of the biology department at Caltech . . . representing backgrounds that ranged from one gentleman with 25 years in medical microbiology to a [participant] who would soon admit that [he] was not exactly sure where 'the ballpark' was."** The advisors were instructed about the field by Berg and Singer, and then Hogness and Curtiss debated the proposed guidelines; the public witnesses were led off by David Baltimore, and others who followed spoke not only for themselves but for various groups, most finding the regulations too lax. Don Brown, a Johns Hopkins scientist whose work with frog genes would be made more difficult by the La Jolla guidelines protested that they were too strict, as reported in the following material.

MICHAEL ROGERS, BIOHAZARD

183–84, 187–90 (1977).

Brown's statement before the Advisory Committee was intense, angry, and cogent. " 'Guidelines' is a terrible word for these," he said. "These aren't guidelines—they're rules that are massive, detailed, forbidding, and above all rigid." He pinpointed accurately the areas in which the guidelines committee had been particularly conservative: It was possible, he pointed out, to work with some whole, infectious viruses under far lower containment conditions than those prescribed by the guidelines for viral DNA removed from its protective vehicle. "Why were such strict and irrational guidelines drawn up?" he asked. "They were produced by scientists who had no choice." And here, strikingly, Brown agreed completely with the critics on the other side of the fence: The problem was insufficient public input, which, in Brown's view, made the scientists bend over backward so as not to appear self-serving. The result was "this kind of

* Decision of the Director, National Institutes of Health to Release Guidelines for Research on Recombinant DNA Molecules, 41 Fed.Reg. 27902 (1976). [Dr. Kutter, a biophysicist from Evergreen State College, a small school in Washington, was a new member of the committee. [Eds.]]

† Wade, Recombinant DNA: NIH Sets Strict Rules to Launch New Technology, 190 Science 1175, 1179 (1975) (quoting an unnamed critic).

** Rogers, Biohazard 178–79 (1977).

rigid, immensely detailed set of rules which encourages people to look for loopholes."

The predominant criticism at the Advisory Committee meeting was, however, just the opposite. A young woman historian from the University of Michigan—who a few months later helped organize an unsuccessful attempt to keep recombinant DNA work off the Ann Arbor campus—argued that the guidelines were flawed from the outset, since there had never been any discussion of whether the work should ever go forward at all. She went on to suggest that the committee should have included no more than two or three people in the field, and that in general, the discussions had "ignored the infinite capacity of living things to change and adapt." Her vaguely vitalistic approach to the science was characteristic of much of the lay criticism leveled at the guidelines; predictably, it did not arouse much sympathy in the hearts of most biologists.

The remainder of the young critics that day had scientific backgrounds and their objections were all similar, focusing on the use of *E. coli* and the guidelines drawn up for shotgunning. . . . One speaker recommended delaying all the experiments indefinitely. "What's the rush?" he said. "After all, we have several billion years of evolution behind us."

Philip Handler, the President of the National Academy of Sciences and a member of the Advisory Committee, remarked later that he was "troubled by the fact that the nay-sayers are far younger than the aye-sayers. Conservatism used to be the role for the elders of the tribe. . . . I'm not sure what it means."

. . .

A few months after the Advisory Committee meeting, I visited a young postdoctoral fellow named Richard Goldstein in his small office at Harvard Medical School. Goldstein had been . . . probably the most effective and articulate of the critics who appeared before the February hearings of the NIH Advisory Committee.

Goldstein had returned from those hearings hurt and a bit angry. The Boston Area Group had, after all, spent two months composing a long and carefully detailed critique of the Woods Hole guidelines, which was sent to each of the members of the NIH Recombinant DNA Molecules Advisory Committee prior to La Jolla. "I never heard a word from any person on that committee other than Stetten, who said thank you. I don't have the faintest idea whether it was even considered." Goldstein shook his head. "And even after the Advisory Committee meeting, I *still* don't know."

As one of the most well-informed of the critics, Goldstein was occasionally embarrassed by some of his unsolicited allies, as at the Advisory Committee hearings. "I wish," he said, "they'd stick to the issues they know." . . .

The selection of magazine articles given as background material to the members of the Advisory Committee was, without question, favorably biased and did not represent the full range of opinions that had already appeared, even in journals as restrained as *Science.* Goldstein felt also that the structure of the meeting—with proponents like Berg and Singer speaking at length in the morning, and the opponents left with only short amounts of time late on a long day—was unfair, and that Fredrickson had been unnecessarily condescending in introducing the young opponents. David Baltimore, on the other hand, had been conspicuously introduced as a new Nobel laureate (to which Baltimore, to his credit, responded quietly, "I don't think that's relevant here").

In scientific circles, of course, such credentials are in fact relevant, and if one's rank is high enough one can rise above the usual red tape that comes with involvement in public processes. After the Advisory Committee meeting, Goldstein was uncertain whether he could continue his own involvement. The long critique had taken much time and now the heads of his department were pointedly suggesting that he make a choice between scientific politics and his own work.

After we'd talked for an hour or so that afternoon, the abrasive, contentious approach that Goldstein had adopted in public had vanished. In odd ways, in fact, he'd come to remind me a bit of Paul Berg. "I'll be sad if the guidelines don't work out," he said. "I think you can work within the system; I don't know if that's an elitist position, but then I have no great faith in government control over anything. That's why I felt that somehow we had to regulate ourselves."

Yet by that time Goldstein clearly felt himself to be irrevocably on the outside. "It's one of the strange strains throughout this," he said finally. "There were plenty of people who knew we were deeply involved in this, and they had a lot more at stake than we did, because they wanted to do the work. Yet they never picked up the phone and said, gee, let's talk about this thing. It seems like that would be the quickest way to get it straightened out—so they'd know where they were going to work for the next year or two."

The criticisms raised by Goldstein and company seemed to have had a minimal effect on the Advisory Committee. The second day of comments provided just about the reaction one might have expected from the group: general agreement with the guidelines, a handful of specific suggestions about enforcement, and regular exhortations toward continued caution. "NIH," said NAS president Handler, "is to be congratulated on getting this far. The question is where you go now." What troubled him most, he said, was that he had found it possible to sit through one-and-a-half days of controversy "and agree with almost everything I heard."

"If Dr. Berg and his colleagues don't deserve the Nobel Prize for medicine," said another member, "they deserve it for Peace"—he paused—"since they don't give one in controversy."

"There's no instant feedback here," lamented one scientist. "With toxic chemicals, it used to be easy: You keeled over."

Other comments expressed real alarm, particularly about the effect public opinion might have on legislation. "You can pat yourselves on the back," said the president of one student organization, "but keep looking over your shoulder. If Congress gets the idea that scientists aren't playing straight, you'll be using your pipettes to pick your teeth."

All of the committee members were to submit written opinions, and Fredrickson announced that he would make his decision on the basis of those and the hearing transcript. But De Witt Stetten probably had the last word in terms of summing up the two days' proceedings. He described a fogbound strait that separates Newfoundland from Canada—a narrow, treacherous passage which sailors navigate by listening for the sound of the surf on the left side and the sound of the surf on the right. When the sound from each side is equal, then they know they are in the middle, and they sail on. "And that," Stetten concluded, "is my best advice to you."

NIH Director Fredrickson smiled and shook his head. "Maybe," he said, "that explains the roaring in my ears."

NOTE

After the February meeting, Dr. Fredrickson met again with the advisory committee on DNA and with selected representatives of industry. Then, on June 23, 1976, he issued the "Final Guidelines for Research Involving Recombinant DNA Molecules." Two weeks later, these guidelines—which ran to 32 triple-column printed pages (counting appendices)—were printed in the Federal Register, along with a ten page explanatory statement by Dr. Fredrickson.

The NIH guidelines have been revised several times since 1976. Among the most important changes were several ordered by HEW Secretary Califano in December 1978, including formal efforts to extend the effect of the guidelines to privately sponsored research (through the use of the regulatory authority of the Food and Drug Administration and of the Environmental Protection Agency) and to enlarge and broaden the membership in the RAC. Mr. Califano later described the benefits of the latter action:

> [W]e sparked [the scientists'] spirited resistance when we added a number of ethicists, clergy, lawyers, and lay persons to the committee. Fredrickson, however, saw the move as enriching the advisory group and strengthening a potential consensus on DNA research. Eventually many of the scientists who originally opposed the action appreciated some of the benefits of broad public participation. Califano, Governing America: An Insider's Report from the White House and the Cabinet 204 (1981).

Along with the increased role for the public in approving and monitoring recombinant DNA experiments has come a progressive relaxation of the restrictions themselves—for example, by exempting certain categories of research and by downgrading the level of biological and physical containment required for most experiments. The most recent revision in the guidelines (reproduced here in abridged form) was issued in May 1983; it amounts to a major recodification of all the rules. What should a lawyer who is not a scientist expect to learn in reading such regulations? Conversely, what is a researcher who is not a lawyer to make of all the detailed regulation of the activities in and around the laboratory?

DEPARTMENT OF HEALTH AND HUMAN SERVICES, NATIONAL INSTITUTES OF HEALTH, GUIDELINES FOR RESEARCH INVOLVING RECOMBINANT DNA MOLECULES

48 Fed.Reg. 24556, 24557–24564, 24567, 24577, 24580 (June 1, 1983).

I. Scope of the Guidelines

I–A. *Purpose.* The purpose of these Guidelines is to specify practices for constructing and handling (i) recombinant DNA molecules and (ii) organisms and viruses containing recombinant DNA molecules.

I–B. *Definition of Recombinant DNA Molecules.* In the context of these Guidelines, recombinant DNA molecules are defined as either (i) molecules which are constructed outside living cells by joining natural or synthetic DNA segments to DNA molecules that can replicate in a living cell, or (ii) DNA molecules that result from the replication of those described in (i) above.

. . .

I–C. *General Applicability.* The Guidelines are applicable to all recombinant DNA research within the United States or its territories which is conducted at or sponsored by an Institution that receives any support for recombinant DNA research from NIH. This includes research performed by NIH directly.

An individual receiving support for research involving recombinant DNA must be associated with or sponsored by an Institution that can and does assume the responsibilities assigned in these Guidelines.

The Guidelines are also applicable to projects done abroad if they are supported by NIH funds. If the host country, however, has established rules for the conduct of recombinant DNA projects, then a certificate of compliance with those rules may be submitted to NIH in lieu of compliance with the NIH Guidelines. NIH reserves the right to withhold funding if the safety practices to be employed abroad are not reasonably consistent with the NIH Guidelines.

I–D. *General Definitions.* The following terms, which are used throughout the Guidelines, are defined as follows:

I–D–1. "Institution" means any public or private entity (including Federal, State, and local government agencies).

I–D–2. "Institutional Biosafety Committee" or "IBC" means a committee that (i) meets the requirements for membership specified in Section IV–B–2, and (ii) reviews, approves, and oversees projects in accordance with the responsibilities defined in Sections IV–B–2 and IV–B–3.

I–D–3. "NIH Office of Recombinant DNA Activities" or "ORDA" means the office within NIH with responsibility for (i) reviewing and coordinating all activities of NIH related to the Guidelines, and (ii) performing other duties as defined in Section IV–C–3.

I–D–4. "Recombinant DNA Advisory Committee" or "RAC" means the public advisory committee that advises the Secretary, the Assistant Secretary for Health, and the Director of the National Institutes of Health concerning recombinant DNA research. The RAC shall be constituted as specified in Section IV–C–2.

. . . .

II. Containment

Effective biological safety programs have been operative in a variety of laboratories for many years. Considerable information, therefore, already exists for the design of physical containment facilities and the selection of laboratory procedures applicable to organisms carrying recombinant DNAs. The existing programs rely upon mechanisms that, for convenience, can be divided into two categories: (i) A set of standard practices that are generally used in microbiology laboratories, and (ii) special procedures, equipment, and laboratory installations that provide physical barriers which are applied in varying degrees according to the estimated biohazard. Four levels of physical containment which are designated as P1, P2, P3, and P4 are described in Appendix G. P4 provides the most stringent containment conditions, P1 the least stringent.

Experiments on recombinant DNAs, by their very nature, lend themselves to a third containment mechanism—namely, the application of highly specific biological barriers. In fact, natural barriers do exist which limit either (i) the infectivity of a *vector,* or *vehicle,* (plasmid or virus) for specific hosts or (ii) its dissemination and survival in the environment.

The vectors that provide the means for replication of the recombinant DNAs and/or the host cells in which they replicate can be genetically designed to decrease by many orders of magnitude the probability of dissemination of recombinant DNA's outside the laboratory.

As these means of containment are complementary, different levels of containment appropriate for experiments with different recombinants can be established by applying various combinations of the physical and biological barriers along with a constant use of the standard practices. We consider these categories of containment separately in order that such combinations can be conveniently expressed in the Guidelines.

In constructing the Guidelines, it was necessary to define boundary conditions for the different levels of physical and biological containment and for the classes of experiments to which they apply. We recognize that these definitions do not take into account all existing and anticipated information on special procedures that will allow particular experiments to be carried out under different conditions than indicated here without affecting risk. Indeed, we urge that individual investigators devise simple and more effective containment procedures and that investigators and institutional biosafety committees recommend changes in the Guidelines to permit their use.

III. Containment Guidelines for Covered Experiments

. . .

III–A. *Experiments that Require RAC Review and NIH and IBC Approval Before Initiation.* Experiments in this category cannot be initiated without submission of relevant information on the proposed experiment to NIH, the publication of the proposal in the Federal Register for thirty days of comment, review by the RAC, and specific approval by NIH. The containment conditions for such experiments will be recommended by RAC and set by NIH at the time of approval. Such experiments also require the approval of the IBC before initiation. Specific experiments already approved in this section and the appropriate containment conditions are listed in Appendices D and F. If an experiment is similar to those listed in Appendices D and F, ORDA may determine appropriate containment conditions according to case precedents under Section IV–C–1–b–(3)–(g).

III–A–1. Deliberate formation of recombinant DNAs containing genes for the biosynthesis of toxic molecules lethal for vertebrates at an LD_{50} of less than 100 nanograms per kilogram body weight (e.g., microbial toxins such as the botulinum toxins, tetanus toxin, diphtheria toxin, *Shigella dysenteriae* neurotoxin). Specific approval has been given for the cloning in *E. Coli* K–12 of DNAs containing genes coding for the biosynthesis of toxic molecules which are lethal to vertebrates at 100 nanograms to 100 micrograms per kilogram body weight. Containment levels for these experiments are specified in Appendix F.

III–A–2. Deliberate release into the environment of any organism containing recombinant DNA, except certain plants as described in Appendix L.

III–A–3. Deliberate transfer of a drug resistance trait to microorganisms that are not known to acquire it naturally, if such acquisition could compromise the use of the drug to control disease agents in human or veterinary medicine or agricultue.

III–B. *Experiments that Require IBC Approval Before Initiation.* Investigators performing experiments in this category must submit to their Institutional Biosafety Committee (IBC), prior to initiation of the experiments, a registration document that contains a description of: (a) The source(s) of DNA, (b) the nature of the inserted DNA sequences, (c) the hosts and vectors to be used, (d) whether a deliberate attempt will be made to obtain expression of a foreign gene, and, if so, what protein will be produced, and (e) the containment conditions specified in these Guidelines. This registration document must be dated and signed by the investigator and filed only with the local IBC. The IBC shall review all such proposals prior to initiation of the experiments. Requests for lowering of containment for experiments in this category will be considered by NIH.

III–B–1. *Experiments Using Human or Animal Pathogens (Class 2, Class 3, Class 4, or Class 5 Agents) as Host-Vector Systems.* *

. . .

III–B–2. *Experiments in Which DNA from Human or Animal Pathogens (Class 2, Class 3, Class 4, or Class 5 Agents) is Closed in Nonpathogenic Prokaryotic or Lower Eukaryotic Host-Vector Systems.*

. . .

III–B–3. *Experiments Involving the Use of Infectious Animal or Plant Viruses or Defective Animal or Plant Viruses in the Presence of Helper Virus in Tissue Culture Systems.*

Caution: Special care should be used in the evaluation of containment levels for experiments which are likely to either enhance the pathogenicity (e.g., insertion of a host oncogene) or to extend the host range (e.g., introduction of novel control elements) of viral vectors under conditions which permit a productive infection. In such cases, serious consideration should be given to raising the physical containment by at least one level.

Note.—Recombinant DNA molecules which contain less than two-thirds of the genome of any eukaryotic virus (all virus from a single Family being considered identical) may be considered defective and can be used, in the absence of helper, under the conditions specified in Section III–C.

. . .

III–B–4. *Recombinant DNA Experiments Involving Whole Animals or Plants.*

III–B–4–a. DNA from any source except for greater than two-thirds of a eukaryotic viral genome may be transferred to any non-human vertebrate organism and propagated under conditions of physical containment comparable to P1 and appropriate to the organism under study. It is important that the investigator demonstrate that the fraction of the viral genome being utilized does not lead to productive infection. A USDA permit is required for work with Class 5 agents.

III–B–4–b. For all experiments involving whole animals and plants and not covered by III–B–4–a, the appropriate containment will be determined by the IBC.

III–B–5. *Experiments Involving More Than 10 Liters of Culture.* The appropriate containment will be decided by the IBC. Where appropriate, the large-scale containment recommendations of the NIH should be used (45 FR 24968).

---

* The reference to organisms as Class 1, 2, 3, 4 or 5 refers to the classification system published in Centers for Disease Control, Dep't of Health, Ed. & Welfare, Classification of Etiologic Agents on the Basis of Hazard (4th ed. 1974). [Eds.]

III–C. *Experiments that Require IBC Notice Simultaneously with Initiation of Experiments.* Experiments not included in Sections III–A, III–B, III–D, and subsections of these Sections are to be considered in Section III–C. All such experiments can be carried out at P1 containment. For experiments in this category, a registration document as described in Section III–B must be dated and signed by the investigator and filed with the local IBC at the time of initiation of the experiment. The IBC shall review all such proposals, but IBC review prior to initiation of the experiment is not required. . . .

. . .

III–D. *Exempt Experiments.* The following recombinant DNA molecules are exempt from these Guidelines and no registration with the IBC is necessary.

III–D–1. Those that are not in organisms or viruses.

III–D–2. Those that consist entirely of DNA segments from a single nonchromosomal or vital DNA source, though one or more of the segments may be a synthetic equivalent.

III–D–3. Those that consist entirely of DNA from a prokaryotic host, including its indigenous plasmids or viruses, when propagated only in that host (or a closely related strain of the same species) or when transferred to another host by well established physiological means; also, those that consist entirely of DNA from an eukaryotic host, including its chloroplasts, mitrochondria, or plasmids (but excluding viruses), when propagated only in that host (or a close related strain of same species).

III–D–4. Certain specified recombinant DNA molecules that consist entirely of DNA segments from different species that exchange DNA by known physiological processes, though one or more of the segments may be a synthetic equivalent. A list of such exchangers will be prepared and periodically revised by the Director, NIH, with advice of the RAC, after appropriate notice and opportunity for public comment. . . .

III–D–5. Other classes of recombinant DNA molecules, if the Director, NIH, with advice of the RAC, after appropriate notice and opportunity for public comment, finds that they do not present a significant risk to health or the environment. . . .

IV. Roles and Responsibilities

IV–A. *Policy.* Safety in activities involving recombinant DNA depends on the individual conducting them. The Guidelines cannot anticipate every possible situation. Motivation and good judgment are the key essentials to protection of health and the environment.

The Guidelines are intended to help the Institution, the Institutional Biosafety Committee (IBC), the Biological Safety Officer, and the Principal Investigator determine the safeguards that should be implemented. These Guidelines will never be complete or final, since all conceivable experiments involving recombinant DNA cannot be foreseen. Therefore, *it is the responsibility of the Institution and those associated with it to adhere to the intent of the Guidelines as well as to their specifics.*

. . .

IV–B. *Responsibilities of the Institution.*

IV–B–1. *General Information.* Each Institution conducting or sponsoring recombinant DNA research covered by these Guidelines is responsible for ensuring that the research is carried out in full conformity with the provisions of the Guidelines. In order to fulfill this responsibility, the Institution shall:

IV–B–1–a. Establish and implement policies that provide for the safe conduct of recombinant DNA research and that ensure compliance with the Guidelines. The Institution, as part of its general responsibilities for implementing the Guidelines, may establish additional procedures, as deemed necessary, to govern the Institution and its components in the discharge of its responsibilities under the Guidelines. This may include (i) statements formulated by the Institution for general implementation of the Guidelines and (ii) whatever additional precautionary steps the Institution may deem appropriate.

IV–B–1–b. Establish an Institutional Biosafety Committee (IBC) that meets the requirements set forth in Section IV–B–2 and carries out the functions detailed in Section IV–B–3.

IV–B–1–c. If the Institution is engaged in recombinant DNA research at the P3 or P4 containment level, appoint a Biological Safety Officer, (BSO), who shall be a member of the IBC and carry out the duties specified in Section IV–B–4.

IV–B–1–d. Require that investigators responsible for research covered by these Guidelines comply with the provisions of Section IV–B–5, and assist investigators to do so.

IV–B–1–e. Ensure appropriate training for the IBC chairperson and members, the BSO, Principal Investigators (PIs), and laboratory staff regarding the Guidelines, their implementation, and laboratory safety. Responsibility for training IBC members may be carried out through the IBC chairperson. Responsibility for training laboratory staff may be carried out through the PI. The Institution is responsible for seeing that the PI has sufficient training, but may delegate this responsibility to the IBC.

IV–B–1–f. Determine the necessity, in connection with each project, for health surveillance of recombinant DNA research personnel, and conduct, if found appropriate, a health surveillance program for the project. [The Laboratory Safety Monograph (LSM) discusses various possible components of such a program—for example, records of agents handled, active investigation of relevant illnesses, and the maintenance of serial serum samples for monitoring serologic changes that may result from the employees' work experience. Certain medical conditions may place a laboratory worker at increased risk in any endeavor where infectious agents are handled. Examples given the LSM include gastrointestinal disorders and treatment with steroids, immunosuppressive drugs, or antibiotics. Workers with such disorders or treatment should be evaluated to determine whether they should be engaged in research with potentially hazardous organisms during their treatment or illness. . . .]

IV–B–1–g. Report within 30 days to ORDA any significant problems with any violations of the Guidelines and significant research-related accidents and illnesses, unless the institution determines that the PI or IBC has done so.

IV–B–2. *Membership and Procedures of the IBC.* The Institution shall establish an Institutional Biosafety Committee (IBC) whose responsibilities need not be restricted to recombinant DNA. The committee shall meet the following requirements:

IV–B–2–a. The IBC shall comprise no fewer than five members so selected that they collectively have experience and expertise in recombinant DNA technology and the capability to assess the safety of recombinant DNA research experiments and any potential risk to public health or the environment. At least two members shall not be affiliated with the Institution (apart from their membership on the IBC) and shall represent the interest of the surrounding community with respect to health and protection of the environment. Members meet this requirement if, for example, they are officials of State or local public health or environmental protection agencies, members of other local governmental bodies, or persons active in medical, occupational health, or environmental concerns in the community. The Biological Safety Officer (BSO), mandatory when research is being conducted at the P3 and P4 levels, shall be a member.

IV–B–2–b. In order to ensure the competence necessary to review recombinant DNA activities, it is recommended that (i) the IBC include persons with expertise in recombinant DNA technology, biological safety, and physical containment; (ii) the IBC include, or have available as consultants, persons knowledgeable in institutional commitments and policies, applicable law, standards of professional conduct and practice, community attitudes, and the environment; and (iii) at least one member be from the laboratory technical staff.

IV–B–2–c. The Institution shall identify the committee members by name in a report to the NIH Office of Recombinant DNA Activities (ORDA) and shall include relevant background information on each member in such form and at such times as ORDA may require.

IV–B–2–d. No member of an IBC may be involved (except to provide information requested by the IBC) in the review or approval of a project in which he or she has been, or expects to be, engaged or has a direct financial interest.

IV–B–2–e. The Institution, who is ultimately responsible for the effectiveness of the IBC, may establish procedures that the IBC will follow in its initial and continuing review of applications, proposals, and activities.

IV–B–2–f. Institutions are encouraged to open IBC meetings to the public whenever possible, consistent with protection of privacy and proprietary interests.

IV–B–2–g. Upon request, the Institution shall make available to the public all minutes of IBC meetings and documents submitted to or received from funding agencies which the latter are required to make available to the public. If comments are made by members of the public on IBC actions, the Institution shall forward to NIH both the comments and the IBC's response.

IV–B–3. *Functions of the IBC.* On behalf of the Institution, the IBC is responsible for:

IV–B–3–a. Reviewing for compliance with the NIH Guidelines recombinant DNA research as specified in Part III conducted at or sponsored by the Institution, and approving those research projects that it finds are in conformity with the Guidelines. This review shall include:

IV–B–3–a–(1). An independent assessment of the containment levels required by these Guidelines for the proposed research, and

IV–B–3–a–(2). An assessment of the facilities, procedures, and practices, and of the training and expertise of recombinant DNA personnel.

IV–B–3–b. Notifying the Principal Investigator (PI) of the results of their review.

IV–B–3–c. Lowering containment levels for certain experiments as specified in Section III–B–2.

IV–B–3–d. Setting containment levels as specified in Sections III–B–4–b and III–B–5.

IV–B–3–e. Reviewing periodically recombinant DNA research being conducted at the Institution, to ensure that the requirements of the Guidelines are being fulfilled.

IV–B–3–f. Adopting emergency plans covering accidental spills and personnel contamination resulting from such research.

IV–B–3–g. Reporting within 30 days to the appropriate institutional official and to the NIH Office of Recombinant DNA Activities (ORDA) any significant problems with or violations of the Guidelines, and any significant research-related accidents or illnesses, unless the IBC determines that the PI has done so.

IV–B–3–h. The IBC may not authorize initiation of experiments not explicitly covered by the Guidelines until NIH (with the advice of the RAC when required) establishes the containment requirement.

IV–B–3–i. Performing such other functions as may be delegated to the IBC under Section IV–B–1.

IV–B–4. *Biological Safety Officer.* The Institution shall appoint a BSO if it engages in recombinant DNA research at the P3 or P4 containment level. The officer shall be a member of the Institutional Biosafety Committee (IBC). . . .

. . .

IV–B–5. *Principal Investigator.* On behalf of the Institution, the PI is responsible for complying fully with the Guidelines in conducting any recombinant DNA research.

IV–B–5–a. *PI—General.* As part of this special responsibility, the PI shall:

IV–B–5–a–(1). Initiate or modify no recombinant DNA research requiring approval by the IBC prior to initiation until that research, or the proposed modification thereof, has been approved by the IBC and has met all other requirements of the Guidelines;

IV–B–5–a–(2). Determine whether experiments are covered by Section III–C and follow the appropriate procedures;

IV–B–5–a–(3). Report within 30 days to the IBC and NIH (ORDA) all significant problems with and violations of the Guidelines and all significant research-related accidents and illnesses;

IV–B–5–a–(4). Report to the IBC and to NIH (ORDA) new information bearing on the Guidelines;

IV–B–5–a–(5). Be adequately trained in good microbiological techniques;

IV–B–5–a–(6). Adhere to IBC-approved emergency plans for dealing with accidental spills and personnel contamination; and

IV–B–5–a–(7). Comply with shipping requirements for recombinant DNA molecules.

IV–B–5–b. *Submissions by the PI to NIH.* The PI shall:

IV–B–5–b–(1). Submit information to NIH (ORDA) in order to have new host-vector systems certified;

IV–B–5–b–(2).   Petition NIH, with notice to the IBC, for exemptions to these Guidelines;

IV–B–5–b–(3).   Petition NIH, with concurrence of the IBC, for approval to conduct experiments specified in Section III–A of the Guidelines;

IV–B–5–b–(4).   Petition NIH for determination of containment for experiments requiring case-by-case review;

IV–B–5–b–(5).   Petition NIH for determination of containment for experiments not covered by the Guidelines.

IV–B–5–c.   *Submissions by the PI to the IBC.*   The PI shall:

IV–B–5–c–(1).   Make the initial determination of the required levels of physical and biological containment in accordance with the Guidelines;

IV–B–5–c–(2).   Select appropriate microbiological practices and laboratory techniques to be used in the research;

IV–B–5–c–(3).   Submit the initial research protocol if covered under Guidelines Section III–A, III–B, or III–C (and also subsequent changes—e.g., changes in the source of DNA or host-vector system) to the IBC for review and approval or disapproval; and

IV–B–5–c–(4).   Remain in communication with the IBC throughout the conduct of the project.

IV–B–5–d.   *PI Responsibilities Prior to Initiating Research.*   The PI is responsible for:

IV–B–5–d–(1).   Making available to the laboratory staff copies of the protocols that describe the potential biohazards and the precautions to be taken;

IV–B–5–d–(2).   Instructing and training staff in the practices and techniques required to ensure safety and in the procedures for dealing with accidents; and

IV–B–5–d–(3).   Informing the staff of the reasons and provisions for any precautionary medical practices advised or requested, such as vaccinations or serum collection.

IV–B–5–e.   *PI Responsibilities During the Conduct of the Research.*   The PI is responsible for:

IV–B–5–e–(1).   Supervising the safety performance of the staff to ensure that the required safety practices and techniques are employed;

IV–B–5–e–(2).   Investigating and reporting in writing to ORDA, the Biological Safety Officer (where applicable), and the IBC any significant problems pertaining to the operation and implementation of containment practices and procedures;

IV–B–5–e–(3).   Correcting work errors and conditions that may result in the release of recombinant DNA materials;

IV–B–5–e–(4).   Ensuring the integrity of the physical containment (e.g., biological safety cabinets) and the biological containment (e.g., purity, and genotypic, and phenotypic characteristics).

IV–C.   *Responsibilities of NIH.*

IV–C–1.   *Director.*   The Director, NIH, is responsible for (i) establishing the NIH Guidelines for Research Involving Recombinant DNA Molecules, (ii) overseeing their implementation, and (iii) their final interpretation.

. . .

IV–C–2.   *Recombinant DNA Advisory Committee.*   The NIH Recombinant DNA Advisory Committee (RAC) is responsible for carrying out specified functions cited below as well as others assigned under its charter or by the Secretary, HHS, the Assistant Secretary for Health, and the Director, NIH.

The members of the committee shall be chosen to provide, collectively, expertise in scientific fields relevant to recombinant DNA technology and biological safety—e.g., microbiology, molecular biology, virology, genetics, epidemiology, infectious diseases, the biology of enteric organisms, botany, plant pathology, ecology, and tissue culture. At least 20 percent of the members shall be persons knowledgeable in applicable law, standards of professional conduct and practice, public attitudes, the environment, public health, occupational health, or related fields. Representatives from Federal agencies shall serve as nonvoting members. . . .

All meetings of the RAC will be announced in the Federal Register, including tentative agenda items, 30 days in advance of the meeting, with final agendas (if modified) available at least 72 hours before the meeting. No item defined as a major action under Section IV–C–1–b–(1) may be added to an agenda after it appears in the Federal Register.

. . .

IV–C–3.   *The Office of Recombinant DNA Activities.*   ORDA shall serve as a focal point for information on recombinant DNA activities and provide advice to all within and outside NIH, including Institutions, Biological Safety Committees, Principal Investigators, Federal agencies, State and local governments, and institutions in the private sector. ORDA shall carry out such other functions as may be delegated to it by the Director, NIH.
. . . .

IV–D.   *Compliance.*   As a condition for NIH funding of recombinant DNA research, Institutions must ensure that such research conducted at or sponsored by the Institution, irrespective of the source of funding, shall comply with these Guidelines. The policies on noncompliance are as follows:

IV–D–1.   All NIH-funded projects involving recombinant DNA techniques must comply with the NIH Guidelines. Noncompliance may result in (i) suspension, limitation, or termination of financial assistance for such projects and of NIH funds for other recombinant DNA research at the Institution, or (ii) a requirement for prior NIH approval of any or all recombinant DNA projects at the Institution.

IV–D–2.   All non-NIH funded projects involving recombinant DNA techniques conducted at or sponsored by an Institution that receives NIH funds for projects involving such techniques must comply with the NIH Guidelines. . . .

IV–D–3.   Information concerning noncompliance with the Guidelines may be brought forward by any person. It should be delivered to both NIH (ORDA) and the relevant Institution. The Institution, generally through the IBC, shall take appropriate action. The Institution shall forward a complete report of the incident to ORDA, recommending any further action indicated.

IV–D–4. In cases where NIH proposes to suspend, limit, or terminate financial assistance because of noncompliance with the Guideline, applicable DHHS and Public Health Service procedures shall govern.

. . .

VI. Voluntary Compliance

VI–A. *Basic Policy.* Individuals, corporations, and institutions not otherwise covered by the Guidelines are encouraged to do so by following the standards and procedures set forth in Parts I–IV of the Guidelines. . . . For purposes of complying with the Guidelines, an individual intending to carry out research involving recombinant DNA is encouraged to affiliate with an institution that has an Institutional Biosafety Committee approved under the Guidelines.

Since commercial organizations have special concerns, such as protection of proprietary data, some modifications and explanations of the procedures in Parts I–IV are provided below, in order to address these concerns.

VI–B. *IBC Approval.* The NIH Office of Recombinant DNA Activities (ORDA) will review the membership of an institution's Institutional Biosafety Committee (IBC) and, where it finds the IBC meets the requirements set forth in Section IV–B–2, will give its approval to the IBC membership.

. . .

VI–D. *Requests for Exemptions and Approvals.* Requests for exemptions or other approvals required by the Guidelines should be requested by following the procedures set forth in the appropriate sections in Part I–IV of the Guidelines.

In order to ensure protection for proprietary data, any public notice regarding a request for an exemption or other approval which is designated by the institution as proprietary under Section VI–E–1 will be issued only after consultation with the institution as to the content of the notice.

VI–E. *Protection of Proprietary Data.* In general, the Freedom of Information Act requires Federal agencies to make their records available to the public upon request. However, this requirement does not apply to, among other things, "Trade secrets and commercial and financial information obtained from a person and privileged or confidential." 18 U.S.C. 1905, in turn makes it a crime for an officer or employee of the United States or any Federal department or agency to publish, divulge, disclose, or make known "in any manner or to any extent not authorized by law any information coming to him in the course of his employment or official duties or by reason of any examination or investigation made by, or return, report or record made to or filed with, such department or agency or officer or employee thereof, which information concerns or relates to the trade secrets, [or processes . . . of any person, firm, partnership, corporation, or association." This provision applies to all employees of the Federal Government, including special Government employees. Members of the Recombinant DNA Advisory Committee are "special Government employees."

VI–E–1. In submitting information to NIH for purposes of complying voluntarily with the Guidelines, an institution may designate those items of information which the institution believes constitute trade secrets or privileged or confidential commercial or financial information.

VI–E–2.   If NIH receives a request under the Freedom of Information Act for information so designated, NIH will promptly contact the institution to secure its views as to whether the information (or some portion) should be released.

VI–E–3.   If the NIH decides to release this information (or some portion) in response to a Freedom of Information request or otherwise, the institution will be advised; and the actual release will not be made until the expiration of 15 days after the institution is so advised, except to the extent that earlier release, in the judgement of the Director, NIH, is necessary to protect against an imminent hazard to the public or the environment.

VI–E–4.   *Presubmission Review.*

VI–E–4–a.   Any institution not otherwise covered by the Guidelines, which is considering submission of data or information voluntarily to NIH, may request presubmission review of the records involved to determine whether, if the records are submitted, NIH will or will not make part or all of the records available upon request under the Freedom of Information Act.

VI–E–4–b.   A request for presubmission review should be submitted to ORDA, along with the records involved.   These records must be clearly marked as being the property of the institution, on loan to NIH solely for the purpose of making a determination under the Freedom of Information Act. . . .

Appendix D—Actions Taken Under the Guidelines

As noted [above], the Director, NIH, may take certain actions with regard to the Guidelines after the issues have been considered by the RAC.

Some of the actions taken to date include the following:

Appendix D–I.   Permission is granted to clone Foot-and-Mouth Disease Virus in the EK1 host-vector system consisting of *E. coli* K-12 and the vector pBR322, all work to be done at the Plum Island Animal Disease Center.

Appendix D–II.   Certain specified clones derived from segments of the Foot-and-Mouth Disease Virus may be transferred from Plum Island Animal Disease Center to the facilities of Genentech, Inc., of South San Francisco, California.   Further development of the clones at Genentech has been approved under P1 ± EK1 conditions.

Appendix D–III.   The Rd strain of *Hemophilus influenzae* can be used as a host for the propagation of the cloned Tn 10 tet R gene derived from *E.coli* K–12 employing the non-conjugative *Haemophilus* plasmid, pRSF0885, under P1 conditions.

. . .

Appendix D–V.   Permission is granted to Dr. Ronald Davis of Stanford University to field test corn plants modified by recombinant DNA techniques under specified containment conditions.

Appendix D–VI.   Permission is granted to clone in *E. coli* K–12, under P1 physical containment conditions, subgenomic segments of Rift Valley Fever Virus subject to conditions which have been set forth by the RAC.

Appendix D–VII.   Attenuated laboratory strains of *Salmonella typhimurium* may be used under P1 physical containment conditions to screen for the *Saccharomyces cerevisiae* pseudouridine synthetase gene. The plasmid YEp13 will be employed as the vector.

Appendix D–VIII.   Permission is granted to transfer certain clones of subgenomic segments of Foot-and-Mouth Disease Virus from Plum Island Animal Disease Center to the laboratories of Molecular Genetics, Inc., Minnetonka, Minnesota, and to work with these clones under P1 containment conditions.   Approval is contingent upon review of data on infectivity testing of the clones by a working group of the RAC.

Appendix D–IX.   Permission is granted to Dr. John Sanford of Cornell University to field test tomato and tobacco plants transformed with bacterial (*E. coli* K–12) and yeast DNA using pollen as a vector.

Appendix D–X.   Permission is granted to Drs. Steven Lindow and Nickolas Panopulos of the University of California, Berkeley, to release under specified conditions *Pseudomonas syringae* pv. *syringae* and *Erwinia herbicola* carrying *in vitro* generated deletions of all or part of the genes involved in ice nucleation.

. . .

Appendix J—Federal Interagency Advisory Committee on Recombinant DNA Research

Appendix J–I.   *Federal Interagency Advisory Committee.*   The Federal Interagency Advisory Committee on Recombinant DNA Research advises the Secretary of the Department of Health and Human Services, the Assistant Secretary for Health, and the Director, National Institutes of Health, on the coordination of those aspects of all Federal programs and activities relating to recombinant DNA research.   The Committee provides for communication and exchange of information necessary to maintain adequate coordination of such programs and activities.   The Committee is responsible for facilitating compliance with a uniform form set of guidelines in the conduct of this research in the public and private sectors and, where warranted, to suggest administrative or legislative proposals.

The Director of the NIH, or his designee, serves as Chairman, and the Committee includes representation from all Departments and Agencies whose programs involve health functions or responsibilities as determined by the Secretary.

Departments and Agencies which have representation on this Committee, as of December 1980, are

Department of Agriculture

Department of Commerce

Department of Defense

Department of Energy

Environmental Protection Agency

Executive Office of the President

Department of Health and Human Services, Office of the Assistant Secretary for Health, Centers for Disease Control, Food and Drug Administration, National Institutes of Health

Department of the Interior

Department of Justice

Department of Labor

National Aeronautics and Space Administration

National Science Foundation

Nuclear Regulatory Commission

Department of State

Department of Transportation

Arms Control and Disarmament Agency

Veterans Administration

At the second meeting of the Committee on November 23, 1976, all of the Federal agencies endorsed the NIH Guidelines, and Departments which support or conduct recombinant DNA research agreed to abide by the NIH Guidelines.

. . .

Appendix L—Release Into the Environment of Certain Plants

Appendix L–1. *General Information.* Appendix L specifies conditions under which certain plants, as specified below, may be approved for release into the environment. Experiments in this category cannot be initiated without submission of relevant information on the proposed experiment to NIH, review by the RAC Plant Working Group, and specific approval by NIH. Such experiments also require the approval of the IBC before initiation. . . .

Experiments which do not meet the specifications of Appendix L–II fall under Section III–A and require RAC review and NIH and IBC approval before initiation.

Appendix L–II. *Criteria Allowing Review by the RAC Plant Working Group Without the Requirement for Full RAC Review.* Approval may be granted by ORDA in consultation with the RAC Plant Working Group without the requirement for full RAC review (IBC review is also necessary) for growing plants containing recombinant DNA in the field under the following conditions:

Appendix L–II–A. The plant species is a cultivated crop of a genus that has no species known to be a noxious weed.

Appendix L–II–B. The introduced DNA consists of well-characterized genes containing no sequences harmful to humans, animals, or plants.

Appendix L–II–C. The vector consists of DNA: (i) From exempt host-vector systems; (ii) from plants of the same or closely related species; (iii) from nonpathogenic prokaryotes or nonpathogenic lower eukaryotic plants; (iv) from plant pathogens only if sequences causing disease have been deleted; or (v) chimeric vectors constructed from sequences defined in (i) to (iv) above. The DNA may be introduced by any suitable method.

Appendix L–II–D. Plants are grown in controlled access fields under specified conditions appropriate for the plant under study and the geographical location. . . .

NOTES

1. Although lengthy and detailed, the 1983 revisions of the recombinant DNA guidelines are briefer and less complex than their predecessors. During 1981, suggestions were made by several leading scientists to replace the guidelines with a nonregulatory "code of laboratory practices." When this move was eventually defeated in the RAC early in 1982, an alternative process was begun to

simplify the guidelines; an *ad hoc* Working Group on Revision of the Guidelines began meeting on April 19, 1982, and published the results of its deliberations for public comment in the May 26, 1982, Federal Register.

2.   Much of the concern over gene splicing centers on the escape of a dangerous microbe into the general environment.   For a thorough review of the risks within a research facility itself and an analysis of alternative means of minimizing those risks (self-regulation, professional regulation, direct governmental regulation, and "participatory mechanisms"), which ends favoring the last, see McGarity, Contending Approaches to Regulating Laboratory Safety, 28 Kan.L.Rev. 183 (1980).   The article recounts that, following the death of a physics graduate student, the Occupational Safety and Health Administration (OSHA) undertook a three week inspection of the Massachusetts Institute of Technology laboratories and turned up 1651 violations of OSHA standards.   Although they have not yet developed any special standards for recombinant DNA work, OSHA and the National Institute of Occupational Safety and Health have found in surveys of labs in private biotechnology companies that some are very good and others manifest obvious problems.   See Six Industry Labs: Only Two Pass NIOSH Test, 15 National J. 2099 (1983).

3.   Detailed regulatory-style guidelines have become such an accepted part of the genetic engineering landscape that it is interesting to remember the reaction of one group of biologists at the time of Asilomar:

> To old guard microbiologists and virologists, long accustomed to working with highly infectious agents, the dangers emanating from DNA experiments with *E. coli* were posed by the technical sloppiness of the new generation of molecular biologists.   To this camp, sound training, discipline, and common sense would be far more efficacious than guidelines in reducing the possible biohazards.

Swazey, Sorenson and Wong, Risks and Benefits, Rights and Responsibilities: A History of the Recombinant DNA Research Controversy, 51 S.Cal.L.Rev. 1019, 1034–35 (1978).   Although the manner by which recombinant DNA and related areas of research are supervised would doubtless be very different today if these views had prevailed, the fact that they did not was apparently not due solely to the dominance of the molecular biologists in the debate; in 1976, a special committee appointed by the American Society of Microbiology reviewed the NIH guidelines and suggested two principal changes (strengthening the containment criteria, and developing additional protection for research workers), and at its annual meeting on May 8, 1977, the ASM Council approved recommendations concerning regulations in this field that supported governance through HEW.

4.   Shortly before the first NIH guidelines were promulgated, Dr. DeWitt Stetten, chairman of the original advisory committee, told his fellow members that "the real hazard is one no one around this table has dreamed of yet, and this you cannot specify against."   Simring, On the Dangers of Genetic Meddling, 192 Science 940 (1976) (letter).   Freeman J. Dyson, a noted physicist at the Institute for Advanced Study in Princeton, N.J., replied that while Stetten was right, "it is equally true that the real benefit to humanity from recombinant DNA will probably be the one no one dreamed of."   Dyson, Costs and Benefits of Recombinant DNA Research, 193 Science 6 (1976) (letter).   Dyson laments that despite the balance of ignorance, legal and public institutions are designed to count the "costs of saying yes" to a new technology and lack procedures for "counting the costs of saying no."   Id.

5.   Coincident with the relaxation of the requirements for federally funded laboratory experiments involving recombinant molecules, the RAC backed away from a major role in developing standards for privately sponsored work in this field, especially because almost all of the proposals submitted by private industry for "voluntary" review involved the specially weakened strain of E. coli called K–12.   The RAC members reasoned that if it was safe at a small scale there was no reason it would be more dangerous at a large scale.   Compare this view with that expressed at the conclusion of the Asilomar conference, supra Sec. B.1.

6. The ambiguous relationship between the RAC and the work of commercial firms in the recombinant DNA business may grow more problematic because such firms are likely to be doing work that involves three areas over which the RAC has retained oversight: (a) cloning toxin-producing genes (agricultural firms are trying to produce pathogens that could kill agricultural pests), (b) introducing drug-resistance into an organism (firms are interested in developing plants and animals resistant to pesticides or drugs), and (c) deliberately releasing genetically engineered organisms into the environment (new developments, especially in agriculture, have to be field-tested before they can be marketed; see Sec. C.1 infra). In September 1983, the RAC held its first closed-door meeting to consider several proposals from commercial gene splicers to release altered organisms into the environment. Opponents of such research were unsuccessful in persuading a federal judge to override NIH's decision that the committee should meet in private to preserve the companies' trade secrets. Hilts, NIH Weighing Plans to Release Altered Bacteria, Washington Post, Sept. 20, 1983, at A1. Is it appropriate to have the body that reviews government-funded research also responsible for the safety of rapidly expanding commercial development in this field? Could its need to protect trade secrets by closed-door meetings seriously compromise its credibility with the public?

7. The Environmental Protection Agency (EPA) has already stated that it intends to move into this field once products are perfected. As of late 1983, however, the EPA had not drawn up standards for the safe testing, manufacture, or use of genetically engineered organisms outside laboratories. EPA bases its jurisdiction on the Federal Insecticide, Fungicide and Rodenticide Act (FIFRA), 7 U.S.C. §§ 136–136y (1976 & Supp. V 1981), and the Toxic Substances Control Act (TOSCA), 15 U.S.C. §§ 2601–2629 (1976 & Supp. V 1981). While TOSCA was intended to give the EPA authority to fill any gaps in federal agencies' ability to protect the environment, doubts have arisen about its applicability to recombinant DNA technology because it regulates only chemical substances and mixtures. EPA's regulation thus depends upon a finding that altered organisms come within the definition of "chemical substances." McGarity & Boyer in Federal Regulation of Emerging Genetic Technologies, 36 Vanderbilt L.Rev. 461, 505–506 (1983), suggest that the DNA molecules in a microorganism fit the TOSCA definition even if the entire microorganism is not a "chemical substance."

8. The Food and Drug Administration has used its existing standards for safety and efficacy in approving the first drugs manufactured by recombinant DNA processes, just as the Agriculture Department has in safety-testing new animal vaccines. One issue of particular importance—will the results of safety tests be available to the public?—is addressed in McGarity & Shapiro, The Trade Secret Status of Health and Safety Testing Information, 93 Harv.L.Rev. 837 (1980).

9. Is divided administrative oversight appropriate different agencies for different functions? Or is centralized expertise needed? And if so, what kind? A comment by Harvey S. Price, executive director of the industry's trade association, illustrates the varied senses of expertise: "NIH already 'regulates' the sorts of functions EPA is starting to look at. It is not clear to a lot of people that there is any need for EPA to look over NIH's shoulder on these kinds of issues. [Yet] because of the expertise they have that NIH does not have, many people in the industry think the agency has something to contribute." Wines, Genetic Engineering—Who'll Regulate the Rapidly Growing Private Sector?, 15 National Journal 2096, 2101 (1983).

3. CONGRESSIONAL OVERSIGHT

Although the major source of governmental action on recombinant DNA research was in the Executive Branch (particularly the National Institutes of Health), Congress was also involved. Indeed, activity on this subject in Congress—in the form of both hearings and proposed legislation—is thought by many observers to have been a major influence on the manner in which executive branch officials approached the subject and particularly on their decision to broaden the membership of the RAC.

Congressional attention began immediately after Asilomar, before the Hogness subcommittee had begun the first draft of the NIH regulations. At hearings on April 22, 1975, on "Examination of the Relationship of a Free Society and Its Scientific Community," Senator Edward M. Kennedy, chairman of the health subcommittee of the Senate Committee on Labor and Public Welfare, heard not only from two of the researchers, who argued for self-regulation, but also from Drs. Halsted Holman of Stanford and Willard Gaylin of the Institute of Society, Ethics and the Life Sciences (Hastings Center), who supported the public's right to be involved in the area as one involving moral as well as technical issues. Although he was not able to generate much congressional interest at the time, Sen. Kennedy continued to speak on the topic; at a widely publicized speech at the Harvard School of Public Health in May he surprised the DNA researchers (especially those who had led the efforts at self-regulation) by criticizing them for "making public policy . . . in private." J. Goodfield, Playing God 148 (1977).

After the NIH guidelines were published in July 1976, the legislators' concerns actually increased because it became apparent that those guidelines applied only to federal grantees and contractors and not to private industry, which was showing an increasing interest in the field. On July 19, 1976, Senators Kennedy and Jacob Javits (then the senior Democratic and Republican members of the health subcommittee) wrote to President Ford that they were "gravely concerned that these relatively stringent guidelines may not be implemented in all sectors of the domestic and international research communities and that the public will therefore be subjected to undue risks." 24 B.U.J. 22 (1976). They were particularly doubtful of industry's response because "some elements of the guidelines, such as limitations on the size of experiments, public disclosure, and non-release of materials into the environment, may be contrary to the interest and practice of researchers in private industry." They noted also the need to go beyond research rules to guidance for the applications of techniques, once experiments had been completed. The senators asked President Ford to make sure the guidelines were implemented, either under existing rulemaking authority or by seeking new legislation. Rather than coming from the Administration, however, legislative initiative over the following 18 months came largely from the Democrats in Congress, with considerable encouragement from critics of the NIH process from outside Washington.

LIBRARY OF CONGRESS, CONGRESSIONAL RESEARCH SERVICE, SCIENCE POLICY RESEARCH DIVISION, GENETIC ENGINEERING, HUMAN GENETICS, AND CELL BIOLOGY *

64–65 (Dec. 1976).

Dr. Susan Wright (University of Michigan), an outspoken critic of the process by which the NIH guidelines evolved, recently summarized her

* DNA Recombinant Molecule Research (Supplemental Report II), Prepared for the Subcomm. on Science, Research and Tech- nology of the House Committee on Science and Technology, 94th Cong., 2d Sess. [Committee Print, Ser. KKK].

concern about reaching public policy decisions on difficult issues general-ly:

> Advocates of the present policy [on DNA recombinant research] maintain that the public has participated in its formation. Let it be clear that expression of views to decision makers is a quite different matter from participation in decisions. Through the mechanism of a technical committee, decision-making power has been concentrated in the hands of front-rank researchers, all of whom are committed to bio-logical research in general and many, to recombinant research in par-ticular. There has been no representation from those most immedi-ately at risk—technicians and maintenance personnel, for example; no representation from public interest and environmental organizations; no representation from the public at large.

> It is questionable whether self-regulation of this type can be relied upon as a means of making public policy . . . . Scientists must recognize that in a democratic society, they do not have special rights to self-government for an activity which carries serious implications for the whole society. . . . Unfortunately, procedures for making poli-cy decision on hazardous areas of science and technology have not yet been developed.

> Accountable commissions at the local and national levels estab-lished to formulate policy for all work that poses biological hazards might afford one path. Such bodies would require access to the wid-est possible range of technical perspectives from both advocates and critics. But their memberships should reflect the fact that their deci-sions would be on matters of public policy.

Whether one agrees with the NIH guidelines or not, there is evidence that there was a deliberate effort to provide for participation by the public at large and by public interest groups. The persistence of this concern by the advocates of a need for even more public participation indicates that further efforts may need to be made. . . .

It is difficult to resolve this complex issue into a minimum of factors for easy evaluation. Fundamentally, however, there appear to be several basic issues. One, there is a strong criticism that the decision to continue the research was made essentially on the basis of a determination that the research could be conducted at an "acceptable" level of safety rather than examining the issue from the perspective of whether the research should be conducted at all. In this respect, the DNA recombinant molecule issue is being likened to the nuclear energy problem. Some would prefer that the reseach had never continued to the technology. Two, there is an even more fundamental question which many wish would receive more attention. This is the issue of society interacting with science and the determination of the basic social responsibilities for the decision making process. The scientist is beginning to acknowledge the right of society to participate in the evaluation of the scope and rate of investment of re-sources in research but still wants to retain certain basic rights of freedom of inquiry. There is a nucleus of resistance to total scientific freedom as the ability to tamper with the most fundamental processes of life chal-lenges the ability of society to perceive the implications of this capability. Perhaps this is fundamentally a fear reaction. The ethicists are finding this aspect of the issue a fertile field for investigation. Third, if the re-search is to continue, there is concern being implied that the investigator is not to be trusted.

This is the basis of the evolution of guidelines and the gradual emergence of stronger criteria such as monitoring, licensing, inspection, education, and training of investigators in this field.

. . .

NOTE

Professor Clifford Grobstein, vice-chancellor at the University of California at San Diego, expanded on the view that public discussion and participation had been "minimal," by arguing there is an "urgent" need for action without waiting "to gain some experience with the [NIH] guidelines" which do not reach issues that go beyond human health hazards.

. . . These issues, probably wisely, were minimized or specifically excluded in formulating the NIH guidelines. Potential ecological hazards, although touched on, were deemphasized by the very selection of NIH as the lead federal agency. What may be loosely called ethical, social, and political issues were avoided entirely. Substantial concern has been expressed about a series of such questions, concerns that remain to be evaluated on balance against potential benefits. Are there some kinds of knowledge, even though they offer health benefits, for which the price in other values is too high? Is it safe, in the present state of our society, to provide means to intervene in the very essence of human individuality, even to achieve humanitarian ends?
. . .

Under what auspices and in what time span should this kind of broad assessment occur? The objective is to inform public understanding and improve further policy decisions that may be necessary. The auspices, therefore, must be chosen to assure complete objectivity and comprehensiveness. On the other hand, the impact of the assessment must be able to feed quickly and efficiently to decision points ranging from the local to the international level.
. . .

The broadest and highest national auspices include the President and the Congress. Moreover, both the executive and legislative branches will have to implement any national and international policy that flows from the analysis— whether it only confirms the NIH guidelines or proposes modification or alternatives. Careful consideration is needed of possible mechanisms, but a joint commission chosen by the President and the Congress, with the Vice President as chairman, would seem eminently suitable. Such a commission should be charged not to conduct the analysis itself but to assure its quality and comprehensiveness. . . .

Is there something to be lost by a "high visibility" assessment? This is again debatable. A Washington-based extravaganza in the polarizing light of the mass media certainly is not needed. The procedures adopted must avoid this. The substantive activity is only in small part suitable for Capitol hearing rooms. In large part it belongs in secluded conference rooms and individual studies. Yet somehow the overall process must be observable and eventually widely shared. Will such visibility elevate public unease to hysteria, thereby cutting off the additional insight that is the only sure antidote to uncertainty? Hopefully not, if the analysis is designed and conducted appropriately. Is this kind of issue better resolved in informed inner circles rather than in the view of a general population that some believe does not have sufficient background for sound judgment? Here the bite of the doctrine of "informed consent" and the weight of "sunshine politics" must take precedence over the nervous concerns of the expert and the professional.

Grobstein, Recombinant DNA Research: Beyond the NIH Guidelines, 194 Science 1133, 1134–1135 (1976).

JUDITH P. SWAZEY, JAMES R. SORENSON AND CYNTHIA B. WONG, RISKS AND BENEFITS, RIGHTS AND RE-SPONSIBILITIES: A HISTORY OF THE RECOM-BINANT DNA RESEARCH CONTROVERSY

51 S.Cal.L.Rev. 1019, 1068–1074 (1978).

The first of many congressional pronouncements on rDNA is introduced in the House on January 19, 1977, in the form of a resolution stating that rDNA research may pose serious health and safety threats to American society. At approximately the same time, Senator Dale Bumpers files legislation in the Senate that requires licensing of rDNA laboratories and holds researchers strictly liable for any and all damages that might result from their research.

On March 4th, the House Subcommittee on Science, Research and Technology, Committee on Science and Technology, begins a series of hearings that continue into September. The same month, major legislation is introduced in the House by Congressman Paul Rogers and in the Senate by Senator Edward Kennedy, Congress' leading figures in the health arena. Rogers' House bill, H.R. 7897, seeks to regulate rDNA research in a fashion that proves acceptable to most scientists, by giving regulatory authority to the Secretary of HEW. The bill expands coverage of the NIH Guidelines to include all federal agencies and calls for the establishment of an advisory committee to assist the Secretary in this regulatory activity. The bill also provides for local variation in regulatory practices, if it can be demonstrated that a special circumstance or need exists.

Kennedy's bill, S. 1217, takes a different stance from Rogers' on most regulatory issues and proves far less acceptable to most researchers. First, fearing a potential conflict of interest in NIH's sponsoring and regulating rDNA research, Kennedy calls for the creation of a new regulatory commission, outside of HEW, to be composed of both nonscientists and scientists. Second, Kennedy does not accept the notion of federal preemption of state and community regulations, and his bill, unlike Rogers', permits local as well as federal controls in the absence of special circumstances.

With input from the Federal Interagency Committee on Recombinant DNA Research, the Administration also formulates legislation. The Administration bill provides for federal preemption of state and local regulations and calls for HEW to take the main role in regulation by placing all other federal agencies under its purview. When this proposed legislation is sent to the Office of Management and Budget (OMB), it encounters stiff opposition, chiefly from federal agencies that do not look favorably on the leadership of HEW. The Administration's approach to rDNA regulation becomes mired in interagency entanglements and does not advance beyond its initial review at OMB.

While Congress is working on legislation and holding hearings, some important developments occur elsewhere and cast new light on the magnitude and nature of the risks associated with rDNA research. Whereas the original NIH Advisory Committee had been charged with first developing a program to assess the risks of rDNA research and then, on the basis of that research, establishing guidelines, in fact the reverse took place. One of the first attempts to assess some of the possible risks associated with using *E. coli* in rDNA research is reported in a letter from Roy Curtiss of the University of Alabama to Donald Fredrickson, Director of NIH, on April 12, 1977. In his letter, Curtiss spells out why he has now concluded that the use of EK1 and EK2 host-vectors poses no danger to human beings. Curtiss' letter is widely circulated among scientists and on Capitol Hill and has a significant impact on the response to legislative proposals.

Another development during this period grows out of criticisms of the procedure by which NIH had developed the Guidelines. . . . [T]here were complaints that the writing of the NIH Guidelines was "dominated by molecular biologists to the exclusion of bacteriologists, virologists, infectious disease specialists, and others whose experience with virulent organisms was far greater than that of any scientist who spends most of the time thinking about [r]DNA." In response to this criticism, NIH forms an ad hoc committee that meets in June 1977 in Falmouth, Massachusetts, to assess the risks of serious infections resulting from rDNA research. The results of the committee's deliberations are reported in a letter to Fredrickson dated July 14, 1977. While the conclusions of the committee are not unanimous, the group generally agrees that the claims of hazards associated with rDNA research are "unsubstantiated." Like the Curtiss letter earlier, this letter receives wide circulation.

A third widely circulated document that shapes or reshapes opinions in Washington about rDNA research is a prepublication draft of a paper by Stanley Cohen and Shing Chang, later published in the Proceedings of the National Academy of Sciences. The paper reports on a study that contravenes prevailing assumptions about evolutionary barriers that block genetic recombinations between lower and higher forms of life in nature, the barriers that Sinsheimer, Chargaff, and others have feared might be breached by rDNA experiments. The work of Cohen, et al., however, indicates that natural recombinants do occur, and hence suggests that rDNA research may not be as novel as had been previously assumed.

On another front, scientists, not known as a group for their political activism, begin to organize themselves into a coalition to oppose legislative proposals that they feel will unduly restrict rDNA research. Harlyn Halvorson, a microbiologist from Brandeis and former president of the American Society of Microbiologists, plays a leading role in developing an effective lobbying effort in Washington. Drawing on the advice of experienced people in Washington, Halvorson decides that because some form of legislation probably will be enacted by Congress, it would be a strategic blunder to oppose all legislation. Working with other scientists, Halvorson brings together a powerful coalition of individuals and societies interested in rDNA research and in favor of having regulatory power remain within HEW. To a large extent, Halvorson's coalition finds its interests most compatible with the House bill introduced by Representative Paul Rogers. Having established a position in the House, Halvorson and colleagues turn their efforts to the Senate. Those efforts will begin to pay off in the fall.

During the last half of 1977, the House Subcommittee on Science, Research and Technology concludes its hearings and publishes a 1293-page volume on science policy implications of rDNA research. The fifty-one individuals who testify before the subcommittee include familiar figures such as Maxine Singer, David Baltimore, and Roy Curtiss together with a broad range of figures from science, law, policymaking groups, federal agencies, and industry, who have not played central roles in the rDNA controversy but who are concerned with the policy issues surrounding the conduct and regulation of such research.

While the major House legislation, Rogers' bill, remains entangled in committee discussions, there are a series of legislative actions in the Senate. In August, Senator Gaylord Nelson, who finds the arguments of Halvorson's congressional lobby persuasive, introduces a bill offered as an alternative to Kennedy's earlier proposal which Nelson did not vote for in committee. In contrast to Kennedy's bill—but much like Rogers'—Nelson's legislation makes HEW the primary regulatory agency for rDNA research and provides for federal preemption of local and state controls.

Members of the scientific community who favor proceeding with rDNA research and oppose legislative controls contact Senate members to urge their support of Nelson's bill. Another senator, supportive of the scientists' appeals, enters the rDNA arena: Senator Adlai Stevenson III, Chairman of the Subcommittee on Science, Technology, and Space, delivers an influential speech on the Senate floor in September. Stevenson describes several developments that suggest rDNA research is not as hazardous as the researchers themselves had once thought. Based in part on these newer assessments of risk, Stevenson suggests that legislative activity at this time would be hasty and might pose a serious threat to the right of freedom of inquiry. He calls for more hearings under the auspices of his subcommittee and urges the Senate to delay action on regulation of rDNA research until the next session.

Less than a week after Stevenson's speech, Senator Kennedy announces he is temporarily withdrawing support for his own bill, although he is not actually withdrawing the bill from the Senate calendar. Apparently influenced by the accumulating evidence that rDNA research is not as risky as had been assumed, and aware of the changing political views in Congress about rDNA research, Kennedy senses that there is less and less support for the type of strict control that had seemed necessary only 6 months earlier. He still feels, however, that there is a demonstrated need for a national commission to review the entire rDNA situation, and he holds to his earlier position that localities should have the option of providing their own regulations of rDNA research, in addition to those that may be imposed by federal mandate.

With congressional action on rDNA legislation reaching an impasse, the Administration's Office of Science and Technology Policy initiates a study of the feasibility of using existing federal statutes to provide coverage beyond that of the NIH's authority.

At NIH, rDNA activities center on drafting proposed revisions of the Guidelines, which are published in the September 27th Federal Register, and on preparing a final draft environmental impact statement which is filed in October. The proposed revisions of the Guidelines are in essence "minor relaxations" of various requirements in the 1976 document that the committee feels are warranted by the reassessment of biohazards.

NIH holds public hearings on the proposed Guidelines in December.
. . . .

In response to much that transpires at the hearings, Fredrickson publicly states his belief that there is some validity to the complaints lodged against the procedures employed by NIH in developing revised Guidelines. In addition, he articulates a position concerning the role of NIH in rDNA regulation that is strikingly close to the one Kennedy had advanced when he proposed his Senate bill. Fredrickson now feels that there was too great a potential conflict of interest for NIH to act at the same time as "sponsor, conductor, and regulator" of rDNA research, and that perhaps the regulatory function should be allotted to some other federal agency. In addition, Fredrickson believes that a simple extension of the existing Guidelines to cover all rDNA research would be legislatively desirable at this time.

NOTE

Curtiss's letter was avowedly political in purpose—he sent a copy to all relevant members of Congress. Would he have said exactly the same in the absence of any political motive? Very possibly, and yet, when the NIH later proposed revising the guidelines in a way that would reduce the use of chi-1776, the disabled *E. coli* developed in Curtiss's laboratory, he asked Fredrickson to veto the revision because "the people now engaged in recombinant DNA research come from a diversity of backgrounds and the same people who have difficulty in using chi-1776 plasmid vector systems are also the same individuals who have never been adequately trained in microbiological techniques. . . ." Curtiss was the most scrupulous and conscientious member of the NIH recombinant DNA committee; and yet even his views of the hazards, like those of many other scientists, could be shaded just a little by the political context in which they were expressed.

N. Wade, The Ultimate Experiment 167 (1977).

PHILIP HANDLER*

HEARINGS BEFORE THE SUBCOMMITTEE ON SCIENCE, RESEARCH AND TECHNOLOGY, HOUSE COMMITTEE ON SCIENCE AND TECHNOLOGY

95th Cong., 2d Sess. 72–79 (April 11, 1978).

MR. THORNTON. Dr. Handler, I want to thank you for a fine presentation.

It seems to me that you may be telling us that it is a difficult matter to propose legislation to protect us against our fears as contrasted with legislation to protect us against dangers?

DR. HANDLER. Yes, sir.

MR. THORNTON. And I want to commend you for your very thoughtful presentation.

MR. McCormack, do you have any questions?

MR. McCormack. Yes, Mr. Chairman.

I am almost inclined to direct this question to you, Mr. Chairman, as well as to Dr. Handler. But as I read the findings of this bill, one can summarize them by saying that while no hazard has been demonstrated, there is an uncertainty about the hazards involved in a certain area of research, and therefore that research should be subject to control.

Dr. Handler, isn't this setting again a precedent, to single out any area of research and say we, a committee of Congress, have decided that this is potentially hazardous, that there may be a hazard associated with doing this research, and therefore the research should be controlled.

* The witness is the late Dr. Philip Handler, then President of the National Academy of Sciences. [Eds.]

Dr. Handler.   That is precisely the way I feel about it, yes.   I think it is a very dangerous precedent, and it must be addressed carefully.

Mr. McCormack.   Do you know of any area where research itself has been subject to control because it might be hazardous, or there might be a hazard associated with it?

Dr. Handler.   No sir.

The analogies that are offered are the controls which we have readily accepted with respect to research on human subjects.

Mr. McCormack.   That is a different matter.

Dr. Handler.   I agree; it is totally different.   But these are the analogies which have been offered.   The other has to do with the controls which have been placed on the use of radioactive material.   But again that was a real hazard, a known hazard.   And we accepted those controls. And we never dictated what experiment one may do provided we live within the protective regulations.

Mr. McCormack.   What about this matter of protecting against contamination or standardizing radiation levels?

Dr. Handler.   I accept this bill in the sense that the guidelines which forbid us to undertake certain experiments—which I venture to say nature is undertaking every day while we are not watching—nevertheless I assume that those guidelines are simply awaiting the day we assure ourselves that such research is entirely safe to undertake, rather than that there are forbidden experiments in the sense that there is some fear about learning the answer.

Mr. McCormack.   I would suggest that recent experience in the public and in Congress doesn't give me much confidence that your assumption is a correct one, Dr. Handler.

Dr. Handler.   It is the only assumption under which I will support the bill.

Mr. McCormack.   The experience has been, as you know, that each control is used as a step to ratchet to the next higher level of control.

Dr. Handler.   Absolutely.

Mr. McCormack.   Witness, for instance, the levels of radiation that we are working with today in nuclear research.

But how does one answer the question that any change, however small, is not acceptable, and that we must be absolutely certain as scientists that there is zero hazard before we go ahead?

Dr. Handler.   Nothing has zero hazard.   There is no process known to me associated with zero hazard.

Mr. McCormack.   Then to turn it the other way, can any law prevent—

Dr. Handler.   I am reminded, for example, since you are going to discuss energy later today, that the largest single known risk associated with the use of coal in our society, the demonstrated clear risk for which the statistics are valid, has to do with the number of people who are killed at grade crossing as that coal goes from the mines to the powerplant. Painful as that is, it is hardly a reason that will lead the country to forgo the use of coal.

MR. MCCORMACK. By the same token, is it possible to prevent DNA research? Couldn't there be bootleg research carried out in spite of any regulations?

DR. HANDLER. Very easily.

MR. MCCORMACK. After all, it is an easy sort of research; it doesn't take a lot of equipment.

DR. HANDLER. It doesn't take a lot of money, it doesn't take elaborate equipment. It can be done.

I find myself somewhat amused at the dilemma faced by the inspectors as to just how they will recognize recombinant DNA itself when they see it.

MR. MCCORMACK. In a large laboratory, hundreds of hoods could be set aside for DNA research, and they would know it only if someone else told them?

You mentioned that a reason for it might be to prevent Balkanization?

DR. HANDLER. Yes.

MR. MCCORMACK. But isn't it true that the practice in most regulatory legislation today is to allow States to establish still more restrictive regulations than the national standard, as in the case of air and water regulations?

DR. HANDLER. Yes; and several versions of this bill did not have preemptive provisions. This one does, qualified by the provision, and says that if a given locality can make a persuasive case of the Secretary that there are some local circumstances which demand yet more stringent regulations, that he can then grant them.

MR. MCCORMACK. The implication is that some States will simply ignore it and go ahead. That is the way it is with nuclear energy; they go ahead and write the laws and nothing is done about it. It is the same effect as if you didn't have a law at all.

DR. HANDLER. In a world of uncertainty the hazards associated with this, if any exist at all, have been blown out of proportion. We have dealt with a lot of science fiction rather than science. And around the country there are well-meaning, thoughtful but frightened individuals. We must do something to allay that concern and assure them that those who are responsible for our national affairs have given this careful consideration.

MR. MCCORMACK. Would you recommend, then, that the NIH guidelines be established under law or not?

DR. HANDLER. I rather wish that we would delay the entire matter for at least a year.

MR. MCCORMACK. Thank you. Mr. Chairman.

MR. THORNTON. Thank you very much, Mr. McCormack.

. . .

Mr. Harkin.

MR. HARKIN. Mr. Chairman, I don't believe I have any questions at this time other than just to state that again I am about half way through your testimony, and I find it a very interesting and very worthwhile addition to our proceedings that we started, I guess, over a couple of years ago in this subcommittee. It is an area that even the people out on the farms, so to speak, are aware of. They are aware of it through the general medium of the newspapers and television. And it is a subject that is approached by the general public that I come in contact with some fear and trepidation.

As you point out in your testimony, it is almost like we are crossing some boundary that man ought not to cross. But I agree with you that scientific inquiry ought not to be stopped because of perceived or social or cultural bias. On the other hand, I share the concern about Government control over this process, over the freedom of inquiry.

Again, we also are charged with the responsibility of providing for the public safety in many different areas. And there must be some form or some measures that can be taken to do both of those things, to accommodate both of those things, legitimate concerns of the public in this area. I know you seem to say that it is a distinctly remote possibility that these strains may get out of the laboratory, and that they might be very harmful to mankind. It may be remote, but it is a possibility.

Dr. Handler. Yes, sir, that is true of almost everything. And the question is, what odds will you take?

Mr. Harkin. That is right. And there are some odds that certainly are great in this area. But there are some things over which we have no control. And there are odds that a foreign body will strike the Earth at sometime and completely disintegrate the planet. There are odds on it, but there is nothing we can do about it.

Dr. Handler. That is correct.

Mr. Harkin. And there are odds that there might be a new strain developed through recombinant DNA that would be harmful to mankind. And there are some things, I believe, that we can do, while not limiting inquiry, while not limiting freedom of thought process, while not eliminating the scientific inquiry, that we can do to try to insure that these things don't happen at some future point in time, by simply trying to make sure that the place of scientific inquiry is secure, making sure that it is not done in a place where those strains could get out into the atmosphere or into the human environment, without some kind of protection.

Dr. Handler. But, sir, I think you should understand that, first, the organism that is being used, *Escherichia coli* K–12, is itself a helpless creature that cannot exist outside of a laboratory, it cannot survive in nature itself. When we add to it a bit of genetic information, from whatever source, it becomes yet further crippled, not benefitted. And the odds we are talking about are chances of the order of 10^{-15}, or some number that is so absurdly small that it can be ignored.

You can't live in a world where you refuse to take risks at those odds. It would close down life. When I say the chance is not zero I am being honest. But you must understand how incredibly small the chance is that we are taking.

Mr. Harkin. Are you saying that we ought not to even concern ourselves at all?

Dr. Handler. No. I think that since the world at large doesn't understand what I mean when I say that the chances, the statistical probability is 10^{-15} or some other very low number, what we need is an orderly demonstration of just what those risks are. And that is what I have encouraged NIH to do. It is the work which they have finally been permitted to attempt. But actually demonstrating the positive event at all, much less assessing the risk has so far proved to be impossible. You can't make one to survive if you want to at this point. No one I know understands how to deliberately make a new disease-forming organism. Not one, two or three genes known to me, introduced into *Escherichia coli* K–12 can possibly convert it into a viable disease-causing organism.

But for me to say, can no one ever do that, is the chance zero, that is not fair; of course I cannot say that. But if you ask me, is the risk so trivial and so tiny that it can be ignored, my answer is yes, sir.

In saying that, however, I may have transgressed. The assessment of risk is a scientific question; the matter of the degree of risk acceptable to society, however, is a political question. And I am here as a scientist.

MR. THORNTON. Anything further?

MR. HARKIN. No, thank you, Mr. Chairman.

MR. THORNTON. Mr. Brown.

MR. BROWN. If I could just raise a question here of a more general nature.

I have been concerned about the general feasibility of risk benefit analysis as it applies to a number of different kinds of cases. I will cite you one example which came up in a hearing last Saturday in Long Island, where the potable water supply of a community had been found to be polluted with organics to a level of 50 parts per billion last year. The water supply has been closed down and the community faces bankruptcy from having to buy potable water from whatever source it can. The organics were apparently placed into the underground supply over a period of years, possibly a generation, from local manufacturers. There were no standards indicating the carcinogenicity of the organics at the time they were being manufactured. And there still aren't sufficient standards of carcinogenicity for particular levels of this organic substance.

DR. HANDLER. Is it a known material?

MR. BROWN. Yes; and the State health department established this level. In accordance with their best wisdom, and relying somewhat on studies, they decided to lower it to 10 parts per billion later on.

The question I have—this is a good example of the general sort of problem that faces us today, where we find a generation later that something we were unaware of had a concentration which we still don't know may present hazards that we don't want to face. And you state that you have considerable evidence that industrial firms with their acute sensitivity to exposure to liability claims will comply with the guidelines in recombinant DNA research.

DR. HANDLER. While there are guidelines in force, yes. A company would have a difficult time were there any untoward event and they hadn't been following those guidelines. They must surely know this.

MR. BROWN. What can we do to protect the public and to insure the responsibility of a private industrial firm which engages in good faith in a legal activity following the guidelines and we find out later that there are costs and damages which were unanticipated? And we seem to be running into more of such cases, I am sure that this is what spurred some of the fear about recombinant DNA research. But the Constitution protects us from ex post facto legislation. We can't hold them accountable for what they did when it was legal . . . when they did it.

DR. HANDLER. I don't know quite how or when that material got into the water supply. But when we can, we make a judgment as to the level of acceptable risk; and then we set standards well below that risk to make sure that there is a big enough margin.   In this case, recombinant DNA, I don't know how to do the assessment of risks.   It is being attempted. But there is a simple guideline which I can put forward for anybody working in this field; the manner in which an experiment should be conducted should be determined by the riskiest component that is being employed and then treat every component as one would the riskiest.

For example, there are some microorganisms which one can handle by the bucket and nothing happens, they are totally harmless.   And if that is all that is involved, you can use the kind of general precautions appropriate to that organism.   If, on the other hand, you are going to deal with the yellow fever virus, or the typhus rickettsia or something of that sort, then treat everything in the system just the way you would handle that one.

I remind you that the materials that are to be used in recombinant DNA research are all harvested from nature, nothing is man-made in these systems but the recombination.   The materials that are alleged to be dangerous have to be obtained from nature by man and without incident, or usually without incident.   And laboratory—I say that carefully— people have died doing this kind of research.   But they know what the hazards are.   And one should handle everything in an experimental system the way one would the most hazardous component being used.   And any sensible laboratory will do that.   I cannot imagine anyone doing it otherwise.

And I will remind you again, sir, that every day in every hospital all over the world nurses, doctors, and technicians deal with sick people who carry the most pathogenic organisms known to us.   We do not regulate that endeavor.   It is self-regulating.   And it is self-regulating on behalf of the people who are doing it.   They are taught techniques which are designed for that kind of activity and similarly I would think we should educate those who are doing this kind of research.

MR. BROWN.   Dr. Handler, I am sure you are also aware that there are some cases in which going to the hospital is more hazardous than staying at home?

DR. HANDLER.   Yes, indeed, that is true.   The reason infants in most hospitals are no longer put into some sort of a big room full of other infants but are kept with their mothers is just that; it has reduced the incidence of staphylococcus infection (impetigo) considerably.

MR. BROWN.   The point of that remark is that the best intentions in the world sometimes do not achieve their purpose.

DR. HANDLER.   Absolutely.

MR. BROWN.   You have suggested here a reasonable proposal that industrial firms or any firm engaged in potentially hazardous research in this field should have a committee on biohazards on which the public should be represented.

DR. HANDLER.   I believe that.

MR. BROWN.   Presumably that would be applicable where the firms are engaged in the production of potentially hazardous chemical compounds?

DR. HANDLER.   Conceivably.

Mr. Brown, that kind of a mechanism is a way of assuring that we are doing what we do with sense of stewardship over the public interest, which is extremely important.   But there are factors such as the desire for running a successful business which sometimes contravene that kind of procedure. However, I think we can work that out. But I remind you that the entire antibiotic industry and the citric acid industry centers about microorganisms grown in 2,000- and 4,000-gallon fermenters. If, today, someone had just discovered how to make penicillin or streptomycin, I could immediately see the same challenges; namely, how do you know you can handle 2,000 or 4,000 gallons of one of those organisms without affecting the public health? There are no such things as completely safe microorganisms. Enough of any organism in your lungs will give you pneumonia. There is no organism which cannot do that, including these, *Escherichia coli.*

If you inspire this organism in a large amount you will surely have a form of pneumonia. But so will the organisms that we use to make streptomycin, penicillin, and chlorotetracycline and all the others. But no one has been injured by that industry, as far as I know. I have never heard of such a thing.

MR. BROWN. May I suggest another approach to this, which is not without flaws. In the nuclear industry we have decided that the Government would provide certain forms of insurance for catastrophic events. Do you think that there is any potential value to generalizing this principle to situations of this sort? And I am not limiting—

DR. HANDLER. I suppose I would agree if I thought there were hazards. But I must confess that I don't agree with the philosophy by which you can buy a license to pollute. That doesn't sit well with me. I would rather protect ourselves against the pollution, using that word in a rather generic sense.

MR. BROWN. I am not even speaking so much of buying a license to pollute as I am providing financial protection against catastrophic events that might occur without intent or knowledge or forewarning.

DR. HANDLER. I think that principle would have merit, sir. . . .

MR. THORNTON. Dr. Handler, I would like to inquire whether or not we in Congress might also consider that while we are examining something difficult in our legislative proposals on recombinant DNA research, that is, scientists have been troubled with that problem, may we not also be concerned with whether, by moving into mandatory regulation of inquiry, we might be producing a "microorganism" (legislation) which, as long as it is tightly contained and limited to a life of 2 years, and subject to regulations which are acceptable, appears to be not very fearful and not very likely to cause harm. But what if that "organism" (legislation) were to be released and did begin to act as a precedent for additional regulation, additional restraints, against fears, when hazards have not been yet demonstrated?

DR. HANDLER. All I can say, sir, is that it has been demonstrated that the virus of regulation is extraordinarily virulent once it has been released.

MR. THORNTON. Thank you.

Are there other questions?

If not, Dr. Handler, I want to thank you for your testimony.

DR. HANDLER. Thank you, sir.

NOTES

1. The interaction among legislators, scientists and their advocates, and the health research bureaucracy is described by science journalist Nicholas Wade, a long-time observer of the DNA research controversy, as follows:

> Persuaded by the scientific lobbyists that the hazards of the research were negligible, Congress lost its appetite for legislation. After two years of intense and often confusing discussion, a dozen bills had been proposed but no law was passed . . . . Meanwhile the guidelines themselves, partly in anticipation of the possibility that they might be turned into law, were reduced in stringency by the NIH recombinant DNA committee.

N. Wade, The Ultimate Experiment 158 (1977). He believes that the outcome of this "political tussle" has set an "important precedent" for future debates over the applications of gene splicing discoveries. Does that seem likely? Why or why not?

2. On June 1, 1978, Senators Edward Kennedy, Jacob Javits, Gaylord Nelson, Adlai Stevenson, Harrison Williams and Richard Schweiker—who had urged a wide variety of approaches to the controversy—wrote Secretary Califano, acknowledging that legislation was unlikely, and urged that deficiencies in the regulatory system be addressed through executive action based on existing authority. Secretary Califano's response, in December 1978, was described, supra, in Sec. B.2. Peter Barton Hutt, a former FDA counsel with extensive experience in the area of recombinant DNA oversight, argued that further legislation was not required because Sec. 361 of the Public Health Service Act, 42 U.S.C. § 264 (1976), provides the Secretary [of what is now Health and Human Services] with adequate authority to require all researchers in this field to comply with the NIH Guidelines. Hutt, Research on Recombinant DNA Molecules: The Regulatory Issues, 51 S.Cal.L.Rev. 1435, 1443 (1978). See also Sec. B.2, supra, regarding federal statutory authority for regulating the products of this research.

3. Professor Sheldon Krimsky of Tufts University provides an excellent history of events, in Washington and elsewhere, in his analysis of the recombinant DNA controversy, Genetic Alchemy (1982).

4. NONFEDERAL REGULATION

Part of the original impetus for Federal intervention came from the realization among Congressional leaders that the field might become very disorderly in the absence of national regulations applicable to all activities undertaken by private enterprise as well as by publicly supported researchers. As part of its report, Genetic Engineering, Human Genetics, and Cell Biology, to the House subcommittee on Science, Research and Technology of the Science and Technology Committee in December 1976, the Library of Congress Research Service warned (at page 53):

> Although the proliferation of interest in this issue has not been totally unexpected, there is some concern about the potential for the evolution of ordinances or regulations on a local basis. Since the research transcends local boundaries, there is a strong interest in the development of standard guidelines. In the discussions held thus far, the NIH guidelines have occupied a central focus of attention. There probably would be no objection by NIH if State or local regulations evolved which utilized these guidelines as the core of any locally enforced regulations. The evolution of a maze of regulations would, on the other hand, contribute to great confusion as to requirements and undoubtedly interfere with effective control over research which crosses not only State but international boundaries. Evidence for this same interest in other Nations is available not only from the statements made by

foreign participants at U.S. meetings but also in the debates which are producing regulations in these other Nations.

Surprisingly, when Congress finally walked away from the subject, leaving it to the Executive branch under existing authority, this issue remained largely unresolved.

SHELDON KRIMSKY, LOCAL MONITORING OF BIOTECHNOLOGY: THE SECOND WAVE OF RECOMBINANT DNA LAWS

5 Recombinant DNA Technical Bulletin 79–84 (No. 2, June 1982).

Between the summer of 1976 and the winter of 1977 national attention was directed to the city council of Cambridge, Massachusetts. The media, public policy experts, members of Congress, and government agencies watched as the city set out to enact legislation that would place recombinant DNA (RDNA) research under the authority of a local biohazards committee and the commissioner of health and hospitals. The city passed an ordinance of an unprecedented nature. It placed under legal restraints a field of basic scientific research, namely molecular biology, by establishing standards for the use of its most promising research technique RDNA molecules and gene splicing.

The ordinance was only slightly more stringent than the guidelines issued by the National Institutes of Health (NIH). In subsequent years, even those differences were removed to bring the Cambridge law into conformity with the current NIH regulations. Nevertheless, the action by the Cambridge city council brought tremors to the scientific community for what it represented. Research scientists and the institutions in which they work were now accountable to public officials at the local level on issues of laboratory safety.

The Cambridge RDNA controversy also stimulated other legislative initiatives. Several congressional leaders were persuaded to introduce bills for regulating RDNA activities. Having first opposed a federal law, some scientists began to view that course of action as a lesser evil to a patchwork of local laws. From 1977 to 1979 two states and five cities and towns followed the precedent set by Cambridge. Laws were enacted in the states of Maryland and New York; ordinances were also passed in the communities of Emeryville and Berkeley, California; Princeton, New Jersey; and Amherst, Massachusetts. . . .

A second wave of RDNA legislation appeared between 1981 and 1982. During this period all the laws were enacted by communities located in the greater Boston metropolitan area. The issue that precipitated the new concerns was the siting of commercial RDNA firms in the respective communities. This new generation of RDNA ordinances received significantly less publicity and media coverage than those passed when the debate focused on university research. Although the cities involved are in close proximity to one another, the laws themselves are important expressions of social concerns and values over the commercial uses of RDNA technology. . . .

During the summer of 1980 the Swiss genetic engineering firm Biogen was seeking a commercial and management headquarters for its research and development activities in the United States. Company officials, which include Harvard biologist and Nobel laureate Walter Gilbert, chairman of Biogen's scientific board, notified the Cambridge City Council that they had selected a site in an industrial area of the city a short distance from M.I.T. The plan for the site showed a facility consisting of approximately 30,000 square feet on which would be located offices, research and development laboratories, and a pilot plant with a fermentor in the 1000–3000 liter range. No manufacturing operations were planned for the facility. Biogen's management was asked why it chose to locate in a community that had an RDNA law, an additional layer of bureaucracy in the form of a municipal biohazards committee, a skeptical city council, and a history of heated debate that left residues of ill feelings among some members of the academic community. In its reply the company stated it preferred to locate in a city which had matured with respect to the RDNA controversy. Cambridge, Biogen surmised, would not have to return to square one in dealing with public attitudes toward genetic research but could build upon its previous citizens' review process. And that is precisely what the city did.

Shortly after Biogen's site was announced, the Cambridge Biohazards Committee (CBC), which was created by the 1977 ordinance, exercising its authority to review present and future RDNA activities, called for a hearing on 28 October 1980. The public turnout at the hearing was light. Community opposition to the site was mild compared to what had taken place when the issues were first raised over university research. Unlike the early hearings in 1976 there were no biologists who testified in support of additional controls in the city for RDNA work. The CBC, however, did receive letters from scientists and public health professionals requesting the biohazards committee to proceed with caution, particularly since large scale RDNA work was being considered.

While the CBC was in the process of preparing a response to Biogen's site request, the issue was placed on the agenda of the Cambridge City Council. City Councillor Alfred Vellucci, who had previously opposed P–3 level recombinant DNA research in Cambridge, tried to block Biogen's plan. Suspecting that the CBC would approve Biogen's request, Vellucci called upon the council to reconvene the Cambridge Experimentation Review Board (CERB) which had been responsible for resolving the 1976 debate. Ironically, Vellucci issued public statements critizing the original decision of the citizen task force that permitted P–3 research in the city ending a six month moratorium.

The council approved of reinstating the CERB. Except for one individual, the make-up of the committee was identical to what it had been four years earlier. The new CERB made a strategic political decision to work together with the CBC in evaluating the Biogen proposal. Instead of having two independent recommendations, the citizens decided to develop a consensus position between the CBC and the CERB before approaching the city council.

For a period of a month and a half members of the two committees met with officials of Harvard, M.I.T. and Biogen to examine safety factors involved with having a research and development facility in an industrial section of the city. Experts in the fields of fermentation engineering and survival of biological hosts and vectors in the environment appeared before the joint committees. Procedures for handling spills, deactivating cells and treating effluent were carefully examined by committee members.

The meetings were open to the general public but attracted few onlookers. Final deliberations took place in an atmosphere supportive of accommodation and negotiation. The community was far less polarized during this second RDNA round and that was reflected in CERB's decision process. The joint committee was particularly sensitive to the prospect of driving away a firm because of regulations that were unworkable or unreasonable. It was generally acknowledged that Biogen wanted to locate in Cambridge so it could be near Harvard and M.I.T. But the company was not willing to locate there at a cost of excessive regulation and an uncertain future.

If the CBC and CERB failed to come up with a set of mutually acceptable and workable standards, Biogen, most likely, would have located in a community that had no mandatory regulations for RDNA technology. Had this occurred city officials undoubtedly would have been viewed as the Luddites of biotechnology.

The result of the deliberations was a new RDNA ordinance that superseded the 1977 law and placed special conditions on the commercial aspects of genetic engineering. Although Biogen and the two universities were not pleased with the result, they agreed that their respective institutions could live with the new law. The citizenry involved in developing the new ordinance welcomed the opportunity to work with representatives of industry and academia in order to give concrete expression to its concerns over health and safety of a burgeoning industry. The ordinance adopted by Cambridge was not intended to replicate or be in conflict with the work of the NIH and its *Guidelines* for research. On the contrary, the function of the new law was to establish safeguards against the promiscuous release of organisms into the environment and to develop some awareness about occupational safety. Without state and federal oversight of biotechnology in the private sector, the citizens in the review process believed that the city had as much responsibility to oversee commercial bioengineering establishments as it had to regulate other commercial activities where public health and safety are at stake. In essence, the city was taking out an insurance policy against an uncertain environmental future in industrial genetic technology.

On 24 March 1981 the city council was advised of the revised RDNA ordinance with little fanfare and no national publicity. The council voted the proposal into law on 27 April. Long term opponent to RDNA research Alfred Vellucci issued the only negative vote.

The new law incorporates the idea that firms introducing risks to the community, whether real or conjectured, shall internalize the costs the municipality must bear *to assure itself* that adverse consequences will not be realized. For Cambridge, those assurances are in the form of external audits and inspections of facilities.

. . .

In response to the new ordinance in Cambridge several other communities in the Boston area that were courted by RDNA firms passed similar laws. The four communities are Boston, Somerville, Waltham and Newton. Except for Somerville, each of these cities has a firm that is currently engaging in RDNA research and development. The Boston and Somerville laws are close derivatives of the Cambridge ordinance. A unique provision in the Boston ordinance calls for community elections to fill four positions on the municipal biohazards committee. Somerville passed its ordinance nearly a year after the Genetics Institute tried to obtain city approval to set up operations in a vacated silver plating factory. When Somerville delayed, Genetics Institute rented space in the old Boston Lying-In Hospital in the heart of the nation's largest medical complex. That event prompted community activists and local officials to adapt the Cambridge ordinance to Boston.

Since Cambridge enacted its second RDNA ordinance, three private firms have applied for permits in the city. Biogen began operating in its new building in February 1982. The facilities of a new firm Repligen have been inspected and given CBC approval to conduct research. A third firm seeking a site is Biotechnica, International. Officials there have applied for a permit and were preparing for an inspection in April 1982. Contrary to the opinion of some, the RDNA law in Cambridge has not repelled firms from taking residence. Meanwhile, public confidence in the fledgling biotechnology industry has improved, at least in part because better channels of communications exist and citizens feel they are adequately represented in the firms' decisions on health and safety standards.

ORDINANCE FOR THE USE OF RECOMBINANT DNA TECHNOLOGY IN THE CITY OF CAMBRIDGE [MASSACHUSETTS]

Ord. No. 955, Final Publication No. 2092 (April 27, 1981).

Section 11-7. GUIDELINES FOR THE REGULATION OF RECOMBINANT DNA USE

I. DEFINITIONS

In the context of this ordinance the following definitions are adopted:

a) Recombinant DNA molecules (RDNA) and organisms and viruses containing RDNA are those defined in the National Institutes of Health Guidelines promulgated in the Federal Register on November 21, 1980, and such amendments thereto as may be approved by the Cambridge Biohazards Committee.

. . .

c) . . . In the event that the National Institutes of Health shall discontinue or abolish their guidelines, those guidelines in effect at the time of such discontinuance shall remain in effect in the City of Cambridge.

II. PURPOSE

All use of RDNA by institutions in the City of Cambridge shall be undertaken only in strict conformity with the "Guidelines", as defined above, and in conformity also with such other health regulations as the Commissioner of Health and Hospitals may from time to time promulgate.

III. CAMBRIDGE BIOHAZARDS COMMITTEE

a) A Cambridge Biohazards Committee (CBC) shall be established for the purpose of overseeing all use of RDNA in the City of Cambridge and of advising the Commissioner of Health and Hospitals and the Health Policy Board.

b) The CBC shall be composed of the Commissioner of Health and Hospitals or his/her designee, the Chairperson of the Health Policy Board or a board member designated by the Chairperson and a minimum of three other members to be appointed by the City Manager. The City Manager is authorized to provide for the adequate staffing of the CBC.

c) The CBC and the Commissioner of Health and Hospitals are empowered to retain competent professional assistance in carrying out their duties under this ordinance.

d) The salaries and expenses of the staff and consultants of the CBC under this ordinance shall be apportioned to the institutions holding permits under this ordinance.

IV. PERMIT REQUIREMENT

a) All institutions proposing to use RDNA must obtain a permit from the Commissioner of Health and Hospitals with the approval of the CBC. Permit requirements include written agreement to:

1) Follow the "Guidelines".

2) Follow other conditions set forth in this ordinance.

3) Allow inspection of facilities and pertinent records by the Cambridge Biohazards Committee.

4) Prepare a Health and Safety manual which contains all procedures relevant to the use of RDNA at all levels of containment in use at the institution. Said manual shall be submitted to the Cambridge Biohazards Committee for review.

5) Establish a training program of safeguards and procedures for personnel using RDNA.

V. The Institutional Biosafety Committee (IBC) required by the National Institutes of Health Guidelines shall have at least one member who is a nondoctoral person from a laboratory technical staff and one representative approved by the Health Policy Board. The IBC shall be the final arbiter within an institution, with regard to the implementation of this Ordinance and the "Guidelines".

VI. All minutes of the IBC meetings must be forwarded to the Commissioner of Health and Hospitals and the CBC. It shall also be the responsibility of the institution to file regular reports with the Cambridge Biohazards Committee, in a manner to be determined by the CBC.

VII. Institutions using RDNA shall perform adequate screening to insure the purity of the strain of host organisms used in the experiments and shall test organisms resulting from such experiments for their resistance to commonly used therapeutic antibiotics.

VIII. All institutions are to provide an appropriate medical surveillance program as determined by the Institutional Biosafety Committee for all persons engaged in the use of RDNA. Such programs must be approved by the CBC.

IX. The institution shall report within thirty (30) days to the CBC and the Commissioner of Health and Hospitals any significant problems with or violations of the "Guidelines" and any significant RDNA related accidents or illnesses.

X. The premises in which RDNA is used must be totally and completely free of rodent and insect infestation.

Section 11–8.   LARGE SCALE

All institutions using RDNA on a "Large Scale" (as defined in the "Guidelines") must adhere to the following requirements in addition to those stated in Section 11–7.

I.   SPECIAL PERMIT.

All institutions must obtain a special Large Scale Permit (LS Permit) from the Commissioner of Health and Hospitals with the approval of the CBC, after the Commissioner and the CBC have conducted an appropriate public hearing.   LS Permit requirements include written agreement to:

a) Identify clearly all large scale RDNA use in the IBC minutes.

b) Development procedures through the IBC for monitoring of large scale operations, for compliance with this ordinance and the "Guidelines".   These procedures shall be approved by the CBC and the Commissioner of Health and Hospitals.

c)

1) Allow an annual inspection and review of the procedures and practices of Large Scale RDNA use for compliance with this ordinance. The scope of this inspection and review shall be mutually agreed upon by the institution and the CBC.

2) The CBC shall retain a professionally competent person, persons, agency or institution to perform this inspection and review.   The results should be reported to the CBC, the Commissioner of Health and Hospitals and the institution involved.

3) The institution shall reimburse the City for the expense of this inspection and review including an apportionment of the salaries of the staff of the CBC under Section 11–7, III subsections (b) and (c).

d) Establish a Health-Safety Program for appropriate employees. Such a program is to include safety training, periodic retraining and periodic health surveillance.   Details and procedures are to be established by each institution and approved by the CBC and the Commissioner of Health and Hospitals.

e) Advance approval must be given by the CBC for Large Scale uses of RDNA requiring P2 or P3 physical containment.

. . .

Section 11–10.   RESTRICTIONS

I.   RDNA use classified by the "Guidelines" as requiring P3 physical containment and biological containment greater than HV2 shall not be permitted without prior approval of the CBC.   RDNA use requiring P4 containment shall not be permitted in the City of Cambridge.

II.   There shall be no deliberate release into the environment, that is, the sewers, drains or the air, of any organism containing recombinant DNA and further that any accidental release shall be reported to the Commissioner of Health and Hospitals within five days.

Section 11–11.   PENALTIES

I.   Violation of the conditions of this ordinance shall subject the violator to a fine of Two Hundred Dollars ($200.00) per day and in addition the facility in which the violation occurs may be closed by the Commissioner of Health and Hospitals. Each day of violation shall constitute a separate and distinct offense.

II.   Once a permit has been issued it may be revoked by the Commissioner of Health and Hospitals only upon a determination (subject to judicial review) by the CBC and the Commissioner of Health and Hospitals after due notice and hearing, that the institution involved has materially failed to comply with the City Ordinance, the permit agreements or the "Guidelines" (notwithstanding reasonable notice and an opportunity to correct such failures to comply with the provisions of this ordinance).

. . . .

NOTES

1.   During the first (and most contentious) debates in Cambridge over the city's attempts to evaluate the risks of genetic research and to impose regulations needed to protect the public health, a great deal of skepticism was expressed about the ability of the people appointed to the first nine-member panel—a former mayor, a community worker, two nurses, a former city councilman, a structural engineer, a professor of urban policy and a physician—to appreciate the complex scientific issues and judgments involved. One answer given was that the process was not a technical one but was addressed to the issues of public policy.

A novel method of gathering information was adopted; on July 16, 1976, a week after the Cambridge City Council had held its second day of public hearings and had created the review panel to make recommendations, the city sponsored a street fair.

Located in two booths, separated by a table at which Mayor Vellucci sits, the two sides are prepared to explain their stances and to argue for support from the Cambridge lay community. The proponents' table is staffed by well-attired scientists, who have brought with them a variety of scientific materials, including a model of DNA. The opponents' table is emptier, containing some pamphlets.

Swazey, Sorenson and Wong, Risks and Benefits, Rights and Responsibilities, 51 S.Cal.L.Rev. 1019, 1060 (1978). Is this a sensible way to gather public opinion? Compare it with the effort of the Environmental Protection Agency, announced in 1983, to hold a series of "town meetings" in Tacoma, Washington, to obtain the public's view on whether to close a local copper smelter that poses a risk of cancer to some residents. (See Ch. 5 for further discussion of such issues of risk.)

2.   Although the debates in Cambridge were probably the most colorful and the most widely reported in the general media, an earlier controversy had occurred at the University of Michigan when it was proposed that the Board of Regents allocate $302,000 to renovate three existing laboratories for low-to-moderate genetic engineering research. The decision sparked six months of often acrimonious debate, at the end of which those favoring the laboratories were victorious.

Madison, Wisconsin; Princeton, New Jersey; Bloomington, Indiana; and San Diego, California, were other university communities in which the local citizenry became involved in reviewing gene splicers' laboratory plans. New York, California, Maryland, New Jersey and Massachusetts have all taken action at the state level. N. Wade, The Ultimate Experiment 127–44 (1977).

3.   International controls have also been discussed and promulgated. One such action, by the Parliamentary Assembly of the Council of Europe, appears in Sec. D.2., infra.

5. FINDING APPROPRIATE INSTITUTIONS

A process that began in individual discussions among a few scientists grew to encompass prestigious scientific organizations and the Federal agencies that support research, governmental health and safety officials, the United States Congress and other elected officials, and—through press coverage and public hearings—members of the general public. To what extent do you think public institutions made up of nonscientists can really play an important part in "controlling" science and medicine? Does it seem that they could have a more effective role in framing policy than in implementing it? In reviewing consequences? Who should decide what, and when?

Specifically regarding genetic engineering, does the process that occurred seem desirable? Likely to be repeated in other areas of science and technology? Capable of being improved through the use of more appropriate institutions at various stages? Are there particular problems that this method is likely to be less successful in addressing? And, in particular, are there roles for courts and legislatures that might be more fully explored?

PAUL SIEGHART ET AL.*, THE SOCIAL OBLIGATIONS OF THE SCIENTIST

1 Hastings Cntr. Studies 7–16 (No. 2, 1973).

. . . [From the atom bomb in 1945 to organ transplants in more recent times, the social consequences of science and technology have become increasingly obvious to the general public.] . . .

High rates of technological growth, so long sought after as a means of bringing Utopia nearer, are coming to be seen as a potential threat to civilization and the quality of life. Because they are associated with progress in the natural sciences, that progress is held to be their cause. So scientists come to be blamed for the use which society makes of their work; in their turn, scientists become troubled about the extent of their moral responsibility, both for the social problems themselves, and for devising solutions for them.

In that situation, the interplay of science and technology on the one hand, and social ethics on the other, is much discussed today. These two are not easy to discuss in a common language: science uses concepts which are in themselves morally neutral, while ethics does not yield readily to analysis by the scientific method. Moral problems cannot be answered by devising an appropriate set of experiments. There may be general agreement about some moral issues, but there will always be large areas of dispute which cannot be resolved by objective tests.

. . .

The terms of reference which we gave ourselves were "to devise practical means, within the framework of the existing social system, for the performance of the social obligations of scientists, both individually and collectively, and to report and make recommendations accordingly."

. . .

* The interdisciplinary working party that drew up this proposal for a "science and society council" for Great Britain consisted of: Dr. B.S. Drasar, bacteriologist, St. Mary's Hospital Medical School, London; J.C.B. Glover, philosopher, New College, Oxford; Dr. V.A.S. Glover, neurochemist, University College, London; Dr. M.J. Hill, biochemist, St. Mary's Hospital Medical School, London; Dr. J. Issroff, psychiatrist, Tavistock Institute for Human Relations; D.A. Parfit, philosopher, All Souls College, Oxford; and Paul Sieghart, retired barrister (convenor). [Eds.]

We first considered a number of possible radical conclusions. Those which have been proposed fall into three broad groups. First, that there should be something in the nature of a Hippocratic Oath or code of ethics for all scientists, whereby they bind themselves not to take part in work which will have socially harmful consequences; second, given that we have an increasingly science-based civilization, that moral and political decisions about the social application of scientific work should be left increasingly to scientists themselves; and third, that there should be radical—if not revolutionary—reform of the whole social system. Of these, we think the first impracticable, the second dangerous, and the third beyond our competence.

(1) The field of science is vast, and the effects of the work done by the people who operate in it are complex and often quite unpredictable. There is nothing inherently good or bad about any advance in the scientific field: the consequences for society will depend on the use which society makes of it. Taking just one example, when antibiotics were first discovered they were rightly hailed as an unqualified boon; now, farmers who feed them to their pigs, and so enhance their profits, may be putting human life at risk by encouraging the evolution of resistant pathogens who first meet them in the pigs' bowels. Because of the diversity and complexity of possible social effects, any attempt to draw up a set of general ethical rules for scientists is bound in the end to reduce to a series of pious generalities, incapable of giving a particular scientist any help or guidance in a particular situation. . . .

(2) We suspect that the idea that scientists should be left to decide how society should use their work is based on a tacit confusion. If decisions of this kind were "scientific" decisions, there might be something to be said for leaving them to scientists. But they are not: they are essentially political and moral decisions. . . .

(3) Many people today think that there is a great deal wrong with our social system. . . . For our part, therefore, we start from the premise that "The System" is with us, and will be with us for some time to come, but that there may be some ways of making it work a little better, and of improving our prospects.

Our concern is therefore to argue the merits of some such ways, and to suggest one in particular which we think might help our society to make better thought-out and better informed choices, and at the same time give scientists a greater opportunity of putting their social consciences to work for the common good. . . .

. . .

The response time available to society for successful adjustment to new techniques seems to be shortening rapidly. There was less time for adapting to an industrial society than there was for adapting to a pastoral or agrarian one. . . .

More and more often, decisions have to be made too late, when there is little time to think them out fully, to discuss them publicly, to have second and even third thoughts, and to hear what people with different points of view have to say. As a result, often nothing is done at all where clearly something should have been done, or else what is done is a hasty measure which has to be altered later, by which time it may be too late to do what should have been done in the first place.

In one other important respect things have changed profoundly in recent times, and that is the extent of the mistakes which we can still afford to make. . . . Not only . . . has it become necessary to reach decisions more quickly; it is often supremely important to get them right the first time.

In our view, the greatest scope for influencing the future of our species favourably lies in a more efficient use of the response time available to society for deciding how new work in the field of science and technology should be used. . . .

It is in this area also that the greatest opportunities arise for scientists themselves to discharge the moral responsibility to society about which they are becoming increasingly concerned. But what does that responsibility amount to? To what extent, if any, has a scientist, as a scientist, special moral obligations to society, over and above those which he owes in his ordinary capacity as a citizen?

Apart from the social obligations which we all share as citizens, there are particular ones which attach to particular activities, relationships or professions. . . . [S]ome responsibilities are moral without being legal: no law forces parents to take an interest in how their children are doing at school, yet most of us would agree that this is part of their responsibility.

Scientists are already subject to a number of special legal duties, such as those imposed by the regulations governing experiments on live animals. We are not here concerned with these, but with the particular moral responsibilities of scientists which are not enforced by any law. How can we decide what these are?

A good starting point for deciding whether anyone has a special moral obligation to others is to ask whether he is especially well placed to benefit or harm them. . . .

The outcome of scientific work can often have a great impact, for good or ill, on other people. Quite frequently, scientists can predict this outcome earlier, and more accurately, than others. Sometimes they can even modify the results. One could claim, therefore, that scientists are in one of those special positions which give rise to special obligations.

Let us consider some possible objections to this claim.

(a) *"Much scientific work has no effect on society."* This may well be true, but it is no answer for those who work in fields which do, in the end, have a significant social effect.

(b) *"The social effects of a piece of scientific work may not be predictable."* This again may be true in many cases but it is not true in all. Besides, predictability is a matter of degree. While some of the practical applications of a piece of theoretical work may well be unpredictable, others can often be foreseen. And even though the kind of effect may not be predictable, the fact that there will be an effect may be clear quite early on. In such cases, whether the scientist can predict better than others what applications are (or might be) technically feasible, that alone could give rise to a special moral obligation.

(c) *"The scientist only provides the knowledge and the techniques: it is society's responsibility how they are used."* Within its limits, this is a good point. In many cases, one's responsibility for the consequences of one's act ends where someone else's act intervenes in the causal chain. The manufacturer of rat poison is not held responsible for the use to which a murderer puts his product. But the explanation is that the act of the other is not reasonably foreseeable; if I put rat poison on the market, I am not expected to foresee that someone will use it to commit murder. It is quite another matter if I sell it to someone whom I know—or have good reason for suspecting—to have homicidal intentions. This objection will therefore not hold where the scientist is in a special position to foresee how others will, or are likely to, use the results of his work. If he places knowledge and skills in the hands of politicians, industrialists and soldiers, it is arguable that he has at least the responsibility of trying to find out what they intend to do with it.

(d) "*If I don't do it, someone else will.*" This is one of the oldest—and in many ways the most difficult—of the objections put up against attempts to make people morally responsible for the consequences of what they do. . . .

If one judges the moral quality of an act solely by its consequences, the objection at first sight looks convincing. In a world containing a fair number of unscrupulous people, someone can probably be found to do almost any bad act. . . . [I]t would follow that no one could be legitimately blamed for doing wrong, and the basis for any moral judgment would disappear.

There are two possible answers to this.

First, we doubt whether the objection is well founded in fact. It may be true in many cases that if one scientist refused to do one piece of work, another might be found to do it in his place. But if such refusals were to become the rule rather than the exception, the moral climate might well be influenced enough to reduce the number of occasions on which anyone was asked to do this kind of work. . . .

Second, there are those who believe that good acts should be done for their own sake, independently of whether they can be shown to have good consequences. . . .

(e) "*As a scientist, I am only concerned to increase knowledge. That must take priority over everything else.*" There are two possible grounds for this objection: either that knowledge is of such value that we must have it at any cost, or that scientists in particular have an overriding obligation to place knowledge first.

The first of these is an extreme position and, like many extreme positions, can be shown to lead to results which most people would regard as absurd. For instance, if knowledge must be enlarged at any cost, then the medical experiments conducted in Hitler's concentration camps were justified. . . .

The second, more moderate ground is that *scientists* should pursue knowledge at any cost, rather than that knowledge itself is worth any cost. This is like saying that judges must adhere scrupulously to the law, even if that may produce injustice in a particular case, or that soldiers have an overriding duty to obey their orders. But there are good reasons for those propositions which do not hold for the scientist: the reason why judges must stick to the law is that, if they did not, there would be more injustice in the law courts than there is already. Again, if soldiers did not obey orders an army would turn into a disorganized rabble: yet even here no one would seriously argue that a soldier must carry out an order to commit rape, or assassinate the Prime Minister—as the German generals discovered to their cost at Nuremberg. In any case, therefore, where a scientist's pursuit of truth might lead to harmful results for mankind, this objection also loses its force.

What the Obligations Are

Accordingly, we conclude that none of these objections is well founded, and that scientists do have special obligations to society. The next question is what these obligations are. The principal ones which have been advanced by others can be conveniently, though loosely, classified as follows: first, to refrain from doing some kinds of work; second, to do some kinds of work; third, to contribute to a greater sense of social responsibility among other scientists; fourth, to think out the social consequences of their own work and of other work in their field; and fifth, to inform the public about what is being done, and its likely consequences.

. . .

Thinking out the consequences. We believe that anyone who engages in an activity which might have harmful social consequences ought to apply his mind to those consequences, and to act on his conclusions. We do not think that it is good enough to put on the conventional blinkers, concentrate on the job in hand, and leave the consequences to others. In the past, there has been a discernible tendency amongst scientists in general to do just that. They were by no means alone, but we suspect that the tendency has contributed to the image of them which is held by many laymen. Whatever virtues academic remoteness may be thought to further, it is not a popular quality. Although it is easy to state this obligation in general terms, its application in particular cases will often be difficult. The social consequences of a particular piece of research or application may be far from obvious, and their evaluation will often lie outside the competence of the scientist concerned. It is this which leads us to consider the last—and, in our view, in practice the most important—of the classes of obligation which we listed at the beginning of this section.

Informing the public. If it appears that work which is being done in a particular field might have a significant social impact, it is in our view of the utmost importance that society at large should be given warning in advance. Sometimes, it may be obvious at an early stage that a particular discovery is likely to have clearly harmful social consequences. In that situation, the rest of society should have the opportunity to begin as soon as possible to work out a response which will minimize or eliminate them. On other occasions, important beneficial consequences may be foreseen Here society should have the opportunity, as soon as possible, to reinforce the research effort, and to prepare the means for utilizing the benefits and making them available to its members. . . .

Of the five classes of social obligation which we have listed, the first two (to refuse to do, or to do, certain kinds of work) are matters for the consciences of individual scientists. . . .

The other three classes of obligation differ from the first two because they can be performed in an organized fashion. . . .

But the most important conclusion to which we have come is that . . . . the institutional machinery available to scientists for the most effective performance of their special social obligations is at present quite inadequate. . . .

What particularly concerns us is that, at present, there appears to be far too little communication between the organs of government on the one hand, and the scientific community on the other. We do not doubt that the government of the day has at its disposal the best scientific advice if it chooses to call for it, but it is not the primary function of those advisers to press on politicians and civil servants unasked-for views, nor to stimulate discussion and planning about possible dangers, at all events before they have become a matter of public concern. . . .

The present position is too often chaotic. Scientific work which may have a great impact on all our lives is being done all over the world. The scientists who are doing the work may well be aware, even if sometimes only dimly, of the possible dangers, but it is no part of their task to work out the appropriate social response, nor are they qualified to do this. To say, as we do, that they have an obligation to inform the public about what they are doing, and its implications, is easy enough. But at the moment there is little the individual scientists can do in this respect between the extremes of a sensational newspaper article, and a discreet letter to a member of the government. It is not until the potential dangers become apparent through some scandal or disaster that they catch the attention of the popular press, and there is a public outcry. At that point, politicians and their advisers begin to take an active interest and look—often frantically—for the appropriate response. But by that time, only too often, it is in one way or another too late, for too many people or organizations have acquired a vested interest in the discovery, or its development, to make it possible to deprive them of its fruits. The response will then be too little and too late, and we either have to put up with the harmful consequences with little or no mitigation, or we are subjected to the constraints of panic measures which are ill thought out and which later prove to be inadequate or to have unexpected side effects.

. . .

We think that this situation could be much improved if there were to be brought into existence a body, organized by the scientific community itself and expressly charged with the task of informing the public in general, and the organs of government in particular, at the earliest possible time, of all scientific work likely to have important social consequences for good or ill. This would serve to lengthen the available response time, and eliminate the present lack of communication. Also, individual scientists would have an opportunity to perform their social obligations in many situations where, as things now are, they can do nothing.

NOTES ON SCIENTIFIC RESPONSIBILITY

1. What is the central responsibility of the scientist according to Sieghart and his colleagues? Is it to anticipate the uses (especially harmful) of his or her scientific findings or merely to publicize what is known? If the former obligation were applied to the rat poison hypothetical, would the results be as stated by Sieghart, namely forbidding sales to someone one knows—or has good reason for suspecting—has an evil purpose? Or would greater foresight (including inquiry into purchasers' purposes) be needed?

2. One American philosopher has expanded on this theme:

If the essence of good scientific research is to leave no stone unturned, it is no less pertinent to moral thought. A scientific researcher would, in strictly scientific terms, be considered poor if he did not allow his mind to roam in all directions during the phase of hypothesis development, taking seriously any idea that might produce a promising lead . . . .. The same is true of moral thinking, particularly when it bears on the future consequences of our actions. We are obliged to explore all possibilities, however vague and remote; and the moral person will also end by throwing most of them out—most, finally, but not all. Since we surely now know that scientific research, whether basic or applied, is a source of enormous power for both good and ill, the scientific researcher has, then, an obligation to be as active in his moral imagination as in his scientific imagination. We ask the same of any person in a position of power.

Callahan, Ethical Responsibility in Science in the Face of Uncertain Consequences, 265 Ann.N.Y.Acad.Sci. 1, 6 (1976).

An example of personal actions apparently based on "moral imagination" occurred early in the development of genetic engineering:

> In 1970, shortly after the first isolation of a DNA fragment which constituted a single identifiable gene, the young scientists involved in the project decided they would not continue their work on DNA. The reason, they reported, was that such work would eventually be put to evil uses by the large corporations and governments that control science. They also believed it would lead to political oppression and the creation of so-called inferior subclasses of beings based on genetic classification. Dr. James Shapiro, who was 26 at the time, announced he would leave science altogether for a career in radical politics; Dr. Jonathan Beckwith, who was then 33, shifted his work to other areas of genetics and became a leader of Science for the People.

> . . .

> Beckwith's and Shapiro's renunciation of their work seem to have had no effect whatever on subsequent developments in molecular genetics, because the dangers they described seemed utterly fantastic to scientists in the field and made no significant impression on public opinion. Only after the discovery of recombinant DNA did concern over genetics research become more widespread, and the political opponents of human genetics then joined forces with those concerned with the environmental and health effects of proposed laboratory experiments.

Gershon, Should Science be Stopped? The Case of Recombinant DNA Research, The Pub. Interest 3, 3–4 (1983).

3. Do the scientists involved in the recombinant DNA controversy seem comfortable with their self-policing role? Are the rewards of that role sufficient to ensure that adequate social control of science will arise when needed?

4. Not everyone who participates in an exercise of "science responsibility" ends up happy to have done so. James Watson, for example, told a December 1977 meeting at NIH that he "apologize[d] to society" for having helped to call the moratorium. "The question now," he stated, "is what is the best way to get out of this political mess? Science is good for society. We are being attacked by everyone who does not have the guts to go ahead." 199 Science 33 (1978).

5. How well does self-policing do in preventing and detecting cheating? Early in the period of the first NIH guidelines on recombinant DNA research, two prominent scientists found themselves involved in apparent violations. In the spring of 1977, a team researching insulin genes at the University of California at San Francisco used a plasmid developed by Herbert Boyer before it had been certified for use by the director of NIH. Although a senior member of the team, William Rutter, insisted that the experiment be destroyed and repeated with certified materials, the UCSF biosafety committee was not immediately notified and instead the second experiment was entered retroactively in the biosafety logbook. When the head of the committee finally learned of the illicit experiment, he blamed NIH for the infraction.

The Senate Subcommittee on Science, Technology and Space summoned Rutter and Boyer to Washington in November 1977 for an inquiry into the affair. What surprised the senators was not the infraction, which they regarded as clearly trivial, but the researchers' attitude. In explaining why he had delayed telling the NIH and the UCSF biosafety committee about the incident, Rutter observed that there was an "inflamed social and political climate that existed with respect to recombinant DNA technology at that time." The press, he said, often fanned the flames of controversy. Also, he told the senators, "Repressive and punitive legislation was considered. We felt that directly informing the NIH would inevitably lead to public disclosure and debate about this incident and that would exacerbate the whole situation."

N. Wade, The Ultimate Experiment 163–64 (1977).

A few months later, Charles A. Thomas of the Harvard Medical School (a member of the RAC at NIH) was told by NIH to halt his genetic research because he had failed to file a necessary description of the safety conditions he was employing.

Science reporter Nicholas Wade believes that the general aura of social responsibility generated by the genetic experimenters served them well; "legislators had no difficulty in seeing the two incidents in proper perspective and nothing was made of them." Id. at 165. Nevertheless, the attitude of the scientists—that their willingness to exercise oversight made it unnecessary (and perhaps improper) for others to do so—clearly did not sit well in Washington. As the Senate Committee that had investigated the UCSF incident stated in its report:

> This assumption of superior judgment . . . threatens not only regulation but also productive scientific inquiry. If even a few scientists ignore the common ground rules of research, they undermine the basis of healthy scientific competition. If they are discovered, they undermine public confidence in their enterprise. It is clearly in the interest of the scientific community to cultivate a willingness to comply with the guidelines.

These concerns are treated in more detail in Ch. 3, Sec. A. 5, infra. For a forceful critique of scientists' performance in policing themselves, and general skepticism about the theory that fraud is automatically weeded out in research, see W. Broad & N. Wade, Betrayers of the Truth (1982).

6.   What, exactly, are we looking to various institutions to do by way of control over science and technology? Does "control" include promotion as well as prohibition and retardation? At what stages in the process—in establishing policies, in applying them to individual situations, and in reviewing the consequences of various policies—are particular formal or informal groups likely to prove most effective in exercising the powers of "control"?

W. HENRY LAMBRIGHT,
GOVERNING SCIENCE AND TECHNOLOGY

3–7 (1976).

Since World War II the federal government has become a dominant force behind scientific and technological change in the United States. Private sector organizations perform most of the nation's technical work, but government increasingly provides research and development (R&D) resources and policy direction. Who controls government policy in relation to science and technology? While the answer is far from simple, what is clear is that a major role is played by the operating agencies and departments of the executive branch. They stand at the nexus of government and science and technology. They make the day-to-day decisions, year-in, year-out, that determine who gets what, when, and how in federal research and development. They play a role not only in the execution of policy but also in its formulation.

The science and technology intensive agencies serve to provide a focus for the broader interactions of government, politics, and R&D . . . . They constitute a subset of the federal bureaucracy.[1] They link scientists

---

1. The executive branch may be conceived as having two parts: the Presidency, including the White House Office and the Executive Office of the President, and the bureaucracy, containing the various agencies, departments, commissions, etc. See Richard Schott, The Bureaucratic State: The Evolution and Scope of the American Federal Bureaucracy (Morristown, N.J.: General Learning Press, 1974), p. 35.

and technologists to public policy. They are "technocratic" bureaucracies or . . . technoscience agencies. These agencies include the Department of Defense (DOD), the National Aeronautics and Space Administration (NASA), the Energy Research and Development Administration (ERDA), the National Science Foundation (NSF), the National Institutes of Health (NIH), and a number of others. Viewed individually and as a group, they are a key locus of science and technology decision-making in the United States. They are among the most important yet least understood or investigated elements in the R&D policy process.

The technoscience agencies are at the heart of the federal R&D function. They represent public administration in its most dramatic role as innovator. The organizations of technoscience have become major agents of change. The amount of money that they control for research, development, and related testing and demonstrations is enormous—over $20 billion in fiscal year 1976. The impact of this money on the people of America and the world, today and tomorrow, is incalculable. These R&D expenditures have significance well beyond their sheer dollar volume. They reach deeply into higher education and the economy. They represent the nation's prime investment in its technological future. Technoscience agencies stand where the interests of the President, his Executive Office, Congress, courts, and other public and private interest groups converge.

Technoscience agencies are where the action is—whether they wish to be or not. The target of others' claims, they are themselves major and independent actors in the policy process. Their semi-autonomy within the governmental system derives from a number of factors. The most important is the Constitution itself. The separation of powers makes Congress as much a "chief executive" over the technoscience agencies as the President. Congress not only creates agencies, it sustains them through authorizations and appropriations. It can make the lives of their personnel unpleasant and precarious through the spotlight of investigations. If dissatisfied with a particular agency's performance, it can destroy that organization. From the perspective of federal science and technology agencies, there is not one man on top but many, for Congress consists of two Houses and many committees and subcommittees. It is 100 Senators, 435 Representatives, and many powerful staffers. The courts are also an omnipresent force in the life of technoscience agencies. Such agencies can never be quite sure who their "chief" executive is. Indeed, who that may be at one point in time may not be at another.

The separation of powers may cause the technoscience agencies to be uncertain as to their governmental master, but it also provides options for them. If the Executive is fragmented, policy guidelines from the "leadership" are likely to be ambiguous at best, inconsistent at worst. The ambiguities in national science and technology policy will invariably have to be resolved at the level of the agencies. How a given agency resolves such matters depends not only on the political pressures of the moment but also on its own sense of institutional mission.

Every agency has a clientele or, at least, seeks to build one as protection against Presidential and congressional vicissitudes. Moreover, every agency has organizational identity, usually defined by professional administrative elites that are concerned with the survival and growth of the agency as an institution. Presidents will be in office for eight years at most. The political lifetimes of Congressmen and Senators vary: some of them are longer, some are shorter than those of Presidents. On the other hand, the agencies have missions that extend for decades, even centuries. A consensus forms within the agency as to what its place in national life should be. Over time, an ideology emerges along with standard operating procedures governing administrative behavior in recurring circumstances. There is, thus, an internal logic to technoscience agencies which is independent of immediate environmental forces. The combination of internal and external influences produces an administrative policy. Such a policy may or may not be in accord with national policy as interpreted by a given President.

The technoscience agencies do not escape the charge that is directed at bureaucracy in general: resistance to change. Bureaucratic inertia, however, is not necessarily always evil. Many policies require long-term administrative persistence and commitment. Such qualities must extend over many elections. What a given partisan administration wants may not be in the public interest, as hindsight can easily reveal. The problem derives from the occasion when a mission is completed and an agency substitutes survival for its own sake as a principal goal. There can be serious discontinuities between what the public and its representatives want (policy change) and what a technoscience agency is, in fact, doing (policy maintenance). Change may not always be desirable, but neither is bureaucratic recalcitrance exercised for self-serving ends.

The once popular notions, that there is a politics/administration dichotomy and that politicians make policy and administrators carry it out, have been abandoned by most theorists. But the *issue* of the appropriate role of administration in politics/policy has not been resolved. Administrators and their agencies do engage in politics in the sense of influencing "authoritative allocations of values." The technoscience agencies influence policy formation as well as policy implementation. But how? With what consequences? To the extent that an administrative politics/policy exists, what is its relationship to national policy/politics?

The technoscience agencies are the cutting edge of federal bureaucracy. They are at bureaucracy's forefront in terms of the *substance* of work— R&D. They bring R&D to bear on their mission responsibilities; for a few, R&D is their mission, at least as they define it. They are also at the forefront of bureaucracy in respect to *organization* of work, particularly in the use of grants and contracts to outside, largely private-sector institutions. . . .

. . . The fact of bureaucracy's politics/policy role creates a critical issue in democracy. The bureaucracy is not elected. It is, in theory, an instrument of democracy: a tool. Who controls this tool? To whom or to what is bureaucracy responsible? . . .

DAVID L. BAZELON, COPING WITH TECHNOLOGY THROUGH THE LEGAL PROCESS

62 Cornell L.Rev. 817, 818–24, 828–29 (1977).

The idea that nonscientists can or should have anything to do with science is a relatively recent one, and one that may not be entirely welcome to the scientific community. Scientists have sometimes likened their profession to an autonomous, self-governing "republic." To qualify for citizenship in this republic, one's scientific credentials would have to be in order. And only its "citizens"—that is, only scientists—would be entitled to a voice in the way the scientific community is governed; only they could participate in the process of mutual criticism that keeps science valid. As Gerard Piel, the publisher of *Scientific American*, recently wrote, "A scientist can accept no authority but his own judgment and conscience . . . ."

For a good many years, the rest of us, the nonscientists, really had no quibble with this view. Scientific and technological progress were seen as inevitable, and as inherently desirable. We were happy to leave the scientists alone—at least as long as science-based technology provided us with a never-ending stream of technological goodies.

Recently, however, we have begun to reexamine our relationship with the so-called "republic of science." Since World War II, government, science, and technology have become increasingly interdependent. The Manhattan Project, Sputnik, the Apollo program, and, most recently, the enactment of significant environmental legislation, are some of the familiar landmarks along this road towards increasing interdependence. The reasons for this new interdependence are also familiar. First, the costs of much modern research and development are so enormous that only the government has the resources to foot most of the bill; and when government pays for research, some governmental supervision of that research is inevitable.

Most importantly, however, we are all becoming increasingly conscious of the extent to which many supposedly scientific or technical decisions involve painful value choices, and pose difficult policy problems. We have come to realize that virtually every technological innovation may carry unwanted consequences, and that technological progress may therefore cause, as well as solve, critical societal problems. We have even begun to ask whether there are certain subjects into which scientists should not inquire at all, because the process of investigation, or the knowledge to be acquired, may bring too many perils along with its promises.

Scientists are not entirely happy to find themselves the target of this scrutiny. When the National Science Foundation recently asked the directors of America's leading research institutions for their views on the current state of American science, one recurring response was an objection to excessive regulation of scientific activities, and to bureaucratic "meddling" in *their* domain. In the words of one participant in the study, "The ever increasing bureaucracy . . . will in the not too distant future completely eradicate our Nation's world position in research and technology."

These complaints are not frivolous. Regulation is costly. Someone has to pay the salaries of the bureaucrats who are looking over the scientists' shoulders, and of the judges who are looking over the bureaucrats' shoulders. And, more importantly, of course, this kind of surveillance *can* impede or even stifle needed research.

The problem, though, is that science and technology are not now—if, indeed, they ever were—the exclusive domain of the scientists and engineers. While their expertise is essential for assessing the costs and benefits of particular innovations, it provides no special qualifications for determining how the balance between costs and benefits should be struck.

How can such decisions be made? . . .

In primitive societies, painful choices of this sort are often made by the tribal witch doctor. . . . By externalizing the decision to the gods, the tribe avoids dangerous internal confrontations. Other ages have achieved the same escape from conflict through their own soothsayers, savants, and oracles. We, too, are not immune from the temptation to turn these decisions over to a shaman—although, instead of a mask and feathers, we might prefer to dress *our* witch doctors in white lab coats or black robes.

Questions of this sort pose difficult—if not impossible—problems for decisionmakers. The experts are likely to disagree about the underlying facts, which are usually both complex and uncertain; they are even more likely to disagree about the inferences to be drawn from those facts. Postponing a decision may sometimes provide the opportunity to reduce uncertainty. But a decision not to decide, or to delay deciding, is still a decision. Both time and information can be costly resources.

. . .

Amidst this swirling uncertainty, one thing seems very clear. Courts are *not* the agency either to resolve the factual disputes, or to make the painful value choices. The problem is not just that these scientific issues are complicated; courts have long grappled with complicated issues in reviewing actions by the FCC, SEC, ICC, CAB, and scores of other governmental regulatory agencies. These more traditional administrative matters, however, involve issues with which all judges have at least a speaking familiarity; but I daresay that almost none have the knowledge and training to assess the merits of competing scientific arguments. And this is hardly a task for on-the-job training.

It follows that, where administrative decisions on scientific issues are concerned, it makes no sense to rely upon the courts to evaluate the agency's scientific and technological determinations; and there is perhaps even less reason for the courts to substitute their own value preferences for those of the agency, to which the legislature has presumably delegated the decisional power and responsibility.

What courts and judges can do, however—and do well when conscious of their role and limitations—is scrutinize and monitor the decisionmaking process to make sure that it is thorough, complete, and rational; that all relevant information has been considered; and that insofar as possible, those who will be affected by a decision have had an opportunity to participate in it. The agencies themselves will usually be in the best position to determine which particular procedures, or combinations of procedures, are best suited to a particular issue. But whatever procedures are used, the important thing is that the agency generate a record in which the factual issues are fully developed.

By articulating both their factual determinations and their value preferences, and by attempting to separate the one from the other, administrators make possible effective professional peer review, as well as legislative and public oversight. With respect to scientific, factual determinations, decisionmakers should disclose where and why the experts disagree as well as where they concur, and where the information is sketchy as well as complete. Other experts who are steeped in the subject matter—in academe, in government, in industry—can then evaluate the agency's factual determinations, bring new data to light, or challenge gaps in reasoning. And if individuals or groups differ with the agency's value choices, they can make their views known in the various public forums. When the reasons for decisions are fully disclosed, there is a genuine opportunity to seek reconsideration in light of new knowledge or changing values.

. . .

Improving the way we make our value choices may prove even more difficult than improving the way we resolve factual disputes. I have long advocated broadened public participation in the administrative process as a technique for ensuring that, insofar as possible, the decisions that are made reflect the divergent interests in our society. But as Professor Richard Stewart has recently pointed out, "interest representation" is no panacea. Various proposals have been made to broaden representation in agency proceedings, by, for example, funding public interest intervenors. I fully support the goal of these proposals, and I think that they are worth a try. But we have to remember that any scheme of this sort raises extraordinarily difficult problems. Who should be represented? Who is entitled to speak for the public interest, and who is entitled to public funds to do so? How do we guard against subsidizing the most vocal representatives of the public interest, instead of the most worthy? And how do we assess the risk that increasing the number of participants in a particular proceeding may simply prolong the decisionmaking process, without necessarily improving, or even changing, the eventual result?

These are valid concerns. But I am not sure that we have much choice. In democratic societies, elected legislatures traditionally make the hard value choices. Indeed, this is precisely what legislatures are designed to do. Increasingly, however, our legislatures have delegated these value choices to administrative agencies—institutions that cannot resolve value conflicts through the relatively simple expedient of a show of hands. I believe that if we are going to ask unelected administrators to make our vital "legislative policy judgments," some sort of "interest representation" is an absolutely essential safeguard.

An alternative, of course, would be to give these decisions back to the legislators. While this has some appeal in theory, I fear that it is not very practical to expect a relative handful of legislators somehow to keep tabs on all the wide-ranging and complex activities in which the government is involved today. . . .

NOTES

1. Both Lambright and Bazelon identify administrative agencies as central in the resolution of science policy disputes. It is worth noting that such agencies are not mentioned in the Constitution or in most thumbnail sketches of American government. Why haven't any of the traditional "three branches of government"—executive, legislative and judicial—seized the initiative in science policy? Is it simply part of a broader delegation of American government to permanent bureaucratic agencies or are science issues particularly ill-suited for the traditional branches?

2. Is there a danger that "technoscience agencies" may approach policy issues from too exclusively scientific a perspective? What corrective might be offered?

The predominant methodological strategy of biological research is reductionism: the isolation of the phenomenon under study from its usual circumstances, thereby reducing the number of variables that affect the analysis. This allows a clearer understanding of the "basic" processes, and has led to important discoveries.

The strength of reductionism is the principle of isolation. This principle, however, is also inherently limiting: the circumstances of the investigation are necessarily "unreal" in everyday terms. Of course, it may be that the isolated phenomena behave similarly under natural circumstances. This assumption, however, is often uncertain and may frequently be untrue. Moreover, the characteristics of those natural circumstances are rarely fully known. In some cases, knowledge of the multiple external influences upon biological processes could lead to a perception of those processes quite different from those obtained in the isolation of laboratory study. A critical understanding of present biological knowledge requires recognition of those methodological weaknesses. Public participation in science, by broadening the range of factors considered at each stage of investigation, provides a means of counteracting biases resulting from reductionist strategy.

Holman and Dutton, A Case for Public Participation in Science Policy Formation and Practice, 51 S.Cal.L.Rev. 1505, 1513–14 (1978). See also D. Nelkin, Technological Decisions and Democracy (1977) for a cross-cultural analysis of the difficulties in—as well as rationales for—various mechanisms by which lay people might participate in technical decisions.

3. If the public is to be involved, it must be informed of the issues. One study of the press coverage of the recombinant DNA debate concluded that, despite the fact that the participants often raised political and philosophical matters, the points reported and statements quoted were largely technical. Yet the same author notes that group considerations of the subject of gene splicing—from Asilomar onward—tended to be narrowly scientific.

Similarly, after several months of deliberation of the Cambridge Experimentation Review Board during which the members heard scientist-advocates on both sides of the issue, the Board made recommendations which "closely approximated those of the NIH." The outcome and the process were widely praised; but from inception, the Board restricted itself to technical matters, the only ones it was wholly unqualified to analyze. Rather than contending with the ethical and political issues raised by R–DNA, the Board appeared to reinforce the notion that this was a technical problem and conferred the legitimacy of the democratic process on such an interpretation. . . .

Not only the defenders of R–DNA research have chosen to disregard the political and philosophical issues, as shown in the following exchange between biologist Ruth Hubbard and U.S. Representative Tim Lee Carter during the 15 March 1977 hearings on Recombinant DNA, held before the Subcommittee on Health and Environment:

Carter: Would you have stopped Fermi in his work?
Hubbard: It depends.
Carter: You remember Enrico Fermi?
Hubbard: Yes.
Carter: He did basic study for the nuclear bomb. He is the man who developed the first chain reaction. Of course, there have been some disastrous results.
Hubbard: That is correct.
Carter: But it may well have saved thousands of lives in World War II. Again, it is quite dangerous. Would you have stopped Enrico Fermi?
Hubbard: Fermi's experiments themselves were not dangerous.
Carter: He is the man who started the chain reaction. He is the first man to do that.
Hubbard: That is right.
Carter: All right.
Hubbard: The experiment itself was not dangerous.

It would be gratuitous to suggest that Hubbard's concerns about science are limited to the immediate safety of experiments. Yet, even this scientist, in an important public forum, retreats to this position when questioned on the one issue, nuclear weaponry, to which all others are compared in discussion of the ethical and political ramifications of scientific research.

The early press coverage of the Recombinant DNA controversy centered on the technical issues, and tended to ignore the important questions that the public dispute might have brought into public focus: What is the role of the scientific expert in policy questions? Can a technical society be governed democratically? Should science be done for the good of the people? Is some knowledge in itself dangerous? . . .

Altimore, The Social Construction of a Scientific Controversy: Comments on Press Coverage of the Recombinant DNA Debate, 7 Sci., Tech. & Hum. Values 24, 27, 29, 30 (1982).

4. At the very least, persistence of vigorous (indeed, heated) debate over the decisions that must be made for or against recombinant DNA experiments points to the lack of agreement about the relevant scientific "facts." Recently, it has been proposed that resolution of similar disagreements about the factual underpinnings of other public policy decisions—for example, whether to promote or restrict supersonic transport planes—would be facilitated by a "science court" to determine the "factual" issues without entering into the value-laden realm of the underlying policy choice. The debate over recombinant DNA, however, serves to illustrate the difficulties with this plan, because the disputants take very different views of what evidence is "admissible" or what would constitute acceptable "proof" of a point. The resolution of issues such as these would necessarily involve the "court" in choosing certain values over others, just as those now debating about recombinant DNA are often separated by unarticulated value differences rather than by differences in their scientific understanding or competence. For example, does the recent escape of foot-and-mouth disease from the Department of Agriculture's high-security Animal Disease Center on Plum Island in Long Island Sound provide evidence of the fallibility of laboratory safety measures that is relevant to recombinant DNA work in a so-called "P3" or "P4" . . . facility? Or what of the uncontrolled spread of some infections in hospitals? Is that a datum one ought to note in thinking about the danger of epidemics, should a novel and untreatable virus begin reproducing outside a laboratory?

More important . . . than the disagreement over scientific premises, the recombinant DNA experience reveals the disarray of legal as well as scientific thinking. As little agreement as there may be about the legal principles most germane to the construction of public policy, even less seems to be known about the expected consequences to society from adopting one mode of dispute resolution, or a particular attitude toward scientific inquiry, over alternative ones. The empirical basis for social decisionmaking is very thin, thus only increasing the tendency to rely on legal and philosophical analysis, which can at least operate on the plane of logic (without worrying too much about our society's irritating habit of behaving "illogically"), once an agreed upon factual starting point can be found.

Capron, Prologue: Why Recombinant DNA?, 51 S.Cal.L.Rev. 973, 975–76 (1978). See Ch. 4, Sec. D.3 infra, for a discussion of the "science court" and other dispute-resolution mechanisms. In the meantime, consider the following case in light of Judge Bazelon's analysis.

DIAMOND v. CHAKRABARTY

Supreme Court of the United States, 1980.
447 U.S. 303, 100 S.Ct. 2204, 65 L.Ed.2d 144.

MR. CHIEF JUSTICE BURGER delivered the opinion of the Court.

We granted certiorari to determine whether a live, human-made micro-organism is patentable subject matter under 35 U.S.C. § 101.

I

In 1972, respondent Chakrabarty, a microbiologist, filed a patent application, assigned to the General Electric Co. The application asserted

36 claims related to Chakrabarty's invention of "a bacterium from the genus *Pseudomonas* containing therein at least two stable energy-generating plasmids, each of said plasmids providing a separate hydrocarbon degradative pathway." This human-made, genetically engineered bacterium is capable of breaking down multiple components of crude oil. Because of this property, which is possessed by no naturally occurring bacteria, Chakrabarty's invention is believed to have significant value for the treatment of oil spills.[2]

Chakrabarty's patent claims were of three types: first, process claims for the method of producing the bacteria; second, claims for an inoculum comprised of a carrier material floating on water, such as straw, and the new bacteria; and third, claims to the bacteria themselves. The patent examiner allowed the claims falling into the first two categories, but rejected claims for the bacteria. His decision rested on two grounds: (1) that micro-organisms are "products of nature," and (2) that as living things they are not patentable subject matter under 35 U.S.C. § 101.

Chakrabarty appealed the rejection of these claims to the Patent Office Board of Appeals, and the Board affirmed the examiner on the second ground.[3] Relying on the legislative history of the 1930 Plant Patent Act, in which Congress extended patent protection to certain asexually reproduced plants, the Board concluded that § 101 was not intended to cover living things such as these laboratory created micro-organisms.

The Court of Customs and Patent Appeals, by a divided vote, reversed on the authority of its prior decision in In re Bergy, 563 F.2d 1031, 1038 (1977), which held that "the fact that microorganisms . . . are alive . . . [is] without legal significance" for purposes of the patent law. . . . After re-examining . . . in the light of our holding in [Parker v.] Flook, [437 U.S. 584, 98 S.Ct. 2522, 57 L.Ed.2d 451 (1978)] that court, with one dissent, reaffirmed its earlier judgments. 596 F.2d 952 (1979).

The Commissioner of Patents and Trademarks again sought certiorari, and we granted the writ . . . .

II

The Constitution grants Congress broad power to legislate to "promote the Progress of Science and useful Arts, by securing for limited Times to Authors and Inventors the exclusive Right to their respective Writings and Discoveries." Art. I, § 8, cl. 8. The patent laws promote this progress by offering inventors exclusive rights for a limited period as an incentive for their inventiveness and research efforts. . . .

The question before us in this case is a narrow one of statutory interpretation requiring us to construe 35 U.S.C. § 101, which provides:

"Whoever invents or discovers any new and useful process, machine, manufacture, or composition of matter, or any new and useful

---

2. At present, biological control of oil spills requires the use of a mixture of naturally occurring bacteria, each capable of degrading one component of the oil complex. In this way, oil is decomposed into simpler substances which can serve as food for aquatic life. However, for various reasons, only a portion of any such mixed culture survives to attack the oil spill. By breaking down multiple components of oil, Chakrabarty's micro-organism promises more efficient and rapid oil-spill control.

3. The Board concluded that the new bacteria were not "products of nature," because *Pseudomonas* bacteria containing two or more different energy-generating plasmids are not naturally occurring.

improvement thereof, may obtain a patent therefor, subject to the conditions and requirements of this title."

Specifically, we must determine whether respondent's microorganism constitutes a "manufacture" or "composition of matter" within the meaning of the statute.

III

In cases of statutory construction we begin, of course, with the language of the statute. And "unless otherwise defined, words will be interpreted as taking their ordinary, contemporary, common meaning." Perrin v. United States, 444 U.S. 37, 42, 100 S.Ct. 311, 314, 62 L.Ed.2d 199 (1979). We have also cautioned that courts "should not read into the patent laws limitations and conditions which the legislature has not expressed." United States v. Dubilier Condenser Corp., 289 U.S. 178, 199, 53 S.Ct. 554, 561, 77 L.Ed. 1114 (1933).

Guided by these canons of construction, this Court has read the term "manufacture" in § 101 in accordance with its dictionary definition to mean "the production of articles for use from raw or prepared materials by giving to these materials new forms, qualities, properties, or combinations, whether by hand-labor or by machinery." American Fruit Growers, Inc. v. Brogdex Co., 283 U.S. 1, 11, 51 S.Ct. 328, 330, 75 L.Ed. 801 (1931). Similarly, "composition of matter" has been construed consistent with its common usage to include "all compositions of two or more substances and . . . all composite articles, whether they be the results of chemical union, or of mechanical mixture, or whether they be gases, fluids, powders or solids." Shell Development Co. v. Watson, 149 F.Supp. 279, 280 (D.C.1957). In choosing such expansive terms as "manufacture" and "composition of matter," modified by the comprehensive "any," Congress plainly contemplated that the patent laws would be given wide scope.

The relevant legislative history also supports a broad construction. The Patent Act of 1793, authored by Thomas Jefferson, defined statutory subject matter as "any new and useful art, machine, manufacture, or composition of matter, or any new or useful improvement [thereof]." Act of Feb. 21, 1793, § 1, 1 Stat. 319. The Act embodied Jefferson's philosophy that "ingenuity should receive a liberal encouragement." . . . In 1952, when the patent laws were recodified, Congress replaced the word "art" with "process," but otherwise left Jefferson's language intact. The Committee Reports accompanying the 1952 Act inform us that Congress intended statutory subject matter to "include anything under the sun that is made by man." S.Rep. No. 1979, 82d Cong., 2d Sess., 5 (1952); H.R. Rep. No. 1923, 82d Cong., 2d Sess., 6 (1952).

This is not to suggest that § 101 has no limits or that it embraces every discovery. The laws of nature, physical phenomena, and abstract ideas have been held not patentable. . . . Thus, a new mineral discovered in the earth or a new plant found in the wild is not patentable subject matter. Likewise, Einstein could not patent his celebrated law that $E=mc^2$; nor could Newton have patented the law of gravity. Such discoveries are "manifestations of . . . nature, free to all men and reserved exclusively to none." Funk [Brothers Seed Co. v. Kalo Inoculant Co., 333 U.S. 127, 130, 68 S.Ct. 440, 441, 92 L.Ed. 588 (1948)].

Judged in this light, respondent's micro-organism plainly qualifies as patentable subject matter. His claim is not to a hitherto unknown natural phenomenon, but to a nonnaturally occurring manufacture or composition of matter—a product of human ingenuity "having a distinctive name, character [and] use." Hartranft v. Wiegmann, 121 U.S. 609, 615, 7 S.Ct. 1240, 1243, 30 L.Ed. 1012 (1887). The point is underscored dramatically by comparison of the invention here with that in *Funk*. There, the patentee had discovered that there existed in nature certain species of root-nodule bacteria which did not exert a mutually inhibitive effect on each other. He used that discovery to produce a mixed culture capable of inoculating the seeds of leguminous plants. Concluding that the patentee had discovered "only some of the handiwork of nature," the Court ruled the product nonpatentable. . . . Here, by contrast, the patentee has produced a new bacterium with markedly different characteristics from any found in nature and one having the potential for significant utility. His discovery is not nature's handiwork, but his own; accordingly it is patentable subject matter under § 101.

IV

Two contrary arguments are advanced, neither of which we find persuasive.

(A)

The petitioner's first argument rests on the enactment of the 1930 Plant Patent Act, which afforded patent protection to certain asexually reproduced plants, and the 1970 Plant Variety Protection Act, which authorized protection for certain sexually reproduced plants but excluded bacteria from its protection. In the petitioner's view, the passage of these Acts evidences congressional understanding that the terms "manufacture" or "composition of matter" do not include living things; if they did, the petitioner argues, neither Act would have been necessary.

We reject this argument. Prior to 1930, two factors were thought to remove plants from patent protection. The first was the belief that plants, even those artificially bred, were products of nature for purposes of the patent law. This position appears to have derived from the decision of the Patent Office in Ex parte Latimer, 1889 Dec.Com.Pat. 123, in which a patent claim for fiber found in the needle of the *Pinus australis* was rejected. . . . The second obstacle to patent protection for plants was the fact that plants were thought not amenable to the "written description" requirement of the patent law. See 35 U.S.C. § 112. Because new plants may differ from old only in color or perfume, differentiation by written description was often impossible.

In enacting the Plant Patent Act, Congress addressed both of these concerns. It explained at length its belief that the work of the plant breeder "in aid of nature" was patentable invention. S.Rep. No. 315, 71st Cong., 2d Sess., 6–8 (1930); H.R. Rep. No. 1129, 71st Cong., 2d Sess., 7–9 (1930). And it relaxed the written description requirement in favor of "a description . . . as complete as is reasonably possible." 35 U.S.C. § 162. No Committee or Member of Congress, however, expressed the broader view, now urged by the petitioner, that the terms "manufacture" or "composition of matter" exclude living things. . . . Congress . . . recognized that the relevant distinction was not between living and inanimate things, but between products of nature, whether living or not, and human-made inventions. . . .

Nor does the passage of the 1970 Plant Variety Protection Act support the Government's position. As the Government acknowledges, sexually reproduced plants were not included under the 1930 Act because new varieties could not be reproduced true-to-type through seedlings. By 1970, however, it was generally recognized that true-to-type reproduction was possible and that plant patent protection was therefore appropriate. The 1970 Act extended that protection. There is nothing in its language or history to suggest that it was enacted because § 101 did not include living things.

In particular, we find nothing in the exclusion of bacteria from plant variety protection to support the petitioner's position. The legislative history gives no reason for this exclusion. As the Court of Customs and Patent Appeals suggested, it may simply reflect congressional agreement with the result reached by that court in deciding In re Arzberger, 27 C.C.P.A. (Pat.) 1315, 112 F.2d 834 (1940), which held that bacteria were not plants for the purposes of the 1930 Act. Or it may reflect the fact that prior to 1970 the Patent Office had issued patents for bacteria under § 101. In any event, absent some clear indication that Congress "focused on [the] issues . . . directly related to the one presently before the Court," SEC v. Sloan, 436 U.S. 103, 120–121, 98 S.Ct. 1702, 1713, 56 L.Ed.2d 148 (1978), there is no basis for reading into its actions an intent to modify the plain meaning of the words found in § 101.

(B)

The petitioner's second argument is that micro-organisms cannot qualify as patentable subject matter until Congress expressly authorizes such protection. His position rests on the fact that genetic technology was unforeseen when Congress enacted § 101. From this it is argued that resolution of the patentability of inventions such as respondent's should be left to Congress. The legislative process, the petitioner argues, is best equipped to weigh the competing economic, social, and scientific considerations involved, and to determine whether living organisms produced by genetic engineering should receive patent protection. In support of this position, the petitioner relies on our recent holding in Parker v. Flook, 437 U.S. 584, 98 S.Ct. 2522, 57 L.Ed.2d 451 (1978), and the statement that the judiciary "must proceed cautiously when . . . asked to extend patent rights into areas wholly unforeseen by Congress." Id., at 596, 98 S.Ct., at 2529.

It is, of course, correct that Congress, not the courts, must define the limits of patentability; but it is equally true that once Congress has spoken it is "the province and duty of the judicial department to say what the law is." Marbury v. Madison, 1 Cranch 137, 177, 2 L.Ed. 60 (1803). Congress has performed its constitutional role in defining patentable subject matter in § 101; we perform ours in construing the language Congress has employed. In so doing, our obligation is to take statutes as we find them, guided, if ambiguity appears, by the legislative history and statutory purpose. Here, we perceive no ambiguity. . . .

Nothing in *Flook* is to the contrary. That case applied our prior precedents to determine that a "claim for an improved method of calculation, even when tied to a specific end use, is unpatentable subject matter under § 101." 437 U.S., at 595, n. 18, 98 S.Ct., at 2528, n. 18. . . . . *Flook* did not announce a new principle that inventions in areas not contemplated by Congress when the patent laws were enacted are unpatentable *per se*.

. . . A rule that unanticipated inventions are without protection would conflict with the core concept of the patent law that anticipation undermines patentability. Mr. Justice Douglas reminded that the inventions most benefiting mankind are those that "pushed back the frontiers of chemistry, physics, and the like." Great A. & P. Tea Co. v. Supermarket Corp., 340 U.S. 147, 154, 71 S.Ct. 127, 131, 95 L.Ed. 162 (1950) (concurring opinion). Congress employed broad general language in drafting § 101 precisely because such inventions are often unforeseeable.

To buttress his argument, the petitioner, with the support of *amicus*, points to grave risks that may be generated by research endeavors such as respondent's. The briefs present a gruesome parade of horribles. Scientists, among them Nobel laureates, are quoted suggesting that genetic research may pose a serious threat to the human race, or, at the very least, that the dangers are far too substantial to permit such research to proceed apace at this time. We are told that genetic research and related technological developments may spread pollution and disease, that it may result in a loss of genetic diversity, and that its practice may tend to depreciate the value of human life. These arguments are forcefully, even passionately, presented; they remind us that, at times, human ingenuity seems unable to control fully the forces it creates—that, with Hamlet, it is sometimes better "to bear those ills we have than fly to others that we know not of."

It is argued that this Court should weigh these potential hazards in considering whether respondent's invention is patentable subject matter under § 101. We disagree. The grant or denial of patents on microorganisms is not likely to put an end to genetic research or to its attendant risks. The large amount of research that has already occurred when no researcher had sure knowledge that patent protection would be available suggests that legislative or judicial fiat as to patentability will not deter the scientific mind from probing into the unknown any more than Canute could command the tides. Whether respondent's claims are patentable may determine whether research efforts are accelerated by the hope of reward or slowed by want of incentives, but that is all.

What is more important is that we are without competence to entertain these arguments—either to brush them aside as fantasies generated by fear of the unknown, or to act on them. The choice we are urged to make is a matter of high policy for resolution within the legislative process after the kind of investigation, examination, and study that legislative bodies can provide and courts cannot. That process involves the balancing of competing values and interests, which in our democratic system is the business of elected representatives. Whatever their validity, the contentions now pressed on us should be addressed to the political branches of the Government, the Congress and the Executive, and not to the courts.

We have emphasized in the recent past that "[o]ur individual appraisal of the wisdom or unwisdom of a particular [legislative] course . . . is to be put aside in the process of interpreting a statute." TVA v. Hill, 437 U.S., at 194, 98 S.Ct., at 2302. Our task, rather, is the narrow one of determining what Congress meant by the words it used in the statute; once that is done our powers are exhausted. Congress is free to amend § 101 so as to exclude from patent protection organisms produced by genetic engineering. Cf. 42 U.S.C. § 2181(a), exempting from patent protection inventions "useful solely in the utilization of special nuclear material or atomic energy in an atomic weapon." Or it may choose to craft a statute specifically designed for such living things. But, until Congress takes such action, this Court must construe the language of § 101 as it is. The language of that section fairly embraces respondent's invention.

Accordingly, the judgment of the Court of Customs and Patent Appeals is affirmed.

MR. JUSTICE BRENNAN, with whom MR. JUSTICE WHITE, MR. JUSTICE MARSHALL, and MR. JUSTICE POWELL join, dissenting.

I agree with the Court that the question before us is a narrow one. Neither the future of scientific research, nor even the ability of respondent Chakrabarty to reap some monopoly profits from his pioneering work, is at stake. Patents on the processes by which he has produced and employed the new living organism are not contested. The only question we need decide is whether Congress, exercising its authority under Art. I, § 8, of the Constitution, intended that he be able to secure a monopoly on the living organism itself, no matter how produced or how used. Because I believe the Court has misread the applicable legislation, I dissent.

The patent laws attempt to reconcile this Nation's deep-seated antipathy to monopolies with the need to encourage progress. Given the complexity and legislative nature of this delicate task, we must be careful to extend patent protection no further than Congress has provided. In particular, were there an absence of legislative direction, the courts should leave to Congress the decisions whether and how far to extend the patent privilege into areas where the common understanding has been that patents are not available.

In this case, however, we do not confront a complete legislative vacuum. The sweeping language of the Patent Act of 1793, as re-enacted in 1952, is not the last pronouncement Congress has made in this area. In 1930 Congress enacted the Plant Patent Act affording patent protection to developers of certain asexually reproduced plants. In 1970 Congress enacted the Plant Variety Protection Act to extend protection to certain new plant varieties capable of sexual reproduction. Thus, we are not dealing—as the Court would have it—with the routine problem of "unanticipated inventions." In these two Acts Congress has addressed the general problem of patenting animate inventions and has chosen carefully limited language granting protection to some kinds of discoveries, but specifically excluding others. These Acts strongly evidence a congressional limitation that excludes bacteria from patentability.

First, the Acts evidence Congress' understanding, at least since 1930, that § 101 does not include living organisms. If newly developed living organisms not naturally occurring had been patentable under § 101, the plants included in the scope of the 1930 and 1970 Acts could have been patented without new legislation. Those plants, like the bacteria involved in this case, were new varieties not naturally occurring.[3] . . . The

---

3. The Court refers to the logic employed by Congress in choosing not to perpetuate the "dichotomy" suggested by Secretary Hyde. But by this logic the bacteria at issue here are distinguishable from a "mineral . . . created wholly by nature" in exactly the same way as were the new varieties of plants. If a new Act was needed to provide patent protection for the plants, it was equally necessary for bacteria. Yet Congress provided for patents on plants but not on these bacteria. In short, Congress decided to make only a subset of animate "human-made inventions" patentable.

Committee Reports contain expansive prose about the previously unavailable benefits to be derived from extending patent protection to plants. Because Congress thought it had to legislate in order to make agricultural "human-made inventions" patentable and because the legislation Congress enacted is limited, it follows that Congress never meant to make items outside the scope of the legislation patentable.

Second, the 1970 Act clearly indicates that Congress has included bacteria within the focus of its legislative concern, but not within the scope of patent protection. Congress specifically excluded bacteria from the coverage of the 1970 Act. 7 U.S.C. § 2402(a). The Court's attempts to supply explanations for this explicit exclusion ring hollow. It is true that there is no mention in the legislative history of the exclusion, but that does not give us license to invent reasons. The fact is that Congress, assuming that animate objects as to which it had not specifically legislated could not be patented, excluded bacteria from the set of patentable organisms.

The Court protests that its holding today is dictated by the broad language of § 101, which cannot "be confined to the 'particular application[s] . . . contemplated by the legislators.'" But as I have shown, the Court's decision does not follow the unavoidable implications of the statute. Rather, it extends the patent system to cover living material even though Congress plainly has legislated in the belief that § 101 does not encompass living organisms. It is the role of Congress, not this Court, to broaden or narrow the reach of the patent laws. This is especially true where, as here, the composition sought to be patented uniquely implicates matters of public concern.

NOTES

1. Should the Court be willing to weigh well-documented proof of a technique's hazards as a factor against granting it a patent if it appears likely that the denial of a patent would seriously curtail research efforts?

2. Ironically, although the opponents of genetic engineering feared that patenting would give the field a great boost, at least some of the leaders in biotechnology doubt the value of either trade secrets or patent law. J. Leslie Glick, president of one genetic engineering firm, has termed these forms of legal protection "anachronisms" because patents involve delays between filing and issuance (in a field that is moving very rapidly) and a virtual requirement of depositing a sample of the novel organism in a cell culture collection (whence competitors seeking to make improvements can obtain it), and trade secrets require physical security (virtually impossible to achieve in academic labs). See 306 Nature 3 (1983). For a further discussion of patent, trade secret and copyright in the area of scientific research, see Ch. 4, Sec. B.4, infra.

3. With or without patents, the ownership of specially altered cells can become a matter of considerable importance. Several lawsuits have been filed in this area (although all were settled before trial); the disputants have included the National Institutes of Health, the biomedical researchers who produced the altered cells, and—in the case of human cell lines—the physicians and institutions that cared for the patients from whom the cells were originally derived. What would it mean for one person to own another person's cells? Should permission be obtained from patients if specimens from them are going to be used for cultured cells? Should they be paid?

4. Diamond v. Chakrabarty opened the door for patent protection for recombinant techniques, microorganisms, and cellular and metabolic products, which in turn suggests that "private ordering"—arrangements among those with proprieta-

ry and other commercial interests in the patented process and products—are another possible institutional arrangement to govern the scope, direction, and methods of research. See generally R. Saliwanchik, Legal Protection for Microbiological and Genetic Engineering Inventions (1982).

A major method of private ordering in science is the licensing agreement. Licenses play an important role in the search for new techniques and products as well as in the commercial exploitation of a discovery. For example, a company in one field (e.g., agricultural chemicals) that develops a product that might be useful in another field (e.g., human medicine) could license a company in the second field to explore the product's suitability and, if successful, to market the product—in return for a royalty on its sales.

In genetic engineering, the laboratories undertaking much of the research are located within academic institutions or small, specialized research companies, neither of which institutions have the capability or inclination to exploit their discoveries commercially through the necessary development, manufacturing, distribution, and marketing. Thus, the institutions holding patents have entered into agreements with licensees to use their discoveries. See Ch. 3, Sec. A.6, infra. To what extent are the issues that were raised from the first expression of concern over the dangers of this field adequately treated by such private arrangements?

STANFORD UNIVERSITY, LICENSE AGREEMENT

Effective as of December 2, 1980, THE BOARD OF TRUSTEES OF THE LELAND STANFORD JUNIOR UNIVERSITY, a body having corporate powers under the laws of the State of California (STANFORD), and _____ a _____ corporation having a principal place of business at _____ (LICENSEE) agree as follows:

1. BACKGROUND

1.1—In the course of fundamental research programs at the University of California and STANFORD (Universities), inventions were conceived jointly which relate to engineering biologically functional replicons possessing desired genetic properties of parent DNA molecules. These research programs were supported by the National Science Foundation, the American Cancer Society, and the National Institutes of Health of the Department of Health, Education and Welfare, now Health and Human Services (HHS). These agencies and the Universities agreed that the intellectual property rights resulting from these inventions (and licensed through this Agreement) would be administered pursuant and subject to the terms of STANFORD's Institutional Patent Agreement (IPA) with HHS.

1.2—The Universities have agreed that Stanford will manage the securing of patent rights and licensing in the public interest, and that any net income arising therefrom will be shared between the Universities, and designated to be used for educational and research purposes.

1.3—By assignment of the inventions from the inventors, STANFORD is the owner of certain U.S. patent rights and desires to grant licenses under those rights to licensees for development of products and processes for public use and benefit.

1.4—LICENSEE desires to develop processes and methods and marketable products for public use and benefit by using Licensed Patent Rights, and it will follow good safety practices in such development work.

2. DEFINITIONS

2.1—*Licensed Patent Rights* means U.S. Patent No. 4,237,224, issued December 2, 1980, and pending U.S. Patent Application Serial No. 959,288, filed November 9, 1978, and any divisions, continuations, and continuations-in-part based thereon, and any patents which may issue therefrom and any reissues or extension thereof.

. . .

2.3—*Licensed Product(s)* means materials (including organisms) which, in the course of manufacture, use, or sale would, in the absence of this license, infringe one or more claims of *Licensed Patent Rights* which have not been held invalid by a court from which no appeal may be taken.

Four categories of *Licensed Products* are designated:

End Products

Basic Genetic Products

Process Improvement Products

Bulk Products . . .

2.8—*Net Sales* means the gross sales, royalties or fees invoiced to customers, less returns and allowances actually granted, packing, insurance, freight out, taxes or excise duties imposed on the transaction (if separately invoiced), wholesaler discounts and cash discounts.

. . .

2.10—"LICENSEE" is understood to include all of its *Affiliates*. An *Affiliate* of LICENSEE shall mean any corporation or other business entity controlled by, controlling, or under common control with LICENSEE. For this purpose, "control" means direct or indirect beneficial ownership of at least fifty percent (50%) of the voting stock, or at least fifty percent (50%) interest in the income of such corporation or other business.

3. GRANT

3.1—STANFORD grants to LICENSEE a non-exclusive, non-transferable right and license to make, have made, use and sell *Licensed Products* under *Licensed Patent Rights*.

4. COMPLIANCE WITH LAWS, REGULATIONS AND STANDARDS

4.1—LICENSEE agrees to comply with all governmental laws and regulations applicable to the use, production and/or sale of *Licensed Products*.

4.2—With respect to operations by the LICENSEE in the United States, its territories and possessions, LICENSEE specifically expresses its intent to comply with the physical and biological containment standards set forth in the NIH Guidelines . . . . . LICENSEE further agrees to cooperate with government agency(ies) authorized to monitor compliance with such containment standards.

. . . .

6. ROYALTIES

6.1—In consideration of the rights granted herein, LICENSEE shall pay to STANFORD upon execution of this agreement a royalty payment of Ten Thousand Dollars ($10,000). Thereafter, LICENSEE shall pay a minimum annual advance on earned royalties of Ten Thousand Dollars ($10,000) on or before the first day of February for each calendar year following execution of this agreement. Said payments are nonrefundable except that they can be credited against earned royalties to the extent provided in paragraph 6.3.

. . .

6.3—Earned royalty payments due under Article 8 in excess of the annual minimum may be reduced up to 50% in any one year by a credit equal in total to five (5) times the cumulative amount of the royalties paid in accordance with paragraph 6.1 in years prior to the calendar year in which the first sale takes place of an *End Product* for other than development purposes, but not for minimum payments made for 1987 and following years, so long as is necessary during the period of royalty payment to amortize the specified multiple (five (5)) of the cumulative royalties paid under paragraph 6.1 prior to the calendar year of such first sale.

6.4—LICENSEE shall pay earned royalties for use of *Licensed Patent Rights* for production and sale of *End Products* based on the *Net Sales* in the United States of *End Products* by LICENSEE. The earned royalty rate for *End Products* shall depend upon the total sales of *End Products* in each calendar year as specified in the following schedule.

Annual Net Sales of End Products in U.S.	Earned Royalty Rate on Net Sales of End Products
up to $5 million	1.00%
$5–$10 million	0.75%
over $10 million	0.50%

6.5—LICENSEE shall pay earned royalties for use of *Licensed Patent Rights* to produce in the United States *End Products* and *Bulk Products* for sale outside of the United States of 0.5% of *Net Sales* of *End Products* and 1% of *Net Sales* of *Bulk Products* regardless of sales volume.

6.6—LICENSEE also shall pay earned royalties for use of *Licensed Patent Rights* for production and sale of *Licensed Products* that are not *End Products* as follows:

6.6.1—The earned royalty rate for *Basic Genetic Products* shall be 10% of *Net Sales*.

6.6.2—The earned royalty rate for *Bulk Products* shall depend upon *Net Sales* by LICENSEE of *Bulk Products* in each calendar year as specified in the following schedule.

Annual Net Sales of Bulk Products in U.S.	Earned Royalty Rate on Net Sales of Bulk Products
up to $5 million	3%
$5–$10 million	2%
over $10 million	1%

6.6.3—The earned royalty rate for *Process Improvement Products* shall be 10% of cost savings and economic benefits enjoyed by LICENSEE.

. . .

7.   MORE FAVORED TERMS

7.1—STANFORD intends that the terms of all licenses under *Licensed Patent Rights* are to be essentially similar to the terms of this license.

. . .

8.   PAYMENTS AND REPORTS

8.1—LICENSEE agrees to notify STANFORD promptly, in writing, of the date of the *First Commercial Sale* of a *Licensed Product* and date of first transaction under paragraph 10.1.

8.2—Beginning with the date of *First Commercial Sale*, royalties from LICENSEE hereunder (less the credits allowed by paragraphs 6.3 and 6.7 and less the minimum annual royalty paid in advance for that calendar year) shall be paid to STANFORD within ninety (90) days after the close of each subsequent calendar quarter.

. . .

8.4—LICENSEE shall provide with each earned royalty payment of paragraph 8.2 a statement of *Net Sales* and the applicable royalties in accordance with Article 6 and a report of each transaction under paragraph 10.1. All such reports shall be held in confidence by STANFORD. Such statements and reports shall be submitted whether or not a payment in excess of the minimum is due.

. . .

10.   OTHER TRANSFERS OF LICENSED PRODUCTS

10.1—It is anticipated that LICENSEE may supply *Licensed Products* to an *Affiliate* (as defined in pararaph 2.10) or to another licensee of STANFORD for further processing and/or sale by the *Affiliate* or other licensee under *Licensed Patent Rights*. No earned royalty shall be payable by LICENSEE with respect to such *Licensed Products*, so long as the *Affiliate* or second licensee shall be obligated to pay STANFORD royalty under *Licensed Patent Rights* on its use or sales thereof. However, reports made by LICENSEE as provided in paragraph 8.4 shall list each such transaction as a non-royalty bearing sale and identify such *Affiliate* or other licensee.

. . .

11.   TERM AND TERMINATION

11.1—The term of this Agreement shall extend from the above effective date until expiration of the last to expire of *Licensed Patent Rights*.

11.2—Upon any breach of, or default under, this License Agreement by LICENSEE, STANFORD may terminate this License Agreement by ninety (90) days written notice to LICENSEE. Said notice shall become effective at the end of such period unless during said period LICENSEE shall cure such defect or default.

11.3—LICENSEE shall have the right to terminate this Agreement at any time upon ninety (90) days written notice to STANFORD.

. . .

13.   NEGATION OF WARRANTIES AND INDEMNITY

13.1—Nothing in this Agreement shall be construed as:

(a) a warranty or representation by STANFORD as to the validity or scope of any *Licensed Patent Rights*; or

(b) a warranty or representation that anything made, used, sold or otherwise disposed of under any license granted in this Agreement is or will be free from infringement of patents of third parties; or

(c) an obligation to bring or prosecute actions or suits against third parties for infringement; or

(d) conferring the right to use in advertising, publicity or otherwise any trademark, trade name, or names, or any contraction, abbreviation, simulation or adaptation thereof, of STANFORD; or

(e) conferring by implication, estoppel or otherwise any license or rights under any patents of STANFORD other than *Licensed Patent Rights*, regardless of whether such patents are dominant or subordinate to *Licensed Patent Rights* (however, STANFORD is not aware of any STANFORD patent or application dominant to *Licensed Patent Rights*); or

(f) an obligation to furnish any know-how not provided in *Licensed Patent Rights*.

13.2—STANFORD makes no representations other than those specified in Article 1. STANFORD MAKES NO EXPRESS OR IMPLIED WARRANTIES OF MERCHANTABILITY OR FITNESS FOR A PARTICULAR PURPOSE.

13.3—LICENSEE shall defend, indemnify and hold STANFORD harmless from and against all liability, demands, damages, expenses and losses for death, personal injury, illness or property damage ("claims and damages") arising (a) out of the use by LICENSEE of any method under *Licensed Patent Rights*, or (b) out of any use, sale or other disposition of *Licensed Products* by LICENSEE or its transferees. . . .

14.   GENERAL

14.1—Neither party may waive or release any of its rights or interests in this Agreement except in writing. Failure to assert any right arising from this Agreement shall not be deemed or construed to be a waiver of such right.

14.2—This License Agreement constitutes the entire agreement between the parties relating to the subject matter thereof, and all prior negotiations, representations, agreements and understandings are merged into, extinguished by, and completely expressed by it.

14.3—This Agreement and its effects are subject to and shall be construed and enforced in accordance with the laws of the State of California.

14.4—Any dispute or controversy arising out of or relating to this License Agreement, its construction or its actual or alleged breach, shall be finally decided by arbitration conducted in San Francisco, California, by and in accordance with the Licensing Agreement Arbitration Rules of the American Arbitration Association. Judgment upon the award rendered may be entered in the highest court or forum, state or federal, having jurisdiction, provided, however, that the provisions of this Article 14 shall not apply to decision of the validity of patent claims or to any dispute or controversy as to which any treaty or law prohibits such arbitration.

C. MAKING DECISIONS: VALUES AND UNCERTAINTY

---

1. ESTIMATING THE IMPACT ON THE WORLD

OFFICE OF THE DIRECTOR, NATIONAL INSTITUTES OF HEALTH, FINAL ENVIRONMENTAL IMPACT STATEMENT ON NIH GUIDELINES FOR RESEARCH INVOLVING RECOMBINANT DNA MOLECULES

Part One, 23–37, (Oct. 1977).

C. DESCRIPTION OF ISSUES RAISED BY RECOMBINANT DNA RESEARCH

Research is, by definition, investigation of the unknown. The results of research, whether beneficial, neutral, detrimental, or some combination of these, cannot be fully predicted ahead of time. The following discussions are assessments based on present knowledge and collective technical judgments. Unexpected benefits and unexpected hazards are possible.

1. Possible Hazardous Situations

The stable insertion of DNA derived from a different species into a cell or virus (and thus the progeny thereof) may change certain properties of the host. The changes may be advantageous, detrimental, or neutral with regard to (a) the survival of the recipient species, (b) other forms of life that come in contact with the recipient, and (c) aspects of the nonliving environment. Current knowledge does not permit accurate assessment of whether such changes will be advantageous, detrimental, or neutral, and to what degree, when considering a particular recombinant DNA experiment. A major part of this uncertainty is derived from the fact that mere insertion of foreign genes does not automatically affect the host. The genes must be "expressed"—that is, must cause a new protein to be produced—or must otherwise alter function. At present it is only possible to speculate on ways in which the presence of recombinant DNA in a cell might change the cell's properties.

It should be emphasized that there is no known instance in which a hazardous agent has been created by recombinant DNA technology. The following discussion considers ways in which hazardous agents might be produced. In principle, the analysis is applicable to animals, including humans, and plants, when potential effects on complex organisms are described.

a. *The effect of foreign DNA on the survival of recipient species (host cell, plasmids, or viruses)*

The effect of foreign DNA on the survival of recipient species is important to the discussion of possible hazards of recombinant DNA experiments. A recipient species may acquire a potential for harmful effects as a result of the foreign DNA, but the possibility of the occurrence of the harmful effects will depend on the survival of the altered recipient and its ability to multiply. If acquisition of foreign DNA increases the probability of survival and multiplication, the possibility of harmful effects will increase. Similarly, if acquisition of foreign DNA decreases the probability of survival or multiplication, the possibility of harmful effects will decrease. It is important to recognize, in evaluating the potential for harmful effects, that significant infections of animals and plants by bacteria or viruses usually require contact with far more than a single organism. The critical number of infectious agents will vary, depending on both the agent and the recipient.

Survival of Host Cell. There are multiple indications that both host bacteria and plasmid or virus vectors containing inserted foreign DNA are less likely to survive and multiply than are the original organisms, except for the very unusual instances where the foreign DNA supplies some function, such as antibiotic resistance, that favors the organism in a particular, non-natural environment. . . . Therefore, it is probable that bacterial cells, plasmids, or viruses containing inserted foreign DNA would multiply more slowly in nature than the same cells or vectors without foreign DNA; and in a natural competitive environment, those organisms containing recombinant DNA would generally be expected to disappear.
. . .

Survival of Vectors. Because potentially useful vectors such as plasmids and viruses may be transferred from cell to cell, independent of the growth and survival of the initial recipient, it is also necessary to consider survival of the vectors. Plasmids and viruses occur widely in nature. Any particular plasmid or virus will normally multiply only within a limited number of species. Thus, for example, viruses that infect particular bacteria neither multiply nor cause disease in the cells of other bacterial species or complex organisms. In many instances, they do not even enter the cells of any organism other than the particular natural host.

Only limited information concerning the effect of foreign DNA insertions on the survival or transferability of plasmid and viral vectors is available. In the case of plasmids, the factors contributing to their maintenance or loss from cells in natural environments, even without insertion of a foreign DNA, are not clearly understood. One exception is the selective advantage for maintenance provided by an antibiotic-resistant gene on the plasmid. Also, some plasmids are known to confer on host cells the ability to manufacture substances poisonous to other, closely related cells, thus giving the poison-producers special advantage in a competitive situation. Insertion of a foreign DNA fragment within the DNA sequence coding for the poison has been shown to eliminate production of the poison, thus decreasing the likelihood that the cells and their resident recombinant DNA will survive in nature. . . .

b.   *The effect of bacteria and viruses containing recombined DNA on other forms of life*

The analysis leading to the Guidelines centered on the possibility of deleterious effects, since the concern was the health and safety of living organisms, including humans, and the environment. Agents constructed by recombinant DNA technology could prove hazardous to other forms of life by becoming pathogenic (disease-producing) or toxigenic (toxin-producing), or by becoming more pathogenic or toxigenic than the original agent.

There are two basic mechanisms by which a recipient microorganism might be altered with regard to its pathogenicity or toxicity as a result of a resident recombinant:

(1) *The recombinant DNA may result in formation of a protein that has undesirable effects*

The case in which bacterial cells are used as carriers of foreign DNA is discussed first. A foreign protein, specified by the foreign DNA, might act after being liberated from the microorganism, or it could function within the microorganism and alter, secondarily, normal microbial cell function in such a way that the cell is rendered harmful to other living things. Either means depends on the expression of the foreign genes; that is, the information in the foreign genes must be used by the recipient bacterium to produce a foreign protein. Examples of proteins that might prove harmful to other organisms are hormones, enzymes, and toxins.

Present evidence suggests that foreign DNA from bacteria of one species, when inserted into bacteria of another species, may be expressed in the recipient, depending on the similarities of the protein synthesis mechanisms in the two organisms: For example, if the donor of the foreign DNA produces a toxic substance, then the recipient cell may produce such a substance, provided the gene for the toxic substance is present in the recombinant. The recipient may or may not be more hazardous than the original donor organism, depending on the relative ability of the two organisms to grow and infect an animal or plant species at risk.

The evidence available at present is insufficient to predict whether or not foreign genes derived from a complex organism (animals, plants, yeasts, and fungi) will be expressed in a bacterium in any particular instance. It may be that specific manipulations will be required to permit bacteria to express information from a foreign DNA efficiently. Faithful expression of a gene requires accurate functioning of the complex bacterial machinery involved in protein synthesis. At each step, specific signals originating in the foreign gene must be recognized by the bacterial machinery. Evolutionary divergence has resulted in different signals in bacteria and complex organisms.

. . .

DNA fragments from yeast have been inserted into a strain of the bacterium *E. coli* which cannot manufacture the amino acid histidine. (Histidine is a component of most proteins and is therefore required for the growth of all organisms.) After insertion, some cells no longer required histidine, the need for which had been overcome by the yeast DNA. This is the first indication that a foreign gene from an organism more complex than bacteria can function in a bacterial cell. (Although yeast is a single-cell organism, it contains an organized nucleus, like cells of higher organisms.)

Analogous issues must be considered for the case in which animal viruses are the carriers of foreign DNA. Many viruses are simply described as DNA molecules enclosed and protected by coats of protein molecules. The protein coat protects the DNA from environmental effects, thus increasing the ability of the viral DNA to infect a cell. If viral DNAs are recombined with foreign DNAs in such a way that necessary viral genes remain intact, then the recombinant DNA may in turn be able to produce, and be packaged in, the coat of the virus. Inadvertent dispersal of such a viral particle outside of the laboratory might then result in entry of the recombinant DNA into cells of living organisms. The foreign genes may be expressed, resulting in the formation of a protein foreign to the infected cell, or the uncontrolled synthesis of a normal protein. The likelihood of expression of the foreign genes will probably depend on the degree of relatedness between its source and the infected organism as well as its location in the viral DNA used as vector. Currently, few relevant experimental data are available.

(2) *The recombined DNA may itself cause pathogenic or toxic effects*

Foreign DNA inserted in a bacterial gene might so alter the microbial cell's properties that it becomes harmful to other organisms. This might happen, for example, through a change in the growth rate and competitive advantage of the recipient microbial cell, resulting in increased virulence of a mildly pathogenic bacteria. In general, one would expect the inserted DNA to result in a reduced growth rate and a selective disadvantage to the organism, as discussed in IV–C–1–a above. Similar issues arise where animal viruses serve as carriers of foreign DNA.

It is also necessary to consider situations in which DNA molecules themselves may escape from the laboratory or from the experimental host cell and enter cells of living organisms with which they come in contact. Although free DNA molecules are themselves relatively fragile (and the probability that they would survive, in a significant form or for a significant time, in air, water, or any other medium, is considered remote), they can be protected in nature in a variety of ways and be released either into, or close to, a living cell.

When a cell or virus dies, or comes close to or invades the tissue of another living organism, the recombinant DNA may effectively enter a new cell. A hazardous situation similar to that described above might ensue if foreign proteins were manufactured in this "secondary" recipient. The recombinant DNA might survive as an independent cellular component, or it could recombine by natural process with the DNA of the secondary recipient. . . .

. . .

2. Expected Benefits of Recombinant DNA Research

Benefits may be divided into two broad categories: an increased understanding of basic biological processes, and practical applications for medicine, agriculture, and industry.

At this time the expected practical applications have not yet been realized and their success remains uncertain. But the ability of recombinant DNA methods to increase understanding of basic biological processes has already been proved. It is important to stress that the most significant results of this work, as with any truly innovative endeavor, are likely to arise in unexpected ways and will almost certainly not follow a predictable path.

a. *Increased Understanding of Basic Biological Processes*

There are many important fundamental biomedical questions that can be answered or approached by DNA recombinant research. In order to advance against inheritable diseases or to understand how man's genetic makeup affects his response to the environment, we need to understand the structure of genes and how they work. The DNA recombinant methodology provides a simple and inexpensive way to prepare large quantities of specific genetic information in pure form. This should permit elucidation of the organization and function of the genetic information in higher organisms. For example, current estimates of the fraction of this information that codes for proteins are simply educated guesses. There are almost no clues about the function of the portions of DNA that do not code for proteins, although these DNA sequences are suspected of being involved in the regulation of gene expression.

The existing state of ignorance is largely attributable to our previous inability to isolate discrete segments of the DNA in a form that permits detailed molecular analysis. Recombinant DNA methodology removes this barrier. Furthermore, ancillary techniques have been developed whereby pure DNA segments that contain particular sequences of interest can be identified and selected. Of particular interest is the isolation of pure DNA segments that contain the genes for the variable and constant portions of the immunoglobin proteins, the substances providing the major resistence of the body to infections or transplants. The analyses of such segments obtained from both germline and somatic cells should be valuable in determining the mechanism of immunologic diversity.

A major problem in understanding the mechanism by which certain viruses cause cancer in animals is how and where the infecting or endogenous viral genomes are integrated into the cell's chromosome. This bears on the question of how the expression of the integrated viral genes affects cellular regulation, thus leading to the abnormal growth characteristics of cancer cells. With the recombinant DNA techniques for isolation and purification of specific genes, this research problem is reduced to manageable proportions. It is possible to isolate the desired DNA segment in pure form. Large quantities can be obtained for detailed study by simply extracting a culture of the bacteria carrying the viral DNA segment in a plasmid. . . .

b. *Potential Practical Applications for Medicine, Agriculture and Industry*

Certain of the potential applications will be realized only if the reproduction of the recombined foreign DNA in a recipient host cell is followed by expression of the genetic information contained in the DNA in the form of synthesis of proteins. Since the efficient translation of genes of higher organisms (eukaryotes) in bacterial hosts (prokaryotes) has yet to be proved, these potential applications are speculative at this time. Applications that depend on the expression of foreign prokaryotic genes in prokaryotic recipient cells are presently more certain.

. . .

3. Long-Range Implications

Another major issue in recombinant DNA research is its long-range implications. The experimental situations treated in the Guidelines are those that appear feasible either currently or in the near future. The experiments primarily involve insertion of recombined DNA into bacteria or into single cells derived from more complex organisms and maintained under special laboratory conditions. It is only in the case of plants that the Guidelines cover experiments involving insertion of DNA into cells capable of developing into complex, multicellular organisms. The Guidelines and the discussions leading to their development have focused on problems of safety.

It is possible that techniques similar to or derived from current recombinant DNA methodology may, in the future, be applicable to the deliberate modification of complex animals, including humans. Such modification might have as its aim correction of an inherited defect in an individual, or alteration of heritable characteristics in the offspring of individuals of a given species. The latter type of alteration has been successfully achieved in agriculture for centuries, by classical breeding techniques. It may be that recombinant DNA methods, should they develop in appropriate ways, will offer new opportunities for specificity and accuracy in animal breeding. It should be noted, however, that the techniques covered by the NIH Guidelines involve the recombining of DNA fragments in the test tube and their insertion into independent single cells only. The techniques do not permit alteration of whole complex organisms.

Application of such methods for the correction of individual genetic defects or the alteration of heritable characteristics in man, should these ever become possible, would pose complex and difficult problems. In addition to questions of concern to individuals, serious societal issues would be involved. Broad discussion in a variety of forums would be indicated.

It would be premature to address these questions in an EIS concerning guidelines for protection against possibly hazardous microorganisms.
. . . .

· · ·

MACK v. CALIFANO

United States District Court for the District of Columbia, 1978.
447 F.Supp. 668.

JOHN LEWIS SMITH, JR., DISTRICT JUDGE.

Plaintiff seeks a preliminary injunction to prevent an experiment testing the biological properties of polyoma DNA (deoxyribonucleic acid) cloned in bacterial cells. The experiment is to be conducted in Building 550, Frederick Cancer Research Center at Fort Detrick, Maryland. Also before the Court is defendants' motion to vacate a voluntary stay.

Defendants are Joseph A. Califano, Jr., Secretary of Health, Education, and Welfare, Donald S. Frederickson, Director of National Institutes of Health, and John E. Nutter, Chief Officer of Specialized Research and Facilities, National Institute of Allergies and Infectious Diseases, National Institutes of Health.

On May 31, 1977 plaintiff, an infant resident of Frederick, Maryland, filed a motion for temporary restraining order and preliminary injunction to enjoin defendants from undertaking the experiments or constructing facilities at Fort Detrick to be used for the research. On July 18th a stipulation was entered into by the parties staying all proceedings pending finalization by the defendants of an Environmental Impact Statement and providing for 30 days notice to plaintiff of any experiments to be conducted at Fort Detrick after such finalization. In accordance with the stipulation, defendants advised plaintiff that an Environmental Impact Statement (EIS) became final on November 28, 1977 when the Council on Environmental Quality published notice of its receipt in the Federal Register. Plaintiff contends that the statement does not comply with the requirements of the National Environmental Policy Act (NEPA), 42 U.S.C. § 4332(2)(C) and other statutes.

A motion of the American Society for Microbiology for leave to file a brief as Amicus Curiae with respect to the public health consequences of the proposed research was granted. Counsel for the Society participated in oral argument and submitted a brief. Dr. Naum S. Bers, Rockville, Maryland, appeared individually as a concerned citizen and was granted permission to file a statement.

Plaintiff asserts that defendants are planning to conduct experiments with polyoma, a virus known to cause cancer in mice. He states that the nature of the organisms to be created by the research is such that even a miniscule quantity, if released, in the environment would represent a threat to life and health. He further contends that the Fort Detrick experiments are to be conducted by defendants without determining the applicability of NEPA and according to the very guidelines of the Department of Health, Education, and Welfare (HEW) classified as "prohibited".

Defendants on the other hand take the position that the EIS and NIH (National Institutes of Health) guidelines reflect the cautious manner in which the scientific community and NIH have considered the new technology involving recombinant DNA molecules. They further state that the final EIS was completed after extensive public comment and discussion of alternatives. Much of plaintiff's concern, they state, is based on an apparent misunderstanding of the nature of the materials to be used in the experiment. Plaintiff's affidavits are based on the belief that the experiment here in question will be conducted utilizing a common strain of escherichia coli (E coli) as the host-vector for the planned studies. Significantly, the NIH guidelines "prohibit certain kinds of recombinant DNA experiments which include virtually all the known hazards—for example, those involving known infectious agents."

The research is now restricted by these guidelines to implanting any new genes into enfeebled strains of E coli, a human gut bacteria that has been modified even further to make it safe as the new DNA's laboratory host. In the planned experiment a derivative of E coli K–12, which has been specifically designed to "self destruct", will be employed. E coli K–12 is unable to colonize within the human intestinal tract and causes no known human or animal disease. This EK2 host-vector system will not survive passage through the intestinal tract of animals and will "die" because of its dependency on chemicals not found in nature.

Defendants further point out that the complete experiment will be conducted in P4 physical containment laboratories which have been shown to safely contain microbes presenting a known and demonstrable hazard to man. For each certified EK2 system, . . . NIH reviews extensive scientific data to determine that the system meets the standards for safety. It is evident, therefore, that there is actually a two step distinction between the common strains of E coli which "do live in people" and the EK2 host-vector system which will be used in these experiments.

Counsel for the American Society for Microbiology states that the weight of scientific opinion now considers that recombinant DNA research in accordance with the NIH guidelines will not have adverse environmental or public health consequences. He contends that the present guidelines are more conservative than necessary and that certain restrictions in these guidelines could be safely modified. He further asserts that these guildelines are *not* in fact the very guidelines of HEW classified as "prohibited" as was asserted by plaintiffs. In the opinion of the Society, the proposed Fort Detrick experiment will specifically advance the public interest and present no risk of harm to the environment.

The research involves dividing and then rejoining the heredity-carrying material of various organisms—deoxyribonucleic acid, or DNA—to make recombinant hybrids that carry some of the traits of two unrelated forms. It is contended that the value of such work is that it may create new medicines, vaccines, industrial chemicals or crops. The risk, some scientists claim, is that it could create unexpectedly dangerous new ailments or epidemics. Many scientists are of the opinion that exaggerations of the hypothetical hazards have gone far beyond any reasoned assessment. They take the position that the experience of the last four years, including many laboratory experiments, has shown no actual hazards.

Recently the Supreme Court has summarized the limited role of the courts in determining whether the agencies have complied with NEPA.

The only role for a court is to insure that the agency has taken a 'hard look' at environmental consequences; it cannot 'interject itself within the area of discretion of the executive as to the choice of the action to be taken'. Kleppe v. Sierra Club, 427 U.S. 390, 410 n. 21, 96 S.Ct. 2718, 2731, 49 L.Ed.2d 576 (1976) citing Natural Resources Defense Council v. Morton, 148 U.S.App.D.C. 5, 16, 458 F.2d 827, 838 (1972).

The EIS does represent a "hard look" by NIH at recombinant DNA research performed in accordance with its guidelines. It appears that compliance with the NIH guidelines will insure that no recombinant DNA molecules will escape from the carefully controlled laboratory to the environment.

Plaintiff requested an extension of time to furnish additional evidence. He submitted supplemental affidavits from four of his previous affiants which reaffirmed their previously expressed opinions. None of the affidavits established that the experiment is likely to cause harm to human health or to the environment. The Recombinant DNA Research Guidelines represent an effort by many scientists to evaluate the hazards and provide safe methods for their control. The record reflects that NIH has carefully considered the potential risks of this experiment under the guidelines and has taken the necessary precautions.

The experiment is designed to provide important and needed information on the possibilities of recombinant DNA technology. Important scientific information relative to the possibilities of this technology would be delayed if a preliminary injunction were granted.

Accordingly, plaintiff's motion for a preliminary injunction is denied. Defendants' motion to vacate stay is granted.

FINDINGS OF FACT

1. Plaintiff's complaint, motion for temporary restraining order and preliminary injunction were filed on May 31, 1977.

2. On July 18, 1977 a stipulation was approved by the Court providing that all matters would be stayed pending the finalization of an Environmental Impact Statement (EIS), that defendants would give plaintiff thirty days notice before proceeding with the experiment, and that no such experiment would be conducted prior to the finalization of an EIS.

3. The National Institutes of Health (NIH) guidelines and final EIS were the result of a lengthy administrative process. The scientific community had operated for several years under voluntary restraints limiting the kinds of recombinant DNA research that could be undertaken.

4. A public meeting was held by NIH on February 9th and 10th, 1976 which was announced to the public in the Federal Register. Thereafter NIH published the decision of the Director, NIH and NIH guidelines on recombinant DNA research on July 7, 1976. At that time NIH announced that it was preparing a draft environmental impact statement. 41 Fed.Reg. 27902 (1976). On September 9, 1976 the draft EIS was published in its entirety in the Federal Register. 41 Fed.Reg. 38426 (1976). The final EIS was prepared and notice of its availability published in the Federal Register on November 28, 1977. 42 Fed.Reg. 6588 (1977).

5. The NIH guidelines govern all facets of NIH-funded research using recombinant DNA techniques. The guidelines provide detailed requirements for both physical and biological containment designed to insure that recombinant DNA molecules will pose no threat to man or the environment. The experiment is to be conducted in accordance with these guidelines.

6. The laboratory at Fort Detrick is a P4 laboratory with extensive safeguards built into its design. The experiment is to be conducted under P4 physical containment requirements—the highest level of physical containment. P4 facilities are governed by rules limiting access, providing for change of clothes before entering and leaving, and numerous other safety features. All recombinant DNA materials are handled in gas-type safety cabinets and removed only after sterilization.

7. The experiment is to be conducted using EK2 host-vector systems. In the planned experiment, a derivative of E coli K–12 which has been specifically designed to self-destruct if removed from the controlled laboratory environment will be used. E coli K–12 itself is safe and has been used for years without known harm to the laboratory workers or to the environment.

8. E coli K–12 is unable to colonize in the human intestinal tract and causes no known human or animal disease. The EK2 system uses a K–12 derivative that must have special chemicals found only in an artificial laboratory setting in order to survive and is safer than ordinary K–12. If these chemicals are not present, the EK2 is designed to self-destruct.

9. Recombinant DNA research has already become a valuable aid in progress against illness. Benefits include applied medical advances and an accelerated understanding of the genetic and biochemical basis of the disease process.

10. The experiment is designed to provide important knowledge concerning recombinant DNA technology.

11. The experiment poses no substantial risk to human health or to the environment because (1) there is little likelihood the materials will escape from the maximum containment of the P4 facility; (2) if such an escape did occur, the recombinant DNA molecules would not survive but would self destruct outside the laboratory environment; and (3) the particular virus being used has never been implicated in human disease.

12. Plaintiff has offered no evidence to show that he will suffer irreparable injury or that there is any significant possibility that the experiment will have an adverse impact on the environment.

CONCLUSIONS OF LAW

1. Plaintiff has not shown that he would be irreparably injured unless a preliminary injunction is granted.

2. Plaintiff has not sustained the burdens imposed upon him by Virginia Petroleum Jobbers Association v. FPC, 104 U.S.App.D.C. 106, 259 F.2d 921 (1958) in that he has failed to demonstrate that he would be irreparably injured in the absence of the issuance of an injunction, that he is likely to prevail upon the merits of the controversy, and that the public interest lies in granting the requested relief.

NOTE ON ENVIRONMENTAL IMPACT LITIGATION

The environmental impact statement (EIS) excerpted here was prepared by the National Institutes of Health in conjunction with its earliest guidelines on recombinant DNA (see Sec. B.2, supra). Five years after Mack v. Califano was decided, a second controversy involving the EIS and the NIH guidelines arose. It concerned an experiment approved by the RAC (pursuant to Sec. III–A–2 of the NIH Guidelines) in which two bacteria that have been altered through recombinant DNA techniques were to be released in a potato field to test their ability to survive and to displace their unaltered brethren. The bacteria in question normally excrete a protein that serves as a nucleation site for ice formation on plants at temperatures slightly below 32 degrees Fahrenheit. Dr. Steven Lindow of the University of California at Berkeley genetically engineered the bacteria to inactivate the synthesis of the frost-forming chemical, so that it is expected the plants on which the bacteria grow will remain frost-free to 23 degrees, a matter of considerable interest for commercial agriculture which suffers an estimated $3 billion in frost damage each year.

Suit was brought in September 1983 in the federal district court in Washington, D.C., by four public interest groups to halt the field-test on the ground that NIH failed to prepare an EIS specifically for this intentional release of bacteria, in violation of the National Environmental Policy Act. The plaintiffs also contend that the RAC does not include any ecologists among its 19 members and that it failed to consider the possibility that the multiplying microbes might affect the formation of rain and snow in the upper atmosphere. The RAC's representatives responded that it makes use of ecological (and other) experts as needed, and that the risks seen by the experiment's opponents are not realistic.

Many knowledgeable scientists were reported to be dubious about such risks, in part because similar bacteria (altered by nonrecombinant techniques) have already been tested in open fields. Dr. Lindow believes the genetically engineered bacteria will probably be safer than the chemically mutated ones because the alterations are more specific, being limited to the frost-genes. Nevertheless, the University of California researchers announced in October that they would postpone the field test until the spring of 1984 because the group suing NIH had threatened to seek a temporary restraining order against the university to halt the experiment; the researchers feared that the delays for review by the courts would in any case make it too late in the year for the project. Budianasky, Frost Damage Trial Halted, 305 Nature 564 (1983).

Are courts better places than the executive branch (and its advisory committees) to resolve these issues? By what standards should the judges weigh the uncertainties involved? In addition to the scientists who have provided affidavits for the plaintiffs in the suit, others who do not oppose the experiment, like Cornell University microbiologist Martin Alexander, admit that some risk remains: "In general, whenever a new technology is introduced, there is a possible hazard. My belief is that the same likely is true of genetically engineered organisms. Most of them introduced into the environment won't survive. But a few will. Most that survive won't have an effect. But a few will. And most of those that have an effect won't do any damage—but a few will." See Wines, Genetic Engineering—Who'll Regulate the Rapidly Growing Private Sector?, 15 Nat'l J. 2096 (1983).

STEPHEN P. STICH,
THE RECOMBINANT DNA DEBATE

7 Phil. & Pub.Aff. 187, 193–194, 196–198 (1978).

In trying to assess costs and benefits, a familiar first step is to set down a list of possible actions and possible outcomes. Next, we assign some measure of desirability to each possible outcome, and for each action we estimate the conditional probability of each outcome given that the action is performed. In attempting to apply this decision-making strategy to the case of recombinant DNA research, the assignment of probabilities poses some perplexing problems. Some of the outcomes whose probabilities we want to know can be approached using standard empirical techniques. Thus, for example, we may want to know what the probability is of a specific enfeebled host E. coli strain surviving passage through the human intestinal system, should it be accidentally ingested. Or we may want to know what the probability is that a host organism will escape from a P−4 laboratory. In such cases, while there may be technical difficulties to be overcome, we have a reasonably clear idea of the sort of data needed to estimate the required probabilities. But there are other possible outcomes whose probabilities cannot be determined by experiment. It is important, for example, to know what the probability is of recombinant DNA research leading to a method for developing nitrogen-fixing strains of corn and wheat. And it is important to know how likely it is that recombinant DNA research will lead to techniques for effectively treating or preventing various types of cancer. Yet there is no experiment we can perform nor any data we can gather that will enable us to *empirically* estimate these probabilities. Nor are these the most problematic probabilities we may want to know. A possibility that weighs heavily on the minds of many who are worried about recombinant DNA research is that this research may lead to negative consequences for human health or for the environment *which have not yet even been thought of.* The history of technology during the last half-century surely demonstrates that this is not a quixotic concern. Yet here again there would appear to be no data we can gather that would help much in estimating the probability of such potential outcomes.

It should be stressed that the problems just sketched are not to be traced simply to a paucity of data. Rather, they are conceptual problems; it is doubtful whether there is *any clear empirical sense* to be made of objective probability assignments to contingencies like those we are considering. . . . A second cluster of problems that confronts us in assessing the risks and benefits of recombinant DNA research turns on the assignment of a measure of desirability to the various possible outcomes. Suppose that we have a list of the various harms and benefits that might possibly result from pursuing recombinant DNA research. The list will include such "benefits" as development of an inexpensive way to synthesize human clotting factor and development of a strain of nitrogen-fixing wheat; and such "harms" as release of a new antibiotic-resistant strain of pathogenic bacteria and release of a strain of *E. coli* carrying tumor viruses capable of causing cancer in man.

Plainly, it is possible that pursuing a given policy will result in more than one benefit and in more than one harm. Now if we are to assess the potential impact of various policies or courses of action, we must assign some index of desirability to the possible *total outcomes* of each policy, outcomes which may well include a mix of benefits and harms. To do this we must confront a tangle of normative problems that are as vexing and difficult as any we are likely to face. We must *compare* the moral desirabilities of various harms and benefits. The task is particularly troublesome when the harms and benefits to be compared are of different kinds. Thus, for example, some of the attractive potential benefits of recombinant DNA research are economic: we may learn to recover small amounts of valuable metals in an economically feasible way, or we may be able to synthesize insulin and other drugs inexpensively. By contrast, many of the risks of recombinant DNA research are risks to human life or health. So if we are to take the idea of cost-benefit analysis seriously, we must at some point decide how human lives are to be weighed against economic benefits.

There are those who contend that the need to make such decisions indicates the moral bankruptcy of attempting to employ risk-benefit analyses when human lives are at stake. On the critics' view, we cannot reckon the possible loss of a human life as just another negative outcome, albeit a grave and heavily weighted one. To do so, it is urged, is morally repugnant and reflects a callous lack of respect for the sacredness of human life.

On my view, this sort of critique of the very idea of using risk-benefit analyses is ultimately untenable. It is simply a fact about the human condition, lamentable as it is inescapable, that in many human activities we run the risk of inadvertently causing the death of a human being. We run such a risk each time we drive a car, allow a dam to be built, or allow a plane to take off. Moreover, in making social and individual decisions, we cannot escape weighing economic consequences against the risk to human life. A building code in the Midwest will typically mandate fewer precautions against earthquakes than a building code in certain parts of California. Yet earthquakes are not impossible in the Midwest. If we elect not to require precautions, then surely a major reason must be that it would simply be too expensive. In this judgment, as in countless others, there is no escaping the need to balance economic costs against possible loss of life. To deny that we must and do balance economic costs against risks to human life is to assume the posture of a moral ostrich.

I have been urging the point that it is not *morally objectionable* to try to balance economic concerns against risks to human life. But if such judgments are unobjectionable, indeed necessary, they also surely are among the most difficult any of us has to face. It is hard to imagine a morally sensitive person not feeling extremely uncomfortable when confronted with the need to put a dollar value on human lives. It might be thought that the moral dilemmas engendered by the need to balance such radically different costs and benefits pose insuperable practical obstacles for a rational resolution of the recombinant DNA debate. But here, as in the case of problems with probabilities, I am more sanguine. For while some of the risks and potential benefits of recombinant DNA research are all but morally incommensurable, the most salient risks and benefits are easier to compare. The major risks, as we have noted, are to human life and health. However, the major potential benefits are *also* to human life and health. The potential economic benefits of recombinant DNA research pale in significance when set against the potential for major break-throughs in our understanding and ability to treat a broad range of conditions, from birth defects to cancer. Those of us, and I confess I am among them, who despair of deciding how lives and economic benefits are to be compared can nonetheless hope to settle our views about recombinant DNA research by comparing the potential risks to life and health with the potential benefits to life and health. Here we are comparing plainly commensurable outcomes. If the balance turns out to be favorable, then we need not worry about factoring in potential economic benefits.

There is a certain irony in the fact that we may well be able to ignore economic factors entirely in coming to a decision about recombinant DNA research. For I suspect that a good deal of the apprehension about recombinant DNA research on the part of the public at large is rooted in the fear that (once again) economic benefits will be weighed much too heavily and potential damage to health and the environment will be weighed much too lightly. The fear is hardly an irrational one. In case after well-publicized case, we have seen the squalid consequences of decisions in which private or corporate gain took precedence over clear and serious threats to health and to the environment. It is the profit motive that led a giant chemical firm to conceal the deadly consequences of the chemical which now threatens to poison the James River and perhaps all of Chesapeake Bay. For the same reason, the citizens of Duluth drank water laced with a known carcinogen. And the ozone layer that protects us all was eroded while regulatory agencies and legislators fussed over the loss of profits in the spray deodorant industry. Yet while public opinion about recombinant DNA research is colored by a growing awareness of these incidents and dozens of others, the case of recombinant DNA is fundamentally different in a crucial respect. The important projected benefits which must be set against the risks of recombinant DNA research are not economic at all, they are medical and environmental.

NOTE

Do you agree with the authors of the environmental impact statement that it is too soon to consider the possibility that recombinant DNA research will lead to the deliberate modification of humans? If that issue is to be considered it is difficult to put it in a cost/benefit framework. Does Stich provide guidance on how that might be done?

LAURENCE H. TRIBE,
WAYS NOT TO THINK ABOUT PLASTIC TREES: NEW
FOUNDATIONS FOR ENVIRONMENTAL LAW

83 Yale L.J. 1315, 1317–22 (1974).

From the start, the aspect of environmental policy analysis that has most concerned students of the matter has been the supposed difficulty of ever incorporating certain *kinds of values* into systematic analyses of environmental problems, whether in the service of legislators, of planning agencies, of litigators, of private enterprises, or of courts. Variously described as fragile, intangible, or unquantifiable, these values have been widely thought to possess peculiar features making them intrinsically resistant to inclusion along with such allegedly "hard" concerns as technical feasibility and economic efficiency. In particular, those dimensions of a choice for which market prices do not exist have seemed to pose intractable obstacles to "objective measurement."

. . .

. . . Despite what appears to be a widely held assumption to the contrary, all [intangible or otherwise "fuzzy"] concerns can in theory be incorporated in a rigorous analysis, either by using various market price or other numerical surrogates to value extramarket costs or benefits, or by the technique of "shadow pricing"—that is, qualitatively describing as best one can the contents of a constraint as intangible as natural beauty or procedural fairness or respect for future generations, and then calculating the tangible benefits that would have to be forgone if one were to insist that one's policy conform to the constraint described.

Thus, even in the relatively unsophisticated (by current standards) cost-benefit analyses performed to evaluate alternative levels of water quality improvement in the Delaware estuary, the enhanced swimming, fishing, and boating possibilities of a cleaner Delaware River were translated into dollar terms. The methods used in that translation were highly questionable in their ability to measure the economically relevant variables (that is, to measure how much prospective swimmers, fishermen, and boaters would willingly sacrifice before becoming indifferent between the enhanced opportunities caused by an improvement and the opportunities previously available to them), and it is true that those variables themselves could not measure the value of enhanced water quality to future generations, or to the aquatic life that inhabits the estuary. But an observer who believes that such values also matter could describe their significance in any terms that seem appropriate, and the analyst could then calculate how costly it would be to raise the water quality to the level demanded by the observer's description. Whether the sacrifice was justified by the values invoked would then have to be determined by whichever individuals or groups were responsible for making the choice in question. That their decision would be a difficult one reflects not any intrinsic weakness of the analytic methodology as applied to nonmonetizable values but rather the universal difficulty of choosing among incommensurables, a difficulty that can be obscured but never wholly eliminated by any method of decisionmaking.

It should be added as a qualifying caveat, however, that the tools of analysis are currently too blunt to be of very great use in this endeavor. If the analytic disciplines are truly to clarify the relations within and among values so as to identify inconsistencies not otherwise perceived and to show that some perceived conflicts are in fact illusory by inventing "policies from which two groups with apparently conflicting interests can both benefit," then the analytic fields, and the scientific disciplines which support them, must sharpen both their capacity to ask and answer probing and imaginative "what if" questions, and their capacity to understand and describe in some detail what each of the nonmonetary values significantly involved in a choice really represents.

Organizations engaged in environmental policy analyses are rarely able today to discover or to articulate the underlying character of the ecological and aesthetic concerns, many of them essentially symbolic, that play so major a role in environmental disputes or to design the models that would be needed to facilitate a thorough search of even mildly novel alternatives. It may be, as Nobel laureate Murray Gell-Mann has proposed, that we must therefore develop a new group of professionals sensitive to the sorts of values and issues that analyses currently tend to slight—diversity, balance, aesthetic quality, reversibility, the claims of the future—and adept at modeling policy impacts in terms of such values. In studying a particular environmental case, such professionals might translate each of the relevant values or concerns into a parameterized constraint designed to show how costly the options for choice would be from the perspective of the value in issue. Thus, for example, a "distortion of natural landscape" index might be studied to determine how slowly or rapidly the other costs associated with a project would rise if that index were constrained within lower and lower levels; an "ecological diversity" index might be examined to ascertain what increments in various cost curves would result as one tightened the ecological constraint by forcing this index ever higher.

The curves generated by this sort of analysis will at times have a more complex structure than those typically assumed by analysts, especially those trained primarily in neoclassical economics. For example, most individuals would probably not trade breathing rights below a certain point for even limitless rights to pollute. And many persons—far from regarding such human capacities as eyesight, hearing and physical mobility as all subject to continuous trade-offs to levels approaching zero—probably have preference orderings that display significant discontinuities, lexicalities, and nonzero thresholds which an adequate analysis would be forced to consider.

However difficult the investigation of such ordering structures might be, and however complex may be the general task of defining the relevant parameterized constraints and generating the associated curves, the effort to move analysis in such directions should at least prove illuminating. And even before anyone is very good at the task of attaching shadow prices to varying levels of constraints as elusive as ecological diversity, the *attempt* to attach them rather than simply incorporating such constraints in an all-or-nothing fashion should lead to better decision processes even if not better outcomes. Whether or not new professions must be developed in order to perform this sort of task sensitively, it seems clear that treating the problem as an *inherent* incapacity of analysis to incorporate the intangible can only retard the needed development of these important abilities.

MARTIN P. GOLDING,
OBLIGATIONS TO FUTURE GENERATIONS

in Responsibilities to Future Generations
69–71 (E. Partridge ed. 1980).

. . . I began by stressing the importance of fixing the purview of obligations to future generations. They comprise the community of the future, a community with which we cannot expect to share a common life. It appears to me that the more *remote* the members of this community are, the more problematic our obligations to them become. That they are members of our moral community is highly doubtful, for we probably do not know what to desire for them.

Let us consider a concrete example, namely, that of the maintenance of genetic quality. Sir Julian Huxley has stated:

> [I]f we don't do something about controlling our genetic inheritance, we are going to degenerate. Without selection, bad mutations inevitably tend to accumulate; *in the long run, perhaps 5,000 to 10,000 years from now,* we [*sic*] shall certainly have to do something about it. . . . Most mutations are deleterious, but we now keep many of them going that would otherwise have died out. If this continues indefinitely . . . then the whole genetic capacity of man will be much weakened.

This statement, and others like it, raise many issues. . . . [G]iven that we do not know the conditions of life of the very distant future generations, we do not know what we ought to desire for them even on such matters as genic constitution. The chromosome is "deleterious" or "advantageous" only relative to given circumstances. And the same argument applies against those who would promote certain social traits by means of genetic engineering (assuming that social traits are heritable). Even such a trait as intelligence does not escape immune. (There are also problems in eugenic programs having nothing to do with remoteness.) One might go so far as to say that if we have an obligation to distant future generations it is an obligation not to plan for them. Not only do we not know their conditions of life, we also do not know whether they will maintain the same (or a similar) conception of the good life for man as we do. Can we even be fairly sure that the same general characterization is true both of them and us?

The moral to be drawn from this rather extreme example is that the more distant the generation we focus upon, the less likely it is that we have an obligation to promote its good. We would be both ethically and practically well-advised to set our sights on more immediate generations and, perhaps, solely upon our immediate posterity. After all, even if we do have obligations to future generations, our obligations to immediate posterity are undoubtedly much clearer. The nearer the generations are to us, the more likely it is that our conception of the good life is relevant to them. There is certainly enough work for us to do in discharging our responsibility to promote a good life for them. But it would be unwise, both from an ethical and a practical perspective, to seek to promote the good of the very distant.

And it could also be *wrong,* if it be granted—as I think it must—that our obligations towards (and hence the rights relative to us of) near future generations and especially our immediate posterity are clearer than those of more distant generations. By "more distant" I do not necessarily mean "very distant." We shall have to be highly scrupulous in regard to anything we do for any future generation that also could adversely affect the rights of an intervening generation. Anything else would be "gambling in futures." We should, therefore, be hesitant to act on the dire predictions of certain extreme "crisis ecologists" and on the proposals of those who would have us plan for mere survival. In the main, we would be ethically well-advised to confine ourselves to removing the obstacles that stand in the way of immediate posterity's realizing the social ideal. This involves not only the active task of cleaning up the environment and making our cities more habitable, but also implies restraints upon us. Obviously, the specific obligations that we have cannot be determined in the abstract. This article is not the place for an evaluation of concrete proposals that have been made. I would only add that population limitation schemes seem rather dubious to me. I find it inherently paradoxical that we should have an obligation to future generations (near and distant) to determine in effect the very membership of those generations.

A final point. If certain trends now apparent in our biological technology continue, it is doubtful that we should regard ourselves as being under an obligation to future generations. It seems likely that the man—humanoid(?)—of the future will be Programmed Man, fabricated to order, with his finger constantly on the Delgado button that stimulates the pleasure centers of the brain. I, for one, cannot see myself as regarding the good for Programmed Man as a good-to-me. That we should do so, however, is a necessary condition of his membership in our moral community . . .. The course of these trends may very will be determined by whether we believe that we are, in the words of Burke, "but a clause in the great primaeval contract of eternal society, linking the lower with the higher natures, connecting the visible and invisible world, according to a fixed compact sanctioned by the inviolable oath which holds all physical and all moral natures, each in their appointed place." We cannot yet pretend to know the outcome of these trends. It appears that whether we have obligations to future generations in part depends on what we do for the present.

NOTES

1. As part of a reasonable cost-benefit analysis could a group of legislators, judges, or the new professionals envisioned by Professor Tribe undertake to figure the impact of genetic engineering on future generations?

2. Despite the strong sense that many people have that they ought to care about future generations, they may find it difficult to know how to go about it, for reasons of uncertainty of the type raised by Golding. Jean-Paul Sartre presents another—rather unflattering—view of why the living might worry about those who come after.

> In order to assure myself that the human race would remember me forever, it was agreed in my head that the species would never end. For me to expire in humanity's bosom was to be born and become infinite, but if anyone put forward, in my presence, the hypothesis that a cataclysm might some day destroy the planet, even in fifty thousand years, I would be panic-stricken. Though I am now disillusioned, I cannot think about the cooling of the sun without fear. I don't mind if my fellowmen forget about me the day after I'm buried. As long as they're alive, I'll haunt them, unnamed, imperceptible, present in every one of them just as the billions of dead who are unknown to me and whom I preserve from annihilation are present in me. But if mankind disappears, it will kill its dead for good.

J. Sartre, The Words 156 (B. Frechtman trans. 1964).

3. One of the greatest difficulties in estimating the impact of a technology that may pose health hazards comes in trying to take appropriate account of possible ill-effects that may take many years to be manifested. See Ch. 3, Sec. B.3, for a current example of this problem (asbestos-related illnesses) and the difficulties it poses for after-the-fact distribution of the resultant costs.

2. CONTRASTING VALUE SYSTEMS

Complicating any attempt to decide about research in and application of genetic engineering are a number of conflicting value systems, occasionally perceived by decisionmakers but often unrecognized or unacknowledged. In this section, we begin with a look at competing moral theories for assessing benefits and harms, and then turn to the contrast between the norms of science and law.

TOM L. BEAUCHAMP, ETHICAL THEORY AND BIOETHICS

in Contemporary Issues in Bioethics
1, 4–11, 13–24, 26–31 (T. Beauchamp & L. Walters 2d ed. 1982).

The Resolution of Moral Disagreements. Can we hope—in light of complex dilemmas and other sources of dispute—to resolve moral disagreements? If so, on what principles and procedures should we rely? Probably no single set of considerations will prove consistently reliable as a means of ending disagreement and controversy (and resolutions of cross-cultural conflicts will always be especially elusive). Nonetheless, several methods for dealing constructively with moral disagreements have been employed in the past, and each deserves recognition as a method of easing and perhaps even settling controversies. . . .

First, many moral disagreements can be at least partially resolved by obtaining factual information concerning points of moral controversy. It has often been uncritically assumed that moral disputes are (by definition) produced solely by differences over moral principles or their application, and not by a lack of information. This assumption is overly simplistic, however, because disputes over what morally ought or ought not to be done often have nonmoral elements as central ingredients. . . .

. . .

Second, controversies have been settled by reaching conceptual or definitional agreement over the language used by disputing parties. In some cases stipulation of a definition or a clear explanation of what is meant by a term may prove sufficient, but in other cases agreement cannot be so conveniently achieved. . . . Although conceptual agreement provides no guarantee that a dispute will be settled, it should at least facilitate discussion of the issues. . . .

Third, resolution of moral problems can be facilitated if disputing parties can come to agreement on a common set of moral principles. If this method requires a complete shift from one starkly different moral point of view to another, agreement will rarely if ever be achieved. Differences that divide persons at the level of their most cherished principles are deep divisions, and conversions are infrequent. Various forms of discussion and negotiation can, however, lead to the adoption of a new or changed moral framework that can serve as a common basis for discussion.

. . .

Fourth, resolution of moral controversies can be aided by a method of example and opposed counterexample. Cases or examples favorable to one point of view are brought forward, and counterexamples to these cases are thrown up by a second person against the examples and claims of the first. Such use of example and counterexample serves as a format for weighing the strength of conflicting considerations. . . .

Fifth and finally, one of the most important methods of philosophical inquiry, that of exposing the inadequacies and unexpected consequences of an argument, can also be brought to bear on moral disagreements. If an argument is inconsistent, then pointing out the inconsistency will change the argument and shift the focus of discussion. There are, in addition, many more subtle ways of attacking an argument than pointing to straightforward inconsistencies. For example, . . . a number of writers have discussed the nature of "persons" when dealing with problems of abortion, fetal rights, and the definition of death. Some of these writers have not appreciated that their arguments about persons—used, for example, to discuss fetuses and those who are irreversibly comatose—were so broad that they carried important but unnoticed implications for both infants and animals. Their arguments implicitly provided reasons they had not noticed for denying rights to infants that adults have, or for granting (or denying) the same rights to fetuses that infants have, and in some cases for granting (or denying) the same rights to animals that infants have. It may, of course, be correct to hold that infants have fewer rights than adults, or that fetuses and animals should be granted the same rights as infants. . . . The point is that if a moral argument leads to conclusions that a proponent is not prepared to defend and did not previously anticipate, then part of the argument will have to be changed, and this process may reduce the distance between those who disagree. This style of argument is often supplemented by one or more of the other four ways of reducing moral disagreement. Much of the work published in philosophical journals takes precisely these forms of attacking arguments, using counterexamples, and proposing alternative frameworks of principles.

Much moral disagreement may not be resolvable by any of the five means discussed. Philosophy need not contend that moral disagreements can always be resolved, or even that every rational person must accept the same method for approaching such problems. There is always a possibility of ultimate disagreement. However, if something is to be done about problems of justification in contexts of disagreement, a resolution is most likely to occur if the methods outlined are used. . . .

Relativism

The fact of moral disagreement raises questions about appropriate criteria for *correct* or *objective* moral judgments. People's awareness of cultural differences relative to moral judgment, and of moral disagreements among friends over issues like abortion, has led many to doubt the possibility that there are correct and objective positions in morals. This doubt is fed by popular aphorisms which assert that morality is more properly a matter of taste than reason, that it is ultimately arbitrary what one believes, and that there is no neutral standpoint from which to view disagreements. . . .

Tension between the belief that morality is purely subjective and the belief that it has an objective grounding leads to issues of relativism in morals. One basic issue is whether an objective morality is possible and whether reason has any substantial role to play in ethics. Proponents of relativism believe that all moral beliefs and principles relate only to individual cultures or individual persons: one person's or one culture's values do not govern the conduct of others. Relativists defend this position by appeal to anthropological data indicating that moral rightness and wrongness vary from place to place. . . . They add that rightness is contingent on individual or cultural beliefs and that the concepts of rightness and wrongness are therefore meaningless apart from the specific contexts in which they arise.

Moral relativism is no newcomer to the scene of moral philosophy. Ancient thinkers were as perplexed by cultural and individual differences as moderns. . . . Nevertheless, it was easier in former times to ignore cultural differences than it is today, because there was once greater uniformity within cultures, as well as less commerce between them. The contrast between ancient Athens and modern Manhattan is evident, and any contemporary pluralistic culture is saturated with individuality of belief and lifestyle. . . . At the same time, we tend to reject the claim that this diversity compels us to tolerate racism, social caste systems, sexism, genocide, and a wide variety of inequalities of treatment that we deeply believe morally wrong but find sanctioned either in our own culture or in others.

Problems of apparent moral diversity offer a serious challenge to moral philosophy. If rightness and wrongness are completely determined or exhausted by particular contexts, a universal ethical system seems a hopeless ideal. Although it has at times been a fashionable view in the social sciences that relativism is a correct and highly significant doctrine, moral philosophers have generally tended to reject relativism. They find relativistic views unconvincing, both because they seem irrelevant to the main task of moral philosophy and because the counterarguments seem at least as good as the arguments defending relativism. Furthermore, there are so many different notions subsumed under the theme of relativism that arguments often seem undirected and confused. In an effort to clarify these notions of relativism, the two main forms it has taken are discussed.

Cultural Relativism. Anthropologists have often asserted that patterns of culture can only be understood as unique wholes. Moral beliefs about normal behavior are thus closely connected in a culture to other cultural characteristics, such as language and fundamental political institutions. Studies show, they maintain, that what is deemed worthy of moral approval or disapproval in one society varies, both in detail and as a whole pattern, from moral standards in other societies. So far as universality is concerned, these anthropologists believe that their data show at most that in all societies persons possess a moral conscience, that is, a general sense of right and wrong. Their reasoning is that although in every culture some actions and intentions are approved as right or good and others are disapproved, the *particular* actions, motives, and rules that are praised and blamed vary greatly from culture to culture. . . .

From the perspective taken by these anthropologists, a moral standard is simply a historical product sanctioned by custom—nothing more, nothing less. Psychological and historical versions of this same thesis hold that the moral beliefs of individuals vary according to historical, environmental, and familial differences. . . .

This form of relativism has plagued moral philosophy, and many philosophical arguments have been advanced against it. Among the best known are arguments that there is a universal *structure* of human nature or at least a universal set of human needs which leads to the adoption of similar or even identical principles in all cultures. This line of argument rests at least partially on empirical claims about what actually is believed across different cultures. More important than this empirical thesis, however, is the claim that even though cultural or individual beliefs vary, it does not follow that people ultimately or fundamentally disagree about moral standards. That is, two cultures may agree about an ultimate *principle of morality,* yet disagree about the "ethics" of a particular situation or practice. If a moral conflict were truly fundamental, then the conflict could not be removed even if there were perfect agreement about the facts of a case, about the analysis of concepts involved, and about background beliefs. Much anthropological evidence suggests that conflicts between moral beliefs across cultures are not basic or fundamental, because disagreements over critical *facts* or *concepts* are the underlying source of "moral" diversity. For example, in many cultures it is thought that people are reborn just as they die; individuals who die in a senile and broken-hearted state will be reborn in the same state. To avoid this condition in the afterlife, people in these cultures execute their parents at what is considered an age immediately prior to senility. Although this practice is vastly different from that sanctioned in nations most familiar to [our] readers . . . the difference in moral judgment at a fundamental level is not as great as it appears at first, because both cultures appeal to a similar ultimate moral principle to justify their treatment of the aged. That is, they both appeal to beneficent concern for the ultimate welfare of their parents.

Mere disagreements or differences in practice do not alone defeat belief in moral objectivity. When two parties argue for or against some moral view—the morality of research involving children as subjects, killing animals, abortion, or withholding information from patients—most people tend to think that at least one party is mistaken or that some genuinely fair compromise can be reached, or perhaps they remain uncertain while on the lookout for a best argument to emerge. But they do not infer from the mere fact of a conflict between beliefs that there is no way to establish one view as correct, or at least as better argued than the other. The more absurd the position advanced by one party, the more convinced they become that some views being defended are mistaken or require supplementation. They are seldom tempted to conclude that there could not be any correct moral theory that might resolve such a dispute among reasonable persons. In fact, the existence of diverse and culturally bound customs is perfectly compatible with each of the nonrelativist ethical theories discussed later . . . utilitarianism and deontology, in particular.

Normative Relativism. Cultural relativists might reasonably be said to hold that "What is right in one place or time may be wrong at another." This statement is ambiguous, however, and can easily be interpreted as a second form of relativism. Some relativists interpret "What is right at one place or time may be wrong at another" to mean that it *is right* in one context to act in a way that it *is wrong* to act in another. This thesis is normative, because it discloses standards, or norms, of right and wrong behavior. One form of this normative relativism asserts that one ought to do what one's *society* determines to be right (a group or social form of normative relativism), and a second form holds that one ought to do what one *personally* believes (an individual form of normative relativism).

This normative position has sometimes crudely been translated as "anything is right or wrong whenever some individual or some group sincerely thinks it is right or wrong." However, less crude formulations of the position can be given, and more or less plausible examples can be adduced. One can hold the slightly more sophisticated view, for example, that in order to be right something must be conscientiously and not merely customarily believed. Alternatively, it might be formulated as the view that whatever is believed is right if it is part of a well-formed traditional moral code of rules in a society.

Support is sometimes claimed for these relativist contentions by appeal to the belief that it is inappropriate to criticize one culture from the perspective of another. Thus, normative relativism has been said to include the following thesis: Because moral norms are valid only when accepted by a group or an individual, it is morally illegitimate to apply any norm to another culture or individual. The claim is that the validity of moral norms is limited in scope and that the norms themselves are binding only in a specific domain, much as principles of etiquette and custom are binding only in certain locations.

The apparent inconsistency of this form of relativism with many cherished moral beliefs is one major source of objections directed at normative relativism by both philosophers and nonphilosophers. For example, most of us believe that better and worse moral beliefs can sometimes be identified, and that moral progress or moral retrogression can occur in cultures and individuals. Moreover, no theory of normative relativism is likely to convince us that we must tolerate all acts of others. . . .

. . .

A final objection is the following: If we interpret normative relativism as requiring tolerance of other views, the theory is imperiled by inconsistency. The proposition that we ought to tolerate the views of others, or that it is right not to interfere with others, is not permitted by the theory itself, for such a proposition bears the marks of a *nonrelative* account of moral rightness—one based on, but not reducible to, the cross-cultural findings of anthropologists. . . . If the relativist holds that a principle of tolerance is demanded by "morality itself," then other fundamental normative propositions cannot be excluded from similar standing in the purportedly relativist theory. . . . But if this moral principle is recognized as valid, it can of course be employed as an instrument for criticizing such cultural practices as the denial of human rights to minorities and beliefs such as that of racial superiority. A moral principle requiring tolerance of other practices and beliefs thus leads inexorably to the abandonment of normative relativism.

Moral Justification

One general and important question implicit . . . thus far is, "Can answers about what is morally good and right be justified?" This question arises repeatedly even in popular discussions of morality. Questions of justification are matters of immediate practical significance, and at the same time they are related to the most theoretical dimensions of philosophy. . . . [A] good case can be made that the central questions in ethics are those of justification. But what is required in order to justify some moral point of view?

Moral judgments are justified by giving reasons for them. Not all reasons, however, are *good* reasons, and not all good reasons are *sufficient* for justification. For example, . . . a good reason for involuntarily committing certain mentally ill persons to institutions is that they present a clear and present danger to other persons. Many believe that this reason is also sufficient to justify various practices of involuntary commitment. By contrast, a reason for commitment that is sometimes *offered* as a good reason, but which many people . . . consider a *bad* reason (because it involves a deprivation of liberty), is that some mentally ill persons are dangerous to themselves. If someone holds that commitment on grounds of danger to self is a good reason and is solely sufficient to justify commitment, that person should be able to give some further account of *why* this reason is good and sufficient. . . . The person might refer, for example, to the dire consequences for the mentally ill that will occur if someone fails to intervene. The person might also invoke certain principles about the importance of caring for the needs of the mentally ill, etc.

In short, the person is expected to give a set of reasons that amounts to an argued defense of his or her perspective on the issues.

. . .

CLASSICAL ETHICAL THEORIES

A structured normative ethical theory is a system of principles by which to determine what ought and ought not to be done. Modern ethical theory has come to be classified in terms of deontological and utilitarian approaches. . . .

Utilitarian Theories

Utilitarianism is rooted in the thesis that an action or practice is right (when compared to any alternative action or practice) if it leads to the greatest possible balance of good consequences or to the least possible balance of bad consequences in the world as a whole. In taking this perspective, utilitarians invite us to consider the whole point or function of morality as a social institution, where "morality" is understood to include our shared rules of justice and other principles of the moral life. The point of the institution of morality, they insist, is to promote human welfare by minimizing harms and maximizing benefits: There would be no point at all in having moral codes and understandings unless they served this purpose. Utilitarians thus see moral rules as the means to the fulfillment of individual needs as well as to the achievement of broad social goals. . . .

Mill's Utilitarianism. The major exposition of utilitarianism has generally been regarded as that of John Stuart Mill in his work *Utilitarianism* (1863). In this work Mill discusses two foundations of utilitarianism: (1) a *normative* foundation in the principle of utility, and (2) a *psychological* foundation in human nature. The principle of utility, or the Greatest Happiness Principle, he proposes as the foundation of morals: "Actions are right in proportion as they tend to promote happiness, wrong as they tend to produce the reverse of happiness, i.e., pleasure or absence of pain." Pleasure and freedom from pain, Mill argues, are alone desirable as ends; all desirable things (which are numerous) are therefore desirable either for the pleasure inherent in them, or as means to the promotion of pleasure and the prevention of pain.

Mill's second foundation of utilitarianism derives from his belief that most and perhaps all persons have a basic desire for unity and harmony with their fellow human beings. Whereas Mill's utilitarian predecessor, Jeremy Bentham, had tried to justify the principle of utility by claiming that it is in our own self-interest to promote everyone's interest, Mill appeals to social feelings of mankind for his justification. Just as we feel horror at crimes, he says, so we have a basic moral sensitivity to the needs of others. In the end his view seems to be that the purpose of morality is at once to tap natural human sympathies so as to benefit others, while at the same time controlling unsympathetic attitudes that cause harm to others. The principle of utility is conceived as the best means to these basic human goals.

For Mill and many other utilitarians, moral theory is grounded in a theory of the general goals of life, which they conceive as the pursuit of pleasure and the avoidance of pain. The production of pleasure and pain assumes moral and not merely personal significance when the consequences of our actions affect the pleasurable or painful states of others.

Moral rules and moral and legal institutions, as they see it, must be grounded in a general theory of value, and morally good actions are alone determined by these final values. Utilitarians . . . have not always agreed on these goals and values, but one main task for any utilitarian is to provide an acceptable theory that explains which things are intrinsically good and why they are so. Additionally, there is a question of *whose* goals are to count in a utilitarian calculation. For example, when discussing the morality of biomedical research, are the pains of animals to count . . . and in considering euthanasia for defective newborns, are the interests of fetuses and newborns to count, and if so, by what utilitarian criteria. . . .

The Theory of Value. Within utilitarian theories of value, a major distinction is drawn between *hedonistic* and *pluralistic* utilitarians. Bentham and Mill are hedonistic, because they conceive utility entirely in terms of pleasure. In effect, they argue that the good life is constituted by happiness, which is equivalent to pleasure (though they did not argue that the word "good" *means* happiness or pleasure in ordinary language). All good things are valuable only as means to the production of pleasure or the avoidance of pain. Hedonistic utilitarianism, then, holds that acts or practices which maximize pleasure are right actions. Pluralistic utilitarian philosophers, by contrast, believe that no single goal or state constitutes *the* good and that many values besides happiness possess intrinsic worth— for example, the values of friendship, knowledge, love, devotion, health, beauty, and perhaps even certain moral qualities such as fairness. Those who subscribe to this pluralistic approach prefer to interpret the principle of utility as demanding that the rightness or wrongness of an action be assessed in terms of the total range of intrinsic values ultimately produced by the action, not in terms of pleasure alone. The greatest aggregate good, then, must be determined by considering multiple intrinsic goods. . . .

Although not as part of the dispute between hedonists and pluralists, Mill went to considerable lengths to clarify his use of the term "happiness." He insisted that happiness does not refer merely to "pleasurable excitement" but rather encompasses a realistic appraisal of the pleasurable moments afforded in life, whether they take the form of tranquillity or passion. Mill and Bentham both believed that pleasure and the freedom from pain could at least in rough ways be measured and compared, and Bentham argued that pleasure and pain can be measured by using a hedonic calculus. To determine the moral value of an action, he said, one must add up the total happiness to be produced, subtract the pains involved, and then determine the balance, which expresses the moral value of the act. Thus, a person literally is able, in Bentham's scheme, to calculate what ought morally to be done.

Many philosophers have objected to such quantification, arguing that it either is impossible or would take too long to be practical for determining what we ought to do in daily life. Whatever the merits of this objection, . . . Mill and Bentham realized that it is unrealistic in our daily practical affairs to pause and rationally calculate in detail on every occasion where choices must be made. They maintained that we must rely heavily on our common sense, our habits, and our past experience, as do contemporary utilitarians. . . .

Both the hedonistic and the pluralistic approaches have nonetheless seemed to some recent philosophers relatively useless for purposes of objectively aggregating widely different interests in order to determine where maximal value, and therefore right action, lies. Many utilitarians thus interpret the good as that which is subjectively desired or wanted; the *satisfaction* of desires or wants is seen as the goal of our moral actions. This third approach is based on individual *preferences,* and utility is analyzed in terms of an individual's actual preferences, not in terms of intrinsically valuable experiences or states of affairs. To maximize an individual's utility is to maximize what he or she has chosen or would choose from the available alternatives. To maximize the utility of those persons affected by an action or policy is to maximize the utility of the aggregate group. . . .

This preference-based utilitarian approach to value has been viewed by many as superior to its predecessors, but it is not trouble free as a general theory of morals. A major theoretical problem arises when individuals have morally unacceptable preferences. For example, a person's strong sexual preference may be to rape young children, but such a preference is morally intolerable. We reject such preferences. Utilitarianism based purely on subjective preferences is satisfactory, then, only if a range of *acceptable* preferences can be formulated. . . .

[E]ven if most persons are not perverse and if the ideals of utilitarianism are well entrenched in society, some rational agents may have preferences that are immoral or unjust, and a major problem for utilitarian theory is that it may stand in need of a supplementary criterion of value in addition to mere preference. (Many critics have suggested that at least a principle of justice must supplement the principle of utility.)

Act and Rule Utilitarianism. A significant dispute has arisen among utilitarians over whether the principle of utility is to be applied to particular *acts* in particular circumstances or to *rules* of conduct that determine which acts are right and wrong. For the *rule* utilitarian, actions are justified by appeal to such rules as "Don't deceive" and "Don't break promises." These rules, in turn, are justified by appeal to the principle of utility. An *act* utilitarian simply justifies actions directly by appeal to the principle of utility.

. . .

Many philosophers object vigorously to act utilitarianism, charging its exponents with basing morality on mere expediency. . . . Many opponents of act utilitarianism have thus argued that strict rules, which cannot be set aside for the sake of convenience, must be maintained. Many of these apparently desirable rules can be justified by the principle of utility, so utilitarianism need not be abandoned even if act utilitarianism is judged unworthy.

Rule utilitarians hold that rules have a central position in morality and cannot be compromised by the demands of particular situations. Such compromise would threaten the very effectiveness of the rules; effectiveness is judged by determining that the observance of a given rule would, in theory, maximize social utility better than would any possible substitute rule (or no rule). . . .

Still, it is necessary to ask whether rule-utilitarian theories can escape the very criticisms they acknowledge as tarnishing act utilitarianism. Dilemmas often arise that involve conflicts among moral rules—for example, rules of confidentiality conflict with rules protecting individual welfare, as in the Tarasoff case. . . . [see Ch. 3, Sec. B.2a, infra.] If the moral life were so ordered that we always knew which rules and rights should receive priority, there would be no serious problem for moral theory. Yet such a ranking of rules seems clearly impossible, and in a pluralistic society there are many rules that some persons accept and others reject. Even if everyone agreed on the same rules and on their interpretation, in one situation it might be better to break a confidence in order to protect someone, and in another circumstance it might be better to keep the information confidential.

Mill briefly considered this problem. He held that the principle of utility should itself decide in any given circumstance which rule is to take priority. However, if this solution is accepted by *rule* utilitarians, then their theory must rely directly on some occasions on the principle of utility to decide *in particular situations* which *action* is preferable to which alternative action in the absence of a governing rule. . . . [D]o all the same criticisms and counterexamples that rule utilitarians (and others) bring against act utilitarians apply to rule utilitarianism itself?

The rule utilitarian can reply to this criticism by asserting that a sense of relative weight and importance should be built directly into moral rules, at least insofar as possible. . . . Rule utilitarians may acknowledge that weights cannot be so *definitely* formulated and built into principles that irresolvable conflicts among rules will *never* arise. What they need not concede is that this problem is unique to rule utilitarianism. Every moral theory, after all, has certain practical limitations in cases of conflict. This is a general problem with the moral life itself, the rule utilitarian will argue, and thus not unique to a particular theory. It will nonetheless be possible to distinguish theories that require strict observance of rules from those, such as act utilitarianism, that do not. . . .

Criticisms of Utilitarianism. Two criticisms of utilitarianism are of major importance for our purposes. The first centers on the suggestion that goods can be measured and comparatively weighed. Because utility is to be maximized, one who makes a utilitarian choice must be in a position to compare the different possible utilities of an action. But can units of happiness or some other utilitarian value be measured and compared so as to determine the best among alternatives? In deciding how to allocate resources, for example, how is a state legislature to compare the value of a good screening program for genetic disease with the value of regular medical examinations at publicly funded clinics for checkups—or either with public health education? It is difficult for individuals to rank their *own* preferences, and still more difficult to compare one person's preferences with the preferences of others. Yet at least a rough comparison is required if the utility of everyone affected by the actions is to be maximized.

The utilitarian reply to these criticisms is that we make crude, rough and ready comparisons of values every day. For example, we decide to go on a picnic rather than have an office party because we think one activity will be more pleasurable or will satisfy more members of a group than the other. Physicians commonly recommend courses of treatment or nontreatment to families based on judgments of pain avoidance and family welfare. It is easy to overestimate the demands of utilitarianism and the precision with which its exponents have thought it could be employed. Accurate measurements of others' goods or preferences can seldom be provided because of limited knowledge and time. In everyday affairs—such as medical practice, hospital administration, or legislative decision-making—prior knowledge about the consequences of our actions is severely limited. What is important, morally speaking, is that a person conscientiously attempt to determine the most favorable action, and then with equal seriousness attempt to perform that action.

A second criticism is that utilitarianism can easily lead to injustices, especially to unjust social distributions. The argument may be expressed as follows: The action that produces the greatest balance of value for the *greatest number* of people may bring about unjustified harm or disvalue to a minority. An ethical theory requiring that the rights of individuals be surrendered in the interests of the majority seems plainly deficient; if a fair opportunity is denied the minority or the sick, the theory supporting such a recommendation is clearly unjust. Moreover, many political philosophers and legal theorists have argued that documents such as the Bill of Rights in the United States Constitution . . . contain a set of rules based on nonutilitarian principles, for such rights rigidly protect citizens from invasions in the name of the public good. . . .

. . .

Utilitarianism, then, conceives the moral life in terms of intrinsic value and the means to produce such value. Deontologists, by contrast, argue that moral standards exist independently of utilitarian ends and that the moral life is wrongly conceived in terms of means and ends. (The Greek word *deon*, or binding duty, is the source of the term "deontology.") An act or rule is right, in their view, insofar as it satisfies the demands of some overriding principle(s) of duty.

Deontological Theories

Deontologists urge us to consider that actions are morally wrong not because of their consequences but because the action type—the class of which the actions are instances—involves a moral violation. A radical deontologist will even argue that consequences are irrelevant to moral evaluations: An act is right if and only if it conforms to an overriding moral duty and wrong if and only if it violates the overriding moral duty or principle. Many deontological theories are not so radical, however, holding that moral rightness is only in part independent of utilitarian conceptions of goodness.

Deontologists believe that our duties to others are manifold and diverse, some springing from special relationships that utilitarians unjustifiably ignore. These relationships include, for example, those of parent and child, physician and patient, and employer and employee. Physicians have obligations to their patients that they do not have to other individuals, no matter the utilitarian outcome of treating their patients and not treating others. Children incur special obligations to their parents, and vice-versa; parents have a moral obligation to oversee and support the health and welfare needs of their children that they do not have in regard to other children in their neighborhood. . . .

Deontologists also believe that utilitarians give too little consideration to the performance of acts in the past that create obligations in the present. If a person has promised something or has entered into a contract, he or she is bound to the terms of the agreement, no matter what the consequences of keeping it. If one person harms another, the person who inflicted the injury is bound to compensate the injured one, whether the compensation serves utilitarian goals or not.

Since deontologists believe that moral standards are independent of utilitarian ends, what is the source of these standards and how is moral duty based on these standards? Throughout the history of philosophy deontologists have identified starkly different ultimate principles of duty as the final moral standards. Although these many different views cannot be surveyed here, it is possible to briefly distinguish several different grounds to which they have appealed. Perhaps the best known deontological account is the Divine Command theory. The will of God is the ultimate standard in this account, and an action or action type is right or wrong if and only if commanded or forbidden by God. Other deontologists hold that some actions or action types are naturally right or wrong, good or evil, requiring no reason having to do with religion, politics, or social organization. . . . Many deontologists believe these principles right as a fundamental matter. (Some claim that the moral value of principles—and therefore actions—can be known through reason, whereas others hold that their value can only be known through intuition.)

Finally, some deontologists appeal to a social contract reached under conditions of absolute fairness as the source of moral duty. The ultimate principle of duty is action in accordance with moral rules fairly derived from a situation of mutual agreement. . . .

. . .

Kant's Ethical Theory. The single most widely studied deontological theory is the rule-oriented theory developed by Immanuel Kant. . . . Kant tries to establish the ultimate basis for the validity of moral rules in pure (practical) reason, not in intuition, conscience, or the production of utility. Morality, he contends, provides a rational framework of principles and rules that constrain and guide everyone, without regard to their own personal goals and interests. Moral rules apply universally, and any rule qualifies as universally acceptable only if it cannot be rationally rejected. The ultimate basis of morality, then, rests on principles of reason that all rational agents possess.

Kant thought all considerations of utility and self-interest secondary, because the moral worth of an agent's action depends exclusively on the moral acceptability of the rule on the basis of which the person is acting— or, as Kant prefers to say, moral acceptability depends on the rule that determines the agent's *will.* An action, therefore, has moral worth only when performed by an agent who possesses what Kant calls a good will, and a person has a good will only if moral duty based on a universally valid rule is the sole motive for the action.

Kant lays great emphasis on performing one's duty for the sake of duty and not for any other reason, and this emphasis is one indicator that he espouses a pure form of deontology. All persons, he insists, must act not only *in accordance with duty* but *for the sake of duty.* That is, the person's motive for acting must rest in a *recognition* of an act as required by duty. It is not good enough, in Kant's view, that one merely perform the morally correct action, for one could perform one's duty for self-interested reasons having nothing to do with morality. If one does what is morally right simply because one is scared, because one derives pleasure from doing that kind of act, because one is selfish, or because the action is in one's own interest, then there is nothing morally praiseworthy about the action. . . .

When a person behaves according to binding moral rules valid for everyone, Kant considers that person to have an *autonomous* will. Kant compares autonomy with what he calls heteronomy—the determination of the will by persons or conditions other than oneself. Autonomy of the will is present when one knowingly governs oneself in accordance with universally valid moral principles. His concept of autonomy, however, does not simply imply personal liberty of action in accordance with a plan chosen by oneself. . . .

The difference between governance of oneself by moral obligation and governance by coercive force is critical to Kant's moral theory. Coerced acts such as being raped at knifepoint are obviously heteronomously produced, but Kant also holds that actions done from desire, impulse, or personal inclination are heteronomous actions. For example, refraining from theft merely out of fear of being caught is clearly an instance of heteronomy. Actions that are autonomous and morally right, by contrast, are based on moral principles that we accept (but have the freedom to reject). It is, however, easy to misunderstand this argument. To say that an agent "accepts" a moral principle does not mean either that the principle is merely subjective or that each individual must wholly create (author or originate) his or her own moral principles. Kant holds only that each individual must *will the acceptance* of the moral principles to be acted upon. A person's autonomy consists in the ability to govern himself or herself according to these moral principles. Moreover, Kant urges, moral relationships between persons are contingent on mutual respect for autonomy by all the parties involved. Kant develops this notion into a fundamental moral demand that persons be treated as ends in themselves and never solely as means to the ends of others. . . .

Kant's supreme principle, also called "the moral law," is actually expressed in several ways in his writings. In what appears to be his favored formulation, the principle is stated as follows: "I ought never to act except in such a way that I can also will *that my maxim should become a universal law.*" This Kantian principle has often been compared to the Golden Rule, but Kant calls it the "categorical imperative." He gives several examples of moral maxims that are made imperative by this fundamental principle: "Help others in distress"; "Do not commit suicide"; and "Work to develop your abilities." The categorical imperative is *categorical*, he argues, because it admits of no exceptions and is absolutely binding. It is *imperative* because it gives instruction about how one must act.

Kant clarifies this basic moral law—the very condition of morality, in his view—by drawing a distinction between a categorical imperative and a *hypothetical* imperative. A hypothetical imperative takes the form "*If* I want to achieve such and such an end, then I must do so and so." These prescriptions—so reminiscent of utilitarian thinking—tell us what we must do provided that we already have certain desires, interests, or goals. An example would be, "If you want to regain your health, then you must take this medication," or "If you want to improve infant mortality rates, then you must improve your hospital facilities." Such imperatives are obviously not commanded for their own sake; they are commanded only as *means* to an end that has already been willed or accepted. Hypothetical imperatives are not *moral* imperatives because moral imperatives tell us what must be done independently of our goals or desires.

Kant's imperative is an unusual ultimate principle because it mentions nothing about the *content* of moral rules. For this reason, it is often said to be a purely formal principle. It does not, for instance, dictate anything so substantive as "An action is right if and only if it produces the greatest good." The categorical imperative offers only the *form* any rule must have in order to be an acceptable rule of morality. As noted earlier, Kant states his categorical imperative in a distinctly different formulation (which many interpreters take to be a wholly different principle). This form is probably more widely quoted and endorsed in contemporary philosophy than the first form, and certainly it is more frequently invoked in biomedical ethics. Kant's later formulation stipulates that "One must act to treat every person as an end and never as a means only." This imperative insists that one must treat persons as having their own autonomously established goals and that one must never treat them solely as the means to one's own personal goals.

It has been widely stated in contemporary textbooks that Kant is arguing categorically that we can never treat another as a means to our ends. This interpretation, however, seems to misrepresent his views. He argues only that we must not treat another *exclusively* as a means to our own ends. When adult human research subjects are asked to volunteer to test new drugs, for example, they are treated as a means to someone else's ends (perhaps society's ends), but they are not exclusively used for others' purposes, because they do not become mere servants or objects. . . . Kant does not prohibit this use of persons categorically and without qualification. His imperative demands only that persons in such situations be treated with the respect and moral dignity to which every person is entitled at all times, including the times when they are used as means to the ends of others. To treat persons merely as means, strictly speaking, is to disregard their personhood by exploiting or otherwise using them without regard to their own thoughts, interests, and needs.

As appealing as his ethical theory may be, Kant has often been criticized on grounds that he leaves unresolved how duty is to be determined when two or more different duties are in conflict. This criticism is similar to the one directed at rule utilitarians. For example, if one rule demands truth telling to patients while another rule demands the protection of patients from unnecessary harm, what ought to be done in a situation where the disclosure of a piece of information the patient has requested will bring him or her great harm—perhaps a heart attack or the end of a treasured marriage? The categorical imperative seems to give no advice in this regard; it seems, in fact, to demand that both relevant duties be fulfilled. As mentioned above, it may be that no ethical theory can resolve this problem. But Kant's philosophy not only seems unable to help; it apparently *obliges* moral agents to perform two or more actions when only one can be performed.

W.D. Ross, a prominent twentieth-century British philosopher, developed a *pluralistic* rule-deontological theory intended to assist in resolving this problem of a conflict of duties. Ross's views are based on an account of what he calls prima facie duties, which he contrasts with *actual* duties. A *prima facie* duty is a duty that is always to be acted upon unless it conflicts on a particular occasion with an equal or stronger duty. A prima facie duty, then, is always right and binding, all other things being equal; it is "conditional on not being overridden or outweighed by competing moral demands." One's *actual* duty, by contrast, is determined by an examination of the respective weights of competing prima facie duties. Prima facie duties are thus not absolute, since they can in principle be overridden, but at the same time they have far greater moral significance than mere rules of thumb.

As Ross admits, neither he nor any other deontologist has ever been able to present a system of moral rules free of conflicts and exceptions. Ross argues that this is no more of a problem for him than for anyone else, Kant included, because the complexity of the moral life simply makes an exception-free hierarchy of rules and principles impossible.

Rawls's Theory. In recent years a book in the Kantian tradition has had great currency in deontological ethics. John Rawls's *A Theory of Justice* presents a deontological theory as a direct challenge to utilitarianism on grounds of social justice. Rawls's basic objection to utilitarianism is that social distributions produced by maximizing utility could entail violations of basic individual liberties and rights that ought to be guaranteed by social justice. Utilitarianism, which is concerned with the *total* satisfaction in a society, is indifferent as to the *distribution* of satisfactions among individuals. This indifference would in Rawls's view, permit the infringment of some people's rights and liberties if the infringement genuinely promised to produce a proportionately greater utility for others.

Rawls therefore sets as his task the development of an alternative ethical theory that is capable of grounding satisfactory principles of justice. Rawls turns for this purpose to a hypothetical social contract procedure that is strongly indebted to what he calls the "Kantian conception of equality." According to this social contract account, valid principles of justice are those to which we would all agree if we could freely and impartially consider the social situation from a standpoint (the "original position") outside any actual society. Impartiality is guaranteed in this situation by a conceptual device Rawls calls the "veil of ignorance." This notion stipulates that in the original position, each person is (at least momentarily) ignorant of all his or her particular fortuitous characteristics. For example, the person's sex, race, IQ, family background, and special talents or handicaps are unrevealed in this hypothetical circumstance.

The veil of ignorance prevents people from promoting principles of justice biased toward their own combinations of talents and characteristics. Rawls argues that under these conditions, people would unanimously agree on two fundamental principles of justice. The first requires that each person be permitted the maximum amount of equal basic liberty compatible with a similar liberty for others. The second stipulates that once this equal basic liberty is assured, inequalities in social primary goods (e.g., income, rights, and opportunities) are to be allowed only if they benefit everyone and only if everyone has fair equality of opportunity. Rawls considers social institutions to be just if and only if they are in conformity with these two basic principles.

Rawls's theory makes equality a basic characteristic of the original position from which the social contract is forged. . . . Nevertheless, Rawls rejects radical egalitarianism, arguing that equal distribution cannot be justified as a sole moral principle. If inequalities were to be introduced that rendered everyone better off by comparison to initial equality, these inequalities would be desirable—as long as they were consistent with equal liberty and fair opportunity. More particularly, if these inequalities work to enhance the position of the most disadvantaged persons in society, then it would be self-defeating for the least advantaged or anyone else to seek to prohibit the inequalities. Rawls thus rejects radical egalitarianism in favor of his second principle of justice.

The first part of his second principle is called the "difference principle." . . .

The difference principle rests on the view that because inequalities of birth, historical circumstance, and natural endowment are undeserved, society should correct them by improving the unequal situation of naturally disadvantaged members. This is a deontologically based demand that Rawls believes fundamental to moral life in society.

. . .

MAJOR ETHICAL PRINCIPLES

How are we to determine, in light of the preceding theories and account of justification, the moral acceptability of a particular act? Understandably, this question is complex, and there is no way to answer it with confident finality. But this much, at least, seems reasonable to assume: If a particular act is wrong, then it will have certain similarities, certain shared features, with other wrong actions; conversely, if a particular act is morally required, it will share similar features with other actions that are morally required. Philosophers who have tried to develop a general normative theory of right and wrong have, of course, tried to discover what these shared features are.

Theories of the two general sorts just discussed have also been used by moral philosophers to support a great many derivative moral principles (and rules—such as the one stating that it is right to keep our promises and wrong to break them). Not all such principles are needed for or even applicable to a discussion of any given moral problem . . . . But in order to take a reasoned approach to these problems, we need principles that permit us to take a consistent position on specific and related issues. Three moral principles have proved to be directly relevant to discussions of [bioethical] issues . . .: autonomy, beneficence, and justice.

. . .

Autonomy

The first principle deserving mention is one commonly referred to as the Principle of Respect for Persons, by which is usually meant something like the following: Because humans act morally and have a capacity for rational choice, they possess value independently of any special circumstances conferring value, and because all human beings and only human beings have such unconditional value, it is always inappropriate to treat them as if they had merely the conditional value possessed by natural objects and (so some believe) by animals. Human beings, as it is sometimes put, have an incalculable worth or moral dignity not possessed by other things or creatures, which are valuable *only under certain conditions*. To respect persons is to see them as unconditionally worthy agents, and so to recognize that they should not be treated as conditionally valued things that serve our own purposes. By contrast, to treat persons as mere means to our own ends is to treat them as if they were not moral agents.

From this perspective, to exhibit a lack of respect for persons is either to reject a person's considered judgments or to deny the person the liberty to act on those judgments. . . . For purposes of this discussion, the import is that individuals should be allowed to be self-determining agents, making their own evaluations and choices when their own interests are at stake. This narrowed version of "respect for persons" will be referred to here as respect for the autonomy of persons—or, more briefly, as the Principle of Autonomy. What is entailed by this principle?

There is an almost uniform agreement in the history of philosophy that a person who lacks critical internal capacities for self-rule in some organized fashion—and not mere freedom from external constraint—lacks something integral to freedom and control. Thus, in order to be autonomous, the person must be both *free of external control* and *in control of his or her own affairs*. One is autonomous in this sense only if one's ruling part is in control, if one is subject to no other governing conditions except those to whose control one has consented, and if one is capable of controlled deliberation and action.

. . .

The *principle of autonomy* can be formulated as follows: Insofar as an autonomous agent's actions do not infringe on the autonomous actions of others, that person should be free to perform whatever action he or she wishes (presumably even if it involves considerable risk to himself or herself and even if others consider the action to be foolish). Some philosophers have believed that autonomy is the primary moral principle and takes precedence over all other moral considerations. However, others consider it merely *one* important principle among others. . . .

The controversial problems with such a noble-sounding principle, as with all moral principles, arise when we must determine precise limits on its application and how to handle situations when it conflicts with such other moral principles as beneficence and justice. . . . Some persons cannot act autonomously because they are immature, incapacitated, ignorant, or coerced. A person of diminished autonomy is highly dependent on others, less than self-reliant, and in at least some respect incapable of choosing a plan on the basis of controlled deliberations. For example, children and institutionalized populations such as the mentally retarded may have diminished autonomy in this sense. For such persons the principle is inapplicable, except perhaps through some principle of proxy consent or substituted judgment. . . .

. . .

Among the most important demands made by the principle of automony is that of telling the truth. . . . [P]rinciples of veracity can be treated as derivative from autonomy, as can several other moral principles—such as those of confidentiality and privacy. Certainly autonomy has often been treated in moral theory as such an umbrella concept.

Beneficence

Among the most quoted principles in the history of codes of medical ethics is the maxim *primum non nocere*—"above all, do no harm." Other duties in medicine, nursing, public health, and research are expressed in terms of a more positive obligation to come to the assistance of those in need of treatment or in danger of injury. . . . The range of duties requiring abstention from harm and positive assistance may be conveniently clustered under the single heading of the Principle of Beneficence.

The term "beneficence" has broad usage in English; its meanings include the doing of good and the active promotion of good, kindness and charity. But in the present context the duty of beneficence has a narrower meaning. In it most general form, the principle of beneficence requires us to abstain from injuring others and to help others further their important and legitimate interests, largely by preventing or removing possible harms. Presumably such acts are required when they can be performed with minimal risk to the actors—not under all circumstances of risk. According to William Frankena, this principle can be expressed as including the following four elements: (1) One ought *not to inflict* evil or harm (a principle of nonmaleficence). (2) One ought to *prevent* evil or harm. (3) One ought to *remove* evil or harm. (4) One ought to *do or promote good*. Frankena suggests that the fourth element may not be a duty at all (being an act of benevolence that is over and above duty) and contends that these elements appear in a hierarchical arrangement so that the first takes precedence over the second, the second over the third, and the third over the fourth.

There are philosophical reasons for separating passive nonmaleficence (as expressed in 1) and active beneficence (as expressed in 2–4), and even ordinary moral discourse expresses the view that certain duties not to injure others are more compelling than duties to benefit them. . . . Nonetheless, the duty expressed in (1) may not always be stronger than those expressed in (2–4), and demands to benefit others and not to injure them can be unified under a single principle of beneficence—taking care to distinguish, as appropriate, between strong and weak requirements of this principle corresponding roughly to the ordering from 1 to 4.

Firmly established in the history of ethics, in practices of international relations, and in public policy formulation in most countries is the conviction that the failure to increase the good of others when one is knowingly in a position to do so is morally wrong. . . .

Still, there are problems with appeals to beneficence, some of which were implicitly encountered in discussing utilitarianism. Because beneficence potentially demands extreme generosity in the moral life, some philosophers have argued that it is commonly *virtuous*, but not a *duty*, to act beneficently. . . .

. . .

Several moral philosophers have offered proposals to resolve this problem by showing that beneficence does, in fact, generate duties. These attempts are too diverse and complex to be considered here, but despite this unresolved problem, it seems reasonable to assume that *some* forms of beneficence are morally required. That we are morally obligated on at least some occasions to assist others or to abstain from harming them is, after all, hardly a matter of moral controversy (even if the exact basis of the obligation is in dispute). For example, we are often morally obligated to benefit someone because of a role we have voluntarily assumed. Beneficent acts are built into our very understanding of the relationship between patients and health care professionals. . . .

. . .

Justice

Some moral philosophers have held that principles of justice have a moral priority over other moral principles, or at least that certain controversial moral issues can only be grounded within the broad framework of a theory of distributive justice. What, then, is justice, and what makes it unique?

Basic notions of both individual and social justice have been explicated in terms of fairness and "what is deserved." A person has been treated justly when he has been given what he or she is due or owed, what he or she deserves or can legitimately claim. What is deserved may be either a benefit or a burden. . . . Naturally, any denial of something to which a person has a right or entitlement is an injustice. It is also an injustice to place an undue burden on the exercise of a right—for example, to make a deserved piece of information unreasonably difficult to obtain. . . .

The more restricted expression "distributive justice" refers to the proper distribution of social benefits and burdens. Usually it refers to the distribution of what Rawls calls "primary social goods," such as economic goods and fundamental political rights. But social burdens must also be considered. Paying taxes and being drafted into the armed services to fight a war are distributed burdens; Medicare checks and grants to do research are distributed benefits. . . .

The notion of justice has been analyzed in different ways in rival theories. But common to all theories of justice is this minimal principle: Like cases should be treated alike—or, to use the language of equality, equals ought to be treated equally and unequals unequally. This elementary principle is referred to as the formal principle of justice, or sometimes as the formal principle of equality—*formal* because it states no particular respects in which people ought to be treated. It merely asserts that whatever respects are under consideration, *if* persons are equal in those respects, they should be treated alike. Thus, the formal principle of justice does not tell us how to *determine* equality or proportion in these matters, and it therefore lacks substance as a specific guide to conduct. In any group of persons there will be many respects in which they are both similar and different, and therefore this account of equality must be understood as "equality in relevant respects."

. . .

Theories of justice attempt to be more specific than the formal principle by systematically and precisely elaborating the notions of equality or proportion in distribution; they specify in detail what counts as a relevant respect in terms of which people are to be compared and what it means to give people their due. Philosophers achieve this specificity by developing *material* principles of justice, so called because they put material content into a theory of justice. Each material principle of justice identifies a relevant property that serves as a basis for distributing burdens and benefits. The following is a sample list of major candidates for the position of valid principles of distributive justice (though longer lists have been proposed): 1. To each person an equal share. 2. To each person according to individual need. 3. To each person according to that person's rights. 4. To each person according to individual effort. 5. To each person according to societal contribution. 6. To each person according to merit. There is no obvious barrier to acceptance of more than one of these principles, and some theories of justice accept all six as valid. Most societies use several in the belief that different rules are appropriate to different situations. . . .

STEPHEN P. STICH, THE RECOMBINANT DNA DEBATE

7 Phil. & Pub.Aff. 187, 199–202 (1978).

. . . Once we have assessed the potential harms and benefits of recombinant DNA research, how should we use this information in coming to a decision? It might be thought that the answer is trivially obvious. To assess the harms and benefits is, after all, just to compute, for each of the various policies that we are considering, what might be called its *expected utility*. The expected utility of a given policy is found by first multiplying the desirability of each possible total outcome by the probability that the policy in question will lead to that total outcome, and then adding the numbers obtained. As we have seen, finding the needed probabilities and assigning the required desirabilities will not be easy. But once we know the expected utility of each policy, is it not obvious that we should choose the policy with the highest expected utility? The answer, unfortunately, is no, it is not at all obvious.

Let us call the principle that we should adopt the policy with the highest expected utility the *utilitarian principle*. The following example should make it clear that, far from being trivial or tautological, the utilitarian

principle is a substantive and controversial moral principle.   Suppose that
the decision which confronts us is whether or not to adopt policy *A*.
What is more, suppose we know there is a probability close to 1 that
100,000 lives will be saved if we adopt *A*.   However, we also know that
there is a probability close to 1 that 1,000 will die as a direct result of our
adopting policy *A*, and these people would survive if we did not adopt *A*.
Finally, suppose that the other possible consequences of adopting *A* are
relatively inconsequential and can be ignored.   (For concreteness, we
might take *A* to be the establishment of a mass vaccination program, using
a relatively risky vaccine.)   Now plainly if we take the moral desirability of
saving a life to be exactly offset by the moral undesirability of causing a
death, then the utilitarian principle dictates that we adopt policy *A*.   But
many people feel uncomfortable with this result, the discomfort increasing with the number of deaths that would result from *A*.   If, to change the
example, the choice that confronts us is saving 100,000 lives while causing the deaths of 50,000 others a significant number of people are inclined to think that the morally right thing to do is to refrain from doing
A, and "let nature take its course."

   If we reject policy *A*, the likely reason is that we also reject the utilitarian principle.   Perhaps the most plausible reason for rejecting the utilitarian principle is the view that our obligation to *avoid doing harm* is stronger
than our obligation to do good.   There are many examples, some considerably more compelling than the one we have been discussing, which
seem to illustrate that in a broad range of cases we do feel that our obligation to avoid doing harm is greater than our obligation to do good.
Suppose, to take but one example, that my neighbor requests my help in
paying off his gambling debts.   He owes $5,000 to a certain bookmaker
with underworld connections.   Unless the neighbor pays the debt immediately, he will be shot.   Here, I think we are all inclined to say, I have no
strong obligation to give my neighbor the money he needs, and if I were
to do so it would be a supererogatory gesture.   By contrast, suppose a
representative of my neighbor's bookmaker approaches me and requests
that I shoot my neighbor.   If I refuse, he will see to it that my new car,
which cost $5,000, will be destroyed by a bomb while it sits unattended at
the curb.   In this case, surely, I have a strong obligation not to harm my
neighbor, although not shooting him will cost me $5,000.

   Suppose that this example and others convince us that we cannot
adopt the utilitarian principle, at least not in its most general form, where
it purports to be applicable to all moral decisions.   What are the alternatives?   One cluster of alternative principles would urge that in some or all
cases we weigh the harm a contemplated action will cause more heavily
than we weigh the good it will do.   The extreme form of such a principle
would dictate that we ignore the benefits entirely and opt for the action
or policy that produces the *least* expected harm.   .   .   .   A more plausible variant would allow us to count both benefits and harms in our deliberations, but would specify how much more heavily harms were to count.

   On my view, some moderate version of a "harm-weighted" principle is
preferable to the utilitarian principle in a considerable range of cases.
However, the recombinant DNA issue is not one of these cases.   Indeed, when we
try to apply a harm-weighted principle to the recombinant DNA case we
run head on into a conceptual problem of considerable difficulty.   The
distinction between doing good and doing harm presupposes a notion of
the normal or expectable course of events.   Roughly, if my action causes
you to be worse off than you would have been in the normal course of
events, then I have harmed you; if my action causes you to be better off

than in the normal course of events, then I have done you some good; and if my action leaves you just as you would be in the normal course of events, then I have done neither. In many cases, the normal course of events is intuitively quite obvious. Thus in the case of the neighbor and the bookmaker, in the expected course of events I would neither shoot my neighbor nor give him $5,000 to pay off his debts. Thus I am doing good if I give him the money and I am doing harm if I shoot him. But in other cases, including the recombinant DNA case, it is not at all obvious what constitutes the "expected course of events," and thus it is not at all obvious what to count as a harm. To see this, suppose that as a matter of fact many more deaths and illnesses will be prevented as a result of pursuing recombinant DNA research than will be caused by pursuing it. But suppose that there *will* be at least some people who become ill or die as a result of recombinant DNA research being pursued. If these are the facts, then who would be harmed by imposing a ban on recombinant DNA research? That depends on what we take to be the "normal course of events." Presumably, if we do not impose a ban, then the research will continue and the lives will be saved. If this is the normal course of events, then if we impose a ban we have *harmed* those people who would be saved. But it is equally natural to take as the normal course of events the situation in which recombinant DNA research is not pursued. And if *that* is the normal course of events, then those who would have been saved are not harmed by a ban, for they are no worse off than they would be in the normal course of events. However, on this reading of "the normal course of events," if we *fail* to impose a ban, then we have harmed those people who will ultimately become ill or die as a result of recombinant DNA research, since as a result of not imposing a ban they are worse off than they would have been in the normal course of events. I conclude that, in the absence of a theory detailing how we are to recognize the normal course of events, harm-weighted principles have no clear application to the case of recombinant DNA research.

Harm-weighted principles are not the only alternatives to the utilitarian principle. There is another cluster of alternatives that take off in quite a different direction. These principles urge that in deciding which policy to pursue there is a strong presumption in favor of policies that adhere to certain formal moral principles (that is, principles which do not deal with the *consequences* of our policies). Thus, to take the example most directly relevant to the recombinant DNA case, it might be urged that there is a strong presumption in favor of a policy which preserves freedom of scientific inquiry. In its extreme form, this principle would protect freedom of inquiry *no matter what the consequences*; . . . .. A much more plausible principle would urge that freedom of inquiry be protected until the balance of negative over positive consequences reaches a certain specified amount, at which point we would revert to the utilitarian principle. On such a view, if the expected utility of banning recombinant DNA research is a bit higher than the expected utility of allowing it to continue, then we would nonetheless allow it to continue. . . .

NOTES

1. The recombinant DNA debate is actually many different controversies—about facts, about politics and economics, and about moral views. Mary Williams, of the University of Delaware, suggests that the proponents of the research are utilitarians, while its opponents build their arguments on a form of Kantian absolutism. Williams, Ethical Theories Underlying the Recombinant DNA Controversy, in Recombinant DNA: Science, Ethics, and Politics 177 (J. Richards ed. 1978).

2. Physician-biologist Leon R. Kass of the University of Chicago has examined questions of distributive justice in the context of bioethics.

The introduction of any biomedical technology presents a new instance of an old problem—how to distribute scarce resources justly. We should assume that demand will usually exceed supply. Which people should receive a kidney transplant or an artificial heart? Who should get the benefits of genetic therapy or of brain stimulation? Is "first-come, first-served" the fairest principle? Or are certain people "more worthy," and if so, on what grounds?

It is unlikely that we will arrive at answers to these questions in the form of deliberate decisions. More likely, the problem of distribution will continue to be decided ad hoc and locally. If so, the consequence will probably be a sharp increase in the already far too great inequality of medical care. The extreme case will be longevity, which will probably be, at first, obtainable only at great expense. Who is likely to be able to buy it? Do conscience and prudence permit us to enlarge the gap between rich and poor, especially with respect to something as fundamental as life itself?

Questions of distributive justice also arise in the earlier decisions to acquire new knowledge and to develop new techniques. Personnel and facilities for medical research and treatment are scarce resources. Is the development of a new technology the best use of the limited resources, given current circumstances? How should we balance efforts aimed at prevention against those aimed at cure, or either of these against efforts to redesign the species? How should we balance the delivery of available levels of care against further basic research? More fundamentally, how should we balance efforts to eliminate poverty, pollution, urban decay, discrimination, and poor education? This last question about distribution is perhaps the most profound. We should reflect upon the social consequences of seducing many of our brightest young people to spend their lives locating the biochemical defects in rare genetic diseases, while our more serious problems go begging. The current squeeze on money for research provides us with an opportunity to rethink and reorder our priorities.

Problems of distributive justice are frequently mentioned and discussed, but they are hard to resolve in a rational manner. We find them especially difficult because of the enormous range of conflicting values and interests that characterizes our pluralistic society. We cannot agree—unfortunately, we often do not even try to agree—on standards for just distribution. Rather, decisions tend to be made largely out of a clash of competing interests. Thus, regrettably, the question of how to distribute justly often gets reduced to who shall decide how to distribute. The question about justice has led us to the question about power.

Kass, The New Biology: What Price Relieving Man's Estate, 174 Science 782 (1971). See generally Ch. 5, Sec. B, infra.

PHILIP HANDLER,
AN INTERVIEW

19 News Rep. Nat'l Acad.Sci. 9 (1969).

NEWS REPORT: Do you feel any constraints should be placed on fundamental research if there is some reason to believe that the results of that research might be harmful to society?

HANDLER: No. No constraints. Let me give you a dramatic illustration. You may know of the demonstration that one can take a fertilized frog egg, discard its nucleus and insert a nucleus from a somatic cell of some other frog, and the egg develops into a frog which is an absolutely perfect twin of the donor frog—the one that provided the transplanted nucleus. Presumably, by that technique we would make an indefinite number of perfect copies of that donor frog. It's merely a matter of time before we can switch from frogs to mammals. When we have the biological technology, we should be able to make perfect copies of the best bull or greatest cow in the world, in whatever number may be desired. This could go a long way toward improving world food production. Obviously, the next step would be man, and perhaps one day we may be able to make copies of a Bunche, Rabi, or Schirra, or of an Eldridge Cleaver, or Lew Alcindor or of any other geno-type identifiable in our population.

I hope that day never comes. I can't imagine any more dangerous tool in the hands of an autocratic, dictatorial, authoritarian government. It would be the most powerful mechanism ever devised—the ultimate despoliation of the human race, degradation of the worst order. We could create an ant-like society that is utterly repugnant. The idea of exploring all of the remarkable variety in the human gene pool is far more attractive. There are all kinds of people we have yet to produce. The human gene pool is colossal in its potential variety. The other idea leads to disaster.

And yet I think there is no alternative but to go down this trail and do the biological experimentation that, one day, may offer this kind of a capability. The idea that, since we can see this end possibility, we should by fiat state, "Thou shalt not in thy laboratory do any experiment which leads down that trail," is an equally repugnant thought. That kind of censorship is as repugnant as censorship of literature in other communities and is as potentially damaging. No constraints. Utilization of scientific information is a political and social decision and we have mechanisms in our society for arriving at such decisions. Let's use those. But no constraints on dissemination of facts, the ideas people are allowed to think, or the search for scientific understanding.

Historically, there isn't much we can do in the future that can compare to the shocks of the past. . . . The search for truth is man's noblest pursuit. Surely man's mind can live comfortably with the knowledge and understanding so gained without damage to man. And what better basis is there for the moral imperatives which guide our society?

NOTES ON SCIENCE AND MORALITY

1. Karl W. Deutsch presents a strong argument for the inherent interrelationship of science and morality:

Science itself depends for its life on the prior acceptance of certain fundamental values, such as the value of curiosity and learning, the value of truth, the value of sharing knowledge with others, the value of respect for facts, and the value of remembering the vastness of the universe in comparison with the finite knowledge of men at any particular moment. . . .

As science rests on certain values, so do almost all values depend on knowledge, and thus to some extent in turn on science, if they are to proceed from the realm of words to that of action. This implies a circular chain of causation or a feedback process, as do many processes of social and cultural development. To act morally is in one sense the opposite of acting blindly. It is acting in the presumed knowledge of what in fact it is that we are doing. Almost every significant action of this kind implies serious assumptions in some field of science. To love one's neighbor requires at the very least that we find out where and who our neighbor is. If we are to respond to his needs we must first ascertain what his needs are and what action in fact is likely to be helpful to him. . . . The duty to have good intentions . . . is meaningless without the duty to try to know the facts and try to foresee correctly the consequences of one's deeds, and it is this latter duty which may distinguish in practice the responsible from the irresponsible statesman, or the well-intentioned doctor from the well-intentioned quack.

Deutsch, Scientific and Humanistic Knowledge in the Growth of Civilization, in Science and the Creative Spirit 18–19 (H. Brown ed. 1958).

2. Theodore Roszak takes a much less benign view of the effects of science:

[T]here exists no way whatever, on strictly scientific grounds, to invalidate *any* objective quest for knowledge, regardless of where it may lead or how it may proceed. The particular project may be unpalatable to the more squeamish among us—for "purely personal reasons"; but it does not thereby cease to be a legitimate exercise of objectivity. After all, knowledge is knowledge; and the more of it, the better. Just as Leigh-Mallory set out to climb Everest simply because it was *there*, so the scientific mind sets out to solve puzzles and unravel mysteries because it perceives them as being *there*. What further justification need there be?

Once an area of experience has been identified as an object of study or experimental interference, there is no rational way in which to deny the inquiring mind its right to know, without calling into question the entire scientific enterprise. In order to do so, one would have to invoke some notion of the "sacred" or "sacrosanct" to designate an area of life that must be closed to inquiry and manipulation. But since the entire career of the objective consciousness has been one long running battle against such suspiciously nebulous ideas, these concepts survive in our society only as part of an atavistic vocabulary. They are withered roses we come upon, crushed in the diaries of a prescientific age.

We are sadly deceived by the old cliché which mournfully tells us that morality has failed to "keep up with" technical progress (as if indeed morality were a "field of knowledge" in the charge of unidentified, but presumably rather incompetent, experts). The expansion of objective consciousness must, of necessity, be undertaken at the expense of moral sensibility. Science deracinates the experience of sacredness wherever it abides, and does so unapologetically, if not with fanatic fervor. And lacking a warm and lively sense of the sacred, there can be no ethical commitment that is anything more than superficial humanist rhetoric. We are left with, at best, good intentions and well-meaning gestures that have no relationship to authoritative experience, and which therefore collapse into embarrassed confusion as soon as a more hard-headed, more objective inquirer comes along and asks, "But why not?" Having used the keen blade of scientific skepticism to clear our cultural ground of all irrational barriers to inquiry and manipulation, the objective consciousness is free to range in all directions. And it so does.

T. Roszak, The Making of a Counter-Culture 272–73 (1969).

THOMAS S. KUHN,
THE STRUCTURE OF SCIENTIFIC REVOLUTIONS

10–11, 52, 84–85, 165–167, 172 (1962).

In this essay, 'normal science' means research firmly based upon one or more past scientific achievements, achievements that some particular scientific community acknowledges for a time as supplying the foundation for its further practice. Today such achievements are recounted, though seldom in their original form, by science textbooks, elementary and advanced. These textbooks expound the body of accepted theory, illustrate many or all of its successful applications, and compare these applications with exemplary observations and experiments. Before such books became popular early in the nineteenth century (and until even more recently in the newly matured sciences), many of the famous classics of science fulfilled a similar function. Aristotle's *Physica*, Ptolemy's *Almagest*,

Newton's *Principia* and *Opticks*, Franklin's *Electricity*, Lavoisier's *Chemistry*, and Lyell's *Geology*—these and many other works served for a time implicitly to define the legitimate problems and methods of a research field for succeeding generations of practitioners. They were able to do so because they shared two essential characteristics. Their achievement was sufficiently unprecedented to attract an enduring group of adherents away from competing modes of scientific activity. Simultaneously, it was sufficiently open-ended to leave all sorts of problems for the redefined group of practitioners to resolve.

Achievements that share these two characteristics I shall henceforth refer to as 'paradigms,' a term that relates closely to 'normal science.' By choosing it, I mean to suggest that some accepted examples of actual scientific practice—examples which include law, theory, application, and instrumentation together—provide models from which spring particular coherent traditions of scientific research. These are the traditions which the historian describes under such rubrics as 'Ptolemaic astronomy' (or 'Copernican'), 'Aristotelian dynamics' (or 'Newtonian'), 'corpuscular optics' (or 'wave optics'), and so on. The study of paradigms, including many that are far more specialized than those named illustratively above, is what mainly prepares the student for membership in the particular scientific community with which he will later practice. Because he there joins men who learned the bases of their field from the same concrete models, his subsequent practice will seldom evoke overt disagreement over fundamentals. Men whose research is based on shared paradigms are committed to the same rules and standards for scientific practice. That commitment and the apparent consensus it produces are prerequisites for normal science, i.e., for the genesis and continuation of a particular research tradition. . . .

Normal science, the puzzle-solving activity we have just examined, is a highly cumulative enterprise, eminently successful in its aim, the steady extension of the scope and precision of scientific knowledge. In all these respects it fits with great precision the most usual image of scientific work. Yet one standard product of the scientific enterprise is missing. Normal science does not aim at novelties of fact or theory and, when successful, finds none. New and unsuspected phenomena are, however, repeatedly uncovered by scientific research, and radical new theories have again and again been invented by scientists. History even suggests that the scientific enterprise has developed a uniquely powerful technique for producing surprises of this sort. If this characteristic of science is to be reconciled with what has already been said, then research under a paradigm must be a particularly effective way of inducing paradigm change. That is what fundamental novelties of fact and theory do. Produced inadvertently by a game played under one set of rules, their assimilation requires the elaboration of another set. After they have become parts of science, the enterprise, at least of those specialists in whose particular field the novelties lie, is never quite the same again. . . .

The transition from a paradigm in crisis to a new one from which a new tradition of normal science can emerge is far from a cumulative process, one achieved by an articulation or extension of the old paradigm. Rather it is a reconstruction of the field from new fundamentals, a reconstruction that changes some of the field's most elementary theoretical generalizations as well as many of its paradigm methods and applications. During the transition period there will be a large but never complete overlap between the problems that can be solved by the old and by the new paradigm. But there will also be a decisive difference in the modes of solution. When the transition is complete, the profession will have changed its view of the field, its methods, and its goals. One perceptive historian, viewing a classic case of a science's reorientation by paradigm change, recently described it as "picking up the other end of the stick," a process that involves "handling the same bundle of data as before, but placing them in a new system of relations with one another by giving them a different framework." Others who have noted this aspect of scientific advance have emphasized its similarity to a change in visual gestalt: the marks on paper that were first seen as a bird are now seen as an antelope, or vice versa. . . .

In its normal state, then, a scientific community is an immensely efficient instrument for solving the problems or puzzles that its paradigms define. Furthermore, the result of solving those problems must inevitably be progress. There is no problem here. Seeing that much, however, only highlights the second main part of the problem of progress in the sciences. Let us therefore turn to it and ask about progress through extraordinary science. Why should progress also be the apparently universal concomitant of scientific revolutions? . . . If authority alone, and particularly if nonprofessional authority, were the arbiter of paradigm debates, the outcome of those debates might still be revolution, but it would not be *scientific* revolution. The very existence of science depends upon vesting the power to choose between paradigms in the members of a special kind of community. Just how special that community must be if science is to survive and grow may be indicated by the very tenuousness of humanity's hold on the scientific enterprise. Every civilization of which we have records has possessed a technology, an art, a religion, a political system, laws, and so on. In many cases those facets of civilization have been as developed as our own. But only the civilizations that descend from Hellenic Greece have possessed more than the most rudimentary science. The bulk of scientific knowledge is a product of Europe in the last four centuries. No other place and time has supported the very special communities from which scientific productivity comes.

What are the essential characteristics of these communities? Obviously, they need vastly more study. In this area only the most tentative generalizations are possible. Nevertheless, a number of requisites for membership in a professional scientific group must already be strikingly clear. The scientist must, for example, be concerned to solve problems about the behavior of nature. In addition, though his concern with nature may be global in its extent, the problems on which he works must be problems of detail. More important, the solutions that satisfy him may not be merely personal but must instead be accepted as solutions by many. The group that shares them may not, however, be drawn at random from society as a whole, but is rather the well-defined community of the scientist's professional compeers. One of the strongest, if still unwritten, rules of scientific life is the prohibition of appeals to heads of state or to the populace at large in matters scientific. Recognition of the existence of a uniquely competent professional group and acceptance of its role as the exclusive arbiter of professional achievement has further implications. The group's members, as individuals and by virtue of their shared training and experience, must be seen as the sole possessors of the rules of the game or of some equivalent basis for unequivocal judgments. To doubt that they shared some such basis for evaluations would be to admit the existence of incompatible standards of scientific achievement.

That admission would inevitably raise the question whether truth in the sciences can be one. . . .

Anyone who has followed the argument this far will nevertheless feel the need to ask why the evolutionary process should work. What must nature, including man, be like in order that science be possible at all? Why should scientific communities be able to reach a firm consensus unattainable in other fields? Why should consensus endure across one paradigm change after another? And why should paradigm change invariably produce an instrument more perfect in any sense than those known before? From one point of view those questions, excepting the first, have already been answered. But from another they are as open as they were when this essay began. It is not only the scientific community that must be special. The world of which that community is a part must also possess quite special characteristics, and we are no closer than we were at the start to knowing what these must be. That problem—What must the world be like in order that man may know it?—was not, however, created by this essay. On the contrary, it is as old as science itself, and it remains unanswered. But it need not be answered in this place. Any conception of nature compatible with the growth of science by proof is compatible with the evolutionary view of science developed here. Since this view is also compatible with close observation of scientific life, there are strong arguments for employing it in attempts to solve the host of problems that still remain.

ROBERT K. MERTON, SOCIAL THEORY AND SOCIAL STRUCTURE

607–615 (1968).

Four sets of institutional imperatives—universalism, communism, disinterestedness, organized scepticism—comprise the ethos of modern science.

Universalism finds immediate expression in the canon that truth claims, whatever their source, are to be subjected to *preestablished impersonal criteria*: consonant with observation and with previously confirmed knowledge. The acceptance or rejection of claims entering the lists of science is not to depend on the personal or social attributes of their protagonist; his race, nationality, religion, class and personal qualities are as such irrelevant. Objectivity precludes particularism. The circumstance that scientifically verified formulations refer to objective sequences and correlations militates against all efforts to impose particularistic criteria of validity. The Haber process cannot be invalidated by a Nuremberg decree nor can an Anglophobe repeal the law of gravitation. The chauvinist may expunge the names of alien scientists from historical textbooks but their formulations remain indispensable to science and technology. However *echt-deutsch* or hundred-per-cent American the final increment, some aliens are accessories before the fact of every new technical advance. The imperative of universalism is rooted deep in the impersonal character of science.

. . .

'Communism,' in the non-technical and extended sense of common ownership of goods, is a second integral element of the scientific ethos. The substantive findings of science are a product of social collaboration and are assigned to the community. They constitute a common heritage in which the equity of the individual producer is severely limited. An

eponymous law or theory does not enter into the exclusive possession of
the discoverer and his heirs, nor do the mores bestow upon them special
rights of use and disposition. Property rights in science are whittled
down to a bare minimum by the rationale of the scientific ethic. The
scientist's claim to 'his' intellectual 'property' is limited to that of recognition and esteem which, if the institution functions with a modicum of efficiency, is roughly commensurate with the significance of the increments
brought to the common fund of knowledge. Eponymy—e.g., the Copernican system, Boyle's law—is thus at once a mnemonic and a commemo-
rative device.

Given such institutional emphasis upon recognition and esteem as the
sole property right of the scientist in his discoveries, the concern with
scientific priority becomes a 'normal' response. Those controversies over
priority which punctuate the history of modern science are generated by
the institutional accent on originality. There issues a competitive cooperation. The products of competition are communized, and esteem accrues
to the producer. Nations take up claims to priority, and fresh entries into
the commonwealth of science are tagged with the names of nationals: witness the controversy raging over the rival claims of Newton and Leibniz
to the differential calculus. But all this does not challenge the status of
scientific knowledge as common property.

The institutional conception of science as part of the public domain is
linked with the imperative for communication of findings. Secrecy is the
antithesis of this norm; full and open communication its enactment. The
pressure for diffusion of results is reenforced by the institutional goal of
advancing the boundaries of knowledge and by the incentive of recognition which is, of course, contingent upon publication. A scientist who
does not communicate his important discoveries to the scientific fraternity—thus, a Henry Cavendish—becomes the target for ambivalent responses. He is esteemed for his talent and, perhaps, for his modesty.
But, institutionally considered, his modesty is seriously misplaced, in view
of the moral compulsive for sharing the wealth of science. Layman
though he is, Aldous Huxley's comment on Cavendish is illuminating in
this connection: "Our admiration of his genius is tempered by a certain
disapproval; we feel that such a man is selfish and anti-social." The epithets are particularly instructive for they imply the violation of a definite
institutional imperative. Even though it serves no ulterior motive, the
suppression of scientific discovery is condemned.

The communal character of science is further reflected in the recognition by scientists of their dependence upon a cultural heritage to which
they lay no differential claims. Newton's remark—"If I have seen farther
it is by standing on the shoulders of giants"—expresses at once a sense of
indebtedness to the common heritage and a recognition of the essentially
cooperative and cumulative quality of scientific achievement. The humility of scientific genius is not simply culturally appropriate but results from
the realization that scientific advance involves the collaboration of past
and present generations. . . .

Science, as is the case with the professions in general, includes disinterestedness as a basic institutional element. Disinterestedness is not to
be equated with altruism nor interested action with egoism. Such
equivalences confuse institutional and motivational levels of analysis. A
passion for knowledge, idle curiosity, altruistic concern with the benefit to
humanity and a host of other special motives have been attributed to the
scientist. The quest for distinctive motives appears to have been misdi-

rected. *It is rather a distinctive pattern of institutional control of a wide range of motives which characterizes the behavior of scientists.* For once the institution enjoins disinterested activity, it is to the interest of the scientists to conform on pain of sanctions and, in so far as the norm has been internalized, on pain of psychological conflict. . . .

Organized scepticism is variously interrelated with the other elements of the scientific ethos. It is both a methodologic and an institutional mandate. The suspension of judgment until 'the facts are at hand' and the detached scrutiny of beliefs in terms of empirical and logical criteria have periodically involved science in conflict with other institutions. Science which asks questions of fact, including potentialities, concerning every aspect of nature and society may come into conflict with other attitudes toward these same data which have been crystallized and often ritualized by other institutions. . . .

NOTES ON THE LOGIC OF SCIENCE

1. The scientific process involves the construction and testing of hypotheses. In a famous discussion of "the task of the logic of scientific discovery, or the logic of knowledge," Karl Popper argued that it is "not the *verifiability* but the *falsifiability* of a system" that is a criterion of its being empirical or scientific.

> Various objections might be raised against the criterion of demarcation here proposed. In the first place, it may well seem somewhat wrong-headed to suggest that science, which is supposed to give us positive information, should be characterized as satisfying a negative requirement such as refutability. However, . . . this objection has little weight, since the amount of positive information about the world which is conveyed by a scientific statement is the greater the more likely it is to clash, because of its logical character, with possible singular statements. (Not for nothing do we call the laws of nature 'laws': the more they prohibit the more they say.) . . .

K. Popper, The Logic of Scientific Discovery 27, 41 (1968).

2. An interesting twist on this apparently neutral scientific method arose early in the recombinant DNA story, during the meeting of the RAC in La Jolla, California, in December 1975. Sydney Brenner suggested doing "a dangerous experiment" (in an appropriately secure laboratory) to see if bacteria with plasmids containing DNA from the polyoma virus could cause tumors (or at least produce polyoma antibodies) in mice that had been fed the bacteria. The appearance of symptoms of polyoma infection would almost certainly require tightening the NIH guidelines. Brenner's view was that the research would at least produce "numbers," whatever its results. But Wallace Rowe, the NIH chief virus researcher declared, "I won't do the experiment," when others said that a negative result would make the NIH guidelines "almost irrelevant." In the end, however, the RAC decided unanimously to authorize the experiment. See Rogers, Biohazard 175–176 (1977). Does it seem appropriate for scientists to refuse to do research because they believe that the results, although accurate, will be "overinterpreted" by others or, especially, will lead to bad public policy?

3. Does the "either-or" approach of falsifiability theory seem an adequate description of the world? According to the distinguished scientist and student of Chinese culture, Joseph Needham, it was not a part of traditional science in China. Indeed, while formal logic is more fully incorporated into the linguistic structure of Chinese than of any Indo-European language, abstract logic never gained the central place in China that it has in the Aristotelian traditions of the West. Needham, History and Human Values: A Chinese Perspective for World Science and Technology, 20 Centennial Rev. 1, 27–30 (1976).

C.P. SNOW,
THE TWO CULTURES

4–7, 10–11 (1964).

Literary intellectuals at one pole—at the other scientists, and as the most representative, the physical scientists. Between the two a gulf of mutual incomprehension—sometimes (particularly among the young) hostility and dislike, but most of all lack of understanding. They have a curious distorted image of each other. Their attitudes are so different that, even on the level of emotion, they can't find much common ground. Non-scientists tend to think of scientists as brash and boastful. They hear Mr. T.S. Eliot, who just for these illustrations we can take as an archetypal figure, saying about his attempts to revive verse-drama that we can hope for very little, but that he would feel content if he and his co-workers could prepare the ground for a new Kyd or a new Greene. That is the tone, restricted and constrained, with which literary intellectuals are at home: it is the subdued voice of their culture. Then they hear a much louder voice, that of another archetypal figure, Rutherford, trumpeting: 'This is the heroic age of science! This is the Elizabethan age!' Many of us heard that, and a good many other statements beside which that was mild; and we weren't left in any doubt whom Rutherford was casting for the role of Shakespeare. What is hard for the literary intellectuals to understand, imaginatively or intellectually, is that he was absolutely right.

And compare 'this is the way the world ends, not with a bang but a whimper'—incidentally, one of the least likely scientific prophecies ever made—compare that with Rutherford's famous repartee, 'Lucky fellow, Rutherford, always on the crest of the wave.' 'Well, I made the wave, didn't I?'

The non-scientists have a rooted impression that the scientists are shallowly optimistic, unaware of man's condition. On the other hand, the scientists believe that the literary intellectuals are totally lacking in foresight, peculiarly unconcerned with their brother men, in a deep sense anti-intellectual, anxious to restrict both art and thought to the existential moment. And so on. Anyone with a mild talent for invective could produce plenty of this kind of subterranean back-chat. On each side there is some of it which is not entirely baseless. It is all destructive. Much of it rests on misinterpretations which are dangerous. . . .

First, about the scientists' optimism. This is an accusation which has been made so often that it has become a platitude. It has been made by some of the acutest non–scientific minds of the day. But it depends upon a confusion between the individual experience and the social experience, between the individual condition of man and his social condition. Most of the scientists I have known well have felt—just as deeply as the non-scientists I have known well—that the individual condition of each of us is tragic. Each of us is alone: sometimes we escape from solitariness, through love or affection or perhaps creative moments, but those triumphs of life are pools of light we make for ourselves while the edge of the road is black: each of us dies alone. Some scientists I have known have had faith in revealed religion. Perhaps with them the sense of the tragic condition is not so strong. I don't know. With most people of deep feeling, however high-spirited and happy they are, sometimes most with those who are happiest and most high-spirited, it seems to be right in the fibres, part of the weight of life. That is as true of the scientists I have known best as of anyone at all.

But nearly all of them—and this is where the colour of hope genuinely comes in—would see no reason why, just because the individual condition is tragic, so must the social condition be. Each of us is solitary: each of us dies alone: all right, that's a fate against which we can't struggle—but there is plenty in our condition which is not fate, and against which we are less than human unless we do struggle.

Most of our fellow human beings, for instance, are underfed and die before their time. In the crudest terms, *that* is the social condition. There is a moral trap which comes through the insight into man's loneliness: it tempts one to sit back, complacent in one's unique tragedy, and let the others go without a meal.

As a group, the scientists fall into that trap less than others. They are inclined to be impatient to see if something can be done: and inclined to think that it can be done, until it's proved otherwise. That is their real optimism, and it's an optimism that the rest of us badly need. . . . If I were to risk a piece of shorthand, I should say that naturally they had the future in their bones. . . .

EDWARD H. LEVI,
AN INTRODUCTION TO LEGAL REASONING

1, 3–5 (1949).

It is important that the mechanism of legal reasoning should not be concealed by its pretense. The pretense is that the law is a system of known rules applied by a judge; the pretense has long been under attack.[1] In an important sense legal rules are never clear, and, if a rule had to be clear before it could be imposed, society would be impossible. The mechanism accepts the differences of view and ambiguities of words. It provides for the participation of the community in resolving the ambiguity by providing a forum for the discussion of policy in the gap of ambiguity. On serious controversial questions, it makes it possible to take the first step in the direction of what otherwise would be forbidden ends. The mechanism is indispensable to peace in a community. . . .

Therefore it appears that the kind of reasoning involved in the legal process is one in which the classification changes as the classification is made. The rules change as the rules are applied. More important, the rules arise out of a process which, while comparing fact situations, creates the rules and then applies them. But this kind of reasoning is open to the charge that it is classifying things as equal when they are somewhat different, justifying the classification by rules made up as the reasoning or classification proceeds. In a sense all reasoning is of this type, but there is an additional requirement which compels the legal process to be this way. Not only do new situations arise, but in addition peoples' wants change. The categories used in the legal process must be left ambiguous in order to permit the infusion of new ideas. And this is true even where legislation or a constitution is involved. The words used by the legislature or the constitutional convention must come to have new meanings. Furthermore, agreement on any other basis would be impossible. In this manner the laws come to express the ideas of the community and even

1. The controlling book is Frank, Law and the Modern Mind (1936).

when written in general terms, in statute or constitution, are molded for the specific case.

But attention must be paid to the process. A controversy as to whether the law is certain, unchanging, and expressed in rules, or uncertain, changing, and only a technique for deciding specific cases misses the point. It is both. Nor is it helpful to dispose of the process as a wonderful mystery possibly reflecting a higher law, by which the law can remain the same and yet change. The law forum is the most explicit demonstration of the mechanism required for a moving classification system. The folklore of law may choose to ignore the imperfections in legal reasoning, but the law forum itself has taken care of them.

What does the law forum require? It requires the presentation of competing examples. The forum protects the parties and the community by making sure that the competing analogies are before the court. The rule which will be created arises out of a process in which if different things are to be treated as similar, at least the differences have been urged. In this sense the parties as well as the court participate in the law-making. In this sense, also, lawyers represent more than the litigants.

Reasoning by example in the law is a key to many things. It indicates in part the hold which the law process has over the litigants. They have participated in the law-making. They are bound by something they helped to make. Moreover, the examples or analogies urged by the parties bring into the law the common ideas of the society. The ideas have their day in court, and they will have their day again. This is what makes the hearing fair, rather than any idea that the judge is completely impartial, for of course he cannot be completely so. Moreover, the hearing in a sense compels at least vicarious participation by all the citizens, for the rule which is made, even though ambiguous, will be law as to them.

BENJAMIN N. CARDOZO, THE PARADOXES OF LEGAL SCIENCE

1–4 (1956).

"They do things better with logarithms." The wail escapes me now and again when after putting forth the best that is in me, I look upon the finished product, and cannot say that it is good. In these moments of disquietude, I figure to myself the peace of mind that must come, let us say, to the designer of a mighty bridge. The finished product of his work is there before his eyes with all the beauty and simplicity and inevitableness of truth. He is not harrowed by misgivings whether the towers and piers and cables will stand the stress and strain. His business is to know. If his bridge were to fall, he would go down with it in disgrace and ruin. Yet withal, he has never a fear. No mere experiment has he wrought, but a highway to carry men and women from shore to shore, to carry them secure and unafraid, though the floods rage and boil below.

So I cry out at times in rebellion, "why cannot I do as much, or at least something measurably as much to bridge with my rules of law the torrents of life?" I have given my years to the task, and behind me are untold generations, the judges and lawgivers of old, who strove with a passion as burning. Code and commentary, manor-roll and year-book, treatise and law-report, reveal the processes of trial and error by which they struggled to attain the truth, enshrine their blunders and their triumphs for warning and example. All these memorials are mine; yet unwritten is my table of logarithms, the index of the power to which a precedent must be raised to produce the formula of justice. My bridges are experiments. I cannot span the tiniest stream in a region unexplored by judges or lawgivers before me, and go to rest in the secure belief that the span is wisely laid.

Let me not seem to cavil at the difficulties that learning can subdue. They are trying enough in all conscience, yet what industry can master, it would be weakness to lament. I am not thinking of the multitude of precedents and the labor of making them our own. The pangs that convulse are born of other trials. Diligence and memory and normal powers of reasoning may suffice to guide us truly in those fields where the judicial function is imitative or static, where known rules are to be applied to combinations of facts identical with present patterns, or, at worst, but slightly different. The travail comes when the judicial function is dynamic or creative. The rule must be announced for a novel situation where competitive analogies supply a hint or clew, but where precedents are lacking with authoritative commands.

I know the common answer to these and like laments. The law is not an exact science, we are told, and there the matter ends, if we are willing there to end it. One does not appease the rebellion of the intellect by the reaffirmance of the evil against which intellect rebels. Exactness may be impossible, but this is not enough to cause the mind to acquiesce in a predestined incoherence. Jurisprudence will be the gainer in the long run by fanning the fires of mental insurrection instead of smothering them with platitudes. "If science," says Whitehead, "is not to degenerate into a medley of *ad hoc* hypotheses, it must become philosophical and must enter upon a thorough criticism of its own foundations." We may say the like of law.

So I keep reaching out and groping for a pathway to the light. The outlet may not be found. At least there may be glimmerings that will deny themselves to a craven *non possumus,* the sterility of ignoble ease. Somewhere beneath the welter, there may be a rationalizing principle revealing system and harmony in what passes for discord and disorder. Modern science is tending to revolutionize our ideas of motion within the atom, and so of motion generally. We had thought of radiation as continuous and flowing. We are told that in truth it is discrete and irregular.
.   .   .   Is it possible that in rationalizing the development of law, in measuring the radiating energy of principle and precedent, we have been hampered by a like illusion? We have sought for a formula consistent with steady advance through a continuum. The continuum does not exist. Instead there are leaps from point to point. We have been beguiled by the ideal of an harmonious progression. Centres of energy exist, of attraction and repulsion. A landing-place is found between them. We make these landing places for ourselves through the methods of the judicial process. How shall they be wrought? Where shall they be found?
.   .   .

NOTES

1. What are the main contrasts between science and the law? Consider in particular their approaches to the universality of knowledge, the nature of "truth," and the role of (and means for resolving) disputes.

2. Are lawyers likely to be particularly pessimistic (or cynical) compared with what Snow says some view as scientists' "shallow optimism?" The subject matter of law—human relations—is certainly capable of giving rise to pessimism. Yet

Snow argues further that scientists are rightly optimistic about improving social conditions. What, if anything, does science tell us, for example, about whether poverty can be eliminated?

3. Are there "paradigms" in law in the sense that Kuhn uses the term? Levi's image of a "moving classification system" responding to changing desires could be seen as presenting law as an evolutionary process somewhat similar to science. But law rarely appears as cumulative and progressive as science. Is it inevitable that legal rules seem to swing back and forth rather than moving forward? Cardozo holds out hope that someday judges may discover a rationalizing principle that will bring order out of chaos. Would the results be permanent or would they change as quickly as society changes?

4. In addition to the contrast between the values of science and the law, other clashes can occur. The involvement of commercial firms in sponsorship of basic research in molecular and microbial genetics in university laboratories poses "dangers to traditional academic values," according to Robert Sinsheimer of the University of California at Santa Cruz. At a closed meeting at Parajo Dunes, California, in March 1982, the presidents of five universities active in biotechnology (along with representatives from their faculties and from businesses with which they had some connection) agreed on a general statement, while leaving the writing of rules to each institution at a later time. President Derek Bok of Harvard found the meeting "reassuring" because a consensus emerged "about the importance of maintaining academic values while acknowledging the possibility of creating sound relationships." Culliton, Pajaro Dunes: The Search for Consensus, 216 Science 155 (1982). See generally Ch. 3, Sec. A.5, infra.

5. What are "academic values," and do they differ at all from "scientific values"? What role should outsiders have in protecting them—indeed, are they capable of being protected by nonacademics, such as legislators? See, e.g., Subcomm. on Investigations and Oversight, and Subcomm. on Science, Research and Technology, House Comm. on Science and Technology, 97th Cong., 2d Sess., Joint Hearings on the Academic-Industrial Complex (1982).

6. The search for "appropriate institutions" in Sec. B.5, supra, revealed the possibility of relying on scientific self-control (individual and collective) or on governmental regulation. Could such regulation include a complete ban on an area of research if the legislature decided it was too risky in its means or in its likely ends? A recent National Science Foundation survey of Americans' attitudes showed that almost two-thirds believe that genetic engineering studies aimed at "new life forms" should not be pursued. 215 Science 270 (1982).

Contrarily, is "scientific freedom" (to think? to test theories? to experiment with people?) protected by the Constitution? Why should science be different from other trades or professions? Is the protection of scientific freedom a matter of settled law or merely custom? See Ch. 4, Sec. A.2 infra, for a fuller exploration of these issues.

Walter Rosenblith has observed that, "scientists and scholars have long had a bargain with society by which they have produced ideas and devices with few constraints, but . . . now this bargain is in danger of breaking down or in need of revision." Graham, Concerns About Science and Attempts to Regulate Industry, 107 Daedalus 1 (Spring 1978). For further discussion of the constitutional dimension of these issues with special attention to gene splicing, see Delgado & Miller, God, Galileo, and Government: Toward Constitutional Protection for Scientific Inquiry, 53 Wash.L.Rev. 349 (1978); Robertson, The Scientist's Right to Research: A Constitutional Analysis, 51 S.Cal.L.Rev. 1203 (1977); Cohen, When May Research Be Stopped?, 296 New Eng.J.Med. 1203 (1977); Stetten, Freedom of Enquiry, 81 Genetics 416 (1975).

D. APPLYING GENETIC ENGINEERING TO HUMAN BEINGS

1. USES: PRESENT AND PROSPECTIVE

The experience with genetic engineering in microorganisms illustrates how difficult it is for any process of reviewing science and medicine to separate concerns about means from those about ends. The same problem arises as we turn to the application of gene splicing techniques to human beings. The question of means—taken up under the title "experimentation with human subjects" in Chapter 6, infra—must be confronted early on in any new medical field.

But often more important is the question: What are the goals in this field? Of the three objectives usually cited for genetic engineering—producing drugs and vaccines, improving genetic screening and prenatal diagnosis, and curing genetic conditions—the third (and most controversial) receives most attention in this section. The specific goals in this area should, however, be just a springboard for a broader inquiry into the goals of the life sciences, which might include the pursuit of knowledge, the relief of suffering, the promotion of health and even of happiness, and the betterment of the whole society.

PRESIDENT'S COMMISSION FOR THE STUDY OF ETHICAL PROBLEMS IN MEDICINE AND BIOMEDICAL AND BEHAVIORAL RESEARCH, SPLICING LIFE

42–48 (1982).

In the immediate future, the most important applications of gene splicing techniques for human health will probably be in the creation of products—hormones, enzymes, vaccines, and so forth—for human consumption and in the development of genetic screening. But in the long run, direct use of the technique in humans can be expected to have an impact that is much more significant in terms of changing people's health and developmental status, and more novel and far-reaching in conceptual and psychological terms. During 1982, the prospect of direct application of gene splicing to cure human genetic diseases moved forward by large steps, although formidable hurdles remain.

The simplest form of human gene splicing would be directed at single gene mutations, which are now known to cause more than 2000 human disorders. Such a defect in just one gene—although each human cell has as many as 100,000 genes—can have tragic and even fatal consequences. Existing treatments of genetic diseases are all palliative rather than curative—that is, they are merely aimed at modifying the consequences of a defective gene. In contrast, gene splicing technology offers the possibility of correcting the defects themselves and thus curing at least some of these diseases. The effects of gene splicing might be limited to the somatic cells of the individual being treated or might, intentionally or otherwise, alter the germ cells, thereby creating a change in the genes that would be passed on to future generations.

Somatic Cells. The basic method proposed for using gene splicing on human beings is termed "gene therapy." This is defined as the introduction of a normal functioning gene into a cell in which its defective counterpart is active. If the mutant gene is not removed but merely supplemented, the cells may continue to produce the defective product alongside the normal product generated by the newly added gene.

Even further in the future is a theoretical possibility, sometimes referred to as "gene surgery," in which not only would the normal gene be added but the defective gene itself would either be excised or its function suppressed, so that it would no longer send out a message for a defective product in competition with the message from the inserted "normal" gene.

The technology, which researchers are now attempting to develop, involves four steps: cloning the normal gene, introducing the cloned genes in a stable fashion into appropriate target cells by means of a vector, regulating the production of the gene product, and ensuring that no harm occurs to the host cells in the patient. Only the first step—cloning a normal counterpart of a defective gene—is a straightforward matter with current knowledge and technology.

Introducing copies of the normal gene specifically to a particular set of target cells can, in theory, be achieved. Gene therapy offers the greatest promise for those single-gene defects in which an identifiable product is expressed in a discrete subpopulation of cells. For example, sickle-cell anemia and beta-thalassemia (also called Cooley's anemia) both involve alterations in the hemoglobin gene that is expressed in an accessible subpopulation of cells (that is, bone marrow cells) that could be removed from the body for gene treatment and then returned to the patient. These two diseases have therefore been among the early objects of attention for researchers designing gene therapy techniques.

In most other cases, it is not practical to remove the target cells (such as brain cells in people with Tay-Sachs disease) for gene repair. A far more promising approach takes advantage of the distinctive properties of different cells, the unique markers each type of cell has on its surface. Once the unique marker for particular cells has been identified, it may be possible to construct a special "package," carrying copies of the normal gene, that will home in on this marker and deliver the new genes exclusively to the cells where the defective gene is active.

Once in the cell, the normal gene may persist as an independent unit, like a plasmid, or may integrate itself randomly somewhere in the DNA. The principal problem is inducing the host cell to produce the proper amount of the desired product. Lack of expression of the normal gene would prevent the "therapy" from being effective, whereas excess production could be deleterious or even fatal. Although transposable elements of the sort that permitted new genetic material to be inserted in a nonrandom fashion and properly expressed in the experiments with fruit flies have not yet been identified in human beings, a comparable set of DNA appears to exist in human beings.

A final worry is that introducing a new gene may disrupt the functioning of the existing cells. For example, were the new piece of DNA to be spliced in the middle of another gene, it could create a gene defect that is worse than the defect the gene therapy was intended to correct.

Despite these technical stumbling blocks, two attempts have already been made at gene therapy. The first—which relied on viral transduction before recombinant DNA techniques were discovered—occurred more than a decade ago and attracted little public attention. Several German sisters had a rare metabolic error that caused them to develop a high level of a substance called arginine in their bloodstream. Left uncorrected, this genetic defect leads to metabolic and neurologic abnormalities, including severe mental retardation. No treatment for argininemia was known, so medical researchers in Germany decided to take advantage of a characteristic of the Shope virus, which, although apparently harmless to human beings, causes people exposed to it to have an unusually low level of arginine. Researchers infected the girls with the virus, in the hope that it would transfer to them its gene for the enzyme that the body needs to metabolize arginine. This attempt to add new genetic material failed— that is, the buildup of arginine continued.

The second attempt at gene therapy in human beings involved a controversial experiment in 1980 on patients suffering from beta-thalassemia. . . .

Popular notions regarding gene therapy range from seeing it as a weapon for fighting *any* disease to hailing it as a tool for changing human characteristics, including removal of a hypothetical "aggression gene" from hardened criminals. These notions are unrealistic. Many diseases have multigenic or unknown etiologies; human attributes such as kindness or aggression are most certainly the result of a complex interaction of multigenic and environmental factors. The forms of genetic treatment now being discussed would be relevant to such conditions only if the effects of specific genes could be identified and particularly if some of these genes prove to be major determinants, since attempts to change a number of genes at the same time would probably be extremely difficult. It is therefore highly unlikely that in the foreseeable future predictable changes in such attributes could be achieved through genetic alterations.

Gene therapy carried out on somatic cells, such as bone marrow cells, would resemble standard medical therapies in that they all involve changes limited to the cells of the person being treated. They differ, however, in that gene therapy involves an inherent and probably permanent change in the body rather than requiring repeated applications of an outside force or substance. An analogy is organ transplantation, which also involves the incorporation into an individual of cells containing DNA of "foreign" origin.

Germ-Line Cells. Thus far, attempts at gene therapy have focused on treating a discrete population of patients' somatic cells. Some researchers believe that certain forms of gene therapy that have been considered, such as the use of a virus to carry the desired gene to the patient's cells, might also affect germinal cells. Furthermore, gene therapy could also be applied to fertilized human eggs (zygotes) in conjunction with *in vitro* fertilization techniques.[31] Whereas the effects of genetic therapy on somatic cells would be expected to be limited to the individual patient treated, DNA therapy to fertilized eggs would probably affect all cells—including the germ cells—of the developing embryo; assuming normal birth, devel-

---

31. The approach would involve the following: (1) isolating and amplifying the desired gene by standard recombinant DNA techniques, (2) removing a mature ovum from a woman and fertilizing it *in vitro*, (3) injecting copies of the cloned gene into the fertilized egg (zygote) using microsurgical techniques, and (4) implanting the genetically altered zygote into the woman's uterus.

opment, and reproduction, the individual would then pass on the altered gene to his or her offspring according to Mendelian rules. Zygote therapy would thus involve an alteration of the genetic inheritance of future generations and a significant departure from standard medical therapy.

To date, genetic engineering experiments using zygotes have been conducted for academic rather than therapeutic reasons. Several laboratories are currently working on fertilized mouse eggs. In one experiment, mice developed from zygotes injected with the rabbit hemoglobin gene were reported to contain rabbit hemoglobin in their red blood cells. The medical significance is obvious. In a case where both parents are carriers of a particular recessive disorder the risk of an affected child is one in four. But if the relevant normal gene could safely be introduced *in vitro* to a fertilized egg of that couple, the individual who resulted from the egg would not have the disease and none of his or her descendants would be at risk for that disease.

Zygote therapy differs significantly from gene therapy on somatic cells in several ways. First, from the standpoint of the individual it may be useful in the treatment of genetic diseases, like cystic fibrosis, that affect many tissues—lungs, pancreas, intestines, and sex organs—rather than a discrete, accessible subpopulation of cells. Successful treatment at a very early stage of development would confer "good" genes to all the organs of an afflicted individual. Second, from the societal standpoint, such therapy if ever practiced on a vast scale could potentially reduce the overall frequency in the population of genes that usually have deleterious consequences, such as the sickle-cell gene.

Although zygote therapy may hold great promise, it is also fraught with technical risks and uncertainties. First of all, the technique itself is largely unproven, even with laboratory animals. For example, the success rate of microinjecting genes into mouse embryos remains low. Increasing the amount of DNA injected into a zygote makes it more likely that a gene will be incorporated, but it also increases the mortality rate of embryos. Microinjection of DNA into zygotes is obviously not a benign procedure.

The second major technical drawback at present is that transferred genes integrate randomly in the genome. Depending on the site of integration and perhaps the physiological state of the embryo, some of the foreign genes may be expressed and others not. Thus far, in experiments with mice, genes are rarely expressed in a tissue-specific way. Even then, expression of the microinjected foreign gene in somatic tissue has not resulted in stable inheritance of that expression, which is essential if the purpose is to introduce a new trait permanently. The consequences of having the wrong tissues producing the products of inserted genes could be disastrous.

Finally, as in gene therapy on somatic cells, introducing foreign DNA into the zygote may affect the regulation of the cell in some undetermined way. Embryological development depends on a precise set of genetic instructions; disruption of this process is therefore much more likely to have serious adverse consequences than a disruption of the regulatory mechanisms operating in a subset of somatic cells. Instead of being therapeutic, therapy on zygotes or on more-developed embryos might be teratogenic and increase the incidence of congenital abnormalities.

. . .

Furthermore, unless the presence or absence of a genetic defect could be established at a very early stage without harm—that is, at or just prior to fertilization or in a 2 to 4 cell zygote—it would be difficult to determine to whom gene therapy ought to be applied. Yet without such a determination, the use of gene splicing as a "treatment" seems dubious. In most cases identified by genetic screening, both parents are carriers of a recessive condition (those who have only a single defective gene of a pair and do not manifest the disease); in such cases, there is only a 25% chance that the disease is present in any zygote. It would not seem appropriate to run the risk of zygote therapy when three out of four of the potential "patients" do not need treatment.

Therefore, the technical uncertainties, the ethical implications, and the low probability of actually treating an affected person are strong contraindications against therapy of fertilized eggs or embryos becoming a useful clinical option in the near future.

NOTES

1. The 1980 experiment on beta-thalassemia resulted in a UCLA physician becoming the first biomedical investigator formally sanctioned by NIH for violating regulations on government-supported research with human beings. Consider how this incident might appear through the eyes of one of the patient-subjects, the physician-investigator, the members of the various review committees, and the officials of NIH.

. . . Dr. Martin J. Cline failed to disclose to the IRB [Institutional Review Board] at Hadassah Hospital in Israel, or to the patients in Israel and Italy, that the bone marrow transplants would contain recombinant DNA material despite the fact that the review board at Hadassah went to considerable length to verify that the procedure would *not* involve recombinant DNA. (There are no review committees in Italy comparable to IRBs.) Moreover, the procedures he used were the same as those submitted to the IRB at UCLA in May 1979 and disapproved on July 16, 1980, after four outside consultants all advised that more animal studies should be conducted prior to human experimentation.

The UCLA general assurance with HHS specifically states that all research performed by UCLA employees (even if performed elsewhere) must be reviewed by an IRB at the collaborating institution; and UCLA must receive a report of that review. Although no NIH funds were used to perform the studies abroad, or to pay the cost of the trip, the materials used in Israel and Italy were prepared at UCLA as part of research supported by NIH.

The Office for Protection from Research Risks at NIH first became aware of the possibility that Dr. Cline had performed research using recombinant DNA and in violation of NIH rules in September 1980. Following a letter from the NIH Director to the UCLA Chancellor, and the Chancellor's reply, the Director established an ad hoc committee to consider the report from UCLA, determine whether NIH regulations had been violated, and recommend appropriate action. Meanwhile Dr. Cline's resignation from his position as Chief of Hematology and Oncology was accepted by the UCLA Chancellor and the Medical School Dean as appropriate under the circumstances.

The NIH ad hoc committee reported in May 1981 that Dr. Cline's activities violated both the NIH Guidelines on use of recombinant DNA and the Department's regulations for the protection of human subjects. The Committee recommended that four actions be taken and NIH Director Fredrickson accepted them all: (1) prior NIH approval will be required for any new application from Dr. Cline for NIH support of research involving human subjects; (2) prior NIH approval will be required for each project of his involving recombinant DNA; (3) the Director of each NIH Institute currently supporting research grants for which Dr. Cline is principal investigator should forward the report of the Ad Hoc Committee to the Institute's Advisory Council for advice regarding continuation of such grants; and (4) for each application for new or competing renewal of NIH grants, the study sections and National Advisory Councils shall consider the report of the Ad Hoc Committee in making decisions regarding support of the research.

All four recommendations were implemented. In September and October 1981, National Advisory Councils of the three NIH institutes that had been funding Dr. Cline's research reviewed the ad hoc committee's report and forwarded their recommendations to the Acting Director, NIH, through the Associate Director for Extramural Research and Training who endorsed all but one recommendation. . . .

Although Dr. Cline had been asked to comment on a *draft* of the NIH ad hoc committee's report and had replied that he had no response to make "at this time," he was not invited to respond at any other time or in any other manner to the charges against him. Finally, knowing the ad hoc committee's negative conclusions but not knowing when the advisory councils would act upon them nor how to contact the councils, Dr. Cline sent a letter to the Executive Secretary of the ad hoc committee on September 17, 1981, to be forwarded to the advisory councils "providing arguments in support of his actions as well as more general comments on review and approval of innovative research." That letter, however, was not received by NIH until September 28 and thus was too late to be taken into consideration by the two National Advisory Councils that reviewed his case on September 24 and 25. Only the National Cancer Advisory Board (which did not meet until October 6) had Dr. Cline's letter at the time of its consideration of the matter.

Authorities cited by NIH for imposition of the sanctions included: (1) grants administration regulations for terminating or suspending a grant and related provisions for appeal of such action to the Department's Grants Appeals Board; (2) HHS regulations for attaching conditions to grants as a consequence of poor performance; (3) the regulations governing research with human subjects that state that the Secretary may withhold or withdraw departmental support of research from investigators or institutions that "fail materially" either to comply with the terms of a grant or to protect human subjects; and (4) similar provisions contained in guidelines governing NIH-funded projects involving recombinant DNA. The regulations setting forth the procedures for debarment and suspension (that provide an accused scientist with notice and an opportunity for a hearing) were not invoked.

President's Commission, Protecting Human Subjects, (Appendix E) 177, 182–85 (1981). On August 30, 1982, the Departmental Grants Appeals Board denied an appeal by Dr. Cline from the decision of the NIH Director to withhold the second and subsequent years' support under his National Heart, Lung, and Blood Institute award. Board Docket No. 82–16, Dec. No. 340. In the course of denying the appeal, the Board discussed Dr. Cline's September 17, 1981, letter in which the Doctor's central contention was that in his experiments the use of nonrecombinant molecules, for which there are no guidelines, would not differ significantly in biological effects from the use of recombinant DNA. The Board regarded this argument as unpersuasive. Do you agree?

2. Would Dr. Cline's experiment have been ethical if it had worked after all? Bob Williamson, a molecular geneticist at the University of London, expresses a negative view:

> Cline's experiments were *fundamentally* unethical. His own work on mice shows that there was no basis for hope that globin gene insertion into marrow cells could give clinical benefit at that time. [The subjects'] families were given hope that the gene therapy might help them in their fight for survival. It is unacceptable that patients should be misled in this way.

Williamson, Gene Therapy, 298 Nature 416, 418 (1982).

3. Chapter 3, Sec. B, reviews the role that an individual can play in controlling research as a consequence of the requirement of "informed consent"; Chap-

ter 6 expands upon this point in the context of human experimentation. The following consent form, signed by the parents of Dr. Cline's Italian patient, is illustrative of the process of obtaining permission for research, although it is much less detailed than the consent form submitted by Dr. Cline to the IRB at UCLA, which nonetheless disapproved his research protocol.

At the Center of Microthemia of the Pediatric Clinic II where our children Maria Addolorata and Andrea, suffering from Cooley's disease, (Homozygotic Thalassemia) were treated, Prof. Nicola and Dr. Gabutti on July 8, 1980 suggested to us that Maria Addolorata should undergo a new therapeutic treatment at the University's Institute of Medical Pathology (Prof. Condorelli) in Naples in cooperation with the University of California in Los Angeles (Prof. Cline).

The procedure calls for the sampling of cells from the bone marrow, their induction for the purpose of synthesizing hemoglobin through the immission of genes by way of the hemoglobinic chain and genes through the "timidichinasi" /term unknown/ and their reintroduction through the intravenous system. The treatment will be preceded by a 200 r radiation of a small surface of the tibia.

The principles, the purpose, the methodology and the possible risks involved in this procedure have been exhaustively and comprehensibly explained. We have been informed that a therapy of this sort has successfully been carried out on animals but never on man.

Fully aware of the importance this new method may have for the treatment of our children and of all others suffering from thalassemia and having heard Maria Addolorata's favorable consciously and freely expressed opinion we agree of our own will and without any duress that our daughter undergo the treatment.

Reprinted in Human Genetic Engineering, Hearings Before the Subcomm. on Investigations and Oversight, House Comm. on Science and Technology, 97th Cong., 2d Sess. 461 (1982) (translated by Paul Vidal, Congressional Reference Service, Language Services).

4. When would it be acceptable to initiate trials of human gene therapy? A scientist and an ethicist at the National Institutes of Health suggest that three conditions should first be met in animal studies: (1) the new gene should be put into target cells and remain in them; (2) the new gene should be regulated appropriately; and (3) the presence of the new gene should not harm the cell. Anderson & Fletcher, Gene Therapy in Human Beings: When is it Ethical to Begin?, 303 New Eng.J.Med. 1293 (1980). For a fuller treatment see Fletcher, Moral Problems and Ethical Issues in Prospective Human Gene Therapy, 69 Va.L.Rev. 515 (1983).

5. For a more detailed account of the therapeutic possibilities, see Roblin, Human Genetic Therapy: Outlook and Apprehensions, in Health Handbook 103 (G. Chacko ed. 1979); Anderson, Genetic Therapy, in The New Genetics and the Future of Man 109 (M. Hamilton ed. 1972); Friedman & Roblin, Gene Therapy for Human Genetic Disease?, 175 Science 949 (1972).

6. The many concerns raised by human gene splicing have been discussed in scores of books, articles and meetings. One writer summed up the general sense of foreboding:

Some thirty-five years ago physicists learned how to manipulate the forces in the nucleus of the atom, and the world has been struggling to cope with the results of that discovery ever since. The ability to penetrate nucleus of the living cell, to rearrange and transplant the nucleic acids that constitute the genetic material of all forms of life, seems a more beneficent power but one that is likely to prove at least as profound in its consequences.

N. Wade, The Ultimate Experiment 2 (1977).

2. POSSIBLE BURDENS AND BENEFITS

a. Ethical and Religious Concerns

MESSAGE FROM THREE GENERAL SECRETARIES

(June 20, 1980) *

We are rapidly moving into a new era of fundamental danger triggered by the rapid growth of genetic engineering. Albeit, there may be opportunity for doing good; the very term suggests the danger. Who shall determine how human good is best served when new life forms are being engineered? Who shall control genetic experimentation and its results which could have untold implications for human survival? Who will benefit and who will bear any adverse consequences, directly or indirectly?

These are not ordinary questions. These are moral, ethical and religious questions. They deal with the fundamental nature of human life and the dignity and worth of the individual human being.

With the Supreme Court decision allowing patents on new forms of life—a purpose that could not have been imagined when patent laws were written—it is obvious that these laws must be reexamined. But the issue goes far beyond patents.

New life forms may have dramatic potential for improving human life, whether by curing diseases, correcting genetic deficiencies or swallowing oil slicks. They may also, however, have unforeseen ramifications, and at times the cure may be worse that the original problem. New chemicals that ultimately prove to be lethal may be tightly controlled or banned, but we may not be able to "recall" a new life form. For unlike DDT or DES—both of which were in wide use before their tragic side effects were discovered—life forms reproduce and grow on their own and thus would be infinitely harder to contain.

Control of such life forms by any individual or group poses a potential threat to all of humanity. History has shown us that there will always be those who believe it appropriate to "correct" our mental and social structures by genetic means, so as to fit their vision of humanity. This becomes more dangerous when the basic tools to do so are finally at hand. Those who would play God will be tempted as never before.

We also know from experience that it would be naive and unfair to ask private corporations to suddenly abandon the profit motive when it comes to genetic engineering. Private corporations develop and sell new products to make money, whether those products are automobiles or new forms of life. Yet when the products are new life forms, with all the risks entailed, should there be broader criteria than profit for determining their use and distribution? Given all the responsibility to God and to our fellow human beings, do we have the right to let experimentation and ownership to new life forms move ahead without public regulation?

These issues must be explored, and they must be explored now. It is not enough for the commercial, scientific or medical communities alone to examine them; they must be examined by individuals and groups who

* Dr. Claire Randall, General Secretary, National Council of Churches; Rabbi Bernard Mandelbaum, General Secretary, Synagogue Council of America; Bishop Thomas Kelly, General Secretary, United States Catholic Conference.

represent the broader public interest. In the long-term interest of all humanity, our government must launch a thorough examination of the entire spectrum of issues involved in genetic engineering to determine before it is too late what oversight and controls are necessary.

We believe, after careful investigation that no government agency or committee is currently exercising adequate oversight or control, nor addressing the fundamental ethical questions in a major way. Therefore, we intend to request that President Carter provide a way for representatives of a broad spectrum of our society to consider these matters and advise the government on its necessary role.

We also intend to ask the appropriate Congressional Committee to begin immediately a process of reviewing our patent laws looking to revisions that are necessary to deal with the new questions related to patenting life forms. In addition, we will ask our government to collaborate with other governments with the appropriate international bodies, such as the UN, to evolve international guidelines related to genetic engineering.

Finally, we pledge our own efforts to examine the religious and ethical issues involved in genetic engineering. The religious community must and will address these fundamental questions in a more urgent and organized way.

LAURENCE H. TRIBE,
TECHNOLOGY ASSESSMENT AND THE FOURTH
DISCONTINUITY: THE LIMITS OF
INSTRUMENTAL RATIONALITY

46 S.Cal.L.Rev. 617, 648–50 (1973).

[A]s one's most intimate nature as a person—one's genetic basis and neurological identity—becomes increasingly subject to deliberate external manipulation and even prior determination, one's ability to conceive of oneself as a free and rational being entitled to resist various societal claims may gradually weaken and might finally disappear altogether. In a society that came to view its members as just so many cells or molecules to be manufactured or rearranged at will, one wonders how easy it would be to recall what all the shouting about "human rights" was supposed to mean.

To be sure, some objections of this form can be regarded as merely adding plausibility to the still speculative fear that these technologies will ultimately enhance the dangers of tyrannical government. But it is not so easy to dismiss the underlying proposition that pursuing the technologies in question, for better or for worse, *will profoundly alter what it means to be a human being* and will do so in ways that matter whether or not particular "abuses" ever take place. As one observer so aptly put it, to "lay one's hands on human generation is to take a major step toward making man himself simply another one of the manmade things." And to mechanize through technology the formation of human character and personality may make that first major step a truly irreversible one. Nobel Laureate Joshua Lederberg looks forward to the day when our mastery over ourselves as well as our environment will be such that we can do "essentially anything that we care to do in the area of biological engineering." But does not that dream at least potentially entail the final transformation of man into an object—a thing to be "engineered" according to technical specifications along with the many other products of human ingenuity?

If, as Marx recognized, man "changes his own nature" by "acting on the external world and changing it," how much clearer it seems that man changes himself by turning his technology inward in order to achieve the ultimate mastery—mastery over his own evolution as a species and his own development as an individual.

What such a change would mean for particular systems of human ends and values is by no means obvious and demands further study; but that it could alter those systems radically seems to me hard to dispute. That a societal choice with respect to technologies responsible for changes this profound ought to address the desirability and moral permissibility of such changes seems equally undeniable. At stake are not merely alterations in the "costs" and "benefits" associated with implementing existing preferences and values but alterations in the very structures of human thought and reality on which all value premises and the choices that embody them—all the frames of reference for defining one thing as a "cost" and another as a "benefit"—must ultimately be based. To conceive of the choice as a selection in terms of a "given" value framework thus begs the question presented by the sorts of cases that have been considered here. . . .

PAUL RAMSEY,
FABRICATED MAN

139–140, 148–151 (1970).

A recent article by the leading Roman Catholic theologian in Germany, Karl Rahner, probes profoundly the question of what, if anything, theology is going to be able to say about schemes for man's indefinite self-modification—so profoundly as to leave us at the heart of the problem.[30] Christianity—or for that matter, all the world's great religions—have taught, Rahner points out, that "man has always had the power to determine his permanent, everlasting orientation." But till now this power was "exercised almost exclusively in the area of the contemplative knowledge of metaphysics and faith," and in moral decisions opening man to the eternal. Now there has taken place an "historical breakthrough from theory to practice—from self-awareness to self-creation." This breakthrough by which men have now grasped and can fundamentally alter the roots of their own existence arises, Rahner believes, essentially from Christianity. This judgment seems to be a spill-over from Rahner's esteem for man's powers of self-awareness and self-determination in contemplation. "Man is essentially a freedom-event. As established by God, and in his very nature, he is unfinished." From the fact that "freedom enables man to determine himself irrevocably, to be for all eternity what he himself has chosen to make himself," Rahner concludes that, in the practical order, the "creature" of this creative freedom is man himself. From the fact that "man determines himself in his innermost depths of his free actions," Rahner moves smoothly to an endorsement of man's modification of the "innermost depths" of his biological, genetic, psychological and historical existence.

This sounds remarkably like a priestly blessing over everything, doing duty for ethics. Rahner envisions "a hominized world, where man dwells as both the experimenter and the experiment—so that he can finally in-

---

30. Karl Rahner, Experiment: Man, Theology Digest 16 (Feb.1968): 57–69.

vent himself." "Man is experimentally manipulable," he writes, "and legitimately so." Since "evil is, in the final analysis, the absurdity of willing the impossible," Rahner concludes that "there is really nothing *possible* for man that he ought not to do" and that "there is no reason why man should not do whatever he is really able to do"—"what he ought not to do is—even today—impractical."

. . . We are not apt to come into the possession of . . . future moral wisdom if now we are utterly deprived of all grounds for judging that some things we *can* do *should* not be done—that we ought not to practice everything that *could* be technically accomplished. . . .

The immanent providence of a morally blind biological technology decrees, of course, that men-gods *must* do what they *can* do. In the end, Fleming voices the justifiable sullenness of the men of the future who are to be worked over by our new deities and creators. "We the manufactured would be everybody and we the manufacturers a minority of scientists and technicians." But this will come, he predicts, with a gradual adjustment of our values "to signify that we approve of what we will actually be getting." . . .

Doubtless the ethics of the future will not be the same as the ethics of the past. But the sine qua non of any morality at all, of any future for humanism, must be the premise that there may be a number of things that we *can* do that *ought* not to be done. Our common inquiry must be to fix upon those things that are worthy of man from among the multitude of things he is more and more capable of doing. Any other premise amounts to a total abdication of human moral reasoning and judgment and the total abasement of man before the relentless advancement of biological and medical technology. . . .

This is the edification to be found in the thought that we should not play God before we have learned to be men, and as we learn to be men we will not want to play God.

NOTES

It has long been apparent that you and I do not enter this world as unformed clay compliant to any mold. Rather, we have in our beginnings some bent of mind, some shade of character. The origin of this structure—of the fiber in this clay—was for centuries mysterious. In earlier times men sought its trace in the conjunction of the stars or perhaps in the momentary combination of the elements at nativity. Today, instead, we know to look within. We seek not in the stars but in our genes for the herald of our fate.

. . . For the first time in all time a living creature understands its origin and can undertake to design its future. . . . Even in the ancient myths man was constrained by his essence. He could not rise above his nature to chart his destiny. Today we can . . . envision that chance—and its dark companion of awesome choice and responsibility.

. . .

I know there are those who find this concept and this prospect repugnant—who fear, with reason, that we may unleash forces beyond human scale and who recoil from this responsibility. I would suggest to them that they do not see our present situation whole. They are not among the losers in that chromosomal lottery that so firmly channels our human destinies. This response does not come from the 250,000 children born each year in this country with structural or functional defects, of which it is estimated 80% involve a genetic component. And this figure counts only those with gross evident defects outside those ranges we choose to call natural. It does not include the 50,000,000 "normal" Americans with an IQ of less than 90.

We who are among those who were favored in the chromosomal lottery and, in the nature of things, it will be our very conscious choice, whether as a species we will continue to accept the innumerable, individual tragedies inherent in the outcome of this mindless, age-old throw of dice, or instead will shoulder the responsibility for intelligent genetic intervention.

As we enlarge man's freedom, we diminish his constraints and that which he must accept as given. Equality of opportunity is a noble aim given the currently inescapable genetic diversity of man. But what does equality of opportunity mean to the child born with an IQ of 50?

Sinsheimer, The Prospect of Designed Genetic Change, 32 Engineering and Science 8, 13 (April 1969).

2. Speaking to several groups of Italian physicians in October 1980, Pope John Paul II voiced disapproval of a number of "technological developments" including genetic engineering. "Certainly," he declared, "scientific knowledge has its own laws by which it must abide. It must also recognize, however, especially in medicine, an impassable limit in respect for the person and in protection of his right to live in a way worthy of a human being. . . . Science . . . is not the highest value to which all others must be subordinated." Pope John Paul II, On Medical Ethics, Hospital Progress 18 (Dec. 1980) (reprinted from L'Osservatore Romano, Oct. 27, 1980).

Two years later, the Pope told the Pontifical Academy of Science's convocation on biological experimentation of his approval and support for gene splicing when its aim is to "ameliorate the conditions of those who are affected by chromosonic diseases" because this offers "hope for the great number of people affected by those maladies." Pope John Paul II, La sperimentozione in biologia deve contribuire al bene integrale dell'uomo, L'Osservatore Romano, Oct. 24, 1982, at 2.

PRESIDENT'S COMMISSION FOR THE STUDY OF ETHICAL PROBLEMS IN MEDICINE AND BIOMEDICAL AND BEHAVIORAL RESEARCH, SPLICING LIFE

53–60 (1982).

Hardly a popular article has been written about the social and ethical implications of genetic engineering that does not suggest a link between "God-like powers" and the ability to manipulate the basic material of life. Indeed, a popular book about gene splicing is entitled *Who Should Play God?*, and in their June 1980 letter to the President, the three religious leaders sounded a tocsin against the lack of a governmental policy concerning "[t]hose who would play God" through genetic engineering.

. . . .

In the view of the theologians, contemporary developments in molecular biology raise issues of responsibility rather than being matters to be prohibited because they usurp powers that human beings should not possess. The Biblical religions teach that human beings are, in some sense, co-creators with the Supreme Creator. Thus, as interpreted for the Commission by their representatives, these major religious faiths respect and encourage the enhancement of knowledge about nature, as well as responsible use of that knowledge.[6] Endorsement of genetic engineering,

---

6. In the Biblical tradition of the major Western religions, the universe and all that exists in it is God's creation. In pagan religion, the gods inhabit nature, which is thus seen as sacrosanct, but the Biblical God transcends nature. However, since God created the world, it has meaning and purpose. God has placed a special being on earth—humans—formed in the image of God and endowed with creative powers of intelligence and freedom. Human beings must accept responsibility for the effects brought about by the use of the great powers with which they have been endowed—for the betterment of the world—to uncover nature's secrets.

which is praised for its potential to improve the human estate, is linked with the recognition that the misuse of human freedom creates evil and that human knowledge and power can result in harm.

While religious leaders present theological bases for their concerns, essentially the same concerns have been raised—sometimes in slightly different words—by many thoughtful secular observers of contemporary science and technology. Concerns over unintended effects, over the morality of genetic manipulation in all its forms, and over the social and political consequences of new technologies are shared by religious and secular commentators. The examination of the various specific concerns need not be limited, therefore, to the religious format in which some of the issues have been raised.

Fully Understanding the Machinery of Life. Although it does not have a specific religious meaning, the objection to scientists "playing God" is assumed to be self-explanatory. On closer examination, however, it appears to the Commission that it conveys several rather different ideas, some describing the power of gene splicing itself and some relating merely to its consequences.

At its heart, the term represents a reaction to the realization that human beings are on the threshold of understanding how the fundamental machinery of life works. A full understanding of what are now great mysteries, and the powers inherent in that understanding, would be so awesome as to justify the description "God-like." In this view, playing God is not actually an objection to the research but an expression of a sense of awe—and concern.

Since the Enlightenment, Western societies have exalted the search for greater knowledge, while recognizing its awesome implications. Some scientific discoveries reverberate with particular force because they not only open new avenues of research but also challenge people's entire understanding of the world and their place in it. Current discoveries in gene splicing—like the new knowledge associated with Copernicus and Darwin—further dethrone human beings as the unique center of the universe. By identifying DNA and learning how to manipulate it, science seems to have reduced people to a set of malleable molecules that can be interchanged with those of species that people regard as inferior. Yet unlike the earlier revolutionary discoveries, those in molecular biology are not merely descriptions; they give scientists vast powers for action.

Arrogant Interference with Nature. By what standards are people to guide the exercise of this awesome new freedom if they want to act responsibly? In this context, the charge that human beings are playing God can mean that in "creating new life forms" scientists are abusing their learning by interfering with nature.

But in one sense *all* human activity that produces changes that otherwise would not have occurred interferes with nature. Medical activities as routine as the prescription of eyeglasses for myopia or as dramatic as the repair or replacement of a damaged heart are in this sense "unnatural." In another sense, human activity cannot interfere with nature—in the sense of contravening it—since all human activities, including gene splicing, proceed according to the scientific laws that describe natural processes. Ironically, to believe that "playing God" in this sense is even possible would itself be hubris according to some religious thought, which maintains that only God can interfere with the descriptive laws of nature (that is, perform miracles).

If, instead, what is meant is that gene splicing technology interferes with nature in the sense that it violates God's prescriptive natural law or goes against God's purposes as they are manifested in the natural order, then some reason must be given for this judgment. None of the scholars appointed to report their views by the three religious bodies that urged the Commission to undertake this study suggested that either natural reason or revelation imply that gene splicing technology as such is "unnatural" in this prescriptive sense. Although each scholar expressed concern over particular applications of gene splicing technology, they all also emphasized that human beings have not merely the right but the duty to employ their God-given powers to harness nature for human benefit. To turn away from gene splicing, which may provide a means of curing hereditary diseases, would itself raise serious ethical problems.

Creating New Life Forms. If "creating new life forms" is simply producing organisms with novel characteristics, then human beings create new life forms frequently and have done so since they first learned to cultivate new characteristics in plants and breed new traits in animals. Presumably the idea is that gene splicing creates new life forms, rather than merely modifying old ones, because it "breaches species barriers" by combining DNA from different species—groups of organisms that cannot mate to produce fertile offspring.

Genetic engineering is not the first exercise of humanity's ability to create new life forms through nonsexual reproduction. The creation of hybrid plants seems no more or no less natural than the development of a new strain of *E. coli* bacteria through gene splicing. Further, genetic engineering cannot accurately be called unique in that it involves the creation of new life forms through processes that do not occur in nature without human intervention. [S]cientists have found that the transfer of DNA between organisms of different species occurs in nature without human intervention. Yet, as one eminent scientist in the field has pointed out, it would be unwarranted to assume that a dramatic increase in the frequency of such transfers through human intervention is not problematic simply because DNA transfer sometimes occurs naturally.

In the absence of specific religious prohibitions, either revealed or derived by rational argument from religious premises, it is difficult to see why "breaching species barriers" as such is irreligious or otherwise objectionable. In fact, the very notion that there are barriers that must be breached prejudges the issue. The question is simply whether there is something intrinsically wrong with intentionally crossing species lines. Once the question is posed in this way the answer must be negative—unless one is willing to condemn the production of tangelos by hybridizing tangerines and grapefruits or the production of mules by the mating of asses with horses.

There may nonetheless be two distinct sources of concern about crossing species lines that deserve serious consideration. First, gene splicing affords the possibility of creating hybrids that can reproduce themselves (unlike mules, which are sterile). So the possibility of self-perpetuating "mistakes" adds a new dimension of concern, although here again, the point is not that crossing species lines is inherently wrong, but that it may have undesirable consequences and that these consequences may multiply beyond human control. As noted, the Commission's focus on the human applications of gene splicing has meant that it does not here address this important set of concerns, which lay behind the original self-imposed moratorium on certain categories of gene splicing research and which have been, and continue to be, addressed through various scientific and public mechanisms, such as RAC.

Second, there is the issue of whether particular crossings of species—especially the mixing of human and nonhuman genes—might not be illicit. The moral revulsion at the creation of human-animal hybrids may be traced in part to the prohibition against sexual relations between human beings and lower animals. Sexual relations with lower animals are thought to degrade human beings and insult their God-given dignity as the highest of God's creatures. But unease at the prospect of human-animal hybrids goes beyond sexual prohibitions.

The possibility of creating such hybrids calls into question basic assumptions about the relationship of human beings to other living things. For example, those who believe that the current treatment of animals—in experimentation, food production, and sport—is morally suspect would not be alone in being troubled by the prospect of exploitive or insensitive treatment of creatures that possess even more human-like qualities than chimpanzees or porpoises do. Could genetic engineering be used to develop a group of virtual slaves—partly human, partly lower animal—to do people's bidding? Paradoxically, the very characteristics that would make such creatures more valuable than any existing animals (that is, their heightened cognitive powers and sensibilities) would also make the moral propriety of their subservient role more problematic. Dispassionate appraisal of the long history of gratuitous destruction and suffering that humanity has visited upon the other inhabitants of the earth indicates that such concerns should not be dismissed as fanciful.

Accordingly, the objection to the creation of new life forms by crossing species lines (whether through gene splicing or otherwise) reflects the concern that human beings lack the God-like knowledge and wisdom required for the exercise of these God-like powers. Specifically, people worry that interspecific hybrids that are partially human in their genetic makeup will be like Dr. Frankenstein's monster. A striking lesson of the Frankenstein story is the uncontrollability and uncertainty of the consequences of human interferences with the natural order. Like the tale of the Sorcerer's apprentice or the myth of the golem created from lifeless dust by the 16th century rabbi, Loew of Prague, the story of Dr. Frankenstein's monster serves as a reminder of the difficulty of restoring order if a creation intended to be helpful proves harmful instead. Indeed, each of these tales conveys a painful irony: in seeking to extend their control over the world, people may lessen it. The artifices they create to do their bidding may rebound destructively against them—the slave may become the master.

Suggesting that someone lacks sufficient knowledge or wisdom to engage in an activity the person knows how to perform thus means that the individual has insufficient knowledge of the consequences of that activity or insufficient wisdom to cope with those consequences. But if this is the rational kernel of the admonition against playing God, then the use of gene splicing technology is not claimed to be wrong as such but wrong because of its potential consequences. Understood in this way, the slogan that crossing species barriers is playing God does not end the debate, but it does make a point of fundamental importance.[11] It emphasizes that

11. [W]hat made the Gallilean and the other major scientific revolutions disturbing is the reductionism, that we become less than what we are. [T]hat is what is so un- certain about gene therapy, because it gets back to a very fundamental question . . . "Is there anything unique about humans?"

any realistic assessment of the potential consequences of the new technology must be founded upon a sober recognition of human fallibility and ignorance. At bottom, the warning not to play God is closely related to the Socratic injunction "know thyself": in this case, acknowledge the limits of understanding and prediction, rather than assuming that people can foresee all the consequences of their actions or plan adequately for every eventuality.

Any further examination of the notion that the hybridization of species, at least when one of the species is human, is intrinsically wrong (and not merely wrong as a consequence of what is done with the hybrids) involves elaboration of two points. First, what characteristics are uniquely human, setting humanity apart from all other species? And second, does the wrong lie in bestowing some but not all of these characteristics on the new creation or does it stem from depriving the being that might otherwise have arisen from the human genetic material of the opportunity to have a totally human makeup? The Commission believes that these are important issues deserving of serious study.

It should be kept in mind, however, that the information available to the Commission suggests that the ability to create interspecific hybrids of the sort that would present intrinsic moral and religious concerns will not be available in the foreseeable future. The research currently being done on experimentation with recombinant DNA techniques through the use of single human genes (for example, the insertion of a particular human hemoglobin gene into mouse cells at the embryonic stage) or the study of cellular development through the combining of human genetic material with that of other species in a way that does not result in a mature organism (for example, *in vitro* fusion of human and mouse cells) does not, in the Commission's view, raise problems of an improper "breaching of the barriers."

NOTE ON ORGANIC [HUMAN?] COMPUTERS

Rather than treating human beings, what of the use of genetic engineering to create something with human-like capabilities—as with the following hypothetical "organic computer"?

On the outside it looks like another ho-hum electronic device, perhaps a hand-held calculator. But inside this garden variety box lurks an alien computer. In place of the usual green plastic boards holding silicone microchips are ultra-thin films of glass crusted over with invisible layers of proteins, linked together in complex crystal patterns . . . Within the delicate protein latticework are organic molecules, called biochips, that dance at the touch of an electric current, winding or unwinding, passing hydrogen atoms from one end to the other. . . .

[B]ecause they are so tiny and so close together, they can perform a calculation in about a millionth the time of today's best chips. One more thing: these molecular diodes, transistors and wires, as well as the protein architecture that holds everything together, were manufactured by simple E. coli bac-

And if there isn't anything unique about humans, there's nothing wrong with doing gene manipulation. But if there is something unique about humans, then it is wrong to pass over the barrier, wherever the barrier is—but we don't know where the barrier is.

But as soon as you ask, "Where is the barrier?" you ask, "Is there a barrier?" And that's frightening. If there's nothing unique about humans—that's not a theological question but a very real one.

Testimony of Dr. French Anderson, transcript of 22nd meeting of the President's Commission (July 10, 1982) at 115–16.

teria fashioned to do the job by genetic engineering. It can almost be said that the computer is alive.

The Organic Computer, Discover 76 (May 1982). For a discussion of computers, see Chapter 10 infra.

b. Concerns about Social Impact

In the United States, genetics has entered public policy in two periods: (1) under the banner of eugenics during the early decades of this century, state laws were enacted to permit sterilization of those thought to have undesirable genes and the federal government moved to exclude them from immigrating into the country; and (2) beginning in the mid-1960's, most states adopted statutes requiring screening for certain genetic conditions, primarily among newborns (see Chapter 8). Although public policy on genetic engineering has thus far been concentrated on the issues of laboratory and environmental safety, some people fear it will lead to a "new eugenics," which could be implemented with less cooperation from the public than would have been required for any of the programs of "selective breeding" that were discussed earlier. Even if such steps are never taken, the medical uses of gene splicing present a number of difficult issues for society to consider.

PRESIDENT'S COMMISSION FOR THE STUDY OF ETHICAL PROBLEMS IN MEDICINE AND BIOMEDICAL AND BEHAVIORAL RESEARCH, SPLICING LIFE

64–68 (1982).

Parental rights and responsibilities. Current attitudes toward human reproductive activity are founded, in part, on several important assumptions, among them that becoming a parent requires a willingness, within very broad limits, to accept the child a woman gives birth to, that parents' basic duties to children are more or less clear and settled, and that reproduction and parenting are and should remain largely private and autonomous spheres of people's lives. The doors that genetic engineering can open challenge all three of these assumptions.

Genetic counseling and screening have already undercut the first assumption by enabling parents to make an informed decision to prevent the occurrence of some genetic defects by terminating pregnancy, by artificial insemination, or by avoiding conception. If gene therapy or gene surgery become available, parents could have more control over their children's characteristics. They will no longer face the stark alternatives of either playing the hand their child has been dealt by the "natural lottery" or avoiding birth or conception. Instead, they could prevent some genetic defects through gene surgery on the zygote and remedy others through gene therapy before the genetic defect produces irreversible changes in the child.

With this increased ability to act for the well-being of the child would come an expansion of parental responsibility. The boundaries of this responsibility—and hence people's conception of what it is to be a good parent—may shift rapidly. It seems safe to say that one important duty of a parent is to prevent or ameliorate serious defects (if it can be done safely) and that the duty to enhance favorable characteristics is less stringent and clear. Yet the new technological capabilities may change people's view of what counts as a defect. For example, if what is now regarded as the normal development of important cognitive skills could be significantly augmented by genetic engineering, then today's "normal" level might be considered deficient tomorrow. Thus ethical uncertainty about the scope of a parent's obligation is linked to conceptual uncertainty about what counts as a defect.

The problem of shifting conceptions of parental responsibility becomes even more complicated when the effects of parents' present actions on descendants beyond their immediate offspring are considered. Deciding whether to engineer a profound change in an expected or newborn child is difficult enough; if the change is inheritable, the burden of responsibility could be truly awesome.

Gene splicing technology may also change people's sense of family and kinship. On the one hand, the possibility of promoting significant inheritable changes through gene surgery may encourage people to think of their family as extending further into the future than they now do. On the other hand, knowing that future generations may employ an even more advanced technology to alter or replace the characteristics passed on to them may weaken people's sense of genetic continuity.

· · ·

Societal obligations. The concept of society's obligation to protect or enhance the health of children and future generations often rests on some notion of an adequate minimum of health care. This benchmark, in turn, depends upon assumptions about what counts as a serious defect or disability, on the one hand, and what constitutes normal functioning or adequate health, on the other. As technological capabilities grow, the boundary between these criteria will blur and shift, and with this will come changes in people's views about what society owes to children and to future generations.

As new technological capabilities raise the standard of normal functioning or adequate health, the scarcity of societal resources may raise anew a very difficult question that theorists of distributive justice have strongly disagreed about: where does justice to future generations end and generosity begin? This question is of vital practical import, for the demands of justice are characteristically thought of as valid claims or entitlements to be enforced by the coercive power of the state, while generosity is usually regarded as a private virtue.

· · ·

The commitment to equality of opportunity. Since the application of the burgeoning recombinant DNA technology will bring benefits as well as costs and since it will be funded at least in part by public resources, it is essential to ask several questions. Who will benefit from the new technology? And will the benefits and costs be distributed equitably? Indeed, what sort of distribution would count as "fair" when the very thing that is being distributed (such as cognitive ability) is itself often the basis for distributing other things of value in society?

The possibilities presented by gene therapy and gene surgery may in fact call into question the scope and limits of a central element of democratic political theory and practice: the commitment to equality of opportunity. One root idea behind the modern concept of equality of opportunity is the belief that because the social assets a person is born with are in no way earned or merited, it is unfair for someone's luck in the "social lottery" to determine that person's most basic prospects in life. Until recently, those who have sought to ground the commitment to equality of opportunity on this belief have only urged that social institutions be designed so as to minimize or compensate for the influence that the "social lottery" exerts on a person's opportunities. Genetic engineering raises the question of whether equality of opportunity requires intervention in the "natural lottery" as well, for people's initial genetic assets, like their initial social assets, are unearned and yet exert a profound influence on opportunities in life. Even to ask this question challenges a fundamental assumption about the scope of principles of distributive justice, namely that they deal only with inequalities in social goods and play no role in regulating natural inequalities.

NOTES

1.   On the issue of fairness in distributing genetic traits, Professor Michael H. Shapiro of the University of Southern California Law Center poses some fundamental questions:

> Suppose, for example, a society distributes certain scarce resources on the basis of merit—e.g., intelligence, diligence, physical abilities. What if intelligence could be engineered upward? Who would merit this increase in merit? The very oddity of the inquiry calls into question the continued use of intelligence as a basis for resolving competing claims—say, for admission to educational institutions or for access to the intelligence-raising technology itself. We could resort to the other coexisting merit attributes—unless they too were alterable by design. Under these conditions, how could we retain our system of merit distribution? If we could not, how would we then distribute the resources? By resort to a standard of efficiency? By leaving matters to a market? Or by designing a lottery?

Shapiro, Introduction to the Issue: Some Dilemmas of Biotechnology Research, 51 S.Cal.L.Rev. 987, 1001–02 (1978) (citations omitted). See also Shapiro, Who Merits Merit? Problems in Distributive Justice and Utility Posed by the New Biology, 48 Col.L.Rev. 318 (1974).

2.   Is it an advantage or a disadvantage of human genetic manipulation that it might be capable of solving an intractable social problem (e.g., racial discrimination) by transforming it into something to be treated medically (by eliminating genes that cause dark skin)? Do technologies have any inherent limits, or only those imposed upon them by their users?

3.   If genetic technology were capable of changing important human characteristics and capabilities, ought it to be embraced as a means of improving society—indeed, all humankind? Herman J. Muller advocated social improvement through selective breeding (by the selection of certain males with desirable traits to be sperm donors), but his list of traits, and the types of men who exemplified them, changed radically over time. Allen, Science and Society in the Eugenic Thought of H.J. Muller, 20 Bio-Science 346 (1970). Science will soon improve on old-fashioned breeding techniques (gene splicing is faster and more precise)—but has society improved on Muller's ideas about the desirability of certain traits? Who would decide? For a more detailed discussion of the relationship of genetic screening to selective breeding, see Ch. 8, Sec. C.1, infra.

4.   Professor Tribe points out that some changes in technology alter our "frames of reference." If the genes responsible for people's central characteristics could be altered, by what set of values should the results be judged—present ones, or those that would accompany the new genes? See Lappé and Martin, The Place of the Public in the Conduct of Science, 52 S.Cal.L.Rev. 1535, 1537 (1978).

5.   Why is there such concern about the changes that genetic engineering might produce, when society accepts so many other factors (education, entertainment, forms of behavior control, etc.) that already affect people's desires, values,

and the way they live? Is it the type of changes, their sources, or their potential heritability?

If any one age really attains, by eugenics and scientific education, the power to make its descendants what it pleases, all men who live after it are patients of that power. They are weaker, not stronger: for though we may have put wonderful machines in their hands we have pre-ordained how they are to use them . . . . The real picture is that of one dominant age . . . which resists all previous ages most successfully and dominates all subsequent ages most irresistibly, and thus is the real master of the human species. But even within this master generation (itself an infinitesimal minority of the species) the power will be exercised by a minority smaller still. Man's conquest of Nature, if the dreams of the scientific planners are realized, means the rule of a few hundreds of men over billions upon billions of men.

C.S. Lewis, The Abolition of Man 70–71 (1965).

6. Who should decide which research on, and application of, genetic engineering ought to be promoted?

This question is not ordinarily raised about medical technology in general. When it is, the assumption is that for the most part the key decisions are to be made by the relevant experts, the research community, and the medical profession, guided by the availability of research funds (which come predominately from Federal agencies) and by the dictates of medical malpractice law and of state and Federal regulatory agencies designed to protect the public from very tangible, unambiguous harms. Yet genetic engineering is more than a new medical technology. Its potential uses . . . extend far beyond intervention to cure or prevent disease or to restore functioning. This more expansive nature makes it unlikely that decisions about the development of gene splicing technology can be made appropriately within institutions that have evolved to control medical technology and the practice of medicine.

President's Commission, Splicing Life 73 (1982).

3. MECHANISMS FOR DECIDING ABOUT GENE SPLICING IN HUMANS

PRESIDENT'S COMMISSION FOR THE STUDY OF ETHICAL PROBLEMS IN MEDICINE AND BIOMEDICAL AND BEHAVIORAL RESEARCH, SPLICING LIFE

82–87 (1982).

The President's Commission believes that the design of any oversight group should be guided by several objectives. First, the group should regard education as a primary responsibility. It is necessary to educate the scientific community about the social and ethical implications of its work as well as to educate the public about science.

Second, the group should have roles both of general oversight and of leadership within the Federal government. For this, it will need direct access, through liaison arrangements, to all Federal departments or agencies with a large stake in sponsoring, regulating, or scrutinizing work in this field. At a minimum it should possess "action-forcing power," whereby departments and agencies are required to publish its regulatory recommendations for comment in the Federal Register within a specified time and then either to adopt or reject the recommendations, with an explanation likewise published in the Federal Register.

Third, the body should be capable of leading, as well as reflecting, public thinking on the important issues before it; it can serve as an intermediary between biomedical scientists and the public, helping to translate and clarify the ideas and concerns of each for the other. To do so, it will need diverse membership. It also ought to conduct its work in public and seek to have it widely disseminated. A policymaking process that draws on nonscientists and avoids unnecessary secrecy is likely not only to lead to better results but also to inspire much greater public confidence in, and support for, research efforts themselves.

Fourth, it should strive to operate on scientifically sound premises. For this it will need a means of drawing on groups of scientists for advice and explanation in a way that does not lead it to be dominated by the scientific community.

Fifth, it should treat—in as unified a framework as possible—all the issues raised by genetic engineering: laboratory and industrial safety, environmental hazards, agricultural and commercial opportunities and pitfalls, international ramifications, biomedical benefits and risks, and social and ethical implications.

Sixth, insofar as possible, the oversight functions should be separated from any sponsoring functions, so that no conflicts of interest, of the sort that plagued the Atomic Energy Commission, will arise.

. . . Recently, Dr. Donald Fredrickson, who presided over the transformation as the Director of NIH, suggested that the time for a "third generation" RAC may have arrived. The President's Commission concurs, since there is plainly great value in building on the history—largely regarded as successful—of RAC. . . .

One means of supplementing RAC, now that it is less active since the laboratory biohazards are no longer regarded as urgent matters, would be through a mixed public-private sector body established outside the Federal government. This format has been employed in the initial work in other fields and there are plainly many organizations, ranging from those with academic and commercial interests to the religious bodies that prompted the present study, from which such a group could draw.

If it is felt that the extent of Federal responsibility is so great, both for safety and for promotion of this field, that a governmental body of greater breadth than the present RAC is needed, the Interagency Committee established in 1976, which has been inactive for the past several years, could be reinvigorated. This would have the advantage of direct involvement of the leading Federal agencies but the disadvantage that its membership is entirely governmental and its meetings are not subject to the Federal Advisory Committees Act.

Rather than creating additions to RAC, it might be preferable to redesign it. The greater scope of work for the new RAC would have two aspects. First, the range of issues must certainly be broadened beyond laboratory and manufacturing hazards. Second, the involvement of other Federal bodies must be greater. Placing the successor to RAC outside of any one department should promote this end, without making it merely a group of Federal agency representatives.

One format would be the creation of a Genetic Engineering Commission (GEC) of 11 to 15 members from outside the government that would meet regularly to deal solely with this field. This group could have a majority of nonscientists—members of the general public as well as experts in ethics and philosophy, law, the social and behavioral sciences, and public and private management. In addition to a small staff, the GEC could have a series of Technical Panels that could provide expertise in (1) laboratory research; (2) agricultural and environmental uses and dangers; (3) manufacturing concerns; (4) human uses; and (5) international controls. It should also be able to draw on a panel of liaison officers from the Department of Agriculture, Commerce, Defense, Energy, Health and Human Services (one each from the Centers for Disease Control, the National Institutes of Health, the Food and Drug Administration, and the National Institute for Occupational Safety and Health), Interior, Labor (including one from the Occupational Safety and Health Administration), and State; the National Science Foundation; the National Endowment for the Humanities; and the Environmental Protection Agency.

An alternative format would be to assign responsibility for oversight of genetic engineering to the body that succeeds the President's Commission. This arrangement could have some advantages. Principally, it would permit the continuing oversight of gene splicing to be integrated into the consideration given to the social, legal, and ethical implications of other important developments in the biomedical arena. . . .

NOTES

1. Rep. Albert Gore, Jr., introduced a bill in the 98th Congress (subsequently reported favorably as part of the Public Health Service Act amendments, H.R. 2350, by the House committee that handles health matters) to create the President's Commission on the Human Applications of Genetic Engineering. This fifteen-member, multidisciplinary body is instructed to

> conduct, and regularly update, comprehensive reviews of developments in genetic engineering that have implications for human genetic engineering, including activities in recombinant DNA technology, and . . . examine the medical, legal, ethical, and social issues presented by the human applications of such developments [Sec. 15(b)(1)].

2. One eloquent physician-essayist probably speaks for many scientists in being skeptical about the public's fondness for commissions:

> The easiest decision for society to make in matters of this kind is to appoint an agency, or a commission, or a subcommittee within an agency to look into the problem and provide advice. And the easiest course for a committee to take, when confronted by any process that appears to be disturbing people or making them uncomfortable, is to recommend that it be stopped, at least for the time being.
>
> I can easily imagine such a committee, composed of unimpeachable public figures, arriving at the decision that the time is not quite ripe for further exploration of the transplantation of genes, that we should put this off for a while, maybe until next century, and get on with other affairs that make us less discomfited. Why not do science on something more popular, say, how to get solar energy more cheaply? Or mental health?
>
> The trouble is, it would be very hard to stop once this line was begun. There are, after all, all sorts of scientific inquiry that are not much liked by one constituency or another, and we might soon find ourselves with crowded rosters, panels, standing committees, set up in Washington for the appraisal, and then the regulation, of research.

L. Thomas, The Medusa and the Snail 71–72 (1979).

Another experienced physician-administrator, no less protective of the mission of biomedical research, takes a different view:

> Some scientists will view the advent of more public governance as evidence that science has passed through its Periclean Age and is in decline. I remind them of Toynbee's comments on the disintegration of the fountainhead of Hellenic society. The failure of Athens, he said, was one of lost initiative. In its dream of sovereignty, the elite and creative city ignored the political and economic dictates of the changing civilization of which it was a part. The

nemesis of creative institutions, Toynbee implies, is the temptation to idolize themselves to the point of failure to accommodate to altered realities. Thus, the isolation of Athens had to end, but its brilliance could have survived.

So it must be true of biomedical science emerging from a more sheltered period. The shift toward public governance does not spell the end of rationalism and scientific optimism—not if the instruments of government receive from the scientific community the full measure of cooperation upon which they desperately depend. Science must anticipate public needs or fears, learn better to explain, and extend interest in and responsibility for its technology beyond what has been traditional. . . .

The public, for its part, has no less a responsibility to understand the perishability of the capital, both human and physical, assembled by a nation's heavy investment in research. It must understand the organic nature of scientific processes and the ease with which they can be stifled by inflexible regulation or commands for discovery.

The interests of the public and of its scientific component can be served jointly. Indeed, they must be served together if our earthly presence is to survive. Ways will be found. Adversary processes need not imply totally adverse interests. Man's genius for discovery is matched by his art in compromise. As Frankfurter wrote, what ties people in friendship is not identity of opinions but harmony of aims.

Fredrickson, The Public Governance of Science, 3 Man and Medicine 77, 87–88 (1978). Have the materials in this chapter suggested a harmony of aims among the various groups in society concerning science and medicine?

3. In June 1983, leaders of numerous American church groups signed a resolution calling for a ban on genetic engineering of human reproductive cells. "The resolution has sparked a sharp controversy because the prohibition it seeks would be so broad that it would preclude attempts to correct some genetic disorders, such as Tay-Sachs disease, by manipulating germline cells. Even some of the signatories seem uncertain that they want to prohibit such work." Norman, Clerics Urge Ban on Altering Germline Cells, 220 Science 1360 (1983). The New York Times criticized the clerics for uttering "so far-reaching a proscription on the basis of so little argument." Genesis and Genetics (Editorial), New York Times, June 11, 1983, at 22. Are inheritable changes so different from past medical treatment that they are obviously unacceptable? If Congress were to act on the ban, but to conclude that certain interventions should be allowed (because of the benefit to people who suffer from otherwise untreatable conditions), it might set up an expert board to decide which genetic manipulations to exempt from the ban. Would this group become a eugenics commission, deciding which diseases were burdensome enough, for individuals and society, to be in which category—in other words, who gets helped and who doesn't? That would seem an ironic end result from a resolution declaring that "no individual, group of individuals, or institutions can legitimately claim the right or authority to make such decisions on behalf of the rest of the species alive today or for future generations."

4. Because national boundaries are not part of the vocabulary of science, must law learn to speak in an international language if appropriate means for encouraging, controlling and using genetic engineering are to be found? One of the arguments raised early in the recombinant DNA debate—and roundly criticized (see, e.g., Weizenbaum, Costs and Benefits of Recombinant DNA Research, 193 Science 2 (1976), which praises Erwin Chargaff for laying bare "the illusion of technological inevitability that is so much part of the current zeitgeist")—was "If we don't do it, someone else will." What could "we" do to stop "them"?

COUNCIL OF EUROPE, PARLIAMENTARY ASSEMBLY, 33RD ORDINARY SESSION, RECOMMENDATION 934 ON GENETIC ENGINEERING

(Jan. 26, 1982).

The Assembly,

1.   Aware of public concern about the use of new scientific techniques for artificially recombining genetic material from living organisms, referred to as "genetic engineering";

2.   Considering that these concerns fall into two distinct categories:

— those arising from uncertainty as to the health, safety and environmental implications of experimental research;

— those arising from the longer-term legal, social and ethical issues raised by the prospect of knowing and interfering with a person's inheritable genetic pattern;

3.   Having regard, in respect of the health, safety and environmental implications of experimental research, to the following considerations:

   i.   the techniques of genetic engineering present an immense industrial and agricultural potential which in coming decades could help to solve world problems of food production, energy and raw materials;

   ii.   radical breakthroughs in scientific and medical understanding (university of the genetic code) are associated with the discovery and development of these techniques;

   iii.   freedom of scientific inquiry—a basic value of our societies and a condition of their adaptability to the changing world environment—carries with it duties and responsibilities, notably in regard to the health and safety of the general public and of fellow scientific workers and to the non-contamination of the environment; . . .

   v.   in the light of new scientific knowledge and experience, uncertainties in regard to experimental research have in recent years been largely clarified and resolved—to the point of allowing substantial relaxation of the control and containment measures initially instituted or envisaged;

   vi.   strict and comparable levels of protection should be provided in all countries for the general public and for laboratory workers against risks involved in the handling of pathogenic microorganisms in general, irrespective of whether techniques of genetic engineering are used;

4.   Having regard, in respect of the legal, social and ethical issues, to the following considerations inspired by the Council of Europe's 7th Public Parliamentary Hearing (Copenhagen, 25 and 26 May 1981) on genetic engineering and human rights:

   i.   the rights to life and to human dignity protected by Articles 2 and 3 of the European Convention on Human Rights imply the right to inherit a genetic pattern which has not been artificially changed;

   ii.   this right should be made explicit in the context of the European Convention on Human Rights;

   iii.   the explicit recognition of this right must not impede development of the therapeutic applications of genetic engineering (gene therapy), which holds great promise for the treatment and eradication of certain diseases which are genetically transmitted;

iv.   gene therapy must not be used or experimented with except with the free and informed consent of the person(s) concerned, or in cases of experiment with embryos, foetuses or minors with the free and informed consent of the parent(s) or legal guardian(s);

v.   the boundaries of legitimate therapeutic application of genetic engineering techniques need to be clearly drawn, brought to the attention of research workers and experimentalists, and subjected to periodical re-appraisal;

vi.   outline regulations should be drawn up to protect individuals against non-therapeutic applications of these techniques;

5.   Expressing the wish that the European Science Foundation should keep under review:

a.   procedures and criteria for licensing the use of products of recombinant DNA techniques in medicine, in agriculture and industry;

b.   the effects of the commercialisation of recombinant DNA techniques on the funding and orientations of fundamental research in molecular biology. . . .

7.   Recommends that the Committee of Ministers:

a.   draw up a European agreement on what constitutes legitimate application to human beings (including future generations) of the techniques of genetic engineering, align domestic regulations accordingly, and work towards similar agreements at world level;

b.   provide for explicit recognition in the European Convention on Human Rights of the right to a genetic inheritance which has not been artificially interfered with, except in accordance with certain principles which are recognised as being fully compatible with respect for human rights (as, for example, in the field of therapeutic applications);

c.   provide for the drawing up of a list of serious diseases which may properly, with the consent of the person concerned, be treated by gene therapy (though certain uses without consent, in line with existing practice for other forms of medical treatment, may be recognised as compatible with respect for human rights in the probability of a very serious disease being transmitted to a person's offspring);

d.   lay down principles governing the preparation, storage, safeguarding and use of genetic information on individuals, with particular reference to protecting the rights to privacy of the persons concerned in accordance with the Council of Europe conventions and resolutions on data protection;

e.   examine whether levels of protection of the health and safety of the general public and of laboratory workers engaged in experiments or industrial applications involving micro-organisms, including micro-organisms subject to recombinant DNA techniques, are adequate and comparable throughout Europe, and whether existing legislation and institutional machinery offer an adequate framework for their periodical verification and revision to this end;

f.   ensure, by periodic reviews in liaison with the European Science Foundation, that national containment measures for recombinant DNA research and required laboratory safety practice continue to converge and to evolve (albeit by different routes) towards harmonization in Europe, in the light of new research findings and risk evaluations;

g. examine the draft recommendation of the Council of the European Communities on the registration and notification to appropriate national and regional authorities of experiments involving recombinant DNA, with a view to the concerted implementation of its provisions in the countries of the Council of Europe;

h. examine the patentability of microorganisms genetically altered by recombinant DNA techniques.

Chapter Two

THE FORMATION OF THE MODERN SCIENCE ESTABLISHMENT: THE GROWTH OF NUCLEAR ENERGY

A. THE SCIENTIFIC BASIS AND HISTORIC IMPACT OF NUCLEAR WEAPONS

1. THE SCIENTIFIC BASIS OF NUCLEAR ENERGY

BANESH HOFFMANN, ALBERT EINSTEIN

69–82 (1972).

Let us now look at the content of his [Einstein's] paper of 1905 on what came to be called the special theory of relativity. . . .

[H]e begins by noting a conflict that goes to the heart of the matter: Maxwell's theory * makes unwarranted distinctions between rest and motion. Einstein gives an example. When a magnet and a loop of wire move past one another, an electric current appears in the wire. Suppose we think of the magnet as moving and the loop as at rest. Then Maxwell's theory gives an excellent explanation. Suppose we now switch and think of the coil as moving and the magnet at rest. Then Maxwell's theory again gives an excellent explanation; but it is a quite different one physically, and this even though the calculated currents are equal.

Having thus aroused our suspicions about Maxwellian rest and motion, Einstein bolsters them by adducing "the unsuccessful attempts to discover any motion of the earth relative to the [ether]." He therefore makes the impossibility-type postulate that no experiment of any sort can detect absolute rest or uniform motion . . . . In view of the evidence, this postulate, which he calls the *principle of relativity*, is certainly plausible. Einstein now quickly adds a second principle that seems, if anything, even more plausible; and with these deft strokes he sets the stage for revolution.

His second principle says that in empty space light travels with a definite speed c that does not depend on the motion of its source. Perhaps this startles us. If, for example, we think of light as consisting of particles, we would naturally say that their speeds depend on the way their sources move. But from the point of view of the wave theory of light, Einstein's second principle takes on the aspect of an utter triviality. For, no matter how a light wave is started, once it is on its way it is carried by

* James Clerk Maxwell's (1831–1879) theory expressed in a unified mathematical form fundamental principles concerning electricity and magnetism. [Eds.]

190

the ether at the standard speed with which waves are transmitted therein. If this is so obvious, why does Einstein state it as a principle? Because early in his paper he says that the introduction of an ether will prove "superfluous." His second principle extracts from the ether the essential that he needs. Note his audacity. Fresh from his quantum proposal that light must somehow consist of particles, he takes as the second principle of his theory of relativity something inherent in the wave theory of light, even as he declares the idea of an ether superfluous. There is in this a striking indication of the sureness of his physical intuition.

Here, then, we have two simple principles, each plausible, each seemingly innocent, each bordering on the obvious. Where is the harm in them? Where the threat of revolution?

In his paper, Einstein speaks of them as "only apparently irreconcilable." *Irreconcilable?* Where is the conflict? Only *apparently* irreconcilable? What can he possibly have in mind?

Watch closely. It will be worth the effort. But be forewarned. As we follow the gist of Einstein's argument we shall find ourselves nodding in agreement, and later almost nodding in sleep, so obvious and unimportant will it seem. There will come a stage at which we shall barely be able to stifle a yawn. Beware. We shall by then have committed ourselves and it will be too late to avoid the jolt; for the beauty of Einstein's argument lies precisely in its seeming innocence.

Consider, then, two similar, well-equipped vehicles in uniform motion, as shown in the accompanying diagram, and imagine them far out in space so that they are unaffected by external influences. The vehicles, named *A* and *B* after their captains, have a uniform relative motion of, shall we say, 10,000 miles per second, as indicated. At the center of each vehicle is a lamp. When *A* and *B* come abreast, they flash their lamps on for an instant, thus sending out pulses of light to left and right. The diagram shows these pulses and the vehicles a moment later. For convenience, we have drawn it as though *A* were "at rest."

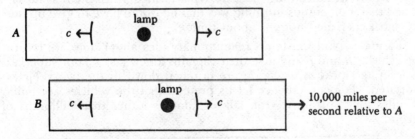

We now set the stage for a question. By Einstein's second principle the speeds of the pulses of light do not depend on the motions of their sources. Therefore—and this is important—the pulses keep abreast as shown. In his vehicle, *A* measures their speeds to the right and the left and finds the value *c* for both. *B* makes corresponding measurements within his own vehicle. He is moving at 10,000 miles per second relative to *A*, while his light pulses keep abreast of *A*'s. Agreed? Then here is the question: What values of the speeds of the pulses relative to himself does *B* obtain?

Because of his motion relative to *A*, we would expect *B* to find his leftward-moving light pulse traveling relative to him with a speed of $c + 10,000$, and the other with the vastly different speed of $c - 10,000$.

But if this were the case, we should run afoul of Einstein's first postulate. How so? Because A and B are performing identical internal experiments within their respective vehicles, and since they are in uniform motion they must obtain identical results. Therefore B, like A, must find that the speeds are both c. Indeed, no matter how fast B may travel relative to A in an attempt to overtake the receding light, it will always recede from him with the same speed c. He cannot catch up with the receding light any more than one can reach the horizon on earth. No material object can travel as fast as light. Here in this startling result we see an unexpected answer to the sixteen-year-old Einstein's question about keeping abreast of light waves. [At age sixteen, Einstein had asked himself what a light wave would look like to someone keeping pace with it].

Since the result is so startling, let us look at it differently, if only to convince ourselves that it necessarily follows from Einstein's two principles. Suppose A found the speed in both directions to be c while B found it to be $c + 10,000$ in one direction and $c - 10,000$ in the other. Then A could legitimately conclude that he was at absolute rest and B could legitimately conclude that he was traveling at an absolute speed of 10,000 miles per second. And this would belie the principle of relativity.

A lesser man finding this calamitous consequence of two seemingly innocent postulates would immediately have abandoned one or the other. But Einstein had chosen his two principles precisely because they went to the heart of the matter, and he boldly retained both. Their very plausibility—taken separately—gave his theory a firm foundation. In such treacherous regions of thought he could not afford to build on quicksands.

We have now seen why Einstein used the word "irreconcilable." Yet he had said that his two principles were only "apparently" irreconcilable, and this meant that he was going to reconcile them nevertheless. But how?

Here we enter the crucial stage of the argument. The remedy obviously had to be something drastic. What flashed on Einstein as he sat up in bed that momentous morning was that he would have to give up one of our most cherished notions about time.

To understand Einstein's revolutionary idea about time, we return to the vehicles A and B and give their captains a new task. Four superlatively accurate clocks a_1, a_2, b_1, b_2 are fastened down in the two vehicles as indicated. For convenience let us pretend that the vehicles are millions of miles long so that we can talk of minutes rather than billionths of a second.

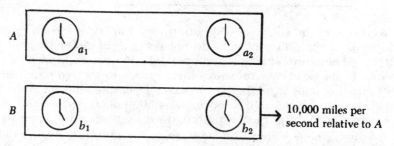

A sends a flash of light from a_1 to a_2, where it is immediately deflected back to a_1. The light leaves a_1 when the hands of a_1 read noon, and reaches a_2 when *its* hands read 3 minutes past noon. We can not be sure from this that the light took 3 minutes to travel from a_1 to a_2: for example, the workmen who installed the clocks may inadvertently have moved the hands. How can we synchronize clock a_2 with clock a_1? Let us consider the double journey. Suppose the light leaves a_1 when the hands of a_1 read noon, reaches a_2 when *its* hands read 3 minutes after noon, and returns to a_1 when a_1's hands read 4 minutes after noon. We immediately suspect that something is wrong. The clocks are alleging that the light took 3 minutes to travel from a_1 to a_2 but only 1 minute to return from a_2 to a_1. We do the obvious thing. We move the minute hand of a_2 back 1 minute. Now, when we perform the experiment, the clocks will indicate that the light took 2 minutes to travel from a_1 to a_2 and 2 minutes to travel back from a_2 to a_1. Since, as we have seen, we want the speed of the light to be c in both directions, we would agree with Einstein that the hands of the clocks a_1 and a_2 are now so set that the clocks are synchronized. And if, a little later, something happens at a_1 when the hands of a_1 read 4:30, and something else happens at a_2 when the hands of a_2 also read 4:30, we would agree with Einstein that the two separated events had occurred simultaneously.

Perhaps all this seems rather pointless—so obvious that we can barely stifle the yawn we spoke about. But, as we have mentioned before, the beauty of Einstein's argument is that it is based on concepts of beguiling acceptability. While politely stifling our yawn, we have unknowingly committed ourselves to a staggering consequence.

As A synchronizes his clocks a_1 and a_2 in the above manner prescribed by Einstein, B observes him in utter amazement. For, relative to B, A is moving to the left at 10,000 miles per second. Thus although A claims that his light is traveling equal distances forward and back like this

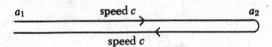

B sees the distances as manifestly unequal, like this

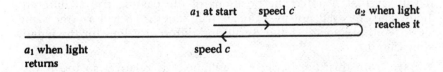

What is B to think? What is he driven to conclude? That since the forward and backward distances are *unequal*, the very fact that the forward and backward journeys of the light take equal times according to a_1 and a_2 is proof to B that clocks a_1 and a_2 are *not* synchronized.

Naturally, when B tells A about this, A is upset. So he asks B to synchronize clocks b_1 and b_2 according to the agreed-upon Einsteinian procedure. B does so, and at once A has his revenge. For, relative to A, B is moving to the right at 10,000 miles per second, and although B claims that his light is traveling equal distances forward and back like this

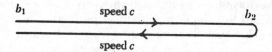

A sees the distances as manifestly unequal, like this

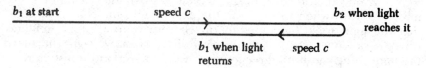

Thus A says that clocks a_1 and a_2 are synchronized, but B says they are not. And B says that clocks b_1 and b_2 are synchronized, but A says they are not. So if A says that events occurring at a_1 and a_2 are simultaneous, B will deny it. And vice versa.

Do we side with A or do we side with B? Einstein's first postulate, the principle of relativity, puts A and B on an equal footing. We must therefore conclude with Einstein that both are right.

Now comes the supreme stroke of genius. Einstein looks on this divergence of views not as a minor squabble but as a characteristic of Time itself. Our common-sense, Newtonian concept of a universal time providing a universal simultaneity has been shattered before our eyes. Time, according to Einstein, is of such a nature that the simultaneity of separated events is relative. Events simultaneous for A are, in general, not simultaneous for B; and events simultaneous for B are, in general, not simultaneous for A. Though this may be shocking, we have to learn to live with it. And to live with further shocks. For time is fundamental, and a drastic change in our conception of it brings the whole structure of theoretical physics tumbling down like a house of cards. Hardly anything remains untouched.

Take length, for instance, that other mainstay of theoretical physics. Imagine a rod moving past A and B. To measure its length as it rushes by, A notes the positions of its ends at a particular instant—which is to say simultaneously. So does B. But since A and B disagree about simultaneity, A will say that B noted the positions of the passing rod at different moments and thus did not measure its true length. B will say the same about A. And in general A and B will find different values for the length thus measured.

We see from this that because simultaneity is relative, so too is distance. And there is obviously no stopping the epidemic. Speed, acceleration, force, energy—all these and more depend on time and distance: the very fabric of physics is changed.

What of the relationship between the measurements of time and space made by A and those made by B? Or by any two observers in vehicles in uniform relative motion? Einstein typically looked for the simplest mathematical relationship deducible from his two principles. In this way he derived from them none other than the Lorentz * transformation [that

---

* Hendrik Antoon Lorentz (1853–1928)
won the 1902 Nobel Prize for physics for his
theory of electromagnetic radiation. [Eds.]

objects contract in the direction of their motion]—a transformation with which, almost certainly, he had not been previously acquainted.

Armed with this transformation, he made further deductions. His two principles may at first have seemed innocent, but their logical consequences are often such as to outrage common sense. For example, as Einstein showed, *A* finds *B*'s clocks going at a slower rate than his own. After recovering from our surprise—for, were not the clocks all equally reliable?—we expect that *B* finds *A*'s clocks going at a faster rate than his own. But no. Each finds that the other's clocks go the more slowly.

Again, we recall the proposal . . . that objects contract in the directions of their motion through the ether. Einstein obtained precisely the same formula for the amount of the contraction. But in Einstein's theory this is a mutual, relative effect: *A* finds that *B*'s longitudinal yardsticks are contracted compared with his own, while *B* finds that *A*'s are the shorter. Nothing could reveal more strikingly the revolutionary boldness of Einstein's ideas compared with those of his elders Lorentz and Poincaré.* All three had the Lorentz transformation, in which the startling consequences were implicit. But, when interpreting it, neither Lorentz nor Poincaré dared to give the principle of relativity full trust. If *A* was at rest, as they put it, then *B*'s yardsticks would be contracted. But nothing was said about *B* finding *A*'s contracted. It was tacitly assumed that *B* would find *A*'s the longer. As for the rates of actual clocks, no such discussion as Einstein's was given.

Poincaré, one of the greatest mathematicians of his time, was a man of subtle philosophical insight. In his major paper of 1905 he had extraordinary command of the detailed mathematical apparatus of the theory of relativity. For years he had preached the purely conventional nature of physical concepts. He had early sensed the probable validity of a principle of relativity. Yet when he came to the decisive step, his nerve failed him and he clung to old habits of thought and familiar ideas of space and time. If this seems surprising, it is because we underestimate the boldness of Einstein in stating the principle of relativity as an axiom and, by keeping faith with it, changing our notions of time and space.

In making this revolutionary change Einstein was greatly influenced by the ideas of Mach,** whose critical book on Newtonian mechanics Besso had brought to Einstein's attention in his student days. Mach will enter our story further, even though Einstein's early enthusiasm for his philosophical ideas did not last. Mach had been profoundly skeptical of concepts like absolute space and absolute time—and atoms. Roughly speaking, he looked on science as a sort of neat cataloguing of data, and he wanted all concepts to be clearly definable in terms of specific procedures. Einstein's treatment of simultaneity in terms of specific synchronizing procedures clearly shows Mach's influence. But others, Poincaré among them, also knew Mach's ideas, yet it was Einstein who made the crucial advance.

The mutual contractions of lengths, like the mutual slowings of clocks, are not self-contradictory. They are closely analogous to effects of perspective. For example, if two people of equal height walk away from one another, stop, and look back, each appears to the other diminished in

---

* Henri Poincaré (1854–1912) was a prominent mathematician, astronomer, and philosopher of science. [Eds.]

** Ernst Mach (1838–1916) was a physicist and a philosopher who was among the founders of scientific positivism. [Eds.]

size; and the reason this particular mutual contraction does not strike us adults as a contradiction is simply that we have grown used to it.

We have told barely enough to give a hint of the revolutionary nature of Einstein's paper of 1905 on relativity. Once the foundations are laid, the paper becomes highly mathematical. Einstein shows how, with the new ideas of time and space, Maxwell's equations conform to the principle of relativity, even as these ideas require a revision of Newtonian mechanics. For example, the faster an object moves relative to an experimenter, the greater will be its mass relative to him. Characteristically, Einstein leads up to a prediction that can be put to experimental test. He gives formulas for the motion of electrons in an electromagnetic field, taking account of the relativistic increases in their masses as their speeds increase relative to the observer. By a different route, Lorentz had made essentially the same prediction in 1904, and had compared it favorably with results already found by an experimenter. The equivalence of the formulas need not surprise us, since; as we have said, Lorentz and Einstein had a common Maxwellian heritage. But there is a difference between the men that is worthy of note. In 1906 the same experimenter, publishing new measurements, categorically declared them incompatible with the prediction of Lorentz and Einstein but compatible with certain rival theories. Lorentz was distinctly disheartened. But Einstein was unperturbed. Looking at the rival theories with aesthetic disapproval, he confidently suggested that the experimenter could be in error. And subsequent measurements by others showed that Einstein was correct.

. . .

But our chapter cannot stop here. Einstein was not yet done with 1905. In late September, three months after the relativity paper, he sent to *Annalen der Physik* a further paper that was published in November. It occupies three printed pages. Using electromagnetic equations taken from his previous paper, Einstein here shows by calculation that if a body gives off an amount E of energy *in the form of light*, its mass diminishes by an amount E/c^2.

With his instinctive sense of cosmic unity he now tosses off a penetrating and crucially important remark: that the fact that the energy is in the form of light "evidently makes no difference." He therefore announces a general law to the effect that if a body gives off or takes in an amount E of energy *of any sort*, it loses or gains an amount of mass E/c^2.

According to this, because c is so large, if a light bulb emitted 100 watts of light for a hundred years it would give off in that time energy whose total mass was less than a millionth of an ounce. But radium, through its radioactivity, gives off relatively enormous amounts of energy, and Einstein suggested that the theory could thus be tested.

In this paper of 1905 Einstein said that all energy of whatever sort has mass. It took even him two years more to come to the stupendous realization that the reverse must also hold: that all mass, of whatever sort, must have energy. He was led to this by aesthetic reasons. Why should one make a distinction in kind between the mass that an object already has and the mass that it loses in giving off energy? To do so would be to imagine two types of mass for no good reason when one would suffice. The distinction would be inartistic and logically indefensible. Therefore all mass must have energy.

With mass and energy thus wholly equivalent, Einstein was able in 1907, in a long and mainly expository paper published in the *Jahrbuch der*

Radioaktivität, to write his famous equation $E = mc^2$. Imagine the audacity of this step: every clod of earth, every feather, every speck of dust becoming a prodigious reservoir of entrapped energy. There was no way of verifying this at the time. Yet in presenting his equation in 1907 Einstein spoke of it as the most important consequence of his theory of relativity. His extraordinary ability to see far ahead is shown by the fact that his equation was not verified quantitatively till some twenty-five years later, and then only in difficult laboratory experiments. He could not foresee the tragic events that were to grow from his artistically motivated $E = mc^2$. . . .

NOTE

Hoffmann's description of Einstein's development of the special theory of relativity provides a glimpse of a great scientific mind at work. Would Einstein's undoubted brilliance have made him a successful judge? Indeed, is brilliance, as contrasted with wisdom or empathy, a necessary characteristic of a good attorney or judge?

When Einstein found two principles in apparent conflict he dared to accept some rather astonishing implications of those principles. Should a judge react similarly when two principles appear to conflict? If judges must resolve value-laden human conflicts, rather than seek timeless truth, should they maintain a greater willingness to reinterpret or refine principles? Consider, in this respect, descriptions of the legal process set forth by Cardozo and Levi in Ch. 1, Sec. C.2, supra.

Whether one sees similarities between legal and scientific reasoning depends in part on whether one views law as a science. Even apart from traditional natural law theories, there have been persistent efforts throughout American history to identify legal reasoning with scientific methods. Thus, for example, Professor G. Edward White has linked the emergence of tort law late in the 19th century in part to "an impulse toward 'conceptualization' . . . [that] stressed 'scientific methodologies' " and that sought to perfect "the law as a science." White, The Intellectual Origins of Torts in America, 86 Yale L.J. 671, 678 (1977). More pointedly, a leader in the field of law and economics has written that "as biology is to living systems, astronomy to the stars, or economics to the price system, so should legal studies be to the legal system: an endeavor to make precise, objective and systematic observations of how the legal system operates in fact and to discover and explain the recurrent patterns in the observations—the 'laws' of the system." Posner, Volume One of the Journal of Legal Studies—An Afterward, 1 J. Legal Stud. 437 (1972). At the other extreme, Grant Gilmore wrote that "the quest for the laws which will explain the riddle of human behavior leads us not toward truth but toward the illusion of certainty, which is our curse. So far as we have been able to learn, there are no recurrent patterns in the course of human events; it is not possible to make scientific statements about history, sociology, economics—or law." G. Gilmore, The Ages of American Law, 99–100 (1977). Do you agree with Posner that legal studies can be like astronomy? Is the only alternative to that a form of nihilism?

Einstein's historic development of $E = mc^2$ also illustrates the role of aesthetics in science. Recall that aesthetic considerations led him to conclude that there should be no distinction between the mass that an object already has and the mass that it loses in giving off energy. The scientist's search for a beautiful order in nature motivated, among many others, J. D. Watson in his search for the double helix. See Ch. 1, Sec. A.1, supra. Can lawyers or legal scholars pursue a comparable search for beauty? In analyzing the views of Posner and Gilmore discussed above, Arthur Leff sided with Gilmore's view that law is not a science, yet Leff concluded:

The truth is, I fear, as Grant Gilmore sees it: all we can understand, and that not very well, are the games we ourselves generate and eventually, but predictably, lose . . ... But at least there is this: on the way to those final defeats, there are, at least for some, some beautiful innings.

Leff, Law And, 87 Yale L.J. 989, 1011 (1978).

MICHAEL POLANYI, THE REPUBLIC OF SCIENCE

1 Minerva 54, 62 (1962).

In January 1945 Lord [Bertrand] Russell and I were together on the BBC Brains Trust. We were asked about the possible technical uses of Einstein's theory of relativity, and neither of us could think of any. This was 40 years after the publication of the theory and 50 years after the inception by Einstein of the work which led to its discovery. . . . But, actually, the technical application of relativity, which neither Russell nor I could think of, was to be revealed within a few months by the explosion of the first atomic bomb. For the energy of the explosion was released at the expense of mass in accordance with the relativistic equation $e = mc^2$, an equation which was soon to be found splashed over the cover of *Time* magazine, as a token of its supreme practical importance.

Perhaps Russell and I should have done better in foreseeing these applications of relativity in January 1945, but it is obvious that Einstein could not possibly take these future consequences into account when he started on the problem which led to the discovery of relativity at the turn of the century. For one thing, another dozen or more major discoveries had yet to be made before relativity could be combined with them to yield the technical process which opened the atomic age.

Any attempt at guiding scientific research towards a purpose other than its own is an attempt to deflect it from the advancement of science. Emergencies may arise in which all scientists willingly apply their gifts to tasks of public interest. It is conceivable that we may come to abhor the progress of science, and stop all scientific research or at least whole branches of it, as the Soviets stopped research in genetics for 25 years. You can kill or mutilate the advance of science, you cannot shape it. For it can advance only by essentially unpredictable steps, pursuing problems of its own, and the practical benefits of these advances will be incidental and hence doubly unpredictable.

NOTE

When Einstein began his work on the special theory of relativity he did not have in mind the practical generation of energy, let alone the atomic bomb. As Polanyi indicates, numerous discoveries followed before the bomb became possible. In particular, experimental and theoretical work involving the bombardment of uranium with neutrons led to the discovery of nuclear fission, the "atom-splitting" that liberates energy in accordance with Einstein's equation. See, e.g., S. Glasstone, Sourcebook on Atomic Energy 473–504 (1967). One of the central difficulties for the social control of science is finding the point at which unwanted consequences of science can be controlled without harming basic science. A judge considering the environmental implications of the breeder reactor, a nuclear technology discussed in Ch. 2, Sec. B.2, infra, put the matter as follows:

I say this: I say there comes a time, we start out with E equals MC^2, we both agreed you don't have to have the impact statement then. Then there comes a time when there are a thousand of these breeder plants in existence all over the country.

Sometime before that, surely as anything under the present law, there has to be an impact statement, and a long time before that, actually.

But the question is, exactly where in this chain do we have to have an impact statement.

Scientists' Institute for Public Information v. Atomic Energy Commission, 481 F.2d 1079, 1093 (D.C.Cir.1973).

2. DEVELOPING AND USING THE ATOMIC BOMB

During World War II, fears that the Germans might develop atomic weapons spurred the United States to undertake a program designed for the same end. The Manhattan Project began in 1942 and led ultimately to the atomic bombing of Hiroshima and Nagasaki in 1945. The Project involved 150,000 people, over $2.2 billion and a remarkable level of scientific and technological expertise. The scientists' experience with the Manhattan Project, as well as with wartime radar research at the MIT Radiation Laboratory, greatly influenced the post-war relation between science and the state. For decades, most of America's leading spokesmen in science policy, including presidential science advisors such as George Kistiakowsky and Jerome Wiesner, were those who had worked in the wartime labs. See Greenberg, The Politics of Pure Science 81–96 (1967).

The wartime experience affected American science in a variety of ways. Government assumed a greater role in supporting science and scientists assumed a greater role in policy debates. Scientists also began to question more sharply the morality of their own endeavor. The materials below raise these issues primarily through the eyes of Robert Oppenheimer, a brilliant theoretical physicist who directed the Los Alamos Scientific Laboratory—the heart of the Manhattan Project—and who later lost his security clearance because of his alleged contacts with Communists and his opposition to the post-war construction of the hydrogen bomb.

ROBERT JUNGK,
BRIGHTER THAN A THOUSAND SUNS
131–132 (1958).

It seemed as though unsuspected physical resources had come to Oppenheimer's aid in those weeks |when he first took over at Los Alamos]. The first thing he had to do was to travel about the country by air or by rail to persuade other physicists to join him at the new secret laboratory on the edge of the desert. In the course of his recruitment tour he had first to dispose of the prejudices of many of his colleagues against Project S–1 [the Manhattan Project]. During the two years and more it had taken people to make up their minds, while the atomic project stuck fast in a deadlock of overlapping authorities, the opinion had gone round among physicists that nothing good could ever come of the affair. In order to silence such doubts Oppie often went further than he should have gone on security grounds in his descriptions of the new studies and aims.

At that time he believed, in common with the most able of the specialists concerned, for example Hans Bethe, that the bomb could be ready within about a year. It is true that he could give no guarantee that the new weapon would be able to do its job. It might quite possibly turn out to be a dud. Nor did he conceal the fact that those who agreed to go to Los Alamos would have to sign, on security grounds, a more or less binding contract to remain there for the entire duration of the war. He added that they and their families would be cut off, as never before, from the outside world, and would be living in less than comfortable conditions.

In spite of Oppenheimer's frank admission of the many difficulties involved his recruiting campaign had an unexpectedly great success. His remarkable capacity for seeing the other point of view enabled him to find the right answer to the doubts expressed. Some physicists he terrified by the prospect of a German atom bomb. Others he attracted by his descriptions of the beauty of New Mexico. But to all he imparted the feeling of how exciting it would be to participate in the pioneering work to be carried out in this still-quite-novel field of research.

Probably, however, many of those he approached, who were mostly very young, agreed to his request for the reason, above all, that it was Oppenheimer who was to be their chief. His personal magnetism, hitherto only exercised upon his students, both male and female, now proved equally irresistible in wider circles. It was only seldom that one came across such inspiring personalities in the learned world. Oppenheimer bore no resemblance to the dry-as-dust specialist. He could quote Dante and Proust. He could refute objections by citing passages from the works of Indian sages which he had read in the original. And he seemed to be aflame with an inward spiritual passion. It would be extraordinarily stimulating to work in such close and intense association as would never have been possible in times of peace, with this and other outstanding atomic-research experts. Oppenheimer in fact possessed, as one of the victims subsequently put it, in irreverent but striking fashion, "intellectual sex appeal." . . .

[The following passage describes the reactions of Oppenheimer and of Nobel Prize winner I.I. Rabi to the testing of "Fat Boy"—the first atomic bomb.]

NUEL PHARR DAVIS, LAWRENCE AND OPPENHEIMER

240–242 (1968).

While the light faded, not abruptly for him, Oppenheimer became conscious again that he was not alone in the blockhouse. "A few people laughed, a few people cried, most people were silent," he said. "There floated through my mind a line from the *Bhagavad-Gita* in which Krishna is trying to persuade the Prince that he should do his duty: 'I am become death, the shatterer of worlds.' I think we all had this feeling more or less."

By their eyes and eardrums physicists could tell at once that Fat Boy's violence was something new to human capabilities. "We felt the world would never be the same again," said Oppenheimer. While searchlights picked at the faded fireball and re-created it as a huge ghostly cloud in the night sky, preliminary instrument reports indicated blast had far exceeded the official hopeful expectation of five thousand tons. From the blockhouse roof Oppenheimer watched the cloud feint frighteningly north. A little after dawn it turned east in the direction it had been expected to take. He and the other physicists went back to the base camp.

. . . .

When the blast came, he [Rabi] was surprised at the response his body made. After a minute he noticed with a scientist's habit of observation that gooseflesh appeared on the backs of his hands. It was not like watching an ordinary explosion scaled up. "The experience was hard to describe," he says. "I haven't got over it yet. It was awful, ominous, personally threatening. I couldn't tell why." Dawn found him still in reverie as he watched the blockhouse party approaching from a long way off across the sand. Oppenheimer parked too far away for Rabi to see his face, but something in his bearing brought Rabi's gooseflesh back again. He moved like a confident stranger, darkly glittering, at ease, in tune with the thing. "I'll never forget his walk," says Rabi. "I'll never forget the way he stepped out of the car."

NOTE

Oppenheimer's excitement at working on the atomic bomb and his ambivalence after seeing its capabilities are not unusual responses for scientists whose work has social consequences. It is difficult to overestimate the impact on post-war scientists in all disciplines of the Manhattan Project experience; an experience that culminated, in Oppenheimer's phrase, with the realization that "the physicists have known sin." P. Goodchild, J. Robert Oppenheimer: Shatterer of Worlds 174 (1981). When the cancer researcher Robert Pollack was asked to help organize the first Asilomar Conference on the dangers of recombinant DNA research, he agreed because he felt that inadequate safety standards posed a "pre-Hiroshima condition—It would be a real disaster if one of the agents now being handled in research should in fact be a real human cancer agent." Swazey, Sorenson and Wong, Risks and Benefits, Rights and Responsibilities: A History of the Recombinant DNA Research Controversy, 51 S.Cal.L.Rev. 1019, 1022 (1978).

Do scientists have any particular responsibility to control scientific projects that may have undesirable social consequences? On the one hand, scientists are often in the best position to know, early on, what consequences might occur. On the other hand, as discussed in Ch. 1, supra, the value system of scientists makes it particularly difficult for them to slow the progressive growth of knowledge. Shortly after the completion of the Manhattan Project, Oppenheimer, in a speech to Los Alamos scientists, stated:

> But when you come right down to it the reason that we did this job is because it was an organic necessity. If you are a scientist you cannot stop such a thing. If you are a scientist you believe that it is good to find out how the world works; that it is good to find out what the realities are, that it is good to turn over to mankind at large the greatest possible power to control the world and to deal with it according to its lights and values.

Smith and Weiner (eds.), Robert J. Oppenheimer: Letters and Recollections 317 (1980).

BARTON J. BERNSTEIN,
THE ATOMIC BOMB

vii (1976).

On August 6, 1945, at 8:15 A.M., the *Enola Gay* dropped a uranium bomb ("Little Boy") on Hiroshima, a major Japanese city, killing about 70,000 and injuring 70,000 others—more than half the city's population. On August 9, the day after Russia declared war on Japan, the United States dropped a second bomb (a plutonium weapon, or "Fat Man"), this time at Nagasaki, killing about 40,000 Japanese, injuring 60,000, and also killing some Dutch prisoners of war. President Harry S. Truman promised that the United States would "continue . . . until we completely destroy Japan's power to make war. Only a Japanese surrender will stop us." On August 14 Japan surrendered, and on September 2 the nations signed the formal papers. Nearly four years after Japan's attack on Pearl Harbor, the war in the Pacific had finally ended.

Most Americans rejoiced that the costly war was over, and few were troubled by the use of the bomb. For most citizens its justification seemed obvious: the bomb was a legitimate weapon, it speeded victory, and it saved American lives. Policymakers publicly shared these views. In future years, Truman often declared that he never had any doubts about using the bomb, that it saved millions of lives, and that he would do it again. . . .

LOUIS BERES, APOCALYPSE

123–126 (1980).

[Hiroshima] was the site of a genuine nuclear attack by one country upon another, although the bomb itself—a weapon with the mere force of less than 20,000 tons of TNT—was certainly a pygmy by today's standards. The bomb created an area of total destruction which extended about two miles in all directions, destroying 60,000 buildings and killing between 78,000 and 200,000 people. At points close to the hypocenter, all metal and stone were melted, and human beings were completely incinerated. According to Robert Jay Lifton, the distinguished Yale psychiatrist:

> The area was enveloped by fires fanned by a violent "firewind;" these broke out almost immediately within a radius of more than three thousand meters (up to two miles). The inundation with death of the area closest to the hypocenter was such that if a man survived within a thousand meters (.6 miles) and was out of doors (that is, without benefit of shielding from heat or radiation), more than nine tenths of the people around him were fatalities. . . . Those closest to the hypocenter could usually recall a sudden flash, an intense sensation of heat, being knocked down or thrown some distance, and finding themselves pinned under debris or simply awakening from an indeterminate period of unconsciousness. *The most striking psychological feature of this immediate experience was the sense of a sudden and absolute shift from normal existence to an overwhelming encounter with death.*

After the initial shock, Lifton points out interestingly, the prevailing atmosphere was one of "deathly silence" rather than wild panic. Amidst an aura of weirdness and unreality, the "survivors" described a ghastly stillness in which the normal line between life and death was blurred beyond distinction. In the words of M. Hachiya's classic *Hiroshima Diary*:

> Those who were able walked silently toward the suburbs in the distant hills, their spirits broken, their initiative gone. When asked whence they had come, they pointed to the city and said, "That way:" and when asked where they were going, pointed away from the city and said, "This way." They were so broken and confused that they moved and behaved like automatons. Their reactions had astonished outsiders who reported with amazement the spectacle of long files of people holding stolidly to a narrow, rough path when close by was a smooth, easy road going in the same direction. The outsiders could not grasp the fact that they were witnessing the exodus of a people who walked in the realm of dreams.

This sort of dreamlike, disoriented behavior was also reportedly characteristic of the Nazi death camp survivors upon their liberation. And in both cases, despite the apparent hopelessness of the situation, numerous survivors—however ineffectually—sought to help others, a factor that probably contributed a great deal to their own survival. This point, that compassion and concern for others in extreme situations is the key to one's own survival, is the main thesis of Terrence Des Pres's account of Hitler's kingdom of death. There are, however, several accounts of the atomic bomb experience which discount this thesis. For example, according to Takashi Nagai, a physician of Nagasaki (the second target of American nuclear attack in August 1945):

> In general, then, those who survived the atom bomb were the people who ignored their friends crying out *in extremis*; or who shook off wounded neighbors who clung to them, pleading to be saved. . . . In short, those who survived the bomb were, if not merely lucky, in a greater or lesser degree selfish, self-centered, guided by instinct and not civilization . . . and we know it, we who have survived. Knowing it is a dull ache without surcease.

This last remark points to the phenomenon of *survivor guilt*, an inevitable and enduring consequence of nuclear attack. Lifton's descriptions of the need of the *hibakusha* (atomic bomb survivors), from the moment of atomic bomb exposure, to justify their own survival in the midst of death for so many others, are paralleled by the death camp accounts of other literary intellectuals.

Survivor guilt, however, is not the only enduring personal consequence of nuclear catastrophe, as the experience of the "Hiroshima Maidens" points out. These twenty-five young women, brought to the United States in 1955 for plastic-surgical treatment of burn scars and hideous accumulations of keloid scar tissue, are still ravaged by their experience of many years ago. Initially tormented by catastrophic injuries that left them with eyes they could not close and mouths that could not speak or eat, they still live in fear that their exposure to radiation might produce deformed children. One of the "maidens," Michiko Sako, expresses her feelings in a poem entitled, "Bring Back My Smile:"

> Though flowers bloom again,
>   Even after blossoms have fallen,
>   Once injured, the body never heals.

Now that some of the more terrible physical deformities have been corrected or relieved, Mrs. Sako still feels that she will never "be able to erase the nonphysical scars, even in the future."

At the time of their suffering, the survivors of Auschwitz and Hiroshima, of Treblinka and Nagasaki, reacted to the otherworldly grotesqueness of their conditions with what Lifton describes as a profound sense of "death in life." Witnessing, in the one case, the thrusting of newly delivered babies, *alive*, into ovens, and in the other, the appearance of long lines of severely burned, literally melting, ghosts, the survivors found themselves, in Bruno Bettelheim's words, an "anonymous mass," or in the Japanese term, *mugamuchū*, "without self, without a center." Such a total disruption of individual and social order, of one's customary personal and community supports, produced consequences that went far beyond immediate physical and emotional suffering. Indeed, this understanding is incorporated in the Japanese term for atomic bomb survivors, *hibakusha*, which delimits four categories of victims. According to Dr. Lifton, these categories include

> those who at the time of the bomb were within the city limits of Hiroshima as then defined . . . those who came into the city within fourteen days and entered a designated area extending to about two thousand meters from the hypocenter; those who came into physical contact with bomb victims, through various forms of aid or disposal of bodies; and those who were *in utero* at the time, and whose mothers fit into any of the first three groups.

The effects of Hiroshima, therefore, are not confined to the immediate or even long-term experiences of those who bore witness, but extend to their rescuers, their progeny, and even to the progeny of their rescuers. Perhaps it would not be unreasonable to expand the category of *habakusha* to include the children of Japanese mothers who do not fit into one of the three above-mentioned groups, as well as several generations of Americans who, willingly or unwillingly, share the burden of national guilt. Perhaps it would not even be unreasonable to include human kind as a whole, since the legacy of Hiroshima is an interloper that can never be fully excluded from our collective destiny.

HERMAN KAHN,
THINKING ABOUT THE UNTHINKABLE

18–19, 22–24 (1962).

In 1960 I published a book [*On Thermonuclear War*] that attempted to direct attention to the possibility of a thermonuclear war, to ways of reducing the likelihood of such a war, and to methods for coping with the consequences should war occur despite our efforts to avoid it. The book was greeted by a large range of responses—some of them sharply critical. Some of this criticism was substantive, touching on greater or smaller questions of strategy, policy, or research techniques. But much of the criticism was not concerned with the correctness or incorrectness of the views I expressed. It was concerned with whether any book should have been written on this subject at all. It is characteristic of our times that many intelligent and sincere people are willing to argue that it is immoral to think and even more immoral to write in detail about having to fight a thermonuclear war. . . .

The arguments against hard thinking by anyone at all about the realities of thermonuclear war break down into a number of categories: First, it is argued that thinking about the indescribable horror of nuclear war breeds callousness and indifference to the future of civilization in our planners and decision makers. It is true that detailed and dispassionate discussion of such questions is likely to look incredibly hard-hearted. It should also be clear, at least to thoughtful readers, that such questions must be considered. The reality may be so unpleasant that decision makers would prefer not to face it; but to a great extent this reality has been forced on them, or has come uninvited. Thanks to our ever-increasing technology we are living in a terrible and dangerous world; but, unlike the lady in the cartoon we cannot say, "Stop the world, I want to get off." We cannot get off. Even the most utopian of today's visionaries will have to concede that the mere existence of modern technology involves a risk to civilization that would have been unthinkable twenty-five years ago. While we are going to make major attempts to change the nature of this reality, accepting great risks if necessary, most of us are unwilling to choose either a pronounced degree of unilateral disarmament or a preventive war designed to "settle" our problems one way or another. We therefore must face the facts that thermonuclear bombs now exist in the hands of at least four powers; that at least one of these powers has announced it is interested in the destruction of our society, albeit by peaceful means if possible; that the number of thermonuclear powers may grow; that the power most likely to obtain these weapons next, China, stands on the thesis that war with us is inevitable; and, finally, that the possibilities of an immediate solution by negotiation are indeed slim. Unless we are willing to abdicate our responsibilities we are pledged to the maintenance of terrifying weapon systems with known and unknown, calculable and incalculable risks, unless and until better arrangements can be made.

If we are to have an expensive and lethal defense establishment, we must weigh all the risks and benefits. We must at least ask ourselves what are the likely and unlikely results of an inadvertent war, the possibilities of accident, irresponsibility, or unauthorized behavior on the other side as well as on our own.

A variation of the objection to careful consideration of these problems focuses on the personality of the thinker. This argument goes: Better no thought than evil thought; and since only evil and callous people can think about this, better no thought. Alternatively, the thinker's motives are analyzed: This man studies war; he must like war—much like the suspicion that a surgeon is a repressed sadist. Even if the charge were true, which in general it is not, it is not relevant. Like the repressed sadist who can perform a socially useful function by sublimating his urges into surgery, the man who loves war or violence may be able to successfully sublimate his desires into a careful and valuable study of war. It does indeed take an iron will or an unpleasant degree of detachment to go about this task. Ideally it should be possible for the analyst to have a disciplined empathy. In fact, the mind recoils from simultaneously probing deeply and creatively into these problems and being conscious at all times of the human tragedy involved.

This is not new. We do not continually remind the surgeon while he is operating of the humanity of his patient. We do not flash pictures of his patient's wife or children in front of him. We want him to be careful, and we want him to be aware of the importance and frailty of the patient; we do not want him to be distracted or fearful. We do not expect illustrations in a book on surgery to be captioned: "A particularly deplorable tumor," or "Good health is preferable to this kind of cancer." Excessive comments such as, "And now there's a lot of blood," or "This particular cut really hurts," are out of place although these are important things for a surgeon to know. To mention such things may be important. To dwell on them is morbid, and gets in the way of the information. The same tolerance needs be extended to thought on national security.

Some feel that we should consider these problems but view them with such awe and horror that we should not discuss them in normal, neutral, professional everyday language. I tend to disagree, at least so far as technical discussions and research are concerned. One does not do research in a cathedral. Awe is fine for those who come to worship or admire but for those who come to analyze, to tamper, to change, to criticize, a factual and dispassionate, and sometimes even colorful, approach is to be preferred. And if the use of everyday language jars, that is all the more reason for using it. Why would one expect a realistic discussion of thermonuclear war not to be disturbing? . . .

NOTE

Kahn supports his view that rigorous cost-benefit analysis should guide our nuclear strategy by arguing that one should not continually remind a surgeon of the humanity of his patient. Do you agree that disinterested physicians provide the best medical care? See Ch. 3, Sec. A.3, infra.

Are nuclear weapons "the first of mankind's technological innovations which are simply not encompassable within the familiar moral world"? See M. Walzer, Just and Unjust Wars 282 (1977). The Nazis killed millions with conventional means. President Truman justified the bombings of Hiroshima and Nagasaki on the ground that they actually saved lives by shortening the war. See Morton, The Decision to Use the Atomic Bomb, in Art and Waltz, The Use of Force (1971). Analysis of Truman's argument should presumably include the effect of the atomic bombings on the survivors, who suffer from increased rates of leukemia and other diseases, and whose offspring have an increased risk of genetic abnormality. See The Committee for the Compilation of Materials on Damage Caused by the Atomic Bombs in Hiroshima and Nagasaki, Hiroshima and Nagasaki: The Physical, Medical, and Social Effects of the Atomic Bombings (1981).

Perhaps nuclear weapons are different in that they would almost inevitably cause extensive civilian casualties as well as a level of destruction that may be disproportionate to the ends of warfare. Would carefully-targeted tactical nuclear weapons be more morally acceptable than large-scale nuclear weapons? Or does nuclear weaponry in any form raise special concerns? Years after the Manhattan Project, Albert Einstein observed that "the unleashed power of the atom has changed everything except our modes of thinking, and thus we drift toward unparalleled catastrophes." Lapp, The Einstein Letter That Started it All, New York Times Magazine, Aug. 2, 1964.

3. PROTECTING THE SECRET OF THE HYDROGEN BOMB

After World War II, the United States began efforts to build a hydrogen bomb, a weapon that fuses together hydrogen isotopes to release, in accordance with $E = mc^2$, far more energy than an atomic bomb releases. Robert Oppenheimer, as Chairman of the General Advisory Committee to the Atomic Energy Commission, questioned whether the hydrogen bomb could be built and whether it was necessary. In 1952, the United States conducted the first successful full-scale test of the hydrogen bomb (sometimes then called the "Super"); not much later the Soviet Union developed its own hydrogen bomb.

In 1954, Oppenheimer appeared in a quasi-judicial proceeding before an Atomic Energy Commission security board chaired by an attorney, Gordon Gray. Oppenheimer was charged with having associated with Communists, having been less than frank in naming certain alleged Soviet agents, and of having opposed the development of the hydrogen bomb. The Gray Board ultimately concluded that Oppenheimer, while loyal, should no longer have access to military secrets, since such access would not be "consistent with the security interests of the United States." P. Goodchild, J. Robert Oppenheimer: Shatterer of Worlds 262 (1981). The excerpt below describes the Gray Board proceeding.

PHILIP M. STERN,
THE OPPENHEIMER CASE: SECURITY ON TRIAL

181–182, 242–244, 273–274, 281–282, 377, 506–507 (1969).

That summer John Walker, a Yale Law School [graduate] . . . joined the staff of the Atomic Energy Committee. One of Walker's assignments was to keep tabs on the progress of the AEC's H-bomb work, and as he set about educating himself in the thermonuclear field, he found one name to be ubiquitous, that of J. Robert Oppenheimer—chairman of this, consultant on that, expert witness on the other. Walker became disturbed at the omnipresence of Oppenheimer, but even more at the manner in which Oppenheimer seemed to exploit his role. For example, he found that Oppenheimer, as a member of a Pentagon policy group, had argued against declaring a military need for the H-bomb since AEC scientists had not yet declared it technically feasible; however, later on the same day, sitting as an AEC adviser, he had discouraged expansion of technical research on the H-bomb, on the ground that the Pentagon had failed to express any military need for such a weapon.

After a nationwide tour of atomic facilities, Walker concluded that Oppenheimer's apparent influence on the H-bomb program was even greater in the scientific community than it was in government councils. As late as October, 1951, even after the unveiling of Edward Teller's promising new approach to the bomb, Walker could find no more than a dozen important scientists who were in favor of the thermonuclear project.

In ensuing months, Walker and his friend William Borden would spend many hours discussing the remarkable Dr. Oppenheimer, whose security file Borden continued to study. . . . .

[After deciding to proceed against Oppenheimer,] the AEC's . . . problem was how the prodigious amount of evidence in the investigative files should be presented to the hearing board, and by whom. Even before a hearing board was picked, it was decided that an outside attorney should be engaged to handle the case for the Commission.

For aid in finding such a person, Lewis Strauss turned to the Department of Justice. There the matter fell largely to Deputy Attorney General William P. Rogers, who, unlike Attorney General Brownell, had previously practiced law in Washington and was therefore well acquainted with the array of local attorneys. Since the case would clearly call for the presentation of a vast amount of information to the board, Rogers sought a man with considerable trial experience, preferably in the role of prosecutor. Prominent among those who seemed to meet Rogers' prerequisites was a native Washingtonian by the name of Roger Robb, who had had seven years of prosecutorial experience as an Assistant United States Attorney. During that time he had tried twenty-three murder cases, obtaining, according to the local newspaper, "an unusually high percentage of convictions," and had won some local renown for his prosecution of Washington gambling czar Sam Beard. Robb had also been the court-appointed attorney for Communist leader Earl Browder in a contempt-of-Congress case, for which he earned Browder's public praise.† William Rogers him-

---

† "Despite his pronounced political opinions, which I would call reactionary," Browder wrote in the preface of a book about the trial, Robb provided "substantial, not merely formal, assistance," and displayed a high "pride of profession."

self had had occasion to observe Robb's courtroom talents at first hand, since Robb had been his legal adversary in a libel action against Drew Pearson. (Rogers, who represented Pearson, had emerged victorious on that occasion.)

When Chairman Strauss received Rogers' suggested list of Washington attorneys, Roger Robb was the one he selected to approach first. After one preliminary conversation with Robb, and after obtaining the approval of the other Commissioners, Strauss asked Robb to take on the case. . . .

Who would be Roger Robb's adversary in the forthcoming hearing? . . .

Early in January, in part at the suggestion of John Lord O'Brian, Oppenheimer called Lloyd K. Garrison [who was to become his counsel], a leading New York attorney whom Oppenheimer had come to know the preceding April, when Garrison joined the board of trustees of the Institute for Advanced Study. Garrison came from a distinguished family. His great-grandfather was abolitionist William Lloyd Garrison, his grandfather literary editor of *The Nation*. Garrison himself had been dean of the Wisconsin Law School and a pioneering expert and activist in government labor relations work. As a private practitioner of the law in New York since the war, and as president of the National Urban League and a leader in the American Civil Liberties Union, Garrison had earned a reputation for unimpeachable integrity and enormous dedication to public causes. Lincolnesque in appearance, mild of manner, Garrison sought weekend respite at a country home where he devoted his sparse leisure time to bird-watching and reading philosophy, Greek literature and books on politics.

[Shortly after the hearing began,] Oppenheimer's account soon reached the crucial 1949 GAC [General Advisory Committee to the AEC] meetings on the H-bomb, and in testifying about the GAC's written reports on those deliberations, he became involved in an apparent conflict of testimony. Had he and the GAC opposed the "Super" *per se*? Or had they merely been against a "crash" development program? Roger Robb had made available to Oppenheimer, not the complete GAC reports, but selected "extracts," and from these the scientist read a statement in the 1949 report to which all eight members of the GAC had agreed:

> We all hope that by one means or another, the development of these weapons [the H-bomb] can be avoided. We are all reluctant to see the United States take the initiative in precipitating this development. We are all agreed that it would be wrong at the present moment to commit ourselves *to an all-out effort towards its development.* [Emphasis added.]

On its face, this passage, which Oppenheimer told the Gray Board was "the crux of it," seemed to argue more against a crash program for the H-bomb than against the bomb itself.

At this time Oppenheimer had before him only those extracts of the 1949 GAC reports that Robb had provided him. Lloyd Garrison, of course, was not allowed to see even the extracts. Neither of them, therefore, could know what Robb knew—namely, that the so-called "majority annex" of the GAC report, which Oppenheimer and five others had signed, contained this passage:

> *We believe a super bomb should never be produced.* Mankind would be far better off not to have a demonstration of the feasibility of such a weap-

on until the present climate of world opinion changes. [Emphasis added.]

Robb waited until the final days of the four-week hearing to unveil this excerpt—to the complete surprise of both Oppenheimer and Garrison.

. . .

Robb quickly established himself as an exacting interrogator. With his very first questions, he sought to manacle Oppenheimer to everything he had said in his lengthy letter of reply to the AEC charges, presumably so that any errors that might later be proven would appear more like deliberate lies than inadvertent mistakes.

Q: Dr. Oppenheimer, did you [with the assistance of counsel] prepare your letter of March 4, 1954, to General Nichols?

A: Yes.

Q: In all events, you were thoroughly familiar with the contents of it?

A: I am.

Q: And have read it over very carefully, I assume?

A: Yes.

Q: Are all the statements which you make in that letter the truth, the whole truth and nothing but the truth?

A: Yes.

Robb then asked about a year-by-year biographical sketch that Lloyd Garrison had given the board. That, said Oppenheimer, had been prepared by his secretary, and he hadn't even read it over very carefully, whereupon Robb, in true prosecutorial style, demanded, "Are you, or are you not prepared to vouch for [its] accuracy?"

Oppenheimer would merely say it was accurate so far as he knew.

Then emerged Roger Robb the bulldog; fiercely tenacious; once set upon a line of questions, impossible to shake off with elliptical answers.

Why, during World War II, had Oppenheimer considered *current* (as distinct from past) Communist Party membership as incompatible with secret war work? Robb inquired. Was it because party members were expected, if so ordered, to commit espionage? "I was never told that," replied Oppenheimer.

Robb was not satisfied. He wanted a direct answer. It required four separate forays, but ultimately he prevailed:

Q: [*First probe*] Doctor, let me ask you a blunt question. Don't you know, and didn't you know certainly by 1943, that the Communist Party was an instrument or a vehicle of espionage in this country?

A: I was not clear about it.

Q: [*Second probe*] Didn't you suspect it?

A: No.

Q: [*Third probe*] Wasn't that the reason why you felt that membership in the party was inconsistent with the work on a secret war project?

A: I think I have stated the reason about right.

Q: [*Fourth probe*] I am asking you now if your fear of espionage wasn't *one of the reasons* why you felt that association with the Communist Party was inconsistent with work on a secret war project. [Emphasis added.]

A: Yes.

Q: [*Success. Now, nail it down*] Your answer is that it was?

A: Yes.

Soon Robb was to catch Oppenheimer in another contradiction. When, he asked, had the physicist been a "fellow traveler"?

A: From late 1936 or early 1937, and then it tapered off, and I would say I traveled much less fellow after 1939 and very much less after 1942.

Then, this exchange:

Q: How long after 1942 did you continue as a fellow traveler?

A: After 1942 I would say not at all.

Q: But you did continue as a fellow traveler until 1942?

A: Well, now, let us be careful.

Q: I want you to be, Doctor.

A: I had no sympathy with the Communist line about [U.S. intervention in] the war between the spring of 1940 and when they changed [from isolationism to interventionism]. . . .

Q: Did you cease to be a fellow traveler at the time of the Nazi-Russian [nonaggression] Pact in 1939?

A: I think I did, yes.

Q: [After one intervening question] Are you now amending your previous answer that you were more or less a fellow traveler until 1942?

A: *Yes, I think I am.* [Emphasis added.] . . .

What must Robert Oppenheimer have felt at these and similar moments during Robb's interrogation? The defendant sits in the witness chair, facing first the prospect and then the reality of being pummeled by skillful, relentless and hostile questions from a tough, adroit trial attorney. The heart pounds; the blood rises into the face. . . .

How much does the prosecutor know? . . . *What will he ask?* . . . *What is he getting at with this question or that?* . . . *Is he leading me into a trap?* . . . *Is my memory correct?* . . . *Can I outguess him?* . . . *Is he closing in on me?* . . . *Has he outsmarted me?* . . . Emotion rises; and as it does, reason and intellect recede. Common sense flees. The interrogator appears more and more omniscient; the beleaguered witness feels growingly impotent. It is, at best, an intimidating experience; at worst, it is terrifying.

Particularly must this have been true for Robert Oppenheimer. Aware that for eleven years his daily life had been under the Federal Government's most high-powered investigative microscope, he nevertheless must have been appalled, as he testified, to realize the full extent of the government's scrutiny. As the hearing proceeded, it became clear that the secretly made tape recordings of the Pash and Lansdale interrogations were only the beginning of the intimate, mysteriously gathered information that Robb had in his possession. Pitted against Robb's hidden reports, in the struggle to recapture the truth about events, people and places after more than a decade's passage of time, was the naked memory of J. Robert Oppenheimer, prey not only to the toll that time itself exacts, but also to the tendency of all humans to permit their recollections to be cosmetically altered by their wishes. As Oppenheimer himself put it, in the Gray Board hearing, "I don't want to remember more than I do remember." . . .

The Gray Board's finding on the H-bomb charge (presented here with interpolations) went roughly as follows: After the presidential go-ahead was made public on January 31, 1950, Oppenheimer "did not oppose the [H-bomb] project in a positive or open manner" (*as had Hans Bethe, Albert Einstein and other leading scientists*), nor did he decline to cooperate in the project (*as Edward Teller had done at Los Alamos during the height of global war, in refusing to work on the projects assigned him by his superiors*). Oppenheimer's sin lay in the supremacy of his personal influence in the scientific community, and in the fact that he "did not make it known that he had abandoned" his well-known anti-H-bomb views. This, the board concluded, "undoubtedly had an adverse effect on recruitment of scientists" for the H-bomb program. . . .

Why should so debasing a tragedy have befallen so extraordinary a man? Oppenheimer himself took a rather fatalistic view of the matter. Not long after the security case, he said to an interviewer, "I think of this as a major accident—much like a train wreck or the collapse of a building. It has no relation or connection with my life. I just happened to be there."

To some extent, Oppenheimer did just happen to be in the way of external forces that had very little relation to his personal life:

• *The "McCarthy era"*: A wave of postwar anxiety and fear of the unorthodox not dissimilar to that which followed World War I. But in the 1950's popular fears were intensified by the emergence of Russia as a hostile power, the revelations of Soviet espionage against Western powers, and by the rise of a superlative and fearsome demagogue—Senator Joseph McCarthy. . . .

• *The emergence of the scientist-as-policy-maker*: Oppenheimer was both the symbol and the victim of a new and perplexing problem in American Government: the sudden transformation of The Scientist from a rumpled, abstracted, ivory-tower figure into a major force in American policy-making. If technology put new tools in the hands of the statesmen and the military, it also made them increasingly dependent on the technical advice of The Scientist. But how does the nonexpert layman who receives such advice distinguish a scientist-adviser's "technical" views from his political, moral or philosophical predilections? For example, when such an adviser gives counsel as to the "technical" feasibility of a new weapon, might not his judgment be clouded—however unconsciously—by his view that the weapon is, say, morally repugnant or, on the contrary, absolutely essential to the survival of the nation?

Statesmen and politicians have long had to wrestle with their reliance, in military matters, on generals and admirals. But the postwar dependence on scientists and their sudden inclusion in the high councils of government was something far newer; and because it was new it was, to many, perplexing. The concern it caused was often reflected in the Oppenheimer proceeding, nowhere more clearly than in the Gray Board's plea that scientist-advisers rely on their "special competence" and their "soundly-based convictions . . . uncolored and uninfluenced by considerations of an emotional character."

NOTE

Do the methods of prosecutor Robb (later a judge of the United States Court of Appeals for the District of Columbia Circuit) and of the Oppenheimer hearing itself bear any resemblance to the methods used by Albert Einstein as described in Ch. 2, Sec. A.1, supra? Do not the trial and the scientist both seek the truth? Why then do the approaches seem so different?

Lawyers often note with pride the ability of someone like Robb to represent ably disparate clients such as Communist leader Earl Browder and the Atomic Energy Commission. Why do you suppose scientists often feel uncomfortable with this aspect of the legal profession?

Oppenheimer arguably used his expertise to attempt to affect United States policy on the hydrogen bomb. Does this constitute a misuse of his expertise? Does Oppenheimer deserve a special role in the hydrogen bomb debate compared with, for example, the engineer who makes the materials used in the bomb? Consider in this light Krauthammer's attack on the use of scientific expertise in policy debate in Ch. 1, Sec. A.3, supra. In addition, Oppenheimer's alleged activities raise questions about the personal responsibility of a scientific "insider" who comes to disagree with government or industrial policy. Should we place special obligations or restrictions on the "whistleblower"? See Ch. 3, Sec. A.5, infra.

The Oppenheimer case also highlights the tension created when scientific research and debate, which rely on the free national and international exchange of ideas, come in conflict with military secrecy. That tension remains a central problem today. See, e.g., Ch. 4, Sec. A.1, infra, on the efforts of the *Progressive* magazine to publish material about the hydrogen bomb.

In the end, apart from all of the security clearance issues, Oppenheimer's hydrogen bomb experience demonstrates, as did his atomic bomb experience, the deep ambivalence felt by a socially conscious scientist toward progress that might lead to dangerous ends. Oppenheimer based his reluctance about the hydrogen bomb partly on its apparent scientific unfeasibility; part of his opposition was undercut by the scientific attractiveness of the ultimate bomb design developed by Edward Teller:

> Oppenheimer later held that if a weapon of this kind had been suggested initially, he would never have opposed it. He described Teller's new development as 'technically so sweet that you could not argue about that' and now he could see only one possible course of action. 'You go ahead and do it and you argue about what to do about it only after you have had your technical success.'

P. Goodchild, J. Robert Oppenheimer: Shatterer of Worlds 210 (1981).

4. RETHINKING THE BOMB: THE NUCLEAR FREEZE MOVEMENT

RANDALL FORSBERG, A BILATERAL NUCLEAR–WEAPON FREEZE

247 Sci. Am. 52 (Nov. 1982).

The proposal of a bilateral nuclear-weapon "freeze" by the U.S. and the U.S.S.R. has excited wide public discussion in this country during the past year. The idea is to stop the nuclear arms race quite literally, by stopping the development and production of all nuclear-weapon systems in the two countries. Public interest (expressed, for example, by votes in numerous town meetings) brought the proposal in the form of an advisory resolution before the U.S. Congress. Whereas a vote on it was blocked in the Senate, it lost in the House in August by the narrow margin of 204 to 202. The proposal is now on the ballot as a referendum question in impending congressional and local elections in enough cities and states to put it before nearly a fourth of the country's population. Next to the depressed state of the economy, the nuclear freeze is said to be the warmest current issue in the country's politics.

First put forward in the "Call to Halt the Nuclear Arms Race" drafted by me and published in April, 1980, by several public-interest groups, the freeze goes beyond other arms-control measures proposed in the past 25 years to put a stop to the production, testing and, implicitly, development of nuclear weapons as well as their deployment. By the same simplicity that has given it wide popular appeal the freeze proposal responds directly to an ominous turn in the arms race. The bilateral freeze would preclude the production of a new generation of "counterforce" weapons by the U.S. and the U.S.S.R. These are weapons designed to attack the opponent's nuclear forces. In the ultimate scenario they would disarm the other nation and hold its population hostage. The quest for improved counterforce capability has driven the arms race far past the point where each contender can destroy the other's society and much else besides. The production of counterforce weapons would increase the risk of a nuclear war. Their deployment would put pressure on leaders to launch their weapons first in time of crisis, before they were attacked, and perhaps to place their nuclear forces in an automatic "launch on warning" status in peacetime. A freeze would prevent these dangerous developments.

A freeze would help to accomplish other desirable goals. The U.S. and the U.S.S.R., by fulfilling the pledge they made in the 1970 Nonproliferation Treaty to stop the arms race, would help to brake the spread of nuclear weapons to countries that do not already have them. A freeze would create an opportunity for the nations of the world to make further progress in arms control and other global issues. It would also save billions of dollars.

The time is propitious for a bilateral freeze. Today the U.S. and the U.S.S.R. are closer to parity in nuclear arms than they have been at any time since World War II. The U.S.S.R. has advantages in some elements of nuclear weaponry, the U.S. has advantages in others. The most frequently cited statistics compare the numbers of "strategic" ballistic missiles and bombers and the numbers of nuclear warheads and free-fall bombs they carry. The U.S.S.R. has more strategic missiles: 1,398 land-based intercontinental ballistic missiles (ICBM's) compared with 1,052 for the U.S. and 950 submarine-launched ballistic missles (SLBM's) compared with 520 for the U.S. In addition a recent buildup has brought the strategic force of the U.S.S.R. abreast of that of the U.S. in the arming of these missiles with multiple independently targetable reentry vehicles (MIRV's). The land-based ICBM's of the U.S.S.R. carry more warheads and larger ones. On the other hand, the U.S. has more warheads in total, owing to the larger number of warheads on its SLBM's. The U.S. also has many more intercontinental bombers, with much larger payloads, and a five-to-10-year lead in the new technology of small, long-range, low-flying cruise missiles.

More meaningful than comparisons of numbers of weapons is the fact that both countries have acquired enormous "overkill," that is, each has many times the number of weapons necessary to annihilate the other's urban population. Thus even if the U.S.S.R destroyed all U.S. ICBM's, all U.S. bombers and all U.S. submarines in port, the U.S. would still have about 2,400 nuclear warheads on submarines at sea, completely invulnerable to such preemptive attack. This is several times the number needed to destroy the 300 largest cities and towns in the U.S.S.R., which have one-third of the population and three-fourths of the industry. Conversely, a U.S. attack on ICBM's, bomber bases and submarine ports in the U.S.S.R. would leave an estimated 1,200 strategic warheads, more than enough to inflict equivalent damage on U.S. urban centers.

RICHARD PERLE,
A FREEZE MEANS THIN ICE

New York Times, Sept. 7, 1982 at 23.

Proponents of a freeze contend that it would reduce the risk of nuclear war and bring about a speedier reduction in nuclear arsenals than can be expected from President Reagan's arms-control proposals. They argue that the freeze would stop the "arms race" and create incentives for the Soviet Union to agree to nuclear-arms reductions. They are wrong.

The various freeze resolutions would apply to the production, testing and further deployment of nuclear warheads, missiles and other delivery systems. That would terminate every current program designed to correct the problems in America's strategic posture that have developed as a result of the Soviet Union's large-scale buildup in arms in recent years. But the freeze would not reach a number of the Soviet programs that have the greatest potential for upsetting the strategic balance. The freeze would bar our developing a survivable intercontinental ballistic missile, but it would not eliminate the threat that makes that effort necessary. The freeze would bar both our development of a modern bomber to replace the venerable B–52 and our deployment of cruise missiles on B–52's, but it would not prevent the Soviet Union from thickening even further its extensive conventional air-defense network, which is a serious threat to our strategic-bomber force. The freeze would stop our Trident submarine program and put on ice our programs for submarine-launched cruise missiles, but it would not halt high-priority Soviet programs aimed at neutralizing our aging submarine fleet. In Europe, the freeze would permit the Russians to continue to menace the North Atlantic Treaty Organization with hundreds of intermediate-range-missile warheads while throttling NATO's plans to deploy even a partial counter.

The freeze would force us to abandon programs for making our nuclear weapons safer—for example, those now under way to render the weapons even less susceptible to detonation through tampering or accidents.

Keeping our strategic deterrent effective requires constant adjustment, repair and modernization. The freeze would stop all that—freezing in all the accumulated problems and vulnerabilities, and freezing out essential corrective programs. This problem would not affect the Kremlin's arsenal as it would America's. Our nuclear-weapons systems generally are older than Soviet systems, and many of ours will soon reach obsolescence while the Russians' systems will remain operational for years. About 85 percent of Moscow's nuclear-missile warheads are on systems deployed in the last 10 years; only 45 percent of ours are on systems deployed in that period.

The concept of the freeze misses the central point about nuclear weapons: They are not inherently good or bad. They are good if they promote stability and contribute to deterrence of war, and bad if they diminish stability and weaken deterrence. The freeze proposal would deal with the "arms race" by benching the good and allowing the bad to run. It would erode the survivability of our strategic forces, thus undermining the policy of deterrence that every Administration since Harry S. Truman's has relied on to keep the peace between the superpowers. That policy has enabled the world to live with nuclear weapons without seeing them used. By damaging deterrence, the freeze would upset the stability of the strategic balance and thus increase the likelihood of war.

"Arms race"—I use quotation marks because the term is misleading. It is not true that the respective numbers of nuclear weapons deployed by the United States and Soviet Union have both been spiraling upward. America has, over the last 15 years, repaired, replaced and improved certain nuclear-weapons systems, but we have not increased the size of our nuclear arsenal. In fact, it is smaller by several thousand nuclear warheads than in 1967. The Soviet arsenal has grown since 1967 by some 6,000 nuclear warheads.

Why have American proponents of the freeze ignored its effect on the stability of the strategic balance? It is because they seek a simple answer to a complex problem, a prescription that can gather political momentum in an understandably anxious but imperfectly informed electorate. . . .

JONATHAN SCHELL,
THE FATE OF THE EARTH

181–182 (1982).

Four and a half billion years ago, the earth was formed. Perhaps a half billion years after that, life arose on the planet. For the next four billion years, life became steadily more complex, more varied, and more ingenious, until, around a million years ago, it produced mankind—the most complex and ingenious species of them all. Only six or seven thousand years ago—a period that is to the history of the earth as less than a minute is to a year—civilization emerged, enabling us to build up a human world, and to add to the marvels of evolution marvels of our own: marvels of art, of science, of social organization, of spiritual attainment. But, as we built higher and higher, the evolutionary foundation beneath our feet became more and more shaky, and now, in spite of all we have learned and achieved—or, rather, because of it—we hold this entire terrestrial creation hostage to nuclear destruction, threatening to hurl it back into the inanimate darkness from which it came. And this threat of self-destruction and planetary destruction is not something that we will pose one day in the future, if we fail to take certain precautions; it is here now, hanging over the heads of all of us at every moment. The machinery of destruction is complete, poised on a hair trigger, waiting for the "button" to be "pushed" by some misguided or deranged human being or for some faulty computer chip to send out the instruction to fire. That so much should be balanced on so fine a point—that the fruit of four and a half billion years can be undone in a careless moment—is a fact against which belief rebels. And there is another, even vaster measure of the loss, for stretching ahead from our present are more billions of years of life on earth, all of which can be filled not only with human life but with human civilization. The procession of generations that extends onward from our present leads far, far beyond the line of our sight, and, compared with these stretches of human time, which exceed the whole history of the earth up to now, our brief civilized moment is almost infinitesimal. And yet we threaten, in the name of our transient aims and fallible convictions, to foreclose it all. If our species does destroy itself, it will be a death in the cradle—a case of infant mortality. The disparity between the cause and the effect of our peril is so great that our minds seem all but powerless to encompass it. In addition, we are so fully enveloped by that which is menaced, and so deeply and passionately immersed in its events, which are the events of our lives, that we hardly know how to get far enough away from it to see it in its entirety. It is as though life itself were one huge distraction, diverting our attention from the peril to life. In its apparent durability, a world menaced with imminent doom is in a way deceptive. It is almost an illusion. Now we are sitting at the breakfast table drinking our coffee and reading the newspaper, but in a moment we may be inside a fireball whose temperature is tens of thousands of degrees. Now we are on our way to work, walking through the city streets, but in a moment we may be standing on an empty plain under a darkened sky looking for the charred remnants of our children. Now we are alive, but in a moment we may be dead. Now there is human life on earth, but in a moment it may be gone. . . .

NOTE

The nuclear freeze movement, like other arms control issues, propels ordinary citizens into an arena dominated by experts. Note that Forsberg praises the freeze and Perle condemns it on the ground that it simplifies the issue. Are the referenda held by the towns and states an appropriate part of a decisionmaking process with national and international dimensions? If not, what institutions can express popular opinion in areas like this?

At the other end of the spectrum there is no shortage of experts taking a stand on the nuclear freeze. Such groups as Physicians for Social Responsibility and the American Physical Society, which includes some scientists who make nuclear weapons, have assumed positions sympathetic to the freeze, while military analysts and other experts have spoken against it. See, e.g., 308 New Eng.J.Med. 338, (1983); Washington Post, Feb. 9, 1983, at A15, col. 5; New York Times, Oct. 31, 1982, at E19, col. 2. Laypeople, of course, can attack these experts by reversing the above argument—nuclear strategy and arms control involve values, not expertise, and experts have no special claim on our attention. See Ch. 1, Sec. A.3, supra. Do you believe any group of experts deserves particular deference in a nuclear arms controversy? Would doctors or scientists be such a group? Would lawyers?

In defending the freeze, Forsberg relies on detailed quantitative arguments about various weapons systems. Is she subject to the same objections raised to Herman Kahn's work in Sec. A.2, supra? Does Schell bring the controversy into sharper focus or merely cloud the issues by playing on human emotion?

As the Hiroshima materials in Sec. A.2, supra, made clear, the prospect of nuclear war makes the use of cost-benefit analysis particularly problematic. Yet the question of whether such analysis is appropriate remains. How do you view the following observation by Senator Howard Baker during an arms treaty debate in 1979?

There is a young man who flies for me in Tennessee He lets me sit in the right seat of that small plane from time to time. The other day we were flying through a thunderstorm, and I was watching the radar screen intently for weather and severe turbulence. I had had my head in the radar-scope. He touched me on the shoulder and said, "Senator, why don't we turn that thing off before we scare ourselves."

You know, I sort of get the feeling that every time we conjure up the idea and the image of nuclear holocaust, if we are not careful, we are going to scare ourselves. We are not here to decide whether the world is going to be faced with nuclear holocaust. We are here to determine whether this treaty better serves the purpose of diminishing that prospect.

The SALT II Treaty: Hearings Before the Senate Committee on Foreign Relations, 96th Cong., 1st Sess. (July 9, 1979).

UNITED STATES BISHOPS, PASTORAL LETTER ON WAR AND PEACE, THE CHALLENGE OF PEACE: GOD'S PROMISE AND OUR RESPONSE

Reprinted in 13 Origins 1, 9–10, 13–14, 18, 29 (May 19, 1983).

The moral theory of the "just-war" or "limited-war" doctrine begins with the presumption which binds all Christians: We should do no harm to our neighbors; how we treat our enemy is the key test of whether we love our neighbor; and the possibility of taking even one human life is a prospect we should consider in fear and trembling. How is it possible to move from these presumptions to the idea of a justifiable use of lethal force?

Historically and theologically the clearest answer to the question is found in St. Augustine. Augustine was impressed by the fact and the consequences of sin in history—the "not yet" dimension of the kingdom. In his view war was both the result of sin and a tragic remedy for sin in the life of political societies. War arose from disordered ambitions, but it could also be used in some cases at least to restrain evil and protect the innocent. The classic case which illustrated his view was the use of lethal force to prevent aggression against innocent victims. Faced with the fact of attack on the innocent, the presumption that we do no harm even to our enemy yielded to the command of love understood as the need to restrain an enemy who would injure the innocent.

The just-war argument has taken several forms in the history of Catholic theology, but this Augustinian insight is its central premise. In the 20th century, papal teaching has used the logic of Augustine and Aquinas to articulate a right of self-defense for states in a decentralized international order and to state the criteria for exercising that right. The essential position was stated by Vatican II: "As long as the danger of war persists and there is no international authority with the necessary competence and power, governments cannot be denied the right of lawful self-defense, once all peace efforts have failed." We have already indicated the centrality of this principle for understanding Catholic teaching about the state and its duties.

Just-war teaching has evolved, however, as an effort to prevent war; only if war cannot be rationally avoided does the teaching then seek to restrict and reduce its horrors. It does this by establishing a set of rigorous conditions which must be met if the decision to go to war is to be morally permissible. Such a decision, especially today, requires extraordinarily strong reasons for overriding the presumption *in favor of peace* and *against* war. This is one significant reason why valid just-war teaching makes provision for conscientious dissent. It is presumed that all sane people prefer peace, never *want* to initiate war and accept even the most justifiable defensive war only as a sad necessity. Only the most powerful reasons may be permitted to override such objection.

. . .

[T]he just-war teaching . . . [is] confronted with a unique challenge by nuclear warfare. This must be the starting point of any further moral reflection: Nuclear weapons particularly and nuclear warfare as it is planned today raise new moral questions. No previously conceived moral position escapes the fundamental confrontation posed by contemporary nuclear strategy. Many have noted the similarity of the statements made by eminent scientists and Vatican II's observation that we are forced today "to undertake a completely fresh reappraisal of war." The task before us is not simply to repeat what we have said before; it is first to consider anew whether and how our religious-moral tradition can assess, direct, contain and, we hope, help to eliminate the threat posed to the human family by the nuclear arsenals of the world. Pope John Paul II captured the essence of the problem during his pilgrimage to Hiroshima: "In the past it was possible to destroy a village, a town, a region, even a country. Now it is the whole planet that has come under threat."

The Holy Father's observation illustrates why the moral problem is also a religious question of the most profound significance. In the nuclear arsenals of the United States or the Soviet Union alone there exists a capacity to do something no other age could imagine: We can threaten the entire planet. For people of faith this means we read the Book of Genesis with a new awareness; the moral issue at stake in nuclear war involves the meaning of sin in its most graphic dimensions. Every sinful act is a confrontation of the creature and the Creator. Today the destructive potential of the nuclear powers threatens the human person, the civilization we have slowly constructed and even the created order itself.

We live today, therefore, in the midst of a cosmic drama; we possess a power which should never be used, but which might be used if we do not reverse our direction. We live with nuclear weapons knowing we cannot afford to make one serious mistake. This fact dramatizes the precariousness of our position, politically, morally and spiritually.

A prominent "sign of the times" today is a sharply increased awareness of the danger of the nuclear arms race. Such awareness has produced a public discussion about nuclear policy here and in other countries which is unprecedented in its scope and depth. What has been accepted for years with almost no question is now being subjected to the sharpest criticism. What previously had been defined as a safe and stable system of deterrence is today viewed with political and moral skepticism.

. . . .

We have had to examine, with the assistance of a broad spectrum of advisers of varying persuasions, the nature of existing and proposed weapons systems, the doctrines which govern their use and the consequences of using them. We have consulted people who engage their lives in protest against the existing nuclear strategy of the United States, and we have consulted others who have held or do hold responsibility for this strategy. It has been a sobering and perplexing experience. In light of the evidence which witnesses presented and in light of our study, reflection and consultation, we must reject nuclear war. But we feel obliged to relate our judgment to the specific elements which comprise the nuclear problem.

Though certain that the dangerous and delicate nuclear relationship the superpowers now maintain should not exist, we understand how it came to exist. In a world of sovereign states devoid of central authority and possessing the knowledge to produce nuclear weapons many choices were made, some clearly objectionable, others well-intended with mixed results, which brought the world to its present dangerous situation.

We see with increasing clarity the political folly of a system which threatens mutual suicide, the psychological damage this does to ordinary people, especially the young, the economic distortion of priorities—billions readily spent for destructive instruments while pitched battles are waged daily in our legislatures over much smaller amounts for the homeless, the hungry and the helpless here and abroad. But it is much less clear how we translate a no to nuclear war into the personal and public choices which can move us in a new direction, toward a national policy and an international system which more adequately reflect the values and vision of the kingdom of God.

. . .

[W]e wish now to make some specific evaluations:

1. If nuclear deterrence exists only to prevent the *use* of nuclear weapons by others, then proposals to go beyond this to planning for prolonged periods of repeated nuclear strikes and counterstrikes, or "prevailing" in nuclear war, are not acceptable. They encourage notions that nuclear war can be engaged in with tolerable human and moral consequences. Rather, we must continually say no to the idea of nuclear war.

2. If nuclear deterrence is our goal, "sufficiency" to deter is an adequate strategy; the quest for nuclear superiority must be rejected.

3. Nuclear deterrence should be used as a step on the way toward progressive disarmament. Each proposed addition to our strategic system or change in strategic doctrine must be assessed precisely in light of whether it will render steps toward "progressive disarmament" more or less likely. . . .

. . .

To Men and Women in Defense Industries

You also face specific questions because the defense industry is directly involved in the development and production of the weapons of mass destruction which have concerned us in this letter. We do not presume or pretend that clear answers exist to many of the personal, professional and financial choices facing you in your varying responsibilities. In this letter we have ruled out certain uses of nuclear weapons, while also expressing conditional moral acceptance for deterrence. All Catholics, at every level of defense industries, can and should use the moral principles of this letter to form their consciences. We realize that different judgments of conscience will face different people, and we recognize the possibility of diverse concrete judgments being made in this complex area. We seek as moral teachers and pastors to be available to all who confront these questions of personal and vocational choice. Those who in conscience decide that they should no longer be associated with defense activities should find support in the Catholic community. Those who remain in these industries or earn a profit from the weapons industry should find in the church guidance and support for the ongoing evaluation of their work.

To Men and Women of Science

At Hiroshima Pope John Paul said:

"Criticism of science and technology is sometimes so severe that it comes close to condemning science itself. On the contrary, science and technology are a wonderful product of a God-given human creativity, since they have provided us with wonderful possibilities and we all gratefully benefit from them. But we know that this potential is not a neutral one: It can be used either for man's progress or for his degradation."

We appreciate the efforts of scientists, some of whom first unlocked the secret of atomic power and others of whom have developed it in diverse ways, to turn the enormous power of science to the cause of peace.

Modern history is not lacking scientists who have looked back with deep remorse on the development of weapons to which they contributed, sometimes with the highest motivation, even believing that they were creating weapons that would render all other weapons obsolete and convince the world of the unthinkableness of war. Such efforts have ever proved illusory. Surely equivalent dedication of scientific minds to reverse current trends and to pursue concepts as bold and adventuresome in favor of peace as those which in the past have magnified the risks of war could result in dramatic benefits for all of humanity. We particularly note in this regard the extensive efforts of public education undertaken by physicians and scientists on the medical consequences of nuclear war.

We do not, however, wish to limit our remarks to the physical sciences alone. Nor do we limit our remarks to physical scientists. In his address at the United Nations University in Hiroshima, Pope John Paul II warned about misuse of "the social sciences and the human behavioral sciences when they are utilized to manipulate people, to crush their mind, souls, dignity and freedom." The positive role of social science in overcoming the dangers of the nuclear age is evident in this letter. We have been dependent upon the research and analysis of social scientists in our effort to apply the moral principles of the Catholic tradition to the concrete problems of our day. We encourage social scientists to continue this work of relating moral wisdom and political reality. We are in continuing need of your insights.

. . .

NOTE

The Catholic Bishops' letter has occasioned lively debate in the Catholic community and elsewhere. See, e.g., Hellwig, Langan, Schall, Winters and O'Brien, From the University: American Catholics and the Peace Debate, The Washington Quarterly 120 (1982). Does the constitutional separation of church and state bear on the propriety of Catholic Bishops speaking out on nuclear weapons? Are the problems here similar to those raised when religious leaders speak out on evolution? See Ch. 4, Sec. A.2, infra. On abortion? See Ch. 8, Sec. A.1, infra. For a survey of the views of non-Catholic religious groups on nuclear weapons, see van Voorst, The Churches and Nuclear Deterrence, 61 Foreign Affairs 827 (1983).

The Bishops state that they were assisted by "a broad spectrum of advisers of varying persuasions . . . ." What expertise did the Bishops themselves bring to bear on the issue of nuclear deterrence?

The Bishops contend that if "scientific minds" turned from developing weapons to the pursuit of "bold and adventuresome" concepts for peace the result would be "dramatic benefits for all of humanity." Do you agree that the scientific approach would be particularly helpful in the quest for peace?

B. THE DEVELOPMENT AND SOCIAL CONSEQUENCES OF CIVILIAN NUCLEAR POWER

1. THE LICENSING OF NUCLEAR REACTORS

DWIGHT D. EISENHOWER, THE ATOM FOR PROGRESS AND PEACE

(December 8, 1953).

It is not enough to take this weapon out of the hands of the soldiers. It must be put into the hands of those who will know how to strip its military casing and adapt it to the arts of peace.

The United States knows that if the fearful trend of atomic military buildup can be reversed, this greatest of destructive forces can be developed into a great boon, for the benefit of all mankind.

The United States knows that peaceful power from atomic energy is no dream of the future. That capability, already proved, is here—now—today. Who can doubt, if the entire body of the world's scientists and engineers had adequate amounts of fissionable material with which to test and develop their ideas, that this capability would rapidly be transformed into universal, efficient, and economic usage. . . .

NOTE

In linking the destructive power of the atom to its peaceful potential, President Eisenhower touched on a common theme in the years after World War II. Just as some seem to oppose civilian nuclear power because of the existence of nuclear weapons, others seem to support it because it somehow cleanses the wartime experience.

While President Eisenhower's predictions appear overly optimistic today, nuclear energy did begin to assume a civilian role in the 1950's. Since that time, the United States has used such power primarily to generate electricity. In a reactor, a controlled fission reaction is used to boil water. After that, the process is just like that in a coal or oil-fired plant—the steam drives a turbine that turns a generator to produce electricity. In 1983, the 76 operating reactors in the United States produced about 12 percent of this country's electricity, while about 65 more reactors were in various stages of construction.

The materials that follow describe the history and present status of government regulation of civilian nuclear energy, as well as some of the issues that have embroiled nuclear power in controversy.

VERMONT YANKEE NUCLEAR POWER CORP. v. NATURAL RESOURCES DEFENSE COUNCIL, INC.

Supreme Court of the United States, 1978.
435 U.S. 519, 98 S.Ct. 1197, 55 L.Ed.2d 460.

MR. JUSTICE REHNQUIST delivered the opinion of the Court.

Under the Atomic Energy Act of 1954, 68 Stat. 919, as amended, 42 U.S.C. § 2011 *et seq.*, the Atomic Energy Commission[2] was given broad

2. The licensing and regulatory functions of the Atomic Energy Commission (AEC) were transferred to the Nuclear Regulatory Commission (NRC) by the Energy

regulatory authority over the development of nuclear energy. Under the terms of the Act, a utility seeking to construct and operate a nuclear power plant must obtain a separate permit or license at both the construction and the operation stage of the project. See 42 U.S.C. §§ 2133, 2232, 2235, 2239. In order to obtain the construction permit, the utility must file a preliminary safety analysis report, an environmental report, and certain information regarding the antitrust implications of the proposed project. See 10 CFR §§ 2.101, 50.30(f), 50.33a, 50.34(a) (1977). This application then undergoes exhaustive review by the Commission's staff and by the Advisory Committee on Reactor Safeguards (ACRS), a group of distinguished experts in the field of atomic energy. Both groups submit to the Commission their own evaluations, which then become part of the record of the utility's application. See 42 U.S.C. §§ 2039, 2232(b). The Commission staff also undertakes the review required by the National Environmental Policy Act of 1969 (NEPA), 83 Stat. 852, 42 U.S.C. § 4321 *et seq.*, and prepares a draft environmental impact statement, which, after being circulated for comment, 10 CFR §§ 51.22–51.25 (1977), is revised and becomes a final environmental impact statement. § 51.26. Thereupon a three-member Atomic Safety and Licensing Board conducts a public adjudicatory hearing, 42 U.S.C. § 2241, and reaches a decision which can be appealed to the Atomic Safety and Licensing Appeal Board, and currently, in the Commission's discretion, to the Commission itself. 10 CFR §§ 2.714, 2.721, 2.786, 2.787 (1977). The final agency decision may be appealed to the courts of appeals. 42 U.S.C. § 2239; 28 U.S.C. § 2342. The same sort of process occurs when the utility applies for a license to operate the plant, 10 CFR § 50.34(b) (1977), except that a hearing need only be held in contested cases and may be limited to the matters in controversy. See 42 U.S.C. § 2239(a); 10 CFR § 2.105 (1977); 10 CFR pt. 2, App. A, V(f) (1977).

. . .

In December 1967, after the mandatory adjudicatory hearing and necessary review, the Commission granted petitioner Vermont Yankee a permit to build a nuclear power plant in Vernon, Vt. See 4 A.E.C. 36 (1967). Thereafter, Vermont Yankee applied for an operating license. Respondent Natural Resources Defense Council (NRDC) objected to the granting of a license, however, and therefore a hearing on the application commenced on August 10, 1971. Excluded from consideration at the hearings, over NRDC's objection, was the issue of the environmental effects of operations to reprocess fuel or dispose of wastes resulting from the reprocessing operations.[6] This ruling was affirmed by the Appeal Board in June 1972.

In November 1972, however, the Commission, making specific reference to the Appeal Board's decision with respect to the Vermont Yankee license, instituted rulemaking proceedings "that would specifically deal

Reorganization Act of 1974, 42 U.S.C. § 5801 *et seq.* (1970 ed., Supp. V). Hereinafter both the AEC and NRC will be referred to as the Commission.

6. The nuclear fission which takes place in light-water nuclear reactors apparently converts its principal fuel, uranium, into plutonium, which is itself highly radioactive but can be used as reactor fuel if separated from the remaining uranium and radioactive waste products. Fuel reprocessing refers to

the process necessary to recapture usable plutonium. Waste disposal, at the present stage of technological development, refers to the storage of the very long lived and highly radioactive waste products until they detoxify sufficiently that they no longer present an environmental hazard. There are presently no physical or chemical steps which render this waste less toxic, other than simply the passage of time.

with the question of consideration of environmental effects associated with the uranium fuel cycle in the individual cost-benefit analyses for light water cooled nuclear power reactors." App. 352. The notice of proposed rulemaking offered two alternatives, both predicated on a report prepared by the Commission's staff entitled Environmental Survey of the Nuclear Fuel Cycle. The first would have required no quantitative evaluation of the environmental hazards of fuel reprocessing or disposal because the Environmental Survey had found them to be slight. The second would have specified numerical values for the environmental impact of this part of the fuel cycle, which values would then be incorporated into a table, along with the other relevant factors, to determine the overall cost-benefit balance for each operating license. See id., at 356–357.

Much of the controversy in this case revolves around the procedures used in the rulemaking hearing which commenced in February 1973. In a supplemental notice of hearing the Commission indicated that while discovery or cross-examination would not be utilized, the Environmental Survey would be available to the public before the hearing along with the extensive background documents cited therein. All participants would be given a reasonable opportunity to present their position and could be represented by counsel if they so desired. Written and, time permitting, oral statements would be received and incorporated into the record. All persons giving oral statements would be subject to questioning by the Commission. At the conclusion of the hearing, a transcript would be made available to the public and the record would remain open for 30 days to allow the filing of supplemental written statements. See generally id., at 361–363. More than 40 individuals and organizations representing a wide variety of interests submitted written comments. On January 17, 1973, the Licensing Board held a planning session to schedule the appearance of witnesses and to discuss methods for compiling a record. The hearing was held on February 1 and 2, with participation by a number of groups, including the Commission's staff, the United States Environmental Protection Agency, a manufacturer of reactor equipment, a trade association from the nuclear industry, a group of electric utility companies, and a group called Consolidated National Intervenors which represented 79 groups and individuals including respondent NRDC.

After the hearing, the Commission's staff filed a supplemental document for the purpose of clarifying and revising the Environmental Survey. Then the Licensing Board forwarded its report to the Commission without rendering any decision. The Licensing Board identified as the principal procedural question the propriety of declining to use full formal adjudicatory procedures. The major substantive issue was the technical adequacy of the Environmental Survey.

In April 1974, the Commission issued a rule which adopted the second of the two proposed alternatives described above. The Commission also approved the procedures used at the hearing, and indicated that the record, including the Environmental Survey, provided an "adequate data base for the regulation adopted." Id., at 392. Finally, the Commission ruled that to the extent the rule differed from the Appeal Board decisions in Vermont Yankee "those decisions have no further precedential significance," id., at 386, but that since "the environmental effects of the uranium fuel cycle have been shown to be relatively insignificant, . . . it is unnecessary to apply the amendment to applicant's environmental reports submitted prior to its effective date or to Final Environmental Statements for which Draft Environmental Statements have been circulated for comment prior to the effective date," id., at 395.

Respondents appealed from both the Commission's adoption of the rule and its decision to grant Vermont Yankee's license to the Court of Appeals for the District of Columbia Circuit.

.   .   .

With respect to the challenge of Vermont Yankee's license, the court first ruled that in the absence of effective rulemaking proceedings,[13] the Commission must deal with the environmental impact of fuel reprocessing and disposal in individual licensing proceedings. 178 U.S.App.D.C., at 344, 547 F.2d, at 641. The court then examined the rulemaking proceedings and, despite the fact that it appeared that the agency employed all the procedures required by 5 U.S.C. § 553 (1976 ed.) * and more, the court determined the proceedings to be inadequate and overturned the rule. Accordingly, the Commission's determination with respect to Vermont Yankee's license was also remanded for further proceedings. 178 U.S.App.D.C., at 358, 547 F.2d, at 655.

Petitioner Vermont Yankee first argues that the Commission may grant a license to operate a nuclear reactor without any consideration of waste disposal and fuel reprocessing. We find, however, that this issue is no longer presented by the record in this case. The Commission does not contend that it is not required to consider the environmental impact of the spent fuel processes when licensing nuclear power plants. Indeed, the Commission has publicly stated subsequent to the Court of Appeals' decision in the instant case that consideration of the environmental impact of the back end of the fuel cycle in "the environmental impact statements for individual LWR's [light-water power reactors] would represent a full and candid assessment of costs and benefits consistent with the legal requirements and spirit of NEPA." 41 Fed.Reg. 45849 (1976). Even prior to the Court of Appeals' decision the Commission implicitly agreed that it would consider the back end of the fuel cycle in all licensing proceedings: It indicated that it was not necessary to reopen prior licensing proceedings because "the environmental effects of the uranium fuel cycle have been shown to be relatively insignificant," and thus incorporation of those effects into the cost-benefit analysis would not change the results of such licensing proceedings. App. 395. Thus, at this stage of the proceedings the only question presented for review in this regard is whether the Commission may consider the environmental impact of the fuel processes when licensing nuclear reactors. In addition to the weight which normally attaches to the agency's determination of such a question, other reasons support the Commission's conclusion.

Vermont Yankee will produce annually well over 100 pounds of radioactive wastes, some of which will be highly toxic. The Commission itself,

---

13. In the Court of Appeals no one questioned the Commission's authority to deal with fuel cycle issues by informal rulemaking as opposed to adjudication. 178 U.S.App.D.C., at 345–346, 547 F.2d, at 642–643. Neither does anyone seriously question before this Court the Commission's authority in this respect.

* This section of the Administrative Procedure Act covers so-called "notice-and-comment" or "informal" rulemaking. The section provides that the agency shall publish notice of a proposed rule in the Federal Register and shall then give interested persons an opportunity to submit written statements concerning the rule. Oral presentations may or may not be allowed, at the agency's discretion. All relevant material presented to the agency is to be considered before promulgation of the final rule. See generally B. Schwartz, Administrative Law (1976) at 165–175. [Eds.]

in a pamphlet published by its information office, clearly recognizes that these wastes "pose the most severe potential health hazard . . .." U.S. Atomic Energy Commission, Radioactive Wastes 12 (1965). Many of these substances must be isolated for anywhere from 600 to hundreds of thousands of years. It is hard to argue that these wastes do not constitute "adverse environmental effects which cannot be avoided should the proposal be implemented," or that by operating nuclear power plants we are not making "irreversible and irretrievable commitments of resources." 42 U.S.C. §§ 4332(2)(C)(ii), (v). As the Court of Appeals recognized, the environmental impact of the radioactive wastes produced by a nuclear power plant is analytically indistinguishable from the environmental effects of "the stack gases produced by a coal-burning power plant." 178 U.S.App.D.C., at 341, 547 F.2d, at 638. For these reasons we hold that the Commission acted well within its statutory authority when it considered the back end of the fuel cycle in individual licensing proceedings.

We next turn to the invalidation of the fuel cycle rule. . . . [T]he majority of the Court of Appeals struck down the rule because of the perceived inadequacies of the procedures employed in the rulemaking proceedings. The court first determined the intervenors' primary argument to be "that the decision to preclude 'discovery or cross-examination' denied them a meaningful opportunity to participate in the proceedings as guaranteed by due process." 178 U.S.App.D.C., at 346, 547 F.2d, at 643. The court then went on to frame the issue for decision thus:

> "Thus, we are called upon to decide whether the procedures provided by the agency were sufficient to ventilate the issues." Ibid.

The court conceded that absent extraordinary circumstances it is improper for a reviewing court to prescribe the procedural format an agency must follow, but it likewise clearly thought it entirely appropriate to "scrutinize the record as a whole to insure that genuine opportunities to participate in a meaningful way were provided . . .." Id., at 347, 547 F.2d, at 644. The court also refrained from actually ordering the agency to follow any specific procedures, id., at 356–357, 547 F.2d at 653–654, but there is little doubt in our minds that the ineluctable mandate of the court's decision is that the procedures afforded during the hearings were inadequate. This conclusion is particularly buttressed by the fact that after the court examined the record, particularly the testimony of Dr. Pittman [Director of the AEC's Division of Waste Management and Transportation], and declared it insufficient, the court proceeded to discuss at some length the necessity for further procedural devices or a more "sensitive" application of those devices employed during the proceedings. Ibid. The exploration of the record and the statement regarding its insufficiency might initially lead one to conclude that the court was only examining the sufficiency of the evidence, but the remaining portions of the opinion dispel any doubt that this was certainly not the sole or even the principal basis of the decision. Accordingly, we feel compelled to address the opinion on its own terms, and we conclude that it was wrong.

In prior opinions we have intimated that even in a rulemaking proceeding when an agency is making a " 'quasi-judicial' " determination by which a very small number of persons are " 'exceptionally affected, in each case upon individual grounds,' " in some circumstances additional procedures may be required in order to afford the aggrieved individuals due process.[16] United States v. Florida East Coast R. Co., 410 U.S., at 242, 245, 93 S.Ct., at 819–821, quoting from Bi-Metallic Investment Co. v. State Board of Equalization, 239 U.S. 441, 446, 36 S.Ct. 141, 142, 60 L.Ed. 372 (1915). It might also be true, although we do not think the issue is presented in this case and accordingly do not decide it, that a totally unjustified departure from well-settled agency procedures of long standing might require judicial correction.

But this much is absolutely clear. Absent constitutional constraints or extremely compelling circumstances the "administrative agencies 'should be free to fashion their own rules of procedure and to pursue methods of inquiry capable of permitting them to discharge their multitudinous duties.'" FCC v. Schreiber, 381 U.S., at 290, 85 S.Ct., at 1467, quoting from FCC v. Pottsville Broadcasting Co., 309 U.S., at 143, 60 S.Ct., at 441. Indeed, our cases could hardly be more explicit in this regard. . . .

Respondent NRDC argues that § 4 of the Administrative Procedure Act, 5 U.S.C. § 553 (1976 ed.), merely establishes lower procedural bounds and that a court may routinely require more than the minimum when an agency's proposed rule addresses complex or technical factual issues or "Issues of Great Public Import." Brief for Respondents in No. 76–419, p. 49. We have, however, previously shown that our decisions reject this view. Supra, at 542 to this page. We also think the legislative history, even the part which it cites, does not bear out its contention. The Senate Report explains what eventually became § 4 thus:

"This subsection states . . . the minimum requirements of public rule making procedure short of statutory hearing. Under it agencies might in addition confer with industry advisory committees, consult organizations, hold informal 'hearings,' and the like. Considerations of practicality, necessity, and public interest . . . will naturally govern the agency's determination of the extent to which public proceedings should go. Matters of great import, or those where the public submission of facts will be either useful to the agency or a protection to the public, should naturally be accorded more elaborate public procedures." S.Rep. No. 752, 79th Cong., 1st Sess., 14–15 (1945).

The House Report is in complete accord:

" '[U]niformity has been found possible and desirable for all classes of both equity and law actions in the courts . . . . It would seem to require no argument to demonstrate that the administrative agencies, exercising but a fraction of the judicial power may likewise operate under uniform rules of practice and procedure and that they may be required to remain within the terms of the law as to the exercise of both quasi-legislative and quasi-judicial power.'

. . .

---

16. Respondent NRDC does not now argue that additional procedural devices were required under the Constitution. Since this was clearly a rulemaking proceeding in its purest form, we see nothing to support such a view. See United States v. Florida East Coast R. Co., 410 U.S. 224, 244–245, 93 S.Ct. 810, 810–821, 35 L.Ed.2d 223 (1973); Bowles v. Willingham, 321 U.S. 503, 64 S.Ct. 641, 88 L.Ed. 892 (1944); Bi-Metallic Investment Co. v. State Board of Equalization, 239 U.S. 441, 36 S.Ct. 141, 60 L.Ed. 372 (1915).

"The bill is an outline of minimum essential rights and procedures. . . . It affords private parties a means of knowing what their rights are and how they may protect them . . . .

". . . [The bill contains] the essentials of the different forms of administrative proceedings . . . ." H.R.Rep. No. 1980, 79th Cong., 2d Sess., 9, 16–17 (1946).

And the Attorney General's Manual on the Administrative Procedure Act 31, 35 (1947), a contemporaneous interpretation previously given some deference by this Court because of the role played by the Department of Justice in drafting the legislation, further confirms that view. In short, all of this leaves little doubt that Congress intended that the discretion of the *agencies* and not that of the courts be exercised in determining when extra procedural devices should be employed.

There are compelling reasons for construing § 4 in this manner. In the first place, if courts continually review agency proceedings to determine whether the agency employed procedures which were, in the court's opinion, perfectly tailored to reach what the court perceives to be the "best" or "correct" result, judicial review would be totally unpredictable. And the agencies, operating under this vague injunction to employ the "best" procedures and facing the threat of reversal if they did not, would undoubtedly adopt full adjudicatory procedures in every instance. Not only would this totally disrupt the statutory scheme, through which Congress enacted "a formula upon which opposing social and political forces have come to rest," Wong Yang Sung v. McGrath, 339 U.S., at 40, 70 S.Ct., at 450, but all the inherent advantages of informal rulemaking would be totally lost.

Secondly, it is obvious that the court in these cases reviewed the agency's choice of procedures on the basis of the record actually produced at the hearing, 178 U.S.App.D.C., at 347, 547 F.2d., at 644, and not on the basis of the information available to the agency when it made the decision to structure the proceedings in a certain way. This sort of Monday morning quarterbacking not only encourages but almost compels the agency to conduct all rulemaking proceedings with the full panoply of procedural devices normally associated only with adjudicatory hearings.

Finally, and perhaps most importantly, this sort of review fundamentally misconceives the nature of the standard for judicial review of an agency rule. The court below uncritically assumed that additional procedures will automatically result in a more adequate record because it will give interested parties more of an opportunity to participate in and contribute to the proceedings. But informal rulemaking need not be based solely on the transcript of a hearing held before an agency. Indeed, the agency need not even hold a formal hearing. See 5 U.S.C. § 553(c) (1976 ed.). Thus, the adequacy of the "record" in this type of proceeding is not correlated directly to the type of procedural devices employed, but rather turns on whether the agency has followed the statutory mandate of the Administrative Procedure Act or other relevant statutes. If the agency is compelled to support the rule which it ultimately adopts with the type of record produced only after a full adjudicatory hearing, it simply will have no choice but to conduct a full adjudicatory hearing prior to promulgating every rule. In sum, this sort of unwarranted judicial examination of perceived procedural shortcomings of a rulemaking proceeding can do nothing but seriously interfere with that process prescribed by Congress.

Respondent NRDC also argues that the fact that the Commission's inquiry was undertaken in the context of NEPA somehow permits a court to require procedures beyond those specified in § 4 of the APA when investigating factual issues through rulemaking. The Court of Appeals was apparently also of this view, indicating that agencies may be required to "develop new procedures to accomplish the innovative task of implementing NEPA through rulemaking." 178 U.S.App.D.C., at 356, 547 F.2d, at 653. But we search in vain for something in NEPA which would mandate such a result. We have before observed that "NEPA does not repeal by implication any other statute." Aberdeen & Rockfish R. Co. v. SCRAP, 422 U.S. 289, 319, 95 S.Ct. 2336, 2355, 45 L.Ed.2d 191 (1975). See also United States v. SCRAP, 412 U.S. 669, 694, 93 S.Ct. 2405, 2419, 37 L.Ed. 2d 254 (1973). In fact, just two Terms ago, we emphasized that the only procedural requirements imposed by NEPA are those stated in the plain language of the Act. Kleppe v. Sierra Club, 427 U.S. 390, 405–406, 96 S.Ct. 2718, 2728–2729, 49 L.Ed.2d 576 (1976). Thus, it is clear NEPA cannot serve as the basis for a substantial revision of the carefully constructed procedural specifications of the APA.

In short, nothing in the APA, NEPA, the circumstances of this case, the nature of the issues being considered, past agency practice, or the statutory mandate under which the Commission operates permitted the court to review and overturn the rulemaking proceeding on the basis of the procedural devices employed (or not employed) by the Commission so long as the Commission employed at least the statutory *minima*, a matter about which there is no doubt in this case.

There remains, of course, the question of whether the challenged rule finds sufficient justification in the administrative proceedings that it should be upheld by the reviewing court. Judge Tamm, concurring in the result reached by the majority of the Court of Appeals, thought that it did not. There are also intimations in the majority opinion which suggest that the judges who joined it likewise may have thought the administrative proceedings an insufficient basis upon which to predicate the rule in question. We accordingly remand so that the Court of Appeals may review the rule as the Administrative Procedure Act provides. We have made it abundantly clear before that when there is a contemporaneous explanation of the agency decision, the validity of that action must "stand or fall on the propriety of that finding, judged, of course, by the appropriate standard of review. If that finding is not sustainable on the administrative record made, then the Comptroller's decision must be vacated and the matter remanded to him for further consideration." Camp v. Pitts, 411 U.S. 138, 143, 93 S.Ct. 1241, 1244, 36 L.Ed.2d 106 (1973). See also SEC v. Chenery Corp., 318 U.S. 80, 63 S.Ct. 454, 87 L.Ed. 626 (1943). The court should engage in this kind of review and not stray beyond the judicial province to explore the procedural format or to impose upon the agency its own notion of which procedures are "best" or most likely to further some vague, undefined public good. . . .

NOTE

As *Vermont Yankee* indicates, the regulation of civilian nuclear power follows a rather traditional administrative law framework. Legislative-style rulemaking proceedings are used to frame general standards, while trial-type adjudications are used for the resolution of specific cases, such as whether a given reactor complies with the general standards. Do issues involving conflicting scientific expertise fit comfortably into this framework? See Ch. 4, Sec. C.1, infra.

Perhaps the most controversial part of *Vermont Yankee* is its holding that legislative-style rulemaking is all that is required to set standards for issues like nuclear waste storage, unless Congress explicity requires more. In reaching this decision, the court relied heavily on the intent of the framers of the 1946 Administrative Procedure Act, a statute that predates the civilian uses of nuclear energy. Is the legislature the only appropriate institution to say whether new procedures are needed? For a diverse set of views on whether *Vermont Yankee* unwisely limits the judicial role, see Stewart, *Vermont Yankee* and the Evolution of Administrative Procedure, 91 Harv.L.Rev. 1805 (1978); Byse, *Vermont Yankee* and the Evolution of Administrative Procedure: A Somewhat Different View, 91 Harv.L.Rev. 1823 (1978); Breyer, *Vermont Yankee* and the Court's Role in the Nuclear Power Controversy, 91 Harv.L.Rev. 1833 (1978).

Although *Vermont Yankee* held that the procedures used in developing the nuclear waste rule were adequate, it remanded the case to the Court of Appeals for a determination of whether the agency had provided adequate substantive justification for the rule. In 1982, the Court of Appeals held that the agency had not provided adequate justification because it had not allowed for proper consideration of the uncertainties involved in long-term waste storage. Natural Resources Defense Council v. United States Nuclear Regulatory Commission, 685 F.2d 459 (D.C.Cir. 1982). The Court of Appeals noted that nuclear waste contains materials that remain radioactive for periods ranging from hundreds of years for the bulk of fission products to millions of years for certain portions of those products. Id., at 467, n. 14. The Supreme Court granted review of this decision and rendered the following opinion.

BALTIMORE GAS AND ELECTRIC CO. v. NATURAL RESOURCES DEFENSE COUNCIL, INC.

Supreme Court of the United States, 1983.
__ U.S. __, 103 S.Ct. 2246, 76 L.Ed.2d 437.

JUSTICE O'CONNOR delivered the opinion of the Court.

Section 102(2)(C) of the National Environmental Policy Act, 42 U.S.C. § 4332(2)(C) (NEPA), requires federal agencies to consider the environmental impact of any major federal action.[1] As part of its generic rulemaking proceedings to evaluate the environmental effects of the nuclear fuel cycle for nuclear power plants, the Nuclear Regulatory Commission (Commission)[2] decided that licensing boards should assume, for purposes of NEPA, that the permanent storage of certain nuclear wastes would have no significant environmental impact and thus should not af-

---

1. Section 102(2)(C) provides:

"The Congress authorizes and directs that, to the fullest extent possible . . . all agencies of the Federal Government shall . . . include in every recommendation or report on proposals for legislation and other major Federal actions significantly affecting the quality of the human environment, a detailed statement by the responsible official on—

(i) the environmental impact of the proposed action,

(ii) any adverse environmental effects which cannot be avoided should the proposal be implemented,

. . . ., and

(v) any irreversible and irretrievable commitments of resources which would be involved in the proposed action should it be implemented."

2. The original Table S–3 rule was promulgated by the Atomic Energy Commission (AEC). Congress abolished the Atomic Energy Commission in the Energy Reorganization Act of 1974, 42 U.S.C. § 5801 et seq., and transferred its licensing and regulatory functions to the Nuclear Regulatory Commission (NRC). The interim and final rules were promulgated by the NRC. This opinion will use the term "Commission" to refer to both the NRC and the predecessor AEC.

fect the decision whether to license a particular nuclear power plant. We conclude that the Commission complied with NEPA and that its decision is not arbitrary or capricious within the meaning of § 10(e) of the Administrative Procedure Act (APA), 5 U.S.C. § 706.[3]

. . .

The environmental impact of operating a light-water nuclear power plant includes the effects of offsite activities necessary to provide fuel for the plant ("front end" activities), and of offsite activities necessary to dispose of the highly toxic and long-lived nuclear wastes generated by the plant ("back end" activities). The dispute in these cases concerns the Commission's adoption of a series of generic rules to evaluate the environmental effects of a nuclear power plant's fuel cycle. At the heart of each rule is Table S–3, a numerical compilation of the estimated resources used and effluents released by fuel cycle activities supporting a year's operation of a typical light-water reactor. . . .

. . .

The Commission first adopted Table S–3 in 1974, after extensive informal rulemaking proceedings. 39 Fed.Reg. 14188 et seq. (1974). This "original" rule, as it later came to be described, declared that in environmental reports and impact statements for individual licensing proceedings the environmental costs of the fuel cycle "shall be as set forth" in Table S–3 and that "[n]o further discussion of such environmental effects shall be required." Id. at 14191. The original Table S–3 contained no numerical entry for the long-term environmental effects of storing solidified transuranic and high-level wastes, because the Commission staff believed that technology would be developed to isolate the wastes from the environment. The Commission and the parties have later termed this assumption of complete repository integrity as the "zero-release" assumption: the reasonableness of this assumption is at the core of the present controversy. . . .

. . .

In 1979, following further hearings, the Commission adopted the "final" Table S–3 rule. 44 Fed.Reg. 45362 et seq. (1979). . . . The Commission . . . continued to adhere to the zero-release assumption that the solidified waste would not escape and harm the environment once the repository was sealed. It acknowledged that this assumption was uncertain because of the remote possibility that water might enter the repository, dissolve the radioactive materials, and transport them to the biosphere. Nevertheless, the Commission predicted that a bedded-salt repository would maintain its integrity, and found the evidence "tentative but favorable" that an appropriate site would be found. Id. at 45368. The Commission ultimately determined that any undue optimism in the assumption of appropriate selection and perfect performance of the repository is offset by the cautious assumption, reflected in other parts of the Table, that *all* radioactive gases in the spent fuel would escape during the initial 6 to 20 year period that the repository remained open, ibid, and thus did not significantly reduce the overall conservatism of the S–3 Table. Id., at 45369.

---

3. 5 U.S.C. § 706 states in part: "The reviewing court shall—

(2) hold unlawful and set aside agency action, findings, and conclusions found to be—

(A) arbitrary, capricious, an abuse of discretion, or otherwise not in accordance with law."

The Commission rejected the option of expressing the uncertainties in Table S–3 or permitting licensing boards, in performing the NEPA analysis for individual nuclear plants, to consider those uncertainties. It saw no advantage in reassessing the significance of the uncertainties in individual licensing proceedings:

"In view of the uncertainties noted regarding waste disposal, the question then arises whether these uncertainties can or should be reflected explicitly in the fuel cycle rule. The Commission has concluded that the rule should not be so modified. On the individual reactor licensing level, where the proceedings deal with fuel cycle issues only peripherally, the Commission sees no advantage in having licensing boards repeatedly weigh for themselves the effect of uncertainties on the selection of fuel cycle impacts for use in cost-benefit balancing. This is a generic question properly dealt with in the rulemaking as part of choosing what impact values should go into the fuel cycle rule. The Commission concludes, having noted that uncertainties exist, that for the limited purpose of the fuel cycle rule it is reasonable to base impacts on the assumption which the Commission believes the probabilities favor, i.e., that bedded-salt repository sites can be found which will provide effective isolation of radioactive waste from the biosphere." 44 Fed.Reg. 45362, 45369 (1979). . . .

. . .

We are acutely aware that the extent to which this Nation should rely on nuclear power as a source of energy is an important and sensitive issue. Much of the debate focuses on whether development of nuclear generation facilities should proceed in the face of uncertainties about their long-term effects on the environment. Resolution of these fundamental policy questions lies, however, with Congress and the agencies to which Congress has delegated authority, as well as with state legislatures and, ultimately, the populace as a whole. Congress has assigned the courts only the limited, albeit important, task of reviewing agency action to determine whether the agency conformed with controlling statutes. As we emphasized in our earlier encounter with these very proceedings, "[a]dministrative decisions should be set aside in this context, as in every other, only for substantial procedural or substantive reasons as mandated by statute . . . ., not simply because the court is unhappy with the result reached." *Vermont Yankee*, 435 U.S., at 558, 98 S.Ct., at 1219.

The controlling statute at issue here is the National Environmental Policy Act. NEPA has twin aims. First, it "places upon an agency the obligation to consider every significant aspect of the environmental impact of a proposed action." *Vermont Yankee*, supra, at 553, 98 S.Ct., at 1216. Second, it ensures that the agency will inform the public that it has indeed considered environmental concerns in its decisionmaking process. Weinberger v. Catholic Action of Hawaii, 454 U.S. 139, 143, 102 S.Ct. 197, 201, 70 L.Ed.2d 298 (1981). Congress in enacting NEPA, however, did not require agencies to elevate environmental concerns over other appropriate considerations. See Stryckers' Bay Neighborhood Council v. Karlen, 444 U.S. 223, 227, 100 S.Ct. 497, 499, 62 L.Ed.2d 433 (1980) (per curiam). Rather, it required only that the agency take a "hard look" at the environmental consequences before taking a major action. See Kleppe v. Sierra Club, 427 U.S. 390, 410, n. 21, 96 S.Ct. 2718, 2730, n. 21, 49 L.Ed.2d 576 (1976). The role of the courts is simply to ensure that the agency has adequately considered and disclosed the environmental impact of its actions and that its decision is not arbitrary or capricious.

See generally Citizens to Preserve Overton Park v. Volpe, 401 U.S. 402, 415–417, 91 S.Ct. 814, 823–824, 28 L.Ed.2d 136 (1971).

In its Table S–3 Rule here, the Commission has determined that the probabilities favor the zero-release assumption, because the Nation is likely to develop methods to store the wastes with no leakage to the environment. The NRDC did not challenge and the Court of Appeals did not decide the reasonableness of this determination, 685 F.2d, at 478, n. 96, and no party seriously challenges it here. The Commission recognized, however, that the geological, chemical, physical and other data it relied on in making this prediction were based, in part, on assumptions which involve substantial uncertainties. Again, no one suggests that the uncertainties are trivial or the potential effects insignificant if time proves the zero-release assumption to have been seriously wrong. After confronting the issue, though, the Commission has determined that the uncertainties concerning the development of nuclear waste storage facilities are not sufficient to affect the outcome of any individual licensing decision.

It is clear that the Commission, in making this determination, has made the careful consideration and disclosure required by NEPA. The sheer volume of proceedings before the Commission is impressive. Of far greater importance, the Commission's Statement of Consideration announcing the final Table S–3 Rule shows that it has digested this mass of material and disclosed all substantial risks. 44 Fed.Reg. 45362, 45367–45369 (1979). The Statement summarizes the major uncertainty of long-term storage in bedded-salt repositories, which is that water could infiltrate the repository as a result of such diverse factors as geologic faulting, a meteor strike, or accidental or deliberate intrusion by man. The Commission noted that the probability of intrusion was small, and that the plasticity of salt would tend to heal some types of intrusions. The Commission also found the evidence "tentative but favorable" that an appropriate site could be found. Table S–3 refers interested persons to staff studies that discuss the uncertainties in greater detail. Given this record and the Commission's statement, it simply cannot be said that the Commission ignored or failed to disclose the uncertainties surrounding its zero-release assumption.

Congress did not enact NEPA, of course, so that an agency would contemplate the environmental impact of an action as an abstract exercise. Rather, Congress intended that the "hard look" be incorporated as part of the agency's process of deciding whether to pursue a particular federal action. It was on this ground that the Court of Appeals faulted the Commission's action, for failing to allow the uncertainties potentially to "tip the balance" in a particular licensing decision. As a general proposition, we can agree with the Court of Appeals' determination that an agency must allow all significant environmental risks to be factored into the decision whether to undertake a proposed action. We think, however, that the Court of Appeals erred in concluding the Commission had not complied with this standard.

As *Vermont Yankee* made clear, NEPA does not require agencies to adopt any particular internal decisionmaking structure. Here, the agency has chosen to evaluate generically the environmental impact of the fuel cycle and inform individual licensing boards, through the Table S–3 rule, of its evaluation. The generic method chosen by the agency is clearly an appropriate method of conducting the hard look required by NEPA. See *Vermont Yankee*, supra, 435 U.S., at 535, n. 13, 98 S.Ct., at 1207, n. 13. The environmental effects of much of the fuel cycle are not plant specific, for any plant, regardless of its particular attributes, will create additional wastes that must be stored in a common long-term repository. Administrative efficiency and consistency of decision are both furthered by a generic determination of these effects without needless repetition of the litigation in individual proceedings, which are subject to review by the Commission in any event. See generally Ecology Action v. AEC, 492 F.2d 998, 1002, n. 5 (CA2 1974) (Friendly, J.) (quoting Administrative Conference Proposed Recommendation 73–6).

The Court of Appeals recognized that the Commission has discretion to evaluate generically the environmental effects of the fuel cycle and require that these values be "plugged into" individual licensing decisions. The court concluded that the Commission nevertheless violated NEPA by failing to factor the uncertainty surrounding long-term storage into Table S–3 and precluding individual licensing decisionmakers from considering it.

The Commission's decision to affix a zero value to the environmental impact of long-term storage would violate NEPA, however, only if the Commission acted arbitrarily and capriciously in deciding generically that the uncertainty was insufficient to affect any individual licensing decision. In assessing whether the Commission's decision is arbitrary and capricious, it is crucial to place the zero-release assumption in context. Three factors are particularly important. First is the Commission's repeated emphasis that the zero-risk assumption—and, indeed, all of the Table S–3 rule—was made for a limited purpose. The Commission expressly noted its intention to supplement the rule with an explanatory narrative. It also emphasized that the purpose of the rule was not to evaluate or select the most effective long-term waste disposal technology or develop site selection criteria. A separate and comprehensive series of programs has been undertaken to serve these broader purposes. In the proceedings before us, the Commission's staff did not attempt to evaluate the environmental effects of all possible methods of disposing of waste. Rather, it chose to analyze intensively the most probable long-term waste disposal method—burial in a bedded-salt repository several hundred meters below ground—and then "estimate its impact conservatively, based on the best available information and analysis." 44 Fed.Reg. 45362, 45363 (1979). The zero-release assumption cannot be evaluated in isolation. Rather, it must be assessed in relation to the limited purpose for which the Commission made the assumption.

Second, the Commission emphasized that the zero-release assumption is but a single figure in an entire Table, which the Commission expressly designed as a risk-averse estimate of the environmental impact of the fuel cycle. It noted that Table S–3 assumed that the fuel storage canisters and the fuel rod cladding would be corroded before a repository is closed and that all volatile materials in the fuel would escape to the environment. Given that assumption, and the improbability that materials would escape after sealing, the Commission determined that the overall Table represented a conservative (i.e., inflated) statement of environmental impacts. It is not unreasonable for the Commission to counteract the uncertainties in post-sealing releases by balancing them with an overestimate of pre-sealing releases. A reviewing court should not magnify a single line item beyond its significance as only part of a larger Table.

Third, a reviewing court must remember that the Commission is making predictions, within its area of special expertise, at the frontiers of science. When examining this kind of scientific determination, as opposed to simple findings of fact, a reviewing court must generally be at its most deferential. See, e.g., Industrial Union Department v. American Petroleum Institute, 448 U.S. 607, 656, 100 S.Ct. 2844, 2871, 65 L.Ed.2d 1010 (1980) (plurality opinion); id., at 705–706, 100 S.Ct., at 2895–2896 (Marshall, J., dissenting).

With these three guides in mind, we find the Commission's zero-release assumption to be within the bounds of reasoned decisionmaking required by the APA. We have already noted that the Commission's Statement of Consideration detailed several areas of uncertainty and discussed why they were insubstantial for purposes of an individual licensing decision. The Table S–3 Rule also refers to the staff reports, public documents that contain a more expanded discussion of the uncertainties involved in concluding that long-term storage will have no environmental effects. These staff reports recognize that rigorous verification of long-term risks for waste repositories is not possible, but suggest that data and extrapolation of past experience allow the Commission to identify events that could produce repository failure, estimate the probability of those events, and calculate the resulting consequences. NUREG–0116, at 4–86. The Commission staff also modelled the consequences of repository failure by tracing the flow of contaminated water, and found them to be insignificant. Id., at 4–89 through 4–94. Ultimately, the staff concluded that

"[t]he radiotoxic hazard index analyses and the modeling studies that have been done indicate that consequences of all but the most improbable events will be small. Risks (probabilities times consequences) inherent in the long term for geological disposal will therefore also be small." NUREG–0116, at 2–11.

We also find significant the separate views of Commissioners Bradford and Gilinsky. These Commissioners expressed dissatisfaction with the zero-release assumption and yet emphasized the limited purpose of the assumption and the overall conservatism of Table S–3. Commissioner Bradford characterized the bedded-salt repository as a responsible working assumption for NEPA purposes and concurred in the zero-release figure because it does not appear to affect Table S–3's overall conservatism. 44 Fed.Reg. 45362, 45372 (1979). Commissioner Gilinsky was more critical of the entire Table, stating that the Commission should confront directly whether it should license any nuclear reactors in light of the problems of waste disposal, rather than hide an affirmative conclusion to this issue behind a table of numbers. He emphasized that the "waste confidence proceeding", see note 14, supra, should provide the Commission an appropriate vehicle for a thorough evaluation of the problems involved in the Government's commitment to a waste disposal solution. For the limited purpose of individual licensing proceedings, however, Commissioner Gilinsky found it "virtually inconceivable" that the Table should affect the decision whether to license, and characterized as "naive" the notion that the fuel cycle effluents could tip the balance in some cases and not in others. Id., at 45374 (1979).

In sum, we think that the zero-release assumption—a policy judgment concerning one line in a conservative Table designed for the limited purpose of individual licensing decisions—is within the bounds of reasoned decisionmaking. It is not our task to determine what decision we, as Commissioners, would have reached. Our only task is to determine whether the Commission has considered the relevant factors and articulated a rational connection between the facts found and the choice made.

Bowman Transportation, Inc. v. Arkansas-Best Freight System, Inc., 419 U.S. 281, 285–286, 95 S.Ct. 438, 441–442, 42 L.Ed.2d 447 (1974); Citizens to Preserve Overton Park v. Volpe, supra. Under this standard, we think the Commission's zero-release assumption, within the context of Table S–3 as a whole, was not arbitrary and capricious. . . .

NOTE

Why should a court give particular deference to an agency which acts "at the frontiers of science"? When uncertainties pervade a policy area, technical expertise often includes implicit policy judgments. On the respective role of agencies and the courts in science policy, see Ch. 4, Secs. C.1 and D.1.

In addition to emphasizing the role of the agency, the Supreme Court decision above stresses that Congress and the state legislatures must make the fundamental policy decisions about nuclear power. If you were a legislator contemplating the long-term effects of nuclear waste, how would you weigh the risk to future generations? See Ch. 1, Sec. C.1, supra.

On January 7, 1983, President Reagan signed the Nuclear Waste Policy Act of 1982, P.L. 97–425. This Act establishes a schedule "for the siting, construction and operation of repositories that will provide a reasonable assurance that the public and the environment will be adequately protected from the hazards of high-level radioactive waste . . . ." Sec. 111(b)(1). Should Congress have provided more specific goals than "reasonable assurance" and "adequate protection"? How would you phrase the goals for a nuclear waste repository?

One of the difficulties in waste storage—a difficulty not limited to the nuclear field—is that while many localities are happy to receive the electricity generated by nuclear energy, few are eager to become waste-storage sites. The Nuclear Waste Policy Act provides an elaborate scheme under which potential sites chosen by the Secretary of Energy and the President can be disapproved by the state involved, but the disapproval can be overturned by Congress. Secs. 115, 116. Would you give the states more authority in this matter? On the relationship between federal and state authority in the licensing of nuclear reactors, see Pacific Gas and Electric Co. v. State Energy Resources Conservation and Development Commission, Ch. 4, Sec. C.2, infra.

Up to this point, we have discussed government regulation of civilian nuclear power. The government has also encouraged the development of nuclear energy in various ways, as the following case demonstrates.

DUKE POWER CO. v. CAROLINA ENVIRONMENTAL STUDY GROUP, INC.

Supreme Court of the United States, 1978.
438 U.S. 59, 98 S.Ct. 2620, 57 L.Ed.2d 595.

MR. CHIEF JUSTICE BURGER delivered the opinion of the Court.

These appeals present the question of whether Congress may, consistent with the Constitution, impose a limitation on liability for nuclear accidents resulting from the operation of private nuclear power plants licensed by the Federal Government.

I

A

When Congress passed the Atomic Energy Act of 1946, it contemplated that the development of nuclear power would be a Government monopoly. See Act of Aug. 1, 1946, ch. 724, 60 Stat. 755. Within a decade, however, Congress concluded that the national interest would be best served if the Government encouraged the private sector to become involved in the development of atomic energy for peaceful purposes under a program of federal regulation and licensing. See H.R.Rep. No. 2181, 83d Cong., 2d Sess., 1–11 (1954). The Atomic Energy Act of 1954, Act of Aug. 30, 1954, ch. 1073, 68 Stat. 919, as amended, 42 U.S.C. §§ 2011–2281 (1970 ed. and Supp. V), implemented this policy decision, providing for licensing of private construction, ownership, and operation of commercial nuclear power reactors for energy production under strict supervision by the Atomic Energy Commission (AEC).[1] See Power Reactor Development Co. v. Electrical Workers, 367 U.S. 396, 81 S.Ct. 1529, 6 L.Ed.2d 924 (1961), rev'g and remanding 108 U.S.App.D.C. 97, 280 F.2d 645 (1960).

Private industry responded to the Atomic Energy Act of 1954 with the development of an experimental power plant constructed under the auspices of a consortium of interested companies. It soon became apparent that profits from the private exploitation of atomic energy were uncertain and the accompanying risks substantial. See Green, Nuclear Power: Risk, Liability, and Indemnity, 71 Mich.L.Rev. 479–481 (1973) (Green). Although the AEC offered incentives to encourage investment, there remained in the path of the private nuclear power industry various problems—the risk of potentially vast liability in the event of a nuclear accident of a sizable magnitude being the major obstacle. Notwithstanding comprehensive testing and study, the uniqueness of this form of energy production made it impossible totally to rule out the risk of a major nuclear accident resulting in extensive damage. Private industry and the AEC were confident that such a disaster would not occur, but the very uniqueness of nuclear power meant that the possibility remained, and the potential liability dwarfed the ability of the industry and private insurance companies to absorb the risk. See Hearings before the Joint Committee on Atomic Energy on Government Indemnity for Private Licensees and AEC Contractors Against Reactor Hazards, 84th Cong., 2d Sess., 122–124 (1956). Thus, while repeatedly stressing that the risk of a major nuclear accident was extremely remote, spokesmen for the private sector informed Congress that they would be forced to withdraw from the field if their liability were not limited by appropriate legislation. Id., at 9, 109–110, 115, 120, 136–137, 148, 181, 195, and 240.

Congress responded in 1957 by passing the Price-Anderson Act, 71 Stat. 576, 42 U.S.C. § 2210 (1970 ed. and Supp. V). The Act had the dual purpose of "protect[ing] the public and . . . encourag[ing] the development of the atomic energy industry." 42 U.S.C. § 2012(i). In its original form, the Act limited the aggregate liability for a single nuclear incident to $500 million plus the amount of liability insurance available on the private market—some $60 million in 1957. The nuclear industry was required to purchase the maximum available amount of privately underwritten public liability insurance, and the Act provided that if damages from a nuclear disaster exceeded the amount of that private insurance coverage, the Federal Government would indemnify the licensee and other "persons indemnified" in an amount not to exceed $500 million. Thus, the actual ceiling on liability was the amount of private insurance coverage plus the Government's indemnification obligation which totaled $560 million.

1. Under the terms of the Energy Reorganization Act of 1974, 42 U.S.C. § 5801 *et seq.* (1970 ed., Supp. V), the Nuclear Regulatory Commission (NRC) has now replaced the AEC as the licensing and regulatory authority.

Since its enactment, the Act has been twice amended, the first occasion being on the eve of its expiration in 1966. These amendments extended the basic liability-limitation provisions for another 10 years, and added a provision which had the effect of requiring those indemnified under the Act to waive all legal defenses in the event of a substantial nuclear accident. This provision was based on a congressional concern that state tort law dealing with liability for nuclear incidents was generally unsettled and that some way of insuring a common standard of responsibility for all jurisdictions—strict liability—was needed. A waiver of defenses was thought to be the preferable approach since it entailed less interference with state tort law than would the enactment of a federal statute prescribing strict liability. See S.Rep. No. 1605, 89th Cong., 2d Sess., 6–10 (1966).

In 1975, Congress again extended the Act's coverage until 1987, and continued the $560 million limitation on liability. However a new provision was added requiring, in the event of a nuclear incident, each of the 60 or more reactor owners to contribute between $2 and $5 million toward the cost of compensating victims. 42 U.S.C. § 2210(b) (1970 ed., Supp. V). Since the liability ceiling remained at the same level, the effect of the "deferred premium" provision was to reduce the Federal Government's contribution to the liability pool. In its amendments to the Act in 1975, Congress also explicitly provided that "in the event of a nuclear incident involving damages in excess of [the] amount of aggregate liability, the Congress will thoroughly review the particular incident and will take whatever action is deemed necessary and appropriate to protect the public from the consequences of a disaster of such magnitude . . .." 42 U.S.C. § 2210(e) (1970 ed., Supp. V).

Under the Price-Anderson Act as it presently stands, liability in the event of a nuclear incident causing damages of $560 million or more would be spread as follows: $315 million would be paid from contributions by the licensees of the 63 private operating nuclear power plants; $140 million would come from private insurance (the maximum now available); the remainder of $105 million would be borne by the Federal Government.

B

Appellant in No. 77–262, Duke Power Co., is an investor-owned public utility which is constructing one nuclear power plant in North Carolina and one in South Carolina. Duke Power, along with the NRC, was sued by appellees, two organizations—Carolina Environmental Study Group and the Catawba Central Labor Union—and 40 individuals who live within close proximity to the planned facilities. The action was commenced in 1973, and sought, among other relief, a declaration that the Price-Anderson Act is unconstitutional. . . .

Specifically, as we read the complaint, appellees are making two basic challenges to the Act—both of which find their moorings in the Fifth Amendment. First, appellees contend that the Due Process Clause protects them against arbitrary governmental action adversely affecting their property rights and that the Price-Anderson Act—which both creates the source of the underlying injury and limits the recovery therefor—constitutes such arbitrary action. And second, they are contending that in the event of a nuclear accident their property would be "taken" without any assurance of just compensation. The Price-Anderson Act is the instrument of the taking since on this record, without it, there would be no power plants and no possibility of an accident. . . .

The District Court held that the Price-Anderson Act contravened the Due Process Clause because "[t]he amount of recovery is not rationally related to the potential losses"; because "[t]he Act tends to encourage irresponsibility in matters of safety and environmental protection . . ."; and finally because "[t]here is no *quid pro quo*" for the liability limitations. 431 F.Supp., at 222–223. An equal protection violation was also found because the Act "places the cost of [nuclear power] on an arbitrarily chosen segment of society, those injured by nuclear catastrophe." Id., at 225. Application of the relevant constitutional principles forces the conclusion that these holdings of the District Court cannot be sustained.

A

Our due process analysis properly begins with a discussion of the appropriate standard of review. Appellants, portraying the liability-limitation provision as a legislative balancing of economic interests, urge that the Price-Anderson Act be accorded the traditional presumption of constitutionality generally accorded economic regulations and that it be upheld absent proof of arbitrariness or irrationality on the part of Congress. See Ferguson v. Skrupa, 372 U.S. 726, 731–732, 83 S.Ct. 1028, 1031–1032, 10 L.Ed.2d 93 (1963); Usery v. Turner Elkhorn Mining Co., 428 U.S. 1, 15, 98 S.Ct. 2882, 2892, 49 L.Ed.2d 752 (1976). Appellees, however, urge a more elevated standard of review on the ground that the interests jeopardized by the Price-Anderson Act "are far more important than those in the economic due process and business-oriented cases" where the traditional rationality standard has been invoked. Brief for Appellees 36. An intermediate standard like that applied in cases such as Craig v. Boren, 429 U.S. 190, 97 S.Ct. 451, 50 L.Ed.2d 397 (1976) (equal protection challenge to statute requiring that males be older than females in order to purchase beer) or United States Trust Co. of New York v. New Jersey, 431 U.S. 1, 97 S.Ct. 1505, 52 L.Ed.2d 92 (1977) (Contract Clause challenge to repeal of statutory covenant providing security for bondholders) is thus recommended for our use here.

As we read the Act and its legislative history, it is clear that Congress' purpose was to remove the economic impediments in order to stimulate the private development of electric energy by nuclear power while simultaneously providing the public compensation in the event of a catastrophic nuclear incident. See, e.g., S.Rep. No. 296, 85th Cong., 1st Sess., 15 (1957). The liability-limitation provision thus emerges as a classic example of an economic regulation—a legislative effort to structure and accommodate "the burdens and benefits of economic life." Usery v. Turner Elkhorn Mining Co., supra, 428 at 15, 96 S.Ct. 2892. "It is by now well established that [such] legislative Acts . . . come to the Court with a presumption of constitutionality, and that the burden is on one complaining of a due process violation to establish that the legislature has acted in an arbitrary and irrational way." Ibid. That the accommodation struck may have profound and far-reaching consequences, contrary to appellees' suggestion, provides all the more reason for this Court to defer to the congressional judgment unless it is demonstrably arbitrary or irrational.

B

When examined in light of this standard of review, the Price-Anderson Act, in our view, passes constitutional muster. The record before us fully supports the need for the imposition of a statutory limit on liability to encourage private industry participation and hence bears a rational relationship to Congress' concern for stimulating the involvement of private enterprise in the production of electric energy through the use of atomic power; nor do we understand appellees or the District Court to be of a different view. Rather their challenge is to the alleged arbitrariness of the *particular figure* of $560 million, which is the statutory ceiling on liability. The District Court aptly summarized its position:

"The amount of recovery is not rationally related to the potential losses. Abundant evidence in the record shows that although major catastrophe in any particular place is not certain and may not be extremely likely, nevertheless, in the territory where these plants are located, damage to life and property for this and future generations could well be many, many times the limit which the law places on liability." 431 F.Supp., at 222.

Assuming, *arguendo,* that the $560 million fund would not insure full recovery in all conceivable circumstances [28] and the hard truth is that no one can ever know—it does not by any means follow that the liability limitation is therefore irrational and violative of due process. The legislative history clearly indicates that the $560 million figure was not arrived at on the supposition that it alone would necessarily be sufficient to guarantee full compensation in the event of a nuclear incident. Instead, it was conceived of as a "starting point" or a working hypothesis.[29] The reasonableness of the statute's assumed ceiling on liability was predicated on two corollary considerations—expert appraisals of the exceedingly small risk of a nuclear incident involving claims in excess of $560 million, and the recognition that in the event of such an incident, Congress would likely enact extraordinary relief provisions to provide additional relief, in accord with prior practice.

"[T]his limitation does not, as a practical matter, detract from the public protection afforded by this legislation. In the first place, the likelihood of an accident occurring which would result in claims exceeding the sum of the financial protection required and the governmental in-

---

28. As the various studies considered by the District Court indicate, there is considerable uncertainty as to the amount of damages which would result from a catastrophic nuclear accident. See 431 F.Supp., at 210–214. The Reactor Safety Study published by the NRC in 1975 suggested that there was a 1 in 20,000 chance (per reactor year) of an accident causing property damage approaching $100 million and having only minor health effects. By contrast, when the odds were reduced to the range of 1 in 1 billion (per reactor year), the level of damages approached $14 billion; and 3,300 early fatalities and 45,000 early illnesses were predicted. NRC, Reactor Safety Study, An Assessment of Accident Risks in U.S. Commercial Nuclear Power Plants 83–85 (Wash–1400, Oct. 1975). For a thorough criticism of the Reactor Safety Study, see EPA, Reactor Safety Study (Wash–1400): A Review of the Final Report (June 1976).

29. What we were thinking about was the magnitude of protection and we set an arbitrary figure because it seemed to be practical at that time and because we didn't think an accident would happen . . . but yet we recognize that it could happen. *We wanted to have a base to work from."* Hearings before the Joint Committee on Atomic Energy on Possible Modification or Extension of the Price-Anderson Insurance And Indemnity Act of 1957 In Order for Proper Planning of Nuclear Power Plants to Continue Without Delay, 93d Cong., 2d Sess., 68 (1974) (remarks of Rep. Holifield) (emphasis added).

demnity is exceedingly remote, albeit theoretically possible. Perhaps more important, in the event of a national disaster of this magnitude, it is obvious that Congress would have to review the problem and take appropriate action. The history of other natural or man-made disasters, such as the Texas City incident, bears this out. The limitation of liability serves primarily as a device for facilitating further congressional review of such a situation, rather than as an ultimate bar to further relief of the public." H.R.Rep. No. 883, 89th Cong., 1st Sess., 6–7 (1965).

See also S.Rep. No. 296, supra, at 21; H.R.Rep. No. 94–648, pp. 12, 15 (1975).

Given our conclusion that, in general, limiting liability is an acceptable method for Congress to utilize in encouraging the private development of electric energy by atomic power, candor requires acknowledgment that whatever ceiling figure is selected will, of necessity, be arbitrary in the sense that any choice of a figure based on imponderables like those at issue here can always be so characterized. This is not, however, the kind of arbitrariness which flaws otherwise constitutional action. When appraised in terms of both the extremely remote possibility of an accident where liability would exceed the limitation [30] and Congress' now statutory commitment to "take whatever action is deemed necessary and appropriate to protect the public from the consequences of" any such disaster, 42 U.S.C. § 2210(e) (1970 ed., Supp. V),[31] we hold the congressional decision to fix a $560 million ceiling, at this stage in the private development and production of electric energy by nuclear power, to be within permissible limits and not violative of due process.

This District Court's further conclusion that the Price-Anderson Act "tends to encourage irresponsibility . . . on the part of builders and owners" of the nuclear power plants, 431 F.Supp., at 222, simply cannot withstand careful scrutiny. We recently outlined the multitude of detailed steps involved in the review of any application for a license to construct or to operate a nuclear power plant, Vermont Yankee Nuclear Power Corp. v. NRDC, 435 U.S. 519, 526–527, and n. 5, 98 S.Ct. 1197, 1203–1204, and n. 5, 55 L.Ed.2d 460 (1978); nothing in the liability-limitation provision undermines or alters in any respect the rigor and integrity of that process. Moreover, in the event of a nuclear accident the utility itself would suffer perhaps the largest damages. While obviously not to be

---

30. Congress' conclusion that "the probabilities of a nuclear incident are much lower and the likely consequences much less severe than has been thought previously," was a key factor in the decision not to increase the $560 million liability ceiling in 1975. S.Rep. No. 94–454, p. 12 (1975).

31. In the past Congress has provided emergency assistance for victims of catastrophic accidents even in the absence of a prior statutory commitment to do so. For example, in 1955, Congress passed the Texas City Explosion Relief Act, 69 Stat. 707, to provide relief for victims of the explosion of ammonium nitrate fertilizer in 1947. Congress took this action despite the decision in Dalehite v. United States, 346 U.S. 15, 73 S.Ct. 956, 97 L.Ed. 1427 (1953), holding the United States free from any liability under the Federal Tort Claims Act for the damages incurred and injuries suffered. More recently Congress enacted legislation to provide relief for victims of the flood resulting from the collapse of the Teton Dam in Idaho. Pub.L. 94–400, 90 Stat. 1211. Under the Act, the Secretary of the Interior was authorized to provide full compensation for any deaths, personal injuries, or property damage caused by the failure of the dam. Ibid.

The Price-Anderson Act is, of course, a significant improvement on these prior relief efforts because it provides an advance guarantee of recovery up to $560 million plus an express commitment by Congress to take whatever further steps are necessary to aid the victims of a nuclear incident.

compared with the loss of human life and injury to health, the risk of financial loss and possible bankruptcy to the utility is in itself no small incentive to avoid the kind of irresponsible and cavalier conduct implicitly attributed to licensees by the District Court.

The remaining due process objection to the liability-limitation provision is that it fails to provide those injured by a nuclear accident with a satisfactory *quid pro quo* for the common-law rights of recovery which the Act abrogates. Initially, it is not at all clear that the Due Process Clause in fact requires that a legislatively enacted compensation scheme either duplicate the recovery at common law or provide a reasonable substitute remedy. However, we need not resolve this question here since the Price-Anderson Act does, in our view, provide a reasonably just substitute for the common-law or state tort law remedies it replaces. Cf. New York Central R. Co. v. White, 243 U.S. 188, 37 S.Ct. 247, 61 L.Ed. 667 (1917); Crowell v. Benson, 285 U.S. 22, 52 S.Ct. 285, 76 L.Ed. 598 (1932).

The legislative history of the liability-limitation provisions and the accompanying compensation mechanism reflects Congress' determination that reliance on state tort law remedies and state-court procedures was an unsatisfactory approach to assuring public compensation for nuclear accidents, while at the same time providing the necessary incentives for private development of nuclear-produced energy. The remarks of Chairman Anders of the NRC before the Joint Committee on Atomic Energy during the 1975 hearings on the need for renewal of the Price-Anderson Act are illustrative of this concern and of the expectation that the Act would provide a more efficient and certain vehicle for assuring compensation in the unlikely event of a nuclear incident:

> "The primary defect of this alternative [nonrenewal of the Act], however, is its failure to afford the public either a secure source of funds or a firm basis for legal liability with respect to new plants. While in theory no legal limit would be placed on liability, as a practical matter the public would be less assured of obtaining compensation than under Price-Anderson. Establishing liability would depend in each case on state tort law and procedures, and these might or might not provide for no-fault liability, let alone the multiple other protections now embodied in Price-Anderson. The present assurance of prompt and equitable compensation under a pre-structured and nationally applicable protective system would give way to uncertainties, variations and potentially lengthy delays in recovery. It should be emphasized, moreover, that it is collecting a judgment, not filing a lawsuit, that counts. Even if defenses are waived under state law, a defendant with theoretically "unlimited" liability may be unable to pay a judgment once obtained. When the defendant's assets are exhausted by earlier judgments, subsequent claimants would be left with uncollectable awards. The prospect of inequitable distribution would produce a race to the courthouse door in contrast to the present system of assured orderly and equitable compensation." Hearings on H.R. 8631 before Joint Committee on Atomic Energy, 94th Cong., 1st Sess., 69 (1975).

Appellees, like the District Court, differ with this appraisal on several grounds. They argue, *inter alia,* that recovery under the Act would not be greater than without it, that the waiver of defenses required by the Act, 42 U.S.C. § 2210(n) (1970 ed., Supp. V), is an idle gesture since those involved in the development of nuclear energy would likely be held strictly liable under common-law principles; that the claim-administration procedure under the Act delays rather than expedites individual recovery; and finally that recovery of even limited compensation is uncertain since the liability ceiling does not vary with the number of persons injured or amount of property damaged. The extension of short state statutes of limitations and the provision of omnibus coverage do not save the Act, in their view, since such provisions could equally well be included in a fairer plan which would assure greater compensation.

We disagree. We view the congressional *assurance* of a $560 million fund for recovery, accompanied by an express statutory commitment, to "take whatever action is deemed necessary and appropriate to protect the public from the consequences of" a nuclear accident, 42 U.S.C. § 2210(e) (1970 ed., Supp. V), to be a fair and reasonable substitute for the uncertain recovery of damages of this magnitude from a utility or component manufacturer, whose resources might well be exhausted at an early stage. The record in this case raises serious questions about the ability of a utility or component manufacturer to satisfy a judgment approaching $560 million—the amount guaranteed under the Price-Anderson Act. Nor are we persuaded that the mandatory waiver of defenses required by the Act is of no benefit to potential claimants. Since there has never been, to our knowledge, a case arising out of a nuclear incident like those covered by the Price-Anderson Act, any discussion of the standard of liability that state courts will apply is necessarily speculative. At the minimum, the statutorily mandated waiver of defenses establishes at the threshold the right of injured parties to compensation without proof of fault and eliminates the burden of delay and uncertainty which would follow from the need to litigate the question of liability after an accident. Further, even if strict liability were routinely applied, the common-law doctrine is subject to exceptions for acts of God or of third parties—two of the very factors which appellees emphasized in the District Court in the course of arguing that the risks of a nuclear accident are greater than generally admitted. All of these considerations belie the suggestion that the Act leaves the potential victims of a nuclear disaster in a more disadvantageous position than they would be in if left to their common law remedies—not known in modern times for either their speed or economy.

Appellees' remaining objections can be briefly treated. The claim-administration procedures under the Act provide that in the event of an accident with potential liability exceeding the $560 million ceiling, no more than 15% of the limit can be distributed pending court approval of a plan of distribution taking into account the need to assure compensation for "possible latent injury claims which may not be discovered until a later time." 42 U.S.C. § 2210(o)(3) (1970 ed., Supp. V). Although some delay might follow from compliance with this statutory procedure, we doubt that it would approach that resulting from routine litigation of the large number of claims caused by a catastrophic accident. Moreover, the statutory scheme insures the equitable distribution of benefits to all who suffer injury—both immediate and latent; under the common-law route, the proverbial race to the courthouse would instead determine who had "first crack" at the diminishing resources of the tortfeasor, and fairness could well be sacrificed in the process. The remaining contention that recovery is uncertain because of the aggregate rather than individualized nature of the liability ceiling is but a thinly disguised version of the contention that the $560 million figure is inadequate, which we have already rejected.

In the course of adjudicating a similar challenge to the Workmen's Compensation Act in New York Central R. Co. v. White, 243 U.S., at 201,

37 S.Ct., at 252, the Court observed that the Due Process Clause of the Fourteenth Amendment was not violated simply because an injured party would not be able to recover as much under the Act as before its enactment. "[H]e is entitled to moderate compensation in all cases of injury, and has a certain and speedy remedy without the difficulty and expense of establishing negligence or proving the amount of the damages." The logic of *New York Central* would seem to apply with renewed force in the context of this challenge to the Price-Anderson Act. The Price-Anderson Act not only provides a reasonable, prompt, and equitable mechanism for compensating victims of a catastrophic nuclear incident, it also guarantees a level of net compensation generally exceeding that recoverable in private litigation. Moreover, the Act contains an explicit congressional commitment to take further action to aid victims of a nuclear accident in the event that the $560 million ceiling on liability is exceeded. This panoply of remedies and guarantees is at the least a reasonably just substitute for the common-law rights replaced by the Price-Anderson Act. Nothing more is required by the Due Process Clause.

Although the District Court also found the Price-Anderson Act to contravene the "equal protection provision that is included within the Due Process Clause of the Fifth Amendment," 431 F.Supp., at 224–225, appellees have not relied on this ground since the equal protection arguments largely track and duplicate those made in support of the due process claim. In any event, we conclude that there is no equal protection violation. The general rationality of the Price-Anderson Act liability limitations—particularly with reference to the important congressional purpose of encouraging private participation in the exploitation of nuclear energy—is ample justification for the difference in treatment between those injured in nuclear accidents and those whose injuries are derived from other causes. Speculation regarding other arrangements that might be used to spread the risk of liability in ways different from the Price-Anderson Act is, of course, not pertinent to the equal protection analysis. See Mourning v. Family Publications Service, Inc., 411 U.S. 356, 378, 98 S.Ct. 1652, 1665, 36 L.Ed.2d 318 (1973).

Accordingly, the decision of the District Court is reversed, and the cases are remanded for proceedings consistent with this opinion. Reversed and remanded.

NOTE

Duke Power involves a form of subsidy—government liability limits—for nuclear power. Do subsidies for research and development differ in principle from the subsidy implicit in a liability limit? As the decision notes, the government has for many years encouraged the development of nuclear power. Should nuclear energy compete in the market place without subsidies? Should solar energy? See Ch. 10, infra. Scientific research and development is not generally left to the private market place since science is a public good with distant and uncertain payoffs. See Ch. 4, Sec. B.2, infra. On the other hand, once science has given birth to a commercially feasible technology, the case for government subsidies weakens. Id. Is nuclear power now at that stage where the government should leave it on its own or are there national security considerations involved in assuring certain forms of energy supply?

The court upheld the liability limit in *Duke Power* in part because it found an analogy to traditional worker's compensation. Do you believe there are differences of constitutional significance between the two situations? Does the traditional judicial technique of looking decades back for precedent, even in cases involving a new technology, trouble you?

The availability of punitive damages under the Price-Anderson Act liability framework is discussed in Silkwood v. Kerr-McGee Corp., 464 U.S. ___, 104 S.Ct. 615, 78 L.Ed.2d 443 (1984).

REPORT OF THE PRESIDENT'S COMMISSION ON THE ACCIDENT AT THREE MILE ISLAND

2, 8–9, 12–14, 28 (October 1979).

At 4:00 a.m. on March 28, 1979, a serious accident occurred at the Three Mile Island 2 nuclear power plant near Middletown, Pennsylvania. The accident was initiated by mechanical malfunctions in the plant and made much worse by a combination of human errors in responding to it. . . . During the next 4 days, the extent and gravity of the accident was unclear to the managers of the plant, to federal and state officials, and to the general public. What is quite clear is that its impact, nationally and internationally, has raised serious concerns about the safety of nuclear power. This Commission was established in response to those concerns.

. . .

[The accident began when] [t]he pilot-operated relief valve (PORV) at the top of the pressurizer opened as expected when pressure rose but failed to close when pressure decreased, thereby creating an opening in the primary coolant system—a small-break loss-of-coolant accident (LOCA).* The PORV indicator light in the control room showed only that the signal had been sent to close the PORV rather than the fact that the PORV remained open. The operators, relying on the indicator light and believing that the PORV had closed, did not heed other indications and were unaware of the PORV failure; the LOCA continued for over 2 hours. The TMI–2 emergency procedure for a stuck-open PORV did not state that unless the PORV block valve was closed, a LOCA would exist. Prior to TMI, the NRC had paid insufficient attention to LOCAs of this size and the probability of their occurrence in licensing reviews. Instead, the NRC focused most of its attention on large-break LOCAs.

The high pressure injection system (HPI)—a major design safety system—came on automatically. However, the operators were conditioned to maintain the specified water level in the pressurizer and were concerned that the plant was "going solid," that is, filled with water. Therefore, they cut back HPI from 1,000 gallons per minute to less than 100 gallons per minute. For extended periods on March 28, HPI was either not operating or operating at an insufficient rate. This led to much of the core being uncovered for extended periods on March 28 and resulted in severe damage to the core. If the HPI had not been throttled, core damage would have been prevented in spite of a stuck-open PORV.

. . .

Just how serious was the accident? Based on our investigation of the health effects of the accident, we conclude that in spite of serious damage to the plant, most of the radiation was contained and the actual release will have a negligible effect on the physical health of individuals. The major health effect of the accident was found to be mental stress.

---

* *Loss-of-coolant accident (LOCA)*—An accident involving a broken pipe, stuck-open valve, or other leak in the reactor coolant system that results in a loss of the water cooling the reactor core.

The amount of radiation received by any one individual outside the plant was very low. However, even low levels of radiation may result in the later development of cancer, genetic defects, or birth defects among children who are exposed in the womb. Since there is no direct way of measuring the danger of low-level radiation to health, the degree of danger must be estimated indirectly. Different scientists make different assumptions about how this estimate should be made and, therefore, estimates vary. Fortunately, in this case the radiation doses were so low that we conclude that the overall health effects will be minimal. There will either be no case of cancer or the number of cases will be so small that it will never be possible to detect them. The same conclusion applies to the other possible health effects. The reasons for these conclusions are as follows.

An example of a projection derived for the total number of radiation-induced cancers among the population affected by the accident at TMI was 0.7. This number is an estimate of an average, such as the one that appears in the statement: "The average American family has 2.3 children."

In the case of TMI, what it really means is that each of some 2 million individuals living within 50 miles has a miniscule additional chance of dying of cancer, and when all of these minute probabilities are added up, they total 0.7. In such a situation, a mathematical law known as a Poisson distribution (named after a famous French mathematician) applies. If the estimated average is 0.7, then the actual probabilities for cancer deaths due to the accident work out as follows: There is a roughly 50 percent chance that there will be no additional cancer deaths, a 35 percent chance that one individual will die of cancer, a 12 percent chance that 2 people will die of cancer, and it is practically certain that there will not be as many as five cancer deaths.

Similar probabilities can be calculated for our various estimates. All of them have in common the following: It is entirely possible that not a single extra cancer death will result. And for all our estimates, it is practically certain that the additional number of cancer deaths will be less than 10.

Since a cancer caused by nuclear radiation is no different from any other cancer, additional cancers can only be determined statistically. We know from statistics on cancer deaths that among the more than 2 million people living within 50 miles of TMI, eventually some 325,000 people will die of cancer, for reasons having nothing to do with the nuclear power plant. Again, this number is only an estimate, and the actual figure could be as much as 1,000 higher or 1,000 lower. Therefore, there is no conceivable statistical method by which fewer than 10 additional deaths would ever be detected. Therefore, the accident may result in *no* additional cancer deaths or, if there were any, they would be so few that they could not be detected.

We found that the mental stress to which those living within the vicinity of Three Mile Island were subjected was quite severe. There were several factors that contributed to this stress. Throughout the first week of the accident, there was extensive speculation of just how serious the accident might turn out to be. At various times, senior officials of the NRC and the state government were considering the possibility of a major evacuation. There were a number of advisories recommending steps short of a full evacuation. Some significant fraction of the population in the immediate vicinity voluntarily left the region. NRC officials contributed to the raising of anxiety in the period from Friday to Sunday (March 30–April 1). On Friday, a mistaken interpretation of the release of a burst of radiation led some NRC officials to recommend immediate evacuation. And on Friday Governor Thornburgh advised pregnant women and preschool aged children within 5 miles of TMI to leave the area. On Saturday and Sunday, other NRC officials mistakenly believed that there was an imminent danger of an explosion of a hydrogen bubble within the reactor vessel, and evacuation was again a major subject of discussion.

We conclude that the most serious health effect of the accident was severe mental stress, which was short-lived. The highest levels of distress were found among those living within 5 miles of TMI and in families with preschool children.

There was very extensive damage to the plant. While the reactor itself has been brought to a "cold shutdown," there are vast amounts of radioactive material trapped within the containment and auxiliary buildings. The utility is therefore faced with a massive cleanup process that carries its own potential dangers to public health. The ongoing cleanup operation at TMI demonstrates that the plant was inadequately designed to cope with the cleanup of a damaged plant. The direct financial cost of the accident is enormous. Our best estimate puts it in a range of $1 to $2 billion, even if TMI–2 can be put back into operation. (The largest portion of this is for replacement power estimated for the next few years.) And since it may not be possible to put it back into operation, the cost could even be much larger.

The accident raised concerns all over the world and led to a lowering of public confidence in the nuclear industry and in the NRC.

From the beginning, we felt it important to determine not only how serious the actual impact of the accident was on public health, but whether we came close to a catastrophic accident in which a large number of people would have died. Issues that had to be examined were whether a chemical (hydrogen) or steam explosion could have ruptured the reactor vessel and containment building, and whether extremely hot molten fuel could have caused severe damage to the containment. The danger was never—and could *not* have been—that of a *nuclear* explosion (bomb).

We have made a conscientious effort to get an answer to this difficult question. Since the accident was due to a complex combination of minor equipment failures and major inappropriate human actions, we have asked the question: "What if one more thing had gone wrong?"

We explored each of several different scenarios representing a change in the sequence of events that actually took place. The greatest concern during the accident was that significant amounts of radioactive material (especially radioactive iodine) trapped within the plant might be released. Therefore, in each case, we asked whether the amount released would have been smaller or greater, and whether large amounts could have been released.

Some of these scenarios lead to a more favorable outcome than what actually happened. Several other scenarios lead to increases in the amount of radioactive iodine released, but still at levels that would not have presented a danger to public health. But we have also explored two or three scenarios whose precise consequences are much more difficult to calculate. They lead to more severe damage to the core, with additional melting of fuel in the hottest regions.   These consequences are, surprisingly, independent of the age of the fuel.

Because of the uncertain physical condition of the fuel, cladding, and core, we have explored certain special and severe conditions that would, unequivocally, lead to a fuel-melting accident.   In this sequence of events fuel melts, falls to the bottom of the vessel, melts through the steel reactor vessel, and finally, some fuel reaches the floor of the containment building below the reactor vessel where there is enough water to cover the molten fuel and remove some of the decay heat.   To contain such an accident, it is necessary to continue removing decay heat for a period of many months.

At this stage we approach the limits of our engineering knowledge of the interactions of molten fuel, concrete, steel, and water, and even the best available calculations have a degree of uncertainty associated with them.   Our calculations show that even if a meltdown occurred, there is a high probability that the containment building and the hard rock on which the TMI–2 containment building is built would have been able to prevent the escape of a large amount of radioactivity.   These results derive from very careful calculations, which hold only insofar as our assumptions are valid.   We cannot be absolutely certain of these results.   .   .   .

NOTE

In assessing the costs and benefits of nuclear energy, how would you weigh the probability of cancer deaths found by the President's Commission on Three Mile Island?   How did the Commission determine that mental stress was a greater health effect of the accident than the potential deaths from cancer?   Almost three years after the Commission's report, a federal court held that the National Environmental Protection Act required that environmental impact statements prepared in connection with the resumption of operations of a reactor at Three Mile Island must include an analysis of the psychological health of the residents living near the reactor.   See People Against Nuclear Energy v. United States Nuclear Regulatory Commission, 678 F.2d 222 (D.C.Cir.1982).   The Supreme Court reversed, stating that, "NEPA does not require the agency to assess *every* impact or effect of its proposed action, but only the impact or effect on the environment."   460 U.S. __, 103 S.Ct. 1556, 1560, 75 L.Ed.2d 534, 541 (1983).   Should Congress amend NEPA to require agencies to consider psychological impacts such as those involved at Three Mile Island?

Given the relatively small direct physical impact of the accident at Three Mile Island, what explains the enormous level of public concern caused by the accident?   Is it the fear that a much larger number of deaths was possible?   Is it a subconscious association of civilian nuclear power with the bomb?   Does it reflect a broader concern with modern science generally?

2.   THE SAFEGUARDING OF NUCLEAR MATERIALS

One potential danger of nuclear energy is that nuclear material might be diverted and made into nuclear weapons.   With current reactors, converting the fuel into weapons is a complex process.   With the proposed breeder reactor, however, the possibility of such conversion increases, in part because the breeder may well use weapons grade material as its initial fuel.   The materials below present varying perspectives on the overall problem of nuclear safeguards.

VICTOR GILINSKY,
THE NEED FOR NUCLEAR SAFEGUARDS

17 Atom. Energy L.J. 143–144, 150–151 (1975).

My main purpose is to discuss issues raised by the need for nuclear safeguards. These safeguards embrace both nuclear material accountability systems and physical protection systems for nuclear facilities. As you know, the main purpose of physical security systems is twofold: (1) to protect facilities containing potentially explosive nuclear materials; and (2) to protect facilities—chiefly reactors—against sabotage of a kind leading to harmful release of radioactive materials. The purpose of the accountability systems is to help keep track of and control special nuclear material—primarily plutonium and highly enriched uranium—to prevent their theft for use in nuclear explosive devices.

Our primary international objectives in this area are to ensure that civilian nuclear materials are not diverted to manufacture of nuclear explosive devices, and also to ensure that all governments protect access to civil nuclear materials from which such devices could be fabricated.

The management of nuclear materials transcends purely economic considerations. The possibility that certain special nuclear materials, in sufficient quantities, can be fashioned into nuclear explosives introduces an inescapable security-related element into the development and commercial exploitation of nuclear energy. This is not only a domestic problem. Although I will not focus here on international safeguards, it is important to point out that material held in other countries can be put to illicit use in the United States and vice versa. In addition, the general advance of civilian nuclear power programs, together with a considerable increase in the extent of international transactions in nuclear materials and technology, serves to bring increasing numbers of countries to the threshold of nuclear weaponry. While this condition has been abstractly talked about for many years, it is becoming a hard reality. . . .

Our recently heightened perception of the vulnerability of nuclear systems to human malevolence is but one example of the general vulnerability of technologically advanced societies to malevolent acts. We need to limit this vulnerability, in part through technological means, in part through shaping our institutions to be consistent with the fundamental philosophy and nature of our society.

It is clear that we need to tighten our security control over some aspects of nuclear energy. But we need to be highly discriminating and rational about how such controls are applied. If we are wise, we shall depend on our technical ingenuity and the resiliency of existing institutions to diminish our vulnerability, and we shall strictly circumscribe further necessary protective measures that tend to increase government intrusion into traditionally private domains.

MASON WILLRICH AND THEODORE TAYLOR,
NUCLEAR THEFT: RISKS AND SAFEGUARDS

20–21, 171 (1974).

As a result of extensive reviews of publications that are available to the general public and that relate to the technology of nuclear explosives, unclassified conversations with many experts in nuclear physics and engineering and a considerable amount of thought on the subject, we conclude:

Under conceivable circumstances, a few persons, possibly even one person working alone, who possessed about ten kilograms of plutonium oxide and a substantial amount of chemical high explosive could, within several weeks, design and build a crude fission bomb. By a "crude fission bomb" we mean one that would have an excellent chance of exploding, and would probably explode with the power of at least 100 tons of chemical high explosive. This could be done using materials and equipment that could be purchased at a hardware store and from commercial suppliers of scientific equipment for student laboratories.

The key persons or person would have to be reasonably inventive and adept at using laboratory equipment and tools of about the same complexity as those used by students in chemistry and physics laboratories and machine shops. They or he would have to be able to understand some of the essential concepts and procedures that are described in widely distributed technical publications concerning nuclear explosives, nuclear reactor technology, and chemical explosives, and would have to know where to find these publications. Whoever was principally involved would also have to be willing to take moderate risks of serious injury or death.

Statements similar to those made above about a plutonium oxide bomb could also be made about fission bombs made with high-enriched uranium or uranium–233. However, the ways these materials might be assembled in a fission bomb could differ in certain important respects.

We have reason to believe that many people, including some who have extensive knowledge of nuclear weapon technology, will strongly disagree with our conclusion. We also know that some experts will not. Why is this a subject of wide disagreement among experts? We suspect that at least part of the reason is that very few of the experts have actually spent much time pondering this question: "What is the easiest way I can think of to make a fission bomb, given enough fission explosive material to assemble more than one normal density critical mass?" The answer to this question may have little to do with the kinds of questions that nuclear weapon designers in the United States, the Soviet Union, the United Kingdom, France, or Peoples Republic of China ask themselves when they are trying to devise a better nuclear weapon for military purposes. But the question is likely to be foremost in the mind of an illicit bomb maker.

Whatever opinions anyone may have about the likelihood that an individual or very small group of people would actually steal nuclear materials and use them to make fission bombs, those opinions should not be based on a presumption that all types of fission bombs are very difficult to make.

EFFECTS OF NUCLEAR EXPLOSIONS

Even a "small" nuclear explosion could cause enormous havoc. A crude fission bomb, as we have described it, might yield as much as twenty kilotons of explosive power—the equal of the Nagasaki A-bomb.

· · · ·

Safeguards should emphasize the *prevention* of theft of any nuclear weapon materials from the nuclear power industry, and the *detection* of any theft attempt in time to prevent its completion. Detection of a completed theft, recovery of stolen nuclear weapon material, and response to any nuclear threat involving stolen material are important supplementary safeguard functions.

The principle of containment should be used as the basis for the design and development of safeguard measures. The physical barriers and security forces employed to contain nuclear weapon materials in order to prevent theft should be capable of defeating the maximum credible threat that can be reasonably expected anywhere in any nuclear fuel cycle. That threat might involve an attack by a group of perhaps five to ten persons using sophisticated firearms and equipment.

Insofar as practical, instruments and techniques should be developed and used to provide a timely and accurate picture of the material flows in authorized channels in the various nuclear fuel cycles. Furthermore, instruments and techniques should be developed and used to detect *immediately* the flow of any nuclear weapon materials out of a material access area through an unauthorized channel.

The *best available technology and institutional mechanisms* should be used in the safeguards system. The technology involved in the nuclear power industry is changing rapidly as a result of intensive research and development efforts. This offers both a challenge and an opportunity with respect to safeguards technology. The challenge is for safeguards technology to keep up with relevant changes in fuel cycle technology, while the opportunity is to take safeguards considerations fully into account initially in developing nuclear power options. . . .

NOTE

If plutonium becomes a more important part of the fuel cycle, some observers worry that the guarding of nuclear materials would substantially burden the liberties of American citizens. Russell Ayres, an attorney, argues that "[v]irtually everyone in society would be called on to make sacrifices of personal liberty in order to assure effective safeguards." Ayres, Policing Plutonium: The Civil Liberties Fallout, 10 Harv.C.R.—C.L.L.Rev. 369, 441 (1975). On the other hand, physicists Robert Avery and Hans Bethe contend that "[t]here is absolutely no reason to fear that the guarding of plutonium in this country would require a large police force and lead to any loss of civil rights." Avery and Bethe, Breeder Reactors: The Next Generation in Nuclear Power: Both Sides 206, 213 (Kaku & Trainer eds. 1982). Does safeguarding nuclear materials differ from safeguarding poisons that might be dropped in a city's water or food supply? In any of these cases, what institutions are best suited to balance the cost to society of increased security against the need for energy, water, safe drugs, and so on? On October 26, 1983, the United States Senate, partly because of safeguards concerns, ended funding for the Clinch River breeder reactor, the major American breeder project. See Dewar, Seemingly Fatal Blow Dealt Breeder Reactor by Senate, Washington Post, Oct. 27, 1983, at A2, Col. 1. Other countries, including France, retain breeder programs.

As the following materials indicate, pursuant to the Nuclear Non-Proliferation Act of 1978, the President can authorize the export of certain nuclear materials even when the Nuclear Regulatory Commission will not grant an export license. Under the Act, Congress can reverse such presidential decisions, though the Supreme Court's decision in Immigration & Naturalization Service v. Chadha, 462 U.S. ___, 103 S.Ct. 2764, 77 L.Ed.2d 317 (1983), invalidating the legislative veto, has called this power into question. See Ch. 4, Sec. C.1, infra. In any event, in the case involving India described below, Congress did not reverse President Carter's decision.

JIMMY CARTER,
AUTHORIZING THE EXPORT OF SPECIAL NUCLEAR
MATERIAL AND COMPONENTS TO INDIA

President's Message to Congress, 16 Weekly Comp. Pres. Doc. 1137–1138
(June 19, 1980).

To the Congress of the United States:

I am transmitting with this message, pursuant to Section 126b(2) of the Atomic Energy Act of 1954, as amended, an Executive Order authorizing the export of 39,718 kgs. of low-enriched uranium to India for use in fueling its Tarapur Atomic Power Station and authorizing the export of replacement parts for this station.

Two applications for licenses to export the fuel were submitted to the Nuclear Regulatory Commission in September 1978 and August 1979 respectively. After a careful review of these applications, and the applications for replacement parts of the Tarapur reactors, the Executive Branch concluded that the proposed exports would not be inimical to the common defense and security, that they met all applicable statutory criteria under the Atomic Energy Act, and that the licenses should be issued. The Commission was notified of these Executive Branch findings and recommendations on March 28, 1979, and on May 7, 1980.

On May 16, 1980, the Nuclear Regulatory Commission decided that it could not find that the criteria for issuing the licenses had been met. Pursuant to the law, the Commission then referred these applications to me. . . .

I have determined that to withhold these exports would be seriously prejudicial to the achievement of United States non-proliferation objectives and would otherwise jeopardize the common defense and security. I have made this determination for the policy reasons discussed below. However, I want to make it clear that I do in fact regard these export applications as having fallen within the statutory grace period before the full-scope safeguards requirement of section 128a takes effect. Thus, my authorization of these exports does not constitute a precedent for an exception to the full-scope safeguards criterion. Further, this action in no way indicates a change in the high priority I attach to preventing the spread of nuclear explosives. On the contrary, this action reflects my judgment that non-proliferation would be set back, not advanced, by withholding these exports, and that our failure to supply this fuel could seriously jeopardize other important U.S. interests.

India's failure to accept international safeguards on all its peaceful nuclear activities and its failure to commit itself not to conduct further nuclear explosions are of serious concern to me. These exports will help us to maintain a dialogue with India in which we try to narrow our differences on these issues.

The exports will avoid the risk of a claim by India that the United States has broken an existing agreement between the two governments and has thereby relieved India of its obligation to refrain from reprocessing the fuel previously supplied by the United States.

Supply of this fuel will also ensure the continuation of safeguards and other U.S. controls on disposition of U.S.-origin fuel that has been supplied to India.

Approval of these exports will help strengthen ties with a key South Asian democracy at a time when it is particularly important for us to do so. Insecurity in South and Southwest Asia has been greatly heightened by the crisis in Iran and the Soviet invasion of Afghanistan. We must do all we reasonably can to promote stability in the area and to bolster our relations with states there, particularly those that can play a role in checking Soviet expansionism.

When I signed the Nuclear Non-Proliferation Act of 1978, I expressed reservations about the constitutionality of provisions of law which purport to allow the Congress to overturn my decisions by actions not subject to my veto power. In transmitting this Executive Order, I also want to make it clear that I am not departing from those reservations.

HON. CHRISTOPHER J. DODD, TESTIMONY BEFORE THE HOUSE COMM. ON FOREIGN AFFAIRS, ON THE RESOLUTIONS OF DISAPPROVAL OF THE SHIPMENT OF NUCLEAR FUEL TO INDIA

96th Cong., 2d Sess. 11–12 (1980).

Mr. Chairman, members of the committee. I am pleased to have the opportunity to appear before you today on a matter of great importance to the future of this nation's non-proliferation policy.

As you know, on June 19, 1980, President Carter issued an Executive order to export low-enriched uranium and various nuclear components to India, thereby overruling an earlier unanimous decision by the Nuclear Regulatory Commission. On that same day, I introduced House Concurrent Resolution 369 disapproving the proposed exports. I am pleased to have as co-sponsors Mr. Long of Maryland and Mr. Ottinger of New York. I am particularly pleased to have their cosponsorship as the three of us had introduced a similar resolution 2 years ago when the President proposed an earlier nuclear fuel export to India.

In order to gain some historical perspective on this issue, I think that it might be useful for me to point out some of the similarities and some of the differences between the proposed exports we are considering today and those of 2 years ago.

Two years ago, the ink on the Nuclear Non-Proliferation Act of 1978 was hardly dry. In order to try to stem the further proliferation of nuclear weapons capability around the world, we made a decision not to export nuclear fuel to nations which had not accepted International Atomic Energy Agency full scope safeguards on all their nuclear facilities.

However, to give our State Department ample time in which to convince other nations to accept full-scope safeguards on their nuclear facilities, we wrote a 2-year grace period into the legislation. At the time, I felt that is was extremely unlikely that we could, in fact, convince the Indian Government to accept safeguards and that we would later be forced into cutting off their fuel supply. It was for this reason that I opposed the sale of uranium to India 2 years ago. The 2-year grace period expired on March 10, 1980, and the Indians have shown absolutely no inclination to accept the required full-scope safeguards. In fact, during that 2-year period the Indian Government has gone from a policy of promising not to explode any further nuclear "devices" to explicitly stating that it reserves the right to do so.

It should be noted that the primary catalyst for developing and passing the Nuclear Non-Proliferation Act was the Indian explosion of a nuclear "device" in 1974. It was not simply the fact that India set off a nuclear explosion, it was the fact that they used Canadian equipment and U.S. supplied heavy water—in violation of the peaceful use agreements—to achieve an explosion which so alarmed the world. In response to the 1974 nuclear test, Canada immediately suspended its nuclear relationship with India. In contrast, the United States continued to supply India with nuclear material while we attempted to convince India to accept safeguards.

In the 6 years since 1974, we have repeatedly failed to convince India to accept I.A.E.A. full-scope safeguards or to sign the nonproliferation treaty. It is time to admit that we have failed in our Nonproliferation Policy towards India. The question now is whether we will continue to supply India with fuel in spite of India's consistent refusal to accept safeguards.

My answer is no—not unless we want to show the world that our nuclear nonproliferation policy is a sham. The foundation of our nonproliferation policy rests on the acceptance of safeguards by nations we supply nuclear fuel to. If we do not enforce our insistence on safeguards, then we have no nonproliferation policy.

I still believe that nonproliferation is one of the most vital foreign policy goals this Nation can pursue. Preventing the continued spread of nuclear's weapons capability around the world is not only vital to our own interest, it may be the most important factor in insuring peace in the world. Over the past 25 years, we have been moderately successful in limiting the spread of nuclear weapons. However, several nations now are standing on the threshold of having a nuclear capability and are probably deciding whether to take the final step. We sent them a message in 1974 when we did not end our nuclear relationship with India after their nuclear test; I sincerely hope that we will not send these threshold nations another signal by approving the currently proposed exports.

As you know, in spite of India's refusal to accept the safeguards mandated by the Nuclear Non-Proliferation Act of 1978, President Carter is proposing that we export to India 38 tons of low-enriched uranium and various nuclear components. Interestingly, the administration is not maintaining that we still have a chance to gain India's acceptance of safeguards; instead, the administration is emphasizing the steps India might take if we do not continue our nuclear fuel exports. India has threatened to lift the current safeguards on U.S. fuel and to reprocess our spent fuel if we cut off their supply. (Reprocessing is the first step towards manufacturing weapons grade plutonium.) In other words, by threatening to reprocess our spent fuel, India is subjecting the United States to a form of blackmail. Submitting to this kind of blackmail, in my opinion, is not likely to strengthen our nonproliferation policy with the rest of the world. And the fact that India is threatening such blackmail should not give us confidence in the future direction of Indian nuclear policy.

The administration has also argued that we need to maintain our nuclear ties to India because of our heightened security concerns in South and Southwest Asia following the Soviet invasion of Afghanistan. While it is evident that this region has taken on greater importance to us since the Soviet invasion, I fail to see how abandoning our nonproliferation policy will help us in combatting Soviet influence in that region. The recently signed $1.6 billion arms deal between the Soviet Union and India should leave us with no illusions about our ability to influence Indian policy in this regard.

If we allow this latest nuclear fuel export to be sent to India, we will be clearly abdicating our leadership in the nonproliferation field. We will also be abdicating the role we in Congress established in the Nuclear Nonproliferation Act of 1978. I would urge this committee in the strongest possible terms to favorably report a resolution of disapproval of the proposed nuclear exports.

NOTE

Because national boundaries do not limit scientific advances, the regulation of science often involves consideration of the international arena. President Carter, in sending fuel to India, relied in part on the familiar argument that if we do not do it, others will. What is the relevance of that argument to areas such as the regulation of DNA research?

The absence of strong sanctions in international law against the sale of nuclear materials to nations that might misuse them has led many to despair of any effective limitations on the proliferation of nuclear weapons. On June 7, 1981, Israeli planes bombed and destroyed a research reactor near Baghdad, Iraq on the ground that the reactor would be used to enable Iraq to manufacture nuclear weapons. New York Times, June 9, 1981, at A1, col. 6. Did proliferation concerns justify Israel's action? Is it relevant that Israel itself may have nuclear weapons? A few weeks after the bombing, President Hussein of Iraq said that "the people who have been aggressed against have a right to retaliation against the aggressor." New York Times, June 29, 1981, at A3, col. 1.

Part Two

CONTROLLING SCIENCE AND MEDICINE: THE ROLES OF INDIVIDUALS, GROUPS AND THE STATE

Chapter Three

PRIVATE CONTROL OF SCIENCE AND MEDICINE

A. PROFESSIONALS AND THEIR ORGANIZATIONS AND INSTITUTIONS

---

1. WHAT IS A PROFESSION?

NEWMARK v. GIMBELS, INC.

Supreme Court of New Jersey, 1969.
54 N.J. 585, 258 A.2d 697.

FRANCIS, J.

This appeal involves the liability of a beauty parlor operator for injury to a patron's hair and scalp allegedly resulting from a product used in the giving of a permanent wave. The action was predicated upon charges of negligence and breach of express and implied warranty. Trial was had before the county district court and a jury. At the close of the proof, the court ruled as a matter of law that the warranty theory of liability was not maintainable because in giving a permanent wave a beauty parlor is engaged in rendering a service and not a sale . . . . The Appellate Division reversed holding that a fact issue existed requiring jury decision as to whether there was an implied warranty of fitness of the lotion applied to Mrs. Newmark's hair and scalp for the purpose of producing the permanent wave. . . .

. . .

. . . For about a year and a half prior to the incident in question, Mrs. Newmark had been a patron of one of defendants' shops where she had a standing appointment every week to have her hair washed and set. She was usually attended by the same operator, one William Valante. During that period . . . she had purchased permanent waves there, at least one having been given by Valante, and she had not experienced any untoward results.

On November 16, 1963, pursuant to an appointment, Mrs. Newmark went to the beauty parlor where she inquired of Valante about a permanent wave that was on special sale. He told her that her fine hair was not right for the special permanent and that she needed a "good" permanent wave. She agreed to accept the wave suggested by him. Valante conceded that the wave she received was given at his suggestion and that in accepting it she relied on his judgment as to what was good for her hair. Both Valante and Mrs. Newmark testified there was nothing wrong with her hair or scalp before the wave was given.

256

Valante proceeded to cut and wash her hair after which he put her head under a dryer for about 10 minutes. The hair was then sectioned off, a permanent wave solution marketed under the name "Helene Curtis Candle Wave" was applied with cotton and the hair was rolled section by section. Following this, more of the waving solution was put on by an applicator-bottle. Then a cream was placed along the hairline and covered with cotton. About three to five minutes after the last of the waving solution had been applied Mrs. Newmark experienced a burning sensation on the front part of her head. She complained to Valante who added more cream along the hairline. This gave some relief but after a few minutes she told him that it was burning again. The burning sensation continued but was alleviated when Valante brought her to a basin and rinsed her hair in lukewarm water. The curlers were then removed, a neutralizing solution was applied and allowed to remain for about seven minutes, and her hair was again rinsed. After this Valante set her hair and again put her under the dryer where she remained for about 25 minutes. The burning sensation returned and she promptly informed Valante who reduced the heat of the dryer thereby giving her partial relief. When the dryer operation was completed her hair was combed, and she left the parlor.

That evening her head reddened, and during the following day her entire forehead was red and blistered. A large amount of hair fell out when it was combed. . . .

. . .

It seems to us that the policy reasons for imposing warranty liability in the case of ordinary sales are equally applicable to a commercial transaction such as that existing in this case between a beauty parlor operator and a patron. Although the policy reasons which generate the responsibility are essentially the same, practical administration suggests that the principle of liability be expressed in terms of strict liability in tort thus enabling it to be applied in practice unconfined by the narrow conceptualism associated with the technical niceties of sales and implied warranties. . . . One, who in the regular course of a business sells or applies a product (in the sense of the sales-service hybrid transaction involved in the present case) which is in such a dangerously defective condition as to cause physical harm to the consumer-patron, is liable for the harm. Consumption in this connection includes all ultimate uses for which the product is intended. 2 Restatement, Torts 2d, § 402A, p. 347 (1965) adopts this view. Obviously the ultimate use of the Helene Curtis permanent wave solution intended by both manufacturer and beauty parlor operator was its application to the hair of a patron. And as Comment l to the Restatement section says, "the customer in a beauty shop to whose hair a permanent wave solution is applied by the shop is a consumer." 2 Restatement, supra, at p. 354.

Defendants claim that to hold them to strict liability would be contrary to Magrine v. Krasnica, 94 N.J.Super. 228, 227 A.2d 539 (Cty.Ct.1967), aff'd sub nom. Magrine v. Spector, 100 N.J.Super. 223, 241 A.2d 637 (App.Div.1968), aff'd 53 N.J. 259, 250 A.2d 129 (1969). We cannot agree. Magrine, a patient of the defendant-dentist, was injured when a hypodermic needle being used, concededly with due care, to administer a local anesthetic broke off in his gum or jaw. The parties agreed that the break resulted from a latent defect in the needle. It was held that the strict liability in tort doctrine was not applicable to the professional man, such as a dentist, because the essence of the relationship with his patient was the furnishing of professional skill and services. We accepted the view that a dentist's bill for services should be considered as representing pay for that alone. The use of instruments, or the administration of medicines or the providing of medicines for the patient's home consumption cannot give the ministrations the cast of a commercial transaction. Accordingly the liability of the dentist in cases involving the ordinary relationship of doctor and patient must be tested by principles of negligence, i.e., lack of due care and not by application of the doctrine of strict liability in tort.

Defendants suggest that there is no doctrinal basis for distinguishing the services rendered by a beauty parlor operator from those rendered by a dentist or a doctor, and that consequently the liability of all three should be tested by the same principles. On the contrary there is a vast difference in the relationships. The beautician is engaged in a commercial enterprise; the dentist and doctor in a profession. The former caters publicly not to a need but to a form of aesthetic convenience or luxury, involving the rendition of non-professional services and the application of products for which a charge is made. The dentist or doctor does not and cannot advertise for patients; the demand for his services stems from a felt necessity of the patient. In response to such a call the doctor, and to a somewhat lesser degree the dentist, exercises his best judgment in diagnosing the patient's ailment or disability, prescribing and sometimes furnishing medicines or other methods of treatment which he believes, and in some measure hopes, will relieve or cure the condition. His performance is not mechanical or routine because each patient requires individual study and formulation of an informed judgment as to the physical or mental disability or condition presented, and the course of treatment needed. Neither medicine nor dentistry is an exact science; there is no implied warranty of cure or relief. There is no representation of infallibility and such professional men should not be held to such a degree of perfection. There is no guaranty that the diagnosis is correct. Such men are not producers or sellers of property in any reasonably acceptable sense of the term. In a primary sense they furnish services in the form of an opinion of the patient's condition based upon their experienced analysis of the objective and subjective complaints, and in the form of recommended and, at times, personally administered medicines and treatment. Practitioners of such callings, licensed by the State to practice after years of study and preparation, must be deemed to have a special and essential role in our society, that of studying our physical and mental ills and ways to alleviate or cure them, and that of applying their knowledge, empirical judgment and skill in an effort to diagnose and then to relieve or to cure the ailment of a particular patient. Thus their paramount function—the essence of their function—ought to be regarded as the furnishing of opinions and services. Their unique status and the rendition of these *sui generis* services bear such a necessary and intimate relationship to public health and welfare that their obligation ought to be grounded and expressed in a duty to exercise reasonable competence and care toward their patients. In our judgment, the nature of the services, the utility of and the need for them, involving as they do, the health and even survival of many people, are so important to the general welfare as to outweigh in the policy scale any need for the imposition on dentists and doctors of the rules of strict liability in tort.

. . .

Accordingly, a factual issue was presented at trial for jury determination as to (1) whether the permanent wave solution was defective, and (2) whether it was the proximate cause of the [plaintiff's injury]. An affirmative answer by the jury would warrant a verdict for the plaintiffs.

The judgment of the Appellate Division is affirmed for the reasons stated, and the cause is remanded for a new trial.

NOTES

1. The *Newmark* court distinguished professions from "commercial enterprises" in part by stating that "the dentist or doctor does not and cannot advertise for patients." Since this 1969 decision, professional advertising restrictions, both statutory and regulatory, have been dramatically reduced. In 1976, the Supreme Court struck down on first amendment grounds a Virginia statute that banned price advertising by pharmacists. Virginia State Board of Pharmacy v. Virginia Citizens Consumer Counsel, 425 U.S. 748, 96 S.Ct. 1817, 48 L.Ed.2d 346 (1976). The Court declared that the state could maintain the professionalism of pharmacists through subsidies or other protections, but not through the "highly paternalistic" approach of abridging the public's right to receive legitimate price information. 425 U.S. at 770, 96 S.Ct. at 1829, 48 L.Ed.2d at 363.

Under a similar first amendment interpretation, "legal clinic" attorneys may now advertise the price of routine services. Bates v. State Bar of Arizona, 433 U.S. 350, 97 S.Ct. 2691, 53 L.Ed.2d 810 (1977). However, a bar association, acting under state authority, may discipline a lawyer who personally solicits business from accident victims, because such solicitation often pressures the potential client into making an ill-advised choice. Ohralik v. Ohio State Bar Association, 436 U.S. 477, 457, 98 S.Ct. 1912, 1919, 56 L.Ed.2d 444, 459 (1978).

In 1978, pursuant to the Magnuson-Moss Act, the Federal Trade Commission promulgated a regulation that dramatically curtailed the ability of states and professional associations to restrict advertising by ophthalmologists. In support of this rule, the FTC pointed to inadequate consumer information and artificially high prices in the opthamological market. The American Optometric Association, the American Medical Association and nine states sought immediate judicial review. American Optometric Association v. FTC, 626 F.2d 896 (D.C.Cir.1980). The court supported the FTC's general policy of relaxing the regulations in this area, but remanded the relevant provisions of the rule to the FTC for revision in light of the *Bates* decision.

What rationale supported the absolute ban on professional advertising? The Virginia State Board of Pharmacy argued that pharmacist advertising would allow "corner-cutters" to threaten the "stable pharmacist-customer relationship," to damage the professional image of pharmacists and to drive truly professional pharmacists out of business. 425 U.S. at 768, 96 S.Ct. at 1828, 48 L.Ed.2d at 362. Could the same be said of legal clinics? See, e.g., Comment, A Critical Analysis of Rules Against Solicitation by Lawyers, 25 U.Chi.L.Rev. 674 (1958).

2. Do you find the rationale of the *Newmark* court persuasive? Should dentists and physicians be held to a higher standard of professional conduct in their dealings with the public than hair stylists? Are they?

3. What are the distinguishing characteristics of professions? Consider Eliot Freidson, Profession of Medicine 71–74, 77 (1973):

> What are the formal characteristics of the profession of medicine? In the most elementary sense, the profession is a group of people who perform a set of activities which provide them with the major source of their subsistence— activities which are called "work" rather than "leisure" and "vocation" rather than "avocation." Such activities are performed for compensation, not for their own sake. They are considered to be useful or productive, which is why those who perform them are compensated by others. When a number of people perform the same activity and develop common methods, which are passed on to new recruits and come to be conventional, we may say that workers have

been organized into an occupational group, or an occupation. In the most general classification, a profession is an occupation.

However, a profession is usually taken to be a special kind of occupation, so that it is necessary to develop analytically useful distinctions between the profession and other occupations. . . . [T]he most strategic distinction lies in legitimate, organized autonomy—that a profession is distinct from other occupations in that it has been given the right to control its own work. Some occupations, like circus jugglers and magicians, possess a de facto autonomy by virtue of the esoteric or isolated character of their work, but their autonomy is more accidental than not and is subject to change should public interest be aroused in it. Unlike other occupations, professions are *deliberately* granted autonomy, including the exclusive right to determine who can legitimately do its work and how the work should be done. Virtually all occupations struggle to obtain both rights, and some manage to seize them, but only the profession is *granted* the right to exercise them legitimately. And while no occupation can prevent employers, customers, clients, and other workers from evaluating its work, only the profession has the recognized right to declare such "outside" evaluation illegitimate and intolerable.

. . .

Consulting and Scholarly Professions

Some kinds of work require for their performance the cooperation of laymen and require for their survival some degree of popularity with laymen: they are practicing or consulting occupations which must sustain a direct, continuous relationship with a lay clientele. . . .

It is in the case of applied work, particularly work involving a broadly based lay clientele, that formal, legal controls are most likely to be imposed. Only applied work is likely to have immediate consequences in human affairs, and some can be serious. When the public is considered too inexpert to be able to evaluate such work, those dominating society may feel that the public needs protection from unqualified or unscrupulous workers. Having been persuaded that one occupation is most qualified by virtue of its formal training and the moral fiber of its members, the state may exclude all others and give the chosen occupation a legal monopoly that may help bridge the gap between it and laymen, if only by restricting the layman's choice. The outcome is support of the profession by licensure or some other formal device of protecting some workers and excluding others. Licensing is much less likely to occur on behalf of the scholar or the scientist, for they are devoted to exploring intellectual systems primarily for the eyes of their colleagues. Nonetheless, in the case of the consulting or practicing professions such a legally exclusive right to work will not assure survival because the work cannot be performed, license or not, without being in some way positively attractive to a lay clientele. . . .

The Formal Criteria of Profession

. . . [The] two core characteristics [of professions] are "a prolonged specialized training in a body of abstract knowledge, and a collectivity or service orientation." Among the "derived characteristics," which are presumably "caused" by the core characteristics, are five which refer to autonomy: "(1) The profession determines its own standards of education and training. . . . (3) Professional practice is often legally recognized by some form of licensure. (4) Licensing and admission boards are manned by members of the profession. (5) Most legislation concerned with the profession is shaped by that profession. . . . (7) The practitioner is relatively free of lay evaluation and control." . . .*

* William J. Goode, "Encroachment,   American Sociological Review, XXV (1960), Charlatanism, and the Emerging Profession: 902–914. Psychology, Medicine, and Sociology,"

MICHAEL POLANYI,
SCIENCE, FAITH AND SOCIETY

63–65 (1946).

Freedom bears an old question-mark across its face. To prevent lawless conflict a paramount power is required: how can this power be prevented from suppressing freedom? How can it indeed fail to suppress it if it is to eliminate lawless strife? Government appears as essentially supreme and absolute, leaving no room for freedom.

But we have said that in the world of science, which is an organized social body, there is freedom and that freedom is even essential to the maintenance of its organization. How can that be true?

Sovereignty over the world of science is vested in no particular ruler or governing body, but is divided into numerous fragments, each of which is wielded by one single scientist. Every time a scientist makes a decision in which he ultimately relies on his own conscience or personal beliefs, he shapes the substance of science or the order of scientific life as one of its sovereign rulers. The power thus exercised may sharply affect the interests of his fellow scientists. Yet there is no need for a paramount supreme power to arbitrate in the last resort between all these individual decisions. There are divisions among scientists, sometimes sharp and passionate, but both contestants remain agreed that scientific opinion will ultimately decide right; and they are satisfied to appeal to it as their ultimate arbiter. Scientists recognize that, inasmuch as each scientist is following the ideals of science according to his own conscience, the resultant decisions of scientific opinion are rightful. This absolute submission leaves each free since each remains acting throughout in accordance to his own conviction. A common belief in the reality of scientific ideals and a sufficient confidence in their fellow scientists' sincerity thus resolves among scientists the apparent internal contradiction in the conception of freedom. It establishes government by scientific opinion, as a General Authority, inherently restricted to the guardianship of the premises of freedom. . . .

This also throws a new light on the nature of the Social Contract. In the case of the scientific community the contract consists of the gift of one's own person—not to a sovereign ruler as Hobbes thought, nor to an abstract General Will as Rousseau postulated—but to the service of a particular ideal. The love of science, the creative urge, the devotion to scientific standards—these are the conditions which commit the novice to the discipline of science. By apprenticing himself to an intellectual process based on a certain set of ultimates, the newcomer enlists as a member of the community holding these ultimates and his commitment to these necessarily involves the acceptance of the rules of conduct indispensable to their cultivation. Each new member undertakes to follow through life an obligation to a particular tradition to which his whole person gives assent.

Since a scientist requires special gifts, lack of these voids the contract. So does also lack of true animus, as in the fraudulent or unsound novice. I have described the disciplinary methods by which the scientific community strives to keep out bunglers, frauds, and cranks and pointed out the grave problems involved in distinguishing from these the great pioneers of revolutionary portent, who desire to enter on the Social Contract of science under modified conditions from the start. However, the difficulties which may arise in this connexion cannot affect the essential clarity of the contract by which the scientist becomes a member of his community. It consists in his dedication to the service of a particular spiritual reality.

We have seen how this dedication, pledging him to act according to his own conscience, represents an obligation to be free. Freedom of this kind, it would seem, must be described in the particular as freedom to act according to particular obligations. Just as a person cannot be obliged in general, so also he cannot be free in general, but only in respect to definite grounds of conscience. . . .

NOTES

1. Mendelsohn, The Emergence of Science as a Profession in Nineteenth-Century Europe, in The Management of Scientists 3, 40–43 (K. Hill, ed.1964):

> Professionalization came to science as the result of numerous forces, some internal to science and long in the making, others much more closely tied to changes taking place in society at large. As men turned to nature they soon learned to respect the old maxim which said "that the more you learn, the more you discover there is to know." This meant in practice that natural philosophers, men such as Robert Hooke and René Descartes, who in the seventeenth century could take all of nature as a field of study, slowly disappeared as the decades of the eighteenth century passed. They were replaced by investigators of more limited range, and with good reason, for the amount of knowledge about nature had increased so that meaningful theories could be constructed and meaningful experiments executed only by those who had begun to specialize. Specialization as it came to full strength made its own definite demands on the institutional structure. . . . [S]pecial laboratories . . . became necessary and [brought] . . . pressures . . . for new kinds of education and training. Whereas the Royal Society or the Académie des Sciences served admirably for the dilettante in science, the new specialist wanted and needed to communicate directly with those who shared the same limited body of knowledge in the same depth. The scientific organizations centering upon a particular field of science served to provide this intimate contact and also often added the specialized journal which brought the latest research findings to those most interested in sharing them. Specialization made one additional and very great demand—it seemed to take the whole man working full time. This required the new positions, the support, the organization for the advancement of science and its practitioners, the professional standards which came to mark science during the nineteenth century. It is difficult to overestimate the impact that specialization had upon the organizational and institutional structure of science. But it is clear that those nations which were best able to accommodate the new requirements were the nations where science flourished. Ultimately the specialist in science became the normal man, and the machinery of every society which made a pretext of harboring a scientific tradition became geared to the needs and used to the language of specialized science.
>
> But specialization was only one cause, albeit an important one, among many for the changes we have lumped together and called professionalization. When men whose livelihood depended upon their daily work became interested in science, means had to be provided for their support or they had to give up anything but a passing interest in scientific research. . . . Although the utility of science had been proclaimed *forte voce* since the days of Francis Bacon, science in actuality had been of little practical use. And, since it was supported most often by individual researchers with private wealth, or by private patrons, there was little real expectation that science would solve many practical problems. But when men had to appeal to the public, to government, to industry for financial reward for work in science, their own image of science changed as did their requirements for the organization of science. If a society is to support the "cultivators of science," its many small contributors, a new

view of the uses of science must be constructed; also, a whole new series of places to put these new men of science must be found.   Groups such as the British Association in England and the Gesellschaft Deutscher Naturforscher in Germany were brought into being to serve, either directly or indirectly, as spokesmen for the new full-time men of science.

The shift in the social origins of scientists from predominantly upper-class practitioners in the early seventeenth century to the middle- and lower-class orientation of science by the beginning of the nineteenth century did, however, reflect the influence of the industrial revolution, a factor external to science itself.   Throughout the course of the century, scientists in increasing numbers were drawn from the recently industrialized cities, a phenomenon common to both England and the continent.   As these men gathered together in their newly organized local scientific societies or as they became active in national groups they definitely reflected the needs and aspirations of the growing industrial classes from which they came.   That science assumed a utilitarian garb in the nineteenth century should surprise no one; that it did not become the "handmaiden" of industry is the real wonder.   The circle is completed, however, only when we recognize that it was not until well into the century that industrial technology had advanced to the stage that it could call upon science for help, or that it in turn could absorb the new advances that science was bringing.   This absorption in its turn was possible only because fairly large numbers of the men called "cultivators of science" had been trained and made available by the changes that occurred in the social organization of science.

. . . .

In appealing to government and industry for support, science slipped most easily into using the rationale of utility; the nation would be made stronger and industries would flourish only if science were encouraged and scientists rewarded; science provided the theoretical background for all those processes necessary to assure the commercial health of the state.   But in attempting to break into the educational system the appeal of utility had limited use.   New institutions might be supported on this basis as providing a necessary alternative to the tradition-ridden older establishments, especially when connected with the appeal for an increase in scientific manpower.   The École Polytechnique in France, the School of Mines, the Royal College of Chemistry in England, and the Polytechnicium in Germany all fit this latter role.   But science very rapidly became aware of the fact that if it were to affect the outlook of society as a whole it would have to penetrate the existing educational structure, from primary school up.   Not only would entrance into the instructional system provide many new positions for scientists, a factor not overlooked by the partisans of the advancement of science, but it would also aid in attaining recognition and appreciation for scientific activity and would serve as a means for recruiting new members to ranks of science.

The attempt to establish science within the university shared many of the general educational goals but partook of several other important ones as well. First, the prestige of the university, even when under attack, was greater than that of any of the alternate institutions which had been established for professional training.   Perhaps most importantly, it was functioning on a scale which made it the only nationally recognized source of advanced learning.   Scientists, however, faced one additional problem as their field grew in size and importance during the nineteenth century: where could they carry on the research which would add to the store of scientific knowledge?   The small private laboratory was no longer feasible and the industrially founded and sponsored laboratory seemed too limited in scope due to the obvious demands for useful invention.   In this sense the university seemed to be the perfect home for science.   Utility had not been the byword in these ancient seats of learning, and yet men had found within them a haven for scholarship.   In a field like science, where the new knowledge which was rapidly being produced had to become part of the training of the new recruits, what relationship could be better than the one offered within the university, of the part-time teacher, part-time research worker. But the university in its turn had to be flexible. The older organizational patterns had to change and new room had to be made for the accommodation of new scientific fields in specialized institutes within the university framework.

Within their university departments and institutes, within their new scientific societies, scientists were in command; they used their newly consolidated positions to establish the traditions within which scientists would be trained, within which scientific research would be carried out and communicated, within which science would respond to the pressures and demands of society, within which the professional aspirations could be transmitted to new generations, and within which science could petition for support, recognition, and appreciation.

2. Science emerged as a profession in the United States later than it did in Europe. While many of the framers of the Constitution had received training in the sciences, see Ch. 4, Sec. B.1, infra, the young nation as a whole produced numerous "inventors" but few "scientists."

What conditions in the United States do you suppose delayed the emergence of science as a profession? Consider the following observation made by Alexis de Tocqueville:

> At (age) fifteen (Americans) enter their calling, and thus their education ends when ours begins. Whatever is done afterwards is with a view to some special and lucrative object; a science is taken up as a matter of business, and the only branch of it which is attended to is such as admits of an immediate practical application. In America, most of the rich men were formerly poor; most of those who now enjoy leisure were absorbed in business during their youth; the consequence of which is, that when they might have had a taste for study they had no time for it, and when time is at their disposal, they have no longer the inclination.

Democracy in America 52 (Cook ed.1900).

2. ESTABLISHING NORMS AND STANDARDS OF CONDUCT

a. Through Codes

PIERCE v. ORTHO PHARMACEUTICAL CORP.

Supreme Court of New Jersey, 1980.
84 N.J. 58, 417 A.2d 505.

POLLOCK, J.

This case presents the question whether an employee at will has a cause of action against her employer to recover damages for the termination of her employment following her refusal to continue a project she viewed as medically unethical. . . .

Plaintiff, Dr. Grace Pierce, sued for damages after termination of her employment with defendant, Ortho Pharmaceutical Corporation. The trial judge granted defendant's motion for summary judgment. The Appellate Division reversed and remanded for a full trial. 166 N.J.Super. 335, 399 A.2d 1023 (1979). We granted defendant's petition for certification. 81 N.J. 266, 405 A.2d 810 (1979). We now reverse the Appellate Division and reinstate the summary judgment granted by the Law Division.

. . . .

Ortho specializes in the development and manufacture of therapeutic and reproductive drugs. Dr. Pierce is a medical doctor who was first employed by Ortho in 1971 as an Associate Director of Medical Research. She signed no contract except a secrecy agreement, and her employment was not for a fixed term. She was an employee at will. In 1973, she became the Director of Medical Research/Therapeutics, one of three major sections of the Medical Research Department. Her primary responsibilities were to oversee development of therapeutic drugs and to establish procedures for testing those drugs for safety, effectiveness, and marketability. Her immediate supervisor was Dr. Samuel Pasquale, Executive Medical Director.

In the spring of 1975, Dr. Pierce was the only medical doctor on a project team developing loperamide, a liquid drug for treatment of diarrhea in infants, children, and elderly persons. The proposed formulation contained saccharin. Although the concentration was consistent with the formula for loperamide marketed in Europe, the project team agreed that the formula was unsuitable for use in the United States. An alternative formulation containing less saccharin might have been developed within approximately three months.

By March 28, however, the project team, except for Dr. Pierce, decided to continue with the development of loperamide. That decision was made apparently in response to a directive from the Marketing Division of Ortho. This decision meant that Ortho would file an investigational new drug application (IND) with the Federal Food and Drug Administration (FDA), continue laboratory studies on loperamide, and begin work on a formulation. FDA approval is required before any new drug is tested clinically on humans. Therefore, loperamide would be tested on patients only if the FDA approved the saccharin formulation.

Dr. Pierce knew that the IND would have to be filed with and approved by the FDA before clinical testing could begin. Nonetheless, she continued to oppose the work being done on loperamide at Ortho. On April 21, 1975, she sent a memorandum to the project team expressing her disagreement with its decision to proceed with the development of the drug. In her opinion, there was no justification for seeking FDA permission to use the drug in light of medical controversy over the safety of saccharin.

Dr. Pierce met with Dr. Pasquale on May 9 and informed him that she disagreed with the decision to file an IND with the FDA. She felt that by continuing to work on loperamide she would violate her interpretation of the Hippocratic oath. She concluded that the risk that saccharin might be harmful should preclude testing the formula on children or elderly persons, especially when an alternative formulation might soon be available.

Dr. Pierce recognized that she was joined in a difference of "viewpoints" or "opinion" with Dr. Pasquale and others at Ortho concerning the use of a formula containing saccharin. In her opinion, the safety of saccharin in loperamide pediatric drops was medically debatable. She acknowledged that Dr. Pasquale was entitled to his opinion to proceed with the IND. On depositions, she testified concerning the reason for her difference of opinion about the safety of using saccharin in loperamide pediatric drops:

> Q   That was because in your medical opinion that was an unsafe thing to do. Is that so?

A No. I didn't know. The question of saccharin was one of potential harm. It was controversial. Even though the rulings presently look even less favorable for saccharin it is still a controversial issue.

After their meeting on May 9, Dr. Pasquale informed Dr. Pierce that she would no longer be assigned to the loperamide project. On May 14, Dr. Pasquale asked Dr. Pierce to choose other projects. After Dr. Pierce returned from vacation in Finland, she met on June 16 with Dr. Pasquale to discuss other projects, but she did not choose a project at that meeting. She felt she was being demoted, even though her salary would not be decreased. Dr. Pierce summarized her impression of that meeting in her letter of resignation submitted to Dr. Pasquale the following day. In that letter, she stated:

> Upon learning in our meeting June 16, 1975, that you believe I have not 'acted as a Director', have displayed inadequacies as to my competence, responsibility, productivity, inability to relate to the Marketing Personnel, that you, and reportedly Dr. George Braun and Mr. Verne Willaman consider me to be non-promotable and that I am now or soon will be demoted, I find it impossible to continue my employment at Ortho.

The letter made no specific mention of her difference of opinion with Dr. Pasquale over continuing the work on loperamide. Nonetheless, viewing the matter most favorably to Dr. Pierce, we assume the sole reason for the termination of her employment was the dispute over the loperamide project. Dr. Pasquale accepted her resignation.

In her complaint . . . Dr. Pierce claimed damages for the termination of her employment. Her complaint alleged:

> The Defendant, its agents, servants and employees requested and demanded Plaintiff follow a course of action and behavior which was impossible for Plaintiff to follow because of the Hippocratic oath she had taken, because of the ethical standards by which she was governed as a physician, and because of the regulatory schemes, both federal and state, statutory and case law, for the protection of the public in the field of health and human well-being, which schemes Plaintiff believed she should honor.

However, she did not specify that testing would violate any state or federal statutory regulation. Similarly, she did not state that continuing the research would violate the principles of ethics of the American Medical Association. She never contended her participation in the research would expose her to a claim for malpractice.

Ortho moved for summary judgment on two theories. The first was that Dr. Pierce's action for wrongful discharge was barred because she resigned. The trial judge denied the motion on that ground because he found that there was a fact question whether Ortho induced Dr. Pierce's resignation. However, the trial court granted Ortho's motion on the alternative ground that because Dr. Pierce was an employee at will, Ortho could end her employment for any reason. . . .

. . .

As discussed below, our careful examination of Dr. Pierce's allegations and the record reveals no genuine issue of material fact requiring disposition at trial. Although this case raises important policy considerations, all the relevant facts are before us, and there is no reason to defer a decision.

Accordingly, we reverse the Appellate Division and reinstate the summary judgment in favor of defendant.

Under the common law, in the absence of an employment contract, employers or employees have been free to terminate the employment relationship with or without cause. . . .

. . .

. . . The twentieth century has witnessed significant changes in socioeconomic values that have led to reassessment of the common law rule. Businesses have evolved from small and medium size firms to gigantic corporations in which ownership is separate from management. Formerly there was a clear delineation between employers, who frequently were owners of their own businesses, and employees. The employer in the old sense has been replaced by a superior in the corporate hierarchy who is himself an employee. . . . Growth in the number of employees has been accompanied by increasing recognition of the need for stability in labor relations.

Commentators have questioned the compatibility of the traditional at will doctrine with the realities of modern economics and employment practices. See, e.g, Blades, Employment at Will vs. Individual Freedom: On Limiting the Abusive Exercise of Employer Power, 67 Colum.L.Rev. 1404 (1967) [hereinafter cited as Blades]. The common law rule has been modified by the enactment of labor relations legislation. The National Labor Relations Act and other labor legislation illustrate the governmental policy of preventing employers from using the right of discharge as a means of oppression. Consistent with this policy, many states have recognized the need to protect employees who are not parties to a collective bargaining agreement or other contract from abusive practices by the employer.

Recently those states have recognized a common law cause of action for employees at will who were discharged for reasons that were in some way "wrongful". . . . Nearly all jurisdictions link the success of the wrongfully discharged employee's action to proof that the discharge violated public policy.

. . .

. . . The interests of employees, employers, and the public lead to the conclusion that the common law of New Jersey should limit the right of an employer to fire an employee at will.

. . .

Although the contours of an exception are important to all employees at will, this case focuses on the special considerations arising out of the right to fire an employee at will who is a member of a recognized profession. One writer has described the predicament that may confront a professional employed by a large corporation:

Consider, for example, the plight of an engineer who is told that he will lose his job unless he falsifies his data or conclusions, or unless he approves a product which does not conform to specifications or meet minimum standards. Consider also the dilemma of a corporate attorney who is told, say in the context of an impending tax audit or antitrust investigation, to draft backdated corporate records concerning events which never took place or to falsify other documents so that adverse legal consequences may be avoided by the corporation; and the predicament of an accountant who is told to falsify his employer's profit and loss statement in order to enable the employer to obtain credit. [Blades, supra at 1408–1409 (footnotes omitted)]

Employees who are professionals owe a special duty to abide not only by federal and state law, but also by the recognized codes of ethics of their professions. That duty may oblige them to decline to perform acts required by their employers. However, an employee should not have the right to prevent his or her employer from pursuing its business because the employee perceives that a particular business decision violates the employee's personal morals, as distinguished from the recognized code of ethics of the employee's profession. See Comment, 28 Vand.L.Rev. 805, 832 (1975).

We hold that an employee has a cause of action for wrongful discharge when the discharge is contrary to a clear mandate of public policy. The sources of public policy include legislation, administrative rules, regulations or decisions, and judicial decisions. In certain instances, a professional code of ethics may contain an expression of public policy. However, not all such sources express a clear mandate of public policy. For example, a code of ethics designed to serve only the interests of a profession or an administrative regulation concerned with technical matters probably would not be sufficient. . . .

. . .

We now turn to the question whether Dr. Pierce was discharged for reasons contrary to a clear mandate of public policy. . . .

As stated above, before loperamide could be tested on humans, an IND had to be submitted to the FDA to obtain approval for such testing. The IND must contain complete manufacturing specifications, details of pre-clinical studies (testing on animals) which demonstrate the safe use of the drug, and a description of proposed clinical studies. The FDA then has 30 days to withhold approval of testing. Since no IND had been filed here, and even giving Dr. Pierce the benefit of all doubt regarding her allegations, it is clear that clinical testing of loperamide on humans was not imminent.

Dr. Pierce argues that by continuing to perform research on loperamide she would have been forced to violate professional medical ethics expressed in the Hippocratic oath. She cites the part of the oath that reads: "I will prescribe regimen for the good of my patients according to my ability and my judgment and never do harm to anyone." Clearly, the general language of the oath does not prohibit specifically research that does not involve tests on humans and that cannot lead to such tests without governmental approval.

We note that Dr. Pierce did not rely on or allege violation of any other standards . . . Similarly, she did not allege that continuing her research would constitute an act of medical malpractice or violate any statute, including N.J.S.A. 45:9–16(h).

In this case, Dr. Pierce has never contended that saccharin would necessarily cause harm to anyone. She alleged that the current controversy made continued investigation an unnecessary risk. However when she stopped work on loperamide, there was no risk. Our point here is not that participation in unethical conduct must be imminent before an employee may refuse to work. The more relevant consideration is that Dr. Pierce does not allege that preparation and filing of the IND was unethical. Further Dr. Pierce does not suggest that Ortho would have proceeded with human testing without FDA approval. The case would be far different if Ortho had filed the IND, the FDA had disapproved it, and Ortho insisted on testing the drug on humans. The actual facts are that Dr. Pierce could not have harmed anyone by continuing to work on loperamide.

Viewing the matter most favorably to Dr. Pierce, the controversy at Ortho involved a difference in medical opinions. Dr. Pierce acknowledged that Dr. Pasquale was entitled to his opinion that the oath did not forbid work on loperamide. Nonetheless, implicit in Dr. Pierce's position is the contention that Dr. Pasquale and Ortho were obliged to accept her opinion. Dr. Pierce contends, in effect, that Ortho should have stopped research on loperamide because of her opinion about the controversial nature of the drug.

Dr. Pierce espouses a doctrine that would lead to disorder in drug research. Under her theory, a professional employee could redetermine the propriety of a research project even if the research did not involve a violation of a clear mandate of public policy. Chaos would result if a single doctor engaged in research were allowed to determine, according to his or her individual conscience, whether a project should continue. An employee does not have a right to continued employment when he or she refuses to conduct research simply because it would contravene his or her personal morals. An employee at will who refuses to work for an employer in answer to a call of conscience should recognize that other employees and their employer might heed a different call. However, nothing in this opinion should be construed to restrict the right of an employee at will to refuse to work on a project that he or she believes is unethical. In sum, an employer may discharge an employee who refuses to work unless the refusal is based on a clear mandate of public policy.

. . .

Under these circumstances, we conclude that the Hippocratic oath does not contain a clear mandate of public policy that prevented Dr. Pierce from continuing her research on loperamide. To hold otherwise would seriously impair the ability of drug manufacturers to develop new drugs according to their best judgment.

. . .

Accordingly, we . . . remand the cause to the trial court for entry of judgment for defendant.

PASHMAN, J., dissenting.

. . .

The majority's analysis recognizes that the ethical goals of professional conduct are of inestimable social value. By maintaining informed standards of conduct, licensed professions bring to the problems of their public responsibilities the same expertise that marks their calling. The integrity of codes of professional conduct that result from this regulation deserves judicial protection from undue economic pressure. Employers are a potential source of this pressure, for they can provide or withhold—until today, at their whim—job security and the means of enhancing a professional's reputation. Thus, I completely agree with the majority's ruling that "an employee has a cause of action for wrongful discharge when the discharge is contrary to a clear mandate of public policy" as expressed in a "professional code of ethics."

The Court pronounces this rule for the first time today. One would think that it would therefore afford plaintiff an opportunity to seek relief

within the confines of this newly announced cause of action. . . .
There are a number of detailed, recognized codes of medical ethics that
proscribe participation in clinical experimentation when a doctor perceives an unreasonable threat to human health. Any one of these codes
could provide the "clear mandate of public policy" that the majority requires.

The "Declaration of Helsinki" of the World Medical Association * established guidelines for conducting medical experimentation on humans.
. . . The House of Delegates of the American Medical Association
gave official endorsement to the principles of this declaration at its annual
convention in 1966. . . .

. . .

The American Medical Association has also drafted and adopted its
own ethical guidelines for clinical investigations. [See Ch. 6, Sec. B.1.]
. . .

A final source of ethical guidelines is what is now called the "Nuremberg Code" a statement of principles included in the Nuremberg Military
Tribunal's decision in *United States v. Karl Brandt.* [See Ch. 6, Sec. B.1.]
. . .

Each of these . . . "codes of professional ethics" establish standards for the participation of doctors in clinical experimentation on
humans. Both the source and the content of each set of guidelines provide persuasive evidence that each is a "clear mandate of public policy."
Each also provides the basis for denying defendant summary judgment.
Plaintiff should receive the opportunity to prove at trial that she was discharged for her refusal to violate one or more of these ethical standards.

. . .

Each of the previously described codes of medical ethics would prohibit plaintiff from conducting clinicial experimentation where unnecessary medical risks have economic profit as their only justification. The
original Declaration of Helsinki proscribes experimentation combined
with professional care unless it "is justified by its therapeutic value for the
patient," . . . Non-therapeutic research may not be conducted if, in
the judgment of the investigator, it would be "harmful to the individual
[test subject]." The 1975 revision of the declaration also prohibits doctors from conducting experiments where they are not satisfied that the
possible hazards are predictable, or where they outweigh the potential
benefits. Where the research program has a therapeutic purpose, the
doctor may conduct experiments only where he weighs the proposal
against other courses of treatment and concludes it is "the best proven
. . . therapeutic method." The American Medical Association's own
guidelines also make participation in clinical experimentation contingent
upon the doctor's professional judgment regarding "the welfare, safety,
and comfort of the [test subject]," and the "best interest of the patient."
Finally, the Nuremberg Code similarly conditions a doctor's participation
on his "good faith, superior skill and careful judgment" that the experiment is safe.

At this stage of the litigation—when all disputed factual issues must be
resolved against defendant—plaintiff is entitled to claim the protection of
one or more of these recognized codes of professional ethics. I therefore
conclude that plaintiff should have an opportunity to prove those facts

_____

* See Ch. 6, Sec. B.1. [Eds.]

which may entitle her to relief under the majority's newly promulgated cause of action.

This opportunity to prove a discharge in violation of public policy is not based solely on recognized codes of professional ethics. There is also a legislative prohibition of conduct by physicians that endangers life or health. To regulate the professional behavior of doctors, the Legislature has empowered the State Board of Medical Examiners to grant, suspend or revoke licenses to practice medicine within the State. See N.J.S.A. 45:9–6, –16. The statute enumerating the Board's powers provides in part:

> The [B]oard may refuse to grant or may suspend or revoke a license
> . . . to practice medicine . . . upon proof . . . of gross
> malpractice or gross neglect in the practice of medicine which has en-
> dangered the health or life of any person . . . .

> [N.J.S.A. 45:9–16(h)]

This statutory prohibition of "gross malpractice or gross neglect" establishes another "clear mandate of public policy" which plaintiff should be allowed to invoke. Assuming without deciding that the infliction of unnecessary medical risks—the specific conduct plaintiff refused to perform—might have constituted "gross malpractice," I find not even the attempt by defendant to refute such a claim. If plaintiff could prove that defendant discharged her for refusing to engage in "gross malpractice," defendant would be liable for its violation of a "clear mandate of public policy." I would permit plaintiff to demonstrate at trial that her discharge was a response to her refusal to violate statutory policy as well as several codes of medical ethics.

The majority denies plaintiff this opportunity. I do not understand why. . . .

The ostensible reason for the majority's rejection is that plaintiff "did not rely on or allege violation of any other standards" besides the Hippocratic Oath. Yet, the majority's own opinion conclusively shows this statement to be inaccurate. As the majority notes, plaintiff asserted in her complaint that her participation in the proposed drug program would have been in violation of "ethical standards" *other than* the broad mandate or her Hippocratic Oath. Thus, the majority's stated reason for upholding summary judgment contradicts its own description of plaintiff's claims. It may be that the majority dismisses these claims because plaintiff did not allege them specifically. But this rationale would reject a possibly valid claim for a formal defect in pleading—a result our courts have long eschewed. . . .

Three other points made by the majority require discussion, for they reflect the majority's failure to follow the well-established rule that the claims of a party opposing summary judgment are to be "indulgently treated." The first is the majority's characterization of the effect of plaintiff's ethical position. It appears to believe that Dr. Pierce had the power to determine whether defendant's proposed development program would continue at all. This is not the case, nor is plaintiff claiming the right to halt defendant's developmental efforts. Interpreted "indulgently," yet realistically, plaintiff claims only the right to her professional autonomy. She contends that she may not be discharged for expressing her view that the clinical program is unethical or for refusing to continue her participation in the project. She has done nothing else to impede continued development of defendant's proposal; moreover, it is undisputed that defendant was able to continue its program by reassigning personnel. Thus, the majority's view that granting doctors a right to be free from abusive discharges would confer on any one of them complete veto power over desirable drug development is ill-conceived.

The second point concerns the role of governmental approval of the proposed experimental program. In apparent ignorance of the past failures of official regulation to safeguard against pharmaceutical horrors, the majority implies that the necessity for administrative approval for human testing eliminates the need for active, ethical professionals within the drug industry. But we do not know whether the United States Food and Drug Administration (FDA) would be aware of the safer alternative to the proposed drug when it would pass upon defendant's application for the more hazardous formula. The majority professes no such knowledge. We must therefore assume the FDA would have been left in ignorance. This highlights the need for ethically autonomous professionals within the pharmaceutical industry—a need which the majority's approach does nothing to satisfy.

The final point to which I must respond is the majority's observation that plaintiff expressed her opposition prematurely, before the FDA had approved clinical experimentation. Essentially, the majority holds that a professional employee may not express a refusal to engage in illegal or clearly unethical conduct until his actual participation and the resulting harm is imminent. This principle grants little protection to the ethical autonomy of professionals that the majority proclaims. Would the majority have Dr. Pierce wait until the first infant was placed before her, ready to receive the first dose of a drug containing 44 times the concentration of saccharin permitted in 12 ounces of soda?[4] The majority minimizes the scope of plaintiff's ethical obligation. The "clear mandate of public policy" was no less clear when she made known her opposition and refusal to participate. A professional's opposition to unethical conduct should not be considered untimely when its unethical nature is apparent. By contrast, the majority's requirement that proposed conduct be imminent would require, for example, an associate in a law firm to withhold his opposition to the preparation of perjured testimony or false evidence, see *DR* 7–102(A)(4), (5) & (6), until he is actually ordered to begin the preparation. This narrow view of an employee's duty to obey codes of ethics does little to promote such clear mandates of public policy. It will allow unscrupulous employers to forestall discussion on proposed unethical conduct, and to evade the spirit of the majority's new principle by carefully timing such conduct to prevent meaningful dissent. Thus, the majority's additional requirement that proposed conduct be imminent is both unnecessary and self-defeating. I would hold that defendant has not eliminated "all genuine disputes as to any material facts" under the majority's principle that an employee may not be discharged for opposing conduct in violation of a "clear mandate of public policy." I would therefore affirm the denial of summary judgment on plaintiff's tort claim.

. . .

4. There is at present undisputed evidence in the record that the amount of saccharin in the proposed drug formulation is this high. This limits [sic] on saccharin in soft drinks are those imposed by the FDA at the time the parties were conducting discovery.

THE HIPPOCRATIC OATH

I swear by Apollo Physician and Asclepius and Hygieia and Panaceia and all the gods and goddesses, making them my witnesses, that I will fulfill according to my ability and judgment this oath and this covenant:

To hold him who has taught me this art as equal to my parents and to live my life in partnership with him, and if he is in need of money to give him a share of mine, and to regard his offspring as equal to my brothers in male lineage and to teach them this art—if they desire to learn it— without fee and covenant; to give a share of precepts and oral instruction and all the other learning to my sons and to the sons of him who has instructed me and to pupils who have signed the covenant and have taken an oath according to the medical law, but to no one else.

I will apply dietetic measures for the benefit of the sick according to my ability and judgment; I will keep them from harm and injustice.

I will neither give a deadly drug to anybody if asked for it, nor will I make a suggestion to this effect. Similarly I will not give to a woman an abortive remedy. In purity and holiness I will guard my life and my art.

I will not use the knife, not even on sufferers from stone, but will withdraw in favor of such men as are engaged in this work.

Whatever houses I may visit, I will come for the benefit of the sick, remaining free of all intentional injustice, of all mischief and in particular of sexual relations with both female and male persons, be they free or slaves.

What I may see or hear in the course of the treatment or even outside of the treatment in regard to the life of men, which on no account one must spread abroad, I will keep to myself holding such things shameful to be spoken about.

If I fulfill this oath and do not violate it, may it be granted to me to enjoy life and art, being honored with fame among all men for all time to come; if I transgress it and swear falsely, may the opposite of all this be my lot.

ROBERT M. VEATCH,
A THEORY OF MEDICAL ETHICS

21–25 (1981).

THE HIPPOCRATIC TRADITION

While some specific, often archaic, features of the Oath were abandoned, many of its essential elements remained as the Oath began to find its place in Western culture. Specific views on surgery, the tripartite division of medicine, and the swearing by Apollo disappeared, but among the significant features retained throughout the history of the Hippocratic tradition is the view that the practice of the physician's art is a calling, something having a quasi-religious overtone. This concept carries with it a sense of loyalty to one's teachers that, by the late Middle Ages, came to mean loyalty to one's professional group.

Even more central to this common tradition is a moral perspective that dominates the Oath. At two points, a fundamental moral principle—what I shall call the Hippocratic principle—is stated. It comes first in the section related to dietetics, but many modern interpreters have generalized it so that it applies to all treatments. The taker of the Oath says, "I will apply . . . measures for the benefit of the sick according to my ability and judgment; I will keep them from harm and injustice." Later, when the Oath refers to visiting the sick, the same theme is repeated: "Whatever houses I may visit, I will come for the benefit of the sick, remaining free of all intentional injustice. . . ." [12]

This I take to be the core of professional physician ethics, the core of the Hippocratic tradition. Those who have stood in that tradition are committed to producing good for their patient and to protecting that patient from harm. (To be sure, this consequentialism was originally given a very peculiar turn in the Hippocratic cult; medicine was viewed as "the art," and special cultic values like purity and holiness heavily influenced the interpretation of what would count as benefit.) Love of the art was a central value. Modern proponents of the tradition loosely related to the Oath still retain, in varying degrees, this special vision of the good. The principle in its core has thus remained, although sometimes there are variants. Avoiding harm may be given priority over benefiting the patient, for example. This version has been given the dignity of latinization into the formula *primum non nocere,* "first do no harm," but this is not Hippocratic. "The Epidemics," the Hippocratic work to which this formula is sometimes attributed, does not really give a priority to avoiding harm. "As to diseases," the author of "The Epidemics" wrote, "make a habit of two things—to help, or at least to do no harm." [13]

Sometimes, especially •in contemporary physician "folk" ethics, the formula is converted into the principle of preventing harm by preserving life. That is a variant without classical roots,[14] and it has received only minority support even in the decades of heroic medical interventionism in the mid-twentieth century. Only one important twentieth-century code commits the physician to the preservation of life, the World Medical Association's International Code of Medical Ethics, and that seems highly qualified with exceptions and seems targeted at the abortion issue rather than at contemporary problems in the care of the terminally ill.

.   .   .

From its position as a minority document for an isolated group of physicians, the Oath, together with related ethical documents from the Hippocratic corpus, gradually emerged as the dominant summary of the physician's own understanding of his ethical responsibility. The works were known to Plato, and many were commented upon by Galen (although apparently not the Oath specifically or the other deontological writings).
.   .   .

.   .   .

.   .   .   [I]nterest in the Hippocratic tradition continued and flourished into the modern period of medical practice. In Elizabethan England, for example, we find four versions of the Hippocratic Oath, all containing variants of what I have identified as the core of the Hippocratic ethic.[23] The major Anglo-American event signaling the emergence of the Hippocratic tradition in the modern period, however, came at the end of

12. [Edelstein, Ancient Medicine], p. 6. The term for injustice is a general term sometimes translated as simply "harm" or "wrongdoing".

13. "The Epidemics," bk. 1, chap. 11, in Hippocrates, p. 165.

14. Darrel W. Amundsen, "The Physician's Obligation to Prolong Life: A Medical Duty without Classical Roots," Hastings Center Report 8 (August 1978): 23–30.

23. Sanford v. Larkey, "The Hippocratic Oath in Elizabethan England," in Legacies

the eighteenth century, when a feud broke out at the Manchester Infirmary.[24] In 1789, an epidemic of typhoid or typhus struck, taxing the infirmary staff. At the time, medical practitioners were divided into three groups: physicians, surgeons, and apothecaries. Tensions among these groups were exacerbated when staff changes were made to respond to the epidemic. Some of the staff resigned, taking the changes to be a negative reflection on their efforts. In order to keep the peace, the trustees of the infirmary approached Thomas Percival, a physician who had been on the infirmary staff but had resigned years earlier because of physical disabilities. He had maintained close relationships with the infirmary and its staff and was asked to draw up a "scheme of professional conduct relative to hospitals and other medical charities."[25] The result was Percival's famous "Medical Ethics; or, a Code of Institutes and Precepts Adapted to the Professional Conduct of Physicians and Surgeons. . . ." Out of these meager beginnings, in a local dispute over intraprofessional division of labor, was to emerge the foundation of Anglo-American medical ethics.[26]

American medical ethics took its lead from Percival. In 1847, at the founding meeting of the American Medical Association in Philadelphia, a code of ethics, which drew heavily upon Percival's pragmatic, problem-solving approach to professional squabbles, was approved. Like its predecessor, it reflected the core of the Hippocratic ethic, pledging physicians to "minister to the sick with due impressions of the importance of their office; reflecting that the ease, the health, and the lives of those committed to their charge, depend on their skill, attention and fidelity."[27]

That code has been revised from time to time over the past century, most significantly in 1957 and 1980. The 1957 revision replaced the detailed compilation of rules and interpretations of the earlier versions with a set of ten principles stating in more general terms the ethical mandate of the physician, and the 1980 update introduced for the first time a rights perspective into professional physician ethics. Only in these very recent versions, as we shall see in due course, did the Hippocratic commitment to benefit exclusively the patient, according to the physician's judgment, begin to give way to other ethical commitments—those that take into account the interests of the rest of society; those that take into account physicians' rights and duties as well as benefits and harms; and those that take into account the judgment of the patients and others beyond the physician.

AMERICAN MEDICAL ASSOCIATION, PRINCIPLES OF MEDICAL ETHICS

(1980)

PREAMBLE

The medical profession has long subscribed to a body of ethical statements developed primarily for the benefit of the patient. As a member of

in Ethics and Medicine, ed. Chester Burns (New York: Science History Publications, 1977), pp. 218–36.

24. Thomas Percival, Percival's Medical Ethics, ed. Chauncey D. Leake (Baltimore, Md.: Williams & Wilkins, 1927), pp. 29–32; Ivan Waddington, "The Development of Medical Ethics—A Sociological Analysis," Medical History 19 (January 1975): 36–51.

25. Waddington, "Development of Medical Ethics," p. 31.

26. Ibid.

27. American Medical Association, Code of Medical Ethics (New York: H. Ludwig and Co., 1848).

this profession, a physician must recognize responsibility not only to patients, but also to society, to other health professionals, and to self. The following Principles adopted by the American Medical Association are not laws, but standards of conduct which define the essentials of honorable behavior for the physician.

PRINCIPLES

I. A physician shall be dedicated to providing competent medical service with compassion and respect for human dignity.

II. A physician shall deal honestly with patients and colleagues, and strive to expose those physicians deficient in character or competence, or who engage in fraud or deception.

III. A physician shall respect the law and also recognize a responsibility to seek changes in those requirements which are contrary to the best interests of the patient.

IV. A physician shall respect the rights of patients, of colleagues, and of other health professionals, and shall safeguard patient confidences within the constraints of the law.

V. A physician shall continue to study, apply and advance scientific knowledge, make relevant information available to patients, colleagues, and the public, obtain consultation, and use the talents of other health professionals when indicated.

VI. A physician shall, in the provision of appropriate patient care, except in emergencies, be free to choose whom to serve, with whom to associate, and the environment in which to provide medical services.

VII. A physician shall recognize a responsibility to participate in activities contributing to an improved community.

NOTES

1. Should there be a code of ethics for scientists? Consider the views of Pigman and Carmichael, An Ethical Code for Scientists, 111 Science 643, 643–644 (1950):

A new phenomenon of our present-day society is the obviously important role played by science. Only a short time ago science was considered by many "practical" men as a plaything of inconsequential importance in contributing to the welfare of society. Although the significance of science was becoming more generally evident before World War II, this war demonstrated to the public in general and to legislators and businessmen in particular that science, especially basic science, is much more than a scholarly pursuit—that it is a vital force for the advancement or destruction of society. Science is now "big business." As a result, the scientist cannot and must not remain a scholarly recluse divorced from the remainder of society. His behavior and that of society toward him will greatly influence the progress of science and, to an increasing extent, that of society itself.

During its long period of development, science has evolved a code of professional tradition and ethics, largely in an unwritten form. This code, really the foundation of the scientific method in many of its aspects, has to a considerable extent been responsible for the achievements of science. . . .

The important achievements of science and its contributions to our civilization seem adequate proof of the basic validity of these traditions. On the other hand, conditions of scientific work have changed greatly, and obviously the traditions must be interpreted in terms of prevailing conditions. Science has emerged from a period in which the predominant effort was made by individuals, sometimes of almost an amateur status, to a period marked by the development of large research groups, many in the pursuit of research for profit. As a result it is timely for the scientist to consider his professional traditions and to relate them in terms of the structure of modern scientific work.

These traditions are essentially an unwritten code of professional ethics. . . . It is true that professional codes at best can only express an ideal; their acceptance and application will depend upon the individual scientists. We believe, however, that the scientist's position in the world today makes it extremely important that his time-proved traditions be reconsidered in terms of modern circumstances and possibly written into a formal code. We believe that such an action would maintain the advance of science, increase its public support, and improve the professional relations of scientists. Improved professional relations would better morale and increase productivity among research men. . . .

The planning of an ethical code for scientists should take into account first the scientist's general obligations as a member of society, and beyond that his special obligation as a scientist to protect society—here, there are many problems related to warfare, to the health and general well-being of mankind, and to nationalism versus internationalism. Such a code should preserve the scientist's ethical traditions and incorporate the scientific method. It should state the scientist's obligation to explain the nature and purposes of science, and the policies in dealing directly with the public. It should clarify the scientist's attitudes toward patents and secrecy restrictions. It should affirm the scientist's obligations to individuals—to his employer, his associates, other scientists, and his assistants and graduates—and scientists' obligation as a group to other professions. . . .

Is this recommendation consistent with the nature of the world of science as Polanyi described it, Sec. A.1., supra? With the characteristics Merton identified, Sec. A.3.c., infra?

2. Compare Gass, Codes of Health Care Professions, 4 Encyclopedia of Bioethics 1725, 1725–26 (1978):

Contrary to what one might expect, namely, a strong emphasis on the resolution of important bioethical issues, we find that the ethical issues usually addressed by health-care professions fall mainly into two categories. The first is characterized by broad moral imperatives reminiscent of the Ten Commandments and the Golden Rule, and the second by detailed statements regarding the commercial aspects of professional practice.

Common Features of Codes

The broad ethical concerns of the major health-care professions—medicine, dentistry, nursing, pharmacy, and psychology—are generally predictable. For example, a typical code exhorts practitioners to preserve human life, to be good citizens, to prevent the exploitation of patients, to promote the highest-quality health care available, to perform their duties with objectivity and accuracy, to strive for professional excellence through continuing education, to avoid discriminatory practices, to promote the interest and ideals of the profession, to expose unethical or incompetent colleagues, to encourage public health through health-care education, to render service in times of public emergencies, to promote harmonious relations with other health-care professions and to protect the welfare, dignity, and confidentiality of patients. Most of these imperatives are vague and of limited value, since they do not go beyond the fundamental humanitarian concerns we would expect of every member of society.

In contrast, the specific though mundane ethical guidelines address advertising, billing procedures, self-aggrandizement, conflicts of interest, professional courtesy, public and media relations, employment and supervision of auxiliary personnel, use of secret remedies and exclusive methods, as well as the location and physical appearance of the office practice.

Frequently, the more elaborate codes of ethics are accompanied by complex peer review mechanisms designed to enforce the code and discipline violators through censure, suspension, or, for particularly heinous conduct, expulsion. While disciplinary actions may prove detrimental to a practitioner's professional reputation, they seldom affect the right to practice. For those professions subject to state licensure, the judicial actions of health-care organizations rarely trigger official investigations, and when they do license revocation is the exception rather than the rule. Control over the unlicensed health-care professions (e.g., in the United States, medical technologists, dieticians, occupational therapists, physical therapists, and social workers) is even less formal.

A few codes specify distinct grounds for disciplinary action, including conviction of a felony or a crime involving moral turpitude, suspension or termination of licensure, self-aggrandizement, improper financial dealings, incompetence, solicitation of patients, unprofessional conduct, violation of the state or local society's bylaws, and even failure to pay dues. While professional organizations rarely report violations of their codes of ethics in forums readily accessible to the public, the limited evidence available suggests that a majority of complaints relate to business practices, especially restrictions on advertising, and not to transgressions of broad ethical principles. The American Physical Therapy Association reported in 1973 that its Judicial Committee adjudicated grievances falling into three general categories: telephone listing violations, improperly printed communications, and miscellaneous infractions including misuse of the association insignia, product endorsements, and failure to give loyalty and support.

Relatively new health-care professions (e.g., physicians' assistants and medical technologists) and subspecialties (e.g., bariatric medicine, legal medicine, endodontics, and nurse midwifery) have sought alternative ways of addressing ethical issues, if they do so at all. Subspecialties tend to endorse, in toto or with slight modifications, the code of ethics that dominates their major health-care field, and only in a few instances are these codes supplemented by the subspecialty's own code and/or policy statements. The American College of Foot Surgeons simply endorses the code of the American Podiatry Association: the Society for Pediatric Radiology endorses the codes of the American College of Radiology (1969) and the American Medical Association; the American College of Apothecaries has adopted its own *Code of Professional Practice* (n.d.) as well as (in 1969) that of the American Pharmaceutical Association; and the interdisciplinary Association for Advancement of Behavior Therapy endorses the codes of the American Medical Association, the American Psychiatric Association, and the American Psychological Association. One rarity is the American College of Legal Medicine (1960), which has adopted the code of a health-care organization, the American Medical Association, as well as that of a non-health-care profession, the American Bar Association's *Code of Professional Responsibility and Code of Judicial Conduct* (adopted, 1969; revised, 1975).

with Caplan, Cracking Codes, 8 Hastings Ctr.Rep. 18 (1978):

All this bemoaning the absence of morality and public spirit from professional codes strikes me as a bit disingenuous. Such complaints ignore the old saw that it is hard to legislate morality; but, even more, I find it surprising that anyone would expect a professional code to serve any goals other than those that are in the self-interest of the professionals who constructed it.

.   .   .

Codes and professions go hand in hand. Not all codes are . . . arbitrary and arcane . . . , but they exist to define and orient the practices and behaviors of a particular group or guild. They are meant to serve its aims, and to provide a reference point for maintaining group cohesion. Public scrutiny and moral aspiration, while not incompatible with codes, rarely enter into the intentions of their creators. Indeed that is why most professional codes so rarely contain sanctions.

The real value of a code for moral and ethical discussion lies in its revealing to the outsider where the group stands, what its intentions are, and what objectives it serves. Thus codes are documents worthy of study and critique not because they provide nuanced moral distinctions or standards for behavioral evaluation but because they make the self-interest of professional groups explicit.

b. Through Education and Training

DOE v. NEW YORK UNIVERSITY

United States Court of Appeals for the Second Circuit, 1981.
666 F.2d 761.

MANSFIELD, Circuit Judge:

In this action under § 504 of the Rehabilitation Act of 1973, 29 U.S.C. § 794, which prohibits a recipient of federal financial assistance from denying benefits to an "otherwise qualified" handicapped person solely because of his or her handicap, defendants, New York University and certain of its administrators (collectively referred to herein as NYU), appeal from an order of the Southern District of New York entered by Judge Gerard L. Goettel granting plaintiff Jane Doe preliminary injunctive relief directing NYU Medical School to readmit her as a first-year medical student and denying defendants' motion for summary judgment dismissing her complaint. We reverse the grant of preliminary injunctive relief and affirm the denial of NYU's motion for summary judgment.

. . . .

Each year approximately 5,000 persons apply for admission as medical students to NYU Medical School, of whom those found best qualified by the Admissions Committee, some 170, are accepted. In 1975 Jane Doe was accepted after falsely representing in her application that she did not have any chronic or recurrent illnesses or emotional problems. In fact she, while gifted academically, had suffered for many years from serious psychiatric and mental disorders, which evidenced themselves in the form of numerous self-destructive acts and attacks upon others, followed by periodic treatments by psychologists and psychiatrists and admissions to various psychiatric hospitals for care and therapy. In the third grade she had trouble with her teacher, requiring the help of a psychologist and psychiatrist. In 1963, at 14 years of age, she tore up a report card and took five Doriden tablets (sleeping pills) in anger at her parents. Beginning in November 1963, she was treated by a psychiatrist on 24 weekly visits. . . . [S]he terminated this treatment in June, 1964.

There is no evidence of further symptoms of psychiatric difficulties on Doe's part until November, 1972, when at the age of 23 she became upset by an interview she had had at the University of San Francisco Medical School and attempted suicide by drinking potassium cyanide. Over her resistance she was taken to the Stanford University Hospital emergency room. There she threatened to kill herself and had to be strapped to a stretcher. She was then moved to Santa Clara Valley Medical Center (Valley), where she stayed for 2½ days. In January, 1973, she injected herself with cytosine arabinoside, a drug for treatment of cancer which attacks certain cells and renders them susceptible to infection. In March, 1973, she carved a hole in her stomach with a kitchen knife, using a local anesthetic stolen from a laboratory. Later in the month, after a counsel-lor at school asked her to accept inpatient treatment at Langley Porter Neuropsychiatric Institute, she severed an artery in her elbow with a razor blade. She was then admitted to Langley Porter, where she stayed for eight days. During her stay there she broke a light bulb, scratched her wrists, attacked a doctor, tore his nameplate off his door, and left against medical advice.

. . .

After starting at NYU Medical School in September, Doe was required as a matriculating student to undergo a medical examination early that month but delayed doing so until October 30, 1975. When the doctor who examined her, Dr. Michael Ruoff, noticed scars on Doe's arm, and inquired as to their cause she for the first time informed the University of some of her history of psychiatric problems. Dr. Ruoff recommended that Doe undergo a psychiatric examination to determine whether she was fit to stay at the school. Her reply was, "It is my body and what I do to it is my concern. If I want to go out and f___ a cat I can." She then walked out without completing the examination.

Shortly thereafter Doe met with Dr. David S. Scotch, Associate Dean of NYU Medical School, and agreed to be examined by a Student Health Service psychiatrist, Dr. Marvin Stern. In an interview with Dr. Stern on November 3, 1975, she gave a more detailed history of her psychiatric problems. Dr. Stern reached the conclusion that Doe had a "fragile personality" and sent her to Dr. Emmanuel Fisher for psychological tests. Doe underwent testing by Fisher on November 5, 1975. On the basis of these tests and his interview of her, Dr. Fisher also concluded that Doe had a serious psychiatric problem. He "noted that she had a grossly detached and alienated personality, with no effective intellectual or emotional contact with the world of things or people."

On November 10 Doe was again examined by Dr. Stern, following which Dr. Fisher recommended to Dr. Scotch that Doe be asked to withdraw from the medical school. Dr. Scotch agreed, and informed Doe of the decision on November 12. Doe asked to discuss the matter with Dr. Ivan Bennett, the Dean of the Medical School, and did so the same day. After reviewing the matter further Scotch and Bennett agreed to permit Doe to remain at NYU on the condition that she undertake psychiatric therapy with a medical follow-up by the Student Health Service. Doe accepted these conditions and was advised that if she had further psychiatric trouble she would be expected to withdraw from the school.

Doe began psychiatric therapy with Dr. Grace Frank of Bellevue Hospital while continuing her medical school program. Apparently this therapy was unsuccessful and it was eventually terminated. . . .

On Friday, January 30, 1976, Doe went to Dr. Scotch's office, apparently by appointment, to discuss with him a conflict in her schedule that would occur the following Monday. Dr. Scotch was not in his office when Doe arrived, and she became distressed and angry. She left the office and attempted to calm herself, but to no avail. She returned and told Dr. Scotch that she would have to revert to her past habits in order to cope with the situation. She retreated to a bathroom, where she bled herself with a catheter. An hour later she returned to Dr. Scotch's office and told him what she had done, explaining that it was the only way she could cope with her stress. Dr. Scotch requested her resignation.

Doe met with Dr. Bennett the following Monday, February 2, discussed her situation with him and made a written proposal for a leave of absence, which was granted on the understanding that she might request reinstatement, which would be considered but not guaranteed in view of the problems she presented. Her tuition and dormitory fee for the second semester were refunded. After going to the University Hospital's psychiatric ward and then refusing to be admitted, on February 9 Doe was told by NYU to move out of her dormitory room and stop attending classes. She finally agreed to enter the Payne-Whitney Psychiatric Clinic (not affiliated with NYU) two days later, but left against medical advice on February 16. Doe apparently wandered around New York during the next three days, sleeping in public restrooms. She returned to Payne-Whitney on February 19, admitting that she was in need of help, and stayed there for 17 more days, after which her insurance ran out, but made no progress. Her condition on discharge was listed as "no improvement," with a diagnosis by Dr. James H. Spencer of "Borderline personality. . . . Personality disorders, other specified types 301.89."

A personality disorder classified as "Borderline Personality" is a serious condition, manifesting itself by a series of five or more recognizable characteristics, according to the American Psychiatric Association's Diagnostic and Statistical Manual (3d ed.) (known as "DSM–III"). A person suffering from it is likely to have it continue through most of his or her adult life, subject to modification only by treatment by well-trained therapists over a period of years and adoption of a lifestyle which avoids situations that subject the person to types of stress with which he or she cannot cope.

After leaving Payne-Whitney in March of 1976, Doe returned to California, where she was treated by two psychiatrists simultaneously on an outpatient basis, one (Dr. Casella) providing individual therapy, the other (Dr. Richards) family therapy in which her husband joined. Doe states that leaving NYU was "a major turning point in my life." She maintains that through the treatment she received in California she was able to master her psychiatric problems, develop healthy ways of dealing with stress, and cease her self-destructive behavior. . . .

Doe and her husband moved to New York in October of 1976, apparently because he had a fellowship there. She took a job with an advertising agency and continued to undergo psychiatric treatment in New York until sometime between April and June of 1977. NYU and Doe disagree about the degree to which this treatment was successful. According to NYU she was unable to handle group therapy sessions at Payne-Whitney. According to Dr. Warren Tanenbaum, with whom she began treatment in February, 1977, which ended in April or May, she was ill at ease with him, hated psychiatrists, was late for her sessions, blamed Dr. Scotch for her difficulties at NYU, had thought of sticking scissors into her ribs, and feared she could not manage medical school.

In June or July of 1977, after having returned to California, Doe applied for readmission to NYU. Her application was supported by both of the psychiatrists who had treated her while she had been in California after leaving NYU, Drs. Richards and Casella, even though the first had seen her at most three times and the second at most two times during that summer. Both sent letters of support to NYU. According to NYU's standards a student seeking readmission

"must demonstrate that the problems that precipitated the leave are resolved, that the applicant must be able to handle all of the academic and emotional stress of attending medical school, and that the school must be satisfied that the applicant will be able to function properly after graduation as a physician."

More specifically NYU states that Doe would be required to show

"(c) that she does not pose a significant risk of reexhibiting her prior disorder either; (i) when readmitted to the same Medical School environment which previously caused her such difficulty; or (ii) when she might in the future be fully licensed and authorized to practice medicine; and

"(d) that in addition to being fully cured, she possesses the additional qualifications of good judgment, personal integrity and truthfulness, and a genuine commitment to the medical profession."

The Payne-Whitney files on Doe were obtained by NYU for purposes of considering her application and turned over to the Medical School's Chairman of the Department of Psychiatry, Dr. Robert Cancro, for a recommendation as to her fitness to return to the school.

Upon Dr. Cancro's recommendation and the judgments of other NYU faculty members, made after considering the letters from Doe's two California psychiatrists, NYU decided not to readmit Doe. . . . At approximately the same time (fall of 1977) Doe was admitted as a graduate student to the Harvard School of Public Health to undertake a course of study leading to a degree of Masters of Science in Health and Policy Management. In her Harvard University medical questionnaire she falsely stated that she had not experienced any nervousness, worry or emotional disturbance causing a loss of time from work or study.

In response to NYU's refusal to readmit her Doe sought legal assistance, and on October 25, 1977, an attorney representing her wrote to NYU requesting that it reconsider Doe's application and threatening to bring legal action if it did not. NYU responded by agreeing to reopen the application on condition that Doe agree to be interviewed by an NYU psychiatrist. . . .

On December 2, 1977, the parties (NYU and Doe) agreed to an interview by Dr. Veva H. Zimmerman, an Associate Professor of Clinical Psychiatry at NYU Medical School. Dr. Zimmerman examined Doe on December 13, 1977, and made a report to Dr. Scotch by letter on December 27, 1977, explaining that she had met with Jane Doe for one hour and 40 minutes and that in order to avoid biasing herself she had not read any reports on Doe before the examination. . . . While recognizing that some progress had been made, Dr. Zimmerman noted that Doe depended greatly on her marriage "to help her maintain psychological equilibrium" and that although Doe might be able to handle a graduate program involving "purely intellectual material," medical school, which required successful interaction with people, was quite a different matter. She therefore recommended against readmitting Doe.

On the basis of the Zimmerman report NYU adhered to its earlier decision and on December 28, 1977, Jane Doe brought this action. . . . The district court, Goettel, J., . . . required Doe to exhaust her administrative remedies with the Office of Civil Rights (OCR) of the Department of Health, Education, and Welfare (HEW). . . .

In June, 1978, Doe successfully completed her course at Harvard, receiving a masters degree, and took a summer internship at the Department of Health, Education and Welfare in Washington. There she successfully served in various capacities from the summer of 1978 until

October, 1981, when the district court required that NYU readmit her. She was promoted from intern to a research assistant in the Office of the Deputy Assistant Secretary of HEW for Planning and Evaluation, which develops policy and manages the decision-making process for major proposals to Congress. In the spring of 1979 her supervisor evaluated her performance as excellent and she, with seven of her colleagues, received an unusual cash award with a statement by the Assistant Secretary that she had worked long hours, producing high quality work under pressure. She then served as liaison with the Food and Drug Administration, attending meetings with the Secretary of HEW (later HHS) and representatives of groups dealing with departmental policy. The high quality of her services was attested to by various officials. There is no evidence that she has engaged in any self-destructive or anti-social behavior since the fall of 1977.

Pursuant to the district court's order of January 3, 1978, Doe filed a complaint with OCR in January, 1978. OCR investigated her claim, and on August 14, 1979, its Regional Director, Charles Tejada, issued a letter to her attorney finding that she had been discriminated against by NYU in violation of § 504. . . . Efforts by OCR to effectuate a conciliation failed. The Department of Education, which had the power to seek enforcement of OCR's ruling, declined to do so or to seek a cut-off of federal funding, in view of the pendency of the present action.

. . . On August 6, 1981, Doe moved for a preliminary injunction and subsequently NYU cross-moved for summary judgment.

. . .

In a decision issued on September 25, 1981, Judge Goettel found that Doe was a "handicapped person" under § 504 and implementing regulations, 34 C.F.R. § 104.3(j) and 45 C.F.R. § 84.3(j). He stated that whether she was "otherwise qualified" for admission to NYU Medical School depended on whether her psychiatric symptoms would recur, preventing her from performing as a medical student and causing her to pose a danger to herself and others. In deciding this issue the judge discounted the testimony of the psychiatrists on both sides and relied upon Doe's "actual behavior and condition over the past five years." He also gave no weight to the findings of the OCR except for its finding that Doe was a handicapped person, since the OCR had not conducted any independent investigation, the Regional Director and Department of Education had backed away from seeking enforcement of its determination, Doe was an HEW employee at the time when the OCR recommendations were made, and there were indications of possible OCR bias in her favor, including the unauthorized disclosure to her counsel of agency action. He concluded that Doe "will more likely than not be able to complete her course of medical studies and serve creditably as a physician," that she was therefore "otherwise qualified" under the Act, and that she had been denied readmission "solely because of the handicap." . . . [H]e further concluded that NYU had failed to sustain its burden of going forward and proving that Doe was not an otherwise qualified handicapped person or that her application for readmission was rejected for reasons other than her handicap. . . .

On the question of whether a preliminary injunction should issue, Judge Goettel found that an additional year's delay in Doe's medical studies would irreparably harm her. . . . Accordingly he issued a mandatory preliminary injunction directing that Doe be readmitted to NYU Medical School pending trial of the action. . . .

DISCUSSION

Preliminary Injunctive Relief

Turning first to the propriety of preliminary injunctive relief, Doe was entitled to a preliminary injunction only upon showing (a) that she would otherwise suffer irreparable injury and (b) either (1) a likelihood of success on the merits or (2) sufficiently serious questions going to the merits.

. . .

Irreparable Injury

On this record Doe did not in our view make a sufficient showing of irreparable injury to entitle her to mandatory injunctive relief. Ordinarily a one-year delay in obtaining admission to a graduate school for the purpose of pursuing professional studies, as distinguished from interruption or termination of attendance already in progress, is insufficient to warrant an injunction in the absence of other circumstances militating in favor of such relief.

. . .

[I]t is clear in the present case that Doe, a handicapped person, was denied readmission because of her handicap. NYU has come forward with evidence that the handicap was relevant to her qualifications for readmission according to its standards which appear reasonable enough and are not challenged. She therefore bears the burden of showing that despite her handicap she is qualified. Since her admission in 1975 was obtained on her false representation that she did not suffer from any recurrent illnesses or emotional problems, that initial admission does not serve to establish that she is "otherwise qualified" under the Act except to indicate that except for her personality disorder, which involved self-destructive and antisocial behavior, she was academically acceptable. . . .

The crucial question to be resolved in determining whether Doe is "otherwise qualified" under the Act is the substantiality of the risk that her mental disturbances will recur, resulting in behavior harmful to herself and others. The district court adopted as its test that she must be deemed qualified if it appeared "more likely than not" that she could complete her medical training and serve as a physician without recurrence of her self-destructive and antisocial conduct. We disagree with this standard. In our view she would not be qualified for readmission if there is a significant risk of such recurrence. It would be unreasonable to infer that Congress intended to force institutions to accept or readmit persons who pose a significant risk of harm to themselves or others, even if the chances of harm were less than 50%. Indeed, even if she presents any appreciable risk of such harm, this factor could properly be taken into account in deciding whether, among qualified applicants, it rendered her less qualified than others for the limited number of places available. In view of the seriousness of the harm inflicted in prior episodes, NYU is not required to give preference to her over other qualified applicants who do not pose any such appreciable risk at all.

The evidence in the record before us indicates that there is a significant risk that Doe will have a recurrence of her mental disorder, with resulting danger to herself and to others with whom she would be associated as a medical student. Several psychiatrists and mental institutions enjoying excellent reputations in their field, . . . have diagnosed her as suffering from a serious condition known as a "Borderline Personality" disorder which is likely to continue through most of her adult life. The seriousness of its manifestations can only be minimized by treatment by well-trained therapists over a long period of time and by the adoption of a lifestyle that avoids stress of the unusual types faced in medical training and practice. . . . The non-recurrence of Doe's self-destructive and antisocial activity for the past four years, during which she has peacefully coexisted with others, is attributed to the fact that the types of stress to which she has been subjected at the Harvard School of Public Health and as an HEW employee do not approximate the seriousness of those which she would experience as a medical student and doctor.[9] Moreover, her history indicates that although there were no manifestations of disorder for seven years after the earlier episodes in 1963–64, they recurred during the period 1972–1977, indicating that despite a period of dormancy they may recur again.

In support of her claim Doe, on the other hand, has offered the opinions of various psychiatrists . . . to the effect that she is fit to pursue a medical career. . . . However, none of these psychiatrists rules out the risk that she may suffer a recurrence. . . .

For the reasons stated by the district court, it acted properly in refusing to give any weight to the findings of the OCR and, if the action is tried, they should not be accepted as evidence. On the other hand, the court erred in ruling that it would disregard for the most part Doe's prior psychiatric history and treat the expert testimony as being of lesser reliability than her recent behavior. In light of the type of behavioral disorder presented, which could result in a recurrence after a dormant period, expert opinion was entitled to greater weight in reaching a decision as to whether Doe was qualified. The court is required to perform the disagreeable task of considering Doe's entire psychiatric history and weighing the expert testimony on each side.

In our view, Doe, in addition to her failure to show threatened irreparable injury, has not on this record established any likelihood of success in proving that despite her handicap she is qualified for acceptance as a medical student or to engage in the practice of medicine. Moreover, while there may possibly be questions going to the merits that are sufficiently serious to make them a fair ground for litigation, the evidence indicates that there is a significant risk of recurrence of her self-destructive and harmful conduct, which NYU should not be required to bear pending trial and that a substantial basis exists for upholding NYU's decision to deny her readmission.[10] . . . Accordingly, the grant of a mandatory preliminary injunction must be reversed.

9. There appears to be a great deal of medical literature supporting the view that medical students and physicians are subject to exceptional stresses. See, e.g., Combs, Mastering Medicine (Free Press, 1978), where the author, based on 10 years of research states:

"The rigors of medical training, especially during the early stages, tend to place a severe strain upon the mental, emotional, and physical well-being of students. . . . (p. 111).

"Many medical recruits who withdraw from medical school do so not because they are academically incompetent but because they succumb to adversity and emotional strain." (p. 133).

See also, Tokarz, Bremer and Peters, *Beyond Survival*, Work-group on Physician Well-Being, Resident Physicians Section, American Medical Association, Chicago (1979).

10. Care must be exercised by schools and employers (and courts assessing their decisions under 504) not to permit prior

Summary Judgment

NYU would be entitled to summary judgment only upon showing that there is no genuine issue as to material facts which would mandate a judgment in its favor as a matter of law. Although on the record before us Doe has not shown a likelihood of success on the merits and, on the contrary, it appears quite likely that NYU would prevail at trial, some material facts relied upon by NYU are not attested to on personal knowledge, as required by F.R.Civ.P. 56(e), but are summaries by counsel of information contained in depositions, medical records and reports. . . .

Accordingly, the district court's denial of NYU's motion for summary judgment is affirmed . . . . .

NOTES

1. Upon remand, New York University moved to dismiss the cause of action with prejudice after the plaintiff had sought extended delays and adjournments. The plaintiff opposed this request, and the district court dismissed without prejudice.

The plaintiff is still seeking admission to medical school. At present, she is a civil servant involved with health policy issues related to the Medicare and Medicaid programs. Telephone interview with plaintiff in Doe v. New York University (Nov. 18, 1983).

2. In Board of Curators, University of Missouri v. Horowitz, 435 U.S. 78, 98 S.Ct. 948, 55 L.Ed.2d 124 (1978), the Supreme Court reviewed the procedures followed when a medical student was expelled for having an abrasive manner and an untidy, unclean appearance along with unsatisfactory performance in her clinical placements. The Court held that the procedures, which included numerous warnings and informal discussion of her unsatisfactory clinical performance, were constitutional despite the absence of a formal, adversarial hearing.

3. In Cannon v. University of Chicago, 441 U.S. 677, 99 S.Ct. 1946, 60 L.Ed. 2d 560 (1979), the plaintiff had alleged that the medical schools' age policies effectively eliminated persons over 35 years of age and that this tendency had a disparate impact on women, who tend to interrupt their studies to raise families. She alleged that these actions were a violation of Title IX of the Education Amendments of 1972. The Supreme Court held that the plaintiff could bring a private cause of action under Title IX against the universities that she alleged had discriminated against her on the basis of sex in denying her admission to their medical schools.

On remand, the district court dismissed the plaintiff's complaint. The Court of Appeals for the Seventh Circuit affirmed 648 F.2d 1104 (1981), and the Supreme Court denied a writ of certiorari 454 U.S. 1128, 102 S.Ct. 981, 71 L.Ed.2d 117 (1981), and ___ U.S. ___, 103 S.Ct. 1254, 75 L.Ed.2d 482 (1983). The Court of Appeals determined that the Supreme Court had held only that Title IX implied a private right of action and that the Court did not reach the sufficiency of her complaint against other Rule 12(b)(6) motions. 648 F.2d at 1106. The court held that the plaintiff's allegations of disparate impact of the medical schools' age policies upon women did not establish a violation of Title IX. Id. at 1109–10. The court said that an "illegal intent to discriminate cannot be posited solely upon a failure to equalize an apparent disparate impact." Id. at 1110.

4. Do admission requirements for law school or the bar raise similar issues? See, e.g., Application of Ronwin, 113 Ariz. 357, 555 P.2d 315 (1976) (Arizona Supreme Court upheld state's Committee on Examinations and Admissions in re-

mental illness to be routinely regarded as a disqualification. This case, however, involves not simply a prior mental illness; Doe has been diagnosed as having a recog- nized disorder for which long-term treatment has been prescribed by competent psychiatrists and Doe has declined to accept such recommended treatment.

fusing to certify applicant as "mentally and physically able" to practice law; Court described admission to the bar as "privilege" and determined Committee had "duty" to exclude persons who could not meet established standards), certiorari denied 430 U.S. 907, 97 S.Ct. 1178, 51 L.Ed.2d 583 (1977). In 1978, Ronwin sued the Committee on Examinations and Admissions, each member of the Committee and each committee member's spouse, seeking $1.2 million dollars in damages. He claimed that the bar examiners' practice of predetermining how many applicants will pass the bar examination and then calculating what will be a passing score violates federal antitrust laws. The district court dismissed his cause of action, but the Court of Appeals for the Ninth Circuit reinstated it against the Committee on Examinations and Admissions members. 686 F.2d 692 (1981). The Supreme Court granted a writ of certiorari in May 1983. Hoover v. Ronwin, ___ U.S. ___, 103 S.Ct. 2084, 77 L.Ed.2d 296 (1983). See generally Browning, Fail the Bar, Sue the Examiners, 69 A.B.A.J. 1656 (1983).

PRESIDENT'S COMMISSION FOR THE STUDY OF ETHICAL PROBLEMS IN MEDICINE AND BIOMEDICAL AND BEHAVIORAL RESEARCH, MAKING HEALTH CARE DECISIONS

130–131, 136–142 (1982).

Some observers have argued that the quickest and most effective way to turn out doctors of broadly humane sympathies who are both committed to and skilled in communicating with patients is to admit to medical school more people likely to have such characteristics. While this strategy is appealing in theory, there is little evidence that such individuals can be readily identified, much less that the characteristics of people admitted to medical school are translated into their traits when they become physicians relating to patients.

. . .

Medical educators, students, and the public have become increasingly critical of medical education. Professional and popular journals abound with articles pointing out the defects in medical education and suggesting ways to correct them.

The traditional medical school curriculum is divided into two years of preclinical course work followed by two years of clinical rotations through various medical and surgical specialties. This division has often been criticized for being unnecessarily sharp and counterproductive. The basic sciences may seem irrelevant when presented outside the patient care context. The transition from preclinical to clinical work is abrupt and stressful, and once in clinical rotations there may be little opportunity to digress into nonclinical areas or to apply behavioral science concepts to the clinical aspects of patient care.

In addition, several other factors are commonly cited as contributing to a general climate that hinders the development of attitudes necessary for the humane practice of medicine. First, the explosion in medical technology has resulted in a massive and rapidly expanding body of facts that must be assimilated by students. . . . [M]any critics contend that students spend too much time memorizing and not enough time learning problem-solving and observation skills. Especially during the first two years of medical school, intellectual thought may be stifled because the expectation (as reflected in examinations) is that students should simply memorize and regurgitate facts rather than learn to apply information and concepts to solving problems.

Second, many physicians and medical educators have noted that students spend relatively little time learning medicine at the bedside with "wise old doctors." Instead, their role models typically are students and house officers with not much more experience than the students have.

. . .

Moreover, due to the large number of medical students, limited faculty, and the need for clinical training to occur in small groups, medical schools typically draw a substantial proportion of their clinical teachers from the surrounding community. Control over what such part-time faculty teach, how it is taught, and the coherence and consistency of the material may be limited. It is particularly difficult to monitor or control the attitudes and implicit values projected by this diverse, numerous, adjunct faculty to ensure that they foster the desired attitudinal changes.

A third problem derives from the fact that typically each health profession carries out its own educational program in isolation from the others. Thus although doctors and nurses eventually practice together, they are rarely trained explicitly to collaborate. As the role of nurses has expanded to include substantial portions of what was traditionally the exclusive domain of medicine, there is an increased need to clarify and coordinate the roles of the two professions. Nowhere is this need greater than in communications with patients to ensure they receive the information they need to make health care decisions.

Finally, concern has been voiced about a disproportionate amount of physicians' training taking place in university hospitals. The principal criticism is that these highly specialized, sophisticated, technological centers prepare doctors poorly for the day-to-day practice of medicine elsewhere. . . .

These are but some of the concrete criticisms of medical education. Each has important implications for the particular elements of physician training that are of greatest concern here, namely the structuring of underlying values and attitudes conducive to the goals of effective patient participation in health care decisionmaking.

Curricular Innovations. Numerous innovations and experiments in medical education have been designed to address these issues. These include course offerings in the behavioral sciences and humanities, increased exposure to outpatient medical care, faculty development, alterations in grading systems designed to reduce competition (for example, the pass-fail grading now used by most schools), the restructuring and reordering of curricula to integrate the basic sciences with patient care, and some limited efforts and combined training of medical and nursing students. Innovations such as these have been introduced in traditional medical schools, in combined six- or seven-year college and medical school programs, and in the new community-based medical schools, where the entire curriculum has often been designed to foster a changed outlook on health care.

The teaching of social and behavioral sciences in medical schools began in the mid-1950s in an attempt to educate physicians about a variety of influences on patient behavior and to train them to assess patient needs. The social sciences tended to be taught in classrooms during the preclinical years; hence, students often found it difficult to appreciate their relevance to medical care. Moreover, the material taught by social scientists was typically not reinforced during clinical training and suffered from a lack of integration with the rest of the curriculum. By the 1970s the programs were beginning to decline, having never overcome some people's initial "romantic overenthusiasm" or others' "skeptical noninvolvement."

About this time, a new movement began in medical education—teaching humanities with a focus on the human values underlying the physician-patient relationship and medical practice. With this came courses in medical ethics, aimed initially at value questions that were being highlighted by rapid technological developments, by shifts in medical care delivery, and by the renewed interest of moral philosophers and lawyers in [such] issues. . . . Unlike the earlier social science movement, this human values movement has been aware since its inception of the need to collaborate with other departments, to educate faculty as well as students, and to integrate its teaching with students' clinical assignments.

Despite impressive modifications of the curricula, most courses in the behavioral sciences and humanities are offered primarily as electives. The students who take them are therefore self-selected and already aware of the importance of the subject.

Half the physicians in the Commission's survey had received "some formal training" in medical ethics while in medical school; 36%, some training in medical law; and 54%, some formal training in physician-patient communications. The exact meaning of "some formal training" is unclear in light of the Medical Student Graduation Questionnaire Survey conducted by the AAMC in 1981, in which only 5% of the 10,795 students questioned reported having taken actual courses in ethical problems in medicine, and less than 3% reported courses in medical jurisprudence and in the behavioral and social sciences. When graduates were asked to assess the adequacy of the time spent in such areas as patient-interviewing skills, management of patients' socioeconomic, educational, and emotional problems, and teamwork with other health professionals, sizable proportions of them felt that too little time had been devoted to each of these topics. Thus it appears that relatively few recent medical graduates have been exposed to these curricular innovations and that many find their training inadequate in a number of areas relevant to informed consent.

Unfortunately, very little is known about the effects of these courses upon the attitudes and behaviors of even the self-selected fraction of medical students who take them. Standard examinations and evaluations by students of their professors and courses only indicate what has been learned and liked, not whether attitudes and behaviors towards patient care have been affected. Unlike clinical techniques, which can be directly observed and assessed, the ultimate effects of these teachings in the behavioral sciences have eluded direct study. . . .

**DAVID E. REISER AND ANDREA K. SCHRODER,
PATIENT INTERVIEWING**

90–93, 96 (1980).

FEARS AND FANTASIES ABOUT WHAT CONSTITUTES
PROFESSIONAL BEHAVIOR

What is a doctor? Even in simpler times than these, people's perceptions of doctors were enigmatic, extreme, and often paradoxical. Is the doctor a wise, sympathetic healer who sits patiently at the bedside sometimes holding his dying patient's hand? Or is he the austere, emotionally unapproachable "brain surgeon" who nevertheless performs brilliant and miraculous operations? Images of the wise, humane physician commingle uneasily in our minds with the image of Dr. Frankenstein, the scientist who flirted with life's ultimate mysteries, who had commerce with forces dark and uncontrollable. In our current social climate, the paradoxes are even more abundant. The glowing accolades that accompany medicine's unparalleled technical advances coexist with an increasingly restive and suspicious public image of physicians as greedy, technologically obsessed, compassionless, incompetent, and grandiose. It is no doubt inevitable that anyone linked as closely with the fundamentals of human existence as a doctor would be perceived with such ambivalence. At no time in history have the paradoxes been more abundant and seemingly irreconcilable.

The physician himself is not immune to these fragmented and conflicting views of what a doctor really is. Doctors at all levels of training and experience are currently experiencing a considerable crisis of identity, self-esteem, and purpose. The beginning student is particularly vulnerable. In the midst of this confusion, the student has a strong and understandable psychological need for an image of stability, coherence, and confidence. Just as societies in times of great turmoil turn to strong charismatic leaders, so do students during a period of major internal upheaval and loss of identity search for some strong, charismatic image of the ideal physician.

The images, myths, and fantasies about this figure change over time for each student and vary considerably in their details from student to student. The common thread that links all students, however, is the wish for a model to aspire to and perhaps initially to imitate until its ideal characteristics can be internalized.

Three "caricatures" of the charismatic physician are identified below—there are doubtless more. They are the wise professor, the humane generalist, and Captain Medicine. Not only do these three images often commingle in a student's mind, but, more importantly, each figure is perceived with some ambivalence, as we shall see.

The Wise Professor

These are older clinicians, usually men, often department heads, almost always full professors. Often they wear long white coats and have at least some distinguished trace of gray. Typically they have achieved national prominence in some specialized area of research, but they also retain stature as senior clinicians.

Viewing them from afar, students see in such mentors symbols of absolute calm, inner equanimity, and unflappable self-assurance. These traits are most appealing at a time in the student's development when they hardly characterize his own experience.

On the other hand, students can perceive these same professors at other times in a very different, and negative way. They are the aloof administrators cut off from real patient care. They are the scientists, more interested in research than in human beings. Finally, like all patriarchal symbols, the wise professor walks perilously close to the "dottering old fool." It is not uncommon for a student's image of one of these heroes to be shattered when he hears younger housestaff say that this professor is, in fact, totally out of date and hasn't written "anything worth a damn" in the last 10 years.

The Compassionate Generalist

Call him Dr. Welby or Dr. Jones. For most medical students, as for much of society, there runs a deep respect and affection for our image of the wise, humane, warm family doctor. The recent resurgence of interest in family medicine among many medical students doubtless reflects this respect and perhaps a longing to get back to "the basics." As the popularity of the TV show makes clear, the basis of our longing for this archetypal hero runs deep.   . . .

. . .

It is often the image of the compassionate generalist that most shapes a student's notion of physicianhood prior to beginning medical training. In most training centers, however, generalists are nowhere to be found. Thus, the image of the generalist's good qualities becomes based more on fantasy than actual exposure to real models. In contrast, students also hear a great deal that is pejorative.

The compassionate generalist is referred to by many housestaff as "the LMD" (local medical doctor)—a dumb jerk who is so out of date with recent journals that he can't order the right tests and sends his disasters to the medical center to be saved when it's all but too late. He is also a money grubber, an excessively affluent business man of medicine who owns two Cadillacs and a funmobile. Finally, he is an ignorant sentimentalist—a hand holder—because he lacks the skills and technical expertise to cure his patients of rare diseases. Many of these negative stereotypes are reinforced by the third charismatic type.

Captain Medicine

In our experience, it is the interns and residents who ultimately exert the most powerful influence as role models for medical students. This is less apparent in the first 2 years of medical education, when a great deal of time is taken up with basic science lectures. The clinical courses that are offered in these first 2 years—notably, introduction to clinical medicine courses—are typically taught by faculty. Early in the student's education, however, the image of the houseofficer emerges vividly. He is the exhausted yet somehow dashing figure toting a bellboy and dressed in surgical greens. He is the one who knows just what to do when that disastrous motorcycle accident is brought into the emergency room. He starts the i.v., gives the bicarb. He administers the cardiac massage. It is he who seems comfortable with the catastrophic, overwhelming, and unimaginable. It is he who has the latest journal article at his fingertips. Always, the student remembers that it is this figure who the student will become in just a few short years.

During the junior and senior years, resident housestaff exert a truly profound influence on medical students. Here is a description by one of the authors of his impression of houseofficers when he was a junior student.

> I remember those weeks vividly. The sounds and smells . . . I have never felt so helpless or inadequate . . . perhaps I was too impressionable. As I look back on the experience, it's clear I wasn't emulating the medical techniques of houseofficers, but rather their style of adaptation to stress. It was very strange. Under normal circumstances I would have seen these people for what they were: students a little older than I with strengths and weaknesses of their own. But somehow my sense of inadequacy at that time made it necessary to take them for models.
>
> Basically what I learned from my young mentors was that preparing oneself for an admitting night . . . is like preparing for battle. We don callousness like a suit of armor.

Houseofficers epitomize both the best and worst of medicine. A seasoned 3rd year surgery resident may well be at the pinnacle of his emergency room prowess; his technical skills, his knowledge of the latest procedures, and his ability to implement them can be awesome. At the same time, he may be callous, brusque, and harsh to the people entrusted to his care. Overwhelmed by the demands placed on him—for omniscience in the face of sleeplessness, omnipotence in the face of overwhelming suffering—the houseofficer is not at a stage in his own development that permits him to be receptive to himself, warm, or well rounded.

Perhaps, partly from his own sense of guilt, this houseofficer is often prone to mock such qualities in other physicians. Generalists are handholders. Older clinicians are "behind the times." Medical students who show too much feeling for their patients are "impressionable" and "green."

. . .

[S]tudents are usually quickly surprised to discover how therapeutic their interactions with patients turn out to be. Usually students quickly rediscover the strength of their own personalities. Positive patient responses and appropriate reinforcement by the preceptor lead to a reawakening of confidence in the student's own natural abilities. It is a vulnerable period, however. Like a seedling, the student's re-emerging self-esteem needs a fertile climate of support, meaningful encouragement, and helpful criticism to grow. A few put-downs or an upsetting or disruptive patient interview can leave the student feeling unsure again. Unfortunately, we all too often witness the phenomenon of students who begin to develop a sense of themselves, only later to feel humiliated by more advanced students and houseofficers.

It is important to remember that, in a world increasingly populated by technologists and machines, the most precious gift a doctor has to offer a patient is still himself. Rediscovering the therapeutic potential of one's own personality, therefore, is one of the important goals of any introductory interviewing experience.

. . .

NOTE

Residents are licensed physicians engaged in postgraduate training at hospitals with approved residency programs. A major element of surgical training is resident participation in surgery under the supervision of specialists or board certified surgeons. Indeed, a physician must have "major operative experience involving senior/chief responsibility" to obtain American Board of Surgery certification. Accordingly, in teaching hospitals attending physicians, whom patients have selected to perform surgery, often permit residents to perform major portions of the surgical procedure. When residents participate in surgery without the patient's knowledge or consent, the practice is commonly called "ghost surgery."

Is ghost surgery a violation of the patient's right to be informed only if the attending physician does not actually supervise the resident? If the patient does not consent to the resident's participation? If patient consent is required, would the requirement result in substantially fewer opportunities for residents to gain experience? Are patient interests satisfied if patients know the names of the persons ultimately responsible for their surgical care? Would your answers change if it could be shown that patients suffer no harm as a result of the practice? Finally, are the physicians who supervise the residents receiving unjustified compensation?

For a discussion of these issues, see Holmes, Ghost Surgery, 56 Bull.N.Y.Acad. Med. 412 (1980); Siegel, Surgical Training, Quality Surgical Care and Informed Consent, 56 Bull.N.Y.Acad.Med. 433 (1980); Joint Commission on Accreditation of Hospitals, Accreditation Manual for Hospitals xiii-xiv (1983 ed.); 2 Directory of Medical Specialists 3592 (20th ed.1981).

For additional discussion of informed consent requirements, see Ch. 3, Sec. B.1., infra.

3.   DISCIPLINING FOR MISCONDUCT AND FRAUD

a.   The Role of Licensure

FORZIATI v. BOARD OF REGISTRATION IN MEDICINE

Supreme Judicial Court of Massachusetts, 1955.
333 Mass. 125, 128 N.E.2d 789.

QUA, C.J. All parties seek a declaratory decree as to the jurisdiction of the board to discipline the plaintiff, a duly registered and licensed doctor of medicine, upon charges made upon information filed with the board by "the Massachusetts Claim Investigation" and the Massachusetts Medical Society and contained in a letter to the plaintiff from the board dated June 3, 1954, as amplified in greater detail in a second letter dated January 25, 1955.

The charges in substance are that in the years 1945 to 1949, inclusive, the plaintiff was engaged in a conspiracy with one Centracchio, an attorney at law, by which the plaintiff solicited persons who had claims for damages for personal injuries and who came to him as patients to employ Centracchio to prosecute their claims, and in return, after paying the plaintiff by check for his medical services, Centracchio paid him in cash further sums representing in each instance the difference between the amount of the medical bill and one half of the combined medical and legal fees. In this way the doctor and the lawyer each received the same amount in each case without regard to the relative amounts of work performed by them. One hundred thirty-eight instances of this form of fee splitting are enumerated in the detailed specifications set forth in the second letter of the board. If true, the figures show that during the entire period the plaintiff received in cash as "kick backs" from the lawyer a total sum considerably in excess of $8,000, while during the same period he received by check as his medical fees a substantially smaller sum.

The jurisdiction of the board to proceed in the matter rests upon G.L. (Ter.Ed.) c. 112, § 61, which provides, among other things, that the board may "suspend, revoke or cancel any certificate, registration, license or authority issued by it" if it appears to the board that the holder thereof "is guilty of deceit, malpractice, gross misconduct in the practise of his profession, or any offence against the laws of the commonwealth relating thereto."

We think it clear that if the charges are established the board can find that the plaintiff was guilty of "gross misconduct in the practice of his profession."

. . . Our . . . decisions and those of other jurisdictions fully recognize the strongly professional and confidential nature of the practice of medicine, as well as the necessity for the observance of high moral standards in connection with it. In Lawrence v. Board of Registration in Medicine, 239 Mass. 424, 132 N.E. 174, this court said through Chief Justice Rugg, "Soundness of moral fibre to insure the proper use of medical learning is as essential to the public health as medical learning itself. . . . Highly trained intelligence combined with disregard of the fundamental virtues is a menace." 239 Mass. at page 429, 132 N.E. at page 176.

. . .

The fee splitting operations of the plaintiff were in plain conflict with his moral obligations as a physician. It might be enough to say that very few of the plaintiff's patients would be pleased to know that the plaintiff had received in addition to his medical bill a further sum out of his patient's money for no service rendered to the patient. The whole scheme was in violation of the trust and confidence reposed in both the lawyer and the doctor. It tended to increase expenses unduly. It was an inducement to the fomenting of litigation, to the exaggeration of claims, to false testimony, and even to the lessening of the proper interest of the doctor in promptly curing his patients, and it diverted patients from honest lawyers to the detriment of the administration of justice. Moreover, the plaintiff's conduct was in violation of G.L. (Ter.Ed.) c. 221, § 43, as appearing in St.1939, c. 197, § 1, which forbids attorneys to employ "runner[s]" and forbids persons to act as "runner[s]" for attorneys. It may be well to add here that the records of this court show that the lawyer member of this medico-legal team has already been disbarred. Matter of Centracchio, Suffolk Law, No. 53628, Order of March 23, 1954.

We are of opinion that the misconduct of the plaintiff, if proved as charged, could be found to have been "gross" within the meaning of c. 112, § 61. The scheme here carried out for a series of years between these two men of different learned professions was no matter of mere peccadillo. It tended seriously to undermine public confidence in both professions. If such conduct became the rule, rather than, fortunately, the exception the effect could be disastrous. The amount of money involved was substantial. That both parties knew this conduct was wrong is strongly suggested by the pains taken through all this time to separate the legitimate payments always made by check from the illegitimate payments always made in cash. Gross misconduct in the practice of his profession is not too indefinite as a ground for discipline of a registered physician by the board. Lawrence v. Board of Registration in Medicine, 239 Mass. 424, 428–430, 132 N.E. 174.

. . .

We are also of opinion that the misconduct of the plaintiff could be found to have been "in the practise of his profession." These words of § 61 are not in our opinion limited, as the plaintiff would have us believe, to that which is done in the diagnosis and treatment of the patient. We are satisfied that they were intended to include all conduct of the practitioner in carrying on his professional activities. Fee splitting was one of the methods adopted by the plaintiff in his practice of medicine. Any narrower interpretation of the statute would leave it inadequate to cope with many conditions that might arise.

. . .

We are of opinion, however, that no separate charge can be made against the plaintiff for acting as a "runner" based on the ground that such conduct was an "offence against the laws of the commonwealth relating" to the practice of medicine. Chapter 221, § 43, forbidding persons to act as "runner[s]" can hardly be described as a law relating to the practice of medicine. See Giroux v. Board of Dental Examiners, 322 Mass. 251, 252, 76 N.E.2d 758. It relates rather to the practice of law. Nevertheless the plaintiff, in common with all other people, was bound by it, and if he violated it, that fact may be considered in determining whether he was guilty of "misconduct in the practise of his profession" and whether such misconduct was "gross."

A final decree is to be entered to the effect that the board has jurisdiction under G.L. (Ter.Ed.) c. 112, § 61, to proceed against the plaintiff on the charge of gross misconduct in the practice of his profession.

So ordered.

MILTON FRIEDMAN, CAPITALISM AND FREEDOM

149–60 (1962).

The medical profession is one in which practice of the profession has for a long time been restricted to people with licenses. Offhand, the question, "Ought we to let incompetent physicians practice?" seems to admit of only a negative answer. But I want to urge that second thought may give pause.

In the first place, licensure is the key to the control that the medical profession can exercise over the number of physicians. To understand why this is so requires some discussion of the structure of the medical profession. The American Medical Association is perhaps the strongest trade union in the United States. The essence of the power of a trade union is its power to restrict the number who may engage in a particular occupation. This restriction may be exercised indirectly by being able to enforce a wage rate higher than would otherwise prevail. If such a wage rate can be enforced, it will reduce the number of people who can get jobs and thus indirectly the number of people pursuing the occupation. This technique of restriction has disadvantages. There is always a dissatisfied fringe of people who are trying to get into the occupation. A trade union is much better off if it can limit directly the number of people who enter the occupation—who ever try to get jobs in it. The disgruntled and dissatisfied are excluded at the outset, and the union does not have to worry about them.

The American Medical Association is in this position. It is a trade union that can limit the number of people who can enter. How can it do this? The essential control is at the stage of admission to medical school. The Council on Medical Education and Hospitals of the American Medical Association approves medical schools. In order for a medical school to get and stay on its list of approved schools it has to meet the standards of the Council. The power of the Council has been demonstrated at various times when there has been pressure to reduce numbers. For example, in the 1930's during the depression, the Council on Medical Education and Hospitals wrote a letter to the various medical schools saying the medical schools were admitting more students than could be given the proper kind of training. In the next year or two, every school reduced the number it was admitting, giving very strong presumptive evidence that the recommendation had some effect.

Why does the Council's approval matter so much? If it abuses its power, why don't unapproved medical schools arise? The answer is that in almost every state in the United States, a person must be licensed to practice medicine, and to get the license, he must be a graduate of an approved school. In almost every state, the list of approved schools is identical with the list of schools approved by the Council on Medical Education and Hospitals of the American Medical Association. That is why the licensure provision is the key to the effective control of admission. It has a dual effect. On the one hand, the members of the licensure commission are always physicians and hence have some control at the step at which men apply for a license. This control is more limited in effectiveness than control at the medical school level. In almost all professions requiring licensure, people may try to get admitted more than once. If a person tries long enough and in enough jurisdictions he is likely to get through sooner or later. Since he has already spent the money and time to get his training, he has a strong incentive to keep trying. Licensure provisions that come into operation only after a man is trained therefore affect entry largely by raising the costs of getting into the occupation, since it may take a longer time to get in and since there is always some uncertainty whether he will succeed. But this rise in cost is nothing like so effective in limiting entry as is preventing a man from getting started on his career. If he is eliminated at the stage of entering medical school, he never comes up as a candidate for examination; he can never be troublesome at that stage. The efficient way to get control over the number in a profession is therefore to get control of entry into professional schools.

Control over admission to medical school and later licensure enables the profession to limit entry in two ways. The obvious one is simply by turning down many applicants. The less obvious, but probably far more important one, is by establishing standards for admission and licensure that make entry so difficult as to discourage young people from ever trying to get admission. Though most state laws require only two years of college prior to medical school, nearly 100 per cent of the entrants have had four years of college. Similarly, medical training proper has been lengthened, particularly through more stringent internship arrangements.

.   .   .

[I]t is the provision about graduation from approved schools that is the most important source of professional control over entry. The profession has used this control to limit numbers. To avoid misunderstanding let me emphasize that I am not saying that individual members of the medical profession, the leaders of the medical profession, or the people who are in charge of the Council on Medical Education and Hospitals deliberately go out of their way to limit entry in order to raise their own incomes. That is not the way it works. Even when such people explicitly comment on the desirability of limiting numbers to raise incomes they will always justify the policy on the grounds that if "too" many people are let in, this will lower their incomes so that they will be driven to resort to unethical practices in order to earn a "proper" income. The only way, they argue, in which ethical practices can be maintained is by keeping people at a standard of income which is adequate to the merits and needs of the medical profession. I must confess that this has always seemed to me objectionable on both ethical and factual grounds. It is extraordinary that leaders of medicine should proclaim publicly that they and their colleagues must be paid to be ethical. And if it were so, I doubt that the price would have any limit. There seems little correlation between poverty and honesty. One would rather expect the opposite; dishonesty may not always pay but surely it sometimes does.

Control of entry is explicitly rationalized along these lines only at times like the Great Depression when there is much unemployment and relatively low incomes. In ordinary times, the rationalization for restriction is different. It is that the members of the medical profession want to raise what they regard as the standards of "quality" of the profession. The defect in this rationalization is a common one, and one that is destructive of a proper understanding of the operation of an economic system, namely, the failure to distinguish between technical efficiency and economic efficiency.

A story about lawyers will perhaps illustrate the point. At a meeting of lawyers at which problems of admission were being discussed, a colleague of mine, arguing against restrictive admission standards, used an analogy from the automobile industry. Would it not, he said, be absurd if the automobile industry were to argue that no one should drive a low quality car and therefore that no automobile manufacturer should be permitted to produce a car that did not come up to the Cadillac standard. One member of the audience rose and approved the analogy, saying that, of course, the country cannot afford anything but Cadillac lawyers! This tends to be the professional attitude. The members look solely at technical standards of performance, and argue in effect that we must have only first-rate physicians even if this means that some people get no medical service—though of course they never put it that way. Nonetheless, the view that people should get only the "optimum" medical service always lead to a restrictive policy, a policy that keeps down the number of physicians. I would not, of course, want to argue that this is the only force at work, but only that this kind of consideration leads many well-meaning physicians to go along with policies that they would reject out-of-hand if they did not have this kind of comforting rationalization.

It is easy to demonstrate that quality is only a rationalization and not the underlying reason for restriction. The power of the Council on Medical Education and Hospitals of the American Medical Association has been used to limit numbers in ways that cannot possibly have any connection whatsoever with quality. The simplest example is their recommendation to various states that citizenship be made a requirement for the practice of medicine. I find it inconceivable to see how this is relevant to medical performance. A similar requirement that they have tried to impose on occasion is that examination for licensure must be taken in English. . . .

. . .

. . . Let me now ask the question: Does licensure have the good effects that it is said to have?

In the first place, does it really raise standards of competence? It is by no means clear that it does raise the standards of competence in the actual practice of the profession for several reasons. In the first place, whenever you establish a block to entry into any field, you establish an incentive to find ways of getting around it, and of course medicine is no exception. The rise of the professions of osteopathy and of chiropractic is not unrelated to the restriction of entry into medicine. On the contrary, each of these represented, to some extent, an attempt to find a way around restriction of entry. Each of these, in turn, is proceeding to get itself licensed, and to impose restrictions. The effect is to create different levels and kinds of practice, to distinguish between what is called medical practice and substitutes such as osteopathy, chiropractic, faith healing and so on. These alternatives may well be of lower quality than medical practice would have been without the restrictions on entry into medicine.

More generally, if the number of physicians is less than it otherwise would be, and if they are all fully occupied, as they generally are, this means that there is a smaller total of medical practice by trained physicians—fewer medical man-hours of practice, as it were. The alternative is untrained practice by somebody; it may and in part must be by people who have no professional qualifications at all. Moreover, the situation is much more extreme. If "medical practice" is to be limited to licensed practitioners, it is necessary to define what medical practice is, and featherbedding is not something that is restricted to the railroads. Under the interpretation of the statutes forbidding unauthorized practice of medicine, many things are restricted to licensed physicians that could perfectly well be done by technicians, and other skilled people who do not have a Cadillac medical training. I am not enough of a technician to list the examples at all fully. I only know that those who have looked into the question say that the tendency is to include in "medical practice" a wider and wider range of activities that could perfectly well be performed by technicians. Trained physicians devote a considerable part of their time to things that might well be done by others. The result is to reduce drastically the amount of medical care. . . .

Even these comments do not go far enough, because they consider the situation at a point in time and do not allow for changes over time. Advances in any science or field often result from the work of one out of a large number of crackpots and quacks and people who have no standing in the profession. In the medical profession, under present circumstances, it is very difficult to engage in research or experimentation unless you are a member of the profession. If you are a member of the profession and want to stay in good standing in the profession, you are seriously limited in the kind of experimentation you can do. A "faithhealer" may be just a quack who is imposing himself on credulous patients, but maybe one in a thousand or in many thousands will produce an important improvement in medicine. There are many different routes to knowledge and learning and the effect of restricting the practice of what is called medicine and defining it as we tend to do to a particular group, who in the main have to conform to the prevailing orthodoxy, is certain to reduce the amount of experimentation that goes on and hence to reduce the rate of growth of knowledge in the area. . . .

. . .

When all this is said, many a reader, I suspect, like many a person with whom I have discussed these issues, will say, "But still, how else would I get any evidence on the quality of a physician.   Granted all that you say about costs, is not licensure the only way of providing the public with some assurance of at least minimum quality?"   The answer is partly that people do not now choose physicians by picking names at random from a list of licensed physicians;   partly, that a man's ability to pass an examination twenty or thirty years earlier is hardly assurance of quality now; hence, licensure is not now the main or even a major source of assurance of at least minimum quality.   But the major answer is very different.   It is that the question itself reveals the tyranny of the status quo and the poverty of our imagination in fields in which we are laymen, and even in those in which we have some competence, by comparison with the fertility of the market.   Let me illustrate by speculating on how medicine might have developed and what assurances of quality would have emerged, if the profession had not exerted monopoly power.

Suppose that anyone had been free to practice medicine without restriction except for legal and financial responsibility for any harm done to others through fraud and negligence.   I conjecture that the whole development of medicine would have been different.   The present market for medical care, hampered as it has been, gives some hints of what the difference would have been.   Group practice in conjunction with hospitals would have grown enormously.   Instead of individual practice plus large institutional hospitals conducted by governments or eleemosynary institutions, there might have developed medical partnerships or corporations— medical teams.   These would have provided central diagnostic and treatment facilities, including hospital facilities.   Some presumably would have been prepaid, combining in one package present hospital insurance, health insurance, and group medical practice.   Others would have charged separate fees for separate services.   And of course, most might have used both methods of payment.

These medical teams—department stores of medicine, if you will— would be intermediaries between the patients and the physician.   Being long-lived and immobile, they would have a great interest in establishing a reputation for reliability and quality.   For the same reason, consumers would get to know their reputation.   They would have the specialized skill to judge the quality of physicians;   indeed, they would be the agent of the consumer in doing so, as the department store is now for many a product. In addition, they could organize medical care efficiently, combining medical men of different degrees of skill and training, using technicians with limited training for tasks for which they were suited, and reserving highly skilled and competent specialists for the tasks they alone could perform. The reader can add further flourishes for himself, drawing in part, as I have done, on what now goes on at the leading medical clinics.

Of course, not all medical practice would be done through such teams. Individual private practice would continue, just as the small store with a limited clientele exists alongside the department store, the individual lawyer alongside the great many-partnered firm.   Men would establish individual reputations and some patients would prefer the privacy and intimacy of the individual practitioner.   Some areas would be too small to be served by medical teams.   And so on.

I would not even want to maintain that the medical teams would dominate the field.   My aim is only to show by example that there are many alternatives to the present organization of practice.   The impossibility of any individual or small group conceiving of all the possibilities, let alone evaluating their merits, is the great argument against central governmental planning and against arrangements such as professional monopolies that limit the possibilities of experimentation.   On the other side, the great argument for the market is its tolerance of diversity; its ability to utilize a wide range of special knowledge and capacity.   It renders special groups impotent to prevent experimentation and permits the customers and not the producers to decide what will serve the customers best.

NOTES

1.   How could a patient distinguish between a Cadillac physician and a Chevy physician?   Even if such distinctions were possible, would anyone chose the Chevrolet version when purchasing health care, as distinguished from purchasing a car?   Does this suggest problems with Friedman's automobile analogy?

2.   Are the licensed professions essentially self-regulating as Friedman suggests?   Compare R. Derbyshire, Medical Licensure and Discipline in the United States 13–17 (1969):

For a long time physicians have prided themselves on the fact that their profession is self-regulated.   But this is true to a limited extent only; self-regulation today is confined to the medical societies which have some disciplinary powers over their members.   However, their actions have no force of law.   As far as the legal aspects of medical practice are concerned, the profession is anything but self-governing.   Although the boards of medical examiners, composed of physicians, ostensibly supervise the practice of medicine, these bodies are controlled in varying degrees by all of the branches of the state governments.

The legislature is the initial body to control the practice of medicine.   Not only does it pass the laws which define the methods of control, it also has the power to modify these by periodically amending the medical practice laws.   The executive branch of the government plays a part in the regulation of medical practice in that in most states the members of the boards of medical examiners are appointed by the governor, are accountable to him, and can be removed by him for sufficient cause.   The boards are also accountable to the judiciary; all of their actions are subject to review by the courts.   The boards of medical examiners are administrative bodies with quasi-judicial functions.   But the rights of the individual cannot be violated by the boards which have little knowledge of law and many board decisions have been reversed by the courts if they find that they have acted arbitrarily or capriciously or have failed to follow proper procedures.

. . . .

The legal control of the practice of medicine was emphasized by Shindell (1966) when he wrote, "While a medical practice act conveys special status on physicians, status is incidental to its primary purpose.   Essentially its purpose is to provide a means by which society may exercise formal control over persons designated to minister to its ills."   Shindell also points out that the importance of the medical practice act is that it is the public and not the profession who makes the rules.   He continues, "Inescapable is the fact that both the privileges and limitations of the profession are in the hands of society."

. . . .

The state, through its medical practice law, not only decides who may practice within its borders but it also defines the conditions under which the physician shall practice. Even after a license has been granted it does not become a permanent property right. The impermanence of a license is emphasized by the fact most states require periodic registration of physicians, many on an annual basis. If a physician fails to meet the registration requirement his license can be suspended and not restored until he has met certain requirements including reexamination in some instances.

. . .

The statutes give the boards of medical examiners the power to revoke licenses as well as to grant them. . . . Although boards are composed of physicians who presumably regulate their own profession, in the case of disciplinary actions, the board members can make only preliminary decisions which can be overturned by the courts and frequently are, sometimes on purely technical grounds. This is particularly true in the case of the malefactor whose crime does not fit neatly into one of the categories of unprofessional and unethical practices enumerated in the law. Complications often arise when the action of the board is based upon the vague term, "unprofessional conduct."

The idea that the medical profession is self-policing is again exploded by the fact that the conduct of disciplinary hearings in all states is carefully prescribed by law. The statutes set forth in detail the procedure which must be followed from the form of the initial notice of contemplated action, through the entire hearing, including the questioning of witnesses and the assurance that the accused be informed that he is entitled to be represented by counsel. The laws require that the findings of fact and the decision of the board be set forth in precise terms. Precautions are taken to protect the rights of the accused. This sometimes results in members of a board emerging from an attempted disciplinary action with a feeling of impotence and frustration. . . .

3. The first statute in America to control the medical profession, enacted in Virginia in 1639, regulated fees. In 1649, Massachusetts attempted for the first time to regulate the practice of medicine. The act was unenforceable, however, because of vagueness. The first act to require a licensing examination, later repealed, was enacted in New York City in 1760. In 1773, Connecticut passed a statute requiring a medical license before a physician could charge fees for treatment of the ill. By the early 1800's, almost all states had licensing boards or permitted medical societies to approve persons for licensure. After that period, however, licensing requirements were steadily diluted. Many states relied on graduation from medical schools, considering that a better indicator of competence. Others repealed their statutes and allowed anyone to practice.

This chaotic period lasted until 1873 when Texas enacted a medical practice act. This revival of licensure was in part due to the rise of professional associations, such as the American Medical Association, founded in 1847, and their desire to restore licensing to combat increases in the number of inferior medical schools and quackery. The Supreme Court gave impetus to this revival in Dent v. West Virginia, 129 U.S. 114, 9 S.Ct. 231, 32 L.Ed. 623 (1889), which upheld the constitutionality of the West Virginia medical practice act. By 1930, all states had some form of a mandatory licensure. See R. Derbyshire, Medical Licensure and Discipline in the United States (1969); R. Shryock, Medical Licensing in America, 1950–1965 (1967). Dentists, optometrists, pharmacists, osteopathic and allopathic physicians, podiatrists, veterinarians, dental hygienists and both practical and registered nurses, in addition to physicians, are currently licensed in all states. Weisfeld, Licensure of Primary Care Practitioners, A Manpower Policy for Primary Health Care (staff paper), Institute of Medicine, National Academy of Sciences 8 (1977).

4. Traditionally, the governor of a state, with the guidance of state medical societies, appoints practicing physicians to be members of the state licensing board. These boards were historically concerned with qualifications and licensing rather than discipline. Derbyshire reports that "from 1963 through 1967 . . . a total of 938 actions against physicians were taken by the boards." Sanctions

imposed varied from revocation of license (334) to reprimands (68). R. Derbyshire, Medical Licensure and Discipline in the United States 77–78 (1969).

A later study revealed that from 1968 through 1972, state boards had taken 1,971 formal actions. This number includes voluntary surrender of licenses. Derbyshire, Medical Ethics and Discipline, 228 J.A.M.A. 59, 61 (1974). Derbyshire further reports:

> During the past five years, seven states with a physician population of more than 23,000 have reported no disciplinary actions whatever. California, with a physician population of approximately 33,000, reported a total of 194. Some of the other large states reported an amazingly small number. For example, one state with a physician population of 17,000 took only six actions, all reprimands. At the opposite extreme, a state with a total of 1,200 physicians reported 25 actions. Excluding California, the five largest states with a total physician population of 104,000 reported only 140 actions. In other words, 0.58% of the California physicians were disciplined, while in the next five states, the percentage was 0.11%. Obviously, there is wide variation in the diligence of the state boards in investigating and punishing unethical physicians.

Id. Criticism of state boards, see, e.g., Report, The Secretary's Commission on Medical Malpractice, HEW Dept. Pub. No. (OS) 73–88 (1973), has resulted in the passage of updated medical practice acts in many states.

In 1969, Florida passed the first statute specifically addressing incompetent physicians, Fla.Stat.Ann. § 455.201 (West 1981). The statute provides guidelines for the Florida Department of Professional Regulation to follow when asked to investigate complaints lodged against physicians. It also specifies who should report incompetent physicians and the types of conduct that should be reported. For a comparison of the Florida, Massachusetts and New York statutes, see Fama, Reporting Incompetent Physicians: A Comparison of Requirements in Three States, 3 L.Med. & Health Care (1983). For a case extending coverage of the state Healing Act to include "extreme incompetency," see Kansas State Board of Healing Acts v. Foote, 200 Kan. 447, 436 P.2d 828 (1968).

5. In addition to licensure, the other methods of credentialing health care providers are certification, a professional organization's recognition of an individual's competence; registration, the listing, with a public or private source, of persons viewed as competent to provide certain services; and finally, accreditation (as Friedman discussed, supra), the approval by public or private institutions to provide designated care or training of individuals. Do you think these other methods are more effective than licensure in controlling entry into a profession? Friedman suggests, for example, that accreditation is more effective than licensure. Do you agree?

b. What Is Fraud?

CHARLES BABBAGE,
REFLECTIONS ON THE DECLINE OF SCIENCE IN ENGLAND, AND SOME OF ITS CAUSES

174–179 (1830).

Scientific inquiries are more exposed than most others to the inroads of pretenders; and I feel that I shall deserve the thanks of all who really value truth, by stating some of the methods of deceiving practised by unworthy claimants for its honours, whilst the mere circumstance of their arts being known may deter future offenders.

There are several species of impositions that have been practised in science, which are but little known, except to the initiated, and which it may perhaps be possible to render quite intelligible to ordinary understandings. These may be classed under the heads of hoaxing, forging, trimming, and cooking.

Of Hoaxing. This, perhaps, will be better explained by an example. In the year 1788, M. Gioeni, a knight of Malta, published at Naples an account of a new family of Testacea, of which he described, with great minuteness, one species, the specific name of which has been taken from its *habitat*, and the generic he took from his own family, calling it Gioenia Sicula. It consisted of two rounded triangular valves, united by the body of the animal to a smaller valve in front. He gave figures of the animal, and of its parts; described its structure, its mode of advancing along the sand, the figure of the tract it left, and estimated the velocity of its course at about two-thirds of an inch per minute. He then described the structure of the shell, which he treated with nitric acid, and found it approach nearer to the nature of bone than any other shell.

The editors of the *Encyclopédie Methodique*, have copied this description, and have given figures of the Gioenia Sicula. The fact, however, is, that no such animal exists. . . .

Such frauds are far from justifiable; the only excuse which has been made for them is, when they have been practised on scientific academies which had reached the period of dotage. . ·. .

Forging differs from hoaxing, inasmuch as in the latter the deceit is intended to last for a time, and then be discovered, to the ridicule of those who have credited it; whereas the forger is one who, wishing to acquire a reputation for science, records observations which he has never made. . . .

Fortunately instances of the occurrence of forging are rare.

Trimming consists in clipping off little bits here and there from those observations which differ most in excess from the mean, and in sticking them on to those which are too small; a species of "equitable adjustment," as a radical would term it, which cannot be admitted in science.

This fraud is not perhaps so injurious (except to the character of the trimmer) as cooking, which the next paragraph will teach. The reason of this is, that the *average* given by the observations of the trimmer is the same, whether they are trimmed or untrimmed. His object is to gain a reputation for extreme accuracy in making observations; but from respect for truth, or from a prudent foresight, he does not distort the position of the fact he gets from nature, and it is usually difficult to detect him. He has more sense or less adventure than the Cook.

Of Cooking. This is an art of various forms, the object of which is to give to ordinary observations the appearance and character of those of the highest degree of accuracy.

One of its numerous processes is to make multitudes of observations, and out of these to select those only which agree, or very nearly agree. If a hundred observations are made, the cook must be very unlucky if he cannot pick out fifteen or twenty which will do for serving up.

Another approved receipt, when the observations to be used will not come within the limit of accuracy, which it has been resolved they shall possess, is to calculate them by two different formulae. The difference in the constants employed in those formulae has sometimes a most happy effect in promoting unanimity amongst discordant measures. If still greater accuracy is required, three or more formulae can be used.

NOTES

1. In addition to falsification of data, three other types of misconduct should be noted. The first is plagiarism, which involves taking credit for another's ideas or data. This category also includes problems of inadequate citation. A recent example of this is the fraud of Elias Al-Sabti. His published papers were plagiaries of others' work. See W. Broad and N. Wade, Betrayers of the Truth 38–56 (1982). The second category encompasses abuse of confidentiality. Officials of universities and funding institutions extensively review most research proposals. In addition, experts in the relevant field of study review articles submitted to professional journals. At any stage in these review processes, reviewers or those with whom reviewing parties communicate may appropriate ideas and data. Helena Wachslicht-Robard, for example, accused Yale researchers Vijay R. Soman and Philip Felig of lifting passages from an unpublished paper she had submitted to the New England Journal of Medicine. Felig had been asked to review the paper and had recommended that the journal reject it. See W. Broad and N. Wade, supra, 161–180 (1982); Hunt, A Fraud that Shook the World of Science, New York Times, Nov. 1, 1981, § 6 (Magazine) at 42. Finally, some researchers have deliberately violated regulations that govern the conduct of research. See, e.g., Ch. 1, Sec. B.3, supra. See generally President's Commission, Protecting Human Subjects 53–60 (1981).

2. If a lawyer deliberately misrepresents the holding of a precedental case, should he or she be disciplined by the bar? By the bench?

c. Can the Profession Stop It?

ROBERT K. MERTON, THE SOCIOLOGY OF SCIENCE

276–277 (N. Stover ed. 1973).

The virtual absence of fraud in the annals of science, which appears exceptional when compared with the record of other spheres of activity, has at times been attributed to the personal qualities of scientists. By implication, scientists are recruited from the ranks of those who exhibit an unusual degree of moral integrity. There is, in fact, no satisfactory evidence that such is the case; a more plausible explanation may be found in certain distinctive characteristics of science itself. Involving as it does the verifiability of results, scientific research is under the exacting scrutiny of fellow experts. Otherwise put—and doubtless the observation can be interpreted as lese majesty—the activities of scientists are subject to rigorous policing, to a degree perhaps unparalleled in any other field of activity. The demand for distinterestedness has a firm basis in the public and testable character of science and this circumstance, it may be supposed, has contributed to the integrity of men of science. There is competition in the realm of science, competition that is intensified by the emphasis on priority as a criterion of achievement, and under competitive conditions there may well be generated incentives for eclipsing rivals by illicit means. But such impulses can find scant opportunity for expression in the field of scientific research. Cultism, informal cliques, prolific but trivial publications—these and other techniques may be used for self-aggrandizement. But, in general, spurious claims appear to be negligible and ineffective. The translation of the norm of disinterestedness into practice is effectively supported by the ultimate accountability of scientists to their compeers. The dictates of socialized sentiment and of expediency largely coincide, a situation conducive to institutional stability.

In this connection, the field of science differs somewhat from that of other professions. The scientist does not stand vis-à-vis a lay clientele in the same fashion as do the physician and lawyer, for example. The possibility of exploiting the credulity, ignorance, and dependence of the layman is thus considerably reduced. Fraud, chicane, and irresponsible claims (quackery) are even less likely than among the "service" professions. To the extent that the scientist-layman relation does become paramount, there develop incentives for evading the mores of science. The abuse of expert authority and the creation of pseudo-sciences are called into play when the structure of control exercised by qualified compeers is rendered ineffectual.

It is probable that the reputability of science and its lofty ethical status in the estimate of the layman is in no small measure due to technological achievements. Every new technology bears witness to the integrity of the scientist. Science realizes its claims. However, its authority can be and is appropriated for interested purposes, precisely because the laity is often in no position to distinguish spurious from genuine claims to such authority. The presumably scientific pronouncements of totalitarian spokesmen on race or economy or history are for the uninstructed laity of the same order as newspaper reports of an expanding universe or wave mechanics. In both instances, they cannot be checked by the man-in-the-street and in both instances, they may run counter to common sense. If anything, the myths will seem more plausible and are certainly more comprehensible to the general public than accredited scientific theories, since they are closer to common-sense experience and to cultural bias. Partly as a result of scientific achievements, therefore, the population at large becomes susceptible to new mysticisms expressed in apparently scientific terms. The borrowed authority of science bestows prestige on the unscientific doctrine.

. . .

NICHOLAS WADE,
MADNESS IN THEIR METHOD

188 The New Republic 13 (June 27, 1983).

. . .

How could a scientist, committed to discovering the truth, even think of betraying the central principle of his profession by publishing false data? Yet fraud is by no means rare in science. Consider the record of cases reported in the last seven months alone:

December 27, 1982. Joseph H. Cort, a researcher trained at Harvard and Yale Universities, was found by a faculty committee of the Mount Sinai School of Medicine to have fabricated data on new drugs he claimed to have synthesized. The committee concluded he had done only a third of the work reported in a successful patent application. "I was under a lot of pressure and things got confused. I had to earn the money for research, or die," Dr. Cort told *The New York Times.*

February 16, 1983. The National Institutes of Health released the report of an inquiry into a major research fraud at the Harvard Medical School. Despite persistent statements from Harvard and a blue-ribbon committee that only one minor cheating incident was involved, the N.I.H.'s inquiry established that John Darsee had probably forged all of his published work since arriving in the laboratory of cardiologist Eugene Braunwald.

March 1, 1983.   Harvey M. Levin, a Philadelphia gynecologist, pleaded guilty to falsifying results of clinical trials on five proposed painkillers. The data, prepared for several leading drug companies, were used by the Food and Drug Administration in evaluating the safety and efficacy of the drugs.

March 23, 1983.   The F.D.A. barred Wilbert S. Aronow from testing drugs because of false evidence he submitted about a drug for possible use against congestive heart failure.   Until his resignation, Aronow was professor of medicine at the University of California, Irvine, and chief of cardiovascular diseases at the Veterans Administration Medical Center in Long Beach.   Aronow is also the author of a study of carbon monoxide and heart disease which has been heavily relied on by those who work to tighten the Clean Air Act's carbon monoxide standard.

April 5, 1983.   Another case of fraud was alleged at Harvard, this time at a hospital associated with the Harvard Medical School.   The case concerns an unnamed research fellow, now on leave of absence, who works in the rheumatology department of the Brigham and Women's Hospital.

May 4, 1983.   A psychology faculty committee at the University of North Carolina found that Arnold Rincover, a member of the department, had plagiarized a student's thesis "virtually word-for-word" in order to obtain a $723,000 grant from the Department of Education.   The committee said that he had also changed details of published research to fit his proposal.

May 6, 1983.   Emory University, where John Darsee worked before going to Harvard, announced the results of an investigation which concluded Darsee had faked eight scientific articles and forty-three research abstracts during his time there.   A professor at Notre Dame, where Darsee did his undergraduate work, discovered that Darsee had forged data in two papers written for the school science journal in 1969.   Darsee's career of successful fakery thus spanned fourteen years, much of it spent at two of the nation's leading centers of heart research.

May 12, 1983.   A report released by the Environmental Protection Agency concluded that 737 safety tests of herbicides and pesticides conducted by Industrial Bio-Test were invalid.   The tests, submitted by manufacturers to gain market approval of their products, involve 212 pesticides, or almost 15 percent of those on the market.   The E.P.A. report was released during the trial in Chicago of four executives of Industrial Bio-Test, formerly one of the country's largest testing laboratories.

The occurrence of these and several other recent cases of fraud in science calls out for explanation. . . .

The science establishment's undeviating line is founded on the following premises: (1) Science is a self-correcting system.   (2) Since any fraud is bound to be detected by the internal checking mechanisms of science, only a madman would try it.   (3) Therefore, the roots of fraud should be sought in individual psychopathology, not in the institutions of science— rotten apples are to blame, not the barrel.   (4) Even the recent spate of cases constitute so small a proportion of all the science that goes on that fraud remains basically irrelevent.

All of these premises of this comfortably insulating hypothesis are seriously flawed. . . .

The system . . . has three components. The first is peer review, the committees of outside scientists that advise the government on the merit of their colleagues' applications for research funds. Peer review is widely considered to be a rigorous test, since applications must describe very fully the methods and rationale of the experiments to be conducted. When a researcher comes to publish his results, the journal to which he submits his manuscript will send it out for review by experts in the field. If the reviewers, or referees, find faults, the manuscript is rejected or returned for revision. Refereeing is the second stage of the self-correcting system. The third, and theoretically most rigorous, is replication. Once an experiment is published, other scientists are able to test its validity by trying to replicate it. But the recent crop of fraud cases was not harvested by these means.

Dr. Cort's omissions came to light only because he walked into a colleague's office one day and confessed that he had fabricated data. The falsifications of Drs. Levin and Aronow were uncovered by the F.D.A.'s drug test auditing system, a kind of external police force that does not exist in academic research. The Industrial Bio-Test scandal was also brought to light by an F.D.A. investigation, triggered when an official looking for something else pulled out a file of I.B.T. data by accident.

Dr. Darsee's fabrications were exposed because his colleagues at Harvard Medical School became suspicious of his enormous productivity. Surreptitiously observing one day, they saw him generate in a few hours data that he later presented as having been gathered over several days. Even with this massive hint that something was wrong, the Harvard authorities were strangely incapable of getting to the bottom of the affair.

Darsee's lab chiefs, Eugene Braunwald and Robert Kloner, spent five months auditing his previous research, which had formed the basis of articles published by the three of them, and informed the dean of the medical school that "No misleading results have been released from our laboratory." The dean, Daniel Tosteson, appointed a blue-ribbon committee, chaired by the dean of the Johns Hopkins School of Medicine, to examine Darsee's work. This committee too concluded that "the previously published work . . . is accurate." Only through the inquiry of a genuinely independent panel appointed by the National Institutes of Health did it emerge that there were statistical implausibilities in Darsee's research that rendered all of it highly suspect. Braunwald and Kroner have now retracted the five scientific papers published under their names that were based on Darsee's data.

. . .

Another recent case of scientific fraud, the grand plagiary of Elias Al-Sabti, illustrates a seldom-recognized feature of the scientific literature: that much of it is as unread as it is unreadable. Al-Sabti, until his public exposure in 1980, amassed an impressive bibliography of some forty-three published papers on the subject of cancer research. It was not his style, however, to endure the tedium of doing experiments. His papers were plagiaries of other scientists' articles.

. . .

. . . Al-Sabti's plagiarism was several times discovered or suspected by the institution that harbored him, but in each case he was simply asked to leave quietly and had little trouble reestablishing himself elsewhere. The pattern was broken only after a diligent reporter, William

Broad, publicized Al-Sabti's methods in several articles in *Science* magazine.

Most often it is through private means—the jealousy or suspicion of a colleague, combined with egregious carelessness on the part of the forger—that fraud is detected. Science is not a self-correcting system. Its checking mechanisms are at best a crude screen, and offer little deterrent to the forger who publishes prudently unambitious claims.

But why should a scientist even contemplate faking data when he has undergone lengthy training for the sole purpose of learning to uncover the truth about nature? Modern science is a career. In addition to the disinterested pursuit of truth, scientists necessarily have another goal—the pursuit of glory, of due credit for their ideas, of the rewards and prestige that will assist in the next step up the career ladder. For the most part the two goals are complementary and reinforce each other. But competitive pressures and the opportunism of certain scientific arrangements seem sometimes to force a disjunction between the scientist's two purposes.

The peer review system awards large grants to senior scientists who use the money to employ doctoral and post-graduate students. At its best, the relationship between a professor and his students is a vital bond through which a research tradition is inculcated and handed on. But some lab chiefs pursue credit at their students' expense. To build up their list of publications, they sign their names to work of their junior colleagues even if they have contributed little to the work in question. Though happy to share the glory, the same lab chiefs are quick to distance themselves when fraud comes to light.

The younger researchers go along with the system, in part because they hope to become lab chiefs in their turn, in part because they have little recourse for complaint. For some lab chiefs, maximizing production of scientific articles becomes a goal in itself. It is scarcely surprising that in such an environment younger researchers should be tempted to shade their results, to tidy up the data so as to give the chief what he wants, and eventually even to invent data out of whole cloth.

. . .

Another case, the writings of Sir Cyril Burt on I.Q. and heredity, affords a glimpse into the role played by nonlogical factors in science. Burt, an educational psychologist, worked his way to the top of his academic profession in Britain and was the first foreigner to receive the American Psychological Association's prestigious Thorndike prize in 1971. His strong belief in the overriding importance of heredity in determining I.Q. was backed by extensive batteries of psychological test reports, all presented in a lucid expository style and with an unusual mastery of statistical technique. Burt's results occupied center stage of a fierce debate for many years, yet it took an outsider, Leon Kamin of Princeton, to spot the glaring statistical implausibilities in Burt's data. These turned out to be the sign of a wholesale invention of data. . . .

. . .

How common is fraud in science? And does it matter?

The first question cannot be answered with precision, because no one knows the number of frauds that escape detection. The outright fabrication of data is probably rare, if only because of the difficulty of endowing a wholly invented experiment with verisimilitude. It is much easier to do some of the work and shade the details to give a sufficiently impressive answer. Minor fraud, such as tidying up data or selective reporting, could be relatively common in science, particularly as the chances of detection by the standard checks are so small. Fraud in science, whatever its exact frequency, is an endemic feature of the system. . . .

Often [in] the testing of chemicals and drugs, fraud has an immediate consequence on public health. With the exception of cases such as Burt's, fraud in academic research is of less practical importance, since most fraudulent papers are specks in the ocean of forgotten research. The importance of academic fraud lies elsewhere, in its warning that the checking mechanisms of science are not as thorough as advertised, and that the skepticism with which we are warned to listen to experts is amply justified. For it is not the checking mechanisms that guarantee the reliability of scientific knowledge, but a more ruthless and impersonal test, that of time.

What should be done about fraud? Faking safety tests is a direct threat to public health and requires urgent corrective action, such as tighter government policing and a policy of holding companies legally responsible for the truth of the data they submit. Fraud in academic research is a different matter entirely. Measures to crack down on fraud might also bring research to a grinding halt. More important is to reduce the temptations to fraud. Protection of graduate students, more honest distribution of credit, reducing the number of vanity press journals, and raising research standards are all steps worth taking in their own right, as well as for their salutary effect in reversing the steady erosion of the academic ethos.

. . .

NOTE

For further discussion of the role of journal editors and publishers in policing unethical behavior, see Ch. 6, Sec. C.3, infra.

ASSOCIATION OF AMERICAN MEDICAL COLLEGES, THE MAINTENANCE OF HIGH ETHICAL STANDARDS IN THE CONDUCT OF RESEARCH (1982)

The primary goal of this document is to set forth guidelines and recommendations that will be useful to medical schools and teaching hospitals in designing their individual institutional approaches to dealing with alleged misconduct by researchers. Although the guidelines and recommendations that follow principally address fraud (i.e., the intentional fabrication, falsification, or "stealing" of research data) they may also be useful in institutional efforts to deal with the violation of existing administrative procedures and ethical codes for the treatment of human and animal subjects of research and other problems that may arise in the conduct of research.

The Prevention of Research Fraud

The primary responsibility for taking steps to prevent research fraud rests with the scientific community. In academic institutions, it can best be executed by the faculties. In a free society, and particularly in the academic milieu where creativity and individual thought are qualities to be fostered and not stifled, aberrant behavior of individuals cannot be completely controlled. It is unrealistic, therefore, to assume that research fraud can be entirely prevented. On the other hand, faculties can create a climate that promotes faithful attention to high ethical standards. This climate should enhance the research process and should not inhibit the productivity and creativity of scientists.

It is recognized that the principal deterrent in research fraud is the overwhelming probability that fraudulent data will be detected soon after their presentation. Virtually all experimentation leading to scientific findings of significance will be repeated, and the likelihood that falsified, fabricated, or plagiarized data will go unquestioned is exceedingly slim. Despite the self-correcting nature of science, however, instances of research fraud have occurred and faculties should explore additional measures to decrease further the likelihood that a researcher will risk the odds and commit fraud. Faculties and institutional officials should consider the following:

- Having in place a conspicuous and understandable mechanism for dealing with instances of alleged fraud.

- Adopting institutional policies that define misrepresentation of research data as a major breach of contract between the faculty or staff member and the institution. (This policy should particularly be articulated in the faculty handbook.)

- Articulating institutional policies that foster openness of research.

- Encouraging faculties to discuss research ethics to heighten awareness and recognition of these issues.

- Establishing institutional policies to provide: 1) an appropriate and clearly defined locus of responsibility for the conduct of research; 2) assurance that individuals charged with supervision of other researchers can realistically execute their responsibility; and 3) particular attention to adequate supervision of large research teams.

- Assuring that quality rather than quantity of research is emphasized as a criterion for the promotion of faculty.

- Examining institutional policies on authorship of papers and abstracts to ensure that named authors have had a genuine role in the research and accept responsibility for the quality of the work being reported.

- Reviewing institutional policies on the recording and retention of research data to ensure that such policies are appropriate and are clearly understood and complied with by all faculty.

- Examining the institutional role and policies in guiding faculty concerning public announcement and publication of research findings.

Institutional Responses to Instances of Alleged Research Fraud

. . .

In developing policies and procedures, institutions and their faculties should recognize that judgments about the substantive questions relating to whether research findings are true or false must largely be made by faculty peers. If action adverse to a faculty member is taken by the institution based upon findings of fraud and such action is later challenged in court, the court ordinarily will look to see if fair procedures have been followed; that the accused had an adequate opportunity to explain and defend his actions, including when appropriate, confronting those persons who presented evidence of fraud; and that the decision was not arbitrary or capricious, but based on credible evidence. If institutional policies and procedures meet these criteria the courts are unlikely to interfere with the institutional decision.

The following guidelines and procedures for dealing with allegations of fraud are offered as a prototype to assist schools in designing a process appropriate to their own situations. Consultations with university counsel in such an effort are strongly recommended. It is recognized that in these procedures a faculty member's reputation is put at risk during the investigation. This is justified since scientists on the university faculty occupy a special place of privilege and responsibility and must be held to a higher standard of conduct. The procedures indeed must be fair to the individuals involved. They must also be designed to be responsive to the special responsibility that science and faculty have to society.

Prototype of Procedures for Dealing with Alleged Research Fraud

A. *Processing Initial Reports of Fraud*

- From the outset, institutions should protect rights and reputations for all parties involved including the individual(s) who report perceived misconduct in good faith.
- Initial reports of alleged fraud should be brought to the attention of the faculty member responsible for the individual whose actions are in question. That person should in turn report the allegations to the department chairperson immediately.
- If the initial report of misconduct is not regarded as blatantly frivolous in nature, the report should promptly be referred to the dean or the chief executive officer of the institution. The dean should in turn immediately initiate a review by individuals at the institution who have been designated to review initial reports of fraud. Such individuals should be selected from among the faculty and administration. Care should be taken to exclude those with personal responsibility for the research under investigation.
- After this initial review, a determination should be made as to whether the report warrants more thorough investigation. If it is determined that there is sufficient basis for pursuing the allegations, the researcher(s) in question should be advised of the allegations and any collaborators should be informed of the pending investigation.

B. *Investigation of Reported Fraud that Appears Substantial*

- Institutions should have in place or be prepared to appoint immediately a committee or other administrative unit to conduct a prompt and thorough investigation of the reported fraud and should consider the merits of involving outside, objective parties in the investigation at this stage.
- The sponsoring agency should be notified that there is an investigation underway.
- During the investigation, consideration should be given to the review of all research with which the individual is involved.
- The investigating committee or unit should determine whether there was fabrication or dishonesty.
- Throughout the investigation, the individual and any collaborators or supervisors whose role in the alleged misconduct is questionable should be advised of the progress of the investigation and be af-

forded the opportunity to respond and provide additional information.

C. *Subsequent Action Following Completed Investigation*

1. If the alleged fraud is substantiated by a thorough investigation the following actions are recommended:

   - The sponsoring agency should be notified of the findings of the investigation and appropriate restitution should be made.

   - All pending abstracts and papers emanating from the fraudulent research should be withdrawn and editors of journals in which previous abstracts and papers appeared should be notified.

   - Institutions and sponsoring agencies with which the individual has been affiliated should be notified if there is reason to believe that the validity of previous research might be questionable.

   - Appropriate action should be taken to terminate or alter the status of faculty members whose misconduct is substantiated.

   - Institutional administrators should consider, in consultation with legal counsel, release of information about the incident to the public press, particularly when public funds were used in supporting the fraudulent research.

2. If the alleged fraud is not substantiated by a thorough investigation, formal efforts should be undertaken to restore fully the reputation of the researcher and others under investigation. In addition, appropriate action should be taken against any parties whose involvement in leveling unfounded charges was demonstrated to have been malicious or intentionally dishonest.

3. Subsequent to the completion of an investigation, faculty practices and institutional policies and procedures for promoting the ethical conduct of research and investigating allegations of misconduct should be scrutinized and modified in light of the experience gained.

NOTES

1. The AAMC guidelines require public disclosure of the investigation of allegations of fraud if the allegations do not appear to be frivolous. Such disclosure could possibly harm the career and reputation of an innocent researcher. In your view, is that risk of harm justified?

2. The AAMC guidelines recommend that sponsoring agencies should be notified of the findings of any investigation. What responsibilities should sponsoring agencies have with respect to the information they receive? Should the sponsoring agency conduct its own investigation? Should results be shared with peer review panels considering the investigated researcher's pending and future proposals? Should the sponsoring agency take the lead in notifying all journals publishing the data in question, or should it publish retractions in relevant journals?

JUDITH P. SWAZEY AND STEPHEN R. SCHER, THE WHISTLEBLOWER AS A DEVIANT PROFESSIONAL: PROFESSIONAL NORMS AND RESPONSES TO FRAUD IN CLINICAL RESEARCH

in President's Commission, Whistleblowing in Biomedical Research
173, 179–181, 187–189 (1981).

. . . [T]he social role of the whistleblower is subject to differing interpretations. The whistleblower may be—and within his group usually is—perceived and treated as a Judas Iscariot who has committed a disloyal, indeed treasonable act. Less frequently, he is seen as a Paul Revere who has sounded a tocsin against an imminent danger or as a Daniel Berrigan acting in civil disobedience for a just cause.

Both the negative responses to and sanctions against the whistleblower . . . seem to have two major sources. First, in terms of group or organizational norms, the whistleblower is seen by those within the group as having violated a moral obligation of loyalty, particularly if he goes public. Second, if whistleblowing occurs in the context of a professional group, such as scientists or physicians, it is seen from within the group as violating professional norms of autonomy and self-regulation.

The obligation of loyalty is one of the obligations created by membership in the scientific community. . . . It is typical for members of a community to respond to a disloyal act by asserting that the disloyal person should have used the means available within the community itself to resolve whatever problem motivated the act. Disloyal acts directly or indirectly threaten the freedom or continued existence of the community or its ability to pursue its explicit purpose or goal. . . . [T]he act of whistleblowing, which calls into question the scientific community's ability to regulate or control its own activities and members, undermines the scientific community's claim of independence from external interference, supervision, and control, i.e. its claim to be a self-regulating company of equals. A loyal member of the scientific community will, other things equal, not engage in such acts; he will attempt to resolve problems through the mechanisms for control accepted by the community as a whole.

. . .

Whistleblowing often occurs when unethical conduct in scientific research is expected to create risks for or cause harm to persons, institutions, or interests outside of the scientific community. In such cases, a person who, in good faith, is considering the act of whistleblowing is in a situation of moral conflict; his obligation of loyalty to the scientific community conflicts with his other moral duties or obligations, for example, his duty to prevent harm to other persons. The central issue is whether the accepted and available forms of social control within the scientific community are adequate to avoid risks or harm to persons or interests outside the community. If the potential whistleblower can act within the scientific community to avoid the harm in question, his obligation of loyalty would require him to use the available internal mechanisms for dealing with the problem about which he is concerned. If the scientific community's standard methods of control are inadequate for purpose of avoiding the harm, then the potential whistleblower's duties or obligations to nonscientists might either override his obligation of loyalty (making it morally required to blow the whistle) or at least make it morally permissible to do so.

. . .

The almost universal experience of whistleblowers . . . is that their actions generate a vehement, angry, and often punitive response by colleagues and superordinates. . . . The reactions of the scientific and medical communities to acts of whistleblowing are quite different in character and intensity . . . from those that would be expected if a physician or scientist had *simply* violated a moral duty or obligation, for example, by committing a crime, embezzling grant funds, or even mistreating human research subjects. While such actions would obviously be condemned, scientists and physicians would not respond to them as being malevolent attacks upon the professional community. What, then, accounts for this response?

Perhaps the most important factor in understanding the intensity of the research community's response to whistleblowing is that researchers value scientific knowledge very highly and value the research community as a means of achieving such knowledge. Researchers typically derive a sense of personal identity from their work, which is a central part of their lives; researchers achieve and maintain self-esteem through their own research achievements and those of the research community as a whole.

The act of whistleblowing calls into question the capacity of scientists and physicians to regulate themselves effectively; this charge implies that the research community has failed to pursue scientific activity autonomously and as a self-regulating group. In addition, the malfeasance of one researcher can be taken by the public as reflecting on the presumed good faith and integrity of all members of the research community. Whistleblowing thus threatens both the individual self-esteem of members of the research community and the continued prestige and existence of that community as a self-regulating company of equals, especially when the whistleblower makes his charges public.

The negative reaction to and sanctions levied against whistleblowers . . . also serve as an *ad hominen* defense by the research community against charges that imply a failure of individual and group norms. That is, by focusing attention on the whistleblower as the deviant group member and attacking his motivations and actions, attention may be diverted, at least for a time, from the substance of the disclosure to the discloser himself.

. . .

The negative reaction to the whistleblower as a violator of group norms of loyalty, autonomy, or self-regulation also seems to be related, in part, to the status of the whistleblower. That is, most cases to date have involved whistleblowing "from the bottom up," i.e. with subordinates calling attention to suspected or known misconduct by superordinates. In business or government. . . . The occasion for whistleblowing "from the top down" is likely to be rare "because it is relatively easy to police lower-echelon employees who step out of line." The same holds true, we suggest, in professional contexts, particularly in a field such as medicine, given the physician's professional dominance.

If whistleblowing becomes accepted within government, industry, professional groups as a normatively appropriate act—which, as we have argued, it should be on moral and sociological grounds—then we would expect an increased incidence of whistleblowing involving persons having comparable professional roles and status. Such a trend should, in turn, change colleagues' reactions to the whistleblower's actions, a change that may result in the replacement of the term "whistleblower" itself.

. . .

NOTES

1. Does whistleblowing support professional norms and autonomy? See generally President's Commission, Whistleblowing in Biomedical Research (1981).

2. A whistleblower, as Swazey and Scher point out, often suffers adverse consequences as a result of his or her activities. Consider Dirks v. SEC, ___ U.S. ___, 103 S.Ct. 3255, 77 L.Ed.2d 911 (1983):

JUSTICE POWELL delivered the opinion of the Court.

. . .

I

In 1973, Dirks was an officer of a New York broker-dealer firm who specialized in providing investment analysis of insurance company securities to institutional investors. On March 6, Dirks received information from Ronald Secrist, a former officer of Equity Funding of America. Secrist alleged that the assets of Equity Funding, a diversified corporation primarily engaged in selling life insurance and mutual funds, were vastly overstated as the result of fraudulent corporate practices. Secrist also stated that various regulatory agencies had failed to act on similar charges made by Equity Funding employees. He urged Dirks to verify the fraud and disclose it publicly.

Dirks decided to investigate the allegations. He visited Equity Funding's headquarters in Los Angeles and interviewed several officers and employees of the corporation. The senior management denied any wrongdoing, but certain corporation employees corroborated the charges of fraud. Neither Dirks nor his firm owned or traded any Equity Funding stock, but throughout his investigation he openly discussed the information he had obtained with a number of clients and investors. Some of these persons sold their holdings of Equity Funding securities, including five investment advisers who liquidated holdings of more than $16 million.

While Dirks was in Los Angeles, he was in touch regularly with William Blundell, the Wall Street Journal's Los Angeles bureau chief. Dirks urged Blundell to write a story on the fraud allegations. Blundell did not believe, however, that such a massive fraud could go undetected and declined to write the story. He feared that publishing such damaging hearsay might be libelous.

During the two-week period in which Dirks pursued his investigation and spread word of Secrist's charges, the price of Equity Funding stock fell from $26 per share to less than $15 per share. This led the New York Stock Exchange to halt trading on March 27. Shortly thereafter California insurance authorities impounded Equity Funding's records and uncovered evidence of the fraud. Only then did the Securities and Exchange Commission (SEC) file a complaint against Equity Funding and only then, on April 2, did the Wall Street Journal publish a front-page story based largely on information assembled by Dirks. Equity Funding immediately went into receivership.

The SEC began an investigation into Dirks' role in the exposure of the fraud. After a hearing by an administrative law judge, the SEC found that Dirks had aided and abetted violations of § 17(a) of the Securities Act of 1933, § 10(b) of the Securities Exchange Act of 1934, and SEC Rule 10b–5, by repeating the allegations of fraud to members of the investment community who later sold their Equity Funding stock. The SEC concluded: "Where 'tippees'—regardless of their motivation or occupation—come into possession of material 'information that they know is confidential and know or should know came from a corporate insider,' they must either publicly disclose that information or refrain from trading."   21 SEC Docket 1401, 1407 (1981). . . . Recognizing, however, that Dirks "played an important role in bringing [Equity Funding's] massive fraud to light," 21 SEC Docket, at 1412, the SEC only censured him.

Dirks sought review in the Court of Appeals for the District of Columbia Circuit. The court entered judgment against Dirks . . .

In view of the importance to the SEC and to the securities industry of the question presented by this case, we granted a writ of certiorari.

. . .

IV

Under the inside-trading and tipping rules . . . we find that there was no actionable violation by Dirks. It is undisputed that Dirks himself was a stranger to Equity Funding, with no pre-existing fiduciary duty to its shareholders. He took no action, directly or indirectly, that induced the shareholders or officers of Equity Funding to repose trust or confidence in him. There was no expectation by Dirk's sources that he would keep their information in confidence. Nor did Dirks misappropriate or illegally obtain the information about Equity Funding. Unless the insiders breached their Cady, Roberts [In Re Cady, Roberts & Co, 40 SEC 907 (1961)] duty to shareholders in disclosing the nonpublic information to Dirks, he breached no duty when he passed it on to investors as well as to the Wall Street Journal.

It is clear that neither Secrist nor the other Equity Funding employees violated their Cady, Roberts duty to the corporation's shareholders by providing information to Dirks. The tippers received no monetary or personal benefit for revealing Equity Funding's secrets, nor was their purpose to make a gift of valuable information to Dirks. As the facts of this case clearly indicate, the tippers were motivated by a desire to expose the fraud. In the absence of a breach of duty to shareholders by the insiders, there was no derivative breach by Dirks. Dirks therefore could not have been "a participant after the fact in [an] insider's breach of a fiduciary duty."

V

We conclude that Dirks, in the circumstances of this case, had no duty to abstain from use of the inside information that he obtained. The judgment of the Court of Appeals therefore is reversed.

Cf. facts in Nixon v. Fitzgerald, 457 U.S. 731, 102 S.Ct. 2690, 73 L.Ed.2d 349 (1982).

4. POLICING CONFLICTS OF INTEREST

WASHINGTON POST CO. v. UNITED STATES DEPARTMENT OF HEALTH AND HUMAN SERVICES

United States Court of Appeals for the District of Columbia Circuit, 1982.
690 F.2d 252.

WALD, CIRCUIT JUDGE:

This appeal involves a request under the Freedom of Information Act (FOIA), 5 U.S.C. § 552, by the Washington Post Company ("Post") for information concerning possible conflicts of interest of scientific consultants employed by the National Cancer Institute (NCI). The Post seeks to compel disclosure, for each consultant, of (1) a list of his non-federal employment and (2) a list of organizations in which the consultant has financial interests related to his consulting duties. The government claims that the information is exempt from disclosure under Exemptions 4 and 6 to FOIA, 5 U.S.C. § 552(b)(4), (6). . . .

. . .

NCI is a division of the National Institutes of Health (NIH), which is in turn administered by appellee Department of Health and Human Services (HHS). It annually disburses approximately $1 billion in grants and contracts for cancer research. In deciding which grant proposals to fund, NCI depends on the advice of scientific consultants who serve on various advisory boards and committees. These consultants are respected scientists, familiar with cancer research, who exercise "peer review" over grant applications.

Pursuant to Executive Order No. 11,222, HHS, in order to monitor conflicts of interest that could affect consultants' judgment of the merits of grant proposals, requires them to complete Form HEW-474. That form, titled "Confidential Statement of Employment and Financial Interests," requires each consultant to list all other federal and non-federal employment and "all organizations in which you, your spouse, minor child, partner, or an organization with which you are connected have financial interests which relate directly or indirectly to your consultancy duties." HHS then reviews this statement to determine whether a conflict exists. Consultants are told that the information on Form 474 will be used to determine whether their consulting duties will involve a conflict of interest, and are given a limited pledge of confidentiality—the information "will not be disclosed except as the Chairman of the Civil Service Commission or the head of the principal operating component or designee may determine for good cause shown."

On February 14, 1980, the Post requested copies of the statements of employment and financial interests filed by members of NCI's advisory boards and committees. HHS refused the request, relying on FOIA Exemption 6, 5 U.S.C., § 552(b)(6), which exempts from disclosure:

> personnel and medical files and similar files the disclosure of which would constitute a clearly unwarranted invasion of personal privacy.

The Post appealed the decision to the Assistant Secretary of HHS for Public Health and Surgeon General, who affirmed the refusal to disclose. Having exhausted its administrative remedies, the Post filed suit to compel disclosure on July 8, 1980.

After a status call, the district court ordered the parties to file cross-motions for summary judgment. The government, in its motion for summary judgment, again relied on Exemption 6 and added a claim that the requested data was confidential financial information within the meaning of Exemption 4, 5 U.S.C. § 552(b)(4), which permits withholding of:

> trade secrets and commercial or financial information obtained from a person and privileged or confidential.

In support of its motion, the government, which has the burden of justifying nondisclosure, see 5 U.S.C. § 552(a)(4)(B), submitted no evidence except an affidavit by Robert Eaglesome, Director of Personnel Policy for HHS. That affidavit states Mr. Eaglesome's "professional opinion" that disclosure "would impair the Department's ability to obtain candid and accurate information in the future" and might deter "significant numbers of persons" from applying for advisory board or committee positions.

The Post argued with respect to Exemption 6 that the public interest in disclosure of conflicts of interest outweighs the consultants' privacy interests. With respect to Exemption 4, it argued that a mere list of organizations in which one has financial interests, without dollar amounts, is not "financial" information within the meaning of Exemption 4, and that in any event the government had not made a factual showing that disclosure would impair its ability to obtain this information in the future.

The government agreed before decision to release the names of NCI consultants, their federal employment, the results of HHS's review of Form 474, and the name of the reviewing official. Thus, the remaining disputed information was the consultants' non-federal employment and their list of financial interests related to their consulting duties.

The district court held that Exemption 4 did not apply because it was not designed to protect "personal financial information as distinguished from economic data relating to corporations or other business entities." With regard to Exemption 6, the district court felt bound by the reasoning of *Women in Science* [Association for Women in Science v. Califano, 566 F.2d 339 (D.C.Cir.1977),] where we held that information contained on Form 474 was privileged from discovery under Rule 26(b)(1) of the Federal Rules of Civil Procedure. In *Women in Science,* for purposes of the confidential report privilege, we balanced the litigants' need for information against the government's need to foster gathering of the information and found the government's need to be greater. The district court recognized that under FOIA Exemption 6, a court must instead balance the public interest in disclosure against the privacy interests of individuals. However, it believed that the general public interest in disclosure was weaker than the specific need of the plaintiffs in *Women in Science,* and that the consultants' personal privacy interests were "identical for purposes of practical analysis" to the government's interest in gathering information. Therefore, the district court found the balance struck in *Women in Science* to be controlling for Exemption 6 purposes, and held that Form 474 was exempt from disclosure.

In this appeal, the Post argues that *Women in Science* is not controlling and that the balancing of interests required by Exemption 6 mandates disclosure. The government contests that proposition and also argues that the disputed information is both "financial" and "confidential," and hence is covered by Exemption 4.

II. EXEMPTION 6

A. *The Limited Relevance of Discovery Rules for Exemption 6*

It is well established that information that is exempt from disclosure to the general public under FOIA may nevertheless be subject to discovery. This case involves the converse question: whether information that is privileged against discovery can nonetheless be obtained under FOIA.

As an initial matter, neither the text nor the legislative history of FOIA suggests that the existence of a discovery privilege should control the determination of whether withholding is warranted under Exemption 6. . . .

. . .

Exemption 6 requires an independent inquiry into whether withholding is proper. . . .

· · ·

B. *The Exemption 6 Balancing of Interests*

Exemption 6 permits withholding of "personnel and medical files and similar files" whose disclosure would be "a clearly unwarranted invasion of personal privacy." The analysis proceeds in two stages. First, we must determine whether the information on Form 474 is contained in personnel, medical, or "similar" files. If so, we must determine whether disclosure would constitute "a clearly unwarranted invasion of personal privacy."

The first stage is fairly minimal and is easily satisfied in this case. All information which "applies to a particular individual" is covered by Exemption 6, regardless of the type of file in which it is contained. United States Department of State v. Washington Post Co., 456 U.S. 595, 102 S.Ct. 1957, 1961, 72 L.Ed.2d 358 (1982). This ensures that FOIA's protection of personal privacy is not affected by the happenstance of the type of agency record in which personal information is stored. Id. at 595, 102 S.Ct. at 1961. Each Form 474 is filled out by a particular consultant and thus meets the threshold criterion for coverage under Exemption 6.

In the second stage—determining whether disclosure is clearly unwarranted—we must balance the public interest in disclosure against the privacy interests of the consultants. Department of the Air Force v. Rose, 425 U.S. 352, 372 (1976). In performing this balance, we must keep in mind Congress's "dominant objective" to provide full disclosure of agency records. Id. at 361. Congress, however, also created nine "carefully structured" exemptions to FOIA "to protect specific confidentiality and privacy interests. But unless the requested material falls within one of these nine statutory exemptions, FOIA requires that . . . [it] be made available on demand to any member of the general public." NLRB v. Robbins Tire & Rubber Co., 437 U.S. 214, 220–21 . . . . .

In addition to Congress's general purpose to make disclosure the dominant practice and withholding the exception, Exemption 6's requirement that disclosure be "clearly unwarranted" instructs us to "tilt the balance [of disclosure interests against privacy interests] in favor of disclosure." Ditlow v. Shultz, 517 F.2d 166, 169 (D.C.Cir.1975); Getman v. NLRB, 450 F.2d 670, 674 (D.C.Cir.1971). . . .

1. *Privacy Interests*

Turning to Form 474, we first consider whether disclosure would create an invasion of privacy at all and, if so, how serious an invasion. We then evaluate the public interest in disclosure. Finally, we balance the competing interests to determine whether the invasion of privacy is clearly unwarranted.

The disputed portions of Form 474 require consultants to list their non-federal employment and any organizations in which the consultant, his spouse, minor children, partners, or organizations with which he is connected have financial interests that relate to his consulting duties. Notably, Form 474 requests only cursory information. For employment, consultants need only list their employer, the "kind of organization (e.g., Manufacturing, research, insurance)" it is, and the title or kind of position they hold. For financial interests, they need only list the name and kind of organization, the nature of the interest, and in whose name it is held. Form 474 does not require information on either rates of pay or the dollar amount of financial interests.

Considering the employment information first, we believe that disclosure would be only a minimal invasion of privacy. . . . In addition, although its brief discusses the privacy interest in Form 474's financial information, the government does not even attempt to explain why the information on consultants' non-federal employment raises privacy concerns. Indeed, the government admits that the employment of most of NCI's consultants is available from the biographical sketches in *American Men and Women of Sciences,* a widely available publication. This omission is especially telling in light of the government's burden to justify nondisclosure.

The government also fails to demonstrate a substantial privacy interest in the limited financial information contained in Form 474. The government asserts that Form 474 contains "intimate details" of personal finances, but does not explain why it reaches that conclusion. . . .

We conclude that release of the list in Form 474 of organizations in which consultants have financial interest, while constituting a greater invasion of privacy than release of the list of their non-federal employment, still does not amount to a serious invasion. It merits emphasis that consultants not only need not disclose dollar amounts, but must disclose only financial interests that relate to their consulting duties. While public knowledge of affiliation with some organizations may, in some circumstances, lead to embarrassment or harm, we perceive little such danger from disclosure of affiliations related to one's scientific consulting.

Several pieces of evidence support this view. First, in response to a questionnaire mailed to NIH consultants by the plaintiffs in *Women in Science,* only 10% of respondents (7/69) stated that they would object to serving or having served on an advisory committee if a "complete list of your professional affiliations and financial holdings such as you provided to NIH" were made public.[32] Presumably even fewer would have objected if the questionnaire had not referred to a "complete list of . . . financial holdings," thus suggesting that *all* financial interests, including dollar amounts, would be made public. This response strongly suggests that most scientific consultants do not regard the information contained in Form 474 as highly personal.[33]

Second, Executive Order 11,222 does not require that consultants' statements be held confidential—it at most *permits* the government to promise confidentiality. The decision not to require a promise of confidentiality was apparently deliberate, for the Order does require that the more extensive disclosure statements of certain high-level officials be kept confidential. This suggests that the President did not view the limited disclosure required of consultants to be a serious invasion of privacy.

32. Joint Appendix at 70–145, *Women in Science.* The plaintiffs received 76 responses to their questionnaire. Sixty-two people replied "no," 7 replied "yes," 4 responded with some variant of "maybe," and 3 did not respond.

33. The dissent argues that this conclusion ignores the interests of the minority who would object. It is intrinsic to a balancing analysis, however, that the views of the majority who do not object receive greater weight than the views of the more sensitive minority. Cf. United States Dep't of State v. Washington Post, 456 U.S. at ___, 102 S.Ct. at 1960 (emphasis added) (noting that "place of birth, date of birth, date of marriage, employment history, and comparable data is not *normally regarded* as highly personal").

Moreover, as we discuss below, most of the confidentiality provisions of the Order were repealed by the Ethics in Government Act of 1978—suggesting Congress's view that financial disclosure is not an undue invasion of privacy.

Third, the consultants are given only a limited promise of confidentiality—the information can be disclosed "for good cause." That vague phrase could mean, for all the consultants know, that conflicts of interest will generally be made public. Yet the government has not suggested that this undefined and potentially broad exception to confidentiality has discouraged scientists from accepting consulting positions.

To be sure, the consultants' expectations of privacy were heightened by the government's pledge of confidentiality. Other things being equal, release of information provided under a pledge of confidentiality involves a greater invasion of privacy than release of information provided without such a pledge. On the other hand, to allow the government to make documents exempt by the simple means of promising confidentiality would subvert FOIA's disclosure mandate. On balance, we believe that a government pledge of confidentiality, made in good faith and consistently honored, should generally be given weight on the privacy side of the scale in accord with its effect on expectations of privacy. However, such a pledge should not be given determinative weight where the public interest in disclosure is high and the privacy interest in the information would otherwise be low. In this case, we believe that the limited pledge of confidentiality does not substantially increase the privacy expectations of most consultants; certainly not enough to tip the balance in favor of withholding.

2. *Disclosure Interests*

In contrast to the limited privacy interests, the public has a singularly strong interest in disclosure of consultants' conflicts of interest. Scientific consultants determine, in large part, who receives roughly $1 billion per year in cancer research funds. While the peer review system provides the government with needed expert advice, it also has undeniable potential for occasional abuse. Unscrupulous consultants could promote the projects of organizations with which they are connected, recommend disapproval of the projects of competitors, or, to curry favor for their own proposals, recommend projects favored by other consultants.

The possibility of such conflicts is more than mere speculation. HHS's program of in-house review is itself evidence that conflicts of interest are a potential problem. Also, there have been recent allegations of and investigations into conflicts of interest on the part of NCI peer reviewers. See National Cancer Institute Contract and Procurement Procedures, 1981: Hearing Before the Senate Comm. on Labor and Human Resources, 97th Cong., 1st Sess. (June 2, 1981) ("NCI Hearing"). . . .

One hopes, of course, that HHS's in-house review is rigorous enough to catch any abuses. But the purpose of FOIA is to permit the public to decide *for itself* whether government action is proper. . . . In light of that purpose, the public interest in disclosure is not diminished by the possibility or even the probability that HHS is doing its reviewing job right.

Our belief that public disclosure of conflict-of-interest information is vital is strengthened by Congress's passage of the Ethics in Government Act of 1978. . . . [T]he Act shows Congress's general belief that public disclosure of conflicts of interest is desirable despite its cost in loss of personal privacy. Indeed, it is hard to see how disclosure of the limited information on Form 474 can be a clearly unwarranted invasion of privacy for a consultant . . . while regular employees with comparable or in some cases lesser responsibility must make far more extensive disclosure under the Ethics in Government Act.

In sum, when the strong interest in disclosure of potential abuses of official position is balanced against the consultants' relatively slight privacy interest in the limited information required by Form 474, we have no trouble concluding that disclosure is not "clearly unwarranted."

III.   EXEMPTION 4

Exemption 4 authorizes withholding of "commercial or financial information obtained from a person and privileged or confidential." 5 U.S.C. § 552(b)(4). Thus, there are two threshold requirements for Exemption 4: the information must be (1) "obtained from a person" and (2) "commercial or financial." If these threshold requirements are met, we must determine whether the information is "privileged or confidential."

A.   *Applicability of Exemption 4 to Personal Financial Information*

We do not see, nor has the government explained, how the list of non-federal employment on Form 474 can be "commercial or financial information." As for the list of financial interests, it was certainly "obtained from a person," but the parties dispute whether it is "financial" information within the meaning of Exemption 4. . . .

. . .

. . . Lacking guidance in the legislative history, we must give the term "financial" its "ordinary meaning[ ]." In our view, the list of organizations required by Form 474 is within the common understanding of the term "financial." Indeed, we cannot think of any description of that information that would not use the word "financial" or a synonym.

B.   *The Meaning of "Confidential" Under Exemption 4*

The remaining issue is whether the list of financial interests is "privileged or confidential." The government has not asserted that Form 474 is "privileged" within the meaning of Exemption 4. . . .

. . .

2.   *The Test for Confidentiality*

Under the standard test in this circuit, commercial or financial information is "confidential" under Exemption 4 if disclosure is likely "(1) to impair the Government's ability to obtain necessary information in the future; or (2) to cause substantial harm to the competitive position of the person from whom the information was obtained." National Parks & Conservation Association v. Morton, 498 F.2d 765, 770 (D.C.Cir.1974) (National Parks I). The test is an objective one and the government's promise of confidentiality is not dispositive. Id. at 766.

In this case, the government concedes that disclosure will not cause competitive harm, and the conflict of interest information is sufficiently important to be "necessary." Thus the only issue is whether disclosure is likely to impair the government's ability to obtain similar information in the future.

. . .

This inquiry [into whether disclosure will impair the government's ability to obtain necessary information] necessarily involves a rough balancing of the extent of impairment and the importance of the information against the public interest in disclosure. We do not decide today the details of the balancing process.

. . .

. . . The decision of the district court is *reversed* as to Exemption 6 and *reversed and remanded* as to Exemption 4.

TAMM, CIRCUIT JUDGE, dissenting: . . .

. . .

[T]here can be, as the majority concedes, no doubt that the information sought by appellant is contained in "personnel . . . [or] similar files" for the purposes of Exemption 6. It is clear that the Forms 474 contain information applicable and directly relating to the financial and employment affairs of individuals, and the majority's rejection of appellant's position on this issue is clearly correct.

I turn, then, to what is in this case the more difficult of the Exemption 6 inquiries—whether the disclosure of the forms would constitute a "clearly unwarranted invasion of personal privacy." . . . [T]he dispositive question . . . is whether "the severity of the invasion of the personal privacy resulting from disclosure would outweigh the public interest in publication." Furthermore, it is clear that the "clearly unwarranted" language of Exemption 6 expresses a " 'carefully considered congressional policy favoring disclosure' which 'instructs the court to tilt the balance in favor of disclosure.' " Ditlow v. Shultz, 517 F.2d 166, 169 (D.C.Cir.1975) (quoting Getman v. NLRB, 450 F.2d 670, 674 & n. 11 (D.C.Cir.1971)).

. . .

. . . I [, however,] am able to discern no fewer than six factors that, in my opinion, militate against disclosure of the financial and employment material found on the Forms 474.

(1) *The sensitive, personal nature of the information.*

. . .

The focus of this and every other court in an Exemption 6 case must be on the respective public and private interests at stake. After carefully studying these interests, I am compelled to conclude that the district judge was eminently correct in upholding the government's claims that Exemption 6 grounded nondisclosure of the Forms 474. For many, if not most, individuals details of personal financial strategies are intensely personal matters. Few individuals publicize, at least voluntarily, the scope of their investments; rather, such matters are typically maintained with the greatest of privacy. Similarly, for a variety of motives, reasonable, law-abiding citizens may be reluctant to disclose their employers; indeed, it is not unreasonable to surmise that that might particularly be the case where the individuals perform ad hoc consulting functions, as undoubtedly do many of those who submit Form 474 to the NCI. . . . [These] concerns of embarrassing revelations are at the heart of the personal privacy exemption to the FOIA.

Thus, I demur strongly to the majority's contention that the revelation of the employment and financial data in question would infringe only minor and insignificant privacy interests of the appointees. The implicit basis of this court's decision in *Women in Science* was the conclusion that the data at issue partook of a sensitive, personal nature that would lead reasonable individuals to desire that the information not be disclosed. We reached that conclusion in *Women in Science* notwithstanding the fact that a poll conducted by appellants in that case indicated that eighty per cent of the NCI appointees would not have objected to the disclosure. Both appellant in the case at bar and, with respect, the majority miss the point of this poll, the accuracy of which no one appears to dispute: *to argue that because four-fifths of those polled would not object to disclosure suggests that the infringement of privacy interests would collectively be minor ignores totally the interests of the forgotten twenty per cent.* It is beyond any cavil that Exemption 6 was drafted and enacted to protect against the disclosure of *embarrassing information;* that eighty per cent of the appointees apparently are not in a position to be embarrassed is, in my opinion, utterly irrelevant to the determination of whether disclosure of the information submitted by the remaining twenty per cent *would* be "clearly unwarranted."

When one combines the fact that many of the appointees apparently *would* object to the disclosure of the Form 474 data with the fact that the government promised *all* of the appointees that the information would not be disclosed without "good cause," the error committed by the majority in declining to recognize the applicability of Exemption 6 to the data is manifest. Thus, even if the majority is correct in straitjacketing the Exemption 6 inquiry to the public interests *favoring* disclosure, ignoring those interests of the public militating against release, I cannot agree that disclosure of the information is proper. . . . .

Moreover, we should not forget—as I believe the majority conveniently does—that the submitter of the Form 474 data does not provide information regarding only his own financial affairs. Rather, he is directed to provide a listing of all organizations the interests of which might relate to his consultancy duties, and in which his spouse, child, partner, or affiliated organization has an interest. That the invasion of privacy affects not simply the provider of the information, but his or her family as well, further militates, in my opinion, against disclosure.

(2) *The pledge of confidentiality.*

. . .

In determining the efficacy of a pledge of confidentiality in a given case, it will usually be necessary to examine all the surrounding circumstances to discover the extent to which the pledge induced the submission of the information. . . .

. . . [T]his situation is one in which the providers of the data might well have placed considerable reliance on the promise of confidentiality. The advisory board and committee members serve as part-time employees of the federal government and presumably could have declined the proffered opportunity to serve if the "conditions" of employment were altered. In a case such as this one, it would thus appear that a pledge of confidence should be given great weight. . . .

(3) *The limited compensation afforded the advisory board members.*

. . . I believe that few individuals would participate on the NCI boards were a selfish commitment to personal gain the primary motivation. Although I harbor no delusions regarding the vagaries of human character, the reports of the demise of altruism are, I believe, exaggerated.

(4) *The internal review scheme.*

Further militating against the release of the Form 474 data is the existence of the NCI's own internal review scheme for ferreting out conflicts of interest. . . .

. . . The important question in the current context is not, of course, whether scrutiny by the Washington Post Company or by any citizen might shed additional light on self-serving practices engaged in by advisory board members. The critical inquiry is rather whether the *marginal* gain from such scrutiny outweighs the significant privacy interests that would be infringed by disclosure of the Form 474 data. . . .

(5) *The incongruity of the release of the Form 474 data with the result in* Women in Science.

. . .

(6) *The "public harm" that might result from disclosure.*

. . .

Perhaps the most troubling and difficult issue in the case at bar is the matter of the weight, if any, that should be accorded the fact that disclosure of the Form 474 data might well deter qualified applicants from accepting NCI advisory board positions and might inhibit the flow of accurate information to the government. . . . [T]his is a matter of no small moment; even individuals with "nothing to hide" might be hesitant to accept an NCI position out of a fear that the details of their financial and work lives would provide the grist for a newspaper reporter's mill. . . .

. . .

Although I do not wish to mandate the inclusion of a new element in the Exemption 6 balancing process, I think it wrong to foreclose completely consideration of the important public interest in securing talented, qualified appointees to staff the NCI advisory boards. . . . To be sure, I would not accord too much significance to this factor, for the contention that the citizenry would be better off not knowing certain matters has a potential for perniciousness that no court should ignore. To ignore the public harm that might result from disclosure, however, is to adopt an ostrich-like approach to the Exemption 6 balancing process that is inconsistent with a full and intelligent consideration of all factors relevant to the "public interest in disclosure."

Accordingly, I would hold that the data at issue in this litigation is exempt from disclosure under Exemption 6.

. . .

NOTES

1. Do you agree with the *Washington Post* majority's analysis of the privacy interests of the NCI consultants? Or do you side with Judge Tamm? What pub-

lic interests would disclosure of the information in question actually serve? Do you think that the material sought would be helpful in uncovering individual conflicts of interest? In what ways would the material be helpful? Do you agree with Judge Tamm that decisionmakers must weigh in the balance any public harm that might result from disclosure?

2. California has recently applied stringent conflict of interest laws to scientists at state universities. These scientists will now be required to disclose their financial ties to a commercial enterprise if that enterprise makes a grant to the scientist or the scientist's institution to underwrite research. A state Fair Political Practice Committee will evaluate any reported connections and determine if the scientist must sever ties with the enterprise. See Washington Post, Feb. 16, 1982, at A3, col. 1. Do you think that this disclosure requirement is significantly different from the one examined in *Washington Post?* If so, how? Some California faculty members have suggested that this requirement could violate academic freedom. Do you agree?

3. In many academic medical centers, medical practice plans have become an important means for retaining the services of full-time faculty members and for generating income for the medical schools. These practice plans represent an accommodation of two sometimes conflicting desires: the teaching physician's desire to treat patients privately to increase his or her earnings and the institution's desire to keep a faculty member available for research and teaching. The plan is structured to centralize billing and collecting procedures, to compensate participants based on their varying activity levels and to provide office space and support services, while at the same time to limit the time a participant can devote to private practice. Although the individual plans take different shapes, most often they are units of the relevant medical school or private corporations which the teaching physicians themselves control. For a more complete discussion, see Association of American Medical Colleges, Medical Practice Plans in 1980 (1981); Schmidt, Zieve and D'Lugoff, A Practice Plan in a Municipal Teaching Hospital, 304 New Eng.J.Med. 263 (1981); Relman, Faculty-Practice Plans, 304 New Eng.J.Med. 292 (1981).

What conflicts of interest do you think might result from medical practice plans? Are they serious enough to require some form of professional regulation? Governmental regulation? How might lawyers involved in setting up medical practice plans anticipate and protect against potential conflicts?

4. The legal profession also has had to police various conflicts of interest. One of the more controversial conflicts is the so-called "revolving door" problem that occurs when a government lawyer leaves his or her position to take a job in a private law firm that represents parties opposing the government in pending or potential legal actions. To avoid improper conflicts, Congress passed the Ethics in Government Act of 1978, Pub.L. No. 95–521, 92 Stat. 1824 (codified as amended at 2, 5, 18, 28 & 39 U.S.C. (Supp. V 1981)). A major provision of the act completely revised the employment restrictions imposed on government officers and employees when they leave government service. 18 U.S.C. § 207 (Supp. V 1981). Section 207 imposes criminal liability on former government officers or employees who violate its operative provisions. Subsection (a) places a lifetime restriction on any former government officer or employee representing in any way a party opposing or petitioning the government in any matter in which he or she had participated personally in any advisory or decisionmaking capacity. § 207(a). Subsection (b) has two provisions. First, it restricts for two years the ability of a former government officer or employee to represent a party opposing or petitioning the government in any matter which had been pending under his or her official responsibility. Second, it forbids for the same two-year period a former government officer or employee from making an appearance on behalf of a party opposing or petitioning the government in any matter in which he or she had "personally and substantially" participated. § 207(b). Finally, subsection (c) makes it illegal for a former government officer or employee to represent a party opposing or petitioning the government in any matter pending before the department or agency with which the officer or employee served within one year after he

or she leaves government service even if he or she was not involved in that matter. § 207(c). The Director of the Office of Government Ethics can permit former officers and employees covered under subsection (c) to appear before and make communications to unrelated agencies if no possibility of unfair advantage or undue influence exists. § 207(d). Less stringent penalties are imposed against partners of former government officers or employees who violate subsection (a), (b) or (c). 207(g).

In addition, to these statutory requirements, courts have imposed other obligations on former government lawyers and their law firms. The courts require a law firm that hires a former government attorney to build up internal safeguards (a "Chinese wall") to insure that he or she does not participate in planning or litigating any matter on which he or she may have worked while serving in the government, does not have access to files of such matters and does not share in any profits derived from such matters. When a court feels that the exclusion of the one attorney would be insufficient protection against a conflict or an appearance of impropriety, it can disqualify the entire firm from participating in the matter.

An influential "Chinese wall" case is Armstrong v. McAlpin, 625 F.2d 433 (2d Cir.1980), vacated on other grounds, 449 U.S. 1106, 101 S.Ct. 911, 66 L.Ed.2d 835 (1981), where a divided U.S. Court of Appeals for the Second Circuit, sitting *en banc*, upheld a district court's denial of disqualification of a law firm representing a securities firm receiver, even though an attorney at the firm had been an assistant director at the SEC. Some courts have reached different results. In *Greitzer & Locks*, 710 F.2d 127, cert. denied 459 U.S. 1010, 103 S.Ct. 364, 74 L.Ed.2d 400 (1982), a panel of the Court of Appeals reversed the district court's disqualification of a six member law firm representing a large number of plaintiffs in asbestos litigation in which the federal government and various federal agencies were defendants. The attorney in question had participated in the government's defense preparation while working at the Department of Justice. In holding that the "Chinese wall" erected would suffice to prevent any conflicts, the panel found that no evidence had been presented to justify the "harsh remedy" of disqualification of the entire firm. The full Court affirmed the District Court, without opinion, on an even vote. See also Analytica Corp. v. NPD Research, Inc., 708 F.2d 1263 (7th Cir.1983) (upholding district court's disqualification of two law firms representing plaintiff in antitrust action when lead law firm had represented former employee of defendant, whose wife had organized plaintiff corporation, in stock transfer matter requiring detailed analysis of defendant's confidential financial and operating data) and LaSalle National Bank v. County of Lake, 703 F.2d 252 (7th Cir.1983) (upholding district court's disqualification of large law firm representing plaintiffs in suit against local governmental bodies where law firm had hired former assistant state's attorney who had reviewed agreements between local and county governments in question and had helped formulate strategy concerning such agreements despite assurances attorney had revealed no confidential material).

The major difference between the judicial and statutory approaches concerns the sanctions involved. The judicial "Chinese wall" doctrine causes the involved former government attorney to lose his or her share of income from the matter in question and can cause the law firm to lose all income from the matter. On the other hand, the statutory approach makes the involved former government officer or employee *and* all of his or her partners criminally liable for actions which Congress has determined to be conflicts of interest. Which approach do you think will be more successful? Why? Do you think either will be successful?

In *Armstrong*, the court discussed disciplinary rule D.R. 5–105(D) of the A.B.A. Model Code of Professional Responsibility, which provides, "If a lawyer is required to decline employment or to withdraw from employment under a disciplinary rule, no partner, or associate, or any other lawyer affiliated with him or his firm, may accept or continue such employment." Consider the language of the

A.B.A. Model Rules of Professional Conduct, which the A.B.A. promulgated in 1983 to replace the Model Code:

RULE 1.11   Successive Government and Private Employment

(a) Except as law may otherwise expressly permit, a lawyer shall not represent a private client in connection with a matter in which the lawyer participated personally and substantially as a public officer or employee, unless the appropriate government agency consents after consultation. No lawyer in a firm with which that lawyer is associated may knowingly undertake or continue representation in such a matter unless:

(1) the disqualified lawyer is screened from any participation in the matter and is apportioned no part of the fee therefrom; and

(2) written notice is promptly given to the appropriate government agency to enable it to ascertain compliance with the provisions of this Rule.

. . .

COMMENT:

The Rule prevents a lawyer from exploiting public office for the advantage of a private client: . . .

A lawyer representing a government agency, whether employed or specially retained by the government, is subject to the Rules of Professional Conduct, including the prohibition against representing adverse interests and to statutes and government regulations regarding conflict of interest. . . .

Where the successive clients are a public agency and a private client, the risk exists that power or discretion vested in public authority might be used for the special benefit of a private client. . . . [U]nfair advantage could accrue to the private client by reason of access to confidential governmental information about the client's adversary obtainable only through the lawyer's government service. However, the rules governing lawyers presently or formerly employed by a government agency should not be so restrictive as to inhibit transfer of employment to and from the government. The government has a legitimate need to attract qualified lawyers as well as to maintain high ethical standards.

. . .

Is the new rule an improvement? Do you think that it is possible to isolate an attorney totally from a matter on which he or she had previously worked? Of what importance is the concern, expressed in the Comment to Model Rule 1.11, that screening provisions should not be so strict as to serve as a determent to lawyers' serving in the government? It should be noted that in Armstrong v. McAlpin, a host of present and former government attorneys asserted these same concerns as *amici curiae.* 625 F.2d at 443. They contended that too stringent restrictions would hamper the government's efforts both to hire and to promote qualified attorneys. Id.

6. Less than a year after enacting the Ethics in Government Act, Congress amended it to exempt former government employees or officers distinguished in "scientific, technological or other technical discipline[s]." 18 U.S.C. § 207(g) (Supp. V 1981). Congress acted because it believed that in scientific and technical areas, especially biomedical and defense-related research, a policy that fosters a mix of career and short-term employees in government positions best serves the public interest. H.R.Rep. No. 115, 96th Cong., 1st Sess. 5 (1979). It accepted the belief expressed in committee testimony that the penalties for which private employers could be liable under the Ethics in Government Act would effectively make the most talented researchers unavailable for government service. Id. at 3–4. How does this action relate to the concerns that the A.B.A. expressed in the Model Rules Comment and the *Armstrong amici curiae* articulated regarding attorneys? Is there justification for treating scientists differently than attorneys?

5.   INSTITUTIONAL RESPONSIBILITIES

a.   Protecting the Search for Knowledge

Universities must face the challenges of financing large-scale scientific research in the contemporary climate of decreasing federal subsidies and of accommodating the interests of faculty members seeking the economic benefits that increased industrial involvement provides.   In so doing, they have sought new ways to generate income and to share in income that faculty members realize through university-related activities.   While reviewing the following materials, consider the various approaches to increase institutions' ability to generate funding to support research activities.   Do you prefer some approaches to others?   Why?   Can you identify each approach's strengths and weaknesses?   What roles should the law and lawyers play in implementing means to support research?

AN ACT TO AMEND THE PATENT AND TRADEMARK LAWS

Public Law No. 96–517 (1980) 35 U.S.C. §§ 200–202, 205.

Sec. 6.   (a) Title 35 of the United States Code, entitled "Patents", is amended by adding after chapter 37 the following new chapter 38:

"CHAPTER 38—PATENT RIGHTS IN INVENTIONS MADE WITH FEDERAL ASSISTANCE

. . .

"§ 200.   Policy and objective

"It is the policy and objective of the Congress to use the patent system to promote the utilization of inventions arising from federally supported research or development; to encourage maximum participation of small business firms in federally supported research and development efforts; to promote collaboration between commercial concerns and nonprofit organizations, including universities; to ensure that inventions made by nonprofit organizations and small business firms are used in a manner to promote free competition and enterprise; to promote the commercialization and public availability of inventions made in the United States by United States industry and labor; to ensure that the Government obtains sufficient rights in federally supported inventions to meet the needs of the Government and protect the public against nonuse or unreasonable use of inventions; and to minimize the costs of administering policies in this area.

"§ 201.   Definitions

"As used in this chapter—

. . .

"(b) The term 'funding agreement' means any contract, grant, or cooperative agreement entered into between any Federal agency . . . and any contractor for the performance of experimental, developmental, or research work funded in whole or in part by the Federal Government. Such term includes any assignment, substitution of parties, or subcontract of any type. . . .

. . .

"(d) The term 'invention' means any invention or discovery which is or may be patentable or otherwise protectable under this title.

"(e) The term 'subject invention' means any invention of the contractor conceived or first actually reduced to practice in the performance of work under a funding agreement.

. . .

"(i) The term 'nonprofit organization' means universities and other institutions of higher education or an organization of the type described in section 501(c)(3) of the Internal Revenue Code of 1954 . . . or any nonprofit scientific or educational organization qualified under a State nonprofit organization statute.

"§ 202. Disposition of rights

"(a) Each nonprofit organization or small business firm may, within a reasonable time after disclosure as required by paragraph (c)(1) of this section, elect to retain title to any subject invention: *Provided, however,* That a funding agreement may provide otherwise (i) when the funding agreement is for the operation of a Government-owned research or production facility, (ii) in exceptional circumstances when it is determined by the agency that restriction or elimination of the right to retain title to any subject invention will better promote the policy and objectives of this chapter or (iii) when it is determined by a Government authority which is authorized by statute or Executive order to conduct foreign intelligence or counter-intelligence activities that the restriction or elimination of the right to retain title to any subject invention is necessary to protect the security of such activities. The rights of the nonprofit organization or small business firm shall be subject to the provisions of paragraph (c) of this section and the other provisions of this chapter.

. . .

"(c) Each funding agreement with a small business firm or nonprofit organization shall contain appropriate provisions to effectuate the following:

"(1) A requirement that the contractor disclose each subject invention to the Federal agency within a reasonable time after it is made and that the Federal Government may receive title to any subject invention not reported to it within such time.

"(2) A requirement that the contractor make an election to retain title to any subject invention within a reasonable time after disclosure and that the Federal Government may receive title to any subject invention in which the contractor does not elect to retain rights or fails to elect rights within such time.

"(3) A requirement that a contractor electing rights file patent applications within reasonable times and that the Federal Government may receive title to any subject inventions in the United States or other countries in which the contractor has not filed patent applications on the subject invention within such times.

"(4) With respect to any invention in which the contractor elects rights, the Federal agency shall have a nonexclusive, nontransferable, irrevocable, paid-up license to practice or have practiced for or on behalf of the United States any subject invention throughout the world, and may, if provided in the funding agreement, have additional rights to sublicense any foreign government or international organization pursuant to any existing or future treaty or agreement.

"(5) The right of the Federal agency to require periodic reporting on the utilization or efforts at obtaining utilization that are being made by the contractor or his licensees or assignees: *Provided*, That any such information may be treated by the Federal agency as commercial and financial information obtained from a person and privileged and confidential and not subject to disclosure under section 552 of title 5 of the United States Code.

"(6) An obligation on the part of the contractor, in the event a United States patent application is filed by or on its behalf or by any assignee of the contractor, to include within the specification of such application and any patent issuing thereon, a statement specifying that the invention was made with Government support and that the Government has certain rights in the invention.

"(7) In the case of a nonprofit organization, (A) a prohibition upon the assignment of rights to a subject invention in the United States without the approval of the Federal agency, except where such assignment is made to an organization which has as one of its primary functions the management of inventions and which is not, itself, engaged in or does not hold a substantial interest in other organizations engaged in the manufacture or sale of products or the use of processes that might utilize the invention or be in competition with embodiments of the invention (provided that such assignee shall be subject to the same provisions as the contractor); (B) a prohibition against the granting of exclusive licenses under United States Patents or Patent Applications in a subject invention by the contractor to persons other than small business firms for a period in excess of the earlier of five years from first commercial sale or use of the invention or eight years from the date of the exclusive license excepting that time before regulatory agencies necessary to obtain premarket clearance unless, on a case-by-case basis, the Federal agency approves a longer exclusive license. If exclusive field of use licenses are granted, commercial sale or use in one field of use shall not be deemed commercial sale or use as to other fields of use, and a first commercial sale or use with respect to a product of the invention shall not be deemed to end the exclusive period to different subsequent products covered by the invention; (C) a requirement that the contractor share royalties with the inventor; and (D) a requirement that the balance of any royalties or income earned by the contractor with respect to subject inventions, after payment of expenses (including payments to inventors) incidental to the administration of subject inventions, be utilized for the support of scientific research or education.

. . . .

"(d) If a contractor does not elect to retain title to a subject invention in cases subject to this section, the Federal agency may consider and after consultation with the contractor grant requests for retention of rights by the inventor subject to the provisions of this Act and regulations promulgated hereunder.

"(e) In any case when a Federal employee is a coinventor of any invention made under a funding agreement with a nonprofit organization or small business firm, the Federal agency employing such coinventor is authorized to transfer or assign whatever rights it may acquire in the subject invention from its employee to the contractor subject to the conditions set forth in this chapter.

"(f)(1) No funding agreement with a small business firm or nonprofit organization shall contain a provision allowing a Federal agency to require the licensing to third parties of inventions owned by the contractor that are not subject inventions unless such provision has been approved by the head of the agency and a written justification has been signed by the head of the agency . . . .

"(2) A Federal agency shall not require the licensing of third parties under any such provision unless the head of the agency determines that the use of the invention by others is necessary for the practice of a subject invention or for the use of a work object of the funding agreement and that such action is necessary to achieve the practical application of the subject invention or work object. . . .

· · ·

"§ 205. Confidentiality

"Federal agencies are authorized to withhold from disclosure to the public information disclosing any invention in which the Federal Government owns or may own a right, title, or interest (including a nonexclusive license) for a reasonable time in order for a patent application to be filed. Furthermore, Federal agencies shall not be required to release copies of any document, which is part of an application for patent filed with the United States Patent and Trademark Office or with any foreign patent office.

· · ·

NOTE

For discussion of the role of patents and licensing in DNA research, see Ch. 1, Sec. B.5, supra.

BERNARD DAVIS,
PROFIT SHARING BETWEEN PROFESSORS
AND THE UNIVERSITY?

304 New Eng. J.Med. 1232 (1981).

The intellectual yield from our country's investment in fundamental biologic research has been tremendous. . . .

. . . [U]nlike earlier experience with the biochemistry of amino acids, vitamins, hormones, and antibiotics, the practical payoffs from molecular genetics were disappointingly slow. . . . [T]he picture has now changed dramatically. Emerging from the integration of three decades of fundamental and even esoteric research, the recombinant-DNA technology now promises innumerable applications in agriculture and in energy production as well as in medicine. Molecular biology has thus burst into the age of high technology, and the resulting acute speculative fever has perhaps been exacerbated by the earlier celebrity of recombinant DNA as a presumed menace.

The new commercial possibilities present universities with both opportunities and risks. . . . In my analysis of these problems, I shall proceed on the following assumptions: first of all, that the university community has a social obligation to try to promote technology transfer, but that it should do so in ways that will not jeopardize the search for knowledge for its own sake; secondly, that in this country the options will continue to lie within the framework of a system of private enterprise; and thirdly, that because of the changing pattern of government support of scientific research, universities are obligated to try to find additional sources of funds, both to preserve their autonomy and to prevent a waste of trained scientific talent. All these assumptions may be questioned, of course, but such questions are beyond the scope of this discussion.

PATENTS

Patents have long been used to provide income for universities. For example, the royalties of the Wisconsin Alumni Research Foundation since the 1920s have made biochemistry an unusually strong field at that university. In general, however, biologists have been much less interested in patents than chemists or engineers have—perhaps because their work has only rarely lent itself to applications. Moreover, in medicine the earlier tradition of charity to the poor raised additional barriers to commercialization. Accordingly, for many years the Harvard Corporation required that any health-related discoveries in its laboratories be dedicated to the public. Meanwhile, there have been major changes in the economics of medical care and in the attitude of federal agencies toward patents. In addition, it has become clear that the absence of a patent often impairs, rather than promotes, the availability of a useful product to the public. . . .

Some object to even this degree of university involvement on the grounds that it may lead to preferential treatment of certain faculty members. However, this problem is not unique to patents. Grants bring in a large overhead. Moreover, faculty salaries are often derived from grants to individual faculty members, and the influence of external funding on appointments may then be considerable. In contrast, any royalties from patents can be distributed without externally imposed restrictions. It is thus hard to see why patents are likely to bias appointments more than grants and contracts do.

Another criticism of patenting is that it encourages secrecy. However, as is well known, secrecy is widespread in highly competitive fields of even the purest research. To be sure, patentability may provide an additional incentive to secrecy over the short term, but in the long run patents eliminate the need for secrecy, since after the date of filing of a patent application, like the date of submission of a publication, the information is released for free discussion and for noncommercial use by others. Indeed, in industry, unpatentable information is the main body of trade secrets.

. . .

PRIVATE CORPORATIONS AND THE SPECIAL PROBLEMS OF BIOLOGY

Another well-established mechanism for the commercial exploitation of science—potentially more profitable for the professor—is the formation of a private corporation. That a number of molecular biologists have initiated such undertakings is not surprising, especially since research in this field has been characterized by unusual boldness in moving to challenging new problems.

Universities have treated such activities much as they treat industrial consulting—a practice that they often encourage because, like part-time practice in medicine, it helps to retain valuable faculty. Consulting time is often limited, either by a formal rule or by an informal agreement, to one day a week. However, the development of a new company is likely to require much more time. Moreover, the impact of such an involvement on academic activities cannot be measured entirely in terms of formal hours of work; a change in what the professor is thinking about when showering or driving may have an even greater effect.

An excessive diversion of time may be only a temporary stage at the start of a new business. Accordingly, in this area universities are justified in continuing their tradition of flexibility and patience in supervising the daily distribution of faculty time. On the other hand, the problem of a substantial diversion for a long period under the umbrella of a full-time university salary cannot be ignored, and I shall return to it.

The collegial academic atmosphere is likely to be even more seriously harmed by competition between faculty colleagues who are associated with different companies, although the tradition of industrial ties in chemistry and in solid-state physics provides a somewhat reassuring model. However, there are important differences, not only in the traditions but also in the content of the fields. Specifically, in recombinant-DNA research the competition may well be much more intense than it is in these other fields, at least for the present, because the range of problems is so much narrower; many groups are inevitably seeking the same product, such as insulin or interferon.

Two other differences between biology and chemistry are also pertinent. In the first place, biology often asks more philosophic questions that are remote from potential applications. Secondly, because of the extraordinary complexity of biologic material, major breakthroughs frequently depend on a happy accident, an unexpected observation, or an unpredictable implication of distant findings. If the search for wealth diverts too many of the best biologists in the next generation from undirected exploration of the nature of life, something precious will be lost.

Clearly, these are serious problems. If research in this new industry becomes more autonomous and developmental, perhaps like research in antibiotics over the past decades, these problems may be only temporary. However, antibiotics arose from an accidental discovery, and their pursuit has remained largely empirical, whereas recombinant DNA has extensive theoretical roots. Hence, its applications are likely to continue to depend heavily on advances in academic laboratories.

The Harvard Proposal and the Future of Institutional Profit Sharing

. . . [U]niversities have generally shared in profits from patents on discoveries made in their laboratories but not in those from companies stemming from such discoveries. However, some European laboratories have recently extended profit sharing to the second arrangement. A similar proposal was made at Harvard last October but was soon withdrawn. It elicited a strongly unfavorable response from some of the faculty and from editorial writers in the news media. Now that the tempest has subsided, it may be useful to reexamine the issues.

The proposal arose when Harvard was considering the possibility of patenting a discovery of Prof. Mark Ptashne in recombinant DNA. The Harvard administration suggested the alternative of setting up a company with outside venture capital and with the university given a minority share (which was subsequently said to be 10 per cent). The company, in return, would have the rights to any patents on Ptashne's discoveries held by the university. In the memorandum that opened the discussion, the Harvard administration carefully spelled out a number of pitfalls in this kind of venture, and it asked the faculty to consider the abstract policy issues and principles involved. However, it did not specify any details of the proposed arrangement or even mention Ptashne's name; it simply informed the faculty that it would be making a decision on a specific arrangement within three weeks.

. . .

In the end, two dangers seem to have caused the greatest concern: pressures on faculty in their choice of research and favoritism of the university toward financially productive faculty members. The memorandum unfortunately presented both these problems as though they were novel, instead of comparing them with the similar problems associated with other sources of funds. As a result, the issues were analyzed rather unrealistically, and an idealized conception of the university was defended: the institution was presumed to be entirely free of restrictions on how it distributes its income in supporting the preservation, advancement, and dissemination of pure knowledge. In fact, research grants from government, foundations, and industry—and many endowments in support of professorial chairs or specialized institutes—generally do not provide such freedom.

. . .

Universities have had a long history of negotiations, especially in medical schools, over academic activities and positions linked to private gain. The members of the Harvard Faculty of Arts and Sciences demonstrated little awareness of this history in their . . . discussion. The emergence of professors as entrepreneurs raises a wide range of problems, but the only one discussed was the prospect of having the university involved as well. In particular, no questions were raised about existing [private] companies that do not contaminate (or benefit) the university. . . .

In the absence of limiting ground rules, it was perfectly proper for enterprising faculty members to have set up such unshared private corporations, but I suggest that the rapid expansion of such activities now demands a broader look. Medical schools have long faced a similar problem with full-time salaried faculty members who collect fees from private patients. Many solutions have been tried, ranging from complete transfer of the money to the institution to no transfer. Unfortunately, this experience does not offer any ideal, universally accepted model for other faculties beginning to face a similar dilemma. Nevertheless, it has certainly not been obvious that complete retention of the income by the faculty member best serves the university, or that it represents the fairest possible arrangement.

CONCLUSIONS

We may all regret the loss of the more Arcadian atmosphere of the past. However, if universities are to protect their financial base in order to advance their academic goals, nostalgia will be no substitute for imaginative adaptations and a tough-minded attitude. There are surely risks in developing industrial connections, but they must be balanced against the increasing financial insecurity of universities today and against a monolithic dependence on an often unsympathetic government.

There is also a question of simple justice. The facilities, the atmosphere, and the financial support of universities have provided an essential background for many commercial developments, and the continued connection of the entrepreneur with the university, like the connection of a physician with a teaching hospital, often gives the entrepreneur a good deal of prestige. It therefore seems just that the university, which can no longer afford to be in the position of a generous parent, should in return receive a share of the profits. In addition, such profit sharing would respond to a widespread and cogent criticism of the present system: that it unfairly allows professors to become rich through developments stemming from tax-supported research. There is still appeal in the basic concept of dedicating a medical discovery (especially a tax-supported discovery) to the public interest, and distribution of part of the profit to the university surely serves the public interest more directly than does distribution only to the other participants.

One could argue that licensing patents is a less entangling way to reimburse the university than is the sharing of equity. However, the advantage of equity in a corporation is not only the possibility of a larger income to the university; it may be even more important as a means of ensuring continued benefits from future discoveries. Once a professor had begun to direct research in an industry as well as in an academic laboratory, he or she would no doubt be tempted to shift to the latter any branch of the academic work that appeared potentially patentable.

Finally, profit sharing could have certain mutually advantageous byproducts that were not mentioned in connection with the Harvard proposal. For example, if the industrial laboratory was nearby, which would be convenient for all concerned, a financial interest by the university could eliminate the question of recompense for access of company scientists to libraries and seminars. Similarly, the specialized instruments and facilities for large-scale preparations in an industrial laboratory could occasionally be useful for university researchers.

. . . [T]he possibility of conflict of interest is real, as is the problem of keeping the business connection at arm's length from the academic activities of the university. In addition, there remains a serious moral issue. Given the rules of the game, the scientist-entrepreneur is free, within the restrictions of the Securities and Exchange Commission, to convert paper profits into a fortune by selling stock at an inflated, speculative price. Similarly, it is legitimate for a university's investment managers to seek capital gains in the open market from fluctuations in the price of such securities. However, if its connection with a company increases public confidence, a university has an additional responsibility not only to protect its reputation but also to protect the public against the creation of a financial bubble.

. . .

NOTES

1. One general phenomenon over the past few years in the area of financial relationships is the growth of industry-university cooperation in research activities. Although some of these relationships date back many years and involve a

wide range of scientific endeavors (see note 3, infra), most contemporary public and professional attention centers on industry-university ties in biomedical research.   The general structure of these relationships is for commercial enterprises to sponsor academic research.   They have triggered a significant public debate, not only about the propriety of each individual cooperative venture and of the notion of industry-sponsored academic research, but also about the nature of a professor's relationship with his or her university when a participant in such cooperative activities and the position of universities as centers for the free flow and exchange of ideas.   Many people question whether these close industry-university ties serve to benefit the public and to increase the general availability of scientific discovery.   For further discussion, see, e.g., New Genetics Industry Tests University Values, 16 The Center Magazine 43 (1983); Peterson, Academic Questions: Campus and Company Partnerships, 123 Sci. News 76 (1983); Culliton, The Academic-Industrial Complex, 216 Science 960 (1983); Culliton, Biomedical Research Enters the Marketplace, 304 New Eng. J.Med. 1195 (1981).

Three programs have attracted significant public attention.   They also illustrate the diversity of industry-university cooperative ventures and their benefits and weaknesses.   The three programs all formally began in the early 1980's, though initial planning and negotiation started earlier.   Each one emphasizes, solely or predominantly, biomedical research.

a.   At Stanford University, the senior members of the university's Department of Medicine organized themselves into a consulting body, the Institute of Biological and Clinical Investigation, in mid-1980.   The Institute's purpose is to cultivate relationships between experienced department researchers and corporations to raise funds to support junior department members' research projects.   Not only does the Institute undertake consulting projects, but also it serves as the reviewing authority for grant proposals of these junior faculty members.   Initially, two companies, Syntex Research and Hewlett-Packard Corp., entered into consulting contracts with the Institute.

No senior department member can consult on Institute business for more than eight days a year, and no potential grant recipient can become involved in consulting projects.   The Institute requires the companies seeking consulting services to make a set donation to the Institute and then charges a *per diem* consulting fee per consultant (initially $500).   Faculty members can apply for grants through their third year in the Department of Medicine.   For a more complete description of the Institute, see Culliton, Stanford Doctors Try Consulting Inc., 217 Science 1122 (1982).

b.   A different arrangement at Massachusetts General Hospital (MGH), a private hospital affiliated with the Harvard Medical School, involves a contract for a West German chemical company, Hoechst AG, to equip and finance a new Department of Molecular Biology at MGH.   In return for its seventy million dollar investment in the department and for the considerable independence which the contract grants MGH and its staff members in undertaking research projects, Hoechst has the right to license for commercial development all patents arising out of research its funds sponsor and a right of first refusal to fund research projects beyond the contractual minimum.   Hoechst also is entitled to at least a nonexclusive license to develop any discoveries resulting from research its funding supports in part.   Hoechst must pay MGH a licensing fee for any patent developed successfully.   Participants in Hoechst-sponsored research have the right to publish research results, subject to Hoechst's review of preliminary drafts of any papers for detection of patentable rights.

The director of MGH's Department of Molecular Biology must be a member of Harvard Medical School's Department of Genetics; other scientists involved in the Hoechst-sponsored research will be staff members at MGH and, if they are academically-oriented, faculty members at Harvard.   Despite MGH's connections to Harvard, neither the Medical School nor the university administration participated in the substantive negotiation of the agreement.   For further discussion of this relationship, see Culliton, The Hoechst Department at Mass General, 216 Science 1200 (1982);   Bouton, Academic Research and Big Business, New York

Times, Sept. 11, 1983, § 6 (Magazine), at 62. For discussion of the congressional investigation this agreement spawned, see note 2, infra.

c. The third major cooperative venture links the Massachusetts Institute of Technology (MIT) with the Whitehead Institute, a nonprofit biomedical research institute. Edwin C. Whitehead, a self-made multimillionaire, offered to donate twenty million dollars for initial establishment, five million dollars annually and one hundred million dollars at his death to set up the Institute. Before the MIT faculty and administration approved the relationship and entered into formal agreement with Whitehead, the MIT–Whitehead link was a source of great controversy at MIT. A principal debate topic was Whitehead's personal stake in the Institute. Because he had made his fortune with a company that manufactures precision instruments for clinical experiments and because he had organized a venture capital company to promote commercialization of biomedical discoveries, some MIT faculty members accused Whitehead of seeking to obtain personal financial gain through the Institute. They argued that he could promote scientific research, if he really desired to do so, by simply donating money to MIT. Others suggested that allowing Institute scientists to become MIT professors and Institute directors to have other corporate connections would give rise to conflicts of loyalty and conflicts of interest.

The Whitehead Institute, under the agreement which MIT and Whitehead eventually concluded, will have an MIT professor as its Director, and Institute scientists will be regular members of the MIT faculty. Revenue from Institute patents will go in equal shares to the two institutions, after deduction of development costs. While MIT will have the power to appoint members to the Institute's board of directors, the two institutions will be administered separately. For a more detailed discussion of the MIT–Whitehead Institute relationship, see Interview with Edwin C. (Jack) Whitehead, 10 SIPI Scope 1 (1982); Interview With David Baltimore, 10 SIPI Scope 11 (1982); Norman, Whitehead–MIT Link Wins Final Approval, 214 Science 1104 (1981); Norman, MIT Agonizes Over Links with Research Unit, 214 Science 416 (1981).

What do you think are the principal benefits of these relationships? The most significant problems? Which of the three approaches do you favor? How do you think government, federal or state, should be involved in the organization and functioning of ventures like these, if at all? How might the drafters of the contracts employed in organizing these relationships anticipate the major problems and provide for them?

2. The growing interrelationship between industry and academia has triggered much reflection on and investigation into the propriety of such relationships. University and corporate officials have formally met at least twice to reach a consensus on how universities can receive the benefits of affiliation with outside corporate entities without sacrificing intellectual values and academic freedom. The first of these conferences, which the presidents of Harvard, Stanford, MIT, University of California and California Institute of Technology organized, was held at Pajaro Dunes, California in March 1982. Faculty members from these institutions and representatives of eleven corporations with which they have ties met to discuss the conflicts between university-industry connections and traditional academic values. On December 14–16, 1982, over four hundred university and corporate officials held a similiar but more broadly-based conference at the University of Pennsylvania. The attendees again discussed how universities can preserve intellectual and academic values while participating in corporate-sponsored research activities. See Culliton, Academe and Industry Debate Partnership, 219 Science 150 (1983); Culliton, Pajaro Dunes: The Search for Consensus, 216 Science 155 (1982).

Harvard University has taken further steps to insure that its relationships with industry do not sacrifice university control. Harvard officials cannot enter into research contracts that would allow corporate sponsors to specify certain goals, including marketability of research results, for research projects or to block publication of research results. The guidelines strongly discourage giving research sponsors exclusive patent licenses. See Harvard Adopts Guidelines on Sponsored

Research, New York Times, May 22, 1983 at 29, col. 1. Would any of the arrangements described in note 1, supra, be acceptable under these guidelines?

The federal government has also expressed concern over the relationships between universities (and other non-profit groups) and scientific and technological corporations. Two congressional committees held hearings on these cooperative ventures in 1981 after announcement of the MGH–Hoechst agreement described in note 1, supra. The paramount federal concern is the fact that much university research is federally funded and therefore the federal government would be subsidizing patent rights that would benefit the corporate research partners. Rep. Albert Gore, Jr., was the key figure in the congressional investigation. The investigation uncovered no misuse of federal funds. See Commercialization of Academic Biomedical Research: Hearings Before the Subcommittees on Investigations and Oversight and Science, Research and Technology of the House Committee on Science and Technology, 97th Cong., 1st Sess. (1981); see also Bouton, Academic Research and Big Business: A Delicate Balance, New York Times, Sept. 11, 1983, § 6 (Magazine) at 62; Government Scrutinizes Link Between Genetics Industry and Universities, New York Times, June 16, 1981 at C1, col. 1.

3. Though much recent debate has centered on university-industry cooperative ventures in biomedical research, similar ventures have existed for many years in other scientific and technological areas. In the 1950's, Procter and Gamble provided partial funding for research at Indiana University into the use of stannous fluoride in toothpaste. The university, through a foundation, received almost three million dollars in royalty income from that one discovery.

Electronics firms are presently increasing their level of university research funding, too. Stanford University has established a Center for Integrated Systems (CIS) with a large amount of funding from corporate contributors. Contributing companies will be able to send researchers to CIS to work, as well as to nominate members to a committee that will advise on CIS's policy and programs.

Other schools are in the process of creating such institutes. Rensselaer Polytechnic Institute set up a Center for Integrated Electronics, which corporate contributors will eventually fund totally. MIT has created a Microsystems Industrial Group, which both large and small corporate contributors will fund. At some state institutions, even though most of the funding for electronics research institutes will come from the relevant state government, corporate contributors provide a significant amount of funding.

Does the multiplicity of corporate donors to these electronic research units make them less objectionable than those discussed in note 1, supra? Why? Is such collaboration among state-supported universities, state governments and private corporations improper? How might these arrangements be structured so that any impropriety could be avoided? For additional discussion, see Electronic Firms Plug Into the Universities, 217 Science 511 (1982).

The federal government has also been a major research underwriter, especially in defense-related areas. Many important universities and institutes, including MIT and Stanford, are involved directly or indirectly in such projects. A recent controversy at Stanford centered around the university's approval of a major radiation research venture to be conducted at the Stanford Synchrotron Radiation Laboratory. The project would unite Stanford and the University of California with researchers from weapons laboratories at Lawrence Livermore, Los Alamos and Sandia. See Stanford Says Yes to Modified Weapons Proposal, 222 Science 146 (1983); Omenn, Taking University Research Into the Marketplace, 307 New Eng.J.Med. 694 (1982). Do you find any significant differences between federally-funded research at universities and research that private corporations support? What conflicts might develop in federally-funded research? Should the federal government concentrate its research funding at a few universities or should it be required to contract with many different universities? See generally Ch. 4, Sec. B.2, infra.

b.   Protecting Individuals

JOHNSON v. MISERICORDIA HOSPITAL

Supreme Court of Wisconsin, 1981.
99 Wis.2d 708, 301 N.W.2d 156.

. . .

This action arose out of a surgical procedure performed at Misericordia [Community Hospital] by Dr. [Lester V.] Salinsky on July 11, 1975, in which he unsuccessfully attempted to remove a pin fragment[2] from Johnson's right hip. During the course of this surgery, the plaintiff's common femoral nerve and artery were damaged causing a permanent paralytic condition of his right thigh muscles with resultant atrophy and weakness and loss of function.

About fifteen months thereafter, on October 13, 1976, the plaintiff filed suit alleging that both Dr. Salinsky and Misericordia Community Hospital were negligent. The hospital was negligent:

"(a) by being imprudent and careless in its selection of Lester V. Salinsky as a member of its staff;

"(b) in allowing Lester V. Salinsky to perform orthopedic surgery within its operative facilities when it knew, or should have known, that Lester V. Salinsky was not qualified to perform such diagnostic and operative procedures;

"(c) in failing to investigate the abilities and qualities of Lester V. Salinsky's capabilities in orthopedic care when said hospital knew, or should have known, that he did not possess such proper capability."

Prior to trial, Salinsky and his insurance carrier settled with the plaintiff and were released from the suit . . . upon payment of $140,000. Although Salinsky was no longer a party to the action, the question of whether he was negligent in the manner in which he performed the operation on July 11, 1975, remained an issue at trial, as it was incumbent upon the plaintiff to prove that Salinsky was negligent in this respect to establish a causal relation between the hospital's alleged negligence in granting Salinsky orthopedic surgical privileges and Johnson's injuries. Further, a determination of Salinsky's causal negligence, if any, was necessary to accomplish a proper allocation of the causal negligence between the two alleged joint tortfeasors, Salinsky and Misericordia.

At trial, undisputed expert testimony established that the surgical procedure utilized by Salinsky in attempting to remove the pin fragment from Johnson's right hip at Misericordia in July of 1975 was not in accord with good orthopedic practice. Accordingly, the jury found that Salinsky was negligent with respect to the medical care and treatment he afforded the plaintiff and attributed twenty percent of the causal negligence to him and eighty percent to the hospital. The jury's finding of negligence on the part of Salinsky has not been challenged on appeal and thus the facts relating thereto are not at issue in this review. Therefore, the only facts material to this review are those connected with Misericordia Hospital in appointing Dr. Salinsky to the medical staff with orthopedic privileges.

---

2. In 1969 Dr. Salinsky inserted two "Knowles" pins into Johnson's right hip in an attempt to correct a condition known as capitofemoral epiphysis. Subsequently, in 1970, Salinsky attempted to remove both pins but one fragmented in the process and thus a portion of the pin was left in the plaintiff's hip.

. . . The hospital known as Misericordia Community Hospital was not and has not been accredited by the Joint Commission on Accreditation of Hospitals.

On March 5, 1973 . . . Dr. Salinsky applied for orthopedic privileges on the medical staff. In his application, Salinsky stated that he was on the active medical staff of Doctors Hospital (Family Hospital), with orthopedic privileges, and held consultant privileges at Northwest General Hospital and New Berlin Community Hospital. He further stated in the application that his privileges at other hospitals had never "been suspended, diminished, revoked, or not renewed." In another part of the application form, he failed to answer any of the questions pertaining to his malpractice insurance, i.e., carrier, policy number, amount of coverage, expiration date, agent, and represented that he had requested privileges only for those surgical procedures in which he was qualified by certification.

In addition to requiring the above information, the application provided that significant misstatements or omissions would be a cause for denial of appointment. Also, in the application, Salinsky authorized Misericordia to contact his malpractice carriers, past and present, and all the hospitals that he had previously been associated with, for the purpose of obtaining any information bearing on his professional competence, as well as his moral, and ethical qualifications for staff membership. The application also contained a consent form for the inspection of Salinsky's medical records at the hospitals that he was presently affiliated with, or had been in the past, and further provided that Salinsky released "from any liability any and all individuals and organizations who provide information to the hospital, or its medical staff, in good faith and without malice concerning my professional competence, ethics, character and other qualifications for staff appointment and clinical privileges."

Mrs. Jane Bekos, Misericordia's medical staff coordinator (appointed April of 1973), testifying from the hospital records, noted that Salinsky's appointment to the medical staff was recommended by the then hospital administrator, David A. Scott, Sr., on June 22, 1973. Salinsky's appointment and requested orthopedic privileges, according to the hospital records, were not marked approved until August 8, 1973. This approval of his appointment was endorsed by Salinsky himself. Such approval would, according to accepted medical administrative procedure, not be signed by the applicant but by the chief of the respective medical section. Additionally, the record establishes that Salinsky was elevated to the position of Chief of Staff shortly after he joined the medical staff. However, the court record and the hospital records are devoid of any information concerning the procedure utilized by the Misericordia authorities in approving either Salinsky's appointment to the staff with orthopedic privileges, or his elevation to the position of Chief of Staff.

Mrs. Bekos, testified that although her hospital administrative duties entailed obtaining all the information available regarding an applicant from the hospitals and doctors referred to in the application for medical staff privileges, she failed to contact any of the references in Salinsky's case. In her testimony she attempted to justify her failure to investigate Salinsky's application because she believed he had been a member of the medical staff prior to her employment in April of 1973, even though his application was not marked approved until some four months later on August 8, 1973. Further, Mrs. Bekos stated that an examination of the

Misericordia records reflected that at no time was an investigation made by anyone of any of the statements recited in his application.

The record indicates that at the Misericordia medical staff meeting on June 21, 1973, Dr. A. Howell, the hospital's medical director, stated that the hospital did not have a functioning credentials committee at this time, and therefore the executive committee must assume the responsibility of evaluating and approving applications for medical staff privileges. Additionally, the minutes of this meeting list Salinsky as an attending member of the defendant's medical staff at the meeting despite the fact that Salinsky's application for staff privileges had neither been recommended for approval, nor approved by the committee as of this date. At trial, the only member of Misericordia's medical staff executive committee to testify was Dr. Louis Maxey who stated that he did not recall ever being at any meeting where Salinsky's application was even considered.

Thus, besides raising a question as to when Salinsky was in fact appointed to Misericordia's medical staff, the testimony of Mrs. Bekos, and Dr. Maxey, together with the minutes of the defendant's medical staff meeting on June 21, 1973, clearly establishes that Misericordia did not investigate Salinsky's application before appointing him to its medical staff. Further, Walter Harden, Family Hospital's administrator, testified that no one from Misericordia, much less an executive committee member, contacted him in regard to Salinsky's statement in his application that he had orthopedic privileges at that institution. In fact, Misericordia concedes this point, stating "In this particular case, the defendant-appellant-petitioner hospital has admitted all along it did not check Dr. Salinsky's credentials. . . ."

At trial, the representatives of two Milwaukee hospitals, Arthur Schmidt, attorney for St. Anthony's Hospital, and Walter Harden, administrator of Family Hospital, together with Charles Taylor, administrative hospital consultant with the Wisconsin Department of Health (Bureau of Quality Compliance), gave testimony concerning the accepted procedure for evaluating applicants for medical staff privileges. Briefly, they stated that the hospital's governing body, i.e., the board of directors or board of trustees, has the ultimate responsibility in granting or denying staff privileges. However, the governing board delegates the responsibility of evaluating the professional qualifications of an applicant for clinical privileges to the medical staff. The credentials committee . . . conducts an investigation of the applying physician's or surgeon's education, training, health, ethics and experience through contacts with his peers in the specialty in which he is seeking privileges, as well as the references listed in his application to determine the veracity of his statements and to solicit comments dealing with the applicant's credentials. Once the credentials committee (or committee of the whole) has conducted their investigation and reviewed all of the information bearing on the applicant's qualifications, it relays its judgment to the governing body, which, as noted, has the final appointing authority.

The record demonstrates that had the executive committee of Misericordia, in the absence of a current credentials committee, adhered to the standard and accepted practice of investigating a medical staff applicant's qualifications and thus examined Salinsky's degree, post graduate training, and contacted the hospitals referred to in his application, it would have found, contrary to his representations, that he had in fact experienced denial and restriction of his privileges, as well as never having been granted privileges at the very same hospitals he listed in his application. This information was readily available to Misericordia, and a review of Salinsky's associations with various Milwaukee orthopedic surgeons and hospital personnel would have revealed that they considered Salinsky's competence as an orthopedic surgeon *suspect*, and viewed it with a great deal of concern.

A short history of Salinsky's hospital contacts in the metropolitan Milwaukee area reflect that on December 19, 1947, Mt. Sinai Hospital granted Salinsky's request for privileges to perform simple orthopedic procedures [11] such as reducing simple fractures. A year and a half later, in August of 1949, Mt. Sinai denied Salinsky's request for additional orthopedic privileges and on December 30, 1963 transferred him to the rank of a courtesy physician in the Department of General Practice. [12]

As to Family Hospital, Salinsky was granted orthopedic surgical privileges on January 22, 1954. Some years later, in December of 1972, the executive committee of Family Hospital, after receiving a report of "continued flagrant bad practices" in the hospital on the part of Dr. Salinsky, recommended that his privileges for hip surgery be temporarily suspended. The hospital administrator then informed Salinsky that the executive committee had temporarily suspended his privileges, and advised him that the suspension would continue pending a review of his cases by a committee of three orthopedic surgeons. Pursuant to the recommendation of this committee the hospital withdrew Salinsky's privileges to perform any hip surgery, and further ordered that he obtain consultation before attempting *any* open surgical procedure. This limitation of Salinsky's surgical privileges at Family Hospital occurred on January 10, 1973, just two months prior to his application for staff privileges at Misericordia. Thus, this information also, was readily available to the Misericordia authorities if they had conducted a proper investigation.

On June 24, 1970, Salinsky applied for orthopedic surgical privileges at St. Anthony's Hospital. In his application, Salinsky stated that he was a member of the active staff at Doctors (now known as Family) Hospital. In the course of accepted investigative procedures of an applicant, the administrator of St. Anthony's Hospital contacted the administrator of Family Hospital, Walter Harden, and requested any and all medical information on Salinsky that might be helpful to the St. Anthony's credentials committee in reviewing and passing judgment on his application. Harden replied that Salinsky did have orthopedic surgical privileges at Family Hospital, although not certified in that specialty, and advised St. Anthony's Hospital to be careful and circumspect in their review of Salinsky's application. St. Anthony's subsequently denied Salinsky's application for orthopedic surgical privileges in January of 1971.

. . .

Drs. Salinsky and Maxey testified for the defense. Salinsky contradicted the testimony of the administrators of Northwest General Hospital and New Berlin Memorial Hospital, stating that he had consultant privi-

---

11. These "simple" orthopedic procedures were defined in a letter from the administrator of Mt. Sinai to Dr. Salinsky on August 31, 1949 as the treatment of superficial lacerations, amputation of digits, reparation of severed tendons in the hands and feet, reduction of simple dislocations of the elbow joint and removal of exostosis of the toes.

12. The Wisconsin Administrative Code defines the courtesy staff as those physicians ". . . who desire to attend patients in the hospital but who, for some reason not disqualifying, are ineligible for appointment in another category of the staff." Wis.Adm. Code sec. H24.04(1)(g)4.

leges with those hospitals. He also testified that he did not approve his own appointment to Misericordia's medical staff and attempted to explain away his signature in the approval section of his application, stating his signature appeared there "Because I was asked to sign the papers, and I signed the papers. . . ." Salinsky further stated that his appointment to Misericordia's medical staff was approved because other members of the staff recommended him.

Dr. Maxey, as noted above, was the only member of Misericordia's medical staff executive committee in 1973 to testify at the trial. Besides testifying that he could not recall ever having participated in the review of Salinsky's application, Maxey stated that he was familiar with Salinsky's ability as an orthopedic surgeon prior to the time Salinsky applied for staff privileges at Misericordia. Further, that he was of the opinion that Salinsky, in 1973, was a competent orthopedic surgeon, even though his own speciality (Maxey's) was in the field of plastic surgery. Maxey testified that the fact that other hospitals had denied, suspended, limited or revoked Salinsky's privileges would not influence his belief in this regard, stating:

". . . if I personally had contacted a hospital and the contact point such as an administrator had given me a negative opinion relative to Dr. Salinsky, or any doctor, particularly a surgeon, I would have a great deal of reservations as to what the source of the criticism was in view of the medical hospital politics that exist today, and so it would not have swayed my opinion relative to his competency at all."

However, on cross examination, Maxey stated that he would be interested in reviewing what other hospitals had done relative to a particular applicant and further limited his endorsement of Salinsky when he stated that he "would have to defer to an orthopedic man's opinion relative to another orthopedic man with due consideration of the medical politics and economic controls that get into surgery."

The jury found that the hospital was negligent in granting orthopedic surgical privileges to Dr. Salinsky and thus apportioned eighty percent of the causal negligence to Misericordia. . . . Misericordia appealed to the court of appeals raising some thirty issues. The appellate court affirmed the decision of the trial court. We granted Misericordia's petition for review but limit our consideration to the following two issues.

Issues

1. Does a hospital owe a duty to its patients to use due care in the selection of its medical staff and the granting of specialized surgical (orthopedic) privileges?

2. What is the standard of care that a hospital must exercise in the discharge of this duty to its patients and did Misericordia fail to exercise that standard of care in this case?

Duty

At the outset, it must be noted that Dr. Salinsky was an independent contractor, not an employee of Misericordia, and that the plaintiff is not claiming that Misericordia is vicariously liable for the negligence of Dr. Salinsky under the theory of *respondeat superior*. Rather, Johnson's claim is premised on the alleged duty of care owed by the hospital directly to its patients.

. . .

. . . . [T]he issue of whether Misericordia should be held to a duty of due care in the granting of medical staff privileges depends upon whether it is foreseeable that a hospital's failure to properly investigate and verify the accuracy of an applicant's statements dealing with his training, experience and qualifications as well as to weigh and pass judgment on the applicant would present an unreasonable risk of harm to its patients. The failure of a hospital to scrutinize the credentials of its medical staff applicants could foreseeably result in the appointment of unqualified physicians and surgeons to its staff. Thus, the granting of staff privileges to these doctors would undoubtedly create an unreasonable risk of harm or injury to their patients. Therefore, the failure to investigate a medical staff applicant's qualifications for the privileges requested gives rise to a foreseeable risk of unreasonable harm and we hold that a hospital has a duty to exercise due care in the selection of its medical staff.

Our holding herein is in accord with the public's perception of the modern day medical scientific research center with its computed axial tomography (CAT-scan), radio nucleide imaging thermography, microsurgery, etc., formerly known as a general hospital. The public is indeed entitled to expect quality care and treatment while a patient in our highly technical and medically computed hospital complexes. The concept that a hospital does not undertake to treat patients, does not undertake to act through its doctors and nurses, but only procures them to act solely upon their own responsibility, no longer reflects the fact. The complex manner of operation of the modern-day medical institution clearly demonstrates that they furnish far more than mere facilities for treatment. They appoint physicians and surgeons to their medical staffs, as well as regularly employing on a salary basis resident physicians and surgeons, nurses, administrative and manual workers and they charge patients for medical diagnosis, care, treatment and therapy, receiving payment for such services through privately financed medical insurance policies and government financed programs known as Medicare and Medicaid. Certainly, the person who avails himself of our modern "hospital facilities" (frequently a medical teaching institution) expects that the hospital staff will do all it reasonably can to cure him and does not anticipate that its nurses, doctors and other employees will be acting solely on their own responsibility.

. . .

One of the leading cases introducing the concept that a hospital, as an institution, has a responsibility for the quality of medical care provided by members of its medical staff was Darling v. Charleston Community Memorial Hospital [33 Ill.2d 326, 211 N.E.2d 253 (1965), cert. denied, 383 U.S. 946 (1965)]. In Darling, the plaintiff broke his leg in a college football game and was taken to the defendant hospital's emergency room where the doctor on emergency call applied traction and placed the leg in a plaster cast. Not long after the application of the cast, the plaintiff was in great pain and his toes, which protruded from the cast, became swollen and dark in color and eventually cold and insensitive. The same doctor who applied the cast removed it just three days later and cut the plaintiff's leg on both sides in the process. At this time, nurses and other witnesses observed "blood and other seepage" and smelled a foul odor in the room. Despite knowledge of these facts, the hospital failed to investigate or review the doctor's work or require consultation. Eleven days thereafter, the plaintiff was transferred to another hospital under the care of an orthopedic surgeon who determined that the fractured leg contained a considerable amount of dead tissue and opined that this resulted from a severe interference with the circulatory system in the limb, caused by the swelling or hemorrhaging of the leg against the cast. He made several attempts to try and save the leg but ultimately had to amputate it below the knee.

The court characterized the central issue as involving the duty that rested upon the defendant hospital in rendering care and treatment to the plaintiff. Accordingly, one of the issues considered on review was whether the hospital was negligent, in the fact situation recited in this case, in failing to:

> ". . . require consultation with or examination by members of the hospital surgical staff skilled in such treatment; or to review the treatment rendered to the plaintiff and to require consultants to be called in as needed." Id. 211 N.E.2d at 258.

The court readily found that the hospital owed a duty to the plaintiff in this regard stating:

> "The Standards for hospital Accreditation, the state licensing regulations and the defendant's bylaws demonstrate that the medical profession and other responsible authorities regard it as both desirable and feasible that a hospital assume certain responsibilities for the care of the patient." Id. 211 N.E.2d 257.

Further, noting that there was no dispute that the hospital failed to review the doctor's treatment or require consultation after having been made aware that serious complications arose in the plaintiff's care and treatment, the court upheld the jury's verdict finding that the hospital was negligent in failing to review the doctor's work or require a consultation. Thus, the Illinois Supreme Court held that hospitals have a duty to monitor the quality of the practice of medicine and surgery that takes place within their facilities.

. . .

Standard

The defendant's primary claim before this court is that the plaintiff failed to meet its burden of proving a breach of duty on the part of the hospital, i.e., that Misericordia did not exercise reasonable care when granting orthopedic surgical privileges to Dr. Salinsky. Misericordia contends that the failure to exercise reasonable care when granting staff privileges can only be shown by proof that Dr. Salinsky was an incompetent orthopedic surgeon before it granted him privileges or before the operation on July 11, 1975, and that the hospital knew or should have known of his incompetency. Even if we were to hold proof of incompetency at the time a physician or surgeon applies for staff privileges to be the standard, there was sufficient testimony to establish that Salinsky used questionable orthopedic procedures as far back as 1973. Dr. Neeseman stated that he had personally reviewed some of Salinsky's cases and found that they "were not the work of a competent orthopedic surgeon." However, in this case, we do not adopt the legal theory that knowledge of incompetency is the standard for determining whether a hospital exercised due care in selecting its staff.

. . . [O]nce a duty is established, the standard of care to be exercised is defined as follows:

" '. . . the degree of care which the great mass of mankind ordinarily exercises under the same or similar circumstances. A person fails to exercise ordinary care when, without intending to do any wrong, he does an act or omits a precaution under circumstances in which a person of ordinary intelligence and prudence ought reasonably to foresee that such act or omission will subject him or his property, or the person or property of another to an unreasonable risk of injury or damage.' " Peters v. Holiday Inns, Inc., supra, 89 Wis.2d at 122–23, 278 N.W.2d 208.

. . . Thus, for Misericordia to be liable for negligence in this case, it must have failed to exercise that degree of care and skill required of a hospital under like or similar circumstances. . . .

. . . Applying this standard to the facts of this case, Johnson was only required to show that the defendant did not exercise reasonable care (that degree of care ordinarily exercised by the average hospital) to determine whether Salinsky was competent. Thus, the defendant's claim that the plaintiff had the burden of showing that Salinsky was actually incompetent and that the hospital knew or should have known of his incompetence before granting him surgical privileges or before the July 11, 1975 operation is in error, as we hold that Johnson *was only obliged to prove that Misericordia did not make a reasonable effort to determine whether Salinsky was qualified to perform orthopedic surgery.* Therefore, the trial court's instruction that the hospital was required to exercise reasonable care in the granting of medical staff privileges and that reasonable care "meant that degree of care, skill and judgment usually exercised under like or similar circumstances by the average hospital," was proper.

. . . .

In summary, we hold that a hospital owes a duty to its patients to exercise reasonable care in the selection of its medical staff and in granting specialized privileges. The final appointing authority resides in the hospital's governing body, although it must rely on the medical staff and in particular the credentials committee (or committee of the whole) to investigate and evaluate an applicant's qualifications for the requested privileges. However, this delegation of the responsibility to investigate and evaluate the professional competence of applicants for clinical privileges does not relieve the governing body of its duty to appoint only qualified physicians and surgeons to its medical staff and periodically monitor and review their competency. The credentials committee (or committee of the whole) must investigate the qualifications of applicants. The facts of this case demonstrate that a hospital should, at a minimum, require completion of the application and verify the accuracy of the applicant's statements, especially in regard to his medical education, training and experience. Additionally, it should: (1) solicit information from the applicant's peers, including those not referenced in his application, who are knowledgeable about his education, training, experience, health, competence and ethical character; (2) determine if the applicant is currently licensed to practice in this state and if his licensure or registration has been or is currently being challenged; and (3) inquire whether the applicant has been involved in any adverse malpractice action and whether he has experienced a loss of medical organization membership or medical privileges or membership at any other hospital. The investigating committee must also evaluate the information gained through its inquiries and make a reasonable judgment as to the approval or denial of each application for staff privileges. The hospital will be charged with gaining and evaluating the knowledge that would have been acquired had it exercised ordinary care in investigating its medical staff applicants and the hospital's failure to exercise that degree of care, skill and judgment that is exercised by the average hospital in approving an applicant's request for privileges is negligence. This is not to say that hospitals are *insurers* of the competence of their medical staff, for a hospital will not be negligent if it exercises the noted standard of care in selecting its staff.

The decision of the Court of Appeals is affirmed.

NOTES

1. For discussions of the dramatic influence the *Darling* case had on the organization of hospitals see, Copeland, Hospital Responsibility for Basic Care Provided by Medical Staff Members: "Am I My Brother's Keeper?," 5 N.Kent L.Rev. 27 (1978); Southwick, The Hospital's New Responsibility, 17 Clev.-Mar.L.Rev. 146 (1968).

The AMA strongly criticized the case, saying "The effect of this decision is unfortunate since it appears to place a hospital in a position where it must exercise control over the practice of medicine by physicians on its attending staff in order to avoid liability. This is apt to encourage control of the practice of medicine by persons who are not licensed physicians. The decision is also unfortunate because it is apt to discourage the adoption of high standards which are intended to improve the level of hospital care, but which may now be ones interpreted as a basis for liability." 12 Citation 82 (1965).

2. There has been a fair amount of litigation on the subject of access to hospital staff privileges. See, e.g., Foster v. Mobile County Hospital, 398 F.2d 227 (5th Cir. 1968) (privileges may not be denied solely for lack of membership in local medical society when membership was closed to black physicians); Fritz v. Huntington Hospital, 39 N.Y.2d 339, 384 N.Y.S.2d 92, 348 N.E.2d 547 (1976) (privileges may not be denied for failure to graduate from AMA approved medical school). See generally Note, Due Process Considerations in Hospital Staff Privileges Case, 7 Hastings Const.L.Q. 217 (1979).

CAMPBELL v. MINCEY

United States District Court, for the Northern District of Mississippi, 1975.
413 F.Supp. 16.

ORMA R. SMITH, DISTRICT JUDGE.

. . .

On August 19, 1974, Ms. Campbell and her son filed suit against the chairman and members of the Board of Trustees of the Marshall County Hospital in Holly Springs, Mississippi, and the Administrator, Chief of Staff, and Director of Nursing at the hospital. The plaintiffs alleged that on the occasion of the birth of her son, Ms. Campbell was refused admittance to the Marshall County Hospital and its emergency room because of her race (she is black) and financial condition (she is indigent). . . .

. . .

The course of events giving rise to this litigation began in the early morning hours of March 21, 1974, when Ms. Campbell was awakened by labor contractions. The child was not expected before April; however, it soon became apparent to Ms. Campbell and her family that delivery would occur somewhat sooner than anticipated. Ms. Campbell, accompanied by her sister, secured the services of a neighbor to drive her from their home some eight miles north of Holly Springs, Mississippi, to Oxford, Mississippi, where Ms. Campbell received prenatal care from a local physician. Upon reaching Holly Springs, the occupants of the automobile concluded that it would not be possible for them to arrive at the Oxford-Lafayette County Hospital, located some thirty miles south of Holly Springs, prior to the birth of Ms. Campbell's child. Ms. Campbell had not previously visited the Marshall County Hospital during the course of the pregnancy here in issue.

Upon arrival at the Marshall County Hospital, Ms. Campbell and her sister entered the emergency room where they encountered a staff nurse. Upon learning that Ms. Campbell was of the opinion that she was about to deliver, the nurse informed Ms. Campbell and her sister that they should go to the hospital in Oxford where Ms. Campbell had received prenatal care and have the baby delivered there. The nurse did call the emergency room doctor, the only physician on duty in the hospital at that time, and informed him that Ms. Campbell's labor contractions were occurring at the rate of one every five minutes, that her water was intact, and that she had been seeing a doctor in Oxford. The emergency room doctor then affirmed the nurse's directive to Ms. Campbell that she should go to Oxford for the delivery of her child.

Following the hospital staff's refusal to admit her, Ms. Campbell and her sister returned to the parking lot where she gave birth on the front seat of the neighbor's automobile.

After Frederick's birth, Ms. Campbell's sister again went into the hospital and requested the nurse to admit Ms. Campbell and her newly-born son. Once again the nurse refused to admit plaintiffs but did go out into the parking lot to look over the mother and child. The only assistance which the nurse provided was in the form of a sheet in which the baby could be wrapped. The nurse did not notify the emergency doctor of the birth of the child and no other post-natal care was afforded mother or child by the staff of the Marshall County Hospital. The staff did, however, summons [sic] a Holly Springs ambulance which delivered the mother and child to the Oxford-Lafayette County Hospital where the plaintiffs were promptly admitted and treated. The evidence shows that the mother and son suffered no physical injury due to their inability to gain admittance to and treatment at the Marshall County Hospital. The report of the attending physician at the Oxford hospital indicates Ms. Campbell's delivery was normal in all respects other than the location and the absence of a doctor at the immediate time of the birth.

. . .

. . . [P]laintiff's claim that defendants' conduct on the night of March 20–21, 1974 constitutes a breach of a common law duty owed plaintiffs . . . that both public and private hospitals in this state operating an emergency room must accept, treat, and admit every individual who comes to them seeking assistance. The court can find no cases in this jurisdiction discussing the duty of a hospital to undertake to render emergency treatment to anyone seeking such aid, nor have the parties cited any decisions relative to that duty to the court. However, the court has noted the existence of what may be described as a "trend" in the common law of this country toward imposing liability upon a hospital which refuses to admit and treat, on an emergency basis, a seriously injured person. 35 A.L.R.3d 841, 844. . . . . [T]he court would observe that, in most instances, liability was predicated upon the defendant's arbitrary refusal to treat the plaintiff in question, which refusal was a marked departure from previous hospital custom and procedure. The refusal of the staff of the Marshall County Hospital to admit or treat the plaintiffs here was in compliance with, rather than a departure from hospital policy not to admit patients who are not referred by local physicians.

The following excerpts from the bylaws of the Marshall County Hospital furnished the motivation underlying the defendants' refusal to treat or admit plaintiffs:

All inpatients shall be admitted and attended only by members of the medical staff. If during an emergency the attending physician is unavailable then the on call or staff physician may be asked to serve in the emergency. All emergency outpatients shall be attended by members of the medical staff, according to the posted call system or by the staff physician on duty in the hospital.

. . .

In the case of an emergency the physician attending the patient shall be expected to do all in his power to save the life of the patient, including the call of such consultation as may be available. For the purpose of this section an emergency is defined as a condition in which the life of the patient is in imminent danger and in which any delay in administering treatment would increase the danger.

. . .

According to hospital policy, when an individual appears at the emergency room seeking treatment between the hours of 6:30 PM and 7:00 AM, and such individual has not been referred for treatment and/or admission by a local physician, the emergency room doctor will see the individual but only for the limited purpose of determining whether the patient should be treated at the Marshall County Hospital or carried to another facility. . . .

Plaintiffs in the case at bar were twice examined by a staff nurse who determined that no "emergency", as that term is defined by the regulations of the hospital, existed. The nurse's determination that no emergency existed prior to Frederick's birth was confirmed by the emergency room doctor. The nurse's conclusion that no emergency existed after Frederick's birth was confirmed by the report of treating physician in Oxford who recorded his observation that Ms. Campbell's delivery and postpartum recovery was "uneventful" except for a loss of blood during the ambulance trip.

While the court is disturbed by the seemingly cursory examinations performed on Ms. Campbell by the staff nurse and by the fact that Ms. Campbell was never examined by the emergency room physician, the court must conclude that plaintiffs suffered no tortious injury at the hands of the defendants on the date in question. This conclusion is primarily compelled by the evidence indicating that the nurse's determination that Ms. Campbell's delivery did not amount to an "emergency" situation, as that term is customarily used in the furnishing of hospital and medical services, was proved substantially correct by subsequent events. Further, neither the emergency room doctor nor the staff nurse was joined as a defendant in the case and the plaintiffs did not allege that their injuries resulted from the failure of this doctor and this nurse to adhere to established hospital procedure. Rather, the basic tenor of plaintiffs' complaint, as the court understands it, is that the hospital regulations concerning operation of the emergency room function in an unconstitutional manner.

Another fact worthy of consideration in determining the propriety of the actions taken by the hospital personnel on the night here in question is that the ambulance which carried Ms. Campbell and her child to the Oxford-Lafayette County Hospital had already arrived at the Marshall County Hospital by the time the nurse became aware that the child had been born. The court feels that the nurse's actions in allowing the plaintiff to proceed to Oxford at that time were reasonable in view of her knowledge that there was no doctor in Holly Springs who accepted obstetric cases and that Ms. Campbell had a regular physician in Oxford, some thirty minutes away by ambulance.

. . .

Turning finally to the constitutional issues raised in the complaint, the plaintiffs claim that they were refused admittance to the hospital and treatment in the emergency room because of their race and indigency. The overwhelming weight of the evidence in the record is to the effect that plaintiffs' race and financial condition had nothing at all to do with the defendants' refusal to admit or treat plaintiffs. The court, as the finder of fact, has concluded that defendants' refusal was based solely on the hospital policy not to admit patients who are not referred by local physicians. . . .

. . .

. . . Plaintiffs maintain that the Equal Protection Clause of the Fourteenth Amendment entitles them to use of the Marshall County Hospital on the same basis as all other individuals and that by refusing them admission and treatment, the defendants infringed this right.

. . .

. . . [D]isposition of this case reduces to a determination of whether the hospital regulations requiring reference of incoming patients by local physicians except in true "emergency" situations operates in a reasonable manner to further a legitimate state objective. On the basis of this record, the court cannot but conclude that the regulation does so function. The operation of the rule in this case resulted in no injury to plaintiffs according to the report of the attending physician at the transferee hospital. There was no evidence introduced which tended to show that true "emergency" cases were refused treatment at the Marshall County Hospital and suffered actual injury thereby. In the absence of some proof that this regulation has or can operate in some manner to inflict an injury upon some individual, the court must accept the considered judgment of the medical specialists who are charged with the responsibility of administering the hospital. Without some concrete evidence to the contrary, the court cannot say that the justification of the regulation offered by the hospital (which was to the effect that a local physician must authorize admission of a patient in order to insure a doctor will be available for follow-up treatment of that patient) is not a reasonable restriction upon the use of this public facility by plaintiffs and other similarly-situated individuals.

. . .

NOTE

The leading case on the question of whether a hospital has a duty to treat patients who present themselves for treatment is Wilmington General Hospital v. Manlove, 54 Del. 15, 174 A.2d 135 (1961). In *Manlove*, the Delaware Supreme Court held that a private hospital could be liable for refusing to treat a patient, but only when the prospective patient's condition was an "unmistakeable emergency." Id., at 25, 174 A.2d, at 140. See, e.g., Guerrero v. Copper Queen Hospital, 112 Ariz. 104, 537 P.2d 1329 (1975) (Arizona Supreme Court relying on *Manlove* upheld cause of action two burned children brought against private hospital when hospital refused to treat them and where practice was to render medical treatment to any seriously injured person). For a case holding that individual physicians do not have to treat even in emergencies, see Hurley v. Eddingfield, Sec. B.1.a.ii, infra.

EDMUND PELLEGRINO, HUMANISM AND THE PHYSICIAN

147–150 (1979).

. . . [I]t seems clear that the institutionalization of so many aspects of medicine increasingly demands a moral relationship between the patient and the hospital which can be very similar to the patient/physician relationship. . . . What is called for is a sharing of the same range of ethical responsibilities which have traditionally been implicit in the relationships between physician and patient. The board of trustees must feel moral as well as legal responsibility for the actions of the professional and nonprofessional workers within the hospital walls. This responsibility, even in presumably professional matters, cannot be delegated. Institutional morality, by necessity, must concern itself with every facet of the corporate life of that institution.

The result should be an overlapping and sharing of moral obligations in which the professional and the institution check and balance each other more intimately than is now customary. . . .

This mutuality of moral obligation becomes even more impelling in remediation of the injured humanity of the patient which illness entails. Both physician and hospital must reduce the inequalities in the relationship as well as the situation allows. . . . The obligation goes well beyond the mere legal requirement for valid consent. It demands consent of the highest quality and fullest sense of self-determination by the patient. The right to refuse specific treatment must be protected as well. The physician, the patient, and the hospital share obligations to each other, but because of the patient's vulnerability his needs are foremost.

. . .

There are clear indications that more and more patients will wish to be their own moral agents and not delegate this agency to physicians as in the past. We live in a democratic society in which there is no uniformity of opinion on most medico-moral issues and no recognized authority to settle differences in ethical beliefs. There is also a growing tendency to distrust experts and institutions. The traditional moral authority of the physician has already been substantially eroded. Under these circumstances, the moral responsibility of hospitals, like that of the physician, must be to make its values clear so the patient can make his own choice among institutions. . . .

There is room for considerable variation in ethical practices among hospitals. A democratic society should offer each patient the possibility of care in institutions that declare the same moral values he holds. This right can be actualized only if boards of trustees are willing to state clearly, in more specific terms than is now the case the ethical principles to which they subscribe.

B. PATIENTS, SUBJECTS AND CITIZENS

1. WHAT CONTROL CAN INDIVIDUALS EXERCISE?

Health care and research involve a human interaction between at least two people, the patient and the health care professional such as a physician. The first section of this chapter dealt with the ways in which control is exercised by—and over—professionals. We turn now to the lay side of the relationship.

It is usual to treat the law's interest in the lay side of the medical relationship under the heading of "informed consent." As we saw in Chapter 1, the term has even been employed when describing the citizens' role in making decisions about scientific developments, such as research using recombinant DNA techniques. This section begins with an examination of this legal doctrine and its ramifications, but it does not linger too long over all of the law's twists and turns on this subject because, unlike a standard work on medical jurisprudence or malpractice law, this chapter is concerned with the question: What types of private control over medicine and science are effective and under what circumstances? The law of informed consent is scrutinized here not as an end in itself but for whatever insights it can shed on the subject at hand, a subject which can also be illuminated by examining other branches of the law (constitutional and criminal, for example), as well as philosophy and the social sciences.

a. The Role of Assent or Refusal

i.   *In Deciding About Medical Care*

SCHLOENDORFF v. SOCIETY OF NEW YORK HOSPITAL

Court of Appeals of New York, 1914.
211 N.Y. 125, 105 N.E. 92.

CARDOZO, J. In the year 1771, by royal charter of George III, the Society of the New York Hospital was organized for the care and healing of the sick. During the century and more which has since passed, it has devoted itself to that high task. It has no capital stock; it does not distribute profits; and its physicians and surgeons, both the visiting and the resident staff, serve it without pay. . . .

To this hospital the plaintiff came in January, 1908. She was suffering from some disorder of the stomach. She asked the superintendent or one of his assistants what the charge would be, and was told that it would be $7 a week. She became an inmate of the hospital, and after some weeks of treatment, the house physician, Dr. Bartlett, discovered a lump, which proved to be a fibroid tumor. He consulted the visiting physician, Dr. Stimson, who advised an operation. The plaintiff's testimony is that the character of the lump could not, so the physicians informed her, be determined without an ether examination. She consented to such an examination, but notified Dr. Bartlett, as she says, that there must be no operation. She was taken at night from the medical to the surgical ward and prepared for an operation by a nurse. On the following day ether was administered, and, while she was unconscious, a tumor was removed. Her testimony is that this was done without her consent or knowledge. She is contradicted both by Dr. Stimson and by Dr. Bartlett, as well as by many of the attendant nurses. For the purpose of this appeal, however, since a verdict was directed in favor of the defendant, her narrative, even if improbable, must be taken as true. Following the operation, and, according to the testimony of her witnesses, because of it, gangrene developed in her left arm, some of her fingers had to be amputated, and her sufferings were intense. She now seeks to charge the hospital with liability for the wrong.

Certain principles of law governing the rights and duties of hospitals, when maintained as charitable institutions have, after much discussion, become no longer doubtful. It is the settled rule that such a hospital is not liable for the negligence of its physicians and nurses in the treatment of patients. . . . .

. . . .

. . . . In the case at hand, the wrong complained of is not merely negligence. It is trespass. Every human being of adult years and sound mind has a right to determine what shall be done with his own body; and a surgeon who performs an operation without his patient's consent commits an assault, for which he is liable in damages. This is true, except in cases of emergency where the patient is unconscious, and where it is necessary to operate before consent can be obtained. The fact that the wrong complained of here is trespass, rather than negligence, distinguishes this case from most of the cases that have preceded it. In such circumstances the hospital's exemption from liability can hardly rest upon implied waiver. Relatively to this transaction, the plaintiff was a stranger. She had never consented to become a patient for any purpose other than an examination under ether. She had never waived the right to recover damages for any wrong resulting from this operation, for she had forbidden the operation. In this situation, the true ground for the defendant's exemption from liability is that the relation between a hospital and its physicians is not that of master and servant. The hospital does not undertake to act through them, but merely to procure them to act upon their own responsibility. . . . .

. . . .

The conclusion, therefore, follows that the trial judge did not err in his direction of a verdict. A ruling would, indeed, be an unfortunate one that might constrain charitable institutions, as a measure of self-protection, to limit their activities. A hospital opens its doors without discrimination to all who seek its aid. It gathers in its wards a company of skilled physicians and trained nurses, and places their services at the call of the afflicted, without scrutiny of the character or the worth of those who appeal to it, looking at nothing and caring for nothing beyond the fact of their affliction. In this beneficent work, it does not subject itself to liability for damages, though the ministers of healing whom it has selected have proved unfaithful to their trust.

The judgment should be affirmed, with costs.

NOTES

1. From its Latin origin, the word "consent" means "to feel together," in other words, to agree or accord with another. The term has moral as well as legal implications. See, for example, the chapter on "Consent as a Canon of Loyalty with Special Reference to Children in Medical Investigations" in Professor Paul Ramsey's The Patient as Person 1–58 (1970), in which he urges partnership as a better term than contract to describe the consensual relation of patient and physician. The term "assent" is sometimes used to distinguish the agreement of a person (such as a child) who lacks the legal capacity to give a binding consent. Likewise, the term "permission" is sometimes used to differentiate consent (what a person may do autonomously on his or her own behalf) from what one, such as a parent, does in deciding on behalf of another. See National Commission for the Protection of Human Subjects of Biomedical and Behavioral Research, Report and Recommendations on Research Involving Children 13 (1977).

Consent may be either express or implied. Health caregivers often have patients sign a form, which is then referred to as "the consent." In fact, it is no such thing. Consent is the agreement between the persons involved; a "consent form" is merely a fairly formal means of documenting express consent and, if the consent itself is valid, the form serves to memorialize that fact. Implied consent occurs routinely in health care, when patients by their conduct, in cooperating with caregivers, provide the necessary authorization for caregivers' actions. See, e.g., O'Brien v. Cunard Steamship Co., 154 Mass. 272, 28 N.E. 266 (1891) (passenger gave implied consent to vaccination by joining line of people receiving injections on ship). It is sometimes said that implied consent also exists for emergency treatment of patients who are incapable of consenting because of age or condition, but this is a misnomer; the exception to the usual rule is better described as presumed consent, which results from the operation of the law (in attributing to the patient the wish of a reasonable person to receive emergency treatment) rather than being implied by the patient's conduct.

2. In legal literature, the relationship of patient and physician is often spoken of as a contract. Not all these contracts are enforceable, however. For example, a release from liability for future negligence imposed as a condition for admission to a charitable research hospital has been held invalid as a matter of public policy. Tunkl v. Regents of University of California, 60 Cal.2d 92, 32 Cal.Rptr. 33, 383 P.2d 441 (1963).

3. Judge Cardozo's ringing (and oft-quoted) declaration of a patient's right of self-determination (in an opinion that actually upholds the verdict for defendant hospital) is, if anything, less sweeping than one opinion he cited, that of Justice Brown of the Illinois Court of Appeals in Pratt v. Davis, in which the patient's rights in the private relationship with the physician are explicitly linked to the civil rights of citizenship. The plaintiff had admitted herself to defendant's hospital, and the defendant had removed her uterus without her prior knowledge or consent. In affirming a judgment for the plaintiff, the court stated:

> [U]nder a free government at least, the free citizen's first and greatest right, which underlies all others—the right to the inviolability of his person, in other words, his right to himself—is the subject of universal acquiescence, and this right necessarily forbids a physician or surgeon, however skillful or eminent, who has been asked to examine, diagnose, advise, and prescribe (which are at least necessary first steps in treatment and care), to violate without permission the bodily integrity of his patient by a major or capital operation, placing him under an anaesthetic for that purpose, and operating on him without his consent or knowledge. . . .

Pratt v. Davis, 118 Ill.App. 161, 166 (1905), affirmed 224 Ill. 30, 79 N.E. 562 (1906). The invocation of "a citizen's first and greatest right" places the issue of unconsented treatment in a different light: May the state command treatment when a physician could not, or does the common law right to personal inviolability have constitutional dimensions too?

JOHN STUART MILL, ON LIBERTY

9, 73–75, 101 (1859).

The object of this essay is to assert one very simple principle, as entitled to govern absolutely the dealings of society with the individual in the way of compulsion and control, whether the means used be physical force in the form of legal penalties or the moral coercion of public opinion. That principle is that the sole end for which mankind are warranted, individually or collectively, in interfering with the liberty of action of any of their number is self-protection. That the only purpose for which power can be rightfully exercised over any member of a civilized community, against his will, is to prevent harm to others. His own good, either physical or moral, is not a sufficient warrant. He cannot rightfully be compelled to do or forbear because it will be better for him to do so, because it will make him happier, because, in the opinions of others, to do so would be wise or even right. These are good reasons for remonstrating with him, or reasoning with him or persuading him, or entreating him, but not for compelling him or visiting him with any evil in case he do otherwise. To justify that, the conduct from which it is desired to deter him must be calculated to produce evil to someone else. The only part of the conduct of anyone for which he is amenable to society is that which concerns others. In the part which merely concerns himself, his independence is, of right, absolute. Over himself, over his own body and mind, the individual is sovereign.

It is, perhaps, hardly necessary to say that this doctrine is meant to apply only to human beings in the maturity of their faculties. We are not speaking of children or of young persons below the age which the law may fix as that of manhood or womanhood. Those who are still in a state to require being taken care of by others must be protected against their own actions as well as against external injury. . . .

. . .

What, then, is the rightful limit to the sovereignty of the individual over himself? Where does the authority of society begin? How much of human life should be assigned to individuality, and how much to society?

Each will receive its proper share if each has that which more particularly concerns it. To individuality should belong the part of life in which it is chiefly the individual that is interested; to society, the part which chiefly interests society.

Though society is not founded on a contract, and though no good purpose is answered by inventing a contract in order to deduce social obligations from it, everyone who receives the protection of society owes a return for the benefit, and the fact of living in society renders it indispensable that each should be bound to observe a certain line of conduct toward the rest. This conduct consists, first, in not injuring the interests of one another, or rather certain interests which, either by express legal provision or by tacit understanding, ought to be considered as rights; and secondly, in each person's bearing his share (to be fixed on some equitable principle) of the labors and sacrifices incurred for defending the society or its members from injury and molestation. These conditions society is justified in enforcing at all costs to those who endeavor to withhold fulfillment. . . .

It would be a great misunderstanding of this doctrine to suppose that it is one of selfish indifference which pretends that human beings have no business with each other's conduct in life, and that they should not concern themselves about the well-doing or well-being of one another, unless their own interest is involved. Instead of any diminution, there is need of a great increase of disinterested exertion to promote the good of others. But disinterested benevolence can find other instruments to persuade people to their good than whips and scourges, either of the literal or the metaphorical sort. I am the last person to undervalue the self-regarding virtues; they are only second in importance, if even second, to the social. It is equally the business of education to cultivate both. But even education works by conviction and persuasion as well as by compulsion, and it is by the former only that, when the period of education is passed, the self-regarding virtues should be inculcated. Human beings owe to each other help to distinguish the better from the worse, and encouragement to choose the former and avoid the latter. They should be forever stimulating each other to increased exercise of their higher faculties and increased direction of their feelings and aims toward wise instead of foolish, elevating instead of degrading, objects and contemplations. But neither one person, nor any number of persons, is warranted in saying to another human creature of ripe years that he shall not do with his life for his own benefit what he chooses to do with it. He is the person most interested in his own well-being: the interest which any other person, except in cases of strong personal attachment, can have in it is trifling compared with that which he himself has; the interest which society has in him individually (except as to his conduct to others) is fractional and altogether indirect, while with respect to his own feelings and circumstances the most ordinary man or woman has means of knowledge immeasurably surpassing those that can be possessed by anyone else. The interference of society to overrule his judgment and purposes in what only regards himself must be grounded on general presumptions which may be altogether wrong and, even if right, are as likely as not to be misapplied to individual cases, by persons no better acquainted with the circumstances of such cases than those are who look at them merely from without. In this department, therefore, of human affairs, individuality has its proper field of action. In the conduct of human beings toward one another it is necessary that general rules should for the most part be observed in order that people may know what they have to expect; but in each person's own concerns his individual spontaneity is entitled to free exercise. Considerations to aid his judgment, exhortations to strengthen his will may be offered to him, even obtruded on him, by others; but he himself is the final judge. All errors which he is likely to commit against advice and warning are far outweighed by the evil of allowing others to constrain him to what they deem his good. . . .

. . .

It was pointed out in an early part of this essay that the liberty of the individual, in things wherein the individual is alone concerned, implies a corresponding liberty in any number of individuals to regulate by mutual agreement such things as regard them jointly, and regard no persons but themselves. This question presents no difficulty so long as the will of all the persons implicated remains unaltered; but since that will may change it is often necessary, even in things in which they alone are concerned,

that they should enter into engagements with one another; and when they do, it is fit, as a general rule, that those engagements should be kept. Yet, in the laws, probably, of every country, this general rule has some exceptions. Not only persons are not held to engagements which violate the rights of third parties, but it is sometimes considered a sufficient reason for releasing them from an engagement that it is injurious to themselves. In this and most other civilized countries, for example, an engagement by which a person should sell himself, or allow himself to be sold, as a slave would be null and void, neither enforced by law nor by opinion. The ground for thus limiting his power of voluntarily disposing of his own lot in life is apparent, and is very clearly seen in this extreme case. The reason for not interfering, unless for the sake of others, with a person's voluntary acts is consideration for his liberty. His voluntary choice is evidence that what he so chooses is desirable, or at least endurable, to him, and his good is on the whole best provided for by allowing him to take his own means of pursuing it. But by selling himself for a slave, he abdicates his liberty; he foregoes any future use of it beyond that single act. He therefore defeats, in his own case, the very purpose which is the justification of allowing him to dispose of himself. He is no longer free, but is thenceforth in a position which has no longer the presumption in its favor that would be afforded by his voluntarily remaining in it. The principle of freedom cannot require that he should be free not to be free. It is not freedom to be allowed to alienate his freedom.
. . .

NOTES

1. Mill's essay, certainly among the most familiar in political philosophy, seems to have several purposes. First, it explores certain implications of the utilitarian philosophy Mill had inherited from Jeremy Bentham (1748–1832) and from his own father James Mill (1773–1836). As the description of utilitarianism in Ch. 1, Sec. C.2, suggests, the measurement of the good (the Greatest Happiness Principle) depends upon a calculation of what gives a person pleasure; in *On Liberty*, Mill argues that the purpose of government is to ensure that each person is free to come to his or her own definition of happiness and to pursue it, so long as he or she does not cause harm to another in the process—comparable to the ancient maxim of property law, *sic utere tuo ut alienum non laedas* (use your own property in such a manner as not to injure that of another).

Second, Mill sees the need to reinterpret aspects of utilitarianism in light of the tensions emerging in mid-19th-century Britain between democracy (the great cause of Bentham and Mill *père*) and minority rights. Like the Jeffersonians in America, the Benthamites were democrats, believing firmly in social equality and majority rule, in place of a society governed by inherited rank and privilege. With the growth of popular democracy, Mill realized something the earlier utilitarians had not: the need to protect individuals from the pressures toward conformity exerted by the masses, often poorly educated and intolerant. See Rapaport, Editor's Introduction, in On Liberty vii–xv (1978).

2. Where—and for what reasons—do you think the line ought to be drawn between individual choice and the insistence of others that another choice would be better for the person in question? Is the answer different when the alternative choice is one put forward by a scientist or physician on the basis of his or her superior knowledge and understanding versus a choice advocated by representatives of the state? Occasionally, the two come together. In Montgomery v. Board of Retirement, 33 Cal.App.3d 447, 109 Cal.Rptr. 181 (1973), the appellant, a county employee, had been denied her nonservice-connected disability retirement benefits because she refused (on religious grounds) to permit her surgeon to operate on her uterine tumor; rejecting the government's argument of a com-

pelling public interest in the preservation of citizens' life and health, the court ruled in her favor on first amendment grounds.

For an informative debate involving these issues, see H.L.A. Hart, Law, Liberty and Morality 31 (1963); P. Devlin, The Enforcement of Morals 132 (1965).

H. TRISTRAM ENGELHARDT, RIGHTS AND RESPONSIBILITIES OF PATIENTS AND PHYSICIANS

in Medical Treatment of the Dying: Moral Issues
9, 24–26 (M. Bayles & D. High eds. 1978).

[T]he social nature of medicine augments the otherwise circumscribed rights of patients, providing a context in terms of which the physician-patient contract can be renegotiated, giving the patient more parity with the physician by sustaining his claims to knowledge and decision, even if sustaining such claims is not conducive to effective treatment.

The point is that, because of societal investment in the development of medical research and education, public health care programs, and individual health care (e.g., Medicare), medicine has become an element of social or civil policy. Medicine, once an enterprise of private citizens, has now become an extension of those citizens through the development of medicine within a political structure. The force of this development is that medicine as a social or political enterprise can legitimately be required to temper its interests in cure and care and make them accord with basic claims of citizens to self-determination and choice. In this sense, rights to health care and the rights listed in patients' bills of rights are civil rights, rights which accrue to an individual in virtue of his membership in a political structure of a certain character. One begins thus to speak of a new quality of patient freedom, even though its quantity, its scope, can never (because of the restraints of disease and the social distribution of knowledge) be comparable to that of the physician. Patient bills of rights involve bringing the pursuit of cure and care on medicine's terms into a social context of basic non-medical concerns for self-determination, so that such concerns are less likely to be overridden. . . .

The socialization of medicine paradoxically implies both less and more freedom. On the one hand, it provides an arena in which general claims to greater parity in physician-patient relationships can be made. That is, patients as citizens can constrain medicine, an enterprise of their society, to allow patients to share in the responsibility for treatment and diagnosis. On the other hand, the socialization of medicine (i.e., the placing of medicine within a political structure and thus in terms of civil policies) implies that an element of general societal concern will extend to general treatment of the population—fluoridation and chlorination of water supplies, the requirement of vaccinations, etc. The socialization of medicine can not only give all persons a civil right to health care and to participation in decisions concerning their treatment, but it can also impose on them civil duties to participate in health maintenance, even in programs which cannot be directly in their self-interest (e.g., rubella vaccinations). In short, the socialization of medicine involves the placing of individual concerns about disease, health, care and cure in terms of general civil goals. It provides a domain within which talk about general rights and duties with regard to health care can take place.

In particular, talk of patients' rights to health care, to full knowledge concerning their prognosis, to terminating life-prolonging therapy, can gain a meaning in terms of duties to society by medicine regarding those patients. They can be viewed as rights from society, as a political institution, regarding medicine. It is not as if a particular physician had a duty to accept a particular patient has his and discharge his general duty to provide health care in the instance of that particular patient. Nor is it really the case that, all things being equal, a physician, *qua* physician, has a duty to let a patient determine the criteria for informing the patient concerning his prognosis or for terminating his treatment. It is rather, I suggest, that such issues arise in terms of the scope of the patients' basic civil rights. Otherwise puzzling talk about rights to health care can thus be given a sense, a social one. Patients' rights, including the rights of the dying patient, are, if they are to be rights at all, civil rights. They are claims that must be formally recognized by society. . . .

NOTE ON, "DEFENSIVE MEDICINE" AND UNWITTING PATIENT CONTROL OF PROFESSIONAL CONDUCT

Physicians (and practitioners of other learned professions such as law) enjoy a protection not accorded to most people when they are accused of having negligently injured another—compliance with the customs of at least a reputable segment of one's professional peers is a complete defense against liability. Although not immune from criticism, this rule has long enjoyed academic as well as judicial approval as "probably the only workable test available," and one unlikely to comfort the quack or truly incompetent. Morris, Custom and Negligence, 42 Colum. L.Rev. 1147, 1164–1165 (1942). The control of medical standards is thus largely in the hands of individual members of the professions and the various bodies through which they operate collectively to educate, test, and discipline themselves (as is detailed in Sec. A, supra).

Yet in a very real sense, the levers of control are in the hands of lay people, for it is they (and their lawyers) who identify which particular conduct by professionals will be challenged in court as negligent. Even when a good defense exists, physicians may be wary of doing (or not doing) things that increase the risk of litigation and liability. Although this fear may be overblown, some physicians are influenced enough to engage in "defensive medicine," conduct dictated by the desire to avoid malpractice liability, not by their professional judgment. See Altman, Poll Indicates 3 in 4 Doctors Order Extra Tests to Protect Against Suits, New York Times, Mar. 28, 1977, at 19, col. 2.

When a field is experiencing rapid innovation, the pressure to overuse new techniques may be very stong—indeed, much stronger than any felt constraints to hold back on steps a physician thinks might be useful although they are not yet fully accepted by the profession. Consider the following illustration of this problem and the ironic implication that a group of patients (unborn children) who are obviously incapable of participating in medical decisionmaking may nevertheless be exercising significant influence on professional conduct.

Electronic fetal monitoring (EFM) has been widely adopted over the past decade in the United States, and is used routinely on all patients during labor in many United States institutions. Nonetheless, it has been suggested that EFM was embraced too rapidly and on the basis of inadequate knowledge about the correlation between the results of monitoring and poor outcomes of pregnancy. "Questions about its efficacy, safety, and cost have been raised by women's groups, in recent newspaper articles, in U.S. Congressional hearings, and in the medical literature."

Faced with a signal of "abnormality" from a monitor, an obstetrician has two choices: either do nothing or intervene to relieve the cause of the disturbing reading. It is here that defensive medicine is said to enter the picture, for the physician fears liability if the fetus suffers harm as a result of inaction.

A basic response to apparent fetal distress is to accelerate delivery, as by cesarean section; not surprisingly, the rate at which cesarean sections are performed has multiplied dramatically of late (for this and other reasons) and now accounts for up to twenty-five to thirty percent of all deliveries in some hospitals.

If fetal monitoring is used inappropriately—for example, if it goes from being a screening technique used to warn of possible danger to being substituted for physicians' and nurses' clinical judgment—unnecessary operations may occur, resulting in needless harm to women during labor. Yet once a technique such as EFM has been widely adopted it is very difficult for a physician in a litigation-conscious world to resist using it even if statistically it is likely to cause more net harm, especially when the harm spreads out in relatively small increments over a large population while the harm avoided would fall dramatically on a few people.

An obstetrician who uses a fetal monitor and consequently performs a cesarean is in a strong position to defend against the patient's claim that she was subjected to unwarranted harm. The obstetrician can rely on the endorsement of the device by leading, indeed vocal, physicians, leaving the plaintiff with the burden of proving, through expert witnesses, that the profession's practices are not supported by adequate scientific data. The defendant can point to the "abnormal" reading on the monitor, while the plaintiff must show that the reading, though irregular, did not mean that the fetus was in danger, and that had the defendant physician held off operating and turned instead to other diagnostic measures there would still have been time enough to operate if those measures confirmed the monitor. Finally, the basic stance of the defendant is sympathetic: "I acted under great pressure to avoid a catastrophic event, which seemed to be impending, at what statistically seemed likely to be only a small cost to the mother-to-be." Even a plaintiff mother who has suffered terribly as a result of the operation is faced with the reproach: "Are you really saying your doctor should have held back from aiding your baby when it was in distress? Should the doctor have run the risk of severe injury, mental retardation, or death, in order to avoid simple abdominal surgery, the only probable risk of which for you was a scar?" Ironically, since a normal baby is more likely to be born when the perceived "distress" was actually a false alarm, the probability that a lawsuit will be instituted against an obstetrician is lower when the intervention was less necessary.

Conversely, an obstetrician who declines to use a fetal monitor routinely is in an unenviable position when sued on behalf of a child injured during labor. Nominally, the burden still rests with the plaintiff, who must show that it is more probable than not that the indications of danger to the fetus which eluded the physician's due care would have been revealed by EFM. But the burden may seem to shift to the defendant, for once the plaintiff's experts have testified to the general acceptance of the technique, the defendant's witnesses may be faced with having to convince the jury that such acceptance is not scientifically justified. To the challenge, "But wouldn't the monitor have displayed the danger signs here?" the defendant's answer, "Yes," will be remembered, while his qualifier, "But I wouldn't have known at that time whether the danger was a real one or whether this was one of the many cases when surgery would have been unnecessary," is forgotten. All the other patients who would undergo unnecessary monitoring and treatment were the plaintiff's rules adopted are not in the courtroom—only this woman and her injured child.

Capron, Tort Liability in Genetic Counseling, 79 Colum.L.Rev. 618, 668–670 (1979) (citations omitted).

Do patients in other treatment settings—like pregnant women, vis-a-vis prenatal diagnosis, or dying patients in intensive care units (see Chs. 7 and 8)—exert similar "control" over physicians fearful of being sued for omitting some technological intervention, no matter how dubious in general cost/benefit terms?

ii. In Forcing versus Resisting Action

ISAIAH BERLIN,
TWO CONCEPTS OF LIBERTY

in Four Essays on Liberty 118 (1969).

To coerce a man is to deprive him of freedom—freedom from what?
. . . [T]he meaning of this term is so porous that there is little interpretation that it seems able to resist. . . . I propose to examine no
more than two of these senses—but those central ones, with a great deal
of human history behind them and, I dare say, still to come. The first of
these political senses of freedom or liberty (I shall use both words to
mean the same), which I shall call the "negative" sense, is involved in the
answer to the question "What is the area within which the subject—a person or group of persons—is or should be left to do or be what he wants
to do or be, without interference by other persons?" The second, which
I shall call the positive sense, is involved in the answer to the question
"What, or who, is the source of control or interference, that can determine someone to do, or be, one thing rather than another?" The two
questions are clearly different, even though the answers to them may
overlap.

The notion of "negative" freedom

. . . If I am prevented by other persons from doing what I want I
am to that degree unfree; and if the area within which I can do what I
want is contracted by other men beyond a certain minimum, I can be described as being coerced, or, it may be, enslaved. Coercion is not, however, a term that covers every form of inability. If I say that I am unable
to jump more than 10 feet in the air, or cannot read because I am blind,
or cannot understand the darker pages of Hegel, it would be eccentric to
say that I am to that degree enslaved or coerced. Coercion implies the
deliberate interference of other human beings within the area in which I
wish to act. You lack political liberty or freedom only if you are prevented from attaining your goal by human beings.

. . .

[T]here ought to exist a certain minimum area of personal freedom
which must on no account be violated, for, if it is overstepped, the individual will find himself in an area too narrow for even that minimum development of his natural facilities which alone makes it possible to pursue,
and even to conceive, the various ends which men hold good or right or
sacred. It follows that a frontier must be drawn between the area of private life and that of public authority. Where it is to be drawn is a matter
of argument, indeed of haggling. Men are largely interdependent, and
no man's activity is so completely private as never to obstruct the lives of
others in any way. "Freedom for the pike is death for the minnows"; the
liberty of some must depend on the restraint of others. Still, a practical
compromise has to be found.

. . .

The notion of "positive" freedom

The "positive" sense of the word "liberty" derives from the wish on
the part of the individual to be his own master. I wish my life and decisions to depend on myself, not on external forces of whatever kind. I

wish to be the instrument of my own, not of other men's, acts of will. I wish to be a subject, not an object; to be moved by reasons, by conscious purposes which are my own, not by causes which affect me, as it were, from outside. I wish to be somebody, not nobody; a doer—deciding, not being decided for, self-directed and not acted upon by external nature or by other men as if I were a thing, or an animal, or a slave incapable of playing a human role, that is, of conceiving goals and policies of my own and realizing them. This is at least part of what I mean when I say that I am rational, and that it is my reason that distinguishes me as a human being from the rest of the world. I wish, above all, to be conscious of myself as a thinking, willing, active being, bearing responsibility for his choices and able to explain them by reference to his own ideas and purposes. I feel free to the degree that I believe this to be true, and enslaved to the degree that I am made to realize that it is not.

. . . [T]he "positive" and "negative" notions of freedom developed in divergent directions until, in the end, they came into direct conflict with each other.

One way of making this clear is in terms of the independent momentum which the metaphor of self-mastery acquired. "I am my own master"; "I am slave to no man"; but may I not . . . be a slave to nature? Or to my own "unbridled" passions? Are these not so many species of the identical genus "slave"—some political or legal, others moral or spiritual? Have not men had the experience of liberating themselves from spiritual slavery, or slavery to nature, and do they not in the course of it become aware, on the one hand, of a self which dominates, and, on the other, of something in them which is brought to heel? This dominant self is then variously identified with reason, with my "higher nature," with the self which calculates and aims at what will satisfy it in the long run, with my "real," or "ideal," or "autonomous" self, or with my self "at its best"; which is then contrasted with irrational impulse, uncontrolled desires, my "lower" nature, the pursuit of immediate pleasures, my "empirical" or "heteronomous" self, swept by every gust of desire and passion, needing to be rigidly disciplined if it is ever to rise to the full height of its "real" nature. Presently the two selves may be represented as divided by an even larger gap: the real self may be conceived as something wider than the individual (as the term is normally understood), as a social "whole" of which the individual is an element or aspect: a tribe, a race, a church, a state, the great society of the living and the dead and the yet unborn. This entity is then identified as being the "true" self which, by imposing its collective, or "organic," single will upon its recalcitrant "members," achieves its own, and, therefore, their, "higher" freedom. The perils of using organic metaphors to justify the coercion of some men by others in order to raise them to a "higher" level of freedom have often been pointed out. But what gives such plausibility as it has to this kind of language is that we recognize that it is possible, and at times justifiable, to coerce men in the name of some goal (let us say, justice or public health) which they would, if they were more enlightened, themselves pursue, but do not, because they are blind or ignorant or corrupt. This renders it easy for me to conceive of myself as coercing others for their own sake, in their, not my, interest, I am then claiming that I know what they truly need better than they know it themselves. What, at most, this entails is that they would not resist me if they were rational, and as wise as I, and understood their interests as I do. But I may go on to claim a good deal more than this. I may declare that they are actually aiming at what in their benighted state they consciously resist, because there exists within them an occult entity—their latent rational will, or their "true" purpose—and that this entity, although it is belied by all that they overtly feel and do and say, is their "real" self, of which the poor empirical self in space and time may know nothing or little; and that this inner spirit is the only self that deserves to have its wishes taken into account. Once I take this view, I am in a position to ignore the actual wishes of men or societies, to bully, oppress, torture them in the name, and on behalf, of their "real" selves, in the secure knowledge that whatever is the true goal of man (happiness, fulfillment of duty, wisdom, a just society, self-fulfilment) must be identical with his freedom—the free choice of his "true," albeit submerged and inarticulate, self.

. . .

This magical transformation, or sleight of hand . . . can no doubt be perpetrated just as easily with the "negative" concept of freedom, where the self that should not be interfered with is no longer the individual with his actual wishes and needs as they are normally conceived, but the "real" man within, identified with the pursuit of some ideal purpose not dreamed of by his empirical self. And, as in the case of the "positively" free self, this entity may be inflated into some super-personal entity—a state, a class, a nation, or the march of history itself, regarded as a more "real" subject of attributes than the empirical self. But the "positive" conception of freedom as self-mastery, with its suggestion of a man divided against himself, lends itself more easily to this splitting of personality into two: the transcendent, dominant controller, and the empirical bundle of desires and passions to be disciplined and brought to heel. This demonstrates (if demonstration of so obvious a truth is needed) that the conception of freedom directly derives from the view that is taken of what constitutes a self, a person, a man. Enough manipulation with the definitions of man, and freedom can be made to mean whatever the manipulator wishes. Recent history has made it only too clear that the issue is not merely academic.

. . .

For if the essence of men is that they are autonomous beings—authors of values, of ends in themselves, the ultimate authority of which consists precisely in the fact that they are willed freely—then nothing is worse than to treat them as if they were not autonomous, but natural objects, played on by causal influences, creatures at the mercy of external stimuli, whose choices can be manipulated by their rulers, whether by threats of force or offers of rewards. To treat men in this way is to treat them as if they were not self-determined. "Nobody may compel me to be happy in his own way," said Kant. "Paternalism is the greatest despotism imaginable." This is so because it is to treat men as if they were not free, but human material for me, the benevolent reformer, to mould in accordance with my own, not their, freely adopted purpose. This is, of course, precisely the policy that the early utilitarians recommended. Helvetius (and Bentham) believed not in resisting, but in using, men's tendency to be slaves to their passions; they wished to dangle rewards and punishments before men—the acutest possible form of heteronomy—if by this means the "slaves" might be made happier. But to manipulate men, to propel them towards goals which you—the social reformer—see, but they may not, is to deny their human essence, to treat them as objects without wills of their own, and therefore to degrade them. That is why to lie to men, or to deceive them, that is, to use them as means for my, not their own, independently conceived ends, even if it is for their own benefit, is, in effect, to treat them as sub-human, to behave as if their ends are less ultimate and sacred than my own. In the name of what can I ever be justified in forcing men to do what they have not willed or consented to? Only in the name of some value higher than themselves. But if, as Kant held, all values are the creation of men, and called values only so far as they are so, there is no value higher than the individual. Therefore to do this is to coerce men in the name of something less ultimate than themselves—to bend them to my will, or to someone else's particular craving for happiness or expediency or security or convenience. I am aiming at something desired by me or my group, to which I am using other men as means. But this is a contradiction of what I know men to be, namely ends in themselves. All forms of tampering with human beings, getting at them, shaping them against their will to your own pattern, all thought control and conditioning, is, therefore, a denial of that in men which makes them men and their values ultimate.

NOTES

1. Could one support a positive view of freedom without being coercive? Consider Walicki, Marx and Freedom, 30 New York Rev. of Books 50 (Nov. 24, 1983):

> In contrast with [the view that freedom is independence of the arbitrary will of another] Marx saw freedom as man's *ability* to exercise conscious rational control over his natural environment and over his own social forces. [He] made liberals increasingly aware that in social life the distinction between objective impossibility and man-made obstacles is not clear enough. If poor people cannot afford to buy a great many things, this can be treated as a lack of capacity, and not as a limitation on their freedom; if, however, social relations and, by the same token, the distribution of national income are seen as man-made, the very fact that poor people are poor can be treated as the result of the man-made social order and, thus, as an enforced limitation of freedom.

2. To what degree does Anglo-American law give individuals "positive" freedom in a legally enforceable sense? Is there a distinction between a court telling the legislature that there is a sphere of medical care into which it should not intrude (via criminal penalties) and a court declaring that a person is to be master of certain decisions about his or her own life?

3. Commentators have pointed to one unwanted implication of the term "consent": that it suggests that what is wanted is the patient's agreement when what is actually at issue is the patient's decision to accept or to decline a proposed intervention. See, e.g., Goldstein, For Harold Lasswell: Some Reflections on Dignity, Entrapment, Informed Consent, and the Plea Bargain, 84 Yale L.J. 683 (1975).

GRAMM v. BOENER

Supreme Court of Indiana, 1877.
56 Ind. 497.

WORDEN, J.—This was an action by the appellee, against the appellant, to recover damages for alleged negligence and unskilfulness on the part of the defendant, in the performance of his undertaking, as a surgeon, to set a broken arm and a broken leg of the plaintiff, whereby the plaintiff lost the use of his arm, and his leg became crooked, deformed and permanently lame.

Trial by jury; verdict and judgment for the plaintiff. . . .

. . .

It seems to us to be the duty of a surgeon, when called upon to perform some surgical operation, to advise against it, if, in his opinion, it is unnecessary, unreasonable, or will result injuriously to the patient. The patient is entitled to the benefit of his judgment, whether asked for or not. If the surgeon, when called upon, should proceed to the performance of the operation, without expressing any opinion as to its necessity or propriety, the patient would have a right to presume, that, in the opinion of the surgeon, the operation was proper.

But if a surgeon, when thus called upon, advises the patient, who is of mature years and of sound mind, that the operation is unnecessary and improper, in short advises against the performance, and patient still insists upon the performance of the operation, in compliance with which the surgeon performs it, we do not see upon what principle the surgeon can be held responsible to the patient for damages, on the ground that the operation was improper and injurious. In such case, the patient relies upon his own judgment, and not upon that of the surgeon, as to the propriety of the operation; and he can not complain of an operation performed at his own instance and upon his own judgment, and not upon that of the surgeon. The maxim, *volenti non fit injuria*, we think, well applies to such a case. The principle is quite analogous to that which prevents a recovery for injuries consequent upon unskillful or negligent treatment by a physician, if the plaintiff's own negligence directly contributed to them.

There is evidence in the record tending to show that the plaintiff, who was a married man and may be supposed to have been of mature years, repeatedly desired to have his arm re-broken, when the defendant visited him. He said positively that he wanted it re-broken. The defendant advised against it. He told them it would be of no use; that it had better be left alone, and that they ought not to think of it. In short, there is enough in the evidence, if the jury believed it, to justify them in finding that the arm was re-broken at the sole instance of the plaintiff, and against the advice of the defendant.

. . .

The judgment below is reversed . . . and the cause remanded, for a new trial.

MARINOFF v. DEPARTMENT OF HEALTH, EDUCATION & WELFARE

United States District Court for the Southern District of New York, 1978.
456 F.Supp. 1120.

Lasker, District Judge.

In her pro se complaint, Roslyn C. Marinoff seeks to compel an investigation by the Department of Health, Education and Welfare (HEW) into whether a certain chemical substance can serve as a cure for cancer. . . . HEW moves to dismiss the complaint for lack of jurisdiction and failure to state a cause of action. . . . HEW's motion is granted.

A district court has original jurisdiction to issue a writ of mandamus compelling an agency of the United States "to perform a duty owed to the plaintiff." This remedy is generally available only where the defendant has failed to perform a specific statutory or regulatory directive. Though HEW has a general duty . . . to undertake cancer research, the agency has not been specifically directed to investigate the possible cancer-curing properties of particular substances. Congress appears instead to have left to the agency's discretion the choice as to what substances purported to cure cancer warrant extensive research.

. . . It cannot . . . be said that HEW exercised its discretionary authority in an impermissible fashion by declining to undertake an investigation of the substance in question here. A large number of substances might profitably be investigated by HEW in its cancer research programs, and considerable federal funds would need to be advanced to study any one of them. A court, less well versed than HEW in scientific matters, must generally defer to the agency's judgment as to what substances should be selected for extensive testing.

For considerations similar to those which make issuance of a writ of mandamus inappropriate, judicial review of HEW's decision not to test the substance is unavailable. The Administrative Procedure Act bars judicial review of an agency action "[that] is committed to agency discretion by law." Agency determinations as to whether scientific research into a matter within the agency's area of expertise should be undertaken or funded have previously been found within the permissible scope of agency discretion. . . .

Plaintiff's motion is denied, defendant's motion is granted, and the complaint is dismissed.

NOTE ON PATIENTS ASSERTING CONTROL

Sometimes a patient may need to assert authority because the direction of his treatment is dispersed among too many physicians, as is illustrated in the autobiography of a patient who survived acute leukemia:

I kept fighting through all the fevers and transfusions. I felt I could only survive it by insisting on control. And there would be plenty of chances to test my resolve. The personnel assigned to monitor various functions never coordinated their blood sample requirements on a given day, so they'd come two or three times to leech my tender, collapsing veins. I finally put my foot down.

"You're not going to take more blood" I shouted. "You take it once a day. Get together and find out how much you want and for what purpose, and, goddam it, in the absence of an emergency, don't you touch my veins. Also, no one's going to draw blood except the intravenous nurse team," I said, "because that's all they do, and they know how to do it."

I got my way in both instances, thereby saving myself considerable pain.

M. Abram, The Day Is Short 209 (1982).

HURLEY v. EDDINGFIELD

Supreme Court of Indiana, 1901.
156 Ind. 416, 59 N.E. 1058.

BAKER, J. The appellant sued appellee for $10,000 damages for wrongfully causing the death of his intestate. The court sustained appellee's demurrer to the complaint, and this ruling is assigned as error.

The material facts alleged may be summarized thus: At and for years before decedent's death appellee was a practicing physician at Mace, in Montgomery county, duly licensed under the laws of the state. He held himself out to the public as a general practitioner of medicine. He had been decedent's family physician. Decedent became dangerously ill, and sent for appellee. The messenger informed appellee of decedent's violent sickness, tendered him his fee for his services, and stated to him that no other physician was procurable in time, and that decedent relied on him for attention. No other physician was procurable in time to be of any use, and decedent did rely on appellee for medical assistance. Without any reason whatever, appellee refused to render aid to decedent. No other patients were requiring appellee's immediate service, and he could have gone to the relief of decedent if he had been willing to do so. Death ensued, without decedent's fault, and wholly from appellee's wrongful act. The alleged wrongful act was appellee's refusal to enter into a contract of employment. Counsel do not contend that, before the enactment of the law regulating the practice of medicine, physicians were bound to render professional service to every one who applied. The act regulating the practice of medicine provides for a board of examiners, standards of qualification, examinations, licenses to those found qualified, and penalties for practicing without license. The act is a preventive, not a compulsive, measure. In obtaining the state's license (permission) to practice medicine, the state does not require, and the licensee does not engage, that he will practice at all or on other terms than he may choose to accept. Counsel's analogies, drawn from the obligations to the public on the part of innkeepers, common carriers, and the like, are beside the mark. Judgment affirmed.

NOTES

1. As already seen, Sec. A.5 supra, hospitals today have responsibilities, established by legislation and court decisions, to render emergency care, and may be held liable for harm that occurs because a person, having sought treatment, is turned away at the hospital emergency room.

2. Once a physician establishes a relationship with a patient, he is normally required to continue providing necessary care or he may be liable for the tort of abandonment. See, e.g., Ascher v. Gutierrez, 533 F.2d 1235 (D.C.Cir. 1976). See generally, Comment, The Action of Abandonment in Medical Malpractice Litigation, 36 Tul.L.Rev. 834 (1962).

This requirement has in turn created problems for physicians faced with treating difficult patients. For a decision holding that it was not abandonment to stop providing dialysis to a disruptive patient suffering from end stage renal disease because she was given "due notice, and an ample opportunity . . . to secure the presence of other medical attendance," see Payton v. Weaver, 131 Cal.App.3d 38, 182 Cal.Rptr. 225 (1982).

3. Physicians who have no prior relationship with a patient and who have not held themselves out as available to provide emergency care when needed cannot be commanded to provide treatment by a person desiring it; a physician who did so would be playing the role of "the Good Samaritan." Many physicians have been unwilling to render such aid, however, apparently out of fear that if their emergency aid led to any bad results, they would later be held liable for medical negligence. As a consequence, all states (beginning with California in 1959) have now adopted statutes that grant immunity from suit for negligence to persons (sometimes limited to licensed health professionals or to physicians) who voluntarily give assistance to the victims of accidents or other emergencies, even though "litigation against Good Samaritans was never a problem to begin with." Emergency Medical Care Liability Law Project, American Bar Association–American Society of Law and Medicine, Current Status and Utility of Emergency Medical Care Liability Law, 15 Forum 377, 391 (1980). This article questions the utility of the statutes in inducing the desired behavior on the part of physicians because the interstate statutory variations are so great as to leave many physicians uncertain of the protection provided. The statutes are analyzed in Note, 27 Wayne L.Rev. 217 (1980).

Only one state statute imposes a duty on physicians to act—at least in some circumstances:

(a) A person who knows that another is exposed to grave physical harm shall, to the extent that the same can be rendered without danger or peril to himself or without interference with important duties owed to others, give reasonable assistance to the exposed person unless that assistance or care is being provided by another.

(b) A person who provides reasonable assistance in compliance with subsection (a) of this section shall not be liable in civil damages unless his acts constitute gross negligence or unless he will receive or expects to receive remuneration. Nothing contained in this subsection shall alter existing law with respect to tort liability of a practitioner of the healing arts for acts committed in the ordinary course of his practice.

(c) A person who wilfully violates subsection (a) of this section shall be fined not more than $100.00.

Vt.Stat.12 § 519, discussed in McClintock, Duty to Aid the Endangered Act: The Impact and Potential of the Vermont Approach, 7 Vt.L.Rev. 143 (1982). See also Weinreb, The Case for a Duty to Rescue, 90 Yale L.J. 247 (1980). Is the penalty provided by the Vermont statute appropriate? Notice that the statute imposes duties on ordinary citizens as well as on health professionals. Is that wise?

b. The Role of Disclosure

NATANSON v. KLINE

Supreme Court of Kansas, 1960.
186 Kan. 393, 350 P.2d 1093.

SCHROEDER, JUSTICE.

This is an action for malpractice against a hospital and the physician in charge of its radiology department to recover for injuries sustained as the result of radiation therapy with radioactive cobalt, alleged to have been given in an excessive amount.

The plaintiff (appellant), Irma Natanson, suffering from a cancer of the breast, had a radical left mastectomy performed on May 29, 1955. At the direction of Dr. Crumpacker, the surgeon who performed that operation, the plaintiff engaged Dr. John R. Kline, a radiologist, for radiation therapy to the site of the mastectomy and the surrounding areas.

Dr. Kline, a licensed physician and specialist in radiation therapy, was head of the radiology department at St. Francis Hospital at Wichita, Kansas. The plaintiff seeks damages for injuries claimed to have been sustained as a result of alleged acts of negligence in the administration of the cobalt radiation treatment. Dr. Kline and the hospital were named as defendants (appellees).

The case was tried to a jury which returned a verdict in favor of both defendants. The plaintiff's motion for a new trial having been denied, this appeal followed specifying various trial errors.

.   .   .

We are here concerned with a case where the patient consented to the treatment, but alleges in a malpractice action that the nature and consequences of the risks of the treatment were not properly explained to her. This relates directly to the question whether the physician has obtained the informed consent of the patient to render the treatment administered.

.   .   .

The conclusion to be drawn from [previous] cases is that where the physician or surgeon has affirmatively misrepresented the nature of the operation or has failed to point out the probable consequences of the course of treatment, he may be subjected to a claim of unauthorized treatment. But this does not mean that a doctor is under an obligation to describe in detail all of the possible consequences of treatment. It might be argued, that to make a complete disclosure of all facts, diagnoses, and alternatives or possibilities which may occur to the doctor could so alarm the patient that it would, in fact, constitute bad medical practice. There is probably a privilege, on therapeutic grounds, to withhold the specific diagnosis where the disclosure of cancer or some other dread disease would seriously jeopardize the recovery of an unstable, temperamental or severely depressed patient. But in the ordinary case there would appear to be no such warrant for suppressing facts and the physician should make a substantial disclosure to the patient prior to the treatment or risk liability in tort.

In our opinion the proper rule of law to determine whether a patient has given an intelligent consent to a proposed form of treatment by a physician was stated and applied in Salgo v. Leland Stanford, Etc. Bd. Trustees [154 Cal.App.2d 560, 317 P.2d 170, (1957)]. This rule in effect compels disclosure by the physician in order to assure that an informed consent of the patient is obtained. The duty of the physician to disclose, however, is limited to those disclosures which a reasonable medical practitioner would make under the same or similar circumstances. How the physician may best discharge his obligation to the patient in this difficult situation involves primarily a question of medical judgment. So long as the disclosure is sufficient to assure an informed consent, the physician's choice of plausible courses should not be called into question if it appears, all circumstances considered, that the physician was motivated only by the patient's best therapeutic interests and he proceeded as competent medical men would have done in a similar situation.

Turning now to the facts in the instant case, the appellant knew she had a cancerous tumor in her left breast which was removed by a radical mastectomy. Pathological examination of the tissue removed did not disclose any spread of the cancer cells into the lymphatics beyond the cancerous tumor itself. As a precautionary measure the appellant's ovaries and fallopian tubes were removed, which likewise upon pathological examination indicated no spread of the cancer to these organs. At the time the appellant went to Dr. Kline as a patient there was no immediate emergency concerning the administration of cobalt irradiation treatment . . . . We think upon all the facts and circumstances here presented Dr. Kline was obligated to make a reasonable disclosure to the appellant of the nature and probable consequences of the suggested or recommended cobalt irradiation treatment, and he was also obligated to make a reasonable disclosure of the dangers within his knowledge which were incident to, or possible in, the treatment he proposed to administer.

. . . Dr. Kline made no disclosures to the appellant whatever. He was silent. This is not to say that the facts compel a verdict for the appellant. Under the rule heretofore stated, where the patient fully appreciates the danger involved, the failure of a physician in his duty to make a reasonable disclosure to the patient would have no causal relation to the injury. In such event the consent of the patient to the proposed treatment is an informed consent. The burden of proof rests throughout the trial of the case upon the patient who seeks to recover in a malpractice action for her injury.

In considering the obligation of a physician to disclose and explain to the patient in language as simple as necessary the nature of the ailment, the nature of the proposed treatment, the probability of success or of alternatives, and perhaps the risks of unfortunate results and unforeseen conditions within the body, we do not think the administration of such an obligation, by imposing liability for malpractice if the treatment were administered without such explanation where explanation could reasonably be made, presents any insurmountable obstacles.

. . .

The judgment of the lower court is reversed with directions to grant a new trial.

NOTES

1. The opinion in *Natanson* was the beginning, not the end, of the Kansas court's struggle to define the duty it had created for physicians. Some months after its first opinion, the Kansas Supreme Court issued a second lengthy opinion denying motions (by the appellees and by a new amicus curiae, the Kansas Medical Society) for rehearing. Natanson v. Kline, 187 Kan. 186, 354 P.2d 670 (1960). The court's purpose in "clarifying" its first opinion seems to have been to emphasize (1) that it regarded "informed consent" as a claim grounded in negligence, not battery, which therefore did not impose an absolute duty upon physicians but a professionally defined one; (2) that negligence was the appropriate standard not only because of plaintiff's allegations but also because the defendants had asserted "assumption of the risk" as a defense, which presupposed a plaintiff "equally competent with the defendant to judge concerning the risks and hazards"; and (3) that when in this particular case, Dr. Kline gave Mrs. Natanson "no explanation whatever" of the risks and hazards inherent in the proposed treatment, he breached his duty "as a matter of law" unless his behavior was justified, through evidence produced by the defendants, as being "in accordance with [the practices] of a reasonable medical practitioner under the same or similar circumstances."

Three years later, the Kansas Supreme Court clarified *Natanson* further. The court asserted that the duty of "reasonable disclosure" it had established "does not mean that a doctor is under an obligation to describe in detail all of the possible consequences of treatment." A "complete disclosure" might "so alarm the patient that it would, in fact, constitute bad medical practice." The disclosure must merely be "sufficient to assure an informed consent" so long as it appears, "all circumstances considered, that the physician was motivated only by the patient's best therapeutic interests and he proceeded as competent medical men would have done in a similar situation." Williams v. Menehan, 191 Kan. 6, 8, 379 P.2d 292, 294 (1963). Is this a clarification of, or a retreat from, *Natanson*? From the philosophical arguments for personal self-determination? Is it helpful to lawyers, judges, juries, and physicians, or ultimately circular?

2. The reluctance of physicians to disclose information to their patients apparently has ancient roots:

Perform [these duties] calmly and adroitly, concealing most things from the patient while you are attending to him. Give necesssary orders with cheerfulness and sincerity, turning his attention away from what is being done to him; sometimes reprove sharply and emphatically, and sometimes comfort with solicitude and attention, revealing nothing of the patient's future or present condition.

Hippocrates, Decorum, in 2 Hippocrates 297 (W.H.S. Jones trans. 2d ed. 1967). What impact ought such factors to have in evaluating whether it is appropriate to use medical custom or the behavior of the "reasonable physician" to measure the adequacy of a physician's effort to enable a patient to become an informed decisionmaker?

3. Physicians insist that patients recall very little of what they are told. Does this suggest that cases involving alleged deficiencies in the consent process will be nothing more than "swearing contests" between physician and patient?

4. What about medications dispensed or prescribed by a physician, but not requiring any physical "touching"? Compare Hamilton v. Hardy, 37 Colo.App. 375, 549 P.2d 1099 (1976), and Sharpe v. Pugh, 270 N.C. 598, 155 S.E.2d 108 (1967) (holding informed consent required), with Malloy v. Shanahan, 280 Pa. Super. 440, 421 A.2d 803 (1980) (holding informed consent requirements inapplicable because no battery).

CANTERBURY v. SPENCE

United States Court of Appeals for the District of Columbia Circuit, 1972.
464 F.2d 772, certiorari denied, 409 U.S. 1064, 93 S.Ct. 560, 34 L.Ed.2d 518.

SPOTTSWOOD W. ROBINSON, III, CIRCUIT JUDGE:

. . .

I

. . .

At the time of the events which gave rise to this litigation, appellant was nineteen years of age, a clerk-typist employed by the Federal Bureau of Investigation. In December, 1958, he began to experience severe pain between his shoulder blades. He consulted two general practitioners, but the medications they prescribed failed to eliminate the pain. Thereafter, appellant secured an appointment with Dr. Spence, who is a neurosurgeon.

. . . Dr. Spence . . . recommended that appellant undergo a myelogram—a procedure in which dye is injected into the spinal column and traced to find evidence of disease or other disorder—at the Washington Hospital Center.

. . . The myelogram revealed a "filling defect" in the region of the fourth thoracic vertebra. Since a myelogram often does no more than pinpoint the location of an aberration, surgery may be necessary to discover the cause. Dr. Spence told appellant that he would have to undergo a laminectomy—the excision of the posterior arch of the vertebra—to correct what he suspected was a ruptured disc. Appellant did not raise any objection to the proposed operation nor did he probe into its exact nature.

Appellant explained to Dr. Spence that his mother was a widow of slender financial means living in Cyclone, West Virginia, and that she could be reached through a neighbor's telephone. Appellant called his mother the day after the myelogram was performed and, failing to contact her, left Dr. Spence's telephone number with the neighbor. When Mrs. Canterbury returned the call, Dr. Spence told her that the surgery was occasioned by a suspected ruptured disc. Mrs. Canterbury then asked if the recommended operation was serious and Dr. Spence replied "not anymore than any other operation." He added that he knew Mrs. Canterbury was not well off and that her presence in Washington would not be necessary. The testimony is contradictory as to whether during the course of the conversation Mrs. Canterbury expressed her consent to the operation.   Appellant himself apparently did not converse again with Dr. Spence prior to the operation.

Dr. Spence performed the laminectomy on February 11 at the Washington Hospital Center.   Mrs. Canterbury traveled to Washington, arriving on that date but after the operation was over, and signed a consent form at the hospital.   The laminectomy revealed several anomalies: a spinal cord that was swollen and unable to pulsate, an accumulation of large tortuous and dilated veins, and a complete absence of epidural fat which normally surrounds the spine.   A thin hypodermic needle was inserted into the spinal cord to aspirate any cysts which might have been present, but no fluid emerged.   In suturing the wound, Dr. Spence attempted to relieve the pressure on the spinal cord by enlarging the dura—the outer protective wall of the spinal cord—at the area of swelling.

For approximately the first day after the operation appellant recuperated normally, but then suffered a fall and an almost immediate setback. Since there is some conflict as to precisely when or why appellant fell, we reconstruct the events from the evidence most favorable to him.   Dr. Spence left orders that appellant was to remain in bed during the process of voiding.   These orders were changed to direct that voiding be done out of bed, and the jury could find that the change was made by hospital personnel.   Just prior to the fall, appellant summoned a nurse and was given a receptacle for use in voiding, but was then left unattended.   Appellant testified that during the course of the endeavor he slipped off the side of the bed, and that there was no one to assist him, or side rail to prevent the fall.

Several hours later, appellant began to complain that he could not move his legs and that he was having trouble breathing; paralysis seems to have been virtually total from the waist down.   Dr. Spence was notified on the night of February 12, and he rushed to the hospital.   Mrs. Canterbury signed another consent form and appellant was again taken into the operating room.   The surgical wound was reopened and Dr. Spence created a gusset to allow the spinal cord greater room in which to pulsate.

Appellant's control over his muscles improved somewhat after the second operation but he was unable to void properly.   .   .   .   For several years after his discharge he was under the care of several specialists, and at all times was under the care of a urologist.   At the time of the trial in April, 1968, appellant required crutches to walk, still suffered from urinal incontinence and paralysis of the bowels, and wore a penile clamp.

In November, 1959 on Dr. Spence's recommendation, appellant was transferred by the F.B.I. to Miami where he could get more swimming and exercise.   Appellant worked three years for the F.B.I. in Miami, Los Angeles and Houston, resigning finally in June, 1962.   From then until the time of the trial, he held a number of jobs, but had constant trouble finding work because he needed to remain seated and close to a bathroom.   The damages appellant claims include extensive pain and suffering, medical expenses, and loss of earnings.

II

Appellant filed suit in the District Court on March 7, 1963, four years after the laminectomy and approximately two years after he attained his majority.   The complaint   .   .   .   alleged, among other things, negligence in the performance of the laminectomy and failure to inform him beforehand of the risk involved.   .   .   .

.   .   .

At the close of appellant's case in chief, each defendant moved for a directed verdict and the trial judge granted both motions.   .   .   .

.   .   .

III

Suits charging failure by a physician adequately to disclose the risks and alternatives of proposed treatment are not innovations in American law.   They date back a good half-century,[7] and in the last decade they have multiplied rapidly.   There is, nonetheless, disagreement among the courts and the commentators on many major questions, and there is no precedent of our own directly in point.   For the tools enabling resolution of the issues on this appeal, we are forced to begin at first principles.

The root premise is the concept, fundamental in American jurisprudence, that "[e]very human being of adult years and sound mind has a right to determine what shall be done with his own body.   .   .   ." True consent to what happens to one's self is the informed exercise of a choice, and that entails an opportunity to evaluate knowledgeably the options available and the risks attendant upon each.   The average patient has little or no understanding of the medical arts, and ordinarily has only his physician to whom he can look for enlightenment with which to reach an intelligent decision.   From these almost axiomatic considerations springs the need, and in turn the requirement, of a reasonable divulgence by physician to patient to make such a decision possible.[15]

A physician is under a duty to treat his patient skillfully but proficiency in diagnosis and therapy is not the full measure of his responsibility.   The cases demonstrate that the physician is under an obligation to communi-

---

7. See, e.g., Theodore v. Ellis, 141 La. 709, 75 So. 655, 660 (1917); Wojciechowski v. Coryell, 217 S.W. 638, 644 (Mo.App. 1920); Hunter v. Burroughs, 123 Va. 113, 96 S.E. 360, 366–368 (1918).

15. The doctrine that a consent effective as authority to form [sic] therapy can arise only from the patient's understanding of alternatives to and risks of the therapy is commonly denominated "informed consent." See, e.g., Waltz & Scheuneman, Informed Consent to Therapy, 64 Nw.U.L.Rev. 628, 629 (1970).   The same appellation is frequently assigned to the doctrine requiring physicians, as a matter of duty to patients, to communicate information as to such alternatives and risks.   See, e.g., Comment, Informed Consent in Medical Malpractice, 55 Calif.L.Rev. 1396 (1967).   While we recognize the general utility of shorthand phrases in literary expositions, we caution that uncritical use of the "informed consent" label can be misleading.   See, e.g., Plante, An Analysis of "Informed Consent," 36 Ford.L. Rev. 639, 671–72 (1968).

In duty-to-disclose cases, the focus of attention is more properly upon the nature and content of the physician's divulgence than the patient's understanding or consent. Adequate disclosure and informed consent are, of course, two sides of the same coin— the former a *sine qua non* of the latter. But the vital inquiry on duty to disclose relates to the physician's performance of an obligation, while one of the difficulties with analysis in terms of "informed consent" is its tendency to imply that what is decisive is the degree of the patient's comprehension. As we later emphasize, the physician discharges the duty when he makes a reasonable effort to convey sufficient information although the patient, without fault of the physician, may not fully grasp it. Even though the factfinder may have occasion to draw an inference on the state of the patient's enlightenment, the factfinding process on performance of the duty ultimately reaches back to what the physician actually said or failed to say. And while the factual conclusion on adequacy of the revelation will vary as between patients—as, for example, between a lay patient and a physician-patient—the fluctuations are attributable to the kind of divulgence which may be reasonable under the circumstances.

cate specific information to the patient when the exigencies of reasonable care call for it. Due care may require a physician perceiving symptoms of bodily abnormality to alert the patient to the condition. It may call upon the physician confronting an ailment which does not respond to his ministrations to inform the patient thereof. It may command the physician to instruct the patient as to any limitations to be presently observed for his own welfare, and as to any precautionary therapy he should seek in the future. It may oblige the physician to advise the patient of the need for or desirability of any alternative treatment promising greater benefit than that being pursued. Just as plainly, due care normally demands that the physician warn the patient of any risks to his well-being which contemplated therapy may involve.

The context in which the duty of risk-disclosure arises is invariably the occasion for decision as to whether a particular treatment procedure is to be undertaken. To the physician, whose training enables a self-satisfying evaluation, the answer may seem clear, but it is the prerogative of the patient, not the physician, to determine for himself the direction in which his interests seem to lie. To enable the patient to chart his course understandably, some familiarity with the therapeutic alternatives and their hazards becomes essential.

A reasonable revelation in these respects is not only a necessity but, as we see it, is as much a matter of the physician's duty. It is a duty to warn of the dangers lurking in the proposed treatment, and that is surely a facet of due care. It is, too, a duty to impart information which the patient has every right to expect.[27] The patient's reliance upon the physician is a trust of the kind which traditionally has exacted obligations beyond those associated with arms-length transactions. His dependence upon the physician for information affecting his well-being, in terms of contemplated treatment, is well-nigh abject. . . . [W]e have found "in the fiducial qualities of [the physician-patient] relationship the physician's duty to reveal to the patient that which in his best interests it is important that he should know." We now find, as a part of the physician's overall obligation to the patient, a similar duty of reasonable disclosure of the choices with respect to proposed therapy and the dangers inherently and potentially involved.

This disclosure requirement, on analysis, reflects much more of a change in doctrinal emphasis than a substantive addition to malpractice law. It is well established that the physician must seek and secure his patient's consent before commencing an operation or other course of treatment. It is also clear that the consent, to be efficacious, must be free from imposition upon the patient. It is the settled rule that therapy not authorized by the patient may amount to a tort—a common law battery—by the physician. And it is evident that it is normally impossible to obtain

---

27. Some doubt has been expressed as to ability of physicians to suitably communicate their evaluations of risks and the advantages of optional treatment, and as to the lay patient's ability to understand what the physician tells him. Karchmer, Informed Consent: A Plaintiff's Medical Malpractice "Wonder Drug," 31 Mo.L.Rev. 29, 41 (1966). We do not share these apprehensions. The discussion need not be a disquisition, and surely the physician is not compelled to give his patient a short medical education; the disclosure rule summons the physician only to a reasonable explanation. That means generally informing the patient in nontechnical terms as to what is at stake: the therapy alternatives open to him, the goals expectably to be achieved, and the risks that may ensue from particular treatment and no treatment. So informing the patient hardly taxes the physician, and it must be the exceptional patient who cannot comprehend such an explanation at least in a rough way.

a consent worthy of the name unless the physician first elucidates the options and the perils for the patient's edification. Thus the physician has long borne a duty, on pain of liability for unauthorized treatment, to make adequate disclosure to the patient.[36] The evolution of the obligation to communicate for the patient's benefit as well as the physician's protection has hardly involved an extraordinary restructuring of the law.

IV

Duty to disclose has gained recognition in a large number of American jurisdictions, but more largely on a different rationale. The majority of courts dealing with the problem have made the duty depend on whether it was the custom of physicians practicing in the community to make the particular disclosure to the patient.

. . .

There are, in our view, formidable obstacles to acceptance of the notion that the physician's obligation to disclose is either germinated or limited by medical practice. To begin with, the reality of any discernible custom reflecting a professional concensus on communication of option and risk information to patients is open to serious doubt. We sense the danger that what in fact is no custom at all may be taken as an affirmative custom to maintain silence, and that physician-witnesses to the so-called custom may state merely their personal opinions as to what they or others would do under given conditions. We cannot gloss over the inconsistency between reliance on a general practice respecting divulgence and, on the other hand, realization that the myriad of variables among patients makes each case so different that its omission can rationally be justified only by the effect of its individual circumstances. Nor can we ignore the fact that to bind the disclosure obligation to medical usage is to arrogate the decision on revelation to the physician alone. Respect for the patient's right of self-determination on particular therapy demands a standard set by law for physicians rather than one which physicians may or may not impose upon themselves.

More fundamentally, the majority rule overlooks the graduation of reasonable-care demands in Anglo-American jurisprudence and the position of professional custom in the hierarchy. The caliber of the performance exacted by the reasonable-care standard varies between the professional and non-professional worlds, and so also the role of professional custom. "With but few exceptions," we recently declared, "society demands that everyone under a duty to use care observe minimally a general standard." . . . "Beyond this," however, we emphasized, "the law requires those engaging in activities requiring unique knowledge and abil-

---

36. We discard the thought that the patient should ask for information before the physician is required to disclose. Caveat emptor is not the norm for the consumer of medical services. Duty to disclose is more than a call to speak merely on the patient's request, or merely to answer the patient's questions: it is a duty to volunteer, if necessary, the information the patient needs for intelligent decision. The patient may be ignorant, confused, overawed by the physician or frightened by the hospital, or even ashamed to inquire. See generally Note, Restructuring Informed Consent: Legal Therapy for the Doctor-Patient Relationship, 79 Yale L.J. 1533, 1545–51 (1970). Perhaps relatively few patients could in any event identify the relevant questions in the absence of prior explanation by the physician. Physicians and hospitals have patients of widely divergent socio-economic backgrounds, and a rule which presumes a degree of sophistication which many members of society lack is likely to breed gross inequities. See Note, Informed Consent as a Theory of Medical Liability, 1970 Wis.L.Rev. 879, 891–97.

ity to give a performance commensurate with the undertaking." Thus physicians treating the sick must perform at higher levels than non-physicians in order to meet the reasonable care standard in its special application to physicians—"that degree of care and skill ordinarily exercised by the profession in [the physician's] own or similar localities." And practices adopted by the profession have indispensable value as evidence tending to establish just what that degree of care and skill is.

We have admonished, however, that "[t]he special medical standards are but adaptions of the general standard to a group who are required to act as reasonable men possessing their medical talents presumably would." There is, by the same token, no basis for operation of the special medical standard where the physician's activity does not bring his medical knowledge and skills peculiarly into play. And where the challenge to the physician's conduct is not to be gauged by the special standard, it follows that medical custom cannot furnish the test of its propriety, whatever its relevance under the proper test may be. The decision to unveil the patient's condition and the chances as to remediation, as we shall see, is ofttimes a non-medical judgment and, if so, is a decision outside the ambit of the special standard. Where that is the situation, professional custom hardly furnishes the legal criterion for measuring the physician's responsibility to reasonably inform his patient of the options and the hazards as to treatment.

The majority rule, moreover, is at war with our prior holdings that a showing of medical practice, however probative, does not fix the standard governing recovery for medical malpractice. Prevailing medical practice, we have maintained, has evidentiary value in determinations as to what the specific criteria measuring challenged professional conduct are and whether they have been met, but does not itself define the standard. . . .

. . . In sum, the physician's duty to disclose is governed by the same legal principles applicable to others in comparable situations, with modifications only to the extent that medical judgment enters the picture. We hold that the standard measuring performance of that duty by physicians, as by others, is conduct which is reasonable under the circumstances.

V

Once the circumstances give rise to a duty on the physician's part to inform his patient, the next inquiry is the scope of the disclosure the physician is legally obliged to make. The courts have frequently confronted this problem but no uniform standard defining the adequacy of the divulgence emerges from the decisions. Some have said "full" disclosure, a norm we are unwilling to adopt literally. It seems obviously prohibitive and unrealistic to expect physicians to discuss with their patients every risk of proposed treatment—no matter how small or remote—and generally unnecessary from the patient's viewpoint as well. . . .

The larger number of courts, as might be expected, have applied tests framed with reference to prevailing fashion within the medical profession. Some have measured the disclosure by "good medical practice," others by what a reasonable practitioner would have bared under the circumstances, and still others by what medical custom in the community would demand. We have explored this rather considerable body of law but are unprepared to follow it. The duty to disclose, we have reasoned, arises from phenomena apart from medical custom and practice. The latter, we think, should no more establish the scope of the duty than its existence. . . .

In our view, the patient's right of self-decision shapes the boundaries of the duty to reveal. That right can be effectively exercised only if the patient possesses enough information to enable an intelligent choice. The scope of the physician's communications to the patient, then, must be measured by the patient's need, and that need is the information material to the decision. Thus the test for determining whether a particular peril must be divulged is its materiality to the patient's decision: all risks potentially affecting the decision must be unmasked. And to safeguard the patient's interest in achieving his own determination on treatment, the law must itself set the standard for adequate disclosure.

Optimally for the patient, exposure of a risk would be mandatory whenever the patient would deem it significant to his decision, either singly or in combination with other risks. Such a requirement, however, would summon the physician to second-guess the patient, whose ideas on materiality could hardly be known to the physician. That would make an undue demand upon medical practitioners, whose conduct, like that of others, is to be measured in terms of reasonableness. Consonantly with orthodox negligence doctrine, the physician's liability for nondisclosure is to be determined on the basis of foresight, not hindsight; no less than any other aspect of negligence, the issue on nondisclosure must be approached from the viewpoint of the reasonableness of the physician's divulgence in terms of what he knows or should know to be the patient's informational needs. . . .

Of necessity, the content of the disclosure rests in the first instance with the physician. Ordinarily it is only he who is in position to identify particular dangers; always he must make a judgment, in terms of materiality, as to whether and to what extent revelation to the patient is called for. He cannot know with complete exactitude what the patient would consider important to his decision, but on the basis of his medical training and experience he can sense how the average, reasonable patient expectably would react. Indeed, with knowledge of, or ability to learn, his patient's background and current condition, he is in a position superior to that of most others—attorneys, for example—who are called upon to make judgments on pain of liability in damages for unreasonable miscalculation.

From these considerations we derive the breadth of the disclosure of risks legally to be required. The scope of the standard is not subjective as to either the physician or the patient; it remains objective with due regard for the patient's informational needs and with suitable leeway for the physician's situation. In broad outline, . . . "[a] risk is thus material when a reasonable person, in what the physician knows or should know to be the patient's position, would be likely to attach significance to the risk or cluster of risks in deciding whether or not to forego the proposed therapy."

The topics importantly demanding a communication of information are the inherent and potential hazards of the proposed treatment, the alternatives to that treatment, if any, and the results likely if the patient remains untreated. The factors contributing significance to the dangerousness of a medical technique are, of course, the incidence of injury and the degree of the harm threatened. A very small chance of death or serious disablement may well be significant; a potential disability which dramatically outweighs the potential benefit of the therapy or the detriments of the existing malady may summons discussion with the patient.[86]

There is no bright line separating the significant from the insignificant; the answer in any case must abide a rule of reason. Some dangers—infection, for example—are inherent in any operation; there is no obligation to communicate those of which persons of average sophistication are aware. Even more clearly, the physician bears no responsibility for discussion of hazards the patient has already discovered, or those having no apparent materiality to patients' decision on therapy.[89] The disclosure doctrine, like others marking lines between permissible and impermissible behavior in medical practice, is in essence a requirement of conduct prudent under the circumstances. Whenever nondisclosure of particular risk information is open to debate by reasonable-minded men, the issue is for the finder of the facts.

VI

Two exceptions to the general rule of disclosure have been noted by the courts. . . . The first comes into play when the patient is unconscious or otherwise incapable of consenting, and harm from a failure to treat is imminent and outweighs any harm threatened by the proposed treatment. . . .

The second exception obtains when risk-disclosure poses such a threat of detriment to the patient as to become unfeasible or contraindicated from a medical point of view. It is recognized that patients occasionally become so ill or emotionally distraught on disclosure as to foreclose a rational decision, or complicate or hinder the treatment, or perhaps even pose psychological damage to the patient. Where that is so, the cases have generally held that the physician is armed with a privilege to keep the information from the patient, and we think it clear that portents of that type may justify the physician in action he deems medically warranted. The critical inquiry is whether the physician responded to a sound medical judgment that communication of the risk information would present a threat to the patient's well-being.

The physician's privilege to withhold information for therapeutic reasons must be carefully circumscribed, however, for otherwise it might devour the disclosure rule itself. The privilege does not accept the paternalistic notion that the physician may remain silent simply because divulgence might prompt the patient to forego therapy the physician feels

---

86. See Bowers v. Talmage, [159 So.2d 888 (Fla.App.1963)], (3% chance of death, paralysis or other injury, disclosure required); Scott v. Wilson, 396 S.W.2d 532 (Tex.Civ.App.1965), aff'd, 412 S.W.2d 299 (Tex.1967) (1% chance of loss of hearing, disclosure required). Compare, where the physician was held not liable. Stottlemire v. Cawood, [213 F.Supp. 897 (D.D.C.), new trial denied, 215 F.Supp. 266 (1963)], (1/800,000 chance of aplastic anemia); Yeates v. Harms, [193 Kan. 320, 393 P.2d 982 (1964), on rehearing, 194 Kan. 675, 401 P.2d 659 (1965)], (1.5% chance of loss of eye); Starnes v. Taylor, 272 N.C. 386, 158 S.E.2d 339, 344 (1968) (1/250 to 1/500 chance of perforation of esophagus).

89. [W]e do not subscribe to the view that only risks which would cause the patient to forego the treatment must be divulged, see Johnson, Medical Malpractice—Doctrines of Res Ipsa Loquitur and Informed Consent, 37 U.Colo.L.Rev. 182, 185–91 (1965); Comment, Informed Consent in Medical Malpractice, 55 Calif.L.Rev. 1396, 1407 n. 68 (1967); Note, 75 Harv.L.Rev. 1445, 1446–47 (1962), for such a principle ignores the possibility that while a single risk might not have that effect, two or more might do so. Accord, Waltz & Scheuneman, Informed Consent to Therapy, 64 Nw.U.L. Rev. 628, 635–41 (1970).

the patient really needs. That attitude presumes instability or perversity for even the normal patient, and runs counter to the foundation principle that the patient should and ordinarily can make the choice for himself. Nor does the privilege contemplate operation save where the patient's reaction to risk information, as reasonable foreseen by the physician, is menacing. And even in a situation of that kind, disclosure to a close relative with a view to securing consent to the proposed treatment may be the only alternative open to the physician.

VII

No more than breach of any other legal duty does nonfulfillment of the physician's obligation to disclose alone establish liability to the patient. An unrevealed risk that should have been made known must materialize, for otherwise the omission, however unpardonable, is legally without consequence. Occurrence of the risk must be harmful to the patient, for negligence unrelated to injury is nonactionable. And, as in malpractice actions generally, there must be a causal relationship between the physician's failure to adequately divulge and damage to the patient.

A causal connection exists when, but only when, disclosure of significant risks incidental to treatment would have resulted in a decision against it. The patient obviously has no complaint if he would have submitted to the therapy notwithstanding awareness that the risk was one of its perils. On the other hand, the very purpose of the disclosure rule is to protect the patient against consequences which, if known, he would have avoided by foregoing the treatment. The more difficult question is whether the factual issue on causality calls for an objective or a subjective determination.

It has been assumed that the issue is to be resolved according to whether the factfinder believes the patient's testimony that he would not have agreed to the treatment if he had known of the danger which later ripened into injury. We think a technique which ties the factual conclusion on causation simply to the assessment of the patient's credibility is unsatisfactory. To be sure, the objective of risk-disclosure is preservation of the patient's interest in intelligent self-choice on proposed treatment, a matter the patient is free to decide for any reason that appeals to him. When, prior to commencement of therapy, the patient is sufficiently informed on risks and he exercises his choice, it may truly be said that he did exactly what he wanted to do. But when causality is explored at a post-injury trial with a professedly uninformed patient, the question whether he actually would have turned the treatment down if he had known the risks is purely hypothetical: "Viewed from the point at which he had to decide, would the patient have decided differently had he known something he did not know?" And the answer which the patient supplies hardly represents more than a guess, perhaps tinged by the circumstance that the uncommunicated hazard has in fact materialized.

In our view, this method of dealing with the issue on causation comes in second-best. It places the physician in jeopardy of the patient's hindsight and bitterness. It places the factfinder in the position of deciding whether a speculative answer to a hypothetical question is to be credited. It calls for a subjective determination solely on testimony of a patient-witness shadowed by the occurrence of the undisclosed risk.

Better it is, we believe, to resolve the causality issue on an objective basis: in terms of what a prudent person in the patient's position would have decided if suitably informed of all perils bearing significance. If adequate disclosure could reasonably be expected to have caused that person to decline the treatment because of the revelation of the kind of risk or danger that resulted in harm, causation is shown, but otherwise not. The patient's testimony is relevant on that score of course but it would not threaten to dominate the findings. And since that testimony would probably be appraised congruently with the factfinder's belief in its reasonableness, the case for a wholly objective standard for passing on causation is strengthened. Such a standard would in any event ease the factfinding process and better assure the truth as its product.

VIII

In the context of trial of a suit claiming inadequate disclosure of risk information by a physician, the patient has the burden of going forward with evidence tending to establish prima facie the essential elements of the cause of action, and ultimately the burden of proof—the risk of nonpersuasion—on those elements. These are normal impositions upon moving litigants, and no reason why they should not attach in nondisclosure cases is apparent. The burden of going forward with evidence pertaining to a privilege not to disclose, however, rests properly upon the physician. This is not only because the patient has made out a prima facie case before an issue on privilege is reached, but also because any evidence bearing on the privilege is usually in the hands of the physician alone. . . .

. . .

There are obviously important roles for medical testimony in such cases, and some roles which only medical evidence can fill. Experts are ordinarily indispensable to identify and elucidate for the factfinder the risks of therapy and the consequences of leaving existing maladies untreated. They are normally needed on issues as to the cause of any injury or disability suffered by the patient and, where privileges are asserted, as to the existence of any emergency claimed and the nature and seriousness of any impact upon the patient from risk-disclosure. Save for relative infrequent instances where questions of this type are resolvable wholly within the realm of ordinary human knowledge and experience, the need for the expert is clear.

The guiding consideration our decisions distill, however, is that medical facts are for medical experts and other facts are for any witnesses—expert or not—having sufficient knowledge and capacity to testify to them.[121] It is evident that many of the issues typically involved in nondisclosure cases do not reside peculiarly within the medical domain. Lay

---

121. Lucy Webb Hayes Nat. Training School v. Perotti, [136 U.S.App.D.C. 122, 127–29, 419 F.2d 704, 709–11 (1969)], (permitting patient to wander from closed to open section of psychiatric ward); Monk v. Doctors Hosp., 131 U.S.App.D.C. [174,] 177, 403 F.2d [580,] 583 (operation of electro-surgical machine); Washington Hosp. Center v. Butler, 127 U.S.App.D.C. 379, 384 F.2d 331 (1967)] (fall by unattended x-ray patient); Young v. Fishback, 104 U.S.App.D.C. 372, 373, 262 F.2d 469, 470 (1958) (bit of gauze left at operative site); Garfield Memorial Hosp. v. Marshall, 92 U.S.App.D.C. [234,] 240, 204 F.2d [721,] 726 (newborn baby's head striking operating table); Goodwin v. Hertzberg, 91 U.S.App. D.C. 385, 386, 201 F.2d 204, 205 (1952) (perforation of urethra); Byrom v. Eastern Dispensary & Cas. Hosp., 78 U.S.App.D.C. [42,] 43, 136 F.2d [278,] 279 (failure to further diagnose and treat after unsuccessful therapy); Grubb v. Groover, 62 App.D.C. 305, 306, 67 F.2d 511, 512 (1933), cert. denied, 291 U.S. 660, 54 S.Ct. 377, 78 L.Ed. 1052 (1934) (burn while unattended during x-ray treatment).

witness testimony can competently establish a physician's failure to disclose particular risk information, the patient's lack of knowledge of the risk, and the adverse consequences following the treatment. Experts are unnecessary to a showing of the materiality of a risk to a patient's decision on treatment, or to the reasonably, expectable effect of risk disclosure on the decision. These conspicuous examples of permissible uses of nonexpert testimony illustrate the relative freedom of broad areas of the legal problem of risk nondisclosure from the demands for expert testimony that shackle plaintiffs' other types of medical malpractice litigation.

. . .

X

. . .   [T]he evidence was clearly sufficient to raise an issue as to whether Dr. Spence's obligation to disclose information on risks was reasonably met or was excused by the surrounding circumstances. Appellant testified that Dr. Spence revealed to him nothing suggesting a hazard associated with the laminectomy. His mother testified that, in response to her specific inquiry, Dr. Spence informed her that the laminectomy was no more serious than any other operation. When, at trial, it developed from Dr. Spence's testimony that paralysis can be expected in one percent of laminectomies, it became the jury's responsibility to decide whether that peril was of sufficient magnitude to bring the disclosure duty into play. There was no emergency to frustrate an opportunity to disclose, and Dr. Spence's expressed opinion that disclosure would have been unwise did not foreclose a contrary conclusion by the jury. There was no evidence that appellant's emotional makeup was such that concealment of the risk of paralysis was medically sound. Even if disclosure to appellant himself might have bred ill consequences, no reason appears for the omission to communicate the information to his mother, particularly in view of his minority. The jury, not Dr. Spence, was the final arbiter of whether nondisclosure was reasonable under the circumstances.

. . .

Reversed and remanded for a new trial.

NOTES

1. President's Commission, Making Health Care Decisions 23–29 (1982): The distinctive role and function of the courts in American society have been major influences in shaping informed consent. . . .

Only by understanding this process and the practical difficulties in carrying it out can the development of the legal doctrine of informed consent be appreciated.

First, the medical malpractice cases that find their way to court invariably involve medical interventions that did not go well. Not only has the patient been physically injured by the intervention, but the patient is sufficiently displeased by the outcome so as to initiate legal action, with its well-known costs and tribulations, which may include the destruction of any positive relationship between patient and professional. When there was a strong preexisting bond between patient and professional, and when the patient was prepared for the possibility of an adverse outcome, litigation is less likely. Thus, the courts' perspective is necessarily shaped by their near-exclusive experience with injured, unhappy patients. The far more numerous instances in which care is provided without serious misadventure do not come before them. . . .

Second, and more specific to informed consent, courts see only those cases in which particular allegedly undisclosed risks associated with medical procedures have led to actual injuries. . . . [S]ignificantly, in such cases attention tends to focus almost automatically on the particular procedure employed and on the risk that resulted in injury . . . rather than whether the overall course of care, and the extended process of disclosure, discussion, and decisionmaking regarding care, were properly respectful of the patient's right of self-determination. . . .

Third, courts must grapple with difficulties posed by the impact of hindsight on the litigation process. Such problems arise in a number of contexts, and if not resolved satisfactorily may endanger the integrity of the courts' truth-seeking function.

Two closely related instances of such difficulties involve the centrally important determinations of whether information that was not disclosed was "material" to the patient . . . and whether the provider's failure to disclose this information "caused" the patient to undertake the course of action that resulted in injury. In both instances, the patient's own testimony about what would have been important to know and how that information would have affected his or her decision may be colored by hindsight, as well as by the patient's recognition that different reconstructions of hypothetical past decisions may help determine whether the case is won or lost. Thus, . . . the courts have understandably tried to limit the impact of possibly speculative and potentially self-serving testimony.

. . .

The fourth influence of the litigation process on the evolution of informed consent law is that courts must determine whether required disclosures were in fact made. . . . As in many other legal contexts, written documentation of disclosure and consent can provide useful evidence—hence, the ubiquitous "informed consent form." Unfortunately, all too often such forms can become a substitute for, rather than merely a record of a continual process of disclosure, discussion, and consent. If providers come to believe (probably incorrectly) that their obligation to obtain the patient's informed consent can be satisfied by securing a signature—even if a patient is drowsy, drugged, or confused or the form is abstruse, jargon-ridden, or largely unintelligible—the law's inclination to rely on written documentation may pervert its central purpose in requiring informed consent.

Finally, the structure of lawsuits requires the naming of particular defendants who will bear financial responsibility in the event of an adverse judgment. . . . [C]laims are typically directed against parties with "deep pockets," usually institutions and individual physicians. This pattern does not necessarily reflect the activities of other members of the health care team, particularly nurses, with regard to informing patients and securing their consent.

Thus, the litigation process has shaped the legal doctrine of informed consent. . . . Taken together, these [factors] have brought the current law to an uneasy compromise among ethical aspirations, the realities of medical practice, and the exigencies of the litigation process.

2. As *Canterbury* makes clear, even when a plaintiff has shown that a physician-defendant breached the duty of disclosure, there is no liability unless "causation" and "materialized risk" are also shown. The barrier for plaintiffs presented by the causation requirement is demonstrated by the *Canterbury* case itself: on retrial, the plaintiff lost after the defense brought out that he had submitted to another laminectomy (between the time of the first and second trials), which made it difficult—albeit not logically impossible, in light of his changed circumstances—for the plaintiff to maintain that had he known the risks he would not have undergone the first operation. Consider also Cunningham v. Charles Pfizer & Co., Inc., 532 P.2d 1377 (Okl.1975), in which the plaintiff obtained a $340,000 judgment against the manufacturer of the polio vaccine that he took during a mass immunization program in Tulsa, Oklahoma, in 1963 and that he claimed caused him to contract a paralytic disease. On appeal, the Oklahoma Supreme Court held that defendant's failure to warn plaintiff (who was 15 years old at the time) or his parents of

the (statistically small) risk of paralysis rendered the consent defective within the meaning of Sec. 402 A of the Second Restatement of Torts. The court acknowledged that a drug company's duty to warn is usually discharged by warning the prescribing physician (because the courts view the choice involved as "essentially a medical one involving an assessment of medical risks in light of the physician's knowledge of his patient's needs and susceptibilities," 399 F.2d at 130), but concluded that in a mass program the company must use available means of oral and written communication directly to the people being immunized. Nonetheless, the Oklahoma court reversed and remanded for a new trial because of the causation issue. Although the court adopted the holding of Reyes v. Wyeth Laboratories, 498 F.2d 1264 (5th Cir.1974), that a plaintiff is entitled to a rebuttable presumption that he or she would have heeded a warning had it been given, in the case before it the "considerable risk of contracting polio from natural sources" at that time in Tulsa created a question for the jury whether a reasonable person in the plaintiff's position would have refused to be vaccinated.

The "materialized risk" requirement has been criticized for failure to recognize "that a citizen can be wronged without being harmed, that his dignity as a human being has been violated and that an assault has taken place the moment the [physician] commences therapy . . . ., even if beneficial . . .." Goldstein, For Harold Lasswell: Some Reflections on Dignity, Entrapment, Informed Consent, and the Plea Bargain, 84 Yale L.J. 683, 691 (1975). Judicial reluctance to respect the dignitary aspects of the requirement of consent predates the informed consent era; in McCandless v. State, 3 A.D.2d 600, 162 N.Y.S.2d 570 (1957), affirmed 4 N.Y.2d 797, 173 N.Y.S.2d 30, 149 N.E.2d 530, an award of $10,000 to a patient in a state mental hospital for an unauthorized abortion was reduced in light of testimony that her condition was improved by the termination of pregnancy. Those cases in which plaintiffs did recover for dignitary harm appear to involve the failure to obtain any consent rather than failure to inform. See, e.g., Lloyd v. Kull, 329 F.2d 168 (7th Cir.1964) ($500 for unauthorized removal of mole); Rolater v. Strain, 39 Okl. 572, 137 P. 96 (1913) ($1,000 for unauthorized removal of foot bone); Mohr v. Williams, 95 Minn. 261, 104 N.W. 12 (1905) ($14,322.50 for unauthorized removal of ear membrane).

3. Nearly every state now has some law on this subject and almost 40 recognize a right to recover for lack of informed consent. Nonetheless, the number of cases in which lack of consent is involved remains small. The National Association of Insurance Commissioners reports that the issue of informed consent was raised in only 3% of the cases resolved over a 12-month period in 1975–76. See S. Law & S. Polan, Pain and Profit 113 (1978).

4. At the time of *Canterbury*, the appellate courts of three states had already adopted a lay standard in place of the professional custom standard for the scope of disclosure. Hunter v. Brown, 4 Wn.App. 899, 484 P.2d 1162 (1971), affirmed 81 Wn.2d 465, 502 P.2d 1194 (1972); Cooper v. Roberts, 220 Pa.Super. 260, 286 A.2d 647 (1971); Berkey v. Anderson, 1 Cal.App.3d 790, 82 Cal.Rptr. 67 (1969). In the wake of *Canterbury* and decisions by the highest courts of two jurisdictions in the same year, Cobbs v. Grant, 8 Cal.2d 229, 104 Cal.Rptr. 505, 502 P.2d 1 (1972) and Wilkinson v. Vesey, 110 R.I. 606, 295 A.2d 676 (1972), it appeared that a patient-based definition of materiality might become widely accepted. Yet between 1975 and 1977 about half of the states, including some that had judicially recognized a patient-based standard, enacted legislation on the requirements for informed consent which typically aimed to reduce physicians' "exposure" to liability by limiting recovery to breaches of well-defined professional obligations. As a result of judicial decisions and statutes, as of 1982, 26 states that had declared law on informed consent had adopted a professional standard of disclosure, 19 a patient-oriented standard, and 6 had no law on the subject. See generally Appendix L in 3 President's Commission, Making Health Care Decisions 193–251 (1982).

5. Although most states have declined to go as far as *Canterbury* in imposing obligations on physicians beyond those customary among medical professionals, it can be argued that the jurisdictions following the *Canterbury* view do not go far enough because disclosure and causation are to be measured by the standard of

the reasonably prudent person not the particular patient. In reaching his conclusions, Judge Robinson relied heavily on the influential article by Waltz and Schueneman, Informed Consent to Therapy, 64 Nw.U.L.Rev. 628, 640–646 (1970), which suggested that it would be too burdensome on physicians and too uncertain for jurors to adopt a "subjective" standard. Yet in place of the preferences of the physician, does the reasonable prudence standard not simply substitute the views of the jurors? What about patients with idiosyncratic notions or unusual preferences or phobias? Since even physicians sometimes disagree about the "right" treatment, why cannot patients? Are patients under a duty to anyone to make reasonable decisions? See Capron, Informed Consent in Catastrophic Disease Research and Treatment, 124 U.Pa.L.Rev. 340, 407–09 (1974).

Several courts have framed their rules in terms of "the patient's need" to know information, which suggests that facts about a particular patient-plaintiff are at least relevant, but only two courts have explicitly adopted a subjective standard. Scott v. Bradford, 606 P.2d 554 (Okl.1979); McPherson v. Ellis, 305 N.C. 266, 287 S.E.2d 892 (1982). *McPherson* concerned an operation performed in 1975. Beginning in 1976, North Carolina by statute required that an objective standard should be followed. N.C.Gen.Stat. § 90–21.13(a)(3).

6. For a thorough review of the states' rules see A. Rosoff, Informed Consent: A Guide for Health Care Providers (1981).

TRUMAN v. THOMAS

Supreme Court of California, 1980.
27 Cal.3d 285, 165 Cal.Rptr. 308, 611 P.2d 902.

Bird, Chief Justice.

This court must decide whether a physician's failure to inform a patient of the material risks of not consenting to a recommended pap smear, so that the patient might make an informed choice, may have breached the physician's duty of due care to his patient, who died from cancer of the cervix.

I

Respondent, Dr. Claude R. Thomas, is a family physician engaged in a general medical practice. He was first contacted in April 1963 by appellants' mother, Rena Truman, in connection with her second pregnancy. He continued to act as the primary physician for Mrs. Truman and her two children until March 1969. During this six-year period, Mrs. Truman not only sought his medical advice, but often discussed personal matters with him.

In April 1969, Mrs. Truman consulted Dr. Casey, a urologist, about a urinary tract infection which had been treated previously by Dr. Thomas. While examining Mrs. Truman, Dr. Casey discovered that she was experiencing heavy vaginal discharges and that her cervix was extremely rough. Mrs. Truman was given a prescription for the infection and advised to see a gynecologist as soon as possible. When Mrs. Truman did not make an appointment with a gynecologist, Dr. Casey made an appointment for her with a Dr. Ritter.

In October 1969, Dr. Ritter discovered that Mrs. Truman's cervix had been largely replaced by a cancerous tumor. Too far advanced to be removed by surgery, the tumor was unsuccessfully treated by other methods. Mrs. Truman died in July 1970 at the age of 30.

Appellants are Rena Truman's two children. They brought this wrongful death action against Dr. Thomas for his failure to perform a pap smear test on their mother. At the trial, expert testimony was presented which indicated that if Mrs. Truman had undergone a pap smear at any time between 1964 and 1969, the cervical tumor probably would have been discovered in time to save her life. There was disputed expert testimony that the standard of medical practice required a physician to explain to women patients that it is important to have a pap smear each year to "pick up early lesions that are treatable rather than having to deal with [more developed] tumor[s] that very often aren't treatable . . .." [1]

Although Dr. Thomas saw Mrs. Truman frequently between 1964 and 1969, he never performed a pap smear test on her. Dr. Thomas testified that he did not "specifically" inform Mrs. Truman of the risk involved in any failure to undergo the pap smear test. Rather, "I said, 'You should have a pap smear.' We don't say by now it can be Stage Two [in the development of cervical cancer] or go through all of the different lectures about cancer. I think it is a widely known and generally accepted manner of treatment and I think the patient has a high degree of responsibility. We are not enforcers, we are advisors." However, Dr. Thomas' medical records contain no reference to any discussion or recommendation that Mrs. Truman undergo a pap smear test.

For the most part, Dr. Thomas was unable to describe specific conversations with Mrs. Truman. For example, he testified that during certain periods he "saw Rena very frequently, approximately once a week or so, and I am sure my opening remark was, 'Rena, you need a pap smear,' . . . I am sure we discussed it with her so often that she couldn't [have] fail[ed] to realize that we wanted her to have a complete examination, breast examination, ovaries and pap smear." Dr. Thomas also testified that on at least two occasions when he performed pelvic examinations of Mrs. Truman she refused him permission to perform the test, stating she could not afford the cost. Dr. Thomas offered to defer payment, but Mrs. Truman wanted to pay cash.

Appellants argue that the failure to give a pap smear test to Mrs. Truman proximately caused her death. Two instructions requested by appellants described alternative theories under which Dr. Thomas could be held liable for this failure. First, they asked that the jury be instructed that it "is the duty of a physician to disclose to his patient all relevant information to enable the patient to make an informed decision regarding the submission to or refusal to take a diagnostic test. [¶] Failure of the physician to disclose to his patient all relevant information including the risks to the patient if the test is refused renders the physician liable for any injury legally resulting from the patient's refusal to take the test if a reasonably prudent person in the patient's position would not have refused the test if she had been adequately informed of all the significant perils." Second, they requested that the jury be informed that "as a matter of law . . . a physician who fails to perform a Pap smear test on a female patient over the age of 23 and to whom the patient has entrusted her general physical care is liable for injury or death proximately caused by the failure to perform the test." Both instructions were refused.

---

1. Dr. Thomas conceded at the trial that it is the accepted standard of practice for physicians in his community to recommend that women of child-bearing age undergo a pap smear each year. His records indicate that during the period in which he acted as Mrs. Truman's family physician he performed between 10 and 20 pap smears per month.

The jury rendered a special verdict, finding Dr. Thomas free of any negligence that proximately caused Mrs. Truman's death. This appeal followed.

II

The central issue for this court is whether Dr. Thomas breached his duty of care to Mrs. Truman when he failed to inform her of the potentially fatal consequences of allowing cervical cancer to develop undetected by a pap smear.

In Cobbs v. Grant (1972) 8 Cal.3d 229, 104 Cal.Rptr. 505, 502 P.2d 1, this court considered the scope of a physician's duty to disclose medical information to his or her patients in discussing proposed medical procedures. Certain basic characteristics of the physician-patient relationship were identified. "The first is that patients are generally persons unlearned in the medical sciences and therefore, except in rare cases, courts may safely assume the knowledge of patient and physician are not in parity. The second is that a person of adult years and in sound mind has the right, in the exercise of control over his own body, to determine whether or not to submit to lawful medical treatment. The third is that the patient's consent to treatment, to be effective, must be an informed consent. And the fourth is that the patient, being unlearned in medical sciences, has an abject dependence upon and trust in his physician for the information upon which he relies during the decisional process, thus raising an obligation in the physician that transcends arms-length transactions."

In light of these factors, the court held that "as an integral part of the physician's overall obligation to the patient there is a duty of reasonable disclosure of the available choices with respect to proposed therapy and of the dangers inherently and potentially involved in each." The scope of a physician's duty to disclose is measured by the amount of knowledge a patient needs in order to make an informed choice. All information material to the patient's decision should be given.

Material information is that which the physician knows or should know would be regarded as significant by a reasonable person in the patient's position when deciding to accept or reject the recommended medical procedure. To be material, a fact must also be one which is not commonly appreciated. If the physician knows or should know of a patient's unique concerns or lack of familiarity with medical procedures, this may expand the scope of required disclosure.

Applying these principles, the court in *Cobbs* stated that a patient must be apprised not only of the "risks inherent in the procedure [prescribed, but also] the risks of a decision not to undergo the treatment, and the probability of a successful outcome of the treatment." This rule applies whether the procedure involves treatment or a diagnostic test. On the one hand, a physician recommending a risk-free procedure may safely forego discussion beyond that necessary to conform to competent medical practice and to obtain the patient's consent. If a patient indicates that he or she is going to *decline* the risk-free test or treatment, then the doctor has the additional duty of advising of all material risks of which a reasonable person would want to be informed before deciding not to undergo the procedure. On the other hand, if the recommended test or treatment is itself risky, then the physician should always explain the potential consequences of declining to follow the recommended course of action.

Nevertheless, Dr. Thomas contends that *Cobbs* does not apply to him because the duty to disclose applies only where the patient *consents* to the recommended procedure. He argues that since a physician's advice may be presumed to be founded on an expert appraisal of the patient's medical needs, no reasonable patient would fail to undertake further inquiry before rejecting such advice. Therefore, patients who reject their physician's advice should shoulder the burden of inquiry as to the possible consequences of their decision.

This argument is inconsistent with *Cobbs*. The duty to disclose was imposed in *Cobbs* so that patients might meaningfully exercise their right to make decisions about their own bodies. The importance of this right should not be diminished by the manner in which it is exercised. Further, the need for disclosure is not lessened because patients reject a recommended procedure. Such a decision does not alter "what has been termed the 'fiducial qualities' of the physician-patient relationship," since patients who reject a procedure are as unskilled in the medical sciences as those who consent. To now hold that patients who reject their physician's advice have the burden of inquiring as to the potential consequences of their decisions would be to contradict *Cobbs*. It must be remembered that Dr. Thomas was not engaged in an arms-length transaction with Mrs. Truman. Clearly, under *Cobbs*, he was obligated to provide her with all the information material to her decision.

Dr. Thomas next contends that, as a matter of law, he had no duty to disclose to Mrs. Truman the risk of failing to undergo a pap smear test because "the danger [is] remote and commonly appreciated to be remote." The merit of this contention depends on whether a jury could reasonably find that knowledge of this risk was material to Mrs. Truman's decision.

The record indicates that the pap smear test is an accurate detector of cervical cancer. Although the probability that Mrs. Truman had cervical cancer was low, Dr. Thomas knew that the potential harm of failing to detect the disease at an early stage was death. This situation is not analogous to one which involves, for example, "relatively minor risks inherent in [such] common procedures" as the taking of blood samples. These procedures are not central to the decision to administer or reject the procedure. In contrast, the risk which Mrs. Truman faced from cervical cancer was not only significant, it was the principal reason why Dr. Thomas recommended that she undergo a pap smear.

Little evidence was introduced on whether this risk was commonly known. Dr. Thomas testified that the risk would be known to a reasonable person. Whether such evidence is sufficient to establish that there was no general duty to disclose this risk to patients is a question of fact for the jury. Moreover, even assuming such disclosure was not generally required, the circumstances in this case may establish that Dr. Thomas did have a duty to inform Mrs. Truman of the risks she was running by not undergoing a pap smear.

Dr. Thomas testified he never specifically informed her of the purpose of pap smear test. There was no evidence introduced that Mrs. Truman was aware of the serious danger entailed in not undergoing the test. However, there was testimony that Mrs. Truman said she would not undergo the test on certain occasions because of its cost or because "she just didn't feel like it." Under these circumstances, a jury could reasonably conclude that Dr. Thomas had a duty to inform Mrs. Truman of the danger of refusing the test because it was not reasonable for Dr. Thomas to assume that Mrs. Truman appreciated the potentially fatal consequences of her conduct. Accordingly, this court cannot decide as a matter of law that Dr. Thomas owed absolutely no duty to Mrs. Truman to make this important disclosure that affected her life.

. . .

. . . The jury was instructed that a "proximate cause of an injury is a cause which, in natural and continuous sequence, produces the injury, and without which the injury would not have occurred." Obviously, this test could not be satisfied if the jury were to conclude that even given adequate disclosure Mrs. Truman would have refused to take the recommended test in time to save her life. Thus, the rejected instruction would have correctly indicated that satisfaction of the prudent person test for causation established in *Cobbs* was necessary but not sufficient for plaintiffs to recover. If the jury were to reasonably conclude that Mrs. Truman would have unreasonably refused a pap smear in the face of adequate disclosure, there could be no finding of proximate cause. Though awkwardly phrased, the rejected instrument accurately reflected the law and a theory of liability applicable to the facts of this case.[5]

Refusal to give the requested instruction meant that the jury was unable to consider whether Dr. Thomas breached a duty by not disclosing the danger of failing to undergo a pap smear. Since this theory finds support in the record, it was error for the court to refuse to give the requested instruction. . . .

III

The other contentions of instructional and evidentiary error urged by appellants are considered because these matters probably will arise at any retrial of the case.

First, the trial court refused to instruct the jury that "as a matter of law . . . a physician who fails to perform a Pap smear test on a female patient over the age of 23 and to whom the patient has entrusted her general physical care is liable for injury or death proximately caused by the failure to perform the test." In support of this instruction plaintiffs relied on the decision of the Supreme Court of Washington in Helling v. Carey (1974) 83 Wash.2d 514, 519 P.2d 981.

That decision involved a suit against two physicians specializing in ophthalmology who *failed to recommend* a test for glaucoma. The court held as a matter of law that the exercise of due care required the administration of that test. That holding has no application to this case since the evidence presented showed that the physician recommended the appropriate test but failed to inform the patient of the risks entailed in refusing to follow his advice. The suggestion that a physician *must* perform a test on a patient, who is capable of deciding whether to undergo the proposed procedure, is directly contrary to the principle that it is the *patient* who

---

5. . . . The prudent person test for causation was established to protect defendant physicians from the unfairness of having a jury consider the issue of proximate cause with the benefit of the "20/20 vision of hindsight . . .." This standard should not be employed to prevent a physician from raising the defense that even given adequate disclosure the injured patient would have made the same decision, regardless of whether a reasonably prudent person would have decided differently if adequately informed.

must ultimately decide which medical procedures to undergo. Accordingly, the trial court did not err in refusing this instruction.

. . .

The judgment is reversed.

TOBRINER, MOSK and NEWMAN, JJ., concur.

CLARK, JUSTICE, dissenting.

I dissent. . . .

A primary consideration in determining whether a new duty should be imposed upon a defendant is the "extent of the burden to the defendant and consequences to the community" in imposing the duty.

The burden of explaining the purposes of a pap smear and the potential risks in failing to submit to one may not appear to be great, but the newly imposed duty upon physicians created by today's majority opinion goes far beyond. The instruction requires disclosure of all "relevant information to enable the patient to make an informed decision regarding the submission to or refusal to take a diagnostic test." In short, it applies not only to pap smears, but to all diagnostic procedures allegedly designed to detect illness which could lead to death or serious complication if not timely treated.

Carried to its logical end, the majority decision requires physicians to explain to patients who have not had a recent general examination the intricacies of chest examinations, blood analyses, X-ray examinations, electrocardiograms, urine analyses and innumerable other procedures. In short, today's ruling mandates doctors to provide each such patient with a summary course covering most of his or her medical education. Most medical tests—like pap smears—are designed to detect illness which might prove fatal absent timely treatment. Explaining the purposes of each procedure to each such patient will obviously take hours if not days.

Few, if any, people in our society are unaware that a general examination is designed to discover serious illness for timely treatment. While a lengthy explanation may result in general examinations for some patients who would otherwise decline or defer them, the onerous duty placed upon doctors by today's decision will result in reduced care for others. Requiring physicians to spend a large portion of their time teaching medical science before practicing it will greatly increase the cost of medical diagnosis—a cost ultimately paid by an unwanting public. Persons desiring treatment for specific complaints will be deterred from seeking medical advice once they realize they will be charged not only for treatment but also for lengthy lectures on the merits of their examination.

The great educational program the majority embark upon, even if justifiable, is a question of public policy for the Legislature to determine: whether the cost warrants the burden, and whether the duty to educate rests with doctors, schools or health departments. Requiring individual doctors to enlighten the public may be found through legislative hearings to be inefficient, not reaching those who need it most—the ones hesitant to consult doctors.

When a patient chooses a physician, he or she obviously has confidence in the doctor and intends to accept proffered medical advice. When the doctor prescribes diagnostic tests, the patient is aware the tests are intended to discover illness. It is therefore reasonable to assume that a patient who refuses advice is aware of potential risk.

Moreover, the physician-patient relationship is based on trust, and forcing the doctor in a hard sell approach to his services can only jeopardize that relationship.

The new duty to explain, imposed by the majority as a matter of law, creates an undue burden on both the doctor and society and should be rejected. . . .

Nothing in Cobbs v. Grant (1972) 8 Cal.3d 229, 104 Cal.Rptr. 505, 502 P.2d 1 warrants imposition of such an onerous duty—to the contrary, that case expressly rejected any such duty. In *Cobbs*, a doctor performed risky ulcer surgery on a patient which resulted in severe complications. While the surgeon explained the nature of the operation to the patient, he did not discuss the inherent risks.

. . .

Thus, *Cobbs* is not helpful to the majority because the duty of disclosure in that case was imposed to assure consent to the intrusion would be effective. When no intrusion takes place, no need for consent—effective or otherwise—arises.

Furthermore, contrary to the express limitations in *Cobbs*, today's decision requires not only an explanation of the risks of a single procedure but also a "mini-course in medical science," if not a maxi-course. Similarly, because discovery of serious illness in a general examination of an apparently healthy person is remote, the doctor, contrary to *Cobbs*, is now required to disclose remote possibilities of illness. Moreover, the *Cobbs* duty to warn in cases where an adequately informed prudent person would have declined treatment shows a concern for preventing over-selling of services by physicians. By contrast, today's duty appears designed to increase selling of medical services.

. . .

Refusal to give the requested instruction does not warrant reversal. I would affirm the judgment.

NOTES

1. What liability should a hospital have if an attending physician fails to obtain valid informed consent for treatment rendered in the hospital?

Consider Fiorentino v. Wenger, 19 N.Y.2d 407, 280 N.Y.S.2d 373, 227 N.E.2d 296 (1967), in which the New York Court of Appeals reversed a verdict against a private proprietary hospital that had been rendered for a plaintiff who claimed her son had been subjected to an unusual, dangerous operation by a private surgeon without informed consent. Holding the physician to be an "independent contractor," the court refused to enlarge the hospital's liability to include ensuring that its physicians obtained informed consent. Although this view has been the dominant one, the Illinois Court of Appeals recently remanded for trial a case in which an injured patient sought to hold liable the hospital where she was treated, as well as her own physician, for failure to ensure an informed consent. Magana v. Elie, 108 Ill.App.3d 1028, 64 Ill.Dec. 511, 439 N.E.2d 1319 (1982). The court held it to be a factual issue whether the hospital should have required physicians to inform patients of the risks of proposed procedures, in order to conform with its duty to act reasonably in light of apparent risks to its patients articulated in the landmark case of Darling v. Charleston Community Memorial Hospital, 33 Ill.2d 326, 211 N.E.2d 253 (1965), certiorari denied 383 U.S. 946, 86 S.Ct. 1204, 16 L.Ed.2d 209 (1966) [discussed in Johnson v. Misericordia Hospital, Sec. A.5.b, supra.] See Greenlaw, Should Hospitals Be Responsible for Informed Consent?, 11 L.Med. & Health Care 173 (1983).

2.   What obligations should nurses or the "patient representatives" now employed by some hospitals have regarding consent?   See Holder & Lewis, Informed Consent and the Nurse, 2 Nursing Law & Ethics 1 (Feb. 1981).   Nurses, in particular, may find themselves faced with a dilemma (ethically speaking, at least) if they are aware that inadequate information has been given to a patient by a physician about a proposed treatment or if a patient asks them for information that the physician has instructed them not to reveal for fear of upsetting the patient.

3.   Should lawyers not only prescribe informed consent as therapy for improving other professionals' relations with their clients but also take some of this medicine themselves?   The new ABA Model Rules of Professional Conduct enlarge on attorneys' traditional obligations to disclose information to their clients and to recognize the clients' right to control their legal affairs.   See Spiegel, Lawyering and Client Decisionmaking, Informed Consent and the Legal Profession, 128 U.Pa.L.Rev. 41 (1979), which argues cogently for an expansion of the client's role in decisions about his rights and interests.

4.   In Chapter 6, infra, we turn to the various "codes" that have been formulated to guide research with human subjects.   Prior to any of the court opinions on informed consent, the United States tribunal in post-war Germany that tried Nazi physicians who had used concentration camp inmates in experiments declared, in what became known as the Nuremberg Code, that the "voluntary consent of the human subject is absolutely essential" and that the "person involved .   .   .   should have sufficient knowledge and comprehension of the elements of the subject matter involved as to enable him to make an understanding and enlightened decision."   (Compare the "elements" specified by the Code, Ch. 6, Sec. B.1.b, infra, with those required in nonresearch settings.)

Remarkably, none of the seminal judicial decisions rely on, or even cite, statements in the Nuremberg, or other research codes.   Nonetheless, although they developed along separate, parallel tracks the two areas—informed consent for research and for therapy—are today basically the same, and commentators and federal regulators draw on the extensive case law from therapeutic settings in elaborating the rules that are appropriate for disclosure and consent in research settings.

President's Commission, Making Health Care Decisions 21, n. 19 (1982).

PRESIDENT'S COMMISSION FOR THE STUDY OF ETHICAL PROBLEMS IN MEDICINE AND BIOMEDICAL AND BEHAVIORAL RESEARCH, MAKING HEALTH CARE DECISIONS

72–76, 80–83 (1982).

In the Commission's survey,* professionals and the public were asked several questions about disclosure in general and about who is responsible for making sure patients are adequately informed.   Nearly all the public (97%) said that patients should have the right to all available information about their condition and treatment that they wish.   Somewhat surprisingly (since patients report that they want virtually all information), when asked "Who do you think is the best judge of the amount of information that should be disclosed to the patient?," 45% of the public said the patient and 44% said the physician.   In addition, 56% of the public

* As part of its study of informed consent, the President's Commission contracted for a number of empirical investigations to be carried out, including parallel national surveys by Louis Harris and Associates of 800 physicians and 1250 adults in the general public, sample sizes sufficiently large to support generalizations about the views of these two populations with 95% confidence that they are correct within 3%.   The results are set forth in 2 President's Commission, Making Health Care Decisions 17–316 (1982).   [Eds.]

thought that some patients should be told less about their treatment than others.[5] Few people (2%) complained that doctors tell patients too much about either routine care or serious illness. However, 38% felt that patients are told too little about routine care and 33% felt the same about serious illness.[6]

Physicians were asked: "How often do you find yourself in a situation where you must make a conscious and deliberate evaluation of how much to tell a patient about his condition or treatment?" Far from being a rare occurrence, 27% said "several times a day," 25% said "daily," 20% said "weekly," 25% said "rarely," and 3% said "never." In an open-ended question, physicians were asked: "What are the primary factors that influence how much you tell a patient about his condition or treatment?" The patient's ability to understand (56%) and to cope with the information (31%), the seriousness of the condition (30%), and the patient's desire to know (25%) were the reasons given most frequently. Time constraints were mentioned by only 2% of the sample.

In terms of responsibility, physicians felt it is primarily their responsibility to make sure that the patient is fully informed (77%) rather than the patient's responsibility to ask for information (3%), although 19% said the doctor and patient are equally responsible. The public, on the other hand, especially those in poor health and with little education, generally placed more of a burden of responsibility on the patient (20%). In general, however, the public agreed with the physicians that it is the latter's responsibility to make sure patients are fully informed.

When asked whether their physicians keep them informed about questions and decisions relating to their medical care that they (the public) consider important, 37% said they are informed on all important issues and another 30% said they are informed on most issues.

What, then, are the substantive issues to be discussed by professional and patient? These have been variously formulated by courts and commentators, and one version has been incorporated in the federal regulations governing the conduct of research with human subjects. In addition, recent surveys have identified a number of elements as particularly important to patients. Without seeking to provide the last word on this much-discussed subject, the Commission believes the core elements fall under three headings: (1) the patient's current medical status, including its likely course if no treatment is pursued; (2) the intervention(s) that might improve the prognosis, including a description of the procedure(s) involved, a characterization of the likelihood and effect of associated risks and benefits, and the likely course(s) with and without therapy; and (3) a professional opinion, usually, as to the best alternative. Furthermore, each of these elements must be discussed in light of associated uncertainties.

---

5. People in poor health, the elderly, and those with little education or low income were most likely (up to 58%) to view the doctor as the best judge. People with a life-threatening illness, those in poor health, those over 35, those with high incomes, and college graduates were more likely (up to 65%) to feel that some people should have less information than others.

6. Young people, women, people without a usual source of medical care or health insurance, the college-educated, and those with high incomes were more likely than others to feel that doctors give too little information about routine care and serious illness. Overall, 11% of the public were uncertain whether doctors give the right amount of information about serious illness.

Current Medical Status. Inaccurate or incomplete information about illness limits patients' understanding of the effects and of what is at stake in any effort to alter the natural course of diseases. . . .

Since informed consent has, in terms of legal requirements, sometimes been equated with a duty to disclose according to the standards of the medical community, it is interesting to learn that on certain points physicians and the public are in substantial agreement. For example, 17% of physicians claimed that all their patients want candid assessments of their diagnosis and prognosis, even unfavorable ones, and an additional 69% perceived that most of their patients felt that way. Of the public, 94% reported that they would "want to know everything." Indeed, the public displayed an unflinching desire for facts about their conditions, even dismal facts. When asked specifically whether they would want to know about a diagnosis of cancer, 96% of the public said yes (with almost no variation across subgroups). When asked "If you had a type of cancer that usually leads to death in less than a year, would you want your doctor to give you a realistic estimate of how long you had to live, or would you prefer that he not tell you?," 85% (again, with little variation) said they would want a realistic estimate.

When, however, physicians were asked "If you had a patient with a fully confirmed diagnosis of lung cancer in an advanced stage, which of the following would you be most likely to tell your patient?," they showed much less willingness to be candid. Only 13% said they would "give a straight statistical prognosis for his class of disease"; 33% said they would say they "couldn't tell how long he might live, but would stress that it could be for a substantial period of time"; 28% would say they "couldn't tell how long, but would stress that in most cases people live no longer than a year"; and 22% would "refuse to speculate on how long the patient might live." Thus it would still appear that physicians are more reluctant to disclose a limited prognosis than patients would like. Nonetheless, the Commission's survey indicates that physicians generally disclose information about patients' diagnosis and prognosis, and that both physicians and the public feel this should be done. These results are consistent with findings from other surveys that have demonstrated a recent trend toward more complete and frank disclosure and even toward more open discussion specifically regarding "bad news." [14]

Treatment Alternatives and the Professional's Recommendation. In order for medical intervention to be warranted, the patient must stand to gain more from some intervention than if none were undertaken at all. As noted previously, the benefit to be gained must be assessed in terms of the patient's own values and goals. Thus, a practitioner should be cautious not to rule out prematurely an alternative that might offer what a particular patient would perceive as a benefit even if the practitioner sees it differently.

The patient's condition and the range of available alternatives will necessarily shape the course of the discussion. In some instances, there may

14. For example, a survey conducted in 1961 found that 90% of physicians preferred not to inform patients of a diagnosis of cancer. See D. Oken, What to Tell Cancer Patients: A Study of Medical Attitudes, 175 J.A.M.A. 1120 (1961). By 1977, 97% of physicians said they routinely disclosed cancer diagnoses. D.H. Novak et al., Changes in Physicians' Attitudes Towards Telling the Cancer Patient, 241 J.A.M.A. 897 (1979). See also Arnold J. Rosoff, Informed Consent: A Guide for Health Care Providers, Aspen Publications, Rockville, Md. (1961) at 340–76.

be only one medically recognized treatment, so that the decision is primarily between that treatment and no treatment at all. . . .

More commonly, there will be a range of medically acceptable responses to a given disease or health condition. The decision then has two components: *whether* to treat and *how* to treat. . . .

Since the judgment about which choice will best serve well-being properly belongs to the patient, a physician is obliged to mention all alternative treatments, including those he or she does not provide or favor, so long as they are supported by respectable medical opinion. . . .

The observational studies conducted by the Commission are most striking in their findings that in hospital settings often little or nothing is actually discussed with patients regarding either alternative treatments or the recommended treatment. Instead, physicians commonly make decisions and proceed to treat the patient. Beyond this generalization, however, there was tremendous variation in the nature of disclosure and decisionmaking that was related to the structure of the medical care setting, the nature of the patient's illness, and the treatment under consideration.

In the study of treatment refusals in medical, surgical, and specialty wards of a university teaching hospital and a community hospital, it was found that most of the treatment refusals were related to the nature and extent of information provided to patients. In many cases there was a total lack of information concerning diagnostic and therapeutic procedures. Typically these were ordered by physicians without patients being alerted to what was to be done, much less being asked. Although most people went along with these tests and procedures, the lack of information served as a trigger for refusals by patients already primed to resist treatment because of ambivalence about the primary procedure for which they had been hospitalized, delays, previous complications, etc. It was not always obvious to patients why something needed to be done and some refused to proceed until they were given some justification. Thus this lack of information was often a precipitating factor, but not generally the sole cause of refusals. In some cases, patients were told that a test or procedure would be performed, but they were not informed about the purpose or the risks. Patients who knew or discovered that certain procedures were potentially very risky refused treatment until reasonable justification and assurances were provided.

Another source of refusals of treatment was conflicting information given to patients by different health care professionals. This is especially likely to occur in hospitals, where patient care is divided among different people, many of whom are not in direct communication with each other. . . .

Some refusals could be traced to a lack of communication on the part of both the doctor and the patient. For example, one patient refused to take a routinely prescribed laxative because she had severe diarrhea. The doctor had failed to ask the patient about her bowels and the patient was hesitant to volunteer the relevant information. Once the patient told the nurse responsible for dispensing medications why she did not want the laxative (which she had previously been taking despite her diarrhea), the medication was withdrawn.

In the Commission's other observational study, the nature of the communication and decisionmaking process varied for cardiology versus surgery patients, for outpatients versus inpatients, and for acute versus chronic disorders. Differences in the nature of disclosures for surgery and cardiology patients derived from differences in the authority structures and daily routines in the two wards and from the nature of the interventions themselves. Surgery is a single event that is relatively easily described by staff and understood by patients. On the surgical ward, a single, readily identifiable physician was usually clearly in charge. Patients had a greater opportunity to ask questions than in cases where responsibility was more diffuse. Cardiology is organized around an organ malfunction, not around a particular treatment. Cardiac care is therefore more process-oriented and ambiguous and may involve numerous forms of treatment and diagnostic tests. The nature of disclosures for cardiology patients varied with the procedure. . . .

Cardiac catheterization patients . . . got detailed explanations of the procedure and its risks. The following is a transcript of part of a typical conversation between one physician and patient. Having explained why the procedure should be done and what information it would provide, the physician went on to describe how it was done and what it would feel like, including that the patient would feel very hot for about 20 seconds.

Patient: Oh, seconds only, that's all right. But I do want this explanation because I knew I would get this for 25 years. I guess I've heard a lot of things about it. Friends of mine have had it and so forth.

Doctor: Yes, some people like it and some say it's the worse thing that happened to them in their lives. I think I ought to tell you that there's some possibility that we may have to do a transeptum catheterization [and he explained what this consisted of]. There's some potential risks. I think you will find they are terrifying, but I want you to remember we weigh the risks both of doing it and not doing it before we recommend it to you.

Patient: Maybe you shouldn't tell me until tomorrow.

Doctor: Well, I could wait until tomorrow, but I do have to tell you this. I want you to know the risk is low. We are talking about a one in a thousand chance of a major risk. There's some minor ones, too. But they can all be dealt with. Some of the major ones can, too, but they're not very likely. Here are some of them. First of all we have to go into the vessel, and we can injure the vessel, and that can sometimes require surgery, which can be difficult in its own right. The second one is that you might have hardening of the arteries already, and some sort of blockage could result from pushing through them. This can require surgery also to make it better, and even so there's a low risk of a heart attack or of stroke from it. Then another thing is that some people are allergic to the dye, and this can put somebody into shock, and usually we can treat that with medicine, but it's quite serious. Another thing it can do is it can cause an irregular heartbeat, and you can even need an electric shock because it can cause your heart to stop. But of course you would be asleep then, and you wouldn't feel it. Another thing is that if we need to do the transeptal catheterization, that can cause a puncture of the heart and bleeding. The blood can get between the heart and the sac around it, and then we would have to drain that. One of the minor risks is that you can have a hematoma around where we put in the catheter.

That's not much of a real problem, but you can get black and blue, and that happens because of the Heparin we put in to prevent the clotting I talked about earlier.

Patient: You know, I can't remember any of that stuff.

Doctor: Well, I know it's scary, but I want you to understand that it's my feeling that it is a higher risk not to have it done. But of course ultimately it's your decision, not mine.

Patient: Do you do this often?

Doctor: Yeah, this is a big center for that sort of thing, for valve replacements, and we see a lot of these.

Patient: You see it's all new to me.

Doctor: And one other thing is that you're going to have to sign a consent form. The nurse'll bring that in later tonight.

Patient: Well, you have to do it because it's the best procedure.

NOTE ON PATIENTS' COMPREHENSION

Might the courts do well to recognize that *informed* consent could refer to the patient's level of comprehension as well as to physician's obligation to disclose? (There is at least negative support in the judicial opinions already for the view that disclosure is valued as a means to an end (patient comprehension) and not as an end in itself because the courts hold that no disclosure is required for risks that are, or are likely to be, known by the patient.)

. . . Thus far the courts have attempted to effectuate patient participation in medical decisionmaking by imposing a duty of disclosure upon physicians. The courts should go beyond this "information approach" to consider whether the physician has taken reasonable measures to ensure that the patient *understands* the information disclosed. Only this "comprehension approach" can guarantee that the patient engages in informed, meaningful participation in medical decisionmaking. . . .

. . . .

. . . At the very least, the comprehension standard should require a dialogue between physician and patient, in which the physician: (1) inquires into the patient's understanding of risk, (2) encourages the patient to ask questions, and (3) repeats risk information to ensure that the patient assimilates it. . . .

The procedures suggested above inject some content into the comprehensive standard. Nevertheless, unless the requirements of the comprehension standard can be set forth in a relatively detailed list of guidelines, physicians might still lack sufficient guidance to ascertain compliance with the requirements of informed consent. . . . These guidelines should include the following elements:

. . . .

8. The physician should offer to answer any questions the patient may have concerning the proposed treatment, its risk, or alternatives. In view of the general reluctance of patients to ask questions, physicians should make special efforts to encourage patient inquiries. Specifically, the physician should offer to answer the patient's questions several times during the disclosure session, expressly inquiring as to whether the patient has any further questions. In conjunction with the offer to answer the patient's questions, the physician should also offer to repeat or supplement the relevant risk information at a later time. The patient may not have particular questions concerning the treatment, but may still desire to hear the relevant risk information again in order to more fully assimilate it. The patient should, therefore, be informed that the physician stands ready to review the information if the patient believes it is necessary.

. . . .

12.   In determining liability under these guidelines, the trial court should consider the duration of the disclosure sessions as a factor. The shorter the sessions, the greater the probability both that the physician gave only a cursory presentation of the relevant information and that the patient had little meaningful opportunity to assimilate and weigh the information in deciding whether to accept or reject the recommended treatment.

13.   The trial court should also take into account the number of disclosure sessions and the number of times the physician reviewed the risk information with the patient. A greater number of sessions and reviews increases the patient's ability to assimilate the relevant information.

14.   Finally, the trial court should consider the point during the preoperative period at which the physician conducted the disclosure sessions. The earlier in treatment that this occurred, the longer the time that the patient had to carefully weigh all the relevant factors and to discuss with his or her family members, and, therefore, the greater the probability that the patient comprehended the nature and risks of treatment when giving consent.

Note, Informed Consent: From Disclosure to Patient Participation in Medical Decisionmaking, 76 Nw.Univ.L.Rev. 172, 172–173, 190–195 (1981). For specific proposals to test patients' knowledge, see Miller & Willner, The Two-Part Consent Form, 290 New Eng.J.Med. 964 (1974); Grabowski, O'Brien & Mintz, Increasing the Likelihood that Consent is Informed, 12 J.Applied Behav.Anal. 283 (1979). For elective procedures, one physician told the President's Commission that he has patients write their own consent forms in order (among other things) to find out how much of what he's told them they understand. Making Health Care Decisions 118 (1982).

JAY KATZ,
INFORMED CONSENT—A FAIRY TALE?

39 U.Pitt.L.Rev. 137, 139–142, 146–147, 155–157, 164, 174 (1977).

Fairy tales are so appealing because ultimately they reduce complex human encounters to enchanting simplicity. In listening to them we suspend judgment and believe that once upon a time it was, and maybe even today it is, possible to utter magic words or perform magic deeds which transform frogs into princes or punish greedy fishermen's wives. The phrase "informed consent" evokes the same magic expectations. Its protagonists often convey that once kissed by the doctrine, frog-patients will become autonomous princes. Its antagonists warn that all the gold of good medical care which physicians now so magnanimously bestow on patients will turn to worthless metal if the curse of informed consent were to remain with us. .   .   .

The common law's vision of informed consent is confusing and confused. Its frequently articulated underlying purpose—to promote patients' decisional authority over their medical fate—has been severely compromised from the beginning. The wish that patients can or should be allowed to make their own decisions, based on the fullest disclosure possible, runs through most of the opinions. But once the wish has been given its separate due, the rest of the opinion ignores that dream and instead defers to those realities of legal, medical, and human life which are opposed to fostering patients' decision-making. Thus the doctrine of informed consent remains a symbol which despite widespread currency has had little impact on patients' decision-making, either in legal theory or medical practice.

Anglo-American law is caught up in a conflict between its vision of human beings as autonomous persons and its deference to paternalism, another powerful vision of man's interaction with man. The conflict created by uncertainties about the extent to which individual and societal well-being is better served by encouraging patients' self-determination or supporting physicians' paternalism is the central problem of informed consent. This fundamental conflict, reflecting a thoroughgoing ambivalence about human beings' capacities for taking care of themselves and need for care-taking, has shaped judicial pronouncements on informed consent more decisively than is commonly appreciated. The assertion of a "need" for physicians' discretion—for a professional expert's rather than a patient's judgment as to what constitutes well-being—reveals this ambivalence. Other oft-invoked impediments to fostering patients' self-determination, such as patients' medical ignorance, doctors' precious time, the threat of increased litigation, or the difficulty of proving what actually occurred in the dialogue between physician and patient are, substantially, rationalizations which obscure the basic conflict over whose judgment is to be respected.

This ambivalence also reflects conflicting legal views about the psychological nature of human beings. In jurisprudential theory, man is said to be autonomous, self-determining and responsible for his actions. Yet law-makers do not place complete faith in such theoretical constructs once man comes into living contact with law. The never-ending debates over criminal responsibility and civil commitment are telling examples of this conflict in other areas of law. It extends, however, from encounters with persons tainted by attributes of "mental illness" to interactions with "normal" persons where, as in most informed consent disputes, no considerations of mental abnormality enter.

Medical law in the United States is a clear case of institutionalized paternalism. In the last fifty years allopathic physicians have been awarded virtually a complete monopoly over the licensure and practice of the healing arts. Similarly, for the "protection" of citizens, the most rigid drug laws in the world have been promulgated, sequestering most of the pharmacopaeia under the control of experts. When judges began to consider the issue of patients' autonomy in medical decision-making, it took place in a climate where the question of self-determination had been neglected by law for centuries. Lawmakers had reduced patients' personal freedom to the right of vetoing unwanted procedures and even this veto power is not always respected.

As will be developed below, the courts' dicta on self-determination as the fundamental principle underlying the informed consent doctrine are misleading if taken to imply a broad duty of physicians to disclose pertinent medical information or to invite active patients' participation in medical decision-making. Such dicta give the unwary reader of informed consent opinions a false sense that they shaped the doctrine's development, when instead other considerations, including strong doubts about the dicta themselves, were more important. There may, however, have been wisdom in judges' reluctance to give full support to patients' self-determination, once having made a symbolic bow to its supposed supremacy. Disclosure and consent may well be deleterious to a patient if, for example, as a consequence of medicine's ubiquitous uncertainties about risks and benefits, physicians' *and* patients' unexamined faith in the curative power of medical interventions contributes significantly to therapeutic success. Even partial awareness of such uncertainties, which an informed consent doctrine based on thoroughgoing self-determination would bring to consciousness, thus could prove detrimental to recovery. Judges, having been patients themselves, may intuitively have appreciated this crucial, though unexplored, issue and decided to avoid it. . . .

. . .

Courts have not acknowledged their failure to place effective authority in patients' hands. Though judges have felt morally bound to announce that patients ought to be enabled to guide their medical fate, they considered this position unsatisfactory in application and subjected it to extensive modifications. . . . Judicial concern about patients' capacity to make medical decisions and about the detrimental impact of disclosure on patients proved to be more influential than self-determination in shaping the informed consent doctrine, even though the validity of these concerns rests more on conjecture than fact.

Physicians, while in recent decades increasingly confused as to what law expected them to do, have continued to exercise their traditional discretion in deciding what to and what not to disclose to patients. They have done so out of a felt necessity that unites most professionals in society. At the same time the fear of malpractice suits has led to an increased flow of words between physicians and patients. But this has not altered greatly the nature of the "informed consent" dialogue, because the information was not conveyed in the spirit of extending greater freedom of choice to patients. To accomplish that objective would have required a significant modification of the physician's deeply held convictions that he must make the ultimate decision about his patient's medical fate and this has not happened. Instead, the "dialogue" between them continues to be subtly and not so subtly punctuated with crucial distortions, not so much guided by enlightenment in order to facilitate patients' participation in decision-making, but by a conviction that doctors' orders should be followed.

. . .

. . . The label "informed consent" is misleading, since violation of the new duty to disclose risks and alternative treatments does not invalidate the patients' consent to the procedure in the great majority of jurisdictions. Rather the law of "informed consent" denotes a cause of action based on negligent failure to warn, i.e., failure to disclose pertinent medical information. While concern over patients' right to self-determination has led judges to entertain the need for greater disclosure of medical information, it did not prompt them to expand the requisites for valid consent. It is important to appreciate this lack of development, for it raises the question: Can patients' right to self-decision-making be safeguarded by merely modifying requirements for disclosure without at the same time expanding the requirement for valid consent? Or put another way, since there is a reciprocal relationship between disclosure and consent, how extensively and substantively must the informational needs of patients be satisfied to insure greater self-decision-making if it is to be accomplished within the matrix of the traditional consent requirement? In theory there is perhaps nothing wrong with leaving consent as it has always been, since self-determination could be protected by amplifying the requirements for mandatory disclosure. In practice, however, judges' sole focus on disclosure, to the exclusion of consent, tends to perpetuate physicians' disengaged monologues and to discourage a meaningful dialogue between doctors and patients. While it is difficult to compel change in the discourse between human beings where so much depends on the spirit in which it is carried on, a focus on the consent process would highlight the need for

being mindful not only of physicians' conduct, standing alone, but of their conduct in relation to their patient. Questions would then arise as to whether physicians have explored what a patient wishes to know by inviting him to ask further questions about treatment options and by ascertaining whether a patient's informational needs have been met to his satisfaction. Consent is more responsive to inquiries into the care taken for facilitating understanding, while disclosure is less so; for the temptation is great to emphasize what is said rather than how it is communicated.
. . .

. . .

The new rule of law laid down in *Canterbury* . . . is far from clear. Judge Robinson, returning to basic principles of expert testimony, had simply said, there is "no basis for operation of the special medical standard whenever the physician's activity does not bring his medical knowledge and skills peculiarly into play," and that ordinarily disclosure was not such a situation. But Judge Robinson left room for such situations, with respect to disclosure: "When medical judgment enters the picture and for that reason the special standard controls, prevailing medical practice must be given its *just due.*" He did not spell out his meaning. In this case, the defendant claimed that "communication of that risk (of paralysis) to the patient is not good medical practice because it might deter patients from undergoing needed surgery and might produce adverse psychological reactions which could preclude the success of the operation." Such claims, we shall see, will almost invariably be raised by physicians since they derive from widely held tenets of medical practice. "Just due," Judge Robinson's enigmatic phrase, in context certainly suggests that the medical professional standard would be applicable in such a case. If so, the plaintiff's failure to produce an expert witness to contradict the defendant's proposed applicable standard of care, expressing an exercise of professional judgment, will demand or strongly invite a directed verdict. Alternatively, the defense of medical judgment could be treated under the "therapeutic privilege" not to disclose, admitted by Judge Robinson and other courts. . . .

At the same time the court paid no deference to the medical judgment, that disclosure of a one percent risk of paralysis is generally unwise where a laminectomy is considered medically necessary; instead the "just due" of that judgment is to be treated like any other testimony. Thus, on what may have seemed to be an easy fact situation, the court did not face the trial problems of respecting medical judgment raised by its statement of the law. Neither did the plaintiff, since on retrial he came equipped with an expert witness to establish the plaintiff's version of the standard of disclosure.

. . .

The therapeutic privilege not to disclose, as Judge Robinson recognized, is merely a procedurally different way of invoking the professional standard of care. The burden of proof of course remains on the plaintiff. Only if a prima facie case of negligent nondisclosure has been made, does the burden of going forward shift to the defendant, to produce evidence that failure to disclose represented a reasonable exercise of medical judgment. The effect of such evidence is as yet unclear. It may be given the status of medical professional evidence, so that failure to produce contralateral expert testimony will demand a directed verdict. If so, there is virtually no difference between the *Natanson* and *Canterbury* lines of cases, since the plaintiff will almost always be obliged to produce expert testimony that non-disclosure was unreasonable. Alternatively, the defendant-doctor's evidence of the therapeutic appropriateness of nondisclosure could be given no special status, and the question of reasonableness of disclosure could be sent to the jury on the testimony of the plaintiff that it was unreasonable to withhold the information at issue. If so, then the therapeutic privilege becomes merely a description of reasonableness, and not a true legal privilege; it would then have no role at trial except as a basis for jury instruction.

The ambiguous status of the standard of care and the therapeutic privilege in informed consent case law brings to surface judges' ambivalence toward both patients' self-determination and medical paternalism. In attempting to resolve their ambivalance, however, courts favored the traditional wisdom of the medical profession. . . .

The law of informed consent has undergone little analytic development since *Canterbury*. In the twenty years following its birth in *Salgo*, legal protection for patients' freedom of choice was not significantly expanded. Whatever promise *Salgo* and the first *Natanson* opinion held out to secure such rights faded in subsequent constructions of the doctrine. . . .

At present the law of informed consent is substantially mythic and fairy tale-like as far as advancing patients' rights to self-decision-making is concerned. It conveys in its dicta about such rights a fairy tale-like optimism about human capacities for "intelligent" choice and for being respectful of other persons' choices; yet in its implementation of dicta, it conveys a mythic pessimism of human capacities to be choice-makers. The resulting tensions have had a significant impact on the law of informed consent which only has made a bow toward a commitment to patients' self-determination, perhaps in an attempt to resolve these tensions by a belief that it is "less important that this commitment be total than that we believe it to be there." It is premature to decide whether society is better served by proclaiming a commitment to patients' autonomy, even though we do not wish to implement it, or by a frank acknowledgment that it is a fairy tale, at least to a considerable extent: but it is not at all clear whether in interactions between physicians and patients both fairy tale and myth cannot be reconciled much more satisfactorily with reality.

NOTES

1. Professor Marcus Plant of the University of Michigan has criticized *Canterbury* and related decisions from the opposite vantage point: in his view, they go too far in imposing obligations on physicians. He argues that the courts have enormously compounded the uncertainty "that has always bedeviled this area of law."

> This vagueness can appear at several levels. For example, how will a lawyer who is consulted by a physician advise his client as to what to disclose in a specific case? Suppose he tells the physician that he must make all disclosures that "a reasonable person, in what the physician knows or should know to be the patient's position, would be likely to attach significance . . . in deciding whether or not to forego the proposed therapy." Can it be thought that this will be meaningful to any person unaccustomed to thinking in broad legal concepts? When the lawyer adds that the physician's effort to comply with this obscure standard is subject to later review by a jury of laymen who are free to disregard any expert evidence he may produce, the physician's distress will be understandable.

As an illustration, take the facts in Cobbs v. Grant, one of *Canterbury's* followers, at least in part. Plaintiff, having undergone surgery for a duodenal ulcer, had to endure three successive subsequent agonies (spleen removal, gastric ulcer, and premature suture absorption). It would be interesting to have the members of the California Supreme Court who signed that opinion, or the judges in *Canterbury*, write out the advice they would have given to the surgeon prior to the original procedure describing his duty to disclose the hazards that later materialized, and to guide him in such a way that a subsequent jury could not find against him.

It is one thing to formulate a verbally attractive rule of law in the quiet of an academic cloister or a judicial chamber; it is another thing for a practicing lawyer to make that rule of law function; and it is still quite another thing for a physician, not versed in the subtleties of the law and its ways, to live and work under it with any reasonable degree of security.

Plant, The Decline of "Informed Consent," 35 Wash. & Lee L.Rev. 91, 97–98 (1978). Other commentators agree that the uncertainties created by the "objective" standard actually increase costs. Riskin, Informed Consent: Looking for the Action, 1975 U.Ill.L.F. 580; Norton, Contract Law as a Viable Alternative to Problems of Informed Consent, 21 Cath.Law. 122 (1975).

2. In light of the complications created by the judicial decisions, consider the following results from the survey of the President's Commission described earlier in this chapter:

[S]everal questions to physicians and the public dealt with the legal doctrine of informed consent. The majority of both groups agreed that patients' rights to information should be protected by law. However, significantly more physicians than patients agreed with the statement "Time spent discussing diagnosis, prognosis, and treatment could be better spent taking care of patients." The public was more likely than physicians to think that the legal requirements for obtaining informed consent were clear and explicit (52% versus 32%), and doctors were more likely than the public to feel that the requirements put too much emphasis on disclosure of remote risks (73% versus 44%).

Finally, both groups were asked which disclosure standard was best. More than 40% of the physicians and the public thought that a standard based on the informational needs of a particular patient was preferable to a reasonable patient or physician standard.

Physicians were then asked whether they knew which standard applied in the state[s] in which they practiced. Only 23% said they did. Surgeons were more likely than any other specialty to say they knew (30%), and older doctors were more likely than younger ones to claim knowledge of their state's standard (27% versus 17%). Overall, of the 23% who claimed to know the standard, 54% of those practicing in states that have a standard gave the correct answer.

Consent forms, which were originally intended as documentation of disclosure and consent, have in many cases come to substitute for the very processes they are intended to substantiate. Furthermore, there appears to be substantial variation among health care professionals about when consent forms are required deriving in many cases from institutional differences in interpretation of the law. And the law is, in fact, often unclear and nonspecific about the requirements for consent.

Several different consent forms are in use. Hospitals often require patients upon admission to sign a blanket consent that purports to give physicians authority to "treat as necessary." The Joint Commission on Accreditation of Hospitals requires that separate consent forms be signed for any procedure or treatment "for which it is appropriate" and that these forms be included in the medical record . . . .

In the Commission's survey, physicians were asked whether they usually obtained consent—and if so, in what form—for a variety of procedures. The frequency with which consent was obtained varied significantly with the nature of the procedure; virtually all doctors reported getting consent for inpatient surgery, and about half those surveyed reported they did not get consent for prescriptions and blood tests (see Table 3). This finding was substantiated in the Commission's two observational studies . . . .

Physicians and the public were asked whether they agreed with several statements regarding consent forms. Nearly four-fifths of the public and 55% of the physicians think the primary purpose of consent forms is to protect physicians from law suits. . . . The majority of physicians (64%) and the public (65%) think that consent forms help doctor-patient communications. Concerning written consent forms, 62% of the physicians and 86% of the public think that a patient's signature establishes that the individual has given consent . . . .

Physicians were asked in an open-ended question what the effect of consent forms had been: 52% thought they had a positive effect (for example, that they improved patient awareness so patients knew more about their treatment and risks and asked more and better questions, encouraged more communication between doctors and patients, and provided legal protection for doctors and hospitals); 23% felt that consent forms had a negative effect (for example, that they increase patients' fears, reduced compliance, caused patients to avoid necessary treatment, made patients distrust their doctors, increased law suits, and provided no legal protection); 18% thought that informed consent forms had no effect; and 7% were not sure whether they had an effect or not.

President's Commission, Making Health Care Decisions 104–108, 111 (1982).

Table 3:
Nature of Consent Obtained for Various Procedures *

Procedure	Written Consent	Oral Consent	Written and Oral Consent	Neither
Inpatient Surgery	81%	3%	15%	0
Minor Office Surgery	26%	58%	9%	7%
Setting Bones	39%	42%	9%	8%
General Anesthesia	83%	3%	12%	1%
Local Anesthesia	21%	57%	7%	15%
Diagnostic X-rays Involving Injections	45%	35%	8%	10%
Blood Tests	2%	52%	0	45%
Prescriptions	1%	43%	2%	54%
Radiation Therapy	63%	18%	11%	4%

* The total number on which figures in this table are based varied for each procedure in order to eliminate physicians who did not perform the particular procedure. Therefore the figures refer to the proportion of physicians performing a procedure who obtained consent.

Source: Commission survey conducted by Louis Harris and Associates.

3. What should patients be told? Are people's answer to this question likely to vary depending on whether they are patients (ranging from those deciding about elective procedures to those offered previously untested treatments for a desperate illness), medical educators, physicians, physicians' or hospitals' lawyers (counseling their clients versus defending them once suit has been brought), judges, or jurors?

Consider the form proposed by Dr. Preston J. Burnham

CONSENT FORM FOR HERNIA PATIENTS:

I, _____, being about to be subjected to a surgical operation said to be for repair of what my doctor thinks is a hernia (rupture or loss of belly stuff—intestines—out of the belly through a hole in the muscles), do hereby give said doctor permission to cut into me and do duly swear that I am giving my informed consent, based upon the following information:

Operative procedure is as follows: The doctor first cuts through the skin by a four-inch gash in the lower abdomen. He then slashes through the other things—fascia (a tough layer over the muscles) and layers of muscle—until he sees cord (tube that brings the sperm from testicle to outside) with all its arteries and veins. The doctor then tears the hernia (thin sac of bowels and things) from the cord and ties off the sac with a string. He then pushes the testicle back into the scrotum and sews everything together, trying not to sew up the big arteries and veins that nourish the leg.

Possible complications are as follows:

1. Large artery may be cut and I may bleed to death.
2. Large vein may be cut and I may bleed to death.
3. Tube from testicle may be cut. I will then be sterile on that side.
4. Artery or veins to testicles may be cut—same result.
5. Opening around cord in muscles may be made too tight.
6. Clot may develop in these veins which will loosen when I get out of bed and hit my lungs, killing me.
7. Clot may develop in one or both legs which may cripple me, lead to loss of one or both legs, go to my lungs, or make my veins no good for life.
8. I may develop a horrible infection that may kill me.
9. The hernia may come back again after it has been operated on.
10. I may die from general anesthesia.
11. I may be paralyzed if spinal anesthesia is used.
12. If ether is used, it could explode inside me.
13. I may slip in hospital bathroom.
14. I may be run over going to the hospital.
15. The hospital may burn down.

I understand: the anatomy of the body, the pathology of the development of hernia, the surgical technique that will be used to repair the hernia, the physiology of wound healing, the dietetic chemistry of the foods that I must eat to cause healing, the chemistry of body repair, and the course which my physician will take in treating any of the complications that can occur as a sequel of repairing an otherwise simple hernia.

_____

Patient

_____

Lawyer for Patient

_____

Lawyer for Doctor

_____

Lawyer for Hospital

_____

Lawyer for Anesthesiologist

_____

Mother-in-Law

_____

Notary Public

Burnham, Medical Experimentation on Humans, 152 Science 448–50 (1966).

In a more serious (albeit somewhat startling) vein, William Bennett describes what he calls "An Arm and a Leg" game he played with his medical school classmates. Imagine that having found a tiny blemish on the fourth toe of your right foot, your physician tells you the choice is between removing the toe (in which case you will be totally cured), and dying (swiftly and relatively painlessly) of a rare and otherwise untreatable cancer. Bennett assumes that all but the very vain would have the toe removed and be "grateful for the opportunity to strike such a favorable bargain with fate." He then changes the rules of the game: What if the blemish were on your thigh (loss of leg), internally in the pelvis (lower half of body must be removed), and so forth, to the futuristic point when all that can be saved is your brain, alive in a bath of fluid. Bennett, The Science Watch, Harv. Mag. 6 (Jan./Feb. 1982). Noting that people draw the line for themselves in varying places, "according to principles I have not divined," Dr. Bennett concludes that decisions in the world about trading longevity for comfort, convenience, bodily integrity, or physical pleasure are even more complex than in his game because in real life physicians cannot make any flat guarantees. He illustrates the tradeoffs involved through the results of research conducted by Barbara J. McNeil, Ralph Weichselbaum, and Stephen G. Pauker, physicians associated with Howard and Tufts medical schools.

To clarify the way their subjects (normal volunteers) feel about the value of life now, as opposed to a few years from now, the investigators invited each volunteer to gamble with the remaining years of his life. First, each player was told that he could flip a coin. If it came up heads, he would be granted 25 more years of expected life; if tails, death would come [in] a few months. In effect, anyone who was about to flip the coin had a life expectancy of twelve and a half years (but would only be able to collect zero or 25 years). But before the flip, the experimenters gave each player a way out: Instead of flipping the coin, he would take a flat guarantee—say, ten more years of life. In this deal, the subject paid for certainty by bargaining away some of his life expectancy (two and a half years, in this example). If a player accepted the ten-year warranty, he was then asked about a shorter period, and so on down to the minimum guarantee of life that he would accept to avoid the gamble.

What McNeil, Weichselbaum, and Pauker found was that subjects varied considerably in their willingness to gamble on the jackpot of 25 years. Many would settle for a short-term sure thing rather than risk the flip. Others were inclined to go for the extra years.

. . .

. . . What McNeil and her colleagues have demonstrated is that . . . people don't all have the same values. Thus, a physician who bases his choice of therapy on his own values, or even those of some imaginary average, may rob his patients of what they want most.

Bennett, The Science Watch, Harv.Mag. 6 (Jan./Feb.1982).

See also McNeil, Pauker, Sox & Tversky, On the Elicitation of Preferences for Alternative Therapies, 306 New Eng. J. Med. 1259 (1982) which suggests that the quality of medical decisionmaking would be improved if physicians (and patients) were aware of the way variations in presenting information affect decisions (such as viewing surgery for lung cancer as more attractive, relative to radiation therapy, when the same data are framed in terms of the probability of living rather than the probability of dying).

4. Compare the approaches of three state legislatures:

Iowa Written Informed Consent Law

Iowa Code Ann. § 147.137 (1975).

A consent in writing to any medical or surgical procedure or course of procedures in patient care which meets the requirements of this section shall create a presumption that informed consent was given. A consent in writing meets the requirements of this section if it:

1. Sets forth in general terms the nature and purpose of the procedure or procedures, together with the known risks, if any, of death, brain damage, quadriplegia, paraplegia, the loss or loss of function of any organ or limb, or disfiguring scars associated with such procedure or procedures, with the probability of each such risk if reasonably determinable.

2. Acknowledges that the disclosure of that information has been made and that all questions asked about the procedure or procedures have been answered in a satisfactory manner.

3. Is signed by the patient for whom the procedure is to be performed, or if the patient for any reason lacks legal capacity to consent, is signed by a person who has legal authority to consent on behalf of that patient in those circumstances.

New York Informed Consent Law

N.Y. Pub. Health Code § 2805–d (1976).

1. Lack of informed consent means the failure of the person providing the professional treatment or diagnosis to disclose to the patient such alternatives thereto and the reasonably foreseeable risks and benefits involved as a reasonable medical practitioner under similar circumstances would have disclosed, in a manner permitting the patient to make a knowledgeable evaluation.

2. The right of action to recover from medical malpractice based on a lack of informed consent is limited to those cases involving either (a) non-emergency treatment, procedure or surgery, or (b) a diagnostic procedure which involved invasion or disruption of the integrity of the body.

3. For a cause of action therefor it must also be established that a reasonably prudent person in the patient's position would not have undergone the treatment or diagnosis if he had been fully informed and that the lack of informed consent is a proximate cause of the injury or condition for which recovery is sought.

4. It shall be a defense to any action for medical malpractice based upon an alleged failure to obtain such an informed consent that:

(a) the risk not disclosed is too commonly known to warrant disclosure; or

(b) the patient assured the medical practitioner he would undergo the treatment, procedure or diagnosis regardless of the risk involved, or the patient assured the medical practitioner that he did not want to be informed of the matters to which he would be entitled to be informed; or

(c) consent by or on behalf of the patient was not reasonably possible; or

(d) the medical practitioner, after considering all of the attendant facts and circumstances, used reasonable discretion as to the manner and extent to which such alternatives or risks were disclosed to the patient because he reasonably believed that the manner and extent of such disclosure could reasonably be expected to adversely and substantially affect the patient's condition.

Texas Medical Disclosure Panel Law

Tex.Civ.Code Ann. art. 45901, §§ 6.03–6.04 (1977).

Sec. 6.03

(a) The Texas Medical Disclosure Panel is created to determine which risks and hazards related to medical care and surgical procedures must be disclosed by health care providers or physicians to their patients or persons authorized to consent for their patients and to establish the general form and substance of such disclosure.

(b) The panel established herein is administratively attached to the Texas Department of Health. The Texas Department of Health, at the request of the panel, shall provide administrative assistance to the panel; and the Texas Department of Health and the panel shall coordinate administrative responsibilities in order to avoid unnecessary duplication of facilities and services. The Texas Department of Health, at the request of the panel, shall submit the panel's budget request to the legislature. The panel shall be subject, except where inconsistent, to the rules and procedures of the Texas Department of Health; however, the duties and responsibilities of the panel as set forth in the Medical Liability and Insurance Improvement Act of Texas, as amended (Article 4590i, Vernon's Texas Civil Statutes), shall be exercised solely by the panel and the board or Texas Department of Health shall have no authority or responsibility with respect to same.

(c) The panel is composed of nine members, with three members licensed to practice law in this state and six members licensed to practice medicine in this state. Members of the panel shall be selected by the Commissioner of Health.

(d) The commissioner shall select members of the panel according to the following schedule:

(1) one attorney and two physicians to serve a term of two years, which term shall begin on September 1, 1979, and expire on August 31, 1981, or until a successor is qualified;

(2) one attorney and two physicians to serve a term of four years, which terms shall begin September 1, 1979, and expire August 31, 1983, or until a successor is qualified;

(3) one attorney and two physicians to serve a term of six years, which term shall begin September 1, 1979, and expire on August 31, 1985, or until a successor is qualified.

Thereafter, at the expiration of the term of each member of the panel so appointed, the commissioner shall select a successor, and such successor shall serve for a term of six years, or until his successor is selected. Any member who is absent for three consecutive meetings without the consent of a majority of the panel present at each such meeting may be removed by the commissioner at the request of the panel submitted in writing and signed by the chairman. Upon the death, resignation, or removal of any member, the commissioner shall fill the vacancy by selection for the unexpired portion of the term.

(e) Members of the panel are not entitled to compensation for their services, but each panelist is entitled to reimbursement of any necessary expense incurred in the performance of his duties on the panel including necessary travel expenses.

(f) Meetings of the panel shall be held at the call of the chairman or on petition of at least three members of the panel.

(g) At the first meeting of the panel each year after its members assume their positions, the panelists shall select one of the panel members to serve as chairman and one of the panel members to serve as vice-chairman, and each such officer shall serve for a term of one year. The chairman shall preside at meetings of the panel, and in his absence, the vice-chairman shall preside.

(h) Employees of the Texas Department of Health shall serve as the staff for the panel.

Sec. 6.04

(a) To the extent feasible, the panel shall identify and make a thorough examination of all medical treatments and surgical procedures in which physicians and health care providers may be involved in order to determine which of those treatments and procedures do and do not require disclosure of the risks and hazards to the patient or person authorized to consent for the patient.

(b) The panel shall prepare separate lists of those medical treatments and surgical procedures that do and do not require disclosure and for those treatments and procedures that do require disclosure shall establish the degree of disclosure required and the form in which the disclosure will be made.

(c) Lists prepared under Subsection (b) of this section together with written explanations of the degree and form of disclosure shall be published in the Texas Register.

(d) At least annually, or at such other period the panel may determine from time to time, the panel will identify and examine any new medical treatments and surgical procedures that have been developed since its last determinations, shall assign them to the proper list, and shall establish the degree of disclosure required and the form in which the disclosure will be made. The panel will also examine such treatments and procedures for the purpose of revising lists previously published. These determinations shall be published in the Texas Register.

5.   Some states have attempted to regulate informed consent in the area of abortion. For example, in 1978, Akron, Ohio enacted Ordinance No. 160–1978, entitled "Regulation of Abortions". Section 1870.06 required written consent, freely given without coercion. The ordinance stipulated that consent must be based on a full disclosure of: (1) the number of weeks elapsed from the probable time of conception; (2) that the fetus is a human life at the moment of conception, including a detailed physical description of the fetus; (3) possible physical and mental complications which could arise from the operation; (4) information on local agencies which would assist the mother during the pregnancy and birth of the child if she wished. Section 1870.07 required a physician to wait at least 24 hours after a woman signed a consent form before performing the abortion. The U.S. Supreme Court struck down the Akron ordinance. City of Akron v. Akron Center for Reproductive Health, Inc., __ U.S. __, 103 S.Ct. 2481, 76 L.Ed.2d 687 (1983). For further discussion of *City of Akron*, see note 4 following Roe v. Wade, Ch. 8, Sec. B.1.a., infra.

6.   As detailed as they are, the statutes on informed consent fail to illuminate many issues. For example, could a patient knowingly consent to a "local" standard of care by a physician in a rural area (that is, one lower than that prevailing "nationally," meaning in the major medical centers where physicians are trained and whence expert witnesses are typically recruited), perhaps because the patient values other aspects of the physician's treatment or simply wishes to avoid having to travel to the city for treatment? And what of the costs of treatment? The President's Commission found that 70% of the public thought physicians should initiate discussion of this subject, but only 38% of the physicians report doing so. Making Health Care Decisions 79 (1982). Furthermore, may a physician withhold information about a treatment alternative that is not worth its costs in the physician's view, or one that is not covered by the patient's health insurance plan? Indeed, are those who sell health insurance or memberships in prepaid group health plans obligated by the law of informed consent to make sure potential buyers receive a comprehensible explanation of the scope of their coverage including all limitations on treatment for all potential illnesses?

BUDD N. SHENKIN AND DAVID C. WARNER, GIVING THE PATIENT HIS MEDICAL RECORD: A PROPOSAL TO IMPROVE THE SYSTEM

289 New Eng.J.Med. 688, 688–691 (1973).

Dissatisfaction with the functioning of the medical-care system has become widespread. Four serious problems are maintaining high quality of care, establishing mutually satisfactory physician-patient relations, ensuring continuity and avoiding excessive bureaucracy. We believe these problems could be alleviated, in part, if patients were given copies of all their medical records. The record to a large extent embodies the informational product of medical consultation and treatment. In most exchanges in society a purchased product becomes the property of the purchaser, who is then free to evaluate the product on his own, have it evaluated by experts and choose freely among suppliers for any further services. Patients, physicians and planners and administrators would all benefit if the conditions of open information and freedom of choice that prevail in the market were to be introduced into the area of medical care.

At present, medical records are not routinely available to either physicians or patients. In theory, records are transferable within the profession; in practice, they are seldom transferred even in summary form, and even within one institution. . . . It is indeed paradoxical that records are available primarily for setting the patient and physician against one another, and in most cases, only through the intervention of another professional!

The Proposal

We propose that legislation be passed to require that a complete and unexpurgated copy of all medical records, both inpatient and outpatient, be issued routinely and automatically to patients as soon as the services provided are recorded. The legislation should also require that physician and hospital qualifications (accreditations, memberships, etc.) and charges for services be recorded.

Hospital records should be available regularly to patients on the ward, and copies sent to them upon termination of the hospitalization. Outpatient records could be issued in two ways: copies could be sent directly from the physician's office; or records could be stored and mailed centrally. Although the latter approach would generate more red tape, centrally stored records could provide data for epidemiologic studies, be coordinated with activities of Professional Standards Review Organizations, and ensure against loss of his records by the patient. In addition, central record storage would facilitate a patient's option to refuse or accept the record anonymously.

Expected Positive Results

The Proposal would benefit most participants in the medical-care system.

Patients

Information. At present, patients generally receive insufficient information on their own case, and their health knowledge is quite poor regardless of socioeconomic status, race, rural or urban background, age group or sex. Both physicians and patients find this undesirable. In addition, inadequate transmittal of understandable information from physician to patient largely accounts for the widespread phenomenon of patient noncompliance with professional recommendations.

With record in hand, the patient would receive more complete information about his medical encounters, a source of satisfaction in itself. Patient compliance would probably improve, since the available record would supplant reliance on memory and would help the patient understand the rationale for treatment. Better records might even result as patients corrected mistakes in the history, and were encouraged by seeing their case described to keep relevant symptomatic notes for the next visit.

The record would serve as an educational tool. Patients would consult books or medical personnel about unfamiliar words, and thus learn professional terminology and concepts. Eventually, increased knowledge would lead to more appropriate utilization of physicians and a greater ability of patients to participate in their own care.

Continuity. The effects of replacing the "whole-person" physician by many specialist referrals have been exacerbated by population mobility, frequent use of emergency rooms, and physicians who cover one another's patients. Even when referred from another physician, patients must give the same history time and time again (a necessarily faulty one, since they are forgetful and do not know the details of their past professional care), and submit to the same laboratory and radiologic procedures repeatedly, because records are not at hand.

In contrast to this situation, implementing the Proposal would always provide a physician direct access to the history of the patient's previous care, complete with base-line data, drug schedules (a major problem), hypersensitivities, etc. Patients would accordingly be subjected to fewer repeat tests, would be required to repeat but little information and would receive more complete, better informed care. The patients would at all times feel less "lost" in the system.

Choice. Patients have little opportunity to exercise informed free choice of physician in either primary or secondary care. The few criteria available for judging physician capability (e.g., specialty certification or hospital affiliations) are often unknown to patients or uninterpretable by them; they must use personalistic, nonprofessional criteria instead. Patients are inhibited from freely changing physicians, in part, by the expense of new work-ups, and by the difficulty of ever returning to the original physician if the new one should request the previous records.

Clearly, adopting the Proposal would free patients to choose and change physicians more easily. Patients would also be able to make better judgments about their physicians, and to differentiate legitimate physicians from quacks. Comparing physicians on professional grounds would become possible to some extent. It would take little sophistication, for example, for the patient to correlate a surgical procedure with the presence or absence of surgical-board certification (as listed on the record). A sophisticated patient might want to research the diagnosis himself, and learn more about it while monitoring the physician. Such personal attempts might have the side effect of emphasizing to a patient the difficulty of medical practice, and enhancing the physician's legitimacy as an authority (on the basis of official status combined with recognized expertise).

Published guides to medical care would soon flourish, and professional consultant services for records "translation," interpretation and evaluation would arise in response to consumer demand. Medical societies, universities, private groups, or Professional Standards Review Organizations could operate such services, which would then function as noncompulsory, decentralized quality-enforcement mechanisms.

Physician-patient relations. The nature of physician-patient relations has conflicted with American cultural norms. Americans demand autonomy; yet patients have been forced into profound dependency on physicians whom they must trust on faith alone, whom they can hardly understand, and to whom they have often had little real alternative. As a result, many patients have acquired paranoid feelings about the medical-care system—

and acted on them. The Women's Health Movement takes matters into its own hands; the thriving business of quacks and cultists reflects a search for friendly attitudes in a hostile professional world, as well as the public's inability to discriminate on a scientific basis.

Availability of records would enable patients to be much more autonomous in making judgments and choices; less dependent, they would feel less paranoid. The increase in patient information would undermine much of the current suspicion of physicians' candor. Since provision of medical records to all patients would be obligatory, no physician would regard any single patient as impeaching his services. As patients became more familiar with medical concepts, physician-patient communication would improve. All these improvements would produce more harmonious physician-patient relations.

Physicians

Quality care. At present physicians have only limited means of evaluating one another's performance. As a result, an incentive for practicing high-quality care is lost, and referring patients to other physicians of known competence is made more difficult.

An effect of implementing the Proposal would be decentralized peer review. After seeing several patients whom another practitioner had seen, in conjunction with their records, a physician could hardly help making an assessment of that physician's abilities and practice. In this way professional reputations would grow according to the concrete criteria of patient care. Anticipating this process, physicians would have a clear incentive to practice high-quality medicine, especially since the practices of the most reputable would probably increase. In many cases, favorable evaluation by a specialist of a primary practitioner's records, or vice-versa, would result in increased trust and more expeditious referral of the patient to the appropriate level.

In addition, the Proposal would provide physicians new opportunities to learn. Just as residents learn by caring for patients and observing how various specialists treat their patients after they themselves have done as much as they can, so physicians in whatever practice setting would have the same experience repeatedly. The freely available record would provide a more "longitudinal" view of a patient, and physicians would appreciate better (and treat better) the course of a disease. Since innovation proceeds mainly by the contagion effect, new knowledge would probably be put into practice more swiftly, and isolated practitioners reached more quickly.

Satisfaction. Practitioners have become less satisfied with their role and status in society. . . .

Decentralized peer review would provide recognition of excellence in the practice of medicine, and hence enhance the prestige of being a practicing physician. Patient records and the care that they reflected would become a source of pride open to the perusal of fellow professionals. The expected improvement in continuity would decrease frustrations, and improved physician-patient relations would add importantly to physician satisfaction. . . .

Objections to the Proposal

A number of objections to the Proposal may be anticipated. To begin with, various objections could arise from so strong a reliance on records.

Records could be falsified, and diagnostic and treatment procedures made to look more complete and exhaustive than they were. A reliance on form rather than substance could develop, with no associated improvement in patient care. Or, conversely, practitioners could be led to do too much and be too complete for the sake of self-protection. With records so public, practitioners might be less free to practice in the most expeditious way possible, and the record might become a real burden. Moreover, judgment of medical-care quality on the basis of records could penalize a good practitioner who happened to keep poor records.

Certainly, records could be falsified, although verification procedures and patient recollection would serve as a check. Adherence to proper form would have little chance of passing for substantive validity in this decentralized system, as explained above.

Less-than-adequate work-ups are more common than more-than-adequate ones, so that a correction of this tendency would be salutary. With records traveling predominantly in the medical realm, despite the patient intermediary, medically warranted shortcuts should prove acceptable.

Finally, it must be stressed that medical records are not merely more red tape like insurance forms. The medical record constitutes an integral and vitally important part of the medical-care process, formalizing and focusing medical logic as well as facilitating memory. If a practitioner can somehow convince his patients that he is good despite records deficiencies (as might be true rarely), the Proposal would allow this relation to continue unhindered, whereas more centralized and routinized procedures would not.

A second objection might be that peer review of any sort can be questioned. . . .

Much of the unwarranted fear of review would be assuaged with experience. Moreover, decentralized review with voluntary sanctions might be easier to accept than centralized alternatives. Decentralized peer review should also be more effective since the medical profession is not really monolithic. After implementation of the Proposal any group could offer patients evaluation services and a majoritarian professional protective interest would accordingly be less effective, whereas the closed-door proceedings of centralized peer review would find dissenters excluded and overwhelmed.

A third possible objection would be fear that open disclosure of records would lead to more malpractice suits. What should be feared, however, is not more suits, but unjustified ones. The Secretary's Commission on Medical Malpractice has found that most suits are generated by poor patient care rather than greed and ". . . the unavailability of medical records without resort to litigation creates needless expense and increases the incidence of unnecessary malpractice litigation."

A fourth objection would be that some might fear that physicians would be called upon to spend more time per patient, both in writing better records and in answering more questions.

NOTES

1. A number of states have statutes that afford patients some access to records—or information abstracted from records—in the possession of health care providers. Many of the statutes that apply to hospital records permit access only after the patient has been discharged, although a few, such as the Massachusetts law, allow hospitalized patients to see their charts if they wish. (Apparently very

few patients take advantage of this statutory right, created by Ch. 214 of Mass. Acts of 1979. See Lipsitt, The Patient and the Record, 302 New Eng.J.Med. 167 (1980).) In order to encourage health care providers to cooperate with patients' requests, some statutes include specified times for compliance and even permit a patient denied access beyond a reasonable time to seek punitive damages. Several states specify that if disclosure of information would be harmful to a patient's health, the information will be given to the patient's representative rather than directly to the patient.

The major reason for allowing patient access to records is not as an aid to decisionmaking during treatment but to permit patients to know what information a hospital or other provider has about them. Where permissible, a patient who finds inaccurate or misleading material in his or her records may request the party holding the records to make modifications or additions, or to include his or her personal statement about the information as part of the record. Because patients must be aware of the fact that a hospital or other record holder may be privileged to disclose their records to third parties—or even required to—it is not clear that the access statutes have yet had much impact on health care.

2. In Gotkin v. Miller, 514 F.2d 125 (2d Cir.1975), plaintiff sued to obtain her records from three mental hospitals where she had been treated as a voluntary patient on several occasions over an eight year period because of a series of suicide attempts; she sought the records because she had contracted to write a book about her experiences and wanted to verify her recollection of various incidents. The hospitals offered to release the records to Mrs. Gotkin's physician, but no request for such a release was made.

> The hospitals explained that they prefer to release records to a designated physician rather than to the patient himself because 1) medical records are often unintelligible to the layman, 2) the revelation of certain information could be detrimental to the individual's current well-being, and 3) the records often contain references to other individuals who might be harmed by disclosure. See New York State Department of Mental Hygiene, Department Policy Manual § 2932 (1974). The designated physician is expected to withhold material which might be harmful to the patient or third parties.

Id. at 127, n. 2.

The trial court granted the hospitals' motion for summary judgment; the court of appeals affirmed, holding that none of her constitutional rights had been violated. Specifically, the court concluded that she had not been deprived of her property without due process of law.

> Appellants argue that under New York case law, patients have a property interest in their hospital records. However, none of the cases cited by appellants indicates that patients have a right to unrestricted access to their records.
> . . .
>
> The only New York decision cited by the parties which deals directly with the question of whether a patient has a property interest in his records is In re Culbertson's Will, 57 Misc.2d 391, 292 N.Y.S.2d 806 (Sur.Ct.1968). In that case the court held that the records were the property of the physician but that a provision in a doctor's will calling for the destruction of his records would not be enforced because it violated public policy. Culbertson is consistent with the cases cited by the appellants. All of them indicate that patients have certain rights in their records short of the absolute property right to unrestricted access which the appellants are claiming here.
>
> New York statutory law also establishes that while patients may exercise a considerable degree of control over their records, they do not have the right to demand direct access to them. Under § 15.13 of the Mental Hygiene Law (McKinney's Consol.Laws, c. 27, Supp.1974), records may not be released to third parties without the consent of the patient, except in certain enumerated situations. Section 17 of the Public Health Law (McKinney's Consol.Laws, c. 45, Supp.1974) provides for the release of medical records to a hospital or physician designated by the patient. These sections indicate the existence of

substantial limitations on the right of access claimed by appellants. We therefore hold that the Fourteenth Amendment does not support appellants' claim that former mental patients have a constitutionally protected, unrestricted property right directly to inspect and copy their hospital records.

Id. at 129.

The court also found that the hospitals' refusal to give Mrs. Gotkin her records did not stigmatize her as mentally ill. Finally, it rejected her contention that her right to privacy and control over her own body was jeopardized by the hospitals' actions.

3. What other sources of information are available for a patient who is curious about aspects of his or her illness or possible treatment? What about medical libraries? Or pharmacists? Some years ago, congressional interest in "patient package inserts" (PPI's) to accompany prescription drugs prompted the FDA to propose that printed information be dispensed with drugs on their nature, purpose, proper use and risks. A study done for the FDA by the Rand Corporation found that PPI's led some patients to have fuller discussions with their physicians about the drugs prescribed. See D. Kanouse et al., Informing Patients about Drugs: Summary Report on Alternative Designs for Prescription Drug Leaflets (1981). After the FDA announced in 1982 that it was not going forward with the PPI program, the American Medical Association began a voluntary system under which it sells information forms to physicians on 20 of the most widely prescribed drugs. Should PPI's be mandated by statute?

2. WHAT LIMITATIONS SHOULD BE PLACED ON INDIVIDUAL CHOICE?

a. Based on Concern for Others

JACOBSON v. MASSACHUSETTS

Supreme Court of the United States, 1905.
197 U.S. 11, 25 S.Ct. 358, 49 L.Ed. 643.

MR. JUSTICE HARLAN . . . . delivered the opinion of the court.

. . . . The defendant insists that his liberty is invaded when the State subjects him to fine or imprisonment for neglecting or refusing to submit to vaccination; that a compulsory vaccination law is unreasonable, arbitrary and oppressive, and, therefore, hostile to the inherent right of every freeman to care for his own body and health in such way as to him seems best; and that the execution of such a law against one who objects to vaccination, no matter for what reason, is nothing short of an assault upon his person. But the liberty secured by the Constitution of the United States to every person within its jurisdiction does not import an absolute right in each person to be, at all times and in all circumstances, wholly freed from restraint. There are manifold restraints to which every person is necessarily subject for the common good. On any other basis organized society could not exist with safety to its members. Society based on the rule that each one is a law unto himself would soon be confronted with disorder and anarchy. Real liberty for all could not exist under the operation of a principle which recognizes the right of each individual person to use his own, whether in respect of his person or his property, regardless of the injury that may be done to others. . . .

. . .

Applying these principles to the present case, it is to be observed that the legislature of Massachusetts required the inhabitants of a city or town to be vaccinated only when, in the opinion of the Board of Health, that was necessary for the public health or the public safety. . . .

. . . Upon the principle of self-defense, of paramount necessity, a community has the right to protect itself against an epidemic of disease which threatens the safety of its members. It is to be observed that when the regulation in question was adopted, smallpox, according to the recitals in the regulation adopted by the Board of Health, was prevalent to some extent in the city of Cambridge and the disease was increasing. If such was the situation—and nothing is asserted or appears in the record to the contrary—if we are to attach any value whatever to the knowledge which, it is safe to affirm, is common to all civilized peoples touching smallpox and the methods most usually employed to eradicate that disease, it cannot be adjudged that the present regulation of the Board of Health was not necessary in order to protect the public health and secure the public safety. . . .

. . . If the mode adopted by the Commonwealth of Massachusetts for the protection of its local communities against smallpox proved to be distressing, inconvenient or objectional to some—if nothing more could be reasonably affirmed of the statute in question—the answer is that it was the duty of the constituted authorities primarily to keep in view the welfare, comfort and safety of the many, and not permit the interests of the many to be subordinated to the wishes or convenience of the few. There is, of course, a sphere within which the individual may assert the supremacy of his own will and rightfully dispute the authority of any human government, especially of any free government existing under a written constitution, to interfere with the exercise of that will. But it is equally true that in every well-ordered society charged with the duty of conserving the safety of its members the rights of the individual in respect of his liberty may at times, under the pressure of great dangers, be subjected to such restraint, to be enforced by reasonable regulations, as the safety of the general public may demand. An American citizen, arriving at an American port on a vessel in which, during the voyage, there had been cases of yellow fever or Asiatic cholera, although apparently free from disease himself, may yet, in some circumstances, be held in quarantine against his will on board of such vessel or in a quarantine station, until it be ascertained by inspection, conducted with due diligence, that the danger of the spread of the disease among the community at large has disappeared. . . .

Did the offers of proof made by the defendant present a case which entitled him, while remaining in Cambridge, to claim exemption from the operation of the statute and of the regulation adopted by the Board of Health? . . .

Could he reasonably claim such an exemption because "quite often" or "occasionally" injury had resulted from vaccination, or because it was impossible, in the opinion of some, by any practical test, to determine with absolute certainty whether a particular person could be safely vaccinated?

It seems to the court that an affirmative answer to these questions would practically strip the legislative department of its function to care for the public health and the public safety when endangered by epidemics of disease. Such an answer would mean that compulsory vaccination could not, in any conceivable case, be legally enforced in a community, even at the command of the legislature, however widespread the epidemic of smallpox, and however deep and universal was the belief of the community and of its medical advisers, that a system of general vaccination was vital to the safety of all.

We are not prepared to hold that a minority, residing or remaining in any city or town where smallpox is prevalent, and enjoying the general protection afforded by an organized local government, may thus defy the will of its constituted authorities, acting in good faith for all, under the legislative sanction of the State. . . . While this court should guard with firmness every right appertaining to life, liberty or property as secured to the individual by the Supreme Law of the Land, it is of the last importance that it should not invade the domain of local authority except when it is plainly necessary to do so in order to enforce that law. The safety and the health of the people of Massachusetts are, in the first instance, for that Commonwealth to guard and protect. They are matters that do not ordinarily concern the National Government. So far as they can be reached by any government, they depend, primarily, upon such action as the State in its wisdom may take; and we do not perceive that this legislation has invaded any right secured by the Federal Constitution.

. . . Until otherwise informed by the highest court of Massachusetts we are not inclined to hold that the statute establishes the absolute rule that an adult must be vaccinated if it be apparent or can be shown with reasonable certainty that he is not at the time a fit subject of vaccination or that vaccination, by reason of his then condition, would seriously impair his health or probably cause his death. No such case is here presented. It is the case of an adult who, for aught that appears, was himself in perfect health and a fit subject of vaccination, and yet, while remaining in the community, refused to obey the statute and the regulation adopted in execution of its provisions for the protection of the public health and the public safety, confessedly endangered by the presence of a dangerous disease.

We now decide only that the statute covers the present case, and that nothing clearly appears that would justify this court in holding it to be unconstitutional and inoperative in its application to the plaintiff in error.

The judgment of the court below must be affirmed.

McINTOSH v. MILANO

Superior Court of New Jersey, 1979.
168 N.J.Super. 466, 403 A.2d 500.

PETRELLA, J.S.C.

Defendant Michael Milano, M.D., a board-certified psychiatrist licensed to practice in New Jersey, seeks summary judgment dismissing the complaint in this wrongful death action on the ground that he owed no duty to plaintiff's decedent and daughter, Kimberly McIntosh (sometimes referred to as decedent). On July 8, 1975 Lee Morgenstein, who by then had been a patient of defendant for slightly more than two years, murdered decedent.

. . . Plaintiff places reliance in her claim of duty and breach thereof on the case of Tarasoff v. Regents of Univ. of California, 17 Cal.3d 425, 131 Cal.Rptr. 14, 551 P.2d 334 (Sup.Ct.1976) (*Tarasoff* II), which is nonbinding authority in this jurisdiction.

Defendant argues that no such duty exists in this State, and that this court should not create one or allow one to be asserted by plaintiff by adopting the *Tarasoff* II rule or one comparable thereto.

. . . Defendant first met Lee Morgenstein, then age 15, and began his treatment on May 5, 1973, after the latter's school psychologist had given Morgenstein's parents defendant's name and that of certain other therapists, partially because of Morgenstein's involvement with drugs. His treatment was on a weekly basis for what he initially diagnosed as "an adjustment reaction of adolescence." During the course of therapy over the approximate two-year period, Morgenstein related many "fantasies" to defendant on various subjects, including fantasies of fear of other people, being a hero or an important villain, and using a knife to threaten people who might intimidate or frighten him.

Morgenstein also related certain alleged experiences and emotional involvements with decedent, who in 1973 was about 20 years old and at that time lived with her parents next door to the Morgensteins. Defendant considered all such "fantasies" referred to above as just that, but he came to accept, after initial reservations, that the experiences related to him by Morgenstein as to his eventual victim represented truth and not fantasy. Dr. Milano stated he was somewhat "nonplussed" initially about the revelations of Morgenstein concerning Miss McIntosh and alleged sexual experiences because of the five-year age difference. However, he said that he came to believe it because the way Morgenstein responded emotionally fit with what he told him, and Milano claimed he never had any reason to doubt Morgenstein. . . . Defendant did indicate in his deposition that he advised Morgenstein to break off the relationship.

Morgenstein had possessive feelings towards Kimberly, according to the doctor, and was "overwhelmed" by the relationship. Although Morgenstein is said to have repeatedly expressed anxiety to defendant over his relationship with Miss McIntosh, defendant asserts she was not the dominant theme of the therapy.[4]

It is undisputed, and Dr. Milano admits, that Morgenstein had confided that he had fired a B.B. gun at what he recalled to be a car (Miss McIntosh's or her boyfriend's) on one occasion when he was upset because she was going on a date with her boyfriend. There is evidence proffered by plaintiff that other windows in the McIntosh house and another vehicle had been shot at and damaged by a B.B. or some other gun, and a factfinder might infer that these were actions of Morgenstein. It is also undisputed that Dr. Milano had been told by Morgenstein that he had purchased and carried a knife to show to people to scare them away if they should attempt to frighten or intimidate him, and brought it to a therapy session to show the doctor.

Although Dr. Milano said that Morgenstein wished Miss McIntosh would "suffer" as he did and had expressed jealousy and a very possessive attitude towards her, was jealous of other men and hateful towards her boyfriends, had difficulty convincing himself that fights or things were really over or finished, he denied that Morgenstein ever indicated or exhibited any feelings of violence toward decedent or said that he intended to kill her or inflict bodily harm. Morgenstein was also very angry that he

---

4. At the criminal trial of *State v. Morgenstein*, supra, Milano diagnosed Morgenstein as a "schizoid personality," which he described as a "personality disorder" and not a mental illness. He indicated that means that "under severe emotional stress, the person tends to withdraw and not show much emotion, and in fact be rather blan [sic], and apparently unemotional on the surface."

had not been able to obtain Miss McIntosh's phone number when she moved from the family home. He may not even have known where she lived in 1975. Plaintiff proffered testimony that Miss McIntosh had told her family of Morgenstein's drug problems, felt sorry for him, and hoped he could get help.

Following an incident in which Morgenstein fell off a bicycle and injured his face the day before the July 8, 1975 therapy session, and after an incident during the course of that day's therapy (apparently when Dr. Milano briefly left the room), he stole a prescription form from the doctor's desk. Later that day he attempted to obtain 30 Seconal tablets [5] from a pharmacist with the stolen form. The pharmacist apparently became suspicious and called Dr. Milano, who instructed him to retain the unauthorized prescription form, not to fill it, and to send Morgenstein home. He later tried to reach Morgenstein at home, but between then and the early evening hours Morgenstein was involved in the tragedy which took Miss McIntosh's life. Whatever exactly transpired thereafter, it would appear that Morgenstein left the pharmacy upset and at some point either late that afternoon or early evening obtained a pistol which he had kept hidden at his home, and knowing Miss McIntosh was expected to visit her parents, waited for her and either got her to go with him, wittingly or unwittingly, to a local park area where he fatally shot her in the back.

Dr. Milano had indicated in his testimony at the criminal trial that sometimes he inquired further when he felt that a patient was in some ways endangering himself or someone else, and in those instances he would contact his patient's parents, school, or people like that. In his deposition in this civil case Dr. Milano said he had spoken to Morgenstein's parents about a problem with a car accident and this resulted in their withholding certain privileges from their son. He also indicated he spoke to a school teacher about one of Morgenstein's problems. Apparently this was usually with Morgenstein's consent. Dr. Milano had said he would "look into it" if he felt the patient was endangering himself or someone else. He apparently talked to Morgenstein's parents in some fashion about the relationship between their son and Miss McIntosh a number of times in late 1974 and in 1975, but never attempted to contact decedent or her parents. Despite Morgenstein's fantasies and the incidents previously recited, and wishes for her suffering, he felt that Morgenstein had never expressed a desire for retaliation or "fantasies" of retaliation.[6] Dr. Milano had said at the criminal trial that Morgenstein

---

5. It is clear from the criminal trial testimony of Dr. Milano that one of the reasons Lee Morgenstein was sent to him for therapy was because of a drug involvement, and that one of the drugs abused was Seconal.

6. Plaintiff also relies on defendant's report to the prosecutor which had certain typed portions crossed out and certain interlineations made by him and by an attorney-friend who he had consulted. For example, in one portion, his report as typed said:

. . . During the latter half of the year, powerful affects of anger and jealousy, ambivalent feelings of affection and desires for retaliation emerged. They accentuated prior conflicts, and centered primarily on fantasies of revenge for Kimberly's dating and sexual experiences

with other men. Lee was able, during 1974, to share some of his experiences with his parents and received their support. He saw her infrequently during 1975, though he did not develop an independent and flourishing social life.

Taking account of handwritten deletions and additions on defendant's report, those sentences, as changed, read:

. . . During the latter half of the *school* year, powerful affects of anger and jealousy, ambivalent feelings of affection and [ ] *fantasies* of retaliation emerged, *he denied any intention of actual retaliation* [ ] centering primarily on fantasies of revenge for Kimberly's dating and sexual experiences with other men. Lee was able, during 1975, to share some of his

had fantasies of magical power and violence, which meant that if somebody said he was a scrawny little runt and wouldn't dare fight back, that he would be able to pull out a gun and shoot them. But he denied that Morgenstein ever had fantasies of pulling out a gun, and claimed that his fantasies apparently related to pulling out a knife and scaring people off. Morgenstein, nevertheless, was quoted as saying that if he had a gun, that would scare men and then nobody would dare threaten him.

In the evening of July 8, 1975 Dr. Milano was called to police headquarters after decedent's death and spoke to Morgenstein, who was then in custody. He asked Morgenstein where he had gotten the gun and why he had not told him about it. Morgenstein responded he was frightened, and was unsure about what the doctor would have done. There was also discussion at that time about earlier events of that day, including Morgenstein's taking of the prescription form.

. . .

Plaintiff instituted this wrongful death action based in large part on the trial testimony of Dr. Milano. She relies also on a report of a psychiatrist retained as an expert witness expressing the opinion that defendant had a duty to warn Kimberly McIntosh, her parents or appropriate authorities that Morgenstein posed a physical threat or danger to decedent. Plaintiff asserts defendant breached that duty.

On the other hand, defendant argues there is no such duty by a therapist to third parties or potential victims, and that *Tarasoff* II should not be applied, and was wrongly decided in that it (1) imposes an "unworkable" duty on therapists to warn another of a third person's dangerousness when that condition cannot be predicted with sufficient reliability; (2) will interfere with effective treatment by eliminating confidentiality; (3) may deter therapists from treating potentially violent patients in light of possible malpractice claims by third persons; and (4) will result in increased commitments of patients to mental or penal institutions.

. . .

Plaintiff, in opposition to the motion, relies on the report of her expert, a psychiatrist, who states that defendant committed a "gross deviation" from accepted medical practice by failing to warn or protect decedent under the factual circumstances he derives from defendant Milano's report to the prosecutor and testimony at the Morgenstein trial. Plaintiff's expert opines that it is clear from the criminal trial testimony of Dr. Milano that Lee Morgenstein was a dangerous individual, and the object of his aggression was Miss McIntosh. Even though a diagnosis of dangerousness is recognized by that proposed expert witness as a complex determination, in his opinion that was not an issue since Morgenstein demonstrated his dangerousness by (a) firing a weapon at Miss McIntosh's car, (b) exhibiting a knife to Dr. Milano, (c) forging a prescription, and (d) verbalizing threats towards Miss McIntosh and her boyfriends. In light of this and the commission of a violent act, i.e., firing the gun, dangerousness was not in his opinion a prediction, but a known fact.

experiences with his parents and received their support. He saw [ ] *Kim* infrequently during 1975, though he did not develop an independent and flourishing social life. [Deleted portions are where brackets appear. Emphasis represents handwritten additions.]

Various other changes by way of deletions and additions appeared throughout that report. Obviously, issues of credibility arise from the report, particularly based on the additions and deletions. See e.g., Evid.R. 20. Any such questions would be for a jury.

Plaintiff's expert indicates there appears to be no doubt as to dangerousness because Dr. Milano admitted in his testimony that Morgenstein had fantasies of violence or feelings of retribution.

I

Duty to Warn of "Dangerousness" and Alleged Inability to Predict

The argument in this case is whether principles analogous to those expressed in *Tarasoff* II apply or should be applied in New Jersey. That case was a lawsuit against university regents, psychotherapists employed by the university hospital, and campus police to recover for the murder of plaintiffs' daughter by a psychiatric patient. It was alleged that the patient had expressly informed his therapist that he was going to kill an unnamed girl (identifiable as plaintiff's decedent) when she returned home from spending the summer in Brazil. The therapist, with the concurrence of two colleagues, decided to commit the patient for observation. The campus police detained the patient at the oral and written request of the therapist, but released him after somehow satisfying themselves that he was rational and exacting his promise to stay away from the girl. The therapist's superior then ordered all copies of his subordinate's letter to the police and therapy notes destroyed and directed that no further steps be taken for commitment or evaluation. After the patient subsequently murdered the girl her parents filed suit alleging, among other things, that the therapists involved had failed either to warn them of the threat to their daughter or to detain the patient as "dangerous." 17 Cal.3d at 432–433, 131 Cal.Rptr. at 21, 551 P.2d at 341. Allegations against the university and its hospital and the campus police were also made, but were disposed of under the California Tort Claims Statute.

A majority of the California Supreme Court imposed a duty on the defendant therapists, holding:

. . . When a therapist determines, or pursuant to the standards of his profession should determine, that his patient presents a serious danger of violence to another, he incurs an obligation to use reasonable care to protect the intended victim against such danger.

The California court concluded that the relationship between the patient and defendant therapists supported an affirmative duty for the benefit of third persons and sustained the second of four stated causes of action in the complaint. They did uphold the therapists' contention that statutory immunity insulated them from liability for failure to confine. One justice concurred only in the result, expressing concern (and a dissent) as to the lack of "standards of the [psychiatric] profession" in terms of reliable prediction of violence and preferring to limit the holding to instances where a therapist actually predicted potential violence. Two dissenting justices argued that policy considerations weighed against imposition of such a duty and that the California Welfare and Institutions Code, §§ 5000 et seq. (that state's commitment statute) required confidentiality and thus imposed a duty not to disclose. The majority had rejected that conclusion because they did not consider the statute applicable.

· · ·

Actionable negligence from which liability may arise consists of various essential elements, including a disregard or violation of a duty imposed by the law.

· · ·

Realistically, . . . duty does partake of many of the characteristics of an abstract term as defined in standard dictionaries, and thus may be difficult or impossible to define in absolute and precise terms, even when applied to specific facts. Similarly, the terms "dangerous" or "dangerousness"[9] have abstract qualities, as do such concepts as reasonableness, beauty and so forth. Even though State v. Krol, 68 N.J. 236, 344 A.2d 289 (1975), discussed dangerous conduct, obviously there will be room for debate as to the definition and application to specific settings.

. . . . Dangerous conduct is not identical with criminal conduct. Dangerous conduct involves not merely violation of social norms enforced by criminal sanctions, but significant physical or psychological injury to persons or substantial destruction of property. Persons are not to be indefinitely incarcerated because they present a risk of future conduct which is merely socially undesirable.

It may be true that there cannot be 100% accurate prediction of dangerousness[10] in all cases. However, a therapist does have a basis for giving an opinion and a prognosis based on the history of the patient and the course of treatment. Where reasonable men might differ and a fact issue exists, the therapist is only held to the standard for a therapist in the particular field in the particular community. Unless therapists clearly state when called upon to treat patients or to testify that they have no ability to predict or even determine whether their treatment will be efficacious or may even be necessary with any degree of certainty, there is no basis for a legal conclusion negating any and all duty with respect to a particular class of professionals. This is not to say that isolated or vague threats will of necessity give rise in all circumstances and cases to a duty.

Whether a duty exists for a therapist to warn or guard against a criminal or tortious event by a patient to some third party, depends, as with other situations giving rise to a possible legal obligation to exercise due care, ultimately on questions of fairness involving a weighing of the relationship of the parties, the nature of the risk involved, and the public interest in imposing the duty under the circumstances.

Generally, a person (the first person) does not have a duty to control the conduct of another person (the second person and the potential tortfeasor) so as to prevent that person from harming a third person unless a

---

9. In Shah, "Dangerousness—A Paradigm for Exploring Some Issues in Law and Psychology," Am.Psych. 224, 225 (March 1978), the author says:

It has been suggested that dangerousness, like beauty, lies in the eye of the beholder. Certainly, the term is rather vague and appears often to receive surplus meanings. As used in this article, *dangerousness* refers to a propensity (i.e., an increased likelihood when compared with others) to engage in dangerous behavior. *Dangerous behavior* refers to acts that are characterized by the application of or the overt threat of force and that are likely to result in injury to other persons. This also defines violent behavior and, in this article, the two are considered synonymous.

. . . .

While dangerousness as used in laws and regulation is clearly a *legal* term re-

quiring determination by courts, such crucial determinations are often actually made by mental health 'experts' as a function of judicial default. [Citation omitted].

10. See von Hirsh, "Prediction of Criminal Conduct and Preventive Confinement of Convicted Persons," 21 Buffalo L.Rev. 717, 725–726 (1972), where the author states:

Failure to provide explicit legal standards of 'dangerousness' creates the unacceptable situation where, for example, one psychiatrist can decide that, only those mental patients who are likely to perpetrate violent crimes ought to be confined, while another psychiatrist, depending upon his personal philosophy, can employ the concept of 'dangerousness' to confine potential minor offenders, as well. . . .

special relationship [11] exists either between the first person and the second person imposing such a duty or between the first person and the third person giving him a right to protection. See Restatement, Torts 2d, § 315 at 122 (1965). Absent some form of special relationship, the general rule to date in most jurisdictions has been that set forth in § 314 of the Restatement, Torts 2d, at 116, which acknowledges that the fact that a person realizes or should realize that action on his part is necessary for another's aid or protection does not of itself impose a duty to take such action.

However, that section indicates that it should be read together with other sections. The comment to § 314 contains the following:

> The result of the rule [that even if an actor realizes or should realize that action is necessary for another's protection does not impose a duty—absent special circumstances or special relationship] has been a series of older decisions to the effect that one human being, seeing a fellow man in dire peril, is under no legal obligation to aid him, but may sit on the dock, smoke his cigar, and watch the other drown. Such decisions have been condemned by legal writers as revolting to any moral sense, but thus far they remain the law. It appears inevitable that, sooner or later, such extreme cases of morally outrageous and indefensible conduct will arise that there will be further inroads upon the older rule.

See also Restatement, Torts 2d, § 314A at 118, which sets forth illustrative "Special Relations Giving Rise to Duty to Aid or Protect," and containing a caveat wherein "[t]he Institute expresses no opinion as to whether there may not be other relations which impose a similar duty."

The *Tarasoff* II duty has received criticism from some, but not all authors mostly those in the medical professions. However, the concept of legal duties for the medical profession is not new. A doctor-patient relationship in some circumstances admittedly places a duty to warn others of contagious diseases. New Jersey recognizes the general rule that a person who negligently exposes another to a contagious disease, which the other contracts, is liable in damages. Specifically, a physician has the duty to warn third persons against possible exposure to contagious or infectious diseases, e.g., tuberculosis, venereal diseases, and so forth. That duty extends to instances where the physician should have known of the infectious disease. . . .

Physicians also must report tuberculosis, venereal disease and various other contagious diseases, as well as certain other conditions.[13] There is, to be sure, a relative certainty and uniformity present in a diagnosis of most physical illnesses, conditions and injuries as opposed to a psychiatric

---

11. *Tarasoff* recognized a special relationship between a therapist and his patient, citing Restatement, Torts 2d, §§ 315–320. Section 319, entitled "Duty of Those in Charge of Person Having Dangerous Propensities," notes a duty to "control" a third person who the actor knows or should know is likely to cause bodily harm to others if not controlled. . . .

13. Physicians are also under a statutory duty to report gunshot wounds to the chief of police and county prosecutor and epilepsy to the Division of Motor Vehicles. The obvious purpose of all such provisions is to protect society and its individual members. In the case of the Motor Vehicle Law, its purpose is to protect not only other drivers and pedestrians, but also property, if an individual might constitute a danger to himself or others while driving a motor vehicle. Confidentiality is to some extent protected where such reports are required consistent with the purpose of the various statutes. Likewise, statutes on controlled dangerous substances also require a certain amount of reporting, together with some requirements and safeguards for confidentiality.

prediction of dangerousness based on symptoms and historical performance. Nevertheless, psychiatrists diagnose, treat and give opinions based on medical probabilities, particularly relying on a patient's history, without any clear indication of an inability to predict that is here asserted.

As a further illustration of types of duties imposed by statutes, N.J.S.A. 2A:97–2 provides that any person who has knowledge of actual commission of high misdemeanors and certain other crimes, but fails to report or disclose same, is himself guilty of a misdemeanor. No exception is set forth therein for a physician. To threaten to take the life of another person is also a crime. . . .

Disclosure is, therefore, required in numerous situations. As noted in Point II, infra, even the Principles of Medical Ethics recognize that confidentiality gives way where "it becomes necessary in order to protect the welfare of the individual or of the community." [17]

Although defendant asserts public policy or public interest in the patient-therapist relationship as a reason for a holding of no duty, such an argument views only one side of the problem. . . . Certainly there also should be protection against frivolous or fraudulent suits, but the remedy lies not in eliminating all causes of action by aggrieved individuals against a certain class, but in improving the competence of the court system to deal with such claims. Groundless claims are always a risk.

Obviously, the courts should not dismiss a complaint on the sole ground that a question or issue is too complex, or may provide a vehicle for an unscrupulous person to assert a frivolous or unfounded claim. . . .

. . . .

There may well be problems of proof. Whether plaintiff will ultimately prevail is an open question on which this court expresses no opinion as to the factual outcome. However, the law in most malpractice cases requires the jury to be aided by an expert. Thus, defendant also has the opportunity of presenting and refuting evidence as to the appropriate applicable standard of care in his field and in the applicable community according to the standards in effect at the time of the alleged occurrences. This type and amount of training received in medical education is an element to be established at trial.

Here, the jury could find that Dr. Milano knew or should have known that Morgenstein presented a clear danger or threat to Miss McIntosh. They could also find, based on the facts adduced, that there was a duty which was indeed recognized by defendant, who indicated that he would inquire when he felt a patient was endangering himself or others and might as a result contact appropriate persons, or as he said, "look into it." A jury might also find that what was originally stated in defendant's report to the prosecutor to the effect that Morgenstein had "desires" for retaliation was fact, even though crossed out of the report, and was supported by other evidence they might well find credible. They might also find that Morgenstein led Dr. Milano on or misled him deliberately for various purposes, such as avoiding penal consequences of drug use or to facilitate obtaining and use of drugs.

To summarize, this court holds that a psychiatrist or therapist may have a duty to take whatever steps are reasonably necessary to protect an

17. Principles of Medical Ethics, § 9 (1957).

intended or potential victim of his patient when he determines, or should determine, in the appropriate factual setting and in accordance with the standards of his profession established at trial, that the patient is or may present a probability of danger to that person. The relationship giving rise to that duty may be found either in that existing between the therapist and the patient, as was alluded to in *Tarasoff* II, or in the more broadly based obligation a practitioner may have to protect the welfare of the community, which is analogous to the obligation a physician has to warn third persons of infectious or contagious disease. That analogy may also be applied in a somewhat different fashion. To an admittedly uncertain but nevertheless sufficient extent, "dangerousness" must be considered identifiable (despite the contrary claims presented by defendant in this matter), and although not a "disease" as that term is commonly used, may affect third persons in much the same sense as a disease may be communicable. The obligation imposed by this court, therefore, is similar to that already borne by the medical profession in another context.

II

Confidentiality Aspect

Certain other aspects of the arguments raised warrant some discussion. Defendant asserts the need for confidentiality in therapy and alleges socially undesirable ramifications, particularly to patients and potential patients arising out of a *Tarasoff* II type duty when therapists may not be able to accurately predict dangerousness. The dissent in *Tarasoff* II embraced that argument. Although New Jersey has recognized the physician-patient privilege by statute and in the context of judicial disclosures, the need for confidentiality cannot be considered either absolute or decisive in this setting. A patient is entitled to freely disclose his symptoms and condition to his physician in confidence "except where the public interest or the private interest of the patient so demands." A patient, therefore, possesses a "limited right" to confidentiality in extra-judicial disclosures, "subject to exceptions prompted by the supervening interest of society," Hague v. Williams, 37 N.J. 328, 336, 181 A.2d 345 (1962), just as a lawyer has no privilege in the lawyer-client relationship to protect or conceal intent to commit a crime. That conclusion is consonant with § 9 of the *Principles of Medical Ethics* (1957), which reads:

> A physician may not reveal the confidences entrusted to him in the course of medical attendance, or the deficiencies he may observe in the character of patients, unless he is required to do so by law or unless it becomes necessary in order to protect the welfare of the individual or of the community.*

Section 9, as well as other sections of the *Principles of Medical Ethics*, has been adopted and accepted by the psychiatric profession as applicable to that specialty with certain annotations pertaining specifically to Psychiatry. Those annotations referable to the quoted § 9 state:

> . . . Because of the sensitive and private nature of the information with which the psychiatrist deals, he must be circumspect in the information that he chooses to disclose to others about a patient. The welfare of the patient must be a continuing consideration.

* Compare 1980 Text, Sec. A.2, Supra.
[Eds.]

A psychiatrist *may* release confidential information only with the authorization of the patient or under proper legal compulsion. The continuing duty of the psychiatrist to protect the patient includes fully apprising him of the connotations of waiving the privilege of privacy.

. . .

III

Other Alleged Implications

Defendant also claims that the imposition of a *Tarasoff* type duty may deter therapists from treating potentially violent patients in light of possible malpractice claims by third persons. However, even the statement of that policy position involves some inconsistency. If the psychiatrist claims inability to predict dangerousness or detect a dangerous person, how will he make the determination to weed out "potentially violent patients"?

. . .

. . . If psychiatrists now say, as is argued in the brief of defendant and the articles submitted in support thereof, that therapists are no more accurate than the average layman, serious questions would arise as to the entire present basis for commitment procedures.

In considering in the absence of statute whether or not there should be a legal duty or a remedy for a wrong, the courts cannot determine legal relationships based only on *ipse dixit* and assumptions that a certain course of action will follow without regard to medical or professional responsibility and ethical considerations, as well as appropriate legal considerations. If accepted, defendant's argument would establish a sphere of immunity from liability "for the foreseeable results" of the action or inaction of a therapist (assuming the factfinder might reasonably find it was a foreseeable result). Whether a duty exists is a question of law. Failure in that duty must be proved as a fact and established by application of the law to the facts. . . .

. . .

Summary judgment in favor of defendant is thus clearly inappropriate. This means no more than that there is a factual question which should be presented to a jury as to whether, based on expert testimony, defendant breached the appropriate duty in this case.

The possibility (or perhaps what could be called a threat) that in some case or cases in the future some therapists may choose not to accept some potential patients for therapy in their private practice (with obvious ramifications, and potential new causes of action) should not forever preclude victims of torts or crimes referable to the breach of duty of such therapists from being without any remedy whatsoever.

The further argument that such a duty would result in increased commitments of individuals rather than a therapist exposing himself to civil suit not only runs counter to the argument of defendant on inability to predict dangerousness, but is an argument which has no reliable statistical support or backing at the present time, if indeed it can even be established. See generally, Huff, How to Lie with Statistics (30th Printing, 1964). There has certainly been inadequate experience or data collection from which any such pronouncement could authoritatively be made, even if relevant to the issue of providing a remedy for a possible wrong.

Defendant's motion for summary judgment is denied.

NOTES

1. Following the decision in *McIntosh v. Milano*, the case was tried before a jury in June 1981. The jury unanimously found that Dr. Milano had not deviated from his profession's standards of conduct. Brennan, Duty to Warn Third Parties, 249 J.A.M.A. 191 (1983) (letter).

2. Information from the physician-patient relationship may be of importance to other people besides those who are immediately at physical risk. The courts have taken divergent views on whether patient information may be revealed to someone investigating a physician. The Arizona Supreme Court has held that disclosure of patient's identities in a malpractice action would be improper when the patients have not consented to the use of their files in the investigation, Ziegler v. Superior Court of Arizona, 131 Ariz. 250, 640 P.2d 181 (1982), and a court in Hawaii reached the same conclusion regarding seizure of a psychologist's records by the Hawaii Attorney General's Medical Fraud Unit. Hawaii Psychiatric Society v. Ariyoshi, ___ F.Supp. ___ (D.Cal.1982). An appellate court in California, however, held that the Division of Medical Quality was entitled to receive the hospital records of patients treated by a physician against whom disciplinary proceedings were being considered, because of a statutory exemption to the physician-patient privilege in investigations aimed at the revocation or suspension of professional licenses. Division of Medical Quality v. Harn, 135 Cal.App.3d 561, 185 Cal.Rptr. 405 (1982).

Confidentiality and disclosure are also implicated in the release of a patient's medical records for research purposes. Epidemiology, the study of the distribution and dynamics of disease in human populations, provides the basis for public health programs designed to prevent disease. Epidemiological research, however, often requires the identification of individuals with specific diseases and the disclosure of detailed medical histories. Requiring patient consent for release of such records could make such research difficult. Often the records are compiled years before any actual study for a particular disease is conducted. In addition, a search of records is often only a first step used to identify patients who may have a given disease so that they may be traced. *Tarasoff* and *Milano* both noted that confidentiality of the patient gives way when "it becomes necessary in order to protect the welfare of the individual or of the community." Principles of Medical Ethics § 9 (1957). Could a physician or other scientist be under a duty to disclose medical records for research in order to protect the community? What "special relationship" does a researcher have with the community as a whole? Is this issue resolved by the shorter revision of the Principles adopted by the American Medical Association in 1980 that states in part that physicians "shall safeguard patient confidences within the constraints of the law" (Principle IV) and also "shall continue to . . . advance scientific knowledge, make relevant information available to . . . colleagues, and the public . . .." (Principle V)?

3. The Principles of Medical Ethics, used by *Tarasoff* and *Milano* to impose liability on psychiatrists for failure to disclose can also be used to impose liability for wrongful disclosure. Can a physician make a rational choice when faced with possible liability no matter which choice is made? What type of guidelines could be formulated to guide a physician in deciding when to disclose?

4. A physician who wrongly discloses a patient's medical records faces potential liability under several headings, including breach of fiduciary duty, invasion of privacy, and other torts, as well as revocation of license for unprofessional conduct. In Berthiaumes Estate v. Pratt, 365 A.2d 792 (Maine 1976), the court found

that a physician could be liable for an invasion of privacy for taking photographs of a patient without permission, even though the photos were never intended to be published. The photographs were compiled to study the progression of the patient's disease, and even though the court acknowledged the need for medical research, the rights of the individual were considered overriding.

5. Lawyers as well as physicians are bound by a duty of confidentiality. The 1983 ABA convention rejected a proposed set of ethical rules that would have increased lawyers' obligations to expose wrongdoing by clients. Under the present Code of Professional Responsibility, a lawyer must keep a client's confidences except to prevent imminent death or substantial harm; an attorney who violates these principles is subject to disciplinary action. Supporters of the current rule stress that a lawyer cannot help a client if the client withholds information and that an effective attorney-client relationship depends on confidentiality. Freedman, Lawyer's Silence is Right, N.Y.Times, Feb. 14, 1983, at A17, col. 1. Of course these same arguments can be made for a physician-patient relationship. Are there any reasons why lawyers should not have to make the choice of when community interests are sufficient to warrant disclosure? Is there a "special relationship" between attorneys and the community?

b. Based on Concern for the Individual

PEOPLE v. PRIVITERA

Supreme Court of California, 1979.
23 Cal.3d 697, 153 Cal.Rptr. 431, 591 P.2d 919.

CLARK, JUSTICE.

Under California Health and Safety Code section 1707.1, it is a misdemeanor to sell, deliver, prescribe or administer any drug or device to be used in the diagnosis, treatment, alleviation or cure of cancer which has not been approved by the designated federal agency or by the state board.[1]

Defendants James Robert Privitera, Jr., a medical doctor, William David Turner, Phyllis Blanche Disney, Winifred Agnes Davis, and Carroll Ruth Leslie were convicted by jury of the felony of conspiracy to sell and to prescribe an unapproved drug—laetrile—intended for the alleviation or cure of cancer. Davis and Turner were also convicted of selling laetrile for the alleviation or cure of cancer.

---

1. Section 1707.1 provides: "The sale, offering for sale, holding for sale, delivering, giving away, prescribing or administering of any drug, medicine, compound or device to be used in the diagnosis, treatment, alleviation or cure of cancer is unlawful and prohibited unless (1) an application with respect thereto has been approved under Section 505 of the Federal Food, Drug and Cosmetic Act, or (2) there has been approved an application filed with the board setting forth: [¶] (a) Full reports of investigations which have been made to show whether or not such drug, medicine, compound or device is safe for such use, and whether such drug, medicine, compound or device is effective in such use; [¶] (b) A full list of the articles used as components of such drug, medicine, compound or device; [¶] (c) A full statement of the composition of such drug, medicine, compound or device; [¶] (d) A full description of the methods used in, and the facilities and controls used for, the manufacture, processing and packing of such drug, medicine or compound or in the case of a device, a full statement of its composition, properties and construction and the principle or principles of its operation; [¶] (e) Such samples of such drug, medicine, compound or device and of the articles used as components of the drug, medicine, compound or device as the board may require; and [¶] (f) Specimens of the labeling and advertising proposed to be used for such drug, medicine, compound or device."

Viewed in the light most favorable to the judgments the evidence amply supports the jury's conclusion that defendants were involved in a common plan to import, prescribe, sell and distribute laetrile (also referred to as amygdalin or vitamin B–17) to cancer patients. Dr. Privitera prescribed laetrile for cancer patients and referred his patients to Turner and Disney as suppliers of laetrile. Disney referred patients to Dr. Privitera for treatment. Leslie and Disney worked as distributors in various residential areas. Defendants told prospective users that laetrile is an effective treatment or cure for cancer. Laetrile has not been approved for that purpose by one of the designated governmental agencies.

Defendants appeal on the ground the statute is unconstitutional. They contend the *right of privacy* protected by the federal and California Constitutions includes a right to obtain laetrile or, more generally, a right of access to drugs not recognized by the government as effective. Fundamental rights, defendants point out, may be regulated only to the extent necessary to achieve a compelling state interest. Defendants argue the purported right to obtain laetrile is fundamental and therefore the regulation challenged here must be reviewed under the compelling state interest standard. Section 1707.1 is found to be unconstitutional, defendants conclude, when measured against that standard.

. . .

The Supreme Court has held that regulations limiting certain fundamental rights may be justified only by a compelling state interest . . . . . . The right of privacy, founded in the Fourteenth Amendment's concept of personal liberty and restriction upon state action, has been declared a fundamental right. (Roe v. Wade [Ch. 8, Sec. A.1].) Thus, if the right of privacy were implicated in this case the challenged statute would, arguably, be judged under the compelling state interest standard.

However, a fundamental privacy right is not at stake here. The interest defendants allege is, apparently, "the interest in independence in making certain kinds of important decisions." (Whalen v. Roe) [Ch. 10 Sec. A] But the kinds of "important decisions" recognized by the high court to date as falling within the right of privacy involve " 'matters relating to marriage, procreation, contraception, family relationships, and child rearing and education' " but do not include medical treatment.

For this reason defendants' reliance on *Roe v. Wade* is misplaced.

. . .

Significantly, when danger to health exists *Roe v. Wade* indicates that state regulation shall be tested under the *rational basis* standard. Indeed, the high court held in *Roe v. Wade* that a state may—without encroaching upon any right of privacy—further its important interests "in the areas of health and safety" by requiring abortions be performed at licensed institutions which "insure maximum safety for the patient" and prohibiting performance of abortion by a person not a physician as defined by state law. The lesson of *Roe v. Wade* for our case is that a requirement that a drug be certified effective for its intended use is a reasonable means to "insure maximum safety for the patient."

In Planned Parenthood of Central Missouri v. Danforth (1976) 428 U.S. 52, 96 S.Ct. 2831, 49 L.Ed.2d 788, the high court struck down a state prohibition of a particular abortion procedure on the ground the prohibition did not reasonably relate to preservation and protection of maternal health. Significantly, in discussing the validity of the statutory prohibition of the medical procedure, the court did not refer to any constitutional considerations of privacy. Rather the procedure was evaluated by the court on the basis of medical evidence of its safety and effectiveness under the rational basis standard. *Planned Parenthood* thus stands for the proposition that although the decision to have an abortion may be within the constitutional zone of privacy deserving the protection provided by the compelling interest standard, the selection of a particular procedure is a medical matter to which privacy status does not attach and which may be regulated by the government, providing a rational basis for such regulation exists.

Whalen v. Roe, supra, 429 U.S. 589, 97 S.Ct. 869, 51 L.Ed.2d 64, provides additional support for our conclusion . . .

. . .

[There] the high court reiterated: "It is, of course, well settled that the State has broad police powers in regulating the administration of drugs by the health professions." (Whalen v. Roe, supra, 429 U.S. at p. 603, fn. 30, 97 S.Ct. at p. 878, fn. 30.) Although it had not done so, the court observed, "the State no doubt could prohibit entirely the use of particular Schedule II drugs." (Id. at p. 603, 97 S.Ct. at p. 878.) If the state has the power to ban a drug with a recognized medical use because of its potential for abuse, then—given a rational basis for doing so—the state clearly has the power to ban a drug not recognized as effective for its intended use.

The legitimate state interest expressed in the challenged statute is set forth in the legislative findings recited in section 1700. "The effective diagnosis, care, treatment or cure of persons suffering from cancer is of paramount public importance. Vital statistics indicate that approximately 16 percent of the total deaths in the United States annually result from one or another of the forms of cancer. It is established that accurate and early diagnosis of many forms of cancer, followed by prompt application of methods of treatment which are scientifically proven, either materially reduces the likelihood of death from cancer or may materially prolong the useful life of individuals suffering therefrom. [¶] Despite intensive campaigns of public education, there is a lack of adequate and accurate information among the public with respect to presently proven methods for the diagnosis, treatment, and cure of cancer. Various persons in this State have represented and continue to represent themselves as possessing medicines, methods, techniques, skills, or devices for the effective diagnosis, treatment, or cure of cancer, which representations are misleading to the public, with the result that large numbers of the public, relying on such representations, needlessly die of cancer, and substantial amounts of the savings of individuals and families relying on such representations are needlessly wasted."

These findings were recently echoed by the Commissioner of the federal Food and Drug Administration with specific reference to laetrile. "In the Commissioner's opinion, the use of Laetrile in the United States has become a genuine public health problem. Increasingly, doctors dealing with cancer patients are finding that the patients are coming to legitimate therapy too late, having delayed while trying Laetrile. It seems clear that another substantial group of persons afflicted with cancer is avoiding effective therapy altogether and using Laetrile instead. The question has become one of life and death for these patients and for others who may be convinced to use Laetrile in the future." (42 Fed.Reg. 39769.)

The commissioner rendered his opinion at the conclusion of a rulemaking proceeding undertaken in compliance with the opinion of the court of appeals in Rutherford v. United States (10th Cir.1976) 542 F.2d 1137, and the order of the district court in Rutherford v. United States (W.D.Okl.1977) 424 F.Supp. 105. "Based upon a careful review of the administrative record," the commissioner found that "Laetrile is not generally recognized by qualified experts as a safe and effective cancer drug." (42 Fed.Reg. 39775.) . . . Distribution of laetrile in interstate commerce, the commissioner concluded, is thus illegal and subject to regulatory activity by the Food and Drug Administration.

Because of defendants' reliance on it, subsequent developments in the *Rutherford* case will now be considered. In Rutherford v. United States (W.D.Okl.1977) 438 F.Supp. 1287, the district court set aside the commissioner's action and enjoined federal authorities from interfering with distribution of laetrile in interstate commerce or with use of laetrile for the treatment of cancer. The decision was based on two grounds: First, contrary to the conclusion reached by the commissioner, the court held that laetrile is exempt from the premarket approval requirement for new drugs by virtue of compliance with the 1962 grandfather clause. Second, contrary to the conclusion we reach today, the court concluded the federal right of privacy encompasses a "right to use a nontoxic substance in connection with one's own personal health-care."

On appeal by the government, the court of appeals addressed neither the grandfather clause question nor the right of privacy issue. Instead, the court held that "the 'safety' and 'effectiveness' terms used in the statute have no reasonable application to terminally ill cancer patients." "We are considering only cancer patients who are terminally ill and only their intravenous use of Laetrile. Thus in this context, what can 'generally recognized' as 'safe' and 'effective' mean as to such persons who are so fatally stricken with a disease for which there is no known cure? What meaning can 'effective' have in the absence of anything which may be used as a standard? Under this record Laetrile is as effective as anything else. What can 'effective' mean if the person, by all prevailing standards . . . is going to die of cancer regardless of what may be done." The permanent injunction granted by the district court was continued but limited only to permit procurement of intravenous injections of laetrile administered by a licensed medical practitioner to persons who are certified by a licensed medical practitioner to be terminally ill of cancer in some form.

Defendants can take no comfort in the court of appeals' decision for, unlike *Rutherford,* this case is not an action on behalf of the class of terminally ill cancer patients. Whatever may be said in favor of permitting "terminal" cancer patients access to laetrile, there is no indication in the record that defendants sought to restrict their activities to that class when prescribing, distributing and administering laetrile. Indeed, the record reflects that Dr. Privitera sometimes neither took a medical history from nor personally examined the patients for whom he prescribed laetrile. The lay defendants, of course, were not qualified to diagnose cancer, much less to determine whether a cancerous condition was "terminal."

Moreover, we are not prepared to reject as unreasonable the explanation given by the commissioner for the Food and Drug Administration's refusal to approve laetrile for use by "terminal" cancer patients. The commissioner concluded: "[A]pproval of Laetrile restricted to 'terminal' patients would lead to needless deaths and suffering among (1) patients characterized as 'terminal' who could actually be helped by legitimate therapy and (2) patients clearly susceptible to the benefits of legitimate therapy who would be misled as to Laetrile's utility by the limited approval program or who would be able to obtain the drug through the inevitable leakage in any system set up to administer such a program." (42 Fed. Reg. 39805.) Substantial evidence in the administrative record appears to support the conclusion reached by the commissioner.[6] Certainly the record in this case does not inspire one with confidence that advocates of laetrile would cooperate with a regulation restricting it to "terminal" cancer patients. In studied defiance of current law, Dr. Privitera prescribed and administered the drug as a cancer cure, advised his patients to discontinue conventional treatment, and warned them not to let their regular physicians know they were taking laetrile.

In conclusion, we emphasize we are not taking sides on the fiercely contested medical questions regarding laetrile's safety or efficacy as a cancer drug. Laetrile advocates may yet be vindicated in the court of scientific opinion, for even as this is being written the National Cancer Institute is seeking approval from the Food and Drug Administration to test laetrile on advanced cancer patients. Nor are we endorsing the decision the Legislature has made on the basis of existing scientific evidence. Whether cancer patients—especially advanced cancer patients who have unsuccessfully sought relief from conventional therapy and who are fully informed as to the consensus of scientific opinion concerning the drug— should have access to laetrile is clearly a question about which reasonable persons may differ. It is not our function to render scientific or legislative judgments. Rather, we must resolve a narrow question: Does the challenged legislation bear a reasonable relationship to the achievement of the legitimate state interest in the health and safety of its citizens? We conclude section 1707.1 does satisfy this standard and that it therefore does not encroach upon the federal constitutional right of privacy.

. . .

We have considered defendants' remaining contentions and find them to lack merit.

The judgments of conviction are affirmed.

BIRD, CHIEF JUSTICE, dissenting.

I respectfully dissent.

I do not question for a moment that the effective treatment of persons suffering from cancer is a matter of paramount public importance. However, we are dealing here with a disease whose causes and treatment continue to baffle the medical community. Among physicians and scientists

---

6. For example, with regard to the impossibility of determining "who is terminal," the commissioner cited Dr. Peter H. Wiernik, Chief of the Clinical Oncology Branch of the National Cancer Institute's Baltimore Cancer Research Center, who stated "One major difficulty in making a particular chemical available for terminal patients only is that no one can prospectively define the term 'terminal' with any accuracy. A patient can be said to be terminal only after he dies. Many patients who are critically ill respond to modern day management of cancer." This opinion was shared by Dr. Joseph F. Ross, Professor of Medicine at the University of California School of Medicine at Los Angeles. Dr. Ross stated "[T]he distinction of 'terminal' patients from 'nonterminal' may not be reliably determined and an assumption that Laetrile may be given to such patients with impunity may deprive such patients of therapeutic measures which could help them." As Helene Brown, Executive Director of Cancer Control/Los Angeles, put it, "No one knows if and when any patient is going to die." (42 Fed.Reg. 39805.) [For further discussion of when a patient is "terminal" see note following Satz v. Perlmutter in Ch. 7, infra. Eds.]

themselves there remains legitimate dispute as to what is truly an effective program of treatment for cancer. So long as there is no clear evidence that laetrile is unsafe to the user, I believe each individual patient has a right to obtain the substance from a licensed physician who feels it appropriate to prescribe it to him.

Cancer is a disease with potentially fatal consequences; this makes the choice of treatment one of the more important decisions a person may ever make, touching intimately on his or her being. For this reason, I believe the right to privacy, recognized under both the state and federal Constitutions, prevents the state from interfering with a person's choice of treatment on the sole grounds that the person has chosen a treatment which the state considers "ineffective."

The right of privacy is a concept of as yet undetermined parameters. Justice Staniforth's opinion for the Court of Appeal in this case provides as decent a map through this difficult terrain as I believe is available. For this reason, I herewith reprint his opinion.

. . .

Dr. Privitera does not challenge the validity of the general or specific regulatory laws to the extent they prohibit the advertisement of amygdalin as a cure for cancer; or require amygdalin be labeled in accordance with state law and regulations; or impose standards on the manufacturing and packing of amygdalin to insure quality and prevent adulteration or deterioration, or the prohibition of the sale of amygdalin to members of the general public for the purpose of treating cancer by persons other than licensed physicians.

Rather, Dr. Privitera's challenge is directed to those laws, specifically the one of which he is convicted, insofar as they prohibit a duly licensed physician from administering amygdalin to cancer patients and which prohibit its sale to either licensed physicians or persons who have obtained prescriptions from a licensed physician.

. . .

Dr. Privitera points out that many cancer victims have investigated and evaluated the merits of surgery, radiation therapy or chemotherapy with the aid of competent medical advice and have made the highly personal decision [that] the benefits from such therapy [are] not sufficient to justify the risks which include disfigurement, debilitation, and accelerated death and for this reason have chosen to seek amygdalin as a treatment; other cancer victims have been advised that their condition is hopeless, their case is terminal and as a last resort before certain death, seek amygdalin.

Privitera contends many conceded cancer victims, competent and responsible adults, seek and use amygdalin as a food substance to ameliorate the horrifying physical wasting away of the body (cachexia) which accompanies cancer. Thus they seek amygdalin not only for its possible cancer curative benefits, but also for its known nutritional benefits. Cancer victims cannot be certain amygdalin will either cure or control cancer but they believe, based upon the anecdotal, personal experience approach, the drug provides relief from the terrible pain, mental malaise, the emotional depression and weight loss which mark the progression of their disease.

The People assert, contrary to Dr. Privitera's contentions, not a single accredited medical school in the State of California teaches amygdalin might be effective in the controlling or curing of cancer. Further the use

of amygdalin as a form of nutritional therapy is officially regarded by the
State Department of Health, the California Medical Association, the National Cancer Institute and a great block of practicing physicians, to be of
no value whatsoever in the controlling or curing of cancer.

. . .

The challenge of Dr. Privitera . . . resolves itself, upon analysis,
into two separate and distinct areas of claimed constitutional rights; there
is the right of privacy of the patient to choose or reject his or her own
treatment, orthodox or unorthodox, approved or unapproved by the
state. The second contention is bifaceted: Dr. Privitera asserts (1) a derivative right—equal in stature to that of his patient, and (2) the doctor's
independent right to practice medicine generally and to prescribe
medicine, use procedures, without unreasonable government restrictions.

. . .

The right to control one's own body is not restricted to the wise; it
includes the "foolish" refusal of medical treatment. Nor is this right limited in its recognition to any single segment of the political, economic, or
social thought spectrum. In commenting upon Justice Brandeis' most
valued of rights, that right to be left alone, now Chief Justice Burger, in
his dissent in Application of President & Directors of Georgetown Col.,
118 U.S.App.D.C. 90, at page 97, 331 F.2d 1010, at page 1017, stated:
"Nothing in this utterance suggests that Justice Brandeis thought an individual possessed these rights only as to *sensible* beliefs, *valid* thoughts, *reasonable* emotions, or *well-founded* sensations. I suggest he intended to include a great many foolish, unreasonable and even absurd ideas which do
not conform, such as refusing medical treatment even at great risk."

Without specific reference to a constitutional basis, the right to choose
what may be a suicidal medical course has been upheld. In Erickson v.
Dilgard, 44 Misc.2d 27, 252 N.Y.S.2d 705, 706, a New York court sustained the unwilling Jehovah's Witness' objection to a needed blood
transfusion despite risk of death. The court there said at page 706:
". . . it is the individual who is the subject of a medical decision who
has the final say and that this must necessarily be so in a system of government which gives the greatest possible protection to the individual in
the furtherance of his own desires."

. . .

Aden v. Younger, 57 Cal.App.3d 662, 129 Cal.Rptr. 535, held unconstitutional the provisions of Welfare and Institutions Code section 5326.4
requiring substantive review by a medical committee of a voluntary, competent patient's consent to choice of electro-shock treatment. It was an
unjustified infringement of the patient's right to privacy. This court stated at page 684, 129 Cal.Rptr. at page 549:

"Where informed consent is adquately insured, there is no justification
for infringing upon the patient's right to privacy in selecting and consenting to the treatment. The state has varied interests which are served
by the regulation of ECT, but these interests are not served where the
patient and his physician are the best judges of the patient's health, safety
and welfare.

". . . Any possible need which exists for the voluntary and competent patient cannot prevail in the face of the serious infringement to the
patient's right to privacy as guaranteed by Roe v. Wade, supra, 410 U.S.
113, 93 S.Ct. 705, 35 L.Ed.2d 147 and Doe v. Bolton, supra, 410 U.S.

179, 93 S.Ct. 739, 35 L.Ed.2d 201." (Aden v. Younger, supra, 57 Cal. App.3d 662, 684, 129 Cal.Rptr. 535, 549.)

This right-of-choice-of-medical-treatment concept reached its quintessence in the Matter of Quinlan, 70 N.J. 10, 355 A.2d 647. [Ch. 7, Sec. B, infra.]

. . .

Dr. Privitera asserts a separate and distinct constitutionally protected right—a zone of privacy—to prescribe, to treat patients whether in the orthodox mode—free from unjustified state interference.

. . .

Doe v. Bolton, 410 U.S. 179, 93 S.Ct. 739, 35 L.Ed.2d 201 . . . speaks specifically of the *doctor's right* to administer medical care. *Bolton* involved a constitutionally defective statute requiring the consent of *two* state licensed physicians other than the patient's own doctor before an abortion could be performed as well as advance approval of three members of the hospital staff where the abortion was to be performed. Concerning this statute the Supreme Court said: "The woman's right to receive medical care in accordance with her licensed physician's best judgment *and the physician's right to administer it* are substantially limited by this statutorily imposed overview."

Dr. Privitera additionally asserts an *independent* right to treat, not derived from or measured by his patient's right of choice, without first obtaining approval of the procedure or drug prescribed from a governmental board. He argues Health and Safety Code section 1707.1 invades this right. Again, as in the right of the patient, the doctor's asserted right must be first examined to determine its nature and thereby select . . . the degree of scrutiny to which the state interference will be put. The right found must be balanced against . . . the public interest protected.

Dr. Privitera's right, in relation to the patient, has been viewed traditionally as a species of economic interest rather than as "fundamental" akin to the privacy right. If a rational basis was found to support an encroachment, the statute was sustained.

While a dispassionate reading of the physician's licensing requirements raises some question concerning the total rationality of the licensing scheme, such standards are generally upheld as reasonable and necessary means of protecting the public health.

The more recent cases hint at the more profound right in the doctor. It is postulated: There exists in the doctor licensed to practice medicine a right, constitutional in nature, as yet ill-defined, to treat and to treat by unorthodox modalities—as yet unapproved by the state board—an informed consenting patient.

Doe v. Bolton, supra, 410 U.S. 179, 200, 93 S.Ct. 739, 751, 35 L.Ed. 2d 201, 217, states if a physician is licensed by the state he is recognized by the state as capable of expressing acceptable clinical judgment. If he fails in this, professional censure and deprivation of his license are remedies available and " '[r]eliance must be placed on the assurance given by his license . . . that he [the physician] possesses the requisite qualifications.' "

. . .

Reason, based on history, experience, supports the doctor's premise. To require prior state approval before advising—prescribing—administering—a new treatment modality for an informed consenting patient is to suppress innovation by the person best qualified to make medical progress. The treating doctor, the clinician, is at the cutting edge of medical knowledge.

To require the doctor to uses only orthodox "state sanctioned" methods of treatment under threat of criminal penalty for variance is to invite a repetition in California of the Soviet experience with "Lysenkoism."[5] The mention of a requirement that licensed doctors must prescribe, treat, within "state sanctioned alternatives" raises the spector of medical stagnation at best, statism, paternalistic Big Brother at worst. It is by the alternatives to orthodoxy that medical progress has been made. A free, progressive society has an enormous stake in recognizing and protecting this right of the physician.

. . .

We have established this premise: The patient's and Dr. Privitera's rights of privacy are of such magnitude only a compelling state interest can justify intrusion in the patient-doctor treatment setting. We now consider the strength of that state interest. Does Health and Safety Code section 1707.1 serve a compelling state interest which overrides the rights so found? Indeed, a state has a profound interest in maintaining medical standards and in protecting health, life. This justifies the testing and licensing of doctors and the limits on the giving of medical advice by qualified practitioners. The regulation of pharmaceuticals, the licensing requirements for pharmacists and other dispensers of drugs are so authorized. Harm to others is readily foreseeable. It is well settled the state has broad police powers in regulating the administering of certain types of drugs by the health professions. . . .

The cases cited by the People in support of this unquestioned power of the state uniformly involve drugs which are narcotic, habit forming, toxic in nature. . . .

. . .

. . . Laetrile is not in this class. It is generally conceded to be a harmless drug. Its alleged evil lies in its "ineffective" treatment of cancer.

. . .

Conclusions

We turn now to the final, the pivotal question: Does the imposition of criminal sanction on the doctor for prescribing amygdalin as a cancer treatment for an informed consenting cancer victim, without first seeking governmental approval of its safety and effectiveness, serve a compelling state interest?

. . .

The doctor in California is licensed to practice only after meeting long rigid education, experience qualifications. He is bound by oath to preserve, to prolong, the life of his patient. He is under a legal duty, under threat of malpractice suit, to act in accordance with the generally accepted

---

5. Soviet geneticist T.D. Lysenko, controversial dictator of "communistic" biology during the Stalin period, stultified the science of genetics in the U.S.S.R. for at least a generation. He imposed the "state sanctioned alternative," the curious idea that environmentally acquired characteristics of an organism could be transmitted to the offspring through inheritance. Thus, the Stalinist concept of ideological conformity politically implanted in genetics paralyzed this important branch of Soviet science.

standards of medical practice in his community in this state. He is required under threat of malpractice to treat only after receiving the informed consent of the patient. These are the "rational means" society through law has imposed to insure a high standard of performance by the California doctor. It follows after such rigid standards are met, the matter of choice of treatment of the informed consenting patient becomes "a purely medical determination, which is within a doctor's professional judgment." . . .

Limiting this exercise of the doctor's professional judgment on some vague suspicion that "various persons" in this state are engaging in quackery does not follow as a matter of logic.

. . .

Dr. Privitera is charged under Health and Safety Code section 1707.1. This statute requires for its breach an intent to prescribe the unauthorized drug or medicine for treatment of cancer. The efficacy of the treatment proposed or medicine prescribed is not an issue under this statute. The truth or veracity of the representations, disclosures, discussions, made in connection with the treatment, by the doctor to the patient are not an issue in a trial of charges made under section 1707.1.

The criminal liability attaches because the doctor in the exercise of his medical judgment has prescribed a drug for treatment of cancer not yet approved under section 505 of the federal Food, Drug and Cosmetic Act or which has not yet received approval of the state board. Whether the doctor in his best medical judgment believes he has a miracle drug, a food supplement or a hope-giving placebo is not an issue. The governmental agencies have not given approval; therefore the doctor cannot prescribe.

The patient's right to receive medical care, and the doctor's right to administer it are substantially limited not because of some established defect in the medication, some danger to the public if this patient is so treated. The doctor becomes a criminal because the government agency has not given its prior approval to the exercise of his best medical judgment.

The statute must be measured against the legislative purpose of frustrating cancer quacks, and for the promotion of the early effective care, diagnosis and cure of cancer. Instead, the immediate and most direct effect of the prohibition of section 1707.1 is to chill, to prevent, innovative treatment by a licensed doctor, the person or in the class of persons most likely to make the hoped-for breakthrough against dreaded cancer. How logically this threat to the innovative physician will increase early effective diagnosis and cure of cancer is difficult to perceive.

. . .

If it be conceded section 1707.1 would theoretically assure some protection to the public or that unfortunate portion of the public who have cancer but who have not yet heard of the need for early treatment, by prohibiting the use of amygdalin or any other unapproved modality by the licensed physician, yet under the law of this state and the United States any individual can possess, use, self-treat, his condition, whatever it may be, by use of amygdalin, to his heart's content without liability. In effect it turns the whole matter of treatment back to the cancer patient himself if he is unwilling to accept the "state sanctioned alternatives."

We conclude not only is there no compelling reason shown to override the patient's or the doctor's fundamental right of choice in the treatment setting but that the statute when sought to be applied to a licensed medical doctor does not pass the test as a rational means of accomplishment of the announced legislative purpose.

There remains one further concern. The evidence in this case shows without exception the cancer victims, whether People's or defense's witnesses, were knowledgeable persons fully aware of the nature of the "state sanctioned alternatives" before seeking treatment from Dr. Privitera. Many were unwilling to accept the orthodox alternatives; many unwilling to accept the verdict of "terminal." These are not wide-eyed country bumpkins seeking to be conned. The class actions filed against governmental authorities to compel the availability of the drug in question illustrate the desperate seeking of the cancer victims. We need cite only one witness as a basis for a composite picture: The patient is a "senior" citizen with diagnosed cancer of the prostate; treatment recommended—prostate removal and castration; female hormone treatment for the rest of his life. The victim simply refused to accept these alternatives and sought amygdalin treatment.

The nineteen witnesses testifying for Dr. Privitera conveyed a felt imminency of death. One senses a mortal fear of both the disease and the orthodox alternatives. This is a desperate utterly human seeking to avoid the pain and to prolong life. . . .

To these nineteen cancer victims the enforcement of Health and Safety Code section 1707.1, the denial to them of medical treatment, albeit unorthodox, albeit unapproved by a state agency, must surely take on a Kafkaesque, a nightmare, quality. No demonstrated public danger, no compelling interest of the state, warrants an Orwellian intrusion into the most private of zones of privacy.

The state has in the name of protecting the cancer victim criminalized the doctor who is willing to innovate, willing to try an unapproved drug with the consent of his patient. From the terminal patient's viewpoint a new depth of inhumanity is reached by a broad sweep of this law so interpreted. No compelling interest of the state requires Dr. Privitera's 19 cancer patients to endure the unendurable, to die, even forbidden hope.

Health and Safety Code section 1707.1 as here sought to be applied invades the patient's and the doctor's zone of privacy without showing of external compelling state interests in violation of the Fourteenth Amendment to the federal Constitution and article I, section 1 of the California Constitution.

. . .

NOTES

1. The California court took note of the FDA litigation in the Rutherford case. In United States v. Rutherford, 442 U.S. 544, 99 S.Ct. 2470, 61 L.Ed.2d 68 (1979), the United States Supreme Court reversed the Tenth Circuit. The Court found no basis in the 1938 Food, Drug, and Cosmetic Act or in the 1962 Amendments, which added the requirements of safety and efficacy, to exempt from premarket approval drugs used to treat terminally ill patients. Recognition of such an exemption should be left to "legislative judgment, not judicial inference."

Only when a literal construction of a statute yields results so manifestly unreasonable that they could not fairly be attributed to congressional design will an exception to statutory language be judicially implied. Here, however, we have no license to depart from the plain language of the Act, for Congress could reasonably have intended to shield terminal patients from ineffectual or unsafe drugs.

Id. at 555, 99 S.Ct. at 2477, 61 L.Ed.2d at 78.

On remand, the court of appeals upheld the district court's finding that the exemption under the 1938 grandfather provisions, 21 U.S.C. § 321(p)(1), was inapplicable, but reversed the lower court's ruling that Laetrile was entitled to an exemption under the 1962 grandfather provision. Rutherford v. United States, 616 F.2d 455 (10th Cir.1980). The court concluded that it is acceptable for the state, through congressional enactment and FDA enforcement, to limit patients' access to medications: "The decision by the patient whether to have a treatment or not is a protected right, but his selection of a particular treatment, or at least a medication, is within the area of governmental interest in protecting public health." Id. at 457.

While the litigation over the FDA's refusal to approve Laetrile was wending its way through the courts, two other developments were occurring. On the one hand, the legislatures in over half the states passed bills legalizing Laetrile therapy within their borders. On the other hand, the National Cancer Institute sponsored a multi-institution clinical trial of Laetrile. That study found that, even when combined with the "metabolic" therapy (vitamins, enzymes, and a special diet) recommended by therapists who oppose conventional cancer treatment, Laetrile provided no substantive benefits in terms of cure, improvement or stabilization of cancer, improvement of symptoms, or extension of life span; several patients did, however, manifest symptoms of, or dangerous blood levels of, cyanide poisoning. Moertel et al., A Clinical Trial of Amygdalin (Laetrile) in the Treatment of Human Cancer, 306 New Engl.J.Med. 201 (1982).

2. The FDA Commissioner expressed concern that a "substantial group of perons afflicted with cancer is avoiding effective therapy altogether and using Laetrile instead." If the latter failing can be outlawed, what about the former? Suppose a patient, diagnosed as suffering from a cancer that will be fatal if not treated, chooses no treatment or only palliative treatment (whether provided by a licensed physician or by, say, the local liquor store). Should the Laetrile cases be read to recognize state authority to keep citizens from making unwise medical choices or merely to regulate the practice of health care and, specifically, behavior that is potentially fraudulent?

3. Both those judges who approved of the ban on Laetrile and those who did not apparently accept governmental regulation of addictive drugs (including prohibition when appropriate). Why is that? Stripped of their association with criminal activity, why are such drugs beyond the realm of individual choice? Is it for the reason that Mill excluded slavery from those things the state must leave alone—that is, one cannot claim the freedom to alienate one's freedom? Or simply for paternalistic reasons, that the drugs in question are deleterious to health?

4. The shortage of kidneys for transplantation has prompted one physician to announce that he is establishing a company to facilitate the sale of kidneys by living donors; on Oct. 5, 1983, Rep. Albert Gore introduced H.R. 4080, which among other things would make such arrangements illegal. Despite the reluctance of most physicians to become involved in the sale of organs, it apparently occurs in other parts of the world. See, e.g., Brooke, Kidney, Cornea Sale Flourishes in Brazil, Washington Post, Oct. 12, 1981, at A22, col. 1. Should selling one's organs be prohibited if the removal of the organ (1) would not endanger life but would restrict functioning or lead to disfigurement (for instance, removal of a cornea); (2) would create a small risk of life-threatening illness (for instance, removal of one kidney); or (3) would cause death (removal of the heart)? What if the money received would ensure health care, education, and long and comfortable lives for the members of the seller's large, destitute family, whom he or she has no other means of supporting?

GERALD DWORKIN, PATERNALISM

56 Monist 1, 64–84 (1972).

I take as my starting point the "one very simple principle" proclaimed by Mill in *On Liberty* . . . . "That principle is, that the sole end for which mankind are warranted, individually or collectively, in interfering with the liberty of action of any of their number, is self-protection. That the only purpose for which power can be rightfully exercised over any member of a civilized community, against his will, is to prevent harm to others. . . . He cannot rightfully be compelled to do or forbear because it will be better for him to do so, because it will make him happier, because, in the opinion of others, to do so would be wise, or even right."

This principle is neither "one" nor "very simple." It is at least two principles; one asserting that self-protection or the prevention of harm to others is sometimes a sufficient warrant and the other claiming that the individual's own good is *never* a sufficient warrant for the exercise of compulsion either by the society as a whole or by its individual members. I assume that no one with the possible exception of extreme pacifists or anarchists questions the correctness of the first half of the principle. This essay is an examination of the negative claim embodied in Mill's principle—the objection to paternalistic interferences with a man's liberty.

I

By paternalism I shall understand roughly the interference with a person's liberty of action justified by reasons referring exclusively to the welfare, good, happiness, needs, interests or values of the person being coerced. . . .

[W]e may . . . divide paternalistic interferences into "pure" and "impure" cases. In "pure" paternalism, the class of persons whose freedom is restricted is identical with the class of persons whose benefit is intended to be promoted by such restrictions. Examples: the making of suicide a crime, requiring passengers in automobiles to wear seat-belts, requiring a Jehovah's Witness to receive a blood transfusion. In the case of "impure" paternalism, in trying to protect the welfare of a class of persons we find that the only way to do so will involve restricting the freedom of other persons besides those who are benefitted. Now it might be thought that there are no cases of "impure" paternalism since any such case could always be justified on non-paternalistic grounds, i.e., in terms of preventing harm to others. Thus we might ban cigarette manufacturers from continuing to manufacture their product, on the grounds that we are preventing them from causing illness to others in the same way that we prevent other manufacturers from releasing pollutants into the atmosphere, thereby causing danger to members of the community. The difference is, however, that in the former, but not the latter case the harm is of such a nature that it could be avoided by those individuals affected, if they so chose. The incurring of the harm requires, so to speak, the active co-operation of the victim. It would be mistaken theoretically, and hypocritical in practice, to assert that our interference in such cases is just like our interference in standard cases of protecting others from harm. At the very least someone interfered with in this way can reply that no one is complaining about his activities. It may be that impure paternalism requires arguments or reasons of a stronger kind in order to be justified, since there are persons who are losing a portion of their liberty and they do not even have the solace of having it be done "in their own interest." Of course in some sense, if paternalistic justifications are ever correct, then we are protecting others, we are preventing some from injuring others, but it is important to see the differences between this and the standard case.

Paternalism then will always involve limitations on the liberty of some individuals in their own interest, but it may also extend to interferences with the liberty of parties whose interests are not in question.

. . .

Now it may be that some legislation of this nature is, in fact, paternalistically motivated. I am not denying that. All I want to point out is that there is another possible way of justifying such measures, which is not paternalistic in nature. It is not paternalistic because, as Mill puts it in a similar context, such measures are "required not to overrule the judgment of individuals respecting their own interest, but to give effect to that judgment: they being unable to give effect to it except by concert, which concert again cannot be effectual unless it receives validity and sanction from the law." [2]

The line of reasoning here is a familiar one, first found in Hobbes and developed with great sophistication by contemporary economists in the last decade or so. There are restrictions which are in the interests of a class of persons taken collectively, but are such that the immediate interest of each individual is furthered by his violating the rule when others adhere to it. In such cases the individuals involved may need the use of compulsion, to give effect to their collective judgment of their own interest by guaranteeing each individual compliance by the others. In these cases compulsion is not used to achieve some benefit which is not recognized to be a benefit by those concerned, but rather because it is the only feasible means of achieving some benefit which *is* recognized as such by all concerned. This way of viewing matters provides us with another characterization of paternalism in general. Paternalism might be thought of as the use of coercion to achieve a good which is not recognized as such by those persons for whom the good is intended. Again, while this formulation captures the heart of the matter—it is surely what Mill is objecting to in *On Liberty*—the matter is not always quite like that. For example, when we force motorcyclists to wear helmets we are trying to promote a good—the protection of the person from injury—which is surely recognized by most of the individuals concerned. It is not that a cyclist doesn't value his bodily integrity; rather, as a supporter of such legislation would put it, he either places, perhaps irrationally, another value or good (freedom from wearing a helmet) above that of physical well-being or, perhaps, while recognizing the danger in the abstract, he either does not fully appreciate it or he underestimates the likelihood of its occurring. But now we are approaching the question of possible justifications of paternalistic measures, and the rest of this essay will be devoted to that question.

V

. . .

An initial feature that strikes one is the absolute nature of Mill's prohibitions against paternalism. It is so unlike the carefully qualified admonitions of Mill and his fellow Utilitarians on other moral issues. He speaks of self-protection as the *sole* end warranting coercion, of the indi-

2. J.S. Mill, Principles of Political Economy (New York: P.F. Collier and Sons, 1900), p. 442.

viduals own goals as *never* being a sufficient warrant. Contrast this with his discussion of the prohibition against lying in *Utilitarianism.*

> Yet that even this rule, sacred as it is, admits of possible exception, is acknowledged by all moralists, the chief of which is where the with-holding of some fact . . . would save an individual . . . from great and unmerited evil.[3]

The same tentativeness is present when he deals with justice.

> It is confessedly unjust to break faith with any one: to violate an en-gagement, either express or implied, or disappoint expectations raised by our own conduct, at least if we have raised these expectations knowingly and voluntarily. Like all the other obligations of justice al-ready spoken of, this one is not regarded as absolute, but as capable of being overruled by a stronger obligation of justice on the other side.[4]

This anomaly calls for some explanation. The structure of Mill's argu-ment is as follows:

1. Since restraint is an evil the burden of proof is on those who propose such restraint.

2. Since the conduct which is being considered is purely self-re-garding, the normal appeal to the protection of the interests of others is not available.

3. Therefore we have to consider whether reasons involving refer-ence to the individual's own good, happiness, welfare, or interests are sufficient to overcome the burden of justification.

4. We either cannot advance the interests of the individual by compulsion, or the attempt to do so involves evil which outweighs the good done.

5. Hence the promotion of the individual's own interests does not provide a sufficient warrant for the use of compulsion.

Clearly the operative premise here is (4) and it is bolstered by claims about the status of the individual as judge and appraiser of his welfare, interests, needs, etc.

> With respect to his own feelings and circumstances, the most ordinary man or woman has means of knowledge immeasurably surpassing those that can be possessed by any one else.[5]

> He is the man most interested in his own well-being: the interest which any other person, except in cases of strong personal attachment, can have in it, is trifling, compared to that which he himself has.[6]

These claims are used to support the following generalizations concern-ing the utility of compulsion for paternalistic purposes.

> The interferences of society to overrule his judgment and purposes in what only regards himself must be grounded on general presumptions; which may be altogether wrong, and even if right, are as likely as not to be misapplied to individual cases.[7]

> But the strongest of all the arguments against the interference of the public with purely personal conduct is that when it does interfere, the odds are that it interferes wrongly and in the wrong place.[8]

3. Mill, *Utilitarianism* and *On Liberty,* p. 174.

4. Ibid., p. 299.

5. Ibid., p. 207.

6. Ibid., p. 206.

7. Ibid., p. 207.

8. Ibid., p. 214.

All errors which the individual is likely to commit against advice and warning are far outweighed by the evil of allowing others to constrain him to what they deem his good.[9]

Performing the utilitarian calculation by balancing the advantages and disadvantages we find that:

Mankind are greater gainers by suffering each other to live as seems good to themselves, than by compelling each other to live as seems good to the rest.[10]

From which follows the operative premise (4).

This classical case of a utilitarian argument with all the premises spelled out is not the only line of reasoning present in Mill's discussion. There are asides, and more than asides, which look quite different and I shall deal with them later. But this is clearly the main channel of Mill's thought, and it is one which has been subjected to vigorous attack from the moment it appeared—most often by fellow Utilitarians. The link that they have usually seized on is, as Fitzjames Stephen put it, the absence of proof that the "mass of adults are so well acquainted with their own interests and so much disposed to pursue them that no compulsion or restraint put upon them by any others for the purpose of promoting their interest can really promote them." [11]   Even so sympathetic a critic as Hart is forced to the conclusion that:

In Chapter 5 of his essay Mill carried his protests against paternalism to lengths that may now appear to us as fantastic. . . . No doubt if we no longer sympathise with this criticism this is due, in part, to a general decline in the belief that individuals know their own interest best.[12]

Mill endows the average individual with "too much of the psychology of a middle-aged man whose desires are relatively fixed, not able to be artificially stimulated by external influences; who knows what he wants and what gives him satisfaction of happiness; and who pursues these things when he can." [13]

Now it is interesting to note that Mill himself was aware of some of the limitations on the doctrine that the individual is the best judge of his own interests. In his discussion of government intervention in general (even where the intervention does not interfere with liberty but provides alternative institutions to those of the market), after making claims which are parallel to those just discussed, e.g.:

People understand their own business and their own interests better, and care for them more, than the government does, or can be expected to do,[14]

he goes on to an intelligent discussion of the "very large and conspicuous exceptions" to the maxim that:

Most persons take a juster and more intelligent view of their own interest, and of the means of promoting it, than can either be prescribed to them by a general enactment of the legislature, or pointed out in the particular case by a public functionary.[15]

---

9. Ibid., p. 207

10. Ibid., p. 138.

11. J.F. Stephens, Liberty, Equality, Fraternity (New York: Henry Holt & Co., n.d.), p. 24.

12. H.L.A. Hart, Law, Liberty and Morality (Stanford: Stanford University Press, 1963), p. 32.

13. Ibid., p. 33.

14. Mill, Principles, II, 448.

15. Ibid., II, 458.

Thus there are things

> of which the utility does not consist in ministering to inclinations, nor in serving the daily uses of life, and the want of which is least felt where the need is greatest. This is peculiarly true of those things which are chiefly useful as tending to raise the character of human beings. The uncultivated cannot be competent judges of cultivation. Those who most need to be made wiser and better, usually desire it least, and, if they desired it, would be incapable of finding the way to it by their own lights.

> . . . A second exception to the doctrine that individuals are the best judges of their own interest, is when an individual attempts to decide irrevocably now what will be best for his interest at some future and distant time. The presumption in favor of individual judgment is only legitimate, where the judgment is grounded on actual, and especially on present, personal experience; not where it is formed antecedently to experience, and not suffered to be reversed even after experience has condemned it.[16]

The upshot of these exceptions is that Mill does not declare that there should never be government interference with the economy but rather that

> . . . in every instance, the burden of making out a strong case should be thrown not on those who resist but on those who recommend government interference. Letting alone, in short, should be the general practice: every departure from it, unless required by some great good, is a certain evil.[17]

In short, we get a presumption, not an absolute prohibition. The question is why doesn't the argument against paternalism go the same way?

I suggest that the answer lies in seeing that in addition to a purely utilitarian argument Mill uses another as well. As a Utilitarian Mill has to show, in Fitzjames Stephen's words, that:

> Self-protection apart, no good object can be attained by any compulsion which is not in itself a greater evil than the absence of the object which the compulsion obtains.[18]

To show this is impossible; one reason being that it isn't true. Preventing a man from selling himself into slavery (a paternalistic measure which Mill himself accepts as legitimate), or from taking heroin, or from driving a car without wearing seat-belts may constitute a lesser evil than allowing him to do any of these things. A consistent Utilitarian can only argue against paternalism on the grounds that it (as a matter of fact) does not maximize the good. It is always a contingent question that may be refuted by the evidence. But there is also a non-contingent argument which runs through On Liberty. When Mill states that "there is a part of the life of every person who has come to years of discretion, within which the individuality of that person ought to reign uncontrolled either by any other person or by the public collectively" he is saying something about what it means to be a person, an autonomous agent. It is because coercing a person for his own good denies this status as an independent entity, that Mill objects to it so strongly and in such absolute terms. To be able to choose is a good that is independent of the wisdom of what is chosen.

---

16. Ibid., II, 459.   18. Stephen, p. 49.

17. Ibid., II, 451.

A man's "mode of laying out his existence is the best, not because it is the best in itself, but because it in his own mode." [19]

> It is the privilege and proper condition of a human being, arrived at the maturity of his faculties, to use and interpret experience in his own way.[20]

As further evidence of this line of reasoning in Mill consider the one exception to his prohibition against paternalism.

> In this and most civilised countries, for example, an engagement by which a person should sell himself, or allow himself to be sold, as a slave, would be null and void; neither enforced by law nor by opinion. The ground for thus limiting his power of voluntarily disposing of his own lot in life, is apparent, and is very clearly seen in this extreme case. The reason for not interfering, unless for the sake of others, with a person's voluntary acts, is consideration for his liberty. His voluntary choice is evidence that what he so chooses is desirable, or at least endurable, to him, and his good is on the whole best provided for by allowing him to take his own means of pursuing it. But by selling himself for a slave, he abdicates his liberty; he foregoes any future use of it beyond that single act.
>
>   He therefore defeats, in his own case, the very purpose which is the justification of allowing him to dispose of himself. He is no longer free; but is thenceforth in a position which has no longer the presumption in its favour, that would be afforded by his voluntarily remaining in it. The principle of freedom cannot require that he should be free not to be free. It is not freedom to be allowed to alienate his freedom.[21]

Now leaving aside the fudging on the meaning of freedom in the last line, it is clear that part of this argument is incorrect. While it is true that *future* choices of the slave are not reasons for thinking that what he chooses then is desirable for him, what is at issue is limiting his immediate choice; and since this choice is made freely, the individual may be correct in thinking that his interests are best provided for by entering such a contract. But the main consideration for not allowing such a contract is the need to preserve the liberty of the person to make future choices. This gives us a principle—a very narrow one—by which to justify some paternalistic interferences Paternalism is justified only to preserve a wider range of freedom for the individual in question. How far this principle could be extended, whether it can justify all the cases in which we are inclined upon reflection to think paternalistic measures justified, remains to be discussed. What I have tried to show so far is that there are two strains of argument in Mill—one a straight-forward Utilitarian mode of reasoning and one which relies not on the goods which free choice leads to, but on the absolute value of the choice itself. The first cannot establish any absolute prohibition but at most a presumption, and indeed a fairly weak one, given some fairly plausible assumptions about human psychology; the second, while a stronger line of argument, seems to me to allow on its own grounds a wider range of paternalism than might be suspected. I turn now to a consideration of these matters.

19. Mill, Utilitarianism and On Liberty,   **21.** Ibid., pp. 235–236.
p. 197.

20. Ibid., p. 186.

VI

We might begin looking for principles governing the acceptable use of paternalistic power in cases where it is generally agreed that it is legitimate. Even Mill intends his principles to be applicable only to mature individuals, not those in what he calls "non-age." What is it that justifies us in interfering with children? The fact that they lack some of the emotional and cognitive capacities required in order to make fully rational decisions. It is an empirical question to just what extent children have an adequate conception of their own present and future interests, but there is not much doubt that there are many deficiencies. For example it is very difficult for a child to defer gratification for any considerable period of time. Given these deficiencies and given the very real and permanent dangers that may befall the child, it becomes not only permissible but even a duty of the parent to restrict the child's freedom in various ways. There is however an important moral limitation on the exercise of such parental power, which is provided by the notion of the child eventually coming to see the correctness of his parent's interventions. Parental paternalism may be thought of as a wager by the parent on the child's subsequent recognition of the wisdom of the restrictions. There is an emphasis on what could be called future-oriented consent—on what the child will come to welcome, rather than on what he does welcome.

The essence of this idea has been incorporated by idealist philosophers into various types of "real-will" theory as applied to fully adult persons. Extensions of paternalism are argued for by claiming that in various respects, chronologically mature individuals share the same deficiencies in knowledge, capacity to think rationally, and the ability to carry out decisions that children possess. Hence in interfering with such people we are in effect doing what they would do if they were fully rational. Hence we are not really opposing their will, hence we are not really interfering with their freedom. The dangers of this move have been sufficiently exposed by Berlin in his Two Concepts of Liberty. I see no gain in theoretical clarity nor in practical advantage in trying to pass over the real nature of the interferences with liberty that we impose on others. Still the basic notion of consent is important and seems to me the only acceptable way of trying to delimit an area of justified paternalism.

Let me start by considering a case where the consent is not hypothetical in nature. Under certain conditions it is rational for an individual to agree that others should force him to act in ways in which, at the time of action, the individual may not see as desirable. If, for example, a man knows that he is subject to breaking his resolves when temptation is present, he may ask a friend to refuse to entertain his requests at some later stage.

A classical example is given in the Odyssey when Odysseus commands his men to tie him to the mast and refuse all future orders to be set free, because he knows the power of the Sirens to enchant men with their songs. Here we are on relatively sound ground in later refusing Odysseus' request to be set free. He may even claim to have changed his mind, but since it is just such changes that he wished to guard against we are entitled to ignore them.

A process analogous to this may take place on a social rather than individual basis. An electorate may mandate its representatives to pass legislation which when it comes time to "pay the price" may be unpalatable. I may believe that a tax increase is necessary to halt inflation, though I may resent the lower pay check each month. However in both this case and that of Odysseus the measure to be enforced is specifically requested by the party involved and at some point in time there is genuine consent and agreement on the part of those persons whose liberty is infringed. Such is not the case for the paternalistic measures we have been speaking about. What must be involved here is not consent to specific measures but rather consent to a system of government, run by elected representatives, with an understanding that they may act to safeguard our interests in certain limited ways.

I suggest that since we are all aware of our irrational propensities, deficiencies in cognitive and emotional capacities, and avoidable and unavoidable ignorance it is rational and prudent for us to in effect take out "social insurance policies." We may argue for and against proposed paternalistic measures in terms of what fully rational individuals would accept as forms of protection. Now clearly, since the initial agreement is not about specific measures, we are dealing with a more-or-less blank check, and therefore there have to be carefully defined limits. What I am looking for are certain kinds of conditions which make it plausible to suppose that rational men could reach agreement to limit their liberty even when other men's interests are not affected.

Of course as in any kind of agreement schema there are great difficulties in deciding what rational individuals would or would not accept. Particularly in sensitive areas of personal liberty, there is always a danger of the dispute over agreement and rationality being a disguised version of evaluative and normative disagreement.

Let me suggest types of situations in which it seems plausible to suppose that fully rational individuals would agree to having paternalistic restrictions imposed upon them. It is reasonable to suppose that there are "goods" such as health which any person would want to have in order to pursue his own good—no matter how that good is conceived. This is an argument that is used in connection with compulsory education for children but it seems to me that it can be extended to other goods which have this character. Then one could agree that the attainment of such goods should be promoted even when not recognized to be such, at the moment, by the individuals concerned.

An immediate difficulty that arises stems from the fact that men are always faced with competing goods and that there may be reasons why even a value such as health—or indeed life—may be overridden by competing values. Thus the problem with the Jehovah's Witness and blood transfusions. It may be more important for him to reject "impure substances" than to go on living. The difficult problem that must be faced is whether one can give sense to the notion of a person irrationally attaching weights to competing values.

Consider a person who knows the statistical data on the probability of being injured when not wearing seat belts in an automobile and knows the types and gravity of the various injuries. He also insists that the inconvenience attached to fastening the belt every time he gets in and out of the car outweighs for him the possible risks to himself. I am inclined in this case to think that such a weighing is irrational. Given his life-plans which we are assuming are those of the average person, his interests and commitments already undertaken, I think it is safe to predict that we can find inconsistencies in his calculations at some point. I am assuming that this is not a man who for some conscious or unconscious reasons is trying to injure himself nor is he a man who just likes to "live dangerously." I am assuming that he is like us in all the relevant respects but just puts an enormously high negative value on inconvenience—one which does not seem comprehensible or reasonable.

It is always possible, of course, to assimilate this person to creatures like myself. I, also, neglect to fasten my seat belt and I concede such behavior is not rational, but not because I weigh the inconvenience differently from those who fasten the belts. It is just that having made (roughly) the same calculation as everybody else I ignore it in my actions. (Note: a much better case of weakness of the will than those usually given in ethics texts.) A plausible explanation for this deplorable habit is that, although I know in some intellectual sense what the probabilities and risks are, I do not fully appreciate them in an emotionally genuine manner.

We have two distinct types of situation in which a man acts in a non-rational fashion. In one case he attaches incorrect weights to some of his values; in the other he neglects to act in accordance with his actual preferences and desires. Clearly there is a stronger and more persuasive argument for paternalism in the latter situation. Here we are really not—by assumption—imposing a good on another person. But why may we not extend our interference to what we might call evaluative delusions? After all in the case of cognitive delusions we are prepared, often, to act against the expressed will of the person involved. If a man believes that when he jumps out the window he will float upwards—Robert Nozick's example—would not we detain him, forcibly if necessary? The reply will be that this man doesn't wish to be injured and if we could convince him that he is mistaken as to the consequences of his action he would not wish to perform the action. But part of what is involved in claiming that a man who doesn't fasten his seat-belts is attaching an irrational weight to the inconvenience of fastening them is that if he were to be involved in an accident and severely injured, he would look back and admit that the inconvenience wasn't as bad as all that. So there is a sense in which if I could convince him of the consequences of his action, he also would not wish to continue his present course of action. Now the notion of consequences being used here is covering a lot of ground. In one case it's being used to indicate what will or can happen as a result of a course of action, and in the other it's making a prediction about the future evaluation of the consequences—in the first sense—of a course of action. And whatever the difference between facts and values—whether it be hard and fast or soft and slow—we are genuinely more reluctant to consent to interferences where evaluative differences are the issue. Let me now consider another factor which comes into play in some of these situations, which may make an important difference in our willingness to consent to paternalistic restrictions.

Some of the decisions we make are of such a character that they produce changes which are in one or another way irreversible. Situations are created in which it is difficult or impossible to return to anything like the initial stage at which the decision was made. In particular, some of these changes will make it impossible to continue to make reasoned choices in the future. I am thinking specifically of decisions which involve taking drugs that are physically or psychologically addictive and those which are destructive of one's mental and physical capacities.

I suggest we think of the imposition of paternalistic interferences in situations of this kind as being a kind of insurance policy which we take out against making decisions which are far-reaching, potentially dangerous, and irreversible. Each of these factors is important. Clearly there are many decisions we make that are relatively irreversible. In deciding to learn to play chess I could predict, in view of my general interest in games, that some portion of my free-time was going to be pre-empted and that it would not be easy to give up the game once I acquired a certain competence. But my whole life-style was not going to be jeopardized in an extreme manner. Further it might be argued that even with addictive drugs such as heroin one's normal life plans would not be seriously interfered with if an inexpensive and adequate supply were readily available. So this type of argument might have a much narrower scope than appears to be the case at first.

A second class of cases concerns decisions which are made under extreme psychological and sociological pressures. I am not thinking here of the making of the decision as being something one is pressured into— e.g., a good reason for making duelling illegal is that unless this is done many people might have to manifest their courage and integrity in ways in which they would rather not do so—but rather of decisions such as that to commit suicide, which are usually made at a point where the individual is not thinking clearly and calmly about the nature of his decision. In addition, of course, this comes under the previous heading of all-too-irrevocable decision. Now there are practical steps which a society could take if it wanted to decrease the possibility of suicide—for example, not paying social security benefits to the survivors or, as religious institutions do, not allowing such persons to be buried with the same status as natural deaths. I think we may count these as interferences with the liberty of persons to attempt suicide, and the question is whether they are justifiable.

Using my argument schema the question is whether rational individuals would consent to such limitations. I see no reason for them to consent to an absolute prohibition but I do think it is reasonable for them to agree to some kind of enforced waiting period. Since we are all aware of the possibility of temporary states, such as great fear or depression, that are inimical to the making of well-informed and rational decisions, it would be prudent for all of us if there were some kind of institutional arrangement whereby we were restrained from making a decision which is (all too) irreversible. What this would be like in practice is difficult to envisage, and it may be that if no practical arrangements were feasible then we would have to conclude that there should be no restriction at all on this kind of action. But we might have a "cooling off" period, in much the same way that we now require couples who file for divorce to go through a waiting period. Or, more far-fetched, we might imagine a Suicide Board composed of a psychologist and another member picked by the applicant. The Board would be required to meet and talk with the person proposing to take his life, though its approval would not be required.

A third class of decisions—these classes are not supposed to be disjoint—involves dangers which are either not sufficiently understood or appreciated correctly by the persons involved. Let me illustrate, using the example of cigarette smoking, a number of possible cases.

1. A man may not know the facts—e.g., smoking between 1 and 2 packs a day shortens life expectancy 6.2 years, the costs and pain of the illness caused by smoking, etc.

2.   A man may know the facts, wish to stop smoking, but not have the requisite will-power.

3.   A man may know the facts but not have them play the correct role in his calculation because, say, he discounts the danger psychologically, because it is remote in time, and/or inflates the attractiveness of other consequences of his decision which he regards as beneficial.

In case 1 what is called for is education, the posting of warnings, etc. In case 2 there is no theoretical problem. We are not imposing a good on someone who rejects it. We are simply using coercion to enable people to carry out their own goals. (Note: There obviously is a difficulty in that only a subclass of the individuals affected wish to be prevented from doing what they are doing.) In case 3 there is a sense in which we are imposing a good on someone since, given his current appraisal of the facts, he doesn't wish to be restricted. But in another sense we are not imposing a good, since what is being claimed—and what must be shown or at least argued for—is that an accurate accounting on his part would lead him to reject his current course of action. Now we all know that such cases exist, that we are prone to disregard dangers that are only possibilities, that immediate pleasures are often magnified and distorted.

If in addition the dangers are severe and far-reaching, we could agree to allowing the state a certain degree of power to intervene in such situations. The difficulty is in specifying in advance, even vaguely, the class of cases in which intervention will be legitimate.

A related difficulty is that of drawing a line so that it is not the case that all ultra-hazardous activities are ruled out, e.g., mountain-climbing, bull-fighting, sports-car racing, etc. There are some risks—even very great ones—which a person is entitled to take with his life.

A good deal depends on the nature of the deprivation—e.g., does it prevent the person from engaging in the activity completely or merely limit his participation—and how important to the nature of the activity is the absence of restriction, when this is weighed against the role that the activity plays in the life of the person. In the case of automobile seat belts, for example, the restriction is trivial in nature, interferes not at all with the use or enjoyment of the activity, and does, I am assuming, considerably reduce a high risk of serious injury. Whereas, for example, making mountain climbing illegal prevents completely a person engaging in an activity which may play an important role in his life and his conception of the person he is.

In general the easiest cases to handle are those which can be argued about in the terms which Mill thought to be so important—a concern not just for the happiness or welfare, in some broad sense, of the individual, but rather a concern for the autonomy and freedom of the person. I suggest that we would be most likely to consent to paternalism in those instances in which it preserves and enhances for the individual his ability rationally to consider and carry out his own decisions.

I have suggested in this essay a number of types of situations in which it seems plausible that rational men would agree to granting the legislative powers of a society the right to impose restrictions on what Mill calls "self-regarding" conduct. However, rational men knowing something about the resources of ignorance, ill-will, and stupidity available to the law-makers of a society—a good case in point is the history of drug legislation in the United States—will be concerned to limit such intervention to a minimum. I suggest in closing two principles designed to achieve this end.

In all cases of paternalistic legislation there must be a heavy and clear burden of proof placed on the authorities to demonstrate the exact nature of the harmful effects (or beneficial consequences) to be avoided (or achieved) and the probability of their occurrence. The burden of proof here is twofold—what lawyers distinguish as the burden of going forward and the burden of persuasion That the authorities have the burden of going forward means that it is up to them to raise the question and bring forward evidence of the evils to be avoided. Unlike the case of new drugs where the manufacturer must produce some evidence that the drug has been tested and found not harmful, no citizen has to show with respect to self-regarding conduct that it is not harmful or promotes his best interests. In addition the nature and cogency of the evidence for the harmfulness of the course of action must be set at a high level. To paraphrase a formulation of the burden of proof for criminal proceedings—better 10 men ruin themselves than one man be unjustly deprived of liberty.

Finally I suggest a principle of the least restrictive alternative. If there is an alternative way of accomplishing the desired end without restricting liberty then, although it may involve great expense, inconvenience, etc., the society must adopt it.

SISSELA BOK,
LYING: MORAL CHOICE IN PUBLIC AND PRIVATE LIFE

221–31, 234–40 (1978).

DECEPTION AS THERAPY

A forty-six-year-old man, coming to a clinic for a routine physical check-up needed for insurance purposes, is diagnosed as having a form of cancer likely to cause him to die within six months. No known cure exists for it. Chemotherapy may prolong life by a few extra months, but will have side effects the physician does not think warranted in this case. In addition, he believes that such therapy should be reserved for patients with a chance for recovery or remission. The patient has no symptoms giving him any reason to believe that he is not perfectly healthy. He expects to take a short vacation in a week.

For the physician, there are now several choices involving truthfulness. Ought he to tell the patient what he has learned, or conceal it? If asked, should he deny it? If he decides to reveal the diagnosis, should he delay doing so until after the patient returns from his vacation? Finally, even if he does reveal the serious nature of the diagnosis, should he mention the possibility of chemotherapy and his reasons for not recommending it in this case? Or should he encourage every last effort to postpone death?

In this particular case, the physician chose to inform the patient of his diagnosis right away. He did not, however, mention the possibility of chemotherapy. A medical student working under him disagreed; several nurses also thought that the patient should have been informed of this possibility. They tried, unsuccessfully, to persuade the physician that this was the patient's right. When persuasion had failed, the student elected to disobey the doctor by informing the patient of the alternative of chemotherapy. After consultation with family members, the patient chose to ask for the treatment.

Doctors confront such choices often and urgently. What they reveal, hold back, or distort will matter profoundly to their patients. Doctors stress with corresponding vehemence their reasons for the distortion or concealment: not to confuse a sick person needlessly, or cause what may well be unnecessary pain or discomfort, as in the case of the cancer patient; not to leave a patient without hope, as in those many cases where the dying are not told the truth about their condition; or to improve the chances of cure, as where unwarranted optimism is expressed about some form of therapy. Doctors use information as part of the therapeutic regimen; it is given out in amounts, in admixtures, and according to timing believed best for patients. Accuracy, by comparison, matters far less.

Lying to patients has, therefore, seemed an especially excusable act. Some would argue that doctors, and *only* doctors, should be granted the right to manipulate the truth in ways so undesirable for politicians, lawyers, and others. Doctors are trained to help patients; their relationship to patients carries special obligations, and they know much more than laymen about what helps and hinders recovery and survival.

. . .

. . . [W]e find very few mentions of veracity in the codes and oaths and writings by physicians through the centuries. This absence is all the more striking as other principles of ethics have been consistently and movingly expressed in the same documents.

The two fundamental principles of doing good and not doing harm—of beneficence and nonmaleficence—are the most immediately relevant to medical practitioners, and the most frequently stressed. To preserve life and good health, to ward off illness, pain, and death—these are the perennial tasks of medicine and nursing. . . .

But there is no similar stress on veracity. It is absent from virtually all oaths, codes, and prayers. The Hippocratic Oath makes no mention of truthfulness to patients about their condition, prognosis, or treatment. Other early codes and prayers are equally silent on the subject. . . . One of the few who appealed to such a principle was Amatus Lusitanus, a Jewish physician widely known for his skill, who, persecuted, died of the plague in 1568. He published an oath which reads in part:

> If I lie, may I incur the eternal wrath of God and of His angel Raphael, and may nothing in the medical art succeed for me according to my desires.

Later codes continue to avoid the subject. Not even the Declaration of Geneva, adopted in 1948 by the World Medical Association, makes any reference to it. And the Principles of Medical Ethics of the American Medical Association still leave the matter of informing patients up to the physician.[5]

Given such freedom, a physician can decide to tell as much or as little as he wants the patient to know, so long as he breaks no law. . . . A great many would choose to be able to lie. They would claim that not only can a lie avoid harm for the patient, but that it is also hard to know whether they have been right in the first place in making their pessimistic diagnosis; a "truthful" statement could therefore turn out to hurt patients unnecessarily. The concern for curing and for supporting those who cannot be cured then runs counter to the desire to be completely

5. See Harry Friedenwald, "The Ethics of the Practice of Medicine from the Jewish Point of View," Johns Hopkins Hospital Bulletin, no. 318 (August 1917), pp. 256–61.

open. This concern is especially strong where the prognosis is bleak; even more so when patients are so affected by their illness or their medication that they are more dependent than usual; perhaps more easily depressed or irrational.

Physicians know only too well how uncertain a diagnosis or prognosis can be. They know how hard it is to give meaningful and correct answers regarding health and illness. They also know that disclosing their own uncertainty or fears can reduce those benefits that depend upon faith in recovery. They fear, too, that revealing grave risks, no matter how unlikely it is that these will come about, may exercise the pull of the "self-fulfilling prophecy." They dislike being the bearers of uncertain or bad news as much as anyone else. And last, but not least, sitting down to discuss an illness truthfully and sensitively may take much-needed time away from other patients.

These reasons help explain why nurses and physicians and relatives of the sick and dying prefer not to be bound by rules that might limit their ability to suppress, delay, or distort information. This is not to say that they necessarily plan to lie much of the time. They merely want to have the freedom to do so when they believe it wise. And the reluctance to see lying prohibited explains, in turn, the failure of the codes and oaths to come to grips with the problems of truth-telling and lying.

But sharp conflicts are now arising. Doctors no longer work alone with patients. They have to consult with others much more than before; if they choose to lie, the choice may not be met with approval by all who take part in the care of the patient. . . .

. . . The fact that these problems have not been carefully thought through within the medical profession, nor seriously addressed in medical education, merely serves to intensify the conflicts.[8] Different doctors then respond very differently to patients in exactly similar predicaments. The friction is increased by the fact that relatives often disagree even where those giving medical care to a patient are in accord on how to approach the patient. Here again, because physicians have not worked out to common satisfaction the question of whether relatives have the right to make such requests, the problems are allowed to be haphazardly resolved by each physician as he sees fit.

THE PATIENT'S PERSPECTIVE

The turmoil in the medical profession regarding truth-telling is further augmented by the pressures that patients themselves now bring to bear and by empirical data coming to light. Challenges are growing to the three major arguments for lying to patients: that truthfulness is impossible; that patients do not want bad news; and that truthful information harms them.

The first of these arguments . . . confuses "truth" and "truthfulness" so as to clear the way for occasional lying on grounds supported by

---

8. Though a minority of physicians have struggled to bring them to our attention. See Thomas Percival, Medical Ethics, 3d ed. (Oxford: John Henry Parker, 1849), pp. 132–41; Worthington Hooker, Physician and Patient (New York: Baker and Scribner, 1849), pp. 357–82; Richard C. Cabot, "Teamwork of Doctor and Patient Through the Annihilation of Lying," in Social Service and the Art of Healing (New York: Moffat, Yard & Co., 1909), pp. 116–70; Charles C. Lund, "The Doctor, the Patient, and the Truth," Annals of Internal Medicine 24 (1946): 955; Edmund Davies, "The Patient's Right to Know the Truth," Proceedings of the Royal Society of Medicine 66 (1973): 533–36.

the second and third arguments. At this point, we can see more clearly that it is a strategic move intended to discourage the question of truthfulness from carrying much weight in the first place, and thus to leave the choice of what to say and how to say it up to the physician. To claim that "since telling the truth is impossible, there can be no sharp distinction between what is true and what is false" is to try to defeat objections to lying before even discussing them. One need only imagine how such an argument would be received, were it made by a car salesman or a real estate dealer, to see how fallacious it is.

In medicine, however, the argument is supported by a subsidiary point: even if people might ordinarily understand what is spoken to them, patients are often not in a position to do so. This is where paternalism enters in. When we buy cars or houses, the paternalist will argue, we need to have all our wits about us; but when we are ill, we cannot always do so. We need help in making choices, even if help can be given only by keeping us in the dark. And the physician is trained and willing to provide such help.

It is certainly true that some patients cannot make the best choices for themselves when weakened by illness or drugs. But most still can. And even those who are incompetent have a right to have someone—their guardian or spouse perhaps—receive the correct information.

The paternalistic assumption of superiority to patients also carries great dangers for physicians themselves—it risks turning to contempt.
. . . .

The argument which rejects informing patients beause adequate truthful information is impossible in itself or because patients are lacking in understanding must itself be rejected when looked at from the point of view of patients. They know that liberties granted to the most conscientious and altruistic doctors will be exercised also in the "Medicaid Mills"; that the choices thus kept from patients will be exercised by not only competent but incompetent physicians; and that even the best doctors can make choices patients would want to make differently for themselves.

The second argument for deceiving patients refers specifically to giving them news of a frightening or depressing kind. . . . On the basis of such a belief, most doctors in a number of surveys stated that they do not, as a rule, inform patients that they have an illness such as cancer.

When studies are made of what patients desire to know, on the other hand, a large majority say that they *would* like to be told of such a diagnosis. All these studies need updating and should be done with larger numbers of patients and non-patients. But they do show that there is generally a dramatic divergence between physicians and patients on the factual question of whether patients want to know what ails them in cases of serious illness such as cancer. In most of the studies, over 80 percent of the persons asked indicated that they would want to be told.

Sometimes this discrepancy is set aside by doctors who want to retain the view that patients do not want unhappy news. In reality, they claim, the fact that patients say they want it has to be discounted. The more someone asks to know, the more he suffers from fear which will lead to the denial of the information even if it is given. Informing patients is, therefore, useless; they resist and deny having been told what they cannot assimilate. According to this view, empirical studies of what patients say they want are worthless since they do not probe deeply enough to uncover this univeral resistance to the contemplation of one's own death.

This view is only partially correct. For some patients, denial is indeed well established in medical experience. A number of patients (estimated at between 15 percent and 25 percent) will give evidence of denial of having been told about their illness, even when they repeatedly ask and are repeatedly informed. And nearly everyone experiences a period of denial at some point in the course of approaching death.[12]   . . .

But to say that denial is universal flies in the face of all evidence. And to take any claim to the contrary as "symptomatic" of deeper denial leaves no room for reasoned discourse. There is no way that such universal denial can be proved true or false. To believe in it is a metaphysical belief about man's condition, not a statement about what patients do and do not want. It is true that we can never completely understand the possibility of our own death, any more than being alive in the first place. But people certainly differ in the degree to which they can approach such knowledge, take it into account in their plans, and make their peace with it.

. . . Some may request to be deceived rather than to see their lives as thus finite; others reject the information which would require them to do so; but most say that they want to know. Their concern for knowing about their condition goes far beyond mere curiosity or the wish to make isolated personal choices in the short time left to them; their stance toward the entire life they have lived, and their ability to give it meaning and completion, are at stake. In lying or withholding the facts which permit such discernment, doctors may reflect their own fears (which, according to one study,[16] are much stronger than those of laymen) of facing questions about the meaning of one's life and the inevitability of death.

Beyond the fundamental deprivation that can result from deception, we are also becoming increasingly aware of all that can befall patients in the course of their illness when information is denied or distorted. Lies place them in a position where they no longer participate in choices concerning their own health, including the choice of whether to be a "patient" in the first place. A terminally ill person who is not informed that his illness is incurable and that he is near death cannot make decisions about the end of his life: about whether or not to enter a hospital, or to have surgery; where and with whom to spend his last days; how to put his affairs in order—these most personal choices cannot be made if he is kept in the dark, or given contradictory hints and clues.

.   .   .

The reason why even doctors who recognize a patient's right to have information might still not provide it brings us to the third argument against telling all patients the truth. It holds that the information given might hurt the patient and that the concern for the right to such information is therefore a threat to proper health care. .   . .

The factual basis for this argument has been challenged from two points of view. The damages associated with the disclosure of sad news

---

12. See Avery Weisman, On Dying and Denying (New York: Behavioral Publications, 1972); Elisabeth Kübler-Ross, On Death and Dying (New York: The Macmillan Co., 1969); Ernest Becker, The Denial of Death (New York: Free Press, 1973); Philippe Ariès, Western Attitudes Toward Death, trans. Patricia M. Ranum (Baltimore and London: Johns Hopkins University Press, 1974); and Sigmund Freud, "Negation," Collected Papers, ed. James Strachey (London: Hogarth Press, 1950), 5: 181–85.

16. Herman Feifel et al., "Physicians Consider Death," Proceedings of the American Psychoanalytical Association, 1967, pp. 201–2.

or risks are rarer than physicians believe; and the *benefits* which result from being informed are more substantial, even measurably so. Pain is tolerated more easily, recovery from surgery is quicker, and cooperation with therapy is greatly improved. The attitude that "what you don't know won't hurt you" is proving unrealistic; it is what patients do not know but vaguely suspect that causes them corrosive worry.

It is certain that no answers to this question of harm from information are the same for all patients. If we look, first, at the fear expressed by physicians that informing patients of even remote or unlikely risks connected with a drug prescription or operation might shock some and make others refuse the treatment that would have been best for them, it appears to be unfounded for the great majority of patients. Studies show that very few patients respond to being told of such risks by withdrawing their consent to the procedure and that those who do withdraw are the very ones who might well have been upset enough to sue the physician had they not been asked to consent beforehand.[17] It is possible that on even rarer occasions especially susceptible persons might manifest physical deterioration from shock; some physicians have even asked whether patients who die after giving informed consent to an operation, but before it actually takes place, somehow expire because of the information given to them.[18] While such questions are unanswerable in any one case, they certainly argue in favor of caution, a real concern for the person to whom one is recounting the risks he or she will face, and sensitivity to all signs of distress.

The situation is quite different when persons who are already ill, perhaps already quite weak and discouraged, are told of a very serious prognosis. Physicians fear that such knowledge may cause the patients to commit suicide, or to be frightened or depressed to the point that their illness takes a downward turn. The fear that great numbers of patients will commit suicide appears to be unfounded.[19] And if some do, is that a response so unreasonable, so much against the patient's best interest that physicians ought to make it a reason for concealment or lies? Many societies have allowed suicide in the past; our own has decriminalized it; and some are coming to make distinctions among the many suicides which ought to be prevented if at all possible, and those which ought to be respected.[20]

Another possible response to very bleak news is the triggering of physiological mechanisms which allow death to come more quickly—a form of giving up or of preparing for the inevitable, depending on one's outlook. . . .

Such a response may be appropriate, in which case it makes the moments of dying as peaceful as those who have died and been resuscitated so often testify. . . .

17. See Ralph Alfidi, "Informed Consent: A Study of Patient Reaction," Journal of the American Medical Association 216 (1971): 1325–29.

18. See Steven R. Kaplan, Richard A. Greenwald, and Arvey I. Rogers, Letter to the Editor, New England Journal of Medicine 296 (1977): 1127.

19. Oken, "What to Tell Cancer Patients"; Veatch, Death, Dying, and the Biological Revolution; Weisman, On Dying and Denying.

20. Norman L. Cantor, "A Patient's Decision to Decline Life-Saving Treatment: Bodily Integrity Versus the Preservation of Life," Rutgers Law Review 26: 228–64; Danielle Gourevitch, "Suicide Among the Sick in Classical Antiquity," Bulletin of the History of Medicine 18 (1969): 501–18; for bibliography, see Bok, "Voluntary Euthanasia."

It is not inconceivable that unhappy news abruptly conveyed, or a great shock given to someone unable to tolerate it, could also bring on such a "dying response," quite unintended by the speaker. There is every reason to be cautious and to try to know ahead of time how susceptible a patient might be to the accidental triggering—however rare—of such a response. One has to assume, however, that most of those who have survived long enough to be in a situation where their informed consent is asked have a very robust resistance to such accidental triggering of processes leading to death.

. . .

Apart from the possible harm from information, we are coming to learn much more about the benefits it can bring patients. People follow instructions more carefully if they know what their disease is and why they are asked to take medication; any benefits from those procedures are therefore much more likely to come about. Similarly, people recover faster from surgery and tolerate pain with less medication if they understand what ails them and what can be done for them.

RESPECT AND TRUTHFULNESS

Taken all together, the three arguments defending lies to patients stand on much shakier ground as a counterweight to the right to be informed than is often thought. The common view that many patients cannot understand, do not want, and may be harmed by, knowledge of their condition, and that lying to them is either morally neutral or even to be recommended, must be set aside. Instead, we have to make a more complex comparison. Over against the right of patients to knowledge concerning themselves, the medical and psychological benefits to them from this knowledge, the unnecessary and sometimes harmful treatment to which they can be subjected if ignorant, and the harm to physicians, their profession, and other patients from deceptive practices, we have to set a severely restricted and narrowed paternalistic view—that *some* patients cannot understand, *some* do not want, and *some* may be harmed by, knowledge of their condition, and that they ought not to have to be treated like everyone else if this is not in their best interest.

Such a view is persuasive. A few patients openly request not to be given bad news. Others give clear signals to that effect, or are demonstrably vulnerable to the shock or anguish such news might call forth. Can one not in such cases infer implied consent to being deceived?

Concealment, evasion, withholding of information may at times be necessary. But if someone contemplates lying to a patient or concealing the truth, the burden of proof must shift. It must rest, here, as with all deception, on those who advocate it in any one instance. They must show why they fear a patient may be harmed or how they know that another cannot cope with the truthful knowledge. A decision to deceive must be seen as a very unusual step, to be talked over with colleagues and others who participate in the care of the patient. Reasons must be set forth and debated, alternatives weighed carefully. At all times, the correct information must go to *someone* closely related to the patient.

The law already permits doctors to withhold information from patients where it would clearly hurt their health. But this privilege has been sharply limited by the courts. Certainly it cannot be interpreted so broadly as to permit a general practice of deceiving patients "for their own good." Nor can it be made to include cases where patients might calmly decide, upon hearing their diagnosis, not to go ahead with the therapy their doctor recommends. Least of all can it justify silence or lies to large numbers of patients merely on the grounds that it is not always easy to tell what a patient wants.

For the great majority of patients, on the contrary, the goal must be disclosure, and the atmosphere one of openness. But it would be wrong to assume that patients can therefore be told abruptly about a serious diagnosis—that, so long as openness exists, there are no further requirements of humane concern in such communication. . . .

Above all, truthfulness with those who are suffering does not mean that they should be deprived of all hope: hope that there is a chance of recovery, however small; nor of reassurance that they will not be abandoned when they most need help.

Much needs to be done, however, if the deceptive practices are to be eliminated, and if concealment is to be restricted to the few patients who ask for it or those who can be shown to be harmed by openness. The medical profession has to address this problem.

PRESIDENT'S COMMISSION FOR THE STUDY OF ETHICAL PROBLEMS IN MEDICINE AND BIOMEDICAL AND BEHAVIORAL RESEARCH, MAKING HEALTH CARE DECISIONS

95–101 (1982).

The final exception to informed consent, which has been the subject of substantial comment, is called therapeutic privilege and permits professionals to refrain from making a disclosure that could so seriously upset a patient that it would be countertherapeutic. . . .

Despite all the anecdotes about patients who committed suicide, suffered heart attacks, or plunged into prolonged depression upon being told "bad news," little documentation exists for claims that informing patients is more dangerous to their health than not informing them, particularly when the informing is done in a sensitive and tactful fashion. . . .

Attitudes toward less than full disclosure. In the Commission's survey an attempt was made to discover how often and why physicians withhold information from patients, the conditions under which the public considers this acceptable, and the justifications for providing information to families when it is not given to patients.

Although physicians reported that they frequently make a conscious and deliberate evaluation of how much to tell patients, relatively few reported that they ultimately withheld information. Physicians who judged that 90–100% of their patients are able to understand most information were generally less likely to withhold details. Interestingly, physicians who had graduated from medical school ten years ago or sooner were more likely than older physicians to withhold information about treatment risks and alternatives and about diagnosis and prognosis.

Physicians were also asked: "What are the most common reasons for you to withhold information about condition or treatment?" Patients' inability to cope with the information (34%), inability to understand it (28%), and the wishes of the patients' families (21%) were the reasons given most frequently. Only 9% mentioned effects on the patients health.

Further questioning revealed that in nearly two-thirds of the cases in which physicians withhold "bad news" the decision to do so is rarely or never based upon the patients' wishes. Moreover, when members of the public were asked "Have you ever asked a doctor not to tell you 'bad news'?," only 2% said yes, although 5% of those who had received care in a setting other than a doctor's office, or who were in poor health, or who had less than a high school education said yes. These figures on the public's request not to be told "bad news" are substantially lower than the physicians' reports of such requests.

Nevertheless, physicians do believe in disclosing information to patients' relatives—a step that may alert them to potential idiosyncratic objections to an intervention or other special facts but that still falls far short of shared decisionmaking with the patient.[39] Of physicians surveyed, 80% said they "usually discussed the withheld information with another family member," 10% said "sometimes," 4% said "rarely," and 3% said "never." In an unusual response 3% said they were "not sure."

The responses of the public, when asked whether a physician would be justified in withholding information about a medical condition or treatment from a patient, more closely parallel existing law than do those in the physician sample. A majority of the public only disapproved of physicians withholding information when the withholding occurs because the information might make the patient unwilling to undergo treatment believed to be medically necessary. However, more than two-thirds of those responding thought a physician would be justified in withholding information if the patient asked for it to be withheld or if the information might significantly harm the patient's health. About half those in the public sample find nondisclosure acceptable if the patient's family asked that the patient not be told (which 8% of the public reports having done) or if the information might make the patient upset or anxious.[41]

NOTES

1. How should the law respond to the patient who does not want to be involved in, or exercise control over, decisions about his or her own health care? Physicians report that it is not unusual for patients to say, "You decide, Doctor," and that many patients indicate they prefer not to be told much if anything about their condition or procedures proposed to treat it. Courts have acknowledged that a patient may elect "to know nothing and instead to rely completely upon the physician," even to the point of being "free to unwisely act in the dark," provided "he is exercising his own 'right of self-determination'." Henderson v. Milobsky, 595 F.2d 654 (D.C.Cir.1978). Nevertheless, the outcome of no case has actually turned on this variety of "waiver," so that predictions about the requisites of a valid waiver must be grounded in analogies to other areas of law. See Meisel, The "Exceptions" to the Informed Consent Doctrine: Striking a Balance Between Competing Values in Medical Decisionmaking, 1979 Wis.L.Rev. 413, 453–460.

The impact of the waiver exception is that if a waiver is properly obtained the patient remains the ultimate decisionmaker, but the content of his decision is shifted from the decisional level to the metadecisional level—from the equiva-

---

39. The legal status of disclosure to patients' relatives when the therapeutic privilege is invoked is uncertain.

41. In general, older, less well educated people and those in poor health were more likely to feel that withholding information was justifiable; these groups were also more likely to express uncertainty than others. There is no recognition in law for withhold-ing information from patients at the request of a family member. Whether or not a physician is entitled to withhold information that might make a patient upset or anxious depends on whether the concern is merely with upsetting the patient or with causing the patient to reject the doctor's therapeutic advice.

lent of "I want this treatment (or that treatment or no treatment)" to "I don't want any information about the treatment."

Id. at 459. Does this mean that courts should respect some waivers as a means of respecting the part of self-determination that encompasses the moral right to formal control over a decision, while recognizing that the patient has chosen to forgo that aspect of self-determination that encompasses an ideal of active participation in decisionmaking. Do you agree that "it is questionable whether patients should be permitted to waive the professional's obligation to disclose fundamental information about the nature and implications of certain procedures (such as, 'when you wake up, you will learn that your limb has been amputated' or 'that you are irreversibly sterile')"? President's Commission, Making Health Care Decisions 94 (1982).

2. May a plaintiff claim that his agreement to treatment was involuntary because he held the physician in such awe he felt unable to refuse the proposed treatment? Would it matter then precisely how the physician's advice had been stated? Is there a difference between, "If I were you, I'd have the operation," and "In light of my professional experience, I believe the benefits of this operation outweigh its risks." Or are such sentiments implicit in any physician's very recommendation?

3. On the problem of stress created by illness or the health care setting itself, see Ch. 7, Sec. B. 3, infra. See also Moore v. Fragatos, 116 Mich.App. 179, 321 N.W.2d 781 (1982) (waiver of access to the courts unconstitutional where signed at the time of plaintiff's admission to the hospital, when plaintiff was in considerable pain).

Consider Rubin, Medical Malpractice Suits Can be Avoided 52 Hospitals, J.A.H.A. 86, 87 (1978):

The hospital often seems to be a threatening, hostile environment to many patients who may be frightened and bewildered by their illnesses. . . .

A hospitalized patient is in a completely dependent, childlike position. His clothes have been removed, his privacy and sense of dignity are constantly intruded upon, and he is removed from the familiar surroundings of his home to a sometimes frightening, frantically busy atmosphere. His concern about his illness, his pain and suffering, and his helplessness are real problems. It is, of course, unrealistic to expect every staff member who interacts with a patient to identify personally with the patient's problems.

4. What can the law do to buttress decisionmaking capacity and authority? Consider Glass, Restructing Informed Consent: Legal Therapy for the Doctor-Patient Relationship, 76 Yale L.J. 1533, 1534 (1970): "[the law should] encourage the development of a partnership mode in doctor-patient relations to replace the prevalent authoritarian pattern." Does the doctrine of informed consent as it has developed in the courts and legislatures move in this direction? One expert argues that the courts have missed the opportunity, in framing informed consent rules, to move toward "a new and unaccustomed dialogue between physicians and patients . . . in which both, appreciative of their respective inequalities, make a genuine effort to voice and clarify their uncertainties and then to arrive at a mutually satisfactory course of action," and instead have imposed primarily a duty-to-warn which merely reinforces "physicians' traditional monologue of talking *at* and not *with* patients." Katz, Disclosure and Consent: In Search of Their Roots, in Genetics and the Law II 122 (A. Milunsky & G. Annas eds., 1980).

5. For consideration of the problems posed in relying on informed consent in researcher-subject relations, see Ch. 6, Sec. C.2, infra.

c. Based on Concern for Those Who Cannot Decide for Themselves

LAKE v. CAMERON

United States Court of Appeals for the District of Columbia Circuit, 1966.
364 F.2d 657.

On Rehearing en banc

BAZELON, CHIEF JUDGE:

Appellant is confined in Saint Elizabeths Hospital as an insane person and appeals from denial of release in habeas corpus. On September 29, 1962, when she was sixty years old, a policeman found her wandering about and took her to the D.C. General Hospital. On October 11, 1962, she filed in the District Court a petition for a writ of habeas corpus. The court transferred her to St. Elizabeths Hospital for observation in connection with pending commitment proceedings, allowed her to amend her petition by naming the Superintendent of Saint Elizabeths as defendant, and on November 2, 1962, dismissed her petition without holding a hearing or requiring a return.

After she filed her appeal from denial of habeas corpus, she was adjudged "of unsound mind" and committed to Saint Elizabeths. At the commitment hearing two psychiatrists testified that she was mentally ill and one of them that she was suffering from a "chronic brain syndrome" associated with aging and "demonstrated very frequently difficulty with her memory . . . . Occasionally, she was unable to tell me where she was or what the date was." Both psychiatrists testified to the effect that she could not care for herself adequately. She did not take a timely appeal from the commitment order. We heard her appeal from the summary dismissal of her petition for habeas corpus and remanded the case to the District Court with directions to require a return and hold a hearing.

At the hearing on remand, the sole psychiatric witness testified that appellant was suffering from a senile brain disease, "chronic brain syndrome, with arteriosclerosis with reaction." The psychiatrist said she was not dangerous to others and would not intentionally harm herself, but was prone to "wandering away and being out exposed at night or any time that she is out." This witness also related that on one occasion she wandered away from the Hospital, was missing for about thirty-two hours, and was brought back after midnight by a police officer who found her wandering in the streets. She had suffered a minor injury which she attributed to being chased by boys. She thought she had been away only a few hours and could not tell where she had been. The psychiatrist also testified that she was "confused and agitated" when first admitted to the Hospital but became "comfortable" after "treatment and medication."

At both the commitment hearing and the habeas corpus hearing on remand, appellant testified that she felt able to be at liberty. At the habeas corpus hearing her husband, who had recently reappeared after a long absence, and her sister said they were eager for her release and would try to provide a home for her. The District Court found that she "is suffering from a mental illness with the diagnosis of chronic brain syndrome associated with cerebral arteriosclerosis"; that she "is in need of care and supervision, and that there is no member of the family able to give the petitioner the necessary care and supervision; and that the family is without sufficient funds to employ a competent person to do so"; that she "is a danger to herself in that she has a tendency to wander about the streets, and is not competent to care for herself." The District Court again denied relief in habeas corpus, but noted appellant's right "to make further application in the event that the patient is in a position to show that there would be some facilities available for her provision." The court thus recognized that she might be entitled to release from Saint Elizabeths if other facilities were available, but required her to carry the burden of showing their availability.

Appellant contends . . . that remand to the District Court is required for a consideration of suitable alternatives to confinement in Saint Elizabeths Hospital in light of the new District of Columbia Hospitalization of the Mentally Ill Act, which came into effect after the hearing in the District Court. . . .

. . .

We are not called upon to consider what action we would have taken in the absence of the new Act, because we think the interest of justice and furtherance of the congressional objective require the application to the pending proceeding of the principles adopted in that Act. It provides that if the court or jury finds that a "person is mentally ill and, because of that illness, is likely to injure himself or other persons if allowed to remain at liberty, the court may order his hospitalization for an indeterminate period, or order any other alternative course of treatment which the court believes will be in the best interests of the person or of the public." D.C.Code § 21–545(b) (Supp. V, 1966). This confirms the view of the Department of Health, Education and Welfare that "the entire spectrum of services should be made available, including outpatient treatment, foster care, halfway houses, day hospitals, nursing homes, etc." The alternative course of treatment or care should be fashioned as the interests of the person and of the public require in the particular case. Deprivations of liberty solely because of dangers to the ill persons themselves should not go beyond what is necessary for their protection.

The court's duty to explore alternatives in such a case as this is related also to the obligation of the state to bear the burden of exploration of possible alternatives an indigent cannot bear. This appellant, as appears from the record, would not be confined in Saint Elizabeths if her family were able to care for her or pay for the care she needs. Though she cannot be given such care as only the wealthy can afford, an earnest effort should be made to review and exhaust available resources of the community in order to provide care reasonably suited to her needs.

. . .

Appellant may not be required to carry the burden of showing the availability of alternatives. Proceedings involving the care and treatment of the mentally ill are not strictly adversary proceedings. Moreover, appellant plainly does not know and lacks the means to ascertain what alternatives, if any, are available, but the government knows or has the means of knowing and should therefore assist the court in acquiring such information.

We remand the case to the District Court for an inquiry into "other alternative courses of treatment." The court may consider, *e.g.*, whether the appellant and the public would be sufficiently protected if she were required to carry an identification card on her person so that the police or others could take her home if she should wander, or whether she should be required to accept public health nursing care, community mental health and day care services, foster care, home health aide services, or whether available welfare payments might finance adequate private care. Every effort should be made to find a course of treatment which appellant might be willing to accept.

. . .

We express no opinion on questions that would arise if on remand the court should find no available alternative to confinement in Saint Elizabeths.[19]

. . . Our decision does no more than require the exploration respecting other facilities to be made by the government for the indigent appellant in the circumstances of this case.

. . .

Remanded for further proceedings in accordance with this opinion.

NOTES

. . .

1. Consider the following comments addressed by Mr. Solicitor General Sobeloff to the Supreme Court:

Associate Justice Robert Houghwout Jackson died suddenly of a heart attack on Saturday, October 9, 1954, at the age of sixty-two and at the height of his brilliant judicial career. . . .

. . .

Justice Jackson had suffered a previous attack in the spring of 1954. . . . His doctors gave him the choice between years of comparative inactivity or a continuation of his normal activity at the risk of death at any time. With characteristic fortitude he chose the second alternative. . . .

In Memory of Mr. Justice Jackson, 349 U.S. XXVII (1955):

2. For consideration of which minors are too "immature" to have the capacity to decide on whether to seek an abortion, see Belotti v. Baird, Ch. 8 Sec. B.1, infra.

DEPARTMENT OF HUMAN SERVICES v. NORTHERN

Court of Appeals of Tennessee, 1978.
563 S.W.2d 197.

TODD, JUDGE.

This is a proceeding under Chapter 23, Title 14, T.C.A. entitled "Protective Services for Elderly Persons."

. . .

. . . On January 24, 1978, the Tennessee Department of Human Services filed this suit alleging that Mary C. Northern was 72 years old, with no available help from relatives; that Miss Northern resided alone under unsatisfactory conditions as a result of which she had been admitted to and was a patient in Nashville General Hospital; that the patient suffered from gangrene of both feet which required the removal of her feet to save her life; that the patient lacked the capacity to appreciate her condition or to consent to necessary surgery.

---

19. Such questions might be whether so complete a deprivation of appellant's liberty basically because of her poverty could be reconciled with due process of law and the equal protection of the laws.

Attached to the complaint are identical letters from Drs. Amos D. Tackett and R. Benton Adkins which read as follows:

"Mrs. Mary Northern is a patient under our care at Nashville General Hospital. She has gangrene of both feet probably secondary to frost bite and then thermal burning of the feet. She has developed infection along with the gangrene of her feet. This is placing her life in danger. Mrs. Northern does not understand the severity or consequences of her disease process and does not appear to understand that failure to amputate the feet at this time would probably result in her death. It is our recommendation as the physicians in charge of her case, that she undergo amputation of both feet as soon as possible."

On January 24, 1978, the Chancellor appointed a guardian ad litem to defend the cause and to receive service of process pursuant to Rule 4.04(2) T.R.C.P.

On January 25, 1978, the guardian ad litem answered as follows:

"The Respondent, by and through her guardian ad litem, states as follows:

1. She is 72 years of age and a resident of Davidson County, Tennessee.

2. She is presently in the intensive care unit of General Hospital, Nashville, Tennessee, because of gangrenous condition in her two feet.

3. She feels very strongly that her present physical condition is improving, and that she will recover without the necessity of surgery.

4. She is in possession of a good memory and recall, responds accurately to questions asked her, is coherent and intelligent in her conversation and is of sound mind.

5. She is aware that the Tennessee Department of Human Services has filed this complaint, knows the nature of the complaint, and does not wish for her feet to be amputated.

6. There is no psychiatric report of her mental capacity, and there is nothing in the hospital or court record to support the statement that she lacks the capacity to realize the need for protective services.

7. The Court should not grant the relief sought by the Department of Human Services until a psychiatric report of the Respondent's present mental state has been made a part of this record, and the Court finds that the Respondent lacks the mental capacity to consent to medical treatment.

8. The Court is without jurisdiction to grant the relief to award physical custody of the respondent to the Department of Human Services absent a finding that the Respondent is guilty of a crime, or absent a finding that the Respondent lacks sufficient mental capacity in accordance with T.C.A. 33–501 et seq., (Mentally Retarded Person), and/or T.C.A. 33–601 et seq., (Mentally Ill Person).

9. The relief sought by the Department of Human Services should be denied.

10. In the event that the court deems it proper to grant the relief sought, the appointment should be limited to allow the Department of Human Services only to consent to the operation and necessary medical care.

11.   Although over fourteen years of age and mentally competent, the Respondent is not physically capable of signing this Answer, and the guardian ad litem signs on her behalf."

On January 25, 1978, the Chancellor entered an order   .   .   .

On the same date, January 25, 1978, at 4:00 P.M., the Chancellor entered a further order staying the effectiveness of the preceding order until further order of Court.

On January 26, 1978, there was filed in this cause a letter from Dr. John J. Griffin, reporting that he found the patient to be generally lucid and sane, but concluding:

"Nonetheless, I believe that she is functioning on a psychotic level with respect to ideas concerning her gangrenous feet. She tends to believe that her feet are black because of soot or dirt. She does not believe her physicians about the serious infection. There is an adamant belief that her feet will heal without surgery, and she refused to even consider the possibility that amputation is necessary to save her life. There is no desire to die, yet her judgment concerning recovery is markedly impaired. If she appreciated the seriousness of her condition, heard her physicians' opinions, and concluded against an operation, then I would believe she understood and could decide for herself. But my impression is that she does not appreciate the dangers to her life. I conclude that she is incompetent to decide this issue. A corollary to this denial is seen in her unwillingness to consider any future plans. Here again I believe she was utilizing a psychotic mechanism of denial.

"This is a schizoid woman who has been urged by everyone to have surgery. Having been self-sufficient previously (albeit a marginal adjustment), she is continuing to decide alone. The risks with surgery are great and her lifestyle has been permanently disrupted. If she has surgery there is a tremendous danger for physical and psychological complications. The chances for a post-operative psychosis are immense, yet the surgeons believe an operation is necessary to save her life. I would advise delaying surgery (if feasible) for a few days in order to attempt some work for strengthening her psychologically. Even if she does not consent to the operation after that time, however, I believe she is incompetent to make the decision."

On January 26, 1978, the Chancellor entered a further order vacating the stay of the first order and reinstating the previous (first) order, and providing further:

".   .   .   The court requested that the guardian ad litem contact the head surgeon and delay surgery as recommended by Dr. Griffin.

.   .   .

On January 27, 1978, the guardian ad litem moved for a new trial and stay of previous orders on grounds of unconstitutionality of Title 14, Chapter 23, T.C.A. and a number of other grounds.

On January 27, 1978, the Chancellor entered a decree overruling the motion for new trial   .   .   .

On January 28, 1978   .   .   .   two members of this Court heard argument on behalf of the parties and on behalf of a proposed amicus curiae, after which it was announced that this Court would act under § 27–327 T.C.A. to investigate the facts.

On the same date two members of this Court heard testimony of the three doctors previously mentioned and visited the patient in the intensive care unit of the hospital. . . .

On the same date, January 28, 1978, this Court entered an order . . . .

The first assignment of error asserts that Title 14, Chapter 23, T.C.A. is unconstitutional.

. . .

Appellant challenges the constitutionality of the provision of the statute authorizing ex parte preliminary orders without hearing. No action of the Chancellor taken without a hearing has been implemented, and all actions by this court have occurred after full hearing. Therefore it would seem unnecessary for this Court to rule upon the validity of such provision in this case. . . .

. . .

Also in respect to the first assignment, the brief of appellant states:

"Such actions by the Court were injurious to the appellant because they deprived her of her right to make her own decisions—regardless as to whether death might be a probable consequence—as to whether she was willing to surrender control of her own person and life."

This controversy arises from the fact that Miss Northern's attending physicians have determined that all of the soft tissue of her feet has been killed by frostbite, that said dead tissue had become infected with gangrene and that the feet must be removed to prevent loss of life from spreading of gangrene and its effects to the entire body. Miss Northern has refused to consent to the surgery.

The physicians have determined, and the Chancellor and this Court have found, that Miss Northern's life is critically endangered; that she is mentally incapable of comprehending the facts which constitute that danger; and that she is, to that extent, incompetent, thereby justifying State action to preserve her life.

[A] member of this Court asked Miss Northern if she would prefer to die rather than lose her feet, and her answer was "possibly." This is the most definitive expression of her desires in this record.

The patient has *not* expressed a desire to die. She evidences a strong desire to live and an equally strong desire to keep her dead feet. She refuses to make a choice.

If the patient would assume and exercise her rightful control over her own destiny by stating that she prefers death to the loss of her feet, her wish would be respected. The doctors so testified; this Court so informed her; and this Court here and now reiterates its commitment to this principle.

For the reasons just stated, this is *not* a "right to die" case.

. . .

The appellant has filed [a] supplemental assignment of error . . . .

"1. The statute, T.C.A. §§ 14–2301, et seq., is impermissibly vague; and, therefore, void and unconstitutional. The two phrases used in the statute, 'imminent danger of death' and 'capacity to consent' have not been defined in the statute nor is the Court given any assistance to determine when either standard has been met in the legal context, rather than a medical context."

In the judgment of this Court, the words "imminent danger of death" are no more vague than is consistent with the nature of the subject matter.

. . .

The words, "imminent danger of death" mean conditions calculated to and capable of producing within a short period of time a reasonably strong probability of resultant cessation of life if such conditions are not removed or alleviated. Such is undoubtedly the legislative intent of the words.

. . .

Appellant also complains of vagueness of the meaning of "capacity to consent." Capacity means mental ability to make a rational decision, which includes the ability to perceive, appreciate all relevant facts and to reach a rational judgment upon such facts.

Capacity is not necessarily synonymous with sanity. A blind person may be perfectly capable of observing the shape of small articles by handling them, but not capable of observing the shape of a cloud in the sky.

A person may have "capacity" as to some matters and may lack "capacity" as to others.

. . .

In the present case, this Court has found the patient to be lucid and apparently of sound mind generally. However, on the subjects of death and amputation of her feet, her comprehension is blocked, blinded or dimmed to the extent that she is incapable of recognizing facts which would be obvious to a person of normal perception.

For example, in the presence of this Court, the patient looked at her feet and refused to recognize the obvious fact that the flesh was dead, black, shriveled, rotting and stinking.

The record also discloses that the patient refuses to consider the eventuality of death which is or ought to be obvious in the face of such dire bodily deterioration.

As described by the doctors and observed by this Court, the patient wants to live and keep her dead feet, too, and refuses to consider the impossibility of such a desire. In order to avoid the unpleasant experience of facing death and/or loss of feet, her mind or emotions have resorted to the device of denying the unpleasant reality so that, to the patient, the unpleasant reality does not exist. This is the "delusion" which renders the patient incapable of making a rational decision as to whether to undergo surgery to have her life or to forego surgery and forfeit her life.

The physicians speak of probabilities of death without amputation as 90 to 95% and the probability of death with surgery as 50–50 (1 in 2). Such probabilities are not facts, but the existence and expression of such opinions are facts which the patient is unwilling or unable to recognize or discuss.

If, as repeatedly stated, this patient could and would give evidence of a comprehension of the facts of her condition and could and would express her unequivocal desire in the face of such comprehended facts, then her decision, however unreasonable to others, would be accepted and honored by the Courts and by her doctors.   The difficulty is that she cannot or will not comprehend the facts.

The supplemental assignment of error is respectfully overrruled.

.   .   .

.   .   .

The order of the Chancellor entered on January 25, 1978, .   .   .   is modified to read as follows:

"The Court is of the opinion that Mary C. Northern is in imminent danger of death if she does not receive certain protective services and she lacks the capacity to consent to said protective services."

"IT IS, THEREFORE, ORDERED, ADJUDGED AND DECREED that

"1.   Mary C. Northern is in imminent danger of death if she does not receive surgical amputation of her lower extremities and she lacks the capacity to consent or refuse consent for such surgery.

"2.   That Honorable Horace Bass, Commissioner of Human Services of the State of Tennessee or his successor in office is hereby designated and authorized to act for and on behalf of said Mary C. Northern in consenting to surgical amputation of her lower extremities and of exercising such custodial supervision as is necessarily incident thereto at any time that Drs. Amos D. Tackett and R. Benton Adkins join in signing a written certificate that Mary C. Northern's condition has developed to such a critical stage as to demand immediate amputation to save her life.   The previous order of this Court is likewise so modified.

As modified, the order of the Chancellor is affirmed.   The cause is remanded for further appropriate proceedings including fixing of such additional guardian ad litem fee as may be appropriate.

Modified, Affirmed and Remanded.

IN RE SEIFERTH

Court of Appeals of New York, 1955.
309 N.Y. 80, 127 N.E.2d 820.

VAN VOORHIS, JUDGE.

This is a case involving a fourteen-year-old boy with cleft palate and harelip, whose father holds strong convictions with which the boy has become imbued against medicine and surgery.   This proceeding has been instituted by the deputy commissioner of the Erie County Health Department on petition to the Children's Court to have Martin declared a neglected child, and to have his custody transferred from his parents to the Commissioner of Social Welfare of Erie County for the purpose of consenting to such medical, surgical and dental services as may be necessary to rectify his condition.   The medical testimony is to the effect that such cases are almost always given surgical treatment at an earlier age, and the older the patient is the less favorable are likely to be the results according to experience.   The surgery recommended by the plastic surgeon called for petitioner consists of three operations: (1) repair of the harelip by bringing the split together; (2) closing the cleft or split in the rear of the palate, the boy being already too late in life to have the front part mended by surgery; and (3) repairing the front part of the palate by dental appliances.   The only risk of mortality is the negligible one due to the use of anesthesia.   These operations would be spaced a few months apart and six months would be expected to complete the work, two years at the outside in case of difficulty. Petitioner's plastic surgeon declined to be precise about how detrimental it would be to the prognosis to defer this work for several years. He said: "I do not think it is emergent, that is has to be done this month or next month, but every year that goes is important to this child, yes." A year and a half has already elapsed since this testimony was taken in December, 1953.

Even after the operation, Martin will not be able to talk normally, at least not without going to a school for an extended period for concentrated speech therapy. There are certain phases of a child's life when the importance of these defects becomes of greater significance. The first is past, when children enter grade school, the next is the period of adolescence, particularly toward the close of adolescence when social interests arise in secondary school. Concerning this last, petitioner's plastic surgeon stated: "That is an extremely important period of time. That child is approaching that age where it is very important that correction, that it is very significant that correction made at this time could probably put him in a great deal better position to enter that period of life than would otherwise. Another thing which is difficult is that we have very excellent speech facilities at the Buffalo Public Schools through grade level. At secondary school level and in higher age groups speech training facilities are less satisfactory, so that it is important that it be done at this age. However, the most important thing of all is this gradually progressive [sic] with time. The earlier done, the better results. Normally the lip is repaired in early infancy, one to three years of age. Speech training would begin at school or earlier. Every year lost has been that much more lost to the boy. Each year lost continues to be lost. The time to repair is not too early." He testified that in twenty years of plastic surgery he had never encountered a child with this boy's defects who had not been operated upon at his age. Nevertheless, he testified that such an operation can be performed "from the time the child is born until he dies." In this doctor's view, the consideation bulked larger than the quality of postoperative results, that the boys increasing social contacts required that he be made to look and to speak normally as he approached adolescence.

Everyone testified that the boy is likeable, he has a newspaper route, and his marks in school were all over 90 during the last year. However, his father did testify that recently the boy had withdrawn a little more from his fellows, although he said that "As soon as anyone contacts Martin, he is so likeable nobody is tempted to ridicule him. . . . Through his pleasantness he overcomes it."

The father testified that "If the child decides on an operation, I shall not be opposed", and that "I want to say in a few years the child should decide for himself . . . whether to have the operation or not." The father believes in mental healing by letting "the forces of the universe work on the body", although he denied that this is an established religion of any kind stating that it is purely his own philosphy and that "it is not classified as religion." There is no doubt, however, that the father is strong minded about this, and has inculcated a distrust and dread of surgery in the boy since childhood.

The Erie County Children's Court Judge caused the various surgical procedures to be explained to Martin by competent and qualified practitioners in the field of plastic surgery and orthodontia. Photographs of other children who had undergone similar remedial surgery were exhibited to him showing their condition both before and after treatment. He was also taken to the speech correction school where he heard the reproduction of his own voice and speech, as well as records depicting various stages of progress of other children. He met other children of his own age, talked to them and attended class in speech correction. Both the boy and the father were given opportunity to ask questions, which they did freely not only of the professional staff but of the different children.

On February 11, 1954, Martin, his father and attorney met after these demonstrations in Judge Wylegala's chambers. Judge Wylegala wrote in his opinion that Martin "was very much pleased with what was shown him, but had come to the conclusion that he should try for some time longer to close the cleft palate and the split lip himself through 'natural forces.'" After stating that an order for surgery would have been granted without hesitation if this proceeding had been instituted before this child acquired convictions of his own, Judge Wylegala summed up his conclusions as follows: "After duly deliberating upon the psychological effect of surgery upon this mature, intelligent boy, schooled as he has been for all of his young years in the existence of 'forces of nature' and his fear of surgery upon the human body, I have come to the conclusion that no order should be made at this time compelling the child to submit to surgery. His condition is not emergent and there is no serious threat to his health or life. He has time until he becomes 21 years of age to apply for financial assistance under County and State aid to physically handicapped children to have the corrections made. This has also been explained to him after he made known his decision to me." The petition accordingly was dismissed.

The Appellate Division, Fourth Department, reversed by a divided court, and granted the petition requiring Martin Seiferth to submit to surgery.

As everyone agrees, there are imporant considerations both ways. The Children's Court has power in drastic situations to direct the operation over the objection of parents. Nevertheless, there is no present emergency, time is less of the essence than it was a few years ago insofar as concerns the physical prognosis, and we are impressed by the circumstance that in order to benefit from the operation upon the cleft palate, it will almost certainly be necessary to enlist Martin's co-operation in developing normal speech patterns through a lengthy course in concentrated speech therapy. It will be almost impossible to secure his co-operation if he continues to believe, as he does now, that it will be necessary "to remedy the surgeon's distortion first and then go back to the primary task of healing the body." This is an aspect of the problem with which petitioner's plastic surgeon did not especially concern himself, for he did not attempt to view the case from the psychological view point of this misguided youth. Upon the other hand, the Children's Court Judge, who saw and heard the witnesses, and arranged the conferences for the boy and his father which have been mentioned, appears to have been keenly aware of this aspect of the situation, and to have concluded that less would be lost by permitting the lapse of several more years, when the boy may make his own decision to submit to plastic surgery, than might be sacrificed if he were compelled to undergo it now against his sincere and frightened antagonism. One cannot be certain of being right under these circumstances, but this appears to be a situation where the discretion of the trier of the facts should be preferred to that of the Appellate Division. Harrington v. Harrington, 290 N.Y. 126, 48 N.E.2d 290.

The order of the Appellate Division should be reversed and that of the Children's Court reinstated dismissing the petition, without prejudice to renew the application if circumstances warrant.

FULD, JUDGE (dissenting).

Every child has a right, so far as is possible, to lead a normal life and, if his parents, through viciousness or ignorance, act in such a way as to endanger that right, the courts should, as the legislature has provided, act on his behalf. Such is the case before us.

The boy Martin, twelve years old when this proceeding was begun, fourteen now, has been neglected in the most egregious way. He is afflicted with a massive harelip and cleft palate which not only grievously detract from his appearance but seriously impede his chances for a useful and productive life. Although medical opinion is agreed that the condition can be remedied by surgery, that it should be performed as soon as possible and that the risk involved is negligible, the father has refused to consent to the essential operation. His reason—which is, as the Appellate Division found, entirely unsubstantial—was that he relies on "forces in the universe" which will enable the child to cure himself of his own accord. He might consent to the operation, he said, if the boy "in a few years" should favor one.

It is quite true that the child's physical life is not at peril—as would be the situation if he had an infected appendix or a growth on the brain—but it may not be questioned, to quote from the opinion below, "What is in danger is his chance for a normal, useful life." Judge Van Voorhis does not, I am sure, take issue with that, but he feels that the boy will benefit, to a greater extent, from the operation if he enters the hospital with a mind favorably disposed to surgery. Therefore he counsels delay, on the *chance*—and that is all it is—on the *chance* that at some future time the boy may make his own decision to submit to plastic surgery.

It would, of course, be preferable if the boy were to accede to the operation, and I am willing to assume that, if he acquiesces, he will the more easily and quickly react to the postoperative speech therapy. However, there is no assurance that he will, either next year, in five years or six, give his consent. Quite obviously, he is greatly influenced by his father, quite plainly a victim of the latter's unfortunate delusions. And, beyond that, it must be borne in mind that there is little if any risk involved in the surgery and that, as time goes on, the operation becomes more difficult.

Be that as it may, though, it is the court which has a duty to perform, Children's Court Act, § 24, and it should not seek to avoid that duty by foisting upon the boy the ultimate decision to be made. Neither by statute nor decision is the child's consent necessary or material, and we should not permit his refusal to agree, his failure to co-operate, to ruin his life and any chance for a normal, happy existence; normalcy and happiness, difficult of attainment under the most propitious conditions, will unquestionably be impossible if the disfigurement is not corrected.

Moreover, it is the fact, and a vital one, that this is a proceeding brought to determine whether the parents are neglecting the child by refusing and failing to provide him with necessary surgical, medical and dental service, Children's Court Act, § 2, subd. 4, cl. (e). Whether the child condones the neglect, whether he is willing to let his parents do as they choose, surely cannot be operative on the question as to whether or not they are guilty of neglect. They are not interested or concerned with whether he does nor does not want the essential operation. They have arbitrarily taken the position that there is to be no surgery. What these parents are doing, by their failure to provide for an operation, however well-intentioned, is far worse than beating the child or denying him food or clothing. To the boy, and his future, it makes no difference that it may be ignorance rather than viciousness that will perpetuate his unfortunate condition. If parents are actually mistreating or neglecting a child, the circumstance that he may not mind it cannot alter the fact that they are guilty of neglect and it cannot render their conduct permissible.

The welfare and interests of a child are at stake. A court should not place upon his shoulders one of the most momentous and far-reaching decisions of his life. The court should make the decision, as the statute contemplates, and leave to the good sense and sound judgment of the public authorities the job of preparing the boy for the operation and of getting him as adjusted to it as possible. We should not put off decision in the hope and on the chance that the child may change his mind and submit at some future time to the operation.

The order of the Appellate Division should be affirmed.

HART v. BROWN

Superior Court of Connecticut, 1972.
29 Conn.Sup. 368, 289 A.2d 386.

TESTO, JUDGE.

This matter is before this court by way of an action for a declaratory judgment.

The plaintiffs are Peter Hart and Eleanor Hart, the parents and natural guardians of Katheleen A. Hart and Margaret H. Hart, minors, identical twins, age seven years and ten months. . . .

The plaintiff minor Katheleen A. Hart is presently a patient in the Yale-New Haven Hospital awaiting a kidney transplant. It is reasonably probable that if such procedure does not occur soon she will die. The defendant physicians have in the past performed successful kidney transplantation operations, and they are of the opinion that a successful transplantation operation can be performed on the plaintiff minors, Katheleen A. Hart as donee and Margaret H. Hart as donor.

The plaintiffs Peter Hart and Eleanor Hart, each of whom had originally offered a kidney, have requested as parents and natural guardians of the identical twins the transplantation operation of the kidney, but the defendant physicians are unwilling to perform this operation and the defendant hospital refuses the use of its facilities unless this court declares that the parents and/or guardians ad litem of the minors have the right to give their consent to the operation upon the minor twins.

. . .

The inherent power of a court of equity to grant the relief sought herein has been decided previously in our American courts. In earlier decisions, the English courts took a broader view of this power, with respect to incompetents. Ex parte Whitebread, 2 Mer. 99, 35 Eng.Rep. 878 (Ch.1816). That case held that a court of equity has the power to make provisions for a needy brother from the estate of an incompetent. This inherent rule was followed in this country in New York; Re Willoughby, 11 Paige 257 (N.Y.Ch.1844); where the court stated that a chancellor has the power to deal with the estate of an incompetent in the same manner as the incompetent if he had his faculties. This rule has been extended to cover not only property matters but also the personal affairs of an incompetent. 27 Am.Jur.2d 592, Equity, § 69. "[A] court of equity has full and complete jurisdiction over the persons of those who labor under any legal disability . . . . The court's action . . . is not limited by any narrow bounds, but it is empowered to stretch forth its arm in whatever direction its aid . . . may be needed. While this indeed is a special exercise of equity jurisdiction, it is beyond question that by virtue thereof the court may pass upon purely personal rights." Ibid. The right to act for an incompetent has been recognized as the "doctrine of substituted judgment" and is broad enough to cover all matters touching on the well-being of legally incapacitated persons. The doctrine has been recognized in American courts since 1844.

This court is not being asked to act where a person is legally incompetent. The matter, however, does involve two minors who do not have the legal capacity to consent. This situation was dealt with in three earlier unreported cases decided in our sister state of Massachusetts. The commonwealth of Massachusetts ruled that a court of equity does have the power to permit the natural parents of minor twins to give their consent to a procedure such as is being contemplated by this court. Masden v. Harrison, No. 68651, Eq.Mass.Sup.Jud.Ct. (June 12, 1957); Hushey v. Harrison, No. 68666, Eq.Mass.Sup.Jud.Ct. (Aug. 30, 1957); Foster v. Harrison, No. 68674, Eq.Mass.Sup.Jud.Ct. (Nov. 20, 1957). Those cases involved minors of the ages of nineteen, fourteen and fourteen. In a similar case, Strunk v. Strunk, 445 S.W.2d 145 (Ky.1969), a court of equity was confronted with whether or not it had the power to permit the natural parent of a twenty-seven-year-old mental incompetent with a mentality of a six-year-old to give her consent to a kidney transplantation operation. The Kentucky case dealt with a transplant from the mental incompetent to his twenty-eight-year-old brother. The court held that a court of equity does have such power, applying also the "doctrine of substituted judgment."

Therefore, this court is of the opinion that it has the power to act in this matter.

The facts of the case as testified to by competent medical witnesses are as follows: Katheleen Hart is a minor of the age of seven years and ten months and is suffering from a hemolytic uremic syndrome. This is a disorder of the kidneys with clots within the small blood vessels. This disease has no known etiology and is prevalent primarily in young children. The diagnosis was confirmed on November 29, 1971, after a kidney biopsy was performed. Hemodialysis treatments were commenced on December 8, 1971, along with other treatment to correct this disorder. On February 1, 1972, her kidney was biopsied for the second time because of the onset of a malignant type of blood pressure elevation, and this biopsy disclosed a new and more disastrous lesion—malignant hypertension—which could prove fatal. On February 17, 1972, a bilateral nephrectomy was performed with removal of both kidneys to control the situation. As of that date, Katheleen became a patient with fixed uremia with no potential kidney function and required dialysis treatments twice weekly. The prospect of survival is, because of her age, at best questionable. It was medically advised that she not continue this dialysis therapy but rather that a kidney transplantation take place.

The types of kidney transplantations discussed in this matter were a parental homograft—transfer of tissue from one human being to another—and an isograft, that is, a one-egg twin graft from one to another. The parental homograft always presents a serious problem of rejection by the donee. Because the human body rejects any foreign organs, the donee must be placed upon a program of immunosuppressive drugs to combat such rejection. An isograft transplantation, on the other hand, is not presented with the problem of rejection. A one-egg twin carries the same genetic material, and, because of this, rejection is not a factor in the success rate of the graft.

The chance of Katheleen's surviving dialysis therapy for a period of five years was estimated at fifty-fifty, with the possibility of many other complications setting in. The ultimate purpose of dialysis treatment in a child this age is to keep the patient alive until a kidney transplant is found. Because of the many complications involved in a transplantation procedure other than with the minor identical twin as donor, it has been medically advised that an isograft transplantation be recommended.

Since 1966, it is reported in the Ninth Report of the Human Renewal Transplant Registry, twelve twin grafts have been performed. All twelve have been successful, as reported by the Registry, at one- and two-year follow-ups. In the identical-twin donations since 1966, grafts are functioning at 100 percent. Before 1966, because of technical matters, the survival rate was about 90 percent. Of all isografts followed since 1966, all are successful. In this type of a graft there is substantially a 100 percent chance that the twins will live out a normal life span—emotionally and physically.

If a parent donates the kidney, the statistics show less success. The average percent of success in that type of transplant has been 70 percent at one year and 65 percent or so over a two-year period. The falloff thereafter runs another 5 to 10 or more percent per year. The long-range survival of a parent transplant runs around 50 to 55 percent over a period of five years and appears to fall off to about 37 percent over a period of seven years.

The side effects of the immunosuppressive drugs in a parental homograft are numerous and include the possibility of bone marrow toxicity, liver damage, and a syndrome called Cushing syndrome—a roundish face, a "buffalo hump" on the back of the neck, and growth retardation. Some less common side effects are a demineralization of the bone mass which will result in the collapsing of bones of the spine; aseptic necrosis of the femoral head of the hip, making a person unable to walk; peptic ulcer disease with bleeding; hairiness; sexual immaturity; and cataracts of the eyes. It has also been reported that two suicides have occurred because of the psychological effect upon young girls resulting from immunosuppressive drugs. An overall percentage of around 70 to 77 percent would be expected to survive two years from a parental graft. It is also possible that 40 to 50 percent of the patients might still be surviving at near ten years with a parental graft.

Of 3000 recorded kidney operations of live donors, there is reported only one death of a donor, and even this death may have been from causes unrelated to the procedure. The short-range risk to a donor is negligible. The operating surgeon testified that the surgical risk is no more than the risk of the anesthesia. The operative procedure would last about two and one-half hours. There would be some minor postoperative pain but no more than in any other surgical procedure. The donor would be hospitalized for about eight days and would be able to resume normal activities in thirty days. Assuming an uneventful recovery, the donor would thereafter be restricted only from violent contact sports. She would be able to engage in all of the normal life activities of an active young girl. Medical testimony indicated that the risk to the donor is such that life insurance actuaries do not rate such individuals higher than those with two kidneys. The only real risk would be trauma to the one remaining kidney, but testimony indicated that such trauma is extremely rare in civilian life.

The tests to be performed on the donor are an intravenous pyelogram and an aortagram. The former would permit the examiner to visualize the structure and anatomy of the kidneys, while the latter would outline the blood vessels that supply the blood to the kidneys. Both tests involve a single needle puncture—one into a vein and one into an artery. There might be a skin graft test performed if necessary to confirm the fact that donor and donee are identical twins. The operation would not be performed if the medical team was not fully satisfied that the donor and the donee are identical twins.

A psychiatrist who examined the donor gave testimony that the donor has a strong identification with her twin sister. He also testified that if the expected successful results are achieved they would be of immense benefit to the donor in that the donor would be better off in a family that was happy than in a family that was distressed and in that it would be a very great loss to the donor if the donee were to die from her illness.

The donor has been informed of the operation and insofar as she may be capable of understanding she desires to donate her kidney so that her sister may return to her. A clergyman was also a witness and his testimony was that the decision by the parents of the donor and donee was morally and ethically sound. The court-appointed guardian ad litem for the donor gave testimony that he conferred with the parents, the physicians, the donor, and other men in the religious profession, and he has consented to the performance of the operation.

The medical testimony given at this hearing clearly indicates that scientifically this type of procedure is a "perfect" transplant.

The court has weighed the testimony of the clergyman who stated that the natural parents are making a morally sound decision. Also, the testimony of the court-appointed guardians ad litem was that they are giving their consent to the procedure. The psychiatric testimony is of limited value only because of the ages of the minors. The testimony of the natural parents was reviewed by this court, and it is apparent that they came to their decision only after many hours of agonizing consideration.

One of the legal problems in this matter presents a balancing of the rights of the natural parents and the rights of minor children—more directly, the rights of the donor child. Because of the unusual circumstances of this case and the fact of great medical progress in this field, it would appear that the natural parents would be able to substitute their consent for that of their minor children after a close, independent and objective investigation of their motivation and reasoning. This has been accomplished in this matter by the participation of a clergyman, the defendant physicians, an attorney guardian ad litem for the donor, the guardian ad litem for the donee, and, indeed, this court itself.

A further question before this court is whether it should abandon the donee to a brief medically complicated life and eventual death or permit the natural parents to take some action based on reason and medical probability in order to keep both children alive. The court will choose the latter course, being of the opinion that the kidney transplant procedure contemplated herein—an isograft—has progressed at this time to the point of being a medically proven fact of life. Testimony was offered that this type of procedure is not clinical experimentation but rather medically accepted therapy.

There is authority in our American jurisdiction that nontherapeutic operations can be legally permitted on a minor as long as the parents or other guardians consent to the procedure. Bonner v. Moran, 75 U.S. App.D.C. 156, 126 F.2d 121 (1941). That case involved skin grafting from a fifteen-year-old boy to his cousin, who was severely burned. The year of the case was 1941, when such skin homografting—transferring tissue from one human being to another—was relatively novel. "[H]ere we have a case of a surgical operation not for the benefit of the person operated on but for another, and also so involved in its technique as to require a mature mind to understand precisely what the donor was offering to give." Id., 123. The court held that the consent of the parent was necessary.

. . .

The court understands that the operation on the donee is a necessity for her continued life; that there are negligible risks involved to both donor and donee; that to subject the donee to a parental homograft may be cruel and inhuman because of the possible side effects of the immunosuppressive drugs; that the prognosis for good health and long life to both children is excellent; that there is no known opposition to having the operations performed; that it will be most beneficial to the donee; and that it will be of some benefit to the donor. To prohibit the natural parents and the guardians ad litem of the minor children the right to give their consent under these circumstances, where there is supervision by this court and other persons in examining their judgment, would be most unjust, inequitable and injudicious. Therefore, natural parents of a minor should have the right to give their consent to an isograft kidney transplantation procedure when their motivation and reasoning are favorably reviewed by a community representation which includes a court of equity.

. . .

Judgment accordingly.

NOTE

There is substantial disagreement about the relative roles of children, parents, health care providers, and the state in decisionmaking about the treatment of children. (See Ch. 7, Sec. B.4, infra.) One position particularly critical of the approach followed in Hart v. Brown is expressed by Prof. Joseph Goldstein of Yale Law School in Medical Care for the Child at Risk: On State Supervention of Parental Authority, 86 Yale L.J. 645, 669–670 (1977):

The doctors recommended and the Hart parents consented to the "unnecessary" surgery on Margaret to provide Katheleen with an opportunity to pursue a relatively normal life. But the hospital administration and the doctors refused to accept parental consent without a court review. They acted out of a concern for their livelihood, not for the lives or well-being of Margaret or of Katheleen. Understandably, they feared becoming liable for money damages because the law might not accept parental consent as a defense to assault and malpractice, were such suits brought.

The Harts were thus forced to turn to the state to establish either their authority to decide on the rightness of their decision. They initiated a declaratory judgment action. There followed hearings and proceedings before Judge Robert Testo which intruded massively on the privacy of the family and set a dangerous precedent for state interference with parental autonomy. There was no *probable cause* to suspect that the parents might be exploiting either of their children, only that the doctors and administrators in refusing to accept the parental choice might be risking the well-being of both children and the family. The court upheld the parental choice, though not their autonomy to decide.

Although Judge Testo's decision avoided tragic consequences for the Harts, he did set a precedent for unwarranted and undesirable intervention by the state. . . .

Had the Hart parents refused to consent to Margaret's surgery and the transplant of her kidney to Katheleen, equally unwarranted proceedings might have been brought to establish their neglect in order to obtain court authority to impose the doctors' recommendation. Doctors can, because of their special training, make diagnoses and prognoses; doctors can indicate the probable consequences for a Margaret or a Katheleen of pursuing one course or another. But absent a societal consensus, nothing in their training, or for that matter in the training of judges, qualifies them to impose upon others their preferred value choices about what the good or better is for such children or for their families. The critical fallacy is to assume as Judge Testo does in his declaratory judgment—as the legislature does in its laws of neglect and abuse—that the training and offices of doctors, legislators, and judges endow them not just with the authority but also with the capacity to determine what risks to take for someone else's child, in circumstances where there is no right or wrong answer or set of answers.

In addition to concern about the integrity of the family, what attitude should the law take about the role of the children themselves in decisions about their own medical care?

The orthodox answer . . . to the question—when the authority to make medical decisions will be denied to children on grounds of "incompetence"—is "always" or "almost always." But a discernible trend has been set in motion by the ever-broadening case and statutory law "exceptions" to the rule of incompetence, pushed forward by constitutional law decisions that give greater scope to the "privacy" and self-determination of minor as well as adult patients, and given credibility by comparable rules in other areas of Amercian law and the jurisprudence of other countries. Projecting its further development, an unorthodox but defensible answer to the question at issue would be: a child with the capacity to give informed consent has the legal authority (i.e., "competence") to do so.

Such a rule would make competence dependent on the individual child's capacity first to understand the procedure, second to reach an intelligent judgment about it in light of its risks, benefits, and alternatives, and third to possess sufficient independence to articulate and maintain any judgment voluntarily made, even when it differs from those taken by others, such as relatives and professionals. In many ways this standard is a difficult one to meet; it goes beyond that established in the law of informed consent regarding adult patients and subjects. The difference is justifiable, for there is no reason for society completely to dismiss a realistic concern to protect people who lack sufficient self-protective ability. But approaching the question from the vantage of competence rather than incompetence means that each child is assumed to be a possible self-decider (if he or she is capable of giving informed consent) rather than being presumed incapable and permitted to show otherwise in only certain limited circumstances.

Formulating the rule of medical decision making for minors in the newer way should not pose a heavy burden on physicians and biomedical scientists. In effect the task of the professional is comparable to that already existing under the law of informed consent. A professional would be reasonable in expecting to find few, if any, seven-, ten-, or even fourteen-year-olds with the requisite ability to give informed consent—but the law need not require the professional to insist on transferring authority to someone else in the case of a child who *does* possess such ability. Conversely, the professional may encourage even older minors to involve their parents (or other relevant adults) in the decision-making process; furthermore, in nonemergent situations, nothing prevents a physician or other professional from declining to go ahead on the sole authority of a minor who asserts, but does not convince the professional of, his or her adequacy as a self-decision maker. As elsewhere, this right of "conscience" can be preserved without jeopardizing the interest of all people in not being deprived of their autonomy by application of state power. Rules of thumb adopted by individuals although occasionally burdensome are seldom as oppressive as rules of law applied across the board. The vantage point discerned to be emerging replaces the rule of law that viewed young people as inherently incapable of understanding and analyzing matters affecting their own welfare with one that begins with at least an open mind about each person's capabilities. Through such a change in official rules may come changes in personal attitudes and behavior, for the law not only symbolizes the present but molds the future.

Capron, The Competence of Children as Self-Deciders in Biomedical Interventions in Who Speaks for the Child 57, 89–90 (W. Gaylin & R. Macklin eds. 1982).

GUARDIANSHIP OF ROE

Supreme Judicial Court of Massachusetts, 1981.
383 Mass. 415, 421 N.E.2d 40.

HENNESSEY, CHIEF JUSTICE.

The ultimate question we address in this case is whether the guardian of a mentally ill person possesses the inherent authority to consent to the forcible administration of antipsychotic medication to his noninstitutionalized ward in the absence of an emergency.

. . .

On April 1, 1980, after a hearing on the petition of Richard Roe, Jr. (the guardian), and his wife, a judge of the Probate Court found that the guardian's son, Richard Roe, III (the ward), was a mentally ill person whose judgment was seriously impaired and who was in need of the immediate appointment of a guardian. At this hearing the ward was represented by a guardian ad litem. The judge appointed the father temporary guardian of the ward, who, since February 19, 1980, had been committed to Northampton State Hospital for observation and report in connection with complaints against him for attempted unarmed robbery and assault and battery. Since the ward was still institutionalized at the time of the hearing, the judge . . . decided that the temporary guardian had the inherent authority to consent to forcible administration of antipsychotic drugs for his ward. On April 4, 1980, prior to the implementation of such medical treatment, the guardian ad litem's motion to stay entry of judgment was allowed by the probate judge . . . as to the administration of antipsychotic drugs. . . .

On May 27 and June 19, 1980, evidentiary hearings on the temporary guardian's petition for appointment as permanent guardian were held in the Probate Court before the same judge. The Commissioner of the Massachusetts Department of Mental Health, represented by the Attorney General, was allowed to intervene in both the Probate Court and this court. On July 30, 1980, the probate judge appointed the temporary guardian to be permanent guardian, stating in his order that upon the vacating of the stay issued by the single justice the permanent guardian would have the authority to consent to the forcible administration of antipsychotic medication to the ward.

In his appeal the guardian ad litem raises several issues. He first contends that the evidence was insufficient to permit the probate judge to make the findings which were used to support the appointments of both the temporary and permanent guardians, and that such evidence must be tested by the "beyond a reasonable doubt" standard of proof. He takes the further position that even if the evidence was sufficient to permit these findings, the challenged findings are insufficient as a matter of law to warrant the guardianship appointments. The guardian ad litem finally contends that even if the evidence was sufficient to support the findings, and the findings are sufficient to warrant the guardianship appointments, it was error for the probate judge to empower the guardian to consent to the forcible administration of antipsychotic drugs for the ward. . . . [W]e hold that both the temporary and permanent guardianship appointments were warranted by the evidence as evaluated under the "preponderance of the evidence" standard of proof, and the findings were legally sufficient, although we agree with the guardian ad litem that to empower the guardian to consent to the challenged medical treatment was error.

. . .

II.   The Decision to Administer Antipsychotic Drugs to the Ward.

. . . We must decide whether the substituted judgment determination to be made in cases such as this may be delegated to the guardian. The probate judge found that the guardian did *not* propose to authorize forcible administration of antipsychotic drugs[7] immediately but rather sought contingent authority to administer such drugs if certain anticipated events took place. Under these circumstances, the question presented by the guardian was hypothetical, and any substituted judgment determination made was premature. However, the judge did in fact authorize the guardian to consent to administration of antipsychotic medication for the ward. We conclude that this was error. [B]ecause of the likelihood of further proceedings in this case and the necessity of making similar determinations in other cases, we establish guidelines regarding the criteria to be used and the procedures to be followed in making a substituted judgment determination. . . .

. . .

A.   Need for a Court Order.

The primary dispute in this case concerns the means by which the ward is to exercise his right to refuse treatment, a right which the ward possesses but is incapable of exercising personally.[9] The guardian's posi-

7. Two drugs—Haldol (haloperidol) and Prolixin (fluphenazine)—were recommended for the ward. Although these drugs are occasionally referred to as "psychotropic" drugs, they are more accurately described as "antipsychotic" drugs. See note 10 infra.

9. That such a right exists is indisputable. "[A] person has a constitutionally protected interest in being left free by the state to decide for himself whether to submit to the serious and potentially harmful medical treatment that is represented by the administration of antipsychotic drugs." *Rogers II,* [634 F.2d 650 (1st Cir.1980)] supra at 653. The source of this right according to *Rogers II,* supra, lies in the "Due Process Clause of the Fourteenth Amendment . . . , most likely as part of the penumbral right to privacy, bodily integrity, or personal security." Id. Other courts have discussed in individual's First Amendment right to maintain the integrity of his mental processes. See Scott

tion is that the power to exercise this right on behalf of the ward is vested in the guardian simply by virtue of his appointment as guardian. The ward claims that he is entitled to a judicial determination of substituted judgment. . . . We think that this question is best resolved by requiring a judicial determination in accordance with the substituted judgment doctrine.

We have in the past stated our preference for judicial resolution of certain legal issues arising from proposed extraordinary medical treatment. Superintendent of Belchertown State School v. Saikewicz, 373 Mass. 728, 759, 370 N.E.2d 417 (1977). Matter of Spring, 380 Mass. 629, 636, 405 N.E.2d 115 (1980). We reaffirm this preference in the circumstances shown here. . . .

The question presented by the ward's refusal of antipsychotic drugs is only incidentally a medical question. Absent an overwhelming State interest, a competent individual has the right to refuse such treatment. To deny this right to persons who are incapable of exercising it personally is to degrade those whose disabilities make them wholly reliant on other, more fortunate, individuals. In order to accord proper respect to this basic right of all individuals, we feel that if an incompetent individual refuses antipsychotic drugs, those charged with his protection must seek a judicial determination of substituted judgment. No medical expertise is required in such an inquiry, although medical advice and opinion is to be used for the same purposes and sought to the same extent that the incompetent individual would, if he were competent. We emphasize that the determination is *not* what is medically in the ward's best interests—a determination better left to those with extensive medical training and experience. The determination of what the incompetent individual would do if competent will probe the incompetent individual's values and preferences, and such an inquiry, in a case involving antipsychotic drugs, is best made in courts of competent jurisdiction.

There is no bright line dividing those decisions which are (and ought to be) made by a guardian, from those for which a judicial determination is necessary. The tension which makes such a line so difficult to draw is apparent. There is an obvious need for broad, flexible, and responsive guardianship powers, but simultaneously there is a need to avoid the serious consequences accompanying a well-intentioned but mistaken exercise of those powers in making certain medical treatment decisions.

We have recently identified the factors to be taken into account in deciding when there must be a court order with respect to medical treatment of an incompetent patient. . . . Without intending to indicate the relative importance of these and other factors in all cases, it is appro-

v. Plante, 532 F.2d 939, 946 (3d Cir.1976); Mackey v. Procunier, 477 F.2d 877, 878 (9th Cir.1973); Rogers I, [478 F.Supp. 1342 (D.Mass.1979)] at 1366–1367. We ground this right firmly in the constitutional right to privacy, which we have previously described as "an expression of the sanctity of individual free choice and self-determination as fundamental constituents of life." Superintendent of Belchertown State School v. Saikewicz, 373 Mass. 728, 742, 370 N.E.2d 417 (1977). We find support as well in the inherent power of the court to prevent mistakes or abuses by guardians, whose authority comes from the Commonwealth and the courts. Buckingham v. Alden, 315 Mass. 383, 389, 53 N.E.2d 101 (1944). Chase v. Chase, 216 Mass. 394, 397, 103 N.E. 857 (1914). Hicks v. Chapman, 10 Allen 463, 465 (1865). The third factor upon which we rely is the common law right of every person "of adult years and sound mind . . . to determine what shall be done with his own body." Schloendorff v. Society of N.Y. Hosp., 211 N.Y. 125, 129, 105 N.E. 92 (1914) (Cardozo, J.). We have held that the incompetence of a ward does not allow his guardian to exercise vicariously this common law right regarding extraordinary treatment. *Saikewicz*, supra.

priate to identify some of those factors which are weighty considerations in this particular case. . . .

(1) *The intrusiveness of the purposed treatment.*   We can identify few legitimate medical procedures which are more intrusive than the forcible injection of antipsychotic medication.[10]   "In general, the drugs influence chemical transmissions to the brain, affecting both activatory and inhibitory functions.   Because the drugs' purpose is to reduce the level of psychotic thinking, it is virtually undisputed that they are mind-altering." [Rogers v. Okin, 478 F.Supp. 1342, 1360 (D.C.Mass.1979) (Rogers I); affirmed in part, reversed in part, 634 F.2d 650 (1st Cir.1980) (Rogers II)]. A single injection of Haldol, one of the antipsychotic drugs proposed in this case, can be effective for ten to fourteen days.   The drugs are powerful enough to immobilize mind and body.   Because of both the profound effect that these drugs have on the thought processes of an individual and the well-established likelihood of severe and irreversible adverse side effects, we treat these drugs in the same manner we would treat psychosurgery or electroconvulsive therapy. . . .   The record in this case indicates that if the drugs were mistakenly administered to a nonpsychotic individual, then that individual might develop a "toxic psychosis," causing him to suffer symptoms of psychosis.   While the actual physical invasion involved in the administration of these drugs amounts to no more than an injection, the impact of the chemicals upon the brain is sufficient to undermine the foundations of personality.

While antipsychotic drugs can actually lessen the amount and intensity of psychotic thinking, among the most important reasons for their continued use is to control behavior.[11] . . .

(2) *The possibility of adverse side effects.*   Although, as we establish above, the intended effects of antipsychotic drugs are extreme, their unintended effects are frequently devastating and often irreversible.   The adverse side effects accompanying administration of antipsychotic drugs have been known since the late 1950's.   Baldessarini & Lapinski, Risks vs. Benefits of Antipsychotic Drugs, 289 New England J.Med. 427, 428 (1973). " '[T]oxic' effects regularly accompany the use of antipsychotic drugs to ameliorate schizophrenic symptoms.   The most common results are the

---

10.   The doctors who testified in the proceedings below used the terms psychotropic ("acting on the mind") and antipsychotic ("tending to alleviate psychosis or psychotic states") interchangeably.   Webster's New Collegiate Dictionary, at 50, 924 (1979). The distinction between the two terms has been subject to confusion in the past.   See *Rogers II*, supra at 653 n. 1.   The specific drugs recommended in this case, Prolixin (fluphenazine) and Haldol (haloperidol), are both classed as "major tranquilizers" or "neuroleptics."   Plotkin, Limiting the Therapeutic Orgy: Mental Patients' Right to Refuse Treatment, 72 Nw.U.L.Rev. 461, 474 n. 75 and n. 77 (1977).   See generally Physicians' Desk Reference 1116–1118, 1728–1733 (35th ed. 1981).   Their use is characterized by "(1) marked sedation, without sleep; (2) effectiveness in the most intensely agitated and excited patient; (3) progressive disappearance of symptoms in acute and chronic psychoses; (4) extra-pyramidal reac-

tion; and (5) subcortical site of action" Plotkin, supra at 474 n. 75.   We refer to these drugs as "antipsychotic" drugs, "a more generally accepted and less confusing designation than other terminology." American   College   of   Neuropsychopharmacology-Food and Drug Administration Task Force, Neurologic Syndromes Associated with Antipsychotic Drug Use, 289 New England J.Med. 20, 20 (1973).

11.   The obvious potential for misuse of these drugs provides an additional reason to require judicial approval prior to the forcible use of antipsychotic drugs upon incompetent individuals.   Another court, which in the past has not required court orders regarding the termination of life support equipment, now requires a court order before administration of treatment which had been "subject to abuse in the past."   In re Grady, 85 N.J. 235, 252, 426 A.2d 467, 475 (1981).

temporary, muscular side effects (extra-pyramidal symptoms) which disappear when the drug is terminated; dystonic reactions (muscle spasms, especially in the eyes, neck, face, and arms; irregular flexing, writhing or grimacing movements; protrusion of the tongue); akathesia (inability to stay still, restlessness, agitation); and Parkinsonisms (mask-like face, drooling, muscle stiffness and rigidity, shuffling gait, tremors). Additionally, there are numerous other nonmuscular effects, including drowsiness, weakness, weight gain, dizziness, fainting, low blood pressure, dry mouth, blurred vision, loss of sexual desire, frigidity, apathy, depression, constipation, diarrhea, and changes in the blood. Infrequent, but serious, nonmuscular side effects, such as skin rash and skin discoloration, ocular changes, cardiovascular changes, and occasionally, sudden death, have also been documented.

"The most serious threat phenothiazines [one type of antipsychotic drug] pose to a patient's health is a condition known as tardive dyskinesia. This effect went unrecognized for years because its symptoms are often not manifested until late in the course of treatment, sometimes appearing after discontinuation of the drug causing the condition. Tardive dyskinesia is characterized by involuntary muscle movements, often in the oral region. The associated rhythmic movements of the lips and tongue (often mimicking normal chewing, blowing, or licking motions) may be grotesque and socially objectionable, resulting in considerable shame and embarrassment to the victim and his or her family. Additionally, hypertrophy of the tongue and ulcerations of the mouth may occur, speech may become incomprehensible, and, in extreme cases, swallowing and breathing may become difficult. To date, tardive dyskinesia has resisted curative efforts, and its disabling manifestations may persist for years.

. . .

(3) *The absence of an emergency.* The evidence presented in the proceedings below makes it quite clear that the probate judge was not presented with a situation which could accurately be described as an emergency. We accept the dictionary definition of "emergency": "an unforeseen combination of circumstances or the resulting state that calls for immediate action." Webster's Third New Int'l Dictionary, at 741 (1961). Medical evidence showed that the ward apparently had been schizophrenic for four years, without more than slight or temporary improvement, and that without treatment his mental health could deteriorate. Expert testimony indicated that the prognosis for most individuals with untreated schizophrenia was "gradual worsening." . . . We think that the possibility that the ward's schizophrenia might deteriorate into a chronic, irreversible condition at an uncertain but relatively distant date does not satisfy our definition of emergency, especially where, as here, the course of the illness is measured by years and no crisis has been precipitated.

We are not called upon here to decide under which circumstances an emergency might relieve a guardian from the obligation of seeking a judicial determination of substituted judgment which would otherwise be required. We do, however, emphasize that in determining whether an emergency exists in terms of requiring "immediate action," the relevant time period to be examined begins when the claimed emergency arises, and ends when the individual who seeks to act in the emergency could, with reasonable diligence, obtain judicial review of his proposed actions. This time period will, of course, be brief—as we noted in *Matter of Spring,* supra at 636, 405 N.E.2d 115, "expedited decision can be obtained when appropriate." We recognize that "the interests of the patient himself would [not] be furthered by requiring responsible [parties] to stand by and watch him slip into possibly chronic illness while awaiting an adjudication." *Rogers II*, supra at 660. However, the evidence shows that this is not such a case—in fact, unless the course of a disease is measured by hours, there need never be such a case in the courts of this Commonwealth. We are certain that every judge recognizes that in any case where there is a possibility of immediate, substantial, and irreversible deterioration of a serious mental illness, even the smallest of avoidable delays would be intolerable.

(4) *The nature and extent of prior judicial involvement.* For the past four years the ward has rejected antipsychotic medication on every occasion on which it has been offered, and there has been no judicial finding of incapacity relative to many of these occasions. It is possible that in some cases, although not in the instant case, a mentally ill ward may retain sufficient competence to make treatment decisions himself, thereby eliminating the need for a substituted judgment determination. It has been held that patients involuntarily committed to State mental hospitals are entitled to a judicial determination of incapacity before they may be forcibly medicated with mind-altering drugs.[14] *Rogers II*, supra, at 661. This is because the "commitment decision itself is an inadequate predicate to the forcible administration of drugs to an individual where the purported justification for that action is the State's *parens patriae* power." Id. at 659. . . . A person is presumed to be competent unless shown by the evidence not to be competent. Lane v. Candura, 6 Mass.App. 377, 382, 376 N.E.2d 1232 (1978). Similarly, in the absence of an independent finding of incompetency to make treatment decisions, we cannot assume that a mentally ill ward lacks the capacity to make a treatment decision of this magnitude.

In a case such as the one before us, some judicial involvement is unavoidable inasmuch as the judge must: (1) appoint the guardian, and (2) determine the ward's competency to make treatment decisions. This significant and inescapable prior judicial involvement eliminates much concern we might otherwise have about requiring a further judicial determination, since one of the factors we consider in deciding whether the guardian is to make the substituted judgment determination is the amount of additional time which will be needed to obtain a judicial determination. While this prior involvement is not conclusive in and of itself, it is a factor to be considered in determining whether a court order must be obtained.

(5) *The likelihood of conflicting interests.* Decisions such as the one the guardian wishes to make in this case pose exceedingly difficult problems for even the most capable, detached, and diligent decisionmaker. We intend no criticism of the guardian when we say that few parents could make this substituted judgment determination—by its nature a self-centered determination in which the decisionmaker is called upon to ignore all but the implementation of the values and preferences of the ward— when the ward, in his present condition, is living at home with other children. . . . Nor do we think that the father was not a suitable person to be appointed guardian. Those characteristics laudable in a parent might often be a substantial handicap to a guardian faced with such a decision but who might in all other circumstances be an excellent guardi-

___

14. We express no opinion concerning whether such a finding is sufficient judicial involvement to permit other persons to make subsequent medical treatment decisions for involuntarily committed patients.

an. A judicial determination also benefits the guardian, who otherwise might suffer from lingering doubts concerning the propriety of his decision.

Each individual involved, when called upon to participate in the substituted judgment determination, is assisting in the attempt to determine the ward's values and preferences. The guardian will usually play a major role in this process. The formalities and discipline inherent in a judicial determination will impress upon all involved the need for objectivity and selflessness. We are convinced that in this case, as in other cases, the regularity of the procedure—guaranteed by a judicial determination—will ensure that objectivity which other processes might lack.

B.   Relevant Factors in the Substituted Judgment Determination.

The immediate question confronting us is resolved by our conclusion that, when a timely determination needs to be made, it is to be made by a judge. . . .

The factors we identify below are to be considered by the probate judge in order to identify the choice "which would be made by the incompetent person, if that person were competent, but taking into account the present and future incompetency of the individual as one of the factors which would necessarily enter into the decision-making process of the competent person." Superintendent of Belchertown State School v. Saikewicz, 373 Mass. 728, 752–753, 370 N.E.2d 417 (1977). The determination must "give the fullest possible expression to the character and circumstances of that individual." Id. at 747, 370 N.E.2d 417. We observe that this is a subjective rather than an objective determination. Cf. id. at 746–747, 370 N.E.2d 417. All persons involved in such an inquiry will readily admit that the bounds of relevance therefor are exceedingly broad. In this search, procedural intricacies and technical niceties must yield to the need to know the actual values and preferences of the ward. In this spirit we briefly identify the following relevant factors, ...

(1) *The ward's expressed preferences regarding treatment.* If the ward has expressed a preference while not subjected to guardianship—and presumably competent, such an expression is entitled to great weight in determining his substituted judgment unless the judge finds that either: (a) simultaneously with his expression of preference the ward lacked the capacity to make such a medical treatment decision, or (b) the ward, upon reflection and reconsideration, would not act in accordance with his previously expressed preference in the changed circumstances in which he currently finds himself.

. . .

(2) *The ward's religious beliefs.* An individual might choose to refuse treatment if the acceptance of such treatment would be contrary to his religious beliefs. If such a reason is proffered by or on behalf of an incompetent, the judge must evaluate it in the same manner and for the same purposes as any other reason: the question to be addressed is whether certain tenets or practices of the incompetent's faith would cause him individually to reject the specific course of treatment proposed for him in his present circumstances. . . . While in some cases an individual's beliefs may be so absolute and unequivocal as to be conclusive in the substituted judgment determination, in other cases religious practices may be only a relatively small part of the aggregated considerations.

(3) *The impact upon the ward's family.* An individual who is part of a closely knit family would doubtless take into account the impact his acceptance or refusal of treatment would likely have on his family. Such a factor is likewise to be considered in determining the probable wishes of one who is incapable of formulating or expressing them himself. In any choice between proposed treatments which entail grossly different expenditures of time or money by the incompetent's family, it would be appropriate to consider whether a factor in the incompetent's decision would have been the desire to minimize the burden on his family. If this factor would have been considered by the individual, the judge must enter it into the balance of making the substituted judgment determination. If an incompetent has enjoyed close family relationships and subsequently is forced to choose between two treatments, one of which will allow him to live at home with his family and the other of which will require the relative isolation of an institution, then the judge must weigh in his determination the affection and assistance offered by the incompetent's family. We note, however, that the judge must be careful to avoid examination of these factors in any manner other than one actually designed and intended to effectuate the incompetent's right to self-determination. . . .

(4) *The probability of adverse side effects.* We have described the adverse side effects of antipsychotic medication. . . . Clearly any competent patient choosing whether to accept such treatment would consider the severity of these side effects, the probability that they would occur, and the circumstances in which they would be endured.

(5) *The consequences if treatment is refused.* If the prognosis without treatment is that an individual's health will steadily, inevitably and irreversibly deteriorate, then that person will, in most circumstances, more readily consent to treatment which he might refuse if the prognosis were more favorable or less certain. This general rule, however, will not always indicate whether an individual would, if competent, accept treatment. . . . This factor must be utilized to reach an individual determination. . . .

(6) *The prognosis with treatment.* We think it can fairly be stated as a general proposition that the greater the likelihood that there will be cure or improvement, the more likely an individual would be to submit to intrusive treatment accompanied by the possibility of adverse side effects. Additionally, professional opinion may not always be unanimous regarding the probability of specific benefits being received by a specific individual upon administration of a specific treatment. Both of these factors— the benefits sought and the degree of assurance that they actually will be received—are entitled to consideration.

Finally, the judge . . . should address, . . . each of the six factors as well as any others relevant in the case before him. He is to make written findings for each factor indicating within each finding those reasons both for and against treatment. Following this he must analyze the relative weight of the findings in that particular case. If the determination is to accept treatment, the judge is to order its administration. If the determination is to refuse treatment, the judge may order treatment only in accordance with the procedures we discuss in Part C, infra.

C. The Accommodation of Overriding State Interests.

There are circumstances in which the fundamental right to refuse extremely intrusive treatment must be subordinated to various State interests.

(1) *The State interests involved.* Among the State interests which we have identified in our prior cases are: "(1) the preservation of life; (2) the protection of the interests of innocent third parties; (3) the prevention of suicide; and (4) maintaining the ethical integrity of the medical profession." *Saikewicz,* supra, at 741, 370 N.E.2d 417. These four State interests are not exhaustive, and other State interests may also deserve consideration. . . .

In the present case the judge found that the State had a vital interest in seeing that its residents function at the maximum level of their capacity and that this interest outweighed the rights of the individual. We disagree. While the State, in certain circumstances, might have a generalized parens patriae interest in removing obstacles to individual development, this general interest does not outweigh the fundamental individual rights here asserted.[20]

. . . In the past we have interpreted the phrase "the protection of the interests of innocent third parties" as representing the State's interest in protecting minor children from the emotional and financial consequences of the decision of a competent adult to refuse life-saving or life-prolonging treatment.[21] Id. at 741–743, 370 N.E.2d 417. We have identified this as a State interest of considerable magnitude. Equally deserving of such regard is the State interest in preventing the infliction of violence upon members of the community by indivuduals suffering from severe mental illness. This is a second aspect of the State interest in protecting innocent third parties. Although few would question that this interest is capable of overriding the individual's right to refuse treatment, a substantial question remains as to the likelihood of violence which must be established in order to support forced administration of antipsychotic medication.

(2) *The standard of proof required to justify administration of antipsychotic drugs to an unconsenting, noninstitutionalized individual.* Once it is recognized that the State's interest in the prevention of violence is capable of overriding the individual's right to refuse, it must also be recognized that the character of the government intrusion then changes. The primary purpose of the treatment is not to implement the substituted judgment of the incompetent, nor is it intended to administer treatment thought to be in his best interests. It bears emphasis that public safety then becomes the primary justification for such treatment. Under these circumstances antipsychotic drugs function as chemical restraints forcibly imposed upon an unwilling individual who, if competent, would refuse such treatment. Ex-

---

20. The factors which concerned the judge—the natural desire to prevent suffering and the need of each individual to maintain and improve his capabilities—are better viewed as likely foundations of individual preference to be considered in the substituted judgment determination. See Part II B(5), supra. Where the medical evidence, unchallenged at every turn and unimpeachable in its sincerity, shows that treatment will maintain or regain competence, this is a weighty factor to be considered by the judge as it would be considered by the affected individual. It is not conclusive, however. If the judge feels that the "best interests" of the ward demand one outcome but concludes that the ward's substituted judgment

would require another, then, in the absence of an overriding State interest, the substituted judgment prevails. In short, if an individual would, if competent, make an unwise or foolish decision, the judge must respect that decision as long as he would accept the same decision if made by a competent individual in the same circumstances. . . . We digress concerning this "right to be wrong" only to establish the relationship between the "best interests" standard and the substituted judgment determination. . . .

21. This particular aspect of the State interest is inapplicable in the instant case because the ward is unmarried and has no minor children.

amined in terms of personal liberty, such an infringement is at least the equal of involuntary commitment to a State hospital. Accordingly, we think that the same standard of proof is applicable in both involuntary commitment and involuntary medication proceedings.

In order to commit an individual to a State hospital without his consent, the likelihood of serious harm must be established beyond a reasonable doubt. In G.L. c. 123, § 1, as amended through St.1980, c. 571, § 1 (the statute governing involuntary commitment), the likelihood of serious harm is defined as "(1) a substantial risk of physical harm to the person himself as manifested by evidence of threats of, or attempts at, suicide or serious bodily harm; (2) a substantial risk of physical harm to other persons as manifested by evidence of homicidal or other violent behavior or evidence that others are placed in reasonable fear of violent behavior and serious physical harm to them; or (3) a very substantial risk of physical impairment or injury to the person himself as manifested by evidence that such person's judgment is so affected that he is unable to protect himself in the community and that reasonable provision for his protection is not available in the community." Absent criminal conduct, this statutory definition establishes the earliest moment at which the State may intervene to deny an individual his liberty based upon a prediction of future harmfulness. The State may not justify its intervention on a lower standard merely because it proposes to utilize antipsychotic drugs rather than physical restraints.

(3) *The extended substituted judgment determination.* Since the standard of proof is the same for both involuntary commitment and involuntary administration of antipsychotic medication, in any case where the State's interest in preventing violence in the community has been found sufficient to override the individual's right to refuse treatment, two means are then available for protecting this State interest.[23] In such cases, that lesser intrusive means of restraint which adequately protects the public safety is to be used.[24] . . . In order to satisfy the least intrusive means test, the incompetent is entitled to choose, by way of substituted judgment, between involuntary commitment and involuntary medication. Such an extended substituted judgment proceeding differs from the substituted judgment determination we describe in Part II B, supra, only in that the outcome is limited to involuntary commitment or involuntary medication.[25]

23. We do not mean to suggest that once an individual has been involuntarily committed he is then subject to involuntary medication because his potential harmfulness had been established by his commitment. We have defined the State interest here as the prevention of violence in the community. By "community" we mean those persons likely to encounter the mentally ill individual outside of an institutional setting. This State interest is extinguished when the individual is institutionalized. We do not address the question of whether and to what extent the State interest in *institutional* order and safety may be capable of overwhelming the right of an involuntarily committed individual to refuse medical treatment.

24. We are unwilling to establish a universal rule as to which is less intrusive—involuntary commitment or involuntary medication with mind-altering drugs. Since we feel that such a determination must be individually made, we conclude that the lesser intrusive means is the means of restraint which would be chosen by the ward if he were competent to choose.

25. We do not perceive any State interest here sufficient to override the incompetent's right to self-determination. Certainly the public safety provides no such interest since it is sufficiently protected by restricting the incompetent's options to these two alternatives.

III.   The Limits of Our Decision.

. . .

While we emphasize those conclusions we have reached and the circumstances in which they are to be utilized, it is prudent to note that our guidelines are not directed toward a single case but rather identify the decisionmaking processes necessary to reach outcomes in a type of case. It is apparent from our decision today that the right of an individual to refuse treatment is not absolute but is, rather, a right to be counterbalanced against State interests. The proper balance to be struck in a given situation can only be determined after examining the specifically defined and precisely articulated interests of those who are or will be actually affected by the decision. The weight to be afforded these interests is impossible to predetermine, and the balance will vary according to the circumstances of those asserting the interests. For these reasons, we decline to strike the balance in any individual case. Specifically, we decline to rule on the right of patients confined against their will to State hospitals to refuse antipsychotic medication. We do not mean to imply that these patients' rights are wholly unprotected or that their circumstances are entirely dissimilar to those we have discussed. We do suggest, however, that it would be imprudent to establish prematurely the relative importance of adverse interests when each may be capable of being controlling and each draws its importance from the circumstances in which it is asserted.

The ward in this case, though institutionalized at the time the temporary guardian was appointed, is currently living at home and has done so for many months. Indeed, the two occasions on which he was institutionalized were for observation and report pursuant to G.L. c. 123, §§ 15(*b*) and 16(*a*), and were not involuntary civil commitments. The guardian cannot now institutionalize the ward unless he establishes beyond a reasonable doubt that failure to commit would create a likelihood of serious harm. Doe v. Doe, 377 Mass. 272, 385 N.E.2d 995 (1979). No antipsychotic medication has yet been administered to him.

In addition to observing that it would be improper to establish the extent to which persons other than a noninstitutionalized individual in a nonemergency situation are entitled to a judicial substituted judgment determination, we wish to emphasize as well that in this case we treat the ward's right to a determination only in so far as it concerns antipsychotic medication. The spectrum of medical care available to individuals and the diverse circumstances in which it may be administered do not permit us to make universal rules in anticipation of cases involving different treatment or different circumstances. Even when a medical treatment decision is confined to a single set of circumstances, it is often difficult to formulate and apply a uniform and predictable standard.

. . . We . . . vacate the order in so far as it allows the ward to be medicated over his objection. The remainder of the order, appointing Richard Roe, Jr., as guardian of his son, Richard Roe, III, is affirmed.

So ordered.

NOTES

1. Rogers II was reversed and remanded by the Supreme Court sub nom. Mills v. Rogers, 457 U.S. 291, 102 S.Ct. 2442, 73 L.Ed.2d 16 (1982). The Court held that Guardianship of Roe raises the possibility that Massachusetts recognizes

liberty interests of incompetent persons that are broader than those protected by the Constitution of the United States.

2. The President's Commission, Making Health Care Decisions 177–178 (1982) states:

. . . [T]wo different standards . . . have traditionally guided decisionmaking for the incapacitated: "substituted judgment" and "best interests." Although these standards are now used in health care situations, they have their origins in a different context—namely, the resolution of family disputes and decisions about the control of the property of legal incompetents. When people become seriously disabled and unable to manage their property, they may be judged incompetent and a guardian appointed to make financial and property decisions. These doctrines were developed to instruct guardians about the boundaries of their powers without issuing detailed and specific guidelines and to provide a standard for guidance of courts that must review decisions proposed by a guardian.

Simply stated, under the substituted judgment standard, the decisions made for an incapacitated person should attempt to arrive at the same choice the person would make if competent to do so (but within boundaries of "reasonableness" intended to protect the incompetent). Under the best interests standard, decisions are acceptable if they would promote the welfare of the hypothetical "average person" in the position of the incompetent, which may not be the same choice the individual would make (but which may still have some aspects of subjectivity to it).

Despite the long legal history of both these standards, they provide only hazy guidance for decisionmaking even in their original contexts, not to mention in the often far more complex, urgent, and personal setting of health care. Although a number of recent cases involving decisions about health care for incapacitated patients have given courts the opportunity to clarify these often vague guidelines, increased confusion may have accompanied some of the attempts to add precision to these doctrines.

In your view, did the courts in the cases above use the appropriate standards? For additional discussion of the standards by which to make judgments for incompetent persons, see Ch. 7, Sec. B.4, infra.

3. Consider Professor John Rawls's justification for use of the "substituted judgment" standard:

In the original position the parties assume that in society they are rational and able to manage their own affairs. Therefore they do not acknowledge any duties to self, since this is unnecessary to further their good. But once the ideal conception is chosen, they will want to insure themselves against the possibility that their powers are undeveloped and they cannot rationally advance their interests, as in the case of children; or that through some misfortune or accident they are unable to make decisions for their good, as in the case of those seriously injured or mentally disturbed. It is also rational for them to protect themselves against their own irrational inclinations by consenting to a scheme of penalties that may give them a sufficient motive to avoid foolish actions and by accepting certain impositions designed to undo the unfortunate consequences of their imprudent behavior. For these cases the parties adopt principles stipulating when others are authorized to act in their behalf and to override their present wishes if necessary; and this they do recognizing that sometimes their capacity to act rationally for their good may fail, or be lacking altogether.

Thus the principles of paternalism are those that the parties would acknowledge in the original position to protect themselves against the weakness and infirmities of their reason and will in society. Others are authorized and sometimes required to act on our behalf and to do what we would do for ourselves if we were rational, this authorization coming into effect only when we cannot look after our own good. Paternalistic decisions are to be guided by the individual's own settled preferences and interests insofar as they are not irrational, or failing a knowledge of these, by the theory of primary goods. As we know less and less about a person, we act for him as we would act for ourselves from the standpoint of the original position. We try to get for him the things he presumably wants whatever else he wants. We must be able to argue that with the development or the recovery of his rational powers the individual in question will accept our decision on his behalf and agree with us that we did the best thing for him.

The requirement that the other person in due course accepts his condition is not, however, by any means sufficient, even if this condition is not open to rational criticism. Thus imagine two persons in full possession of their reason and will who affirm different religious or philosophical beliefs; and suppose that there is some psychological process that will convert each to the other's view, despite the fact that the process is imposed on them against their wishes. In due course, let us suppose, both will come to accept conscientiously their new beliefs. We are still not permitted to submit them to this treatment. . . .

J. Rawls, A Theory of Justice 248–250 (1971).

4. Should there be formal review procedures in some circumstances when others have made health care decisions for incompetent persons? What form should such review take? Consider the statement of the President's Commission, Making Health Care Decisions 187–188 (1982):

To provide an alternative that is more responsive to the needs of all parties, "institutional ethics committees" [21] are increasingly being used. Because they are closer to the treatment setting, because their deliberations are informal and typically private (and are usually regarded by the participants as falling within the general rules of medical confidentiality), and because they can reconvene easily or can delegate decisions to a separate subgroup of members, ethics committees may have some marked advantages over judicial review when it comes to decisionmaking that is rapid and sensitive to the issues at hand. Furthermore, testimony presented to the Commission indicated that these committees have had a valuable educational role for professionals.

Very little is known, however, about the actual effectiveness of institutional ethics committees, especially in comparison with private, informal mechanisms or with judicial decisionmaking for patients who lack decisionmaking capacity. The composition and functions of existing ethics committees vary substantially from one institution to another. Not enough experience has accumulated to date to know the appropriate and most effective functions and hence the suitable composition of such committees. If their role is to serve primarily as "prognosis committees" to pass on the accuracy of an attending physician's judgment, then committees composed largely of physicians would seem appropriate. If the ethics committees are supposed to reach decisions that best reflect the individually defined well-being of patients or the ethicality of decisions, however, it seems doubtful that an exclusively medical group would be suitable. And if the appropriate role of such review bodies should be to determine whether a surrogate decisionmaker is qualified to make medical decisions on a patient's behalf (and to set only outer boundaries on the nature of the decision reached rather than second-guessing the choice), membership should be diverse.

Alternative institutional and private arrangements, formal and informal, deserve careful examination and evaluation. Furthermore, important details, such as means of case referral, range of functions, committee composition, protection of privacy, and legal status, have not been debated, much less resolved. From what little is already known, it seems that ethics committees may be able to take a leading role in formulating and disseminating policy on decisionmaking for incapacitated patients, assisting in the resolution of difficult sit-

---

21. The Commission uses the term "institutional ethics committee" rather than "hospital ethics committee" because such committees could well function in other health care institutions such as nursing homes.

uations, and protecting the interests of incapacitated patients. Although committees can be reasonably prompt, efficient, sensitive, and private, having many of the decisions about health care for the incapacitated made in an informal manner between surrogate and provider is plainly a desirable objective as well, just as routine decisions for competent patients should be made by patient and provider without any outside intervention. Furthermore, just as judicial review may sometimes be an unnecessarily onerous means of reviewing medical decisions, review by an ethics committee may also sometimes be inappropriate.

The Commission believes there should be various kinds of review mechanisms available. Thus, the Commission recommends that health care institutions not only develop appropriate mechanisms but also encourage and cooperate in comparative evaluations of such approaches. The results of these studies will have particular importance for society because one presumed advantage of institutional mechanisms is that they avoid the undesirable aspects of having to turn to more formal means of review. Assurance that any new mechanisms have been well thought out and are appropriate to the task is needed before widespread official sanctions can be expected.

3. WHAT MATTERS REQUIRE COLLECTIVE ACTION—AND HOW?

PRESIDENT'S COMMISSION FOR THE STUDY OF ETHICAL PROBLEMS IN MEDICINE AND BIOMEDICAL AND BEHAVIORAL RESEARCH, IMPLEMENTING HUMAN RESEARCH REGULATIONS

45–48 (1983).*

The Role of the Nonscientific and Unaffiliated Members of the IRB. HHS regulations require that each IRB [Institutional Review Board] be "sufficiently qualified through the experience and expertise of its members, and the diversity of the members' backgrounds . . . and sensitivity to such issues as community attitudes, to promote respect for its advice and counsel." More specifically,

> In addition to possessing the professional competence necessary to review specific research activities, the IRB shall be able to ascertain the acceptability of proposed research in terms of institutional commitments and regulations, applicable law, and standards of professional conduct and practice. The IRB shall therefore include persons knowledgeable in the these areas. If an IRB regularly reviews research that involves a vulnerable category of subjects, . . . the IRB shall include one or more individuals who are primarily concerned with the welfare of these subjects.[37]

Furthermore, each IRB must include at least one member whose primary concerns are in nonscientific areas (for example, lawyers, ethicists, members of the clergy) and each IRB must include at least one member who is not otherwise affiliated with the institution.

Although the regulations would appear to require considerable diversity among IRB members, they are apparently satisfied if the IRB includes one member who is a layperson, lawyer, or clergy unaffiliated with the institution. How many IRBs fulfill the requirement in this way is un-

---

* The relevant regulations are set forth in   **37.**   45 CFR 46.107.
ch. 6, Sec. A.3 infra [Eds.]

known. In addition, it is not clear what role such an individual should serve.

A variety of purposes or roles of nonscientist and community members on IRBs have been suggested: (1) to provide additional perspectives and offset professional narrowness of focus; (2) to provide advice on local laws, customs, values and attitudes; (3) to provide ethical analysis and guidance; (4) to represent the human subjects' interests; (5) to force scientists to examine their work—and their defense of their work—more critically; (6) to open the review process to community participation; (7) to enhance the confidence of the community in the research enterprise; and (8) to assist in assuring the adequacy and understandability of the information to be conveyed to prospective subjects. One might well ask whether a single individual can be expected to perform so many functions. One might also question the extent to which the inclusion of a single lawyer, member of the clergy, or a "community representative" (as they are sometimes called) fulfills any useful function in an IRB that may number as many as 15–25 people.

When local review was first initiated, it was in the form of peer review (i.e., review by other scientists). In the mid-1960s, however, scholars began to examine more carefully the need for adequate review of research with human subjects and the concept that nonscientists should be included on review boards began to gain support. . . .

. . . .

In the 1969 issue of *Daedalus,* in one of the earliest published materials on research with human subjects, William Curran suggested that perhaps NIH should encourage institutions to widen the membership of their review committees. He noted that lawyers would be useful for assuring adequate procedures and advising on matters of local law. The role of philosophers in discussing ethical issues was, he thought, equally clear; similarly, he believed that members of the clergy might be interested not only in ethical principles but also in particular religious beliefs and in the welfare of individuals (presumably, the research subjects). The role of other professionals, businessmen, and laymen he viewed as equally important, as

> forcing the professionals to interpret their deliberations and decisions to these general community representatives. Lay members will thus tend to transform the committee from closed associations of like-minded professionals who 'understand' one another into a more open forum of community responsibility.[40]

Curran also viewed IRB lay members as "consumers" sharing in community decisionmaking; and he suggested that perhaps research subjects should be included among members of review committees.[41]

The regulations and earlier NIH policy statements suggest that someone on the IRB should represent community attitudes. As Bernard Barber and his colleagues observed in 1973, however, it is hard to see how any one person could represent the "full diversity of the local community or the society." [42] Barber recommended that IRBs include "informed ousiders," knowledgeable about relevant laws, codes, and norms, as well as about the nature and purposes of biomedical research and survey tech-

---

40. William Curran, The Approach of Two Federal Agencies, 98 Daedalus 583–84 (Spring 1969).

41. Id.

42. Bernard Barber et al., Research on Human Subjects, Russell Sage Foundation, New York (1973) at 195.

niques (useful for discovering the attitudes and values of a representative sample of the population). They also suggested that active participation of community members on such committees "might forestall the possibility of a hostile public reaction against biomedical research."[43]

The National Commission for the Protection for Human Subjects believed that "to guard against self-interest influencing or appearing to influence IRB determinations," at least one-third of the IRB members should be nonscientists.[44] They further noted that "it is desirable that the IRB show awareness and appreciation of the various qualities, values and needs of the diverse elements of the community served by the institution or in which it is located."[45] In Denmark, half the members of ethics review committees must be nonscientists; these lay members are appointed by the local county councils.[46]

More recently, attention has focused on the usefulness of lay members in assuring that the information to be conveyed to prospective subjects is both adequate and clearly presented.[47] Many IRBs seek the advice of their lay members on the wording of consent documents; indications are that they can be very helpful in this regard.

NOTE

Should the federal regulations require more than one lay member on each IRB? More than one member unaffiliated with the institution? How likely is a lay member to make an extensive contribution to IRB deliberations? Should lay members be expected to focus primarily on the adequacy of informed consent forms? Are lay members likely to perform effectively where deliberations concern complex scientific and technical data? See, e.g., Ch. 1, Sec. B.2, supra for a discussion of the inclusion of lay members on the Recombinant DNA Advisory Committee (RAC). See also DuVal, The Human Subjects Protection Committee: An Experiment in Decentralized Federal Regulation, American Bar Foundation Journal 571 (1979).

BOREL v. FIBREBOARD PAPER PRODUCTS CORP.

United States Court of Appeals for the Fifth Circuit, 1973.
493 F.2d 1076.

WISDOM, CIRCUIT JUDGE:

This product liability case involves the scope of an asbestos manufacturer's duty to warn industrial insulation workers of dangers associated with the use of asbestos,

. . .

I.

Clarence Borel began working as an industrial insulation worker in 1936. During his career, he was employed at numerous places, usually in

43. Id. at 196–97.

44. Report and Recommendations: Institutional Review Boards, supra note 2, at 14.

45. Id.

46. Povl Riis, Experience with Committees and Councils for Research Ethics in Scandinavia, paper presented at the Research Ethics Symposium, Oslo, Norway (Aug. 1982).

47. W.E. Waters, Role of the Public in Monitoring Research With Human Subjects, in National Institutes of Health, Issues in Research With Human Subjects, U.S. Government Printing Office, Washington (1980); Joan M. Ghio, Inquiry: What is the Role of a Public Member on an IRB?, 2 IRB 7 (Feb. 1980).

Texas, until disabled by the disease of asbestosis in 1969. Borel's employment necessarily exposed him to heavy concentrations of asbestos dust generated by insulation materials. In his pre-trial deposition, Borel testified that at the end of a day working with insulation material containing asbestos his clothes were usually so dusty he could "just barely pick them up without shaking them." Borel stated: "You just move them just a little and there is going to be dust, and I blowed this dust out of my nostrils by handfuls at the end of the day, trying to use water too, I even used Mentholatum in my nostrils to keep some of the dust from going down in my throat, but it is impossible to get rid of all of it. Even your clothes just stay dusty continually unless you blow it off with an air hose."

Borel said that he had known for years that inhaling asbestos dust "was bad for me" and that it was vexatious and bothersome, but that he never realized that it could cause any serious or terminal illness. Borel emphasized that he and his fellow insulation workers thought that the dust "dissolves as it hits your lungs". He said:

A. Yes, I knew the dust was bad but we used to talk [about] it among the insulators, [about] how bad was this dust, could it give you TB, could it give you this, and everyone was saying no, that dust don't hurt you, it dissolves as it hits your lungs. That was the question you get all the time.

Q. Where would you have this discussion, in your Union Hall?

A. On the jobs, just among the men.

Q. In other words, there was some question in your mind as to whether this was dangerous and whether it was bad for your health?

A. There was always a question, you just never know how dangerous it was. I never did know really. If I had known I would have gotten out of it.

Q. All right, then you did know it had some degree of danger but you didn't know how dangerous it was?

A. I knew I was working with insulation.

Q. Did you know that it contained asbestos?

A. Yes, sir, but I didn't know what asbestos was.

When asked about the use of respirators, Borel replied that they were not furnished during his early work years. Although respirators were later made available on some jobs, insulation workers usually were not required to wear them and had to make a special request if they wanted one. Borel stated that he and other insulation workers found that the respirators furnished them were uncomfortable, could not be worn in hot weather, and—"you can't breathe with the respirator." Borel further noted that no respirator in use during his lifetime could prevent the inhalation of asbestos dust. As an alternative precaution, therefore, he would sometimes wear a wet handkerchief over his nostrils or apply mentholatum, but these methods were also unsatisfactory and did not exclude all the dust.

Borel stated that throughout his early working life and until the mid-1960's he was in good health, except for pains caused by lung congestion that his doctor attributed to pleurisy. In 1964, a doctor examined Borel in connection with an insurance policy and informed him that x-rays of his lung were cloudy. The doctor told Borel that the cause could be his occupation as an insulation worker and therefore advised him to avoid asbestos dust as much as he possibly could.

On January 19, 1969, Borel was hospitalized and a lung biopsy performed. Borel's condition was diagnosed as pulmonary asbestosis. Since the disease was considered irreversible, Borel was sent home. Borel testified in his deposition that this was the first time he knew that he had asbestosis.

Borel's condition gradually worsened during the remainder of 1969. On February 11, 1970, Borel underwent surgery for the removal of his right lung. The examining doctors determined that Borel had a form of lung cancer known as mesothelioma, which had been caused by asbestosis. As a result of these diseases, Borel later died before the district case reached the trial stage.

The medical testimony adduced at trial indicates that inhaling asbestos dust in industrial conditions, even with relatively light exposure, can produce the disease of asbestosis. The disease is difficult to diagnose in its early stages because there is a long latent period between initial exposure and apparent effect. This latent period may vary according to individual idiosyncrasy, duration and intensity of exposure, and the type of asbestos used. In some cases, the disease may manifest itself in less than ten years after initial exposure. In general, however, it does not manifest itself until ten to twenty-five or more years after initial exposure. This latent period is explained by the fact that asbestos fibers, once inhaled, remain in place in the lung, causing a tissue reaction that is slowly progressive and apparently irreversible. Even if no additional asbestos fibers are inhaled, tissue changes may continue undetected for decades. By the time the disease is diagnosable, a considerable period of time has elapsed since the date of the injurious exposure. Furthermore, the effect of the disease may be cumulative since each exposure to asbestos dust can result in additional tissue changes. A worker's present condition is the biological product of many years of exposure to asbestos dust, with both past and recent exposures contributing to the overall effect. All of these factors combine to make it impossible, as a practical matter, to determine which exposure or exposures to asbestos dust caused the disease.

A second disease, mesothelioma, is a form of lung cancer caused by exposure to asbestos. It affects the pleural and peritoneal cavities, and there is a similarly long period between initial contact and apparent effect. As with asbestosis, it is difficult to determine which exposure to asbestos dust is responsible for the disease.

At issue in this case is the extent of the defendants' knowledge of the dangers associated with insulation products containing asbestos. We pause, therefore, to summarize the evidence relevant to this question.

Asbestosis has been recognized as a disease for well over fifty years.[3] The first reported cases of asbestosis were among asbestos textile workers. In 1924, Cooke in England discovered a case of asbestosis in a person who had spent twenty years weaving asbestos textile products. In the next decade, numerous similar cases were observed and discussed in medical journals. . . . In the United States, the first official claim for compensation associated with asbestos was in 1927.[6] By the mid-1930's

---

3. Asbestos has been known to man since ancient times. As a generic term, it applies to a number of inorganic, fibrous, silicate minerals that possess a crystaline structure. Asbestos is incombustible in air and separable into filaments. It was used as an insulator against heat as early as 1866, and asbestos cement was introduced about 1870. Asbestos insulation material has been commercially produced since at least 1874.

6. Lanza, Asbestosis, 106 J.A.M.A. 368 (1936).

the hazard of asbestosis as a pneumoconiotic dust was universally accepted.[7] Cases of asbestosis in insulation workers were reported in this country as early as 1934.[8] The U.S. Public Health Service fully documented the significant risk involved in asbestos textile factories in a report by Dreessen et al., in 1938.[9] The authors urged precautionary measures and urged elimination of hazardous exposures.

The first large-scale survey of asbestos insulation workers was undertaken in the United States by Fleischer-Drinker et al., in 1945.[10] The authors examined insulation workers in eastern Navy shipyards and found only three cases of asbestosis. They concluded that "asbestos covering of naval vessels is a relatively safe operation." Significantly, ninety-five percent of those examined had worked at the trade for less than ten years. Since asbestosis is usually not diagnosable until ten to twenty years after initial exposure, the authors' conclusion has been criticized as misleading.[11] Perhaps recognizing this possibility, the authors cautioned that the study did not "give a composite picture of the asbestos dust that a worker may breathe over a period of years", and that "if pipe coverers had worked steadily [under conditions] where the amount of asbestos dust in the air was consistently high, the incidence of asbestosis among these workers would have been considerably greater." The authors stated that "the suggestions relative to exhaust ventilation and respiratory protection are therefore of value in maintaining this low incidence of asbestosis".[12]

In 1947, the American Conference of Governmental Industrial Hygienists, a quasi-official body responsible for making recommendations concerning industrial hygiene, issued guidelines suggesting threshold limit values for exposure to asbestos dust. In its first report, the ACGIH recommended that there should be no more than five million parts per cubic foot of air. It later determined in 1968 that the threshold limit value should be reduced to two million.[13]

Throughout the 1950's and 1960's, further studies and medical reports on asbestosis were published. In 1965, I.J. Selikoff and his colleagues published a study entitled "The Occurrence of Asbestosis Among

7. H.R.Rep. No. 14816, 90th Cong., 2d Sess. 349, 355 (1968). Dr. I. J. Selikoff of the School of Environmental Sciences Laboratory, Mount Sinai School of Medicine, City University of New York, stated:

. . . It is an unhappy reflection on all of us—government, public health authorities, and my own medical profession—that at this time in the United States in the 1960's 7 percent of all deaths among insulation workers in this country are due to a completely preventable cause, pulmonary asbestosis.

8. Ellman, Pneumoconiosis, 14 Brit.J. Radiol. 361 (1934).

9. Dreessen et al., A Study of Asbestosis in the Asbestos Textile Industry, Public Health Bull. No. 241 (1938).

10. Fleischer, Viles, Gade and Drinker, A Health Survey of Pipe-Covering Operations in Constructing Naval Vessels, 28 J.Indust. Hyg. 9–16.

11. Selikoff et al., Asbestosis and Neoplasia, 42 Am.J.Med. 487 (1967).

12. Fleischer, supra note 10 at 15.

13. See Documentation of the Threshold Limit Values for Substances in Workroom Air, A.C.G.I.H. (3 ed. 1971) The A.C. G.I.H. has described the threshold limit values as "conditions under which it is believed that nearly all workers may be repeatedly exposed, day after day, without adverse effect. The values list refer to time-weighted average concentrations for a normal workday. The amount by which these figures may be exceeded for short periods without injury to health depends upon a number of factors such as the nature of the contaminant, whether very high concentrations even for short periods produce acute poisoning, whether the effects are cumulative, the frequency with which high concentrations occur, and the duration of such periods."

See Threshold Limit Values for 1961, A.C. G.I.H. (1961).

Insulation Workers in the United States." [14]   The authors examined 1,522 members of an insulation workers union in the New York-New Jersey metropolitan area.   Evidence of pulmonary asbestosis was found in almost half the men examined.   Among those with more than forty years experience, abnormalities were found in over ninety percent.   The authors concluded that "asbestosis and its complications are significant hazards among insulation workers."   Other studies have since confirmed these findings.[16]

The plaintiff introduced evidence tending to establish that the defendant manufacturers either were, or should have been, fully aware of the many articles and studies on asbestosis.   The evidence also indicated, however, that during Borel's working career no manufacturer ever warned contractors or insulation workers, including Borel, of the dangers associated with inhaling asbestos dust or informed them of the ACGIH's threshold limit values for exposure to asbestos dust.   Furthermore, no manufacturer ever tested the effect of their products on the workers using them or attempted to discover whether the exposure of insulation workers to asbestos dust exceeded the suggested threshold limits.

On October 20, 1969, Borel initiated the present diversity action in the United States District Court for the Eastern District of Texas.   Borel named as defendants eleven manufacturers of asbestos insulation materials used by him during his working career.   He settled with four defendants before trial.   The trial court instructed a verdict as to a fifth. . . .   Borel died before trial and his widow was substituted as plaintiff under the Texas wrongful death statutes.

The plaintiff sought to hold the defendants liable for negligence, gross negligence, and breach of warranty or strict liability.   The negligent acts alleged in the complaint were: (1) failure to take reasonable precautions or to exercise reasonable care to warn Borel of the danger to which he was exposed as a worker when using the defendants' asbestos insulation products; (2) failure to inform Borel as to what would be safe and sufficient wearing apparel and proper protective equipment and appliances or method of handling and using the various products; (3) failure to test the asbestos products in order to ascertain the dangers involved in their use; and (4) failure to remove the products from the market upon ascertaining that such products would cause asbestosis.   The plaintiff also alleged that the defendants should be strictly liable in warranty and tort.   The plaintiff contended that the defendants' products were unreasonably dangerous because of the failure to provide adequate warnings of the foreseeable dangers associated with them.

The defendants denied the allegations in the plaintiff's complaint and interposed the defenses of contributory negligence and assumption of risk.

The trial court submitted the case to the jury on general verdicts accompanied by a special interrogatory as to Borel's contributory negligence.   As to the negligence count, the jury found that all the defendants, except [two] were negligent but that none of the defendants had been

14. Selikoff, Churg, and Hammond, The Occurrence of Asbestosis Among Industrial Insulation Workers, 132 Ann. New York Acad.Sc. 139 (1965).

16. Recognition of the grave occupational health problem posed by asbestos and other toxic and physically harmful substances has led to the passage of the Occupational Safety and Health Act of 1970, 29 U.S.C. § 651 et seq., 84 Stat. 1590.   The Act gives the Secretary of Labor the authority to establish standards for permissible concentrations of airborne asbestos fibers.

grossly negligent. It found also, however, that Borel had been contributorily negligent.

As to the strict liability count, the jury found that all the defendants were liable and determined that the total damages were $79,436.24. The defendants appealed.

II.

At the outset, we meet the question whether the trial court properly instructed the jury on strict liability.

. . .

. . . In general, "[t]he rule of strict liability subjects the seller to liability to the user or consumer even though he has exercised all possible care in the preparation and sale of the product". Section 402A, Comment a [Restatement (Second) of Torts (1964)]. This is not the case where the product is alleged to be unreasonably dangerous because of a failure to give adequate warnings. Rather, a seller is under a duty to warn of only those dangers that are reasonably foreseeable. The requirement of foreseeability coincides with the standard of due care in negligence cases in that a seller must exercise reasonable care and foresight to discover a danger in his product *and to warn users and consumers of that danger.* Davis v. Wyeth Laboratories, Inc., 9 Cir.1968, 399 F.2d 121.

As the plaintiff has argued, insulation materials containing asbestos may be viewed as "unavoidably unsafe products". As explained in comment k to section 402A of the Restatement, "unavoidably unsafe products" are those which, in the present state of human knowledge, are incapable of being made safe for their ordinary and intended use. Strict liability may not always be appropriate in such cases because of the important benefits derived from the use of the product. This is especially so with respect to new drugs that are essential in treating disease but involve a high degree of risk. It may also be so with respect to other commercial products possessing both unparalled utility and unquestioned danger. As a practical matter, the decision to market such a product requires a balancing of the product's utility against its known or foreseeable danger. But, as comment k makes clear, even when such balancing leads to the conclusion that marketing is justified, the seller still has a responsibility to inform the user or consumer of the risk of harm. The failure to give adequate warnings in these circumstances renders the product unreasonably dangerous. . . . The rationale for this rule is that the user or consumer is entitled to make his own choice as to whether the product's utility or benefits justify exposing himself to the risk of harm. Thus, a true choice situation arises, and a duty to warn attaches, whenever a reasonable man would want to be informed of the risk in order to decide whether to expose himself to it.

. . .

So it is with the case at bar. The utility of an insulation product containing asbestos may outweigh the known or foreseeable risk to the insulation workers and thus justify its marketing. The product could still be unreasonably dangerous, however, if unaccompanied by adequate warnings. An insulation worker, no less than any other product user, has a right to decide whether to expose himself to the risk.

. . .

For the reasons stated, the decision of the district court is affirmed.

ON PETITION FOR REHEARING AND PETITION
FOR REHEARING EN BANC

All of the defendants-appellants have moved for a rehearing en banc.

I.

Three of the movants, Johns-Manville Corporation, Fibreboard Corporation, and Ruberoid Company contend that the Court erred in basing its opinion on "the overriding factor" of "the alleged failure of the defendants to at any time warn Borel of the dangers involved in working with asbestos insulation while employed by various independent contractors". They state that the record shows that Johns-Manville placed a warning label on packages of its products in 1964, and that Fibreboard and Ruberoid placed warning labels on their products in 1966. (Borel filed suit in 1969.) The three warnings were substantially the same. Johns-Manville's read as follows:

"This product contains asbestos fiber.

"Inhalation of asbestos in excessive quantities over long periods of time may be harmful.

"If dust is created when this product is handled, avoid breathing the dust.

"If adequate ventilation control is not possible wear respirators approved by the U.S. Bureau of Mines for pneumoconiosis producing dusts."

It should be noted that none of these so-called "cautions" intimated the gravity of the risk: the danger of a fatal illness caused by asbestosis and mesothelioma or other cancers. The mild suggestion that inhalation of asbestos in excessive quantities over a long period of time "*may* be harmful" conveys no idea of the extent of the danger. The admonition that a worker should "avoid breathing the dust" is black humor: There was no way for insulation workers to avoid breathing asbestos dust. As for wearing respirators if adequate ventilation control is not possible, Borel and other insulators never worked in any place where there was adequate ventilation, and respirators were ineffective: "you can't breathe with the respirator".

Within the trial judge's instructions, the jury could have concluded that the "cautions" were not warnings in the sense that they adequately communicated to Borel and other insulation workers knowledge of the dangers to which they were exposed so as to give them a choice of working or not working with a dangerous product. . . .

. . .

NOTES

1. *Borel* illustrates two types of problems with relying on individuals to control technology: difficulties individuals face in exercising choice before an injury and difficulties they face in affecting others' conduct through litigation after an injury has occurred. On the first point, does Judge Wisdom seem to believe that it is possible for workers to control their exposure to asbestos? If not, why is it wrong to fail to warn them of the dangers involved? The Occupational Safety and Health Administration now requires this warning: "Caution—Contains Asbestos Fibers—Avoid Creating Dust—Breathing Asbestos Dust May Cause Serious Bodily Harm." 29 C.F.R. § 1910.1001(g)(2)(ii) (1983).

2.   Suits to redress workers' injuries until recently have been brought primarily under state workers compensation laws, which make damages easier to collect by eliminating the need to prove negligence or product defects and defenses based on workers' misconduct.   Yet the amounts awarded under workers compensation are usually much less than awards similar injuries would receive in tort suits.   In addition there are institutional differences between workers compensation and tort suits: workers compensation cases are typically decided before commissions, not juries; and contingent fees that attorneys receive in workers compensation suits are usually in the range of 10 percent, rather than the 33–50 percent in tort suits.   It is not surprising, therefore, that injured workers and their attorneys have turned increasingly to the tort system—usually through suits against manufacturers or suppliers of products used in the workplace—as a source of redress.

Nevertheless, plaintiff's counsel faces formidable problems in such cases.   See T. Henderson, Product Liability Disease Litigation: Blueprint for Occupational Safety and Health, 16 Trial 25 (1980).

3.   Some important changes are occurring in "toxic tort" litigation, however. For example, the New Jersey Supreme Court struck down the "medical state of the art" defense in Beshada v. Johns-Manville Products Corp., 90 N.J. 191, 447 A.2d 539 (1982).   The court ruled that such a defense is a negligence defense, while in strict liability "culpability is irrelevant."   Therefore the state of the art defense is invalid in strict liability actions.   Some courts have attempted to ease the burden on plaintiffs (and to increase judicial economy) through procedural changes, e.g., limiting the available defenses.   One federal district court had extended the plaintiff's use of collateral estoppel in holding that manufacturers who were not parties to previous suits could nonetheless be barred from relitigating certain issues in subsequent actions.   This decision was reversed in Hardy v. Johns-Manville Sales Corp., 681 F.2d 334 (5th Cir.1982).   (For a proposed Standard Procedure for Handling Asbestos Cases, see the opinion's appendix, 681 F.2d at 348.)   Jeffrey Trauberman, Director of the Toxic Substances Program, Environmental Law Institute, has proposed a model statute for litigating actions arising from toxic substance injury, which suggests an expansion of evidentiary rules, modification of causation principles, creation of a government- and industry-financed compensation fund, and establishment of "no-fault" compensation. Trauberman, Statutory Reform of "Toxic Torts": Relieving Legal, Scientific, and Economic Burdens on the Chemical Victim, 7 Harv.Envtl.L.Rev. 177 (1983).   The statute was drafted for state adoption, but could, with modification, become a federal statute.   Would federal enactment be preferable to a state-by-state approach?

4.   For an analysis of the various legislative proposals considered by the 97th Congress, see Relief For Asbestos Victims: A Legislative Analysis, 20 Harv.J. Legis. 179 (1983).

5.   Perhaps the greatest problem facing defendants is the number of suits filed coupled with an entity's potentially overwhelming liability.   In the summer of 1982, the Manville Corporation was faced with some 16,500 claims and potential liability of more than $2 billion.   Citing a growing financial drain, Manville filed under Chapter 11 of the Bankruptcy Act to halt pending lawsuits and prevent the filing of new ones.   How can the asbestos manufacturers have failed to anticipate their potential tort liability?   Professor Richard A. Epstein argues that they "were subject to no discernible risk of tort liability" up to the 1960s under prevailing legal and medical theories.   Prior to *Borel*, Epstein writes, "Asbestosis was regarded preeminently as an occupational disease, and it was thought that control of the level of exposure within the workplace, often by direct regulation, was the proper approach to the problem."   Epstein, Manville: The Bankruptcy of Product Liability Law, Regulation 14, 17–18 (Sept./Oct. 1982).

Professor Epstein is especially critical of Judge Wisdom's failure to "do justice to the historical ambiguities and uncertainties."   Id. at 19.

If the only question relevant to the legal inquiry was the association between asbestos and disease—any disease—then the affirmative connection was clearly recognized by the time of the 1938 Dreessen study on the asbestos textile industry and the 1946 Fleischer-Drinker study of insulation workers in naval vessels during World War II. Yet the apparent simplicity of this conclusion should not be allowed to conceal the essential point that the early studies thought that the permissible levels of exposure to asbestos products were far greater than those which are today generally regarded to be safe, by a factor of perhaps 50 to 100.

That such represented the prevailing scientific wisdom of the time is, moreover, reinforced by looking again at the subsequent classical work on the relationship of asbestos to disease by Dr. I.J. Selikoff and his colleagues. In three studies published in 1964–65, they repeatedly stated that proper analysis of the problem requires a breakdown of asbestos workers by particular types and that any inferences to be drawn from textile workers, the chief object of the early studies, to other types of workers must be heavily guarded. . . .

[W]hen in . . . the opinion Wisdom did comment on the soundness of the earlier work, he was quite happy to condemn the 1945 studies on the basis of . . . criticisms published some twenty years later—as if it were expected for manufacturers to be twenty years ahead of established medical knowledge. Nor does his opinion disclose any evidence that the suppliers possessed any private knowledge that they withheld from the public at large. The kindest thing that can be said about the summary of the medical evidence in *Borel* is that it is one-sided and incomplete, written far more like an over-argued brief than a judicial opinion.

Id. at 18–19 and 43.

6. If a major purpose of tort liability is to induce appropriate action by the party in the best position to avoid or reduce a risk most efficiently, on whom ought that pressure be placed in the context of scientific or technological risks in the work environment? In the asbestos case, is the wrong of the manufacturers, assuming that they did not know the full risks of asbestos for many years, their failure to undertake studies about the possible risks in light of what they did know? Should the antitrust laws apply to efforts by the multiple manufacturers of a product to conduct such studies, compared to the industries in which the product is put to varied uses under varying conditions? Would it then make a difference how large a percentage of the product is used by each industrial purchaser— that is, whether there are many small users or a few large ones who purchase from a number of manufacturers?

ROBERT S. MORISON,
BIOETHICS AFTER TWO DECADES

11 Hastings Center Rpt. 8, 8–9, 12 (April 1981).

Like Sigmund Freud I was brought up as a biologist and have never overcome it. Also like the great man, and long before I read *Civilization and its Discontents,* I had been impressed by the tension between the two sides of human biological nature—one's needs as an individual and one's dependence on a society. . . .

A biologist who influenced me more directly than Freud . . . was the geneticist C.H. Waddington. Particularly memorable in his essays on the relationship between biology and ethics was his elaboration of the concept of "stochastic morality." Conventional ethics and morals, he said, deal largely with one-to-one situations; the ethics of the future must take into account actions at a distance of varying probability. Paradigmatically, the Ten Commandments tell particular individuals to honor particular fathers and mothers and to avoid stealing identifiable maid-servants from identifiable neighbors. Waddington was among the first to formulate explicitly a new kind of crime, the victims of which could be identified only as statistics. . . .

It was not crime in the conventional legal sense nor the interest in ethical problems involving probable damage to unidentifiable persons that primarily attracted attention to the new field of bioethics. Advances in biology and medicine were creating new problems about conduct of the traditional person-to-person sort. Even more frequently, old ethical concerns were brought forth in new dress, more strikingly colored and more precisely cut. . . .

The greatest achievement so far may be methodological. Current biomedical ethics has shown the academy that interdisciplinary scholarship really is possible. Perhaps, success was in part due to the active participation of physicians, clergy, and lawyers with practical experience in decision making involving several different interests. It may also be significant that much of the early activity originated in partially or completely independent institutes or societies unencumbered with traditional academic rules and prejudices. Two recent developments may work against this interdisciplinary approach. The first is the growing tendency to professionalize the field. . . .

Equally ominous is the tendency to turn ethical principles into legal regulations. . . . Further contributing to the regulatory edicts was the rapid decline in respect for all authority figures that has characterized the last two decades of American life. On the whole, doctors have fared better in the polls than most others; even so, they are too suspect to be allowed to follow their traditional ways unrestrained except by conscience. Finally, the growing interest in stochastic morality led naturally to a search for ways to protect unidentifiable people from the acts of corporations and other faceless entities.

[M]edical ethics was designed to help doctors to make the right choices in the moral problems that confronted them and their patients. In this primitive view one readily acknowledged that doctors carried a particular kind of power and authority. This in turn placed upon them the obligation to use this power with wisdom and due respect for the dignity of those in their care. This would now be regarded as an elitist conception, and as such it is suspect in our egalitarian society.

Whether one likes it or not, however, in any society some individuals are more equal than others. In the case of doctors the primary sources of authority and power are the possession of special knowledge and the inheritance of a particular tradition. There is also an awareness that doctors are acquainted with death and have made many decisions involving the life and death of others.

This special position of those in authority has not made them immune from social control, nor should it. Two broad approaches are commonly employed. The first seeks to control the individual from the inside by making him or her a better person. The second tries to achieve the same end by means of laws, constitutions, licensing arrangements, and the like. . . .

One looked to the resurgence of bioethics primarily for an enrichment of the understanding and a quickening of the sense of responsibility in individual physicians. It rapidly became obvious that the same movement could help lay people to know more about the potential effects of advances in biology and medicine so that they could share in the decisions affecting themselves and their loved ones. . . .

Perhaps the most serious difficulty with the general principles underlying such matters as abortion, euthanasia, suicide, or genetic engineering is the lack of general agreement about them. . . . Our pluralistic society was founded on the proposition that differences of opinion of this kind are in fact irresolvable by argument or political compromise. Well aware of the melancholy history of European efforts to use the temporal power to enforce religious consistency, the Founding Fathers of the United States wisely declared religious differences beyond the reach of government action. Why have we not followed their example and been willing to leave these currently urgent bioethical questions involving individuals to the individual conscience? Perhaps their apparent novelty and the technical trappings with which they are surrounded have deluded us into thinking that they are primarily technical questions subject to a "technological fix". . . .

[S]everal areas of biomedical ethics do transcend the purview of the individual conscience and may properly be dealt with on a national, as well as an individual, basis. Particularly appropriate are areas of stochastic morality, as suggested above. Some formal regulation of the use of human subjects and animals in medical experimentation is already in force and seems in principle to be appropriate, although it is doubtful if it can ever take the place of an acute ethical sense on the part of the researcher. Many issues involved in the equitable distribution of medical care require a societal rather than an individual frame of reference. Particularly worthy of a broader analysis are the social consequences of the "medicalization" of human problems. . . .

There is certainly enough to do at every level without reaching down to regulate matters better left to the individual conscience, quickened and deepened by philosophical discussion but unconfined by the metaphysical conviction of a vocal minority or even a moral majority.

NOTE

Robert Morrison identifies those areas in bioethics that he believes should be regulated on a public basis rather than being left to lay control (or to the conscience of the professional). Are there other areas, in your view, in which private control is inadequate? Consider the shortcomings of tort litigation revealed in *Borel* and discussed further in Ch. 5, Sec. B.1. Consider also the proper role for the criminal law in protecting individuals from wrongdoing. See, e.g., People v. Phillips, 64 Cal.2d 574, 51 Cal.Rptr. 225, 414 P.2d 353 (1966) (affirming murder conviction of chiropractor who had represented to parents of eight year old victim that he could cure her eye cancer without the surgery recommended by physicians at UCLA). For more detailed discussion of when the government should regulate risks to life and health, see Ch. 5, Sec. A.

Chapter Four

PUBLIC CONTROL OF SCIENCE AND MEDICINE

A. LIMITS ON GOVERNMENT CONTROL OF SCIENCE AND MEDICINE: THE FIRST AMENDMENT FRAMEWORK

1. FREE SPEECH

UNITED STATES v. THE PROGRESSIVE, INC.

United States District Court for the Western District of Wisconsin, 1979.
467 F.Supp. 990.

MEMORANDUM AND ORDER

WARREN, DISTRICT JUDGE.

On March 9, 1979, this Court, at the request of the government, but after hearing from both parties, issued a temporary restraining order enjoining defendants, their employees, and agents from publishing or otherwise communicating or disclosing in any manner any restricted data contained in the article: "The H–Bomb Secret: How We Got It, Why We're Telling It."

In keeping with the Court's order that the temporary restraining order should be in effect for the shortest time possible, a preliminary injunction hearing was scheduled for one week later, on March 16, 1979. At the request of the parties and with the Court's acquiescence, the preliminary injunction hearing was rescheduled for 10:00 A.M. today in order that both sides might have additional time to file affidavits and arguments. The Court continued the temporary restraining order until 5:00 P.M. today.

In order to grant a preliminary injunction, the Court must find that plaintiff has a reasonable likelihood of success on the merits, and that the plaintiff will suffer irreparable harm if the injunction does not issue. In addition, the Court must consider the interest of the public and the balance of the potential harm to plaintiff and defendants.

Jurisdiction in this action is grounded on 42 U.S.C. § 2280, the Atomic Energy Act and 28 U.S.C. § 1345.

Under the facts here alleged, the question before this Court involves a clash between allegedly vital security interests of the United States and the competing constitutional doctrine against prior restraint in publication.

In its argument and briefs, plaintiff relies on national security, as enunciated by Congress in The Atomic Energy Act of 1954, as the basis for classification of certain documents. Plaintiff contends that, in certain areas, national preservation and self-interest permit the retention and classification of government secrets. The government argues that its national security interest also permits it to impress classification and censorship upon information originating in the public domain, if when drawn together, synthesized and collated, such information acquires the character of presenting immediate, direct and irreparable harm to the interests of the United States.

Defendants argue that freedom of expression as embodied in the First Amendment is so central to the heart of liberty that prior restraint in any form becomes anathema. They contend that this is particularly true when a nation is not at war and where the prior restraint is based on surmise or conjecture. While acknowledging that freedom of the press is not absolute, they maintain that the publication of the projected article does not rise to the level of immediate, direct and irreparable harm which could justify incursion into First Amendment freedoms.

Hence, although embodying deep and fundamental principles of democratic philosophy, the issue also requires a factual determination by a federal court sitting in equity. At the level of a temporary restraining order, or a preliminary injunction, such matters are customarily dealt with through affidavits.

Thus far the affidavits filed are numerous and complex. They come from individuals of learning and renown. They deal with how the information at issue was assembled, what it means, and how injurious the affiant believes it to be.

The Court notes the *amici curiae* briefs filed by the American Civil Liberties Union, the Wisconsin Civil Liberties Union, the Federation of American Scientists and the Fund for Open Information and Accountability, Inc., and expresses thanks for them. The Court gave consideration to the suggestion that a panel of experts be appointed to serve as witnesses for the Court to assist it in determining whether the dangers of publication are as great as the government asserts or as inconsequential as *The Progressive* states. However, the Court concluded that such a procedure really would merely proliferate the opinions of experts arrayed on both sides of the issue.

Both parties have already marshalled impressive opinions covering all aspects of the case. The Court has read all this material and has now heard extensive argument. It is time for decision.

From the founding days of this nation, the rights to freedom of speech and of the press have held an honored place in our constitutional scheme. The establishment and nurturing of these rights is one of the true achievements of our form of government.

Because of the importance of these rights, any prior restraint on publication comes into court under a heavy presumption against its constitutional validity. New York Times v. United States, 403 U.S. 713, 91 S.Ct. 2140, 29 L.Ed.2d 822 (1971).

However, First Amendment rights are not absolute. They are not boundless.

Justice Frankfurter dissenting in Bridges v. California, 314 U.S. 252, 282, 62 S.Ct. 190, 203, 86 L.Ed. 192 (1941), stated it in this fashion: "Free speech is not so absolute or irrational a conception as to imply paralysis of the means for effective protection of all the freedoms secured by the Bill of Rights." In the *Schenck* case, Justice Holmes recognized: "The character of every act depends upon the circumstances in which it is done." Schenck v. United States, 249 U.S. 47, 52, 39 S.Ct. 247, 249, 63 L.Ed. 470 (1931).

In Near v. Minnesota, 283 U.S. 697, 51 S.Ct. 625, 75 L.Ed. 1357 (1931), the Supreme Court specifically recognized an extremely narrow area, involving national security, in which interference with First Amendment rights might be tolerated and a prior restraint on publication might be appropriate. The Court stated:

> "When a nation is at war many things that might be said in time of peace are such a hindrance to its effort that their utterance will not be endured so long as men fight and that no Court could regard them as protected by any constitutional right." No one would question but that a government might prevent actual obstruction to its recruiting service or the publication of the sailing dates of transports or the number and location of troops. Id. at 716, 51 S.Ct. at 631 (citation omitted).

Thus, it is clear that few things, save grave national security concerns, are sufficient to override First Amendment interests. A court is well admonished to approach any requested prior restraint with a great deal of skepticism.

Juxtaposed against the right to freedom of expression is the government's contention that the national security of this country could be jeopardized by publication of the article.

The Court is convinced that the government has a right to classify certain sensitive documents to protect its national security. The problem is with the scope of the classification system.

Defendants contend that the projected article merely contains data already in the public domain and readily available to any diligent seeker. They say other nations already have the same information or the opportunity to obtain it. How then, they argue, can they be in violation of 42 U.S.C. §§ 2274(b) and 2280 which purport to authorize injunctive relief against one who would disclose restricted data "with reason to believe such data will be utilized to injure the United States or to secure an advantage to any foreign nation . . ." ?

Although the government states that some of the information is in the public domain, it contends that much of the data is not, and that the Morland article contains a core of information that has never before been published.

Furthermore, the government's position is that whether or not specific information is "in the public domain" or has been "declassified" at some point is not determinative. The government states that a court must look at the nature and context of prior disclosures and analyze what the practical impact of the prior disclosures are as contrasted to that of the present revelation.

The government feels that the mere fact that the author, Howard Morland, could prepare an article explaining the technical processes of thermonuclear weapons does not mean that those processes are available to everyone. They lay heavy emphasis on the argument that the danger lies in the exposition of certain concepts never heretofore disclosed in conjunction with one another.

In an impressive affidavit, Dr. Hans A. Bethe, whose affidavit was introduced by the government and whose article, *The Hydrogen Bomb: II,* was a source document for Theodore Postol's affidavit I filed by the defendants states that sizeable portions of the Morland text should be classified as restricted data because the processes outlined in the manuscript describe the essential design and operation of thermonuclear weapons. He later concludes "that the design and operational concepts described in the manuscript are not expressed or revealed in the public literature nor do I believe they are known to scientists not associated with the government weapons programs."

The Court has grappled with this difficult problem and has read and studied the affidavits and other documents on file. After all this, the Court finds concepts within the article that it does not find in the public realm—concepts that are vital to the operation of the hydrogen bomb.

Even if some of the information is in the public domain, due recognition must be given to the human skills and expertise involved in writing this article. The author needed sufficient expertise to recognize relevant, as opposed to irrelevant, information and to assimilate the information obtained. The right questions had to be asked or the correct educated guesses had to be made.

The ability of G.I. Taylor to calculate the yield of the first nuclear explosion from a *Life* magazine photo demonstrates that certain individuals with some knowledge, ability to reason and extraordinary perseverance may acquire additional knowledge without access to classified information, even though the information thus acquired may not be obvious to others not so equipped or motivated. All of this must be considered in resolving the issues before the Court.

Does the article provide a "do-it yourself" guide for the hydrogen bomb? Probably not. A number of affidavits make quite clear that a *sine qua non* to thermonuclear capability is a large, sophisticated industrial capability coupled with a coterie of imaginative, resourceful scientists and technicians. One does not build a hydrogen bomb in the basement. However, the article could possibly provide sufficient information to allow a medium size nation to move faster in developing a hydrogen weapon. It could provide a ticket to by-pass blind alleys.

The Morland piece could accelerate the membership of a candidate nation in the thermonuclear club. Pursuit of blind alleys or failure to grasp seemingly basic concepts have been the cause of many inventive failures.

For example, in one of the articles submitted to the Court, the author described how, in the late 1930's physicists in various countries were simultaneously, but independently, working on the idea of a nuclear chain reaction. The French physicists in their equation neglected to take full account of the fact that the neutrons produced by fission could go on to provoke further fissions in a many-step process—which is the essence of a chain reaction. Even though this idea seems so elementary, the concept of neutron multiplication was so novel that no nuclear physicists saw through the French team's oversight for about a year.

Thus, once basic concepts are learned, the remainder of the process may easily follow.

Although the defendants state that the information contained in the article is relatively easy to obtain, only five countries now have a hydrogen bomb. Yet the United States first successfully exploded the hydrogen bomb some twenty-six years ago.

The point has also been made that it is only a question of time before other countries will have the hydrogen bomb. That may be true. However, there are times in the course of human history when time itself may be very important. This time factor becomes critical when considering mass annihilation weaponry—witness the failure of Hitler to get his V–1 and V–2 bombs operational quickly enough to materially affect the outcome of World War II.

Defendants have stated that publication of the article will alert the people of this country to the false illusion of security created by the government's futile efforts at secrecy. They believe publication will provide the people with needed information to make informed decisions on an urgent issue of public concern.

However, this Court can find no plausible reason why the public needs to know the technical details about hydrogen bomb construction to carry on an informed debate on this issue. Furthermore, the Court believes that the defendants' position in favor of nuclear non-proliferation would be harmed, not aided, by the publication of this article.

The defendants have also relied on the decision in the *New York Times* case. In that case, the Supreme Court refused to enjoin the *New York Times* and the *Washington Post* from publishing the contents of a classified historical study of United States decision-making in Viet Nam, the so-called "Pentagon Papers."

This case is different in several important respects. In the first place, the study involved in the *New York Times* case contained historical data relating to events that occurred some three to twenty years previously. Secondly, the Supreme Court agreed with the lower court that no cogent reasons were advanced by the government as to why the article affected national security except that publication might cause some embarrassment to the United States.

A final and most vital difference between these two cases is the fact that a specific statute is involved here. Section 2274 of The Atomic Energy Act prohibits anyone from communicating, transmitting or disclosing any restricted data to any person "with reason to believe such data will be utilized to injure the United States or to secure an advantage to any foreign nation."

Section 2014 of the Act defines restricted data. " 'Restricted Data' means all data concerning 1) design, manufacture, or utilization of atomic weapons; 2) the production of special nuclear material; or 3) the use of special nuclear material in the production of energy, but shall not include data declassified or removed from the Restricted Data category pursuant to section 2162 of this title."

As applied to this case, the Court finds that the statute in question is not vague or overbroad. The Court is convinced that the terms used in the statute—"communicates, transmits or discloses"—include publishing in a magazine.

The Court is of the opinion that the government has shown that the defendants had reason to believe that the data in the article, if published, would injure the United States or give an advantage to a foreign nation. Extensive reading and studying of the documents on file lead to the conclusion that not all the data is available in the public realm in the same fashion, if it is available at all.

What is involved here is information dealing with the most destructive weapon in the history of mankind, information of sufficient destructive potential to nullify the right to free speech and to endanger the right to life itself.

Stripped to its essence then, the question before the Court is a basic confrontation between the First Amendment right to freedom of the press and national security.

Our Founding Fathers believed, as we do, that one is born with certain inalienable rights which, as the Declaration of Independence intones, include the right to life, liberty and the pursuit of happiness. The Constitution, including the Bill of Rights, was enacted to make those rights operable in everyday life.

The Court believes that each of us is born seized of a panoply of basic rights, that we institute governments to secure these rights and that there is a hierarchy of values attached to these rights which is helpful in deciding the clash now before us.

Certain of these rights have an aspect of imperativeness or centrality that make them transcend other rights. Somehow it does not seem that the right to life and the right to not have soldiers quartered in your home can be of equal import in the grand scheme of things. While it may be true in the long-run, as Patrick Henry instructs us, that one would prefer death to life without liberty, nonetheless, in the short-run, one cannot enjoy freedom of speech, freedom to worship or freedom of the press unless one first enjoys the freedom to live.

Faced with a stark choice between upholding the right to continued life and the right to freedom of the press, most jurists would have no difficulty in opting for the chance to continue to breathe and function as they work to achieve perfect freedom of expression.

Is the choice here so stark? Only time can give us a definitive answer. But considering another aspect of this panoply of rights we all have is helpful in answering the question now before us. This aspect is the disparity of the risk involved.

The destruction of various human rights can come about in differing ways and at varying speeds. Freedom of the press can be obliterated overnight by some dictator's imposition of censorship or by the slow nibbling away at a free press through successive bits of repressive legislation enacted by a nation's lawmakers. Yet, even in the most drastic of such situations, it is always possible for a dictator to be overthrown, for a bad law to be repealed or for a judge's error to be subsequently rectified. Only when human life is at stake are such corrections impossible.

The case at bar is so difficult precisely because the consequences of error involve human life itself and on such an awesome scale.

The Secretary of State states that publication will increase thermonuclear proliferation and that this would "irreparably impair the national security of the United States." The Secretary of Defense says that dissemination of the Morland paper will mean a substantial increase in the risk of thermonuclear proliferation and lead to use or threats that would "adversely affect the national security of the United States."

Howard Morland asserts that "if the information in my article were not in the public domain, it should be put there . . . so that ordinary citizens may have informed opinions about nuclear weapons."

Erwin Knoll, the editor of *The Progressive,* states he is "totally convinced that publication of the article will be of substantial benefit to the United States because it will demonstrate that this country's security does not lie in an oppressive and ineffective system of secrecy and classification but in open, honest, and informed public debate about issues which the people must decide."

The Court is faced with the difficult task of weighing and resolving these divergent views.

A mistake in ruling against *The Progressive* will seriously infringe cherished First Amendment rights. If a preliminary injunction is issued, it will constitute the first instance of prior restraint against a publication in this fashion in the history of this country, to this Court's knowledge. Such notoriety is not to be sought. It will curtail defendants' First Amendment rights in a drastic and substantial fashion. It will infringe upon our right to know and to be informed as well.

A mistake in ruling against the United States could pave the way for thermonuclear annihilation for us all. In that event, our right to life is extinguished and the right to publish becomes moot.

In the *Near* case, the Supreme Court recognized that publication of troop movements in time of war would threaten national security and could therefore be restrained. Times have changed significantly since 1931 when *Near* was decided. Now war by foot soldiers has been replaced in large part by war by machines and bombs. No longer need there be any advance warning or any preparation time before a nuclear war could be commenced.

In light of these factors, this Court concludes that publication of the technical information on the hydrogen bomb contained in the article is analogous to publication of troop movements or locations in time of war and falls within the extremely narrow exception to the rule against prior restraint.

Because of this "disparity of risk," because the government has met its heavy burden of showing justification for the imposition of a prior restraint on publication of the objected-to technical portions of the Morland article, and because the Court is unconvinced that suppression of the objected-to technical portions of the Morland article would in any plausible fashion impede the defendants in their laudable crusade to stimulate public knowledge of nuclear armament and bring about enlightened debate on national policy questions, the Court finds that the objected-to portions of the article fall within the narrow area recognized by the Court in *Near v. Minnesota* in which a prior restraint on publication is appropriate.

The government has met its burden under section 2274 of The Atomic Energy Act. In the Court's opinion, it has also met the test enunciated by two Justices in the *New York Times* case, namely grave, direct, immediate and irreparable harm to the United States.

The Court has just determined that if necessary it will at this time assume the awesome responsibility of issuing a preliminary injunction against *The Progressive's* use of the Morland article in its current form. . . .

NOTE

After the district court handed down the above decision, another journal obtained and published the Morland article. The 7th Circuit therefore viewed the case as moot and dismissed The Progressive's appeal. United States v. The Progressive, Inc., 610 F.2d 819 (7th Cir.1979). It is not known whether publication of the Morland article has brought any nation closer to building a hydrogen bomb.

As Chapter 2 indicates, the government's concern over hydrogen bomb secrets dates back to the immediate post-World War II period and, in particular, to the Oppenheimer affair. The protection of military secrets often hampers scientific progress as well as public debate on science policy issues. Did the district court properly strike this extraordinarily difficult balance in *The Progressive*?

As the district court decision assumes, the First Amendment protects scientific speech, including the publication of articles. Thus, for example, in its obscenity decisions, the United States Supreme Court has carefully noted that the "First Amendment protects works, which taken as a whole, have serious . . . scientific value." Miller v. California, 413 U.S. 15, 34, 93 S.Ct. 2607, 2620, 37 L.Ed.2d 419, 437 (1973). As the opinion in *The Progressive* makes clear, the First Amendment does not afford absolute protection to scientific speech, but does provide a substantial barrier to government regulation.

Most commentators agree that the First Amendment affords less protection for the actual conduct of scientific or medical experiments, as opposed to the writing of papers, since experiments involve action as well as speech. The approach set forth in United States v. O'Brien, 391 U.S. 367, 88 S.Ct. 1673, 20 L.Ed.2d 672 (1968), probably applies to the regulation of experiments. *O'Brien* upheld the conviction of a draft card burner on grounds that "when 'speech' and 'nonspeech' elements are combined in the same course of conduct, a sufficiently important governmental interest in regulating the nonspeech element can justify incidental limitations on First Amendment freedoms." Id. at 376, 88 S.Ct. at 1678, 20 L.Ed. 2d at 679. Thus, for example, the state could regulate a scientific experiment involving poisons so as to protect the public health and safety. See, e.g., Robertson, The Scientists' Right to Research: A Constitutional Analysis, 51 S.Cal.L.Rev. 1203, 1254–1256 (1978); Delgado and Millen, God, Galileo and Government: Toward Constitutional Protection for Scientific Inquiry, 53 Wash.L.Rev. 349, 390–392 (1978); Ferguson, Scientific Inquiry and the First Amendment, 64 Cornell L.Rev. 639, 655 (1979). Such regulation is common when hazardous substances are involved—the Atomic Energy Act, for example, restricts private research involving certain nuclear materials. See 42 U.S.C. § 2061(1) (1976). Could the federal government restrict experiments involving recombinant DNA on the ground that such experiments will lead to decreased respect for such values as individuality and human freedom?

There are problems involving national security and science that are less dramatic but far more pervasive than the publication of the design for a hydrogen bomb. For many years, American national security experts have suspected that U.S.–U.S.S.R. university exchange programs and U.S. publications freely available to Soviet readers have provided valuable information with military implications to the Soviet Union. Many American scientists have feared, however, that restrictions on their ability to work and publish in the international arena would hamper the development of American science, including science useful to the military. The following report describes certain existing restrictions on American scientific freedom and presents recommendations that seek to balance the values at stake.

PANEL ON SCIENTIFIC COMMUNICATION AND NATIONAL SECURITY, A JOINT PANEL OF THE NATIONAL ACADEMY OF SCIENCES, THE NATIONAL ACADEMY OF ENGINEERING, AND THE INSTITUTE OF MEDICINE, SCIENTIFIC COMMUNICATION AND NATIONAL SECURITY

2–3, 5–6 (1982).

THE CURRENT CONTROL SYSTEM

The government can restrict scientific communication in various ways. First, information bearing a particularly close relationship to national security may be subject to classification. This is the most stringent of the control systems because it serves to bar all unauthorized access.

Second, communications with foreign nationals may be restricted by export controls, such as those established by the Export Administration Act (EAA) and its associated Export Administration Regulations (EAR) and by the Arms Export Control Act and its associated International Traffic in Arms Regulations (ITAR). Unless an exemption (or "general license") applies, both systems require prior governmental approval for transfer of technical data—either in written or oral communication—to foreign nationals. Neither EAR nor ITAR is aimed at general scientific communication, and the Constitution limits the government's ability to restrain such communication. Nonetheless, some of the current discussion has focused on the application of export controls to scientific communication. This has proved particularly troubling to the research community in that the current control system appears to be vague in its reach, potentially disruptive, and hard to understand.

Third, the government can include controls on communications in the legal instrument defining the obligations of a recipient of government research funds. A proposal currently under consideration by the Department of Defense would require a DOD funding recipient to allow the government the opportunity for prepublication review of manuscripts dealing with certain research areas of national security concern.

Fourth, the government could attempt to influence conduct by seeking a voluntary agreement with researchers to limit the flow of technical information. Such an agreement is in place to enable the National Security Agency to review manuscripts dealing with cryptography and to negotiate alterations before publication.

Finally, communication with foreign nationals might be inhibited indirectly by limiting their access to the United States. The government can deny a visa request or impose restrictions on activities in this country. In addition, the government can directly regulate the admission of Soviet and East European visitors under particular scientific exchange agreements. . . .

The Panel recommends that no restriction of any kind limiting access or communication should be applied to any area of university research, be it basic or applied, unless it involves a technology meeting *all* the following criteria:

- The technology is developing rapidly, and the time from basic science to application is short;

- The technology has identifiable direct military applications; or it is dual-use and involves process or production-related techniques;
- Transfer of the technology would give the U.S.S.R. a significant near-term military benefit; and
- The U.S. is the only source of information about the technology, or other friendly nations that could also be the source have control systems as secure as ours.

Classification

The Panel recommends that if government-supported research demonstrably will lead to military products in a short time, classification should be considered. It should be noted that most universities will not undertake classified work, and some will undertake it only in off-campus facilities.

Gray Areas

The Panel recommends that in the limited number of instances in which all of the above four criteria are met but classification is unwarranted, the values of open science can be preserved and the needs of government can [be] met by written agreements no more restrictive than the following:

a. Prohibition of direct participation in government-supported research projects by nationals of designated foreign countries, with no attempt made to limit physical access to university space or facilities or enrollment in any classroom course of study. Where such prohibition has been imposed by visa or contractually agreed upon, it is not inappropriate for government-university contracts to permit the government to ask a university to report those instances coming to the university's attention in which the stipulated foreign nationals seek participation in any such activities, however supported. It is recognized that some universities will regard such reporting requests as objectionable. Such requests, however, should not require surveillance or monitoring of foreign nationals by the universities.

b. Submission of stipulated manuscripts simultaneously to the publisher and to the federal agency contract officer, with the federal agency then having 60 days to seek modifications in the manuscript. The review period is not intended to give the government the power to order changes: The right and freedom to publish remain with the university, as they do with all unclassified research. This does not, of course, detract from the government's ultimate power to classify in accordance with law any research it has supported.

The Panel recommends that in cases where the government places such restrictions on scientific communication through contracts or other written agreements, it should be obligated to record and tabulate the instances of those restrictions on a regular basis. . . .

NOTE

Can you improve on the panel's effort to balance national security and scientific freedom? How? How would you determine which types of research have military implications? In one recent controversy, developments in prime number theory and computer science made possible the development of codes that are difficult to break. See Gardner, Mathematical Games: A New Kind of Cipher

That Would Take Millions of Years to Break, 237 Scientific American 120 (1977); Wallerstein, Voluntary Restraints on Research With National Security Implications: The Case of Cryptography, 1975–1982, in Scientific Communication and National Security, supra, at 120.

The free international exchange of scientific ideas raises problems in areas other than national security. Would you favor restricting access to scientific advances developed by Americans in order to help American industry compete with Japan and Western Europe?

2. SCIENCE AND RELIGION: CAN THE GOVERNMENT CHOOSE SIDES?

EPPERSON v. ARKANSAS

Supreme Court of the United States, 1968.
393 U.S. 97, 89 S.Ct. 266, 21 L.Ed.2d 228.

MR. JUSTICE FORTAS delivered the opinion of the Court.

I.

This appeal challenges the constitutionality of the "anti-evolution" statute which the State of Arkansas adopted in 1928 to prohibit the teaching in its public schools and universities of the theory that man evolved from other species of life. The statute was a product of the upsurge of "fundamentalist" religious fervor of the twenties. The Arkansas statute was an adaption of the famous Tennessee "monkey law" which that State adopted in 1925. The constitutionality of the Tennessee law was upheld by the Tennessee Supreme Court in the celebrated *Scopes* case in 1927.[2]

The Arkansas law makes it unlawful for a teacher in any state-supported school or university "to teach the theory or doctrine that mankind ascended or descended from a lower order of animals," or "to adopt or use in any such institution a textbook that teaches" this theory. Violation is a misdemeanor and subjects the violator to dismissal from his position.[3]

2. Scopes v. State of Tennessee, 154 Tenn. 105, 289 S.W. 363 (1927). The Tennessee court, however, reversed Scopes' conviction on the ground that the jury and not the judge should have assessed the fine of $100. Since Scopes was no longer in the State's employ, it saw "nothing to be gained by prolonging the life of this bizarre case." It directed that a *nolle prosequi* be entered, in the interests of "the peace and dignity of the state." 154 Tenn., at 121, 289 S.W., at 367.

3. Initiated Act No. 1, Ark.Acts 1929; Ark.Stat.Ann. §§ 80–1627, 80–1628 (1960 Repl.Vol.).

The text of the law is as follows:

"§ 80–1627.—Doctrine of ascent or descent of man from lower order of animals prohibited.—It shall be unlawful for any teacher or other instructor in any University, College, Normal, Public School, or other institution of the State, which is supported in whole or in part from public funds derived by State and local taxation to teach the theory or doctrine that mankind ascended or descended from a lower order of animals and also it shall be unlawful for any teacher, textbook commission, or other authority exercising the power to select textbooks for above mentioned educational institutions to adopt or use in any such institution a textbook that teaches the doctrine or theory that mankind descended or ascended from a lower order of animals.

"§ 80–1628.—Teaching doctrine or adopting textbook mentioning doctrine—Penalties—Positions to be vacated.—Any teacher or other instructor or textbook commissioner who is found guilty of violation of this act by teaching the theory or doctrine mentioned in section 1 hereof, or by using, or adopting any such textbooks in any such educational institution shall be guilty of a misdemeanor and upon conviction shall be fined not exceeding five hundred dollars; and upon conviction shall vacate the position thus held in any educational institutions of the character above mentioned or any commission of which he may be a member."

The present case concerns the teaching of biology in a high school in Little Rock. According to the testimony, until the events here in litigation, the official textbook furnished for the high school biology course did not have a section on the Darwinian Theory. Then, for the academic year 1965–1966, the school administration, on recommendation of the teachers of biology in the school system, adopted and prescribed a textbook which contained a chapter setting forth "the theory about the origin . . . of man from a lower form of animal."

Susan Epperson, a young woman who graduated from Arkansas' school system and then obtained her master's degree in zoology at the University of Illinois, was employed by the Little Rock school system in the fall of 1964 to teach 10th grade biology at Central High School. At the start of the next academic year, 1965, she was confronted by the new textbook (which one surmises from the record was not unwelcome to her). She faced at least a literal dilemma because she was supposed to use the new textbook for classroom instruction and presumably to teach the statutorily condemned chapter; but to do so would be a criminal offense and subject her to dismissal.

She instituted the present action in the Chancery Court of the State, seeking a declaration that the Arkansas statute is void and enjoining the State and the defendant officials of the Little Rock school system from dismissing her for violation of the statute's provisions. H.H. Blanchard, a parent of children attending the public schools, intervened in support of the action.

The Chancery Court, in an opinion by Chancellor Murray O. Reed, held that the statute violated the Fourteenth Amendment to the United States Constitution. The court noted that this Amendment encompasses the prohibitions upon state interference with freedom of speech and thought which are contained in the First Amendment. Accordingly, it held that the challenged statute is unconstitutional because, in violation of the First Amendment, it "tends to hinder the quest for knowledge, restrict the freedom to learn, and restrain the freedom to teach." In this perspective, the Act, it held, was an unconstitutional and void restraint upon the freedom of speech guaranteed by the Constitution.

On appeal, the Supreme Court of Arkansas reversed. Its two-sentence opinion is set forth in the margin.[7] It sustained the statute as an exercise of the State's power to specify the curriculum in public schools. It did not address itself to the competing constitutional considerations.

Appeal was duly prosecuted to this Court under 28 U.S.C. § 1257(2). Only Arkansas and Mississippi have such "anti-evolution" or "monkey" laws on their books. There is no record of any prosecutions in Arkansas under its statute. It is possible that the statute is presently more of a

---

7. "Per Curiam. Upon the principal issue, that of constitutionality, the court holds that Initiated Measure No. 1 of 1928, Ark. Stat.Ann. § 80–1627 and § 80–1628 (Repl. 1960), is a valid exercise of the state's power to specify the curriculum in its public schools. The court expresses no opinion on the question whether the Act prohibits any explanation of the theory of evolution or merely prohibits teaching that the theory is true; the answer not being necessary to a decision in the case, and the issue not having been raised.

"The decree is reversed and the cause dismissed.

"Ward, J., concurs. Brown, J., dissents.

"Paul Ward, Justice, concurring. I agree with the first sentence in the majority opinion.

"To my mind, the rest of the opinion beclouds the clear announcement made in the first sentence."

curiosity than a vital fact of life in these States.[9]　Nevertheless, the present case was brought, the appeal as of right is properly here, and it is our duty to decide the issues presented.

II.

At the outset, it is urged upon us that the challenged statute is vague and uncertain and therefore within the condemnation of the Due Process Clause of the Fourteenth Amendment.　The contention that the Act is vague and uncertain is supported by language in the brief opinion of Arkansas' Supreme Court.　That court, perhaps reflecting the discomfort which the statute's quixotic prohibition necessarily engenders in the modern mind,[10] stated that it "expresses no opinion" as to whether the Act prohibits "explanation" of the theory of evolution or merely forbids "teaching that the theory is true."　Regardless of this uncertainty, the court held that the statute is constitutional.

On the other hand, counsel for the State, in oral argument in this Court, candidly stated that, despite the State Supreme Court's equivocation, Arkansas would interpret the statute "to mean that to make a student aware of the theory . . . just to teach that there was such a theory" would be grounds for dismissal and for prosecution under the statute; and he said "that the Supreme Court of Arkansas' opinion should be interpreted in that manner."　He said: "If Mrs. Epperson would tell her students that 'Here is Darwin's theory, that man ascended or descended from a lower form of being,' then I think she would be under this statute liable for prosecution."

In any event, we do not rest our decision upon the asserted vagueness of the statute.　On either interpretation of its language, Arkansas' statute cannot stand.　It is of no moment whether the law is deemed to prohibit mention of Darwin's theory, or to forbid any or all of the infinite varieties of communication embraced within the term "teaching."　Under either interpretation, the law must be stricken because of its conflict with the constitutional prohibition of state laws respecting an establishment of religion or prohibiting the free exercise thereof.　The overriding fact is that Arkansas' law selects from the body of knowledge a particular segment which it proscribes for the sole reason that it is deemed to conflict with a particular religious doctrine; that is, with a particular interpretation of the Book of Genesis by a particular religious group.

III.

The antecedents of today's decision are many and unmistakable. They are rooted in the foundation soil of our Nation.　They are fundamental to freedom.

Government in our democracy, state and national, must be neutral in matters of religious theory, doctrine, and practice.　It may not be hostile

---

9.　Clarence Darrow, who was counsel for the defense in the *Scopes* trial, in his biography published in 1932, somewhat sardonically pointed out that States with anti-evolution laws did not insist upon the fundamentalist theory in all respects.　He said: "I understand that the States of Tennessee and Mississippi both continue to teach that the earth is round and that the revolution on its axis brings the day and night, in spite of all opposition."　The Story of My Life 247 (1932).

10.　R. Hofstadter & W. Metzger, in The Development of Academic Freedom in the United States 324 (1955), refer to some of Darwin's opponents as "exhibiting a kind of phylogenetic snobbery [which led them] to think that Darwin had libeled the [human] race by discovering simian rather than seraphic ancestors."

to any religion or to the advocacy of no-religion; and it may not aid, foster, or promote one religion or religious theory against another or even against the militant opposite. The First Amendment mandates governmental neutrality between religion and religion, and between religion and nonreligion.

As early as 1872, this Court said: "The law knows no heresy, and is committed to the support of no dogma, the establishment of no sect." Watson v. Jones, 13 Wall. 679, 728, 20 L.Ed. 666. This has been the interpretation of the great First Amendment which this Court has applied in the many and subtle problems which the ferment of our national life has presented for decision within the Amendment's broad command.

Judicial interposition in the operation of the public school system of the Nation raises problems requiring care and restraint. Our courts, however, have not failed to apply the First Amendment's mandate in our educational system where essential to safeguard the fundamental values of freedom of speech and inquiry and of belief. By and large, public education in our Nation is committed to the control of state and local authorities. Courts do not and cannot intervene in the resolution of conflicts which arise in the daily operation of school systems and which do not directly and sharply implicate basic constitutional values. On the other hand, "[t]he vigilant protection of constitutional freedoms is nowhere more vital than in the community of American schools," Shelton v. Tucker, 364 U.S. 479, 487, 81 S.Ct. 247, 251, 5 L.Ed.2d 231 (1960). As this Court said in Keyishian v. Board of Regents, the First Amendment "does not tolerate laws that cast a pall of orthodoxy over the classroom." 385 U.S. 589, 603, 87 S.Ct. 675, 683, 17 L.Ed.2d 629 (1967).

The earliest cases in this Court on the subject of the impact of constitutional guarantees upon the classroom were decided before the Court expressly applied the specific prohibitions of the First Amendment to the States. But as early as 1923, the Court did not hesitate to condemn under the Due Process Clause "arbitrary" restrictions upon the freedom of teachers to teach and of students to learn. In that year, the Court, in an opinion by Justice McReynolds, held unconstitutional an Act of the State of Nebraska making it a crime to teach any subject in any language other than English to pupils who had not passed the eighth grade. The State's purpose in enacting the law was to promote civic cohesiveness by encouraging the learning of English and to combat the "baneful effect" of permitting foreigners to rear and educate their children in the language of the parents' native land. The Court recognized these purposes, and it acknowledged the State's power to prescribe the school curriculum, but it held that these were not adequate to support the restriction upon the liberty of teacher and pupil. The challenged statute it held, unconstitutionally interfered with the right of the individual, guaranteed by the Due Process Clause, to engage in any of the common occupations of life and to acquire useful knowledge. Meyer v. Nebraska, 262 U.S. 390, 43 S.Ct. 625, 67 L.Ed. 1042 (1923). See also Bartels v. Iowa, 262 U.S. 404, 43 S.Ct. 628, 67 L.Ed. 1047 (1923).

For purposes of the present case, we need not re-enter the difficult terrain which the Court, in 1923, traversed without apparent misgivings. We need not take advantage of the broad premise which the Court's decision in *Meyer* furnishes, nor need we explore the implications of that decision in terms of the justiciability of the multitude of controversies that beset our campuses today. Today's problem is capable of resolution in the narrower terms of the First Amendment's prohibition of laws respecting an establishment of religion or prohibiting the free exercise thereof.

There is and can be no doubt that the First Amendment does not permit the State to require that teaching and learning must be tailored to the principles or prohibitions of any religious sect or dogma. In Everson v. Board of Education, this Court, in upholding a state law to provide free bus service to school children, including those attending parochial schools, said: "Neither [a State nor the Federal Government] can pass laws which aid one religion, aid all religions, or prefer one religion over another." 330 U.S. 1, 15, 67 S.Ct. 504, 511, 91 L.Ed. 711 (1947).

At the following Term of Court, in People of State of Ill. ex rel. McCollum v. Board of Education, 333 U.S. 203, 68 S.Ct. 461, 92 L.Ed. 649 (1948), the Court held that Illinois could not release pupils from class to attend classes of instruction in the school buildings in the religion of their choice. This, it said, would involve the State in using tax-supported property for religious purposes, thereby breaching the "wall of separation" which, according to Jefferson, the First Amendment was intended to erect between church and state. Id., at 211, 68 S.Ct., at 465. See also Engel v. Vitale, 370 U.S. 421, 428, 82 S.Ct. 1261, 1265, 8 L.Ed.2d 601 (1962); Abington School District v. Schempp, 374 U.S. 203, 83 S.Ct. 1560, 10 L.Ed.2d 844 (1963). While study of religions and of the Bible from a literary and historic viewpoint, presented objectively as part of a secular program of education, need not collide with the First Amendment's prohibition, the State may not adopt programs or practices in its public schools or colleges which "aid or oppose" any religion. Id., at 225, 83 S.Ct., at 1573. This prohibition is absolute. It forbids alike the preference of a religious doctrine or the prohibition of theory which is deemed antagonistic to a particular dogma. As Mr. Justice Clark stated in Joseph Burstyn, Inc. v. Wilson, "the state has no legitimate interest in protecting any or all religions from views distasteful to them . . . .." 343 U.S. 495, 505, 72 S.Ct. 777, 782, 96 L.Ed. 1098 (1952). The test was stated as follows in Abington School District v. Schempp, supra, 374 U.S. at 222, 83 S.Ct., at 1571: "[W]hat are the purpose and the primary effect of the enactment? If either is the advancement or inhibition of religion then the enactment exceeds the scope of legislative power as circumscribed by the Constitution."

These precedents inevitably determine the result in the present case. The State's undoubted right to prescribe the curriculum for its public schools does not carry with it the right to prohibit, on pain of criminal penalty, the teaching of a scientific theory or doctrine where that prohibition is based upon reasons that violate the First Amendment. It is much too late to argue that the State may impose upon the teachers in its schools any conditions that it chooses, however restrictive they may be of constitutional guarantees. Keyishian v. Board of Regents, 385 U.S. 589, 605–606, 87 S.Ct. 675, 684–685, 17 L.Ed.2d 629 (1967).

In the present case, there can be no doubt that Arkansas has sought to prevent its teachers from discussing the theory of evolution because it is contrary to the belief of some that the Book of Genesis must be the exclusive source of doctrine as to the origin of man. No suggestion has been made that Arkansas' law may be justified by considerations of state policy other than the religious views of some of its citizens.[15] It is clear that

---

15. Former Dean Leflar of the University of Arkansas School of Law has stated that "the same ideological considerations under- lie the anti-evolution enactment" as underlie the typical blasphemy statute. He says that the purpose of these statutes is an "ideolog-

fundamentalist sectarian conviction was and is the law's reason for existence.[16] Its antecedent, Tennessee's "monkey law," candidly stated its purpose: to make it unlawful "to teach any theory that denies the story of the Divine Creation of man as taught in the Bible, and to teach instead that man has descended from a lower order of animals." Perhaps the sensational publicity attendant upon the *Scopes* trial induced Arkansas to adopt less explicit language. It eliminated Tennessee's reference to "the story of the Divine Creation of man" as taught in the Bible, but there is no doubt that the motivation for the law was the same: to suppress the teaching of a theory which, it was thought, "denied" the divine creation of man.

Arkansas' law cannot be defended as an act of religious neutrality. Arkansas did not seek to excise from the curricula of its schools and universities all discussion of the origin of man. The law's effort was confined to an attempt to blot out a particular theory because of its supposed conflict with the Biblical account, literally read. Plainly, the law is contrary to the mandate of the First, and in violation of the Fourteenth, Amendment to the Constitution.

The judgment of the Supreme Court of Arkansas is reversed.

Reversed.

STEVEN GOLDBERG,
THE CONSTITUTIONAL STATUS OF AMERICAN SCIENCE

1979 U.Ill.L.F. 1, 7–10 (1979).

The evolution controversy came before the Supreme Court in *Epperson v. Arkansas*, a 1968 challenge to the constitutionality of an Arkansas statute prohibiting the teaching of evolution. The challenge was successful

ical" one which "involves an effort to prevent (by censorship) or punish the presentation of intellectually significant matter which contradicts accepted social, moral or religious ideas." Leflar, Legal Liability for the Exercise of Free Speech, 10 Ark.L.Rev. 155, 158 (1956). See also R. Hofstadter & W. Metzger, The Development of Academic Freedom in the United States 320–366 (1955) (passim); H. Beale, A History of Freedom of Teaching in American Schools 202–207 (1941); Emerson & Haber, The *Scopes* Case in Modern Dress, 27 U.Chi.L. Rev. 522 (1960); Waller, The Constitutionality of the Tennessee Anti-Evolution Act, 35 Yale L.J. 191 (1925) (passim); ACLU, The Gag on Teaching 7 (2d ed., 1937); J. Scopes & J. Presley, Center of the Storm 45–53 (1967).

16. The following advertisement is typical of the public appeal which was used in the campaign to secure adoption of the statute:

"THE BIBLE OR ATHEISM, WHICH?

"All atheists favor evolution. If you agree with atheism vote against Act No. 1. If you agree with the Bible vote for Act No. 1. . . . Shall conscientious church members

be forced to pay taxes to support teachers to teach evolution which will undermine the faith of their children? The Gazette said Russian Bolshevists laughed at Tennessee. True, and that sort will laugh at Arkansas. Who cares? Vote FOR ACT NO. 1." The Arkansas Gazette, Little Rock, Nov. 4, 1928, p. 12, cols. 4–5.

Letters from the public expressed the fear that teaching of evolution would be "subversive of Christianity," id., Oct. 24, 1928, p. 7, col. 2; see also id., Nov. 4, 1928, p. 19, col. 4; and that it would cause school children "to disrespect the Bible," id., Oct. 27, 1928, p. 15, col. 5. One letter read: "The cosmogony taught by [evolution] runs contrary to that of Moses and Jesus, and as such is nothing, if anything at all, but atheism. . . . Now let the mothers and fathers of our state that are trying to raise their children in the Christian faith arise in their might and vote for this anti-evolution bill that will take it out of our tax supported schools. When they have saved the children, they have saved the state." Id., at cols. 4–5.

. . .

because the case was a dispute between religion and science. An amicus brief demonstrated to the Court that science was in fact at stake by including a statement signed by 179 biologists asserting that evolution "is firmly established even as the rotundity of the earth is firmly established." The brief for the appellants, in a passage with roots in the eighteenth century, argued that the uninformed use "all forms of physical and mental torture, to maintain the status quo of their unenlightenment and their accepted beliefs." During oral argument, counsel for the State was asked, "What if Arkansas would forbid the theory that the world is round?" And the Court's opinion, in striking down the statute under the establishment clause, featured excerpts from arguments against fundamentalist religion generally.

Commentary on *Epperson* has tended to focus on the doctrinal point that the Court found the statute unconstitutional because it had been enacted for a religious purpose. Such inquiries into purpose or motive are quite rare in religion cases, and *Epperson* hardly seemed a likely candidate. The Court's proof of an illegal purpose consisted merely of citation to newspaper advertisements, letters to the editor, and law review articles. No statement of any legislator was included. In other cases where a religious purpose seems likely, the Court has declined to find one or even to look very hard for one. Academic emphasis on purpose or motive in the usual sense is misplaced here. The Court's scrutiny of the statute was more intense than in the usual establishment case because the competing value at stake was science. Indeed, the Court said as much: "The State's undoubted right to prescribe the curriculum for its public schools does not carry with it the right to prohibit, on pain of criminal penalty, the teaching of a scientific theory or doctrine where that prohibition is based upon reasons that violate the First Amendment." The Arkansas statute's improper purpose was not to aid religion, but rather to aid religion at the expense of science.

Subsequent decisions have made this point more clear. Disputes about evolution continue in part because of the resurgence in recent years of American fundamentalism, including a "creationist" movement which has leveled continuing attacks on the theory of evolution. In 1975, the United States Court of Appeals for the Sixth Circuit reviewed a Tennessee statute requiring the teaching of evolution in public schools to be accompanied both by a disclaimer that it is "theory" not "scientific fact," and by an explanation of the Genesis account in the Bible without such disclaimer. The court held that putting science at this disadvantage compared to religion was, under *Epperson,* a violation of the establishment clause.

Epperson was extended further in a North Carolina case involving a substitute teacher who was asked by a student if he believed man descended from monkeys. The teacher said yes, challenged some other Biblical stories as unscientific, and was fired the next day when students complained. The district court held in favor of the teacher on various grounds, including the establishment clause. The court's opinion traces the persecution of Galileo and the contributions of Newton, and concludes that the "United States Constitution was drafted after these and similar events had occurred, but not so long after that they had been forgotten."

To analyze these decisions as religion cases, without reference to the role of science, is misleading. Consider, by comparison, application of the establishment clause to state laws against homosexuality. Those laws, at least as much as evolution laws, are religious in origin in every meaningful sense. They derive directly from specific Biblical passages, and the offense in question was defined traditionally as "the abominable sin not fit to be named among Christians." Furthermore, homosexuality laws cannot be analogized for constitutional purposes to criminal laws, like those against murder, which have religious roots but have taken on a secular purpose. Unlike laws against murder, laws against homosexuality are retained in larger measure because of religious pressure, and many homosexual crimes affect only consenting adults. Yet establishment clause challenges to the laws against homosexuality have failed uniformly. Moreover, in decisions involving homosexuality, courts often go out of their way to *rely* on the Biblical origins of the laws. Citations to Leviticus are routine; sodomy cases are replete with references to Sodom and Gomorrah.

If a teacher were fired for teaching that homosexuality is acceptable, the establishment clause would not protect him in court. Similarly, if a textbook presents slanted arguments against homosexuality, establishment clause challenges would fail. The establishment clause cannot be understood solely as a statement about religion; its content depends upon the context in which religion is operating. When religion shapes our moral standards, constitutional scrutiny is more lax than when religion shapes our scientific standards. Analayzing the evolution decisions without reference to the constitutional status of science is like analyzing a steam engine without reference to the steam.

NOTE

Disputes over the teaching of the theory of evolution remain quite lively. At present, those who oppose evolution often urge public schools to teach, along with evolution, the views of those who believe that there is scientific evidence for creationism, the theory that life developed as described in the Book of Genesis. Creationists argue that *Epperson* does not forbid this approach because they are not establishing religion but simply urging the teaching of a rival scientific theory. A federal court found unconstitutional a 1981 Arkansas statute requiring the teaching of both evolution and creationism on the ground that creationism is merely a religious doctrine masquerading as a scientific theory. McLean v. Arkansas Board of Education, 529 F.Supp. 1255 (E.D.Ark.1982). The establishment of religion clause makes the difficult judicial task of deciding whether creationism is science or religion unavoidable. The teaching of transcendental meditation (TM) in public schools presented a similar issue in Malnak v. Yogi, 592 F.2d 197 (3d Cir.1979). The court found a violation of the establishment of religion clause because, notwithstanding the claims of its proponents that TM is a science, the particular course was religious in nature. Perhaps the most important aspect of these disputes is the way they reveal the centrality of science in American culture. The attempt to justify Genesis or TM in terms of science can be seen as a victory for those who believe science is the sole or most important truth system in existence.

Many, of course, regard the theory of evolution as fully compatible with religious belief and would happily leave the latter out of the public schools. Nonetheless, the continued opposition to evolution reflects in part an undeniable tension between a scientific theory that closely links humans with nonhumans and traditional ethical and theological beliefs that humans are fundamentally different from nonhumans, for example, in being capable of good and evil acts. A similar tension may well accompany scientific advances relating to genetic engineering, see Ch. 1, supra, and artificial intelligence, see Ch. 10, infra.

B. GOVERNMENT SUPPORT FOR SCIENCE AND MEDICINE

1. THE HISTORICAL BACKGROUND: THE FRAMERS AND SCIENCE

RICHARD DELGADO AND DAVID R. MILLEN, GOD, GALILEO, AND GOVERNMENT: TOWARD CONSTITUTIONAL PROTECTION FOR SCIENTIFIC INQUIRY

53 Wash.L.Rev. 349, 354–355, 358–361 (1978).

Several colonial figures were leading exponents of Enlightenment thought, the principal source of the American revolutionary spirit. Central to Enlightenment thought are the notions of toleration and liberalism, and a concept of truth-seeking as a continual process subject to objective verification and correction. Because these are also some of the basic values of science, the development and growing influence of science during the same period reinforced the rationalistic, anti-authoritarian tenor of social and political thought. Political theory borrowed basic values and assumptions from science, while politics contributed such metaphors as the "laws" which all physical bodies were assumed to obey. John Locke believed that natural laws for government could be derived empirically by studying nature. Madison saw the United States Constitution as a gigantic machine for the regulation of interest groups, by means of which the struggles among social classes would be balanced by political structures in much the same manner in which the physical universe remained in equilibrium under the influence of the laws of dynamics discovered by Newton. . . .

[Thomas Jefferson, who was interested in a variety of scientific pursuits, including natural history,] described freedom as "the first-born daughter of science," and equated scientific progress with forward development in government and morals. His beloved University of Virginia was to be based on the "illimitable freedom of the human mind" and was to include a medical school as well as a curriculum rich in mathematics and natural science. He was convinced that nothing was so conducive to intellectual and moral development as the study of science, and in language reminiscent of the account of the education of philosopher kings in Plato's *Republic* he wrote, "When your mind shall be well improved with science, nothing will be necessary to place you in the highest points of view, but to pursue the interests of your country . . . with the purest integrity, the most chaste honor." Indeed, Jefferson concluded that the American reaction against "monkish ignorance and superstition" in favor of the natural rights of man was caused by the general spread of the light of science. . . .

[Benjamin] Franklin was one of the leading experimental scientists of his day. His studies embraced electricity, magnetism, light, sound, geology, and human and animal physiology. His papers were read before learned societies in many countries and translated into several foreign languages. He founded, with Jefferson, the American Philosophical Society, whose members included leading colonial scientists and intellectuals. The organization's charter was granted in 1743 by the Pennsylvania General Assembly and signed by clerk Thomas Paine. Like Jefferson, Franklin wrote of the importance of including mathematical and scientific training in the curricula of colonial schools and universities, urging that these studies would help students develop habits of tolerance, practicality, and respect for truth. Although as a careful experimentalist he avoided over-literal importation of Newtonian metaphors into political theory, it is clear that he believed in a physically and politically ordered universe, with science as the method by which this order was to be ascertained. . . .

A thoroughgoing rationalist and exponent of Enlightenment thought, [James] Madison conceived of the Constitution in Newtonian terms, as a collection of devices to balance and to maintain equilibrium among opposing groups and forces. Among these devices was the first amendment, of which Madison was the principal author. He worked with Thomas Jefferson in planning the University of Virginia, a strictly secular institution which would serve as a "temple dedicated to science and liberty." Outside politics, his chief interests were science and philosophy. He read widely the work of Pascal, Montesquieu, Locke, and other leading natural scientists and economists. He carried out his own investigations of natural history, and at his death there was found among his papers an unfinished essay titled *The Symmetry of Nature*, in which he described the harmony of the physical and human realms under the universal rule of law. His maxim was "Dare to Know." He saw the scientific method as offering the only sure guide to progress in both social and physical spheres. . . .

Other leading colonial figures evidenced in either their personal lives or their writings the same respect for science held by Franklin, Jefferson, and Madison. Adams and Taylor corresponded about constitutional arrangements, agreeing that the idea of checks and balances borrowed from physical theory offered the best hope for political stability. Adams was influenced by the work of Montesquieu, whose book applied Cartesian and Newtonian ideas to sociopolitical problems. Rush, an eminent physician and signer of the Declaration of Independence, served as trustee of Princeton University, an early center of scientific education and liberal thought.

Scientific ideas and the scientific spirit were thus central to the thinking of leading colonial figures and integral to the Revolutionary idea. The political thinking of the colonial era was steeped in the heritage of the Enlightenment, including the ideals of liberty, zeal for truth-seeking, humility in the face of error, and hatred of authoritarianism. Many of the Revolution's leaders and theorists were leading scientists in their own right; others borrowed from the prevailing scientific climate metaphors and assumptions which they applied to politics, sometimes almost uncritically. . . .

NOTE

The list of colonial figures who combined interests in science and government could be extended considerably. Alexander Hamilton studied medicine and urged his friends to master chemistry to improve their thinking. J. Flexner, The Young Hamilton: A Biography 47, 62 (1978); B. Mitchell, Alexander Hamilton: Youth to Maturity 54 (1957). David Rittenhouse, the leading American astronomer of the Revolutionary period, was a member of the Pennsylvania General Assembly and of that state's constitutional convention. See generally, B. Hindle, David Rittenhouse (1964). In the 18th century, the word "science"—often used in the excerpts from Delgado and Millen—referred to knowledge generally. W. Bell, Early American Science: Needs and Opportunities for Study 8 (1955). Many of the Framers believed that areas as disparate as politics and physics would yield to a Newtonian approach. Why is that view less prevalent today? Why are fewer modern presidents and cabinet members scientists?

In addition to the protections afforded science by the First Amendment, see Ch. 4, Sec. A.1, supra, the Constitution framed by these 18th century science enthusiasts provided support for science in several ways. The patent clause, discussed in Ch. 4, Sec. B.4, infra, gave an important incentive for scientific research. The first administrator of the patent law, Thomas Jefferson, personally inspected various inventions soon after passage of the law in 1790. A.H. Dupree, Science in the Federal Government 12–13 (1957). The federal power over weights and measures led to the creation in 1901 of the National Bureau of Standards. 31 Stat. 1449 (1901) (current version codified at 15 U.S.C. § 271 (1977)). Through its census provision, the Constitution required the federal government to "make the largest collection of social-science data in the world . . ." D. Price, Government and Science 5 (1962).

It cannot be denied, however, that in the early years of the republic, direct federal spending to support scientific research and development was sharply limited. Strict constructionists, including Thomas Jefferson, believed the Constitution left such activities to the states, not to the federal government. See, e.g., A.H. Dupree, Science in the Federal Government at 22. Thus, before the Civil War, federal science spending was generally tied to specific Congressional powers, such as those relating to national defense. The Constitution does not list scientific and medical research among Congress' enumerated powers. The central constitutional question for science was whether Congress' spending power was limited to the powers enumerated in Article 1, or whether Congress could spend for the general welfare, which would undoubtedly include science. The breakthrough for scientists came in 1862 when Congress created the Department of Agriculture pursuant to the power to spend for the general welfare and directed the Department to employ "chemists, botanists, entomologists, and other persons skilled in the natural sciences pertaining to agriculture." 12 Stat. 388 (1862) (current version codified at 7 U.S.C. § 2201 (1977)). The Supreme Court's later decision in United States v. Butler, 297 U.S. 1, 56 S.Ct. 312, 80 L.Ed. 477 (1936), holding that federal spending could be for the general welfare, resolved the constitutional controversy and provided a solid constitutional basis for federal spending for scientific and medical research. See generally Goldberg, The Constitutional Status of American Science, 1979 U.Ill.L.F. 1 (1979). Such spending has increased throughout this century, particularly after World War II.

Given the existence of free enterprise in America, the government's ability to spend for science does not settle the issue of whether it should. There is, however, remarkable agreement among economists and politicians of all parties that the private marketplace alone will not produce enough basic research. Science is a public good; producers of science cannot fully appropriate the benefits of what they have created. See, e.g., G. Tullock, Private Wants, Public Means 224–225 (1970). But that, of course, does not determine how much the federal government should spend for science. As the following sections discuss, the federal government currently spends about $40 billion a year on research and development in a variety of areas including defense, energy and health. The size and distribution of that pie is a continual subject of political debate, the importance of which is highlighted by the fact that federal funding today accounts for about two-thirds of all American spending on research and development.

2. GOVERNMENT SPENDING FOR SCIENCE AND MEDICINE: THE FEDERAL BUDGET PROCESS

a. Presidential Control of Agency Budget Requests

THE NATIONAL SCIENCE AND TECHNOLOGY POLICY, ORGANIZATION, AND PRIORITIES ACT OF 1976

Public Law No. 94–282 (1976).
42 U.S.C. §§ 6601, 6611, 6613.

TITLE II—OFFICE OF SCIENCE AND TECHNOLOGY POLICY

Short Title

Sec. 201. This title may be cited as the "Presidential Science and Technology Advisory Organization Act of 1976".

Establishment

Sec. 202. There is established in the Executive Office of the President an Office of Science and Technology Policy (hereinafter referred to in this title as the "Office").

Director; Associate Directors

Sec. 203. There shall be at the head of the Office a Director who shall be appointed by the President, by and with the advice and consent of the Senate, and who shall be compensated at the rate provided for level II of the Executive Schedule in section 5313 of title 5, United States Code. The President is authorized to appoint not more than four Associate Directors, by and with the advice and consent of the Senate, who shall be compensated, at a rate not to exceed that provided for level III of the Executive Schedule in section 5314 of such title. Associate Directors shall perform such functions as the Director may prescribe.

Functions

Sec. 204. (a) The primary function of the Director is to provide, within the Executive Office of the President, advice on the scientific, engineering, and technological aspects of issues that require attention at the highest levels of Government.

(b) In addition to such other functions and activities as the President may assign, the Director shall—

(1) advise the President of scientific and technological considerations involved in areas of national concern including, but not limited to, the economy, national security, health, foreign relations, the environment, and the technological recovery and use of resources;

(2) evaluate the scale, quality, and effectiveness of the Federal effort in science and technology and advise on appropriate actions;

(3) advise the President on scientific and technological considerations with regard to Federal budgets, assist the Office of Management and Budget with an annual review and analysis of funding proposed for research and development in budgets of all Federal agencies, and

aid the Office of Management and Budget and the agencies throughout the budget development process; and

(4) assist the President in providing general leadership and coordination of the research and development programs of the Federal Government.

EXCERPTS FROM HOUSE REPORT ON PUBLIC LAW NO. 94–282

U.S. Code Congressional and Administrative News Vol. 2, 898–900.
94th Congress, 2d Sess. (1976).

TITLE II

Title II would make available to the President a new organizational entity to assist in using science and technology in national decision-making—an Office of Science and Technology Policy, whose Director also serves as science adviser. The basic premise is not to insist upon a particular style of scientific support for the President, but to provide a way of mobilizing expertise in the President's behalf. The President can use the Director of the Office, and such Assistant Directors as are appointed, in whatever manner he chooses. In any case, the Office would speak for the best public use and understanding of science and technology and not as an advocate for science and technology per se.

Numerous witnesses have contended that as the Federal role and support structure for R&D has grown, so has grown the need for better awareness and attention at the highest levels of government. Increasingly complex scientific and technological issues confront the President. Off and on since the beginning of World War II, the nation has been debating the issue of how best to incorporate science and technology into national decision-making.

World War II led to widespread use of science and technology by our allies, our enemies and ourselves. For the first time, a President had what amounted to a "science adviser"—Dr. Vannevar Bush, who marshalled the U.S. scientific and technological effort and worked closely with President Roosevelt.

Dr. John Steelman was designated by President Truman to head a Scientific Research Board in the Executive Office of the President. Close personally to the President, Steelman also acted as the President's liaison with the scientific community.

From 1952 until late 1957, science advice for President Eisenhower was provided by a Science Advisory Committee through the Director of the Office of Defense Mobilization. With the launch of Sputnik in October 1957, science and technology came once again to center stage and President Eisenhower created the position of Special Assistant to the President for Science and Technology. Dr. James R. Killian, Jr. was appointed to the post. Also, ODM's Science Advisory Committee was reconstituted as the President's Science Advisory Committee (PSAC).

In time, Congress became dissatisfied with these steps and pushed for a more formal arrangement. In mid-1962 President Kennedy established an Office of Science and Technology (OST) and his Science Adviser then wore several "hats," including Science Adviser to the President and Director of OST in the Executive Office of the President.

Most agree that the role of presidential science adviser was strong and influential from Roosevelt through Kennedy. Beginning with President Johnson and continuing with President Nixon, it was "downhill" to January 1973.

At that time President Nixon announced Reorganization Plan No. 1 of 1973 which abolished OST and PSAC, and transferred the function of Science Adviser to the Director of the National Science Foundation as an additional duty. Hearings were held by the Government Operations Committees, but the prevailing mood seemed different from that of 1961–1962 when President Kennedy was more or less persuaded to establish OST. The view in 1973 seemed to be, "If the President doesn't want a science advisory capability in the Executive Office, there is no point in making him keep one."

This Committee's inquiries have produced very few outside the Administration (in '73) who really approved the present setup. Virtually all of the Committee's other testimony indicated a conviction that the dual role of the Science Adviser and the Director of the National Science Foundation was not tenable. It is particularly noteworthy that Dr. McElroy, who had preceded Dr. Stever in the post of Director of the Science Foundation, was quite emphatic on this point. Since Dr. McElroy is the only former Director to have held that post during NSF's modern history, his views carried quite a bit of weight. . . .

Hence the substance of Title II. That Title encompasses the duties and functions of the proposed Office of Science and Technology Policy and its Director. The number of statutory Assistants may run from 0 to 4 depending on the President's desire.

Among the important features of this Title are (1) evaluating the quality and effectiveness of the Federal R&D effort; (2) advising the President with regard to scientific and technological considerations in all major fields including national security; (3) advising and assisting in the development of Federal R&D budgets; (4) developing criteria for optimum levels of Federal R&D support in accordance with the principles established in Title I.

It is also important to note the reorganization feature which would permit the President to reorganize the advisory setup within his own Executive Office, unless vetoed by both houses of Congress. However, the President could not simply abolish the advisory setup and replace it with nothing. He could alter it, but he would be obliged to establish something in the place of whatever advisory arrangements were in existence.

EDWARD J. BURGER, SCIENCE AT THE WHITE HOUSE

114–115 (1980).

There has been an evolution in character of the scientific advisory machinery in the Office of the President. It has been led in directions that were not considered by its early scientific advocates and practitioners. However, the ultimate relationship between scientists and professionals and the public policy apparatus perhaps has still not clearly been defined. In latter years, from the scientists' side, there has been a steadily increasing attempt toward proximity to politics and toward useful articulation with the political machinery. From the politicians' point of view, the desire for scientific and technical counsel is not as compelling, and is inevitably tempered by political liabilities.

The early relationships between scientists and the White House were generally ones marked by modest and hesitating advice on strictly technical issues. The periods of advice were characteristically discrete and limited to specific questions. Scientists were generally fearful of too close an approximation to the political system and to politicians. Periods of substantial and sustained collaboration were unusual and were marked principally by the recognized importance to the nation of the successful pursuit of specific national projects or goals. The notable marriage between universities and government in behalf of agriculture remains perhaps the most outstanding example of cooperation—a concept born not of the imagination of the scientific and academic community but of politicians. The other area of successful collaboration was in time of war—especially during World War II.

The period since World War II might well be described as one in which scientists have been trying to find out *if* and *how* they can be useful to politicians and to the public policy machinery. Increasingly, members of the scientific and professional community have endeavored to prove their utility alongside others *at court*. All of this has been done, however, not without some ambivalence. Scientists in the service of the President still do not wish to compromise their ties to their own fraternity—especially those ties to academic settings. . . .

NOTE

The President's science advisor, typically a prominent scientist, heads the Office of Science and Technology Policy (OSTP), which provides the President with technical advice independent of the views of other government agencies. The science advisor thus inevitably becomes embroiled in political disputes over matters such as the effectiveness of weapons systems, the environmental impact of pesticides, and the risks involved in mass inoculation programs. If you were a leading scientist, would you accept the job of science advisor to the President? What relevance would your scientific knowledge have in such a job? Consider, in this light, the materials on the role of expertise in Ch. 1, Sec. A.3, supra.

The OSTP is a presidential staff operation with advisory power. Huge mission agencies, such as Defense, Energy and the National Institutes of Health (NIH), actually spend the vast bulk of federal research and development funds. Although there have been various efforts throughout American history to create a centralized science agency, none has succeeded—there is no Department of Science. See A. H. Dupree, Science in the Federal Government 377–379 (1957). The National Academy of Sciences, established by Congress in 1863, is a private group that advises the federal government when it is requested to do so. The National Science Foundation, created by Congress in 1950, funds basic research in a variety of fields but has never become dominant in federal research and development. The leading actors in science spending are the agencies created by Congress over the years to perform particular tasks. In 1983, federal research and development spending totalled about $40 billion, $6 billion of which was allotted for basic research. The leading agencies in spending that $40 billion were, in order, Defense, Energy, NIH, the National Aeronautics and Space Administration, the National Science Foundation, and Agriculture. Special Analyses, Budget of the United States Government, Fiscal Year 1984, K–4, K–5 (1983).

The President, of course, appoints the top officials of these agencies. Needless to say, however, that power alone does not guarantee that agency budget requests will reflect presidential priorities. The agencies are large and the appointees may have priorities of their own. Accordingly, the President, through the OSTP and through another White House agency—the Office of Management and Budget (OMB)—reviews and revises agency budget requests relating to science before those requests go to Congress. The materials that follow describe this interplay among the agencies, OSTP and OMB.

DR. FRANK PRESS, DIRECTOR, OFFICE AND SCIENCE AND TECHNOLOGY POLICY, TESTIMONY BEFORE THE SUBCOMMITTEE ON HUD–INDEPENDENT AGENCIES OF THE SENATE COMMITTEE ON APPROPRIATIONS

95th Congress, 1st Sess. (March 22, 1978).

Mr. Chairman and Members of the Committee: I appreciate the opportunity to appear before you to discuss the work of the Office of Science and Technology Policy. I am accompanied by my three Assistant Directors—Ben Huberman, Gil Omenn, and Phil Smith—and the OSTP Executive Officer, Bill Montgomery. They will join me in responding to your questions.

President Carter asked me to be his Science and Technology Adviser and to be the Director of the Office of Science and Technology Policy in March 1977. I have therefore been on the job about a year. . . .

The Work of OSTP in the FY 1979 Budget Process

I think that it is fair to say that the FY 1979 budget was developed with a special sensitivity to research and development issues. This reflects the President's interest in science and technology, the awareness of officials in OMB of the importance of research and development, as well as the special concern of OSTP in this aspect of the budget. Indeed, the importance of R&D in the budget is reflected in the fact that the President chose to highlight research and development in his Budget Message to the Congress. The President said:

"The Federal Government must lead the way in investing in the Nation's technological future. Shortly after taking office, I determined that investment in basic research on the part of the Federal Government had fallen far too low over the past decade. Accordingly, I directed that a careful review be undertaken of appropriate basic research opportunities. As a result of that review, this budget proposes a real rate of growth of almost 5% for basic research in 1979. I believe this emphasis is important to the continued vitality of our economy."

In this Administration—from the President on down—we are pursuing the belief that science and technology will play an increasingly important role in helping us meet the physical, economic and social challenges that we see ahead—and in helping us to anticipate and avoid new problems that could arise.

To convey to you the way that the Administration has worked, and the way in which my office and I have worked with others in the Executive Office and with the agencies, I would like to dwell for a moment on the formulation of the fiscal year 1979 budget.

We could see in examining many of the issues we have looked at this year that we have been living off past research results. We clearly need to stimulate new research and allow the entry of more young scientists and engineers into the system. The declines of research support over the past decade or so were fairly obvious—as was the beginning of the reversal of that trend two years ago. But what has probably given most impetus to our determination to strengthen research has been its association with our current state of affairs in such areas as agriculture, industry and economic growth, world trade, national security needs and energy and environmental matters. In each case, it can be seen that new ideas and fundamental changes are clearly in order.

— In agriculture, where the best land is already in use, our future increases in crop productivity will depend principally on advances in photosynthesis, biological nitrogen fixation, genetic improvements and protection of plants from adverse environmental stresses.

— In health, there is a need for more focus on basic research in such disciplines as genetics, cell biology, immunology and virology to get closer to the causes and prevention of diseases, rather than to continue to emphasize the development and use of costly medical technologies directed at advanced complications of diseases. More and better research is also needed in such areas as mental health, alcohol and drug abuse, and in biomedical and behavioral research in reproduction and family planning.

— In defense, basic research is essential to maintain our technological superiority in strategic and tactical weapons systems and to improve our intelligence systems, worldwide communications and test and evaluation capabilities.

— In the environmental field, there is increasing need to provide a strong scientific basis to develop standards and effective controls and to identify long-range problems.

— In many other R&D areas ranging through such interests as energy, climate, space, and others with a strong bearing on the country's health and growth, there is a need for the extension of fundamental knowledge to serve as the basis for new advances.

Hence the President's Budget definitely leans toward investments in fundamental science—the basic research that is an investment for the future strength of the nation.

The budget process started during the spring preview when certain issues were identified in the OMB planning sessions with the President. My staff and I participated in all of those discussions. Subsequently, OMB and OSTP met with a number of leaders in science and engineering from universities, industry and the government to review their impressions of trends, issues and alternatives. In the summer the Director of OMB, with my concurrence, wrote to each of the heads of the mission agencies asking them to assess and, if necessary, correct the balance between long-term and short-term research in their agency's programs. The letter reflected OMB's concern that in some agencies the emphasis on meeting short-term goals may have been squeezing out funding for longer-term research. Bowman Cutter of OMB and I met with heads of the major agencies to discuss our perceptions and to gain their perspectives. We then submitted a memorandum to the President describing the problem briefly and suggesting that basic research funding should grow 3–5% above inflation. The President agreed to this approach, emphasizing however, his interest in strengthening the research capability of the universities.

In the Fall budget review my staff and I worked closely with the OMB staff on various aspects of agency budget submissions, but with a particular focus on basic research. The outcome, as the President's budget message emphasized, is that the proposed Federal obligational authority for support of the conduct of basic research will total over $3.6 billion, a 10.9% growth over FY78 (about 5% real growth).

The growth of funding for the conduct of development activity is much more modest, about 4.6% over FY78. The outcome was not the product of a special effort as in basic research, but rather arose chiefly from the joint analytical efforts of OMB, OSTP, and the other Executive Office units. Analysis of some proposed demonstration projects, such as solar heating and hot water demonstrations, were seen as warranting decreased Federal funding because of the private sector capacity that has developed over recent years, and because the incentive provided through tax credits replaced the need for direct Federal funding. Other demonstration activities were foregone because of the likelihood that the technology would be unacceptable or uneconomic or because the demonstration did not promise significant advances. Thus, as part of the hard look at proposed projects there has been somewhat of a pause or slowdown in some demonstration activities. The net effect is that the proposed overall obligational support for the conduct of research and development in FY 1979 is about 6.1% above that of FY 1978. . . .

JOHN WALSH AND BARBARA CULLITON, OFFICE OF MANAGEMENT AND BUDGET: SKEPTICAL VIEW OF SCIENTIFIC ADVICE

in Science, Technology and National Policy
274–294 (T. Kuehn and A. Porter eds. 1981).

The phase "men with a passion for anonymity" was coined in a 1937 report of the President's Commission on Administrative Management and was used, often with malice, to describe the presidential advisers and top bureaucrats who manned the machinery of the New Deal and who accepted anonymity in exchange for power. Today, the phrase and its overtones might be applied to the officials of the Office of Management and Budget (OMB), who are as influential in the U.S. government as the gentlemen of the Treasury in Britain or the inspectors of finance in France.

Because the agency operates behind the scenes and because it appears to have the last word with the President on decisions which often result in cuts in program funds, OMB is blamed for goring a lot of congressional oxen, is a source of fear and anxiety to federal agencies, and is looked on by many members of the scientific community as the scourge of the science budget. . . .

The Office of Management and Budget is the agent of the President. Its officials are paid to make sure that legislation and budgets proposed by government agencies conform to Presidential wishes.

They are also supposed to see to it that the agencies interpret and carry out presidential policy correctly. In fact, one important feature of the OMB's Reorganization Plan No. 1 of 1973 was ". . . the goal of reorienting the Office to focus on its original mission as a staff to the President for top-level policy formulation and for monitoring policy execution—where reliance could not appropriately be placed on individual departments and agencies." At least that's what John C. Sawhill told Congress.

The OMB is set apart from the rest of the government. Its officials are not paid to make people in government agencies happy. Nor are they

paid to please the people on Capitol Hill. Frequently, they don't. Staffers at OMB are not hired to be popular. By and large, they aren't.
. . .

The OMB's activities with respect to the National Institutes of Health and biomedical research policy and funding are revealing of the way in which the office works and of its relationships with the scientific community generally.

On the whole, OMB and NIH are not on very good terms. One apparent reason is that their respective leaders do not spend enough time talking to each other. Former NIH director Robert Q. Marston complained about that last fall, when he debated OMB associate director Paul H. O'Neill at the Institute of Medicine of the National Academy of Sciences. Marston, alleging that "the source and scope of expert advice used by the executive branch is very limited," said, "I think Paul brought out one of the reasons for this when he said that he has been distracted by other things. I suspect, Paul, that we will probably spend as much time today together talking about major NIH problems as we did during the whole time that I was director of NIH."

It is no wonder that O'Neill becomes distracted from the problems of biomedical research. A glance at the list of agencies for which he is responsible puts things in perspective. The NIH is not even mentioned by name; its presence is subsumed under the listing for HEW.

If biomedical scientists are unhappy that O'Neill does not listen to them, O'Neill also is unhappy with the quality of advice he receives when he does listen. In his opinion, scientists often implicitly ask for special treatment but do nothing to deserve it. He says he hears too frequently the idea that what scientists say should be accepted just because they are scientists. "I don't think we can turn our world over to people who couch their reasoning in terms of their expertise or their degrees," he says.

When it comes to broad recommendations, O'Neill finds that panels of scientists, like panels of any special group, first propose that "a new organizational element be attached, either in the Office of the President or in the Office of the Secretary, to deal with the subject." Having done that, "They will recommend more money for their thing without looking out across the broader world."

O'Neill is also wary of much of the advice he gets from scientists because he believes he cannot always trust it. Simply put, the same people who stand up in public and declare that budget cuts are destroying American science say, in private, that there are excesses in the biomedical research budget. The national cancer program, in particular, has prompted individuals to follow this kind of double standard. Says O'Neill, ". . . while I have had people tell me quietly and privately, 'Look, we think, you are doing too much in one area of biomedical research,' they have not been willing to stand up where it counts in public or in the Congress and say, 'You are doing too much.' They turn the argument around and say, 'You are not doing enough in other areas.'" He wishes, he says, that scientists could learn to think in terms of options or alternatives, especially in view of the fact that national resources are limited and that biomedical research is competing for them at the margin. "There is a fundamental notion in economics that says we live in a world of finite resources," he says. People who want them are going to have to be pretty good at justifying their claim. O'Neill thinks that research scientists are not doing a very good job of that.

Science looks different to different people. The OMB wants to know, first and foremost, what good a given scientific enterprise is, what will come of it. Even though many OMB people concede that the products of scientific research cannot be anticipated the way those of an automobile plant can, the prevailing philosophy at the OMB is that science, like everything else, should pay off if it is going to get public support.

Most scientists hold as an article of faith that science deserves public support because it contributes to the advancement of man's understanding of himself and his world. The unhappy truth is that not everyone shares this faith, or, in any case, not as completely. Some of those people are in influential positions in the Nixon Administration. It is not an easy matter to resolve, but the fact that the two sides enter budget negotiations with different first premises does not help.

With respect to the Administration's willingness to support biomedical research, it is worth noting that the NIH budget has been going up, not down. Granted, its increases have been selective, going only to the cancer and heart institutes, but from the Administration's point of view its support of research has not declined. The argument is over how those additional funds are allocated, which brings one back to the issue of whether research should be expected to pay off in order to justify receiving large amounts of federal funds. . . . .

When government scientists are not busy defending their programs in reports and memos to ranking OMB officials, they are justifying their activities to its budget examiner. There is one budget examiner for all of NIH. Her name is Ann Stone. She has been a budget examiner for 2 years. A fairly recent graduate of Duke University, where she studied social sciences, she worked for HEW before joining the staff of OMB. As part of an internship program at HEW, she took a few management courses, but she has never had any formal training in hard science. Stone recognizes that this is a sore point with many of the scientists with whom she deals at NIH, but she believes that her lack of an academic background in science is an asset to doing her job. Many officials at NIH would, of course, prefer to see a scientist in her position, but most of them are realistic enough to know that is not going to happen.

Stone is involved in the budget process from the very beginning of its yearly cycle, and as she goes from institute to institute to review its programs, she asks a lot of questions that make people uncomfortable. (O'Neill says that OMB is asking questions today that are a lot tougher than the ones it asked in 1967, when he first worked in the budget office; NIH scientists agree.)

As Ann Stone makes her rounds, she asks for a description of institute programs, demanding a definition of what they are and where they are supposed to be going. She asks institute officials how they measure progress. She asks what the alternatives to any given program are and, as part of that, suggests that scientists start asking whether the federal government should be supporting certain programs at all.

The latter question has become something of a refrain for this Administration. It was the question OMB asked when it decided to phase out NIH training grants. Scientists defended the program that supported young biologists, but OMB decided that there was no reason taxpayers should pick up the bill for individuals who will go on to earn good incomes, especially since they believe the nation is not facing a shortage of biomedical researchers. When the Administration was subsequently persuaded to relent a little and restore some of the training money, OMB was there to make sure NIH executed the "new" training program in accordance with policy. The Administration had decided that training money should go only to persons working in areas in which there is a shortage of researchers, and NIH was instructed to determine which ones they are.

Instead of trusting NIH to do that job, OMB stepped in and asked a slew of detailed questions about what the areas of shortage are and how anybody had determined that and what scientific accomplishments might be anticipated by training persons in one field rather than another. The questions offended many NIH scientists who believe that no one at OMB knows enough to evaluate such scientific judgments. Officials at OMB say that the people at NIH have it all wrong. It was never their intention to ask NIH to make substantive changes as far as its scientific assessment goes. Rather, OMB asked those questions to force the scientists to think about what they were doing, to force them to consider alternatives and to set goals. The OMB intends to keep asking such questions until everybody learns.

Although Stone's questions are offensive, at times, to scientists who are put off by her cross-examination, what galls them more is their conviction that she and her immediate supervisor, Victor Zafra, are ultimately making decisions about what NIH is going to do. At the very least, they think that O'Neill should be directly involved every step of the way, and they are not happy about having their point of view filtered through Stone and Zafra, who also lacks academic credentials in science. In short, senior NIH scientists resent the fact that individuals whom they sometimes refer to as "just a couple of young kids" can tell them what to do.
. . .

NOTE

Should OMB hire staff with strong science credentials to study science-related budget requests? Would such scientific expertise help or hinder implementation of OMB's budgetary function?

Some perceive the President's science advisor as an advocate for science in the budget process. Is that an appropriate role? George Keyworth, the head of OSTP under President Reagan, has said that "[i]t is to the decided advantage of the science and engineering communities to have a Presidential advisor that is looked upon by the White House, not as a political pleader for those communities—an 'inside lobbyist' if you will—but as an objective advisor who can act as an effective link to them." Remarks at the 6th Annual American Association for the Advancement of Science R&D Colloquium, Washington, D.C., June 25, 1981. Is this simply another way of being an advocate for science?

b. The Congressional Budget Process

After White House review, the budget requests of the agencies, including the components of those budgets that involve science, go to Congress. Because there is no "Department of Science," there is no single "science budget" for Congress to consider. Congress decides on science spending as it acts on the budget requests of the various agencies. Thus, science spending on cancer research, for example, does not compete for funds with science spending for solar energy; it competes instead with non-science programs such as anti-cancer publicity campaigns. This system allows for few generalizations about Congressional attitudes toward science. One common reality is that Members of Congress, understandably concerned about their political futures, often prefer programs promising immediate payoffs over those with only long-term prospects. Thus, one study found that over a multi-year period, Congress was harder on budget requests from the National Science Foundation than from the National Institutes of Health, in part because the former requests involved more pure science with its relatively distant and uncertain benefits. See Roback, Congress and the Science Budget, 160 Science 964–971 (1968). See also Ch. 9, Sec. B.2, infra.

Beyond this, however, the story of Congressional treatment of science is largely a story of fragmentation. Budget requests wend their way through various subcommittees, often with overlapping jurisdictions and conflicting points of view, in both the House of Representatives and the Senate. Members of Congress obtain help in understanding technical issues from their staff, some of whom may be scientists, from the Congressional Research Service of the Library of Congress, and from outside groups such as the National Academy of Sciences and its offshoot the National Research Council. Nonetheless, in the late 1960's and early 1970's, Congress came to believe that it needed more in order to participate effectively on issues involving science and technology. As a result it created the Office of Technology Assessment. The analysis below of the purposes and performance of that Office presents an insight into Congressional control of science generally.

TECHNOLOGY ASSESSMENT ACT OF 1972

Public Law No. 92–484 (1972).
2 U.S.C. §§ 471, 472.

To establish an Office of Technology Assessment for the Congress as an aid in the identification and consideration of existing and probable impacts of technological application; to amend the National Science Foundation Act of 1950; and for other purposes.

Be it enacted by the Senate and House of Representatives of the United States of America in Congress assembled, That this Act may be cited as the "Technology Assessment Act of 1972".

Findings and Declaration of Purpose

Sec. 2. The Congress hereby finds and declares that:

(a) As technology continues to change and expand rapidly, its applications are—

(1) large and growing in scale; and

(2) increasingly extensive, pervasive, and critical in their impact, beneficial and adverse, on the natural and social environment.

(b) Therefore, it is essential that, to the fullest extent possible, the consequences of technological applications be anticipated, understood, and considered in determination of public policy on existing and emerging national problems.

(c) The Congress further finds that:

(1) the Federal agencies presently responsible directly to the Congress are not designed to provide the legislative branch with adequate and timely information, independently developed, relating to the potential impact of technological applications, and

(2) the present mechanisms of the Congress do not and are not designed to provide the legislative branch with such information.

(d) Accordingly, it is necessary for the Congress to—

(1) equip itself with new and effective means for securing competent, unbiased information concerning the physical, biological, economic, social, and political effects of such applications; and

(2) utilize this information, whenever appropriate, as one factor in the legislative assessment of matters pending before the Congress, particularly in those instances where the Federal Government may be called upon to consider support for, or management or regulation of, technological applications.

Establishment of the Office of Technology Assessment

Sec. 3. (a) In accordance with the findings and declaration of purpose in section 2, there is hereby created the Office of Technology Assessment (hereinafter referred to as the "Office") which shall be within and responsible to the legislative branch of the Government.

(b) The Office shall consist of a Technology Assessment Board (hereinafter referred to as the "Board") which shall formulate and promulgate the policies of the Office, and a Director who shall carry out such policies and administer the operations of the Office.

(c) The basic function of the Office shall be to provide early indications of the probable beneficial and adverse impacts of the applications of technology and to develop other coordinate information which may assist the Congress. In carrying out such function, the Office shall:

(1) identify existing or probable impacts of technology or technological programs;

(2) where possible, ascertain cause-and-effect relationships;

(3) identify alternative technological methods of implementing specific programs;

(4) identify alternative programs for achieving requisite goals;

(5) make estimates and comparisons of the impacts of alternative methods and programs;

(6) present findings of completed analyses to the appropriate legislative authorities;

(7) identify areas where additional research or data collection is required to provide adequate support for the assessments and estimates described in paragraph (1) through (5) of this subsection; and

(8) undertake such additional associated activities as the appropriate authorities specified under subsection (d) may direct.

(d) Assessment activities undertaken by the Office may be initiated upon the request of:

(1) the chairman of any standing, special, or select committee of either House of the Congress, or of any joint committee of the Congress, acting for himself or at the request of the ranking minority member or a majority of the committee members;

(2) the Board; or

(3) the Director, in consultation with the Board.

(e) Assessments made by the Office, including information, surveys, studies, reports, and findings related thereto, shall be made available to the initiating committee or other appropriate committees of the Congress. In addition, any such information, surveys, studies, reports, and findings produced by the Office may be made available to the public except where—

(1) to do so would violate security statutes; or

(2) the Board considers it necessary or advisable to withhold such information in accordance with one or more of the numbered paragraphs in section 552(b) of title 5, United States Code. . . .

SUBCOMMITTEE ON SCIENCE, RESEARCH AND TECHNOLOGY OF THE HOUSE COMMITTEE ON SCIENCE AND TECHNOLOGY, REVIEW OF THE OFFICE OF TECHNOLOGY ASSESSMENT AND ITS ORGANIC ACT

95th Congress, 2d Sess. 1, 13–14 (1978).

The Office of Technology Assessment, upon its creation in 1972, was only the third service organization set up by the Congress for its own use. The others were the Congressional Research Service, organized within the Library of Congress, in 1915—and the General Accounting Office, formed from the amalgamation of a number of Executive department audit units in 1921 and placed in the Legislative branch. . . .

It is important to understand that nothing quite like OTA has been tried before. It is a unique institution. Among the characteristics which distinguish OTA are the following:

OTA—

(1) Was not formed within an existing organization, as was CRS, nor by the union of a number of already operational offices, as was GAO; it was totally new and untried;

(2) Exists only to serve the needs of the committees of Congress—though the value of its work may range much further;

(3) Has no officials, administrators or staff who have been appointed by the President or recommended by any Executive entity;

(4) Is governed by a bipartisan all-Congressional Board, composed equally of members from the House and Senate and of members from each political party;

(5) Does not depend on in-house personnel for the production of most of its work but utilizes the services and talents of the private sector, in addition to public sources, in carrying out its mission.

(6) Delivers an end-product which is not advisory in character but presents a variety of choices for Congress to consider and/or as complete a range of options as possible for potential legislative action. . . .

The OTA was established within the legislative branch by the Technology Assessment Act of 1972 (Public Law 92–484, approved Oct. 13, 1972). It was created to provide the Congress with an effective means for securing competent, unbiased information concerning the large-scale physical, biological, economic, social, and political effects of the increasingly extensive applications of technology. This information represents one factor in the legislative decision-making process, particularly in those legislative areas where Congress must manage or regulate technological applications.

The OTA consists of a Technology Assessment Board, which formulates the policies of the Office; a Director, who implements these policies and manages the Office; and an Advisory Council, which reviews activities of the Office and makes recommendations to the Board concerning these activities. The Board consists of 12 Members of Congress, 6 from each house, and the Director of the Office, who is a non-voting member. Senators are appointed to the Board by the President pro tempore of the Senate, and Representatives are appointed by the Speaker of the House, 3 from each party in each House. The Board elects a Chairman and a Vice Chairman, and appoints the Director. The Act stipulates that the Chairman must be elected from the Senate Members of the Board in odd-numbered Congresses, and from the Representatives in even-numbered Congresses.

BARRY M. CASPER,
THE RHETORIC AND REALITY OF CONGRESSIONAL TECHNOLOGY ASSESSMENT

Bulletin of Atomic Scientists 20–31 (1978).

Congress created the Office of Technology Assessment (OTA) in 1972 with much fanfare and optimistic predictions. Now, five years later, one can begin to compare the reality with the rhetoric and to assess the impact of OTA on the politics of technology. OTA's record to date, particularly in the area of military technology, will be examined here. In that area especially it is largely, but not totally, a record of omission. . . .

The record contrasts with the conception of OTA enunciated by OTA Board Chairman Edward Kennedy:

The impetus for OTA was congressional inability to assess major federal programs involving complex technology. The executive branch, with its vast resources, would develop complex programs which Congress had no capability to properly evaluate. So when the time came to vote on issues such as the ABM, the SST, or the Space Shuttle, it was extremely difficult for Congress to marshall the facts and arguments effectively.

The most striking feature of OTA's record so far is the systematic exclusion from its agenda of controversial new programs of the sort mentioned by Senator Kennedy. In 1976 and 1977, for example, several such issues came to the floor, including the B–1 Bomber, the Liquid Metal Fast Breeder Reactor, and a number of provisions of the Clean Air Act. OTA studies could have helped members of Congress to marshall the facts and arguments effectively. But none were prepared. There is little indication in OTA's record that Congress will be any better off the next time it has to vote on a controversial major program involving complex technology. . . .

Two principal rationales were advanced for the creation of OTA. The first was the need to redress an imbalance of technical expertise between the Congress and the executive branch. Rep. Charles Mosher made this argument persuasively when the OTA bill was being debated on the House floor in 1972:

Let us face it, Mr. Chairman, we in the Congress are constantly outmanned and outgunned by the expertise of the executive agencies.

We desperately need a stronger source of professional advice and information, more immediately and entirely responsible to us and responsive to the demands of our own committees, in order to more nearly match those resources in the executive agencies.

Many, perhaps most of the proposals for new or expanding technologies come to us from the executive branch; or at least it is the representatives of those agencies who present expert testimony to us concerning such proposals. We need to be much more sure of ourselves, from our own sources, to properly challenge the agency people, to probe deeply their advice, to more effectively force them to justify their testimony—to ask sharper questions, demand more precise answers, to pose better alternatives.

The notion was that Congress was dependent on executive agencies for technical information and expertise but, as Sen. Kennedy has noted, those are "the very agencies having the most to gain or lose by the decisions made by Congress." To challenge executive branch programs, Congress needed its own independent technical capability.

A second rationale for OTA was to introduce a unique new element into technology policy development. One of its principal functions would be an aspect of "technology assessment" termed "early warning." OTA would attempt to ascertain early in the development of a new technology what its full range of impacts was likely to be and, in particular, provide an early warning of potentially adverse consequences.

More generally, OTA was to attempt to anticipate future national problems such as the one we face today in energy and direct long-term planning of technology so as to avoid or at least mitigate those problems. In the language of the Technology Assessment Act, signed into law on October 13, 1972, "It is essential that to the fullest extent possible, the consequences of technological applications be anticipated, understood, and considered in the determination of public policy on existing or emerging national problems." . . .

In order to cope with the wide diversity of policy issues that come before it, Congress delegates responsibility to its various specialized committees. And it is at the committee level where technology policy is usually decided upon in the Congress. A striking feature of the operation of many of those committees is the phenomenon of "cozy triangles." The congressional committees often develop close working relationships with the federal agencies and sub-agency units they oversee and with related industry. An obvious example is the strategic weapons triumvirate, consisting of the Armed Services and Defense Appropriations committees in the Congress, Pentagon planners, and defense contractors. The chief promoters of the ABM were not just the Army and Western Electric; Congress' defense committees were close, powerful allies.

Thus, one often finds not an adversary relationship at all between Congress and the executive agencies, but rather close cooperation in pursuit of mutually agreed-upon goals. A principal source of a committee's power, vis-à-vis the rest of Congress, is its access to technical expertise and information about new technologies through its agency and industry contacts. For example, former congressional staffer Alton Frye has described how Congress dealt with the development of multiple, independently targetable warheads (MIRVs) for intercontinental missiles:

Throughout this period [1962–68], the fact of an American MIRV program had registered but slightly in Congress, the significance of the effort not at all. MIRV had reached the flight stage with an invisibility scarcely imaginable for a program expected to cost upwards of $10 billion. The members cognizant of the Minuteman III and Poseidon programs were those on the Armed Services Committees and the Joint Committee on Atomic Energy—men who, it must be said, inclined to skepticism about the possibilities for international arms control and who evaluated MIRV less as a threat to the stability of mutual deterrence than as a hopeful means of protecting U.S. strategic superiority. Outside the still closed circles of the national security cognoscenti, members of Congress were generally ignorant of MIRV, although sizeable sums had already been appropriated for the program in previous defense bills.

Similar remarks would apply to almost any new technology. The vast majority of members of Congress are simply unaware of the implications of most new technologies as they pass through the research and development stage. Awareness and sometimes controversy comes (if at all) only years after the critical decisions have been made to proceed to the advanced development stage of a new technology such as MIRV, ABM, cruise missiles, the B–1, the liquid metal fast breeder reactor, the space shuttle, the SST, and so forth. At that point, of course, reconsideration is much more difficult. Muscle and money have been invested, jobs are at stake; a politically potent constituency for the technology has developed to resist the economic and bureaucratic dislocation that would then accompany significant modification of the program.

On the other hand, some members of Congress—those serving on the specialized committees—are aware of new technologies and are party to the decisions as to whether to proceed to advanced development. As the MIRV example illustrates, however, they tend to be close to the agency promoting the development and sympathetic to its objectives and outlook. This is the reality in Congress: the institutional setting in which OTA has been placed.

This reality calls into question some of the tacit assumptions underlying the creation of OTA, including the notions that Congress would *want* to

- reduce its dependence on the executive agencies in many areas of technology,
- create a new center of authoritative information and expertise in these areas,
- probe deeply the secondary consequences of new technologies before they are deployed, and
- provide a public forum for individuals and groups, such as the science advisers, operating outside present governmental and industrial institutions.

The tensions between rhetoric and reality began to be reconciled when the way OTA was to be organized was debated in the Congress. The part of the original bill dealing with how OTA would be controlled had been written by Harvey Brooks, working with the staff of the Science and Astronautics Committee. It called for an OTA governing board consisting of 13 members: two Senators, two Representatives, the directors of the General Accounting Office and the Congressional Research Service, and seven public members appointed by the President. That is, the "public members" (presumably including eminent scientists) would be a majority of the board.

But Congress, acutely sensitive to the allocation of political power, would have none of that. When the OTA bill was debated on the floor of the House in February 1972, Rep. Jack Brooks asserted, "I am convinced that in our representative system the experts should be on tap, not on top." His colleagues ratified his proposal to substitute a board composed entirely of members of Congress. The final version of the bill established a bipartisan 12-member Technology Assessment Board (hereafter the Board) composed of six Senators and six Representatives, with an equal number from each political party. The bill contained only vestigial remains of the public board; it established a 12–member Technology Assessment Advisory Council (hereafter the Advisory Council), including 10 representatives of the public. The responsibilities of the Advisory Council, clearly subsidiary to the Board, were not spelled out.

During the debate, a concerted attempt was made to allay the concerns of those who feared that OTA might be a Frankenstein monster that would rise up and challenge the authority of the committees. It was emphasized that OTA (1) would remain small (less than about 100 persons), (2) would be a servant of the committees, and (3) would not become an independent center of authoritative expertise. Rep. Charles Mosher, a senior member of the House Science and Astronautics Committee and later the first vice-chairman of the OTA Board, described the relation of OTA to the Congress:

> It is absolutely fundamental to our entire concept, and it is the very essence of this bill, that the OTA shall not in any way usurp any of the intrinsic powers or functions of the Congress itself, nor of any of the Congressional committees; it will only be supplemented. The OTA shall be solely a servant of the Congress.

In particular, OTA would serve the committees. In Mosher's words:

> Now it will be asked, who shall have the privilege of asking or demanding assessment reports from the new Office of Technology Assessment? As we conceive it, in the bill before us, the OTA shall be responsive only to official requests from the committees of the Congress, acting through their respective chairmen; or, of course, the OTA could also respond to requests and instructions from the Congressional leadership.

Fears that OTA might itself become an independent center of authority were assuaged by assurances that the OTA staff would not itself perform assessments, but rather would merely administer contracted studies that congressional committees requested. Witness this exchange between Rep. James Rhodes of Arizona and Science and Astronautics Committee member Rep. Marvin Esch:

> *Mr. Rhodes.* Mr. Chairman, as I read the committee report on this bill, there is no intent to allow this office to develop an in-house scientific capability. In other words it is not intended to be a scientific resource. It is to be a clearinghouse and a purveyor of knowledge which has been gathered by other governmental bodies and which is made available for this office for that particular purpose.
>
> *Mr. Esch.* The gentleman from Arizona is correct. It is intended that it would be a filtering or channeling of information down to specific committees rather than conducting intensive research 'in-house.'

Rep. Mosher spelled out the limited function envisioned for the staff:

> It is very important to recognize that the staff of the new OTA will not themselves do the actual assessment studies and reports that Congress

will ask of them. The essential function of the OTA staff will be administrative. They will be expected to identify, recruit, and employ the best available expert talent, wherever it may be found, to do the actual assessment studies and reports.

It took nearly a year and a half following passage of the Act before OTA actually went into operation in early 1974. During that time, the 12 members of the Board were named, with Sen. Kennedy chosen as the chairman for the 93rd Congress. The Board then selected former Rep. Daddario to serve as director. . . . To be sure, many committees would prefer that OTA stay off their turf. But this may not be nearly the constraint that OTA's record of omission suggests. In most areas of technology policy, Congress is not totally monolithic; jurisdiction is frequently shared among a number of congressional committees. Thus, in the case of strategic weapons doctrine, not only the Armed Services committees, but also the Senate Foreign Relations Committee had a legitimate interest. Similarly, in the case of nuclear proliferation, the Government Operations Committee could claim some jurisdiction. This suggests that even if OTA were to maintain a strict policy of awaiting a committee request before taking on an assessment, few topics would really be out of bounds. As one senior OTA official put it: "I don't see that as an insuperable constraint. All you need is one committee to get it through." . . . So far, the most successful mode of operation for OTA has proved to be the ad hoc expert panel. For OTA to take on many important topics with optimal links to the technical community, the large ratio of outside experts to in-house staff and the flexibility to choose appropriate personnel for each topic makes ad hoc panels attractive. They are particularly well suited to short-term policy issues, as exemplified by the Wiesner panel critique of the Defense Department calculations. Such panels can also aid in "early warning" assessments. The panels can propose questions congressional committees might put to agencies and industry, challenging assumptions and structuring the inquiry, but leaving detailed analyses to the respondents. . . .

NATIONAL AERONAUTICS AND SPACE ACT
OF 1958, AS AMENDED

Public Law No. 85–568 (1958).
42 U.S.C. §§ 2451, 2452.

An act to provide for research into problems of flight within and outside the earth's atmosphere, and for other purposes.

Be it enacted by the Senate and House of Representatives of the United States of America in Congress assembled,

TITLE I—SHORT TITLE, DECLARATION OF
POLICY, AND DEFINITIONS

Public Law 85–568, 85th Congress, H.R. 12575, July 29, 1958,
72 Stat. 426

Short Title

Sec. 101. This Act may be cited as the "National Aeronautics and Space Act of 1958".

Declaration of Policy and Purpose

42 U.S.C. 2451

Sec. 102.   (a) The Congress hereby declares that it is the policy of the United States that activities in space should be devoted to peaceful purposes for the benefit of all mankind.

(b) The Congress declares that the general welfare and security of the United States require that adequate provision be made for aeronautical and space activities.   The Congress further declares that such activities shall be the responsibility of, and shall be directed by, a civilian agency exercising control over aeronautical and space activities sponsored by the United States, except that activities peculiar to or primarily associated with the development of weapons systems, military operations, or the defense of the United States (including the research and development necessary to make effective provision for the defense of the United States) shall be the responsibility of, and shall be directed by, the Department of Defense; and that determination as to which such agency has responsibility for and direction of any such activity shall be made by the President in conformity with section 201(e).

(c) The aeronautical and space activities of the United States shall be conducted so as to contribute materially to one or more of the following objectives:

(1) The expansion of human knowledge of phenomena in the atmosphere and space;

(2) The improvement of the usefulness, performance, speed, safety, and efficiency of aeronautical and space vehicles;

(3) The development and operation of vehicles capable of carrying instruments, equipment, supplies, and living organisms through space;

(4) The establishment of long-range studies of the potential benefits to be gained from, the opportunities for, and the problems involved in the utilization of aeronautical and space activities for peaceful and scientific purposes;

(5) The preservation of the role of the United States as a leader in aeronautical and space science and technology and in the application thereof to the conduct of peaceful activities within and outside the atmosphere;

(6) The making available to agencies directly concerned with national defense of discoveries that have military value or significance, and the furnishing by such agencies, to the civilian agency established to direct and control nonmilitary aeronautical and space activities, of information as to discoveries which have value or significance to that agency;

(7) Cooperation by the United States with other nations and groups of nations in work done pursuant to this Act and in the peaceful application of the results thereof; and

(8) The most effective utilization of the scientific and engineering resources of the United States, with close cooperation among all interested agencies of the United States in order to avoid unnecessary duplication of effort, facilities, and equipment.

(d) The Congress declares that the general welfare of the United States requires that the unique competence in scientific and engineering systems of the National Aeronautics and Space Administration also be directed toward ground propulsion systems research and development. Such development shall be conducted so as to contribute to the objectives of developing energy- and petroleum-conserving ground propulsion systems, and of minimizing the environmental degradation caused by such systems.

(e) The Congress declares that the general welfare of the United States requires that the unique competence in scientific and engineering systems of the National Aeronautics and Space Administration also be directed toward the development of advanced automobile propulsion systems. Such development shall be conducted so as to contribute to the achievement of the purposes set forth in section 302(b) of the Automotive Propulsion Research and Development Act of 1978.

(f) The Congress declares that the general welfare of the United States requires that the unique competence of the National Aeronautics and Space Administration in science and engineering systems be directed to assisting in bioengineering research, development, and demonstration programs designed to alleviate and minimize the effects of disability.

(g) It is the purpose of this Act to carry out and effectuate the policies declared in subsections (a), (b), (c), (d), (e) and (f).

Definitions

42 U.S.C. 2452

Sec. 103. As used in this Act—

(1) the term "aeronautical and space activities" means (A) research into, and the solution of, problems of flight within and outside the earth's atmosphere, (B) the development, construction, testing, and operation for research purposes of aeronautical and space vehicles, and (C) such other activities as may be required for the exploration of space; and

(2) the term "aeronautical and space vehicles" means aircraft, missiles, satellites, and other space vehicles, manned and unmanned, together with related equipment, devises, components, and parts. . . .

NOTE

If there had been an Office of Technology Assessment before the beginning of the space program, would that Office have favored the program? If so, would it have favored wording the National Aeronautics and Space Act as it appears above?

The space program can focus attention on the purposes of technology assessment as well as on Congressional attitudes toward science generally. What kind of technical advice, if any, does a legislature need to decide if a nation should undertake a space program? Scientists and Members of Congress often justify the space program in immediate cost-benefit terms, emphasizing, for example, the "spin-off" of useful devices or the possible military importance of space research. One suspects that scientists may in fact be more motivated by a desire to expand knowledge for its own sake, while Members of Congress may be particularly concerned with considerations of national prestige. Are either of these factors appropriate grounds for spending the taxpayers' money?

Congress usually provides support for research and development in areas where the private sector fails to generate adequate funding. Thus as an area of scientific research leads to a commercially feasible technology, some argue that government should reduce its support. See Ch. 2, Sec. B.1, infra. Valuable areas of research may slip between the cracks under this approach. In 1983, for example, Congress passed the Orphan Drug Act which provides that 50 percent of the expenses of conducting certain clinical research can be used as a credit against taxes. 26 U.S.C. § 44H. Do the following excerpts from the House Report that accompanied this bill adequately justify this program?

HOUSE COMMITTEE ON ENERGY AND COMMERCE, REPORT ON ORPHAN DRUG ACT

H.R.Rep.No. 97–840, 97th Cong., 2d Sess. 6–9 (1983).

BACKGROUND AND NEED FOR THE LEGISLATION

The people of the United States are affected by a broad array of diseases and conditions. Some of these, like hypertension, affect tens of millions of people. Pharmaceutical companies are willing to invest substantial research funds and personnel into the development of drugs for such prevalent diseases because of the tremendous return of investment which could be expected. There are other diseases and conditions, though, such as Huntington's Disease, ALS (Lou Gehrig's Disease) and muscular dystrophy, which affect such a small number of persons that there is virtually no commercial value to any drug which is useful against them. Under these circumstances, it is not financially feasible, except as a public service, for a pharmaceutical manufacturer to expend research and development funds on drugs for these rare diseases or conditions. As a result, drugs for rare diseases and conditions are commonly referred to as "orphan drugs." They generally lack a sponsor to undertake the necessary research and development activities to attain their approval by the Food and Drug Administration (FDA).

Though the Federal government and the private pharmaceutical industry spend millions of dollars a year in biomedical research and drug development, this country's system of financing and conducting biomedical research and for discovering and developing new drugs does not adequately account for the inherent disincentives in orphan drug development. The system has three components: the Federal government, the nonprofit medical research centers which are mainly in medical schools and other affiliated hospitals, and the pharmaceutical industry's research laboratories. The Federal government conducts medical research in its own laboratories and clinics and it also finances medical research and research training programs conducted by academic institutions through competitively awarded grants. The government also regulates the pharmaceutical industry's drug development and marketing activities.

The academic medical research centers conduct mainly basic medical and clinical research. The role of systematic discovery and development of new drugs has been relegated to the private, profit-oriented pharmaceutical industry. Almost all new drugs brought out in the last 20 years were discovered in the pharmaceutical industry's laboratories.

This system is based on an assumption that the necessarily market-oriented activities of the pharmaceutical industry will produce the drugs and vaccines that the advance of basic medical science makes possible. Unfortunately, there is no governmental policy, and therefore no governmental mechanism, to facilitate the development of those drugs or vaccines, such as orphan drugs, for which the market offers no financial rewards.

There has been interest for many years in the problem of inadequate motivation, and resources, for the development and distribution of drugs for rare diseases. The FDA has established two committees, in 1975 and again in 1979, to study and report on this matter. The 1979 report contained a thorough analysis of the problems and an extensive list of recommendations. In a 1977 report to the Congress the Office of Technology Assessment indicated that the problem had existed for some time but had not received adequate attention. And in another 1977 report to the Secretary of Health, Education and Welfare the Commission for the Control of Huntington's Disease and its Consequences recommended the formation of a task force to propose recommendations.

The Subcommittee on Health and the Environment, after conducting initial hearings in June 1980, designed and conducted an extensive survey of pharmaceutical companies, Federal research agencies (including the National Institutes of Health, the Alcohol, Drug Abuse and Mental Health Administration, and the Centers for Disease Control), the FDA and several independent university scientists. The purpose of the survey was to identify as many drugs for rare diseases as possible and to gather information about them. The survey covered 196 different drug products.

The initial results of the survey were published on March 8, 1982, in the Subcommittee's "Preliminary Report of the Survey on Drugs for Rare Diseases." Of the 196 drugs surveyed, 134 were identified as drugs for rare diseases; and of these 134 drugs, 47 are approved for use in the United States. Of the 47 approved drugs, 34 are marketed by pharmaceutical companies and 13 are made available through government agencies.

The major findings of the survey can be summarized as follows:

Orphan drugs are predominantly used in the treatment of rare diseases.

They are not profitable.

It is difficult to conduct human clinical trials to prove their effectiveness because there are so few people with any given disease.

Many are not patentable.

They cause more adverse side effects, on average, than drugs for common diseases.

There are many drugs for rare diseases which are not approved and on the market.

The Committee favorably reported this bill because it believes that many more drugs for rare diseases can be developed if private drug companies become more actively involved. The Committee was told by FDA at the March 8, 1982 hearing held by the Subcommittee on Health and the Environment that since 1970 approximately 960 drugs had been approved by FDA. The Subcommittee's survey found that only 34 of these have been developed and marketed by pharmaceutical companies; and in 24 of the 34 drugs, either a government agency or a university assisted by providing funds or participating in discovery or development or both. The Committee concluded that in order to encourage greater involvement by private companies, changes should be made in applicable Federal laws to reduce the costs of developing drugs for rare diseases, and to provide financial incentives for their development, and to better coordinate government agencies involved in drug development and regulation and those agencies and private pharmaceutical firms.

In formulating legislation to encourage orphan drug development, the Committee recognized that the determination that a drug is for a rare

disease or condition, and therefore lacks the potential for an adequate
return on investment, can occur at different stages of a drug's development. In perhaps the best known orphan drugs, it has occurred after the
essential research has been done, but before practical development can
prove its safety and efficacy. These drugs need a sponsor to test the drug
and seek FDA approval for marketing.

This determination also occurs during the earlier research stage of the
drug research and development process as new insights occur and new
substances are discovered to have potential as therapies for rare diseases
and disorders. Research on these drugs needs to be continued until additional knowledge is gained.

Orphan drug legislation needs to encourage pursuit of both kinds of
orphan drugs to practical fruition in patient care as rapidly as possible.
The Committee believes H.R. 5238, as amended, accomplishes this goal
by establishing new governmental policy and appropriate governmental
mechanisms to facilitate the development of drugs for rare diseases and
conditions.

PROPOSED LEGISLATION

The Committee's bill amends the Federal Food, Drug and Cosmetic
Act (FFDCA), the Public Health Service Act (PHSA) and the Internal Revenue Code (IRC). The Committee hopes and expects that the amendments to the FFDCA will encourage private pharmaceutical companies to
develop and make available drugs for rare diseases and conditions. Included in the Committee's definition of drugs are any biologicals, such as
vaccines which are used for rare diseases or conditions.

Designation of Drugs for Rare Diseases or Conditions

In order to assure that the financial incentives and other regulatory
provisions of the bill apply only to drugs for rare diseases and conditions,
the bill establishes a "designation" procedure at the Food and Drug Administration (FDA). Under this procedure, the manufacturer or sponsor
of a drug may, at its discretion, request that its drug be designated as a
drug for a disease or condition which is rare in the United States. The
decision to request the designation is exclusively within the discretion of
the sponsor and may be made at any time during the drug development
process or while the FDA is reviewing the sponsor's new drug application.
Once FDA designates the drug, then the provisions of the bill are applicable to the drug. . . .

Upon the request of a sponsor, the FDA would make a determination
of whether the drug (or biological) is in fact for a rare disease or condition. The FDA would evaluate (1) what specific indication or use the
drug will be, is, or has been tested for, and (2) whether the drug would be
used for a rare disease or condition if it were approved (or in the case of a
biological, a license were issued) by the FDA as safe and effective for the
indication or use for which it will be, is being, or was tested. If the FDA
determines that drug or biological is for a rare disease or condition, the
FDA would be required to designate it.

The FDA is given broad latitude in determining whether a disease or
condition is "rare in the States." The Committee chose not to define this
term because of the difficulty of predicting the variety of circumstances
which might arise. Establishing a population number as a definition was
considered and rejected as too inflexible to accomplish the goal of more

orphan drug development. Listing all rare diseases and conditions also
was rejected as impractical. . . .

NOTE

If Congress desires to fund research on orphan drugs, why doesn't Congress
itself decide which drugs are needed or which diseases are rare? In delegating
these functions to an administrative agency, Congress followed a familiar pattern
in the science policy field. See Ch. 4, Sec. C.1, infra.

Why did Congress fund the orphan drug program through tax credits rather
than direct grants? The tax system is often used to further social policies, including policies relating to science. Congress has, for example, designed tax provisions to promote solar energy. See Ch. 9, Sec. A.1, infra. This approach makes
it even harder for Congress and the public to get an overview of what in fact
constitutes American science policy.

Would consolidating all federal research and development spending in one
Department of Science, with a unified annual science budget for Congress to consider, better serve national goals or those of science? The practical chances of
such a Department coming about are limited, since huge agencies like Defense
and Health and Human Services (which contains the National Institutes of Health)
would not likely give up their science programs without an enormous political
fight. Nonetheless, proposals surface from time to time—in 1983, President Reagan's science advisor reportedly began a study of the wisdom of merging some
civilian science programs into a new department. Norman, NSF, Do You Take
NBS . . ., 221 Science 1363 (1983).

c. Spending the Money: Who Gets It and What Strings are Attached

GRASSETTI v. WEINBERGER

United States District Court for the Northern District of California, 1976.
408 F.Supp. 142.

CONTI, DISTRICT JUDGE.

Plaintiff Davide R. Grassetti, Director of Research for the Arequipa
Foundation, San Francisco, Clinical Associate Professor of Biochemistry,
School of Dentistry, University of the Pacific, San Francisco, and holder of
a Ph.D. degree in chemistry from the University of Lausanne, Switzerland,
brings this action against various individuals associated with the federal
government's cancer research program, alleging that at their hands he received unfair treatment in their denial of research grant money to enable
him to study and develop a certain chemical compound, CPDS,[1] and a
family of compounds related thereto, which he discovered, and which he
claims "impede the spread of existing cancer." [2] He labels their decisions
to disapprove his grant applications arbitrary and capricious and without
factual foundation, and as being the product of invidious discrimination
practiced against him because, *inter alia,* he held patents covering the series of compounds, and he had made various public statements, some of
which were critical of National Cancer Institute funding procedures, and

---

1. "CPDS", or carboxypridine disul-
phide, according to plaintiff, retards the
growth or spread of cancer by reacting with
cancer cells in such manner as to form a stable compound on the surface of such cell.
In a sense, then, the theory of the anti-meta-

static (or anti-growth or spread) mechanism
of CPDS is that it forms a hard wall around
cancer cells, which does not admit of further
growth.

2. See Complaint at p. 1.

others which tended to disparage an FDA-approved antibiotic known as Rifampicin.[3]

In addition to the challenges brought against the disapprovals of his grant applications, Grassetti alleges that the defendants arbitrarily refused adequately to test CPDS for its alleged anti-metastatic effects,[4] or to provide for its testing by others, in order that it could be considered for possible development by other scientists if the government would not fund plaintiff to do so. Further, he makes general claims that various agencies within the National Institutes of Health (NIH), which are charged by Congress with the responsibility of waging a comprehensive war on cancer, are failing to do so, in contravention of the statutory mandates. The crux of this contention as it relates to the instant controversy seems to be that since the government's cancer research apparatus has "blocked" the development of plaintiff's life-prolonging drug for improper reasons or for no reasons at all, the agencies and individuals responsible are not living up to their statutory duty, as plaintiff states it, "to comprehensively and energetically exploit scientific leads which may aid in the treatment of cancer". One specific violation of this duty is purported to lie in defendants' failure to promulgate regulations which set forth specific guidelines and standards to be applied in the process by which applications for cancer research grants are reviewed for scientific merit. Had such regulations been in existence, asserts plaintiff, there would have been no opportunity for the kind of arbitrary and discriminatory treatment to which his grant applications allegedly were subjected. Finally, plaintiff challenges the entire administrative scheme which allocates, as between the NIH and the National Cancer Institute (NCI), decision-making power in the area of scientific review of grant applications. These claims will be dealt with in detail below. . . .

I. *Facts*

Over the past several years, Dr. Grassetti has applied on numerous occasions for grant support in the areas of chemistry, pharmacology, and cancer, and has several times been successful in receiving funds. The last award was made in the amount of $105,850 for the period October 1, 1971, through September 30, 1973, on an application entitled "Prevention of the Spread of Cancer", under which Dr. Grassetti was to study and document the chemical and pharmacological properties of CPDS and related compounds as they affect the growth of cancer On April 6, 1973, as the above grant was nearing the end of its term, Dr. Grassetti submitted an application (CA 12469–03A1) in order to obtain additional funds in the amount of $538,041 for five years to continue his research and exploration of the same family of compounds, the specific purpose of the new request being "to determine the precise mechanism through which

---

3. Some biomedical theorists suggest, Dr. Grassetti among them that Rifampicin actually favors the formation of metastases (or secondary cancer tumors) due to its immunosuppressant properties. See Attachments 1 and 2 to Plaintiff's Supplemental Response to Defendants' Motion for Summary Judgment. Plaintiff made several public statements expressing his beliefs in 1972 and 1973 in an attempt to bring them to the attention of the FDA and Institutes of Health. National Cancer Institute testing of the drug gave negative results.

4. Metastasis is the growth or spread of cancer cells. Dr. Grassetti claims that the National Cancer Institute's screening of compounds submitted for anti-cancer testing is inadequate in that only toxicity and anti-tumor activity, and not anti-metastatic activity, are measured, and thus that CPDS did not get a fair chance to exhibit positive beneficial results. This matter is taken up in part IV.B. infra.

the spread of cancer is prevented by this type of compound." Consistent with the procedure which is followed by NIH upon receipt of grant applications, see infra, plaintiff's application was sent for scientific merit review to a study section chosen for its particular expertise in the technical field concerned—in this case, the Experimental Therapeutics Study Section. This proposal was reviewed during the Section's September, 1973, meeting, and disapproval was unanimously recommended to the National Cancer Advisory Board "because of the lack of meaningful progress in Dr. Grassetti's research and his failure to follow previous Study Section recommendations relative to obtaining data to support the biological and pharmacological aspects of his research". Dr. Grassetti was subsequently advised of the Study Section's recommendation.

Dr. Grassetti submitted another research proposal on October 1, 1973 (CA 16150–01) which the Division of Research Grants (DRG) of the NIH, see infra, determined to be not significantly different from the April 6, 1973, proposal (CA 12469–03A1) previously reviewed by the Experimental Therapeutics Study Section. DRG did not, therefore, send this proposal on to that Study Section or to another for review, but rather ruled that further review would be repetitious. Having been advised of this disposition, Dr. Grassetti sent a letter to all members of the NCAB [National Cancer Advisory Board] expressing disappointment; nevertheless, the NCAB at its November, 1973, meeting concurred with the Study Section's recommendations concerning application CA 12469–03A1, and, by necessary implication (assuming the DRG's assessment of CA 16150–01 was correct), the latter application as well.

On March 11, 1974, another application, entitled "Metastasis Prevention by Cell Surface Modification" (CA 16150–01A1), was submitted by plaintiff. In view of Dr. Grassetti's expressed dissatisfaction with the recommendations of the Experimental Therapeutics Study Section concerning the earlier proposal, a Special Study Section was formed, composed of five scientists with expertise in relevant fields, none of whom were members of the Experimental Therapeutics Study Section, who conducted a visit of Dr. Grassetti's laboratory at the University of the Pacific to obtain first-hand information concerning plaintiff's facilities and research support, in the light of which the grant application could be comprehensively evaluated. Following their scientific review of this latest proposal, the Section unanimously recommended that the application be disapproved, which decision was communicated to plaintiff. Plaintiff thereupon requested of the Executive Secretary of the NCAB that he be allowed to make an oral presentation at the next NCAB meeting. While this request was denied, in the exercise of the Board's discretion over the scope and content of its proceedings, plaintiff was informed that he could submit a written statement which would be circulated to the Board's members. So far as the record shows, plaintiff submitted no such statement.

Upon further requests by Dr. Grassetti for the NCAB to conduct a special review of his latest application (CA 16150–01A1), the Chairman of the Board appointed two members to conduct an independent review of the administrative details of the Special Study Section's actions. These doctors reported to the NCAB that "the administrative peer review procedures followed by both the Special Study Section and the NCI staff were proper and fair."

On December 27, 1974, plaintiff submitted a further grant application (CA 16150–01A2) entitled "Mechanism of Metastasis Prevention", which was reviewed by the Experimental Therapeutics Study Section during its

April, 1975, meeting, and unanimously recommended by that Section for disapproval by the NCAB. That recommendation was followed. Shortly thereafter, plaintiff requested and received a report of the Study Section's reasons for its action, which stated in part that "lack of detail in [the application] was indicative of a lack of appreciation by Dr. Grassetti for biomedical and pharmacological studies."

Concurrent with plaintiff's various submissions of grant proposals, he sent to NCI several compounds for testing, among them CPDS, which were screened for anti-cancer activity, without significant positive results.

II. *The Issues*

While the instant complaint, its prayer for relief and the supporting papers are extremely prolix and wide-ranging, it is the opinion of this court that the issues meritorious of our consideration separate along two major lines of inquiry, the first having several subparts.

First, we must consider whether the various administrative determinations respecting plaintiff's grant applications were made in accordance with law. Resolution of this issue necessarily includes consideration of plaintiff's allegations of (1) conflicts of interest on the part of scientists assigned to evaluate the applications, (2) discrimination against plaintiff because he had patents, (3) discrimination against plaintiff because of his exercise of rights guaranteed by the First Amendment, (4) defendants' failure to promulgate adequate regulations as required by law setting forth standards for scientific review, (5) the NCI's and the NCAB's improper delegation of scientific merit review functions to the Division of Research Grants (DRG) of NIH, and (6) defendants' refusal to make full disclosure to plaintiff of the contents of all reports, documents and files concerning his grant applications, as he claims is required by the Freedom of Information Act.

Second, independent of the relationship between the various agencies and plaintiff as a grant applicant, we must consider whether the federal agencies and individuals charged under the National Cancer Act with various responsibilities in administering the government's war on cancer have lived up to their statutory duties in their handling of the chemical compounds submitted by plaintiff for testing.

Resolution of the important issues raised by the first inquiry necessarily requires a complete understanding of the administrative and scientific schemata pursuant to which a grant application is evaluated and a decision whether or not to fund it is made. This background will be presented first. The court will then pass to the testing issue.

III. *The Grant Application Review Process*

A. *Statutes and Regulations:*

Subchapter III of Title 42 of the U.S. Code provides the statutory framework for the formation of the National Research Institutes, one of which is the National Cancer Institute, created under Part A, 42 U.S.C. §§ 281–286g. The NCI is a division of the National Institutes of Health, which is composed of ten other institutes and various support divisions, all dedicated to research and development activities in the area of public health and welfare. NIH is in turn a component of the Public Health Service, a part of the Department of Health, Education and Welfare (HEW). [Now Health and Human Services (HHS).]

Section 301(c) of the Public Health Service Act, 42 U.S.C. § 241(c), authorizes the Secretary of HEW to:

Make grants-in-aid to universities, hospitals, laboratories, and other public or private institutions, and to individuals for such research projects as are . . ., with respect to cancer, recommended by the National Cancer Advisory Board . . .

The award of research grants under the above provision is governed by 42 C.F.R. Part 52. With respect to evaluation and disposition of research grant applications, 42 C.F.R. § 52.13(a) states:

(a) Evaluation. All applications filed in accordance with § 52.12 shall be evaluated by the Secretary through such officers and employees and such experts or consultants engaged for this purpose as he determines are specially qualified in the areas of research involved in the project, including review by an appropriate National Advisory Council or other body as may be required by law. The Secretary's evaluation shall take into account among other pertinent factors the scientific merit and significance of the project, the competency of the proposed staff in relation to the type of research involved, the feasibility of the project, the likelihood of its producing meaningful results, the proposed project and the amount of grant funds necessary for completion, and in the case of applications for support of research in emergency medical services, special consideration shall be given to applications for grants for research relating to the delivery of emergency medical services in rural areas.

In the case of cancer research grant applications, the direct costs of which do not exceed $35,000, the Director of NCI, under procedures approved by the Director of NIH, may approve grants after "appropriate review for scientific merit" without the necessity for review and recommendation by the NCAB. Where direct costs exceed that figure, the NCAB must review and recommend approval to the Director of NCI. See 42 U.S.C. § 282(b)(1) and (2). In this manner, requests for small grants can receive expedited treatment. See 1971 U.S.Code Congressional & Administrative News, pp. 2356–57. When the NCAB recommends approval, it in effect certifies to the Secretary of HEW that the application "show[s] promise of making valuable contributions to human knowledge with respect to the cause, prevention, or methods of diagnosis or treatment of cancer". 42 U.S.C. § 284(c). The NCAB's decision to approve reflects the Board's assessment of the proposal's technical and scientific merit as well as its determination that the proposed project fits into the NCI's mission and research priorities and into the total pattern of research in universities and other institutions. The determination whether or not to grant funding must still be made after approval of the Director of NCI, on the basis of budget and priorities existing within the Institute as a whole, by the Secretary of HEW, who considers the Institute's own assessment of the application, in light of Institute policies and program priorities and availability of appropriations. The power to make a final decision is, by operation of the statutory scheme, lodged in the Secretary, HEW.

B. *Administrative Grant Application Processes within NIH.*

Applications for research grants received at NIH, are sent to the NIH's Division of Research Grants, which normally assigns them to one of a number of regularly constituted advisory committees (referred to as "study sections") responsible for initial scientific review and recommendation. At the same time, DRG designates the appropriate awarding unit or Institute (such as NCI), to which the proposed research grant application will be referred. DRG makes the study section assignments and the awarding unit designation on the basis of the scientific or technical area into which the application's subject matter falls. Often, of course, the subject of a given application reaches across many technical disciplines, in which case an ad hoc study group may be formed, composed of scientists and biomedical experts from all relevant areas of technical expertise. In such a case DRG designates more than one Institute as the appropriate awarding units. It is presumably in response to the obvious need for coordination of all research activities within NIH that a central clearing house of grant applications, namely DRG, is maintained separate from any particular Institute.

The scientist administrators in DRG who assign applications to study sections are organizationally separate from the Institutes and their programs. Each study section is made up of experts in the biomedical sciences and other scientific areas relevant to the particular inquiry, who come, with few exceptions, from universities and other organizations outside the federal government.

Following the initial study section review a "summary statement" is prepared by the executive secretary, a DRG staff member, in which the salient features of the members' deliberations, recommendations, and substantive conclusions relating to the application are documented. Upon request, the applicant is provided with reasons abstracted from the "summary statement" for the action recommended on the application.

The study section's recommendation on the application represents an assessment of scientific and technical merit only. It is not intended as a competitive review in relation to other applications being reviewed by the same group or other groups. If approval is recommended, the study section is required to assign to the application a rating of its scientific merit, which can aid the appropriate national council (such as the NCAB) in making its decision on relative priorities of approved projects.

Whether the study section advises approval or disapproval, the recommendation as to cancer research proposals goes to the NCAB, which, considering not only technical merit but also the needs of the Institute and NIH as a whole, the need for the initiation of research in new areas, the degree of relevance of the proposed research to the mission of the Institute, and other matters of policy, can make an independent decision on the application. If the study section has recommended disapproval, the NCAB can "remand" for reconsideration, or simply recommend approval in the exercise of its own judgment. Applications, with their attached study section recommendations, are reviewed by the NCAB at three of its four yearly meetings, in March, June and November. The October NCAB meeting is generally reserved for review of ongoing NCI research programs.

As noted, NCAB approval is communicated to the Director, NIH and eventually the Secretary, HEW, who makes the final decision and disburses the funds.

IV. *The Law Governing Plaintiff's Claims.*

A. *Denial of Research Funding.*

In this aspect of the case, plaintiff is basically alleging that the administrative determinations made by first the study sections and eventually the NCAB, the Director, NIH, and the Secretary, HEW, in disapproving his grant applications were arbitrary, discriminatory, without factual basis, were made as a reprisal for his exercise of his First Amendment rights or because he held patents on his chemical compounds and thus constituted an abuse of administrative discretion.

These charges require the court to inquire into whether it is given jurisdiction to review such an administrative determination, and, if so, the scope of that review. The answer is found in the provisions of the Administrative Procedure Act dealing with judicial review of administrative action, namely, 5 U.S.C. §§ 701 and 702. Section 702 states:

A person suffering legal wrong because of agency action, or adversely affected or aggrieved by agency action within the meaning of a relevant statute, is entitled to judicial review thereof.

Section 701(a) states, in pertinent part: This chapter applies . . . except to the extent that—

(1) statutes preclude judicial review; or

(2) agency action is committed to agency discretion by law.

Since neither the Public Health Service Act nor the National Cancer Act contains any provision expressly precluding review, jurisdiction exists here to the extent that the action undertaken ultimately by the Secretary, HEW, is not of a type committed to his agency's or his delegate agency's discretion by law. See 4 Davis, Admin.Law, § 28.16.

While we need not go so far as to decide the question, it is probable that the medical merits of agency decisions on research grant applications are committed to the unreviewable discretion of the agency, subject to judicial scrutiny only where it is alleged that the agency has transgressed a constitutional guarantee or violated an express statutory or procedural directive. See, e.g., Apter v. Richardson, 510 F.2d 351 (7th Cir. 1975); Kletschka v. Driver, 411 F.2d 436 (2d Cir. 1969); Cappadora v. Celebrezze, 356 F.2d 1 (2d Cir. 1966); see generally, Saferstein, Nonreviewability: A Functional Analysis of "Committed to Agency Discretion", 82 Harv.L. Rev. 367 (1968) In cases such as these, and the one at bar here, were a substantial evidence or abuse of discretion standard held to apply, the result would be to place a tremendous burden on the courts to digest masses of technical data before it could be decided that one grant application was so superior that it was an abuse of discretion to reject it in favor of others. A much more important consideration is that, unfortunate as it might be, it is a fact of life that courts are simply not competent to step into the role of a medical research scientist faced with having to evaluate an applicant's technical expertise, the theoretical chemical and pharmacological underpinnings of his study methodology, the statistical validity of his test results and the conclusions drawn therefrom, or just about any other factor of importance to NCI in deciding who should get its research money. But in this court's opinion the preeminent consideration militating against general judicial review of research grant decisions is that such review would place a heavy burden of litigation on an agency with more important matters at hand, would delay the funding process to the detriment of potential grantees, and would perforce place in jeopardy a program designed to combat cancer.

Even assuming, however, that a substantial evidence standard should be applied, it is amply satisfied here. Some of the reasons given for the denial of research funds were that: (1) The application "indicates a lack of appreciation for experiments which should be conducted, and those which have been done have in nearly every respect been inadequately presented both in the application and in the discussion during the site visit. There are serious questions of the significance and reproducibility of the test system, as used here, to detect effects upon metastases and the entire program is dependent upon this;" (2) Proposed experiments to determine, among other things, the interaction of CPDS with the surface of cancer cells, were presented "in a diffuse way with the details either not settled upon or not presented in a manner to permit evaluation;" (3) "There are reservations on the chemical interpretation of what the principal investigator observes in his studies in cellular systems . . ." Plaintiff's interpretations of the relevant chemical phenomena were in many cases contrary to hard results obtained by other experimenters; (4) "In summary, the results are interesting, however, appropriate design of experiments has not been made and a rather naive chemical view of the reaction of CPDS (or related derivatives) with cells has been adopted. The applicant failed to present well thought out ideas about his short-term goals and did not project the insight to pursue a longer term planned series of experiments to warrant project support. It does not appear that he is familiar with the chemistry of unsymmetrical disulfides nor the principles which govern their reactions. This proposal did not generate confidence that the applicant could work with chemically modified macromolecules in a careful and meaningful series of experiments." See particularly, Attachments O and W to Affidavit of Richard A. Tjalma, Assistant Director for Board and Panel Affairs, NCI, Defendants' Motion for Summary Judgment. The record more than adequately shows that the determination to disapprove the applications was made after careful review by expert medical and scientific professionals, who, in the exercise of their best technical judgment, simply were not satisfied that the proposals had such scientific merit as to justify funding.

The court's only legitimate function in a case such as this is the extremely limited one of insuring that the agency's determination was arrived at through procedures which were reasonable and fair. After a careful review of the record, the court finds that there was no deviation here from the usual procedures under which grant applications are processed, and those procedures, which have been in existence for a number of years in NCI and NIH, are eminently fair in guaranteeing to the maximum extent possible that the best ideas in the field of cancer research are highlighted for government support, and that notwithstanding plaintiff's allegations to the contrary, the administrative decision here is sufficiently supported by the medical and scientific evidence. This case bears striking similarity to *Kletschka*, supra, in which the court upheld a denial of research funds in affirming the district court's grant of defendants' motion for summary judgment, against plaintiff's charge that the agency action was undertaken in retaliation against him for his having exercised certain of his legal rights. Id. at 441–42.

Apart from the reviewability or nonreviewability of the decision not to award plaintiff a grant, however, plaintiff charges that the defendants' action constituted certain violations of law, as to which a reviewing court may take cognizance and in the appropriate case, substitute its own judicial judgment as to what the law is and whether a violation has occurred. See 4 Davis, Administrative Law § 30.01 et seq. Specifically, plaintiff has charged (1) that certain individuals who had a part in reviewing his applications were acting with conflicts of interest, violative of 18 U.S.C. § 208, 43 C.F.R. § 73.735–1202, and Executive Order 11222, including Section

302 thereof; (2) that the National Cancer Act, specifically Section 410A thereof, 42 U.S.C. § 286e, requires the Director, NCI, to promulgate certain regulations, which he has not done; and (3) that the delegation by NCI to the Division of Research Grants, NIH, of initial responsibility for review of grant applications is violative of the express provisions of the National Cancer Act whereunder scientific review is to be accomplished by NCI and not by NIH or its divisions. We now turn to these contentions.

(1) The conflict of interest provisions above require that one with a financial interest in the outcome of a given decision to be made by a government agency not be allowed to contribute in any way to making that decision. Plaintiff claims that the three members of the study group which initially evaluated application CA 16150–01A1 in May of 1974 were acting with conflicts of interest in that these individuals or the institutions with which they were associated were recipients of NCI funded grants. Suffice to say that this fact in itself does not create a conflict of interest within the meaning of the relevant statutes and regulations. In no way would the individuals involved benefit financially by denying grant money to Dr. Grassetti, unless it be argued that their denial to him would leave more money in the pot for future proposals from themselves, a possibility of conflict of interest which the court deems to be much too remote. As a practical matter, high-level cancer research probably cannot be carried forward with the kind of vigor needed to solve this important and complex problem without government funding on a large scale; and probably in some way every doctor or scientist meeting the extremely high standards of technical competence required to be named to a study group has in the past been or is in the present on the receiving end of government support.

Putting this issue in its correct context, conflicts of interest in the grant review process would arise when a study section or NCAB member contributed to a decision as to whether to award himself or his institution a funding grant. This is assiduously avoided by NIH, NCI and NCAB policies and directives which disqualify such individuals from serving on study groups or being in attendance at NCAB meetings during which the individual's or his institution's proposal is being discussed and reviewed. See Release 4506, NIH Manual, "Review of Research Grant Applications" at par. G.1.b. and Attachment E to Affidavit of Dr. Tjalma, Defendants' Motion for Summary Judgment.

The court finds the above procedures designed to avoid conflicts of interest in the grant application review process adequate and reasonable, and finds that there was no violation of law in defendants' actions with respect to Dr. Grassetti's applications.

(2) Section 410A of the National Cancer Act, as amended, 42 U.S.C. § 286e(a) states:

The Director of the National Cancer Institute shall, by regulation, provide for proper scientific review of all research grants and programs over which he has authority (1) by utilizing, to the maximum extent possible, appropriate peer review groups established within the National Institutes of Health and composed principally of non-Federal scientists and other experts in the scientific and disease fields, and (2) when appropriate, by establishing, with the approval of the National Cancer Advisory Board and the Director of the National Institutes of Health, other formal peer review groups as may be required.

Subsection (b) directs the Director, NCI, to prepare annual reports to the President for transmittal to the Congress on the "activities, progress, and accomplishments" under the National Cancer Program.

Citing subsection (a), plaintiff asserts that the Director, NCI, has failed to obey the duty contained therein by virtue of his not having promulgated a regulation providing objective standards and criteria under which applications for research grants can be reviewed for scientific merit.

This contention is without merit. First, as a matter of statutory construction, it is by no means clear that subsection (a) requires such a regulation. The thrust of the provision seems to cover only existing grants and programs, that is to say, those as to which a decision to fund has been made and which at that point actually constitute an element of the National Cancer Program's research activities. This would not include potential grants, those as to which a decision to fund has not been made. Support for this construction is found in subsection (b) in that the duties placed on the Director, NCI, in subsection (a) seem to look to the requirement that that official make an annual comprehensive report on on-going activities and accomplishments to the President and Congress. The Director must have some means of apprising himself of these activities, through the mechanism of scientific review thereof.

It is not necessary to so hold, however, because in the opinion of this court, the Director, NCI, has, in fact, promulgated regulations governing review for scientific merit, through NIH and its grant application review component, DRG. See Referral Handbook, NIH, DRG (Attachment A to Tjalma Affidavit, Defendants' Motion for Summary Judgment); Orientation Handbook for New Members of Study Sections, NIH, DRG (Attachment B to Tjalma Affidavit); Releases 4506 and 4507, NIH Manual, "Review of Research Grant Applications" and "Exchange of Information between Initial Review Groups and Awarding Units" (Attachment C to Tjalma Affidavit); Handbook for Executive Secretaries, 3d ed., NIH, DRG (February 1973) (Attachment D to Tjalma Affidavit). The court finds that the guidelines for scientific merit review contained in these publications go just about as far as is practicably possible in setting forth "objective criteria" for evaluations on scientific bases. What the plaintiff seems to request is something much more specific in the way of exact pre-established standards for deciding a proposal has the requisite "scientific merit" to justify funding it. As a scientist, plaintiff surely realizes that a great deal of independent scientific judgment must go into an assessment of a given proposal, and that hard and fast rules against which can be tested "scientific merit" simply do not exist. The only way there can be assurance that those proposals with "scientific merit" are recommended for funding and those without it are not, is to pick the best qualified experts in the relevant technical fields to make the decision on the basis of their well-informed judgment. There is absolutely no indication in the record that NIH is doing other than that, and plaintiff has made no challenge of the credentials of the scientists assigned to evaluate his proposals.

In view of the foregoing, the court holds that defendant Director, NIH, has in Dr. Grassetti's case complied in every respect with the law, particularly section 410A of the National Cancer Act.

(3) Plaintiff also challenges the delegation by NCI of initial review for scientific merit to NIH and its component, DRG. Plaintiff's position basically is that NCI and NCAB should perform the entire review function where research proposals in the cancer area are concerned. Plaintiff can-

not reasonably challenge the use of peer groups for initial review purposes, given the strong congressional approbation their use received, as is shown in the legislative history. See 1971 U.S.Code Congressional & Administrative News, pp. 2356–57. It is also evident from that history that Congress contemplated the coordination of all health-related research by a group within NIH:

> One of the important concerns of the biomedical research community had to do with preserving the integrity of the peer review system now applied across all biomedical research areas. The concern, expressed by a number of witnesses before the Committee, was that the latitude allowed in the Senate bill for the creation of special cancer review bodies would lead to the development of two peer review systems applying disparate standards; and that, further, a dual system in this area would effectively fragment the biomedical research community. . . . The hazards of evaluating the scientific merit of research projects are many, but the Committee has received abundant testimony that no system has yet surpassed the study section system of the National Institutes of Health in assuring that high standards of quality and scientific merit—in addition to program relevance—are applied before public funds are expended. The Committee, therefore, has taken steps to assure that these advantages of the NIH study section system will be applied to the effort to find a cure for cancer . . .

Id. The history also unequivocally indicates that Congress intended the attack on cancer to be undertaken in the "interdisciplinary setting" provided by NIH coordination. Id. at 2339. See also id. at 2348–49.

In view of these strong indications of Congressional intent that cancer research activities be coordinated by NIH and that the existing peer review or study group systems be utilized, plaintiff's contention is seen to be untenable. The procedure employed by NIH, NCI and the NCAB in evaluating grant applications is exactly what Congress hoped for, indeed, mandated, in the National Cancer Act. The court finds no violation of law in the method by which cancer research grant applications in general, and plaintiff's in particular, are processed through NIH, DRG, NCI and NCAB. . . .

B.   *Testing of CPDS*

As noted, plaintiff claims that defendants failed adequately to test CPDS, which, he asserts, they are legally required to do if they are to obey their statutory command to exploit every available lead showing promise in the treatment or cure of cancer. The contention basically is that CPDS is an antimetastatic compound, whose beneficial effects are seen only in the retardation or termination of growth or spread of cancer, whereas defendants have tested it only for its toxicity and its anti-tumor effects, which Dr. Grassetti never intimated that it had.

Apart from whatever legal duty may lie on defendants to test compounds submitted to them, the court finds that defendants did in fact perform various standard tests, and the treatment accorded plaintiff's chemical compounds was reasonable and non-arbitrary. Tests are conducted by the Division of Cancer Treatment of NCI in the following manner: Tumor cells are injected into two groups of mice. One group is treated with the subject substance (test group), the other group is left untreated (control group). The prime criterion used to assess potential anti-cancer activity is the effect of the substance on mortality. If there is no difference in survival between the test and control groups, or if there is no shrinking of visible tumor masses, the substance is not tested further unless something unique is known about the compound or class of compounds which would lead to further tests.

NCI does not routinely screen substances *specifically* for their anti-metastatic (prevention of cancer spread) activity. This is because, if anti-cancer effects are observed during regular screening, NCI proceeds with drug development regardless of the anti-cancer mechanism involved. In its screening activity, NCI is interested in the net outcome of the test (i.e., survival rate and tumor shrinkage) and not the precise mechanism involved. Thus, the NCI approach is a "black box" approach; that is, total anti-cancer activity, including one or both of two possible factors, anti-tumor and anti-metastatic effects, is measured, without careful differentiation between the two. Differentiation is not absolutely necessary, since it is the total anti-cancer effect which is the most significant variable.

The Director of the Division of Cancer Treatment, Vincent T. DeVita, M.D., states:

> Although there are tests which could perhaps be utilized to determine specifically the anti-metastatic effects of drugs, in the judgment of NCI scientists these approaches would be no more reliable for predicting the potential utility of anti-cancer drugs than those currently employed to screen for overall anti-cancer activity. In other words, if no anti-cancer activity is observed for a substance tested, as evidenced by the absence of a reduction in mortality or of tumor shrinkage, there is no scientific purpose served by testing for added results of anti-metastatic activity of hundreds of thousands of compounds, most of which will not be shown to inhibit tumor growth in any site. Furthermore, currently there is no *generally* accepted test that directly measures anti-metastatic effects of drugs which does not also show an effect on either the primary lesion (shrinkage) or on metastasis (survival).

Affidavit of Dr. DeVita, Exhibit D of Defendants' Reply to Plaintiff's Opposition.

NCI tests approximately 50,000 compounds each year in the fashion described above. The annual cost of this program is five million dollars. In order to test 50,000 compounds each year specifically for anti-metastatic activity, it would cost much more because the tests are apparently more complex. Defendants state "The NCI staff believes the added cost to be prohibitive and not of high enough priority in view of the questionable value of such testing and other scientific opportunities competing for the same funds."

Under the above procedures, Dr. Grassetti's compounds were tested by NCI. According to the defendants, all were found to be inactive by criteria routinely applied to all compounds regardless of their source. In addition, a special test was performed on CPDS, at the repeated requests of Dr. Grassetti. While "slight activity" was shown, it was defendants' judgment that this activity was not of sufficient magnitude to be considered worth pursuing, under normal criteria.

Defendants' determination of which test to use and of how extensive such testing should be is a matter clearly outside the scope of this court's jurisdiction to review. Likewise, defendants' assessment that a test specifically picking up anti-metastatic activity is cost-prohibitive when weighed against the advantages thereof, is not reviewable here. These are matters for the judgment of medical experts, not courts. At the risk of being pedantic, the court reiterates that which was said before. The only role for this court to play on this issue of testing, like the other issues presented here, is to see that normal procedures were followed and that plaintiff received fair treatment. This he clearly did. If anything, defendants have gone to greater lengths than usual to explore any possible beneficial effects of CPDS and its derivatives. They found none.

For this court to order defendants to perform certain tests on CPDS, or any other compound, would not only be ludicrous, but would also constitute interference of a most egregious sort with an administrative agency trying to do an important job. This the court will not do.

Accordingly, it is the order of this court that defendants' motion for summary judgment be, and hereby is, granted.

NOTE

As we have seen, agencies begin the science funding process by sending their budget requests to the White House and then to Congress. After Congress appropriates the money, the agency then has the task of deciding which projects get funded within the guidelines established by Congress. As *Grassetti* suggests, when the agency grants money to private applicants, it typically employs a peer review process in which scientists select the applications which have the most merit. As one can see from *Grassetti*, courts are reluctant to second-guess these judgments, unless an applicant can show not a scientific error, but rather a grant decision infected with prejudice involving, for example, race or gender. See, e.g., Apter v. Richardson, 510 F.2d 351 (7th Cir. 1975).

Scientists judging other scientists in this way obviously raises some dangers. As the court concedes in *Grassetti*, in most cases only scientists who engage in the very type of research involved in the application can adequately assess its merits. Therefore, truly novel ideas may go unnoticed, and unknown but talented applicants may go unrewarded. On the other hand, all of the scientists in a given field would rarely agree on whether to fund a particular proposal. An applicant's chance of approval often turns on which scientists happen to sit on the peer review panel. Indeed, a National Science Foundation study concluded that "the fate of a particular grant application is roughly half determined by the characteristics of the proposal and the principal investigator, and about half by apparently random elements which might be characterized as the 'luck of the reviewer draw.' " Cole, Cole and Simon, Chance and Consensus in Peer Review, 214 Science 881, 885 (1981). Would you want to reduce the importance of the "luck of the reviewer draw"?

Government support for some science projects at the expense of others also effects the first amendment values discussed in Ch. 4, Sec. A.1, supra. Under the first amendment, Dr. Grassetti has the right to publish articles claiming that his theories concerning cancer are correct and the government's theories are wrong. This vital right keeps open the possibility that Dr. Grassetti and others like him can persuade Congress or other responsible institutions to change the nation's cancer policy. But Dr. Grassetti's right to free speech hardly puts him on an equal footing with those who share the government's views on cancer and who therefore receive funding. Writing an article is one thing; actually doing research requires money and, for basic scientific research, government money is often the only realistic source. Doesn't the government's choice to fund research in one area rather than another inevitably disrupt the free market place of scientific ideas? We would, after all, be deeply troubled if the government allowed free speech to all political parties, but provided government funding only to Democrats. See Goldberg, The Constitutional Status of American Science, 1979 U.Ill. L.F. 1 (1979).

This distortion may be inevitable since not all conceivable scientific theories can be funded. But the dangers involved here can provide guidelines for government action. Diverse, broad-ranging funding policies can help alleviate the dangers of an inbred, narrow view becoming the dominant scientific approach even though that view may turn out to be mistaken. Indeed, one of the most important current protections in this regard may be America's diverse, even disorganized, set of federal agencies engaged in science. The "Department of Science" idea, Ch. 4, Sec. B.2, supra, may be particularly dangerous if it involves an increased centralization of views on what constitutes good science.

Government funding for scientific research raises another set of concerns with constitutional implications. When the government provides money it often attaches conditions on how that money is to be used. See, e.g., Robertson, The Law of Institutional Review Boards, 26 UCLA L.Rev. 484 (1979). The courts often uphold this use of the conditional spending power when the conditions relate to the purpose of the spending program. See Comment, The Federal Conditional Spending Power: A Search for Limits, 70 Nw.U.L.Rev. 293 (1975). Thus, when the government funds research involving human subjects it can almost surely require the institution receiving the funds to establish an institutional review board (IRB) to assure the protection of the subjects' rights. See Ch. 6, Secs. B.3 and C.2, infra. But can the government also require the institution to set up IRB's for that portion of its research unsupported by government funds? Such proposals have brought forth vigorous protest. See, e.g., de Sola Pool, The New Censorship of Social Research, Pub. Interest 57 (Spring 1980). While restrictions of this type may well be constitutional, see Robertson, The Scientists' Right to Research: A Constitutional Analysis, 51 S.Cal.L.Rev. 1203, 1275 (1978), they certainly raise important questions of Congressional intent and of sound administrative policy. See, e.g., Swazey, Professional Protectionism Rides Again: A Commentary on Exempted Research and Responses to DHEW's Proposed Regulations, IRB 4 (1980).

These concerns focus on classic fears of centralized government power. But stiff competition for American technology from Japan, Western Europe and elsewhere has led some to call for a more unified American approach to research and development, including increased government scientific support for carefully chosen portions of the private sector and antitrust immunity for private concerns that work together on scientific research. See, e.g., Behr, R&D Immunity Weighed, Washington Post, June 29, 1983, at F1, col. 4. Would such steps help or hinder productivity? The motivation for these proposals appears to stem from the belief that the United States, while strong in basic research, has lagged behind other countries in applying such research to commercial enterprises such as the auto and steel industries. At the same time, there are reports that the Japanese government is concerned that too large a portion of Japanese research money is going into applied research and not enough into basic research. See Science in Japan, 305 Nature 361 (1983).

3. STATE SPENDING FOR SCIENCE AND MEDICINE

State spending on scientific research cannot measure up to the federal effort. In fiscal year 1977, the last year for which full statistics are available, the states combined spent about $600 million on research and development; federal expenditures that year totalled over $20 billion. See National Science Foundation, Research and Development in State and Local Governments, Fiscal Year 1977, at 7; National Science Foundation, Expenditures for Scientific Activities at Universities and Colleges, Fiscal Year 1977, Detailed Statistical Tables 1 (1978); Office of Management and Budget, Special Analyses: Budget of the United States Government, 1979, at 306 (1978).

Perhaps the most important area in which states play a major role in funding research is agriculture. The McCalla excerpt below sets forth the history of this role and something of its current structure. The Hightower piece that follows presents a vigorous attack on the alleged undue influence of business interests on state agricultural research.

ALEX F. McCALLA,
POLITICS OF THE AGRICULTURAL
RESEARCH ESTABLISHMENT

in The New Politics of Food.
77–78, 81, 86–87 (D. Hadwiger and W. Browne eds. 1978).

Most discussions of the current agricultural research arrangement in the United States begin with the year 1862. In that year the Morrill Act established federal land grants to the states for the establishment of Land-Grant Colleges. In the same year the U.S. Department of Agriculture (USDA) was created. Early emphasis of both organizations was on education. Formal recognition of the need for direct support of research came 25 years later in the Hatch Act of 1887, which established federal matching support to state experiment stations to be established in conjunction with the land grants. That act with subsequent amendments also authorized direct federal support for in-house research in an organization that later became the Agricultural Research Service (ARS). Thus the two major public components of the agricultural research establishment have been in place since before the turn of the century. The original justifications of public support for agricultural research were that farms were too small to support their own research and that productivity increases in agriculture benefited both farmers and consumers and therefore society.
. . . .

The current form and magnitude of the agricultural research enterprise, as seen by a National Academy of Science study team, are presented in two categories: sources of funds and research performers. The four major sources of funds are the federal government, state governments, private industry, and foundations. It is estimated that in 1976 these sources provided $1.9 billion for food research. About half of this came from federal and state sources. The federal government provided $645 million, state governments $425 million, industry $800 million, and foundations $100 million. . . .

At the state level, the dominant spenders of research dollars are the State Experiment Stations. Here the situation varies from state to state with respect to organizational structure and the form of state appropriations. These appropriations could come either as a lump-sum budget as part of a university's organized research budget or as rather specific line items from the legislature. The means by which other federal, industry, and foundation funds enter the university system also vary. In some cases, this money will come to the university via general research administrations as opposed to Agricultural Experiment Station administration. This further complicates an already complex arrangement in the land grants where teaching, extension, and state public service functions compete for faculty time and institutional rewards. Of particular importance in the large university is the relative importance of state-appropriated funds, federal formula funds, and extramural public or private funds. Those who provide the most funding are likely to have the most influence. . . .

Money is, after all, the lifeblood of a research organization. It influences the number and quality of people that can be employed. It provides the wherewithal to buy equipment, conduct field trials, and disseminate results. Given the decentralized fragmented system we are discussing, competition for monetary support becomes a continuing concern of all involved in the system. It follows, then, that actors in a position to directly influence the level of monetary support are vitally important. In this category fall the appropriations subcommittees in both federal houses, state legislatures, granting agencies, Office of Management and Budget (OMB), Congressional Budget Office (CBO), GAO, commodity groups and industrial firms which provide direct support, and foundations. All these actors can and do have powerful influences on the overall magnitude of research budgets. Therefore it follows that individuals who hold positions of power in these groups can by the amount of funding and the conditions attached thereto influence annual and longer-term directions of research. These, then, are the most important political forces influencing macro research priorities and in many instances micro priorities.

These funding entities are obviously influenced in their judgments by other actors in the system, and it is worth noting briefly the potential influence of some of these. Agricultural organizations and lobby groups have potential but likely declining influence on research outcomes. Research funding, particularly at the federal level, tends to be general rather than commodity-specific. Thus general farm organizations like the Bureau and the Farmers' Union could influence general funding levels. However, as the overall political process relating to agricultural policy has become more commodity-fractionated and at the same time more macro (i.e., involving many other groups besides agriculture), the analyses in this regard have been conducted by Bonnen, Youngberg, Hadwiger and Fraenkel, and Barton, all of whom argue that the control of the agricultural political agenda is rapidly shifting. Given that research tends to be general and not immediately obvious in terms of its specific or commodity outcome, it tends to attract less attention from groups with specific objectives. At the state level, however, commodity groups continue to have potential influence. But in general it is my judgment that the influence of farm organizations on macro priorities and general funding levels is not strong. . . .

JIM HIGHTOWER,
HARD TOMATOES, HARD TIMES

43, 47–49 (1973).

The most distressing examples of land grant college research for agribusiness are those that work against the farmer. Chief among these are projects to assist vertical integration of agriculture—a system whereby the in-put and out-put industries usurp from the farmer control of production. Vertical integration is a key component in the land grant college community's effort to achieve total food systems, with one corporation maintaining effective control of a crop from seed to supermarket. Vertical integration of the broiler industry was effected during the sixties by such feed corporations as Ralston Purina, and the impact was devastating to thousands of independent poultry producers. Ralston Purina and others are moving now toward vertical integration of the hog industry. Given the experience of broiler raisers, it is easy to understand the chagrin of hog producers today when they learn that their tax dollars are being expended at land grant colleges for these projects:

— Vertical coordination in the hog industry. (Purdue)

— Economic evaluation of alternative forms of vertical coordination in the livestock meat industry. (Auburn)

— Development of an integrated procurement and production control system for feed manufacturers. (Purdue)

Throughout the land grant system, research projects such as these are underway, designed principally to increase the profits of the corporate input and out-put industries surrounding agriculture. A 1969 Minnesota symposium on resource allocation in agricultural research stated that the "essential rationale" for investing tax dollars in agricultural research is that "publicly supported units are less constrained by the need to relate research expenditures to their ability to capture the economic gains from the research they perform. These examples of research underway indicate that the land grant colleges are not as constrained as might be thought. Through the research efforts of these institutions, the public is subsidizing corporate profits. . . .

Land grant researchers do not confront this question of quality impact, choosing instead to dwell on the benefits that food engineering offers agribusiness. The University of Florida, for example, recently has developed a new fresh market tomato (the MH–1) for machine harvesting. In describing the characteristics that make this tomato so desirable for machine harvest, the University pointed to "the thick walls, firm flesh, and freedom from cracks." It may be a little tough for the consumer, but they can't please everyone. The MH–1, which will eliminate the jobs of thousands of Florida farm workers who now hand-pick tomatoes for the fresh market, also is designed to be harvested green and to be "ripened" in storage by application of ethylene gas. . . .

Then there is meat. Land grant college research has played a key role in the development of integrated meat systems that have successfully brought huge quantities of beef, pork, lamb and poultry to American dinner tables. Land grant scientists, economists, and management and marketing experts have all assisted corporations in the creation of mass production centers, where livestock and poultry are closely confined, constantly fed to achieve a standard weight, and slaughtered for quick sale. Again, the effort is to short-circuit nature's design by accelerating "maturity." Profits flow to the agribusiness firms that own the production centers. Increasingly these owners are major feed companies, supermarket chains and even oil conglomerates. The consumer is benefitted by an abundance of meat, but, as one writer put it, "Americans buy at high prices, cook poorly, and eat in incredible quantities the lowest quality meat possible. . . ."

NOTE

There are no bright lines along the continuum from basic research to development of a technology to commercial application of a device. Nonetheless, as one moves away from basic research, the justifications for government funding decrease. With some state funding of agricultural research, taxpayer dollars may unduly subsidize business interests. What kinds of agricultural research do you believe the states should fund?

Hightower contends that agricultural developments pursued for the profit of big business shortchange the consumer. Do consumers have the ability to purchase agricultural products of higher quality, thus affecting business decisions on what to produce? Do consumers of food occupy a stronger or weaker position in this respect than consumers of medical services?

A lawsuit against the University of California seeking to halt funding for research on agricultural mechanization processes that convey "a special economic benefit to narrow, private agribusiness interests . . ." is due to come to trial in 1984. The case is California Agrarian Action Project v. The Regents of the University of California, Civ. Docket No. 516427–5 (Sup.Ct. Alameda County, filed Jan. 17, 1979).

4. INDIRECT INCENTIVES FOR RESEARCH AND DEVELOPMENT: PATENT, TRADE SECRET AND COPYRIGHT

DIAMOND v. DIEHR

Supreme Court of the United States, 1981.
450 U.S. 175, 101 S.Ct. 1048, 67 L.Ed.2d 155.

JUSTICE REHNQUIST delivered the opinion of the Court.

We granted certiorari to determine whether a process for curing synthetic rubber which includes in several of its steps the use of a mathematical formula and a programmed digital computer is patentable subject matter under 35 U.S.C. § 101.

I

The patent application at issue was filed by the respondents on August 6, 1975. The claimed invention is a process for molding raw, uncured synthetic rubber into cured precision products. The process uses a mold for precisely shaping the uncured material under heat and pressure and then curing the synthetic rubber in the mold so that the product will retain its shape and be functionally operative after the molding is completed.[1]

Respondents claim that their process ensures the production of molded articles which are properly cured. Achieving the perfect cure depends upon several factors including the thickness of the article to be molded, the temperature of the molding process, and the amount of time that the article is allowed to remain in the press. It is possible using well-known time, temperature, and cure relationships to calculate by means of the Arrhenius equation[2] when to open the press and remove the cured product. Nonetheless, according to the respondents, the industry has not been able to obtain uniformly accurate cures because the temperature of the molding press could not be precisely measured, thus making it difficult to do the necessary computations to determine cure time.[3] Because

1. A "cure" is obtained by mixing curing agents into the uncured polymer in advance of molding, and then applying heat over a period of time. If the synthetic rubber is cured for the right length of time at the right temperature, it becomes a usable product.

2. The equation is named after its discoverer Svante Arrhenius and has long been used to calculate the cure time in rubber-molding presses. The equation can be expressed as follows:

$$\ln v = CZ + x$$

wherein ln v is the natural logarithm of v, the total required cure time; C is the activa-

tion constant, a unique figure for each batch of each compound being molded, determined in accordance with rheometer measurements of each batch; Z is the temperature in the mold; and x is a constant dependent on the geometry of the particular mold in the press. A rheometer is an instrument to measure flow of viscous substances.

3. During the time a press is open for loading, it will cool. The longer it is open, the cooler it becomes and the longer it takes to reheat the press to the desired temperature range. Thus, the time necessary to raise the mold temperature to curing tem-

the temperature *inside* the press has heretofore been viewed as an uncontrollable variable, the conventional industry practice has been to calculate the cure time as the shortest time in which all parts of the product will definitely be cured, assuming a reasonable amount of mold-opening time during loading and unloading. But the shortcoming of this practice is that operating with an uncontrollable variable inevitably led in some instances to overestimating the mold-opening time and overcuring the rubber, and in other instances to underestimating that time and undercuring the product.

Respondents characterize their contribution to the art to reside in the process of constantly measuring the actual temperature inside the mold. These temperature measurements are then automatically fed into a computer which repeatedly recalculates the cure time by use of the Arrhenius equation. When the recalculated time equals the actual time that has elapsed since the press was closed, the computer signals a device to open the press. According to the respondents, the continuous measuring of the temperature inside the mold cavity, the feeding of this information to a digital computer which constantly recalculates the cure time, and the signaling by the computer to open the press, are all new in the art.
. . .

Last Term in Diamond v. Chakrabarty, 447 U.S. 303, 100 S.Ct. 2204, 65 L.Ed.2d 144 (1980), [see Ch. 1, Sec. B.5, supra] this Court discussed the historical purposes of the patent laws and in particular 35 U.S.C. § 101. As in *Chakrabarty*, we must here construe 35 U.S.C. § 101 which provides:

"Whoever invents or discovers any new and useful process, machine, manufacture, or composition of matter, or any new and useful improvement thereof, may obtain a patent therefor, subject to the conditions and requirements of this title."

In cases of statutory construction, we begin with the language of the statute. Unless otherwise defined, "words will be interpreted as taking their ordinary, contemporary, common meaning," Perrin v. United States, 444 U.S. 37, 42, 100 S.Ct. 311, 314, 62 L.Ed.2d 199 (1979), and, in dealing with the patent laws, we have more than once cautioned that "courts 'should not read into the patent laws limitations and conditions which the legislature has not expressed.'" Diamond v. Chakrabarty, supra, at 308, 100 S.Ct., at 2207 quoting United States v. Dubilier Condenser Corp., 289 U.S. 178, 199, 53 S.Ct. 554, 561, 77 L.Ed. 1114 (1933).

The Patent Act of 1793 defined statutory subject matter as "any new and useful art, machine, manufacture or composition of matter, or any new or useful improvement [thereof]." Act of Feb. 21, 1793, ch. 11, § 1, 1 Stat. 318. Not until the patent laws were recodified in 1952 did Congress replace the word "art" with the word "process." It is that latter word which we confront today, and in order to determine its meaning we may not be unmindful of the Committee Reports accompanying the 1952 Act which inform us that Congress intended statutory subject matter to "include anything under the sun that is made by man." S.Rep.No.1979, 82d Cong., 2d Sess., 5 (1952); H.R.Rep.No.1923, 82d Cong., 2d Sess., 6 (1952).

perature is an unpredictable variable. The respondents claim to have overcome this problem by continuously measuring the actual temperature in the closed press through the use of a thermocouple.

Although the term "process" was not added to 35 U.S.C. § 101 until 1952, a process has historically enjoyed patent protection because it was considered a form of "art" as that term was used in the 1793 Act. In defining the nature of a patentable process, the Court stated:

"That a process may be patentable, irrespective of the particular form of the instrumentalities used, cannot be disputed. . . . A process is a mode of treatment of certain materials to produce a given result. It is an act, or a series of acts, performed upon the subject-matter to be transformed and reduced to a different state or thing. If new and useful, it is just as patentable as is a piece of machinery. In the language of the patent law, it is an art. The machinery pointed out as suitable to perform the process may or may not be new or patentable; whilst the process itself may be altogether new, and produce an entirely new result. The process requires that certain things should be done with certain substances, and in a certain order; but the tools to be used in doing this may be of secondary consequence." Cochrane v. Deener, 94 U.S. 780, 787–788, 24 L.Ed. 139 (1877).

Analysis of the eligibility of a claim of patent protection for a "process" did not change with the addition of that term to § 101. Recently, in Gottschalk v. Benson, 409 U.S. 63, 93 S.Ct. 253, 34 L.Ed.2d 273 (1972), we repeated the above definition recited in *Cochrane v. Deener*, adding: "Transformation and reduction of an article 'to a different state or thing' is the clue to the patentability of a process claim that does not include particular machines." 409 U.S., at 70, 93 S.Ct., at 256.

Analyzing respondents' claims according to the above statements from our cases, we think that a physical and chemical process for molding precision synthetic rubber products falls within the § 101 categories of possibly patentable subject matter. That respondents' claims involve the transformation of an article, in this case raw, uncured synthetic rubber, into a different state or thing cannot be disputed. The respondents' claims describe in detail a step-by-step method for accomplishing such, beginning with the loading of a mold with raw, uncured rubber and ending with the eventual opening of the press at the conclusion of the cure. Industrial processes such as this are the types which have historically been eligible to receive the protection of our patent laws.

Our conclusion regarding respondents' claims is not altered by the fact that in several steps of the process a mathematical equation and a programmed digital computer are used. This Court has undoubtedly recognized limits to § 101 and every discovery is not embraced within the statutory terms. Excluded from such patent protection are laws of nature, natural phenomena, and abstract ideas. See Parker v. Flook, 437 U.S. 584, 98 S.Ct. 2522, 57 L.Ed.2d 451 (1978); Gottschalk v. Benson, supra, at 67, 93 S.Ct., at 255; Funk Bros. Seed Co. v. Kalo Inoculant Co., 333 U.S. 127, 130, 68 S.Ct. 440, 441, 92 L.Ed. 588 (1948). "An idea of itself is not patentable," Rubber-Tip Pencil Co. v. Howard, 20 Wall. 498, 507, 22 L.Ed. 410 (1874). "A principle, in the abstract, is a fundamental truth; an original cause; a motive; these cannot be patented, as no one can claim in either of them an exclusive right." Le Roy v. Tatham, 14 How. 156, 175, 14 L.Ed. 367 (1853). Only last Term, we explained:

"[A] new mineral discovered in the earth or a new plant found in the wild is not patentable subject matter. Likewise, Einstein could not patent his celebrated law that $E=mc^2$; nor could Newton have patented the law of gravity. Such discoveries are 'manifestations of . . .

nature, free to all men and reserved exclusively to none.'" Diamond v. Chakrabarty, 447 U.S., at 309, 100 S.Ct., at 2208, quoting Funk Bros. Seed Co. v. Kalo Inoculant Co., supra, at 130, 68 S.Ct., at 441.

Our recent holdings in *Gottschalk v. Benson*, supra, and *Parker v. Flook*, supra, both of which are computer-related, stand for no more than these long-established principles. In *Benson*, we held unpatentable claims for an algorithm used to convert binary code decimal numbers to equivalent pure binary numbers. The sole practical application of the algorithm was in connection with the programming of a general purpose digital computer. We defined "algorithm" as a "procedure for solving a given type of mathematical problem," and we concluded that such an algorithm, or mathematical formula, is like a law of nature, which cannot be the subject of a patent.

Parker v. Flook, supra, presented a similar situation. The claims were drawn to a method for computing an "alarm limit." An "alarm limit" is simply a number and the Court concluded that the application sought to protect a formula for computing this number. Using this formula, the updated alarm limit could be calculated if several other variables were known. The application, however, did not purport to explain how these other variables were to be determined, nor did it purport "to contain any disclosure relating to the chemical processes at work, the monitoring of process variables, or the means of setting off an alarm or adjusting an alarm system. All that it provides is a formula for computing an updated alarm limit." 437 U.S., at 586, 98 S.Ct., at 2523.

In contrast, the respondents here do not seek to patent a mathematical formula. Instead, they seek patent protection for a process of curing synthetic rubber. Their process admittedly employs a well-known mathematical equation, but they do not seek to pre-empt the use of that equation. Rather, they seek only to foreclose from others the use of that equation in conjunction with all of the other steps in their claimed process. These include installing rubber in a press, closing the mold, constantly determining the temperature of the mold, constantly recalculating the appropriate cure time through the use of the formula and a digital computer, and automatically opening the press at the proper time. Obviously, one does not need a "computer" to cure natural or synthetic rubber, but if the computer use incorporated in the process patent significantly lessens the possibility of "overcuring" or "undercuring," the process as a whole does not thereby become unpatentable subject matter.

Our earlier opinions lend support to our present conclusion that a claim drawn to subject matter otherwise statutory does not become non-statutory simply because it uses a mathematical formula, computer program, or digital computer. In *Gottschalk v. Benson* we noted: "It is said that the decision precludes a patent for any program servicing a computer. We do not so hold." 409 U.S., at 71, 93 S.Ct., at 257. Similarly, in *Parker v. Flook* we stated that "a process is not unpatentable simply because it contains a law of nature or a mathematical algorithm." 437 U.S., at 590, 98 S.Ct., at 2526. It is now commonplace that an *application* of a law of nature or mathematical formula to a known structure or process may well be deserving of patent protection. See, e.g., Funk Bros. Seed Co. v. Kalo Inoculant Co., 333 U.S. 127, 68 S.Ct. 440, 92 L.Ed. 588 (1948); Eibel Process Co. v. Minnesota & Ontario Paper Co., 261 U.S. 45, 43 S.Ct. 322, 67 L.Ed. 523 (1923); Cochrane v. Deener, 94 U.S. 780, 24 L.Ed. 139 (1877); O'Reilly v. Morse, 15 How. 62, 14 L.Ed. 601 (1854);

and Le Roy v. Tatham, 14 How. 156, 14 L.Ed. 367 (1853). As Justice Stone explained four decades ago:

> "While a scientific truth, or the mathematical expression of it, is not a patentable invention, a novel and useful structure created with the aid of knowledge of scientific truth may be." Mackay Radio & Telegraph Co. v. Radio Corp. of America, 306 U.S. 86, 94, 59 S.Ct. 427, 431, 83 L.Ed. 506 (1939).

We think this statement in *Mackay* takes us a long way toward the correct answer in this case. Arrhenius' equation is not patentable in isolation, but when a process for curing rubber is devised which incorporates in it a more efficient solution of the equation, that process is at the very least not barred at the threshold by § 101. . . .

In this case, it may later be determined that the respondents' process is not deserving of patent protection because it fails to satisfy the statutory conditions of novelty under § 102 or nonobviousness under § 103. A rejection on either of these grounds does not affect the determination that respondents' claims recited subject matter which was eligible for patent protection under § 101. . . .

JUSTICE STEVENS, with whom JUSTICE BRENNAN, JUSTICE MARSHALL, and JUSTICE BLACKMUN join, dissenting.

[T]he starting point in the proper adjudication of patent litigation is an understanding of what the inventor claims to have discovered. Indeed, the outcome of such litigation is often determined by the judge's understanding of the patent application. This is such a case.

In the first sentence of its opinion, the Court states the question presented as "whether a process for curing synthetic rubber . . . is patentable subject matter." Of course, that question was effectively answered many years ago when Charles Goodyear obtained his patent on the vulcanization process. The patent application filed by Diehr and Lutton, however, teaches nothing about the chemistry of the synthetic rubber-curing process, nothing about the raw materials to be used in curing synthetic rubber, nothing about the equipment to be used in the process, and nothing about the significance or effect of any process variable such as temperature, curing time, particular compositions of material, or mold configurations. In short, Diehr and Lutton do not claim to have discovered anything new about the process for curing synthetic rubber.

As the Court reads the claims in the Diehr and Lutton patent application, the inventors' discovery is a method of constantly measuring the actual temperature inside a rubber molding press. As I read the claims, their discovery is an improved method of calculating the time that the mold should remain closed during the curing process. If the Court's reading of the claims were correct, I would agee that they disclose patentable subject matter. On the other hand, if the Court accepted my reading, I feel confident that the case would be decided differently.

There are three reasons why I cannot accept the Court's conclusion that Diehr and Lutton claim to have discovered a new method of constantly measuring the temperature inside a mold. First, there is not a word in the patent application that suggests that there is anything unusual about the temperature-reading devices used in this process—or indeed that any particular species of temperature-reading device should be used in it. Second, since devices for constantly measuring actual temperatures—on a back porch, for example—have been familiar articles for quite some time, I find it difficult to believe that a patent application filed in

1975 was premised on the notion that a "process of constantly measuring the actual temperature" had just been discovered. Finally, the Patent and Trademark Office Board of Appeals expressly found that "the only difference between the conventional methods of operating a molding press and that claimed in [the] application rests in those steps of the claims which relate to the calculation incident to the solution of the mathematical problem or formula used to control the mold heater and the automatic opening of the press." This finding was not disturbed by the Court of Customs and Patent Appeals and is clearly correct. . . .

Parker v. Flook, 437 U.S. 584, 98 S.Ct. 2522, 57 L.Ed.2d 451 (1978), involved the use of a digital computer in connection with a catalytic conversion process. During the conversion process, variables such as temperature, pressure, and flow rates were constantly monitored and fed into the computer; in this case, temperature in the mold is the variable that is monitored and fed into the computer. In *Flook,* the digital computer repetitively recalculated the "alarm limit"—a number that might signal the need to terminate or modify the catalytic conversion process; in this case, the digital computer repetitively recalculates the correct curing time—a number that signals the time when the synthetic rubber molding press should open.

The essence of the claimed discovery in both cases was an algorithm that could be programmed on a digital computer. . . .

NOTE

Patents are available for inventions that are useful, novel and nonobvious. Because patents give the inventor an exclusive opportunity for 17 years to exploit the invention, while simultaneously making the invention public, they provide important incentives for the development of science and technology. As noted in Ch. 4, Sec. B.2, supra, the Constitution is the source of the federal patent power.

Why are patents unavailable for so-called "laws of nature" like $E=mc^2$? Some contend that it is because these vital building blocks of science should be available to all. Do you believe that patents would provide incentive to scientists who seek to discover laws of nature? Consider the materials on Einstein's discovery of $E=mc^2$ in Ch. 2, Sec. A.1, supra.

Does the Court's opinion in *Diehr* persuade you that the patent in question was something more than a patent for a formula? In both this case and in *Chakrabarty,* see Ch. 1, Sec. B.5, supra, the Court read broadly the scope of the patent laws in areas where Congress had not spoken directly. Should Congress decide in the first instance whether to make patents available in areas such as computer science and recombinant DNA research?

KEWANEE OIL CO. v. BICRON CORP.

Supreme Court of the United States, 1974.
416 U.S. 470, 94 S.Ct. 1879, 40 L.Ed.2d 315.

MR. CHIEF JUSTICE BURGER delivered the opinion of the Court.

. . .

I.

Harshaw Chemical Co., an unincorporated division of petitioner, is a leading manufacturer of a type of synthetic crystal which is useful in the detection of ionizing radiation. In 1949 Harshaw commenced research into the growth of this type crystal and was able to produce one less than two inches in diameter. By 1966, as the result of expenditures in excess of $1 million, Harshaw was able to grow a 17-inch crystal, something no one else had done previously. Harshaw had developed many processes, procedures, and manufacturing techniques in the purification of raw materials and the growth and encapsulation of the crystals which enabled it to accomplish this feat. Some of these processes Harshaw considers to be trade secrets.

The individual respondents are former employees of Harshaw who formed or later joined respondent Bicron. While at Harshaw the individual respondents executed, as a condition of employment, at least one agreement each, requiring them not to disclose confidential information or trade secrets obtained as employees of Harshaw. Bicron was formed in August 1969 to compete with Harshaw in the production of the crystals, and by April 1970, had grown a 17-inch crystal.

Petitioner brought this diversity action in United States District Court for the Northern District of Ohio seeking injunctive relief and damages for the misappropriation of trade secrets. The District Court, applying Ohio trade secret law, granted a permanent injunction against the disclosure or use by respondents of 20 of the 40 claimed trade secrets until such time as the trade secrets had been released to the public, had otherwise generally become available to the public, or had been obtained by respondents from sources having the legal right to convey the information.

The Court of Appeals for the Sixth Circuit held that the findings of fact by the District Court were not clearly erroneous, and that it was evident from the record that the individual respondents appropriated to the benefit of Bicron secret information on processes obtained while they were employees at Harshaw. Further, the Court of Appeals held that the District Court properly applied Ohio law relating to trade secrets. Nevertheless, the Court of Appeals reversed the District Court, finding Ohio's trade secret law to be in conflict with the patent laws of the United States. The Court of Appeals reasoned that Ohio could not grant monopoly protection to processes and manufacturing techniques that were appropriate subjects for consideration under 35 U.S.C. § 101 for a federal patent but which had been in commercial use for over one year and so were no longer eligible for patent protection under 35 U.S.C. § 102(b).

We hold that Ohio's law of trade secrets is not preempted by the patent laws of the United States, and, accordingly, we reverse.

II

Ohio has adopted the widely relied-upon definition of a trade secret found at Restatement of Torts § 757, comment *b* (1939). B. F. Goodrich Co. v. Wohlgemuth, 117 Ohio App. 493, 498, 192 N.E.2d 99, 104 (1963); W. R. Grace & Co. v. Hargadine, 392 F.2d 9, 14 (C.A.6 1968). According to the Restatement,

> "[a] trade secret may consist of any formula, pattern, device or compilation of information which is used in one's business, and which gives him an opportunity to obtain an advantage over competitors who do not know or use it. It may be a formula for a chemical compound, a process of manufacturing, treating or preserving materials, a pattern for a machine or other device, or a list of customers."

The subject of a trade secret must be secret, and must not be of public knowledge or of a general knowledge in the trade or business. B. F.

Goodrich Co. v. Wohlgemuth, supra, at 499, 192 N.E.2d, at 104; National Tube Co. v. Eastern Tube Co., 3 Ohio Cir.Ct.R., N.S., 459, 462 (1902), aff'd, 69 Ohio St. 560, 70 N.E. 1127 (1903). This necessary element of secrecy is not lost, however, if the holder of the trade secret reveals the trade secret to another "in confidence, and under an implied obligation not to use or disclose it." Cincinnati Bell Foundry Co. v. Dodds, 10 Ohio Dec. Reprint 154, 156, 19 Weekly Law Bull. 84 (Super.Ct.1887). These others may include those of the holder's "employees to whom it is necessary to confide it, in order to apply it to the uses for which it is intended." National Tube Co. v. Eastern Tube Co., supra, 3 Ohio Cir.Ct.R., N.S., at 462. Often the recipient of confidential knowledge of the subject of a trade secret is a licensee of its holder. See Lear, Inc. v. Adkins, 395 U.S. 653, 89 S.Ct. 1902, 23 L.Ed.2d 610 (1969).

The protection accorded the trade secret holder is against the disclosure or unauthorized use of the trade secret by those to whom the secret has been confided under the express or implied restriction of nondisclosure or nonuse. The law also protects the holder of a trade secret against disclosure or use when the knowledge is gained, not by the owner's volition, but by some "improper means," Restatement of Torts § 757(a), which may include theft, wiretapping, or even aerial reconnaissance. A trade secret law, however, does not offer protection against discovery by fair and honest means, such as by independent invention, accidental disclosure, or by so-called reverse engineering, that is by starting with the known product and working backward to divine the process which aided in its development or manufacture.

Novelty, in the patent law sense, is not required for a trade secret. W. R. Grace & Co. v. Hargadine, 392 F.2d, at 14. "Quite clearly discovery is something less than invention." A. O. Smith Corp. v. Petroleum Iron Works Co., 73 F.2d 531, 538 (C.A.6 1934), modified to increase scope of injunction, 74 F.2d 934 (1935). However, some novelty will be required if merely because that which does not possess novelty is usually known; secrecy, in the context of trade secrets, thus implies at least minimal novelty.

The subject matter of a patent is limited to a "process, machine, manufacture, or composition of matter, or . . . improvement thereof," 35 U.S.C. § 101, which fulfills the three conditions of novelty and utility as articulated and defined in 35 U.S.C. §§ 101 and 102, and nonobviousness, as set out in 35 U.S.C. § 103. If an invention meets the rigorous statutory tests for the issuance of a patent, the patent is granted, for a period of 17 years, giving what has been described as the "right of exclusion." R. Ellis, Patent Assignments and Licenses § 4, p. 7 (2d ed. 1943). This protection goes not only to copying the subject matter, which is forbidden under the Copyright Act, 17 U.S.C. § 1 et seq., but also to independent creation. . . .

IV.

The question of whether the trade secret law of Ohio is void under the Supremacy Clause involves a consideration of whether that law "stands as an obstacle to the accomplishment and execution of the full purposes and objectives of Congress." Hines v. Davidowitz, 312 U.S. 52, 67, 61 S.Ct. 399, 404, 85 L.Ed. 581 (1941). See Florida Lime & Avocado Growers, Inc. v. Paul, 373 U.S. 132, 141, 83 S.Ct. 1210, 1216, 10 L.Ed.2d 248 (1963). We stated in Sears, Roebuck & Co. v. Stiffel Co., 376 U.S. 225,

229, 84 S.Ct. 784, 11 L.Ed.2d 661 (1964), that when state law touches upon the area of federal statutes enacted pursuant to constitutional authority, "it is 'familiar doctrine' that the federal policy 'may not be set at naught, or its benefits denied' by the state law. Sola Elec. Co. v. Jefferson Elec. Co., 317 U.S. 173, 176, 63 S.Ct. 172, 173, 87 L.Ed. 165 (1942). This is true, of course, even if the state law is enacted in the exercise of otherwise undoubted state power."

The laws which the Court of Appeals in this case held to be in conflict with the Ohio law of trade secrets were the patent laws passed by the Congress in the unchallenged exercise of its clear power under Art. I, § 8, cl. 8, of the Constitution. The patent law does not explicitly endorse or forbid the operation of trade secret law. However, as we have noted, if the scheme of protection developed by Ohio respecting trade secrets "clashes with the objectives of the federal patent laws," Sears, Roebuck & Co. v. Stiffel Co., supra, 376 U.S., at 231, 84 S.Ct., at 789, then the state law must fall. To determine whether the Ohio law "clashes" with the federal law it is helpful to examine the objectives of both the patent and trade secret laws.

The stated objective of the Constitution in granting the power to Congress to legislate in the area of intellectual property is to "promote the Progress of Science and useful Arts." The patent laws promote this progress by offering a right of exclusion for a limited period as an incentive to inventors to risk the often enormous costs in terms of time, research, and development. The productive effort thereby fostered will have a positive effect on society through the introduction of new products and processes of manufacture into the economy, and the emanations by way of increased employment and better lives for our citizens. In return for the right of exclusion—this "reward for inventions," Universal Oil Co. v. Globe Co., 322 U.S. 471, 484, 64 S.Ct. 1110, 1116, 88 L.Ed. 1399 (1944)—the patent laws impose upon the inventor a requirement of disclosure. To insure adequate and full disclosure so that upon the expiration of the 17-year period "the knowledge of the invention enures to the people, who are thus enabled without restriction to practice it and profit by its use," United States v. Dubilier Condenser Corp., 289 U.S. 178, 187, 53 S.Ct. 554, 77 L.Ed. 1114 (1933), the patent laws require that the patent application shall include a full and clear description of the invention and "of the manner and process of making and using it" so that any person skilled in the art may make and use the invention. 35 U.S.C. § 112. When a patent is granted and the information contained in it is circulated to the general public and those especially skilled in the trade, such additions to the general store of knowledge are of such importance to the public weal that the Federal Government is willing to pay the high price of 17 years of exclusive use for its disclosure, which disclosure, it is assumed, will stimulate ideas and the eventual development of further significant advances in the art. The Court has also articulated another policy of the patent law: that which is in the public domain cannot be removed therefrom by action of the States.

> "[F]ederal law requires that all ideas in general circulation be dedicated to the common good unless they are protected by a valid patent."
> Lear, Inc. v. Adkins, 395 U.S., at 668, 89 S.Ct., at 1910.

See also Goldstein v. California, 412 U.S. at 570–571, 93 S.Ct., at 2316–2317; Sears, Roebuck & Co. v. Stiffel Co., supra; Compco Corp. v. Day-Brite Lighting, Inc., 376 U.S. 234, 237–238, 84 S.Ct. 779, 781–782, 11 L.Ed.2d 669 (1964); International News Service v. Associated Press, 248

U.S. 215, 250, 39 S.Ct. 68, 76, 63 L.Ed. 211 (1918) (Brandeis, J., dissenting).

The maintenance of standards of commercial ethics and the encouragement of invention are the broadly stated policies behind trade secret law. "The necessity of good faith and honest, fair dealing, is the very life and spirit of the commercial world." National Tube Co. v. Eastern Tube Co., 3 Ohio Cir.Ct.R., N.S., at 462. In A. O. Smith Corp. v. Petroleum Iron Works Co., 73 F.2d, at 539, the Court emphasized that even though a discovery may not be patentable, that does not

> "destroy the value of the discovery to one who makes it, or advantage the competitor who by unfair means, or as the beneficiary of a broken faith, obtains the desired knowledge without himself paying the price in labor, money, or machines expended by the discoverer."

In Wexler v. Greenberg, 399 Pa. 569, 578–579, 160 A.2d 430, 434–435 (1960), the Pennsylvania Supreme Court noted the importance of trade secret protection to the subsidization of research and development and to increased economic efficiency within large companies through the dispersion of responsibilities for creative developments.

Having now in mind the objectives of both the patent and trade secret law, we turn to an examination of the interaction of these systems of protection of intellectual property—one established by the Congress and the other by a State—to determine whether and under what circumstances the latter might constitute "too great an encroachment on the federal patent system to be tolerated." Sears, Roebuck & Co. v. Stiffel Co., 376 U.S., at 232, 84 S.Ct., at 789. . . .

. . . .

The final category of patentable subject matter to deal with is the clearly patentable invention, i.e., that invention which the owner believes to meet the standards of patentability. It is here that the federal interest in disclosure is at its peak; these inventions, novel, useful and nonobvious, are " 'the things which are worth to the public the embarrassment of an exclusive patent.' " Graham v. John Deere Co., supra, at 9, 86 S.Ct., at 689 (quoting Thomas Jefferson). The interest of the public is that the bargain of 17 years of exclusive use in return for disclosure be accepted. If a State, through a system of protection, were to cause a substantial risk that holders of patentable inventions would not seek patents, but rather would rely on the state protection, we would be compelled to hold that such a system could not constitutionally continue to exist. In the case of trade secret law no reasonable risk of deterrence from patent application by those who can reasonably expect to be granted patents exists.

Trade secret law provides far weaker protection in many respects than the patent law. While trade secret law does not forbid the discovery of the trade secret by fair and honest means, e.g., independent creation or reverse engineering, patent law operates "against the world," forbidding any use of the invention for whatever purpose for a significant length of time. The holder of a trade secret also takes a substantial risk that the secret will be passed on to his competitors, by theft or by breach of a confidential relationship, in a manner not easily susceptible of discovery or proof. Painton & Co. v. Bourns, Inc., 442 F.2d, at 224. Where patent law acts as a barrier, trade secret law functions relativel ' as a sieve. The possibility that an inventor who believes his invention meets the standards of patentability will sit back, rely on trade secret law, and after one year of use forfeit any right to patent protection, 35 U.S.C. § 102(b), is remote indeed.

Nor does society face much risk that scientific or technological progress will be impeded by the rare inventor with a patentable invention who chooses trade secret protection over patent protection. The ripeness-of-time concept of invention, developed from the study of the many independent multiple discoveries in history, predicts that if a particular individual had not made a particular discovery others would have, and in probably a relatively short period of time. If something is to be discovered at all very likely it will be discovered by more than one person. Singletons and Multiples in Science (1961), in R. Merton, The Sociology of Science 343 (1973); J. Cole & S. Cole, Social Stratification in Science 12–13, 229–230 (1973); Ogburn & Thomas, Are Inventions Inevitable?, 37 Pol.Sci.Q. 83 (1922).[19] Even were an inventor to keep his discovery completely to himself, something that neither the patent nor trade secret laws forbid, there is a high probability that it will be soon independently developed. If the invention, though still a trade secret, is put into public use, the competition is alerted to the existence of the inventor's solution to the problem and may be encouraged to make an extra effort to independently find the solution thus known to be possible. The inventor faces pressures not only from private industry, but from the skilled scientists who work in our universities and our other great publicly supported centers of learning and research.

We conclude that the extension of trade secret protection to clearly patentable inventions does not conflict with the patent policy of disclosure. Perhaps because trade secret law does not produce any positive effects in the area of clearly patentable inventions, as opposed to the beneficial effects resulting from trade secret protection in the areas of the doubtfully patentable and the clearly unpatentable inventions, it has been suggested that partial pre-emption may be appropriate, and that courts should refuse to apply trade secret protection to inventions which the holder should have patented, and which would have been, thereby, disclosed. However, since there is no real possibility that trade secret law will conflict with the federal policy favoring disclosure of clearly patentable invention partial pre-emption is inappropriate . . . .

NOTE

After *Kewanee Oil*, an inventor has a choice between using trade secret law or patent law to protect a technological development. In some areas, a third choice—copyright law—may be available. One such area is computers; a 1980 amendment to the Copyright Act establishes the copyrightability of computer programs, although it does not resolve all of the issues—litigation has arisen, for example, concerning the copyrightability of programs embodied in chips in the computer's circuitry and of programs that control the inner workings of a computer as opposed to those that control tasks, such as word processing, performed for the user. See P.L. 96–517 § 10, 94 Stat. 3028; Williams Electronics, Inc. v. Arctic International, Inc., 685 F.2d 870 (3d Cir. 1982); Apple Computer, Inc. v. Franklin Computer Corp., 714 F.2d 1240, 219 U.S.P.Q. 113 (3d Cir. 1983).

If you were an inventor who had developed a new device relying heavily on computer programs, which form of protection would you choose? Patents are difficult to obtain. You must meet the tests of novelty, utility and nonobvious-

---

19. See J. Watson, The Double Helix (1968). If Watson and Crick had not discovered the structure of DNA it is likely that Linus Pauling would have made the discovery soon. Other examples of multiple discovery are listed at length in the Ogburn and Thomas article.

ness, and you must fall under Diamond v. Diehr rather than Parker v. Flook on the issue of whether you are attempting simply to patent a formula. On the other hand, the 17-year patent monopoly protects you from people who independently make the same discovery you did. Copyright protects you from copying, not from independent discovery, but you can obtain copyright much more easily and it lasts for the life of the author plus 50 years. The trade secret approach also does not protect you from independent discovery, but you can obtain it more easily than patent protection and, unlike patents, trade secrets are not made public. How does your decision on what protection to seek depend on your predictions concerning the rate and nature of growth in the computer science field? At present, no one form of protection dominates the computer industry. See, e.g., Tunick, Computer Law: An Overview, 13 Loy.L.A.L.Rev. 315, 338, 345 (1980).

C. GOVERNMENT REGULATION OF SCIENCE AND MEDICINE

1. FEDERAL REGULATION: THE CENTRAL ROLE OF THE ADMINISTRATIVE AGENCY

We have already noted the importance of administrative agencies—primarily Cabinet departments such as Defense, Energy and Health and Human Services—in federal science spending. These agencies formulate budget requests and dispense large sums in accordance with their own judgment, often guided only by quite broad legislative language, as to what research projects deserve support. Judicial review in the funding area is typically quite limited. See Ch. 4, Sec. B.2, supra.

Federal regulation of science and medicine also relies heavily on administrative agencies. Congressional legislation again often provides only broad guidance—"protect the public health and safety"—and then gives the job of implementation to an agency. The agencies involved include the Environmental Protection Agency, the Nuclear Regulatory Commission, the Food and Drug Administration, the Occupational Safety and Health Administration, and many others. In every case the regulatory agency must comply with the statute that defined its mission as well as with the general requirements of administrative law. Courts review regulatory decisions more often than funding matters, although, as we shall see, even in the regulatory arena the courts at times show considerable deference to the agencies.

As we noted in discussing Vermont Yankee v. Natural Resources Defense Council, Ch. 2, Sec B.1, supra, agencies use two basic approaches in performing their regulatory mission. Legislative-type rulemaking involves publication of a proposed rule, receipt of written and sometimes oral comments, followed by publication of a final rule. Trial-type adjudication involves application of a rule or statutory standard to a specific case. Evidence is introduced, cross-examination is held, and a final opinion is rendered.

One of the major reasons for the creation of administrative agencies was to provide organizations with expertise that could study the information available and, on the basis of that information, render fair decisions. Thus it is not surprising that Congress often delegates to agencies issues involving a high level of scientific or technical data. It may have once been hoped that agency decisions would be purely technical, that is, non-political. But because Congress often gives only general guidance and because it is so difficult to separate scientific judgments from policy judgments in areas of uncertainty, it cannot be denied that agencies today often make vital policy decisions, particularly in areas of scientific and medical dispute. Moreover, just as there is no single Department of Science making funding decisions, there is no single regulatory agency, and thus a variety of approaches to regulation are used throughout the federal government. See National Research Council, Risk Assessment in the Federal Government: Managing the Process (1983). Since agency heads are appointed by the President, not elected, and since agency personnel are often career civil servants, this central role for regulatory agencies poses vital questions about American democracy. To approach these questions in a context involving controversial technical issues, the materials in this section begin with an examination of the Occupational Safety and Health Administration's decision on occupational exposure to cotton dust.

OCCUPATIONAL EXPOSURE TO COTTON DUST

43 Fed.Reg. 27,350, 27,351–27,355 (1978).

AGENCY: Occupational Safety and Health Administration, Department of Labor.

ACTION: Final Standard.

SUMMARY: This final standard establishes occupational safety and health requirements for occupational exposure to cotton dust. It reflects OSHA's determination, based on evidence that has been placed in the public record in this rulemaking proceeding, that exposure to cotton dust presents a significant health hazard to employees. The standard establishes permissible exposure limit of 200 $\mu g/m^3$ for yarn manufacturing, 750 $\mu g/m^3$ for slashing and weaving operations, and 500 $\mu g/m^3$ for all other processes in the cotton industry and for non-textile industries where there is exposure to cotton dust. Cotton ginning is the subject of a separate regulation, § 1910.1040, published today also in Part III of this Federal Register. The harvesting of cotton and the manufacture of garments from cotton fabrics are not covered by this standard. The cotton dust standard, which is promulgated as 29 CFR 1910.1043, also provides for employee exposure monitoring, engineering controls and work practices, respirators, employee training, medical surveillance, signs and recordkeeping. . . .

B.   History of the Regulation

(1) Early developments. Substantial improvement in working conditions in the cotton textile industry did not occur until well into the twentieth century. The most important early improvements came in England as a result of legislative acts requiring medical inspection of workplaces, compulsory reporting of industrial diseases and compensation of diseased and disabled workers. In 1942 a compensation scheme was introduced in England as a means of implementing the Factory Act of 1937 and associated legislation which for the first time recognized byssinosis as an occupational disease.

In 1934 the American Conference of Governmental Industrial Hygienists (ACGIH) placed cotton dust on its tentative list of threshold limit values (TLV), and in 1966 they adopted a 1000 $\mu g/m^3$ of total cotton dust as their recommended value for exposure. This TLV was based upon the work of Roach and Schilling in the Lancashire cotton mills. Exposure to cotton dust was not regulated in the United States until 1968, when the Secretary of Labor under the Walsh-Healey Act (41 U.S.C. 35 et seq.), promulgated the 1968 ACGIH list of Threshold Limit Values which included for "Cotton dust (raw)" the limit of 1000 $\mu g/m^3$. This standard was subsequently adopted as an established Federal standard under section 6(a) of the Occupational Safety and Health Act of 1970. In 1972, the British Occupational Hygiene Society (BOHS) published a report, largely based upon Molyneux and Berry's "Correlation of Cotton Dust Exposure with the Prevalence of Respiratory Symptoms," recommending a new standard of 500 $\mu g/m^3$ less "fly"; the term fly meaning dust particles removed by a 2-mm wire screen. In addition, in 1972, on the basis of BOHS and others, a revision of the ACGIH TLV was recommended that would measure respirable dust rather than "total dust". In 1974, a TLV of 200 $\mu g/m^3$ of cotton dust as measured by the vertical elutriator was adopted by ACGIH.

On September 26, 1974, pursuant to section 20(a)(3) of the Act, the Director of the National Institute for Occupational Safety and Health (NIOSH) submitted to the Secretary of Labor a criteria document which contained NIOSH's recommendations for a new cotton dust standard.

On December 27, 1974, OSHA published an Advance Notice of Proposed Rulemaking (39 FR 44769) requesting that interested persons submit their views on specific issues relating to cotton dust, particularly the NIOSH Criteria Document.

Thereafter, in January 1975, the Textile Worker's Union of America filed a petition with the Secretary urging the Secretary to propose a modified standard for occupational exposure to cotton dust, setting an exposure limit of 100 $\mu g/m^3$. They were joined in this petition by the North Carolina Public Interest Research Group.

(2) The Proposal. On December 28, 1976, OSHA published a proposal to revise the existing standard for occupational exposure to cotton dust (41 FR 56498). The proposal called for a permissible exposure limit of 200 $\mu g/m^3$ of vertical elutriated cotton dust for all segments of the cotton industry.

The proposal allowed 90 days for interested parties to submit written comments, views, and arguments and announced that an informal public hearing for the submission of oral testimony would begin on April 5, 1977. Additional hearing dates were set by notice published March 15, 1977 (42 FR 14134). There were 263 comments and 109 notices of intent to appear at the hearings.

(3) The Hearing. The OSHA rulemaking hearing was conducted in Washington, D.C. from April 5–8, May 2–6, and 16–17; in Greenville, Mississippi on April 12; and in Lubbock, Texas on May 10–12, 1977.

Numerous persons appeared at the hearings as witnesses. Among the witnesses were large corporate and small business employers, manufacturers, representatives from the affected workforce, experts in every relevant field including physicians, scientists, statisticians, economists, industrial hygienists, representatives from agriculture, and other interested parties. Public participation was representative of virtually the entire "cotton community." The written and oral testimony of all participants was made part of the rulemaking record. The hearing record was originally scheduled to close on July 17, 1977, but at the request of several parties it was kept open until September 2, 1977 (42 FR 39120).

(4) Environmental Impact Statement.   In conjunction with the development of the proposed standard, OSHA prepared a draft environmental impact statement.   The draft environmental impact statement was published in the FEDERAL REGISTER (41 FR 56498) on December 28, 1976, along with the proposal.

Prior to the promulgation of this final standard, OSHA prepared a final environmental impact statement (FEIS) in accordance with 29 CFR 1999.5.   Notice of the availability of the FEIS was published by the Environmental Protection Agency on December 30, 1977 (42 FR 65263).

(5) The Record.   This final cotton dust standard is based on careful consideration of the entire record in this proceeding, including materials relied on in the proposal and the record of the informal rulemaking hearing including the transcript, exhibits pre-hearing and post-hearing written comments and briefs.   Copies of the official list of hearing exhibits, comments, and notices of intent to appear at the hearing can be obtained from the Docket Office, Docket No. H–052, Room 56212, U.S. Department of Labor, Third Street and Constitution Avenue NW., Washington, D.C. 20210. . . .

III.   OCCUPATIONAL HEALTH IMPLICATIONS OF EXPOSURE TO COTTON DUST

A.   General

The preamble to the proposed standard for exposure to cotton dust presented detailed scientific evidence demonstrating the health hazard to workers in the various cotton industries and the extent of that risk (41 FR 56498, Ex. 6 #1, 2, 3, 7, 13, 14, 15, 16, 17, 18, 19, 20, 21, 42, 43, 44, 51, 54, 55).   The provisions of the proposed standard were based on this evidence.   Upon reviewing the complete body of data compiled in the record, including a thorough discussion of the underlying evidence, OSHA has determined that the basic conclusions advanced in the proposed regulations have withstood critical scrutiny by the public, the cotton industry and the scientific community.   Accordingly, the evidence set forth in detail in the preamble to the proposal, will not be repeated here.

The overwhelming scientific evidence in the record supports the finding that cotton dust produces adverse health effects among cotton workers (Ex. 1, Ex. 11, Ex. 13, Ex. 19, Ex. 12, Ex. 38, d).   The disorders range from an acute reaction manifested by a depression of pulmonary function indicators, or by subjective symptoms such as chest-tightness, shortness of breath, or cough, to a stage characteristic of chronic obstructive pulmonary disease which is often disabling (Ex. 48, p.1; Ex. 6, #17, 20, 21, 42, 43, 57, 54, 56).   The chronic stages of cotton dust induced respiratory disease are, as a clinical entity, similar to chronic bronchitis or emphysema (Ex. 41, p. 5).   While gaps exist in the understanding of the etiology of respiratory disease caused by cotton dust and their progression from acute to chronic stages, the evidence in the record supports the fundamental connection between cotton dust and various respiratory disorders in both the textile and the non-textile industries (Ex. 1, Ex. 38d, Ex. 11).

Byssinosis is the specific respiratory disease attributable to the action of cotton dust on the respiratory passages.   The essential hallmark of byssinosis is the Monday phenomenon, the cyclic disorder characterized by cough, breathlessness or tightness of the chest experienced on the first day of the work week (Ex. 48, p. 1). The Schilling grading scheme for byssinosis discussed in the proposal inherently reflects the differences in duration and degree of the Monday morning symptoms (41 FR 56498).

In addition to the familiar subjective symptoms, objective measurements sometimes indicate the presence of airways obstruction (Ex. 41, pp. 8–10). Pulmonary function measurements such as Forced Expiratory Volume in one second (FEV_1), or Forced Vital Capacity (FVC) are frequently used to indicate deviation from normal breathing. As the NIOSH statement (Ex. 38, a) introduced at the hearing explains:

> Pooled data on groups of workers with byssinosis consistently show a strong association between byssinosis and drops in expiratory flow rates on Monday . . . ., both also clearly attributable to cotton dust exposure. Among individuals, however, it has been observed repeatedly that those with Monday chest tightness do not necessarily show a drop in FEV_1, and conversely, individuals with clearcut drops in Monday FEV_1 will not necessarily have a history of byssinosis.

There is further testimony that, if large groups of workers are surveyed for subjective symptoms and for pulmonary function changes, approximately the same proportion exhibit both subjective symptoms and decrements of pulmonary function (Ex. 38d). OSHA also agrees with NIOSH that "characteristic respiratory symptoms and drops in flow rates are useful epidemiologic and clinical tools and are highly associated with cotton dust concentration (Ex. 38d)."

From the description of its manifestations, it is clear that byssinosis represents a constellation of respiratory effects (Ex. 38d, Ex. 11, Ex. 6, Ex. 1, Ex. 12, Ex. 13). These effects range from acute to chronic and from reversible to disabling, and may be described by diverse terminology, such as reactor state or chronic bronchitis, but these respiratory diseases have been conclusively shown to be causally related to exposure to cotton dust (Ex. 1, Ex. 11, Ex. 38a, b, d).

B.   Chronic Obstructive Pulmonary Disease

It was the overwhelming opinion of the medical experts testifying at the hearings that byssinosis can develop into chronic obstructive pulmonary disease which is, in most cases, irreversible and disabling (Ex. 38d, Ex. 11, Ex. 41, Ex. 46). The preamble to the proposal describes Grade 3 byssinosis as follows:

> "In this advanced stage the clinical picture often becomes confused, as the chronic disease process is neither well understood nor well defined. Workers frequently manifest symptoms consistent with chronic bronchitis and emphysema. This stage is generally considered to be irreversible, with work in dusty atmospheres becoming extremely difficult or impossible. The rate at which a worker progresses to this stage, if at all, depends upon the amount of the causative agent contained in the dust inhaled, and the susceptibility of the individual."

In human terms, the affected worker frequently loses the ability to function normally on or off the job. Members of the Carolina Brown Lung Association (CBLA) testified at the hearing that the respiratory disease contracted in the textile mills typically resulted in premature retirement often after futile and painful attempts to continue on the job (Ex. 51, Ex. 54).

Testimony pointed out that several terms were being used interchangeably to describe the final clinical stage of cotton dust induced respiratory disease. These include: grade 3 byssinosis, chronic or advanced byssinosis, chronic obstructive lung disease, or the specific names of chronic obstructive pulmonary diseases (i.e. chronic bronchitis and emphysema). Among textile workers "brown lung" appears to be a synonym for disabling respiratory disease. In that sense, Dr. Russell Harley's suggestion that the term chronic obstructive pulmonary disease (COPD) constituted a generally accepted clinical definition of chronic lung disease that described the clinical end product of cotton dust induced lung disease without becoming entangled in definitions of preceding stages of the disease has merit (Ex. 41, p. 2).

The record strongly indicates that chronic bronchitis, one form of COPD, is prevalent among byssinotics (Ex. 6, #8, 17, 19, 20). Data on groups of workers with byssinosis consistently demonstrate a strong association between byssinosis and drops in expiratory flow rates on Monday and chronic cough and phlegm (bronchitis), which are both also clearly related to cotton dust exposure (Ex. 6, #17, Ex. 38d, Ex. 6, #22, 23, 25; Ex. 11). Chronic bronchitis which is not specifically related to cotton dust exposure has also been found to be far more common along cotton textile workers than among workers in mills processing only synthetic fibers (Ex. 6, #17, 21, 22, 23, 24, 32).

Since exposure to environmental pollutants such as cigarette smoke has also been identified as a causative agent of COPD, parties to the hearings representing industry argued that COPD caused by cotton dust was a minor fraction of COPD prevalence among textile workers and that most was caused by smoking (Ex. 41, p. 6; Ex. 47, #18; Ex. 46, p. 1). Dr. Mario Battigelli, testifying on behalf of the American Textile Manufacturers Institute (ATMI), stated that the background level of chronic bronchitis among the general population, estimated by him at between 10 and 40%, easily explained the observed high prevalence of chronic bronchitis, 3–50%, among cotton textile workers (Ex. 48, p. 8). It should be noted that Dr. Battigelli's estimate of background chronic bronchitis, based as it is on autopsy studies, is not comparable with other studies of relatively healthy men and women (Ex. 6, #17).

OSHA recognizes that smoking is an influential variable in the production of COPD among cotton workers (Ex. 6). Indeed, the co-existence of exposure to cotton dust and exposure to cigarette smoke has been shown to result in increased risk of COPD (Ex. 41, p. 6; Ex. 47, Ref. #18; Ex. 46, p. 1; Ex. 38d; Ex. 11). However, persuasive evidence demonstrates that the cigarette smoking variable, rather than overwhelming the cotton dust variable, is merely related to it. Indeed, there are no studies in the literature attributing the high prevalence of respiratory disease found among cotton workers primarily to smoking, or, in other words, there is no documentation for Dr. Battigelli's statement. Conversely, where the relationship between exposure to cotton dust and smoking has been explored scientifically, substantial evidence characterizes the increased risk from smoking to be additive or multiplicative to the risk due to exposure to cotton dust (Ex. 11). Dr. Arend Bouhuys of Yale University, a preeminent authority on pulmonary function, described the relationship as follows (Ex. 11, p. 16):

. . . . in our statistical analysis of symptom prevalence among large numbers of cotton textile workers and appropriate controls we found that, for all symptoms, work in textile mills was by far the largest factor in determining the prevalence of respiratory symptoms. For shortness of breath, mill work was the only significant variable. For chronic cough, sputum and wheezing, cigarette smoking was an additional important variable, but of lesser degree of significance than work in the mills. In other studies where similar analyses have been performed, cigarette smoking has also emerged as a contributing factor to chronic symptoms. But in these studies no control group was considered at the same time, so that the preponderant effect of exposure to dust in mills (in comparison with the absence of such exposure among persons not employed in textile mills) could not be assessed. It is also important to point out that shortness of breath is an important factor in disability among cotton textile workers, and that this symptom was not significantly affected by smoking. Although it should be considered an additional risk for cotton textile workers, the extent of the risk of smoking is not clearly different for cotton workers and for others not employed in the cotton textile industry. In fact, we found that the effects of cotton dust exposure and of smoking on chronic lung function loss were additive, and there is no indication in our data for any synergism between the two exposures with respect to long-term lung function.

Other evidence is consistent with Dr. Bouhuys' findings. One particularly striking feature is the high prevalence of respiratory disease among women textile workers who have never smoked (Ex. 6, #17, p. 427). Finally, it has generally been found that bronchitis prevalence is proportional to level of dust wherever this parameter has been studied.

Undoubtedly some COPD exists in the cotton worker population which is independent of exposure to cotton dust. Neither Dr. Battigelli's figures nor morbidity data from a study done in a Colorado community appear to shed light on the normal state of employee health. However, Merchant's control population consisting of textile workers in wool and synthetic industries provides a reasonable estimate of the prevalence of bronchitis among textile workers not exposed to cotton dust (Ex. 6, #17). These levels of chronic bronchitis varied from 2–3% to approximately 12% depending upon age, sex and smoking habit (Ex. 6, #17). As Merchant's work made clear, compared to these controls, workers exposed to cotton dust exhibit a significantly greater prevalence of chronic bronchitis, i.e. 24% (Ex. 6, #43, p. 173); in this study, not only cotton dust exposure but also smoking (Ex. 6, #43) and age (Ex. 6, #17, p. 427) were found to be determinants of chronic bronchitis frequency and severity. . . .

IV. PERMISSIBLE EXPOSURE LIMITS

A. General Considerations

OSHA believes that the causal relationship between exposure to cotton dust and the development of byssinosis and other respiratory diseases has been clearly established. It follows, then, that the most important step in reducing the risk of cotton dust induced respiratory disease is to reduce employee exposure to cotton dust (Ex. 6, #1, 19, 30, 51, 55, 57, 58; Ex. 124).

At the same time, OSHA recognizes that cotton dust is a heterogeneous mixture containing an as yet unidentified active agent or agents.

Cotton dust is defined in this standard as "dust present during the handling or processing of cotton which may contain a mixture of substances including ground-up plant matter, fiber, bacteria, fungi, soil, pesticides, non-cotton plant matter and other contaminants which may have accumulated during the growing, harvesting and subsequent processing or storage periods." As the preamble to the proposal states, the relative proportion of these substances in "cotton dust" can vary depending upon the type of plant, harvesting and storage methods, and cleaning operations, both at the gin and in subsequent processing (41 FR 56503).

Some parties at the hearings argued that the standard should be delayed until an active agent was isolated (e.g. Ex. 65a). OSHA has concluded that the weight of evidence in the record requires the implementation of a standard based on "cotton dust," as broadly defined, to all the segments within the scope of the cotton industry in order to prevent further and widespread development of acute and chronic respiratory disease including irreversible and disabling chronic obstructive pulmonary disease. The continuing scientific debate over the identity of the specific agent does not detract from the conclusion that "cotton dust," as defined and regulated by this standard, has been shown to cause a constellation of respiratory illnesses (Ex. 11, Ex. 38a, d; Ex. 124; Ex. 6, #1, 30, 17, 31, 32, 33, 34, 51, 55, 57, 58). Protection of employees cannot await resolution of all the points of scientific debate. . . .

NOTE

The excerpts above provide only a glimpse at OSHA's cotton dust decision. The Federal Register notice concerning the final cotton dust rule also discussed a host of other matters, including why OSHA selected the specific exposure level over various alternatives, an estimate of compliance costs for industry, an analysis of applicable legal standards, and so on. The entire notice occupies 69 pages of the Federal Register; the record compiled by the agency in the course of the cotton dust proceeding exceeded 100,000 pages. See American Textile v. Donovan, 452 U.S. 490, 501, 101 S.Ct. 2478, 2486, 69 L.Ed.2d 185, 197 (1981).

Does the agency's reasoning in the above excerpt persuade you? Do you think a ban on cigarette smoking would cause the problem to disappear or decrease greatly? How can the agency assert that "the causal relationship between exposure to cotton dust and the development of byssinosis . . . has been clearly established," and yet admit that the "active agent or agents" in cotton dust have not been identified?

Judicial review of agency decisions typically takes place in a federal court of appeals. The record—in this case, over 100,000 pages long—goes to the court, along with briefs from the opposing parties. No new evidence is submitted to the court. The court must decide if the agency complied with the relevant statutory standards. On the substance of the rule, various formulations are used, but the net result is that many judges accord considerable deference to the agency's view if that view is well-explained and defended. See Ch. 4, Sec. D.1, infra. Courts will more often review legal issues *de novo*. The United States Court of Appeals for the District of Columbia Circuit upheld the cotton dust rule in all major respects. AFL–CIO v. Marshall, 617 F.2d 636 (D.C.Cir. 1979). The case was then taken by the United States Supreme Court. At this stage, the issues involved covered only a few aspects of the original 69-page Federal Register notice. As is usually the case, a variety of largely factual matters argued at the agency level were not being pursued by the parties in the judicial filings. Accordingly, the Supreme Court's decision focused on a central issue of statutory construction.

AMERICAN TEXTILE MANUFACTURERS INSTITUTE, INC. v. DONOVAN

Supreme Court of the United States, 1981.
452 U.S. 490, 101 S.Ct. 2478, 69 L.Ed.2d 185.

JUSTICE BRENNAN delivered the opinion of the Court.

. . .

The principal question presented in these cases is whether the Occupational Safety and Health Act requires the Secretary, in promulgating a standard pursuant to § 6(b)(5) of the Act, 29 U.S.C. § 655(b)(5), to determine that the costs of the standard bear a reasonable relationship to its benefits. Relying on §§ 6(b)(5) and 3(8) of the Act, 29 U.S.C. §§ 655(b)(5) and 652(8), petitioners urge not only that OSHA must show that a standard addresses a significant risk of material health impairment, see Industrial Union Dept. v. American Petroleum Institute, 448 U.S., at 639, 100 S.Ct., at 2863 (plurality opinion), but also that OSHA must demonstrate that the reduction in risk of material health impairment is significant in light of the costs of attaining that reduction. See Brief for Petitioners in No. 79–1429, pp. 38–41. Respondents on the other hand contend that the Act requires OSHA to promulgate standards that eliminate or reduce such risks "to the extent such protection is technologically and economically feasible." Brief for Federal Respondent 38; Brief for Union Respondents 26–27. To resolve this debate, we must turn to the language, structure, and legislative history of the Act.

The starting point of our analysis is the language of the statute itself. Steadman v. SEC, 450 U.S. 91, 97, 101 S.Ct. 999, 1005, 67 L.Ed.2d 69 (1981); Reiter v. Sonotone Corp., 442 U.S. 330, 337, 99 S.Ct. 2326, 2330, 60 L.Ed.2d 931 (1979). Section 6(b)(5) of the Act, 29 U.S.C. § 655(b)(5) (emphasis added), provides:

"The Secretary, in promulgating standards dealing with toxic materials or harmful physical agents under this subsection, shall set the standard which most adequately assures, *to the extent feasible*, on the basis of the best available evidence, that no employee will suffer material impairment of health or functional capacity even if such employee has regular exposure to the hazard dealt with by such standard for the period of his working life."

Although their interpretations differ, all parties agree that the phrase "to the extent feasible" contains the critical language in § 6(b)(5) for purposes of these cases.

The plain meaning of the word "feasible" supports respondents' interpretation of the statute. According to Webster's Third New International Dictionary of the English Language 831 (1976), "feasible" means "capable of being done, executed, or effected." Accord, the Oxford English Dictionary 116 (1933) ("Capable of being done, accomplished or carried out"); Funk & Wagnalls New "Standard" Dictionary of the English Language 903 (1957) ("That may be done, performed or effected"). Thus, § 6(b)(5) directs the Secretary to issue the standard that "most adequately assures . . . that no employee will suffer material impairment of health," limited only by the extent to which this is "capable of being done." In effect then, as the Court of Appeals held, Congress itself defined the basic relationship between costs and benefits, by placing the "benefit" of worker health above all other considerations save those making attainment of this "benefit" unachievable. Any standard based on a balancing of costs and benefits by the Secretary that strikes a different balance than that struck by Congress would be inconsistent with the command set forth in § 6(b)(5). Thus, cost-benefit analysis by OSHA is not required by the statute because feasibility analysis is. See Industrial Union Dept. v. American Petroleum Institute, 448 U.S., at 718–719, 100 S.Ct., at 2902–2903 (Marshall, J., dissenting).

When Congress has intended that an agency engage in cost-benefit analysis, it has clearly indicated such intent on the face of the statute. One early example is the Flood Control Act of 1936, 33 U.S.C. § 701:

"[T]he Federal Government should improve or participate in the improvement of navigable waters or their tributaries, including watersheds thereof, for flood-control purposes if the *benefits to whomsoever they may accrue are in excess of the estimated costs,* and if the lives and social security of people are otherwise adversely affected." (Emphasis added.)

A more recent example is the Outer Continental Shelf Lands Act Amendments of 1978, 43 U.S.C. § 1347(b) (1976 ed., Supp. III), providing that offshore drilling operations shall use

"the best available and safest technologies which the Secretary determines to be economically *feasible,* wherever failure of equipment would have a significant effect on safety, health, or the environment, except where the Secretary determines that the *incremental benefits are clearly insufficient to justify the incremental costs of using such technologies.*"

These and other statutes demonstrate that Congress uses specific language when intending that an agency engage in cost-benefit analysis. See Industrial Union Dept. v. American Petroleum Institute, supra, at 710, n. 27, 100 S.Ct., at 2898, n. 27 (Marshall, J., dissenting). Certainly in light of its ordinary meaning, the word "feasible" cannot be construed to articulate such congressional intent. We therefore reject the argument that Congress required cost-benefit analysis in § 6(b)(5). . . .

When Congress passed the Occupational Safety and Health Act in 1970, it chose to place pre-eminent value on assuring employees a safe and healthful working environment, limited only by the feasibility of achieving such an environment. We must measure the validity of the Secretary's actions against the requirements of that Act. For "[t]he judicial function does not extend to substantive revision of regulatory policy. That function lies elsewhere—in Congressional and Executive oversight or amendatory legislation." Industrial Union Dept. v. American Petroleum Institute, supra, 448 U.S., at 663, 100 S.Ct., at 2875 (Burger, C. J., concurring); see TVA v. Hill, 437 U.S. 153, 185, 187–188, 194–195, 98 S.Ct. 2279, 2297, 2298, 2301, 57 L.Ed.2d 117 (1978).

. . .

JUSTICE REHNQUIST, with whom THE CHIEF JUSTICE joins, dissenting.

A year ago I stated my belief that Congress in enacting § 6(b)(5) of the Occupational Safety and Health Act of 1970 unconstitutionally delegated to the Executive Branch the authority to make the "hard policy choices" properly the task of the legislature. Industrial Union Dept. v. American Petroleum Institute, 448 U.S. 607, 671, 100 S.Ct. 2844, 2878, 65 L.Ed.2d 1010 (1980) (concurring in judgment). Because I continue to believe that the Act exceeds Congress' power to delegate legislative authority to nonelected officials, see J. W. Hampton & Co. v. United States,

276 U.S. 394, 48 S.Ct. 348, 72 L.Ed. 624 (1928), and Panama Refining Co. v. Ryan, 293 U.S. 388, 55 S.Ct. 241, 79 L.Ed. 446 (1935), I dissent.

I will repeat only a little of what I said last Term. Section 6(b)(5) provides in pertinent part:

> "The Secretary, in promulgating standards dealing with toxic materials or harmful physical agents under this subsection, shall set the standard which most adequately assures, *to the extent feasible*, on the basis of the best available evidence, that no employee will suffer material impairment of health or functional capacity even if such employee has regular exposure to the hazard dealt with by such standard for the period of his working life." (Emphasis added.)

As the Court correctly observes, the phrase "to the extent feasible" contains the critical language for the purpose of these cases. We are presented with a remarkable range of interpretations of that language. Petitioners contend that the statute *requires* the Secretary to demonstrate that the benefits of its "Cotton Dust Standard," in terms of reducing health risks, bear a reasonable relationship to its costs. Brief for Petitioners in No. 79–1429, pp. 38–41. Respondents, including the Secretary of Labor at least until his postargument motion, counter that Congress itself balanced costs and benefits when it enacted the statute, and that the statute *prohibits* the Secretary from engaging in a cost-benefit type balancing. Their view is that the Act merely requires the Secretary to promulgate standards that eliminate or reduce such risks "to the extent . . . technologically or economically feasible." Brief for Federal Respondent 38; Brief for Union Respondents 26–27. As I read the Court's opinion, it takes a different position. It concludes that, at least as to the "Cotton Dust Standard," the Act does not require the Secretary to engage in a cost-benefit analysis, which suggests of course that the Act *permits* the Secretary to undertake such an analysis if he so chooses.

Throughout its opinion, the Court refers to § 6(b)(5) as adopting a "feasibility standard" or a "feasibility requirement." Ante, at 2490–2497. But as I attempted to point out last Term in Industrial Union Dept. v. American Petroleum Institute, supra, at 681–685, 100 S.Ct., at 2883–2885, the "feasibility standard" is no standard at all. Quite the contrary, I argued there that the insertion into § 6(b)(5) of the words "to the extent feasible" rendered what had been a clear, if somewhat unrealistic, statute into one so vague and precatory as to be an unconstitutional delegation of legislative authority to the Executive Branch. Prior to the inclusion of the "feasibility" language, § 6(b)(5) simply required the Secretary to "set the standard which most adequately assures, on the basis of the best available professional evidence, that no employee will suffer any impairment of health . . . ." Legislative History, Occupational Safety and Health Act of 1970, p. 943 (Comm. Print 1971) (hereinafter Leg. Hist.). Had that statute been enacted, it would undoubtedly support the result the Court reaches in these cases, and it would not have created an excessive delegation problem. The Secretary of Labor would quite clearly have been authorized to set exposure standards without regard to any kind of cost-benefit analysis

But Congress did not enact that statute. The legislative history of the Act reveals that a number of Members of Congress, such as Senators Javits, Saxbe, and Dominick, had difficulty with the proposed statute and engaged Congress in a lengthy debate about the extent to which the Secretary should be authorized to create a risk-free work environment. Congress had at least three choices. It could have required the Secretary to engage in a cost-benefit analysis prior to the setting of exposure levels, it could have prohibited cost-benefit analysis, or it could have permitted the use of such an analysis. Rather than make that choice and resolve that difficult policy issue, however, Congress passed. Congress simply said that the Secretary should set standards "to the extent feasible." Last year, Justice Powell reflected that "one might wish that Congress had spoken with greater clarity." *American Petroleum Institute*, 448 U.S., at 668, 100 S.Ct., at 2877 (Powell, J., concurring in part and in judgment). I am convinced that the reason that Congress did not speak with greater "clarity" was because it could not. The words "to the extent feasible" were used to mask a fundamental policy disagreement in Congress. I have no doubt that if Congress had been required to choose whether to mandate, permit, or prohibit the Secretary from engaging in a cost-benefit analysis, there would have been no bill for the President to sign.

The Court seems to argue that Congress *did* make a policy choice when it enacted the "feasibility" language. Its view is that Congress required the Secretary to engage in something called "feasibility analysis." But those words mean nothing at all. They are a "legislative mirage, appearing to some Members [of Congress] but not to others, and assuming any form desired by the beholder." *American Petroleum Institute*, supra, at 681, 100 S.Ct., at 2883. Even the Court does not settle on a meaning. It first suggests that the language requires the Secretary to do what is "capable of being done." But, if that is all the language means, it is merely precatory and "no more than an admonition to the Secretary to do his duty . . .." Leg. Hist. 367 (remarks of Sen. Dominick). The Court then seems to adopt the Secretary's view that feasibility means "technological and economic feasibility." But there is nothing in the words of § 6(b)(5), or their legislative history, to suggest why they should be so limited. One wonders why the "requirement" of § 6(b)(5) could not include considerations of administrative or even political feasibility. As even the Court recognizes, when Congress has wanted to limit the concept of feasibility to technological and economic feasibility, it has said so. Thus the words "to the extent feasible" provide no meaningful guidance to those who will administer the law.

In believing that § 6(b)(5) amounts to an unconstitutional delegation of legislative authority to the Executive Branch, I do not mean to suggest that Congress, in enacting a statute, must resolve all ambiguities or must "fill in all of the blanks." Even the neophyte student of government realizes that legislation is the art of compromise, and that an important, controversial bill is seldom enacted by Congress in the form in which it is first introduced. It is not unusual for the various factions supporting or opposing a proposal to accept some departure from the language they would prefer and to adopt substitute language agreeable to all. But that sort of compromise is a far cry from this case, where Congress simply abdicated its responsibility for the making of a fundamental and most difficult policy choice—whether and to what extent "the statistical possibility of future deaths should . . . be disregarded in light of the economic costs of preventing those deaths." *American Petroleum Institute*, supra, at 672, 100 S.Ct., at 2879. That is a "quintessential legislative" choice and must be made by the elected representatives of the people, not by nonelected officials in the Executive Branch. As stated last Term:

"In drafting § 6(b)(5), Congress was faced with a clear, if difficult, choice between balancing statistical lives and industrial resources or authorizing the Secretary to elevate human life above all concerns save massive dislocation in an affected industry. That Congress recognized the difficulty of this choice is clear . . .. That Congress chose, intentionally or unintentionally, to pass the difficult choice on to the Secretary is evident from the spectral quality of the standard it selected." 448 U.S., at 685, 100 S.Ct., at 2885.

In sum, the Court is quite correct in asserting that the phrase "to the extent feasible" is the critical language for the purposes of these cases. But that language is critical, not because it establishes a general standard by which those charged with administering the statute may be guided, but because it has precisely the opposite effect: in failing to agree on whether the Secretary should be either mandated, permitted, or prohibited from undertaking a cost-benefit analysis, Congress simply left the crucial policy choices in the hands of the Secretary of Labor. As I stated at greater length last Term, I believe that in so doing Congress unconstitutionally delegated its legislative responsibility to the Executive Branch.

NOTE

Does Justice Brennan's opinion that Congress meant to place the " 'benefit' of worker health above all other considerations save those making attainment of this 'benefit' unachievable" persuade you? Does this mean that if reducing the exposure level further would improve the health of one worker while throwing hundreds out of work, the agency must reduce the exposure level? For a more detailed look at the role of cost-benefit assessment in public regulation, see Ch. 5, infra.

The Court has not used the non-delegation doctrine invoked by Justice Rehnquist to strike down legislation since the New Deal. Does Congress' action in this case justify such a resurgence of judicial activism? If Congress had to make particularized decisions on health issues, would the substance of those decisions improve? The Supreme Court's 1983 invalidation of the legislative veto may lead to fewer Congressional delegations of broad, legislative-type authority. Immigration and Naturalization Service v. Chadha, 462 U.S. ___, 103 S.Ct. 2764, 77 L.Ed.2d 317 (1983). Before *Chadha*, Congress may at times have been willing to delegate because it retained the veto power. In some instances, a legislative veto was present in delegations involving technical issues, see, e.g., Nuclear Non-Proliferation Act of 1978, 42 U.S.C. §§ 2160(f), 2155(b), 2157(b), 2153(d) (Supp. III 1979) (cooperative agreements concerning spent nuclear fuel, proposed export of nuclear materials, and proposed agreements for international cooperation in nuclear reactor development may be disapproved by concurrent resolution), although Congress often delegated broadly without retaining a veto.

At present, given the Court's willingness to uphold extensive Congressional delegations of authority, the agencies play the central role in regulatory matters involving technical issues. Indeed, in practice, White House and Congressional figures often find themselves "lobbying" agencies in a striking reversal of the textbook depiction of elected officials as the target of lobbyists. In upholding the Environmental Protection Agency's authority to receive certain informal contacts while formulating rules for emission standards for coal-fired power plants, the United States Court of Appeals for the District of Columbia Circuit allowed lobbying by then-majority leader Senator Robert Byrd: "[W]e believe it entirely proper for Congressional representatives vigorously to represent the interests of their constituents before administrative agencies engaged in informal, general policy rulemaking . . ." Sierra Club v. Costle, 657 F.2d 298, 409 (D.C.Cir. 1981). The court also upheld the propriety of certain agency contacts with the executive branch. See Ch. 5, Sec. A.5, infra. Does this make you feel better or worse about having agencies perform "general policy rulemaking"?

PAUL J. QUIRK,
FOOD AND DRUG ADMINISTRATION

In The Politics of Regulation.
191, 211–217 (J. Q. Wilson ed. 1980).

The impact of external influences on the FDA is a disputed subject: some critics argue that the FDA is subjected to intense pressures primarily by industry; others see the main pressures as favoring tighter regulatory controls. Some features of the FDA's environment support each of these views; it is hard to say which is correct.

Undoubtedly the most significant pressure on the FDA to approve drugs results directly from industry lobbying of the agency. In the drug-evaluation process there are necessarily frequent contacts between agency officials and representatives of drug companies. The issues and information involved are too complex for efficient handling in writing alone. According to FDA medical officers responding to a survey, industry usually behaves itself during such contacts, using factual and reasoned arguments in support of its positions, rather than hard-sell tactics, threats, or bribes. Nevertheless, having frequent contacts with industry representatives, getting to know and perhaps like them personally, and seeing their anxiousness to have drugs approved obviously will tend to create some sympathy for industry viewpoints and interests. Such contacts on a regular basis over a period of years may strongly shape the attitudes of FDA officials. Moreover, there are no regular, direct contacts between reviewing officials and any parties inclined to oppose drug approvals. In addition to its psychological effects, this lobbying imbalance also creates an imbalance of information and analysis—arguments favorable to a drug approval will be discovered and articulately put by company representatives while criticisms must be discovered by the reviewer unassisted.

In addition to this direct lobbying, industry might employ indirect lobbying as well. A company executive might ask the commissioner, the secretary of HEW, a key congressman, or even the president to use his leverage with the Bureau of Drugs to bring about favorable action. Although such political intervention might be hard to observe, it is evidently rare. Very few instances have come to light. The most notable case concerned Panalba—a very popular combination antibiotic that was pronounced ineffective in the review of drugs retroactively subject to the proof-of-efficacy requirement of the 1962 amendments. The Upjohn Company, producers of Panalba, objected to the FDA's decision in May 1969 to decertify the drug by a summary procedure, without a prior hearing, and took its complaint to HEW Secretary Robert Finch. Finch ordered the FDA to grant the prior hearing. However, news of the secretary's intervention immediately leaked to Representative Lawrence Fountain's subcommittee of the Government Operations Committee. The subcommittee staff expressed interest in the matter, and the secretary's order was reversed before it was a day old. Perhaps partly for partisan reasons, Fountain, a Democrat, held hearings on the case which produced publicity embarrassing to the Nixon administration. The Panalba case is the kind of exception that proves the rule: it suggests that attempts to intervene in favor of industry are likely to be politically unrewarding. In interviews with the author, FDA officials have described such political intervention as extremely uncommon.

In some cases, industry can obstruct or at least delay FDA regulatory action by use of administrative and judicial appeals. The effectiveness of these tactics, however, is dependent on the circumstances. The courts generally allow the FDA wide administrative discretion, especially with regard to its scientific and policy judgments on drug safety and efficacy. Judicial limitations on the agency usually concern matters of jurisdiction and procedure. Thus, appeals can be useful to industry primarily to prevent or to delay agency action.

Delay cannot help companies seeking to market a new product, and therefore attempts to secure marketing approval by judicial appeal are rare. Appeals are most useful to industry when the FDA seeks to withdraw an already marketed drug or to change its labeling. Even then, however, a company will not appeal if it believes that the FDA's case is so strong that resisting it would result in bad publicity or that sales would decline anyway. Indeed, most product withdrawals sought by the FDA are accomplished voluntarily.

Some critics have argued that drug companies gain influence with the FDA because officials have often left the agency for jobs in industry. The assumption is that, while they are in the FDA, officials might want to preserve or enhance future opportunities for industry employment and therefore might make more lenient regulatory decisions than they otherwise would. FDA officials do go on to industry jobs with significant frequency—former commissioners Herbert Ley and Charles Edwards, former Bureau of Drugs Director Henry Simmons, and former head of the Office of New Drug Evaluation George Leong all subsequently accepted direct or indirect drug-industry employment. Nevertheless, the contribution of this career pattern to industry influence is evidently very limited. FDA officials believe that industry employment is offered primarily on the basis of experience in the agency and scientific or managerial competence. Only that small fraction of the agency's lower-level officials who take extremely strong antiindustry positions, of a sort considered factually unsupported by most of the agency, are believed to lose opportunities for future industry employment. For the range of policy views covering most of the agency, and all of its high officials, policy is considered irrelevant to such opportunities. In support of this position, some officials point out that both Edwards and Simmons were noted for a tough attitude toward industry, but still were offered industry employment. Thus, even for FDA officials interested in industry employment, the incentives to adopt industry views are negligible as long as they avoid identification as extremists.

On some issues, the main opposition to FDA action is not from the drug industry, but from the medical profession. The FDA has attempted to discourage or prevent certain prescribing practices; it has required "patient labels" for some drugs, which serve to give the patient medical advice; and it has threatened to withdraw drugs whose frequent misuse makes them a public health hazard. The AMA and other medical organizations object strenuously to such efforts, which are perceived as medically and legally unwarranted. They argue that the individual physician can determine patient needs better than a distant and slow-moving bureaucracy such as the FDA, and they argue that Congress intended the FDA to regulate only the production and marketing of drugs—not the practice of medicine. Moreover, the organized medical profession has supported the criticism that burdensome FDA regulation has kept valuable drugs off the American market.

By the mid-1970s, disaffection of the medical profession with the FDA had become quite severe. State and national medical conventions passed resolutions calling for reduction of the agency's authority. On a wide range of issues, the medical profession was acting in concert with the drug industry in pursuit of more lenient regulation.

On rare occasions, the principal resistance to FDA regulation comes from the mass public. The attempted banning of saccharin (a food additive, and thus not strictly our concern here), the attempt to strengthen labeling and dosage restrictions on vitamins and minerals, and the denial of marketing approval to the purported cancer cure, laetrile, have all stimulated intense opposition from a significant segment of public opinion. Apparently, such public opposition occurs when the FDA takes action to prohibit or restrict sale or discourage use of a product that has gained substantial public acceptance. In the cases of saccharin and of vitamins, public opposition was intensified by the presence of obvious disagreement among responsible experts concerning the merits of the FDA's decision. In the case of laetrile, respectable opinion was more unanimously in the FDA's favor, but apparently sympathy for the frustrating and desperate circumstances of cancer victims made many people willing to ignore or disregard the experts.

When FDA actions offend public opinion, other institutions, particularly Congress, are ready to consider reversing them. Congress legislatively reversed the FDA's vitamin and mineral regulations and delayed implementation of the saccharin ban. A bill was introduced, with over one hundred cosponsors in the House, to legalize laetrile by eliminating proof-of-efficacy as a requirement for drug-marketing approval. And a U.S. District Court in Oklahoma enjoined the FDA from interfering with the prescribing or sale of laetrile to patients certified by their doctors to be terminally ill with cancer.

These cases of intense public opposition are significant not only because of the possibility of legislative or judicial reversal, but also because they threaten the agency's political support and its access to needed resources. Some analysts have argued that regulatory agencies must avoid doing serious harm to regulated industry interests in order to assure survival and to permit growth. They have budgetary incentives to adopt policies favored by industry. In interviews designed to test this hypothesis, however, FDA officials perceived no threats to the agency budget resulting from actions opposed by industry alone or by industry along with the medical profession. Except for some issues on which agency decisions affect agriculture, the only actions seen as bearing a risk of budgetary damage were those that led to *public* protest and opposition. Thus the agency has strong incentives to minimize the number of decisions likely to generate mass resistance.

The drug industry might learn to exploit this FDA vulnerability by using tactics designed to stimulate public protest. Bureau of Drugs Director Richard Crout argues that industry has attempted to hasten approval of new drugs by applying for approval early, before acceptable evidence of safety and efficacy has been assembled, and then generating stories suggesting that the FDA is sitting on an application for a valuable new drug. This criticism leads to intense pressure on the agency to approve the drug from patients wishing to use it, their families, and their doctors. One such example is sodium valproate, a promising drug for children's epilepsy that was available abroad for several years but was not available in the United States until intense public and congressional pressure provoked accelerated FDA approval. From another perspective, this tactic is helpful rather than harmful if it serves as a means of alerting the public to the damage that can be done by excessive testing requirements and unnecessary delays.

Counteracting any pressures in favor of swift or lax drug approvals are important forces tending to produce strict or even burdensome regulation. Consumer groups such as the Ralph Nader-affiliated Health Research Group and the Consumer Federation of America actively promote stricter regulatory standards and criticize FDA decisions that they consider weak or irresponsible. Although the financial resources and personnel of these organizations are completely eclipsed by the resources that the drug industry is able to devote to regulatory affairs, consumer groups have certain advantages over industry. Their news releases make good copy and are often picked up by the press, they have a generally favorable public image and can often count on rallying significant public support for their actions, and they have powerful allies in Congress (and, during the Carter administration, in the White House). Their resource limitations are partly compensated for by the willingness of some FDA officials, who are critical of the agency's leadership, to supply them with information and tips about potentially controversial issues.

The positions consumer groups advocate do not necessarily represent the objective interests of consumers. Because they must gain publicity and persuade the public of their importance in order to remain in business, such groups have reason to exaggerate industry's irresponsibility and to depict the FDA as completely "captured" by the industry. This enables them to assume the role of lone protector of the public interest. The demands of this role lead consumer groups to argue consistently for more and tougher regulatory control and therefore to ignore or deny the costs of regulation.

Probably the most important pressures on the FDA to regulate strictly result from congressional oversight. For two decades a number of congressmen—especially Senators Estes Kefauver, Gaylord Nelson, and Edward Kennedy and Representatives Lawrence Fountain and Paul Rogers—have headed almost continuous investigations of the FDA and the drug industry. These investigations have often gained national attention and have helped the congressmen involved rise in prominence. With rare exceptions, these congressional hearings have criticized FDA decisions and enforcement as lax, have attributed this laxness (directly or by implication) to agency subservience to industry, and have demanded tougher regulation. According to then-Commissioner Alexander Schmidt, testifying before Congress in 1974:

> By far the greatest pressure that the Bureau of Drugs or the Food and Drug Administration receives with respect to the new drug approval process is brought to bear through Congressional hearings. In all our history, we are unable to find one instance where a Congressional hearing investigated the failure of FDA to approve a new drug . . . the message conveyed by this situation could not be clearer. . . . Until perspective is brought to the legislative oversight function, the pressure from Congress for FDA to disapprove new drugs will continue to be felt, and could be a major factor in health care in this country.

Congressional oversight of drug regulation is affected by some of the same biases that influence consumer groups, for similar reasons. Thus, in 1973 and 1974, Senators Nelson and Kennedy tended to dismiss all evidence that high regulatory barriers were creating a significant disincentive to new drug development and keeping useful drugs, available abroad, off the American market.   In part, such behavior simply reflects the necessity for congressmen to decide who will be their friends, and who their enemies—an attitude of judicious moderation is likely to gain the support of no one.

The importance of these congressional pressures is worth examining: Schmidt's estimate, suggesting their preeminent effectiveness, need not be taken at face value.   Interestingly, FDA officials do not consider consumer-oriented congressional criticism of the FDA threatening to the agency's budgetary stability and growth.   It is not the appropriations committees that make this criticism; nor are they perceived as being negatively influenced by it.   More to the point, criticism often has the effect of supporting FDA claims for more resources and authority.   Accordingly, the congressmen who are most critical are those who most support strengthening the agency.   In short, it is not clear that consumerist congressional pressures carry with them any credible threat of sanctions—at least of the kinds usually supporting congressional influence with administrators.   There are, however, other reasons why the FDA might respond to them, including the need to protect the president from adverse publicity, to maintain agency morale and reputation, and to avoid painful accusations and conflict.   . . .

NOTE

One could formulate two extreme positions on the role of agencies in making science and health policy.   On the one hand, if the purpose of having the agencies is to emphasize expertise, pressures from non-expert sources presumably should be minimized.   If the agency receives public input just as a legislature does, why not give all of these decisions back to Congress?   On the other hand, if expertise and policy cannot be wholly separated, and if Congress simply cannot deal with the number and complexity of modern science policy issues, the agencies should presumably foster input—pressure, if you will—from all sides.   How else can agency decisions properly serve a democratic society?   Which of these extremes— or what compromise between them—do you favor?

2.   STATE REGULATION

PACIFIC GAS AND ELECTRIC CO. v. STATE ENERGY RESOURCES CONSERVATION AND DEVELOPMENT COMMISSION

Supreme Court of the United States, 1983.
460 U.S. ___, 103 S.Ct. 1713, 75 L.Ed.2d 752.

JUSTICE WHITE delivered the opinion of the Court.

. . .

This case emerges from the intersection of the federal government's efforts to ensure that nuclear power is safe with the exercise of the historic state authority over the generation and sale of electricity.   At issue is whether provisions in the 1976 amendments to California's Warren-Alquist Act, Cal.Pub.Res.Code § 25524.2 (West 1977), which condition the construction of nuclear plants on findings by the State Energy Resources Conservation and Development Commission that adequate storage facilities and means of disposal are available for nuclear waste, are preempted by the Atomic Energy Act of 1954, 42 U.S.C. § 2011, et seq.   . . .

Section 25524.2 deals with the long-term solution to nuclear wastes. This section imposes a moratorium on the certification of new nuclear plants until the Energy Commission "finds that there has been developed and that the United States through its authorized agency has approved and there exists a demonstrated technology or means for the disposal of high-level nuclear waste." "Disposal" is defined as a "method for the permanent and terminal disposition of high-level nuclear waste . . . ." Cal.Pub.Res.Code § 25524.2(a), (c). Such a finding must be reported to the state legislature, which may nullify it. . . .

It is well-established that within Constitutional limits Congress may preempt state authority by so stating in express terms. Jones v. Rath Packing Co., 430 U.S. 519, 525, 97 S.Ct. 1305, 1309, 51 L.Ed.2d 604 (1977). Absent explicit preemptive language, Congress' intent to supercede state law altogether may be found from a "scheme of federal regulation so pervasive as to make reasonable the inference that Congress left no room to supplement it," "because the Act of Congress may touch a field in which the federal interest is so dominant that the federal system will be assumed to preclude enforcement of state laws on the same subject," or because "the object sought to be obtained by the federal law and the character of obligations imposed by it may reveal the same purpose." Fidelity Federal Savings & Loan Ass'n v. de la Cuesta, 458 U.S. 141, 153, 102 S.Ct. 3014, 3022, 73 L.Ed.2d 664 (1982); Rice v. Santa Fe Elevator Corp., 331 U.S. 218, 230, 67 S.Ct. 1146, 1152, 91 L.Ed. 1447 (1947). Even where Congress has not entirely displaced state regulation in a specific area, state law is preempted to the extent that it actually conflicts with federal law. Such a conflict arises when "compliance with both federal and state regulations is a physical impossibility," Florida Lime & Avocado Growers, Inc. v. Paul, 373 U.S. 132, 142–143, 83 S.Ct. 1210, 1217–1218, 10 L.Ed.2d 248 (1963), or where state law "stands as an obstacle to the accomplishment and execution of the full purposes and objectives of Congress." Hines v. Davidowitz, 312 U.S. 52, 67, 61 S.Ct. 399, 404, 85 L.Ed. 581 (1941).

Petitioners, the United States, and supporting *amici*, present three major lines of argument as to why § 25524.2 is preempted. First, they submit that the statute—because it regulates construction of nuclear plants and because it is allegedly predicated on safety concerns—ignores the division between federal and state authority created by the Atomic Energy Act, and falls within the field that the federal government has preserved for its own exclusive control. Second, the statute, and the judgments that underlie it, conflict with decisions concerning the nuclear waste disposal issue made by Congress and the Nuclear Regulatory Commission. Third, the California statute frustrates the federal goal of developing nuclear technology as a source of energy. We consider each of these contentions in turn.

A

Even a brief perusal of the Atomic Energy Act reveals that, despite its comprehensiveness, it does not at any point expressly require the States to construct or authorize nuclear power plants or prohibit the States from deciding, as an absolute or conditional matter, not to permit the construction of any further reactors. Instead, petitioners argue that the Act is intended to preserve the federal government as the sole regulator of all matters nuclear, and that § 25524.2 falls within the scope of this impliedly preempted field. But as we view the issue, Congress, in passing the

1954 Act and in subsequently amending it, intended that the federal government should regulate the radiological safety aspects involved in the construction and operation of a nuclear plant, but that the States retain their traditional responsibility in the field of regulating electrical utilities for determining questions of need, reliability, cost and other related state concerns.

Need for new power facilities, their economic feasibility, and rates and services, are areas that have been characteristically governed by the States. Justice Brandeis once observed that the "franchise to operate a public utility . . . is a special privilege which . . . may be granted or withheld at the pleasure of the State." Frost v. Corporation Commission, 278 U.S. 515, 534, 49 S.Ct. 235, 242, 73 L.Ed. 483 (1929) (Brandeis, J. dissenting). "The nature of government regulation of private utilities is such that a utility may frequently be required by the state regulatory scheme to obtain approval for practices a business regulated in less detail would be free to institute without any approval from a regulatory body." Jackson v. Metropolitan Edison Co., 419 U.S. 345, 357, 95 S.Ct. 449, 456, 42 L.Ed.2d 477 (1974). See Central Hudson Gas & Electric Corp. v. Public Service Commission of New York, 447 U.S. 557, 569, 100 S.Ct. 2343, 2353, 65 L.Ed.2d 341 (1980) ("The state concern that rates be fair and efficient represents a clear and substantial governmental interest.") With the exception of the broad authority of the Federal Power Commission, now the Federal Energy Regulatory Commission, over the need for and pricing of electrical power transmitted in interstate commerce, see Federal Power Act, 16 U.S.C. § 824 (1976), these economic aspects of electrical generation have been regulated for many years and in great detail by the states. As we noted in Vermont Yankee Nuclear Power Corp. v. NRDC, 435 U.S. 519, 550, 98 S.Ct. 1197, 1215, 55 L.Ed.2d 460 (1977), "There is little doubt that under the Atomic Energy Act of 1954, state public utility commissions or similar bodies are empowered to make the initial decision regarding the need for power." Thus, "Congress legislated here in a field which the States have traditionally occupied . . . . so we start with the assumption that the historic police powers of the States were not to be superseded by the Federal Act unless that was the clear and manifest purpose of Congress." Rice v. Santa Fe Elevator Corp., supra, 331 U.S., at 230, 67 S.Ct., at 1152.

The Atomic Energy Act must be read, however, against another background. Enrico Fermi demonstrated the first nuclear reactor in 1942, and Congress authorized civilian application of atomic power in 1946, Atomic Energy Act of 1946, see Act of Aug. 1, 1946, ch. 724, 60 Stat. 755, at which time the Atomic Energy Commission (AEC) was created. Until 1954, however, the use, control and ownership of nuclear technology remained a federal monopoly. The Atomic Energy Act of 1954, Act of Aug. 30, 1954, ch. 1073, 68 Stat. 919, as amended, 42 U.S.C. §§ 2011–2281 (1976), grew out of Congress' determination that the national interest would be best served if the Government encouraged the private sector to become involved in the development of atomic energy for peaceful purposes under a program of federal regulation and licensing. See H.R. Rep. No. 2181, 83d Cong., 2d Sess., 1–11 (1954). The Act implemented this policy decision by providing for licensing of private construction, ownership, and operation of commercial nuclear power reactors. Duke Power Co. v. Carolina Environmental Study Group, Inc., 438 U.S., at 63, 98 S.Ct., at 2625. The AEC, however, was given exclusive jurisdiction to license the transfer, delivery, receipt, acquisition, possession and use of

nuclear materials. 42 U.S.C. §§ 2014, (e), (z), (aa), 2061–2064, 2071–
2078, 2091–99, 2111–14 (1976 and Supp. IV 1980). Upon these subjects, no role was left for the states.

The Commission, however, was not given authority over the generation of electricity itself, or over the economic question whether a particular plant should be built. We observed in *Vermont Yankee*, supra, 435 U.S.,
at 550, 98 S.Ct., at 1215, that "The Commission's prime area of concern
in the licensing context, . . . is national security, public health, and
safety." See also Power Reactor Development Corp. v. International
Union of Electrical, Radio and Machine Workers, 367 U.S. 396, 415, 81
S.Ct. 1529, 1539, 6 L.Ed.2d 924 (1961) (utility's investment not to be
considered by Commission in its licensing decisions). The Nuclear Regulatory Commission (NRC), which now exercises the AEC's regulatory authority, does not purport to exercise its authority based on economic considerations, 10 CFR § 8.4, and has recently repealed its regulations
concerning the financial qualifications and capabilities of a utility proposing to constuct and operate a nuclear power plant. 47 Fed.Reg. 13751.
In its notice of rule repeal, the NRC stated that utility financial qualifications are only of concern to the NRC if related to the public health and
safety. It is almost inconceivable that Congress would have left a regulatory vacuum; the only reasonable inference is that Congress intended the
states to continue to make these judgments. Any doubt that ratemaking
and plant-need questions were to remain in state hands was removed by
§ 271, 42 U.S.C. § 2018 which provided:

"Nothing in this chapter shall be construed to affect the authority or
regulations of any Federal, State or local agency with respect to the
generation, sale, or transmission of electric power produced through
the use of nuclear facilities licensed by the Commission . . ."

The legislative reports accompanying this provision do little more than
restate the statutory language, S.Rep. No. 1699, 83d Cong., 2d Sess. 31;
H.R.Rep. No. 2181, 83d Cong., 2d Sess. 31 (1954), U.S.Code Cong. &
Admin.News 1954, p. 3456, but statements on the floor of Congress confirm that while the safety of nuclear technology was the exclusive business
of the federal government, state power over the production of electricity
was not otherwise displaced.

The 1959 Amendments reinforced this fundamental division of authority. In 1959, Congress amended the Atomic Energy Act in order to
"clarify the respective responsibilities . . . of the States and the Commission with respect to the regulation of byproduct, source, and special
nuclear materials." 42 U.S.C. § 2021(a)(1). See S.Rep. No. 870, 86th
Cong., 1st Sess. 8, 10–12 (1959), U.S. Code Cong. & Admin.News 1959,
p. 2872. The authority of the states over the planning for new power-
plants and ratemaking were not at issue. Indeed, the point of the 1959
Amendments was to heighten the states' role. Section 274(b), 42 U.S.C.
§ 2021(b), authorized the NRC, by agreements with state governors to
discontinue its regulatory authority over certain nuclear materials under
limited conditions. State programs permitted under the amendment
were required to be "coordinated and compatible" with that of the NRC.
§ 2021(g); S.Rep. No. 870, supra, at 11. The subject matters of those
agreements were also limited by § 274(c), 42 U.S.C. § 2021(c), which
states that:

"The Commission shall retain authority and responsibility with respect
to regulation of

(1) the construction and operation of any production or utilization facility; . . . .

(4) the disposal of such . . . byproduct, source or special nuclear material as the Commission determines . . . should, because of the hazards or potential hazards thereof, not be so disposed of without a license from the Commission."

Although the authority reserved by Section 274(c) was exclusively for the Commission to exercise, See S.Rep. No. 870 at 8, 9; H.R.Rep. No. 1125, 86th Cong., 1st Sess. 8, 9 (1959), Congress made clear that the section was not intended to cutback on preexisting state authority outside the NRC's jurisdiction. Section 274(k), 42 U.S.C. § 2021(k) states:

"Nothing in this section shall be construed to affect the authority of any state or local agency to regulate activities for purposes other than protection against radiation hazards."

§ 274(k), by itself, limits only the preemptive effect of "this section," that is, § 274, and does not represent an affirmative grant of power to the states. But Congress, by permitting regulation "for purposes other than protection against radiation hazards" underscored the distinction drawn in 1954 between the spheres of activity left respectively to the federal government and the states.

This regulatory structure has remained unchanged, for our purposes, until 1965, when the following proviso was added to § 271:

"*Provided*, that this section shall not be deemed to confer upon any Federal, State or local agency any authority to regulate, control, or restrict any activities of the Commission."

The accompanying report by the Joint Committee on Atomic Energy makes clear that the amendment was not intended to detract from state authority over energy facilities. Instead, the proviso was added to overrule a Court of Appeals opinion which interpreted § 271 to allow a municipality to prohibit transmission lines necessary for the AEC's own activities. Maun v. United States, 347 F.2d 970 (CA9 1965). There is no indication that Congress intended any broader limitation of state regulatory power over utility companies. Indeed, reports and debates accompanying the 1965 Amendment indicate that § 271's purpose "was to make it absolutely clear that the Atomic Energy Act's special provisions on licensing of reactors did not disturb the status quo with respect to the then existing authority of Federal, State, and local bodies to regulate generation, sale, or transmission of electric power." 111 Cong.Rec. 19822 (statement of Sen. Hickenlooper).

This account indicates that from the passage of the Atomic Energy Act in 1954, through several revisions, and to the present day, Congress has preserved the dual regulation of nuclear-powered electricity generation: the federal government maintains complete control of the safety and "nuclear" aspects of energy generation; the states exercise their traditional authority over the need for additional generating capacity, the type of generating facilities to be licensed, land use, ratemaking, and the like.

The above is not particularly controversial. But deciding how § 25524.2 is to be construed and classified is a more difficult proposition. At the outset, we emphasize that the statute does not seek to regulate the construction or operation of a nuclear powerplant. It would clearly be impermissible for California to attempt to do so, for such regulation, even if enacted out of non-safety concerns, would nevertheless directly conflict with the NRC's exclusive authority over plant construction and operation. Respondents appear to concede as much. Respondents do broadly argue, however, that although safety regulation of nuclear plants by states is forbidden, a state may completely prohibit new construction until its safety concerns are satisfied by the federal government. We reject this line of reasoning. State safety regulation is not preempted only when it conflicts with federal law. Rather, the federal government has occupied the entire field of nuclear safety concerns, except the limited powers expressly ceded to the states. When the federal government completely occupies a given field or an identifiable portion of it, as it has done here, the test of preemption is whether "the matter on which the state asserts the right to act is in any way regulated by the federal government." Rice v. Santa Fe Elevator Corp., supra, 331 U.S., at 236, 67 S.Ct., at 1155. A state moratorium on nuclear construction grounded in safety concerns falls squarely within the prohibited field. Moreover, a state judgment that nuclear power is not safe enough to be further developed would conflict directly with the countervailing judgment of the NRC, see, infra, at 1729–1730, that nuclear construction may proceed notwithstanding extant uncertainties as to waste disposal. A state prohibition on nuclear construction for safety reasons would also be in the teeth of the Atomic Energy Act's objective to insure that nuclear technology be safe enough for widespread development and use—and would be preempted for that reason. Infra, at 1731–1732.

That being the case, it is necessary to determine whether there is a non-safety rationale for § 25524.2. California has maintained, and the Court of Appeals agreed, that § 25524.2 was aimed at economic problems, not radiation hazards. The California Assembly Committee On Resources, Land Use, and Energy, which proposed a package of bills including § 25524.2, reported that the waste disposal problem was "largely economic or the result of poor planning, *not* safety related." Reassessment of Nuclear Energy in California: A Policy Analysis of Proposition 15 and its Alternatives (1976) (Reassessment Report) at 18 (emphasis in original). The Committee explained that the lack of a federally approved method of waste disposal created a "clog" in the nuclear fuel cycle. Storage space was limited while more nuclear wastes were continuously produced. Without a permanent means of disposal, the nuclear waste problem could become critical leading to unpredictably high costs to contain the problem or, worse, shutdowns in reactors. "Waste disposal *safety*," the Reassessment Report notes, "is not directly addressed by the bills, which ask only that a method [of waste disposal] be chosen and accepted by the federal government." Id., at 156 (emphasis in original).

The Court of Appeals adopted this reading of § 25524.2. Relying on the Reassessment Report, the court concluded:

"[S]ection 25524.2 is directed towards purposes other than protection against radiation hazards. While Proposition 15 would have required California to judge the safety of a proposed method of waste disposal, section 25524.2 leaves that judgment to the federal government. California is concerned not with the adequacy of the method, but rather with its existence." 659 F.2d, at 925.

Our general practice is to place considerable confidence in the interpretations of state law reached by the federal courts of appeals. Cf. Mills v. Rogers, 457 U.S. 291, 306, 102 S.Ct. 2442, 2452, 73 L.Ed.2d 16 (1982); Bishop v. Wood, 426 U.S. 341, 346, 96 S.Ct. 2074, 2078, 48 L.Ed.2d 684 (1976). Petitioners and *amici* nevertheless attempt to upset this interpretation in a number of ways. First, they maintain that § 25524.2 evinces no concern with the economics of nuclear power. The statute states that the "development" and "existence" of a permanent disposal technology approved by federal authorities will lift the moratorium; the statute does not provide for considering the economic costs of the technology selected. This view of the statute is overly myopic. Once a technology is selected and demonstrated, the utilities and the California Public Utilities Commission would be able to estimate costs; such cost estimates cannot be made until the federal government has settled upon the method of long-term waste disposal. Moreover, once a satisfactory disposal technology is found and demonstrated, fears of having to close down operating reactors should largely evaporate.

Second, it is suggested that California, if concerned with economics, would have banned California utilities from building plants outside the state. This objection carries little force. There is no indication that California utilities are contemplating such construction; the state legislature is not obligated to address purely hypothetical facets of a problem.

Third, petitioners note that there already is a body, the California Public Utilities Commission, which is authorized to determine on economic grounds whether a nuclear power plant should be constructed. While California is certainly free to make these decisions on a case-by-case basis, a state is not foreclosed from reaching the same decision through a legislative judgment, applicable to all cases. The economic uncertainties engendered by the nuclear waste disposal problems are not factors that vary from facility to facility; the issue readily lends itself to more generalized decisionmaking and California cannot be faulted for pursuing that course.

Fourth, petitioners note that Proposition 15, the initiative out of which § 25524.2 arose, and companion provisions in California's so-called nuclear laws, are more clearly written with safety purposes in mind. It is suggested that § 25524.2 shares a common heritage with these laws and should be presumed to have been enacted for the same purposes. The short answer here is that these other state laws are not before the Court, and indeed, Proposition 15 was not passed; these provisions and their pedigree do not taint other parts of the Warren-Alquist Act.

Although these specific indicia of California's intent in enacting § 25524.2 are subject to varying interpretation, there are two further reasons why we should not become embroiled in attempting to ascertain California's true motive. First, inquiry into legislative motive is often an unsatisfactory venture. United States v. O'Brien, 391 U.S. 367, 383, 88 S.Ct. 1673, 1682, 20 L.Ed.2d 672 (1968). What motivates one legislator to vote for a statute is not necessarily what motivates scores of others to enact it. Second, it would be particularly pointless for us to engage in such inquiry here when it is clear that the states have been allowed to retain authority over the need for electrical generating facilities easily sufficient to permit a state so inclined to halt the construction of new nuclear plants by refusing on economic grounds to issue certificates of public convenience in individual proceedings. In these circumstances, it should be up to Congress to determine whether a state has misused the authority left in its hands.

Therefore, we accept California's avowed economic purpose as the rationale for enacting § 25524.2. Accordingly, the statue lies outside the occupied field of nuclear safety regulation.

B

Petitioners' second major argument concerns federal regulation aimed at the nuclear waste disposal problem itself. It is contended that § 25524.2 conflicts with federal regulation of nuclear waste disposal, with the NRC's decision that it is permissible to continue to license reactors, notwithstanding uncertainty surrounding the waste disposal problem, and with Congress' recent passage of legislation directed at that problem.

Pursuant to its authority under the Act, 42 U.S.C. §§ 2071–2075, 2111–2114, the AEC, and later the NRC, promulgated extensive and detailed regulations concerning the operation of nuclear facilities and the handling of nuclear materials. The following provisions are relevant to the spent fuel and waste disposal issues in this case. To receive an NRC operating license, one must submit a safety analysis report, which includes a "radioactive waste handling system." 10 CFR 50.34(b)(20)(i), (ii). See also 10 CFR 150.15(a)(1)(i). The regulations specify general design criteria and control requirements for fuel storage and handling and radioactive waste to be stored at the reactor site. 10 CFR Part 50, App. A, Criteria 60–64, at 412. In addition, the NRC has promulgated detailed regulations governing storage and disposal away from the reactor. 10 CFR Part 72. NRC has also promulgated procedural requirements covering license applications for disposal of high-level radioactive waste in geologic repositories. 10 CFR Part 60.

Congress gave the Department of Energy the responsibility for "the establishment of temporary and permanent facilities for the storage, management, and ultimate disposal of nuclear wastes." 42 U.S.C. § 7133(a)(8)(C). No such permanent disposal facilities have yet to be licensed, and the NRC and the Department of Energy continue to authorize the storage of spent fuel at reactor sites in pools of water. In 1977, the NRC was asked by the Natural Resources Defense Council to halt reactor licensing until it had determined that there was a method of permanent disposal for high-level waste. The NRC concluded that, given the progress toward the development of disposal facilities and the availability of interim storage, it could continue to license new reactors. Natural Resources Defense Council, Inc. v. NRC, 528 F.2d 166, 168–169 (CA2 1978).

The NRC's imprimatur, however, indicates only that it is safe to proceed with such plants, not that it is economically wise to do so. Because the NRC order does not and could not compel a utility to develop a nuclear plant, compliance with both it and § 25524.2 are possible. Moreover, because the NRC's regulations are aimed at insuring that plants are safe, not necessarily that they are economical, § 25524.2 does not interfere with the objective of the federal regulation.

Nor has California sought through § 25524.2 to impose its own standards on nuclear waste disposal. The statute accepts that it is the federal responsibility to develop and license such technology. As there is no attempt on California's part to enter this field, one which is occupied by the federal govenment, we do not find § 25524.2 preempted any more by the NRC's obligations in the waste disposal field than by its licensing power over the plants themselves.

After this case was decided by the Court of Appeals, a new piece was added to the regulatory puzzle. In its closing week the 97th Congress passed the Nuclear Waste Policy Act of 1982, Pub.L. 97–425, 96 Stat. 2201 (1982), a complex bill providing for a multi-faceted attack on the problem. *Inter alia,* the bill authorizes repositories for disposal of high-level radioactive waste and spent nuclear fuel, provides for licensing and expansion of interim storage, authorizes research and development, and provides a scheme for financing. While the passage of this new legislation may convince state authorities that there is now a sufficient federal commitment to fuel storage and waste disposal that licensing of nuclear reactors may resume, and, indeed, this seems to be one of the purposes of the Act, it does not appear that Congress intended to make that decision for the states through this legislation. Senator McClure attempted to do precisely that with an amendment to the Senate bill providing that the Act satisfied any legal requirements for the existence of an approved technology and facilities for disposal of spent fuel and high-level nuclear waste. The amendment was adopted by the Senate without debate. 128 Cong. Rec. S4310 (April 29, 1982). During subsequent House hearings, it was strongly urged that this language be omitted so as not to affect this case. See Nuclear Waste Disposal Policy, Hearings Before the Subcomm. on Energy Conservation and Power, Committee on Energy and Commerce, 97th Cong., 2d Sess., 356, 406, 553–554 (1982). The bill which emerged from the House Committee did omit the Senate language, and its manager, Rep. Ottinger, stated to the House that the language was deleted "to insure that there be no preemption." 128 Cong.Rec. H8797 (December 2, 1982). The bill ultimately signed into law followed the House language. While we are correctly reluctant to draw inferences from the failure of Congress to act, it would, in this case, appear improper for us to give a reading to the Act that Congress considered and rejected. Moreover, it is certainly possible to interpret the Act as directed at solving the nuclear waste disposal problem for existing reactors without necessarily encouraging or requiring that future plant construction be undertaken.

C

Finally, it is strongly contended that § 25524.2 frustrates the Atomic Energy Act's purpose to develop the commercial use of nuclear power. It is well established that state law is preempted if it "stands as an obstacle to the accomplishment of the full purposes and objectives of Congress." Hines v. Davidowitz, 312 U.S. 52, 67, 61 S.Ct. 399, 404, 85 L.Ed. 581 (1941); Florida Lime & Avocado Growers v. Paul, 373 U.S. 132, 142–143, 83 S.Ct. 1210, 1217–18, 10 L.Ed.2d 248 (1963); Fidelity Federal Savings & Loan Ass'n v. de la Cuesta, 458 U.S. at 153, 102 S.Ct., at 3022.

There is little doubt that a primary purpose of the Atomic Energy Act was, and continues to be, the promotion of nuclear power. The Act itself states that it is a program "to encourage widespread participation in the development and utilization of atomic energy for peaceful purposes to the maximum extent consistent with the common defense and security and with the health and safety of the public." 42 U.S.C. § 2013(b). The House and Senate Reports confirmed that it was "a major policy goal of the United States" that the involvement of private industry would "speed the further development of the peaceful uses of atomic energy." H.R. Rep. No. 883, 89th Cong., 1st Sess. 4 (1965); H.R.Rep. No. 2181, 83d Cong., 2d Sess. 9 (1954); S.Rep. No. 1699, 83d Cong., 2d Sess. 9 (1934). The same purpose is manifest in the passage of the Price-Anderson Act, 42 U.S.C. § 2210, which limits private liability from a nuclear accident. The Act was passed "in order to protect the public and to encourage the development of the atomic energy industry . . . " 42 U.S.C. § 2012(i).

Duke Power Co. v. Carolina Environmental Study Group, Inc., 438 U.S., at 63–67, 98 S.Ct., at 2625–2627.

The Court of Appeals' suggestion that legislation since 1974 has indicated a "change in congressional outlook" is unconvincing. The court observed that Congress reorganized the Atomic Energy Commission in 1974 dividing the promotional and safety responsibilities of the AEC, giving the former to the Energy Research and Development Administration (ERDA) and the latter to the NRC. Energy Reorganization Act of 1974, 88 Stat. 1233, 42 U.S.C. § 5801, *et seq.* The evident desire of Congress to prevent safety from being compromised by promotional concerns does not translate into an abandonment of the objective of promoting nuclear power. The legislation was carefully drafted, in fact to avoid any anti-nuclear sentiment. The continuing commitment to nuclear power is reflected in the extension of the Price-Anderson Act's coverage until 1987, Pub.L. No. 94–197, § 2–14, 89 Stat. 1111–1115, as well as in Congress' express preclusion of reliance on natural gas and petroleum as primary energy sources in new power plants, Powerplant and Industrial Fuel Act of 1978, 92 Stat. 3291, 42 U.S.C. §§ 8301(b)(3), 8311, 8312(a). It is true, of course, that Congress has sought to simultaneously promote the development of alternative energy sources, but we do not view these steps as an indication that Congress has retreated from its oft-expressed commitment to further development of nuclear power for electricity generation.

The Court of Appeals is right, however, that the promotion of nuclear power is not to be accomplished "at all costs." The elaborate licensing and safety provisions and the continued preservation of state regulation in traditional areas belie that. Moreover, Congress has allowed the States to determine—as a matter of economics—whether a nuclear plant vis-a-vis a fossil fuel plant should be built. The decision of California to exercise that authority does not, in itself, constitute a basis for preemption. Therefore, while the argument of petitioners and the United States has considerable force, the legal reality remains that Congress has left sufficient authority in the states to allow the development of nuclear power to be slowed or even stopped for economic reasons. Given this statutory scheme, it is for Congress to rethink the division of regulatory authority in light of its possible exercise by the states to undercut a federal objective. The courts should not assume the role which our system assigns to Congress.

NOTE

Does the Court persuade you that California sought to regulate the economic, as opposed to safety, aspects of nuclear power? Can the two types of regulation be so neatly separated? Consider, in this light, Silkwood v. Kerr-McGee Corp. 464 U.S. ___, 104 S.Ct. 615, 78 L.Ed.2d 443 (1984), in which the Supreme Court held that federal law did not preempt the award of punitive damages in a state law tort action brought against a federally licensed nuclear facility.

As a policy matter, do you favor the current allocation of authority between state and federal governments on nuclear power? Should there be a similar allocation with recombinant DNA research? See Ch. 1, Sec. B.4, supra. These questions pose problems because, while state or local control brings decisions closer to home, state boundaries do not confine the costs and benefits of a technology. Thus a complete absence of federal regulation can lead to the state with the lowest safety standards attracting activities that might endanger neighboring states. Where the federal government sets minimum standards that the state can raise, a state may shield its citizens from the costs of research or power generation by setting very high safety standards, yet still draw the ultimate benefits from the activity in question. Everyone would like to have dangerous cancer research done elsewhere, as long as the resulting cure for cancer is available to all.

At present no one approach pervades the federal-state regulation issue in major areas of scientific and medical activity. Overlapping state and federal regulatory regimes are common. For example, the Food and Drug Administration has not approved Laetrile, see United States v. Rutherford, 442 U.S. 544, 99 S.Ct. 2470, 61 L.Ed.2d 68 (1979), but several states allow its use in the intrastate market. See Comment, The Uncertain Application of the Right of Privacy in Personal Medical Decisions: The Laetrile Cases, 42 Ohio St.L.J. 523, 530 (1981). The Department of Health and Human Services regulates fetal research conducted with Departmental support, yet the regulations provide that state laws are not displaced and state laws on the subject have been enacted. See 45 C.F.R. § 46.201 (Oct. 1, 1982); Mass.Gen.Laws, Ann., Ch. 112, § 12J (West 1980). In the environmental field, a host of federal and state statutes interact in a variety of ways. See generally Environmental Legislation: A Sourcebook (M. Sive ed. 1976). Assuming the federal government has authority under the Constitution—a reasonable assumption in most cases, given the modern scope of the commerce and spending powers—would you favor complete federal preemption in any of these areas?

D. JUDICIAL CONTROL OF SCIENTIFIC AND MEDICAL RESEARCH

1. JUDICIAL REVIEW OF AGENCY ACTION

With agencies making key decisions involving science and medicine, the most important aspect of judicial involvement in scientific and medical policy comes through judicial review of agency action. As noted above, see Ch. 4, Sec. C.1, supra, judicial review in such cases typically takes place in a federal court of appeals. The agency's record is before the court; no new evidence is taken. Perhaps the central question for judges confronting such cases is the extent to which they should immerse themselves in the complexities of the agency's decision. The opinions that follow embody a debate on that issue between judges of the United States Court of Appeals for the District of Columbia Circuit, a court which is particularly important in this area because it hears so many cases involving administrative agencies. As you read these opinions, formulate your own views on how you would approach technical issues if you were a judge in these cases.

INTERNATIONAL HARVESTER CO. v. RUCKELSHAUS

United States Court of Appeals for the District of Columbia Circuit, 1973.
478 F.2d 615.

LEVENTHAL, CIRCUIT JUDGE:

These consolidated petitions of International Harvester and the three major auto companies, Ford, General Motors and Chrysler, seek review of a decision by the Administrator of the Environmental Protection Agency denying petitioners' applications, filed pursuant to Section 202 of the Clean Air Act, for one-year suspensions of the 1975 emission standards prescribed under the statute for light duty vehicles in the absence of suspension.

I. STATEMENT OF THE CASE

The tension of forces presented by the controversy over automobile emission standards may be focused by two central observations:

(1) The automobile is an essential pillar of the American economy. Some 28 per cent of the nonfarm workforce draws its livelihood from the automobile industry and its products.

(2) The automobile has had a devastating impact on the American environment. As of 1970, authoritative voices stated that "[a]utomotive pollution constitutes in excess of 60% of our national air pollution problem" and more than 80 per cent of the air pollutants in concentrated urban areas. . . .

On December 31, 1970, Congress grasped the nettle and amended the Clean Air Act to set a statutory standard for required reductions in levels of hydrocarbons (HC) and carbon monoxide (CO) which must be achieved for 1975 models of light duty vehicles. Section 202(b) of the Act added by the Clean Air Amendments of 1970, provides that, beginning with the 1975 model year, exhaust emission of hydrocarbons and carbon monoxide from "light duty vehicles" must be reduced at least 90 per cent from the permissible emission levels in the 1970 model year. In accordance with the Congressional directives, the Administrator on June 23, 1971, promulgated regulations limiting HC and CO emissions from 1975 model light duty vehicles to .41 and 3.4 grams per vehicle mile respectively. 36 Fed.Reg. 12,657 (1971). At the same time, as required by section 202(b)(2) of the Act, he prescribed the test procedures by which compliance with these standards is measured.

Congress was aware that these 1975 standards were "drastic medicine," designed to "force the state of the art." There was, naturally, concern whether the manufacturers would be able to achieve this goal. Therefore, Congress provided, in Senator Baker's phrase, a "realistic escape hatch": the manufacturers could petition the Administrator of the EPA for a one-year suspension of the 1975 requirements, and Congress took the precaution of directing the National Academy of Sciences to undertake an ongoing study of the feasibility of compliance with the emission standards. The "escape hatch" provision addressed itself to the possibility that the NAS study or other evidence might indicate that the standards would be unachievable despite all good faith efforts at compliance. This provision was limited to a one-year suspension, which would defer compliance with the 90% reduction requirement until 1976. . . .

On March 13, 1972, Volvo, Inc., filed an application for suspension and thereby triggered the running of the 60 day period for a decision. 37 Fed.Reg. 5766 (March 21, 1972.) Additional suspension requests were filed by International Harvester on March 31, 1972, and by Ford Motor Company, Chrysler Corporation, and General Motors Corporation on April 5, 1972. Public hearings were held from April 10–27, 1972. Representatives of most of the major vehicle manufacturers (in addition to the applicants), a number of suppliers of emission control devices and materials, and spokesmen from various public bodies and groups, testified at the hearings and submitted written data for the public record. The decision to deny suspension to all applicants was issued on May 12, 1972.

The Decision began with the statement of the grounds for denial: ". . . I am unable, on the basis of the information submitted by the applicants or otherwise available to me, to make the determinations required, by section 202(b)(5)(D)(i), (iii), or (iv) of the Act." The EPA Decision specifically focused on requirement (iii) that:

> the applicant has established that effective control technology, processes, operating methods, or other alternatives are not available or have not been available for a sufficient period of time to achieve compliance prior to the effective date of such standards . . . .

A Technical Appendix, containing the analysis and methodology used by the Administrator in arriving at his decision, was subsequently issued on July 27, 1972. . . .

IV. THE REQUIRED SHOWING ON "AVAILABLE TECHNOLOGY"

It is with utmost diffidence that we approach our assignment to review the Administrator's decision on "available technology." The legal issues are intermeshed with technical matters, and as yet judges have no scientific aides. Our diffidence is rooted in the underlying technical complexities, and remains even when we take into account that ours is a judicial review, and not a technical or policy redetermination, our review is channeled by a salutary restraint, and deference to the expertise of an agency that provides reasoned analysis. Nevertheless we must proceed to the task of judicial review assigned by Congress. . . .

The multiple assumptions used by the Administrator in making his prediction are subject to serious doubts.

The basic formula used to make the prediction that each of the manufacturers could meet the 1975 standards was based on 1975 certification requirements, so that in part it paralleled testing procedures which would be used in 1975 to certify automobiles for sale. The formula is:

50,000 mile emissions = 4000 mile emissions × deterioration factor

Four kinds of assumptions were used in making the 50,000 mile emission prediction: (1) regulatory, (2) engineering or scientific, (3) techniques of application of basic formula to particular companies, and (4) statistical reliability of the final prediction.

1. *Regulatory assumptions*

First, EPA assumed that certain types of maintenance would have to be performed on 1975 model year cars, if its 50,000 miles emission predictions were to be meaningful. Subsequent to the issue of its Technical Appendix, a Proposed Rule Making formulated these requirements as part of 1975 certification procedure. This assumption was necessary because much of the data supplied by the companies was obtained from cars that were under rigid controls during testing. The problem with such maintenance assumptions is whether the ordinary driver will actually pay for this kind of maintenance just to reduce the emission levels of his automobile. It is one thing to build maintenance into the 1975 certification procedure, when fleet samples are durability tested. It is another to posit that such standards will be maintained, or are reasonably likely to be maintained by consumers. A hard question is raised by the use of a methodological assumption without evidence that it will correspond to reality, or a reasonable and forthright prediction based on expertise.

Secondly, the predicted emission level assumes that there will be one total replacement of the catalytic converter at some time after 25,000 miles. This entered into the formula as an adjustment to the predicted deterioration factor. The critical question is how much will the one replacement reduce emissions otherwise obtainable by use of a single catalyst. This relationship had to be assumed because manufacturers had not used catalytic converter replacements in their testing. The Administrator admitted that this factor was imprecise. Yet, in the case of General Motors, the use of the assumed value of this factor was critical in allowing the Administrator to make a 50,000 mile emission prediction under the 1975 standards.

The third regulatory assumption relates to the average lead level which will exist in gasoline available for 1975 model year cars. Lead levels in gasoline contribute to the levels of HC and CO both in terms of normal emission control achievable (the 4000 mile emission) and to the deterioration in emissions over time (deterioration factor). Thus, in the case of the Chrysler car used to predict conformity with the 1975 standards, a .03 lead in gasoline produced 4000 mile emissions of .27 grams HC and 1.51 CO, whereas a .05 level of lead resulted in .29 and 1.66 grams respectively. Similarly .03 lead produced a corrected deterioration factor of .67 HC and 1.5 CO, whereas a .05 level produced .73 HC and 1.65 CO.

On December 27, 1972, a regulation was promulgated "designed to assure general availability by July 1, 1974, of suitable gasolines containing no more than .05 grams per gallon of lead. . . ." It was the assumption of the Administrator that the .05 maximum would result in gas containing on the average .03 grams per gallon of lead. The discrepancy between the maximum and average is accounted for by the contamination of lead free gasoline from its point of production to its marketing outlet. Thus EPA will allow a maximum of .05 but anticipates that on the average fuel will be at .03. This assumption is, however, subject to testimony in the record indicating a difference between companies in their ability to achieve gasoline with a low lead level complying with the proposed regulation. Amoco said that its proposal for a .07 maximum "should result in effective lead levels of .02 to .03 grams of lead per gallon." Texaco did not think it could deliver gas to service stations at a lead level below .07. We cannot resolve whether a differential ability really exists, but we also have no refinement and resolution by the EPA (as distinguished from the briefs of its counsel). We do not say this matter is a critical defect; still it leaves a residue of uncertainty that beclouds the EPA assumption of a .03 average, needed in its methodology to predict conformity with the 1975 standards.

2. *Engineering and scientific assumptions*

Engineering or scientific assumptions are made in predicting 4000 mile emissions and deterioration factors, and we shall give separate consideration to each independent variable.

a. *The 4000 mile emission factor*

The use of 4000 mile emissions as a starting point is based on certification procedures. No challenge has been made to this mileage as a base point, largely because it appears that at this mileage the engine is broken in and emission levels are relatively stabilized. EPA decided to adjust raw data supplied, at least in the case of Ford and Chrysler, of emissions at 4000 miles to take account of a "Lead Adjustment Factor." This was done because in most cases emissions data reflected fuels with a close to zero lead level which had been used by the manufacturers in their testing programs.

Lead adjustment factor

This Lead Adjustment Factor was calculated using only Ford cars, but the value of the factor was assumed to be the same in adjusting Chrysler 4000 mile emissions with this factor. The cars had been tested with a dynamometer, a type of test equipment used for laboratory testing of an engine. A measurement of the efficiency of the catalytic converter at the 4000 mile mark was the critical value which had to be obtained from the dynamometer since this would indicate what the proper lead adjustment factor would be.

EPA assumed that 200 hours on the dynamometer corresponded to 4000 miles usage, based on a critical and contested EPA assumption that the tests were conducted at 1000 RPM. Petitioners claim that the high temperature readings on the dynamometer reflect a higher RPM, and hence that a testing below 200 hours corresponded to 4000 miles of use. EPA disputes the steps in that chain of reasoning, and argues that a higher temperature may be attributable not to a RPM in excess of 1000, but to a heavy load on the vehicle, and in the alternative contends that even if there was a RPM greater than 1000, the speed may not have increased, due to a shift in gear.

The cause of higher than expected temperature readings cannot be ascertained from the record, and we are left with the alternative contentions of the parties. It is up to EPA, however, to support its methodology as reliable, and this requires more than reliance on the unknown, either by speculation, or mere shifting back of the burden of proof.

b. *Deterioration factor*

Methodological problems also existed with the calculation of the deterioration factor, which took account of possible deterioration in emission quality from 4000 miles to 50,000 miles. Different questions arose as to the calculation of this factor for Ford and Chrysler.

In the case of Ford, the Administrator predicted that emissions would *improve* from 4000 to 50,000 miles, and arrived at a deterioration factor of less than 1. He calculated average deterioration factors for Ford vehicles of .80 HC and .83 CO. This is to be compared with a deterioration factor of 2.5 used by NAS. The Administrator never explained why there should be no deterioration. Nor does EPA explain how this result can be squared with other data on Ford catalyst efficiencies, which was used in the case of the General Motors prediction, showing 50,000 mile catalyst efficiencies ranging from 21% to 53% for HC and 47% to 72% for CO.

In the case of Chrysler, the deterioration factor was also calculated to be less than 1, but this figure was only arrived at after eliminating some data points from the emission measurement on the tested car #333, due to what EPA claimed were unrepresentative points resulting from non-catalyst malfunctions. Although it may be, as EPA argues here, that including the data points would still produce predicted 50,000 emission levels in conformity with the 1975 standard, the fact remains that these data points were removed. Moreover, it is not apparent why one should ignore malfunctions of a car which contribute to high emissions, even if they are not malfunctions of the converter. Malfunctions of cars occur to some degree, and cars operating in 1975 will undoubtedly be subject to them.

Lead adjustment factor

A lead adjustment factor is applied to the deterioration factor, as well as to 4000 mile emissions. EPA estimated on the basis of the questionable Ford dynamometer data, that lead levels had no observable effect, which was contrary to industry testimony on the subject. The Administrator evidently had doubts as to the dependability of these results as well, and therefore assumed a 10% factor for lead adjustment. No explanation is given of the origins of this 10% figure. If the willingness to take some factor evidences distrust in the data, the question then becomes whether 10% is enough

3.   *EPA methodology for General Motors*

In the case of General Motors an entirely different methodology from that used for Ford and Chrysler was employed. This was adopted due to limited testing by GM of noble metal catalysts.

The methodology was to take the raw emission values produced by a GM car prior to catalyst treatment of any kind multiplied by a factor representing the efficiency of the catalyst, i.e., the percentage of a given pollutant that the catalyst converts to harmless vapor, in order to obtain the projected overall emission performance at 50,000 miles. These methods of calculation were developed by the Administrator and were not used by NAS in their evaluation.

The catalyst efficiency data were taken from Engelhard converters used principally on Ford cars and applied against the raw emissions of a General Motors engine. This assumed, with no explanation of the validity of such an assumption, that Engelhard catalysts will function as efficiently in General Motors cars as in those of Ford. A prediction was made on the basis of a hypothetical case. One cannot help be troubled by the adoption of this technique for General Motors. It was apparently recognized as at best a second best approach, in terms of the reliability of the prediction, or the same catalyst efficiency procedure would also have been used for Ford and Chrysler.

4.   *Statistical reliability of assumptions*

In this case the Administrator is necessarily making a prediction. No tests exist on whether this prediction is or is not reliable. It would, therefore, seem incumbent on the Administrator to estimate the possible degree of error in his prediction. The NAS, for example, said that the data of the manufacturers were subject to ± 20–30% margin of error, and this is separate from any margin of error that may be due to the various assumptions made by the Administrator. It is not decisive to say, as EPA argues in its brief, that this is just a matter of quality control in production. The first issue is whether the automobile built with rigid adherence to specifications will perform as predicted. The issue of quality control, whether cars will indeed be built in accordance with specifications, raises a separate and additional problem.

The possibility of error must take into account that only 1 Ford car, 1 Chrysler car, and 1 hypothetical General Motors car form the foundation for predicted conformity with the 1975 standard. The Administrator would say that it is enough to validate the principle of the electric light bulb if only one is seen at work. But we do not yet have one that has worked; instead we have four predictions. Questions like these arise: (1) For how many different types of engines will these predictions be valid? (2) Does it make a difference that the tested cars were experimental and driven under the most controlled conditions? The best car analysis of EPA raises even further doubts when considered alongside the NAS Report which used 55 vehicles in arriving at its recommended interim standard.

V. CONCLUSION AND DISPOSITION

We may sensibly begin our conclusion with a statement of diffidence. It is not without diffidence that a court undertakes to probe even partly into technical matters of the complexity of those covered in this opinion. It is with even more diffidence that a court concludes that the law, as judicially construed, requires a different approach from that taken by an official or agency with technical expertise. Yet this is an inescapable aspect of the judicial condition, though we stay mindful of the overarching consideration that a court's role on judicial review embraces that of a constructive cooperation with the agency involved in furtherance of the public interest.

A court does not depart from its proper function when it undertakes a study of the record, hopefully perceptive, even as to the evidence on technical and specialized matters, for this enables the court to penetrate to the underlying decisions of the agency, to satisfy itself that the agency has exercised a reasoned discretion, with reasons that do not deviate from or ignore the ascertainable legislative intent.

In this case technical issues permeate the "available technology" determination which the Administrator made the focal point of his decision. In approaching our judicial task we conclude that the requirement of a "reasoned decision" by the Environmental Protection Agency means, in present context, a reasoned presentation of the reliability of a prediction and methodology that is relied upon to overcome a conclusion, of lack of available technology, supported prima faciely by the only actual and observed data available, the manufacturers' testing.

The number of unexplained assumptions used by the Administrator, the variance in methodology from that of the Report of the National Academy of Sciences, and the absence of an indication of the statistical reliability of the prediction, combine to generate grave doubts as to whether technology is available to meet the 1975 statutory standards. We say this, incidentally, without implying or intending any acceptance of petitioners' substitute assumptions. These grave doubts have a legal consequence. This is customarily couched, by legal convention, in terms of "burden of proof." We visualize the problem in less structured terms although the underlying considerations, relating to risk of error, are related. As we see it the issue must be viewed as one of legislative intent. And since there is neither express wording or legislative history on the precise issue, the intent must be imputed. The court must seek to discern and reconstruct what the legislature that enacted the statute would have contemplated for the court's action if it could have been able to foresee the precise situation. It is in this perspective that we have not flinched from our discussion of the economic and ecological risks inherent in a "wrong decision" by the Administrator. We think the vehicle manufacturers established by a preponderance of the evidence, in the record before us, that technology was not available, within the meaning of the Act, when they adduced the tests on actual vehicles; that the Administrator's reliance on technological methodology to offset the actual tests raised serious doubts and failed to meet the burden of proof which in our view was properly assignable to him, in the light of accepted legal doctrine and the intent of Congress discerned, in part, by taking into account that the risk of an "erroneous" denial of suspension outweighed the risk of an "erroneous" grant of suspension. We do not use the burden of proof in the conventional sense of civil trials, but the Administrator must sustain the burden of adducing a reasoned presentation supporting the reliability of EPA's methodology.

EPA's diligence in this proceeding, fraught with questions of statutory interpretation, technical difficulties and burdensome time constraints placed on the decision-making process, has been commendable. The agency was presented with a prickly task, but has acted expeditiously to carry out what it perceived to be a drastic mandate from Congress. This statute was, indeed, deliberately designed as "shock treatment" to the industry. Our central difference with the Administrator, simply put, stems from our view concerning the Congressional intent underlying the one year suspension provision. That was a purposeful cushion—with the twin purpose of providing "escape hatch" relief for 1975, and thus establishing a context supportive of the rigor and firmness of the basic standards slated for no later than 1976. In our view the overall legislative firmness does not necessarily require a "hard-nosed" approach to the application for suspension, as the Administrator apparently supposed, and may indeed be furthered by our more moderate view of the suspension issue, particularly in assigning to the Administrator the burden of producing a reasoned presentation of the reliability of his methodology. This is not a matter of clemency, but rather a benign approach that moderates the "shock treatment" so as to obviate excessive and unnecessary risk of harm.

Our decision is also responsive to the differences between the EPA decision and the NAS Report. Although in some instances "the factual findings and technical conclusions" are consistent with those of the Administrator, the NAS conclusion was that technology was not available to meet the standards in 1975. Congress called on NAS, with presumed reliance on the knowledge and objectivity of that prestigious body, to make an independent judgment. The statute makes the NAS conclusion a necessary but not sufficient condition of suspension. While in consideration of the other conditions of suspension, EPA was not necessarily bound by NAS's approach, particularly as to matters interlaced with policy and legal aspects, we do not think that it was contemplated that EPA could alter the conclusion of NAS by revising the NAS assumptions, or injecting new ones, unless it states its reasons for finding reliability—possibly by challenging the NAS approach in terms of later-acquired research and experience.

These factors combine to convince us that, under our view of Congressional intent, we cannot affirm the EPA's denial of suspension as stated. That is not necessarily to assume, as at least some petitioners do, that the EPA's process must be brought to nullity.

The procedures followed in this case, whether or not based on rulings that were "mistaken" when made, have resulted in a record that leaves this court uncertain, at a minimum, whether the essentials of the intention of Congress were achieved. This requires a remand whereby the record as made will be supplemented by further proceedings. In the interest of justice, see 28 U.S.C. § 2106, and mutual regard for Congressional objective, the parties should have opportunity on remand to address themselves to matters not previously put before them by EPA for comment, including material contained in the Technical Appendix filed by EPA in 1972 subsequent to its Decision.

It is contemplated that, in the interest of providing a reasoned decision, the remand proceeding will involve some opportunity for cross-examination. In the remand proceeding—not governed by the same time congestion as the initial Decision process—we require reasonable cross-examination as to new lines of testimony, and as to submissions previously made to EPA in the hearing on a proffer that critical questions could not be satisfactorily pursued by procedures previously in effect. There is, however, still need for expedition, both by virtue of our order and the "lead time" problem, and the EPA may properly confine cross-examination to the essentials, avoiding discursive or repetitive questioning.

Following our suggestion in Environmental Defense Fund, Inc. v. EPA, 150 U.S.App.D.C. 348, 465 F.2d 528 (1972), the Administrator may consider possible use of interim standards short of complete suspension. The statute permits conditioning of suspension on the adoption, by virtue of the information adduced in the suspension proceeding, of interim standards, higher than those set for 1974.

We cannot grant petitioners' request that this court order a suspension since determinations which Congress made necessary conditions of suspension, as to the public interest and good faith, have not been made by the Administrator. The Administrator's decision did not reach these questions and accordingly we must remand for further consideration. The initial requirement that an EPA decision on the suspension, aye or nay, be made within 60 days of the application, obviously does not preclude further consideration following remand by the court. In the interest of justice, 28 U.S.C. § 2106, and the Congressional intention that decisions be made timely in the light of considerations of "lead time" for 1975 model year production, we require the suspension deliberations by EPA to be completed within 60 days. The Administrator's decision on remand must, of course, be consistent with our legal rulings herein—including the need for redefinition of light duty vehicles, and promulgation of an appropriate regulation.

In conformance to the Congressional contemplation of expedition, and our responsibilities as an appellate court, we further require that the Administrator render a decision, on the basis of the best information available, which extends to all the determinations which the statute requires as a condition of suspension. We do not preclude further consideration of the question of "available technology," especially if developments in the art provide enlightenment. Last but not least, especially in view of Ford's submission and the NAS Report concerning interim standards, we reiterate that the EPA's determination may consist of a conditional suspension that results in higher standards than an outright grant of applications for suspension.

The case is remanded for further proceedings not inconsistent with this opinion.

BAZELON, CHIEF JUDGE (concurring in result):

Socrates said that wisdom is the recognition of how much one does not know. I may be wise if that is wisdom, because I recognize that I do not know enough about dynamometer extrapolations, deterioration factor adjustments, and the like to decide whether or not the government's approach to these matters was statistically valid. Therein lies my disagreement with the majority.

The court's opinion today centers on a substantive evaluation of the Administrator's assumptions and methodology. I do not have the technical know-how to agree or disagree with that evaluation—at least on the basis of the present record. My grounds for remanding the case rest upon the Administrator's failure to employ a reasonable decision-making process for so critical and complex a matter. At this time I cannot say to what extent I could undertake an evaluation of the Administrator's findings if they were based on an adequate decisional process.

I cannot believe that Congress intended this court to delve into the substance of the mechanical, statistical, and technological disputes in this case. Senator Cooper, the author of the judicial review provision, stated repeatedly that this court's role would be to "determine the question of due process." Thus the court's proper role is to see to it that the agency provides "a framework for principled decision-making." Such a framework necessarily includes the right of interested parties to confront the agency's decision and the requirement that the agency set forth with clarity the grounds for its rejection of opposing views.

The majority's interpretation of the present statute and the administrative precedents would give us no right to establish these procedural guidelines. Their opinion maintains that the strict deadlines in the Clean Air Act preclude any right to challenge the Administrator until after the decision has been made. It indicates that, since this hearing was "rule-making" rather than "adjudicatory", cross-examination and confrontation are not required under traditional rules of administrative law.

I understand this viewpoint, but I do not share it. I do not think the authors of the Clean Air Act intended to put such strict limits on our review of the Administrator's decision-making process. Further, the interests at stake in this case are too important to be resolved on the basis of traditional administrative labels. We recognized two years ago that environmental litigation represents a "new era" in administrative law. We are dealing here not with an airline's fares or a broadcaster's wattage, but with all humanity's interest in life, health, and a harmonious relationship with the elements of nature.

This "new era" does not mean that courts will dig deeper into the technical intricacies of an agency's decision. It means instead that courts will go further in requiring the agency to establish a decision-making process adequate to protect the interests of all "consumers" of the natural environment. In some situations, traditional rules of "fairness"—designed only to guard the interests of the specific parties to an agency proceeding—will be inadequate to protect these broader interests. This is such a case. Whether or not traditional administrative rules require it, the critical character of this decision requires at the least a carefully limited right of cross-examination at the hearing and an opportunity to challenge the assumptions and methodology underlying the decision.

The majority's approach permits the parties to challenge the Administrator's methodology only through the vehicle of judicial review. I do not think this is an adequate substitute for confrontation prior to the decision. I reach this position not only out of concern for fairness to the parties (". . . for if a party first learns of noticed facts through the final report

. . . the burden of upsetting a decision announced as final is a heavy one.") but also out of awareness of the limits of our own competence for the task. The petitioners' challenges to the decision force the court to deal with technical intricacies that are beyond our ken. These complex questions should be resolved in the crucible of debate through the clash of informed but opposing scientific and technological viewpoints.

It is true that courts occasionally find themselves in the thick of technological controversies—e.g., in patent cases. But those are different circumstances. We do not review patent disputes until they have been through a full panoply of procedures involving full rights of confrontation. Further, unlike our decision in a patent case, our decision on the Administrator's action here is sure to be tested by analysis and challenge in Congress, in the scientific community, and among the public.

My brethren and I are reaching for the same end—a "reasoned decision"—through different means. They would have us examine the substance of the decision before us. There are some areas of administrative law—involving issues of liberty and individual rights—where judges are on firm ground in undertaking a substantive review of agency action. But in cases of great technological complexity, the best way for courts to guard against unreasonable or erroneous administrative decisions is not for the judges themselves to scrutinize the technical merits of each decision. Rather, it is to establish a decision-making process which assures a reasoned decision that can be held up to the scrutiny of the scientific community and the public. "[T]he best test of truth is the power of the thought to get itself accepted in the competition of the market." If we were to require procedures in this case that open the Administrator's decision to challenge and force him to respond, we could rely on an informed "market" rather than on our own groping in the dark to test the validity of that decision.

Candor requires the admission that the process of confrontation and challenge might not be possible within the statutory decision period of 60 days. My response would be to permit an extension of the time limit—perhaps 30 days more. This would put less strain on the overall statutory scheme—and on the manufacturers' lead time—than the months that have been expended in litigation, and now a remand, over the decision. Congress did not intend for us to enforce this relatively minor time restriction so strictly as to do major damage to the statute as a whole.

My brethren argue that the 60-day time limit in the statute precluded any opportunity for cross-examination or confrontation at the time of the original decision. But their opinion would apparently permit these procedural rights on the remand. This bit of judicial legerdemain confounds me. I can find nothing in the statute or common sense to support this distinction. If anything, the statute, with its obvious emphasis on reaching a final decision quickly, would dictate procedures at the original decision which were sufficient to produce a reasoned decision without the need for a remand. . . .

ETHYL CORP. v. ENVIRONMENTAL PROTECTION AGENCY

United States Court of Appeals for the District of Columbia Circuit, 1976.
541 F.2d 1.

[This *en banc* decision reversed a decision by a panel of the D.C. Circuit. The panel, looking closely at the substantive issues, had determined that the Environmental Protection Agency had improperly found that leaded gasoline automotive emissions present "a significant risk of harm" to the public health.   See Ch. 5, Sec A.3, infra.]

BAZELON, CHIEF JUDGE, with whom McGOWAN, CIRCUIT JUDGE, joins (concurring):

I concur in Judge Wright's opinion for the court, and wish only to further elucidate certain matters.

I agree with the court's construction of the statute that the Administrator is called upon to make "essentially legislative policy judgments" in assessing risks to public health.   But I cannot agree that this automatically relieves the Administrator's decision from the "procedural . . . rigor proper for questions of fact."   Quite the contrary, this case strengthens my view that

> . . . in cases of great technological complexity, the best way for courts to guard against unreasonable or erroneous administrative decisions is not for the judges themselves to scrutinize the technical merits of each decision.   Rather, it is to establish a decision-making process that assures a reasoned decision that can be held up to the scrutiny of the scientific community and the public.

This record provides vivid demonstration of the dangers implicit in the contrary view, ably espoused by Judge Leventhal, which would have judges "steeping" themselves "in technical matters to determine whether the agency 'has exercised a reasoned discretion'".   It is one thing for judges to scrutinize FCC judgments concerning diversification of media ownership to determine if they are rational.   But I doubt judges contribute much to improving the quality of the difficult decisions which must be made in highly technical areas when they take it upon themselves to decide, as did the panel in this case, that "in assessing the scientific and medical data the Administrator made clear errors of judgment."   The process making a de novo evaluation of the scientific evidence inevitably invites judges of opposing views to make plausible-sounding, but simplistic, judgments of the relative weight to be afforded various pieces of technical data.

It is true that, where, as here, a panel has reached the result of invalidating agency action by undue involvement in the uncertainties of the typical informal rulemaking record, the court *en banc* will be tempted to justify its affirmation of the agency by confronting the panel on its own terms.   But this is a temptation which, if not resisted, will not only impose severe strains upon the energies and resources of the court but also compound the error of the panel in making legislative policy determinations alien to its true function.   We would be wiser to heed the admonition of the Supreme Court that: "[e]xperience teaches . . . that the affording of procedural safeguards, which by their nature serve to illuminate the underlying facts, in itself often operates to prevent erroneous decisions on the merits from occurring."

Because substantive review of mathematical and scientific evidence by technically illiterate judges is dangerously unreliable, I continue to believe we will do more to improve administrative decision-making by concentrating our efforts on strengthening administrative procedures:

> When administrators provide a framework for principled decision-making, the result will be to diminish the importance of judicial review by enhancing the integrity of the administrative process, and to im-

prove the quality of judicial review in those cases where judicial review is sought.

It does not follow that courts may never properly find that an administrative decision in a scientific area is irrational. But I do believe that in highly technical areas, where our understanding of the import of the evidence is attenuated, our readiness to review evidentiary support for decisions must be correspondingly restrained.

As I read the court's opinion, it severely limits judicial weighing of the evidence by construing the Administrator's decision to be a matter of "legislative policy," and consequently not subject to review with the "substantive rigor proper for questions of fact." Since this result would bar the panel's close analysis of the evidence, it satisfies my concerns.

. . .

An additional matter which emerges from this record deserves comment: namely, the failure of the record to clearly disclose the procedural steps followed by EPA. As a result, an onerous, time-consuming burden was cast upon the court to reconstruct these steps by inference and surmise. It is not enough for an agency to prepare a record compiling all the evidence it relied upon for its action; it must also organize and digest it, so that a reviewing court is not forced to scour the four corners of the record to find that evidence for itself. These principles apply with no less force to judicial review of agency procedures. In informal rule-making, the record should clearly disclose when each piece of new information is received and when and how it was made available for comment. If information is received too late for comment, the agency must at least clearly indicate how the substance of its consideration would be affected.

It is regrettable that EPA did not give the same care to clearly setting forth procedural matters for the record as it gave to substantive matters. It may well be that this court's 30-day order interfered with the opportunity to do so. Based on that possibility, and the court's own reconstruction of the procedural record (albeit at the expense of much judicial time and effort), I am persuaded that the petitioner's rights were not prejudiced. Ordinarily, however, I think a record which so burdens judicial review would require a remand for clarification.

Statement of CIRCUIT JUDGE LEVENTHAL:

I concur without reservation in the excellent opinion for the court.

I write an additional word only because of observations in the concurring opinion authored by Chief Judge Bazelon. I would not have thought they required airing today, since they in no way relate, so far as I can see, to the court's en banc opinion. But since they have been floated I propose to bring them to earth, though I can here present only the highlights of analysis.

What does and should a reviewing court do when it considers a challenge to technical administrative decision-making? In my view, the panel opinion in this case overstepped the bounds of proper judicial supervision in its willingness to substitute its own scientific judgments for that of the EPA. In an effort to refute that approach convincingly the panel dissent may have over-reacted and responded too much in kind. In a kind of sur-rebuttal against such overzealousness, Judge Bazelon has also over-reacted. His opinion—if I read it right—advocates engaging in no substantive review at all, whenever the substantive issues at stake involve technical matters that the judges involved consider beyond their individual technical competence.

If he is not saying that, if he agrees there must be some substantive review, then I am at a loss to discern its significance. Certainly it does not help those seeking enlightenment to recognize when the difference in degree of substantive review becomes a difference in kind.

Taking the opinion in its fair implication, as a signal to judges to abstain from any substantive review, it is my view that while giving up is the easier course, it is not legitimately open to us at present. In the case of legislative enactments, the sole responsibility of the courts is constitutional due process review. In the case of agency decision-making the courts have an additional responsibility set by Congress. Congress has been willing to delegate its legislative powers broadly—and courts have upheld such delegation—because there is court review to assure that the agency exercises the delegated power within statutory limits, and that it fleshes out objectives within those limits by an administration that is not irrational or discriminatory. Nor is that envisioned judicial role ephemeral, as *Overton Park* makes clear.

Our present system of review assumes judges will acquire whatever technical knowledge is necessary as background for decision of the legal questions. It may be that some judges are not initially equipped for this role, just as they may not be technically equipped initially to decide issues of obviousness and infringement in patent cases. If technical difficulties loom large, Congress may push to establish specialized courts. Thus far, it has proceeded on the assumption that we can both have the important values secured by generalist judges and rely on them to acquire whatever technical background is necessary.

The aim of the judges is not to exercise expertise or decide technical questions, but simply to gain sufficient background orientation. Our obligation is not to be jettisoned because our initial technical understanding may be meagre when compared to our initial grasp of FCC or freedom of speech questions. When called upon to make de novo decisions, individual judges have had to acquire the learning pertinent to complex technical questions in such fields as economics, science, technology and psychology. Our role is not as demanding when we are engaged in review of agency decisions, where we exercise restraint, and affirm even if we would have decided otherwise so long as the agency's decisionmaking is not irrational or discriminatory.

The substantive review of administrative action is modest, but it cannot be carried out in a vacuum of understanding. Better no judicial review at all than a charade that gives the imprimatur without the substance of judicial confirmation that the agency is not acting unreasonably. Once the presumption of regularity in agency action is challenged with a factual submission, and even to determine whether such a challenge has been made, the agency's record and reasoning has to be looked at. If there is some factual support for the challenge, there must be either evidence or judicial notice available explicating the agency's result, or a remand to supply the gap.

Mistakes may mar the exercise of any judicial function. While in this case the panel made such a mistake, it did not stem from judicial incompetence to deal with technical issues, but from confusion about the proper stance for substantive review of agency action in an area where the state of current knowledge does not generate customary definitiveness and certainty. In other cases the court has dealt ably with these problems, without either abandoning substantive review or ousting the agency's action for lack of factual underpinning.

On issues of substantive review, on conformance to statutory standards and requirements of rationality, the judges must act with restraint. Restraint, yes, abdication, no.

NOTE

Are you comfortable with Judge Leventhal's technical analysis in *International Harvester* or do you feel, as Judge Bazelon apparently did, that the court was in over its head? Judge Bazelon argues that a court should dig more deeply into the substance of a first amendment claim than into the substance of a scientific issue. But don't first amendment cases often rest on assumptions, such as whether a given speech will cause a riot, that rely on complex psychological, empirical or statistical theories?

Vermont Yankee, discussed in Ch. 2, Sec. B.2, supra, largely blunts Judge Bazelon's call for judicial imposition of increased procedural requirements in rulemaking, but the policy issue of whether Congress should impose such requirements on agencies remains. Moreover, judges intent on emphasizing the procedural over the substantive can still often find procedural issues in the various statutes involved in a particular agency action.

From the point of view of the agency contemplating review of its actions in the court of appeals, there may be relatively little difference between the substantive and procedural scrutiny recommended by Judges Leventhal and Bazelon—both judges and their followers are obviously tough on agencies in cases such as those presented above. Should courts look so closely at technical issues?

2. COURTROOM USE OF SCIENTIFIC AND MEDICAL EVIDENCE

Certain traditional functions of the courts have long involved judges and juries in scientific disputes. Consider, for example, the continuing controversies over whether the results of various criminal investigation techniques should be admissible in court. The materials below on lie detector evidence are representative of this type of problem.

JOHN A TRULIK, THE COURTROOM STATUS OF THE POLYGRAPH

14 Akron L.Rev. 133, 134–141, 144–145 (1980).

A polygraph is a machine which, according to its proponents, allows a trained operator to detect lies in the statements of a person attached to the machine. The polygraph machine used by the Akron Police Department, for example, consists of a blood pressure cuff similar to that used by a doctor, two pneumograph tubes (one fastened around the subject's abdomen to measure stomach breathing and the other attached to his chest to measure chest breathing) and a galvanic skin reflex unit which electronically measures sweat gland activities when attached to a person's fingers. Although there are various types of machines, the theory behind them is the same:

> that there is a definite relationship between willful lying and an elevation of blood pressure, fluctuations and the depth of respiration and variations in the resistance to electric current; that such relationship

could be ascertained by means of a polygraph which simultaneously records these reactions on paper.

This theory is supported by a consensus of opinion in the medical profession. Thus, by interpreting changes which occur in these four measurements as the subject is questioned, the polygraph operator is able to determine the truthfulness of the subject's answers.

Although lying is a voluntary action, a person's physiological reaction to his lies is not. Whenever someone encounters an emergency situation the sympathetic autonomic nervous system becomes activated to help meet the emergency. This reaction is most noticeable in fear situations. For example, if a person were to step into the street in front of a truck, he would receive a rush of energy which would allow him to react quickly. Safe on the curb, his heart would be pounding ferociously. It was the autonomic nervous system which increased his heart beat in order to speed fuel and oxygen throughout his body, thus increasing his speed and strength. Other organs in the body react in a similar manner.

Being questioned concerning the commission of a crime creates a fear situation, the fear of being sanctioned. As in the earlier example, the autonomic nervous system is triggered. Respiration, pulse and sweat gland activity are all affected. But instead of aiding one's escape, these reactions, when recorded by a polygraph, may cause these fears to be realized.

Unfortunately, professional acceptance of the theory behind the polygraph is not universal. According to Professor Jerome Skolnick:

[T]he scientific basis for lie detection is questionable. There seems to be little evidence that upholds the claim to a regular relationship between lying and emotion; there is even less to support the conclusion that precise inferences can be drawn from the relationship between emotional change and physiological response.

Moreover, "the autonomic response to the critical question will always be influenced by individual difference variables which are not a function of the subject's guilt or innocence." For example, being accused of a crime and taking a polygraph test, whether guilty or not, will in itself create a fear situation. This would activate one's autonomic nervous system, and register a response during testing. The extent of the response would vary with the individual. On the other hand, a guilty person with no fear of criminal sanctions may register no response at all. An illustration of this occurs where a subject is given a placebo and told it will immunize him from detection; if he believes it, he would 'beat' the test.

The theory of the polygraph can be impaired by other characteristics of a test subject. Test results can be detrimentally affected if the subject suffers from a heart condition, excessively high or low blood pressure, hiccups, allergies, asthma, hay fever, or coughs. The feebleminded and mentally retarded, morons, psychotics, sociopaths, psychoneurotics and psychopaths can all cause test interpretation problems. The potential for error is increased in tests involving young children, regular drug users who are presently 'straight,' and persons under the influence of drugs or alcohol. Other factors include overanxiety, anger, concern over a neglected duty (e.g., a night watchman who was asleep at the time of a burglary may react to a question because of guilt feelings for letting the theft happen), involvement in similar acts or offenses, extensive or suggestive prior interrogation, prior testing, physical discomfort, adrenal exhaustion from being tested too soon after an emergency, psychological evasion, rationalization and self-deceit. It has been suggested that the polygraph can even brainwash or subconsciously persuade a subject of his guilt through physiological feedback.

Proponents of the polygraph contend that most of these problems can be minimized by a properly trained examiner. . . .

The scientific basis of the polygraph is further eroded by reliance on the examiner's subjective evaluation of the test subject. In their widely read and judicially recognized polygraph handbook, *Truth and Deception—The Polygraph ("Lie-Detector") Technique*, Reid and Inbau instruct examiners to note various listed symptoms of lying and truthfulness. Their list includes delays in answering a question, attitude towards the test, body movements, etc. They state that:

> No final conclusions should be drawn from the subject's answers or reactions which we have pointed out as indications of probable deception or truthfulness. Nevertheless, they are very helpful as factors to be considered in the ultimate decision to be made of truthfulness or deception. At the very least, they may place the examiner on his guard against a positive opinion based upon the test results alone whenever these various pretest answers and reactions point to an opposite indication.

Thus, despite claims to the contrary, it appears as if:

> the professional polygrapher almost never arrives at his final diagnosis on the basis of the polygraphic records alone. . . . [I]n the vast majority of field examinations, the final diagnosis results from a subjective blending in the mind of the examiner of what he has observed in the charts, in the demeanor of the subject during the test, and in the preexamination interview, what he knows of the evidence against the suspect and what he may infer from the suspect's prior history, and even any prejudices he may hold about the subject's race, age, appearance, and the like.

Obviously, a critique of the polygraph does not leave its basic theory unscathed; consider this point:

> there does not appear to be general scientific acceptance of a theory to explain all the phenomena of aspirin. But even though aspirin's theoretical underpinnings may never be elucidated to the satisfaction of the scientific community, the fact is that it works.

The next inquiry will be to determine if the same statement can be made of the polygraph.

Various studies of the polygraph estimate its accuracy from a high of 100 percent to a low of 63 percent, with any errors which occur favoring the innocent. In addition to the doubt generated merely by the large range of accuracy estimates, there are other reasons for withholding credence in these studies. Laboratory studies are unreliable because they can not adequately evoke the fear factor on which a diagnosis is made. Actual case studies can not be properly verified because confessions are rare and not necessarily reliable. Reference to the findings of the jury does not help gauge the accuracy of the polygraph. The unreliability of jury findings is highlighted by the perceived need for some sort of mechanical 'lie detector.' Thus, all that can safely be said about the accuracy of the polygraph is that: 1) valid diagnoses of truthfulness are often made; and 2) errors can occur. . . .

The judicial regulation of the polygraph began in 1923, when the Circuit Court for the District of Columbia held in *Frye v. United States* that polygraphic evidence is not generally admissible at trial. The defendant in *Frye* attempted to introduce the results of a polygraph test conducted solely by systolic blood pressure which vindicated him of the second degree murder charges. The appellate court held that, to be admitted, the polygraph "must be sufficiently established to have gained general acceptance in the particular field in which it belongs." Placing it in the fields of physiology and psychology, the court noted the polygraph's less than general acceptance by experts in these fields. Ironically, Frye spent three years in prison before he was cleared by the confession of a third person.

Criticism of *Frye* has been plentiful. McCormick feels that the general scientific standard of *Frye:*

is a proper condition for taking judicial notice of scientific facts but not a criterion for the admissibility of scientific evidence. Any relevant conclusions which are supported by a qualified expert witness should be received unless there are other reasons for exclusion.

Others contend that polygraphy is a science in itself and that the only required acceptance should be that of the polygraph community, noting that, "Not many psychologists or psychiatrists are actually in an advantageous position to evaluate the lie detector. Very few have done any applied work with it, or even experimental studies." Mention is also made of the increased sophistication of both the machine and its operators since 1923.

Despite these attacks on the rationale of *Frye,* the case has, with rare exceptions, been followed in Ohio and throughout the nation. The Ohio Supreme Court, however, has hinted that the day may eventually come when Ohio courts will admit polygraph results despite objections from opposing counsel. Unfortunately, the high court did not give any indication as to what type of a showing would be needed to freely admit polygraph evidence. They only stated, without explanation, that a claim that defendant was denied his constitutional right of compulsory process for attaining witnesses in his behalf is an inadequate ground for admission.

Ohio courts of appeals have held that exclusion of polygraph evidence will be the rule in Ohio until its proponents can show an advancement in the reliability of the polygraph's diagnosis, or until counsel can show its "scientific recognition and public acceptance." Notably, the latter test did not mention whether the scientific recognition was to come from the field of polygraphy itself or from the fields of physiology and psychology as designated in *Frye.* These showings must be made on the record at the point counsel lays his foundation for the introduction of the evidence. However, the trial court may refuse to even hear the profert.

III. THE RIGHT TO TAKE OR REFUSE A POLYGRAPH TEST

Frye has been narrowly interpreted so that it does not preclude every courtroom use of the polygraph. Before approaching the court or the prosecutor concerning the polygraph, a wise criminal attorney will first have the test administered secretly to his client. The element of surprise is most damaging when it comes from the defendant himself. Although not conclusive, if a first test is passed it is likely that the accused will pass a second test. Most prosecutors will assume a prior test has been taken before they are contacted concerning one. Still, some will even accept the results. For instance, Summit County, Ohio prosecutors are known to accept the results of a prior test subject to their approving of the test examiner. This practice, however, has been questioned because of potential inaccuracies caused by a lessened fear of detection. . . .

The complement to any real or theoretical right to take a polygraph is the right not to take the test. Police departments regularly suggest the polygraph to a suspect as a quick way to vindication without further involvement in the criminal process. The United States Supreme Court, in dicta, has stated that the polygraph is "essentially testimonial," making the normal fifth amendment waiver rules applicable. Logically, if a defendant is in custody, he must be given his *Miranda* rights before testing can proceed. Before Ohio courts admit polygraphic evidence against a *pro se* defendant, there must be an affirmative showing on the record that the test was taken with full knowledge of his constitutional rights. The better view is that prior to any testing which is later to be used in court, the judge should advise the defendant of his rights and affirmatively determine that his waiver is voluntarily, knowingly and intelligently made, regardless of any status as to counsel. Surely the same guardian rationale for judicial inquiry that underlies Federal Rule of Criminal Procedure 11(C) and (D) and Ohio Rule of Criminal Procedure 11(C) and (D) in the guilty plea setting would require such inquiry prior to polygraph tests as well. . . .

As discussed, the results of a polygraph examination are generally not admitted at trial. The major exception to this rule is when both parties stipulate to its admission. Although many courts note the polygraph's unreliability and state that the rule against admissibility can not be circumvented by agreement, the trend is to accept the stipulated evidence at trial. Ohio, in *State v. Souel*, became one of at least twenty states accepting stipulations. Souel, accused of a robbery-murder, entered into a written stipulation with the prosecutor which on its face permitted the results of a polygraph test to be introduced as evidence at the trial. Souel was implicated in the crime by the test results and objected to their introduction. The objection overruled, the prosecutor then called the polygraph examiner to the stand who, before disclosing the test results, testified as to his polygraph training and experience and also as to how the test was administered to the defendant. On cross-examination, defense counsel reviewed that testimony and further questioned the examiner as to the conditions under which the test had been administered and the various possibilities for error. The court's jury instruction emphasized the point that the polygraph results should be weighed with all the other evidence and that it can not in and of itself be deemed conclusive on any point. Souel was thereafter convicted. . . .

CHRIS GUGAS, THE SILENT WITNESS

5–6 (1979).

World War II accounted for quantum leaps in technology. Wide use of the polygraph by the armed services not only produced a whole new breed of carefully trained examiners, but in a few short years it took testing and analysis techniques a long way toward standardization. In 1953, when two outstanding examiners, John Reid and Fred Inbau, tested 4,280 criminal suspects, their accuracy rate was 95 percent. And in 1971, Reid, working with F.S. Horvath, in a striking demonstration of the new exactness and uniformity of polygraph data showed examiners the charts of forty tests in which they had not been involved. Trained but inexperienced examiners scored 79 percent accuracy, experienced examiners 91.4 percent!

Yet the courtroom doors that slammed on polygraph evidence in 1923 remain shut still, with few exceptions. The root argument against admitting such evidence is that it results in self-incrimination. No one, says the Fifth Amendment to our Constitution, "shall be compelled in any criminal case to be a witness against himself." And what about the drunk driving suspect made to walk a chalk line, to close his eyes and touch his nose with a fingertip? Has he become a witness against himself? If not, then how can anyone be said to have done so in taking a polygraph test?

No, speech is not the issue. A polygraph test can be given without either examiner or subject uttering a word. . . . And on the subject of words, lawyers opposed to the polygraph like to say, "You can't cross-examine a machine." This is true. It's true of most of the equipment in today's big-city crime laboratories. But medical examiners and others able to use such equipment are cross-examined every day in courtrooms all over the country.

As recently as 1958, three California Supreme Court justices ruled that the polygraph examination "is offensive to the traditions of the law." But what is traditional about the electron microscope, semen-typing, voiceprints, and the hundred other scientific advances law enforcement uses today, and which trial lawyers and judges accept? Less than a hundred years ago, fingerprinting was still a novelty! The word of witnesses, physical evidence, circumstantial evidence—these are traditional. It's safe to say they reach back beyond written history. Yet what judge or attorney of today would ban every other means but these of determining guilt or innocence, because they are "offensive to the traditions of our law"?

In their Stone Age attitude toward the polygraph, the courts stand almost alone. Every major police force in the United States uses the polygraph, not as a substitute for investigating crimes, but to help sort out lies from truth. Much time and many tax dollars are saved. And countless citizens every year have polygraph tests to thank for clearing them of mistaken suspicions of wrongdoing. Attorneys, public and private, regularly call on polygraph examiners to determine the truth or falsehood of stories told them by clients, witnesses, suspects. . . .

NOTE

If juries are thought to be capable of evaluating demeanor evidence, why not allow them to evaluate polygraph evidence? Is demeanor evidence always more reliable? Is there fear that because polygraphs are "scientific" juries will be afraid to question them? Is that fear justified? Proposals to provide juries with certain statistical propositions concerning the probability that a particular defendant is linked to particular evidence have caused controversy reminiscent of the polygraph dispute. See M. Finklestein, Quantitative Methods in Law 288–311 (1978); Tawshunsky, Admissibility of Mathematical Evidence in Criminal Trials, 21 Am. Crim.L.R. 55 (1983).

The *Frye* case, discussed by Trulik, set forth the general standard for the admissibility of scientific evidence for many years. *Frye* holds that scientific evidence can be admitted only if it has been "sufficiently established to have gained general acceptance in the particular field in which it belongs." Frye v. United States, 293 F. 1013 (D.C.Cir. 1923). The Federal Rules of Evidence, which became effective in 1975, contain several provisions that arguably set forth a less rigorous standard for admissibility of scientific evidence, although the courts are split on whether the Rules in fact changed the *Frye* test. See McCormick, Scientific Evidence: Defining a New Approach to Admissibility, 67 Iowa L.Rev. 879 (1982). Do you view the *Frye* test as too stringent?

The use of scientific evidence and the use of expert witnesses to present that evidence raise the concern that the experts will usurp the jury's role. In short, the problem is a standard one in the social control of science—confining expertise to its proper domain. Consider in this respect the following statement by the American Psychiatric Association on the insanity defense.

AMERICAN PSYCHIATRIC ASSOCIATION, STATEMENT ON THE INSANITY DEFENSE

12–17 (1982).

Should psychiatric testimony be limited to statements of mental condition?

This area for potential reform of the insanity defense is one of the most controversial. Some proposals would limit psychiatric testimony in insanity defense trials to statements of mental condition, i.e., to statements of conventional psychiatric diagnoses, to provision of accounts of how and why the defendant acted as he did at the time of the commission of the act, to explanations in medical and psychological terms about how the act was affected or influenced by the person's mental illness. However, under this approach, psychiatrists would not be permitted to testify about so-called "ultimate issues" such as whether or not the defendant was, in their judgment, "sane" or "insane," "responsible" or not, etc. A further limitation upon psychiatric "ultimate issue" testimony would be to restrict the psychiatrist from testifying about whether a defendant did or did not meet the particular legal test for insanity at issue. Thus the law could prevent psychiatrists from testifying in a conclusory fashion whether the defendant "lacked substantial capacity to conform his behavior to the requirements of law," "lacked substantial capacity to appreciate the criminality of his act," was not able to distinguish "right from wrong" at the time of the act, and so forth.

The American Psychiatric Association is not opposed to legislatures restricting psychiatric testimony about the aforementioned ultimate legal issues concerning the insanity defense. We adopt this position because it is clear that psychiatrists are experts in medicine, not the law. As such, the psychiatrist's first obligation and expertise in the courtroom is to "do psychiatry," i.e., to present medical information and opinion about the defendant's mental state and motivation and to explain in detail the reason for his medical-psychiatric conclusions. When, however, "ultimate issue" questions are formulated by the law and put to the expert witness who must then say "yea" or "nay," then the expert witness is required to make a leap in logic. He no longer addresses himself to medical concepts but instead must infer or intuit what is in fact unspeakable, namely, the *probable relationship* between medical concepts and legal or moral constructs such as free will. These impermissible leaps in logic made by expert witnesses confuse the jury. Juries thus find themselves listening to conclusory and seemingly contradictory psychiatric testimony that defendants are either "sane" or "insane" or that they do or do not meet the relevant legal test for insanity. This state of affairs does considerable injustice to psychiatry and, we believe, possibly to criminal defendants. These psychiatric disagreements about technical, legal and/or moral matters cause less than fully understanding juries or the public to conclude that psychiatrists cannot agree. In fact, in many criminal insanity trials both prosecution and defense psychiatrists do agree about the nature and even the extent of mental disorder exhibited by the defendant at the time of the act.

Psychiatrists, of course, must be permitted to testify fully about the defendant's psychiatric diagnosis, mental state and motivation (in clinical and commonsense terms) at the time of the alleged act so as to permit the jury or judge to reach the ultimate conclusion about which they, and only they, are expert. Determining whether a criminal defendant was legally insane is a matter for legal factfinders, not for experts.

What should be done with defendants following "not guilty by reason of insanity" verdicts?

This is the area for reform where the American Psychiatric Association believes that the most significant changes can and should be made in the present administration of the insanity defense. We believe that neither the law, the public, psychiatry, or the victims of violence have been well-served by the general approach and reform of the last ten years, which has obscured the quasi-criminal nature of the insanity defense and of the status of insanity acquittees.

The American Psychiatric Association is concerned particularly about insanity acquittals of persons charged with violent crime. In our view, it is a mistake to analogize such insanity acquitees as fully equivalent to civil committees who, when all has been said and done, have not usually already demonstrated their clear-cut potential for dangerous behavior because they have not yet committed a highly dangerous act. Because mental illness frequently affects the patient's ability to seek or accept treatment, we believe that civil commitment, as a system of detention and treatment, should be predicated on the severity of the patient's illness and/or in some instances on the mental patient's potential for perpetrating future violence against others. The usual civil committee has not, however, committed nor will he commit in the future a major crime. Most mentally ill persons are not violent. By contrast, the "dangerousness" of insanity acquittees who have perpetrated violence has already been demonstrated. Their future dangerousness need not be inferred; it may be assumed, at least for a reasonable period of time. The American Psychiatric Association is therefore quite skeptical about procedures now implemented in many states requiring periodic decisionmaking by mental health professionals (or by others) concerning a requirement that insanity acquittees who have committed previous violent offenses be repetitively adjudicated as "dangerous," thereupon provoking their release once future dangerousness cannot be clearly demonstrated in accord with the standard of proof required.

While there are no easy solutions to these problems, the following are some potential alternatives for the future.

First, the law should recognize that the nature of inhospital psychiatric intervention has changed over the last decade. Greater emphasis is now placed upon psychopharmacological management of the hospitalized person. Such treatment, while clearly helpful in reducing the overt signs and symptoms of mental illness, does not necessarily mean, however, that "cure" has been achieved—nor that a patient's "nondangerousness" is assumed. Continuing, even compelled, psychiatric treatment is often required for this population once the patient is released from the hospital.

Although some insanity acquittees will recover in such facilities, there can be no public guarantee. Therefore, the presumption should be that after initial hospitalization a long period of conditional release with careful supervision and outpatient treatment will be necessary to protect the public and to complete the appropriate treatment programs. Unfortunately however, many jurisdictions have neither the trained personnel nor appropriate outpatient facilities and resources to provide for such close management of previously violent persons who are conditionally released. Where statutes provide for conditional release and judges allow it without these necessary resources, the public is subjected to great risk and the insanity acquittee is deprived of an opportunity for a necessary phase of treatment.

At any hearing that might order the conditional release of an insanity acquittee, the following questions must be answered affirmatively. Has a coherent and well structured plan of supervision, management, and treatment been put into place? Is this plan highly likely to guarantee public safety while maximizing the chances for rehabilitation of the insanity acquittee? Are the necessary staff and resources available to implement the plan? Is there in place a procedure to reconfine the insanity acquittee who fails to meet the expectations of the plan?

For some acquittees contingent release is not possible because of the risk to society, the lack of resources, or other relevant legal considerations. Yet because psychiatry has no more to offer the acquittee, continued confinement cannot be justified on therapeutic or psychiatric grounds. When there exists no realistic therapeutic justification for confinement, the psychiatric facility becomes a prison. The American Psychiatric Association believes this hypocrisy must be confronted and remedied. One appropriate alternative is to transfer the locus of responsibility and confinement for such acquittees to a nontreatment facility that can provide the necessary security.

The American Psychiatric Association believes that the decision to release an insanity acquittee should not be made *solely* by psychiatrists or *solely* on the basis of psychiatric testimony about the patient's mental condition or predictions of future dangerousness. While this may not be the only model, such decisions should be made instead by a group similar in composition to a parole board. In this respect, the American Psychiatric Association is impressed with a model program presently in operation in the State of Oregon under the aegis of a Psychiatric Security Review Board. In Oregon a multidisciplinary board is given jurisdiction over insanity acquittees. The board retains control of the insanity acquittee for a period of time as long as the criminal sentence that might have been awarded were the person to have been found guilty of the act. Confinement and release decisions for acquittees are made by an experienced body that is not naive about the nature of violent behavior committed by mental patients and that allows a quasi-criminal approach for managing such persons. Psychiatrists participate in the work of the Oregon board, but they do not have primary responsibility. The Association believes that this is as it should be since the decision to confine and release persons who have done violence to society involves more than psychiatric considerations. The interest of society, the interest of the criminal justice system, and the interest of those who have been or might be victimized by violence must also be addressed in confinement and release decisions.

. . .

NOTE

Is this statement motivated by a desire to reduce the role of psychiatrists for the good of the criminal justice system or for the good of the psychiatric profession? Do you agree that "in many criminal insanity trials both prosecution and defense psychiatrists do agree about the nature and even the extent of mental disorder exhibited by the defendant at the time of the act" ? The medical, legal and ethical issues raised by the insanity defense have spawned an enormous literature. Good starting places include A. Goldstein, The Insanity Defense (1967); and Goldstein and Katz, Abolish the Insanity Defense—Why Not?, 72 Yale L.J. 872 (1963).

The American Psychiatric Association statement expresses concern that expert witnesses might "confuse" the jury. This possibility is obviously not limited to the insanity defense. In recent years, considerable debate has arisen over the ability of juries to handle complex cases involving, for example, patent law, and about the scope of the constitutional right to a jury trial in such cases. See, e.g., Kirst, The Jury's Historic Domain in Complex Cases, 58 Wash.L.Rev. 1 (1982).

3. A BROADER ROLE FOR THE JUDICIAL MODEL? THE SCIENCE COURT PROPOSAL

RICHARD E. TALBOTT, "SCIENCE COURT": A POSSIBLE WAY TO OBTAIN SCIENTIFIC CERTAINTY FOR DECISIONS BASED ON SCIENTIFIC "FACT"?

8 Envtl.L. 827–833 (1978).

The news regularly reports decisions which affect the public at large and which have been largely dominated by scientific determinations. Recent examples include: whether SST landing rights should be permitted at Kennedy Airport in New York; whether recombinant DNA research should be allowed in the city of Cambridge, Massachusetts; whether nerve gas should be stored in the eastern part of the state of Oregon; whether high-rise buildings should be built over earthquake faults; whether some effluent from a factory is detrimental to human health or to the environment; whether a local water supply should be fluoridated. All of these involved policy decisions which were affected to greater or lesser degrees by the existence of some level of scientific certainty that the particular cause for concern did, in fact, exist. The general question is, therefore: How does the decision maker—individual citizen, elected official, administrator, businessman, judge—obtain the data needed to reach the decision, and how does the decision maker know that those data are really "the facts" unadorned and uncolored by particular points of view regarding their significance?

There are many ways one might try to get the "facts". Within the sphere of "big issues" at the national level there has developed a variety of scientific advice-rendering mechanisms including advisory committees, individual science advisors, congressional hearings, regulatory hearings and court suits. The recent addition of congressional science fellows provides another form of science advice. Of course, trial courts might get scientific facts from expert witnesses or from masters, and it has been suggested that the appellate courts might get scientific aides to assist in their interpretation of technical material contained in the hearing records made by an agency. However, concerns have been expressed about the objectivity of these various forms of scientific advice; more particularly, the concerns focus on the purity of the factual basis for the advice, that is to say, whether the facts are tainted by the values of the advisor.

One of the most consistent voices expressing concern about the need for morally neutral facts in the decision making process has been that of Dr. Arthur Kantrowitz. In 1967 Dr. Kantrowitz explicitly proposed "institutionalizing the scientific advisory function with a view toward increasing the *presumptive validity* of the scientific input." Specifically, Dr. Kantrowitz was concerned about what he called "mixed decisions"—decisions which have considerable political and moral implications as well as an important scientific input or component, but in an area of science which does not yet have a consensus regarding the state of that particular branch of science. Kantrowitz was concerned that the moral responsibility which the scientist feels could very easily affect his judgment as to the state of scientific facts when the scientific facts were not yet crystal clear.

Kantrowitz made three recommendations which he believed would overcome the tainting of scientific with moral aspects of a so-called fact in the decision-making process. First, Kantrowitz recommended separating the scientific from the political and moral components of a mixed decision since Kantrowitz contended that facts could always be separated from values. His primary concern was that objectivity not be overcome by strongly held moral or political values. Second, Kantrowitz recommended separation of the judge and the advocate roles in the decision making process. Third, Kantrowitz suggested for this new system of institutionalized decision making that any resulting scientific judgments must be published.

In 1976 the Task Force of the Presidential Advisory Group on Anticipated Advances in Science and Technology produced what they called *The Science Court Experiment: An Interim Report* (hereinafter Task Force). The proposal of the Task Force, and the comments and controversy which have followed from it, constitute the bulk of the remainder of this paper.

THE PROPOSED "SCIENCE COURT" PROCESS

Although a science court does not yet exist, the concept has generated much discussion. Past proposals for other specialized courts have not succeeded well on the whole.

The basic product of the Task Force was a complex outline of proposed procedures for resolving scientific disputes. The gist of the Task Force proposal, however, is contained in the following:

There are many cases in which technical experts disagree on scientific facts that are relevant to important public decisions. As a result, there is a pressing need to find better methods for resolving factual disputes to provide a sounder basis for public decisions. We accordingly propose a series of experiments to develop *adversary proceedings* and test their value in resolving technical disputes over questions of scientific fact. One such approach is embodied in a proposed *Science Court* that is to be concerned solely with questions of scientific fact. It will leave social value questions—the ultimate policy decisions—to the normal decision making apparatus of our society, namely the executive, legislative and judicial branches of the government as well as popular referenda.

The Task Force had at least one explicit purpose in mind, namely: "the Science Court is to create a situation in which the adversaries direct their best arguments at each other and at a panel of sophisticated scientific judges rather than at the general public." The Task Force further provided: "The basic mechanism proposed here is an *adversary hearing,* open to the public, governed by a distinterested referee, in which expert proponents of the opposing scientific positions argue their cases before a panel of scientist/judges. The judges themselves will be established experts in areas adjacent to the dispute."

JAMES A. MARTIN,
THE PROPOSED SCIENCE COURT

75 Mich.L.Rev. 1058, 1069–1976 (1977).

IV.   SPECIFICS OF THE SCIENCE COURT PROPOSAL

A.   *Who Would Use a Science Court?*

The best case for a science court can be made when it is invoked by Congress or the Executive for assistance in the determination of global policy issues. The science court proposals, if viewed as sets of procedures rather than as an institution, might very well assist various administrative agencies in finding methods to resolve issues within their administrative jurisdiction. However, although its significance as a set of procedures is noteworthy, greater attention here will be paid to an institutionalized science court that could serve presidential and congressional needs.

It should be noted that the Executive is less likely to make use of a science court than are administrative agencies or the Congress, since the President already has a science adviser and will often have a political stake in a decision of a science court that could be undermined if the decision were adverse to the Executive's interest. Congress, on the other hand, is not monolithic, and if, as proposed below, minorities in Congress are allowed to present issues to the science court, political factors are likely to encourage rather than discourage submission of such issues from Congress. Also suggested below is a system of intervention by Congress when issues are submitted by the President, and vice versa, based on the notion that once Congress has submitted an issue, allowing intervention would minimize the danger that either the President or Congress could manipulate results by presenting a set of one-sided questions to a science court.

B.   *Who Will Select the Issues?*

One of the original purposes of the science court proposal is to separate the scientific questions from the policy or political issues in problems involving science. Consistent with that goal it ought to be reasonably clear that the selection of the issues that a science court would consider is itself a political function. If Congress does not want to know what the effects of the SST may be on the upper atmosphere, there is little need for advice on the subject from a science court. The selection of the issues must come from the body that needs to know their answers. This may severely limit the utility of the science court. If a public issue touching on a scientific question involves attacks on some established practice, such as the production of freon, there may be little incentive for the "establishment" and its friends in Congress to invoke the assistance of a science court, for that interest could only lose. Other issues, such as which energy source should receive research funding, may not involve questions in which one side or another is the "established" interest.

The existence of a possible institutional bias against submission of a particular issue to a science court does not, of course, eliminate the utility

of the court. First, as noted above, many public questions will not involve entrenched positions which can only lose by answers to scientific
questions. Second, although there may be institutional resistance to submission of questions in certain cases, the resistance is by no means insured of success. On important issues there will be pressure to get answers to the underlying scientific questions and there may be
embarrassment to those resisting such a course. It is, of course, obvious
that it would take a majority of close-minded policymakers on the "establishment" side of the issue, standing against the votes of those with fixed
opinions on the opposite side plus the votes of those with open minds,
simply to defeat the submission of an issue.

A device for submitting issues that might preserve some of the benefits of a science court when Congress is the policymaker would be to allow
a minority of defined size (such as one-third) to submit an issue. The size
of the minority should be large enough to make it likely that significant
interest exists in answers to the questions submitted. If there remain issues that should be submitted to a science court but for political reasons
are not, it does not follow that the science court idea has failed. On
these issues that are not submitted, we will have to "muddle through"
with our current procedures, but at least we will not have fallen behind
our present position.

A problem similar to that of choosing the general issues for consideration by the science court will be insuring that issues are not submitted in
such a way as to distort the court's contribution. To take an extreme
example, if the issue of the safety of nuclear reactors between now and
the year 2000 were submitted to a science court without submission of the
issue of the safety of alternative energy sources, a distorted picture could
emerge, even though the scientific questions were answered quite accurately. The stamp of a science court, intended to isolate scientific issues
to allow for informed and democratic policymaking, might have the opposite result. Unlike the problem discussed above of congressional majori-
ties blocking issue submission, the harm from such issue distortion could
be affirmative—not merely having the effect of preserving the status quo.

Fortunately, however, the solution to the two problems is the same:
allow congressional minorities to submit questions that round out the issues submitted by the majority or by other minorities. A congressional
technical staff, such as the Office of Technological Assessment, could assist in the specific framing of the issues involved for greater protection
against issue distortion.

Unfortunately, no similar, obvious device exists when the entity referring issues to the science court is the executive branch of the government.
There might be a great temptation on the part of a particular administration to "load the dice" by submitting carefully tailored issues—designed
carefully enough so that the one-sidedness would not be blatant but
might affect the political impact. The structure of the Executive is such
that minority views within it are not likely to surface the way they do in
Congress, and thus no internal, general "watchdog" exists to check any
bias of the administration.

Here a strong argument emerges for an institutionalized, rather than
ad hoc, science court, since a single institution available to Congress and
the executive could allow intervention (borrowing further from the
courts) by congressional minorities (or a congressional majority) when it
is felt that the Executive has submitted distorted issues. Such a course

would be difficult if the President were free to convene his or her own science court panel not made available to Congress. And, of course, it would be especially troublesome to have *two* (or more) science courts considering factual questions involved in the same overall issue, especially if they were to produce inconsistent results or at least were to give inconsistent impressions by answering somewhat different but related questions. Similarly, the Executive should be able to intervene when issues are submitted by Congress.

. . .

D.   *Selection of the Advocates*

In many ways, the selection of the advocates is the most difficult task in designing the science court—even more difficult than the selection of judges, discussed below. In a law suit, plaintiffs choose both themselves and the defendants as parties. Intervention is a rather rare event. Plaintiffs become such because they think they have something to gain from the litigation. In all but a few cases (such as class actions and so-called public interest cases) plaintiffs represent only their own interests. Defendants are chosen by plaintiffs because defendants have or can do something plaintiffs want. (Again, in a small number of cases, for example those challenging the constitutionality of a law, choosing the right defendant may be more of a problem.) The analogy between the law courts and the proposed science court breaks down badly here, however, since in the latter, in most cases, advocates on at least one side of an issue would be representing interests much wider than those of a single person or company. How, then, can advocates be chosen so that they will be representative, capable, and vigorous?

The problem can be diminished somewhat when there is a natural adversary in a given controversy—for example, companies producing or intending to produce freon would be the obvious candidates to choose the advocates on one side of the freon issue. But what about the other side? Who should represent the atmosphere? The Task Force has suggested an idea that may prove workable in many (but not all) contexts. Under the proposal, chief adversaries or "case managers" would be appointed by the science court or the "collaborating agency"—the agency seeking the scientific advice. Both selection processes may cause difficulties. If the collaborating agency is seen as biased, its selection of case managers may be suspect. If the science court selects the case managers, it has involved itself closely with the adversaries. A neutral institution, such as the National Science Foundation, may be a preferable agency for choosing case managers. Whatever the choosing agency, the selection would be accomplished after "requests for proposals" for case managers (already dubbed "RFPs") had been issued. The Task Force states that

> Each submitted proposal should exhibit that the bidder has the expertise and constituency to speak for one side of the issue and name its case manager. For example, a group such as the Union of Concerned Scientists, the Sierra Club, or Friends of the Earth might be a reasonable bidder to represent the antinuclear side of that issue. It might form an alliance with a scientific institution such as a nonprofit analysis group, with individual consultants, or both. In any case, the objective is to exhibit that the bidder can provide the best case for its side of the issue. Combinations of groups opposing nuclear energy would be encouraged, and the RFP would point out that such coalitions would be favored to receive the contract . . . .

The scientific credentials and constituency of the proposers will be examined carefully by the Science Court, the collaborating agency, or both, and a selection will be made by processes similar to those used in selecting contractors for other purposes.

Nothing in the Task Force's proposal inherently limits it to issues involving only two sides, and one can well imagine disputes—such as a debate over the source of energy whose development ought to be most heavily funded in the next twenty years—in which three or more sides, each with a case manager, might participate.

The Interim Report of the Task Force leaves unanswered what is to be done when there is *no* natural adversary, such as in the case of drug testing. The problem is not merely one of selecting advocates, but rather also involves the workability of the whole factfinding concept itself, since the central purpose of the proposal is to borrow the adversary process from the legal model on the assumption that the truth would emerge after an encounter between disputing parties.

An approach that may be worth trying when natural adversaries are lacking is what might be called the "canonization model," making use of a devil's advocate. Any agency, such as the FDA, whose task it is to make determinations about a specific product as to which there is no organized opposition, might seek out a competent "hired gun" as an advocate—a kind of lawyer without a client. The weakness in such an approach is that there is little incentive to keep the devil's advocate advocating devilishly. A lazy or complacent devil's advocate will do little good but will help create the false appearance of a useful proceeding.

In favor of the science court proposal, even when a devil's advocate is necessary, it might be noted that public prosecutors bear some similarities to the devil's advocate. Prosecutors theoretically "win" either way the case comes out—but that fact has not generally prevented them from gaining an emotional attachment (and thus some adversarial zeal) to "winning" in the more common sense. However, since prosecutors get to choose the cases they pursue, it is much easier for them to believe that the defendant is guilty whenever prosecuted—making emotional involvement all the easier. A devil's advocate against the efficacy or safety of a randomly chosen drug, on the other hand, would have no such ready-made moral crutch.

A second argument in favor of the science court approach, even with the devil's advocate, is that a supposedly adversarial process with an ineffective advocate on the "anti" side may still be more effective in finding the truth than the ordinary inquisitorial process it would displace. This conclusion is sufficiently doubtful, however, to make it clear that a science court approach will require particular scrutiny when the devil's advocate must be used. Fortunately, by the nature of things, such situations are likely to arise only on issues that are not important enough to have generated much public controversy. For the "big" issues, the Interim Report's method of choosing adversaries seems reasonably likely to be successful.

E.　*Selection of the Judges*

The Task Force's Interim Report says:

It is currently envisioned that the Science Court with consultation from appropriate scientific societies and organizations will produce a list of prospective judges certified as unusually capable scientists having no obvious connections to the disputed issue. These will then be examined by the case managers for prejudice. After acceptance, a panel of judges, say, three for the first experiment, will be formed.

The Interim Report makes no mention of the idea that judges be drawn from an allied field so that, while they cannot be personally interested, they are readily educable as to the issues. At the experimental stage it might be interesting to see whether biologists, for example, could function well in the context of a dispute involving physics. Even if that proves possible, however, it would seem likely that time and effort could be saved by choosing judges whose training allowed readier understanding of a given set of arguments. Moreover, the opinions of such judges would probably command more respect than would those of judges with less expertise.

A possible alternative to the selection of unbiased judges would be the selection of a panel containing representatives of various viewpoints. Rather obviously the judges should not have taken sides on the issues being presented, but it might be possible to select representatives of various general political persuasions—conservative, moderate, liberal, radical, and the like. Although there are obvious pitfalls with such an approach, it might be tempting to use it in the effort to achieve wide popular acceptance of science court opinions. In homespun terms, officials might fear that Ralph Nader would not accept the opinion of a panel of Edward Tellers on any issue, whether or not it had to do with nuclear energy.

Although philosophical balance on the panel is desirable, it should not be pursued by attempting to weigh various extremes against each other. The virtue of the science court proposal is that it harnesses bias and self-interest through the use of advocates, while judges remain as impartial as possible in considering scientific questions. In all but a very few cases [18] the political motivations of a science court judge could not legitimately affect the answers to scientific questions. Thus, injecting political considerations would invite trouble. If some people are left unsatisfied by such an approach and the science court's opinion on a question does not achieve universal acceptance, so be it. It is still open to all to point out weaknesses in the science court's reasoning, and it is still open to the policymakers—the ones who are to use the science court's opinion—to assess its work product in light of the criticism.

BARRY M. CASPER,
IS THE PROPOSED SCIENCE COURT WHAT WE NEED?

194 Science 29–30 (1976).

The political context in which the science court would operate cannot be ignored. Issues like the ABM (antiballistic missile), the SST (supersonic transport), or nuclear power involve very large stakes for very powerful interest groups. One thing that can be said for certain about the implementation of this proposal is that interested parties would try to use it to promote their own ends.

18. It is possible that a science court judge of a particular political persuasion could be motivated by political views to probe certain arguments more vigorously than would others more politically neutral, and in the process turn up faults in the analysis that even the politically neutral would agree were weaknesses. The incidence of such a happening should be minimized by the use of adequate advocates, however, since the science court judge described above would really be performing the function of an advocate.

Consider the question of when the science court would be brought into play. To get some feeling for the importance of this decision, one has only to look back to recent debates such as that over the ABM. If the science court had been functioning in the late 1960's, it might have entered the ABM debate at any one of a large number of critical times. By way of illustration, consider two possibilities:

In September 1967 Secretary of Defense McNamara announced that the United States would deploy a limited number of ABM interceptors, with the principal aim of protecting against a limited attacked by Chinese missiles. Soon thereafter two physicists, Richard Garwin and Hans Bethe, published an article criticizing the proposed system on the grounds that it could be penetrated by even relatively unsophisticated decoys that the Chinese could deploy. If opponents of the ABM could have brought this criticism to a science court, almost certainly the court would have found it valid. This would have been a great political setback for proponents of ABM deployment, perhaps undermining the credibility of the project altogether.

As it happened, however, this technical criticism went largely unnoticed by the public and it might well have been insufficient to activate the court's attention. Another ABM issue did generate widespread public concern, however. In late 1968, citizens in several of the cities where the ABM's nuclear-armed interceptors were to be located became frightened by the perceived danger of "H-bombs in our backyards." If ABM proponents had been able to bring this issue before a science court, the court would almost certainly have found the chances of an accidental detonation to be exceedingly small. This judgment might well have defused public concern over the ABM right from the start and the congressional debate over the project might then never have taken place.

All this is speculation, of course. But it illustrates the potential political power that lies in the hands of those who decide what issues the court will consider and when it will come into play. All that the task force guidelines have to say about the question is that "it is important to have involvement of an agency in whose jurisdiction the issue falls so that it can help in formulating the issue" and "it is most important that the issue be stated in a manner as close as possible to the actual decision that must be made by the agency". The guidelines say nothing about who would decide when the court would become involved. As the ABM example clearly illustrates, however, this might greatly influence the issue the court would consider: in 1967, the decision before the Department of Defense was whether or not to deploy a limited ABM system; in 1969, the decision was whether or not to move the proposed ABM sites away from the cities. It is relevant to note in this regard that the agencies in whose jurisdiction the issue falls are rarely disinterested parties in disputes over technology policy.

Prior Consideration of Scientific Questions

Let us now turn to the principal new features of the court proposal. Consider first the practicability and desirability of separating out questions of science and technology for prior consideration. Is it possible to make such a separation? In matters of public policy are there questions of science and technology that are completely separate from political and value questions? Of course there are. In the case of the ABM many such questions could be identified, ranging from the two already mentioned to the vulnerability of the ABM radar installations and Minuteman missiles, the adequacy of the computer codes, the relative cost of additional Soviet missiles and U.S. interceptors, and so on. These questions are quite distinct from such political and value questions as how the Soviets would be likely to respond to U.S. deployment of ABM's, how important Minuteman vulnerability is if our other strategic offense systems, the submarines and bombers, remain invulnerable, how many deliverable nuclear weapons are required for deterrence how many civilian casualties would be "acceptable," and so on. Clearly there are many questions which can be identified as strictly technical, without reference to normative considerations.

But of all the possible technical questions the court will choose only those that by some process of selection are deemed the significant questions. Is this choice of the significant questions independent of political and value judgments? In general it is not.

For example, in the case of the ABM, for some participants in the debate the potential vulnerability of the U.S. Minuteman missiles was of grave concern. For others the additional U.S. strategic weapons systems, the invulnerable submarines and the bombers, by themselves constituted a more than sufficient deterrent; some even suggested that we unilaterally scrap Minuteman. Clearly, these individuals would differ over the significance of the questions of how vulnerable the Minuteman force was likely to become and how much protection for it the proposed ABM system would buy. Some would have judged these to be the central questions to be considered by the science court. Others would have thought them of minor importance.

The point is simply that political and value judgments will generally enter into the decision concerning which of the many possible technical questions associated with an issue the court will address. Thus, the very process of separating technical from political and value questions could well involve political and value choices. The conception of a linear process of first judging the scientific issues and then integrating this judgment into the political process overlooks these significant choices. It is well to be aware of the potential political power that lies in the hands of those who frame the questions the court will address.

According to the task force guidelines, the questions will be framed by "case managers" selected to represent opposing positions on an issue. The case managers each prepare "a series of factual statements which they regard as most important to their cases". But different candidates for case manager on a given side of an issue might well have quite different conceptions of which technical questions are most important. For example, consider the anti-ABM position in the 1969 or 1970 congressional debates. A case manager concerned about the vulnerability of Minuteman to a Soviet first strike would have considered very important the question of how much (or, from his point of view, how little) Minuteman protection the Safeguard system would provide. Another might have felt that the vulnerability of Minuteman was a highly peripheral if not virtually irrelevant question, and would have addressed instead the question of the vulnerability of the entire U.S. deterrent force, the submarines and bombers as well as Minuteman. It is clear from this example that implicit political and value choices will be introduced into the process with the selection of case managers.

Finally, there is an even more important question concerning the proposed separation of scientific and nonscientific elements of policy issues encompassing both: is it *desirable* to separate the scientific questions for prior consideration? In general it is not. For major public policy issues with technical facets, the political and social value questions are almost invariably far more significant than those relating to science and technology. If the science and technology questions are isolated for separate consideration by a science court, they are likely to acquire a greater political impact than they deserve.

This is just the reverse of what is needed. Our present institutions for involving scientists in public policy decision making already tend to bring about this separation of and overemphasis on technical matters. This tendency is a major contributor to the current syndrome of crisis reaction, narrow technical debate, and piecemeal "technical fixes" which fail to address basic long-range problems. New institutions based on adversary proceedings are definitely needed, but they should have a broader rather than a narrower perspective.

NOTE

Are there "neutral experts" who could serve on a science court? If so, would they necessarily agree on the issues before the tribunal?

How does a science court differ from an administrative agency? In theory, agencies, through the use of expertise, implement policy choices made by Congress; in practice, the agencies themselves make numerous policy decisions. Would a science court similarly find itself immersed in policy questions?

Although the science court Task Force discussed by Talbott was dissolved when President Carter took office, there have been occasional trials of similar ideas. One of the problems that has emerged is the question of the status of science court decisions. If they are merely advisory, it is hard to see how a science court differs from the host of advisory committees and the like that already exist. When the Food and Drug Administration (FDA) considered the safety of the artificial sweetener aspartame, the parties agreed to let a Public Board of Inquiry made up of scientists hear the case. The board had enough doubt about aspartame to prohibit its use. The Commissioner of the FDA reversed the Board and approved aspartame. One commentator has concluded that the Commissioner gave no more weight to the Board's findings than he would have given to the findings of "a lay administrative law judge." Brannigan, The First FDA Public Board of Inquiry: The Aspartame Case in Nyart and Carrow, Law and Science in Collaboration 181, 201 (1983).

OFFICE OF TECHNOLOGY ASSESSMENT, UNITED STATES CONGRESS, TECHNOLOGY TRANSFER AT THE NATIONAL INSTITUTES OF HEALTH

44–47 (1982).

On May 11, 1977, the Director of NIH initiated a request to the Department of Health, Education, and Welfare (HEW) to establish the Office for Medical Applications of Research (OMAR).

. . .

OMAR is a relatively small office, with five professional and four support staff members. During its first 2 years, the program cost approximately $700,000 per year. In 1981, $1.2 million was the approximate figure, exclusive of staff costs and evaluation studies (83).

. . .

OMAR's primary activity has been the administration of the consensus development program at NIH and support of the actual consensus conferences. The consensus development conferences bring together scientists, practitioners, consumers, and others in an effort to reach general agreement on the safety and efficacy of medical technologies. The technologies of interest may be emerging or may be in general use. Recent conferences have tended toward examining emerging technologies, while early conferences generally focused on existing—and sometimes controversial—technologies. The technologies studied may be drugs, devices, or medical, surgical, or dental procedures. Since the first conference in September 1977, there have been 32 conferences held and four more are currently scheduled. Table 12 lists the topics, dates, and sponsors.

The first step in planning a consensus development conference is the selection of the technology to be assessed. Since this activity occurs at the individual institute or division level, procedures vary widely. Before a conference topic is finally selected and scheduled at OMAR, it will have been discussed and reviewed for 2 to 15 months at the institute level. It will also have been discussed by the OMAR Advisory Committee to generate suggestions and interest from other institutes that may have escaped the original sponsors. Should the case arise (and it has not to date) that there are more topics identified for conferences than OMAR has the resources to support, the OMAR Advisory Committee would be the body to recommend a priority order in which the conferences would be held.

Once the conference topic has been identified, the planning process begins. OMAR provides the initiative and logistic support and offers guidance based on the experiences with previous consensus development exercises. The planning period typically lasts 9 to 18 months. A number of planning meetings, first involving only NIH and OMAR staff, and later involving outside experts, are usually held to delineate the key issues. Also determined during the meetings are the specific questions surrounding the technology under discussion and the approaches to be used in reaching consensus. Individual experts may prepare papers prior to the meeting summarizing the state of the science; alternatively, or in addition, task forces are asked to produce draft documents for consideration at the conferences.

Consensus development panels are carefully constituted to reflect the range of individuals and organizations with expertise and interest in the use of the technologies. They include researchers in relevant fields, members of the pertinent clinical specialties, health care consumers, and others. Without question, however, the panel is overwhelmingly scientific, often reflecting the orientation of its sponsor. The conference is open to the public and audience participation is encouraged.

Most NIH consensus development conferences have used some variation of the following general format. The conference begins with a plenary session, during which individual experts or representatives of task forces present information on the state of the science. Comments by panelists may follow. Also, members of the audience may ask questions or provide comments. In some cases, work groups or task forces then meet to discuss specific aspects of the technology. In a closed session, the panel then convenes in an attempt to reach a consensus on the relevant issues. At the final plenary session, the consensus statement is presented to the audience for comment. At times, the audience comments are incorporated. Panel members who disagree with major conclusions may issue a minority report. A minority report has only been issued once.

**Table 12.—NIH Consensus Development Meetings, September 1977
Through November 1982, Office for Medical
Applications of Research**

Sponsors	Title	Dates held
NCI	Breast Cancer Screening	Sept. 14–16, 1977
NCI	Educational Needs of Physicians and the Public Regarding Asbestos Exposure	May 22, 1978
NIDR	Dental Implants Benefit and Risk	June 13–14, 1978
NCI	Mass Screening for Colo-Rectal Cancer	June 26–28, 1978
NIA	Treatable Brain Diseases in the Elderly	July 10–11, 1978
NINCDS	Indications for Tonsillectomy and Adenoidectomy: Phase I	July 20, 1978
NIAID	Availability of Insect Sting Kits to Nonphysicians	Sept. 14, 1978
NCI	Mass Screening for Lung Cancer	Sept. 18–20, 1978
NIGMS	Supportive Therapy in Burn Care	Nov. 10–11, 1978
NIAMDD	Surgical Treatment of Morbid Obesity	Dec. 4–5, 1978
Interagency Committee on New Therapies for Pain and Discomfort (Organizer)	Pain, Discomfort, and Humanitarian Care	Feb. 16, 1979
NICHD	Antenatal Diagnosis	Mar. 5–7, 1979
NHLBI	Transfusion Therapy in Pregnant Sickle Cell Disease Patients	Apr. 23–24, 1979
NHLBI	Improving Clinical and Consumer Use of Blood Pressure Measuring Devices	Apr. 26–27, 1979
NCI	The Treatment of Primary Breast Cancer: Management of Local Disease	June 5, 1979
NCI	Steroid Receptors in Breast Cancer	June 27–29, 1979
NEI	Intraocular Lens Implantation	Sept. 10–11, 1979
NIA	Estrogen Use and Postmenopausal Women	Sept. 13–14, 1979
NIAID	Amantadine: Does It Have a Role in the Prevention and Treatment of Influenza?	Oct. 15–16, 1979

**Table 12.—NIH Consensus Development Meetings, September 1977
Through November 1982, Office for Medical
Applications of Research**—Continued

Sponsors	Title	Dates held
DRS	The Use of Microprocessor-Based "Intelligent" Machines in Patient Care	Oct. 17–19, 1979
NIDR	Removal of Third Molars	Nov. 28–30, 1979
NHLBI	Thrombolytic Therapy in Thrombosis	Apr. 10–12, 1980
NINCDS	Febrile Seizures	May 19–21, 1980
NCI	Adjuvant Chemotherapy of Breast Cancer	July 14–16, 1980
NCI, NIA, NICHD, NCHCT	Cervical Cancer Screening: The Pap Smear	July 23–25, 1980
NIAMDD	Endoscopy in Upper GI Bleeding	Aug. 20–22, 1980
NICHD	Childbirth by Cesarean Delivery	Sept. 22–23, 1980
NCI	CEA and Immunodiagnoses	Sept. 29–Oct. 1, 1980
NHLBI, NCHCT	Coronary Bypass Surgery	Dec. 3–5, 1980
NINCDS, NIAID, NIAMDD, NICHD, NEIHS, DRS	Reye's Syndrome Diagnosis and Treatment	Mar. 2–4, 1981
NINCDS, NCI	CT Scanning of the Brain	Nov. 4–6, 1981
NIAID	The Effect of Diet on Hyperactivity	Jan. 13–15, 1982
NIADDK	Hip Joint Replacement	Mar. 1–3, 1982
CC	Critical Care Medicine	Summer 1982
NIAID	Immunotherapy-Treatment of Insect Sting Allergy	Oct. 6–8, 1982
DRS	Validation of Biomaterials	Nov. 1–3, 1982

SOURCE: Office for Medical Applications of Research, National Institutes of Health.

Consensus statements are not, and do not attempt to be, regulations on the "proper" pratice of medicine. Rather they are attempts to represent the best current thinking by a group of scientific experts and others in a position to make judgments on safety and efficacy. Consensus conferences differ from standard state-of-the-art meetings in that consensus panels must consider and seek closure on specific sets of questions, and the format of the conference has been predetermined.

. . .

Those conducting consensus development conferences hope that by supplying practitioners with critiques of complex medical technologies, the consensus reports will contribute to an improvement in the quality of medical practice. Dissemination of the consensus statements and supporting materials is thus an essential part of the program. Practicing physicians and others in the health care system, the biomedical research community, and the public are the groups targeted to receive the statements. OMAR assists in the actual dissemination and in the monitoring of the following dissemination activities. Consensus materials and information have been published in the three American medical journals with the largest circulation—the *Journal of the American Medical Association,* the *New England Journal of Medicine,* and the *Annals of Internal Medicine.* Distribution through State medical journals, other scientific publications, mainstream periodicals, and the general press is encouraged, though such distribution is not directly initiated by OMAR.

DRUMMOND RENNIE,
CONSENSUS STATEMENTS

304 New Eng.J.Med. 665–666 (1981).

If you wanted to know whether a new unproved clinical test or operation or a new health program was any good, how would you proceed to find out? The best way would be to set up a controlled clinical trial, comparing the new with the old in everything from morbidity to dollar cost. Such essential trials, however, are always lengthy and very expensive. Each may focus on different aspects of the problem, and although the results of some may be available, others may still be brewing. In the meantime, as a practicing physician you want to advise your patients prudently and you need some help.

Most of us would then compromise by asking someone whom we considered to be an expert. This interim approach is the one that the National Institutes of Health resolved to take when their Office of Medical Applications of Research (OMAR) held, in September 1977, the first of a lengthy series of consensus-development conferences. Each institute identifies important topics, and OMAR (no doubt with loaf of bread and jug of wine) makes these conferences happen.

At first the idea was to assemble experts on developing biomedical technologies to decide what we knew and what directions we should take for the future, but it soon became apparent that many such technologies were already generally used but had never been subjected to appropriate scientific scrutiny, and that others were worthy of more general attention.

This journal and the *British Medical Journal* have published the statements produced by assembled panels of participating experts. The *Journal of the American Medical Association* has taken another tack, publishing summaries of the conferences in its "Medical News" section. Among other journals and newspapers, *Science* has published a preliminary report on a consensus conference on coronary-artery bypass, the full statement of which appears in this issue of the *Journal.*

No more appropriate topic could have been chosen by the NIH. If the indications for the operation, the workup necessary beforehand, the morbidity following surgery, the long-term survival, and the long-term quality of life are all vigorously debated, and if 110,000 such operations are performed annually at a cost of $1.6 billion, then who can argue that this is not a reasonable topic for an attempt to define the areas where we can all agree and, equally important, where gaps in our knowledge impede agreement?

This particular panel statement concludes that "Coronary-artery bypass represents a major advance in the treatment of patients with coronary-artery disease." Not a very startling conclusion, and at first glance, surely one that did not require the efforts of at least 17 panelists—cardiologists, cardiac surgeons, biostatisticians, a radiologist, a cost-benefit analyst, and a philosopher. The facts are much more complicated than that, however, and the statement gives general and specific guidance on who shall have workups, when, and how, and on what to expect from operations given different degrees of coronary-artery disease. This consensus statement, like some others, poses as many questions as it answers, but it provides us with a bench mark. In that sense it is an event: though each of us may differ with the panel's conclusions on one point or another, we can see what this distinguished panel thinks of this subject, and so the statement is useful.

Since their theoretical benefits are so obvious, why doesn't the *Journal* publish every one of the consensus statements? The reasons range from the feeling that our readership has heard it all before to the impression that the panel has come up with nothing useful. There are, however, other difficulties with this sort of consensus statement. As I read such statements I have the sensation that I am being provided with the bland generalities that represent the lowest common denominator of a debate— the only points on which the experts can wholeheartedly agree—and that these points must be so mild, so far from the cutting edge of progress, and so well established that surely everyone must already know them. We are kept from the debate: there is little sense of doubt and disagreement in the statements; yet the debate, as we know from many panelists, is immensely stimulating and instructive to the participants. Moreover, because of the "event," the statements may be taken to embalm a set of truths—an idea that the scientists who develop these statements would be horrified to consider. This spurious stamp of approval would be very hard for the individual physician to resist, and it might have legal as well as other practical implications.

Furthermore, one has only to compare the Statement on Breast Cancer Screening with a short, but far more interesting comment by the panel's chairman to realize how difficult it is for any committee to draft a useful document to which all members of a panel can attach their names, and how bland such statements must inevitably be.

This feeling of received truth that is conveyed by consensus statements reminds us that most explorations of nature would have been stillborn if the scientists or navigators or climbers had heeded the advice of consensus panels. I fear lest these statements will act like a dead hand, discouraging thought. After all, in the nature of things, they can only rehash, codify, and grade work already done. Although this has great importance because we should indeed know where we stand, I wish that fewer topics were chosen more discriminately and that ways could be found to generate new knowledge, for example, by making fuller recommendations about future research and by keeping the panels intact to obtain their opinion on funding research projects in their areas.

For all that, we are happy to publish this particular consensus statement and hope that our readers will learn something from it. I believe that physicians will be critical and sophisticated enough not to accept what statements contain simply because of their govenmental imprimatur or their august authorship. I hope that readers will take such documents for no more and no less than what they profess to be: an attempt by a panel of honest experts to reach agreement on what we think we know and what we do not know about important medical topics.

NOTE

Could consensus development conferences benefit fields other than medicine? Would they serve a useful purpose in areas such as nuclear waste disposal?

Consensus conferences would likely fail to resolve difficult social issues because such issues usually involve matters in which experts have reached nothing resembling a consensus. Even when there is broad agreement among experts in a relatively noncontroversial area, do government-approved consensus conferences pose any danger? Cf. the discussion of the dangers raised by a lack of diversity in government science funding in Ch. 4, Sec. B.2, supra.

*

Part Three

ACHIEVING THE GOALS OF PUBLIC POLICY: AVOIDING HARM AND PROMOTING FAIRNESS

Chapter 5

REDUCING RISKS AND DISTRIBUTING
BENEFITS

A. DECIDING WHEN AND HOW
TO REGULATE RISK

The first section of this chapter addresses two of the central problems of modern government: deciding when and how to reduce risks to life and health. The last two chapters focused primarily on the strengths and weaknesses of different mechanisms for control of science and medicine, ranging from the doctrine of informed consent to congressional legislation. In this section, by contrast, the focus is on recent efforts to use systematic decision techniques for assessing and managing risks, techniques that may be used by a variety of regulatory institutions.

The chapter begins with two recent case studies in regulatory decisionmaking. The first concerns saccharin; the second, the pesticides heptachlor and chlordane. These two case studies were chosen because they illustrate two of the different approaches that Congress has adopted in delegating authority to regulatory agencies. The two do not exhaust the universe of models of delegation, of course, but they do demonstrate some of the consequences of providing more or less discretion to agency decisionmakers. As you read the case studies, ask yourself how you would have decided the issues presented at each step in the decisionmaking process, whether as a member of Congress, as head of the agency, or as a federal judge. The balance of this part of the chapter examines two of the techniques (risk assessment and cost-benefit analysis) that have been proposed for making such regulatory decisions on what are said to be more objective bases. As you learn more about these two techniques consider what help, if any, they would have been to you if you had been one of the public officials who had to make the decisions about saccharin, heptachlor or chlordane.

1. TWO CASE STUDIES OF RISK REGULATION

a. Saccharin and the Delaney Clause

---

i. Congress Sets the Standard

FOOD ADDITIVES AMENDMENT, FEDERAL FOOD,
DRUG AND COSMETIC ACT § 409(c)(3)(A)

21 U.S.C. § 348(c)(3)(A) (1958).

[N]o such regulation [authorizing use of a food additive] shall issue if a fair evaluation of the data before the Secretary—

644

(A) fails to establish that the proposed use of the food additive, under the conditions of use to be specified in the regulation, will be safe: *Provided, That no additive shall be deemed to be safe if it is found to induce cancer when ingested by man or animal, or if it is found, after tests which are appropriate for the evaluation of the safety of food additives, to induce cancer in man or animal* . . ..

NOTE

The italicized portion of the Food Additives Amendment is known as the Delaney Clause. Comparable provisions appear in two other sections of the Act as well: the Color Additives Amendments of 1960 (§ 706(b)(5)(B), 21 U.S.C. § 376(b)(5)(B) (1970)) and the Animal Drug Amendments of 1968 (§ 512(d)(1) (H), 21 U.S.C. § 360b(d)(1)(H) (1970)), so there are in fact three Delaney Clauses. The remaining text is termed the "general safety clause." Other parts of Section 409 require the submission to FDA of a petition demonstrating a food additive's safety. Only after FDA has approved the petition and promulgated a food additive regulation may a substance defined in the statute as a "food additive" be used in food. See generally R. Merrill and P. Hutt, Food and Drug Law 65–68 (1980).

SENATE REPORT NO. 85–2422

85th Cong., 2d Sess. (1958).

. . . [U]nder existing law the Federal Government is unable to prevent the use in foods of a poisonous or deleterious substance until it first proves that the additive is poisonous or deleterious. To establish this proof through experimentation with generations of mice or other animals may require 2 years or even more on the part of the relatively few scientists the Food and Drug Administration is able to assign to a particular problem. Yet, until that proof is forthcoming, an unscrupulous processor of foodstuffs is perfectly free to purvey to millions of our people foodstuffs containing additives which may or may not be capable of producing illness, debility, or death.

. . . This huge loophole is 1 of 2 flaws in existing law which, through this measure, we are attempting to fill. This bill, if enacted, will require the processor who wants to add a new and unproven additive to accept the responsibility now voluntarily borne by all responsible food processors of first proving it to be safe for ingestion by human beings.

. . .

The concept of safety used in this legislation involves the question of whether a substance is hazardous to the health of man or animal. Safety requires proof of a reasonable certainty that no harm will result from the proposed use of an additive. It does not—and cannot—require proof beyond any possible doubt that no harm will result under any conceivable circumstances. . . .

In determining the "safety" of an additive, scientists must take into consideration the cumulative effect of such additive in the diet of man or animals over their respective life spans together with any chemically or pharmacologically related substances in such diet. Thus, the safety of a given additive involves informed judgments based on educated estimates by scientists and experts of the anticipated ingestion of an additive by man and animals under likely patterns of use. . . .

The report of the Secretary of Health, Education, and Welfare . . . follows:

> . . . We would like . . . to call attention to the fact that the Committee on Interstate and Foreign Commerce of the House of Representatives, before bringing the bill to a vote in the House, decided to add to its previously approved bill the [Delaney Clause]. . . . We have no objections to that amendment whatsoever, but we would point out that in our opinion it is the intent and purpose of this bill, even without that amendment, to assure our people that nothing shall be added to the foods they eat which can reasonably be expected to produce any type of illness in humans or animals. . . . In short, we believe, the bill reads and means the same with or without the inclusion of the clause referred to. This is also the view of the Food and Drug Administration. . . .

ii. FDA Proposes a Ban

FOOD AND DRUG ADMINISTRATION, SACCHARIN AND ITS SALTS: PROPOSED RULEMAKING

42 Fed.Reg. 19,996–20,002 (1977).

Summary: The Commissioner of Food and Drugs is proposing to revoke the interim food additive regulation under which saccharin and its salts (saccharin) are currently permitted as ingredients in prepackaged foods, such as soft drinks, and as tabletop nonnutritive sweeteners. The Commissioner is also inviting comments on a proposal to accept and promptly review new drug applications for the marketing of saccharin as a single-ingredient drug, available without a physician's prescription. . . .

. . .

The Commissioner's determination that saccharin must be banned as a food additive is based on a series of scientific studies conducted in accordance with currently accepted methods for determining whether compounds can cause cancer. The most recent of these studies, conducted by Canadian scientists under the auspices of the Canadian Government, confirms what earlier American studies have suggested: that saccharin poses a significant risk of cancer for humans. Under these circumstances, conscientious concern for the public health requires that FDA prohibit the continued general use of saccharin in foods.

This conclusion is also dictated by the so-called Delaney clause of the Federal Food, Drug, and Cosmetic Act . . . . .

The Delaney clause does not apply to human drugs, however, and it therefore does not prohibit the approval of a drug that has been shown to cause cancer in laboratory animals if the drug provides medical benefits that outweigh the potential risk. For many individuals, including diabetics who must limit their intake of sugar and other carbohydrates, the availability of a nonnutritive sweetener, may serve a legitimate medical need. The Commissioner is therefore proposing to permit the submission of new drug applications for the marketing of saccharin as a single-ingredient OTC drug, which applications must be accompanied by legally sufficient evidence of the effectiveness of saccharin for its labeled indications.

. . .

A. HISTORY OF THE USE AND SAFETY OF SACCHARIN

Saccharin is a nonnutritive, artificial sweetener that is approximately 350 times sweeter than sugar. . . .

. . .

Saccharin use today is widespread. Approximately 6 to 7.6 million pounds of saccharin were used in the United States in 1976. It is used in food and beverages, cosmetics, drugs, animal feed, and industrial processes. Food and beverage uses are by far the most extensive, accounting for over 70 percent of the saccharin used.

The soft drink industry accounts for about 74 percent of the saccharin consumed in food and beverages in the United States. Other dietary uses, which account for 14 percent of the saccharin consumed, include powdered juices and drinks, other beverages, sauces and dressings, canned fruits, dessert toppings, cookies, gums, jams, candies, ice cream, and puddings. About 12 percent of the saccharin consumed is as a sweetener in place of nutritive sweeteners (e.g., sugar) in coffee and tea and on cereal.

Although saccharin's predominant use is in foods, it is also used in drugs—both prescription and OTC—especially those intended for pediatric use and for use by diabetics. Saccharin is also found in a variety of cosmetics, including lipsticks, dentifrices, mouthwashes, aftershave lotions, moisturizing skin preparations, hair tonics, skin cleansers, bubble baths, colognes, face powders, and douches. Saccharin is also used to a limited extent in animal feed and animal drugs.

[I]n 1955 the Committee on Food Protection of the National Academy of Sciences reviewed the literature bearing on the safety of saccharin and concluded that the "maximum probable tolerance level for saccharin in the human diet is at least as great as 1.0 gram per day." The National Academy of Sciences (NAS) committee further concluded that the substitution of saccharin for the average daily consumption of sugar in the United States would amount to about 0.3 gram of saccharin, and that "the maximal amount of saccharin likely to be consumed was not hazardous."

Because of greatly increased use of saccharin and cyclamate, another nonnutritive sweetener, as well as *drastic changes in the patterns of their con sumption during the 1960's,* in 1967 FDA requested the National Academy of Sciences again to evaluate the safety of these nonnutritive sweeteners. In response to this request, an ad hoc committee was formed under the NAS Committee on Food Protection. In 1968, the committee issued an interim report in which it concluded that the intake of 1 gram or less per day of saccharin by an adult should present no hazard. However, the committee also recognized at that time that the existing carcinogenesis studies on saccharin, judged by current standards, were inadequate, and it therefore recommended that comtemporary studies be undertaken.

During the late 1960's, saccharin was being widely used competitively or in combination with cyclamates. Consequently, when the use of cyclamate was banned by FDA in 1969, it was anticipated that the daily intake of saccharin by users of nonnutritive sweeteners would increase substantially. An ad hoc subcommittee of the NAS Committee on Food Protection was once again requested by FDA to review all available toxicity data on saccharin in the light of the projected sharp increase in use.

The NAS subcommittee issued its final report in July 1970. It arrived at conclusions regarding the safety of saccharin very similar to the assessments of 1955 and 1968. The subcommittee again recommended that chronic toxicity studies, designed according to modern protocols, be completed. It further recommended that: (a) epidemiologic studies should be carried out with emphasis on the diabetic segment of the population and in relation to pregnancy; (b) comparative metabolism studies should be done in man and in animals; and (c) toxicologic interactions with other selected chemicals should be explored.

Although the then existing studies raised some questions about whether saccharin could cause cancer, no firm conclusions could be reached on the basis of those data. In 1972, because of the questions about the safety of saccharin, FDA removed saccharin from the list of substances generally recognized as safe (GRAS) and imposed limits on the use of saccharin to discourage general use by consumers and to inhibit an increase in its use by the general population. At that time, FDA also issued an interim food additive regulation to permit continued limited use of saccharin pending completion of studies to resolve the questions concerning the safety of saccharin. . . .

B. HISTORY OF SCIENTIFIC AND MEDICAL INQUIRY INTO THE CAUSES OF CANCER

Sir Percival Potts' description, almost 200 years ago, of the relationship between exposure to soot and cancer of the scrotum in chimney sweeps is usually cited as marking the beginning of studies in environmental carcinogenesis. It was not until the late 19th century, however, that the association between exposure to aromatic amines and the production of bladder cancer among workers in the German dye industry was established, and only in the early part of this century that the production of skin cancer by X-radiation and radium became evident.

Modern research on chemical carcinogenesis dates from the classic studies of Yamagiwa and Itchikawa. They successfully induced cancer by applying coal tar to the ears of rabbits and thereby produced the first experimental animal analogy of a type of chemically induced human cancer. . . .

The known causes of human cancer include physical, chemical, and biological agents. According to Boyland:

> Reasonable estimates are that not more than 5% of human cancer is due to viruses and less than 5% to radiations. Some 90% of cancer in man is therefore due to chemicals, but we do not know how much is due to endogenous carcinogens and how much to environmental factors. An expert committee (WHO, 1965) has concluded that at least half of all cancer in man is due to environmental factors. It should therefore be possible to prevent a great deal of human cancer by finding and removing chemical carcinogens from the environment.

In 1960, Dr. G.B. Mider prepared for a committee of the United States Congress a summary of the current state of scientific knowledge about the causes of cancer. Despite major subsequent advances in our understanding of the role of microsomal enzyme metabolism in the action of carcinogens, in molecular biology, in virology, in our knowledge of the immunological aspects of cancer, and in the development of in vitro models for carcinogenesis, the summary of the causes of cancer prepared by Dr. Mider more than a decade ago is still essentially correct:

(1) Although cancer can be caused by extraneous agents, not all members of the exposed population will develop cancer. Those who are most susceptible can be identified only by experience.

(2) Even a powerful carcinogen requires weeks or months to elicit cancer in mice or rats and probably requires years in man.

(3) No change need be recognizable in the organ or tissue destined to become cancerous before the cancer itself appears.

(4) Experience in the laboratory does not predict unequivocally the reaction of humans to the same agent. On the other hand, those few chemical and physical agents known to produce cancer in man, with the possible exception of inorganic arsenical compounds, have elicited cancers in animals.

(5) No one at this time can tell how much or how little of a carcinogen would be required to produce cancer in any human being, or how long it would take the cancer to develop.

(6) The effect of certain chemical carcinogens can be markedly increased by other compounds with little or no carcinogenic power.

(7) The accumulated evidence suggests the irreversibility of the cancerous response once it has been initiated and further suggests a cumulative effect.

(8) The most potent carcinogens, by their very strength, are almost sure to be discovered clinically. It is assuredly the less potent carcinogens that seem most important in human cancer and provide the real problem for evaluation. A major objective of experimental carcinogenesis is, therefore, the bioassay for the presence of weak carcinogens.

(9) Chemical configuration alone cannot be used to predict the ability of a new compound to produce cancer.

(10) Possession (by a substance) of a biological effect, known to be associated with a particular type of cancer production, may be of importance in assessing potential carcinogenicity. Examples are: estrogenic activity, goitrogenic activity, production of liver cirrhosis.

The special attention given to the prevention of cancer is reflected in the Food Additives Amendment of 1958 and Color Additive Amendments of 1960. In principle, both laws recognize that all substances have a potential for harm and that, conversely, there are conditions under which most substances may be used safely. However, both laws also provide that under no conditions are cancer-producing substances to be considered safe. This Congressional expression of concern about cancer-producing agents indicates the need to know about the cancer-producing potential of food additives.

USE OF ANIMAL TESTS TO IDENTIFY
RISKS TO HUMAN HEALTH

. . .

Questions are frequently raised about the significance of carcinogenesis observed in animal experiments based on the belief that the high dosages to which animals are customarily exposed have no relevance in the assessment of human risk. . . .

It should be recognized that, generally, only high dosages will produce tumors in animals under the experimental conditions that must customarily be employed. In setting up model experimental systems, scientists have no choice but to use relatively small numbers of animals in comparison to the human population likely to be exposed. In order to obtain meaningful, consistent, and reproducible results, studies must be designed to produce a significant number of cancers in the animals under test.

Even as low an incidence of cancer as 10 percent in a group of 100 experimental animals, which would approach the limit of reproducibility, would exceed any acceptable human risk. An incidence of 0.01 percent would represent 20,000 out of the total U.S. population of 200 million, and would certainly be considered unacceptably high. But to detect such a low incidence in experimental animals using dosage levels comparable to those administered to humans would require literally tens of thousands of animals. For this reason, scientists administer large doses to relatively small groups of experimental animals and then extrapolate the results to estimate the risk of cancer at low dosages.

Several methods for making such calculations of risk have been employed, but based on present knowledge and experience, the Commissioner believes the proper conservative approach is to assume a direct proportionality between the size of the dose and the incidence of tumors. For example, if a daily dosage of 1 gram per kilogram (kg) fed to experimental animals over a 2-year period produces a 10 percent incidence of tumors, FDA would assume that there would be a 1 percent incidence with 0.1 gram per kg dose, or a 0.1 percent incidence with a 0.01 gram per kg dose. Using this method of calculation, the agency would estimate, conservatively, that if a substance produces a 10 percent incidence of cancer in the rat at a dose of 1 gram per kg, it would produce a 0.01 percent incidence, representing 20,000 persons out of a total population of 200 million, if ingested by man at a dose of 1 milligram per kg.

. . .

D. CARCINOGENICITY TESTING OF SACCHARIN

. . .

Because of the continuing questions about the carcinogenicity of saccharin, in June 1972, FDA once more called upon the Academy to review the results of all experiments on the issue. To be able to provide FDA with a complete and up-to-date report, the Academy delayed completing its review until several studies, including the FDA study, then underway, were completed.

The Academy's report was received by FDA in December 1974. The report's primary conclusion was that the data then available had "not established conclusively whether saccharin is or is not carcinogenic when administered orally to test animals." This conclusion was based in part on the uncertainty about the role of orthotoluenesulfonamide (OTS) [a contaminant of commercial saccharin] in the induction of tumors. The Academy recommended that additional research on saccharin be conducted to determine whether saccharin is a carcinogen. The Academy recommended further that FDA reconsider the question when a substantial portion of the additional data became available.

E. CANADIAN STUDY

The recently reported Canadian study was initiated in February 1974 under the sponsorship of the Department of Health and Public Welfare of the Canadian Government (Toxicity and Carcinogenicity Study of Orthotoluenesulfonamide and Saccharin, Project E405/405E). Two generations of test animals (the F_0 and F_1 generations) were fed OTS and OTS-free saccharin to evaluate the toxicity and carcinogenicity of these compounds. The study on saccharin was the third experiment in which rats were exposed to saccharin during their period of development in the uterus and then throughout their entire life span. [Earlier] studies had shown an increased incidence of bladder tumors in male rats, but had left unresolved the question whether the tumors were caused by saccharin itself or by OTS. The Canadian study was designed to clarify this question by testing the OTS by itself as well as by testing purified saccharin containing only minimal amounts of the impurity. The Canadian study was thus designed to resolve the uncertainties noted by the NAS in its 1974 report.

. . .

The results of the Canadian study have been evaluated by expert pathologists, including scientists from FDA and other institutions in the United States, from Great Britain, and from other European countries, as well as from Canada. *The findings indicate unequivocally that saccharin causes bladder tumors in the test animals.* . . .

. . .

F. ASSESSMENT OF HUMAN RISK

An important question raised about the animal studies on saccharin is their relevance to human beings. Public reaction to recent publicity about the Canadian study suggests considerable misunderstanding about the nature of toxicity testing in animals and the interpretation of results. For example, it has been widely publicized that the dose of saccharin found to be carcinogenic in rats is about 1,000 times that ingested by a human in a single diet beverage (when both doses are adjusted for the difference in body weight between rats and humans). Since this amount of saccharin would clearly never be ingested chronically by any person, some have suggested that these results have no pertinence whatsoever to human risk. In the judgment of FDA, this conclusion is not valid for the reasons to be described in this section.

Before dealing with the saccharin data specifically, however, the principles of appraising the risk of chemical carcinogenic substances should be explicitly stated. Those principles are as follows:

1. Certain substances can be shown in validly controlled animal experiments to increase the incidence of benign and/or malignant tumors. This result does not occur with all chemicals, only with certain ones.

2. Those substances that cause benign or malignant tumors in one species often also do so in other species. Therefore, any substance that causes such tumors in any species must be considered a potential carcinogen in man.

3. Chemical carcinogens, like other toxic substances, generally demonstrate a dose-response relationship, i.e., the greater the dose the greater the tendency to produce tumors, and vice versa. The predomi-

nant opinion among experts in the field of carcinogenesis is that the dose-response principle extends to very low doses of the carcinogen—that is, that there is no dose, however small, at which one can be certain there is no risk. In other words, there is no threshold dose below which a carcinogen may be considered safe in the absolute sense.

4. Estimation of the risk of a low dose of a carcinogen in animals requires that one test the carcinogen at a dose high enough to produce tumors in the group of animals tested and then calculate what the risk is likely to be at a very small dose. The intent of animal testing is not only to identify potential risks such as carcinogenesis but also to estimate whether such an effect is likely to occur with a frequency, e.g., of 1 in 100, 1 in 1,000, 1 in 10,000, 1 in a 100,000, 1 in a million, etc. Since the actual measurement of a single event once in e.g., 1,000 times, requires several thousand animals, it is evident that direct measurement of low frequency events cannot feasibly be done because of limitations on cost, the difficulty of handling large numbers of animals, etc. The problem is thus currently solved, albeit imperfectly and not without difference of opinion among experts, by conducting tests with a feasible number of animals at high doses and extrapolating the results to low doses.

5. The method of extrapolation of results obtained at high doses to low doses should be a "conservative" method, i.e., it should err in the direction of overstating risk rather than understating it. Two accepted methods that meet this principle are the linear extrapolation method and the Mantel-Bryan procedure. In the dose range under consideration, the two methods give similar results for saccharin. The linear extrapolation method has been used in the FDA calculation on saccharin because it is easier to explain and understand.

6. The results of animal tests and their extrapolation to low doses provides an estimate of the risk of developing a tumor in the species tested. If one is to assume that such results are directly applicable to man, one must assume that one lifetime in the test animal is equal to a lifetime in man and that the test animal and humans are equally sensitive to the carcinogen. These assumptions are clearly open to debate, but in the absence of data to the contrary, the opinion of most experts is to assume that they are applicable. In the case of some carcinogens, wide variation among species in their sensitivity to the chemical has been demonstrated. The current view of experts is that these differences are due, at least in part, to species differences in the way the carcinogen is metabolized. In the case of saccharin, the drug is metabolized little, if at all, in either the rat or man. This fact supports the assumption that results from testing in rats are applicable to human risk assessment. The FDA risk estimates are then based on the principle that risk estimates in the rat are directly applicable to man.

Current scientific methods are not capable of determining the exact risk to humans of a chemical found to be carcinogenic in animals. However, techniques are available for estimating the upper limits of the risk. The Food and Drug Administration estimates that the lifetime ingestion of the amount of saccharin in one diet beverage per day results in a risk to the individual of somewhere between zero and 4 in 10,000 of developing a cancer of the bladder. If this risk is transposed to the population at large and if everyone in the United States drank one such beverage a day, this would result in anywhere between zero and 1,200 additional cases of bladder cancer per year. . . .

In the Canadian study, a 24 percent incidence of bladder tumors (12 of 50) was noted in the second generation male rats fed saccharin in a dose of 5 percent of the diet. This was the most sensitive group in the study to the carcinogenic effect of saccharin. Thus, in the absence of evidence that factors involved in its sensitivity are not relevant to the human population, this group is used to estimate the upper limit of human risk. There were no bladder tumors in an untreated control group of comparable size. Although the observed incidence of bladder tumors was 24 percent, the upper limit of risk in this study at the 95 percent confidence level is 36 percent. A 5 percent dietary level of saccharin in the rat is equivalent to 2,500 milligrams/kilogram/day of saccharin. If a 60-kilogram human (approximately 132 pounds) were to ingest 150 milligrams/day of saccharin (i.e., 2.5 milligrams/kilogram/day over a lifetime, he or she would thus receive the equivalent of one one-thousandth of the rat dose per day. This dose is approximately that contained in one large diet beverage drink (12½ ounces) per day.

Since rats fed 2,500 milligrams/kilogram/day may have as high as a 36 percent incidence of bladder tumors, ingestion by rats of one one-thousandth of that dose could yield, by linear extrapolation, an incidence of 0.036 percent or 4 cases per 10,000.

The lifetime risk of bladder cancer in humans in the United States is 1.5 percent; that is, of every 10,000 persons, it is expected that 150 will develop bladder cancer sometime during their lives. Extrapolating from the Canadian rat study, and if one assumes a direct correlation between the estimate of maximum risk of saccharin in rats and humans, if a human ingests 150 milligrams/day of saccharin for a lifetime, he could increase the risk of bladder cancer by 0.036 percent, for a total risk of approximately 1.54 percent. That is, of every 10,000 persons, 154 might develop bladder cancer (if they all use 150 milligrams/day of saccharin) and if the assumptions are valid.

The risk from use of 150 milligrams/day of saccharin over a lifetime can be assessed in another fashion. The annual case rate of bladder cancer in the United States is given by the NCI as approximately 30,000. If everyone in the United States ingested 150 milligrams of saccharin per day (e.g., from one large diet drink) over a lifetime, and if the other assumptions are correct, there could be approximately an additional 1,200 cases per year (or an increase in risk of 4 percent over the basal risk). If only half the population ingested 150 milligrams of saccharin per day over a lifetime, an additional 600 cases per year could occur (or an increase in risk of 2 percent over the basal risk).

The estimated increased risk from this moderate use of saccharin cannot be detected in human epidemiological studies. Such studies usually can only detect increased risks of 200 to 300 percent (i.e., 2 to 3 times the baseline rate) or greater. Even the best feasible epidemiologic study is not likely to detect an increased risk of only 2 to 4 percent over background incidence. . . .

. . .

Although the risk from consumption of saccharin is small compared to that of other health hazards, e.g., cigarette smoking, saccharin is only one of a potentially large number of hazards present in our environment. The Commissioner believes that reduction of prolonged, general exposure to a number of weakly carcinogenic substances in our environment as they are discovered may be essential to reduce the total incidence of cancer.

G.   LEGAL BASIS FOR ACTION

Press reports of the announcement of FDA's intention to withdraw approval of saccharin as an ingredient in foods and beverages have given the impression that the Commissioner is acting reluctantly, based exclusively on the Delaney anticancer clause . . . ..

. . .

The discussion in the previous section makes clear that the human risk of cancer indicated by these findings is significant and cannot be ignored. The Commissioner believes that conscientious protection of the public health is not consistent with continued general use in foods of a compound shown to present the kind of risk of cancer that has been demonstrated for saccharin—regardless of the asserted benefits of its use for some individuals in the population.

Section 409(c) of the act (21 U.S.C. 348(c)) requires that any food additive must be found to be safe for human consumption before it can be approved or, in case of an additive already approved, continue to be used in foods. Based on the accumulated evidence of hazard associated with ingestion of saccharin, culminated by the Canadian study, the Commissioner concludes that the finding required by the statute can no longer be made, and that the interim food additive regulation approving the use of saccharin should be repealed.

. . . [A]lthough FDA has acted on a number of occasions to remove carcinogenic substances from the food supply during the past 25 years, only two previous actions—both involving minor indirect food additives— have been based on the Delaney clause.

Those actions, like this one, were based on certain well-recognized postulates about chemical carcinogenesis: (1) there is reason to believe that those substances which cause cancer in animals may also cause cancer in man; (2) animal tests, despite inadequacies, provide the best evidence currently available about the potential of chemicals to cause cancer in humans; (3) there is no reliable basis for concluding that there is a completely "safe" level of a carcinogen, i.e., a threshold level that will not cause cancer in some members of the population; and (4) cancer appears to be an irreversible process, in both test animals and in man.

It is of course true that the present law would afford the Commissioner no choice but to prohibit the marketing of saccharin as an ingredient in foods even if he were not persuaded that the scientific evidence independently warranted such action. . . .

. . . [U]nder both the general safety requirement of the Food Additives Amendment of 1958 and the Delaney anticancer clause, the Commissioner concludes that saccharin may no longer be approved as a food additive. . . .   The Commissioner welcomes comments on any facet of this proposal, including the reasonableness of his judgment about the safety of saccharin under the law. He feels constrained to point out, however, that the wisdom of the Delaney clause is not at issue in this proceeding. FDA could not ignore that provision even if the Commissioner were persuaded that the risks to human health were less than they appear. He further notes that under the provisions of the law relating to food additives, FDA is not empowered to take into account the asserted benefits of any food additive in applying the basic safety standard of the act.

NOTES

1. As the proposed rulemaking makes clear, saccharin could have been banned by the FDA even if there were no Delaney Clause. Have critics of food safety legislation been wrong, therefore, in focusing on the Delaney Clause?

2. Who did Congress intend should bear the burden of proving the safety of a food additive? Who in practical effect had the burden of proof on the safety of saccharin?

3. Did the proposed rulemaking persuade you that the FDA was justified in drawing the conclusion it did about risk to humans on the basis of animal tests? Why was it not possible to study the risks in humans? Alternative methods for identifying carcinogens and the limitations inherent in each method are examined in more detail in Section A.3b, infra.

4. It has recently been reported that Americans consume 10,000 times more cancer-causing chemicals naturally in their daily diet than from man-made pesticides. Certain foods also naturally contain cancer-preventing chemicals. Ames, Dietary Carcinogens and Anticarcinogens, 221 Science 1256 (1983). Ames predicts that because scientists soon will be able to identify both the cancer-causers and the cancer-preventers in the human diet and will try to bring them into balance, an era is near in which people will be able to "fine-tune" their diets to avoid many major causes of cancer. Washington Post, Sept. 16, 1983, at A1, col. 6. In light of these facts, was it appropriate to devote limited regulatory resources to a ban on saccharin? Did Congress give the FDA any choice? If the FDA had decided not to initiate regulatory action against the food additive uses of saccharin, could a consumer group have successfully sued the agency? What arguments could FDA have made in court to defend such a position? What ruling should a court have made?

iii.   The Reaction of the Public and Congress

RICHARD MERRILL, REGULATING CARCINOGENS IN FOOD: A LEGISLATOR'S GUIDE TO FOOD SAFETY PROVISIONS OF THE FEDERAL FOOD, DRUG AND COSMETIC ACT

77 Mich.L.Rev. 171, 171–172 (1978).

The FDA's announcement triggered public incredulity and congressional demands for revision of the nation's legal framework for regulating food safety. Critics of the agency's action focused on the much publicized Delaney Clause of the Federal Food, Drug, and Cosmetic Act. They characterized this provision, which forbids the approval of any "food additive" shown to induce cancer in man or in animals, as outdated and several critics also ridiculed the test methods used to evaluate the safety of food ingredients.[4] Reacting to these criticisms and to the public's apparent indignation at the imminent abolition of the only non-nutritive sweetener approved in this country for use in foods, Congress in late

---

4. For descriptions of the reaction, see, e.g., The Great Saccharin Snafu, Consumer Rep., July 1977, at 410; Demkovich, Saccharin's Dead, Dieters Are Blue, What Is Congress Going To Do?, Natl. J., June 4, 1977, at 856; Wolff, Of Rats and Men, N.Y. Times, May 15, 1977, § 6, (Magazine), at 88; Hines & Randal, Behind the Saccharin Uproar, The Progressive, June 1977, at 13.

Epitomizing the exaggerated reaction of many nonscientists was the proposal of Congressman Andrew Jacobs to amend the law to permit the continued sale of saccharin accompanied by the warning: "The Canadians have determined saccharin is dangerous to your rat's health." See Cancer and Your Sweet Tooth, New Republic, March 26, 1977, at 7, 8.

1977 enacted the Saccharin Study and Labeling Act.[5] This legislation forbade any FDA action against saccharin for eighteen months and directed the Secretary of Health, Education, and Welfare to arrange for separate studies of the safety and benefits of saccharin and of the current laws regulating food safety. The latter study and a major part of the former were subsequently undertaken by the Institute of Medicine of the National Academy of Sciences.

NOTES

1. The 1977 legislation forbidding FDA from acting against saccharin has been repeatedly extended by Congress, most recently by P.L. 98–22 (1983). Does it still make sense for Congress to prevent regulatory action against saccharin by again extending the moratorium?

2. Was it appropriate for Congress to limit FDA's rulemaking authority with respect to a specific substance? Should Congress attempt to review every regulatory decision? Compare the discussion of the legislative veto in Section A.7c, infra.

3. In 1983, an alternative artificial sweetener, aspartame, was approved for the full spectrum of uses of saccharin. Washington Post, July 13, 1983, at Al, col. 1. See also Ch. 4, Sec. D.3, supra.

How should the availability of aspartame affect the regulatory status of saccharin? Is it relevant that it would cost approximately $1.04 to sweeten a case of 24 twelve ounce cans of soft drinks with aspartame versus 3 cents for saccharin and 55 cents for sugar?

iv.   The Delaney Clause Reconsidered

As the proposed rulemaking on saccharin makes clear, the FDA is not permitted under either the Delaney Clause or the general safety clause to consider the possible benefits of a food additive in assessing its safety: the law directs FDA to analyze risk, but forbids the use of cost-benefit analysis in deciding how to manage that risk. The materials in this section address the question of whether the law should be changed to include consideration of benefits as well as risks by the FDA.

COMMITTEE FOR A STUDY ON SACCHARIN AND FOOD SAFETY POLICY, NATIONAL ACADEMY OF SCIENCES, FOOD SAFETY POLICY: SCIENTIFIC AND SOCIETAL CONSIDERATIONS

S1–S7, 9.12–9.21, MS2–MS4 (1979).

This report was prepared in response to the "Saccharin Study and Labeling Act," P.L. 95–203, November 23, 1977.

. . . .

Briefly, the law requested the National Academy of Sciences to conduct a study, based on available information, of:

A.   current technical capabilities to predict carcinogenicity or other toxicity in humans of food additives, contaminants and natural components which have been found to cause cancer in animals

---

5. Pub.L. No. 95–203, 91 Stat. 1451 (codified in sections of 21 U.S.C.A. (West 1977)). For discussions of Congress's motives, see H.R.Rep. No. 658, 95th Cong., 1st Sess. 6–11 (1977); S.Rep. No. 353, 95th Cong., 1st Sess. 2–10 (1977).

B. health benefits and risks from foods that contain carcinogens or other toxins

C. existing means of evaluating risks and benefits of foods containing such substances and existing statutory authority for, and appropriateness of, weighing risks and benefits

D. instances in which restriction or prohibition of substances do not accord with relationship between risks and benefits

E. relationship between existing federal regulatory policy for carcinogens and toxins in food and non-food areas . . ..

A further portion of the law required a study that dealt specifically with the technical means of assessing risks and benefits of saccharin and its impurities. In responding to the congressional charge, the National Academy of Sciences formed a Committee for the Study of Saccharin and Food Safety Policy. The technical report on saccharin appeared in November 1978 as Part 1 of the committee's report, under the title Saccharin: Technical Assessment of Risks and Benefits.

At the turn of this century, the major causes of illness and death were infectious diseases. Socioeconomic and scientific advances—better nutrition, sanitation measures, immunizations, among others—have so reduced the toll from infectious diseases, that today's major health concerns in the United States and other industrially developed nations are chronic diseases with multiple causes, particularly cardiovascular diseases and cancer.

Industrial development, however, also has brought changes in the human environment, which in recent years have been recognized as possible risks to health. The strongest evidence for environmental-health links for non-infectious diseases has come from studies of populations who have left their country of birth and whose traditional disease patterns have shifted to those of their new host countries within one or two generations, suggesting that environmental factors play an important role. To the extent that a disease is environmentally produced, the prospects for prevention would appear fairly good. Most chronic diseases, however, are caused by a combination of hereditary and environmental factors, and the details of interactions among such factors to produce disease are not yet well understood.

The concomitants of industrialization have parallels in the specific area of food. Technical advances have shifted concern about food hazards away from the microbial contamination that produced acute disease soon after exposure. Foodborne infections are now relatively well controlled through improved technology and appropriate regulation and inspection of food preparation and storage. The contemporary concern is with chemicals in small quantities and other hazards introduced by environmental contamination as well as by food production and processing. These substances may form part of a hazardous environmental background contributing to chronic diseases. Many foods are now processed in some way, and the proportion of the American diet composed of such foods has greatly increased. However, even unprocessed, raw foods may contain residues of potentially hazardous substances—pesticides, growth hormones, antibiotics, contaminants from packaging, or other diverse environmental contaminants. Furthermore many edible plants and animals contain naturally-occurring carcinogens or other toxic substances. Examples are spinach which contain[s] nitrates and potatoes which contain potential toxins such as solanine alkaloids. For nitrates, exposure from natural sources far exceeds that resulting from food processing.

Individuals are largely unable to control their exposure to these potential hazards. The substances in question are ubiquitous and information is lacking on which substances are likely to pose a risk and which foods contain these substances in hazardous amounts. Federal regulation of foods has attempted to control exposure to some substances. But public support for this effort, even when it is aimed at preventing a disease as feared as cancer, has become increasingly difficult. The scientific advances that have made possible the detection of contaminants in even smaller quantities, and the animal testing that can give early warning of possible human problems, have sometimes been greeted by the public with skepticism.

Difficulties in Present Food Safety Policy and Some Specific Recommendations

. . . Four cases are examined in Chapter 3 of this report.

- *Saccharin*—a non-nutritive sweetener added to many foods, for which there is no approved substitute; a low potency carcinogen in animals; some possible health and non-health benefits. Regulatory status: ban proposed in 1977, but ban prohibited by Congress pending outcome of the present study.

- *Mercury*—a contaminant, primarily of fish, which present technology can only partly eliminate; toxic effects on the human nervous system. Regulatory status: permitted concentrations established by FDA now being litigated.

- *Nitrites*—substances used to cure, color, and preserve meats, for some of which uses there is now no approved substitute, but the greatest human exposure is from nitrates occurring naturally and reduced in the body to nitrites; possibly carcinogens of themselves, nitrites can form substances (nitrosamines) that are high potency carcinogens in animals; nitrites prevent growth of botulism organisms. Regulatory status: unclear; nitrites continue in use, usually at permitted concentrations, although their use is currently under intense scrutiny.

- *Aflatoxin*—a natural contaminant of such common foods as peanuts, corn, and milk; a proved animal carcinogen of high potency and therefore a suspected human carcinogen. Regulatory status: formal tolerance levels proposed in 1974, pending completion of regulatory requirements; meanwhile, a higher, temporary action level in effect.

An obvious problem illustrated by the four cases is the presence of gaps in scientific information when a regulatory decision needs to be taken. In none of the four cases is current information adequate to remove uncertainty as to appropriate action. We do not know total individual exposure to either aflatoxin or nitrites, we cannot fully evaluate the significance of saccharin as a cancer promoter, and the multiple natural and industrial sources of mercury and its movement through the atmosphere and oceans need more detailed assessment.

Another major problem presented by the current law is the exclusion, in most cases, of both health and non-health benefits as explicit factors for regulatory consideration. This is especially troublesome when no substitute for a food with a suspected or actual risk exists. Also especially troublesome is the weighing of hard-to-assess economic and commercial benefits against uncertain or low levels of health hazards. The difficulty of accurately assessing both risks and benefits is a theme that pervades this report . . . . Nevertheless, the committee noted that in fact a regulatory agency often tacitly takes benefits into account in making its decision. The committee believes that it is better to have benefits defined, evaluated and openly considered when that is possible. Subjective factors (perceived benefits) also need explicit attention even though they may defy accurate quantification. Nonetheless, the committee reasserts that it should still primarily be risk that triggers government intervention in the food supply and the government must remain cognizant of the centrality of risks in food safety regulation.

. . .

Chapter 9

CURRENT POLICY ISSUES AND RECOMMENDATIONS

. . .

A statute permitting a comprehensive approach should define broadly the categories and degrees of risk, and should relate these to appropriate risk containment, the permissible type of regulatory activity, and the type of accountability to which regulation would be subject, by executive, legislative, and judicial review. The FDA should have statutory authority and resources to assess . . . the risk of all constituents in the food supply.

Degrees of risk can rarely be defined in numerical terms because of the complexity and constantly changing nature of the problem. . . . This report will not attempt to define risk categories with any precision. In arriving at risk categories, or sub-categories, the FDA will need to consider not only potency of the harmful substances, but the levels at which it is present in foods, the number and susceptibilities of people who consume the foods or food ingredients of concern, the amounts of such foods consumed by various segments of the population, and the type of health threat posed. A potent substance present in exceedingly low concentrations in some foods might not represent a health risk to consumers, but the same substance might be a hazard if it were present in other foods or in high concentration.

Categorizing substances by health risk will aid the regulatory agency in setting priorities so it can devote its efforts to areas of greatest concern. Certain kinds of harmful effects, such as irreversible effects and intergenerational effects, would be weighted very heavily. Even when these affect only a small portion of the population, or have a low probability of occurring, they would merit greater concern than would less serious effects that might occur with greater frequency. For instance, the equal probability of a mild allergic reaction and a carcinogenic effect call for rather different responses.

In order to act, a regulatory agency must take each item—for example, a particular food additive—and consider how to put it in some rank order, among the tremendous number and variety of others. For purposes of food regulation, this cannot be done by grading the items with precise numbers, on some linear scale, on the basis of scientific tests. This impossibility results not only from the uncertainty of some of our testing techniques, but also from the fact that various factors have to be taken into account—how probable an adverse effect may be, how severe the effect, how long it may take to develop, whether it affects everyone or only certain types of people, and whether its dangers may be averted by one or another type of prohibition, restriction, provision of alternative substances, or educational effort.

The problem is similar to those encountered in other contexts, such as the grading of meats (prime, choice, good) and the grading of students' performance (A, B, C, D, F). In cases such as these, the grader must consider many factors, not all of which are quantifiable along a single dimension. Furthermore, the boundaries between categories cannot be sharply defined.

Although the problem is complex, it seems necessary, in order to permit practical action, to authorize the Food and Drug Administration to assign each substance under review to one of a limited number of categories—three, for example—primarily on the basis of judgment about both degree and type of risk.

a. *Categories of risk. Without suggesting precise statutory language, the committee proposes that the FDA should be authorized to act differently for several broadly defined risk categories, such as high, moderate, and low. These categories at present cannot be defined by precise quantitative scientific standards, but would depend on informed judgment. Their function would be to provide a rating scale to help determine regulatory response and priorities.*

The committee emphasizes that risk and response are frequently multidimensional, non-linear, and hard to define. Nonetheless, practical considerations make useful the designation of a small number of general categories that can be readily understood by consumers. Three categories might indicate high or serious risk, moderate or intermediate risk, low or slight risk. The number of categories and the names actually attached to them should be chosen to be easily recognized and understood by the general public. They also should convey some sense of how the consumer should respond to the warning—for example "Dangerous. Use only when necessary and as directed in attached information." Each of the major categories could be subdivided for practical purposes. For simplicity this report uses merely the relative designations "high," "moderate," and "low." The designations would be based both on the toxicity or potency of the substances and the estimated level of exposure of the general population or various special subpopulations. The boundaries between the categories would presumably be defined so as to leave some latitude for discretionary judgment.

High risk foods or ingredients are materials demonstrated by experience, or suitable scientific testing, to be likely to result in severe (irreversible, incapacitating, or lethal) damage to humans, either in general or in susceptible subpopulations, with appreciable frequency.*

Moderate risk foods or ingredients are materials that, as shown by experience or suitable scientific tests, may cause appreciable harm to humans, either in general or in susceptible subpopulations, with sufficient frequency to justify regulatory action designed to modify their use.

Low risk foods or ingredients are those for which there is evidence of some risk, but the risk is neither serious nor frequent enough for placement in the moderate risk category.

Other food Outside of these three risk categories would be food and food ingredients that, under current knowledge, individually neither pose

---

* As an extreme example, food obtained in highly contaminated run-off waters from a mercury processing plant would be high risk for continuous consumption.

known risk nor the presumption of any significant risk under reasonable patterns of consumption.

b.   *Response of regulatory system based on risk categories.   Once the risk of a particular food or food substance has been established according to its potency and exposure level, and a risk category has been assigned, the optimal regulatory strategy must be selected.   This should take into account not only the risk of continued use but the risk of limiting or discontinuing use.*

In some cases, this may mean assessing the objective or perceived benefits so as to weigh them against risks.   But, the range of regulatory options for a given risk category should be broad so that the option selected can be carefully matched to the particular case.   In many instances an option lying between total discontinuance of use and unrestricted use may be optimal either temporarily or indefinitely.

The committee suggests that standard symbols (as have been used to warn of poisonous or radioactive materials) for each risk category may be useful as a means to alert consumers of the need for further information.   Such logos would require little space or cost.   Depending upon the risk category, further information might be required to be attached to the product or made available on request by the distributor.   Experimentation with such logos is necessary to establish their effectiveness.

The committee believes that, whether through logos or other means, consumers must be given the opportunity to play a larger role in food safety decisions.   Further research on the most effective means of providing warning and information to consumers is urgently required.

High risk—Regardless of health or other benefits, FDA should be authorized to ban high risk substances from the food supply.   A ban will be most appropriate when a satisfactory substitute for the high risk food or food ingredient is available.   If no such substitute is available, and the risk is clearly outweighed in well defined circumstances by significant benefits that are not available from safer sources, the FDA should be authorized to permit marketing of such substances, through restricted channels or with appropriate labeling, for limited purposes, to limited categories of the population, or under other restrictions.   Such high risk but essential foods or ingredients could be identified with a conspicuous and distinctive high risk logo, requiring an attached circular outlining the nature of the risk and the prescribed appropriate use.   The number of high risk substances made available for such restricted distribution would be expected to be small.

Moderate risk—If moderate risk foods are to be marketed, they could be required to display a conspicuous distinctive logo, designed uniformly to identify clearly the moderate risk category for all purchasers.   If foods or ingredients involving moderate risk have suitable alternatives or offer no significant health benefits FDA should be authorized to exercise discretion to deter their use by means that could include restricted distribution, financial disincentives, or outright ban.   Purchasers of moderate risk foods should be provided by sellers, on request, with a descriptive circular explaining the risk entailed and special precautions to be taken in consuming the particular food.

Low risk—Low risk foods should be exempt from special regulatory control, but not necessarily from educational efforts to reduce the risk still further by acquainting the public with the risks they may pose, particularly in combination with other substances.

General reduction of risk—Besides devoting its efforts to circumstances of greatest risk, FDA should take other effective actions to reduce risks where desirable. It should set tolerance levels that encourage or require efforts to develop new technologies to reduce risks. Such technology-forcing tolerance levels could focus on reducing the amount of risky substances in a food, or in [sic] seeking substitutes for the risky food or ingredient.

   c. *The consideration of benefits. When benefits can be estimated or objectively assessed so as to assist the judgment of the consumer and of the agency, FDA should be responsible for obtaining such assessment. However, it should continue primarily to be risk that triggers government intervention in the food supply, and the government must remain cognizant of the centrality of risks in food safety regulation.*

   As difficult as it is to get an authoritative assessment of risks, it is often still more difficult to make a precise estimate of aggregated benefits that may include components that are physiologically, psychologically, or economically defined. Physiological health benefits are sometimes easier to measure than other types of benefits, but any complete risk and benefit assessment presumably should include all benefits. . . .

   In a few, unusual cases, FDA may find that high risk foods or substances may have offsetting benefits of such importance, especially for specific segments of the population, that their distribution through special channels should be permitted, at least for special purposes. Under those unusual circumstances, such high risk foods or substances could be accompanied by a logo and circular as described earlier. . . .

MINORITY STATEMENT

January 31, 1979.

Fred P. Abramson (Panel I)   Helen E. Nelson (Panel II)
T. Colin Campbell (Panel II)   Sheldon W. Samuels (Panel I)
Joyce McCann (Panel I)

   The following points represent those major areas of disagreement with Panel II's report. The first six deal with food safety policy in general; the last two deal with saccharin specifically.

I. CLASSIFICATION OF FOOD ADDITIVES INTO RISK CATEGORIES SUCH AS HIGH OR MODERATE FOR REGULATORY PURPOSES CANNOT BE DONE USING CURRENT SCIENTIFIC DATA AND THEORIES

   There is no scientifically defensible way to divide carcinogens or other irreversible toxins into different risk categories. This was the conclusion of Panel I's report on saccharin, and is the predominant scientific opinion for carcinogens in general. The ability of science to quantify human risk has not advanced sufficiently since the formulation of the Delaney Amendment to permit the construction of a scientific rationale for such a scheme. Massive *post facto* human epidemiological experiments lasting for at least a full generation might accurately assess toxic risks in a quantitative fashion. Otherwise, we can only determine the qualitative potential for human risk. Having reached that judgement, we have reached the limits of scientific knowledge. An appropriate use of a categorization scheme is to prioritize possible hazards for additional studies.

II. IRREVERSIBLE TOXICITIES ARE DESERVING OF
SPECIAL REGULATIONS

The characteristics of a regulatory system for compounds causing irreversible toxicities, frequently highlighted by cancer, should be distinguished from the characteristics of a system for compounds causing lesser and reversible toxicities. A single policy which fails to separate these two widely different consequences is dangerous and unrealistic.

III. RISKS FROM FOODS SHOULD BE LOWER THAN
OTHER TYPES OF RISKS

The public has a right to food that is as free of serious health hazards as possible. The exposure group is enormous and the mode of exposure is by chronic ingestion—the optimal way for carcinogenesis. Applications of standards for occupational health, or comparison of food risks to risks from other sources is improper.

IV. DIRECT FOOD ADDITIVES SHOULD BE REGULATED
DIFFERENTLY THAN OTHER CLASSES OF FOOD
ADDITIVES OR CONTAMINANTS

The obvious reason is that it is easier to do something about a hazardous substance that is purposely added to food than it is to do something about a substance, whether natural or unnatural, which is already in food. Certainly, in the ultimate control of cancer, one wants to pinpoint the most important sources of hazard, and it is clear that some of these may be natural substances in food. However, it is not clear that this is the role of the FDA.

V. A FOOD SAFETY POLICY SHOULD INVOLVE
LITTLE AGENCY DISCRETION

The FDA has taken many actions in areas of food safety which indicate the tremendous pressures and complexities generated in the present decision-making process. It is hard to imagine that a policy which contains so few specific guidelines as that contained in the report could be a step forward. The proposed ability to consider benefits, while an attractive idea, is so vague that it appears to offset risks by unquantified benefits. The relative simplicities of our current food safety policy cannot be tampered with because the structure of which it is a part can only support regulatory decisions no more complicated than a stop sign on the street corner.

VI. A COMPARISON OF THE ISSUES RAISED IN THE CASE
STUDIES IN CHAPTER THREE WITH THE RECOM-
MENDED POLICIES IN CHAPTER NINE POINT
OUT THE WEAKNESS OF THE
PROPOSED SYSTEM

The four case studies presented—saccharin, nitrite, mercury and aflatoxin—were selected because each presents important problems which should be taken into account in directing food safety. The report is so non-specific that one cannot, with the possible exception of saccharin, deduce from it how these substances should be regulated.

Alternative Recommendations for Saccharin

VII. THERE IS LITTLE REASON TO POSTPONE A DECISION ON SACCHARIN UNTIL THE ONGOING EPIDEMIOLOGY STUDIES ARE COMPLETED

An examination of present day bladder cancer cases represents saccharin ingestion at much lower doses than the current dose, especially when the younger age of current saccharin users and the singular availability of saccharin as a non-nutritive sweetener are considered. Thus any presently detectable increase in bladder cancer based on past saccharin use should be viewed with considerable alarm because it could be a gross under-estimation.

VIII. THE CLASSIFICATION OF SACCHARIN AND ITS REGULATORY STATUS ARE UNACCEPTABLE

This minority report already has rejected the classification of risks into categories. A policy decision which requires only labeling, logos and/or brochures for saccharin is too weak. Although the committee feels that a total, immediate ban on saccharin would be undesirable, the health hazards posed by saccharin indicate that stronger measures be taken to protect the public. Both existing and new food additives should be expected to meet the same criteria. If not already on the market, saccharin would not be allowed as a food additive and therefore should be removed. However, the institutionalization of this and other already existing products suggests that a phase-out period be recommended in such cases. A fully advertised time limit, together with vigorous education of the rationale for the eventual ban will prepare the consuming public and the manufacturers. A period of three years for the phase-out is recommended.

NOTES

1. Consider the feasibility and desirability of each position advanced by the majority. How persuasive are the dissenters on each point?

2. If the NAS proposal had been law when the FDA confronted saccharin, would the agency have taken any action? What action would you have recommended if you had been the chief counsel of FDA?

WILLIAM B. SCHULTZ, TESTIMONY ON FOOD SAFETY LAWS, OVERSIGHT OF FOOD SAFETY HEARINGS BEFORE THE SENATE COMMITTEE ON LABOR AND HUMAN RESOURCES

98th Cong. 1st Sess. 292–303 (June 10, 1983).

. . . For the past seven years I have been an attorney with the Public Citizen Litigation Group, which is a public interest law firm founded by Ralph Nader. . . .

The purpose of these hearings is to review the adequacy of laws enacted more than 20 years ago. . . . Congress recognized when it passed these laws, as it implicitly recognizes when it enacts any statute, that they might some day become outdated. For example, the Delaney Clause . . . is based on the scientific assumption that an animal carcinogen poses a risk of cancer to humans. The question which we should be answering today is not whether the food safety laws, including the Delaney Clause, will work forever. Instead, the relevant questions are, have those laws worked in the past, and are they working today.

We submit that the facts support an affirmative answer to both of these questions. Only once in the past 25 years has Congress concluded that the result dictated by these statutes was inappropriate. In that instance, it intervened and reversed the FDA's decision to ban the use of saccharin as a food additive. In our view, the only justification for permitting the continued sale of saccharin was that Congress perceived there to be an [overwhelming] public demand for the substance. However, before deciding whether to support proposals to amend the food safety laws, the question which you should ask is whether there are examples of other additives which the FDA has banned or refused to approve, but which you believe should be available to consumers. If the answer is "no," as we believe it is, then in our view the single example of saccharin should not be used as a justification for adopting wholesale changes in the laws regulating food and food additives.

I would now like to turn briefly to the arguments advanced in support of repealing the Delaney Clause, since this issue seems to be a central focus of every discussion [of] food safety legislation. The Delaney Clause reflects Congress' view that the possible "benefits" of food additives do not outweigh the risk of cancer, however small. Thus, in the Delaney Clause, Congress required the removal from the market of any substance shown to cause cancer in animals.

There are essentially three arguments which are made in support of such a repeal. The first is that the Delaney Clause does not allow the FDA sufficient scientific discretion. As the argument goes, the Delaney Clause requires the FDA to ban an additive where a single animal test has shown the additive to be a carcinogen, even if the animal study is flawed. This is not correct. In fact, the Delaney Clause retains a large amount of scientific discretion for the FDA to determine whether a substance is an animal carcinogen. For example, even after its own study had found that saccharin causes bladder tumors in laboratory animals, the FDA waited five years until additional studies had reached the same conclusion before it banned saccharin as a food additive. Thus, the Delaney Clause gives the FDA authority to determine the quantity and quality of scientific evidence that must be provided before such a decision is made. However, once the agency has concluded that a substance is an animal carcinogen, Congress, through the Delaney Clause, has removed the agency's discretion to allow it to continue to be sold.

The second argument is that modern science has made the Delaney Clause obsolete because we can now measure minute quantities of substances, such as food packaging materials, which can migrate to foods and are considered food additives subject to the Delaney Clause. The argument is that the amounts, which often involve only a few parts per billion or even a few parts per trillion, are so small that there is no genuine health concern.

While it is true that it is possible to read the statute as requiring that such substances be banned, it is now clear that such an interpretation is legally incorrect. In Monsanto v. Kennedy, 613 F.2d 947 (1979), the United States Court of Appeals for the District of Columbia held that the FDA had inherent authority to exempt small quantities of substances from the food additive amendments, and thus from the Delaney Clause. This exception, sometimes called "the *de minimus* exception," applies only where the amount which has migrated is very small, for example one part per billion. In addition, under the *de minimus* exception, the Commissioner must find that, based on the small amount of substance found in the product, allowing the substance to remain on the market "clearly present[s] no public health or safety concerns." Therefore, the second argument for repealing the Delaney Clause depends on an incorrect reading of the statute, which has already been clarified in the *Monsanto* case.

The third argument for repealing the Delaney Clause is that the scientific assumptions underlying the provision are no longer valid. In essence, the argument is that it is no longer appropriate to assume that an animal carcinogen is likely also to be a human carcinogen. My understanding of the science is that this argument simply is not correct today. We may come to a point in the future where we are able to identify animal carcinogens that are not human carcinogens, and if that happens it will be appropriate to modify the Delaney Clause to take that scientific fact into account. However, insofar as I am aware, no one has yet identified a single example of a food additive which falls into that category, and it is unlikely that we will be able to identify such substances in the future.

When Congress was considering the Delaney Clause in the late 1950's and early 1960's, officials from the Department of Health, Education and Welfare and the Food and Drug Administration testified that the clause was essentially redundant of the general safety clause, which prohibits the sale of additives which are unsafe. They pointed out that, under this provision, even without the Delaney Clause, they would be compelled to ban any food additive shown to be an animal carcinogen. This analysis has turned out to be accurate by and large. In every major instance, including the case of saccharin, where the FDA has banned a significant additive on the ground that it is an animal carcinogen, it would have been required under the general safety clause to ban that additive in any event.

This redundancy does not mean that the Delaney Clause is unimportant. To a certain extent, the Delaney Clause sets the priorities for the FDA by requiring the agency to give elimination of carcinogens serious attention. For Congress to repeal the Delaney Clause would send the wrong signal to the agency, and could result in additional delay in banning dangerous additives, even if such legislative action would not affect the ultimate result.

Although it is not 100% certain that all animal carcinogens are also human carcinogens, this relationship has been shown in numerous instances. Moreover, our current scientific knowledge does not allow us ever to rule out the possibility that an animal carcinogen used as a food additive will cause additional human cancers. In the face of this uncertainty, Congress must decide who should bear the risk: the consumers who could develop cancer and die from ingesting carcinogenic food additives; or the food industry which could be financially harmed as a result of an incorrect decision by the Food and Drug Administration.

Depending on the product, Congress has traditionally struck this balance differently. For example, in the regulation of drugs, Congress has directed the Food and Drug Administration to balance the benefits of drugs against the risks. In certain cases, even carcinogenic substances are allowed in drugs because the therapeutic benefits outweigh the risk of cancer.

Food additives, however, are a different matter. In general, they are either interchangeable or unnecessary. For example, it matters little to the consumer whether the manufacturer uses Red Dye No. 2, another red dye, or no dye at all in manufacturing processed foods. Similarly, most preservatives are interchangeable, and not essential. Therefore, 25 years ago Congress enacted a statute which makes the assumption that any particular food additive has no unique benefits and therefore should not be allowed in food if it is a carcinogen. The theory of the provision is that we ought to eliminate the risk of cancer where we can. Through the Delaney Clause and other provisions of the Food, Drug and Cosmetic Act, we reduce human cancers by lowering our exposure to carcinogenic additives. One can admit that exposure to some carcinogens is unavoidable and still take the position that we ought to have strong laws regulating food additives to minimize our risk of cancer, when possible.

Hearings on the Delaney Clause in 1960 offer an educational example of why it is important to be cautious and of just how wrong the experts can sometimes be. As you will recall, the first Delaney Clause was passed in 1958, but there were no hearings or debate on the provision in that year. Therefore, the hearings on the 1960 Color Additive Amendments contain the first Congressional discussion of the Delaney Clause.

Among the witnesses was Dr. Thomas Carney, a Vice President for Eli Lilly Company.[1] The gist of his testimony was that Congress should not adopt the Delaney Clause because the assumption that animal carcinogens are human carcinogens was simply incorrect. As an example he cited diethylstilbestrol ("DES") which he pointed out had been found to cause cancer in a few species of animals.[2] However, Dr. Carney argued that this substance had been used in human drugs for more than 20 years and was so safe that doctors were prescribing it to thousands of women to prevent miscarriages. He then quoted experts who had concluded that in 1960 DES was safe for humans and that any correlation between DES and human cancer was "most probably mythical." [3]

Twenty years later we know much more. We know that DES causes a rare form of vaginal and cervical cancer in daughters of the pregnant women who took the drug. We also know that approximately 80% of those daughters have an abnormal vaginal condition called "adenosis" as a result of their mother's ingestion of the drug. In addition, a significant percentage of daughters will experience problems during pregnancy as a result of DES, and both DES daughters and DES sons may experience fertility problems. It seems to me that the DES tragedy is an excellent argument for erring on the side of caution, and assuming that if a chemical causes cancer in animals, it is likely, if not certain, to cause cancer in humans as well.

It may be true that Dr. Carney did not know in 1960, when he and his company vigorously promoted the use of DES as a drug and as an additive for animal feed, that the product would injure so many victims. But the whole point of the Delaney Clause is that in general food additives are not particularly important and, because there is so much we do not know,

1. Hearings on H.R. 7624 and S. 2197 Before the Comm. on Interstate and Foreign Commerce, 86th Cong. 2d Sess. 265–95 (1960) (hereinafter "Color Additive Hearings").

2. Color Additive Hearings 266–70.

3. Color Additive Hearings 268.

our laws are designed to require federal agencies to err on the side of safety.

. . .

I would like to close with several additional points. First, it is important to recognize that no law is perfect. It will always be possible to find [examples of substances] at the edges of regulatory statutes which do not quite fit into the statutory scheme. If saccharin is such a substance, then it may have been appropriate for Congress to overrule the FDA's saccharin decision. But I do not think we should allow this single example to justify a complete overhaul of the statute that would allow numerous other additives on the market for which an exception of the kind made in the saccharin case simply would not be justified.

Second, I hope that Congress will persist in asking anyone who advocates lowering the safety standards applicable to food additives to identify exactly what the problem is. In particular, advocates of statutory change should be required to identify which past FDA decisions the amendments would overturn. If there are very few such decisions, then in my view the statute should not be amended. In other words, "don't fix what ain't broke."

DONALD KENNEDY, TESTIMONY ON FOOD SAFETY LEGISLATION, OVERSIGHT OF FOOD SAFETY, HEARINGS BEFORE THE SENATE COMMITTEE ON LABOR AND HUMAN RESOURCES

98th Cong., 1st Sess. 29–46 (June 8, 1983).

Mr. Chairman and members of the committee, I am Donald Kennedy, President of Stanford University; from April of 1977 to July of 1979, I served as Commissioner of the Food and Drug Administration.

. . .

Levels of Risk

The general standards of safety for food additives are wise, and surely should be retained. They put upon the proponents of use the burden of demonstrating that the substance is safe. To those basic provisions have been added some more explicit ones, the best-known of which—the Delaney Clause—embodies a number of scientific assumptions. In prohibiting any amount of a substance that has been shown to "induce cancer in man or animals," for example, the Delaney Clause states a very strong hypothesis about the biological significance of very low doses.

My own view . . . is that the Delaney Clause is undesirably inflexible in two different ways. First, it leaves no headroom for scientific progress. Second, by increasingly requiring Agency action under conditions where the risks appear to be trivial, it invites public ridicule and disregard for the food safety laws. More generally, I thought then that the Delaney amendment should be made more flexible before it breaks, and I still hold that view.

Let me give a specific example of the sort of difficulty I have in mind. It seems almost certain to me, as a biologist, that some carcinogenic substances will be shown to behave as though there were a biological threshold for their action. Suppose a substance's role is to promote the release of a hormone, like estrogen, that itself increases the likelihood of cancer.

It would not be surprising at all to find that such a promoting substance has no effect on hormone release at low levels, but requires a certain concentration in order to trigger the critical event. Similarly, it is likely to emerge that certain species of test animals are simply inappropriate for demonstrating carcinogenicity in humans of certain classes of chemicals, because they lack the enzyme systems that, in man, serve to detoxify those compounds. The Delaney Clause in the present law provides no incentive whatever to seek out such exceptions and justify them scientifically. Accordingly, I believe that the language of the Delaney Clause should be revised to permit more scientific discretion in deciding whether a substance causes cancer. This could be done by changing the absolute character of its prohibition, so as to permit exceptions if there is a showing that the concentrations to be found or expected contribute no added risk.

"Acceptable" Risk

A more difficult question is whether the general standard of safety should be changed so as to permit risks that are insignificant, trivial, or negligible—all terms that can be found in recent legislative efforts to modify the food safety laws, and all of which imply the acceptability of some very small amount of risk.

This is a difficult question to talk about, partly because the language is itself confusing. The current standard is "reasonable certainty of no harm." You will note that this is essentially a probabilistic assertion: it concedes the possibility of error in our judgment about risk, but stops short of suggesting that a small but certain risk would be acceptable. Efforts to reinterpret or rephrase this concept, it seems to me, ought to be forthright. It is one thing to say that we can accept some small probability that our judgment is incorrect, but quite another to say that we are prepared to accept certain risks as long as they are small; the second formulation raises, directly and immediately, the question "how small is small enough?"

I think it is essential for Congress to face up to this question. For too long, all of our risk statutes have been almost deliberately vague on this point, sending Agency heads out with instructions that sound a little like: "keep the people safe, but be reasonable about it." That simply requires the Agency head to guess at Congressional intent, and then to take the heat for the Congress if the guess turns out to be wrong.

Risk estimation is still a poorly-understood science, and it adds to all the uncertainties of toxicology the additional difficulty of translating from animal effects to human risks. Nevertheless useful—though broad—approximations are possible. I would think that Congress might want to consider establishing a definition for negligible—say, one estimated incremental cancer death, lifetime, per million population. This risk would be quite modest with respect to others that could be prevented by very modest legislative intervention, e.g., by lowering the speed limit by a very small amount. I am not so naive as to believe that it will be easy, or even likely, for the Congress to legislate in this way. I introduce it here because I think it is a legitimate part of the debate.

Consideration of Benefits

I expect that you will be urged by some quarters to include consideration of benefits as a part of the regulatory process for food additives. This is a matter that, it seems to me, ought to be approached with a great deal of caution. Both the saccharin and nitrite * cases show that health benefits can enter the consideration of food additive safety in significant ways. Unfortunately, "health benefits" is a difficult term to define, and it can be made either so narrow as to be useless or so broad as to be limitless. My own inclination is to recommend that health benefits be considered and defined fairly broadly. But that health benefits should be considered only for those additives with a substantial history of use in the food supply, and where there is no practical substitute for the already-used additive; and there should be a stringent requirement that the health benefit be demonstrated, not just shown to be plausible.

Arguments will no doubt be made for the extension of risk/benefit comparisons to include economic benefits. I think that is a very slippery slope indeed, and I would urge you not to wander far onto it. Risk/ benefit balancing can only be carried out successfully in a limited universe where risks and benefits are measured in the same kinds of units. It is difficult to compare the health benefits associated with the protection nitrites provide against botulism with the health risks they impose. But at least we are talking about the same thing. Consider how much more difficult it would be if we were asked to weigh the health risks of a food additive against its distributed economic benefits! If Congress were to give serious consideration to such a provision, it should be prepared to state at the same time what dollar value it places upon a single human life. Without that, Congress will be making agencies accountable for a process Congress is itself unwilling to define.

NOTES

1. Commissioner Kennedy proposes a specific level of risk as acceptable, namely "one estimated incremental cancer death, lifetime, per million population." That is the level FDA has proposed for carrying out its statutory duties to regulate food additives or drugs given to food-producing animals. See generally 44 Fed.Reg. 17,070 (1979).

Congress in 1962 had directed the FDA to ensure that "no residue [of a carcinogenic compound] will be found (by methods of examination prescribed or approved by [FDA]) in any edible portion of such animal after slaughter or in any food yielded by or derived from the living animal . . .." Sec. 409(c)(3)(A) of the Federal Food, Drug and Cosmetic Act. No "method of examination," however, can assure that literally no residue is present. Every method of examination has a limited sensitivity and cannot detect the presence of a substance at levels below its limit. Therefore, FDA explained that to interpret the statute literally as requiring no—i.e. "zero"—residue would be inconsistent with the relevant legislative history, which plainly reflected an intent to permit the safe use of carcinogenic additives and drugs in food-producing animals. (Such additives and drugs are economically very important because they promote growth and efficient use of feed, and prevent or treat disease.) FDA concluded that what was needed was a standard for determining what levels of carcinogenic substances are "safe." With such a standard, the agency could require the development of methods of examination adequate to detect residues of levels equal to or greater than the "safe" level. Yet Congress had not itself prescribed a safe level.

FDA proposed to apply a standard of "safety" roughly as follows. It would require the conduct of studies to identify the metabolites and breakdown products that result from administration of carcinogenic substances to animals. These by-products or a suitable representative of them would be tested in a bioassay to determine carcinogenic potency. The resulting quantitative data on potency plus

* See Committee for a Study on Saccharin and Food Safety Policy of the National Academy of Sciences, supra. [Ed.]

data on human consumption of meat or dairy products from treated animals would enable FDA to project probable maximum extra human cancer deaths attributable to the carcinogenic substance. The remaining issue was what rate of deaths should be considered "safe"? Once that rate was specified, FDA would require the party proposing to use a carcinogenic additive or drug in food processing animals to develop a "method of examination" sensitive enough to detect residues so small that the rate of cancer deaths attributable to them would not exceed the "safe" level. If a method so sensitive found no residue, FDA would deem the statutory requirement of "no residue" satisfied. But what is the "safe" level?

Initially FDA proposed a level of one added death per hundred million people over a lifetime. 38 Fed.Reg. 19226 (1973). In response to comments that this would be unduly restrictive of needed additives and drugs, the proposed level was later lowered to 1 in 1 million. 42 Fed.Reg. 10412 (1977). On reconsideration, FDA adhered to the 1 in 1 million level and explained:

(a) The risk level of 1 in 1 million is an increased risk over the entire lifetime of a human being. . . .

(b) . . . [T]he extrapolation procedure [used] is conservative by nature. [Therefore] the maximum concentration of residues of carcinogenic concern that will go undetected in edible tissues is expected to increase the lifetime risk of excess cancer in humans by less than 1 in 1 million.

(c) This 1 in 1 million *lifetime* risk is expected only if the maximum concentration of residues potentially undetected in edible tissues is consumed every day over a lifetime. Because there is so little likelihood that these residues will be so consumed . . . the actual risk is likely to be lower than 1 in 1 million . . . . . .

. . .

(g) . . . It is difficult to choose between 1 in 1 million and 1 in 10,000 but the agency chose the more conservative number in the general interest of protecting human health.

44 Fed.Reg. 17070, 17072 (1979).

Despite going through several Federal Register proceedings on these issues, FDA has never adopted a final rule—principally because the costs of developing the data necessary to apply its proposed approaches appear to be prohibitively high. Are you persuaded that FDA's choice of the one lifetime death per million people is a sound one? Compare the proposal of EPA in July, 1983, to permit a risk as high as 9 cases of lung cancer for each 100 people exposed to arsenic emissions, which is discussed in Sec. A.5, infra. Reportedly, EPA had approved risks higher than the one in one million or one in 100,000 only once or twice prior to 1980, and then the level was one in 10,000. New York Times, Sept. 18, 1983, at A1, col. 1.

2. The Senate Oversight Committee pursued the issue of what level of risk is small enough to be acceptable in a colloquy that followed the presentation by Dr. Kennedy and one by Jere Goyan, his successor as Commissioner of FDA:

The Chairman [Senator Orrin Hatch]

Let me turn to you, Dr. Goyan.

Tommorow, eight distinguished scientists will appear before this committee, and one of the issues that they have been asked to discuss is the meaning of risk when it is defined as, quote, less than one chance in a million over a lifetime, unquote.

Now, could you tell us your understanding of what this standard means and explain why you believe, quote, among most people there is an inherent feeling that such a level of increased risk is reasonable, unquote.

Are you in fact saying that a risk of one in a million is so low that no public health consequence would result?

Mr. Goyan. Well, perhaps I am in danger of behaving in an anecdotal fashion as a former Commissioner, for which I would apologize up front.

However, in discussing these sorts of issues over a period of the last few years with a number of groups, if you tell them that you are talking about an increased risk of 1 in 1,000, people get very concerned; 1 in 100,000, they still show some concern. But there seems to be something a little bit magic about the one in a million. I confess, I feel it myself.

The important thing, though, is something I said earlier, and that is that by one in a million, we don't mean that you can then multiply that by the 200 million people in the United States and say that there will be 200 additional cases of cancer due to this substance over the next year. It probably means that we will never know—because there is usually no way of tracing back, because of the time difference between when you ingest a substance and when you develop the cancer—that there has been an increase. But all of our approaches to it are, as I say, so conservative that rather than being one in a million—although that would be our estimate—in most cases it is considerably less than that, and I really don't know what the difference is between 1 in 10 million and 1 in 100 million when you get down to that low a level.

The Chairman. Would you care to comment on that, Dr. Kennedy?

Dr. Kennedy. Well, it is a very difficult world. We live in a society, as you well know, Senator, which will spend large amounts of resources to save the life of a particular identified human being who is in danger, but feels quite differently about the spending of resources to save a marginal expected life, identity uncertain, over the next year.

I think that people understand that certain risks that are taken voluntarily are very substantially larger than one-in-a-million risks, but I think that we also understand that people have a right to take those risks where they are patent and obvious and where they can understand them, even if they cannot estimate them quantitatively.

When we talk about the food additive laws, however, we are talking about involuntarily assumed risks. We are talking about people who cannot be expected to memorize all the hazards and cannot be expected to avoid substances based on those risks; rather, we are talking about a general standard that we would apply to the entire food supply.

So I think it is reasonable for us to be quite cautious and conservative about those risks, simply because we are asking people to assume them involuntarily.

I don't think there is anything particularly magic about one in a million/ lifetime incremental cancer risk, but it is a number that strikes me, for the same reasons it strikes Jere, as a reasonable place to start. . . .

Are you persuaded that one in a million is small enough?

3. Would it be preferable, as suggested by the NAS committee, to permit the FDA to engage in cost-benefit decisionmaking in regulating the safety of the food supply? The next case study examines the experience of another regulatory agency (EPA) in regulating under a statute that explicitly directs cost-benefit decisionmaking. As you read the materials, consider how FDA would have dealt with saccharin under such a statute.

b. Heptachlor/Chlordane and Risk-Benefit Assessment

---

i. Congress Sets the Standard

THE FEDERAL INSECTICIDE, FUNGICIDE, AND RODENTICIDE ACT ("FIFRA")

7 U.S.C. §§ 136(1), 136(bb).

§ 2(b) **Imminent Hazard.**—The term 'imminent hazard' means a situation which exists when the continued use of a pesticide during the time required for cancellation proceeding would be likely to result in unreasonable adverse effects on the environment . . . .

§ 2(bb) **Unreasonable Adverse Effects on the Environment.**—The term 'unreasonable adverse effects on the environment' means any unreasonable risk to man or the environment, taking into account the economic, social, and environmental costs and benefits of the use of any pesticide.

ii. EPA Takes Action

ENVIRONMENTAL PROTECTION AGENCY, CONSOLIDATED HEPTACHLOR/CHLORDANE HEARING

41 Fed. Reg. 7552 (1976).

NOTICE OF INTENT TO SUSPEND AND FINDINGS OF THE IMMINENT HAZARD POSED BY REGISTRATIONS OF PESTICIDES CONTAINING HEPTACHLOR OR CHLORDANE

On November 18, 1974, I determined that the continued registration and use of pesticides containing heptachlor or chlordane posed a substantial question of safety and accordingly I issued "Notice of Intent to Cancel" such registrations pursuant to Section 6(b) of the Federal Insecticide, Fungicide, and Rodenticide Act, as amended ("FIFRA"). New evidence has recently come to my attention which confirms and heightens the human cancer hazard posed by these pesticides. In addition it is now apparent that the ongoing cancellation proceedings would not be concluded in time to avert substantial additions of these pertinent and ubiquitous compounds to already serious human and environmental burdens. In view of these recent developments which are discussed in greater detail below, I find that continued use of these pesticides during the time required for completion of the cancellation proceedings would be likely to result in unreasonable adverse effects on the environment. Accordingly, pursuant to FIFRA Section 6(c), I hereby issue notice of intent to suspend the registrations and prohibit the production for use of all pesticides containing heptachlor or chlordane other than those registrations exempted from the heptachlor/chlordane cancellation order. This suspension order shall become effective within five days of the receipt by affected registrants unless the registrants request an expedited hearing . . . .

. . . . The Notice of Intent To Cancel Registrations Of Certain Pesticide Products Containing Heptachlor Or Chlordane was based upon the following:

Data from human monitoring studies showing that more than 90% of the American people have residues of heptachlor epoxide and oxychlordane in their tissues;

Data from human stillborn infant monitoring studies showing that heptachlor epoxide is transferred from mother to child across the placenta;

Data from human milk monitoring studies showing that heptachlor epoxide is present in a substantial percentage of mothers' milk at levels ranging from trace amounts to 0.49 ppm;

Data from human food monitoring studies showing that heptachlor epoxide is commonly found in the dairy, meat, fish and poultry components of the human diet at levels ranging from 0.001 to 0.03 ppm;

Data from two test animal feeding studies showing that heptachlor and heptachlor epoxide caused cancer and the conclusion of the Carcinogenicity Panel of the HEW Secretary's Commission on Pesticides and their Relationship to Environmental Health that heptachlor epoxide was "positive for tumor induction"; and

Data from nationwide residue monitoring studies indicating that heptachlor and chlordane are highly persistent, lipid soluble and ubiquitous.

Additional Cancer Evidence

Since the issuance of the cancellation notice in November, 1974, I have received additional evidence which confirms the cancer hazard posed by these chemicals.

First, additional expert pathologists have reviewed both of the 1959 and the 1965 test animal feeding studies referred to in the cancellation notice. Their reviews support and strengthen the finding that these two studies demonstrate the carcinogenicity of heptachlor and heptachlor epoxide.

Second, new evidence of the results of additional 1973 test animal feeding studies conducted for Velsicol Chemical Corporation with heptachlor and chlordane have been submitted to EPA.[2] The heptachlor study reported a statistically significant increase of hyperplastic nodules in exposed animals with relatively few carcinomas. This result is itself indicative of carcinogenic action. In recent months, independent review of selected heptachlor and heptachlor epoxide tissue slides from this study by EPA consultant pathologists found substantial numbers of carcinomas. The analysis of the EPA consultant pathologist who reviewed all of the more than 650 heptachlor and heptachlor epoxide tissue slides found statistically significant increases in carcinomas of exposed animals over controls. In addition, a review of the animal tissues by pathologists consulted by Velsicol which has recently been brought to my attention found that substantial numbers of lesions originally reported as hyperplastic nodules were carcinomas.

The chlordane study reported a statistically significant increase in hyperplastic nodules and a substantial increase in carcinomas. Independent statistical analysis by EPA consultants demonstrates that at one feeding level (25 ppm) male mice exhibited statistically significant increases in carcinomas. Independent review of selected slides by the EPA consultant

2. Technical chlordane contains approximately 7% heptachlor and technical heptachlor contains approximately 20% of the gamma isomer of chlordane.

pathologists also found substantial numbers of carcinomas. A review of virtually all of the chlordane test slides by an EPA consultant pathologist demonstrated statistically significant increases in carcinomas of exposed animals over controls in both sexes at two feeding levels (25 ppm and 50 ppm). Selected tissue review by the Velsicol consultants also found substantial numbers of carcinomas in animals exposed to chlordane.

Third, human adipose tissue studies for FY 1973 have now been completed and confirm the residues discovered in prior years samplings, finding heptachlor epoxide in 97.71% and oxychlordane in 98.35% of the people sampled. Similarly, whereas the cancellation notice referred to a 1972 human milk study which found heptachlor epoxide residues in mothers' milk, new evidence from an EPA survey shows heptachlor epoxide residues in 35.09% and oxychlordane residues in 45.61% of human milk samples taken.

Fourth, it is now anticipated that the cancellation hearing could require as much as 18 months of additional litigation before a final decision could be reached. During that period more than 38 million pounds of technical heptachlor and chlordane are likely to be released into the environment through uses contested in the cancellation proceeding.

In view of the mounting evidence that these compounds cause cancer and in view of the large quantity which will be added to human and environmental burdens in the interim, I find that the continued registration of the contested uses of heptachlor and chlordane pending completion of the cancellation proceeding poses an unreasonable risk to the American people and thus constitutes an "imminent hazard" under Sections 6(c) and 2(e) of FIFRA.

. . .

Dated: July 29, 1975

Russell E. Train
Administrator

VELSICOL CHEMICAL CORPORATION ET AL., REGISTRANTS

Preliminary Statement; Recommended Decision

This is a proceeding under the Federal Insecticide, Fungicide, and Rodenticide Act, as amended . . . .

Velsicol Chemical Corporation, the sole manufacturer of the pesticides involved, filed timely objections to the notice of intention to suspend and prior and subsequent thereto many other registrants also filed objections. In addition, the Secretary of Agriculture of the United States, Environmental Defense Fund, Louisiana State Pest Control Association, Mississippi State Pest Control Association, Florida Nurserymen and Growers Association, Inc., New England Pest Control Association, Georgia State Pest Control Association, Long Island Pest Control Association, North Carolina Pest Control Association, Alabama State Pest Control Association, National Pest Control Association, Inc., United Pesticide Formulators and Distributors Association, Tennessee Pest Control Association, Pest Control Operators of California, New Jersey Pest Control Association, Maryland Pest Control Association, the State of Hawaii and the Pineapple Growers Association of Hawaii, were granted leave to intervene herein

. . . .

[Administrative Law Judge Perlman at the end of the proceeding refused to recommend suspension because he was "hesitantly unwilling at this time" to find that heptachlor and chlordane are *conclusively* carcinogenic in laboratory animals. Recognizing that the Administrator might disagree with this conclusion, he also made a series of detailed factual findings.—Eds.]

. . .

Findings

. . .

73. Hawaii is the world's largest producer of pineapple. The canned pineapple production in 1974 of 7.9 million cases represents 28 percent of the total world production. The gross income reported from the production of pineapple in Hawaii in 1974 amounted to 124.3 million dollars. Hawaii's pineapple, grown on 43,300 acres, employs approximately 3,700 people year around and an additional 7,000 during the peak of the season. The Hawaiian pineapple industry has experienced a decline in recent years.

74. The mealybug wilt disease is a highly devastating malady of pineapple. The affected plants do not produce marketable fruit. If no control measure is applied, the disease can spread rapidly and extensively, often over the entire field. The Hawaiian pineapple industry suffered a tremendous loss years ago from this disease prior to the development of effective control measures.

75. Mealybugs are the principal cause of mealybug wilt. Mealybugs suck sap from the pineapple plants. If the mealybugs are not controlled, the root systems of the pineapple plant will collapse. Ants have a commensal relationship with mealybugs. Ants carry mealybugs to and from pineapple plants, particularly from the wild growth in the outfield area to pineapple plants in the field, and ants attend or protect mealybug colonies on pineapple plants. All mealybugs excrete a sweet-tasting product referred to as honeydew. Ants particularly have developed the capacity to exploit honeydew as a food resource. Certain ant species such as the big-headed ant, *Pheidole megacephala* (Fabrioius) and the Argentine ant, *Iridomyrmex humilis* (Mayr), aggressively seek out honeydew producers such as mealybugs. The active solicitation of honeydew by ants increases the volume of sap imbibed and the amount of honeydew produced by individual mealybugs. In Hawaii heavy populations of mealybugs are associated with attendant ants. Elimination of these ants allows natural enemies, such as predators and parasites to greatly reduce mealybug infestations. In the absence of ants, the mealybug becomes surrounded with masses of honeydew which is a substate for fungi that will cover and eventually kill the mealybugs. Mealybugs on pineapple can be largely controlled by eliminating the ants which tend them.

. . .

77. Heptachlor is effective for the control of ants in Hawaii's pineapple fields. Heptachlor may be applied to the soil at a rate of one to three pounds of active ingredient per acre and as a foliar spray for the control of the ants at a rate of one to two pounds of active ingredient per acre. Applications of this chemical may be made at monthly intervals to the foliage for as long a period as is required provided that it is not applied

within 60 days of harvest. Chlordane also will give effective control of the ants. However, by label restrictions it can only be applied to the soil and only when there is no fruit present.

78. The only registered alternative for the control of ants in pineapple in Hawaii is mirex. Mirex, as a broadcast treatment of pineapple fields, may be applied only once in any twelve-month period. Mirex is applied at the rate of 2.5 pounds of Harvester Ant Bait "300" which contains 3.4 grams of active ingredient per acre per year. Wet ground or rain may make the bait worthless as an ant control measure. Oil in the bait is the attractant and moisture washes the oil out of the bait. Heptachlor can be used under those weather conditions where rainfall has rendered the mirex treatment worthless.

79. Without the control of ants the spread of mealybug wilt can accelerate and the commercial growing of pineapple could be in serious jeopardy. Mealybugs, as distinguished from the ants, can be partially controlled using diazinon or malathlon. Mealybug infestation at subterranean level, however cannot be reached with these insecticides. Without ant control, mealybug control by these two chemicals would be only a temporary restraint on the rapid acceleration of wilt.

. . . .

Conclusions

. . .

3. The Hawaiian pineapple industry has presented a very striking need for a pesticide to deal with ants having a commensal relationship with the mealybug, which is the principal cause of mealybug wilt, a potentially devastating disease in pineapple fields. It seems to us that mirex presents an effective and, perhaps, preferable alternative to heptachlor due to the small amount of chemical utilized although its use is not as flexible as the use of heptachlor by reason of label restrictions, that is, mirex, as a broadcast treatment of pineapple fields, may be applied only once in any 12-month period. Such restriction may, of course, be altered and mirex appears to be the preferred treatment of pineapple growers. However, mirex is the subject of a proceeding under section 6(b)(2) of the act and its continued use is in question although the fact that action was instituted under section 6(b)(2) would indicate less cause for questioning safety as distinguished from a suspension proceeding or a notice of intent to cancel under section 6(b)(1) of the act, the source of the cancellation notice with respect to heptachlor and chlordane. In any event, because, in part of the uncertainty as to the status of mirex under the act, the availability of supplies of mirex is questionable. In the absence of mirex, heptachlor need be available for this use and a great amount of heptachlor is not required. Heptachlor is applied in relatively small quantities, within prescribed boundaries, under close, professional supervision and at infrequent intervals. In addition, a zero tolerance exists for residues of heptachlor on raw pineapples. It seems to us that continued heptachlor use indirectly against the mealybug should be allowed during a period of suspension with the *proviso* that should mirex use be continued for this purpose at the conclusion of the proceedings . . . with respect thereto and the supply of mirex is once again assured, this suspension proceeding could, if deemed appropriate by the Administrator, be held open or reopened to consider the effect of mirex availability on these conclusions. The consequences of the absence of mirex and heptachlor

could potentially be very great to an industry which is already hard pressed. It is not certain that mealybug wilt would reoccur in devastating fashion absent chemical control, but the possibility is too real for the risk of no chemical treatment.

. . .

Herbert L. Perlman,
Chief Administrative Law Judge.

December 12, 1975.

Decision of the Administrator on the Suspension of Heptachlor-Chlordane

This is a proceeding . . . to suspend the registrations of the pesticides heptachlor and chlordane pending a final decision on the question of whether to cancel these registrations. As set forth in this decision and Order, I have concluded that the registrations of heptachlor and chlordane should be and are hereby suspended for some, but not all uses.

. . .

B. *The Recommended Decision.* In a 122-page Recommended Decision, Judge Perlman has set forth 95 Findings of Fact and 50 pages of Conclusions, leading to a proposed Order, which states: "By reason of the foregoing, the notice of intention to suspend is dismissed." For the reasons stated herein, I adopt all 95 Findings of Fact set forth in the Recommended Decision and hereby specifically incorporate them by reference in this final Decision. Notwithstanding my agreement with the facts as found by Judge Perlman, I have reached different conclusions on some of the issues presented and, therefore, partially accept and partially reject his recommendations.

. . .

1. *Hawaiian Pineapples.* Heptachlor is employed by Hawaiian pineapple growers to control ants, and thereby control the spread of mealy bug wilt. This disease rises out of a virus in the pineapple plant which is activated by the saliva of the feeding mealy bug. The mealy bug depends for transport from plant to plant and for survival upon the ant which feeds upon the sweet tasting exudate of the bug, which but for this removal would drown or suffocate in the exudate. Effective ant control, therefore, is essential to the control of the mealy bug wilt. This has been generally and successfully effected by the use of mirex baits. Mirex bait has generally replaced the earlier method of control through heptachlor soil treatments. To the limited extent that these baits are rendered ineffective by the excessive rainfall, foliar applications of heptachlor are made upon the matured plant.

Diazinon and malathlon, as alternative foliar applications, are considered ineffective against subterranean infestation. Mealy bugs, as distinguished from ants, can be partially controlled by these pesticides. Were these the only factors to be considered, the case for continued availability, of heptachlor for mealy bug wilt control would lack strong basis. However, a serious question exists regarding the safety of mirex which is presently being examined in an ongoing hearing under Section 6(b)(2) of FIFRA. As a result, there is some doubt cast upon the continued availability of mirex baits, as evidenced by a letter received late in the mirex hearing from the chemical manufacturer of the bait, representing that production of these baits has ceased as of July 1975, with no present manufacturer intention to resume that production.

The record clearly reveals that heptachlor is used on pineapples in minimal amounts within prescribed boundaries, under close professional supervision, and at infrequent intervals. In addition, a zero tolerance exists for residues of heptachlor on raw pineapples. Annual use of heptachlor for the Hawaiian pineapple crop is projected at only 7700 pounds, subject to the continued availability of mirex and the findings and recommendations which may emerge from the hearing bearing upon its safety.

While it is undisputed that mealy bug wilt is under control, this factor obviously does not eliminate the need to continue certain agricultural practices which appear to have achieved this condition. Indeed, this fact militates toward continuance of such practices.

In view of the uncertainties involving the availability of mirex, the fact that at the present time the amount of heptachlor used is very small, and the fact that existing alternative chemicals lack efficacy as substitutes, I must conclude that the benefits attendant upon the use of heptachlor outweigh any risks associated with its use on pineapples during the period required to complete the cancellation proceeding.

. . .

Conclusions

1. Based on the testimony of record in the suspension hearing and the considerations set forth in Part II of this Decision, I have concluded that the continued use of heptachlor and chlordane during the time required to reach a final decision in the cancellation proceeding presents a substantial likelihood that serious harm to man or the environment will be experienced during that period. I also conclude based on the record of the hearing and taking into account the economic, social, and environmental costs and benefits of the use of heptachlor and chlordane, that the continued use of heptachlor and chlordane during the time required to reach a final decision in the cancellation proceeding would be likely to result in an unreasonable human health risk and, therefore, that an "imminent hazard" within the meaning of section 2(1) of FIFRA would result during the pendency of the cancellation proceeding.

2. I have concluded further . . . that the benefits of continued use of heptachlor and chlordane for household, garden, lawn and turf purposes (both by private homeowners and by pesticide control operators), against ticks and chiggers, and as a constituent in shelf paper, during the time required to reach a final decision in the cancellation proceeding, are not sufficient to outweigh the human health risks identified, and that, in any event, alternative registered and recommended pesticides do exist and will be available to provide effective, economical pest control for these purposes.

3. I have concluded further . . . that the benefits of continued use of heptachlor and chlordane to control cutworms on corn crops during the time which may be required to reach a final decision in the cancellation proceeding are not sufficient to outweigh the human health risks identified; *provided, however,* that particularly in view of the difficult transition required to implement alternative cutworm control methods, the use of heptachlor and chlordane to control cutworm on corn crops should be permitted during the 1976 corn growing season. Accordingly, I have

concluded that the registration for use of heptachlor and chlordane to control cutworms on corn crops should be suspended effective August 7, 1976.

4. Notwithstanding the foregoing conclusion regarding the existence of an "imminent hazard," I have concluded that the benefits of continued use of heptachlor for control of the (1) narcissus bulb fly, (2) seed treatment, and (3) the pineapple mealybug, and the continued use of chlordane for the (1) Federal-State quarantine programs for Japanese beetle and imported fire ant, (2) the Michigan quarantine program for black vine weevil, (3) the harvester ant (in Oklahoma), (4) the imported fire ant, (5) the white fringed beetle (except on tobacco), (6) the Fuller Rose Beetle and other root weevils on Florida citrus crops, (7) the root-destroying pests on strawberry crops, and (8) white grubs in the State of Michigan, during the time required to reach a final decision in the cancellation proceeding outweigh the human health risks identified, particularly in view of the unavailability and cost of alternative treatment methods and the relatively small amounts of heptachlor or chlordane used for these purposes.

. . .

6. The effect of this decision is greatly to restrict the amount of heptachlor and chlordane which will be introduced into the environment during the time required to reach a final decision in the cancellation proceeding. The suspension of heptachlor use for household, garden, lawn, and turf purposes, together with the registrant's voluntary commitment to restrict domestic shipment of heptachlor to uses for termites, seed treatment, fire ants, and pineapples pending completion of the cancellation proceeding (i.e., most significantly, eliminating its use on corn), means that the amount of heptachlor will be reduced (by comparison to 1974 use levels) by almost 85 percent. Moreover, the amount of chlordane will be reduced (by comparison to 1974 use levels) by more than 70 percent immediately and, after August 1, 1976 (the effective date for suspension of chlordane use on corn crops), by over 90 percent.

While these reductions are the best estimates which can now be made, it should be noted that some additional heptachlor and chlordane will be available during 1976 from existing stocks. As set forth in the notice of intention to suspend issued on July 29, 1975, the continued use of stocks of heptachlor and chlordane in existence as of that date will be permitted. Although the precise amount of existing stocks was not determined in the suspension hearing, it was clear that at the time the notice of intent to suspend was issued that the continued use of these stocks would be environmentally safer than attempting to retrieve them, transport them, and then somehow dispose of the consolidated and remaining supplies. I also do not think it would be appropriate to penalize farmers, growers, and other users who have already purchased these pesticides with the expectation of being able to use them.

                                        Russell E. Train.

December 24, 1975.

iii. The Judiciary Reviews

ENVIRONMENTAL DEFENSE FUND v. ENVIRONMENTAL PROTECTION AGENCY

United States Court of Appeals for the District of Columbia Circuit, 1977.
548 F.2d 998.

LEVENTHAL, CIRCUIT JUDGE:

This case involves the pesticides heptachlor and chlordane. Consolidated petitions seek review of an order of the Environmental Protection Agency (EPA) suspending the registration of those pesticides under the Federal Insecticide, Fungicide and Rodenticide Act (FIFRA) for certain uses. . . . The order prohibited further production of these pesticides for the suspended uses, but permitted the pesticides' continued production and sale for limited minor uses. Even as to the suspended uses, the Order tempered its impact in certain respects: It delayed until August 1, 1976, the effective date of the prohibition of production for use on corn pests; and it permitted the continued sale and use of existing stocks of registered products formulated prior to July 29, 1975.

One petition to review was filed by Earl L. Butz, Secretary of Agriculture of the United States (U.S.D.A.). Secretary Butz and intervenor Velsicol Chemical Corporation, the sole manufacturer of heptachlor and chlordane, urge that the EPA order as to chlordane be set aside on both substantive and procedural grounds.[2]

. . .

The other petition, filed by Environmental Defense Fund, urges that the Order did not go far enough to protect against the hazards of heptachlor and chlordane use.

. . .

What is involved here is a suspension of registration of two pesticides during the pendency of the more elaborate cancellation of registration proceeding, initiated in this case by a November 18, 1974, notice of intent to cancel. This 1974 notice stated that there existed "substantial questions of safety amounting to an unreasonable risk to man and the environment" from continued use of heptachlor and chlordane.

On July 29, 1975, the Administrator issued a Notice of Intent to Suspend the registrations of most uses of the two pesticides.

. . .

[T]he primary challenge raised by Velsicol and USDA goes to the adequacy of the evidentiary basis of EPA's finding that the suspended pesticides present an imminent hazard during the time required for cancella-

---

2. Velsicol has voluntarily ceased production of heptachlor for the uses suspended by the Administrator, and has not really attacked the Administrator's decision suspending those uses. USDA urges that this makes the heptachlor issues moot. Although we put more emphasis on chlordane than heptachlor in this opinion, we cannot agree with USDA that voluntary cessation of production moots our consideration of the order of suspension as to heptachlor, since this voluntary acquiescence does not bind Velsicol; nor does it resolve the challenges EDF makes to EPA's failure to recall heptachlor stocks from the distributive chain and its refusal to suspend heptachlor's use on pineapples and for seed treatment.

tion. The standard against which we test that challenge is defined in Section 16(b) of FIFRA:

> The court shall consider all evidence of record. The order of the Administrator shall be sustained if it is supported by substantial evidence when considered on the record as a whole.

The standard of substantial evidence has been defined as:

> something less than the weight of the evidence . . . . [T]he possibility of drawing two inconsistent conclusions from the evidence does not prevent an administrative agency's finding from being supported by substantial evidence.

In applying this principle of review in the specific context of a suspension of pesticides, this court has reiterated that "the function of the suspension decision is to make a preliminary assessment of evidence, and probabilities, not an ultimate resolution of difficult issues. We cannot accept the proposition . . . that the Administrator's findings . . . [are] insufficient because controverted by respectable scientific authority. . . .

These decisions of our court also point out that the Administrator is not required to establish that the product is unsafe in order to suspend registration, since FIFRA places "[t]he burden of establishing the safety of a product requisite for compliance with the labeling requirements . . . at all times on the applicant and registrant."

SUBSTANTIAL EVIDENCE SUPPORT FOR THE ADMINISTRATOR'S DECISION

To evaluate whether use of a pesticide poses an "unreasonable risk to man or the environment," the Administrator engages in a cost-benefit analysis that takes "into account the economic, social, and environmental costs and benefits of the use of any pesticide." 7 U.S.C. § 136(bb). We have previously recognized that in the "preliminary assessment of probabilities" involved in a suspension proceeding, "it is not necessary to have evidence on . . . a specific use or area in order to be able to conclude on the basis of substantial evidence that the use of [a pesticide] in general is hazardous." EDF v. EPA, 160 U.S.App.D.C. at 130, 489 F.2d at 1254, quoted in EDF v. EPA [Shell Chemical Co.], 167 U.S.App. D.C. at 80, 510 F.2d at 1301. "Reliance on general data, consideration of laboratory experiments on animals, etc." has been held a sufficient basis for an order cancelling or suspending the registration of a pesticide. Id. Once risk is shown, the responsibility to demonstrate that the benefits outweigh the risks is upon the proponents of continued registration. Conversely, the statute places a "heavy burden" of explanation on an Administrator who decides to permit the continued use of a chemical known to produce cancer in experimental animals. Applying these principles to the evidence adduced in this case, we conclude that the Administrator's decision to suspend most uses of heptachlor and chlordane and not to suspend others is supported by substantial evidence and is a rational exercise of his authority under FIFRA.

Risk Analysis—Carcinogenicity of Heptachlor and Chlordane

Velsicol and USDA contend that the laboratory tests on mice and rats do not "conclusively" demonstrate that chlordane is carcinogenic to those animals; that mice are too prone to tumors to be used in carcinogenicity testing in any case; and that human exposure to chlordane is insufficient to create a cancer risk. They place strong reliance on the Administrative Law Judge's refusal to recommend suspension . . .. While adopting the ALJ's factual findings, the Administrator concluded that the ALJ had applied an erroneous legal standard in requiring a conclusive rather than probable showing that the pesticides were animal carcinogens, and concluded in any case that the evidence showed heptachlor and chlordane to be animal carcinogens. We affirm.

1. *Mice and Rat Studies*

An ultimate finding in a suspension proceeding that continued use of challenged pesticides poses a "substantial likelihood of serious harm" must be supported by substantial, but not conclusive, evidence. In evaluating laboratory animal studies on heptachlor and chlordane there was sufficient "respectable scientific authority" upon which the Administrator could rely in determining that heptachlor and chlordane were carcinogenic in laboratory animals.

We start by rejecting Velsicol's argument that the "cancer principles" EPA relied on in structuring its analysis of the mice and rat studies improperly biased the agency's open-minded consideration of the evidence. In brief form, the principles accept the use of animal test data to evaluate human cancer risks; consider a positive oncogenic effect in test animals as sufficient to characterize a pesticide as posing a cancer risk to man; recognize that negative results may be explained by the limited number and sensitivity of the test animals as compared to the general human population; note that there is no scientific basis for establishing a no-effect level for carcinogens; and view the finding of benign and malignant tumors as equally significant in determining cancer hazard to man given the increasing evidence that many "benign" tumors can develop into cancers. The Agency's reliance on these principles did not come as a surprise to Velsicol; they were included in the Administrator's Notice of Intent to Suspend; and as recognized in EDF v. EPA, 167 U.S.App.D.C. at 77–78, 510 F.2d at 1298–99, form part of the Agency's "scientific expertise." Velsicol was properly given an opportunity to put in evidence contesting those principles, but failed to demonstrate anything more than some scientific disagreement with respect to them. Velsicol's principal complaint—that mice are inappropriate test animals—was specifically rejected by the Administrator, citing statements by the National Academy of Sciences' Food Protection Committee, the World Health Organization, HEW's Commission on Pesticides and their Relationship to Environmental Health, FDA Advisory Panel on Carcinogenesis, International Agency for Research on Cancer, and Director of the National Cancer Institute's Carcinogenesis Program. Unlike the failure to adduce critical methodology that we criticized in *International Harvester*, EPA's specific enunciation of its underlying analytic principles, derived from its experience in the area, yields meaningful notice and dialogue, enhances the administrative process and furthers reasoned agency decisionmaking.

The animal experiments the Administrator relied on tested heptachlor, its chief metabolite heptachlor epoxide and chlordane. Technical or commercial heptachlor and chlordane both contain the substances tested. Five studies involved mice and one involved rats. Velsicol urges that only the chlordane studies can be relied on to support a findng of carcinogenicity for chlordane, and more broadly, that there was insufficient objective evidence of carcinogenicity in laboratory animals to find a cancer risk to man. The objective evidence Velsicol charges is lacking is evidence that the tumors induced during the feeding studies had properties of invasion (spreading of a tumor into adjacent tissues) and metastasis (spreading of malignant cells into nonadjacent tissues)—characteristics two of their witnesses considered essential definitional elements of "cancer." By contrast, the other pathologists consulted during the suspension proceeding generally believe that cancer can be reliably diagnosed by observation of tissue cells under a microscope (histopathological evidence) without evidence, or very much evidence, of invasion or metastasis. The Administrator concluded, on what we view as respectable scientific authority, that evidence of invasion and metastasis is not essential to the diagnosis of cancer in mice, and also found that metastasis and invasion had been reported in some of the studies where protocols for the study did not preclude such analysis. That a low percentage of metastasis was found in those studies was also explained by the failure to use the more sensitive examination techniques developed since the studies relied on here were carried out.

In reviewing and evaluating the studies relied on by the Administrator, five EPA witnesses and five Velsicol consultants agreed that animals fed chlordane and animals fed heptachlor/heptachlor epoxide in fact underwent cellular changes indicating malignancy. . . . The Administrator has adequately explained his reliance on these test results which show significant carcinoma development in treated animals. None of the tests yielded negative results; chlordane was shown to be independently carcinogenic, as well as to contain a carcinogenic component (heptachlor/heptachlor epoxide). We think it plain that the foregoing establishes substantial evidence supporting the Administrator's result, and that Velsicol cannot be said to have met its burden of overcoming EPA's prima facie case by showing that chlordane and heptachlor are not carcinogenic in laboratory animals.

2. *Extrapolation of Animal Data to Man*

Human epidemiology studies so far attempted on chlordane and heptachlor gave no basis for concluding that the two pesticides are safe with respect to the issue of cancer. To conclude that they pose a carcinogenic risk to humans on the basis of such a finding of risk to laboratory animals, the Administrator must show a causal connection between the uses of the pesticides challenged and resultant exposure of humans to those pesticides. He made that link by showing that widespread residues of heptachlor and chlordane are present in the human diet and in human tissues. Their widespread occurrence in the environment and accumulation in the food chain is explained by their chemical properties of persistence, mobility and high solubility in lipids (the fats contained in all organic substances). Residues of chlordane and heptachlor remain in soils and in air and aquatic ecosystems for long periods of time. They are readily transported by means of vaporization, aerial drift, and runoff of eroding soil particles. The residues have been consistently found in meat, fish, poultry and dairy products monitored in the FDA Market Basket Survey and are also frequent in components of animal feeds. This evidence supports a finding that a major route of human exposure is ingestion of contaminated foodstuffs. EPA's National Human Monitoring Survey data shows that heptachlor epoxide and oxychlordane, the principal metabolites of heptachlor and chlordane respectively, are present in the adipose tissue of over 90% of the U.S. population.

The population's exposure to these pesticides, in large part involuntary, can be divided into agricultural and nonagricultural related routes. Seven million pounds of heptachlor and chlordane were used as corn soil insecticide in 1975, producing residues which persist in the soil for several years after application. These residues are taken up by such food, feed, and forage crops as soybeans, barley, oats, and hays typically rotated with corn. . . .

There are several non-agricultural uses which involve a large volume of heptachlor and chlordane as well as significant human exposures. For example, the record shows that approximately six million pounds of chlordane are used annually on home lawns and gardens. The Administrator found that these uses involve high risks of human intake "due to the many avenues which exist for direct exposure, through improper handling and misuse, inhalation, and absorption through the skin from direct contact." Velsicol asserts that the mice studies showing carcinogenic effects after ingestion of chlordane do not warrant an inference about the carcinogenic effects of inhaling it or absorbing it through the skin, and that consequently nonagricultural routes of exposure cannot be considered to present a cancer risk. They rely on Reserve Mining Co. v. EPA, 514 F.2d 492 (8th Cir. 1975) (en banc). That reliance is misplaced. In that case, the court was concerned with the propriety of the district court's granting the immediate relief of shutting down a plant discharging asbestos fibers into the City of Duluth's drinking water source. It instead ordered cesssation of dumping within a "reasonable time" pursuant to the unstructured equitable discretion given the court under the Federal Water Pollution Control Act, even though it had concluded that continued discharge posed a hazard to health. By contrast, the FIFRA statutory scheme mandates explicit relief—the suspension of registration—when an unreasonable risk to health is made out. We have previously held that it is not necessary to have evidence on a specific use to be able to conclude that the use of a pesticide in general is hazardous. Once the initial showing of hazard is made for one mode of exposure in a suspension proceeding, and the pesticide is shown to be present in human tissues, the burden shifts to the registrant to rebut the inference that other modes of exposure may also pose a carcinogenic hazard for humans. Velsicol has totally failed to meet that burden here. Although it was put on notice in the Notice to Suspend of EPA's intent to rely on direct inhalation and dermal exposure as reasons to suspend household lawn and turf uses of chlordane, it failed to offer even a medical theory as to why the significant inhalation or dermal exposure associated with such uses would *not* pose a carcinogenic threat. In view of the general failure to understand the mechanics of carcinogenicity, the lack of hypothetical explanation may be based on Velsicol's own data that exposure to vapors of chlordane and heptachlor in the work place, leads (as dietary exposure leads) to storage of oxychlordane, heptachlor epoxide, and other components in the fat tissue, and to circulation of these compounds in the blood, with consequent exposure to other organs in the body. Nor did Velsicol focus on the individual user's intense inhalation exposure associated with lawn and turf uses in its response to the point made in the EPA Staff's exceptions to the ALJ recommended decision, that the evidence showed that an individual using these chemicals for lawn and turf applications is subjected to a marked intensity of inhalation. Instead Velsicol attacked as inconsistent with the minimal amounts of chlordane and heptachlor normally found in ambient air, the EPA Staff's proposed reliance on inhalation as a major route of human exposure for the general population. However, the Administrator did not proceed on this basis. And if Velsicol hypothesized that chlordane residues are safe so long as they reach the tissue only through inhalation (even intense inhalation) it should have presented witnesses expressing that hypothesis. Instead they argue, in general and procedural terms, that the evidence presented by the Administrator was not sufficient to meet his full burden, and this in our view seeks to impose a broader burden on the Administrator than is appropriate in a suspension proceeding.

Benefits

Velsicol and USDA challenge the Administrator's finding that the benefits derived from the suspended uses of chlordane do not outweigh the harms done. EDF urges that the Administrator's decision to continue some uses was not justified by evidence that the risk of harm was outweighed by benefits from the continued uses.

1.   *Use on Corn*

Heptachlor and chlordane were used on an estimated 3.5% of the total corn acreage in the United States in 1975, largely in an effort to control black cutworm. Cutworms sporadically infest 2 to 8% of total U.S. corn farms, and occur most often in lowland, river bottom areas. Chlordane and heptachlor are used as preplant treatments to insure against possible infestations. The Administrator found, with record support, that no macro-economic impact will occur as a result of suspending those pesticides. He also found that crop surveillance or "scouting" for infestations during the early weeks of plant growth, together with application of post-emergence baits or sprays where necessary, provide an effective alternative to the more indiscriminate prophylactic use of chlordane and heptachlor. Velsicol urges that this approach is not as effective as the persistent protection provided by chlordane. Especially in the absence of proof of a serious threat to the nation's corn, there is no requirement that a pesticide can be suspended only if alternatives to its use are absolutely equivalent in effectiveness. The Administrator reasonably took into account that a transition period would be necessary to implement post-emergent techniques of control and concluded that the challenged pesticides could continue in use for corn protection until August 1, 1976. This evaluation of alternatives and the time required to implement them is supported by substantial evidence, and we find no basis to disturb the Administrator's balancing of costs and benefits.

2.   *Miscellaneous Agricultural Uses*

The Administrator suspended a number of agricultural uses where the record was insufficient to support any finding that benefits outweigh costs of continued use of heptachlor or chlordane on these crops. Possibly the lack of benefits evidence reflected readily available alternatives, possibly a relative lack of interest in lesser-volume uses. In any event, the registrant's failure to carry its burden of adducing sufficient evidence on benefits in effect leaves the Administrator nothing to weigh in his cost-benefit analysis except the evidence that the use of the challenged pesticides in general is hazardous. That evidence of general hazard is sufficient to support a suspension of uses.

3. *Non-Agricultural Uses Suspended by the Administrator*

Chlordane is a common household, lawn, garden, and ornamental turf insecticide, with over 7.5 million pounds (36% of total use) so employed in 1974. The ALJ and Administrator found on the basis of substantial evidence that the "efficaciousness of the substitutes for control of household and lawn insects is not really at issue" and that when lack of evidence of substantial benefits from continued use is weighed against the special hazards of exposure presented by the possibilities of inhalation, dermal absorption, and the increased dangers associated with improper handling, suspension of those uses was justified. Similarly, on the basis of evidence in the record, the Administrator could reasonably find that the residual capacity of chlordane was not necessary to control either structural pests or ticks and chiggers, given the existence of effective alternatives to each of those uses.

4. *The Administrator's Refusal to Suspend Certain Uses*

EDF challenges the Administrator's refusal to suspend use of chlordane or heptachlor on strawberries, for seed treatment, pineapples, the white fringed beetle, Florida citrus, white grubs in Michigan, narcissi bulbs, harvester ants, imported fire ant, Japanese beetle quarantine, and black vine weevil quarantine in Michigan. Following the recommendations of the ALJ, the Administrator found that for each use the benefits outweighed the risks for the limited time under consideration, effective alternatives were generally not available, and that the exposure risk arising from the use was minimal. EDF counters that the total exposure resulting from these "minor" uses is in fact significant, and that the Administrator continued these uses whenever a "colorable" case of benefits had been made out.

Once the Administrator has found that a risk inheres in the use of a pesticide, he has an obligation to explain how the benefits of continued use outweigh that risk. We are satisfied that he has met that obligation here, and that substantial evidence supports his decision. We note, however, that we come to this conclusion in the context of a suspension proceeding where perforce the Administrator is engaged in making a "preliminary assessment" of the evidence; a more careful exploration of economic impact and available alternatives would be required to support continued registration in a cancellation proceeding.

Continued Sale and Use of Existing Stocks of Chlordane and Heptachlor for Suspended Uses

Although we have no doubt that the Administrator has the power under FIFRA to exempt from a suspension order the use of existing stocks (in this case stocks existing as of July 29, 1975), the Administrator acted arbitrarily when he failed to even inquire into the amount of stocks left, and the problem of returning and disposing of them. *Some* evidence must be adduced before an exemption decision is made, and it is the responsibility of the registrant to provide it. It may be that the lapse of time has lessened the current significance of this issue but we are in no position to do other than remand for further consideration.

We affirm the Agency's suspension order of December 24, 1975, as clarified by the order of January 19, 1976, except for the exemption of the sale and use of existing stocks. The record is remanded for further consideration of that issue.

So ordered.

iv.   Aftermath

R. JEFFREY SMITH,
HAWAIIAN MILK CONTAMINATION CREATES ALARM

217 Science 137–139 (1982).

The analysis of milk samples at Albert Oda's laboratory was usually a routine matter. Every 6 months, colleagues of his in the Hawaii health department would collect some samples from local dairies to determine whether the milk was contaminated by pesticides. Roughly 9 million pounds of pesticides are used in Hawaii each year, and contamination is regarded as an ever-present threat but an unlikely occurrence. Oda says that the tests were always negative—until 21 January.

On that day, samples from several dairy farms and a milk plant on Oahu were shown to contain extraordinarily high levels of heptachlor . . . . Remarkably, health department officials reacted to this discovery as if nothing was seriously amiss. They allowed the milk to be sold and consumed. They sent the samples to a federal laboratory in San Francisco for confirmation. They waited. When the results were confirmed, they thought about it for awhile. They decided to collect more samples. When it was determined that these too contained heptachlor, still more samples were sought.

The public was finally informed 57 days after the initial discovery, when inquiries from a Honolulu newspaper forced the department to admit that milk supplies were contaminated. A limited recall was announced, and the remaining stocks were certified as pesticide-free. Within a few days, it developed that remaining stocks were also contaminated, and a more sweeping recall was issued. In this manner, department officials repeatedly certified milk and milk products, backtracked, and issued additional recalls.

After 11 successive milk recalls, public confidence in the dairy industry and state regulators has been shaken. . . . And many of Oahu's 19 dairy farms are reeling in the face of enormous financial losses.

The parties involved are all anxious to blame someone else. The dairymen have sued one of the state's principal pineapple growers, the Del Monte Corporation, for $31 million, and another grower, Castle and Cooke Inc. (Dole), for unspecified damages, claiming that their cattle ingested the heptachlor in feed made from pineapple leaves. The state attorney general is weighing suits against the dairies and the pineapple growers. A citizen is suing the dairies and the state, seeking an injunction against the continued sale of contaminated milk. And there is a good chance that the entire country will foot the bill, through an obscure program in the federal Department of Agriculture, designed expressly to compensate dairy farmers for the loss of milk due to contamination by pesticides.

In the weeks after the contamination was revealed, health department officials sought vigorously to calm public fears that milk consumed during the regulatory delay was harmful. They did so in large part on the advice of scientists at the University of Hawaii, several of whom argued that the threat to public health was less serious than the potentially adverse consequences for the dairy industry. The medical consequences of the heptachlor exposure—if any—will not be manifest for years, but several other experts are concerned that infants in particular will suffer a heightened risk of leukemia or liver disorders. Studies of infant mortality during the period of exposure and potential liver enlargements in the subsequent period are being organized at a children's hospital and a state research center.

. . .

Pineapple growers discovered in the 1940's that wilt could best be controlled by pesticides that eliminated the ant, and since then have sprayed millions of pounds of DDT, mirex, and heptachlor on their crops.

When the growers ultimately received federal permission to continue using heptachlor until an alternative was developed, they were supposed to abide by a requirement that green chop [pineapple leaves] would not be collected and fed to cattle within a year of the most recent pesticide spraying. Heptachlor does not degrade significantly in a year, but it becomes more dilute as the plant continues growing. The purpose of the requirement was apparently to ensure that the resultant heptachlor levels in a single batch of milk would be less than the maximum permitted by federal Food and Drug Administration (FDA) regulations. Now, in two lawsuits against the growers, the dairymen claim that this regulaton was not followed—that Dole and Del Monte illegally sold leaves that had been recently sprayed. The state's agriculture department recently examined this charge at the request of the federal Environmental Protection Agency (EPA), but forwarded its report to the state's attorney general and to EPA without official comment. The irony is that it was the dairymen themselves, acting through their cooperative, who physically cleared the fields, and the growers who merely let them in, possibly too soon.

The state is still uncertain how long the feed, and thus the state's milk and milk products, have been contaminated. Stored samples of chop that were harvested as long ago as April 1981 were recently shown to contain levels of heptachlor as high as those that appeared last January. Oda maintains that the state's monitoring program picked up no signs of heptachlor contamination in milk in June 1981, although he cannot explain the discrepancy between this result and the high level of contamination in the feed then. He says that he cannot recheck the milk data from last June because the gas chromatograph slides were discarded in accordance with standard office procedure. If Oda's results from last June are somehow incorrect, or if the sampling was not truly representative of the market, there is a considerable likelihood that Hawaiian citizens have consumed highly contaminated milk and milk products for a year, and possibly longer. Lower, but still significant, quantities of heptachlor have been found in chop samples more than 2 years old.

NOTES

1. What practical alternatives to the regulatory scheme of FIFRA are available for the regulation of pesticides? Could pesticides be sensibly regulated under a Delaney Clause-type standard?

2. Are any techniques available to Congress to reduce the discretion vested in EPA by FIFRA short of a ban on the weighing of benefits exemplified by the Delaney Clause? Would it be preferable, for example, for Congress to decide in advance how much a human life is worth by specifying what costs might be imposed on industry to reduce the risk by a given amount?

3.   Did the court effectively review EPA's weighing of risks and benefits in the heptachlor decision? Judge Levanthal in Ethyl Corp. v. EPA, see Ch. 4, Sec. D.1, supra, argued that "[o]nce the presumption of regularity in an agency action is challenged with a technical submission, and even to determine whether such a challenge has been made, the agency's record and reasoning has to be looked at." Did he comply with his own standard in this case?

4.   Does the subsequent history of heptachlor in Hawaii show that EPA was wrong to permit the use of heptachlor on pineapples? Does it suggest that the FIFRA standard vests too much discretion in EPA?

2. UNDERSTANDING RISK: THE TENSION BETWEEN OBJECTIVE AND SUBJECTIVE RISK IDENTIFICATION

a. Defining Risk

WILLIAM LOWRANCE, THE NATURE OF RISK

in Societal Risk Assessment
5–8 (R. Schwing and W. Albers, Jr. eds. 1980).

We begin to be taught about risks from a very early age: "Don't run; you'll skin your knees!" "Don't go near the water!" "Don't chase your ball into the street!" "Stay away from the stove!" We are taught moderation: "Don't swing so high; you'll fall out." We learn that Nature is capricious: "Bring your umbrella; it may rain." "Don't aggravate the dog; he'll bite you." At the beach, the tide comes in and, to our tears, washes away our sandcastles. We learn that technology has its limits: higher and higher we stack our building blocks, until they topple. Our board-bridge over the creek works fine the first summer, but the second summer it becomes rotten, cracks, and dumps somebody in the water. Generality is imparted by classical teachings: the Careless Little Pig builds his house of straw, but the Wise Little Pig builds his of brick. . . . We get safety instruction in swimming class. We are taught to be careful in using household appliances and tools. As we become of independent age we learn about the risks in driving automobiles and fooling around with sex, alcohol, and drugs. In all of this we learn about particular risks and become sensitized to the nature of risk-taking. Then, of course, as we grow into adults, it all gets terribly complicated.

WHAT IS "RISK?"

I prefer to define "risk" as a compound measure of the probability and magnitude of adverse effect.

Thus a statement about "risk" is a description of the likelihood and consequences of harmful effect. We are familiar with parallels from financial investment and from gambling: "There is a very small chance that you will win the jackpot, but a large chance that you will simply contribute to that jackpot", and from weather prediction: "The chance of a snowstorm is 80%".

Risk may be expressed in many ways: number of lives lost per year, or average shortening of lifespan, or degree of loss of hearing, or frequency of chromosomal mutations.

Once the size of a risk is estimated, whether by intuitive guestimate or by formal empirical analysis, larger personal and social decisions have to be made about whether to bear that risk, taking into account many normative factors. . . .

From our dreary experience with personal misjudgments and technological surprises, it is only too clear that we are not able to size up all threats with equal precision and accuracy. At one extreme are untoward events that are so familiar that they can be expressed actuarially: the classic example is highway fatalities, the statistics on which are tallied regularly and which do not vary in number or pattern very much from year to year. (Of course, although we know these numbers for groups of people, and can use them in calculating the odds of misfortune for given individuals, we are helpless to know for sure what will happen to particular people.) At this extreme, then, for risks that have a long recorded history of repeated events, we know the odds. That is, this knowledge is recorded within our social ledgers; indivduals may or may not avail themselves of this knowledge, and even those who bother to enquire about the numbers may not be able to grasp what the numbers really mean or how they compare with other such risk numbers. At the other extreme are risks about which we have almost no knowledge. Surely we in this room are exposed to unknown or barely-known hazards at this very moment: trace chemicals unknown to the best chemists, antigens not yet identified, ultrasonic vibrations, microscopic flora breeding luxuriously in the carpets and in the dark crannies of the ventilating system, weak electromagnetic radiation. . . . Even hazards we partially understand, we have trouble predicting with specificity: how bad the 'flu epidemic will turn out to be, when the earthquake will occur.

Notice that across this entire range, from well-known hazards to ones only imagined, estimates of risk can be made using the tools of science: empirical knowledge, developed systematically within the prevailing orthodoxy of the scientific community, subject to the tests of repeatability, control, and the other guides of Western science, and evaluatable in retrospect on grounds of predictive power. . . .

[E]stimates of risk, whether made by scientists or by laypeople, cannot escape containing elements of "subjectivity", of human opinion. Subjectivity enters into the very defining of the questions, and into the designing of the experiments used in assembling evidence, and then into the weighing of the social importance of the risk. Therefore we should not be surprised when scientists disagree among themselves or when the lay public views a risk differently from the experts. Non-scientist officials are fond of ridiculing scientists for failing to reach internal agreement, and sometimes make the assumption that lack of scientific consensus allows the conclusion that the hazard is negligible: "Danger I don't know, must be trivial". Science is a matter of voting, directly as experts debate, or indirectly as they adopt, refine, or ignore putative "facts". Organizations of scientists are not much different, as they exert collective judgment and develop communal biases. . . .

The U.S. Weather Bureau performs a useful educational function as it announces its forecasts. These predictions are naturally the butt of many jokes—surely this is an occupational hazard of the meteorological profession—but I would argue that the basic approach is sound and is a model for other risk predictions. What does it mean to say that "there is a 30% chance of rain"? This statement is defined to mean that for a given geographic area, on 30% of the days for which such a forecast is made, it actually does rain a predefined minimum amount; on seven out of ten such days it should not be expected to rain. Contrary to cynics' beliefs it is possible for the weatherfolks to find themselves "wrong". Periodically the National Weather Records Center's computers evaluate individual weather stations' forecasting records and recommend adjustments: "On such-and-such kinds of days you tend to underestimate snow by 10%". Thus what is striven for is predictive validity.

Unfortunately, especially with infrequent or "freak" events, many people have trouble interpreting risk estimates. There are those who criticize what they call hysteria and overanxiousness in the 1976 rush campaign to immunize all Americans against swine 'flu. The single early swine influenza fatality at Fort Dix did not turn out to presage an epidemic, or, worse, a repeat of the 1918 pandemic that took twenty million lives around the world. I don't approve of the particular actions the Ford Administration took. But our hindsight—the knowledge that the pandemic did not in fact materialize—does not at all give us license to say that it was foolish for public health experts, the President, and others to become quite apprehensive about the disease and seek precautions; had the 1976 epidemic slaughtered the number of people it did in 1918, the 1976 precautions would have seemed irresponsibly slight.

More complicated issues surround the nuclear fiasco at Three Mile Island. Toward the end of the crisis period, as the reactor cooled down and the hydrogen bubble shrank, two extreme views emerged. One view was that the accident was a terrible event that showed that the nuclear technocrats had gone entirely too far, had failed to take account of human operator error and incompetence, had come within a hair's breadth of totally losing control of the machine, and had finally given the nation reason to close down the entire nuclear industry. Opposed to that was a conviction that the system had "worked", had vindicated the prior risk assessments, had demonstrated that the reactor could be kept under control even through a series of unprecedented and unanticipated extreme disturbances. Which opinion people favor seems to depend a lot on whether they like nuclear power in the first place. I admit that I took advantage of the Three Mile affair's extraordinary coincidence with Jane Fonda's movie, and adopting columnist Herb Caen's witticism, entitled several lectures on the accident, "Best Supporting Reactor". But I was quite offended by those who pooh-poohed it as simply a "media event", as Edward Teller did and as the National Enquirer did with its screaming headline, "EXCLUSIVE: NUCLEAR PLANT CRISIS A HOAX." How serious the threat was depends on how close to disaster the accident came, how many people might have been hurt how badly, how quickly help could have been rendered, and so on. What should not be overlooked is the probabilistic nature of the whole affair. What also should not be overlooked, in the large view, is how the risks of the entire nuclear industry compare with the risks of alternative energy sources.

HAROLD GREEN,
THE ROLE OF LAW IN DETERMINING
ACCEPTABILITY OF RISK

in Societal Risk Assessment
255, 256–258, 266 (R. Schwing and W. Albers, Jr. eds. 1980).

A useful starting point is to consider the manner in which the common law handles the acceptability of risk. . . .

The area of the common law most relevant to acceptability of risk is the law of torts, which deals primarily with the liability of defendants whose conduct causes injury to plaintiffs. Not every injury to another gives rise to liability, but only those injuries caused by the fault—primarily negligence—of the defendant. Liability is imposed to compensate the innocent plaintiff for her injuries, and, by example, to deter dangerous conduct by others in the future. Negligence is "conduct which falls below the standard established by law for the protection of others against unreasonable risk of harm"[1]. "Risk" is the "chance of harm"[2]. Since it is only conduct that creates an "unreasonable risk of harm" to others that gives rise to liability, such conduct, although not "unacceptable" in the sense that society prohibits it, is "unacceptable" in the sense that society disfavors it by penalizing the actor if the conduct results in harm to others.

It is, moreover, only "unreasonable" risk that is unacceptable in this sense. This means that the actor would be liable only if a fictitious "reasonable" person applying a mythical community standard would recognize that the conduct involves unreasonable risk to others[3]. The risk is "unreasonable" if it is of "such magnitude as to outweigh what the law regards as the utility of the act or of the particular manner in which it is done"[4]. The magnitude of the risk is a function of the social value the law attaches to the interests imperiled, the probabilities that the conduct will cause injury, the magnitude of the likely injury, and the number of persons who may be injured[5]. The utility of the actor's conduct is a function of the social value the law attaches to the interest to be advanced or protected by the conduct, the probability that this interest will be advanced or protected by the conduct, and the availability of other less dangerous alternatives to advance or protect the interest[6].

It is the legal, and not the popular, opinion that is controlling with respect to utility of the conduct, although courts frequently reexamine and correct the law's view of utility when such view is inconsistent with public conviction[7].

These formulations involve a kind of risk-benefit assessment to determine the reasonableness of the defendant's conduct. Although the principles discussed above do not preclude the use of techniques for measuring and assessing relevant factors in objective, quantified terms, they do not contemplate or require such techniques, and, indeed, assessments based on purported objective quantifications are rare. Thus, for example, the operation of railroads and utilities, the conduct of commerce, and the free use of highways are all regarded, without objective evidence, as having sufficient utility to justify acceptance of some injuries to the public. Indeed, the law's reliance on such concepts as "reasonable", "social value", and "opinion" clearly evidences a *qualitative* or common sense, rather than a quantitative, approach.

Let me offer two examples of this. In a 1934 decision, the Wisconsin Supreme Court suggested that a careful driver should not be liable to a pedestrian splashed with muddy water on a rainy day, because the benefit of allowing people to travel under such circumstances clearly outweighs the probable injury to pedestrians. Such a conclusion made no pretense at quantification of the competing considerations, but was derived from the wisdom and experience of the court and the traditions of the people, as perceived by the court. Similarly, one of the most eminent federal

---

1. Restatement (Second) of Torts 282, 1965.

2. Id. § 282(g).

3. Id. § 283.

4. Id. § 291.

5. Id. § 293.

6. Id. § 292.

7. Id. § 291(d).

judges, Learned Hand, in a case involving liability for injury resulting from the breaking loose of a vessel from its pier, reduced the question to algebraic terms with three variables:

P—the probability that the vessel will break away

L—the gravity of the injury

B—the burden of adequate precautions,

so that liability would depend on whether $B > PL$. Nevertheless, Judge Hand gave content to the algebraic terms in a purely non-quantitative analysis that included consideration of custom in the industry [9].

In the interest of completeness, it should be mentioned in passing that the common law recognizes strict liability, i.e., liability without fault, in cases involving "abnormal risk"; and in some cases extraordinarily hazardous or unpleasant conduct may be prohibited by injunction. The same general approach to assessment of risk, and balancing of utility against risk, as is discussed above with respect to negligence is applicable in these special situations. . . .

The perceived inadequacies of the common law in protecting society against hazardous activities frequently lead to legislative action resulting in statutes that merely set standards of general applicability, that also prescribe penalties for violation of the standards, or that prescribe a regulatory pattern to be administered by a regulatory agency. Such statutes are based on some kind of determination as to the acceptability of risk that is made by legislatures. Where a legislature enacts a statute dealing with protection of people against risks, such legislation, unlike a judicial decision, is a positive, deliberate making of law intended to control conduct in the future.

Sometimes the statute flatly prohibits the conduct of an activity regarded as hazardous. For example, statutes may prohibit the sale, use, or possession of certain items such as fireworks, heroin, or pornographic materials, reflecting a legislative judgment that the risks associated with the activity are of such magnitude that the activity should be banned notwithstanding the magnitude of any possible offsetting benefits. In most such cases, the activity in fact is perceived as having very little, if any, social utility; but there are some cases in which the activity is flatly prohibited even though substantial offsetting benefits are present. A leading example of this is the Delaney Amendment which prohibits the use of any chemical in food where the chemical is known to cause cancer when ingested by animals.

The important point with respect to these examples is that the legislature has made a determination that the activity in question involves a risk that is unacceptable from the standpoint of society, and should therefore be prohibited. The evidence on the basis of which such a determination is made is invariably more anecdotal than objective or empirical, and there usually is no effort on the part of the legislature to consider either risk or benefit in quantitative terms. There is, moreover, no satisfactory rationale to explain why the legislature prohibits some activities involving risk and not others. It appears anomalous, to say the least, that a statute might prohibit sale or possession of marijuana or pornography, but not of liquor and tobacco.

9. United States v. Carroll Towing Co., 159 F.2d 169 (2d Cir.1947).

NOTE

How, if at all, does a decision by EPA as to whether a pesticide poses a risk of unreasonable adverse effects on the environment differ from a jury's decision whether a defendant in a tort case acted unreasonably? Is it significant that EPA is required to justify its decision in writing?

For a discussion of some of the different standards of risk followed in the law see note 58 in Ethyl Corp. v. EPA, Section A.3, infra.

EDMUND CROUCH AND RICHARD WILSON, RISK/BENEFIT ANALYSIS

9–11, 12–16, 19–21 (1982).

Although there are uses of the word *risk* that are more inclusive, . . . we associate risks with events or actions. (Note that inaction, whether it is conscious or unconscious, is also susceptible to analysis—for example, the effects of a decision to take no action on CO_2 buildup in the atmosphere might be analyzed). The events and actions may be small or large, from digging one shovel of dirt to creating new seas, from creating a one-way street to decisions on whole highway construction programs. For each event or action we associate some units of risk, leading to a risk per street crossing, for example, or a risk per ton of copper ore mined. Thus in some way we have a visualization as follows:

Total risk = (How much or how often) ⊗ (Some risk per unit of action, or per event).

In a more useful form, we can write:

Risk = Probability ⊗ Severity.

Notice that we have carefully refrained from putting an ordinary multiplication sign (×) in the equation, for in some practical cases risk perceptions may not be truly multiplicative. Most risks do have some multiplicative features, though, which we shall use in our first attempt to introduce objectivity.

Thus far, the discussion has been concerned mainly with single events or actions. Since the definition has been left open, such single events or actions could cover most cases, but in essence they consist of the most elementary actions to be analyzed with respect to their risk content. To associate a risk with more complex events or actions, it is necessary to break down the actions into individual smaller actions, the summation of which is usually assumed to be possible.

Risk=S (Probability ⊗ Severity ⊗ Weight),

where the S stands for whatever form of addition (unknown) is actually used by individuals. The weight factor is included separately here; it could perhaps be included in the severity term if the equation relates perceptions, but it is convenient for later discussion to isolate it. It is included to account for the possibility that in evaluating a problem consisting of many different parts, risks of apparently similar magnitude may be accorded very different weights in consideration of the totality.

Any inappropriate assignment of weight or erroneous perception of the risk of any section of a problem may lead to inappropriate ("wrong") actions or decisions. Such actions or decisions would result in end results different from those planned and thus not optimum from some point of view.   One attempt at reducing such possibilities is the objective analysis of risk   .   .   ..

To make any start on objective assessment it is necessary to realize what is being measured. Death is one clear objective measure. The total annual risk of death at any age is just the probability of dying within one year.   In the absence of any extra causes, population averages for this measure are obtained from national mortality tables   .   .   .. But in risk assessments we are interested in additional risks of death or components of the total risk of death due to some specific actions undertaken either voluntarily or involuntarily.   More often, we are interested in how much of an action to undertake, so that we wish to evaluate measures such as extra probability of death per unit of action (per cigarette smoked, or per ton of coal mined, for example).

Death is not the only measure of risk of interest, for, although it is probably the most objective one and for this reason often used, it may not capture large components of what are perceived as risks.   In balanced decisions it may become vital to consider other measures.   A few possible such measures are:

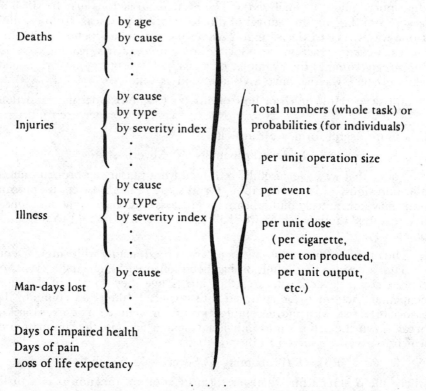

Although we shall not concern ourselves much with it, the distinction between risks and measures of risk is not totally academic.   A simple example is the American coal industry, taken as a whole, between 1950 and 1970.   Figure 2–1 is a plot of one measure of risk in this industry—the number of accidental deaths per million tons of coal mined.   Clearly this measure steadily declined during this period, so that, if we follow the industry through successive years, it appears to be getting safer.   Looking at Figure 2–2, which shows the behavior of another measure of risk—the number of accidental deaths per thousand persons employed—one might naively assert that the industry is getting more dangerous, not safer.

Figure 2-1. Accidental Deaths per Million Tons of Coal Mined in the United States.

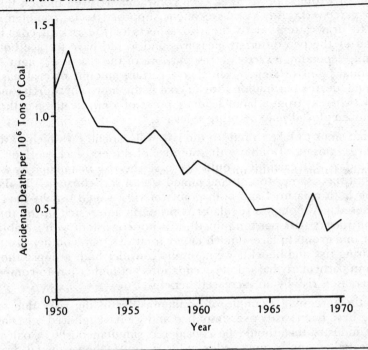

Figure 2-2. Accidental Deaths per Thousand Coal Mine Employees in the United States.

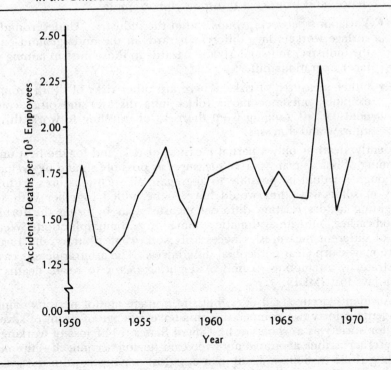

Evidently the two measures illustrated might be used to support opposing views on the safety of coal mining. Neither measure taken alone is right or wrong, nor are they even contradictory even though they may be so perceived. Any risk assessment supposed to be complete would have to draw attention to the two aspects of the risk of coal mining gauged by the two different measures and would have to take both into account, depending exactly on the purpose of the risk assessment. From a national point of view, given that a certain amount of coal has to be obtained, deaths per million tons of coal is the more appropriate measure of risk, whereas from a labor leader's point of view, deaths per thousand persons employed may be more relevant.

What steps to take to reduce the risk will depend on which of the two measures is used. Doubling the number of miners, each working on alternate days, for example, would decrease the risk per miner by a factor of 2, but the risk per ton of coal mined would stay constant. In decision making both measures and both points of view would usually have to be considered. Although a regulator is primarily interested in the total impact on society (risk per ton mined), it is not consistent with a stable society for one group to face a much larger total risk than another group. In comparing risk and benefits we naturally consider both groups; those engaged in particularly hazardous occupations get higher pay to compensate the increased risk by an increased benefit.

In the foregoing example of accidental death, the risks due to coal mining have been vastly oversimplified and we have ignored other aspects of the industry that should be considered simultaneously. Coal mining was treated as one homogeneous industry, and only accidental deaths of employees were included in the measures of risk used. We have completely ignored, inter alia:

- Risk to the public—from dust and water emissions, from subsidence, and from coal transport, for example.

- Variations between groups within the industry. Underground and surface workers face different hazards in the underground part of the industry, and similarly the hazards to those in strip mining (surface) operations differ.

- Other measures of risk. There are other risks of death from, for example, pneumoconiosis (black lung disease) and other components of risk ranging from the risks of traveling to work, through injuries and illnesses.

Evidently, death is only a partial measure of risk, and for the best understanding of risk as many partial measures as possible should be evaluated. Although it would be possible to aggregate all such measures arithmetically in some way, they would have to be added together with some weighting factors relating different measures, as by using the formulas stated earlier, but with arithmetic summation and multiplication. Weighting of different measures is necessarily somewhat arbitrary and furthermore may usurp clear perceptual differences. The arbitrariness is easy to illustrate by attempting to find a weighting factor to relate deaths and man-days lost (MDL).

Accidents occur at all ages, but the average age of persons dying of accidents is forty-two compared with an average age of death of seventy-two for society as a whole in the United States. The loss of working life expectancy is thus about twenty-five years (taking account of retirement), leading to $25 \times 300 = 7,500$ man-days lost per death. But the average

age for cancer deaths is about fifty-four, so the loss of working life expectancy is thirteen years or 3,900 MDL per death. Any weighting factor would thus strictly have to depend on the cause of death, although an average of 6,000 MDL per death is often used—and whether such an average is adequate will depend on the particular case. These estimates do not assist in our problem particularly, for we do not necessarily perceive death as being simply equivalent to a loss of a certain number of working days! The measure takes no account of nonworking time, for one thing. Moreover, depending on the question being answered by the risk assessment, the average may not be of interest—it may be that individual variations are of more importance.

With these caveats on measures of risk we return to objective risk assessment. . . .

. . .

It would appear that, having broken the action or event into components, analyzed each component, and summed again, one has obtained the measure of risk for the complete action or event. This statement is not quite true, however, or, rather, it is incomplete. Consider a single action, with the possibility of its being either carried out or not. In the first case, the procedure evaluates some measure(s) of risk for performing the action. Even if the action is not carried out, it is likely that there will still be some risks to the persons who would be affected by the action. There is thus an arbitrary choice in a risk assessment: Should such a "background level" of risk be subtracted from each evaluated measure to account for the risks that would be present even in the absence of the action or event being assessed?

The problem posed refers to the case of a simple decision: to do or to refrain. If the decision is between two or more alternatives, a similar problem arises as soon as any attempt is made to make any comparison: Should the comparison be based on absolute or on incremental measures of risk? The importance of this question becomes obvious when it is realized that comparisons based on the first may give different results from those based on the second.

. . .

Some apparent ambiguities may be resolved by careful attention to the problem actually under study. Consider the problem of evaluating some measure of total societal impact of risks in the production of iron in the United States, and note that perhaps one-third of the iron ore used is imported. Evidently some of the risk in producing iron ore comes from the risk of mining, milling, and transporting iron ore, but what risk measure should be assigned to imported iron ore to account for these risks in its production? There are at least three possibilities.

1. Assigning zero risk might be appropriate if the measure of risk required referred to the total risk of iron production to the population of the United States. Since import of iron ore causes no risk to any of the domestic population, any actual risks incurred in its production can be ignored. (Note that risk attribution to imports is not zero on a differential risk basis, because paying for the imports requires some actions that are not risk free.)

2. Assigning a risk measure equal to that incurred in production of ore in the United States is the simplest procedure and leads to indifference (from the point of view of total risk) between imports

and domestic production. This assignment is equivalent to assuming that all variations in production occur in U.S. sources.

3. Assigning a risk measure equal to that actually incurred in overseas production is the most difficult option of the three because it requires much more analysis. It might be apporpriate if the total risk of iron production to the global population were required.

In practice, the option usually chosen is (2), because the measure is available (it has to be computed in analysis of domestic production anyway), requires no decisions to be made on the domestic/import split (as would be required for (1)), and is an approximation to (3), if it may be assumed that risks are not too disparate between countries.

The position of system boundaries is of crucial concern also for risk comparisons between different systems (or projects, events, actions). For any use to be made of such comparisons, the systems under consideration should presumably be designed to perform similarly or to produce the same or similar results. An example that has attracted considerable attention recently is the relative risks of systems for generating or converting energy, especially electricity, with special attention to comparisons between the so-called conventional systems (using coal, oil, gas, hydropower, or nuclear energy) and unconventional systems (such as various solar technologies, wind, biomass). Most of these technologies may be used for generating electricity, but comparison of the risks of different systems may be easily and grossly affected by alteration of system boundaries. The choice of system boundaries should, of course, be predicated on the exact question required to be answered in any such comparison. Some of the problems that must be faced are illustrated in the following list:

1. What risk measures are to be chosen? [I]t would be usual in this case to normalize to some unit size so as to get a risk per megawatt hour (MWh) generated, or per megawatt (MW) installed capacity, or per MW firm capacity (*firm* means available for use with some defined (high) probability). As before, choice of a particular measure or set of measures may not be straightforward.

2. Is total risk or incremental risk to be measured?

3. Should possible contributions to global effects be included or excluded? (Burning of fossil fuels contributes to carbon dioxide buildup in the atmosphere, which may lead to large-scale deleterious effects, but the best scientific opinions are currently divided as to the size and character of such effects.)

4. How are geographical siting factors to be taken into account? (Many of the "unconventional" systems produce results that would be strongly dependent on geographical siting: Wind systems require a windy environment; solar systems outputs vary with the availability of sunshine.)

5. Is the comparison to be made between typical systems, between averages taken over large numbers of systems or between marginal systems (the next to be built)? For the unconventional systems there is the problem that few, if any, have actually been built, so that unless care is exercised an attempt will be made to compare mature, optimized technologies with nonoptimized technologies. Whether this is of importance depends on what the risk compari-

son is supposed to show. Are such systems comparable from the point of view of the question to be answered?

. . .

NOTES

1. How likely is it that in making decisions about risk, governmental decision-makers will have reliable data on the various kinds of issues identified by Crouch and Wilson? How should they act in the absence of such data?

2. Who should bear the cost of generating the data needed for good risk assessments: those whose products or services create risks? taxpayers? others?

3. For more detailed discussion of risk assessment see generally W. Lowrance, Of Acceptable Risk: Science and the Determination of Safety (1978); W. Rowe, An Anatomy of Risk (1977); Quantitative Risk Assessment in Regulation (L. Lave, ed. 1982); Societal Risk Assessment: How Safe is Safe Enough (R.C. Schwing and W.A. Albers, Jr., ed. 1980); Subcommittee on Science, Research and Technology of the Committee on Science and Technology of the U.S. House of Representatives, Hearings on Comparative Risk Assessment, 96th Cong. 2d Sess., May 14–15 (1980); see also Lowrance, Choosing Our Pleasures and Our Poisons: Risk Assessment for the 1980's, in Science, Technology and the Issues of the Eighties: Policy Outlook (A.H. Teich and R. Thornton, ed. 1983); McGarity, Substantive and Procedural Discretion in Administrative Resolution of Science Policy Questions: Regulating Carcinogens in EPA and OSHA, 67 Geo.L.J. 729 (1979); Starr, Social Benefit v. Technological Risk, 165 Science 1232 (1969).

b. Perceiving Risk

COMMITTEE ON RISK AND DECISION MAKING, NATIONAL ACADEMY OF SCIENCES* RISK AND DECISION MAKING: PERSPECTIVES AND RESEARCH

2–5, 11–13 (1982).

The first sentence of a recent report (U.S. Surgeon General, 1979) proclaimed that "the health of the American people has never been better." The surgeon general documents improvement in many indices of

* Members of the Committee responsible for this report were:

HOWARD RAIFFA (Chair), Graduate School of Business, Harvard University

A. KARIM AHMED, Natural Resources Defense Council, Inc., New York

DAVID COHEN, Common Cause, Washington, D.C.

JAMES S. COLEMAN, Department of Sociology, University of Chicago

ROBERT W. KATES, Graduate School of Geography, Clark University

CHARLES E. LINDBLOM, Institute for Social and Policy Studies, Yale University. (Charles E. Lindblom does not approve this report).

GLENN C. LOURY, Department of Economics, University of Michigan

ROY RADNER, Bell Telephone Laboratories, Inc., Murray Hill, N.J. (December 1979–June 1981)

WILLIAM D. RUCKELSHAUS, Weyerhauser Corporation, Tacoma, Wash.

JACK P. RUINA, Department of Electrical Engineering, Massachusetts Institute of Technology

PETER SCHUCK, Law School, Yale University

EILEEN SERENE, Department of Philosophy, Yale University

AMOS TVERSKY, Department of Psychology, Stanford University

JAMES H. WARE, School of Public Health, Harvard University

RICHARD WILSON, Energy and Environmental Center, Harvard University

ROSALYN YALOW, Veterans Administration Medical Center, Bronx, N.Y.

illness, non-fatal conditions, and mortality. We would like to emphasize primarily the progress made against mortality, since, in the absence of a comprehensive statistical measure of risk, the single best indicator is perhaps that provided by mortality statistics. The decline in U.S. mortality rates since the turn of the century has been steady and, on a cumulative basis, dramatic.

Life expectancy at birth has increased in the United States from 47 years in 1900 to 74 years in 1979. The age-adjusted death rate has fallen by two-thirds, from 18 per 1,000 in 1900 to under 6 per 1,000 in 1979. The probability of "early" death—death before age 65—has declined from over 60 percent at 1900 mortality rates to under 25 percent at 1979 rates.

Mortality reductions in the 1970s have been especially impressive. For example, in the United States the likelihood that a person age 65 would live at least another decade has increased by 14 percentage points from 1900 to 1970 (from 55 to 69 percent) and then by another 5 percentage points by 1979 (to 74 percent). In 1979, the age-adjusted death rate at all ages was 18 percent lower than it was 9 years earlier. Similar improvements have occurred in other countries as well, including dramatic ones in the less developed countries considered as a group.

According to one poll (Louis Harris and Associates, 1980) most Americans believe life is getting riskier: 78 percent of the public surveyed agreed that "people are subject to more risk today than they were twenty years ago" (p. 9); only 6 percent thought there was less risk. Furthermore, 55 percent felt that "the risks to society stemming from various scientific and technological advances will be somewhat greater 20 years from now than they are today" (p. 10), as opposed to only 18 percent who felt that the risks will be somewhat less.

The degree of concern about risk has increased sharply since about 1960. For example:

- The enactment of more than 30 major laws by the U.S. Congress from 1965 to 1980 (and numerous laws by state legislatures) aimed at coping with occupational, consumer product, environmental, transportation, and other sources of risks;

- The establishment or strengthening of at least a dozen regulatory agencies with broad legal authority and rising budgets throughout the 1970s;

- The growth of litigation related to health, safety, and environmental risks in the 1970s in both the tort-liability system and the arena of judicial review of agency decision making;

- The creation and growth of numerous public interest groups concerned with health, safety, and environmentl risks, a movement that has significantly changed the politics of risk and the politics of regulation;

- The emergence of various forms of business-sponsored efforts to improve risk management by the private sector, to publicize these efforts, and to coordinate them with those being taken by local, state, and federal governments . . . .;

- The expanded media coverage of scientific findings about risks, corporate risk-management activities, and political activity related to risk;

• The increase in funding for health, safety, and environmental research and the emergence of a relatively new field of "risk analysis."

SOME POSSIBLE INTERPRETATIONS

Multiple hypotheses have been proposed for the apparent contradiction between increased longevity and increased concern with risk. . . .

One source of concern about risk may be a growing realization that certain groups in society suffer from higher than ordinary rates of early death. Despite historical progress, it is increasingly apparent that there are numerous opportunities for further longevity gains.

For example, two types of mortality differentials suggest that it may still be possible to substantially reduce mortality rates in the United States: the high rates of mortality among disadvantaged groups in the United States and the higher rates of mortality for the entire U.S. population compared with that of many other developed nations.

Blacks, Hispanic Americans, American Indians, and the poor and poorly educated in general suffer from substantially higher death rates than do middle- and upper-class whites. These disparities should be understood in the context of a period of dramatic improvement, at least for some disadvantaged groups. Between 1950 and 1975, for example, both whites and nonwhites experienced sharply reduced rates of infant mortality as well as general increases for all ranges of age-specific mortality except for the very old. Although these improvements were greater for nonwhites than for whites, mortality differentials between the two groups remain large. For example, if current mortality rates remain unchanged, two of five nonwhites will die before reaching age 65, compared with one of five whites. Although data are sparse, mortality and morbidity rates among migrant workers in the United States appear to be especially high.

The United States fares poorly compared with other developed countries in terms of a variety of health indicators, including infant mortality, life expectancy, cardiovascular disease rates, cancer death rates, and homicide rates. For instance, the United States is 26th on a list of countries in the probability of death before age 65. In terms of reported mortality rates, the United States ranks close to countries with less than half the U.S. per-capita income.

The likelihood of death before age 65 for selected countries is:

Rank	Country	Probability
1	Sweden	.183
10	Canada	.235
26	United States	.275
37	Mexico	.419
41	Liberia	.665

Persistent differences in life expectancies, between nations and between different groups in the United States (e.g., whites and nonwhites), may mean that, for the lagging populations, achievable mortality gains are not being realized. These attainable gains also imply inequities in the distribution of risk; some groups carry higher burdens of risks. The persistence of mortality differentials and the linked issue of equity in the sharing of risks are surely part of the reason for increased concern with risk despite general increases in life expectancies.

Anxiety about risk is a product of people's beliefs and attitudes. People often form such beliefs and attitudes on the basis of incomplete and often biased information using fallible modes of inference, which sometimes result in systematic distortions and misperceptions of reality. . . .

For example, scientific progress identifies new risks, which are reported to the public. There are reports on the risks of the Three Mile Island accident, hazardous chemical wastes in the Love Canal, DC–10s, benzene, saccharin, asbestos, tampons, PCBs, the pill, recombinant DNA, nuclear waste, and so forth. These reports may make certain risks more memorable or imaginable, thereby increasing perceived probabilities of risk regardless of the total scientific evidence about or trends in actual indices of risk. If this phenomenon is occurring on a large scale, it may explain part of the rising public concern about risk.

As people become better informed about various health and safety risks, levels of concern can be expected to rise. This process is accelerated by scientific advances that detect more and more previously unknown sources of risk.

In addition, certain attributes of risks that concern people are not reflected in mortality statistics or in typical quantitative risk assessments. The catastrophic nature of some risks and the uncontrollability of other risks are not easily communicated by simple tallies of deaths and injuries. This is not an argument against quantitative risk estimates but rather an argument for a broader risk analysis in combination with numerical risk estimates. Consider two examples. The expected annual number of deaths from nuclear power plants may be extremely small, but some people may be especially concerned about the catastrophic nature of a major accident if it were to occur. The number of annual highway deaths far exceeds the annual expected death toll from nuclear plant meltdown, yet there is a widespread perception that highway accident risks are more controllable by the individual, even though one-fourth of the accidents occur in such a way that they cannot be controlled. Factors such as the geographical concentration of risk and the individual controllability of risk influence social concern about risk even though such factors do not influence typical quantitative risk assessments. . . .

As per-capita income in a society rises, the desire for risk reduction will generally increase. Rising levels of affluence in the United States may therefore be contributing to accelerating public concern about risk. In addition, aspirations are related to faith in science and technology. While technological progress often creates new risks, it also provides society with new opportunities to reduce old and emerging risks. If expectations about science and technology have increased in recent decades, it may explain part of the increasing attention to risk. Finally, while many of the risks of the early 1900s appeared to be acts of nature or God, today's risks may appear to be more subject to individual human control. The fatalistic attitudes of the past are increasingly, though unevenly, replaced by concern about risks viewed as manageable.

Public concern about risk may be rising because business and government, the major risk-management institutions in society, have suffered from a loss of public confidence in the past 20 years. The decline in public confidence in businesses during the late 1960s and early 1970s is well-documented by survey data. While in 1968 more than two-thirds of Americans believed business was, according to one poll, striking a "fair balance" between profits and the broader interests of the public, only 16 percent believed it by 1976 . . . .. Increased public skepticism of government began in the Vietnam years of the 1960s, and was paralleled by the perceived failure of the Great Society programs, accelerated by the Watergate scandal, and remained throughout the 1970s at a high level.

PAUL SLOVIC, BARUCH FISCHHOFF, AND SARAH LICHTENSTEIN, FACTS AND FEARS: UNDERSTANDING PERCEIVED RISK

in Societal Risk Assessment
190–194, 208–212 (R. Schwing and W. Albers, Jr., eds. 1980).

In one study, we asked four different groups of people to rate 30 activities (e.g., smoking, fire fighting), substances (e.g., food coloring), and technologies (e.g., railroads, aviation) according to the present risk of death from each. Three groups were from Eugene, Oregon; they included 30 college students, 40 members of the League of Women Voters (LOWV), and 25 business and professional members of the "Active Club." The fourth group was composed of 15 persons selected nationwide for their professional involvement in risk assessment. This "expert" group included a geographer, an environmental policy analyst, an economist, a lawyer, a biologist, a biochemist, and a government regulator of hazardous materials.

All these people were asked, for each of the 30 items, "to consider the risk of dying (across all U.S. society as a whole) as a consequence of this activity or technology. . . ." Respondents were told first to study the items individually, thinking of all the possible ways someone might die from each (e.g., fatalities from nonnuclear electricity were to include deaths resulting from the mining of coal and other energy production activities as well as electrocution; motor vehicle fatalities were to include collisions with bicycles and pedestrians). Next, they were to order the items from least to most risky and, finally, to assign numerical risk values by giving a rating of 10 to the least risky item and making the other ratings accordingly. . . .

Table 2 shows how the various groups ranked these 30 activities and technologies according to riskiness. There were many similarities between the three groups of laypeople. For example, each group believed that motorcycles, motor vehicles and handguns were highly risky, while vaccinations, home appliances, power mowers, and football posed relatively little risk. However, there were strong differences as well. Active Club members viewed pesticides and spray cans as relatively much safer than did the other groups. Nuclear power was rated as highest in risk by the LOWV and student groups, but only eighth by the Active Club. The students viewed contraceptives as riskier and mountain climbing as safer than did the other lay groups. Experts' judgments of risk differed markedly from the judgments of laypeople. The experts viewed electric power, surgery, swimming and X rays as more risky than did the other groups and they judged nuclear power, police work and mountain climbing to be much less risky.

What Determines Risk Perception?—What did people mean, in this study, when they said that a particular technology was quite risky? A series of additional studies was conducted to answer this question.

Perceived Risk Compared to Frequency of Death—When people judge risk, are they simply estimating frequency of death? To answer this question, we collected the best available technical estimates of the annual number of deaths for the activities included in our study. For some, such as commercial aviation and handguns, there is good statistical evidence based on counts of known victims. For others, such as nuclear or fossil-fuel power plants, available estimates are based on uncertain inferences about incompletely understood processes, such as the effect of low doses of radiation on latent cancers. For still others, such as food coloring, we could find no estimates of annual fatalities.

TABLE 2

Ordering of Perceived Risk for 30 Activities and Technologies [a]

	Group 1 LOWV	Group 2 College Students	Group 3 Active Club Members	Group 4 Experts
Nuclear power	1	1	8	20
Motor vehicles	2	5	3	1
Handguns	3	2	1	4
Smoking	4	3	4	2
Motorcycles	5	6	2	6
Alcoholic beverages	6	7	5	3
General (private) aviation	7	15	11	12
Police work	8	8	7	17
Pesticides	9	4	15	8
Surgery	10	11	9	5
Fire fighting	11	10	6	18
Large construction	12	14	13	13
Hunting	13	18	10	23
Spray cans	14	13	23	26
Mountain climbing	15	22	12	29
Bicycles	16	24	14	15
Commercial aviation	17	16	18	16
Electric power	18	19	19	9
Swimming	19	30	17	10
Contraceptives	20	9	22	11
Skiing	21	25	16	30
X rays	22	17	24	7
High school & college football	23	26	21	27
Railroads	24	23	20	19
Food preservatives	25	12	28	14
Food coloring	26	20	30	21
Power mowers	27	28	25	28
Prescription antibiotics	28	21	26	24
Home appliances	29	27	27	22
Vaccinations	30	29	29	25

a. *The ordering is based on the geometric mean risk ratings within each group. Rank 1 represents the most risky activity or technology.*

For the 25 cases for which we found technical fatality estimates, we compared these estimates with perceived risk. The experts' judgments of risk were so closely related to these statistical or calculated frequencies that it seems reasonable to conclude that they both knew what the technical estimates were and viewed the risk of an activity or technology as synonymous with them. The risk judgments of laypeople, however, were only moderately related to the annual death rates, raising the possibility that, for them, risk may not be synonymous with fatalities. In particular, the perceived risk of nuclear power was remarkably high compared to its estimated number of fatalities.

Lay Fatality Estimates—[W]e investigated the possibility that laypeople based their risk judgments on subjective fatality estimates which were inaccurate. To test this hypothesis, we asked additional groups of students and LOWV members "to estimate how many people are likely to die in the U.S. in the next year (if the next year is an average year) as a consequence of . . . 30 activities and technologies."

. . . If laypeople really equate risk with annual fatalities, their own estimates of annual fatalities, no matter how inaccurate, should be very similar to their judgments of risk. There was, however, only a low to moderate agreement between these two sets of judgments . . . . Of particular importance was nuclear power, which had the *lowest* fatality estimate and the *highest* perceived risk for both LOWV members and students. Overall, laypeople's risk perceptions were no more closely related to their own fatality estimates than they were to the technical estimates. Thus we can reject the idea that laypeople wanted to equate risk with annual fatalities, but were inaccurate in doing so. . . .

Disaster Potential—One striking result is the fact that the LOWV members and students assigned nuclear power the highest risk values and the lowest annual fatality estimates. One possible explanation is that they expected nuclear power to have a low death rate in an average year, but considered it to be a high risk technology because of its potential for disaster.

In order to understand the role played by expectations of disaster in determining lay people's risk judgments, we asked these same respondents to indicate for each activity and technology "how many times more deaths would occur if next year were particularly disastrous rather than average." . . . For most activities, people saw little potential for disaster. The striking exception is nuclear power, with a mean disaster multiplier in the neighborhood of 100.

For any individual, an estimate of the expected number of fatalities in a disastrous year could be obtained by applying the disaster multiplier to the estimated fatalities for an average year. When this was done for nuclear power, almost 40% of the respondents expected more than 10,000 fatalities if next year were a disastrous year. More than 25% expected 100,000 or more fatalities. An additional study, in which people were asked to describe their mental images of the consequences of a nuclear accident, showed an expectation that a serious accident would likely result in hundreds of thousands, even millions, of immediate deaths. These extreme estimates can be contrasted with the Reactor Safety Study's conclusion that the maximum credible nuclear accident, coincident with the most unfavorable combination of weather and population density, would cause only 3,300 prompt fatalities. Furthermore, that study estimated the odds against an accident of this magnitude occurring next year to be about 3,000,000:1.

Disaster potential seems to explain much of the discrepancy between the perceived risk and the annual fatality estimates for nuclear power. Yet, because disaster plays only a small role in most of the other activities and technologies, it provides only a partial explanation of the perceived risk data.

Qualitative Characteristics—Are there other determinants of risk perceptions besides frequency estimates? We asked experts, students, LOWV members and Active Club members to rate the 30 technologies and activities on nine qualitative characteristics that have been hypothesized to be important . . . .

The "risk profiles" made from mean ratings on these characteristics showed nuclear power to have the dubious distinction of scoring at or near the extreme on all of the characteristics associated with high risk. Its risks were seen as involuntary, delayed, unknown, uncontrollable, unfamiliar, potentially catastrophic, dreaded, and severe (certainly fatal). . . . Both electric power and X rays were judged more voluntary, less catastrophic, less dreaded, and more familiar than nuclear power.

Across all 30 items, ratings of dread * and of the severity of consequences were closely related to lay judgments of risk. . . .

Judged Seriousness of Death—In a further attempt to improve our understanding of perceived risk, we examined the hypothesis that some hazards are feared more than others because the deaths they produce are much worse than deaths from other activities. We thought, for example, that deaths from risks imposed involuntarily, from risks not under one's control, or from hazards that are particularly dreaded might be given greater weight in determining people's perceptions of risk.

However, when we asked students and LOWV members to judge the relative seriousness to society of a death from each of . . . 30 activities and technologies, the differences were slight. The most serious forms of death (from nuclear power and handguns) were judged only about 2 to 4 times worse than the least serious forms of death (from alcoholic beverages and smoking). Furthermore, across all 30 activities, judged seriousness of death was not closely related to perceived risk of death.

. . .

We are led to conclude that beliefs about the catastrophic nature of nuclear power are a major determinant of public opposition to that technology. This is not a comforting conclusion because the rarity of catastrophic events makes it extremely difficult to resolve disagreements by recourse to empirical evidence. . . . As a result, the "perception gap" between pro-nuclear experts and the anti-nuclear public is likely to persist, leaving frustration, distrust, conflict, and costly hazard management as its legacy. We suspect that the potential for similar disputes exists with other low-probability, high-consequence hazards such as LNG, pesticides, industrial chemicals, and recombinant DNA research.

Weighing Catastrophes—Any attempt to control accidents must be guided by assessments of their probability and severity. As we have seen, probability assessment poses serious difficulties, particularly for rare

---

* "Dread" is used by the authors as a term of art. The ratings of dread were obtained by characterizing risks on a scale, from those that people have learned to live with and can think about reasonably calmly ("common"), to those for which people have "great dread" ("on the level of a gut reaction"). Slovic, Fischhoff and Lichtenstein, Facts and Fears: Understanding Perceived Risk, in Societal Risk Assessment 195 (Schwing & Albers, eds. 1980). [ed.]

events. Unfortunately, weighing of the severity or social cost of an accident is also problematic.

Society appears to react more strongly to infrequent large losses of life than to frequent small losses. This has led analysts to propose a weighting factor that accommodates the greater impact of N lives lost at one time relative to the impact of one life lost in each of N separate incidents. Risk/benefit analysts would then apply this weighting factor when evaluating the expected social costs of a proposed activity.

The precise nature of the fatality weighting factor has been the subject of some speculation. Wilson suggested that N lives lost simultaneously were N^2 times more important than the loss of one life. Ferreira and Slesin hypothesized, on the basis of observed frequency and severity data, that the function might be a cubic one.

We believe that a single weighting function cannot adequately explain, predict, or guide social response to catastrophe. For one, we have found that people hold, simultaneously, several conflicting attitudes about the weighting function. They believe that the function relating social impact to N lives lost should be (a) concave, because they recognize that the same additional number of lives lost seems more important in a small accident than in a large accident; (b) linear, because each unidentified life is equally important; and (c) convex, because large losses of life have important higher order consequences and may even threaten the resilience of a community or society. Clearly any attempt to model the impact of a multiple fatality event will need to consider how situational factors will interact with these multiple values . . . . .

Signal Value—Another complication is that the occurrence of a rare, catastrophic event contains information regarding the probability of its reoccurrence. As a result, the impact of an accident may be determined as much by its signal value as by its toll of death and destruction.

The importance of accidents as signals is demonstrated by a study in which we asked 21 women (median age = 37) to rate the seriousness of 10 hypothetical accidents. Several aspects of seriousness were rated including:

a. The total amount of suffering and grief caused by the loss of life in each mishap,

b. The number of people who need to be made aware of the mishap via the media,

c. The amount of effort (and money) that should be put into investigating the cause of the mishap and preventing its recurrence, and

d. The degree to which hearing about the mishap would cause one to be worried and upset during the next few days.

The accident scenarios were constructed so as to vary on total fatalities and informativeness (see Table 10). The five uninformative accidents represented single incidents, generated by reasonably well-known and understood processes, and limited to a particular time and locale. The high-information mishaps were designed to signal a change in riskiness, potential for the proliferation of similar mishaps, or some breakdown in the system controlling the hazard. Thus a bus skidding on ice represented a low-information mishap because its occurrence did not signal a change in motor-vehicle risks, whereas an accident caused by a poorly designed steering system in a new model automobile would be informative about all such vehicles. To check our intuitions our respondents also judged informativeness, defined as the degree to which the mishap told them (and society) something that may not have been known about the hazardousness of the specific activity.

All ratings were on a seven-point scale. The means ratings are shown in Table 10. Note that the five mishaps designed to be high in signal value were all judged more informative than the most informative mishap in the low-information category. As expected, the judged amount of suffering and grief was closely related to the number of people killed. However, all other aspects of seriousness were more closely related to the information content of the accident. Accidents signaling either a possible breakdown in safety control systems or the possibility that the mishap might proliferate were judged more worrisome and in need of greater awareness and greater public effort to prevent reoccurrences. The number of people killed appeared to be relatively unimportant in determining these aspects of seriousness.

For this study we conclude that risk analyses, designed to anticipate public reaction or to aid in decision making, need to consider what accidents indicate about the nature and controllability of risk. An accident that takes many lives may have little or no impact on perceived risk if it occurs as part of a familiar, well-understood and self-limiting process. In contrast, a small accident may greatly enhance perceived risk and trigger strong corrective action because it increases the judged probability of future accidents. The great impact of the accident at Three Mile Island (which caused no immediate fatalities) would seem to reflect such considerations.

TABLE 10

Effect of Informativeness on the Impact of Catastrophic Mishaps

	Inform- ativeness	Suffering and Grief	Need for Awareness	Effort to Prevent Recurrence	Worry
Less Informative Mishaps					
Bus skids on ice and runs off road (27 killed)	1.8	4.4	2.5	3.1	1.8
Dam collapse (40 killed)	4.7	4.9	4.7	5.9	3.8
Two jumbo jets collide on runway (600 killed)	4.8	6.1	5.8	6.5	4.5
Hundred year flood (2,700 killed)	2.8	6.1	5.3	3.5	2.7
Meteorite hits stadium (4,000 killed)	2.2	6.2	5.7	2.1	2.5
More Informative Mishaps					
Nuclear reactor accident: Partial core meltdown releases radiation inside plant but not to outside (1 killed)	6.5	4.5	6.5	7.0	6.1
Botulism in well-known brand of food (2 killed)	5.7	3.7	5.2	6.1	4.6
New model auto steering fails (3 killed)	5.2	3.8	5.2	6.3	4.6
Recombinant DNA workers contract mysterious illness (10 killed)	6.1	4.6	5.9	6.3	5.1
Jet engine falls off on takeoff (300 killed)	5.7	6.0	6.1	6.9	5.5

ADAM SMITH, THE WEALTH OF NATIONS

108 (New York 1937) (1st ed. London 1776).

The overwhelming concept which the greater part of men have of their own abilities is an ancient evil remarked by the philosophers and moralists of all ages. Their absurd presumption in their own good fortune has been less taken notice of. It is, however, if possible, still more universal. There is no man living who, when in tolerable health and spirits, has not some share of it. The chance of gain is by every man more or less over-valued and the chance of loss is by most men undervalued, and by scarce any man, who is in tolerable health and spirits, valued more than it is worth.

PAUL SLOVIC, BARUCH FISCHHOFF, AND SARAH LICHTENSTEIN, INFORMING PEOPLE ABOUT RISK

in Banbury Report 6: Product Labeling and Health Risks
165, 170–175 (L. Morris, M. Mazis, and I. Barofsky eds. 1980).

Subtle changes in the way that risks are expressed can have major impact on our perceptions and behaviors. There is a large amount of psychological research documenting this assertion. Here, we shall present only a brief introduction to the topic. Our first example is based on two problems that Tversky and Kahneman gave to a group of physicians. Each problem had two options and the physicians were asked to indicate which option they would choose.

1. Problem 1. Imagine that the U.S. is preparing for the outbreak of an unusual Asian disease, which is expected to kill 600 people. Two alternative programs to combat the disease have been proposed. Assume that the consequences of the programs are as follows: If Program A is adopted, 200 people will be saved. If Program B is adopted, there is $1/3$ probability that 600 people will be saved, and $2/3$ probability that no people will be saved. Which of the two programs would you favor?

2. Problem 2. (Same cover story as Problem 1.) If Program C is adopted, 400 people will die. If Program D is adopted, there is $1/3$ probability that nobody will die, and $2/3$ probability that 600 people will die. Which of the two programs would you favor?

Seventy-five percent of the physicians chose Program A over Program B and 67% chose Program D over Program C. On closer examination: one can see that A and C are identical options, as are B and D. The preference patterns of many physicians were inconsistent, reversed by the simple change from lives saved to lives lost.

A second demonstration of the importance of the presentation format comes from a study of attitudes towards the use of automobile seat belts. Drawing upon previous research showing that probability of loss was more important than the magnitude of loss in triggering protective action, Slovic and colleagues argued that the reluctance of people to wear seat belts voluntarily was understandable in light of the extremely small probability of a fatal accident on a single automobile trip. Given the fact that only about one in every 3.5 million person trips ends in a fatal accident and about one in every 100,000 person trips results in a disabling injury, failure to buckle one's seat belt cannot be considered an unreasonable action. Slovic et al. further argued that voluntary use of seat belts depends on motorists believing that their personal likelihood of being in an accident is high enough to make wearing a belt seem sensible. They suggested that motorists be informed that over a 50-year lifetime of driving (about 40,000 trips), the probability of a fatal accident rises to .01 and the probability of experiencing at least one disabling injury is .33. Their research showed that people induced to consider the lifetime perspective did, in fact, respond more favorably (compared to people induced to consider a trip-by-trip perspective) towards use of seat belts and towards the enactment of laws that required the wearing of seat belts or the installation of air bags. Whether the favorable attitudes towards seat belts engendered by a lengthened time perspective would be maintained and translated into behavior, remains to be seen.

Numerous other format effects have been documented in the psychological literature. For example, people have been found to evaluate gambles much differently when they consider them in pairs than when they judge them singly. Schoemaker and Kunreuther have shown that decisions to buy insurance are frequently reversed when the problem is instead portrayed as a choice between facing a gamble versus accepting a certain loss of a small amount of money.

The fact that subtle differences in how risks are presented can have marked effects in how they are perceived suggests that people who inform others have considerable ability to manipulate perceptions. The possibility of manipulating people's beliefs without their knowledge or consent raises ethical problems that must be addressed by any responsible risk-information program.

Cross-Hazard Comparisons May Be Misleading

One of the most valued approaches for deepening people's perspectives is to present quantified risk estimates for a variety of hazards. Presumably, the sophistication gleaned from examining such data will be useful for personal and societal decision making. Wilson observed that we should "try to measure our risks quantitatively . . . . Then we could compare risks and decide which to accept or reject." Likewise, Sowby argued that to decide whether or not we are regulating radiation hazards properly, we need to pay more attention to "some of the other risks of life," and Lord Rothschild recently added, "There is no point in getting into a panic about the risks of life until you have compared the risks which worry you with those that don't, but perhaps should."

Typically, such exhortations are followed by elaborate tables and even catalogs of risks in which diverse indices of death or disability are displayed for a broad spectrum of life's hazards. Thus Sowby provided extensive data on risks per hour of exposure, showing, for example, that 1 hour riding a motorcycle is as risky as 1 hour of being 75 years old. Wilson developed Table 1, which displays a set of activities, each of which is estimated to increase one's chances of death (during any year) by one in one million (which in the case of accidental death would decrease one's life expectancy by an average of about 15 minutes). Wilson claimed that ". . . these comparisons help me evaluate risks and I imagine that they may help others to do so, as well. But the most important use of these comparisons must be to help the decisions we make, as a nation, to improve our health and reduce our accident rate." In similar fashion, Cohen and Lee ordered many hazards in terms of their expected reduction in life expectancy (Table 2) on the assumption that "to some approximation, the ordering (in this table) should be society's order of priorities. However, we see several very major problems that have received very little attention . . . . whereas some of the items near the bottom of the list, especially those involving radiation, receive a great deal of attention".

TABLE 1

Risks Which Increase the Chance of Death in Any Year by One Part in One Million (.000001)

Event	Risk
Smoking 1.4 cigarettes	cancer, heart disease
Drinking .5 liter of wine	cirrhosis of the liver
Spending 1 hour in a coalmine	black lung disease
Spending 3 hours in a coalmine	accident
Living 2 days in New York or Boston	air pollution
Traveling 6 minutes by canoe	accident
Traveling 10 miles by bicycle	accident
Traveling 150 miles by car	accident
Flying 1000 miles by jet	accident
Flying 6000 miles by jet	cancer caused by cosmic radiation
Living 2 months in Denver on vacation from N.Y.	cancer caused by cosmic radiation
Living 2 months in average stone or brick building	cancer caused by natural radioactivity
One chest X ray taken in a good hospital	cancer caused by radiation
Living 2 months with a cigarette smoker	cancer, heart disease
Eating 40 tablespoons of peanut butter	liver cancer caused by aflatoxin B
Drinking Miami drinking water for 1 year	cancer caused by chloroform
Drinking 30 12–oz cans of diet soda	cancer caused by saccharin
Living 5 years at site boundary of a typical nuclear power plant in the open	cancer caused by radiation
Drinking 1000 24–oz soft drinks from recently banned plastic bottles	cancer from acrylonitrile monomer
Living 20 years near PVC plant	cancer caused by vinyl chloride (1976 standard)
Living 150 years within 20 miles of a nuclear power plant	cancer caused by radiation
Eating 100 charcoal broiled steaks	cancer from benzopyrene
Risk of accident by living within 5 miles of a nuclear reactor for 50 years	cancer caused by radiation

Data from Wilson (1979).

Properly speaking, comparing hazards is not a decision-making procedure, but merely an aid to intuition. The logic of the calculations does not require any particular conclusion to be drawn, say, from the contrast between the risks of motorcycling and advanced age. Moreover, cross-hazards comparisons have a number of inherent limitations. For example, although some people feel enlightened upon learning that a single takeoff or landing in a commercial airliner takes an average of 15 minutes off one's life expectancy, others find themselves completely bewildered by such information. On landing, one will either die prematurely (almost certainly by more than 15 minutes) or one will not. To many people, averages seems inadequate to capture the essence of such risks.

TABLE 2

Loss of Life Expectance (△E) Due to Various Causes

Cause	Days	Cause	Days
Being unmarried (male)	3500	Job with radiation exposure	40
Cigarette smoking (male)	2250	Falls	39
Heart disease	2100	Accidents to pedestrians	37
Being unmarried (female)	1600	Safest job (accidents)	30
Being 30% overweight	1300	Fire (burns)	27
Being a coal miner	1100	Generation of energy	24
Cancer	980	Illicit drugs (U.S. average)	18
20% Overweight	900	Poison (solid, liquid)	17
<8th Grade education	850	Suffocation	13
Cigarette smoking (female)	800	Firearms accidents	11
Low socioeconomic status	700	Natural radiation (BEIR)[a]	8
Stroke	520	Medical X rays	6
Living in unfavorable state	500	Poisonous gases	7
Army in Vietnam	400	Coffee	6
Cigar smoking	330	Oral contraceptives	5
Dangerous job (accidents)	300	Accidents to pedal cycles	5
Pipe smoking	220	All catastrophes combined	3.5
Increasing food intake		Diets drinks	2
100 calories/day	210	Reactor accidents (UCS)[b]	2[c]
Motor vehicle accidents	207	Reactor accidents	
Pneumonia (influenza)	141	(Rasmussen)	0.02[c]
Alcohol (U.S. average)	130	Radiation from nuclear	
Accidents in home	95	industry	0.02[c]
Suicide	95	PAP test	−4
Diabetes	95	Smoke alarm in home	−10
Being murdered (homicide)	90	Air bags in car	−50
Legal drug misuse	90	Mobile coronary care units	−125
Average job (accidents)	74	Safety improvements	
Drowning	41	1966–76	−110

Data from Cohen and Lee (1979).
a. Biological Effects of Ionizing Radiation.
b. Union of Concerned Scientists, the most prominent group of nuclear critics.
c. These items assume that all U.S. power is nuclear.

Summary statistics like those in Tables 1 and 2 often mask some important characteristics of risk. Where there is lack of knowledge of disagreement about the facts, some indication of uncertainty is needed. Since people are particularly concerned about the potential for catastrophic accidents, some indication of the probability and magnitude of extreme losses is needed. Other characteristics important in determining people's reactions to hazards, but neglected in Tables 1 and 2, are the voluntariness, controllability, and familiarity of the risk, the immediacy of the consequences, the degree to which benefits are distributed equitably to those who bear the risk, the possibility of damage to future generations, and the ease of reducing the risk.

It is all too easy for arithmetically facile analysts to get carried away by the ease of computing risk statistics. Statements such as "the risk from nuclear power is equal to the risk of riding in automobiles an extra 3 miles," because they ignore differences between automobiles and nuclear power with regard to level of uncertainty, catastrophic potential, equity, and other important characteristics, produce outrage rather than enlightenment and lead some to characterize the arithmetic of cross-hazards comparisons as "only the kindergarten of risk". Some faults, such as the omission of uncertainty bands, are easy to correct; however, determining the proper weight to assign to the other important considerations will require a serious research effort.

NOTE

In Metropolitan Edison Co. v. People Against Nuclear Energy, __ U.S. __, 103 S.Ct. 1556, 75 L.Ed.2d 534 (1983), a unanimous United States Supreme Court held that the Nuclear Regulatory Commission did not need to consider whether the risk of a nuclear accident might cause psychological harm to the surrounding community in preparing an Environmental Impact Statement on whether to resume operation of one of the two nuclear power plants at Three Mile Island. See Ch. 2, Sec. B.1, supra. In the Court's words:

> Renewal Operation of TMI–1 may well cause psychological health problems for . . . people . . . . However, this harm is simply too remote from the physical environment to justify requiring the NRC to evaluate the psychological health damage to these people . . . .

> Risk is a pervasive element of modern life; to say more would belabor the obvious . . . . Medical experts apparently agree that risk can generate stress in human beings, which in turn may rise to the level of serious health damage. For this reason among many others, the question whether the gains from any technological advance are worth its attendant risks may be an important public policy issue. Nonetheless it is quite different from the question whether the same gains are worth a given level of alteration of our physical environment or depletion of our natural resources. The latter question rather than the former is the central concern of NEPA.

Id. at __, 103 S.Ct. at 1562, 75 L.Ed.2d at 543.

Does the holding suggest Congress should require preparation of a "psychological impact statement" for controversial technological projects? How much weight, if any, should public officials give to public fears about such things as nuclear power if most experts think that the fears of the public are greater than justified by more objective methods of assessing risk?

3. ASSESSING RISK

a. What Constitutes an Adequate Assessment?

ETHYL CORP. v. ENVIRONMENTAL PROTECTION AGENCY

United States Court of Appeals for the District of Columbia Circuit, en banc, 1976.
541 F.2d 1.

J. SKELLY WRIGHT, CIRCUIT JUDGE:

Man's ability to alter his environment has developed far more rapidly than his ability to foresee with certainty the effects of his alterations. It is only recently that we have begun to appreciate the danger posed by unregulated modification of the world around us, and have created watchdog agencies whose task it is to warn us, and protect us, when technological "advances" present dangers unappreciated—or unrevealed—by their supporters. Such agencies, unequipped with crystal balls and unable to read the future, are nonetheless charged with evaluating the effects of unprecedented environmental modifications, often made on a massive scale. Necessarily, they must deal with predictions and uncertainty, with developing evidence, with conflicting evidence, and, sometimes, with little or no evidence at all. Today we address the scope of the power delegated one such watchdog, the Environmental Protection Agency (EPA). We must determine the certainty required by the Clean Air Act before EPA may act to protect the health of our populace from the lead particulate emissions of automobiles.

Section 211(c)(1)(A) of the Clean Air Act authorizes the Administrator of EPA to regulate gasoline additives whose emission products "will endanger the public health or welfare . . . ." 42 U.S.C. § 1857f–6c(c) (1)(A). Acting pursuant to that power, the Administrator, after notice and comment, determined that the automotive emissions caused by leaded gasoline present "a significant risk of harm" to the public health. Accordingly, he promulgated regulations that reduce, in step-wise fashion, the lead content of leaded gasoline. We must decide whether the Administrator properly interpreted the meaning of Section 211(c)(1)(A) and the scope of his power thereunder, and, if so, whether the evidence adduced at the rule-making proceeding supports his final determination. . . .

In making his threshold determination that lead particulate emissions from motor vehicles "will endanger the public health or welfare," the Administrator provided his interpretation of the statutory language by couching his conclusion in these words: such emissions "present a significant risk of harm to the health of urban populations, particularly to the health of city children." . . .

Petitioners argue that the "will endanger" standard requires a high quantum of factual proof, proof of actual harm rather than of a "significant risk of harm. . . ."

Since, according to petitioners, regulation under Section 211(c)(1)(A) must be premised upon factual proof of actual harm, the Administrator has, in their view, no power to assess risks or make policy judgments in deciding to regulate lead additives. . . . It is our view that the Administrator's interpretation of the standard is the correct one.

The meaning of "endanger" is not disputed. Case law and dictionary definition agree that endanger means something less than actual harm. When one is endangered, harm is *threatened*; no actual injury need ever occur. Thus, for example, a town may be "endangered" by a threatening plague or hurricane and yet emerge from the danger completely unscathed. A statute allowing for regulation in the face of danger is, necessarily, a precautionary statute. Regulatory action may be taken before the threatened harm occurs; indeed, the very existence of such precautionary legislation would seem to *demand* that regulatory action precede, and, optimally, prevent, the perceived threat. As should be apparent, the "will endanger" language of Section 211(c)(1)(A) makes it such a precautionary statute.

The Administrator read it as such, interpreting "will endanger" to mean "presents a significant risk of harm." 38 Fed.Reg. 33734. We agree with the Administrator's interpretation. . . .

Petitioners further argue that Section 211 requires the Administrator to make a "threshold factual determination" that automobile emissions "will endanger" the public health . . . and dispute EPA's claim that the Administrator may make "an essentially legislative policy judgment, rather than a factual determination, concerning the relative risks of underprotection as compared to overprotection." Industrial Union Department, AFL–CIO v. Hodgson, 162 U.S.App.D.C. 331, 339, 499 F.2d 467, 475 (1974). We must reject petitioners' argument, since the power to assess risks, without relying solely on facts, flows inexorably from the nature of the "will [en]danger" standard.

We find that deletion of the findings requirement for action under Section 211(c)(1)(A) was a recognition by Congress that a determination of endangerment to public health is necesarily a question of policy that is to be based on an assessment of risks and that should not be bound by either the procedural or the substantive rigor proper for questions of fact.

This conclusion follows not only from the language of Section 211(c) (1)(A) and its legislative history, but from the nature of the Administrator's charge: to protect the public from danger. Regulators such as the Administrator must be accorded flexibility, a flexibility that recognizes the special judicial interest in favor of protection of the health and welfare of people, even in areas where certainty does not exist.

Questions involving the environment are particularly prone to uncertainty. Technological man has altered his world in ways never before experienced or anticipated. The health effects of such alterations are often unknown, sometimes unknowable. While a concerned Congress has passed legislation providing for protection of the public health against gross environmental modifications, the regulators entrusted with the enforcement of such laws have not thereby been endowed with a prescience that removes all doubt from their decision-making. Rather, speculation, conflicts in evidence, and theoretical extrapolation typify their every action. How else can they act, given a mandate to protect the public health but only a slight or nonexistent data base upon which to draw? Never before have massive quantities of asbestiform tailings been spewed into the water we drink. Never before have our industrial workers been occupationally exposed to vinyl chloride or to asbestos dust. Never before has the food we eat been permeated with DDT or the pesticides aldrin and dieldrin. And never before have hundreds of thousands of tons of lead emissions been disgorged annually into the air we breathe. Sometimes, of course, relatively certain proof of danger or harm from such modifications can be readily found. But, more commonly, "reasonable medical concerns" and theory long precede certainty. Yet the statutes— and common sense—demand regulatory action to prevent harm, even if the regulator is less than certain that harm is otherwise inevitable.

Undoubtedly, certainty is the scientific ideal—to the extent that even science can be certain of its truth.[52] But certainty in the complexities of environmental medicine may be achievable only after the fact, when scientists have the opportunity for leisurely and isolated scrutiny of an entire mechanism. Awaiting certainty will often allow for only reactive, not preventive, regulation. Petitioners suggest that anything less than certainty, that any speculation, is irresponsible. But when statutes seek to avoid environmental catastrophe, can preventive, albeit uncertain, decisions legitimately be so labeled?

The problems faced by EPA in deciding whether lead automotive emissions pose a threat to the public health highlight the limitations of

---

52. Even scientific "facts" are not certain, but only theories with high probabilities of validity. Scientists typically speak not of certainty, but of probability; they are trained to act on probabilities that statistically constitute "certainties." See generally T. Kuhn, The Structure of Scientific Revolutions. While awaiting such statistical certainty may constitute the typical mode of scientific behavior, its appropriateness is questionable in environmental medicine,

where regulators seek to prevent harm that often cannot be labeled "certain" until after it occurs. See note 58 infra.

The uncertainty of scientific fact parallels the uncertainty of all fact. In a metaphysical sense, at least, facts are themselves nothing more than risks, or statistical probabilities. See D. Hume, A Treatise of Human Nature, bk. I, pt. III, § 6, at 87 (L.A. Selby-Bigge ed. 1958).

awaiting certainty. First, lead concentrations are, even to date, essentially low-level, so that the feared adverse effects would not materialize until after a lifetime of exposure. Contrary to petitioners' suggestion, however, we have not yet suffered a lifetime of exposure to lead emissions. At best, emissions at present levels have been with us for no more than 15–20 years.[54] Second, lead exposure from the ambient air is pervasive, so that valid control groups cannot be found against which the effects of lead on our population can be measured. Third, the sources of human exposure to lead are multiple, so that it is difficult to isolate the effect of automobile emissions. Lastly, significant exposure to lead is toxic, so that considerations of decency and morality limit the flexibility of experiments on humans that would otherwise accelerate lead exposure from years to months, and measure those results. . . .

The scientific techniques for attempting to overcome these limitations are several: toxicology can study the distribution and effect of lead in animals; epidemiological techniques can analyze the effects of lead emissions on entire populations; clinical studies can reproduce in laboratories atmospheric conditions and measure under controlled circumstances the effects on humans. All of these studies are of limited usefulness, however. . . . The best biomedical evidence will be derived from relating all three research approaches. This EPA did. That petitioners, and their scientists, find a basis to disagree is hardly surprising, since the results are still uncertain, and will be for some time. But if the statute accords the regulator flexibility to assess risks and make essentially legislative policy judgments, as we believe it does, preventive regulation based on conflicting and inconclusive evidence may be sustained.

Of course, we are not suggesting that the Administrator has the power to act on hunches or wild guesses. *Amoco* makes it quite clear that his conclusions must be rationally justified. Amoco Oil Co. v. EPA, 163 U.S. App.D.C. [162,] 180–181, 501 F.2d [722,] 740–741 [(1974).] However, we do hold that in such cases the Administrator may assess risks. He must take account of available facts, of course, but his inquiry does not end there. The Administrator may apply his expertise to draw conclusions from suspected, but not completely substantiated, relationships between facts, from trends among facts, from theoretical projections from imperfect data, from probative preliminary data not yet certifiable as "fact," and the like. We believe that a conclusion so drawn—a risk assessment—may, if rational, form the basis for health-related regulations under the "will endanger" language of Section 211.[58]

54. According to [an] NAS Panel, present air lead concentrations, which over the largest American cities are 2,000 times greater than air lead concentrations over the mid-Pacific Ocean, have existed for 15 years. . . . The Panel attributed these high concentrations primarily to automotive emissions. . . .

58. It bears emphasis that what is herein described as "assessment of risk" is neither unprecedented nor unique to this area of law. To the contrary, assessment of risk is a normal part of judicial and administrative fact-finding. Thus EPA is not attempting to expand its powers; rather, petitioners seek to constrict the usual flexibility of the fact-finding process. Petitioners argue that the Administrator must decide that lead emis-

sions "will endanger" the public health solely on "facts," or, in the words of the division majority, by a "chain of scientific facts or reasoning leading [the Administrator] ineluctably to this conclusion . . . ." Petitioners demand sole reliance on *scientific* facts, on evidence that reputable scientific techniques certify as certain. Typically, a scientist will not so certify evidence unless the probability of error, by standard statistical measurement, is less than 5%. That is, scientific fact is at least 95% certain.

Such certainty has never characterized the judicial or the administrative process. It may be that the "beyond a reasonable doubt" standard of criminal law demands 95% certainty. Cf. McGill v. United States, 121 U.S.App.D.C. 179, 185 n. 6, 348 F.2d

All of this is not to say that Congress left the Administrator free to set policy on his own terms. To the contrary, the policy guidelines are largely set, both in the statutory term "will endanger" and in the relationship of that term to other sections of the Clean Air Act. These prescriptions direct the Administrator's actions. Operating within the prescribed guidelines, he must consider all the information available to him. Some of the information will be factual, but much of it will be more speculative—scientific estimates and "guesstimates" of probable harm, hypotheses based on still-developing data, etc. Ultimately he must act, in part on "factual issues," but largely "on choices of policy, on an assessment of risks, [and] on predictions dealing with matters on the frontiers of scientific knowledge . . . ." Amoco Oil Co. v. EPA, supra, 163 U.S.App. D.C. at 181, 501 F.2d at 741. A standard of danger—fear of uncertain or unknown harm—contemplates no more.

Petitioners vigorously attack both the sufficiency and the validity of the many scientific studies relied upon by the Administrator, while advancing for consideration various studies allegedly supportive of their position. The record in this case is massive—over 10,000 pages. Not surprisingly, evidence may be isolated that supports virtually any inference one might care to draw. Thus we might well have sustained a determination by the Administrator *not* to regulate lead additives on health grounds. That does not mean, however, that we cannot sustain his determination to so regulate. As we have indicated above, we need not decide whether his decision is supported by the preponderance of the evidence, nor, for that matter, whether it is supported by substantial evidence. To the contrary, we must sustain if it has a rational basis in the evidence. Keeping in mind the precautionary "will endanger" standard under which the Administrator acted, we have no difficulty in terming his decision rational.

A word about our approach to the evidence may be in order. Contrary to the apparent suggestion of some of the petitioners, we need not seek a single dispositive study that fully supports the Administrator's determination. Science does not work that way; nor, for that matter, does

791, 797 n. 6 (1965). But the standard of ordinary civil litigation, a preponderance of the evidence, demands only 51% certainty. A jury may weigh conflicting evidence and certify as adjudicative (although not scientific) fact that which it believes is more likely than not. Since *Reserve Mining* was adjudicated in court, this standard applied to the court's fact-finding. Inherently, such a standard is flexible; inherently, it allows the fact-finder to assess risks, to measure probabilities, to make subjective judgments. Nonetheless, the ultimate finding will be treated, at law, as fact and will be affirmed if based on substantial evidence, or, if made by a judge, not clearly erroneous.

The standard before administrative agencies is no less flexible. Agencies are not limited to scientific fact, to 95% certainties. Rather, they have at least the same fact-finding powers as a jury, particularly when, as here, they are engaged in rule-making.

Looking to the future, and commanded by Congress to make policy, a rule-making agency necessarily deals less with "evidentiary" disputes than with normative conflicts, projections from imperfect data, experiments and simulations, educated predictions, differing assessments of possible risks, and the like.

Amoco Oil Co. v. EPA, supra, 163 U.S.App. D.C. at 175, 501 F.2d at 735. An agency's finding of fact differs from that of a jury or trial judge primarily in that it is accorded more deference by a reviewing court. Thus, as a matter of administrative law, the Administrator found *as fact* that lead emissions "will endanger" the public health. That in so doing he did not have to rely solely on proved scientific fact is inherent in the requirements of legal fact-finding. Petitioners' assertions of the need to rely on "fact" confuse the two terminologies. We must deal with the terminology of law, not science. At law, unless the administrative or judicial task is peculiarly factual in nature, or Congress expressly commands a more rigorous finding . . . assessment of risks as herein described typifies both the administrative and the judicial fact-finding function, and is not the novel or unprecedented theory that petitioners contend.

adjudicatory fact-finding. Rather, the Administrator's decision may be fully supportable if it is based, as it is, on the inconclusive but suggestive results of numerous studies. By its nature, scientific evidence is cumulative: the more supporting, albeit inconclusive, evidence available, the more likely the accuracy of the conclusion. If, as petitioners suggest, one single study or bit of evidence were sufficient independently to mandate a conclusion, there would, of course, be no need for any other studies. Only rarely, however, is such limited study sufficient. Thus, after considering the inferences that can be drawn from the studies supporting the Administrator, and those opposing him, we must decide whether the cumulative effect of all this evidence, and not the effect of any single bit of it, presents a rational basis for the low-lead regulations. . . . We find the Administrator's analysis of the evidence and assessment of the risks to be well within the flexibility allowed by the "will endanger" standard.

[Concurring opinions by Judge Bazelon and Judge Leventhal are reprinted in Ch. 4, Sec. D.1, supra]

WILKEY, CIRCUIT JUDGE, with whom joined TAMM and ROBB, CIRCUIT JUDGES (dissenting): We think that the statute does require that, before the Administrator can prescribe the regulations involved here, he must find that the lead from auto emissions by itself or alone contributes a *measurable increment of lead* to the human body, and that *this measurable increment causes a significant health hazard.* . . .

To us all analysis leads inescapably to this conclusion, yet the court's opinion endeavors to avoid this by resorting to two obfuscating dichotomies (perhaps the same distinction expressed in two ways). First, the opinion attempts to separate *actual* from *potential* harm, and, second, to separate *risk* from *fact.* "[T]he 'will endanger' standard is precautionary in nature and does not require proof of actual harm before regulation is appropriate." "[T]he power to assess risks, without relying solely on facts, flows inexorably from the nature of the 'will [en-]danger' standard." We submit no such separation occurs in the real world, and if the Administrator proceeded on any such fanciful theory, it is an instance of his failure to discern the intent of Congress manifested by the words "will endanger."

As to the first distinction, there is no distinction possible here between actual and potential, between past and future harm. The Administrator is dealing with a *continuing situation.* If there can be found potential harm from lead in exhaust emissions, the best (and only convincing) proof of such potential harm is what has occurred in the past (either in 50 years of practical usage or in laboratory experimentation), from which the Administrator can logically deduce that the same factors will produce the same harm in the future. For the court's opinion to hold that the Administrator can dispense with proof of actual harm, i.e., what has occurred in the past, and can nevertheless somehow determine *potential* harm, is to grant the plainest license for the wildest speculation. We have always thought scientific conclusions, above all, demanded proof by events recorded and observed.

The court's second asserted dichotomy, risks versus facts, is equally indefensible in logic. All true risk assessment is based on facts and nothing else.[121] Those professional risk-assessors, the professional sports

---

121. In all games of chance in which theoretically the factor of human control is not present, e.g., roulette, dice, the fall of cards, the risk of a given event occurring or not occurring can be calculated with mathematical certainty. In those games in which human

gambling fraternity, would smile at any other theory. To the extent that hunch and intuition enter into any final decision, these are separate factors outside of any scientific risk calculation.

Our colleagues apparently find it necessary to legitimatize the Administrator playing hunches. They assert, "Danger is a risk and so must be decided by assessment of risks *as well as* by proof of facts." Of course the Administrator assesses risk—from the facts as he knows them. The question here is how much he knows. To the extent the agency found it necessary to make an "assessment of risks as well as [rely on] proof of facts," the agency was frankly just speculating. No reviewing court can countenance this. If such agency decision is not "arbitrary and capricious," what decision could be? It is precisely a devotion to *facts*, not hunches, that distinguishes the professionals from the amateurs in assessing risks; we deem the Administrator to have been intended by Congress to be a "professional."

NOTE

Which opinion has a more accurate understanding of what constitutes risk assessment? Compare R. Kasper, Perceptions of Risk and their Effects on Decision Making, in Societal Risk Assessment 73 (R.C. Schwing & W.A. Albers, Jr. eds. 1980):

> There have been a number of attempts to observe or calculate the risk of particular activities. Some involve collection of data to describe the risk; highway fatality statistics fall in this class. The generation of such data allows a fairly accurate picture of certain kinds of risks, most notably those that involve easily recognized and countable risks (such as death) for which the cause is clear and for which there exists a body of available statistics . . . . Unfortunately, few risks fall into this class. For some the relationship between cause and effect is clear . . . . For other[s], experience may be only a very partial guide and assessors are forced to use elaborate methods to project or predict highly uncertain effects.

How demanding should judicial review be when the assessment in question is of the more speculative sort?

GULF SOUTH INSULATION v. UNITED STATES CONSUMER PRODUCT SAFETY COMMISSION

United States Court of Appeals for the Fifth Circuit, 1983.
701 F.2d 1137.

CLARK, CHIEF JUDGE:

On April 2, 1982, the Consumer Product Safety Commission (Commission) concluded a six-year investigation and rulemaking with the issuance of a final rule banning urea-formaldehyde foam insulation (UFFI) in residences and schools. 47 Fed.Reg. 14,366 . . . . The Commission found that UFFI presents an unreasonable risk of injury from irritation and cancer and that no feasible product standard exists that would adequately protect the public from these hazards. . . .

---

or animal skill is presumed to predominate, e.g., football, basketball, horse racing, the *facts* as to the physical conditions and mental attitude of the contestants are avidly sought by the professional risk-assessors; it is on the basis of known *facts* that the initial odds are fixed.

I. THE PRODUCT

UFFI is a thermal insulation material used in residences and other buildings. It is manufactured at the job site by mixing a liquid resin containing formaldehyde, a foaming agent, and compressed gas. The resulting liquid foam, which resembles shaving cream, is pumped into the walls of the building being insulated. After a time the mixture solidifies.

According to the industry, UFFI exhibits several characteristics that make it a particularly attractive insulation alternative. Although relatively inexpensive, it has excellent thermal resistance and energy conservation properties. Unlike some other insulation materials, it is resistant to fire. Perhaps most important, UFFI is well suited for installations in existing structures, termed by the industry the "retrofit" market.

The attribute of UFFI that spawned this rulemaking is its propensity to emit formaldehyde gas. Formaldehyde is a colorless gas composed of carbon, hydrogen, and oxygen. It is present in every cell in the human body and in the atmosphere. Formaldehyde has been in widespread commercial use for almost a century. Seven billion pounds per year are produced in the United States. According to the industry, formaldehyde is a component of products aggregating 8% of this country's Gross National Product. Approximately half of the formaldehyde produced in the United States is used in preparing bonding resins. These resins are used in producing plywood, particleboard, fiberboard and permanent press products, in addition to UFFI. Such products as shampoo, toothpaste, cosmetics, and paper towels also contain formaldehyde.

II. THE RULEMAKING

. . .

A. Formaldehyde Levels

The Commission's initial step was to determine the average levels of formaldehyde in UFFI homes and non-UFFI homes. The agency obtained results of formaldehyde measurements in 1,164 UFFI homes. The tests showed that formaldehyde levels are highest for several months after installation. They then decrease gradually over a several-year period, eventually approaching ambient levels. The Commission determined that the average level of formaldehyde over a nine-year period after installation of UFFI is .08 parts per million. In tests of 103 non-UFFI homes, an average level of .03 ppm was found.

To obtain more data, the Commission arranged tests on a number of commercially available UFFI products in simulated wall panels. The tests were conducted by the Franklin Institute Research Laboratory (Franklin Lab), the Oak Ridge National Laboratory (Oak Ridge Lab), and the Commission Engineering Laboratory. The Oak Ridge Lab concluded that the panels emitted formaldehyde at levels ranging from .03–.44 ppm sixteen months after foaming. The average level was .13 ppm.

B. Acute Irritant Effects

The Commission's primary concern when it began investigating UFFI was the link between formaldehyde exposure and acute irritant symptoms. According to the agency, these symptoms include eye, nose, and throat irritation, persistent cough, respiratory distress, skin irritation, nausea, headaches, and dizziness.

From 1979 to 1981 the Commission investigated 350 homes whose occupants had complained of adverse health effects related to UFFI. The agency obtained information about the particular UFFI product installed, the method of installation, the surrounding environment, and the symptoms suffered by household members. According to the Commission, numerous families were forced to evacuate their homes after installation of UFFI, and in several cases acute symptoms were so severe that hospitalization was required. The agency concluded that "taken as a whole, the complaints do identify a real problem."

The agency commissioned the National Academy of Sciences to determine whether there is a level of formaldehyde exposure below which no acute symptoms will be experienced. After reviewing the available scientific literature, the Committee on Toxicology, a group of experts empaneled by the academy, concluded that there is no threshold for the irritant effects of formaldehyde. According to the committee, even at concentrations of formaldehyde below .25 ppm somewhat less than 20% of the population may experience some degree of irritation.

Based on this finding and its own complaint data, the Commission reached the conclusion that formaldehyde emitted from UFFI poses an unreasonable risk of acute irritant effects.

C. Carcinogenicity

While the investigation of acute effects was ongoing, the industry apprised the Commission of the preliminary results of a Chemical Industry Institute for Toxicology (Chemical Institute) study linking formaldehyde exposure at high levels to nasal cancer in rats. The agency subsequently established the Federal Panel on Formaldehyde, a group of sixteen scientists from various government agencies, to evaluate the Chemical Institute findings. The panel concluded that the Chemical Institute study was valid and that formaldehyde should be presumed to pose a carcinogenic risk to humans.

The Commission's next step was to extrapolate from the high exposure rat data in order to quantify the risk of cancer to humans at the low levels of formaldehyde exposure associated with UFFI. To perform this task, the agency selected a computerized mathematical risk assessment model called Global 79. Global 79 was chosen over a number of other predictive models because it incorporated several assumptions the Commission believed were applicable to formaldehyde carcinogenesis. Unlike some other models, Global 79 does not predict an actual or most likely risk. Rather it predicts a range of risk within which there is a 95% possibility the actual risk will fall. Based on the actual formaldehyde levels found in the tests of 1,164 homes, the model predicted that the increased risk of cancer to a person living in a UFFI home for 9 years, 16 hours a day, would range from 0 to 51 in 1,000,000. From the results of the Franklin and Oak Ridge Labs studies, Global 79 predicted a risk range of between 0 and 37 in 1,000,000.[6]

---

6. As we have noted, the Commission concluded from the in-home tests that the average formaldehyde level in a UFFI home over a nine-year period is .08 ppm. The average level found in the Franklin/Oak Ridge Lab studies was .13 ppm. It seems anomalous, then, that Global 79 predicted a higher risk from the in-home data than from the Franklin/Oak Ridge Lab data. The explanation for this discrepancy apparently lies in the Commission's use of the declining curve of formaldehyde levels found in the in-home tests, not the average level, in the Global 79 risk assessment.

From the Global 79 analysis of the Chemical Institute rat study, the Commission concluded that UFFI poses an unreasonable risk of cancer to humans. This determination, coupled with the agency's finding of an unreasonable risk of acute irritant effects, is the reason for the ban. The Commission acknowledges that unless substantial evidence supports both its carcinogenicity and acute effects findings the ban was not proper.

The industry challenges both of these findings and the procedures employed by the Commission in reaching them.

In attacking the UFFI ban, the industry and amici leave very few stones unturned. They take issue with numerous aspects of the Commission's findings with respect to acute irritant effects. The bigger salvo, however, is aimed at the finding that UFFI poses an unreasonable risk of injury from cancer. We therefore address the Commission's cancer risk assessment first.

IV. THE RISK OF CANCER FROM UFFI

As we have noted, the Commission incorporated the results of the Chemical Institute high-exposure rat study into its Global 79 computerized risk assessment model in order to predict the cancer risk to humans at the low levels of formaldehyde exposure associated with UFFI. . . .

According to the industry, these predictions are flawed for a number of reasons. The industry argues that: (1) neither the formaldehyde levels found in the 1,164 test homes nor the Franklin/Oak Ridge Labs test results are accurate indicators of the formaldehyde levels in average UFFI homes; (2) the Commission erred in relying exclusively on the Chemical Institute rat data in its risk assessment model and ignored numerous epidemiologic studies indicating that formaldehyde is not a human carcinogen; (3) the Commission ignored the real explanation for the incidence of tumors at the high levels of formaldehyde exposure involved in the Chemical Institute study; (4) no substantial evidence supports the Commission's assumption that the effective formaldehyde dose for humans is the same as that for rats; (5) Global 79 incorporates several assumptions about formaldehyde carcinogenicity that are not supported by substantial evidence; (6) Global 79 predicts only an upper limit of risk and does not constitute substantial evidence that "it is at least more likely than not that [UFFI] presents a significant risk of [cancer]," Industrial Union Dept. AFL–CIO v. American Petroleum Inst., 448 U.S. 607, 653, 100 S.Ct. 2844, 2869, 65 L.Ed.2d 1010 (1980); and (7) other federal agencies have determined that formaldehyde does not pose a substantial health risk to man. We need examine only the first two contentions in detail.

A. Formaldehyde Levels

At the outset, the industry asserts that the average formaldehyde level attributed by the Commission to UFFI homes is inaccurate and grossly exaggerates the true level. In fact, the industry contends that there is no significant difference between formaldehyde levels in UFFI homes and non-UFFI homes.

According to the industry, the in-home measurements, which resulted in a predicted additional risk of cancer of 51 in a million, were scientifically invalid and do not constitute substantial evidence. The industry points out that the great majority of the tests were conducted by state agencies, not Commission personnel. Measurement methodologies differed from state to state. Twenty percent of the test homes were located in Massachusetts and Minnesota, where measurement techniques of questionable accuracy were used. More important, the test homes were not randomly chosen. A large percentage of the measurements taken were in residences whose occupants had complained about UFFI-related health problems.[10] According to the industry, this tended to overstate the actual average level. Additionally, the high formaldehyde levels that were recorded in many of the "complaint" homes were the result of faulty installation. These problems could be eliminated by a product standard. The industry concludes that the Commission should have conducted its own tests of randomly selected UFFI homes before taking the draconian step of a product ban.

The industry also asserts that the Franklin/Oak Ridge Labs test data do not accurately predict formaldehyde levels in actual homes. It notes that only nine panels were tested and that the results varied widely around the mean of .13 ppm.[12] The industry also argues that storage of the panels in exteme conditions invalidated the test results. Additionally, the industry contends that the test did not account for the air flow and exchange that occurs in actual homes and that Oak Ridge Lab recognized that this failure could lead to errors of two- to threefold. According to the industry, even the Commission recognized that in-home measurements could not be extrapolated from the Franklin/Oak Ridge Labs data.

The industry bases its claim that formaldehyde levels in UFFI homes do not differ significantly from levels in non-UFFI homes on three studies. . . .

The Commission contends that the . . . studies were invalid. None of the three considered the length of time that had elapsed since installation of the UFFI, a vital factor in the level of formaldehyde emitted. . . .

The agency also defends its use of Franklin/Oak Ridge Labs data. It argues that the conditions to which the panels were exposed before testing were no worse than would exist in a home without heating or air-conditioning. The Commission does not address other concerns raised by the industry about the Franklin/Oak Ridge Labs studies, but nevertheless concludes that the study was valid because its results were similar to those obtained in the in-home tests. Two significant omissions with respect to the in-home tests cloud this conclusion. The Commission does not explain its reliance on a data base comprised largely of complaint houses. Nor does the agency justify its failure to conduct a study of randomly selected UFFI homes before issuing the product ban.

. . . The studies relied on by the industry do not demonstrate conclusively that formaldehyde levels in UFFI and non-UFFI homes are essentially the same. As the Commission notes, age is a vital factor in the level of formaldehyde emitted by UFFI. The in-home and Franklin/Oak Ridge Labs studies do suggest that UFFI appreciably raises in-home formaldehyde levels.

But the Commission did not use the studies only to support such a generalized finding. They were also incorporated into an exacting, precise, and extremely complicated risk assessment model. The goal of the

10. Of the 1,164 in-home measurements, 827 were conducted in complaint homes, 337 in non-complaint homes. were considerably higher, however, and raised the mean for the entire group to .13 ppm.

12. Seven of the nine panels produced a mean result of .07 ppm. The other two

model was to determine the risk of cancer to a consumer living in an average UFFI home. The difficulty in reaching this goal is that neither the in-home nor the Franklin/Oak Ridge Labs studies were consistent with this aim. The in-home study focused on complaint residences, not average residences, not randomly selected residences. The Franklin/Oak Ridge Labs studies reflected conditions similar to an unheated, unair-conditioned home, not an average home. The similar results achieved by the two studies validate neither. The studies were inadequate to serve as a data base for the Global 79 risk assessment.

B. Evidence of Carcinogenicity: Epidemiologic Data and the Chemical Institute Study

The industry next contends that the numerous studies of humans exposed to formaldehyde in the workplace discredit the Commission's finding that formaldehyde is carcinogenic at low levels. Eleven epidemiologic studies involving a total of 10,000 workers were introduced into the record. None of the studies' authors found a statistically significant increase in the number of cancers among workers exposed to formaldehyde compared to the general population. . . .

The industry also relies on studies that were not completed until after the close of the record. The Federal Panel on Formaldehyde, which was convened by the Commission to assess the carcinogenicity of formaldehyde, stated in its recommendations to the agency that three pending studies of embalmers would "provide a good estimate of potential risk from formaldehyde exposure." Results in two of the three have now been released. In neither were nasal cancers or excess respiratory cancers found.

Finally, the industry points to statements made by Dr. Higginson, former director of the International Agency for Research on Cancer, in a letter submitted to the Commission shortly before issuance of the ban. Dr. Higginson stated that the epidemiologic data "are insufficient to exclude a minimal risk, but certainly they weigh heavily against the view that formaldehyde constitutes any considerable risk for nasal cancer to man." He also wrote that "[e]xact estimates as to the number of cases of a cancer that might be expected to occur in man based on a single experiment [the Chemical Institute rat study] are silly and simply ignore biological realities."

The Commission defends its reliance on the Chemical Institute rat data by reminding us that the Federal Panel found the study valid and concluded that formaldehyde should be presumed to pose a carcinogenic risk to humans. The agency rejects the industry's contention that the available epidemiologic evidence demonstrates that formaldehyde is safe. The Commission points to the small number of workers involved in the epidemiologic studies and their failure to account for the duration and concentration of formaldehyde exposure.

Again, the truth appears to lie somewhere between the positions taken by the Commission and the industry. We agree with the agency that the epidemiologic studies cited by the industry do not demonstrate conclusively that formaldehyde poses no cancer risk to man. The Commission concluded that the increased risk of cancer from formaldehyde exposure (at the levels it attributed to UFFI) was *up to* approximately 1 in 20,000 (51 in a million). It is highly unlikely that studies involving a total of 10,000 workers would detect such a small risk. Additionally, the failure to consider either the length of time the workers were exposed to formaldehyde or the levels to which they were exposed diminishes the studies' usefulness.

While the Commission correctly notes that the epidemiologic evidence is not conclusive, its exclusive reliance on the Chemical Institute study in its Global 79 risk assessment is equally unsupportable. In the study 240 rats were exposed to an average of 14.3 ppm formaldehyde for six hours a day, five days a week. After 24 months 103 of the rats developed nasal carcinomas. This was the only empirical datum with respect to formaldehyde carcinogenicity that was incorporated into the Global 79 model. But in a study as small as this one the margin of error is inherently large. For example, had 20 fewer rats, or 20 more, developed carcinomas, the risk predicted by Global 79 would be altered drastically.[19]

The element of doubt present here is similar to that with respect to formaldehyde levels. The Federal Panel's findings that the Chemical Institute study was valid and that formaldehyde should be presumed to pose a cancer risk to man do not authenticate the use of the study's results, and only those results, to predict exactly the cancer risk UFFI poses to man. As Dr. Higginson aptly stated, it is not good science to rely on a single experiment, particularly one involving only 240 subjects, to make precise estimates of cancer risk.

This problem is exacerbated by concerns about the Chemical Institute study raised by the industry. Although the average level of formaldehyde exposure in the experiment was 14.3 ppm, the rats in fact were exposed regularly to much higher doses. The average daily high was a near-lethal 32.4 ppm. We do not have to agree with the industry that this disparity renders the study invalid for all purposes to conclude that the Commission could not properly use the study as it did. To make precise estimates, precise data are required.

C. Other Contentions

The industry attacks the Commission's cancer findings on several other grounds. Most of these relate to assumptions made by the Commission in its risk assessment. Although several of these contentions present substantial questions,[20] we do not address them. The predictions made by the risk assessment model are no better than the data base. We have concluded that this base was inadequate. The Commission improperly relied on in-home data gathered largely from complaint homes. It failed to conduct a controlled study of randomly selected residences. The result is that the Commission's finding that UFFI poses an unreasonable

---

19. A more recent study has been conducted at New York University. Of 200 rats exposed to 14.6 ppm formaldehyde for 18 months, only approximately 10% developed nasal carcinomas. The Commission does not explain the wide gap between the results of this study and the Chemical Institute study. Nor does it apprise us how many tumors the Global 79 model would have predicted under the conditions of the NYU study. The NYU study shows it is doubtful that an experiment replicating the conditions of the Chemical Institute study would achieve identical results.

20. At least two of the assumptions are of questionable validity. The Commission assumed that at identical exposure levels the effective dose for rats is the same as that for humans. The industry points out that the effective dose for mice is much less than that for rats and argues that it is far more sensible to assume that rats equal mice than that rats equal humans.

Probably the most controversial assumption incorporated into Global 79 is that the risk of cancer from formaldehyde is linear at low dose—in other words that there is no threshold below which formaldehyde poses no risk of cancer. As the Commission acknowledges, this assumption leads inescapably to the conclusion that ambient air is carcinogenic, albeit to a lesser extent than UFFI.

risk of cancer is not supported by substantial evidence on the record as a whole.[21]

V. ACUTE IRRITANT EFFECTS

. . .

From its in-depth investigations, the Commission concluded that inhabitants of UFFI homes suffer eye, nose, and throat irritation, persistent cough, respiratory distress, skin irritation, nausea, headaches, and dizziness. The industry asserts that "in-depth" is a misleading misnomer. It points out that very few of the reported symptoms, which resemble those of influenza and colds, were diagnosed by physicians to be related to formaldehyde. Additionally, the industry notes that formaldehyde measurements were taken in very few homes. The industry takes the position that the complaint data are worthless and do not establish a causal relationship between UFFI and the symptoms reported. The Commission responds to this assessment with the following facts: Symptoms (1) were reported by more than one family member in many homes; (2) normally manifested themselves immediately after installation and often persisted for months or even years; (3) frequently dissipated outside the home; and (4) in several cases were verified to be linked to formaldehyde by physicians.

Certainly the investigations do not establish that all the reported symptoms were caused by formaldehyde emitted by UFFI. But the Commission's defense of its investigations persuades us that UFFI is not completely innocent. We agree that "taken as a whole, the complaints do identify a real problem." 47 Fed.Reg. at 14,382.

The problem is the complaints do no more. Specifically, they do not answer the question whether the risk of injury from acute irritant effects is unreasonable. This inquiry involves "a balancing test like that familiar in tort law: The regulation may issue if the severity of the injury that may result from the product, factored by the likelihood of the injury, offsets the harm the regulation imposes upon manufacturers and consumers." Southland Mower v. CPSC, 619 F.2d 499, 508–09 (5th Cir.1980).

. . . What the complaints fail to demonstrate is how likely it is that acute symptoms will occur.

To fill this gap in the equation, the Commission points to the conclusion reached by the National Academy of Sciences' Committee on Toxicology. That committee found that somewhat less than 20% of healthy adults may respond to the irritant effects of formaldehyde at .25 ppm. For the Commission's purposes and ours, this finding is worth exactly

---

21. The industry also refers to findings of other government agencies that are inconsistent with those of the Commission. After reviewing the Chemical Institute study and much of the other evidence relied on by the Commission, the Environmental Protection Agency concluded that formaldehyde does not present a significant risk of serious or widespread harm. The Food and Drug Administration made a similar determination. The Occupational Safety and Health Administration denied an emergency petition seeking to lower the present workplace standard from the present 3 ppm, a level many times that attributed by the Commission to UFFI.

These contrary pronouncements of course do not prove the Commission wrong, and we do not rely on them in reaching our decision. But they are disconcerting. Regulatory agencies such as these were created primarily to protect the public from latent risks. For them to be effective, the public must be confident in their ability to determine which products are unsafe, which drugs are dangerous, and which substances are carcinogenic. Interagency disagreement undermines such confidence.

nothing. First, it does not state whether the response at .25 ppm is expected to be slight or severe. All record evidence indicates the former. Second, with the exception of the first few months after installation, .25 ppm is much higher than the formaldehyde level associated with UFFI. The committee did not address the risk at the appropriate level. Third, the agency states that the committee predicted that "somewhat less than 20%" of the population may respond at .25%. This, like the Commission's cancer prediction of "up to 51 in a million," provides us no basis for review under the substantial evidence standard.

We conclude that the Commission's finding that UFFI poses an unreasonable risk of injury from acute irritant effects is not supported by substantial evidence. The failure to quantify the risk at the exposure levels actually associated with UFFI is the finding's Achilles heel. Predicting how likely an injury is to occur, at least in general terms, is essential to a determination of whether the risk of that injury is unreasonable.

. . .

VII. CONCLUSION

We are not unmindful that regulating in the face of scientific uncertainty within ever-tightening budgetary constraints presents the Commission with a difficult task. We nevertheless cannot abdicate our role in the regulatory process. Congress and our circuit's precedents require us to take a "harder look" to determine whether rules adopted under the Consumer Product Safety Act are supported by substantial evidence. That look discloses that the evidence is lacking here. The Commission's rule banning UFFI is vacated.

NOTES

1. Can the approaches of the D.C. Circuit in *Ethyl Corp.* and the Fifth Circuit in *Gulf South Insulation* be reconciled? Has the Fifth Circuit established a Catch 22: a demand for a quantitative risk assessment supported at each step by substantial evidence where such evidence is currently unavailable? If so, does it follow that the court erred?

2. In Baltimore Gas and Electric Co. v. Natural Resources Defense Council, __ U.S. __, 103 S.Ct. 2246, 76 L.Ed.2d 437 (1983), the Supreme Court upheld the decision of the Nuclear Regulatory Commission that licensing boards should assume that the permanent storage of certain nuclear waste would have no significant environmental impact and that therefore concerns about storage should not affect the decision whether to license a particular nuclear power plant. See Ch. 2, Sec. B.1, supra. In reaching its decision, the Court explained:

. . . . a reviewing court must remember that the Commission is making predictions, within its area of special expertise, at the frontiers of science. When examining this kind of scientific determination, as opposed to simply findings of fact, a reviewing court must generally be at its most deferential."

Id. at 4682.

Is the decision in *Gulf South Insulation* consistent with the mandate of *Baltimore Gas and Electric*? At a minimum, *Gulf South Insulation* suggests the extent to which courts (and lawyers) are likely to be drawn into the middle of technical debates about the quality of particular risk assessments. As you read the material in this section on assessing risks, consider what use a judge should make of this material and whether courts as presently constituted are appropriate forums for resolving debates about risk assessments.

3. On August 25, 1983, Solicitor General Rex Lee announced that, despite the request of the Consumer Product Safety Commission to seek Supreme Court

review of the Fifth Circuit's decision in *Gulf South Insulation*, the United States would not do so. Nancy H. Steorts, chairman of the CPSC stated that she was "still convinced" that the insulation "presents a risk of injury to consumers" and added "I would not put it in my own home." New York Times, Aug. 26, 1983 at A.1, col. 4. On October 20, 1983, the CPSC announced it would establish a warning program about urea formaldehyde foam. Washington Post, Friday, Oct. 21, 1983, at A.17, col. 3. On the merits of warnings versus bans for managing risk see Sec. A.4, infra.

b. Uncertainties Inherent in Alternative Methods of Testing for Carcinogens, Mutagens and Teratogens

OFFICE OF TECHNOLOGY ASSESSMENT OF THE CONGRESS OF THE UNITED STATES, ASSESSMENT OF TECHNOLOGIES FOR DETERMINING CANCER RISKS FROM THE ENVIRONMENT

113–117, 120–127, 136–139 (1981).

There are four major methods for detecting and identifying carcinogens:

1. molecular structure analysis,

2. short-term tests,

3. long-term chronic bioassays in laboratory animals (termed "bioassays" or "animal tests" hereafter), and

4. epidemiology.

The first two methods produce information about potential carcinogenicity; the third provides direct evidence of carcinogenicity in animals; the fourth produces direct evidence about cancer in man. These categories are briefly described in table 23.

Probably no statement made in the last column of table 23 is free from dispute. Results may be, and frequently are, challenged for several reasons: because the test was incorrectly designed or executed (all methods); because the method does not directly measure carcinogenicity (methods 1 and 2); because the test is too sensitive and produces false positives (methods 2 and 3); because the test is too insensitive and produces false negatives (method 4); and because the test does not measure human experience (all methods but 4), etc.

ANALYSIS OF MOLECULAR STRUCTURE AND OTHER PHYSICAL CONSTANTS

Some information about the likelihood of a chemical being a carcinogen may be obtained by comparing its structure and chemical and physical characteristics with those of known carcinogens and noncarcinogens.
. . .

. . .

Certain molecular structures have been associated with carcinogenicity, and structural similarity is used in making decisions about which agents are more or less suspect. For instance, 8 of the first 14 carcinogens regulated by the Occupational Safety and Health Administration (OSHA) are aromatic amines. . . .

Table 23.—General Classification of Tests Available To Determine Properties Related to Carcinogenicity

Method	System	Time required	Basis for test	Result	Conclusion, if result is positive
Molecular structure analysis	"Paper chemistry"	Days	Chemicals with like structures interact similarly with DNA	Structure resembles (positive) or does not resemble (negative) structure of known carcinogen	Chemical may be hazardous. That determination requires further testing.
	Basic laboratory tests	Weeks			
Short-term tests	Bacteria, yeast, cultured cells, intact animals	Generally few weeks (range 1 day to 8 months)	Chemical interaction with DNA can be measured in biological systems	Chemical causes (positive) or does not cause (negative) a response known to be caused by carcinogens	Chemical is a potential carcinogen.
Bioassay	Intact animals (rats, mice)	2 to 5 years	Chemicals that cause tumors in animals may cause tumors in humans	Chemical causes (positive) or does not cause (negative) increased incidence of tumors	Chemical is recognized as a carcinogen in that species and as a potential human carcinogen.
Epidemiology	Humans	Months to lifetimes	Chemicals that cause cancer can be detected in studies of human populations	Chemical is associated (positive) or is not associated (negative) with an increased incidence of cancer	Chemical is recognized as a human carcinogen.

Source: Office of Technology Assessment.

A number of proposals have been made that chemicals be divided up into classes depending on their structural similarities and that testing be done on a number of members in each class. Unfortunately, carcinogens are known in several chemical classes, and ". . . the dozen or more known classes of these agents [carcinogens] share no common structural features". Furthermore, even within classes, closely related chemicals may differ with respect to carcinogenicity—e.g., 2-acetylaminofluorene (2-AAF) is a well-documented carcinogen; its chemical relative, 4-acetylaminofluorene (4-AAF), is not a carcinogen.

SHORT–TERM TESTS

Short-term tests are so named because of the relatively short time needed to conduct the experiments. Some studies involving micro-organisms require less than 1 day to complete, most require a few days to a few weeks, and the longest, using mice, requires 8 to 9 months. These times may be compared to the more than 3 years required to complete a bioassay and the months to years required to complete epidemiologic studies.

A number of reasons account for the growing interest in using short-term tests to predict a chemical's carcinogenic potential:

- shorter time period required for the tests;
- low cost ($100 to a few thousand dollars for each test compared to $400,000 to $1 million for a bioassay);
- evidence that the majority of chemical carcinogens are mutagens and that many mutagens are carcinogens;
- growing opinion that short-term tests can predict which chemicals may be carcinogens.

The third point is important because many short-term tests determine whether or not a chemical causes mutations (mutagenicity) rather than if it causes cancer (carcinogenicity). The postulated relationship between mutagenicity and carcinogenicity stems from biological properties common to all living organisms. The genetic information in both germ cells (egg and sperm) and somatic cells (nongerm or "body cells") is composed of deoxyribonucleic acid (DNA), and agents that cause mutations in germ cells are also expected to cause mutations in somatic cells. A germ cell mutation may prevent the formation of viable offspring, cause a genetic malformation, or produce subtle defects in the progeny, such as minimal depression in intelligence or increased susceptibility to disease.

The consequences of somatic cell mutations are quite different from those in germ cells. Somatic cells do not contribute genetic information to succeeding generations, but as each somatic cell grows and divides, copies of its DNA are passed on to its two "daughter" cells. Some somatic cell mutations result in uncontrolled cellular growth: The normal tightly controlled growth pattern of the somatic cell is broken down, the cell grows and divides more quickly than it should, progeny cells exhibit the same uncontrolled growth, and cancer results.

The hypothesis that assigns genetic changes in somatic cells a role in cancer initiation is referred to as "the somatic mutation theory of cancer." . . .

The short-term tests that depend on mutagenicity can detect only materials that interact with DNA. Some cancers may be caused by other, "epigenetic," pathways that may not involve alterations in genetic information. Short-term tests cannot detect such activities. Additionally, short-term tests do not detect promoters that do not interact with DNA. The generally good correlation between mutagenic and carcinogenic activity as well as the bulk of results from basic cancer biological research support the notion that carcinogens generally interact with DNA.

The Ames Test

The most widely used and best-studied short-term test, the "Ames test," is named for its developer, Bruce Ames, a molecular biologist. The test measures the capacity of a chemical to cause mutations in the bacterium *Salmonella typhimurium*, a favorite tool for laboratory investigations since the 1940's. Salmonella's genetics and biochemistry are well understood: it is quickly and easily grown; it presents few manipulative problems in the laboratory, and test results are easily interpretable and reproducible between laboratories.

Basically, the Ames test involves mixing the chemical under test with a bacterial culture and then manipulating the culture so that only mutated bacteria will grow. The number of mutated bacteria is a measure of the potency of the tested material as a mutagen.

It is well known that some chemicals must be altered before they interact with DNA and that in humans and other mammals these changes are often accomplished by enzymes in the liver. The addition of liver extracts to the Ames test system and to other short-term tests provides a mechanism for these metabolic activation changes to be accomplished. Generally, extracts are prepared from rats, hamsters, or other laboratory animals. The source of the extracts and the amount used in the tests affect results, and careful experiments report these specifics so that others can replicate the tests. Some chemicals are "activated" by bacteria normally present in the intestine rather than by the liver. The addition of extracts of such bacteria to Ames test mixtures has been shown to activate some chemicals to mutagenic forms.

As of early 1979, more than 2,600 Ames test results had been published. . . .

Short-term tests are still in their infancy; development of the Ames test began about 15 years ago. The major factor influencing the acceptance or rejection of any short-term test as a method for identifying carcinogens is a demonstration that the test can discriminate between carcinogens and noncarcinogens.

The crux of validation experiments is determining: 1) how frequently carcinogens are correctly identified by short-term tests (sensitivity) and 2) how frequently noncarcinogens are correctly identified (specificity). Ideally the frequency for both sensitivity and specificity would be 100 percent. If the Ames test worked perfectly, every tested carcinogen would be a mutagen; every tested noncarcinogen would be a nonmutagen in the test.

The difference between the ideal and the measured performance can be expressed in terms of sensitivity. If the test identified 90 of 100 carcinogens as mutagens, it would have a sensitivity of 90 percent. The same observation can be described in terms of its false-negative rate. In the example, 10 carcinogens were falsely negative in the mutagenicity test, so it had a 10-percent false-negative rate.

Similarly for noncarcinogens, the test's success can be expressed as a specificity rate. If it identified 90 of 100 noncarcinogens as nonmutagens, its specificity was 90 percent. Alternatively, the result can be expressed in terms of the false-positive rate, which is 10 percent in the example.

Ames and his associates tested agents that had been classified as carcinogens or noncarcinogens in bioassays. They found that 156 of 174 animal carcinogens (90 percent) were mutagenic, and, equally important, 96 of 108 (88 percent) chemicals classified as noncarcinogens were not mutagenic. Ames has suggested that some of the "noncarcinogenic" chemicals that were detected as mutagens might have been incorrectly classified as noncarcinogens on the basis of bioassay results. His suggestion points up a problem inherent in "validating" any test against the results of other tests: There is no guarantee that the results of the tests that are used as standards are completely accurate.

Other researchers have investigated the correlation between Ames test mutagenicity and animal carcinogenicity in efforts to validate the mutagenicity test for predicting carcinogenicity. . . . There is general agreement that the tests are predictive, but some disagreement about whether they are 70-, 80-, or 90-percent sensitive.

Other Short-Term Tests

The number of short-term tests has proliferated rapidly. Purchase et al. included only six short-term tests in a 1976 review of the published literature; less than 1 year later, OTA had saccharin tested in 12 short-term tests. Two years after that, in the summer of 1979, a review by Hollstein et al. reported that over 100 short-term tests had been described in the scientific literature. The proliferation of tests reflects the great interest in cheaper, faster tests for identifying chemical carcinogens.

Hollstein et al. divided short-term tests into eight classes, according to what they can detect:

1. mutagenesis in bacteria (including Salmonella) and bacterial viruses;

2. mutagenesis in yeast;

3. mutagenesis in cultured (laboratory-grown) mammalian cells;

4. mutagenesis affecting mouse hair color;

5. mutagenesis in fruit flies (*Drosophila melanogaster*);

6. effects on chromosomal mechanics in intact mammals and in mammalian cells in culture;

7. disruption of DNA synthesis and DNA repair mechanisms in bacteria and other organisms; and

8. in vitro transformation of cultured cells.

One of the powerful tools available to biology is the use of cell culture systems, which allows cells obtained from animal or human tissues to be grown and manipulated in the laboratory. Cell cultures can be manipulated to serve as assays for mutagens (# 3 above) and for chemicals that interfere with chromosomal mechanics (# 6 above), but the most directly applicable use of cultured cells for carcinogen identification involves in vitro transformation (# 8 above).

Cells grown in culture exhibit characteristic morphologies and growth patterns. Exposing cultured cells to known tumor-causing viruses or to chemical carcinogens causes changes in morphology and growth characteristics. The changes are collectively called "transformation." Transformed cells resemble cells from tumors and have the important property of causing tumors when they are injected into animals, thus demonstrating a direct relationship between transformation and oncogenicity (tumor formation). Transformation of cell cultures is biologically more closely related to oncogenicity than is mutation, and transformation assays may take on major importance in testing programs.

Use of Short-Term Test Results and Policy Statements About the Tests

How best to utilize short-term tests in carcinogen identification is hotly debated. The majority view is that the tests are most useful as a screen to determine a chemical's potential carcinogenicity. As a new chemical is developed or as an old one comes under suspicion, an inexpensive short-term test or battery of tests can provide information about whether it is or is not likely to be a carcinogenic hazard. If the results of the test are negative, the chemical is considered less likely to be a hazard than a chemical that is positive. In the case of a chemical being commercially developed, a positive result might suggest that the chemical not be produced or that the cost of testing it in a bioassay should be considered in deciding whether or not to produce it. A positive short-term test result on a commercially produced chemical most likely causes more of a problem. The manufacturer is faced with having to begin other tests and to warn his employees and customers of potential hazard.

Opinions differ about the weight to be placed on short-term test results. Peter Hutt, former General Counsel at the Food and Drug Administration (FDA), and now in private law practice says that he advises his clients not to continue the development of a product which is positive in a short-term test. He maintains that, "life is too short" to invest time and effort in a chemical that is more likely than not to be considered a suspect carcinogen. Near the other end of the spectrum of opinion, Leon Golberg, in reviewing poor correlations between results of Ames testing and bioassays of components of hair dyes, concludes ". . . it is very hard to accept the fact that the Ames test is a predictor of carcinogenic potential".

The OSHA document "Identification, Classification and Regulation of Potential Occupational Carcinogens"[279], accepts the results of short-term tests as supportive evidence for deciding whether a chemical will be classified as a carcinogen or noncarcinogen. TSCA test standards and Federal Insecticide, Fungicide, and Rodenticide Act (FIFRA) guidelines accept short-term tests as measures for mutagenicity but do not consider them in making decisions about carcinogenicity. However, they mention that test developments are promising.

The problem of the carcinogens that are not detected (false negatives; lack of sensitivity) and the noncarcinogens that are falsely detected (false positives; lack of specificity) by any one test might be solved with additional short-term tests. The great attractiveness of a battery of short-term tests is that it might correctly identify all carcinogens and noncarcinogens. Unfortunately, no such battery has yet been defined. The composition of the battery will depend on validation studies and acceptance of each component test.

The growing use of short-term tests shows that short-term tests have moved to an important position in toxicology. The speed with which they have been incorporated into Government and private sector programs reflects the importance of the need to which they are addressed.

BIOASSAYS

Chemicals cannot be tested for carcinogenicity in humans because of ethical considerations. A substantial body of experimentally derived knowledge and the preponderance of expert opinion support the conclusion that testing of chemicals in laboratory animals provides reliable information about carcinogenicity. Animal tests employ whole mammal systems, and although they differ one from another, all mammals, including humans, share many biological features.

Effects in animals, properly qualified, are applicable to man. This premise underlies all of experimental biology and medicine, but because it is continually questioned with regard to human cancer, it is desirable to point out that cancer in men and animals is strikingly similar. Virtually every form of human cancer has an experimental counterpart, and every form of multicellular organism is subject to cancer, including insects, fish, and plants. Although there are differences in susceptibility between different animal species, and between individuals of the same strain, carcinogenic chemicals will affect most test species, and there are large bodies of experimental data that indicate that exposures that are carcinogenic to animals are likely to be carcinogenic to man, and vice versa.

In comparison to short-term tests and epidemiology, bioassays have had a longer development period and enjoy greater acceptance than the short-term tests; they are more easily manipulated to produce evidence linking a particular substance to cancer than epidemiology, and they can predict human risks rather than relying on cases of human cancer to

279.   . . . 45 Fed.Reg. 5001 (1980).

demonstrate risk. On the other hand, they take longer and cost much more than short-term tests.

The bioassay's apparent simplicity belies the difficulty of executing such experiments. Briefly, the suspect chemical is administered to a population of laboratory animals. As animals die or are killed during the course of the study, they are examined for the presence of tumors. At the end of the treatment and observation period (generally about 2 years), the surviving animals are killed and examined. A control group of animals is treated exactly the same except that they are not exposed to the suspect substance. The type and number of tumors and other relevant pathologies present in the exposed animals are compared with those in the control group, and statistically analyzed.

A statistical expression commonly used to describe a positive result is ". . . it has a p value less than 0.05" (5 percent). The p value is the probability that the observed effect might be explained by chance; in this case, the expression means that the probability of the observed carcinogenic effect being due to chance is less than 5 percent. A p value of 0.05 or less is commonly required to decide that a test result was statistically positive.

Finally a conclusion is drawn about whether or not the evidence indicates that the substance caused cancer in the exposed animals.

. . . Most chemicals which are presently known to cause cancer in humans are also carcinogens in animals. . . .

Standard Protocols for Bioassays

An important event in bioassay design was the development of NCI's Guidelines for Carcinogenic Bioassay in Small Rodents. The guidelines describe minimum requirements for the design and conduct of a scientifically valid bioassay and discuss important considerations in undertaking such studies. They are written to provide flexibility in experimental design while setting certain minimal requirements:

1. Each chemical should be tested in at least two species and both sexes. Rats and mice are usually the species of choice.

2. Each bioassay should contain at least 50 animals in each experimental group. When both sexes of two species are used and two treatment levels are administered and a third group is used as controls, a total of 600 animals is needed (see table 26).

3. Exposure to the chemical should start when the animals are 6 weeks old or younger and continue for the greater part of their lifespan. Mice and rats are usually exposed for 24 months.

4. One treatment group should receive the maximum tolerated dose (MTD), which is defined as the highest dose that can be given that would not alter the animals' normal lifespan from effects other than cancer. The other treatment group is treated with a fraction of MTD.

5. The route by which a chemical is administered should be the same or as close as possible to the one by which human exposure occurs.

6. Animals are closely monitored throughout the study for signs of toxic effects and other causes affecting their health.

7. Examination of animals is conducted by or under the direction of a pathologist qualified in laboratory animal pathology.

The guidelines also specify that special procedures (e.g., organ function tests, body burden determinations, absorption and excretion tests) may be needed for evaluating certain chemicals.

Table 26.—Distribution and Number of Animals in a Typical Bioassay Study of Carcinogens

Experimental groups	Species A		Species B	
	Males	Females	Males	Females
Dosage MTD[a] group	50	50	50	50
Dosage MTD/x group	50	50	50	50
Control group	50	50	50	50

[a] Maximum tolerated dose. Source: National Cancer Institute.

Objections to the Usefulness of Bioassays

Some general aspects of test design are seldom disputed. Examples of such provisions are the requirement of a minimum number of animals in the test groups and that (generally) both sexes be tested. On the other hand, consensus does not exist about some aspects of experimental design, for instance: How high a dose is to be administered? The policy of the agency that draws up the guidelines is reflected in what it says about the arguable aspects of experimental design. Tomatis has discussed five debated issues about bioassay . . . .

. . . .

2. Routes of exposure in animal tests do not correspond to routes of human exposure.

Chemicals are administered to laboratory animals in either food, water, by inhalation, force-feeding (gavage), skin-painting, or injection. Few objections are raised to administration in food, water, or by inhalation when the chosen route mimics the route of human exposure. More objections are raised to gavage, skin-painting, injection, or ingestion when that is not the normal human exposure route. However, such methods are sometimes necessary and, furthermore, carcinogens appear to be distributed throughout the body regardless of the route of exposure. . . .

3. Some animals used for testing are so biologically different from humans that results from them have no value.

Choice of animals for bioassays represents a compromise. Most current guidelines require or suggest that chemicals be tested in two rodent species, generally rats and mice. The advantages of these species are their small size, reducing the space necessary for housing, short lifespans (2 to 3 years), reducing the time needed for a lifetime study, and a large amount of information about the genetics, breeding, housing, and health of these animals. Rats and mice are cheap to buy, feed, and house, as compared with larger animals.

Primates are sometimes used for certain toxicological testing. They are certainly more like humans than rodents but their supply is limited. They are expensive, live up to 25 years, and require large areas for housing. . . .

Differences in metabolism, bioaccumulation, and excretion between rodents and humans should be considered in interpreting the significance of animal results for humans. There is no question that further research in the comparative biochemistry and physiology of man and rodents is necessary, but the comparisons will ultimately be limited by restrictions on what can be determined by experimentation in humans. Moreover, metabolic studies have shown that most differences between humans and experimental animals are quantitative rather than qualitative and support the idea that animal results can be used to predict human responses.

4. Some test animals or organs of test animals are exquisitely sensitive to carcinogens, and such sensitivity invalidates use of results from such animals.

Griesemer and Cueto have analyzed the results of testing 190 chemicals in the NCI Bioassay Program . . . .. They identified 35 chemicals that were "strongly carcinogenic" in either the rat or the mouse and non-carcinogenic in the other species. Of the 35, 18 were positive in the mouse and negative in the rat, and 17 were positive in the rat and negative in the mouse, which indicates that neither animal was much more often the sensitive species. However, 12 chemicals caused mouse liver tumors, no other lesion in the mouse and no lesions in rats. Taken by themselves these results suggest that the mouse liver is a sensitive organ.

Liver tumors are often found in mice but are infrequently found in U.S. citizens, although they occur frequently in human populations in other parts of the world. Should a chemical that causes mouse liver tumors be considered a hazard? An approach to resolving the mouse liver question was to review how predictive such results are for tumors in other animals. Tomatis, Partensky, and Montesano showed positive correlation between a chemical's being oncogenic in the mouse liver and its being oncogenic either in the liver or at some other site in rats or hamsters.

. . .

Despite the finding of Tomatis, Partensky, and Montesano that mouse liver carcinogens were often positive at other sites or in other animals, IARC* considers mouse liver and lung tumors as "limited evidence" for carcinogenicity. However, OSHA accepts mouse liver tumors as "indicators of carcinogenicity" if "scientific experience and judgment" are used in interpreting the data.

. . .

5. Finding benign tumors in test animals has no value in defining carcinogenicity.

Tumors can be divided into two classes, benign and malignant. Benign tumors do not metastasize, the tumor cells remain in contact with each other and do not invade other tissues or organs. Malignant tumors can invade other tissues and metastasize, spreading to distant parts of the body and causing other tumors. Both types of tumors are found in experimental animals.

. . .

The position that a benign tumor may later become malignant, that the line of demarcation between benign and malignant is unclear, and that benign tumors can also be life-threatening has prevailed in regulatory agencies. Therefore, no distinction is made in regulatory decisions between benign and malignant tumors. This is clearly reflected in FIFRA

---

* International Agency for Research on Cancer. [Eds.]

guidelines and TSCA test standards in which the endpoint is oncogenicity (tumor causation) rather than carcinogenicity (which emphasizes malignancy).

. . .

Expert Review of Bioassay Results

In addition to the general objections to bioassay procedures that have been discussed, specific objections may be raised to particular tests. For instance, animals may have been inadvertently exposed to more than one chemical, to pathogenic micro-organisms, to extreme temperature, or to temporary deprivation of food or water, any one of which might influence results.

EPIDEMIOLOGY

Lilienfeld defined epidemiology as the study of the distribution of disease in human populations and of the factors that influence disease distribution. Epidemiologic techniques are useful for identifying causative agents and conditions that predispose for cancer. Studies can determine associations in populations between exposure to carcinogenic agents or between aspects of lifestyle and increased cancer risk.

. . .

For the purpose of this discussion, epidemiologic studies are divided into three general types: 1) experimental, 2) descriptive, and 3) observational. While several basic strategies exist, there are no rigid study designs within any of these categories. Flexibility is important since, unlike laboratory experiments, epidemiology examines groups of unpredictable people living in dynamic environments.

Experimental Epidemiology

The ideal procedure for investigating cause-and-effect hypotheses is through experimental epidemiology. This type of study requires the deliberate application or withholding of a factor and observing the appearance or lack of appearance of any effect. Given the severity of cancer, ethical considerations preclude the administration of suspected carcinogens to people, though it is possible to test agents thought to aid in prevention.

Experimental epidemiology studies are difficult to conduct because of the need to secure the cooperation of a large group of people willing to permit an experimenter to intervene in their lives. The investigator must have reason to believe that the proposed intervention, whether a deliberate application or withholding, will be beneficial, but at the same time, he must be somewhat skeptical of the effects. Once sufficient evidence leads to the conclusion that the intervention is or is not beneficial, the experiment must be terminated.

Descriptive Epidemiology

Descriptive epidemiology studies examine the distribution and extent of disease in populations according to basic characteristics—e.g., age, sex, race, etc. The primary purpose of conducting descriptive epidemiologic studies is to provide clues to the etiology of a disease which may then be investigated more thoroughly through more detailed studies. Descriptive studies have focused on international comparisons and comparisons among smaller geographical regions, such as U.S. counties.

The identification of high bladder cancer rates in New Jersey males and excess mortality rates from cancer of the mouth and throat, esophagus, colon, rectum, larynx, and bladder in the industrialized Northeast have suggested that occupational factors might be incriminated and have prompted additional investigations. . . . Examination of age-specific rates of disease occurrence or mortality across time is another example of descriptive epidemiology.

Observational Epidemiology

Observational epidemiology depends on data derived from observations of individuals or relatively small groups of people. These studies are analyzed using generally accepted statistical methods to determine if an association exists between a factor and a disease and, if so, the strength of the association. Often the hypothesis to be investigated arises from the results of a descriptive study.

Cohort Studies

Two types of observational epidemiology studies, cohort and case-control studies, differ in the selection of the population groups for study.

A cohort study starts with a group of people, a cohort, considered free of the disease under study, and whose disposition regarding the risk factor under consideration is known. Usually the risk factor is an exposure to a suspect carcinogen or a personal attribute or behavior. The group is then studied over time and the health status of the individual members observed. This type of study is sometimes referred to as "prospective" because it looks forward from exposure to development of the disease characteristic. Cohort studies can be either concurrent or nonconcurrent in design. Concurrent cohort studies depend on events which will occur in the future, while nonconcurrent cohort studies rely on past data or past events.

Case-Control Studies

In a case-control study, individuals with the disease under study (cases) are compared to individuals without the disease (controls) with respect to risk factors which are judged relevant. Some authors label this study design "retrospective" because the presence or absence of the predisposing risk factor is determined for a time in the past. However, in some cases the presence or absence of the factor and the disease are ascertained simultaneously.

The choice of appropriate controls is rarely without problems. Often, for practical reasons, controls are chosen from hospital records. However, they may not be representative of the population, and they therefore may introduce "selection bias." . . . .

In case-control and cohort studies, the groups selected should be comparable in all characteristics except the factor under investigation. In case-control studies, the groups should resemble each other except for the *presence* of the disease, while in cohort studies, the study and comparison groups should be similar except for *exposure* to the suspect factor. Since this rarely is possible in practice, comparability between groups can be improved by either matching individual cases and controls (in case-control studies) or by standard statistical adjustment procedures (in either case-control or cohort studies). Demographic variables, e.g., age, sex, race, socioeconomic status, are most commonly used for adjustment or matching.

There are advantages and disadvantages with both the case-control and cohort studies. Case-control studies tend to be less expensive to conduct, require relatively fewer individuals, and many have been especially useful in studying cancer. The great advantage of cohort studies is that they allow observation of all outcomes, not only those originally anticipated. Bias is somewhat reduced in cohort studies since classification into an exposure category cannot be influenced by prior knowledge that the disease exists. In a concurrent cohort study, it is often necessary to wait many years for the manifestation of enough disease cases to conduct an analysis. The cost and time of the study can be reduced if conducted nonconcurrently. Cohort studies tend to require many more subjects than case-control studies and assignment of individuals to the correct cohort for analysis is difficult.

Causal Associations

A pragmatic view of causality is necessary, particularly when studying complex, multifactorial diseases such as cancer. Analysis of the association between exposure and disease in an epidemiologic study depends on tests of statistical significance. However, finding a positive statistically significant association is not sufficient to conclude a causal relationship. Artifactual and indirect associations must be considered. As MacMahon and Pugh state, ". . . only a minority of statistical associations are causal within the sense of the definition, which requires that change in one party to the association alters the other."

Policy Considerations About Epidemiology

While short-term tests and bioassays are used to evaluate a chemical's carcinogenic potential in the laboratory, the effect on humans is directly assessed by epidemiologic techniques. Well-conducted and properly evaluated epidemiology studies which show a positive association are accepted as the most convincing evidence about human risks.

Negative epidemiologic results show that exposure of a certain number of people to a substance at a specified level did not cause cancer. From such results, it is possible to calculate that human risk is no higher than what the study could have detected. For instance, a study of 1,000 people which showed no excess cancer would be "more negative" than one of 100 people exposed at the same level. Neither study would show that a risk exists, and neither shows that no risk exists, but the larger study shows a lower probability of risk.

The OSHA position, and that of Federal Government regulatory agencies in general, is to use epidemiology to estimate limits of risk, but not to weigh negative human evidence against other positive evidence in deciding whether or not a substance is a carcinogen.

NOTES

1. The Fifth Circuit in *Gulf South Insulation* focused on the fact that the rats in the key study were exposed to nearly lethal doses of formaldehyde. If you were representing the CPSC in court, what arguments would you make to reassure the judges on dose level? What rejoinder would you make if you were a lawyer representing Gulf South Insulation.

2. One of the major sources of uncertainty in current risk assessments is deciding how to extrapolate from animal tests or epidemiological studies. Consider the choices facing a risk assessor posed by the information presented by Office of

Technology Assessment in its report, Assessment of Technologies for Determining Cancer Risks from the Environment 172, 169–70, 157–58, 160–64 (1981):

Animal tests or epidemiologic studies yield data that relate cancer (or tumor) incidence to exposure levels (dosage) of the substance under study. The accuracy of the relation between exposure and incidence is always limited. Practical restraints on the number of animals that can be tested means that the data are always subject to significant experimental error; it also means that only relatively high incidences, almost always greater than 10 percent, can be measured in the experiments. Epidemiologic studies may be limited by small numbers of people available for study, or by unknown or uncertain exposure levels. In all cases, deficiencies in experimental design and execution may further limit the accuracy of relating incidence to dose. . . .

Accepting that experimental animals provide appropriate data for extrapolation to estimates of human risk, a decision has to be made about how to adjust the dose measured in the bioassay to the dose experienced by humans. A mouse or rat, of course, is much smaller than a human, and the dose necessary to cause a carcinogenic response is less than that required in humans. Three "scaling factors" are in general use to make allowance for the different sizes and rates of metabolism between experimental animals and humans. The three are listed below in order from least conservative, that is the one that predicts the lowest human risk, to the most conservative. The fourth scaling factor is less often used, ...

. . . For rats and mice, the most commonly used laboratory animals, the relationship between scaling factors and estimated risk in man for the same doses are shown in table 33.

1. Exposures may be adjusted on the basis of relative body weights, milligram of agent/kilogram of body weight/day (mg/kg/day), for animals and humans. This method is most generally used by toxicologists.

2. In cases where the experimental dose is measured as parts per million in food, air, or water and human exposure is through ingestion, the dose of the chemical is expressed as parts per million. This method is generally used by FDA and in some cases by EPA.

3. Exposure may be adjusted on the basis of the relative surface areas of the test animal and humans: milligram of agent/surface area/day, for animals and humans. It is generally expressed as milligram of substance/square meter of surface area/day or mg/m^2/day. EPA uses this scaling factor.

4. Exposures may be adjusted on the basis of relative body weight over lifetime, milligrams of agent/kilogram of body weight/lifetime (mg/kg/lifetime).

As can be seen from table 33, the choice of scaling factor can make a difference of up to fortyfold in estimating human risks. The mg/kg/day scaling factor was arbitrarily set equal to 1.0. Use of the mg/m^2/day factor (for instance) projects that humans would have 14 times the risk of a mouse for equivalent doses measured in mg/kg/day. The information given in table 33 allows a comparison to be made among the scaling factors. However, it is important to remember that great uncertainties surround biologic extrapolation because of possible differences between laboratory animals and man, and no great assurance is attached to any number in table 33.

Table 33.—Relative Human Risk Depending on How Dose Rate Is Scaled From Experimental Animals to Humans

| Experimental animal | Risk projected for humans when an identical dose is scaled by different factors | | | |
	Milligram Kilogram body weight/day	Parts per million In diet	Milligram m² body area	Milligram Kilogram body weight/lifetime
Mouse	1	6	14	40
Rat	1	3	6	35

SOURCE: Office of Technology Assessment.

[There is also no agreement about which mathematical models best extrapolate from the exposure levels measured in studies to those encountered in the environment.]

Toxicity testing produces data relating tumor incidence (I) to dosage (D) as shown in figure 21. Generally, a smooth curve drawn between the experimental points, P_1-P_5, (solid line in figure 21) is sigmoidal, or S-shaped. It can be seen that the incidence of tumor formation decreases with decreasing dosage. The crux of the extrapolation problem is what sort of line best approximates the response in the region for which data are not available. Or, what kind of line should be drawn from point P_1 to lower, unmeasured, response levels.

Graphic representations such as figure 21 do not fully show the difficulties in estimating incidence at very low doses. The first division on the vertical incidence scale is 10 percent, which means that 1 human or animal out of 10 developed cancer. For many agents, especially those present in air or water, we are interested in knowing what dose is projected to cause an incidence orders of magnitude less, e.g., 1 tumor in 100,000 animals or humans. Such small fractions cannot be seen on the figure, but they can be calculated using any extrapolation method.

**Figure 21.—A Stylized Dose-Response Curve
and Some Extrapolated Curves**

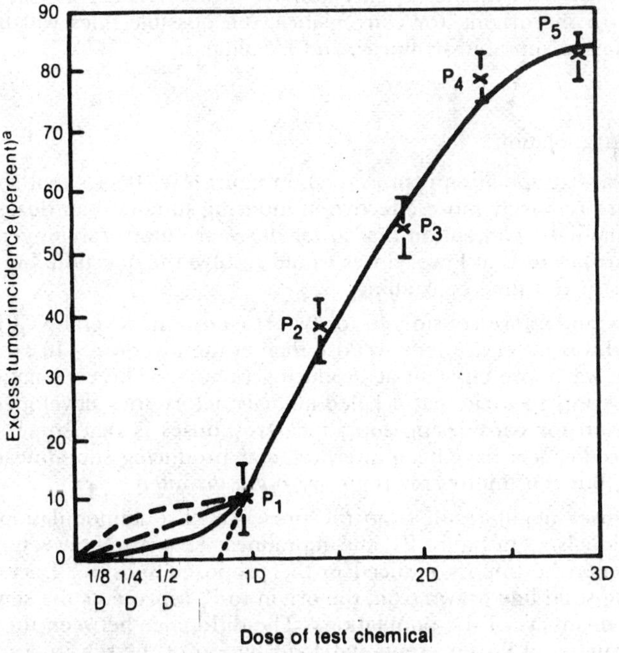

^aExcess tumor incidence (percent) is defined as:

$$\frac{\text{tumors in exposed population}}{\text{number of exposed population}} - \frac{\text{tumors in control population}}{\text{number of exposed population}} \times 100$$

——— a sigmoid dose-response curve; infralinear between O and P₁
—·—·— linear extrapolation
— — — supralinear extrapolation
------- line projected to a threshold

SOURCE: Office of Technology Assessment.

The solid curved line drawn from point P_1 to the origin is a continuation of the curve constructed between the experimentally determined points. It was drawn by eye, and it is representative of a number of smooth, concave upward lines that can connect P_1 and the origin as a continuation of the sigmoidal curve constructed between P_1 and P_5.

The Question of Thresholds

The solid line on figure 21 embodies the premise that there is no threshold. A threshold model would have the curve hit zero incidence at some dose greater than zero, as is shown in figure 21.

The threshold argument contends that there are doses of carcinogens so low that they will not cause cancer, and that no matter how many animals are exposed to doses that low or lower, no tumors will result. The counterargument is that any dose of a carcinogen, no matter how small, has a finite although small, chance of causing a tumor, and, if an experiment were performed with a sufficiently large number of animals, such risk would be detectable.

. . .

It is difficult, if not impossible, to marshal more evidence on one side of the threshold question than on the other. The ascendancy of the more conservative view, that thresholds cannot be identified for human populations can be taken as a policy decision made in the interest of protecting the public health. Such a general policy can not exclude the possibility that a threshold may someday be demonstrated.

Numeric Extrapolation To Project Risk at Doses Below Those Tested

The shape of the line in figure 21 depends on the number of tumors observed at points P_1-P_5. No matter what method is used to extend the line below P_1, that extension represents an estimate. Any number of smooth curves can be drawn from point P_1 to the origin; for convenience, the possible lines will be divided into three families: supralinear, linear, and infralinear.

. . .

Supralinear Extrapolation

A supralinear extrapolation is presented on figure 21. It says that some doses less than 1D are relatively more effective in inducing tumors than doses equal to 1D. Conceptually the contention that lower doses are more carcinogenic is easy to address. Further tests at lower doses would resolve the question, but additional tests are costly and time consuming.

Supralinear models are considered for two reasons. In several NCI bioassays, the tumor yield was lower at the high dose than at the low dose. In other words, the lower dose was more efficient at producing tumors. The explanation is that the higher dose was so toxic that it killed animals before they developed tumors. The other reason for considering supralinear responses is that some studies of radiation-induced cancer have been interpreted as producing supralinear dose-response curves, but those interpretations are hotly disputed.

Such responses might result from the presence of a subpopulation of more sensitive individuals. On figure 21, the supralinear response between the origin and P_1 represents the tumors induced in the proposed sensitive fraction of the population; the solid line drawn from the origin to P_5 represents the sensitivity of the remaining members of the population. The difference between the two lines between the origin and P_1 represents the contribution of the sensitive subpopulation to the total response at doses below 1D. It can be seen that the sensitive subpopulation accounts for the majority of tumors that occur below P_1.

. . .

Nonartifactual, supralinear dose responses have rarely been observed in bioassays but neither would they be expected. Laboratory animals are highly inbred and each animal should be more nearly equally sensitive than are members of human populations. Supralinear response models have been advanced but do not now receive the acceptance accorded to the other two general models.

Linear Extrapolation

A linear model is shown by the straight line that extends from P_1 to the origin on figure 21. If the true dose-response curve is represented by the solid curved line from P_1 to the origin, then the linear model is "conservative" and overestimates the number of tumors at all doses between P_1 and the origin.

The paper by Crump et al.* is an often-cited and important argument for linear dose responses at low doses. The paper points out that 25 percent of the U.S. population will develop cancer as a result of existing carcinogenic influences. Crump et al. propose that any new carcinogenic substance interacts additively with exposures and behaviors already present in the environment. Their mathematical theories predict that regardless of the shape of the dose-response curve at high exposures, at low doses cancer incidence should be proportional (linear) with exposure to the substance under study.

Gaylor and Kodell argue that no risk estimate can be very reliable for doses below that associated with the lowest data point (P_1 in figure 21) because there is no information available below point P_1. They propose the use of "linear interpolation" and the 95-percent upper confidence level to estimate the *maximum* risk posed by a substance.

Error is associated with any experimental determination, and standard methods can be used to calculate "confidence limits" for each estimate. Usually "95-percent confidence limits" are calculated for carcinogenicity experiments; they are plotted as vertical bars extending from the data points, as shown on the figure. The 95-percent confidence limit says that given the experimentally determined incidence and the size of the experiment, we can be 95-percent certain that the actual incidence represented by the point estimate lies inside the error limits.

In the method of Gaylor and Kodell a line is drawn from the upper limit of the error bar on the lowest data point to the origin. Inspection of figure 21 shows that this method projects a larger risk than does linear interpolation from the point P_1 to the origin. This is not an estimate of risk; it is an estimate of the upper bound of risk.

Objections to including upper confidence levels in extrapolation are frequently voiced. The practice of including them is seen as introducing a "safety factor." Industry spokesmen and others contend that the best risk estimate should be made and the safety factors added after the estimate is made.

As a practical matter, there is often no alternative to the linear model. The dose-response curve in figure 21 is an outrageous overstatement of the data that are generally available. Bioassays carried out according to NCI's cancer testing guidelines produce only two data points. The Environmental Protection Agency's (EPA) analysis of many such tests showed that tumor incidence was sometimes higher and sometimes only measurable at the lower of the two doses because other toxic effects killed animals at the higher dose. Left with only the response at the lower dose, there is little choice available but to estimate responses at still lower doses on the basis of simple proportionality. Such calculations produce a straight line from the experimental point to the origin.

. . .

A linear extrapolation model from the lowest positive data point to zero dose was used by EPA's Carcinogen Assessment Group (CAG) until the summer of 1980. At that time, CAG (48) announced it was going to discontinue use of the linear model and subsequently employ a model developed by Crump. The CAG decision was not made because evidence had shown the linear model was poorer than the new one:

> There is no really solid scientific basis for any mathematical extrapolation model which relates carcinogen exposure to cancer risks at the extremely low

* Crump, K.S. et al., Fundamental Carcinogenic Processes and Their Implication for Low Dose Risk Assessment, 36 Cancer Res. 2973 (1976). [Eds.]

level of concentration that must be dealt with in evaluating the environmental hazards.

The now-adopted model is linear at low doses, and, in practice, produces estimates of risk at low doses which ". . . are not markedly different from those obtained with the former procedure based on the one-hit [linear] model". However, the new model does allow consideration of data produced above the linear part of the curve (points P_4 and P_5 on figure 21) to influence the slope of the line and the range of error associated with each point.

Infralinear Extrapolation

The curved line between P_1 and the origin on figure 21 or any curved line which remains below the straight line is infralinear. Such models predict lower tumor incidence than the linear model. If it were decided that a certain level of risk were acceptable, higher exposure to the chemical would be allowable under infralinear than under linear models.

. . .

QUANTITATIVE EFFECTS OF SELECTING A MODEL

Selection of the appropriate model for estimating risks at low doses would be made easier if some models clearly did not fit the observed data points. As mentioned above, hardly ever is it possible to select the best model or even to reject the worst on the basis of fit to observed data points. The low end of the dose-response curve is most informative for selecting the correct model but it is the part that is most difficult to measure. In practice, incidence rates in animal tests much below 10 percent (5 tumor-bearing animals in a test population of 50) can seldom be distinguished from the rate of spontaneous tumors.

Table 32, derived from a paper by Brown, shows that two infralinear models and the one-hit model, which is essentially linear at doses that cause an incidence of 10 percent or less, are indistinguishable at high doses. For the table, a dose level of one was set as sufficient to cause an incidence of 50 percent. The expected incidence using higher doses or doses as low as one-sixteenth are nearly equal regardless of the model. Brown points out that no experiment of practical size could distinguish among the three models at those dose levels.

Table 32.—Expected Incidence of Tumors Calculated by Three Models When a Dose of 1.0 Caused Tumors in 50 Percent of the Tested Animals

Dose level	Projected percentage of tumor bearing animals		
	Log-normal model (Infralinear)	Log-logistic model (Infralinear)	Single-hit model (linear at incidence below 10%)
16	98	96	100
4	84	84	94
1	50	50	50
1/4	16	16	16
1/16	2	4	4
1/100	0.05	0.4	0.7
1/1,000	0.00035	0.026	0.07
1/10,000	0.0000001	0.0016	0.007

SOURCE: Adapted from Brown (35).

However, at much lower dose levels of 1/100, 1/1,000, and 1/10,000, the models diverge greatly in their projections of incidence. These greatly lower dose and response levels are often the ones of most interest for estimating human risks, but they cannot be measured. The incidences measured at higher doses do not provide sufficient information to choose the appropriate model. These problems plague all extrapolation efforts.

In general, either a linear or infralinear model is used for extrapolation. The linear model predicts a higher incidence at low doses than does the infralinear model.

Selection of the correct extrapolation model is important for only one of the three possible regulatory strategies for carcinogens. The first strategy is to accept either human or animal evidence as sufficient to identify carcinogens, and once the identification is made, try to eliminate the exposure. This approach requires no quantitative or numeric extrapolation. The second approach uses biologic and numeric extrapolation to rank substances in order from that expected to be most carcinogenic to those that are noncarcinogenic. This relative ranking can be accomplished by consistently applying any model, and the numerical accuracy of the estimated incidence is not critical. The third approach, which includes a quantitative estimate of human risk to be used in risk-benefit computations or to consider levels of acceptable risk requires the most accurate numerical estimate. Clearly, in this case, the selection of models is important because the numbers produced by different models vary across a wide range.

Virtually Safe Doses

A very low risk of cancer, say, one chance in a million lifetimes, is sometimes suggested as a virtually safe dose. Any extrapolation model can be used to calculate the dose which will produce such a risk, and different models produce very different estimates for the virtually safe dose (see table 32). As shown on figure 21, infralinear models predict higher virtually safe doses (i.e., lower risks at any dose) than does the linear model.

. . .

OTHER EXTRAPOLATION MODELS

The supralinear, linear, and infralinear models are all dichotomous. They compare the number of tumors or tumor-bearing animals in the exposed population to the number in the controls. In both populations, the analysis depends on the presence or absence of tumors. Other models can be used to make inferences about the times (or ages) at which animals develop tumors in response to exposures.

Two of these models have been used extensively to describe animal and human "time-to-tumor" data. The lognormal model described in Chand and Hoel, predicts that the average time-to-tumor is longer at low doses. An important outcome of this model is that at sufficiently low doses, the time necessary for tumor development may exceed the expected lifespan. Such a long latent period would produce a "practical threshold." The Weibull model . . . predicts that the average time-to-tumor is nearly independent of dose. This prediction means that an increase in dose simply causes more cancers; it does not shift the age distribution at which they occur. The assumptions and predictions of these two models are quite different. Unfortunately both are apt to give adequate fits to any available data set, making it difficult to reject one in favor of the other. . . . The mathematics for these models is sophisticated, and the interested reader is referred to Chand and Hoel.*

. . .

3. Assume you are asked to select the "best" extrapolation model for assessing the risk posed by a particular pesticide that has been found to produce tumors in mice. What recommendation would you make to the Administrator of EPA? to a federal judge? to Congress? Why?

---

* N. Chand and D.G. Hoel, A Comparison of Models for Determining Safe Levels of Environmental Agents, in Reliability and Biometry: Statistical Analysis of Life Length (1974). [Eds.]

c. On the Significance of Significance

FOOD AND DRUG ADMINISTRATION, NOTICE OF INTERLOCUTORY DECISION ON CYCLAMATE

Docket No. 76F–0392, June 29, 1979.*

The data from most of the carcinogenicity studies on cyclamate were analyzed to determine the incidence of bladder tumors. Other effects, however, such as lung, liver, lymphoid tissue and mammary tumors, in certain instances, do not appear to have been explored by the parties. The results of analyses of those data submitted in evidence but apparently not analyzed by the parties are summarized in the tables in Appendix A.** At this time, these analyses are not evidence, nor do I rely on them for any purpose. I ask the parties to review Appendix A, adopt, modify, or reject the data contained therein, decide whether to offer those data into evidence, and make clear on the record their positions with respect to those data. I further ask the parties to submit any other evidence and arguments relating to those data.

In particular, the parties should consider the matter of evaluation of significance. The terms "negative study" and "positive study" are used by both parties throughout their briefs. Abbott† contends that to be positive, i.e., to raise an inference that cyclamate is unsafe within the meaning of 21 U.S.C. 348, the results of a study must be "statistically significant". The term "statistically significant" does not, however, appear to have been discussed in sufficient detail for me to reach a fully informed decision on this issue.

The term "statistically significant" is generally understood to refer to a conclusion that there is a small probability of an event occurring due to chance alone. In other words, if an event happens frequently enough in a suitable test conducted under controlled circumstances, scientists will conclude that the event is not an accidental or random occurrence, but rather is caused by one or more controlled circumstances. With respect to evidence on the carcinogenicity of cyclamate, studies are examined to determine whether cancer found in cyclamate-treated animals is due to cyclamate or is, instead, a spontaneous event. This procedure involves comparing the incidence of cancer in those animals treated with cyclamate to the incidence of cancer in those animals that are not treated with cyclamate.

A statistical test is employed to determine the probability that the incidence of cancer found in the cyclamate-treated group is caused by cyclamate. No matter what the results of the study, one can never be absolutely certain that the results seen are not due solely to chance. The greater the difference between the incidence of cancer in the cyclamate-treated group and the control group, the greater the likelihood that the cancers in the cyclamate group are caused by cyclamate. It is the degree

---

* This is a decision by the Commissioner of Food and Drugs on review of an initial decision by an administrative law judge after an evidentiary hearing. The analyses referred to in the first paragraph were prepared by scientific advisors to the Commissioner on the basis of data in the record of the hearing. [Eds.]

** The analyses showed varying associations between cyclamate and cancer incidence, but below the 95% confidence level. [ed.]

† Abbott Laboratories, the manufacturers of cyclamate. [Eds.]

of certainty that should be required before attributing carcinogenic results to cyclamate over which Abbott and the Bureau* disagree.

Abbott appears to argue that the agency should be at least 95% certain, i.e., the probability (P) that the observed results are due to chance alone should be equal to or less than .05. . . . The Bureau, on the other hand, appears to argue that something less than 95% certainty is sufficient to lend support to the conclusion that cyclamate has not been shown to be safe. . . .

The use of "statistical significance" in the scientific community has not had the degree of inflexibility that the parties in these proceedings have assumed it has. Although the ".05" confidence level has often been used in the scientific literature to determine whether a result is positive, there is no fixed convention on the matter, and in fact it is more usual for scientists simply to give a result and supply the level of statistical significance, leaving judgments about *biological* significance to others.

This practice underscores the independence of the two kinds of significance. On the one hand, a result that is highly significant statistically owing to large sample size may lack biological significance if the parameter measured contributes trivially to the total variance. On the other hand, a result that is only at the 90% confidence level could have great biological significance. Thus, a conclusion of biological significance may be drawn by collective consideration of several related biological results, each of which may have a different level of statistical significance.

There is always a temptation to adopt the highest possible confidence level, particularly in the scientific community where a very high value is given to the avoidance of a false positive result. Especially high reliance is placed on reports of positive results because they are used to construct new hypotheses and theories and will be incorporated into the body of assumed scientific knowledge. But no particular value of significance constitutes a law of nature; it is a matter of scientific custom, reflecting human value judgments about the purposes of the scientific enterprise. And in some contexts we are especially troubled by the prospect of mistakenly declaring that the results of a study are negative, i.e., of mistakenly concluding that a study demonstrates safety. Such a decision, if incorrect, could result in the widespread marketing of a carcinogen. A regulatory agency may therefore have less reason than scientists do to insist on a very high degree of certainty before concluding that a study is positive. Similarly, there may be reason for a regulatory agency to require greater stringency than other scientists require before concluding that a study is negative. I am not now expressing any final view on this matter. Moreover, resolution of this issue *may* not be necessary to a final decision in this case. It is also possible, however, that resolution of this issue will be important once the record has been completed on remand. I find that this issue has not been sufficiently developed by the parties and therefore I seek further comment and evidence elaborating in detail upon each party's position on it.

. . .

Donald Kennedy
Commissioner of the Food
and Food Administration

---

* FDA's Bureau of Foods, the party supporting the ban on cyclamate. [Eds.]

MITCHELL LAZARUS,
ON STATISTICAL SIGNIFICANCE

Scientists like to say that they design and conduct experiments in order to test hypotheses. Often that is not quite true; especially in basic research, many experiments amount to a kind of sophisticated puttering, with only vague goals in mind. But even in those cases, scientists do develop hypotheses afterward, and report the experiments as though the goal all along had been to test them. Let us, then, stay with the party line. We shall suppose that the hypothesis came first, and that the experiment was indeed constructed for the purpose of testing it.

In thinking about what it means to test a hypothesis, we find an interesting asymmetry: it is possible to *dis*prove a hypothesis, but never possible to prove one.[1] Consider, for example, a simple hypothesis from the theory of gravitation. Hypothesis: dropped stones fall down. If one stone ever were to fall upward, that would disprove the hypothesis once and for all. No matter how many stones fall down, in contrast, there is still no guarantee that the next stone will do likewise. Each next stone is likely to fall down, of course, but not certain to. Thus, each downward-falling stone tends to confirm the hypothesis, but no number of them can absolutely prove it. After a million stones have fallen down, there always remains that possibility that the millionth-and-first stone will not.

In testing a hypothesis, then, a scientist does not attempt to prove it. Rather, he attempts to disprove it. Generally he hopes to fail in the attempt, for a failed effort to disprove the theory will tend to confirm it. In our gravitational example, we attempt to disprove the hypothesis by dropping a stone. We observe that it does not fall upward. The hypothesis is once again not yet disproved, and that finding tends once again to confirm it.

If the attempt to disprove the hypothesis is a half-hearted one, it does not tell us much when it fails. For the experiment to mean anything, we must drop enough stones. How many stones do we need? And once we have dropped them, and noted that all of them fall downward, how confident can we be of the hypothesis that all stones fall down? Those are the questions that statistical significance answers, as we shall see in the following example.

The Gender Detector

It used to be the custom, and it may still be, for the engineering students at McGill University in Montreal to give a dance every February for the entire school. A highlight of the event was the judging of a competition among the various departments of the engineering school. One year in the early 1960s, the electrical engineering students unveiled a device that looked much like the scales in a doctor's office. Whenever a person stood on the platform, a sign overhead would light up either MALE or

---

1. We use "prove" here in its mathematical sense, not in its legal sense. For example, a lawyer working under the proponderance-of-the-evidence rule has proved a fact when he has shown it to be more likely true than not. The standards are stiffer under the clear-and-convincing rule, and stiffer still under the reasonable-doubt rule. But a lawyer is never called upon to prove that a fact must absolutely be so. That is precisely what mathematicians do attempt to prove, and they are never satisfied with less. Any doubt whatsoever will invalidate a mathematical proof. Scientists attempt the same standard as the mathematicians, but as we see infra, can never achieve it.

FEMALE, according to the person's gender. The machine functioned flawlessly all evening, and no one could figure out how it worked.

Our immediate concern here is not *how* the machine worked, but *whether* it worked. We go back in time to a few days before the dance. We are in a basement laboratory. Amidst a debris of parts and tools, the newly constructed machine is plugged in for the first time. One of the students who built it, a man, stands on the platform. The sign lights up MALE. "Look at that," he says. "It works!"

Not so fast. Suppose that the machine were lighting up at random. There would be a 50–50 chance of its giving the right answer. That is not much in the way of proof. And so a second student stands on the platform, this time a woman. The sign flashes FEMALE. Better; but there is still that nagging possibility that the machine is responding by chance.

We can work it out easily enough. For two students in turn, the machine could have responded in any of four ways:

male	male
female	male
male	female
female	female

If the machine is operating at random, all of these four sequences are equally likely. There is, then, fully one chance in four that the machine is not responding to gender at all, but merely picking answers out of the air.

We are tempted to ask how many students we must test to be certain that the machine really works. But the question is fallacious. We can never be certain. In principle, the machine might be answering at random, yet still give the right responses for a million students in a row. That is outrageously improbable, to be sure, but not impossible.

Let us put the question differently. How many students must we test to be *reasonably confident* that the machine works? That question leads immediately to another: how confident is "reasonably confident"? We were not satisfied with two students, and properly so—one chance in four of being misled is not good enough. Might we be content if the machine works for, say, a thousand students? We should be; to write out the odds against obtaining those responses by chance would take a one followed by 301 zeros![2]

There is a way to ask the "reasonably confident" question more precisely, but we must first rephrase the discussion in terms of probabilities. Suppose once more that the machine is operating at random, and gives the right answers by chance. With two students tested, the probability of our being misled into thinking that the machine really works is one in four, or 0.25—too high. But if the probability were low enough, we could be reasonably confident that the results are *not* due to chance—in other words, that the machine works.

The probability we are looking at has a name: it is the level of significance for the experiment—here, 0.25. *The level of significance is the probability that the experimental results were due to chance, rather than to whatever the experimenter did.*[3] The level of significance is a most useful thing to

---

2. The odds against correct responses by chance for N students are one in 2^N. Here 2^N means $2 \times 2 \times \ .\ .\ .\ \times 2$, with N 2s in the expression. When N is over 10 or so, 2^N is approximately equal to a one followed by N/3.3 zeros.

3. The usual mathematician's disclaimer: there is really more to it than that. But this

know, because it helps us decide how much faith to put in the results. Unless the results are very probably *not* due to chance, they are scarcely worth our attention.

The lower the level of significance, the better it is. The smaller that number, the lower the probability that the results occurred by chance. Hence, the higher becomes the probability that the results are due to the actual gender of the person standing on the platform. Telescoping that: a low level of significance means that the machine probably works.

We first tested one student, and then two. Let us now test a few more. It is not hard to construct a table that shows the levels of significance for different numbers of students tested. We assume that the machine gives the right answer evey time:

Number of Students	Level of Significance
1	.50
2	.25
3	.13
4	.06
5	.03
6	.016
7	.008
8	.004
9	.002
10	.001

The more students we test, the lower and better the level of significance becomes. That is generally true, and it is very important in more elaborate studies. Ordinarily it costs more money to test more subjects, and sometimes it costs a great deal more. Good significance, then, costs money. We shall take up below the question of just how low the level of significance must be, in order to be considered satisfactory.

Even very good levels of significance can give unwarranted faith in an experiment. Suppose that our machine does not work properly at all. In fact, it is stuck; no matter who is on the platform, it responds MALE. Suppose further that we test it with 10 students—and all of them are men. The machine will respond perfectly every time. From the table, the level of significance will be .001. That is low enough to give us great confidence in the machine, even though in fact it is not functioning. We can deduce from this a warning: the level of significance is meaningful only if the experiment is designed and executed soundly. Here, we should test approximately equal numbers of men and women, and they should step onto the machine in random order. Scientists often use tables of random numbers in designing such experiments.[4]

simple definition can take us a very long way nonetheless. The level of significance is sometimes also called "level of confidence," and may be symbolized by the letter *p*. There are differences in meaning among the terms, but they need not concern us here.

4. How did the machine work? In those days, men always wore dark suits to dances, and women wore dresses. It is very cold in Montreal, in February; women needed stockings. In the early 1960s, women's dresses came approximately to the knee. The machine sent out a horizontal beam of light about one foot above the platform, and used an electric eye to measure what came back. A woman's stocking reflects more light than a man's trouser leg, and on that basis the machine made its decision.

The machine, in other words, did not detect gender at all, no matter how low the level of significance. It merely detected reflectivity of a person's garments. Under the particular conditions of that place and time, the correlation with gender was quite good. Today, or in a different climate, the results might be different. This points up yet an-

Additives and Remedies

The preceding example was inherently a simple one. We added a further simplification, in assuming that the machine either worked perfectly or responded at random. That is, we left out the possibility that the gender of the person on the platform might influence the machine's answer, but only partially.

Nature rarely allows us that kind of assumption. Suppose, for example, that a scientist wishes to determine whether a particular drug relieves headaches. First problem: no drug will relieve every headache every time. Second problem: a great many factors in addition to the drug will affect each patient's headache. The most that the scientist can hope for, then, is a finding that the drug has some therapeutic influence on the pain—that it helps to relieve some headaches some of the time.

Let us design an experiment to test the drug. We round up 100 people with headaches and give the drug to all of them. Fifty-one of the patients report that their headaches are better. To an unsophisticated observer, that might seem impressive. But some number of the patients—we do not know how many—would probably have felt better even without the drug. The mere fact that 51 felt better with the drug tells us nothing.

We must refine the experiment. This time, we round up 200 people with headaches. To 100 of them, we give the drug; we call them the "experimental group." To the other 100, we give nothing; they are the "control group." The results:

Experimental group: 47 improved
Control group: 16 improved

That looks promising, but it is still not good enough. For many people, the mere act of taking a pill can give psychological relief from pain—even if the pill contains no medication whatsoever. Such a pill is called a "placebo." Improvement from it is called the "placebo effect"; and the phenomenon works only if the patient does not know that the pill is a placebo. In our last experiment, the experimental group took a pill, while the control group did not. Perhaps, then, the difference between the groups is due to the placebo effect.

We try once more. We find another 200 sufferers and again divide them into equal groups. Again, the 100 in the experimental group receive the drug. This time, we give the control group a pill also; but a placebo. For both groups to be equally subject to the placebo effect, we must make sure that none of the 200 people knows whether his pill is the drug or the placebo. Such an experiment is called a "blind study." If the staff members working with the patients know what pill each is taking, they might unconsciously influence the patients' responses, and so we keep it a secret from them, too. That makes our experiment a "double-blind study." All of the pills look the same; they come in individually numbered bottles; and the piece of paper saying whether each numbered bottle contains a pill or a placebo is locked away in a sealed envelope. We will not break the code until all of the results are in.

Now, finally, we are in a position to learn something. We tot up the results, open the envelope, and summarize the findings:

other potential problem with levels of significance: we must always make sure that they are telling us about the correct phenomenon.

Experimental group: 48 improved
Control group: 39 improved

The control group did better with placebos than without. But the experimental group is still doing better than the control group. Perhaps the drug is effective after all.

Or perhaps it is not. If we work through the mathematics, we find that the level of significance for this experiment is 0.10.[5] That means there is still one chance in ten (0.10) of obtaining the results we did—even if the drug had no more medicinal effect than the placebo (none) and the patients were merely getting better at random. With that degree of doubt, we might hesitate before spending millions of dollars to promote the drug, or even applying for FDA approval.

We are now in a quandary. Either the drug does not work at all, and we hit that one chance in ten of good results, or the drug does work, but the experiment did not show it convincingly. The only way to find out for sure is to repeat the experiment, using more subjects. And so we try it again, this time tripling the number of people in each group. Although it is unlikely to happen, let us suppose for illustration that the proportions of people helped in the two groups remain exactly the same. The numbers in each group are simply tripled:

Experimental group: 144 improved
Control group: 117 improved

Again we calculate the level of significance, and we find it has dropped to 0.013.[6] That is far better. Now there is only about one chance in 77 of the results coming about by chance. That should be good enough to give us considerable confidence in the drug. Note once again, however, that the improved level of significance came at a cost. We had to test 600 patients instead of 200, which is roughly three times as expensive. For some very rare diseases, there may not be enough patients available anywhere to reach a low enough level of significance.

A real drug study would be considerably more elaborate. The experimenters would not look for all-or-none relief, as we have here, but instead would attempt to quantify, however crudely, the degree of pain before and after taking the medication or placebo. They would keep track of the type of headache and its location, hoping to learn if the drug is more effective for some kinds of pain than others. Different groups of patients would be given different doses of the new drug, and the effects compared. Some groups in the study might take aspirin or acetaminophen, to see if the new drug is any more effective than the remedies commonly available today. In their analysis, the experimenters would calculate levels of significance among all pairs of groups.

Again, the warning: levels of significance can be relied upon only if the experiment itself is properly conducted. Should the control group accidentally learn that they are receiving placebos, for example, they will obtain less relief, and the level of significance will spuriously improve.

A more troubling problem arises when the test of a new drug involves an affliction more serious than headache. In the design we used here, members of the control group received only placebos, and so they went untreated for the duration of the experiment. We were sacrificing the

---

5. For the cognoscenti: the normal approximation to the binomial distribution yields $z = 1.284$, which on a one-tailed test gives an alpha of .09964.

6. $z = 2.223$; alpha $= .01310$.

welfare of a few for the possible benefit of many, and that raises a difficult ethical question. Perhaps the fairest solution is not to use a placebo group at all, but to treat the control group with the most effective medication available, short of the new drug. The level of significance would then tell us something different—whether the new drug is reliably better than the best existing treatment. That is not an unreasonable question to ask, and it ensures that all patients participating in the experiment will receive one treatment or another.

Levels of significance work much the same way in many other studies—those in which the experimental treatment is but one of many factors which affect the result. Suppose, for example, that we wish to determine whether a particular food additive causes cancer in rats. There are, of course, many potential causes of cancer besides the additive. We obtain two groups of rats, as genetically alike as possible. One, the control group, subsists on laboratory rat food, while the other group receives the additive as well. We count up the cancers in both groups, run through the mathematics, and decide if the level of significance is low enough to warrant a finding that the additive is indeed carcinogenic.

Cancers are not all that common, and so we may well not achieve respectable levels of significance in a study of moderate size. There are basically two ways to solve the problem: we can use more rats, or we can try to increase the number of cancers in the rats that we have. One way to increase the number of cancers in the experimental group, and hence to improve the level of significance, is to use very large doses of the additive. Indeed, unless we either do that or use millions of rats, the results will usually be close to random.[7]

How Low is Low Enough?

Teachers of statistics invariably tell their students to determine the appropriate level of significance first, before they run the experiment; and then, when the data are in, to accept or reject the findings accordingly. Sometimes government regulations or university guidelines specify particular levels of significance for particular kinds of experiments. With experience, it is possible to estimate how large the experiment must be in order to achieve the levels of significance sought. But in the absence of such outside constraints, most scientists first run the experiment, look at the resulting levels of significance, and only then draw their conclusions.

Two main factors determine what levels of significance will be acceptable. One is the consequence of being wrong. If the public health or large sums of money are at stake, those responsible for making the decision will insist on very low levels of significance. Suppose, for example, that a promising new pain reliever has potentially harmful side effects. Unless its proponents can show at very low levels of significance that the new drug relieves pain better than aspirin does, there is little point to introducing it. The second factor is the financial cost of making the experiment larger, in order to bring the level of significance down. A new drug might be thought useful in alleviating a very rare blood disease. A thorough test would require us to locate patients all over the country and subject them to long, costly courses of treatment. If the drug is other-

---

7. Note, however, that once we have used large doses of the additive in the rats, the level of significance we find is then valid only for those same large doses, and only in rats. Whether that result can be extended to the lower doses that humans ingest over longer periods of time is an entirely separate question.

wise safe, we might be willing to accept it provisionally on the basis of a relatively poor level of significance.

The extremes are easy to find. A level of significance at .001 is generally considered to be excellent; 0.20 is never to be relied upon. Scientists working in pharmacology, physiology, and the like ordinarily insist on a level at least as low as 0.05. That varies among fields of study, however. Psychologists working in certain aspects of human vision use techniques so precise that they do not take seriously anything higher than .001, and levels at .0001 are not uncommon. (Below that, the mathematical techniques become unreliable.) In sociology, on the other hand, researchers must sometimes be content with 0.10, and with the relatively high probability of error that it entails.

The level of significance is only one indication of whether we should trust an experimental result. It can never replace a hard look at the experiment itself. Moreover, the level of significance helps to rule out only one kind of flaw: that of good results by chance. Experimental data can be misleading in many other ways, and still give a low level of significance. In a word, there is no safety in numbers.

NOTES

1. What is the difference between statistical and biological significance?

2. On September 16, 1980, Commissioner Jere Goyan of the FDA announced that cyclamate would not be approved as a food additive. 45 Fed.Reg. 61,474. In explaining his decision, he made the following findings on statistical significance and biological significance:

4. *Commissioner's Findings on Statistical Significance. Although P<.05 has in the past been used as a standard, this usage is grounded in history, not in science or law. Before the advent of computer technology, statisticians relied on statistical tables to determine statistical significance. These tables generally reported only three significance levels: .01, .05, and .1.* The use of P<.05 as a reference point evolved from the use of these tables. Indeed, Abbott's witnesses seem to recognize the lack of scientific basis for use of P<.05. One of these witnesses, Dr. Smuckler, stated that "it is true that (the use of the .05 confidence level) is an arbitrary decision, and, from a strictly mathematical standpoint, the selection of this limit could be criticized . . . ." Dr. Oser, another Abbott witness, could say only that the .05 confidence level is "commonly used." Dr. Carlborg, a third Abbott witness who is a statistician, did not articulate any rationale for use of P<.05, but rather stated that "NCI regularly uses the .05 level". Traditional usage of a scientific method is not necessarily, however, a valid reason for usage of that method in a particular case.

Moreover, although use of the P<.05 as a standard is grounded in tradition, it is no longer the method used by most statisticians. Most statisticians, with the use of computers, now can and do report to the precise P-value for an observed result and allow toxicologists and other scientists to make a judgment for themselves on whether or not the level of statistical significance obtained is sufficient for them to reach a conclusion that the effect seen is the real effect of the substance tested.

In deciding how to apply the concepts of statistical and biological significance in proceedings under Section 409 of the act, we do well to keep in mind the fact, adverted to earlier, that evidence not conclusive enough to confirm harm may yet be probative enough of harm to negate safety. . . . It is that distinction which is mandated by the statute. We are commanded to seek proof of safety, not merely to accept as proof of safety anything falling minutely short of proof of harm.

Commissioner Kennedy put it another way in pointing out that one's choice of a P value may depend on the purpose to which it will be put. In some cases, the consequences of a false positive are very serious. Suppose, for example, that we are testing a new component for a rocket to be used in a moon shot, and that that component's survival is critical to success of the mission. In such a circumstance, we would want to be virtually 100% certain that the new component is more reliable than the component it is replacing. Thus, a P-value of .000001 might be desirable.

Where, however, it is a false negative that presents a problem, a test with a P-value higher than .05 may supply important information. In this proceeding, there is good reason to be seriously concerned about an incorrect finding of safety, for the consequence is the marketing of a carcinogen. Using this principle, there is a valid reason for FDS to consider effects that are not significant at P$<$.05 even though scientists or regulators engaged in different endeavors may not. In so doing I emphasize that the difference between a confidence level of P$<$.05 and P$=$.06 is merely a matter of the degree of certainty. In the former case, one is 95 percent certain that the observed result is not due to chance. In the latter case, one is 94 percent certain. There is no valid scientific rationale for concluding that there is a substantial difference between these two confidence levels. In the latter case, one is a little less certain about whether the carcinogenic effect is associated with treatment. I cannot, however, ignore such an effect. It may not be conclusive, but it is at least suggestive of a carcinogenic effect and therefore supports the conclusion that the tested substance has not been shown to be safe. Such suggestive results are especially important where they recur in a number of studies, for as a scientific matter, several inconclusive but suggestive studies containing similar results increase the likelihood that the effect observed is real. Adopting Abbott's suggested use of P$<$.05 for all studies would preclude consideration of such inconclusive but suggestive results and therefore would be both scientifically and legally inappropriate. Ethyl Corp. v. EPA, 541 F.2d 1, 28 n. 58 (D.C.Cir.) (en banc) cert. denied, 426 U.S. 941 (1976).

I also reject Abbott's argument that in evaluating other food additive petitions, the Bureau of Foods always uses P$<$.05 as a standard. There is no evidence in this record to that effect. . . .

Moreover, even if the Bureau had in the past used P$<$.05 as a standard, the Bureau's past practice is not controlling because the Bureau does not set the *agency's* standards for approval of food additive petitions. . . .

Finally, it is important to note that, although I find that it is appropriate to rely on effects that are not significant at the P$<$.05 level, I am not relying solely on such effects in denying approval of the food additive petition for cyclamate. . . . Thus, even if I were to use P$<$.05 as a standard, as Abbott has suggested, I would nevertheless find that Abbott has failed to show that cyclamate is safe.

5. *Position of the Parties, Findings of the ALJ and Commissioner's Findings On Biological Significance.* Abbott agrees that "evaluating effects for their biological significance, if any, is a valid scientific and regulatory exercise". Moreover, it is undisputed that to determine whether a tumor incidence is biologically significant, the consideration of biological factors, such as methodology of the study involved, chemical structure, length of use, dose response, rarity of tumors, and the presence of similar results in other studies is involved. The ALJ found that "biological significance must be attached to study findings where borderline statistically significant effects occur (e.g. P$=$.06), but additional factors exist."

Abbott contends, however, that the concept of biological significance can be applied only to reject effects that are statistically significant at P$<$.05 . . . ., but cannot be applied to attribute significance to effects that are not statistically significant at P$<$.05. I find Abbott's "one way" test to be untenable, for it would operate only to prove safety, not to disprove it. Scientifically, it is just as appropriate to rely on biological factors to conclude that an effect has biological significance, even though it is not statistically significant at

P$<$.05, as it is to rely on biological factors to reject effects that are significant at P$<$.05.

Consideration of biological factors can add further credence to or detract from the weight that would normally be given to findings with a particular P-value. For example, two different types of tumors may occur at the same P-value in a particular study. If only one of these tumor types recurs in other studies, the recurring tumor type will be considered to have greater biological significance than the tumor type that does not recur in other similar studies. (The latter tumor type may be found to be insignificant if it does not recur in any studies.)

Similarly, an effect may occur at P-value that, when viewed by itself, does not appear to be significant. However, consideration of biological factors may result in a conclusion that the effect has biological significance. For example, in a number of direct cyclamate feeding studies in rats more bladder tumors occurred in cyclamate treated rats than occurred in controls. The occurrence of these tumors in each of the individual studies is not statistically significant at P$<$.05. However, because bladder tumors are historically rare in the strains of animals used in these studies, because the occurence of these tumors in cycla-mate-treated animals is consistent with a small treatment effect, because the occurrence of these tumors in control animals is consistent with the incidence of these tumors in historical controls, and because these bladder tumors have recurred in a number of studies involving different strains of rats, these blad-der tumors are biologically significant.[14]

To summarize, the concepts of statistical significance and biological signifi-cance should be viewed together in determining the significance of a treatment related incidence of tumors. The closer the P-value is to P$<$.05 the greater the confidence that can be placed in the results of the study. The factors to be considered in determining biological significance may increase or decrease that confidence. This evaluation results in a decision as to how much, if any, weight a study should be given.

Moreover, each study is not only considered independently, but also is con-sidered as part of the totality of the evidence. An individual study, standing alone, may not raise a serious question as to the safety of a substance. When that study is viewed with other similar studies, a trend of a particular effect may become apparent. Where several studies, viewed together, point in the direction of carcinogenicity, those studies, even though inconclusive, are a val-id and objective basis for concluding that a food additive has not been shown to be safe. This is particularly true when the inability to demonstrate a statisti-cally significant treatment effect in the individual studies is a result of the in-sensitivity of the studies.

Courts have consistently upheld decisions made by federal agencies where those decisions have been based on evidence that was inconclusive but sugges-tive.

The District of Columbia Circuit Court of Appeals recently reaffirmed the opinion in *Ethyl Corp.* and further recognized that a regulatory agency could not carry out its statutory mandate to protect the public from incompletely understood dangers such as cancer if the agency could not rely on suggestive results:

> . . . [R]egulations [prohibiting marketing of a suspected carcinogen] may jeopardize plants or whole industries, and the jobs depending on them. In such circumstances, the temptation to demand that the agency furnish conclusive proof of carcinogenicity as support for the regulations is great. However, the decision to delegate authority to an agency to control suspected carcinogens is a legislative judgment that is not open to question in this court. Congress's direction to EPA to protect against incompletely

---

14. It should be emphasized that the great majority of substances do not cause cancer when tested in the types of animal studies contained in this record. Attention is therefore properly paid to such studies whenever cancerous tumors are found.

understood dangers could not be carried out if we were to adopt the proof requirements advocated by industry petitioners.

Environmental Defense Fund v. EPA, supra, 598 F.2d at 89. Accord, *Color Mfg. Ass'n v. Mathews,* 543 F.2d 284, 297 (D.C.Cir.1976). See *Hercules v. EPA,* 598 F.2d 91, 110 (D.C.Cir.1978).

Commissioner Goyan's views on significance are examined and for the most part criticized in Havender, The Science and Politics of Cyclamate, 71 The Public Interest 17 (Spring 1983).

3. Should regulators use a less rigorous standard of statistical significance than research scientists? If so, how should they decide what level of significance to use? What standards of significance are used elsewhere in the law? Consider the discussion by Judge Skelly Wright at n. 58 in *Ethyl Corp. v. EPA, supra.*

4. MANAGING RISK

a. The Relevance of the Distinction Between Voluntary and Involuntary Exposure To Risk

STATE v. ALBERTSON

Supreme Court of Idaho, 1970.
93 Idaho 640, 470 P.2d 300.

SHEPARD, JUSTICE.

This cause presents for decision the constitutionality of our Idaho statute requiring motorcycle riders to wear a helmet while operating a motorcycle upon a public street or highway.

. . .

In capsule form the position of respondent may be stated as follows: The statute in question and others like it are designed solely and completely to protect the well-being of persons who are operating a motorcycle and bear no relationship whatsoever to the health, safety and welfare of the *general* public. . . .

The courts across the nation have adopted various approaches in pointing out that protective helmet statutes are designed to protect the general public's welfare and safety, as well as that of the motorcycle rider. Some have found legislative intention to confer benefits to highway users as a class on the basis that since the motorcycle rider is in an exposed position, he may be struck by flying objects causing loss of control and thereby endangering pedestrians or other motorists; others suggest that such statutes protect motorists who might otherwise become involved in automobile-motorcycle accidents and be charged with negligent homicide; others suggest that since the use of highways is only a conditional privilege a helmet requirement may be legitimately imposed; others suggest that helmet laws are simply equipment regulations similar to those requiring other safety devices on other types of motor vehicles; others, such as the court in Washington, suggest that the public expense of providing emergency ambulance, medical and hospital care for persons injured upon the public highways justify the initiation of measures by the legislature to reduce such burdens upon the general public; others suggest that a disabling head injury usually results in the diminished ability of an individual to support himself and the possibility of another addition to the already overloaded public welfare rolls; still others cite the probability of increased insurance rates.

Whatever approach other courts have taken by way of holding their statutes of this same type constitutional, the authority is overwhelming and the reasons therefor many and varied.   There can be no doubt that certain interests of the general public in its welfare and safety are served by statutes of the type presented herein.   We believe that the general traveling public is benefited as a class in that the protective helmet reduces to some extent the possibility of a motorcycle rider losing control of his vehicle and endangering other highway users.   It further reduces the need for and therefore the costs of providing police, ambulance and other emergency personnel and equipment at accident scenes.   While the interest of the general public may be secondary as compared with the importance of wearing a helmet to the motorcycle rider, those rights of the general public are nevertheless real, ascertainable, and needful of protection.   In such cases the right of the individual as asserted by the respondent to "be let alone" must be considered subservient to the real necessities of protection of the general public.   . . .

. . .

The decision of the district court ruling I.C. § 49–761A unconstitutional is reversed and the case remanded for such further proceedings as may be appropriate.

COMMITTEE ON RISK AND DECISION MAKING, NATIONAL ACADEMY OF SCIENCES, RISK AND DECISION MAKING: PERSPECTIVES AND RESEARCH

14–17 (1982).

RISK-GENERATING AND RISK-COPING PROCESSES

In this report, the phrase the "generation of risks" is used broadly to refer to the manner by which risks are caused, created, triggered, and aggravated in society.   The phrase refers not only to the chemical, biological, and physical sources of risk but also to economic, behavioral, and organizational factors that create risks.   Similarly, the phrase "coping with risks" is used broadly to refer to the many ways in which individuals and organizations respond to risks in life.   These responses are often deliberate preventive actions; more often, however, they are reactive, ad hoc actions by individuals, businesses, agencies, legislatures, courts, etc. Careful study of both risk-generating and risk-coping processes is essential to improving society's ability to control risks in an optimal or acceptable manner.

The Generation of Risks

The committee's investigation of risk generation suggests that (1) not all risks require social intervention, (2) the rationales for social intervention are strikingly different depending on how a risk is perceived to be generated, and (3) although society frequently must respond to risks without conclusive scientific evidence about causation, the development of effective, long-term coping strategies is possible only if the generation of risks is better understood.   To provide organization to the analysis of risk generation, the committee used a simple classification scheme (see Figure 1).[8] Although it is an imperfect model of risk generation, the scheme is useful in elucidating some broad perspectives about social intervention and risk-coping strategies.

Social Intervention to Reduce Risks: When and Why?

Some risks, such as those generated by criminal behavior and by certain production externalities, are widely regarded as important social problems of widespread public concern. In both cases, those who incur risks are suffering from an imposition by other individuals or productive enterprises, an imposition that the victims of such risks cannot easily control. In contrast, the risks generated by self-hazardous behavior—although they may produce more deaths, injuries, and illnesses than those created by productive enterprises or by criminals—are not so widely regarded as an appropriate subject of social intervention. Advocating social intervention to reduce risks from self-hazardous behavior quickly triggers debates about freedom and the role of government in society. Similar concerns, albeit to a lesser degree, apply to co-generated risks (see Figure 1).

There are certainly plausible arguments both for or against intervention in self-hazardous behavior. The self-hazardous aspects of smoking, alcoholism, suicide, motor vehicle accidents, obesity, etc. are of such an enormous magnitude that they sometimes defy explanation in terms of purely "rational" behavior. Many but not all adult smokers, drinkers, overeaters, and nonexercisers, after due and deliberate reflection, like to do what they are doing (at least in the short run), making the rationales for intervention to influence behavior complex and controversial. The rationales for social intervention can be compelling when the social costs of self-hazardous behavior are considered, such as the effects on children and adolescents. This is particularly important for those risks that are habit-forming, such as taking drugs and smoking. Moreover, some self-hazardous activities, such as smoking and drinking, also create risks for others (i.e., passive smoking, fires, and accidents), strengthening the case for some form of social intervention. However, since some self-hazardous behavior is often the result of conscious, informed decisions by adults who bear the consequences of their actions, the case for intervention becomes complex, requiring the balancing of opposing objectives.

---

8. One member of the committee, while agreeing that risks can be classified in this way, argues that other classifications may be more useful. He argues that the important classifications are the way the risk is calculated and the magnitude of the risk. Specifically:

1. Can the risk be directly calculated from historical data with a clear cause and effect?

2. Is the risk a historical one, but with a weak cause and effect relationship, so that it is not easily recognized?

3. Risks of new technologies have to be calculated by factoring the problem, such as is done in "event free" analysis.

4. Some risks have such a delayed cause and effect relationship that direct calculation is very hard; cancer is in this category. The risk has to be calculated by an analogy of people and experimental animals.

Each of these categories leads to difficult strategies for risk prevention and to different public perceptions. Each also leads to a great deal of argument about words; for example, the risk posed by air pollution falls in the second category. That risk is often discounted as being "unknown" or "hypothetical" even if the magnitude is as large as other risks in the first category.

FIGURE 1

The Generation of Risks: A Simple Classification Scheme

Self-Hazardous Behavior: Situations in which an individual creates and incurs the same risk. Illustrative examples: smoking, alcohol abuse, not using seat belts, or hang gliding.

Co-generation of Risks: When the combined actions of two or more parties impose a risk on one of the parties. Illustrative examples: risks imposed on a worker resulting from combined actions of worker and employer or risks imposed on consumers by the combined actions of producer and consumer.

Risks Generated by Production Externalities: When productive enterprises generate risks that are incurred by people not directly involved in the production or consumption of a good. Illustrative examples: air and water pollution, nuclear accidents, and hazardous wastes.

Risks Imposed by Particular Individuals on Others: When individuals generate risks that are imposed on others. Illustrative examples: crime, speeding, drunken driving, child abuse, and smoking in public places.

Risks Generated by Nature: A category including natural hazards such as earthquakes, droughts, and floods as well as certain physical conditions generated by nature (e.g., diseases of old age, genetic mutations, and disease from natural ionizing radiation). Of course, the degree of possible risk can be tempered by individual or social actions: deciding to live near a fault zone, earthquake-resistant design or construction, construction of dams, and so on.

Risks Generated by Economic Conditions: Individuals and communities create and incur risks due to various economic conditions. Financial insecurity itself is a risk that also creates risk for health and safety. Illustrative examples: poverty-induced disease and unemployment-induced stress.

Risks Generated by Government Policies: Public policies sometimes subsidize, encourage, or force individuals or organizations to create risks. For example, some national energy policies create risks to human health, safety, and the environment as well as to national security and the likelihood of war.

The class of co-generated risks is somewhat of an intermediate case with regard to justification for social intervention. Workers and consumers co-generate risks with employers and sellers; furthermore, in their consensual nature, co-generated risks are somewhat similar to self-hazardous behavior. But workers and consumers are often unaware of the risks they incur. For example, employers and sellers sometimes have an incentive to withhold information about risks in order to prevent subsequent liability or regulation. The information problem may be particularly acute for consumers engaged in one-time purchases or for consumers and workers who are exposed to risks that become apparent only after long latency periods. For these reasons and others, co-generated risks should be important targets of social intervention.

PAUL SLOVIC, BARUCH FISCHHOFF, AND SARAH LICHTENSTEIN, FACTS AND FEARS: UNDERSTANDING PERCEIVED RISK

in Societal Risk Assessment
205–207 (R. Schwing and W. Albers, Jr. eds. 1980).

The Voluntariness Hypothesis — By examining statistical and economic indicators of benefit and risk for eight hazards, Starr proposed several hypotheses about the nature of acceptable risk:

- The acceptable level of risk is roughly proportional to the third power (cube) of the benefits.

- The public seems willing to accept risks from voluntary activities, such as skiing, that are roughly a thousand times greater than it would tolerate from involuntarily imposed hazards providing the same level of benefit.

Although Starr acknowledged the preliminary nature of his data and hypotheses, the voluntary/involuntary distinction has been widely cited as relevant for standard setting. Attempts to derive quantitative criteria for acceptable levels of risk often recommend stricter standards on hazards imposed involuntarily.

The judgments of current and acceptable risks in our own studies provide a test of Starr's hypotheses with very different methodology and data. Our first study, in which members of the League of Women Voters rated the risks and benefits of 30 hazards, produced results supportive of Starr's. Our respondents appeared to believe that greater risk should be tolerated for more beneficial activities and that a double standard is appropriate for voluntary and involuntary activities. However, these people also seemed to desire similar double standards based on characteristics such as controllability, knowledge, familiarity, and immediacy. We concluded that, in addition to benefits and voluntariness, a number of other psychological and physical characteristics of risk might need to be incorporated into risk standards.

The results of our extended study have clarified these tentative conclusions. Consider first the role of voluntariness: the correlation matrix shows that involuntariness is closely related to many other risk characteristics and particularly to lack of control ($r = .68$), global catastrophe* ($r = .69$), inequity ($r = .76$), and catastrophe ($r = .74$). For example, six of the ten most involuntary hazards (nuclear weapons, nerve gas, terrorism, warfare, nuclear power, and DDT) are also among the 10 most cata-

---

* "Global catastrophe" is used by the authors to mean the potential that the pursuit of an activity, or the use of a substance or a technology, will cause catastrophic death and destruction across the whole world.

Slovic, Fischhoff, and Lichtenstein, Facts and Fears: Understanding Perceived Risk in Societal Risk Assessment 198 (Schwing & Albers, eds. 1980). [Eds.]

strophic hazards. These relationships suggest that much, if not all, of the observed aversion to involuntary risks may be due to other characteristics that are closely associated with voluntariness.

Support for this interpretation comes from the following data analyses conducted on the extended study. An estimate of the acceptable level of risk was calculated for each of the 90 hazards by dividing the hazard's mean risk level by its mean adjustment factor. This index of acceptable risk was found to correlate positively with perceived benefit ($r = .58$) as Starr hypothesized and as our previous studies had also demonstrated. Furthermore, deviations from the best-fit line relating benefit and acceptable risk were significantly correlated with voluntariness, in the direction predicted by Starr's hypothesis. However, these deviations were much more strongly related to characteristics such as catastrophic potential, dread, and equity than to voluntariness. In fact, when the effects of any of these other characteristics were removed statistically, voluntariness no longer was related to acceptable risk.

These doubts about the importance of voluntariness have been reinforced by other considerations, such as the following thought experiment. Suppose that you own and ride in two automobiles. One is needed for your work and when you ride in it, you are chauffeured (thus your exposure to risk is involuntary and relatively uncontrollable). The second auto is driven by you for pleasure, thus the risks you take while driving it are voluntary and somewhat controllable. Consider the standards of safety you would wish for the two vehicles. Would you demand that standards be much safer for the first car than for the second? If you are like us, then you would desire equivalent safety standards for both vehicles.

Lave expressed similar doubts about the intrinsic significance of involuntary risks. He noted that involuntary hazards typically affect larger numbers of people so that stricter safety standards for such hazards merely reflect the greater amount of money that groups would be willing to pay for safety, relative to what an individual would be willing to pay.

We conclude that society's apparent aversion to involuntary risks may be mostly an illusion, caused by the fact that involuntary risks are often noxious in more important ways, such as being inequitable or potentially catastrophic.

b. **Selecting the Appropriate Regulatory Response**

COMMITTEE ON RISK AND DECISION MAKING, NATIONAL ACADEMY OF SCIENCES, RISK AND DECISION MAKING: PERSPECTIVES AND RESEARCH

20–24 (1982).

Selecting Risk-Coping Strategies

The diversity of risk-coping strategies, including those listed in Figure 2, leads to a difficult question: What criteria should be used to select coping strategies in a given situation? Generic rules or formulas are inapplicable because the nature of risks differs, the rationales for social intervention differ, and the consequences of various coping strategies differ. The committee can only suggest several themes that might illuminate the strategy-selection process.

FIGURE 2

Strategies for Coping with Some Categories of Risks

Self-Hazardous Behavior
Insurance Premium Adjustments
Educational Campaigns
Incentives/Disincentives
Legal Restrictions
Automatic Protection Strategies
Liability Rules

Co-Generated Risks
Occupational Risks
Wage Premiums for Risky Jobs
Worker Compensation Programs
Liability Rules
Union Bargaining
Informational Approaches
Taxing Occupational Risks
Employee Protective Measures
Standard Setting for Health and Safety
Consumer Product Risks
Product Safety Research and Development
Regulation of Advertising
Product Labels and Warnings
Consumption Goals and Guidelines
Liability Rules
Regulating Standards and Bans

Risks From Production Externalities
Government Standard Setting
Sale of Pollution Licenses
Effluent Fees
Liability Rules
Governmental Compensation Programs
Negotiation Processes
Compulsory Liability Insurance

The first theme is that while all strategies for coping with risks—individual, market, legislative, regulatory, and judicial—have strengths, they also have serious and systematic defects. The task is to define those combinations of risk-coping strategies that can offer the flexibility and effectiveness necessary to respond to risks. Most strategies for coping with risks are not mutually exclusive. Occupational injury taxes can complement selective safety standards by providing incentives for firms to reduce the full range of causes of injury. Meanwhile, the regulatory approach can partially compensate for the tort-liability system's inability to disentangle multiple causes of risks involving toxic substances, especially for health risks that occur only after long latency periods. A more sophisticated understanding of the strengths and weaknesses of different coping methods can help society develop creative combinations of such methods.

Society must be concerned not only with risk reduction and risk prevention but also with compensating those who suffer losses as a result of certain imposed and co-generated risks. In recent decades the tort-liability system for compensating those who have suffered has been adapted to the consequences of new risks, e.g., pollution from factories affecting people, nearby farms, etc. Compensation is designed both to discourage risk-generating conduct and to provide relief to those who suffer losses from imposed and co-generated risks. Effective and equitable compensation is needed for three reasons: First, some risks are the inevitable result of public- or private-sector activities that are vital to achieving societal goals, such as a police force to maintain local safety and a military force to maintain national security. Second, some imposed and co-generated risks that should be reduced or eliminated will inevitably persist due to imperfections in regulation, society's lack of knowledge of appropriate methods of risk reduction, and the insensitivity of people in businesses, government agencies, legislatures, and other institutions. Third, some risks might be so costly to eliminate entirely that it may be more prudent to invest resources elsewhere. For these reasons, it is important to improve mechanisms for compensating the victims of certain kinds of risks; however, victims may not be compensated at all in nonnegligent accidents, that is, those accidents in which the risk was considered too remote to be worth the cost of prevention.*

A second theme is the need to experiment with new or modified processes for coping with risks. Coping strategies such as education campaigns, the sale of pollution licenses, and revisions in tort law should not be adopted on a national scale without careful analysis, experimentation, evaluation, and adaptation. Yet innovations will rarely be adopted if decision makers and the public do not have confidence that such approaches will be effective. Needed are pilot projects or social experiments in which small-scale introduction of new coping processes, careful monitoring and evaluation of performance, and modifications or original innovations precede adoption of new methods on a large scale. This approach is sometimes used (e.g., in environmental policy), but could be used more extensively and more productively.

Pilot projects are important not only for coping with persistent risks, such as smoking and air pollution, but also for emerging environmental threats, such as inadequate disposal of hazardous wastes. Traditional coping strategies are ill-equipped to deal with risks posed by toxic substances in the air, food, water, homes, and workplaces and thereby em-

---

* Compensation is discussed in more detail in Section B.1, infra. [Eds.]

phasize the need to experiment with and learn from multiple strategies for attacking this problem. We add the caveat that it is very difficult to make social experiments truly representative of potential social policies.

A third theme is that coping methods that preserve or increase free choice by individuals should be considered. Sometimes informing the individual of ways to cope with particular risks is the best tactic, enabling free choice and avoiding direct constraints. Media campaigns to improve nutritional habits or to reduce smoking are examples of an information strategy. In other cases, more direct action is needed, such as banning certain food additives for their carcinogenic potential.

The committee does not posit individual choice as an absolute value but rather suggests that for decisions by which individuals generate risks for themselves, there should be persuasive reasons to override the results of individual decision making. Of course, when freedom is exercised by some to generate risks that are incurred by others, the case for considering social intervention is widely accepted.

Finally, the mere existence of deficiencies in individual and market decision making about risks does not establish the claim that social institutions should intervene to reduce risks. Government decision making is also imperfect and costly, and governmental failures must be considered when deciding whether social intervention should be employed and what forms intervention should take.

NOTE

When the Consumer Product Safety Commission had its ban on urea-formaldehyde foam insulation overturned by the Fifth Circuit, it turned to a system of warning consumers. Similarly, when Congress rejected FDA's proposed ban of saccharin, it substituted warnings. In order to minimize intrusion on personal freedom, should the government rely more frequently on warnings to the general public? Entirely? The next selection considers some of the problems with such a strategy.

RICHARD M. COOPER,
FREEDOM OF CHOICE IN THE REAL WORLD

34 Food Drug Cosmetic L.J. 612, 618–24 (1979).

. . . . To see what broad freedom of choice on safety matters in the real world of foods would mean, we shall leave the philosophers of freedom of choice in their offices and studies, and shall venture into a supermarket.

I frequently do the shopping for my family. I do it after work, when I am rather worn down; or on the weekend, when I am more relaxed. Sometimes I take my children with me. When I enter a supermarket I do not expect to make BIG, LIFE-AND-DEATH DECISIONS; and I am not mentally or emotionally prepared to do that.

It normally takes me about an hour or so to reach the check-out counter. I am concerned about quality and, on a civil servant's salary, I have to be concerned about price. My hour includes some time comparing different kinds of products and different brands of the same product from the perspectives of quality and price. I generally don't choose products on the basis of safety; I simply don't worry about that; I have enough trouble making sure of freshness and price and keeping my kids from running all over the store. And, for the most part, I simply buy the same items week after week, without thinking too much about it and without examining the fine print on labels. I certainly don't do my food shopping on a zero-base principle by re-examining each and every food purchasing decision.

Shopping is a chore, but it's not really unpleasant (except for the price increases every week). The store is bright and clean; the foods are attractively packaged; choosing foods from the shelves is modestly enjoyable. And the whole process doesn't take very long; I'd much rather spend my free time with my wife and kids, playing basketball or tennis, taking walks, reading, and so on. That's how I shop today.[17]

The Freedom-of-Choice Supermarket

Let us go then, you and I, on a shopping trip to the future world of the freedom-of-choice supermarket. I have learned from the TV that the government no longer tries to prevent very many risky substances from getting into food. The point is reinforced by a sign over the supermarket door (required by law): "Abandon confidence in the food supply, all you who enter here."

When I enter the store, I know that somewhere inside those thousands of jars and cans and boxes are substances that are risky, but that were approved because they provide economic benefits to farmers and food processors or to their employees or to towns where they have mills or plants. Others were approved because members of the public *perceived* them to have benefits, although these benefits could not be scientifically demonstrated. Still others were approved to protect my personal autonomy, for which I thank the free market philosophers. So now safety is something I've got to be concerned about along with quality and price.

I'm not paranoid, and I don't worry more than the average person. But I don't want to buy food that will harm my wife and kids or that will harm me. Fortunately, the new system of freedom-of-choice food safety regulation pursues an "information strategy." All the foods in the supermarket contain a logo that signifies high risk, moderate risk, or low risk. The high risk logo, I know, is a skull-and-crossbones. The other two logos I sometimes confuse in my mind, even though I saw them on TV a couple of nights ago. I'm in luck, however, because my store has posted a sign explaining the logos.

---

17. In a recent survey, the Food and Drug Administration (FDA) asked respondents, "Aside from prices, please tell me about any particular problems, difficulties, or concerns which you have with food these days." About half the respondents (49%) reported no problems other than price; 14% mentioned generalized concerns about quality; another 14% mentioned adverse health implications; 8% thought food is not as fresh as it should be; another 8% mentioned labeling problems; and 3% had miscellaneous concerns. Nearly three-fifths of consumers, when asked directly about information on food labels, said they were satisfied. Among the dissatisfied (33%), most wanted full ingredient labeling. FDA, 1978 Consumer Food Labeling Survey (Summary Report) 3, 5 (May, 1979). There is no evi-

dent demand for additional information about risks.

When the FDA proposed to announce its defect action levels for foods (which limit, for example, the quantity of mold or insect fragments that may be present in food), 37 F.R. 6497 (Mar. 30, 1972), it received more than 600 comments, about 98% of which were from consumers. The FDA reported that most of these comments "objected to the existence of any level of defects in food or maintained that the levels allow an excessive amount of defects in food." 38 F.R. 854 (Jan. 5, 1973). It is safe to say that the public is not eager for food package labels to disclose the number of insect fragments permitted in processed foods.

Early on, it was found that the logos didn't mean much to people. Surveys showed that the simple message—"high risk," "moderate risk," or "low risk"—merely produced an attitude of "So what?" In addition, people were confused because some traditional foods that they had been eating all their lives, and their parents and grandparents before them, were labeled "high risk;" and new foods they'd never heard of and that had lots of chemicals in them were labeled "low risk."

Since one of the premises of freedom-of-choice is *informed* decision-making, the government attempted to solve this problem by requiring that additional information be provided to consumers. At one point this approach did get out of hand: some bureaucrat took seriously the notion that consumers should be permitted to make their own judgments about risks on the basis of *complete* and *accurate* information about the hazards involved, and the government started to require that the packages of all high risk products contain a "brief and succinct" explanation of the principles of toxicology. But, after a lawsuit, that approach was abandoned. Now, a "reasonable" amount of information is provided. Here are some examples of statements on food packages:

"This product contains a substance that has been found to cause cancer in rats."

"This product contains a substance that has been found to cause cancer in one species of mice and that is positive in 3 out of 5 screening tests."

"This product contains a substance that has been found to cause cancer in rats, but the effect was barely significant statistically. The product has also been found to cause reproductive effects in monkeys."

"This product contains a substance that, when given in high doses in laboratory animals, has been found to cause cancer. There is no epidemiological evidence that it causes cancer in humans."

"This product contains a substance that causes toxic effects in animals, but there is no accepted way to estimate its risk to humans."

"This product contains one substance that has been found to cause cancer in rats and another that has been found to cause cancer in two species of mice."

"This product *may* contain a contaminant that is a potent carcinogen."

"This product contains a substance that has raised concerns about whether it causes cancer or interferes with the body's immune system. It is known to combine with other substances to form a potent carcinogen. However, certain kinds of products without this substance may present a risk of botulism if they are not handled properly."

"This product contains a substance that has been found to cause cancer, but the U.S. Government has determined that the risk of cancer it presents is acceptable."

"This product contains a substance that has been found to cause cancer, but the U.S. Government has determined that the substance is an essential nutrient, necessary for maintaining life."

In the aisles the shoppers come and go, talking of angiosarcomas.

I do many things in my life that I suppose are relatively risky, but I have no idea what the statistical risks are and I hardly ever think about them. As I wheel my shopping cart down the aisles, I pick out packages from the shelves to see whether there is any safety information I should be aware of. I have to check every package I consider buying because you never know what it will say. Then I have to think about all those descriptions of risk, figure out what they really mean, and decide which risks my wife and kids and I should take. The most intense agony comes when I have to decide whether to pay more for a product that seems less risky.

Swarms of foods carry some sort of risk information—even the fresh fruits and vegetables, due to pesticides. (Do I dare to eat a peach?) I had not known the information strategy had undone so many. And it's never easy to make these risk decisions. Some people talk as though I carry around in my head a set of risk-benefit decision rules and a set of food safety indifference curves; but I don't.

Standing there in the aisle trying to make these important decisions isn't easy because people are always rushing past you, grabbing things from in front of you or asking you to step aside. The kids yank at my sleeve and ask whether they can buy this candy or that cake, or they complain that they're bored. At least I don't have to carry an infant with me when I shop, as I used to do.

Shopping is no longer any fun at all. I certainly don't enjoy making all those decisions. I'm never satisfied that I've made them correctly. I never feel that I have enough information, but I don't know that more information would make it any easier. Some theorists talk as though I'm able to process an indefinite quantity of information about every one of the large number of consumption decisions I make in the supermarket. But the advertisers know that isn't true. And, even with the quite small amount of risk information that is provided on the packages, my shopping seems to take forever. I'd much rather spend my limited time on this earth doing other things.

I leave it to you to judge, given a social policy of freedom-of-choice, how much of my description of the freedom-of-choice supermarket is impossible fantasy. I will, though, make one claim for it—that it illustrates how freedom of choice philosophers have lost their sense of proportion and how they fundamentally misconceive and misapply our society's strong but selective commitment to individual autonomy and freedom of choice.

We are committed to freedom of choice in the important matters of life, about which we believe individual autonomy should govern. In religion, in morals, in politics, in arts, sciences and ideas generally, we believe that people should be free to choose as their inner lights guide them. We believe that people do not need or want to be protected from the risk of error in such matters, and that the history of governmental efforts to say what is error and to seek to prevent it demonstrates that such efforts are the essence of tyranny. We also believe that people should be free to make fundamental decisions about their lives—where to live, where to work, whom to marry, whether to have children, how to spend free time, and so on. Here, too, we as a society believe with Augustine that the value of free choice outweighs all the harms and unhappiness that may result from decisions that may prove to have been wrong.

When we come to choices among foods, however, the claims of individual autonomy are very different. Certainly the government shouldn't tell me what to eat; that would be unthinkable. Free exercise, however, is a quite different matter. The banning of food additives cannot be compared to the banning of religious sects or political parties or literary clubs. Mr. Hutt contends, however, that decisions about foods raise "the most basic questions of personal beliefs and human values."[18]   I simply disagree.

When Patrick Henry said, "Give me liberty or give me death", he wasn't talking about the composition of foods.   Some things in life are vastly more important than others.   Our human dignity, our distinctively human faculties, our spiritual, moral, political, emotional, intellectual, aesthetic and social values *are* expressed in decisions about religion, politics, art, science, and the course of our lives.   But, in general, they are not expressed in decisions about additives in foods.

I enjoy consumption about as much as the next person, but I am quite content to leave it to the government to decide on safety grounds what substances may not be added to the food I eat, or what pollutants may not be added to the air I breathe (should there be freedom of choice in pollutants?), or what defective parts may not be included in the engines of airplanes I fly in.   In general, I believe that when the government bans an additive or a pollutant or a defective part, it doesn't interfere with my ability to live in accordance with my personal beliefs and values.

I say "in general" because there are exceptions.   There *are* some substances that are peculiarly important and that people feel strongly about. Such substances are, as a practical matter, unbannable.   Examples are alcohol and tobacco.   I suspect we are learning that saccharin—or, at least, the last non-nutritive sweetener—is a third.   In this democracy, if a majority of the people (as reflected by their elected representatives) want to go on consuming these substances, they should be able to.

But the public demand for these substances that have special appeal does not justify any general argument that the centerpiece of food safety policy should be freedom of choice.   I submit that, as to the generality of risks that may arise in the food supply, the public wants protection, not information and not freedom of choice.[19]   People would rather spend their time and energy on the areas of life where freedom is really important and not have to worry about the toxicology of the food supply.   Indeed, freedom of choice on food safety matters would distract time and energy away from activities that are expressions of far more important freedoms.

The general and strong presumption in food safety policy should be for protection and against freedom of choice.[20]   Where the public regis-

18. P. Hutt, Public Policy Issues in Regulating Carcinogens in Food, 33 Food Drug Cosmetic Law Journal 541, 548 (1978).

19. The public's views when asked about public policy toward carcinogens are ambivalent and complex.   When asked about carcinogens generally, about 1/4 of the population favors a total ban, and 3/4 favors letting people make their own decisions.   When asked specifically about additives to foods and drugs, about 3/4 favor a ban on carcinogens, and 1/4 oppose it.   See Cambridge Reports, Inc., Public and Worker Attitudes Toward Carcinogens and Cancer Risk 42, 46, 47 (April, 1978) (prepared for Shell Oil Co.).

20. I am, of course, referring to the policy toward risks that foods pose to the generality of the population and that under current law would warrant a ban (e.g., risks of cancer, risks of acute poisoning).   Foods that present risks only to a relatively small and relatively well-defined group within the population (e.g., people allergic to a particular additive, people on salt-free diets, people with certain nutritional diseases) warrant a different policy.   In general, such people have been told by their doctors to avoid certain substances.   Consequently, they are not looking for information with which to make complex risk-benefit decisions; they simply want a complete list of ingredients: if a food contains the substance to be avoided, they won't buy the food.   Here, an information strategy is tolerably effective; although a ban would protect those who should avoid the substance but whose condition has not been diagnosed, it would impose an unacceptable loss on the rest of society.   A recent survey by the FDA found that among

ters its determined preference to keep a particular risky substance in the food supply, our democratic political system can and should find a way to keep it in. I would expect such cases to be quite rare.

NOTES

1. In another part of his article, Richard Cooper raises the additional problem that substantial segments of our population are functionally illiterate, noting:

> A recent study of adult functional competence reported that "approximately one-fifth of U.S. adults are functioning with difficulty." University of Texas at Austin, Industrial and Business Training Bureau, Adult Performance Level Project, Adult Functional Competence: A Summary 6 (1975). The conclusion was based on consideration of the following areas of knowledge and skills: occupational knowledge, consumer economics, government and law, health, community resources, reading, problem solving, computation, and writing. The report further commented: "In terms of the general knowledge areas, the greatest area of difficulty appears to be Consumer Economics. . . . [S]ome 34.7 million adult Americans function with difficulty and an additional 39 million are functional (but not proficient) in coping with basic requirements that are related to Consumer Economics. . . . A greater proportion of people is unable to perform basic computations than the other skills. Approximately one-third of the population, or 39 million adults, functions with difficulty, and a little over one-fourth, or 29.5 million adults, is functional but not proficient in task performance on items requiring mathematical manipulation." Id., 6–7.
>
> Moreover, the U.S. population includes millions of people whose language is other than English and who have difficulty with English. See, e.g., U.S. Department of Commerce, Bureau of the Census, Language Usage in the United States: July, 1975 (Current Population Reports, Special Studies, Series P–23, No. 60 (Revised), July, 1976).

Does this state of affairs justify greater reliance on bans of dangerous substances in the food supply than on a labeling strategy of providing warnings only? Compare the views of Peter Barton Hutt, who like Richard Cooper, is a former chief counsel of the FDA:

Three Levels of Risk

Conceptually, there are three levels of risk. For lack of better terminology, I shall call them high, moderate, and low.

For high risks, we impose a ban. Examples of high risks that are banned in our society include putting frank poisons in the food supply, attempted suicide, and going over Niagara Falls in a barrel. In each instance the probability of death is extremely high. The only high risks that we might tolerate would be those with an extraordinary potential benefit, such as the use of a highly toxic anticancer drug for otherwise terminal cancer patients.

For moderate risks, we provide information and appropriate warnings to the public, but do not ban the activity, where individual choice is feasible. We advise mountain climbers, canoers, swimmers, and Indianapolis Speedway drivers, to take all appropriate safety cautions, and we warn them about the risks of serious injury and death, but we do not ban that kind of activity. We place appropriate warnings on aerosolized food containers about intentional misuse that can result in death, but we do not ban them. Many other consumer products bear appropriate directions for use and warnings against misuse. Even though none of these activities and products is essential to human life,

consumers who pay any attention to food labeling (apart from product information, brand name, and price) by far the most frequent use of labeling is use of the ingredients list to avoid particular substances thought to be harmful or hazardous. The ingredients most often mentioned were sugars (by far the number one item), salt, fats and oils, and preservatives. FDA, 1978 Food Labeling Survey (Summary Report), 6 (May, 1979).

individuals are permitted to make their own choice whether or not to accept the risk involved. Only in situations where individual choice is not feasible—such as the purity of the air we breathe and the water we drink—are moderate risks banned as unacceptable to society as a whole.

For low risks, there is little or no attempt even to disseminate information about the risks or how to avoid them. Virtually all consumer products can produce low-level allergic reactions, irritation, cuts and scratches, and other mild injuries, and undoubtedly all of them could be misused in one way or another to result in serious injury or death. For none of these types of risks, however, is there any significant effort to provide warnings or information about safety precautions.

Differentiation Among Levels of Risk

At least until now, the differentiation between these three levels of risk has been made on an entirely ad hoc basis. Regulatory agencies have determined which regulatory response should be invoked more on the basis of intuition than by application of any systematic policy rationale. Perhaps the largest task facing us in the future will be at least a rough approximation of the dividing lines between these three risk categories in order to forge a consistent rationale for regulatory action.

Dr. Richard Wilson of Harvard has suggested that any substance or activity that represents a risk of 10^{-2} or greater should be banned; 10^{-5} or less should raise no concern; and between 10^{-2} and 10^{-5} should be the subject of appropriate information to the individuals involved so that they can make their own benefit-risk decisions. This concept deserves serious consideration. Whether or not it or some variation is ultimately accepted, it unquestionably represents an important attempt to approach the issue on a rational basis, rather than the more emotional and intuitive approaches that have been used up to now.

The FDA has experimented with a mathematical approach by advancing a modification of the Mantel-Bryan model to determine unacceptable residue levels of carcinogenic animal drugs in human food. That particular approach suffers, however, from an all-or-nothing philosophy. It does not permit a middle ground where information is given to consumers and they are allowed to make their own free choice. Its application should therefore be restricted to those situations where individual choice is not feasible.

Whatever method is ultimately chosen to differentiate between these three risk categories, it is essential that it result in consistent handling of equivalent risks. The public will not understand or tolerate a continuation of our present ad hoc approach, under which one chemical is banned, another is labeled with a warning, and a third is allowed to be marketed freely, even though they present essentially equivalent risks.

Public Policy Issues in Regulating Carcinogens in Food, 33 Food Drug Cosmetic L.J. 541, 554–55 (1978). See also Hutt, Unresolved Issues in the Conflict Between Individual Freedom and Government Control of Food Safety, 33 Food Drug Cosmetic L.J. 558 (1978); Hutt, Food and Drug Regulation in Transition, 35 Food Drug Cosmetic L.J. 283 (1980); Cooper, A Time to Warn and a Time to Ban, in Banbury Report 6: Product Labeling and Health Risks (L. Morris, M. Mazis and I. Barofsky eds. 1980).

2. Does the right of privacy constrain governmental decisionmaking about food safety? Other risks to life and health? Compare the debate over regulation of Laetrile in Ch. 3 Sec. B.2b, supra.

3. Three important aspirin-like drugs were withdrawn recently from the market for causing unacceptable side-effects and even deaths. One of the drugs, Zomax, made by Johnson & Johnson, was withdrawn after 1,100 allergic reactions and five deaths had been associated with it. A new British study of some 9,272 patients, however, by Dr. William Inman of Southampton University found that serious sensitivity to Zomax was rare—and never fatal. But in the 23 weeks after the drug's withdrawal, 29 deaths were recorded that may be related to the with-

drawal. The Economist 103 (Nov. 19, 1983). Should the government be held liable for deaths associated with a drug's compulsory withdrawal?

c. The Use of Cost-Benefit Analysis

This section takes up a second analytic technique—cost-benefit analysis—which has been widely recommended as the best method for deciding when to regulate risk. This recommendation became a requirement for Executive agencies in 1981. Although cost-benefit analysis is often performed in conjunction with risk assessment, it need not be. The Delaney Clause, for example, directs FDA to regulate a particular category of risk without comparing the costs and benefits of such action.

Cost-benefit analysis is the more controversial of the two: its critics charge that it is often misleading if not immoral. Proponents retort that it is no more subject to manipulation than other decision techniques and the best there is for making certain decisions about risk regulation. As you read the material in this section consider whether the critics successfully make a case for abandoning cost benefit analysis or only for limiting its role to being merely one factor in the decision process rather then the sole or principal determinant.

RONALD REAGAN, EXECUTIVE ORDER NO. 12291

3 C.F.R. § 127 (1981), reprinted in 5 U.S.C. § 601.

By the authority vested in me as President by the Constitution and laws of the United States of America, and in order to reduce the burdens of existing and future regulations, increase agency accountability for regulatory actions, provide for presidential oversight of the regulatory process, minimize duplication and conflict of regulations, and insure well-reasoned regulations, it is hereby ordered as follows:

Section 1. *Definitions.* For the purposes of this Order:

(a) "Regulation" or "rule" means an agency statement of general applicability and future effect designed to implement, interpret, or prescribe law or policy or describing the procedure or practice requirements of an agency. . . .

(b) "Major rule" means any regulation that is likely to result in:

(1) An annual effect on the economy of $100 million or more;

(2) A major increase in costs or prices for consumers, individual industries, Federal, State, or local government agencies, or geographic regions; or

(3) Significant adverse effects on competition, employment, investment, productivity, innovation, or on the ability of United States-based enterprises to compete with foreign-based enterprises in domestic or export markets.

(c) "Director" means the Director of the Office of Management and Budget.

(d) "Agency" means any authority of the United States that is an "agency" under 44 U.S.C. 3502(1), excluding those agencies specified in 44 U.S.C. 3502(10).

(e) "Task Force" means the Presidential Task Force on Regulatory Relief.

Sec. 2. *General Requirements.* In promulgating new regulations, reviewing existing regulations, and developing legislative proposals concerning regulation, all agencies, to the extent permitted by law, shall adhere to the following requirements:

(a) Administrative decisions shall be based on adequate information concerning the need for and consequences of proposed government action;

(b) Regulatory action shall not be undertaken unless the potential benefits to society for [sic] the regulation outweigh the potential costs to society;

(c) Regulatory objectives shall be chosen to maximize the net benefits to society;

(d) Among alternative approaches to any given regulatory objective, the alternative involving the least net cost to society shall be chosen; and

(e) Agencies shall set regulatory priorities with the aim of maximizing the aggregate net benefits to society, taking into account the condition of the particular industries affected by regulations, the condition of the national economy, and other regulatory actions contemplated for the future.

Sec. 3. *Regulatory Impact Analysis and Review.*

(a) In order to implement Section 2 of this Order, each agency shall, in connection with every major rule, prepare, and to the extent permitted by law consider, a Regulatory Impact Analysis. . . .

. . .

(d) To permit each proposed major rule to be analyzed in light of the requirements stated in Section 2 of this Order, each preliminary and final Regulatory Impact Analysis shall contain the following information:

(1) A description of the potential benefits of the rule, including any beneficial effects that cannot be quantified in monetary terms, and the identification of those likely to receive the benefits;

(2) A description of the potential costs of the rule, including any adverse effects that cannot be quantified in monetary terms, and the identification of those likely to bear the costs;

(3) A determination of the potential net benefits of the rule, including an evaluation of effects that cannot be quantified in monetary terms;

(4) A description of alternative approaches that could substantially achieve the same regulatory goal at lower cost, together with an analysis of this potential benefit and costs and a brief explanation of the legal reasons why such alternatives, if proposed, could not be adopted; and

(5) Unless covered by the description required under paragraph (4) of this subsection, an explanation of any legal reasons why the rule cannot be based on the requirements set forth in Section 2 of this Order.

(e) (1) The Director, subject to the direction of the Task Force, which shall resolve any issues raised under this Order or ensure that they are presented to the President, is authorized to review any preliminary or final Regulatory Impact Analysis, notice of proposed rulemaking, or final rule based on the requirements of this Order.

(2) The Director shall be deemed to have concluded review unless the Director advises an agency to the contrary under subsection (f) of this Section:

(A) Within 60 days of a submission under subsection (c)(1) or a submission of a preliminary Regulatory Impact Analysis or notice of proposed rulemaking under subsection (c)(2);

(B) Within 30 days of the submission of a final Regulatory Impact Analysis and a final rule under subsection (c)(2); and

(C) Within 10 days of the submission of a notice of proposed rulemaking or final rule under subsection (c)(3).

(f) (1) Upon the request of the Director, an agency shall consult with the Director concerning the review of a preliminary Regulatory Impact Analysis or notice of proposed rulemaking under this Order, and shall, subject to Section 8(a)(2) of this Order, refrain from publishing its preliminary Regulatory Impact Analysis or notice of proposed rulemaking until such review is concluded.

(2) Upon receiving notice that the Director intends to submit views with respect to any final Regulatory Impact Analysis or final rule, the agency shall, subject to Section 8(a)(2) of this Order, refrain from publishing its final Regulatory Impact Analysis or final rule until the agency has responded to the Director's views, and incorporated those views and the agency's response in the rulemaking file.

(3) Nothing in this subsection shall be construed as displacing the agencies' responsibilities delegated by law.

(g) For every rule for which an agency publishes a notice of proposed rulemaking, the agency shall include in its notice:

(1) A brief statement setting forth the agency's initial determination whether the proposed rule is a major rule, together with the reasons underlying that determination; and

(2) For each proposed major rule, a brief summary of the agency's preliminary Regulatory Impact Analysis.

(h) Agencies shall make their preliminary and final Regulatory Impact Analyses available to the public.

(i) Agencies shall initiate reviews of currently effective rules in accordance with the purposes of this Order, and perform Regulatory Impact Analyses of currently effective major rules. The Director, subject to the direction of the Task Force, may designate currently effective rules for review in accordance with this Order, and establish schedules for reviews and Analyses under this Order.

.   .   .

Sec. 6.   *The Task Force and Office of Management and Budget.*

(a) To the extent permitted by law, the Director shall have authority, subject to the direction of the Task Force, to:

(1) Designate any proposed or existing rule as a major rule in accordance with Section 1(b) of this Order;

(2) Prepare and promulgate uniform standards for the identification of major rules and the development of Regulatory Impact Analyses;

(3) Require an agency to obtain and evaluate, in connection with a regulation, any additional relevant data from any appropriate source;

. . .

Sec. 9. *Judicial Review.*   This Order is intended only to improve the internal management of the Federal government, and is not intended to create any right or benefit, substantive or procedural, enforceable at law by a party against the United States, its agencies, its officers or any person.   The determinations made by agencies under Section 4 of this Order, and any Regulatory Impact Analyses for any rule, shall be made part of the whole record of agency action in connection with the rule.

NOTES

1.   The heart of Exec. Order 12291 is the mandate in Sec. 2(b) that "[r]egulatory action shall not be undertaken unless the potential benefits to society for [*sic*] the regulation outweigh the costs to society. . . . ."   This mandate is qualified, however, to apply only "to the extent permitted by law."

The distinction between what is permitted and what is required becomes crucial in understanding the impact of the Order.   For example, in American Textile Manufacturers Institute v. Donovan, Chapter 4, Sec. C.1, supra, the Supreme Court held that the relevant statutes did not require OSHA to do a cost-benefit analysis for deciding whether to regulate cotton dust.   By contrast, in Donovan v. Castle & Cooke Foods, 692 F.2d 641 (9th Cir. 1983), the Fifth Circuit upheld the use of cost—benefit analysis in determining whether a cannery should be required to reduce the noise levels to which employees were exposed at the source of the noise rather than merely having the employees wear ear plugs and muffs.   The Fifth Circuit explained that the relevant regulatory body in *Castle and Cooke Foods* had chosen to do cost-benefit analysis, and although such analysis might not be required as a matter of law it was *permitted.*

2.   In *American Textile Manufacturers,* OSHA had explained the roughness of its analysis by noting that the industry had refused to make more of its own data available.   How should an agency confronted with such industry behavior comply with Executive Order 12291?   In March of 1982, Commissioner Arthur Hayes of the Food and Drug Administration reported to a congressional subcommittee that the Order was the main reason the FDA did not prevent the marketing of a dangerously defective infant formula.   FDA had prepared regulations that would have prevented the problem, but their issuance was delayed in order to complete the economic impact analysis required by the Order.   He added that the FDA had tried unsuccessfully for two months to obtain from industry the information necessary to do the economic analysis.   Washington Post, March 12, 1982, at A.12, Col. 3.   Is this example an argument for abolishing the Order?   Compare the statement of Howard Raiffa to the Subcommittee on Science, Research and Technology of the U.S. House of Representatives Committee on Science and Technology, Hearings on Comparative Risk Assessment, 96th Cong., 2nd Sess. 253 (May 14, 1980):

> We must not pay attention to those voices that say one life is just as precious as 100 lives, or that no amount of money is as important as saving one life. Numbers do count.   Such rhetoric leads to emotional, irrational inefficiencies and when life is at stake we should be extremely careful lest we fail to save lives that could have easily been saved with the same resources, or lest we force our disadvantaged poor to spend money that they can ill afford in order to gain a measure of safety that they don't want in comparison to their other more pressing needs.

3.   Ronald Reagan was not the first President to require some cost-benefit analysis as a way of constraining agency discretion.   In 1975, Gerald Ford issued Executive Order 11821, which required agencies to prepare "inflation impact statements" for major federal actions.   3 C.F.R. 203, reprinted in 12 U.S.C. § 1904 (1976).   Jimmy Carter, in Executive Order 12044, required agencies to

prepare a draft regulatory analysis before proposing major rules, and to issue a final analysis with the final rule. 3 C.F.R. 152 (1979), reprinted in 5 U.S.C. § 553 (Supp. III 1979). In contrast to the Reagan order, Carter's order required agencies to analyze the costs of alternative ways of dealing with the problem and to provide a detailed explanation of the reasons for choosing one alternative over the others. Thus, Carter's order focused on cost—effectiveness rather than cost-benefit analysis. See generally Note, Regulatory Analyses and Judicial Review of Informal Rulemaking, 91 Yale L.J. 739, 746–49 (1982).

A more significant difference between the orders is the approach to enforcement. The Reagan Order, unlike its predecessors, gives extensive enforcement powers to OMB, including the power to order an agency not to publish a proposed rule until OMB review is completed. OMB is part of the Executive Office of the President. If regulatory agencies make major decisions, involving substantial elements of judgment and discretion, for which the President will be held politically responsible, should the President have greater control than in the past over regulatory decisions? If so, how should that control be structured, and how should it be made accountable to congressional and public oversight? For a provocative discussion of whether this significant shift in decision-making authority to OMB may be unconstitutional see Rosenberg, Presidential Control of Agency Rulemaking: An Analysis of Constitutional Issues That May be Raised by Executive Order 12291, 23 Ariz.L.Rev. 1199 (1981).

4. Does Section 9 of the Reagan Order preclude judicial review of claims that agencies have violated the Order? For a forceful argument that it may not, see Raven-Hansen, Making Agencies Follow Orders: Judicial Review of Agency Violations of Executive Order 12291, 1983 Duke L.J. 285 (1983).

STEVEN KELMAN,
COST–BENEFIT ANALYSIS: AN ETHICAL CRITIQUE

5 Regulation 33–40 (January-February 1981).

At the broadest and vaguest level, cost-benefit analysis may be regarded simply as systematic thinking about decision-making. Who can oppose, economists sometimes ask, efforts to think in a systematic way about the consequences of different courses of action? The alternative, it would appear, is unexamined decision-making. But defining cost-benefit analysis so simply leaves it with few implications for actual regulatory decision-making. Presumably, therefore, those who urge regulators to make greater use of the technique have a more extensive prescription in mind. I assume here that their prescription includes the following views:

(1) There exists a strong presumption that an act should not be undertaken unless its benefits outweigh its costs.

(2) In order to determine whether benefits outweigh costs, it is desirable to attempt to express all benefits and costs in a common scale or denominator, so that they can be compared with each other, even when some benefits and costs are not traded on markets and hence have no established dollar values.

(3) Getting decision-makers to make more use of cost-benefit techniques is important enough to warrant both the expense required to gather the data for improved cost-benefit estimation and the political efforts needed to give the activity higher priority compared to other activities, also valuable in and of themselves.

My focus is on cost-benefit analysis as applied to environmental, safety, and health regulation. In that context, I examine each of the above propositions from the perspective of formal ethical theory, that is, the study of what actions it is morally right to undertake. My conclusions are:

(1) In areas of environmental, safety, and health regulation, there may be many instances where a certain decision might be right even though its benefits do not outweigh its costs.

(2) There are good reasons to oppose efforts to put dollar values on non-marketed benefits and costs.

(3) Given the relative frequency of occasions in the areas of environmental, safety, and health regulation where one would not wish to use a benefits-outweigh-costs test as a decision rule, and given the reasons to oppose the monetizing of non-marketed benefits or costs that is a prerequisite for cost-benefit analysis, it is not justifiable to devote major resources to the generation of data for cost-benefit calculations or to undertake efforts to "spread the gospel" of cost-benefit analysis further.

I

How do we decide whether a given action is morally right or wrong and hence, assuming the desire to act morally, why it should be undertaken or refrained from? Like the Molière character who spoke prose without knowing it, economists who advocate use of cost-benefit analysis for public decisions are philosophers without knowing it: the answer given by cost-benefit analysis, that actions should be undertaken so as to maximize net benefits, represents one of the classic answers given by moral philosophers—that given by utilitarians. To determine whether an action is right or wrong, utilitarians tote up all the positive consequences of the action in terms of human satisfaction. The act that maximizes attainment of satisfaction under the circumstances is the right act. . . .

Before proceeding further, the subtlety of the utilitarian position should be noted. The positive and negative consequences of an act for satisfaction may go beyond the act's immediate consequences. A facile version of utilitarianism would give moral sanction to a lie, for instance, if the satisfaction of an individual attained by telling the lie was greater than the suffering imposed on the lie's victim. Few utilitarians would agree. Most of them would add to the list of negative consequences the effect of the one lie on the tendency of the person who lies to tell other lies, even in instances when the lying produced less satisfaction for him than dissatisfaction for others. They would also add the negative effects of the lie on the general level of social regard for truth-telling, which has many consequences for future utility. A further consequence may be added as well. It is sometimes said that we should include in a utilitarian calculation the feeling of dissatisfaction produced in the liar (and perhaps in others) because, by telling a lie, one has "done the wrong thing." Correspondingly, in this view, among the positive consequences to be weighed into a utilitarian calculation of truth-telling is satisfaction arising from "doing the right thing." This view rests on an error, however, because it *assumes* what it is the purpose of the calculation to *determine*—that telling the truth in the instance in question is indeed the right thing to do. . . . The logical error discussed . . . appears to suggest that we have a notion of certain things being right or wrong that *predates* our calculation of costs and benefits. Imagine the case of an old man in Nazi Germany who is hostile to the regime. He is wondering whether he should speak out against Hitler. If he speaks out, he will lose his pension. And his action will have done nothing to increase the chances that the Nazi regime will be overthrown: he is regarded as somewhat eccentric by those around him, and nobody has ever consulted his views on political questions. Recall that one cannot add to the benefits of speaking out any satisfaction from doing "the right thing," because the purpose of the exercise is to determine whether speaking out *is* the right thing. How would the utilitarian calculation go? The benefits of the old man's speaking out would, as the example is presented, be nil, while the costs would be his loss of his pension. So the costs of the action would outweigh the benefits. By the utilitarians' cost-benefit calculation, it would be *morally wrong* for the man to speak out.

Another example: two very close friends are on an Arctic expedition together. One of them falls very sick in the snow and bitter cold, and sinks quickly before anything can be done to help him. As he is dying, he asks his friend one thing, "Please, make me a solemn promise that ten years from today you will come back to this spot and place a lighted candle here to remember me." The friend solemnly promises to do so, but does not tell a soul. Now, ten years later, the friend must decide whether to keep his promise. It would be inconvenient for him to make the long trip. Since he told nobody, his failure to go will not affect the general social faith in promise-keeping. And the incident was unique enough so that it is safe to assume that his failure to go will not encourage him to break other promises. Again, the costs of the act outweigh the benefits. A utilitarian would need to believe that it would be *morally wrong* to travel to the Arctic to light the candle.

A third example: a wave of thefts has hit a city and the police are having trouble finding any of the thieves. But they believe, correctly, that punishing someone for theft will have some deterrent effect and will decrease the number of crimes. Unable to arrest any actual perpetrator, the police chief and the prosecutor arrest a person whom they know to be innocent and, in cahoots with each other, fabricate a convincing case against him. The police chief and the prosecutor are about to retire, so the act has no effect on any future actions of theirs. The fabriction is perfectly executed, so nobody finds out about it. Is the *only* question involved in judging the act of framing the innocent man that of whether his suffering from conviction and imprisonment will be greater than the suffering avoided among potential crime victims when some crimes are deterred? A utilitarian would need to believe that it is *morally right to punish the innocent man* as long as it can be demonstrated that the suffering prevented outweighs his suffering.

And a final example: imagine two worlds, each containing the same sum total of happiness. In the first world, this total of happiness came about from a series of acts that included a number of lies and injustices (that is, the total consisted of the immediate gross sum of happiness created by certain acts, minus any long-term unhappiness occasioned by the lies and injustices). In the second world the same amount of happiness was produced by a different series of acts, none of which involved lies or injustices. Do we have any reason to prefer the one world to the other? A utilitarian would need to believe that the choice between the two worlds is a *matter of indifference.*

To those who believe that it would not be morally wrong for the old man to speak out in Nazi Germany or for the explorer to return to the Arctic to light a candle for his deceased friend, that it would not be morally right to convict the innocent man, or that the choice between the two worlds is not a matter of indifference—to those of us who believe these things, utilitarianism is insufficient as a moral view. We believe that some acts whose costs are greater than their benefits may be morally right and, contrariwise, some acts whose benefits are greater than their costs may be morally wrong.

This does not mean that the question whether benefits are greater than costs is morally irrelevant. Few would claim such. Indeed, for a broad range of individual and social decisions, whether an act's benefits outweigh its costs is a sufficient question to ask. But not for all such decisions. These may involve situations where certain duties—duties not to lie, break promises, or kill, for example—make an act wrong, even if it would result in an excess of benefits over costs. Or they may involve instances where people's rights are at stake. We would not permit rape even if it could be demonstrated that the rapist derived enormous happiness from his act, while the victim experienced only minor displeasure. We do not do cost-benefit analyses of freedom of speech or trial by jury. . . . As the United Steelworkers noted in a comment on the Occupational Safety and Health Administration's economic analysis of its proposed rule to reduce worker exposure to carcinogenic coke-oven emissions, the Emancipation Proclamation was not subjected to an inflationary impact statement. The notion of human rights involves the idea that people may make certain claims to be allowed to act in certain ways or to be treated in certain ways, even if the sum of benefits achieved thereby does not outweigh the sum of costs. It is this view that underlies the statement that "workers have a right to a safe and healthy work place" and the expectation that OSHA's decisions will reflect that judgment.

In the most convincing versions of nonutilitarian ethics, various duties or rights are not absolute. But each has a *prima facie* moral validity so that, if duties or rights do not conflict, the morally right act is the act that reflects a duty or respects a right. If duties or rights do conflict, a moral judgment, based on conscious deliberation, must be made. Since one of the duties non-utilitarian philosophers enumerate is the duty of beneficence (the duty to maximize happiness), which in effect incorporates all of utilitarianism by reference, a non-utilitarian who is faced with conflicts between the results of cost-benefit analysis and non-utility-based considerations will need to undertake such deliberation. But in that deliberation, additional elements, which cannot be reduced to a question of whether benefits outweigh costs, have been introduced. Indeed, depending on the moral importance we attach to the right or duty involved, cost-benefit questions may, within wide ranges, become irrelevant to the outcome of the moral judgment.

In addition to questions involving duties and rights, there is a final sort of question where, in my view, the issue of whether benefits outweigh costs should not govern moral judgment. I noted earlier that, for the common run of questions facing individuals and societies, it is possible to begin and end our judgment simply by finding out if the benefits of the contemplated act outweigh the costs. This very fact means that one way to show the great importance, or value, attached to an area is to say that decisions involving the area should not be determined by cost-benefit calculations. This applies, I think, to the view many environmentalists have of decisions involving our natural environment. When officials are deciding what level of pollution will harm certain vulnerable people—such as asthmatics or the elderly—while not harming others, one issue involved may be the right of those people not to be sacrificed on the altar of somewhat higher living standards for the rest of us. But more broadly than this, many environmentalists fear that subjecting decisions about clean air or water to the cost-benefit tests that determine the general run of decisions removes those matters from the realm of specially valued things.

II

In order for cost-benefit calculations to be performed the way they are supposed to be, all costs and benefits must be expressed in a common measure, typically dollars, including things not normally bought and sold on markets, and to which dollar prices are therefore not attached. The most dramatic example of such things is human life itself; but many of the other benefits achieved or preserved by environmental policy—such as peace and quiet, fresh-smelling air, swimmable rivers, spectacular vistas—are not traded on markets either.

Economists who do cost-benefit analysis regard the quest after dollar values for non-market things as a difficult challenge—but one to be met with relish. They have tried to develop methods for imputing a person's "willingness to pay" for such things, their approach generally involving a search for bundled goods that *are* traded on markets and that vary as to whether they include a feature that is, *by itself*, not marketed. Thus, fresh air is not marketed, but houses in different parts of Los Angeles that are similar except for the degree of smog are. Peace and quiet is not marketed, but similar houses inside and outside airport flight paths are. The risk of death is not marketed, but similar jobs that have different levels of risk are. Economists have produced many often ingenious efforts to impute dollar prices to non-marketed things by observing the premiums accorded homes in clean air areas over similar homes in dirty areas or the premiums paid for risky jobs over similar nonrisky jobs.

These ingenious efforts are subject to criticism on a number of technical grounds. It may be difficult to control for all the dimensions of quality other than the presence or absence of the non-marketed thing. More important, in a world where people have different preferences and are subject to different constraints as they make their choices, the dollar value imputed to the non-market things that most people would wish to avoid will be lower than otherwise, because people with unusually weak aversion to those things or unusually strong constraints on their choices will be willing to take the bundled good in question at less of a discount than the average person. Thus, to use the property value discount of homes near airports as a measure of people's willingness to pay for quiet means to accept as a proxy for the rest of us the behavior of those least sensitive to noise, of airport employees (who value the convenience of a near-airport location) or of others who are susceptible to an agent's assurances that "it's not so bad." To use the wage premiums accorded hazardous work as a meaure of the value of life means to accept as proxies for the rest of us the choices of people who do not have many choices or who are exceptional risk-seekers.

A second problem is that the attempts of economists to measure people's willingness to pay for non-marketed things assume that there is no difference between the price a person would require for *giving up* something to which he has a preexisting right and the price he would pay to *gain* something to which he enjoys no right. Thus, the analysis assumes no difference between how much a homeowner would need to be paid in order to give up an unobstructed mountain view that he already enjoys and how much he would be willing to pay to get an obstruction moved once it is already in place.   Available evidence suggests that most people would insist on being paid far more to assent to a worsening of their situation than they would be willing to pay to improve their situation.   The difference arises from such factors as being accustomed to and psychologically attached to that which one believes one enjoys by right.   But this creates a circularity problem for any attempt to use cost-benefit analysis to determine *whether* to assign to, say, the homeowner the right to an unobstructed mountain view.   For willingness to pay will be different depending on whether the right is assigned initially or not.   The value judgment about whether to assign the right must thus be made first.   (In order to set an upper bound on the value of the benefit, one might hypothetically assign the right to the person and determine how much he would need to be paid to give it up.)

Third, the efforts of economists to impute willingness to pay invariably involve bundled goods exchanged in *private* transactions.   Those who use figures garnered from such analysis to provide guidance for *public* decisions assume no difference between how people value certain things in private individual transactions and how they would wish those same things to be valued in public collective decisions.   In making such assumptions, economists insidiously slip into their analysis an important and controversial value judgment, growing naturally out of the highly individualistic microeconomic tradition—namely, the view that there should be no difference between private behavior and the behavior we display in public social life.   An alternative view—one that enjoys, I would suggest, wide resonance among citizens—would be that public, social decisions provide an opportunity to give certain things a higher valuation than we choose, for one reason or another, to give them in our private activities.

Thus, opponents of stricter regulation of health risks often argue that we show by our daily risk-taking behavior that we do not value life infinitely, and therefore our public decisions should not reflect the high value of life that proponents of strict regulation propose.   However, an alternative view is equally plausible.   Precisely because we fail, for whatever reasons, to give life-saving the value in everyday personal decisions that we in some general terms believe we should give it, we may wish our social decisions to provide us the occasion to display the reverence for life that we espouse but do not always show.   By this view, people do not have fixed unambiguous "preferences" to which they give expression through private activities and which therefore should be given expression in public decisions.   Rather, they may have what they themselves regard as "higher" and "lower" preferences.   The latter may come to the fore in private decisions, but people may want the former to come to the fore in public decisions.   They may sometimes display racial prejudice but support antidiscrimination laws.   They may buy a certain product after seeing a seductive ad, but be skeptical enough of advertising to want the government to keep a close eye on it.   In such cases, the use of private behavior to impute the values that should be entered for public decisions, as is done by using willingness to pay in private transactions, commits grievous offense against a view of the behavior of the citizen that is deeply engrained in our democratic tradition.   It is a view that denudes politics of any independent role in society, reducing it to a mechanistic, mimicking recalculation based on private behavior.

Finally, one may oppose the effort to place prices on a non-market thing and hence in effect incorporate it into the market system out of a fear that the very act of doing so will reduce the thing's perceived value. To place a price on the benefit may, in other words, reduce the value of that benefit. Cost-benefit analysis thus may be like the thermometer that, when placed in a liquid to be measured, itself changes the liquid's temperature.

Examples of the perceived cheapening of a thing's value by the very act of buying and selling it abound in everyday life and language. The disgust that accompanies the idea of buying and selling human beings is based on the sense that this would dramatically diminish human worth. Epithets such as "he prostituted himself," applied as linguistic analogies to people who have sold something, reflect the view that certain things should not be sold because doing so diminishes their value. Praise that is bought is worth little, even to the person buying it. A true anecdote is told of an economist who retired to another university community and complained that he was having difficulty making friends. The laconic response of a critical colleague—"If you want a friend why don't you buy yourself one"—illustrates in a pithy way the intuition that, for some things, the very act of placing a price on them reduces their perceived value. . . .

The second way in which placing a market price on a thing decreases its perceived value is by removing the possibility of proclaiming that the thing is "not for sale," since things on the market by definition are for sale. The very statement that something is not for sale affirms, enhances, and protects a thing's value in a number of ways. . . .

. . .

III

An objection that advocates of cost-benefit analysis might well make to the preceding argument should be considered. I noted earlier that, in cases where various non-utility-based duties or rights conflict with the maximization of utility, it is necessary to make a deliberative judgment about what act is finally right. I also argued earlier that the search for commensurability might not always be a desirable one, that the attempt to go beyond expressing benefits in terms of (say) lives saved and costs in terms of dollars is not something devoutly to be wished.

In situations involving things that are not expressed in a common measure, advocates of cost-benefit analysis argue that people making judgments "in effect" perform cost-benefit calculations anyway. If government regulators promulgate a regulation that saves 100 lives at a cost of $1 billion, they are "in effect" valuing a life at (a minimum of) $10 million, whether or not they say that they are willing to place a dollar value on a human life. Since, in this view, cost-benefit analysis "in effect" is inevitable, it might as well be made specific.

This argument misconstrues the real difference in the reasoning processes involved. In cost-benefit analysis, equivalencies are established *in advance* as one of the raw materials for the calculation. One determines costs and benefits, one determines equivalencies (to be able to put various costs and benefits into a common measure), and then one sets to toting things up—waiting, as it were, with bated breath for the results of the calculation to come out. The outcome is determined by the arithmetic; if the outcome is a close call or if one is not good at long division, one does not know how it will turn out until the calculation is finished. In the kind of deliberative judgment that is performed without a common measure, no establishment of equivalencies occurs in advance. Equivalencies are not aids to the decision process. In fact, the decision-maker might not even be aware of what the "in effect" equivalencies were, at least before they are revealed to him afterwards by someone pointing out what he had "in effect" done. The decision-maker would see himself as simply having made a deliberative judgment; the "in effect" equivalency number did not play a causal role in the decision but at most merely reflects it. Given this, the argument against making the process explicit is the one discussed earlier in the discussion of problems with putting specific quantified values on things that are not normally quantified—that the very act of doing so may serve to reduce the value of those things.

My own judgment is that modest efforts to assess levels of benefits and costs are justified, although I do not believe that government agencies ought to sponsor efforts to put dollar prices on non-market things. I also do not believe that the cry for more cost-benefit analysis in regulation is, on the whole, justified. If regulatory officials were so insensitive about regulatory costs that they did not provide acceptable raw material for deliberative judgments (even if not of a strictly cost-benefit nature), my conclusion might be different. But a good deal of research into costs and benefits already occurs—actually, far more in the U.S. regulatory process than in that of any other industrial society. The danger now would seem to come more from the other side.

JAMES V. DeLONG,
DEFENDING COST–BENEFIT ANALYSIS—REPLIES TO STEVEN KELMAN
5 Regulation 39–42 (March-April 1981).

Steven Kelman's "Cost-Benefit Analysis—An Ethical Critique" presents so many targets that it is difficult to concentrate one's fire. However, four points seem worth particular emphasis:

(1) The decision to use cost-benefit analysis by no means implies adoption of the reductionist utilitarianism described by Kelman. It is based instead on the pragmatic conclusion that any value system one adopts is more likely to be promoted if one knows something about the consequences of the choices to be made. The effort to put dollar values on noneconomic benefits is nothing more than an effort to find some common measure for things that are not easily comparable when, in the real world, choice must be made. Its object is not to write a computer program but to improve the quality of difficult social choices under conditions of uncertainty, and no sensible analyst lets himself become the prisoner of the numbers.

(2) Kelman repeatedly lapses into "entitlement" rhetoric, as if an assertion of a moral claim closes an argument. Even leaving aside the fundamental question of the philosophical basis of those entitlements, there are two major problems with this style of argument. First, it tends naturally toward all-encompassing claims.

Kelman quotes a common statement that "workers have a right to a safe and healthy workplace," a statement that contains no recognition that safety and health are not either/or conditions, that the most difficult questions involve gradations of risk, and that the very use of entitlement language tends to assume that a zero-risk level is the only acceptable one. Second, entitlement rhetoric is usually phrased in the passive voice, as if the speaker were arguing with some omnipotent god or government that is maliciously withholding the entitlement out of spite. In the real world, one person's right is another's duty, and it often clarifies the discussion to focus more precisely on who owes this duty and what it is going to cost him or her. For example, the article posits that an issue in government decisions about acceptable pollution levels is "the right" of such vulnerable groups as asthmatics or the elderly "not to be sacrificed on the altar of somewhat higher living standards for the rest of us." This defends the entitlement by assuming the costs involved are both trivial and diffused. Suppose, though, that the price to be paid is not "somewhat higher living standards," but the jobs of a number of workers?

Kelman's counter to this seems to be that entitlements are not firm rights, but only presumptive ones that prevail in any clash with nonentitlements, and that when two entitlements collide the decision depends upon the "moral importance we attach to the right or duty involved." So the above collision would be resolved by deciding whether a job is an entitlement and, if it is, by then deciding whether jobs or air have greater "moral importance."

I agree that conflicts between such interests present difficult choices, but the quantitative questions, the cost-benefit questions, are hardly irrelevant to making them. Suppose taking X quantity of pollution from the air of a city will keep one asthmatic from being forced to leave town and cost 1,000 workers their jobs? Suppose it will keep 1,000 asthmatics from being forced out and cost one job? These are not equivalent choices, economically or morally, and the effort to decide them according to some abstract idea of moral importance only obscures the true nature of the moral problems involved.

(3) Kelman also develops the concept of things that are "specially valued," and that are somehow contaminated if thought about in monetary terms. As an approach to personal decision making, this is silly. There are many things one specially values—in the sense that one would find the effort to assign a market price to them ridiculous—which are nonetheless affected by economic factors. I may specially value a family relationship, but how often I phone is influenced by long-distance rates. I may specially value music, but be affected by the price of records or the cost of tickets at the Kennedy Center.

When translated to the realm of government decisions, however, the concept goes beyond silliness. It creates a political grotesquerie. People specially value many different things. Under Kelman's assumptions, people must, in creating a political coalition, recognize and accept as legitimate everyone's special value, without concern for cost. Therefore, everyone becomes entitled to as much of the thing he specially values as he says he specially values, and it is immoral to discuss vulgar questions of resource limitations. Any coalition built on such premises can go in either of two directions: It can try to incorporate so many different groups and interests that the absurdity of its internal contradictions becomes manifest. Or it can limit its membership at some point and decide that the special values of those left outside are not legitimate and should be sacrificed to the special values of those in the coalition. In the latter case, of course, those outside must be made scapegoats for any frustration of any group member's entitlement, a requirement that eventually leads to political polarization and a holy war between competing coalitions of special values.

(4) The decisions that must be made by contemporary government indeed involve painful choices. They affect both the absolute quantity and the distribution not only of goods and benefits, but also of physical and mental suffering. It is easy to understand why people would want to avoid making such choices and would rather act in ignorance than with knowledge and responsibility for the consequences of their choices. While this may be understandable, I do not regard it as an acceptable moral position. To govern is to choose, and government officials—whether elected or appointed—betray their obligations to the welfare of the people who hired them if they adopt a policy of happy ignorance and nonresponsibility for consequences.

The article concludes with the judgment that the present danger is too much cost-benefit analysis, not too little. But I find it hard to believe, looking around the modern world, that its major problem is that it suffers from an excess of rationality. The world's stock of ignorance is and will remain quite large enough without adding to it as a matter of deliberate policy.

ROBERT M. SOLOW

I am an economist who has no personal involvement in the practice of cost-benefit analysis, who happens to think that modern economics underplays the significance of ethical judgments both in its approach to policy and its account of individual and organizational behavior, and who once wrote in print:

> It may well be socially destructive to admit the routine exchangeability of certain things. We would prefer to maintain that they are beyond price (although this sometimes means only that we would prefer not to know what the price really is).

You might expect, therefore, that I would be in sympathy with Steven Kelman's ethical critique of cost-benefit analysis. But I found the article profoundly, and not entirely innocently, misleading. I would like to say why.

First of all, it is not the case that cost-benefit analysis works, or must work, by "monetizing" everything from mother love to patriotism. Cost-benefit analysis is needed only when society must give up some of one good thing in order to get more of another good thing. In other cases the decision is not problematical. The underlying rationale of cost-benefit analysis is that the cost of the good thing to be obtained is precisely the good thing that must or will be given up to obtain it. Wherever he reads "willingness to pay" and balks, Kelman should read "willingness to sacrifice" and feel better. In a choice between hospital beds and preventive treatment, lives are traded against lives. I suppose it is only natural that my brethren should get into the habit of measuring the sacrifice in terms of dollars forgone. In the typical instance in which someone actually does a cost-benefit analysis, the question to be decided is, say, whether the public should be taxed to pay for a water project—a context in which it does not seem far-fetched to ask whether the project will provide services for which the public would willingly pay what it would have to give up in taxes. But some less familiar unit of measurement could be used.

Let me add here, parenthetically, that I do agree with Kelman that there are situations in which the body politic's willingness to sacrifice may be badly measured by the sum of individuals' willingnesses to sacrifice in a completely "private" context. But that is at worst an error of technique, not a mistaken principle.

Second, Kelman hints broadly that "economists" are so morally numb as to believe that a routine cost-benefit analysis could justify killing widows and orphans, or abridging freedom of speech, or outlawing simple evidences of piety or friendship. But there is nothing in the theory or the practice of cost-benefit analysis to justify that judgment. Treatises on the subject make clear that certain ethical or political principles may irreversibly dominate the advantages and disadvantages capturable by cost-benefit analysis. Those treatises make a further point that Kelman barely touches on: since the benefits and the costs of a policy decision are usually enjoyed and incurred by different people, a distributional judgment has to be made which can override any simple-minded netting out.

. . .

Third, Kelman ends by allowing that it is not a bad thing to have a modest amount of cost-benefit analysis going on. I would have supposed that was a fair description of the state of affairs. Do I detect a tendency to eat one's cost-benefit analysis and have it too? If not, what is the point of all the overkill? As a practical matter, the vacuum created by diminished reliance on cost-benefit analysis is likely to be filled by a poor substitute for ethically informed deliberation. Is the capering of Mr. Stockman more to Mr. Kelman's taste.

_____

GERARD BUTTERS, JOHN CALFEE, PAULINE IPPOLITO

. . .

. . . Cost-benefit analysis is not a means for judging private decisions. It is a guide for decision making involving others, especially when the welfare of many individuals must be balanced. It is designed not to dictate individual values, but to take them into account when decisions must be made collectively. Its use is grounded on the principle that, in a democracy, government must act as an agent of the citizens.

We see no reason to abandon this principle when health and safety are involved. Consider, for example, a proposal to raise the existing federal standards on automobile safety. Higher standards will raise the costs, and hence the price, of cars. From our point of view, the appropriate policy judgment rests on whether customers will value the increased safety sufficiently to warrant the costs. Any violation of a cost-benefit criterion would require that consumers purchase something they would not voluntarily purchase or prevent them from purchasing something they want. One might argue, in the spirit of Kelman's analysis, that many consumers would want the government to impose a more stringent standard than they would choose for themselves. If so, how is the cost-safety trade-off that consumers really want to be determined? Any objective way of doing this would be a natural part of cost-benefit analysis.

Kelman also argues that the process of assigning a dollar value to things not traded in the marketplace is rife with indignities, flaws, and biases. Up to a point, we agree. It *is* difficult to place objective dollar values on certain intangible costs and benefits. Even with regard to intangibles which have been systematically studied, such as the "value of life," we know of no cost-benefit advocate who believes that regulatory staff economists should reduce every consideration to dollar terms and simply supply the decision maker with the bottom line. Our main concerns are twofold: (1) to make the major costs and benefits explicit so that the decision maker makes the trade-offs consciously and with the prospect of being held accountable, and (2) to encourage the move toward a more consistent set of standards.

The gains from adopting consistent regulatory standards can be dramatic. If costs and benefits are not balanced in making decisions, it is likely that the returns per dollar in terms of health and safety will be small for some programs and large for others. Such programs present opportunities for saving lives, and cost-benefit analysis will reveal them. Perhaps, as Kelman argues, there is something repugnant about assigning dollar values to lives. But the alternative can be to sacrifice lives needlessly by failing to carry out the calculations that would have revealed the means for saving them. It should be kept in mind that the avoidance of cost-benefit analysis has its own cost, which can be gauged in lives as well as in dollars.

Nonetheless, we do not dispute that cost-benefit analysis is highly imperfect. We would welcome a better guide to public policy, a guide that would be efficient, morally attractive, and certain to ensure that governments follow the dictates of the governed. Kelman's proposal is to adopt an ethical system that balances conflicts between certain unspecified "duties" and "rights" according to "deliberate reflection." But who is to do the reflecting, and on whose behalf? His guide places no clear limits on the actions of regulatory agencies. Rather than enhancing the connections between individual values and state decisions, such a vague guideline threatens to sever them. Is there a common moral standard that every regulator will magically and independently arrive at through "deliberate reflection"? We doubt it. Far more likely is a system in which bureaucratic decisions reflect the preferences, not of the citizens, but of those in a peculiar position to influence decisions. What concessions to special interests cannot be disguised by claiming that it is degrading to make explicit the trade-offs reflected in the decision? What individual crusade cannot be rationalized by an appeal to "public values" that "rise above" values revealed by individual choices?

STEVEN KELMAN, LETTER TO THE EDITOR

5 Regulation 2, 3 (May-June 1981).

. . .

Let me start by noting where my critics and I *agree.* We agree that decisions about what levels of regulatory protection to require are difficult ones. We agree that consequences of decisions should be sketched out and analyzed systematically. We agree that explanations for decisions should be given, so that decision makers can be accountable for the balancing judgments they make.

I mention these areas of agreement partly because a number of those replying to me suggest that to criticize cost-benefit analysis is to attack the above propositions. If all that cost-benefit analysis did were to systematically sketch out the effects of regulatory alternatives and explain why a certain alternative was chosen, it would hardly be the powerful tool that "regulatory reformers" clearly believe it to be, EPA and OSHA, for example, have long carried out such analyses and explanations.

Honesty requires us to recognize that cost-benefit analysis implies more: It implies a rule ("maximize net benefits") that dictates, or very strongly suggests, *what decisions should be made at the end of the analysis.* It also requires, if the rule is to be applied, reducing costs and benefits to a common metric for purposes of comparison.

James DeLong is correct to note that I spoke of rights as an alternative to the "maximize net benefits" test as a justification for decisions. In this brief space, I can only suggest the outlines of an argument regarding the nature of rights. The notion of human rights rests, I think, on the suggestion that all people may legitimately make certain claims simply because they are human beings. The strength of a claim to a right is therefore based on the strength of its connection to the maintenance of human life, human dignity, or the elements of our common humanity (such as the ability to reason) that make humans unique among forms of life. Since this basis of claims to human rights is something we all share equally, there is also an egalitarian thrust to the notion.

Proponents of cost-benefit analysis offer an entirely different test for the strength of a claim: They ask whether the cost of meeting the claim is greater than the claimant's willingness to pay for it. But rights such as those to freedom of speech are granted on the former basis, not the latter, which is why we do not do cost-benefit analyses of the Bill of Rights, Costs, and the willingness to pay of various parties, are part of any moral deliberation, but far from the *only* factors. There is where I profoundly differ from cost-benefit advocates.

.   .   .

James DeLong notes that "I may specially value a family relationship, but how often I phone is influenced by long-distance rates." I must confess that my reaction is: "So what?" If he means to suggest that we should put dollar values on family relationships, then he ought to make this argument explicitly. He doesn't, and therefore I fail to see the significance of his point.

Robert Solow notes that using units of measurement other than dollars might reduce the costs of monetizing non-market things. This is an interesting point. But all except one of the arguments my article makes against monetizing non-market benefits would hold just as well if the accounting unit were doughnuts. Only my last argument—that the process of pricing can itself diminish the perceived value of the previously non-priced thing—is partly dependent on dollars as the unit of account. I believe that part of this decrease comes from the very fungibility of *any* standard unit of account. Many years ago, Emile Durkheim argued that the very nature of sacredness is that we do not treat the sacred thing in ways that we treat the normal run of things. I also believe that if some unit of account other than dollars were invented for use in cost-benefit analysis, similar problems would soon attach to this new unit.

Finally, a number of my critics suggest that I attacked a "straw man." Much of Solow's reply, for example, argued not so much against points I made as against the idea that any serious advocate of cost-benefit analysis would suggest a simple decision rule of maximizing net benefits.

I urge Solow to look at cost-benefit analyses economists have done, say of OSHA regulations, in search of the kind of recognitions he says all serious practitioners accept. President Reagan's executive order states that regulation "shall not be undertaken unless the potential benefits to society for the regulation outweigh the potential costs to society" and that "[r]egulatory objectives shall be chosen to maximize the net benefits to society." The "straw man" does indeed seem real.

If my comments serve to chasten cost-benefit enthusiasts about the ethical implications of methods they appear to feel are mere "neutral science," I believe I will have achieved an important purpose.

NOTES

1. Laurence Tribe, in writing on the weaknesses of cost-benefit analysis, see Ch. 1, Sec. C.1, supra, has suggested the development of "a new group of professionals sensitive to the sorts of values and issues that analyses currently tend to slight—diversity, balance, aesthetic quality, reversibility, [and] the claims of the future." Does this answer all of Kelman's objections to cost-benefit analysis? Some of them?

2. For generally favorable assessments of cost-benefit analysis see generally E. Mishan, Cost Benefit Analysis (1973); D. Pearce, The Valuation of Social Cost (1978); Leonard and Zeckhauser, Cost-Benefit Analysis Applied to Risks: Its Philosophy and Legitimacy, Center for Philosophy and Public Policy of the University of Maryland Working Paper (1983).

For more critical views see Baram, Cost-Benefit Analysis: An Inadequate Basis for Health, Safety and Environmental Regulatory Decision-Making, 8 Ecol.L.Q. 473 (1980); Bogen, Quantitative Risk-Benefit Analysis in Regulatory Decision-Making: A Fundamental Problem and an Alternate Proposal, 8 J. of Health Politics, Policy and Law 1 (Spring 1983); Fischhoff, Cost Benefit Analysis and the Art of Motorcycle Maintenance, 8 Policy Sciences 177 (1977); Kennedy, Cost-Benefit Analysis of Entitlement Problems: A Critique, 33 Stan.L.Rev. 387 (1981); Ricci and Molton, Risk and Benefit in Environmental Law, 214 Science 1096 (Dec. 4, 1981); Rogers, Benefits, Costs, and Risks: Oversight of Health and Environmental Decisionmaking, 4 Harv.Envir.L.Rev. 191 (1980); Shaw & Wolfe, A Legal and Ethical Critique of Using Cost-Benefit Analysis in Public Law, 19 Houston L.R. 899 (1982).

3. Two major criticisms are commonly made of cost-benefit analysis: (1) that it is not sensitive to the distribution (as opposed to the total) of costs or benefits to different individuals or groups of individuals, and (2) that it discriminates against considering long-term as opposed to short-term costs, particularly costs imposed on future generations. Both are embodied in the continuing debate on how to put a price tag on human life. The final selections in this section introduce the two most popular approaches to valuing life and examine their strengths and weaknesses.

MOLLY SINCLAIR,
HOW DOES SOCIETY PUT A PRICE TAG
ON HUMAN LIFE?

The Washington Post, Sunday, March 22, 1981 at B1, Col. 1.

In a recent D.C. court case, the estate of an unborn fetus was awarded damages totaling $75,000.

The federal government is willing to pay $30,000 a year to provide dialysis treatment for a kidney patient, but refuses to pay $70,000 for a heart transplant.

And an economic index used by the government for health planning puts the "value" of a 34-year-old white man at $328,475 and an 85-year-old black woman at $236.

How is it, in a society where life is supposedly priceless, that the courts and government have come regularly and routinely to place price tags on human life, particularly price tags that vary so enormously?

In part, the answer is that there really is no choice. Judges and juries have to make those decisions in everything from airline crashes to night-club fires. In the case of government, as a federal economist has put it, "whenever public spending decisions are made, values are implicitly attached to life," whether it be for public health or highway safety appropriations.

And, as the same economist, Dorothy P. Rice, said in one study:

"Attaching a dollar figure to death—that is, determining how much a life is worth—is an emotion-laden issue."

How, then, is it done?

Essentially, economists calculate the earnings that a person can expect to collect over a lifetime, based on normal life expectancy as well as sex and race. The earnings figures, which in this case do not attempt to take into account such variables as education and type of job, typically are available through the U.S. Census Bureau and the Department of Labor. Since many women are full-time homemakers who don't have a salary, economists traditionally have factored into the earnings chart a "value" for housewives' services. Without that added value, the price tag for women would be even lower than it is.

Economists also determine the pattern of earnings for a person from birth to old age. They plot the point in midlife when a person's maximum earnings are still ahead. For a white man, for example, that tends to be around the ages of 30 to 34; for a woman, 20 to 24. Then, working backward from that point, the economists assign a presentday value to the lifetime earnings for the very young who, like a bottle of newly made wine, haven't reached their prime. Finally, working forward from the midlife point, the economists take into account the gradual decline in earnings as the person ages.

The result of all that is a chart, such as the one accompanying this article.

Critics say such charts are discriminatory because they imply that men are more valuable than women, whites more valuable than blacks and the middle-aged more valuable than the very young and the very old.

But the earnings approach, which dates to 1915, still is the most common formal method used by economists to compute the value of life. And despite complaints about its shortcomings, it is regarded by economists like Rice as the only method that yields consistent, reliable numbers.

There is one other way that value is sometimes attached to life for statistical or legal reasons. It is called "willingness to pay," and it reflects how much a person or an institution will spend to combat accident, illness or death. For example, a sick person may be willing to pay $25 for a doctor's help but not $50. And an institution may be willing to spend $10,000 to install a safety device but not $100,000.

It was the life earnings calculation that formed the basis for the decision in the case of the fetus. And it was the earnings index that represents the chasm between the assigned value of the 34-year-old white man and the elderly black woman.

WHAT ECONOMISTS SAY YOU ARE WORTH

AGE	MEN TOTAL	WHITE	NON-WHITE	WOMEN TOTAL	WHITE	NON-WHITE
Under 1	$ 89,645	$ 93,860	$ 57,467	$ 56,996	$ 58,065	$ 49,887
1-4 yrs.	101,997	106,650	65,813	64,672	65,808	56,838
5-9	136,929	143,143	88,471	86,739	88,246	76,285
10-14	183,525	191,844	118,603	116,236	118,251	102,254
15-19	238,035	248,661	154,477	148,282	150,909	130,073
20-24	288,217	300,783	185,851	167,650	170,815	145,586
25-29	314,613	328,409	198,394	166,408	169,716	143,152
30-34	314,250	328,475	191,689	155,504	158,936	131,076
35-39	296,372	310,241	173,865	142,624	146,177	116,295
40-44	265,345	277,663	152,278	127,356	130,888	99,651
45-49	224,215	234,140	128,038	108,904	112,376	80,184
50-54	176,931	184,060	102,981	86,692	89,926	58,690
55-59	124,634	129,036	76,884	62,238	64,983	37,442
60-64	71,002	73,287	45,934	39,387	41,281	21,532
65-69	33,317	34,281	23,287	21,878	22,892	11,899
70-74	18,190	18,739	12,716	12,140	12,624	6,780
75-79	9,999	10,442	5,829	6,249	6,488	3,599
80-84	5,905	6,171	3,384	2,773	3,874	1,678
85-over	955	999	535	357	363	236

Source: Based on a 1976 Social Security Administration paper. The figures here have been updated to 1981.

STEVEN E. RHOADS,
HOW MUCH SHOULD WE SPEND TO SAVE A LIFE?

in Valuing Life
285, 287–295, 301–303, 306–309 (S. Rhoads ed. 1979).

Can't we think sensibly about life-saving programs without trying to put a dollar value on human life? One possibility would be to do cost-effectiveness analyses. We could estimate how many lives could be saved at various levels of expenditure and then leave it up to the responsible political officials to determine how much we could afford, given the other demands on the budget. Most economists, however, think we should try to go further. After all, if we have a successful cost-effectiveness analysis in hand, we know that if we had spent additional dollars, we could have saved additional lives. By not spending the money, we are saying that saving those lives is not worth that amount. We are implicitly putting a value on lives—so why not determine whether our implicit value is reasonable? Furthermore, if the inevitable valuing process is done implicitly by each agency, there are likely to be indefensible differences in the values used throughout the government. The central budget staff could prevent this by sending out a memorandum announcing that "X is as high as the government will go to save a life in 1978." But in a sense "X" then becomes society's value for life. Besides, it is not clear that all differences in life valuations are indefensible. Differences depending on age and lingering disabilities might be relevant. As Richard Zeckhauser and Donald Shepard have suggested, these could be compensated for by comparing the costs of a program with the number of additional "quality-adjusted life-years" it produces.[9] But perhaps there are other relevant differences. For example, should the government spend more per "quality-adjusted life-year" on defense or air travel, where the individual has less control over his safety, than it spends on highway safety or lung can-

9. Richard Zeckhauser and Donald Shep-   Law and Contemporary Problems 11–15
ard, Where Now For Saving Lives? in 40   (Autumn 1976).

cer, where by wearing seat belts or abstaining from smoking individuals could do much to reduce their risks without government spending? A persuasive way of valuing life-saving programs could be of real assistance.

Though there is considerable agreement among economists about the need to calculate a value for life, there is no consensus as to how it should be done. There are two fundamentally different general approaches: One focuses on the "discounted future earnings" of potential decedents, while the other tries to determine the willingness of individuals to pay for risk reduction. The advocates of the "willingness-to-pay" (WTP) approach argue, with considerable justification, that only their methodology can correctly be traced to the normative branch of economics. There have, however, been few attempts to apply this methodology, and all the dozens of government studies that place a value on life use a variant of the discounted future earnings (DFE) approach.

Discounted Future Earnings

The basic DFE approach takes the average age at which death of people killed by a certain type of disease or accident occurs and computes what their expected future income would have been if they had lived a normal term. This future income is discounted, since a dollar received today can be invested and is thus worth more than a dollar received in future years. The "present-value" figure that results is taken as the value of life for the average member of the group in question. Though the procedure is simple enough, the actual figures can range from under $100,000 to over $400,000. Significant differences result from the use of different discount rates, or from studying different groups. (Air travelers make more money than motorists, and the value of their lives is consequently higher.) However, the highest values are explained mainly by a decision of many economists to use the DFE amount only as a base figure to which other values are added. And there are also economists who use DFE as a base from which individual consumption is subtracted.

[One analyst] defended DFE as an indicator of "output loss" from early death: "The individual's marginal product is measured by his earnings. That's his contribution to G.N.P., his contribution to the market place."

But of what interest is "contribution to G.N.P." or "output loss" if one wants to determine an appropriate value of life? Does society's welfare increase whenever more people earn more money? Those who support Zero Population Growth and limitations on immigration do not think so. Moreover, if the rest of society is concerned about economic output, it is concerned only with what the potential decedent would earn *less* what he would consume.

Proponents of the basic DFE approach respond by arguing that the potential decedent is himself a part of society, and his consumption should be seen as an end in itself. However, if a DFE figure is also meant to reflect the utility loss to the individual, it is too small to use as a societal value for life. An economist must presume that an individual experiences pleasure from *all* uses of his income, whether he spends it on himself, his wife, or his alma mater. But if the whole of DFE is needed to represent the decedent's utility loss, how can it also incorporate the losses of wife, family, and alma mater?

This seems to be the objection of the school that adds other values such as family-income loss and employer restaffing costs to a DFE base. Gary Fromm started this approach, and it is still being used by the National Highway Traffic Safety Administration in recent analyses. It does about as well as can be done if one begins with DFE. There is, however, no economic justification for beginning in that way.

In his work on F.A.A. problems, Fromm indicates his belief in the fundamental importance of consumer sovereignty and in the resulting obligation of the F.A.A. to base its activities on an estimate of consumers' willingness to pay for F.A.A. services. Yet by using a modified version of DFE, Fromm has left himself open to the charge that he has ignored those crucial principles of welfare economics. By his own admission, Fromm's modified DFE approach ignores all costs of fear of the risk of death, as well as the nonmonetary suffering that death causes. More importantly, DFE does not in fact reflect the individual's utility loss from death. We cannot assume that a man who will earn 10 times more than another values his life 10 times more. Very rich men can be near suicide, and there are life-loving hobos.

DFE figures often yield bizarre guideposts for policy. For example, since men on the average earn more than women, DFE figures show men's lives to be of far more value than women's. Critics of the DFE approach have had great fun asking if there really are husbands and wives in their 30s who would want to pay twice as much to reduce the risk of death for the husband as for the wife, or if families would pay $60,000 to save a baby boy but only $35,000 to save a baby girl.[13]

From the point of view of discounted earnings, the most valuable people in society are young adult white males. All that feeding and education for no return is at last completed, and society can look forward to 40 to 50 years of good productive output. This view of societal preferences was dramatically illustrated when HEW conducted cost-benefit analyses on a number of programs in the mid-1960s. Studies suggested that a media campaign encouraging the wearing of motorcycle helmets might save a life for $3,000. A cervix cancer program could do almost as well—$3,520 per life saved. Yet DFE figures prevented the programs from being close competitors. The benefit-cost ratio for the motorcycle program was 55.6, while for the cervix cancer program it was only 8.9.

Of course, DFE proponents never claimed that they were capturing a person's full worth with their figures. The earnings numbers were a "floor" value, and costs such as pain and grief were not taken into account. Still, these brief disclaimers did not affect the benefit-cost ratios, and were quickly forgotten. Indeed, they almost had to be because the whole point of valuing life was to go beyond cost-effectiveness analysis—which by itself could tell only which programs would save lives at least cost—to use cost-benefit analysis to indicate society's preferences for saving lives in different population groups and to determine how much might justifiably be spent to save people in each of these groups. . . .

. . .

13. . . . Matters might be even worse had not Dorothy Rice, an early friend of women's liberation, tried to ameliorate this problem by placing a value on a housewife's labor. Rice decided to value such labor at the weekly wage level of domestic servants, though she realized that this was still not altogether fair since "it makes no allowance for the housewife's longer work week." However, women bounce back in later life: Those over 65 are still valued at a good housekeeper's wages, while retired men's lives are worth nothing at all!

Willingness To Pay

Almost all economists would agree with Ezra Mishan's view that in normative economics "the worth or value of a thing to a person is determined simply by what a person is willing to pay for it." [18]   Unlike their DFE counterparts, those who subscribe to the "willingness-to-pay" approach take this precept very seriously.   The WTP school does not focus on how much people would pay to avoid certain death, for in such a situation most would pay almost all they could get their hands on, and thus the WTP figure would reveal more about absolute wealth than about the relative preference for a particular good or service.

WTP proponents point out, however, that most safety and health programs lower the risk of death, but we do not know *who* would have died without the program.   In the typical case, the government must decide if it should spend money to make a small probability of death even smaller for a large number of individuals.   In such cases, the sum of the willingness to pay for reduced risk of all those affected is seen as reflecting their preferences.   This aggregate WTP is divided by the number of deaths prevented to determine what government might justifiably spend to save a life in the program under consideration.

Though all proponents of WTP agree that the preferences of consumers are the best guide for public policy, they disagree about the best means of determining WTP.   Some favor consumer polls, while others look to decisions that individuals make when their lives are actually at risk.   Although many have advocated one method or the other, there have been only three serious published attempts to apply either approach: One used polling, while the other two made deductions from decisions in the job market.

Jan Acton polled 100 people in Boston about heart attacks and risk reduction.   He thought his most "basic" question was the following:

> Let's suppose that your doctor tells you that the odds are 99:1 against your having a heart attack.   If you have the attack, the odds are 3:2 that you will live.   The heart-attack program would mean that the odds are 4:1 that you live after a heart attack.   How much are you willing to pay in taxes per year to have this heart-attack program which would cut your probability of dying from a heart attack in half (i.e., the chances are two per 1,000 you will have a heart attack and be saved by the program this year)?

In the community sample Acton thought most typical of the general citizenry, the average response to this question was $56.   This implies a value of life of $28,000 (1,000/2 x $56).

There are two standard criticisms of using polling to determine WTP. The first is the possibility that respondents may engage in strategic behavior: Taking account of their likely tax burden and other respondents' likely responses, they may understate or overstate their real WTP in order to shift the average WTP and the resulting tax burden in ways helpful to them.   Like Acton, I do not think such behavior is likely to be a serious problem in preliminary efforts to assess people's preferences.   The second problem is more fundamental: Many wonder if poll respondents will be able to understand and give consistent answers to questions such as those Acton asked.   In other areas, economists have found that people's stated preferences and actual behavior often differ widely.

18.   Ezra Mishan, Cost-Benefit Analysis
(New York: Praeger, 1976), p. 24.

Acton acknowledges these potential problems. He also notes that the order in which his questions were asked seemed to affect responses, and that respondents frequently gave identical WTP answers for different changes in the probability of death. Still, he believes that most people "thought rather carefully" about his "basic" question, and he thinks the polling approach to WTP "a better guide to true preferences than any of the alternatives."

It is unclear why Acton thought the question above more "basic" than another he asked:

> They are thinking about putting ambulances and other devices in communities around the country, but only if people are willing to pay enough for them. This program would be for you and 10,000 people living around you. In your area, there are about 100 heart attacks per year. About 40 of these persons die. With the heart-attack program, only 20 of these people would die. How much would you be willing to pay in taxes per year for the ambulance so that 20 lives could be saved in your community?

This question focuses on community-wide benefits, while the earlier one emphasizes benefits to the individual. Both questions, however, describe the same program—one where the respondent and others in the community are .002 less likely to die the year after implementation than before. Yet in the community sample most representative of the public—in which Acton had the most confidence—the average response was $56 to the first question, and $33 to the second. This means that small changes in the way the same program was described led to WTP values varying from $28,000 to $16,500.

Risky Business

Applications of the alternative WTP methodology have also run into serious problems. The two studies of this type, by Robert Smith and by Richard Thaler and Sherwin Rosen, have examined decisions made in the job market. Since people spend much of their lives on the job, the authors believe that workers have an incentive to acquire decent information about their work-related risks. And since risky jobs will be less attractive, the expectation is that after controlling for education, race, experience, unionization, region, etc., wage rates will be higher in high-risk occupations.

Both studies have found this to be the case. Smith used data on injury rates among hourly workers in manufacturing industries and found that where the yearly death rate is 16 per 100,000 workers, employees receive approximately 1.5 percent more in annual wages than do employees of comparable skills in industries with an average rate of eight deaths per 100,000 workers. Smith's estimates imply that workers are collectively willing to forego $1.5 million in pay if employers undertake steps that will save one life.[23] Thaler and Rosen's study used actuarial data to compare the expected number of deaths for those of a certain age with actual deaths in 37 hazardous occupations. The authors found that 1,000 workers in an occupation associated with an extra death risk of .001 per year will each sacrifice $200 per year if the extra death probability is reduced to zero. This implies a value for life of $200,000.[24]

23. Robert Smith, The Occupational Safety and Health Act (Washington: American Enterprise Institute, 1976), pp. 30, 93.

24. Richard Thaler and Sherwin Rosen, "The Value of Saving a Life: Evidence from the Labor Market," in Nester Terleckyj,

Because of inadequate data neither Smith nor Thaler and Rosen have great confidence in the WTP figures they have come up with.[25] But even if the data were as good as one could wish, information from the job market may never produce a decent WTP estimate for programs that reduce the risk of death. The figures that result will omit the WTP of most white collar employees and all nonworkers. Moreover, the society's WTP for life-saving programs may depend on how painful the pre-death stages of a disease are, or whether the program is preventive or curative. (We would pay more for a program that would prevent kidney or heart failure than for one that allowed some sort of life after such failures.) Indeed, even within the same life-saving program, similar improvements in program effectiveness will not necessarily lead to the same value for life. A thousand workers might collectively give up in pay more to save one life if their annual risk of death was .01 than they would if the risk was .001.

It would be hard to know how the job market figures should be adjusted to take account of these factors when varying life-saving programs and probabilities are involved. But two other difficulties are more significant. First, the method might ignore important external effects on nonworkers. Second, workers may not be aware of the real risks of occupations, and thus wage differentials may not really tell us what we want to know about workers' attitudes toward their job-related risks.[26]

Household Production and Consumption (New York: National Bureau of Economic Research, Columbia, 1975), p. 294.

25. Smith's data lump together all hourly workers within an industry. This introduces a large measurement error for individuals, because job risks in each industry are not uniform across occupations. Thaler and Rosen do have data showing death rates by occupations, but only for very risky occupations, and there is reason to believe that those attracted to such jobs are more tolerant of risks than are most Americans. For this reason, the Thaler and Rosen figures will underestimte most people's willingness to pay for risk reduction. Moreover, Thaler and Rosen have no information on cause of death, and they simply assume that unusually high death rates in the occupations studied are caused by real work-related dangers. For most of the listed occupations where death rates are high (such as that of lumberman or boilermaker) this assumption seems plausible, but for others (such as cook, waiter, or bartender) it seems much less so. Perhaps cooks, waiters, and bartenders die sooner than most not because they are engaged in risky occupations, but because they are more likely to be transients, alcoholics, or whatever.

26.   . . . Bailey suggests that workers judge job risks accurately enough for empirical work that makes use of that assumption to be useful. W. Kip Viscusi has investigated this subject recently and concluded that there is "a strong positive relationship between the worker's danger perceptions and both the pertinent Bureau of Labor Standards industry injury rate and his direct injury experiences." [Employment Hazards: An Investigation of Market Performance, Harvard Economic Studies Series (Cambridge: Harvard University Press, in press), Ch. 14.] On the other hand, in an earlier work Guido Calabresi argued that, for psychological reasons, people underestimate the risks of injury and death. [The Costs of Accidents: A Legal and Economic Analysis (New Haven: Yale, 1970), pp. 91, 220.] One unpleasant way to test Calabresi's argument is for my readers to ask themselves how likely they think they are to die within the year. Average probabilities for different age groups are in Table 1.

Table 1

U.S. DEATH RATES BY AGE

Age	20–30	30–35	35–40	40–45	45–50	50–55	55–60	60–65	65–70
Annual Death Rate in U.S. (from all causes)	.0015	.0020	.0025	.004	.006	.009	.013	.02	.04

Source: J. Hirshleifer, T. Bergstrom, E. Rappaport, Applying Cost-Benefit Concepts to Projects which Alter Human Mortality, UCLA-Eng-7478 (Los Angeles: UCLA, 1974), appendix I, p. 74.

In any case, WTP proponents do not yet have an alternative figure to substitute for the DFE numbers in various government studies.   The work of Smith and of Thaler and Rosen suggests that DFE is too low to use as a value for life. But the Acton study suggests that most DFE figures are too high.

Still, one could make too much of the disagreements among WTP figures at this early stage.   Acton had a very small sample, and his WTP results were for a program that might allow one to live a possibly crippled life *after* a heart attack.   One would expect people to be willing to pay less for such a program than for death-preventing job-related programs. Moreover, three informal applications of the polling approach to WTP have yielded value-of-life figures of $1 million or more.[27]   Since other more theoretical work also suggests that WTP should be much greater than DFE,[28] a WTP proponent could argue that our current knowledge is sufficient to support a WTP figure two or three times DFE.   And the government should be doing more polling and collecting information on occupational death rates and cause of death, so that statistical studies of risk premiums in the job market could make more accurate estimates.

. . .

NOTE ON DATA PROBLEMS

After pointing to its failure to consider issues of distributive justice, critics of cost-benefit analysis commonly also point to the fact that the data employed are simply not reliable.   Consider the assessment of the Hastings Center * prepared for the Office of Technology Assessment of the Congress of the United States:

> This criticism appears to be legitimate to an undetermined, possibly large, extent.   It is a very serious criticism, chiefly because it conflicts with the quantitative and scientific trappings of CBA [cost-benefit analysis]. . . .
>
> The general problem here . . . is that CBA is a form of modeling, and, like all other attempts at modeling, expresses only certain aspects (and those perhaps not wholly accurately) of a very complex world.   CBA is "irretrievably" second-best; that is, CBA seeks to explore the consequences of particular actions in the imperfect economy as it exists and in which the insights of theories applicable to a first-best world may be misleading.   "Its practitioners are frequently tempted to simplify their problem by making first-best assumptions . . . ."[475]

The Problem of Defining Outcomes and Goals

Criticisms of data are made on a number of different grounds.   Most obvious are the simple inadequacies of our current reporting and data systems.   In a very real sense, of course, such inadequacies are technical problems that can be improved once they are identified and someone in a position of power decides to deal with them and improve the system.

27. Thomas C. Schelling, "The Life You Save May Be Your Own," in Problems in Public Expenditure Analysis, ed., Samuel Chase (Washington, D.C.: Brookings Institution, 1969), p. 157; H.C. Joksch, "A Critical Appraisal of the Applicability of Benefit-Cost Analysis to Highway Traffic Safety," Accident Analysis and Prevention, vol. 7, p. 144; M. Jones-Lee, The Value of Life: An Economic Analysis (Chicago: Univ. of Chicago Press, 1976), chs. 6 and 7.

28. J. Hirshleifer, T. Bergstrom, E. Rappaport, Applying Cost-Benefit Concepts to Projects Which Alter Human Mortality, UCLA-ENG-7478 (Los Angeles: UCLA, 1974), 39 and Appendix II, p. 16.

* The Hastings Center, Values, Ethics and CBA in Health Care in Office of Technology Assessment, The Implications of Cost-Effectiveness Analysis of Medical Technology 168, 175–178, 180–181 (August 1980).

475. Parish, R.M., "The Scope of Benefit-Cost Analysis," Econ. Record., September 1976.

Fein, however, has identified a number of much more difficult data problems. One concerns the measurement of outcomes which are conceptually amorphous (e.g., higher levels of health) and to which many factors contribute (e.g., housing, income, nutrition, environment, and medical care of all kinds). In addition, there are many factors whose relative contribution may differ for different persons, and whose proportional importance is largely unknown. Another problem is how to measure the goals of a health program that exist on a continuum. It is more difficult to measure continuous states with a wide range of effect, like pain or impairment of functional ability, than to measure discontinuous states like life and death. Furthermore, difficulties in measurement create a bias in favor of programs that have easily measurable goals.

Most discussions of CBA mention the selection of goals and objectives as a problem. Many critics and even some proponents of CBA feel that the goals are often vague and nonspecific (e.g., "health"). Kenneth Boulding points out that we often agree on major goals. We disagree on how to reach the goals, and in some cases, on what the alternative approaches might be. Mishan, for example, criticizes Klarman's study of syphilis by pointing out that the calculations were based on the goal of eradicating the disease. There was no comparison with a defined control program to reduce the disease to some prespecified level.

. . .

Economists may also make naive assumptions about the practicality of stated goals and outcomes, Klarman says. At least in the early days of CBA, he notes, there was a tendency by economists to attribute greater efficacy to medical care than we now believe is warranted

The Problem of Uncertainty About the Future

The whole area of uncertainty about the future—guesswork about costs and benefits of technological innovations and unanticipated shifts in demand—continues to plague CBA. According to Mishan:

> The problem of how to make decisions in any situation where the past affords little or any guidance is not one that can be satisfactorily resolved either by logic or empiricism, and what moves have been formulated are either of limited application or of no practical value.

To cope with uncertainty, one can figure an arbitrary cutoff period, adjust the discount rates, or simply pick a subjective probability. A number of recent articles recommend using sensitivity analysis [627]:

> . . . In this method, the most uncertain features and assumptions in the cost-effectiveness calculation are varied one at a time over the range of possible values. If the basic conclusions do not change when a particular feature or assumption is varied, confidence in the conclusion is increased. If, instead, the basic conclusions are sensitive to variations in a particular feature or assumption, further research to learn more about that feature may be especially valuable. . . .

> . . . Examples of sensitivity analyses that are often useful are to vary the estimates of the degree of clinical efficacy of the procedure in question, to vary the weights assigned to various quality levels in computing quality-adjusted life expectancy, and to test a range of discount rates, say, from 0 to 10 percent per year.

The Problem of Using Proxy Goals and Measures

Another problem comes from the use of proxy goals and measures that may bias the number and variety of options for action. Fein cites as an example measuring the health of children by counting school days missed. A program designed to improve children's health so that they miss fewer days, he argues, is

627. Weinstein, M., and Stason, W.B., Hypertension, A Policy Perspective, Cam-   bridge, Mass.: Harvard University Press, 1976.

different from one that focuses so heavily on reducing days of absence that its success results in sick children being sent to school.

In fact, some argue that one of the deficiencies of CBA is that it is a complete exercise in proxy measures, since, as Fein himself points out, monetary benefits are only a part (and in some cases a small part) of all benefits, and they do not represent a stable or constant fraction of all benefits. . . .

For Fein, the choice of data is very important because budget officials will tend to focus on those outcomes that have numbers, or more specifically, economic values, attached to them. Programs that affect future productivity thus come to be overvalued because they can be quantified, and programs that relieve pain and suffering but do not affect productivity come to be undervalued. According to Fein:

> It may, indeed, be that programmes addressed to disabling conditions and to disease involving mortality, rather than to conditions that do not remove the person from economic activity, should be favored. That conclusion, however, should not be reached primarily because some things can be measured while others cannot. The analyst may discount the nature of the difficulty and the likelihood that this might occur, believing that his description of the items (particularly, benefits) that cannot be measured will suffice to alert the decision-maker to the inadequacy of the numbers. I suggest, however, that the analyst may underestimate the problem. He would do well to consider how compelling numbers are to finance officials and how high a rate of discount is applied to words, however well-turned the phrases may be.

. . .

The Problem of Infinite Externalities

Boulding points out that almost everything we do turns out differently from what we expect; both the bad and good are often unintentional. So, it is not surprising that a major problem with assessing cost and benefits are so-called externalities, otherwise known as external effects, neighborhood effects, side effects, spillover effects, or spillovers. Externalities include such things as the effect of building a road on esthetic sensibilities, on noise and pollution, on loss of life as a result of increased traffic accidents, and so forth.

What characterizes all these effects, Mishan says, is that they are unintentional and not subject to control by the people who experience them (at least not unless there is some way such people can spend money to avoid them). Mishan suggests that the number of external effects in the real world is virtually unlimited. He believes society is obliged to limit them for the economist.

The number of effects that can be internalized into the pricing mechanism, Mishan says, is limited. According to Mishan, the costs of spillovers such as traffic noises, pollution, radioactive waste, and diseases of the nerves, heart, and stomach caused by high-tension living cannot be internalized. Internalization would require that the potential victim of the spillover have a legal property right to some measure of quiet or clean air, freedom from tension, and so forth. For that right to be enforceable, it would be necessary to delineate a territory around each individual that belongs solely to that person, so that an intrusion subject to legal compensation procedures could be identified. Since it is impossible to create a market, even an artificial one, that would make pricing them possible, such spillovers must ultimately be evaluated by the victims' subjective estimate.

Deriving his argument from John Stuart Mill, a 19th century British disciple of Bentham, Mishan thinks compensatory sums should actually be paid to victims of spillovers. He rejects the social engineering approach to spillovers which seeks to formulate tolerance levels for society:

> If the liberal economist rejects social engineering norms such as "tolerance level," it is not merely because the choice of such a level for society is necessarily arbitrary, but because the adoption of such tolerance norms on behalf of all members of society runs counter to the doctrine that each man is deemed

to be the best judge of his interests, particularly in matters that affect him intimately.

A good portion of Mishan's book is devoted to a discussion of possible compensation and legal liability in such situations.

Prest and Turvey argue that CBA is not relevant to decisions on large investments because such large investments spill over so much that they may end up altering the whole economy. The example they use is the building of a dam in an underdeveloped country. Prest and Turvey's argument, however, might apply equally well to health care.

Grosse recounts that HEW's study of the possibilities for comprehensive health care programs for young children looked good enough that Congress became very interested. It was clear, however, that if children who then lacked access to good medical care were to be provided with conventional pediatric services, an acute shortage of doctors would result. Ways had to be found to use medical manpower more efficiently. Thus, the Social Security Amendments of 1967, which provided for early case finding and treatment of birth defects and chronic conditions in children, also provided for a research and demonstration program to train and use physicians' assistants.

Training physicians' assistants is an example of a side effect, because such training was not counted as a cost in the original HEW study. Nor was it anticipated how a CBA of this sort, translated by law into public policy, can influence the practice of medicine. This analysis led fairly directly to an increase in interest in physicians' assistants, which may change the whole hierarchical structure of medicine in the United States. It is not clear whether such a development should be counted as a cost or a benefit, or possibly a bit of each. Ordinarily, however, a massive (usually entirely unforeseen) ultimate effect such as this simply does not figure into the calculations.

The Problem of Pricing the Unpriceable

Finally, there is the stubborn problem of valuing intangibles, or pricing the unpriceable. In discussing intangible costs like pain, discomfort, and grief, Klarman notes that one difficulty in valuing them is that they accrue partly to patients, but also partly to their friends, relatives, and to society. One way of valuing such intangibles is to ask what an individual would be willing to pay to avoid them. But Klarman believes the measurement problems here are major. Although he describes a number of different ways such intangibles have been valued, he is not very enthusiastic about any. Mishan points out that Klarman himself, when he did his 1965 calculations on syphilis, attributed more than 40 percent of the final benefit to "reduction of stigma," which was valued (essentially arbitrarily) at either 1 or 0.5 percent of earnings subsequent to the discovery of syphilis.

. . .

The Fictional "Facts"

All of these quite genuine measurement difficulties mean that CBA can never really tell the unvarnished truth, and that it is therefore at bottom a kind of systematic misrepresentation of the world it purports to measure. Self goes so far as to accuse cost-benefit analysts of:

. . . unwittingly or not, playing a confidence trick with the symbols of monetary exchange. Of course the theoretical welfare economist is not a confidence trickster, in fact he is often high-minded, but he is committed to the discovery of some ideal ("optimum") set of economic conditions that transcend the ordinarily market economy, with the aid of which he can measure intrinsic value.

Many commentators believe that fact saddles economists with a heavy moral responsibility, and speak of it in exactly such terms. Mishan, for instance, ultimately characterizes CBA as horse-and-rabbit stew, the rabbit representing costs and benefits that really can be quantified, and the horse representing other considerations, including environmental spillovers. [410]   "No matter how carefully the scientific rabbit is chosen, the flavor of the resulting stew is sure to be swamped by the horse flesh," he concludes.   Economists should resist the temptation to ignore the horse.

5. WHO SHOULD DECIDE: ALTERNATIVES TO AGENCY DISCRETION

a. Individuals

WHIRLPOOL CORP. v. MARSHALL

Supreme Court of the United States, 1980.
445 U.S. 1, 100 S.Ct. 883, 63 L.Ed.2d 154.

MR. JUSTICE STEWART delivered the opinion of the Court.

The Occupational Safety and Health Act of 1970 (Act) prohibits an employer from discharging or discriminating against any employee who exercises "any right afforded by" the Act.   The Secretary of Labor (Secretary) has promulgated a regulation providing that, among the rights that the Act so protects, is the right of an employee to choose not to perform his assigned task because of a reasonable apprehension of death or serious injury coupled with a reasonable belief that no less drastic alternative is available.[3]   The question presented in the case before us is whether this regulation is consistent with the Act.

410. Mishan, E.J., Cost-Benefit Analysis, Washington, D.C.: Praeger Publications, 1976.

3. The regulation, 29 CFR § 1977.12 (1979), provides in full:

"(a) In addition to protecting employees who file complaints, institute proceedings, or testify in proceedings under or related to the Act, section 11(c) also protects employees from discrimination occurring because of the exercise 'of any right afforded by this Act.'   Certain rights are explicitly provided in the Act; for example, there is a right to participate as a party in enforcement proceedings (sec. 10).   Certain other rights exist by necessary implication. For example, employees may request information from the Occupational Safety and Health Administration; such requests would constitute the exercise of a right afforded by the Act.   Likewise, employees interviewed by agents of the Secretary in the course of inspections or investigations could not subsequently be discriminated against because of their cooperation.

"(b)(1) On the other hand, review of the Act and examination of the legislative history discloses that, as a general matter, there is no right afforded by the Act which would entitle employees to walk off the job because of potential unsafe conditions at the workplace.   Hazardous conditions which may be violative of the Act will ordinarily be corrected by the employer, once brought to his attention.   If corrections are not accomplished, or if there is dispute about the existence of a hazard, the employee will normally have opportunity to request inspection of the workplace pursuant to section 8(f) of the Act, or to seek the assistance of other public agencies which have responsibility in the field of safety and health.   Under such circumstances, therefore, an employer would not ordinarily be in violation of section 11(c) by taking action to discipline an employee for refusing to perform normal job activities because of alleged safety or health hazards.

"(2) However, occasions might arise when an employee is confronted with a choice between not performing assigned tasks or subjecting himself to serious injury or death arising from a hazardous condition at the workplace.   If the employee, with no reasonable alternative, refuses in good faith to expose himself to the dangerous condition, he would be protected against subsequent discrimination.   The condition causing the employee's apprehension of death or injury must be of such a nature that a reasonable person, under the circumstances then confronting the employee, would conclude that there is a real danger of death or serious injury and that there is insufficient time, due to the urgency of the situation, to eliminate the danger through resort to regular statutory enforcement channels.   In addition, in such circumstances, the employee, where possible, must also have sought from his employer, and been unable to obtain, a correction of the dangerous condition."

I

The petitioner company maintains a manufacturing plant in Marion, Ohio, for the production of household appliances. Overhead conveyors transport appliance components throughout the plant. To protect employees from objects that occasionally fall from these conveyors, the petitioner has installed a horizontal wire-mesh guard screen approximately 20 feet above the plant floor. This mesh screen is welded to angle-iron frames suspended from the building's structural steel skeleton.

Maintenance employees of the petitioner spend several hours each week removing objects from the screen, replacing paper spread on the screen to catch grease drippings from the material on the conveyors, and performing occasional maintenance work on the conveyors themselves. To perform these duties, maintenance employees usually are able to stand on the iron frames, but sometimes find it necessary to step onto the steel mesh screen itself.

In 1973, the company began to install heavier wire in the screen because its safety had been drawn into question. Several employees had fallen partly through the old screen and on one occasion an employee had fallen completely through to the plant floor below but had survived. A number of maintenance employees had reacted to these incidents by bringing the unsafe screen conditions to the attention of their foremen. The petitioner company's contemporaneous safety instructions admonished employees to step only on the angle-iron frames.

On June 28, 1974, a maintenance employee fell to his death through the guard screen in an area where the newer, stronger mesh had not yet been installed. Following this incident, the petitioner effectuated some repairs and issued an order strictly forbidding maintenance employees from stepping on either the screens or the angle-iron supporting structure. An alternative but somewhat more cumbersome and less satisfactory method was developed for removing objects from the screen. This procedure required employees to stand on power-raised mobile platforms and use hooks to recover the material.

On July 7, 1974, two of the petitioner's maintenance employees, Virgil Deemer and Thomas Cornwell, met with the plant maintenance superintendent to voice their concern about the safety of the screen. The superintendent disagreed with their view, but permitted the two men to inspect the screen with their foreman and to point out dangerous areas needing repair. Unsatisfied with the petitioner's response to the results of this inspection, Deemer and Cornwell met on July 9 with the plant safety director. At that meeting, they requested the name, address, and telephone number of a representative of the local office of the Occupational Safety and Health Administration (OSHA). Although the safety director told the men that they "had better stop and think about what [they] were doing," he furnished the men with the information they requested. Later that same day, Deemer contacted an official of the regional OSHA office and discussed the guard screen.

The next day, Deemer and Cornwell reported for the night shift at 10:45 p.m. Their foreman, after himself walking on some of the angle-iron frames, directed the two men to perform their usual maintenance duties on a section of the old screen.[6] Claiming that the screen was un-

6. This order appears to have been in direct violation of the outstanding company

safe, they refused to carry out this directive. The foreman then sent them to the personnel office, where they were ordered to punch out without working or being paid for the remaining six hours of the shift.[7] The two men subsequently received written reprimands, which were placed in their employment files.

A little over a month later, the Secretary filed suit in the United States District Court for the Northern District of Ohio, alleging that the petitioner's actions against Deemer and Cornwell constituted discrimination in violation of § 11(c)(1) of the Act.

. . .

Following a bench trial, the District Court found that the regulation in question justified Deemer's and Cornwell's refusals to obey their foreman's order on July 10, 1974. . . . The District Court nevertheless denied relief, holding that the Secretary's regulation was inconsistent with the Act and therefore invalid. Usery v. Whirlpool Corp., 416 F.Supp. 30, 32–34.

The Court of Appeals for the Sixth Circuit reversed the District Court's judgment. . . .

. . .

We granted certiorari, 444 U.S. 823, 100 S.Ct. 43, 62 L.Ed.2d 29, because the decision of the Court of Appeals in this case conflicts with those of two other Courts of Appeals on the important question in issue. . . . That question, as stated at the outset of this opinion, is whether the Secretary's regulation authorizing employee "self-help" in some circumstances, 29 CFR § 1977.12(b)(2) (1979), is permissible under the Act.

II

. . . [T]he Secretary is obviously correct when he acknowledges in his regulation that, "as a general matter, there is no right afforded by the Act which would entitle employees to walk off the job because of potential unsafe conditions at the workplace." By providing for prompt notice to the employer of an inspector's intention to seek an injunction against an imminently dangerous condition, the legislation obviously contemplates that the employer will normally respond by voluntarily and speedily eliminating the danger. And in the few instances where this does not occur, the legislative provisions authorizing prompt judicial action are designed to give employees full protection in most situations from the risk of injury or death resulting from an imminently dangerous condition at the worksite.

As this case illustrates, however, circumstances may sometimes exist in which the employee justifiably believes that the express statutory arrangement does not sufficiently protect him from death or serious injury. Such circumstances will probably not often occur, but such a situation may arise when (1) the employee is ordered by his employer to work under conditions that the employee reasonably believes pose an imminent risk of death or serious bodily injury, and (2) the employee has reason to believe that there is not sufficient time or opportunity either to seek effective redress from his employer or to apprise OSHA of the danger.

---

directive that maintenance work was to be accomplished without stepping on the screen apparatus.

7. Both employees apparently returned to work the following day without further incident.

A

The regulation clearly conforms to the fundamental objective of the Act—to prevent occupational deaths and serious injuries.

To accomplish this basic purpose, the legislation's remedial orientation is prophylactic in nature.

The Act does not wait for an employee to die or become injured. It authorizes the promulgation of health and safety standards and the issuance of citations in the hope that these will act to prevent deaths or injuries from ever occurring. It would seem anomalous to construe an Act so directed and constructed as prohibiting an employee, with no other reasonable alternative, the freedom to withdraw from a workplace environment that he reasonably believes is highly dangerous.

Moreover, the Secretary's regulation can be viewed as an appropriate aid to the full effectuation of the Act's "general duty" clause. That clause provides that "[e]ach employer . . . shall furnish to each of his employees employment and a place of employment which are free from recognized hazards that are causing or are likely to cause death or serious physical harm to his employees." 29 U.S.C. § 654(a)(1). As the legislative history of this provision reflects, it was intended itself to deter the occurrence of occupational deaths and serious injuries by placing on employers a mandatory obligation independent of the specific health and safety standards to be promulgated by the Secretary. Since OSHA inspectors cannot be present around the clock in every workplace, the Secretary's regulation ensures that employees will in all circumstances enjoy the rights afforded them by the "general duty" clause.

The regulation thus on its face appears to further the overriding purpose of the Act, and rationally to complement its remedial scheme. In the absence of some contrary indication in the legislative history, the Secretary's regulation must, therefore, be upheld, particularly when it is remembered that safety legislation is to be liberally construed to effectuate the congressional purpose.

B

In urging reversal of the judgment before us, the petitioner relies primarily on two aspects of the Act's legislative history.

. . .

1

Representative Daniels of New Jersey sponsored one of several House bills that led ultimately to the passage of the Act. As reported to the House by the Committee on Education and Labor, the Daniels bill contained a section that was soon dubbed the "strike with pay" provision. This section provided that employees could request an examination by the Department of Health, Education, and Welfare (HEW) of the toxicity of any materials in their workplace. If that examination revealed a workplace substance that had "potentially toxic or harmful effects in such concentration as used or found," the employer was given 60 days to correct the potentially dangerous condition. Following the expiration of that period, the employer could not require that an employee be exposed to toxic concentrations of the substance unless the employee was informed of the hazards and symptoms associated with the substance, the employee was instructed in the proper precautions for dealing with the substance, and the employee was furnished with personal protective equipment. If these conditions were not met, an employee could "absent himself from such risk of harm for the period necessary to avoid such danger without loss of regular compensation for such period."

This provision encountered stiff opposition in the House. . . .

The petitioner argues that Congress' overriding concern in rejecting the "strike with pay" provision was to avoid giving employees a unilateral authority to walk off the job which they might abuse in order to intimidate or harass their employer. Congress deliberately chose instead, the petitioner maintains, to grant employees the power to request immediate administrative inspections of the workplace which could in appropriate cases lead to coercive judicial remedies. As the petitioner views the regulation, therefore, it gives to workers precisely what Congress determined to withhold from them.

We read the legislative history differently. Congress rejected a provision that did not concern itself at all with conditions posing real and immediate threats of death or severe injury. The remedy which the rejected provision furnished employees could have been invoked only after 60 days had passed following HEW's inspection and notification that improperly high levels of toxic substances were present in the workplace. Had that inspection revealed employment conditions posing a threat of imminent and grave harm, the Secretary of Labor would presumably have requested, long before expiration of the 60-day period, a court injunction pursuant to other provisions of the Daniels bill. Consequently, in rejecting the Daniels bill's "strike with pay" provision, Congress was not rejecting a legislative provision dealing with the highly perilous and fast-moving situations covered by the regulation now before us.

It is also important to emphasize that what primarily troubled Congress about the Daniels bill's "strike with pay" provision was its requirement that employees be paid their regular salary after having properly invoked their right to refuse to work under the section. It is instructive that virtually every time the issue of an employee's right to absent himself from hazardous work was discussed in the legislative debates, it was in the context of the employee's right to continue to receive his usual compensation.

When it rejected the "strike with pay" concept, therefore, Congress very clearly meant to reject a law unconditionally imposing upon employers an obligation to continue to pay their employees their regular paychecks when they absented themselves from work for reasons of safety. But the regulation at issue here does not require employers to pay workers who refuse to perform their assigned tasks in the face of imminent danger. It simply provides that in such cases the employer may not "discriminate" against the employees involved. An employer "discriminates" against an employee only when he treats that employee less favorably than he treats others similarly situated.

2

The second aspect of the Act's legislative history upon which the petitioner relies is the rejection by Congress of provisions contained in both the Daniels and the Williams bills that would have given Labor Department officials, in imminent-danger situations, the power temporarily to shut down all or part of an employer's plant. These provisions aroused considerable opposition in both Houses of Congress. The hostility engendered in the House of Representatives lead Representative Daniels to delete his version of the provision in proposing amendments to his original bill. The Steiger bill that ultimately passed the House gave the Labor Department no such authority. The Williams bill, as approved by the Senate, did contain an administrative shutdown provision, but the Conference Committee rejected this aspect of the Senate bill.

The petitioner infers from these events a congressional will hostile to the regulation in question here. The regulation, the petitioner argues, provides employees with the very authority to shut down an employer's plant that was expressly denied a more expert and objective United States Department of Labor.

As we read the pertinent legislative history, however, the petitioner misconceives the thrust of Congress' concern. Those in Congress who prevented passage of the administrative shutdown provisions in the Daniels and Williams bills were opposed to the unilateral authority those provisions gave to federal officials, without any judicial safeguards, drastically to impair the operation of an employer's business. Congressional opponents also feared that the provisions might jeopardize the Government's otherwise neutral role in labor-management relations.

Neither of these congressional concerns is implicated by the regulation before us. The regulation accords no authority to Government officials. It simply permits private employees of a private employer to avoid workplace conditions that they believe pose grave dangers to their own safety. The employees have no power under the regulation to order their employer to correct the hazardous condition or to clear the dangerous workplace of others. Moreover, any employee who acts in reliance on the regulation runs the risk of discharge or reprimand in the event a court subsequently finds that he acted unreasonably or in bad faith. The regulation, therefore, does not remotely resemble the legislation that Congress rejected.

C

For these reasons we conclude that 29 CFR § 1977.12(b)(2) (1979) was promulgated by the Secretary in the valid exercise of his authority under the Act. Accordingly, the judgment of the Court of Appeals is affirmed.

It is so ordered.

NOTES

1. One of the areas of growing controversy in the workplace is the use of genetic testing. On the one hand, such tests may be used to identify susceptible workers and interfere with their ability to earn a living. Compare the revelation that four women at an American Cyanamid Company plant had themselves sterilized in order to keep their jobs in the pigments section. The company acknowledged it had a policy of prohibiting fertile women from working in certain areas. Washington Post, Oct. 11, 1979 at A18, col. 1. See generally Williams, Firing the Woman to Protect the Fetus, 69 Geo.L.J. 641 (1981).

On the other hand, tests might benefit workers by identifying and protecting them from certain workplace hazards. Significantly, OSHA has included medical removal protection (MRP) in some of its standards that set exposure limits in the workplace. See, e.g., 29 C.F.R. § 1910.1017(k)(5) (1981) [vinyl chloride standard]. MRP means that when a periodic medical examination indicates that an employee is showing symptoms of the adverse effects of exposure, the employee is to be removed from exposure—to a "safe" job if there is one available—until it is medically advisable for the employee to return.

The extent of genetic testing is uncertain. A 1982 survey of the Fortune 500 largest U.S. industrial companies conducted for the Office of Technology Assessment (OTA) of the U.S. Congress concluded that it is being used by a few, that its use has declined in the past 12 years, but that it may be used by many more companies in the future. Of the 18 companies that have ever conducted genetic testing, more screened for preexisting genetic conditions (sickle cell trait was the most frequently used screening) than monitored for genetic changes occurring during employment. Office of Technology Assessment, The Role of Genetic Testing in the Prevention of Occupational Disease 39 (1983).

2. In July 1983, the Environmental Protection Agency (EPA) announced that it would ask the residents of Tacoma, Washington, to play a major part in deciding whether to close a local copper smelter. See 48 Fed.Reg. 3312 (July 20, 1983). Inorganic arsenic has been identified in several studies as carcinogenic to humans. On June 5, 1980, EPA therefore listed it as a hazardous air pollutant under Section 112 of the Clean Air Act, 44 Fed.Reg. 37886, and began a series of studies of the sources of inorganic emissions in order to establish appropriate emission restrictions.

The ASARCO copper smelter, located in Tacoma, Washington, is the largest single source of arsenic emissions in the United States; it produces some 311 tons per year. The standards proposed by EPA in July, if applied to the ASARCO smelter, would require that its emissions be reduced to some 189 tons per year. EPA estimated this change would reduce the cases of lung cancer for the 370,000 people living within 20 kilometers (12.5 miles) of the smelter from a range of 1.1 to 17.6 cases per year to a range of 0.2 to 3.4 cases per year. The risks posed by the smelter could be reduced further, according to EPA, only by undermining the economic viability of the smelter, which provides some 800 jobs. William Ruckelshaus, the Administrator of EPA, said that although the final decision on the proposed standard would be his, he would give the views of citizens heavy weight adding "[f]or me to sit here in Washington and tell the people of Tacoma what is an acceptable risk would be at best arrogant and at worst inexcusable." Ruckelshaus stated that EPA was not taking a referendum to ascertain the views of citizens but would see whether a consensus emerged from public meetings and mail after the people of Tacoma had been informed of the choice. Shabecoff, A City Weighs Cancer Risk Against Lost Jobs, New York Times, Wed. July 13, 1983 at Al, Col. 3.

Do you think that public meetings and mail results constitute reliable measures of public views on such an issue? What if anything could EPA do to identify the views of informed as opposed to uninformed citizens? What information would a citizen of Tacoma need to be "informed" on this issue? If public views should be given greater weight in the future on such issues, should we replace administrative agencies with procedures for conducting a referendum of the "affected public"? If the hazard at issue can travel large distances in the air or in water, who should be included in the referendum?

If there is strong public feeling that a risk is acceptable and that an agency should not act against it, what recourse do citizens have? Compare the case of saccharin, supra.

3. Under the EPA proposal, the maximum lifetime risk from exposure to airborne inorganic arsenic around the ASARCO smelter would be reduced from a range of 2.3 to 37 cases of lung cancer in 100 to a range of 0.58 to 9.2 cases in 100. Compare this to the proposal for modifying the Delaney Clause to permit lifetime risks of less than 1 *death* (not merely case of cancer) in a million discussed in Sec. A.l, supra. The director of the National Cancer Institute recently reported that the five year survival rate for lung cancer is now 12 percent, versus a fifty percent survival rate for all cancers. Cohn, Cancer Survival Rate is Reported at 50 percent, Washington Post, Nov. 29, 1983 at Al, col. 2.

b. Experts

COMMITTEE ON RISK AND DECISION MAKING, NATIONAL ACADEMY OF SCIENCES RISK AND DECISION MAKING: PERSPECTIVES AND RESEARCH

27–33, 36–38 (1982).

THE ROLES OF SCIENCE AND ANALYSIS

. . . Given the scientific complexity of many risk problems, it might be argued that ideal policy would be made by scientists and professional analysts. The committee rejects such a model of policy making as both unattainable and incompatible with democratic principles. We do so for several reasons.

First, decisions about social problems—such as those involving risks—almost always involve some conflict of interest. Rarely can a decision be simultaneously the best for all parties concerned. Even if all people benefit by a decision, some win more while others win less. While analysis can help identify the total benefits and costs of various policy alternatives, it cannot objectively resolve these conflicts of interest. Furthermore, policy choices cannot always be made politically acceptable by compensating apparent losers. In a democracy, these imbalances between efficiency and equity are left to be sorted out in the political process.

Second, some policy problems that are in principle analyzable—that is to say, would respond to an intellectual resolution if they could be pursued long and painstakingly enough—are not in fact analyzable because they run beyond anyone's cognitive capacities or beyond society's store of information. Again, these issues need political as well as intellectual contributions to their solution. The difficulties are enlarged by the facts that policy questions involve contributions from many different disciplines and that it is extremely difficult to blend these different perspectives in any formal way.

Third, analysis can be done and is done by persons other than policy analysts or risk analysts. For example, public servants would be better off, on some kinds of issues, to conduct their own informal analysis of a risk problem—without any professional analysis—since they can draw on a fund of practical experience and can better cope with and respond to the realities of a particular organization.

Fourth, professional analysis, even when it is more competent than any other method of assessment or evaluation, is fallible and inconclusive. How far to trust it, when to trust it, and when not, are questions that should be decided by appropriate political authorities; in a democratic society, that means the use of analysis should be subject to the control of the electorate and political officials.

Finally, professional risk analysis is expensive and time-consuming. It is simply impossible to subject every important aspect of a policy decision to professional analysis. There are not enough professionals to go around, nor would there be if their numbers were many times multiplied. The cost of analysis may exceed the benefits of the decision, or the issues may have to be decided before an analysis can be completed.[12]

___

12. A member of the committee points out that professional risk analysis need not be expensive or time-consuming. A risk analysis can be professional and useful and still cheap and rapid. For example, the analysis of risk for occupational exposure to

Given the inherently limited role of analysis in decision making, how can it help? The committee believes that formal analyses can often be useful to decision makers at various levels of interaction by providing needed information or by helping decision makers to structure their thinking. One goal of this report is to articulate how analysis can be useful and how it can be made more useful. . . .

Many decision makers must do more than decide what risk-coping strategy to advocate. They must often decide how to enlist the support of interest groups for a particular policy, how to enforce risk-coping strategies, how to defend policy positions in court and at legislative hearings, what new information to gather, what kinds of authority to delegate and to whom, and so forth. Tailor-made analyses, if responsive, judicious, and incisive, can help decision makers with this entire range of choices.

Some analyses are conducted for multiple purposes and for multiple audiences. These analyses, which are often done in universities or research organizations or in some cases by the government, can usefully serve to raise the level of political discourse on some policy issue. They are often, however, not only used but misused as political weapons in the adversarial process. Hence, it is important that such analyses be reviewed by others and not be viewed as above the political battle.[13]

In addition to aiding a decision maker in the selection of an alternative within a specific range of choices, analysis can be useful in two other important but neglected ways. First, situations are frequent in which adversarial parties in, say, an environmental dispute are not in a zero-sum game (i.e., what one party wins the other loses). Analysis can help organize and lay the groundwork for bargaining between parties so that potential joint gains are actually realized. Second, analysis can sometimes lead to the design of superior policy alternatives. By better understanding the reasons why various alternatives are relatively strong or weak in their details, creative new alternatives can be devised. The policy debate may not be resolved, but instead of a dispute between lackluster policy alternatives A and B, the debate could lead to a dispute between innovative and superior alternatives C and D. Moreover, analyses are not always intended to resolve well-formulated questions; sometimes the aim of analysis is to help formulate the right questions. That goal is often approached iteratively: a deeper insight into the right questions is achieved by struggling with what turn out to be the wrong questions.

A preliminary back-of-the-envelope analysis about whether a formal analysis is worthwhile may often be helpful but often is not done. Such an analysis of whether or not to do analysis may quickly reach a point of diminishing returns; nevertheless, informal, preliminary thinking can oft-

benzene took four working days. It is doubtful that more work would have changed the court's decision denying OSHA's reduction of occupational exposure to benzene permitted during a work day. The emphasis should not be on professionalism but on detail and precision. A risk analysis that leads to a risk of death of 1 in a billion years with an uncertainty of a factor of 10 is small enough that no further precision is necessary. Yet, one that leads to 1 in 50 years (the risk of automobile use) is large enough that improved precision and subdi-

viding of the groups at risk may be worthwhile.

13. At least one committee member feels that publication in the open scientific literature allows the best possible scope for peer review. Often, the risk analysis for a specific chemical is performed to meet a regulatory deadline. However, this is no reason why the general procedure for the analysis, with examples of other chemicals, should not be properly published.

en indicate the potential gains that one might expect from deeper analysis.

People differ sharply on the value of formal analysis: to some analysis is to be avoided, while to others analysis is to be embraced regardless of its cost. Both of these attitudes are misguided since the value of analysis will tend to vary widely depending on the problem, the institution, and the cast of actors involved in the decision. The committee believes that a case-by-case examination of the value of analysis is more sensible and productive. Analysis, whenever it is done, should clearly state its basic assumptions and biases to enable users to evaluate it.

Analysis, it should also be noted, sometimes can exacerbate controversy rather than relieve it, by enabling protagonists to fully understand that their interests are deeply opposed to those of others. Thus, it is not the case that more information and more knowledge always help resolve conflicts about risks.

TWO ASPECTS OF RISK ANALYSIS: ASSESSMENT AND EVALUATION

Individuals who must frequently decide between complex alternatives—doctors, business executives, investment analysts, judges, and juries—rarely decompose their thinking into separate compartments and formalize each component task separately. They generally do not, for example, formally assess probability distributions of key uncertainties and systematically combine these assessments with value trade-offs. Rather, they gather bits and pieces of facts and somehow synthesize them. They would be hard pressed to explain how they reached a decision, and, if forced to justify their action, their rationales may not accurately reflect their deeper insights. Even those decision analysts who espouse the divide-and-conquer philosophy of decomposition and recomposition acknowledge that formal analysis requires experience and, at least initially, that it may not be better than informal musings.

In a complex policy problem for which no single individual has command of all its facets, a decision maker and his or her advisers may wish to decompose the overall problem into parts and call on experts to help advise on the various facets. Decomposition has several benefits. It provides a formal structure for collating expertise on different facets of a problem. It also makes explicit the rationales in reasoning about the problem. Such explicitness, by facilitating peer review and providing insights into the problem, both elevates the quality of the risk analyses and points to needed research. Also, an assessment free of overt policy values may be useful to a wide range of decision makers, inside and outside the government. There is a decomposition of tasks that seems quite natural and that is extensively employed by such federal agencies as the Environmental Protection Agency, the Food and Drug Administration, and the Nuclear Regulatory Commission. This decomposition divides analysis into assessment and evaluation. Given their importance, a definition of these terms and a discussion of their interrelationship is warranted.

One task of analysis is to identify the main uncertainties present in a given problem and to assess their magnitude. Is a given chemical carcinogenic? If so, what is its severity? How many people will be exposed? What are the potential health effects? What is the risk of a rupture of a dam, of a nuclear meltdown, of an LNG-induced fire? Uncertainties are particularly important in the categories of risk that society is now considering: risks in which cause and effect are ill-defined and the risks of new technologies. The policy maker may want not only a single estimate of the magnitudes of these risks but also some information about the range of uncertainty of these estimates. This is risk assessment. There are also assessments of consequences not involving risks to health and safety, such as effects on productivity, people's happiness, and people's confidence in institutions.

After the various uncertainties are assessed, the policy choice may still be far from obvious. The policy maker has to consider, formally or informally, the alternative actions he or she might pursue, the institutional and political constraints, value and ideological judgments, and so on. This is risk evaluation.[14] It can be viewed as a subset of what some people call policy evaluation or policy analysis.

. . .

Value Trade-Offs and Ethical Considerations in Risk Evaluation

. . .

Much of the disagreement today about how to cope with a variety of risks stems from uncertainty about their magnitude: how hazardous is benzene or saccharin or ionizing radiation? Extrapolations from observable to nonobservable conditions, either in dose level or from animals to humans, will probably remain contentious. If, however, contrary to all expectations all such scientific imprecision could be resolved, controversy would still abound and perhaps would be even more vehement. Instead of a heated argument about linear versus nonlinear extrapolations from high to low dose rates, the dispute might be about the role of government in a free society.

A few simplified examples of some of the most perplexing problems involving ethics and value trade-offs are sketched below.

How much of society's limited resources should be allocated to life-saving activities versus other pressing social concerns?

If you had to make the uncomfortable choice of saving an anonymous 1-year-old's life or that of an anonymous 20-year-old or 60-year-old, which would you choose?

How important is the psychological well-being associated with clean air and blue skies compared with various levels of economic well-being?

How should an asthma attack suffered by a 30-year-old be compared with a bout of emphysema suffered by a 60-year-old?

How should our society decide whether to save the lives of inhabitants of North America 100 years from now versus saving starving Sahelians now?

Do we have the responsibility of maintaining ecological balances for nature's sake rather than—or in addition to—for people's sake?

To what extent should society be willing to impose costs and risks on a few members of society in order to benefit most members of society?[15]

---

14. This terminology is not standard: What we refer to as assessment others call estimation or, more broadly, the compilation of the relevant empirical facts.

15. A variation of this is: To what extent should society be willing to impose small costs and risks to a large number of members of society in order to greatly benefit a few members of society? There would be a large societal consensus on the answer if the above question were changed to say, imposing great costs to many that modestly benefit a few.

When should heroic measures be taken to prolong life?

When should governments restrict individuals from self-hazardous behaviors?

These long-standing issues of value are common in risk and decision making. While science and professional analysis may contribute to a more informed debate concerning these trade-offs, they cannot resolve them; they may, however, help to define and structure those value trade-offs. This perspective is important because it highlights the limited albeit important role of science and professional analysis in resolving disputes over decisions about acceptable risk.

c. Other Institutions of Government

---

i. *The Courts*

INDUSTRIAL UNION DEPARTMENT, AFL–CIO v. AMERICAN PETROLEUM INSTITUTE

Supreme Court of the United States, 1980.
448 U.S. 607, 100 S.Ct. 2844, 65 L.Ed.2d 1010.

Mr. Justice Stevens announced the judgment of the Court and delivered an opinion in which The Chief Justice and Mr. Justice Stewart join and in Parts I, II, III–A–C and E of which Mr. Justice Powell joins.

The Occupational Safety and Health Act of 1970, 29 U.S.C. § 651 et seq. (the Act), was enacted for the purpose of ensuring safe and healthful working conditions for every working man and woman in the Nation. This case concerns a standard promulgated by the Secretary of Labor to regulate occupational exposure to benzene, a substance which has been shown to cause cancer at high exposure levels. The principal question is whether such a showing is a sufficient basis for a standard that places the most stringent limitation on exposure to benzene that is technologically and economically possible.

. . .

III

Our resolution of the issues in this case turns, to a large extent, on the meaning of and the relationship between § 3(8), which defines a health and safety standard as a standard that is "reasonably necessary and appropriate to provide safe or healthful employment," and § 6(b)(5), which directs the Secretary in promulgating a health and safety standard for toxic materials to "set the standard which most adequately assures, to the extent feasible, on the basis of the best available evidence, that no employee will suffer material impairment of health or functional capacity . . . ."

A

Under the Government's view, § 3(8), if it has any substantive content at all, merely requires OSHA to issue standards that are reasonably calculated to produce a safer or more healthy work environment. Tr. of Oral Arg. 18, 20. Apart from this minimal requirement of rationality, the Government argues that § 3(8) imposes no limits on the Agency's power, and thus would not prevent it from requiring employers to do whatever would be "reasonably necessary" to eliminate all risks of any harm from their workplaces. With respect to toxic substances and harmful physical agents, the Government takes an even more extreme position. Relying on § 6(b)(5)'s direction to set a standard "which most adequately assures . . . that no employee will suffer material impairment of health or functional capacity," the Government contends that the Secretary is required to impose standards that either guarantee workplaces that are free from any risk of material health impairment, however small, or that come as close as possible to doing so without ruining entire industries.

If the purpose of the statute were to eliminate completely and with absolute certainty any risk of serious harm, we would agree that it would be proper for the Secretary to interpret §§ 3(8) and 6(b)(5) in this fashion. But we think it is clear that the statute was not designed to require employers to provide absolutely risk-free workplaces whenever it is technologically feasible to do so, so long as the cost is not great enough to destroy an entire industry. Rather, both the language and structure of the Act, as well as its legislative history, indicate that it was intended to require the elimination, as far as feasible, of significant risks of harm.

B

By empowering the Secretary to promulgate standards that are "reasonably necessary or appropriate to provide safe or healthful employment and places of employment," the Act implies that, before promulgating any standard, the Secretary must make a finding that the workplaces in question are not safe. But "safe" is not the equivalent of "risk-free." There are many activities that we engage in every day—such as driving a car or even breathing city air—that entail some risk of accident or material health impairment; nevertheless, few people would consider these activities "unsafe." Similarly, a workplace can hardly be considered "unsafe" unless it threatens the workers with a significant risk of harm.

Therefore, before he can promulgate *any* permanent health or safety standard, the Secretary is required to make a threshold finding that a place of employment is unsafe—in the sense that significant risks are present and can be eliminated or lessened by a change in practices.

. . .

Section 6(b)(8) lends additional support to this analysis. That subsection requires that, when the Secretary substantially alters an existing consensus standard, he must explain how the new rule will "better effectuate" the purposes of the Act. If this requirement was intended to be more than a meaningless formality, it must be read to impose upon the Secretary the duty to find that an existing national consensus standard is not adequate to protect workers from a continuing and significant risk of harm. Thus, in this case, the Secretary was required to find that exposures at the current permissible exposure level of 10 ppm present a significant risk of harm in the workplace.

In the absence of a clear mandate in the Act, it is unreasonable to assume that Congress intended to give the Secretary the unprecedented power over American industry that would result from the Government's view of §§ 3(8) and 6(b)(5), coupled with OSHA's cancer policy. Expert testimony that a substance is probably a human carcinogen—either because it has caused cancer in animals or because individuals have contracted cancer following extremely high exposures—would justify the conclusion that the substance poses some risk of serious harm no matter how minute the exposure and no matter how many experts testified that they regarded the risk as insignificant. That conclusion would in turn justify pervasive regulation limited only by the constraint of feasibility. In light of the fact that there are literally thousands of substances used in the workplace that have been identified as carcinogens or suspect carcinogens, the Government's theory would give OSHA power to impose enormous costs that might produce little, if any, discernible benefit.[51]

. . .

If the Government was correct in arguing that neither § 3(8) nor § 6(b)(5) requires that the risk from a toxic substance be quantified sufficiently to enable the Secretary to characterize it as significant in an understandable way, the statute would make such a "sweeping delegation of legislative power" that it might be unconstitutional under the Court's reasoning in Schechter Poultry Corp. v. United States, 295 U.S. 495, 539, 55 S.Ct. 837, 847, 79 L.Ed. 1570, and Panama Refining Co. v. Ryan, 293 U.S. 388, 55 S.Ct. 241, 79 L.Ed. 446. A construction of the statute that avoids this kind of open-ended grant should certainly be favored.

C

The legislative history also supports the conclusion that Congress was concerned, not with absolute safety, but with the elimination of significant harm. The examples of industrial hazards referred to in the committee hearings and debates all involved situations in which the risk was unquestionably significant. . . .

Moreover, Congress specifically amended § 6(b)(5) to make it perfectly clear that it does not require the Secretary to promulgate standards that would assure an absolutely risk-free workplace. Section 6(b)(5) of the initial Committee bill provided that

"The Secretary in promulgating standards under this subsection, shall set the standard which most adequately and feasibly assures, on the basis of the best available evidence, that no employee will suffer *any* impairment of health or functional capacity, or diminished life expectancy even if such employee has regular exposure to the hazard dealt with by such standard for the period of his working life." (Emphasis supplied.) S. 2193, 91st Cong., 2d Sess., at 40; Legis.Hist., at 243.

---

51. OSHA's proposed generic cancer policy, 42 Fed.Reg. 54148 (1977), indicates that this possibility is not merely hypothetical. Under its proposal, whenever there is a certain quantum of proof—either from animal experiments, or, less frequently, from epidemiological studies—that a substance causes cancer at any exposure level, an emergency temporary standard would be promulgated immediately, requiring employers to provide monitoring and medical examinations and to reduce exposures to the lowest feasible level. A proposed rule would then be issued along the same lines, with objecting employers effectively foreclosed from presenting evidence that there

is little or no risk associated with current exposure levels. Id., at 54154–54155; 29 CFR, Part 1990 (1977).

The scope of the proposed regulation is indicated by the fact that NIOSH has published a list of 2,415 potential occupational carcinogens, NIOSH, Suspected Carcinogens: A Subfile of the Registry of Toxic Effects of Chemical Substances (HEW Pub.No. 77–149, 2d ed. 1976). OSHA has tentatively concluded that 269 of these substances have been proved to be carcinogens and therefore should be subject to full regulation. See OSHA Press Release, USDL 78–625 (July 14, 1978).

On the floor of the Senate, Senator Dominick questioned the wisdom of this provision, stating

> "How in the world are we ever going to live up to that? What are we going to do about a place in Florida where mosquitoes are getting at the employee—perish the thought that there may be mosquitoes in Florida? But there are black flies in Minnesota and Wisconsin. Are we going to say that if employees get bitten by those for the rest of their lives they will not have been done any harm at all? Probably they will not be, but do we know?" Legis.Hist., at 345.

He then offered an amendment deleting the entire subsection.[52] After discussions with the sponsors of the Committee bill, Senator Dominick revised his amendment. Instead of deleting the first sentence of § 6(b)(5) entirely, his new amendment limited the application of that subsection to toxic materials and harmful physical agents and changed "any" impairment of health to "material" impairment.[53] In discussing this change, Senator Dominick noted that the Committee's bill read as if a standard had to "assure that, no matter what anybody was doing, the standard would protect him for the rest of his life against any foreseeable hazard." Such an "unrealistic standard," he stated, had not been intended by the sponsors of the bill. Rather, he explained that the intention of the bill, as implemented by the amendment, was to require the Secretary

> ". . . to use his best efforts to promulgate the best available standards, and in so doing, . . . he should take into account that anyone working in toxic agents and physical agents which might be harmful may be subjected to such conditions for the rest of his working life, so that we can get at something which might not be toxic now, if he works in it a short time, but if he works in it the rest of his life might be very dangerous; and we want to make sure that such things are taken into consideration in establishing standards." Legis.Hist., at 502–503.

52. In criticizing the Committee bill, Senator Dominick also made the following observations:

"It is unrealistic to attempt, as this section apparently does, to establish a utopia free from any hazards. Absolute safety is an impossibility and it will only create confusion in the administration of this act for the Congress to set clearly unattainable goals." Legis.Hist., at 480.

. . .

"But I ask, Mr. President, just thinking about that language let us take a fellow who is a streetcar conductor or a bus conductor at the present time. How in the world, in the process of the automobile accidents that we have all during a working day of any one driving a bus or trolley car, or whatever it may be, can we set standards that will make sure he will not have any risk to his life for the rest of his life? It is totally impossible for this to be put in a bill: and yet it is in the committee bill." Legis.Hist., at 423.

As an opponent of the legislation, Senator Dominick may have exaggerated the signifi-

cance of the problem since the language in § 3(8) already was sufficient to prevent the Secretary from trying "to establish a utopia free from any hazards." Nevertheless, the fact that Congress amended the bill to allay Senator Dominick's concern demonstrates that it did not intend the statute to achieve "clearly unattainable goals."

53. Senator Dominick had also been concerned that the placement of the word "feasibly" could be read to require the Secretary to "ban all occupations in which there remains *some* risk of injury, impaired health, or life expectancy," since the way to most "adequately" and "feasibly" assure absolute protection might well be to prohibit the occupation entirely. Legis.Hist., at 366–367. In his final amendment, he attempted to cure this problem by relocating the feasibility requirement, changing "the standard which most adequately and feasibly assures" to "the standard which most adequately assures, to the extent feasible."

Senator Williams, one of the sponsors of the Committee bill, agreed with the interpretation, and the amendment was adopted.

In its reply brief the Government argues that the Dominick amendment simply means that the Secretary is not required to eliminate threats of insignificant harm; it argues that § 6(b)(5) still requires the Secretary to set standards that ensure that not even one employee will be subject to any risk of serious harm—no matter how small that risk may be.[55] This interpretation is at odds with Congress' express recognition of the futility of trying to make all workplaces totally risk-free. Moreover, not even OSHA follows this interpretation of § 6(b)(5) to its logical conclusion. Thus, if OSHA is correct that the only no-risk level for leukemia due to benzene exposure is zero and if its interpretation of § 6(b)(5) is correct, OSHA should have set the exposure limit as close to zero as feasible. But OSHA did not go about its task in that way. Rather, it began with a 1 ppm level, selected at least in part to ensure that employers would not be required to eliminate benzene concentrations that were little greater than the so-called "background" exposures experienced by the population at large. Then, despite suggestions by some labor unions that it was feasible for at least some industries to reduce exposures to well below 1 ppm, OSHA decided to apply the same limit to all, largely as a matter of administrative convenience.

OSHA also deviated from its own interpretation of § 6(b)(5) in adopting an action level of 0.5 ppm below which monitoring and medical examinations are not required. In light of OSHA's cancer policy, it must have assumed that some employees would be at risk because of exposures below 0.5 ppm. These employees would thus presumably benefit from medical examinations, which might uncover any benzene-related problems. OSHA's consultant advised the Agency that it was technologically and economically feasible to require that such examinations be provided. Nevertheless, OSHA adopted an action level, largely because the insignificant benefits of giving such examinations and performing the necessary monitoring did not justify the substantial cost.

OSHA's concessions to practicality in beginning with a 1 ppm exposure limit and using an action level concept implicitly adopt an interpretation of the statute as not requiring regulation of insignificant risks. It is entirely consistent with this interpretation to hold that the Act also requires the Agency to limit its endeavors in the standard-setting area to eliminating significant risks of harm.

Finally, with respect to the legislative history, it is important to note that Congress repeatedly expressed its concern about allowing the Secretary to have too much power over American industry. Thus, Congress refused to give the Secretary the power to shut down plants unilaterally because of an imminent danger, see Whirlpool Corp. v. Marshall, 445 U.S. 1, 100 S.Ct. 883, 63 L.Ed.2d 154, and narrowly circumscribed the Secretary's power to issue temporary emergency standards. This effort by Congress to limit the Secretary's power is not consistent with a view that the mere possibility that some employee somewhere in the country may confront some risk of cancer is a sufficient basis for the exercise of

---

55. Reply Brief, at 24–26. While it is true that some of Senator Dominick's comments were concerned with the relative unimportance of minor injuries (see his "fly" example quoted at p. 2867, supra), it is clear that he was also concerned with the remote possibility of major injuries, see n. 52, supra.

the Secretary's power to require the expenditure of hundreds of millions of dollars to minimize that risk.

. . .

D

Contrary to the Government's contentions, imposing a burden on the Agency of demonstrating a significant risk of harm will not strip it of its ability to regulate carcinogens, nor will it require the Agency to wait for deaths to occur before taking any action. First, the requirement that a "significant" risk be identified is not a mathematical straitjacket. It is the Agency's responsibility to determine, in the first instance, what it considers to be a "significant" risk. Some risks are plainly acceptable and others are plainly unacceptable. If, for example, the odds are one in a billion that a person will die from cancer by taking a drink of chlorinated water, the risk clearly could not be considered significant. On the other hand, if the odds are one in a thousand that regular inhalation of gasoline vapors that are 2% benzene will be fatal, a reasonable person might well consider the risk significant and take appropriate steps to decrease or eliminate it. Although the Agency has no duty to calculate the exact probability of harm, it does have an obligation to find that a significant risk is present before it can characterize a place of employment as "unsafe."[62]

Second, OSHA is not required to support its finding that a significant risk exists with anything approaching scientific certainty. Although the Agency's findings must be supported by substantial evidence, 29 U.S.C. § 655(f), § 6(b)(5) specifically allows the Secretary to regulate on the basis of the "best available evidence." As several Courts of Appeals have held, this provision requires a reviewing court to give OSHA some leeway where its findings must be made on the frontiers of scientific knowledge. See Industrial Union Dept., AFL–CIO v. Hodgson, 162 U.S.App.D.C. 331, 340, 499 F.2d 467, 476 (1974); Society of the Plastics Industry, Inc. v. OSHA, 509 F.2d 1301, 1308 (CA2 1975), cert. denied, 421 U.S. 992, 95 S.Ct. 1998, 44 L.Ed.2d 482. Thus, so long as they are supported by a body of reputable scientific thought, the Agency is free to use conservative assumptions in interpreting the data with respect to carcinogens, risking error on the side of overprotection rather than underprotection.[63]

---

62. In his dissenting opinion, Mr. Justice Marshall states: "[W]hen the question involves determination of the acceptable level of risk, the ultimate decision must necessarily be based on considerations of policy as well as empirically verifiable facts. Factual determinations can at most define the risk in some statistical way; the judgment whether that risk is tolerable cannot be based solely on a resolution of the facts." We agree. Thus, while the Agency must support its finding that a certain level of risk exists by substantial evidence, we recognize that its determination that a particular level of risk is "significant" will be based largely on policy considerations. At this point we have no need to reach the issue of what level of scrutiny a reviewing court should apply to the latter type of determination.

63. Mr. Justice Marshall states that, under our approach, the Agency must either wait for deaths to occur or must "deceive the public" by making a basically meaningless determination of significance based on totally inadequate evidence. Mr. Justice Marshall's view, however, rests on the erroneous premise that the only reason OSHA did not attempt to quantify benefits in this case was because it could not do so in any reasonable manner. As the discussion of the Agency's rejection of an industry attempt at formulating a dose-response curve demonstrates, however, the Agency's rejection of methods such as dose-response curves was based at least in part on its view that nothing less than absolute safety would suffice.

Finally, the record in this case and OSHA's own rulings on other carcinogens indicate that there are a number of ways in which the Agency can make a rational judgment about the relative significance of the risks associated with exposure to a particular carcinogen.[64]

It should also be noted that, in setting a permissible exposure level in reliance on less-than-perfect methods, OSHA would have the benefit of a backstop in the form of monitoring and medical testing. Thus, if OSHA properly determined that the permissible exposure limit should be set at 5 ppm, it could still require monitoring and medical testing for employees exposed to lower levels. By doing so, it could keep a constant check on the validity of the assumptions made in developing the permissible exposure limit, giving it a sound evidentiary basis for decreasing the limit if it was initially set too high. Moreover, in this way it could ensure that workers who were unusually susceptible to benzene could be removed from exposure before they had suffered any permanent damage.[67]

.   .   .

NOTES

1. In American Textile Manufacturers v. Donovan (known as the Cotton Dust case), Ch. 4, Sec. C.1, *supra*, the Supreme Court of the United States held that OSHA is not required to use *cost-benefit analysis* in regulating risks in the workplace. But as this opinion makes clear, a *risk assessment* is required in order to determine that the risk in question is significant—at least when it is *possible* to

64. For example, in the coke-oven emissions standard, OSHA had calculated that 21,000 exposed coke-oven workers had an annual excess mortality of over 200 and that the proposed standard might well eliminate the risk entirely. 41 Fed.Reg. 46742, 46750 (1976), upheld in American Iron & Steel Inst. v. OSHA, 577 F.2d 825 (CA3 1978), cert. granted 448 U.S. 909, 100 S.Ct. 3054, 65 L.Ed.2d 1139. In hearings on the coke-oven emissions standard, the Council on Wage and Price Stability estimated that 8 to 35 lives would be saved each year, out of an estimated population of 14,000 workers, as a result of the proposed standard. Although noting that the range of benefits would vary depending on the assumptions used, OSHA did not make a finding as to whether its own staff estimate or CWPS's was correct, on the ground that it was not required to quantify the expected benefits of the standard or to weigh those benefits against the projected costs.

In other proceedings, the Agency has had a good deal of data from animal experiments on which it could base a conclusion on the significance of the risk. For example, the record on the vinyl chloride standard indicated that a significant number of animals had developed tumors of the liver, lung, and skin when they were exposed to 50 ppm of vinyl chloride over a period of 11 months. One hundred out of 200 animals died during that period. 39 Fed.Reg. 35890, 35891 (1974). Similarly, in a 1974 standard regulating 14 carcinogens, OSHA found that one of the substances had caused

lung cancer in mice or rats at 1 ppm and even 0.1 ppm, while another had caused tumors in 80% of the animals subjected to high doses. Id., at 3756, 3757, upheld in Synthetic Organic Chemical Mfrs. Assn. v. Brennan, 503 F.2d 1155 (CA3 1974), cert. denied, 420 U.S. 973, 95 S.Ct. 1396, 43 L.Ed.2d 653, and Synthetic Organic Chemical Mfrs. Assn. v. Brennan, 506 F.2d 385 (CA3 1974), cert. denied, 423 U.S. 830, 96 S.Ct. 50, 46 L.Ed.2d 48.

In this case the Agency did not have the benefit of animal studies, because scientists have been unable as yet to induce leukemia in experimental animals as a result of benzene exposure. It did, however, have a fair amount of epidemiological evidence, including both positive and negative studies. Although the Agency stated that this evidence was insufficient to construct a precise correlation between exposure levels and cancer risks, it would at least be helpful in determining whether it is more likely than not that there is a significant risk at 10 ppm.

67. In its explanation of the final standard OSHA noted that there was some testimony that blood abnormalities would disappear after exposure had ceased. 43 Fed. Reg. 5946 (1978). Again, however, OSHA refused to rely on the hypothesis that this would always occur. Yet, in requiring medical examinations of employees exposed to between 0.5 ppm and 1 ppm, OSHA was essentially providing itself with the same kind of backstop.

quantify the risk. See Marshall, J., dissenting, 448 U.S. at 690, 100 S.Ct. at 2888:
"It is fortunate indeed that—a majority of the Justices reject the view that the
Secretary is prevented from taking regulatory action when the magnitude of a
health risk cannot be quantified on the basis of current techniques." While a
majority of the Justices held that the determination of whether a risk is significant
can be based largely on policy considerations, note 62, supra, the only guidance
given as to magnitude are the observations of *three* justices that a one in a billion
risk of death "clearly could not be considered significant", while a one in a thousand risk "might well be consider[ed] significant. . . ." 448 U.S. at 655, 100
S.Ct. at 2870. Compare the discussion of a one in million lifetime risk of death as
insignificant enough to be an acceptable risk for a food additive in Sec. A.1, supra.

2. The plurality opinion in the main case supported in part its requirement
that the risks OSHA singles out for regulation must be "significant" by finding
that it would be inconsistent with the Act's legislative history to authorize the Secretary "to require the expenditure of hundreds of millions of dollars" to minimize
an insignificant risk. 448 U.S. at 652. But what if that risk could be eliminated
for a few cents?

3. If you were the general counsel of OSHA, and were asked to advise the
agency as to what should be done in order to promulgate a 1 ppm benzene standard that would not be overturned in the courts, what would you advise? Cf.
Comment, The Significant Risk Requirement in OSHA Regulation of Carcinogens, 33 Stan.L.Rev. 551 (1981). Would your answer be altered after June 6,
1983, when the Supreme Court decided Baltimore Gas and Electric Co. v. Natural
Resources Defense Council, discussed in the note following *Gulf South Insulation*, in
Sec. A.3.a, supra.

4. For an example of more aggressive judicial decision-making see United
States v. Anderson Seafoods, Inc., 447 F.Supp. 1151 (N.D.Fla.1978). The case
concerned the proper adulteration level of mercury-contaminated swordfish. The
FDA claimed fish containing more than .05 ppm (parts per million) of mercury
should be considered adulterated. The company claimed that 2 ppm was the correct level. The court, after reviewing the evidence, effectively set the level at 1
ppm or less. FDA acquiesced in that decision and did not seek appellate review.

ii. The Executive Office of the President

RONALD REAGAN, EXECUTIVE ORDER 12291

[The text of the Order is printed in Sec. A.4.c, supra]

NOTE

Although the primary thrust of the Executive Order was to impose a requirement of cost-benefit decision-making on regulatory agencies, the Order may in
fact have further politicized the decision-making process. In September of 1983,
the former chief of staff of the Environmental Protection Agency told an oversight
subcommittee of the House of Representatives that OMB, in the course of reviewing pending regulations pursuant to the Order, had leaked proposed changes in
environmental regulation to the affected industries. He further alleged that OMB
had brought "tremendous pressure" on EPA to make changes in the regulations
desired by industry. Washington Post, Sept. 28, 1983, at Al, col. 2.

Would it be good or bad for OMB to act in a political way in implementing the
Order? Consider the views expressed by Judge Wald for the court in Sierra Club
v. Costle, 657 F.2d 298, 406 (D.C.Cir. 1981) in response to a challenge that the
White House had improperly interfered with another regulatory decision:

. . . In the particular case of EPA, Presidential authority is clear since it
has never been considered an "independent agency," but always part of the
Executive Branch.

The authority of the President to control and supervise executive policymaking is derived from the Constitution; the desirability of such control is

demonstrable from the practical realities of administrative rulemaking. Regulations such as those involved here demand a careful weighing of cost, environmental and energy considerations. They also have broad implications for national economic policy. Our form of government simply could not function effectively or rationally if key executive policymakers were isolated from each other and from the Chief Executive. Single mission agencies do not always have the answers to complex regulatory problems. An overworked administrator exposed on a 24-hour basis to a dedicated but zealous staff needs to know the arguments and ideas of policymakers in other agencies as well as in the White House.

In light of the political purpose of Presidential control of regulatory agency decisions through OMB, what procedural requirements and constraints should apply to OMB? Consider available decision-making models, including (i) the legislative process, (ii) informal rulemaking on the record by an agency, and (iii) the judicial process. Should it matter whether the agency decision being reviewed was reached after an on-the-record process?

iii. The Congress

RICHARD COOPER,
THE ROLE OF REGULATING AGENCIES IN
RISK/BENEFIT DECISION MAKING

33 Food, Drug, Cosmetic Law Journal 755, 766–773 (1978).

. . .

The value judgments inherent in administrative risk-benefit decision-making as we know it today do not fit into the mold of traditional regulatory decision-making. The weighing of health risks to one group against economic benefits to another cannot be justified by reference to expertise, in whatever fancy dress the exercise may be clothed. The making of such value judgments pursuant to FIFRA and similar statutes is not an interstitial activity subject to effective statutory guidance. It is a free activity, subject to no effective statutory constraint at all. Administrative procedures do not provide a record on the basis of which risk-benefit value judgments can be justified and evaluated in the way that other administrative determinations can be justified and evaluated. Therefore, judicial review cannot perform its usual function.

Today, regulatory agencies are required under some statutes to make unstructured risk-benefit evaluations. Consequently, the agencies have no alternative but to make fundamental value judgments as best they can. These judgments involve very high economic stakes, running into the hundreds of millions or even billions of dollars. Quantitative methods for assessing risks and benefits are widely used despite very serious methodological shortcomings. In many instances, the health risks at issue would be devastating if they were fulfilled, but the occurrence of actual harm is uncertain. Commonly, the existence of health risks is not supported by human epidemiological data; and clear and present economic dislocations have to be weighed against inferences and theories of health risk, rather than against demonstrable, actual harms. This state of affairs produces regulatory decisions that the public finds it difficult to understand or to accept.

The notion is abroad that the regulatory agencies are somehow out of control. In large measure, I think the notion is false. The head or heads of agencies are appointed by the President with the advice and consent of the Senate (or by a Cabinet officer appointed by the President). With respect to most of their decisions, the agencies are subject to adequate statutory criteria, vigorous industry and public participation, meticulous judical review based on a record, and effective congressional oversight. But with respect to the value judgments in risk-benefit decision-making, the notion of loss of control is close to the mark. When an agency is free to express its own subjective value judgments in determining what is an "unreasonable risk" or in making some other equally unstructured determination, it is outside the controls that normally apply to administrative action.

Regulatory agencies are like planets, created to move in orbits determined by statutes enacted by Congress and the President and authoritatively interpreted by the courts. The agencies move along their orbits by issuing decisions in accordance with procedures suited to their respective paths. If they carry out their statutory mandate adequately, they will move on a course that reflects the prevailing political forces in the solar system. When making risk-benefit value judgments, however, an agency is no longer subject to statutory guidance and is likely to move off its assigned orbit. In astronomical terms, it undergoes a perturbation. Its procedures may not correct its course because to maintain a true course the agency needs to come back under the legitimate influence of directives emanating from the political system. An agency cannot create legitimate directives itself. Its procedures are designed to adduce evidence of facts and considerations drawn from *established* law and policy, and are not designed to produce politically ratified value judgments.

For this and no doubt other reasons, there have been suggestions that other units of government move into a perceived political vacuum surrounding regulatory agencies, that these units increase one kind of control or another over regulatory agencies, that they reimpose something akin to the checks and balances that operate elsewhere in our political system. It is characteristic of recent regulatory statutes to give agencies fairly broad and unstructured powers, but then to burden their exercise with elaborate, time-consuming and expensive procedures. During recent years, the courts have imposed increasingly exquisite and burdensome procedural requirements. The courts are not permitted, of course, to substitute their own value judgments openly for those of the agencies. As the Supreme Court pointed out in a recent case, however, the courts have used increased procedural requirements to achieve indirectly what they cannot achieve directly. We have also witnessed the emergence of requirements for published impact analyses—environmental, economic and urban; and proposals, for example, for analyses of impacts on government administration, the courts, paperwork, and society generally. Proposals abound for a legislative veto and for increasing oversight of regulatory activities by the Executive Office of the President.

But all of these efforts address the symptoms and not the causes. A principal cause, it seems to me, is the opportunity for free, uncontrolled value choices presented by risk-benefit, decision-making, which these efforts do not address. They ignore the real need: for usable value judgments bearing the imprimatur of the democratic political process. They bring with them other problems as well.

Increasingly refined procedural requirements imposed by Congress and the courts may improve the regulatory process at the margin. But the slight improvement is far outweighed by the opportunities they provide for delay and abuse and by the sheer difficulty of getting anything done. As the procedural requirements mount higher and higher, the regulatory process slows down and becomes more expensive, and invites public and political denunciation.

Increased politicization of regulatory decisions, the vast majority of which do not need further political controls, could further undermine public confidence in the fairness and expertness of regulatory decisions, particularly those, not involving risk-benefit value judgments, that may fairly be regarded as based on expertise and accepted notions of fairness.

I agree that risk-benefit decision-making is unavoidable. It makes no sense to ignore the consequences of decisions, and it is becoming increasingly evident that the public will not accept a regulatory system that ignores economic and, perhaps, social and other impacts as well. But I submit that the public and our political system will not accept fundamental risk-benefit value judgments made by regulatory agencies.

I see two realistic alternatives to the kind of decision-making exemplified by FIFRA. The first, suggested by some segments of industry and the private bar, is to subject those regulatory decisions that by some standard are "major" to some form of frankly political review. The review might be congressional, in the form of a legislative veto or in some other form; or, it could be executive, through some mechanism established in the Executive Office of the President, or perhaps involving the President himself.

Such a review system would require the politically responsible reviewing body to be accountable for the end product of the reviewing process. If an FDA regulation were reviewed, the reviewing body would be responsible for approving it, modifying it, or vetoing it; and agency responsibility would be reduced.

I do not suggest that such review decisions would be haphazard or entirely ad hoc. I would expect that, over time, despite the political variations from one case to another, a rough "common law" of political acceptability would develop, and operational value judgments would be hammered out, in a more or less articulated fashion, on a case-by-case basis.

But this system would pay a high price. Every regulatory decision reviewed would be "major". Thus, in every case the interests at stake would be major. Massive lobbying would occur because the final decision-maker would be, and would be perceived to be, politically responsible. The losing side would be likely to feel ill-treated by the system because its individual case was decided, not on the basis of the record made in an administrative process, but rather on the basis of whatever went on in a political process. Some interest groups would succeed in winning disparate treatment, and their success would generate a perception of unfairness in the whole enterprise. It is one thing to lose in an open, on-the-record process conducted in accordance with known rules; it is quite another thing to lose in a closed, off-the-record process conducted in accordance with unknown rules, particularly when the closed process follows on the heels of and supplants an open process.

Certainly, the administrative record made pursuant to most current statutes (even when supplemented by impact statements) would not provide a sufficient basis for judicial review of the political review process. If a regulation were vetoed or modified to reduce costs, how would a court determine whether the veto or modification was supported by substantial evidence or was arbitrary and capricious? Or would this sort of judicial review go by the boards? How would congressional oversight function?

When an agency head is asked to defend his action or failure to act, he often would have to say that the committee has the wrong person before it.

Finally, the system would build in a good deal of inefficiency: a great virtue of the administrative process is its capacity to resolve subordinate policy questions definitively (subject to judicial review) and move on. Even if a process of political review created *a de facto* political common law, it would not have definitive status; and the ground rules would always be open to challenge by interests clamoring for special treatment. (If the policies were definitive, they could be incorporated into the agencies' substantive law and be implemented by the agencies, subject to judicial review and congressional oversight; there would no longer be a need for political review.)

Before leaving this approach to controlling regulatory cost-benefit decisions, I want to emphasize that the difficulties I have pointed out arise from political review *after* the regulatory agency has conducted its public process and made its decision. They do not arise from review early in the regulatory process, before the commencement of public procedures and the making of agency decisions. At the planning stage, some form of consultation or review within the Executive Branch can give regulators a heightened awareness of the economic and social consequences of contemplated actions, and of alternative ways to achieve health protection goals. Review at that stage also does not subvert on-the-record regulatory proceedings, judicial review, or congressional oversight. Moreover, where the review is conducted by a consortium of regulatory agencies, as in the new Regulatory Council established by President Carter,[37] the undesirable aspects of political review are avoided. This form of review has major advantages over post-decisional political review, and it is likely to make a very useful contribution to the regulatory process, particularly through elimination of inconsistencies between regulatory requirements, duplicative regulations, and unforeseen adverse impacts from multiple regulations issued by different agencies. In this way, such review can eliminate or reduce some undesirable economic impacts of regulations. Nevertheless, it does not address the root cause of the current malaise.

The second alternative to risk-benefit decision-making by regulatory agencies (and one that could be combined with Executive Branch review) is for Congress and the President to make the necessary value judgments in legislation. If regulatory decisions are to be broadly acceptable, the governing statutes must do more than provide for decisions about what is safe or what is an unreasonable risk. They must also do more than merely list factors to be considered. The legislative process must make the basic value judgments and tell the agencies how to make the necessary trade-offs.

The perception that agencies are out of control arises from the fact that in being called on to make fundamental value judgments they have moved outside their accustomed sphere of activity, outside their expertise, and outside the established system of controls. This perturbation of the regulatory process will not be corrected until the regulatory agencies are relieved of the necessary of making judgments they are not equipped to make.

---

37. See 14 Weekly Compilation of Presidential Documents 1839, 1841–42 (1978) (address to the Nation on anti-inflation program, Oct. 24, 1978); id., 1905 (memorandum for the heads of executive departments and agencies on strengthening regulatory management, Oct. 31, 1978).

Value judgments are the heartland of the political process: they are what it exists for. Politics is the very process of making authoritative allocations of social values for the conduct of public affairs. Neither the administrative process nor the judicial process is appropriate for the making of basic social value judgments. That is a responsibility of the people's elected officials. The electoral and legislative processes give social value judgments an objective validity that the judicial and administrative processes cannot provide.

Making social value judgments to help resolve current health controversies will be a difficult and painful task—no one will feel comfortable deciding what a human life is worth or how much risk to one person is worth how much economic benefit to another, how much risk-reduction is worth how much cost, how the difference between voluntary and involuntary exposure to risk is to be treated and so on. But the task will be less painful and difficult if carried out statute-by-statute rather than in some form of ad hoc political review, decision-by-decision.

It may be that our political system is not yet ready to face the awesome task of establishing useful, concrete value judgments for conducting risk-benefit evaluations. This task is as difficult intellectually, morally, and politically as any a legislature can be called on to make. We might all be tempted to say with Hamlet, "The time is out of joint. O cursed spite/ That ever I was born to set it right." But the time for avoiding those hard issues is ebbing away, and I hope all of us who participate in the legislative process will try to achieve a viable solution there.

NOTE

The legislative veto mentioned in Richard Cooper's article is a procedure under which one or both Houses of Congress can nullify, by resolution or otherwise, decisions made pursuant to authority delegated by statute. Although only five statutes included such provisions as of 1937, between 1970 and 1975 more than 160 such provisions were included in some 89 laws as Congress came increasingly to rely on the device as a check on agency decision-making.

In INS v. Chadha, ___ U.S. ___, 103 S.Ct. 2764, 77 L.Ed.2d 317 (1983), the Supreme Court held unconstitutional a legislative veto provision in an opinion so broad that it appears to invalidate all such provisions. In an opinion written by the Chief Justice, the Court held that the veto in question violated both the requirement for bicameralism contained in Art. 1, § 1 of the Constitution, and the requirement of presentment to the President contained in Art. 1, § 7 of the Constitution.

The broad reading of *Chadha* was confirmed one week later when the Court affirmed two lower court decisions striking down other legislative veto provisions. Consumer Energy Council of America v. FERC, 673 F.2d 425 (D.C.Cir. 1982), affirmed ___ U.S. ___, 103 S.Ct. 3556, 77 L.Ed.2d 1402 (1983), struck down a veto provision that unlike *Chadha* involved a decision by an independent regulatory commission. Consumers Union of United States v. Federal Trade Commission, 691 F.2d 575 (D.C.Cir. 1982), affirmed ___ U.S. ___, 103 S.Ct. 3556, 77 L.Ed.2d 1402 (1983), held unconstitutional a legislative veto that applied to a a rulemaking rather than an adjudication as in *Chadha*, and one that required action by both Houses of Congress, rather than only one.

A major question now is what alternative (or alternatives) to the legislative veto Congress will adopt. Within days after the decision in *Chadha*, Congressman Waxman proposed an amendment to the pending reauthorization bill for the Consumer Product Safety Commission (CPSC) that would require all CPSC rules to be reported to Congress and thereafter remain ineffective for sixty days, during which time Congress could overturn the rule by legislative action. Under another amendment proposed by Congressman Levitas (a major proponent in the past of the legislative veto), the CPSC rules would not take effect *unless* they were specifically approved by both Houses and the President. Both amendments were adopted by the House. Washington Post, June 30, 1983, at B1, col. 5.

Congress need not take all discretion away from agencies now that the legislative veto is no longer available. For one thing, Congress remains free to overturn any proposed agency rule the way it did with saccharin—by passing a law denying the agency authority to act. *Chadha* may be seen, in other words, as merely forbidding the Congress to take shortcuts (that bypass the President) when overturning agency action. Congress might also make more specific initial delegations of authority, for example by taking a position on such issues as how much a human life is worth for purposes of making cost-benefit decisions as suggested in Richard Cooper's article. Recall also the dissent of Justice Rehnquist in the Cotton Dust case, Ch. 4, Sec. C.1, supra.

B. ALLOCATING BURDENS AND BENEFITS

Even after the most scrupulous attempts have been made to assess and then to reduce risks, some will remain. Moreover, the process of avoiding risks itself may not operate evenly; in avoiding or reducing one person's risks, those to which another person is exposed may grow larger in relative (and perhaps even absolute) terms. Thus, science and technology, in generating benefits and burdens, also create the need for distributive decisions. Indeed, these questions begin as soon as the scientific process begins, because the choice to study certain questions in certain ways itself involves the likelihood that some individuals and groups in society will benefit disproportionately—although because science proceeds in unpredictable ways, it is not always possible at the outset to know *which* individuals or groups.

Any attempt to answer questions of distribution immediately confronts some of the same questions explored earlier in this chapter, namely: how are burdens and benefits to be measured? Beyond this, the issues can be analyzed in two ways: what distribution is desirable, and what method of distribution is desirable? The former question often seems more difficult to answer in a satisfactory way then the latter, so it is not surprising that discussions of distribution often become examinations of the alternative means available to make allocative decisions; some people might even claim that in a diverse society governed by democratic ideals it is preferable to concentrate on finding the right means to allocate risks and benefits because there will never be full agreement on the fairness of the results but even the people who do not get the allocation they desire are more likely to be satisfied if they can see that the process of arriving at a decision was appropriately designed and carefully applied.

The section begins by looking at society's response when an activity that has exposed a few people to an unusual level of risks results in their being injured. By what standards should their claims be judged? Is it possible to find a system that provides justice to the claimants in a way that is fair to others in society, both those (such as the taxpayers) who may be called on to redress the injuries and those who suffer equally severe injuries from other sources that cannot so easily be identified or brought into court?

The materials then turn to the distribution of benefits, such as medical care. As an initial matter, this division of the subject itself raises a question: can an ethical (or legal) distinction be drawn between imposing burdens on someone and giving (or taking away) benefits to them? (This issue also foreshadows a concern that arises in Chapter 7 about a possible difference between death that follows cessation of treatment and death that follows administration of a poison.) Another question underlies these materials: is there something unique, or at least special, about health care? Are conclusions reached here applicable to the distribution of other valuable resources, such as computers (see Chapter 10)?

The ways in which institutions in our society distribute direct benefits to people are quite varied. We make no attempt here to examine the complex processes by which such allocations are made on a legislative level not only directly through the appropriation of funds and the framing of tax policy but also through laws that affect how much certain activities occur (e.g., the effect of licensure statutes on the distribution of health care professionals in different places in the country). Instead, we examine basic principles about distribution and their application in institutions at various levels, from the national to the local, as they grapple with decisions such as whether to perform (and fund) heart transplantation. This decision is merely illustrative of many others explored in later chapters, such as the question (examined in Chapter 8) whether limitations on eligibility for prenatal disgnosis are matters to be determined by technical data and reasoning or otherwise. Hard choices of this sort have always been with us, but the burgeoning powers of science and medicine make them even more acute today.

1. DISTRIBUTING SPECIAL RISKS

a. The DES Experiment

The late 1940's and early 1950's marked the beginning of a great technological explosion in aid of human reproduction (a topic pursued more fully in Chapter 8). Because the social expectation for American women of childbearing age during the "baby boom" era was that they would have babies, those who had difficulties doing so sought the aid of a medical profession eager to bring to bear on patients' problems the sort of scientific creativity that had just proven itself in the war effort.

One of the innovations employed was the development and use of diethylstilbestrol (a synthetic nonsteroidal estrogen, usually called DES) early in pregnancy as therapy against repeated or threatened miscarriages. After the drug had been in general use for several years, its manufacturer, responding to questions about the value of the drug for this use, sponsored a "double blind" clinical trial.[1] Eventually, the research showed that DES was not an effective means of preventing miscarriages, and its widespread use for this purpose ended.

That might have been the end of the story had not physicians begun in the late 1960's to observe a surprising number of adenocarcinomas among teenage girls and young women. Their puzzlement over the growing frequency of this previously rare disease ended in 1971 with the publication in the New England Journal of Medicine of a report showing the correlation between the disease and the ingestion of DES by the patients' mothers early in pregnancy. Once this information was disseminated within the medical community, efforts were begun by physicians

---

1. This is a study design in which neither a patient-subject nor the physician-investigators know whether any particular pill, injection, etc., is the agent being studied or a "control" substance, such as an existing drug or an inert "placebo." Chapter 6 addresses the issues of human experimentation in more detail. [Eds.]

and women's health organizations to ensure that the people at risk (who turned out to include the sons as well as the daughters of DES patients) were made aware of the need to seek appropriate diagnostic and preventative measures. Additionally, many injured persons filed lawsuits against physicians and drug companies. Our interest here, however, is directed at the women who participated in the research on DES.

MINK v. UNIVERSITY OF CHICAGO

United States District Court for the Northern District of Illinois, 1978.
460 F.Supp. 713.

GRADY, DISTRICT JUDGE.

Plaintiffs have brought this action on behalf of themselves and some 1,000 women who were given diethylstilbestrol ("DES") as part of a medical experiment conducted by the defendants, University of Chicago and Eli Lilly & Company, between September 29, 1950, and November 20, 1952. The drug was administered to the plaintiffs during their prenatal care at the University's Lying-In Hospital as part of a double blind study to determine the value of DES in preventing miscarriages. The women were not told they were part of an experiment, nor were they told that the pills administered to them were DES. Plaintiffs claim that as a result of their taking DES, their daughters have developed abnormal cervical cellular formations and are exposed to an increased risk of vaginal or cervical cancer. Plaintiffs also allege that they and their sons have suffered reproductive tract and other abnormalities and have incurred an increased risk of cancer.

The complaint further alleges that the relationship between DES and cancer was known to the medical community as early as 1971, but that the defendants made no effort to notify the plaintiffs of their participation in the DES experiment until late 1975 or 1976 when the University sent letters to the women in the experiment informing them of the possible relationship between the use of DES in pregnant women and abnormal conditions in the genital tracts of their offspring. The letter asked for information to enable the University to contact the sons and daughters of the plaintiffs for medical examination.

The complaint seeks recovery on three causes of action. The first alleges that the defendants committed a series of batteries on the plaintiffs by conducting a medical experiment on them without their knowledge or consent. The administration of DES to the plaintiffs without their consent is alleged to be an "offensive invasion of their persons" which has caused them "severe mental anxiety and emotional distress due to the increased risk to their children of contracting cancer and other abnormalities." The second count is grounded in products liability and seeks to recover damages from defendant Lilly premised on its manufacture of DES as a defective and unreasonably dangerous drug. Finally, the plaintiffs allege that the defendants breached their duty to notify plaintiffs that they had been given DES while pregnant and that children born from that pregnancy should consult a medical specialist. Throughout the complaint plaintiffs claim the defendants intentionally concealed the fact of the experiment and information concerning the relationship between DES and cancer from the plaintiffs.

Both defendants have moved to dismiss the complaint for failure to state a claim. We will deny the motions as to the first cause of action, and grant the motions as to the second and third causes of action.

Battery

We must determine whether the administration of a drug, DES, to the plaintiffs without their knowledge or consent constitutes a battery under Illinois law. The defendants argue that the plaintiffs' first count is really a "lack of informed consent" case premised on negligence. Because the named plaintiffs have not alleged specific physical injury to themselves, the defendants contend they have failed to state a claim for negligence and the count should be dismissed. However, if we find the action to be based on a battery theory, it may stand notwithstanding the lack of an allegation of personal physical injury.

. . .

Illinois courts have adopted the modern approach to true informed consent cases, and have treated them as negligence actions. However, they have not overruled earlier cases which recognize a cause of action in battery for surgery performed without a patient's consent. Pratt v. Davis, 224 Ill. 300, 79 N.E. 562 (1906). Thus, it appears the two separate theories continue to exist in Illinois, and battery may be the proper cause of action in certain situations, for example, where there is a total lack of consent by the patient.

The question thus becomes whether the instant case is more akin to the performance of an unauthorized operation than to the failure to disclose the potential ramifications of an agreed to treatment. We think the situation is closer to the former. The plaintiffs did not consent to DES treatment; they were not even aware that the drug was being administered to them. They were the subjects of an experiment whereby nonemergency treatment was performed upon them without their consent or knowledge.

. . .

Battery is defined as the unauthorized touching of the person of another. To be liable for battery, the defendant must have done some affirmative act, intended to cause an unpermitted contact.

. . .

The administration of DES to the plaintiffs was clearly intentional. It was part of a planned experiment conducted by the defendants. The requisite element of intent is therefore met, since the plaintiffs need show only an intent to bring about the contact; an intent to do harm is not essential to the action.

The act of administering the drug supplies the contact with the plaintiffs' persons. . . . Had the drug been administered by means of a hypodermic needle, the element of physical contact would clearly be sufficient. We believe that causing the patient to physically ingest a pill is indistinguishable in principle.

Finally, there is the question of consent.

. . .

The defendants argue that the plaintiffs consented to treatment when they admitted themselves to the University's Lying-In Hospital for prenatal care. The scope of the plaintiffs' consent is crucial to their ultimate recovery in a battery action. The defendants' privilege is limited at least to acts substantially similar to those to which the plaintiffs consented. If the defendants went beyond the consent given, to perform substantially different acts, they may be liable. The time, place and circumstances will affect the nature of the consent given. . . . These questions, however, are questions of fact which are to be determined by the jury, not by this court on a motion to dismiss. The plaintiffs have alleged sufficient lack of consent to the treatment involved to state a claim for battery against both defendants.

Strict Liability

In their second cause of action, plaintiffs allege that the DES ingested by them was "defective and unreasonably dangerous at the time it was manufactured, and Lilly is therefore strictly liable to the plaintiffs for their damages." . . .

. . .

Clearly, one of the essential elements in a claim for strict liability is physical injury to the plaintiff. The closest the complaint comes to alleging physical injury is the allegation of a "risk" of cancer. . . .

. . .

The plaintiffs argue that they have alleged personal physical injury in paragraph 1, which states that DES "has or may cause reproductive tract and other abnormalities in themselves." There is no indication that any of the named plaintiffs have suffered any of these "abnormalities." Without more concrete allegations of injury to the named plaintiffs, the second count must be dismissed for failure to state a claim.

Failure to Notify

In their third cause of action, plaintiffs assert that the defendants breached their duty to inform plaintiffs and their children of the experiment and of the precautions which the children should take to minimize the risk of contracting cancer. This duty allegedly arose in 1971 when the defendants learned of the relationship between DES and cancer. Plaintiffs claim that defendant Lilly had made no attempt to contact the plaintiff class, and that the notice given by the University in 1975 and 1976 was insufficient to fulfill the obligation because of the delay, and because it failed to advise of the precautions which should be taken by DES children.[9] This failure to notify has allegedly "injured some plaintiffs, increasing the risk of cancer to their children by depriving them of the ability to take the medically recommended precautions, including frequent check-ups."

We agree that both defendants had a duty to notify the plaintiff patients of the risks inherent in DES treatment when they became aware, or should have become aware, of the relationship between DES and cancer. . . . The University's duty to notify is simply an extension of the duty of physicians to warn their patients of the risks inherent in treatment. Canterbury v. Spence, 150 U.S.App.D.C. 263, 464 F.2d 772 (1972), cert. denied, 409 U.S. 1064, 93 S.Ct. 560, 34 L.Ed.2d 518 (1972). The fact the knowledge of the risk was obtained after the patient was treated does not alter the obligation. If the defendant fails to notify the patient when the risk becomes known, he has breached this duty.

Defendant Lilly has a continuing obligation as a manufacturer of drugs to warn of risks inherent in its drugs. . . . [T]o state a claim against

---

9. The plaintiffs also take issue with the University's failure to inform patients that they did not consent to taking DES and therefore might have a legal claim against the defendants. There is no duty in these circumstances to inform potential litigants of possible legal claims. Moreover, each patient should know whether or not she consented to DES treatment.

either defendant, the plaintiffs must allege injury to themselves attributable to the breach of the duty to notify. The required injury differs from that in the previous counts in that this injury must be caused by the delay in notice, or failure to notify the plaintiffs in 1971—for example, aggravation of a prior injury, or increase in damage caused by the failure to seek treatment. However, the only injury alleged by the plaintiffs in this count is the increased risk of cancer to their children. Due to the lack of any allegations of physical injury to the named plaintiffs caused by the defendants' breach of their duty to notify, the third cause of action must be dismissed for failure to state a claim.

[The court rejected defendants' contentions that the actions were barred as a matter of law by the statute of limitations and by the doctrine of charitable immunity. The plaintiffs were permitted to amend the second and third counts of their complaint. The court dismissed the amended complaint, however, ruling that plaintiffs could not recover damages based on their new allegations that many of the women in the experiment were physically injured or have died as a result of ingesting DES, because class representatives must show that they personally, and not merely unidentified members of their class, have suffered an injury.]

NOTE

On February 26, 1982, the district court approved a settlement between the parties in which defendants, without admitting any wrongdoing, paid plaintiffs a lump sum of $225,000 and agreed to provide lifetime treatment of adenocarcinoma without charge to any daughter of a subject in the Chicago DES experiment. The defendants also promised to keep open for five years the free DES clinics they had been operating.

NOTE ON RISK–SPREADING AS A SOCIAL PROBLEM

Is there an irony—or merely an inherent and forseeable problem—in the harm that comes to a few people in research? After all, research often aims at finding ways of reducing life's risks, including those (as in the use of DES to prevent miscarriages) that are imposed by health care itself. Yet in the process, new risks may be generated. In this particular case, the fact that the drug causes serious disease for some of those exposed to it underlines not only the harm they have suffered but also the great importance of the research, which resulted in many times as many people later being saved unnecessary exposure to DES.

Putting aside the additional factor that the women in the Chicago study were not aware that they were research subjects, what is a fair way to adjust the distribution of burdens after-the-fact? Plainly, the tort system may not prove adequate from a victim's viewpoint. Might it also harm society by discouraging important research? While "carefulness" is usually a virtue in legal terms, one commentator is worried that scientists at the University of Chicago and elsewhere "will be more careful in the future, thus increasing the risk that new cancer sources will go undetected." Kinsey, Fate and Lawsuits, 182 The New Republic 20, 25 (June 14, 1980).

At the very least, situations like the *Mink* case—or the harm that occurs to a few, random victims in other activities that benefit society as a whole, like the vaccination program in Cunningham v. Charles Pfizer & Co., Inc. (discussed following Canterbury v. Spence in Ch. 3, Sec. B.1. supra)—serve as reminders that the means used to prevent and to spread risk have developed piecemeal and are far from consistent. Should we try to make arrangements for each new problem as it presents itself or insist on first developing an overall approach?

At one time in history, injuries could be clearly divided into two groups, those caused by a human agency and those attributed to "fate." For the former, redress could be sought through the law (criminal as well as tort law), provided that the person responsible could be identified, as was usually the case. For the latter, the expected response was uncomplaining acceptance of this personal working out of the grand scheme of things—or, perhaps, a search for the personal fault that might explain an "act of God." The world then may not have been a better place to live, but it was surely simpler.

Neither the old paradigms of injury nor the responses they engendered seem to work well today. In particular, tort litigation is in many ways ill suited to assigning responsibility for a large portion of modern injuries. The individual nature of tort cases—often employing a jury—works well when a determination of personal wrongdoing is needed, both to assess the amount the defendant must pay to make the plaintiff whole and also to declare the community's standard of conduct as a warning to individuals in the future. But many injuries arise today which do not seem to have been caused directly by a single individual: numerous separate actions, some by institutions rather than individuals, often widely separated in time and space from the injury, must coincide for an injury to occur. The instrumentalities of harm are like the boy in the rhyme who "shot an arrow in the air, it fell to earth [he] knew not where." The chain of causation and responsibility may become so tangled as to preclude anything other than an arbitrary assignment of liability on the parites seen as best able to bear the costs. Although the growth of nonfault liability in several areas (most notably, for injuries caused by consumer products) has removed the additional burden of trying the issue of negligence, the complex problems of causation still remain.

The collapse of the second part of the ancient paradigm of risk—the uncomplaining acceptance of a divinely ordained fate—is well illustrated in the recent litigation over risks of cancer allegedly imposed by use of DES. It is well nigh impossible for an individual plaintiff in a DES case to prove that *her* vaginal cancer resulted biologically from her mother's having been given DES while the plaintiff was *in utero*. Instead, causation is established as a statistical matter, by showing that it is more probable than not that the injury came from the administration of DES.

To women with other forms of cancer, the compensation of the DES daughters, rather than seeming a great triumph, may appear instead a failure of science and society to establish the cause of *their own* grievous harm and to provide compensation. It does not matter that for many (perhaps even for most), there is no single "cause," in the legal sense of the word as employed in the DES ligitation, but rather a coincidence of factors from genes to workplace environment, from health care to personal habits. What matters is that redress is available to some, while others are told that it is just fate. Yet, as a commentator recently pointed out, it is nonsensical to rule that cancer is a matter of fate only insofar as its cause is unknown.

Any attempt to spread *some* risks has the danger of seeming unfair for failing to spread *all* risks. Risks in the biomedical sphere have posed special problems of late for the existing means of cost-allocation. Although partiality is, thus, always in danger, there may be reasons for special attention to providing compensation for research injuries. . . .

[P]olicymakers in the United States are not alone in considering this problem. In Sweden, insurance coverage has been available since 1975 to provide compensation to subjects injured as a result of participation in biomedical research. Similarly, accident insurance has been available at the University of Leiden (The Netherlands) since 1976 for medical research projects determined by the Committee on Medical Ethics to warrant such coverage. In March 1978, a Royal Commission (the "Pearson Commission") reported to the British Parliament its recommendation that "any volunteer from medical research or clinical trials who suffers severe damage as a result should have a cause of action, on the basis of strict liability, against the authority to whom he has consented to make himself available." Finally, in 1980, a World Health Organization working group to develop international guidelines for human experimentation concluded that "natural justice demands that every subject participating in medical research should have automatic entitlement to reasonable and expeditious compensation for any injury sustained as a result of participation." Proposed guidelines reflecting that conclusion are under consideration by the World Health Organization and the Council for International Organizations of Medical Sciences.

President's Commission, Compensating for Research Injuries 17–19 (1982).

Additional complications arise in dealing with the compensation of victims of vaccine-related injuries because vaccines are manufactured by private companies but vaccination provides a benefit to society at large and may even be required by law. See Jacobsen v. Massachusetts, Ch. 3, Sec. B.2a; see generally Office of Technology Assessment, Compensation for Vaccine-Related Industries, A Technical Memorandum (1980).

PRESIDENT'S COMMISSION FOR THE STUDY OF ETHICAL PROBLEMS IN MEDICINE AND BIOMEDICAL AND BEHAVIORAL RESEARCH, COMPENSATING FOR RESEARCH INJURIES

49–64 (1982).

The basic case for a program of compensation for injured subjects can be stated briefly: Medical and scientific experimentation, even if carefully and cautiously conducted, carries certain inherent dangers. Experimentation has its victims, people who would not have suffered injury and disability were it not for society's desire for the fruits of research. Society does not have the privilege of asking whether this price should be paid; it is being paid. In the absence of a program of compensation of subjects, those who are injured bear both the physical burdens and the associated financial costs. The question of justice is why it should be these persons, rather than others, who are to be expected to absorb the financial, as well as the unavoidable human costs of the societal research enterprise which benefits everyone.

The argument in favor of compensating injured subjects proceeds from a simple rule of thumb for determining the justice of the distribution of burdens and benefits in contexts like that of medical research: those who receive the benefits should be those who undertake the risks. In some medical research, the subjects are patients who volunteer precisely because the experiment offers the greatest chance of cure; prospective benefits outweigh prospective risks and distributive justice is not a major concern. When, however, as is often the case in research with human subjects, those who bear the risks are not the direct beneficiaries of the research, it is felt that the scales of justice are out of balance. . . .

The Argument from Fairness. The ethical norm underlying most of the literature favoring a program of compensation is that of fairness, a key element in the concept of justice. . . .

> If there is a "mutually beneficial scheme of social cooperation," then "a person who has accepted the benefits of the scheme is bound by a duty of fair play to do his part and not to take advantage of the free benefits by not cooperating."

Stated as such, this is a principle of distributive justice: it dictates an assignment of benefits and burdens that is held to be just. This principle is invoked, for example, by moral and political theorists to justify the extraction of taxes from those who may never have signed an actual agreement to contribute to the state's budget. The idea is simply that if one benefits while others take their turns, then one too must take his or her turn. This notion of fairness appeals to an ideal of reciprocity in social relations . . . . In the research context, it is the government, representing the society, which must "take its turn." The research subject has contributed by exposing himself to risks, and the government must do its part.

. . .

The point of the argument from fairness, then, is that the potential beneficiaries of medical research—which includes the entire citizenry—ought not have a "free ride" at the expense of injured research subjects. If the human costs of research are low—say, a matter of a little time and inconvenience—then the allocation of costs is not a serious ethical issue. When, however, higher costs are occasionally imposed, as in the case of injured subjects, the question "Who pays?" becomes important. Research subjects are already doing more than their share, merely by the fact of having volunteered. Those who are injured bear the greatest burden of all. According to this view, certainly, they are the *least* appropriate parties to have to bear the financial costs of injury. Let those costs be shouldered by the potential beneficiaries who have contributed neither time nor health to the research effort. The society ought to meet this expense, through government action if necessary, in order to compensate the injured subjects.

The Gift of Security: Consenting Subjects as Free Agents. There is, however, another view which denies that a failure to compensate injured research subjects is necessarily an injustice. This view attempts to rebut the argument from fairness by stressing the possibility of informed consent to the risk of injury. Professor H. Tristram Engelhardt [has] stated that

> [F]ree and informed consent would seem in most cases equivalent to waiver of any moral basis for a claim to recover for damages. Respect for freedom of the individual would include, so this argument would go, respect for that individual's freedom to choose to risk and suffer the consequences. When a human subject, who is sufficiently informed and who is free to choose, chooses in the absence of coercion to participate in an experiment, it would appear that the subject has given up any strict moral claim to compensation for damages incident to being a subject in an experiment.

The moral principle underlying [such] statements is often given in its Latin formulation: *volenti non fit injuria*—there is no injury (for which another party is responsible) to one who consents. Its application in the research context appears straightforward: the subject is told of the risks; he consents to joining the experiment even though those risks are present, and he has not been promised any compensation. Why, then, would society be obligated to compensate in the case of injury?

The Task Force, after much debate, took a strong stand on this question:

> Informed consent in the research setting functions as a recognition of and a protection for a person's integrity and autonomy, but does not imply a waiver of the right of the person to compensation in the event of injury . . . . Even if a subject perfectly understands a research procedure and agrees to participate in that procedure, the subject's consent does not, in and of itself, include, explicitly or implicitly, a waiver of compensation. [V]olunteers may give informed consent to

participation in biomedical and behavioral research without thereby surrendering the right to be compensated should injury occur.[10]

But if, as the Task Force stated, one ought to respect the autonomy of the potential subject, it is at least initially difficult to understand why there is a moral requirement to compensate a subject who consents to participation without the expectation of compensation in case of injury. If "respect for autonomy" requires the subject's consent to be secured before using him or her as a research subject, why would that same "respect" not also require that the subject be permitted to agree to shoulder the risk of injury without the possibility of compensation?

The Task Force, it must be recalled, was speaking of a consent form (and process) that merely listed the risks and benefits of procedures, together with a statement of certain rights of the patient having nothing to do with compensation. Perhaps it could be said of that consent form, and of the process of obtaining consent which the form records, that the signing and consenting did not amount to an assumption of responsibility for risk. Shortly after the Task Force's report, however, institutions receiving Federal funds for research were told to include an explicit statement on their policy of providing or not providing medical care and other compensation. Thus the consent form became something closer to an explicit assumption of risk. And the forms could be made even clearer on this score—for example, with the addition of a sentence such as: "In signing this form I knowingly and freely assume all risks attendant to the nonnegligent conduct of this experiment and do not expect, and will not seek to hold others liable for, compensation in case of injury not resulting from negligence." In this latter instance, if not at present, it is difficult to understand a contention that the subject's consent did not entail an assumption of risk.

Thus, there would seem to be an inconsistency in a position that would allow a subject of medical research to volunteer his or her time and comfort but not to assume the risk of possible injury. When the subject agrees to participate in an experiment, he or she voluntarily makes a gift to society of the time and inconvenience involved in participation, and agrees to bear any discomfort, which may be quite substantial. In some cases, subjects are paid for their time and trouble, but often they are not. One does not think that unless they are paid a sum proportional to their contribution, they have been treated unjustly. Indeed, subjects who are not paid may be especially admired. Their participation in the research is simply accepted as a gift.

A subject is, moreover, in a position to give still another gift. This is the gift of security, the assumption of the risk of injury without guarantee of compensation. Some potential subjects might be willing to give only the gift of their time and trouble, but others are willing to give not only that gift but also the gift of security. Why should it be considered unjust to accept the second gift if it is perfectly ethical to accept the first?

Whereas the Task Force asked whether volunteers must be compensated, the "free agent" view asks whether the government should be considered unjust if it refuses to accept volunteers who are unwilling to make the additional gift of their security. . . .

10. HEW Secretary's Task Force on the Compensation of Injured Research Subjects, Report, U.S. Department of Health, Education, and Welfare, Washington (1977) (hereinafter cited as Task Force Report) at VI-4, 5, 6.

Fairness vs. Consent.   . . .

Which of these two perspectives ought to be adopted in the case of research-related injuries?   . . .

. . .

Several serious reservations about the consent that is obtained from subjects make the latter view less convincing to the Commission.   First, the consent argument's appeal to the notion of a gift freely offered would be strongest if the research subject were offered at the time he or she agreed to participate the alternatives of either having or not having compensation available should injury result.   If subjects then reject the promise of compensation, they would appear to wish to donate both their time and their security.   But in the absence of such an offer of future compensation, one cannot conclude that the consent of subjects who wish to aid research indicates their desire to make the additional gift of their security. Moreover, if injured subjects would accept compensation were it offered, then it would appear that they did not wish to make the gift of their security.   This is not to say that consent could not be valid without an offer of compensation, but it does suggest that an element of capitalizing on subjects' desire to help science may sometimes occur.

Many subjects will have an altruistic desire to aid research by offering their time, together with a personal desire not to put their security at risk. If the research investigator and the government can afford to offer compensation for injury, but refuse to do so knowing that they will still obtain volunteers, they thereby exploit the altruistic motivation of volunteers: when a subject gives the willing gift of his or her time, the unwilling gift of his or her security is extracted as well.   If exploitation is a form of unfair taking advantage of another, then the government or researcher may act unfairly in asking for volunteers while refusing them the possibility of compensation for injury.

In particular cases, there may be no ground for concern over the moral sufficiency of consent—for example, when an intelligent, financially secure, educated adult agrees to undertake a small, accurately estimated risk of a minor harm of known character.   But rules concerning compensation of subjects will not, as a practical matter, be able to distinguish these simple cases from the more difficult ones and the conditions of less-than-ideal consent are present often enough that the difficulties should be taken into account in formulating policy.

In many experiments, the risks are not well known.   A treatment may be so new that the pattern of adverse reactions or side effects has not been established, nor will it be possible to determine whether a given subject is at especially high risk for these harms.   Remote risks of serious harms are especially likely to attend experimental procedures.   Consent in such cases is necessarily somewhat blind, and true appreciation of risk is doubtful, even for ideally competent subjects.   Further, there is accumulating evidence that people do not perform well in calculating the expected utilities of events with small probabilities of occurrence.   Events of different orders of magnitude of probability may be given the single rating of "unlikely."   Assigning full responsibility to the subject for assumption of remote, but serious, risks of research thus takes on the air of exploitation of known weaknesses.

. . .

To these difficulties may be added a host of standard complaints about the consent process.   . . .

It can be presumed that under the current regulatory system, consent to treatment in most research involving human subjects meets the standards upon which society insists for valid transactions in other contexts, such as commerce. Indeed, the knowledge, competence, and independence of the contracting parties in society generally are seldom scrutinized as closely as are those qualities of potential subjects in biomedical research. Nevertheless, it is fitting to use a higher moral standard in the research context. The goals of human health and well-being that motivate research ought to be reflected as well in a higher moral standard than the *caveat emptor* of the marketplace.

In addition to arguments based upon justice, there are at least two other moral grounds for a program of compensation.

Appropriate Regard for Patient-Subjects' Well-Being. Justice is not the only standard of morality. There are acts, or failures to act, that are surely wrong even though they violate no one's rights and are not instances of injustice. Acts can be mean-spirited, selfish, cheap, irresponsible, though they comply with the rules of conduct required by justice.

Ordinary English does not provide a precise vocabulary in which to distinguish these sorts of wrongs, nor does moral theory itself speak with one voice—in part because the classifications are matters of substance as well as semantics. Still, it is worthwhile to make a rough distinction between considerations of justice and other, still important, moral considerations. As regards the present subject, the most important such consideration would be the distress of anyone injured in the course of research who was faced with large medical bills and loss of income due to research-related disability. Such instances of need suggest the simplest of all arguments for a program of compensation: the serious need of those few injured in research can be met without untoward expense or difficulty by a program administered through research institutions. If, as Henry Beecher wrote, medical experimentation must be "ethical in its inception," then, one may add, it must also be ethical in its consequences. A program of compensation for research-related injuries would help to ensure that the consequences of research would be good ones rather than bad. In this view, not to adopt such a program would be a selfish and cheap or even irresponsible disregard of patient-subjects' well-being.

Of course, this argument is unduly simple. The claim advanced is not in itself sufficient to establish the rightness of enacting a compensation program, although it *may* lend support to a decision that rests on a stronger moral claim. But it depends on showing that a serious need of injured subjects can be met without imposing disproportionate burdens on others. One is, after all, not considered irresponsible for failing to do something heroic, only for failing to meet a great need without great cost to oneself.

Public Conceptions of Justice. Although the moral sensibilities of the public on this issue are not known, there are certain indirect indications that lack of compensation of injured subjects is, or would be, seen as wrong. . . .

Thus, whether or not the moral argument in favor of an obligation to compensate is compelling, many members of the public subscribe to it. Even those who are not themselves convinced that failing to compensate injured subjects is a true injustice may not wish to see their government involved in an action that has even the appearance of an injustice.

. . .

Research on human subjects, if done as part of a broad attack on disease, is of necessity risk-laden. The public, if it is to support this enterprise, must find the human costs tolerable. It will be more likely to do so if the costs are widely shared through a program of compensation of subjects who are injured in research. The moral importance of medical research—a value worthy of respect and protection—thus adds weight to a conclusion in favor of compensation for research injuries.

Obligations to Subjects in Therapeutic Research

A crucial issue is whether compensation is owed to all subjects whose medical condition worsens in some respect in the course of research. The ethical arguments already developed are premised upon some notion of sacrifice, of giving a benefit to the whole. This situation is met most clearly by subjects in "nontherapeutic research" who undergo procedures unconnected with their own condition (indeed, they are often "normal volunteers").

At first sight, "therapeutic research"—that is, an experiment designed to gain generalizable knowledge about a medical intervention by employing it under controlled conditions with a group of patient-subjects— would appear to be disqualified ethically because participating subjects may be seeking benefit for themselves as patients rather than being solely vessels through which knowledge can flow to others. This view would treat therapeutic research as an example of ordinary (albeit innovative) therapy for purposes of compensation; patients who become subjects are seen as taking no greater risk than they would otherwise face in dealing with their illness.

The distinction between therapeutic research and innovative therapy is a narrow one. In innovative therapy, a physician is simply trying something new to benefit the patient often because existing remedies have failed. In therapeutic research, a physician-investigator follows a research protocol in order to produce generalizable knowledge through testing out a medical intervention that, it is hoped, may be of benefit. This goal creates at least a potential conflict of interest on the part of the physician-investigator, over and above any hazards inherent in the particular study design. Each patient who is also a research subject is exposed to the possibility that the procedures most conducive to his recovery will be altered so that the research program can best be carried out (for example, that random assignment will remove the possibility of access to certain procedures). The patient could avoid this jeopardy by seeking the innovative therapy outside of the research context, where this is available. Where the patient instead decides to become the subject of therapeutic research, he or she makes a gift (however slight) of some of his or her security to the larger society.

Moreover, some therapeutic research will not offer a patient his or her best chance for recovery. It is, furthermore, quite common for therapeutic experiments to involve procedures, especially tests, that are performed only for scientific reasons. In all of these cases, the medical intervention being studied may be intended to be "therapeutic" for the patient-subject, but compensation for injuries would rest on the same footing as for nontherapeutic research: the patient is making a contribution to society.

Conclusions

A program of compensating for research injuries will help to equalize the burdens of progress in this field that would otherwise fall very unevenly on people. Competing conceptions of justice lead to contrary conclusions about whether justice requires that such a program be adopted. Fairness argues for compensation, but the alternative argument from the consent of free agents denies this. Although, for both philosophical and practical reasons, it is not persuaded by the latter argument, the Commission does not hold that compensation is a basic right (such as the right to a fair trial), to be provided regardless of cost, practicality, or other policy considerations. The arguments for compensation of injured subjects on fairness grounds simply do not establish so strict an obligation.

Several additional considerations add weight to the arguments for compensation beyond the notion of fairness, both in ethical theory and in the public perception of the government's stance. First, the moral claims of charity and generosity ought not to be ignored—although the obligations they create have inherent limits, for one is not judged wrong in failing to be heroic. Second, the frailties of the consent process, especially with regard to small risks of serious harm, weigh heavily as a reason for added "protection" in the form of after-the-fact recompense at least for any serious harms experienced by subjects.

The Commission concludes that compensation of injured subjects is appropriate to the research enterprise. . . .

b. Open-Air Nuclear Testing

It is not only medical research that generates uneven risks. Scientific and technological activities that can be justified on a risk-benefit basis may nonetheless cause severe harm to a few people. The issue of who should bear the cost of such risk is illustrated in a class action suit brought under the Federal Tort Claims Act (FTCA) for injuries allegedly suffered as a result of the federal government's open-air testing of nuclear weapons in Nevada between 1951 and 1962.

In Allen v. United States, 527 F.Supp. 476 (C.D.Utah 1981) (*Allen I*), the court denied the government's motion to dismiss based on the discretionary function exception to the FTCA, 28 U.S.C. § 2680(a), and declined to hear further evidence on the discretionary issue prior to a full trial on the merits. At trial, Allen v. United States, No. C–79–0515, C.D. Utah (*Allen II*), the government contended that international events at the time of tests, especially the acquisition of nuclear weapons by the Soviet Union, made continental testing of nuclear weapons necessary for national defense. The choice of the Nevada site, based on extensive studies conducted by the Atomic Energy Commission and the Department of Defense, was made by the President for reasons of national need, and hence the suit should be barred by § 2680(a).

The plaintiffs argued that they were not attacking the validity of the President's decision itself, but rather the government's failure to carry it out in a non-negligent manner. Their major contention was that the government failed to take adequate precautionary measures to protect the residents from the dangers of exposure to fallout. The government pointed to the absence of clear proof that anyone was injured by the tests, and argued that even if some few people were injured, the federal government cannot be held liable.

Should the court accept the government's arguments, the effect would be to place the costs of weapons testing primarily on the victims rather than to spread them among all taxpayers. As the court in *Allen I* noted:

> Considering initially the injured party, the court should review the nature of the loss imposed by the governmental injury. The more serious, in terms of physical or mental impairment, and isolated the loss the closer the question becomes as to whether the individual can be expected to absorb the loss as incident to an acceptable social or political risk of governmental activities . . . . The interests of the injured party are of particular concern, according to *Payton* [v. United States, 636 F.2d 132 (5th Cir.1981)] because 'the spread of monetary losses among the taxpayers is the principal concern' of the Federal Tort Claims Act.

527 F.Supp. at 482.

The *Allen* case also serves as a reminder of the difficulties the traditional tort system has when faced with litigation of this sort. The major difficulty arises from the requirement that plaintiffs prove that defendants' wrongful conduct was the proximate cause of their injuries. Radiation cases, like most other "toxic torts," are characterized by a long latency period between exposure and significant signs of disease. Consequently, the existence (or the lack) of causation must be determined through dosimetry, a method of measuring the amount of radiation emitted from a given source. In a case such as *Allen*, this dose rate must then be translated into an exposure rate for persons in the vicinity of the fallout (i.e., the translation of data on a substance's *toxicity* into particular *risk* data). The amount of radiation present in a cloud of fallout must be measured as it moves away from the blast site, and then modified by many factors to yield the amount of radiation received by each individual (whether he or she was indoors or outdoors, the type of clothing worn, his or her food and water supply during the exposure period, and so forth).

The government did keep records of the radiation exposure as the fallout clouds traveled away from the test area. At trial the government contended that these records demonstrate that none of the plaintiffs were exposed to levels of radiation which were considered dangerous at the time of the test, while the plaintiffs attempted to establish that the government's tests were wholly inadequate and could not be relied on to determine the levels each of the plaintiffs had been exposed to. To complicate matters further, it is not at all clear today just what amount of low-level radiation is harmful to humans.

In 1980, an Interagency Task Force on the Health Effects of Ionizing Radiation conducted a study on the alternatives to the tort system in dealing with radiation problems. The task force looked at the possibility of maintaining the present system of tort litigation based on the FTCA, legislatively modifying the FTCA to remove the issues of negligence and causation, or establishing an administrative program that would serve to compensate the victims. The Task Force concluded that, although an administrative compensation program has disadvantages,

> it may well be the best mechanism for addressing the health issues arising from the atmospheric weapons testing program. Such a remedy could include eligibility criteria which would reflect current and future scientific knowledge of radiation effects, while at the same time providing a reasonable level of benefits. Further, given the nature of

the illness, and the underlying national security reasons for the nuclear tests, resolution of the claims in a non-adversial context is very much in the public interest. Finally, since veterans and federal employees exposed to radiation from atmospheric tests presently have an administrative forum for resolution of their injury claims, the establishment of the suggested program would place the downwind residents in a position of substantial parity.

Report of the Interagency Task Force on Compensation for Radiation-Related Illness 56 (Feb. 1980).

Failures in the existing means of redressing injuries caused by such environmental health hazards as asbestos (discussed in more detail in Ch. 3, Sec. B.3, supra), Agent Orange, and radiation can be traced to several sources. First, individual causation is difficult to fit within usual tort rules; second, corporate defendants may be financially unable to provide adequate compensation; and third, the expansion of strict liability in tort law increases the perceived injustice if large numbers of injured people go without redress. Yet the pressure to substitute the federal government as the source of compensation through nonfault, administrative mechanisms has also caused concern in some quarters. One analysis by the Department of Labor, for example, shows potential outlays of up to $500 billion over the next 30 years for toxic injuries to people, with potential annual expenditures as high as $30 billion per year by 2015.

2. DISTRIBUTING SPECIAL BENEFITS

a. Access to Medical Care

CAMPBELL v. MINCEY

United States District Court for the Northern District of Mississippi, 1975.
413 F.Supp. 16.

(The opinion is set forth in Ch. 3, Sec. A.5b, supra).

CHARLES FRIED,
EQUALITY AND RIGHTS IN MEDICAL CARE

6 Hastings Center Report 29–34 (February 1976).

The notion of some kind of a right to health care is not likely to be found in any but the most recent writings, not to mention legislation. After all, even the much more well-established institution of free, universal public education has not achieved the status of a federal constitutional right, is not a constitutional right by the law of many states, and stands as a right more as an inference from the practices and legislation of states, counties, and municipalities. The federal constitutional litigation regarding rights in that area has been restricted to the provision *equally* of whatever public education is in fact provided. So it should not be surprising that the notion of a right to health care is something of a novelty. Moreover, it is only fairly recently that health care could deliver a product which was as unambiguously beneficial as elementary schooling. Nevertheless, if one looks to the laws, practices, and understandings of states, counties, and municipalities, one sees growing up through the last century, and certainly in the twentieth century, an understanding which might be thought of as the inchoate recognition of a right to health care. . . .

. . .

[S]omething should be said by way of at least informal definition of [the] term "right." A right is more than just an interest that an individual might have, a state of affairs or a state of being which an individual might prefer. A claim of right invokes entitlements; and when we speak of entitlements, we mean not those things which it would be nice for people to have, or which they would prefer to have, but which they must have, and which if they do not have they may demand, whether we like it or not. Although I would not want to say that a right is something we must recognize "no matter what," nevertheless a right is something we must accord unless _____ and what we put in to fill in the unless clause should be tightly confined and specific.

This notion of rights has interesting and not altogether obvious relations to the concept of equality, and confusions about those relations are very likely to lead to confused arguments about the very area before us—rights to health care and equality in respect to health care.

First, it should be noted that equality itself may be considered a right. Thus, a person can argue that he is not necessarily entitled to any particular thing—whether it be income, or housing, or education, or health care—but that he is entitled to equality in respect to that thing, so that whatever anyone gets he should get, too. And this is a nice example of my previous proposition about the notion of rights generally. For to recognize a right to equality may very well be—I suppose it often is—contrary to many other policies that we may have, and particularly contrary to attempts to attain some kind of efficiency. Yet, by the very notion of rights, if there is a right to equality, then granting equality cannot depend on whether or not it is efficient to do so.

Second, there is the relation between rights and equality which runs the other way, too: to say that a class of persons, or all persons, have a certain right implies that they all have that right equally. If it is said that all persons within the jurisdiction of the United States have a constitutionally protected right to freedom of speech, whatever that may mean, one thing seems clear: that this right should not depend on what it is one wants to say, who one is, and the like. Indeed, if the government against whom this right is protected were to make such distinctions, for instance, subjecting to constraints the speech of "irresponsible persons," that would be the exact concept of denial of freedom of speech to those persons.

. . .

Now this analogy is offered as more than a distant irrelevance. Is it not very similar to many things that are said in the area of health? For analogous to the claim that the right to freedom of speech really implies a right to be heard by the multitude, is the notion that whatever rights might exist in respect to health care are rights to health, rather than to health *care*. And of course the claim is equally absurd in both instances. We may sensibly guarantee that all will be equally free of constraints on the speaking they wish to do, but we should not guarantee that all will be equally effective in getting their views across. Similarly, we may or may not choose to guarantee all equality of access to health care, but we cannot possibly guarantee to all equality of health.

. . .

[I]f we commit ourselves to the notion that there is a right to whatever health care might be available, we do indeed get ourselves into a difficult situation where overall national expenditure on health must reach absurd proportions—absurd in the sense that far more is devoted to health at the expense of other important social goals than the population in general wants. Indeed, more is devoted to health than the population wants relative not only to important social goals—for example, education or housing—but relative to all the other things which people would like to have money left over to pay for. And if we recognize that it would be absurd to commit our society to devote more than a certain proportion of our national income to health, while at the same time recognizing a "right to health care," we might then be caught on the other horn of the dilemma. For we might then be required to say that because a right to health care implies a right to equality of health care, then we must limit, we must lower the quality of the health care that might be purchased by some lest our commitment to equality require us to provide such care to all and thus carry us over a reasonable budget limit.

. . .

Now it might be said that I am exaggerating. The case put forward is the British National Health Service, which is alleged to provide a model of high level care at reasonable costs with equality for all. But I would caution planners and enthusiasts from drawing too much from this example. The situation in Great Britain is very different in many ways. The country is smaller and more homogeneous. Moreover, even in Great Britain there are disparities between the care available between urban and rural areas; there are long waits for so-called "elective procedures"; and there is a small but significant and distinguished private sector outside of National Health which is the focus of great controversy and rancor. Finally, Great Britain is a country where a substantial portion of the citizenry is committed to the socialist ideal of equalizing incomes and nationalizing the provisions of all vital services. Surely this is a very different situation from that in the United States. . . .

. . .

[I]s health care so special? Is it different from education, housing, food, legal assistance? In respect to all of these things, we recognize in our society a right whose enjoyment may not be made wholly dependent upon the ability to pay. But just as surely in respect to all these things, we do not believe that this right entails equality of enjoyment, so that whatever diet one person or class of persons enjoys must be enjoyed by all. . . . Rather, in all of these areas—education, housing, food, legal assistance—there obtains a notion of a decent, fair standard, such that when this standard is satisfied all that exists in the way of *rights* has been accorded. And it is necessarily so; were we to insist on equality all the way up, that is, past this minimum, we would have committed ourselves to a political philosophy which I take it is not the dominant one in our society.

. . . The real task before us is not, therefore, I think, to explain why there must be complete equality in medicine, but the more subtle and perilous task of determining the decent minimum in respect to health which accords with sound ethical judgments, while maintaining the virtues of freedom, variety, and flexibility which are thought to flow from a mixed system such as ours. The decent minimum should reflect some conception of what constitutes tolerable life prospects in general. It should speak quite strongly to things like maternal health and child health, which set the terms under which individuals will compete and develop. On the other hand, techniques which will offer some remote relief from conditions that rarely strike in the prime of life, and which strike late in the life because something must, might be thought of as too esoteric to be part of the concept of minimum decent care.

On the other hand, the notion of a decent minimum should include humane and, I would say, worthy surroundings of care for those whom we know we are not going to be able to treat. Here, it seems to me, the emphasis on technology and the attention of highly trained specialists is seriously mistaken. Not only is it unrealistic to imagine that such fancy services can be provided for everyone "as a right," but there is serious doubt whether these kinds of services are what most people really want or can benefit from.

In the end, I will concede very readily that the notion of minimum health care, which it does make sense for our society to recognize as a right, is itself an unstable and changing notion. As my initial historical remarks must have suggested, the concept of a decent minimum is always relative to what is available over all, and what the best which is available might be. I suppose that if we allowed an artificial heart to be developed under private auspices and to be available only to those who could pay for it, or who could obtain it from specialized eleemosynary institutions, then the time might well come when it would have been so perfected that it would be a reasonable component of what one would consider minimum decent care. And the process of arriving at this new situation would be a process imbued with struggle and political controversy. But since I do not believe in utopias or final solutions, a resolution of the problem of the right to health care having these kinds of tensions within it neither worries me nor leads me to suspect that I am on the wrong track. To my mind, the right track consists in identifying what it is that health care can and cannot provide, in identifying also the cost of health care, and then in deciding how much of this health care, what level of health care, we are ready to underwrite as a floor for our citizenry.

. . .

ROBERT M. VEATCH, WHAT IS A "JUST" HEALTH CARE DELIVERY?

in Ethics and Health Policy
131–142 (Veatch and Branson, eds 1976).

The Utilitarian Theory of a Just Health Care Delivery

At first it seems reasonable to distribute health care so as to maximize the health of the society. The goal should be to improve the major social measures of health—infant mortality, average life expectancy, days of hospitalization, days of morbidity by disease—as much as possible. This is a health application of classical utilitarianism. According to the utilitarian position, the objective is to increase the net good in society to the greatest possible amount without regard to how that good is distributed except insofar as the distribution itself contributes to the total amount of good (through decreasing marginal utility or decreasing social unrest).

. . . . The argument that utilitarian theory cannot account for our sense of justice is an old one. Suppose that in some hypothetical society the National Health Planning Council was considering ways of improving the health of the nation's citizens. Suppose also that the professional staff for the council had gathered data and made computer projections and had reached the conclusion that one particular plan would most improve the aggregate health indicators for the nation. It was the case in this society that one small group could be identified as having multiple chronic diseases consuming huge amounts of health resources. These individuals tended to be lower class, of low intelligence, and often brain damaged, so that health instruction had little usefulness. The proposed plan is to identify this group, amounting to 0.1 percent of the population, and ban them from the health care delivery system. The computers indicated that even though this would lower life expectancy for this particular group, it would in aggregate increase not only average life expectancy, but also all the other measures of health.

A second part of the plan would be the identification of the healthiest 10 percent of the population. This group would be encouraged to double their reproduction. Since their contribution to the health statistics would increase, all of the averages would improve.

The utilitarian theory of a just health care delivery would support the plan. In fact, since the sickest in the population would soon die off, morbidity (as opposed to mortality) would be directly improved.

Now utilitarian members of the National Health Planning Council may object. They may point out that the harm of death is critical and must be added to the calculation of goods and harms. Nonhealth harms also might have to be taken into account, such as social malaise or rebellion of the relatives of the sickest ones. It is not logical, however, that the feelings of social guilt would be one such harm, because one would not or should not feel guilty about doing what morality requires. Put more cautiously, the utilitarian should feel even more guilty if he fails to exclude the sickest, because he is consciously choosing to avoid producing the greatest good for the greatest number. One cannot appeal to nonconsequentialist feelings of justice, since those are ruled out by definition in the theory being advocated.

These additional harms would indeed increase the burden of the professional staff of the council—provided they conceded that nonhealth harms could be traded off against health goods. New computer projections, however, might add in these nonhealth harms. It is conceivable that even after these are added in, the banning of the one in a thousand still turns out to be utility maximizing.

It is the conclusion of nonutilitarians—and I would include myself—that such an outcome would not in itself be sufficient to justify the plan. Furthermore, even if it were the case that adding in enough social harms would always reveal that those policies we find morally objectionable were also not utility maximizing, it does not follow that they are morally wrong because they are not utility maximizing. It could be that they are not utility maximizing because they are wrong (and therefore generate guilt, which is a disutility).

I am convinced the plan of banning the sick is wrong because it is unjust. I am much more convinced that it is wrong than I am convinced of its disutility. In fact, since utility calculations in an area as complex as health care are so intricate, we should always be very uncertain of our judgments—much more uncertain than we actually are—if we based them on the utilitarian theory of a just health care delivery.

The Egalitarian Theory of a Just Health Care Delivery

I propose as an alternative to utilitarianism an egalitarian theory of a just health care delivery. An egalitarian theory of justice is . . . based on the premise that, at least insofar as health goes, every human being has an equal claim. Since it is health care we are trying to distribute we can formulate the principle as follows: (1) Everyone has a claim to the amount of health care needed to provide a level of health equal to other persons' health.

This sounds much like the first principle (that justice requires that everyone get the resources needed to be healthy). In this form, however, it [is] recognized that healthiness as a goal can generate infinite demands so the egalitarian dimension is made more explicit: those whose health is worst are entitled to enough health care to get them as healthy as others. We would target our efforts on the sickest.

. . .

[P]rinciple (1) . . . sounds rather similar to Outka's.* Beginning with the formal principle that justice requires similar treatment for similar cases, Outka maintains that this leads to the substantive principle that access to health care should be equal for people with similar categories of illness. However, he recognizes a fundamental problem with the formula of this type. To return to our [first] formula, if everyone has a claim to the amount of health care needed to provide a level of health equal to other persons' health, the system will collapse as soon as the person most in need of health care is in need because he has a condition that cannot be treated. If health care is distributed strictly in proportion with ill health, . . . a group of the incurably sick who are the most ill must end up with *all* the medical resources. This is certainly inefficient. Furthermore, if they do not benefit from the commitment of resources, it is hard to see why it is just that they get those resources. Outka apparently recognized that and thus allows for discrimination according to categories of illness. In doing so, however, his formula of treating similar categories of illness similarly could justify the National Health Planning Council's scheme to ban the 0.1 percent with serious multiple illnesses. Similar cases are treated similarly, but the priority for the neediest can be lost.

A modification might be to recognize that the neediest have a just claim only when something fruitful can come from the resource commitment. Thus: (2) Everyone has a claim to the amount of health care needed to provide a level of health equal, insofar as possible, to other persons' health. This principle still will have to be both clarified and modified, but that is the principle in its stark form.

Another qualification is to shift from the duty to actually produce equal health (as far as possible) to a duty to provide an opportunity of equal health. One should not be required to improve his health (if, for instance, he prefers to abjure exercise or proper diet), and justice does not demand that we impose health care or that we provide repeated treatments because an individual does not take advantage of treatments rendered. Thus: (3) Justice requires everyone has a claim to health care

* See Gene Outka, Social Justice and
Equal Access to Health Care, 1 J. of Relig.
Ethics 23 (1974) [Eds.]

needed to provide an opportunity for a level of health equal, as far as possible, to other persons' health.

. . .

The Least Well Off: Generally and Medically

The principle that justice requires that everyone has a claim to the amount of health care needed to provide an opportunity for a level of health equal, as far as possible, to the health of other persons produces a priority for health care for the sickest insofar as health care can improve their health, qualified by individual freedom to reject that health care if it is not desired. This forces us to deal with the question why the medically least well off ought to be the focus of our distribution principle rather than the generally least well off. . . .

. . . The question is, Why should the wealthy, even the sick wealthy, be included in a health care program at all?

Two answers seem appropriate. First, it could be argued that health is a prior requirement for receipt of any other goods. Rawls has argued that liberty is such a good. One cannot trade off liberty for other goods, because liberty by its very nature is required for enjoyment of the others. Health is, in some ways, like liberty. Certainly death-preventing medical care is like liberty in this respect. However, other forms of health care are not always prior in this way. I think it is meaningful to say that one is generally well off or well off on balance though sick, while it is not meaningful to say that with regard to either death or lack of liberty. Thus it appears that some kinds of health care could receive an absolute priority, taking them out of the general calculation of goods, but by itself is not an altogether convincing argument for separating all health care allocation from the general allocation of goods.

Another argument is a more pragmatic one. While I am not convinced that all with a particular illness, in principle, have an equal claim to health care at government expense without regard to their general financial means, I am convinced that adopting a practice of behaving as if they *did* have an equal claim will serve the interests of the generally least well off as well as the medically least well off, and may promote equality as well. . . .

. . . First, to support the policy of giving funds to the generally least well off one has to be convinced that distribution of a more generalized medium (money) would really be the policy adopted as an alternative. There is strong reason to believe that that is not the case. It is dangerous to assume that if a national health program is not adopted the funds saved will be allocated so as to be more beneficial to the generally least well off. The generally least well off should take what they can get, even if it also benefits those who are not generally least well off. . . .

[Second, there] is reason to believe that having the more wealthy included in the same health system as the poor directly benefits the health care given to the poor. There are at least two ways the poor might benefit from including the wealthy. First, some goods are what might be called social or collective goods. They are not readily divisible. Some practices count as good if, and only if, a critical mass of people participate in the practice. The good of voting or of not walking on the grass accrues only if a critical mass join in the practice. Not everyone need participate, but a large number must. Those who do not will be "free riders." Society can tolerate a certain number of these free riders, but when the critical threshold is crossed, it is not simply the free riders who lose, it is everyone.   Some elements of a national health care program may be social or collective goods of this type.   Support for health research, for complex equipment, and for highly specialized skilled workers requires a large base of support.   If the mass of the middle class were excluded it is quite possible there would not be sufficient support for the social good to result.

This is not the only, or even the primary, way that the poor will benefit by the participation of the relatively wealthy in a national health care program.   If those in powerful places must participate in the same health care system as those least well off, the quality of that system may improve not because it adds a critical mass, but because it adds a group with sufficient power to make sure that the care is of high quality and that the patient is treated with respect and dignity.   .   .   .

Merit

One historically significant qualifier of the egalitarian principle of distribution is merit.   Merit (or some modification of it) can, in principle, be a legitimate qualifier to the egalitarian principle that everyone should have an equal claim to health care sufficient to provide an opportunity to achieve a level of health equal, as far as possible, to other persons'.   Consider two individuals (say identical twins) who have had equal genetic and environmental opportunities.   Both open small grocery stores, but one works diligently, putting in a sixteen-hour day for twenty years, while the other is slothful, working short days and squandering his resources.   It seems to me to be fair (or just) that the first brother has more accumulated goods at the end of the twenty years (even if the memories of experiences may possibly have been richer for the slothful brother).

In principle, justice requires taking into account effort or merit as a consideration of a fair or just distribution of health care.   At the same time, I see the gravest danger in including effort or merit as a qualifier of a principle for just distribution of health care.   ("Merit" is a confusing term because it seems to include not only the subjective component of effort, but also native abilities as well.   "Diligence" or "effort" seems to me to generate the stronger claim.)   It seems almost impossible to separate merit or effort from class privilege, inherited wealth and skills, and the social and value biases of those who would be doing the classifying. The error rate in ranking on the basis of effort or merit would seem to be extremely great.   Furthermore, the enterprise of ranking individuals on the basis of merit or effort is itself potentially malicious and degrading. Qualifying the egalitarian distribution principle for merit or effort could be justified for some practices in some forms of social organization. However, we are talking about a national policy on the distribution of health care.   The dangers appear so great that, with one qualification, any such effort ought to be abandoned.

That one exception is the case of health need resulting from what is seen as a voluntary decision to take a health risk to engage in behavior that is not worthy of public subsidy, such as professional automobile racing, alcohol consumption, smoking, and recreational stunt flying.   All are presumed to be voluntary behavior and are thus radically different from health needs as they are normally conceptualized.   (If alcoholism were judged a nonvoluntary genetically or psychiatrically determined "disease," it would be excluded from the list.)   Furthermore, all are generally not considered activities worthy of public subsidy. This separates them from professional fire fighting, which is voluntary behavior but worthy of subsidy.

Even if these voluntary health-risky behaviors not worthy of public support are thought to generate a lower claim for just health care allocation, humaneness still requires including treatment for such conditions in a national health system. The source of funding for such care, however, might be radically different because of the nature of the medical condition. I have elsewhere supported the view that while all such conditions should be covered by national health insurance, the behaviors should be taxed, where possible, in an amount that would equal the projected costs of the medical treatment.

Compensatory Justice

. . . Do we have a special obligation of justice to provide health care to those who are sick because of previous social wrongs over and above the obligation to distribute health care on the basis of equality for opportunities for health? Of course, those who have suffered significant social wrongs will often rank high solely on this criterion of need, but is there an additional claim for those whose need derives from previous social harms? In general there is. The duty to provide compensatory justice is a legitimate modifier of the general principle of egalitarian justice. I am not persuaded, however, that the compensatory justice qualifier ought to have significant bearing on the general egalitarian principle for purposes of health care distribution. The question is once again a pragmatic one. If we assume that health need alone will tend to identify those who have suffered previous social wrong, we must compare the justice resulting from the established preference for health care to the wronged group with the risks of singling that group out for an additional priority. I see a great danger in singling out any group for special health care on any basis other than ability to meet medical need. Creating a special class will once again create a two-class health system, with all of the risks involved. . . .

Which Diseases Have Priority?

The thrust of the entire argument has been toward the position that priority go to the diseases or disease combinations that create the most hardship or suffering—to those which make one medically the least well off. The medically worst off have a complete claim of justice on health care resources in order to bring them, as far as possible, up to the level of health of others. This is strikingly different from the usual criteria of distribution in most of the national health insurance proposals, which for the most part focus heavily not on the nature of the diseases or medical conditions but on absolute limits on health care consumption in dollars or days or, in the case of catastrophic illness proposals, the size of the medical bill. . . .

The task of ranking diseases from worst to most benign is rather repulsive as well as gargantuan. Fortunately much of the ranking is unnecessary. We have the capacity to provide available health care necessary to improve the health, insofar as possible of the medically least well off. In fact we can probably work our way up the list of the worst diseases before the question of limits is even raised—if we approach the allocation of health care from this medical egalitarian perspective. Furthermore, we probably can agree on some medical conditions that impose (or ought to impose) so slight a burden that they should not be included in any national health program at this point in history. Alopecia (baldness), most cosmetic surgery, and personal attendance by a physician-traveling companion for general reasons of health safety are examples. The use of certain futuristic biomedical technologies for the satisfaction of medical tastes such as *in vitro* fertilization, prenatal sex selection, or electrical stimulation of the brain's "pleasure centers" might be others.

The real difficulties come in a fairly narrow range. We may not be sure whether patients claiming a need for hemodialysis, semiannual or annual physical examinations, nuclear-powered artificial hearts, dental prostheses, experimental treatments of the aging process, or psychoanalysis have the greatest medical need. If our task is to identify those most in need of health care we need not choose between penicillin for pneumonia and insulin for the diabetic. Certainly both qualify. Only when we get to the borders of our capacity to provide health care does the problem arise. Here the egalitarian claim is that, difficult though it may be, we must include those conditions which constitute the greatest assault on one's health—however that may be defined. The answer will clearly require an understanding of the human norms of healthiness, something requiring arduous philosophical reflection. This, however, is the appropriate task, rather than arbitrarily assigning dollar or day limits to the use of health care resources in a national program. To choose the latter is to distribute health in proportion to the luck of the natural and social lottery and according to our ability to buy health care in the private market.

NOTES

1. How would Mrs. Campbell's need for obstetrical services be judged under each of the theories discussed by Professors Veatch and Fried? See also the June 1979 issue of The Journal of Medicine and Philosophy, which contains nine enlightening essays under the heading "Rights to Health Care." A strong defense of the "free market" approach to health care allocation is Sade, Medical Care as a Right: A Refutation, 285 New Eng.J.Med. 1288 (1971).

Rather than speaking in terms of a "right," the President's Commission concluded that society has an ethical obligation to ensure equitable access to health care for all. In defining equitable access, it rejected treating equity as equality or as access solely according to a person's benefit from, or need for, care, because these concepts were unworkable; instead, it held that equity requires that all citizens be able to secure an adequate level of care without excessive burdens in obtaining it. While adequacy would have to be defined in the context of comparing the effects of alternative policies and programs and in the context of a society's resources, the Commission did not equate it with "basic" or "minimal" care. See President's Commission, Securing Access to Health Care 16–47 (1983).

2. To the extent that any theory of a fair distribution of health care resources depends on some people being satisfied with having less than others, is it subject to failure in the real world?

> The proportion of any population that report themselves satisfied with their economic performance rises not at all as that population's average income rises. Those happiest with their economic circumstances have above-average incomes. There is no minimum absolute standard of living that will make people content. Individual wants are not satiated as incomes rise, and individuals do not become more willing to transfer some of their resources to the poor as they grow richer. If their income rises less rapidly than someone else's, or less rapidly than they expect, they may even feel poorer as their incomes rise.

L. Thurow, The Zero-Sum Society 18 (1980).

3. Obligations to provide health care have been found as a result of certain statutes and constitutional provisions. For example, the Hill-Burton Act, adopted by Congress in July 1946, provided hospitals funds for construction and renovation, in exchange for which the hospitals assured the federal government that services would be provided in their community on a nondiscriminatory basis to indigent patients. For many years, the assurances were met through an "open door" policy, under which hospitals certified that no one would be denied medical attention based on inability to pay. During the 1970s, the Hill-Burton regulations were extensively revised into strict guidelines that obligate hospitals to provide uncompensated treatment. See Wyoming Hospital Association v. Harris, 527 F.Supp. 551 (D.Wyo.1981) (upholding new regulations). These obligations have in turn been held to create enforceable rights in indigent patients to hospital services. See, e.g., Euresti v. Stenner, 458 F.2d 1115 (10th Cir.1972).

In certain contexts, the right to health care may even be constitutionally based. For example, to knowingly deprive a prisoner of vital medical treatment has been held to violate his constitutionally protected rights, including the right to be free of cruel and unusual punishment. Estelle v. Gamble, 429 U.S. 97, 97 S.Ct. 285, 50 L.Ed.2d 251 (1976). As a general proposition, however, the Supreme Court has made clear that there is no legally enforceable right to health care at state expense, even in instances in which the state may not directly restrict access to a particular service (such as abortion, see notes following Roe v. Wade in Ch. 8, Sec. A.1 infra) through health regulations or criminal penalties.

4. What role should a theory of "just deserts" play in allocating care? See Veatch, Voluntary Risks to Health: The Ethical Issues, 243 J.A.M.A. 50 (1980).

---

b. Access to Very Expensive Treatment

i. Selection of Treatment Modalities

J.L. PENNOCK, P.E. OYER, D.A. REITZ, S.W. JAMIESON, C.P. BIEBER, J. WALLWORK, E.B. STINSON, and N.E. SHUMWAY, CARDIAC TRANSPLANTATION IN PERSPECTIVE FOR THE FUTURE

83 J.Thorac.Cardiovasc.Surg. 168 (February, 1982).

We are now into the second decade of clinical cardiac transplantation at Stanford University Medical Center and have entered the fourteenth year of the program. . . . The overall scientific goal has been and remains the assessment of the long-term therapeutic value of cardiac transplantation in patients with advanced heart disease for whom standard forms of medical or surgical treatment offer no realistic expectation of any benefit.

A predictable resurgence of interest in clinical heart transplantation is evolving in this country and around the world. It is realistic to expect that by the end of this calendar year ten to twelve major referral centers in this country will be conducting clinically active programs in heart transplantation. . . .

Two hundred twenty-seven cardiac transplant procedures have been performed at Stanford University in 206 patients from January, 1968, to April, 1981. . . . The purpose of this report is to validate heart transplantation as a realistic mode of treatment to be considered in the strategy of clinical management of selected patients. We have examined the causes of transplant failure and report the common features of patients dying of these causes. In addition, we report the cost of hospitalization and long-term care of cardiac transplant recipients at Stanford University. Utilizing current methods of recipient selection and management and current state-of-the-art immune suppression, we believe clinical cardiac transplantation is therapeutic. Moreover, recent evidence from the experimental laboratory has documented Cyclosporin-A as an efficacious and possibly superior agent in cardiac allograft recipients, and we report here our early clinical experience with Cyclosporin-A in human cardiac transplantation.

Survival following cardiac transplantation

The proportion of patients surviving at 1 year following cardiac transplantation increased from 22% in 1968 to 67% in 1979 (Fig. 1). This increase resulted primarily from improvement in survival achieved during the first 3 postoperative months . . . ., an effect reflecting changes in early postoperative management. These protocol changes included refinement of criteria for patient selection (Table II), the introduction of rabbit antihuman thymocyte globulin for immune suppression, T-lymphocyte monitoring for the early diagnosis of rejection, liberal use of transvenous right ventricular endomyocardial biopsy to diagnose and confirm the severity of graft rejection, and retransplantation.

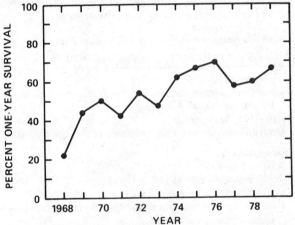

Fig. 1. One-year survival rates for each year of the Stanford program.

One hundred six of the total patient population of 206 (51%) have survived 1 year or more after transplantation. One hundred forty-eight patients (72%) have survived the initial 3 month postoperative period. Survival beyond 3 months has prognostic value, since these patients achieve postoperative survival rates of 78%, 66%, 58%, 48%, and 42% at 1, 2, 3, 4, and 5 years, respectively.

Postoperative survival rates, calculated by the actuarial method for combined program years from January, 1968, to April, 1981 (206 patients), are 57%, 48%, 42%, 35%, and 30% at 1 through 5 years, respectively. By 1974 rabbit antithymocyte globulin was substituted for equine antithymocyte globulin as a prophylactic and augmentative immune suppressive agent. . . . A more accurate appraisal of the current prognosis for cardiac transplant recipients, therefore, is provided by comparing survival data in patients from the first 6 years of the program with survival in patients receiving cardiac transplants since 1974.

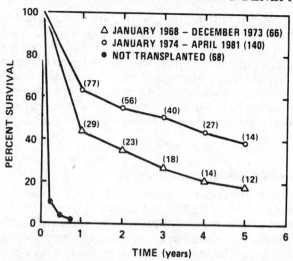

Fig. 3. Actuarial survival curves for Stanford cardiac transplantation program. *Triangles* include all patients treated from January 1968 through December 1973. *Open circles* include all patients treated from January, 1974, through April, 1981. *Closed circles* include patients chosen as potential recipients but not receiving a heart transplant.

Table II. *Recipient selection criteria and donor matching for orthotopic cardiac transplantation*

Primary selection criteria
    Irremediable terminal cardiac disease with less than 10% likelihood of survival for 6 months
    Age—50 years or younger
    Normal function or reversible dysfunction of liver and kidneys

Contraindications
    Active infection
    Recent pulmonary infarction
    Diabetes mellitus necessitating insulin
    Pulmonary vascular resistance greater than 8 Wood units and unresponsive to vasodilator drugs
    Symptomatic or documented severe peripheral or cerebrovascular disease
    Active peptic ulcer disease
    Drug addiction
    Psychosis or mental deficiency unrelated to low cardiac output or metabolic status
    Alcoholic cardiomyopathy
    Absence of adequate external psychosocial support
    Presence of any systemic illness that would limit recovery or survival

Donor matching
    ABO compatibility
    Absence of donor-specific lymphocyte cytotoxicity
    Appropriate size match
    HLA-A2 compatibility

Postoperative survival rates for program years from 1968 to 1974 (66 patients) are 44%, 35%, 27%, 21%, and 18% at 1 through 5 years, respectively (Fig. 3).   Postoperative survival rates for patients receiving transplants since 1974 (140 recipients) are 63%, 55%, 51%, 44%, and 39% at 1 through 5 years, respectively (Fig. 3).   Statistical significance for the differences between the two subgroups is present at all comparable years (p < 0.01).

The survival rate of an additional 68 patients selected for transplantation during all program years and for whom no donor organ became available is less than 5% at 6 months.   Thus the therapeutic efficacy of cardiac transplantation in terms of patient survival in our opinion, is not disputable.

Rehabilitation

The quality of life of surviving recipients is of equal importance to survival in the assessment of the therapeutic value of clinical heart transplantation.   At the present time, 106 patients in our series have survived for 1 year or more after transplantation.   . . .

Eighty-two percent (87) of these patients have enjoyed active rehabilitation, defined simply as restoration of overall functional capacity sufficient to provide the patient an unrestricted option for return to active employment or an activity of choice.   The majority, 73% (Table V), have returned to employment, activity as homemakers, or continuing education.   Factors accounting for unsatisfactory rehabilitation in 18% of 1 year survivors have been debilitating cachexia or remote neurologic deficits, present at the time of transplantation and unreversed postoperatively, and recurrent infections or metabolic complications of corticosteroid treatment.   The therapeutic efficacy in terms of patient rehabilitation has been most rewarding.

Table V. *Rehabilitation following cardiac transplantation: One-year survivors (N = 106)*

	No.	Percent
. . .		
Rehabilitated		
Yes	87	82
No	19	
Work activity		
Employed full time	45	
Employed part time	14	
Homemaker	8	
Student	10	
	77	73
Retired by choice	19	
Medical disability	10	

Costs

An analysis of the costs of cardiac transplantation at Stanford for 97 patients undergoing transplantation between October, 1973, and April, 1979, is summarized in Table VI.   The primary focus throughout our program in cardiac transplantation has been the development of methods for patient management necessary to achieve long-term survival. The accumulation of a large amount of scientific and clinical data pertinent to successive improvements in patient care made control of costs a secondary goal. Thus this phase of early research and development does not reflect the true costs of cardiac transplantation but represents an approximate upper limit to such costs at our institution.

All figures are reported in terms of 1980 dollars. . . .

Table VI. *Stanford cardiac transplantation costs expressed in terms of 1980 dollars*

Transplant hospitalization
  October 1973 to April 1979, 97 patients
    Average length of stay

Intensive care unit			41 days (range 14-99 days)
General ward			24 days (range 1-93 days)
Total			65 days

Costs	Average per day	Average per admission	Median per admission
Room and nursing	$652	$42,380 ± 20,709	$39,342
Ancillary	$883	$57,395 ± 24,405	$51,397
Totals		$99,775 ± 45,114	$90,739

  May 1980 to December 1980, 13 patients
    Average length of stay

Intensive care unit			47 days (range 23-105 days)
General ward			19 days (range 5- 40 days)
Total			66 days

Costs	Average per day	Average per admission	Median per admission
Room and nursing	$619	$41,494 ± 16,123	$36,427
Ancillary	$625	$41,938 ± 15,598	$40,464
Totals		$83,432 ± 31,721	$73,852

Follow-up hospitalizations
  October 1973 to April 1979, 97 patients

	Year 1	Year 2	Year 3	Year 4
Average length of stay	22 days	19 days	11 days	15 days
Median length of stay	11 days	6 days	4 days	4 days
Costs				
Room and nursing	$ 8,243	$ 5,869	$ 4,180	$ 4,993
Ancillary	$13,571	$ 8,035	$ 9,528	$ 8,098
Average total	$21,814 ± 21,393	$13,724 ± 15,774	$13,708 ± 15,967	$13,091 ± 15,940
Median total	$10,392	$ 7,028	$ 5,895	$ 5,353

Outpatient visits
  October 1973 to April 1979, 82 patients

	Year 1	Year 2	Year 3	Year 4
Average number of visits	35	19	21	15
Average cost per visit	$ 217	$ 236	$ 213	$ 141
Average cost per patient	$7,510 ± 4,470	$4,593 ± 5,749	$4,574 ± 6,597	$2,154 ± 2,211

The development of new immunosuppressive techniques (currently Cyclosporin-A) may contribute to cost reductions in the near future by virtue of a decrease in complications related to infection and rejection. Such complications have been responsible, in large measure, for the high costs of cardiac transplantation.

Discussion

. . . The principal reason for strict definition of candidacy for cardiac transplantation is identification of potential recipients for whom the probability of survival and rehabilitation is maximal. Thus only 11.3% of 1,125 patients referred to Stanford for evaluation from 1977 to 1981 were ultimately accepted for transplantation. One hundred eight (9.6%) patients died while under active consideration or awaiting a donor after acceptance. Five hundred forty patients had incomplete follow-up. Historical documentation has revealed that in the majority of these cases death occurred prior to complete transmission of medical records to Stanford. Upon the basis of recipient selection criteria previously advanced, the number of potential heart transplant recipients in this country probably ranges from 1,000 to 5,000 annually.

Cardiac transplantation in perspective for the future must be viewed from the standpoint of objectives that are both forward and realistic. Estimates for the total first year costs of a national heart transplant program have ranged from $212.2 million to $3.2 billion, depending on whether 2,000 or 30,000 transplants are performed. It is our opinion that 30,000 potential heart transplant recipients in the United States per year represent a gross exaggeration of the true number of patients for whom the current state of technology offers a high expectation of success. Even if immune suppression improved (i.e., Cyclosporin-A), there is at present no convincing evidence for wide liberalization of current recipient selection criteria.

The final limit upon potential numbers of cardiac transplant recipients is clearly the number of suitable donors. Cadaver donors for kidney transplantation, an accepted therapy for end-stage renal disease, reached 1,533 in 1979. This represented a 10% increase per year since 1977. The total number of living related and cadaver kidney transplants performed in the United States in 1979 was 4,271. (The number of patients receiving renal dialysis during 1979 was 45,565.) It is estimated that at least 20,000 Americans die from brain injury, brain tumor, or stroke each year under circumstances that could permit removal of viable organs for transplantation. The reality of actual cadaver organ donations is far less, as reflected by current numbers.

A realistic number of potential cadaver cardiac donors per year in the United States is difficult to ascertain. Upon the basis of the renal transplant experience, however, the number of potential cadaver cardiac donors would appear to be slightly less than 2,000 per year. This estimate, in combination with our average historical cost data ($130,000 first-year costs per patient including transplant hospitalization, follow-up hospitalization, and outpatient visits), yields an estimate of the first-year costs of a national heart transplant program in the range of $260 million. The first-year costs of such a program based upon current average cost data would be $226 million, based upon current median cost data, $184 million.

. . . Unlike end-stage renal disease, there is no alternative therapy for end-stage cardiac disease. On the basis of this consideration and the survival and rehabilitation data presented, we believe that the cost of cardiac transplantation is justified in selected individuals.

NOTES

1. Should public funds be provided for heart transplants? The federal government is currently studying whether the Medicare program should pay for heart transplants. The study was ordered in June 1980 by Health and Human Services Secretary Patricia Roberts Harris after her earlier reversal of the decision the Health Care Financing Administration had announced in November 1979 that it would reimburse for the operation, but only at Stanford University, the heart transplant program with the world's largest and most successful record in this field. Secretary Harris announced that the assessment of heart transplantation would be "the prototype" of the evaluations HHS would henceforth require of the "social consequences" of new technologies before "financing their wide distribution." Knox, Heart Transplants: To Pay or Not to Pay, 209 Science 570 (1980). The new requirements are intended to give more content to the statutory stan-

dards that federal reimbursement will be provided only for treatments that are "reasonable and necessary" 42 U.S.C. § 1862(a)(1). In the meantime heart transplants were defined as "experimental" and Medicare funding was therefore denied; of course, the National Heart, Lung and Blood Institute has since the 1960's provided tens of millions of dollars for heart transplants as research.

2.   Many people have criticized the willingness of both governmental and private insurance plans to pay for palliative care but not for organ transplantation, even when the latter might be less costly and has a chance of a good outcome (while palliative care just keeps the patient comfortable until death occurs). What reasons can you see for and against such a policy?

3.   Recent developments in immunosuppression (with the drug Cyclosporin-A) make it likely that heart transplantation (as well as liver, pancreas, and heart-lung transplants) will seem much more attractive to cardiologists and their seriously ill patients. Obviously, this would increase pressure for a program of the sort that now pays for hemodialysis and renal transplantation. If kidney failure is given special coverage, why not heart failure? If such coverage were provided, what is likely to occur to the medical criteria by which "suitability" is determined, judging by the experience with kidney failure under Medicare since 1972?

By the early 1970s—as the number of people treated moved beyond the small percentage it had been during the early, experimental stages to a greater (though still fractional) portion of the total need—the contrasting fates of those treated and the larger number who died untreated became intolerable. Rather than continue to seek methods of allocating the resource fairly, a decision was made to make it available to every American with end-stage renal disease under a special provision in the Medicare program.

This response to the dilemma of limited resources is understandable. Indeed, it may have been inevitable, given the drama of identifiable patients who died because they could not obtain life-saving medical treatment. Moreover, the cost of overcoming the tragedy seemed acceptable—in part because of the way in which the number of "eligible" patients was estimated. Over the past decade, however, expenditures on the End Stage Renal Dialysis Program (now totaling approximately $2 billion per year) have exceeded the original estimates manyfold and the standards for eligibility for dialysis, no longer constrained by a scarcity of resources, have expanded to include many patients whose age or concurrent diseases would have left them out of the calculations of the relevant "pool" of patients in 1972. [Note: This serves as another reminder of the interaction of "facts" and "values"—in this case, the understandable (and probably unconscious) tendency of physicians to exclude from eligibility for dialysis those patients whose characteristics made their prognosis least favorable. Unlike choices between patients based on such social factors as wealth, education, marital and parental status, and the like, the criteria of "medical suitability" were regarded as "objective." With sufficient resources, it proved possible to redefine "suitability" since the patients with less favorable prognoses were no longer competing with those who "deserved" the treatment more because their prognoses were better. Though few would argue with a decision to use scarce resources for the most likely to benefit from them, any decision based on people's deserts is plainly one that involves values, not merely objective facts.]

President's Commission, Summing Up 73–74 (1983).

ALEXANDER LEAF,
THE MGH TRUSTEES SAY NO TO HEART TRANSPLANTS *

302 New Eng.J.Med. 1087–88 (1980).

[T]he recent decision by the trustees of the Massachusetts General Hospital that their institution would not engage in human heart transplantation . . . demonstrates two important principles: that physicians may not make independent final decisions regarding what professional services they provide, and that with the rapid proliferation of expensive medical technology, there is a clear responsibility to evaluate new procedures in terms of the greatest good for the greatest number.

Since the preservation of useful, meaningful life is the goal of the medical profession, the decision to pass up the opportunity to save even one life by cardiac transplantation was very difficult to make. It is this ethical issue that today sparks divergent views not only among the staff of the MGH but among physicians and the public in general. As one trustee stated, "It would have been easier to say 'Yes' to the request to do heart transplantations."

The request to do heart transplantations came from the chief of the General Surgical Services. He noted that he was bringing to the General Executive Committee of service chiefs a request for permission to carry out a surgical procedure. Previously, new therapeutic modalities could be introduced at will by each clinical service, depending on its own assessment of the value of the procedure. Recognizing that heart transplantation would require the collaboration and resources of many services and departments in the hospital, he requested approval from his peers to proceed with the operation. A previous request in 1974 had been considered but regarded as premature. In the interval, further experimental work by his cardiac surgical colleagues and by transplantation immunologists, as well as the Stanford experience, made the procedure clinically feasible, he argued, and his request was to do only six cases a year. His arguments won support from nearly all the service chiefs, and all agreed that the excellent record of the hospital's cardiac surgeons and the immunologic research of the kidney-transplant unit warranted doing the procedure at the MGH.

The debate over heart transplantation centered about three basic issues: the therapeutic efficacy of the procedure, the possible scientific fallout from conducting the procedure, and the effects of the procedure on the allocation of costly and limited resources.

The possibility of saving even six lives a year was weighed against the potential impact of this procedure, now and in the foreseeable future, on the incidence of cardiovascular deaths in our society. Estimates of the number of potential candidates for this operation nationwide vary from a few thousand to over 40,000 a year. No one knows the real figure, of course, and with some four million Americans suffering from clinically manifest heart disease, the number of potential candidates would clearly depend on the evolving surgical and medical indications for the procedure. But the availability of donor hearts must also be considered. The number obtainable will be considerably lower than the number needed.

* Dr. Leaf is Chief of the Medical Service at Massachusetts General Hospital; he is discussing here the decision reached by the hospital's trustees on Feb. 1, 1980, against allowing the hospital's cardiac surgical service to begin a limited program of heart transplantation. [ed.]

The situation contrasts with that of kidney transplants. Nature has generously provided us with two kidneys, only one of which is necessary for normal life, and technology has provided renal dialysis—a procedure that allows the recipient to be kept alive almost indefinitely, until the appropriate live or cadaver kidney can be procured for transplantation. Such abundance of donor organs and leeway to temporize is not available for heart transplantation.

Most important is the fact that the problem of tissue rejection has not been solved. . . . It was chiefly this consideration that led to the conclusion that for the present, human heart transplantation cannot be considered routine clinical therapy. To conclude otherwise would be to raise false hopes among the many patients who suffer from heart disease and to create serious public-relations problems when applicants would have to be denied inclusion in the program.

To assess what potential scientific knowledge might accrue from establishing a heart-transplantation program, the trustees turned to the hospital's committee on research. The committee interrogated a number of expert immunologists and clinical cardiac physiologists within and outside the hospital. Most thought that there was little likelihood that a new clinical transplantation program would add appreciably to understanding of tissue rejection. There was already so much motivation to solve this problem in relation to transplantation of kidney and other tissues that a further clinical program was not needed. Many laboratories around the world are intensely pursuing the problem. New important knowledge about cardiovascular function did not seem a likely consequence of the procedure either. All witnesses indicated, however, that important scientific advances might emerge unexpectedly from the serious study of almost any problem.

Another major concern is the impact on overall patient care that the assumption of a heart-transplantation program would entail. Such a program would commit costly and scarce resources to a procedure that at best would benefit a very few patients; these are the same resources that public demand has kept available for the benefit of many. A heart-transplantation program would further load the already overburdened intensive-care facilities with prospective transplant recipients as well as postoperative patients. Many of the former would die while awaiting a donor heart. To deny many patients the services of the hospital for procedures and care known to improve survival and the quality of life in an effort to help a few through the very difficult and resource-consuming procedure of heart transplantation was considered by the trustees to be unjustified at present.

. . . .

The very success of technology is responsible for the considerations involved in this decision. Before we had the capability for such demanding procedures, we were not confronted as a profession by the need to make these hard choices. We are now in an era when the decision to act in one way reduces or forecloses our options to do other things that we may want to do or have to do. In recent years we have often been admonished that with resources becoming limited, we as a profession must set our priorities or others will do it for us. Not all will agree with the decision of the trustees, and some will argue that only the profession should be involved in such determinations. If one considers that the medical profession has historically been fostered and supported to serve a societal need and not to supply physicians with a privileged status, one can find little argument with the course that the MGH trustees thoughtfully and responsibly followed.

NOTE

The publication of Dr. Leaf's description of the MGH decision provoked a number of letters to the editor. Dr. Muir Gray of Oxford, England, praised the trustees' "courage" but saw a weakness in their main rationale, "the greatest good for the greatest number."

The Utilitarian principle has many good aspects, but it has one serious drawback: some people must suffer so that others may enjoy some "good." Would the MGH trustees put to death a small number of people a month or two before they were due to die of disease, for "the benefit of many"?

Of course, it can be argued that letting people die is not the same as killing them; however, I have been persuaded by the arguments of Glover that the distinction between active and passive euthanasia, or between death by commission and by omission, is not ethically defensible although it needs to be maintained for the sanity and emotional survival of those who must allocate limited resources or those who practice clinical medicine. There is no single ethical principle on which such allocation decisions can be made. It is important to emphasize (as the MGH trustees have done) that there is always an ethical aspect to such decisions, for the ethics of resource allocation will be an increasingly important topic.

Dr. Francis D. Moore of Harvard Medical School, who as Surgeon-in-Chief at Peter Bent Brigham Hospital, Boston, had been a pioneer in organ transplantation, regretted that Boston, with its "historic position . . . in transplant surgery, immunology, cardiology, and hepatology, along with its record of close collaboration between the laboratory and the clinic and between disciplines," would not be playing a role as one of the four or five American centers of cardiac transplantation.

Although the costs of this type of episodic transplantation activity seem high, the procedure will not lead to repetitive readmission. In all the major teaching hospitals in Boston (including the MGH) patients with much rarer and more costly diseases are undergoing only occasionally effective treatment every day. Why was cardiac transplantation singled out for the negative vote?

It seems an unfortunate precedent when a group of trustees (even very distinguished ones) sitting in a board room decide against treatment that needs exactly the sort of aggressive, sophisticated clinical exploration characteristic of the MGH since that bright October day in 1846, now so frequently celebrated.

As the final decade of the 20th century nears, are we really beginning to lose compassion for those suffering from rare illnesses, merely because such illnesses are costly?

303 New Eng.J.Med. 998, 999 (1980).

———————

ii. Selection of Treatment Recipients

JAY KATZ AND ALEXANDER MORGAN CAPRON, CATASTROPHIC DISEASES: WHO DECIDES WHAT?

185–193 (1975).

i. **The Market.** Perhaps it would be simplest to make the treatment resources available to those who wish to purchase them. . . .

Rather than having individuals bid for the limited number of treatment slots available, an alternative market system would extend the right to each person for a portion of the treatment, the size of the portion calculated so that the number of options would use up, but not exceed, treatment capacity. Those who needed the treatment and had the funds would then buy from others the portions necessary to get treated. Although the price would lead some of the poorer patients to sell their options rather than purchasing the whole treatment, this market system, however unacceptable, is slightly better than the first, "since the effect of income distribution is somewhat mitigated where people are allowed to sell rights to life instead of having to buy them." Calabresi goes on to note that nevertheless,

> as the choice more obviously involves lives, even the right-to-sell market becomes unacceptable. We can, for instance, usefully contrast whether we allow (1) people to sell their blood (minimal risk to life), (2) sell a kidney (somewhat greater risk to life), (3) be one of three people who for a price take one chance in three of having to give their heart for a transplant ($1/3$ chance of selling a life) and (4) a straight deal under which a man sells his heart for a transplant.

In the present hypothetical case, of course, the confrontation with life-selling is less direct than in Calabresi's examples, since what is being sold is an option on a portion of a potentially lifesaving treatment. On balance, however, this distinction, and indeed the distinction between the "selling" and "buying" markets, probably makes little difference in our evaluation of the primary characteristic of the market: While it permits individuals to give expression to their desire to expend their resources on preserving their own lives versus other expenditures, the spectacle of desperate patients bidding against each other for limited treatment facilities would be destructive of the myth of our collective attachment to the incomparable value of human life.

The market could also be modified from one in which catastrophic disease treatment is purchased to one trading in "contingent claims," that is, the purchase of insurance so that treatment resources will be available if one needs them. Since people would not be in actual need at the time of purchase, the problems of desperation bidding and of placing a dollar value on life would be avoided. The future nature of the payoff creates some difficulties, however. For one, there is the practical difficulty of knowing the quantity of treatment resources needed at any future time. Second, a contingent claims market is biased in favor of the cautious person, the person willing to forego present enjoyment for future safety. Consequently, a third problem arises: At the time of the "payoff," treatment resources may be devoted to saving A, who is only moderately attached to living but enough so that he will accept treatment since he has already paid for it through insurance, rather than saving B, who wants desperately to live but who failed to insure against catastrophic illness. If the "contingent claims" market is strictly enforced so that there is no way for B to obtain treatment, there would probably be few public reverberations from his desire to do so, since there would be no present forum in which he could make a spectacle of himself frantically bidding (against C and D and other noninsureds) the price of treatment higher and higher. But an open system of sales, or a black market, could arise in which some "winners" in the insurance scheme (i.e., those who purchased a contingent claim on catastrophic disease treatment and then developed such a disease) would sell their rights to the highest bidder. That practice could be equally, or more, destructive than ordinary "desperation bidding." To avoid this phenomenon, the payoff could be in monetary terms (like the "major medical" coverage some people now have), rather than directly as a share of treatment resources. Unfortunately, such a system would not guarantee adequate facilities and would therefore leave open the danger of desperation bidding, by both the insured and (depending on their means) the uninsured.

As disconcerting as the spectacle would be, it might still be tolerable if we felt that it were the method most likely to reach the "right" allocation of treatment resources. But it does not represent a true expression of a desire to live, since a rich person would have to devote only a small percentage of his wealth to offer a price for the treatment which would exceed the amount which could be offered by a poor person who was willing to give all that he possessed to purchase the treatment. The economist's theory of the market in part postulates that through the expression of individual choice a distribution of goods and services can be arrived at which is optimal for society. Thus the market in catastrophic disease treatment would be less bothersome if we were confident that a man's wealth accurately reflected his worth to society, so the fact that a large percentage of rich people received the scarce lifesaving treatment could be said to result from their being more valuable. Yet such a premise would be dismissed out of hand by most people today, both as a factual matter and as a deviation from our collective ethic of equality of all persons.

To eliminate the distortion of wealth variation a number of alternatives could be tried. The modification closest to the simple market model would be the creation of a wealth distribution neutral market, as described by Calabresi in the following terms:

> The price at which scarce lifesaving resources were allocated would vary with the wealth of the recipient. . . . Wealth neutrality could only be achieved by setting rules for each wealth category so that the same proportion of potential users would buy the scarce resource in each wealth category. The prices would be set so that only the total resources allocated would be bought.

[T]his method of treatment distribution faces many practical objections. First, there is the general problem of cheating or falsification of wealth status, and particularly the likelihood of black markets. More important, it would be exceedingly difficult to construct such a system, and the more precisely it was calculated the more offensive the regulation would seem. There is something very unattractive about a governmental agency expending great energy and intellectual resources to be constantly adjusting the price of the treatment for each wealth category (and perhaps redefining categories as well) so as to be able to announce that "we have found just the price where enough of you, whether rich or poor, will choose to die rather than avail yourselves of this treatment."

In sum, modifications in the market—by changing what is bargained for or people's ability to bargain—do not seem likely to solve the problems inherent in the market system. In particular, we doubt that people's own willingness to pay for and undergo a lifesaving treatment corresponds very exactly to the value of their lives to society, and, even if it did, the market does a poor job of allowing them to express their valuation. . . .

ii. **Collective Decisions.** Rather than leaving the allocation of treatment resources to individual decisions in the marketplace, we could assign this task to a group appointed by the community which would pick treatment recipients according to their importance to society. There are two ways to go about this: either to formulate standards openly and then employ them to select among the applicants for treatment or to combine these two steps and have a single body make the selections according to whatever criteria it finds appropriate for judging the case before it. The defining characteristic of the second method is that no set of standards is ever publicly articulated by the selecting group; indeed, that is the advantage of such a system in its proponents' eyes.

. . .

"Social value" can play an explicit role in administrative standards, both in the case of companies (e.g., in deciding which broadcaster should be licensed for a channel because he will best serve the "public interest, convenience or necessity," etc.) and of individuals (e.g., exemptions from military service for men employed in defense industries or otherwise "in the national interest," etc.). On a similar basis, standards might be established to select for lifesaving treatment those persons whose continued lives would provide the greatest "return" to society for each dollar invested in their treatment. Depending on the precision with which standards could be promulgated, more or less discretion might be left to the administering body to apply them according to its "expertise" and free of judicial review.

The ominous social reverberations which would inevitably resound from such a scheme hardly require expatiation. The drafting of soldiers provides an illuminating comparison. In times of national emergency, when everyone or nearly everyone (especially males) is called upon to make sacrifices and take some risks, the drafting of some people into active service, with its accompanying higher probability (but not, of course, certainty) of death or injury, gives rise to some uneasiness but is generally accepted. When the effort in which the draftees are called upon to fight is, like the conflict in Southeast Asia, unpopular, the system of selection may come in for a great deal of criticism; otherwise, abuses of the system, rather than the system itself, are more likely to become the subject of disapproval. On the other hand, where the need for a method of selection is not based on national survival but on the accident of disease and where an adverse selection means certain death, a societally based ranking of persons would be difficult to accept. If the ranking were believed, it would be hard to confine it to the sphere of catastrophic diseases. More likely, the ranking would be doubted and criticized for being too arbitrary and lacking in ability to differentiate between people on any number of important points—in other words, it would be hard to reach collective agreement on what is a truly "valuable" life. Furthermore, any explicit ranking would either undermine, or be undermined by, our society's proclaimed devotion to the concept of human equality, adherence to which is very important for the just and efficient operation of many of our social institutions.

To overcome these difficulties a second alternative has been suggested, namely, reliance on a body which will select recipients without publicly declaring why it favors *A* over *B*. Probably the most notable example of this type of decisionmaking is the jury (particularly in a criminal case); judges in sentencing convicts and, to a lesser extent, local draft boards and hospital clinical investigation committees also provide useful analogues of this model.

> To the extent they are representative they may reflect societal rankings of value of lives. To the extent that they make individual decisions they can consider individual . . . desire to live (if they so choose) more readily than can be done under responsibly promulgated general standards. To the extent they are local, individualized and a-responsible (i.e., they do not need to give the reasons for their decisions and answer for them), they avoid many of the demoralization costs. . . .

These advantages seem to have recommended this model to the physicians at the Swedish Hospital in Seattle when they sought to establish a method for selecting patients for their pioneering chronic hemodialysis program in 1961. The device they developed was to give the power of choice to

> seven humble laymen. They are all high-minded, good-hearted citizens, much like the patients themselves, who were selected as a microcosm of society-at-large. They were appointed to their uncomfortable post by Seattle's King County Medical Society, and for more than a year now they have remained there voluntarily, anonymously and without pay.

Without any formal guidelines and relying solely on their own opinions and consciences, they were assigned the task of selecting patients among those whom the physicians said were medically and psychiatrically suitable candidates for the limited number of dialysis beds available in the artificial kidney center. The Seattle committee drew up a list of factors it would weigh in making its selections, but since it was an "a-responsible" body, it did not have to publicize its criteria nor explain their interrelationship nor even provide assurance that they were adhered to in each case. In her *Life* article Shana Alexander did reveal some of the committee's thinking, particularly the broad exclusions it had adopted.

> For example, the doctors recommended that the committee begin by passing a rule to reject automatically all candidates over 45 years of age. Older patients with chronic kidney disease are too apt to develop other serious complications, the medical men explained. Also, the doctors thought that the committee should arbitrarily reject children. The nature of the treatment itself might cruelly torment and terrorize a child, and there were other purely medical uncertainties, such as whether a child forced to live under the dietary restrictions would be capable of growth. In any case, the doctors believed it would be a mistake to accept children and thereby be forced to reject heads of families with children of their own.
>
> . . . Finally they agreed to consider only those applicants who were residents of the state of Washington at the time the feasibility trial got under way. They justified this stand on the grounds that, since the basic research to develop the U-shaped tube had been done at the University of Washington Medical school and its new University Hospital—both state-supported institutions—the people whose taxes had paid for the research should be the first beneficiaries. . . .

Plainly these rules vary a great deal in their underlying rationale: To exclude all patients over 45 because "older patients" tend to have other diseases which complicate treatment seems quite a different rationale than excluding children because they would be taking up space which could be used for "heads of families with children of their own." In all likelihood none of the rules would meet the standards applicable to officially promulgated regulations. Yet, of course, they did not have to; they were arbitrary judgments made in an area in which rationally articulated decisions seemed to the committee either impossible of attainment or destructive in their impact. Even the *Life* coverage, which exposed the workings of the Seattle "Life or Death Committee" to greater scrutiny than is typical for an a-responsible body, served mainly to focus attention on the fact that such a group had to make the decisions it did, rather than to criticize the basis on which the group's decisions had been reached.

Although one does not want to admit it, however, even "high-minded, good-hearted citizens" make mistakes and may even be

> unrepresentative, corruptible, or simply arbitrary. Unless one knows why a decision is made to prefer *A* over *B*, or unless one has substantial faith in the decider's ability to know and apply societal values, one is bound to suspect that the preference did not reflect a sensible or even honest scale of values.

A fine line separates the exercise of reasonable, albeit a-responsible, discretion from irresponsible and arbitrary judgment. On the other hand, if a pattern emerges from the choices made, so that a committee's criteria can be discerned by piecing together the characteristics of the people it selects, then such difficulties as having a system with an explicit societal ranking reappear, with the added problem that the ranking has not been subject to review and correction by agencies responsible to the community and sensitive to its wishes.

iii. **The Lottery.** When the burdens of using a selection system which depends on conscious choice, made either by those selected or by society or a combination of the two, seem too great, decisionmakers have sometimes turned to chance as a basis for making choices. . . . As Calabresi has succinctly observed:

> The principal advantages of the lottery are that it is extremely cheap administratively, and that it fails to rank people's lives. Its principal disadvantage stems from its second advantage. The lottery treats the man who wants to live desperately, even with an artificial kidney, exactly in the same way as the man who other things being equal might prefer to live but for whom the burden of an artificial kidney (or of life in general) is such that he would almost as soon die.

On this analysis, the "fairness" of the lottery may be seen to be deceptive—it is more blind than fair, for an evenhanded approach is desirable only insofar as it deals with like classes of individuals. A lottery probably represents the method of selection which causes the fewest pangs of conscience and which is the least destructive of fundamental values, but it is certainly not likely to produce the optimal set of treatment recipients, whether judged by individual or societal standards, unless it is used to select among a group of applicants who are relatively equal on relevant criteria.

GUIDO CALABRESI and PHILIP BOBBITT, TRAGIC CHOICES

186–187 (1978).

Allocation of Artificial Kidneys in America. The procedures by which artificial kidneys and transplants have been allotted in the United States present an interestingly different pattern. As befits a land of plenty and a society convinced that an orgastic future awaits it if only the proper plans are made, the principal object of the tragic allocation in America has been to avoid owning up to having made a first-order determination.* From this as much as from our democratic ideology follows the consistent reliance on limiting second-order criteria to those which seem unchosen, and correcting second-order results before they reveal discriminations which offend a qualified egalitarianism, that is, that persons ought to be treated as equals if they are similar according to generalized efficiency criteria, but also if not treating them as equals displays a disfavored group in some prominent way. Here then, as in America's approach to military conscription and to education, efficiency plays a significant role, but becomes suspect when it results in an obvious discrimination against a well-defined socioeconomic group.

Our first approach was a purely technical one: Kidneys went to those people in whom the kidneys were likeliest to work, or to those in whom there was a substantial experimental interest. These decisions were left up to doctors and hospitals which faced a scarcity not of their own making. If it appeared that every patient who was really likely to benefit would get a kidney, then attention was never focused on the first-order determination and no decisions threatening egalitarian or humanistic values needed to be made.

This approach broke down because it did not fit the facts of the matter. On the one hand, the use of a customary approach to the first-order determination quickly drove the number of artificial kidneys available up to levels sufficient to provide more than enough to that group for whom successful dialysis was almost a sure bet, as well as for justifiable experimentation. The existence of a perimeter enclosing a group of sure bets became rather unconvincing as the line was advanced and the enclosure expanded; suspicion was voiced that some medical bets were surer than others because of previous or present wealth advantages. On the other hand, it became apparent that the remaining scarcity was very much the product of a societal decision.

The first difficulty was met by a variety of measures—none of them completely successful. A first-come-first-served basis was tried. But some of the patients first to come asking were poor recipients. A modification by which a first-come-first-served approach was limited to equally good recipients ran into the problem that there was a continuum between better and worse recipients. It was not easy simply to draw a line and treat all those above the line as equally good and those below the line as unacceptable (though this too was suggested). Trade-offs between relatively good recipients and relatively first in time were almost impossible to administer and accordingly raised doubts about the nature of what had become aresponsible, unrepresentative, and technically uncontrollable decisions. Were the doctors favoring friends? Or those who could pay? Or those they deemed worthiest? Doctors themselves tended to refuse to be put in so vulnerable a role.

Of course many doctors and hospital groups recognize that a first-come-first-served approach made choices, and made them mindlessly. Some of these physicians and administrators attempted to confront the problem of second-order determinations directly. The Seattle God Com-

---

* The authors early assert that society must make two sorts of decisions about a scarce good: (1) how much of it will be produced (within the limits set by natural scarci-ty) and (2) who shall get what is made. The former decision is called a first-order determination, and the latter a second-order determination or decision. Id. at 19. [Eds.]

mittee was a courageous attempt to do this, and its experience illustrated both the advantages and dangers of thinking too clearly in this area.
. . .

JAMES F. CHILDRESS, WHO SHALL LIVE WHEN NOT ALL CAN LIVE?

53 Soundings 339–362 (Winter 1970).

. . .

A significant example of the distribution of scarce medical resources is seen in the use of penicillin shortly after its discovery. Military officers had to determine which soldiers would be treated—those with venereal disease or those wounded in combat. In many respects such decisions have become routine in medical circles. Day after day physicians and others make judgments and decisions "about allocations of medical care to various segments of our population, to various types of hospitalized patients, and to specific individuals," for example, whether mental illness or cancer will receive the higher proportion of available funds. Nevertheless, the dramatic forms of "Scarce Life-Saving Medical Resources" (hereafter abbreviated as SLMR) such as hemodialysis and kidney and heart transplants have compelled us to examine the moral questions that have been concealed in many routine decisions. I do not attempt in this paper to show how a resolution of SLMR cases can help us in the more routine ones which do not involve a conflict of life with life. Rather I develop an argument for a particular method of determining who shall live when not all can live. . . .

. . .

Analogous Conflict Situations

An especially interesting and pertinent [analogous case] is U.S. v. Holmes.[5] In 1841 an American ship, the *William Brown*, which was near Newfoundland on a trip from Liverpool to Philadelphia, struck an iceberg. The crew and half the passengers were able to escape in the two available vessels. One of these, a longboat, carrying too many passengers and leaking seriously, began to founder in the turbulent sea after about twenty-four hours. In a desperate attempt to keep it from sinking, the crew threw overboard fourteen men. Two sisters of one of the men either jumped overboard to join their brother in death or instructed the crew to throw them over. The criteria for determining who should live were "not to part man and wife, and not to throw over any women." Several hours later the others were rescued. Returning to Philadelphia, most of the crew disappeared, but one, Holmes, who had acted upon orders from the mate, was indicted, tried, and convicted on the charge of "unlawful homicide."

We are interested in this case from a moral rather than a legal standpoint, and there are several possible responses to and judgments about it. Without attempting to be exhaustive I shall sketch a few of these. The judge contended that lots should have been cast, for in such conflict situations, there is no other procedure "so consonant both to humanity and to justice." Counsel for Holmes, on the other hand, maintained that the

5. [36] Fed.Cas. 360 (C.C.E.D.Pa.1842)
. . . . .

"sailors adopted the only principle of selection which was possible in an emergency like theirs,—a principle more humane than lots."

Another version of selection might extend and systematize the maxims of the sailors in the direction of "utility"; those are saved who will contribute to the greatest good for the greatest number. Yet another possible option is defended by Edmond Cahn in The Moral Decision. He argues that in this case we encounter the "morals of the last day." By this phrase he indicates that an apocalyptic crisis renders totally irrelevant the normal differences between individuals. He continues:

> In a strait of this extremity, all men are reduced—or raised, as one may choose to denominate it—to members of the genus, mere congeners and nothing else. Truly and literally, all were "in the same boat," and thus none could be saved separately from the others. I am driven to conclude that otherwise—that is, if none sacrifice themselves of free will to spare the others—they must all wait and die together. For where all have become congeners, pure and simple, no one can save himself by killing another.

Cahn's answer to the question "who shall live when not all can live" is "none" unless the voluntary sacrifice by some persons permits it.

Few would deny the importance of Cahn's approach although many, including this writer, would suggest that it is relevant mainly as an affirmation of an elevated and, indeed, heroic or saintly morality which one hopes would find expression in the voluntary actions of many persons trapped in "borderline" situations involving a conflict of life with life. It is a maximal demand which some moral principles impose on the individual in the recognition that self-preservation is not a good which is to be defended at all costs. The absence of this saintly or heroic morality should not mean, however, that everyone perishes. Without making survival an absolute value and without justifying all means to achieve it, we can maintain that simply letting everyone die is irresponsible. This charge can be supported from several different standpoints, including society at large as well as the individuals involved. Among a group of self-interested individuals, none of whom volunteers to relinquish his life, there may be better and worse ways of determining who shall survive. One task of social ethics, whether religious or philosophical, is to propose relatively just institutional arrangements within which self-interested and biased men can live. The question then becomes: which set of arrangements—which criteria and procedures of selection—is most satisfactory in view of the human condition (man's limited altruism and inclination to seek his own good) and the conflicting values that are to be realized?

· · ·

Criteria of Selection for SLMR

· · ·

We need two sets of criteria which will be applied at two different stages in the selection of recipients of SLMR. First, medical criteria should be used to exclude those who are not "medically acceptable." Second, from this group of "medically acceptable" applicants, the final selection can be made. Occasionally in current America medical practice, the first stage is omitted, but such an omission is unwarranted. Ethical and social responsibility would seem to require distributing these SLMR only to those who have some reasonable prospect of responding to the treatment. Furthermore, in transplants such medical tests as tissue and blood typing are necessary, although they are hardly full developed.

"Medical acceptability" is not as easily determined as many non-physicians assume since there is considerable debate in medical circles about the relevant factors (e.g., age and complicating diseases). Although ethicists can contribute little or nothing to this debate, two proposals may be in order. First, "medical acceptability" should be used only to determine the group from which the final selection will be made, and the attempt to establish fine degrees of prospective response to treatment should be avoided. Medical criteria, then, would exclude some applicants but would not serve as a basis of comparison between those who pass the first stage. For example, if two applicants for dialysis were medically acceptable, the physicians would *not* choose the one with the *better* medical prospects. Final selection would be made on other grounds. Second, psychological and environmental factors should be kept to an absolute minimum and should be considered only when they are without doubt critically related to medical acceptability (e.g., the inability to cope with the requirements of dialysis which might lead to suicide).

The most significant moral questions emerge when we turn to the final selection. Once the pool of medically acceptable applicants has been defined and still the number is larger than the resources, what other criteria should be used? How should the final selection be made? First, I shall examine some of the difficulties that stem from efforts to make the final selection in terms of social value   .   .   . .

Occasionally criteria of social worth focus on past contributions but most often they are primarily future-oriented. The patient's potential and probable contribution to the society is stressed, although this obviously cannot be abstracted from his present web of relationships (e.g., dependents) and occupational activities (e.g., nuclear physicist). Indeed, the magnitude of his contribution to society (as an abstraction) is measured in terms of these social roles, relations, and functions. Enough has already been said to suggest the tremendous range of factors that affect social value or worth.   .   .   . How do we determine the relevant criteria of social value?

How does one quantify and compare the needs of the spirit (e.g., education, art, religion), political life, economic activity, technological development? Joseph Fletcher suggests that "some day we may learn how to 'quantify' of 'mathematicate' to 'computerize' the value problem in selection, in the same careful and thorough way that diagnosis has been." I am not convinced that we can ever quantify values, or that we should attempt to do so. But even if the various social and human needs, in principle, could be quantified, how do we determine how much weight we will give to each one? Which will have priority in case of conflict? Or even more basically, in the light of which values and principles do we recognize social "needs"?

One possible way of determining the values which should be emphasized in selection has been proposed by Leo Shatin. He insists that our medical decisions about allocating resources are already based on an unconscious scale of values (usually dominated by material worth). Since there is really no way of escaping this, we should be self-conscious and critical about it. How should we proceed? He recommends that we discover the values that most people in our society hold and then use them as criteria for distributing SLMR. These values can be discovered by attitude or opinion surveys. Presumably if fifty-one percent in this testing period put a greater premium on military needs than technological development, military men would have a greater claim on our SLMR than experimental researchers. But valuations of what is significant change, and the student revolutionary who was denied SLMR in 1970 might be celebrated in 1990 as the greatest American hero since George Washington.

Shatin presumably is seeking criteria that could be applied nationally, but at the present, regional and local as well as individual prejudices tincture the criteria of social value that are used in selection. Nowhere is this more evident than in the deliberations and decisions of the anonymous selection committee of the Seattle Artificial Kidney Center where such factors as church membership and Scout leadership have been deemed significant for determining who shall live. As two critics conclude after examining these criteria and procedures, they rule out "creative nonconformists, who rub the bourgeoisie the wrong way but who historically have contributed so much to the making of America. The Pacific Northwest is no place for a Henry David Thoreau with bad kidneys."

Closely connected to this first problem of determining social values is a second one. Not only is it difficult if not impossible to reach agreement on social values, but it is also rarely easy to predict what our needs will be in a few years and what the consequences of present actions will be. Furthermore it is difficult to predict which persons will fulfill their potential function in society. Admissions committees in colleges and universities experience the frustrations of predicting realization of potential. For these reasons, as someone has indicated, God might be a utilitarian, but we cannot be. We simply lack the capacity to predict very accurately the consequences which we then must evaluate. Our incapacity is never more evident than when we think in societal terms.

Other difficulties make us even less confident that such an approach to SLMR is advisable. Many critics raise the spectre of abuse, but this should not be overemphasized. The fundamental difficulty appears on another level: the utilitarian approach would in effect reduce the person to his social role, relations, and functions. Ultimately it dulls and perhaps even eliminates the sense of the person's transcendence, his dignity as a person which cannot be reduced to his past or future contribution to society. It is not at all clear that we are willing to live with these implications of utilitarian selection. Wilhelm Kolff, who invented the artificial kidney, has asked: "Do we really subscribe to the principle that social standing should determine selection? Do we allow patients to be treated with dialysis only when they are married, go to church, have children, have a job, a good income and give to the Community Chest?"

. . .

The Values of Random Selection

My proposal is that we use some form of randomness or chance (either natural, such as "first come, first served", or artificial, such as a lottery) to determine who shall be saved. Many reject randomness as a surrender to non-rationality when responsible and rational judgments can and must be made. [O]ther critics see randomness as a surrender to "non-human" forces which necessarily vitiates human values (e.g., it is important to have persons rather than impersonal forces determining who shall live). Sometimes they are identified with the outcome of the process (e.g., the features such as creativity and fullness of being which make human life what it is are to be considered and respected in the decision). [I]t must be admitted that the use of chance seems cold and impersonal. But presumably the defenders of utilitarian criteria in SLMR want to make their application as objective and impersonal as possible so that subjective bias does not determine who shall live.

Such criticism, however, ignores the moral and nonmoral values which might be supported by selection by randomness or chance. A more important criticism is that the procedure that I develop draws the relevant moral context too narrowly. That context, so the argument might run, includes the society and its future and not merely the individual with his illness and claim upon SLMR. But my contention is that the values and principles at work in the narrower context may well take precedence over those operative in the broader context both because of their weight and significance and because of the weaknesses of selection in terms of social worth. As Paul Freund rightly insists, "The more nearly total is the estimate to be made of an individual, and the more nearly the consequence determines life and death, the more unfit the judgment becomes for human reckoning. . . . Randomness as a moral principle deserves serious study." Serious study would, I think point toward its implementation in certain conflict situations, primarily because it preserves a significant degree of *personal dignity by providing equality* of opportunity. Thus it cannot be dismissed as a "non-rational" and "non-human" procedure without an inquiry into the reasons, including human values, which might justify it. Paul Ramsey stresses this point about the *Holmes* case:

> Instead of fixing our attention upon "gambling" as the solution—with all the frivolous and often corrupt associations the word raises in our minds—we should think rather of equality of opportunity as the ethical substance of the relations of those individuals to one another that might have been guarded and expressed by casting lots.

The individual's personal and transcendent dignity, which on the utilitarian approach would be submerged in his social role and function, can be protected and witnessed to by a recognition of his equal right to be saved. Such a right is best preserved by procedures which establish equality of opportunity. Thus selection by chance more closely approximates the requirements established by human dignity than does utilitarian calculation. It is not infallibly just, but it is preferable to the alternatives of letting all die or saving only those who have the greatest social responsibilities and potential contribution.

NOTE ON SELECTION OF DONORS

According to Dr. David Ogden, President of the National Kidney Foundation, testifying before a committee of the U.S. House of Representatives on April 14, 1983, more than 24,000 kidneys would have been available for transplantation in 1981 had donations been made in all suitable cases; in fact, only 3,425 cadaver kidneys were transplanted in the United States that year. (Similar shortages exist for other organs.) What do you think of these alternatives for increasing the number of donations: More extensive education and advertising? Federal support for a computerized national system to allow matching of donors and recipients around the clock, and for local "transplant coordinators" to work with health care personnel and the families of potential donors, encouraging and facilitating organ donation? Personal appeals in the media for organs by potential recipients and their families, or even by the President (as Mr. Reagan did in July 1983 on behalf of several children who were dying of liver failure)? Making all adults choose either to donate or not, by placing the option on all federal tax forms or on all state drivers' license applications and renewals? Making donation automat ic unless a person has "opted out" during his or her lifetime? Taking organs at death in all suitable cases, without opportunity for the decedent or relatives to opt out? What are the limits of the moral and legal obligation to donate?

One court, faced with a petition from a man dying of aplastic anemia to order his unwilling cousin to be a bone marrow donor, concluded that there is no duty to be unselfish (even when taking a small risk could save a life), and denied the petition. McFall v. Shimp, 10 Pa.D. & C.3d 90 (Allegheny Cty.C.P.1978). For a strong argument that the judge's decision was correct because an involuntary invasion of the body of one individual to aid another would be utterly intolerable see Meisel & Roth, Must a Man Be His Cousin's Keeper? 8 Hastings Cntr.Rpt. 5 (Oct. 1978). Compare Hart v. Brown, Ch. 3, Sec. B.2 (approved removal of kidney for transplantation to twin from child too young to give consent).

3. EXPORTING RISKS AND BENEFITS

Most of this chapter, indeed, most of this book, has focused on problems of science and medicine in the United States. But many of these issues do not follow national boundaries. Whether it is the risk of fall-out from nuclear explosions, or the revelation that some $5 million worth of Tris-treated children's sleepwear was exported after it had been removed from the domestic market because of mounting evidence that the flame retardant would cause cancer in children exposed to it, the international dimension of these issues raises some of the most difficult problems of all.

One aspect of the problem is that the benefits posed by a particular substance may vary from nation to nation. It might be appropriate, in short, to ban a substance in one nation, but not in another after balancing risks and benefits. Consider whether Depo-Provera is such a substance.

a. A Specific Product

DONALD KENNEDY, STATEMENT, HEARINGS ON U.S. EXPORT OF BANNED PRODUCTS, SUBCOMMITTEE OF THE HOUSE COMMITTEE ON GOVERNMENT OPERATIONS

95th Cong., 2d Sess, 91–108 (July 12. 1978).

The main question being examined at these hearings is whether the U.S. Government should allow the export of useful but potentially hazardous substances not approved for marketing in this country. It is one that evokes strong views on both sides.

On the one hand, there is concern that current export policy for some products results in the "dumping" of inferior or even dangerous substances in countries poorly equipped to evaluate the potential risks involved.

On the other hand, it is claimed that export restrictions deprive citizens of foreign countries [of] the benefits of important products that, for often rather special reasons, have been deemed unsuitable for use by U.S. citizens.

Like other Federal agencies that regulate chemicals, the Food and Drug Administration sometimes finds itself at the center of controversy between representatives of these divergent, but equally legitimate, positions.

Over the years, through participation in a number of debates on this issue, we have reexamined the export provisions of our laws to determine if changes were in order.

For example, recently as part of an overall revision of our drug laws, we submitted to Congress significant amendments to the current export provisions regarding drugs.

Because of the importance of this change, I would like to discuss it here in some detail, with your permission, including the ways in which it would modify current law and why we believe it is necessary. . . .

Under current law, a new drug may not be exported for commercial use unless it is approved for marketing domestically and complies with all the requirements of title V of the Federal Food, Drug, and Cosmetic Act and the drug's new drug application.

An unapproved new drug may be exported only under an investigational new drug protocol approved by the Food and Drug Administration. That investigational study must comply with all the conditions and requirements that attend a clinical study conducted in this country.

But certain categories of drugs that are not classifed as new drugs—like antibiotics, insulin, and pre–1938, or grandfather, drugs—may be exported without any prior notice to the Food and Drug Administration, even when these products may be adulterated or misbranded under domestic standards. These drugs must simply comply with the specifications of the foreign purchaser and the laws of the importing countries and be labeled for export only.

Our proposed new law—the Drug Regulation Reform Act of 1978—would revise the current export rules applicable to drugs. Under the act, two standards for export would apply to all drugs.

Approved drugs in compliance with domestic requirements could be freely exported. Unapproved drugs or approved drugs not in compliance with domestic requirements could be exported only after an export permit had been approved by the Secretary.

An export permit would be granted only when the exporter of an unapproved or noncomplying drug demonstrates that the importing government has assented to its importation after being informed of its legal status here and the basis for it.

The scientific and medical data concerning the drug's unapproved status would be made available to the importing government to assure an informed decision. The Secretary would have authority to deny an export permit where such export would be contrary to public health.

Currently, we provide information on the safety and efficacy of many drugs to the World Health Organization and to individual foreign countries.

For example, when a drug is withdrawn from the market for reasons of safety we notify the World Health Organization and all those countries which have requested to receive information of this kind.

The World Health Organization, in turn, issues special bulletins to all its member governments.

Because we have limited authority and resources to provide technical assistance of this kind to foreign countries, we have included a provision in the Reform Act authorizing the Secretary to provide assistance to foreign governments that lack the resources to evaluate the medical and scientific information about a drug.

. . .

In sum, our proposed change in the law would provide greater protection against the export of some drug product, such as adulterated and misbranded antibiotics, insulin, and pre-1938 drugs.

At the same time, it would make more drug products available to foreign countries that are needed in those countries.

. . .

In our view, the relative safety and efficacy of a drug or medical device is a composite judgment which must be made by each country based upon many factors, such as the status of the health care system in that country, patient compliance with dosage regimens, alternative therapies that may be available, and other health-related and social characteristics of that nation's population.

A number of diseases prevalent through the world—especially in the tropics where most of the developing nations are found—are rare or nonexistent in this country. A drug that is useful against such a disease may never receive adequate testing in this country to warrant its approval here.

Again, under the existing law, such a drug could not be exported from the United States for general use in other countries of the world—even if it had received approval in these other nations. Neither could a qualified drug company in this country contract to produce a drug for a foreign country.

Our recent decision not to approve the drug Depo Provera for use as an injectable contraceptive was a benefit/risk determination made in terms of the U.S. population for whom the drug was intended.

In announcing our decision, I made it clear that the drug, which is approved for use as a contraceptive in nearly 70 nations, may well have favorable benefit/risk ratios in those other countries.

Animal studies have demonstrated that the drug may pose serious potential risks in long-term usage.

The availability in this country of many safe and effective alternative methods of contraception and sterilization precludes the need in the United States for a long-term, potentially high-risk injectable contraceptive.

However, in nations with serious overpopulation and related health problems, these potential risks could very well be acceptable when weighed against the potential benefits of the use of Depo Provera as one element in a comprehensive family planning program.

We are writing a letter to the foreign governments involved and the international health organizations to explain that our decision was made solely in terms of the U.S. population.

I would like to provide a copy of this letter for the record.

DEPARTMENT OF HEALTH, EDUCATION, AND WELFARE
PUBLIC HEALTH SERVICE
FOOD AND DRUG ADMINISTRATION
ROCKVILLE, MARYLAND 20852

Monsieur le Ministre de la Sante
de la Republique populaire d'Angola
Luanda,
ANGOLA

Gentlemen:

On March 7, 1978 the United States Food and Drug Administration (FDA) notified the Upjohn Company that approval
had been denied to market Depo-Provera (medroxyprogesterone acetate) Sterile Aqueous Suspension, 150 milligrams,
for use as an intramuscular contraceptive for women in the
United States. The decision was based on the grounds that
the benefits of Depo-Provera for contraception in the
United States do not justify the potential risks to the
user.

For the information of World Health Organization members,
and all other interested parties, the considerations on
which FDA made this decison are as follows:

1. Safety questions raised by studies in beagle dogs
    showing an increased incidence of mammary tumors as-
    sociated with the drug have not been resolved. Be-
    nign tumors in the dogs occurred at the human dose
    (on a mg/kg basis), and benign and malignant tumors
    occurred at 25 times the human dose over a period of
    three years. No intermediate doses were studied.
    Although the tumors at the human dose level were be-
    nign there were too few animals to ascertain the
    propensity for malignancy at doses lower that 25
    times the human dose. Of the 4 dogs studied at this
    dose level only 2 survived for as long as 5 years.

    The U. S. manufacturer of Depo-Provera claims that
    there does not appear to be an increased incidence
    of mammary tumors in women exposed to Depo-Provera,
    but studies have been inadequate to make such a
    claim with any degree of confidence.

2. The availability in this country of many safe and
    effective alternative method of contraception and
    sterilization lessens the need for a long-term, po-
    tential high-risk injectable contraceptive. No clear
    evidence has been submitted to show that a signifi-
    cant patient population in need of the drug exists
    in the United States. Since October 1974, when FDA
    stayed the order providing for patient labeling for
    Depo-Provera for contraception, to the present time,
    there has been no clear demand from the medical com-
    munity for Depo-Provera for contraceptive use.

3. Irregular bleeding disturbances caused by the drug
   often result in the administration of estrogen, imposing an added risk factor and decreasing the benefits of a progestrogen-only contraceptive. . . .

4. Exposure of the fetus to medroxyprogesterone, if the
   drug fails and pregnancy occurs, poses a risk of
   congenital malformations. This risk is enhanced by
   the prolonged action of the drug.

We wish to emphasize that the benefit-risk judgment made
for the United States *is not necessarily appropriate for
other countries*, and the FDA's failure to appove a drug
does not necessarily signify that it is unsafe for contraceptive use in other countries. The balancing of risks
and benefits in deciding on a product's appropriateness
should be undertaken by each nation in light of its own
circumstances and needs. We recognize that the benefit-
risk considerations may not be the same in other countries
of the world as they are in the United States. Nations
with a higher birth rate, lower physician-to-patient ratio, and less readily available or acceptable alternative
contraceptive methods, would of course have different benefit-risk considerations. The Administration recently
submitted to Congress major new drug legislation that
would, among other things, change the current law governing the export of drugs from the U.S. Under the proposed Act, a drug unapproved for use in this country could
be exported provided that the drug meets the specification
of the foreign purchaser, and that the Government of the
country of destination has approved the importation and
distribution of the drug. . . .

. . .

Even without the proposed new authorities, we are in a
position to provide assistance to foreign governments in
helping them to make decisions about drugs. In the case
of Depo-Provera, for example, we recently met with a representative of the World Health Organization and offered
to provide summaries of our evaluations of the safety and
efficacy data of this drug. Transcripts of advisory committee meetings during which benefit/risk considerations
were weighed, and other data that might assist foreign
countries in deciding whether to import it. To the extent
we are able, we will continue to cooperate with the World
Health Organization and other appropriate organizations by
providing data on this or any other drug or device being
considered for use in other nations.

Sincerely yours,

Donald Kennedy
Commissioner of Food and
Drugs

STEPHEN MINKIN,*
DEPO-PROVERA: A CRITICAL ANALYSIS
HEARINGS ON EXPORT OF HAZARDOUS PRODUCTS BEFORE
THE SUBCOMMITTEE ON INTERNATIONAL ECONOMIC
POLICY AND TRADE OF THE HOUSE COMMITTEE
ON FOREIGN AFFAIRS

96th Cong., 2nd Sess., 302 (Sept. 9, 1980).

Currently Depo-Provera is being used as a contraceptive in more than 82 countries. An estimated five million women have been injected with the drug in the course of the last 15 years. In the United States, Depo-Provera is indicated for "adjunctive therapy and palliative treatment of inoperable, recurrent and metastatic endometrial carcinoma." It is not approved by the Food and Drug Administration (FDA) for use as a contraceptive. Many physicians, however, disagree with the FDA and continue to prescribe it as one.

This report presents documentation showing that doctors, family planning professionals and patients do not have access to the information necessary for making a scientific assessment of Depo-Provera. . . . .

. . .

Depo-Provera (DP) is a long-acting injectable contraceptive manufactured by the Upjohn Company. Depending on the dose, DP makes woman infertile for three to six months or longer. Depo-Provera . . . acts on the hypothalamus-pituitary axis to suppress ovulation. It interferes with the normal pattern of hormonal changes usually associated with the menstrual cycle. Principally, it inhibits the surge of luteinizing hormone (LH) which precedes ovulation. It has also been suggested that when the drug is injected, the initial blood levels of DP are high enough to "produce a shock" to the hypothalamus, disrupting the menstrual cycle for three months or longer.

Depo-Provera also acts on the ovaries and the endometrium—the uterine lining—as well as the mammaries, the clitoris, the blood and other glands and tissues.

The Food and Drug Administration rejected Upjohn's application to approve DP as a contraceptive on the grounds that "studies in beagle dogs have shown an increased incidence of mammary carcinoma." Hence, the benefits did not outweigh the risks.

In rejecting Upjohn's request, the FDA took the extraordinary step of informing the company that the assessment of the risks of DP was not necessarily applicable to other countries . . . ..

The reference to other countries appears to be a response to pressure by Congress and international population control agencies, including the U.S. Agency for International Development (AID) and the International Planned Parenthood Federation. The Drug Regulation Reform Act before Congress would allow U.S. drug companies to export directly to other countries drugs not approved by the FDA. . . . Depo-Provera has had an important role in the development of key provisions of this bill. An informal survey of several legislative assistants and FDA officials re-

---

* Health Policy Analyst, National Women's Health Network.

vealed that DP was the only drug known to fall within the category—"Required by other countries but not approved by the FDA."

. . .

This year three "scientific judges" constituting a FDA Board of Inquiry must decide whether Depo-Provera should be marketed as a contraceptive in the United States. If the board votes for approval, the United States Agency for International Development (AID) will attempt to export the drug on a vast scale. Past experience has shown that as many as 90 percent of the recruits to AID-sponsored contraceptive inundation campaigns are lactating mothers.

Apparently the health and safety of women and children have a lower priority in AID and many other international organizations than does population control. Even after the cancers were discovered in monkeys, AID, WHO, and International Planned Parenthood continued to pressure the FDA to approve the drug. The WHO toxicology review panel, for instance, "expressed reservations about the relevance of the findings of endometrial cancer in monkeys to women using DMPA (Depo-Provera)." The panel also reaffirmed its conclusion "that there were no toxicological reasons for discontinuing the use of Depo-Provera in current and planned WHO studies or family planning programmes." The official position of these agencies on Depo-Provera is not necessarily scientific nor well informed. It clearly reflects the political orientation, the male dominance and, perhaps, the undue influence of the pharmaceutical industry at the policymaking levels.

The continued use of Depo-Provera for birth-control is unjustified and unethical. A healthy woman on Depo-Provera prematurely ages. She takes on the characteristic profile of a post-menopausal woman who is at high risk of developing endometrial carcinoma. Her uterus atrophies, she stops ovulating and is sterile. Most women stop menstruating, but many experience excessive bleeding, some requiring D&Cs and hospitalization. Intermittent bleeding from the vagina commonly occurs after the first few injections. A significant proportion develops abnormal glucose tolerance curves or becomes diabetic.

The animal studies strongly suggest that the incidence of endometrial cancer will be higher with Depo-Provera than with oral contraceptives. Does the fact the two surviving monkeys developed cancer mean that two women in 100, or 1,000, or 10,000 or 100,000 will develop the disease? Obviously, the answer will depend on the age of women, length of treatment, dietary, environmental and possibly genetic factors. The cancers may not develop for 20 to 30 years after the initial exposure. It is unlikely that the relationship between Depo-Provera and cancer will ever be studied in the countries where it is widely used. The estimation of risks decades later will provide little comfort to women dying of uterine disease.

For many women the chance of surviving until menopause will be decreased by the use of Depo-Provera. The presence of viral particles in the endometrium is *proof* of the immunosuppressive effect in women at contraceptive doses. The alteration of immune response increases the vulnerability of women to serious illness particularly in countries where mortality from infectious diseases remains high.

In 40 Egyptian women on Depo-Provera liver function tests showed "a significant decrease in the prothrombin activity" and a significant impairment of hepatic excretion. The exact mechanism whereby liver function is weakened by Depo-Provera is not known.   The livers of DP treated monkeys were astrophied, however, and liver disfunction as well as liver cell adenomas were reported in dogs at relatively low doses of Depo-Provera.

Depo-Provera inhibits bone growth.   It produced skeletal abnormalities in monkeys in *all* treatment groups.   The drug should be withdrawn from family planning programs on these grounds alone.   Furthermore, treatment with Depo-Provera resulted in the degeneration of the adrenals and produced lesions in the urogenital tract, gallbladder and the endocrine glands.

Finally, all arguments about the suitability of Depo-Provera during lactation collapse when child growth and development are taken into consideration.   Daily microgram doses of the contraceptive are carried in the breast milk for three months or longer after injection.   Does the harm caused by the drug pass from the mother to her nursing infant?   Does Depo-Provera damage the hypothalamus and higher centers in the brain?   Does it retard bone growth or produce skeletal abnormalities?   Does it lower resistence to infection and interfere with the normal development of the sexual organs during infancy, causing a threat of cancer later in life?   The promoters of the drug have not asked these questions, yet they claim Depo-Provera is safe.   Do you believe them?   Would you give this contraceptive to your child, to any child, or to tens of millions of women and children?

THE UPJOHN CO., COMMENTARY ON DEPO–PROVERA, HEARINGS ON EXPORT OF HAZARDOUS PRODUCTS BEFORE THE SUBCOMMITTEE ON INTERNATIONAL ECONOMIC POLICY AND TRADE OF THE HOUSE COMMITTEE ON FOREIGN AFFAIRS

96th Cong., 2nd Sess., 313 (Sept. 9, 1980).

For some time, now, a number of "consumerist" groups (e.g., National Women's Health Network, Institute for Food and Development Policy) have been challenging the use of Depo-Provera as a contraceptive.   While the concern of such groups is primarily social and political, they raise medical and scientific issues in support of their arguments.   A recent example is "Depo-Provera: A Critical Analysis," written by Mr. Stephen Minkin. . . .   The paper has not been published in a reputable medical or scientific journal and therefore has not received scientific peer review.

The Upjohn Company has been aware of drafts of Mr. Minkin's paper for some time—and aware of the misleading interpretations of data it may suggest to the uninformed, uncritical reader.   Communications such as this . . . paper, which contain many inaccuracies and unsubstantiated allegations, use faulty scientific arguments in an attempt to legitimize predetermined social and political points of view. . . .

The letter and paper raise issues which have been considered many times before, both by the U.S. Food and Drug Administration (FDA), the U.S. Congress, the World Health Organization (WHO) and by health ministries around the world. . . .

Nevertheless, we will (1) review the full range of evidence of Depo-Provera's safety and efficacy as a long-acting injectable contraceptive; and (2) put into perspective the biased allegations made by Mr. Minkin.

CLINICAL PERSPECTIVE

. . .

First studied clinically as a contraceptive as early as 1963, Depo-Provera has now been administered as a contraceptive to more than 10 million women around the world. With its high degree of efficacy and low reported incidence of side effects, Depo-Provera is probably the safest hormonal contraceptive drug available. The rate of contraceptive failures among Depo-Provera users is extremely low. The women who receive Depo-Provera for contraception report an incidence of side effects comparable in numbers to reports for oral contraceptives (OC's). However, Depo-Provera's side effects are less serious; unlike OC's, there has never been a death reported which was ascribed to the contraceptive use of Depo-Provera.

Unique properties associated with Depo-Provera allow a single injection to provide contraceptive efficacy for 3 months. This method of contraceptive is particularly suitable for women who for various reasons do not accept the responsibility demanded by dosage schedules of contraceptive methods such as the pill. Depo-Provera is an optional method for women who cannot tolerate the estrogenic side effects associated with OC's or the pain and bleeding associated with intrauterine devices (IDU's), or who wish to avoid demonstrated life threatening complications. Depo-Provera does not suppress lactation, which is important in those developing countries where infant survival is dependent on breast-feeding. It also has little, if any, effect on suppression of vitamin levels or mineral metabolism, important in many developing countries where nutrition is marginal. Excessive menstrual flow is common with IUD's, resulting in iron deficiency anemia. Iron deficiency anemia has not been a problem with Depo-Provera, even in cases where menstrual irregularity occurs. The amenorrhea associated with Depo-Provera prevents this anemia. The method is easily administered by paramedical personnel, in contrast to the IUD which requires a physician or highly skilled paramedical personnel for insertion. This is important in locales where such personnel are scarce.

Thorough study by competent investigators has shown the drug to be at least as safe and efficacious as the OC's. Most serious adverse reactions from OC's have generally been attributed to the estrogen component. Depo-Provera contains no estrogen, nor has it been shown to be metabolized to estrogen as are other currently available progestogens. Adverse effects such as suppression of adrenal and pituitary function have not been encountered clinically. There has been no demonstrable increase in breast, cervical, or endometrial pathology; and although there has been a slight delay in return to fertility reported after discontinuation of therapy, fertility rates are the same as those for OC's, IUD's, and diaphrams 18 months after discontinuation of treatment.

No increase in the frequency of anomalies occurs among infants born after discontinuation of Depo-Provera contraception, nor has there been an increase in the rate of spontaneous abortion following Depo-Provera use. No anomalies have been reported among infants born as a result of conceptions occurring during the use of Depo-Provera.

A potential disadvantage of Depo-Provera is the inability to withdraw the drug promptly in the event of a serious adverse reaction. In actual clinical experience, however, this has not presented a problem. Other disadvantages include disturbed menstrual patterns, possible slight delay in return to fertility upon discontinuation, and the impracticality of self-administration. The latter also may be considered an advantage, because required regular visits to medical personnel can result in better monitoring of a woman's overall health status.

Depo-Provera is presently approved for use as a contraceptive in over 80 countries, including such scientifically advanced countries as West Germany, France, Belgium, Denmark, Holland, New Zealand, and Switzerland. In the U.S., where a hearing on the registration of Depo-Provera's use as a contraceptive is still pending, it has been estimated that 5–9% of the women of childbearing age are potential users of Depo-Provera. It is currently approved for treatment of endometrial and renal carcinoma in the U.S.

. . .

Mr. S. Minkin's paper . . . attempts to paint a bleak picture of Depo-Provera's utility as a contraceptive, based largely on alleged toxicities Mr. Minkin claims to have discovered in Depo-Provera animal data. The effects he points to are typically overstated. . . .

None of the alleged toxicities have been observed in clinical use of Depo-Provera for contraception. It is not appropriate to extrapolate, as Mr. Minkin does, from animal toxicity data to the contraceptive use of Depo-Provera in humans. We do know a great deal about the effects of Depo-Provera in women, from over 15 years of safe, effective and responsible experience throughout the world.

Mr. Minkin's accusation that "Depo-Provera's effect on growth can be particularly disastrous for the breast-feeding child," is totally speculative. There is no factual material cited by him to back up this claim. No adverse effects have been observed in ongoing clinical studies of children who have been nursed by mothers who received Dp for contraception. He then implies that the drug is being administered without proper care, and goes on to make the gratuitous statement that those administering the drug would be "callous and cruel." A remark of this nature, unsupported by any facts, is only argumentative and inflammatory.

. . .

Among the concerns that have arisen about FDA's dog toxicology guidelines is a long-standing controversy about the appropriateness of using the dog for toxicity studies of steroidal contraceptives. Following a meeting in London in February, 1979, held by the Committee on the Safety of Medicines (CSM) of the United Kingdom which was attended by representatives of 14 countries together with a number of scientific experts, the CSM issued a statement which reads as follows (Dept. of Health and Social Security, U.K., 1979, p. 2):

"1. Because of differences between the beagle bitch and the human female in the sensitivity to and the metabolism of progestogens, positive carcinogenicity studies in the beagle bitch can no longer be considered as indicative of significant hazards to women; and

2. The beagle bitch should no longer be a mandatory species for the long term testing of progestogens/contraceptive steroids."

Numerous investigators have questioned the suitability of the female beagle dog as a model for predicting mammary dysplasia in the human female for the following reasons:

(1) the beagle dog is highly susceptible to mammary malignancy;

(2) the dog is far more sensitive to progesterone analogs than to testosterone analogs;

(3) there are differences between the dog and human in metabolism of progestogens; and

(4) other than the ferret, the dog is the only known species in which considerable mammary lobular-alveolar growth can be produced by progesterone or its analogs alone. Other species require a pituitary or placental factor in addition to progesterone.

. . .

Since one purpose of the long-term toxicity studies is to predict potential toxic effects in women, it should be noted that by 1977, worldwide use of Depo-Provera for contraception totaled more than 6 million women-years of experience (Select Comm. Hearing Report No. 12, 1978, p. 281). No hint of an increased frequency of breast tumors or cancer has emerged from this experience.

. . .

It is difficult to speculate on the significance of reported liver and gallbladder toxicity in the Depo-Provera dog studies. Dr. Hansel et al. reported that MPA-treated dogs showed more liver and gallbladder toxicity than did control or even progesterone-treated dogs.

On the other hand, Drs. Goyings and Sokolowski specifically searched for gallbladder abnormalities in dogs treated with MPA, but concluded that their data showed no evidence of abnormality.

. . .

Although Mr. Minkin conjectures that "Depo-Provera has had an important role in the development of key provisions in [the Drug Regulation Reform Act] ", it in fact does not fall within the scope of the bill because the drug is manufactured overseas in countries where it is licensed for use as a contraceptive. The contraceptive dosage form is not exported from the U.S. The Drug Regulation Reform Act would only allow manufacture of the drug within the U.S., but Mr. Minkin fails to mention the critical restrictions contained within the proposed Act which would allow export of a nonapproved drug from the U.S. only if the recipient country's authorities formally indicated to FDA that they did not object to the importation. The U.S. FDA could also refuse to allow export of any drug if the Secretary judged that it presented a public health problem. . . .

In the case of contraceptive agents, the basic observation must be made that in *developed* countries, approximately 25 women die as a result of each 100,000 pregnancies. In developing countries, the average mortality as a result of childbearing approximates 500 per 100,000 pregnancies.

By contrast, the oral contraceptives and IUD's are estimated to have mortalities associated with their use ranging from 1 to 4 per 100,000 users. In the case of Depo-Provera use as a long-term contraceptive, no death has ever been reported from the method itself. Legal abortions have about the same overall mortality rates as OC's, while illegal abortions are estimated to result in a minimum of 100 mortalities per 100,000 abortions.

The characterization of Depo-Provera as "potentially high risk" has stemmed from animal toxicity studies. Use in *women* has to date shown little serious morbidity with Depo-Provera and has not borne out the breast findings in the beagle dog model or the endometrial tumors in high-dose monkeys. The risks of Depo-Provera in U.S. women should, of course, be assessed in controlled studies, such as the post-marketing study planned by The Upjohn Company at the FDA's request. In the meantime, data amassed in the rest of the world should not be ignored.

.   .   .

NOTES

1. FDA's refusal in 1978 to approve Depo-Provera had repercussions abroad. Five countries—Korea, Taiwan, Egypt, Jordan and Yemen—which had approved the drug, reversed their positions. Marjorie Sun, Depo-Provera Debate Revs Up at FDA, 217 Science 424,426 (1982).

The economic stakes are large. The international market for oral contraceptives totals some $700 million annually. One market analyst estimates that Depo-Provera sales have already reached $25 million annually, and further noted that oral and injectable contraceptives "have an incredible profit margin." Id. at 427.

2. There is as yet no decision by the panel of scientists reviewing FDA's decision to deny approval to Depo-Provera. This is only the second use of such a science panel by FDA. The recommendation of the first, on Aspartame, was reversed by the FDA Commissioner. See Ch. 4, Sec. D.3, supra.

At the hearing on Depo-Provera before the science panel, Robert Hoover, chief of the environmental epidemiology branch of the National Cancer Institute, called Upjohn's sale of the contraceptive to 10 million women around the world "unconscionable." Hilts, FDA Consultant Assails Upjohn's Lack of Contraceptive Studies, Washington Post, Jan. 12, 1983, at A.16, col. 1. Spokesmen for Upjohn and FDA acknowledged that carefully controlled studies are needed that follow women who take the drug over a long time. Both agreed that no such studies exist. Hoover cited a number of drugs that appeared to be without severe side effects until such studies were done, such as the hormone DES. Id.

Is the issue of whether to approve Depo-Provera in the United States for contraceptive use one that should be submitted to a science panel? Consider that the "benefits" to be weighed in the case of a contraceptive, unlike those of most drugs, are not health benefits, but reproductive benefits. Is a policy of warning consumers rather than banning the product more appropriate in the case of a contraceptive? Less appropriate? See generally Ch. 8, Sec. B.1, infra, for more detailed consideration of reproductive rights.

3. If you were a member of Congress, would you vote in favor of changing the law on the export of unapproved drugs as proposed by FDA in 1978? Why or why not?

b. Hazardous Substances Export Policy

INTERAGENCY WORKING GROUP ON A HAZARDOUS SUBSTANCES EXPORT POLICY, DRAFT REPORT

45 Fed. Reg. 53754, August 12, 1980.

In early summer of 1978, an Interagency Working Group was established to consider Federal policy on the export of hazardous substances which are banned or whose use is significantly restricted in the United States.

The export of TRIS-treated sleepwear *was not* an isolated incident. Congressional hearings in July 1978 pointed out numerous instances in which American firms exported, without restriction on the part of the U.S. government, substances that had been banned or strictly limited for use in this country. In some of these cases, the risks and benefits of using the exported products in the importing countries may have been different from those in the United States due to differing economic, social, and cultural conditions. However, in most instances, there was little evidence of a special U.S. government effort to share with importing countries the information which had led the United States to ban or strictly limit the use of the products, so that the importing countries could make their own informed judgments. The unrestrained export of hazardous substances by U.S. firms raised questions about this country's ethical responsibility for the hazards arising from hazardous exports, questions that have important implications for U.S. trade and foreign relations. One result of this concern was that in 1978 Congress amended several regulatory acts to provide notification to importers and/or to the government of the importing nation when certain banned products are exported from the United States.

U.S. manufacturers have a strong stake in fostering a positive attitude among foreign governments and consumers toward products bearing the label "Made in USA." Sale abroad of banned products tends to undermine foreign confidence in American-made products. Among the potential consequences are losses in export trade and thus negative effects on our balance of payments, and possible adverse long-term effects on foreign markets.

Uncontrolled export of hazardous substances also tends to damage our relations with foreign countries. Importing countries—generally the poorer, less developed nations of the world—have urged that exporting countries exercise restraint in sending abroad products that are banned for use at home and provide full information on the products' effects. . . . To these countries, a U.S. government policy that tolerates unrestrained export of banned products could appear callous or hostile and thus be detrimental to U.S. foreign policy interests.

. . .

II. Definition of Banned and Significantly Restricted Substances

The Working Group found that careful definition of terms was necessary, to make clear what substances should be considered for purposes of a policy to control export of banned and significantly restricted substances. The Working Group has generically defined these substances to mean a pesticide, chemical food (including meat, meat product, or poultry), food additive, drug, cosmetic, medical device, electronic product, biological product, color additive, or consumer product for which a Federal agency has taken any of the following types of regulatory actions in order to protect against an actual or potential threat to the health or safety of the United States public or to the environment:

(1) Final rulemaking or adjudicatory action (including emergency or interim binding action) which denies or revokes approval for, or prohibits, the manufacture, production, use, or sale in the United States.

(2) Final rulemaking or adjudicatory action (including emergency or interim binding action) which prohibits or revokes approval of most significant uses in the United States.

(3) Withholding, or absence of registration or approval for any substance for which Federal law requires Federal agency registration or approval before manufacture, production, use, or sale in the United States.

. . .

Certain categories of products were excluded from the Working Group report because of their special legislative history or because of the special problems they raise: alcohol, tobacco, and firearms; military weapons and equipment; narcotic and pyschotropic substances; and nuclear fuels. . . .

III. Nature and Scope of the Problem

Since there are only limited controls at present on export of banned and significantly restricted substances, the government has no mechanisms for monitoring or valuing such exports. Further, many firms resist disclosure of the extent or destination of export products. Some of them consider their marketing plans trade secrets. Thus, no estimates are available of the dollar value of such substances exported from the United States.

. . .

Several examples . . . suggest the nature and scope of the problem. . . .

. . .

• In March 1978, the Food and Drug Administration (FDA) issued a final rule prohibiting the nonessential uses of certain chlorofluorocarbons (CFCs) as propellants in self-pressurized containers of foods, drugs and cosmetics. EPA at the same time prohibited domestic production, processing, and use of CFCs for nonessential aerosol propellant use. These actions were taken because chlorofluorocarbons may deplete stratospheric ozone, leading to an increase in skin cancer, climatic changes, and other adverse effects. EPA also banned the processing of CFCs into aerosols for export, though it did not ban the export of unprocessed CFCs. Subsequently, some manufacturers requested information from FDA as to whether or not it was legal to export cosmetics (e.g., hair sprays) containing chlorofluorocarbons as propellants. FDA advised these firms that shipping cosmetic products to other countries was lawful as long as they were not prohibited by the country to which they are shipped.

• The very powerful and very hazardous pesticide, Leptophos, never registered by EPA for domestic use, was manufactured in the United States principally for export. According to Congressional testimony, nearly 14 million pounds was exported to 50 countries between 1971 and 1976. In 1971 and 1972 a number of Egyptian farmers were found to be suffering from hallucinations and impairment of vision and speech after using Leptophos, and 1,200 water buffalos were reported to have died from exposure to the pesticide.

• According to the General Accounting Office, over 500 million pounds of pesticides were exported from the United States in 1976. Of these exports, approximately 30 percent (more than 160 million pounds) were pesticides not registered for use in the United States. . . . Un-registered pesticides may lawfully be exported provided that the product is labeled as unregistered (and meets other labeling requirements) and that importers are notified and acknowledge that the pesticide is unregistered. A copy of the acknowledgement is sent to EPA for transmittal to the foreign government.

. . .

• Chloramphenicol is an extremely potent antibiotic used in the United States only against typhoid fever and a few other life-threatening infections because of its serious potential side effects, such as aplastic anemia. The FDA indicated in Congressional testimony that an American firm had labelled and exported it to Spanish-speaking countries as suitable for treatment of much more routine disease for which there had been no substantiation of its effectiveness, including measles, mumps, and chicken pox, with no warnings as to its dangerous side effects.

. . .

Besides the concerns about health and safety effects of hazardous substances exports on foreign citizens, effects on our own citizens are also a cause of concern. Export of hazardous substances can have a direct effect on U.S. citizens by more than one route: through adverse effects on workers in the plant where the product is manufactured; through the reimportation of the original substances or their traces or derivatives; through the illegal diversion into domestic commerce of restricted products originally produced for export; or through transport of hazardous substances back to this country via the air or oceans. The world environment itself could suffer through release of hazardous substances to the global commons.

A General Accounting Office report concluded that many kinds of imported foods may be contaminated with pesticides not allowed in the United States. FDA spot checks (examining about 1 percent of shipments) of imported raw agricultural commodities found that about 5 percent of the shipments tested in 1977 through 1979 contained residues of pesticides for which no U.S. tolerance levels exist. . . . Pesticides banned in the United States but used in other countries, especially nearby countries like Canada and Mexico, can also travel by water or air to enter the environment of the United States.

. . .

If current economic trends continue, exports are likely to increase. In 1970, total U.S. exports of goods and services were $62.5 billion or 6.4 percent of gross national product. By 1978, the percentage had risen to 9.7 percent and the dollar value was $205 billion. . . .

IV. Existing Statutory Authority and Procedures

. . .

The provisions of existing statutes pertaining to export of substances which are banned or significantly restricted in the United States are of five general types, although some statutes fit more than one category. In addition there are a good many qualifications and exceptions in the laws. As the following outline shows, the regulatory scheme is complex.

(1) *Substances for which there are no export limitations or for which exports must be in accord with the laws of the importing nation:*

Federal Food, Drug and Cosmetic Act—adulterated or misbranded foods (except meat and poultry subject to controls), cosmetics, drugs, and antibiotics.

Public Health Service Act—noncomplying electronic products.

Federal Insecticide, Fungicide and Rodenticide Act—registered pesticides composed of active ingredients for which major uses have been cancelled or suspended.

(2) *Substances for which notification of the importing country of any export is required:*

Federal Insecticide, Fungicide, and Rodenticide Act—pesticides not registered for use in the United States.

Toxic Substances Control Act—certain regulated chemical substances.

Consumer Product Safety Act—consumer products which are banned or do not meet federal safety standards.

Flammable Fabrics Act—fabric-type products which do not conform to federal safety standards.

Federal Hazardous Substances Act—toxic, flammable, corrosive and otherwise hazardous products, including children's articles which fail to meet federal requirements.

(3) *Substances for which prior approval by the importing country must be sought:*

Federal Food, Drug and Cosmetic Act—unapproved medical devices and investigational drugs.

(4) *Substances for which an agency can ban exports if there is a risk to health or the environment of the United States:*

Toxic Substances Control Act—chemical substances

Consumer Product Safety Act—consumer products

Flammable Fabrics Act—fabric-type products

Federal Hazardous Substances Act—household chemicals

(5) *Substances for which there is a total ban on export:*

Federal Food, Drug and Cosmetic Act—unapproved new drugs, unapproved new animal drugs

Public Health Service Act—unapproved biological products (serums, vaccines, etc.)

Meat Inspection Act—meat failing to meet U.S. quality standards (except for preservation)

Poultry Products Inspection Act—poultry failing to meet U.S. standards.

. . .

In addition to the laws regulating specific products or practices, two additional authorities are relevant to export policy.

First, the Export Administration Act of 1979 (Pub.L. 96–72) authorizes the President to use export controls to restrict the export of goods and technology where such export might prove detrimental to the national security of the United States; restrict export where necessary to prevent the excessive drain of scarce materials from the United States or to reduce the serious inflationary impact of foreign demand; and restrict export where necessary to further significantly the foreign policy of the United States or to fulfill its declared international obligations. This recently enacted statute extends and revises the Export Administration Act of 1969.

Second, Executive Order No. 12114, issued by President Carter on January 4, 1979, requires that agencies analyze the environmental effects abroad of certain types of major Federal actions that may significantly affect the environment. This analysis will help guide decisions by the responsible agency officials. However, the grant or denial of an export license under the Export Administration Act is not considered a major Federal action for the purposes of Executive Order No. 12114.

. . .

V. Policy

. . .

A. Policy Considerations

The Working Group agreed on the need to establish a more consistent, practical Federal policy to govern the export of banned and significantly restricted substances. Participating agencies identified the following considerations that should be taken into account:

(1) As a nation exporting banned and significantly restricted substances, the United States has a moral obligation to recognize and assist in controlling the potential effects of these substances on the health and safety of citizens abroad and on the world environment.

(2) Nations differ substantially in their economic and cultural conditions and in their use of, and need for, hazardous substances. It is difficult for one nation to make decisions on the acceptability of risks for another nation. Such assessments require extensive information regarding economic, political, and social conditions which U.S. regulatory agencies do not have and cannot readily obtain.

(3) U.S. relations with other countries could be harmed by unrestrained export of substances which are banned or significantly restricted in the United States.

(4) The unrestrained export of hazardous products could undermine confidence of foreign buyers in U.S.-made goods, and could jeopardize their sale abroad.

(5) Excessively restrictive limitations on the export of products which a foreign country may decide it needs could place U.S. firms at a competitive disadvantage and harm U.S. relations with the government of that country.

(6) Excessively restrictive limitations could also place significant economic burdens on the U.S. economy, including adverse effects on the balance of trade and payments, on output and jobs, and perhaps on domestic competition (if smaller firms suffer disproportionately from reduced ability to compete in foreign markets).

(7) An export policy should be administratively simple and inexpensive to implement, and should recognize the complexities of international commerce.

(8) The United States should encourage and participate actively in international initiatives to develop consistent policies for hazardous substance exports, and for the sharing of data, analysis, and information.

The effectiveness of unilateral United States action could be substantially diminished if foreign facilities or firms were to become alternative suppliers of substances which U.S. policies seek to control.

(9) The United States should attempt to protect American citizens against the dangers to their health and safety of importing hazardous substances and their derivatives or residues, and of damage to the world environment.

B.   Proposed Policy

. . .

(1) *Hazard Notification:* The Working Group concluded that in most circumstances the international responsibilities of the United States could be met by an effective hazard notification system. . . .

Most of the laws requiring notification, including those contained in the Consumer Product Safety Act, the Federal Hazardous Substances Act, the Flammable Fabrics Act, and the Federal Insecticide, Fungicide, and Rodenticide Act, are less than 2 years old; some of the regulations implementing them are not yet final, and those in effect are very recent. The notification schemes in the various laws differ in terms of timing, frequency, and content of the notice, and experience with them is minimal. Accordingly, the Working Group is not able at this point to recommend the best scheme for notification.

The Working Group does not recommend any changes in existing law at this time. As we gain experience with the requirements of present laws, the Administration will assess their effectiveness, any important omissions they may have left, and any burdens they may impose. . . .

. . .

The Working Group agreed that there was a need for greater procedural uniformity in the notification process as used by Federal agencies. It would be more effective and more efficient, for the United States and for other countries, to establish an official government-to-government contract for transmission of information concerning hazardous substances.

The Working Group recommends that the State Department be designated the official conduit of notifications concerning exports of banned and significantly restricted hazardous substances for all Federal agencies.
. . .

. . .

In addition to greater uniformity in procedure, it is also desirable to achieve greater uniformity in the content of the notices sent to foreign governments. The Working Group recommends that the information to be provided by the State Department to the foreign government include, at a minimum:

(a) The name of the hazardous substance to be exported;

(b) A concise summary of the agency's regulatory actions regarding that substance, including the statutory authority for such actions and the timetable for any further actions that are planned; and

(c) A concise summary of the potential risks to human health or safety or to the environment that are the grounds for the agency's actions.

In addition, to the extent deemed appropriate by the agency with jurisdiction, copies of additional documents could be forwarded to a foreign country to assist that country in its assessment of the risks associated with the substance. Trade secret data would not be sent to the foreign country except as authorized by domestic statute and deemed appropriate by the agency with jurisdiction.

. . .

(3) *Export Control:* The Working Group concluded that the responsibilities of the United States concerning the export of hazardous substances would be fulfilled in most cases through notification. There are some limited circumstances, however, where additional safeguards are needed to assure good and stable relations with other nations in the world community. If the United States does not exercise special vigilance over the export of some banned or significantly restricted products which are particularly hazardous, our economic and diplomatic ties with other countries could be jeopardized. . . .

As indicated . . . existing law already prohibits the export of some substances in particular circumstances. Another mechanism that can be used to prohibit hazardous exports where such exports would prove detrimental to the foreign policy interests of the United States is the Export Administration Act of 1979 (Pub.L. No. 96–72, 93 Stat. 503, 50 U.S.C. App. § 2401 et seq. (the Act)). . . .

. . .

The Working Group recommends that the Secretary of Commerce require a validated export license for those prohibited and significantly restricted products which, if exported, would prove detrimental to the foreign policy interests of the United States. The products on which such export controls would be imposed would be chosen in the following manner. First, the appropriate regulatory agencies would prepare lists of substances, products, and classes of products which have been banned or significantly restricted in the United States . . .. These prohibited and restricted substances, with the exception of certain unregistered pesticides and "medicines and medical supplies" as the term is used in the Act, would constitute the universe from which those substances to be subjected to export controls would be chosen. . . .

Next, these lists of substances and products would be brought before an interagency task force. . . . This task force would advise the State Department as to which of the listed substances should be considered, because of the especially severe hazards that their export would pose to human health or safety or to the environment, candidates for inclusion on the Commodity Control List. In doing so, the task force would consider, to the extent possible within the limits of available information, the type, extent, and severity of the potential detrimental effects of each substance proposed for inclusion on the Commodity Control List, by a member of the task force; the likelihood of the effects; the duration of the effects; the ability of foreign countries to avoid or mitigate the effects; the availability of the substance from sources other than the United States; the availability of other substances or methods that would serve the same purpose as the substance to be exported; and the importance of the beneficial uses of the substance (this is not intended to require a rigorous, quantitative analysis of costs and benefits, however, as is usually performed in domestic regulatory procedures).

. . .

The Working Group believes that the economic consequences of invoking expert controls would not be great. The categories of products which would be candidates for Commodity Control List are well defined and readily identifiable. The number of substances which would be chosen for the CCL is expected to be small. In addition, it is quite possible that a U.S. firm may have or could develop a substitute product offering the same benefits without posing severely hazardous risks.

. . .

(6) *Labeling of Hazardous Exports:* The Working Group recommends that regulatory agencies give continuing attention to improvements in labeling, as a technique for dealing with hazardous exports. In some cases, it may be possible to develop simplified, more readily understandable labels. Agencies may also want to consider new requirements that pesticide, drug and toxic substance labels on exported products include more information on the nature of possible hazards associated with their use. The Administration might propose legislation, if appropriate, to impose such requirements.

. . .

PRESIDENT CARTER, EXECUTIVE ORDER 12264

46 Fed.Reg. 4659 (January 15, 1981).

By the authority vested in me as President by the Constitution of the United States of America, and in order to further the foreign policy interests of the United States and to provide for effective and responsible implementation of the Export Administration Act of 1979 (50 U.S.C.App. 2401 et seq.) and other statutes insofar as they relate to the export of banned or significantly restricted substances, it is hereby ordered as follows:

. . .

1–201. Each agency that is required by statute to notify, or to be apprised of notifications to, foreign countries regarding exports of banned or significantly restricted substances to those countries shall adhere, to the extent not inconsistent with applicable law, to the following procedures:

(a) Each agency shall promptly provide to the Department of State such information regarding an export of banned or significantly restricted substances to a foreign government as is required by statute or agency regulation to be forwarded to the foreign government, either by the agency or by another party required to apprise the agency of its notification, and by the notification forms and procedures to be established by the Department of State pursuant to Subsection 1–201(b). As soon as feasible after the receipt of the required information from an agency, the Department of State shall transmit the information to the government of the foreign country to which the banned or significantly restricted substance is to be exported.

(b) The Department of State shall consult with affected agencies regarding the format and content appropriate for required notifications to foreign governments and shall establish, within 90 days after the issuance of this Order, notification forms and procedures. At a minimum, the following information shall be transmitted to foreign governments regarding banned or significantly restricted substances to be exported to them from the United States:

(1) the name of the substance to be exported;

(2) a concise summary of the agency's regulatory actions regarding that substance, including the statutory authority for such actions and the timetable for any further actions that are planned; and,

(3) a concise summary of the potential risks to human health or safety or to the environment that are the grounds for the agency's actions.

In addition, to the extent deemed appropriate by the agency with jurisdiction over the banned or significantly restricted substance to be exported, copies of additional documents may be forwarded to a foreign government, either at the same time as or subsequent to the required notification, to assist the foreign government in its assessment of the nature and extent of the risks associated with the substance.

(c) With respect to each required notification regarding an export of a banned or significantly restricted substance, each agency shall identify for the Department of State the persons or offices within that agency to be contacted in the event that the foreign government receiving the notification wishes to obtain through the Department of State additional information regarding the risks of, or regulatory actions taken with respect to, the banned or significantly restricted substance that is the subject of the notification.

. . .

1-3. Export Control Procedures

1-301. It is the intent of this Order to rely primarily on the notification procedures, annual report, and participation in international efforts provided for in Sections 1-2, 1-4, and 1-5, respectively, in implementing the Order, and to resort to the imposition of export controls only in a very few instances. Specifically, export controls should be limited to extremely hazardous substances, as determined by the agency primarily responsible for regulating a substance on the basis of the record compiled in connection with regulatory action taken by that agency concerning that substance—

(a) which represent a substantial threat to human health or safety or to the environment,

(b) the export of which would cause clear and significant harm to the foreign policy interest of the United States, and

(c) for which export licenses would be granted only in exceptional cases.

Export controls shall not be applied to . . . "medicine or medical supplies," which are excluded from such controls by Section 6(f) of the Export Administration Act of 1979 (50 U.S.C.App. 2405(f)). . . .

1-302. Within 90 days after the issuance of this Order, the Department of Commerce shall develop for interagency review proposed regulations to govern its consideration of applications for licenses to export banned or significantly restricted substances included on the Commodity Control List. Within 120 days after the issuance of this Order, the Department of Commerce shall publish the proposed regulations in the Federal Register for public comment.

1-303. In accord with its statutory role under the Export Administration Act, and consistent with the policy and standards enunciated in Subsection 1-301, the Department of State shall identify, subject to the concurrence of the Department of Commerce, candidates for inclusion on the Commodity Control List. If the Department of State and Department of Commerce are unable to agree on the inclusion on the Commodity Control List of a particular substance, the matter shall be referred to the President.

1-304. In order to assist the Department of State in the development of its advice to the Department of Commerce under subsection 1-303, there is hereby established an interagency task force, to be chaired by the Department of State. . . .

1-305. To the extent possible, within the limits of available information and consistent with the policy and standards enunciated in Subsection 1-301, the task force shall consider, with respect to each banned or significantly restricted substance that is proposed for inclusion on the Commodity Control List by a member of the task force:

(a) the type, extent, and severity of the potential detrimental effects of the substance;

(b) the likelihood of the effects;

(c) the duration of the effects;

(d) the ability of foreign countries to avoid or mitigate the effects; .

(e) the availability of the substance from sources other than the United States;

(f) the availability of other substances or methods that would serve the same purposes as the substance; and

(g) the importance of the beneficial uses of the substances.

1-306. . . . The Department of State shall not recommend issuing a license unless (1) it has determined that the export would not cause clear and significant harm to the foreign policy interests of the United States and (2) after appropriate consultations, it has received no objections to the export from the government of the foreign country to which the banned or significantly restricted substance is to be exported. The findings and recommendations of the Department of State shall be conveyed in writing to the Department of Commerce.

. . .

1-7. Trade Secret Protection

1-701. Trade secrets or other confidential commercial or financial information that pertain to a banned or significantly restricted substance to be exported shall not be forwarded to a foreign government in the notifications or other documents prepared pursuant to this Order unless authorized or required by existing law.

PRESIDENT REAGAN, EXECUTIVE ORDER 12290

46 Fed.Reg. 12943 (Feb. 17, 1981).

By the authority vested in me as President by the Constitution of the United States of America, and in order to ensure that the Export Administration Act of 1979 is implemented with the minimum regulatory burden, Executive Order No. 12264 of January 15, 1981, entitled "On Federal Policy Regarding the Export of Banned or Significantly Restricted Substances," is hereby revoked.

NOTE

Is the policy of relying primarily on notification when exporting hazardous substances an appropriate policy? What standards should the government follow in deciding when to prohibit the export of a particular product?

*

Part Four

EXPLORING PROBLEMS AT
THE FRONTIER

Chapter 6

MEDICAL EXPERIMENTATION WITH HUMAN SUBJECTS

A. OVERVIEW

HANS JONAS,
PHILOSOPHICAL REFLECTIONS ON EXPERIMENTING WITH HUMAN SUBJECTS

in Experimentation with Human Subjects
1–4, 9–14 (P. Freund ed. 1970).

Experimenting with human subjects is going on in many fields of scientific and technological progress. It is designed to replace the over-all instruction by natural, occasional experience with the selective information from artificial, systematic experiment which physical science has found so effective in dealing with inanimate nature. Of the new experimentation with man, medical is surely the most legitimate; psychological, the most dubious, biological (still to come), the most dangerous. I have chosen here to deal with the first only, where the case *for* it is strongest and the task of adjudicating conflicting claims hardest. . . .

The Peculiarity of Human Experimentation

Experimentation was originally sanctioned by natural science. There it is performed on inanimate objects, and this raises no moral problems. But as soon as animate, feeling beings become the subjects of experiment, as they do in the life sciences and especially in medical research, this innocence of the search for knowledge is lost and questions of conscience arise. The depth to which moral and religious sensibilities can become aroused over these questions is shown by the vivisection issue. Human experimentation must sharpen the issue as it involves ultimate questions of personal dignity and sacrosanctity. One profound difference between the human experiment and the physical (beside that between animate and inanimate, feeling and unfeeling nature) is this: The physical experiment employs small-scale, artificially devised substitutes for that about which knowledge is to be obtained, and the experimenter extrapolates from these models and simulated conditions to nature at large. Something deputizes for the "real thing"—balls rolling down an inclined plane for sun and planets, electric discharges from a condenser for real lightning, and so on. For the most part, no such substitution is possible in the biological sphere. We must operate on the original itself, the real thing in the fullest sense, and perhaps affect it irreversibly. No simulacrum can take its place. Especially in the human sphere, experimentation loses entirely the advantage of the clear division between vicarious model and true object. Up to a point, animals may fulfill the proxy role of the classical physical experiment. But in the end man himself must furnish knowledge about himself, and the comfortable separation of noncommittal experiment and definitive action vanishes. . . . Human experimentation for whatever purpose is always *also* a responsible, nonexperimental, definitive dealing with the subject himself. And not even the noblest purpose abrogates the obligations this involves.

This is the root of the problem with which we are faced: Can both that purpose and this obligation be satisfied? If not, what would be a just compromise? Which side should give way to the other? The question is inherently philosophical as it concerns not merely pragmatic difficulties and their arbitration, but a genuine conflict of values involving principles of a high order. May I put the conflict in these terms. On principle, it is felt, human beings *ought not* to be dealt with in that way (the "guinea pig" protest); on the other hand, such dealings are increasingly urged on us by considerations, in turn appealing to principle, that claim to override those objections. . . .

Before going any further, we should give some more articulate voice to the resistance we feel against a merely utilitarian view of the matter. It has to do with a pecularity of human experimentation quite independent of the question of possible injury to the subject. What is wrong with making a person an experimental subject is not so much that we make him thereby a means (which happens in social contexts of all kinds), as that we make him a thing—a passive thing merely to be acted on, and passive not even for real action, but for token action whose token object he is. His being is reduced to that of a mere token or "sample." This is different from even the most exploitative situations of social life: there the business is real, not fictitious. The subject, however much abused, remains an agent and thus a "subject" in the other sense of the word. The soldier's case is instructive: Subject to most unilateral discipline, forced to risk mutilation and death, conscripted without, perhaps against, his will—he is still conscripted with his capacities to act, to hold his own or fail in situations, to meet real challenges for real stakes. Though a mere "number" to the High Command, he is not a token and not a thing. (Imagine what he would say if it turned out that the war was a game staged to sample observations on his endurance, courage, or cowardice.)

These compensations of personhood are denied to the subject of experimentation, who is acted upon for an extraneous end without being engaged in a real relation where he would be the counterpoint to the other or to circumstance. Mere "consent" (mostly amounting to no more than permission) does not right this reification. Only genuine authenticity of volunteering can possibly redeem the condition of "thinghood" to which the subject submits. . . . Let us now look at the nature of the conflict, and especially at the nature of the claims countering in this matter those on behalf of personal sacrosanctity.

The setting for the conflict most consistently invoked in the literature is the polarity of individual versus society—the possible tension between the individual good and the common good, between private and public welfare. . . .

. . . We do not normally—that is, in nonemergency conditions—give the state the right to conscript labor, while we do give it the right to "conscript" money, for money is detachable from the person as labor is not. Even less than forced labor do we countenance forced risk, injury, and indignity.

But in time of war our society itself supersedes the nice balance of the social contract with an almost absolute precedence of public necessities over individual rights. In this and similar emergencies, the sacrosanctity of the individual is abrogated, and what for all practical purposes amounts to a near-totalitarian, quasi-communist state of affairs is *temporarily* permitted to prevail. In such situations, the community is conceded the right to make calls on its members, or certain of its members, entirely different in magnitude and kind from the calls normally allowed. It is deemed right that a part of the population bears a disproportionate burden of risk of a disproportionate gravity; and it is deemed right that the rest of the community accepts this sacrifice, whether voluntary or enforced, and reaps its benefits—difficult as we find it to justify this acceptance and this benefit by any normal ethical categories. We justify it transethically, as it were, by the supreme collective emergency, formalized, for example, by the declaration of a state of war.

Medical experimentation on human subjects falls somewhere between this overpowering case and the normal transactions of the social contract. On the one hand, no comparable extreme issue of social survival is (by and large) at stake. And no comparable extreme sacrifice or foreseeable risk is (by and large) asked. On the other hand, what is asked goes decidedly beyond, even runs counter to, what it is otherwise deemed fair to let the individual sign over of his person to the benefit of the "common good." Indeed, our sensitivity to the kind of intrusion and use involved is such that only an end of transcendent value or overriding urgency can make it arguable and possibly acceptable in our eyes.

Health as a Public Good

The cause invoked is health and, in its more critical aspect, life itself—clearly superlative goods that the physician serves directly by curing and the researcher indirectly by the knowledge gained through his experiments. There is no question about the good served nor about the evil fought—disease and premature death. But a good to whom and an evil to whom? Here the issue tends to become somewhat clouded. In the attempt to give experimentation the proper dignity (on the problematic view that a value becomes greater by being "social" instead of merely individual), the health in question or the disease in question is somehow predicated on the social whole, as if it were society that, in the persons of its members, enjoyed the one and suffered the other.

In trying to resolve some of the complexities and ambiguities lurking in these conceptualizations, I have pondered a particular statement, made in the form of a question, which I found in the *Proceedings* of the earlier *Daedalus* conference: "Can society afford to discard the tissues and organs of the hopelessly unconscious patient when they could be used to restore the otherwise hopelessly ill, but still salvageable individual?" And somewhat later: "A strong case can be made that society can ill afford to discard the tissues and organs of the hopelessly unconscious patient; they are greatly needed for study and experimental trial to help those who can be salvaged." [7] . . . Let me, for a moment, take the question literally. "Discarding" implies proprietary rights—nobody can discard what does not belong to him in the first place. Does society then own my body? "Salvaging" implies the same and, moreover, a use-value to the owner.

7. Proceedings of the Conference on the Ethical Aspects of Experimentation on Human Subjects, November 3–4, 1967 (Boston Massachusetts).

Is the life-extension of certain individuals then a public interest? "Affording" implies a critically vital level of such an interest—that is, of the loss or gain involved. And "society" itself—what is it? When does a need, an aim, an obligation become social? Let us reflect on some of these terms.

What Society Can Afford

"Can Society afford . . .?" Afford what? To let people die intact, thereby withholding something from other people who desperately need it, who in consequence will have to die too? These other, unfortunate people indeed cannot afford not to have a kidney, heart, or other organ of the dying patient, on which they depend for an extension of their lease on life; but does that give them a right to it? And does it oblige society to procure it for them? What is it that *society* can or cannot afford—leaving aside for the moment the question of what it has a *right* to? It surely can afford to lose members through death; more than that, it is built on the balance of death and birth decreed by the order of life. This is too general, of course, for our question, but perhaps it is well to remember. The specific question seems to be whether society can afford to let some people die whose death might be deferred by particular means if these were authorized by society. Again, if it is merely a question of what society can or cannot afford, rather than of what it ought or ought not to do, the answer must be: Of course, it can. If cancer, heart disease, and other organic, noncontagious ills, especially those tending to strike the old more than the young, continue to exact their toll at the normal rate of incidence (including the toll of private anguish and misery), society can go on flourishing in every way.

Here, by contrast, are some examples of what, in sober truth, society cannot afford. It cannot afford to let an epidemic rage unchecked; a persistent excess of deaths over births, but neither—we must add—too great an excess of births over deaths; too low an average life expectancy even if demographically balanced by fertility, but neither too great a longevity with the necessitated correlative dearth of youth in the social body; a debilitating state of general health; and things of this kind. These are plain cases where the whole condition of society is critically affected, and the public interest can make its imperative claims. The Black Death of the Middle Ages was a *public* calamity of the acute kind; the life-sapping ravages of endemic malaria or sleeping sickness in certain areas are a public calamity of the chronic kind. Such situations a society as a whole can truly not "afford," and they may call for extraordinary remedies, including, perhaps, the invasion of private sacrosanctities.

. . .

Society and the Cause of Progress

Much weaker is the case where it is a matter not of saving but of improving society. Much of medical research falls into this category. As stated before, a permanent death rate from heart failure or cancer does not threaten society. So long as certain statistical ratios are maintained, the incidence of disease and of disease-induced mortality is not (in the strict sense) a "social" misfortune. I hasten to add that it is not therefore less of a human misfortune, and the call for relief issuing with silent eloquence from each victim and all potential victims is of no lesser dignity. But it is misleading to equate the fundamentally human response to it with what is owed to society: it is owed by man to man—and it is thereby owed by society to the individuals as soon as the adequate ministering to these concerns outgrows (as it progressively does) the scope of private spontaneity and is made a public mandate. It is thus that society assumes responsibility for medical care, research, old age, and innumerable other things not originally of the public realm (in the original "social contract"), and they become duties toward "society" (rather than directly toward one's fellow man) by the fact that they are socially operated.

Indeed, we expect from organized society no longer mere protection against harm and the securing of the conditions of our preservation, but active and constant improvement in all the domains of life: the waging of the battle against nature, the enhancement of the human estate—in short, the promotion of progress. This is an expansive goal, one far surpassing the disaster norm of our previous reflections. It lacks the urgency of the latter, but has the nobility of the free, forward thrust. It surely is worth sacrifices. It is not at all a question of what society can afford, but of what it is committed to, beyond all necessity, by our mandate. Its trusteeship has become an established, ongoing, institutionalized business of the body politic. As eager beneficiaries of its gains, we now owe to "society," as its chief agent, our individual contributions toward its *continued pursuit.* I emphasize "continued pursuit." Maintaining the existing level requires no more than the orthodox means of taxation and enforcement of professional standards that raise no problems. The more optional goal of pushing forward is also more exacting. We have this syndrome: Progress is by our choosing an acknowledged interest of society, in which we have a stake in various degrees; science is a necessary instrument of progress; research is a necessary instrument of science; and in medical science experimentation on human subjects is a necessary instrument of research. Therefore, human experimentation has come to be a societal interest.

The destination of research is essentially melioristic. It does not serve the preservation of the existing good from which I profit myself and to which I am obligated. Unless the present state is intolerable, the melioristic goal is in a sense gratuitous, and this not only from the vantage point of the present. Our descendants have a right to be left an unplundered planet; they do not have a right to new miracle cures. We have sinned against them, if by our doing we have destroyed their inheritance—which we are doing at full blast; we have not sinned against them, if by the time they come around arthritis has not yet been conquered (unless by sheer neglect). And generally, in the matter of progress, as humanity had no claim on a Newton, a Michelangelo, or a St. Francis to appear, and no right to the blessings of their unscheduled deeds, so progress, with all our methodical labor for it, cannot be budgeted in advance and its fruits received as a due. Its coming-about at all and its turning out for good (of which we can never be sure) must rather be regarded as something akin to grace.

The Melioristic Goal, Medical Research, and Individual Duty

Nowhere is the melioristic goal more inherent than in medicine.

. . .

. . .

[W]e must look outside the sphere of the social contract, outside the whole realm of public rights and duties, for the motivations and norms by which we can expect ever again the upwelling of a will to give what nobody—neither society, nor fellow man, nor posterity—is entitled to. There are such dimensions in man with trans-social wellsprings of conduct, and I have already pointed to the paradox, or mystery, that society cannot prosper without them, that it must draw on them, but cannot command them.

PRESIDENT'S COMMISSION FOR THE STUDY OF ETHICAL PROBLEMS IN MEDICINE AND BIOMEDICAL AND BEHAVIORAL RESEARCH, COMPENSATING FOR RESEARCH INJURIES

11–13, 72–75, 79–80 (1982).

The Role of Biomedical and Behavioral Research. Since World War II, the magnitude of biomedical and behavioral research in the United States has increased tremendously, as has the Federal government's participation. By 1980, health research had become an $8-billion-a-year enterprise, with over half the funding coming from the Federal government, through the National Institutes of Health and over twenty other agencies; furthermore, a large proportion of the privately sponsored research on drugs, medical devices, other consumer products, and pesticides is conducted pursuant to extensive Federal regulation, although not supported by public funds.

The centrality of research in medicine, particularly in American society in recent decades, makes it easy to forget that the role of the professional clinical investigator and the institutionalization of clinical research are historically recent, 20th century developments. Nevertheless, over the past fifty years and particularly since World War II, certain changes are discernible in the settings and modes of organization of biomedical and behavioral research. A progressive shift has occurred from the type of small, collegial, personally directed units such as those depicted in the 1950s by Means and Fox to massive, sprawling institutions which often dominate the academic environments they inhabit or which are conducted under industrial and governmental control.

Americans generally share the benefits of enhanced understanding of human physiology and advances in therapy. Similarly, although contributions to the public purse are not strictly proportionate, it is the citizenry as a whole that sponsors publicly supported research. Research, then, is an enterprise that is collectively sponsored and responsive to the collective good.

The widespread enthusiasm shown in recent decades for medical research can be at least partly explained by one single fact: all of us are threatened by disease and disability. The risks of nature affect everyone, rich or poor, black or white, male or female (though some risks are higher for less-advantaged groups). Research offers the promise of reducing some of these risks. Research can also help to reduce some of the risks imposed by health care itself, for a significant amount of clinical research is designed to test the safety and efficacy of currently accepted medical practices. For example, two clinical trials which spawned widely publicized litigation by injured subjects—the University of Chicago study of the use of diethylstilbestrol (DES) during pregnancy to prevent miscarriage, and the multi-center clinical trial with premature infants examining the relationship of oxygen therapy to the incidence of blindness resulting from retrolental fibroplasia—provided the scientific basis for rejecting or modifying those therapies. Were such research never conducted, these therapies might still be employed in general medical practice. Thus, acceptance of controlled risks in clinical research can, and regularly does, result in knowledge which reduces the "risks of everyday life," including those risks associated with standard medical care, for all members of the society.

Increased freedom from risks is, then, one promise of research. But there is no easy path toward this goal. Scientists must test out hypotheses, and they must sometimes use human beings—meaning their own bodies or others'—as a laboratory to understand normal physiology as well as abnormal conditions, and to fill in important gaps in knowledge about the efficacy and safety of new medical interventions. Thus, in its pursuit of preventive, diagnostic, and therapeutic interventions which are intended to *reduce* the risks caused both by nature and by human activities, research *imposes* other risks. These risks of research are borne by only a tiny fraction of the number of persons who face the risks of disease and disability that research is designed to combat. More importantly, the manifestation of these research risks as actual injuries is *not* spread evenly over the entire population; they occur for an unfortunate few among those who serve as subjects.

. . .

Government-Reported Incidence of Harm. The Commission has found that data on research-related injuries and on research subjects generally are extremely limited in terms of both the amount of information available and its generalizability. Despite the very major role of the government in research, there is no comprehensive Federal mechanism for collecting data on injuries. In response to direct inquiries, officials from FDA and NIH testified that neither agency compiles such information. In addition, of the more than twenty other Federal agencies that conduct or support research with human subjects, only one (the National Bureau of Standards) was able to provide the Commission with information on either the nature or the incidence of injuries experienced by subjects in research conducted under its auspices. Neither the government as a whole nor the individual agencies have data on the number or kind of injuries sustained by subjects of Federally conducted, supported, or regulated research.

The only Federal attempt to collect and analyze data on research injuries was a special study conducted in 1976 by Philippe Cardon and his associates for the HEW Secretary's Task Force on the Compensation of Injured Research Subjects. In a telephone survey, investigators were asked to report the number of subjects involved in therapeutic and in nontherapeutic studies, the nature and incidence of injuries "that could be attributed to the conduct of the experimental regimen," and whether those injuries were experienced by subjects of therapeutic or nontherapeutic research. Injuries were classified as: trivial, temporarily disabling, permanently disabling, and fatal.

Investigators reported on a total of 132,615 subjects. Overall, 3.0% of the subjects experienced trivial adverse effects, 0.7% experienced temporarily disabling injuries, less than 0.1% were permanently disabled and 0.03% died. (All of the fatalities occurred in patient-subjects in therapeutic research.) Of the more than 39,000 subjects participating in therapeutic research studies, 10.8% experienced adverse affects or injuries most of which were trivial in nature. Only 2.4% of subjects were temporarily disabled, less than 0.1% were permanently disabled and approximately 0.1% died. Most of the 43 fatalities were not clearly related to the research. In fact, 37 (86%) of the reported deaths were in cancer chemotherapy trials. In the other categories as well, many of the "injured" were cancer patients who experienced familiar side effects of standard treatment. The incidence of injury for subjects participating in nontherapeutic research was even lower. Of 93,399 subjects, only 8.8% experienced injuries, most of which were trivial. Thirty-seven people (0.1%) were temporarily disabled, one person was permanently disabled and there were no fatalities. The authors correctly point out: "the data are a gross summation of the many interactions and perceptions of patients and subjects, principal investigators and probably others involved in the conduct of their research, the authors of the questionnaire and the telephone interviewers. Other approaches and assumptions might give different results."

Furthermore, it is likely that in a retrospective telephone interview there will be some underreporting of injuries because of incomplete records, problems of recall, and unwillingness to disclose such information. How large a bias this introduces into the data is not known. . . .

. . .

Number of subjects. Very little information is available about the numbers of people serving as research subjects at any given time who are at risk of injury. Neither the funding agencies nor the recipient institutions are required to collect such information. Thus, although it is known, for example, that the Public Health Service (PHS) supports approximately 80% of the Federally funded biomedical research that is conducted throughout the country, the number of subjects involved in such studies is not known. This is also true of other Federal agencies supporting research.

In the 1977 HEW Task Force Report it was estimated that approximately 600,000 subjects are involved annually in PHS-supported clinical trials (i.e., controlled studies of new therapies). Such trials are only a part of the research supported by the Public Health Service; a large amount of research involves studies of basic physiology, normal growth and development, and a variety of other inquiries utilizing normal volunteers.

Other partial estimates include the Food and Drug Administration's figure of 375,000 subjects per year participating in research designed to test new drugs and medical devices; this figure is expected to increase as a result of the recent promulgation of regulations governing the testing of medical devices.

It seems unlikely that a firm estimate of the number of subjects at risk for injury at a given time could be prepared from figures currently available; any such conclusions would be based on too many levels of approximations, extrapolations and assumptions to be reliable. Thus, without either the numerator or the denominator with which to determine the incidence of research-related injuries, neither the absolute magnitude of the problem nor the size of the universe from which it emanates can be known with certainty.

Subject characteristics. Although the PHS and FDA have not provided direct assessments of the characteristics of subjects and of the projects in which they are involved, some data were collected by the University of Michigan's Survey Research Center in the study of IRBs it performed for the National Commission for the Protection of Human Subjects in 1975. These data provide the best available description of the characteristics of subjects participating in biomedical and behavioral research. Principal investigators were asked to estimate the age, sex, racial and income distributions of their experimental subjects. Projects were then weighted, based on the number of subjects, to produce overall estimates of demographic characteristics of research subjects.

Table 1.   Demographic Characteristics of Biomedical and Behavioral Research Subjects

Sex	Female	51.0%
	Male	48.0%
Race	White	71.2%
	Black	20.7%
	Other	7.1%
Income	Higher	11.7%
	Middle	51.3%
	Lower	31.5%
Age	Newborn	5.8%
	3 months–6 years	9.2%
	7–12 years	5.3%
	13–18 years	7.6%
	19–40 years	42.0%
	41–64 years	20.8%
	65 + years	7.4%

. . .

It is evident from the preceding discussion that full data do not exist with which to answer the questions posed initially. One has neither broad-based retrospective data on overall incidence of injury nor adequate data with which to calculate the extent of expected injury in the research universe because none of the components is known with precision. Federal agencies do not know how many subjects there are nor how they are distributed across the different kinds of research endeavors.

What studies there are do show that most research involves minimal or no risk of physical harm. Yet it is also apparent that risk is a composite of many factors, such that for those procedures which do entail risk its magnitude cannot be specified.

Although the evidence consistently suggests that the incidence of serious injury is small, nonetheless, it is clear that at least some subjects sustain injuries as a result of their participation in Federally funded or regulated research.

NOTE

In its report the President's Commission concludes that available studies show that most research on human subjects involves minimal risk or no risk of physical harm. Why then is this an area more suitable for government regulation, than say, auto racing or sky diving?

One way to understand at least the origins of the present system of public regulation is to examine some of the more famous research abuses of the recent past. The next section therefore begins with the revelations of Nuremberg.

B. THE EVOLUTION OF PUBLIC REGULATION OF MEDICAL EXPERIMENTATION

---

1. THE NAZI WAR CRIMES TRIALS *

a. United States v. Karl Brandt

This case is often referred to as the "Medical Case" because 20 of the 23 defendants were doctors, including Karl Brandt, personal physician to Adolph Hitler. The case was tried at the Palace of Justice in Nuremberg from December 1946 to July 1947 before a tribunal consisting of Walter Beals, the Chief Justice of the Supreme Court of the State of Washington; Harold Sebring, an Associate Justice of the Supreme Court of Florida; and Johnson Crawford, former Judge of a District Court of Oklahoma.

The authority of the tribunal derived from a series of agreements among the Allied Powers reached in the aftermath of World War II. In May of 1945, President Truman authorized Robert Jackson, an Associate Justice of the Supreme Court of the United States, to represent the United States "in preparing or prosecuting charges of atrocities and war crimes against such of the leaders of the European Axis powers and their principal agents and accessories as the United States may agree with any of the United Nations to bring to trial before an international military tribunal." Exec. Order No. 9547, 3 C.F.R. 703 (1945).

On August 8, 1945, the London Agreement was signed by Jackson for the United States. U.S. EAS 472, 59 Stat. 1544, 82 UNTS 279. The Agreement, made with France, Great Britain and the U.S.S.R., established an International Military Tribunal to try war crimes. It also affirmed the right of the participants to establish their own courts to try war criminals in their zone of occupation.

On December 20, 1945, representatives of the same four nations signed Control Council Law No. 10, which was designed to implement the London Agreement. The Law established uniform definitions of certain war crimes and procedures for each nation to follow when prosecuting suspected war criminals in its zone of occupation.

OPENING STATEMENT BY TELFORD TAYLOR, BRIGADIER GENERAL, FOR THE PROSECUTION

. . .

CRIMES COMMITTED IN THE GUISE OF SCIENTIFIC RESEARCH

I turn now to the main part of the indictment and will outline at this point the prosecution's case relating to those crimes alleged to have been committed in the name of medical or scientific research. . . . What I

---

* All the materials relating to the Nuremberg Trials are from Trials of War Criminals Before the Nuernberg Military Tribunals Under Control Council Law No. 10 (1949), unless otherwise noted. [Eds.]

will cover now comprehends all the experiments charged as war crimes [1] in paragraph 6 and as crimes against humanity [2] in paragraph 11 of the indictment, and the murders committed for so-called anthropological purposes which are charged as war crimes in paragraph 7 and as crimes against humanity in paragraph 12 of the indictment.

Before taking up these experiments one by one, let us look at them as a whole. Are they a heterogeneous list of horrors, or is there a common denominator for the whole group?

A sort of rough pattern is apparent on the face of the indictment. Experiments concerning high altitude, the effect of cold, and the potability of processed sea water have an obvious relation to aeronautical and naval combat and rescue problems. The mustard gas and phosphorous burn experiments, as well as those relating to the healing value of sulfanilamide for wounds, can be related to air-raid and battlefield medical problems. It is well known that malaria, epidemic jaundice, and typhus were among the principal diseases which had to be combated by the German Armed Forces and by German authorities in occupied territories.

To some degree, the therapeutic pattern outlined above is undoubtedly a valid one, and explains why the Wehrmacht, and especially the German Air Force, participated in these experiments. Fanatically bent upon conquest, utterly ruthless as to the means or instruments to be used in achieving victory, and callous to the sufferings of people whom they regarded as inferior, the German militarists were willing to gather whatever scientific fruit these experiments might yield.

But our proof will show that a quite different and even more sinister objective runs like a red thread through these hideous researches. We will show that in some instances the true object of these experiments was not how to rescue or to cure, but how to destroy and kill. The sterilization experiments were, it is clear, purely destructive in purpose. The prisoners at Buchenwald who were shot with poisoned bullets were not guinea pigs to test an antidote for the poison; their murderers really wanted to know how quickly the poison would kill. This destructive objective is not superficially as apparent in the other experiments, but we will show that it was often there.

Mankind has not heretofore felt the need of a word to denominate the science of how to kill prisoners most rapidly and subjugated people in large numbers. This case and these defendants have created this gruesome question for the lexicographer. For the moment we will christen this macabre science "thanatology," the science of producing death. The thanatological knowledge, derived in part from these experiments, supplied the techniques for genocide, a policy of the Third Reich, exempli-

---

1. Defined by Control Council Law 10, Art. II § 1(b) as:

Atrocities or offences against persons or property constituting violations of the laws or customs of war, including but not limited to, murder, ill treatment or deportation to slave labour or for any other purpose, of civilian population from occupied territory, murder or ill treatment of prisoners of war or persons on the seas, killing of hostages, plunder of public or private property, wanton destruction of cities, towns, or devastation not justified by military necessity. [Eds.]

2. Defined by Control Council Law 10, Art. II § 1(c) as:

Atrocities and offences, including but not limited to murder, extermination, enslavement, deportation, imprisonment, torture, rape or other inhumane acts committed against any civilian population, or persecutions on political, racial or religious grounds whether or not in violation of the domestic laws of the country where perpetrated. [Eds.]

fied in the "euthanasia" program and in the widespread slaughter of Jews, gypsies, Poles, and Russians. This policy of mass extermination could not have been so effectively carried out without the active participation of German medical scientists.

I will now take up the experiments themselves. . . .

A.   High-Altitude Experiments

The experiments known as "high-altitude" or "low-pressure" experiments were carried out at the Dachau concentration camp in 1942. According to the proof, the original proposal that such experiments be carried out on human beings originated in the spring of 1941 with a Dr. Sigmund Rascher. Rascher was at that time a captain in the medical service of the German Air Force, and also held officer rank in the SS. He is believed now to be dead.

The origin of the idea is revealed in a letter which Rascher wrote to Himmler in May 1941 at which time Rascher was taking a course in aviation medicine at a German Air Force headquarters in Munich. According to the letter, this course included researches into high-altitude flying and

"considerable regret was expressed at the fact that no tests with human material had yet been possible for us, as such experiments are very dangerous and nobody volunteers for them."

Rascher, in this letter, went on to ask Himmler to put human subjects at his disposal and baldly stated that the experiments might result in death to the subjects but that the tests theretofore made with monkeys had not been satisfactory.

Rascher's letter was answered by Himmler's adjutant, the defendant, Rudolf Brandt, who informed Rascher that—

". . . Prisoners will, of course, gladly be made available for the high-flight researches."

Subsequently Rascher wrote directly to Rudolf Brandt asking for permission to carry out the experiments at the Dachau concentration camp, and he mentioned that the German Air Force had provided "a movable pressure chamber" in which the experiments might be made. Plans for carrying out the experiments were developed at a conference late in 1941, or early in 1942, attended by Dr. Rascher and by the defendants Weltz, Romberg, and Ruff, all of whom were members of the German Air Force Medical Service. The tests themselves were carried out in the spring and summer of 1942, using the pressure chamber which the German Air Force had provided. The victims were locked in the low-pressure chamber, which was an airtight ball-like compartment, and then the pressure in the chamber was altered to simulate the atmospheric conditions prevailing at extremely high altitudes. The pressure in the chamber could be varied with great rapidity, which permitted the defendants to duplicate the atmospheric conditions which an aviator might encounter in falling great distances through space without a parachute and without oxygen.

The reports, conclusions, and comments on these experiments, which were introduced here and carefully recorded, demonstrate complete disregard for human life and callousness to suffering and pain. These documents reveal at one and the same time the medical results of the experiments, and the degradation of the physicians who performed them. The first report by Rascher was made in April 1942, and contains a description of the effect of the low-pressure chamber on a 37-year-old Jew. I quote:

"The third experiment of this type took such an extraordinary course that I called an SS physician of the camp as witness, since I had worked on these experiments all by myself. It was a continuous experiment without oxygen at a height of 12 kilometers conducted on a 37-year-old Jew in good general condition. Breathing continued up to 30 minutes. After 4 minutes the experimental subject began to perspire and wiggle his head, after 5 minutes cramps occurred, between 6 and 10 minutes breathing increased in speed and the experimental subject became unconscious; from 11 to 30 minutes breathing slowed down to three breaths per minute, finally stopping altogether.

"Severest cyanosis developed in between and foam appeared at the mouth.

"At 5 minute intervals electrocardiograms from three leads were written. After breathing had stopped Ekg (electrocardiogram) was continuously written until the action of the heart had come to a complete standstill. About ½ hour after breathing had stopped, dissection was started."

Rascher's report also contains [a] record of the "autopsy". . . .

After seeing [the] report Himmler ironically ordered that if a subject should be brought back to life after enduring such an experiment, he should be "pardoned" to life imprisonment in a concentration camp. Rascher's reply to this letter, dated 20 October 1942, reveals that up to the time the victims of these experiments had all been Poles and Russians, that some of them had been condemned to death, and Rascher inquired whether Himmler's benign mercy extended to Poles and Russians. A teletyped reply from the defendant, Rudolf Brandt, confirmed Rascher's belief that Poles and Russians were beyond the pale and should be given no amnesty of any kind.

· · ·

C. Malaria Experiments

Another series of experiments carried out at the Dachau concentration camp concerned immunization for and treatment of malaria. Over 1,200 inmates of practically every nationality were experimented upon. The malaria experiments were carried out under the general supervision of a Dr. Schilling, with whom the defendant Sievers and others in the box collaborated. The evidence will show that healthy persons were infected by mosquitoes or by injections from the glands of mosquitoes. Catholic priests were among the subjects. The defendant Gebhardt kept Himmler informed of the progress of these experiments. Rose furnished Schilling with fly eggs for them, and others of the defendants participated in various ways which the evidence will demonstrate.

After the victims had been infected, they were variously treated with quinine, neosalvarsan, pyramidon, antipyrin, and several combinations of these drugs. Many deaths occurred from excessive doses of neosalvarsan and pyramidon. According to the findings of the Dachau court, malaria was the direct cause of 30 deaths and 300 to 400 others died as a result of subsequent complications.

· · ·

I. Sterilization Experiments

In the sterilization experiments conducted by the defendants at Auschwitz, Ravensbrueck, and other concentration camps, the destructive nature of the Nazi medical program comes out most forcibly. The Nazis were searching for methods of extermination, both by murder and sterilization, of large population groups, by the most scientific and least conspicuous means. They were developing a new branch of medical science which would give them the scientific tools for the planning and practice of genocide. The primary purpose was to discover an inexpensive, unobtrusive, and rapid method of sterilization which could be used to wipe out Russians, Poles, Jews, and other people. Surgical sterilization was thought to be too slow and expensive to be used on a mass scale. A method to bring about an unnoticed sterilization was thought desirable.

Medicinal sterilizations were therefore carried out. A Dr. Madaus had stated that caladium seguinum, a drug obtained from a North American plant, if taken orally or by injection, would bring about sterilization. In 1941 the defendant Pokorny called this to Himmler's attention, and suggested that it should be developed and used against Russian prisoners of war. I quote one paragraph from Pokorny's letter written at that time:

"If, on the basis of this research, it were possible to produce a drug which after a relatively short time, effects an imperceptible sterilization on human beings, then we would have a powerful new weapon at our disposal. The thought alone that the 3 million Bolsheviks, who are at present German prisoners, could be sterilized so that they could be used as laborers but be prevented from reproduction, opens the most far-reaching perspectives."

As a result of Pokorny's suggestion, experiments were conducted on concentration camp inmates to test the effectiveness of the drug. At the same time efforts were made to grow the plant on a large scale in hothouses.

At the Auschwitz concentration camp sterilization experiments were also conducted on a large scale by a Dr. Karl Clauberg, who had developed a method of sterilizing women, based on the injection of an irritating solution. Several thousand Jewesses and gypsies were sterilized at Auschwitz by this method.

Conversely, surgical operations were performed on sexually abnormal inmates at Buchenwald in order to determine whether their virility could be increased by the transplantation of glands. Out of 14 subjects of these experiments, at least 2 died.

The defendant Gebhardt also personally conducted sterilizations at Ravensbrueck by surgical operation. The defendant Viktor Brack, in March 1941, submitted to Himmler a report on the progress and state of X-ray sterilization experiments. Brack explained that it had been determined that sterilization with powerful X-rays could be accomplished and that castration would then result. The danger of this X-ray method lay in the fact that other parts of the body, if they were not protected with lead, were also seriously affected. In order to prevent the victims from realizing that they were being castrated, Brack made the following fantastic suggestion in his letter written in 1941 to Himmler, from which I quote:

. . . .

"One way to carry out these experiments in practice would be to have those people who are to be treated line up before a counter.

There they would be questioned and a form would be given them to be filled out, the whole process taking 2 or 3 minutes. The official attendant who sits behind the counter can operate the apparatus in such a manner that he works a switch which will start both tubes together (as the rays have to come from both sides). With one such installation with two tubes about 150 to 200 persons could be sterilized daily, while 20 installations would take care of 3,000 to 4,000 persons daily. In my opinion the number of daily deportations will not exceed this figure."

.   .   .

M.   Jewish Skeleton Collection

I come now to charges stated in paragraphs 7 and 11 of the indictment. These are perhaps the most utterly repulsive charges in the entire indictment. They concern the defendants Rudolf Brandt and Sievers. Sievers and his associates in the Ahnenerbe Society were completely obsessed by all the vicious and malignant Nazi racial theories. They conceived the notion of applying these nauseous theories in the field of anthropology. What ensued was murderous folly.

In February 1942, Sievers submitted to Himmler, through Rudolf Brandt, a report from which the following is an extract:

"We have a nearly complete collection of skulls of all races and peoples at our disposal. Only very few specimens of skulls of the Jewish race, however, are available with the result that it is impossible to arrive at precise conclusions from examining them. The war in the East now presents us with the opportunity to overcome this deficiency. By procuring the skulls of the Jewish-Bolshevik Commissars, who represent the prototype of the repulsive, but characteristic subhuman, we have the chance now to obtain a palpable, scientific document.

"The best, practical method for obtaining and collecting this skull material could be handled by directing the Wehrmacht to turn over alive all captured Jewish-Bolshevik Commissars to the Field Police. They in turn are to be given special directives to inform a certain office at regular intervals of the number and place of detention of these captured Jews and to give them special close attention and care until a special delegate arrives. This special delegate, who will be in charge of securing the 'material' has the job of taking a series of previously established photographs, anthropological measurements, and in addition has to determine, as far as possible, the background, date of birth, and other personal data of the prisoner. Following the subsequently induced death of the Jew, whose head should not be damaged, the delegate will separate the head from the body and will forward it to its proper point of destination in a hermetically sealed tin can, especially produced for this purpose and filled with a conserving fluid.

"Having arrived at the laboratory, the comparison tests and anatomical research on the skull, as well as determination of the race membership of pathological features of the skull form, the form and size of the brain, etc., can proceed. The basis of these studies will be the photos, measurements, and other data supplied on the head, and finally the tests of the skull itself."

After extensive correspondence between Himmler and the defendants Sievers and Rudolf Brandt, it was decided to procure the skulls from inmates of the Auschwitz concentration camp instead of at the front. The hideous program was actually carried out, as is shown by a letter from Sievers written in June 1943, which states in part:

"I wish to inform you that our associate, Dr. Beger, who was in charge of the above special project, has interrupted his experiments in the concentration camp Auschwitz because of the existing danger of epidemics. Altogether 115 persons were worked on, 79 were Jews, 30 were Jewesses, 2 were Poles, and 4 were Asiatics. At the present time these prisoners are segregated by sex and are under quarantine in the two hospital buildings of Auschwitz."

After the death of these wretched Jews had been "induced" their corpses were sent to Strasbourg. A year elapsed, and the Allied armies were racing across France and were nearing Strasbourg where this monstrous exhibit of the culture of the master race reposed. Alarmed, Sievers sent a telegram to Rudolf Brandt in September 1944, from which I quote:

"According to the proposal of 9 February 1942, and your approval of 23 February 1942, Professor Dr. Hirt has assembled a skeleton collection which has never been in existence before. Because of the vast amount of scientific research that is connected with this project, the job of reducing the corpses to skeletons has not yet been completed. Since it might require some time to process 80 corpses, Hirt requested a decision pertaining to the treatment of the collection stored in the morgue of the Anatomy, in case Strasbourg should be endangered. The collection can be defleshed and rendered unrecognizable. This, however, would mean that the whole work had been done for nothing—at least in part—and that this singular collection would be lost to science, since it would be impossible to make plaster casts afterwards. The skeleton collection, as such is inconspicuous. The flesh parts could be declared as having been left by the French at the time we took over the Anatomy and would be turned over for cremating. Please advise me which of the following three proposals is to be carried out:

(1) The collection as a whole is to be preserved.

(2) The collection is to be dissolved in part.

(3) The collection is to be completely dissolved."

The final chapter of this barbaric enterprise is found in a note in Himmler's files addressed to Rudolf Brandt stating that:

"During his visit at the Operational Headquarters on 21 November 1944, Sievers told me that the collection in Strasbourg had been completely dissolved in conformance with the directive given him at the time. He is of the opinion that this arrangement is for the best in view of the whole situation."

These men, however, reckoned without the hand of fate. The bodies of these unfortunate people were not completely disposed of, and this Tribunal will hear the testimony of witnesses and see pictorial exhibits depicting the charnel house which was the Anatomy Institute of the Reich University of Strasbourg.

TESTIMONY OF PROSECUTION EXPERT WITNESS
DR. ANDREW C. IVY

DIRECT EXAMINATION

. . .

MR. HARDY: Now, Professor Ivy, before adjournment you were beginning to discuss medical ethics in the United States.

. . .

Do you have there . . . the principles and rules as set forth by the American Medical Association to be followed?

WITNESS DR. IVY: Yes.

Q. What was the basis on which the American Medical Association adopted those rules?

A. I submitted to them a report of certain experiments which had been performed on human subjects along with my conclusions as to what the principles of ethics should be for use of human beings as subjects in medical experiments. I asked the association to give me a statement regarding the principles of medical ethics and what the American Medical Association had to say regarding the use of human beings as subjects in medical experiments.

. . .

Q. Well now, you have, first of all, a basic requirement for experimentation on human beings, "(1) the voluntary consent of the individual upon whom the experiment is to be performed must be obtained."

A. Yes.

Q. "(2) The danger of each experiment must be previously investigated by animal experimentation," and "(3) the experiment must be performed under proper medical protection and management."

Now, does that purport to be the principles upon which all physicians and scientists guide themselves before they resort to medical experimentation on human beings in the United States?

A. Yes. They represent the basic principles approved by the American Medical Association for the use of human beings as subjects in medical experiments.

JUDGE SEBRING: How do the principles which you have just enunciated comport with the principles of the medical profession over the civilized world generally?

A. They are identical, according to my information. It was with that idea in mind that I cited the principles which were mentioned in [a] letter from the Reich Minister of the Interior dated 28 February 1931 to indicate that the ethical principles for the use of human beings as subjects in medical experiments in Germany in 1931 were similar to those which I have enunciated and which have been approved by the House of Delegates of the American Medical Association.

. . .

MR. HARDY: Dr. Ivy, in medical science and research is the use of human subjects necessary?

WITNESS DR. IVY: Yes, in a number of instances.

Q. Is it frequently necessary and does it perform great good to humanity?

A. Yes. That is right.

Q. Do you have an opinion that the state, for instance, the United States of America, could assume the responsibility of a physician to his patient or experimental subject, or is that responsibility solely the moral responsibility of the physician or scientist?

A. I do not believe the state can assume the moral responsibility that a physician has for his patient or experimental subject.

DR. SEIDL: I object to this question in that it is a purely legal question which the Court has to answer.

DR. SAUTER (for the defendants Ruff and Romberg): If I am not mistaken, a document was read this morning which said that the state assumes the responsibility. I believe that I am not mistaken in this. I also want to point out something else, gentlemen, in order to supplement what Dr. Seidl just said.

The question asked here is always what the opinion of the medical profession in America is. For us in this trial, in the evaluation of German defendants, that is not decisive. In my opinion the decisive question is for example, in 1942, when the altitude experiments were undertaken at Dachau, what the attitude of the medical profession in Germany was. From my point of view as a defense counsel I do not object if the prosecution asks Professor Ivy what the attitude or opinion of the medical profession in Germany was in 1942. If he can answer that question, all right, let him answer it, but we are not interested in finding out what the ethical attitude of the medical profession in the United States was. In my opinion a German physician who in Germany performed experiments on Germans cannot be judged exclusively according to an American medical opinion, which moreover dates from the year 1945 and was coded in the years 1945 and 1946 for future use; it can also have no retroactive force.

PRESIDING JUDGE BEALS: The first objection imposed by Dr. Seidl might be pertinent if the question of legality was concerned, a legal responsibility, that would be a question for a court. The question of moral responsibility is a proper subject to inquire of the witness.

As to Dr. Sauter's objection, the opinion of the witness as to medical sentiment in America may be received. The counsel's objection goes to its weight rather than to admissibility. The witness could be asked if he is aware of the sentiment in America in 1942 and whether it is different from this of the present day or whether it does not differ. The witness may also be asked whether he is aware of the opinion as to medical ethics in other countries or throughout the civilized world. But the objections are both overruled.

MR. HARDY: It is your opinion, then, that the state cannot assume the moral responsibility of a physician to his patient or experimental subject?

WITNESS DR. IVY: That is my opinion.

Q. On what do you base your opinion? What is the reason for that opinion?

A. I base that opinion on the principles of ethics and morals contained in the oath of Hippocrates. I think it should be obvious that a state cannot follow a physician around in his daily administration to see that the moral responsibility inherent therein is properly carried out. This moral responsibility that controls or should control the conduct of a physician should be inculcated into the minds of physicians just as moral responsibility of other sorts, and those principles are clearly depicted or enunciated in the oath of Hippocrates with which every physician should be acquainted.

Q. Is the oath of Hippocrates the Golden Rule in the United States and to your knowledge throughout the world?

A. According to my knowledge it represents the Golden Rule of the medical profession. It states how one doctor would like to be treated by another doctor in case he were ill. And in that way how a doctor should treat his patient or experimental subjects. He should treat them as though he were serving as a subject.

Q. Several of the defendants have pointed out in this case that the oath of Hippocrates is obsolete today. Do you follow that opinion?

A. I do not. The moral imperative of the oath of Hippocrates I believe is necessary for the survival of the scientific and technical philosophy of medicine.

. . .

CROSS–EXAMINATION

Dr. Sauter: Witness, you are an expert in the field of aviation medicine?

Witness Dr. Ivy: Yes.

Q. May I ask you what fields within aviation medicine you have worked on specifically, because my clients, who are recognized specialists in this field, attach importance to ascertaining precisely what fields you have worked in particularly?

A. I have worked particularly in the field of decompression or pressure drop sickness, and I have also worked in the field of anoxia or exposure to altitude repeatedly at a level of 18,000 feet to ascertain if that has any effect in the causation of pilots' fatigue.

Q. At what time did you specifically concern yourself with the fields you have just named? Was that before the Second World War, during the Second World War, or was it earlier than that?

A. My interest in these fields of aviation medicine, including free fall which I did not mention, started in 1939.

Q. Regarding your specific work in this field, Witness, you have also issued publications. I believe you spoke of two publications. Did I understand you correctly, or were there more?

A. There were two in the field of decompression sickness. There was one publication in the field of the effects of repeated exposure to a mild degree of oxygen lack. My other work has not yet been published but was submitted in the form of reports to the Committee on Aviation Medicine of the National Research Council of the United States.

Q. When were these two papers published of which you just told us; when, and were they printed by a publishing house? Did they appear in a journal or a periodical?

A. One appears in the Journal of Aviation Medicine either in September or October of 1946. The other appears in the Journal of the American Medical Association in either December or January 1946 or 1947. The publication on the effect of repeated exposure to mild degrees of oxygen lack at altitude appears in the quarterly bulletin of Northwestern University Medical School and part of the work, insofar as its effect on the elimination of the basis in the urine is concerned, appeared in the Journal of Biological Chemistry around 1944 or 1945, I am not sure of that date.

Q. Theretofore, Witness, you had thus made no publication in the field of aviation medicine before the papers of which you just gave the dates of publication?

A. The question is not clear.

Q. You just gave us the titles of the publications you have published and when; now I ask whether before the dates you just gave, you did not have any publications in the field of aviation medicine?

A. No. My first research started in 1939.

Q. You, yourself, have carried out experiments too; is that not so?

A. Yes.

Q. With human experimental subjects, of course?

A. Yes, and on myself.

Q. And with a lower pressure chamber?

A. Yes.

Q. Were these frequent experiments, or were the experiments in which you, yourself, took part only infrequent in number?

A. The experiments in which I took part were infrequent in number compared to the total number of experiments which I performed.

Q. Did you take part in these experiments as the director of the experiments, as the person responsible, or were you usually the experimental subject yourself?

A. I served in both capacities. For example, I have frequently gone to the altitude of 40,000 feet to study the symptoms of bends with an intermediate pressure device, which we produced in our laboratory. I have been to 47,500 feet on three or four occasions, on one occasion at 52,000 feet for half an hour. I have frequently been to 18,000 feet without supplemental oxygen in order to study the effect of the degree of oxygen lack present there for my ability to perform psycho-motor tests.

. . . .

In your own experiments, Witness, you also used conscientious objectors, is that not so? Did I understand you correctly?

A. Yes, in some of the experiments.

Q. Will you tell us why you used conscientious objectors? Were they particularly adapted for these experiments; or what was the reason for you, as one conducting experiments, to use especially conscientious objectors?

A. It was their duty, their volunteer duty to render public service. They had nothing else to do but to render public service. In the experiments in which we used the conscientious objectors, they could devote their full attention to the experiments. Many of the subjects, which I have used, have been medical students or dental students, who besides serving as subjects had to attend their studies in schools. In the experiments we did on the conscientious objectors, they could not attend school at the same time and carry on or perform all the tests they were supposed to perform. For example, we used a group of conscientious objectors for repeated exposure to an altitude of 18,000 feet without the administration of supplemental oxygen. These tests involved the following of a strict diet, they involved the performance of work tests and psycho-motor tests, which required several hours every day to perform. Another group of conscientious objectors that I used were used for vitamin studies in relation to fatigue.

These conscientious objectors had to do a great deal of carefully measured work during the day as well as to perform psycho-motor tests so medical students or dental students could not be used. We had to have subjects who could spend their full time on the experiments.

. . .

Q. Witness, from the answers that you have given so far, I am still not clear in my mind precisely why you hit upon conscientious objectors in particular as the experimental subjects. You said there were two groups of them: some were in prison and some had to perform public service. From the latter group you took your experimental subjects, but please give me a clear answer to the question: Why did you specifically use such conscientious objectors for your altitude experiments?

A. They could devote full time to the experimental requirements. They did not have to do any other work as was the case of medical students or dental students, the only other type of subjects that I had available to me.

Q. Doctor, these persons were obliged to perform public service. If these conscientious objectors had not been there or if they had been used for public service, then you would not have had any experimental subjects. There must be a specific reason why you specifically used conscientious objectors and I ask you, please, to tell me that reason.

A. Well, we could not have done the experiments unless the conscientious objectors had been available. That is the answer to your question.

Q. Could you not have used prisoners, even conscientious objectors who refused to do public service and were therefore in prison without doing any work? Could you not have used them?

A. Well, that would have meant that I and my assistants would have to go to the prison which was quite a distance away. The conscientious objectors could come to us at the university where they could live in the university dormitory or in the university hospital.

Q. Doctor, if your experiments were really important—perhaps important in view of the state of war—then it is difficult to understand why the experiments could not have been carried out in a prison, let us say. Other experiments have been carried out in prisons to a large extent, and on another occasion. Doctor, you told us that you simply had to get in touch with the prisoners; you simply wrote them a letter or you put up a notice on the bulletin board and then, to a certain extent, you had prisoners available. Can you give me no other information as to why you used specifically and only conscientious objectors?

A. No. If it had been convenient and necessary for me to use prisoners, I believe that we could have had prisoner volunteers for this work.

. . .

Q. Are inmates of Federal penitentiaries used for experiments too, as far as you know?

A. Yes. They may be.

Q. In other words, political prisoners too, that is, prisoners who were condemned by a court martial or by another court?

A. We have no political prisoners in the United States.

Q. Are not prisoners condemned for high treason or treason and the like? Those are political crimes.

A. Not to my knowledge.

Q. For conspiring with the enemy during the war; such cases have not only arisen but they have also been punished, and you must know that from reading your newspaper, Professor; those are political prisoners. Do you not have those in America?

A. Not to my knowledge.

Q. Doctor, if I understood you correctly, you stated this morning that a medical experiment with fatal consequences is to be designated either as an execution or as a murder; is that what you said?

A. I did not say that.

Q. What did you say then?

A. It was more or less as I quoted it, as I remember, I said that under the circumstances which surrounded the first death in high altitude experiments at Dachau, which Dr. Romberg is alleged to have witnessed, Dr. Rascher killed the subject; that the death could be viewed only as an execution or as a murder; and if the subject were a volunteer, then his death could not be viewed as an execution.

Q. Witness, in your opinion, is there a difference whether the experiments are to be traced back to the initiative of the experimenter himself, or whether they are ordered by some authoritative office of the state which also assumes the responsibility for them?

A. Yes. There is a difference, but that difference does not pertain, in my opinion, to the moral responsibilities of the investigator toward his experimental subject.

Q. I cannot understand that, Doctor. I can imagine that the state gives an experimenter the order, particularly during wartime, to carry out certain experiments, and that in peacetime, on his own initiative, the researcher would not carry out such experiments unless he was ordered to by the state. You must recognize this difference yourself.

A. That does not carry over to the moral responsibility of the individual to his experimental subject. I do not believe that the state can assume the responsibility of ordering a scientist to kill people in order to obtain knowledge.

Q. Witness, that is not the question. I am not interested in whether the state can order some one to murder; I am interested in the question whether, in your opinion, the state can order, let us say dangerous experiments, experiments in which perhaps fatalities may occur. In America, too, deaths occurred several times in experiments; what is your view on this?

A. The state, as far as I know, in the United States of America has never ordered scientists to perform any experiment where death is likely to occur.

Q. Doctor, I did not say where death was probable, I said where death is possible, and I ask you to answer the question I put to you. If deaths are probable, then you are correct, then it is murder. If deaths are possible, then I want to know what you say to that. And, let me remind you, Doctor, that even in the American Air Force deaths did occur; in other words, death was possible.

A. Yes, I agree that it is possible for deaths to occur accidentally in experiments which are hazardous. As I said in my testimony under such conditions when they do occur, their cause is investigated very thoroughly as well as the circumstances surrounding the death.

. . .

Q. Witness, you spoke yesterday of a number of experiments carried out in the United States and in other countries outside of Germany. For example, pellagra, swamp fever, beri-beri, plague, etc. Now, I should like to have a very clear answer from you to the following question. In these experiments which you heard of partly from persons involved in them and partly from international literature, did deaths occur during the experiments and as a result of the experiments or not? Professor, I ask you this question because you said yesterday that you examined all international literature concerning this question and, therefore, have a certain specialized knowledge on this question.

A. I also said that when one reviews the literature, he cannot be sure that he has done a complete or perfect job.

So far as the reports I have read and presented yesterday are concerned, there were no deaths in trench fever. There were no deaths mentioned, to my knowledge, in the article on pellagra. There were no deaths mentioned, to my knowledge, in the article on beri-beri, and there were no deaths in the article, according to my knowledge, in Colonel Strong's article on plague. I would not testify that I have read all the articles in the medical literature involving the use of human beings as subjects in medical experiments.

Q. And, in the literature which you have read, Witness, there was not a single case where deaths occurred? Did I understand you correctly?

A. Yes. In the yellow fever experiments I indicated that Dr. Carroll and Dr. Lazare died.

Q. That is the only case you know of?

A. That's all that I know of.

. . .

CLOSING STATEMENT OF THE PROSECUTION

It is the most fundamental tenet of medical ethics and human decency that the subjects volunteer for the experiment after being informed of its nature and hazards. This is a clear dividing line between the criminal and what may be noncriminal. If the experimental subjects cannot be said to have volunteered, then the inquiry need proceed no further. Such is the simplicity of this case.

What then is a volunteer? If one has a fertile imagination, suppositious cases might be put which would require a somewhat refined judgment. No such problem faces this Tribunal. The proof is overwhelming that there was never the slightest pretext of using volunteers. It was for the very reason that volunteers could not be expected to undergo the murderous experiments which are the subject of this trial that these defendants turned to the inexhaustible pool of miserable and oppressed prisoners in the concentration camps. Can anyone seriously believe that Poles, Jews, and Russians, or even Germans, voluntarily submitted themselves to the tortures of the decompression chamber and freezing basin in Dachau, the poison gas chamber in Natzweiler, or the sterilization X-ray machines of Auschwitz? Is it to be held that the Polish girls in Ravensbrueck gave their unfettered consent to be mutilated and killed for the glory of the Third Reich? Was the miserable gypsy who assaulted the defendant Beiglboeck in this very courtroom a voluntary participant in the sea-water experiments? Did the hundreds of victims of the murderous typhus stations in Buchenwald and Natzweiler by any stretch of the imagination consent to those experiments? The preponderance of the proof leaves no doubt whatever as to the answer to these questions. The testimony of experimental subjects, eyewitnesses, and the documents of the defendant's own making, establish beyond a shadow of a doubt that these experimental subjects were nonvolunteers in every sense of the word.

This fact is not seriously denied by the defendants. Most of them who performed the experiments themselves have admitted that they never so much as asked the subjects whether they were volunteering for the experiments. As to the legal and moral necessity for consent, the defendants pay theoretical lip service, while at the same time leaving the back door ajar for a hasty retreat. Thus, it is said that the totalitarian "State" assumed the responsibility for the designation of the experimental subjects, and under such circumstances the men who planned, ordered, performed, or otherwise participated in the experiment cannot be held criminally responsible even though nonvolunteers were tortured and killed as a result. This was perhaps brought out most clearly as a result of questions put to the defendant Karl Brandt by the Tribunal. When asked his view of an experiment, which was assumed to have been of highest military necessity and of an involuntary character with resultant deaths, Brandt replied:

> "In this case I am of the opinion that, considering the circumstances of the situation of the war, this state institution, which has laid down the importance of the interest of the state, at the same time takes the responsibility away from the physician if such an experiment ends fatally, and such responsibility must then be borne by the state."

Further questioning elicited the opinion that the only man possibly responsible in this suppositious case was Himmler, who had the power of life and death over concentration camp inmates, even though the experiment may have been ordered, for example, by the Chief of the Medical Service of the Luftwaffe and executed by doctors subordinated to him. Most of the other defendants took a similar position, that they had no responsibility in the selection of the experimental subjects.

This defense is, in the view of the prosecution, completely spurious. The use of involuntary subjects in a medical experiment is a crime, and if it results in death it is the crime of murder. Any party to the experiment is guilty of murder and that guilt cannot be escaped by having a third person supply the victims. The person planning, ordering, supporting, or executing the experiment is under a duty, both moral and legal, to see to it that the experiment is properly performed. This duty cannot be delegated. It is surely incumbent on the doctor performing the experiment to satisfy himself that the subjects volunteered after having been informed of the nature and hazards of the experiment. If they are not volunteers, it is his duty to report to his superiors and discontinue the experiment. These defendants have competed with each other in feigning complete ignorance about the consent of the experimental victims. They knew, as the evidence proves, that the miserable inmates did not volunteer to be tortured and killed. But even assuming the impossible, that they did not know, it is their damnation not their exoneration. Knowledge could have been obtained by the simple expedient of asking the subjects. The duty of inquiry could not be clearer and cannot be avoided by such lame excuses as "I understood they were volunteers," or, "Himmler assured me they were volunteers."

In this connection, it should never be lost sight of that these experiments were performed in concentration camps on concentration camp inmates. However little, some of these defendants say they knew of the lawless jungles which were concentration camps, where violent death, torture, and starvation made up the daily life of the inmates, they at least knew that they were places of terror where all persons opposed to the Nazi government were imprisoned without trial, where Jews and Poles and other so-called "racial inferiors" were incarcerated for no crime whatever, unless their race or religion be a crime. These simple facts were known during the war to people all over the world. How much greater then was the duty of these defendants to determine very carefully the voluntary character of these experimental subjects who were so conveniently available. True it is that these defendants are not charged with responsibility for the manifold complex of crimes which made up the concentration camp system. But it cannot be held that they could enter the gates of the Inferno and say in effect: "Bring forward the subjects. I see no evil; I hear no evil; I speak no evil." They asked no questions. They did not inquire of the inmates as to such details as consent, nationality, whether a trial had been held, what crime had been committed, and the like. They did not because they knew that the wretched inmates did not volunteer for their experiments and were not expected to volunteer. They embraced the Nazi doctrines and the Nazi way of life. The things these defendants did were the result of the noxious merger of German militarism and Nazi racial objectives. When, in the face of a critical shortage of typhus vaccines to protect the Wehrmacht in its Eastern invasions, Handloser and his cohorts decided that animal experimentation was too slow, the inmates of Buchenwald were sacrificed by the hundreds to test new vaccines. When Schroeder wanted to determine the limit of human tolerance of sea water, he trod the path well-worn by the Luftwaffe to Dachau and got forty gypsies. These defendants with their eyes open used the oppressed and persecuted victims of the Nazi regime to wring from their wretched and unwilling bodies a drop of scientific information at a cost of death, torture, mutilation, and permanent disability. For these palpable crimes justice demands stern retribution.

. . .

CLOSING BRIEF FOR DEFENDANT KARL BRANDT

. . .

Voluntary Participation

Experiments on persons who offer themselves voluntarily have always been considered admissible. In literary works care is always taken *to note this voluntariness;* where it is not mentioned, one may conclude that it was nonexistent.

The interest taken in the voluntariness of the person experimented upon has various reasons.

First of all the compulsory experiment—in contrast to the voluntary experiment—means an additional, very heavy mental strain, for the experimenter since the health and life of a human being may be at stake and the future existence of the person experimented upon may be imperiled.

But the experimenter has not only a purely human interest in having the person to be experimented upon offer himself with a certain voluntariness; in many cases he must absolutely depend on the *cooperation of the person experimented on;* he needs truthful information about observations made during the experiment, which cannot otherwise be carried out properly. . . .

Finally there may exist the wish to be protected against *claims for damages* and to prevent the *uncovering* of legal provisions, as well as to guard against the possible *political odium* that might result from having given orders for a forced experiment.

However, one look at the literature shows that the notion of *voluntariness is strongly suspect,* and every critical reader will in most cases associate himself with such suspicions.

The subjection to an experiment which is dangerous or even only painful or temporarily onerous must be based on a special motive.

Ethical reasons alone can give rise to voluntariness strictly speaking only in the case of the researcher himself, that is in self-experiments, and in the case of persons who for ethical reasons consciously wish to support by their cooperation the aims of the researcher.

. . .

However, if a declaration of voluntariness is made for reasons of *inexperience, thoughtlessness,* or *distress,* then it is unethical. Into this category fall cases where persons are induced to undergo experiments through promise of money or other advantages, while they do not foresee the meaning of the experiments. These are the weak, who, unprotected, are made to serve the interests of humanity. Compare with this the case of the use of immigrants for experiments. . . . The *category* here of particular interest is that of *prisoners* who offer themselves voluntarily.

First of all, one cannot assume that the *ethical level in a penitentiary* is so high above that of free men that here a great number of prisoners would offer themselves for participation in an experiment voluntarily only for purely ethical reasons. On the contrary, one can say that *all prisoners* are living under a certain *compulsion.* They expect from their participation in the experiment an improvement of their position or fear a worsening in case of refusal. Even though the regulations about the treatment of prisoners may be fixed, in practice there remains in this particular world a very wide scope for the punishment of prisoners with measures which, as experience shows, may hit the prisoner much more severely and more grievously than the sentence of the judge itself.

If the motive of the prisoner for his "voluntary offer" is merely a general *and vague hope,* in any direction, then there is no genuine declaration of voluntariness, but the consent is merely the off-shoot of his condition of constraint.

Two things have to be considered with regard to the prisoner's declaration of voluntary consent; the *risk* which he undergoes and the *advantage* that is offered him. One can only give one's consent to something of which one knows the full *meaning* and *importance.* The prisoner must therefore have been fully informed of the possible consequences. Here only lies the real problem of "voluntariness." It is not enough that the person to be experimented upon knows that, for instance, a malaria experiment is to be made; he must also know just how the particular person is to be used. The first easy series of experiments cannot be compared with the daring final experiments. Who is going to offer himself for the ultimate experiment necessary if the other persons to be experimented on get off more lightly? What was the nature of the consent?

Professor Ivy as expert witness has said nothing about this problem.

As a matter of fact a person to be experimented on can hardly estimate the risk, and the recruiting officer will not be inclined to give a frightful description of what may happen. Professor Ivy, who has recruited volunteers himself, does not consider experiments to be an evil. If you add that the "volunteer prisoner" has to forego all claims in case of injury to his health, then the consent of the prisoner cannot be considered as valid.

On the other hand the prisoner must know the advantage promised him as his *compensation* must be in suitable relation to the severity of the experiment and the reward must be assured to the prisoner. If the advantage is strikingly disproportionate to the risk and given as an act of grace without claim after the conclusion of the experiment, then there is no voluntary experiment; it remains a forced experiment.

Only if both basic conditions are fully met will it be possible for the prisoner to make a free decision. He may then allow his possible death to be included in the bargain in order to gain the chance of shortening the time of his imprisonment by years.

Such a case is depicted in the well known pellagra experiments, where with the collaboration of attorneys as defense counsellors, the conditions were agreed upon by the prison administration.*

This is the *classical case of a voluntary experiment in prison.* It will not always be possible or necessary to fix the advantage in the same manner; the official promise of the prison institute may be sufficient to exclude an arbitrary denial of the promise. Examples for that are the leprosy experiments on a person condemned to death, and the continuous experiments in the penitentiary Bilibid.

These experiments must be considered admissible as *experiments where a chance is given.*

The examples from medical literature, however, show that these general conditions for voluntariness were not always fulfilled. So we refer only to the experiments in the penitentiary San Quentin with streptococci on 25 convicts in 1946.

Accordingly, even experiments carried out on persons without their consent must be considered admissible.

. . .

b. The Judgment of the Court and the Establishment of the Nuremberg Code

. . .

THE PROOF AS TO WAR CRIMES AND CRIMES AGAINST HUMANITY

Judged by any standard of proof the record clearly shows the commission of war crimes and crimes against humanity substantially as alleged in counts two and three of the indictment. Beginning with the outbreak of World War II criminal medical experiments on non-German nationals, both prisoners of war and civilians, including Jews and "asocial" persons,

* Additional experiments with prisoners in this country are described in the National Commission staff paper reprinted in Sec. D. 4, infra. [Eds.]

were carried out on a large scale in Germany and the occupied countries. These experiments were not the isolated and casual acts of individual doctors and scientists working solely on their own responsibility, but were the product of coordinated policy-making and planning at high governmental, military, and Nazi Party levels, conducted as an integral part of the total war effort. They were ordered, sanctioned, permitted, or approved by persons in positions of authority who under all principles of law were under the duty to know about these things and to take steps to terminate or prevent them.

PERMISSIBLE MEDICAL EXPERIMENTS

The great weight of the evidence before us is to the effect that certain types of medical experiments on human beings, when kept within reasonably well-defined bounds, conform to the ethics of the medical profession generally. The protagonists of the practice of human experimentation justify their views on the basis that such experiments yield results for the good of society that are unprocurable by other methods or means of study. All agree, however, that certain basic principles must be observed in order to satisfy moral, ethical and legal concepts:

1. The voluntary consent of the human subject is absolutely essential.

This means that the person involved should have legal capacity to give consent; should be so situated as to be able to exercise free power of choice, without the intervention of any element of force, fraud, deceit, duress, over-reaching, or other ulterior form of constraint or coercion; and should have sufficient knowledge and comprehension of the elements of the subject matter involved as to enable him to make an understanding and enlightened decision. This latter element requires that before the acceptance of an affirmative decision by the experimental subject there should be made known to him the nature, duration, and purpose of the experiment; the method and means by which it is to be conducted; all inconveniences and hazards reasonably to be expected; and the effects upon his health or person which may possibly come from his participation in the experiment.

The duty and responsibility for ascertaining the quality of the consent rests upon each individual who initiates, directs or engages in the experiment. It is a personal duty and responsibility which may not be delegated to another with impunity.

2. The experiment should be such as to yield fruitful results for the good of society, unprocurable by other methods or means of study, and not random and unnecessary in nature.

3. The experiment should be so designed and based on the results of animal experimentation and a knowledge of the natural history of the disease or other problem under study that the anticipated results will justify the performance of the experiment.

4. The experiment should be so conducted as to avoid all unnecessary physical and mental suffering and injury.

5. No experiment should be conducted where there is an *a priori* reason to believe that death or disabling injury will occur; except, perhaps, in those experiments where the experimental physicians also serve as subjects.

6. The degree of risk to be taken should never exceed that determined by the humanitarian importance of the problem to be solved by the experiment.

7. Proper preparations should be made and adequate facilities provided to protect the experimental subject against even remote possibilities of injury, disability, or death.

8. The experiment should be conducted only by scientifically qualified persons. The highest degree of skill and care should be required through all stages of the experiment of those who conduct or engage in the experiment.

9. During the course of the experiment the human subject should be at liberty to bring the experiment to an end if he has reached the physical or mental state where continuation of the experiment seems to him to be impossible.

10. During the course of the experiment the scientist in charge must be prepared to terminate the experiment at any stage, if he has probable cause to believe, in the exercise of the good faith, superior skill and careful judgment required of him that a continuation of the experiment is likely to result in injury, disability, or death to the experimental subject.

Of the ten principles which have been enumerated our judicial concern, of course, is with those requirements which are purely legal in nature—or which at least are so clearly related to matters legal that they assist us in determining criminal culpability and punishment. To go beyond that point would lead us into a field that would be beyond our sphere of competence. However, the point need not be labored. We find from the evidence that in the medical experiments which have been proved, these ten principles were much more frequently honored in their breach than in their observance. Many of the concentration camp inmates who were the victims of these atrocities were citizens of countries other than the German Reich. They were non-German nationals, including Jews and "asocial persons", both prisoners of war and civilians, who had been imprisoned and forced to submit to these tortures and barbarities without so much as a semblance of trial. In every single instance appearing in the record, subjects were used who did not consent to the experiments; indeed, as to some of the experiments, it is not even contended by the defendants that the subjects occupied the status of volunteers. In no case was the experimental subject at liberty of his own free choice to withdraw from any experiment. In many cases experiments were performed by unqualified persons; were conducted at random for no adequate scientific reason, and under revolting physical conditions. All of the experiments were conducted with unnecessary suffering and injury and but very little, if any, precautions were taken to protect or safeguard the human subjects from the possibilities of injury, disability, or death. In every one of the experiments the subjects experienced extreme pain or torture, and in most of them they suffered permanent injury, mutilation, or death, either as a direct result of the experiments or because of lack of adequate follow-up care.

Obviously all of these experiments involving brutalities, tortures, disabling injury, and death were performed in complete disregard of international conventions, the laws and customs of war, the general principles of criminal law as derived from the criminal laws of all civilized nations, and Control Council Law No. 10. Manifestly human experiments under such conditions are contrary to "the principles of the law of nations as they result from the usages established among civilized peoples, from the laws of humanity, and from the dictates of public conscience."

[*Signed*] Walter B. Beals
Presiding Judge.

Harold L. Sebring
Judge

Johnson T. Crawford
Judge

Note on Modern Professional Codes

In 1964, the 18th World Medical Assembly, meeting in Helsinki, Finland, adopted what became known as the Declaration of Helsinki. Revised in 1975 and 1983, the Declaration provides:

INTRODUCTION

It is the mission of the physician to safeguard the health of the people. His or her knowledge and conscience are dedicated to the fulfillment of this mission.

The Declaration of Geneva of the World Medical Association binds the physician with the words, "The health of my patient will be my first consideration," and the International Code of Medical Ethics declares that a physician shall act only in the patient's interest when providing medical care which might have the effect of weakening the physical and mental condition of the patient.

The purpose of biomedical research involving human subjects must be to improve diagnostic, therapeutic and prophylactic procedures and the understanding of the aetiology and pathogenesis of disease.

In current medical practice most diagnostic, therapeutic or prophylactic procedures involve hazards. This applies especially to biomedical research.

Medical progress is based on research which ultimately must rest in part on experimentation involving human subjects.

In the field of biomedical research a fundamental distinction must be recognized between medical research in which the aim is essentially diagnostic or therapeutic for a patient, and medical research, the essential object of which is purely scientific and without implying direct diagnostic or therapeutic value to the person subjected to the research.

Special caution must be exercised in the conduct of research which may affect the environment, and the welfare of animals used for research must be respected.

Because it is essential that the results of laboratory experiments be applied to human beings to further scientific knowledge and to help suffering humanity, the World Medical Association has prepared the following recommendations as a guide to every physician in biomedical research involving human subjects. They should be kept under review in the future. It must be stressed that the standards as drafted are only a guide to physicians all over the world. Physicians are not relieved from criminal, civil and ethical responsibilities under the laws of their own countries.

I. BASIC PRINCIPLES

1. Biomedical research involving human subjects must conform to generally accepted scientific principles and should be based on adequately performed laboratory and animal experimentation and on a thorough knowledge of the scientific literature.

2. The design and performance of each experimental procedure involving human subjects should be clearly formulated in an experimental protocol which should be transmitted to a specially appointed independent committee for consideration, comment and guidance.

3. Biomedical research involving human subjects should be conducted only by scientifically qualified persons and under the supervision of a clinically competent medical person. The responsibility for the human subject must always rest with a medically qualified person and never rest on the subject of the research, even though the subject has given his or her consent.

4. Biomedical research involving human subjects cannot legitimately be carried out unless the importance of the objective is in proportion to the inherent risk to the subject.

5. Every biomedical research project involving human subjects should be preceded by careful assessment of predictable risks in comparison with foreseeable benefits to the subject or to others. Concern for the interests of the subject must always prevail over the interests of science and society.

6. The right of the research subject to safeguard his or her integrity must always be respected. Every precaution should be taken to respect the privacy of the subject and to minimize the impact of the study on the subject's physical and mental integrity and on the personality of the subject.

7. Physicians should abstain from engaging in research projects involving human subjects unless they are satisfied that the hazards involved are believed to be predictable. Physicians should cease any investigation if the hazards are found to outweigh the potential benefits.

8. In publication of the results of his or her research, the physician is obliged to preserve the accuracy of the results. Reports of experimentation not in accordance with the principles laid down in this Declaration should not be accepted for publication.

9. In any research on human beings, each potential subject must be adequately informed of the aims, methods, anticipated benefits and potential hazards of the study and the discomfort it may entail. He or she should be informed that he or she is at liberty to abstain from participation in the study and that he or she is free to withdraw his or her consent to participation at any time. The physician should then obtain the subject's freely-given informed consent, preferably in writing.

10. When obtaining informed consent for the research project the physician should be particularly cautious if the subject is in a dependent relationship to him or her or may consent under duress. In that case the informed consent should be obtained by a physician who is not engaged in the investigation and who is completely independent of this official relationship.

11. In case of legal incompetence, informed consent should be obtained from the legal guardian in accordance with national legislation. Where physical or mental incapacity makes it impossible to obtain informed consent, or when the subject is a minor, permission from the responsible relative replaces that of the subject in accordance with national legislation.

Whenever the minor child is in fact able to give a consent, the minor's consent must be obtained in addition to the consent of the minor's legal guardian.

12. The research protocol should always contain a statement of the ethical considerations involved and should indicate that the principles enunciated in the present Declaration are complied with.

II. MEDICAL RESEARCH COMBINED WITH PROFESSIONAL CARE (CLINICAL RESEARCH)

1. In the treatment of the sick person, the physician must be free to use a new diagnostic and therapeutic measure, if in his or her judgement it offers hope of saving life, reestablishing health or alleviating suffering.

2.   The potential benefits, hazards and discomfort of a new method should be weighed against the advantages of the best current diagnostic and therapeutic methods.

3.   In any medical study, every patient—including those of a control group, if any—should be assured of the best proven diagnostic and therapeutic method.

4.   The refusal of the patient to participate in a study must never interfere with the physician-patient relationship.

5.   If the physician considers it essential not to obtain informed consent, the specific reasons for this proposal should be stated in the experimental protocol for transmission to the independent committee (I, 2).

6.   The physician can combine medical research with professional care, the objective being the acquisition of new medical knowledge, only to the extent that medical research is justified by its potential diagnostic or therapeutic value for the patient.

III.   NON–THERAPEUTIC BIOMEDICAL RESEARCH INVOLVING HUMAN SUBJECTS (NON–CLINICAL BIOMEDICAL RESEARCH)

1.   In the purely scientific application of medical research carried out on a human being, it is the duty of the physician to remain the protector of the life and health of that person on whom biomedical research is being carried out.

2.   The subjects should be volunteers—either healthy persons or patients for whom the experimental design is not related to the patient's illness.

3.   The investigator or the investigating team should discontinue the research if in his/her or their judgment it may, if continued, be harmful to the individual.

4.   In research on man, the interest of science and society should never take precedence over considerations related to the wellbeing of the subject.

In 1982, the Judicial Council of the American Medical Association published revised guidelines on clinical investigation which provide in pertinent part:

The following guidelines are intended to aid physicians in fulfilling their ethical responsibilities when they engage in the clinical investigation of new drugs and procedures.

(1) A physician may participate in clinical investigation only to the' extent that those activities are a part of a systematic program competently designed, under accepted standards of scientific research, to produce data which is scientifically valid and significant.

(2) In conducting clinical investigation, the investigator should demonstrate the same concern and caution for the welfare, safety, and comfort of the person involved as is required of a physician who is furnishing medical care to a patient independent of any clinical investigation.

(3) In clinical investigation primarily for treatment—

A.   The physician must recognize that the physician-patient relationship exists and that professional judgment and skill must be exercised in the best interest of the patient.

B.   Voluntary written consent must be obtained from the patient, or from his legally authorized representative if the patient lacks the capacity to consent following: (a) disclosure that the physician intends to use an investigational drug or experimental procedure, (b) a reasonable explanation of the nature of the drug or procedure to be used, risks to be expected, and possible therapeutic benefits, (c) an offer to answer any inquiries concerning the drug or procedure, and (d) a disclosure of alternative drugs or procedures that may be available.

i.   In exceptional circumstances and to the extent that disclosure of information concerning the nature of the drug or experimental procedure or risks would be expected to materially affect the health of the patient and would be detrimental to his best interests, such information may be withheld from the patient. In such circumstances, such information shall be disclosed to a responsible relative or friend of the patient where possible.

ii.   Ordinarily, consent should be in writing, except where the physician deems it necessary to rely upon consent in other than written form because of the physical or emotional state of the patient.

iii.   Where emergency treatment is necessary, the patient is incapable of giving consent, and no one is available who has authority to act on his behalf, consent is assumed.

(4) In clinical investigation primarily for the accumulation of scientific knowledge—

A.   Adequate safeguards must be provided for the welfare, safety and comfort of the subject. It is fundamental social policy that the advancement of scientific knowledge must always be secondary to primary concern for the individual.   .   .   .

B.   Consent, in writing, should be obtained from the subject, or from his legally authorized representative if the subject lacks the capacity to consent, following: (a) a disclosure of the fact that an investigational drug or procedure is to be used, (b) a reasonable explanation of the nature of the procedure to be used and risks to be expected, and (c) an offer to answer any inquiries concerning the drug or procedure.

C.   Minors or mentally incompetent persons may be used as subjects only if:

i.   The nature of the investigation is such that mentally competent adults would not be suitable subjects.

ii.   Consent, in writing, is given by a legally authorized representative of the subject under circumstances in which an informed and prudent adult would reasonably be expected to volunteer himself or his child as a subject.

D.   No person may be used as a subject against his will.

E.   The overuse of institutionalized persons in research is an unfair distribution of research risks. Participation is coercive and not voluntary if the participant is subjected to powerful incentives and persuasion.

c. Epilogue

Fifteen of the twenty-three defendants were found guilty of war crimes and crimes against humanity. Seven, including Karl Brandt and Karl Gebhardt, were sentenced to death by hanging; five were imprisoned for life; and three were given prison terms of fifteen to twenty years. On February 16, 1948, the United States Supreme Court denied petitions for writs of habeas corpus filed on behalf of Karl Brandt and three other defendants. 333 U.S. 827, 836. The death sentences were carried out on June 2, 1948, at Landsberg prison. Some of the major criminals, such as Dr. S. Rascher, died before the trials. Others, including Dr. J. Mengele, escaped to other countries. See generally Redlich, Medical Ethics Under National Socialism, in 3 Encyclopedia of Bioethics 1015 (W. Reich ed. 1978).

In 1976, Telford Taylor provided more background on the evolution of the Nuremberg Code. He reported that:

we were educated in large part by our opponents. We had ample opportunity to interrogate, and in the course of interrogating doctors, of whom some were sophisticated and very able physicians, we began to realize the kind of problems that we would be up against in presenting the case. That led to our getting two well-known American doctors as medical consultants to the prosecution: one, a Boston psychiatrist, Dr. Leo Alexander, and the other, the better-known Dr. Andrew Ivy, who was later involved in a controversial cancer cure . . . . But it was all quite hasty and improvised. If we had been able to do it over again three years later, we would have done it in a much more sophisticated way, that is, with a greater awareness of the implications of the positions we were taking.

Conference on the Proper Use of the Nazi Analogy in Ethical Debate, Hastings Center Report Special Supplement 6, August 1976.

Dr. Alexander, in 1966, reported that he had prepared a memorandum that was submitted to Telford Taylor and the court on April 15, 1947, and that this memorandum with additions from Dr. Ivy's testimony, became the basis of the Nuremberg Code. Dr. Alexander further reported that in preparing the memorandum he relied on what he termed an unequivocal statement in the German literature [Ebermayer, Der Arzt in Recht, Leipzig (Georg Thieme trans.) 1 (1930)]; American statutes and court decisions involving the use of new drugs or new medical or surgical techniques [Pratt v. Davis, 118 Ill.App. 161 (1905); Arthur, Some Liabilities of the Physician in the Use of Drugs, 17 Rocky Mt.L.Rev. 131 (1945)]; and the Hippocratic Oath. Alexander, Limitations in Experimental Research on Human Beings, 3 Lex et Scienta 8, 15 (1966).

Of Dr. Ivy's testimony, Professor Taylor has remarked:

It was quite interesting that Dr. Ivy . . . raised questions which the German lawyers did not feel competent to answer on their own. The lawyers requested permission from the court for Dr. Ivy to be examined by the defendants themselves, which, of course, was a very unusual thing in a trial. The court saw no objection, and the result was that several of the defendants, including Dr. Gerhard Rose, who in medical intellectual terms was by far the strongest of the defendants, themselves cross-examined Ivy, testing in a very illuminating way his ability to distinguish what was done in Illinois prisons and what was done in Germany. I think those parts of the record in some ways give the most illuminating feeling about the clash of opinion and standards that the case projected.

Conference on the Proper Use of the Nazi Analogy in Ethical Debate 6.

NOTES

1. In 1981, American journalists first reported analogous abuses that grew out of experiments conducted on human beings in World War II by a unit of the Japanese Imperial Army, headquartered in Manchuria. The revelations are important for another reason; they raise the question of when, if ever, it is acceptable to profit from information derived from unethically conducted research. A number of the Japanese experimenters agreed to cooperate with their American captors; in exchange for their information about biological warfare, the Japanese were never publicly tried or punished. See Gomer, Powell and Rolino, Japan's Biological Weapons: 1930–1945, Bulletin of Atomic Scientists 43 (Oct. 1981); Dahlby, Japan's Germ Warriors, Washington Post, May 26, 1983, at 1, col. 1.

2. Was Judge Beals correct in overruling the objections of Dr. Seidl and Dr. Sauter?

3. How should one apply the sixth principle of the Nuremberg Code?

4. You are a staff attorney for a multi-national pharmaceutical manufacturer whose head office is in the United States. Previously, the company had conducted most of its research on human subjects in the United States. As a result of changes in FDA's regulations governing research on humans, the company plans

to shift the bulk of its human research to third world countries that do not regulate such research. You have been told that the principal reason for the shift is that compliance with the FDA's regulatory requirements is too expensive, and that the company is seeking to allocate as much of its research budget as reasonably possible to actual scientific work rather than to regulatory paperwork. You are asked to draft form contracts to govern such research, including provisions that define the obligations to your company of the physicians and other scientists who will conduct the research. What requirements, if any, would you insist be included as obligations of the researchers to protect the human subjects. If you failed to include any such requirements, and non-therapeutic research were conducted without informed consent from the subjects and with grave harm to some of them, should you be found guilty of a crime against humanity? Why or why not?

5. The judgment at Nuremberg establishes, at the very least, that physicians conducting medical experiments on human beings cannot escape legal responsibility for their participation by pointing to the involvement of the state. What then should be the responsibility of the state for experiments on human beings which it (a) orders performed; (b) requires to be performed as a condition for regulatory approval of, e.g., drugs; (c) funds; or (d) permits to be performed on persons within its custody, e.g., prisoners? Cf. Nevin v. United States, 696 F.2d 1229 (9th Cir. 1983) (wrongful death action brought under the Federal Tort Claims Act claiming that death occurred as a result of government's negligence in conducting simulated biological warfare attack on San Francisco in 1950; held that chief chemical officer's decision to use particular strain of bacterium was exempt as discretionary function under the Act so government immune from suit).

6. When research on human subjects conducted outside the United States is submitted to an agency of the United States government in fulfillment of a regulatory requirement, what obligation, if any, should the agency have to review the conduct of the study to determine whether the rights of the subjects were adequately protected? Is it necessarily adequate that the research was conducted in full compliance with all national laws and standards of the country in which it was conducted? Does it matter whether that country is a developed country sophisticated in medical matters, or a less developed country unsophisticated in such matters? Can a federal agency make evaluations of, and principled distinctions between, foreign countries? Should a federal agency apply one body of law to research conducted in the United States and a different body to research conducted abroad?

7. Would it be morally acceptable for the United States to establish requirements for the protection of human subjects of medical research in the United States that are so stringent that an appreciable portion of such research is driven overseas to countries providing less protection? On the other hand, should American regulatory bodies reduce the level of protection they would otherwise require for American research subjects in order not to drive research abroad?

2. EXPERIMENTAL ABUSES SINCE WORLD WAR II

a. A Physician Blows the Whistle

HENRY BEECHER,* ETHICS AND CLINICAL RESEARCH

274 N.Eng.J.Med. 1354 (1966).

Human experimentation since World War II has created some difficult problems with the increasing employment of patients as experimental subjects when it must be apparent that they would not have been available if they had been truly aware of the uses that would be made of them. Evidence is at hand that many of the patients in the examples to follow

* Dr. Beecher was the Henry Isaiah Dorr
Professor of Research in Anaesthesia at
Harvard University. [Eds.]

never had the risk satisfactorily explained to them, and it seems obvious that further hundreds have not known that they were the subjects of an experiment although grave consequences have been suffered as a direct result of experiments described here. There is a belief prevalent in some sophisticated circles that attention to these matters would "block progress." But, according to Pope Pius XII, ". . . science is not the highest value to which all other orders of values . . . should be subordinated."

I am aware that these are troubling charges. They have grown out of troubling practices. They can be documented as I propose to do, by examples from leading medical schools, university hospitals, private hospitals, governmental military departments (the Army, the Navy and the Air Force), governmental institutes (the National Institutes of Health), Veterans Administration hospitals and industry. The basis for the charges is broad.

I should like to affirm that American medicine is sound, and most progress in it soundly attained. There is, however, a reason for concern in certain areas, and I believe the type of activities to be mentioned will do great harm to medicine unless soon corrected. It will certainly be charged that any mention of these matters does a disservice to medicine, but not one so great, I believe, as a continuation of the practices to be cited.

Experimentation in man takes place in several areas: in self-experimentation; in patient volunteers and normal subjects; in therapy; and in the different areas of *experimentation on a patient not for his benefit but for that, at least in theory, of patients in general.* The present study is limited to this last category.

. . .

Frequency of Unethical or Questionably Ethical Procedures

Nearly everyone agrees that ethical violations do occur. The practical question is, how often? A preliminary examination of the matter was based on 17 examples, which were easily increased to 50. These 50 studies contained references to 186 further likely examples, on the average 3.7 leads per study; they at times overlapped from paper to paper, but this figure indicates how conveniently one can proceed in a search for such material. The data are suggestive of widespread problems but there is need for another kind of information, which was obtained by examination of 100 consecutive human studies published in 1964, in an excellent journal; 12 of these seemed to be unethical. If only one quarter of them is truly unethical, this still indicates the existence of a serious situation.

. . .

The Problem of Consent

All so-called codes are based on the bland assumption that meaningful or informed consent is readily available for the asking. As pointed out elsewhere, this is very often not the case. Consent in any fully informed sense may not be obtainable. Nevertheless, except, possibly, in the most trivial situations, it remains a goal toward which one must strive for sociologic, ethical, and clear-cut legal reasons. There is no choice in the matter.

If suitably approached, patients will accede, on the basis of trust, to about any request their physician may make. At the same time, every experienced clinician investigator knows that patients will often submit to inconvenience and some discomfort, if they do not last very long, but the usual patient will never agree to jeopardize seriously his health or his life for the sake of "science."

In only 2 of the 50 examples originally compiled for this study was consent mentioned. Actually, it should be emphasized in all cases for obvious moral and legal reasons, but it would be unrealistic to place much dependence on it. In any precise sense statements regarding consent are meaningless unless one knows how fully the patient was informed of all risks, and if these are not known, the fact should also be made clear. A far more dependable safeguard than consent is the presence of a truly *responsible* investigator.

Examples of Unethical or Questionably Ethical Studies

These examples are not cited for the condemnation of individuals; they are recorded to call attention to a variety of ethical problems found in experimental medicine, for it is hoped that calling attention to them will help to correct abuses present. During ten years of study of these matters it has become apparent that thoughtlessness and carelessness, not a willful disregard of the patient's rights, account for most of the cases encountered. Nonetheless, it is evident that in many of the examples presented, the investigators have risked the health or the life of their subjects. No attempt has been made to present the "worst" possible examples; rather, the aim has been to show the variety of problems encountered.

References to the examples presented are not given, for there is no intention of pointing to individuals, but rather, a wish to call attention to widespread practices. All, however, are documented to the satisfaction of the editors of the *Journal*.

Known Effective Treatment Withheld

Example 1. It is known that rheumatic fever can usually be prevented by adequate treatment of streptococcal respiratory infections by the parenteral administration of penicillin. Nevertheless, definitive treatment was withheld, and placebos were given to a group of 109 men in service, while benzathine penicillin G was given to others.

The therapy that each patient received was determined automatically by his military serial number arranged so that more men received penicillin than received placebo. In the small group of patients studied 2 cases of acute rheumatic fever and 1 of acute nephritis developed in the control patients, whereas these complications did not occur among those who received the benzathine penicillin G.

. . .

Example 3. This involved a study of the relapse rate in typhoid fever treated in two ways. In an earlier study by the present investigators chloramphenicol had been recognized as an effective treatment for typhoid fever, being attended by half the mortality that was experienced when this agent was not used. Others had made the same observations, indicating that to withhold this effective remedy can be a life-or-death decision. The present study was carried out to determine the relapse rate under the two methods of treatment; of 408 charity patients 251 were treated with chloramphenicol, of whom 20, or 7.97 percent died. Symptomatic treatment was given, but chloramphenicol was withheld in 157, of whom 36 or 22.9 percent died. According to the data presented, 23 patients died in the course of this study who would not have been expected to succumb if they had received specific therapy.

. . .

Physiologic Studies

Example 5. In this controlled, double-blind study of the hematologic toxicity of chloramphenicol, it was recognized that chloramphenicol is "well known as a cause of aplastic anemia" and that there is a "prolonged morbidity and high mortality of aplastic anemia" and that "chloramphenicol-induced aplastic anemia can be related to dose. . . ." The aim of the study was "further definition of the toxicology of the drug. . . ."

Forty-one randomly chosen patients were given either 2 or 6 gm. of chloramphenicol per day; 12 control patients were used. "Toxic bone-marrow depression, predominantly affecting erythropoiesis, developed in 2 of 20 patients given 2.0 gm. and in 18 of 21 given 6 gm. of chloramphenicol daily." The smaller dose is recommended for routine use.

. . .

Example 16. This study was directed toward determining the period of infectivity of infectious hepatitis. Artificial induction of hepatitis was carried out in an institution for mentally defective children in which a mild form of hepatitis was endemic. The parents gave consent for the intramuscular injection or oral administration of the virus, but nothing is said regarding what was told them concerning the appreciable hazards involved.

A resolution adopted by the World Medical Association states explicitly: "Under no circumstances is a doctor permitted to do anything which would weaken the physical or mental resistance of a human being except from strictly therapeutic or prophylactic indications imposed in the interest of the patient." There is no right to risk an injury to 1 person for the benefit of others.

Example 17. Live cancer cells were injected into 22 human subjects as part of a study of immunity to cancer. According to a recent review, the subjects (hospitalized patients) were "merely told they would be receiving 'some cells'"—". . . the word cancer was entirely omitted. . . ."

Example 18. Melanoma was transplanted from a daughter to her volunteering and informed mother, "in the hope of gaining a little better understanding of cancer immunity and in the hope that the production of tumor antibodies might be helpful in the treatment of the cancer patient." Since the daughter died on the day after the transplantation of the tumor into her mother, the hope expressed seems to have been more theoretical than practical, and the daughter's condition was described as "terminal" at the time the mother volunteered to be a recipient. The primary implant was widely excised on the twenty-fourth day after it had been placed in the mother. She died from metastatic melanoma on the four hundred and fifty-first day after transplantation. The evidence that this patient died of diffuse melanoma that metastasized from a small piece of transplanted tumor was considered conclusive.

. . .

Publication

In the view of the British Medical Research Council it is not enough to ensure that all investigation is carried out in an ethical manner: it must be made unmistakably clear in the publications that the proprieties have been observed. This implies editorial responsibility in addition to the investigator's. The question rises, then, about valuable data that have been improperly obtained. It is my view that such material should not be published. There is a practical aspect to the matter: failure to obtain publication would discourage unethical experimentation. How many would carry out such experimentation if they *knew* its results would never be published? Even though suppression of such data (by not publishing it) would constitute a loss to medicine, in a specific localized sense, this loss, it seems, would be less important than the far-reaching moral loss to medicine if the data thus obtained were to be published. Admittedly, there is room for debate. Others believe that such data, because of their intrinsic value, obtained at a cost of great risk or damage to the subjects, should not be wasted but should be published with stern editorial comment. This would have to be done with exceptional skill, to avoid an odor of hypocrisy.

NOTE

1. Do you agree that medical and scientific journals should regulate the ethical aspects of research the reports of which are submitted for publication? If so, how should such regulation be carried out? If not, should journals simply disregard blatant violations of ethical norms? Consider the observations of Jay Katz:

> [A policy of publishing only ethical reports] would impose an inordinate amount of work on the editors of journals, for publication of articles would now indicate that the investigators have complied with "ethical standards," at least to the satisfaction of the editors. In the light of complex "ethical" problems raised by contemporary research practices—problems which have as yet hardly been subjected to careful and relentless analysis—this is quite an extraordinary and staggering assignment.

Editorial Rewritten, 22 Clin.Res. 10, 11 (1974).

2. What if a proffered report presents an important discovery that was obtained in an unethical manner? Should a journal ever attempt to balance its ethical responsibility against the need to communicate knowledge? What of the argument that the harm has already been done? What of the risk that without dissemination of the results, the research may be repeated by another investigator, causing additional subjects to be exposed to unnecessary risk?

3. If a journal refuses to publish such a report, should it also publish the fact of its rejection to bring the problem to the attention of the public?

b. The Tuskegee Syphilis Study

At almost the same time that the abuses at Dauchau and Auschwitz began, the United States Public Health Service was recruiting participants for a long term study of syphilis. Almost 400 black males were the unwitting subjects of this experiment, which was to continue for more than 40 years.

ALLAN M. BRANDT,
RACISM AND RESEARCH: THE CASE OF
THE TUSKEGEE SYPHILIS STUDY

8 Hastings Ctr. Rep. 21 (December 1978).

In 1932 the U.S. Public Health Service (USPHS) initiated an experiment in Macon County, Alabama, to determine the natural course of untreated, latent syphilis in black males. The test comprised 400 syphilitic men, as well as 200 uninfected men who served as controls. The first published report of the study appeared in 1936 with subsequent papers issued every four to six years, through the 1960s. When penicillin became widely available by the early 1950s as the preferred treatment for syphilis, the men did not receive therapy. In fact on several occasions, the USPHS actually sought to prevent treatment. Moreover, a committee at the federally operated Center for Disease Control decided in 1969 that the study should be continued. Only in 1972, when accounts of the study first appeared in the national press, did the Department of Health, Education and Welfare halt the experiment. At that time seventy-four of the test subjects were still alive; at least twenty-eight, but perhaps more than 100, had died directly from advanced syphilitic lesions. . . .

. . .

Racism and Medical Opinion

A brief review of the prevailing scientific thought regarding race and heredity in the early twentieth century is fundamental for an understanding of the Tuskegee Study. By the turn of the century, Darwinism had provided a new rationale for American racism. Essentially primitive peoples, it was argued, could not be assimilated into a complex, white civilization. Scientists speculated that in the struggle for survival the Negro in America was doomed. Particularly prone to disease, vice, and crime, black Americans could not be helped by education or philanthropy. Social Darwinists analyzed census data to predict the virtual extinction of the Negro in the twentieth century, for they believed the Negro race in America was in the throes of a degenerative evolutionary process.

The medical profession supported these findings of late nineteenth- and early twentieth-century anthropologists, ethnologists, and biologists. Physicians studying the effects of emancipation on health concluded almost universally that freedom had caused the mental, moral, and physical deterioration of the black population. They substantiated this argument by citing examples in the comparative anatomy of the black and white races. . . .

. . .

According to [some] physicians, lust and immorality, unstable families, and reversion to barbaric tendencies made blacks especially prone to venereal diseases. One doctor estimated that over 50 percent of all Negroes over the age of twenty-five were syphilitic. Virtually free of disease as slaves, they were now overwhelmed by it, according to informed medical opinion. Moreover, doctors believed that treatment for venereal disease among blacks was impossible, particularly because in its latent stage the symptoms of syphilis become quiescent. . . . . Even the best educated black, according to Murrell, could not be convinced to seek treatment for syphilis. Venereal disease, according to some doctors, threatened the future of the race. The medical profession attributed the low birth rate among blacks to the high prevalance of venereal disease which caused stillbirths and miscarriages. Moreover, the high rates of syphilis were thought to lead to increased insanity and crime. One doctor writing at the turn of the century estimated that the number of insane Negroes had increased thirteen-fold since the end of the Civil War. Dr. Murrell's conclusion echoed the most informed anthropological and ethnological data:

> So the scourge sweeps among them. Those that are treated are only half cured, and the effort to assimilate a complex civilization driving their diseased minds until the results are criminal records. [sic] Perhaps here, in conjunction with tuberculosis, will be the end of the negro problem. Disease will accomplish what man cannot do.

This particular configuration of ideas formed the core of medical opinion concerning blacks, sex, and disease in the early twentieth century. Doctors generally discounted socio-economic explanations of the state of black health, arguing that better medical care could not alter the evolutionary scheme. These assumptions provide the backdrop for examining the Tuskegee Syphilis Study.

The Origins of the Experiment

In 1929, under a grant from the Julius Rosenwald Fund, the USPHS conducted studies in the rural South to determine the prevalence of syphilis among blacks and explore the possibilities for mass treatment. The USPHS found Macon County, Alabama, in which the town of Tuskegee is located, to have the highest syphilis rate of the six counties surveyed. The Rosenwald Study concluded that mass treatment could be successfully implemented among rural blacks. Although it is doubtful that the necessary funds would have been allocated even in the best economic conditions, after the economy collapsed in 1929, the findings were ignored. It is, however, ironic that the Tuskegee Study came to be based on findings of the Rosenwald Study that demonstrated the possibilities of mass treatment.

Three years later, in 1932, Dr. Taliaferro Clark, Chief of the USPHS Venereal Disease Division and author of the Rosenwald Study report, decided that conditions in Macon County merited renewed attention. Clark believed the high prevalence of syphilis offered an "unusual opportunity" for observation. From its inception, the USPHS regarded the Tuskegee Study as a classic "study in nature," rather than an experiment. As long as syphilis was so prevalent in Macon and most of the blacks went untreated throughout life, it seemed only natural to Clark that it would be valuable to observe the consequences. He described it as a "ready-made situation." Surgeon General H.S. Cumming wrote to R.R. Moton, Director of the Tuskegee Institute:

> The recent syphilis control demonstration carried out in Macon County, with the financial assistance of the Julius Rosenwald Fund, revealed the presence of an unusually high rate in this county and, what is more remarkable, the fact that 99 per cent of this group was entirely without previous treatment. This combination, together with the expected cooperation of your hospital, offers an unparalleled opportunity for carrying on this piece of scientific research which probably cannot be duplicated anywhere else in the world.

Although no formal protocol appears to have been written, several let-ters of Clark and Cumming suggest what the USPHS hoped to find. Clark indicated that it would be important to see how disease affected the daily lives of the men:

> The results of these studies of case records suggest the desirability of making a further study of the effect of untreated syphilis on the human economy among people now living and engaged in their daily pursuits.

It also seems that the USPHS believed the experiment might demonstrate that antisyphilitic treatment was unnecessary. As Cumming noted: "It is expected the results of this study may have a marked bearing on the treat-ment, or conversely the non-necessity of treatment, of cases of latent syphilis."

The immediate source of Cumming's hypothesis appears to have been the famous Oslo Study of untreated syphilis. Between 1890 and 1910, Professor C. Boeck, the chief of the Oslo Venereal Clinic, withheld treat-ment from almost two thousand patients infected with syphilis. He was convinced that therapies then available, primarily mercurial ointment, were of no value. When arsenic therapy became widely available by 1910, after Paul Ehrlich's historic discovery of "606," the study was aban-doned. E. Bruusgaard, Boeck's successor, conducted a follow-up study of 473 of the untreated patients from 1925 to 1927. He found that 27.9 percent of these patients had undergone a "spontaneous cure," and now manifested no symptoms of the disease. Moreover, he estimated that as many as 70 percent of all syphilitics went through life without inconve-nience from the disease. His study, however, clearly acknowledged the dangers of untreated syphilis for the remaining 30 percent.

Thus every major textbook of syphilis at the time of the Tuskegee Study's inception strongly advocated treating syphilis even in its latent stages, which follow the initial inflammatory reaction. In discussing the Oslo Study, Dr. J.E. Moore, one of the nation's leading venereologists wrote, "This summary of Bruusgaard's study is by no means intended to suggest that syphilis be allowed to pass untreated." If a complete cure could not be effected, at least the most devastating effects of the disease could be avoided. Although the standard therapies of the time, arsenical compounds and bismuth injection, involved certain dangers because of their toxicity, the alternatives were much worse. As the Oslo Study had shown, untreated syphilis could lead to cardiovascular disease, insanity, and premature death. Moore wrote in this 1933 textbook:

> Though it imposes a slight though measurable risk of its own, treat-ment markedly diminishes the risk from syphilis. In latent syphilis, as I shall show, the probablity of progression, relapse, or death is re-duced from a probable 25–30 percent without treatment to about 5 percent with it; and the gravity of the relapse if it occurs, is markedly diminished.

"Another compelling reason for treatment," noted Moore, "exists in the fact that every patient with latent syphilis may be, and perhaps is, infec-tious for others." In 1932, the year in which the Tuskegee Study began, the USPHS sponsored and published a paper by Moore and six other syphilis experts that strongly argued for treating latent syphilis.

The Oslo Study, therefore, could not have provided justification for the USPHS to undertake a study that did not entail treatment. . . .

Selecting the Subjects

Clark sent Dr. Raymond Vonderlehr to Tuskegee in September 1932 to assemble a sample of men with latent syphilis for the experiment. The basic design of the study called for the selection of syphilitic black males between the ages of twenty-five and sixty, a thorough physical examination including x-rays, and finally, a spinal tap to determine the incidence of neuro-syphilis. They had no intention of providing any treatment for the infected men. The USPHS originally scheduled the whole experiment to last six months; it seemed to be both a simple and inexpensive project.

The task of collecting the sample, however, proved to be more difficult than the USPHS had supposed. Vonderlehr canvassed the largely illiterate, poverty-stricken population of sharecroppers and tenant farmers in search of test subjects. If his circulars requested only men over twenty-five to attend his clinics, none would appear, suspecting he was conducting draft physicals. Therefore, he was forced to test large numbers of women and men who did not fit the experiment's specifications. This involved considerable expense since the USPHS had promised the Macon County Board of Health that it would treat those who were infected, but not included in the study. Clark wrote to Vonderlehr about the situation: "It never once occurred to me that we would be called upon to treat a large part of the county as return for the privilege of making this study. . . . I am anxious to keep the expenditures for treatment down to the lowest possible point because it is the one item of expenditure in connection with the study most difficult to defend despite our knowledge of the need therefor." Vonderlehr responded: "If we could find from 100 to 200 cases . . . we would not have to do another Wassermann on useless individuals. . . ."

Significantly, the attempt to develop the sample contradicted the prediction the USPHS had made initially regarding the prevalence of the disease in Macon County. Overall rates of syphilis fell well below expectations; as opposed to the USPHS projection of 35 percent, 20 percent of those tested were actually diseased. Moreover, those who had sought and received previous treatment far exceeded the expectations of the USPHS. Clark noted in a letter to Vonderlehr:

I find your report of March 6th quite interesting but regret the necessity for Wassermanning [sic] . . . such a large number of individuals in order to uncover this relatively limited number of untreated cases.

Further difficulties arose in enlisting the subjects to participate in the experiment, to be "Wassermanned," and to return for a subsequent series of examinations. Vonderlehr found that only the offer of treatment elicited the cooperation of the men. They were told they were ill and were promised free care. Offered therapy, they became willing subjects. The USPHS did not tell the men that they were participants in an experiment; on the contrary, the subjects believed they were being treated for "bad blood"—the rural South's colloquialism for syphilis. They thought they were participating in a public health demonstration similar to the one that had been conducted by the Julius Rosenwald Fund in Tuskegee several years earlier. In the end, the men were so eager for medical care that the number of defaulters in the experiment proved to be insignificant.

To preserve the subjects' interest, Vonderlehr gave most of the men mercurial ointment, a noneffective drug, while some of the younger men apparently received inadequate dosages of neoarsphenamine. This required Vonderlehr to write frequently to Clark requesting supplies. He feared the experiment would fail if the men were not offered treatment.

It is desirable and essential if the study is to be a success to maintain the interest of each of the cases examined by me through to the time when the spinal puncture can be completed. Expenditure of several hundred dollars for drugs for these men would be well worth while if their interest and cooperation would be maintained in so doing. . . . It is my desire to keep the main purpose of the work from the negroes in the county and continue their interest in treatment. That is what the vast majority wants and the examination seems relatively unimportant to them in comparison. It would probably cause the entire experiment to collapse if the clinics were stopped before the work is completed.

On another occasion he explained:

Dozens of patients have been sent away without treatment during the past two weeks and it would have been impossible to continue without the free distribution of drugs because of the unfavorable impression made on the negro.

The readiness of the test subjects to participate of course contradicted the notion that blacks would not seek or continue therapy.

The final procedure of the experiment was to be a spinal tap to test for evidence of neuro-syphilis. The USPHS presented this purely diagnostic exam, which often entails considerable pain and complications, to the men as a "special treatment." Clark explained to Moore:

We have not yet commenced the spinal punctures. This operation will be deferred to the last in order not to unduly disturb our field work by any adverse reports by the patients subjected to spinal puncture because of some disagreeable sensations following this procedure. These negroes are very ignorant and easily influenced by things that would be of minor significance in a more intelligent group.

The letter to the subjects announcing the spinal tap read:

Some time ago you were given a thorough examination and since that time we hope you have gotten a great deal of treatment for bad blood. You will now be given your last chance to get a second examination. This examination is a very special one and after it is finished you will be given a special treatment if it is believed you are in a condition to stand it. . . .

REMEMBER THIS IS YOUR LAST CHANCE FOR SPECIAL FREE TREATMENT. BE SURE TO MEET THE NURSE.

The HEW investigation did not uncover this crucial fact: the men participated in the study under the guise of treatment.

. . .

The USPHS offered several inducements to maintain contact and to procure the continued cooperation of the men. Eunice Rivers, a black nurse, was hired to follow their health and to secure approval for autopsies. She gave the men noneffective medicines—"spring tonic" and aspirin—as well as transportation and hot meals on the days of their examinations. More important, Nurse Rivers provided continuity to the project over the entire forty-year period. By supplying "medicinals," the USPHS was able to continue to deceive the participants, who believed that they were receiving therapy from the government doctors. Deceit was integral to the study. . . .

. . .

Finally, because it proved difficult to persuade the men to come to the hospital when they became severely ill, the USPHS promised to cover their burial expenses. The Milbank Memorial Fund provided approximately $50 per man for this purpose beginning in 1935. This was a particularly strong inducement as funeral rites constituted an important component of the cultural life of rural blacks. One report of the study concluded, "Without this suasion it would, we believe, have been impossible to secure the cooperation of the group and their families."

Reports of the study's findings, which appeared regularly in the medical press beginning in 1936, consistently cited the ravages of untreated syphilis. The first paper, read at the 1936 American Medical Association annual meeting, found "that syphilis in this period [latency] tends to greatly increase the frequency of manifestations of cardiovascular disease." Only 16 percent of the subjects gave no sign of morbidity as opposed to 61 percent of the controls. Ten years later, a report noted coldly, "The fact that nearly twice as large a proportion of the syphilitic individuals as of the control group has died is a very striking one." Life expectancy, concluded the doctors, is reduced by about 20 percent.

A 1955 article found that slightly more than 30 percent of the test group autopsied had died *directly* from advanced syphilitic lesions of either the cardiovascular or the central nervous system. Another published account stated, "Review of those still living reveals that an appreciable number have late complications of syphilis which probably will result, for some at least, in contributing materially to the ultimate cause of death." In 1950, Dr. Wenger had concluded, "We now know, where we could only surmise before, that we have contributed to their ailments and shortened their lives." As black physician Vernal Cave, a member of the HEW panel, later wrote, "They proved a point, then proved a point, then proved a point."

During the forty years of experiment the USPHS had sought on several occasions to ensure that the subjects did not receive treatment from other sources. To this end, Vonderlehr met with groups of local black doctors in 1934, to ask their cooperation in not treating the men. Lists of subjects were distributed to Macon County physicians along with letters requesting them to refer these men back to the USPHS if they sought care. The USPHS warned the Alabama Health Department not to treat the test subjects when they took a mobile VD unit into Tuskegee in the early 1940s. In 1941, the Army drafted several subjects and told them to begin antisyphilitic treatment immediately. The USPHS supplied the draft board with a list of 256 names they desired to have excluded from treatment, and the board complied.

In spite of these efforts, by the early 1950s many of the men had secured some treatment on their own. By 1952, almost 30 percent of the test subjects had received some penicillin, although only 7.5 percent had received what could be considered adequate doses. Vonderlehr wrote to one of the participating physicians, "I hope that the availability of antibiotics has not interfered too much with this project." A report published in 1955 considered whether the treatment that some of the men had obtained had "defeated" the study. The article attempted to explain the relatively low exposure to penicillin in an age of antibiotics, suggesting as a reason: "the stoicism of these men as a group; they still regard hospitals and medicines with suspicion and prefer an occasional dose of time-honored herbs or tonics to modern drugs." The authors failed to note that the men believed they already were under the care of the government doctors and thus saw no need to seek treatment elsewhere. Any treatment which the men might have received, concluded the report, had been insufficient to compromise the experiment.

When the USPHS evaluated the status of the study in the 1960s they continued to rationalize the racial aspects of the experiment. For example, the minutes of a 1965 meeting at the Center for Disease Control recorded:

> Racial issue was mentioned briefly. Will not affect the study. Any questions can be handled by saying these people were at the point that therapy would no longer help them. They are getting better medical care than they would under any other circumstances.

A group of physicians met again at the CDC in 1969 to decide whether or not to terminate the study. Although one doctor argued that the study should be stopped and the men treated, the consensus was to continue. Dr. J. Lawton Smith remarked, "You will never have another study like this; take advantage of it." A memo prepared by Dr. James B. Lucas, Assistant Chief of the Venereal Disease Branch, stated: "Nothing learned will prevent, find, or cure a single case of infectious syphilis or bring us closer to our basic mission of controlling venereal disease in the United States." He concluded, however, that the study should be continued "along its present lines." When the first accounts of the experiment appeared in the national press in July 1972, data were still being collected and autopsies performed.

. . .

TESTIMONY OF FRED GRAY,
HEARINGS BEFORE THE SUBCOMMITTEE ON HEALTH OF
THE SENATE COMMITTEE ON LABOR AND
PUBLIC WELFARE

93rd Cong., 1st Sess., 1033–1039 (1973).

MR. GRAY. Mr. Chairman and members of the committee, as has been indicated I am Fred Gray, a member of the Alabama Legislature, representing Barbour, Bullock, and Macon Counties. Tuskegee is the county seat of Macon County. I am also an attorney and as such I represent about 40 of the living participants in the Tuskegee Study. It is in that capacity that I appear before this committee today.

We also represent heirs of approximately 15 families of the deceased participants. . . .

. . .

[O]n behalf of these participants, I would like to thank Senator Kennedy, Chairman of this Subcommittee, for the opportunity to present the views of the participants in the Tuskegee Study.

This is the first time that any governmental agency has permitted them to present their side of the story. I have brought with me two of the participants, Mr. Pollard and Mr. Scott.

According to the participants, this is how they became involved in the Tuskegee Study. In 1932, notices were issued by Dr. Smith and Nurse Rivers, announcing a new health program in Macon County.

These notices were circulated throughout the county by mail and at churches and schools. The new program consisted of taking blood tests. Only blacks were given notices and only black males subsequently participated in the program. They were uneducated, poor, and lived in rural areas. No whites were selected to participate in the study.

After the blood tests were taken the men were told various things by those in charge. Some were told they had bad blood. However, they did not know what bad blood meant at that time.

Others were told nothing of what they had. None were ever told they had syphilis. Most knew nothing about syphilis. They were not told they were involved in a study.

The participants never signed any written consent nor were they asked to sign one. Some were told they would receive money but some never did. Many, however, received $25 and a 25-year certificate of appreciation in 1958.

. . .

. . . Sometime in the late 40's or early 50's, there was a massive effort to get all persons in Macon County treated who had syphilis. Most of the whites and many blacks were sent to Birmingham to receive such treatment.

However, those who participated in the Tuskegee Study were not permitted to receive such treatment. It was not until the summer of 1972 that the participants learned through the news media that they were part of the Tuskegee Study and many of those persons even today still do not know that they have syphilis or that they are part of a study.

. . .

SENATOR KENNEDY. . . . Let's start with you, Mr. Pollard. Would you tell us a little bit about how you heard about this study, how you became involved?

MR. POLLARD. Back in 1932, I was going to school back then and they came around and said they wanted to have a clinic blood testing up there.

SENATOR KENNEDY. How old were you then?

MR. POLLARD. How old was I? Well, I was born in 1906. I had been married—no, I hadn't been married. Anyhow, they came around and give us the blood tests. After they give us the blood tests, all up there in the community, they said we had bad blood. After then they started giving us the shots and give us the shots for a good long time. I don't remember how long it was. But after they got through giving us those shots, they give me a spinal tap. That was along in 1933. They taken me over to John Henry Hospital.

SENATOR KENNEDY. That is rather unpleasant, isn't it, a spinal tap?

MR. POLLARD. It was pretty bad with me.

SENATOR KENNEDY. I have had a spinal tap myself. They stick that big, long needle into your spine.

MR. POLLARD. That is right, at John Andrew Hospital. After that, we went over early that morning, a couple of loads of us, and they taken us upstairs after giving us the spinal shot. They sit me down in the chair and the nurse and the doctor got behind and give me the shot. Then they take us upstairs in the elevators, our heels up and head down. They kept us there until five o'clock that evening, and then the nurse brought us back home.

After then, I stayed in the bed. I had taken down a day or two after I got through with the spinal tap. I stayed in bed 10 days or two weeks and the nurse came out there and give me some pills. I don't think she give me any of the medicine at that time, but just gave me some of the pills. Anyhow, she made several trips out there and I finally got in pretty good shape afterwards. It looked like my head was going back.

So after then they went to seen us once a year. They sent out notices for us to meet at Shiloh School. Sometimes they would just take the blood sample and give us some medicine right there at the school, under the oak tree where we met at Shiloh.

SENATOR KENNEDY. This is a small community?

MR. POLLARD. It is a small community.

SENATOR KENNEDY. How many people are in the community?

MR. POLLARD. Well, Tuskegee is about 12,000, but this other little place up there I imagine is a couple thousand people there. I am about three and a half miles out.

SENATOR KENNEDY. What would you do, come into town?

MR. POLLARD. That is right, go into town.

SENATOR KENNEDY. Did they have a little clinic there or a little hospital?

MR. POLLARD. They didn't have any of that.

SENATOR KENNEDY. What did you do, just meet under the tree?

MR. POLLARD. Yes, at Shiloh School. It was about two and a half miles out. It is 10 miles between there and Tuskegee.

SENATOR KENNEDY. What did they do, ask you to come back once in a while or every couple of weeks?

MR. POLLARD. That is it. They would give us the date to come back and take those shots.

SENATOR KENNEDY. What were the shots for, to cure the bad blood?

MR. POLLARD. Bad blood, as far as I know of.

SENATOR KENNEDY. Did you think they were curing bad blood?

MR. POLLARD. I didn't know. I just attended the clinic.

SENATOR KENNEDY. They told you to keep coming back and you did?

MR. POLLARD. When they got through giving the shots, yes. Then they give us that spinal puncture.

SENATOR KENNEDY. Did they tell you why they were giving a spinal puncture?

MR. POLLARD. No.

SENATOR KENNEDY. Did you think it was because they were trying to help you?

MR. POLLARD. To help me, yes.

SENATOR KENNEDY. You wanted some help?

MR. POLLARD. That is right. They said I had bad blood and they was working on it.

SENATOR KENNEDY. How long did they keep working on it?

MR. POLLARD. After that shot, that spinal shot—

SENATOR KENNEDY. When was that?

MR. POLLARD. That was in 1933.

SENATOR KENNEDY. 1933?

MR. POLLARD. That is right. I don't remember what month it was in, but I know it was in 1933.

SENATOR KENNEDY. Did they treat you after that? Did they treat you after 1933?

MR. POLLARD. Yes. They treat me every year. They would come down and see us every year. Of course, during that time, after I taken that spinal puncture, I wore a rubber belt around my stomach. It had a long strand around it and I would run it around, come back in front and tie it in a bow knot. They used a little ointment or salve that I rubbed on my stomach. I reckon I wore it a year or six months, something like that. After then they would see us once a year up to 25 years.

SENATOR KENNEDY. During this time, did they indicate to you what kind of treatment they were giving you, or that you were involved in any kind of test or experiment?

MR. POLLARD. No, they never did say what it was.

SENATOR KENNEDY. What did you think they were doing, just trying to cure the bad blood?

MR. POLLARD. That is all I knew of.

SENATOR KENNEDY. Did they ever take any more blood and examine it and tell you the blood was getting better?

MR. POLLARD. They would take out blood, though.

SENATOR KENNEDY. What did they tell you after they would take the blood?

MR. POLLARD. They would just give us the pills and sometimes they would give us a little tablet to put under our tongue for sore throats. Then they would give us the green medicine for a tonic to take after meals.

SENATOR KENNEDY. You thought they were treating the bad blood?

MR. POLLARD. That is right.

SENATOR KENNEDY. During this time did they ever give you any compensation or any money?

MR. POLLARD. After that 25 years they gave me $25, a $20 and a $5 bill.

SENATOR KENNEDY. After 25 years?

MR. POLLARD. That is it. They give me a certificate.

SENATOR KENNEDY. They gave you a what?

MR. POLLARD. They gave me a certificate and a picture with six of us on there.

SENATOR KENNEDY. What did the certificate say, do you remember?

MR. POLLARD. This is one of them here in my hand.

SENATOR KENNEDY. It is a certificate of merit, is it?

"U.S. Public Health Service. This certificate is awarded in grateful recognition of 25 years of participation in the Tuskegee Medical Research Study."

MR. POLLARD. I have one of these and then I have one with a picture of five more on it.

SENATOR KENNEDY. Were you glad to get it? Were you glad to get that certificate?

MR. POLLARD. Yes.

SENATOR KENNEDY. You were glad to get the $25.

MR. POLLARD. That is right. I used the $25.

FINAL REPORT OF THE TUSKEGEE SYPHILIS STUDY AD HOC PANEL TO THE DEPARTMENT OF HEALTH, EDUCATION AND WELFARE

5–15 (1973).

Facts and Documentation Pertaining to Charge 1-A

1. There is no protocol which documents the original intent of the study. . . .

   . . .

2. There is no evidence that informed consent was gained from the human participants in this study. Such consent would and should have included knowledge of the risk of human life for the involved parties and information re possible infections of innocent, nonparticipating parties such as friends and relatives. Reports such as "Only individuals giving a history of infection who submitted voluntarily to examination were included in the 399 cases" are the only ones that are documentable. Submitting voluntarily is not informed consent.

3. In 1932, there was a known risk to human life and transmission of the disease in latent and late syphilis was believed to be possible. Moore 1932 reported satisfactory clinical outcome in 85% of patients with latent syphilis that were treated in contrast to 35% if no treatment is given.

4. The study as announced and continually described as involving "untreated" male Negro subjects was not a study of "untreated" subjects. Caldwell in 1971 reported that: All but one of the originally untreated syphilitics seen in 1968–1970 have received therapy, although heavy metals and/or antibiotics were given for a variety of reasons by many non-study physicians and not necessarily in doses considered curative for syphilis. Heller in 1946 reported "about one-fourth of the syphilitic individuals received treatment for their infection. Most of these, however, received no more than 1 or 2 arsenical injections; only 12 received as many as 10." The "untreated" group in this study is therefore a group of treated *and* untreated male subjects.

5. There is evidence that control subjects who became syphilitic were transferred to the "untreated" group. This data is present in the patient files at the Center for Disease Control in Atlanta. Caldwell reports 12 original controls either acquired syphilis or were found to have reactive treponemal tests (unavailable prior to 1953). Heller, also, reported that "It is known that some of the control group have acquired syphilis although the exact number cannot be accurately determined at present." Since this transfer of patients from the control group to the syphilitic

group did occur, the study is not one of late latent syphilis. Also, it is not certain that this group of patients did in fact receive adequate therapy.

6. In the absence of a definitive protocol, there is no evidence or assurance that standardization of evaluative procedures, which are essential to the validity and reliability of a scientific study, existed at any time. This fact leaves open to question the true scientific merits of a longitudinal study of this nature. Standardization of evaluative procedures and clinical judgment of the investigators are considered essential to the valid interpretation of clinical data. It should be noted that, in 1932, orderly and well planned research related to latent syphilis was justifiable since (a) Morbidity and mortality had not been documented for this population and the significance of the survey procedure had just been reported in findings of the prevalence studies for 6 southern counties; (b) Epidemiologic knowledge of syphilis at the time had not produced facts so that it could be scientifically documented "just how and at what stage the disease is spread." (c) There was a paucity of knowledge re clinical aspects and spontaneous cure in latent syphilis and the Oslo study had just reported spontaneous remission of the disease in 27.7% of the patients studied. If perhaps a higher "cure" rate could have been documented for the latent syphilitics, then the treatment priorities and recommendations may have been altered for this community where funds and medical services were already inadequate.

The retrospective summary of the "Scientific Contributions of the Tuskegee Study" from the Chief, Venereal Disease Branch, USPHS (dated November 21, 1972) includes the following merits of the study:

Knowledge already gained or potentially able to be gained from this study may be categorized as contributing to improvements in the following areas:

1. Care of the surviving participants,
2. Care of all persons with latent syphilis,
3. The operation of a national syphilis control program,
4. Understanding of the disease of syphilis,
5. Understanding of basic disease producing mechanisms.

Panel Judgments on Charge 1–A

1. In retrospect, the Public Health Service Study of Untreated Syphilis in the Male Negro in Macon County, Alabama, was ethically unjustified in 1932. This judgment made in 1973 about the conduct of the study in 1932 is made with the advantage of hindsight acutely sharpened over some forty years, concerning an activity in a different age with different social standards. Nevertheless one fundamental ethical rule is that a person should not be subjected to avoidable risk of death or physical harm unless he freely and intelligently consents. There is no evidence that such consent was obtained from the participants in this study.

2. Because of the paucity of information available today on the manner in which the study was conceived, designed and sustained, a scientific justification for a short term demonstration study cannot be ruled out. However, the conduct of the longitudinal study as initially reported in 1936 and through the years is judged to be scientifically unsound and its results are disproportionately meager compared with known risks to human subjects involved. Outstanding weaknesses of this study, supported by the lack of written protocol, include lack of validity and reliabil-

ity assurances; lack of calibration of investigator responses; uncertain quality of clinical judgments between various investigators; questionable data base validity and questionable value of the experimental design for a long term study of this nature.

The position of the Panel must not be construed to be a general repudiation of scientific research with human subjects. It is possible that a scientific study in 1932 of untreated syphilis, properly conceived with a clear protocol and conducted with suitable subjects who fully understood the implications of their involvement, might have been justified in the pre-penicillin era. This is especially true when one considers the uncertain nature of the results of treatment of late latent syphilis and the highly toxic nature of therapeutic agents then available.

. . .

To: The Assistant Secretary for Health and Scientific Affairs
From: Jay Katz, M.D.
Yale Law School
New Haven, Connecticut
Topic: Reservations about the Panel Report on Charge 1

I should like to add the following findings and observations to the majority opinion:

1. There is ample evidence in the records available to us that the consent to participation was not obtained from the Tuskegee Syphilis Study subjects, but that instead they were exploited, manipulated, and deceived. They were treated not as human subjects but as objects of research. The most fundamental reason for condemning the Tuskegee Study at its inception and throughout its continuation is not that all the subjects should have been treated, for some might not have wished to be treated, but rather that they were never fairly consulted about the research project, its consequences for them, and the alternatives available to them. Those who for reasons of intellectual incapacity could not have been so consulted should not have been invited to participate in the study in the first place.

. . .

6. The Tuskegee Syphilis Study finally was reviewed in 1969. A lengthier transcript of the proceedings, not quoted by the majority, reveals that one of the five members of the reviewing committee repeatedly emphasized that a moral obligation existed to provide treatment for the "patients." His plea remained unheeded. Instead the Committee, which was in part concerned with the possibility of adverse criticism, seemed to be reassured by the observation that "if we established good liaison with the local medical society, there would be no need to answer criticism."

7. The controversy over the effectiveness and the dangers of arsenic and heavy metal treatment in 1932 and of penicillin treatment when it was introduced as a method of therapy is beside the point. For the real issue is that the participants in this study were never informed of the availability of treatment because the investigators were never in favor of such treatment. Throughout the study the responsibility rested heavily on the shoulders of the investigators to make every effort to apprise the subjects of what could be done for them if they so wished. In 1937 the then Surgeon General of the USPHS wrote: "(f)or late syphilis no blanket prescription can be written. Each patient is a law unto himself. For every syphilis patient, late and early, a careful physical examination is necessary

before starting treatment and should be repeated frequently during its course." Even prior to that, in 1932, ranking USPHS physicians stated in a series of articles that adequate treatment "will afford a practical, if not complete guaranty of freedom from the development of any late lesions. . . . ."

In conclusion, I note sadly that the medical profession, through its national association, its many individual societies, and its journals, has on the whole not reacted to this study except by ignoring it. One lengthy editorial appeared in the October 1972 issue of the Southern Medical Journal which exonerated the study and chastised the "irresponsible press" for bringing it to public attention. When will we take seriously our responsibilities, particularly to the disadvantaged in our midst who so consistently throughout history have been the first to be selected for human research?

NOTES

1. Fred Gray later filed a $1.8 billion damage suit on behalf of all participants in the study against the federal government. Pollard v. United States, No. 4126–N (M.D.Ala. July 24, 1973). A settlement was reached under which the government agreed to pay each survivor $37,500 and the estate of each deceased syphilitic participant $15,000. New York Times, Feb. 6, 1975, at 35, col. 6.

2. Did the researchers in the Tuskegee Study and the responsible officials of the United States Public Health Service and the Department of Health, Education and Welfare comply with the Nuremberg Code? Did they commit a crime against humanity?

3. Was the settlement for the participants adequate? If not, what amount would have been? How should one determine what is adequate in such a case?

3. THE ADOPTION OF INFORMED CONSENT TO PROTECT SUBJECTS

a. The Common Law Standard

HALUSHKA v. UNIVERSITY OF SASKATCHEWAN

Saskatchewan Court of Appeals, 1965.
53 D.L.R.2d 436.

HALL, J.A.:—The appellants Wyant and Merriman were medical practitioners employed by the appellant University of Saskatchewan. The appellant Wyant was professor of anaesthesia and chief of the department of anaesthetics at the University Hospital. The appellant Merriman was director of the cardio-pulmonary laboratory. As part of their duties in the employ of the appellant University of Saskatchewan, the appellants Wyant and Merriman conducted and carried out medical research projects, some of which involved the comparative study of anaesthetics. When anaesthetics were administered the subjects were obtained from the employment office.

The respondent, a student at the University of Saskatchewan, had attended summer school in 1961. On August 21, 1961, he went to the employment office to find a job. At the employment office he was advised that there were no jobs available but that he could earn $50 by being the subject of a test at the University Hospital. The respondent said that he was told that the test would last a couple of hours and that it was a "safe test and there was nothing to worry about".

The respondent reported to the anaesthesia department at the University Hospital and there saw the appellant Wyant. The conversation which ensued concerning the proposed test was related by the respondent as follows:

Doctor Wyant explained to me that a new drug was to be tried out on the Wednesday following. He told me that electrodes would be put in my both arms, legs and head and that he assured me that it was a perfectly safe test it had been conducted many times before. He told me that I was not to eat anything on Wednesday morning that I was to report at approximately nine o'clock, then he said it would take about an hour to hook me up and the test itself would last approximately two hours, after the time I would be given fifty dollars, pardon me, I would be allowed to sleep first, fed and then given fifty dollars and driven home on the same day.

The appellant Wyant also told the respondent that an incision would be made in his left arm and that a catheter or tube would be inserted into his vein.

The respondent agreed to undergo the test and was asked by the appellant Wyant to sign a form of consent. This form, entered as ex. D.1, reads as follows:

INTENSIVE CARE
460–57–2

Halushka, Walter
72756 Jan 2'40 Mr.
Dr. Nanson

CONSENT FOR TESTS ON VOLUNTEERS

I, WALTER HALUSHKA, age 21 of 236—3rd Street Saskatoon hereby state that I have volunteered for tests upon my person for the purpose of study of

"Heart & Blood Circulation
Response under General
Anaesthesia"

The tests to be undertaken in connection with this study have been explained to me and I understand fully what is proposed to be done. I agree of my own free will to submit to these tests, and in consideration of the remuneration hereafter set forth, I do release the chief investigators, Drs.

Drs. G.M. Wyant and J.E. Merriman

their associates, technicians, and each thereof, other personnel involved in these studies, the University Hospital Board, and the University of Saskatchewan from all responsibility and claims whatsoever, for any untoward effects or accidents due to or arising out of said tests, either directly or indirectly.

I understand that I shall receive a remuneration of $50.00 for each test a series of One tests.

Witness my hand and seal.
"WALTER HALUSHKA" (signed)
"IRIS ZAECHTOWSKI" (Witness)

Date: Aug. 22/61

The respondent described the circumstances surrounding the signing of ex. D.1, saying:

> He then gave me a consent form, I skimmed through it and picked out the word "accident" on the consent form and asked Doctor Wyant what accidents were referred to, and he gave me an example of me falling down the stairs at home after the test and they trying to sue the University Hospital as a result. Being assured that any accident that would happen to me would be at home and not in the Hospital I signed the form.

The test contemplated was known as "The Heart and Blood Circulation Response under General Anaesthesia", and was to be conducted jointly by the appellants Wyant and Merriman, using a new anaesthetic agent known commercially as "Fluoromar". This agent had not been previously used or tested by the appellants in any way.

The respondent returned to the University Hospital on August 23, 1961, to undergo the test. The procedure followed was that which had been described to the respondent and expected by him, with the exception that the catheter, after being inserted in the vein in the respondent's arm, was advanced towards his heart. When the catheter reached the vicinity of the heart, the respondent felt some discomfort. The anaesthetic agent was then administered to him. The time was then 11:32 a.m. Eventually the catheter tip was advanced through the various heart chambers out into the pulmonary artery where it was positioned.

The appellants Wyant and Merriman intended to have the respondent reach medium depth of surgical anaesthesia. However, an endotracheal tube which had been inserted to assist the respondent in breathing caused some coughing. In the opinion of the appellant Wyant the coughing indicated that the respondent was in the upper half of light anaesthesia—on the verge of waking up. At 12:16, therefore, the concentration of the mixture of the anaesthetic was increased. The respondent then descended into deeper surgical anaesthesia.

At about 12:20 there were changes in the respondent's cardiac rhythm which suggested to the appellants Wyant and Merriman that the level of the anaesthetic was too deep. The amount of anaesthetic was then decreased, or lightened.

At 12:25 the respondent suffered a complete cardiac arrest.

The appellants Wyant and Merriman and their assistants took immediate steps to resuscitate the respondent's heart by manual massage. To reach the heart an incision was made from the breastbone to the line of the arm-pit and two of the ribs were pulled apart. A vasopressor was administered as well as urea, a drug used to combat swelling of the brain. After one minute and thirty seconds the respondent's heart began to function again.

The respondent was unconscious for a period of four days. He remained in the University Hospital as a patient until discharged 10 days later. On the day before he was discharged the respondent was given fifty ($50) dollars by the appellant Wyant. At that time the respondent asked the appellant Wyant if that was all he was going to get for all he went through. The appellant said that fifty dollars was all that they had bargained for but that he could give a larger sum in return for a complete release executed by the respondent's mother or elder sister.

As a result of the experiment the appellants concluded that as an anaesthetic agent "Fluoromar" had too narrow a margin of safety and it was withdrawn from clinical use in the University Hospital.

The respondent brought action against the appellants, basing his claim for damages on two grounds, namely, trespass to the person and negligence. The action came on for trial before Balfour, J., sitting with a jury. The respondent called Dr. Mark Baltzan, whose testimony regarding medical practice and whose expert opinion were supplemented by, and in some areas confirmed by questions and answers from the examinations for discovery of the appellants, Wyant and Merriman.

The medical evidence established that the use of any anaesthetic agent involves a certain amount of risk and should be accompanied by care and caution. In general medical practice the risk involved in the use of an anaesthetic agent is balanced against the threat to life presented by the ailment to be treated. It is standard procedure to obtain a medical history of the patient and in some cases to conduct a complete physical examination before administering a general anaesthetic. The medical history is for the most part obtained by interrogating the patient himself. The taking of a medical history usually involves investigation of the functioning of certain of the organic systems. Included are questions primarily related to the heart to ascertain whether the patient has had any specific heart disease, such as high blood pressure or rheumatic fever in the past.

In the instant case the appellants Wyant and Merriman admit that the cardiac arrest would not have occurred if the respondent had not undergone the test, the arrest being caused by the anaesthetic agent used. Dr. Baltzan was of the opinion that the test itself had been well conducted. He also gave his opinion that the insertion of a catheter into the heart is not a dangerous procedure.

If a patient does not die immediately from cardiac arrest, the damage which might ensue can vary in degree from none at all to eventual death with all intermediate degrees possible. Brain damage is the usual cause of death and most of the intermediate damage occurring will be to the brain. The brain cells can be damaged either permanently or temporarily. The portion of the brain most susceptible to damage under these circumstances is that which controls the highest functions, that is, the thinking functions as contrasted to the lowest or automatic functions. Major damage is objective as the patient is totally oblivious to his surroundings. Minor degrees of damage are more subjective as they are confined to emotional and intellectual attributes and are difficult to detect clinically. Dr. Baltzan had examined the respondent prior to the trial and could find no abnormality but he stated that he knew of no equipment available today which would necessarily and unequivocally determine whether there had been minor brain damage.

In Dr. Baltzan's opinion a certain amount of pain would be associated with the incision necessary for the open massage of the heart and expected general discomfort at the site of the incision for a month or two. The respondent himself testified that he experienced a considerable amount of pain in the chest area and that a portion of his left arm was numb for approximately six weeks.

The respondent testified that in public school his marks were mostly "A's". After entering high school he had an "A" average in grade nine. He stood first in his class in grade 10. In grades 11 and 12 he had a "B" average. In 1959 he enrolled in the College of Engineering at the University of Saskatchewan. In his first year he received four "D's" in the regular examinations. He passed in three more subjects by writing supplemental examinations. The respondent explains this relatively poor showing by pointing out that during this academic year he worked in the Post Office four nights a week until 10 or 11 o'clock until the end of December and that he was ill with influenza at examination time. He was away for the week before the final examinations and was not able at that time to write the three which he later passed by writing the supplemental examinations. In his second year at the University the respondent received three "C's", four "D's" and an "A" in the summer school class.

The respondent returned to the University in the fall of 1961. He testified that he became very tired every day and that he had to rest for about three hours before doing his homework. Although this condition did gradually improve, the respondent said that he was never able to complete his homework because of it. The respondent failed in six or seven subjects that year. He said he could not think or concentrate on problems as he had before. He therefore did not try to continue with his University course.

At the time of the trial the respondent was employed as an electrician at Thompson, Manitoba, earning $376 per month. He stated that it was difficult for him to think or concentrate and that he could not understand instructions given to him in the course of the employment unless they were given very slowly.

The appellants, at the close of the respondent's case, moved a nonsuit. The motion was denied by the trial Judge. The questions then put to the jury and the answers to them were as follows:

Q. 1. Did the plaintiff consent to the performance of the test made by the defendant doctors? A. No.

Q. 2. If the answer to Question 1 is no, did the defendant doctors commit a trespass in the performance of the test? A. Yes.

Q. 3. Were the defendant doctors or either of them negligent in the performance of the test? A. Yes.

Q. 4. If the answer to Question 3 is yes, in what respect was there negligence? A. (1) Lack of full explanation to the plaintiff of the test at the time of the so-called "consent". (2) Failure to acquire medical history of the plaintiff and to perform a Physical examination of the plaintiff. (3) Lack of liaison between the two defendant doctors throughout this test.

Q. 5. If the answer to Question 2 or Question 3 is yes, then at what amount do you assess the plaintiff's damage? A. $22,500.00.

From these findings and the judgment thereon the appellants appeal on the grounds:

1. That the learned trial judge erred in refusing to withdraw the plaintiff's claim from the jury on the ground that there was no evidence upon which the jury could find liability against the defendants or either of them.

2. That the learned trial judge misdirected the jury in respect of the consent which had been signed by the plaintiff and further erred in instructing them that this was a case of a doctor and patient relationship whereas he should have charged the jury that it was a contractual relationship.

3. That the findings of the jury on all the questions submitted to them were perverse.

4. That in any event damages awarded were excessive.

The main issue before the jury concerning the respondent's claim of trespass to the person was that of consent. The attachment of the electrodes, the administration of anaesthetic and the insertion of the catheter were each an intentional application of force to the person of the respondent. When taken as a whole they certainly constitute a trespass which would be actionable unless done with consent. . . . The appellants rely upon ex. D.1 and the conduct of the respondent as evidence of consent.

In ordinary medical practice the consent given by a patient to a physician or surgeon, to be effective, must be an "informed" consent freely given. It is the duty of the physician to give a fair and reasonable explanation of the proposed treatment including the probable effect and any special or unusual risks. The relationship between the physician and patient under such circumstances was described by Hodgins, J.A., in Kenny v. Lockwood, [1932] 1 D.L.R. 507 at pp. 519–20, [1932] O.R. 141, where he said:

> The relationship of surgeon and patient is naturally one in which trust and confidence must be placed in the surgeon. His knowledge, skill and experience are not and cannot be known to the patient, and within proper limits it would seem to require that when an operation is contemplated or proposed a reasonable clear explanation of it and of the natural and expected outcome should be vouchsafed.

A similar view has been adopted in some of the United States of America, and has been referred to in Wall v. Brim (1943), 138 F.2d 478; Mitchell v. Robinson (1960), 334 S.W.2d 11; and Natanson v. Kline (1960), 350 P.2d 1093. In the latter case the position was stated at p. 1106 of the report as follows:

> In our opinion the proper rule of law to determine whether a patient has given an intelligent consent to a proposed form of treatment by a physician was stated and applied in Salgo v. Leland Stanford, Etc. Bd. Trustees, 1957, 154 Cal.App.2d 560, 317 P.2d 170. This rule in effect compels disclosure by the physician in order to assure that an informed consent ot the patient is obtained. The duty of the physician to disclose, however, is limited to those disclosures which a reasonable medical practitioner would make under the same or similar circumstances. How the physician may best discharge his obligation to the patient in this difficult situation involves primarily a question of medical judgment. So long as the disclosure is sufficient to assure an informed consent, the physician's choice of plausible courses should not be called into question if it appears, all circumstances considered, that the physician was motivated only by the patient's best therapeutic interests and he proceeded as competent medical men would have done in a similar situation.

It was on the basis of the oridinary physician-patient relationship that the learned trial Judge charged the jury on the matter of consent. In dealing with this part of the case he said:

> In the circumstances of this case I will say that before signing such a document the plaintiff was entitled to a reasonably clear explanation of the proposed test and of the natural and expected results from it.

In my opinion the duty imposed upon those engaged in medical research, as were the appellants Wyant and Merriman, to those who offer themselves as subject for experimentation, as the respondent did here, is at least as great as, if not greater than, the duty owed by the ordinary physician or surgeon to his patient. There can be no exceptions to the ordinary requirements of disclosure in the case of research as there may well be in ordinary medical practice. The researcher does not have to balance the probable effect of lack of treatment against the risk involved in the treatment itself. The example of risks being properly hidden from a patient when it is important that he should not worry can have no application in the field of research. The subject of medical experimentation is entitled to a full and frank disclosure of all the facts, probabilities and opinions which a reasonable man might be expected to consider before giving his consent. The respondent necessarily had to rely upon the special skill, knowledge and experience of the appellants, who were, in my opinion, placed in the fiduciary position described by Lord Shaw of Dunfermline in Nocton v. Lord Ashburton, [1914] A.C. 932, when he said, at p. 969:

> Once . . . the relation of parties has been so placed, it becomes manifest that the liability of an adviser upon whom rests the duty of doing things or making statements by which the other is guided or upon which that other justly relies can and does arise irrespective of whether the information and advice given have been tendered innocently or with a fraudulent intent.

And at p. 972:

> . . . once the relations of parties have been ascertained to be those in which a duty is laid upon one person of giving information or advice to another upon which that other is entitled to rely as the basis of a transaction, responsibility for error amounting to misrepresentation in any statement made will attach to the adviser or informer, although the information and advice have been given not fraudulently but in good faith.

Although the appellant Wyant informed the respondent that a "new drug" was to be tried out, he did not inform him that the new drug was in fact an anaesthetic of which he had no previous knowledge, nor that there was risk involved with the use of an anaesthetic. Inasmuch as no test had been previously conducted using the anaesthetic agent "Fluoromar" to the knowledge of the appellants, the statement made to the respondent that it was a safe test which had been conducted many times before, when considered in the light of the medical evidence describing the characteristics of anaesthetic agents generally, was incorrect and was in reality a nondisclosure.

The respondent was not informed that the catheter would be advanced to and through his heart but was admittedly given to understand that it would be merely inserted in the vein in his arm. While it may be correct to say that the advancement of the catheter to the heart was not in itself dangerous and did not cause or contribute to the cause of the cardiac arrest, it was a circumstance which, if known, might very well have prompted the respondent to withhold his consent. The undisclosed or misrepresented facts need not concern matters which directly cause the ultimate damage if they are of a nature which might influence the judgment upon which the consent is based.

. . .

In view of the foregoing, there was no misdirection on the question of consent of which the appellants can complain and there was evidence upon which the jury could find that the respondent gave no effectual consent or release to the appellants. The appellants cannot, therefore, succeed on their first three grounds of appeal in so far as they relate to the respondent's claim of trespass.

. . .

[The court next held that the damages, while "generous" were not excessive].

Appeal dismissed.

NOTE

What standard did the court adopt in *Halushka* for determining whether the subject had the information necessary to give informed consent? Compare the debate about the appropriate standard when a doctor is treating a patient with nonexperimental therapy in Ch. 3, Sec. B., supra.

b. Federal Regulations

i. First Stage: Early Actions by Congress, FDA and NIH

Following the disclosure of deformities caused by Thalidomide in infants born in 1961 and 1962 primarily in Western Europe, Congress directed the Food and Drug Administration (FDA) to impose stricter controls on the clinical testing of new drugs in this country.[1] The new law specifically directed FDA to issue regulations to ensure that investigators "will inform any human beings to whom [investigational] drugs, or any controls used in connection therewith, are being administered, or their representatives, that such drugs are being used in investigational purposes and will obtain the consent of the human being or their representatives except where they deem it not feasible or, in their professional judgment, contrary to the best interests of such human beings."[2]

Initially, FDA implemented its mandate by issuing regulations that did not elaborate on the statutory language.[3] By 1967, amid growing indications of failure to obtain subject consent in many investigations, FDA proposed stronger regulations governing consent.[4] The new regulations provided in pertinent part:

> (b) This means that the consent of such humans (or the consent of their representatives) to whom investigational drugs are administered primarily for the accumulation of scientific knowledge, for such purposes as studying drug behavior, body processes, or the course of disease, must be obtained in all cases and, in all but exceptional cases, the consent of patients under treatment with investigational drugs or the consent of their representatives must be obtained.

. . .

> (d) "Exceptional cases" as used in paragraph (b) of this section are those relatively rare cases in which it is not feasible to obtain the pa-

---

1. More than a dozen cases of Thalidomide deformities occurred in this country. Ley, Federal Law and Patient Consent, 169 Annals N.Y. Acad. Sci. 523 (1970).

2. Drug Amendments of 1962, P.L. No. 87–781, 76 Stat. 780.

3. 21 C.F.R. §§ 130–37 (1963).

4. See generally, Curran, Government Regulation of the Use of Human Subjects, in Medical Research: The Approach of Two Federal Agencies in Experimentation With Human Subjects 402 (P. Freund, ed. 1970).

tient's consent or the consent of his representative, or in which as a matter of professional judgment exercised in the best interest of a particular patient under the investigator's care, it would be contrary to that patient's welfare to obtain his consent.

. . . .

(f) "Not feasible" is limited to cases wherein the investigator is not capable of obtaining consent because of inability to communicate with the patient or his representative; for example, the patient is in a coma or is otherwise incapable of giving consent, his representative cannot be reached, and it is imperative to administer the drug without delay.

(g) "Contrary to the best interests of such human beings" applies when the communication of information to obtain consent would seriously affect the patient's well-being and the physician has exercised a professional judgment that under the particular circumstances of this patient's case, the patient's best interests would suffer if consent were sought.

(h) "Consent" means that the person involved has legal capacity to give consent, is so situated as to be able to exercise free power of choice, and is provided with a fair explanation of pertinent information concerning the investigational drug. This latter element means that before the acceptance of an affirmative decision by such person the investigator should carefully consider and make known to him (taking into consideration such person's well-being and his ability to understand) the nature, expected duration, and purpose of the administration of said investigational drug; the method and means by which it is to be administered; the hazards involved; the existence of alternative forms of therapy, if any; and the beneficial effects upon his health or person that may possibly come from the administration of the investigational drug.

When consent is necessary under the rules set forth in this section, the consent of persons receiving an investigational new drug in Phase 1 and Phase 2 investigations (or their representatives) shall be in writing. When consent is necessary under such rules in Phase 3 investigations, it is the responsibility of investigators, taking into consideration the physical and mental state of the patient, to decide when it is necessary or preferable to obtain consent in other than written form. When such written consent is not obtained, the investigator must obtain oral consent and record that fact in the medical record of the person receiving the drug.[5]

Thus the new regulations allowed no exceptions to the consent requirement in non-therapeutic studies. The adopted definition of in-

---

5. 32 Fed.Reg. 3994, (1967), codified as 21 C.F.R. §§ 136–37. The three phases of drug testing have been described by the FDA as follows:

"a. Clinical Pharmacology. This is ordinarily divided into two phases: Phase 1 starts when the new drug is first introduced into man—only animal and in vitro data are available—with the purpose of determining human toxicity, metabolism, absorption, elimination, and safe dosage range; phase 2 covers the initial trials on a limited number of patients for specific disease control or prophylaxis purposes

. . . . [Phases 1 and 2 ordinarily are conducted in highly controlled settings.]

"b. Clinical Trial. This phase 3 provides the assessment of the drug's safety and effectiveness and optimum dosage schedules in the diagnosis, treatment or prophylaxis of groups of subjects involving a given disease or condition." FDA Form 1571 (10/82). [Phase 3 ordinarily involves the administration of the experimental drug in normal clinical settings to patients who have the illness or condition for which the drug, if approved, would be used.]

formed consent combined concepts from both the Nuremberg Code and the Declaration of Helsinki.

In 1966, the Surgeon General of the United States directed that all research proposals submitted for financial support from the Public Health Service undergo prior review by an investigator's institutional associates "to assure an independent determination of the protection of the rights and welfare of the individual or individuals involved, of the appropriateness of the methods used to secure informed consent and of the risks and potential medical benefits of the investigation." [6] In 1971, the Public Health Service extended the directive into a formal Institutional Guide to DHEW [Department of Health, Education and Welfare] Policy on Protection of Human Subjects, and strengthened the requirement that the research undergo peer review at the investigator's institution by requiring that the peer committee "be composed of sufficient members with varying backgrounds to assure complete and adequate review of projects." [7] In addition, the 1971 Guide established that no "member of an institutional committee shall be involved in either the initial or continuing review of an activity in which he has a professional responsibility." [8]

In 1972, the national press reported on the Tuskegee Syphilis Study. Congress became increasingly active as well, holding hearings on Tuskegee and other controversial areas of research, including psychosurgery and fetal research. The result was the National Research Act of 1974, Pub.L. No. 93–348, 88 Stat. 342, which established the National Commission for the Protection of Human Subjects of Biomedical and Behavioral Research. The Act also imposed a moratorium on non-therapeutic research conducted or funded by HEW on any living human fetus. The moratorium was to remain in effect until the National Commission recommended whether and under what circumstances research on fetuses should be conducted. The Commission was directed by the Act to make its report on fetal research within four months after the members took office.

The mandated report was submitted to the Secretary of HEW on July 25, 1975. It was the first of a series of reports submitted by the Commission covering such related topics as research on children and research on prisoners, all of which played a very influential role both in shaping later federal regulations and in justifying the establishment in 1978 of a second national commission, entitled the President's Commission for the Study of Ethical Problems in Medicine and Biomedical and Behavioral Research. [9]

The spurt of congressional activity in 1974 coincided with the release by HEW of its first regulations governing research involving human subjects. [10] The regulations provided that HEW would fund no research involving human subjects unless an appropriate committee of the sponsoring institution had approved the research as being in accordance with relevant federal regulations designed to ensure that informed consent would be obtained from all participants.

6. President's Commission, Compensating for Research Injuries 33 (1982).

7. Id. at 36.

8. Id.

9. Title III, Pub.L. 95–622 (1978) as amended by Pub.L. 97–377 (1982).

10. 39 Fed.Reg. 18,914 (May 10, 1974).

ii. Second Stage: Current Regulations of the United States Department of Health and Human Services

A number of changes have been made in the HHS (formerly HEW) regulations since they were first promulgated in 1974. Most were directed at providing additional protection for particularly vulnerable subjects. Thus, regulations providing additional protection for fetuses and pregnant women [11] and for children [12] have been promulgated. Regulations governing research on the institutionalized mentally disabled have been proposed but never finalized.[13]

On August 8, 1978, FDA proposed more detailed standards for the institutional review committees, now termed Institutional Review Boards (IRB's).[14] On January 26, 1981, HHS published the current regulations with the intent of providing a common regulatory framework for IRB's whether they are reviewing research conducted or funded by HHS or within the jurisdiction of FDA.[15] The current regulations, reflecting the general trend toward deregulation, also exempt from their requirements certain kinds of research that normally present little or no risk of harm to subjects, such as surveys, interviews, or observations of public behavior, and studies of data or documents.

DEPARTMENT OF HEALTH AND HUMAN SERVICES, REGULATIONS ON PROTECTION OF HUMAN SUBJECTS

45 C.F.R. 46 (1983).

§ 46.101 To what do these regulations apply?

(a) Except as provided in paragraph (b) of this section, the subpart applies to all research involving human subjects conducted by the Department of Health and Human Services or funded in whole or in part by a Department grant, contract, cooperative agreement or fellowship.

(1) This includes research conducted by Department employees, except each Principal Operating Component head may adopt such nonsubstantive, procedural modifications as may be appropriate from an administrative standpoint.

(2) It also includes research conducted or funded by the Department of Health and Human Services outside the United States, but in appropriate circumstances, the Secretary may, under paragraph (e) of this section waive the applicability of some or all of the requirements of these regulations for research of this type.

(b) Research activities in which the only involvement of human subjects will be in one or more of the following categories are exempt from these regulations unless the research is covered by other subparts of this part:

(1) Research conducted in established or commonly accepted educational settings, involving normal educational practices, such as (i) research on regular and special education instructional strategies, or (ii) research on the effectiveness of or the comparison among instructional techniques, curricula, or classroom management methods.

---

11. 45 C.F.R. 46 subpart B (1983).

12. Reprinted in § D, infra.

13. 43 Fed.Reg. 53,956 (1978).

14. 43 Fed.Reg. 35,186 (Aug. 8, 1978).

15. 46 Fed.Reg. 8366 (Jan. 26, 1981).

(2) Research involving the use of educational tests (cognitive, diagnostic, aptitude, achievement), if information taken from these sources is recorded in such a manner that subjects cannot be identified, directly or through identifiers linked to the subjects.

(3) Research involving survey or interview procedures, except where all of the following conditions exist: (i) responses are recorded in such a manner that the human subjects can be identified, directly or through identifiers linked to the subjects, (ii) the subject's responses, if they became known outside the research, could reasonably place the subject at risk of criminal or civil liability or be damaging to the subject's financial standing or employability, and (iii) the research deals with sensitive aspects of the subject's own behavior, such as illegal conduct, drug use, sexual behavior, or use of alcohol. All research involving survey or interview procedures is exempt, without exception, when the respondents are elected or appointed public officials or candidates for public office.

(4) Research involving the observation (including observation by participants) of public behavior, except where all of the following conditions exist: (i) observations are recorded in such a manner that the human subjects can be identified, directly or through identifiers linked to the subjects, (ii) the observations recorded about the individual, if they became known outside the research, could reasonably place the subject at risk of criminal or civil liability or be damaging to the subject's financial standing or employability, and (iii) the research deals with sensitive aspects of the subject's own behavior such as illegal conduct, drug use, sexual behavior, or use of alcohol.

(5) Research involving the collection or study of existing data, documents, records, pathological specimens, or diagnostic specimens, if these sources are publicly available or if the information is recorded by the investigator in such a manner that subjects cannot be identified, directly or through identifiers linked to the subjects.

. . .

(c) The Secretary has final authority to determine whether a particular activity is covered by these regulations.

(d) The Secretary may require that specific research activities or classes of research activities conducted or funded by the Department, but not otherwise covered by these regulations, comply with some or all of these regulations.

(e) The Secretary may also waive applicability of these regulations to specific research activities or classes of research activities, otherwise covered by these regulations. Notices of these actions will be published in the *Federal Register* as they occur.

(f) No individual may receive Department funding for research covered by these regulations unless the individual is affiliated with or sponsored by an institution which assumes responsibility for the research under an assurance satisfying the requirements of this part, or the individual makes other arrangements with the Department.

(g) Compliance with these regulations will in no way render inapplicable pertinent federal, state, or local laws or regulations.

. . .

§ 46.102 Definitions.

(a) "Secretary" means the Secretary of Health and Human Services and any other officer or employee of the Department of Health and Human Services to whom authority has been delegated.

(b) "Department" or "HHS" means the Department of Health and Human Services.

(c) "Institution" means any public or private entity or agency (including federal, state, and other agencies).

(d) "Legally authorized representative" means an individual or judicial or other body authorized under applicable law to consent on behalf of a prospective subject to the subject's participation in the procedure(s) involved in the research.

(e) "Research" means a systematic investigation designed to develop or contribute to generalizable knowledge. Activities which meet this definition constitute "research" for purposes of these regulations, whether or not they are supported or funded under a program which is considered research for other purposes. For example, some "demonstration" and "service" programs may include research activities.

(f) "Human subject" means a living individual about whom an investigator (whether professional or student) conducting research obtains (1) data through intervention or interaction with the individual, or (2) identifiable private information. "Intervention" includes both physical procedures by which data are gathered (for example, venipuncture) and manipulations of the subject or the subject's environment that are performed for research purposes. "Interaction" includes communication or interpersonal contact between investigator and subject. "Private information" includes information about behavior that occurs in a context in which an individual can reasonably expect that no observation or recording is taking place, and information which has been provided for specific purposes by an individual and which the individual can reasonably expect will not be made public (for example, a medical record). Private information must be individually identifiable (i.e., the identity of the subject is or may readily be ascertained by the investigator or associated with the information) in order for obtaining the information to constitute research involving human subjects.

(g) "Minimal risk" means that the risks of harm anticipated in the proposed research are not greater, considering probability and magnitude, than those ordinarily encountered in daily life or during the performance of routine physical or psychological examinations or tests.

(h) "Certification" means the official notification by the institution to the Department in accordance with the requirements of this part that a research project or activity involving human subjects has been reviewed and approved by the Institutional Review Board (IRB) in accordance with the approved assurance on file at HHS. (Certification is required when the research is funded by the Department and not otherwise exempt in accordance with § 46.101(b)).

§ 46.103 Assurances.

(a) Each institution engaged in research covered by these regulations shall provide written assurance satisfactory to the Secretary that it will comply with the requirements set forth in these regulations.

(b) The Department will conduct or fund research covered by these regulations only if the institution has an assurance approved as provided in this section, and only if the institution has certified to the Secretary that the research has been reviewed and approved by an IRB provided for in the assurance, and will be subject to continuing review by the IRB. This assurance shall at a minimum include:

(1) A statement of principles governing the institution in the discharge of its responsibilities for protecting the rights and welfare of human subjects of research conducted at or sponsored by the institution, regardless of source of funding. This may include an appropriate existing code, declaration, or statement of ethical principles, or a statement formulated by the institution itself. This requirement does not preempt provisions of these regulations applicable to Department-funded research and is not applicable to any research in an exempt category listed in § 46.101.

(2) Designation of one or more IRBs established in accordance with the requirements of this subpart, and for which provisions are made for meeting space and sufficient staff to support the IRB's review and record-keeping duties.

(3) A list of the IRB members identified by name; earned degrees; representative capacity; indications of experience such as board certifications, licenses, etc., sufficient to describe each member's chief anticipated contributions to IRB deliberations; and any employment or other relationship between each member and the institution; for example: full-time employee, part-time employee, member of governing panel or board, stockholder, paid or unpaid consultant. Changes in IRB membership shall be reported to the Secretary.

(4) Written procedures which the IRB will follow (i) for conducting its initial and continuing review of research and for reporting its findings and actions to the investigator and the institution; (ii) for determining which projects require review more often than annually and which projects need verification from sources other than the investigators that no material changes have occurred since previous IRB review; (iii) for insuring prompt reporting to the IRB of proposed changes in a research activity, and for insuring that changes in approved research, during the period for which IRB approval has already been given, may not be initiated without IRB review and approval except where necessary to eliminate apparent immediate hazards to the subject; and (iv) for insuring prompt reporting to the IRB and to the Secretary of unanticipated problems involving risks to subjects or others.

(c) The assurance shall be executed by an individual authorized to act for the institution and to assume on behalf of the institution the obligations imposed by these regulations, and shall be filed in such form and manner as the Secretary may prescribe.

(d) The Secretary will evaluate all assurances submitted in accordance with these regulations through such officers and employees of the Department and such experts or consultants engaged for this purpose as the Secretary determines to be appropriate. The Secretary's evaluation will take into consideration the adequacy of the proposed IRB in light of the anticipated scope of the institution's research activities and the types of subject populations likely to be involved, the appropriateness of the proposed initial and continuing review procedures in light of the probable risks, and the size and complexity of the institution.

(e) On the basis of this evaluation, the Secretary may approve or disapprove the assurance, or enter into negotiations to develop an approvable one. The Secretary may limit the period during which any particular approved assurance or class of approved assurances shall remain effective or otherwise condition or restrict approval.

(f) Within 60 days after the date of submission to HHS of an application or proposal, an institution with an approved assurance covering the proposed research shall certify that the application or proposal has been reviewed and approved by the IRB. Other institutions shall certify that the application or proposal has been approved by the IRB within 30 days after receipt of a request for such a certification from the Department. If the certification is not submitted within these time limits, the application or proposal may be returned to the institution.

. . .

§ 46.107   IRB membership.

(a) Each IRB shall have at least five members, with varying backgrounds to promote complete and adequate review of research activities commonly conducted by the institution. The IRB shall be sufficiently qualified through the experience and expertise of its members, and the diversity of the members' backgrounds including consideration of the racial and cultural backgrounds of members and sensitivity to such issues as community attitudes, to promote respect for its advice and counsel in safeguarding the rights and welfare of human subjects. In addition to possessing the professional competence necessary to review specific research activities, the IRB shall be able to ascertain the acceptability of proposed research in terms of institutional commitments and regulations, applicable law, and standards of professional conduct and practice. The IRB shall therefore include persons knowledgeable in these areas. If an IRB regularly reviews research that involves a vulnerable category of subjects, including but not limited to subjects covered by other subparts of this part, the IRB shall include one or more individuals who are primarily concerned with the welfare of these subjects.

(b) No IRB may consist entirely of men or entirely of women, or entirely of members of one profession.

(c) Each IRB shall include at least one member whose primary concerns are in nonscientific areas; for example: lawyers, ethicists, members of the clergy.

(d) Each IRB shall include at least one member who is not otherwise affiliated with the institution and who is not part of the immediate family of a person who is affiliated with the institution.

(e) No IRB may have a member participating in the IRB's initial or continuing review of any project in which the member has a conflicting interest, except to provide information requested by the IRB.

(f) An IRB may, in its discretion, invite individuals with competence in special areas to assist in the review of complex issues which require expertise beyond or in addition to that available on the IRB. These individuals may not vote with the IRB.

§ 46.108   IRB functions and operations.

In order to fulfill the requirements of these regulations each IRB shall:

(a) Follow written procedures as provided in § 46.103(b)(4).

(b) Except when an expedited review procedure is used (see § 46.110), review proposed research at convened meetings at which a majority of the members of the IRB are present, including at least one member whose primary concerns are in nonscientific areas. In order for the research to be approved, it shall receive the approval of a majority of those members present at the meeting.

(c) Be responsible for reporting to the appropriate institutional officials and the Secretary any serious or continuing noncompliance by investigators with the requirements and determinations of the IRB.

§ 46.109 IRB review of research.

(a) An IRB shall review and have authority to approve, require modifications in (to secure approval), or disapprove all research activities covered by these regulations.

(b) An IRB shall require that information given to subjects as part of informed consent is in accordance with § 46.116. The IRB may require that information, in addition to that specifically mentioned in § 46.116, be given to the subjects when in the IRB's judgment the information would meaningfully add to the protection of the rights and welfare of subjects.

(c) An IRB shall require documentation of informed consent or may waive documentation in accordance with § 46.117.

(d) An IRB shall notify investigators and the institution in writing of its decision to approve or disapprove the proposed research activity, or of modifications required to secure IRB approval of the research activity. If the IRB decides to disapprove a research activity, it shall include in its written notification a statement of the reasons for its decision and give the investigator an opportunity to respond in person or in writing.

(e) An IRB shall conduct continuing review of research covered by these regulations at intervals appropriate to the degree of risk, but not less than once per year, and shall have authority to observe or have a third party observe the consent process and the research.

§ 46.110 Expedited review procedures for certain kinds of research involving no more than minimal risk, and for minor changes in approved research.

(a) The Secretary has established, and published in the *Federal Register*, a list of categories of research that may be reviewed by the IRB through an expedited review procedure. The list will be amended, as appropriate, through periodic republication in the *Federal Register*.

(b) An IRB may review some or all of the research appearing on the list through an expedited review procedure, if the research involves no more than minimal risk. The IRB may also use the expedited review procedure to review minor changes in previously approved research during the period for which approval is authorized. Under an expedited review procedure, the review may be carried out by the IRB chairperson or by one or more experienced reviewers designated by the chairperson from among members of the IRB. In reviewing the research, the reviewers may exercise all of the authorities of the IRB except that the reviewers may not disapprove the research. A research activity may be disapproved only after review in accordance with the non-expedited procedure set forth in § 46.108(b).

(c) Each IRB which uses an expedited review procedure shall adopt a method for keeping all members advised of research proposals which have been approved under the procedure.

(d) The Secretary may restrict, suspend, or terminate an institution's or IRB's use of the expedited review procedure when necessary to protect the rights or welfare of subjects.

§ 46.111 Criteria for IRB approval of research.

(a) In order to approve research covered by these regulations the IRB shall determine that all of the following requirements are satisfied:

(1) Risks to subjects are minimized: (i) By using procedures which are consistent with sound research design and which do not unnecessarily expose subjects to risk, and (ii) whenever appropriate, by using procedures already being performed on the subjects for diagnostic or treatment purposes.

(2) Risks to subjects are reasonable in relation to anticipated benefits, if any, to subjects, and the importance of the knowledge that may reasonably be expected to result. In evaluating risks and benefits, the IRB should consider only those risks and benefits that may result from the research (as distinguished from risks and benefits of therapies subjects would receive even if not participating in the research). The IRB should not consider possible long-range effects of applying knowledge gained in the research (for example, the possible effects of the research on public policy) as among those research risks that fall within the purview of its responsibility.

(3) Selection of subjects is equitable. In making this assessment the IRB should take into account the purposes of the research and the setting in which the research will be conducted.

(4) Informed consent will be sought from each prospective subject or the subject's legally authorized representative, in accordance with, and to the extent required by § 46.116.

(5) Informed consent will be appropriately documented, in accordance with, and to the extent required by § 46.117.

(6) Where appropriate, the research plan makes adequate provision for monitoring the data collected to insure the safety of subjects.

(7) Where appropriate, there are adequate provisions to protect the privacy of subjects and to maintain the confidentiality of data.

(b) Where some or all of the subjects are likely to be vulnerable to coercion or undue influence, such as persons with acute or severe physical or mental illness, or persons who are economically or educationally disadvantaged, appropriate additional safeguards have been included in the study to protect the rights and welfare of these subjects.

§ 46.112 Review by institution.

Research covered by these regulations that has been approved by an IRB may be subject to further appropriate review and approval or disapproval by officials of the institution. However, those officials may not approve the research if it has not been approved by an IRB.

§ 46.113 Suspension or termination of IRB approval of research.

An IRB shall have authority to suspend or terminate approval of research that is not being conducted in accordance with the IRB's requirements or that has been associated with unexpected serious harm to subjects. Any suspension or termination of approval shall include a statement of the reasons for the IRB's action and shall be reported promptly to the investigator, appropriate institutional officials, and the Secretary.

. . .

§ 46.116 General requirements for informed consent.

Except as provided elsewhere in this or other subparts, no investigator may involve a human being as a subject in research covered by these regulations unless the investigator has obtained the legally effective informed consent of the subject or the subject's legally authorized representative. An investigator shall seek such consent only under circumstances that provide the prospective subject or the representative sufficient opportunity to consider whether or not to participate and that minimize the possibility of coercion or undue influence. The information that is given to the subject or the representative shall be in language understandable to the subject or the representative. No informed consent, whether oral or written, may include any exculpatory language through which the subject or the representative is made to waive or appear to waive any of the subject's legal rights, or releases or appears to release the investigator, the sponsor, the institution or its agents from liability for negligence.

(a) *Basic elements of informed consent.* Except as provided in paragraph (c) or (d) of this section, in seeking informed consent the following information shall be provided to each subject:

(1) A statement that the study involves research, an explanation of the purposes of the research and the expected duration of the subject's participation, a description of the procedures to be followed, and identification of any procedures which are experimental;

(2) A description of any reasonably foreseeable risks or discomforts to the subject;

(3) A description of any benefits to the subject or to others which may reasonably be expected from the research;

(4) A disclosure of appropriate alternative procedures or courses of treatment, if any, that might be advantageous to the subject;

(5) A statement describing the extent, if any, to which confidentiality of records identifying the subject will be maintained;

(6) For research involving more than minimal risk, an explanation as to whether any compensation and an explanation as to whether any medical treatments are available if injury occurs and, if so, what they consist of, or where further information may be obtained;

(7) An explanation of whom to contact for answers to pertinent questions about the research and research subjects' rights, and whom to contact in the event of a research-related injury to the subject; and

(8) A statement that participation is voluntary, refusal to participate will involve no penalty or loss of benefits to which the subject is otherwise entitled, and the subject may discontinue participation at any time without penalty or loss of benefits to which the subject is otherwise entitled.

(b) *Additional elements of informed consent.* When appropriate, one or more of the following elements of information shall also be provided to each subject:

(1) A statement that the particular treatment or procedure may involve risks to the subject (or to the embryo or fetus, if the subject is or may become pregnant) which are currently unforeseeable;

(2) Anticipated circumstances under which the subject's participation may be terminated by the investigator without regard to the subject's consent;

(3) Any additional costs to the subject that may result from participation in the research;

(4) The consequences of a subject's decision to withdraw from the research and procedures for orderly termination of participation by the subject;

(5) A statement that significant new findings developed during the course of the research which may relate to the subject's willingness to continue participation will be provided to the subject; and

(6) The approximate number of subjects involved in the study.

(c) An IRB may approve a consent procedure which does not include, or which alters, some or all of the elements of informed consent set forth above, or waive the requirement to obtain informed consent provided the IRB finds and documents that:

(1) The research is to be conducted for the purpose of demonstrating or evaluating: (i) Federal, state, or local benefit or service programs which are not themselves research programs, (ii) procedures for obtaining benefits or services under these programs, or (iii) possible changes in or alternatives to these programs or procedures; and

(2) The research could not practicably be carried out without the waiver or alteration.

(d) An IRB may approve a consent procedure which does not include, or which alters, some or all of the elements of informed consent set forth above, or waive the requirements to obtain informed consent provided the IRB finds and documents that:

(1) The research involves no more than minimal risk to the subjects;

(2) The waiver or alteration will not adversely affect the rights and welfare of the subjects;

(3) The research could not practicably be carried out without the waiver or alteration; and

(4) Whenever appropriate, the subjects will be provided with additional pertinent information after participation.

(e) The informed consent requirements in these regulations are not intended to preempt any applicable federal, state, or local laws which require additional information to be disclosed in order for informed consent to be legally effective.

(f) Nothing in these regulations is intended to limit the authority of a physician to provide emergency medical care, to the extent the physician is permitted to do so under applicable federal, state, or local law.

§ 46.117   Documentation of informed consent.

(a) Except as provided in paragraph (c) of this section, informed consent shall be documented by the use of a written consent form approved by the IRB and signed by the subject or the subject's legally authorized representative. A copy shall be given to the person signing the form.

(b) Except as provided in paragraph (c) of this section, the consent form may be either of the following:

(1) A written consent document that embodies the elements of informed consent required by § 46.116. This form may be read to the subject or the subject's legally authorized representative, but in any event, the investigator shall give either the subject or the representative adequate opportunity to read it before it is signed; or

(2) A "short form" written consent document stating that the elements of informed consent required by § 46.116 have been presented orally to the subject or the subject's legally authorized representative. When this method is used, there shall be a witness to the oral presentation. Also, the IRB shall approve a written summary of what is to be said to the subject or the representative. Only the short form itself is to be signed by the subject or the representative. However, the witness shall sign both the short form and a copy of the summary, and the person actually obtaining consent shall sign a copy of the summary. A copy of the summary shall be given to the subject or the representative, in addition to a copy of the "short form."

(c) An IRB may waive the requirement for the investigator to obtain a signed consent form for some or all subjects if it finds either:

(1) That the only record linking the subject and the research would be the consent document and the principal risk would be potential harm resulting from a breach of confidentiality. Each subject will be asked whether the subject wants documentation linking the subject with the research, and the subject's wishes will govern; or

(2) That the research presents no more than minimal risk of harm to subjects and involves no procedures for which written consent is normally required outside of the research context.

In cases where the documentation requirement is waived, the IRB may require the investigator to provide subjects with a written statement regarding the research.

. . .

NOTES

1. The regulations were revised in 1983 to add an exemption to § 46.101 for research on "Social Security Act or other public benefit or service programs." 48 Fed.Reg. 9269 (March 4, 1983), effectively overturning Crane v. Mathews, 417 F.Supp. 532 (N.D.Ga.1976). There are additional regulations not excerpted here that govern research on certain subjects thought to need additional protection. The regulations governing research on fetuses are set forth in Sec. D.3., infra. Those pertaining to prisoners are discussed in Sec. D.4., infra. The regulations governing research on children are set forth in Sec. D.3., infra.

2. On August 14, 1979, the Secretary of HHS proposed amending the existing federal regulations governing research involving human subjects by directing all Institutional Review Boards to approve research only if "the research methods are appropriate to the objectives of the research and field of study." 44 Fed.Reg. 47,688. When the final regulations were published on January 26, 1981, this requirement was omitted. See § 46.111 of the HHS regulations, supra.

HHS explained the change as follows:

"Many commentators [during the public comment period] objected to an IRB determining if the research methods are appropriate to the objectives of the research and field of study . . . . [M]any argued that the IRB does not have the expertise to make judgments on the scientific merit, since it is primarily designed to insure the protection of human subjects. This requirement, some commentators indicated, could subvert academic freedom and possibly stifle innovative research."   46 Fed.Reg. 8377 (1981).

HHS concluded:

"[T]he requirement that the IRB review the appropriateness of the scientific methods is withdrawn.   HHS feels that this is accomplished through mechanisms such as peer review and need not be addressed by these regulations." 46 Fed.Reg. 8378.

If you had been the Secretary of HHS, how would you have resolved this issue?

3. The elements of informed consent required by HHS are set forth in § 46.116. If you were deciding whether to become a subject in an experiment designed to test a new drug, what would you want to know about the drug? About the researcher?   Are your concerns covered by the HHS regulations?

4. On the federal government's ability to regulate private parties through the use of mechanisms such as the Institutional Review Board, see Ch. 4, Sec. B.2., supra.

5. The HHS regulations apply to social science research as well as to biomedical.   Some critics have argued that because the regulations were designed primarily for biomedical research, they fail to address special issues raised by social science research.   Consider, for example, the problem of deception.

There were two studies performed in the 1960's that demonstrate aspects of the deception debate.   In the first, Stanley Milgram conducted a series of experiments at Yale University designed to study obedience to authority.   Each subject was told only that he was to be a "teacher" in a study designed to determine the effects of punishment on memory.   The "learner" was an accomplice of the experimenter.   Each subject was instructed to teach the "learner" certain paired words by giving electric shocks of increasing intensity for wrong answers.   The accomplice was told to protest with increasing intensity as the shocks became more "severe."   At "150 volts" on the fake generator, the "learner" would ask to be excused from the experiment; at 180, he or she cried out that the pain was intolerable; at 300, the learner refused to give any more answers and asked to be freed.   Each time a subject hesitated about giving a stronger shock, the experimenter would state "You have no other choice, you must go on!"   The experiment would end only when a subject refused to administer a stronger shock.

Milgram found that 65% of the subjects continued to shock the accomplice even when the "danger: severe shock" level was reached on the fake generator. See generally, S. Milgram, Obedience to Authority: An Experimental View (1974); Milgram, Some Conditions of Obedience and Disobedience to Authority, 18 Human Relat. 57 (1965).

Laud Humphreys, another social scientist, played the role of "watch queen", or look-out, in order to observe the behavior of men engaging in anonymous homosexual encounters in public restrooms.   He traced subjects by using their car license numbers, then took a job as a public health pollster to obtain personal data from them.   See generally L. Humphreys, Tearoom Trade: Impersonal Sex in Public Places (1975).

Do either of these standards meet the requirements of the current HHS regulations?   If not, does this mean that the regulations are too restrictive?

Consider the views of the two social scientists.   Humphreys has asserted that the benefits of his study outweigh any risks of harm it might have produced, because its findings should help to correct cruel stereotypes about homosexuals.

Milgram has reported that his post-experimental treatment (interview and questionaires), designed to measure and prevent any harm to subjects, was successful.   Some 84% of the subjects reported that they were glad to participate and some 74% indicated that they had learned something of personal value.   Only 1.3% reported any negative feelings.   But see Warwick, Types of Harm in Social Research in Ethical Issues in Social Science Research 106 (T. Beauchamp, R. Faden, R. Wallace, and L. Walters ed. 1982): "Writers such as Stanley Milgram vehemently deny that subjects suffer any lasting harm from such experiences, but the strength of their convictions is much greater than the rigor of the corroborating data."

For more discussion of the ethical issues raised in social research, see generally R. Bower and P. de Gasparis, Ethics in Social Science Research: Protecting the Interests of Human Subjects (1978); E. Diener and R. Crandall, Ethics in Social and Behavioral Research (1978); Ethical Issues in Social Science Research (T. Beauchamp, R. Faden, R. Wallace and L. Walters, eds. 1982); P. Reynolds, Ethical Dilemmas and Social Science Research: An Analysis of Moral Issues Confronting Investigators in Research Using Human Participants (1979).

c. State Regulations

New York and California are the only states that have enacted laws governing research on human subjects in general. McKinney's N.Y. Public Health Law §§ 2440–44 (1975); West's Ann.Calif. Health & Safety Code §§ 24171–78 (1978). A number of states have statutes designed to protect particular categories of subjects on the other hand. See, e.g., D.C.Code § 6–1969 (1981) (special restrictions on research involving institutionalized mentally retarded persons).

The New York law applies only to nontherapeutic research or investigation but specifically includes psychological as well as physical interventions in its scope. § 2441. Such research may be conducted in New York only with the written, voluntary, informed consent of the subject, with two exceptions. First, if the subject is a minor, his parent or legal guardian may give consent. If the subject is "otherwise legally unable to render consent," the consent may be given by another person "legally empowered" to act on the subject's behalf. § 2442.

Informed consent is defined to include:

"(a) a fair explanation to the individual of the procedures to be followed, and their purposes, including identification of any procedures which are experimental;

(b) a description of any attendant discomforts and risks reasonably to be expected;

(c) a description of any benefits reasonably to be expected;

(d) a disclosure of any appropriate alternative procedures that might be advantageous for the individual;

(e) an offer to answer any inquiries by the individual concerning the procedures; and

(f) an instruction that the individual is free to withdraw his consent and to discontinue participation in the human research at any time without prejudice to him." § 2441.

In addition, only a bona fide researcher within an appropriate institutional format may conduct research involving humans in New York. Each such institution must establish a human research review committee composed of at least five persons of varied backgrounds and institutional affiliation, and approved by the State Commissioner of Health. Committee members may not have any conflicting interest in the experiment.

"The human research review committee in each institution or agency shall require that institution or agency to promulgate a statement of principle and policy in regard to the rights and welfare of human subjects in the conduct of human research, and the committee and the commissioner shall approve that statement prior to its taking effect. The committee shall review each proposed human research project to determine: 1) its necessity; 2) that the rights and welfare of the human subjects involved are adequately protected; 3) that the risks to the human subjects are outweighed by the potential benefits to them or by the importance of the knowledge to be gained; 4) that the voluntary informed consent is to be obtained by methods that are adequate and appropriate; and 5) that the persons proposed to conduct the particular medical research are appropriately competent and qualified." § 2444.

Any violations of the law are to be reported by the committee to the commissioner. Additional protection for minors, incompetent persons, the mentally disabled and prisoners is provided by requiring the consent of both the committee and commissioner for experiments which involve them.

The 1978 California law, like New York's, applies only to nontherapeutic experiments. It is more limited in scope than New York's, however, for it applies only to experiments that involve:

"the severance or penetration or damaging of tissues of a human subject or the use of a drug or device . . . electromagnetic radiation, heat or cold, or a biological substance or organism, in or upon a human subject in the practice or research of medicine in a manner not reasonably related to maintaining or improving the health of such subject or otherwise directly benefiting such subject." § 24174.

Informed consent is required in writing from the subject or, if the subject is incompetent or disabled, from a guardian or conservator.

When a guardian or conservator gives consent, it can be given only for experiments "related to maintaining or improving the health of the human subject, or related to obtaining information about a pathological condition of the human subject." § 24175.

Informed consent is defined to mean that, in writing in a language in which the subject is fluent, he or she must:

"(a) Be informed of the nature and purpose of the experiment.

(b) Be given an explanation of the procedures to be followed in the medical experiment, and any drug or device to be utilized.

(c) Be given a description of any attendant discomforts and risks reasonably to be expected from the experiment.

(d) Be given an explanation of any benefits to the subject reasonably to be expected from the experiment, if applicable.

(e) Be given a disclosure of any appropriate alternative procedures, drugs or devices that might be advantageous to the subject, and their relative risks and benefits.

(f) Be informed of the avenues of medical treatment, if any, available to the subject after the experiment if complications should arise.

(g) Be given an opportunity to ask any questions concerning the experiment or the procedures involved.

(h) Be instructed that consent to participate in the medical experiment may be withdrawn at any time and the subject may discontinue participation in the medical experiment without prejudice.

(i) Be given a copy of the signed and dated written consent form
. . . ..

(j) Be given the opportunity to decide to consent or not to consent to a medical experiment without the intervention of any element of force, fraud, deceit, duress, coercion, or undue influence on the subject's decision." § 24172.

California, unlike New York, does not require review committees. Instead, the California statute establishes fines of up to $10,000 and makes it a misdemeanor punishable by up to one year in prison if a researcher willfully fails to obtain the required informed consent. It also establishes similar penalties for any representative or employee of a pharmaceutical company who is responsible for contracting for a medical experiment but wilfully withholds knowledge of risks or hazards associated with the experiment. A researcher who negligently fails to obtain informed consent is made civilly liable to any subject for damages ranging from a minimum of $50 to a maximum of $1,000. § 24176.

C. ASSESSMENT OF CURRENT REGULATIONS

---

1. RESEARCH OR INNOVATIVE THERAPY?: THE SCOPE OF CURRENT REGULATIONS

KARP v. COOLEY

United States Court of Appeals for the Fifth Circuit, 1974.
493 F.2d 408.

BELL, CIRCUIT JUDGE:

Medical history was made in 1969 when Dr. Denton A. Cooley, a thoracic surgeon, implanted the first totally mechanical heart in 47-year-old Haskell Karp. This threshold orthotopic cardiac prosthesis[1] also spawned this medical malpractice suit by Mr. Karp's wife, individually and as executrix of Mr. Karp's estate, and his children, for the patient's wrongful death. Grounded on diversity jurisdiction, and thus Texas substantive law, novel questions concerning experimentation, as well as issues of informed consent, fraud, and negligence are presented. After nine days of trial and numerous ancillary proceedings outside the jury's presence, the district court in a carefully considered opinion directed a verdict for the defendant-appellees, Dr. Denton A. Cooley and Dr. Domingo S. Liotta. For reasons stated herein, we affirm.

. . .

FACTS

There is no dispute that prior to entering St. Luke's Episcopal Hospital in Houston on March 5, 1969, Haskell Karp had a long and difficult ten-year history of cardiac problems. He suffered a serious heart attack in 1959 and was hospitalized approximately two months because of dif-

---

1. The mechanical heart implant was actually the second stage of a three stage procedure. On April 4, 1969, Dr. Cooley first attempted a ventriculoplasty, or as sometimes termed a wedge excision, or wedge resection. That proved unsuccessful, and it was then that the mechanical heart was implanted in Mr. Karp, where it sustained Mr. Karp for approximately sixty-four hours. A donor heart was then available, and the transplant operation was performed on the morning of April 7, 1969. Mr. Karp died at 4:10 p.m., April 8, 1969, some thirty-two hours after the transplant surgery.

fuse anterior myocardial infarction. He had incurred four heart attacks, thirteen cardiac hospitalizations and considerable medical care culminating in the insertion of an electronic demand pacemaker in May, 1968. Subsequent hospitalization in September and October, 1968 occurred, and finally the decision was made to seek the assistance of Dr. Cooley. . . .

MRS. KARP'S TESTIMONY

Mrs. Karp's testimony in relevant part was that at the time of his hospital admission March 5, Mr. Karp's physical condition was "as normal as any man in the courtroom" and that he was in no pain or discomfort. She testified Dr. Homer L. Beazley, a cardiologist, examined Mr. Karp on March 6 and on a daily basis after that. She said Dr. Cooley first saw Haskell Karp on Tuesday, March 11. She said Dr. Cooley recommended a heart transplant, but that Mr. Karp rejected this suggestion. She said Dr. Cooley next saw Mr. Karp about a week later when he began to talk about a "wedge procedure" and an aneurysm.[3] She then testified that she next saw Dr. Cooley the day before Mr. Karp's surgery on April 3, 1969, although she admitted that Dr. Cooley had seen Mr. Karp the night before on April 2 when she was not present. Mrs. Karp testified Dr. Cooley came into the hospital room about 6:30 or 7:00 p.m. on April 3. As Mrs. Karp described this meeting:

"When Dr. Cooley came in, he said, 'I have a paper here for you to sign for Mr. Karp's surgery,'[4] and I looked at him, and said, 'Why do you want to operate,' you know, 'tomorrow after keeping us here so long? Can you tell me about it?'

"And he said, 'Mr. Karp has taken a sudden turn for the worse. His aneurysm is about to burst. If we wait too long, we may not be able to get into his heart to repair anything.'

3. Mrs. Karp said Dr. Cooley told Mr. Karp and her that an aneurysm

". . . . is like a ballooning out of a section of this [tire tube]. It's like a weak wall. And when you put pressure on it or drive it, it could break open."

4. This consent form was prepared by Dr. Cooley and Mr. Henry Reinhard, Assistant Administrator of St. Luke's Episcopal Hospital, on April 3 especially for the Karp operation. While there is a conflict in the testimony between Mrs. Karp, Dr. Cooley, and Mr. Reinhard as to *when* Mr. Karp signed the form, there is no dispute that Mr. Karp signed it, and that both Mr. and Mrs. Karp's signatures were verified consequently by Mr. Reinhard. The consent form reads as follows:

CONSENT TO OPERATION

April 3, 1969

1. I, Haskell Carp, [sic] request and authorize Dr. Denton A. Cooley and such other surgeons as he may designate to perform upon me, in St. Luke's Episcopal Hospital of Houston, Texas, cardiac surgery for advanced cardiac decompensation and myocar-

dial insufficiency as a result of numerous coronary occlusions. The risk of this surgery has been explained to me. In the event cardiac function cannot be restored by excision of destroyed heart muscle and plastic reconstruction of the ventricle and death seems imminent, I authorize Dr. Cooley and his staff to remove my diseased heart and insert a mechanical cardiac substitute. I understand that this mechanical device will not be permanent and ultimately will require replacement by a heart transplant. I realize that this device has been tested in the laboratory but has not been used to sustain a human being and that no assurance of success can be made. I expect the surgeons to exercise every effort to preserve my life through any of these means. No assurance has been made by anyone as to the results that may be obtained.

. . .

Signature s/ <u>Haskell Karp</u>
Haskell Karp.

WITNESSES:
s/ <u>Mrs. Haskell Karp</u>
Mrs. Haskell Karp (wife)
s/ <u>Henry C. Reinhard, Jr.</u>
Henry D. Reinhard, Jr.

"He says, 'I still don't know whether we can even wait till to-morrow.'

"I said to him, 'You once told me, Dr. Cooley, that . . . you thought he needed a transplant.' I said, 'Do you still think that's the answer.'

"And Dr. Cooley said to me, 'Mrs. Karp, there is a donor heart that will be available and that we will use if there's that need for it.' . . .

"He says, 'Will you sign this now?' And I looked at my husband, and I guess he was in tears because I was shaking. And Dr. Cooley said to me, 'don't worry about the shock element to your husband be-cause I told him exactly what I told you now last night.'

"So then my husband said, 'Honey, he told me this last night.' He said, 'Go ahead. We'll sign the agreement.'

"And that's what happened. My husband signed it—. . . . Then he gave it to me to sign. And I says, 'I got to read it first.'

"And I started to go down it and I was glancing at the—it was all too bewildering and all of a sudden I came across some sort of a mechanical device, and I said, 'Dr. Cooley, what's this thing here that you have?'

"I said, 'what's mechanical device?'

"And he said, 'well you know, Mrs. Karp, when we operate on a heart we have to take the heart out of the body. So what we do is use what's commonly known as a heart lung machine and we attach the pipes from the machine to the different arteries that they sever to take the heart out. And this here keeps the flow of blood going through the body and the oxygen so that there will not be any damage to the body.'

"So he says the reason that he put that into the consent was be-cause the one that they had in the operating room, I believe he said, worked for a matter of maybe two hours or something and this here one was a new model and it was proven in the laboratory, but he [sic] hasn't been used on a human being yet. But that this here should sustain him if he should die on the table. He says it would sustain him for at least thirty minutes in order to get the donor heart into my husband's body."

Mrs. Karp also testified that Dr. Cooley did not state that the device was any different from the heart-lung device ordinarily used for open heart surgery, stating that it was a "newer model" that had not been used be-fore. She said Dr. Cooley told her there was a donor heart available in a nearby hospital, and that the mechanical device would be used for only 30 minutes while the donor was being prepared. Mrs. Karp said Mr. Rein-hard came to the room early the next morning to verify the signatures. She also testified that Mr. Karp at the time of the April 3 meeting with Dr. Cooley was as normal as when he entered the hospital, that his physical appearance was the same and there was no appearance of pain; and that Mr. Karp was able to walk around the hospital even the morning of the operation. She said both Dr. Beazley and Dr. Cooley had said the wedge excision had a 70 per cent chance of success, and that Dr. Cooley had said that in his own personal experience he had less than a five per cent chance of failure and that it "seemed like it hardly ever failed."

DR. COOLEY'S TESTIMONY

Dr. Cooley testified that he first saw Mr. Karp on or about March 5, 1969 and that he recommended a heart transplant which Mr. Karp rejected, preferring "some alternative procedure." Dr. Cooley said tests then showed Mr. Karp had triple vessel disease where all three coronary arteries were occluded. He said electrocardiograms showed evidence of extensive scarring and damage and that his chest x-rays showed enormous cardiac enlargement. In addition, said Dr. Cooley, he had a pacemaker which was about to fail. Dr. Cooley said he estimated that Karp's chances of dying in the operating room as a result of the wedge procedure were approximately thirty per cent. He testified that as some three weeks passed, Mr. Karp grew increasingly impatient waiting for a donor's availability in the event the wedge excision failed. Dr. Cooley said it was the custom of medical doctors in the community to advise a patient of risks of surgery "within certain boundaries . . . but not every contingency can be explained to a layman about the threat and the risk of open heart surgery or the type of device which we are using, many of which are being used for the first time in a patient." About a week before the operation of April 4, 1969, Dr. Cooley said he began to discuss with Mr. Karp the possibility of another alternative "which I did not think was proper when he initially came to the hospital."

"I told him we had no heart donor available, had no prospect of one . . . I told him that there was a possibility that we had a device which would sustain his life in the event that he would die on the operating table. We had a device which would sustain his life, hopefully, until we could get a suitable donor. I had told him that I did not know whether it would take a matter of hours or days, weeks, or maybe not at all, but it would sustain his life and give us another possibility of salvaging him through heart transplantation."

Dr. Cooley said he did not recall who was present when these discussions began. Dr. Cooley described his discussion of this device:

"I told him that it was a heart pump similar to the one that we used in open-heart surgery; that it was a reciprocating-type pump with the membrane, in which the pumping element never became in contact with the bloodstream; that it was designed in such a manner that it would not damage the bloodstream or it would cause minimal damage to the bloodstream; that it would be placed in his body to take over the function of the dead heart and to propel blood throughout his body during this interim until we could have a heart transplant. . . . I told him this device had not been used in human beings; that it had been used in the laboratory; that we had been able to sustain the circulation in calves and that it had not been used in human beings."

Dr. Cooley said that it took about 20 minutes to make the resection repair. He said that after the repair the clamp was taken off the ascending aorta to attempt to restart the myocardium. He stated that there was fibrillation and that he attempted an electrical countershock at least once.[8]

---

8. Dr. Cooley said the electrical shock stopped the fibrillation, a sinus type or a nodal rhythm then began, but the rhythm contraction was too weak to support Mr. Karp's life. Dr. Keats said he believed more than one shock attempt was made, basing this on both memory and the anesthetic record that three attempts were made during this time

He stated that there was a sinus type or nodal rhythm at that point but that the rhythm contraction was too weak to support life due to the fact that there simply was too much scar tissue in the heart. Dr. Hallman testified that some thirty minutes elapsed between the end of the repair and the decision to remove the heart. Mr. Karp's heart was then removed and the mechanical device was inserted. Dr. Cooley said that the mechanical heart functioned very well and Mr. Karp responded to stimulation within 15 or 20 minutes after the incision was closed. His blood pressure was well sustained according to Dr. Cooley and he showed signs of cerebral activity. Dr. Keats said that Mr. Karp was amazingly well following the operation, that the records reflect that he was responding reasonably to commands within 20 minutes postoperatively. Dr. Keats testified that the endotracheal tube was removed about 1:20 a.m., and that he saw Mr. Karp some time the next morning at which time he was responsive and could communicate.

After the mechanical heart had been inserted, Dr. Cooley said he went to Mrs. Karp and told her that the wedge procedure had been unsuccessful; that he had proceeded with the use of the mechanical device and that they were going to try to get a donor. The transplant operation was performed on the morning of April 7, 1969, aproximately 64 hours after the mechanical device had been implanted in Mr. Karp. He died the next day, April 8, 1969, some 32 hours after the transplant surgery.

DR. JOHN D. MILAM

Dr. John D. Milam, a pathologist who participated in both the pathological examination of Mr. Karp's diseased heart and the autopsy performed on Mr. Karp, testified that in reasonable medical probability the immediate cause of Mr. Karp's death was pneumonia, and the secondary or contributing factor was renal failure. In testifying about the "cause of the causes", Dr. Milam said that the cause of the pneumonia was a germ or bacteria called pseudomonas, which he said was a type of pneumonia that has shown up in other patients undergoing heart transplants as well as non-transplant and non-cardiovascular patients. He said that the cause of the renal dysfunction could have been either a state of shock as a result of the surgery, an infectious process such as pneumonia, the use of the heart-lung machine, or the mechanical heart. Dr. Milam said that because of the rarity of hemoglobin casts in Mr. Karp's kidney tubules, the mechanical heart and heart-lung by-pass were less likely causes of the renal shutdown than shock or pneumonia. Based on his examination of Mr. Karp's heart, Dr. Milam said that Mr. Karp would have died in a few hours.

DR. DONALD ROCHELLE

Dr. Donald Rochelle, a cardiologist who first examined Karp some two hours after the transplant, and who also observed the autopsy, said at that initial examination Karp was critically ill with two major problems, pneumonia and renal failure. Dr. Rochelle also expressed the opinion the chief or primary cause of Mr. Karp's death was pneumonia, and he felt

period immediately after the wedge excision to take Karp off the heart-lung by-pass. Dr. Keats confirmed that the shock restarted the beat, but not the heart's pumping action. Apparently one of the plaintiffs' theories of negligence, and also asserted as one of the circumstantial factors supporting the experimentation count, was an alleged lack of medical effort on Dr. Cooley's part to revive Mr. Karp after the wedge resection. Appellants' theory has no evidentiary foundation.

that the renal problem was a contributing or weakening factor. He said that it was "possible" that the renal failure was a result of the first surgery while Karp was on the heart-lung machine, or that the mechanical heart could have been a contributing factor. Asked how long damage to the red blood cells could exist before it became irreversible, Dr. Rochelle said it could exist for a long time—10 days to a month and still become reversible. Dr. Rochelle said there was some damage to the blood caused by the mechanical device. He said the record indicated the rate of blood cell destruction was measured frequently while the mechanical heart was in place, and the longer the mechanical device was in Karp, the rate and severity of the blood cell destruction diminished as the innerlining of the mechanical device became coated with a substance mimicking the interior of blood vessels and the heart. He said that "some" of the renal shutdown was caused by damage to the blood.

. . .

INFORMED CONSENT

Suits charging failure by a physician adequately to disclose the risks and alternatives of proposed treatment are not innovations in American law. They date back a good half-century and in the last decade have increased in number. The courts and commentators have not been in agreement on the substantive requirements or the nature of the proof required, but the Texas requirements are reasonably well-settled and stringent.

. . .

The Texas standard against which a physician's disclosure or lack of disclosure is tested is a medical one which must be proved by expert medical evidence of what a reasonable practitioner of the same school of practice and the same or similar locality would have advised a patient under similar circumstances. . . . As we understand appellants' contention, it is that Mr. Karp was not told about the number of animals tested or the results of those tests; that he was not told there was a chance of permanent injury to his body by the mechanical heart, that complete renal shutdown could result from the use of the prosthesis, that the device was "completely experimental;" and that Dr. Cooley failed to tell Mr. Karp that Dr. Beazley had said Mr. Karp was not a suitable candidate for surgery. Nine physicians testified, but none suggested a standard of disclosure required by Texas law under these circumstances. . . . Dr. Cooley's admitted failure to tell Mr. Karp of Dr. Beazley's March 6 notation is of no import; Dr. Leachman testified he did not think the notation made any difference; the March 6 notation, made during the course of an initial evaluation, was in Dr. Beazley's view not a medical opinion but a reservation about the psychological or emotional acceptance of less than a perfect result.

What is missing from the evidence presented is the requisite expert testimony as to *what* risks under these circumstances a physician should disclose. . . . Dr. Cooley's undisputed testimony is that he began discussing with Mr. Karp the proposed wedge excision and the alternative procedure of a mechanical heart as a stopgap to a transplant about a week before the April 4 operation. He said he next talked with Mr. Karp the evening of April 2. The consent form was prepared on April 3 and although there is a dispute as to *when* it was signed, there is no question it was signed by Mr. Karp. Thus it was against the backdrop of at least two conversations with Dr. Cooley, at which Mrs. Karp was not present, that Mr. Karp was presented and signed the consent document. The consent form is consistent with Dr. Cooley's testimony of what he told Mr. Karp. Although not necessarily conclusive, what Haskell Karp consented to and was told is best evidenced by this document. . . . It is of considerable import that each step of the three-stage operation, objected to due to an alleged lack of informed consent, was specifically set out in the consent document signed by the patient. . . .

A second important reason to affirm the directed verdict on the issue of informed consent here is the absence of substantial evidence on the requisite causal connection between the lack of informed consent and harm. . . . When the only medical expert in a malpractice case, where expert testimony is, as here, the *sine qua non,* is of the opinion that the defendant's treatment was not a proximate cause of the injury complained of, and there is no expert opinion to the contrary, a directed verdict for the defendants is proper.

In the instant case it is difficult to determine exactly what injury appellants complain of as resulting from a lack of informed consent. . . .

. . .

The only expert testimony was that Mr. Karp was near death prior to the wedge excision operation. Mrs. Karp says she does not complain of the informed consent for the wedge excision. The only expert testimony was that death was also imminent after the wedge excision. There is no expert evidence that says as a reasonable medical probability the mechanical heart caused Karp's death. The expert testimony at best links the mechanical heart as only one of the "possible" but less likely causes of the secondary cause of death, renal failure.

Finally, there is no proof that Mr. Karp would *not* have consented to the operative procedures had the alleged undisclosed material risks been disclosed.

Appellants failed to produce substantial evidence establishing a medical standard as to what disclosures should have been made to Mr. Karp, any violation of that standard, or causation. Thus, the trial court properly directed a verdict for defendants on the informed consent question.

. . .

Appellants contend that the trial court erred in directing a verdict on the issue of experimentation. They acknowledge that no Texas case has expressly dealt with a cause of action based on experimentation, but assert that our court's decision in Bender v. Dingwerth, 5 Cir., 1970, 425 F.2d 378, suggests that the decision as to what is actionable experimentation should be left to a jury. We do not agree.

A Texas court bound in traditional malpractice actions to expert medical testimony to determine how a reasonably careful and prudent physician would have acted under the same or similar circumstances . . . would not likely vary that evidentiary requirement for an experimentation charge. This conclusion is also suggested by the few reported cases where experimentation has been recognized as a separate basis of liability.[22] The record contains no evidence that Mr. Karp's treatment was oth-

22. See Salgo v. Leland Stanford Univ. Bd. of Trustees, 1957, 154 Cal.App.2d 560, 577, 317 P.2d 170; Fortner v. Koch, 1935, 272 Mich. 273, 261 N.W. 762; Owens v. McCleary, 1926, 313 Mo. 213, 223, 281 S.W. 682, 685; Carpenter v. Blake, 1872, 60 Barb. (N.Y.) 488, rev'd on other grounds, 50 N.Y. 696.

er than therapeutic and we agree that in this context an action for experimentation must be measured by traditional malpractice evidentiary standards. Whether there was informed consent is necessarily linked to the charge of experimentation, and Mr. Karp's consent was expressly to all three stages of the operation actually performed—each an alternative in the event of a preceding failure. As previously discussed, appellants have not shown an absence of Mr. Karp's informed consent. Causation and proximate cause are also requisite to an actionable claim of experimentation. Even if . . . [other testimony] were admitted and did establish a standard and a departure from that standard in using this prosthetic device, substantial evidence . . . on causation and proximate cause simply is not reflected in the record. That alone would warrant the directed verdict on this issue.

NOTES

1. Consider the conclusions of the National Commission for the Protection of Human Subjects of Biomedical Research in its Belmont Report 2–4 (1978):

It is important to distinguish between biomedical and behavioral research, on the one hand, and the practice of accepted therapy on the other, in order to know what activities ought to undergo review for the protection of human subjects of research. The distinction between research and practice is blurred partly because both often occur together (as in research designed to evaluate a therapy) and partly because notable departures from standard practice are often called "experimental" when the terms "experimental" and "research" are not carefully defined.

For the most part, the term "practice" refers to interventions that are designed solely to enhance the well-being of an individual patient or client and that have a reasonable expectation of success. The purpose of medical or behavioral practice is to provide diagnosis, preventive treatment or therapy to particular individuals.* By contrast, the term "research" designates an activity designed to test a hypothesis, permit conclusions to be drawn, and thereby to develop or contribute to generalizable knowledge (expressed, for example, in theories, principles, and statements of relationships). Research is usually described in a formal protocol that sets forth an objective and a set of procedures designed to reach that objective.

When a clinician departs in a significant way from standard or accepted practice, the innovation does not, in and of itself, constitute research. The fact that a procedure is "experimental," in the sense of new, untested or different, does not automatically place it in the category of research. Radically new procedures of this description should, however, be made the object of formal research at an early stage in order to determine whether they are safe and effective. Thus, it is the responsibility of medical practice committees, for example, to insist that a major innovation be incorporated into a formal research project.

Research and practice may be carried on together when research is designed to evaluate the safety and efficacy of a therapy. This need not cause

* Although practice usually involves interventions designed solely to enhance the well-being of a particular individual, interventions are sometimes applied to one individual for the enhancement of the well-being of another (e.g., blood donation, skin grafts, organ transplants) or an intervention may have the dual purpose of enhancing the well-being of a particular individual, and, at the same time, providing some benefit to others (e.g., vaccination, which protects both the person who is vaccinated and socie-ty generally). The fact that some forms of practice have elements other than immediate benefit to the individual receiving an intervention, however, should not confuse the general distinction between research and practice. Even when a procedure applied in practice may benefit some other person, it remains an intervention designed to enhance the well-being of a particular individual or groups of individuals; thus, it is practice and need not be viewed as research.

any confusion regarding whether or not the activity requires review; the general rule is that if there is any element of research in an activity, that activity should undergo review for the protection of human subjects.

2. In The Artifical Heart, 12 Hastings Ctr.Rep. 22 (February 1982), Arthur Caplan questions the role played by several federal agencies

On July 23, 1981, Willebrordus Meuffels, a retired bus driver from the Netherlands, became the third person to receive an artificial heart in the United States. Meuffels, who had been flown to Houston at the expense of the Dutch government, had suffered a heart attack during a triple bypass procedure on his failing heart. His physician, Dr. Denton Cooley of the Texas Heart Institute, decided to implant an artificial device to keep Meuffels alive until a suitable heart transplant donor could be located. . . .

Meuffels survived for fifty-four hours with the implant. He then received a heart from a donor who had suffered brain death during a surgical procedure at another hospital. Eight days later he succumbed to what a hospital representative termed "other complications that simply overwhelmed him; kidney problems developed which required dialysis . . . there were pulmonary problems and some infection." The previous recipients of the artificial heart—a forty-seven-year-old man implanted by Cooley in 1969, and a brain-dead woman implanted in May 1981 at the Temple University Hospital in Philadelphia—were maintained on the device for sixty-five hours and two hours respectively. If the artificial heart is, in Life's breathless prose, "here," it has made an inauspicious appearance.

. . .

Buried . . . in the various newspaper accounts of the events surrounding Meuffels's death, was a sentence or two stating that Cooley appeared to have violated FDA regulations concerning new medical devices in implanting an artificial heart into his patient's chest. . . .

. . .

Like the rest of the world, the FDA learned of Dr. Cooley's activity through reports in the media. Victor Zafra, acting head of FDA's Bureau of Medical Devices, quickly sent a letter dated July 30, 1981, to Newell France, executive director of the Texas Heart Institute, in which he noted the FDA's view that ". . . the clinical use of a total artificial heart requires an investigational device exemption approved by the Food and Drug Administration" and requested that "if you anticipate implanting another artificial heart in a patient in the future . . ." an IDE be submitted to FDA. In a response dated August 26, 1981, France noted that the implantation had only been undertaken as a final desperate measure to save a man's life:

All conventional resuscitative measures had been exhausted. The total artificial heart was used as a bridge to cardiac allografting. The alternative was to pronounce the patient dead.

According to France, the Texas Heart Institute considered the heart "a custom device . . . used solely for therapeutic purposes." Pursuant to federal regulations governing custom medical devices, an IRB meeting had been convened within five working days after the implantation. The IRB had approved the emergency use of the device for a therapeutic purpose.

The FDA disagreed. According to the federal regulations governing exemptions from IDEs, a custom device must be "intended for use by an individual patient . . . and is to be made in a specific form for that patient; is not generally available to or generally used by other physicians or dentists, and, is not offered for commercial distribution through labelling or advertising" (Federal Register, January 18, 1980, Vol. 45, 21 CFR 812.3(b)). In his final response to Mr. France, Zafra observed, in a letter dated Sept. 25, 1981:

FDA believes that this artificial heart was not intended or designed for implantation solely in a specific patient. It was fabricated in advance and would appear to be appropriate for any of a number of patients. It does not appear that this device was designed specifically for Dr. Cooley's use in his professional practice. The federal government, through the NIH, has supported the development of an artificial heart for many years. The purpose of that program in which the Texas Heart Institute participated, is to develop a totally implantable total [sic] artificial heart for commercial distribution. Given NIH's program for the development of a total artificial heart and its plans for implantation of such a device, once fully developed, in potentially thousands of patients each year, FDA does not agree that this, or any, total artificial heat is a custom device.

Zafra also noted, however, that Cooley had placed the artificial heart into Meuffels in an emergency. FDA rules permit one emergency use of an investigational device, provided the existence of an emergency "is documented and the use is reported to the IRB within five working days." The Texas Heart Institute had complied with these requirements. Accordingly, Zafra concluded by repeating FDA's position that an artificial heart is not a custom device and that any subsequent implantations at the Texas Heart Institute that lacked full compliance with existing regulations would be in violation of the Federal Food, Drug, and Cosmetic Act.

This correspondence clarifies a number of important ethical and regulatory issues regarding the artificial heart. Dr. Cooley implanted an artificial heart in Meuffels as an emergency measure. He did not believe that the heart would be the sole means of extending Meuffels's life. Rather, he intended the heart to keep his patient alive until a suitable transplant donor could be found.
. . .

Why has the FDA's response to Cooley's use of the artificial heart been so little publicized? Since its inception in 1965 the artificial heart program has been plagued by social and moral ambiguities. This case reveals some of those conflicts.

The artificial heart program of the National Heart, Lung, and Blood Institute at NIH has been something of a disappointment to those involved with it over the past fifteen years. Despite optimistic pronouncements by scientists and NIH officials during the mid-60s that, given adequate funds, a totally implantable artificial heart could be produced by the end of the decade, sixteen years of research and $160 million of federal money have failed to produce such a device. While great progress has been made since 1965 in many technical areas, significant problems still must be overcome before a viable artificial heart can be produced and implanted. These include problems in locating suitable biomaterials, which do not produce clotting and hemolysis, for lining the artificial heart, and in developing a total implantable power source for the mechanical pump. Many researchers have concluded that a totally implantable artificial heart is at least a decade away.[3]

Because of its failure to meet its own initial optimistic forecasts, the artificial heart program has been criticized by some scientists, scholars, and government officials as a paradigm case of misguided, "moon-shot" medicine. Critics have questioned the wisdom of targeting funds for the development of a totally implantable heart when the costs of such "half-way" technologies are so high, the quality of life that will be afforded recipients is uncertain, the selection and distribution mechanisms that ought to be utilized in allocating the device are unclear, and when other approaches to heart disease, such as prophylaxis, transplantation, drugs, or less ambitious mechanical aids such as the left ventricle assist device (LVAD), may be more efficacious and less costly. Indeed, over the years as a result of such criticisms, less money has been allocated to the artificial heart program, while more funding has been given to alternate therapeutic approaches, particularly the LVAD.[4]

3. Robert K. Jarvik, "The Total Artificial Heart," Scientific American 244 (January 1981), 79.

4. See Barton J. Bernstein, "The Artificial Heart Program," The Center Magazine, XIV, No. 3 (May 1981), 22–41.

Against this context of disappointment, apprehension, and frustration, consider the response to Cooley's surgery on Meuffels. Medical researchers directly involved with the artificial heart have surely not been pleased with the NIH's seeming loss of faith in the totally implantable artificial heart. Any event that can help restore the waning enthusiasm of a public grown wary about the escalating costs of medical care, and a federal research agency grown tired of overly optimistic predictions of imminent success is likely to receive a positive reception in concerned medical circles. Cooley's peers in cardiology, surgery, and biomedical engineering are not, given such circumstances, likely either to criticize the actions of one of their own members, or to dwell upon the technological differences involved in utilizing an artificial heart as a desperate stop-gap solution rather than as a permanent therapeutic remedy. Cooley's implantation of an artificial heart might appear to cross over the borderline from desperate medical therapy to research, but the distinction may seem trivial when the surgery can be depicted as concrete evidence of technological advance in a field lacking empirical examples of success.

The press also apparently sees little that is suspect, or even newsworthy, in Cooley's action. The artificial heart is, after all, an old story; the distinctions between therapy and research and between a custom device and an investigational one may appear mere technicalities, not the stuff of headlines. By contrast, Martin Cline's recent difficulties with the UCLA IRB and with NIH over his attempts to perform gene therapy on research subjects were widely reported. Like the scientific community, and no doubt the general public, the press apparently finds the Cooley-FDA matter an intramural squabble.

But if the FDA had wished to publicize its own actions in the Cooley case, surely it could have convinced some reporters that a story does exist. Yet the FDA has remained silent. Why?

Dr. Glenn Rahmoeller of the Bureau of Medical Devices responded to a telephone inquiry about FDA's relative silence concerning the Meuffels case by noting that "FDA is not a public information agency; it is a regulatory agency. There is no formal mechanism within FDA for going public about the interactions we have had with Dr. Cooley. Portions of the public know about our activities vis-à-vis Dr. Cooley and the information is there for those who want to know about it."

As a regulatory agency, FDA maintains delicate relationships with both the NIH and the biomedical research community. FDA's mandates regarding new medical devices, as set out in the 1976 Medical Device Amendments to the Federal Food, Drug, and Cosmetic Act, are to assure that the benefits from the use of a new device, in terms of therapy and knowledge, outweigh the risks to a potential recipient; that informed consent is obtained from prospective patients; and that investigations of new devices are conducted in a scientifically sound manner. FDA must ensure that adequate tests have been conducted on animals and that adequate provisions have been made for monitoring human subjects in order to collect data on a new device's safety and efficacy.

These public policy requirements often put the agency at odds with individual researchers or with NIH since, in Rahmoeller's words, the NIH goal is "research optimization." FDA is totally dependent upon both medical researchers and the NIH in carrying out its regulatory goals; it needs both researcher compliance and NIH data.[5] This dependency makes the agency an unlikely source of negative publicity concerning either medical research or its sister federal agencies.

In 1969, when Denton Cooley implanted an artificial heart in a patient, a storm of moral controversy ensued. In 1981 the same act produced a view in many quarters of a tough-minded renegade, forced by circumstances to buck an overly zealous bureaucracy. The change in the response reveals a great deal about changes in social attitudes and institutions in that time.

5. See John C. Petricciani, "An Overview of FDA, IRBs and Regulations," IRB: A Review of Human Subjects Research, Vol. 3, No. 10 (December 1981), 1–3.

3. On December 2, 1982, at the University of Utah Medical Center in Salt Lake City, Dr. Barney J. Clark, a 61 year old retired dentist, became the first recipient of a permanent artificial heart. New York Times, Dec. 3, 1982, at Al, col. 2.

Dr. Clark appeared to have been near death with an inoperable heart condition known as cardiomyopathy. Until June 1982, a patient with such a condition would not, according to FDA requirements, have been eligible for this particular procedure. The FDA had determined that implant surgery should be performed only on a patient who was already receiving conventional open heart surgery and who was not functioning sufficiently well to remain alive. In June 1982, the FDA approved an amendment to enable patients with inoperable cardiomyopathy to be able to take advantage of artificial heart implantation.

Dr. Clark was chosen by a six member selection committee, which carefully scrutinized his emotional and physical health and reached the conclusion that he was both sufficiently stable to withstand the surgery and its aftermath and sufficiently motivated by a desire to contribute to the advancement of science.

The University's Institutional Review Board (IRB), a panel of doctors, nurses, lawyers and philosophers, drafted the consent form that Dr. Clark signed for the $7\frac{1}{2}$ hour operation.

On March 23, the 112th day after surgery, Dr. Clark died. His death was a result of the total collapse and failure of his circulatory system and other organs of his body. The polyurethane heart, which had beat 13 million times, was finally turned off with a key by members of the medical team. New York Times, March 25, 1983 at Al, col. 5.

The period of time during which Dr. Clark had lived with the artificial heart had been riddled with medical problems. On December 4, surgery had been performed to correct leaks in a malfunctioning lung; on December 11, Dr. Clark had suffered seizures; on December 14, the surgeons had replaced the left side of the heart after a crack had developed; and on March 3, the patient began to deteriorate seriously, developing aspiration pneumonia, kidney failure, and infection of the bowel. Note that the doctors felt compelled by medical ethics to conduct the artificial heart experiment on someone who was in poor health from the start. New York Times, March 25, 1983, at A20, col. 3. Why is this true? Do you agree?

The designer of the Jarvik heart remained optimistic about its future use, claiming that a more portable model is being developed and will be available within the next few years. The expectation is that the demand for such hearts could reach 50,000 annually, and that the cost for each will exceed $50,000. Washington Post, Dec. 6, 1982, at A2, col. 1.

On Friday, September 16, 1983, KUTV, a Salt Lake City affiliate of NBC, made public a transcript of the June 1 meeting of the IRB. The transcript shows that several Board members believe that the doctors were too eager to find a recipient for the mechanical heart and thus failed to consider Clark's other health problems. The Board has not yet decided whether to allow a second implant. Washington Post, Sept. 18, 1983 at A.16, col. 2.

4. Alexander M. Capron, The Law of Genetic Therapy in The New Genetics and the Future of Man 133, 150–152 (M. Hamilton ed. 1972):

A distinction is sometimes drawn between the kind of consent needed from a patient in treatment and that required of a subject in research. Others have argued that there is no basis for such a distinction. A.C. Ivy has written:

Even after the therapy of a disease is discovered, its application to the patient remains, in part, experimental. Because of the physiological variations in the response of different patients to the same therapy, the therapy of disease is, and will always be, an experimental aspect of medicine. . . . . The patient is always to some extent an experimental subject of the physician. . . .

Jay Katz has carried this argument one step further. He finds in physicians' collective "reluctance to examine" the ethics of medical experimentation a "conscious or unconscious realization that any resolution of the problems posed by human experimentation cannot be limited to research settings, but instead has far-reaching consequences for medical practice."

It is true in a certain sense that all treatment is experimentation, and yet I believe there is a distinction between the conditions for consent in the two settings. Those who make such a distinction usually set higher requirements for the consent of experimental subjects than for that of patients. Accordingly, many physicians fear that the standards developed for subjects will be extended to their patients, for whom physicians have traditionally been allowed to make many decisions on the ground of the patient's best interests.

Yet if we look at the contexts carefully and focus on the psychological situation of the patient or subject, it seems to me that the usual approach has it backwards. Higher requirements for informed consent should be imposed in therapy than in investigation, I am convinced, particularly when an element of honest experimentation is joined with the therapy.[33] The "normal volunteer" solicited for an experiment is in a good position to consider the physical, psychological, and monetary risks and benefits to him when he consents to participate. How much harder that is for the patient to whom an experimental technique is offered during a course of treatment! The man proposing the experiment is one to whom the patient may be deeply indebted for past care (emotionally as well as financially) and on whom he is probably dependent for his future well-being. The procedure may be offered, despite unknown risks, because more conventional methods have proved ineffective. Even when a successful but slow recovery is being made, patients offered new therapy often have eyes only for its novelty and not for its risks. Dr. Francis D. Moore has observed, "People in this country have been weaned on newspaper accounts of exciting new cures." In the field of genetics as in other fields, "patients are pressing their doctors to be the subject of innovation."

     . . . Certainly, part of the difference in response between healthy subjects and patient-subjects is due to the obviously greater potential benefits which the latter may derive from participation. But that does not entirely explain their far more favorable response. While, as I argued previously we may not wish *in any particular instance* to disregard the consent of a patient whose strong desire for treatment causes him to overrate the benefits and underestimate the risks of a research technique, I believe we should nevertheless decide *as a general rule* to set higher requirements for consent and to impose additional safeguards on therapy combined with experimentation, lest investigators even unwittingly expose "consenting" patient-subjects to unreasonable risks.

5. Compare the views of Robert J. Levine, set forth in Informed Consent in Research and Practice, 143 Arch.Intern.Med. 1229 (1983). Dr. Levine there observes "[w]hile informed consent [in the practice of medicine] fosters the interest of patients or subjects by empowering them to pursue and protect these interests, the consent form [to research] is an instrument designed to protect the interests of investigators and their institutions, to defend them against civil or criminal liability." Id. at 1229. He also argues there is a need for greater flexibility in practice than research, for while a relatively unflexible protocol for research is good science, in practice one must be responsive to the needs of patients. In research, he observes, "an appropriate question might be: 'What is the antihypertensive effect of administration of this thiazide diuretic in a specified dose range for six weeks to patients with moderately severe hypertension?' In medical practice a more appropriate question is: 'What is the best way to control the BP of the patient who not only has moderately severe hypertension but also has diabetes, congestive heart failure, and recently lost her job?'" Id. at 1231. Would Professor

---

33. I exclude from the meeting of "experimentation" here the trivial sense in which we might say that giving aspirin to a new patient is an experiment. I conclude only those situations in which a doctor is concerned with the person before him not only as a patient but also as a means for discovering something about human beings and their illnesses, or for finding new ways of diagnosing and treating a disease (usually, but not always, the disease which has brought the patient to him).

Capron's suggestion of higher requirements for consent in the practice of medicine than in research unduly interfere with the doctor-patient relationship?

2. SHOULD WE RELY ONLY ON INFORMED CONSENT TO PROTECT SUBJECTS?

CARL H. FELLNER AND JOHN R. MARSHALL, KIDNEY DONORS—THE MYTH OF INFORMED CONSENT

126 Am.J. of Psych. 1245, 1245–51 (1970).

. . .

[W]e undertook to study all available previous [kidney] donors to find out how they had become involved [and] how they had made their decision. . . .

. . .

Of the 20 donors interviewed, 14 were seen at five weeks to 24 months after surgery, with a mean of 11 months, and six were seen before as well as after surgery. In addition, a number of potential donors were interviewed who were subsequently rejected as medically unsuitable. Another ten potential donors who were interviewed are currently awaiting surgery.

. . .

The process of making a decision to give up a kidney for a close relative begins when the first communication about the seriousness of the recipient's illness is received. It continues when the first demand for participation in the medical selection process is made and must be sustained through the long-drawn-out medical investigation and usually through a waiting period even after the decision-making process of the renal transplantation team has been concluded, the potential donor is considered a candidate for transplantation, and has been permitted to give his consent. In addition, there appears to be a third or family system, which also tends to influence the selection of a donor but which is very difficult to demonstrate.

1. The medical selection system. When a transplant situation arises, all possible donor relatives of the patient are asked to come to the clinic for blood tests (ABO typing). Great care is taken at this point by the medical staff to inform the volunteer subjects that this is an exceedingly preliminary procedure and that no commitment whatsoever is involved by their appearing at this clinic, or elsewhere, to have their blood samples drawn. Those potential donors who are not ruled out on the basis of blood grouping are then asked to come to the renal clinic for a brief history-taking and complete physical examination, including routine laboratory studies.

Somewhat later, those of the possible donors who still remain are asked to return to the clinic for histocompatability tests. The results of the mixed leucocyte culture tests (MLCT) are not known until several weeks later and may have to be repeated before they can be read conclusively. Only after this stage does it become possible for the renal transplant team to select from among the available possible donors that most suitable one. He is then asked to come to the special studies unit at the hospital for a complete work-up, careful evaluation of renal status, and so on. During this brief hospitalization he is evaluated independently by at least three of the team physicians. Only at the end of this evaluation and after intensive, repeated briefing on the risks involved and the chances for success is the potential donor asked to make a decision, and permitted, if he desires, to give his informed consent. A final chance to refuse any time in a dignified and comfortable manner is offered in the team's expressed willingness to supply a plausible medical excuse to the recipient and family.

2. *Donor decision.* The medical selection system as described assumes that the future donor will make his decision only at the conclusion of the medical work-up and after intensive and repeated briefing. It is assumed that the decision will occur only at the end of adequate information-gathering and weighing of the pros and cons. Actually, members of the renal transplant team were aware that most of the potential donors were ready to make a commitment earlier than that and had to be held off until the team had made its selection. It was thought that this point of commitment was reached perhaps halfway through the evaluation process.

Our findings were surprising. *Not one* of the donors weighed alternatives and *rationally decided.* Fourteen of the 20 donors and nine of the ten donors waiting for surgery stated that they had made their decision immediately when the subject of the kidney transplant was first mentioned over the telephone, "in a split-second," "instantaneously," and "right away." Five said they just went along with the tests hoping it would be someone else. They could not recall ever really having made a clear decision, yet they never considered refusing to go along either. As it became clear to each of them toward the end of the selection process that he was going to be the person most suited to be the donor, each had finally committed himself to the act. However, this decision too occurred before the sessions with the team doctors in which all the relevant information and statistics were put before these individuals and they were finally asked to decide.

Of all the subjects who made their initial decision on the telephone upon first hearing of the possibility of the kidney transplant, none had consulted his or her spouse. When questioned about this particular circumstance each explained that the spouse later on had either been neutral or reinforced the decision. To the hypothetical question of "What would you have done if your spouse had said no?" each answered, "I would have gone ahead and done it anyway." One 48-year-old woman had a good deal of trouble in making her decision. The recipient was her son and the first communication that a renal transplantation would be necessary came from the doctor who had treated her son for some time. The immediate family consisted of the donor, her husband, and four children, two of whom were under 18. The older daughter, who might have been a potential donor, immediately refused to participate in any way. The husband was a diabetic and was therefore disqualified. The woman's own doctor advised her not to do it. However, she went along with the preliminary tests, feeling very ambivalent about them. All her tests were fine and she was finally asked to make a decision before the renal arteriograms would be taken. At that point she felt she wanted to go home for another family conference to ask her husband what she should do. This was a very frightened woman, organized along strict obsessive-compulsive lines, who said, "I get worked up over every little thing, and I have never had surgery before." In the end she did decide to donate her kidney after her family consultation, saying, "I guess I had some encouragement from my husband now."

Of all the people asked to come for the preliminary blood tests, there were about eight who did not show up. Of all those who participated in the initial screening tests, only one subject later refused to participate in further tests. None of the final potential donors availed themselves of the "last-out" opportunity, although there were one or two subjects who seemed glad when they were rejected for medical reasons after the last test (arteriogram). This leads us to believe that for all participants, and by the same token for all those who refused to participate from the beginning, decision making is an early event preceding all information-gathering and clarification offered by the renal team.

Supportive evidence for the instantaneous character of the decision making came from a rather unexpected quarter. We spoke to a resident physician whose blood had been used as a control in the MLC test. By the merest chance he had proved to be compatible with the potential kidney recipient patient. When he was informed of this finding he immediately refused without even having been asked to be a donor. He was subsequently able to tell us that this had been an immediate decision and that he had later spent much time marshalling evidence in support of this decision.

The immediacy of the decision making with regard to donorship often contrasts markedly with the usual way in which the person makes other important decisions. When questioned more closely about this contrast, all our subjects clearly expressed their opinion that this was a rather special situation that could not be compared to ordinary decision making.

3. *The family system of donor selection.* The role the family plays in the selection of donors was very difficult to demonstrate. In retrospect, this difficulty arose perhaps from the general feeling, which we shared, that the family would tend to select a likely donor in the sense of a sacrifice or scapegoat under threat of family ostracism. We could not demonstrate such dynamics in our sample, except possibly in one case.

What we did see, once we have become aware of its possibility, was that a family would *exclude* certain members from participation. This was done most commonly at the level of the initial contact. In only one case was the donor given the first communication about the possibility of renal transplant by a member of the transplant team, and in two cases by the family physician. All the others heard about it first from a family member. Usually the communication was by telephone call, the informant telling the future donor about the seriousness of the future recipient's illness and explaining that the doctors were considering a kidney transplantation and that all close relatives would be invited in the near future to come to the clinic or the hospital for some blood samples to be taken for initial tests. Usually, the informant followed this up with a brief discussion of who among the other family members should be asked to participate, who should not, and for what reasons. The same route was subsequently used to transmit the results of tests and make further appointments and could also serve to discourage further participation.

. . .

The fact remains that all the donors and potential donors interviewed by us reported a decision-making process that was immediate and "irrational" and could not meet the requirements adopted by the American Medical Association to be accepted as an "informed consent." Actually, the medical renal transplant team did not permit these donors to volunteer until a prolonged process of repeated information (or indoctrination?) had been completed. The effectiveness of this procedure must, however, be questioned by the investigators, if for no other reason than that it did not dissuade one single volunteer.

. . .

FRANZ J. INGELFINGER,
INFORMED (BUT UNEDUCATED) CONSENT

287 New Eng.J.Med. 465–466 (1972).

The trouble with informed consent is that it is not educated consent. Let us assume that the experimental subject, whether a patient, a volunteer, or otherwise enlisted, is exposed to a completely honest array of factual detail. He is told of the medical uncertainty that exists and that must be resolved by research endeavors, of the time and discomfort involved, and of the tiny percentage risk of some serious consequences of the test procedure. He is also reassured of his rights and given a formal, quasilegal statement to read. No exculpatory language is used. With his written signature, the subject then caps the transaction, and whether he sees himself as a heroic martyr for the sake of mankind, or as a reluctant guinea pig dragooned for the benefit of science, or whether, perhaps, he is merely bewildered, he obviously has given his "informed consent." Because established routines have been scrupulously observed, the doctor, the lawyer, and the ethicist are content.

But the chances are remote that the subject really understands what he has consented to—in the sense that the responsible medical investigator understands the goals, nature, and hazards of his study. How can the layman comprehend the importance of his perhaps not receiving, as determined by the luck of the draw, the highly touted new treatment that his roommate will get? How can he appreciate the sensation of living for days with a multi-lumen intestinal tube passing through his mouth and pharynx? How can he interpret the information that an intravascular catheter and radiopaque dye injection have an 0.01 per cent probability of leading to a dangerous thrombosis or cardiac arrhythmia? It is moreover quite unlikely that any patient-subject can see himself accurately within the broad context of the situation, to weigh the inconveniences and hazards that he will have to undergo against the improvements that the research project may bring to the management of his disease in general and to his own case in particular. The difficulty that the public has in understanding information that is both medical and stressful is exemplified by [a] report [in the New England Journal Of Medicine, August 31, 1972, page 433]—that only half the families given genetic counseling grasped its impact.

Nor can the information given to the experimental subject be in any sense totally complete. It would be impractical and probably unethical for the investigator to present the nearly endless list of all possible contingencies; in fact, he may not himself be aware of every untoward thing that might happen. Extensive detail, moreover, usually enhances the subject's confusion. Epstein and Lasagna showed that comprehension of medical information given to untutored subjects is inversely correlated with the elaborateness of the material presented.[1] The inconsiderate investigator, indeed, conceivably could exploit his authority and knowledge

1. Epstein, L.C., and Lasagna, L. "Obtaining informed consent: form or substance." Arch.Intern.Med. 123:682–688, 1969.

and extract "informed consent" by overwhelming the candidate-subject with information.

Ideally, the subject should give his consent freely, under no duress whatsoever. The facts are that some element of coercion is instrumental in any investigator-subject transaction. Volunteers for experiments will usually be influenced by hopes of obtaining better grades, earlier parole, more substantial egos, or just mundane cash. These pressures, however, are but fractional shadows of those enclosing the patient-subject. Incapacitated and hospitalized because of illness, frightened by strange and impersonal routines, and fearful for his health and perhaps life, he is far from exercising a free power of choice when the person to whom he anchors all his hopes asks, "Say, you wouldn't mind, would you, if you joined some of the other patients on this floor and helped us to carry out some very important research we are doing?" When "informed consent" is obtained, it is not the student, the destitute bum, or the prisoner to whom, by virtue of his condition, the thumb screws of coercion are most relentlessly applied; it is the most used and useful of all experimental subjects, the patient with disease.

When a man or woman agrees to act as an experimental subject, therefore, his or her consent is marked by neither adequate understanding nor total freedom of choice. The conditions of agreement are a far cry from those visualized as ideal. Jonas would have the subject identify with the investigative endeavor so that he and the researcher would be seeking a common cause: "Ultimately, the appeal for volunteers should seek . . . free and generous endorsement, the appropriation of the research purpose into the person's [i.e., the subject's] own scheme of ends." [2] For Ramsey, "informed consent" should represent a "covenantal bond between consenting man and consenting man [that] makes them . . . joint adventurers in medical care and progress." [3] Clearly, to achieve motivations and attitudes of this lofty type, an educated and understanding, rather than merely informed, consent is necessary.

Although it is unlikely that the goals of Jonas and of Ramsey will ever be achieved, and that human research subjects will spontaneously volunteer rather than be "conscripted," [2] efforts to promote educated consent are in order. In view of the current emphasis on involving "the community" in such activities as regional planning, operation of clinics, and assignment of priorities, the general public and its political leaders are showing an increased awareness and understanding of medical affairs. But the orientation of this public interest in medicine is chiefly socio-economic. Little has been done to give the public a basic understanding of medical research and its requirements not only for the people's money but also for their participation. The public, to be sure, is being subjected to a bombardment of sensation-mongering news stories and books that feature "breakthroughs," or that reveal real or alleged exploitations—horror stories of Nazi-type experimentation on abused human minds and bodies. Muckraking is essential to expose malpractices, but unless accompanied by efforts to promote a broader appreciation of medical research and its methods, it merely compounds the difficulties for both the investigator and the subject when "informed consent" is solicited.

2. Jonas, H.: "Philosophical reflections on experimenting with human subjects." Daedalus 98:219–247, Spring 1969.

3. Ramsey, P.: "The ethics of a cottage industry in an age of community and research medicine." N.Engl.J.Med. 284:700–706, 1971.

2. Jonas, H.: "Philosophical reflections on experimenting with human subjects." Daedalus 98:219–247, Spring 1969.

The procedure currently approved in the United States for enlisting human experimental subjects has one great virtue: patient-subjects are put on notice that their management is in part at least an experiment. The deceptions of the past are no longer tolerated. Beyond this accomplishment, however, the process of obtaining "informed consent," with all its regulations and conditions, is no more than elaborate ritual, a device that, when the subject is uneducated and uncomprehending, confers no more than the semblance of propriety on human experimentation. The subject's only real protection, the public as well as the medical profession must recognize, depends on the conscience and compassion of the investigator and his peers.

DAVID D. RUTSTEIN,
THE ETHICAL DESIGN OF HUMAN EXPERIMENTS

in Experimentation with Human Subjects
383–385, 387–389 (P. Freund ed. 1970).

This analysis of the ethical considerations governing human experiments is based on the assumption that it is ethical under carefully controlled conditions to study on human beings mechanisms of health and disease and to test new drugs, biological products, procedures, methods, and instruments that give promise of improving the health of human beings, of preventing or treating their diseases, or postponing their untimely deaths. Without such an assumption, there can be no systematic method of medical advance. Progress would have to depend on the surreptitious, illegal, or unsupervised research and testing of new modes of prevention and treatment of disease. The ethical standards of such irregular activities would certainly be at a far lower level than can be guaranteed when the testing of new methods of treatment is openly practiced.

Proceeding on that assumption, how can one design experiments upon human beings that will yield the desired scientific information and yet avoid or keep ethical contraindications to a minimum? This question is asked in the belief that in the design of the experiment itself many ethical dilemmas may be resolved. Attention must be given to the ways an experiment can be designed to maintain its scientific validity, meet ethical requirements, and yet yield the necessary new knowledge.

Let us concentrate on laying out new guidelines that might lead to the solution of ethical problems rather than on focusing our attention on the difficulties that these problems present. The ethical requirements that have created the most difficulty are obtaining informed consent from the potential subject; the need for the subject to derive a health benefit from the experiment; and keeping the risk to the subject as small as possible. Such questions are important and relevant because ethical considerations are paramount when experiments are to be performed on human subjects. It is the thesis of this essay that in the design of a human experiment it is mandatory to select those experimental conditions, subjects, and methods of measurement that impose the fewest ethical constraints. Such an approach will not cause the ethical problems of human experiments to disappear. If a definitive attempt is made, during the planning stages of an experiment on human beings, to keep the ethical as well as scientific criteria in mind, it is possible often to perform the necessary research to yield the desired information.

Scientifically Unsound Studies Are Unethical

It may be accepted as a maxim that a poorly or improperly designed study involving human subjects—one that could not possibly yield scientific facts (that is, reproducible observations) relevant to the question under study—is by definition unethical. Moreover, when a study is in itself scientifically invalid, all other ethical considerations become irrelevant. There is no point in obtaining "informed consent" to perform a useless study. A worthless study cannot possibly benefit anyone, least of all the experimental subject himself. Any risk to the patient, however small, cannot be justified. In essence, the scientific validity of a study on human beings is in itself an ethical principle.

How, then, can the experimental human subject be protected from incompetent investigators so that he will not become a victim in feckless studies? There are two lines of defense. The research committee of a medical school, institution, or hospital must be concerned with the ethical principles as well as the scientific validity of the proposals placed before them. To perform this task effectively, every committee must have among its membership a biostatistician to insure scientific validity and an expert (for whom there is as yet no name) who is concerned with the ethical aspects of human experimentation. The biostatistician can assist the committee in evaluating the scientific quality of the proposed investigation and make recommendations for improvement of the scientific aspects of the study design. Experiments on human beings must not be performed without a carefully drawn protocol, which in turn can best be prepared in consultation with experts in study design. In the same way, experts in the ethical aspects of human experimentation should assist the committee in passing on the ethical issues of proposed studies and in recommending modifications that might make the studies ethically acceptable.

The second line of defense can be provided by editors and editorial boards of journals that publish scientific reports of human experiments. If higher scientific standards of publication were established and adhered to, it would soon become clear to investigators that there would be small likelihood that improperly designed studies would be published. Automatically, many human subjects would be protected against participation in unsound and unethical medical research.

. . .

Asking the Right Question

The design of an experiment depends at first on the question asked by the investigator. Some questions are in themselves unethical. One cannot ask whether plague bacilli are more virulent in human beings when injected into the bloodstream than when they are sprayed into the throat. One may obtain hints as to the answer to such a question by epidemiologic comparison of the spread of pneumonic plague (spread from the lungs into the air) and bubonic plague (spread by insect bite). Anecdotal information on the spread of plague can also be obtained through the study of laboratory accidents. But a deliberate experiment to answer this question cannot be performed.

The human experiments performed by the Nazis during World War II horrified the world because they were designed to answer unethical questions. "How long can a human being survive in ice cold water?" will, it is to be hoped, never again be a question to be answered by a scientific experiment. Thus, as a first step in the design of any human experiment, we must first be sure that the question itself is an ethical one.

Moreover, an unethical experiment can sometimes be converted into an ethical one by rephrasing the question. In drug testing, for example, it is not ethical to design an experiment to answer the question: "Is treatment of the disease with the new drug more effective than no treatment at all?" In answering such a question, the patients in the control group would literally have to receive "no treatment" and that is completely unacceptable. Instead, if the patients in the control group are given the best possible current treatment of the disease, we may now ask an ethical question: "Is treatment with the new drug more effective than the generally accepted treatment for this particular disease?"

. . .

When designing a human experiment, the question under study must not be so trivial as not to justify any risk to the human subject. One may not ask whether large doses of a cortico-steroid agent would remove freckles. Nor may there be an excessive risk when compared with the possible benefit of a successful experiment. One may not test in humans a "sure cure" for the common cold which causes paralysis in experimental animals. Thus, in selecting a question for human experimentation, the expectation of benefit to the subject and to mankind must clearly far exceed the risk to the human subject.

Ethical considerations that prohibit certain human experiments are similar in their effects as are scientific constraints on the design of experiments. At the moment, much research on infectious hepatitis, a serious human disease, is impossible because there is no method for isolating infectious hepatitis virus. No laboratory animal has been found which is susceptible to it and no other procedure for its isolation has been developed. This scientific constraint is serious because without isolation of the virus a vaccine cannot be made for the protection of susceptible human beings. Human beings are susceptible and theoretically could be used for the growth of large quantities of virus needed for vaccine manufacture, but now we face the ethical constraint. It is not ethical to use human subjects for the growth of a virus for any purpose. Here, then, we have an example of a scientific constraint that in turn creates an ethical constraint, both of which interfere with the conduct of experiments important to life and health. When asking a question that might be answered by human experimentation, both the scientific and ethical demands must carefully be taken into account. Unless both are satisfied, the experiment cannot be performed.

NOTES

1. Is it true that a scientifically invalid study *cannot possibly* benefit anyone? Consider Cooper, Snake Venom—of Hope and the Scientific Method, 38 Food Drug Cosmetic L.J. 13 (1983). See also the debate in letters to the Editor in Sec. C.3, infra.

2. If a study design is scientifically valid, should it nonetheless be within the jurisdiction of the institutional review board to insist that, because human subjects are involved, the study must be modified to yield even more and/or better information than the investigation is seeking?

E.L. PATTULLO,
INSTITUTIONAL REVIEW BOARDS AND THE
FREEDOM TO TAKE RISKS

307 New Eng.J.Med. 1156–1158 (1982).

This article treats lightly a topic that usually receives more sober treatment. Since the Surgeon General of the United States first issued regulations in 1966 governing the use of human subjects in research funded by the National Institutes of Health, the problems that prompted his action have been discussed widely, exhaustively, and earnestly. Also since 1966, however, concern for protecting subjects has been extended beyond research that threatens bodily harm to include research that threatens the subject's ego, and even further, to include studies that threaten the principles espoused by those who make applied ethics their profession. The research enterprise has proved to be fertile ground on which to nurture a new discipline, complete with journals, professorships, advanced-degree programs, and an assigned role in the control of biomedical and behavioral research.

The fertility of the ground cannot be accounted for by the record of injury to subjects. Of 2384 research projects surveyed in 1974–1975, 3 per cent were reported to have caused harmful effects to a total of 158 subjects, with most of the harm characterized as "trivial or only temporarily disabling." [4] Given the size of the research enterprise ($8 billion of health-related research in 1980) and the number of subjects involved annually, the incidence of injury appears extremely small. A few highly publicized cases involving the abuse of subjects have combined with a precipitate decline in popular esteem for science and medicine to make research a plausible target for some who—newly conscious of the social costs of modern technology—blindly seek reform. A full understanding of the phenomenon, however, awaits a future historian of science.

The Department of Health and Human Services now has reasonable, if not exemplary, regulations governing the use of human subjects in the research it sponsors. Other federal agencies generally follow the Department's lead. The rules require that before research proceeds, an institutional review board (IRB), functioning in accordance with specifications of the Department of Health and Human Services, must review and approve studies that might harm subjects. These regulations were adopted in 1981, only after a version first proposed in 1979 was vigorously protested. In 1979, spurred by the emerging community of "ethicists," the Department of Health and Human Services had published tentative rules that would have given the IRBs authority to control all studies (however funded and whatever the topic) in which subjects were individually identifiable, without regard to risk. Thus, over a period of 13 years the surgeon general's laudable effort to preclude rare instances of carelessness and contempt for subjects (one instance, of course, is too many) had evolved into a plan that would make all scientific inquiry into human affairs uniquely subject to federal control.

If procedures to protect research subjects from abuses of the kind detailed by Beecher in the Journal nearly 20 years ago are to be permanent-

---

4. The National Commission for the Protection of Human Subjects of Biomedical and Behavioral Research, Appendix to report and recommendations: institutional review boards. Washington, D.C.: United States Department of Health, Education, and Welfare, 1977. (DHEW publication no. (OS) 78–0009). 1–73.

ly integrated into the research process, they must be fashioned to that purpose. To use the same procedures in an attempt to improve society's general standards of ethics—however laudable that goal—will hobble research unnecessarily and defeat the original aim. The two objectives are best kept separate by distinguishing between research that threatens bodily harm and research that is harmless or harmful in less palpable ways. If that distinction is coupled with another—the distinction between autonomous and dependent subjects—a basis is thereby created for determining proper limits to third-party intervention in the research process. I have addressed this problem in more detail elsewhere.[9] Here, I speak of research that bridges these distinctions, presents interesting, nontrivial problems, and yet permits, I think, the lighter tone I will adopt.

Thanks to having on our liberal-arts institutional review board a member who serves also on the IRB of a teaching hospital, we recently stumbled on a question none had previously asked: What is the role of an IRB when fully informed subjects, well qualified to weigh the risks, assert their readiness (perhaps their "right") to participate in research?

Our board seldom reviews projects that pose a risk of physical harm, and as experienced IRB members know, psychological and social risks are notoriously difficult to assess. In consequence, perhaps, we have become accustomed, when confronted with a "risky" project, to focusing on the subjects' competence and the adequacy of the consent process. I can't recall that we have ever withheld approval once we have been satisfied that subjects would be fully informed and qualified to judge the risks and benefits. But the hospital IRB, our double-barreled member (whom I will refer to as DB) explained, interprets the rules of the Department of Health and Human Services to require that IRBs determine the risk, calculate the benefit, and decide which outweighs the other. If board members think the risks exceed benefits they must disapprove; even if the harm risked is minor and its occurrence unlikely, the research may not proceed if the IRB judges the benefit to be negligible; the judgment of the subjects is irrelevant.

I find DB's reading of the rules disturbing as well as surprising. Unfortunately, it appears plausible. If it is the correct interpretation I am chagrined, having fancied myself an eager student of the regulations. But let me give bare details of the case that prompted our discussion. (Actually I've indulged in more than a bit of poetic license for the sake of readability, so it is best to read this "case" as historical fiction.)

Once upon a time, a physicist applied to an IRB for approval of his plan to have subjects spend various periods in a room warmed by a microwave field. His purpose was to conduct an informal survey of subjective reactions to this unusual environment. The subjects were to be the principal investigator and members of his laboratory (including graduate students), colleagues in the field, and others who were professionally involved with problems of electromagnetic radiation. All would know the levels of radiation used, and all would spend only as much or as little time in the experimental room as they chose. In fact, the investigator did not think of himself as using subjects at all; it was simply a matter of his own research cohort's trying something out on themselves.

9. Pattullo EL. Modesty is the best policy: the federal role in social research. In: Beauchamp TL, Faden RR, Wallace RJ, Walters, J. eds. Ethical issues in social science research. Baltimore, Md.: The Johns Hopkins University Press, 1982:373–90.

Members of the IRB knew that some people who claim expertise hold that any exposure to microwaves is hazardous. The illusion that this view prevails was quickly dispelled as the principal investigator, invited to the meeting, discussed the topic and canvassed the literature. Although no one questions the fact that microwaves are lethal under some conditions, the dangers (if any) that they pose in other circumstances remain uncertain. Opinions differ and feelings run high. Most of the subjects of the proposed research would be plausible members of any expert panel the IRB might turn to for advice. (We have two M.D.s but no physicists on our board.) Presumably, anyone who volunteered to participate in the project would be among those who minimize the possibility of harm under the conditions proposed.

"Fine," said a member whom I will call MCP. "Let's make sure the subjects are what the principal investigator claims and that the consent form lays it all out, then declare them at risk, give our approval—and turn our attention to that marvelously salacious sex survey that's next on the agenda."

"Wait a minute!" said DB. "Is it conceivable that the inspiring words of 45 CFR 46.111(a)(2) [the Department of Health and Human Services regulations] have gone clean out of your heads?"

"Yes," chorused the rest of the board, sheepishly.

"Ah ha!" trumpeted DB. "I just happen to have them here, engraved on my heart, complete with added emphasis:

In order to approve research . . . *the IRB shall determine* that . . . risks to subjects are reasonable in relation to anticipated benefits, if any, to subjects, and to the importance of the knowledge that may reasonably be expected to result.

"I will be grateful," he continued, "if any of you will point out to me where it is written that an idle, irresponsible, lily-livered IRB is authorized to delegate *to the subjects* authority to make that determination. There is no way," he concluded rather unkindly, "that this board can sidestep responsibility for forming its own conclusions about both risks and benefits. It is only if *we* determine that the latter outweigh the former that Professor Principal Investigator and his colleagues may decide whether or not they wish to volunteer."

"Damn!" said MCP, consulting his watch and ruefully noting that we'd now never get to the one agenda item that excited his interest.

Obviously, as always, this case presents a tangle of issues (each of which, concerned readers will be relieved to know, was seriously debated by the board before it arrived at its decision): Graduate students, though often well informed, are heavily dependent on the good will of their professors, whose very invitation to participate in an experiment may thus constitute an undue inducement. What levels of radiation are we talking about? How does the sponsoring agency feel about risk taking? What constitutes expertise in a field full of unknowns? The problem that fascinates me, however—one that is seldom presented so starkly as in this case—is that of the ethical differences between research involving autonomous subjects and research involving dependent subjects. "Autonomous" here means nothing fancier than healthy, adult, and unfettered by institutional constraints; "dependent" describes those who, usually implicitly, have agreed to forgo some of their usual range of choice by availing themselves of institutional facilities.

It is no accident that it was the double-barreled member to whom the words of the Department of Health and Human Service's basic charge were so salient. Presumably, hospital IRBs concentrate much of their attention on research protocols that raise issues of life and death involving the hospital's patients. Research hospitals (as I shall define the teaching hospitals that serve the principal centers of medical research) have a complex relation to their clientele and to society. It is a dual relation for two reasons—first of all, because patient and subject have discrete social roles; secondly, because such institutions exist to expand knowledge, in the process of which they must also serve patients. Thus, many patients will also be subjects. A research hospital that fails to produce new knowledge loses its special distinction even if it serves its patients well. In this (highly limited) sense, therefore, society has decreed that research is more important for these hospitals than is medical care. (Need I add that a research hospital that failed to provide good care would receive little sympathy within or outside the medical community if it tried to invoke its research mission in defense?)

If the requirements of therapy usually parallel or complement those of research, the needs of the two objectives can conflict. Society's charge to research hospitals is inherently ambiguous. The history of medicine and the moral values of contemporary culture argue that the needs of the patient take precedence over the search for knowledge. But great social pressure is also exerted to encourage the conquest of disease. To maintain the delicate balance these potentially contradictory goals imply, it is essential that the institution determine what research may proceed and when, where, and how it may be carried out. It has reason (and the right) to deny patients the privilege of volunteering for studies the hospital deems too risky. Patients denied the privilege of serving as subjects have no cause to claim that their rights have been abridged; just as we willingly sacrifice autonomy to dine at the Ritz (gentlemen must wear ties; ladies may not wear trousers), so we sacrifice accustomed freedoms when we enter a hospital. Keen though some may be to pass the idle hours serving in notably perilous experiments, it is part of the bargain that hospital authorities should decide which studies may solicit volunteers.

But the scientist has made no such bargain in accepting an appointment to a university or research hospital, nor should he or she be forced to, in my opinion. Citizens at large are entirely free to take grave risks in the pursuit of fame, pleasure, or purpose (sky diving, drag-racing, mountain climbing, starving themselves, or jogging at night in Central Park). Similarly, many kinds of employment offer rewards to those who are willing to take risks that others judge foolhardy (firefighting, law enforcement, lion taming, or entering the military). Why should research be singled out as the one arena in which those most knowledgeable are deterred from taking risks they think reasonable, because others think the risk exceeds the benefit? For a society that once set out to maximize the freedom accorded scientists it is, at least, a curious turn of events. I would extend this argument to include nonscientists who are fully informed and able to comprehend the risks associated with research that interests them.

It will be argued that, in excluding research that fails its IRB's risk-benefit analysis (without reference to the judgment of subjects), an institution is simply deciding what work it wants to sponsor. Any infringement on the subjects' autonomy is an unfortunate necessary consequence of the organization's right to manage its own affairs. That is more persuasive for General Motors than it is for a university or research hospital. A principal purpose of these peculiar places is to provide a setting in which members, individually, may do what they think is important. The history of "academic freedom" consists almost entirely of cases in which colleges struggled to push back the boundaries imposed by law and by mores. It would be a strange academy that used its right of self-management to deny its members permission to conduct lawful studies—even those that pressed hard against the outer limits of popular approval.

I am not sure exactly what the rule should be; perhaps it is just a matter of arriving at a sensible common interpretation of the present language. Presumably we do not want to permit suicidal acts disguised as research, however knowledgeable the subjects or otherwise legal the proposed procedures. On the other hand, every time we hand our 18-year-old the car keys we give him or her approval to act in a way that poses a statistically significant risk of serious harm. (And ask any parent whether that lovely, fresh-faced child can weigh the risks of driving as well as Professor Principal Investigator and his colleagues can weigh those of microwaves.) Do we intend to exercise a kind of paternalism toward responsible physicists that most would regard as overprotective for their own children? Is it quixotic to think that something important would be lost if men and women of science were denied the choice of modest heroism? [10]

In the example that I have used to illustrate my point it is clear that at least a question existed about the possibility of physical risk. It was wholly appropriate for the study described to be reviewed by the IRB. The IRB's mandate, however, should have enabled it to give full respect to the judgment of the scientist-subjects; having satisfied itself that they were well qualified to judge the risks and that they were acting freely, the board should have been loath to substitute its judgment for theirs. In general, those who would protect research subjects without infringing on valuable liberties are well advised to refer to the twin distinctions I have made: between research that poses a threat of bodily harm and research that does not, and between autonomous and dependent subjects. Legislators, bureaucrats, institutions, and IRBs should take care not to impose on the many the ethical standards favored or understood by the few who claim expertise in an area in which the role of expert is properly limited.

3. THE PROBLEMS OF RANDOMIZED CLINICAL TRIALS

CHARLES FRIED,
MEDICAL EXPERIMENTATION: PERSONAL
INTEGRITY AND SOCIAL POLICY

25–36 (1974).

At the outset we must distinguish between therapeutic and nontherapeutic experimentation. Experimentation is clearly nontherapeutic when it is carried out on a person solely to obtain information of use to others, and in no way to treat some illness that the experimental subject might have. Experimentation is therapeutic when a therapy is tried with the sole view of determining the best way of treating that patient. There is a sense, as a number of commentators have observed, in which so far as there is more or less uncertainty about the best way to proceed in the

---

10. Altman LK. Autoexperimentation, an unappreciated tradition in medical science.   In: Bulger RJ. ed. Hippocrates revisited. New York, MEDCOM Press, 1973:193–210.

patient's case, treatment is often experimental. Also what is learned in treating one patient will be of use in treating others. This may be so, but it in no way obscures the distinction between therapeutic and nontherapeutic research, since therapeutic research is carried out only and only so far as that subject's interests require. Any benefits to others are incidental to this dominant goal. These are the clear cases at the extreme.

There are in practice large numbers of gradations in between. Much research is mainly therapeutic, in the sense that the patients' interests are foremost, but nevertheless things may be done which are not dictated solely by the need to treat that patient: tests may be continued even after all the information needed to determine the best treatment of the particular patient has already been gathered; or substances may be injected for a period or in doses not strictly necessary for the cure of that patient, but with the motive of developing information of use to others. Moving in from the clear case at the other extreme, that of nontherapeutic research, it must be recognized that persons who become research subjects in nontherapeutic experimentation may often be the beneficiaries of a degree of medical attention which they might not otherwise enjoy, and which thus redounds to their benefit. And there are all possible degrees and gradations in between.

Nontherapeutic Experimentation

No special doctrines apply to nontherapeutic experimentation. Indeed, to the extent that the experimentation is nontherapeutic, the fact that it is being carried out by doctors should be entirely irrelevant. The usual privileges under which doctors work, and the usual special doctrines according to which the liabilities of doctors are judged, should not be applicable, since they proceed from the premise that the doctor must be given considerable latitude as he works in the presumed interests of his patient. But that is not the case in nontherapeutic research. The doctor confronts his subject simply as a scientist.

In general, the law imposes a strict duty of disclosure, wherever an individual with a great deal to lose is exposed to a risk or is asked to relinquish rights by someone with considerably greater knowledge. And this is true, whether the relation is one of buyer and seller or involves some public interest. Persons selling cosmetics, automobiles, or pharmaceuticals are required to make full disclosures of all the hazards involved in the products they sell. But policemen seeking damaging admissions from suspects are also required to issue a warning of constitutional rights and to offer legal assistance before those rights are waived. There is no reason why the case should be any different where a researcher asks an experimental subject to risk his health.

Indeed the case might be made that the developing doctrines of strict liability would argue for the imposition of liability without fault, and regardless of disclosures for harm occasioned in the course of nontherapeutic experimentation.[58] In general, it is coming to be believed that those who are in a better position to appreciate the risks of a course of conduct,

---

58. See Calabresi, "Reflections on Medical Experimentation" in Daedalus; Freund, in Daedalus; Havighurst, "Compensating Persons Injured in Human Experimentation" 169 Science 153 (1970); Note, "Medical Experimentation Insurance" 70 Colum. L.Rev. 965 (1970); cf. Ehrenzweig "Compulsory Hospital-Accident Insurance: A Needed First Step Toward the Displacement of Liability for Medical Malpractice" 31 U.Chi.L.Rev. 279 (1964); R. Keeton, "Compensation for Medical Accidents" 121 U.Pa. L.Rev. 590 (1973); Note, "Medical Malpractice Litigation: Some Suggested Improvements and a Possible Alternative" 18 U.Fla. L.Rev. 623 (1966).

who are in a better position to ensure against those risks or otherwise spread their cost to the broadest group of beneficiaries, and finally whose responsible decisions in evaluating the propriety of the risks we can influence by imposing upon them the costs of those decisions, should be strictly liable (that is liable without fault) for the risks that their conduct imposes. These conditions are amply met in the case of nontherapeutic experimentation. Finally, if the financial pressures of caring for and compensating subjects injured in nontherapeutic experiments meant that experimenters exercised greater caution and carefully evaluated the benefits to be expected from the research, this would be a highly desirable consequence. It is for this reason that a number of commentators have suggested either strict liability for nontherapeutic experimentation or some form of compulsory medical experimentation insurance. In either case the experimental subject would be assured of proper medical care as well as compensatory payments for any injuries he suffers in the experiment. Since most subjects of nontherapeutic experimentation are either idealistic persons for whom the small amounts of compensation are not a significant inducement, or disadvantaged persons for whom the small compensation acts as an all too significant inducement, this added responsibility would seem fair and appropriate.

Therapeutic Experimentation

Legal decisions and commentators have always stated that a practitioner is only justified in using "accepted remedies," unless his patient specifically consents to the use of an "experimental" remedy.[60] This statement has seemed reactionary and unreasonable to doctors, but if one puts it in the context of general doctrine one might say that its teeth are quite effectively drawn. General principles require the consent of the patient to any therapy, usual or unusual. It is just that as the therapy moves away from the standard and accepted, the need for explicit consent, full disclosure of risks and alternatives, becomes more acute, and more likely to pose an issue. The doctor who prescribes an accepted remedy, under the principles set forth so far, might have a good defense to the claim that he should have told his client about alternative, untried, or experimental remedies.

The obligation to advise the patient of alternative therapies does not extend to all the hypothetical, untried, or experimental remedies that various researchers are in the process of developing. Where, however, the therapy used is in itself experimental, this fact and the existence of either alternatives or professional doubts become material facts, which like all material facts should be disclosed. Beyond this, where the experimentation is truly and exclusively therapeutic, there are no particular legal constraints that do not apply to the practice of medicine generally.[63] It is simply that the implication of those general doctrines may take on a special coloring in this context.

---

60. Slater v. Baker, 2 Wils. K.B. 359, 95 Eng.Rep. 860 (1767); Carpenter v. Blake, 60 Barb. N.Y. 488 (1871); Langford v. Kosterlitz, 107 Cal.App. 175, 290 P. 80 (1930); [24] Syr.L.Rev., [1060] 1069–1071.

63. There may come a point, of course, where the procedure is so risky, the benefits so uncertain, and the basis of the treatment so speculative that to use it even with consent is tantamount to unprofessional conduct and quackery. The vagueness of the boundary is, of course, a cause for disquiet for practitioners working with new therapies.

Mixed Therapeutic and Nontherapeutic Research: the Problem of the Randomized Clinical Trial

The kind of medical experimentation which causes the greatest legal and ethical perplexities is what might be called mixed therapeutic and nontherapeutic experimentation: The patient is indeed being treated for a particular illness, and a serious effort is being made to cure him. The systems of treatment, however, are not chosen solely with the view to curing the particular patient of his particular ills. Rather, the treatment takes place in the context of an experiment or a research program to test new procedures or to compare the efficacy of various established procedures. Nor is it the case that this research purpose is limited to carefully reporting the results of treatments in particular cases. Rather, therapies are tried, continued, or varied, and patients are assigned to treatment categories partially in response to the needs of the research design, i.e., not exclusively by considering the particular patient's needs at the particular time. Usually it will be the case that there is genuine doubt about which is the best treatment, or the best treatment modality, so that the doctors participating in the experiment do not believe they are compromising the interests of their patients. Or where this is not completely true, it is often the case that no serious or irreversible harms or risk are imposed in pursuing the research design rather than pursuing single-mindedly the interests of the particular patient. The clearest case, and the one which is the focus of our concern in this essay, is the randomized clinical trial (RCT), in which patients are assigned to treatment categories by some randomizing device, with the thought that in this way any bias of the experimenter and any unsuspected interfering factor can be eliminated by the statistical method used. And generally it is said that the alternative therapies between which patients are randomized both have a great deal to recommend them, so that there is no real sense in which one or the other group is being deliberately disadvantaged—at least until the results of the experiments are in.[67]

What is the legal status of experimentation having both therapeutic and nontherapeutic aspects? Since there is a general obligation to obtain consent to a therapy, and since that obligation becomes more exigent as the treatment to be used departs from the ordinary and the accepted, there is at least the legal obligation to obtain consent for the use of the treatment contemplated, with full disclosure of the expected benefits and hazards. This much is straightforward, and not peculiar to the area of mixed therapeutic and nontherapeutic experimentation and RCTs. Moreover, as we have seen, a number of courts have insisted that the disclosure made in obtaining consent include a disclosure of the existence and characteristics of alternative therapies.[68] Certainly if the therapy proposed is experimental in the sense of innovative, this fact along with some description of more traditional alternatives should be part of the disclosure.

---

67. Thus, for instance, in a major RCT of the efficacy of simple as compared to radical mastectomy for cancer of the breast, Sir John Bruce writes: "One of the important ethical necessities before a random clinical is undertaken is a near certainty that none of the treatment options is likely to be so much inferior that harm could accrue to those allocated to it. In the present instance . . . . it looked as if the mode of primary treatment make no significant difference, at least in terms of survival." "Operable Cancer of the Breast—A Controlled Clinical Trial," 28 Cancer 1443 (1971).

68. [Canterbury v. Spence; Durham v. Wright, 432 F.2d 940 (3rd Cir.1970); Campbell v. Oliva, 424 F.2d 1244 (6th Cir.1970)].

The crucial question, and one as to which there is no decided case, asks whether it is also necessary to disclose first that an experiment is being conducted, and second and more delicately the nature of the experiment and the experimental design.

Specifically, in the case of the RCT must the doctor disclose the fact that the patient's therapy will be determined by a randomizing procedure rather than by an individualized judgment on the part of the physician? Some physicians active in mixed therapeutic and nontherapeutic experimentation have argued that it is both unnecessary and undesirable to make this last disclosure: It is undesirable because some patients might be scared off, withdraw from the experiment, and seek help elsewhere. It is also undesirable because of those patients who, while remaining in the experiment, might be caused such a degree of distress and anxiety that it would interfere with their cure. The disclosure of randomization is argued to be unnecessary since the medical evidence regarding the alternative treatments will often be evenly balanced (that is why the experiment is being conducted—to help resolve the doubts) so that it is in no way inaccurate to tell the patient that medical opinion is divided on the best therapy, and that the patient will receive the best available therapy according to current medical judgments. To tell the patient that he is being randomized, on this view, would add nothing of relevance regarding the expected outcome of his treatment, and thus nothing of relevance to his choice whether or not to consent to the treatment.

There are no authoritative decisions holding that consent in the absence of a disclosure that the patient is being randomized or that his treatment is being determined by reference to factors other than his individual concerns is invalid consent because of incomplete disclosure. The general principle holds that a person must be given all material information relating to the proposed therapy. But is the fact of randomization, or of the existence of an experiment such material information? The information would seem to deal rather with the way in which the therapy is chosen than with the characteristics of the therapy itself. Nevertheless, it would seem that most patients would consider the information regarding the choice of mechanism as highly relevant, and would feel that they had been "had" upon discovering that they had received or not received surgery because of a number in a random number table. But does this sentiment create a duty; does it mean, for instance, that consent to the treatment was ineffective and the participating doctors are guilty of a battery?

Though there is no authoritative decision to point to, there are analogies from other areas of law which would suggest that full candid disclosure should include disclosure of randomization. The very fact that the doctor acts in the dual capacity of therapist and researcher, and that his role as researcher to some degree does or may influence his decisions as a therapist, would argue that the fullest disclosure of all circumstances relating to that dual role, and to the basis on which functions are exercised and decisions made, would be required. If the relation were not that of doctor and patient, but of lawyer and client, or of trustee and beneficiary of a trust fund, or of a director or officer of a corporation and the corporation, there would be a strict duty to disclose the existence of any interest which the fiduciary has that may conflict with or influence the exericse of his functions in his fiduciary capacity. The fiduciary owes a duty of strict and unreserved loyalty to his client.

Imagine the case of a lawyer for a public defender organization who has agreed to participate in a foundation-sponsored research project on sentencing. As part of the research protocol his decision as to whether to plead certain categories of offenders guilty or to go to trial is determined at random. This is intended to discover how that decision affects the eventual outcome of the case at the time of sentencing and parole. His clients are not told that this is how the lawyer's "advice" as to plea is determined.[79]

The law of conflict of interests and of fiduciary relations clearly provides that the fiduciary may not pursue activities that either do in fact conflict with the exercise of his judgment as a fiduciary, or might conflict with or influence the exercise of his judgment, or might appear to do so, without the explicit consent of his client. And if the consent is obtained other than on the basis of the fullest disclosure of all facts not only which the fiduciary deems relevant but which he knows his client might consider relevant, the disclosure is incomplete, the consent is fraudulently obtained, and the fiduciary is in breach of his fiduciary relationship. There is no reason why the doctor should not be held to be in a fiduciary relationship to his patient, and therefore why the same fiduciary obligations that obtain for a lawyer, a money manager, a corporation executive or director should not obtain for a doctor.

However the issue of informing patients of the fact of randomization might be resolved, it would seem that there is a continuing duty on the part of the patient's physician to inform himself about the progress of the experiment and to inform his patient about any significant new information coming out of the experiment that might bear on the patient's choice to remain in the study or to seek other types of therapy. This is an important issue in RCTs involving long-term courses of treatment. If patients abandon one alternative on the basis of early, inconclusive results, no definitive conclusion can be drawn from the trial. Failure to make continuing disclosures and to offer continuing options to the patient in the light of developing information may not constitute the tort of battery, however, since there may be no physical contact requiring a new consent. The wrong which is done to the patient would be in the nature of negligent practice, and as to that the determinative standard is the standard of practice of a respected segment of the profession. The physician who does not keep his patient continuously informed may argue that to do so would interfere with the experiment, and he might find experts to testify that such continuing disclosure in the course of an experiment is not thought to be good practice. The argument should not be accepted uncritically, since the practice which the doctor in the case of an RCT would refer to would not be traditional therapeutic practice, but rather the practice of experimentation itself. Indeed it would seem that the doctrine of the case, holding that a physician had a duty to inform his patient that his broken leg was not healing properly and that there was another method of treatment available in a nearby city which was more likely to result in cure,[83] is equally applicable to the case of a participant in an RCT who has been assigned to a treatment category which, as the experiment progresses and the data come in, appears to be the less successful treatment. Nor would the device by which only a supervising committee and not the patient's physician has access to the results of the experiment for a determined period of time insulate the physician from the consequences of this doctrine.

---

79. Hammonds v. Aetna Cas. & Sur. Co., 237 F.Supp. 96 (N.D.Ohio 1965), motion denied, 243 F.Supp. 79 (1965); Stafford v. Schultz, 42 Cal.2d 767, 270 P.2d 1 (1954); Lockett v. Goodill, 71 Wash.2d 654, 430 P.2d 589 (1967).

83. Tvedt v. Haugen, [70 N.D. 338, 294 N.W. 183 (1940).]

LETTERS TO THE EDITOR

303 New Eng.J.Med. 1067 (1980).

Henry Sacks, Sherman Kupfer, Thomas C. Chalmers

To the Editor: The publication in the June 5 and 19 issues of two thera-peutic studies, by Antman and Dzau and their colleagues, that lack control groups raises serious questions about the conduct of such trials. Both articles are written as though they provided strong evidence for the effec-tiveness of a new drug for a life-threatening condition but in fact both are collections of anecdotal experience, uncontrolled and unblinded. Both papers acknowledge this important defect with a line or two in the Discus-sion, but obviously neither the investigators nor the reviewers thought that the conclusions were compromised. The use of controls is a basic principle of scientific inquiry; in fact, just one year earlier, the Journal published a history of the placebo effect in one of the conditions (angina), which clearly documented the danger in relying on uncontrolled observa-tions.[1]

Publication of such studies may create problems for other investigators and their patients. If they are convinced by these articles of the effective-ness of the drugs, can they ethically do blinded and randomized trials, as was called for in an accompanying editorial,[2] when to do so would mean withholding a "proved" drug from a patient with a life-threatening dis-ease?

Why were these studies approved by human-experimentation commit-tees at major centers? Good experimental design is the sine qua non of ethical research in human beings. The Food and Drug Administration recognizes this necessity when it includes in the proposed rules for human research the requirement that "the research methods are appro-priate to the objectives of the research and the field of study."[3] To us, such a statement implies that human-research review committees should ensure that adequate controls are included when sick patients are placed at risk in the investigation of new drugs.

The above letter was referred to the authors of the articles in question, three of whom offer the following reply (Antman et al. replied to a similar letter in the issue of October 16):

Norman K. Hollenberg, Victor J. Dzau, Gordon H. Williams

To the Editor: The letter from Sacks et al. raises not one issue but two. Should open, uncontrolled clinical trials be performed? If so, should the results be published?

When the possibility of a new therapy is raised, it is necessary to per-form a preliminary study. Because of the enormous cost and demands of large, controlled clinical trials, some preliminary evidence of efficacy is mandatory. In the absence of such information, the necessary referral of patients for the study is unlikely. How can one encourage a patient to enter a controlled study unless at least some preliminary indication of ef-

1. H. Benson, and D.P. McCallie, Jr., "Angina Pectoris and the Placebo Effect," New England Journal of Medicine, vol. 300, p. 1424, 1979.

2. J.N. Cohn, "Progress in Vasodilator Therapy for Heart Failure," New England Journal of Medicine, vol. 302, p. 1414, 1980.

3. "Proposed Regulations Amending Ba-sic HEW Policy for Protection of Human Research Subjects," Federal Register, vol. 44, p. 47688, 1979.

ficacy is available? Without the encouragement provided by such preliminary evidence, the resources required for a large, controlled clinical trial simply cannot be mobilized.

The second question is, When should the results of such trials be published? The answer is not straightforward. Perhaps the stance adopted by Sacks et al.—Never publish such observations because they cannot prove efficacy—is reasonable. On the other hand, on occasion one sees such dramatic evidence of therapeutic benefit that it seems reasonable to provide this preliminary information to the medical community. Indeed, one may feel an obligation to present the information, not as final evidence—which clearly requires a controlled clinical trial—but rather as an indication that patients who fall into the category under study may benefit.

The promising results in our initial trial have made it possible for us to undertake a controlled clinical trial, which is now under way. We expect the trial will require two years. Should we have waited the two years before providing the medical community with some notion of the efficacy of the drug? We think not. How dramatic and compelling should the results be to merit publication? To that, we find no easy answer.

MARVIN ZELEN,
A NEW DESIGN FOR RANDOMIZED CLINICAL TRIALS

300 New Eng.J.Med. 1242–1245 (1979).

I propose a new way to plan randomized clinical trials. My design has the feature that, before consent is obtained, both patient and physician know whether an experimental treatment will be assigned. Nevertheless, the subsequent clinical trial is a true randomized study.

Consider a clinical trial that compares two therapies. One therapy, designated as A, is a control. The control treatment could be the best standard treatment for that disease. If the standard treatment is to do nothing, then no treatment is given. The other therapy is an experimental therapy designated as B. The object of the clinical study is to evaluate the therapeutic effect of B relative to A.

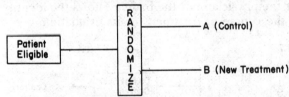

Figure 1. Conventional Randomized Experimental Design
before Requirement for Informed Patient Consent.

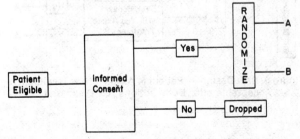

Figure 2. Conventional Randomized Experimental Design
with Informed Patient Consent.

Figure 1 shows the schema for such a randomized study before the federal regulations for human experimentation were promulgated (details of stratification are omitted from this discussion since they would unnecessarily complicate the points at issue).   Figure 2 shows how the schema is modified by the requirement for informed consent.   Patients declining to participate are dropped and generally have no role in evaluation of the therapies.

Figure 3 shows the schema for the new type of experimental design suggested in the paper.   After the patient's eligibility is established, the patient is randomized into one of two groups.   One group (G_1) is called a "do not seek consent" group.   Patients randomized for this group are not approached for consent to enter the clinical trial—they receive the best standard therapy (A).   Patients assigned to the second group (G_2) are asked for their informed consent.   These patients are asked if they wish to participate in the clinical trial and are willing to receive the experimental therapy B.   All potential risks, benefits and treatment options are explained.   If the patient agrees, the experimental treatment (B) will be given; if the patient declines to receive the experimental treatment, the patient will (presumably) receive the best standard treatment (A).

The proposed new design has the desirable feature that the physician need only approach the patient to discuss a single therapy.   The physician need not leave himself open, in the eyes of the patient, to not knowing what he is doing and "tossing a coin" to decide the treatment.   Thus, the patient-physician relation is not compromised.   On the patient's side, there is also an important advantage: before providing consent the patient knows which treatment will be given.   Many patients agree to participate in a randomized study but have reservations about continuing after the treatment is made known to them.   At this point, some decline treatment and are considered "cancelled patients."   However, others may continue the treatment, despite their reservations, because of the build-up momentum to do so and their reluctance to renege on their consent.   My design requires a decision by the patient only on the experimental treatment.   Hence, the patient's decision-making processes should be more straightforward.   This new design cannot be used when there are important reasons for conducting a "double-blind" experiment—i.e., a trial in which neither the physician nor the patient knows the identity of the treatment during the course of treatment or its evaluation.

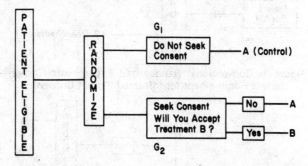

Figure 3. New Design — Patient Is Asked If New Treatment Is Acceptable after Both Options Are Discussed.

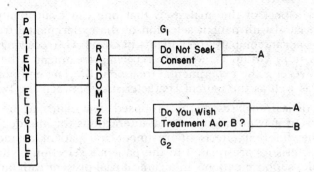

Figure 4. New Design — Patient Is Given Opportunity to Choose Treatment A or B after Both Options Are Discussed.

By a minor extension the experimental plan in Figure 3 can be modified so that a patient assigned to the seek-consent group (G_2) is given a choice between treatments A and B. That is, instead of being presented with the opportunity to receive an experimental therapy, the patient is presented with the two therapies and asked to make a choice (Fig. 4). this approach may be particularly appropriate if one of the therapies is especially disfiguring or disabling. Selection of treatment would be based on the "value system" of the particular patient. At the same time, the clinical study would be a valid, randomized trial.

The analysis of this new design requires that Group G_1 (receiving only treatment A) is compared with Group G_2) (receiving treatment A or B). In other words, the comparison must be made with all patients in Group G_2, regardless of which treatment each received. It is clear that including all patients dilutes the measurable effect of treatment B. Nevertheless, all patients must be included if the analysis is to provide a valid comparison with treatment A. If only a small proportion of patients are willing to take treatment B, this experimental plan may be useless in evaluation of this treatment. However, the refusal of a large proportion of patients to agree to accept B may be interpreted to indicate that it is premature to introduce the experimental therapy into a clinical trial.

There is an apparent loss in statistical efficiency with the proposed new design. If P denotes the proportion of patients in the new plan who accept treatment B, the efficiency of the new design relative to a conventional experimental plan is P^2. This formulation assumes that, in both the conventional and new designs, half the patients are randomized to each group. There is no advantage to randomizing a disproportionate number of patients to either group. The efficiency of P^2 means, for example, that if 90 per cent ($P = 0.9$) accept treatment B, 81 patients (100 P^2) would be needed in a conventional randomized design, as compared to 100 patients for this new design, to permit the same sensitivity in detecting treatment differences.

This loss in efficiency may be illusory, and the new design may be more efficient than a conventional randomized trial. Usually only a proportion of the eligible patients within an institution are approached by the clinical investigator to enter a trial. If adoption of the new design results in the entry of more patients into a study, it can be more efficient than a conventional design.

.   .   .

Another aspect of the analysis is that one can evaluate the possible biases associated with patient selection of the experimental treatment B. Note that one can compare the patients in Group G_1 (receiving treatment A) with those in Group G_2 who are receiving treatment A because they declined to receive the experimental treatment B. The end points can be compared as well as the patient characteristics between the two groups.

The statistical analyses of the proposed new plan may be limited in that the design may not readily reveal interactions (or interdependencies) between the different effects of treatment and patient characteristics if these characteristics are related to the patient's selection of the therapy. For example, suppose patients in a clinical trial present with an important prognostic characteristic that takes two possible values, such as premenopause or postmenopause, two cell types, prior or no prior treatment and the like. For convenience I shall refer to the condition of this characteristic as α or β. Suppose that experimental treatment B has a better outcome than treatment A only in patients with characteristic β. In addition, consider the extreme situation in which all patients with characteristic β decline to accept treatment B. A comparison of the two groups would show no difference in response. If such a situation did indeed arise, it would be possible to recognize the problem by comparing the characteristics of patients who did and did not consent. Of course, such an extreme situation is unlikely, but the example serves to illustrate the problem.

There can be many variations of this new design. For example, the physician could seek consent from the G_1 group after randomization, thus assuring consent from all participants in the study. If a patient in this group preferred the experimental treatment to the best standard treatment, the physician would have little choice but to give the experimental treatment. Clearly, there would be a serious loss in efficiency in evaluation of the therapies if more than a small fraction of patients decided on the change.

ETHICAL PROBLEMS

The design proposed in this paper introduces several ethical problems that were not present in conventional, randomized clinical trials. The evaluation of experimental treament B requires use of the data in the "do not seek consent group" (G_1). These patients are randomly assigned to this group without their knowledge. At least three questions arise. Should these patients be informed about their assignment to best standard treatment? Is it proper to offer only the experimental treatment to a subset of patients? Should permission be obtained to use the patient data?

Should the patient be informed about assignment to Group G_1? One view is that every patient expects to receive best standard therapy. It is only when there are departures from this expectation that the patient should be so informed. The patients in Group G_1 are receiving the therapy that they had every right to expect.

Is it ethical not to offer the experimental treatment to all patients? Receiving an experimental treatment is a privilege that cannot be extended to all patients. Usually, because of limitations in facilities, drugs, personnel and other factors, the experimental treatment can only be given to a subset of available patients. However, as noted above, it is every patient's right to receive best standard therapy. Physicians participating in conventional, randomized or nonrandomized clinical trials do not necessarily invite every eligible patient to participate. In general, the physician approaches those patients who are most likely to consent. A patient may fully understand the therapeutic issues and consent because he considers it in his best interest or wishes to participate in the accumulation of scientific knowledge; consent may be given out of ignorance if the patient is "doing what the doctor thinks best." In some institutions, patients from the higher socioeconomic groups are approached because the physician believes that they will better understand the risks and benefits. In other institutions, patients from the lower socioeconomic groups are approached because they may be more likely to leave the final decision with the physician. The use of the new design avoids this problem. Every eligible patient will have the same opportunity to be assigned to the group with the privilege of receiving an experimental treatment. There is no selection by the physician. This method seems to offer the fairest way to extend a privilege.

Finally, should the patient be informed about the use of the data being generated? The data from Group G_1 will be used, in aggregate, to compare the collective outcome in this group with that in Group G_2. This method is necessary for a statistical analysis of the results. No patient identification is required. The use of these data is no different from the possible uses of data from tumor registries or the retrospective reviews that clinical departments periodically perform to assess their experiences. In general, patients are not consulted about such reviews. In fact, the report of the Privacy Protection Study Commission specifically exempts statistical and epidemiologic research from the requirement for the patient's explicit authorization before use of the data. (This exemption applies only under certain conditions that would be satisfied in research that used the new design.) Alternatively, the patients in this group could be informed that data on their treatment will be ultimately used to evaluate a new therapy. The federal regulations on patient consent only refer to the seeking of consent when a patient is "at risk" because of participation in a clinical trial. The use of the patient data, without identification, would not appear to place the patient at risk.

One further point should be mentioned. Patients in Group G_1, who receive the best standard treatment, will generally be managed better than they would be if a clinical trial were not in progress. Procedures for work-up and patient evaluation will be outlined in great detail. Times of follow-up study will be specified. The quality of the patient record will certainly be superior. Usually, a quality-control committee will determine whether the best standard treatment is given in an optimal manner. Thus, patients in the "do not seek consent group" will also benefit. Their involvement in the study will increase the quality of their care.

. . .

To implement this innovation in planning randomized clinical trials, it is necessary for protocols containing such designs to be reviewed favorably by institution review boards. It is hoped that these boards can hear the issues discussed objectively. In my opinion, the adoption of the new design will lead to better clinical research and, at the same time, help the patient become more fully informed. The implementation of conventional randomized designs raises many questions about how informed patient consent is really obtained, whereas the proposed design provides a realistic method to comply with the spirit of the present federal regulations for informed patient consent.

NOTES

1. Consider Fost, Consent as a Barrier to Research, 300 New Eng.J.Med. 1272 (1979):

> . . . Often the patient's best interests, as well as society's, are served when the patient is a research subject. It is the possibility that a physician-investigator will favor the general welfare at the expense of the individual patient that has given rise to the ever-growing regulations in this area.
>
> In a provocative article in this issue, Marvin Zelen claims that one such requirement—that subjects be informed if their treatment has been chosen by randomization—has inhibited investigators and patients from participating in clinical trials and thereby seriously reduced the rate at which new knowledge is acquired. He proposes a procedural change, wherein consent would be obtained after randomization into experimental and control groups. The control patients would usually not be told that they were part of a study and would not be advised of the alternative treatment.
>
> It is clear that knowledge could advance more rapidly if there were fewer regulations. The rules not only deter some physicians from initiating studies but complicate recruitment of subjects and delay or prevent attainment of sufficient numbers of subjects. But the rules derive from ancient and fundamental sources, and they ultimately revolve around a single principle that is the source of Zelen's concern and the reason why clinical research must always be less efficient than it might be. That principle is called autonomy. "Anglo-American law starts with the premise of thoroughgoing self-determination." What a doctor may do to a competent adult is solely for that adult to decide. It matters not what the doctor perceives to be in society's interest, or even in the patient's interest, unless the patient presents a danger to others.
>
> The mechanism for acknowledging this fundamental right is informed consent. To initiate any treatment, standard or experimental, without the patient's fully informed consent is to fail to respect him as a person with a right to autonomy. It is in recognition of this right that tort law considers it malpractice to treat patients without fully informing them of all relevant information, and the regulations from the Department of Health, Education, and Welfare are simply an attempt to translate the principle into usable guidelines.
>
> Zelen's proposal tests the boundary of the term "relevant." Specifically, he suggests that the act of randomization can ethically be concealed from a patient, and that an awareness of alternative treatments can also be withheld from the group receiving the control, or standard, treatment.
>
> When there is a known difference in the benefits or risks involved in the two treatments, it would be a deception to conceal this fact. Even when the five-year survival rates are identical, there may be other factors that patients would value differently, including the average survival time, differences in drug toxicities and other quality-of-life considerations. Consenting to treatment without knowledge of the existence and details of alternative treatments would be similar to voting on a candidate for election without knowing that there were other candidates.
>
> Even in the hypothetical and unlikely situation in which two treatments were identical in all regards, the patient would have an interest in knowing that he was involved in an experiment. One reason is that the physician has a dual role as personal care-giver and investigator. The latter role may create conflicts in which the patient's welfare must be weighed against the investigator's interest in new knowledge or even in his own personal advancement.
>
> Among the justifications for limiting or waiving informed consent is the patient's expressed wish not to be informed of the detailed choices before him. It is undoubtedly true that some patients would prefer to be randomized or to have their treatment selected in any other way that the doctor chooses, without being asked for informed consent. This "doctor knows best" attitude de-

serves the same respect as an autonomous, assertive posture, but the burden is on the physician-investigator to identify these preferences rather than to assume that all patients are in the former category.

It may be true that the average patient, or "reasonable man," would not perceive concealment of randomization as an infringement of the right to autonomy, or might consider it an infringement that he would accept to maintain the tranquillity of ignorance. Some might find comfort in the belief that the doctor knows which treatment is best, even though this belief would be false. An approximation of what the reasonable person would want could be achieved by surveying a surrogate population of subjects. But even if a clear majority of this group favored a policy of randomization without consent, the thorny problem of the minority who desired full information would remain. One cannot deny that respecting the rights of the few may interfere with the interests of the many, but as Fried has reminded us, "It is the essence of rights to work as constraints on the pursuit of social goods."

In the real world, it is difficult to achieve the ideal of autonomy through the means of obtaining informed consent. In many instances the process serves only a ritual function, leaving patients no more informed or autonomous than they would have been if no information had been disclosed. More research is needed to discover better mechanisms for closing the gap between the ideal and the practical. The difficulty of the task, however, does not seem to offer sufficient justification for deceiving those patients who are capable and desirous of exercising their right to decide how they will be treated.

2.   William J. Curran, Reasonableness and Randomization in Clinical Trials: Fundamental Law and Governmental Regulations, 300 New Eng.J.Med. 1273 (1979):

. . . . At early public meetings after the Drug Amendments became law, the FDA said that informed consent would require that patients be told if they were in a randomized trial, and also be told that they might not know whether they had received one treatment or another. More attention was given at that time to the latter requirement for truth-telling than the former. Many clinical investigators and drug companies could not see how the legal requirement of informed consent to treatment could be reconciled with single-blind or double-blind studies. However, the FDA was heavily committed to blind trials as well as to randomization because both were scientifically advisable. The agency thus decided to reconcile the fundamental law of informed consent with the regulatory policy of controlled clinical trials.

Investigators have apparently followed the FDA requirements, although perhaps with some reluctance. The FDA has generally not insisted that the exact methods of randomization be disclosed at the outset of the conversation over methodology. In their public briefings they have required that investigators tell subjects that they will receive the standard treatment or the new drug, although they will not know which, or that "some of them" will receive the regular therapy whereas "others" will receive the experimental drug not approved by the FDA for general use, and that neither the patient nor the doctor will know which patients are given which drug. Notice that these illustrations again combine randomization and blindness. The method of randomization is often not mentioned before further questioning by the subject, if the exact method is even known by the investigator.

The proposal by Dr. Zelen can be viewed as an attempt to remove the patient from unnecessary participation in the randomization process and as a return to reasonableness, in that it allows the patient to choose between the accepted and the experimental. The proposal eliminates blindness entirely, thus separating out what was considered the more difficult issue of truth-telling. The proposed design moves the randomization process up front, before any contact with patients.

The patients in the investigational drug group would be entitled to know that they were selected at random, and would be given other information—that they have the disease under study, that certain other treatments have not been helping them, that the side effects have been serious and so forth. Knowledge of the randomization may well have no particular effect on the patient's decision to accept or reject the experimental therapy since it is not coupled with blindness about the treatment.

Either of the new designs that Dr. Zelen outlines in Figures 3 and 4 is legally supportable. Each provides for adequate informed consent since, in each instance, the experimental treatment, as well as other treatment options, is explained, and the randomization method is also disclosed. Of course, no undue pressure should be exerted to encourage patients to accept the experimental treatment. When more than one accepted method exists, these other reasonable and available options should be put to the patients. (I assume that Dr. Zelen accepts these points and suggests the alternative of treatment A only as a matter of simplification for purposes of discussion.)

A further question is whether the investigator would have any legal duty to the control group of patients with the same clinical characteristics as those in the experimental group. There are two aspects to this issue. The investigator would not, as an investigator, have any duty of a therapeutic nature to these patients. There is no recognized legal right to be included in an experimental study of a new drug. There is reasonable support for randomization as a means of selecting those to whom the limited resources of drug testing can be offered. Also, Dr. Zelen proposes that patients treated in the standard manner be handled as controls to be observed by the investigator. He asserts that they may, in fact, benefit from better management. It can be argued that these patients need not be asked either to consent to enter the study or to consent to having their records reviewed simultaneously with those in the experimental group or after the study is completed. Record review of patient management is a common research practice that does not involve patient consent when no identifiable information is retained or published. Of course, some institutions may not follow this practice and may require the patient's consent before examining the records. Patient consent is most frequently required when the researchers plan personal follow-up observation by interview or questionnaire. Dr. Zelen's proposal does not provide for this situation.

Under federal regulations and from the standpoint of most institutional ethical-review boards, a key issue regarding this up-front control group would be whether these patients should be considered "members of a study." If they are, they may be entitled to know it. This group is "at risk" only minimally, of course, in terms of the privacy and confidentiality of their records. One could argue strongly that these patients should be informed because their records would be reviewed simultaneously with those of the experimental group. To this extent, the proposal is different from the usual record study, in which a researcher enters to examine the data only at a later time, usually after the patient has left the hospital.

I do not, however, believe that federal regulations would require that this control group be given the opportunity to receive the new drug. They could, nevertheless, refuse to allow examination of their records and comparison of their course of treatment with that of the experimental group. If they asked questions about alternative treatments, it would be proper and necessary to tell them of the randomization. The degree of disclosure would be up to the investigators. They must not be untruthful. They must not actively deceive patients or fail to correct a false impression.

The fundamental law of reasonableness discussed earlier relates to treatment decisions placed before the patient. Here, the patients are approached only in regard to observation of their records and are told the truth about the reasons for the observation. Only if they had a right to engage in the study would they be entitled to delve into the investigator's reasons for observing rather than treating them. There must be a limit to inquiry into an investigator's motivations for research. Why did he pick this hospital or decide to study this disease rather than another? The researcher's freedom is important also. When there is no further duty to the person, there is no further need to disclose motivations.

Within the limitations noted above, the proposal of Dr. Zelen is worthy of serious consideration. As a new approach to randomized trials, it removes a great deal of the uncertainty that surrounds some randomized, double-blind studies now commonly imposed on patients. It allows more patients an opportunity to choose or reject an experimental treatment and to know when they are receiving an experimental drug. In terms of reasonable choices under law, such an approach has definite merit.

D. PROTECTING THE MOST VULNERABLE SUBJECTS

---

1. OVERVIEW

In this section, we consider special issues raised by experiments on categories of subjects who, for one reason or another, are particularly vulnerable to coercion or other abuse. As you read these materials and examine the issues they raise concerning the protection of rights, you should bear in mind one stark set of facts: to the extent that categories of vulnerability are defined in terms that are relevant for medical care (e.g., in most instances in prescribing a drug for a person it is relevant to know whether he is a child, but not whether he is a prisoner), and to the extent that additional requirements are established that burden research on such vulnerable persons, the availability of drugs and other treatments for such persons will be reduced. It is true today that, due to the difficulties of testing drugs in children, for example, there are fewer drugs than there otherwise would be whose effectiveness, safety, and proper dosing regimen in children are known, so that they can be administered to children. Sick children suffer as a result.

HANS JONAS,
PHILOSOPHICAL REFLECTIONS ON EXPERIMENTING WITH HUMAN SUBJECTS

in Experimentation with Human Subjects
1, 18–21, 24–26 (P. Freund ed. 1970).

"Identification" as the Principle of Recruitment in General

. . . [O]ne should look for . . . subjects where a maximum of identification, understanding, and spontaneity can be expected—that is, among the most highly motivated, the most highly educated, and the least "captive" members of the community. From this naturally scarce resource, a descending order of permissibility leads to greater abundance and ease of supply, whose use should become proportionately more hesitant as the exculpating criteria are relaxed. An inversion of normal "market" behavior is demanded here—namely, to accept the lowest quotation last (and excused only by the greatest pressure of need); to pay the highest price first.

The ruling principle in our considerations is that the "wrong" of reification can only be made "right" by such *authentic identification with the cause* that it is the subject's as well as the researcher's cause—whereby his role in its service is not just permitted by him, but *willed*. That sovereign will of his which embraces the end as his own restores his personhood to the otherwise depersonalizing context. To be valid it must be autonomous and informed. The latter condition can, outside the research community, only be fulfilled by degrees; but the higher the degree of the understanding regarding the purpose and the technique, the more valid becomes the endorsement of the will. A margin of mere trust inevitably remains. Ultimately, the appeal for volunteers should seek this free and generous endorsement, the appropriation of the research purpose into the person's own scheme of ends.

. . . .

The Rule of the "Descending Order" and Its Counter-Utility Sense

We have laid down what must seem to be a forbidding rule to the number-hungry research industry. Having faith in the transcendent potential of man, I do not fear that the "source" will ever fail a society that does not destroy it—and only such a one is worthy of the blessings of progress. But "elitistic" the rule is (as is the enterprise of progress itself), and elites are by nature small. The combined attribute of motivation and information, plus the absence of external pressures, tends to be socially so circumscribed that strict adherence to the rule might numerically starve the research process. This is why I spoke of a descending order of permissibility, which is itself permissive, but where the realization that it is a *descending* order is not without pragmatic import. Departing from the august norm, the appeal must needs shift from idealism to docility, from high-mindedness to compliance, from judgment to trust. Consent spreads over the whole spectrum. I will not go into the casuistics of this penumbral area. I merely indicate the principle of the order of preference: The poorer in knowledge, motivation, and freedom of decision (and that, alas, means the more readily available in terms of numbers and possible manipulation), the more sparingly and indeed reluctantly should the reservoir be used, and the more compelling must therefore become the countervailing justification.

Let us note that this is the opposite of a social utility standard, the reverse of the order by "availability and expendability": The most valuable and scarcest, the least expendable elements of the social organism, are to be the first candidates for risk and sacrifice. It is the standard of *noblesse oblige;* and with all its counter-utility and seeming "wastefulness," we feel a rightness about it and perhaps even a higher "utility," for the soul of the community lives by this spirit. It is also the opposite of what the day-to-day interests of research clamor for, and for the scientific community to honor it will mean that it will have to fight a strong temptation to go by routine to the readiest sources of supply—the suggestible, the ignorant, the dependent, the "captive" in various senses.[9] I do not believe that heightened resistance here must cripple research, which cannot be permitted; but it may indeed slow it down by the smaller numbers fed into experimentation in consequence. This price—a possibly slower rate

---

9. This refers to captives of circumstance, not of justice. Prison inmates are, with respect to our problem, in a special class. If we hold to some idea of guilt, and to the supposition that our judicial system is not entirely at fault, they may be held to stand in a special debt to society, and their offer to serve—from whatever motive—may be accepted with a minimum of qualms as a means of reparation.

of progress—may have to be paid for the preservation of the most precious capital of higher communal life.

Experimentation on Patients

So far we have been speaking on the tacit assumption that the subjects of experimentation are recruited from among the healthy. To the question "Who is conscriptable?" the spontaneous answer is: Least and last of all the sick—the most available of all as they are under treatment and observation anyway. That the afflicted should not be called upon to bear additional burden and risk, that they are society's special trust and the physician's trust in particular—these are elementary responses of our moral sense. Yet the very destination of medical research, the conquest of disease, requires at the crucial stage trial and verification on precisely the sufferers from the disease, and their total exemption would defeat the purpose itself. In acknowledging this inescapable necessity, we enter the most sensitive area of the whole complex, the one most keenly felt and most searchingly discussed by the practitioners themselves. No wonder, it touches the heart of the doctor-patient relation, putting its most solemn obligations to the test.

. . .

No Experiments on Patients Unrelated to Their Own Disease

Although my ponderings have, on the whole, yielded points of view rather than definite prescriptions, premises rather than conclusions, they have led me to a few unequivocal yeses and noes. The first is the emphatic rule that patients should be experimented upon, if at all, *only* with reference to *their disease*. Never should there be added to the gratuitousness of the experiment as such the gratuitousness of service to an unrelated cause. This follows simply from what we have found to be the *only* excuse for infracting the special exemption of the sick at all—namely, that the scientific war on disease cannot accomplish its goal without drawing the sufferers from disease into the investigative process. If under this excuse they become subjects of experiment, they do so *because*, and only because, of *their* disease.

This is the fundamental and self-sufficient consideration. That the patient cannot possibly benefit from the unrelated experiment therapeutically, while he might from experiment related to his condition, is also true, but lies beyond the problem area of pure experiment. I am in any case discussing nontherapeutic experimentation only, where *ex hypothesi* the patient does not benefit. Experiment as part of therapy—that is, directed toward helping the subject himself—is a different matter altogether and raises its own problems, but hardly philosophical ones. As long as a doctor can say, even if only in his own thought: "There is no known cure for your condition (or: You have responded to none); but there is promise in a new treatment still under investigation, not quite tested yet as to effectiveness and safety; you will be taking a chance, but all things considered, I judge it in your best interest to let me try it on you"—as long as he can speak thus, he speaks as the patient's physician and may err, but does not transform the patient into a subject of experimentation. Introduction of an untried therapy into the treatment where the tried ones have failed is not "experimentation on the patient."

Generally, and almost needless to say, with all the rules of the book, there is something "experimental" (because tentative) about every individual treatment, beginning with the diagnosis itself; and he would be a poor doctor who would not learn from every case for the benefit of future cases, and a poor member of the profession who would not make any new insights gained from his treatments available to the profession at large. Thus, knowledge may be advanced in the treatment of any patient, and the interest of the medical art and all sufferers from the same affliction as well as the patient himself may be served if something happens to be learned from his case. But this gain to knowledge and future therapy is incidental to the *bona fide* service to the present patient. He has the right to expect that the doctor does nothing to him just in order to learn.

In that case, the doctor's imaginary speech would run, for instance, like this: "There is nothing more I can do for you. But you can do something for me. Speaking no longer as your physician but on behalf of medical science, we could learn a great deal about future cases of this kind if you would permit me to perform certain experiments on you. It is understood that you yourself would not benefit from any knowledge we might gain; but future patients would." This statement would express the purely experimental situation, assumedly here with the subject's concurrence and with all cards on the table. In Alexander Bickel's words: "It is a different situation when the doctor is no longer trying to make [the patient] well, but is trying to find out how to make others well in the future." [10]

But even in the second case, that of the nontherapeutic experiment where the patient does not benefit, at least the patient's own disease is enlisted in the cause of fighting that disease, even if only in others. It is yet another thing to say or think: "Since you are here—in the hospital with its facilities—anyway, under our care and observation anyway, away from your job (or, perhaps, doomed) anyway, we wish to profit from your being available for some other research of great interest we are presently engaged in." From the standpoint of merely medical ethics, which has only to consider risk, consent, and the worth of the objective, there may be no cardinal difference between this case and the last one. I hope that the medical reader will not think I am making too fine a point when I say that from the standpoint of the subject and his dignity there is a cardinal difference that crosses the line between the permissible and the impermissible, and this by the same principle of "identification" I have been invoking all along. Whatever the rights and wrongs of any experimentation on any patient—in the one case, at least that residue of identification is left him that it is his own affliction by which he can contribute to the conquest of that affliction, his own kind of suffering which he helps to alleviate in

10. . . . . To spell out the difference between the two cases: In the first case, the patient himself is meant to be the beneficiary of the experiment, and directly so; the "subject" of the experiment is at the same time its object, its end. It is performed not for gaining knowledge, but for helping him—and helping him in the *act* of performing it, even if by its results it also contributes to a broader testing process currently under way. It is in fact part of the treatment itself and an "experiment" only in the loose sense of being untried and highly tentative. But whatever the degree of uncertainty, the motivating anticipation (the wager if you like) is for success, and success here means the subject's own good. To a pure experiment, by contrast, undertaken to gain knowledge, the difference of success and failure is not germane, only that of conclusiveness and inconclusiveness. The "negative" result has as much to teach as the "positive." Also, the true experiment is an act distinct from the uses later made of the findings. And, most important, the subject experimented on is distinct from the eventual beneficiaries of those findings: He lets himself be used as a means toward an end external to himself (even if he should at some later time happen to be among the beneficiaries himself). With respect to his own present needs and his own good, the act is gratuitous.

others; and so in a sense it is his own cause. It is totally indefensible to rob the unfortunate of this intimacy with the purpose and make his misfortune a convenience for the furtherance of alien concerns. The observance of this rule is essential, I think, to at least attenuate the wrong that nontherapeutic experimenting on patients commits in any case.

. . .

2. PATIENTS

PHILIP BLAIBERG,
LOOKING AT MY HEART

56–57, 65–66, 69, 70 (1968).

. . .

. . . December 3 . . . was the day the world learned that 45-year-old Professor Christiaan N. Barnard, head of a specially trained and selected team, had transplanted a new heart, taken from a car accident victim, Denise Darvall, into Louis Washkansky, a sufferer like myself.

I was feeling particularly ill and despondent at the time, but when I heard the momentous news over the radio at the lunch hour I called [my wife] Eileen. She hurried to the bedroom to find me wildly excited.

"Did you hear the news?" I asked her.

"No, what news?" she said.

"A man," I said, "has been given a new heart. Right here in Cape Town, in the Groote Schuur Hospital. His name is Louis Washkansky. Isn't that terrific?" At first, I thought, the implications of the operation did not seem to register with her.

Let her take up the story of the events of that day:

"I thought Phil's remark interesting, but somehow I could not comprehend exactly what had happened. Though I knew he was desperately ill, I had no thought that he could also be given a new heart and he certainly didn't mention it. But he remained excited and said he hoped Louis Washkansky would pull through. He just could not stop talking about it.

"By four o'clock, however, he was so ill that I was more anxious than usual. I had never telephoned Professor Schrire directly before, but I believed a call was warranted now. He walked in while I was talking to his wife. He took the receiver from her and inquired what was the matter. I replied that Phil was very ill indeed. He asked whether I had not received his message—that he had told our family doctor Phil was being considered for a second heart transplant. It appeared later that our doctor had telephoned several times but he had missed me.

"Anyhow, Professor Schrire repeated that Phil was next on the list. I was astounded. . . ."

. . .

The day after my admission to Ward D 1, I was lying in bed with eyes closed, feeling drowsy and thoroughly miserable when I sensed someone at the head of my bed. I opened my eyes and saw a man. He was tall, young, good-looking with features that reminded me a lot of General Jan Christian Smuts in his later years. His hands were beautiful; the hands of the born surgeon.

"Don't you know me?" he asked.

"No," I said with little interest, "I don't."

"I'm Professor Chris Barnard," he said.

"I'm sorry, Professor," I replied, "but I didn't recognize you. I have never seen you in person, and you look so different from your photographs in the Press."

He spoke earnestly, "Dr. Blaiberg, how do you feel about the prospect of a heart transplant operation? You probably know, don't you, that I am prepared to do you next?"

"The sooner the better," I said fervently, "and I promise you my full cooperation at all times."

Though our conversation was brief and he stayed only a few minutes, I was immediately impressed with the stature of the man and his air of buoyant optimism. He inspired me with the greatest confidence, an invaluable asset in the relations between a surgeon and his patient.

I felt somewhat better. Here was a man to whom I would willingly entrust my life. I came to know him well in the weeks and months that followed. He is a vital, determined, somewhat mercurial, personality, utterly dedicated to his profession.

.   .   .

On the morning of December 21, 1967, I was surprised to see my wife walk into my ward at about 9:30. Her visits had always been in the afternoons because of her morning job.

"Aren't you working today?" I asked.

"No," she said. "I just felt I wanted to see you."

"The nurses have told me that Professor Barnard is also coming to see me this morning," I said.

It seemed strange and unusual, but I did not give the matter further thought. I accepted Eileen's explanation and believed Professor Barnard's visit would be mere routine. Soon afterward he walked in. Eileen rose to excuse herself.

"No, don't go," Professor Barnard said to her, "I want to speak to you together." I looked more closely at him. He was haggard and drawn as though he had not slept all night. He no longer resembled the handsome Smuts, to whom I had compared him, but more a martyred Christ. I felt a twinge of pity for him when I noticed the pain in his face and eyes. Something, I was sure, had happened to dampen the gaiety and boundless optimism I had seen before.

.   .   .

Professor Barnard spoke in low tones. "I feel like a pilot who has just crashed," he said. "Now I want you, Dr. Blaiberg, to help me by taking up another plane as soon as possible to get back my confidence."

Still I did not know what he was driving at. "Professor," I said, puzzled, "why are you telling me this? You know I am prepared to undergo a heart transplant operation at any time you wish."

"But don't you know that Louis Washkansky is dead?" he asked. "He died this morning, of pneumonia."

It dawned on me why Eileen and Professor Barnard had paid me this unexpected visit. Now I knew the reason for his distress and agitation.

"Professor Barnard," I said at once, "I want to go through with it now more than ever—not only for my sake but for you and your team who put so much into your effort to save Louis Washkansky."

. . .

"Don't worry," he said a little more cheerfully now, "everything is going to be fine."

. . .

ALEXANDER I. SOLZHENITSYN,
THE CANCER WARD

164 (1968).

How he craved to be healed!—despite those harrowing months and years of by now hopeless treatments, he would suddenly recover completely. His back would heal and he would stand up straight and walk with a firm step, feeling like a new man. Greetings, Dr. Lyudmila Afanasyevna! I'm well—see?

How they all craved to hear of such a wonder-working doctor, of a medicine unknown to the doctors here! These people might have admitted or denied that they believed in such a thing, but all of them, to a man, felt, deep in their hearts, that there really was such a doctor, such a dispenser of herbs or such an old village woman living somewhere, and that they only had to learn where, take that medicine, and they would be saved.

It was impossible that their lives were already doomed!

Laugh as we may at miracles as long as we are strong, healthy and flourishing, let life become hopelessly wedged and crushed so that only a miracle can save us—and we shall believe in that one and only and altogether extraordinary miracle.

NOTE

A good examination of the dynamics of the patient-researcher relationship is in Fletcher, Realities of Patient Consent to Medical Research, 1 Hastings Ctr.Stud. 39 (1973). See generally P. Ramsey, The Patient as Person: Explorations in Medical Ethics (1970).

NOTE ON THE DYING PATIENT

In late 1981, The Washington Post published a series of articles alleging various abuses in the way terminally ill cancer patients were recruited for the testing of new drugs. Congressional hearings soon followed. The Assistant Secretary for Health of the Department of HHS established a task force to examine the issue.

This task force issued a Report on Anticancer Drugs on January 28, 1982, which stated in pertinent part:

The Task Force heard widely disparate views on whether "therapeutic intent" exists in the initiation and conduct of Phase I clinical trials involving cytotoxic drugs. The Task Force understands this phrase to mean an intention, in some degree, to improve or to stabilize the condition of a specific patient to be inducted into a research protocol.

It is important that such an intent exists. Because the drugs used are so aversive, and because the patients are so dependent and vulnerable, it is more difficult to justify ethically Phase I cancer trials if there is no therapeutic intent.

There is no doubt that the medical community involved in the development of cancer drugs believes that there is a real and substantial therapeutic intent involved in the initiation and conduct of Phase I trials. Members of the medical community note that—(1) subjects are recruited into protocols only if they are terminally ill and conventional treatment has failed; (2) drugs are used only after animal testing has shown evidence of anticancer activity and review has deemed a drug to be promising; and, (3) since 1975, there has been an overall response rate of approximately 9.5 percent in Phase I trials.

On the other hand, critics point to the fact that preclinical animal testing is of little predictive value relative to particular human cancers, that response rate figures include minimal responses that should not be considered therapeutic in any real sense, and that, therefore, while there may be some small hope of benefit to patients, generally any benefit which occurs to a specific patient is mere "happenstance."

Two points confuse this discussion. First, there is a perception that a trial cannot be both therapeutic and experimental. The Task Force believes that perception is wrong. While in some cases an investigator may be interested solely in acquiring generalizable knowledge (as is the case when dealing with normal volunteers with other classes of drugs), when dealing with terminally ill patients and drugs which have shown some anticancer potential, it is possible to pursue *both* therapeutic and experimental goals. In fact, true singleness of purpose may be difficult to find even when physicians administer accepted drugs from their offices to patients to evaluate the impact of the drug not only for the effect on a particular patient but also for the usefulness of the drug on other patients.

The more difficult problem exists when a tension arises between the pursuit of experimental goals and the pursuit of therapeutic goals. For example, it may be that after initial doses of a certain cytotoxic drug, it becomes apparent that the toxicity in a patient is no longer acceptable, but that it is not clear that studies of the drug should be abandoned. Even in this case, conflict is avoidable. In such an event, the patient may be removed from the trial, but the trial may continue with additional patients. The second point of confusion is that Phase I trials are characterized by FDA procedures themselves as being for the purpose of establishing toxicity. [See for example, 21 CFR 312.1(a) form FD 1571]. For most Phase I trials, which involve solely normal volunteers, that characterization is correct. The case, however, is significantly different in Phase I cancer trials. Drugs are administered to sick patients to help them combat illness. To ignore that difference and merely point to a general characterization of Phase I trials is inappropriate.

On the basis of its deliberations, the Task Force has concluded that the real issue before it is not whether some measure of therapeutic intent exists in Phase I trials—clearly, for the reasons set out above, it is possible to establish such an intent. Rather, the concern is whether the low probability of response and the risk of toxic effects of the drug are made clear to the patient through the informed consent process.

We have heard considerable evidence that desperately ill patients are anxious to enter Phase I trials as a last resort. While the Task Force recognized that people do not have an absolute right to harm themselves consciously, neither should they be absolutely precluded from seeking treatment which holds out hope of benefit. If patient or family choice is to be the determinative factor, however, then ensuring that such a choice is a reasonably informed one is critical. A special problem in achieving informed consent in Phase I cancer trials is the physical condition of the patient and desperation of the patient and family. Thus, attention must be given not only to the information being conveyed, but also to whether the information is being "heard," or undue influence of physician on patient exists. Although there are extensive regulations governing the consent process as it relates to experiments involving human subjects, both NCI and FDA officials admitted that they have no means for ascertaining whether the actual interaction between the patient and the physician is conducted in an appropriate manner (see section on Protection of Human Subjects).

In summary, the Task Force found that therapeutic intent exists in Phase I trials. This conclusion acknowledges that—(1) the patients receiving the investigational drugs are terminally ill, and conventional treatment has failed; (2) these drugs are administered to patients only after animal testing has demonstrated evidence of anticancer activity and screening has shown a drug to be promising (although the validity of the screening process has not been proven); and, (3) since 1975, there has been an overall response rate of approximately 9.5 percent in the cancer patients receiving new anticancer drugs.

. . .

PROTECTION OF HUMAN SUBJECTS— INFORMED CONSENT AND IRBs

The clinical investigator, IRBs, institutions, NCI, FDA, and the Office of Protection from Research Risks (OPRR), all have responsibilities to protect human subjects of research through the use, review, and monitoring of consent and investigative procedures. . . .

Problems with Informed Consent for Cancer Patients

There are still many questions and concerns about the adequacy [of] informed consent for terminal cancer patients requested to participate in research with investigational new drugs.

At the House of Representatives Hearing chaired by Representatives Waxman and Gore on October 27, 1981, Dr. Gail Povar, clinical internist and teacher of medical ethics at George Washington University, described the particular problems of informed consent with cancer patients. According to Povar, patients asked to participate in Phase I trials are vulnerable to coercion because of the certainty of death without a new treatment. Dr. Povar questioned whether these fearful, angry, and desperate people are, in fact, free to choose. She further explored the impact of the doctor/patient relationship on the informed consent process, and the doctor's inherent desire to *do something*. She concluded that all these factors affect the objectivity of the information conveyed, the specific competency of the patient, and the freedom to choose.

A contrasting view on informed consent was expressed in the Hearing record by oncologist Dr. Solomon Garb, himself a cancer patient:

"Informed consent is as adequate as human ingenuity can make it. The problem is not in the informed consent form or in what the doctor tells the patient, but in what the patient understands or is willing to understand. Obviously, I knew that cancer protocols can produce all kinds of side effects, some of them lethal, but I also knew that the outlook for stomach cancer had been dismal. I just skimmed over the form I signed. As a patient, my key question was, and is—'Doctor, if you had my illness would you want this treatment for yourself?' When the answer was 'yes,' I signed. I don't think that the informed consent procedure is a serious problem."

Some individuals feel that cancer patients (particularly those in Phase I trials) are extremely vulnerable and need special assistance in giving informed consent because of their physical condition, their anxiety (which may affect the ability to understand information disclosed), the extreme toxicity of anticancer drugs, and the small possibility of significant benefit. Those individuals studying the informed consent process in a variety of medical treatment and research situations have offered suggestions to minimize the possibility of coercion on the part of the physician and to enhance the decision-making capacity of the patient through a variety of special mechanisms, including utilizing a third party to present or to discuss the information, utilizing a patient advocate, allowing time between disclosure of information and patient decision, and testing patient understanding of consent information.

The cancer patient faces extremely difficult treatment decisions in traditional and research situations. It is crucial, therefore, that patient decisions be made on the basis of complete and frank information. In Phase I trials, for example, the physician disclosing information to the potential research participant must be particularly careful to describe fully "reasonably foreseeable risks and discomforts," "any benefits to the subject or other which may reasonably be expected," and to include a statement that "participation is voluntary, refusal to participate will involve no penalty or loss of benefits to which the subject is otherwise entitled." (HHS 45 CFR 46.116) The Task Force concurs that information disclosed for Phase I must include a statement about the small possibility of direct benefit to the patient him/herself.

The informed consent form and process should reflect the different proportions of risks and benefits anticipated as the investigational new drug passes from the first use in human subjects in Phase I through Phases II, III, and beyond. Some Task Force members felt that the patient should also be told how many subjects had preceded him/her in the protocol and what the results were.

NOTES

1. What would it mean for a physician to give a patient/research subject "complete information"?

2. Is it realistic to conceive of a physician-researcher as giving his patient/subject information on the basis of which the latter will make an independent decision? Will not the patient/subject almost always regard the physician as a source of advice and guidance, more than as a source of information, and will not the patient almost always give great weight to that advice? Is it desirable or feasible to reduce the influence a physician has over a patient? See generally Ch. 3, Sec. B.1, supra.

3. Should the government regulate the use of unorthodox methods, drugs and devices to treat terminally ill patients? See United States v. Rutherford, 442 U.S. 544, 99 S.Ct. 2470, 61 L.Ed.2d 68 (1979) discussed in Ch. 3, Sec. B.2, supra.

3. CHILDREN AND FETUSES

MARGARET S. v. EDWARDS

United States District Court for the Eastern District of Louisiana, 1980.
488 F.Supp. 181.

ROBERT F. COLLINS, DISTRICT JUDGE.

This case presents a constitutional challenge to a recently enacted Louisiana statute regulating abortion. La.Rev.Stat.Ann. §§ 40:1299.35.1 et seq. (West Supp.1979).

. . .

[One] section states: "No person shall experiment upon or sell a live child or unborn child unless such experimentation is therapeutic to the child or unborn child." La.Rev.Stat.Ann. § 40:1299.35.13 (West Supp. 1979). The plaintiffs have challenged this section as unconstitutionally vague and allege that it burdens the doctors' right to practice medicine or do medical research. The Court finds that these arguments are not supported by the evidence.

. . .

Plaintiffs . . . contend that the section is so vague that it will inhibit valuable medical experimentation and preclude the use of certain procedures, such as amniocentesis and fetal fluoroscopy. This is a legitimate concern worthy of careful consideration. "[I]ndividual States have broad latitude in experimenting with possible solutions to problems of vital local concern." Whalen v. Roe, 429 U.S. 589 (1977). This is especially so where matters of social policy, such as health regulations are involved, *Whalen*, 429 U.S. at 597, and "whether or not [the Court believes it to be] wise. . . ." Wynn v. Scott, 449 F.Supp. 1302, 1322 (N.D.Ill. 1978), aff'd sub nom. Wynn v. Carey, 599 F.2d 193 (7th Cir.1979). On the other hand, a criminal statute must be carefully scrutinized where allegations of vagueness have been raised. . . .

This section precludes experimentation which is not "therapeutic." Does this wording sweep so broadly that doctors will be unable to conduct tests or perform operations merely because there is a chance that the patient may be harmed or fail to benefit? The Court finds that this question must be answered in the negative. Therapeutic is defined as "of or relating to the treatment of disease or disorders by remedial agents . . . ." Webster's Third New International Dictionary 2372 (1976) (hereinafter cited Webster's); see also Dorland's Illustrated Medical Dictionary 1597 (25th ed. 1974) (hereinafter cited Dorland's). . . . Since experimentation itself involves the chance of failure, the legislature could not have meant that only *successful* experimentation would be therapeutic or it would have said so. The legislature must have meant that it wished to permit only experimentation that is designed to benefit, either in the short or the long term, the individual upon whom it is conducted.[120] Regardless of whether he can calculate the odds of success, a doctor knows whether an experiment is intended to help a patient. If it is so intended, then it is therapeutic. The Court holds that "therapeutic" is not "so indefinite that the line between innocent and condemned conduct becomes a matter of guesswork." L. Tribe, American Constitutional Law at 718 (1978). . . .

Plaintiffs have also suggested that this section will burden medical researchers. "[T]he rights of medical researchers are not fundamental under the Constitution . . . .", Wynn v. Scott, 449 F.Supp. 1302, 1322 (N.D.Ill.1978), aff'd sub nom. Wynn v. Carey, 599 F.2d 193 (7th Cir. 1979). This is true especially when the experiments involved are to be done on minors [122] and fetuses [123] and are *designed* to be non-therapeutic. The Court notes that this section will not proscribe important medical procedures such as amniocentesis. Amniocentesis is not a therapeutic procedure for those fetuses which are defective since discovery of a seri-

---

120. See 45 C.F.R. § 46.102(a), (b), (c); .201–11 (1979). Whether the State can prohibit all nontherapeutic human experimentation is open to question. Rational adults, capable of informed consent, may wish to participate in experiments or to engage in occupations harmful to their health for many reasons: money, fame, idealism, or, in the case of prisoners, the hope of freedom. See, for example, B.A. Franklin, Nuclear Plants Hiring Stand-Ins to Spare Aides Radiation Risks, N.Y. Times, July 16, 1979, at A1, Col. 5. The decision in favor of danger may be a thoughtful part of a desire "to shape a life—to plan its pattern and its style—at a higher than ordinary level of risk." TRIBE [American Constitutional Law] at 938. An activity such as being a guinea pig for a dangerous drug can surely

be as "expressive" as refusing to wear a motorcycle helmet or demanding the right to have access to saccharin. Id. at 940.

122. Note, however, that Louisiana minors can given their consent to treatment, including presumably, experimental methods thereof, under La.Rev.Stat.Ann. § 40:1095 (West 1977).

123. Plaintiffs have made a strenuous attack on the statute on the grounds that it will prevent scientific research which depends on live fetal tissue. However, § 40:1299.35.13 does not prohibit experimentation on fetal tissue, as did the statute in Wynn v. Scott, 449 F.Supp. at 1322 ("no exploitation of or experimentation with the aborted tissue"). The Louisiana statute deals with fetuses while they are still *in utero*.

ous defect will presumably lead to their death *via* abortion. Neither, is it an experiment upon a fetus. It is a *test* as for diabetes or pregnancy or night blindness, rather than an experiment. Doctors do not experiment upon people when they conduct such routine tests. Amniocentesis is used to discover certain inherent defects of a fetus. Physicians recognize the uses of this procedure, its limits, and its risks to both the mother and the fetus. If amniocentesis is not an experiment, La.Rev.Stat.Ann. § 40:1299.35.13 will be inapplicable. No obstacle has been placed in the path of the woman seeking an abortion or of her doctor. Furthermore, neither doctors nor women seeking abortions need non-therapeutic *in utero* experimentation in order to decide upon or to effectuate an abortion. Therefore, plaintiff's argument that this section intrudes upon a woman's fundamental right of privacy is without merit.

Since this provision does not infringe on a fundamental right, it is subject to the less demanding test of rationality. Statutes regulating human experimentation and *in utero* fetal experimentation are a reasonable exercise of the State's police powers. Given the dangers of abuse inherent in any rapidly developing field, it is rational for a State to act to protect the health and safety of its citizens. The Court notes that several states have joined Louisiana in regulating this area.[128] The Court holds that La.Rev. Stat.Ann. § 40:1299.35.13 is rationally related to the promotion of a legitimate state interest, and La.Rev.Stat.Ann. § 40:1299.35.13 is therefore constitutional.

. . .

NOTES

1. It has been argued by some commentators that no one should be able to consent for a child to undergo a nontherapeutic medical procedure. Paul Ramsey in The Patient as Person 14 (1970), for example, contends:

"To attempt to consent for a child to be made an experimental subject is to treat a child as not a child. It is to treat him as if he were an adult person who has consented to become a joint adventurer in the common cause of medical research. If the grounds for this are alleged to be the presumptive or implied consent of the child, that must simply be characterized as a violent and a false presumption. Nontherapeutic, nondiagnostic experimentation involving human subjects must be based on true consent if it is to proceed as a human enterprise."

Richard McCormick, by contrast, in Proxy Consent in the Experimental Situation, 18 Perspectives in Biology and Medicine 2, 13–14 (1974), uses the natural law tradition to argue:

To pursue the good that is human life means not only to choose and support this value in one's own case, but also in the case of others when the opportunity arises . . . ... To share in the general effort and burden of health maintenance and disease control is part of our flourishing and growth as humans. To the extent that it is good for all of us to share this burden, we all *ought* to do so. And to the extent that we ought to do so, it is a reasonable construction or presumption of our wishes to say that we would do so. The reasonableness of this presumption validates vicarious consent.

. . . . Concretely, when a particular experiment would involve no discernible risks, no notable pain, no notable inconvenience and yet hold promise of considerable benefit, should not the child be constructed to wish this in the

128. See Ill.Ann.Stat. Ch. 38, § 81–32 (Smith-Hurd Supp.1977); Ind.Code Ann. § 35–1–58.5–6 (Burns 1979); S.D. Compiled Laws Ann. § 34–23A–17 (Smith Supp. 1976); Utah Crim.Code Ann. § 76–7–310 (Smith 1977). See also 45 C.F.R. §§ 46.201–211 (1979).

same way we presume he chooses his own life, because he *ought* to?   I believe so.

The way Ramsey and McCormick evaluate particular experiments is not necessarily as far apart as their philosophic explanations might suggest.   McCormick, for example, defines "no discernible risk" quite strictly and concludes that parental consent for a kidney transplant from one 3-year-old to another is without moral justification.   Cf. Hart v. Brown, Ch. 3, Sec. A, supra.   Ramsey, on the other hand, expands his definition of "therapeutic" procedures to cover "epidemic conditions" and thus concludes a parent was justified in having the Salk polio vaccine tested on his healthy child.

2.   Charles Fried in Children as Subjects for Medical Experimentation, in Research on Children 107, 111–115 (J. van Eys ed. 1978) also disagrees with Paul Ramsey's position, but for different reasons.   Fried observes:

> A variety of recent [court] decisions have affirmed a moral equal status for the rights of children.   The [principal] case, of course, is the Gault decision, which held that children are entitled to the full panoply of rights in juvenile proceedings, and that they cannot be deprived of these rights—the right to counsel, the right to confront accusers, the privilege against self-incrimination—on the grounds that the state in these proceedings is acting in loco parentis.   That is to say, children have rights even though a guardian purports to be acting in their best interests and to be better able to further the child's interests if the child's rights are ignored.   A variety of decisions stating that minors may obtain abortions and that parental consent may not be made a condition of an abortion represent another convergent thread in this developing strain.
>
> .   .   .
>
> The general theme seems to be that, so far as possible, the autonomy of children should not be compromised by those purporting to act in their best interests, any more than the autonomy of mental patients or those accused of crime.   If we now apply this developing tendency in common and constitutional law to the subject before us, we see how it differs from and resembles the decided cases.   The theme of the decided cases would seem to be that a minor should determine his or her own life-style.   Assume that an institutional review board has found that an experiment does not involve undue risk and that, in any case, the risk is justified by the benefits to others.   Why should a minor have less autonomy to make the altruistic decision to enter an experiment than to make decisions relating to the use of his or her reproductive functions, education, or exercise of legal rights?   It would be ironic indeed if a child were granted greater autonomy in respect to sexual conduct or misconduct or legal rights than about a decision to perform a marginally risky altruistic act.
>
> The trend we notice is surely a sound one.   Surely the common law concept of majority and minority never did have much to justify it, and probably catered as much to the authority of parents as to the autonomy and rights of their children.   Whether we like it or not, children are asserting greater autonomy at an earlier age.   And if this is the trend, should we accept it?   Well, this reminds me of Margaret Fuller's statement that she had finally decided to accept the universe, to which the response was, she had better.   Well, we had better accept the fact that children have both the opportunity and the determination to exercise more autonomy.   All we can do is respond in ways that will make the exercise of that autonomy creative, instructive, and fruitful for the future.   To allow children from the age of 11 onward, let us say, to decide whether to participate in reasonable, but somewhat hazardous experimentation would seem to be not a crucial, but a reasonable manifestation of such a program.   To put the matter differently, it seems to me to tell the worst of all possible stories, a story favoring self-indulgence and selfishness, to say to young people that they are free to have sex with whom they want, to have or not to have abortions, to wear what clothes they wish and hair of whatever length they wish, but that they may not perform a reasonable and useful act of generosity.

The real difficulty, of course, relates to children before the age of nascent responsibility. I cannot give you the precise age I am talking about, but surely children below the age of 8, 7, 6 years old. I suggest that, to the extent that these children can understand at all what they are doing, they, too, should have some opportunity to make a contribution to medical research. Of course, their consent can never be sufficient. Their parents must also consent, but it must be understood that their parents are consenting to something that is an act of generosity on the part of the child. In this instance, however, one would want to make a much closer connection between that child and the benefit he or she is producing. One would want to make a connection of the sort that requires the research to benefit a close relative, or perhaps those suffering from a disease this child is also suffering from. For there the community of interests is tightly drawn. Indeed, if one considers a disease such as cystic fibrosis or one of the juvenile cancers, it is fairly certain that whatever help the potential subject-child is presently receiving comes itself as the result of similar sacrifices by earlier children.

Now as judgment and understanding recede and we approach true infancy, the old flat-footed common law theorem has much more power. In the case of a baby, not only is the educational and self-determination value totally missing, but the safeguard against abuse and imposition, achieved by making the child's consent a necessary condition, no longer obtains. Without that safeguard, I think one has a right to be concerned. And yet I would not make an absolute of this matter. . . .

Now as an inveterate believer in rights, someone who has an allergy to reducing everything to weighing and balancing, someone who believes in moral absolutes, this may seem an unsatisfactory state in which to leave matters. But I do not believe it is so. Certainly in respect to those children who are above the age of infancy, I move in the direction I suggest as much out of a concern for the rights of children as out of a desire to advance medical research. However, in general, I do not see that rights are violated where a minimally risky and useful invasion of the body occurs with the consent of a guardian and at least not against the consent of the subject. In other words, the right I recognize is a right to be free from bodily intrusions *against* consent one has not given, but might have given.

Here I must add a comparison between my view and that which Professor Ramsey set forth before me. The way I would schematize my view is this: First, the basic principle is: do not intentionally impose on a person against that person's will. Second, parents should care for their children. Third, to contribute to others is good. Fourth, it is open to parents as part of their care to enlist their children to do a reasonable and good thing, which as parents they themselves would have done, so long as this is not against the will of the child.

Now Professor Ramsey has a different view, and if we try to locate that difference we locate it in the first and the second of my propositions. It must be that Professor Ramsey has the view that the first premise is not, as I would say, do not intentionally impose on another against that person's will, but rather, do not intentionally impose upon another without that person's consent. If you state it that way, the rest of his argument follows. However, the question is why do it that way, and Ramsey does not tell us why. I propose a different premise, which strikes me as at least as reasonable, and which has to recommend it the fact that it does not lead to what seems a fanatical conclusion. My premise is: do not impose upon another against that person's will. I am prepared to be just as absolute about that as he is about his, but I invite you to consider which of these premises seems to you to be more reasonable. I think it is open to ask, in deciding on the reasonableness of the premise, how reasonable the conclusions are that you draw from that premise. In my view, the conclusions that Ramsey draws from his premise are unreasonable, even though, when stated in the abstract, they may not seem noticeably different from my own. I therefore suggest that my premise is more acceptable.

Then we may differ on the meaning of the proposition that parents should care for their children. Ramsey would draw from this proposition the corollary that a parent who exposes a child to even a minimal risk except solely for that child's own, if you like, selfish benefit is not caring for that child. Once again, stated in that way, the conclusions he draws from that premise flow logically, but one should examine whether that is a premise we should accept. I do not believe any reason was given by Ramsey. What was given was a demonstration that his conclusions follow, if you accept that premise. I would like to suggest that is not a premise we should accept.

In research on children, excesses must be doubly guarded against. However, given justified research, executed in a responsible manner, children can be considered appropriate subjects as long as being part of a research project is not intentionally imposed on them against their will, and as long as participation is a reasonable and good thing that their parents themselves would have done if appropriate.

3. "[I]ntellectual virtue in the main owes both its birth and its growth to teaching . . . while moral virtue comes about as a result of habit . . . . [O]f all things that come to us by nature we first acquire the potentiality and later exhibit the activity . . . ; but the virtues we get by first exercising them, as also happens in the case of the arts as well. For one thing we have to learn before we can do them, we learn by doing them, e.g., men become builders by building and lyre-players by playing the lyre; so too we become just by doing just acts, temperate by doing temperate acts, brave by doing brave acts." Aristotle, Nicomachean Ethics, Bk. II, Ch. 1, § 1103a–b.

DEPARTMENT OF HEALTH AND HUMAN SERVICES, ADDITIONAL PROTECTIONS FOR CHILDREN INVOLVED AS SUBJECTS IN RESEARCH

48 Fed.Reg. 9814 (1983).*

§ 46.401 To what do these regulations apply?

(a) This subpart applies to all research involving children as subjects, conducted or supported by the Department of Health and Human Services.

§ 46.402 Definitions.

(a) "Children" are persons who have not attained the legal age for consent to treatments or procedures involved in the research, under the applicable law of the jurisdiction in which the research will be conducted.

(b) "Assent" means a child's affirmative agreement to participate in research. Mere failure to object should not, absent affirmative agreement, be construed as assent.

(c) "Permission" means the agreement of parent(s) or guardian to the participation of their child or ward in research.

(d) "Parent" means a child's biological or adoptive parent.

(e) "Guardian" means an individual who is authorized under applicable State or local law to consent on behalf of a child to general medical care.

---

* These regulations augment the basic regulations on human experimentation in 45 C.F.R., which are set forth in Sec. B.3, supra. [Eds.]

§ 46.403   IRB duties.

In addition to other responsibilities assigned to IRBs under this part, each IRB shall review research covered by this subpart and approve only research which satisfies the conditions of all applicable sections of this subpart.

§ 46.404   Research not involving greater than minimal risk.

HHS will conduct or fund research in which the IRB finds that no greater than minimal risk to children is presented, ony if the IRB finds that adequate provisions are made for soliciting the assent of the children and the permission of their parents or guardians, as set forth in § 46.408.

§ 46.405   Research involving greater than minimal risk but presenting the prospect of direct benefit to the individual subjects.

HHS will conduct or fund research in which the IRB finds that more than minimal risk to children is presented by an intervention or procedure that holds out the prospect of direct benefit for the individual subject, or by a monitoring procedure that is likely to contribute to the subject's well-being, only if the IRB finds that:

(a) The risk is justified by the anticipated benefit to the subjects;

(b) The relation of the anticipated benefit to the risk is at least as favorable to the subjects as that presented by available alternative approaches; and

(c) Adequate provisions are made for soliciting the assent of the children and permission of their parents or guardians, as set forth in § 46.406.

§ 46.406   Research involving greater than minimal risk and no prospect of direct benefit to individual subjects, but likely to yield generalizable knowledge about the subject's disorder or condition.

HHS will conduct or fund research in which the IRB finds that more than minimal risk to children is presented by an intervention or procedure that does not hold out the prospect of direct benefit for the individual subject, or by a monitoring procedure which is not likely to contribute to the well-being of the subject, only if the IRB finds that:

(a) The risk represents a minor increase over minimal risk;

(b) The intervention or procedure presents experiences to subjects that are reasonably commensurate with those inherent in their actual or expected medical, dental, psychological, social, or educational situations;

(c) The intervention or procedure is likely to yield generalizable knowledge about the subjects' disorder or condition which is of vital importance for the understanding or amelioration of the subjects' disorder or condition; and

(d) Adequate provisions are made for soliciting assent of the children and permission of their parents or guardians, as set forth in § 46.408.

§ 46.407   Research not otherwise approvable which presents an opportunity to understand, prevent, or alleviate a serious problem affecting the health or welfare of children.

HHS will conduct or fund research that the IRB does not believe meets the requirements of §§ 46.404, 46.405, or 46.406 only if:

(a) The IRB finds that the research presents a reasonable opportunity to further the understanding, prevention, or alleviation of a serious problem affecting the health or welfare of children; and

(b) The Secretary, after consultation with a panel of experts in pertinent disciplines (for example: science, medicine, education, ethics, law) and following opportunity for public review and comment, has determined either: (1) That the research in fact satisfies the conditions of §§ 46.404, 46.405, or 46.406, as applicable, or (2) the following:

(i) The research presents a reasonable opportunity to further the understanding, prevention, or alleviation of a serious problem affecting the health or welfare of children;

(ii) The research will be conducted in accordance with sound ethical principles;

(iii) Adequate provisions are made for soliciting the assent of children and the permission of their parents or guardians, as set forth in § 46.408.

§ 46.408   Requirements for permission by parents or guardians and for assent by children.

(a) In addition to the determinations required under other applicable sections of this subpart, the IRB shall determine that adequate provisions are made for soliciting the assent of the children, when in the judgment of the IRB the children are capable of providing assent. In determining whether children are capable of assenting, the IRB shall take into account the ages, maturity, and psychological state of the children involved. This judgment may be made for all children to be involved in research under a particular protocol, or for each child, as the IRB deems appropriate. If the IRB determines that the capability of some or all of the children is so limited that they cannot reasonably be consulted or that the intervention or procedure involved in the research holds out a prospect of direct benefit that is important to the health or well-being of the children and is available only in the context of the research, the assent of the children is not a necessary condition for proceeding with the research. Even where the IRB determines that the subjects are capable of assenting, the IRB may still waive the assent requirement under circumstances in which consent may be waived in accord with § 46.116 of Subpart A.

(b) In addition to the determinations required under other applicable sections of this subpart, the IRB shall determine, in accordance with and to the extent that consent is required by § 46.116 of Subpart A, that adequate provisions are made for soliciting the permission of each child's parents or guardian. Where parental permission is to be obtained, the IRB may find that the permission of one parent is sufficient for research to be conducted under § 46.404 or § 46.405. Where research is covered by §§ 46.406 and 46.407 and permission is to be obtained from parents, both parents must give their permission unless one parent is deceased, unknown, incompetent, or not reasonably available, or when only one parent has legal responsibility for the care and custody of the child.

(c) In addition to the provisions for waiver contained in § 46.116 of subpart A, if the IRB determines that a research protocol is designed for conditions or for a subject population for which parental or guardian permission is not a reasonable requirement to protect the subjects (for example, neglected or abused children), it may waive the consent requirements in Subpart A of this part and paragraph (b) of this section, provided an appropriate mechanism for protecting the children who will participate as subjects in the research is substituted, and provided further that the waiver is not inconsistent with federal, state or local law. The choice of an appropriate mechanism would depend uon the nature and purpose of the activities described in the protocol, the risk and anticipated benefit to the research subjects, and their age, maturity, status, and condition.

(d) Permission by parents or guardians shall be documented in accordance with and to the extent required by § 46.117 of Subpart A.

(e) When the IRB determines that assent is required, it shall also determine whether and how assent must be documented.

§ 46.409   Wards.

(a) Children who are wards of the state or any other agency, institution, or entity can be included in research approved under § 46.406 or § 46.407 only if such research is:

(1) Related to their status as wards; or

(2) Conducted in schools, camps, hospitals, institutions, or similar settings in which the majority of children involved as subjects are not wards.

(b) If the research is approved under paragraph (a) of this section, the IRB shall require appointment of an advocate for each child who is a ward, in addition to any other individual acting on behalf of the child as guardian or in loco parentis. One individual may serve as advocate for more than one child. The advocate shall be an individual who has the background and experience to act in, and agrees to act in, the best interests of the child for the duration of the child's participation in the research and who is not associated in any way (except in the role as advocate or member of the IRB) with the research, the investigator(s), or the guardian organization.

NOTE

The regulations governing research on children are based in large part on the recommendations of the National Commission for the Protection of Human Subjects of Biomedical and Behaviorial Research Commission that was established in 1974 by Pub.L. 93–348. See National Commission, Report and Recommendations: Research Involving Children (Report) (1977). There are, however, three significant differences between the regulations adopted and the Commission's recommendations.

First, the Commission recommended that research on children should be conducted or supported only "where appropriate, studies have been conducted first on animals and adult humans, then on older children, prior to involving infants . . . ." Report at 2. The regulations include this recommendation in the preamble only rather than as a specific regulatory requirement.

Next, the Commission recommended that a permanent National Ethics Advisory Board be established to determine the propriety of research "not otherwise approvable . . . ." The regulations instead only require the Secretary to consult a "panel of experts." § 46.407.

Finally, in order to ensure that children are consulted when appropriate, the Commission recommended (1) requiring a child's assent if he or she is more than six years old, and (2) that a child's objection to participation should be binding unless there is a direct benefit to the child. The regulations deleted the second point, and left the question of when children are capable of providing assent to the IRB.

What position would Charles Fried take on the issue of when to require assent?

ALEXANDER M. CAPRON, LEGAL CONSIDERATIONS AFFECTING CLINICAL PHARMACOLOGICAL STUDIES IN CHILDREN

21 Clinical Research 141 (1973).

. . .

Children cannot be regarded simply as "little people" pharmacologically. Their metabolism, enzymatic and excretory systems, skeletal development and so forth differ so markedly from adults' that drug tests for the latter provide inadequate information about dosage, efficacy, toxicity, side effects, and contraindications for children. . . .

. . .

Limiting the Participants

As with the questions of need and risks, the question "who should participate in drug tests?" must be answered on two levels. First, one has to formulate general rules about the categories of subjects who are, and are not, acceptable experimental subjects. Then there must be mechanisms (i.e., people and institutions operating according to certain rules) to choose individual subjects by applying the formulations to the groups in question. Here we find ourselves facing again the toughest hurdle on the course: the need to choose subjects for experimentation from among a group whose members are incapable of volunteering themselves. . . .

As one way of finessing the problem, some have suggested that only *Phase Two* and *Three* tests (on sick children) but not *Phase One* tests (on normal children) be conducted.[7, 16] This alternative raises a number of questions, however. First, would the outcome of such a procedure be an adequate, well-controlled study as required by the FDA? There are sound scientific reasons for conducting *Phase One* investigations, to determine a drug's pharmacological and toxicological effects, free of the complications imposed by disease; there may also be need to conduct placebo studies. If the absence of such steps reduce the certainty of efficacy and safety, this added risk factor must be recognized as an additional cost which has been assumed because normal testing procedures have not been followed. This leads to a second question: is it proper to place additional risks (in drug testing and use) on sick children? A *yes* answer to this question, if carried to its logical end, would suggest that drugs should be tested *only* on the basis of need for an individual child, without formal approval (basically the present state of affairs, which is seen as needing repair). Third, has the dilemma of using children for "nonbeneficial" research actually been avoided? Even with sick children, certain procedures (from placebo studies to various evaluations of the experimental drug's effect) may not be of any direct benefit to the patient-subject; we are still likely to be left with a number of situations in which some testing will be necessary although not beneficial to the pediatric patient-subjects involved.

7. Lockhart J.D.: The information gap in pediatric drug therapy. Mod. Med. **38**:56–68, Nov. 16, 1970.

16. American Academy of Pediatrics, Committee on Drugs: Drug testing in children—FDA regulations. Ped. **43**:463–465, 1969.

Who, then, should participate in these studies? First, a limitation: no studies should be done on institutionalized subjects or on other subjects whose freedom is severely limited (unless the disease or disorder occurs only in these subjects). The reasons for this restriction seem obvious; the annals of medicine are replete with examples of the ways in which concern over risks and respect for the subject as a human being slowly erode when investigators rely on this class of subject. . . . Moreover, if consent is to play a role in the selection mechanism, the representatives of children under physical, mental, or economic constraint are poorly positioned to exercise unfettered choice.

Accepting this broad limitation, what means are available for selecting participants?

1. *Selection by Guardian.* [T]he present means of choosing subjects operates on a variation of informed consent model in which the child's guardians (usually his parents) are said to exercise their power of consent for him. This preserves some of the intent of the informed consent system, in that the person given the power is one who presumptively understands and identifies with the child and can therefore be expected to act so as to protect him in a manner similar to the one which he would himself have chosen. Nevertheless, the fundamental purpose of informed consent—to assure that one suffers only those risks he has chosen—is not met by substituted consent . . . .

One result of this perspective is to highlight the fact that putting this power of selection in parents, as we now do, is as much a matter of history or of convenience as it is a matter of principle. There are any number of explanations for this societal allocation of authority: respect for the family and a desire to foster the diversity which it brings; the fitness of giving the power to decide to the same people who created the child and have the duty to support and protect him; the belief that a child cannot be much harmed by parental choices which fall within the range permitted by society and a willingness to bear the risks of harm this allocation entails or a belief that in most costs "harm" would be hard for society to distill and measure anyway; or simply the conclusion that the administrative costs of giving authority to anyone but the parents outweigh the risks for children and for society unless the parents are shown to be unable to exercise their authority adequately. While the authority assigned parents may be framed in terms of a right on their part, such right is far from absolute, howsoever it may be justified in terms of the foregoing or other rationales.

Even if society continues to assume, as a general rule, that parents are the best (in whatever sense) representatives of their children, it may wish to place certain checks on their decisions—for example, by inquiring into the grounds for the decisions. The common law had the habit of taking things at face value, and it seldom probed the background of a decision or agreement, much less the parties' states of mind. Depending on the type of experiment for which the child is being volunteered, properly trained personnel should be employed to analyze the basis of the parents' decision and their motivation so as to rule out cases in which the decision was made on a faulty basis, with a desire to punish or hurt the child, or with other pathological intent. So as to prevent the spectacle of pharmacologists exploiting the economic deprivation (and even desperation) which occurs in our country, no economic incentives should be attached to the system of parental choice, or any incentives should be graduated to make them "wealth-neutral" (a very difficult task). A further danger in using a system of selection based on economic rewards is that "the market" in this situation does not behave according to standard theory because parents' responsiveness to a monetary incentive is based on their own relative need for money, which (in the usual market rationale) is said to reflect society's valuation of their worth, yet cannot similarly be said to reflect society's valuation of the child-subject.

2. *Selection on Basis of Fitness*

It is also possible that other persons, perhaps those who work with large numbers of children, would make good selectors for experimentation. While it would be difficult to assure that such persons would act with the level of concern and attention which is normative in the parent-child relationship, their greater familiarity with children might make them more perceptive in identifying those who, for physiological or psychological reasons, would be best suited for testing. It would, of course, be possible to use this method in conjunction with the method of monitored parental selection previously set forth. Those charged with making the decisions could be individuals or groups with varying representation, depending on the expertise that was sought. Their determinations of fitness could be stated in summary form, or through an open, public process. Provided that public confidence existed for the grounds on which the decisions were to be made and for the integrity of the decision-makers—and given both the significance and distasteful nature of the decisions, this is a large assumption—it would probably make little difference whether the deliberations were public or private, since the final outcome would contain the value judgments which inhere in the system as to who is a proper experimental subject. This "rational" process differs from the processes of juries and draft-boards, who operate with broad discretion and need not provide "reasons" for their decisions; the revelation of their processes would probably disturb the public by making clear the value-laden grounds on which they act.

3. *Random Choice*

If we are, in fact, speaking of a definable group and if all members of the group have a roughly equal chance of being afflicted with the diseases which are to be treated in the group, then consideration should also be given to selecting experimental subjects from the group on a random basis. There is something in us which rebels at this notion, but once the field of experiments has been properly limited this alternative cannot be dismissed out of hand. There are many other situations in which membership in a group imposes obligations in return for sharing in the benefits conferred by membership (such as the availability of improved and adequately tested pharmaceuticals). The drafting of young men into the armed services provides a current example. Although I for one would prefer a system which achieved its ends through voluntary heroism rather than obligatory sacrifice, such a system may not produce enough volunteers and, in the case of children, it makes no sense to speak of volunteerism anyway. One can object to random selection on pragmatic grounds, however, for it fails to distinguish those children who are best suited for testing (although it could be used in combination with the second alternative just discussed), and it may make adverse test sequelae more difficult for the parents to bear than would a more rational system, especially one in which they exercised the decision-making power. Nevertheless, the randomness of the procedure itself is less bothersome than the alternative which many favor of using sick children as test subjects, since to the randomness of being afflicted with the disease and its accompanying suffering would be added the risk of further suffering from a drug whose safety and efficacy are unknown.

Thus far, these alternatives have been discussed entirely in functional terms, but it is obvious that they would bring about important changes in the rights and duties of the various participants: children, parents, investigators, and society. Yet I suspect that what makes one uncomfortable about the second and third alternatives is neither their deliberateness (in the case of selection by fitness) nor their arbitrariness (in the case of random selection), but their allocation of authority to officers of the state. We attempt to protect our liberties by placing limitations on the powers of the state; yet, not always trusting the state to be so self-limiting, we also seek protection by dispersing power as widely as possible and, when it is necessary to place power in the government, by putting as many internal checks on its exercise as possible without disabling the system entirely. These liberty-protecting devices are enshrined in our constitution, as prohibitions on "involuntary servitude," guarantees of "due process," and the like. While the selective service system has withstood challenge on constitutional grounds,[22-24] any system of drafting children for medical experimentation would certainly be subject to attack,[25] and its necessity would have to be rather compelling for it to be upheld. One interesting aspect of this is that the result desired (conducting adequate tests) might also be achieved through the first alternative, that of giving parents more freedom in volunteering their children for research for the benefit of children generally rather than of their child in particular. And yet our doubts about such a method would probably not be framed in constitutional terms but in terms of private rights (the parents' v. the child's) in civil law terms.[26]

NOTES

1. In connection with the idea of random selection, consider the notion that acceptance of a benefit (here, medical care based on the sacrifice of others) carries with it an obligation to contribute to its production (here, through service as a subject of research). See, e.g., R. Nozick, Anarchy, State and Utopia 90–95 (1974); Hart, Are There Any Natural Rights?, 44 Phil.Rev. 175 (1955).

2. On the authority of parents to make decisions for their children generally, see J. Areen, Cases and Materials on Family Law 864–929 (1978).

NOTE ON FETAL RESEARCH

The federal government has promulgated regulations governing fetal research that provide in pertinent part:

45 C.F.R. § 46.206   General Limitations

(a) No activity to which this subpart is applicable may be undertaken unless:

(1) Appropriate studies on animals and nonpregnant individuals have been completed;

22. Selective Draft Law Cases, 245 U.S. 366 (1918).

23. Lichter v. United States, 334 U.S. 742 (1948).

24. United States v. O'Brien, 391 U.S. 367 (1968).

25. Cf. Black, C., Jr.: "Constitutional problems in compulsory national service." Yale Law Report, Summer 1967, pp. 19–20.

26. But see Prince v. Massachusetts, 321 U.S. 158 (1944) (limiting parents' authority to make a child a "martyr" to religion, a constitutionally based argument).

(2) Except where the purpose of the activity is to meet the health needs of the mother or the particular fetus, the risk to the fetus is minimal and, in all cases, is the least possible risk for achieving the objectives of the activity.

(3) Individuals engaged in the activity will have no part in: (i) Any decisions as to the timing, method, and procedures used to terminate the pregnancy, and (ii) determining the viability of the fetus at the termination of the pregnancy; and

(4) No procedural changes which may cause greater than minimal risk to the fetus or the pregnant woman will be introduced into the procedure for terminating the pregnancy solely in the interest of the activity.

(5) No inducements, monetary or otherwise, may be offered to terminate pregnancy for purposes of the activity.

§ 46.208   Activities directed toward fetuses in utero as subjects.

(a) No fetus *in utero* may be involved as a subject in any activity covered by this subpart unless: (1) The purpose of the activity is to meet the health needs of the particular fetus and the fetus will be placed at risk only to the minimum extent necessary to meet such needs, or (2) the risk to the fetus imposed by the research is minimal and the purpose of the activity is the development of important biomedical knowledge which cannot be obtained by other means.

(b) An activity permitted under paragraph (a) of this section may be conducted only if the mother and father are legally competent and have given their informed consent, except that the father's consent need not be secured if: (1) His identity or whereabouts cannot reasonably be ascertained, (2) he is not reasonably available, or (3) the pregnancy resulted from rape.

§ 46.209   Activities directed toward fetuses ex utero, including nonviable fetuses, as subjects.

(a) No fetus *ex utero* may be involved as a subject in an activity covered by this subpart until it has been ascertained whether the particular fetus is viable, unless: (1) There will be no added risk to the fetus resulting from the activity, and (2) the purpose of the activity is the development of important biomedical knowledge which cannot be obtained by other means.

(b) No nonviable fetus may be involved as a subject in an activity covered by this subpart unless: (1) Vital functions of the fetus will not be artificially maintained except where the purpose of the activity is to develop new methods for enabling fetuses to survive to the point of viability, (2) experimental activities which of themselves would terminate the heartbeat or respiration of the fetus will not be employed, and (3) the purpose of the activity is the development of important biomedical knowledge which cannot be obtained by other means.

(c) In the event the fetus *ex utero* is found to be viable, it may be included as a subject in the activity only to the extent permitted by and in accordance with the requirements of other subparts of this part.

(d) An activity permitted under paragraph (a) or (b) of this section may be conducted only if the mother and father are legally competent and have given their informed consent, except that the father's informed consent need not be secured if: (1) his identity or whereabouts cannot reasonably be ascertained, (2) he is not reasonably available, or (3) the pregnancy resulted from rape.

§ 46.210   Activities involving the dead fetus, fetal material, or the placenta.

Activities involving the dead fetus, mascerated fetal material, or cells, tissue, or organs excised from a dead fetus shall be conducted only in accordance with any applicable State or local laws regarding such activities.

§ 46.211   Modification or waiver of specific requirements.

Upon the request of an applicant or offeror (with the approval of its Institutional Review Board), the Secretary may modify or waive specific requirements of this subpart, with the approval of the Ethical Advisory Board after such opportunity for public comment as the Ethical Advisory Board considers appropriate in the particular instance. In making such decisions, the Secretary will consider whether the risks to the subject are so outweighed by the sum of the benefit to the subject and the importance of the knowledge to be gained as to warrant such modification or waiver and that such benefits cannot be gained except through a modification or waiver. Any such modifications or waivers will be published as notices in the Federal Register.

These regulations have been criticized by some as too stringent. Willard Gaylin and Marc Lappe in Fetal Politics: The Debate on Experimenting with the Unborn, Atlantic, May 1975 at 66, argue:

> The most justifiable experiment would seem to us to be that which is closest to the therapeutic model. Of course, in the case of abortion the fetus cannot be "helped" by being experimented upon since it is doomed to death anyhow, but perhaps its death can be ennobled because it serves those more fortunate. If the doomed fetus could be used to supply the information that would permit those same parents, or similar parents, a greater opportunity for a healthy wanted child, we would have a persuasive argument for experimentation. The classic example would involve a disease lethal or damaging to the gestating child and a vaccine or drug that would prevent the disease in an expectant mother. The vaccine has been proved harmless or the drug efficacious to adults, though its effect on the developing fetus is unknown, i.e., it may be harmless or therapeutic or it may be more destructive than the disease.

> The development of the rubella vaccination against German measles is a prototypic example. Exposure to German measles causes serious abnormalities in 20 to 40 percent of exposed fetuses. To protect the developing fetus against infection, mothers must be immunized, but for many years no one knew whether the rubella vaccine would harm the fetus itself. Pre-abortion studies were virtually the only way to determine quickly the safety of rubella vaccine. The alternatives would be to give the vaccine to an exposed expectant mother who wanted her child, running the risk of seriously damaging or killing the child; not to give her the vaccine, allowing her the option of carrying to term a possibly congenitally defective child; to abort what might be a healthy fetus to avoid the roughly one-out-of-three odds of having a child with some defect. (We now bypass these dilemmas by vaccinating pre-adolescent girls or a maximal portion of the population of grade-schoolers.)

> The alternative, to do research on fetuses seems clearly the most humane solution. Since we know we are going to destroy, dismember and discard the fetus in a procedure known as abortion, it seems a small indignity to expose it to the rubella vaccine just prior to that termination, and in the process determine whether or not there is an effect on the unborn child, at best the vaccine would not affect the child, and if the woman were to change her mind, the pregnancy would have been protected; at worst, the fetus would have been exposed to an attenuated form of a virus which otherwise causes abnormalities in one case out of three.

In contrast, LeRoy Walters supports the position ultimately adopted in the federal regulations. Ethical and Public-Policy Issues in Fetal Research: A Report to the National Commission for the Protection of Human Subjects of Biomedical and Behavioral Research, reprinted in Research on the Fetus: Appendix. In his words:

> Richard McCormick has presented what seems to me to be a very cogent argument for including children in certain kinds of no-risk or low-risk nontherapeutic research. McCormick's central thesis is that all members of society owe certain minimal debts to society; among these debts is one's obligation to take part in low-risk biomedical or behavioral research. He concludes that parents should be authorized to consent to a child's taking part in experiments which the child *should* be willing to take part in if the child *could* understand and consent.

If one accepts this position on pediatric research, one can easily extend it to cover the prenatal period in the life of a fetus which will be carried to term and be born. The parent or parents of such a fetus can be expected to have the interests of the fetus in view, just as parents of already-born children normally consider the interests of their offspring. Thus, proxy consent for nontherapeutic research on a fetus prior to birth is both possible and ethically consistent with consent for nontherapeutic pediatric research.

In the case of a fetus which will be aborted or has been aborted, the situation is somewhat more complex. The mother has decided, perhaps for good reason, that the life of the fetus should be terminated. Because she will not be obliged to consider the interests of the child on a long-term basis, she cannot give proxy consent *in the same sense* as the mother or both parents of an already-born child or a fetus-to-be-born. There is, in addition, an inherent difficulty in conceptualizing what "risk" or "harm" might mean when one is speaking of an organism which will shortly die at a previable stage of life. I suggest that it is possible to skirt these difficult problems as well as to be ethically consistent if one adopts the general rule: Nontherapeutic research procedures which are permissible in the case of fetuses which will be carried to term are also permissible in the case of (a) live fetuses which will be aborted and (b) live fetuses which have been aborted.

The fundamental presupposition of the position here advocated is that there is a substantial measure of continuity between previable fetal life and viable fetal life or pediatric life. This continuity cannot, in my view, be conclusively demonstrated by means of factual arguments. However, a proponent of the continuity-thesis can point to a series of considerations which render the thesis at least not implausible. It seems clear, for example, that the living previable fetus has a qualitatively different potential from a living tissue or a living sub-human animal. One notes, too, that Anglo-American law has displayed a certain ambivalence vis-a-vis the previable fetus, according to the fetus some, but not all, of the legal protections enjoyed by children or adults. It can also be argued that in form or general appearance the 12- or 16-week-old previable fetus resembles the viable fetus more closely than it resembles the embryo or blastocyst. Finally, one is struck by both the technology-dependence and the somewhat arbitrary character of the viability watershed: fetuses which twenty years ago would have been correctly classified as previable are now surviving in neonatal intensive-care units; today the immaturity of a single organ system, the lungs, constitutes the major barrier between a 450-gram fetus and viability.

In your view, which is the more persuasive argument? Why?

4. PRISONERS

Until now, the categories of subjects under consideration were determined by medical criteria, i.e., because children do not react to some drugs in the same way as adults, some testing must be done on children. Prisoners, on the other hand, are not usually recruited because of their medical needs. Consider, therefore, what justification, if any, there is for testing drugs or medical devices on prisoners.

BAILEY v. LALLY

United States District Court for the District of Maryland, 1979.
481 F.Supp. 203.

FRANK A. KAUFMAN, DISTRICT JUDGE:

Plaintiffs, . . . current and former state prisoners, initiated this class action under 42 U.S.C. § 1983 and its jurisdictional counterpart, 28 U.S.C. § 1343(3), on behalf of all prisoners who were incarcerated at the

Maryland House of Correction (MHC), a medium security penal institution, on or after December 7, 1973, and who participated in any medical research tests in the Medical Research Unit (MRU) of the MHC. Defendants are prison administrators, officials of the University of Maryland and the University of Maryland School of Medicine under whose auspices the medical research was sponsored, and doctors on the faculty of the University of Maryland School of Medicine who were responsible for conducting the research studies at the MRU. Presented herein . . . is the issue of whether conditions of incarceration at the MHC were so bad and the inducements to participate in the MRU so great that the prisoners' participation in the medical research program was not voluntary and therefore in violation of constitutional rights to due process, privacy and protection against cruel and unusual punishment.

Findings of Fact

The MHC was opened in 1879. Various additions and new facilities have been since incorporated. Conditions at the institution often have been the subject of controversy; certain of those conditions related to overcrowding have been declared unconstitutional.

The design capacity of the MHC is approximately 1100. The population of the MHC on January 1 during the years 1971 to 1975 ranged from 1498 to 1617. Approximately 978 prisoners were housed two men to a cell at any one time from 1971 through 1975. The cells which housed two men measured about 40 square feet and were designed for one person. There were sometimes time-consuming problems in finding compatible cellmates. Prior to 1976 there was no hot water in the cells at the MHC. Heat in the winter was inadequate and the institution was very hot in the summer. The building suffered from lack of repairs; the environment has been described as dreary and some have characterized the living conditions as barbaric. Overcrowding resulted in an excessive noise level, sanitation problems, and adverse psychological effects, including increased stress, anxiety and fear. On January 1 of the years 1971–75, the percentage of prisoners on idle status ranged from 16.2% in 1971 to 37.3% in 1974 to 18.5% in 1975. Prisoners on idle status or undergoing job classification did not have a job, educational or vocational assignment, spent between 16 and 17 hours per day in their cells, and were otherwise restricted as to the activities in which they participated. Prisoners with jobs spent approximately 10 hours per day in their cells. Prisoners with jobs (either institutional or State Use Industries) earned, as of April 1975, between $0.63 and $1.46 per day with the exception of those prisoners working in the laundry who earned $2.22 per day. Prior to 1974 prisoners attending the educational program were also allowed to maintain an institutional job but were not paid for their participation in the educational program. After 1974, prisoners in the educational program were paid $0.70 per day but were not permitted to maintain a job. Most jobs and educational programs were active only 5 days per week; about 85 percent of the prisoners who worked earned less than $1.10 per day.

Money earned by a prisoner was used by him to buy items at the commissary not regularly provided to prisoners, to save, or to send home. Indigent prisoners, those with less than $2.00 in their prison accounts, were given certain basic items such as toothpaste and shaving cream which were available to others only for purchase at the commissary. All prisoners were permitted to receive money from outside sources.

Medical research involving prisoners in the MHC started in 1958. The medical research unit (MRU) at the MHC was established by doctors on the staff of the University of Maryland School of Medicine, Division of Infectious Diseases. Between 1971 and 1976, Dr. Richard Hornick, Professor of Medicine and Chief of the Division of Infectious Diseases, was responsible for the MRU and also the principal investigator in many of the experiments conducted. The MRU was approved by prison administrators at the state and institutional level. When the MRU was formed, the then Commissioner of Corrections of the State of Maryland determined that prisoners should be paid for their participation in medical research projects, and set the rate at $2.00 per each day, including any Saturdays or Sundays if an experiment spanned such a day. That rate of pay was recognized as higher than the average prison wage, and as an inducement. The $2.00 per day rate remained constant through 1976 until the MRU was closed.[7] At the outset, it was determined by those in charge that participation in the MRU by any prisoner would have no impact upon any decision regarding his parole.

Some of the studies conducted at the MRU required prisoners to "live in" as patients in a specially designated section of the MRU; other studies were conducted on prisoners who remained in their cells. The former can be described as in-patients, the latter as out-patients. Approximately two-thirds of the prisoner participations (number of prisoners participating times number of times each participated) during the relevant period of time were out-patient participations. The percentage of prisoner volunteers on idle status prior to becoming volunteers ranged from 5.7% in 1971 to 35.2% in 1975. Twenty-nine percent of the volunteers on idle status became in-patients as compared to 20 percent of the volunteers with jobs who became in-patients. After 1972, prisoners on in-patient studies or those on out-patient studies who became sick and had to be admitted to the MRU for treatment lost their right to return to their same cells or dormitories and their right to retain their jobs. A prisoner on an out-patient study could retain his cell and his job, if he had one. Thus, prisoners on out-patient studies could supplement job income and obtain additional time outside their cells.

The MRU live-in section contained 34 beds, which were generally 70–75 percent occupied. The unit was air conditioned, adequately heated, and quiet. It had hot water at all relevant times, color television, and three separate bathroom facilities. The new MRU facilities were opened in 1972 and complied with all relevant public health regulations. Prisoners participating on in-patient studies and confined to the MRU had certain advantages: "[T]he physical set-up . . . is considered superior in many ways to the normal correctional situation. Not only is the volunteer free to do as he wishes, but he associates with persons who are not inmates nor guards and has a definite break in routine."

Prisoners found out about the MRU through several methods, including word of mouth.[9] Participation by prisoners in the MRU was initiated

---

7. Prisoners also received one to five dollars additional pay for various medical procedures necessary for a study, e.g., being subjected to mosquito bites in order to expose the subject to malaria.

9. An information sheet for prisoners contained the following description of the studies conducted in the MRU:

VOLUNTEER STUDIES

For almost 15 years now volunteer studies have been carried out at the House of Correction by doctors from the University of Maryland and the National Institutes of Health. From these studies we have learned a tremendous amount about diseases which affect most of the world. These have in-by application. Application forms were published in the prison newspaper and, during some periods, those forms were given to prisoners when they entered the MHC. There was no other solicitation of volunteers. The defendant doctors testified that there was always a shortage of volunteers and that some studies had to be aborted because of insufficient volunteers. On the other hand, those who did volunteer seemed generally willing to participate again, usually, apparently, because the prisoner who volunteered wanted to make the extra money.

. . . MRU (male) nurses reviewed applications and called in the prisoner volunteers. Either a nurse or the doctor in charge of the study would speak to the prisoners as a group about the study in general, including reasons for the study, the nature of the experiment, and possible hazards.[11] If the prisoner indicated he was interested in taking part in the study, he would then be given a physical examination. Repetitive oral explanations, including questions and answers, were given to the volunteers in layman's language.

The most common question raised by prisoners involved their pay for participation. Other questions concerned retention of jobs, cell arrange-

---

cluded the common cold, flu, malaria, and different types of diarrhea. All of these diseases only occur in man. They don't occur in monkeys or mice or any other animal. Therefore they can only be studied effectively in man. As we have learned more and more about these illnesses we have been able to develop better ways of treating them. But even more important, we have been able to make better vaccines that prevent the disease from ever happening. Some of the new vaccines that have been tested at Jessup are now being used in the United States and all over the world. This would not have been possible without the cooperation of hundreds of volunteers over the years.

When we say volunteer studies, we mean just that. You are volunteers. You are not forced to do anything. If you apply to be on a study and then later on you want to drop out, you can do it. It won't go on your record and you can apply for another study at any time. You can even drop out in the middle of a study. It is your choice. You can choose the kind of study you want to be on. For example, you can choose a so-called "walking test" where you are not admitted to the hospital and you won't risk losing your job.

Above all, you are not guinea pigs. We will explain every study to you at least twice before it starts. This means we will tell you why we are doing the study, what exactly is going to happen, and what risks are involved. If you have any questions, we will answer them. There will be no operations or special tests that would be hard on you. Every study has to be approved ahead of time by a special committee at our university.

We feel that all this is important, especially because some of you have been worried

in the past. None of the studies will make you sick for a long time or sterilize anyone or do any of the things that get spread around by rumors. Some of you may get sick, but we will provide early and complete medical care. In 15 years of these studies we have never had a serious complication.

If you want to join, fill out the application. The assistant warden's office will approve it if you are at least 21 years old. Then we will call you down to our ward and explain the studies to you, including how much we pay for each study.

11. Two examples of the type of consent information apparently used by Dr. Hornick are the following. The second example contained the introductory proviso: "This in no way represents the full explanation given the volunteers."

Protocol: "Study of Shigella Vaccines in Man"

In these diarrheal studies the hazards and symptoms of each disease are explained in detail to the volunteers before the study is begun. They are told they may develop severe diarrhea, abdominal cramping, bloody mucoid stools or high fever. The volunteers may withdraw at anytime and specific antibiotic therapy is available.

Protocol: "Intestinal Biopsy Studies of Volunteers with Acute Non Bacterial Gastroenteritis:

You may develop acute "viral diarrhea". You may have fever, abdominal pain, diarrhea and vomiting. If you agree we would like to obtain a small piece of small or large intestine. On rare occasions following such a procedure small amounts of intestinal bleeding might result and even more rare is the occurrence of intestinal perforation which might require blood transfusions and surgery.

ments, visitation rights, and disease-related questions such as whether the disease would be contagious. Some doctors specifically told the inmates as part of the oral explanations that participation by an inmate would have no impact on parole. Other doctors did not volunteer that information but did reveal it in answers to questions by the prisoners.

For various reasons some volunteers would not be accepted for a particular study. Those accepted were again told what they should expect while on the study and were again asked if they wanted to be on the study and told that they could withdraw without any adverse consequence if they so desired. Many did withdraw for various reasons and at various stages both before and during a study.[13] One doctor characterized attrition as "out-of-sight."

The doctors considered a written consent form insufficient and relied on the repetitive oral explanations to inform the prisoners, though at some time after the initial oral explanation the volunteer would be asked to read and sign a written consent form similar to a standard hospital consent form.

The MRU conducted nontherapeutic studies involving various infectious diseases.[15] With the exception of the common cold and flu, there were known cures for all the infectious diseases studied. Doctors in the field of course do not usually know in advance the disease which they will encounter. In the MRU the doctors knew which disease had been administered to a volunteer and could thus diagnose and treat it at a very early stage if the volunteer developed symptoms of the disease.

The MRU was not a unique facility. Similar facilities conducting similar tests on prisoners were operated in numerous other states.[16] Similar studies were still in being when the trial of this case was commenced in January 1979 at prisons in Jackson, Michigan; Deer Lodge, Montana; and Vacaville, California.

The MRU research studies were largely funded by federal agencies after submission to and review by those agencies of protocols describing all aspects of the proposed research. The principal sponsor was the United States Department of Health, Education and Welfare (HEW) and the United States Department of the Army. There were periodic reviews by those federal agencies as well as by the Maryland Department of Health. The Warden of the MHC and other prison administrators were also kept generally informed. Additionally, the MRU studies were subject to continuous review and approval by the Human Volunteers Research Committee (HVRC) of the University of Maryland School of Medicine.

---

13. Thus, for example, in a typhoid study in which volunteers who have received a vaccine are then administered live organisms to challenge the effectiveness of that vaccine, some would drop out before being vaccinated, others before receiving the live organisms, and one inmate dropped out after receiving the challenge.

15. The principal diseases studied at the MRU were Malaria (118), Cholera (55), Shigella (34), Viral Diarrhea (31), Influence (28), Typhoid (17), E. Coli (17), and Rhinovirus (16). The numbers in parentheses indicate the number of studies of that particular disease from January 1970 until the MRU was closed in 1976.

16. States in which some medical research was conducted on prisoner volunteers during at least some period of time after 1970 include Michigan, Montana, California, Texas, Indiana, Connecticut, Missouri, Oklahoma, Illinois, Florida, Georgia, Massachusetts, New Jersey, Ohio, Rhode Island, Nebraska, and Kentucky. Nontherapeutic biomedical research was conducted in state prisons in the following states in 1975: California, Indiana, Maryland, Michigan, Montana, Texas, Virginia, Connecticut, and Massachusetts.

The HVRC was a multidisciplinary committee composed of physicians and non-physicians, including professors of law, social work, pharmacology, and psychology. The HVRC had final review authority over all medical research on human subjects conducted by faculty members of the University of Maryland School of Medicine (not just the studies conducted at the MRU). The HVRC was responsible for protecting the rights of human subjects, making sure the risks to them were outweighed by the benefits of a proposed study, and assuring that the individual subject's consent had been appropriately obtained. Starting in 1973, the HVRC, in addition to preliminary review, required individuals conducting experiments on human subjects to file six-month reports and final reports describing progress, results, and unusual occurrences.

The HVRC was substantially more than a rubber stamp for research proposals by doctors. It was an integral part of the review process. The committee carefully reviewed proposed studies and took a very strict stand on the issue of informed consent. . . . .

[The court next quotes from letters sent by the HVRC to Dr. Hornick in 1973, 1974 and 1975 criticizing his provisions for informed consent].

In December 1971, HEW issued "The Institutional Guide to DHEW Policy on Protection of Human Subjects," DHEW Publication No. 72–102 (December 1, 1971), applicable to federally funded medical research. That publication addressed, among other matters, institutional review of projects (such as the review processes of the HVRC which predated that 1971 HEW guide) and informed consent. In 1973, HEW published a Notice of Proposed Rulemaking, 38 Fed.Reg. 27882 (October 9, 1973), which indicated HEW's intention to expand and codify its December 1, 1971 policy. In November 1973, HEW published a Draft of Proposed Policies and Procedures, prepared by a study group appointed by the National Institutes of Health, which focused on problems involving research on particular categories of human volunteers, including prisoners. 38 Fed.Reg. 31738 (November 16, 1973). That draft was published prior to final governmental review in recognition of the fact that it would provoke "debate and controversy" and in order to invite "early public comment and participation." 38 Fed.Reg. at 31738. The draft articulated the rationale for using prisoners and observed (at 31743):

> V. *Prisoners*—A. *Policy considerations*. Clinical research often requires the participation of normal volunteers; for example, in the early stages of drug or vaccine evaluation. Sometimes, the need for standardization [of] certain variables, or for monitoring responses over an extended period of time, requires that the subjects of research remain in a controlled environment for the duration of the project. Prisoners may be especially suitable subjects for such studies, since, unlike most adults, they can donate their time to research at virtually no cost to themselves. However, the special status of prisoners requires that they have special protection when they participate in research.

> While there is no legal or moral objection to the participation of normal volunteers in research, there are problems surrounding the participation of volunteers who are confined in an institution. Many aspects of institutional life may influence a decision to participate; the extent of that influence might amount to coercion, whether it is intended or not. Where there are no opportunities for productive activity, research projects might offer relief from boredom. Where there

are no opportunities for earning money, research projects offer a source of income. Where living conditions are unsatisfactory, research projects might offer a respite in the form of good food, comfortable bedding, and medical attention. While this is not necessarily wrong, the inducement (compared to the deprivation) might cause prisoners to offer to participate in research which would expose them to risks of pain or incapacity which, under normal circumstances, they would refuse. In addition, there is always the possibility that the prisoner will expect participation in research to be viewed favorably, and to his advantage, by prison authorities (on whom his other few privileges depend) and by the parole board (on whom his eventual release depends). This is especially true when the research involves behavior modification and may be termed "therapeutic" with respect to the prisoner. In such instances, participation inevitably carries with it the hope that a successful result will increase the subject's chances for parole. Thus, the inducement involved in therapeutic research might be extremely difficult to resist; and for this reason, special protection is necessary for prisoners participating in research whether or not the research is therapeutic.

Further HEW notices of proposed rulemaking were published in 1974, . . . followed by published rules on November 16, 1978, 43 Fed.Reg. 53652, restricting research on prisoners (45 C.F.R. §§ 46.301–46.306). Permitted research involving prisoners was limited to the following (45 C.F.R. § 46.306):

(A) Study of the possible causes, effects, and processes of incarceration, and of criminal behavior, provided that the study presents no more than minimal risk and no more than inconvenience to the subjects;

(B) Study of prisons as institutional structures or of prisoners as incarcerated persons, provided that the study presents no more than minimal risk and no more than inconvenience to the subjects;

(C) Research on conditions particularly affecting prisoners as a class (for example, vaccine trials and other research on hepatitis which is much more prevalent in prisons than elsewhere; and research on social and psychological problems such as alcoholism, drug addiction and sexual assaults) provided that the study may proceed only after the Secretary has consulted with appropriate experts including experts in penology medicine and ethics, and published notice, in the Federal Register, of his intent to approve such research; or

(D) Research on practices, both innovative and accepted, which have the intent and reasonable probability of improving the health or well-being of the subject. In cases in which those studies require the assignment of prisoners in a manner consistent with protocols approved by the IRB to control groups which may not benefit from the research, the study may proceed only after the Secretary has consulted with appropriate experts, including experts in penology medicine and ethics, and published notice, in the Federal Register, of his intent to approve such research.

(b) Except as provided in paragraph (a) of this section, biomedical or behavioral research conducted or supported by DHEW shall not involve prisoners as subjects.

. . .

The reasons for the limitations on prisoner participation in medical research were set forth in HEW's response to comments suggesting broader prisoner participation (43 Fed.Reg. at 53654):

Response: The Department is well aware of the past contributions of prison research . . . to the general health and welfare of the Nation . . . . However, it finds that there are substantial reasons for prohibiting continuation of such research and does not find any demonstrable need for continuing such research except as provided in § 46.306 . . . .

The Department again notes that medical and medically related research:

— Has already been prohibited in all Federal prisons;

— Has been prohibited in eight States;

— Is conducted in only about seven of the States that either permit it or don't regulate it;

— And is not conducted in countries outside the United States.

In general, these prohibitions have been based on the demonstrable inequities of such research and on the questionable voluntariness of prisoner consent. Though in theory the benefits of such research are usually to society as a whole, prisoners included, only one segment of society, prisoners, is asked to accept the research risks. Even if prisoner consent is obtained, the circumstances of that consent in a confined, restrictive, unattractive and boring environment, raise questions as to the voluntary nature of that consent. In addition, other nations active in biomedical and behavioral research have been able to conduct investigations without involving prisoners. . . .

Comment: One respondent felt that the allowable research on practices as stated in § 46.306(a)(2)(D) of the final regulations, appears to allow a broader range of "therapeutic" research than the preamble would lead one to expect. The respondent noted that there is not even a "minimal risk" ceiling on this type of research.

Response: The Commission would permit research on practices which have the intent and reasonable probability of improving the health or well-being of the subject when a prisoner benefits from a practice, no limit on the inherent, medically related risk was intended. [Sic] The Commission felt that a research subject should not be deprived of health benefits (even experimental ones) simply because the subject is a prisoner. The Department agrees.

While this debate was taking place, numerous articles concerning the medical research at the MHC were accepted and published in medical journals. Over 100 articles concerning that research have been published since 1971, 45 since 1974. The articles appeared in such highly regarded journals as the New England Journal of Medicine and the Journal of Infectious Diseases. The acceptance of an article for publication apparently implies that the study discussed by the article is viewed as having been conducted in accordance with medically ethical standards. No article concerning a study at the MHC was ever refused because the study had been conducted in an unethical manner.

. . .

Constitutional Issues

. . .

Plaintiffs contend that the poor prison conditions, idleness, and high level of pay relative to other prison jobs render the prisoners' participation in the studies conducted in the MRU coerced and in violation of their Eighth and Fourteenth Amendment rights.

The tests as to whether defendants' conduct subjected plaintiffs to cruel and unusual punishment or deprived plaintiffs of substantive due process are well established. In Estelle v. Gamble, 429 U.S. 97, 102–03, (1976), Mr. Justice Marshall wrote concerning cruel and unusual punishment:

. . .

Our more recent cases . . . ., have held that the Amendment proscribes more than physically barbarous punishments. See, e.g., Gregg v. Georgia, supra [428 U.S.] at 171 [96 S.Ct. 2909] (joint opinion); Trop v. Dulles, 356 U.S. 86, 100–101 (1958); Weems v. United States, 217 U.S. 349, 373 (1910). The Amendment embodies "broad and idealistic concepts of dignity, civilized standards, humanity, and decency . . . ," Jackson v. Bishop, 404 F.2d 571, 579 (CA8 1968), against which we must evaluate penal measures. Thus, we have held repugnant to the Eighth Amendment punishments which are incompatible with "the evolving standards of decency that mark the progress of a maturing society," Trop v. Dulles, supra [356 U.S.] at 101; see also Gregg v. Georgia, supra [428 U.S.] at 172–173 (joint opinion); Weems v. United States, supra [217 U.S.] at 378 [30 S.Ct. 544], or which "involve the unnecessary and wanton infliction of pain," Gregg v. Georgia, supra [428 U.S.] at 173 (joint opinion). . . .

. . . None of the actions of the defendants herein rises to the levels described in *Estelle* . . . . That is true despite the fact that certain of the conditions which existed at the MHC during the time period involved have been held unconstitutional, and that as many as one-third of the prisoners was idle at certain given times. Medical research studies offered at least a partial escape from those conditions since the MRU provided a clean, less-restrictive environment, and those who took part in its experiments were paid more than were prisoners generally except in a few other prison jobs. Additionally, some volunteers who did not live in the MRU and who had other jobs were able to earn money from both endeavors. The prisoners testified (and the doctors did not contest) that prisoners volunteered principally because of the money inducement and because they also hoped that their participation in the MRU would influence their chances for parole. While prisoner volunteers were told, either as a matter of course or upon a question being raised, that participation in the MRU program would have no impact on parole, "hope springs eternal in the human breast" [21A] and almost surely so did in the breast of each volunteer at the MRU. Nevertheless, it is to be noted that while some of the plaintiffs have stated that parole was never raised as a subject and that they were not told that participation would not affect parole, no prisoner has stated that parole was ever promised to any volunteer or that any volunteer was ever told that his parole would be facilitated through participation in the MRU. Additionally, the testimony of the prisoners

21A. A. Pope, An Essay on Man, Epistle I, line 95.

indicates that they understood that they were free to withdraw from the studies at any time and that indeed some of them did withdraw for various reasons. Some prisoners participated only in out-patient studies and withdrew upon learning that a study would be in-patient; some stopped participating after 1972 when they apparently risked loss of their jobs or cells if they became in-patients.

The doctors made diligent, continuing efforts orally to inform the prisoner volunteers concerning the various studies. They did not simply rely on a written consent form. They also made it clear to the inmates that the latter were free to withdraw at any time. Prisoners participating in studies were regularly and carefully examined and any volunteer who became ill received prompt, high-grade medical attention.

Accordingly, nothing in defendants' conduct of these studies is "incompatible with evolving standards of decency" nor "shocks the conscience" of mankind. That does not mean that there is not strong reason to question or disapprove of the use of prison inmates for research purposes. The issue of informed consent is a most thorny one. Informed consent consists of two elements: information and voluntariness. There is no question that the prisoner volunteers were informed. Each doctor who testified detailed the procedures already described to provide information to the applicants. Plaintiffs' allegation of coercion thus hinges on lack of voluntariness growing out of unconstitutional conditions such as overcrowding and other undesirable aspects of regular institutional life at the MHC. Those conditions may well have caused inmates to value even a few additional hours outside of their cells as worth the risk of participation in the MRU. That plus the high level of pay may have made such participation very attractive to certain inmates. Yet, while the level of pay was an inducement, some prisoners did not find it sufficiently attractive so as to be worth the risk of losing the right to return to their cells or their jobs. Further, there was always a shortage of volunteers. Only some 14 percent of all prisoners who went through the MHC during the years here involved participated in the medical studies. Thus, the program was hardly universally or overwhelmingly attractive to most inmates.

Plaintiffs have cited numerous cases for the proposition that in evaluating the voluntariness of a prisoner's actions, the impact of the totality of circumstances affecting his ability to make a decision must be carefully scrutinized. Those cases involve coerced confessions, consents to search and the like, given in factual situations which do not in any way approximate the conditions under scrutiny herein. Some of those cases refer not only to oppressive physical environment but to repeated interrogations and in certain instances bodily abuses. They do not address the question of the constitutionality of offering a choice to an inmate to participate in a worthwhile but unpleasant activity which may be more attractive to him because of his environment. Prisoners at the MHC were not subject to physical abuse, or confined in segregated cells, or restricted to meagre diets, until they consented to participate in MRU studies. Prisoners were not pressured to participate. To the contrary, prisoners had a viable choice and, even after choosing to participate, had the option to withdraw from the medical studies. The defendant doctors, closely watched by the HVRC and other review committees, took the necessary measures to assure that the prisoners were exercising their free choice.

. . .

One case cited by plaintiffs which does require particular note is Kaimowitz v. Department of Mental Health of the State of Michigan, Civil Action No. 73–19434–AW, Circuit Court for Wayne County, 42 U.S.L.W. 101 (1973). In *Kaimowitz*, the issue was whether a[n] involuntarily confined mental patient suffering from uncontrollable aggression could consent "to an innovative or experimental surgical procedure on the brain . . . [where] the procedure is designed to ameliorate [the anti-social] behavior." (Slip op. at 8). The court's opinion focused on the nature of psychosurgery, its "experimental" status, the "substantial danger" it poses (slip op. at 16), and the "particularly vulnerable" position of the involuntarily confined mental patient (slip op. at 25).

The infectious diseases studied in the MRU were *non* therapeutic. In that sense, they would appear even more vulnerable to attack than the therapeutic surgery found wanting in *Kaimowitz*. But they did not involve the uncertainties inherent in experimental psychosurgery; neither were they "dangerous, intrusive, irreversible, and of uncertain benefit to the patient and society." (Slip op. at 20). Rather, they were well-known diseases for which readily-available, effective cures were easily administered. Dr. Hornick testified that he permitted his own daughter, while a college student, to engage in controlled contagious disease research under appropriately skilled medical direction, as a means of earning money through a part-time job. All of the doctors testified to the almost complete lack of danger to life or to future health and stressed that only temporary illness and discomfort were involved. The record fully discloses that great care was taken to explain all of that to the inmates who indicated any desire to participate in the program.

Nor was there any connection between participation in the MRU and release from the MHC. In point of fact, those performing and administering the experiments in the MRU had absolutely no connection with the institutional release process except that, on occasion, an MRU doctor did write, upon an inmate's request, a letter to be included in the inmate's parole file about the latter's MRU participation. However, none of the MRU doctors seemingly received any feedback concerning the effect, if any, of any such letter. In addition, after a rather major general riot, several prisoners asked one or more doctors to write letters about those inmates' involvement in the MRU and, to the extent of those doctors' knowledge, the particular inmate's noninvolvement in the riot. None of such letters would appear to have overstepped appropriate boundaries.

In sum, though the MRU may have appeared attractive to some prisoners, the totality of the record fails to disclose any violation of the fundamental right of every person, including each inmate, to be free from undue coercion.

. . .

. . . Assuming *arguendo* the existence of violations of plaintiffs' constitutional rights, plaintiffs still may not prevail. That is because a defendant in a 1983 case is entitled to the defense of good faith if he objectively and subjectively so acted. This Court finds that each of the defendants acted in good faith.

. . .

. . . The legal status of the impact of prison environment on the prisoners' ability to give voluntary consent to medical experiments being conducted on them as volunteers had certainly not reached an adverse settled basis during the period of operation of the MRU. Indeed, the within case is the first case instituted in any court in the United States aimed at testing the legality of nontherapeutic medical experiments on prisoners. The HEW Guidelines for the Protection of Human Subjects (1971) mentioned a special concern for "those subjects in groups with limited civil freedom . . . [which] include prisoners." (at 2). That same publication mandated that "[c]ompensation to volunteers should never be such as to constitute an undue inducement." What is "undue" was not defined. Prior to 1973 there was infrequent mention and little, if any, public debate over conditions of confinement as an element to be considered in evaluating consents. Efforts were begun by HEW in 1973 to develop regulations focusing upon prisoner subjects. Comments received were on both sides of the issue. Not until November 1978, some two months prior to the trial of this case and some two years after the closing of the MRU, were negative, restrictive-type regulations promulgated.

During the course of the MRU experiments, all proposals for studies were subject to review by the interdisciplinary HVRC and governmental agencies providing funding. Beginning in 1974, ongoing studies were subject to periodic and final review by the HVRC. Those review committees knew the level of pay and never questioned it as too seductive; the committees knew further that the studies were to be conducted using prisoner volunteers and never raised the issue of the prison environment.

Medical journals accepted articles describing the results of the experiments and their methods. Experiments were being simultaneously conducted in prisons in numerous states, and the fact that some states discontinued medical experiment programs while others continued similar experiments only served to further the debate rather than to indicate the emergence of well-settled principle. To the contrary, throughout the period the MRU was in existence, there was no consensus regarding the importance to be attached to institutional conditions in evaluating a prisoner's consent to participate.

Plaintiffs, stressing the bad conditions prevailing at the MHC, contend that defendants should have been aware of such conditions and should have realized the impact of those conditions upon any prisoner's voluntary participation. However, the defendant doctors testified to a shortage of volunteers and to a preference for out-patient studies, especially after 1972 when a prisoner participating in an in-patient study risked loss of his job and/or his cell. As the law was unsettled as to the importance of conditions of confinement generally—and perhaps still is . . . it is not reasonable to conclude that the defendants should have had the foresight to single out one institution in which conditions vitiated consent. There is no basis to conclude that the defendants knew or should reasonably have known that their conduct of the medical experiments violated plaintiffs' constitutional rights. Rather, the record compels the conclusion that the defendants reasonably concluded that they were not violating any legal principle, constitutional or other. . . .

. . .

. . . Some persons may prefer that if society's needs require that human beings be subjects of non-dangerous, temporarily disabling, unpleasant medical experiments, such subjects should either be chosen by lot or at least not come solely from the ranks of the socially or economically underprivileged, including prison inmates. Such preference, however, even if valid, does not add up to a presently established constitutional absolute. Accordingly, judgments will be entered for defendants.

NATIONAL COMMISSION FOR THE PROTECTION OF HUMAN SUBJECTS OF BIOMEDICAL AND BEHAVIORAL RESEARCH

Staff Paper on Prisoners as Research Subjects

2–23 (October 31, 1975).

The use of prisoners for nontherapeutic research has a long history. Ancient Persian kings and the Ptolemys of Egypt are said to have employed the practice. . . .   At the turn of this century, criminals under sentence of death in the [Philippines] were infected with plague (without their knowledge) by Richard P. Strong, who later became Professor of Tropical Medicine at Harvard. Colonel Strong used another group of [Filipino] convicts to study beri-beri, reportedly rewarding them with tobacco in return for their submitting to a disease which caused paralysis, mental disturbance and heart failure. In 1915, Goldberger induced pellagra in twelve white Mississippi convicts in an attempt to develop a cure. In this instance, formal contracts for subsequent parole were written with the assistance of the prisoners' attorneys. In 1934, a program was established at Leavenworth Prison to assess the abuse potentiality of narcotic analgesics (analogues of morphine, codeine, etc.).

During World War II prisoner participation in research increased considerably in this country. Hundreds of inmates in Chicago and New Jersey prisons volunteered to be infected with malaria to test the safety and efficacy of experimental drugs in treating that disease. This involvement of prisoners in research was considered acceptable and even praiseworthy, since malaria was a serious threat to our military men during the war, and the research project afforded the prisoners an opportunity to contribute to the war effort. . . .

In the years following the Nuremburg Trials, a number of countries decided that prisoners are not acceptable subjects for certain kinds of experimentation. Thus, in 1955, the Public Health Council of the Netherlands stated that:

> Experiments on children; in institutions for children, old people, etc.; on the insane; or on prisoners, which involve dangerous risks, inconvenience or pain are not approved.

. . .

Renée Fox has described a number of factors which contributed to the interest of the United States in continuing its use of prisoners in nontherapeutic research. In the decade following the war, clinical research came into its own. The United States enthusiastically supported biomedical research through government and private grants, and the establishment of prestigious university positions, in a manner which was apparently unique to this country. We were committed heavily (both emotionally and financially) to clinical research.

. . .

Prison research was also endorsed during this period. Governor Green of Illinois convened a committee to study the ethical issues surrounding the participation of prisoners in projects such as the malaria study. In 1948 that committee reported that:

> Since one of the purposes of the parole system is reformative, the reformative value of serving as a subject in a medical experiment should be considered. Serving as a subject in a medical experiment is obviously an act of good conduct, if frequently unpleasant and occasionally hazardous, and demonstrates a type of social consciousness of high order when performed primarily as a service to society.

In like manner, the Deputy Commissioner of Institutions and Agencies of New Jersey said, of the prisoners who had participated in research during the war, that:

> All prisoners who had participated in medical experiments were given certificates of merit, copies of which were put into their records and called to the special attention of the Court of Pardons or the Board of Managers when parole was under consideration. Apparently no definite policy was ever formulated, and the participation in a medical experiment was considered only as one favorable factor in the whole case.

In 1949, after a prisoner from an Iowa penitentiary was enlisted by chance as a subject for their metabolic research ward, two investigators set up a formal arrangement with the Iowa state board of control to provide inmates on a regular basis for their research. When a state attorney general questioned the legality of their arrangement, they suspended operation for two years while they obtained enactment of legislation specifically permitting inmates to participate in medical research at the University Hospitals. They report, in retrospect, that:

> We feel that the use of prison volunteers for medical research is justified and highly desirable for the investigator, for the subjects, and for society.

Prisoner participation in research appeared to be such a salutary experience that the American Medical Association's House of Delegates passed a resolution in 1952 expressing its disapproval "of the participation in scientific experiments of persons convicted of murder, rape, arson, kidnapping, treason or other heinous crimes . . . ." The concern was that such prisoners might receive a pardon or parole through their participation in research, and they were deemed to be unworthy of such consideration.

Impetus was also provided by the Kefauver-Harris amendments to the Food and Drug Act in 1962, which established additional requirements for testing the safety and efficacy of all drugs to be sold in interstate commerce. Phase I of such testing involves evaluation of the safety of new drugs in normal volunteers. The Deputy Director of the FDA's Bureau of Drugs has been quoted as saying that "virtually all" of Phase I tests involve prisoners. (Prisoners may also participate in Phase II tests, by submitting to a disease in order to test the effectiveness of a new drug in [combatting] the illness, as in the malaria studies of the 1940's). The business arrangements between large pharmaceutical manufacturers, individual investigators, and state prisons have been described in detail by Jessica Mitford. She suggests that biomedical research in prisons is a big business, precipitated in large part by the requirements of the Food and Drug Administration and perpetuated by the economic self-interest of the drug firms, the investigators, the prison authorities, and the inmates, themselves.

. . .

[T]he central question concerning the participation of prisoners in nontherapeutic research is whether or not they are so situated as to be able to volunteer, or whether the nature of a prison is such that free choice is impossible. Much has been written on this subject, and the issue does not simply position the ethicists against the scientists. Rather, reasonable people from various disciplines see the same conditions differently.

Hans Jonas believes that those who are poorer in knowledge, motivation, and freedom of decision (the "captive" in various senses) should be the last candidates for research. This, he explains, is the opposite of a standard of availability. On the other hand, Paul Ramsey has written that it is possible to arrange matters so that prisoners "*may* be as free in volunteering as persons in normal life." Agreeing that there are circumstances in which their participation may be unacceptable (for example, when prison authorities are corrupt), he still concludes that with proper precautions, "since we have deprived a prisoner of a large number of his consents, we should yield to his consent to do good if it is an understanding, voluntary consent."

Similarly, Paul Freund has written:

The basic standard ought to be that [the prisoner's] will should not be overborne either by threats of punishment or by promises of reward. Within those limits, although some investigators rule out prisoners as subjects, there seems to be no good reason for depriving this group of the satisfactions of participation on an informed basis, satisfactions that to them are often great, indeed, bolstering their self-esteem and furnishing links to the general community and its values.

Others see the prison setting itself as so coercive and dehumanizing that the promise of better food, more comfortable quarters, additional contact with outsiders, and relief from the boredom (and fear) of the cell block all constitute coercion. This is said to be true even if no reduction in sentence is promised, and even if the payment for participation is comparable to that of other jobs in the same facility.

In a study of why prisoners volunteer to participate in research, John Arnold and his colleagues found that over 50% of the prisoners volunteered, at least in part, out of a desire for better living conditions. Moreover, many of them were "loners", and sought membership in "the only group that would take them—the research project." Altruism and patriotism have also been cited by prisoners as motivating factors. In addition, the relative security of the research ward has been cited, but on the other hand, the research (at least in the perception of the inmate) seemed to offer the status and personal satisfaction associated with risk-taking. Finally, it appeared that money had great appeal, for paying legal fees, supporting families, purchasing items at the canteen or for savings to use after discharge.

. . .

An additional complication is that prisoners are not always adults, nor are they always free of mental disabilities. In fact, according to a survey conducted in the mid 1960's, approximately 9.5% of the individuals in all correctional institutions in this country (except local jails and workhouses) had I.Q.'s below 70. The actual number of retarded individuals (based on the total prison population at that time) would have been 20,000. Similarly, 1.6% of the surveyed population had I.Q.'s below 55, which would indicate a total number of approximately 3,300 moderately to severely retarded inmates. (The range of I.Q. scores reported for 90,477 inmates was from 17 to 145.) The first critical issue identified by the NIMH report for which the survey was undertaken is "the lack of awareness of the complex legal, sociological and psychological problems of the mentally retarded offender." This factor must be kept in mind when considering the competence of prisoners to consent to participation in research.

. . .

PAT DUFFY, JR.,
DRUG TESTING IN PRISONS: THE VIEW FROM INSIDE

in Troubling Problems in Medical Ethics
79–89 (M. Basson, R. Lipson, D. Ganos eds. 1981).

Good morning. I was informed about this seminar about two days ago, and I wasn't told what to prepare for except to come down and look at you and answer a lot of questions that you might have about testing in a prison. My area of expertise, of course, is all kinds of criminal acts, how to survive in Jackson prison (a maximum security facility), how to get along, how to make money within the prison structure, and various and sundry other things you only read about in the newspaper. . . .

I've been at Jackson Prison for approximately 7 years, got another 6 or 7 years to go unless the judge in Detroit takes mercy on me. I've been involved in Phase I testing at Parke Davis and Upjohn and in fact I'm participating in a test right now. It's a test on ointments. (I have both arms wrapped, I can pull it down and let you see what's happening with the ointments. I went over and asked the people at Parke Davis and Upjohn and they were very cooperative.)

First of all you have to understand the philosophy of prison, and you can't do that unless you've been in prison. There's a lot of do-gooders that come in and take what we call the ten dollar tour. The prison officials take them through, and they say, "Oh, this is maximum security; this is where we keep the bad guys, and these are the guys that aren't so bad." People walk through, they walk around and have a cup of coffee and a stale donut from the mess, and now they're expert on prisons. They go out and tell all their friends, "Yeah, I've been to Jackson Prison. I know what it's all about." But you don't know what it's all about. You don't have to walk in the yard. You don't have to have your neck on a ball-bearing so you can see 360° around so that you can protect your life. You don't know what its all about to be without phones in prison. You don't know what it's like to be without visits in prison, to be without your family, without your friends. You don't know what it's like to lock up every night at nine before it's dark outside and get up at six in the morning, and so consequently, the whole spectrum of what goes on in prison— it's not yours to know. It's my world and it's my friends' world that are up at Jackson or Marquette or any other prison in the United States.

The thing of informed consent and free choice as regards a prisoner's life and the programs we participate in can't be approached in the context that a person on the street would use. We make choices in prison. We make our own choices. We are a very definite breed of person. We know what we are going to do, why we are going to do it, what the consequences are, the profit that's involved in it. This is a big part of prison life and all these are choices that only we can make. When we go over to Upjohn or Parke Davis and we volunteer for a test (and that's what it is; they don't recruit, we volunteer), we are informed as to what the test is going to involve. In fact, we are given quite a bit of information about it. We are free to get up and walk out, say we don't want the test. We can start and quit half way through or a quarter of the way through. There's to my mind no coercion involved at all. I can tell them to stuff it. It's not going to inhibit me from future tests. It's not going to inhibit me from telling my friends to go over and volunteer for tests. In fact, Upjohn and Parke Davis, in the minds of most prisoners, is one of the positive aspects of life in the prison. Parke Davis and Upjohn are like an oasis in a desert. You go over there when you want to hide out a little bit, when you want to talk to some people from the streets, when you want to talk to people that are going to treat you half way decent. Now, you may say, "Well, the doctor said that. He said all of these things are in the form of bribes—better conditions, etc." But when you look at prison life, you're looking at something completely different from what you have on the outside, a completely different society. It's turned around. Out in the street, when you walk around, you say, "Well, someone might knock me in the head and take my wallet. Someone may sneak up on me at night by my car and molest me." And you're right, someone might do that. But when you are walking around Jackson Prison, you have 300 jerks up there that you *know* have done something wrong. When you look at the guy next to you, he's in maximum security because he's already done something. You know he's capable of tearing your head off at any moment. So, Upjohn and Parke Davis, far from being coercive, far from being something that would be a detriment to me or my colleagues up there, is looked on almost like a chapel. We go to those tests, and it's pure enjoyment. The little bit of irritation that you might be exposed to on Phase 1 testing is nothing compared to the madness that goes on in the yard. So you take yourself a little vacation and then maybe you can face maybe six or seven more months in the yard or some of these other programs that they have in the prison system. Dr. Levine said it's unskilled labor, being on the tests. That's true. No skill involved. We present our limbs, they put a little ointment on, then we lay around and watch television, and we drink coffee, gamble, swear at one another, whatever convicts do. What you have to understand is that while the labor itself is unskilled, convicts are very skilled when it comes to whimpering and snivelling. We get along real good at that. If my arms itch, I won't sit there quiet, you know. I go tell the guy, "Look man, this is killing me. You gotta do something." We're not bashful at all in that regard.

Also, within the prison system in seven years, from Upjohn and Parke Davis is probably the only time I've received a complete physical, and I mean they go over you from head to toe. I'm sure you all know what's involved in a full physical. There's some things I was a little skeptical about, thought maybe the guy was a little freaky, but he's supposed to know what he's doing. But that's one of the benefits. About every six months or so you get a physical. You know your ticker is in halfway decent shape. You know you're going to be able to hold your own in the yard or whatever, and a lot of guys like it for that reason. They like to go over and participate just because of the physicals. The pay is not commensurate with prison wages; it's better. The money, if you just want to get down to the basics of how much you get, I can go lay over at Parke Davis for a day and they will pay me $20 for a skin test. It takes me a third of a month to earn $20 on my job, and I'm considered skilled labor in prison. I know you don't like that but, I'm a tool and die maker. Four year program, one of the college programs. The pay for the tests is much better than what's paid in the prison. There's been talk among the convicts there at Jackson Prison that at one time Parke Davis and Upjohn did pay even more for the testing and that the system within Michigan did not want more money kicked out by the two facilities because it caused problems within the prison. The problem that this causes is that if you have money in your pocket, someone is going to rob you if they can, and if you don't have money you're going to rob someone else. So, usually when a guy's got a bit of jingle in his jeans, everybody knows about it. When I get broke, I know who I'm gonna borrow from. Prison grapevine is fantastic. You won't believe it. Ten minutes after I'm back today, probably sixty guys in the yard will know it and I'll be getting a thousand questions when I walk out.

Anyway, there's a lot of questions I'd like to answer concerning the testing; I'd like you to be just as forward as you want. Before anybody asks me, I'm doing 30–50 years. That's my sentence, so anybody who had that question on the tip of their tongue, that's it. Don't ask me what for because I won't tell you. At this time if anybody has any questions, I'll be glad to answer.

Q: What do prisoners buy with the money?

A: The prisoners (I'm not used to calling us prisoners) we have two stores. We have a resident store which sells coffee, canned goods, all the things you would buy in a supermarket. We have a resident annex which sells clothes, television sets, radios, tape decks, tapes, socks, underwear, anything that you might find at K-Marts. Not all of the items, but the approved items that will not constitute a security risk in the prison. The prices are generally what you would pay on the street. I think we get a break on cigarettes and coffee. Anybody that smokes can get cigarettes a little cheaper and coffee maybe a little bit cheaper. Tax is eliminated. We don't pay tax. But those are the items that are available. Shoes can be ordered out of a catalogue—we have one vendor and you can order from that vendor only. If you have visits, your people can send you sneakers and it's limited to that. Basically, that's what the money is spent for, other than gambling, dope, etc.

Q: When I visited there, I heard that a lot of people think that the black prisoners are especially exploited. When I visited there, the black prisoners told us that two thirds of the prisoners there were black and yet only one third of the research subjects were black. They said that was because the white people are in control of the subject selection, white prisoners and white guards, and they discriminate against the blacks. They don't let them be research subjects. Is that still the case?

A: Okay, the testing that is done naturally is picked by Parke Davis and Upjohn. The prison, the guards, and the officers up front at the control center, the lieutenants, the captains, the warden, and so on, really have nothing to do with the subjects that are picked for testing. The only time that they will intervene on a test is if one of the subjects constitutes a security risk. They give a list, and it says "X amount of subjects", usually name, number and lock, are on that list. The list is screened, and they may send a memo back to Parke Davis or Upjohn saying that this man cannot participate on the test because he constitutes a security risk for a certain reason. We don't want him over there at this time. The prison population is predominantly black. Seventy percent of Jackson Prison in the maximum security area, the inside, the central complex, is black. Consequently, it's the whites, the Chicanos, and the Indians who are the minorities in Jackson Prison. The black population by and large runs things in the North Yard, the South Yard, the gymnasium, etc. Most of the workers, the guys that work over at Parke Davis and Upjohn are black, the ones that do all maintenance over there, etc. I couldn't get a job at Parke Davis if I wanted one, and it's one of the better paying jobs in the institution. I wouldn't be able to say and I couldn't say whether or not the choice is prejudiced. It well may be. But most of the black guys I know have participated on the studies, and you've got one of them in the case report, the one with the messed up head. He's a good friend of mine. The tests that they can participate on, they participate on. Usually, like they have one coming up now on cough syrup—they'll be participating on that test. The one that I'm on, because of the skin pigmentation, they can't test with black subjects. So I think it's really determined by the test. My experience with the people at Parke Davis and Upjohn is that they don't exhibit to my mind too much prejudice. They seem to me like they are pretty open and accommodating to anybody that comes over.

Q: How do you know about a project that is coming up? How are you included?

A: Grapevine. A lot of times we know about a test before the guys that work over there. There's guys—they have people working at the facilities in Kalamazoo and they'll come in the yard and say, "Hey, there's a new hair test coming down. It's a 120 day walk-in." And the guys'll be in the block shaving their head bald to get on the test. Usually the test that you are going to volunteer for is determined by how much money is involved or a lay-in. The guys like to lay-in. The test that I'm on is called a walk-in test. I go over three times a week, you know, and they read the patches on my arms and they determine whether or not the ointment is helping it. They put another patch on, or they say 24 hours off, and I split. The guys like the ones where they can go over and put their legs up and drink coffee and watch color television, you know, all that kind of thing. If you can get out of the mainstream of the prison population for a while, that's what you do, and that's what Parke Davis and Upjohn offer.

. . .

Q: Are you aware of the risk? Do they inform you of the risks, and have you ever refused an experiment? If not, where would you draw the line? Where would you in fact refuse?

A: I'll answer the last part first. I will not take anything internally. That's where I draw the line. I'm not swallowing anything that Parke Davis or Upjohn gives me, or anyone else, for that matter. In fact, when I go to the infirmary, I don't want to swallow anything they give me, either. And the worst place to swallow anything is in the mess hall.

So, would you restate the first part of your question?

Q: Do they inform you of the risks?

A: Always. You always know what the risk is. And in Phase I testing . . . . the risk is minimal. I'm probably experiencing right now on a Phase I test the most severe reaction that anyone's ever experienced, and it's not from the medication, it's from the tape.

Q: You have refused tests, then?

A: I have refused tests when they involved any medication internally. And that includes cough syrup or cough drops; anything that I gotta put in my gib and swallow.

NOTES

1. The regulations proposed by HEW (now HHS) in 1978 that were excerpted in the *Bailey* opinion would have banned all nontherapeutic research on prisoners. On May 5, 1978, the Food and Drug Administration (FDA) proposed comparable regulations to govern all clinical investigations submitted to FDA. 43 Fed. Reg. 19,417.

Shortly before the FDA regulations were to go into effect on June 1, 1981, four prisoners in the State Prison of Southern Michigan at Jackson filed a law suit alleging that the ban violated their constitutional rights. The effective date of the ban was then stayed until after the law suit was resolved. 46 Fed.Reg. 18,951 (March 27, 1981). In July 1981, FDA announced that it was reconsidering the ban and that it would therefore extend the stay until final action was taken on a reproposal. 46 Fed.Reg. 35,085.

On December 18, 1981, FDA reproposed regulations governing research on prisoners. 46 Fed.Reg. 61,666. The reproposal would permit research on prisoners so long as the conditions in the prison meet the standards recommended in 1977 by the National Commission for the Protection of Human Subjects of Biomedical and Behavioral Research. 42 Fed.Reg. 3076 (1977). According to the FDA, sponsors of proposed research would be required to establish: (1) that the research serves an important social or scientific need and the reasons for using prisoners are compelling, (2) that the involvement of prisoners in this type of research satisfies conditions of equity, and (3) that prison conditions permit voluntary and informed consent. Sponsors of proposed research would have the burden of establishing that the research meets each of these conditions. FDA investigators might, however, be sent to the sites of proposed research to assist the IRB in determining whether the National Commission's requirements have been met.

The IRB would make the determination whether the requirements have been met, after consulting with the Research Involving Human Subjects Committee, an ethical review committee established by the agency (see FDA Staff Manual Guide, 2111.3), whose members include agency officials and members of the public.

The FDA has taken no final action as of May 1984 on the reproposal.

2. There are other categories of vulnerable subjects that have not been singled out by the HHS regulations for special protection. See, e.g., the regulations governing research on the institutionalized mentally disabled that were proposed in 1978 but have never been finalized. 43 Fed.Reg. 53,950 (1978). Should the institutionalized mentally disabled be singled out for protection? Elderly subjects? Poor subjects?

3. Assume you are a member of an IRB. You are asked to approve research to test whether a particular drug is helpful in treating alcoholism. The research protocol submitted proposes to test the drug on a control group of nonalcoholic persons, and on a group of persons determined to be suffering from "alcohol dementia." With alcohol dementia, you learn, there is global intellectual decline characterized by deficits in abstracting ability and problem solving. What additional safeguards, if any, would you want the researcher to meet to ensure that the interests of the persons suffering from alcohol dementia are safeguarded? Would you require the researcher to limit his study to those who have had a legal guardian appointed (and then only if the legal guardian consents to the participation)? Would you further limit the amount of risk to which the persons suffering from alcohol dementia could be exposed even with the permission of their guardian? Cf. the regulations governing research on children, Ch. 6, Sec. C.3., supra. Even

when parents consent, the research can not pose more than a "minor increase over minimal risk" unless the consent of the Secretary of HHS is also obtained.

E. THE PROPER ROLE FOR EXPERIMENTATION ON ANIMALS

LEROY WALTERS, RESEARCH INVOLVING ANIMALS

in Contemporary Issues in Bioethics
569–570 (T. Beauchamp, L. Walters eds. 1982).

Perhaps the first question to be clarified in any discussion of animal research is: Which animals are to be included within the scope of consideration? The books and articles on the ethics of animal research have devoted surprisingly little attention to this question. One can usually infer from these writings that nonhuman mammals—such as monkeys, dogs, and rats—are to be included in the protected group. Indeed, Christina Hoff explicitly refers to "mammals and other highly organized creatures." A somewhat broader class would be all vertebrates, that is, mammals plus birds, reptiles, amphibians, and fish. Peter Singer's essay cites statistics on the extent of research involving vertebrates. Not included in these statistics, of course, are numerous other categories of animals such as protozoa (for example, paramecia), flatworms, shellfish, or insects. In the discussion which follows, it is assumed that the term "animals" refers to nonhuman vertebrates, although the question of research involving invertebrates may also deserve ethical analysis in its own right.

Two primary issues can be identified in the animal research debate: (1) the consequences of the research and (2) the moral status of animals. Proponents of animal research usually advance arguments that appeal rather straightforwardly to the principle of beneficence. The weak form of the argument can be formulated as follows: Good consequences are achieved through the use of animals in research. A somewhat stronger claim is that at least some of these good consequences can be achieved *only* by means of animal research; that is, no alternative (nonhuman) means to the desired end exists.

The empirical background for the strong claim by proponents of animal research is that intact, live animals respond to research interventions in complex ways that cannot be simulated through any other research technique involving nonanimal systems. For example, administering a drug to a dog or presenting a learning stimulus to a rat may produce a complex reaction that affects multiple physiological systems. At present, such a response simply cannot be duplicated through the manipulation of cells in tissue culture or even through the use of sophisticated computer simulations. In theory at least, human subjects could be substituted for animal subjects and would be capable of producing the same kinds of complex response. However, given the painful, invasive, and even lethal character of much animal research, the use of humans in such research would itself pose serious ethical problems.

Critics of animal research can also appeal to the principle of beneficence. In response to the weak form of the proponents' argument, the critics urge that alternatives to animal research be more vigorously explored and more actively employed. . . . The strong form of the proponents' argument presents a more formidable challenge, however. If animal research is the only means for achieving a desirable consequence, then the critic can respond by insisting on a conscientious weighing of research benefits against harms to animals. Indeed, reformers like Singer . . . recommend the use of precisely this kind of calculus.

A complicating factor in any such effort to assess consequences is the problem of animal sentience, or sensitivity to pain. The notion of sentience raises both conceptual and empirical issues. A broad construal of the concept of sentience might conceivably include primitive "avoidance" reactions to aversive stimuli, for example, a paramecium's response to a toxic chemical or a rabbit's reflex reaction to cold. However, a narrower construal of sentience might require the presence of anticipatory or retrospective psychological states, such as fear or regret. Even if one were able to agree on a definition of sentience, there would remain the formidable empirical problem of measuring exactly how much pain is being inflicted upon, or in some sense being experienced by, animal subjects. . . .

The second major issue in the animal research debate is the moral status of animals. This issue closely parallels the problem of personhood and the question of fetal status. In an influential essay, Joel Feinberg has argued that animals can have rights because they have, or can have, interests. Among the rights ascribed to animals by Feinberg is the right to be treated humanely. In his view, such treatment is owed to animals as their due and therefore involves the principle of justice. . . . Singer prefers to avoid the language of rights in discussing animals but nonetheless asserts that humans have an obligation not to inflict suffering on animals. Other philosophers—including Thomas Aquinas, Descartes, and Immanuel Kant—have ascribed no moral status whatever to animals. Descartes regarded animals as mere machines, while Kant argued that because animals lack rationality they need not be treated as ends in themselves.

Kant's position points to the difficult problem of relating the descriptive properties of animals, such as consciousness, to their moral status. For example, Hoff considers whether humans with extremely limited intellectual capacities—for example, severely retarded individuals—should be involved in painful or fatal research, as animals often are. Her negative answer is based on the premise that we cannot "safely permit anyone to decide which human beings fall short of worthiness." To Singer, positions such as Hoff's are discriminatory. In his words, "Our respect for the interests of [infants and mentally retarded humans], and our neglect of the members of other species with equal or superior capacities, is mere 'speciesism'—a prejudice in favor of 'our own kind' that is analogous to, and no more justifiable than, racism."

**PETER SINGER,
ANIMAL EXPERIMENTATION: PHILOSOPHICAL
PERSPECTIVES**

in Encyclopedia of Bioethics
79–81 (W.T. Reich ed. 1978).

Although the practice of conducting scientific experiments on living animals, vivisection, goes back at least to Galen (A.D. 130?–200?), the modern period of experimentation stems from the seventeenth century, when scientific inquiries were beginning to be made in many fields. This was the period of the philosopher and scientist René Descartes (1596–1650). For Descartes and the physiologists who declared themselves his followers, cutting open a fully conscious animal posed no ethical problem, since, Descartes said, animals are mere machines, more complex than clocks but no more capable of feeling pain.

If this convenient view of the nature of nonhuman animals is rejected, however, a serious ethical problem about experimenting on animals does arise, because the infliction of suffering and death on an animal seems, in itself, to be an evil. On the other hand, supporters of vivisection argue that such experiments provide great benefits for humans. Animal experimentation, therefore, raises the issue of whether the end justifies the means (an issue also raised by experiments on humans) and in addition forces us to consider what place nonhuman animals have in our ethical deliberations.

THE NATURE AND EXTENT OF
EXPERIMENTS ON ANIMALS

The number of experiments performed on animals has increased remarkably in the last hundred years. The present extent of experimentation, worldwide, is impossible to ascertain with accuracy, since few countries compile the necessary statistics. In the United Kingdom, according to an annual statement published by the Home Office, more than five million experiments "calculated to cause pain" are performed on live vertebrate animals every year. This figure is low compared to that of the United States, where the number of animals used yearly has been reliably estimated as being in excess of sixty million. Other countries using large numbers of animals include Russia, Japan, West Germany, and France. The worldwide tendency of smaller nations to follow Western scientific techniques has meant that there are now very few nations in which animal experiments are not being performed.

The animals most often used are mice and rats, but dogs, cats, and monkeys are also used in large numbers. It is commonly assumed that animals are experimented upon only for important medical research, but closer scrutiny reveals that only a minority of experiments can be classified as "medical" at all. Many of the most painful experiments are carried out by psychologists and are intended to test theories about learning, punishment, maternal deprivation, and so on. Millions of animals are used to test foodstuffs, pesticides, industrial products, weapons, and even nonessential items like cosmetics, shampoos, and food-coloring agents.

Many of these experiments involve severe and lasting pain for the animals. To test the safety of a foodstuff or cosmetic, the substance is fed in concentrated doses to a group of animals, until a level is found at which half of the sample dies. This means that most of the animals become very sick before some die and others pull through. The dose at which half of the sample dies is supposed to give an indication of the toxicity of the substance, but, since different species have different tolerances, it is at best a very rough guide to the safety of the product for humans (thalidomide, for instance, was tested on several species of animals before being released to humans, and no deformities were found).

. . .

On the other hand, it is true that many experiments involve little or no suffering for the animals involved. This may be because the experiment is of a harmless nature (such as running a rat through a maze) or because the animal is totally anesthetized during the operation and killed painlessly afterward.

Moreover, some animal experimentation has been of considerable benefit to humans. In such areas as the identification of necessary vitamins and minerals and the development of new surgical techniques and new drugs, discoveries have been made through animal experimentation that could not have been made, or would have been much more difficult to make, had animals not been used. Diabetes is often cited as an example of a disease that has lost its terror through a cure first developed on animals.

LEGISLATION

Laws governing experiments on animals vary from country to country, but in no country does the law prohibit outright painful experiments or require that the experiment be of sufficient importance to outweigh the pain inflicted.

The first law specifically regulating experiments was the British Cruelty to Animals Act of 1876. This law which has never been amended, requires the use of an anesthetic, except where "insensibility cannot be produced without necessarily frustrating the object of such experiments"; but neither the statute itself nor the officials who administer it make any attempt to assess whether the object of the experiment is itself worth the pain caused. Clearly, a psychologist wishing to test the effects of electric shock on the behavior of dogs cannot anesthetize the animals without frustrating the object of his experiment. Even in toxicity tests of cosmetics anesthetics are not used, because it is thought that they might distort the result of the test. Therefore such experiments are permitted in Britain.

In the United States, the Animal Welfare Act of 1970 sets standards for the housing, transportation, and handling of animals; but the Act does not control the nature of the experiments performed, except to the extent of requiring research facilities to lodge a report stating that, when painful experiments were performed without the use of pain-relieving drugs, this was necessary to achieve the objectives of the research project. Again, no attempt is made to assess the importance of these objectives, and in fact one section of the law specifically disavows any intention of interfering with the design or performance of research or experimentation. Moreover, since the law is a federal one, facilities not receiving federal funds and not involved in interstate commerce do not have to comply.

A 1972 West German law requires the use of alternatives to experiments on animals whenever possible. Amendments to the same effect have been proposed in Britain, Denmark, and Holland, but it remains to be seen how effective the West German provision will be. Much depends on what is deemed to be a "possible alternative." Many countries, including France, Spain, Brazil, and Japan still have no legislation regulating experiments on animals.

THE CASE FOR EXPERIMENTING ON ANIMALS

The simplest argument for the permissibility of experiments on animals is the Cartesian one: animals do not suffer, and so there is nothing wrong with experimenting upon them. But both common sense and the great majority of experts agree that mammals and probably other vertebrate animals, at least, are capable of suffering both physical pain and some kinds of emotional distress, such as fear.

If animals do suffer, how is their suffering to be justified? The usual justification offered is that the suffering of animals is outweighed by the benefits, for humans, of the discoveries made by the use of animals. Sometimes, however, it is said that the goal of increasing our understanding of the universe is sufficient justification.

Behind these justifications may lie one of a variety of philosophical positions. For instance, it may be said that, as related in Genesis, God has given man "dominion" over the other animals to use as man pleases. Combined with other theological notions, such as the idea that man, alone of all animals, has an immortal soul, this idea has been influential throughout the Christian world. But it can also be turned the other way: as long ago as 1713, Alexander Pope argued against cruel experiments on the grounds that man's dominion requires him to play the role of the good shepherd, caring for his flock.

It has also been said, by writers as diverse as St. Thomas Aquinas, Immanuel Kant, and D.G. Ritchie, that animals are not "ends in themselves" or that they have no rights. In support of this it is alleged that the status of a being that is an "end in itself," or has rights, belongs only to a being that is rationale, capable of autonomous action, or a moral agent. Whereas humans satisfy this requirement, animals, it is alleged, do not. A difficulty with this argument is that *some* humans come no closer to satisfying the requirement than the animals experimented upon. Mentally retarded human beings, for instance, may be no more rational than a dog; yet we do not consider that they are entirely devoid of rights. Other writers have denied that rationality, autonomy, or moral agency is required before we can grant that a being has rights. Still others have taken the approach that we have obligations not to inflict suffering, irrespective of whether we can meaningfully attribute rights to the being in question.

A utilitarian case for animal experimentation is based on the idea that more suffering is alleviated by it than is caused by it. The classical utilitarian writers, however, all accepted that a utilitarian must take *all* suffering—human and animal—into consideration, and this makes the factual claim that animal experimentation relieves more suffering than it causes more difficult to defend. Nevertheless, there are probably some experiments—those that do not involve much suffering for the animals and promise major benefits for humans or animals—that can be defended on this ground.

Finally, defenders of experimentation often accuse their opponents of inconsistency in objecting to the deaths of animals in laboratories while continuing to participate in the practice of rearing and killing animals for food. This argument holds no validity for antivivisectionists who are also vegetarians. Even when directed against someone who does eat meat, it hardly amounts to a positive defense of experimentation.

THE CASE AGAINST EXPERIMENTING ON ANIMALS

Opponents of experiments on animals tend to divide into two groups: absolute abolitionists and reformers. Absolute abolitionists usually rely on the principle that the end does not justify the means. To inflict pain and death on an innocent being is, they maintain, always wrong. They point out that we do not think the possibility of advancing scientific knowledge justifies us in taking healthy human beings and inflicting painful deaths upon them; similarly, they say, the infliction of suffering on animals cannot be justified by reference to future benefits for human or other animals.

The weakness of the absolutist position is that, when the end is sufficiently important, we do sometimes think otherwise unacceptable means are justifiable if there is no other way of achieving the end. We do not like invasions of privacy, but we countenance telephone taps on suspected criminals. Similarly, if the prospects of finding a cure for cancer depended upon a single experiment, should we have any doubt about its justification?

Reformers usually take a more utilitarian line. They concede that some experiments may be justifiable but contend that most are not, because the experiments bring certain suffering and death to animals with no likelihood of significant benefits. In reply to the general argument that experiments on animals benefit humans, the reformers demand that any such benefits be sufficient to offset the costs to the animal subjects; they urge that every experiment come under close prior scrutiny to determine if the benefits are likely to outweigh the costs. Were this done, they maintain, only a small fraction of the experiments now performed would be seen to be justifiable.

Reformers claim that alternative methods, not involving animals, could replace many of the experiments now being carried out on animals. Techniques using tissue cultures, for instance, have already replaced animals in the production of certain vaccines, and opponents of animal experimentation suggest that other alternative methods would be developed more rapidly if they were to receive government support.

Although the absolutists and reformers disagree in important respects, they are united in seeking to narrow the ethical gulf that now separates humans from other animals in our conventional morality. This may be the most philosophically interesting question raised by the vivisection controversy, and it has implications that go beyond experimentation to our treatment of animals in general.

Chapter Seven

DEATH AND DYING

A. DEFINING DEATH

1. SHOULD WE DEFINE?

SMITH v. SMITH

Supreme Court of Arkansas, 1958.
229 Ark. 579, 317 S.W.2d 275.

HARRIS, CHIEF JUSTICE.

Hugh Smith and Lucy Coleman Smith, his wife, lived at Siloam Springs, Arkansas. They had no children. On April 22, 1947, Mrs. Smith executed a will leaving all property to her husband. On November 3, 1952, Mr. Smith executed a will leaving all property to his wife. On April 19, 1957, while riding together in an automobile, the Smiths had an accident. Hugh Smith was dead when assistance arrived at the scene, and Lucy Coleman Smith was unconscious, and remained so until her death seventeen days later on May 6th. Clint Smith, appellant herein, and brother of the deceased, was named administrator, with the will annexed, of the estate of Hugh Smith. A.L. Smith, appellee herein, was named administrator, with the will annexed, of the estate of Lucy Coleman Smith. . . . The administrator of the Hugh Smith estate filed a petition asking for a construction of the two wills. A.L. Smith, administrator of the estate of Lucy Coleman Smith, demurred to the petition, setting out that the petition with exhibits thereto, showed on its face that the two wills were not ambiguous, that appellant had no right or interest in the estate of Lucy Coleman Smith that would entitle him to a construction of her will; that the petition showed that the estate of Hugh Smith, under the terms of his will, became the property of Lucy Coleman Smith at his death, and since her decease, had become the property of her heirs, named in the petition; that the petition set forth no facts which would authorize the consolidation of the cases for the purpose of construing the wills of Hugh Smith and Lucy Coleman Smith and asked that the demurrer be sustained and the petition dismissed. . . . On hearing, the court sustained the demurrers, and dismissed the petition of appellant for construction of the wills. From such order, comes this appeal.

. . .

The petition for construction contains a quite unusual and unique allegation. We quote:

"That the said Hugh Smith and his wife, Lucy Coleman Smith, were in an automobile accident on the 19th day of April, 1957, said accident being instantly fatal to each of them at the same time, although the doctors maintained a vain hope of survival and made every effort to revive and resuscitate said Lucy Coleman Smith until May 6th, 1957, when it was finally determined by the attending physicians that their hope of resuscitation and possible restoration of human life to the said Lucy Coleman Smith was entirely vain, and

"That as a matter of modern medical science, your petitioner alleges and states, and will offer the Court competent proof that the said Hugh Smith, deceased, and said Lucy Coleman Smith, deceased, lost their power to will at the same instant, and that their demise as earthly human beings occurred at the same time in said automobile accident, neither of them ever regaining any consciousness whatsoever."

. . .

. . . It is pointed out that the petition for construction of the wills . . . was disposed of by demurrer, which means that the facts alleged in the petition are admitted to be true; that if such facts are true, a cause of action is stated, and appellant accordingly should be permitted to proceed with his proof. Let it first be observed that in reading appellant's petition, as a whole, the assertion of the death of Lucy Coleman Smith appears to be predicated on the theory that such demise occurred "as a matter of medical science", . . . Black's Law Dictionary, 4th Edition, page 488, defines death as follows:

"The cessation of life; the ceasing to exist; defined by physicians as a total stoppage of the circulation of the blood, and a cessation of the animal and vital functions consequent thereon, such as respiration, pulsation, etc., ..."

Admittedly, this condition did not exist, and as a matter of fact, it would be too much of a strain on credulity for us to believe any evidence offered to the effect that Mrs. Smith was dead, scientifically or otherwise, unless the conditions set out in the definition existed. The trial court was entirely justified in sustaining the demurrers. . . . [W]e take judicial notice that one breathing, though unconscious, is not dead.

. . .

Accordingly, the order sustaining the demurrers, and dismissing the petition for the construction of the wills is affirmed.

NOTE

The standard used by the court in Smith v. Smith to determine whether death has occurred has been called into question by advances in medical technology that permit artificial maintenance of respiratory and circulatory functions. The first significant challenge to that standard occurred in 1968 with the publication of a report of an ad hoc committee of the Harvard Medical School. That report suggested that death occurs when an individual sustains irreversible coma as a result of permanent brain damage. The committee argued that irreversible coma could be diagnosed by satisfying the following three conditions which are generally known as the "Harvard criteria":

1. Unreceptivity and Unresponsitivity—the patient exhibits a total unawareness to externally applied stimuli and inner need and complete unresponsiveness even when exposed to intensely painful stimuli.

2. No Movements or Breathing—total absence of spontaneous breathing or muscular movements or response to stimuli.

3. No Reflexes—absence of elicitable reflexes, e.g., the pupil of the eye is fixed and dilated and does not respond to bright light from a direct source.

The ad hoc committee further recommended that a flat electroencephalogram be used to confirm the absence of discernible central nervous system activity. All tests are to be repeated in twenty-four hours. Ad Hoc Committee of the Harvard Medical School to Examine the Definition of Brain Death, A Definition of Irreversible Coma, 205 J.A.M.A. 337 (1968).

The "Harvard criteria" have proved reliable over time although they have been subject to criticism; proposals have been made to correct deficiencies. See President's Commission, Defining Death 25–29 (1981).

The uncertainty and confusion surrounding the question of what is the appropriate standard to use in determining death resulted in many proposals to redefine it. See, e.g., Capron and Kass, A Statutory Definition of the Standards for Determining Human Death: An Appraisal and a Proposal, 121 Pa.L.Rev. 87 (1972); President's Commission, Defining Death (1981). Such proposals are challenged by Roger Dworkin in the selection that follows.

Do you agree with Dworkin that a unitary definition of death is not needed for legal purposes? Even if a unitary definition of death is not a legal necessity, is such a definition nevertheless desirable?

ROGER B. DWORKIN, DEATH IN CONTEXT

48 Ind.L.J. 623, 628–631, 638–639 (1973).

The effort devoted to defining death is wasted at best, counterproductive at worst. The modern writers on death have failed to ask the most basic question about the death definition problem: What difference does it make whether somebody is dead? That question places the issue of death into the only posture in which it can be of relevance to the law—the posture of context or consequences. Whatever may be the needs of the philosopher or the ethicist, the lawyer needs only to know what consequences follow upon a given determination. Only if we are persuaded that one definition of death will *always* lead to the correct resolution of legal problems do we need to search for such a definition.

. . .

As a practical matter the questions of whether and when death has occurred control many legal problems. Obviously, all wrongful death actions, whether or not they involve special situations such as transplantation or cessation of extraordinary care can be brought only after death. Similarly, death is a prerequisite to a successful prosecution for homicide, in many states the time of death is critically important because a murder conviction can only be obtained if death occurs within a year and a day of the fatal blow. . . .

Numerous property and wealth transmission issues raise death questions: When may an estate be probated? When may property of a testate or intestate decedent be distributed? When does a life estate end? When does property pass to a surviving joint tenant? When do life insurance benefits become payable and health insurance benefits cease to accrue? When may property escheat? When do agents, conservators, attorneys and trustees lose their authority to act, and when do banks become liable for admitting persons to safe deposit boxes and paying money out of accounts? When is an estate tax due? When is a gift within three years of death so that it may be said to be in contemplation of death? And perhaps most importantly, who died first in the event that persons with interests in one another's estates perished in a common disaster?

Status relationships often turn on whether someone is dead. For example, whether a person who remarries is a bigamist and whether the remarriage is valid may both turn on whether the prior spouse is or is deemed to be alive or dead. Whether one may be a voter or elected to an office may depend on whether and when he died. In addition crimes besides homicide and bigamy may depend on someone's being dead or alive. Coroners' obligations and the mandatory contents of death certificates require determinations of the time of death. And occasional unusual statutes make other matters turn on whether and when someone died, and even in one situation, on whether a physician thinks his patient is "at the point of death."

It would be odd indeed if all these different situations were susceptible to resolution by one definition of death. They involve different consequences and resolutions of different policy questions. In all of them death is not important in its own right but is merely a shorthand description of when certain events are to occur. When everyone agreed on what death meant, the shorthand might have been convenient, although even then different meanings attached to the notion of death in different contexts. Now that agreement no longer exists and that an awakened sense of medical progress may suggest continuing evolution in our understanding of death, any potential convenience has been lost. . . .

. . .

. . . [T]he case in favor of defining death comes down to a feeling that the lack of definition offends a sense of neatness in allowing the law to use a term whose meaning no one knows. I agree that it is confusing and aesthetically displeasing to define "death" as meaning different things in different contexts. However, in view of the manifold advantages of avoiding definition, a different route to aesthetic satisfaction should be pursued. The simplest solution lies in recognizing that as there is no need to define death, so too there is no need for the law to use the term at all. . . . What is important . . . are the consequences, not the conclusory determination. The law must be able to determine when each consequence is to occur. Confusion only arises if the word "death" is used to set the time and if it has several meanings. No confusion relevant to this discussion inheres in legal rules such as: "No person's heart may be removed from his body until it has stopped beating (with or without mechanical assistance);" or "Any person who, for the purpose of depriving another of his ability to function as an integrated conscious being, causes another person to lose that ability (or to lose the functional ability of his brain) shall be punished (by the most severe sanction available in this jurisdiction)." The confusion lies in the use of the concept of death. If the law stops using the concept and seeks only to describe the circumstances under which given consequences are to flow, we shall be able to avoid confusion, face problems head-on with the hope of resolving them correctly and, of course, obviate the need for the tidiness of a definition. Such an approach would also relieve us of the need to distinguish the question of whether a person is dead from the question whether to allow him to die. Neither question has meaning for the law, which only needs to know whether a defendant may be convicted of the most serious crime, a doctor may remove a heart or an estate may be probated etc. The concept of death may remain useful for philosophy, religion and literature, but for the law placing death in context should prove the mortality of death.

NOTES

1. A definition of death based on brain death criteria clearly facilitates organ transplantation, because chances of successful transplantation are increased by the

use of viable organs which are nourished by intact respiratory and circulatory systems. Kidneys obtained from those declared dead using brain death criteria and sustained by artificial means are virtually indistinguishable in terms of successful transplantation rates from kidneys obtained from living donors. Many physicians are reluctant, however, to remove organs from patients who are dead by brain death criteria but whose hearts continue to beat, albeit with artificial support, because they fear civil or criminal liability. See, e.g., New York City Health and Hospitals Corp. v. Sulsona, 81 Misc.2d 1002, 367 N.Y.S.2d 686 (Sup.Ct.1975); Tucker v. Lower, No. 831 (Richmond, Va., L. & Eq.Ct., May 23, 1972) discussed in Capron and Kass, A Statutory Definition of the Standards for Determining Human Death: An Appraisal and A Proposal, 121 U.Pa.L.Rev. 87, 98–100. Moreover, the Uniform Anatomical Gift Act, 8 U.L.A. 15 (1968), which establishes procedures for organ donation and has been adopted by 50 states and the District of Columbia, does not contain a definition of death. Sec. 7(b) does provide that "the time of death shall be determined by a physician who attends the donor at his death, or, if none, the physician who certifies the death," but the act is silent with respect to the standard by which a physician is to determine the time of death. Most commentators have been careful to point out that organ transplantation concerns alone are not sufficient to justify a revised or special purpose definition of death. See, e.g., Capron and Kass, supra, at 106–108 (1972); President's Commission, Defining Death 23–24 (1981).

2. A few courts have considered the impact of brain based criteria of death on criminal and civil law. In Commonwealth v. Golston, 373 Mass. 249, 366 N.E.2d 744 (1977), the defendant argued that he was not able to show that the victim would have lived for a year and a day after the fatal blow was struck because the doctors with permission of the family removed the victim from the respirator. The Supreme Judicial Court of Massachusetts held that the trial court "correctly accepted the medical concept of 'brain death' for purposes of the law of homicide." The court's holding was limited, however, to criminal cases. See also Lovato v. District Court, 198 Colo. 419, 601 P.2d 1072 (1979) (en banc) (Colorado Supreme Court adopted Uniform Death Act as alternative definition to cessation of respiration and circulation). Courts do not necessarily have to adopt brain-based criteria of death in order to hold defendants responsible for committing homicide. Defendants may be held responsible on the grounds that they caused the victim's death. See, e.g., People v. Olson, 59 Ill.App.3d 643, 16 Ill. Dec. 660, 375 N.E.2d 533 (1978); People v. Saldana, 47 Cal.App.3d 954, 121 Cal. Rptr. 243 (1975); State v. Fierro, 124 Ariz. 182, 603 P.2d 74 (1974); State v. Brown, 8 Or.App. 72, 491 P.2d 1193 (1971).

For civil cases updating the common law definition of death, see New York City Health and Hospital Corp. v. Sulsona, 81 Misc.2d 1002, 367 N.Y.S.2d 686 (Sup.Ct.1975) (defining death for purpose of applying New York Anatomical Gift Act); In re Bowman, 94 Wn.2d 407, 617 P.2d 731 (1980) (adopting provisions of Uniform Determination of Death Act).

3. Professor Dworkin's views have been criticized. See Capron, The Purpose of Death: A Reply to Professor Dworkin, 48 Ind.L.J. 640 (1973); President's Commission, Defining Death 60 (1981). Are Professor Dworkin's views of greater relevance to the issue of defining when life begins? See Ch. 8, Sec. A.1., infra.

2. HOW TO DEFINE?

H. TRISTRAM ENGELHARDT, MEDICINE AND THE CONCEPT OF PERSON

in Contemporary Issues in Bioethics
94, 94–99 (T. Beauchamp and L. Walters eds. 1982).

Recent advances in medicine and the biomedical sciences have raised a number of ethical issues that medical ethics or, more broadly, bioethics have treated. Ingredient in such considerations, however, are fundamentally conceptual and ontological issues. To talk of the sanctity of life, for example, presupposes that one knows (1) what life is, and (2) what makes for its sanctity. More importantly, to talk of the rights of persons presupposes that one knows what counts as a person. In this paper I will provide an examination of the concept of person and will argue that the terms "human life" and even "human person" are complex and heterogeneous terms. I will hold that human life has more than one meaning and that there is more than one sense of human person. I will then indicate how the recognition of these multiple meanings has important implications for medicine.

KINDS OF LIFE AND SANCTITY OF LIFE

Whatever is meant by life's being sacred, it is rarely held that all life is equally sacred. Most people would find the life of bacteria, for example, to be less valuable or sacred than the life of fellow humans. . . . Moreover, distinctions are made with respect to humans. Not all human life has the same sanctity. The issue of brain-death, for example, turns on such a distinction. Brain-dead, but otherwise alive, human beings do not have the sanctity of normal adult human beings. That is, the indices of brain-death have been selected in order to measure the death of a person. As a legal issue, it is a question of when a human being ceases to be a person before the law. In a sense, the older definition of death measured the point at which organismic death occurred, when there was a complete cessation of vital functions. The life of the human organism was taken as a necessary condition for being a person, and, therefore, such a definition allowed one to identify cases in which humans ceased to be persons.

The brain-oriented concept of death is more directly concerned with human *personal* life. It makes three presuppositions: (1) that being a person involves more than mere vegetative life, (2) that merely vegetative life may have value but it has no rights, (3) that a sensory-motor organ such as the brain is a necessary condition for the possibility of experience and action in the world, that is, for being a person living in the world. Thus in the absence of the possibility of brain-function, one has the absence of the possibility of personal life—that is, the person is dead. . . . The brain-oriented concept of death is of philosophical significance, for, among other things, it implies a distinction between human biological life and human personal life, between the life of a human organism and the life of a human person. That human biological life continues after brain death is fairly clear: the body continues to circulate blood, the kidneys function; in fact, there is no reason why the organism would not continue to be cross-fertile (e.g. produce viable sperm) and, thus, satisfy yet one more criterion for biological life. Such a body can be a biologically integrated reproductive unit even if the level of integration is very low. And, if such a body is an instance of human biological but not human personal life, then it is open to use merely as a subject of experimentation without the constraints of a second status as a person. . . .

We are brought then to a set of distinctions: first, human life must be distinguished as human personal and human biological life. Not all instances of human biological life are instances of human personal life. Brain-dead (but otherwise alive) human beings, human gametes, cells in human cell cultures, all count as instances of human biological life. Further, not only are some humans not persons, there is no reason to hold that all persons are humans, as the possibility of extraterrestrial self-conscious life suggests.

Second, the concept of the sanctity of life comes to refer in different ways to the value of biological life and the dignity of persons. Probably much that is associated with arguments concerning the sanctity of life really refers to the dignity of the life of persons. In any event, there is no unambiguous sense of being simply "pro-life" or a defender of the sanctity of life—one must decide what sort of life one wishes to defend and on what grounds. To begin with, the morally significant difference between biological and personal life lies in the fact, to use Kant's idiom, that persons are ends in themselves. Rational, self-conscious agents can make claims to treatment as ends in themselves because they can experience themselves, can know that they experience themselves, and can determine and control the circumstances of such experience. Self-conscious agents are self-determining and can claim respect as such. That is, they can claim the right to be respected as free agents. Such a claim is to the effect that self-respect and mutual respect turn on self-determination, on the fact that self-conscious beings are necessary for the existence of a moral order—a kingdom of ends, a community based on mutual self-respect, not force. Only self-conscious agents can be held accountable for their actions and thus be bound together solely in terms of mutual respect of each other's autonomy.

.   .   .

It is only respect for persons in this strict sense that cannot be violated without contradicting the idea of a moral order in the sense of the living with others on the basis of a mutual respect of autonomy. The point to be emphasized is a distinction between value and dignity, between biological life and personal life. These distinctions provide a basis for the differentiation between biological or merely animal life, and personal life, and turn on the rather commonsense criterion of respect being given that which can be respected—that is, blamed or praised. Moral treatment comes to depend, not implausibly, on moral agency. The importance of such distinctions for medicine is that they can be employed in treating medical ethical issues. As arguments, they are attempts to sort out everyday distinctions between moral agents, other animals, and just plain things. They provide a conceptual apparatus based on the meaning of obligations as respect due that which can have obligations.

The distinctions between human biological life and human personal life, and between the value of human biological life and the dignity of human personal life, involve a basic conceptual distinction that modern medical science presses as an issue of practical importance. Medicine after all is not merely the enterprise of preserving human life—if that were the case, medicine would confuse human cell cultures with patients who are persons. In fact, a maximum "to treat patients as persons" presupposes that we do or can indeed know who the persons are. These distinctions focus not only on the newly problematic issue of the definition of death, but on the question of abortion as well: issues that turn on when persons end and when they begin. In the case of the definition of death, one is saying that even though genetic continuity, organic function, and reproductive capability may extend beyond brain death, personal life does not. Sentience in an appropriate embodiment is a necessary condition for being a person. One, thus, finds that persons die when this embodiment is undermined.

With regard to abortion, many have argued similarly that the fetus is not a person, though it is surely an instance of human biological life. Even if the fetus is a human organism that will probably be genetically and organically continuous with a human person, it is not yet such a person. Simply put, fetuses are not rational, self-conscious beings—that is, given a strict definition of persons, fetuses do not qualify as persons. One sees this when comparing talk about dead men with talk about fetuses. When speaking of a dead man, one knows of whom one speaks, the one who died, the person whom one knew before his death. But in speaking of the fetus, one has no such person to whom one can refer. There is not yet a person, a "who," to whom one can refer in the case of the fetus (compare: one can keep promises to dead men but not to men yet unborn). In short, the fetus in no way singles itself out as, or shows itself to be, a person. . . .

. . . By the terms of the argument, infants, as well as fetuses, are not persons—thus, one finds infants as much open to infanticide as fetuses are left open to abortion. The question then is whether one can recoup something for infants or perhaps even for fetuses. . . .

. . .

. . . [T]hough we have sorted out a distinction between the value of human biological life and the dignity of human personal life, this distinction does not do all we want, or rather it may do too much. That is, it goes against an intuitive appreciation of children, even neonates, as not being open to destruction on request. We may not in the end be able to support that intuition, for it may simply be a cultural prejudice; but I will now try to give a reasonable exegesis of its significance.

TWO CONCEPTS OF PERSON

I shall argue in this section that a confusion arises out of a false presupposition that we have only one concept of person: we have at least two concepts (probably many more) of person. I will restrict myself to examining the two that are most relevant here. First, there is the sense of person that we use in identifying moral agents: individual, living bearers of rights and duties. That sense singles out entities who can participate in the language of morals, who can make claims and have those claims respected: the strict sense we have examined above. We would, for example, understand "person" in this sense to be used properly if we found another group of self-conscious agents in the universe and called them persons even if they were not human, though it is a term that usually applies to normal adult humans. This sense of person I shall term the strict sense, one which is used in reference to self-conscious, rational agents. But what of the respect accorded to infants and other examples of non-self-conscious or not-yet-self-conscious human life? How are such entities to be understood?

A plausible analysis can, I believe, be given in terms of a second concept or use of person—a social concept or social role of person that is invoked when certain instances of human biological life are treated as if they were persons strictly, even though they are not. A good example is the mother-child or parent-child relationship in which the infant is treated as a person even though it is not one strictly. That is, the infant is treated as if it had the wants and desires of a person—its cries are treated as a call for food, attention, care, etc., and the infant is socialized, placed within a social structure, the family, and becomes a child. The shift is from merely biological to social significance. The shift is made on the basis that the infant is a human and is able to engage in a minimum of social interaction. With regard to the latter point, severely anencephalic infants may not qualify for the role *person* just as brain-dead adults would fail to qualify; both lack the ability to engage in minimal social interaction. This use of person is, after all, one employed with instances of human biological life that are enmeshed in social roles as if they were persons. Further, one finds a difference between the biological mother-fetus relation and the social mother-child relation. The first relation can continue whether or not there is social recognition of the fetus, the second cannot. The mother-child relation is essentially a social practice.

This practice can be justified as a means of preserving trust in families, of nurturing important virtues of care and solicitude towards the weak, and of assuring the healthy development of children. Further, it has a special value because it is difficult to determine specifically when in human ontogeny persons strictly emerge. Socializing infants into the role *person* draws the line conservatively. Humans do not become persons strictly until some time after birth. Moreover, there is a considerable value in protecting anything that looks and acts in a reasonably human fashion, especially when it falls within an established human social role as infants do within the role *child*. This ascription of the role *person* constitutes a social practice that allows the rights of a person to be imputed to forms of human life that can engage in at least a minimum of social interaction. The interest is in guarding anything that could reasonably play the role *person* and thus to strengthen the social position of persons generally.

The social sense of person appears as well to structure the treatment of the senile, the mentally retarded, and the otherwise severely mentally infirm. Though they are not moral agents, persons strictly, they are treated as if they were persons. The social sense of person identifies their place in a social relationship with persons strictly. It is, in short, a practice that gives to instances of human biological life the status of persons. Unlike persons strictly, who are bearers of both rights and duties, persons in the social sense have rights but no duties. That is, they are not morally responsible agents, but are treated with respect (i.e., rights are imputed to them) in order to establish a practice of considerable utility to moral agents: a society where kind treatment of the infirm and weak is an established practice. The central element of the utility of this practice lies in the fact that it is often difficult to tell when an individual is a person strictly (i.e., how senile need one be in order no longer to be able to be a person strictly), and persons strictly might need to fear concerning their treatment (as well as the inadvertent mistreatment of other persons strictly) were such a practice not established. The social sense of person is a way of treating certain instances of human life in order to secure the life of persons strictly.

. . .

It should be stressed that the social sense of person is primarily a utilitarian construct. A person in this sense is not a person strictly, and hence not an unqualified object of respect. Rather, one treats certain instances of human life as persons for the good of those individuals who are persons strictly. As a consequence, exactly where one draws the line between persons in the social sense and merely human biological life is not crucial as long as the integrity of persons strictly is preserved. Thus there is a somewhat arbitrary quality about the distinction between fetuses and infants. One draws a line where the practice of treating human life as human personal life is practical and useful. Birth, including the production of a viable fetus through an abortion procedure, provides a somewhat natural line at which to begin to treat human biological life as human personal life. One might retort, Why not include fetuses as persons in a social sense? The answer is, Only if there are good reasons to do so in terms of utility. One would have to measure the utility of abortions for the convenience of women and families, for the prevention of the birth of infants with serious genetic diseases, and for the control of population growth against whatever increased goods would come from treating fetuses as persons. . . .

One is thus left with at least two concepts of person. On the one hand, persons strictly can and usually do identify themselves as such— they are self-conscious, rational agents, respect for whom is part of valuing freedom, assigning blame and praise, and understanding obligation. That is, one's duty to respect persons strictly is the core of morality itself. The social concept of person is, on the other hand, more mediate, it turns on central values but is not the same as respect for the dignity of persons strictly. It allows us to value highly certain but not all instances of human biological life, without confusing that value with the dignity of persons strictly. That is, we can maintain the distinction between human biological and human personal life. We must recognize, though, that some human biological life is treated as human personal life even though it does not involve the existence of a person in the strict sense.

NOTE

The concept of personhood is intimately related to issues raised throughout this book. In addition to the role it plays in concerns about the definition of death and prolongation of life, the concept of personhood arises whenever there are questions about what members of the human species should be considered persons. See discussions of abortion and the beginning of life, Ch. 8, Sec. A.1., infra; human experimentation, Ch. 6, Secs. B.1 and B.2, supra; and genetic engineering, Ch. 1, Sec. D., supra. At other times the concept of personhood is important because there is a need to determine if the concept is applicable to entities that are not members of the human species. See Ch. 10, infra, for a discussion of artificial intelligence.

Engelhardt discusses the concept by describing the properties that entities must have before they can properly be called persons. Calling entities persons suggests to Engelhardt, though by no means to all, that we should respect them and be obligated to them; therefore, those who approach the problem using a descriptive method are often influenced by their views of how particular entities should be treated. This phenomenon is apparent especially in discussions of abortion. See Ch. 8, Sec. A.2, infra. Obviously, among philosophers there is little agreement about what constitute the significant properties of persons. See, e.g., Fletcher, Indicators of Humanhood, 2 Hastings Ctr.Rep. 1 (Nov. 1972); The Morality of Abortion: Legal and Historical Perspectives (Noonan ed. 1970).

Do you agree with Engelhardt about the attributes of persons? Do members of society need to agree about the attributes of persons before reaching a consensus on the criteria by which to determine when death has occurred?

ROBERT M. VEATCH,
DEATH, DYING AND THE BIOLOGICAL REVOLUTION:
OUR LAST QUEST FOR RESPONSIBILITY

21 (1976).

It seems strange to ask what death means. Throughout history men have had a good enough idea to transact the business of society—to cover the corpse, bury the dead, transmit authority. But now that technology permits us to treat the body organ by organ, cell by cell, we are forced to develop a more precise understanding of what it means to call a person dead. There is a complex interaction between the technical aspects of deciding a person is dead . . . and the more fundamental philosophical considerations which underlie the judgment that a person in a particular condition should be called dead.

. . .

Four separate levels in the definition of death debate must be distinguished. First, there is the purely formal analysis of the term *death*, an analysis that gives the structure and specifies the framework that must be filled in with content. Second, the *concept* of death is considered, attempting to fill the content of the formal definition. At this level the question is, What is is [sic] so essentially significant about life that its loss is termed *death?* Third, there is the question of the locus of death: where in the organism ought one to look to determine whether death has occurred? Fourth, one must ask the question of the criteria of death: what technical tests must be applied at the locus to determine if an individual is living or dead? . . .

NOTE

How specific should policymakers be in trying to establish guidelines by which to determine that death has occurred? How many of Veatch's levels are incorporated in the Uniform Determination of Death Act, infra?

ALEXANDER MORGAN CAPRON AND LEON R. KASS,
A STATUTORY DEFINITION OF THE STANDARDS FOR
DETERMINING HUMAN DEATH: AN APPRAISAL
AND A PROPOSAL

121 U.Pa.L.Rev. 87, 93–95, 97, 100–101(1972).

. . . [W]hile it is true that the application of particular criteria or tests to determine the death of an individual may call for the expertise of a physician, there are other aspects of formulating a "definition" of death that are not particularly within medical competence. . . . The formulation of a concept of death is neither simply a technical matter nor one susceptible of empirical verification. The idea of death is at least partly a philosophical question, related to such ideas as "organism," "human," and "living." Physicians *qua* physicians are not expert on these philosophical questions, nor are they expert on the question of which physiological functions decisively identify a "living, human organism." They, like other scientists, can suggest which "vital signs" have what significance for which human functions. They may, for example, show that a person in an irreversible coma exhibits "total unawareness to externally applied stimuli and inner need and complete unresponsiveness," and they may predict that when tests for this condition yield the same results over a twenty-four hour period there is only a very minute chance that the coma will ever be "reversed." Yet the judgment that "total unawareness . . . and complete unresponsiveness" are the salient characteristics of death, or that a certain level of risk of error is acceptable, requires more than technical expertise and goes beyond medical authority, properly understood.

The proposed departure from the traditional standards for determining death not only calls attention to the extra-medical issues involved, but is itself a source of public confusion and concern. The confusion can perhaps be traced to the fact that the traditional signs of life (the beating heart and the expanding chest) are manifestly accessible to the senses of the layman, whereas some of the new criteria require sophisticated intervention to elicit latent signs of life such as brain reflexes. Furthermore, the new criteria may disturb the layman by suggesting that these visible and palpable traditional signs, still useful in most cases, may be deceiving him in cases where supportive machinery is being used. The anxiety may also be attributable to the apparent intention behind the "new definition," which is, at least in part, to facilitate other developments such as the transplantation of cadaver organs. Such confusion and anxiety about the standards for determining death can have far-reaching and distressing consequences for the patient's family, for the physician, for other patients, and for the community at large. If the uncertainties surrounding the question of determining death are to be laid to rest, a clear and acceptable standard is needed. And if the formulation and adoption of this standard are not to be abdicated to the medical fraternity under an expanded view of its competence and authority, then the public and its representatives ought to be involved. Even if the medical profession takes the lead—as indeed it has—in promoting new criteria of death, members of the public should at least have the opportunity to review, and either to affirm or reject the standards by which they are to be pronounced dead.

There are a number of potential means for involving the public in this process of formulation and review, none of them perfect. The least ambitious or comprehensive is simply to encourage discussion of the issues by the lay press, civic groups, and the community at large. . . . As important as it is to ventilate the issues, studies and public discussions alone may not be adequate to the task. They cannot by themselves dispel the ambiguities which will continue to trouble decisionmakers and the public in determining whether an artificially-maintained, comatose "patient" is still alive.

A second alternative, reliance upon the judicial system, goes beyond ascertaining popular attitudes and could provide an authoritative opinion that might offer some guidance for decisionmakers. Reliance on judge-made law would, however, neither actively involve the public in the decisionmaking process nor lead to a prompt, clear, and general "definition." The courts, of course, cannot speak in the abstract prospectively, but must await litigation, which can involve considerable delay and expense, to the detriment of both the parties and society. A need to rely on the courts reflects an uncertainty in the law which is unfortunate in an area where private decisionmakers (physicians) must act quickly and irrevocably. An ambiguous legal standard endangers the rights—and in some cases the lives—of the participants. In such circumstances, a person's choice of one course over another may depend more on his willingness to test his views in court than on the relative merits of the courses of action.

. . .

Uncertainties in the law are, to be sure, inevitable at times and are often tolerated if they do not involve matters of general applicability or great moment. Yet the question of whether and when a person is dead plainly seems the sort of issue that cannot escape the need for legal clarity on these grounds. Therefore, it is not surprising that although they would be pleased simply to have the courts endorse their views, members of the medical profession are doubtful that the judicial mode of lawmaking offers them adequate protection in this area. There is currently no way to be certain that a doctor would not be liable, criminally or civilly, if he ceased treatment of a person found to be dead according to the Harvard Committee's criteria but not according to the "complete cessation of all vital functions" test presently employed by the courts. . . . A statutory "definition" of death would have notable advantages as an alternative to a judicial promulgation. Basically, the legislative process permits the public to play a more active role in decisionmaking and allows a wider range of information to enter into the framing of criteria for determining death. Moreover, by providing prospective guidance, statutory standards could dispel public and professional doubt, and could provide needed reassurance for physicians and patients' families, thereby reducing both the fear and the likelihood of litigation for malpractice (or even for homicide).

The legislative alternative also has a number of drawbacks, however. Foremost among these is the danger that a statute "defining" death may be badly drafted. It may be either too general or too specific, or it may be so poorly worded that it will leave physicians or laymen unsure of its intent. There is also the danger that the statutory language might seem to preclude future refinements that expanding medical knowledge would introduce into the tests and procedures for determining death. The problem of bad draftsmanship is compounded by the fact that a statute once enacted may be difficult to revise or repeal, leaving to the slow and uncertain process of litigation the clarification of its intent and meaning. By contrast, although judges usually espouse the doctrine of stare decisis, flexibility over time is a hallmark of the common law. An additional practical problem is the possibility that the statutes enacted may reflect primarily the interests of powerful lobbying groups—for example, state medical societies or transplant surgeons. This possibility—similar to the danger of judicial "rubberstamping" of medical experts' opinions—may be avoided by legislatures' holding open and well-publicized hearings at which sociologists, lawyers, theologians, and representatives of various viewpoints are also called upon to testify.

Professor Ian Kennedy [1] has suggested the further danger that a statutory "definition," rather than protecting the public may leave it vulnerable to physicians who through "liberal interpretation and clever argument" might take actions "just within the letter if not the spirit of the law." Kennedy would rely instead on the medical profession's generalized "consensus view" [2] of the proper "definition of death." It is, however, far from clear why physicians who would violate a statute are unlikely to depart from such an informal "consensus," which may or may not

1. Kennedy, The Kansas Statute on Death: An Appraisal, 285 New Eng.J.Med. 946, 947 (1971). [Eds.]

2. Id.

eventually be sanctioned by the courts. Legislation will not remove the need for reasoned interpretation—first by physicians and perhaps then by judges—but it can restrict the compass within which they make their choices to one which has been found acceptable by the public.

Finally, the legislative route may reduce the likelihood that conflicting "definitions" of death will be employed in different jurisdictions in this country. Theoretically, uniformity is also possible in judicial opinions, but it occurs infrequently. . . .

In sum, then, official action, as opposed to mere discussion of the issues, is needed if the conflict between current medical practice and present law is to be eliminated. A reformulation of the standards for determining death should thus be undertaken by either courts or legislatures. There are strengths and weaknesses in both law-creating mechanisms, but on balance we believe that if legislators approach the issues with a critical and inquiring attitude, a statutory "definition" of death may be the best way to resolve the conflicting needs for definiteness and flexibility, for public involvement and scientific accuracy. . . .

UNIFORM DETERMINATION OF DEATH ACT

12 U.L.A. 236 (Supp.1983).

An individual who has sustained either (1) irreversible cessation of circulatory and respiratory functions, or (2) irreversible cessation of all functions of the entire brain, including the brain stem, is dead. A determination of death must be made in accordance with accepted medical standards.

NOTES

1. The Uniform Determination of Death Act (UDDA) was recommended to the states for adoption by the President's Commission. The Commission had been directed to study the "ethical and legal implications of the matter of defining death, including the advisability of developing a uniform definition of death." 42 U.S.C. § 1802 (1978). In formulating the proposal, the Commission worked with three organizations, the American Medical Association, the American Bar Association and the National Conference of Commissioners on Uniform State Laws, which had previously proposed model legislation on the subject. These groups have now endorsed the Uniform Determination of Death Act in place of their earlier proposals. President's Commission, Defining Death 2 (1981).

2. Fifteen jurisdictions have adopted the UDDA. Thirteen adopted it by legislation while another two have adopted it by judicial decision.[1] In six of these jurisdictions, California, Colorado, Idaho, Maryland, Montana and Tennessee, the UDDA replaces previously existing statutes. There are twenty-three jurisdictions that have enacted other statutory formulations recognizing brain death criteria.[2]

1. Those jurisdictions adopting the UDDA by legislation are California, Colorado, Idaho, Maine, Maryland, Mississippi, Montana, Pennsylvania, Rhode Island, Tennessee, Vermont, Wisconsin and the District of Columbia. Those states adopting the UDDA by judicial decision are Indiana and Washington.

2. Alabama, Alaska, Arkansas, Connecticut, Florida, Georgia, Hawaii, Illinois, Iowa, Kansas, Louisiana, Michigan, Missouri, Nevada, New Mexico, North Carolina, Ohio, Oklahoma, Oregon, Texas, Virginia, West Virginia and Wyoming. See President's Commission, Defining Death, Appendix C 109–134; President's Commission Deciding to Forego Life-Sustaining Treatment 9, n. 7 (1983). In addition, two states, Massachusetts in Commonwealth v. Golston, 373 Mass. 249, 366 N.E.2d 744 (1977), certiorari denied 434 U.S. 1039, 98 S.Ct. 777, 54 L.Ed.2d 788 (1979), and Arizona in State v. Fierro, 124 Ariz. 182, 603 P.2d 74 (1979), have judicially adopted brain death criteria updating common law criteria. The Massachusetts Supreme Judicial Court explicitly limited its holding to criminal cases.

In view of the many statutory formulations, judicial decisions, and common law criteria still existing in some thirteen jurisdictions, would uniformity have been better achieved by the passage of federal legislation? See Ch. 8, Sec. A.2., infra, for a discussion of congressional efforts to establish a uniform definition of when life begins.

3. The President's Commission's proposal rejected "higher brain" formulations of death as suggested by Engelhardt. It was the Commission's view that (1) current medical knowledge and criteria are not sufficiently developed to translate into "higher brain" formulations; (2) "higher brain" formulations were too radical a departure from traditional standards; and (3) patients declared dead by "whole brain" criteria would also be considered dead by those advocating "higher brain" formulations President's Commission, Defining Death 40–41. Do you agree with the Commission's conclusions? Would you consider an irreversibly comatose patient a corpse in the traditional sense? See In re Quinlan, 70 N.J. 10, 355 A.2d 647 (1976), Sec. B.2., infra.

B. FOREGOING AND TERMINATING TREATMENT

1. DYING IN THE TWENTIETH CENTURY

LEWIS THOMAS, DYING AS FAILURE

447 Annals 1, 2–4
(Renée Fox, Spec.Ed. 1980).

It is true, as everyone says these days, that doctors do not know what to do about death. Patients who are known to be dying are segregated as much as possible from all the others, and as the clinically unmistakable process of dying gets under way the doctors spend as little time in attendance as they can manage.

What is not so generally recognized is that doctors, especially young doctors, are as frightened and bewildered by the act of death as everyone else. When they avert their eyes it is not that they have lost interest, or find their attendance burdensome because wasteful of their talents; it is surely not because of occupational callousness. Although they are familiar with the business, seeing more of it at first hand than anyone else in our kind of society, they never become used to it. Death is shocking, dismaying, even terrifying.

A dying patient is a kind of freak. It is the most unacceptable of all abnormalities, an offense against nature itself.

Why is this? You'd think that this event, the most universal and inevitable of all aspects of human life, would be taken in professional stride. Was it always like this?

I think not, although I cannot be sure. My own recollection of medicine at the time when I was a medical student, in the mid-1930s, is hazy enough from this distance, but the thing I remember most clearly from the wards of the old Boston City Hospital is death as an everyday, everynight event, occurring up and down the open wards. The white curtains around each bed were usually kept drawn to one side, but when a death was about to occur the head nurse would make the rounds of the ward, moving fast, pulling each curtain across the foot of every bed. I remember the zinging sound of those curtains being yanked across on their metal rings, bed after bed. It was a commonplace ceremony, part of the working day. The sound was the sound of dying, and all the other patients, the day's survivors, knew what it signified.

The difference from a modern hospital, apart from the change from open wards to mostly private rooms, was in the age of the patients who died. Dying could occur, and did, at any age. It was not an event reserved for the very old, or for the middle-aged patients who had reached the end of their long battles with cancer or heart disease or strokes. Many of the patients who died on the open wards of the City Hospital were young people, overwhelmed by an infectious disease—lobar pneumonia, meningitis, septicemia, tuberculosis—for which there was no effective treatment of any kind.

The inevitability of death was plainer to see in those days. For a great many of the ordinary illnesses that brought patients into the hospital, dying was the expected outcome, beyond the control of any doctor. Death was more normal.

This was only forty-odd years ago. There is a difference, and it is reflected in the emotional impact of death on everyone, doctors included. But it is nothing like the difference between this century in the western world and all previous periods of human existence. Sebastian Bach had 7 brothers and sisters, of whom only 3 survived into adult life; of Bach's own 20 offspring, 11 died in childhood. I do not know what destroyed so many 18th century children, for the records of medicine are imprecise; most likely, it was the tubercle bacillus, the streptococcus and any number of other bacterial pathogens. It is only within the last 150 years that human beings have discovered that this kind of dying can be prevented— by sanitation, less crowding, plumbing, better housing, better nutrition, public health quarantine measures and the like.

In Bach's time, death was a perfectly normal event, part of the environment, expected, even looked forward to. He lived to be 65, and was called "Old Bach" by Frederick the Great when he improvised "The Musical Offering" three years earlier. Most of his immediate family, his friends, the residents of the various prosperous towns where he lived, people in general, died young. Everyone knew about death at first hand; there was nothing unfamiliar or even queer about the phenomenon. People seem to have known a lot more about the process itself than is the case today. The "deathbed" was a real place, and the dying person usually knew where he was and when it was time to assemble the family and call for the priest.

It was easier, indeed necessary, to accept the idea of an afterlife, and the power of religion was amplified by the high visibility of dying, especially by the deaths of so many young people. Bach's cantatas are filled with reassurances about this matter, celebrations of the transitory nature of human life, the welcoming of death because of the reward to come.

Today, the average span of human life in our society stands at around 73 years, the longest run at living yet achieved. Obviously, most of the dying is done by old people. It makes a different sort of problem for the human mind. Dying is not so often the tragic striking-down that it was; it is more like the end of a slow process of running-down, more like a slow collapse. We know about its inevitability, but we do not have the same apprehension that it is there, waiting just around the corner, ready to leap.

And so we have come, just in the past 40 years, to view death as a sort of failure, just as we now look at the process of aging itself as failure. We have lost, in this changed view, the old feeling of respect for dying, and all the awe.

I do not know what we are doing to the first-hand experience of dying itself with our technology, but I suspect we may often be interfering with an important process. The awareness of dying can be an extraordinary sensation, described from time to time as a feeling of exaltation. In the days when tuberculosis was the commonest disease, causing death after a prolonged, exhausting illness, doctors could tell when death was near by a remarkable change in the patient's attitude. It was called "*spes phthisica*", the hope of the tuberculous, and it was marked by a sense of tranquility and great peace, and something like pleasure.

Dying *is* a process, I believe. I'm not sure of it, but I think so. The organism seems to come apart in orderly stages. Sometimes patients know when the process has begun and they recognize the manifestations before the doctor is aware of them. I've seen this happen a few times. Once, on rounds, I stood at the bedside of a middle-aged man who had just been brought to the hospital with a coronary. He was lying in bed, propped up comfortably by pillows, and his chest pain had been relieved completely. The intern was describing the details of his condition, concluding that he seemed in stable condition, that all vital signs were good, when the patient interrupted in a tone of mild, rather gentle protest: "But Doctor," he said quietly but with absolute certainty, "I am dying; I'm going." And so he did, within two hours.

Most of the time, it is not a bad feeling. Sir William Osler wrote about it, pointing out that the popular notion of death agony was a fiction; people died, at the moment of the dying, in tranquility.

The act of dying was, at one time, a rather splendid event to behold, a great family occasion. Children grew up knowing all about it, observing the event, over and over again in the normal process of growing into maturity. It took place at the end of a struggle, often a short fight, against infection. When it was the result of lobar pneumonia it would usually occur after 10 days or so of violent illness, with shaking chills at the outset, then incessant coughing, chest pain, a high fever, and, finally, collapse into unconsciousness. But it was known that this disease could be recovered from, and when recovery took place it did so all at once, in a spectacular episode called the "crisis." This might happen, if the patient was lucky, on any day from the seventh on; suddenly, within a matter of a few hours, the temperature would cascade from 105° down to normal, accompanied by profuse sweating, and the patient would, just as suddenly, be well again, ready to resume normal living. The crisis, we now know, was caused by the sudden appearance in the patient's blood of antibodies against the capsular polysaccharide of the pneumococcus, and as soon as this happened the bacteria were destroyed all at once. It was one of the triumphs of human biology, no longer observable in hospitals because of penicillin's capacity to kill off the bacteria at the onset. But before antibiotics, back in the days when medicine possessed no real technology for treating infection, recovery from lobar pneumonia was the body's own accomplishment, and whether the patient lost out or survived it was a spectacular display of combat.

The time may come when medicine will have found out enough about disease mechanisms to think its way around all of today's other lethal human diseases, as effectively as by the techniques for treating infection. We may be left then with no way of dying except by wearing out in old age, barring trauma. It will be the kind of event we now call natural death, ending the lives of very old people in their sleep.

Meanwhile, we are part way along. We have not lost our fear of dying, nor our sense of its ultimate inevitability. But I am afraid that we have lost something else—our respect for it. In a sense quite new to our culture we have become ashamed of death, and we try to hide it, or hide ourselves away from it. It is, to our way of thinking, failure.

NOTES

1. Life spans for both men and women are projected to increase substantially. It is now estimated that the average life span in the year 2,000 will be 74 for men and 86 for women. Washington Post, May 31, 1983, at A2, col. 1. For a discussion concerning whether the number of elderly people, the average period of diminished vigor, the health care needs of the elderly, and the proportion of the life span occupied by chronic disease will increase or decrease in the future, see Fries, Aging, Natural Death, and the Compression of Morbidity, 303 New Eng. J.Med. 130 (1980); Schneider and Brody, Aging, Natural Death, and the Compression of Morbidity: Another View, 309 New Eng. J.Med. 854 (1983).

2. As Thomas points out, death frequently occurs in hospitals and other medical facilities, often in the absence of family members or friends, attended only by medical specialists trained to combat disease and death. Hospice care, deliberately created as an alternative to traditional long-term care institutions, is increasingly perceived as a means to restore dignity to and respect for death.

The hospice concept began in 1842 with the establishment in Lyon, France, of an institution for the care of poor women suffering from cancer. The establishment of modern hospice care was marked by the opening of St. Christopher's Hospital in Syndenham, England, in July 1967, as a result of the pioneering efforts of the British physician Cicely Saunders. The first hospice in the United States was opened in New Haven, Connecticut, in 1974. Since 1974 the number of hospice programs in the United States has increased substantially. In 1978 the National Hospice Organization (NHO) counted 71 operating hospices. Coverage of Hospice Care Under the Medicare Program: Hearings on H.R. 5180 Before the Subcomm. on Health of the House Committee on Ways and Means, 97th Cong., 2d Sess. 22 (1982) (testimony of Edwin Olsen) [hereinafter cited as Hearings]. The NHO estimates that there now may be as many as 800 hospice programs. President's Commission, Deciding to Forego Life-Sustaining Treatment 112, n. 59 (1983).

Hospices exist to assist dying patients—typically cancer patients—to spend their remaining time free of symptoms and as much in control as possible.

Provisions of the recently enacted Tax Equity and Fiscal Responsibility Act of 1982, Pub.Law No. 97–248, codified as 42 U.S.C.A. §§ 1395(c)–(f) (1982) authorize reimbursement under Medicare for hospice care for a trial period from November 1, 1983 through October 1, 1986. Essentially, the act provides for an election of hospice care during up to two periods of 90 days each and one subsequent period of 30 days. 42 U.S.C.A. § 1395(d)(a)(4). The act promises to give hospices a firm financial base, which they have lacked, although some find shortcomings in the legislation. See President's Commission, Deciding to Forego Life-Sustaining Treatment 115–117 (1983). Others fear that the recently passed legislation will lead to an explosion of facilities that will be "hospices" in name only because of the promise of reimbursement. See Butterfield-Piccard and Magno, Hospice the Adjective, Not the Noun, 37 Am.Psycho. 1254, 1259 (1982).

2. INTRODUCING TRADITIONAL MORAL CONCEPTS

a. As Used By Courts

IN RE QUINLAN

Supreme Court of New Jersey, 1976.
70 N.J. 10, 355 A.2d 647, certiorari denied 429 U.S. 922,
97 S.Ct. 319, 50 L.Ed.2d 289.

HUGHES, C.J.

THE LITIGATION

The central figure in this tragic case is Karen Ann Quinlan, a New Jersey resident. At the age of 22, she lies in a debilitated and allegedly moribund state at Saint Clare's Hospital in Denville, New Jersey. . . .

The issues are before this Court following its direct certification of the action prior to hearing in the Superior Court, Appellate Division, to which the appellant (hereafter "plaintiff") Joseph Quinlan, Karen's father, had appealed the adverse judgment of the Chancery Division.

Due to extensive physical damage fully described in the able opinion of the trial judge, Judge Muir, supporting that judgment, Karen allegedly was incompetent. Joseph Quinlan sought the adjudication of that incompetency. He wished to be appointed guardian of the person and property of his daughter. It was proposed by him that such letters of guardianship, if granted, should contain an express power to him as guardian to authorize the discontinuance of all extraordinary medical procedures now allegedly sustaining Karen's vital processes and hence her life, since these measures, he asserted, present no hope of her eventual recovery. A guardian *ad litem* was appointed by Judge Muir to represent the interest of the alleged incompetent.

By a supplemental complaint, in view of the extraordinary nature of the relief sought by plaintiff and the involvement therein of their several rights and responsibilities, other parties were added. These included the treating physicians and the hospital, the relief sought being that they be restrained from interfering with the carrying out of any such extraordinary authorization in the event it were to be granted by the court. Joined, as well, was the Prosecutor of Morris County (he being charged with responsibility for enforcement of the criminal law), to enjoin him from interfering with, or projecting a criminal prosecution which otherwise might ensue in the event of, cessation of life in Karen resulting from the exercise of such extraordinary authorization were it to be granted to the guardian.

The Attorney General of New Jersey intervened as of right . . . . Its basis, of course, was the interest of the State in the preservation of life, which has an undoubted constitutional foundation.

. . .

[It was stipulated below that] [u]nder any legal standard recognized by the State of New Jersey and also under standard medical practice, Karen Ann Quinlan is presently alive.

. . .

It was further stipulated during trial that Karen was indeed incompetent and guardianship was necessary, although there exists a dispute as to the determination later reached by the court that such guardianship should be bifurcated, and that Mr. Quinlan should be appointed as guardian of the trivial property but not the person of his daughter.

After certification the Attorney General filed as of right a cross-appeal challenging the action of the trial court in admitting evidence of prior statements made by Karen while competent as to her distaste for continuance of life by extraordinary medical procedures, under circumstances not unlike those of the present case. These quoted statements were made in the context of several conversations with regard to others terminally ill and being subjected to like heroic measures. The statements were advanced as evidence of what she would want done in such a contingency as now exists. She was said to have firmly evinced her wish, in like circumstances, not to have her life prolonged by the otherwise futile use of extraordinary means. Because we agree with the conception of the trial court that such statements, since they were remote and impersonal, lacked significant probative weight, it is not of consequence to our opinion that we decide whether or not they were admissible hearsay. . . .

. . .

THE FACTUAL BASE

. . .

On the night of April 15, 1975, for reasons still unclear, Karen Quinlan ceased breathing for at least two 15 minute periods. She received some ineffectual mouth-to-mouth resuscitation from friends. She was taken by ambulance to Newton Memorial Hospital. There she had a temperature of 100 degrees, her pupils were unreactive and she was unresponsive even to deep pain. The history at the time of her admission to that hospital was essentially incomplete and uninformative.

Three days later, Dr. Morse examined Karen at the request of the Newton admitting physician, Dr. McGee. He found her comatose with evidence of decortication, a condition relating to derangement of the cortex of the brain causing a physical posture in which the upper extremities are flexed and the lower extremities are extended. She required a respirator to assist her breathing. Dr. Morse was unable to obtain an adequate account of the circumstances and events leading up to Karen's admission to the Newton Hospital. Such initial history or etiology is crucial in neurological diagnosis. Relying as he did upon the Newton Memorial records and his own examination, he concluded that prolonged lack of oxygen in the bloodstream, anoxia, was identified with her condition as he saw it upon first observation. When she was later transferred to Saint Clare's Hospital she was still unconscious, still on a respirator and a tracheotomy had been performed. On her arrival Dr. Morse conducted extensive and detailed examinations. An electroencephalogram (EEG) measuring electrical rhythm of the brain was performed and Dr. Morse characterized the result as "abnormal but it showed some activity and was consistent with her clinical state." Other significant neurological tests, including a brain scan, an angiogram, and a lumbar puncture were normal in result. Dr. Morse testified that Karen has been in a state of coma, lack of consciousness, since he began treating her. He explained that there are basically two types of coma, sleep-like unresponsiveness and awake unresponsiveness. Karen was originally in a sleep-like unresponsive condition but soon developed "sleep-wake" cycles, apparently a normal improvement for comatose patients occurring within three to four weeks. In the awake cycle she blinks, cries out and does things of that sort but is still totally unaware of anyone or anything around her.

Dr. Morse and other expert physicians who examined her characterized Karen as being in a "chronic persistent vegetative state." Dr. Fred Plum, one of such expert witnesses, defined this as a "subject who remains with the capacity to maintain the vegetative parts of neurological function but who . . . no longer has any cognitive function."

Dr. Morse, as well as the several other medical and neurological experts who testified in this case, believed with certainty that Karen Quinlan is not "brain dead." They identified the Ad Hoc Committee of Harvard Medical School report as the ordinary medical standard for determining brain death, and all of them were satisfied that Karen met none of the criteria specified in that report and was therefore not "brain dead" within its contemplation.

In this respect it was indicated by Dr. Plum that the brain works in essentially two ways, the vegetative and the sapient. He testified:

We have an internal vegetative regulation which controls body temperature which controls breathing, which controls to a considerable degree blood pressure, which controls to some degree heart rate, which controls chewing, swallowing and which controls sleeping and waking. We have a more highly developed brain which is uniquely human which controls our relation to the outside world, our capacity to talk, to see, to feel, to sing, to think. Brain death necessarily must mean the death of both of these functions of the brain, vegetative and the sapient. Therefore, the presence of any function which is regulated or governed or controlled by the deeper parts of the brain which in laymen's terms might be considered purely vegetative would mean that the brain is not biologically dead.

Because Karen's neurological condition affects her respiratory ability (the respiratory system being a brain stem function) she requires a respirator to assist her breathing. From the time of her admission to Saint Clare's Hospital Karen has been assisted by an MA-1 respirator, a sophisticated machine which delivers a given volume of air at a certain rate and periodically provides a "sigh" volume, a relatively large measured volume of air designed to purge the lungs of excretions. Attempts to "wean" her from the respirator were unsuccessful and have been abandoned.

The experts believe that Karen cannot now survive without the assistance of the respirator; that exactly how long she would live without it is unknown; that the strong likelihood is that death would follow soon after its removal, and that removal would also risk further brain damage and would curtail the assistance the respirator presently provides in warding off infection.

It seemed to be the consensus not only of the treating physicians but also of the several qualified experts who testified in the case, that removal from the respirator would not conform to medical practices, standards and traditions.

The further medical consensus was that Karen in addition to being comatose is in a chronic and persistent "vegetative" state, having no awareness of anything or anyone around her and existing at a primitive reflex level. Although she does have some brain stem function (ineffective for respiration) and has other reactions one normally associates with being alive, such as moving, reacting to light, sound and noxious stimuli, blinking her eyes, and the like, the quality of her feeling impulses is unknown. She grimaces, makes sterotyped cries and sounds and has chewing motions. Her blood pressure is normal.

Karen remains in the intensive care unit at Saint Clare's Hospital, receiving 24-hour care by a team of four nurses characterized, as was the medical attention, as "excellent." She is nourished by feeding by way of a nasal-gastro tube and is routinely examined for infection, which under these circumstances is a serious life threat. The result is that her condition is considered remarkable under the unhappy circumstances involved.

Karen is described as emaciated, having suffered a weight loss of at least 40 pounds, and undergoing a continuing deteriorative process. Her posture is described as fetal-like and grotesque; there is extreme flexion-rigidity of the arms, legs and related muscles and her joints are severely rigid and deformed.

From all of this evidence, and including the whole testimonial record, several basic findings in the physical area are mandated. Severe brain and associated damage, albeit of uncertain etiology, has left Karen in a chronic and persistent vegetative state. No form of treatment which can cure or improve that condition is known or available. As nearly as may be determined, considering the guarded area of remote uncertainties characteristic of most medical science predictions, she can *never* be restored to cognitive or sapient life. Even with regard to the vegetative level and improvement therein (if such it may be called) the prognosis is extremely poor and the extent unknown if it should in fact occur.

She is debilitated and moribund and although fairly stable at the time of argument before us (no new information having been filed in the meanwhile in expansion of the record), no physician risked the opinion that she could live more than a year and indeed she may die much earlier. Excellent medical and nursing care so far has been able to ward off the constant threat of infection, to which she is peculiarly susceptible because of the respirator, the tracheal tube and other incidents of care in her vulnerable condition. Her life accordingly is sustained by the respirator and tubal feeding, and removal from the respirator would cause her death soon, although the time cannot be stated with more precision.

. . .

. . . When plaintiff and his family, finally reconciled to the certainty of Karen's impending death, requested the withdrawal of life support mechanisms, [Dr. Morse] demurred. His refusal was based upon his conception of medical standards, practice and ethics described in the medical testimony, such as in the evidence given by another neurologist, Dr. Sidney Diamond, a witness for the State. Dr. Diamond asserted that no physician would have failed to provide respirator support at the outset, and none would interrupt its life-saving course thereafter, except in the case of cerebral death. . . .

. . .

We turn to that branch of the factual case pertaining to the application for guardianship, as distinguished from the nature of the authorization sought by the applicant. The character and general suitability of Joseph Quinlan as guardian for his daughter, in ordinary circumstances, could not be doubted. The record bespeaks the high degree of familial love which pervaded the home of Joseph Quinlan and reached out fully to embrace Karen, although she was living elsewhere at the time of her collapse. The proofs showed him to be deeply religious, imbued with a morality so sensitive that months of tortured indecision preceded his belated conclusion (despite earlier moral judgments reached by the other family members, but unexpressed to him in order not to influence him) to seek the termination of life-supportive measures sustaining Karen. A communicant of the Roman Catholic Church, as were other family members, he first sought solace in private prayer looking with confidence, as he says, to the Creator, first for the recovery of Karen and then, if that were not possible, for guidance with respect to the awesome decision confronting him.

To confirm the moral rightness of the decision he was about to make he consulted with his parish priest and later with the Catholic chaplain of Saint Clare's Hospital. He would not, he testified, have sought termination if that act were to be morally wrong or in conflict with the tenets of the religion he so profoundly respects. He was disabused of doubt, however, when the position of the Roman Catholic Church was made known to him as it is reflected in the record in this case. While it is not usual for matters of religious dogma or concepts to enter a civil litigation . . . they were rightly admitted in evidence here. The judge was bound to measure the character and motivations in all respects of Joseph Quinlan as prospective guardian; and insofar as these religious matters bore upon them, they were properly scrutinized and considered by the court.

Thus germane, we note the position of that Church as illuminated by the record before us. We have no reason to believe that it would be at all discordant with the whole of Judeo-Christian tradition, considering its central respect and reverence for the sancity of human life. It was in this sense of relevance that we admitted as *amicus curiae* the New Jersey Catholic Conference, essentially the spokesman for the various Catholic bishops of New Jersey, organized to give witness to spiritual values in public affairs in the statewide community. The position statement of Bishop Lawrence B. Casey, reproduced in the *amicus* brief, projects these views:

(a) The verification of the fact of death in a particular case cannot be deduced from any religious or moral principle and, under this aspect, does not fall within the competence of the church; — that dependence must be had upon traditional and medical standards, and by these standards Karen Ann Quinlan is assumed to be alive.

(b) The request of plaintiff for authority to terminate a medical procedure characterized as "an extraordinary means of treatment" would not involve euthanasia. This upon the reasoning expressed by Pope Pius XII in his "allocutio" (address) to anesthesiologists on November 24, 1957, when he dealt with the question:

Does the anesthesiologist have the right, or is he bound, in all cases of deep unconsciousness, even in those that are completely hopeless in the opinion of the competent doctor, to use modern artificial respiration apparatus, even against the will of the family?

His answer made the following points:

1. In ordinary cases the doctor has the right to act in this manner, but is not bound to do so unless this is the only way of fulfilling another certain moral duty.

2. The doctor, however, has no right independent of the patient. He can act only if the patient explicitly or implicitly, directly or indirectly gives him the permission.

3. The treatment as described in the question constitutes extraordinary means of preserving life and so there is no obligation to use them nor to give the doctor permission to use them.

4. The rights and the duties of the family depend on the presumed will of the unconscious patient if he or she is of legal age and the family, too, is bound to use only ordinary means.

5. This case is not to be considered euthanasia in any way; that would never be licit. The interruption of attempts at resuscitation, even when it causes the arrest of circulation, is not more than an indirect cause of the cessation of life, and we must apply in this case the principle of double effect.

So it was that the Bishop Casey statement validated the decision of Joseph Quinlan:

> Competent medical testimony has established that Karen Ann Quinlan has no reasonable hope of recovery from her comatose state by the use of any available medical procedures. The continuance of mechanical (cardiorespiratory) supportive measures to sustain continuation of her body functions and her life constitute extraordinary means of treatment. *Therefore, the decision of Joseph . . . Quinlan to request the discontinuance of this treatment is, according to the teachings of the Catholic Church, a morally correct decision.* (emphasis in original)

. . .

. . . [W]e feel it essential to reiterate that the "Catholic view" of religious neutrality in the circumstances of this case is considered by the Court only in the aspect of its impact upon the conscience, motivation and purpose of the intending guardian, Joseph Quinlan, and not as a precedent in terms of the civil law.

If Joseph Quinlan, for instance, were a follower and strongly influenced by the teachings of Buddha, or if, as an agnostic or atheist, his moral judgments were formed without reference to religious feelings, but were nevertheless formed and viable, we would with equal attention and high respect consider these elements, as bearing upon his character, motivations and purposes as relevant to his qualification and suitability as guardian.

It is from this factual base that the Court confronts and responds to three basic issues:

1. Was the trial court correct in denying the specific relief requested by plaintiff, *i.e.* authorization for termination of the life-supporting apparatus, on the case presented to him? Our determination on that question is in the affirmative.

2. Was the court correct in withholding letters of guardianship from the plaintiff and appointing in his stead a stranger? On that issue our determination is in the negative.

3. Should this Court, in the light of the foregoing conclusions, grant declaratory relief to the plaintiff? On that question our Court's determination is in the affirmative.

This brings us to a consideration of the constitutional and legal issues underlying the foregoing determinations.

CONSTITUTIONAL AND LEGAL ISSUES

. . .

I. *The Free Exercise of Religion*

We think the contention as to interference with religious beliefs or rights may be considered and dealt with without extended discussion, given the acceptance of distinctions so clear and simple in their precedential definition as to be dispositive on their face.

Simply stated, the right to religious beliefs is absolute but conduct in pursuance thereof is not wholly immune from governmental restraint. . . . The public interest is . . . considered paramount, without essential dissolution of respect for religious beliefs.

We think, without further examples, that, ranged against the State's interest in the preservation of life, the impingement of religious belief, much less religious "neutrality" as here, does not reflect a constitutional question, in the circumstances at least of the case presently before the Court. Moreover, like the trial court, we do not recognize an independent parental right of religious freedom to support the relief requested.
. . .

. . .

III. *The Right of Privacy*

It is the issue of the constitutional right of privacy that has given us most concern, in the exceptional circumstances of this case. Here a loving parent, *qua* parent and raising the rights of his incompetent and profoundly damaged daughter, probably irreversibly doomed to no more than a biologically vegetative remnant of life, is before the court. He seeks authorization to abandon specialized technological precedu005 which can only maintain for a time a body having no potential for resumption or continuance of other than a "vegetative" existence.

We have no doubt, in these unhappy circumstances, that if Karen were herself miraculously lucid for an interval (not altering the existing prognosis of the condition to which she would soon return) and perceptive of her irreversible condition, she could effectively decide upon discontinuance of the life-support apparatus, even if it meant the prospect of natural death. . . .

. . . We have no hesitancy in deciding . . . that no external compelling interest of the State could compel Karen to endure the unendurable, only to vegetate a few measurable months with no realistic possibility of returning to any semblance of cognitive or sapient life. We perceive no thread of logic distinguishing between such a choice on Karen's part and a similar choice which, under the evidence in this case, could be made by a competent patient terminally ill, riddled by cancer and suffering great pain; such a patient would not be resuscitated or put on a respirator . . . and *a fortiori* would not be kept *against his will* on a respirator.

Although the Constitution does not explicitly mention a right of privacy, Supreme Court decisions have recognized that a right of personal privacy exists and that certain areas of privacy are guaranteed under the Constitution. The Court has interdicted judicial intrusion into many aspects of personal decision, sometimes basing this restraint upon the conception of a limitation of judicial interest and responsibility, such as with regard to contraception and its relationship to family life and decision. Griswold v. Connecticut, 381 U.S. 479, 85 S.Ct. 1678, 14 L.Ed.2d 510 (1965).

. . . . Presumably this right is broad enough to encompass a patient's decision to decline medical treatment under certain circumstances, in much the same way as it is broad enough to encompass a woman's decision to terminate pregnancy under certain conditions.

Nor is such right of privacy forgotten in the New Jersey Constitution. N.J.Const. (1947), Art. I, par. 1.

The claimed interests of the State in this case are essentially the preservation and sanctity of human life and defense of the right of the physician to administer medical treatment according to his best judgment. In this case the doctors say that removing Karen from the respirator will conflict with their professional judgment. The plaintiff answers that Karen's present treatment serves only a maintenance function; that the respirator cannot cure or improve her condition but at best can only prolong her inevitable slow deterioration and death; and that the interests of the patient, as seen by her surrogate, the guardian, must be evaluated by the court as predominant, even in the face of an opinion *contra* by the present attending physicians. Plaintiff's distinction is significant. The nature of Karen's care and the realistic chances of her recovery are quite unlike those of the patients discussed in many of the cases where treatments were ordered. In many of those cases the medical procedure required (usually a transfusion) constituted a minimal bodily invasion and the chances of recovery and return to functioning life were very good. We think that the State's interest *contra* weakens and the individual's right to privacy grows as the degree of bodily invasion increases and the prognosis dims. Ultimately there comes a point at which the individual's rights overcome the State interest. It is for that reason that we believe Karen's choice, if she were competent to make it, would be vindicated by the law. Her prognosis is extremely poor,—she will never resume cognitive life. And the bodily invasion is very great,—she requires 24 hour intensive nursing care, antibiotics, the assistance of a respirator, a catheter and feeding tube.

Our affirmation of Karen's independent right of choice, however, would ordinarily be based upon her competency to assert it. The sad truth, however, is that she is grossly incompetent and we cannot discern her supposed choice based on the testimony of her previous conversations with friends, where such testimony is without sufficient probative weight. Nevertheless we have concluded that Karen's right of privacy may be asserted on her behalf by her guardian under the peculiar circumstances here present.

If a putative decision by Karen to permit this non-cognitive, vegetative existence to terminate by natural forces is regarded as a valuable incident of her right of privacy, as we believe it to be, then it should not be discarded solely on the basis that her condition prevents her conscious exercise of the choice. The only practical way to prevent destruction of the right is to permit the guardian and family of Karen to render their best judgment, subject to the qualifications hereinafter stated, as to whether she would exercise it in these circumstances. If their conclusion is in the affirmative this decision should be accepted by a society the overwhelming majority of whose members would, we think, in similar circumstances, exercise such a choice in the same way for themselves or for those closest to them.   It is for this reason that we determine that Karen's right of privacy may be asserted in her behalf, in this respect, by her guardian and family under the particular circumstances presented by this record.

. . .

IV.   *The Medical Factor*

. . .

The existence and nature of the medical dilemma need hardly be discussed at length, portrayed as it is in the present case and complicated as it has recently come to be in view of the dramatic advance of medical technology.   The dilemma is there, it is real, it is constantly resolved in accepted medical practice without attention in the courts, it pervades the issues in the very case we here examine.   The branch of the dilemma involving the doctor's responsibility and the relationship of the court's duty was thus conceived by Judge Muir:

> Doctors . . . to treat a patient, must deal with medical tradition and past case histories.   They must be guided by what they do know. The extent of their training, their experience, consultation with other physicians, must guide their decision-making processes in providing care to their patient.   The nature, extent and duration of care by societal standards is the responsibility of a physician.   The morality and conscience of our society places this responsibility in the hands of the physician.   What justification is there to remove it from the control of the medical profession and place it in the hands of the courts?   [137 N.J.Super. at 259, 348 A.2d at 818].

Such notions as to the distribution of responsibility, heretofore generally entertained, should however neither impede this Court in deciding matters clearly justiciable nor preclude a re-examination by the Court as to underlying human values and rights.   Determinations as to these must, in the ultimate, be responsive not only to the concepts of medicine but also to the common moral judgment of the community at large.   In the latter respect the Court has a nondelegable judicial responsibility.

Put in another way, the law, equity and justice must not themselves quail and be helpless in the face of modern technological marvels presenting questions hitherto unthought of.   Where a Karen Quinlan, or a parent, or a doctor, or a hospital, or a State seeks the process and response of a court, it must answer with its most informed conception of justice in the previously unexplored circumstances presented to it.   That is its obligation and we are here fulfilling it, for the actors and those having an interest in the matter should not go without remedy.

. . .

[I]nsofar as a court, having no inherent medical expertise, is called upon to overrule a professional decision made according to prevailing medical practice and standards, a different question is presented. . . .

The medical obligation is related to standards and practice prevailing in the profession.   The physicians in charge of the case, as noted above, declined to withdraw the respirator.   That decision was consistent with the proofs below as to the then existing medical standards and practices.

Under the law as it then stood, Judge Muir was correct in declining to authorize withdrawal of the respirator.

However, in relation to the matter of the declaratory relief sought by plaintiff as representative of Karen's interests, we are required to reevaluate the applicability of the medical standards projected in the court below. The question is whether there is such internal consistency and rationality in the application of such standards as should warrant their constituting an ineluctable bar to the effectuation of substantive relief for plaintiff at the hands of the court. We have concluded not.

.   .   .

The modern proliferation of substantial malpractice litigation and the less frequent but even more unnerving possibility of criminal sanctions would seem, for it is beyond human nature to suppose otherwise, to have bearing on the practice and standards as they exist. The brooding presence of such possible liability, it was testified here, had no part in the decision of the treating physicians. As did Judge Muir, we afford this testimony full credence. But we cannot believe that the stated factor has not had a strong influence on the standards, as the literature on the subject plainly reveals. Moreover our attention is drawn not so much to the recognition by Drs. Morse and Javed of the extant practice and standards but to the widening ambiguity of those standards themselves in their application to the medical problems we are discussing.

.   .   .

We glean from the record here that physicians distinguish between curing the ill and comforting and easing the dying; that they refuse to treat the curable as if they were dying or ought to die, and that they have sometimes refused to treat the hopeless and dying as if they were curable. In this sense .   .   . many of them have refused to inflict an undesired prolongation of the process of dying on a patient in irreversible condition when it is clear that such "therapy" offers neither human nor humane benefit. We think these attitudes represent a balanced implementation of a profoundly realistic perspective on the meaning of life and death and that they respect the whole Judeo-Christian tradition of regard for human life. No less would they seem consistent with the moral matrix of medicine, "to heal," very much in the sense of the endless mission of the law, "to do justice."

Yet this balance, we feel, is particularly difficult to perceive and apply in the context of the development by advanced technology of sophisticated and artificial life-sustaining devices. For those possibly curable, such devices are of great value, and, as ordinary medical procedures, are essential. Consequently, .   .   . they are necessary because of the ethic of medical practice. But in light of the situation in the present case (while the record here is somewhat hazy in distinguishing between "ordinary" and "extraordinary" measures), one would have to think that the use of the same respirator or like support could be considered "ordinary" in the context of the possibly curable patient but "extraordinary" in the context of the forced sustaining by cardio-respiratory processes of an irreversibly doomed patient. And this dilemma is sharpened in the face of the malpractice and criminal action threat which we have mentioned.

We would hesitate, in this imperfect world, to propose as to physicians that type of immunity which from the early common law has surrounded judges and grand jurors, .   .   .

.   .   .

Nevertheless, there must be a way to free physicians, in the pursuit of their healing vocation, from possible contamination by self-interest or self-protection concerns which would inhibit their independent medical judgments for the well-being of their dying patients. We would hope that this opinion might be serviceable to some degree in ameliorating the professional problems under discussion.

A technique aimed at the underlying difficulty (though in a somewhat broader context) is described by Dr. Karen Teel, a pediatrician and a director of Pediatric Education, who writes in the Baylor Law Review under the title "The Physician's Dilemma: A Doctor's View: What The Law Should Be." Dr. Teel recalls:

> Physicians, by virtue of their responsibility for medical judgments are, partly by choice and partly by default, charged with the responsibility of making ethical judgments which we are sometimes ill-equipped to make. We are not always morally and legally authorized to make them. The physician is thereby assuming a civil and criminal liability that, as often as not, he does not even realize as a factor in his decision. There is little or no dialogue in this whole process. The physician assumes that his judgment is called for and, in good faith, he acts. Someone must and it has been the physician who has assumed the responsibility and the risk.

> I suggest that it would be more appropriate to provide a regular forum for more input and dialogue in individual situations and to allow the responsibility of these judgments to be shared. Many hospitals have established an Ethics Committee composed of physicians, social workers, attorneys, and theologians, . . . which serves to review the individual circumstances of ethical dilemma and which has provided much in the way of assistance and safeguards for patients and their medical caretakers. Generally, the authority of these committees is primarily restricted to the hospital setting and their official status is more that of an advisory body than of an enforcing body.

> The concept of an Ethics Committee which has this kind of organization and is readily accessible to those persons rendering medical care to patients, would be, I think, the most promising direction for further study at this point. . . .

> . . . [This would allow] some much needed dialogue regarding these issues and [force] the point of exploring all of the options for a particular patient. It diffuses the responsibility for making these judgments. Many physicians, in many circumstances, would welcome this sharing of responsibility. I believe that such an entity could lend itself well to an assumption of a legal status which would allow courses of action not now undertaken because of the concern for liability. [27 Baylor L.Rev. 6, 8–9 (1975)].

The most appealing factor in the technique suggested by Dr. Teel seems to us to be the diffusion of professional responsibility for decision, comparable in a way to the value of multi-judge courts in finally resolving on appeal difficult questions of law. Moreover, such a system would be protective to the hospital as well as the doctor in screening out, so to speak, a case which might be contaminated by less than worthy motivations of family or physician. In the real world and in relationship to the momentous decision contemplated, the value of additional views and diverse knowledge is apparent.

We consider that a practice of applying to a court to confirm such decisions would generally be inappropriate, not only because that would be a gratuitous encroachment upon the medical profession's field of competence, but because it would be impossibly cumbersome. Such a requirement is distinguishable from the judicial overview traditionally required in other matters such as the adjudication and commitment of mental incompetents. This is not to say that in the case of an otherwise justiciable controversy access to the courts would be foreclosed; we speak rather of a general practice and procedure.

And although the deliberations and decisions which we describe would be professional in nature they should obviously include at some stage the feelings of the family of an incompetent relative. Decision-making within health care if it is considered as an expression of a primary obligation of the physician, *primum non nocere,* should be controlled primarily within the patient-doctor-family relationship, ...

If there could be created not necessarily this particular system but some reasonable counterpart, we would have no doubt that such decisions, thus determined to be in accordance with medical practice and prevailing standards, would be accepted by society and by the courts, at least in cases comparable to that of Karen Quinlan.

The evidence in this case convinces us that the focal point of decision should be the prognosis as to the reasonable possibility of return to cognitive and sapient life, as distinguished from the forced continuance of that biological vegetative existence to which Karen seems to be doomed.

. . .

V. *Alleged Criminal Liability*

Having concluded that there is a right of privacy that might permit termination of treatment in the circumstances of this case, we turn to consider the relationship of the exercise of that right to the criminal law. We are aware that such termination of treatment would accelerate Karen's death. The County Prosecutor and the Attorney General maintain that there would be criminal liability for such acceleration. Under the statutes of this State, the unlawful killing of another human being is criminal homicide. N.J.S.A. 2A:113–1, 2, 5. We conclude that there would be no criminal homicide in the circumstances of this case. We believe, first, that the ensuing death would not be homicide but rather expiration from existing natural causes. Secondly, even if it were to be regarded as homicide, it would not be unlawful.

These conclusions rest upon definitional and constitutional bases. The termination of treatment pursuant to the right of privacy is, within the limitations of this case, *ipso facto* lawful. Thus, a death resulting from such an act would not come within the scope of the homicide statutes proscribing only the unlawful killing of another. There is a real and in this case determinative distinction between the unlawful taking of the life of another and the ending of artificial life-support systems as a matter of self-determination.

. . .

VI. *The Guardianship of the Person*

The trial judge bifurcated the guardianship, as we have noted, refusing to appoint Joseph Quinlan to be guardian of the person and limiting his guardianship to that of the property of his daughter. Such occasional division of guardianship, as between responsibility for the person and the property of an incompetent person, has roots deep in the common law and was well within the jurisdictional capacity of the trial judge.

. . .

The trial court was apparently convinced of the high character of Joseph Quinlan and his general suitability as guardian under other circumstances, describing him as "very sincere, moral, ethical and religious." The court felt, however, that the obligation to concur in the medical care and treatment of his daughter would be a source of anguish to him and would distort his "decision-making processes." We disagree, for we sense from the whole record before us that while Mr. Quinlan feels a natural grief, and understandably sorrows because of the tragedy which has befallen his daughter, his strength of purpose and character far outweighs these sentiments and qualifies him eminently for guardianship of the person as well as the property of his daughter. . . .

. . .

DECLARATORY RELIEF

We thus arrive at the formulation of the declaratory relief which we have concluded is appropriate to this case. Some time has passed since Karen's physical and mental condition was described to the Court. At that time her continuing deterioration was plainly projected. Since the record has not been expanded we assume that she is now even more fragile and nearer to death than she was then. Since her present treating physicians may give reconsideration to her present posture in the light of this opinion, and since we are transferring to the plaintiff as guardian the choice of the attending physician and therefore other physicians may be in charge of the case who may take a different view from that of the present attending physicians, we herewith declare the following affirmative relief on behalf of the plaintiff. Upon the concurrence of the guardian and family of Karen, should the responsible attending physicians conclude that there is no reasonable possibility of Karen's ever emerging from her present comatose condition to a cognitive, sapient state and that the life-support apparatus now being administered to Karen should be discontinued, they shall consult with the hospital "Ethics Committee" or like body of the institution in which Karen is then hospitalized. If that consultative body agrees that there is no reasonable possibility of Karen's ever emerging from her present comatose condition to a cognitive, sapient state, the present life-support system may be withdrawn and said action shall be without any civil or criminal liability therefor on the part of any participant, whether guardian, physician, hospital or others. We herewith specifically so hold.

CONCLUSION

We therefore remand this record to the trial court to implement (without further testimonial hearing) the following decisions:

1. To discharge, with the thanks of the Court for his service, the present guardian of the person of Karen Quinlan, Thomas R. Curtin, Esquire, a member of the Bar and an officer of the court.

2. To appoint Joseph Quinlan as guardian of the person of Karen Quinlan with full power to make decisions with regard to the identity of her treating physicians.

. . .

By the above ruling we do not intend to be understood as implying that a proceeding for judicial declaratory relief is necessarily required for the implementation of comparable decisions in the field of medical practice.

Modified and remanded.

NOTE

The general public probably first became aware of issues raised by decisions to forego or terminate treatment in the *Quinlan* case. Although there was some initial confusion, the *Quinlan* opinion makes clear that while Karen Quinlan was irreversibly comatose, she was not brain dead by the "Harvard Criteria" because she retained vegetative functions of the brain. See discussion at Sec. A.1., supra. Karen Quinlan remains alive at the time of writing. Her survival was for the most part an unexpected result although a few experts had testified that she might possibly survive and breathe spontaneously after removal from the respirator. In re Quinlan, 137 N.J.Super. at 247, 348 A.2d at 812; Testimony of Julius Korein, M.D., In the Matter of Karen Quinlan 321 (2 vol.) (1977); Testimony of Fred Plum, M.D., id. at 480, 483–85.

The initial view that Karen Quinlan was dead by brain death criteria and her unexpected survival after removal from the respirator raise concerns about the accuracy of diagnosis and reliability of medical prognosis with an unconscious patient. These issues are of course intertwined with questions about appropriate care of long-term unconscious patients. For a discussion of the problems of diagnosis and prognosis, see President's Commission, Deciding to Forego Life Sustaining Treatment 174–81 (1983).

The Supreme Court of New Jersey and the trial court differed on the question of who should make the decision whether to remove Karen Quinlan from the respirator. The trial court approached the question within the framework of equitable concepts;

> The judicial conscience and morality involved in considering whether the Court should authorize Karen Quinlan's removal from the respirator are inextricably involved with the nature of medical science and the role of the physician in our society and his duty to . . . his patient.
>
> . . . . The nature, extent and duration of care by societal standards is the responsibility of a physician. The morality and conscience of our society places this responsibility in the hands of the physician. What justification is there to remove it from the control of the medical profession and place it in the hands of the courts?

137 N.J.Super. at 257, 259, 348 A.2d at 818.

The trial court judge found none. The judge concluded that the court in exercise of its *parens patriae* powers could not, consistent with its obligation to protect incompetent persons, permit Karen Quinlan's death. The trial court consequently refused to appoint Karen's father as the guardian of her person. Do you prefer the conclusion of the trial court judge to that of the Supreme Court of New Jersey? In view of the fact that the trial court held that the determination whether to remove Karen from the respirator was a medical decision and one to be made by her physician, would Karen's parents have been wiser to have changed physicians rather than to seek appointment as Karen's guardian with the express power to authorize the discontinuance of life support systems?

Are issues raised by the care of irreversibly comatose patients different from those of other incompetent patients? Consider the decision In re Conroy, 190 N.J.Super. 453, 464 A.2d 303 (App.Div.1983). Claire Conroy was an 84 year old resident of a nursing home. She had never married and had been devoted to her sisters and cats. Her last sister died in 1975 leaving her nephew as her only living relative. Ms. Conroy was afflicted with organic brain syndrome. She was described as "severely demented." At the time of initiation of the court proceedings she was bed-bound with severe contractions of her lower legs. She did not respond to verbal stimuli, but according to the court's opinion, "she followed movements with her eyes, used her hands to scratch herself, and was able to move her head, neck, arms and hands voluntarily." Id. at 457–58, 464 A.2d at 305. She smiled when someone massaged her or combed her hair. She also moaned while being fed. Her nephew and legal guardian petitioned the court to authorize the removal of Ms. Conroy's nasogastric feeding tube. The trial court granted the petition. In re Conroy, 188 N.J.Super. 523, 457 A.2d 1232 (1983). Its order was stayed pending appeal.

Although Claire Conroy died before the appellate court could rule, it held the case was not moot because the appeal presented issues of great public importance. The appellate court reversed because it believed the trial court order was an act of euthanasia, 190 N.J.Super. at 476, 464 A.2d at 315,

> The distinction between an "awake" but confused patient like Conroy and an "asleep," vegetative patient like Karen Quinlan is material and determinative in this case, ... [I]t is plain that *Quinlan* applies only to noncognitive, vegetative patients . . . . In our view, the right to terminate life-sustaining treatment based on a guardian's substituted judgment should be limited to incurable and terminally ill patients who are brain dead, irreversibly comatose or vegetative, and who would gain no medical benefit from continued treatment. *A fortiori*, there can be no justification for withholding nourishment, which is really not "treatment" at all, from a patient who does not meet these criteria.

Id. at 466, 310.

Quinlan suggests that in appropriate circumstances it is legally permissible to remove an irreversibly comatose patient from a respirator. Should it also be permissible to discontinue intravenous feeding or to refuse to treat infections?

BARBER v. SUPERIOR COURT

Court of Appeal of California, Second District, Division 2, 1983.
147 Cal.App.3d 1006, 195 Cal.Rptr. 484.

COMPTON, J.

. . .

Deceased Clarence Herbert underwent surgery for closure of an ileostomy. Petitioner Robert Nejdl, M.D., was Mr. Herbert's surgeon and petitioner Neil Barber, M.D. was his attending internist. Shortly after the successful completion of the surgery, and while in the recovery room, Mr. Herbert suffered a cardio-respiratory arrest. He was revived by a team of physicians and nurses and immediately placed on life support equipment.

Within the following three days, it was determined that Mr. Herbert was in a deeply comatose state from which he was not likely to recover. Tests and examinations performed by several physicians, including petitioners herein, each specializing in relevant fields of medicine indicated that Mr. Herbert had suffered severe brain damage, leaving him in a vegetative state, which was likely to be permanent.

At that time petitioners informed Mr. Herbert's family of their opinion as to his condition and chances for recovery. While there is some dispute as to the precise terminology used by the doctors, it is clear that they communicated to the family that the prognosis for recovery was extremely poor. At that point, the family convened and drafted a written request to the hospital personnel stating that they wanted "all machines taken off that are sustaining life" (sic). As a result, petitioners, either directly or as a result of orders given by them, caused the respirator and other life-sustaining equipment to be removed. Mr. Herbert continued to breathe without the equipment but showed no signs of improvement. The family remained at his bedside and requested of the nursing staff that Mr. Herbert not be disturbed. They even objected to certain routine procedures followed by hospital personnel in caring for comatose patients.

After two more days had elapsed, petitioners, after consulting with the family, ordered removal of the intravenous tubes which provided hydration and nourishment. From that point until his death, Mr. Herbert received nursing care which preserved his dignity and provided a clean and hygienic environment.

The precise issue for determination by this court is whether the evidence presented before the magistrate was sufficient to support his determination that petitioners should not be held to answer to the charges of murder (Pen.Code, § 187), and conspiracy to commit murder (Pen.Code, § 182).

. . .

Murder is the *unlawful* killing of a human being, . . . with malice aforethought." . . . Malice may be express or implied. It is express when there is an intent *unlawfully* to take any life. It is implied when the circumstances show an abandoned and malignant heart. . . .

The magistrate who heard the evidence made written findings of fact and concluded that (1) petitioners did not "kill" the deceased since their conduct was not the proximate cause of death—the proximate cause (the principal cause listed on the death certificate) being diffuse encephalomalacia, secondary to anoxia, (2) the petitioners' conduct under the circumstances, being the result of good faith, ethical and sound medical judgment, was not unlawful, and (3) the petitioners' state of mind did not amount to "malice."

The superior court judge, as he was required to do under the statute before ordering reinstatement of the complaint, concluded *as a matter of law* that petitioners' conduct, however well motivated, and however ethical or sound in the eyes of the medical profession, was, under California law, "unlawful." This conclusion was reached despite his determination that the magistrate's findings were supported by substantial evidence.

The judge opined that, since everyone, sooner or later will die, homicide is simply the shortening of life by some measurable period of time and inasmuch as the petitioners' intentional conduct, which shortened Mr. Herbert's life, was not authorized by law, it constituted murder.

. . .

For the purposes of this decision, however, we accept the superior court judge's analysis that if petitioners unlawfully and intentionally killed Mr. Herbert, the malice could be presumed regardless of their motive.

The use of the term "unlawful" in defining a criminal homicide is generally to distinguish a criminal homicide from those homicides which society has determined to be "justifiable" or "excusable." Euthanasia, of course, is neither justifiable nor excusable in California.

In California, homicide is excusable, inter alia, "when committed by *accident* or *misfortune*, . . . in doing any . . . lawful act by lawful means, with usual and ordinary caution, and without any unlawful intent." . . . Since petitioners conduct, whether lawful or unlawful, was intentional, if it resulted in the shortening of Mr. Herbert's life, it was not a matter of *accident* and *misfortune*.

Since "justifiable" homicide, by a person other than a peace officer, in California is limited essentially to cases of self-defense and defense of others . . . , that concept has no application here.

Obviously the above mentioned concepts evolved and were codified at a time well prior to the development of the modern medical technology which is involved here, which technology has caused our society to re-think its concepts of what constitutes "life" and "death."

This gap between the statutory law and recent medical developments has resulted in the instant prosecution and its attendant legal dispute. That dispute in order to be resolved within the framework of existing criminal law must be narrowed to a determination of whether petitioners' conduct was unlawful. That determination, as indicated above, must be made on the basis of principles other than those limited ones set forth in Penal Code sections 195 and 197.

. . .

We deal here with the physician's responsibility in a case of a patient who, though not "brain dead," faces an indefinite vegetative existence without any of the higher cognitive brain functions. . . .

. . .

. . . To our knowledge . . . this case is the first instance in which the issue has been presented in the context of a criminal prosecution.

Of course, the only long-term solution to this problem is necessarily legislative in nature. It is that body which must address the moral, social, ethical, medical and legal issues raised by cases such as the one at bench. Manifestly, this court cannot attempt to rewrite the statutory definition of death or set forth guidelines covering all possible future cases. Due to legislative inaction in this area, however, we are forced to evaluate peti-tioners' conduct within the context of the woefully inadequate framework of the criminal law.

. . .

We . . . turn to an analysis of the superior court's determination that petitioners' conduct was "unlawful" as a matter of law.

In this state a . . . long line of cases, approved by the Supreme Court in Cobbs v. Grant (1972) 8 Cal.3d 229, 104 Cal.Rptr. 505, 502 P.2d 1, have held that where a doctor performs treatment in the absence of an informed consent, there is an actionable battery. The obvious corollary to this principle is that a competent adult patient has the legal right to refuse medical treatment.

It is clear from the legislative findings and declaration provided in Health and Safety Code section 7186 [the Natural Death Act], that the Legislature recognized such a right to control one's medical treatment, especially in circumstances such as presented here.

. . .

. . . [W]e conclude that Health and Safety Code section 7188 does not represent the exclusive basis for terminating life-support equipment in this state. Nor is a diagnosis of "brain dead" a condition precedent to the cessation of such treatment.

As a predicate to our analysis of whether the petitioners' conduct amounted to an "unlawful killing," we conclude that the cessation of "heroic" life support measures is not an affirmative act but rather a withdrawal or omission of further treatment.

Even though these life support devices are, to a degree, "self-propelled," each pulsation of the respirator or each drop of fluid introduced into the patient's body by intravenous feeding devices is comparable to a manually administered injection or item of medication. Hence "disconnecting" of the mechanical devices is comparable to withholding the manually administered injection or medication.

Further we view the use of an intravenous administration of nourishment and fluid, under the circumstances, as being the same as the use of the respirator or other form of life support equipment.

The prosecution would have us draw a distinction between the use of mechanical breathing devices such as respirators and mechanical feeding devices such as intravenous tubes. The distinction urged seems to be based more on the emotional symbolism of providing food and water to those incapable of providing for themselves rather than on any rational difference in cases such as the one at bench. . . .

Medical nutrition and hydration may not always provide net benefits to patients. Medical procedures to provide nutrition and hydration are more similar to other medical procedures than to typical human ways of providing nutrition and hydration. Their benefits and burdens ought to be evaluated in the same manner as any other medical procedure.

. . .

In the final analysis, since we view petitioners' conduct as that of omission rather than affirmative action, the resolution of this case turns on whether petitioners had a duty to continue to provide life sustaining [sic] treatment.

There is no criminal liability for failure to act unless there is a legal duty to act. . . . Thus the critical issue becomes one of determining the duties owed by a physician to a patient who has been reliably diagnosed as in a comatose state from which any meaningful recovery of cognitive brain function is exceedingly unlikely.

. . .

In examining this issue we must keep in mind that the life-sustaining technology involved in this case is not traditional treatment in that it is not being used to directly cure or even address the pathological condition. It merely sustains biological functions in order to gain time to permit other processes to address the pathology.

The question presented by this modern technology is, once undertaken, at what point does it cease to perform its intended function and who should have the authority to decide that any further prolongation of the dying process is of no benefit to either the patient or his family?

A physician has no duty to continue treatment, once it has proved to be ineffective. Although there may be a duty to provide life-sustaining machinery in the *immediate* aftermath of a cardio-respiratory arrest, there is no duty to continue its use once it has become futile in the opinion of qualified medical personnel.

. . .

Of course, the difficult determinations that must be made under these principles is the point at which further treatment will be of no reasonable benefit to the patient, who should have the power to make that decision and who should have the authority to direct termination of treatment.

No precise guidelines as to when or how these decisions should be made can be provided by this court since this determination is essentially a medical one to be made at a time and on the basis of facts which will be unique to each case. If specific procedural rules are to be adopted in this area in order to protect the public interest, they must necessarily come from that body most suited for the collection of data and the reaching of a consensus—the Legislature. However, we would be derelict in our duties if we did not provide some general guidelines for future conduct in the absence of such legislation.

.   .   .

Several authorities have discussed the issue of which life-sustaining procedures must be used and for how long their use must be maintained in terms of "ordinary" and "extraordinary" means of treatment.   .   .   . The use of these terms begs the question. A more rational approach involves the determination of whether the proposed treatment is proportionate or disproportionate in terms of the benefits to be gained versus the burdens caused.

Under this approach, proportionate treatment is that which, in the view of the patient, has at least a reasonable chance of providing benefits to the patient, which benefits outweigh the burdens attendant to the treatment. Thus, even if a proposed course of treatment might be extremely painful or intrusive, it would still be proportionate treatment if the prognosis was for complete cure or significant improvement in the patient's condition. On the other hand, a treatment course which is only minimally painful or intrusive may nonetheless be considered disproportionate to the potential benefits if the prognosis is virtually hopeless for any significant improvement in condition.   .   .   .

Several authorities have struggled with this issue and some concensus has been reached on the theory if not the terminology.

.   .   .

[T]he determination as to whether the burdens of treatment are worth enduring for any individual patient depends on facts unique to each case, namely, how long the treatment is likely to extend life and under what conditions.   .   .   .

Of course the patient's interests and desires are the key ingredients of the decision making process. When dealing with patients for whom the possibility of full recovery is virtually non-existent, and who are incapable of expressing their desires, there is also something of a consensus on the standard to be applied.

"[T]he focal point of decision should be the prognosis as to the reasonable possibility of return to cognitive and sapient life, as distinguished from the forced continuance of that biological vegetative existence .   .   . ." (*Matter of Quinlan* [355 A.2d 647, 669]).

" 'Prolongation of life,'   .   .   . does not mean a mere suspension of the act of dying, but contemplates, at the very least, a remission of symptoms enabling a return towards a normal, functioning, integrated existence." (*Matter of Dinnerstein* (1978) 380 N.E.2d 134, at p. 138.)

The evidence presented at the preliminary hearing supports the conclusion that petitioners reasonably concluded that Mr. Herbert had virtually no chance of recovering his cognitive or motor functions. The most optimistic prognosis provided by any of the testifying experts was that the patient had an excellent chance of "recovery." However, recovery was defined in terms of a spectrum running from a persistent vegetative state to full recovery. A persistent vegetative state was described as that state in which the patient would have no contact with the environment but parts of the brain would continue to live. The doctor who was of course approaching the case after the fact and from a hindsight view, was unable to predict where on this continuum Mr. Herbert was likely to end up. Several studies on which the expert relied, however, indicated that the chances for unimpaired or full recovery were miniscule. The results of these studies coincided with the diagnoses of the physicians who had actually examined and dealt with the patient before his demise.

Given the general standards for determining when there is a duty to provide medical treatment of debatable value, the question still remains as to who should make these vital decisions. Clearly, the medical diagnoses and prognoses must be determined by the treating and consulting physicians under the generally accepted standards of medical practice in the community and, whenever possible, the patient himself should then be the ultimate decision-maker.

When the patient, however, is incapable of deciding for himself, because of his medical condition or for other reasons, there is no clear authority on the issue of who and under what procedure is to make the final decision.

It seems clear, in the instant case, that if the family had insisted on continued treatment, petitioners would have acceded to that request. The family's decision to the contrary was, as noted, ignored by the superior court as being a legal nullity.

In support of that conclusion the People argue that only duly appointed legal guardians have the authority to act on behalf of another. While guardianship proceedings might be used in this context, we are not aware of any authority *requiring* such procedure. In the case at bench, petitioners consulted with and relied on the decisions of the immediate family, which included the patient's wife and several of his children. No formal guardianship proceedings were instituted.

In the absence of legislation requiring such legal proceedings, we cannot say that failure to institute such proceedings made petitioners' conduct unlawful. Whether such proceedings are to be required in the future is again a question for the Legislature to decide.

The authorities are in agreement that any surrogate, court appointed or otherwise, ought to be guided in his or her decisions first by his knowledge of the patient's own desires and feelings, to the extent that they were expressed before the patient became incompetent. . . .

If it is not possible to ascertain the choice the patient would have made, the surrogate ought to be guided in his decision by the patient's best interests. Under this standard, such factors as the relief of suffering, the preservation or restoration of functioning and the quality as well as the extent of life sustained may be considered. Finally, since most people are concerned about the well-being of their loved ones, the surrogate may take into account the impact of the decision on those people closest to the patient. . . .

There was evidence that Mr. Herbert had, prior to his incapacitation, expressed to his wife his feeling that he would not want to be kept alive by machines or "become another Karen Ann Quinlan." The family made its decision together (the directive to the hosptial was signed by the wife and eight of his children) after consultation with the doctors.[2]

Under the circumstances of this case, the wife was the proper person to act as a surrogate for the patient with the authority to decide issues regarding further treatment, and would have so qualified had judicial approval been sought. There is no evidence that there was any disagreement among the wife and children. Nor was there any evidence that they were motivated in their decision by anything other than love and concern for the dignity of their husband and father.

Furthermore, in the absence of legislative guidance, we find no legal requirement that prior judicial approval is necessary before any decision to withdraw treatment can be made.

. . .

. . . [W]e conclude that the petitioners' omission to continue treatment under the circumstances, though intentional and with knowledge that the patient would die, was not an unlawful failure to perform a legal duty. In view of our decision on that issue, it becomes unnecessary to deal with the further issue of whether petitioners' conduct was in fact the proximate cause of Mr. Herbert's ultimate death.

The evidence amply supports the magistrate's conclusion. The superior court erred in determining that as a matter of law the evidence required the magistrate to hold petitioners to answer.

Let a peremptory writ of prohibition issue. . . .

NOTE

Are there substantive principles that can be used to judge whether life and death decisions concerning appropriate care are morally justified? That is the question we explore in the materials that immediately follow. In addition, there are three types of questions raised by the treatment of incompetent patients which are considered in more detail in later parts of the chapter. See Sec. B.4., infra. One category of questions concerns the proper legal standard to use in making decisions to forego treatment. The second category involves the "interests" of third parties—families, health care providers, the state—and the extent to which, if any, these "interests" can appropriately be considered in the decisionmaking process. The third category of questions raises the process issues of who should decide.

For additional discussion of issues concerning artificial provision of nutrition and fluids, see Steinbock, The Removal of Mr. Herbert's Feeding Tube, 13 Hastings Ctr.Rep. 13 (Oct. 1983); Lynn and Childress, Must Patients Always Be Given Food and Water? 13 Hastings Ctr.Rep. 17 (Oct. 1983); Paris and Fletcher, Infant Doe Regulations and the Absolute Requirement to Use Nourishment and Fluids for the Dying Infant, 11 Law Med. & Health Care 210 (1983); Weiser, 2 Doctors Take Controversial Stand on Feeding Those Near Death, Washington Post, Nov. 2, 1983, at A3, col. 1.

---

2. The People urge that petitioners were obligated to consult Mr. Herbert's sister-in-law rather than his wife and children for this most important decision. Despite the fact that Mr. Herbert apparently entered the name of his sister-in-law on a hospital form (the purpose of which was unclear from the evidence), his wife and children were the most obviously appropriate surrogates in this case. They were the people who would be most affected by the decision and were in the best position to know Mr. Herbert's own feelings and desire. In addition, there was clear evidence that they were concerned for his comfort and welfare and some or all of them were present at the hospital nearly around the clock.

b. The Distinction Between Active and Passive Euthanasia

JAMES RACHELS,
ACTIVE AND PASSIVE EUTHANASIA

292 New Eng. J.Med. 78–80 (1975).

The distinction between active and passive euthanasia is thought to be crucial for medical ethics. The idea is that it is permissible, at least in some cases, to withhold treatment and allow a patient to die, but it is never permissible to take any direct action designed to kill the patient. This doctrine seems to be accepted by most doctors, and it is endorsed in a statement adopted by the House of Delegates of the American Medical Association on December 4, 1973:

> The intentional termination of the life of one human being by another—mercy killing—is contrary to that for which the medical profession stands and is contrary to the policy of the American Medical Association.

> The cessation of the employment of extraordinary means to prolong the life of the body when there is irrefutable evidence that biological death is imminent is the decision of the patient and/or his immediate family. The advice and judgment of the physician should be freely available to the patient and/or his immediate family.

However, a strong case can be made against this doctrine. . . .

To begin with a familiar type of situation, a patient who is dying of incurable cancer of the throat is in terrible pain, which can no longer be satisfactorily alleviated. He is certain to die within a few days, even if present treatment is continued, but he does not want to go on living for those days since the pain is unbearable. So he asks the doctor for an end to it, and his family joins in the request.

Suppose the doctor agrees to withhold treatment, as the conventional doctrine says he may. The justification for his doing so is that the patient is in terrible agony, and since he is going to die anyway, it would be wrong to prolong his suffering needlessly. But now notice this. If one simply withholds treatment, it may take the patient longer to die, and so he may suffer more than he would if more direct action were taken and a lethal injection given. This fact provides strong reason for thinking that, once the initial decision not to prolong his agony has been made, active euthanasia is actually preferable to passive euthanasia, rather than the reverse. To say otherwise is to endorse the option that leads to more suffering rather than less, and is contrary to the humanitarian impulse that prompts the decision not to prolong his life in the first place.

. . .

My second argument is that the conventional doctrine leads to decisions concerning life and death made on irrelevant grounds.

Consider . . . the case of the infants with Down's syndrome who need operations for congenital defects unrelated to the syndrome to live. Sometimes, there is no operation, and the baby dies, but where there is no such defect the baby lives on. Now, an operation such as that to remove an intestinal obstruction is not prohibitively difficult. The reason why such operations are not performed in these cases is, clearly, that the child has Down's syndrome and the parents and doctor judge that because of that fact it is better for the child to die.

But notice that this situation is absurd, no matter what view one takes of the lives and potentials of such babies. If the life of such an infant is worth preserving, what does it matter if it needs a simple operation? Or, if one thinks it better that such a baby should not live on, what difference does it make that it happens to have an unobstructed intestinal tract? In either case, the matter of life and death is being decided on irrelevant grounds. It is the Down's syndrome, and not the intestines, that is the issue. The matter should be decided, if at all, on that basis, and not be allowed to depend on the essentially irrelevant question of whether the intestinal tract is blocked.

. . .

One reason why so many people think that there is an important moral difference between active and passive euthanasia is that they think killing someone is morally worse than letting someone die. But is it? Is killing, in itself, worse than letting die? To investigate this issue, two cases may be considered that are exactly alike except that one involves killing where-as the other involves letting someone die. Then, it can be asked whether this difference makes any difference to the moral assessments. It is important that the cases be exactly alike, except for this one difference, since otherwise one cannot be confident that it this difference and not some other that accounts for any variation in the assessments of the two cases. So, let us consider this pair of cases:

In the first, Smith stands to gain a large inheritance if anything should happen to his six-year-old cousin. One evening while the child is taking his bath, Smith sneaks into the bathroom and drowns the child, and then arranges things so that it will look like an accident.

In the second, Jones also stands to gain if anything should happen to his six-year-old cousin. Like Smith, Jones sneaks in planning to drown the child in his bath. However, just as he enters the bathroom Jones sees the child slip and hit his head, and fall face down in the water. Jones is delighted; he stands by, ready to push the child's head back under if it is necessary, but it is not necessary. With only a little thrashing about, the child drowns all by himself, "accidentally," as Jones watches and does nothing.

Now Smith killed the child, whereas Jones "merely" let the child die. That is the only difference between them. Did either man behave better, from a moral point of view? If the difference between killing and letting die were in itself a morally important matter, one should say that Jones's behavior was less reprehensible than Smith's. But does one really want to say that? I think not. In the first place, both men acted from the same motive, personal gain, and both had exactly the same end in view when they acted. It may be inferred from Smith's conduct that he is a bad man, although that judgment may be withdrawn or modified if certain further facts are learned about him—for example, that he is mentally de-ranged. But would not the very same thing be inferred about Jones from his conduct? And would not the same further considerations also be rel-evant to any modification of this judgment? Moreover, suppose Jones pleaded, in his own defense, "After all, I didn't do anything except just stand there and watch the child drown. I didn't kill him; I only let him die." Again, if letting die were in itself less bad than killing, this defense should have at least some weight. But it does not. Such a "defense" can only be regarded as a grotesque perversion of moral reasoning. Morally speaking, it is no defense at all.

. . .

Many people will find this judgment hard to accept. One reason, I think, is that it is very easy to conflate the question of whether killing is, in itself, worse than letting die, with the very different question of whether most actual cases of killing are more reprehensible than most actual cases of letting die. Most actual cases of killing are clearly terrible (think, for example, of all the murders reported in the newspapers), and one hears of such cases every day. On the other hand, one hardly ever hears of a case of letting die, except for the actions of doctors who are motivated by humanitarian reasons. So one learns to think of killing in a much worse light than of letting die. But this does not mean that there is something about killing that makes it in itself worse than letting die, for it is not the bare difference between killing and letting die that makes the difference in these cases. Rather, the other factors—the murderer's motive of personal gain, for example, contrasted with the doctor's humanitarian motivation—account for different reactions to the different cases.

I have argued that killing is not in itself any worse than letting die; if my contention is right, it follows that active euthanasia is not any worse than passive euthanasia. . . .

. . .

TOM L. BEAUCHAMP,
A REPLY TO RACHELS ON ACTIVE AND
PASSIVE EUTHANASIA *

in Ethical Issues in Death and Dying
246, 249–253 (T. Beauchamp and S. Perlin eds. 1978).

III

. . . I wish now to provide what I believe is the most significant argument that can be adduced in defense of the active/passive distinction. I shall develop this argument by combining (1) so-called wedge or slippery slope arguments with (2) recent arguments in defense of rule utilitarianism. I shall explain each in turn and show how in combination they may be used to defend the active/passive distinction.

(1) *Wedge arguments* proceed as follows: if killing were allowed, even under the guise of a merciful extinction of life, a dangerous wedge would be introduced which places all "undesirable" or "unworthy" human life in a precarious condition. Proponents of wedge arguments believe the initial wedge places us on a slippery slope for at least one of two reasons: (i) It is said that our justifying principles leave us with no principled way to avoid the slide into saying that all sorts of killings would be justified under similar conditions. Here it is thought that once killing is allowed, a firm line between justified and unjustified killings cannot be securely drawn. It is thought best not to redraw the line in the first place, for redrawing it will inevitably lead to a downhill slide. It is then often pointed out that as a matter of historical record this is precisely what has occurred in the darker regions of human history, including the Nazi era, where euthanasia began with the best intentions for horribly ill, non-Jewish Germans and gradually spread to anyone deemed an enemy of the people. (ii) Second, it is said that our basic principles against killing will

* This paper is a heavily revised version of an article by the same title first published in [Social Ethics (T. Mappes & J. Zembaty eds. 1976)]. . . . Copyright © 1975, 1977 by Tom L. Beauchamp.

be gradually eroded once some form of killing is legitimated. For example, it is said that permitting voluntary euthanasia will lead to permitting involuntary euthanasia, which will in turn lead to permitting euthanasia for those who are a nuisance to society (idiots, recidivist criminals, defective newborns, and the insane, e.g.). Gradually other principles which instill respect for human life will be eroded or abandoned in the process.

I am not inclined to accept the first reason (i). If our justifying principles are themselves justified, then any action they warrant would be justified. Accordingly, I shall only be concerned with the second approach (ii).

(2) *Rule utilitarianism* is the position that a society ought to adopt a rule if its acceptance would have better consequences for the common good (greater social utility) than any comparable rule could have in that society. Any action is right if it conforms to a valid rule and wrong if it violates the rule. Sometimes it is said that alternative rules should be measured against one another, while it has also been suggested that whole moral *codes* (complete sets of rules) rather than individual rules should be compared. While I prefer the latter formulation (Brandt's), this internal dispute need not detain us here. The important point is that a particular rule or a particular code of rules is morally justified if and only if there is no other competing rule or moral code whose acceptance would have a higher utility value for society, and where a rule's acceptability is contingent upon the consequences which would result if the rule were made current.

Wedge arguments, when conjoined with rule utilitarian arguments, may be applied to euthanasia issues in the following way. We presently subscribe to a no-active-euthanasia rule (which the AMA suggests we retain). Imagine now that in our society we make current a restricted-active-euthanasia rule (as Rachels seems to urge). Which of these two moral rules would, if enacted, have the consequence of maximizing social utility? Clearly a restricted-active-euthanasia rule would have *some* utility value, as Rachels notes, since some intense and uncontrollable suffering would be eliminated. However, it may not have the highest utility value in the structure of our present code or in any imaginable code which could be made current, and therefore may not be a component in the ideal code for our society. If wedge arguments raise any serious questions at all, as I think they do, they rest in this area of whether a code would be weakened or strengthened by the addition of active euthanasia principles. For the disutility of introducing legitimate killing into one's moral code (in the form of active euthanasia rules) may, in the long run, outweigh the utility of doing so, as a result of the eroding effect such a relaxation would have on rules in the code which demand respect for human life. If, for example, rules permitting active killing were introduced, it is not implausible to suppose that destroying defective newborns (a form of involuntary euthanasia) would become an accepted and common practice, that as population increases occur the aged will be even more neglectable and neglected than they now are, that capital punishment for a wide variety of crimes would be increasingly tempting, that some doctors would have appreciably reduced fears of actively injecting fatal doses whenever it seemed to them propitious to do so, and that laws of war against killing would erode in efficacy even beyond their already abysmal level.

A hundred such possible consequences might easily be imagined. But these few are sufficient to make the larger point that such rules permitting killing could lead to a general reduction of respect for human life. Rules against killing in a moral code are not *isolated* moral principles; they are pieces of a web of rules against killing which forms the code. The more threads one removes, the weaker the fabric becomes. And if, as I believe, moral principles against active killing have the deep and continuously civilizing effect of promoting respect for life, and if principles which allow passively letting die (as envisioned in the AMA statement) do not themselves cut against this effect, then this seems an important reason for the maintenance of the active/passive distinction. (By the logic of the above argument passively letting die would also have to be prohibited if a rule permitting it had the serious adverse consequence of eroding acceptance of rules protective of respect for life. While this prospect seems to me improbable, I can hardly claim to have refuted those conservatives who would claim that even rules which sanction letting die place us on a precarious slippery slope.)

A troublesome problem, however, confronts my use of utilitarian and wedge arguments. Most all of us would agree that both killing and letting die are justified under some conditions. Killings in self-defense and in "just" wars are widely accepted as justified because the conditions excuse the killing. If society can withstand these exceptions to moral rules prohibiting killing, then why is it not plausible to suppose society can accept another excusing exception in the form of justified active euthanasia? This is an important and worthy objection, but not a decisive one. The defenseless and the dying are significantly different classes of persons from aggressors who attack individuals and/or nations. In the case of aggressors, one does not confront the question whether their lives are no longer *worth living*. Rather, we reach the judgment that the aggressors' morally blameworthy actions justify counteractions. But in the case of the dying and the otherwise ill, there is no morally blameworthy action to justify our own. Here we are required to accept the judgment that their lives are no longer *worth living* in order to believe that the termination of their lives is justified. It is the latter sort of judgment which is feared by those who take the wedge argument seriously. We do not now permit and never have permitted the taking of morally blameless lives. I think this is the key to understanding why recent cases of intentionally allowing the death of defective newborns .   .   . have generated such protracted controversy. Even if such newborns could not have led meaningful lives (a matter of some controversy), it is the wedged foot in the door which creates the most intense worries. For if we once take a decision to allow a restricted infanticide justification or any justification at all on grounds that a life is not meaningful or not worth living, we have qualified our moral rules against killing. That this qualification is a matter of the utmost seriousness needs no argument. I mention it here only to show why the wedge argument may have moral force even though we *already* allow some very different conditions to justify intentional killing.

There is one final utilitarian reason favoring the preservation of the active/passive distinction. Suppose we distinguish the following two types of cases of wrongly diagnosed patients:

1. Patients wrongly diagnosed as hopeless, and who will survive even if a treatment *is* ceased (in order to allow a natural death).

2. Patients wrongly diagnosed as hopeless, and who will survive only if the treatment is *not ceased* (in order to allow a natural death).

If a social rule permitting only passive euthanasia were in effect, then doctors and families who "allowed death" would lose only patients in class 2, not those in class 1; whereas if active euthanasia were permitted, at least some patients in class 1 would be needlessly lost. Thus, the consequence of a no-active-euthanasia rule would be to save some lives which could not be saved if both forms of euthanasia were allowed. This reason is not a *decisive* reason for favoring a policy of passive euthanasia, since these classes (1 and 2) are likely to be very small and since there might be counterbalancing reasons (extreme pain, autonomous expression of the patient, etc.) in favor of active euthanasia. But certainly it is *a* reason favoring only passive euthanasia and one which is morally relevant and ought to be considered along with other moral reasons.

. . .

NOTE

Are you persuaded by Rachels's argument that there is no morally relevant distinction between active and passive euthanasia? Assuming that you are persuaded, what sorts of circumstances justify actively taking the life of another? Would it be permissible to give Karen Quinlan a lethal drug?

Even if there is no moral basis for drawing a distinction between active and passive euthanasia, should society nevertheless retain the distinction for other purposes? Does the distinction serve a useful function in singling out certain cases for closer scrutiny? Should any decision to retain the distinction depend in part on whether there are legal ways to accommodate actions that may be justified which result in death? An excellent debate that further develops these issues took place between Glanville Williams and Yale Kamisar. See Williams, The Sanctity of Life and the Criminal Law (1975); Kamisar, Some Non-religious Views Against Proposed Mercy-Killing Legislation, 42 Minn.L.Rev. 969 (1958); Williams, Mercy-Killing Legislation—A Rejoinder, 43 Minn.L.Rev. 1 (1958).

c. The Principle of Double Effect

EIKE-HENNER W. KLUGE,
THE ETHICS OF DELIBERATE DEATH

15–18 (1981).

One of the concepts frequently used to justify what would otherwise be considered a morally objectionable act of euthanasia is the principle of double effect. This principle is best known from the context of abortion situations where saving the life of the mother must entail killing the fetus. There it supposedly shows that this killing, which would otherwise be morally objectionable, does not contravene moral and theological tenets.

. . .

The principle itself is that if one act has two consequences, the one good and the other evil, where both consequences are inevitable outcomes of the initial act itself, then the act is morally acceptable (and, presumably, the bad result morally excusable) if these four conditions are met:

(1) Considered in and by itself, the act as such is not morally objectionable.

(2) The agent's intention in performing the act is directed towards the good to be achieved only and does not include the bad result as a desideratum.

(3) The bad result is merely the inevitable concomitant and not a means to the good result or a condition of it.

(4) There are grave reasons for engaging in the act itself such that failure to perform the act would result in at least as bad a state of affairs as the bad effect of the performance of the act.

The application of the principle to justify euthanasia is relatively clear. The cases fall into two general categories: those involving an element of triage and those focusing on the agonizing, "undignified" but in any case irremedial condition of the patient. In the case of triage the reasoning is this: Since by the very nature of the situation it is impossible to save both individuals by supplying adequate medical care; and since the nondistribution as well as equal distribution of the available resources will result in the death of both, the selective allocation of the resources (and the pleasant or at least painless demise of one of the individuals) is justified by all four conditions. In situations involving irremediable agony, that state is used as a grave reason for justifying the administration of an analgesic (or other appropriate drug or technique) in amounts that will appreciable shorten the life of the individual or even kill him outright then and there.

. . .

However, the principle is ultimately unacceptable because it is inherently incoherent. The morally acceptable act itself presents no difficulty. But the condition that the agent's intention in performing the act must not include as a desideratum the accompanying bad result cannot be met consistently with the other conditions.

Why is this so? It is already clear that an act in itself is not identical with the physical activity that may be involved in performing it. Thus, the act of murdering a person is not identical with the physical activity of slipping a knife into his heart, the act of stealing is not identical with that of taking certain goods, and so on. In all these cases the mere physical activity must be the result of intention and must occur in a certain context. In fact, all other things being equal, the nature and identity of a given act resides precisely in its context and in the person's intention. Someone may stumble, have a muscle spasm, or simply be careless; he may take something by accident or be a kleptomaniac. Without these conditions—or with different ones operative—the acts would be different.

Since this holds for acts in general, the act referred to in the second clause above is no exception. Being an act, it too takes its nature and identity from the context and the intention associated with it. That fact, however, calls into question the very first requirement, the moral acceptability of the act. For the same act must meet all four conditions. But the moral status of the act referred to in the second clause is precisely the double-resultant act whose moral status is here in question. Therefore, in characterizing it as morally acceptable, the first condition begs the question at issue since it is in the nature of the act that it be double-resultant and involve the particular intention of bringing about the good result despite the bad.

This introduces the second difficulty: The intention can never be confined solely to effecting the good result without the bad. This is so because the agent must be at least aware of the results of the action in order to evaluate the requisite grave reasons. Otherwise, the whole clause would be meaningless and the argument collapse. Furthermore, in this situation the bad result is inevitable. (Otherwise the problem would be entirely different.) Therefore given the agent's awareness of this close connection between good and bad results, his intention in performing the act cannot be confined to bringing about the good result only but must include the bad as well.

. . .

Finally, it should be noted that the whole principle of double effect involves an inherent appeal to the general moral principle of utility, or the principle of greatest good for the greatest number. While this is not a logical reason for rejecting it, that principle is essentially confused and unacceptable . . . . Therefore, even if the preceding analysis were faulty the principle of double effect would still not establish anything about the moral status of an act of euthanasia.

NOTE

The principle of double effect, primarily but not exclusively part of the Roman Catholic tradition, is often invoked to justify a course of conduct when two obligations are perceived to be in conflict. For example, morphine given in doses large enough to relieve severe pain often has the side effect of hastening a patient's death. The Washington Post in a recent article reported that "a physician gave morphine to patients suffering from respiratory insufficiency, a terrifying drawn-out suffocation process in which the patient struggles to breathe, gasping 50 to 60 times a minute." Struggling to Set Standards at Life's Edge, Washington Post, Apr. 21, 1983, at A18, col. 5. The physician explained:

> If you decide that the right thing to do is give enough morphine to depress the breathing—thereby relieving the suffering—then there is an almost direct correlation with an earlier death, as close to one-to-one as man gets, as close to a borderline case as I would want medicine to get to.

Even if you agree with Kluge's criticisms of the principle of double effect, does the principle nevertheless serve a practical purpose in helping to evaluate the behavior of health care professionals? Is it useful, for example, to distinguish the giving of morphine to relieve suffering from the giving of poison? For some of the literature on the principle of double effect, see R. McCormick, Ambiguity in Moral Choice (1973); Boyle, Toward Understanding the Principle of Double Effect, 90 Ethics 527 (1980); Mangan, An Historical Analysis of the Principle of Double Effect, 10 Theological Stud. 4 (1949).

Consider also the distinction between intended versus unintended but foreseeable consequences, see President's Commission, Deciding to Forego Life-Sustaining Treatment 77–82 (1983). Do you prefer the Commission's conclusion (at 82):

> The relevant distinction, then, is not really that death is forbidden as a means to relieve suffering but is sometimes acceptable if it is merely a foreseeable consequence. Rather, the moral issue is whether or not the decisionmakers have considered the full range of foreseeable effects, have knowingly accepted whatever risk of death is entailed, and have found the risk to be justified in light of the paucity and undesirability of other options.

d. The Distinction Between Ordinary and Extraordinary Treatment

PAUL RAMSEY,
THE PATIENT AS PERSON

120–23 (1970).

[W]e need in preliminary fashion to notice some important differences between the moralist's meaning and the physician's meaning when each uses the terms *ordinary* and *extraordinary*. It is, of course, difficult to generalize, and no doubt there are some doctors who are closer than others to the moralists on the point in question. . . .

First, the doctor is apt to use the distinction to mean customary as opposed to unusual procedures. Physicians use these terms relative to the state of medical science and the healing art, by reference to whether or not a remedy has become a part of customary medical practice. In contrast, the moralists are somewhat more likely than doctors to use these terms relative to a patient's particular medical condition. While an unusual practice may become customary and the medical imperative change as medicine advances, it is also the case that the medical imperative ought to change according to the patient's condition and its "advances," no matter how usual the remedy may be for other patients or for this patient at other times. The first relativity is to the disease and to what is ordinarily done to remedy it. The second relativity is to the condition of the man who has the disease; these relative meanings lead to a definition of optional remedies in terms of what would be "extraordinary" for this individual.

. . .

Second, for the moralist, a decision to stop "extraordinary" life-sustaining treatments requires no greater and in fact the same moral warrant as a decision not to begin to use them. Again if I have understood the medical literature, a physician can make the decision not to institute such treatments with an easier conscience than he can make the decision to stop them once begun. . . . But there should be no greater reluctance to judge that continuation of treatments is no longer indicated than to judge that they should not be begun. The moralists would support physicians in this conclusion. Since a trial treatment is often a part of diagnosis of a patient's condition, one might expect there to be greater reluctance on the part of physicians in not starting than in stopping extraordinary efforts to save life. As I understand them, physicians often have the contrary difficulty.

. . .

Third, moralists almost always understand the distinction between ordinary and extraordinary procedures to refer decisively to morally relevant, nonmedical features of a particular patient's care: his "domestic economy," his familial obligations, the neighborhood that has become a part of his human existence, the person and the common good, and whether a man's fiduciary relations with God and with his fellow man have been settled. The difference between an imperative and an elective effort to save life will vary according to evaluations of these features of a human life, and a moralist's terms for expressing this final verdict are *ordinary* and *extraordinary*.

Thus, the standard definition reads as follows: "*Ordinary* means of preserving life are all medicines, treatments, and operations, which offer a reasonable hope of benefit for the patient and which can be obtained and used without excessive expense, pain, or other inconvenience. . . . *Extraordinary* means of preserving life . . . mean all medicines, treatments, and operations, which cannot be obtained without excessive expense, pain or other inconvenience, or which, if used, would not offer a reasonable hope of benefit." . . . . It is evident that theologians mean to counsel first the patient and his family and then the physician that, in deciding concerning an elective effort to save life or elective death, it is quite proper to make a balancing judgment involving decisive reference to a number of human (nonmedical) factors that constituted the worth for which that life was lived and that may discharge it from imperative continuation. Speaking as men who are doctors and in their practice, physicians may also say the same; but it is not strictly a medical judgment to say this. This is certainly not what a physician usually means when he distinguishes between ordinary and extraordinary procedures for saving life.

NOTE

The distinction between extraordinary and ordinary care, like the distinctions between acts and non-acts and direct and indirect effects, is often used to distinguish between acts that constitute homicide and suicide and those that do not. The distinction has a long history in Catholic tradition where it was used to categorize patient decisions about surgery prior to the discovery of antisepsis and anesthesia. Beauchamp and Childress, Principles of Biomedical Ethics 126 (2d ed. 1983). As the Ramsey selection suggests, however, the distinction has various meanings. Some doctors focus on the proposed therapy and label its use ordinary or customary as opposed to extraordinary or unusual. In accordance with this view the use of antibiotics, for example, would probably constitute ordinary and therefore mandatory medical care. Not all physicians would agree. See footnote 90 in note 2 following California Health and Safety Code, The Natural Death Act, infra. To others the distinction suggests that society should examine whether the proposed care in terms of expense, pain or inconvenience is useful or burdensome to the patient. Still others would argue that in assessing non-medical factors such as expense, inconvenience or pain, interests of third parties in addition to those of the patient can be considered. Depending upon what is considered "useful" and "burdensome" and to whom such considerations are significant, the artificial provision of food and use of antibiotics therefore may or may not be extraordinary in specific circumstances.

Catholic tradition allows the burden to the family to be taken into account in determining whether a particular treatment is ordinary or extraordinary. See the *Quinlan* decision, supra. The precise words of Pope Pius XII's statement were:

> The rights and duties of the family depend in general upon the presumed will of the unconscious patient if he is of age and *sui juris*. Where the proper and independent duty of the family is concerned, they are usually bound only to the use of ordinary means.

> Consequently, if it appears that the attempt at resuscitation constitutes in reality such a burden for the family that one cannot in all conscience impose it upon them, they can lawfully insist that the doctor should discontinue these attempts, and the doctor can lawfully comply.

The Prolongation of Life, 4 The Pope Speaks 393, 397 (1958).

This view was apparently affirmed in the "Declaration on Euthanasia," issued May 5, 1980 by the Sacred Congregation for the Doctrine of the Faith and approved by Pope John Paul II. It states:

> It is also permitted, with the patient's consent, to interrupt these means [provided by the most advanced medical techniques], where the results fall short of expectations. But for such a decision to be made, account will have to be taken of the reasonable wishes of the patient and the patient's family, and also of the doctors who are specially competent in the matter. The latter may, in particular, judge that the investment in instruments and personnel is disproportionate to the results foreseen; they may also judge that the techniques applied impose on the patient strain or suffering out of proportion with the benefits which he or she may gain from such techniques.

With respect to determining what is useful or burdensome for irreversibly co-matose patients, how should we weigh the interests of fetuses? See Washington Post, Mar. 2, 1982, at A2, col. 5 (woman gave birth to live child while comatose and on life support system for four months); Dillon, Life Support and Maternal Brain Death During Pregnancy, 248 J.A.M.A. 1089 (1982). To what extent should we consider society's "interests" in preserving life, research, or reducing health costs? See Field and Romanus, A Decerebrate Patient: Eighteen Years of Care, 45 Conn.Med. 720 (1981) (care of patient treated from Oct. 28, 1956 to Mar. 31, 1974, estimated to be $6,104,590).

Despite the confusion over the meaning of the distinction, it nonetheless has been used by the medical profession (see AMA statement discussed in the Rachels selection, supra) and by many courts (see *Quinlan*, supra). Most often questions have arisen concerning the use of respirators; more recently, however, harder questions have arisen with respect to nasogastric feeding, In Re Conroy, 190 N.J. Super. 453, 464 A.2d 303 (1983) (denying petitioner's request that nasogastric feeding be discontinued); antibiotics; blood transfusions, In Re Storar, 52 N.Y.2d 363, 438 N.Y.S.2d 266, 420 N.E.2d 64 (1981), (granting petitioner's request to give blood transfusions to terminally ill patient over guardian's objection); and intravenous feeding, Barber v. Superior Court, 147 Cal.App.3d 1006, 195 Cal. Rptr. 484 (1983) (prohibiting trial court from reinstating criminal complaint against defendant doctors who had ordered intravenous feeding and other life sustaining measures terminated on irreversibly comatose patient). The confusion over meaning has resulted, however, in many questioning its usefulness in moral judgments and in setting public policy. See, e.g., P. Ramsey, Ethics at the Edge of Life 153 (1978); President's Commission, Deciding to Forego Life-Sustaining Treatment 87–89 (1983).

3. THE COMPETENT PATIENT

Should individuals under some circumstances have the right to decline life-sustaining treatments? What are the circumstances? These questions are explored in this section with respect to competent patients and formerly competent patients who make their views known while competent. The special problems posed by patients who have always been incompetent or have never expressed their views on the subject while competent are explored in Section 4.

While reading the following materials, consider whether we can clinically and legally determine that individuals are competent. To what extent, if any, should the patient's wishes, expressed before the onset of illness, be taken into account? Should we recognize oral as well as written forms of communication? Should written communication be in specific predetermined form? Finally, are there circumstances that justify overriding the wishes of these patients? What are the circumstances?

PLEASE LET ME DIE *

DR. WHITE: The 27-year old unmarried man whom you have just seen [on the videotape from which this transcript is taken] has always been an active, independent person with a mind of his own. An athlete in high school and college, he has been physically active since, riding in rodeos and with a love of the outdoors. After three years as a jet pilot in the Air Force, he was discharged in May of 1973 and returned to his hometown

* Transcript of a videotaped interview of   University of Texas Medical Branch, May 8, Donald Cowart by Robert B. White, M.D.,   1974. [Eds.]

to enter a successful real estate business with his father, to whom he was very close.

. . .

I'm most grateful, Mr. C., that you were willing to talk with me today while we make the videotape, and before we get into our discussion, I'd like to just very briefly review some of the sequence of events that have happened to you since last July. Correct me if I get the sequence mixed up.

MR. C.: OK.

DR. WHITE: That was in July of 1973 that you and your father were in a very terrible explosion that occurred with no warning. As I understand it, you and your father were out looking at some real estate property since you were both involved in the real estate business. And when you started to start your car, it wouldn't start. Your father got out to fiddle with the carburetor, and then when he told you to go ahead and try it again and you switched the key to the on slot the whole landscape just went up in one big ball of fire, because there was a gas line nearby that was leaking and you all didn't know it and the ignition of the car set the whole countryside off. You were both very badly burned and your father died on the way to the hospital. You were admitted to the hospital in Dallas with about 66–67 percent total body burns. And you remained in the hospital there in Dallas from July until about the 15th of March when they transferred you to the Texas Rehab Unit there in Houston, where you were for about a month and were transferred here then on about the 15th of April and have been here now from the 15th of April until today, which is the 8th of May of 1974. I have the sequence, I think, essentially correct there, do I not?

MR. C.: Yes, all right.

DR. WHITE: Now, from the very beginning of your admission to the hospital there in Dallas you felt great despair about your future and really have been pretty clear and explicit that you were not sure that you wanted to continue to live. Can you tell me about those feelings and what you recall feeling right at the first when you were first admitted to Parkland?

MR. C.: First of all, I didn't want to go to Parkland or any other hospital. But I was picked up and put in the ambulance anyway, as was my father, and taken to the hospital in Kilgore, and of course they couldn't handle us there. That our burns, they sent us to Parkland, and Parkland told them again that I was burned bad enough that I didn't want them to try to do anything for me and to keep me on a thing. But they did go ahead and treat me and, although they didn't think I was going to make it at the time, they pulled me through. Since then, there's no way I could begin to explain the nightmares and the excruciating pain involved in the first events at Parkland that I can barely remember it myself. It was sort of like a dream, a real bad dream. And, I might add that I had a lot of nightmares at the time and I couldn't tell what was really happening and what I was dreaming. I was dreaming that one of the interns there was using me as a guinea pig for his experiments, and him and one of the nurses would get together and at night would cut on me and do other things that were quite painful. And I thought this was really happening and only now, you know, that I can look back on it with a clear mind, you know, can I say that I know it didn't happen.

DR. WHITE: But it was very real to you at the time and hard for you to tell what was a nightmarish dream and what was the actualities as to what was really happening.

MR. C.: Right. I swore up and down that all the nurses were drinking on duty and that I heard them whooping it up. I was right near the nurses' station and I'm sure that they were laughing and talking a lot, but I thought they were, you know, partying it up with booze.

DR. WHITE: Now, from the very beginning, according to what you told me and what's written in your hospital records, you've had some very strong feelings that you did not want the doctors to go on with your treatment, that you wanted them to leave you alone and not to attempt to sustain your life. How do you feel about that at this point?

MR. C.: At this point I feel much the same way. If I could, if I felt that I could be rehabilitated to where I could walk and do other things normally, I might have a different feeling about it, I don't know, but, being blind itself is one big factor that influences my thinking on that. I know there's no way that I want to go on as a blind and a cripple.

DR. WHITE: Now, of course, your right eye is completely lost and it's unclear at this point as to how much sight might be restored to your left eye. But it's possible that some degree of vision—useful vision—may be restored there, though of course there is no way to know that until some of the operations are done.

Your hands, the surgeons feel likely can be restored to some degree of reasonable, useful function, that is, where you can pick up things, use a pencil, dress yourself and that sort of thing. But up until today, anyway, in our other conversations, you have indicated that you did not want anyone to do any surgery on your hands to see to what degree function can be restored there. How do you feel about that at this point—the surgery on your hands, that is?

MR. C.: Well, I feel like while it's probably right that I'll have some degree of usefulness out of them, I know right now there is a sort of numb feeling and I think this is something that I don't think that surgery is going to correct. I think that it's just because my hands are burned so bad that they feel this way and that they'll probably continue to feel this way from now on.

DR. WHITE: Let me see your right hand, can you move it over here? Can you move that at the elbow at all?

MR. C.: No, I can't.

DR. WHITE: Hold it straight up for me? Is that as high up as you can get it?

MR. C.: This is, yes.

DR. WHITE: And how about your left hand? Can you hold it up as high as you can for me?

Now, you see, they have folded all of your fingers down, though you've lost the most distal part of your fingers, and put a skin graft around the whole thing and the surgery would be a matter of freeing those fingers up so that they could move again individually and be used to pick things up, [and] such as that. But you've had some pretty strong feelings and, indeed, said you would not sign the operative permit for the surgery on your hands. Tell me some about the feelings that you had about that matter of the surgery on your hands and how you feel about it now.

Mr. C.: First of all, I think that I had lots more faith in what a surgeon could do before this accident than, since I've been in the hospital, this right arm was just exactly the same as the left. It was contracted to the same amount and all, and they performed surgery on me there and left me in traction for several weeks. When it came out my arm was straight all right, it wasn't contracted any more, but I couldn't bend it in. And, I heard a doctor at Parkland say that it was out of, that my arm was out of joint, that it wasn't right, and it's obviously not right. It's not working as it should because of something. You know, what it is, I don't know, or it's cause it's out of place or what, but I know I could just barely move my arm after the surgery.

Dr. White: But, how do you feel about the matter of possible future surgery on your hands, now?

Mr. C.: Well, I don't have, like I said, I had more faith in it before I had this operation on my arm than now. And now I really *(interrupted by Dr. White)*

Dr. White: You're pretty skeptical as to *(interrupted by Mr. G)*

Mr. C.: I am. I'm skeptical and maybe this is just a, my arm is just a freak accident or something like this, but *(interrupted by Dr. White)*

Dr. White: Now, just a few days ago you were really pleading to be allowed to leave the hospital and to go home and die, which, of course, you would if you were to leave the hospital at this point. The tubbing each morning was terribly painful and so on, and you thought you could not go on with that painful experience every day. How do you feel about that now?

Mr. C.: The injections that I'm getting now have decreased the pain a whole lot to where while I can remember somewhat some things after I get out of the tank and after I wake up from and am out from under the influence of drugs, I can think back and remember being in some pain but just as soon as they quit well I just drop off to sleep again and so it's not nearly as bad as it was before. I still want out, and I'm working right now to get out.

Dr. White: In what way are you working to get out? What steps are you taking to try to get out of the hospital?

Mr. C.: Well, right now I'm trying to exhaust every legal means that I can find. And I'm working through attorneys and so far I haven't had much luck, it's something that I found out attorneys, at least ethical ones, don't want to touch, probably for the fear of getting bad publicity.

Dr. White: Now, it's, I think, beyond much question that if you were to leave the hospital and simply go home that within a short time you would die from the infections that would spring up in the open burn areas that still remain. Is that what you intend and want, to go home and to die?

Mr. C.: Actually, I just want a very brief visit to home and I don't intend to die from the infection. I'd use some other means.

Dr. White: That is, you would intend to do away with your own life?

Mr. C.: Yes.

Dr. White: Can you tell me what there is as you envision your own future that makes it seem so bleak to you that you do not want to live?

Mr. C.: Probably one of the big reasons is because all my life I've been active in sports. I've played golf, surfed and rodeo and these are things and all that I'm doing now. I played football, basketball in school, ran track and I've been very oriented towards athletics in general. And now I think at best I could just be rehabilitated to the extent where I could make it along rather than I would be, be able to do the things I really enjoy. If I were to enjoy myself after being rehabilitated, I think it would have to be by just changing completely the things that I'm interested in. I don't think that this is very likely that I would become interested in other things as I have been before.

DR. WHITE: Do you have any willingness to wait and see so at least you would be able to be up and around sufficiently, to handle things with your hands sufficiently, that if at that point you simply did not want to go on with your life you would be in a position to terminate it if you wish? Because, as it is now, you would be bedfast and it would be hard put to do away with yourself even if you were strongly inclined to do so.

MR. C.: Well, to me, I feel that the chances are so small that the pain, I mean that the end result isn't worth the pain involved to be able to get to the point where I could try it out. Ideally, this would be the best thing to do if I could go ahead and just see what things are going to be like after I did get out. And, if I didn't like them, as you said, terminate my life then. But, I don't wish to go through the pain of having my hands and fingers in traction and learning to walk again, which I never would have thought of as being a painful thing to do, but, especially with my legs, it's turned out to be quite painful and *(interrupted by Dr. White)*

DR. WHITE: Of course, you're so completely helpless, that is, unable to get out of the bed even by yourself, that you're pretty much at the mercy of all the people around you now as to whether you stay or leave. How do you feel about that?

MR. C.: It's a really sinking feeling. I've always been real independent and I like to do things for myself, and I've had my own ways of doing things, and pretty much done as I wished up to this point. And now I have to rely on someone else to feed me; all my private functions I need help with. And it, what really, I guess, astounds me, I guess I'd say, is that I; in a country like this where freedom has been stressed so much and civil liberties especially during the last few years, how a person can be made to stay under a doctor's care and be subjected to painful treatment, such as the tankings which were very painful, against this person's wishes, especially if he's demonstrated the ability to reason.

DR. WHITE: Even where discontinuing those tankings and the like would be a circumstance that would mean infection would set in that would end your life?

MR. C.: Even then. It's the way I see it, who is a doctor to decide whether a person lives or dies just because someone's put him under your care as a doctor. As long as the patient is willing to be treated I certainly think that a doctor should do everything they should, they could.

DR. WHITE: But you feel that you properly should have the legal right to say, "No, I do not want to be treated"?

MR. C.: Yes. I don't see how anyone else could possibly have this right, justifiably have this right. That's what, like I said, really astounds me, I don't know whether I'm being kept here because of next-of-kin has said they want me here and want me treated, or whether I would be held even irregardless of this. But, I think it's something that's, it's something that if it's been happening in the past—which I am sure it has and I just wasn't aware of it—that something should be done about it in the future so that a person that did not want the care could be left alone and would not have to do, undergo the painful treatment, like I'm having to go, undergo this painful treatment and regardless of my feelings if I am not willing to go to the tank, I am picked up out of bed and just bodily placed on a stretcher and taken away, even if I have to be tied down to it.

DR. WHITE: Well that poses an important issue, of course, for you, for the physicians and for the attorneys.   Let's talk about it some further again soon.

MR. C.: OK.

NOTES

1. After 14 months of excruciatingly painful treatment at several hospitals, Mr. Cowart was released to his mother's home. He is blind, with impaired hearing and limited use of his arms and hands, including only one mobile joint in one thumb. His once handsome face bears the scars of the burns and skin grafts. Plagued by sleeplessness for many years, he tried to commit suicide on several occasions; the insomnia has since been overcome. He had to drop graduate courses in law and business because of his physical limitations.   Nonetheless, he runs a small business, is active in his community and in February, 1983, almost 10 years after the explosion, he married a high-school acquaintance. Because his poor hearing led him to confuse names such as John or Ron with his own name, he changed it to the distinctive Dax. He describes his experience as follows:

> Even though I am now enjoying life and am glad to be alive, I still would not want to be forced to undergo the same treatment if I should once again be critically burned.   I feel strongly that it is the individual affected, and he alone, that has the right to make such decisions.   As long as one has the ability to reason and at least a short time to reflect upon his or her decision, no one else should be allowed to force unwanted treatment on that individual.   If there exists any such thing as self-evident or naturally endowed rights, the right to control over one's own body must surely be among them.

Letter from Dax S. Cowart (Sept. 19, 1983).

For other commentary on this transcript, see R. Burt, Taking Care of Strangers (1979); White and Engelhardt, A Demand to Die, 5 Hastings Ctr.Rep. 9 (June 1975); Platt, Commentary: On Asking to Die, 5 Hastings Ctr.Rep. 9 (Dec. 1975). See also A Happy Life Afterward Doesn't Make Up for Torture, Washington Post, June 26, 1983, at D3, col. 1.

2. For an alternative approach to the management of severely burned patients, consider Imbus and Zawacki, Autonomy for Burned Patients When Survival Is Unprecedented, 297 New Eng.J.Med. 308, 308–309 (1977):

> No burn is certainly fatal until the patient dies; the most severely burned patient may speak of hope with his last breath. . . . Every year, however, several patients are admitted to our burn center with injuries so severe that survival is not only unexpected but, to our knowledge, unprecedented. . . .
>
> . . .
>
> Our approach, developed empirically over several years, is based on our conviction that the decision to begin or to withhold maximal therapeutic effort is more of an ethical than a medical judgment.   The physician and his colleagues on the burn-care team present to the patient the appropriate medical and statistical facts together with authoritative medical opinion about the available therapeutic alternatives and their consequences.   Thus informed, the patient may give or withhold his consent to receive a particular form of therapy, but it is his own decision based on his value system, and it is arrived at before communication and competence are seriously impaired by intubation or altered states of consciousness.

Definitions and Methods

The patient whose management this paper addresses is characterized by some combination of massive burns, severe smoke inhalation or advanced age. Such a patient's condition is designated by "1" on the Bull Mortality Probability Chart and "0" in the National Burn Information Exchange Survival Analysis Diagrams, both indicating nonsurvival from the indexes of age and percentage of body-surface area burned. Furthermore, our staff members cannot, from their own experience, our burn-unit statistics, or references from the literature, recall survival in a similar patient.

To allow the patient maximal clarity of thought in decision making, several points must be communicated to the paramedic teams in the field and to local hospitals who transfer burned patients to our burn center immediately after injury: no administration of morphine or other narcotics before arrival; prompt fluid resuscitation; oxygen administration in treatment of possible carbon monoxide intoxication; avoidance of tracheostomy or endotracheal-tube insertion unless absolutely necessary to preserve the airway and maintain ventilation; and rapid transportation to the burn center.

Upon admission of a patient for whom survival seems in doubt, the burn center's most experienced physician is consulted, day or night, to evaluate the patient. His assessment, combined with a social and family history, is presented to all involved team members. Standard works are rechecked to determine if there has ever been a precedent for survival.

When the diagnosis is confirmed, the physician and other team members enter the room. Family members are not invited into the room to ensure that the decision of the patient is specifically his own. In an attempt to establish a relation with the patient, the attending physician or resident under his guidance tries to assume the role of a compassionate friend who is willing to listen. Hands are often held, and an effort is made to look deeply into the patient's eyes to perceive the unspoken questions that may lie there. Nonverbal cues are watched for closely. The presence of the burn team serves to witness and validate the patient's desires and requests, gives consensus to the gravity of the situation and supports the physician member of the team in this delicate, painful task.

At times, when the question of impending death does not spontaneously arise, suggestions such as "You are seriously ill", "You are sicker than you have ever been" or "Your life is in immediate danger" may be made, always in a caring, gentle way.

Some patients will not respond because of coma or mental incompetency. In those circumstances, the burn team and the family confer, again in a compassionate, concerned relation. All attempts are made to determine and do what the patient would be most likely to want if he were able to communicate.

A few patients will hear but not listen because of a need to deny their predicament. In general, such denials, if persistent, are considered an expression of a strong desire to live, and the patients are treated accordingly with maximal therapeutic effort.

A large majority of patients, however, understand the gravity of their situation and make further inquiries. The very frequent question—"Am I going to die?"—is answered truthfully by the statement, "We cannot predict the future. We can only say that, to our knowledge, no one in the past of your age and with your size of burn has ever survived this injury, either with or without maximal treatment." At this point, those who interpret this diagnosis of a burn without precedent of survival as an indication to avoid heroic measures typically become quite peaceful. Regularly, they then try to live their lives completely and fully to the end, saying things that they must say to those important to them, making proper plans, reparations and apologies and, in general, obtaining what Kavanaugh refers to as "permission to die." These patients receive only ordinary medical measures and sufficient amounts of pain medication to assure comfort after their choice is made explicit. Fluid resuscitation is discontinued, they are admitted to a private room, and visiting hours become unlimited. An experienced nurse and, frequently, a chaplain are in constant attendance, using their expertise to comfort and sustain the patient and his family, chiefly by their continued presence and willingness to listen.

The patients who understand that survival is unprecedented in their case but, nevertheless, choose a maximal therapeutic effort are admitted to the burn intensive-care unit. Fluid resuscitation is continued, and full treatment measures are instituted, as with any other patient in the unit. As with those who choose only ordinary care, however, they may change their minds at any time; their decision is reviewed with them on a daily basis.

In general, when patients are mentally incompetent on admission because of head injury or inhalation injury or some other injury and may reasonably be expected to remain so indefinitely, the socially designated next of kin or other relatives are allowed to speak for the patient. With children who are legally incompetent because of age, however, we have for the past five years been unwilling to declare any burn as being without precedent of survival, chiefly because mortality rates for very large burns in pediatric patients appear to be improving more rapidly than can be reported.

After interviewing the patient or his family, the physician is responsible for recording the salient points and decision in the patient's chart. Accurate documentation serves to clarify communication with other team members and avoids legal ambiguity.

"Postvention," described by Shneidman as "those activities which serve to reduce the aftereffects of a traumatic event in the lives of survivors," is now being evolved on our unit. Nurses are learning how to help survivors comfort each other and, together with the chaplain and social worker, are arranging for safe transportation of the bereaved to their homes, counseling families on the difficult matters of explaining death to children and explaining such points as legal necessity of an unwanted autopsy. Our hospital chaplain is available to conduct the funeral services if the family does not have its own pastor. He gets in touch with the families on the first anniversary of their loved one's death to answer any unfinished questions that may have been bothering them. The social worker also offers her continuing services to the bereaved.

. . . .

The following case [history] illustrate[s] our approach.

Two sisters, 68 and 70 years of age, and their husbands were searching for a schizophrenic daughter who had disappeared after her discharge from a psychiatric hospital. While their car waited for a stoplight, a nearby construction machine hit a gasoline line. The spraying gas exploded, leveling a city block and igniting the car.

The sisters arrived in our burn center two hours later. The younger sister had 91 percent full-thickness, 92 percent total-body burn, with moderate smoke inhalation; the older had 94.5 percent full-thickness, 95.5 percent total-body burn, with severe smoke inhalation. The burn team agreed that survival was unprecedented in both cases. Both women were alert and interviewed separately.

The younger sister asked about death directly, looking intently into the physician's eyes. When he answered, she replied matter-of-factly, "Well, I never dreamed that life would end like this, but since we all have to go sometime, I'd like to go quietly and comfortably. I don't know what to do about my daughter . . ."

After she was made comfortable, the nurse obtained a description of the missing daughter and possible whereabouts. The social worker alerted the police to look for her, and telephoned relatives, informing them of the accident as gently as could be conveyed by telephone. The husbands were located at another burn unit. An attempt was made to arrange a final spousal conversation, but both husbands were intubated.

Meanwhile, the older sister doubted whether her injuries were as serious as reported. "I feel so good, wouldn't I be hurting horribly if I were going to die?" The effect of full-thickness burns on nerve endings was explained. The physician reiterated that we wished to do what she thought was best for her. She hedged, "What did my sister say? I'll go along with her decision." Since the patient seemed unsure of her decision, she was offered full therapy in the room with her sister. She then refused the therapy adamantly but denied that she was dying.

The sisters' beds were placed next to each other so that they could see and touch each other easily. They discussed funeral arrangements and then joked, in the next breath, about the damage done to their hair. The hospital chaplain prayed with them. By active listening, he was able to convey to the older that her husband was not to blame for the accident as she had thought. "It's good to go out not cursing him after all our years together," she said. The younger sister died several hours later after her sister lapsed into a coma; the older died the next day. The daughter was not located.

SATZ v. PERLMUTTER

District Court of Appeal of Florida, Fourth District, 1978.
362 So.2d 160, affirmed 379 So.2d 359.

LETTS, JUDGE.

The State here appeals a trial court order permitting the removal of an artificial life sustaining device from a competent, but terminally ill adult.

.   .   .

Seventy-three year old Abe Perlmutter lies mortally sick in a hospital, suffering from amyotrophic lateral sclerosis (Lou Gehrig's disease) diagnosed in January 1977. There is no cure and normal life expectancy, from time of diagnosis, is but two years. In Mr. Perlmutter, the affliction has progressed to the point of virtual incapability of movement, inability to breathe without a mechanical respirator and his very speech is an extreme effort. Even with the respirator, the prognosis is death within a short time. Notwithstanding, he remains in command of his mental faculties and legally competent. He seeks, with full approval of his adult family, to have the respirator removed from his trachea, which act, according to his physician, based upon medical probability, would result in "a reasonable life expectancy of less than one hour". Mr. Perlmutter is fully aware of the inevitable result of such removal, yet has attempted to remove it for himself (hospital personnel, activated by an alarm, reconnected it). He has repeatedly stated to his family, "I'm miserable take it out" and at a bedside hearing, told the obviously concerned trial judge that whatever would be in store for him if the respirator were removed, "it can't be worse than what I'm going through now."

Pursuant to all of the foregoing, and upon the petition of Mr. Perlmutter himself, the trial judge entered a detailed and thoughtful final judgment which included the following language:

ORDERED AND ADJUDGED that Abe Perlmutter, in the exercise of his right of privacy, may remain in defendant hospital or leave said hospital, free of the mechanical respirator now attached to his body and all defendants and their staffs are restrained from interfering with Plaintiff's decision.

We agree with the trial judge.

The State's position is that it (1) has an overriding duty to preserve life, and (2) that termination of supportive care, whether it be by the patient, his family or medical personnel, is an unlawful killing of a human being under the Florida Murder Statute Section 782.04, Florida Statutes (1977) or Manslaughter under Section 782.08. The hospital, and its doctors, while not insensitive to this tragedy, fear not only criminal prosecution if they aid in removal of the mechanical device, but also civil liability. In the absence of prior Florida law on the subject, their fears cannot be discounted.

The pros and cons involved in such tragedies which bedevil contemporary society, mainly because of incredible advancement in scientific medicine, are all exhaustively discussed in Superintendent of Belchertown v. Saikewicz, Mass., 370 N.E.2d 417 (1977). As *Saikewicz* points out, the right of an individual to refuse medical treatment is tempered by the State's:

1. Interest in the preservation of life.

2. Need to protect innocent third parties.

3. Duty to prevent suicide.

4. Requirement that it help maintain the ethical integrity of medical practice.

In the case at bar, none of these four considerations surmount the individual wishes of Abe Perlmutter. Thus we adopt the view of the line of cases discussed in *Saikewicz* which would allow Abe Perlmutter the right to refuse or discontinue treatment based upon "the constitutional right to privacy . . . an expression of the sanctity of individual free choice and self-determination." (Id. 426.) We would stress that this adoption is limited to the specific facts now before us, involving a competent adult patient. The problem is less easy of solution when the patient is incapable of understanding and we, therefore, postpone a crossing of that more complex bridge until such time as we are required to do so.

PRESERVATION OF LIFE

There can be no doubt that the State *does* have an interest in preserving life, but we again agree with *Saikewicz* that "there is a substantial distinction in the State's insistence that human life be saved where the affliction is curable, as opposed to the State interest where, as here, the issue is not whether, but when, for how long and at what cost to the individual [his] life may be briefly extended." (Id. 425–426.) In the case at bar the condition is terminal, the patient's situation wretched and the continuation of his life temporary and totally artificial.

Accordingly, we see no compelling State interest to interfere with Mr. Perlmutter's expressed wishes.

PROTECTION OF THIRD PARTIES

Classically, this protection is exemplified in the case Application of the President and Directors of Georgetown College, Inc., 118 U.S.App.D.C. 80, 331 F.2d 1000, cert. denied, 377 U.S. 978 (1964), where the patient, by refusing treatment, is said to be abandoning his minor child, which abandonment the State as *parens patriae* sought to prevent. We point out that Abe Perlmutter is 73, his family adult and all in agreement with his wishes. The facts do not support abandonment.

PREVENTION OF SUICIDE

As to suicide, the facts here unarguably reveal that Mr. Perlmutter would die, but for the respirator. The disconnecting of it, far from causing his unnatural death by means of a "death producing agent" in fact will merely result in his death, if at all, from natural causes, *Saikewicz*, Id., 426, fn. 11. The testimony of Mr. Perlmutter, like the victim in the *Georgetown College* case, supra, is that he really wants to live, but do so, God and Mother Nature willing, under his own power. This basic wish to live, plus the fact that he did not self-induce his horrible affliction, precludes his further refusal of treatment being classed as attempted suicide.

Moreover we find no requirement in the law that a competent, but otherwise mortally sick, patient undergo the surgery or treatment which constitutes the only hope for temporary prolongation of his life. This being so, we see little difference between a cancer ridden patient who declines surgery, or chemotherapy, necessary for his temporary survival and the hopeless predicament which tragically afflicts Abe Perlmutter. It is true that the latter appears more drastic because affirmatively, a mechanical device must be disconnected, as distinct from mere inaction. Notwithstanding, the principle is the same, for in both instances the hapless, but mentally competent, victim is choosing not to avail himself of one of the expensive marvels of modern medical science.

The State argues that a patient has *no right* to refuse treatment and cites several of the familiar blood transfusion cases. However, a reading of these reveal substantial distinctions between them and the case at bar. In the blood transfusion cases, the patient is either incompetent to make a medical decision, equivocal about making it ("he would not agree to be transfused but would not resist a court order permitting it because it would be the court's will and not his own.") or it is a family member making the decision for an inert or minor third party patient. By contrast, we find, and agree with, several cases upholding the right of a competent adult patient to refuse treatment for himself. From this agreement, we reach our conclusion that, because Abe Perlmutter has a right to refuse treatment in the first instance, he has a concomitant right to discontinue it.

ETHICS OF MEDICAL PRACTICE

Lastly, as to the ethical integrity of medical practice, we again adopt the language of *Saikewicz*:

> . . . Prevailing medical ethical practice does not, without exception, demand that all efforts toward life prolongation be made in all circumstances. Rather, as indicated in *Quinlan*, the prevailing ethical practice seems to be to recognize that the dying are more often in need of comfort than treatment. Recognition of the right to refuse necessary treatment in appropriate circumstances is consistent with existing medical mores; such a doctrine does not threaten either the integrity of the medical profession, the proper role of hospitals in caring for such patients or the State's interest in protecting the same. It is not necessary to deny a right of self-determination to a patient in order to recognize the interests of doctors, hospitals, and medical personnel in attendance on the patient. . . .

It is our conclusion, therefore, under the facts before us, that when these several public policy interests are weighed against the rights of Mr.

Perlmutter, the latter must and should prevail. Abe Perlmutter should be allowed to make his choice to die with dignity, notwithstanding over a dozen legislative failures in this state to adopt suitable legislation in this field. It is all very convenient to insist on continuing Mr. Perlmutter's life so that there can be no question of foul play, no resulting civil liability and no possible trespass on medical ethics. However, it is quite another matter to do so at the patient's sole expense and against his competent will, thus inflicting never ending physical torture on his body until the inevitable, but artifically suspended, moment of death. Such a course of conduct invades the patient's constitutional right of privacy, removes his freedom of choice and invades his right to self-determine.

The judgment of the trial court is hereby affirmed. . . .

ERIC CASSEL,
THE NATURE OF SUFFERING AND THE
GOALS OF MEDICINE

306 New Eng.J.Med. 639 (1982).

The obligation of physicians to relieve human suffering stretches back into antiquity. Despite this fact, little attention is explicitly given to the problem of suffering in medical education, research, or practice. I will begin by focusing on a modern paradox: Even in the best settings and with the best physicians, it is not uncommon for suffering to occur not only during the course of a disease but also as a result of its treatment. To understand this paradox and its resolution requires an understanding of what suffering is and how it relates to medical care.

Consider this case: A 35-year-old sculptor with metastatic disease of the breast was treated by competent physicians employing advanced knowledge and technology and acting out of kindness and true concern. At every stage, the treatment as well as the disease was a source of suffering to her. She was uncertain and frightened about her future, but she could get little information from her physicians, and what she was told was not always the truth. She had been unaware, for example, that the irradiated breast would be so disfigured. After an oophorectomy and a regimen of medications, she became hirsute, obese, and devoid of libido. With tumor in the supraclavicular fossa, she lost strength in the hand that she had used in sculpturing, and she became profoundly depressed. She had a pathologic fracture of the femur, and treatment was delayed while her physicians openly disagreed about pinning her hip.

Each time her disease responded to therapy and her hope was rekindled, a new manifestation would appear. Thus, when a new course of chemotherapy was started, she was torn between a desire to live and the fear that allowing hope to emerge again would merely expose her to misery if the treatment failed. The nausea and vomiting from the chemotherapy were distressing, but no more so than the anticipation of hair loss. She feared the future. Each tomorrow was seen as heralding increased sickness, pain, or disability, never as the beginning of better times. She felt isolated because she was no longer like other people and could not do what other people did. She feared that her friends would stop visiting her. She was sure that she would die.

. . .

What can this case tell us about the ends of medicine and the relief of suffering? Three facts stand out: The first is that this woman's suffering was not confined to her physical symptoms. The second is that she suffered not only from her disease but also from its treatment. The third is that one could not anticipate what she would describe as a source of suffering; like other patients, she had to be asked. Some features of her condition she would call painful, upsetting, uncomfortable, and distressing, but not a source of suffering. In these characteristics her case was ordinary.

In discussing the matter of suffering with lay persons, I learned that they were shocked to discover that the problem of suffering was not directly addressed in medical education. My colleagues of a contemplative nature were surprised at how little they knew of the problem and how little thought they had given it, whereas medical students tended to be unsure of the relevance of the issue to their work.

The relief of suffering, it would appear, is considered one of the primary ends of medicine by patients and laypersons, but not by the medical profession. As in the care of the dying, patients and their friends and families do not make a distinction between physical and nonphysical sources of suffering in the same way that doctors do.

A search of the medical and social-science literature did not help me in understanding what suffering is; the word "suffering" was most often coupled with the word "pain," as in "pain and suffering." . . .

This phenomenon reflects a historically constrained and currently inadequate view of the ends of medicine. Medicine's traditional concern primarily for the body and for physical disease is well known, as are the widespread effects of the mind-body dichotomy on medical theory and practice. I believe that this dichotomy itself is a source of the paradoxical situation in which doctors cause suffering in their care of the sick. Today, as ideas about the separation of mind and body are called into question, physicians are concerning themselves with new aspects of the human condition. The profession of medicine is being pushed and pulled into new areas, both by its technology and by the demands of its patients. Attempting to understand what suffering is and how physicians might truly be devoted to its relief will require that medicine and its critics overcome the dichotomy between mind and body and the associated dichotomies between subjective and objective and between person and object.

. . . [I] am going to make three points. The first is that suffering is experienced by persons. In the separation between mind and body, the concept of the person, or personhood, has been associated with that of mind, spirit, and the subjective. However, as I will show, a person is not merely mind, merely spiritual, or only subjectively knowable. Personhood has many facets, and it is ignorance of them that actively contributes to patients' suffering. The understanding of the place of the person in human illness requires a rejection of the historical dualism of mind and body.

The second point derives from my interpretation of clinical observations: Suffering occurs when an impending destruction of the person is perceived; it continues until the threat of disintegration has passed or until the integrity of the person can be restored in some other manner. It follows then, that although suffering often occurs in the presence of acute pain, shortness of breath, or other bodily symptoms, suffering extends beyond the physical. Most generally, suffering can be defined as the state of severe distress associated with events that threaten the intactness of the person.

The third point is that suffering can occur in relation to any aspect of the person, whether it is in the realm of social roles, group identification, the relation with self, body, or family, or the relation with a transpersonal, transcendent source of meaning. . . .

. . .

NOTES

1. Would the court that decided *Perlmutter* have permitted Dax Cowart to terminate his lifesaving treatment? Recall the words of the *Quinlan* court: "There is a real and in this case determinative distinction between the unlawful taking of the life of another and the ending of artificial lifesupport systems as a matter of self determination." Sec. B.2, supra. See also Superintendent of Belchertown State School v. Saikewicz (fn. 11), Sec. B.4, infra.

Should a court order feeding of a competent person who refuses food and has chosen starvation as a method of bringing about death? At least two courts have decided cases involving the issue of whether patients may decide to stop eating. Judge Donald H. Miller of the New York State Supreme Court ruled that a nursing home was neither obliged nor had the authority to force feed G. Ross Henninger, an 85-year old former college president, who had been fasting in order to hasten his death. New York Times, Feb. 3, 1984, at A1, col. 3. The California Supreme Court let stand a lower court decision denying the request of Elizabeth Bouvia, a 26-year old victim of cerebral palsy, for an injunction to prevent Riverside County General Hospital in Riverside, California, from discharging her, force-feeding her or denying her pain relieving drugs. Washington Post, Dec. 17, 1983, at A3, col. 1. Ms. Bouvia, who has virtually no control over her body movements, wanted to stay in the hospital and starve herself to death. After the decision Ms. Bouvia resisted being fed. For example, she removed her feeding tubes and had to be restrained so that the tubes could be reinserted. Washington Post, Feb. 2, 1984, at A5, col. 1. See also Goodman, Judging the Right to Die, Washington Post, Feb. 11, 1984, at A23, col. 1. Elizabeth Bouvia discharged herself from Riverside General on April 7, 1984, and checked into the Hospital Del Mar at Playas de Tijuana in Tijuana, Mexico on the same day. She was told by the hospital director that the staff would not watch her die. After trying to starve herself for three days, she changed her mind, returned to the hospital and took her first solid food in seven months. New York Times, Apr. 24, 1984, at A14, col. 1. Where a competent patient's condition can be treated or ameliorated but the patient refuses treatment, many courts have overruled the patient's wishes. See, e.g., Application of President and Directors of Georgetown College, 331 F.2d 1000 (D.C.Cir. 1964), certiorari denied 377 U.S. 978, 84 S.Ct. 1883, 12 L.Ed.2d 746 (1964) (state's interest in protecting minor children); United States v. George, 239 F.Supp. 752 (D.C.Conn.1965) (state's interest in protecting integrity of medical profession); Commissioner of Correction v. Myers, 379 Mass. 255, 399 N.E.2d 452 (1979) (state's interest in orderly prison administration); John F. Kennedy Memorial Hospital v. Heston, 58 N.J. 576, 292 A.2d 670 (1971) (state's interest in preservation of life); Raleigh Fitkin-Paul Morgan Memorial Hospital v. Anderson, 42 N.J. 421, 201 A.2d 537, certiorari denied 377 U.S. 978, 84 S.Ct. 1894, 12 L.Ed.2d 1032 (1964) (state's interest in protecting lives of unborn).

What does it mean to say that a patient has a terminal condition or is terminally ill? See President's Commission, Deciding to Forego Life-Sustaining Treatment, 26 (1983). For results of a survey of how doctors define "terminal illness," see footnotes 88, 89 and 92 in note 2 following California Health and Safety Code, The Natural Death Act, Sec. B.3., infra.

2. There are groups, believing that the individual has a fundamental right to choose the time of his death, that "counsel" persons on how to commit suicide. The two most prominent of these groups are the Voluntary Euthanasia Society in Great Britain (formerly known as the Society for the Right to Die With Dignity and as "EXIT") and its counterpart in the United States, the Hemlock Society.

The Voluntary Euthanasia Society (still commonly known as EXIT) received wide attention in 1980 with its announcement that it planned to publish a handbook for would-be suicides. EXIT's publication, available only to members after a three-month waiting period, is a primer on how to commit suicide written by a group of doctors and lawyers, all EXIT members. The booklet describes various methods of suicide that are relatively painless and foolproof (such as combining certain nonprescription medicines with alcohol) and includes an appendix that lists various medicines, with medical opinions of how much of each constitutes a lethal dose. The book also contains advice on how to deal with family and friends, as well as a section arguing against suicide in cases where the desire for it grows out of some non-medical problem such as loneliness. New York Times, Mar. 7, 1980 at A18, col. 1.

In 1980 an elderly member of EXIT committed suicide in Great Britain. The then-Director of EXIT, Nicholas Reed, was subsequently convicted of two counts of conspiracy to aid and abet a suicide, for which he received a sentence of two years imprisonment, and two counts of aiding and abetting actual suicide, for which he also received a sentence of two and a half years imprisonment, sentences to run concurrently. R. v. Reed, [1982] Crim.App. 819. On appeal his sentence was reduced to 18 months. His co-defendant, Dr. Mark Lyons, another EXIT member, was convicted of five counts of aiding and abetting suicide and was sentenced to a total of two years imprisonment, which was then suspended. There was evidence that Reed, whom the Society has since disowned, put Lyons in touch with people so that he could actually assist them in committing suicide. Attorney General v. Able, [1983] 3 W.L.R. 845. Although attempted suicide is no longer a crime in Britain, aiding and abetting a suicide is still illegal. Committing suicide is still a crime in many U.S. jurisdictions; the last reported prosecution, however, was in 1961. See President's Commission, Deciding to Forego Life-Sustaining Treatment 37–39, n. 73 (1983).

After distribution of the booklet, it was ascertained that within 18 months there were 15 cases of suicide linked to the booklet and an additional 19 suicides where documents were found which showed that the deceased was a member of, or had corresponded with, the Voluntary Euthanasia Society. Attorney General v. Able, [1983] 3 W.L.R. 845. It was this information that induced Her Majesty's Attorney General to bring an action for declaratory relief to declare the distribution of the booklet as being either an offense or an attempted offense contrary to the provisions of the Suicide Act of 1961, 9 & 10 Eliz. 2, ch. 60 § 1 (1961). Section II(1) of that act provides: "A person who aids, abets, counsels or procures the suicide of another, or an attempt by another to commit suicide, shall be liable on conviction on indictment to imprisonment for a term not exceeding fourteen years."

The court found that there was no form of declaratory relief that could be granted; however, it also stated that under certain circumstances distribution of the booklet could be an offense. To establish an offense, it must be proved that (1) the alleged offender had the necessary intent (that he intended the booklet to be used by someone contemplating suicide and intended that the person would be assisted by the book's contents, or otherwise encouraged to attempt to take or actually to take his own life); (2) that while he still had that intention he distributed the booklet to such a person who read it; and (3) in addition, that reading the booklet assisted or encouraged such a person to attempt to take or actually to take his own life. Attorney General v. Able, [1983] 3 W.L.R. 845. Otherwise the alleged offender cannot be guilty of more than an attempt. Id.

Derek Humphrey, a freelance journalist, established in the United States an euthanasia group called the Hemlock Society. Rather than issue a blunt "how-to" manual on suicide, the Hemlock Society has published a book that is a series of case histories of terminally ill people who ended their lives—"Let Me Die Before I Wake." Would the publication of a booklet as explicit as the EXIT publication be protected by the First Amendment? Cf., United States v. The Progressive Inc., 467 F.Supp. 990 (W.D.Wis.1979), Ch. 4, Sec. A.1., supra.

DAVID JACKSON AND STUART YOUNGNER, PATIENT AUTONOMY AND "DEATH WITH DIGNITY"

299 New Eng.J.Med. 404 (1979).

. . .

Physicians have approached the difficult problem of decision making for critically ill patients in various ways. Attempts have been made to establish reliable clinical criteria for predicting outcome in critically ill patients. This effort has been most successful in defining brain death, where clear-cut clinical criteria can predict with certainty a fatal outcome. Efforts at predicting outcome in "vegetative" brain states and other serious "terminal" conditions have been less successful.

Another approach has been to develop systems for classifying patient-care categories. This triage approach is designed to permit direction of maximal effort toward the care of "viable" patients, stressing daily re-evaluation of medical status and treatment options and open communication among medical personnel, patient and family.

Many hospitals have established ethics or "optimal-care" committees that serve in an advisory capacity to physicians, patients and families when difficult decisions arise about stopping or withholding life-support systems.

. . .

Little has been written, however, about the specific clinical and psychological problems that may complicate the concept of patient autonomy and the right to die with dignity. . . .

The issues of patient autonomy and the right to die with dignity are without question important ones that require further discussion and clarification by our society as a whole. However, there is a danger that in certain cases, preoccupation with these dramatic and popular issues may lead physicians and patients to make clinically inappropriate decisions— precisely because sound clinical evaluation and judgment are suspended. This article will attempt to illustrate this concept by use of clinical examples from a medical intensive-care unit. Each case will demonstrate a specific clinical situation where concerns about patient autonomy and the right to die with dignity posed a potential threat to sound decision making and the total clinical (medical, social and ethical) basis for the "optimal" decision.

Case Reports

Case 1—Patient Ambivalence

An 80-year-old man was admitted to the Medical Intensive-Care Unit (MICU) with a three-week history of progressive shortness of beath. He had a long history of chronic obstructive lung disease. He had been admitted to a hospital with similar problems four years earlier and had required intubation, mechanical respiratory support and eventual tracheostomy. The patient remained on the respirator for two months before weaning was successfully completed. During the four years after discharge, his activity had been progressively restricted because of dyspnea on exertion. He required assistance in most aspects of self-care.

On admission, he was afebrile, and there was no evidence of an acute precipitating event. Maximum attempts at pulmonary toilet, low-flow supplemental oxygen and treatment of mild right-sided congestive heart failure and bronchospasm were without effect. After four days of continued deterioration, a decision had to be made about whether to intubate and mechanically ventilate the patient. His private physician and the director of the MICU discussed the options with this fully conversant and alert patient. He initially decided against intubation. However, 24 hours later, when he became almost moribund, he changed his mind and requested that respiratory support be initiated. He was unable to be weaned from the respirator and required tracheostomy—a situation reminiscent of his previous admission. Two months later, he had made no progress, and it became obvious that he would never be weaned from respiratory support.

Attempts were made to find extended-care facilities that could cope with a patient on a respirator. Extensive discussions with the patient and his family about the appropriate course to follow revealed striking changes of mind on an almost daily basis. The patient often expressed to the MICU staff his wish to be removed from the respirator and said, "If I make it, I make it." However, when his family was present, he would insist that he wanted maximal therapy, even if it meant remaining on the respirator indefinitely. The family showed similar ambivalence. The patient was regularly the center of conversation at the MICU weekly interdisciplinary conference (liaison among medical, nursing, social-work and psychiatric staff). There was great disagreement among MICU staff members concerning which side of the patient's ambivalence should be honored. Ultimately (after $4\frac{1}{2}$ months on the respirator), the patient contracted a nosocomial pulmonary infection, became hypotensive and experienced ventricular fibrillation. No efforts were made at cardiopulmonary resuscitation. In this difficult case, the concept of patient "autonomy" became impossible to define.

Case 2—Depression

A 54-year-old married man with a five-year history of lymphosarcoma was admitted to the hospital intensive-care unit for progressive shortness of breath and a one-week history of nausea and vomiting. Over the past five years, he had received three courses of combination-drug chemotheraphy, which resulted in remission. His most recent course occurred four months before admission. On admission, x-ray examination of the chest showed a diffuse infiltrate, more on the left than on the right. Eight hours after admission, he was transferred to the MICU because of hypotension and increasing dyspnea. Initially, it was not clear whether these findings indicated interstitial spread of lymphosarcoma or asymmetric pulmonary edema. Physical findings were compatible with a diagnosis of congestive heart failure, and he was treated for pulmonary edema, with good response. His neurologic examination was normal, except for a flat, depressed affect. Deep-tendon reflexes were $2+$ and symmetric. Laboratory examination revealed only a mildly elevated blood urea nitrogen, with a normal creatinine and a slightly elevated calcium of 11.8 mg per deciliter (2.95 mmol per liter). There were no objective signs of hypercalcemia. His respirtory status improved rapidly.

The patient refused his oncologist's recommendation for additional chemotherapy. Although his cognitive abilities were intact, he steadfastly refused the pleas of his wife and the MICU staff to undergo therapy.

Over the six days in the MICU with treatment by rehydration, his calcium became normal, his nausea and vomiting slowly improved, and his affect brightened. At that time, he agreed to chemotherapy, stating that, "Summer's coming and I want to be able to sit in the backyard a little longer." During this course of chemotherapy, the patient discussed his previous refusal of therapy. In his opinion, the nausea and vomiting had made "life not worth living." No amount of reassurance that these symptoms were temporary could convince him that it was worthwhile to continue his fight. Only when this reassurance was confirmed by clinical improvement did the patient overcome his reactive depression and concur with the reinstitution of vigorous therapy.

Case 3—Patient Who Uses a Plea for Death with Dignity to Identify a Hidden Problem

A 52-year-old married man was admitted to the MICU after an attempt at suicide. He had retired two years earlier because of progressive physical disability related to multiple sclerosis during the 15 years before admission. He had successfully adapted to his physical limitations, remaining actively involved in family matters with his wife and two teenage sons. However, during the three months before admission, he had become morose and withdrawn but had no vegetative symptoms of depression. On the evening of admission, while alone, he ingested an unknown quantity of diazepam. When his family returned six hours later, they found the patient semiconscious. He had left a suicide note.

On admission to the MICU, physical examination showed several neurologic deficits, including spastic paraparesis, right-arm monoparesis, cortical sensory deficits, bilateral ophthalmoplegia and bilateral cerebellar dysfunction. This picture was unchanged from recent neurologic examinations. The patient was alert and fully conversant. He expressed to the MICU house officers his strong belief in a patient's right to die with dignity. He stressed the "meaningless" aspects of his life related to his loss of function, insisting that he did not want vigorous medical intervention should serious complications develop. This position appeared logically coherent to the MICU staff. However, a consultation with members of the psychiatric liaison service was requested.

During the initial consultation, the patient showed that the onset of his withdrawal and depression coincided with a diagnosis of inoperable cancer in his mother-in-law. His wife had spent more and more time satisfying the needs of her terminally ill mother. In fact, on the night of his suicide attempt, the patient's wife and sons had left him alone for the first time to visit his mother-in-law, who lived in another city. The patient had "too much pride" to complain to his wife about his feelings of abandonment. He was able to recognize that his suicide attempt and insistence on death with dignity were attempts to draw the family's attention to his needs. Discussions with all four family members led to improved communication and acknowledgment of the patient's special emotional needs. After these conversations, the patient explicitly retracted both his suicidal threats and his demand that no supportive medical efforts be undertaken. He was discharged, to have both neurologic and psychiatric follow-up examinations.

Case 4—Patient Demands Out of Fear That Treatment Be Withheld or Stopped

An unmarried 18-year-old woman, 24 weeks pregnant and with a history of chronic asthma, was admitted to the hospital with a two-day histo-

ry of increasing shortness of breath. She was found to have a left lobar
pneumonia and a gram-negative urinary-tract infection. She was transferred to the MICU for worsening shortness of breath and hypoxia resistant to therapy with supplemental oxygen. Despite vigorous pulmonary
toilet and antiasthmatic and antibiotic therapy, her condition continued to
deteriorate. She was thought to require intubation for positive end-ex-
piratory pressure respiratory therapy. Initially, she refused this modality
of treatment. She was alert, oriented and clearly legally competent. After several discussions with physicians, nurses, family and friends, she
openly verbalized her fears of the imposing and intimidating MICU
equipment and environment. She was able to accept reassurance and
consented to appropriate medical therapy. She showed slow but progressive improvement and was discharged eight days later.

Case 5—Family's Perception Differs from Patient's Previously Ex-
pressed Wishes

A 76-year-old retired man was transferred to the MICU four days after
laparotomy for diverticulitis. Before hospitalization, he had enjoyed
good health and a full and active life-style. He sang regularly in a barber-
shop quartet until one week before admission. The patient's hospital
course was complicated by a urinary-tract infection, with sepsis and aspiration pneumonia requiring orotracheal intubation to control pulmonary
secretions.

Before intubation, he had emphasized to the medical staff his enjoyment of life and expressed a strong desire to return, if possible, to his
previous state of health. After intubation, he continued to cooperate vigorously with his daily care, including painful procedures (e.g., obtaining
samples of arterial-blood gas). However, he contracted sepsis and became delirious, and at this time his wife and daughter expressed strong
feelings to the MICU staff that no "heroic" measures be undertaken.
Thus, serious disagreement arose concerning the appropriate level of
supportive care for this patient. The professional staff of the MICU felt
that the medical problems were potentially reversible and that the patient
had both explicitly and implicitly expressed a wish to continue the struggle for life. Because this view conflicted with the family's wishes, the
MICU visiting physician called a meeting of the Terminal Care Committee (a hospital committee with broad representation that meets at the request of any physician, nurse or family member who would like advice
concerning the difficult decision to initiate, continue, stop or withhold intensive care for critically ill patients). Meeting with the committee were
the private physician, the MICU attending physician, as well as representatives from the MICU nursing and house-officer teams. The family was
given the opportunity to attend but declined. The committee supported
the judgment of the MICU staff that because of the patient's previously
expressed wishes and the medical situation, vigorous supportive intervention should be continued. A meeting was then held between medical
staff and the patient's family, during which it was agreed by all that appropriate medical intervention should be continued but that the decision
would be reviewed on a daily basis. Five days later, the patient contracted a superinfection that did not respond to maximal antibiotic therapy.
He became transiently hypotensive and showed progressive renal failure.
In the face of a progressing multilobe pneumonia and sepsis caused by a
resistant organism, the decision to support the patient with maximum intervention was reviewed. The family concurred with the professional

staff's recommendation that cardiopulmonary resuscitation should not be attempted if the patient suffered a cardiopulmonary arrest. On the 18th day in the MICU, the patient died.

Decision making in this case became more difficult because the patient's deteriorating condition made him unable to participate. The advice of the Terminal Care Committee was critically important in this situation, where the family's perception of death with dignity conflicted not only with the patient's own wishes but also with the professional judgment of the MICU staff.

Case 6—Misconception by Some of MICU Staff of Patient's Concept of Death with Dignity

A 56-year-old woman was receiving chemotherapy on an outpatient basis for documented bronchogenic carcinoma metastatic to the mediastinal lymph nodes and central nervous system when she had a sudden seizure, followed by cardiorespiratory arrest. Resuscitation was accomplished in the outpatient department, and she was transferred to the MICU. She had been undergoing combination-drug chemotherapy as an outpatient for six months but continued to work regularly.

In the MICU, her immediate management was complicated by "flail chest" and a tension pneumothorax requiring tube drainage of the chest. She was deeply comatose and hypotensive. Several MICU staff members raised questions about the appropriateness of continued intensive care. After initial medical stabilization, including vasopressor therapy and mechanical respiration, her clinical status was reviewed in detail with the family. Because of the patient's ability to continue working until the day of admission, her excellent response to chemotherapy and her family's perception of her often-stated wish to survive to see the birth of her first grandchild (her daughter was seven months pregnant), maximal efforts were continued. She remained deeply comatose for three days. Her course was complicated by recurrent tension pneumothoraces, gram-negative sepsis caused by a urinary-tract infection and staphylococcal pneumonia. She gradually became more responsive and by the seventh hospital day was able to nod "yes" or "no" to simple questions. Her hospital course was similar to that of many critically ill patients. As soon as one problem began to improve, a major setback occurred in another organ system. With each setback, there was growing dissension among the MICU staff about the appropriate level of supportive care. The vast majority of the MICU staff felt strongly that continued maximum intervention was neither warranted nor humane. A smaller group of staff, supported by the patient's daughter and (once she was able to communicate) the patient herself, felt that as long as there was any chance for the patient to return to the quality of life she had enjoyed before cardiorespiratory arrest, maximum therapy was indicated.

The patient was the subject of many hours of debate and was a regular topic of conversation at the weekly interdisciplinary conference. She survived all her medical complications and was discharged home after seven weeks in the MICU, awake, alert and able to walk and engage in daily activities around her home without limitation. She saw the birth of her granddaughter, and spent Thanksgiving, Christmas and New Year's Day at home with her family. She died suddenly at home 11 weeks after discharge.

Discussion

Our purpose is not to refute the importance of patient autonomy or discredit the more complex concept of death with dignity. Rather, we have attempted to provide a specific clinical perspective that may help clarify the difficult and often conflicting factors underlying the decisions made daily at the bedsides of critically ill patients.

. . .

We heartily support the plea by Imbus and Zawacki for "more and earlier communication with the patient." However, their question, "Who is more likely to be totally and lovingly concerned with the patient's best interest than the patient himself?" may be somewhat naive and, in certain clinical situations, potentially dangerous. Physicians must not use "professional responsibility" as a cloak for paternalism, but they must be alert not to let the possibility of abuse keep them from the appropriate exercise of professional judgment. Physicians who are uncomfortable or inexperienced in dealing with the complex psychosocial issues facing critically ill patients may ignore an important aspect of their professional responsibility by taking a patient's or family's statement at face value without further exploration or clarification.

The cases presented in this article illustrate specific situations in which superficial preoccupation with the issues of patient autonomy and death with dignity could have led to inappropriate clinical and ethical decisions. They suggest a checklist that may aid the clinician in evaluating such difficult situations.

Case 1—Patient Ambivalence

One must be cautious not to act precipitously on the side of the patient's ambivalence with which one agrees, while piously claiming to be following the principle of patient autonomy. Ambivalence may not be detected if communication is not a continuing feature of the situation or if the physician makes clear to the patient the answer he expects to hear. Ideally, one hopes for resolution of the ambivalence through clarification of the issues or changes in the course of the illness. However, in some instances, ambivalence may not resolve despite a protracted course and maximal communicative efforts.

Case 2—Depression

A patient's refusal or request for cessation of treatment may be influenced by depression. If the depression is adequately treated or, as is more frequently encountered, is reactive to physical discomfort that can be relieved, the patient may well change his or her mind. The astute clinician must be alert for a history of endogenous depression, vegetative signs of depression and any acute conditions to which the patient may be reacting. Vigorous attempts to treat the causes of the depression should be made before automatically acquiescing to the patient's wishes.

Case 3—Patient Who Uses a Plea for Death with Dignity to Identify a Hidden Problem

As demands for autonomy and death with dignity become acceptable and even popular, patients may use them to mask other less "acceptable" problems or complaints. As Case 3 illustrates, a thorough psychosocial history and clinical interview with the patient and family may identify the real problem. If the MICU team can deal effectively with the underlying "real" problems, the plea for death with dignity may radically change.

Case 4—Patient Demands Out of Fear That Treatment Be Withheld or Stopped

Situations do exist in which fear is rational, unshakable and ultimately a reasonable basis for refusing treatment. On the other hand, fear is often transient and based on misperception or misinformation. When a patient refuses treatment, the physician should try to identify any fears that may underlie the refusal of therapy. The physician can attempt to overcome the fear by means of honest, open explanation and reassurance and by efforts from family, friends and members of the health-care team.

Case 5—Family's Perception Differs from Patient's Previously Expressed Wishes

Case 5 illustrates this difficult problem. In the absence of a legal document specifically expressing the patient's wishes, who has the right to decide? Clearly, the family represents the interest of the patient, but must a physician comply if both his medical judgment and his assessment of the patient's wishes conflict with the family's view? Of course, the issue could be decided in court. Fortunately, in this case, consultation with the ethics committee of the hospital led to a compromise satisfactory to both family and the MICU staff.

Case 6—Misconception by Some of MICU Staff of Patient's Concept of Death with Dignity

In Case 6, some of the MICU staff assumed that a comatose patient with metastatic cancer would not want intensive "heroic" treatment. They were mistaken. This patient's will to live was revealed in her desire to see her grandchild born. In such cases, efforts must be made to ascertain the patient's wishes, rather than to make assumptions by the test "what would I want." Questioning family or waiting until the patient can communicate are methods of discovering the wishes of the patient. Supportive therapy must be continued until this information can be gathered.

This checklist describes six patients we have seen in a busy MICU. It is by no means complete but we hope it will help to clarify situations in which superficial and automatic acquiescence to the concepts of patient autonomy and death with dignity threaten sound clinical judgment. As physicians, we strongly support the principles of patient autonomy and death with dignity and welcome any dialogue that promotes them. Spencer highlighted the importance of judiciously balancing the role of patient and family input into these often difficult decisions with the exercise of sound professional judgment. We must continue to emphasize our professional responsibility for thorough clinical investigation and the exercise of sound judgment. Living up to this responsibility can only enhance the true autonomy and dignity of our patients.

NOTES

1. Patients who wish treatment to be terminated are able to do so on their own. Many patients, however, need the cooperation of others. If those from whom assistance is sought have reason to presume that the patient is competent to make decisions that are consistent with the patient's values and life goals, they have two options. They can take the patient's words literally or, recognizing that words are only one form of communication, explore further the patient's wishes.

This latter approach is, however, fraught with difficulty. Which approach do you prefer?

2. It sometimes happens that "interested parties" question a patient's competence because they disagree with the views that the patient expresses or because they are concerned that the patient's disease or condition, immaturity, inexperience or a combination of these factors may have impaired his or her reasoning. Are all of the above acceptable reasons for questioning competence?

3. Should we presume incapacity when a patient is below the age of majority? The Tennessee Supreme Court refused to hear the argument of the Rev. Larry Hamilton that his daughter, Pamela, should not receive chemotherapy for her disease, Ewing's Sarcoma, over his religious objections. The 12 year old girl reportedly agreed with her father. New York Times, Sept. 30, 1983, at A14, col. 1. Cf. Schowalter, Ferholt and Mann, The Adolescent Patient's Decision to Die, 51 Pediatrics 97 (1973) (16-year-old Catholic girl with irreversible kidney malfunction who had undergone unsuccessful attempt at kidney transplant decided with her parents' concurrence to discontinue life support devices).

4. Should we presume incapacity where a patient's competence might be affected by the underlying disease or treatment? See In the Matter of Spring, 380 Mass. 629, 405 N.E.2d 115 (1980). The Massachusetts Supreme Judicial Court approved a lower court order permitting petitioner, the ward's temporary guardian, to stop dialysis of a 79-year-old man believed to be incompetent due to "chronic organic brain syndrome" or senility. As two authors point out:

> No psychiatric testimony was heard. Two written affidavits from physicians were presented which described Mr. Spring as suffering from chronic organic brain syndrome or senility. The signature on one affidavit was completely illegible; the other affidavit was based upon an examination of Mr. Spring conducted nearly 15 months prior to the appointment of Mr. Spring's wife and son as temporary guardians and their filing of the petition to terminate his hemodialysis treatments. While the report of the guardian *ad litem* indicates that Mr. Spring was confused and disoriented as to time and place when interviewed by the guardian *ad litem*, it is somewhat disturbing that the guardian did not call for periodic psychiatric evaluations. The only medical testimony concerning Mr. Spring's competency, or lack thereof, came from a kidney specialist at the institution where Mr. Spring received his hemodialysis treatments. He testified that, in his opinion, Mr. Spring suffered from irreversible dementia and was incompetent. Based on this evidence, Mr. Spring was found incompetent and his family was authorized to order that his dialysis treatments be withdrawn, despite the absence of any evidence of Mr. Spring's wishes with regard to treatment or his ability to comprehend the nature of his illness and the consequence of discontinuing dialysis.

Dunn and Ator, *Vox Clamantis in Deserto:* Do You *Really* Mean What You Say in *Spring?* in Legal and Ethical Aspects of Treating Critically and Terminally Ill Patients 177, 178 (Doudera and Peters, eds. 1982).

5. If we do not presume incapacity as a result of immaturity or the impact of a disease or underlying conditions, how should we make these determinations? See President's Commission, Making Health Care Decisions 169–188 (1982) for a general discussion of assessing incapacity. At least one author, after examining four cases where patients suffered from gangrene and needed an amputation, (Lane v. Candura, 6 Mass.App.Ct. 377, 376 N.E.2d 1232 (1978), In re Quackenbush, 156 N.J.Super. 282, 383 A.2d 785 (1978), State Department of Human Services v. Northern, 563 S.W.2d 197 (Tenn.App.1978), and In re Schiller, 148 N.J. Super. 163, 372 A.2d 360 (1977)), has concluded that the legal test for determining competence is "the patient's ability to make the choice with recognition of the two alternatives, i.e. loss of limbs or death." In addition, "the patient must be able to indicate knowledge and acceptance of the certainty of death." Clarke, The Choice to Refuse or Withhold Medical Treatment: The Emerging Technology and Medical Ethical Consensus, 13 Creighton L.Rev. 795, 807 (1980). For additional discussion of competence and incapacity, see Ch. 3, Sec. B.2, supra.

The widow of Earle Spring, the patient in *Spring,* discussed above, later sued the Geriatric Authority of Holyoke, alleging that nurses at the institution invaded Mr. Spring's privacy. The nurses had written to a newspaper about his case, stating that Mr. Spring had told them that he did not wish to die. As a result, the care and treatment of Mr. Spring became a matter of much public debate. The jury awarded Mrs. Spring $1 million in damages. Right-to-Die Debate Held to Invade Privacy, New York Times, Aug. 4, 1983 at A12, col. 6.

CALIFORNIA HEALTH AND SAFETY CODE, THE NATURAL DEATH ACT

§ 7186. Legislative findings and declaration

The Legislature finds that adult persons have the fundamental right to control the decisions relating to the rendering of their own medical care, including the decision to have life-sustaining procedures withheld or withdrawn in instances of a terminal condition.

The Legislature further finds that modern medical technology has made possible the artificial prolongation of human life beyond natural limits.

The Legislature further finds that, in the interest of protecting individual autonomy, such prolongation of life for persons with a terminal condition may cause loss of patient dignity and unnecessary pain and suffering, while providing nothing medically necessary or beneficial to the patient.

The Legislature further finds that there exists considerable uncertainty in the medical and legal professions as to the legality of terminating the use or application of life-sustaining procedures where the patient has voluntarily and in sound mind evidenced a desire that such procedures be withheld or withdrawn.

In recognition of the dignity and privacy which patients have a right to expect, the Legislature hereby declares that the laws of the State of California shall recognize the right of an adult person to make a written directive instructing his physician to withhold or withdraw life-sustaining procedures in the event of a terminal condition.

§ 7187. Definitions

The following definitions shall govern the construction of this chapter:

(a) "Attending physician" means the physician selected by, or assigned to, the patient who has primary responsibility for the treatment and care of the patient.

(b) "Directive" means a written document voluntarily executed by the declarant in accordance with the requirements of Section 7188. The directive, or a copy of the directive, shall be made part of the patient's medical records.

(c) "Life-sustaining procedure" means any medical procedure or intervention which utilizes mechanical or other artificial means to sustain, restore, or supplant a vital function, which, when applied to a qualified patient, would serve only to artificially prolong the moment of death and where, in the judgment of the attending physician, death is imminent whether or not such procedures are utilized. "Life-sustaining procedure" shall not include the administration of medication or the performance of any medical procedure deemed necessary to alleviate pain.

(d) "Physician" means a physician and surgeon licensed by the Board of Medical Quality Assurance or the Board of Osteopathic Examiners.

(e) "Qualified patient" means a patient diagnosed and certified in writing to be afflicted with a terminal condition by two physicians, one of whom shall be the attending physician, who have personally examined the patient.

(f) "Terminal condition" means an incurable condition caused by injury, disease, or illness, which, regardless of the application of life-sustaining procedures, would, within reasonable medical judgment, produce death, and where the application of life-sustaining procedures serve only to postpone the moment of death of the patient.

§ 7188. Directive to withhold or withdraw life-sustaining procedures; signature; witnesses; form; contents

Any adult person may execute a directive directing the withholding or withdrawal of life-sustaining procedures in a terminal condition. The directive shall be signed by the declarant in the presence of two witnesses not related to the declarant by blood or marriage and who would not be entitled to any portion of the estate of the declarant upon his decease under any will of the declarant or codicil thereto then existing or, at the time of the directive, by operation of law then existing. In addition, a witness to a directive shall not be the attending physician, an employee of the attending physician or a health facility in which the declarant is a patient, or any person who has a claim against any portion of the estate of the declarant upon his decease at the time of the execution of the directive. The directive shall be in the following form:

DIRECTIVE TO PHYSICIANS

Directive made this _____ day of _____ (month, year).

I _____, being of sound mind, willfully, and voluntarily make known my desire that my life shall not be artificially prolonged under the circumstances set forth below, do hereby declare:

1. If at any time I should have an incurable injury, disease, or illness certified to be a terminal condition by two physicians, and where the application of life-sustaining procedures would serve only to artificially prolong the moment of my death and where my physician determines that my death is imminent whether or not life-sustaining procedures are utilized, I direct that such procedures be withheld or withdrawn, and that I be permitted to die naturally.

2. In the absence of my ability to give directions regarding the use of such life-sustaining procedures, it is my intention that this directive shall be honored by my family and physician(s) as the final expression of my legal right to refuse medical or surgical treatment and accept the consequences from such refusal.

3. If I have been diagnosed as pregnant and that diagnosis is known to my physician, this directive shall have no force or effect during the course of my pregnancy.

4. I have been diagnosed and notified at least 14 days ago as having a terminal condition by _____, M.D., whose address is _____, and whose telephone number is _____. I understand that if I have not filled in the physician's name and address, it shall be presumed that I did not have a terminal condition when I made out this directive.

5. The directive shall have no force or effect five years from the date filled in above.

6.   I understand the full import of this directive and I am emotionally and mentally competent to make this directive.

Signed _____

City, County and State of Residence _____

The declarant has been personally known to me and I believe him or her to be of sound mind.

Witness _____

Witness _____

§ 7188.5.   Patient in skilled nursing facility;   witnesses to directive

A directive shall have no force or effect if the declarant is a patient in a skilled nursing facility as defined in subdivision (c) of Section 1250 at the time the directive is executed unless one of the two witnesses to the directive is a patient advocate or ombudsman as may be designated by the State Department of Aging for this purpose pursuant to any other applicable provision of law.   The patient advocate or ombudsman shall have the same qualifications as a witness under Section 7188.

The intent of this section is to recognize that some patients in skilled nursing facilities may be so insulated from a voluntary decisionmaking role, by virtue of the custodial nature of their care, as to require special assurance that they are capable of willfully and voluntarily executing a directive.

§ 7189.   Revocation of directive;   failure to act upon revocation;   civil or criminal liability

(a)   A directive may be revoked at any time by the declarant, without regard to his mental state or competency, by any of the following methods:

(1)   By being canceled, defaced, obliterated, or burnt, torn, or otherwise destroyed by the declarant or by some person in his presence and by his direction.

(2)   By a written revocation of the declarant expressing his intent to revoke, signed and dated by the declarant.   Such revocation shall become effective only upon communication to the attending physician by the declarant or by a person acting on behalf of the declarant.   The attending physician shall record in the patient's medical record the time and date when he received notification of the written revocation.

(3)   By a verbal expression by the declarant of his intent to revoke the directive.   Such revocation shall become effective only upon communication to the attending physician by the declarant or by a person acting on behalf of the declarant.   The attending physician shall record in the patient's medical record the time, date, and place of the revocation and the time, date, and place, if different, of when he received notification of the revocation.

(b)   There shall be no criminal or civil liability on the part of any person for failure to act upon a revocation made pursuant to this section unless that person has actual knowledge of the revocation.

§ 7189.5. Duration of directive; reexecution; extension during comatose condition or period of incapability of communication

A directive shall be effective for five years from the date of execution thereof unless sooner revoked in a manner prescribed in Section 7189. Nothing in this chapter shall be construed to prevent a declarant from reexecuting a directive at any time in accordance with the formalities of Section 7188, including reexecution subsequent to a diagnosis of a terminal condition. If the declarant has executed more than one directive, such time shall be determined from the date of execution of the last directive known to the attending physician. If the declarant becomes comatose or is rendered incapable of communicating with the attending physician, the directive shall remain in effect for the duration of the comatose condition or until such time as the declarant's condition renders him or her able to communicate with the attending physician.

§ 7190. Civil liability or guilt of criminal act or unprofessional conduct

No physician or health facility which, acting in accordance with the requirements of this chapter, causes the withholding or withdrawal of life-sustaining procedures from a qualified patient, shall be subject to civil liability therefrom. No licensed health professional, acting under the direction of a physician, who participates in the withholding or withdrawal of life-sustaining procedures in accordance with the provisions of this chapter shall be subject to any civil liability. No physician, or licensed health professional acting under the direction of a physician, who participates in the withholding or withdrawal of life-sustaining procedures in accordance with the provisions of this chapter shall be guilty of any criminal act or of unprofessional conduct.

§ 7191. Effectuation of directive by attending physician

(a) Prior to effecting a withholding or withdrawal of life-sustaining procedures from a qualified patient pursuant to the directive, the attending physician shall determine that the directive complies with Section 7188, and, if the patient is mentally competent, that the directive and all steps proposed by the attending physician to be undertaken are in accord with the desires of the qualified patient.

(b) If the declarant was a qualified patient at least 14 days prior to executing or reexecuting the directive, the directive shall be conclusively presumed, unless revoked, to be the directions of the patient regarding the withholding or withdrawal of life-sustaining procedures. No physician, and no licensed health professional acting under the direction of a physician, shall be criminally or civilly liable for failing to effectuate the directive of the qualified patient pursuant to this subdivision. A failure by a physician to effectuate the directive of a qualified patient pursuant to this division shall constitute unprofessional conduct if the physician refuses to make the necessary arrangements, or fails to take the necessary steps, to effect the transfer of the qualified patient to another physician who will effectuate the directive of the qualified patient.

(c) If the declarant becomes a qualified patient subsequent to executing the directive, and has not subsequently reexecuted the directive, the attending physician may give weight to the directive as evidence of the patient's directions regarding the withholding or withdrawal of life-sustaining procedures and may consider other factors, such as information from the affected family or the nature of the patient's illness, injury, or disease, in determining whether the totality of circumstances known to the attending physician justify effectuating the directive. No physician, and no licensed health professional acting under the direction of a physician, shall be criminally or civilly liable for failing to effectuate the directive of the qualified patient pursuant to this subdivision.

§ 7192. Compliance with chapter not to constitute suicide; effect on life insurance; prohibition of execution of directive as condition for being insured for, or receiving, health care services

(a) The withholding or withdrawal of life-sustaining procedures from a qualified patient in accordance with the provisions of this chapter shall not, for any purpose, constitute a suicide.

(b) The making of a directive pursuant to Section 7188 shall not restrict, inhibit, or impair in any manner the sale, procurement, or issuance of any policy of life insurance, nor shall it be deemed to modify the terms of an existing policy of life insurance. No policy of life insurance shall be legally impaired or invalidated in any manner by the withholding or withdrawal of life-sustaining procedures from an insured qualified patient, notwithstanding any term of the policy to the contrary.

(c) No physician, health facility, or other health provider, and no health care service plan, insurer issuing disability insurance, self-insured employee welfare benefit plan, or nonprofit hospital service plan, shall require any person to execute a directive as a condition for being insured for, or receiving, health care services.

§ 7193. Impairment or supersession of legal right or responsibility to withhold or withdraw life-sustaining procedures by this chapter

Nothing in this chapter shall impair or supersede any legal right or legal responsibility which any person may have to effect the withholding or withdrawal of life-sustaining procedures in any lawful manner. In such respect the provisions of this chapter are cumulative.

§ 7194. Willful concealment, cancellation, or defacement; falsification or forgery of directive, or willful concealment or withholding knowledge of revocation

Any person who willfully conceals, cancels, defaces, obliterates, or damages the directive of another without such declarant's consent shall be guilty of a misdemeanor. Any person who, except where justified or excused by law, falsifies or forges the directive of another, or willfully conceals or withholds personal knowledge of a revocation as provided in Section 7189, with the intent to cause a withholding or withdrawal of life-sustaining procedures contrary to the wishes of the declarant, and thereby, because of any such act, directly causes life-sustaining procedures to be withheld or withdrawn and death to thereby be hastened, shall be subject to prosecution for unlawful homicide . . . . .

§ 7195. Inapplicability of chapter to condone, authorize or approve mercy killing or to permit other than natural process of dying

Nothing in this chapter shall be construed to condone, authorize, or approve mercy killing, or to permit any affirmative or deliberate act or omission to end life other than to permit the natural process of dying as provided in this chapter.

NOTES

1. The California Natural Death Act, the first statute of its kind in the United States, became law on September 3, 1976. The Act received national publicity and has inspired similar legislative efforts around the country. As of June 1983, thirteen states and the District of Columbia had followed California's lead. See Code of Ala., Tit. 22, §§ 8A–1 to 8A–10 (May 27, 1981); Ark.Stat.Ann. § 82–3804 (Mar. 30, 1977); 16 Del.Code Ann. § 2501 through 2508 (July 12, 1982); D.C.Code Ann. § 6–2401 (Supp.1982); Idaho Code §§ 29–4501 through 29–4508 (Mar. 1977); Kan.Stat.Ann. 65–28,101 through 65–28,109 (July 1, 1979); Nev.Rev.Stat. 449.550 through 449.590 (May 6, 1977); N.Mex.Comp.Laws §§ 24–7–1 through 24–7–10 (Apr. 7, 1977); N.C.Gen.Stat. §§ 90–320 through 90–322 (July 1, 1977); Or.Rev.Stat. §§ 97.050 through 97.090 (June 9, 1977); Vernon's Ann.Tex.Civ.St. art. 4590h (Aug. 29, 1977); 18 Vt.Stat.Ann. §§ 5251 through 5262 and 13 Vt.Stat.Ann. § 1801 (Apr. 8, 1982); Virginia (Passed by the Virginia Assembly Feb. 1983 and signed into law in Apr. 1983); Rev.Code Wash. Ann. 70.122.010 through 70.122.905 (June 7, 1979). The acts are reprinted in President's Commission, Deciding to Forego Life-Sustaining Treatment (Appendix D) 309–387 (1983).

a. Are Natural Death Acts a good idea? Will provisions be specific enough to give guidance without loss of flexibility? Can persons make informed choices prior to the onset of illness or before death is very near? California approached this issue by creating advisory and binding directives and establishing a waiting period before a binding directive takes effect. The majority of states enacting statutes have not followed California's lead on this issue, however. Would it be preferable to name a proxy in the directive?

b. Under the California statute, a directive is binding only if it is signed by a "qualified patient". The act, moreover, does not apply to children or pregnant women, § 7188, and imposes special requirements on nursing home residents who because of the custodial nature of their care may not be capable of making a voluntary and free choice, § 7188.5. Are the California requirements too restrictive? Would the act have covered Karen Quinlan if she had executed a directive? The North Carolina statute, by contrast, defines a qualifying patient as merely "a person." § 90–321.

c. What should happen to a physician who fails to follow a properly executed directive? The California statute stipulates that a physician's failure to effectuate a binding directive (though not an advisory directive) or to transfer a patient to another physician who will effectuate the directive of the qualified patient, shall constitute unprofessional conduct. Is that an adequate penalty?

d. What happens to a patient with a terminal condition in California who has not issued a directive in accordance with the statute? What should happen? An alternative to natural death acts suggested by the President's Commission, is the use of durable powers of attorney statutes. See Deciding to Forego Life-Sustaining Treatment 145–147, (Appendix E1) 390–437 (1983). A power of attorney is a document by which a person (principal) appoints another person (agent) to act on the principal's behalf, usually with respect to property matters, but often concerning personal matters as well. At common law, the power terminated when the principal became incapacitated. To avoid this result, many states have enacted statutes that create a "durable" power of attorney. In other words, the agent's authority continues despite the principal's incapacity. The Commission suggests that these statutes can accommodate decisionmaking for incompetent patients, although the members recognize the possibility of abuse. The Commission consequently urges that these durable powers of attorney statutes be studied further. Id. at 147. In light of the Commission's recommendations, California adopted a statute (S.B. 762) amending its Civil Code to make explicit provision for a "durable power of attorney for health care." See Cal.Civ.Code §§ 2430–2443. The new law, which went into effect on September 29, 1983, without the

Governor's signature, was introduced by Sen. Barry Keene, who as an Assembly-man had been the sponsor of the Natural Death Act.

2.   A survey employing a mailed questionnaire has been conducted to assess physicians' knowledge and understanding of the California Natural Death Act. Note, 31 Stan.L.Rev. 913 (1979). The questionnaire was mailed to 920 physicians of whom 284 responded. Id. at 925. The survey results are excerpted below:

1.   *Accuracy of the legislative model.*

. . . Because the Act allows the withholding or withdrawal only of *artificial* life-support, we asked whether terminal patients are commonly kept alive artificially. We found that doctors seldom use artificial life-support: Our survey indicated that only approximately 17% of dying patients receive such treatment. Thus, the majority of terminal patients do not fall within the scope of the Act.

Because patients cannot execute binding directives or reaffirm advisory ones until 14 days after learning they are terminally ill, we asked whether the respondent's patients remain conscious and competent for two weeks after it is possible to diagnose them as terminally ill. We found that only about half of the dying patients remain conscious this long. Thus, a large number of terminally ill patients, who otherwise fit within the boundaries of the Act, can never make their wishes binding on physicians.

The practices of individual physicians could also have a substantial effect on whether terminal patients are able to execute binding directives. Because patients must be aware they are terminally ill before executing binding directives, we inquired whether doctors inform patients of terminal illnesses. Most doctors indicated they do disclose this information: Only 7% said they sometimes do not tell patients of terminal illness even if neither the patient nor the patient's family knows. But doctors sometimes assume the patient knows of the terminal condition without being told, or tell the patient's family but fail to tell the patient. Those who do tell the patient often communicate in euphemisms, such as suggesting patients "begin putting their affairs in order." These findings suggest that some patients may be left uncertain about the exact nature of their condition and thus not realize the need to execute a directive.

2.   *Physicians' knowledge and interpretation of the Act.*

. . .

The survey indicates that doctors are generally aware of the existence of the Act: Only 8% said they were unacquainted with it, while 42% had read the text of the Act. But the survey also indicated that general familiarity with the Act is no guarantee that a doctor will know the Act's technical requirements. First, only 22% of the respondents claimed to know the circumstances under which directives are binding or nonbinding. Second, most physicians either did not answer or said they did not know whether the Act permits withholding or withdrawal of life-sustaining procedures only if the patient would die regardless of such procedures. And most of those who did respond answered incorrectly. Third, most doctors said they did not know how long a patient must wait after being diagnosed as terminally ill before executing a binding directive or affirming an advisory one to make it binding. Of those who did respond, more gave the incorrect answer of 1 month than the correct answer of 2 weeks. Thus, although doctors are generally familiar with the Act, most have only a vague understanding of its key technical provisions.

Doctors' ignorance of the details of the Act cannot be explained by a lack of familiarity with it. Indeed, those doctors who have read the Act and those who keep directive forms for their patients fared no better in answering the three questions on the technical requirements than did their colleagues who had only passing acquaintance with the Act. Perhaps doctors feel uncomfortable with the legal jargon in the Act, or think that knowledge of the legal requirements is a lawyer's duty, not theirs. Whatever the reason, this lack of technical knowledge about the Act suggests that some physicians may not be following its specific provisions. Instead they may mistakenly feel bound to stop treatment when technically they are free to continue it, or they may keep patients on life-support when they are required to withdraw treatment.

Even if doctors were familiar with the requirements of the Act, their behavior might vary substantially depending on their interpretation of the Act's often vague terms. In the survey, we asked physicians to decide among several possible definitions of the Act's key terms, or to provide their own definitions. First, we asked the doctors to define "terminal illness." Because patients can execute binding directives only after they are diagnosed as terminally ill, the practical effect of the Act may turn on physicians' interpretation of that term. The survey suggests that "terminal illness" does not have a uniform meaning for doctors. While the majority of the respondents defined terminal illness as "an illness that progresses to death regardless of what is done," a substantial number, including many of those same doctors, also indicated that its meaning "changes with each patient and illness." [88] Nineteen percent of the respondents defined "terminal illness" in terms of the length of time likely to pass before death, giving durations ranging from less than 1 month to 1 year.[89] The Act's application, then, may vary depending on the particular physician's definition of the term "terminal illness."

Second, because the Act allows the withholding or withdrawal of only "artificial life-sustaining procedures," we asked doctors what treatments they thought fell into this category. Doctors generally agreed that respirators, dialysis, and resuscitators constitute "artificial life-support." But they split evenly in their views on intravenous feeding, and only about one-third considered insulin, antibiotics, or chemotherapy to be "artificial." [90] These responses reveal that most doctors find mechanical systems to be more artificial than drugs or other treatments. Nevertheless, a significant minority of doctors classify medications such as antibiotics and insulin as artificial. The Act's application, then, may also vary depending on the particular physician's definition of the term "artificial."

Finally, because treatment of a terminal patient may be stopped only when death is imminent regardless of treatment, we asked physicians their understanding of the term "imminent." According to 46% of the doctors, death is imminent only when it will occur in 24 hours or less. Over 80% of the doctors consider death imminent when it will occur in 1 week or less. Few doctors indicated a longer period.[92] Given this consensus on the meaning of "imminent death," a legislative requirement that doctors withhold treatment only

---

88. We asked doctors: "What, if any, is your working definition of terminal illness?" We gave them several alternative answers and allowed them to choose more than one. Of the respondents, 56% defined a terminal illness as "an illness that progresses to death regardless of what is done," and 47% said "its meaning changes with each patient and illness."

89. 8.4% indicated 6 months, 6.5% indicated 1 year, and another 2.5% wrote in a variety of specific durations.

90. We asked doctors which of a list of treatments they considered to be "artificial life-sustaining procedures." Each of the treatments we suggested could be called "life-sustaining," for patients can die from failure to receive them. Each is "artificial" in the sense that it is an achievement of modern medicine, though only respirators, resuscitation, intravenous feeding, and dialysis involve mechanical means.

TABLE 3

What Treatment Constitutes "Artificial Life-Support"?

	% of doctors reporting
Respirators	96.4
Dialysis	90.2
Resuscitation	89.9
Intravenous feeding	50.9
Antibiotics	38.2
Chemotherapy	36.7
Insulin	34.5

92. TABLE 4

When Is Death Imminent?

	Cumulative % of doctors reporting
24 hrs or less	45.9
1 week or less	83.4
2 weeks or less	91.5
1 month or less	96.1
6 months or less	100.0

when "death is imminent" may spare most terminal patients little more than a few hours or days of artificial life-support.

3. *Physicians' willingness to stop treatment.*

The effect of the California Natural Death Act may ultimately depend on the willingness of doctors to follow their patients' wishes that treatment be stopped. To indirectly assess potential compliance, we presented doctors with four hypothetical clinical situations in which patients had asked that treatment be withheld. We asked the doctors in each case whether they would still give treatment. We varied the type of illness, the age of the patient, and the extent of family involvement in order to note the effect of these factors on treatment decisions. Most important, we also varied the manner in which the patients expressed their wish that treatment be stopped to test the relative effect of oral requests, advisory directives, and binding directives.

The first hypothetical situation allowed us to compare the effect of a patient's oral request made to the doctors shortly before becoming unconscious, with the effect of an advisory directive executed under the Act. Interestingly, the relative effect of the oral and written requests varied with the severity of the patient's injuries. If the patient's life could be saved by treatment, an advisory directive had practically no influence on doctors' decisions: Almost all said they would still give treatment. A prior oral request, however, would persuade about 6% of the doctors, who otherwise would have treated, to withhold care. If the patient was so severely injured that recovery was unlikely—though not impossible—regardless of treatment, an oral request and an advisory directive were equally influential: Each persuaded about 15% of the doctors who otherwise would have treated, to withhold treatment. Finally, an oral request and an advisory directive proved quite influential if the patient had no chance of recovery: Each persuaded about 20% of the doctors, who otherwise would have treated, to withhold care.

A second hypothetical compared the effect of a binding directive with that of an oral request. Binding directives—in contrast with advisory directives—had a significantly greater effect on physicians' decisions than did oral requests. The relative effect of the two forms of request varied substantially depending on the wishes of the patient's family. If the patient had no family, only about one-quarter of the doctors said they would violate the patient's oral request to stop treatment. Similarly, if the family acquiesced to the patient's wish that treatment be stopped, only one-fifth of the doctors would violate the oral request. In both cases, a binding directive increased doctors' rate of compliance by about 10%. A binding directive had the greatest effect when the family disagreed with the patient's request that treatment be withheld and insisted that "everything be done." In this situation nearly three-quarters of the physicians said they would violate the patient's oral request, while only about one-third would violate a binding directive. These findings reveal that a binding directive is generally more effective than a request not in directive form, particularly when the family opposes the patient's wishes. Such a result is not surprising: A doctor's fear of legal liability for honoring a patient's desire to forego treatment would naturally be greater when the family opposes that course of action, because the family, unlike the patient, is in a position to bring legal action against the doctor.

Although most doctors indicated that under at least some circumstances they would comply with a patient's requests that treatment be withheld, a significant minority indicated they would administer artificial life-support every time, regardless of the medical circumstances or the form of the patient's request. For example, 11% of the doctors would give artificial life-support to an 80-year-old heart attack victim in violation of a legally binding directive, even when the patient's family acquiesced in the patient's desire that treatment be withheld. Similarly, a third hypothetical revealed that 14% of the respondents would ignore an advisory directive and put a severely brain-damaged patient on a respirator, even though the patient's lack of cortical activity indicated he was legally dead under California law. Finally, a fourth hypothetical revealed that 19% of the respondents would actively try to contravene a terminal cancer patient's request that blood transfusions given to save him from dying of a severe bleeding ulcer be withheld. These doctors would ask the hospital to take legal steps to see that the patient was transfused even though the patient remained conscious and continued to refuse treatment.

Statistical analyses reveal that the minority who would administer artificial life-support was composed of many of the same doctors in each case. About 10% of the respondents were "interventionists" who indicated they would administer artificial life-support at every opportunity. These physicians do not ignore binding and advisory directives out of fear of legal liability, since the questionnaire explained that such directives relieve doctors of legal liability for stopping treatment. Whether they base their decisions to continue to treat on hopes of miraculous cures or on belief in the sanctity of life, these doctors represent a significant minority whom legislative mandates apparently do not move.

4. *Effect of the Act on physicians' practices.*

A final group of questions directly assessed the effect of the California Natural Death Act on physicians' practices. The results suggest that physicians themselves may be creating practical barriers to application of the Act. First, although doctors themselves are aware of the existence of the nontreatment right, they may not be passing on that information to their patients. Only about 15% of the doctors take an active role in discussing directives. The majority discuss the subject only when patients ask, but few patients apparently do so: Nearly 40% of the doctors reported that no patient has ever asked about directives. Second, fewer than 30% of the physicians surveyed said they have directive forms available for patients.

Despite such attitudes, some patients apparently are exercising their nontreatment right. Nearly two-thirds of the doctors reported that some of their patients have executed directives, and 40% report that at least one patient has died subsequent to filling out a directive. But few of these directives have actually affected the disposition of a case: Only 6.5% of the doctors reported that in the year since the Act went into effect they have withdrawn or withheld treatment when previously they would have administered it.

Although the Act has had only a small effect on actual cases so far, other responses to the survey suggest that its potential effect is great. Two-thirds of the doctors reported that a directive would make a difference in their decision to withhold or withdraw treatment. Moreover, a substantial number say the Act has clarified the legal requirements for stopping treatment: Twenty-one percent indicated the Act has assured them they are acting legally when they withdraw or withhold treatment; 47% indicated that it has made it easier for them to honor their patients' wishes.

A significant number of doctors, however, found the Act more confusing than clarifying. Sixteen percent indicated the Act has increased their fear of malpractice liability for stopping treatment, and 27% say it has made them uncertain about their criminal and civil liability if they do so. This uncertainty about the Act may, to some extent, be reflected in doctors' actions: Ten percent of the doctors report that since the Act took effect they have administered treatment in situations in which they previously would have withheld care. Perhaps doctors who are uncertain about the legal ramifications of treatment decisions consider administering treatment to be the safest course.

Id. at pp. 927–940.

3. What effect should be given to oral or written directives in the absence of enabling legislation? Although decisions to terminate life sustaining care for terminally-ill, comatose patients have been permitted, see Sec. B.2., supra, no court has permitted such termination based upon the execution of a living will (i.e., a document stating patient preferences with respect to manner of dying) in the absence of court approval. At least one court has stated that a living will, executed during the time a person is competent, is "persuasive evidence" of an incompe-

tent patient's wishes and accordingly should be afforded great weight by persons who are permitted to substitute their judgment on behalf of the incompetent patient. John F. Kennedy Memorial Hospital, Inc. v. Bludworth, ___ So.2d ___ (Fla. 1984). For an example of a "living will" proposed by an ethicist, see Bok, Personal Directions for Care at the End of Life, 295 New Eng.J.Med. 367 (1976).

At least one court has given effect to prior oral statements in a case involving a permanently unconscious patient not covered by a natural death act. Brother Fox was an 83 year old member of the Society of Mary. He was in good health, but after he developed a hernia, his physician advised surgery. During the operation he suffered cardiac arrest and substantial brain damage. He was placed on a respirator and remained in a vegetative state. Father Philip Eichner, the supervisor of Br. Fox's religious community, petitioned the court for authorization to remove Br. Fox from the respirator. The New York Court of Appeals authorized removal from the respirator on the ground that the common law permitted a competent patient to decline lifesaving treatment: there was uncontested evidence that Br. Fox had indicated these were his views before he became incompetent. In the Matter of Storar, 52 N.Y.2d 363, 438 N.Y.S.2d 266, 420 N.E.2d 64 (1981) (consolidated appeal). Compare this result with the result in John F. Kennedy Memorial Hospital v. Heston, 58 N.J. 576, 279 A.2d 670 (1971) and In re Osborne, 294 A.2d 372 (D.C.App.1972) where prior expressions of patients in opposition to blood transfusions based upon religious beliefs were not dispositive.

SIDNEY H. WANZER, S. JAMES ADELSTEIN, RONALD E. CRANFORD, DANIEL E. FEDERMAN, EDWARD D. HOOK, CHARLES G. MOERTEL, PETER SAFER, ALAN STONE, HELEN TAUSSIG AND JAN VAN EYS, THE PHYSICIAN'S RESPONSIBILITY TOWARD HOPELESSLY ILL PATIENTS *

310 New Eng.J.Med. 955, 958–959 (1984).

THE PROVISION OF APPROPRIATE CARE

Although relief of pain and suffering is the primary consideration in the care of all hopelessly ill patients, differences in patients' disabilities dictate differences in the appropriate form and intensity of their care.

. . .

General levels of care can be described as follows: (1) emergency resuscitation; (2) intensive care and advanced life support; (3) general medical care, including antibiotics, drugs, surgery, cancer chemotherapy, and artificial hydration and nutrition; and (4) general nursing care and efforts to make the patient comfortable, including pain relief and hydration and nutrition as dictated by the patient's thirst and hunger. Although the program of care must be individualized, since every patient is unique, these four levels of treatment should be considered and discussed with the patient, the family, and other health-care personnel. Certainly, the competent patient has a right to know that such variations in approach exist.

. . .

The Competent Patient

In treating patients who are generally alert but are dying of a progressive illness, such as cancer, the physician must be especially sensitive to

* The authors of this article, physicians from eight institutions across the United States, prepared this statement at a meeting sponsored by the Society for the Right to Die. [Eds.]

their need for relief from pain and suffering. Aggressive treatment in response to this need is often justified even if under other circumstances the risk of such treatment would be medically undesirable (e.g., it would result in respiratory depression). The level of care to be provided should reflect an understanding between patient and physician and should be reassessed from time to time. In many cases neither intensive care nor emergency resuscitation is desired by the patient and his or her family; there may be a wish only for comfort, with general medical treatment given solely to provide relief from distress.

When the facilities provided by an acute-care hospital are not essential to the comfort and dignity of the dying patient, he or she should be moved to a more appropriate setting, if possible. Care at home or in a less regimented environment, such as a hospice, should be encouraged and facilitated.

The Incompetent Patient

Patients with brain death. Patients with irreversible cessation of all functions of the brain, determined in accordance with accepted medical standards, are considered medically and legally dead, and no further treatment is required.

Patients in a persistent vegetative state. In this state the neocortex is largely and irreversibly destroyed, although some brain-stem functions persist. When this neurologic condition has been established with a high degree of medical certainty and has been carefully documented, it is morally justifiable to withhold antibiotics and artificial nutrition and hydration, as well as other forms of life-sustaining treatment, allowing the patient to die. This obviously requires careful efforts to obtain knowledge of the patient's prior wishes and the understanding and agreement of the family. Family attitudes will clearly influence the type of care given in these cases.

Severely and irreversibly demented patients. Patients in this category, most of them elderly, are at one end of the spectrum of decreasing mental capacity. They do not initiate purposeful activity but passively accept nourishment and bodily care.

When the severely demented patient has previously made his or her wishes known and when there is intercurrent illness, it is ethically permissible for the physician to withhold treatment that would serve mainly to prolong the dying process. When there is no prior expression or living will and when no family or advocate is available, the physician should be guided by the need to provide the most humane kind of treatment and the need to carry out the patient's wishes insofar as they are ascertainable.

Severely and irreversibly demented patients need only care given to make them comfortable. If such a patient rejects food and water by mouth, it is ethically permissible to withhold nutrition and hydration artificially administered by vein or gastric tube. Spoon feeding should be continued if needed for comfort. It is ethically appropriate not to treat intercurrent illness except with measures required for comfort (e.g., antibiotics for pneumonia can be withheld). For this category of patients, it is best if decisions about the handling of intercurrent illness are made prospectively, before the onset of an acute illness or threat to life. The physician must always bear in mind that senseless perpetuation of the status quo is decision by default.

Elderly patients with permanent mild impairment of competence. Many elderly patients are described as "pleasantly senile." Although somewhat limited in their ability to initiate activities and communicate, they often appear to be enjoying their moderately restricted lives. Freedom from discomfort should be an overriding objective in the care of such a patient. If emergency resuscitation and intensive care are required, the physician should provide these measures sparingly, guided by the patient's prior wishes, if known, by the wishes of the patient's family, and by an assessment of the patient's prospects for improvement.

4. THE INCOMPETENT PATIENT

Considering the difficulty courts, legislatures and health care providers have in recognizing explicit refusals of treatment by competent and formerly competent patients, it is not surprising that an even greater debate has arisen concerning patients who have never been competent or at least have never expressed their views on the subject while competent. Issues raised by their care and treatment are explored in this section.

SUPERINTENDENT OF BELCHERTOWN v. SAIKEWICZ

Supreme Judicial Court of Massachusetts, 1977.
373 Mass. 728, 370 N.E.2d 417.

LIACOS, JUSTICE.

On April 26, 1976, William E. Jones, superintendent of the Belchertown State School (a facility of the Massachusetts Department of Mental Health), and Paul R. Rogers, a staff attorney at the school, petitioned the Probate Court for Hampshire County for the appointment of a guardian of Joseph Saikewicz, a resident of the State school. Simultaneously they filed a motion for the immediate appointment of a guardian ad litem, with authority to make the necessary decisions concerning the care and treatment of Saikewicz, who was suffering with acute myeloblastic monocytic leukemia. The petition alleged that Saikewicz was a mentally retarded person in urgent need of medical treatment and that he was a person with disability incapable of giving informed consent for such treatment.

On May 5, 1976, the probate judge appointed a guardian ad litem. On May 6, 1976, the guardian ad litem filed a report with the court. The guardian ad litem's report indicated that Saikewicz's illness was an incurable one, and that although chemotherapy was the medically indicated course of treatment it would cause Saikewicz significant adverse side effects and discomfort. The guardian ad litem concluded that these factors, as well as the inability of the ward to understand the treatment to which he would be subjected and the fear and pain he would suffer as a result, outweighed the limited prospect of any benefit from such treatment, namely, the possibility of some uncertain but limited extension of life. He therefore recommended "that not treating Mr. Saikewicz would be in his best interests."

A hearing on the report was held on May 13, 1976. Present were the petitioners and the guardian ad litem. . . . [T]he judge entered findings of fact and an order that in essence agreed with the recommendation of the guardian ad litem. . . . An application for direct appellate review was allowed by this court. . . .

I.

The judge below found that Joseph Saikewicz, at the time the matter arose, was sixty-seven years old, with an I.Q. of ten and a mental age of approximately two years and eight months. He was profoundly mentally retarded. The record discloses that, apart from his leukemic condition, Saikewicz enjoyed generally good health. He was physically strong and well built, nutritionally nourished, and ambulatory. He was not, however, able to communicate verbally—resorting to gestures and grunts to make his wishes known to others and responding only to gestures or physical contacts. In the course of treatment for various medical conditions arising during Saikewicz's residency at the school, he had been unable to respond intelligibly to inquiries such as whether he was experiencing pain. It was the opinion of a consulting psychologist, not contested by the other experts relied on by the judge below, that Saikewicz was not aware of dangers and was disoriented outside his immediate environment. As a result of his condition, Saikewicz had lived in State institutions since 1923 and had resided at the Belchertown State School since 1928. Two of his sisters, the only members of his family who could be located, were notified of his condition and of the hearing, but they preferred not to attend or otherwise become involved.

On April 19, 1976, Saikewicz was diagnosed as suffering from acute myeloblastic monocytic leukemia. Leukemia is a disease of the blood. It arises when organs of the body produce an excessive number of white blood cells as well as other abnormal cellular structures, in particular undeveloped and immature white cells. Along with these symptoms in the composition of the blood the disease is accompanied by enlargement of the organs which produce the cells, e.g., the spleen, lymph glands, and bone marrow. The disease tends to cause internal bleeding and weakness, and, in the acute form, severe anemia and high susceptibility to infection. . . . The disease is invariably fatal.

Chemotherapy, as was testified to at the hearing in the Probate Court, involves the administration of drugs over several weeks, the purpose of which is to kill the leukemia cells. This treatment unfortunately affects normal cells as well. One expert testified that the end result, in effect, is to destroy the living vitality of the bone marrow. Because of this effect, the patient becomes very anemic and may bleed or suffer infections—a condition which requires a number of blood transfusions. In this sense, the patient immediately becomes much "sicker" with the commencement of chemotherapy, and there is a possibility that infections during the initial period of severe anemia will prove fatal. Moreover, while most patients survive chemotherapy, remission of the leukemia is achieved in only thirty to fifty per cent of the cases. Remission is meant here as a temporary return to normal as measured by clinical and laboratory means. If remission does occur, it typically lasts for between two and thirteen months although longer periods of remission are possible. Estimates of the effectiveness of chemotherapy are complicated in cases, such as the one presented here, in which the patient's age becomes a factor. According to the medical testimony before the court below, persons over age sixty have more difficulty tolerating chemotherapy and the treatment is likely to be less successful than in younger patients.[4] This prognosis may

---

4. On appeal, the petitioners have collected in their brief a number of recent empirical studies which cast doubt on the view that patients over sixty are less successfully treated by chemotherapy. . . . None of these authorities was brought to the consid-

be compared with the doctors' estimates that, left untreated, a patient in Saikewicz's condition would live for a matter of weeks or, perhaps, several months. According to the testimony, a decision to allow the disease to run its natural course would not result in pain for the patient, and death would probably come without discomfort.

An important facet of the chemotherapy process, to which the judge below directed careful attention, is the problem of serious adverse side effects caused by the treating drugs. Among these side effects are severe nausea, bladder irritation, numbness and tingling of the extremities, and loss of hair. The bladder irritation can be avoided, however, if the patient drinks fluids, and the nausea can be treated by drugs. It was the opinion of the guardian ad litem, as well as the doctors who testified before the probate judge, that most people elect to suffer the side effects of chemotherapy rather than to allow their leukemia to run its natural course.

. . . The Judge below found:

"5. That the majority of persons suffering from leukemia who are faced with a choice of receiving or foregoing such chemotherapy, and who are able to make an informed judgment thereon, choose to receive treatment in spite of its toxic side effects and risks of failure.

"6. That such toxic side effects of chemotherapy include pain and discomfort, depressed bone marrow, pronounced anemia, increased chance of infection, possible bladder irritation, and possible loss of hair.

"7. That administration of such chemotherapy requires cooperation from the patient over several weeks of time, which cooperation said JOSEPH SAIKEWICZ is unable to give due to his profound retardation.[5]

"8. That, considering the age and general state of health of said JOSEPH SAIKEWICZ, there is only a 30–40 percent chance that chemotherapy will produce a remission of said leukemia, which remission would probably be for a period of time of from 2 to 13 months, but that said chemotherapy will certainly not completely cure such leukemia.

"9. That if such chemotherapy is to be administered at all it should be administered immediately, inasmuch as the risks involved will increase and the chances of successfully bringing about remission will decrease as time goes by.

"10. That, at present, said JOSEPH SAIKEWICZ's leukemia condition is stable and is not deteriorating.

"11. That said JOSEPH SAIKEWICZ is not now in pain and will probably die within a matter of weeks or months a relatively painless death due to the leukemia unless other factors should intervene to themselves cause death.

eration of the probate judge. We accept the judge's conclusion, based on the expert testimony before him and in accordance with substantial medical evidence, that the patient's age weighed against the successful administration of chemotherapy.

5. There was testimony as to the importance of having the full cooperation of the patient during the initial weeks of the chemotherapy process as well as during follow-up visits. For example, the evidence was that it would be necessary to administer drugs in-travenously for extended periods of time—twelve or twenty-four hours a day for up to five days. The inability of Saikewicz to comprehend the purpose of the treatment, combined with his physical strength, led the doctors to testify that Saikewicz would probably have to be restrained to prevent him from tampering with the intravenous devices. Such forcible restraint could, in addition to increasing the patient's discomfort, lead to complications such as pneumonia.

"12. That it is impossible to predict how long said JOSEPH SAIKEWICZ will probably live without chemotherapy or how long he will probably live with chemotherapy, but it is to a very high degree medically likely that he will die sooner without treatment than with it."

Balancing these various factors, the judge concluded that the following considerations weighed *against* administering chemotherapy to Saikewicz: "(1) his age, (2) his inability to cooperate with the treatment, (3) probable adverse side effects of treatment, (4) low chance of producing remission, (5) the certainty that treatment will cause immediate suffering, and (6) the quality of life possible for him even if the treatment does bring about remission."

The following considerations were determined to weigh in *favor* of chemotherapy: "(1) the chance that his life may be lengthened thereby, and (2) the fact that most people in his situation when given a chance to do so elect to take the gamble of treatment."

Concluding that, in this case, the negative factors of treatment exceeded the benefits, the probate judge ordered on May 13, 1976, that no treatment be administered to Saikewicz for his condition of acute myeloblastic monocytic leukemia except by further order of the court. The judge further ordered that all reasonable and necessary supportive measures be taken, medical or otherwise, to safeguard the well-being of Saikewicz in all other aspects and to reduce as far as possible any suffering or discomfort which he might experience.

. . .

Saikewicz died on September 4, 1976, at the Belchertown State School hospital. Death was due to bronchial pneumonia, a complication of the leukemia. Saikewicz died without pain or discomfort.

II.

We recognize at the outset that this case presents novel issues of fundamental importance that should not be resolved by mechanical reliance on legal doctrine. . . . [T]he principal areas of determination are:

A. The nature of the right of any person, competent or incompetent, to decline potentially life-prolonging treatment.

B. The legal standards that control the course of decision whether or not potentially life-prolonging, but not life-saving, treatment should be administered to a person who is not competent to make the choice.

C. The procedures that must be followed in arriving at that decision.

. . .

There is implicit recognition in the law of the Commonwealth, as elsewhere, that a person has a strong interest in being free from nonconsensual invasion of his bodily integrity. . . .

Of even broader import, but arising from the same regard for human dignity and self-determination, is the unwritten constitutional right of privacy found in the penumbra of specific guaranties of the Bill of Rights. Griswold v. Connecticut, 381 U.S. 479, 484, 85 S.Ct. 328, 13 L.Ed.2d 339 (1965). As this constitutional guaranty reaches out to protect the freedom of a woman to terminate pregnancy under certain conditions, so it encompasses the right of a patient to preserve his or her right to privacy against unwanted infringements of bodily integrity in appropriate circumstances. In re Quinlan, [70 N.J. 10, 38–39, 355 A.2d 647, 663–64]. In the case of a person incompetent to assert this constitutional right of privacy, it may be asserted by that person's guardian in conformance with the standards and procedures set forth [in] . . . this opinion. . . .

The question when the circumstances are appropriate for the exercise of this privacy right depends on the proper identification of State interests. . . .

. . . .

. . . [A] survey of recent decisions involving the difficult question of the right of an individual to refuse medical intervention or treatment indicates that a relatively concise statement of countervailing State interests may be made. As distilled from the cases, the State has claimed interest in: (1) the preservation of life; (2) the protection of the interests of innocent third parties; (3) the prevention of suicide; and (4) maintaining the ethical integrity of the medical profession.

It is clear that the most significant of the asserted State interests is that of the preservation of human life. Recognition of such an interest, however, does not necessarily resolve the problem where the affliction or disease clearly indicates that life will soon, and inevitably, be extinguished. The interest of the State in prolonging a life must be reconciled with the interest of an individual to reject the traumatic cost of that prolongation. There is a substantial distinction in the State's insistence that human life be saved where the affliction is curable, as opposed to the State interest where, as here, the issue is not whether but when, for how long, and at what cost to the individual that life may be briefly extended. Even if we assume that the State has an additional interest in seeing to it that individual decisions on the prolongation of life do not in any way tend to "cheapen" the value which is placed in the concept of living, we believe it is not inconsistent to recognize a right to decline medical treatment in a situation of incurable illness. The constitutional right to privacy, as we conceive it, is an expression of the sanctity of individual free choice and self-determination as fundamental constituents of life. The value of life as so perceived is lessened not by a decision to refuse treatment, but by the failure to allow a competent human being the right of choice.

A second interest of considerable magnitude, which the State may have some interest in asserting, is that of protecting third parties, particularly minor children, from the emotional and financial damage which may occur as a result of the decision of a competent adult to refuse life-saving or life-prolonging treatment. . . .

The last State interest requiring discussion [11] is that of the maintenance of the ethical integrity of the medical profession as well as allowing hospitals the full opportunity to care for people under their control. The force and impact of this interest is lessened by the prevailing medical ethical standards. . . . Prevailing medical ethical practice does not, without exception, demand that all efforts toward life prolongation be made

---

11. The interest in protecting against suicide seems to require little if any discussion. In the case of the competent adult's refusing medical treatment such an act does not necessarily constitute suicide since (1) in refusing treatment the patient may not have the specific intent to die, and (2) even if he did, to the extent that the cause of death was from natural causes the patient did not set the death producing agent in motion with the intent of causing his own death. Furthermore, the underlying State interest in this area lies in the prevention of irrational self-destruction. What we consider here is a competent, rational decision to refuse treatment when death is inevitable and the treatment offers no hope of cure or preservation of life. There is no connection between the conduct here in issue and any State concern to prevent suicide.

in all circumstances. Rather, as indicated in *Quinlan*, the prevailing ethical practice seems to be to recognize that the dying are more often in need of comfort than treatment. Recognition of the right to refuse necessary treatment in appropriate circumstances is consistent with existing medical mores; such a doctrine does not threaten either the integrity of the medical profession, the proper role of hospitals in caring for such patients or the State's interest in protecting the same. It is not necessary to deny a right of self-determination to a patient in order to recognize the interests of doctors, hospitals, and medical personnel in attendance on the patient. . . .

Applying the considerations discussed in this subsection to the decision made by the probate judge in the circumstances of the case before us, we are satisfied that his decision was consistent with a proper balancing of applicable State and individual interests. Two of the four categories of State interests that we have identified, the protection of third parties and the prevention of suicide, are inapplicable to this case. The third, involving the protection of the ethical integrity of the medical profession was satisfied on two grounds. The probate judge's decision was in accord with the testimony of the attending physicians of the patient. The decision is in accord with the generally accepted views of the medical profession, as set forth in this opinion. The fourth State interest—the preservation of life—has been viewed with proper regard for the heavy physical and emotional burdens on the patient if a vigorous regimen of drug therapy were to be imposed to effect a brief and uncertain delay in the natural process of death. To be balanced against these State interests was the individual's interest in the freedom to choose to reject, or refuse to consent to, intrusions of his bodily integrity and privacy. We cannot say that the facts of this case required a result contrary to that reached by the probate judge with regard to the right of any person, competent or incompetent, to be spared the deleterious consequences of life-prolonging treatment. We therefore turn to consider the unique considerations arising in this case by virtue of the patient's inability to appreciate his predicament and articulate his desires.

B.

The question what legal standards govern the decision whether to administer potentially life-prolonging treatment to an incompetent person encompasses two distinct and important subissues. First, does a choice exist? That is, is it the unvarying responsibility of the State to order medical treatment in all circumstances involving the care of an incompetent person? Second, if a choice does exist under certain conditions, what considerations enter into the decision-making process?

We think that principles of equality and respect for all individuals require the conclusion that a choice exists. For reasons discussed at some length in subsection A, supra, we recognize a general right in all persons to refuse medical treatment in appropriate circumstances. The recognition of that right must extend to the case of an incompetent, as well as a competent, patient because the value of human dignity extends to both.

. . . Whatever the merits of such a policy where life-saving treatment is available—a situation unfortunately not presented by this case—a more flexible view of the "best interests" of the incompetent patient is not precluded under other conditions. . . .

The "best interests" of an incompetent person are not necessarily served by imposing on such persons results not mandated as to competent persons similarly situated. It does not advance the interest of the State or the ward to treat the ward as a person of lesser status or dignity than others. To protect the incompetent person within its power, the State must recognize the dignity and worth of such a person and afford to that person the same panoply of rights and choices it recognizes in competent persons. If a competent person faced with death may choose to decline treatment which not only will not cure the person but which substantially may increase suffering in exchange for a possible yet brief prolongation of life, then it cannot be said that it is always in the "best interests" of the ward to require submission to such treatment. Nor do statistical factors indicating that a majority of competent persons similarly situated choose treatment resolve the issue. The significant decisions of life are more complex than statistical determinations. Individual choice is determined not by the vote of the majority but by the complexities of the singular situation viewed from the unique perspective of the person called on to make the decision. To presume that the incompetent person must always be subjected to what many rational and intelligent persons may decline is to downgrade the status of the incompetent person by placing a lesser value on his intrinsic human worth and vitality.

. . . This leads us to the question of how the right of an incompetent person to decline treatment might best be exercised so as to give the fullest possible expression to the character and circumstances of that individual.

The problem of decision-making presented in this case is one of first impression before this court, and we know of no decision in other jurisdictions squarely on point. The well publicized decision of the New Jersey Supreme Court in In re Quinlan, 70 N.J. 10, 355 A.2d 647 (1976), provides a helpful starting point for analysis. . . .

. . .

Karen Quinlan's situation, however, must be distinguished from that of Joseph Saikewicz. Saikewicz was profoundly mentally retarded. His mental state was a cognitive one but limited in his capacity to comprehend and communicate. Evidence that most people choose to accept the rigors of chemotherapy has no direct bearing on the likely choice that Joseph Saikewicz would have made. Unlike most people, Saikewicz had no capacity to understand his present situation or his prognosis. The guardian ad litem gave expression to this important distinction in coming to grips with this "most troubling aspect" of withholding treatment from Saikewicz: "If he is treated with toxic drugs he will be involuntarily immersed in a state of painful suffering, the reason for which he will never understand. Patients who request treatment know the risks involved and can appreciate the painful side-effects when they arrive. They know the reason for the pain and their hope makes it tolerable." To make a worthwhile comparison, one would have to ask whether a majority of people would choose chemotherapy if they were told merely that something outside of their previous experience was going to be done to them, that this something would cause them pain and discomfort, that they would be removed to strange surroundings and possibly restrained for extended periods of time, and that the advantages of this course of action were measured by concepts of time and mortality beyond their ability to comprehend.

To put the above discussion in proper perspective, we realize that an inquiry into what a majority of people would do in circumstances that truly were similar assumes an objective viewpoint not far removed from a "reasonable person" inquiry. While we recognize the value of this kind of indirect evidence, we should make it plain that the primary test is subjective in nature—that is, the goal is to determine with as much accuracy as possible the wants and needs of the individual involved.[15] This may or may not conform to what is thought wise or prudent by most people. The problems of arriving at an accurate substituted judgment in matters of life and death vary greatly in degree, if not in kind, in different circumstances. For example, the responsibility of Karen Quinlan's father to act as she would have wanted could be discharged by drawing on many years of what was apparently an affectionate and close relationship. In contrast, Joseph Saikewicz was profoundly retarded and noncommunicative his entire life, which was spent largely in the highly restrictive atmosphere of an institution. While it may thus be necessary to rely to a greater degree on objective criteria, such as the supposed inability of profoundly retarded persons to conceptualize or fear death, the effort to bring the substituted judgment into step with the values and desires of the affected individual must not, and need not, be abandoned.

The "substituted judgment" standard which we have described commends itself simply because of its straightforward respect for the integrity and autonomy of the individual. We need not, however, ignore the substantial pedigree that accompanies this phrase. The doctrine of substituted judgment had its origin over 150 years ago in the area of the administration of the estate of an incompetent person. Ex parte Whitbread in re Hinde, a Lunatic, 35 Eng.Rep. 878 (1816). The doctrine was utilized to authorize a gift from the estate of an incompetent person to an individual when the incompetent owed no duty of support. The English court accomplished this purpose by substituting itself as nearly as possible for the incompetent, and acting on the same motives and considerations as would have moved him. In essence, the doctrine in its original inception called on the court to "don the mental mantle of the incompetent." In re Carson, 39 Misc.2d 544, 545 (N.Y.Sup.Ct.1962).

In modern times the doctrine of substituted judgment has been applied as a vehicle of decision in cases more analogous to the situation presented in this case. In a leading decision on this point, Strunk v. Strunk, 445 S.W.2d 145 (Ky.Ct.App.1969), the court held that a court of equity had the power to permit removal of a kidney from an incompetent donor for purposes of effectuating a transplant. The court concluded that, due to the nature of their relationship, both parties would benefit

---

15. In arriving at a philosophical rationale in support of a theory of substituted judgment in the context of organ transplants from incompetent persons, Professor Robertson of the University of Wisconsin Law School argued that "maintaining the integrity of the person means that we act toward him 'as we have reason to believe [he] would choose for [himself] if [he] were [capable] of reason and deciding rationally.' It does not provide a license to impute to him preferences he never had or to ignore previous preferences. . . . If preferences are unknown, we must act with respect to the preferences a reasonable, competent person in the incompetent's situation would have." Robertson, Organ Donations by Incompetents and the Substituted Judgment Doctrine, 76 Colum.L.Rev. 48, 63 (1976), quoting J. Rawls, A Theory of Justice 209 (1971). In this way, the "free choice and moral dignity" of the incompetent person would be recognized. "Even if we were mistaken in ascertaining his preferences, the person [if he somehow became competent] could still agree that he had been fairly treated, if we had a good reason for thinking he would have made the choices imputed to him." Robertson, supra at 63.

from the completion of the procedure, and hence the court could presume that the prospective donor would, if competent, assent to the procedure.

With this historical perspective, we now reiterate the substituted judgment doctrine as we apply it in the instant case. We believe that both the guardian ad litem in his recommendation and the judge in his decision should have attempted (as they did) to ascertain the incompetent person's actual interests and preferences. In short, the decision in cases such as this should be that which would be made by the incompetent person, if that person were competent, but taking into account the present and future incompetency of the individual as one of the factors which would necessarily enter into the decision-making process of the competent person. Having recognized the right of a competent person to make for himself the same decision as the court made in this case, the question is, do the facts on the record support the proposition that Saikewicz himself would have made the decision under the standard set forth. We believe they do.

The two factors considered by the probate judge to weigh in favor of administering chemotherapy were: (1) the fact that most people elect chemotherapy and (2) the chance of a longer life. Both are appropriate indicators of what Saikewicz himself would have wanted, provided that due allowance is taken for this individual's present and future incompetency. We have already discussed the perspective this brings to the fact that most people choose to undergo chemotherapy. With regard to the second factor, the chance of a longer life carries the same weight for Saikewicz as for any other person, the value of life under the law having no relation to intelligence or social position. Intertwined with this consideration is the hope that a cure, temporary or permanent, will be discovered during the period of extra weeks or months potentially made available by chemotherapy. The guardian ad litem investigated this possibility and found no reason to hope for a dramatic breakthrough in the time frame relevant to the decision.

The probate judge identified six factors weighing against administration of chemotherapy. Four of these—Saikewicz's age, the probable side effects of treatment, the low chance of producing remission, and the certainty that treatment will cause immediate suffering—were clearly established by the medical testimony to be considerations that any individual would weigh carefully. A fifth factor—Saikewicz's inability to cooperate with the treatment—introduces those considerations that are unique to this individual and which therefore are essential to the proper exercise of substituted judgment. The judge heard testimony that Saikewicz would have no comprehension of the reasons for the severe disruption of his formerly secure and stable environment occasioned by the chemotherapy. He therefore would experience fear without the understanding from which other patients draw strength. The inability to anticipate and prepare for the severe side effects of the drugs leaves room only for confusion and disorientation. The possibility that such a naturally uncooperative patient would have to be physically restrained to allow the slow intravenous administration of drugs could only compound his pain and fear, as well as possibly jeopardize the ability of his body to withstand the toxic effects of the drugs.

The sixth factor identified by the judge as weighing against chemotherapy was "the quality of life possible for him even if the treatment does bring about remission." To the extent that this formulation equates the value of life with any measure of the quality of life, we firmly reject it. A reading of the entire record clearly reveals, however, the judge's concern that special care be taken to respect the dignity and worth of Saikewicz's life precisely because of his vulnerable position. The judge, as well as all the parties, were keenly aware that the supposed ability of Saikewicz, by virtue of his mental retardation, to appreciate or experience life had no place in the decision before them. Rather than reading the judge's formulation in a manner that demeans the value of the life of one who is mentally retarded, the vague, and perhaps ill-chosen, term "quality of life" should be understood as a reference to the continuing state of pain and disorientation precipitated by the chemotherapy treatment. Viewing the term in this manner, together with the other factors properly considered by the judge, we are satisfied that the decision to withhold treatment from Saikewicz was based on a regard for his actual interests and preferences and that the facts supported this decision.

C.

We turn now to a consideration of the procedures appropriate for reaching a decision where a person allegedly incompetent is in a position in which a decision as to the giving or withholding of life-prolonging treatment must be made. . . .

. . .

. . . The first step is to petition the court for the appointment of a guardian or a temporary guardian. The decision under which of these two provisions to proceed will be determined by the circumstances of the case, that is, whether the exigencies of the situation allow time to comply with the seven-day notice requirement prior to the hearing on the appointment of a guardian. If appointment of a temporary guardian is sought, the probate judge will make such orders regarding notice as he deems appropriate. At the hearing on the appointment of a guardian or temporary guardian, the issues before the court are (1) whether the person involved is mentally retarded within the meaning of the statute and (2), if the person is mentally retarded, who shall be appointed guardian. As an aid to the judge in reaching these two decisions, it will often be desirable to appoint a guardian ad litem, sua sponte or on motion, to represent the interests of the person. Moreover, we think it appropriate, and highly desirable, in cases such as the one before us to charge the guardian ad litem with an additional responsibility to be discharged if there is a finding of incompetency. This will be the responsibility of presenting to the judge, after as thorough an investigation as time will permit, all reasonable arguments in favor of administering treatment to prolong the life of the individual involved. This will ensure that all viewpoints and alternatives will be aggressively pursued and examined at the subsequent hearing where it will be determined whether treatment should or should not be allowed. The report of the guardian or temporary guardian will, of course, also be available to the judge at this hearing on the ultimate issue of treatment. Should the probate judge then be satisfied that the incompetent individual would, as determined by the standards previously set forth, have chosen to forego potentially life-prolonging treatment, the judge shall issue the appropriate order. If the judge is not so persuaded, or finds that the interests of the State require it, then treatment shall be ordered.

Commensurate with the powers of the Probate Court . . ., the probate judge may, at any step in these proceedings, avail himself or herself of the additional advice or knowledge of any person or group. We note here that many health care institutions have developed medical ethics committees or panels to consider many of the issues touched on here. Consideration of the findings and advice of such groups as well as the testimony of the attending physicians and other medical experts ordinarily would be of great assistance to a probate judge faced with such a difficult decision. We believe it desirable for a judge to consider such views wherever available and useful to the court. We do not believe, however, that this option should be transformed by us into a required procedure. We take a dim view of any attempt to shift the ultimate decision-making responsibility away from the duly established courts of proper jurisdiction to any committee, panel or group, ad hoc or permanent. Thus, we reject the approach adopted by the New Jersey Supreme Court in the *Quinlan* case of entrusting the decision whether to continue artificial life support to the patient's guardian, family, attending doctors, and hospital "ethics committee." . . . For its part, the New Jersey Supreme Court concluded that "a practice of applying to a court to confirm such decisions would generally be inappropriate, not only because that would be a gratuitous encroachment upon the medical profession's field of competence, but because it would be impossibly cumbersome. Such a requirement is distinguishable from the judicial overview traditionally required in other matters such as the adjudication and commitment of mental incompetents. This is not to say that in the case of an otherwise justiciable controversy access to the courts would be foreclosed; we speak rather of a general practice and procedure."

We do not view the judicial resolution of this most difficult and awesome question—whether potentially life-prolonging treatment should be withheld from a person incapable of making his own decision—as constituting a "gratuitous encroachment" on the domain of medical expertise. Rather, such questions of life and death seem to us to require the process of detached but passionate investigation and decision that forms the ideal on which the judicial branch of government was created. Achieving this ideal is our responsibility and that of the lower court, and is not to be entrusted to any other group purporting to represent the "morality and conscience of our society," no matter how highly motivated or impressively constituted.

III.

Finding no State interest sufficient to counterbalance a patient's decision to decline life-prolonging medical treatment in the circumstances of this case, we conclude that the patient's right to privacy and self-determination is entitled to enforcement. Because of this conclusion, and in view of the position of equality of an incompetent person in Joseph Saikewicz's position, we conclude that the probate judge acted appropriately in this case. . . .

IN THE MATTER OF STORAR

Court of Appeals of New York, 1981.
52 N.Y.2d 363, 438 N.Y.S.2d 266, 420 N.E.2d 64, certiorari denied 454 U.S. 858, 102 S.Ct. 309, 70 L.Ed.2d 153.

WACHTLER, JUDGE.

. . .

John Storar was profoundly retarded with a mental age of about 18 months. At the time of this proceeding he was 52 years old and a resident of the Newark Development Center, a State facility, which had been his home since the age of 5. His closest relative was his mother, a 77-year-old widow who resided near the facility. He was her only child and she visited him almost daily.

In 1979 physicians at the center noticed blood in his urine and asked his mother for permission to conduct diagnostic tests. She initially refused but after discussions with the center's staff gave her consent. The tests, completed in July, 1979, revealed that he had cancer of the bladder. It was recommended that he receive radiation therapy at a hospital in Rochester. When the hospital refused to administer the treatment without the consent of a legal guardian, Mrs. Storar applied to the court and was appointed guardian of her son's person and property in August, 1979. With her consent he received radiation therapy for six weeks after which the disease was found to be in remission.

However in March, 1980 blood was again observed in his urine. The lesions in his bladder were cauterized in an unsuccessful effort to stop the bleeding. At that point his physician diagnosed the cancer as terminal, concluding that after using all medical and surgical means then available, the patient would nevertheless die from the disease.

In May the physicians at the center asked his mother for permission to administer blood transfusions. She initially refused but the following day withdrew her objection. For several weeks John Storar received blood transfusions when needed. However, on June 19 his mother requested that the transfusions be discontinued.

The director of the center then brought this proceeding, pursuant to section 33.03 of the Mental Hygiene Law, seeking authorization to continue the transfusions, claiming that without them "death would occur within weeks." Mrs. Storar cross-petitioned for an order prohibiting the transfusions, and named the District Attorney as a party. The court appointed a guardian ad litem and signed an order temporarily permitting the transfusions to continue, pending the determination of the proceeding.

At the hearing in September the court heard testimony from various witnesses including Mrs. Storar, several employees at the center, and seven medical experts. All the experts concurred that John Storar had irreversible cancer of the bladder, which by then had spread to his lungs and perhaps other organs, with a very limited life span, generally estimated to be between 3 and 6 months. They also agreed that he had an infant's mentality and was unable to comprehend his predicament or to make a reasoned choice of treatment. In addition, there was no dispute over the fact that he was continuously losing blood.

The medical records show that at the time of the hearing, he required two units of blood every 8 to 15 days. The staff physicians explained that the transfusions were necessary to replace the blood lost. Without them there would be insufficient oxygen in the patient's blood stream. To compensate for this loss, his heart would have to work harder and he would breathe more rapidly, which created a strain and was very tiresome. He became lethargic and they feared he would eventually bleed to death. They observed that after the transfusions he had more energy. He was able to resume most of his usual activities—feeding himself, showering, taking walks and running—including some mischievous ones, such as stealing cigarette butts and attempting to eat them.

It was conceded that John Storar found the transfusions disagreeable. He was also distressed by the blood and blood clots in his urine which apparently increased immediately after a transfusion. He could not comprehend the purpose of the transfusions and on one or two occasions had displayed some initial resistance. To eliminate his apprehension he was given a sedative approximately one hour before a transfusion. He also received regular doses of narcotics to alleviate the pain associated with the disease.

On the other hand several experts testified that there was support in the medical community for the view that, at this stage, transfusions may only prolong suffering and that treatment could properly be limited to administering pain killers. Mrs. Storar testified that she wanted the transfusions discontinued because she only wanted her son to be comfortable. She admitted that no one had ever explained to her what might happen to him if the transfusions were stopped. She also stated that she was not "sure" whether he might die sooner if the blood was not replaced and was unable to determine whether he wanted to live. However, in view of the fact that he obviously disliked the transfusions and tried to avoid them, she believed that he would want them discontinued.

The court held that the center's application for permission to continue the transfusions should be denied. It was noted that John Storar's fatal illness had not affected his limited mental ability. He remained alert and carried on many of his usual activities. However, the court emphasized that the transfusions could not cure the disease, involved some pain and that the patient submitted to them reluctantly. The court held that a person has a right to determine what will be done with his own body and, when he is incompetent, this right may be exercised by another on his behalf. In this case, the court found that John Storar's mother was the person in the best position to determine what he would want and that she "wants his suffering to stop and believes that he would want this also."

The Appellate Division affirmed in a brief memorandum.

. . .

. . . [W]e do not have any proof [of the patient's wishes]. John Storar was never competent at any time in his life. He was always totally incapable of understanding or making a reasoned decision about medical treatment. Thus it is unrealistic to attempt to determine whether he would want to continue potentially life prolonging treatment if he were competent. As one of the experts testified at the hearing, that would be similar to asking whether "if it snowed all summer would it then be winter?" Mentally John Storar was an infant and that is the only realistic way to assess his rights in this litigation . . . .

A parent or guardian has a right to consent to medical treatment on behalf of an infant (Public Health Law, § 2504, subd. 2). The parent, however, may not deprive a child of live saving treatment, however well intentioned. Even when the parents' decision to decline necessary treatment is based on constitutional grounds, such as religious beliefs, it must yield to the State's interests, as *parens patriae*, in protecting the health and welfare of the child. Of course it is not for the courts to determine the most "effective" treatment when the parents have chosen among reasonable alternatives. But the courts may not permit a parent to deny a child all treatment for a condition which threatens his life. The case of a child who may bleed to death because of the parents' refusal to authorize a blood transfusion presents the classic example.

In the *Storar* case there is the additional complication of two threats to his life. There was cancer of the bladder which was incurable and would in all probability claim his life. There was also the related loss of blood which posed the risk of an earlier death, but which, at least at the time of the hearing, could be replaced by transfusions. Thus, as one of the experts noted, the transfusions were analogous to food—they would not cure the cancer, but they could eliminate the risk of death from another treatable cause. Of course, John Storar did not like them, as might be expected of one with an infant's mentality. But the evidence convincingly shows that the transfusions did not involve excessive pain [7] and that without them his mental and physical abilities would not be maintained at the usual level. With the transfusions on the other hand, he was essentially the same as he was before except of course he had a fatal illness which would ultimately claim his life. Thus, on the record, we have concluded that the application for permission to continue the transfusions should have been granted. Although we understand and respect his mother's despair, as we respect the beliefs of those who oppose transfusions on religious grounds, a court should not in the circumstances of this case allow an incompetent patient to bleed to death because someone, even someone as close as a parent or sibling, feels that this is best for one with an incurable disease.

JONES, JUDGE (dissenting in part).

I.

. . .

The generic issue presented is not of broad scope. We all recognize the right of a competent adult to make decisions with respect to his own medical or surgical care even if the consequence of the particular decision be to hasten death. The question before us is whether, and under what circumstances, a surrogate decision can be made on behalf of the patient when he is incompetent to make it himself, where he has been diagnosed as incurably ill, and where the decision relates to the withholding or withdrawal of extraordinary life support medical procedures. The question poses the problem of judicial involvement in passive euthanasia (sometimes called "dysthanasia")—the deliberate withholding or withdrawal of available clinical means for the prolongation of the life of a patient for whom there is little or no hope of recovery or survival. Treating as the subject does with irreversible decisions affecting life and death, we approach, and even may be thought by some to trespass on, the domain of Providence. Few areas of judicial activity present such awesome questions or demand greater judicial wisdom and restraint.

---

7. Whether the presence or absence of excessive pain would be determinative with respect to the continuation of a life sus- taining measure need not be reached under the facts of this case.

I identify two aspects of the problem so fundamental as to call for exposition by this court, neither of which receives express attention in the writing of the majority. The first is explicit acknowledgment that the problem is one which the judicial system is unsuited and ill-equipped to solve and which should not usually be made the subject of judicial attention. The lapse of time necessarily consumed in appellate review before there can be a final judicial determination will almost always be unacceptable and makes recourse to judicial proceedings impractical. The methodology and the techniques for our classic adversary system are not best suited to the resolution of the issues presented. The courts can claim no particular competence to reach the difficult ultimate decision, depending as it necessarily must not only on medical data, but on theological tenets and perceptions of human values which defy classification and calibration.

There is reliable information that for many years physicians and members of patients' families, often in consultation with religious counselors, have in actuality been making decisions to withhold or to withdraw life support procedures from incurably ill patients incapable of making the critical decisions for themselves.[3] While, of course, there can be no categorical assurance that there have been no erroneous decisions thus reached, or even that in isolated instances death has not been unjustifiably hastened for unacceptable motives, at the same time there is no empirical evidence that either society or its individual members have suffered significantly in consequence of the absence of active judicial oversight. There is no indication that the medical profession whose members are most closely aware of current practices senses the need for or desires judicial intervention.

For all the foregoing reasons I would explicitly affirm the proposition that judicial approval is not required for discontinuance of life support procedures in situations such as those now before us and that neither civil

---

3. (Levisohn, Voluntary Mercy Deaths, 8 J. For Med. 57, 68 [Levisohn conducted a survey of the Chicago Medical Convention which revealed that 61% of the physicians present believed that euthanasia was being practiced by members of the profession]; Euthanasia Questions Stir New Debate, Med. World News, Sept. 14, 1973, p. 75 [87% of respondents to a poll of the Association of American Physicians reported they approved of passive euthanasia]; see also, e.g., Harrison's Principles of Internal Medicine (9th ed.), pp. 6–7; Survey, Euthanasia: Criminal, Tort, Constitutional and Legislative Considerations, 48 Notre Dame Lawyer 1202, 1213; Wilkes, When Do We Have The Right To Die?, Life, Jan. 14, 1972, p. 48; Medical Ethics: The Right To Survival, Hearings Before The Subcommittee On Health Of The Committee On Labor & Public Welfare, 93 Cong.2d Sess. 9 [1979].)

Luis Kutner, Chief Justice of the World Court of Human Rights, has recently written that doctors' attitudes toward euthanasia have changed: "Surprisingly, in a survey reported in mid-1974, 79% of physicians responding expressed some belief in the right of the patient to have a say about his death.

The subject of death has also become an important part of medical school curriculum, whereas in the past there was a tendency to neglect it in other than a strictly clinical sense. Moreover, at its annual conference, the austere American Medical Association formally adopted the following policy statement: 'The cessation of the employment of extraordinary means to prolong the life of the body where there is irrefutable evidence that biological death is imminent is the decision of the patient and-or his immediate family . . . .'. This provided doctors with a sanction for what many had actually been doing for some time, since the practice of turning off machines, for example, to allow death to come to a patient whom only the machine is keeping alive is a fairly common practice for hospitals. As a matter of fact, doctors at the Yale University School of Medicine willingly acknowledged that they had quietly allowed 43 severely deformed infants to die by withholding treatment after the parents agreed there was little chance for 'meaningful life.' The doctors disclosed this in hopes of breaking down 'a major social taboo'." (Kutner, Euthanasia: Due Process For Death With Dignity; The Living Will, 54 Ind.L.J. 201, 223.)

nor criminal liability attaches simply by reason of the absence of a court order of authorization.

As to the second aspect, I nevertheless recognize that there will be occasions in which the courts will have thrust on them cases such as the [one] now before us. It is not difficult to anticipate instances in which for one or more of a variety of reasons a member of the patient's family or a close friend might desire to seek formal judicial approval of a proposal to withhold or to withdraw a particular extraordinary life support procedure. I would therefore explicitly affirm the authority of our courts, in proper cases and in proceedings appropriately instituted, to grant authorization for withholding or withdrawal of extraordinary life support medical procedures, notwithstanding the absence of evidence of an anticipatory expression of the attitude or wishes of the particular patient . . . .

. . .

As to the merits in *Storar,* I find no sufficient ground, as a matter of law, to reverse the determination made by Supreme Court, now affirmed at the Appellate Division, and I perceive no other predicate on which the court can disturb the order of the Appellate Division; it cannot consider the matter *de novo* or make new determinations of fact except where the evidence in the record is so overwhelming as to require a particular determination as a matter of law.

While there was evidence to which the majority refers, that the discontinuation of blood transfusions would have "eventually" led to John Storar's death (and inferentially perhaps before death would otherwise have been caused by his cancer of the bladder), no finding was made as to what extension of life would attend the continuation of transfusions. Supreme Court made the ambiguous finding, undisturbed by the Appellate Division, that "Storar has a life expectancy of from two to six months regardless of whether the blood transfusions are continued or not". Similarly, although evidence was introduced that following transfusions Storar had more energy and was able to resume most of his usual, limited activities, the courts below made no finding that continued transfusions would improve the quality of his life or, if so, in what respects or to what extent. In the absence of factual determinations with respect to these matters (and in my view the evidence in the record is not sufficient to justify this court's now supplying such findings as a matter of law), I cannot conclude as a matter of law that the courts below erred in authorizing discontinuance of the blood transfusions in the light of the factual determinations which the courts did make, to wit:

That John had cancer of the bladder which was both inoperable and incurable, with a life expectancy of from two to six months; that one who has cancer of the bladder suffers severe pain and the need for medication increases as the cancer spreads; that John had been in frequent pain and as his pain had increased his need for medication had also increased;

That the blood transfusions were painful although not excessively so; that because of John's apprehension and manifest dislike of the procedure the nurse had been giving him a shot approximately one hour before the transfusion; that he submitted to the blood transfusions reluctantly and because of the force that compelled him to submit; . . . [T]hat recently he had had to be physically restrained and to have his arm tied down to prevent him from pulling out the needle used for the transfusion; that in contrast to his behavior prior to the commencement of the transfusions, he thereafter ventured outside his room infrequently; that he had appeared to be progressively more uncomfortable during the procedures; that as a result of the transfusions there was frequent clotting in his urine which made urination more painful; that the blood contributed to increased levels of sensitivity to the pain he was experiencing and contributed to his discomfort;

That the transfusions did not serve to reduce John's pain or to make him more comfortable; that the blood forced on him did not serve a curative purpose or offer a reasonable hope of benefit;

That if the transfusions were stopped John would suffer no additional pain, his discomfort would not increase, and indeed cessation might serve to make him less aware of the physical sensations he was experiencing and even lead to a subsiding of the bleeding from his bladder lesions;

That in the circumstances the blood transfusions were extraordinary treatments;

That because of his lifelong profound mental retardation John was incompetent to refuse or consent to the continuation of the blood transfusions or to make a reasoned choice as to his own wishes or best interests;

That his mother over his lifetime had come to know and sense his wants and needs and was acutely sensitive to his best interests; that she had provided more love, personal care, and affection for John than any other person or institution, and was closer to feeling what John was feeling than anyone else; that his best interests were of crucial importance to her;

That in his mother's opinion it would have been in John's best interests to discontinue the transfusions, and she believed that he would wish to have them stopped.

No one suggests that there is not sufficient evidence in this record to support each of these factual findings.

I would hold that the courts below had power to authorize the withdrawal of extraordinary life support measures and that, in the circumstances of this case, there was no error of law when the courts below exercised that power to grant Mrs. Storar's cross application to discontinue blood transfusions for her son, John.

NOTES

1. In *Saikewicz* the court discussed the appropriate principle of decisionmaking for incapacitated persons. It determined that the appropriate standard was "substituted judgment." This standard requires that the decisionmaker attempt to reach the decision that the incapacitated person would have made based upon what is known about the incapacitated patient's previously-expressed values, and to that extent the substituted judgment standard is subjective in nature. In your view did the Massachusetts Supreme Judicial Court appropriately apply the "substituted judgment" standard? Consider the following:

Unwillingness to enter into a direct struggle with an apparently dying person was an explicit, and ultimately the most clearly dispositive, reason offered by Joseph Saikewicz's physicians for their decision to withhold treatment from him. The transcript of the trial proceeding makes this clear. At the end of this proceeding, the trial judge determined that chemotherapy should be withheld. But virtually moments before he reached this determination—in the typed version, on page 43 of the total transcript length of 45 pages—the judge stated his contrary inclination. After hearing the formal testimony, the judge worked toward his conclusion in this way:

THE COURT: There is evidence that chemotherapy treatment is apparently the only treatment, but by giving it to him he may have some discomfiture at the time of the treatment that may prolong his life.

DR. DAVIS: That is one thing and if they don't give it to him at all, then he may die in a matter of days or weeks.

THE COURT: That is the choice I have to make.

DR. DAVIS: That is it. I don't know. I don't have that deep knowledge.

THE COURT: I am inclined to give treatment.

DR. JONES: One thing that concerns me is the question about his ability to cooperate. I think it's been made clear that he doesn't have the capability to understand the treatment and he may or may not be cooperative, therefore greatly complicating the treatment process. . . . That has to be weighed, whether [the treatment] could be administered.

THE COURT: Dr. Davis, do you agree?

DR. DAVIS: I think it's going to be virtually impossible to carry out the treatment in the proper way without having problems. You have to see him. When you approach him in the hospital, he flails at you and there is no way of communicating with him and he is quite strong; so he will have to be restrained and that increases the chances of pneumonia, to restrain him if he can't be up and around.

MR. MELNICK [Court-appointed guardian for Saikewicz, who concurred in the physicians' determination to withhold treatment]: With no treatment he may live longer; with treatment, the treatment itself may terminate his life sooner. There is some risk because of the toxic nature of the treatment, so in effect, by ordering the treatment there is a possibility that you may shorten his life and there is a chance that you may be prolonging it.

THE COURT: Maybe I should change my judgment.

DR. DAVIS: One other factor. Though we will get a remission, we are not through at that point. He'd have to be under medical care weekly and continue treatment and he may be in the hospital for four to five weeks initially and will have to be coming back on a regular basis. That enters the picture.

MR. ROGERS [Attorney for the state institution]: The issue boils down to, as Dr. Davis said, the quality of life now and when he goes through it and he certainly will suffer. The low probility [sic] that he will go into remission has to be measured against any person's life and to gamble for success which he can't do for himself.

THE COURT: Do I have to form a written judgment?

MR. ROGERS: Yes, I will draft it.

THE COURT: After a full hearing with medical specialists and doctors being present and their testimony being taken, the Court determines and adjudges that chemotherapy treatment should not be given at this time.

This proceeding occurred on May 13; the Massachusetts Supreme Judicial Court affirmed the trial court's judgment on July 9; and Saikewicz died on September 4, 1976. The decision to withhold chemotherapy during this time may have saved Saikewicz from needless pain and perhaps even quicker death. But this decision was reached with no effort to test a central factual premise on which it rested—whether Saikewicz's acquiescence in the treatment could somehow be obtained, perhaps through heavy sedation or through continuous intensive efforts by institutional staff familiar to him to keep him calm. All such efforts might have failed. But, at least according to the available record of the proceedings, none was tried.

Most fundamentally, this omission reflected everyone's unwillingness to enter into sustained interaction with Joseph Saikewicz, everyone's wish to absent themselves from any transaction with him. The trial transcript shows this if we attempt to identify from it precisely who decided to withhold treatment from Saikewicz—the doctor or the judge. The judge claimed power to decide, to which the doctor deferred on the ground that he lacked "that deep knowledge"—until the judge suggested that his decision would require the doctor to treat. The doctor then objected, "You have to see him. . . . [H]e flails at you and there is no way of communicating with him and he is quite strong." The judge had thus succeeded in obtaining a highly explicit recommendation from the doctor and then encircled his decision to withhold treatment with the rhetorical flourishes "after a full hearing with medical specialists and doctors being present and their testimony being taken, the Court determines and adjudges. . . ." Who then was responsible for this decision? No one was prepared to speak the final word with Joseph Saikewicz, to cut off any imagined conversation with him. Death was inflicted as if it took force on its own. We have seen this confidence game before regarding another "uncooperative learner-victim."

But if this effort by others to enter the mind of Joseph Saikewicz or Karen Quinlan leads only in such circles, can a sensible path be found by abandoning the fiction of substituted judgment and by frankly acknowledging that, because their purposes and interests are inscrutable, others' interests regarding them should explicitly prevail? The trial judge in Saikewicz's case appeared to adopt this view in one portion of his ultimate written order by stating that "the quality of life possible for him even if the treatment does bring about remission" counted against the treatment. The appellate court struggled, somewhat unconvincingly, to interpret this observation as referring only to Saikewicz's continued suffering from the direct effect of the chemotherapy, notwithstanding remission, and thus to avoid the implication that the trial judge viewed the life of this profoundly retarded man as lacking sufficient "quality" to warrant treatment efforts. But if Joseph's perspective . . . is inherently unknowable, why shouldn't courts acknowledge that they face a connundrum [sic] and turn to a calculus that would account for the identifiable emotional and financial costs to others of the continuation or termination of treatment?

R. Burt, Taking Care of Strangers 155–158 (1979).

2. In *Storar* the court treated John Storar as if he were an infant. The "best interests" principle is the standard by which decisions have traditionally been made for infants. The principle is commonly used in cases involving questions of child care and custody because the child has not matured to the point where he or she is capable of assessing his or her own interests. This standard requires a decisionmaker to select in a highly-individualized process an alternative that is optimal for the child. See Mnookin, Child-Custody Adjudication: Judicial Functions in the Face of Indeterminacy, 39 Law & Contemp.Prob. 226, 255–268 (1975). In the medical context, application of the principle might require a decisionmaker to make an objective assessment of what is best for the patient, taking into account the patient's pain and suffering, the possibility of preserving physical and mental functioning and the quality of future life.

Is the best interests principle preferable to the substituted judgment principle when dealing with an adult patient who has always been incompetent? The President's Commission recommended the following:

[D]ecisionmaking for incapacitated patients should be guided by the principle of substituted judgment. . . . When a patient's likely decision is unknown, however, a surrogate decisionmaker should use the best interests standard and choose a course that will promote the patient's well being as it would probably be conceived by a reasonable person in the patient's circumstances . . . . [No] consensus may exist about what most people would prefer, and surrogates retain discretion to choose among a range of acceptable choices.

President's Commission, Deciding to Forego Life-Sustaining Treatment 136 (1983). For further discussion of the best interests principle, see Note 4, following Jonsen, Ethics, The Law, and The Treatment of Seriously Ill Newborns, infra.

3. Who should make decisions for incompetent persons? As the selections in this chapter suggest, the responsibility might be lodged in the hands of physicians,

family members, committees, courts or legislatures. Where would you place the responsibility?

Consider the views expressed by the Washington Supreme Court in In the Matter of Colyer, 99 Wn.2d 114, 660 P.2d 738 (en banc) (1983). The husband of Bertha Colyer petitioned the court for an order to discontinue life support. She had suffered a cardiopulmonary arrest on March 8, 1982 at age 69, was resuscitated after ten minutes and placed on a respirator. The Supreme Court found that she would never recover to a sapient state and, after oral argument on April 1, 1982, sustained the order of the lower court that allowed withdrawal from life support systems. In its opinion the Supreme Court of Washington stated:

> . . . [We] hold that judicial intervention in every decision to withdraw life sustaining treatment is not required. . . .
>
> . . .
>
> In cases where physicians agree on the prognosis and a close family member uses his best judgment as a guardian to exercise the rights of the incompetent, intervention by the courts would be little more than a formality. Therefore, as a general principle, we hold that a decision to terminate life sustaining treatment, under the circumstances presented here, does not require judicial intervention. We in no way abdicate, however, the authority of the courts to hear and decide any such case brought before it. Nor do we maintain that judicial intervention would not be required under facts similar to *Saikewicz;* such is not the issue before us now.

V

> While we hold that courts need not be involved in individual decisions, we recognize that the court, or the Legislature, must establish guidelines to be followed to ensure that the rights of all parties are adequately protected. Therefore, we turn now to the issue of the procedures to be followed in reaching a decision to withdraw life sustaining treatment. We approach this task by examining separately the roles of (a) the guardian, (b) the guardian ad litem, (c) the physicians, and (d) the courts.

A. The Guardian

> Under the laws governing guardianships, a guardian is required to assert the "rights and best interests" of the incompetent person. RCW 11.92.040(3). We hold now that this provision also enables a guardian to use his best judgment and exercise, when appropriate, an incompetent's personal right to refuse life sustaining treatment. . . .
>
> Although the appointment of a guardian is a judicial process, once a guardian is appointed, the courts need not be involved in the substantive decision to refuse life sustaining treatment. . . .
>
> Our guardianship statute provides that a guardian of a person has the power "to care for and maintain the incompetent or disabled person, *assert his or her rights and best interests,* and provide timely, informed consent to necessary medical procedures". (Italics ours.) As refusal of life sustaining treatment is an individual's personal right, we conclude that under this provision the guardian has the power to assert such a right.
>
> . . .
>
> Once appointed, the guardian's duty is to use his best judgment in deciding whether or not to assert the *personal* right of the incompetent to refuse life sustaining treatment. The guardian's familiarity with the incompetent's character and personality, prior statements, and general attitude towards medical treatment will assist in making that judgment.
>
> . . .
>
> . . . We conclude that prior statements may be probative in determining the wishes of an incompetent patient, with the age and maturity of the patient,

the context of the statements, and the connection of the statements to the debilitating event being factors to be weighed by the guardian.

. . .

B. The Guardian Ad Litem

The guardian ad litem serves an important safeguard function. Appointed during the guardianship proceeding, a guardian ad litem represents the best interests of the incompetent. To fulfill this role, the statute requires such a person "be free of influence from anyone interested in the result of the proceeding".

Among the guardian ad litem's duties enumerated in the statute is the duty to provide the court with a written "evaluation of the appropriateness of the guardian . . . whose appointment is sought". Under circumstances such as these, this evaluation should focus on the closeness of the relationship between the petitioning party and the incompetent, and any evidence of less than salutary motives. The guardian ad litem need not necessarily play an adversarial role with respect to the guardian's petition; his role is rather to ensure that the incompetent's interests are being protected.

While the petition is pending, the guardian ad litem has the authority to consent to emergency lifesaving medical services. . . .

If judicial intervention subsequent to the guardianship appointment is required, however, a guardian ad litem would again be appointed to protect the interests of the incompetent in that proceeding. . . . The guardian ad litem's function in this context would be to discover all the facts relevant to the decision to withdraw life sustaining treatment and present them to the court. Such facts would include, but are not necessarily limited to: (a) facts about the incompetent: i.e., age, cause of incompetency, relationship with family members and other close friends, attitude and prior statements concerning life sustaining treatment; (b) medical facts: i.e., prognosis for recovery, intrusiveness of treatment, medical history; (c) facts concerning the state's interest in preserving life: i.e., the existence of dependents, other third party interests; and (d) facts about the guardian, the family, other people close to the incompetent, and the petitioner: i.e., their familiarity with the incompetent, their perceptions of the incompetent's wishes, any potential for ill motives. Thus, the guardian ad litem would not necessarily play a true adversarial role, but would serve as an investigator and a reporter of relevant facts to the court.

C. The Physicians

Concomitant with the guardian's exercise of the patient's right to refuse treatment is the medical determination that the patient is incurable and will not return to a sapient state. If the patient's condition is hopeless or there is "no reasonable possibility of returning to a cognitive, sapient state," the patient's right of privacy outweighs the state's interest in preserving life.

The prognosis determination is a medical one. Nonetheless, this prong of the decisionmaking process must also incorporate safeguards. While the vast majority of physicians conscientiously adhere to their professional oaths and view their patients' interests as paramount, such a momentous decision requires some protection against those who might be motivated by other interests. The *Quinlan* court recommended a hospital ethics committee, made up of physicians, social workers, attorneys and theologians, to oversee this decision. This type of a committee has been criticized, however, for its amorphous character, for its use of nonmedical personnel to reach a medical decision, and for its bureaucratic intermeddling. We agree that such an administrative body does not best serve the desired function.

In actuality, what is needed is a prognosis board to confirm the attending physician's diagnosis. Concurrence by professional colleagues, who are not attending physicians but who nonetheless have an understanding of the patient's condition, would protect against erroneous diagnoses as well as questionable motives. Thus, we recommend that in future decisions of this nature, there should be unanimous concurrence from a prognosis board or committee. Such a committee should consist of no fewer than two physicians with qualifications relevant to the patient's condition, plus the attending physician.[7] These physicians should agree there is no reasonable medical probability that the patient will return to a sapient state.[8]

Disagreement among the physicians on the prognosis committee may foreclose any action to withhold or withdraw treatment without court intervention. In instances of disagreement, application could be made to the court to resolve the dispute with the aid of expert testimony. Should the testimony show, by clear and convincing evidence, that the patient's condition was incurable and there was no reasonable medical probability of returning to a cognitive, sapient state, the court could then assert the patient's right to refuse treatment.

. . .

D. The Court

The final safeguard in this procedure is the court itself. The court will always be involved in the appointment of the guardian. Moreover, while the court need not play a role in every substantive decision to withhold treatment, there will be instances when the detached opinion of the judiciary will be required. For example, if there is disagreement among family members as to the incompetent's wishes or among the physicians as to the prognosis, if the patient has always been incompetent so that his wishes cannot be known, if there is evidence of wrongful motives or malpractice, or if there is no family member to serve as guardian, the court may be required to intervene. Any participant in the decision, the guardian, a physician or the hospital, may petition for court intervention, as may a member of the incompetent's family.

If a court determination is required, a guardian ad litem must be appointed to ascertain and protect the interests of the patient. At such a proceeding, the focus would be a determination of the rights and wishes of the incompetent. The appointment of the guardian would be presumed valid, unless there is a showing of clear error or an abuse of discretion, and the conclusion of the prognosis board would also be presumed correct. On the basis of information presented to it, the court would determine, in its best judgment, whether the facts demonstrated that the incompetent would have chosen to exercise his or her right to refuse treatment, if he or he were able to do so.

660 P.2d at 746–51. Cf. John F. Kennedy Memorial Hospital, Inc. v. Bludworth, ___ So.2d ___ (Fla.1984) (holding that right of irreversibly comatose patient to refuse treatment may be exercised by close family members without court involvement or guardian of person appointed by court where physicians certify that patient is in permanent vegetative state).

. . .

4. The Supreme Judicial Court of Massachusetts has attempted to clarify some of the procedural questions left open in *Saikewicz*. The court in In the Mat-

---

7. We choose not to dictate selection of the members of a prognosis board. A case-by-case selection would be preferable to a standing committee, however, since a professional understanding of the patient's condition would be an important factor to consider. Selection may be administered by the hospital or another appropriate body. In addition, if no selection mechanism existed, the court may appoint a committee.

8. The dissent prefers an ethics committee to a prognosis committee. We perceive, however, that a determination of the likelihood of a patient's recovery to a cognitive, sapient state is a uniquely medical one. Although the presence of theologians and so-

cial workers would serve to diffuse responsibility for the decision, such a committee may be unable to reach a consensus, or in the alternative, it may use the bureaucratic format, wherein no one is singularly responsible, to treat marginal cases too lightly. Either way, the use of such a committee has many substantive and procedural problems and serves to bureaucratize an essentially personal and private decision. Therefore, we take heed of the criticisms in the literature leveled against such a committee, and choose instead to institute a prognosis board which will focus solely on the medical determination. . . .

ter of Spring, 380 Mass. 629, 405 N.E.2d 115 (1980), first discussed the holding in *Dinnerstein*, Sec. B.5., infra, that the validity of the no code order did not depend on prior court approval and held:

> Without approving all that is said in the opinion of the Appeals Court, we think the result reached on the facts shown in that case was consistent with our holding in *Saikewicz*.

380 Mass. at 635, 405 N.E.2d at 120. The court went on to state that *Saikewicz* did not establish "any requirement of prior judicial approval that would not otherwise exist," and listed the following factors to be considered in deciding when a court order is required:

> The extent of impairment of the patient's mental faculties, whether the patient is in the custody of a State institution, the prognosis without the proposed treatment, the prognosis with the proposed treatment, the complexity, risk and novelty of the proposed treatment, its possible side effects, the patient's level of understanding and probable reaction, the urgency of decision, the consent of the patient, spouse, or guardian, the good faith of those who participate in the decision, the clarity of professional opinion as to what is good medical practice, the interests of third persons, and the administrative requirements of any institution involved.

380 Mass. at 637, 405 N.E.2d at 121. If you were a physician practicing in Massachusetts, would you still seek court approval before terminating treatment of a terminally ill patient?

RAYMOND DUFF AND A.G.M. CAMPBELL, MORAL AND ETHICAL DILEMMAS IN THE SPECIAL–CARE NURSERY

289 New Eng.J.Med. 890 (1973).

. . .

The experiences described in this communication document some of the grave moral and ethical dilemmas now faced by physicians and families. They indicated some of the problems in a large special-care nursery where medical technology has prolonged life and where "informed" parents influence the management decisions concerning their infants.

Background and Methods

The special-care nursery of the Yale New Haven Hospital not only serves an obstetric service for over 4000 live births annually but also acts as the principal referral center in Connecticut for infants with major problems of the newborn period. From January 1, 1970, through June 30, 1972, 1615 infants born at the Hospital were admitted, and 556 others were transferred for specialized care from community hospitals. During this interval, the average daily census was 26, with a range of 14 to 37.

For some years the unit has had a liberal policy for parental visiting, with the staff placing particular emphasis on helping parents adjust to and participate in the care of their infants with special problems. By encouraging visiting, attempting to create a relaxed atmosphere within the unit, exploring carefully the special needs of the infants, and familiarizing parents with various aspects of care, it was hoped to remove much of the apprehension—indeed, fear—with which parents at first view an intensive-care nursery. At any time, parents may see and handle their babies. They commonly observe or participate in most routine aspects of care and are often present when some infant is critically ill or moribund. They may attend, as they choose, the death of their own infant. Since an average of two to three deaths occur each week and many infants are critically ill for long periods, it is obvious that the concentrated, intimate social interactions between personnel, infants and parents in an emotionally charged atmosphere often make the work of the staff very difficult and demanding. However, such participation and recognition of parents' rights to information about their infant appear to be the chief foundations of "informed consent" for treatment.

. . .

For several years, the responsibilities of attending pediatrician have been assumed chiefly by ourselves, who, as a result, have become acquainted intimately with the problems of the infants, the staff, and the parents. Our almost constant availability to staff, private pediatricians and parents has resulted in the raising of more and more ethical questions about various aspects of intensive care for critically ill and congenitally deformed infants. The penetrating questions and challenges, particularly of knowledgeable parents (such as physicians, nurses, or lawyers), brought increasing doubts about the wisdom of many of the decisions that seemed to parents to be predicated chiefly on technical considerations. Some thought their child had a right to die since he could not live well or effectively. Others thought that society should pay the costs of care that may be so destructive to the family economy. Often, too, the parents' or siblings' rights to relief from the seemingly pointless, crushing burdens were important considerations. It seemed right to yield to parent wishes in several cases as physicians have done for generations. As a result, some treatments were withheld or stopped with the knowledge that earlier death and relief from suffering would result. Such options were explored with the less knowledgeable parents to ensure that their consent for treatment of their defective children was truly informed. . . . In lengthy, frank discussions, the anguish of the parents was shared, and attempts were made to support fully the reasoned choices, whether for active treatment and rehabilitation or for an early death.

To determine the extent to which death resulted from withdrawing or with-holding treatment, we examined the hospital records of all children who died from January 1, 1970, through June 30, 1972.

Results

In total, there were 299 deaths; each was classified in one of two categories; deaths in Category 1 resulted from pathologic conditions in spite of the treatment given; 256 (86 per cent) were in this category. Of these, 66 per cent were the result of respiratory problems or complications associated with extreme prematurity (birth weight under 1000 g). Congenital heart disease and other anomalies accounted for an additional 22 per cent (Table 1).

Table 1. Problems Causing Death in Category 1.

Problem	No. of Deaths	Percentage
Respiratory	108	42.2
Extreme prematurity	60	23.4
Heart disease	42	16.4
Multiple anomalies	14	5.5
Other	32	12.5
Totals	256	100.0

Deaths in Category 2 were associated with severe impairment, usually from congenital disorders (Table 2): 43 (14 per cent) were in this group. These deaths or their timing was associated with discontinuance or withdrawal of treatment. The mean duration of life in Category 2 (Table 3) was greater than that in Category 1. This was the result of a mean life of 55 days for eight infants who became chronic cardiopulmonary cripples but for whom prolonged and intensive efforts were made in the hope of eventual recovery. They were infants who were dependent on oxygen, digoxin and diuretics, and most of them had been treated for the idiopathic respiratory-distress syndrome with high oxygen concentrations and positive-pressure ventilation.

Table 2.   Problems Associated with Death in Category 2.

Problem	No. of Deaths	Percentage
Multiple anomalies	15	34.9
Trisomy	8	18.6
Cardiopulmonary	8	18.6
Meningomyelocele	7	16.3
Other central-nervous-system defects	3	7.0
Short-bowel syndrome	2	4.6
Totals	43	100.0

Some examples of management choices in Category 2 illustrate the problems. An infant with Down's syndrome and intestinal atresia, like the much-publicized one at Johns Hopkins Hospital, was not treated because his parents thought that surgery was wrong for their baby and themselves. He died seven days after birth. Another child had chronic pulmonary disease after positive-pressure ventilation with high oxygen

Table 3.   Selected Comparisons of 256 Cases
in Category 1 and 43 in Category 2.

Attribute	Category 1	Category 2
Mean length of life	4.8 days	7.5 days
Standard deviation	8.8	34.3
Range	1–69	1–150
Portion living for < 2 days	50.0%	12.0%

concentrations for treatment of severe idiopathic respiratory-distress syndrome. By five months of age, he still required 40 per cent oxygen to survive, and even then, he was chronically dyspneic and cyanotic. He also suffered from cor pulmonale, which was difficult to control with digoxin and diuretics. The nurses, parents and physicians considered it cruel to continue, and yet difficult to stop. All were attached to this child, whose life they had tried so hard to make worthwhile. The family had endured high expenses (the hospital bill exceeding $15,000), and the strains of the illness were believed to be threatening the marriage bonds and to be causing sibling behavioral disturbances. Oxygen supplementation was stopped, and the child died in about three hours. The family settled down and 18 months later had another baby, who was healthy.

A third child had meningomyelocele, hydrocephalus and major anomalies of every organ in the pelvis. When the parents understood the limits of medical care and rehabilitation, they believed no treatment should be given. She died at five days of age.

We have maintained contact with most families of children in Category 2. Thus far, these families appear to have experienced a normal mourning for their losses. Although some have exhibited doubts that the choices were correct, all appear to be as effective in their lives as they were before this experience. Some claim that their profoundly moving experience has provided a deeper meaning in life, and from this they believe they have become more effective people.

Members of all religious faiths and atheists were participants as parents and as staff in these experiences. There appeared to be no relation between participation and a person's religion. Repeated participation in these troubling events did not appear to reduce the worry of the staff about the awesome nature of the decisions.

Discussion

That decisions are made not to treat severely defective infants may be no surprise to those familiar with special-care facilities. All laymen and professionals familiar with our nursery appeared to set some limits upon their application of treatment to extend life or to investigate a pathologic process. For example, an experienced nurse said about one child, "We lost him several weeks ago. Isn't it time to quit?" In another case, a house officer said to a physician investigating an aspect of a child's disease, "For this child, don't you think it's time to turn off your curiosity so you can turn on your kindness?" Like many others, these children eventually acquired the "right to die."

Arguments among staff members and families for and against such decisions were based on varied notions of the rights and interests of defective infants, their families, professionals and society. They were also related to varying ideas about prognosis. Regarding the infants, some contended that individuals should have a right to die in some circumstances such as anencephaly, hydranencephaly, and some severely deforming and incapacitating conditions. Such very defective individuals were considered to have little or no hope of achieving meaningful "humanhood." For example, they have little or no capacity to love or be loved. They are often cared for in facilities that have been characterized as "hardly more than dying bins," an assessment with which, in our experience, knowledgeable parents (those who visited chronic-care facilities for placement of their children) agreed. With institutionalized well children, social participation may be essentially nonexistent, and maternal deprivation severe; . . . . . To escape "wrongful life," a fate rated as worse than death, seemed right. In this regard, Lasagna notes, "We may, as a society, scorn the civilizations that slaughtered their infants, but our present treatment of the retarded is in some ways more cruel."

Others considered allowing a child to die wrong for several reasons. The person most involved, the infant, had no voice in the decision. Prognosis was not always exact, and a few children with extensive care might live for months, and occasionally years. Some might survive and function satisfactorily. To a few persons, withholding treatment and accepting death was condemned as criminal.

Families had strong but mixed feelings about management decisions. Living with the handicapped is clearly a family affair, and families of deformed infants thought there were limits to what they could bear or should be expected to bear. Most of them wanted maximal efforts to sustain life and to rehabilitate the handicapped; in such cases, they were supported fully. However, some families, especially those having children with severe defects, feared that they and their other children would become socially enslaved, economically deprived, and permanently stigmatized, all perhaps for a lost cause. . . . In some cases, families considered the death of the child right both for the child and for the family. They asked if that choice could be theirs or their doctors.

As Feifel has reported, physicians on the whole are reluctant to deal with the issues. Some, particularly specialists based in the medical center, gave specific reasons for this disinclination. There was a feeling that to "give up" was disloyal to the cause of the profession. Since major research, teaching and patient-care efforts were being made, professionals expected to discover, transmit and apply knowledge and skills; patients and families were supposed to co-operate fully even if they were not always grateful. Some physicians recognized that the wishes of families went against their own, but they were resolute. They commonly agreed that if they were the parents of very defective children, with-holding treatment would be most desirable for them. However, they argued that aggressive management was indicated for others. Some believed that allowing death as a management option was euthanasia and must be stopped for fear of setting a "poor ethical example" or for fear of personal prosecution or damage to their clinical departments or to the medical center as a whole. . . . Some persons were concerned about the loss through death of "teaching material." They feared the training of professionals for the care of defective children in the future and the advancing of the state of the art would be compromised. . . .

Practicing pediatricians, general practitioners and obstetricians were often familiar with these families and were usually sympathetic with their views. However, since they were more distant from the special-care nursery than the specialists of the medical center, their influence was often minimal. As a result, families received little support from them, and tension in community-medical relations was a recurring problem.

Infants with severe types of meningomyelocele precipitated the most controversial decisions. Several decades ago, those who survived this condition beyond a few weeks usually became hydrocephalic and retarded, in addition to being crippled and deformed. Without modern treatment they died earlier. Some may have been killed or at least not resuscitated at birth. From the early 1960's, the tendency has been to treat vigorously all infants with meningomyelocele. As advocated by Zachary and Shurtleff, aggressive management of these children became the rule in our unit as in many others. Infants were usually referred quickly. Parents routinely signed permits for operation though rarely had they seen their children's defects or had the nature of various management plans and their respective prognoses clearly explained to them. Some physicians believed that parents were too upset to understand the nature of the problems and the options for care. Since they believed informed consent had no meaning in these circumstances, they either ignored the parents or simply told them that the child needed an operation on the back as the first step in correcting several defects. As a result, parents often felt completely left out while the activities of care proceeded at a brisk pace.

Some physicians experienced in the care of these children and familiar with the impact of such conditions upon families had early reservations

about this plan of care. More recently, they were influenced by the pessimistic appraisal of vigorous management schemes in some cases. Meningomyelocele, when treated vigorously, is associated with higher survival
rates, but the achievement of satisfactory rehabilitation is at best difficult
and usually impossible for almost all who are severely affected. Knowing
this, some physicians and some families decide against treatment of the
most severely affected. If treatment is not carried out, the child's condition will usually deteriorate from further brain damage, urinary-tract infections and orthopedic difficulties, and death can be expected much earlier. Two thirds may be dead by three months, and over 90 per cent by
one year of age. However, the quality of life during that time is poor,
and the strains on families are great, but not necessarily greater than with
treatment. Thus, both treatment and nontreatment constitute unsatisfactory dilemmas for everyone, especially for the child and his family. When
maximum treatment was viewed as unacceptable by families and physicians in our unit, there was a growing tendency to seek early death as a
management option, to avoid that cruel choice of gradual, often slow, but
progressive deterioration of the child who was required under these circumstances in effect to kill himself. Parents and the staff then asked if his
dying needed to be prolonged. If not, what were the most appropriate
medical responses?

   Is it possible that some physicians and some families may join in a
conspiracy to deny the right of a defective child to live or to die? Either
could occur.. . . On the other hand, from the fatigue of working long
and hard some physicians may give up too soon, assuming that their
cause is lost. Families, similarly, may have mixed motives. They may
demand death to obtain relief from the high costs and the tensions inherent in suffering, but their sense of guilt in this thought may produce the
opposite demand, perhaps in violation of the sick person's rights. Thus,
the challenge of deciding what course to take can be most tormenting for
the family and the physician. Unquestionably, not facing the issue would
appear to be the easier course, at least temporarily; no doubt many patients, families, and physicians decline to join in an effort to solve the
problems. They can readily assume that what is being done is right and
sufficient and ask no questions. But pretending there is no decision to be
made is an arbitrary and potentially devastating decision of default.
Since families and patients must live with the problems one way or another in any case, the physician's failure to face the issues may constitute a
victimizing abandonment of patients and their families in times of greatest
need. . . .

   Can families in the shock resulting from the birth of a defective child
understand what faces them? Can they give truly "informed consent" for
treatment or with-holding treatment? Some of our colleagues answer no
to both questions. In our opinion, if families regardless of background
are heard sympathetically and at length and are given information and
answers to their questions in words they understand, the problems of
their children as well as the expected benefits and limits of any proposed
care can be understood clearly in practically all instances. Parents *are*
able to understand the implications of such things as chronic dyspnea,
oxygen dependency, incontinence, paralysis, contractures, sexual handicaps and mental retardation.

   Another problem concerns who decides for a child. It may be acceptable for a person to reject treatment and bring about his own death. But
it is quite a different situation when others are doing this for him. We do

not know how often families and their physicians will make just decisions for severely handicapped children. Clearly, this issue is central in evaluation of the process of decision making that we have described. But we also ask, if these parties cannot make such decisions justly, who can?

We recognize great variability and often much uncertainty in prognoses and in family capacities to deal with defective newborn infants. We also acknowledge that there are limits of support that society can or will give to assist handicapped persons and their families. Severely deforming conditions that are associated with little or no hope of a functional existence pose painful dilemmas for the laymen and professionals who must decide how to cope with severe handicaps. We believe the burdens of decision making must be borne by families and their professional advisers because they are most familiar with the respective situations. Since families primarily must live with and are most affected by the decisions, it therefore appears that society and the health professions should provide only general guidelines for decision making. Moreover, since variations between situations are so great, and the situations themselves so complex, it follows that much latitude in decision making should be expected and tolerated. Otherwise, the rules of society or the policies most convenient for medical technologists may become cruel masters of human beings instead of their servants. Regarding any "allocation of death" policy we readily acknowledge that the extreme excesses of Hegelian "rational utility" under dictatorships must be avoided. Perhaps it is less recognized that the uncontrolled application of medical technology may be detrimental to individuals and families. . . . Physicians may hold excessive power over decision making by limiting or controlling the information made available to patients or families. It seems appropriate that the profession be held accountable for presenting fully all management options and their expected consequences. Also, the public should be aware that professionals often face conflicts of interest that may result in decisions against individual preferences.

What are the legal implications of actions like those described in this paper? Some persons may argue that the law has been broken, and others would contend otherwise. Perhaps more than anything else, the public and professional silence on a major social taboo and some common practices has been broken further. That seems appropriate, for out of the ensuing dialogue perhaps better choices for patients and families can be made. If working out these dilemmas in ways such as those we suggest is in violation of the law, we believe the law should be changed.

NOTE

The Duff and Campbell article, by revealing the fact that decisions to forego treatment for some disabled newborns were being made in at least one respected health care institution, helped trigger legal and ethical debate on the care and treatment of disabled newborns. Is it appropriate in some circumstances to discontinue treatment for disabled newborns? Can those circumstances be described objectively? Should the family have responsibility for these decisions? Should any decision to forego treatment be subject to review? If so, who should conduct the review and under what procedures? Consider the following materials in attempting to resolve these issues.

ROBERT AND PEGGY STINSON,
ON THE DEATH OF A BABY

244 The Atlantic 64 (July 1979).

Andrew was a desperately premature baby, weighing under two pounds. He died after months of "heroic" efforts in an intensive care facility. The story of his short, cruel, institutionalized life is a case study in the limits and excesses of modern medicine.

The night he told us our son, Andrew, was about to die, the doctor who had taken charge of him six months before also told us we were "intellectually tight," that we had "no feelings, only thoughts and words and strategies." We were "bad parents." As the parents of a five-year-old daughter, we knew the love a mother and father feel for children. Yet, as Andrew's parents, we were used to condemnation and insult.

Andrew was a baby born 15½ weeks prematurely, weighing only 1 lb. 12 oz., and in a state of painful deterioration almost from the start. We wanted him to be allowed to die a natural death. Andrew's story is the story of what can happen when a baby becomes hopelessly entrapped in an intensive care unit where the machinery is more sophisticated than the codes of law and ethics governing its use.

The letter printed below was sent to the administrator and numerous personnel of the hospital that controlled the life and death of our son. The physician in chief of that hospital characterized it as a "carefully documented critique." The letter appears here somewhat edited and abridged; the names of people and institutions have been changed, all but our own. It is the personal record of what happened to our baby and to us.

August 29, 1977

Dear Mr. Clark:

This letter concerns the case of Andrew Stinson, who was a patient in the Infant Intensive Care Unit (IICU) of Pediatric Hospital from December 24, 1976, to June 14, 1977.

Andrew was born at Community Hospital in our town on December 17, 1976, at a gestational age of 24½ weeks and a weight of 800 grams (1 lb. 12 oz.), at the extreme margin of human viability. He was admitted to the Pediatric Hospital Center (PHC) weighing 600 grams (1 lb. 5 oz.) on December 24, was placed on a respirator against our wishes and without our consent on January 13, and remained dependent on the respirator until he was finally permitted to die on the evening of June 14.

The sad list of Andrew's afflictions, almost all of which were iatrogenic, reveals how disastrous this hospitalization was. Andrew had a month-long, unresolved case of bronchopulmonary dysplasia, sometimes referred to as "respirator lung syndrome." He was "saved" by the respirator to endure countless episodes of bradycardia and cyanosis, countless suctionings and tube insertions and blood samplings and blood transfusions, "saved" to develop retrolental fibroplasia, numerous infections, demineralized and fractured bones, an iatrogenic cleft palate, and, finally, as his lungs became irreparably diseased, pulmonary artery hypertension and seizures of the brain. He was, in effect, "saved" by the respirator to die five long, painful and expensive months later of the respirator's side effects.

The IICU's attempt to nourish Andrew artificially was nearly as successful as its attempt to breathe for him. His bone problems, which included severe rickets secondary to hyperalimentation, testify to the large amount of research still required before the nutritional needs of extremely premature, crucially ill infants can be competently met. The notes in the medical record by those called in to consult about Andrew's problems show that research interest in our baby's problems was indeed high. "The incidence of rickets here and in other IICU units is very interesting," one consultant began, "and points out the need for data. . . . The endocrine section, with your help, would be interested in exploring this area."

"Thank you," another note reads, "for interesting consult on this 'syndrome'. . . . The only time I have seen X-rays of more fractured bones was in an air force crash victim." One of the reasons a doctor once gave to explain Andrew's dependence on the respirator and lack of effort to breathe for himself was that, with all those broken ribs, it "hurts like hell everytime he takes a breath."

Andrew's fractures did heal, but he continued to suffer from "severe failure to thrive"—his height, weight, and head circumference were listed as "much less than third percentile," and by the final six weeks his head (i.e., brain) had stopped growing altogether. Clearly, no one really knew how to provide our baby with the nourishment he needed for normal growth and development. The extraordinary technology that was marshaled to keep Andrew from dying was sufficient only to the production of new, "interesting" problems which no one as yet understands.

Complicating Andrew's respiratory and nutritional difficulties was the fact that the IICU could not protect him from recurring rounds of infection. During his stay at Pediatric Hospital, Andrew suffered through a prolonged case of E. coli septicemia, related abscesses at the arterial line sites which necessitated surgical removal of gangrene and necrotic muscle down to the bone of his right leg (it was noted in the record in May that "right foot remains limited due to severed and removed muscle tissue"), several urinary tract infections, and "multiple courses of pneumonia."

And this was not yet the end of Andrew's problems. He also suffered from a heart defect and possible stress ulcers. He experienced a pulmonary hemorrhage in January. The question of whether there were also intracranial hemorrhages in December or January was never successfully settled, but as the months went by, the record noted cortical atrophy, enlarged ventricles, chronic encephalopathy, microcephaly, and "severe developmental delay."

We have begun with a chronicle of Andrew's afflictions because we think the magnitude of the medical failure involved is quite obviously staggering. It can be argued, of course, that this could all have turned out differently. But the only reality now is that it turned out disastrously for all of us. And the meager statistics available in this very new, still largely experimental effort to save babies at 800 grams and 25 weeks or less of gestation who need extensive respiratory support indicate that the chances for survival, and certainly for intact neurological survival, were and are grim.

It was our position at the beginning of this case that medical knowledge was not sufficient to justify the no-holds-barred, heroic attempt to simulate the last 15½ weeks of pregnancy. It is hard to feel now that our pessimism was unreasonable. We can only hope that Andrew's case has been, for the doctors involved, an object lesson in humility—a reminder of how pathetically doctors can still fail and how much suffering that failure can inflict on other human beings, on tiny patients and on their families.

We think the question must be raised as to whose interests were really served by this six months of imposed hospitalization. Certainly not Andrew's. He had the misfortune of being declared "salvageable" (the IICU's word) by people who knew neither how to "salvage" him nor when or how to stop. Certainly not ours. Those six months were for us a nightmare of anguish, frustration, and despair. It seems clear to us that all the benefits in this case went to Pediatric Hospital and its staff. The medical residents got a chance to broaden their education by working with a baby with malfunctions of virtually every system of his body, the specialists took part in some "interesting consults" and gathered some data, and the hospital collected the mind-boggling sum of $102,303.20 from our insurance company.

Although we signed a general consent form when Andrew was admitted to the hospital, we did not know that we were signing away control over the events of the next months or, until later, that we could withdraw our consent. However, in our opinion, the hospital did not accord us, Andrew's parents and legal guardians, our rights of informed consent in decisions about his care. From the very first, we were treated as wholly external to the case. Our wishes, judgments, and thoughts were rarely of interest to the IICU's medical staff, who arrogated decisions to themselves as though we did not exist.

Thus, we often telephoned the hospital or arrived for a conference to discover that major decisions, literally involving life and death, had been taken with little effort to explain the problem, let alone to obtain our specific consent one way or the other. On our first visit to the hospital in December, for example, we met Dr. Carvalho, the IICU's attending physician, and explained that we opposed extraordinary efforts to keep Andrew alive. If his troubled breathing failed, we opposed placing him on a respirator. Dr. Carvalho told us that he and his colleagues had already decided that if the baby's severe episodes of apnea and bradycardia continued to worsen, Andrew would be ventilated (put on a respirator). When parents dissented from its decisions, he said, the hospital's policy was to obtain a court order.

A few days later we drove the many miles to Pediatric Hospital again, and this time a doctor we had not met before explained that Andrew had suffered an intracranial hemorrhage and that Dr. Craft, now the IICU's attending physician, had decided that the baby would *not* be attached to a respirator after all.

Again a few more days passed, and now we met Dr. Farrell. Dr. Craft, we discovered, had been attending physician only over the New Year's weekend; now it was January and Dr. Farrell's turn, and he had already made yet another decision. Andrew *would* be ventilated after all, Dr. Farrell said, for he was not so sure now that the baby had had an intracranial bleed. There was no effort made to win our consent to this reversal; we couldn't determine whether the reversal was due to a change in Andrew's prognosis or to the change in personnel. When we objected to the decision, Dr. Farrell accused us of wanting to "play God" and to "go back to the law of the jungle." Apparently not recognizing his responsibility to obtain our informed consent to Andrew's treatment, he reduced the issue to its most absurd level. "I would not presume," he told us, "to tell my auto mechanic how to fix my car."

Drs. Carvalho, Craft, and Farrell did not even discuss with us the long list of risks they knew were involved in ventilating infants as tiny as Andrew. Within a few more days, Andrew's breathing collapsed and he was attached to the mechanical respirator upon which he would be dependent for the rest of his life.

The EMI scan performed on April 19 is another example of serious blocking out of parental knowledge and consent. The baby's medical record shows that the staff was attempting to schedule a computer scan of Andrew's brain for nearly two weeks before it was done, but no one told us about it until it was over. The anesthetist cautioned in the record for April 18, "Plan & risk of anes. will be discussed w. parents." But *no one called*—not an attending physician, not a resident, not an anesthetist—to discuss the "plan and risk" which were obviously present in their minds but were kept from us.

One curious deviation from this pattern of exclusion occurred in May. When we sought out Dr. Craft during a visit to the hospital on May 5, he told us of several new developments in Andrew's case and said he now regarded Andrew as terminally ill, though Andrew could remain on the respirator for a long time before his respirator-caused lung and heart disease progressed to the point where he would die. Meanwhile, his current case of pneumonia was being successfully treated with antibiotics, and Dr. Craft was close to ordering a tracheostomy because the tube connecting Andrew to the respirator kept coming out and it was becoming more difficult to get it back in.

Then Dr. Craft amazed us by doing something no one at PHC had ever done: he asked our consent. When we refused to give it, we were assured that the hospital had the power to go ahead and operate anyway. But we were by this time more cognizant of our rights—and of the hospital's penchant for not advising us fully and accurately of those rights—than we had been at the beginning of Andrew's case, and after Dr. Craft received a call from our lawyer, plans for the tracheostomy were dropped.

When, at the beginning of Andrew's hospitalization, we asked specific questions about the prognosis for a baby of Andrew's severe prematurity—what, in other words, was the theoretical basis justifying the decision to place Andrew on a respirator?—the medical staff's answers were vague and unrealistically optimistic. Dr. Farrell assued us that statistics show that, thanks to modern medical expertise, almost all premature babies survive and grow up to have no problems of any kind. When we pointed out that such "statistics" were skewed because they lumped together babies of 800 grams with babies of 2000 grams and everything in between, his answer was that we should not adopt this sort of adversary relationship with the medical staff.

Dr. Craft did cite evidence to support his optimism about Andrew: the "Vanderbilt study," which, he said, showed that of 22 babies born at under 1000 grams who survived, 18 turned out to be totally normal. This seemed encouraging until we went, two months later, to the medical school library and discovered that there was no "Vanderbilt study" showing anything of the kind. There had been a study of premature infants done at Vanderbilt, but it dealt with another question. We did discover the study (done in Seattle) dealing with 22 babies born at under 1000 grams (the study included 161 babies, but 87 percent died); it showed that *none* of the babies of Andrew's weight, gestational age, and respiratory status had been successfully "salvaged." (The results of other studies we found later were not quite so bleak, but the prognosis in January 1977 for a baby in Andrew's condition could hardly be seen as encouraging.)

Should a parent have to spend hours in the library of a medical school to obtain answers to his or her questions? We were told later that our questions were inappropriate because the effort to save babies like Andrew is still too new for reliable data to exist, but that was, of course, precisely our point. The attending physicians were not, as they had at first maintained, guided by data; they were creating it.

Nor were our questions about the specifics of Andrew's case answered fully and candidly. Andrew was making good progress, Dr. Farrell assured one of us in late January (though he had developed a major infection, couldn't breathe without the respirator, was off his regu
alar feedings, and had problems with a distended abdomen); he might, said Dr. Farrell, be a "colicky baby" when he came home. Andrew was still "doing all right" on February 9 when we talked to Dr. Craft, though the baby was still dependent on the respirator, still hadn't been cured of the weeks-long bloodstream infection, still hadn't resumed his feedings, and hadn't been gaining weight. All this was, we were assured, "just a technical management problem." In March, Dr. Carvalho was "optimistic" about Andrew, though his bones were breaking because of then unresolved dietary deficiencies and he had developed more infection. Andrew, Dr. Carvalho said, should be off the respirator in "a couple weeks."

The situation became particularly grotesque at the end of March. The resident then in charge discussed with us the high risk that Andrew had by that time suffered serious brain damage. But when we sought an assessment of Andrew's problems and how they would affect his future from Dr. Carvalho, he replied that premature babies tend to be shorter than their siblings, though we shouldn't worry that Andrew's shortness would be so pronounced as to affect him socially.

A severe crisis of confidence developed as we despaired of getting any believable information. And evidence confirms that our cynicism was not out of place. Even *we* were surprised when we obtained a copy of Andrew's medical record and compared the information there with the version we had been given. Andrew's bronchopulmonary dysplasia had first been noted nearly two months before we were informed of it. He had had more infections than had been reported to us, had been on more drugs of a seemingly experimental nature than we knew of, and had bone problems more severe and fractures more numerous than we had been told. We found out that Andrew had developed an iatrogenic cleft palate. We learned for the first time about the gangrene that had developed in his infected leg and of the tissue and muscle that had been cut away down to the bone; we had been told only that Andrew had an abscess which had been drained and which had "healed nicely."

Perhaps most serious was our discovery that pessimistic assessments of Andrew's condition and prognosis had been made by the Neurology Department, though they were never mentioned to us by anyone. How many other parents would discover such omissions and distortions in what they were told about their children's cases, we wonder, if they too were to request their children's medical records?

We recognize that there are very real legal and ethical problems in the area of consent for medical treatment when children are involved. We were told repeatedly that "someone must be the child's advocate." But how is it possible to be sure in a case like Andrew's just what that means? Who can determine whether or at what point the child's true advocate is the person proclaiming his right to life or the person proclaiming his right to death? We felt that we as the child's parents were more likely to have feelings of concern for his suffering than the necessarily detached medical staff busy with scores of other cases and "interesting" projects.

However, the "someone" who became our child's self-appointed advocate was the attending physician of the IICU. It was argued that we were not the baby's advocates but merely the parents' advocates. By that logic, why are Drs. Farrell, Craft, and Carvalho not recognized as the *doctors'* advocates? For it is useless to pretend that there was ever such a thing as an objective advocate of Andrew's rights. Is any neonatologist, who has, in addition to his ethical commitments as a human being, a professional interest in a baby's problems, a pride in his expertise and in the statistics of success in his unit, and concerns about protecting his reputation in the eyes of his associates, really the right person to be trusted as the baby's sole advocate?

Of course, we were self-interested too. As Andrew's parents, we had a heightened sense of his suffering. Also, we feared the prospect of having to care for the rest of our lives for a pathetically handicapped, retarded child. If this is considered less than noble, what then is the appropriate label for the willingness to apply the latest experimental technology to salvage such a high-risk child and then to hand him over to the life-long care of someone else?

We believe there is a moral and ethical problem of the most fundamental sort involved in a system which allows complicated decisions of this nature to be made unilaterally by people who do not have to live with the consequences of their decisions. A minister—to whom we went for counseling when our family life began to fall apart under the pressures of the hospital's handling of Andrew's case—was direct in his assessment: "This tragedy is not an act of God but an act of man. Don't let yourselves be its victims."

The tube connecting Andrew to the respirator came out of his throat on the night of June 9, and when he began breathing on his own, the decision was made that when his breathing proved inadequate, as it surely must in a baby with "irreversible lung disease," Andrew would not be reattached to the respirator even though that meant he would die. All of this happened without our knowing anything about it. Only the accident of our telephone call to the hospital on the afternoon of June 10 revealed that Andrew was off the respirator and that the attending physicians had conferred and made their decision. It should not have surprised us that none of them thought it useful to have explicit, current expressions of our opinion or to include us in their conference. Andrew was more their baby than ours.

One of the ironic "Catch-22's" of our relationship with PHC is that we were treated in a way practically guaranteed to produce profound psychological upset and then blamed and dismissed from further consideration because we were upset. We were categorized as "hostile," "emotionally fragile," "under psychiatric care."

When Andrew was transferred from our community hospital to PHC, he was already one week old. During that first week we visited him each day, brought him breast milk, talked with both doctor and nurses daily, and together worked out a plan for his care. We agreed that Andrew would be made comfortable and given a chance to thrive if he was able, but that there would be no heroics. Community Hospital, his physician there advised us, had all the equipment and staff necessary to safeguard the baby if he should be strong enough to do well. But, unlike an intensive care center, they did not have so much equipment that he could be subjected to extraordinary measures which might keep alive a baby whose prognosis didn't warrant aggressive intervention.

After Andrew had done surprisingly well for a week, he developed what was described to us as a minor fluid adjustment and measurement problem. "The time for heroics is past," his doctor assured us, and we agreed to his transfer to PHC. Three obstetricians, a pediatrician, and numerous nurses at Community Hospital had taken our viewpoints and our anguish seriously and had treated us with competence and concern and simple human understanding. We signed the transfer paper in the naive belief that the same atmosphere would prevail at PHC.

Our initial visit to Andrew at Pediatric Hospital gave us the first shocking insight into the error we had made. When we tried to raise the same issues of extraordinary treatment and quality of life that we had all been discussing at Community Hospital, Dr. Carvalho responded coolly that "these children are precious to most parents."

The succession of six principal residents, and others on night or weekend and holiday assignment, created a major obstacle to effective parent-doctor communication. Having to depend for crucial information on people we hardly knew, and having to express our deepest frustrations and most vulnerable feelings to a new stranger every month, built a special and destructive tension through all the months of Andrew's crisis.

We were told that continuity was assured by the presence of the IICU's three attending physicians, but they rotated too, and it was common knowledge that the philosophy of neonatal care varied from one attending doctor to the next. The medical record ought to have been a guarantor of continuity for Andrew. But even the record contains surprising errors and discontinuities, while basic facts concerning the circumstances of Andrew's birth and our family life are creatively elaborated from one resident to the next like whispered stories in a parlor game.

The residents' written comments reflect the lack of understanding we felt from many of them as we were dealing with them. The doctor who wrote the "discharge summary" at the end of Andrew's life felt qualified to state definitively that we "clearly never wanted to have Andrew." That was not true. Another doctor concluded a discussion of Andrew's birth with: "Not to worry tho. The parents were assured by the obstetrician that the child would die and everyone could be happy."

What possible excuse can there be for this sort of callousness becoming a part of the official information that is reported from one doctor to another just coming on the case? How can anyone be so insensitive to the pain involved when the parents' hope for a new baby takes such a disastrous turn? We wondered frequently how many of the young doctors and nurses who felt so qualified to judge us and our feelings had ever experienced a problem pregnancy, had ever had a child at all, had ever been in a situation even remotely like the one that befell us after Andrew's birth and during his stay at Pediatric Hospital.

We do not entirely blame the residents for all of this. They too were in a real sense victims of the rotation system. It was hard for them to know us, though some tried. But in the end they all went on to other cases. We were the only ones who were not allowed to rotate. (The situation was made bearable only by the chance fact that the first resident with whom we dealt was an unusually understanding person who was willing to remain in contact with us and with Andrew's case for all the months which followed his official tour of duty in the IICU. We are grateful to Dr. Perlman for his attempt to reach out beyond the confines of an impersonal system.)

The medical record contains the following brief summary of Andrew's case, dated only June: "6 months bronchopulmonary dysplasia, pulmonary artery hypertension, cerebal atrophy now with seizures—? current status. Difficult parents as per chart."

We asked ourselves again and again what the staff at PHC could have expected people in our situation to do. Did they think we didn't really mean it when we said we believed it was morally wrong to keep Andrew alive? Did anyone consider the impossible psychological position we were put into when we were systematically and casually overruled?

The whole sad case of Andrew Stinson could have been avoided if we had been given complete, accurate information about the policies and ideologies of those in charge of the IICU of Pediatric Hospital *before* we signed the admission forms, for then we would certainly never have allowed Andrew's transfer.

We recognize, of course, that providing accurate, candid information about hospital policies is not so simple as it sounds. But after spending six months agonizing over what was right and what was wrong at every stage of Andrew's medical treatment, after extensive reading in the field of bioethics, after discussions with acquaintances and colleagues who are by profession philosophers, ministers, theologians, biologists, psychologists, lawyers, and doctors, we can perhaps be excused for saying quite frankly that we are fed up with simplistic discussions of this problem. We are fed up with having to listen to the self-righteous and self-protective rhetoric of "brain death" and "flat EEG's"—as if those concepts weren't irrelevant to the way deaths must really be "orchestrated" (as one more candid doctor put it) in intensive care units. We are fed up with being told that it is illegal and immoral to turn off a respirator at PHC when it is somehow both legal and moral to turn it off somewhere else. We are fed up with the assumption that people disagree on "right-to-life" issues because some of us are moral and some of us are not.

After the responses we got for daring to raise the question of when or in what circumstances Andrew's respirator could be turned off ("what do you want me to do?" asked Dr. Farrell on one memorable occasion. "Go in and put a pillow over his head?"), is it any wonder that we were surprised (and bitter about the hypocrisy of it all) when a variant of respirator withdrawal was in fact arranged—while most of the staff pretended officially that Andrew's death on June 14 was an inevitable occurrence and not arranged at all? Is waiting for a baby who is described as respirator-dependent to dislodge his own breathing tube, chance to breathe for a while for himself, and then, predictably, fail to survive, either moral or "dignified"?

The situation now exists in which it is very easy to turn on a respirator—no one's consent is even needed—and almost impossible to turn one off. Until our legal and moral codes become sophisticated enough to cope with our machinery, parents must have the right to decide whether or in what circumstances their tiny babies should be attached to respirators. Meanwhile, patients, families, hospitals, and society as a whole will continue to be plagued by new and agonizing problems created by the boom in life-support technology. As one attending physician remarked of Andrew's case after it was finally over: "We were all lucky to get out of this as easily as we did."

At the end came a notice from the PHC business office, announcing in passionless figures that the hospital costs alone for Andrew Stinson's treatment came to $104,403.20 (of which all but $2100 has been paid). The bill is more than an accounting of charges for daily treatment. It is a reminder that through the six months of hospital experiments, failures, and arrogance, the meter was ticking—but someone else would pay. The IICU could continue to operate in splendid isolation, not only from our protests, but also from any sense of the financial impact of their solitary decisions.

The bill also reminds us of other financial burdens, and of the many times we tried to give attending physicians, residents, nurses, and business office clerks a sense of how financially destructive this experience was. Our marriage and family life came under substantial pressure, and we began to run up uninsured bills with a family counselor. At the same time we were forced to incur the cost of enunciating and protecting our legal rights when we retained an attorney. Hanging over our heads throughout the spring was the thought that while our medical insurance would probably pay most of the bills that were strictly medical, it listed exclusions and deductions. No matter how expensive our daily lives had become, we knew there would be hundreds and hundreds more to pay at the end.

When this nightmare began, we had a small savings account, but this spring we saw it dwindle to nothing. An annual salary of $13,600 was enough in normal times to maintain a modest living for our family. Since December, when Andrew entered PHC, we have not been able to make ends meet and will do no better in the foreseeable future.

None of this seemed intelligible to the personnel of PHC. It was a problem, perhaps, but it was, again, someone else's problem. We tried, during an extraordinary meeting with him in February, to make Dr. Craft see how serious the situation was. Andrew's hospitalization seemed completely open-ended, we said, and we were afraid that the expenses would run over the limit of our insurance. "What will they do?" we asked. "Will they make us declare bankruptcy and lose everything?" His reply left us speechless: "I guess they will," was all he said. What we needed at that moment was assurance, intercession, or, at the very least, recognition that something fundamentally intolerable could happen, was happening, to other human beings. Instead we saw but one more token of the isolation in which doctors often operate. They do not know how their business offices work and, we suspect, they do not want to know, because knowledge implies responsibility. Ignorance conveniently narrows the focus and enables them to legitimize the disowning of painful problems. Someone else will pay.

What happened at Pediatric Hospital has had a final bitter psychological cost: we have been robbed of the opportunity to grieve at the death of our child. We have friends whose baby son, brain-damaged and unable to breath on his own, died a day after birth in a community hospital. No respirators were available to prolong the suffering of everyone concerned, and the family was able to grieve for the baby in a normal way. The baby is buried in an old country cemetery where the parents, their older child, and their year-old normal, healthy son gather now and then to think of the child who might have been.

There can be no such scene for Andrew. By the time he was finally permitted to die, the death itself could bring only feelings of profound relief: relief that Andrew's pain, as well as our own, was finished at last; relief that we had all escaped the clutches of Pediatric Hospital at last.

We have taken the money that might have gone under different circumstances for a graveside marker and committed it to the only memorial which can have any meaning for us now: to the sponsorship of a living child, an impoverished child whose only problem at birth was that he was born into an affluent society that does not choose to put his well-being at very high priority. For we believe Andrew's case raises broad and difficult questions which the medical profession in particular and society as a whole must face up to.

What sort of memories or thoughts could we have of Andrew? By the time he was allowed to die, the technology being used to "salvage" him had produced not so much a human life as a grotesque caricature of a human life, a "person" with a stunted, deteriorating brain and scarely an undamaged vital organ in his body, who existed only as an extension of a machine. This is the image left to us for the rest of our lives of our son, Andrew.

Sincerely yours   .   .   .

How did the hospital reply?

The administration agreed to drop the $2100 charge and think about ways of improving parent-staff relations, but Mr. Clark's response did not address seriously any of the issues Andrew's case raised. The official reply cited the progress in infant survival that had come about "because of perseverance in units such as ours," and regretted that we had interpreted Dr. Farrell's behavior as offensive. His "very behavior reflects the hospital's mission of providing tertiary care," Mr. Clark explained.

No one can deny that there has been progress in saving premature infants, and we are happy for the children and families who can benefit from the experimentation that made this possible. But there will always be a frontier to challenge neonatologists—an "Andrew" of 600 grams, or 300; of 20 weeks, or 16, or 12. Success even at these levels may someday be possible, but as doctors press onward they will inflict pain and heavy costs on tiny subjects and their families.

Who will set the limits? Can society afford to pay? If research must proceed, can't we at least limit it to consenting families?

We referred Andrew's case to the hospital's patient care committee, but without apparent result. We sent twenty copies of our letter to people involved in Andrew's life and death and asked most for a response, but only two replied.

Aren't these issues of interest? Shouldn't we all be discussing them? If there are others who do not wish to deal with hospitals whose mission is to act as Pediatric Hospital did, they must make their wishes known.

NOTES

1. Robert and Peggy Stinson have written a more complete account of their ordeal based upon the journals they kept during the time that Andrew was alive. They edited and juxtaposed their entries and added bracketed information from medical records and other sources. The reader is therefore able to reflect upon the events, crises and decisions in the lives of the Stinsons as they unfold. R. & P. Stinson, The Long Dying of Baby Andrew (1983). Compare the Stinsons' perspective with that of Sondra Diamond, infra.

2. In addition to the family, do other third parties, such as health care providers, have interests that should be considered? Consider the following:

> In addition to the factors weighed by Judge Wright in Georgetown [Application of President & Directors of Georgetown College, Inc., 331 F.2d 1000 (D.C.Cir.1964)], one consideration is added to the scale. In the difficult realm of religious liberty it is often assumed only the religious conscience is imperiled. Here, however, the doctor's conscience and professional oath must also be respected. In the present case the patient voluntarily submitted himself to and insisted upon medical care. Simultaneously he sought to dictate to treating physicians a course of treatment amounting to medical malpractice. To require these doctors to ignore the mandates of their own conscience, even in the name of free religious exercise, cannot be justified under these circumstances. The patient may knowingly decline treatment, but he may not demand mistreatment. Therefore, this Court, as Judge Wright, "determined to act on the side of life" in the pending emergency.

United States v. George, 239 F.Supp. 752, 754 (D.Conn.1965).

**JOHN LORBER,
EARLY RESULTS OF SELECTIVE TREATMENT
OF SPINA BIFIDA CYSTICA**

4 Brit.Med.J. 201, 202–204 (1973).

Introduction

Two major revolutions have occurred in the past 15 years in the treatment of myelomeningocele. The first was the enthusiasm or moral compulsion to treat all infants, irrespective of the degree of their handicap—largely the result of the insistence of the Sheffield team. The main reason for this enthusiasm was the introduction of the ventriculoatrial shunt in 1958. This procedure was able to control hydrocephalus effectively for the first time.

The second event was the disillusionment which occurred because the technical advances, especially the use of unidirectional valve systems to control the associated hydrocephalus, led to hopes that were unfortunately not fulfilled. Analysis of the results have shown that treating all infants still resulted in a high mortality rate in those cases severely affected at birth and yet led to the prolonged survival of many severely handicapped children, with gross paralysis, multiple deformities of the legs, fractures, kyphosis, scoliosis, incontinence of urine and faeces with frequent secondary effects of hydronephrosis, chronic pyelonephritis, and arterial hypertension. Hydrocephalus was usually well controlled with shunt therapy—in those who needed operation—but the complications of shunt therapy are extremely common, requiring repeated operations. The mortality rate from these complications alone was 20% within seven years of the first shunt operation in a large group of children. Over half of the shunt-treated survivors were mentally handicapped and very few had an I.Q.

over 100. At best not more than 10% of all the survivors (with and without hydrocephalus) were likely to have a chance of earning a living in competitive employment.

The survival of so many severely handicapped children gave rise to progressively greater anxiety among doctors, nurses, parents, teachers, and the general public. This became evident with the rising tide of comments on television, radio, in newspapers, and other media. The ethical validity of prolongation of profoundly handicapped lives, consisting of frequent operations, hospital admissions, and absence from home and school and with no prospect of marriage or employment, became less and less tenable. The cost of maintaining each such child is now about £3,000 a year. A change in policy was bound to come.

Though most infants were offered active treatment during the 1960's this practice was not universal, but those who did not treat all patients or were reluctant to do so did not report their views or results until recently. Nevertheless, in Oxford and in Edinburgh a policy of selection was carried out and, though exact criteria were not laid down where the line should be drawn, very few selectively untreated infants survived to two years of age and the condition of these survivors was probably no worse than if they had been treated. In Stark and Drummond's . . . treated patients the condition of the survivors was more favourable than in those series in which all patients were treated without selection. . . .

In my experience a detailed correlation between the physical findings soon after birth and the results of therapy has clearly indicated that it is possible to define a line of division as criteria for treatment. No infant among 400 consecutive cases treated from the first day of life who had any one or any combination of the adverse features shown in the appendix survived with less than very severe combined handicaps, while in the absence of these criteria many children survived with only "moderate" handicaps. Only half of the latter were treated with a shunt, their average intelligence was normal, and they had far fewer operations. Only 16% without adverse criteria died by 7 years compared with 59% of those with adverse criteria. In view of the predictability of the minimal likely handicap, I proposed, first at the 14th Annual General Meeting of the Society for Research in Hydrocephalus and Spina Bifida in Freiburg in 1970, that these criteria should be adopted for selection. The publication of these results led to the second revolution in the management of myelomeningocele—namely, an almost universal acceptance of selection which has been officially recognized as legitimate practice . . . .

Present Investigation

This study describes the experiences and results of a policy of selection based on the proposed line of division (see appendix) and examines the validity of this dividing line. In the current investigation it was necessary only to use the criteria for selection which were present at birth.

Patients and Methods

Between May 1971, when my policy of "selection" was put into practice, and 31 January 1973, 37 newborn infants born with spina bifida cystica were referred to the medical paediatric unit for assessment, and for treatment if thought appropriate. . . .

All the infants were assessed fully from every point of view. . . . If an infant had one or more of the "adverse criteria" (see appendix)

. . . the father or both parents were interviewed by me (or in my absence by my senior assistant) in the presence of a member of the junior medical staff and a member of the nursing staff.

The infant's condition was fully explained and the facts were repeated, so as to leave no doubt in the parent's mind. The many possible therapeutic actions were described to them and a prognosis was given as to the *likely minimal handicap* their child might have if he was offered total treatment and *if everything went well.* The risks and possible complications were also explained without bias. Finally, a recommendation was made together with an offer for a second opinion. The interview took up to two hours and, if necessary, was repeated later.

No parent was asked to sign a consent form for operation without fully understanding what it would mean to the infant and the family. All but one couple accepted the doctor's recommendation. In one instance where the infant's condition was near the borderline treatment was advised, but the parents refused to give permission. The infant died shortly afterwards.

. . .

Results

Active treatment was recommended for and accepted by the parents of 12 infants. Twenty-five were not treated.

Treated Infants

Of the 12 treated infants 11 had no adverse criteria on admission, but one had a large thoracolumbosacral lesion. At examination within an hour of birth this infant had normal power in her legs, had no outward deformity, her head was of normal size, and the fontanelle was of normal tension. It was such a "good baby" that in spite of the size of her lesion operation was advised and closure of the back was carried out at 4 hours of age. Soon afterwards she lost practically all power in her legs. An intravenous pyelogram and micturating cystourethrogram showed gross hydronephrosis. An x-ray picture of her spine disclosed hemivertebrae at the thoracolumbar junction. This led to progressive scoliosis by 1 year of age. Severe progressive hydrocephalus gradually became apparent. This was treated successfully with isosorbide.

There was progressive deterioration in her renal condition and function studies showed little renal reserve. Thus the size and site of her spina bifida was an accurate prognostic sign, yet had she not been operated on at an early stage the gross loss of muscle function and her other problems might well have been attributed to failure of treatment.

The remaining 11 patients' spina bifida was upper thoracic (1), lumber (1), low lumbosacral (6), and sacral (3). One treated infant died on the surgical ward from respiratory arrest on the second day of life. This infant had no paralysis or hydrocephalus, but at necrosy an exceptionally large Arnold-Chiari malformation was found. All the remaining 10 infants are alive and are between 5 and 18 months of age at the time of writing. None have severe sequelae. Three are fully normal. Seven have slight paraplegia but four of these pass a normal stream of urine and have good anal tone. Three have dribbling incontinence and patulous anus as well as having mild paraplegia.

Four of the 11 survivors have no hydrocephalus, two had moderate hydrocephalus which required no treatment, two other infants' moderate hydrocephalus was fully controlled with isosorbide, and the remaining three have shunt-treated hydrocephalus. None have an abnormally large head. None have required a revision of shunt treatment, so far. All have normal milestones of development.

The 12 treated infants had 16 operations, including the primary closure, three shunt operations, and one foot correction during a total of 160 months of observation.

Untreated Infants

One infant had no adverse criteria, though she had moderately severe asymmetrical paraplegia, was incontinent, and had hydrocephalus. After much discussion with both parents they decided against treatment and the infant died at home under 1 month of age. . . . Most patients (21 out of 25) had two or more adverse criteria. These consisted mostly of gross paralysis (24) and thoracolumbosacral lesions (20), but clinical kyphosis or scoliosis was also very common (13). Intravenous pyelography and echo-encephalography was carried out as a routine.

Once a decision was made not to treat these infants they were looked after as normal babies, given normal nursing-care, and were fed on demand. Analgesics were given as required, but no other treatment was offered: no oxygen, tube feeding, antibiotic drugs, or resuscitation. No painful investigations were carried out: no ventriculography, blood tests, etc. The parents could take the infant home (including for weekends), but they were not expected to do so. Infants born in Sheffield were kept on the ward. The others were returned to their base unit under their own paediatrician's care. (This was invariably agreed to before the infant's transfer to Sheffield.)

Death occurred within nine months in all 25 (table V): three died within a week and 18 (72%) by 3 months of age. Three infants lived for six months or longer. Two went home from the local hospital, and the third was unfortunately being tube-fed for months before dying of oesophageal ulceration and aspirated vomit.

Table V—Age at Death in 25 Untreated Infants

Alive at:	No. of Patients
1 Day	25
1 Week	22
1 Month	14
3 Months	7
6 Months	2
9 Months	0

The most common immediate cause of death was ventriculitis (10 infants) followed by the hydrocephalus itself (six infants); four died of associated congenital anomalies of the heart and other organs; respiratory infection was the last illness in three; but there is no definite information about the remaining two. Necropsy was carried out in 19 infants. All had multiple potential causes of death.

Discussion

The fear that some untreated severe cases of myelomeningocele might survive for long has not been substantiated, and so far the strict criteria for selection have proved reliable. The parents were invariably appreciative of the painless and humane nursing of their untreated infants. Everyone realizes that the solution offered by "selection" is not a good one. There is no "good solution" to a desperate, insoluble problem, merely a "least bad solution," which is being offered.

Selection has also led to an undoubtedly better quality of the survivors than was the case for the less severely affected infants in the past. None have "severe handicaps" so far, except the one treated infant who did have adverse criteria (thoracolumbosacral lesion) at birth. This shows the need for the utmost strictness in applying the criteria for selection.

The results in the untreated infants are similar to the larger series reported from Oxford, but where the decision not to treat was not based on exact criteria and the subsequent management of the infants was not necessarily uniform. This may explain why 4% of the patients survived to two years of age.

One of the advantages of the proposed criteria for selection is that the infants are so severely affected at birth that no appreciable functional loss can result from failure to treat on the first day. On the contrary, at least their hydrocephalus is less likely to be rapidly progressive. If an occasional infant were to survive in good general condition for over six months and seemed likely to live, then he could be "brought back into the fold" and be treated for his hydrocephalus and for his renal, orthopaedic, and other problems as necessary.

If it is the open objective of "no treatment" that the infant should die soon and painlessly, then why cannot euthanasia be carried out? I wholly disagree with euthanasia. Though it is fully logical, and in expert and conscientious hands it could be the most humane way of dealing with such a situation, legalizing euthanasia would be a most dangerous weapon in the hands of the State or ignorant or unscrupulous individuals. One does not have to go far back in history to know what crimes can be committed if euthanasia were legalized. The best hope for the future is to discover the cause or causes of spina bifida and to prevent its occurrence. Already there is a chink of hope on the horizon, and the recent dramatic decline in the incidence of spina bifida in Sheffield gives us the hope that one day it will not be such a major problem for our children and their families.

. . .

Appendix—Contraindications to Active Therapy

At birth:

(1) Gross paralysis of the legs (paralysis below 3rd lumbar segmental level with at most hip flexors, adductors, and quadriceps being active).

(2) Thoracolumbar or thoracolumbosacral lesions related to vertebral levels.

(3) Kyphosis or scoliosis.

(4) Grossly enlarged head, with maximal circumference of 2 cm or more above the 90th percentile related to birth weight.

(5) Intracerebral birth injury.

(6) Other gross congenital defects—for example, cyanotic heart disease, ectopia of bladder, and mongolism.

After closure, in the newborn period:

Meningitis or ventriculitis in an infant who already has serious neurological handicap and hydrocephalus.

Later:

In any life-threatening episode in a child who is severely handicapped by gross mental and neurological defects.

R.B. ZACHARY, LIFE WITH SPINA BIFIDA

2 Brit.Med.J. 1460, 1460–1462 (1977).

Spina bifida is a broad term that includes minimal lesions such as spina bifida occulta and cystic swellings not containing any neural tissue (spina bifida with meningocele). Our main concern, however, is spina bifida with open myelomeningocele, in which the neural tissue is exposed on the surface of the cystic swelling.

The neural tissue in this exposed plaque is abnormal and defective, so that the muscles innervated by it, and indeed distal to the plaque, may be partly or completely paralysed. Naturally, innervation of the bladder and bowels is almost always defective.

In addition, about 90% of the children with open myelomeningocele have hydrocephalus, but the degree of ventricular dilatation and intracranial tension varies and is not directly related to the appearance of the back lesion. If an infant had an operation to close the back wound in the neonatal period he might require a valve for the hydrocephalus within the first six to eight weeks. Complete paralysis of the legs may lead to no deformity whatever, but partial paralysis may lead to dislocation of the hip and to foot deformities. If it is decided to encourage the child to walk with appliances several operations may be needed on the feet and also a muscle transplant at the hip to keep the hip in joint after reduction. The other serious orthopaedic problem is the spinal deformity caused by unopposed action of certain muscles, which leads to kyphosis or kyphoscoliosis and which may require major surgery for partial correction.

In treating the hydrocephalus the excess ventricular fluid can be shunted through the Holter valve back into the bloodstream, and although some patients require revision of the valve several times in the first ten years, the hydrocephalus can be reasonably well controlled. We are learning in Sheffield how to prevent, and also recognise and treat, infection of the valve system; but as with any foreign body, the risk of infection remains.

Defective bladder emptying may lead to stasis of urine within the renal tract and a tendency to infection, and in certain cases may lead to high pressures that cause the upper tract to dilate. Careful and frequent monitoring of the renal tract has enabled us to detect the early signs of trouble and give appropriate treatment, and there is no doubt that young children under treatment now have better kidneys than did children ten years ago. Even so, a ten-year review of survivors of an unselected series showed that nearly a quarter of them had normal or nearly normal bladder control.

Expression of the bladder every two hours may enable the incontinent to be socially dry; but, if not, a penile appliance will help the boys, and an indwelling Foley catheter has been a tremendous boon in many girls. We still, however, have to undertake a urinary diversion in many of these patients.

A typical 10-year-old with severe spina bifida will therefore spend most of his time in a wheelchair but can make some progress in long calipers; his hydrocephalus is controlled with a valve that may have needed two or three revisions during the growth period. Most children have an IQ within the normal range but below the mean; intellectual attainment will depend on the degree of hydrocephalus at the time when treatment was started, whether there has been infection, the speed with which obstruction has been relieved, and the opportunities for intellectual stimulation. I noticed a remarkable change in the children when the spina bifida school was first opened in Sheffield, because many were receiving stimulation that had not been been possible before. A boy will probably have a good upper renal tract and may be wearing a penile appliance if he cannot be kept dry by expression of the bladder. A girl may have an indwelling Foley catheter or may have needed an ileal conduit. This is not an unusual picture of the young person with spina bifida and hydrocephalus. I would emphasise that this is a *person* who has spina bifida, and it is very important that we alway refer to them and treat them as persons. The picture at 15 or 20 years is unlikely to change significantly, unless there is an untreated obstruction of the valve system or an uncorrected stasis and back pressure in the renal tract.

Should they be allowed to die?

At the end of the 1960s my medical colleague Dr. John Lorber became very concerned about the degree of handicap of these young people and the morbidity and hospital admissions that resulted. His extensive study showed that those who have a gross lesion at birth are likely to be severely handicapped when they grow up. He came to the view that the degree of handicap could be forecast at birth, and became strongly opposed to any treatment at all of severely affected babies in the newborn period. He proposed certain criteria for selecting those infants who should be allowed to die, and these were widely accepted—partly because of the human appeal of the view that these children should not be allowed to suffer, and that their parents should not have the burden of looking after them. It was also attractive to administrative authorities because the burden of the financial support needed to treat and care for children with spina bifida would be greatly reduced.

The cardinal error in these proposals is the expression, they should be allowed to die. Thirty years ago I was concerned with the care of many patients with spina bifida at the Children's Hospital in Boston, Mass., under Dr. Franc Ingraham. The policy was that *none* of these children should have a neonatal operation. The lesion was covered by a simple dressing and protected by a ring; and after about a week or ten days the children went home to be looked after by their parents and the local paediatrician, with monthly visits to the neurosurgical and orthopaedic clinics. I have seen many children with severe lesions that epithelialised spontaneously, who then had the operation to close the back wound at about 18 months. Several of the very severely affected ones died at home, but I myself have handled many survivors with serious lesions. I thought it was an unduly heavy burden for the mother to have to look after the swelling on the back, and when I first came to Sheffield I decided to remove the swelling in the neonatal period if possible. Even so, for several years I continued to see children with quite obvious severe lesions who had not undergone any operation immediately after birth.

There is a widespread myth that if you operate on a child with spina bifida the child will live, and if you do not operate he will die. This is nonsense. They will not all die spontaneously.

"No treatment" methods

How is it then that those who write about the value of selection can point to a high mortality, usually 100%, in those that they have selected out? I am sure it has nothing to do with the administration of antibiotics, because those young patients in Boston had no antibiotics 30 years ago. We must look at the exact method of management of those who have no treatment.

One paediatrician has said that they receive the same care and attention as any other baby, being fed and picked up and loved, and even taken out into the sunshine in a pram. Yet these babies are receiving 60 mg/kg body weight of chloral hydrate, not once but four times a day. This is eight times the sedative dose of chloral hydrate recommended in the most recent volume of *Nelson's Paediatrics* and four times the hypnotic dose, and it is being administered four times every day. No wonder these babies are sleepy and demand no feed, and with this regimen most of them will die within a few weeks, many within the first week.

It is sometimes said that the chloral hydrate is being administered for pain, either in the back or due to the hydrocephalus, but I personally have seen little evidence that the babies have pain in the newborn period, nor have I found them unable to sleep. And if chloral hydrate is such a good drug why is it not given to those who are intended to survive?

There is nothing secret or confidential about this method of management, for the paediatrician has stated that he has published the details of management for all to see. At a meeting of doctors, social workers, and theologians another paediatrician explained his method of asking the registrar to administer morphine. He claimed that the parents were taken fully into his confidence and were 100% behind him. When closely questioned he admitted that he did not tell them that the child would receive morphine—merely that the child would die.

In another centre only one out of 24 patients was operated on—all the others died. When asked, "Did they fall or were they pushed"—into death—the reply was, "They were pushed of course." At another meeting I attended a paediatrician was asked by a medical student what was his method of management, and the reply was, "We don't feed them."

I have mentioned the various problems that a person with a moderately severe spina bifida might have in his life, and emphasised that the duration of life would depend on the attitude of the doctor in charge. Some have been prepared to say in public that they would administer drugs, whose direct purpose and effect is the death of the child in a relatively short time. I think there are some paediatricians who have misunderstood the likely consequences of simply withholding surgery, and I have had to deal with children at 6 months of age in whom the total drug treatment part of the regimen had been omitted. I have indeed treated some who have had chloral hydrate, later phenobarbitone, and later morphine and have still survived to require operation. Such doctors are entitled to their view that their actions are best for the child and family, but there should not be any pretence that all these babies are dying spontaneously. Indeed, one must ask, "Are not these actions outside the law?"

I think it is extremely important from a strictly scientific point of view that we cannot regard the non-operative mortality figures as indicating accurately how many babies who are selected for no treatment will die spontaneously—there is, so to speak, an inbuilt insurance policy. There is one further worrying aspect. The editors of medical journals are conscious of their responsibility not to publish papers that are clearly unethical—for example, reporting research that required unnecessary operation or any appreciable risk. How much more carefully should they look at contributions based on studies that include the administration of drugs to accomplish the death of a child?

Criteria for operation

It may be asked whether I would advocate operation on every baby with spina bifida. Of course not. As with every aspect of surgery, there are criteria for selection, which should be based on sound medical and surgical principles and a knowledge of the prospects with and without surgery. My scheme for selection for operation in open myelomeningocele is as follows, babies in categories 1 and 2 having no operation.

Category 1

This category includes those patients who are judged likely to die within a few days or a week or so—for example, babies with severe intracranial haemorrhage or another major life-threatening anomaly. There will be no operation on the back in these children because it could have no bearing at all on whether they lived or died.

Category 2

Some of the children who seem unlikely to die spontaneously in a short time will have a serious lesion of the back—for example, a very wide lesion or one producing a severe kyphosis, in which the chances of primary healing after surgery would be small: there would be a risk of wound breakdown, which would be far worse than no operation at all. Epithelium is likely to grow over the exposed plaque with simple protection of the wound, and this would be the method of treatment.

Category 3

Other babies are judged to have a good chance of primary wound healing after operation, and these are placed in the three grades of severity.

Grade 1—Active movement of the legs has been observed after birth. These babies need urgent operation because otherwise some of that active movement may be lost.

Grade 2—Babies in the intermediate group have certain active muscles such as hip flexors and adductors, and perhaps quadriceps. I think these are important muscles to preserve for the orthopaedic surgeon to use, and I would advocate urgent surgery.

Grade 3—At the other extreme there are babies who make no observed leg movements after birth; in these infants operation on the back will have no effect upon the muscular power in the legs. They can be treated either by a non-urgent operation (but within 24 to 48 hours to minimise infection) or by conservative means such as simple dressings.

The survivors, whether they have been operated on or not, will be offered surgery for hydrocephalus or for renal tract or orthopaedic problems to improve the quality of life or prevent deterioration.

Under no circumstances would I administer drugs to cause the death of the child. There is no doubt that those who are severely affected at birth will continue to be severely handicapped. But I conceive it to be my duty to overcome that handicap as much as possible and to achieve the maximum development of their potential in as many aspects of life as possible—physical, emotional, recreational, and vocational—and I find them very nice people. If in the *neonatal* period you are looking for opportunities to make sure they will die I am sure this attitude is likely to persist even when they are older. Some have been regarded as living completely miserable and unhappy lives. Yet when I see them I find them happy people who can respond to concern for their personal welfare.

One final point, It has often been said by those who oppose abortion that the disregard for the life of a child within the uterus would spill over into postnatal life. This suggestion has been "pooh-poohed," yet in spina bifida there is a clear example of this. The equanimity with which the life of a 17-week-gestation spina bifida infant is terminated after the finding of a high level of x-fetoprotein in the amniotic fluid has, I think, spilled over to a similar disregard for the life of the child with spina bifida after birth.

Much of my surgical life over the past 30 years has been devoted to improving the quality of life of those who have been born with spina bifida. The attitude of mind that would eliminate all the severely handicapped reminds me of the poster issued by Christian Aid some years ago, which said "Ignore the hungry and they will go away"—to their graves. If we eliminate all the severely affected children with spina bifida there will be no more problem; but why stop at spina bifida, why not all the severely affected spastics, all those with muscular dystrophy, and all those with Down's syndrome? Why stop at the neonatal period? Our aim should be that life with spina bifida is the best possible life for that person in the family and in the community.

NOTE

In addition to the materials printed here, Lorber also carried on an extensive debate with J.M. Freeman. Freeman, To Treat or Not to Treat: Ethical Dilemmas of Treating the Infant with a Myelomeningocele, 20 Clinical Neurosurgery 134 (1973); Lorber, Selective Treatment of Myelomeningocele: To Treat or Not to Treat? 53 Pediatrics 307 (1974); Freeman, Shortsighted Treatment of Myelomeningocele, 53 Pediatrics 311 (1974).

PAUL RAMSEY,
ETHICS AT THE EDGES OF LIFE

192–93, 201–03, 212–16, 218–19 (1978).

Surely there is a distinction to be made between, on the one hand, children permitted to die whose deaths "resulted from pathological conditions in spite of the treatment given" (category 1), and, on the other hand, those permitted to die who simply had severe impairments, usually from congenital disorders (category 2). The latter more than likely died *because* they were not treated. Of the former alone could it correctly be said, as physicians report nurses saying, "We lost him several weeks ago; isn't it time to quit?" or "For this child, don't you think it's time to turn off your curiosity so you can turn on your kindness?" or that the facilities in which they were treated are "hardly more than *dying* bins." . . . In medical care, we rightly compare treatments in order to decide what is indicated as responsible activity on the part of those who are still living toward those who are now dying. But we ought not to compare and contrast the persons—the patients who are dying—with one another in other respects. We have no moral right to choose that some live and others die, when the medical indications for treatment are the same.

That means that the standard for letting die must be the same for the normal child as for the defective child. If an operation to remove a bowel obstruction is indicated to save the life of a normal infant, it is also the indicated treatment of a mongoloid infant. The latter is certainly not dying because of Down's syndrome. Like any other child with an obstruction in its intestinal tract, it will starve to death unless an operation is performed to remove the obstruction to permit normal feeding.

Dr. John Lorber of Sheffield, England, is now famous for choosing to let some spina bifida or myelomeningocele babies die while others undergo a series of operations over many years. The latter lead impaired lives, but lives Lorber judges to be worth living. He claims he is able to make this determination on the first day of a baby's life by applying five measurements or tests. Now, I do not think that a series of ordinary treatments—closing the open spine, antibiotics, a contraption to deal with urinary incontinence, and a shunt to prevent hydrocephalus—today adds up to extraordinary medical care, except perhaps in the case of a conscious, competent patient who is able himself to refuse treatment. But the point is that Dr. Lorber does not claim that the infants he chooses to "let die" are now dying, or that to intervene medically only prolongs their dying. Indeed, those babies are heavily sedated. Is the reason for that to keep pain at bay? I doubt it. There is rather some ground for suspicion that, since drowsy babies need to be fed less frequently, the spina bifida babies chosen not be treated are sedated so that they will begin dying of hunger and slowly sleep away. At least, that would be one way of avoiding the notorious case of allowing a defective infant to starve to death in fifteen days, as was done at Johns Hopkins Hospital a few years ago when a Down's baby was refused an operation to remove its intestinal obstruction. So my first point is clear: the fact that dying patients sometimes need no more attempts to be made to save them ought not to be carelessly applied to the case of defective newborns. Sometimes the neglected infants are not born dying. They are only born defective and in need of help. The question whether no treatment is the indicated treatment cannot legitimately be raised, unless there is special medical reason for saying that treatment might make them worse and in any case could not help. The comparison should be between treatments measured to the need. As God is no respecter of persons of high degree, neither should we be. The proper form of the question to be asked is: Should we not close a wound in a newborn expected to be normal? Should we not provide him with devices correcting his incontinence? Should not physical conditions likely to impair any child's mental capacity be stopped if possible; or if not, subdued?

. . .

There is still another moral aspect of the practice of neglect. This is a question of justice. Some physicians who have reported that they let some babies die (perhaps hasten their dying) also report that they make such life or death decisions not only on the basis of the newborn's medical condition and prognosis, but on the basis of familial, social, and economic factors as well. If the marriage seems to be a strong one, an infant impaired to *x* degree may be treated, while an infant with the same impairment may not be treated if the marriage seems about to fall apart. Treatment may be given if the parents are wealthy; not, if they are poor. Now, life may be unfair, as John Kennedy said; but to deliberately make medical care a function of inequities that exist at birth is evidently to add injustice to injury and fate.

Wiser and more righteous is the practice of Dr. Chester A. Swinyard of the New York University medical school's rehabilitation center. Upon the presentation to him of a defective newborn, he immediately tries to make clear to the mother the distinction between the question of ultimate custody of the child and questions concerning the care it needs. The mother must consent to operations, of course. But she is asked only to make judgments about the baby's care, while she is working through the problem of whether to accept the defective child as a substitute for her "lost child," i.e., the perfect baby she wanted. In the prism of the case, when the question is, Shall this open spine be closed? Shall a shunt be used to prevent further mental impairment? the mothers can usually answer correctly. In the case of spina bifida babies, Dr. Swinyard also reports very infrequent need of institutionalization or foster parents. That results from concentrating the mother's attention on what medical care requires, and not on lifelong burdens of custody. One must entirely reject the contention of Duff and Campbell that parents, facing the prospect of oppressive burdens of care, are capable of making the most morally sensible decisions about the needs and rights of defective newborns. There is a Jewish teaching to the effect that only disinterested parties may, by even so innocuous a method as prayer, take any action which may lead to premature termination of life. Husband, children, family and those charged with the care of the patient may not pray for death.

One can understand—even appreciate—the motives of a physician who considers an unhappy marriage or family poverty when weighing the tragedy facing one child against that facing another; and rations his help accordingly. Nevertheless, that surely is a species of injustice. Physicians are not appointed to remove all life's tragedy, least of all by lessening medical care now and letting infants die who for social reasons seem fated to have less care in the future than others. That's one way to remove every evening the human debris that has accumulated since morning.

.   .   .

One could perhaps construct some exceptions to the principle of giving equally vigorous treatment to defective newborns as to normals.
.   .   .

My first thought is a proposed *redescription* of one sort of defective newborn, not logically an "exception"; moreover, it is a hypothetical and moot point, worth mentioning anyway. It is not at all necessary to take an anencephalic baby (born without a brain in its brain chamber) as the demonstration case of a defective newborn that certainly ought not to be treated, and then build up from there other cases of gross defects that should not be treated.   .   .   .

But, for one thing, an anencephalic baby is born dying, and here the morality of letting die clearly applies as it does to a Tay-Sachs baby when it is seized by irreversible degeneration. For another thing, even if it were possible to treat anencephalic babies, this should not be done—but not because they would be the demonstration case in support of a policy of not treating nondying defective newborns. Instead we could and should, consistent with our present understanding of brain life and death, take the definitional route in resolving that hypothetical case. Such an infant is "human," of course, in a generic sense; also it was unique individual of our species. However, it has not been born *alive.* If we use here at the beginning of life the same physiological signs of the difference between life and death which we use at the end of life, an anencephalic baby does not have the unitary function of major organ systems within which the brain has primacy. That is why they soon "die," as we say. Such infants demonstrate their status by dying, in all senses, rather quickly. So an anencephalic baby, it could be argued, no more enters the human community to claim our care and protection than a patient remains in the human community when his brain death (and consequent heart death and lung death) is only disguised behind a heart-lung machine.

. . .

My second suggestion would be a true exception or qualification attached to our moral duty to treat all defective infants who are not born dying and who, of course, cannot for themselves refuse treatment. If care cannot be conveyed, it need not be extended. A mongoloid can receive care. So can a Tay-Sachs baby while it is dying. For the latter we may choose how it will live while dying. In the case of the former, we can add life to its years. But we face an entirely different issue if there is a sort of birth defect for which there is no therapy and if the suffering infant is in insurmountable pain. In such a suppositive case, care cannot be conveyed. Indeed, in regard to adult patients I have elsewhere argued that those circumstances abolish the moral distinction between only caring for the dying (allowing to die) and directly dispatching them.

So now I must ask, is there a birth defect comparable to insurmountable pain or to such deep and prolonged unconsciousness that places terminal patients beyond the reach of the caring human community? From my limited knowledge of it, I am inclined to say that the Lesch-Nyhan syndrome seems a good candidate for this comparison, and that such a suffering infant *may* be an exception to the foregoing ethical analysis. Not, of course, to the moral rule that if possible we should always treat nondying defective newborns: there is no therapy for Lesch-Nyhan genetic illness. It is rather an exception to the rule that, when attempted remedy fails or there is no available remedy, when instead we should move to affirmative caring and comforting action, there is never any reason for stopping caring actions. From cure to care: but then does care never cease? Such a limit, if there is one, would have to be found in the nature of care itself, not in anything extrinsic. Care itself reaches or posits that limit. The fact that there is no remedy for Lesch-Nyhan disease, for example, would not be a reason for ceasing care. But it did seem to me, in the abstract, that giving palliative comfort could not be effectively conveyed to these babies. That seemed a barrier one runs up against by caring until one *can* care no longer.

Lesch-Nyhan disease is a genetic defect, identified and described in a series of cases in 1964, which is passed on only to male children. Its victims are unable to walk or sit up unassisted; they suffer uncontrollable spasms and mental retardation. Initially, I should say, care can and should always be conveyed to such victims, though as yet there is no cure. When, however, the babies' teeth appear they will gnaw through their lips, gnaw their hands and shoulders; they often bite off a finger and mutilate any part of their bodies they can reach. There they lie, bloody and irremediable. Is this not a close approximation to the supposable case of insurmountable pain which in the terminal adult patient places him beyond human caring action and abolishes the moral significance of the distinction between always continuing to care and direct dispatch? When care cannot be conveyed, it need not be extended.

A pediatrician who read these pages expressed dismay over the idea of ever introducing into the special-care nursery the practice of promoting dying; and he told me something about the human care that can be extended to Lesch-Nyhan babies despite the fact that there is now no curative treatment. If he is correct, then my thought experiment need be pursued no further. At any rate, my remarks on this case are exploratory—an extended question. . . .

. . .

. . . I want it understood that my understanding of care was and is what might be called (to borrow philosophical terminology) a "role and relations" ethics. It was and is a question of *agent* morality. The sole question raised was whether there ever comes a time when the care of a human agent (parent, physician) no longer reaches the subject cared for, when the eyes of faith and love no longer see, and it would be fanaticism to think so. If such a time does come, care for the dying would become as aimless as earlier further medical attempts to save or cure that life became purposeless. A gift is not a gift unless received; care is not what we suppose unless received, even if minimally. If not at all, there is no obligation to continue to do the useless. Since mine was and is an ethics of agent agape and, in medical ethics, a strong sense of agent care, I never suggested that one should base moral judgments in any degree upon an evaluation of the patient-subject as such. There was not the slightest suggestion that one should decide *first* whether the patient-subjects are so overwhelmed by their struggle for existence that they have lost effective capacity for meaningful relationship. No quality-of-life judgments were given entrance; only uselessness of agent care was suggested. These outlooks may seem very similar, but the accent is quite different.

"I AM NOT WHAT YOU SEE"*
A FILM DIALOGUE BETWEEN SONDRA DIAMOND AND ROY BONISTEEL

in Decision Making and the Defective Newborn
465, 466–476 (C. Swinyard ed. 1978).

. . . When Sondra [Diamond] was born, doctors suggested to her parents that she not be kept alive. They said there was little or no hope of her ever achieving a meaningful existence. She would always be a human vegetable, a burden to society and to the people around her. Sondra was born with cerebral palsy thirty-six years ago. She cannot walk, she has never been able to dress herself, toilet herself or write a letter, but she is a practicing psychologist and is working on her Ph.D.

* Reproduced with the permission of the Canadian Broadcasting Corporation, Toronto, Canada.

Her fight to be accepted as a full human being has been a tough one, but with the support of loving parents and sheer determination, she has overcome her physical disability. In tonight's repeat program, Sondra talks about her joy of being alive, and she reflects on her moments of despair. Sondra, why have you been considered a vegetable?

SONDRA DIAMOND: When I was born, I was born with extensive brain damage. The extent of the brain damage indicated by medical prognosis that I would not be able to speak, hear, see, or move around, and of course I would be severely retarded, if I had any perceptions at all. The term *vegetable* has been coined. I resent the term very much. It has been coined to refer to human beings that will not live up to the expectations of what people believe a human being is.

ROY BONISTEEL: How did you progress over the years?

SONDRA DIAMOND: Well, initially when my parents were told this, they did not accept it. I was, they tell me, a beautiful child to look at. It was true that I could not sit up, I could not hold my head up, I could not grasp anything, I could not do the tasks that the older children could do, but they loved me very much and they did not accept this vegetable concept. So they went to innumerable doctors, in Philadelphia, Baltimore, and New York, and continually got the same diagnosis until they found a doctor who said that I had cerebral palsy. He gave it a name instead of vegetable and said that he thought that I could be educated and rehabilitated with a great deal of learning and work, so that process was begun at the age of two. I was put in a special school for disabled children and progressed through high school, through college, through to graduate school, with constant rehabilitation.

ROY BONISTEEL: You were also involved with a burn, were you not?

SONDRA DIAMOND: Yes, in 1952 I was again performing a task that a vegetable cannot perform—I was smoking. And I needed to fill my cigarette lighter. I filled it and I lit it to test it to see if there was enough fluid in it. Unfortunately, some had spilled on my clothing and I went up in flames. Because of my disability I could not do very much about it. The fire more or less put itself out, with the help of my mother who was nearby. I was then hospitalized and expected to die.

ROY BONISTEEL: As I understand it, at that point too, there were some doctors who were reluctant to treat you, feeling that perhaps the effort was not worth it.

SONDRA DIAMOND: Yes, the normal procedure when you are burned—I was burned over 60 percent of my body—the normal procedure if you are not disabled is to begin to graft skin on these areas. The physicians told my parents there was no point to this. Since I was so severely disabled, what was the point of spending X number of thousands of dollars and X number of hours on this process? We had a difficult time explaining to them that I was a sophomore in college by that time and I was a functioning human being, although I have a lot of physical contortions, as you can see, and in a burned condition you have extreme pain, so that the severity of my disability looked even worse. And we had to convince the doctors first of all to give me intravenous feeding—they were not feeding me—and we also had to convince them to start to graft some skin. It took a lot of work to convince them, a lot of loud work.

ROY BONISTEEL: Was there a time in your life when you realized that some people—society—considered you less than human?

SONDRA DIAMOND: I remember a particular incident that happened when I was about nine. I was bussed to and from the special school. I got off the bus one day and there was a lady standing there, staring at the process of getting me off the bus and my mother welcoming me home. And the lady was standing there saying, "O my God, O my God," and shaking more than I shake. I was extremely upset. And my mother said to her, "I charge a quarter for this." So we got in the house and I said, "What happened? What is this about?" And she explained to me—I had been to the circus as a child—and she said, "Sondra, this lady is looking at what she thinks is a freak." And I asked her "Is that how you see me?" And she said, "No, we had never seen you this way, but this is how other people will see you."

ROY BONISTEEL: Sondra, if it had not been for your parents, if it had not been for money and doctors that finally did believe in you, you likely would have died, or treatment would certainly have been withheld, because you would have been considered less than a human being. And I am wondering, what does being human mean to you?

SONDRA DIAMOND: It was suggested very early in my life to my parents by the medical profession and well-meaning friends that I be placed in a state institution for children who were such as me. My parents said, "No, we want to keep this child home. We want to keep this child we love. She is our child and we love her." For me the word humanness primarily means, are you loved?—does someone love you? And I know that I personally am loved a great deal by my family, so that I know that I am a human being.

ROY BONISTEEL: So, to be truly human is possible for a severely incapacitated person?

SONDRA DIAMOND: I assume that an incapacitated person is a human being because he is loved. He may not be loved by his parents, as we are finding today—parents are rejecting a child because of severe abnormalities—but we have to begin to accept this as normal.

ROY BONISTEEL: So society then really has to redefine what it means by humanness.

SONDRA DIAMOND: Humanness in our society, as I see it, is to have a beautiful body, blue eyes, blond hair, and to be structurally straight. It means that you are expected to do certain tasks, self-help tasks, to toilet yourself, and to feed yourself, most of which I cannot do. I certainly do not have a beautiful body. Society again says that to be human is to live up to the expectations of the parents. Society also says that one of the requirements of humanness is success, and I think that we need to examine what success is. If I were not a psychologist—for example, when I wanted to go to college, my high school advisor said to me and my parents, "Why do you want to throw the money away? It is only going to be a waste of money. She is not going to be able to do anything with the college education." And my parents and I said, "It does not make any difference what she does with it. She wants a college education, she wants to learn something, and what she does with it is not the point."

ROY BONISTEEL: Sondra, can science determine the humanness of an individual?

SONDRA DIAMOND: I think that science is wrestling with the question at the moment of what is humanness. I think they are beginning—almost too late—but I think they are beginning to do some self-examination in terms of how far we have come in maintaining life, and for what reason science has gotten so well developed. I think that it is science's responsibility to diagnose clinically, to develop the instruments to diagnose, and to develop techniques to rehabilitate, but I do not think we can allow science to make the decision as to what is humanness. My own bias says that I would sooner trust a theologian and his definition of what is humanness, because I think, that theology is based on humanness. That is not being fair to science, I recognize that, but I think that theologians come a little bit closer to saying that we are all God's children. When you asked before about who loves me and am I loved, am I human because I am loved—when I was very very ill in the hospital with the burns, I kept remembering that God above all is loving; if no one could love this charcoaled body who was dying, I really believed that God did love me, so my bias says that I trust the theologian's thinking about it, because I do not think he is in as critical a position to control life and death as the scientist is.

ROY BONISTEEL: There must have been times when you had a great despair in this battle, really, to be recognized as a human being.

SONDRA DIAMOND: It happens about every six months. My family has come to know that I go into my room and lock the door and I sit for a couple of hours and wonder why am I fighting and why am I shouting and why am I pushing? Inside of me I am not a disabled person; I am not what you see visually. I am a woman, inside of me, a woman with professional drives, with sexual drives, with all kinds of drives inside of me. About every six months, I cannot stand the fact that people say, "no, you cannot do this"; "stop, this is as far as you can go." So I need to sit down and cry for awhile and get that over with. Self-pity is very therapeutic for me. And I need to say, "Okay, let's go on from here, let's keep going."

ROY BONISTEEL: Sondra, do you accept the fact that in any case of disability, a person should be considered not worth the effort of saving, or just a vegetable? Is there any condition?

SONDRA DIAMOND: I do not believe that any human being does not deserve the opportunity to live.

ROY BONISTEEL: But do you not agree that there are moments when society and people look and say, "This is not a human being, despite the fact this may be breathing."

SONDRA DIAMOND: I am not sure that we have developed sophisticated enough instruments to measure that yet. I am not sure that we know what is going on inside of that child. If that child is enjoying the sensation of the bedsheets against his skin, as I do, he is enjoying a part of life. If that child enjoys the sensation of someone touching him when he changes his diapers, he is knowing life. Can we deny the knowledge of what it is to live to anyone?

ROY BONISTEEL: Are there still people, Sondra, who consider you less than human? Do you run into them even yet?

SONDRA DIAMOND: Yes, unfortunately, there are people who still consider me less than human. Primarily I would say prospective employers because that is one of my primary goals—to have a competitive position. Socially, people consider me less than human so that I have a limited number of friends. When I am out in public places, people treat me sometimes quite cruelly. What I have to do is again remember, "Do I want to go through life teaching people to relate to me and being the educator all the time, or do I want to react as a human being?" As a human being I react in one of two ways: Sometimes it is with extreme anger, and sometimes it is with extreme humor. May I take the time to give you an example? I was in a restaurant a few months ago and a woman came up to me—a perfectly normal, physically normal woman—came up to me and she did this—and I hope you do not find it offensive—but she did this. She said, "Why are you doing this?" and she shook, trying to imitate me, somehow. And I said, "Pardon me?" She said, "Why are you doing this?" and she shook her whole body and arms in gross movements. And I said, "I am sorry, I do not know what you mean." And she said, "Why are you in the wheelchair then?" And I said, "Wheelchair? What wheelchair? I am sorry, I do not see a wheelchair." And she said some profanity and walked away. Okay, we did not interact very well, but I felt really tremendous. I am sure this sounds a little crazy. But it was my way of making myself feel more comfortable in that situation.

ROY BONISTEEL: Sondra, I think, you could help me and my viewers a great deal to understand what we can do to be more human. I think we are missing a great deal of what you have found. How can we come to an understanding of what being human really means?

SONDRA DIAMOND: To come to an understanding as to how to be human or to decide who is human, the only essential thing to do is to make no assumptions; whomever you meet, whomever you look at, do not make the assumption of what they are until you interact with them. I do not know how you felt when you saw me, but I am sure you had some initial gut reaction which I would like you to share with me if we have time. I am interested enough, because people tell me, "Gee, when I first met you, I thought you were an idiot. I thought you did not have a brain in your head. I had no idea how you possibly got here." And I said, "Why didn't you wait until we interacted a bit and then make those assumptions? [sic] So to be human and to decide who or what is human, I think, essentially is to make no assumptions, to do the best we can medically, educationally, psychologically, lovingly, without making any assumptions, or hiding a set of expectations.

ROY BONISTEEL: You had the potential when you were born to be a human being, but without the care and love of your parents, I wonder how you would have succeeded. I am suggesting, I guess, that it is human relations that makes humanness possible. You would not have gotten very far without the love and care and understanding of your parents.

SONDRA DIAMOND: That is true. When I am asked who I most credit for my development and for whatever I am, I say it is my parents and my family. They have been very supportive. But what if I had not had that family? What will happen when I do not have them any longer? They are not immortal. I think that society needs to take this responsibility—that if they had not wanted me, then I should have been placed in a foster home or adopted. I know disabled children who have been adopted by families who knew they were disabled children. What happens when my parents are no longer able to care for me? At the moment it concerns me greatly because there are no other facilities available. Whether or not I would be financially able to live independently and hire someone to help me is questionable.

ROY BONISTEEL: Well, you asked what my reaction was to you. You suggested that one should wait and interact with a person making up

one's mind and not have any assumptions. I had an idea of what you
were going to be like, so that did not bother me when I first met you,
but I ~~~~ what you would say or how you would respond or how
~~~~ You said earlier in the interview that you certainly
~~~~ person. I would like to contradict that. I think you
~~~~ person. Thank you very much for coming on our

[handwritten margin note: In neonatology, is a serious ? is the extent to which this baby can become fully integrated]

Thank you.

NOTE

...plegic woman filed suit seeking to prevent a hospital from force-feeding her. Elizabeth Bouvia, 26, a cerebral palsy victim, who has earned a bachelor's degree in social work, had refused food for three weeks. Prior to entering
the hospital for a checkup, she had been living on her own. She was estranged
from her mother and her husband, with whom she had lived for one month.
"Mrs. Bouvia said she did not want her father to take on the burden of caring for
her, did not want to spend the rest of her life in a hospital or convalescent home
and had realized she could not live independently." New York Times, Oct. 30,
1983 at A38, col. 1. According to her lawyer she cannot feed herself and apparently has no control over body movements. Washington Post, Nov. 4, 1983 at
A1, col. 4. Her request was denied. Judge John H. Hews, a California Superior
Court judge, ruled that Ms. Bouvia "does have a fundamental . . . right to
terminate her own life . . . but that this right has been overcome by the
strong interest of the state and the society [for] preservation of life." Washington
Post, Dec. 17, 1983 at A3, col. 1. The Supreme Court of California upheld Judge
Hews's decision on January 19, 1984. Washington Post, Jan. 20, 1984 at A15,
col. 1. See Sec. B.3., supra.

ALBERT R. JONSEN,
ETHICS, THE LAW, AND THE TREATMENT OF
SERIOUSLY ILL NEWBORNS

in Legal and Ethical Aspects of Treating Critically and Terminally Ill Patients
236, 237–241 (A. Doudera and J. Peters, eds. 1982).

The law and ethics relative to the care of newborns are unexplored
territory. Like Mount Everest before Hillary and the explorers, there are
several high peaks but there are also many unknown crevices. The problem with ethics and law in neonatology is that lawyers and philosophers
have been looking at the peaks and have very little awareness of the crevices into which one can easily fall.

The reason for this limited view is that the issues which have reached
the courts deal with a certain kind of case which is not typical of the nursery's problems. The legal and philosophical discussions about withholding treatment from the defective or seriously ill newborn (the title under
which a veritable flood of articles has appeared during the last decade)
are almost exclusively devoted to two kinds of cases atypical to the everyday problems of neonatologists.

The first kind is the case of a child who, when born, is immediately
recognized to be suffering from Down Syndrome and is then diagnosed as
having a minor physical anomaly such as an intestinal obstruction, which
could be corrected surgically. The question is whether the child should
go to surgery for correction of the anomaly. Such a decision is not problematic in the ordinary child, but the issue becomes clouded when the
child has Down Syndrome. A number of these cases have reached the

courts in the form of a request for an order to operate, generally because the parents would not consent to the surgery. To my knowledge, the courts have granted such orders in every case.*

The second problem which has been discussed in the philosophical and legal literature as a typical case is posed by a child born with my-elomeningocele or spina bifida. Here a question is also asked about surgery: should the child's lesion be closed surgically to prevent imminent death from infection, even though the underlying problem will not be corrected? . . .**

The legal and philosophical discussions relative to neonatology are almost exclusively devoted to these two kinds of cases. In both, there is the question over a surgical intervention for the immediate saving of the child's life (as in the Down child with duodenal atresia) or to protect the child from a life-threatening infection (as in spina bifida). This problem has captured the attention of commentators. . . . [Y]et I have never found any mention of the problem which is the most prominent in the nursery. There is an entire area of pediatrics which is not cited in these legal articles, and because there is no mention of the prominent problem, the legal analysis of neonatology misses the point.

The dominant problem in the newborn nursery is prematurity: children born prematurely and of low birthweight, usually defined as less than 38 weeks of gestation and below 2500 grams (about 5½ lbs.). Their primary problem is that their lungs are not yet mature enough to breathe from the ambient air, resulting in severe deprivation of oxygen and subsequent acute and chronic lung disease. While prematurity causes a variety of problems, respiratory problems and their consequences are the most serious. At present, about 200,000 infants pass through neonatal intensive care units each year in the United States. Of these 200,000, about 75,000 suffer from the problems attending prematurity and 25,000 of these will die from respiratory diseases even with the best care. Contrast this with the approximately 5000 babies born each year with spina bifida, and the very small proportion of the 3000 or so Down Syndrome babies who require life-saving surgery. Simply in terms of numbers, the children with respiratory disease are the dominant problem in the nursery, and this sort of child poses the most agonizing and difficult questions.

The peculiar ethical and legal problems facing the neonatologist can be summed up by describing three particular issues. The first is the nature of prematurity and of intensive care for the premature. The premature infant is essentially unfinished. It is not ready to face the challenge of the new environment into which it is untimely thrust. The last two or three weeks in the womb are very important in the development and intergration of an organ system ready to meet the world. This is particularly so with the premature lung, but it is true of the fetus' entire organ system. Basically, it suffers from a problem of incomplete integration when it comes into the world. The intensive care brought to bear upon the premature infant allows time for its organ systems to begin to function in an integrated manner. For the premature, the question is how long do we keep trying in order to see whether this unfinished organ sys-

---

* But see In re Infant Doe, No. GU 8204-00 (Cir.Ct. Monroe Cty., Ind., Apr. 12, 1982), writ of mandamus dismissed sub. nom., State ex rel. Infant Doe v. Baker, No. 482–S–140 (Ind.Sup.Ct., May 27, 1982). [Eds.]

** In this regard, see Weber v. Stony Brook Hospital, 60 N.Y.2d 208, 469 N.Y. S.2d 63, 456 N.E.2d 1186 (1983), cert. denied — U.S. —, 104 S.Ct. 560, 78 L.Ed.2d 732 (1983), and United States v. University Hospital, infra. [Eds.]

tem will get going on its own. The question of "how long" is indicative
of the particular sort of questions asked about the neonate.

The second issue is directly related to the first. I call it by a horrendous title: endemic iatrogenicity. Iatrogenic problems are those caused
by the doctor. Any kind of physical intervention into the body for the
sake of healing has side effects which can harm. In some cases, iatrogenic harm is the result of negligence. However, a great deal of iatrogenic
harm has nothing to do with negligence, but simply with the very nature
of an intervention into the physical body, either with drugs or with a
knife. In neonatology, iatrogenicity is epidemic because an organism that
is not yet finished has a peculiar vulnerability. Introducing powerful
agents like drugs and oxygen into the newborn organism can do severe
damage. The most dramatic instance of iatrogenicity occurred some 25
or 30 years ago in the early days of pediatric intensive care, when the first
attempts were made to tide over the premature newborn by administration of oxygen. It was slowly recognized that such massive administration
of oxygen appeared to cause blindness in many of these newborns. It
was a shock to realize that this life-giving element was dangerous. Since
oxygen must be used for the premature newborn, it is used now with particular care. However, this discovery illustrates that the help given to the
newborn during this period of crisis can be dangerous in itself.

One organ which is particularly vulnerable to the kinds of insults that
can arise, both from the intervention and from the general nature of prematurity, is the brain. The brain of the premature infant can be damaged, sometimes severely, while the rest of the immature organs get pulled together fairly well. The lungs can heal, the kidneys begin to
function, but often the insult to the to the brain is irreversible. While the
baby may be pulled through this period of nonintegration, a severe gap
may be left in the organ we esteem most highly in our culture: the brain.
The result of intensive care, therefore, may be a person who becomes
mature enough in the lungs and in the heart, but who never develops
intellectually. That poses a very serious problem in neonatology.

The third issue follows directly from the nature of the premature infant. I call it prognostic perplexity. It is the very nature of medicine to
make a prognosis. A diagnosis is nothing but the first step in prognosis.
Prognosis is difficult in all areas of medicine, although much of it has
become second nature because certain diseases are familiar to the practitioner and have well-known courses. In neonatology however, prognosis
is extraordinarily difficult. The future course of a child may be cloudy
because as he or she grows, many new factors must be considered. The
immediate prognosis for the next day or the next week is rather difficult,
but no more difficult than in intensive care generally. However, long-
term prognosis is extremely difficult in neonatology, particularly with the
child who has suffered an insult to the brain. For example, although a
terrible intercerebral hemorrhage may be diagnosed in the third or fourth
day of a child's life, at age five the child may be acting quite normally.
But another child with a hemorrhage of the same size and in the same
place may become severely retarded. While there may be some agreement, there is a great deal of uncertainty and disagreement about the
prognosis of future development of premature newborns.

These three issues—the nature of the premature infant and the nature
of intensive care for the premature infant, iatrogenicity, and prognostic
perplexity—leave us in a strange and unfamiliar place in regard to the
law. Articles seeking to represent the state of the law to the neonatolo-

gist are, I find, deficient and perhaps unduly threatening. For example, John Robertson's article in the Journal of Pediatrics exposes the theoretical liability in great detail.[3] In fact, the article might be subtitled, "57 Ways in Which a Physician Can Become a Felon." Every possibility for the physician to step off the very small ground of legality is detailed. Professor Robertson asserts that the physician must provide extraordinary and ordinary care, but notes that since it has not been tested legally, the distinction is unclear and the final result uncertain. He concludes by saying that the "clearest and most indisputable grounds for withholding care must exist" if liability is to be avoided. However, he fails to recognize that the clearest and most indisputable grounds will never exist in the most difficult cases, which are intrinsically unclear and very disputable.

The questions posed to conscientious neonatologists are: to what extent they should try to treat and how extreme the deficiencies in the neonate are. Since these are questions of contingent facts and guesses, there are no rules to answer them. The experiences of other neonatologists, to whom one might look for answers, are often not well correlated. Further, each year we see improvements in the science of neonatology, but the disagreements still exist. Assessments of children who were treated five years ago cannot be applied to current neonatology because the technology has changed so dramatically. Thus, the neonatologist's judgment is one of contingent fact and depends little on science. It is a "judgment call"—an informed guess based on one's own experience and on what can be learned from one's colleagues. The law review articles, however, ask for clear criteria for withholding care from newborns, failing to realize that such legal standards of care are not clinically realistic. The standard of practice of other physicians in the community has come under a great deal of criticism, and although recent court decisions have modified that standard in other areas, the old standard is still used in neonatology: the physician's best judgment in accordance with the best standards of practice either in the medical community generally or in the subspecialty of neonatology.

A second problem is the parents' role in making treatment decisions for their seriously ill neonate. About 10 years ago, Dr. Raymond Duff started much of the debate about neonatology by publishing a very frank article in the New England Journal of Medicine, in which he acknowledged that he lets babies die in his nursery. This caused a great deal of concern to everyone who did not know what went on in nurseries. Dr. Duff continues to assert that the decision must be the parents'. In his view, the physician should inform the parents and then the parents should decide whether or not to continue treatment. This approach, in fact, is advocated by many people when discussing the withdrawing or withholding of life-sustaining treatment from incompetent patients. In neonatology, this still remains a serious ethical problem. If the criterion or standard to be followed is the medical one—the physician's best judgment about whether or not this baby can be fully integrated—then no one but a neonatologist should attempt to use the criterion and make that decision. If society turns the decision over to the parents, saying, "You make up your own mind," we risk the possibility that decisions will be made on irrelevant grounds or inappropriate motives. If we permit families to

3. [Robertson and Fost,] Passive Euthanasia of Defective Newborns, [58 J. Pediatrics 883 (1976)]. Also see Robertson, Legal Aspects of Withholding Medical Treatment from Handicapped Children, [in Legal and Ethical Aspects of Treating Critically and Terminally Ill Patients 213 (Doudera and Peters, eds. 1982).]

make these decisions, then we must confront a problem of values which is unsettled in our society: to whom does the infant belong? What are the roles of the family and of society? Can or should parents decide if their seriously ill newborn will live or die? As I said, we do not have answers, only unsettled problems of values that need discussion and debate.

I will conclude by suggesting that as long as neonatologists are told by lawyers that their exposure to both civil and criminal liability is great (which is probably theoretically true), then the decisions in the nursery will be inappropriately made. This threat of liability arises from an unsuitable analysis; that is, the wrong kinds of cases have been used to develop the legal analysis. I think the courts have correctly responded, in both legal and ethical terms by ordering the surgery and thereby saving the life of the Down child with duodenal atresia. To decide otherwise simply because the child has Down Syndrome is discriminatory and barbaric. But, to apply that thinking to the daily problems of decision making in the nursery is inappropriate. An inappropriate analysis will not only lead to inappropriate conclusions, but will also inhibit the development of a legal and ethical analysis more appropriate to the peculiar problems faced by those who dare to try to finish a job unfinished by nature: to make the premature baby live and live well.

UNITED STATES v. UNIVERSITY HOSPITAL

United States Court of Appeals, Second Circuit, 1984.
729 F.2d 144.

PRATT, CIRCUIT JUDGE:

This expedited appeal presents the question whether Section 504 of the Rehabilitation Act of 1973, as amended, 29 U.S.C. § 794 (Supp. V 1981), and one of its implementing regulations, 45 C.F.R. § 84.61 (1982) (incorporating 45 C.F.R. § 80.6(c) (1982)), authorize the United States Department of Health and Human Services (HHS) to obtain access to medical records maintained by defendant University Hospital concerning a seriously deformed newborn infant, identified only as Baby Jane Doe, whose parents have refused to consent to certain surgical procedures necessary to prolong the infant's life. The United States District Court for the Eastern District of New York (Leonard D. Wexler, Judge) ruled that HHS was not entitled to the records and entered summary judgment in favor of University Hospital. For the reasons set forth below, we affirm.

I.

Baby Jane Doe was born on October 11, 1983 at St. Charles Hospital in Port Jefferson, New York. She was suffering from multiple birth defects, the most serious of which were myelomeningocele, commonly known as spina bifida, a condition in which the spinal cord and membranes that envelop it are exposed; microcephaly, an abnormally small head; and hydrocephalus, a condition characterized by an accumulation of fluid in the cranial vault. In addition, she exhibited a "weak face", which prevents the infant from closing her eyes or making a full suck with her tongue; a malformed brain stem; upper extremity spasticity; and a thumb entirely within her fist.

As a result of the spina bifida, the baby's rectal, bladder, leg, and sensory functions were impaired. Due to the combination of microcephaly and hydrocephalus, there was an extremely high risk that the child would be so severely retarded that she could never interact with her environment or with other people.

At the direction of the first pediatric neurosurgeon to examine her, the baby was immediately transferred to University Hospital for dual surgery to correct her spina bifida and hydrocephalus. Essentially, this would entail excising a sac of fluid and nerve endings on the spine and closing the opening, and implanting a shunt to relieve pressure caused by fluid build-up in the cranial cavity. The record indicates that these dual, corrective surgical procedures were likely to prolong the infant's life, but would not improve many of her handicapping conditions, including her anticipated mental retardation.

After consulting with several physicians, nurses, religious advisors, a social worker, and members of their family, the parents of the baby decided to forego the corrective surgery. Instead, they opted for a "conservative" medical treatment consisting of good nutrition, the administration of antibiotics, and the dressing of the baby's exposed spinal sac.

Litigation surrounding Baby Jane Doe began on October 16, when A. Lawrence Washburn, Jr., a Vermont attorney unrelated to the child and her family, commenced a proceeding in New York State Supreme Court seeking appointment of a guardian *ad litem* for the child and an order directing University Hospital to perform the corrective surgery. The court appointed William E. Weber as guardian *ad litem* and held an evidentiary hearing on October 19 and 20 to determine whether Baby Jane Doe was "in need of immediate surgical procedures to preserve her life". Following the hearing, at which University Hospital and the parents of the child were represented, the court concluded that surgery was necessary and ordered that it be performed.

One day later the Appellate Division of the New York Supreme Court reversed the decision of the trial court and dismissed the proceeding. The Appellate Division found that the "concededly concerned and loving parents have made an informed, intelligent, and reasonable determination based upon and supported by responsible medical authority." As the court elaborated:

> The record confirms that the failure to perform the surgery will not place the infant in imminent danger of death, although surgery might significantly reduce the risk of infection. On the other hand, successful results could also be achieved with antibiotic therapy. Further, while the mortality rate is higher where conservative medical treatment is used, in this particular case the surgical procedures also involved a great risk of depriving the infant of what little function remains in her legs, and would also result in recurring urinary tract and possibly kidney infections, skin infections and edemas of the limbs.

Thus, the Appellate Division determined that the parents' decision was in the best interest of the infant and that there was, therefore, no basis for judicial intervention.

On October 28, the New York Court of Appeals affirmed the decision of the Appellate Division, relying on different grounds. Since the petitioner had no direct interest in or relationship to any party and had failed to contact the State Department of Social Services, which has primary responsibility under New York law for initiating child neglect proceedings, and since the trial court also had failed to seek that department's investigative assistance, the Court of Appeals found "no precedent or authority" for the proceeding. Accordingly, the Court of Appeals ruled that the trial court had abused its discretion by permitting the proceeding to go forward.

While the state court proceedings were still in progress, the federal government entered the picture. On October 19, HHS received a complaint from an unidentified "private citizen" that Baby Jane Doe was being discriminatorily denied medically indicated treatment on the basis of her handicaps. HHS referred the complaint to the New York State Child Protection Services, the state agency specifically responsible for investigating suspected incidents of child abuse, mistreatment, and neglect. On November 7, that agency concluded that there was no cause for state intervention.

Meanwhile, HHS obtained a copy of the record of the state court proceedings, which contained the child's medical records through October 19. The record was forwarded to and personally reviewed by the Surgeon General of the United States, who determined, among other things, that:

> An appropriate determination concerning whether the current care of Infant Jane Doe is within the bounds of legitimate medical judgment, rather than based solely on a handicapping condition which is not a medical contraindication to surgical treatment, cannot be made without immediate access to, and careful review of, current medical records and other sources of information within the possession or control of the hospital.

Beginning on October 22, HHS repeatedly requested University Hospital to make available for inspection all of Baby Jane Doe's medical records since October 19. HHS based its authority to conduct an investigation on section 504 of the Rehabilitation Act, which provides in pertinent part that "[n]o otherwise qualified handicapped individual . . . shall, solely by reason of his handicap, . . . be subjected to discrimination under any program or activity receiving Federal financial assistance . . .". HHS further relied on 45 C.F.R. § 80.6(c), as incorporated by 45 C.F.R. § 84.61, which states:

> (c) *Access to sources of information.* Each recipient [of Federal financial assistance] shall permit access by the responsible Department official or his designee during normal business hours to such of its books, records, accounts, and other sources of information, and its facilities as may be pertinent to ascertain compliance with this part. . . . Asserted considerations of privacy or confidentiality may not operate to bar the Department from evaluating or seeking to enforce compliance with this part. . . .

University Hospital refused to honor HHS's requests, basing its decision in part on the refusal of the parents to release the records and in part on "serious concerns both as to the Department's jurisdiction and the procedures the Department has employed in initiating an inquiry."

The government then brought this action on November 2, alleging that University Hospital had violated section 504 and 45 C.F.R. § 80.6(c) by refusing to allow HHS access to information concerning the medical care and hospital services being rendered to Baby Jane Doe. After the parents had intervened as defendants, and after the district court had granted the government's request to expedite the proceedings, both the hospital and the parents moved to dismiss the complaint, arguing, among other things, that (1) congress did not intend section 504 to reach decisions regarding health care services provided to infants; (2) section 504 imposes no affirmative treatment obligations on the hospital beyond providing handicapped persons equal access to its facilities, which the hospital had done; (3) medicare and medicaid reimbursements do not constitute "Federal financial assistance" within the meaning of section 504; (4) Baby Jane Doe's medical records were protected from disclosure by both her and her parents' federal constitutional privacy rights; and (5) the failure of the federal government to intervene in the state court proceedings barred the instant action under the doctrine of laches. . . .

The government cross-moved for summary judgment, contending that HHS was entitled to the requested records because (1) the hospital's neonatal unit was a "recipient" of "Federal financial assistance" in the form of medicaid and (2) under 45 C.F.R. § 80.6(c) any such "recipient" was required to allow HHS access to information necessary to the discharge of the agency's statutory obligation to insure compliance with section 504.

Following oral argument on November 17, during which the government conceded that it had found no evidence of discrimination in the records covering the period through October 19, the district court ruled that defendants were entitled to summary judgment. The court first rejected defendants' claims that (1) the suit was barred by laches; (2) access to the records was barred by New York's physician-patient evidentiary privilege; and (3) medicare and medicaid do not constitute "Federal financial assistance" within the meaning of section 504. Further, the court ruled that the entire hospital, not just its neonatal unit, was the "program or activity" covered by the statute.

. . .

II.

. . .

. . . [W]hile the philosophical, social, and ethical implications of this case may be far-reaching, the precise issue presented for our review is one of statutory construction: Did congress intend section 504 to reach the conduct HHS seeks to investigate? If the investigation is within the scope of section 504, then HHS is entitled to access to Baby Jane Doe's medical records (unless they are protected from disclosure by some statutory or constitutional provision). On the other hand, if the investigation is beyond the scope of section 504, then the district court properly denied access.

III.

. . . [I]t is first necessary to examine the theory upon which the government predicates its request for the records under section 504. The theory rests on two premises. First, the government draws a distinction between decisionmaking based on a "bona fide medical judgment", which without definition it concedes to be beyond the reach of section 504, and decisionmaking based solely on an individual's handicap, which it argues is covered by section 504. Second, the government identifies Baby Jane Doe's microcephaly, which the record indicates will result in severe mental retardation, as the handicapping condition. From these premises, the government reasons that if a newborn infant suffering from spina bifida and hydrocephalus, but not microcephaly, would receive treatment or services that differ from those provided to an infant suffering from all three defects, or alternatively, if the hospital would seek a state court order compelling surgery in the former case, but not in the latter, then a violation of section 504 would have been established. Without the requested records, the government concludes, it is impossible to determine whether any such unlawful discrimination has occurred here, at least after October 19.

A.

. . . [W]e . . . assume, without deciding, that the district judge properly determined both that the hospital was a recipient of "Federal financial assistance" within the meaning of the statute, and that the "program or activity" to which the statute applies, if at all, is the entire hospital. Were we forced to confront these unsettled questions, ... summary judgment could not properly be granted in favor of either side at this juncture. Far from being undisputed, many of the material facts bearing on those issues have simply not been developed in the record.
. . . .

. . . .

Given an understandable desire on both sides to resolve this dispute expeditiously, however, we are reluctant to remand the case to the district court for further factual development on these important issues. In the interest of justice, we shall therefore bypass them and proceed directly to the dispositive question whether, assuming the entire hospital is covered by section 504, the statute authorizes the type of investigation initiated here.

B.

While the question whether section 504 authorizes HHS to investigate medical treatment decisions involving defective newborn infants is technically one of first impression, we do not write on an entirely clean slate. The regulatory history of the statute reveals that the question has already received considerable attention.

In its original notice of intent to issue proposed rules under section 504, published in May 1976, HHS's predecessor, the Department of Health, Education and Welfare (HEW), requested comment on fifteen "critical issues", see 41 Fed.Reg. 29548, including "[w]hether a regulation should contain provisions concerning [institutionalized] patients' rights to receive or refuse treatment . . .". 41 Fed.Reg. 20296 at 20297. Subsequently, in a July 1976 notice of proposed rulemaking, HEW indicated that it had received several comments urging "that the department did *not* have authority to regulate in this area" (emphasis added). 41 Fed.Reg. 29548 at 29559. HEW embraced this position, announcing that "[t]he Secretary is of the opinion that to promulgate rules on these subjects is beyond the authority of section 504." Id.

This limited view of the scope of section 504 was reflected in the first set of proposed regulations promulgated by HEW. The applicable provision, the proposed version of 45 C.F.R. § 84.52, emphasized the *"[a]vailability of services"* to handicapped persons and required that services be made "accessible" through use of methods such as "making house calls, referring patients, arranging to meet patients in accessible facilities, and modifying facilities." 41 Fed.Reg. at 29567 (emphasis in original).

Notwithstanding comments that its proposed health services regulation "lacks specificity", 42 Fed.Reg. at 22693, in its final section 504 regulations, issued in May 1977, HEW created a general "Health, welfare, and other social services" provision, 45 C.F.R. § 84.52, which emphasizes "the basic requirement of equal opportunity to receive benefits . . .". 45 C.F.R., Part 84, Appendix A, ¶ 36.   The agency did, however, also offer more specific guidance on the nature of the nondiscrimination requirement imposed by the regulation:

> One common misconception about the regulation is that it would require specialized hospitals and other health care providers to treat all handicapped persons. The regulation makes no such requirement. Thus, a burn treatment center need not provide other types of medical treatment to handicapped persons unless it provides such medical services to nonhandicapped persons. It could not, however, refuse to treat the burns of a deaf person because of his or her deafness.

Id.

It was not until five years later that HHS first took the position that section 504 made it unlawful for hospitals receiving "Federal financial assistance" to withhold nutrition, or medical, or surgical treatment from handicapped infants if required to correct a life-threatening condition. See American Academy of Pediatrics v. Heckler, 561 F.Supp. 395, 397 (D.D.C.1983) (describing the circumstances leading to this shift in agency policy). This new position was reflected in a "notice . . . to remind affected parties of the applicability of section 504 of the Rehabilitation Act of 1973", dated May 18, 1982 and published on June 16, 1982. 47 Fed.Reg. 26027.   In the notice, HHS "recognize[d] that recipients of Federal financial assistance may not have full control over the treatment of handicapped patients when, for instance, parental consent has been refused." Id.   Nevertheless, referring to 45 C.F.R. § 84.4(b)(1)(v), which provides that a recipient may not aid or perpetuate discrimination by significantly assisting the discriminatory actions of another person, the notice admonished that:

> • Counseling of parents should not discriminate by encouraging parents to make decisions which, if made by the health care provider, would be discriminatory under section 504.

> • Health care providers should not aid a decision by the infant's parents or guardian to withhold treatment or nourishment discriminatorily by allowing the infant to remain in the institution.

Id.

Nearly a year after this notice was published, in March 1983, HHS issued an interim final rule "to meet the exigent needs that can arise when a handicapped infant is discriminatorily denied food or other medical care." 48 Fed.Reg. 9630. This "novel and far-reaching" regulation, American Academy of Pediatrics v. Heckler, 561 F.Supp. at 397, would have required "each recipient that provides covered health services to infants" to display posters in conspicuous places "in each delivery ward, each maternity ward, each pediatric ward, and each nursery, including each intensive care nursery" declaring that "DISCRIMINATORY FAILURE TO FEED AND CARE FOR HANDICAPPED INFANTS IN THIS FACILITY IS PROHIBITED BY FEDERAL LAW". 48 Fed.Reg. at 9631, amending 45 C.F.R. § 84.61. The interim regulation also established a confidential "Handicapped Infant Hotline", "[a]vailable 24 hours a day", which "*[a]ny person having knowledge that a handicapped infant is being discriminatorily denied food or customary medical care should immediately contact*" (emphasis in original). Id. Further, the regulation stated that the required access to records "shall not be limited to normal business hours when, in the judgment of the responsible Department official, immediate access is necessary to protect the life or health of a handicapped individual." Id.

The preamble to the interim rule made clear that HHS believed it could conduct immediate investigations and make immediate referrals to the Department of Justice for appropriate legal action. 48 Fed.Reg. at 9631. However, without eschewing "a vigorous federal role in enforcing the federal civil rights at issue", it also indicated that "[t]he Secretary intends to rely heavily on the voluntary cooperation of State and local agencies, which are closest to the scene of violations, and which have traditionally played the key role in the investigation of complaints of child abuse and neglect." Id. at 9630.

On April 14, 1983, this interim final rule was struck down by the United States District Court for the District of Columbia. American Academy of Pediatrics v. Heckler, supra. In a thorough and informative opinion, Judge Gesell held that the regulation failed to satisfy the requirements of the Administrative Procedure Act, 5 U.S.C. § 551 et seq. (1982), in two respects. First, since the rulemaking record indicated the regulation was a product of "haste and inexperience", 561 F.Supp. at 400, and that many relevant factors, including the scope of section 504, were not considered, the court ruled that the interim final rule was arbitrary and capricious under 5 U.S.C. § 706(2)(A). As the court explained:

> Government intervention into the difficult medical and human decisions that must be made in the delivery rooms and newborn intensive care units of our hospitals involves a profound change in the manner in which these decisions affecting the quality of life are made. Any intervention by an agency of the Federal Government should obviously reflect caution and sensitivity, given the present absence of a clear congressional directive.

561 F.Supp. at 403.

Second, the court ruled that the regulation was invalid due to the secretary's failure to follow the procedural requirements of 5 U.S.C. § 553(b) and (d). In this regard, Judge Gesell reasoned that the interim final rule could not properly be viewed as a restatement of preexisting law or policy, as the government had alleged:

> As [HHS's] counsel acknowledged in argument, the regulation is intended, among other things, to change the course of medical decision-making in these cases by eliminating the parents' right to refuse to consent to life-sustaining treatment of their defective newborn. Moreover, the regulation provides for an intrusive on-premises enforcement mechanism that can be triggered by a simple anonymous call. Thus it clearly is more than a "clarification or explanation of an existing rule or statute" and affects substantive rights.

561 F.Supp. at 401 (footnote and citation omitted).

Following this decision, on July 5, 1983 HHS published a proposed rule in which the notice requirement was slightly revised, and a provision was added declaring that "... each recipient State child protective services agency shall establish and maintain written methods of administration and procedures to assure that the agency utilizes its full authority pursuant to State law to prevent instances of medical neglect of handicapped infants." 48 Fed.Reg. 30846 at 30851. In the appendix to the proposed rule, HHS listed several examples of decisions that would, in its view, constitute violations of section 504. These included:

> (3) Denial of treatment for medically correctable physical anomalies in children born with Spina Bifida, when such denial is based on anticipated mental impairment, paralysis, or incontinence of such child, rather than on reasonable medical judgments that treatment would be futile or too unlikely of success given complications in the particular case.

Id. at 30852.

More recently, on January 12, 1984, after oral argument of this appeal, HHS issued its "final rules on procedures and guidelines relating to non-discrimination on the basis of handicap in connection with health care for handicapped infants." 49 Fed.Reg. 1622. These final rules modified the proposed rules in several major respects. Id. For example, HHS adopted the recommendation of several commenters [sic] that the federal government encourage, but not require, hospitals to establish Infant Care Review Committees "to assist the health care provider in the development of standards, policies and procedures for providing treatment to handicapped infants and in making decisions concerning medically beneficial treatment in specific cases." 45 C.F.R. § 84.55(a), 49 Fed.Reg. 1651; see id. at 1623–25. These committees are not, however, designed to be substitutes for mechanisms to enforce section 504. Id. at 1624.

Under the final rules, the notice requirement is also significantly modified. Among other things, the final rules require only that the notice be posted

> at location(s) where nurses and other medical professionals who are engaged in providing health care and related services to infants will see it. To the extent it does not impair accomplishment of the requirement that copies of the notice be posted where such personnel will see it, the notice need not be posted in area(s) where parents of infant patients will see it.

45 C.F.R. § 84.55(b)(2), 49 Fed.Reg. 1651.

In sum, the regulatory history of section 504 is inconclusive. HHS's current view of the scope of the statute is flatly at odds with the position originally taken by HEW. Notwithstanding HHS's claims to the contrary, see 49 Fed.Reg. at 1635, the current view also represents something of a retreat from the interpretation HHS adopted just last year. In determining whether congress intended section 504 to apply to treatment decisions involving defective newborn infants, we therefore lack the benefit of an administering agency's longstanding, consistent interpretation to which we otherwise might have looked for guidance.

C.

With this unsettled regulatory background in mind, we turn to the statutory language, which is fundamental to any issue of statutory construction. Section 504 provides in pertinent part as follows:

> No otherwise qualified handicapped individual in the United States, as defined in section 706(7) of this title, shall, solely by reason of his handicap, be excluded from the participation in, be denied the benefits of, or be subjected to discrimination under any program or activity receiving Federal financial assistance.

Under 29 U.S.C. § 706(7)(B), "the term 'handicapped individual' means . . . any person who (i) has a physical or mental impairment which substantially limits one or more of such person's major life activities, (ii) has a record of such an impairment, or (iii) is regarded as having such an impairment."

The initial inquiry is whether Baby Jane Doe is properly considered a "handicapped individual" within the meaning of section 706(7). The issue is not as simple as it first seems. While there can be no question that Baby Jane Doe currently suffers from "physical or mental impairments", see 45 C.F.R. § 84.3(j)(2)(i), it is less clear whether these impairments substantially limit "major life activities".

Defendants and some of the *amici* contend that the phrase "major life activities", undefined in the Rehabilitation Act, should be interpreted to exclude newborn infants from the coverage of section 504. In support, they rely on congress's declaration in section 122(a)(1) of the Rehabilitation, Comprehensive Services, and Developmental Disabilities Amendments of 1978, Pub.L. No. 95–602, 92 Stat. 2984, codified at 29 U.S.C. § 701, that the purpose of the Rehabilitation Act "is to develop and implement, through research, training, services, and the guarantee of equal opportunity, comprehensive and coordinated programs of vocational rehabilitation and independent living." This purpose, they assert, is inapplicable to newborn infants, since: "By definition, such infants cannot be eligible for programs of employment, vocational rehabilitation or training. Indeed, no program of independent living can be seriously comprehended for any infant, let alone an infant who has a life-threatening disorder."

Further support for the view that section 504 does not apply to newborn infants can be found in the regulations HHS inherited from HEW. Under 45 C.F.R. § 84.3(j)(2)(ii), " 'Major life activities' means functions such as caring for one's self, performing manual tasks, walking, seeing, hearing, speaking, breathing, learning, and working." With or without corrective surgery, Baby Jane Doe's impairments unquestionably will substantially limit some of these functions in the future. However, the same cannot necessarily be said of the present, since newborn infants simply cannot perform many of these representative functions.

Notwithstanding this ambiguity in the phrase "major life activities", we hold that Baby Jane Doe falls within the definition of a "handicapped individual" in section 706(7)(B). The record indicates that Baby Jane Doe's rectal, bladder, leg, and sensory functions are all presently impaired. Further, the record suggests that, with or without corrective surgery, Baby Jane Doe will experience severe mental retardation for however long she lives. Absent any explicit indication in the statute or regulations that "major life activities" should be defined only with reference to adults, under these circumstances it would defy common sense to rule that she is not presently *regarded* as handicapped under section 706(7)(B)(iii).

Moreover, while congress may not have had handicapped children squarely in mind when it first formulated the definition of a "handicapped individual" in section 706(7)(B) in 1974, see infra, it has subsequently evinced its intent that such children receive at least some of the benefits of the Rehabilitation Act. In 1978, as part of the Rehabilitation, Comprehensive Services, and Developmental Disabilities Amendments of 1978, congress authorized the Director of the Interagency Committee on Handicapped Research to make grants for research into "services for preschool age handicapped children." Pub.L. No. 95–602, § 111, 92 Stat. 2967, codified at 29 U.S.C. § 762(11). The fact that congress recognized the needs of preschool age handicapped children in section 762(11) undercuts defendants' argument that, since the declared purpose of the entire Rehabilitation Act set forth in section 701 focuses on activities available only to adults, the "major life activities" referred to in section 706(7) should be similarly limited.

Having determined that Baby Jane Doe is a "handicapped individual" under section 706(7)(B), we next consider whether she possibly can be considered an "otherwise qualified" handicapped individual or to have been "subjected to discrimination" under section 504. These two issues are intertwined.

The leading cases construing the "otherwise qualified" criterion of section 504 have involved allegedly discriminatory denials of admission to certain educational programs. Southeastern Community College v. Davis, 442 U.S. 397 (1979); Doe v. New York University, 666 F.2d 761 (2d Cir. 1981). In that context, this court in Doe v. New York University recognized that:

> . . . it is now clear that [the phrase "otherwise qualified handicapped individual"] refers to a person who is qualified *in spite of* her handicap and that an institution is not required to disregard the disabilities of a handicapped applicant, provided the handicap is relevant to reasonable qualifications for acceptance, or to make substantial modifications in its reasonable standards or program to accommodate handicapped individuals but may take an applicant's handicap into consideration, along with all other relevant factors, in determining whether she is qualified for admission.

Id. at 775 (emphasis in original). Cf. 45 C.F.R. 84.3(k).

Doe establishes that section 504 prohibits discrimination against a handicapped individual only where the individual's handicap is unrelated to, and thus improper to consideration of, the services in question. As defendants here point out, however, where medical treatment is at issue, it is typically the handicap itself that gives rise to, or at least contributes to, the need for services. Defendants thus argue, and with some force, that the "otherwise qualified" criterion of section 504 cannot be meaningfully applied to a medical treatment decision. Similarly, defendants argue that it would be pointless to inquire whether a patient who was affected by a medical treatment decision was, "solely by reason of his handicap, . . . subjected to discrimination".

The government's answer to both these arguments is that Baby Jane Doe can be viewed as suffering from not one, but multiple handicaps. Indeed, the crux of the government's case is that her microcephaly is the operative handicap, and that the requested records are necessary to determine whether she has been discriminated against solely for that reason.

Despite its superficial logic, the government's theory is flawed in at least two respects. First, the government's view of "otherwise qualified" is divorced from the statutory language. As the mainstream of cases under section 504 exemplifies, the phrase "otherwise qualified" is geared toward relatively static programs or activities such as education, employment, and transportation systems. As a result, the phrase cannot be applied in the comparatively fluid context of medical treatment decisions without distorting its plain meaning. In common parlance, one would not ordinarily think of a newborn infant suffering from multiple birth defects as being "otherwise qualified" to have corrective surgery performed or to have a hospital initiate litigation seeking to override a decision against surgery by the infant's parents. If congress intended section 504 to apply in this manner, it chose strange language indeed.

Second, in arguing that Baby Jane may have been "subjected to discrimination" the government has taken an oversimplified view of the medical decisionmaking process. Where the handicapping condition is related to the condition(s) to be treated, it will rarely, if ever, be possible to say with certainty that a particular decision was "discriminatory". It is at this point that the analogy to race, relied on so heavily by the dissent, breaks down. Beyond the fact that no two cases are likely to be the same, it would invariably require lengthy litigation primarily involving conflicting expert testimony to determine whether a decision to treat, or not to treat, or to litigate or not to litigate, was based on a "bona fide medical judgment", however that phrase might be defined. Before ruling that congress intended to spawn this type of litigation under section 504, we would want more proof than is apparent from the face of the statute.

The legislative history, moreover, indicates that congress never contemplated that section 504 would apply to treatment decisions of this nature. . . . Each version of the legislation approved by congress contained a provision prohibiting discrimination against the handicapped by federal grantees. However, this provision, which had been closely patterned after Title VI of the Civil Rights Act of 1964 and Title IX of the Education Amendments of 1972, was never a matter of controversy. Consequently, there is little discussion of it in the volumes of legislative history that were generated.

.   .   .

Since the primary purpose of the 1973 legislation was to extend and expand the 53-year old federal-state vocational rehabilitation program, it is not surprising that congress initially defined the phrase "handicapped individual" in terms of employment:

> The term "handicapped individual" means any individual who (A) has a physical or mental disability which for such individual constitutes or results in a substantial handicap to employment and (B) can reasonably be expected to benefit in terms of employability from vocational rehabilitation services .   .   ..

Pub.L. No. 93–112, § 7(6), 87 Stat. 355, 361.

However, because "[i]t was clearly the intent of the Congress in adopting section 503 (affirmative action) and section 504 (nondiscrimination) that the term 'handicapped individual' in those sections was not to be narrowly limited to employment (in the case of section 504), nor to the individual's potential benefit from vocational rehabilitation services under titles I and III (in the case of both sections 503 and 504) of the Act", S.Rep. No. 1297, 93d Cong., 2d Sess., reprinted in [1974] U.S.Code Cong. & Ad.News 6373, 6388, congress expanded the definition to its current version, focusing on "major life activities", in the Rehabilitation Act Amendments of 1974, Pub.L. No. 93–516, § 111(a), 88 Stat. 1619. As the senate report accompanying the 1974 amendments elaborated:

> Thus, it was not intended that an employer-government contractor should condition its hiring of handicapped individuals under an affirmative action plan on such individuals' having benefitted, or having a reasonable expectation of benefitting, from vocational rehabilitation services. Similarly, a test of discrimination against a handicapped individual under section 504 should not be couched either in terms of

whether such individual's disability is a handicap to employment, or whether such individual can reasonably be expected to benefit, in terms of employment, from vocational rehabilitation services. Such a test is irrelevant to the many forms of potential discrimination covered by section 504.

Section 504 was enacted to prevent discrimination against all handicapped individuals, regardless of their need for, or ability to benefit from, vocational rehabilitation services, in relation to Federal assistance in employment, housing, transportation, education, health services, or any other Federally-aided programs. Examples of handicapped individuals who may suffer discrimination in receipt of Federally-assisted services but who may have been unintentionally excluded from the protection of section 504 by the references to enhanced employability in section 7(6) are as follows: physically or mentally handicapped children who may be denied admission to Federally-supported school systems on the basis of their handicap; handicapped persons who may be denied admission to Federally-assisted nursing homes on the basis of their handicap; those persons whose handicap is so severe that employment is not feasible but who may be denied the benefits of a wide range of Federal programs; and those persons whose vocational rehabilitation is complete but who may nevertheless be discriminated against in certain Federally-assisted activities.

S.Rep. No. 1297, supra at 6388–89.

This passage provides the best clue to congressional intent regarding section 504's coverage of "health services". As Judge Gesell noted in American Academy of Pediatrics v. Heckler, 561 F.Supp. at 401:

The legislative history . . . [on this subject] focuses on discrimination against adults and older children and denial of access to federal programs. As far as can be determined, no congressional committee or member of the House or Senate ever even suggested that section 504 would be used to monitor medical treatment of defective newborn infants or establish standards for preserving a particular quality of life. No medical group appeared alert to the intrusion into medical practice which some doctors apprehend from such an undertaking, nor were representatives of parents or spokesmen for religious beliefs that would be affected heard.

The post-enactment legislative history also indicates both that congress was primarily concerned with affording the handicapped access to federally-funded programs and activities, and that congress never envisioned that HEW (or HHS) would attempt to apply section 504 to treatment decisions. On April 28, 1977, the day the original set of final section 504 regulations were promulgated by HEW, then Secretary Califano sent congress an explanatory letter. After observing that the regulation "calls for dramatic changes in the actions and attitudes of institutions and individuals who are recipients of HEW funds", and "opens a new era of civil rights in America", Secretary Califano stated that "[i]n light of the limited legislative history, I think it especially important that Congress evaluate the regulation, and the implementation process, to ensure that they conform to the will of Congress." (letter reprinted in Hearings Before the Subcommittee on Select Education of the Committee on Education and Labor of the House of Representatives, 95th Cong., 1st Sess. 76 (hereinafter referred to as "Oversight Hearings")).

Thereafter, the House Subcommittee on Select Education conducted oversight hearings on the section 504 regulations in September 1977. During these hearings, the subcommittee heard testimony covering a wide range of topics from witnesses representing the federal government, state governments, education agencies, and organizations serving handicapped people. Throughout the hearings, the issue of program accessibility was a recurrent theme. See Oversight Hearings at 1 (remarks of Congressman Brademas) ("Central to the implementation of these regulations must be the realization that what handicapped people want is access to programs"); 36–37 (remarks of Thomas P. Carroll); 246 (remarks of Debbie Kaplan); 248 (remarks of Ralph Hotchkiss); 295, 358–59, 361 (remarks of David S. Tatel).

On the other hand, although several witnesses echoed Secretary Califano's remark that the newly-issued regulations ushered in a "new era" of civil rights for handicapped citizens, . . . at no point did any witness even remotely suggest that section 504 could or would be applied to treatment decisions involving defective newborn infants. . . .

We are aware, of course, that "[w]here the words and purpose of a statute plainly apply to a particular situation, . . . the fact that the specific application of the statute never occurred to Congress does not bar us from holding that the situation falls within the statute's coverage." United States v. Jones, 607 F.2d 269, 273 (9th Cir. 1979), cert. denied, 444 U.S. 1085 (1980). Here, however, the government's theory not only strains the statutory language but also goes well beyond congress's overriding concern with guaranteeing handicapped individuals access to programs or activities receiving federal financial assistance. Further, the situation in question is dramatically different in kind, not just in degree, from the applications of section 504 discussed in the legislative history. Under these circumstances, the failure of congress to focus on treatment decisions involving defective newborn infants strikes a telling blow to the government's position.

This void in the legislative history is conspicuous for another reason. Prior to the enactment of the Rehabilitation Act, congress had passed a number of measures limiting federal involvement in medical treatment decisions. For example, the very first section of the medicare law, first enacted in 1965, Pub.L. No. 89–97, § 102(a), 79 Stat. 291, codified at 42 U.S.C. § 1395, ironically one of the laws under which the government purports to exercise jurisdiction in this case, provides that "[n]othing in this subchapter shall be construed to authorize any Federal officer or employee to exercise any supervision or control over the practice of medicine or the manner in which medical services are provided . . . .". Similarly, when it enacted the Professional Standards Review Organization (PSRO) provisions of the Social Security Act in 1972, Pub.L. No. 92–603, § 249F(b), 86 Stat. 1429, codified at 42 U.S.C. § 1320c et seq., congress reiterated its view that determinations regarding the quality and appropriateness of medical treatment should not be undertaken by federal officials. See S.Rep. No. 1230, 92nd Cong., 2d Sess. 256–58 (1972); see also Public Citizen Health Research Group v. HEW, 668 F.2d 537, 542 (D.C.Cir. 1981).

In view of this consistent congressional policy against the involvement of federal personnel in medical treatment decisions, we cannot presume that congress intended to repeal its earlier announcements in the absence of clear evidence of congressional intent to do so. . . .

Along the same lines, we cannot presume that by enacting section 504, congress intended the federal government to enter the field of child care, which, as HHS has recently acknowledged, has traditionally been occupied by the states. See 49 Fed.Reg. 1626–27, 1629–31; 48 Fed.Reg. 9630. Had congress intended to displace state police power functions, it surely would have made that intention explicit.

Finally, case law construing section 504, while not directly on point, also suggests that the government's new interpretation of the statute exceeds the authority conferred by congress. In Southeastern Community College v. Davis, 442 U.S. 397 (1979), the Supreme Court emphasized that "[t]he language and structure of the Rehabilitation Act of 1973 reflect the recognition by Congress of the distinction between the even-handed treatment of qualified handicapped persons and affirmative efforts to overcome the disabilities caused by handicaps." Id. at 410. The Court concluded that "neither the language, purpose, nor history of § 504 reveals an intent to impose an affirmative-action obligation on all recipients of federal funds." Id. at 411. See American Public Transit Association v. Lewis, 655 F.2d 1272 (D.C.Cir. 1981), cf. Dopico v. Goldschmidt, 687 F.2d 644 (2d Cir. 1982).

In the present case, Baby Jane Doe has been treated in an evenhanded manner at least to the extent that the hospital has always been and remains willing to perform the dual, corrective surgeries if her parents would consent. Requiring the hospital either to undertake surgery notwithstanding the parents' decision or alternatively, to petition the state court to override the parents' decision, would impose a particularly onerous affirmative action burden upon the hospital. Cf. American Academy of Pediatrics v. Heckler, 561 F.Supp. at 402 ("section 504 was never intended by Congress to be applied blindly and without any consideration of the burdens and intrusions that might result").

IV.

. . . Our view of the legislative history has shown that congress never contemplated that section 504 of the Rehabilitation Act would apply to treatment decisions involving defective newborn infants when the statute was enacted in 1973, when it was amended in 1974, or at any subsequent time. Further, neither the articulated purposes of the statute, which concern access and admission to federally-funded programs and activities for otherwise qualified handicapped individuals, nor any fair and reasonable projections of those purposes, nor the applicable case law interpreting the statute, support the far-reaching position advanced by the government in this case.

"[G]iven the present absence of a clear congressional directive", American Academy of Pediatrics v. Heckler, 561 F.Supp. at 403, we agree with Judge Gesell that "[a]ny intervention by an agency of the Federal Government should obviously reflect caution and sensitivity". Id. We go one step further, however, and hold that under these circumstances it is congress, rather than an executive agency, that must weigh the competing interests at stake in this context in the first instance. Until congress has spoken, it would be an unwarranted exercise of judicial power to approve the type of investigation that has precipitated this lawsuit.

The judgment of the district court is therefore affirmed.

WINTER, CIRCUIT JUDGE, dissenting:

. . .

. . . The only ambiguity relevant to the present case, I respectfully suggest, is whether the hospital is such a recipient [of federal financial assistance] with regard to its obligations to Baby Jane Doe and not whether Section 504 includes the provision of medical services to handicapped infants.

. . . It hardly needs stating that the underlying issues brim with political and moral controversy and portend to extend the hand of the federal government into matters traditionally governed by an interaction of parental judgment and state authority. Were I able to conclude that Congress had no reason to address these issues in its consideration of Section 504, I would concur with the majority on the grounds that specific consideration by the Congress of this political and moral minefield would be appropriate before applying the statute as written.

However, such a conclusion is untenable since Section 504 is no first step into a hitherto uncharted legal wilderness. As the Senate Report stated:

> Section 504 was patterned after, and is almost identical to, the antidiscrimination language of section 601 of the Civil Rights Act of 1964, 42 U.S.C. 2000d–1 (relating to race, color, or national origin), and section 901 of the Education Amendments of 1972, 42 U.S.C. 1683 (relating to sex). The section therefore constitutes the establishment of a broad government policy that programs receiving Federal financial assistance shall be operated without discrimination on the basis of handicap.

S.Rep. No. 1297, 93d Cong., 2d Sess., reprinted in 1974 U.S.Code Cong. & Ad.News 6373, 6390. Section 504 was thus enacted against a background of well understood law which was explicitly designated as a guide to interpretation. Congress was persuaded that a handicapped condition is analogous to race and that, so far as the administration of federal financial assistance is concerned, discrimination on the basis of a handicap should be on statutory par with discrimination on the basis of race.

Once Section 504's legislative heritage is acknowledged, the "void" in the legislative history is eliminated and the many issues raised by defendants with regard to medical decisions, parental judgments and state authority simply evaporate. The government has never taken the position that it is entitled to override a medical judgment. Its position rather is that it is entitled under Section 504 to inquire whether a judgment in question is a *bona fide* medical judgment. While the majority professes uncertainty as to what that means, application of the analogy to race eliminates all doubt. A judgment not to perform certain surgery because a person is black is not a *bona fide* medical judgment. So too, a decision not to correct a life threatening digestive problem because an infant has Down's Syndrome is not a *bona fide* medical judgment. The issue of parental authority is also quickly disposed of. A denial of medical treatment to an infant because the infant is black is not legitimated by parental consent. Finally, once the legislative analogy to race is acknowledged, the intrusion on state authority becomes insignificant.

. . . Any doubt must stem not from a deficiency in the argument based on the analogy to Title VI of the Civil Rights Act but from a disagreement as to whether a handicapped condition is fully analogous to race. Whether that doubt is justified or not, however, courts are not the proper fora in which the reasonableness of the analogy to race is to be judged.

Selective refusals to be guided by precedents under Title VI of the Civil Rights Act are likely to lead to an incoherent body of interpretative law under Section 504. Ambiguity pervades the majority opinion as to exactly which services and which handicapped persons are excluded from the statute. All one can know for certain is that some medical services may be denied to some handicapped persons, without running afoul of Section 504. . . .

Also, I would respectfully suggest that we act outside our legitimate area of authority in declining to follow the path staked out by Title VI of the Civil Rights Act. Congress did not adopt the analogy to race merely as a legislative means to a policy goal but was persuaded and politically energized by the view that the analogy was correct. A judicial failure to follow the analogy where it leads is an outright disagreement with Congress' judgment and an unconstitutional act in itself.

Finally, we facilitate the democratic legislative process by applying the analogy to race as adopted by the Congress. A political temptation to avoid confrontations with issues of moral or prudential controversy is an inevitable aspect of legislative deliberations. If courts are perceived as ready to "correct" overbroad legislation, Congress will find it ever more tempting to avoid its responsibility to address and resolve the highly delicate issues which may lurk in seemingly unobjectionable legislative proposals. Rhetorical flourishes will be substituted for statutory precision and "voids" in legislative histories will be ever more frequent. This is particularly so in cases involving legislative analogies to race. The moral and legal successes of the civil rights movement have prompted many groups to seek legislation which puts a particular characteristic or condition on a legal par with race. So long as the courts are perceived to stand ready to consider tempering such legislation where it leads to controversial results, the path of least political resistance will always be for the Congress to avoid serious consideration of the actual consequences of legislating particular analogies to race. Only an apprehension that such legislative analogies will be enforced by courts as written can provide a counter incentive to induce Congress to address its legislative responsibilities.

II

I agree with that portion of the discussion in Part IIA of Judge Pratt's opinion which concludes that we cannot determine on the present record whether the defendant hospital is a recipient of "financial federal assistance" within the meaning of Section 504 and whether the "program or activity" to which that section applies is the entire hospital. I would, therefore, reverse and remand so that the record can be amplified. . . .

NOTES

1. Traditionally, the law has presumed that parents act with the best interests of their children in mind; consequently, we are very deferential to parental decisions about children and are reluctant to intervene. See, e.g., Wisconsin v. Yoder, 406 U.S. 205, 92 S.Ct. 1526, 32 L.Ed.2d 15 (1972); Pierce v. Society of Sisters, 268 U.S. 510, 45 S.Ct. 571, 69 L.Ed. 1070 (1925); Meyer v. Nebraska, 262 U.S. 390, 43 S.Ct. 625, 67 L.Ed. 1042 (1923). This deference, however, has never been absolute. Prince v. Massachusetts, 321 U.S. 158, 64 S.Ct. 438, 88 L.Ed. 2d 645 (1944). Where it can be shown that parents have abused or neglected their children or where there is substantial reason to believe that they will do so, the state acting under its *parens patriae* powers can intervene.

With respect to health care matters, courts have intervened and ordered life-saving treatment over parental objection. See, e.g., In re Hamilton, 657 S.W.2d 425 (Tenn.App.1983); State v. Perricone, 37 N.J. 463, 181 A.2d 751, certiorari denied 371 U.S. 890, 83 S.Ct. 189, 9 L.Ed.2d 124 (1962); People ex rel. Wallace v. Labrenz, 411 Ill. 618, 104 N.E.2d 769, certiorari denied 344 U.S. 824, 73 S.Ct. 24, 97 L.Ed. 642 (1952); Maine Medical Center v. Houle, No. 74–145 (Super.Ct., Cumberland Cty., Me., Feb. 14, 1974). Courts traditionally have been reluctant, however, to intervene where life is not in imminent danger. See, e.g., In re Seiferth, 309 N.Y. 80, 127 N.E.2d 820 (1955); In re Phillip B., 92 Cal.App.3d 796, 156 Cal.Rptr. 48 (1979); In re Hofbauer, 65 A.D.2d 108, 411 N.Y.S.2d 416 (1978), affirmed 47 N.Y.2d 648, 419 N.Y.S.2d 936, 393 N.E.2d 1009 (1979). This reluctance is perhaps explained by the fact that it has been difficult to distinguish these parental decisions from a number of other decisions parents are allowed to make about education, religion and discipline which may also adversely affect the future growth and development of the child.

This is not to suggest that the traditional legal line has always been a satisfactory one. In those instances where the judgment of the relevant medical community is that a child's physical health will be seriously impaired and cannot be satisfactorily treated at a later time, courts have increasingly intervened to order treatment even where life is not in imminent danger. See, e.g., In re Sampson, 65 Misc.2d 658, 317 N.Y.S.2d 641 (1970), affirmed 29 N.Y.2d 900, 328 N.Y.S.2d 686, 278 N.E.2d 918 (1972); Custody of a Minor, 375 Mass. 733, 379 N.E.2d 1053 (1978); Matter of Jensen, 54 Or.App. 1, 633 P.2d 1302 (1981).

If courts have been so consistent in ordering lifesaving treatment for children over parental objection, why then have we spent the last decade or more debating questions concerning appropriate care for newborns with congenital disabilities who need lifesaving treatment? One explanation is that the behavior of health care professionals and parents at times has been at odds with legal standards and not subject to judicial review. Several surveys of physicians have indicated their willingness to withhold treatment in accordance with parental wishes where children suffering from Down's syndrome needed operative care. See, e.g., Treating the Defective Newborn: A Survey of Physicians' Attitudes, 6 Hastings Ctr.Rep. 2 (1976); Shaw, Randolph, and Manard, Ethical Issues in Pediatric Surgery: A National Survey of Pediatricians and Pediatric Surgeons, 60 Pediatrics 588 (1977); Todres et al., Pediatricians' Attitudes Affecting Decisionmaking in Defective Newborns, 60 Pediatrics 197 (1977).

In addition, we have come to realize that decisions about appropriate medical care for the majority of disabled newborns, particularly those born prematurely, involve more than the issue of whether lifesaving operative treatment should be given. The decisions are extremely complex because prognosis is uncertain and adverse consequences may result from the treatment as well as the underlying condition.

In such circumstances who makes decisions for the child is of great importance. Are parents best situated to make medical care decisions about newborns? Will they be able to disregard considerations such as costs, concerns for family stability and impact on siblings? Should they? Will they be able to overcome their own sense of guilt or loss that the birth of a seriously ill infant may cause when they expected a normal child? Should we favor parental decisionmaking but make the decisions subject to review and careful monitoring? If review is desirable, what form should it take? Should monitoring be done at an institutional level or is governmental involvement desirable?

2. In April 1982, "Baby Doe," a newborn male with Down's syndrome and a blocked esophagus, was allowed to die with court approval after his parents refused treatment. In re Infant Doe, No. GU 8204–00 (Cir.Ct. Monroe Cty., Ind., Apr. 12, 1982), writ of mandamus dismissed sub nom. State ex rel. Infant Doe v. Baker, No. 482 S 140 (Indiana Supreme Court, May 27, 1982). Efforts to seek United States Supreme Court review were mooted because the child died. The records in this case are sealed so some pertinent facts are not available. For a

description of the medical circumstances, see Correspondence, 309 New Eng.J. Med. 664 (1983).

The public outcry surrounding this incident was so intense that on April 30, 1982, President Ronald Reagan sent a memorandum to the Attorney General and the Secretary of Health and Human Services (HHS) citing the "Baby Doe" case and noting that federal law prohibits discrimination against the handicapped. In response, HHS issued on May 18, 1982, the "notice" to health care providers to "remind affected parties of the applicability of § 504 of the Rehabilitation Act of 1973" that was discussed in United States v. University Hospital, supra.

3. The President's Commission concluded that hospitals that care for seriously ill newborns should have explicit policies on decisionmaking procedures in cases involving life-sustaining treatment for seriously ill newborns. Deciding to Forego Life-Sustaining Treatment at 227. The Commission recommended that such decisions be made by reviewing panels:

> Such policies should provide for internal review whenever parents and the attending physician decide that life-sustaining therapy should be foregone. Other cases, such as when the physician and parents disagree, might well also be reviewed. The policy should allow for different types of review and be flexible enough to deal appropriately with the range of cases that could arise. Some cases may require only a medical consultant to confirm a diagnosis of an inevitably fatal condition, for example. In other cases, when the benefits of therapy are less clear, an "ethics committee" or similar body might be designated to review the decisionmaking process. This approach would ensure that an individual or group whose function is to promote good decisionmaking reviews the most difficult cases. Cases included in this category should certainly encompass those in which a decision to forego life-sustaining therapy has been proposed because of a physical or mental handicap, as well as cases where a dispute has arisen among care givers and surrogates over the proper course of treatment . . . .
>
> Insofar as possible, infants' lives should be sustained long enough to gather the best information and to permit expeditious review. When the parents and physicians feel justified in acting without either or both of these conditions, as might happen with a rapidly deteriorating medical status, retrospective review should be undertaken.

Id. at 227–228.

The Commission expressly rejected the imposition of financial sanctions, which the federal regulations issued under § 504 of the Rehabilitation Act of 1973 provide, but also questioned the efficacy of its own recommendations inasmuch as such internal review of the decisionmaking process has remained largely untried. Id. at 228.

A number of individuals and professional medical organizations were firmly opposed to the revised proposed rule. See, e.g., Strain, Special Report, The American Academy of Pediatrics comments on the "Baby Doe II" Regulation, 309 New Eng.J.Med. 443 (1983); Angell, Handicapped Children: Baby Doe and Uncle Sam, 309 New Eng.J.Med. 659 (1983); Weir, The Government and Selective Nontreatment of Handicapped Infants, 309 New Eng.J.Med. 661 (1983). By contrast a number of child advocacy groups support the basic thrust of the revised proposed rule and object only to the method of enforcement. Holden, HHS Preparing to Issue New Baby Doe Rules, 221 Science 1269 (1983). The American Medical Association, several other medical organizations and individual physicians have brought suit against the United States seeking to declare invalid and to enjoin permanently enforcement of final rules on "Procedures and Guidelines Relating to Health Care for Handicapped Infants" that HHS issued on January 12, 1984 and which became effective on February 13, 1984. Washington Post, Mar. 13, 1984, at A13, col. 3. Plaintiffs' allegations in their complaint included the argument that the rules are invalid under the holding in *University Hospital.* On May 23, 1984, the court entered a memorandum order holding the final rules invalid.

American Hospital Association v. Heckler, ___ F.Supp. ___ (D.N.Y.1984); American Hospital Association v. Heckler, No. 84–Civ. 1724–CLB.

3. The "best interests" principle is the standard ordinarily used to make decisions for children. Is it possible to give substantive content to this principle as applied to newborns? The President's Commission recommends placing individual newborns into one of three categories in order to facilitate the determination of what is in a child's best interests:

Clearly beneficial therapies. The Commission's inquiries indicate that treatments are rarely withheld when there is a medical consensus that they would provide a net benefit to a child. Parents naturally want to provide necessary medical care in most circumstances, and parents who are hesitant at first about having treatment administered usually come to recognize the desirability of providing treatment after discussions with physicians, nurses, and others. Parents should be able to choose among alternative treatments with similarly beneficial results and among providers, but not to reject treatment that is reliably expected to benefit a seriously ill newborn substantially, as is usually true if life can be saved.

. . .

Clearly futile therapies. When there is no therapy that can benefit an infant, as in anencephaly or certain severe cardiac deformities, a decision by surrogates and providers not to try predictably futile endeavors is ethically and legally justifiable. Such therapies do not help the child, are sometimes painful for the infant (and probably distressing to the parents), and offer no reasonable probability of saving life for a substantial period. The moment of death for these infants might be delayed for a short time—perhaps as long as a few weeks—by vigorous therapy. Of course, the prolongation of life—and hope against hope—may be enough to lead some parents to want to try a therapy believed by physicians to be futile. As long as this choice does not cause substantial suffering for the child, providers should accept it, although individual health care professionals who find it personally offensive to engage in futile treatment may arrange to withdraw from the case.

Just as with older patients, even when cure or saving of life are out of reach, obligations to comfort and respect a dying person remain. Thus infants whose lives are destined to be brief are owed whatever relief from suffering and enhancement of life can be provided, including feeding, medication for pain, and sedation, as appropriate. Moreover, it may be possible for parents to hold and comfort the child once the elaborate means of life-support are withdrawn, which can be very important to all concerned in symbolic and existential as well as physical terms.

Ambiguous cases. Although for most seriously ill infants there will be either clearly a beneficial option or no beneficial therapeutic options at all, hard questions are raised by the smaller number for whom it is very difficult to assess whether the treatments available offer prospects of benefit—for example, a child with a debilitating and painful disease who might live with therapy, but only for a year or so, or a respirator-dependent premature infant whose long-term prognosis becomes bleaker with each passing day.

Much of the difficulty in these cases arises from factual uncertainty. For the many infants born prematurely, and sometimes for those with serious congenital defects, the only certainty is that without intensive care they are unlikely to survive; very little is known about how each individual will fare with treatment. Neonatology is too new a field to allow accurate predictions of which babies will survive and of the complications, handicaps, and potentials that the survivors might have . . . . When a child's best interests are ambiguous, a decision based upon them will require prudent and discerning judgment. Defining the category of cases in a way that appropriately protects and encourages the exercise of parental judgment will sometimes be difficult.

Table 1:

Treatment Options for Seriously Ill Newborns—Physician's Assessment in Relation to Parent's Preference

Physician's Assessment of Treatment Options *	Parents Prefer to Accept Treatment **	Parents Prefer to Forego Treatment **
Clearly beneficial	Provide treatment	Provide treatment during review process
Ambiguous or uncertain	Provide treatment	Forego treatment
Futile	Provide treatment unless provider declines to do so	Forego treatment

    * The assessment of the value to the infant of the treatments available will initially be by the attending physician. Both when this assessment is unclear and when the joint decision between parents and physician is to forego treatment, this assessment would be reviewed by intra-institutional mechanisms and possibly thereafter by court.
    ** The choice made by the infant's parents or other duly authorized surrogate who has adequate decisionmaking capacity and has been adequately informed, based on their assessment of the infant's best interests.

Deciding to Forego Life-Sustaining Treatment at 217–223.

    Do you agree with the President's Commission that treatment should always be continued when parents request it except where the child is in great suffering? How do we know that treatment is beneficial? Consider the views of the President's Commission on the issue. Do you find their statement helpful?

    Though inevitably somewhat subjective and imprecise in actual application, the concept of "benefit" excludes honoring idiosyncratic views that might be allowed if a person were deciding about his or her own treatment. Rather, net benefit is absent only if the burdens imposed on the patient by the disability or its treatment would lead a competent decisionmaker to choose to forego the treatment. As in all surrogate decisionmaking, the surrogate is obligated to try to evaluate benefits and burdens from the infant's own perspective. The Commission believes that the handicaps of Down Syndrome, for example, are not in themselves of this magnitude and do not justify failing to provide medically proven treatment, such as surgical correction of a blocked intestinal tract.

    This is a very strict standard in that it excludes consideration of the negative effects of an impaired child's life on other persons, including parents, siblings, and society. Although abiding by this standard may be difficult in specific cases, it is all too easy to undervalue the lives of handicapped infants; the Commission finds it imperative to counteract this by treating them no less vigorously than their healthy peers or than older children with similar handicaps would be treated.

Id. at 218–219.

    5. According to news reports, Baby Jane Doe, whose real name is Keri-Lynn, was discharged from the hospital after undergoing an operation to implant a shunt (or drainage tube) to allow fluid to drain from her head. Her parents had originally refused to consent to operations to drain the fluid and to close the opening in her spine. They reportedly decided to give permission for the implant because the fluid build-up was continuing despite the fact that she was otherwise progressing well. Her skin had grown naturally over the opening in her spine. Washington Post, Apr. 7, 1984, at A1, col. 4.

5. THE PATIENT IN NEED OF RESUSCITATION

Whether to resuscitate a patient—restore breathing and heartbeat—is a question of special concern. Because resuscitation efforts must be started quickly if they are to have a good chance of succeeding, there is little opportunity to decide when such efforts are initiated whether they are warranted. Should all patients experiencing cardiac arrest be resuscitated? If not, under what circumstances, by whom and by what process should decisions not to resuscitate be made?

IN RE DINNERSTEIN

Appeals Court of Massachusetts, Norfolk, 1978.
6 Mass.App.Ct. 466, 380 N.E.2d 134.

ARMSTRONG, JUSTICE.

This case, which comes to us on a report (without decison but with extensive findings of fact) from a judge of a Probate Court, turns on the question whether a physician attending an incompetent, terminally ill patient may lawfully direct that resuscitation measures be withheld in the event of cardiac or respiratory arrest where such a direction has not been approved in advance by a Probate Court.

The patient is a sixty-seven year old woman who suffers from a condition known as Alzheimer's disease. It is a degenerative disease of the brain of unknown origin, described as presenile dementia, and results in destruction of brain tissue and, consequently deterioration in brain function. The condition is progressive and unremitting, leading in stages to disorientation, loss of memory, personality disorganization, loss of intellectual function, and ultimate loss of all motor function. The disease typically leads to a vegetative or comatose condition and then to death. The course of the disease may be gradual or precipitous, averaging five to seven years. At this time medical science knows of no cure for the disease and no treatment which can slow or arrest its course. No medical breakthrough is anticipated.

The patient's condition was diagnosed as Alzheimer's disease in July, 1975, although the initial symptoms of the disease were observed as early as 1972. She entered a nursing home in November, 1975, where her (by that time) complete disorientation, frequent psychotic outbursts, and deteriorating ability to control elementary bodily functions made her dependent on intensive nursing care. In February, 1978, she suffered a massive stroke, which left her totally paralysed on her left side. At the present time she is confined to a hospital bed, in an essentially vegetative state, immobile, speechless, unable to swallow without choking, and barely able to cough. Her eyes occasionally open and from time to time appear to fix on or follow an object briefly; otherwise she appears to be unaware of her environment. She is fed through a naso-gastric tube, intravenous feeding having been abandoned because it came to cause her pain. It is probable that she is experiencing some discomfort from the naso-gastric tube, which can cause irritation, ulceration, and infection in her throat and esophageal tract, and which must be removed from time to time, and that procedure itself causes discomfort. She is catheterized and also, of course, requires bowel care. Apart from her Alzheimer's disease and paralysis, she suffers from high blood pressure which is difficult to control;

there is risk in lowering it due to a constriction in an artery leading to a kidney. She has a serious, life-threatening coronary artery disease, due to arteriosclerosis. Her condition is hopeless, but it is difficult to predict exactly when she will die. Her life expectancy is no more than a year, but she could go into cardiac or respiratory arrest at any time. One of these, or another stroke, is most likely to be the immediate cause of her death.

In this situation her attending physician has recommended that, when (and if) cardiac or respiratory arrest occurs, resuscitation efforts should not be undertaken. Such efforts typically involve the use of cardiac massage or chest compression and delivery of oxygen under compression through an endotracheal tube into the lungs. An electrocardiogram is connected to guide the efforts of the resuscitation team and to monitor the patient's progress. Various plastic tubes are usually inserted intravenously to supply medications or stimulants directly to the heart. Such medications may also be supplied by direct injection into the heart by means of a long needle. A defibrillator may be used, applying electric shock to the heart to induce contractions. A pacemaker, in the form of an electrical conducting wire, may be fed through a large blood vessel directly to the heart's surface to stimulate contractions and to regulate beat. These procedures, to be effective, must be initiated with a minimum of delay as cerebral anoxia, due to a cutoff of oxygen to the brain, will normally produce irreversible brain damage within three to five minutes and total brain death within fifteen minutes. Many of these procedures are obviously highly intrusive, and some are violent in nature. The defibrillator, for example, causes violent (and painful) muscle contractions which, in a patient suffering (as this patient is) from osteoporosis, may cause fracture of vertebrae or other bones. Such fractures, in turn, cause pain, which may be extreme.

The patient's family, consisting of a son, who is a physician practicing in New York City, and a daughter, with whom the patient lived prior to her admission to the nursing home in 1975, concur in the doctor's recommendation that resuscitation should not be attempted in the event of cardiac or respiratory arrest. They have joined with the doctor and the hospital in bringing the instant action for declaratory relief, asking for a determination that the doctor may enter a "no-code" order [3] on the patient's medical record without judicial authorization or, alternatively, if such authorization is a legal prerequisite to the validity of a "no-code" order, that that authorization be given. The probate judge appointed a guardian ad litem, who has taken a position in opposition to the prayers of the complaint.

---

3. The terminology derives from the development in recent years, in acute care hospitals, of specialized "teams" of doctors and nurses trained in the administration of cardiopulmonary resuscitative measures. If a patient goes into cardiac or respiratory arrest, the nurse in attendance causes a notice to be broadcast on the hospital's intercommunications system giving a code word and the room number. The members of the code team converge on the room immediately from other parts of the hospital. In the hospital in question, if the code is broadcast at night, all doctors then in the hospital for whatever reason are expected to respond to the code. A "no-code" order entered in a patient's medical record instructs the nursing staff, as part of the attending physician's ongoing instructions to the nursing staff for the care of the patient, not to summon the code team in the event of cardiac or respiratory arrest. A no-code order is sometimes called ONTR (order not to resuscitate); (Rabkin, Gillerman, & Rice, Orders Not to Resuscitate, 295 New Eng.J. Med. 364 [1976]) or DNR (do not resuscitate) (In re Quinlan, 70 N.J. 10, 29, 355 A.2d 647, cert. denied sub nom. Garger v. New Jersey, 429 U.S. 922, 97 S.Ct. 319, 50 L.Ed.2d 289 [1976]).

By their action for declaratory relief, the plaintiffs seek a resolution of some uncertainties which have arisen in the aftermath of Superintendent of Belchertown State Sch. v. Saikewicz, [Sec. B.4. supra], which has been interpreted by some in the medical profession as casting doubt upon the lawfulness of an order not to attempt resuscitation of an incompetent, terminally ill patient except where the entry of such an order has been previously determined by a Probate Court to be in the best interests of the patient. . . . The practical results of such a reading would, of course, be very far reaching, since it is obvious on reflection that cardiac or respiratory arrest will signal the arrival of death for the overwhelming majority of persons whose lives are terminated by illness or old age; indeed, they are part of the normal act of death.

The *Saikewicz* case, in the range of situations to which it applies, requires "judicial resolution of this most difficult and awesome question— whether potentially life-prolonging treatment should be withheld from a person incapable of making his own decision . . .." In this respect the case represents more than a definition of the procedure which must be followed if the doctor or the family or both feel that an available life-prolonging treatment should not be administered to the incompetent patient. It also, implicitly, would appear to establish a rule of law that unless such a court determination has been obtained, it is the duty of a doctor attending an incompetent patient to employ whatever life-saving or life-prolonging treatments the current state of the art has put in his hands. As it cannot be assumed that legal proceedings such as the present one will be initiated in respect of more than a small fraction of all terminally ill or dying elderly patients, the *Saikewicz* case, if read to apply to the natural death of a terminally ill patient by cardiac or respiratory arrest, would require attempts to resuscitate dying patients in most cases, without exercise of medical judgment, even when that course of action could aptly be characterized as a pointless, even cruel, prolongation of the act of dying.

We think it clear that such a result is neither intended nor sanctioned by the *Saikewicz* case. . . . It is apparent . . . from the factual situation to which the principles of law announced in the case were addressed, from the precedent cited in support of those principles, and from the inherent sense of the case read as a whole, that, when the court spoke of life-saving or life-prolonging treatments, it referred to treatments administered for the purpose, and with some reasonable expectation, of effecting a permanent or temporary cure of or relief from the illness or condition being treated. "Prolongation of life," as used in the *Saikewicz* case, does not mean a mere suspension of the act of dying, but contemplates, at the very least, a remission of symptoms enabling a return towards a normal, functioning, integrated existence.

It must be borne in mind that the *Saikewicz* case, while discussing incidentally the scope of the doctor's duty to administer treatment, was primarily concerned with the patient's right to refuse treatment and the manner in which the exercise of that right may be secured to persons unable to make the decision for themselves. . . .

The same is true of the many cases discussed in the *Saikewicz* decision in reference to the application of the various interests the State might claim in opposition to the individual's right to decline treatment. They all involved a situation of *choice* presented by the availability of a treatment offering hope of restoration to normal, integrated, functioning, cognitive existence.

That is not the situation that presents itself in this case, or in the case of any patient in the terminal stages of an unremitting, incurable mortal illness. The judge's findings make it clear that the case is hopeless and that death must come soon, probably in the form of cardiac or respiratory arrest. Attempts to apply resuscitation, if successful, will do nothing to cure or relieve the illnesses which will have brought the patient to the threshold of death. The case does not, therefore, present the type of significant treatment choice or election which, in light of sound medical advice, is to be made by the patient, if competent to do so. The latter is the type of lay decision which the court in the *Saikewicz* case had in mind when it required judical approval of a negative decision . . . by the physician in attendance and by the family or guardian of a patient unable to make the choice for himself. This case does not offer a life-saving or life-prolonging treatment alternative within the meaning of the *Saikewicz* case. It presents a question peculiarly within the competence of the medical profession of what measures are appropriate to ease the imminent passing of an irreversibly, terminally ill patient in light of the patient's history and condition and the wishes of her family. That question is not one for judicial decision, but one for the attending physician, in keeping with the highest traditions of his profession, and subject to court review only to the extent that it may be contended that he has failed to exercise "the degree of care and skill of the average qualified practitioner, taking into account the advances in the profession."

The case is remanded to the Probate Court, where a judgment is to enter in accordance with the prayers of the complaint for declaratory relief, declaring that on the findings made by the judge the law does not prohibit a course of medical treatment which excludes attempts at resuscitation in the event of cardiac or respiratory arrest and that the validity of an order to that effect does not depend on prior judicial approval.

So ordered.

MITCHELL T. RABKIN, GERALD GILLERMAN AND NANCY R. RICE, ORDERS NOT TO RESUSCITATE

295 New Eng.J.Med. 364 (1976).

Medical opinions on the inappropriateness of cardiopulmonary resuscitation of certain patients are now openly discussed, as acknowledged by the New Jersey Supreme Court in its recent Quinlan decision. As early as 1974 the AMA proposed that decisions not to resuscitate be formally entered in patients' progress notes and communicated to all attending staff. There has been little open discussion, however, of the process by which a decision not to resuscitate is formulated. Within a single institution, practices may vary among physicians, in part from the lack of a clearly articulated hospital policy.

An apparent need for hospital definitions of the process by which decisions not to resuscitate should be made led to the development of the following statement, which is proposed as a policy statement for hospitals concerned with regulating the process whereby Orders Not to Resuscitate may be considered and then implemented. . . .

. . . .

Notwithstanding the hospital's pro-life policy, the right of a patient to decline available medical procedures must be respected. For example, if a competent patient who is not irreversibly and irreparably ill issues instructions that under stated circumstances, he is opposed to the use of certain procedures, the following guidelines should be observed. The physician should explore thoroughly with the patient the types of circumstances that might arise, and warn that the consequences of a generalized prohibition may be to allow an unintended termination of life. If after a careful disclosure the patient persists in some form of order declining use of certain medical procedures when otherwise applicable, the physician is legally required to respect such instructions. Such situations are not unknown to hospitals that have treated Jehovah's Witnesses and other persons with fixed opinions unlikely to be affected by unforeseen medical exigencies. If the physician finds the medical program as ordered by the patient so inconsistent with his own medical judgment as to be incompatible with his continuing as the responsible physician, he may attempt to transfer the care of the patient to another physician more sympathetic to the patient's desires.

The specific issue of the appropriateness of cardiopulmonary resuscitation arises frequently with the irreversibly, irreparably ill patient whose death is imminent. We refer to the medical circumstance in which the disease is "irreversible" in the sense that no known therapeutic measures can be effective in reversing the course of illness; the physiologic status of the patient is "irreparable" in the sense that the course of illness has progressed beyond the capacity of existing knowledge and technic to stem the process; and when death is "imminent" in the sense that in the ordinary course of events, death probably will occur within a period not exceeding two weeks.

When it appears that a patient is irreversibly and irreparably ill and that death is imminent, the question of the appropriateness of cardiopulmonary resuscitation in the event of sudden cessation of vital functions may be considered by the patient's physician, if not already raised by the patient, to avoid an unnecessary abuse of the patient's presumed reliance on the physician and hospital for continued life-supporting care. The initial medical judgment on such question should be made by the primarily responsible physician for the patient after discussion with an ad hoc committee consisting not only of the other physicians attending the patient and the nurses and others directly active in the care of the patient, but at least one other senior staff physician not previously involved in the patient's care. The inquiry should focus on whether the patient's death is so certain and so imminent that resuscitation in the event of sudden cessation of vital functions would serve no purpose. Although the unanimous opinion of the ad hoc committee in support of the decision of the responsible physician is not necessarily required (for some may be uncertain), a strongly held dissenting view not negated by other staff members should generally dissuade the responsible physician from his or her initial judgment on the appropriateness of resuscitation efforts.

Even if a medical judgment is reached that a patient is faced with such an illness and imminence of death that resuscitation is medically inappropriate, the decision to withhold resuscitation (Orders Not to Resuscitate, "ONTR") will become effective only upon the informed choice of a competent patient or, with an incompetent patient, by strict adherence to the guidelines discussed below, and then only to the extent that all appropriate family members are in agreement with the views of the involved staff. In this context, "appropriate" means at least the family members who would be consulted for permission to perform a post-mortem examination if the patient died.

"Competence" in this context is not to be restricted to the legal and medical tests to determine competence to stand trial or to form a criminal intent. For the purpose of making an informed choice of medical treatment, "competence" is understood to rest on the test of whether the patient understands the relevant risks and alternatives, and whether the resulting decision reflects a deliberate choice by the patient. Caution should be exercised that a patient does not unwittingly "consent" to an ONTR, as a result of temporary distortion (for example, from pain, medication or metabolic abnormality) in his ability to choose among available alternatives.

It is recognized that it may be inappropriate to introduce the subject of withholding cardiopulmonary resuscitation efforts to certain competent patients when, in the physician's judgment, the patient will probably be unable to cope with it psychologically. In such event, Orders Not to Resuscitate may not be directed because of the absence of an informed choice. Appropriate family members should be so informed, and the physician should explain the course that will thus follow in the event of sudden cessation of the patient's vital functions. This discussion with the family should be noted by the physician in the medical record. If, however, the physician is able to discuss the essential elements of the case with a competent patient without violating the principles of reasonable and humane medical practice, a valid consent may follow.

If the competent patient thus chooses the ONTR alternative, this is his choice, and it may not be overridden by contrary views of family members. Nevertheless, it is important to inform the family members of the patient's decision (with the patient's permission and in accordance with his directions) so that the failure to resuscitate or to take other heroic measures is not unanticipated. In any event, the decision should be documented by the responsible physician and at least one witness. Such decisions shall remain in effect if the patient subsequently becomes incompetent and if the clinical circumstances for Orders Not to Resuscitate otherwise remain in existence.

Minors who are not emancipated by state law will be deemed incompetent to make a decision not to resuscitate. Such persons, however, will be kept informed if such a communication is appropriate, and have the right to reject a decision not to resuscitate, despite their presumed incompetence.

If a patient is incompetent, he should not be denied the benefits of the evaluation process described above. The physician and the ad hoc committee will consider initially whether the conditions of irreversibility, irreparability and imminence of death are satisfied in their opinion. The basis for a final decision for Orders Not to Resuscitate must be concern from the patient's point of view, and not that of some other person who might present what he regards as sufficient reasons for not resuscitating the patient. It is only the clinical interest of the patient that must be considered; consideration of other factors would violate the fundamental policy of the hospital. An additional condition for the issuance of Orders Not to Resuscitate for an incompetent patient is approval of at least the same family members who are required to consent to postmortem examination. Failure to obtain and record family approval of Orders Not to Resuscitate may expose those involved to charges of negligent or unlawful conduct. Thus, the failure to obtain such approval would foreclose further consideration of Orders Not to Resuscitate in cases in which the patient is incompetent.

To prevent any uncertainty or confusion over the status of a patient's treatment, the decision for Orders Not to Resuscitate and its accompanying consent by the competent patient or the appropriate family members should be recorded promptly in the medical chart. In addition to the formal consent, the written and dated record must include the following: a summary of the staff discussion and decision; the disclosures to the patient, which must include the elements of informed consent, the patient's response, the responsible physician's documentation of the patient's competence, the patient's decision to inform appropriate family members and the resulting discussion with them that may then follow. Each hospital must specify what it deems to be the elements of informed consent and the formats in which consent must be witnessed and documented. Whether or not the patient's signature must be required invariably should also be decided; the signature removes ambiguity, but the physical act of signing may be deemed unpalatable by certain patients and therefore unacceptable to them as a necessary or appropriate formalization of the meaningful discussion and their resulting verbal consent.

It is the responsibility of the physician to convey the meaning of the Orders Not to Resuscitate to all medical, nursing and other staff as appropriate, and, simultaneously, to insist upon being notified immediately if the patient's condition should change so that the orders seem no longer applicable. If the circumstances described to such a patient do not change, a subsequent resuscitation would constitute treatment without consent.

After the issuing of Orders Not to Resuscitate, the patient's course, including continued evaluation of competence and consent, must be reviewed by the responsible physician at least daily, or at more frequent intervals, if appropriate, and documentation made in the medical chart to determine the continued applicability of such orders. If the patient's condition alters in such a way that the orders are no longer deemed applicable, the Orders Not to Resuscitate must be revoked, and the revocation communicated without delay.

Nothing in the entire procedure leading to Orders Not to Resuscitate, nor the ONTR itself, should indicate to the medical and nursing staff or to the patient and family any intention to diminish the appropriate medical and nursing attention to be received by the patient. It is the responsibility of the physician in charge to be certain that no diminution of necessary and appropriate measures for the patient's care and comfort follows from this decision.

When the incompetent patient is sufficiently alert to appreciate at least some aspects of the care he is receiving (the benefit of doubt must always assign to the patient the likelihood of at least partial alertness or receptivity to verbal stimuli), and especially with a child, whose "incompetence" by legal definition may not be supported by clinical observation, every effort must be made to provide the comfort and reassurance appropriate to the patient's state of consciousness and emotional condition regardless of the designation of incompetence.

In every case in which Orders Not to Resuscitate are issued, the hospital shall make available to the greatest extent practicable resources to provide counseling, reassurance, consolation and other emotional support as appropriate, for the patient's family and for all involved hospital staff, as well as for the patient.

Occasionally, a proposal for Orders Not to Resuscitate may be initiated by family members. It is essential to recognize that a family member's instructions not to resuscitate are not to be viewed as the choice of the patient. Thus, the attending physician and the ad hoc committee must not simply concur in the Orders Not to Resuscitate suggested by the family, but such concurrences shall be forthcoming only upon the timing and conditions described above.

NOTES

1. A recent study indicated that of 294 patients studied, only forty-one patients (14%) of the resuscitated patients lived long enough to go home. Only 11% were alive six months after discharge. Moreover, patients with certain characteristics (pneumonia, hypotension, renal failure, cancer and a homebound life style prior to hospitalization) fared less well than others. On the other hand, at the time of discharge and again six months later, 93% of the survivors were mentally intact, although there was some decrease in functional capacity. Bedell, Delbanco, Cook and Epstein, Survival After Cardiopulmonary Resuscitation in the Hospital, 309 New Eng.J.Med. 571 (1983). See also Fox and Lipton, The Decision to Perform Cardiopulmonary Resuscitation, 309 New Eng.J.Med. 607 (1983).

2. Do you agree that where medical judgment indicates that cardiopulmonary resuscitation is inappropriate, the competent patient's wishes should always be respected even when the patient elects to be resuscitated? Would your answer be the same if the patient is in an intensive care unit and beds are scarce? At least one religious tradition apparently calls for aggressive treatment of terminally ill patients. See Meier, Code and No-Code: A Psychological Analysis and the Viewpoint of Jewish Law, in Legal and Ethical Aspects of Treating Critically and Terminally Ill Patients (Doudera and Peters, eds. 1982).

Suppose the patient is incompetent and the immediate family is divided or there is no immediate family; how should we decide whether no-code status is appropriate? A slow-code is a deliberately slow response to a patient who has suffered cardiopulmonary arrest. Because a person without a heartbeat will die within a very short time and any delay in resuscitation greatly reduces the efficacy of the effort, is the use of the "slow-code" ever justified? The slow-code has been used when a patient's prognosis suggests that resuscitation is medically inappropriate and the family has refused to approve "do not resuscitate" status or the health care team believes that the family would refuse. Bassom, The Decision to Resuscitate Slowly, Troubling Problems in Medical Ethics: The Third Volume in a Series on Ethics, Humanism and Medicine 116 (1981). For an argument that a slow-code determination is an aspect of decisionmaking about appropriate care for a dying patient and that a code/no-code approach to the issue is too simple, see commentary by Dantzker, id. at 122.

A growing number of governmental bodies, institutions and professional societies have drafted policies to cover situations where attempts at cardiopulmonary resuscitation may be inappropriate. What should be the content of these policies? For a compilation of such policies, see President's Commission, Deciding to Forego Life-Sustaining Treatment 493–545 (Appendix I) (1983). The Veterans Administration, which had previously held that "no code" orders are "inappropriate," id. at 519, responded to the Commission's report by adopting a new policy based on its recommendation. See New VA Policy Allows Right-to-Die Instructions, Washington Post, Sept. 20, 1983, at Al, col. 1.

Chapter Eight

REPRODUCTION AND THE NEW GENETICS

A. DEFINING LIFE

---

1. SHOULD WE DEFINE?

ROE v. WADE

Supreme Court of the United States, 1973.
410 U.S. 113, 93 S.Ct. 705, 35 L.Ed.2d 147.

MR. JUSTICE BLACKMUN delivered the opinion of the Court.

This Texas federal appeal presents constitutional challenges to state criminal abortion legislation. The Texas statutes under attack here are typical of those that have been in effect in many States for approximately a century. . . .

We forthwith acknowledge our awareness of the sensitive and emotional nature of the abortion controversy, of the vigorous opposing views, even among physicians, and of the deep and seemingly absolute convictions that the subject inspires. One's philosophy, one's experiences, one's exposure to the raw edges of human existence, one's religious training, one's attitudes toward life and family and their values, and the moral standards one establishes and seeks to observe, are all likely to influence and to color one's thinking and conclusions about abortion.

In addition, population growth, pollution, poverty, and racial overtones tend to complicate and not to simplify the problem.

Our task, of course, is to resolve the issue by constitutional measurement, free of emotion and of predilection. We seek earnestly to do this, and, because we do, we have inquired into, and in this opinion place some emphasis upon, medical and medical-legal history and what that history reveals about man's attitudes toward the abortion procedure over the centuries. . . .

. . .

I

The Texas statutes that concern us here are Arts. 1191–1194 and 1196 of the State's Penal Code. These make it a crime to "procure an abortion," as therein defined, or to attempt one, except with respect to "an abortion procured or attempted by medical advice for the purpose of saving the life of the mother." . . .

. . .

II

Jane Roe, a single woman who was residing in Dallas County, Texas, instituted this federal action in March 1970 against the District Attorney of the county. She sought a declaratory judgment that the Texas criminal abortion statutes were unconstitutional on their face, and an injunction restraining the defendant from enforcing the statutes.

Roe alleged that she was unmarried and pregnant; that she wished to terminate her pregnancy by an abortion "performed by a competent, licensed physician, under safe, clinical conditions"; that she was unable to get a "legal" abortion in Texas because her life did not appear to be threatened by the continuation of her pregnancy; and that she could not afford to travel to another jurisdiction in order to secure a legal abortion under safe conditions. She claimed that the Texas statutes were unconstitutionally vague and that they abridged her right of personal privacy, protected by the First, Fourth, Fifth, Ninth, and Fourteenth Amendments. By an amendment to her complaint Roe purported to sue "on behalf of herself and all other women" similarly situated.

. . .

VII

Three reasons have been advanced to explain historically the enactment of criminal abortion laws in the 19th century and to justify their continued existence.

It has been argued occasionally that these laws were the product of a Victorian social concern to discourage illicit sexual conduct. Texas, however, does not advance this justification in the present case, and it appears that no court or commentator has taken the argument seriously. . . .

A second reason is concerned with abortion as a medical procedure. When most criminal abortion laws were first enacted, the procedure was a hazardous one for the woman. This was particularly true prior to the development of antisepsis. . . . Thus, it has been argued that a State's real concern in enacting a criminal abortion law was to protect the pregnant woman, that is, to restrain her from submitting to a procedure that placed her life in serious jeopardy.

Modern medical techniques have altered this situation. . . . Of course, important state interests in the areas of health and medical standards do remain. The State has a legitimate interest in seeing to it that abortion, like any other medical procedure, is performed under circumstances that insure maximum safety for the patient. This interest obviously extends at least to the performing physician and his staff, to the facilities involved, to the availability of after-care, and to adequate provision for any complication or emergency that might arise. The prevalence of high mortality rates at illegal "abortion mills" strengthens, rather than weakens, the State's interest in regulating the conditions under which abortions are performed. Moreover, the risk to the woman increases as her pregnancy continues. Thus, the State retains a definite interest in protecting the woman's own health and safety when an abortion is proposed at a late stage of pregnancy.

The third reason is the State's interest—some phrase it in terms of duty—in protecting prenatal life. Some of the argument for this justification rests on the theory that a new human life is present from the moment of conception. The State's interest and general obligation to protect life then extends, it is argued, to prenatal life. Only when the life of the pregnant mother herself is at stake, balanced against the life she carries within her, should the interest of the embryo or fetus not prevail. Logically, of course, a legitimate state interest in this area need not stand or fall on acceptance of the belief that life begins at conception or at some other point prior to live birth. In assessing the State's interest, recognition may be given to the less rigid claim that as long as at least *potential* life is involved, the State may assert interests beyond the protection of the pregnant woman alone.

. . .

VIII

The Constitution does not explicitly mention any right of privacy. In a line of decisions . . . the Court has recognized that a right of personal privacy, or a guarantee of certain areas or zones of privacy, does exist under the Constitution. . . .

This right of privacy, whether it be founded in the Fourteenth Amendment's concept of personal liberty and restrictions upon state action, as we feel it is, or, as the District Court determined, in the Ninth Amendment's reservation of rights to the people, is broad enough to encompass a woman's decision whether or not to terminate her pregnancy. The detriment that the State would impose upon the pregnant woman by denying this choice altogether is apparent. Specific and direct harm medically diagnosable even in early pregnancy may be involved. Maternity, or additional offspring, may force upon the woman a distressful life and future. Psychological harm may be imminent. Mental and physical health may be taxed by child care. There is also the distress, for all concerned, associated with the unwanted child, and there is the problem of bringing a child into a family already unable, psychologically and otherwise, to care for it. In other cases, as in this one, the additional difficulties and continuing stigma of unwed motherhood may be involved. . . .

On the basis of elements such as these, appellant and some *amici* argue that the woman's right is absolute and that she is entitled to terminate her pregnancy at whatever time, in whatever way, and for whatever reason she alone chooses. With this we do not agree. . . . In fact, it is not clear to us that the claim asserted by some *amici* that one has an unlimited right to do with one's body as one pleases bears a close relationship to the right of privacy previously articulated in the Court's decisions. The Court has refused to recognize an unlimited right of this kind in the past. Jacobson v. Massachusetts, 197 U.S. 11, 25 S.Ct. 358, 49 L.Ed. 643 (1905) (vaccination); Buck v. Bell, 274 U.S. 200, 47 S.Ct. 584, 71 L.Ed. 1000 (1927) (sterilization).

We, therefore, conclude that the right of personal privacy includes the abortion decision, but that this right is not unqualified and must be considered against important state interests in regulation.

. . .

IX

A. The appellee and certain *amici* argue that the fetus is a "person" within the language and meaning of the Fourteenth Amendment. In support of this, they outline at length and in detail the well-known facts of fetal development. If this suggestion of personhood is established, the appellant's case, of course, collapses, for the fetus' right to life would then be guaranteed specifically by the Amendment. The appellant conceded as much on reargument. On the other hand, the appellee conceded on reargument that no case could be cited that holds that a fetus is a person within the meaning of the Fourteenth Amendment.

The Constitution does not define "person" in so many words. Section 1 of the Fourteenth Amendment contains three references to "person." The first, in defining "citizens," speaks of "persons born or naturalized in the United States." The word also appears both in the Due Process Clause and in the Equal Protection Clause. "Person" is used in other places in the Constitution: in the listing of qualifications for Representatives and Senators, Art. I, § 2, cl. 2, and § 3, cl. 3; in the Apportionment Clause, Art. I, § 2, cl. 3; in the Migration and Importation provision, Art. I, § 9, cl. 1; in the Emolument Clause, Art. I, § 9, cl. 8; in the Electors provisions, Art. II, § 1, cl. 2, and the superseded cl. 3; in the provision outlining qualifications for the office of President, Art. II, § 1, cl. 5; in the Extradition provisions, Art. IV, § 2, cl. 2, and the superseded Fugitive Slave Clause 3; and in the Fifth, Twelfth, and Twenty-second Amendments, as well as in §§ 2 and 3 of the Fourteenth Amendment. But in nearly all these instances, the use of the word is such that it has application only postnatally. . . .

All this, together with our observation, supra, that throughout the major portion of the 19th century prevailing legal abortion practices were far freer than they are today, persuades us that the word "person," as used in the Fourteenth Amendment, does not include the unborn. . . . .

. . . .

B. The pregnant woman cannot be isolated in her privacy. She carries an embryo and, later, a fetus, if one accepts the medical definitions of the developing young in the human uterus. See Dorland's Illustrated Medical Dictionary 478–479, 547 (24th ed.1965). The situation therefore is inherently different from marital intimacy, or bedroom possession of obscene material, or marriage, or procreation, or education, ... As we have intimated above, it is reasonable and appropriate for a State to decide that at some point in time another interest, that of health of the mother or that of potential human life, becomes significantly involved. The woman's privacy is no longer sole and any right of privacy she possesses must be measured accordingly.

Texas urges that, apart from the Fourteenth Amendment, life begins at conception and is present throughout pregnancy, and that, therefore, the State has a compelling interest in protecting that life from and after conception. We need not resolve the difficult question of when life begins. When those trained in the respective disciplines of medicine, philosophy, and theology are unable to arrive at any consensus, the judiciary, at this point in the development of man's knowledge, is not in a position to speculate as to the answer.

It should be sufficient to note briefly the wide divergence of thinking on this most sensitive and difficult question. There has always been strong support for the view that life does not begin until live birth. This was the belief of the Stoics. It appears to be the predominant, though not the unanimous, attitude of the Jewish faith. It may be taken to represent also the position of a large segment of the Protestant community, insofar as that can be ascertained; organized groups that have taken a formal position on the abortion issue have generally regarded abortion as a matter for the conscience of the individual and her family. As we have noted, the common law found greater significance in quickening. Physicians and their scientific colleagues have regarded that event with less interest and have tended to focus either upon conception, upon live birth, or upon the interim point at which the fetus becomes "viable," that is, potentially able to live outside the mother's womb, albeit with artificial aid. Viability is usually placed at about seven months (28 weeks) but may occur earlier, even at 24 weeks. The Aristotelian theory of "mediate animation," that held sway throughout the Middle Ages and the Renaissance in Europe, continued to be official Roman Catholic dogma until the 19th century, despite opposition to this "ensoulment" theory from those in the Church who would recognize the existence of life from the moment of conception. The latter is now, of course, the official belief of the Catholic Church. As one brief *amicus* discloses, this is a view strongly held by many non-Catholics as well, and by many physicians. Substantial problems for precise definition of this view are posed, however, by new embryological data that purport to indicate that conception is a "process" over time, rather than an event . . . . .

In areas other than criminal abortion, the law has been reluctant to endorse any theory that life, as we recognize it, begins before live birth or to accord legal rights to the unborn except in narrowly defined situations and except when the rights are contingent upon live birth. For example, the traditional rule of tort law denied recovery for prenatal injuries even though the child was born alive. That rule has been changed in almost every jurisdiction. In most States, recovery is said to be permitted only if the fetus was viable, or at least quick, when the injuries were sustained, though few courts have squarely so held. In a recent development, generally opposed by the commentators, some States permit the parents of a stillborn child to maintain an action for wrongful death because of prenatal injuries. Such an action, however, would appear to be one to vindicate the parents' interest and is thus consistent with the view that the fetus, at most, represents only the potentiality of life. Similarly, unborn children have been recognized as acquiring rights or interests by way of inheritance or other devolution of property, and have been represented by guardians *ad litem*. Perfection of the interests involved, again, has generally been contingent upon live birth. In short, the unborn have never been recognized in the law as persons in the whole sense.

X

In view of all this, we do not agree that, by adopting one theory of life, Texas may override the rights of the pregnant woman that are at stake. We repeat, however, that the State does have an important and legitimate interest in preserving and protecting the health of the pregnant woman, whether she be a resident of the State or a nonresident who seeks medical consultation and treatment there, and that it has still *another* important and legitimate interest in protecting the potentiality of human life. These interests are separate and distinct. Each grows in substantiality as the woman approaches term and, at a point during pregnancy, each becomes "compelling."

With respect to the State's important and legitimate interest in the health of the mother, the "compelling" point, in the light of present medical knowledge, is at approximately the end of the first trimester. This is so because of the now-established medical fact . . . . that until the end of the first trimester mortality in abortion may be less than mortality in normal childbirth. It follows that, from and after this point, a State may regulate the abortion procedure to the extent that the regulation reasonably relates to the preservation and protection of maternal health. Examples of permissible state regulation in this area are requirements as to the qualifications of the person who is to perform the abortion; as to the licensure of that person; as to the facility in which the procedure is to be performed, that is, whether it must be a hospital or may be a clinic or some other place of less-than-hospital status; as to the licensing of the facility; and the like.

This means, on the other hand, that, for the period of pregnancy prior to this "compelling" point, the attending physician, in consultation with his patient, is free to determine, without regulation by the State, that, in his medical judgment, the patient's pregnancy should be terminated.
. . .

With respect to the State's important and legitimate interest in potential life, the "compelling" point is at viability. This is so because the fetus then presumably has the capability of meaningful life outside the mother's womb. State regulation protective of fetal life after viability thus has both logical and biological justifications. If the State is interested in protecting fetal life after viability, it may go so far as to proscribe abortion during that period, except when it is necessary to preserve the life or health of the mother.

Measured against these standards, Art. 1196 of the Texas Penal Code, in restricting legal abortions to those "procured or attempted by medical advice for the purpose of saving the life of the mother," sweeps too broadly. The statute makes no distinction between abortions performed early in pregnancy and those performed later, and it limits to a single reason, "saving" the mother's life, the legal justification for the procedure. The statute, therefore, cannot survive the constitutional attack made upon it here.

. . .

XI

To summarize and to repeat:

1. A state criminal abortion statute of the current Texas type, that excepts from criminality only a *life-saving* procedure on behalf of the mother, without regard to pregnancy stage and without recognition of the other interests involved, is violative of the Due Process Clause of the Fourteenth Amendment.

(a) For the stage prior to approximately the end of the first trimester, the abortion decision and its effectuation must be left to the medical judgment of the pregnant woman's attending physician.

(b) For the stage subsequent to approximately the end of the first trimester, the State, in promoting its interest in the health of the mother, may, if it chooses, regulate the abortion procedure in ways that are reasonably related to maternal health.

(c) For the stage subsequent to viability, the State in promoting its interest in the potentiality of human life may, if it chooses, regulate, and even proscribe, abortion except where it is necessary, in appropriate medical judgment, for the preservation of the life or health of the mother.

2. The State may define the term "physician," as it has been employed in the preceding paragraphs of this Part XI of this opinion, to mean only a physician currently licensed by the State, and may proscribe any abortion by a person who is not a physician as so defined.

. . .

This holding, we feel, is consistent with the relative weights of the respective interests involved, with the lessons and examples of medical and legal history, with the lenity of the common law, and with the demands of the profound problems of the present day. The decision leaves the State free to place increasing restrictions on abortion as the period of pregnancy lengthens, so long as those restrictions are tailored to the recognized state interests. The decision vindicates the right of the physician to administer medical treatment according to his professional judgment up to the points where important state interests provide compelling justifications for intervention. Up to those points, the abortion decision in all its aspects is inherently, and primarily, a medical decision, and basic responsibility for it must rest with the physician. If an individual practitioner abuses the privilege of exercising proper medical judgment, the usual remedies, judicial and intra-professional, are available.

XII

Our conclusion that Art. 1196 is unconstitutional means, of course, that the Texas abortion statutes, as a unit, must fall. . . .

It is so ordered.

Mr. Justice Rehnquist and Mr. Justice White dissented.

NOTE

The Supreme Court in *Roe* decided not to define when life begins because there is no consensus on the issue. Sissela Bok argues, however, that there is no disagreement on the factual matters concerning fetal development, only differences in views "about the names and moral consequences we attach to the changes in this [human] development and the distinctions we consider important." She concludes, therefore, that we should abandon "the quest for a definition of humanity capable of showing us who has a right to live" and focus instead on the reasons for protecting life and on whether those reasons are applicable to the fetus at some stage of its development. Bok, Ethical Problems of Abortion, 2 Hastings Center Studies 33, 38–41 (1974).

Do you find Bok's view persuasive? Consider again the views expressed by Dworkin and Engelhardt on defining death and persons in Ch. 7, Secs. A.1. and A.2., supra. What are society's reasons for protecting life? At what stage of fetal development do these reasons become compelling?

Consider whether a definition of when life begins would help you to resolve the conflict between fetal and maternal interests in the following case.

JEFFERSON v. GRIFFIN SPALDING COUNTY HOSPITAL AUTHORITY

Supreme Court of Georgia, 1981.
247 Ga. 86, 274 S.E.2d 457.

PER CURIAM.

On Thursday, January 22, 1981, the Griffin Spalding County Hospital Authority petitioned the Superior Court of Butts County, as a court of equity, for an order authorizing it to perform a caesarean section and any necessary blood transfusions upon the defendant, an out-patient resident of Butts County, in the event she presented herself to the hospital for delivery of her unborn child, which was due on or about Monday, January 26. The superior court conducted an emergency hearing on Thursday, January 22, and entered the following order:

"This petition and rule nisi were filed and served on defendant today. When the Court convened at the appointed hour, defendant did not appear, in spite of the fact that both she and her husband had notice of the hearing.

"Defendant is in the thirty-ninth week of pregnancy. In the past few weeks she has presented herself to Griffin Spalding County Hospital for pre-natal care. The examining physician has found and defendant has been advised that she has a complete placenta previa; that the afterbirth is between the baby and the birth canal; that it is virtually impossible that this condition will correct itself prior to delivery; and that it is a 99% certainty that the child cannot survive natural childbirth (vaginal delivery). The chances of defendant surviving vaginal delivery are no better than 50%.

"The examining physician is of the opinion that a delivery by caesarean section prior to labor beginning would have an almost 100% chance of preserving the life of the child, along with that of defendant.

"On the basis of religious beliefs, defendant has advised the Hospital that she does not need surgical removal of the child and will not submit to it. Further, she refuses to take any transfusion of blood.

"The Hospital is required by its own policies to treat any patient seeking emergency treatment. It seeks authority of the Court to administer medical treatment to defendant to save the life of herself and her unborn child.

"The child is, as a matter of fact, viable and fully capable of sustaining life independent of the mother (defendant). The issue is whether this unborn child has any legal right to the protection of the Court.

. . .

"Because the life of defendant and of the unborn child are, at the moment, inseparable, the Court deems it appropriate to infringe upon the wishes of the mother to the extent it is necessary to give the child an opportunity to live.

"Accordingly, the plaintiff hospitals are hereby authorized to administer to defendant all medical procedures deemed necessary by the attending physician to preserve the life of defendant's unborn child. This authority shall be effective only if defendant voluntarily seeks admission to either of plaintiff's hospitals for the emergency delivery of the child.

"The Court has been requested to order defendant to submit to surgery before the natural childbirth process (labor) begins. The Court is reluctant to grant this request and does not do so at this time. However, should some agency of the State seek such relief through intervention in this suit or in a separate proceeding, the Court will promptly consider such request."

On Friday, January 23, the Georgia Department of Human Resources, acting through the Butts County Department of Family and Children Services, petitioned the Juvenile Court of Butts County for temporary custody of the unborn child, alleging that the child was a deprived child without proper parental care necessary for his or her physical health . . .

and praying for an order requiring the mother to submit to a caesarean section. After appointing counsel for the parents and for the child, the court conducted a joint hearing in both the superior court and juvenile court cases and entered the following order on the afternoon of January 23:

"This action in the Superior Court of Butts County was heard and decided yesterday, January 22, 1981.

"This morning, the Georgia Department of Human Resources, acting through the Butts County Department of Family and Children Services, filed a complaint in the Juvenile Court of Butts County alleging deprivation and seeking temporary custody of Jessie Mae Jefferson's unborn child.

"Because of the unusual nature of the relief sought in these cases and because the Juvenile Court of Butts County may not have the authority needed effectively to grant the relief sought, the Court consolidates these cases and renders the following judgment both as a Juvenile Court and under the broad powers of the Superior Court of Butts County. The Court readopts its findings contained in the Order dated January 22, 1981.

"At the proceeding held today, Jessie Mae Jefferson and her husband, John W. Jefferson were present and represented by counsel, Hugh Glidewell, Jr. Richard Milam, Attorney at Law, represented the interests of the unborn child.

"Based on the evidence presented, the Court finds that Jessie Mae Jefferson is due to begin labor at any moment. There is a 99 to 100 percent certainty that the unborn child will die if she attempts to have the child by vaginal delivery. There is a 99 to 100 percent chance that the child will live if the baby is delivered by Caesarean section prior to the beginning of labor. There is a 50 percent chance that Mrs. Jefferson herself will die if vaginal delivery is attempted. There is an almost 100 percent chance that Mrs. Jefferson will survive if a delivery by Caesarean section is done prior to the beginning of labor. The Court finds that as a matter of fact the child is a human being fully capable of sustaining life independent of the mother.

"Mrs. Jefferson and her husband have refused and continue to refuse to give consent to a Caesarean section. This refusal is based entirely on the religious beliefs of Mr. and Mrs. Jefferson. They are of the view that the Lord has healed her body and that whatever happens to the child will be the Lord's will.

"Based on these findings, the Court concludes and finds as a matter of law that this child is a viable human being and entitled to the protection of the Juvenile Court Code of Georgia. The Court concludes that this child is without the proper parental care and subsistence necessary for his or her physical life and health.

"Temporary custody of the unborn child is hereby granted to the State of Georgia Department of Human Resources and the Butts County Department of Family and Children Services. The Department shall have full authority to make all decisions, including giving consent to the surgical delivery appertaining to the birth of this child. The temporary custody of the Department shall terminate when the child has been successfully brought from its mother's body into the world or until the child dies, whichever shall happen.

"Because of the unique nature of these cases, the powers of the Superior Court of Butts County are invoked and the defendant, Jessie Mae Jefferson, is hereby Ordered to submit to a sonogram (ultrasound) at the Griffin Spalding County Hospital or some other place which may be chosen by her where such procedure can be given. Should said sonogram indicate to the attending physician that the complete placenta privia is still blocking the child's passage into this world, Jessie Mae Jefferson, is Ordered to submit to a Caesarean section and related procedures considered necessary by the attending physician to sustain the life of this child.

"The Court finds that the State has an interest in the life of this unborn, living human being. The Court finds that the intrusion involved into the life of Jessie Mae Jefferson and her husband, John W. Jefferson, is outweighed by the duty of the State to protect a living, unborn human being from meeting his or her death before being given the opportunity to live.

"This Order shall be effective at 10:00 a.m. on Saturday, January 24, 1981, unless a stay is granted by the Supreme Court of Georgia or some other Court having the authority to stay an Order of this Court."

The parents filed their motion for stay in this court at about 5:30 p.m. on January 23 . . . [T]his court entered the following order on the evening of January 23:

"It is ordered that the Motion for Stay filed in this matter is hereby denied. The trial court's orders are effective immediately . . ."

Motion for stay denied.

All the Justices concur.

HILL, PRESIDING JUSTICE, concurring.

The power of a court to order a competent adult to submit to surgery is exceedingly limited. Indeed, until this unique case arose, I would have thought such power to be nonexistent. Research shows that the courts generally have held that a competent adult has the right to refuse necessary lifesaving surgery and medical treatment (i.e., has the right to die) where no state interest other than saving the life of the patient is involved. . . .

On the other hand, one court has held that an expectant mother in the last weeks of pregnancy lacks the right to refuse necessary life saving surgery and medical treatment where the life of the unborn child is at stake. Raleigh Fitkin-Paul Morgan Memorial Hospital v. Anderson, [42 N.J. 421, 201 A.2d 537, cert. den. 377 U.S. 985, 84 S.Ct. 1894, 12 L.Ed.2d 1032 (1964)]; see also Re Melideo, 88 Misc.2d 974, 390 N.Y.S.2d 523 (1976); Re Yetter, 62 Pa.D.&C.2d 619, 623 (1973).

The Supreme Court has recognized that the state has an interest in protecting the lives of unborn, viable children (viability usually occurring at about 7 months, or 28 weeks). . . .

The mother here was in her last week of normal pregnancy (the 39th week). She had diligently sought prenatal care for her child and herself, except for her refusal to consent to a caesarean section. She was due to deliver on Monday, January 26, and the medical testimony showed that the birth could occur at any time within 2 weeks of that date. . . .

In denying the stay of the trial court's order and thereby clearing the way for immediate reexamination by sonogram and probably for surgery, we weighed the right of the mother to practice her religion and to refuse surgery on herself, against her unborn child's right to live. We found in favor of her child's right to live.

Although we are not called upon here to decide whether the intervention of the juvenile court was necessary, I for one approve the trial court's action in exercising jurisdiction over the unborn child as juvenile judge and over the mother as judge of a court of equity. According to the testimony, this child was facing almost certain death, and was being deprived of the opportunity to live. For this reason, Code Ann. § 24A–401(h)(5) is inapplicable.[1]

I am authorized to state that MARSHALL, J., joins in this concurring opinion.

SMITH, JUSTICE, concurring.

1. "The free exercise of religion is, of course, one of our most precious freedoms. . . . The courts have, however, drawn a distinction between the free exercise of religious belief which is constitutionally protected against any infringement and religious practices that are inimical or detrimental to public health or welfare which are not." . . .

. . .

In the instant case, it appears that there is no less burdensome alternative for preserving the life of a fully developed fetus than requiring its mother to undergo surgery against her religious convictions. Such an intrusion by the state would be extraordinary, presenting some medical risk to both the mother and the fetus. However, the state's compelling interest in preserving the life of this fetus is beyond dispute. Moreover, the medical evidence indicates that the risk to the fetus *and* the mother presented by a Caesarean section would be minimal, whereas, in the absence of surgery, the fetus would almost certainly die and the mother's chance of survival would be no better than 50 per cent. Under these circumstances, I must conclude that the trial court's order is not violative of the First Amendment, notwithstanding that it may require the mother to submit to surgery against her religious beliefs. See *Raleigh Fitkin-Paul Memorial Hospital v. Anderson,* supra; see also Green v. Green, 448 Pa. 338, 292 A.2d 387 (1972).

2. We deal here with an apparent life and death emergency; questions relating to the jurisdiction of the lower court are not our primary concern.

. . . I believe the legislature intended that the juvenile courts exercise jurisdiction only where a child has seen the light of day. I am aware of no "child deprivation" proceeding wherein the "child" was unborn. See Patty v. Department of Human Resources, 154 Ga.App. 455, 269 S.E.2d 30 (1980).

This is a case of first impression, and the trial court, in an attempt to cover all possible ground, rendered its judgment "both as a Juvenile Court and under the broad powers of the Superior Court of Butts County." As the trial court's action was a proper exercise of its equitable jurisdiction with respect to both the mother and the fetus (see *Raleigh Fitkin-Paul Memorial Hospital v. Anderson,* supra), and its decision on the merits a correct one, I fully concur in the denial of appellant's motion for stay.

. . .

---

1. According to newspaper reports, ". . . a third ultrasound test performed Friday night showed the placenta had moved—a most unusual occurrence . . ." Atlanta Journal/Constitution, January 25, 1981.

NOTES

1. As the decision in *Jefferson* demonstrates, conflicts between maternal and fetal interests do arise where the decision whether to abort is not at issue. Does the *Jefferson* decision violate the constitutional rights of the mother? Does *Roe* mean that the mother's wishes should prevail? If *Roe* does not resolve the conflict, as a matter of policy should any pregnant woman be required by law to assist her fetus over her objection in comparable situations? In all circumstances? Should it make a difference if the proposed therapy is a routinely accepted procedure rather than an experimental one? That the pregnant woman is incompetent to make the decision? Should the requirement extend beyond the medical context and include conflicts posed by the mother's lifestyle such as her using drugs or driving recklessly? Would we require a father to donate a kidney to his ill daughter? Bone marrow? Blood? Would a definition of when life begins help you to resolve the conflicts between the pregnant woman and her fetus? For an interesting discussion suggesting that resolution of the fetal status issue would still leave the question of the mother's obligation to her fetus unresolved, see Thompson, A Defense of Abortion, 1 Phil. and Pub. Affairs 47 (1971).

2. For other cases involving therapeutic conflicts between the pregnant woman and her fetus, see Taft v. Taft, 388 Mass. 331, 446 N.E.2d 395 (1983) (court refused to order, as her husband requested, pregnant woman to submit to operation to suture her cervix to hold pregnancy because record failed to show state interest sufficiently compelling to override her right to privacy); Grodin v. Grodin, 102 Mich.App. 396, 301 N.W.2d 869 (1980) (court ruled that son could sue mother for taking tetracycline during pregnancy, allegedly causing damage to son's teeth); Reyes v. Superior Court, 75 Cal.App.3d 214, 141 Cal.Rptr. 912 (1977) (court refused to apply California felony child-endangering statute to pregnant woman using heroin because word "child" does not include fetus). See also Bowes and Selgestad, Fetal Versus Maternal Rights: Medical and Legal Perspectives, 58 Obstet.Gynecol. 209 (1981).

3. Growing medical knowledge about fetal growth and development and the development of a variety of techniques to diagnose and ameliorate fetal disabilities *in utero* will probably serve to increase the potential for conflicts between fetal and maternal interests. See generally Harrison, Golbus and Filly, Management of the Fetus With a Correctable Congenital Defect, 246 J.A.M.A. 774 (1981). There is some indication, however, that at least one diagnostic technique, ultrasound, which permits parental viewing of the fetus by means of ultrasound imaging, may increase the likelihood of early maternal-fetal bonding, thereby potentially reducing conflicts between maternal and fetal interests. See Fletcher and Evans, Maternal Bonding in Early Fetal Ultrasound Examinations, 308 New Eng.J.Med. 392 (1983); contra, Grace, Correspondence, 309 New Eng.J.Med. 561 (1983).

4. Should a mother or couple be able to determine the manner and place of birth? In all circumstances? Only when a normal delivery is expected? Should these decisions be viewed as raising potential conflicts between parental and fetal interests, or alternatively should they be understood as raising conflicts between the interests of parents and the medical profession?

2. HOW TO DEFINE

JOHN T. NOONAN, JR.,
AN ALMOST ABSOLUTE VALUE IN HISTORY

in The Morality of Abortion: Legal and Historical Perspectives
1, 51–58 (J. T. Noonan, ed. 1970).

The most fundamental question involved in the long history of thought on abortion is: How do you determine the humanity of a being? To phrase the question that way is to put in comprehensive humanistic terms what the theologians either dealt with as an explicitly theological question under the heading of "ensoulment" or dealt with implicitly in their treatment of abortion. The Christian position as it originated did not depend on a narrow theological or philosophical concept. It had no relation to theories of infant baptism. It appealed to no special theory of instantaneous ensoulment. It took the world's view on ensoulment as that view changed from Aristotle to Zacchia. There was, indeed, theological influence affecting the theory of ensoulment finally adopted, and, of course, ensoulment itself was a theological concept, so that the position was always explained in theological terms. But the theological notion of ensoulment could easily be translated into humanistic language by substituting "human" for "rational soul"; the problem of knowing when a man is a man is common to theology and humanism.

If one steps outside the specific categories used by the theologians, the answer they gave can be analyzed as a refusal to discriminate among human beings on the basis of their varying potentialities. Once conceived, the being was recognized as man because he had man's potential. The criterion for humanity, thus, was simple and all-embracing: if you are conceived by human parents, you are human.

The strength of this position may be tested by a review of some of the other distinctions offered in the contemporary controversy over legalizing abortion. Perhaps the most popular distinction is in terms of viability. Before an age of so many months, the fetus is not viable, that is, it cannot be removed from the mother's womb and live apart from her. To that extent, the life of the fetus is absolutely dependent on the life of the mother. This dependence is made the basis of denying recognition to its humanity.

There are difficulties with this distinction. One is that the perfection of artificial incubation may make the fetus viable at any time: it may be removed and artificially sustained . . . This hypothetical extreme case relates to an actual difficulty: there is considerable elasticity to the idea of viability. Mere length of life is not an exact measure. The viability of the fetus depends on the extent of its anatomical and functional development. The weight and length of the fetus are better guides to the state of its development than age, but weight and length vary. Moreover, different racial groups have different ages at which their fetuses are viable. Some evidence, for example, suggests that Negro fetuses mature more quickly than white fetuses. If viability is the norm, the standard would vary with race and with many individual circumstances.

The most important objection to this approach is that dependence is not ended by viability. The fetus is still absolutely dependent on someone's care in order to continue existence; indeed a child of one or three or even five years of age is absolutely dependent on another's care for existence; uncared for, the older fetus or the younger child will die as surely as the early fetus detached from the mother. The unsubstantial lessening in dependence at viability does not seem to signify any special acquisition of humanity.

A second distinction has been attempted in terms of experience. A being who has had experience, has lived and suffered, who possesses memories, is more human than one who has not. Humanity depends on formation by experience. The fetus is thus "unformed" in the most basic human sense.

This distinction is not serviceable for the embryo which is already experiencing and reacting. The embryo is responsive to touch after eight weeks and at least at that point is experiencing. At an earlier stage the zygote is certainly alive and responding to its environment. The distinction may also be challenged by the rare case where aphasia has erased adult memory: has it erased humanity? More fundamentally, this distinction leaves even the older fetus or the younger child to be treated as an unformed inhuman thing. Finally, it is not clear why experience as such confers humanity. It could be argued that certain central experiences such as loving or learning are necessary to make a man human. But then human beings who have failed to love or to learn might be excluded from the class called man.

A third distinction is made by appeal to the sentiments of adults. If a fetus dies, the grief of the parents is not the grief they would have for a living child. The fetus is an unnamed "it" till birth, and is not perceived as personality until at least the fourth month of existence when movements in the womb manifest a vigorous presence demanding joyful recognition by the parents.

Yet feeling is notoriously an unsure guide to the humanity of others. Many groups of humans have had difficulty in feeling that persons of another tongue, color, religion, sex, are as human as they. Apart from reactions to alien groups, we mourn the loss of a ten-year-old boy more than the loss of his one-day-old brother or his 90-year-old grandfather. The difference felt and the grief expressed vary with the potentialities extinguished, or the experience wiped out; they do not seem to point to any substantial difference in the humanity of baby, boy, or grandfather.

Distinctions are also made in terms of sensation by the parents. The embryo is felt within the womb only after about the fourth month. The embryo is seen only at birth. What can be neither seen nor felt is different from what is tangible. If the fetus cannot be seen or touched at all, it cannot be perceived as man.

Yet experience shows that sight is even more untrustworthy than feeling in determining humanity. By sight, color became an appropriate index for saying who was a man, and the evil of racial discrimination was given foundation. Nor can touch provide the test; a being confined by sickness, "out of touch" with others, does not thereby seem to lose his humanity. To the extent that touch still has appeal as a criterion, it appears to be a survival of the old English idea of "quickening"—a possible mistranslation of the Latin *animatus* used in the canon law. To that extent touch as a criterion seems to be dependent on the Aristotelian notion of ensoulment, and to fall when this notion is discarded.

Finally, a distinction is sought in social visibility. The fetus is not socially perceived as human. It cannot communicate with others. Thus, both subjectively and objectively, it is not a member of society. As moral rules are rules for the behavior of members of society to each other, they cannot be made for behavior toward what is not yet a member. Excluded from the society of men, the fetus is excluded from the humanity of men.

By force of the argument from the consequences, this distinction is to be rejected. It is more subtle than that founded on an appeal to physical sensation, but it is equally dangerous in its implications. If humanity depends on social recognition, individuals or whole groups may be dehumanized by being denied any status in their society. Such a fate is fictionally portrayed in *1984* and has actually been the lot of many men in many societies. In the Roman empire, for example, condemnation to slavery meant the practical denial of most human rights; in the Chinese Communist world, landlords have been classified as enemies of the people and so treated as nonpersons by the state. Humanity does not depend on social recognition, though often the failure of society to recognize the prisoner, the alien, the heterodox as human has led to the destruction of human beings. Anyone conceived by a man and a woman is human. Recognition of this condition by society follows a real event in the objective order, however imperfect and halting the recognition. Any attempt to limit humanity to exclude some group runs the risk of furnishing authority and precedent for excluding other groups in the name of the consciousness or perception of the controlling group in the society.

A philosopher may reject the appeal to the humanity of the fetus because he views "humanity" as a secular view of the soul and because he doubts the existence of anything real and objective which can be identified as humanity. One answer to such a philosopher is to ask how he reasons about moral questions without supposing that there is a sense in which he and the others of whom he speaks are human. Whatever group is taken as the society which determines who may be killed is thereby taken as human. A second answer is to ask if he does not believe that there is a right and wrong way of deciding moral questions. If there is such a difference, experience may be appealed to: to decide who is human on the basis of the sentiment of a given society has led to consequences which rational men would characterize as monstrous.

The rejection of the attempted distinctions based on viability and visibility, experience and feeling, may be buttressed by the following considerations: Moral judgments often rest on distinctions, but if the distinctions are not to appear arbitrary fiat, they should relate to some real difference in probabilities. There is a kind of continuity in all life, but the earlier stages of the elements of human life possess tiny probabilities of development. Consider for example, the spermatozoa in any normal ejaculate: There are about 200,000,000 in any single ejaculate, of which one has a chance of developing into a zygote. Consider the oocytes which may become ova: there are 100,000 to 1,000,000 oocytes in a female infant, of which a maximum of 390 are ovulated. But once spermatozoon and ovum meet and the conceptus is formed, such studies as have been made show that roughly in only 20 percent of the cases will spontaneous abortion occur. In other words, the chances are about 4 out of 5 that this new being will develop. At this stage in the life of the being there is a sharp shift in probabilities, an immense jump in potentialities. To make a distinction between the rights of spermatozoa and the rights of the fertilized ovum is to respond to an enormous shift in possibilities. For about twenty days after conception the egg may split to form twins or combine with another egg to form a chimera, but the probability of either event happening is very small.

It may be asked, What does a change in biological probabilities have to do with establishing humanity? The argument from probabilities is not aimed at establishing humanity but at establishing an objective discontinuity which may be taken into account in moral discourse. As life itself is a matter of probabilities, as most moral reasoning is an estimate of probabilities, so it seems in accord with the structure of reality and the nature of moral thought to found a moral judgment on the change in probabilities at conception. The appeal to probabilities is the most commonsensical of arguments, to a greater or smaller degree all of us base our actions on probabilities, and in morals, as in law, prudence and negligence are often measured by the account one has taken of the probabilities. If the chance is 200,000,000 to 1 that the movement in the bushes into which you shoot is a man's, I doubt if many persons would hold you careless in shooting; but if the chances are 4 out of 5 that the movement is a human being's, few would acquit you of blame. Would the argument be different if only one out of ten children conceived came to term? Of course this argument would be different. This argument is an appeal to probabilities that actually exist, not to any and all states of affairs which may be imagined.

The probabilities as they do exist do not show the humanity of the embryo in the sense of a demonstration in logic any more than the probabilities of the movement in the bush being a man demonstrate beyond all doubt that the being is a man. The appeal is a "buttressing" consideration, showing the plausibility of the standard adopted. The argument focuses on the decisional factor in any moral judgment and assumes that part of the business of a moralist is drawing lines. One evidence of the nonarbitrary character of the line drawn is the difference of probabilities on either side of it. If a spermatozoon is destroyed, one destroys a being which had a chance of far less than 1 in 200 million of developing into a reasoning being, possessed of the genetic code, a heart and other organs, and capable of pain. If a fetus is destroyed, one destroys a being already possessed of the genetic code, organs, and sensitivity to pain, and one which had an 80 percent chance of developing further into a baby outside the womb who, in time, would reason.

The positive argument for conception as the decisive moment of humanization is that at conception the new being receives the genetic code. It is this genetic information which determines his characteristics, which is the biological carrier of the possibility of human wisdom, which makes him a self-evolving being. A being with a human genetic code is man.

This review of current controversy over the humanity of the fetus emphasizes what a fundamental question the theologians resolved in asserting the inviolability of the fetus. To regard the fetus as possessed of equal rights with other humans was not, however, to decide every case where abortion might be employed. It did decide the case where the argument was that the fetus should be aborted for its own good. To say a being was human was to say it had a destiny to decide for itself which could not be taken from it by another man's decision. But human beings with equal rights often come in conflict with each other, and some decision must be made as whose claims are to prevail. Cases of conflict involving the fetus are different only in two respects: the total inability of the fetus to speak for itself and the fact that the right of the fetus regularly at stake is the right to life itself.

The approach taken by the theologians to these conflicts was articulated in terms of "direct" and "indirect." Again, to look at what they were doing from outside their categories, they may be said to have been drawing lines or "balancing values." "Direct" and "indirect" are spatial metaphors; "line-drawing" is another. "To weigh" or "to balance" values is a metaphor of a more complicated mathematical sort hinting at the process which goes on in moral judgments. All the metaphors suggest that, in the moral judgments made, comparisons were necessary, that no value completely controlled. The principle of double effect was no doctrine fallen from heaven, but a method of analysis appropriate where two relative values were being compared. In Catholic moral theology, as it developed, life even of the innocent was not taken as an absolute. Judgments on acts affecting life issued from a process of weighing. In the weighing, the fetus was always given a value greater than zero, always a value separate and independent from its parents. This valuation was crucial and fundamental in all Christian thought on the subject and marked it off from any approach which considered that only the parents' interests needed to be considered.

Even with the fetus weighed as human, one interest could be weighed as equal or superior: that of the mother in her own life. The casuists between 1450 and 1895 were willing to weigh this interest as superior. Since 1895, that interest was given decisive weight only in the two special cases of the cancerous uterus and the ectopic pregnancy. In both of these cases the fetus itself had little chance of survival even if the abortion were not performed. As the balance was once struck in favor of the mother whenever her life was endangered, it could be so struck again. The balance reached between 1895 and 1930 attempted prudentially and pastorally to forestall a multitude of exceptions for interests less than life.

The perception of the humanity of the fetus and the weighing of fetal rights against other human rights constituted the work of the moral analysts. But what spirit animated their abstract judgments? For the Christian community it was the injunction of Scripture to love your neighbor as yourself. The fetus as human was a neighbor; his life had parity with one's own. The commandment gave life to what otherwise would have been only rational calculation.

The commandment could be put in humanistic as well as theological terms: Do not injure your fellow man without reason. In these terms, once the humanity of the fetus is perceived, abortion is never right except in self-defense. When life must be taken to save life, reason alone cannot say that a mother must prefer a child's life to her own. With this exception, now of great rarity, abortion violates the rational humanist tenet of the equality of human lives.

NOTES

1. There are other points in fetal development that have been advocated as marking the beginning of human life. Implantation, which occurs within one week of fertilization, is often suggested because pregnancy cannot be diagnosed before this time. Moreover, some contraceptives, such as the IUD, are only effective after fertilization. The West German Constitutional Court prohibited abortion beginning two weeks from fertilization. Judgment of February 25, 1975, Bundesverfassungsgericht, W.Ger., 39 BVerge 1, translated in Gorky and Jonas, West German Abortion Decision: A Contrast to Roe v. Wade, 9 J.Mar.J.Proc. & Pro. 551 (1976) (life begins "according to definite biological physiological knowledge," at 14 days after conception at latest, since at that point implantation in uterus occurs and twinning is no longer possible). Others would urge that viability is the critical point, while still others continue to prefer birth. Finally, as medical technology continues to improve, we will possibly be able to pinpoint with great accuracy the onset of brain activity. At that time it could be argued that the criteria for defining both life and death should depend upon the presence of detectable brain activity.

What point in development do you find significant? For what reasons? For further discussion of these issues, see King, The Juridical Status of the Fetus: A Proposal for Legal Protection of the Unborn, 77 Mich.L.Rev. 1647 (1979). For an excellent description of fetal development, see Hellegers, Fetal Development, 31 Theological Studies 3 (1970).

2. For some years bills and resolutions have been introduced in Congress that would either define life or eliminate the right to privacy insofar as it permits a woman to decide whether she will have an abortion. In the 97th Congress, for example, S. 158 was introduced. It would have favored the view that life begins at conception, recognized a compelling state interest in protecting fetal life under the fourteenth amendment, and limited lower federal court jurisdiction to issue certain orders against state abortion laws. Is such legislation constitutional? See generally, Galebach, a Human Life Statute, 7 The Hum. Life Rev. 3 (1981); Estreicher, Congressional Power and Constitutional Rights: Reflections on Proposed "Human Life" Legislation, 68 Va.L.Rev. 333 (1982); Uddo, The Human Life Bill: Protecting the Unborn Through Congressional Enforcement of the Fourteenth Amendment, 27 Loyola L.Rev. 1079 (1981); Emerson, The Power of Congress to Change Constitutional Decisions of the Supreme Court: The Human Life Bill, 77 Nw.U.L.Rev.129 (1982).

3. Do "experts" have a role to play in determining when life begins? The following resolution was passed by the National Academy of Sciences on April 28, 1981:

> It is the view of the National Academy of Sciences that the statement in Chapter 101, Section 1, of U.S. Senate Bill S. 158, 1981, cannot stand up to the scrutiny of science. This section reads "The Congress finds that present day scientific evidence indicates a significant likelihood that actual human life exists from conception." This statement purports to derive its conclusions from science, but it deals with a question to which science can provide no answer. The proposal in S. 158 that the term "person" shall include "all human life" has no basis within our scientific understanding. Defining the time at which the developing embryo becomes a "person" must remain a matter of moral or religious values.

Are the members of the academy "experts" on the question of when life begins? Several of the scientists who testified at the subcommittee hearings on S. 158 argued that scientific evidence has established that life begins at conception. See, e.g., Testimony of Lejeune, Gordon and Mathews, Hearings on S. 158, before the Subcomm. on Separation of Powers, of the Senate Comm. on the Judiciary, 97th Cong., 1st Sess. 7–17 (1981). How should policymakers resolve these differences in views among the "experts"? For additional discussion on the role of experts, see Ch. 1, Sec. A.3., supra.

4. For further discussion of the principle of double effect, see Ch. 7, Sec. B. 2.C., supra.

B. DECIDING WHETHER, WHEN OR HOW TO REPRODUCE

---

1. THE RIGHTS OF PROSPECTIVE PARENTS

a. Competent Parents

GRISWOLD v. CONNECTICUT

Supreme Court of the United States, 1965.
381 U.S. 479, 85 S.Ct. 1678, 14 L.Ed.2d 510.

MR. JUSTICE DOUGLAS delivered the opinion of the Court.

Appellant Griswold is Executive Director of the Planned Parenthood League of Connecticut. Appellant Buxton is a licensed physician and a professor at the Yale Medical School who served as Medical Director for the League at its Center in New Haven—a center open and operating from November 1 to November 10, 1961, when appellants were arrested.

They gave information, instruction, and medical advice to *married persons* as to the means of preventing conception. They examined the wife and prescribed the best contraceptive device or material for her use. Fees were usually charged, although some couples were serviced free.

The statutes whose constitutionality is involved in this appeal are §§ 53–32 and 54–196 of the General Statutes of Connecticut (1958 rev.). The former provides:

> "Any person who uses any drug, medicinal article or instrument for the purpose of preventing conception shall be fined not less than fifty dollars or imprisoned not less than sixty days nor more than one year or be both fined and imprisoned."

Section 54–196 provides:

> "Any person who assists, abets, counsels, causes, hires or commands another to commit any offense may be prosecuted and punished as if he were the principal offender."

The appellants were found guilty as accessories and fined $100 each, against the claim that the accessory statute as so applied violated the Fourteenth Amendment. . . .

. . .

Coming to the merits, we are met with a wide range of questions that implicate the Due Process Clause of the Fourteenth Amendment. . . . We do not sit as a super-legislature to determine the wisdom, need, and propriety of laws that touch economic problems, business affairs, or social conditions. This law, however, operates directly on an intimate relation of husband and wife and their physician's role in one aspect of that relation.

The association of people is not mentioned in the Constitution nor in the Bill of Rights. The right to educate a child in a school of the parents' choice—whether public or private or parochial—is also not mentioned. Nor is the right to study any particular subject or any foreign language. Yet the First Amendment has been construed to include certain of those rights.

By *Pierce v. Society of Sisters*, the right to educate one's children as one chooses is made applicable to the States by the force of the First and Fourteenth Amendments. By *Meyer v. Nebraska*, the same dignity is given the right to study the German language in a private school. . . . Without those peripheral rights the specific rights would be less secure. And so we reaffirm the principle of the *Pierce* and the *Meyer* cases.

In NAACP v. Alabama, 357 U.S. 449, 462, 78 S.Ct. 1163, 1172, we protected the "freedom to associate and privacy in one's associations," noting that freedom of association was a peripheral First Amendment right. . . .

. . . The right of "association," like the right of belief (Board of Education v. Barnette, 319 U.S. 624, 63 S.Ct. 1178), is more than the right to attend a meeting; it includes the right to express one's attitudes or philosophies by membership in a group or by affiliation with it or by other lawful means. Association in that context is a form of expression of opinion; and while it is not expressly included in the First Amendment its existence is necessary in making the express guarantees fully meaningful.

The foregoing cases suggest that specific guarantees in the Bill of Rights have penumbras, formed by emanations from those guarantees that help give them life and substance. Various guarantees create zones of privacy. The right of association contained in the penumbra of the First Amendment is one, as we have seen. The Third Amendment in its prohibition against the quartering of soldiers "in any house" in time of peace without the consent of the owner is another facet of that privacy. The Fourth Amendment explicitly affirms the "right of the people to be secure in their persons, houses, papers, and effects, against unreasonable searches and seizures." The Fifth Amendment in its Self-Incrimination Clause enables the citizen to create a zone of privacy which government may not force him to surrender to his detriment. The Ninth Amendment provides: "The enumeration in the Constitution, of certain rights, shall not be construed to deny or disparage others retained by the people."

. . .

The present case . . . concerns a relationship lying within the zone of privacy created by several fundamental constitutional guarantees. And it concerns a law which, in forbidding the *use* of contraceptives rather than regulating their manufacture or sale, seeks to achieve its goals by means having a maximum destructive impact upon that relationship. Such a law cannot stand in light of the familiar principle, so often applied by this Court, that a "governmental purpose to control or prevent activities constitutionally subject to state regulation may not be achieved by means which sweep unnecessarily broadly and thereby invade the area of protected freedoms." NAACP v. Alabama, 377 U.S. 288, 307, 84 S.Ct. 1302, 1314, 12 L.Ed.2d 325. Would we allow the police to search the sacred precincts of marital bedrooms for telltale signs of the use of contraceptives? The very idea is repulsive to the notions of privacy surrounding the marriage relationship.

We deal with a right of privacy older than the Bill of Rights—older than our political parties, older than our school system. Marriage is a coming together for better or for worse, hopefully enduring, and intimate to the degree of being sacred. It is an association that promotes a way of life, not causes; a harmony in living, not political faiths; a bilateral loyalty, not commercial or social projects. Yet it is an association for as noble a purpose as any involved in our prior decisions.

Reversed.

MR. JUSTICE GOLDBERG, whom THE CHIEF JUSTICE and MR. JUSTICE BRENNAN join, concurring.

. . . Although I have not accepted the view that "due process" as used in the Fourteenth Amendment incorporates all of the first eight Amendments . . . I do agree that the concept of liberty protects those personal rights that are fundamental, and is not confined to the specific terms of the Bill of Rights. My conclusion that the concept of liberty is not so restricted and that it embraces the right of marital privacy though that right is not mentioned explicitly in the Constitution is supported both by numerous decisions of this Court, referred to in the Court's opinion, and by the language and history of the Ninth Amendment. . . . I add these words to emphasize the relevance of that Amendment to the Court's holding.

. . . .

The Ninth Amendment reads, "The enumeration in the Constitution, of certain rights, shall not be construed to deny or disparage others retained by the people." . . .

. . .

. . . To hold that a right so basic and fundamental and so deeprooted in our society as the right of privacy in marriage may be infringed because that right is not guaranteed in so many words by the first eight amendments to the Constitution is to ignore the Ninth Amendment and to give it no effect whatsover. . . .

. . .

In determining which rights are fundamental, judges are not left at large to decide cases in light of their personal and private notions. Rather, they must look to the "traditions and [collective] conscience of our people" to determine whether a principle is "so rooted [there] . . . as to be ranked as fundamental." Snyder v. Massachusetts, 291 U.S. 97, 105, 54 S.Ct. 330, 332. The inquiry is whether a right involved "is of such a character that it cannot be denied without violating those 'fundamental principles of liberty and justice which lie at the base of all our civil and political institutions' . . . ." Powell v. Alabama, 287 U.S. 45, 67, 53 S.Ct. 55, 63, 77 L.Ed. 158. . . .

I agree fully with the Court that, applying these tests, the right of privacy is a fundamental personal right, emanating "from the totality of the constitutional scheme under which we live." [Poe v. Ullman, 367 U.S. 497, 521, 81 S.Ct. 1752, 1765, 6 L.Ed.2d 989 (dissenting opinion of Mr. Justice Douglas).]

. . .

The Connecticut statutes here involved deal with a particularly important and sensitive area of privacy that of the marital relation and the marital home. . . .

I agree with Mr. Justice Harlan's statement in his dissenting opinion in Poe v. Ullman, 367 U.S. 497, 551–552, 81 S.Ct. 1752, 1781: "Certainly the safeguarding of the home does not follow merely from the sanctity of property rights. The home derives its pre-eminence as the seat of family life. And the integrity of that life is something so fundamental that it has been found to draw to its protection the principles of more than one explicitly granted Constitutional right. . . . Of this whole 'private realm of family life' it is difficult to imagine what is more private or more intimate than a husband and wife's marital relations."

. . .

MR. JUSTICE HARLAN, concurring in the judgment.

. . .

In my view, the proper constitutional inquiry in this case is whether this Connecticut statute infringes the Due Process Clause of the Fourteenth Amendment because the enactment violates basic values "implicit in the concept of ordered liberty," Palko v. Connecticut, 302 U.S. 319, 325, 58 S.Ct. 149, 152, 82 L.Ed. 288. For reasons stated at length in my dissenting opinion in *Poe v. Ullman*, I believe that it does. . . .

. . .

Mr. Justice White, concurring in the judgment.

In my view this Connecticut law as applied to married couples deprives them of "liberty" without due process of law, as that concept is used in the Fourteenth Amendment. . . .

It would be unduly repetitious, and belaboring the obvious, to expound on the impact of this statute on the liberty guaranteed by the Fourteenth Amendment against arbitrary or capricious denials or on the nature of this liberty. Suffice it to say that this is not the first time this Court has had occasion to articulate that the liberty entitled to protection under the Fourteenth Amendment includes the right "to marry, establish a home and bring up children," Meyer v. Nebraska, 262 U.S. 390, 399, 43 S.Ct. 625, 626, 67 L.Ed.2d 1042 and "the liberty . . . to direct the upbringing and education of children," Pierce v. Society of Sisters, 268 U.S. 510, 534–535, 45 S.Ct. 571, 573, 69 L.Ed. 1070, and that these are among "the basic civil rights of man." Skinner v. Oklahoma, 316 U.S. 535, 541, 62 S.Ct. 1110, 1113, 86 L.Ed. 1655. These decisions affirm that there is a "realm of family life which the state cannot enter" without substantial justification. Prince v. Massachusetts, 321 U.S. 158, 166, 64 S.Ct. 438, 442, 88 L.Ed. 645. Surely the right invoked in this case, to be free of regulation of the intimacies of the marriage relationship, "come[s] to this Court with a momentum for respect lacking when appeal is made to liberties which derive merely from shifting economic arrangements." Kovacs v. Cooper, 336 U.S. 77, 95, 69 S.Ct. 448, 458, 93 L.Ed. 513 (opinion of Frankfurter, J.).

The Connecticut anti-contraceptive statute deals rather substantially with this relationship. For it forbids all married persons the right to use birth-control devices, regardless of whether their use is dictated by considerations of family planning, Trubek v. Ullman, 147 Conn. 633, 165 A.2d 158, health, or indeed even of life itself, Buxton v. Ullman, 147 Conn. 48, 156 A.2d 508. . . .

An examination of the justification offered, however, cannot be avoided by saying that the Connecticut anti-use statute invades a protected area of privacy and association or that it demeans the marriage relationship. The nature of the right invaded is pertinent, to be sure, for statutes regulating sensitive areas of liberty do, under the cases of this Court, require "strict scrutiny," . . . But such statutes, if reasonably necessary for the effectuation of a legitimate and substantial state interest, and not arbitrary or capricious in application, are not invalid under the Due Process Clause. Zemel v. Rusk, 381 U.S. 1, 85 S.Ct. 1271.

As I read the opinions of the Connecticut courts and the argument of Connecticut in this Court, the State claims but one justification for its anti-use statute. . . . [T]he statute is said to serve the State's policy against all forms of promiscuous or illicit sexual relationships, be they premarital or extramarital, concededly a permissible and legitimate legislative goal.

Without taking issue with the premise that the fear of conception operates as a deterrent to such relationships in addition to the criminal proscriptions Connecticut has against such conduct, I wholly fail to see how the ban on the use of contraceptives by married couples in any way reinforces the State's ban on illicit sexual relationships. . . .

. . .

MR. JUSTICE BLACK, with whom MR. JUSTICE STEWART joins, dissenting.

. . . I do not to any extent whatever base my view that this Connecticut law is constitutional on a belief that the law is wise or that its policy is a good one. In order that there may be no room at all to doubt why I vote as I do, I feel constrained to add that the law is every bit as offensive to me as it is to my Brethren of the majority and my Brothers Harlan, White and Goldberg who, reciting reasons why it is offensive to them, hold it unconstitutional. There is no single one of the graphic and eloquent strictures and criticisms fired at the policy of this Connecticut law either by the Court's opinion or by those of my concurring Brethren to which I cannot subscribe—except their conclusion that the evil qualities they see in the law make it unconstitutional.

. . .

The Court talks about a constitutional "right of privacy" as though there is some constitutional provision or provisions forbidding any law ever to be passed which might abridge the "priva ," of individuals. But there is not. . . .

. . .

. . . I like my privacy as well as the next one, but I am nevertheless compelled to admit that government has a right to invade it unless prohibited by some specific constitutional provision. For these reasons I cannot agree with the Court's judgment and the reasons it gives for holding this Connecticut law unconstitutional.

. . .

NOTES

1. After *Griswold*, but before *Roe*, the Court decided Eisenstadt v. Baird, 405 U.S. 438, 92 S.Ct. 1029, 31 L.Ed.2d 349 (1972), another significant case involving the control and distribution of contraceptives. The opinion in *Eisenstadt* clarified and expanded what the Court had said about the right of privacy in *Griswold*. While *Griswold* involved the use of contraceptives by married persons, *Eisenstadt* overturned a law banning the distribution of contraceptives to single persons. Appellee Baird had been convicted under a Massachusetts statute for having given a young woman a package of vaginal foam at the close of a lecture on contraception delivered to a group of students at Boston University.

The statutory scheme created three distinct classes of distributees: (1) married persons, who could obtain contraceptives to prevent pregnancy, but only from doctors or pharmacists on prescription; (2) single persons, who could not obtain contraceptives to prevent pregnancy; and (3) married or single persons, who could obtain contraceptives from anyone to prevent the spread of disease.

Justice Brennan, writing for the Court, held that the statute, viewed as a prohibition on contraception *per se*, violated the rights of single persons under the equal protection clause of the fourteenth amendment. Although the fourteenth amendment does not deny to states the power to treat different classes of persons in different ways, such classifications must pass scrutiny under the equal protection clause. A classification, to be constitutional, "must be *reasonable*, not arbitrary, and must rest upon some ground of difference *having a fair and substantial relation to the object of the legislation*, so that all persons similarly circumstanced shall be treated alike." 405 U.S., at 447, 90 S.Ct., at 1035 (citing Royster Guano Co. v. Virginia, 253 U.S. 412, 415, 40 S.Ct. 560, 561 (1920)) (emphasis added). The Court concluded that no rational basis had been offered to explain the different treatment accorded married and unmarried persons under the Massachusetts law.

Explaining the outcome in *Eisenstadt*, the Court stated, "If under *Griswold* the distribution of contraceptives to married persons cannot be prohibited, a ban on the distribution [of contraceptives] to unmarried persons would be equally impermissible . . .. If the right of privacy means anything, it is the right of the *individual,* married or single, to be free from unwarranted governmental intrusion into matters so fundamentally affecting a person as the decision whether to bear or beget a child." 405 U.S., at 453, 90 S.Ct., at 1038.

While the Court could find no rational ground for the distinction between the three classes, the Court declined to answer the question of whether the Massachusetts law could be upheld simply as a prohibition on contraception, stating simply that "whatever the rights of the individual to access to contraceptives may be, the rights must be the same for the unmarried and married alike."

The Court did, however, shed light on the question in a case decided after *Roe.* In Carey v. Population Services International, Inc., 431 U.S. 678, 97 S.Ct. 2010, 52 L.Ed.2d 675 (1977), the Court invalidated a number of restrictions on the distribution of non-prescription contraceptives. One provision of the challenged law prohibited the distribution of contraceptives to persons over 16 by anyone other than a licensed pharmacist.

In invalidating the restriction, Justice Brennan, writing for a majority, quoted from the earlier *Eisenstadt* opinion and stated that *Griswold,* read in light of its progeny, may no longer be read as holding only that a state may not prohibit a married couple's use of contraceptives.

2. What impact, if any, will the development of convenient inexpensive, effective and safe contraceptives have on society's views on abortion? On the use of sterilization as a method of birth control, especially with incompetent persons? See Sec. B.1.b., infra. For a comprehensive evaluation of the risks and benefits of various birth control methods published by the Alan Guttmacher Institute, see H. Ory, J. Forrest and R. Lincoln, Making Choices (1983).

ROE v. WADE

Supreme Court of the United States, 1973.
410 U.S. 113, 93 S.Ct. 705, 35 L.Ed.2d 147.

[The opinion is printed in Sec. A.1., supra.]

NOTES

1. There are several points of ambiguity in the *Roe* holding. What does the term "viability" mean? Because viability can not be fixed at a specific point in the gestation period for all fetuses and will advance over time toward conception as medical capability improves, how do we determine whether a particular fetus is viable? In subsequent decisions, the Supreme Court has recognized that viability will advance and has stated that individual determinations are left to the reasonable judgment of physicians. Planned Parenthood of Central Missouri v. Danforth, 428 U.S. 52, 96 S.Ct. 2831, 49 L.Ed.2d 788 (1975); Colautti v. Franklin, 439 U.S. 379, 99 S.Ct. 675, 58 L.Ed.2d 596 (1979); see also King, The Juridical Status of the Fetus: A Proposal for Legal Protection of the Unborn, 77 Mich.L.Rev. 1647 (1979). The Supreme Court in *Roe* held that after viability a state may proscribe abortion "except where necessary, in appropriate medical judgment, for the preservation of the life and health of the mother." 410 U.S., at 165, 93 S.Ct., at 732. What does the Court mean by "health"? Finally, what did the Court in *Roe* mean when it used the term "abortion"? Until recently most discussions of abortion have assumed that induced termination of pregnancy would result in the death of the fetus. Some fetuses, however, have survived attempts at abortions late in pregnancy. See American College of Obstetricians and Gynecologists, Technical Bulletin No. 56, Methods of Mid-Trimester Abortion (Dec.1979) (as high as 7 percent live-birth rate for intrauterine instillation of uterotonic agents). The question, therefore, arises whether a woman is entitled only to the removal of the fetus from her womb or whether she can expect death of the fetus as well. Should a woman's expectation determine the choice of method to be used in late abortions

and determine the extent to which physicians should be obligated to treat live-born infants?

2. The Supreme Court heard its first major post-*Roe* challenge to abortion regulations in Planned Parenthood of Missouri v. Danforth, which involved not only the interests of the mother and of the fetus, but of the father as well. One provision of the challenged statute required that before submitting to an abortion during the first 12 weeks of pregnancy, a woman must obtain, "the written consent of [her] spouse, unless the abortion is certified by a licensed physician to be necessary in order to preserve the life of the mother." 428 U.S., at 58, 96 S.Ct., at 2836. This statutory requirement effectively barred a married woman from obtaining an abortion in most circumstances without her husband's written consent—irrespective of the condition of her marriage. The Court invalidated this requirement. Justice Blackmun, writing for the majority, explained that "since the state cannot [prohibit] abortion during the first stage [of pregnancy], the State cannot delegate the authority to any particular person, even the spouse, to prevent abortion during that same period." 428 U.S., at 69, 96 S.Ct., at 2841.

Justice Blackmun acknowledged that the decision in *Danforth* made the unilateral choice of the woman dispositive, irrespective of the husband's "deep and abiding concern and interest [in] his wife's pregnancy." Because the woman "is the more directly and immediately affected by the pregnancy as between the two," Blackmun found that "the balance weighs in her favor." Id. at 71, 96 S.Ct., at 2842. In his view, the statute at issue in *Danforth* rested on the false premise that the husband's interest is always superior.

While the Constitution protects "a woman's decision whether or not to terminate her pregnancy," Roe v. Wade, 410 U.S. 113, 153, 93 S.Ct. 705, 35 L.Ed.2d 147 (1973), previous decisions of the Court have also recognized that a man's right to father children and enjoy the association of his offspring is constitutionally protected. See, e.g., Stanley v. Illinois, 405 U.S. 645, 92 S.Ct. 1208, 31 L.Ed. 2d 551 (1972) (voiding scheme that declared children of unmarried father, upon death of mother, dependents of state without any hearing on parental fitness and without proof of neglect). In assessing the validity of Missouri's spousal consent requirement in *Danforth*, the Court was forced to choose between competing interests. Should the father's interest have been given weight? In his dissent in *Danforth*, Justice White expressed the view that "[a] father's interest in having a child—perhaps his only child—may be unmatched by any other interest in his life." 428 U.S., at 93, 96 S.Ct., at 2852. White explained that even though the state cannot proscribe abortion [during the first 12 weeks of pregnancy] because the mother's interest in deciding "whether or not to terminate her pregnancy" outweighs the state's interest in the potential life of the fetus, it does not logically follow that the husband's interest is also outweighed and may not be protected by the state. Id.

Given the decision in *Danforth*, would a requirement that the father be given notification before an abortion be constitutional?

3. In three companion cases decided in 1977, the Supreme Court held that neither the Constitution nor federal law required states to fund nontherapeutic abortions for women with financial need. In Beal v. Doe, the Court found that Title XIX of the Social Security Act, which established Medicaid, did not require Pennsylvania to fund "nontherapeutic" abortions as a precondition to receiving funds in a joint federal-state medical assistance program. 432 U.S. 438, 97 S.Ct. 2366, 53 L.Ed.2d 464 (1977). Maher v. Roe held that Connecticut's refusal to pay for nontherapeutic abortions did not violate the equal protection clause. This was true, the Court said, even though Medicaid support was being provided to cover the expenses of childbirth. 432 U.S. 464, 97 S.Ct. 2376, 53 L.Ed.2d 484 (1977). And in Poelker v. Doe, the Court rejected a constitutional attack upon the decision of city-owned hospitals in St. Louis to finance services for childbirth while failing to provide corresponding services for nontherapeutic abortion. 432 U.S. 519, 97 S.Ct. 2391, 53 L.Ed.2d 528 (1977). But cf. Nyberg v. City of Virginia, 667 F.2d 754 (8th Cir.1982) (city could not prohibit staff physician from per-

forming nontherapeutic abortions for paying patients at publicly-owned hospital when hospital was sole hospital in community).

In 1979, access to federal monies for abortions was restricted even further with the passage of the "Hyde Amendment," that prohibited payment for most medically necessary abortions. The amendment excepted abortions performed where the life of the mother would be endangered if the fetus were carried to term and where pregnancy was the result of rape or incest which had been promptly reported to a law enforcement agency or public health service. P.L. 96–123, § 109, 93 Stat. 926 (1979). In Harris v. McRae, 448 U.S. 297, 100 S.Ct. 2671, 65 L.Ed.2d 784 (1980), the constitutionality of the amendment was challenged on the grounds that it violated the substantive due process and equal protection clauses of the Constitution. The Court found that it placed no undue restriction on a woman's right to have an abortion, however, because the due process clause does not require states to provide funds to enable people to avail themselves of constitutionally protected choices. Like the Connecticut welfare regulation at issue in *Maher*, the Hyde Amendment placed no obstacle in the path of a woman who desired to terminate her pregnancy, but rather, "by means of unequal subsidization of abortion and other medical services, encourages alternative activity deemed in the public interest." Id., at 315, 100 S.Ct., at 2687. The failure to fund the full range of a woman's protected choices, the Court stated, was not constitutionally prohibited. Although "government may not place obstacles in the path of a woman's exercise of her freedom of choice, it need not remove those not of its own creation." Id., at 316, 100 S.Ct., at 2687. The Court found indigency to be in the latter category, and of itself not a suspect classification triggering greater scrutiny.

4. The Supreme Court decided three cases in 1983 concerning state and local laws enacted to regulate abortion. The cases are significant because they explicitly reaffirm the Court's decision in Roe v. Wade, 410 U.S. 113, 93 S.Ct. 705, 35 L.Ed.2d 147 (1973), and continue the Court's reliance on the pregnancy trimester framework in determining what abortion regulations are constitutionally permissible.

In City of Akron v. Akron Center for Reproductive Health, Inc., ___ U.S. ___, 103 S.Ct. 2481, 76 L.Ed.2d 687 (1983), the Court struck down as unconstitutional provisions of an Akron city ordinance that included requirements that all abortions after the first trimester be performed in a hospital, that a physician notify and obtain consent of a parent or guardian before performing an abortion on an unmarried minor, that the attending physician provide certain information to an abortion patient so that she could give "informed consent" for the procedure, that the physician allow a 24-hour waiting period between the patient's written consent to and performance of an abortion and that fetal remains be "disposed of in a humane and sanitary manner." Id., at ___-___, 103 S.Ct., at 2488–89.

The Court began by upholding its determination in *Roe* that a state's interest in maternal health becomes compelling at approximately the end of the first trimester, despite medical evidence that such a dividing point might no longer be appropriate. Id., at ___, 103 S.Ct., at 2491–92. The Court said in a footnote:

> *Roe* identified the end of the first trimester as the compelling point because until that time—according to the medical literature available in 1973—"mortality in abortion may be less than mortality in normal childbirth." 410 U.S., at 163, 93 S.Ct., at 731. There is substantial evidence that developments in the past decade, particularly the development of a much safer method for performing second-trimester abortions . . . have extended the period in which abortions are safer than childbirth. See, e.g., LeBolt, *et al.*, Mortality from Abortion and Childbirth: Are the Populations Comparable?, 248 J.A.M.A. 188, 191 (1982) (abortion may be safer than childbirth up to gestational ages of 16 weeks).

> We think it prudent, however, to retain *Roe's* identification of the beginning of the second trimester as the approximate time at which the State's interest in maternal health becomes sufficiently compelling to justify significant regulation of abortion. . . .

The *Roe* trimester standard . . . continues to provide a reasonable legal framework for limiting a State's authority to regulate abortions. Where the State adopts a health regulation governing the performance of abortions during the second trimester, the determinative question should be whether there is a reasonable medical basis for the regulation. . . . The comparison between abortion and childbirth mortality rates may be relevant only where the State employs a health rationale as a justification for a complete prohibition on abortions in certain circumstances.

Id., at ___ n. 11, 103 S.Ct., at 2492 n. 11.

In declaring the hospitalization requirement unconstitutional, the Court said that even though the state interest in maternal health becomes compelling after the first trimester, state health regulations concerning abortion must further that state interest. Id., at ___, 103 S.Ct., at 2495. After lengthy discussion of changes in abortion techniques and professional standards since *Roe*, the Court concluded that the ordinance's requirement of hospitalization for all second trimester abortions constituted "a significant obstacle in the path of women seeking an abortion." Id. The Court felt that the ordinance's application to all second trimester abortions, in light of medical evidence that early second trimester abortions could be performed safely in a "minimally equipped facility" was unreasonable. Id., at ___, 103 S.Ct., at 2496–97.

The Court held that its recognition in *Danforth*, see Note 2, supra, that a state could require giving information about the procedure and its consequences to a woman seeking an abortion could not support the requirements the Akron ordinance imposed. Id., at ___, 103 S.Ct., at 2500. Although Akron conceded that three subsections were unconstitutional (subsections requiring disclosure of detailed information concerning fetal development, fetal viability and possible physical and psychological complications), the Court refused to sever these subsections from four which it found "unobjectionable." Id., at ___ and n. 37, 103 S.Ct., at 2500–01 and n. 37. Additionally, the Court held that the ordinance's requirement that the attending physician provide the information was unreasonable. Id., at ___, 103 S.Ct., at 2503.

In overturning the 24-hour waiting period requirement, the Court found that Akron had "failed to show that any legitimate state interest [would be] furthered by an arbitrary and inflexible waiting period." Id. The Court placed reliance on a physician's willingness to advise a patient to defer an abortion decision when he or she feels deferral is in the patient's best interests. Id.

The Court invalidated the "humane and sanitary" disposal requirement because it felt that "humane" was an impermissibly vague term, not providing physicians with "fair notice" of proscribed behavior. It rejected Akron's argument that the ordinance merely forebade "mindless dumping of aborted fetuses on garbage piles," a power that the Court had confirmed in the states in affirming Planned Parenthood Association v. Fitzpatrick, 401 F.Supp. 554 (E.D.Pa.1975), affirmed mem. sub nom. Franklin v. Fitzpatrick, 428 U.S. 901, 96 S.Ct. 3202, 49 L.Ed.2d 1205 (1976). Id., at ___, 103 S.Ct., at 2504.

In Planned Parenthood Association of Kansas City, Mo., Inc. v. Ashcroft, ___ U.S. ___, 103 S.Ct. 2517, 76 L.Ed.2d 733 (1983), a fragmented Court struck down a second trimester hospitalization requirement similar to that invalidated in *City of Akron*, but upheld Missouri laws requiring the presence of a second physician at abortions after the fetus is viable, pathological analysis of fetal remains and parental consent for minors' abortions. Relying on the *Roe* recognition that a state has a compelling interest in the life of a viable fetus, Justice Powell, joined only by Chief Justice Burger,[1] determined that the second physician requirement is constitutional. Id., at ___, 103 S.Ct., at 2521–22. He reasoned that the second physician's presence would further protect the state's interest in protecting viable fetal life because the first physician's responsibility would be toward the mother. Id., at ___, 103 S.Ct., at 2521–22.

---

1. Justices O'Connor, White and Rehnquist concurred in the judgment. [Eds.]

Nothing in the requirement of a pathology tissue examination, Justice Powell wrote, imposed an unreasonable burden on a pregnant woman's abortion decision, no matter when in her pregnancy a woman should choose to abort. Id., at ___, 103 S.Ct., at 2523–24. He specifically viewed the pathology report as comparable to the record-keeping requirement unanimously upheld in *Danforth* and, therefore, insignificant. Id., at ___, 103 S.Ct., at 2524–25.

The third case of the day, Simopoulos v. Virginia, ___ U.S. ___, 103 S.Ct. 2532, 76 L.Ed.2d 755 (1983), dealt with a physician's criminal conviction for performing a second trimester abortion in an unlicensed clinic, in violation of a Virginia statute requiring that second trimester abortions be performed in a hospital licensed by the state department of health. In upholding the conviction, which the defendant had challenged on the grounds that the hospitalization requirement presented an unconstitutional burden on the right to privacy, the Court distinguished the definition of "hospital" under Virginia law from that applicable in *City of Akron* and *Ashcroft*. Id., at ___, 103 S.Ct., at 2538. Because outpatient facilities performing surgical procedures would be hospitals under the Court's reading of the Virginia definition, Id., at ___, 103 S.Ct., at 2536–38, the Court found that a state's interest in its citizens' health would support establishment of licensing standards and procedures for medical facilities. Id., at ___, 103 S.Ct., at 2539. As long as licensing standards do not require abortion procedures departing from standard abortion procedures, they are not "unreasonable means of furthering the State's compelling interest in 'protecting the woman's own health and safety.'" Id., at ___, 103 S.Ct., at 2539–40, quoting *Roe*, 410 U.S., at 150, 93 S.Ct., at 725.

Justice O'Connor, with Justices White and Rehnquist joining, dissented in *City of Akron* and wrote separately, each time with White and Rehnquist, in *Ashcroft* and *Simopoulos*. Her opinion in *City of Akron* set out the basic principles upon which all three opinions rested.

Fundamental to her analysis of the cases was her view that the trimester approach that the Court upheld in *City of Akron* is "a completely unworkable method of accommodating the conflicting personal rights and compelling state interests that are involved in the abortion context." ___ U.S., at ___, 103 S.Ct. at 2505. She evaluated the medical evidence which the Court had considered and concluded that:

[j]ust as improvements in medical technology inevitably will move *forward* the point at which the State may regulate for reasons of maternal health, different technological improvements will move *backward* the point of viability at which the State may proscribe abortions except when necessary to preserve the life and health of the mother.

Id., at ___, 103 S.Ct., at 2507. She said that the *Roe* trimester/viability framework was "on a collision course with itself" and that such a framework ties courts and legislatures too closely to prevailing scientific and medical trends. Id., at ___, 103 S.Ct., at 2507.

Rejecting the Court's adherence to the *Roe* framework on the basis of *stare decisis*, Justice O'Connor saw *City of Akron* as an opportunity for the Court to correct a "former error" and to reexamine its rationale for the trimester/viability framework. Id., at ___, 103 S.Ct., at 2508. She determined that "there is no justification in law or logic for the trimester framework." Id., at ___, 103 S.Ct., at 2508.

b. Minors and Incompetent Persons

BELLOTTI v. BAIRD

Supreme Court of the United States, 1979.
443 U.S. 622, 99 S.Ct. 3035, 61 L.Ed.2d 797.

MR. JUSTICE POWELL announced the judgment of the Court and delivered an opinion, in which THE CHIEF JUSTICE, MR. JUSTICE STEWART, and MR. JUSTICE REHNQUIST joined.

These appeals present a challenge to the constitutionality of a state statute regulating the access of minors to abortions. . . .

I

A

On August 2, 1974, the Legislature of the Commonwealth of Massachusetts passed, over the Governor's veto, an Act pertaining to abortions performed within the State. . . . Shortly before the Act was to go into effect, the class action from which these appeals arise was commenced in the District Court [1] to enjoin, as unconstitutional, the provision of the Act now codified as Mass.Gen. Laws Ann., ch. 112, § 12S (West Supp. 1979).

Section 12S provides in part:

"If the mother is less than eighteen years of age and has not married, the consent of both the mother and her parents [to an abortion to be performed on the mother] is required. If one or both of the mother's parents refuse such consent, consent may be obtained by order of a judge of the superior court for good cause shown, after such hearing as he deems necessary. Such a hearing will not require the appointment of a guardian for the mother. If one of the parents has died or has deserted his or her family, consent by the remaining parent is sufficient. If both parents have died or have deserted their family, consent of the mother's guardian or other person having duties similar to a guardian, or any person who had assumed the care and custody of the mother is sufficient. The commissioner of public health shall prescribe a written form for such consent. Such form shall be signed by the proper person or persons and given to the physician performing the abortion who shall maintain it in his permanent files."

Physicians performing abortions in the absence of the consent required by § 12S are subject to injunctions and criminal penalties. . . .

. . .

Following three days of testimony, the District Court issued an opinion invalidating § 12S. . . .

. . .

B

Appellants sought review in this Court, and we noted probable jurisdiction. Bellotti v. Baird, 423 U.S. 982, 96 S.Ct. 390, 46 L.Ed.2d 301

---

1. The court promptly issued a restraining order which remained in effect until its decision on the merits. Subsequent stays of enforcement were issued during the complex course of this litigation, with the result that Mass.Gen. Laws Ann., ch. 112, § 12S (West Supp. 1979), never has been enforced by Massachusetts.

(1975). After briefing and oral argument, it became apparent that § 12S was susceptible of a construction that "would avoid or substantially modify the federal constitutional challenge to the statute." Bellotti v. Baird, 428 U.S. 132, 148, 96 S.Ct. 2857, 2866, 49 L.Ed.2d 844 (1976) (*Bellotti I*). We therefore vacated the judgment of the District Court, concluding that it should have abstained and certified to the Supreme Judicial Court of Massachusetts appropriate questions concerning the meaning of § 12S, pursuant to existing procedure in that State. . . .

On remand, the District Court certified nine questions to the Supreme Judicial Court. These were answered in an opinion styled Baird v. Attorney General, 371 Mass. 741, 360 N.E.2d 288 (1977) (*Attorney General*). . . .

. . .

C

Following the judgment of the Supreme Judicial Court, . . . The District Court again declared § 12S unconstitutional and enjoined its enforcement. . . .

. . .

II

. . . The Court long has recognized that the status of minors under the law is unique in many respects. . . . We have recognized three reasons justifying the conclusion that the constitutional rights of children cannot be equated with those of adults: the peculiar vulnerability of children; their inability to make critical decisions in an informed, mature manner; and the importance of the parental role in child rearing.

A

The Court's concern for the vulnerability of children is demonstrated in its decisions dealing with minors' claims to constitutional protection against deprivations of liberty or property interests by the State. . . .

. . . [O]ur cases show that although children generally are protected by the same constitutional guarantees against governmental deprivations as are adults, the State is entitled to adjust its legal system to account for children's vulnerability and their needs for "concern, . . . sympathy, and . . . paternal attention." [McKeiver v. Pennsylvania, 403 U.S. 528, 550, 91 S.Ct. 1976, 29 L.Ed.2d 647 (1971) (plurality opinion)].

B

Second, the Court has held that the States validly may limit the freedom of children to choose for themselves in the making of important, affirmative choices with potentially serious consequences. These rulings have been grounded in the recognition that, during the formative years of childhood and adolescence, minors often lack the experience, perspective, and judgment to recognize and avoid choices that could be detrimental to them.

. . .

C

Third, the guiding role of parents in the upbringing of their children justifies limitations on the freedoms of minors. The State commonly protects its youth from adverse governmental action and from their own immaturity by requiring parental consent to or involvement in important decisions by minors. But an additional and more important justification for state deference to parental control over children is that "[t]he child is not the mere creature of the State; those who nurture him and direct his destiny have the right, coupled with the high duty, to recognize and prepare him for additional obligations." Pierce v. Society of Sisters, 268 U.S. 510, 535, 92 S.Ct. 1526, 1542, 32 L.Ed.2d 15 (1925). "The duty to prepare the child for 'additional obligations' . . . must be read to include the inculcation of moral standards, religious beliefs, and elements of good citizenship." Wisconsin v. Yoder, 406 U.S. 205, 233, 92 S.Ct. 1526, 1542, 32 L.Ed.2d 15 (1972). This affirmative process of teaching, guiding, and inspiring by precept and example is essential to the growth of young people into mature, socially responsible citizens.

We have believed in this country that this process, in large part, is beyond the competence of impersonal political institutions. Indeed, affirmative sponsorship of particular ethical, religious, or political beliefs is something we expect the State *not* to attempt in a society constitutionally committed to the ideal of individual liberty and freedom of choice. Thus, "[i]t is cardinal with us that the custody, care and nurture of the child reside first in the parents, whose primary function and freedom include *preparation for obligations the state can neither supply nor hinder."* Prince v. Massachusetts [321 U.S. 158, 166, 64 S.Ct. 438, 442 (1944)] (emphasis added).

Unquestionably, there are many competing theories about the most effective way for parents to fulfill their central role in assisting their children on the way to responsible adulthood. While we do not pretend any special wisdom on this subject, we cannot ignore that central to many of these theories, and deeply rooted in our Nation's history and tradition, is the belief that the parental role implies a substantial measure of authority over one's children. Indeed, "constitutional interpretation has consistently recognized that the parents' claim to authority in their own household to direct the rearing of their children is basic in the structure of our society." Ginsberg v. New York, [390 U.S. 629, 639, 88 S.Ct. 1274, 1280 (1968)].

Properly understood, then, the tradition of parental authority is not inconsistent with our tradition of individual liberty; rather, the former is one of the basic presuppositions of the latter. Legal restrictions on minors, especially those supportive of the parental role, may be important to the child's chances for the full growth and maturity that make eventual participation in a free society meaningful and rewarding. . . .

III

With these principles in mind, we consider the specific constitutional questions presented by these appeals. . . .

Appellees and intervenors contend that even as interpreted by the Supreme Judicial Court of Massachusetts § 12S does unduly burden [the right to seek an abortion]. They suggest, for example, that the mere requirement of parental notice constitutes such a burden. As stated in Part II above, however, parental notice and consent are qualifications that typically may be imposed by the State on a minor's right to make important decisions.   .   .   .

But we are concerned here with a constitutional right to seek an abortion.   The abortion decision differs in important ways from other decisions that may be made during minority.   The need to preserve the constitutional right and the unique nature of the abortion decision, especially when made by a minor, require a State to act with particular sensitivity when it legislates to foster parental involvement in this matter.

A

The pregnant minor's options are much different from those facing a minor in other situations, such as deciding whether to marry.   A minor not permitted to marry before the age of majority is required simply to postpone her decision.   She and her intended spouse may preserve the opportunity for later marriage should they continue to desire it.   A pregnant adolescent, however, cannot preserve for long the possibility of aborting, which effectively expires in a matter of weeks from the onset of pregnancy.

Moreover, the potentially severe detriment facing a pregnant woman, see Roe v. Wade, 410 U.S., at 153, 93 S.Ct., at 726, is not mitigated by her minority.   Indeed, considering her probable education, employment skills, financial resources, and emotional maturity, unwanted motherhood may be exceptionally burdensome for a minor.   In addition, the fact of having a child brings with it adult legal responsibility, for parenthood, like attainment of the age of majority, is one of the traditional criteria for the termination of the legal disabilities of minority.   In sum, there are few situations in which denying a minor the right to make an important decision will have consequences so grave and indelible.

Yet, an abortion may not be the best choice for the minor.   The circumstances in which this issue arises will vary widely.   In a given case, alternatives to abortion, such as marriage to the father of the child, arranging for its adoption, or assuming the responsibilities of motherhood with the assured support of family, may be feasible and relevant to the minor's best interests.   Nonetheless, the abortion decision is one that simply cannot be postponed, or it will be made by default with far-reaching consequences.

For these reasons, as we held in Planned Parenthood of Central Missouri v. Danforth, 428 U.S., at 74, 96 S.Ct., at 2843, "the State may not impose a blanket provision   .   .   .   requiring the consent of a parent or person *in loco parentis* as a condition for abortion of an unmarried minor during the first 12 weeks of her pregnancy."   Although, as stated in Part II, supra, such deference to parents may be permissible with respect to other choices facing a minor, the unique nature and consequences of the abortion decision make it inappropriate "to give a third party an absolute, and possibly arbitrary, veto over the decision of the physician and his patient to terminate the patient's pregnancy, regardless of the reason for withholding the consent."   428 U.S., at 74, 96 S.Ct., at 2843.   We therefore conclude that if the State decides to require a pregnant minor to obtain one or both parents' consent to an abortion, it also must provide an alternative procedure [22] whereby authorization for the abortion can be obtained.

22.   As § 12S provides for involvement of the state superior court in minors' abortion decisions we discuss the alternative procedure described in the text in terms of judi-

A pregnant minor is entitled in such a proceeding to show either: (1) that she is mature enough and well enough informed to make her abortion decision, in consultation with her physician, independently of her parents' wishes;[23] or (2) that even if she is not able to make this decision independently, the desired abortion would be in her best interests. The proceeding in which this showing is made must assure that a resolution of the issue, and any appeals that may follow, will be completed with anonymity and sufficient expedition to provide an effective opportunity for an abortion to be obtained. . . .

B

It is against these requirements that § 12S must be tested. We observe initially that as authoritatively construed by the highest court of the State, the statute satisfies some of the concerns that require special treatment of a minor's abortion decision. It provides that if parental consent is refused, authorization may be "obtained by order of a judge of the superior court for good cause shown, after such hearing as he deems necessary." A superior court judge presiding over a § 12S proceeding "must disregard all parental objections, and other considerations, which are not based exclusively on what would serve the minor's best interests." *Attorney General*, 371 Mass., at 748, 360 N.E.2d, at 293. The Supreme Judicial Court also stated: "Prompt resolution of a [§ 12S] proceeding may be expected. . . . The proceeding need not be brought in the minor's name and steps may be taken, by impoundment or otherwise, to preserve confidentiality as to the minor and her parents. . . . [W]e believe that an early hearing and decision on appeal from a judgment of a Superior Court judge may also be achieved." Id., at 757–758, 360 N.E.2d, at 298. The court added that if these expectations were not met, either the superior court, in the exercise of its rulemaking power, or the Supreme Judicial Court would be willing to eliminate any undue burdens by rule or order. Ibid.

Despite these safeguards, which avoid much of what was objectionable in the statute successfully challenged in *Danforth*, § 12S falls short of constitutional standards in certain respects. We now consider these.

(1)

Among the questions certified to the Supreme Judicial Court was whether § 12S permits any minors—mature or immature—to obtain judicial consent to an abortion without any parental consultation whatsoever. The state court answered that, in general, it does not. "[T]he consent required by [§ 12S must] be obtained for every nonemergency abortion where the mother is less than eighteen years of age and unmarried." *At-*

cial proceedings. We do not suggest, however, that a State choosing to require parental consent could not delegate the alternative procedure to a juvenile court or an administrative agency or officer. Indeed, much can be said for employing procedures and a forum less formal than those associated with a court of general jurisdiction.

23. The nature of both the State's interest in fostering parental authority and the problem of determining "maturity" makes clear why the State generally may resort to objective, though inevitably arbitrary, criteria such as age limits, marital status, or membership in the Armed Forces for lifting some or all of the legal disabilities of minority. Not only is it difficult to define, let alone determine, maturity, but also the fact that a minor may be very much an adult in some respects does not mean that his or her need and opportunity for growth under parental guidance and discipline have ended. As discussed in the text, however, the peculiar nature of the abortion decision requires the opportunity for case-by-case evaluations of the maturity of pregnant minors.

torney General, supra, at 750, 360 N.E.2d, at 294. The text of § 12S itself states an exception to this rule, making consent unnecessary from any parent who has "died or has deserted his or her family." The Supreme Judicial Court construed the statute as containing an additional exception: Consent need not be obtained "where no parent (or statutory substitute) is available." 371 Mass., at 750, 360 N.E.2d, at 294. The court also ruled that an available parent must be given notice of any judicial proceedings brought by a minor to obtain consent for an abortion.[27] Id., at 755–756, 360 N.E.2d, at 297.

We think that, construed in this manner, § 12S would impose an undue burden upon the exercise by minors of the right to seek an abortion. As the District Court recognized, "there are parents who would obstruct, and perhaps altogether prevent, the minor's right to go to court." *Baird III,* 450 F.Supp., at 1001. There is no reason to believe that this would be so in the majority of cases where consent is withheld. But many parents hold strong views on the subject of abortion, and young pregnant minors, especially those living at home, are particularly vulnerable to their parents' efforts to obstruct both an abortion and their access to court. It would be unrealistic, therefore, to assume that the mere existence of a legal right to seek relief in superior court provides an effective avenue of relief for some of those who need it the most.

We conclude, therefore, that under state regulation such as that undertaken by Massachusetts, every minor must have the opportunity—if she so desires—to go directly to a court without first consulting or notifying her parents. If she satisfies the court that she is mature and well enough informed to make intelligently the abortion decision on her own, the court must authorize her to act without parental consultation or consent. If she fails to satisfy the court that she is competent to make this decision independently, she must be permitted to show that an abortion nevertheless would be in her best interests. If the court is persuaded that it is, the court must authorize the abortion. If, however, the court is not persuaded by the minor that she is mature or that the abortion would be in her best interests, it may decline to sanction the operation.

There is, however, an important state interest in encouraging a family rather than a judicial resolution of a minor's abortion decision. Also, as

---

27. This reading of the statute requires parental consultation and consent more strictly than appellants themselves previously believed was necessary. In their first argument before this Court, and again before the Supreme Judicial Court, appellants argued that § 12S was not intended to abrogate Massachusetts' common-law "mature minor" rule as it applies to abortions. See 428 U.S., at 144, 96 S.Ct., at 2864. They also suggested that, under some circumstances, § 12S might permit even immature minors to obtain judicial approval for an abortion without any parental consultation. See 428 U.S., at 145, 96 S.Ct., at 2865; *Attorney General,* supra, at 751, 360 N.E.2d, at 294. The Supreme Judicial Court sketched the outlines of the mature minor rule that would apply in the absence of § 12S: "The mature minor rule calls for an analysis of the nature of the operation, its likely benefit, and the capacity of the particular minor to understand fully what the medical procedure involves. . . . Judicial intervention is not required. If judicial approval is obtained, however, the doctor is protected from a subsequent claim that the circumstances did not warrant his reliance on the mature minor rule, and, of course, the minor patient is afforded advance protection against a misapplication of the rule." Id., at 752, 360 N.E.2d, at 295. "We conclude that, apart from statutory limitations which are constitutional, where the best interests of a minor will be served by not notifying his or her parents of intended medical treatment and where the minor is capable of giving informed consent to that treatment, the mature minor rule applies in this Commonwealth." Id., at 754, 360 N.E.2d, at 296. The Supreme Judicial Court held that the common-law mature minor rule was inapplicable to abortions because it had been legislatively superseded by § 12S.

we have observed above, parents naturally take an interest in the welfare of their children—an interest that is particularly strong where a normal family relationship exists and where the child is living with one or both parents. These factors properly may be taken into account by a court called upon to determine whether an abortion in fact is in a minor's best interests. If, all things considered, the court determines that an abortion is in the minor's best interests, she is entitled to court authorization without any parental involvement. On the other hand, the court may deny the abortion request of an immature minor in the absence of parental consultation if it concludes that her best interests would be served thereby, or the court may in such a case defer decision until there is parental consultation in which the court may participate. But this is the full extent to which parental involvement may be required.[28] For the reasons stated above, the constitutional right to seek an abortion may not be unduly burdened by state-imposed conditions upon initial access to court.

(2)

Section 12S requires that both parents consent to a minor's abortion. . . .

We are not persuaded that, as a general rule, the requirement of obtaining both parents' consent unconstitutionally burdens a minor's right to seek an abortion. The abortion decision has implications far broader than those associated with most other kinds of medical treatment. At least when the parents are together and the pregnant minor is living at home, both the father and mother have an interest—one normally supportive—in helping to determine the course that is in the best interests of a daughter. . . . As every pregnant minor is entitled in the first instance to go directly to the court for a judicial determination without prior parental notice, consultation, or consent, the general rule with respect to parental consent does not unduly burden the constitutional right. Moreover, where the pregnant minor goes to her parents and consent is denied she still must have recourse to a prompt judicial determination of her maturity or best interests.[29]

(3)

Another of the questions certified by the District Court to the Supreme Judicial Court was the following: "If the superior court finds that the minor is capable [of making], and has, in fact, made and adhered to, an informed and reasonable decision to have an abortion, may the court refuse its consent based on a finding that a parent's, or its own, contrary decision is a better one?" *Attorney General*, 371 Mass., at 747 n. 5, 360 N.E.2d, at 293 n. 5. To this the state court answered:

"[W]e do not view the judge's role as limited to a determination that the minor is capable of making, and has made, an informed and reasonable decision to have an abortion. Certainly the judge must make a determination of those circumstances, but, if the statutory role of the judge to determine the best interests of the minor is to be carried out,

---

28. Of course, if the minor consults with her parents voluntarily and they withhold consent, she is free to seek judicial authorization for the abortion immediately.

29. There will be cases where the pregnant minor has received approval of the abortion decision by one parent. In that event, the parent can support the daughter's request for a prompt judicial determination, and the parent's support should be given great, if not dispositive, weight.

he must make a finding on the basis of all relevant views presented to him. We suspect that the judge will give great weight to the minor's determination, if informed and reasonable, but in circumstances where he determines that the best interests of the minor will not be served by an abortion, the judge's determination should prevail, assuming that his conclusion is supported by the evidence and adequate findings of fact." Id., at 748, 360 N.E.2d, at 293.

The Supreme Judicial Court's statement reflects the general rule that a State may require a minor to wait until the age of majority before being permitted to exercise legal rights independently. . . . But we are concerned here with the exercise of a constitutional right of unique character. . . . As stated above, if the minor satisfies a court that she has attained sufficient maturity to make a fully informed decision, she then is entitled to make her abortion decision independently. We therefore agree with the District Court that § 12S cannot constitutionally permit judicial disregard of the abortion decision of a minor who has been determined to be mature and fully competent to assess the implications of the choice she has made.[30]

IV

Although it satisfies constitutional standards in large part, § 12S falls short of them in two respects: First, it permits judicial authorization for an abortion to be withheld from a minor who is found by the superior court to be mature and fully competent to make this decision independently. Second, it requires parental consultation or notification in every instance, without affording the pregnant minor an opportunity to receive an independent judicial determination that she is mature enough to consent or that an abortion would be in her best interests.[31] Accordingly, we affirm the judgment of the District Court insofar as it invalidates this statute and enjoins its enforcement.

Affirmed.

MR. JUSTICE REHNQUIST, concurring.

I join the opinion of Mr. Justice Powell and the judgment of the Court. At such time as this Court is willing to reconsider its earlier decision in Planned Parenthood of Central Missouri v. Danforth, 428 U.S. 52, 96 S.Ct. 2831, 49 L.Ed.2d 788 (1976), in which I joined the opinion of Mr. Justice White, dissenting in part, I shall be more than willing to partici-

---

30. Appellees and intervenors have argued that § 12S violates the Equal Protection Clause of the Fourteenth Amendment. As we have concluded that the statute is constitutionally infirm for other reasons, there is no need to consider this question.

31. Section 12S evidently applies to all nonemergency abortions performed on minors, without regard to the period in pregnancy during which the procedure occurs. As the court below recognized, most abortions are performed during the early stages of pregnancy, before the end of the first trimester. See *Baird III*, 450 F.Supp., at 1001; *Baird I*, 393 F.Supp., at 853. This coincides approximately with the pre-viability period during which a pregnant woman's right to decide, in consultation with her physician, to

have an abortion is most immune to state intervention. See Roe v. Wade, 410 U.S., at 164–165, 93 S.Ct., at 732.

The propriety of parental involvement in a minor's abortion decision does not diminish as the pregnancy progresses and legitimate concerns for the pregnant minor's health increase. Furthermore, the opportunity for direct access to court which we have described is adequate to safeguard throughout pregnancy the constitutionally protected interests of a minor in the abortion decision. Thus, although a significant number of abortions within the scope of § 12S might be performed during the later stages of pregnancy, we do not believe a different analysis of the statute is required for them.

pate in that task. But unless and until that time comes, literally thousands of judges cannot be left with nothing more than the guidance offered by a truly fragmented holding of this Court.

MR. JUSTICE STEVENS, with whom MR. JUSTICE BRENNAN, MR. JUSTICE MARSHALL, and MR. JUSTICE BLACKMUN join, concurring in the judgment.

. . .

. . . Because the statute has been once authoritatively construed by the Massachusetts Supreme Judicial Court, and because it is clear that the statute as written and construed is not constitutional, I agree with Mr. Justice Powell that the District Court's judgment should be affirmed. Because his opinion goes further, however, and addresses the constitutionality of an abortion statute that Massachusetts has not enacted, I decline to join his opinion.

MR. JUSTICE WHITE, dissenting.

I was in dissent in Planned Parenthood of Central Missouri v. Danforth, 428 U.S. 52, 94–95, 96 S.Ct. 2831, 2853, 49 L.Ed.2d 788 (1976), on the issue of the validity of requiring the consent of a parent when an unmarried woman under 18 years of age seeks an abortion. I continue to have the views I expressed there and also agree with much of what Mr. Justice Stevens said in dissent in that case. Id., at 101–105, 96 S.Ct., at 2855–2857. I would not, therefore, strike down this Massachusetts law.

But even if a parental consent requirement of the kind involved in *Danforth* must be deemed invalid, that does not condemn the Massachusetts law, which, when the parents object, authorizes a judge to permit an abortion if he concludes that an abortion is in the best interests of the child. Going beyond *Danforth*, the Court now holds it unconstitutional for a State to require that in all cases parents receive notice that their daughter seeks an abortion and, if they object to the abortion, an opportunity to participate in a hearing that will determine whether it is in the "best interests" of the child to undergo the surgery. Until now, I would have thought inconceivable a holding that the United States Constitution forbids even notice to parents when their minor child who seeks surgery objects to such notice and is able to convince a judge that the parents should be denied participation in the decision.

With all due respect, I dissent.

NOTE

The Court first addressed the issue of whether a minor can make reproductive decisions in Planned Parenthood of Central Missouri v. Danforth, 428 U.S. 52, 96 S.Ct. 2831, 49 L.Ed.2d 788 (1976). In *Danforth*, the Court invalidated a provision requiring an unmarried woman under 18 to obtain the consent of a parent or a person *in loco parentis* as a prerequisite to obtaining an abortion unless the abortion was certified by a licensed physician to be necessary in order to preserve the life of the mother. Just as with the spousal consent requirement, the Court found that "the State does not have the constitutional authority to give a third party," even a parent, "an absolute, and possibly arbitrary, veto over the decision of the physician and his patient's pregnancy, regardless of the reason for withholding the consent."

In a dissent, however, Justice White thought that the purpose of Missouri's parental consent requirement was to vindicate the very right created in Roe v. Wade—the right of the pregnant woman to decide "whether or *not* to terminate her pregnancy." White found that Missouri was entitled "to protect the minor unmarried woman from making the decision in a way which is not in her own best

interests, and [to seek] to achieve this goal by parental consultation and consent."
428 U.S. at 95, 96 S.Ct., at 2853.

Justice Stevens, in his dissent, also found the parental consent requirement
consistent with the Court's holding in *Roe*. Stevens stated, "[T]he holding in Roe
v. Wade that the abortion decision is entitled to constitutional protection merely
emphasizes the importance of the decision; it does not lead to the conclusion that
the state legislature has no power to enact legislation for the purpose of protecting a young pregnant woman from the consequences of an incorrect decision."
Id. at 102. Stevens emphasized that the decision was one that should be exercised wisely "with [a] full understanding of the consequences of either alternative," and that a legislative determination that such a choice will be made more
wisely with the advice and support of a parent was not irrational.

In Carey v. Population Services International, a divided Court invalidated a
number of restrictions on the distribution and advertising of non-prescription
contraceptives. 431 U.S. 678, 97 S.Ct. 2010, 52 L.Ed.2d 675 (1977). The
prohibitions at issue included a ban on the distribution and sale of "any contraceptive of any kind to a minor under the age of 16 years." New York Educ. Law
§ 6811(8) (McKinney 1972). Justice Brennan, writing for a plurality, found that a
minor could claim a right of privacy in decisions affecting contraception. He recognized, however, that simply because "the constitutionally protected right of privacy extends to an individual's liberty to make choices regarding contraception, 'it
does not' automatically invalidate every state regulation in this area. The business of manufacturing and selling contraceptives may be regulated in ways that do
not infringe protected individual choices. And even a burdensome regulation
may be validated by a sufficiently compelling state interest." 431 U.S. at 685–86,
97 S.Ct., at 2016.

Justice Brennan continued, "[T]he same test must be applied to state regulations that burden an individual's right to decide to prevent conception or terminate pregnancy by substantially limiting access to the means of effectuating that
decision as is applied to state statutes that prohibit the decision entirely. Both
types of regulation 'may be justified only by a compelling state interest' . . .
and . . . must be narrowly drawn to express only the legitimate state interests
at stake." Id. at 688 (citing Roe v. Wade, 410 U.S. 113, 155, 93 S.Ct. 727
(1973)).

In *Carey*, the State argued that significant state interests were served by the
statute restricting minors' access to contraceptives because it would decrease sexual activity among the young—the argument being that minors' sexual activity
may be deterred by increasing the hazards attendant on it. Justice Brennan found
that such a justification was not a "compelling" state interest deserving of constitutional protection, expressed substantial doubt that limiting access to contraceptives would in fact discourage early sexual behavior and refused to ascribe to the
State a "scheme of values" that would prescribe pregnancy and the birth of an
unwanted child as punishment for fornication.

Although the Court invalidated the statute at issue, the concurring opinions of
Justices White, Powell and Stevens indicate that under the right circumstances restrictions on minors' access to contraceptives may be constitutionally permissible.
Justice White concurred in the result primarily because the state had failed to
show that the prohibition measurably contributed to the deterrent purposes for
which it is advanced. White agreed with Justice Stevens, who indicated that there
may be a significant state interest in discouraging sexual activity among unmarried
persons under 16 years of age, stating, "I would describe as frivolous appellee's
argument that a minor has the constitutional right to put contraceptives to their
intended use, notwithstanding the combined objection of both parents and the
state." 431 U.S., at 713, 97 S.Ct., at 2030. Justice Powell also found that there
was considerably more room for state regulation in the area than the plurality
opinion would seem to allow, stating that requiring minors to seek parental guidance would be consistent with prior cases. Powell concluded, "As long as parental distribution is permitted, a state should have substantial latitude in regulating
the distribution of contraceptives to minors." Id. at 710, 97 S.Ct., at 2029.

In H. L. v. Matheson, 450 U.S. 398, 101 S.Ct. 1164, 67 L.Ed.2d 388 (1980), the Supreme Court again addressed the issue of whether a state can require that parents participate in their child's abortion decision. *Matheson* involved a child's privacy challenge to a Utah statute requiring a physician to "[n]otify, if possible, the parents or guardian of the women upon whom [an] abortion is to be performed, if she is a minor . . . ." Utah Code Ann. § 76–7–304(2) (1978). In a 6–3 decision upholding the notification requirement, the Court found it was supported by two significant state interests: the necessity of protecting a minor against an improvident decision and the reinforcement of the parental role in child-rearing matters. Particularly significant for the Court was that the law granted no "veto power over the minor's abortion decision." As applied to immature and dependent minors only, the Court found the statute clearly serves the important consideration of family integrity and protecting adolescents. In City of Akron v. Akron Center for Reproductive Health, Inc., ___ U.S. ___, 103 S.Ct. 2481, 76 L.Ed.2d 687 (1983), the Court made it clear that under *Bellotti*, the City of Akron could not make "a blanket determination that *all* minors under the age of 15 are too immature to make this decision [to abort] or that an abortion never may be in the minor's best interests without parental approval." The Court in *City of Akron* recounted that *Bellotti* indicated that a state's interest in protecting immature minors will sustain a requirement of a consent substitute, either parental or judicial; however, the state must also provide a procedure whereby a pregnant minor may demonstrate she is mature enough to make the abortion decision or that, despite immaturity, an abortion would be in her best interests.

In *City of Akron*, the Court determined that the parental notice and consent section of the Akron ordinance was unconstitutional even though the ordinance contained the judicial alternative required by *Bellotti*. The judicial substitute did not suffice here, the Court said, because the municipal ordinance could not guarantee that Ohio state courts could or would assert jurisdiction over matters relating to a minor's ability to consent to an abortion. Id., at ___, 103 S.Ct., at 2496–99. In Planned Parenthood Association of Kansas City, Missouri, Inc. v. Ashcroft, ___ U.S. ___, 103 S.Ct. 2517, 76 L.Ed.2d 733 (1983) (opinion of Powell, J.), because Justice Powell believed that the Missouri statute adequately provided for a judicial consent alternative, he differentiated the parental consent requirement in the Missouri statute from that overturned in *City of Akron*. Id., at ___, 103 S.Ct., at 2525–26. He construed the statutory language in question as not allowing a court to deny a minor's petition to allow her to give her own consent or to have the court give its consent in place of her parent's consent unless the court found that the minor was not mature enough to make her own decision. Id., at ___, 103 S.Ct., at 2525–26.

At issue most recently has been the validity of the so-called "squeal-rule"—regulations issued by the Secretary of the Department of Health and Human Services (HHS) requiring all providers of family planning services that receive federal funds under Title X of the Public Health Service Act to (1) notify parents or guardians within 10 working-days of prescribing contraceptives to unemancipated minors; and (2) to comply with state laws requiring parental notice of, or consent to, the provision of any family planning services to minors. 48 Fed.Reg. 3600, 3614 (1983). The United States Court of Appeals for the District of Columbia Circuit, in Planned Parenthood Federation of America, Inc. v. Heckler, 712 F.2d 650 (D.C.Cir.1983), affirmed a district court decision invalidating the HHS regulations. The regulations arose out of Title X of the Public Health Service Act, enacted in 1970 to establish a nationwide program with the express purpose of making "comprehensive family planning services readily available to all persons desiring such services." P.L. 91–572, § 2, 84 Stat. 1506 (1970). Later amendments added language that clearly reflected Congress' intent to place "a special emphasis on preventing unwanted pregnancies among sexually active adolescents." S.Rep. No. 822, 95th Cong., 2d Sess. 24 (1978). In 1981, Congress again amended Title X, this time to authorize the Secretary to "encourage family participation in projects [under Title X]." 42 U.S.C. § 300(a). HHS proposed the notification requirements at issue as a means of implementing Congress' 1981 mandate to encourage "family participation."

The Court of Appeals invalidated the regulations, finding that they violated Congress' specific intent as to the issue of parental notification and undermined the fundamental purposes of the Title X programs.   The court's analysis of the statute indicated to it that Congress did not intend to *mandate* family involvement. The court determined that the relevant legislative history clearly showed that the regulations did not comport with the intent of Congress to make family planning services available to adolescents.   In this regard, the Secretary of HHS had exceeded her authority in promulgating the regulations.   Particularly noteworthy for the court was Congress' finding that confidentiality was essential to attract adolescents to family planning clinics.   The court concluded that a notification requirement would abandon HHS's longstanding policy of protecting teenagers' confidences.

BUCK v. BELL

Supreme Court of the United States, 1927.
274 U.S. 200, 47 S.Ct. 584, 71 L.Ed. 1000.

MR. JUSTICE HOLMES delivered the opinion of the Court.

This is a writ of error to review a judgment of the Supreme Court of Appeals of the State of Virginia, affirming a judgment of the Circuit Court of Amherst County, by which the defendant in error, the superintendent of the State Colony for Epileptics and Feeble Minded, was ordered to perform the operation of salpingectomy upon Carrie Buck, the plaintiff in error, for the purpose of making her sterile.   143 Va. 310. The case comes here upon the contention that the statute authorizing the judgment is void under the Fourteenth Amendment as denying to the plaintiff in error due process of law and the equal protection of the laws.

Carrie Buck is a feeble minded white woman who was committed to the State Colony above mentioned in due form.   She is the daughter of a feeble minded mother in the same institution, and the mother of an illegitimate feeble minded child.   She was eighteen years old at the time of the trial of her case in the Circuit Court, in the latter part of 1924.   An Act of Virginia, approved March 20, 1924, recites that the health of the patient and the welfare of society may be promoted in certain cases by the sterilization of mental defectives, under careful safeguard, &c.; that the sterilization may be effected in males by vasectomy and in females by salpingectomy, without serious pain or substantial danger to life; that the Commonwealth is supporting in various institutions many defective persons who if now discharged would become a menace but if incapable of procreating might be discharged with safety and become self-supporting with benefit to themselves and to society; and the experience has shown that heredity plays an important part in the transmission of insanity, imbecility, &c.   The statute then enacts that whenever the superintendent of certain institutions including the above named State Colony shall be of opinion that it is for the best interests of the patients and of society that an inmate under his care should be sexually sterilized, he may have the operation performed upon any patient afflicted with hereditary forms of insanity, imbecility, &c., on complying with the very careful provisions by which the act protects the patients from possible abuse.

· · ·

The attack is not upon the procedure but upon the substantive law.   It seems to be contended that in no circumstances could such an order be justified.   It certainly is contended that the order cannot be justified upon the existing grounds.   The judgment finds the facts that have been recited and that Carrie Buck "is the probable potential parent of socially inadequate offspring, likewise afflicted, that she may be sexually sterilized without detriment to her general health and that her welfare and that of society will be promoted by her sterilization," and thereupon makes the order. In view of the general declarations of the legislature and the specific findings of the Court, obviously we cannot say as matter of law that the grounds do not exist, and if they exist they justify the result. We have seen more than once that the public welfare may call upon the best citizens for their lives. It would be strange if it could not call upon those who already sap the strength of the State for these lesser sacrifices, often not felt to be such by those concerned, in order to prevent our being swamped with incompetence. It is better for all the world, if instead of waiting to execute degenerate offspring for crime, or to let them starve for their imbecility, society can prevent those who are manifestly unfit from continuing their kind. The principle that sustains compulsory vaccination is broad enough to cover cutting the Fallopian tubes. Jacobson v. Massachusetts, 197 U.S. 11, 25 S.Ct. 358, 49 L.Ed. 643, 3 Ann.Cas. 765. Three generations of imbeciles are enough. . . .

Judgment affirmed.

NOTES

1. At the time *Buck* was decided, eugenic sterilization was a relatively new practice. It was only in the 1890's that relatively safe and morally acceptable sterilization methods were developed. Murdock, Sterilization of the Retarded: A Problem or a Solution, 62 Calif.L.Rev. 917, 920 (1974). Once developed, however, those procedures provided the impetus for a wave of sterilization legislation, in which 32 states had passed sterilization statutes by the end of the 1930's. See O'Hara and Sanks, Eugenic Sterilization, 45 Geo.L.J. 20, 22 (1956). Prior to *Buck*, many state sterilization laws were declared unconstitutional, on a variety of grounds. See O'Hara and Sanks, supra, at 23–28 (describing decisions invalidating sterilization laws on cruel and unusual punishment, equal protection and due process grounds).

By the 1930's, however, the eugenic sterilization movement began to subside, largely due to new scientific theories showing that the theory of eugenic sterilization was incorrect and to the negative influence of the Nazi eugenics movement on public sentiment. Vukowich, The Dawning of the Brave New World—Legal, Ethical and Social Issues of Eugenics, 1971 U.Ill.L.F. 189, 190. As a result, the number of eugenic sterilizations has sharply declined since the 1940's. Ferster, Eliminating the Unfit, 27 Ohio St.L.J. 591, 599 (1966). Today, the eugenic motivation is probably insufficient to justify sterilization legislation. See Murdock, supra, at 924–28 (describing flaws in eugenic sterilization theory).

2. In Skinner v. Oklahoma, 316 U.S. 535, 62 S.Ct. 1110, 86 L.Ed. 1655 (1942), decided after *Buck*, the Supreme Court invalidated on equal protection grounds a state statute allowing the sterilization of persons convicted more than once of certain offenses. Other offenses, such as embezzlement, were specifically exempted from the statute. Despite the broad language in the last paragraph of Justice Holmes's *Buck* opinion, the *Skinner* court struck down the statute. *Buck* was distinguished as follows:

In *Buck v. Bell* . . . the Virginia statute was upheld though it applied only to feeble-minded persons in institutions of the State. But it was pointed out that "so far as the operations enable those who otherwise must be kept confined to be returned to the world, and thus open the asylum to others, the equality aimed at will be more nearly reached". . . . Here there is no such saving feature. Embezzlers are forever free. Those who steal or take in other ways are not.

Skinner, 316 U.S., at 542 62 S.Ct., at 1113. Is this distinction between *Buck* and *Skinner* convincing? Is there any force left to the *Buck* decision after *Skinner*? Consider the decision in In re Moore, 289 N.C. 95, 221 S.E.2d 307 (1976):

MOORE, JUSTICE.

The only question before us on this appeal is the constitutionality of G.S. 35–36 through G.S. 35–50, inclusive.

The respondent attacks these statutes on the grounds that they are violative of the Due Process Clause of the Fourteenth Amendment to the United States Constitution . . . from procedural and substantive standpoints, that they deny the respondent equal protection of the law, are unconstitutionally vague and arbitrary, and provide for cruel and unusual punishment. . . .

The right of a state to sterilize retarded or insane persons was first upheld by the United States Supreme Court in Buck v. Bell. . . . Since *Buck,* many states have passed sterilization laws. . . .

Most of these statutes have been declared constitutional. . . .

Our research does not disclose any case which holds that a state does not have the right to sterilize an insane or a retarded person if notice and hearing are provided, if it is applied equally to all persons, and if it is not prescribed as a punishment for a crime.

. . .

Respondent . . . contends that the statutes in question deny him substantive due process. . . .

The traditional substantive due process test has been that a statute must have a rational relation to a valid state objective. In a growing series of decisions, the United States Supreme Court has recognized a right of privacy emanating from the Fourteenth Amendment's concept of personal liberty or encompassed within the penumbra of the Bill of Rights that includes the abortion decision, *Roe v. Wade,* certain marital activities, Loving v. Virginia, 388 U.S. 1, 18 L.Ed.2d 1010, 87 S.Ct. 1817 (1967) and *Griswold v. Connecticut,* and procreation, *Eisenstadt v. Baird,* and *Skinner v. Oklahoma.*

. . .

The right to procreate is not absolute but is vulnerable to a certain degree of state regulation. *Roe v. Wade, Buck v. Bell.* The two state interests recognized as paramount to the individual's freedom of choice in *Roe v. Wade,* at least after the first trimester of pregnancy, were the state's concern with the health of the mother and the potential life of the child. The welfare of the parent and the future life and health of the unborn child are also the chief concerns of the State of North Carolina in authorizing sterilization of individuals under certain circumstances.

The interest of the unborn child is sufficient to warrant sterilization of a retarded individual. "The state's concern for the welfare of its citizenry extends to future generations and when there is overwhelming evidence . . . that a potential parent will be unable to provide a proper environment for a child because of his own mental illness or mental retardation, the state has sufficient interest to order sterilization." Cook v. State, 9 Or.App. 224, 495 P.2d 768 (1972). The people of North Carolina also have a right to prevent the procreation of children who will become a burden on the State.

. . .

The United States Supreme Court has also held that the welfare of all citizens should take precedence over the rights of individuals to procreate. . . .

Furthermore, the sterilization of a mentally ill or retarded individual at certain times may be in the best interest of that individual. The mentally ill or retarded individual may not be capable of determining his inability to cope with children. In addition, he may be capable of functioning in society and caring for his own needs but may be unable to handle the additional responsibility of children. This individual also may not be able to practice other forms of birth control and therefore sterilization is the only available remedy. Sterilization itself does not prevent the normal sex drive of the person, it only prevents procreation. Therefore, the State may only be providing for the welfare of the individual when this individual is unable to do so for himself.

We hold that the sterilization of mentally ill or retarded persons under the safeguards as set out in G.S. 35–36 through G.S. 35–50, inclusive, is a valid and reasonable exercise of the police power, and that these state interests rise to the level of a compelling state interest.

The equal protection clauses of the United States and North Carolina Constitutions impose upon lawmaking bodies the requirement that any legislative classification "be based on differences that are reasonably related to the purposes of the Act in which it is found." Morey v. Doud, 354 U.S. 457, 465, 1 L.Ed.2d 1485, 1491, 77 S.Ct. 1344, 1350 (1957) . . .

The object of G.S. 35–36 through G.S. 35–50, inclusive, is to prevent the procreation of children by a mentally ill or retarded individual who because of physical, mental or nervous disease or deficiency which is not likely to materially improve, would probably be unable to care for a child or children or who would likely, unless sterilized, procreate a child or children who probably would have serious physical, mental or nervous diseases or deficiencies. Considering this object, the classification under these statutes is reasonable.

. . .

Since the North Carolina law applies to all those named in the statute (G.S. 35–43), these statutes, G.S. 35–36 through G.S. 35–50, inclusive, do not violate the equal protection clauses of the United States Constitution or the Constitution of North Carolina.

Respondent next asserts that this legislation provides no adequate judicial standard to guide the court in reaching a decision whether to authorize the sterilization of an individual. Respondent points to the indefiniteness of the terms found in G.S. 35–43:

". . . If the judge of the district court shall find from the evidence that the person alleged to be subject to this section is subject to it and that because of a physical, mental, or nervous disease or deficiency which is not *likely* to materially improve, the person would *probably* be unable to care for a child or children; or, because the person would be *likely*, unless sterilized, to procreate a child or children which *probably* would have serious physical, mental, or nervous diseases or deficiencies, he shall enter an order and judgment authorizing the physician or surgeon named in the petition to perform the operation." (Emphasis added.)

Defendant contends that these indefinite terms render the statute unconstitutionally vague and arbitrary; that there exists no standard at all, except the subjective determination of an individual judge.

. . .

. . . [W]e believe that G.S. 35–36 through G.S. 35–50 meet [the] constitutional standard. The definitions of "mental disease," "mental illness" and "mental defective" are found in G.S. 35–1.1, the same chapter as the sterilization procedure, and are capable of being understood and complied with by the triers of fact with the help of experts in the field. . . . The statute does not specify the burden of proof that the petitioner must meet before the order authorizing the sterilization can be entered. In keeping with the intent of the General Assembly, clearly expressed throughout the article, that the rights of the individual must be fully protected, we hold that the evidence must be clear, strong and convincing before such an order may be entered. . . . [W]e hold that G.S. 35–36 through G.S. 35–50, inclusive, provide a sufficient judicial standard and are not unconstitutionally vague or arbitrary.

The respondent's next contention that sterilization amounts to cruel and unusual punishment is without basis in law in this case. The cruel and unusual punishment clause of the Constitution refers to those persons convicted of a crime. Since this is not a criminal proceeding, there is no basis for the cruel and unusual argument. . . .

This unfortunate respondent and his mother both consented to the performance of a vasectomy. While we do not attach much importance to the respondent's consent due to his mental condition, his mother unquestionably is in a position to know what is best for the future of her child. Under the provisions of G.S. 35–36 through G.S. 35–50, inclusive, the rights of respondent and the State will be fully protected at hearing.

We hold, therefore, that the trial court erred in declaring these statutes unconstitutional. The judgment so entered is reversed.

Reversed.

See also North Carolina Association for Retarded Children v. North Carolina, 420 F.Supp. 451 (M.D.N.C.1976) (statute authorizing sterilization of mentally retarded constitutional because of compelling state interest in preventing birth of defective or neglected children); In re Truesdell, 63 N.C.App. 258, 304 S.E.2d 793 (1983) (application of state sterilization statute constitutional only when state or other petitioner shows by "clear, strong and convincing" evidence that individual is mentally ill or retarded, likely to voluntarily or otherwise engage in sexual conduct; capable of procreating and; unable or unwilling to control procreation through other means and that procedure is least offensive bodily invasion). Cf. Wyatt v Aderholt, 368 F.Supp. 1382 (M.D.Ala.1978) (state statute permitting sterilization of inmates of state institutions unconstitutional due to insufficient procedural safeguards).

Following the Supreme Court of North Carolina's decision in *Moore*, an interesting course of events occurred, as evidenced in the following letter from Moore's attorney (reprinted from J. Areen, Family Law, Cases and Materials 257 (1978)):

"1.   After the Supreme Court of North Carolina declared the statute constitutional, the case was sent back to the District Court of Forsyth County for a hearing on the merits to determine whether sterilization was appropriate for this young man.

"2.   The Petitioner, the Director of the Forsyth County Department of Social Services, had contacts with the actual moving party in the Petition, the mother of Moore, and she indicated to agents of the Department of Social Services that the young man was doing much better from a conduct standpoint, in her opinion, and she wished to just forget about the sterilization proceeding.

"3.   With the consent of the mother, the Director of the Department of Social Services, by and through counsel, took a Voluntary Dismissal of the Special Proceeding in July of 1976. This brought the matter to a close.

"This brings you up to date on the outcome of the proceeding in which I participated. It had a 'happy outcome' from my standpoint, particularly in light of the fact that the young man, during the approximate one-year period between the initial hearing and the dismissal, matured to such an extent that he was not the problem his mother had formerly encountered."

Letter of March 4, 1977, from James Armentrout, attorney for Moore.

3.   The Department of Health and Human Services has authority over the use of federal funds for sterilization operations. See 42 CFR §§ 441.250–441.259 (1978); 42 CFR §§ 50.201–50.210. The regulations prohibit the use of federal funds for the sterilization of institutionalized persons and those declared incompetent by a state or federal court. § 441.254. In addition, the regulations require the informed consent of the patient and that the patient be at least 21 years old. §§ 441.253, 441.257, 441.258. Earlier regulations, proposed in 1974, were invalidated by court order because they failed to prevent sterilization of incompetent persons and to accommodate state laws governing the ability of incompetent persons to consent to sterilization. Relf v. Weinberger, 372 F.Supp. 1196 (D.D.C.

1974). After the district court rejected modifications to the regulations, Relf v. Mathews, 403 F.Supp. 1235 (D.D.C.1975), HEW (predecessor of Health and Human Services) withdrew the regulations and began new rulemaking proceedings. Relf v. Weinberger, 565 F.2d 722, 726 (D.C.Cir.1977). Subsequently, the court of appeals ruled moot the action concerning the withdrawn regulations and dismissed the complaints. Id. at 727.

4. Mr. Justice Holmes's remark that, "three generations of imbeciles are enough," may have been misapplied. Carrie Buck's child "was reported to have been very bright and had completed the second grade in school." She died of measles in 1932. Cynkar, Buck v. Bell: "Felt Necessities" v. Fundamental Values?, 81 Col.L.Rev. 1418, 1458 (1981).

In 1980, it was reported that Virginia had sterilized 7,500 people from 1924 until 1972. Moreover, in addition to Carrie Buck, her younger sister Doris was also sterilized. Dr. Roy Nelson, Director of the Lynchburg Hospital, who had located Carrie and Doris as adults, reported that neither is mentally retarded by today's standards. Washington Post, Feb. 23, 1980, at A1, col. 1.

WENTZEL v. MONTGOMERY GENERAL HOSPITAL, INC.

Court of Appeals of Maryland, 1982.
293 Md. 685, 447 A.2d 1244, certiorari denied ___ U.S. ___, 103 S.Ct. 790, 74 L.Ed.2d 995, 1983.

MURPHY, CHIEF JUDGE.

This case presents the question whether a trial court of general jurisdiction is empowered to grant a guardian's petition to sterilize an incompetent minor through the performance of a subtotal hysterectomy.

I

The child who is the subject of this litigation, Sonya Star Flanary, is a severely retarded 13-year-old with an I.Q. of about 25 to 30 (the equivalent of a mental age of 1 to 2 years), blind and with pronounced neurological problems. Sonya was born a normal child. At the age of 5 months, she was severely injured in an automobile accident, suffering brain and other physical damage. After an initial paralysis, Sonya's physical condition greatly improved but her mental development was seriously retarded. Unable to cope with the event, Sonya's mother took her to live with her grandmother, Nancy Wentzel, who is now 61 years old. Sonya, her two sisters, and Gail Sheppard, Sonya's aunt, have been living with Mrs. Wentzel since shortly after the accident. This case began when Mrs. Wentzel and Gail Sheppard, who together provide Sonya's principal care, sought the performance of a hysterectomy upon Sonya, which would terminate her menstrual cycle and result in her sterilization. The medical staff of Montgomery General Hospital refused to perform the operation without a court order authorizing the procedure. Consequently, Mrs. Wentzel and Ms. Sheppard filed a petition in the Circuit Court for Montgomery County, seeking appointment as Sonya's guardians with authority to consent to the proposed surgical procedure. The petition recited that Sonya "is currently in need of additional medical care (hysterectomy) and that the medical staff and petitioners request an Order of Court approving said medical procedure for therapeutic reasons."

Pursuant to Maryland Rule R76, the court appointed an attorney to represent Sonya and conducted an evidentiary hearing. The evidence disclosed that Sonya regularly attended a special school, although missing many sessions because of illness. It was established that Sonya had reached puberty and was experiencing pain connected with menstruation. It was shown that Sonya could not care for her most basic hygenic needs, that she would not wear sanitary napkins and was irritable and disoriented during the menstruation process.   There was evidence showing that the guardianship petition was motivated by a sincere desire to free Sonya of the pain and other consequences suffered by her during menstruation and because of genuine concern that Sonya was an easy subject for rape and resulting pregnancy.   Sonya's mother testified in support of the guardianship petition, stating that sterilization was in Sonya's best interest.

The petitioners produced testimony of a child psychiatrist who, although he had never treated Sonya and had only seen her twice, said that a subtotal hysterectomy would be in Sonya's best interest.   The psychiatrist was unable to say, however, that such a procedure was necessary for Sonya's physical or mental health.   On cross-examination, the witness admitted that Sonya would not be in any medical danger if the operation were not performed, and he also agreed that some pain and irritation connected with the menstrual cycle is normal.   The psychiatrist agreed that no life threatening consequences would occur if Sonya were to have offspring and further that Sonya was perfectly capable of having a normal baby.   The evidence disclosed that there was no reasonable expectation that Sonya's mental condition would improve.

It was argued that Maryland Code (1974, 1981 Cum.Supp.), § 13–708 of the Estates and Trusts Article empowered the court to grant the guardianship petition and to authorize the guardians to consent to the operation. . . .

The trial judge (Bell, J.) found from the evidence that Sonya was totally lacking in capacity to consent to the operation;   that "Sonya cannot care for herself, let alone a baby";   and that "Sonya's menstruation further burdens an already over-burdened family."   The court noted the sincerity of the family's belief that the operation was in Sonya's best interest, and it also recognized the possibility that Sonya could become pregnant if sexually abused.   The court observed that the psychiatrist did not testify that the operation was necessary for Sonya's medical health or that refusal to authorize it would cause such a mental hardship as would justify the surgery for therapeutic reasons.   The court concluded that § 13–708 of the Estates and Trusts Article "could not be interpreted to provide a hysterectomy in a case such as Sonya's."   It noted that "the alternative to the hysterectomy is not life threatening."   The court said.

"In the absence of such statutory authority and guide lines, this Court cannot find that it has the authority to grant the relief sought."

The court appointed the petitioners as co-guardians of the person and property of Sonya but denied permission to consent to the hysterectomy. The guardians appealed to the Court of Special Appeals.   We granted certiorari prior to decision by the intermediate appellate court to consider the profound issues raised in the case.

II

The guardians claim that the lower court erroneously denied the petition on the ground that it was not empowered, absent express statutory authorization, to order sterilization unless for therapeutic reasons.   They maintain that under § 13–708 of the Estates and Trusts Article the court, upon a showing of "demonstrated need," is authorized to approve the sterilization of a minor incompetent for nontherapeutic reasons. . . .

. . . Sterilization would be in Sonya's best interests, the guardians say, because Sonya is unable to communicate effectively with others; to understand or handle her own bodily functions; to know the difference between sexes, much less the needs of a potential child; and to understand the menstrual cycle or pregnancy. Moreover, the guardians point out that they are presently 61 and 33 years old, respectively, and that Sonya's life expectancy far exceeds their own. In these circumstances, it is contended that it is in the best interests of Sonya and those who assume responsibility for her care, both in the present and in the future, that Sonya be sterilized. The guardians maintain that acting under the *parens patriae* doctrine, equity courts have traditionally exercised their powers in the best interests of incompetent minors, and that accordingly the lower court should have granted their petition in order to preserve Sonya's physical and mental well-being. It is emphasized that should Sonya have a child, both she and the child will become wards of the State, if her family cannot care for both. It is argued that this will place a financial burden on the State, and it therefore has a compelling interest justifying granting the guardians' petition authorizing the giving of consent to Sonya's sterilization.

III

A number of jurisdictions hold that in the absence of express legislative authorization, courts are totally devoid of subject matter jurisdiction to consider petitions seeking sterilization of incompetent minors. See, e.g., Hudson v. Hudson, 373 So.2d 310 (Ala.1979); Guardianship of Tulley, 83 Cal.App.3d 698, 146 Cal.Rptr. 266 (1978), cert. denied, 440 U.S. 967, 99 S.Ct. 1519, 59 L.Ed.2d 783 (1979); Matter of S. C. E., 378 A.2d 144 (Del.Ch.1977); A. L. v. G. R. H., 163 Ind.App. 636, 325 N.E.2d 501 (1975); Holmes v. Powers, 439 S.W.2d 579 (Ky.1968); In Interest of M. K. R., 515 S.W.2d 467 (Mo.1974) (en banc); Frazier v. Levi, 440 S.W.2d 393 (Tex.Civ.App.1969). . . . Regardless of the asserted need, these courts have denied sterilization, deferring on jurisdictional grounds to what they consider to be exclusively a legislative prerogative.

Other cases hold that trial courts of general jurisdiction, either by statute, the exercise of inherent equity powers, including application of the *parens patriae* doctrine, or the doctrine of substituted consent, have subject matter jurisdiction to grant petitions authorizing sterilization of incompetent persons in appropriate cases. Some of these cases, independent of statute, impose strict procedural and substantive safeguards upon the determination of such petitions. For example, in Matter of C. D. M., 627 P.2d 607 (Alaska 1981), the parents of a 19-year-old mildly retarded female with Down's Syndrome filed a petition for her sterilization. By statute, guardians were authorized to "give any consents . . . that may be necessary to enable the ward to receive medical or other professional care." 627 P.2d at 612. The evidence showed a high probability that the child's offspring, if any, would be born with Down's Syndrome. Relying upon the equity powers vested in trial courts of general jurisdiction, which encompassed the *parens patriae* power over incompetents, the court concluded that the trial judge, contrary to his holding, had subject matter jurisdiction to act on the petition. However, it withheld approval of the operation because adequate safeguards had not been observed in the proceedings below. The court established the following minimum standards to govern the determination of a petition for sterilization of incompetent persons:

(1) Those advocating sterilization bear the heavy burden of proving by clear and convincing evidence that sterilization is in the best interests of the incompetent;

(2) The incompetent must be afforded a full judicial hearing at which medical testimony is presented and the incompetent, through a guardian *ad litem*, is allowed to present proof and cross-examine witnesses;

(3) The trial judge must be assured that a comprehensive medical, psychological, and social evaluation is made of the incompetent;

(4) The trial court must determine that the individual is legally incompetent to make a decision whether to be sterilized and that this incapacity is in all likelihood permanent;

(5) The incompetent must be capable of reproduction and unable to care for the offspring;

(6) Sterilization must be the only practicable means of contraception;

(7) The proposed operation must be the least restrictive alternative available;

(8) To the extent possible, the trial court must hear testimony from the incompetent concerning his or her understanding and desire, if any, for the proposed operation and its consequences, and finally,

(9) The court must examine the motivation behind the petition. Id. at 612–13.

The Supreme Court of Washington reached similar conclusions in Matter of Guardianship of Hayes, 93 Wash. 228, 608 P.2d 635 (1980) (en banc). It reversed the judgment of the trial court which had declined to authorize the sterilization of a 16-year-old severely retarded female on the ground of lack of subject matter jurisdiction. In that case, it was shown that the relevant guardianship statute neither authorized nor prohibited sterilization procedures at a guardian's request. . . . It held that a statute was not required to empower the trial court to exercise its jurisdiction, because that power was vested in the court under the state's constitution. The court was unwilling, however, to *sua sponte* approve an order of sterilization absent compliance with most of the safeguards outlined in *Matter of C.D.M.*, supra, to which it added a requirement that it be shown by clear, cogent, and convincing evidence that the current state of scientific and medical knowledge does not suggest either (a) that a reversible procedure or other less drastic contraceptive method will shortly be available, or (b) that science is on the threshold of an advance in treatment of the individual's disability. Id. 608 P.2d at 641. Furthermore, the court stated that the heavy presumption against sterilization will be even more difficult to overcome in the case of an incompetent minor, whose youth may "make it difficult or impossible to prove by clear and convincing evidence that he or she will never be capable of making an informed judgment about sterilization or of caring for a child." Id. The court expressed the belief that only in rare cases would sterilization be in the best interests of the retarded person.

In the case of In Re Grady, 85 N.J. 235, 426 A.2d 467 (1981), the parents of 19-year-old Lee Ann, a mentally retarded woman with Down's Syndrome, sought a court order authorizing the performance of a tubal ligation. Lee Ann had been taking birth control pills for four years but her parents wanted her to become less dependent on their supervision. The court attempted to reconcile the conflict between Lee Ann's diverse privacy rights—her right to bodily integrity and to be free from sterilization on the one hand, and on the other, her "right" to be sterilized, id. 426 A.2d at 471–73. . . . Stating that courts which decline to assume jurisdiction do not reflect "adequate sensitivity to the constitutional rights of the incompetent person," the New Jersey court resolved the conflict in favor of Lee Ann's "right" to be sterilized, premising its decision on the doctrines of *parens patriae* and substituted consent, . . .

In yet another case, In re Penny N., 120 N.H. 269, 414 A.2d 541 (1980), the court held that the trial judge had jurisdiction to consider a petition for sterilization, but it refused to order the procedure because sufficient safeguards had not been utilized. . . .

Matter of A. W., Colo., 637 P.2d 366 (1981) (en banc), involved a severely mentally retarded 15-year-old female whose parents had petitioned the district court (a court of general jurisdiction) to authorize a hysterectomy. The parents were concerned over the child's fear and fright of the menstrual process and also because of the possibility that she could become pregnant. The evidence showed that the child was physiologically normal and therefore perfectly capable of conceiving a child. The child's physician recommended a hysterectomy to avoid pregnancy and to discontinue the menstrual cycle. The trial court granted the petition on the basis of a Colorado statute generally empowering parents to request medical or surgical care for their child. The Supreme Court of Colorado reversed, concluding "that sterilization of a mentally retarded minor is a special case not covered by the general parental consent statute." 637 P.2d at 368. . . . In determining the merits of the sterilization petition, the Colorado court adopted standards to guide the discretion of the trial judge similar to those adopted in *Matter of C.D.M.*, *Hayes*, and *Grady*, all supra. Another standard required the trial judge to find by clear and convincing evidence that the sterilization was "medically essential," as to which the court said:

> "A sterilization is medically essential if clearly necessary, in the opinion of experts, to preserve the life or physical or mental health of the mentally retarded person. The term 'medically essential' is reasonably precise and provides protection from abuses prevalent in this area in the past. The term also avoids confusion as to whose interests are to be considered. It is not the welfare of society, or the convenience or peace of mind of parents or guardians that these standards are intended to protect. The purpose of the standards is to protect the health of the minor retarded person, and to prevent that person's fundamental procreative rights from being abridged. In some circumstances, the possibility of pregnancy, if supported by sufficient evidence that it would threaten the physical or mental health of the person and that no less intrusive means of birth control would prove safe and effective, could justify granting a petition for sterilization as medically essential." Id. at 375–76.

Another view of the problem was taken in Matter of Guardianship of Eberhardy, 102 Wis.2d 539, 307 N.W.2d 881 (1981). That case involved a petition for sterilization by the guardians/parents of Joan, a 22-year-old mentally retarded woman. The petition was motivated by Joan's parents' belief that she had engaged in sexual activity at a summer camp for the mentally retarded and because Joan's physician recommended sterilization as "she would be unable to care for a child and the chances of a child being severely handicapped were considerable." Id. 307 N.W.2d at 883. Joan's parents rejected her usage of an I.U.D. and sought court approval of a tubal ligation. In reversing the judgment of the circuit court that no jurisdiction existed to act on the petition, the Supreme Court of Wisconsin held that the state constitution vested in such courts "jurisdiction in all matters civil and criminal." Id. 307 N.W.2d at 885. . . . [T]he court, although acknowledging the jurisdiction of circuit courts in such cases, concluded that they were not the appropriate forum to resolve such delicate issues of public policy. . . .

. . . In the Matter of Mary Moe, 385 Mass. 555, 432 N.E.2d 712, decided March 16, 1982, involved a petition to sterilize a severely retarded adult woman. The Supreme Judicial Court of Massachusetts concluded that the trial court—a court of general equity jurisdiction—possessed inherent equitable power to grant a petition for sterilization, shown to be in the best interest of the mentally incompetent ward. In so holding, the court said "that the [trial] court is to determine whether to authorize sterilization when requested by the parents or guardian by finding the incompetent would so choose if competent." 385 Mass. at ___, 432 N.E.2d 712. It indicated that medical necessity was but one relevant factor to be assessed in evaluating whether sterilization was in the best interests of the disabled ward. As to this factor, the court indicated that medical necessity could be demonstrated by proof that pregnancy would threaten the physical or mental health of the incompetent person, with the weight given this factor being dependent upon the facts of the case and the degree of medical necessity. . . .

IV

There is no Maryland statute explicitly authorizing courts to approve petitions for the sterilization of any person. . . .

. . . .

. . . [I]t is evident that § 13–708 does not apply to guardianship of the person of a minor. . . . We think, however, that the statutory formulation of § 13–708 essentially parallels and is declaratory of the common law *parens patriae* powers of circuit courts over incompetent minors.
. . . .

The *parens patriae* jurisdiction of circuit courts in this State is well established. . . . It is a fundamental common law concept that the jurisdiction of courts of equity over such persons is plenary so as to afford whatever relief may be necessary to protect the individual's best interests.
. . . We conclude, therefore, that as to incompetent minors circuit courts, acting in pursuance of their inherent *parens patriae* authority, have subject matter jurisdiction to consider a petition for an order authorizing a guardian to consent to the sterilization of an incompetent minor. See Stump v. Sparkman, 435 U.S. 349, 98 S.Ct. 1099, 55 L.Ed.2d 331 (1978).

V

In determining whether a petition to authorize a guardian to consent to sterilization of an incompetent minor is in the minor's best interest, it is essential that the circuit court take into account and be guided by the following minimal standards, which we adopt today in order to safeguard and secure the rights of the ward.

First, the court must appoint an independent guardian *ad litem* to act on the disabled ward's behalf, with full opportunity to meet with the ward and to present evidence and cross-examine witnesses at a full judicial hearing. Second, the court must receive independent medical, psychological and social evaluations by competent professionals and may, if deemed advisable, appoint its own experts to assist in the evaluation of the ward's best interests. Third, the court should personally meet with the minor ward to obtain its own impression of the individual's competency, affording the ward a full opportunity to express his or her personal views or desires with respect to the judicial proceedings and the prospect of sterilization. Fourth, the trial judge must find, by clear and convincing evidence, that the individual lacks competency to make a decision about sterilization and, further, that the incapacity is not likely to change in the foreseeable future. Fifth, the court must be satisfied by clear and convincing evidence that sterilization is in the best interests of the incompetent minor. This determination involves a number of factors, including whether the incompetent minor is capable of reproduction, the child's age and circumstances at the time of the petition, the extent of the child's exposure to sexual contact that could result in pregnancy, the feasibility of utilizing effective contraceptive procedures in lieu of sterilization, the availability of alternative and less intrusive sterilization procedures, and the possibility that scientific advances may occur in the foreseeable future, which could result in improvement of the ward's mental condition. In addition to these factors, the trial court, before authorizing sterilization as being in the best interests of the incompetent minor, must find by clear and convincing evidence that the requested operative procedure is medically necessary to preserve the life or physical or mental health of the incompetent minor.

VI

In refusing to authorize sterilization in this case, the trial judge concluded from the evidence that sterilization by hysterectomy to terminate Sonya's menstrual cycle and to prevent her pregnancy was not, within the contemplation of § 13–708's "demonstrated need" formulation, necessary to preserve her life or physical or mental health. While the court noted the absence of any statutory authority or guidance other than that contained in § 13–708, it did not, as we read its opinion, find an absence of subject matter jurisdiction to determine the merits of the petition; it simply found, in light of the evidence in the case, a lack of justification for granting the petition, i.e., that no "demonstrated need" was established.

. . . We think the trial judge properly concluded that Sonya lacked the mental capacity to herself consent to the operation. Moreover, we think the trial judge was correct in determining that the evidence failed to disclose that sterilization by hysterectomy was in Sonya's best interest as being necessary for her medical or mental health. Manifestly, the fact that Sonya experiences pain and irritation during her menstrual cycle, which she does not understand and with which she has difficulty in coping, does not in itself provide any basis for authorizing a hysterectomy. Nor does the mere fact that Sonya could become pregnant and give birth to a child, for whom she could not care, provide justification to authorize the operation. Indeed, in considering the best interests of an incompetent minor, the welfare of society or the convenience or peace of mind of the ward's parents or guardian plays no part.

Considering Sonya's age and present circumstances, the absence of any evidence, much less clear and convincing evidence, of any medical necessity for the sterilization procedure at this time, no useful purpose would be served by remanding the case to the trial court for further proceedings in light of today's opinion.

We recognize, of course, that declaration of the public policy of this State is normally a function of the legislative branch of government. Felder v. Butler, 292 Md. 174, 438 A.2d 494 (1981). In view of the profound and recurring nature of the issue here involved, and its obvious importance to the public, the legislature may deem it appropriate at this time to declare the law of the State by enacting a statute governing the granting of consent for sterilization of mentally incompetent minors.

Judgment affirmed, with costs.

SMITH, JUDGE, concurring in part and dissenting in part.

I fully agree with much of what Chief Judge Murphy has said in his excellent opinion for the majority. I disagree with the final result, however. . . .

[W]e need to remember as the majority opinion states, that we know that this young woman cannot exercise what some call "the fundamental right to bear and beget children" with any degree of understanding. This is so because her brain injury is irreversible; the psychiatrist in his testimony estimated that her IQ is "[t]wenty-five to thirty," and said that given this IQ she would be comparable to an individual "of around the age of one or two, one and a half to two." We know full well that a two year old would not understand the act of copulation. Thus, logic indicates that if she becomes pregnant it will not be the result of any conscious decision on her part, but will be the consequence of some illegitimate act.

. . . [I]t was the difficulties connected with menstruation, not the problems arising from pregnancy, which apparently have motivated the aunt in her request for the operation. This is what she dwelt upon in her testimony on direct examination. (The aunt and the grandmother were the petitioners for guardianship. On the day of the hearing the grandmother was hospitalized.) The record states:

"Q Now, in living in the home in the last three years I would assume you had the observation—opportunity to observe Sonya before the menstrual cycle began and when it began, during and after; can you characterize her attitude for us prior to, during and after the menstrual cycle?

"A Well, as I stated before, Sonya is ill a lot but during that time it caused confusion for her. She appeared disoriented and uncomfortable.

"Sonya cannot communicate where her discomforts are and the family has to more or less determine what's wrong with her when she seems to be ill or uncomfortable.

"We have to determine what is hurting her. It could be her head, and yet we would think it might have been her stomach that is hurting. She can't—I suppose she doesn't know where pain comes from. She feels uncomfortable, but she cannot communicate where the pain is coming from."

One would not expect more from a person of Sonya's mental age. The only time on direct examination of the aunt that pregnancy was even mentioned was this single question and answer:

"Q Do you think Sonya could care for a child if she were to conceive and have a child?

"A Not at all."

Fourthly, the psychiatrist made it abundantly clear that the *principal* reason for this proposed "subtotal hysterectomy" was not the fear of pregnancy.[1] Aside from that which we have quoted in n.1, no other reference to pregnancy was made on direct examination of the psychiatrist. Rather, the matter of pregnancy was a theory that Sonya's court-appointed counsel developed on cross-examination. The record reflects on direct examination:

"Q Within a reasonable degree of medical certainty, do you have an opinion of whether or not this hysterectomy would be in the child's best interest?

"A I believe it would be.

"Q Can you support it for any reason, sir?

"A Well, when Sonya has her period, which you must know I have not observed, it is strictly the history, and in pyschiatry we have to rely on the history of those who are around, the description that I have is that she— . . . . When she has her period, she doesn't come downstairs. She wants to stay in bed much of the day, and she can't go to school.

"She whimpers, and she gets cross. She hollers to quote Mrs. Wentzel. She doesn't wear her napkin. She may get up to go to the bathroom, and she takes her napkin off, and she doesn't quite understand what it's all about.

"She has pain that she cannot really tell us about or tell her parents about anytime. It's always been a problem when she's febrific or ill that she has not been able to indicate where she's having difficulty except through careful questioning and a woman's intuition to understand.

"In view of the fact that she's unable to communicate these matters it makes it difficult for those who are caring for her to understand always what is happening because she does not have the capacity to speak her mind when something is wrong, and in view of the fact that she is not able to give an indication when she is ill as to what the matter might be, and in view of the fact that she has such a great deal of discomfort with her periods it would seem to me reasonable to recommend this from a medical point of view.

"The emotional stirs inside of her and she doesn't understand it, to me that is sufficient reason to recommend this."

---

1. He explained the nature of a subtotal hysterectomy:

"Q Could you characterize from a medical standpoint how this hysterectomy would benefit the child?

"A Well, a subtotal hysterectomy would be a hysterectomy in which her uterus would be removed, her ovaries would not be, she will not thereby be castrated.

"She would have ovarian function. She would ovulate regularly. She would not have menses, and she would not have the problems that youngsters her age or women would have, menstrual cramps, premenstrual tension, difficulties of that kind because she does not understand what is going on and has this kind of difficulty and does not comprehend all of this. It would seem that she would be happier without having all of that.

"Q Could you repeat, once again, the label that you gave to this operation?

"A It would be a subtotal hysterectomy.

"Q Subtotal hysterectomy?

"A Yes.

"Q Would you give us your opinion of what effect a subtotal hysterectomy would have on her capability to bear children?

"A She would not be able to bear children period."

The record on cross-examination states:

"Q   Isn't it the truth that the principal reason why the family desires the hysterectomy is because they feel that Sonya Star Flanary is incapable of caring for a child; isn't that correct?

"A   No, sir.   That's not correct.

"Q   You didn't tell me that?

"A   No.

"Q   Doctor—

"A   There is a problem there.

"Q   Well, let's hear the problem.   The Court would like to know.

"A   Well, you seem to have the problem, not I, about that.

"Q   Isn't it a fact, Doctor, that the reality of the situation and the tragedy of the situation is that Sonya is in a situation daily going to school and so forth that she could have an unwanted pregnancy; isn't that correct?

"A   That's true.   She could become pregnant, no doubt about that.   There is no doubt that the parents are concerned about that possibility.   I did not say that was the principal reason, okay.   I said it's multidetermined.   Naturally.   Of course.   All right.

"Q   And if Sonya had a child and you told me that she was perfectly capable from what you can understand of having a child and a normal child?

"A   That's correct.

"Q   Because her disability is traumatically induced; if she had a child obviously she cannot take care of that child at all?

"A   That's correct.

"Q   Then the burden and the decision would be, one, to abort or if to have the child this would be an added burden on the Wentzel/Flanary family, would it not?

"A   That's correct.

"Q   And the Wentzel/Flanary family, Wentzel being the grandmother and Flanary being the mother, is very concerned about this fact, are they not, about the unwanted child?

"A   They voiced concerns to me about the possibility, right.   I think the reasons are obvious when you see her that she is rather an attractive girl even though she has limitations with the left side of her hemiparesis, the concern of the family is not so much at the present time but later on when Mrs. Wentzel is no longer able to care for her because of her age and so forth.   I think that's another subject concerning guardianship—I don't care to be concerned, but when she is being treated by other people or taken care of by other people that's a reasonable question.   It is not the principal one.

"Q   You think that the—

"A   I don't know that there is a principal one.   I think that is a concern of theirs, but they also wish to see her free of a lot of discomfort and pain.

"Q   But the freedom from discomfort and pain does not make this surgical procedure medically necessary, does it?

"A   Not in itself.

"Q Well, is there anything life threatening about her having a child?

"A No, there is not a life threatening issue there.

"Q It just becomes medically more convenient to have the sub-total hysterectomy; is that correct, Doctor?

"A It is convenient in the sense that she would not have the discomfort and the emotional turmoil thereby surrounding it and other aspects of this are quite obvious in terms of her hygenic care and so on.

"Q Am I correct in characterizing this subtotal hysterectomy as an operation of convenience? Rather than an operation of necessity?

"A Well, it's a matter of what one means by that.

"Q Well, then let's break down necessity. Necessity means something you cannot do without, isn't that true?

"A That's true. If we take it in the strictest sense of the word, that's true.

"Q Is this an operation that is necessitous in that respect?

"A No.

"Q Then it is then more an operation of convenience, am I correct, Doctor?

"A In that 'medical sense' yes. Can we take into consideration emotions. Is that all right? We couldn't say this is necessary. She's not going to go crazy emotionally if she doesn't have a hysterectomy, but from an emotional point of view we can't compare her to other women with average intelligence and who can understand things and who can speak and walk and talk."

One could hardly expect to achieve toilet training of a child by the time he or she reaches the mental age of this young woman. It thus becomes obvious that she cannot be expected to understand the difficulties and the bodily functions associated with menstruation.

.   .   .

Do my colleagues doubt for one instant what Sonya's choice would be under the circumstances here if she "were in a position to make a sound judgment"? I am certain she would give her assent. From the testimony of the aunt and the psychiatrist which we have set forth, one can see how Sonya is completely unable to cope with menstruation. Furthermore, it would be a terrible thing for this young lady to become pregnant. Imagine what it would be like for a person with a mental age comparable to that of a one and a half to a two year old child to be pregnant. She would not have the mentality to understand that which was taking place, just as she does not understand relative to menstruation and her hygenic care. The process of childbirth undoubtedly would be a terrifying one for her.

This case crys out to the conscience of an equity court for relief. This young woman, her mother, her aunt, and her grandmother are all suffering as a result of the accidental injuries inflicted upon the girl a number of years ago. They are all entitled, as the New York court put it in *In re Weberlist,* "to the promise of the Declaration of Independence for 'Life, Liberty and the pursuit of Happiness.'" Most of the members of this Court are parents. Each of us certainly has some conception of what may be expected from a child of the mental age of this young lady. No one questions the brain injury, the irreversible nature of the injury, and the mental age of the court's ward. All agree as to the accuracy of this statement. Indeed, the majority says, "We think the trial judge properly concluded that Sonya lacked the mental capacity to herself consent to the operation." Therefore, I am of the view that the testimony here of the aunt and the psychiatrist relative to the problems concerning menstruation make out a case by clear and convincing evidence that it is in this young lady's best interests that the surgical procedures which the psychiatrist advocates be performed. Although the problems which would be associated with her becoming pregnant are strong and compelling reasons for authorizing the procedure, these problems are merely additional reasons for granting the requested relief.

. . .

The difficulty inherent in the majority's establishment of "medical necessity" as a controlling factor in determining whether to authorize sterilization is that a trial court is compelled to place primary emphasis on a single objective standard irrespective of the decision that the incompetent minor would make if he or she were competent. In my view, treating medical necessity as a controlling factor results in an unacceptable degree of interference with an incompetent minor's right to make decisions concerning sterilization because such a controlling factor might well prevent an individual who would wish to be sterilized if competent from being sterilized.

. . .

NOTES

1. Because it is impossible to know what Sonya wants, should we speculate, as the dissenting judge invites us to do? Cf. the invocation of a substituted judgment standard in *Saikewicz*, and notes following in Ch. 7, Sec. B.4., supra.

2. Consider the holding in Stump v. Sparkman, 435 U.S. 349, 98 S.Ct. 1099, 55 L.Ed.2d 331 (1978):

MR. JUSTICE WHITE delivered the opinion of the Court.

This case requires us to consider the scope of a judge's immunity from damages liability when sued under 42 U.S.C. § 1983.

I

The relevant facts underlying respondents' suit are not in dispute. On July 9, 1971, Ora Spitler McFarlin, the mother of respondent Linda Kay Spitler Sparkman, presented to Judge Harold D. Stump of the Circuit Court of DeKalb County, Ind., a document captioned "Petition To Have Tubal Ligation Performed On Minor and Indemnity Agreement." The document had been drafted by her attorney, a petitioner here. In this petition Mrs. McFarlin stated under oath that her daughter was 15 years of age and was "somewhat retarded," although she attended public school and had been promoted each year with her class. The petition further stated that Linda had been associating with "older youth or young men" and had stayed out overnight with them on several occasions. As a result of this behavior and Linda's mental capabilities, it was stated that it would be in the daughter's best interest if she underwent a tubal ligation in order "to prevent unfortunate circumstances . . . ." In the same document Mrs. McFarlin also undertook to indemnify and hold harmless Dr. John Hines, who was to perform the operation, and the DeKalb

Memorial Hospital, where the operation was to take place, against all causes of action that might arise as a result of the performance of the tubal ligation.[1]

The petition was approved by Judge Stump on the same day. He affixed his signature as "Judge, DeKalb Circuit Court," to the statement that he did "hereby approve the above Petition by affidavit form on behalf on Ora Spitler McFarlin, to have Tubal Ligation performed upon her minor daughter, Linda Spitler, subject to said Ora Spitler McFarlin covenanting and agreeing to indemnify and keep indemnified Dr. John Hines and the DeKalb Memorial Hospital from any matters or causes of action arising therefrom."

On July 15, 1971, Linda Spitler entered the DeKalb Memorial Hospital, having been told that she was to have her appendix removed. The following day a tubal ligation was performed upon her. She was released several days later, unaware of the true nature of her surgery.

Approximately two years after the operation, Linda Spitler was married to respondent Leo Sparkman. Her inability to become pregnant led her to discover that she had been sterilized during the 1971 operation. As a result of this revelation, the Sparkmans filed suit in the United States District Court for the Northern District of Indiana against Mrs. McFarlin, her attorney, Judge Stump, the doctors who had performed and assisted in the tubal ligation, and

---

1. The full text of the petition presented to Judge Stump read as follows:

"State of Indiana ⎱ ss:
County of DeKalb ⎰

"PETITION TO HAVE TUBAL LIGATION PERFORMED ON MINOR AND INDEMNITY AGREEMENT

"Ora Spitler McFarlin, being duly sworn upon her oath states that she is the natural mother of and has custody of her daughter, Linda Spitler, age fifteen (15) being born January 24, 1956 and said daughter resides with her at 108 Iwo Street, Auburn, DeKalb County, Indiana.

"Affiant states that her daughter's mentality is such that she is considered to be somewhat retarded although she is attending or has attended the public schools in DeKalb Central School System and has been passed along with other children in her age level even though she does not have what is considered normal mental capabilities and intelligence. Further, that said affiant has had problems in the home of said child as a result of said daughter leaving the home on several occassions to associate with older youth or young men and as a matter of fact having stayed overnight with said youth or men and about which incidents said affiant did not become aware of until after such incidents occurred. As a result of this behavior and the mental capabilities of said daughter, affiant believes that it is to the best interest of said child that a Tubal Ligation be performed on said minor daughter to prevent unfortunate circumstances to occur and since it is impossible for the affiant as mother of said minor child to maintain and control a continuous observation of the activities of said daughter each and every day.

"Said affiant does hereby in consideration of the Court of the DeKalb Circuit Court approving the Tubal Ligation being performed upon her minor daughter does hereby [sic] covenant and agree to indemnify and keep indemnified and hold Dr. John Hines, Auburn, Indiana, who said affiant is requesting perform said operation and the DeKalb Memorial Hospital, Auburn, Indiana, whereas [sic] said operation will be performed, harmless from and against all or any matters or causes of action that could or might arise as a result of the performing of said Tubal Ligation.

"In witness whereof, said affiant, Ora Spitler McFarlin, has hereunto subscribed her name this 9th day of July, 1971.

"/S/ ORA SPITLER McFARLIN
Ora Spitler McFarlin
Petitioner

"Subscribed and sworn to before me this 9th day of July, 1971.

"/S/ WARREN G. SUNDAY
Warren G. Sunday
Notary Public

"My commission expires January 4, 1975.

"I, Harold D. Stump, Judge of the DeKalb Circuit Court, do hereby approve the above Petition by affidavit form on behalf of Ora Spitler McFarlin, to have Tubal Ligation performed upon her minor daughter, Linda Spitler, subject to said Ora Spitler McFarlin covenanting and agreeing to indemnify and keep indemnified Dr. John Hines and the DeKalb Memorial Hospital from any matters or causes of action arising therefrom.

"/S/ HAROLD D. STUMP
Judge, DeKalb Circuit Court

"Dated July 9, 1971"

the DeKalb Memorial Hospital. Respondents sought damages for the alleged violation of Linda Sparkman's constitutional rights; also asserted were pendent state claims for assault and battery, medical malpractice, and loss of potential fatherhood.

. . . The District Court . . . held that no federal action would lie against any of the defendants because Judge Stump, the only state agent, was absolutely immune from suit under the doctrine of judicial immunity. . . .

On appeal the Court of Appeals for the Seventh Circuit reversed . . .

We granted certiorari to consider the correctness of this ruling. We reverse.

II

The governing principle of law is well established and is not questioned by the parties. As early as 1872, the Court recognized that it was "a general principle of the highest importance to the proper administration of justice that a judicial officer, in exercising the authority vested in him, [should] be free to act upon his own convictions, without apprehension of personal consequences to himself." Bradley v. Fisher, [13 Wall. 335, 347 (1872)]. For that reason the Court held that "judges of courts of superior or general jurisdiction are not liable to civil actions for their judicial acts, even when such acts are in excess of their jurisdiction, and are alleged to have been done maliciously or corruptly." 13 Wall., at 351. Later we held that this doctrine of judicial immunity was applicable in suits under § 1 of the Civil Rights Act of 1871, 42 U.S.C. § 1983. . . . Pierson v. Ray, 386 U.S. 547, 87 S.Ct. 1213, 18 L.Ed. 2d 288 (1967).

The Court of Appeals correctly recognized that the necessary inquiry in determining whether a defendant judge is immune from suit is whether at the time he took the challenged action he had jurisdiction over the subject matter before him. . . .

2. AIDING REPRODUCTION

a. Artificial Insemination

PEOPLE v. SORENSEN

Supreme Court of California, 1968.
68 Cal.2d 280, 66 Cal.Rptr. 7, 437 P.2d 495.

McComb, Justice.

Defendant appeals from a judgment convicting him of violating section 270 of the Penal Code (willful failure to provide for his minor child), a misdemeanor.

The settled statement of facts recites that seven years after defendant's marriage it was medically determined that he was sterile. His wife desired a child, either by artificial insemination or by adoption, and at first defendant refused to consent. About 15 years after the marriage defendant agreed to the artificial insemination of his wife. Husband and wife, then residents of San Joaquin County, consulted a physician in San Francisco. They signed an agreement, which is on the letterhead of the physician, requesting the physician to inseminate the wife with the sperm of a white male. The semen was to be selected by the physician, and under no circumstances were the parties to demand the name of the donor. The agreement contains a recitation that the physician does not represent that pregnancy will occur. The physician treated Mrs. Sorensen, and she became pregnant. Defendant knew at the time he signed the consent that when his wife took the treatments she could become pregnant and that if a child was born it was to be treated as their child.

A male child was born to defendant's wife in San Joaquin County on October 14, 1960. The information for the birth certificate was given by the mother, who named defendant as the father. Defendant testified that he had not provided the information on the birth certificate and did not recall seeing it before the trial.

For about four years the family had a normal family relationship, defendant having represented to friends that he was the child's father and treated the boy as his son. In 1964, Mrs. Sorensen separated from defendant and moved to Sonoma County with the boy. At separation, Mrs. Sorensen told defendant that she wanted no support for the boy, and she consented that a divorce be granted to defendant. Defendant obtained a decree of divorce, which recites that the court retained "jurisdiction regarding the possible support obligation of plaintiff in regard to a minor child born to defendant."

In the summer of 1966 when Mrs. Sorensen became ill and could not work, she applied for public assistance under the Aid to Needy Children program. The County of Sonoma supplied this aid until Mrs. Sorensen was able to resume work. Defendant paid no support for the child since the separation in 1964, although demand therefor was made by the district attorney. The municipal court found defendant guilty of violating section 270 of the Penal Code and granted him probation for three years on condition that he make payments of $50 per month for support through the district attorney's office.

. . .

. . . [T]he only question for our determination is:

Is the husband of a woman, who with his consent was artificially inseminated with semen of a third-party donor, guilty of the crime of failing to support a child who is the product of such insemination, in violation of section 270 of the Penal Code?

The law is that defendant is the lawful father of the child born to his wife, which child was conceived by artificial insemination to which he consented, and his conduct carries with it an obligation of support within the meaning of section 270 of the Penal Code.

Under the facts of this case, the term "father" as used in section 270 cannot be limited to the biologic or natural father as those terms are generally understood. The determinative factor is whether the legal relationship of father and child exists. A child conceived through heterologous artificial insemination does not have a "natural father," as that term is commonly used. The anonymous donor of the sperm cannot be considered the "natural father," as he is no more responsible for the use made of his sperm than is the donor of blood or a kidney. Moreover, he could not dispute the presumption that the child is the legitimate issue of Mr. and Mrs. Sorensen, as that presumption "may be disputed only by the people of the State of California . . . or by the husband or wife, or the descendant of one or both of them." (Evid.Code, § 661.) With the use of frozen semen, the donor may even be dead at the time the semen is used. Since there is no "natural father," we can only look for a lawful father.

It is doubtful that with the enactment of section 270 of the Penal Code and its amendments the Legislature considered the plight of a child conceived through artificial insemination. However, the intent of the Legislature obviously was to include every child, legitimate or illegitimate, born or unborn, and enforce the obligation of support against the person who could be determined to be the lawful parent.

. . .

. . . [A] reasonable man who, because of his inability to procreate, actively participates and consents to his wife's artificial insemination in the hope that a child will be produced whom they will treat as their own, knows that such behavior carries with it the legal responsibilities of fatherhood and criminal responsibility for nonsupport. One who consents to the production of a child cannot create a temporary relation to be assumed and disclaimed at will, but the arrangement must be of such character as to impose an obligation of supporting those for whose existence he is directly responsible. As noted by the trial court, it is safe to assume that without defendant's active participation and consent the child would not have been procreated.

. . .

The question of the liability of the husband for support of a child created through artificial insemination is one of first impression in this state and has been raised in only a few cases outside the state, none of them involving a criminal prosecution for failure to provide. Although other courts considering the question have found some existing legal theory to hold the "father" responsible, results have varied on the question of legitimacy. In Gursky v. Gursky, 39 Misc.2d 1083, 242 N.Y.S.2d 406 (Sup.Ct. 1963), the court held that the child was illegitimate but that the husband was liable for the child's support because consent to the insemination implied a promise to support.

In Strnad v. Strnad, 190 Misc. 786, 78 N.Y.S.2d 390 (Sup.Ct.1948), the court found that a child conceived through artificial insemination was not illegitimate and granted visitation rights to the husband in a custody proceeding.

It is less crucial to determine the status of the child than the status of defendant as the father. Categorizing the child as either legitimate or illegitimate does not resolve the issue of the legal consequences flowing from defendant's participation in the child's existence. Under our statute, both legitimate and illegitimate minors have a right to support from their parents. The primary liability is on the father, and if he is dead or for any reason whatever fails to furnish support, the mother is criminally liable therefor. To permit defendant's parental responsibilities to rest on a voluntary basis would place the entire burden of support on the child's mother, and if she is incapacitated the burden is then on society. Cost to society, of course, is not the only consideration which impels the conclusion that defendant is the lawful father of the offspring of his marriage. The child is the principal party affected, and if he has no father he is forced to bear not only the handicap of social stigma but financial deprivation as well.

. . .

The public policy of this state favors legitimation (Estate of Lund, 26 Cal.2d 472, 481, 490, 159 P.2d 643, 162 A.L.R. 606), and no valid public purpose is served by stigmatizing an artificially conceived child as illegitimate. . . .

In the absence of legislation prohibiting artificial insemination, the offspring of defendant's valid marriage to the child's mother was lawfully begotten and was not the product of an illicit or adulterous relationship. Adultery is defined as "the voluntary sexual intercourse of a married person with a person other than the offender's husband or wife." (Civ. Code, § 93.) It has been suggested that the doctor and the wife commit adultery by the process of artificial insemination. Since the doctor may be a woman, or the husband himself may administer the insemination by a syringe, this is patently absurd; to consider it an act of adultery with the donor, who at the time of insemination may be a thousand miles away or may even be dead, is equally absurd. Nor are we persuaded that the concept of legitimacy demands that the child be the actual offspring of the husband of the mother and if semen of some other male is utilized the resulting child is illegitimate.

In California, legitimacy is a legal status that may exist despite the fact that the husband is not the natural father of the child. The Legislature has provided for legitimation of a child born before wedlock by the subsequent marriage of its parents, for legitimation by acknowledgment by the father and for inheritance rights of illegitimates, and since the subject of legitimation as well as that of succession of property is properly one for legislative action, we are not required in this case to do more than decide that, within the meaning of section 270 of the Penal Code, defendant is the lawful father of the child conceived through heterologous artificial insemination and born during his marriage to the child's mother.

The judgment is affirmed.

C. M. v. C. C.

Juvenile and Domestic Relation Court, Cumberland County, New Jersey, 1977.
152 N.J. Super. 160, 377 A.2d 821.

TESTA, J.C.C., Temporarily Assigned.

This is a case of first impression, presenting a unique factual situation with no reported legal precedents directly on point, in this or any other jurisdiction.

C.C. had a child who was conceived through the use of sperm donated by C.M. C.C. testified that she had been discussing with C.M. the possibility of having a child by artificial insemination, inquiring of him whether she should ask one of his friends to supply the sperm. C.M. suggested that he provide it and C.C. agreed to his suggestion. C.M. testified that he and C.C. had been seeing each other for some time and were contemplating marriage. She wanted a child and wanted him to be the father, but did not want to have intercourse with him before their marriage. Therefore, he agreed to provide the sperm.

After the decision to have the child was made, the testimony of both parties are substantially the same. C.C. and C.M. went to a doctor who referred them to a sperm bank. The doctor at the sperm bank refused to allow its facilities to be used. However, C.C. learned, as a result of her conversation with the doctor, of a procedure for artificial insemination using a glass syringe and a glass jar.

Over a period of several months, C.C. went to C.M.'s apartment where they attempted the artificial insemination. C.M. would stay in one room while C.C. went to another room to attempt to inseminate herself with semen provided by C.M.   After several attempts over a period of several months, C.C. did conceive a child.

C.M. testified that until C.C. was about three months pregnant, he assumed he would act toward the child in the same manner as most fathers act toward their children.   C.C. denies this, testifying that C.M. was to be only a visitor in her home—much as any of her other friends.   In either case, at that point the relationship between C.M. and C.C. broke off. This present application is a request by C.M. for visitation rights to the baby.   His request is strenuously opposed by C.C.

A natural father is entitled to visitation rights with respect to his illegitimate children.   The key issue in this case is whether C.M. is the natural father of a child or whether he should be considered not to be such because the sperm used to conceive was transferred to C.C. by other than natural means.   C.C. does not dispute that the sperm used to conceive the child was provided by C.M.

The question of who is the father of a child conceived by artificial insemination has been addressed by a few courts in the United States and has been addressed by authorities in the field of family law.   In most cases the donor is unknown, and the issue involves whether the husband of the mother is, in fact, the father.   . . .

. . .

It is clear that the situation in the case at bar is different . . . . There is no married couple.   There is no anonymous donor.   Rather, we have a woman who chooses to have a baby and a man who chooses to provide the needed sperm, who are not married to each other and who choose a method of conception other than sexual intercourse.   If the conception took place by intercourse, there would be no question that the "donor" would be the father.   The issue becomes whether a man is any less a father because he provides the semen by a method different from that normally used.

In the cases above, there are at least three people involved in the conception of the child—a woman, her husband and an anonymous donor. The cases mention a second possible situation—where a woman is artificially inseminated by her husband's own sperm.   . . .   In that situation the husband is clearly the father of the child.

The case at bar is more analogous to the second situation.   In the first, there is competition over whether the husband or donor has the legal responsibility of fatherhood.   The donor is unknown.   In the second, there is no such competition.   The husband and donor are the same person—and dictum, at least, tells us that there would be no question that such husband-donor would be the father.

. . .

The courts have consistently shown a policy favoring the requirement that a child be provided with a father as well as a mother.   In a situation where there is an anonymous donor the courts have required that the person who consents to the use of sperm, not his own, be responsible for fathering the child.

In this case there is a known man who is the donor.   There is no husband.   If the couple had been married and the husband's sperm was used artificially, he would be considered the father.   If a woman conceives a child by intercourse, the "donor" who is not married to the mother is no less a father than the man who is married to the mother.   Likewise, if an unmarried woman conceives a child through artificial insemination from semen from a known man, that man cannot be considered to be less a father because he is not married to the woman.

When a husband consents to his wife's artificial insemination from an anonymous donor, he takes upon himself the responsibilities of fatherhood. By donating his semen anonymously, the donor impliedly gives it without taking on such responsibilities for its use. But here C.C. received semen from C.M., who was a friend—someone she had known for at least two years. The court finds that the evidence supports C.M.'s contention that he and C.C. had a long-standing dating relationship and he fully intended to assume the responsibilities of parenthood. There was no one else who was in a position to take upon himself the responsibilities of fatherhood when the child was conceived. The evidence does not adequately support C.C.'s contention, as argued by her attorney in his brief and stated in her testimony, that C.M. waived his parental rights.

It is in a child's best interests to have two parents whenever possible. The court takes no position as to the propriety of the use of artificial insemination between unmarried persons, but must be concerned with the best interests of the child in granting custody or visitation, and for such consideration will not make any distinction between a child conceived naturally or artificially. In this situation a man wants to take upon himself the responsibility of being a father to a child he is responsible for helping to conceive. The evidence does not support C.C.'s argument that he is unfit. The evidence demonstrates that C.M. attempted to establish a relationship with the child but was thwarted in his attempts by C.C. Contrary to C.C.'s argument, C.M. has shown a genuine interest in the child; he is a teacher and educationally able to aid his development, and is financially capable of contributing to his support. C.M.'s consent and active participation in the procedure leading to conception should place upon him the responsibilities of fatherhood. The court will not deny him the privileges of fatherhood. His motion for the right of visitation is granted. The court reserves the right to hold a hearing as to the period and manner of visitation on behalf of C.M.

Inasmuch as the court has found C.M. to be the natural father, the court must consider support and maintenance of the child and payment of any expenses incurred in his birth. Proper application shall be made by the parties to effect the above.

MARTIN CURIE-COHEN, LESLEIGH LUTTRELL AND SANDER SHAPIRO, CURRENT PRACTICE OF ARTIFICIAL INSEMINATION BY DONOR IN THE UNITED STATES

300 New Eng.J.Med. 585 (1979)

Numerous articles have appeared in scientific and popular journals discussing the moral and ethical aspects of artificial insemination with donor semen as well as the personal experiences of physicians who perform it. Despite the general interest in the subject little is known about its scope or its current methods. . . . In this paper, we report the results of a survey that comprehensively describe the practices and policies of a large group of physicians who perform artificial insemination by donor in the United States.

Methods

In December, 1977, we sent a questionnaire to each physician named in a listing of the American Fertility Society of physicians performing artificial insemination by donor. We also sent questionnaires (9 per cent of our mailing) to authors of recent articles on the subject and to all medical-school departments of obstetrics and gynecology. Most of those surveyed were obstetricians and gynecologists (94 per cent). A second mailing was sent in January, 1978, to all physicians who had not replied initially, but not to medical-school departments.

. . .

We requested those surveyed to return the questionnaires whether or not they performed artificial insemination by donor. Forms were coded to protect the confidentiality of the respondents. . . .

Results

We received 346 out of 711 questionnaires from the first mailing and 125 out of 354 from the second mailing, yielding a total return rate of 471 of 711 mailings, or 66 per cent. Of the 471 respondents, 379 (80 per cent) actually performed artificial insemination by donor; a higher proportion of the respondents from the first mailing (287 of 346) performed the procedure than those from the second mailing (92 of 125, $P<0.03$), suggesting that even a smaller proportion of the non-respondents performed artificial insemination. Not all respondents completed every question, so that the total number of responses varied for each question. Our respondents were located in 46 states and the District of Columbia; 27.8 per cent of them were from New York and California.

. . .

Reasons for Artificial Insemination by Donor

The primary reason for administering artificial insemination is infertility of the husband, accounting for over 95 per cent of almost all respondents' practices. However, at least 40 per cent of the doctors have provided this service for reasons other than infertility. At least 33 per cent (125 of 379) have inseminated women whose husbands feared transmitting a genetic disease. The most frequently cited was Rh-factor incompatibility (11.9 per cent), followed by cystic fibrosis, diabetes, hemophilia, Huntington's disease, muscular dystrophy and Tay-Sachs disease. Surprisingly enough, the third most cited reason was to provide natural children to women without a male partner. Despite societal pressure discouraging artificial insemination for single women, at least 9.5 per cent of the respondents (36 of 379) have done so. Less frequent reasons for performing the procedure included impotence, paraplegia and exposure of the husband to environmental mutagens.

As might be expected, most women who seek artificial insemination are childless. However, successfully inseminated women often return for additional children by this means. In our sample, approximately 11 per cent of the inseminations were performed for women returning after a first child obtained by this method. . . .

Methods of Obtaining Semen Donors

Donors are usually selected by the doctor who performs the insemination. The majority of doctors (91.8 per cent) do not allow recipients to select their own donors, and the rest have done so only rarely. Rather than find their own donors, some doctors (15 per cent) used frozen semen obtained from sperm banks; others used donors selected by urologists or other personal associates.

Most doctors (62 per cent) used medical students or hospital residents; 10.5 per cent used other university or graduate students, and 17.8 per cent used both. The remaining 9.7 per cent of the doctors who selected their own donors obtained donors from military academies, husbands of obstetric patients, hospital personnel and friends of the physician. Consequently, donors are not a random sampling of the general population but are a select group with presumably above-average health and intelligence. Beyond the use of this select donor pool, there is little further screening. Most respondents took family medical histories (96 per cent), but this questioning was often merely asking a donor if any genetic diseases existed in his family or presenting him with a short checklist of common familial diseases. A number of doctors expected medical students and hospital residents to screen themselves before donating semen.

.   .   .

In conjunction with genetic screening, donors were selected to match the husband's physical appearance. .   .   .

Virtually all respondents paid donors for their semen. Almost half the doctors (45.7 per cent) paid $25 per ejaculate; most (87.9 per cent) paid between $20 and $35, and only 5.4 per cent paid less than $20 and 6.7 per cent more than $35, up to $100 per ejaculate.

Use of Frozen Semen

Frozen semen was used by 31.4 per cent (119 of 379) of our respondents but accounted for only 12.7 per cent of total donor semen. Of those who used frozen semen, 43.7 per cent (52 of 119) used it in less than 10 per cent of their inseminations, and 41.2 per cent (49 of 119) used it in most (average of 90 per cent) of them. Surprisingly enough, the use of frozen semen was independent of the size of the practice and the size of the population served. Even more striking was the fact that the use of frozen semen was independent of whether the respondent treated a woman with the same donor for every cycle or different donors in a single cycle.

Among users of frozen semen, 42.4 per cent had never stored semen over three months, and 87 per cent had never stored it over 24 months. Again, these results were independent of the frequency of frozen-semen use. Of those who never or rarely used frozen semen, only 8 per cent used donors from outside their own geographic area, whereas 68.1 per cent of those who usually used frozen semen obtained outside donors.

Performance of Artificial Insemination

Most doctors inseminated women twice per cycle; others did so either once or three times per cycle. Of those who inseminated more than once per cycle, 74.9 per cent did so every other day, and 20.8 per cent on consecutive days. Women who became pregnant were inseminated for an average of about 3.7 months, and those who did not become pregnant discontinued the program after an average of about 6.4 months.

Half the respondents (51.1 per cent) used the same donor for each insemination of a single cycle but different donors for each cycle, whereas

17.1 per cent used the same donor for each cycle. However, 31.8 per cent used different donors within a single cycle. Although it was once common practice, only two doctors in our sample mixed donor semen with the husband's semen.

When asked for the maximum number of pregnancies produced by a single donor, only 249 (65.7 per cent) of the respondents answered—significantly fewer than those replying to any other question, suggesting that this information was frequently unobtainable. Of those who answered, most (77.1 per cent) had never used a donor for more than six pregnancies, whereas 5.7 per cent had used a donor for 15 or more. One respondent had used a single donor for 50 pregnancies. Although most doctors (50.7 per cent) used each donor for an average of one or two pregnancies, 10.3 per cent used each donor for an average of nine or more pregnancies. The multiple use of donors was usually pragmatic since most doctors (88.4 per cent) had no policies concerning the maximum use of a donor. The doctors who did restrict the use of a single donor usually limited the number of pregnancies to six or less.

The success rate of inseminations . . . was significantly associated with the sizes of the doctor's practice, the larger practices having higher success rates. Of interest was the fact that the success rates were independent of the number of times women were inseminated in a single cycle or of the timing with which inseminations were spaced. Weighting each response with the size of the respondent's practice (measured by the number of monthly inseminations), the national success rate for artificial insemination by donor is approximately 57 per cent.

Records

At least 190 of our respondents (50.1 per cent) provided obstetric care for their inseminated patients; 71 more (18.7 per cent) routinely determined the outcome of the pregnancies when they did not perform delivery. The remaining 31.2 per cent did not follow up recipients systematically. Most physicians (92.2 per cent) kept permanent records on recipients, and fewer (36.9 per cent) kept permanent records on children born after artificial insemination, and only 30.4 per cent did so on donors. It was not surprising that 82.6 per cent were opposed to legislation requiring that records be kept on children or donors. The doctors who opposed such legislation usually did so to ensure privacy or to protect the anonymity of the donor.

Discussion

Our respondents accounted for approximately 3576 donor births per year. Extrapolating from our survey return rate (66 per cent), we would expect about 5400 births to be represented in our total survey. Although our sample covered only 5.5 per cent of the 12,848 members of the American College of Obstetricians and Gynecologists and 13.1 per cent of the American Fertility Society, it consisted of the doctors who were most likely to perform artificial insemination. Even among this select group 19 per cent (91 of 480) did not perform artificial insemination by donor, and those who did perform it did so on a relatively small scale. If we assume that our survey reached the doctors who perform at least half the artificial inseminations by donor in this country, we can safely conclude that between 6000 and 10,000 children are born annually as a result of the procedure. Previous estimates have varied from 5000 to over 20,000, but we are unaware of any data to support these estimates.

Donor Selection

Some experts believe that genetic "screening of donors falls into the category of preventive medicine . . . , to reduce the risk of transmitting a disease during the procedure to the extent that our technology will allow." However, the donors in our sample were subjected to very little genetic screening. Family histories were usually superficial, and biochemical tests were rarely performed. Most screening was performed by physicians who were not trained for this task. For example, the list of traits used for rejecting donors included conditions with varied patterns of inheritance: autosomal recessive (Tay-Sachs disease, for which carriers are detectable, and cystic fibrosis, for which carriers are not detectable), dominant (Huntington's disease), X-linked (hemophilia) and multigenic (mental retardation). However, the severity and genetic risk of the conditions were not reflected in the frequency of use for donor rejection. Most notably, 71.4 per cent would reject a donor who had hemophilia in his family, even though it would be impossible to transmit this X-linked gene unless the donor were affected. In addition, screening was not actively carried out for most traits. For example, 92 per cent said they would reject a donor with a translocation or trisomy, but only 12.5 per cent examined the donor's karyotype to determine if such a condition existed; 94.7 per cent would reject a carrier of Tay-Sachs disease, but less than 1 per cent indicated that they tested donors for the carrier state. In fact, only 28.8 per cent performed any biochemical tests on donors other than blood typing, and these tests were primarily for communicable diseases.

Genetic screening depends upon the donor's recognition of inherited traits in reconstructing his family history, since he must volunteer pertinent information. This screening also depends upon the donor's honesty. However, the financial incentive to be a donor may make this procedure less reliable. By analogy, paid blood donors appear less honest than volunteers. Some physicians rely upon sperm banks to screen donors, but wide variation exists in the criteria for rejection used by different sperm banks.

Donor selection tends to promote positive eugenics (genetic improvement) as well as negative eugenics (prevention of genetic diseases), since donors are usually healthy university or medical students. This restricted donor pool may be responsible for the low frequency of congenital abnormalities and spontaneous abortions reported among pregnancies resulting from artificial insemination. The practice of matching the donor to the husband's phenotype reduces the dangers inherent in positive eugenics by limiting the number of characteristics that physicians are free to select.

Multiple Use of Donors

Using a single donor for many recipients may result in inadvertent consanguinity or inbreeding. This complication could occur if two people mated who unknowingly shared the same genetic father (i.e., were half-sibs), or if a recipient was inseminated with the semen of a relative. Either may occur accidentally, since the identity of the semen donor is almost always concealed.

. . . As a result of donor matching, a single donor may make a large contribution to a local ethnic community. Intra-marriage within such a community would result in increased inbreeding due to artificial insemination. In fact, several half-sib matings have nearly occurred already, and our data further suggests that inbreeding may be more frequent than expected. The probability of consanguinity between donor and recipient may also be increased since donors have the same approximate age and socioeconomic background as recipients.

Confidentiality

As compared to other medical practices, artificial insemination by donor is highly secretive. For example, some respondents asked patients to conceal the donor inseminations from their obstetricians, thus allowing the obstetrician to place the husband's name on the birth certificate in good faith. Confidentiality is also reflected in the incomplete records kept by many physicians. Such secrecy can seriously impede a critical examination of artificial insemination and its consequences.

Central to the issue of confidentiality is anonymity of the donor. Respondents were concerned about this issue for several reasons. Donor anonymity allegedly protects the donor, the child and the parents from excessive emotional stress. Anonymity also protects the donor from legal involvement in the legitimacy and inheritance rights of children born through artificial insemination—issues that are not completely resolved.
. . . . Finally, doctors who have difficulty in obtaining donors promise anonymity to encourage donors to participate.

Respondents usually guaranteed donor anonymity by intentionally keeping inadequate records or by inseminating patients with multiple donors in a single cycle, making the identity of the genetic father uncertain. Respondents justified these practices in the light of recent court orders to open the records of adoption agencies.

. . . Nevertheless, accurate records of genetic paternity are important. For the children born through artificial insemination, accessibility to these records not only may satisfy psychologic needs but may be critical in the process of genetic counseling, which is an increasingly useful tool in preventive medicine. For the doctor performing artificial insemination, paternity records are needed to evaluate semen fertility and the eugenic value of a donor through "progeny testing."

. . .

Sources of Error

Our results are offered as representative of current practices of artificial insemination by donor in the United States. However, they depend highly on the respondents' knowledge of their own practices. In some cases, this knowledge was necessarily limited. For example, almost one third did not follow up their patients after the beginning of pregnancy; thus, these respondents could only approximate the number of resultant children. Respondents often commented that their records were inadequate to answer many of the questions and that their responses were only guesses. Anticipating their lack of accurate records, most of our questions had multiple-choice answers (e.g., 0 to 10 per cent or 11 to 20 per cent), with an option to specify more exactly. This format probably sacrificed accuracy but facilitated response.

. . .

NOTES

1. Artificial insemination by donor (AID) permits deliberate separation of the biological act of producing a child from the psychological process of nurturing

and raising the child. For that reason, should the practice be prohibited? Discouraged? Limited to married couples who cannot have children? Is the fact that the sperm contributor is usually anonymous relevant to your answers? Is the practice of keeping the sperm contributor anonymous a sound policy?

Little has been written about what emotional and psychological effects children conceived through AID experience as they grow into adulthood. A recent Phil Donahue television interview program highlighted some of these problems.* The guests on the program included two women in their mid-thirties who had been conceived through AID. Both expressed anger over their inability to gain knowledge about their genetic background and personal identity:

Phil Donahue: Right. [W]hy are you angry . . . ? Why wouldn't you think your mother's 1948 herculean effort to become pregnant would be applauded? She certainly wanted a baby.

[Guest No. 1]: Well, as I got into this and started developing and studying this research—it's not just my family that ended in divorce. There's evidence regular adoptive families are ending in divorce a lot.—the AI doesn't solve all the infertile couple's problems. It's really the beginning.

Phil Donahue: O.K. But I still don't know why you're upset.

[Guest No. 1]: I want to know who I am. I want to know my name. I want to know my medical history. I had two miscarriages. And when I found out on the radio that a man or his—or a woman's father might have left the sperm bad to cause the miscarriages, I want to know, is it a guilt trip on me that people put on me? What did I eat wrong that caused these babies to die? What about these fifty unknown numbers of other children my father was and maybe is still producing through AI. Are all of my half sisters also having miscarriages? . . . I want to contact my father anonymously if need be and ask him, please, he's got weak sperm. I've got bad feet, bad nearsighted eyes—

Phil Donahue: And you want to know—

[Guest No. 1]: —what did he get out of this picture?

Audience: (Laughter).

Phil Donahue: —you want to know if there's any genetic information that might explain the difficulties you've sustained, huh?

[Guest No. 1]: With my miscarriages, yeah.

. . .

Phil Donahue: Do you understand [the first guest's] anger?

[Guest No. 2]: Absolutely.

Phil Donahue: You feel it, too?

[Guest No. 2]: Absolutely.

Phil Donahue: What is it that you're angry about?

[Guest No. 2]: It has to do with betrayal. It has to do with—

Phil Donahue: Well, who's betrayed?

[Guest No. 2]: —my parents in keeping this a secret, for a start. It has to do with the medical establishment in thinking that a person's genetic background is so unimportant that it can simply be ignored. It has to do with a falsified birth certificate which is routine in artificial insemination. This donor is not named on the birth certificate; the wife's husband is simply named.

Phil Donahue: Yeah. So this is a—

[Guest No. 2]: It's a conspiracy.

Phil Donahue: —a conspiracy by a lot of educated professional people—

[Guest No. 2]: Yes.

* Donahue, Transcript No. 08033.

Phil Donahue: —with the cooperation and the contribution of your own mother and stepfather, I guess—

[Guest No. 2]: Absolutely.

Phil Donahue: —to deny you information which—

[Guest No. 2]: The truth.

Phil Donahue: —you think is essential.

[Guest No. 2]: Absolutely.

. . .

Is the women's anger at their parents justified? Their anger at the medical people involved? In neither case was a lawyer involved; should there have been? What might a lawyer have done to anticipate the concerns expressed by these women? When a lawyer participates in AID arrangements does the lawyer owe primary allegiance to the mother (and her spouse, if she is married), to the donor or to the child conceived? What potential conflicts might develop for the lawyer?

The President's Commission made the following recommendations:

The Commission concludes that a genetic history should be obtained on all potential sperm donors and, where appropriate, the results of genetic screening should be available to prospective recipients.

. . .

The Commission believes that safeguards could be put in place to minimize the risk that recordkeeping would violate confidentiality interests. Law reform groups, as part of a much-needed reformulation of law in this field, should include provisions that will allow the source of donor samples to be identified and the results of genetic tests to be recorded in a way that protects the confidentiality of the donor to the greatest extent possible.

Screening and Counseling for Genetic Conditions 70 (1983). Do you agree? How would you implement their proposal?

For an excellent discussion of comparable problems raised by confidentiality in adoption, see Black, Genetics and Adoption: A Challenge for Social Work in Social Work in a Turbulent World (M. Dinerman ed. 1983).

2. Would it be more accurate to refer to the sperm contributor as the "sperm vendor" as opposed to "sperm donor"? Should payments to sperm contributors be prohibited? Should our policy on compensation be the same for sperm contributors and surrogates? See Annas, Fathers Anonymous: Beyond the Best Interests of the Sperm Donor in Genetics and the Law II (Milunsky and Annas, eds. 1980).

3. When a physician chooses to perform artificial insemination by donor using frozen semen, another participant becomes involved in the procedure—the sperm bank. The sperm bank in such circumstances has principal responsibility for screening semen donors, collecting and preserving the donated semen and distributing semen to the physicians needing it. Frozen semen is an important alternative to the use of fresh semen because requiring the donor's proximity would often prove too restrictive for repeated attempts at fertilization and because it relieves the physician of the responsibility for finding and screening potential donors. Researchers endorse use of frozen semen because they believe that it offers a greater potential for compatibility between the donor and the parents' expectations than does a physician's limited ability to find fresh semen donors. They also believe that sperm banks are more capable of screening potential donors than are individual physicians. See National Academy of Sciences, The Integrity of Frozen Spermatozoa: Proceeding of a Roundtable Conference (1978).

The establishment of sperm banks offers, however, a greater potential for carrying out eugenic objectives than does use of sperm which individual physicians provide. A recent development suggesting such consequences is the attempt by Robert Graham, a California industrialist, to organize a sperm bank, known as the Repository for Germinal Choice, with deposits from Nobel Prize laureates and other highly intelligent people. Four prize winners, including Dr. William Shockley, the scientist controversial for his views of inheritance and intelligence, made "repeated" donations. Shockley specifically endorsed the project's goal of "increasing the people at the top of the population." See Nobel Winner Says He Gave Sperm For Women to Bear Gifted Babies, New York Times, Mar. 1, 1981 at A6, col. 2. Commentators were quick to attack the sperm bank's purpose, pointing out that environment, as well as heredity, controls human intellectual development and relating the sperm bank to the views of Shockley and his supporters that overreproduction by persons "genetically disadvantaged" has weakened American society. See id.; How to Win a Nobel: Step 1, New York Times, Mar. 20, 1980, at A26, col. 4; Jacob, Fish Got to Swim, Man Got to Fly, New York Times, Mar. 25, 1980, at A19, col. 1; O'Toole, Hers, New York Times, June 4, 1981, at C2, col. 1. In the latter piece, the author recounts George Bernard Shaw's refusal of dancer Isadora Duncan's request that he father her child, fearing that the child would have his looks and her intelligence; she concludes that proposals such as the Graham/Shockley sperm bank overlook such genetic possibilities.

In addition to concerns about the eugenic objectives of the establishment of the Repository for Germinal Choice, should society also be concerned about the clients of such establishments? The parents of the first child conceived through the Repository for Germinal Choice had lost custody of the wife's children from an earlier marriage because they overworked the children with schoolwork and beat them when they made mistakes. See Parents of 'Nobel Sperm' Baby Lost Custody of Earlier Children, Washington Post, July 14, 1982, at A6, col. 1.

What interest might a state assert in attempting to regulate sperm banks such as the Repository for Germinal Choice? Sperm banks in general?

4. Cryopreserved semen has other uses than in AID situations. Researchers believe that by storing and later concentrating several of a husband's ejaculates, they will be able to assist a couple to conceive a child when a husband suffers from a low sperm count. These researchers also anticipate being able to store a husband's semen so that they can later inseminate his wife with it should he be away or unavailable when she is at the stage in her menstrual cycle when she could conceive. Finally, husbands who for whatever reasons undergo sterilization procedures can deposit semen for cryopreservation while they are still fertile; should these men later desire to have a child, physicians can use the frozen semen in artificial insemination. Do the legal complications surrounding artificial insemination with frozen sperm abate when the semen donor is the woman's husband? What complications, if any, remain? For a general discussion, see Wadlington, Artificial Conception: The Challenge of Family Law, 69 U.Va.L.Rev. 465 (1983).

5. How might the use of frozen semen deposits affect property laws and the canons of descent? See Leach, Perpetuities in the Atomic Age: The Sperm Bank and the Fertile Decedent, 48 A.B.A.J. 942 (1962) (analyzing effect of sperm cryopreservation on Rule Against Perpetuities).

UNIFORM PARENTAGE ACT
9A U.L.A. 587, 592–593 (1979).

§ 7005.   Artificial insemination of wife;   husband as natural father; donor not natural father

(a) If, under the supervision of a licensed physician and with the consent of her husband, a wife is inseminated artificially with semen donated by a man not her husband, the husband is treated in law as if he were the natural father of a child thereby conceived. The husband's consent must be in writing and signed by him and his wife. The physician shall certify their signatures and the date of the insemination, and file the husband's consent with the [State Department of Health], where it shall be kept confidential and in a sealed file. However, the physician's failure to do so does not affect the father and child relationship. All papers and records pertaining to the insemination, whether part of the permanent record of a court or of a file held by the supervising physician or elsewhere, are subject to inspection only upon an order of the court for good cause shown.

(b) The donor of semen provided to a licensed physician for use in artificial insemination of a woman other than the donor's wife is treated in law as if he were not the natural father of a child thereby conceived.

NOTES

1. What provisions, if any, would you add to § 7005 of the Uniform Parentage Act? Would a single statute covering all the new reproductive techniques be a better approach? Does the Uniform Parentage Act, for example, have an adverse impact on surrogate arrangements? See Doe v. Kelley and Syrkowski v. Appleyard, infra. Cf. Washington State statute that would appear to permit surrogate arrangements. Wash. Rev. Code Ann. § 26.26.052(2) (Supp. 1982).

2. The following states have statutes that cover some facet of AID: Alaska Stats. 25.20.045 (Supp. 1982); West's Ann.Cal.Civ.Code § 7005 (1982); Colo.Rev.Stat., 78, 19–6–106; Conn.Gen.Stat.Ann. § 45–69f–n (West 1981); Fla. Stat.Ann. § 742.11 (West 1976); Ga.Code § 19–7–21 (1982); Kan.Stat.Ann.1981 §§ 23–128 to –130; La.Stat.Ann.Civ.Code Ann. art. 188 (West Supp. 1983); Md. Est. & Trusts Code Ann. § 1–206(b) (1974); Mass.Gen.Laws Ann. c. 46, § 4B (West Supp. 1982–1983); Mich.Comp.Laws 1980 § 700.111(2); Minn.Stat. § 257.56 (1982); Rev.Code Mont. 1981, § 40–6–106; Nev.Rev.Stat. 126.061 (1981); McKinney's N.Y. Dom.Rel.Law § 73 (1977); N.C.Gen.Stat. § 49A–1 (1976); 10 Okl.Stat.1981, §§ 551–553; Or.Rev.Stat. 109.239 to .247, 677.355 to .370 (Supp. 1981); Tenn. Code Ann. § 53–446 (Supp. 1981); Vernon's Tex. Codes Ann. Fam. § 12.03 (1975); Va.Code Ann. 1980 § 64.1–7.1; Rev.Code Wash.Ann. 26.26.050 (Supp. 1982); Wis.Stat.Ann. 891.40 (West Supp. 1982–1983); Wyo.Stat.1979 § 14–2–103.

b. Surrogates

DOE v. KELLEY

Court of Appeals of Michigan, 1981.
106 Mich.App. 169, 307 N.W.2d 438, certiorari denied ___ U.S. ___, 103 S.Ct. 834,
74 L.Ed.2d 1027, 1983.

KELLY, JUDGE.

In this case, we are asked to declare unconstitutional those sections of the Michigan Adoption Code, M.C.L. § 710.54; M.S.A. § 27.3178 (555.54) and M.C.L. § 710.69; M.S.A. § 27.3178 (555.69), which prohibit the exchange of money or other consideration in connection with adoption and related proceedings.[1] The plaintiffs appeal of right from a Janu-

1. The statutory provisions sought to be declared invalid provide:

"Sec. 54. (1) Except for charges and fees approved by the court, a person shall not offer, give, or receive any money or other consideration or thing of value in connection with any of the following:

"(a) The placing of a child for adoption.

"(b) The registration, recording, or communication of the existence of a child available for adoption or the existence of a person interested in adopting a child.

"(c) A release.

"(d) A consent.

"(e) A petition.

"(2) Before the entry of the final order of adoption, the petitioner shall file with the court a sworn statement describing money or other consideration or thing of value paid to or exchanged by any party in the adoption proceeding, including anyone consenting to the adoption or adopting the adoptee, any relative of a party or of the adoptee, any physician, attorney, social worker or member of the clergy, and any other person, corporation, association, or other organization. The court

ary 29, 1980, order of the lower court, denying their motion for summary judgment . . . and granting the defendants' own motion . . . . The parties are in agreement as to the pertinent facts in this decision.

Jane Doe and John Doe are pseudonyms for a married couple residing in Wayne County. . . .

It is alleged that Jane Doe has undergone a tubal ligation, rendering her biologically incapable of bearing children and that the Does "wish to have a child biologically related to JOHN DOE". Mary Roe is employed as a secretary by John Doe and also resides in Wayne County. The complaint alleges that these parties contemplate and intend to enter into the following agreement:

"(a) That JANE DOE and JOHN DOE will pay MARY ROE a sum of money in consideration for her promise to bear and deliver JOHN DOE's child by means of artificial insemination.

"(b) That a licensed physician will conduct the artificial insemination process.

"(c) That prior to the delivery of said child, JOHN DOE will file a notice of intent to claim paternity.

"(d) That at the time the child is born, JOHN DOE will formally acknowledge the paternity of said child.

"(e) That MARY ROE will acknowledge that JOHN DOE is the father of said child.

"(f) That MARY ROE will consent to the adoption of said child by JOHN DOE and JANE DOE".

The agreement also provided that plaintiffs would pay to Mary Roe the sum of $5,000 plus medical expenses. In addition, Mary Roe would be covered by sick leave, pregnancy disability insurance, and medical insurance from her employment while she is off work having the child and recuperating from the delivery.

The plaintiffs allege that the disputed statutory provisions impermissibly infringe upon their constitutional right to privacy. This right, first recognized in Griswold v. Connecticut, 381 U.S. 479, (1965) was more recently described in Carey v. Population Services International, 431 U.S. 678 (1977). In *Carey*, the Court specifically held that the decision "whether or not to bear or beget a child" was among those protected by the constitutional right of privacy.

While the decision to bear or beget a child has thus been found to be a fundamental interest protected by the right of privacy, see Maher v. Roe, 432 U.S. 464 (1977), we do not view this right as a valid prohibition

shall approve or disapprove fees and expenses. Acceptance or retention of amounts in excess of those approved by the court constitutes a violation of this section.

"(3) To assure compliance with limitations imposed by this section, by section 14 of Act No. 116 of the Public Acts of 1973, being section 722.124 of the Michigan Compiled Laws, and by section 4 of Act No. 263 of the Public Acts of 1913, as amended, being section 331.404 of the Michigan Compiled Laws, the court may require sworn testimony from persons

who were involved in any way in informing, notifying, exchanging information, identifying, locating, assisting, or in any other way participating in the contracts or arrangements which, directly or indirectly, led to placement of the person for adoption."

"Sec. 69. A person who violates any of the provisions of sections 41 and 54 of this chapter shall, upon conviction, be guilty of a misdemeanor, and upon any subsequent conviction shall be guilty of a felony."

to state interference in the plaintiff's contractual arrangement. The statute in question does not directly prohibit John Doe and Mary Roe from having the child as planned. It acts instead to preclude plaintiffs from paying consideration in conjunction with their use of the state's adoption procedures. In effect, the plaintiffs' contractual agreement discloses a desire to use the adoption code to change the legal status of the child—i.e., its right to support, intestate succession, etc. We do not perceive this goal as within the realm of fundamental interests protected by the right to privacy from reasonable governmental regulation.

The plaintiffs also allege that the state has no compelling interest sufficient to justify the prohibitions embodied in the disputed statutes and, in addition, that the provisions are drawn too wide to reflect any legitimate state interests in this area. Our disposition of the foregoing issue, however, renders consideration of this issue unnecessary.

Affirmed.

SYRKOWSKI v. APPLEYARD

Court of Appeals of Michigan, 1983.
122 Mich.App. 506, 333 N.W.2d 90.

CYNAR, P.J.

. . .

On June 8, 1981, George Syrkowski filed a complaint pursuant to § 4(f) of The Paternity Act, MCL 722.714(f); MSA 25.494(f). Syrkowski alleged that he had reason to believe that defendant Corinne Appleyard was pregnant with a child conceived by him on or about March 23, 24, or 25, 1981, in the City of Dearborn Heights, Michigan. It was alleged that the complaint was filed during Mrs. Appleyard's pregnancy. Mr. Syrkowski requested an order of filiation pursuant to § 7(a) of The Paternity Act, MCL 722.717(a); MSA 25.497(a), and entry of his name as the natural father on the child's birth certificate.

On June 23, 1981, Mrs. Appleyard answered admitting all the allegations. She also requested an order of filiation and entry of Mr. Syrkowski's name as the natural and legal father on the child's birth certificate.

Pursuant to § 33 of the Michigan Adoption Code, MCL 710.33; MSA 27.3178 (555.33), Mr. Syrkowski filed a notice of intent to claim paternity on July 9, 1981. That same month, the parties filed a proposed consent order of filiation and scheduled a hearing on July 24, 1981, for the entry of that order. The proposed consent order of filiation stated the interests of the child and all parties would be best served by a determination by the circuit judge that: (1) Mr. Syrkowski is the natural and legal father of the child to be born to Mrs. Appleyard in December, 1981, (2) Mr. Syrkowski be awarded full custody and responsibility for the child, (3) Mr. Syrkowski's name be entered as the father on the child's birth certificate, and (4) the child bear the surname Syrkowski.

In support of the motion for entry of the consent order of filiation, Mr. Syrkowski submitted the affidavit of Mrs. Appleyard and her husband, Roger Appleyard, and the affidavit of Dr. Warren J. Ringold, M.D. Dr. Ringold in his affidavit stated:

"That on March 23, 24, and 25, 1981 in his professional offices, he inseminated Corinne Appleyard with the semen of George Syrkowski, and subsequent thereto she became and is pregnant; and that in his professional medical opinion, George Syrkowski is the father of the child or children to be born to Corinne Appleyard as a result of the pregnancy . . . ."

The Appleyards in their affidavit stated:

"That Roger Appleyard and Corinne Appleyard voluntarily abstained from having sexual intercourse for a period of six weeks prior to March 23, 1981.

"That Corinne Appleyard was artificially inseminated with the semen of George Syrkowski by Warren J. Ringold, M.D., on March 23, 24, and 25, 1981.

"That Roger Appleyard and Corinne Appleyard voluntarily abstained from sexual intercourse on the above insemination dates and for a period of four weeks subsequent to March 25, 1981.

"That Corinne Appleyard affirmatively states she did not have sexual intercourse with any person during the above-mentioned ten week period."

. . .

On November 9, 1981, the Michigan Attorney General filed a notice of intervention, a motion for accelerated judgment . . . a brief in support of that motion, and a notice of hearing for November 13, 1981.

In his motion, the Attorney General alleged that the circuit court did not have jurisdiction over Mr. Syrkowski's action pursuant to The Paternity Act as the action involved a "surrogate mother" arrangement. The Attorney General alleged that Mr. Appleyard was the legal father of the child because he was married to Mrs. Appleyard when she conceived the child and he consented to the artificial insemination. The Attorney General argued that . . . Mr. Appleyard must be deemed the father of his wife's child.

Mr. Syrkowski replied to the motion and filed a brief in opposition to accelerated judgment on November 13, 1981. In support of this reply, Mr. Syrkowski submitted Mr. Appleyard's April 22, 1981, statement of nonconsent. In that statement, Mr. Appleyard said:

"I, Roger A. Appleyard, husband of Corinne A. Appleyard, who is to become a surrogate mother for an unknown man, acknowledge the existence of Public Act 356 of 1978, Section 2824(6) which provides, 'A child born to a married woman as a result of artificial insemination, with consent of her husband, is considered to be the legitimate child of the husband and wife.' I expressly revoke and withhold my consent for any artificial insemination of my wife in connection with the surrogate arrangements and recognize that by doing so I cannot be declared or considered to be the legal father of said child."

. . .

In his November 25, 1981, opinion granting the Attorney General's motion for accelerated judgment, the trial judge found that neither the law nor the facts in this case support the Attorney General's argument that a child conceived and born of Mrs. Appleyard during the marriage is conclusively presumed to be the legitimate child of her husband. However, the trial court also observed The Paternity Act was enacted to impose financial responsibility for illegitimate children upon those who fathered them and to protect the children from becoming a public charge.

It was the opinion of the trial court that the relief requested in Mr. Syrkowski's petition was beyond the scope and purpose of The Paternity Act. Accordingly, the motion for accelerated judgment was granted.

Mrs. Appleyard gave birth to Theresa Mary Syrkowski on November 22, 1981, in Sinai Hospital of Detroit.[2]

This action was not commenced as an adversary proceeding but was submitted to the trial court for approval of a consent order of filiation which Mr. Syrkowski, Mrs. Appleyard, and their respective counsel had approved as to form and content. The record does not contain a copy of the agreement entered into between Mr. Syrkowski and Mrs. Appleyard. Although the facts submitted for our consideration are limited, we infer that Mr. Syrkowski's inducement for entering into this agreement with Mrs. Appleyard was based on the inability of Mr. Syrkowski and his wife to have children. We recognize the forces which motivate human beings seeking to have children. To assume Mr. Syrkowski's intentions are a pure and a noble attempt to fulfill the wish to have a child in his family is not sufficient for reaching a result in this appeal. In addition to determining the applicability of the legislation relied upon, we must consider the impact of this decision.

We agree with the trial court's decision to permit intervention by the Attorney General. The issues raised by Mr. Syrkowski and Mrs. Appleyard involve significant matters of state interest and public policy. It is noted that the child in this case has been without legal representation. Interest in the welfare of the child must continue to be of paramount importance to the people of this state.

. . .

The Paternity Act was enacted to provide for support of illegitimate children. . . . The purpose and intent of The Paternity Act is to provide support for a child "born out of wedlock". No amendment to the act has altered the general purpose and intent of the act to the extent that it encompasses the circumstances in this case.

A question is raised whether "surrogate parent arrangements" are contrary to public policy. Public policy may be constitutionally, legislatively, or judicially declared. Public policy may also abide in the customs and conventions of the people. . . .

In *Doe v. Attorney General* [Doe v. Kelley, supra] a case involving a surrogate mother arrangement, this Court held that the trial court had properly granted summary judgment where the plaintiffs contemplated entering into an agreement whereby they would pay a third party $5,000 plus medical expenses to have a child by Mr. Doe. . . .

. . .

While we do not decide whether surrogate mother contracts are against public policy, we conclude The Paternity Act's purpose of providing support for children born out of wedlock does not encompass the monetary transaction proposed in this case.

2. There is reason to believe that Mr. Syrkowski now has provisional custody of Theresa pursuant to § 405 of the Probate Code, MCL 700.405; MSA 27.5405. That statute says:

"A parent or a guardian of a minor or legally incapacitated person, by a properly executed power of attorney, may delegate to another person for a period not exceeding 6 months, any of the parent's or guardian's powers regarding care, custody, or property of the minor child or ward, except the power to consent to marriage or adoption of a minor ward and the power to release a minor ward for adoption."

We view the surrogate mother arrangements with caution as we approach an unexplored area in the law which, without a doubt, can have a profound effect on the lives of our people. The courts should not be called upon to enlarge the scope of The Paternity Act to encompass circumstances never contemplated thereby. Studied legislation is needed before surrogate arrangements are recognized as proposed under the facts submitted herein.

Affirmed.

N.J. KAUFMAN, J., concurred.

NOTES

1. A central issue in surrogate parenting arrangements is the legality of the contract that exists among the surrogate mother, her husband (if she is married) and the biological father. The Attorney General of Kentucky has given an official opinion that surrogate parenting contracts are illegal and contrary to public policy. 18 Op.Att'y Gen. 2 (1981). The Attorney General of Kentucky later challenged the right to do business of the Surrogate Parenting Associates, Inc., of Louisville, a corporation created to set up surrogate parenting arrangements, on the basis of three Kentucky statutes regulating adoption and termination of parental rights. The court held that none of the statutes afforded a basis for granting the relief sought because the Kentucky statute governing termination of parental rights had not been violated and because the legal relationship between the father and child prevented the father's activities from being described "as either adopting or buying his own baby." The court also declined to characterize surrogate arrangements as unlawful in the absence of legislation. Kentucky ex rel. Beshear v. Surrogate Parenting Associates, Inc., No. 81–CI–429 (Franklin Cir. Ct. Oct. 26, 1983).

2. In another case, In re Baby Girl, No. 83AD (Jefferson Cir. Ct. Mar. 8, 1983) the Jefferson Circuit Court in Kentucky denied a termination of parental rights motion that a mother and her husband had made as part of a surrogate parenting arrangement. Included in the motion were petitions for the court to declare the alleged biological father the child's natural father, to award the alleged biological father custody of the child as his natural child and to compel state authorities to enter the alleged biological father's name on the child's birth certificate. Id., slip op. at 1–2.

The court held that because the state law allowing a natural parent to terminate parental rights had been enacted specifically to facilitate adoptions through licensed child-placement agencies and because state law recognized a woman's husband as her children's father when the two were married and had capacity to conceive, it had no power to grant the relief which the plaintiffs had requested. The court declared that the Kentucky termination statute could not reach the plaintiffs' situations.

3. The American College of Obstetricians and Gynecologists (the College) issued guidelines covering surrogate parenting arrangements in May 1983, advising its members not to participate in them if there was a possibility that any participant could suffer economic exploitation. The guidelines suggest that any physician who has misgivings about the procedure decline to participate; they specifically recognize that such behavior is "justified" given the uncertainties surrounding surrogate parenting. Furthermore, they recommend that a participating physician accept no finder's or referral fee for setting up a surrogate parenting arrangement and screen all potential participants carefully. Finally, the guidelines require that physicians give surrogate mothers the same medical care that they would give a woman who conceived her child under normal circumstances or refer these women to physicians who will provide such care.

In the report accompanying the guidelines, the College compared surrogate parenting to artificial insemination by donor (AID), which it recognized in many ways is surrogate parenting's "logical counterpart." The College pointed out six common legal and ethical issues: depersonalization of reproduction; creation of stress in the infertile couple; creation of psychological risk for both sperm donor and surrogate mother; potentiality for genetic manipulation; creation of psychological risk for the children involved; and maintenance of donor and surrogate anonymity. Also, the College highlighted what it felt were significant distinctions between the two procedures. These include the increased risk, both physical and psychological, that the surrogate faces; the possibility of the surrogate regaining custody of the child; and the availability of abortion or retention of the child should the surrogate change her mind.

One difference that the College emphasized, and one with which some do not agree, is the financial aspect of the surrogate parenting arrangement. This aspect takes two forms, in the College's view: payment to the surrogate and payment of a finder's fee to the physician or a physician's investment in an enterprise to promote surrogate parenting arrangements. Payment to surrogates is objectionable to the College because it found no clear way to distinguish paying the surrogate for her services as opposed to paying for her baby. The College saw the physician's financial involvement as creating conflict of interest problems.

Another distinguishing feature the College reported was the confusion surrounding who makes decisions that might affect the fetus. The College said that the surrogate mother should be the source of consent with respect to any decisions involving the management of the pregnancy. Involvement of prospective parents in management decisions can only be done with the agreement of the surrogate mother. What arguments could be made for allowing the prospective parents to involve themselves in this decisionmaking?

Are the distinctions that the College drew between surrogate parenting and AID persuasive? Does the fact that sperm donors are often compensated for their services/donations make any difference? Is the critical aspect in this analysis what actually is "donated," with sperm having less legal and ethical significance than ova? Is the fact that the College has no official position or has issued no guidelines regarding AID relevant?

The British Medical Association, by contrast, has told physicians that it would be unethical for them to become involved in surrogate arrangements. 308 Nature 220 (1984).

4. Complications in one recent surrogate parenting situation served to highlight some of the many legal and ethical uncertainties involved in these arrangements. Judy Stiver, a Michigan woman, entered into a surrogate parenting contract with Alexander Malahoff, a New York accountant, to have Malahoff's child through artificial insemination. Noel Keane, a Michigan attorney actively involved in arranging surrogate parenting agreements, drafted the contract that the parties signed.

When the child, a boy, was born on January 10, 1983, he suffered from both microcephaly and strep infection. Microcephaly is a congenital disorder that caused the boy's head to be smaller than normal. Usually the disease indicates some degree of mental retardation. Hospital officials were forced to obtain a court order allowing them to treat the strep infection, which the baby's physicians feared threatened his life. The officials claimed that Malahoff ordered the hospital and doctors not to treat the infection or care for the baby, a claim Malahoff later denied. Malahoff based his orders, the hospital officials claimed, on a clause in the surrogate parenting contract giving him custody of the child. See Washington Post, Jan. 21, 1983, at A11, col. 3; New York Times, Jan. 23, 1983, § 1 at 19, col. 1.

Sometime later, Malahoff denied paternity of and responsibility for the child. Stiver and her husband Ray disputed these claims. In a unique spectacle, the results of blood tests to determine paternity were announced on an episode of the Phil Donahue television show entitled "The Case of the Layaway Baby." The tests proved that Malahoff could not be the father and that Ray Stiver was the probable father. Later in the episode, Stiver admitted having fathered a child whose head stopped developing in infancy during a previous marriage. That child died a few years after birth. See, Washington Post, Feb. 3, 1983, at A8, col. 1; New York Times, Feb. 7, 1983, at A10, col. 1.

5. Several state legislatures have considered attempts to regulate surrogate parenting through comprehensive legislation. The Alaska legislature has been considering surrogate parenting proposals since 1980, the Michigan legislature since 1981 and the California legislature since 1982. Nat'l L.J., July 12, 1982, at 5. col. 1.

If you were asked to draft legislation regulating surrogate arrangements, what provisions would you include?

c.   In Vitro Fertilization

DEL ZIO v. THE PRESBYTERIAN HOSPITAL

United States District Court for the Southern District of New York, Nov. 14, 1978.
74 Civ. 3588 (memorandum decision).

STEWART, DISTRICT JUDGE:

Plaintiffs, husband and wife, allege in their complaint that the defendants wrongfully caused plaintiff Mrs. Del Zio severe emotional distress and tortiously damaged or converted personal property of plaintiffs. Plaintiff Dr. Del Zio claims damages for loss of services and severe emotional distress. Defendants, who generally deny the allegations, are Presbyterian Hospital ("Presbyterian"), Dr. Raymond L. Vande Wiele ("Vande Wiele") and Trustees of Columbia University ("Columbia"). . . . Defendants have moved pursuant to Rule 50 (b) of the Federal Rules of Civil Procedure to set aside the verdict for plaintiffs or for a new trial.

Most of the facts are undisputed. Mrs. Del Zio had a child by a prior husband in 1963 and Dr. Del Zio had two children by a prior marriage. The Del Zios, after their marriage in 1968, unsuccessfully tried to have children. In 1970, Mrs. Del Zio learned that her fallopian tubes were blocked and Dr. William Sweeney of New York Hospital, her physician, performed an operation to remove the blockage. It appeared to be successful, Mrs. Del Zio became pregnant in October, 1970, but suffered a miscarriage in December, 1970. Two further operations on her fallopian tubes were performed by Dr. Sweeney in 1971 and in 1972, each of which were unsuccessful.

In 1972, Dr. Sweeney advised Mrs. Del Zio of a procedure known as in vitro fertilization, which would in effect by-pass her fallopian tubes. The procedure would involve preparing a culture which would include ova removed from Mrs. Del Zio and semen obtained from Dr. Del Zio and placing the culture in a test tube which would then be placed in an incubator to accomplish fertilization. Thereafter, the fertilized ova would be reimplanted into Mrs. Del Zio's uterus and, if all went well, she would become pregnant. Although the procedure had been successfully accomplished in animals, there was not known to be any prior successful attempt in man and Dr. Sweeney so advised the Del Zios. He also advised the Del Zios that Dr. Landrum Shettles of defendant Presbyterian Hospital who was experienced in the field of in vitro fertilization would participate in the procedure. Dr. Shettles was an attending obstetrician-gynecologist at Presbyterian and associate professor of clinical obstetrics and gynecology at College of Physicians and Surgeons of defendant Columbia; Dr. Vande Wiele was his immediate supervisor in both capacities. The Del Zios decided to undergo the procedure and gave Dr. Sweeney their consent.

On September 12, 1973, after a substantial period of preparation, the procedure was undertaken. Dr. Sweeney removed the ova at New York Hospital, the ova was taken to Presbyterian Hospital where Dr. Shettles obtained semen from Dr. Del Zio, prepared the culture and placed it in an incubator (owned by defendant Columbia) at Presbyterian where it was to remain for four days.

The following day, September 13, 1973, defendant Vande Wiele learned of the test tube and its contents, ordered it removed from the incubator and brought to his office, and then had it placed in a deep freeze. These actions effectively terminated the procedure and destroyed the culture. At the time, Dr. Vande Wiele was Chairman of the Department of Obstetrics and Gynecology at Columbia and Chief of the Obstetrical and Gynecological Service at Presbyterian. At the time Dr. Vande Wiele gave instructions to remove the test tube and before it was brought to his office, he called Dr. Tapley, then Acting Dean of the College of Physicians and Surgeons, the medical school of defendant Columbia, and Mr. Alvin Binkert President and chief executive of Presbyterian. He advised each of them of what he was doing and each concurred that the procedure or experiment should be stopped. All of these events occurred between about eight and nine o'clock in the morning of September 13. Thereafter, Dr. Vande Wiele called Dr. Shettles and told him to come to his office at two o'clock in the afternoon. At that time, when Dr. Shettles arrived in his office, Dr. Vande Wiele informed Dr. Shettles of the actions he had taken and the latter thereafter notified Dr. Sweeney.

Dr. Sweeney testified that, because of the numerous operations on Mrs. Del Zio's abdomen, he would not after the September 1973 operaton perform any further such operations unless it were a matter of life or death and that he believed the 1973 operation was her last chance to become pregnant. After that operation, there was evidence that Mrs. Del Zio suffered and continues to suffer substantial mental distress and that she was treated by a psychiatrist on a number of occasions over an extensive period of time. There was also evidence that Dr. Del Zio had suffered emotional distress.

Our charge contained the following instructions:

As I mentioned, the first theory under which the plaintiffs claim is intentional infliction of emotional distress. One who intentionally or recklessly conducts himself toward another person in a manner so shocking and outrageous that it exceeds all bounds of decency, such person is liable to such other person for any resulting severe mental distress and consequential expenses.

.   .   .

The charge further stated, substantially as requested, the contentions of the parties as to this claim in considerable detail . . .

.   .   .   [T]he plaintiffs contend that the conduct of Dr. Vande Wiele in terminating the procedure without considering alternatives and without first informing Dr. Shettles, Dr. Sweeney or the plaintiffs constitutes extreme and outrageous conduct.

The plaintiffs further contend that absent an emergency and they contend that no emergency existed here, a medical procedure being performed in a hospital upon a patient by her physician at her express request and with her fully informed consent may not be terminated by a doctor at another institution unless that doctor first informs her physician of his intention and permits the patient's physician to exercise such alternatives that may be available to him to avoid termination of the procedure.

Plaintiffs further contend that it is no defense that the termination of the procedure may have appeared to be justified to the intervening doctor. Plaintiffs further contend that Dr. Vande Wiele had a duty to inform Dr. Shettles or Dr. Sweeney of his intention to terminate the procedure. And to permit either of them to remove the culture from Columbia University to another place in order to avoid the termination.

The defendants . . . contend that Dr. Vande Wiele's actions were reasonable and justified in light of his responsibilities as Chairman of the Department of Obstetrics and Gynecology at Columbia University and as Chief of Services of Obstetrics and Gynecology at Presbyterian Hospital. His obligation to insure that the proper standards of medical care prevailed in both the hospital and the university and his obligations as a physician [sic].

Further, the defendants contend that the in vitro experiment presented a subtantial possibility of danger to the patient.

The defendants further contend the experiment represented an unwarranted practice which posed danger to any human life resulting from such experimentation and that the state of the art of in vitro fertilization in September, 1973 offered no assurance against possible malformation and damage to any life resulting from such procedure.

The defendants further contend that Dr. Vande Wiele knew that the procedure had not been cleared by any committees and review boards whose purpose at the hospital and the university was to adequately review proposed human experimentation. As such, the defendants contend that the Del Zio experiment was in violation of the rules of the Department of Obstetrics and Gynecology protecting subjects of human experimentation and insuring that such experiments are conducted in conformity with the highest standards of medical practice and in addition, was in violation of the assurance filed by the College of Physicians and Surgeons with the Department of Health, Education and Welfare promising that the University would comply with its guidelines concerning experimentation on human beings.

The defendants further contend that the experiment was carried out by individuals who had no competence to carry out such procedure and whose scientific methods were not sufficient in that there was no adequate protocol or notes which could insure proper review. And the defendants also contend that Dr. Vande Wiele's supervisor at the hospital and the university specifically ordered that the experiments be stopped.

In assessing the reasonableness of the medical judgment exercised by Dr. Vande Wiele, you may consider his duties and responsibilities as a physician and as Chairman of the Department of Obstetrics and Gynecology of Columbia and as Chief of the Obstetrical and Gynecological Service of Presbyterian and his medical judgment as to the procedures as reflected in the contentions I have just outlined, and the state of accepted medical knowledge and published medical literature, but only, as I have told you, that [which] in fact was available on or before September 13, 1973. You may not consider the articles published after September 1973 in considering whether Dr. Vande Wiele acted reasonably in 1973.

As you may recall, there were certain articles admitted on post-1973 medical knowledge. I am sure you will remember what I told you, that these were admitted solely on the issue of whether the procedure followed by Dr. Shettles and Dr. Sweeney in 1973, in September, were scientifically sound, and cannot be considered by you in assessing the reasonableness of the medical judgment exercised at that time by Dr. Vande Wiele.

With respect to the conversion theory, the jury was instructed:

Now the second claim, conversion of property, broadly stated, one who, without authority, intentionally exercises control over the property of another and thereby interferes with the other's right of possession, is guilty of conversion and liable for the value of the property.

. . .

At the outset of their deliberations, the jury requested and were given copies of the charge.

After deliberating approximately 13 hours, the jury found for the plaintiffs on the first claim and awarded Mrs. Del Zio "the amount of $50,000 to be awarded in the amount of $12,500 from Presbyterian Hospital, $12,500 from Columbia University and $25,000 from Dr. Raymond L. Vande Wiele". As to Dr. Del Zio on this claim, the jury awarded him $3.00, one dollar for each defendant. The jury found for the defendants on the conversion claim.

Defendants have moved pursuant to Rule 50(b) of the Federal Rules of Civil Procedure, for judgment notwithstanding the verdict or for a new trial. The following arguments are made in support of these motions:

1. No reasonable juror could find that the defendants' conduct was "so extreme, outrageous and shocking that it exceeded all reasonable bounds of decency".

2. The verdict in favor of defendants on the cause of action for conversion is inconsistent with the verdict in favor of plaintiffs on the cause of action for intentional infliction of emotional distress.

. . .

In addition, defendant Presbyterian contends that the verdict should be set aside because the defendants were prejudiced by adverse publicity, and because of the doctrine of *respondeat superior*. In opposition, plaintiffs ask that the motions be denied.

As to defendants' first contention, there was sufficient credible evidence from which the jury could reasonably find that plaintiffs had met their burden of establishing each of the three elements of the intentional tort cause of action. Even if the jury concluded that Dr. Vande Wiele was justified in directing that the experiment not be continued in his hospital, his decision to destroy the contents of the test tube without giving Mrs. Del Zio's physician any prior notice, or an opportunity to remove the test tube to some other location, or to consider other alternatives, could reasonably support under all the circumstances a finding by the jury of the kind of deliberate, shocking and reckless conduct required under New York law. The jury might well have also taken into account the evidence tending to indicate that Dr. Vande Wiele and Dr. Shettles (both of whom testified at length) had sharply conflicting personalities and the evidence that on several occasions Dr. Vande Wiele chose to admonish Dr. Shettles about his professional conduct, admonitions which Dr. Shettles believed to be unjustified. From these circumstances the jury could have found that Dr. Vande Wiele had some antipathy, at least, towards his subordinate, Dr. Shettles.

Although the defendants were not aware of the precise identity of the plaintiffs, they knew that a particular man and woman were involved in the procedure. It is undisputed that the defendants intended to stop the procedure and that this was done deliberately and without notice; thus, the jury could reasonably have concluded that the defendants acted "with utter disregard" of the substantial certainty that severe emotional distress would follow from the decision to destroy the contents of the test tube and that the defendants' actions were the proximate cause of the emotional distress which plaintiffs suffered.

The principal objection raised by defendants to the charge on the claim of intentional tort was our refusal to charge as one of the elements that the procedure or experiment have a "reasonable probability or reasonable substantial possibility of success". We have found no support in New York cases for defendants' position on this contention. The gist of the tort is conduct deliberately undertaken which predictably caused severe emotional distress. To be sure, if the experiment indisputably and demonstrably had no chance of success and this was known and understood by the plaintiffs, it would seem that the plaintiffs might not be entitled to recover. That was not the situation here. The jury could reasonably find from the medical evidence, the successful animal experiments and the evidence of a successful "dry run" [2] in 1972, that there was more than an insignificant or remote possibility of success and that plaintiffs and Dr. Sweeney were reasonably justified in having an expectation that the experiment might work. The subsequent successful human in vitro fertilization, implantation and pregnancy accomplished by Drs. Steptoe and Edwards in England in 1975 confirm this.[3] We think the high degree of likelihood of success which the defendants['] requested charge on liability would require was inappropriate and improper.

As to the asserted inconsistency between the verdicts on intentional tort and on conversion, they are entirely consistent under the charge. The jury could reasonably have found liability on the conversion claim, but rendered a verdict for defendants on the basis that the amount of damage for conversion was too speculative to be determinable. . . .

Finally, Presbyterian argues that the defendants were prejudiced by adverse publicity. . . . In denying the application, [for an adjournment] we had in mind the following considerations:

. . .

3. The likelihood and, indeed, virtual certainty that the attendant publicity would be just as extensive if the trial were postponed another two or three months.

Moreover, in the voir dire of the jury panel, particular attention was paid to the possibility that individuals might have been infected by the publicity. We found no indication that this had happened.

2. There was evidence of a successful in vitro fertilization performed by Dr. Shettles and Dr. Sweeney in 1972 following substantially the same procedure as that used in September 1973 except that no attempt was made to implant in Mrs. Del Zio the fertilized ova.

3. See Ex. 44. This is not to be confused with the reported birth in England in July, 1978. The record contains no evidence as to the latter.

When the media announced the birth of the "test tube baby" in England on July 26, defendants asked only that the jury be instructed that that event had nothing to do with the case on trial. With the consent of all parties, the jury was instructed as follows:

> In that connection I also want to mention that there have been some events in the last—well, overnight, and I suspect that it is very likely that some of you, if not all of you, are aware of what I am talking about. Of course I am talking about the fact that a baby was born in England. I want you to be aware, as I think you already are, that that event has nothing to do with this case, is totally unrelated to the issues in this case. It is not evidence in this case, and it will have nothing to do with your consideration of the evidence in this case, or in your deliberations after the evidence is all in. It is an unrelated event which you may not consider in any way with respect to the issues in this case which are, as I say, totally unrelated.

Moreover, we instructed counsel that no evidence with respect thereto should be offered or would be received. Consequently, except for the above admonition there was no mention of the English episode in the presence of the jury. The jury was also instructed by us constantly, almost every day throughout the five-week trial, that they were to pay no attention to publicity about the case. We have no reason to think that the jury's verdict was tainted by the publicity and we think the amount awarded to plaintiffs supports our view.

We conclude that the verdict was fair; reasonable and lawful. Accordingly, the motions are denied. The Clerk is directed to enter judgment.

So ordered.

———

Current regulations of the Department of Health and Human Services (HHS) prohibit support of research involving fertilization of a woman's ovum outside her body until the application or proposal has been received by the Ethics Advisory Board (EAB) and the EAB has given its advice. In 1978 the EAB of the Department of Health, Education and Welfare (now HHS) agreed to review a grant application for *in vitro* research. After the birth of a baby following *in vitro* fertilization, HEW Secretary Califano asked the EAB to study the broader social, legal and ethical issues involved in human *in vitro* fertilization. The EAB issued its report in 1979 and was dissolved shortly thereafter. The EAB has not been re-established. The recommendations in the report were never acted upon by Secretary Califano or any of his successors through June 1984. Accordingly, there is no official policy governing either federally or privately funded research. Are the report's conclusions still applicable? Do its conclusions go far enough? Too far?

DEPARTMENT OF HEALTH, EDUCATION AND WELFARE, PROTECTION OF HUMAN SUBJECTS: HEW SUPPORT OF HUMAN IN VITRO FERTILIZATION AND EMBRYO TRANSFER

44 Fed.Reg. 35033 (1979).

A. After much analysis and discussion regarding both scientific data and the moral status of the embryo, the Board is in agreement that the human embryo is entitled to profound respect; but this respect does not necessarily encompass the full legal and moral rights attributed to persons. In addition, the board noted the high rate of embryo loss that occurs in the natural process of reproduction. It concluded that some embryo loss associated with attempts to assist otherwise infertile couples to bear children of their own through *in vitro* fertilization be regarded as acceptable from an ethical standpoint, under certain conditions, as more fully described below.

B. The Board is concerned about still unanswered questions of safety for both mother and offspring of *in vitro* fertilization and embryo transfer; it is concerned, as well, about the physical and mental health of the children born following such a procedure and about their legal status. Many women have told the Board that in order to bear a child of their own they will submit to whatever risks are involved. The Board believes that while the Department should not interfere with such reproductive decisions, it has a legitimate interest in developing and disseminating information regarding safety and health so that fully informed choices about reproduction can be made.

C. A number of fears have been expressed with regard to adverse effects of technological intervention in the reproductive process: fears that such intervention might lead to genetic manipulation or encourage casual experimentation with human embryos, or bring with it the use of surrogate mothers, cloning, or the creation of genetic hybrids. Some have suggested that such research might also have a dehumanizing effect on investigators, the families involved, and society generally.

Although the Board recognizes that there is an opportunity for abuse in the application of this technology as other technologies, it concluded that a broad prohibition of research involving human *in vitro* fertilization is neither justified nor wise. Among the developments warned against by some who testified before the Board, a few (e.g., the cloning of human beings and the creation of animal/human hybrids) are of uncertain or remote risk. Other possible developments, such as the use of surrogate mothers, may be contained by regulation or legislation. Other abuses may be avoided by the use of good judgment based upon accurate information of the type collected by the Board and now being disseminated in this report. Finally, where reproductive decisions are concerned, it is important to guard against unwarranted governmental intrusion into personal and marital privacy.

D. The question of Federal support of research involving human *in vitro* fertilization and embryo transfer was troublesome for the Board in view of the uncertain risks, the dangers of abuse and because funding the procedure is morally objectionable to many. In weighing these considerations, the Board noted that the procedures may soon be in use in the private sector and that Departmental involvement might help to resolve questions of risk and avoid abuse by encouraging well-designed research by qualified scientists. Such involvement might also help to shape the use of the procedures through regulation and by example. The Board concluded that it should not advise the Department on the level of Federal support, if any, of such research; but it concluded that Federal support, if decided upon after due consideration of all that is at issue, would be acceptable from an ethical standpoint.

Evidence presented to the Board indicates that human *in vitro* fertilization and embryo transfer techniques may, in the near future, be employed throughout the world in both research and clinical practice settings. The Board believes that data from these activities as well as related types of animal research should be collected, analyzed and, when appropriate, given wide public dissemination. Accordingly, the Board recommends . . . that the Department take the primary initiative in carrying out these functions.

. . .

Conclusion (1). —The department should consider support of carefully designed research involving *in vitro* fertilization and embryo transfer in animals, including nonhuman primates, in order to obtain a better understanding of the process of fertilization, implantation and embryo development, to assess the risks to both mother and offspring associated with such procedures, and to improve the efficacy of the procedure.

. . .

Conclusion (2). —The ethics advisory board finds that it is acceptable from an ethical standpoint to undertake research involving human *in vitro* fertilization and embryo transfer provided that:

A.   If the research involves human *in vitro* fertilization without embryo transfer, the following conditions are satisfied:

1.   The research complies with all appropriate provisions of the regulations governing research with human subjects.   . . .

2.   The Research [sic] is designed primarily: (A) To establish the safety and efficacy of embryo transfer and (B) to obtain important scientific information toward that end not reasonably attainable by other means;

3.   Human gametes used in such research will be obtained exclusively from persons who have been informed of the nature and purpose of the research in which such materials will be used and have specifically consented to such use;

4.   No embryos will be sustained *in vitro* beyond the stage normally associated with the completion of implantation (14 days after fertilization); and

5.   All interested parties and the general public will be advised if evidence begins to show that the procedure entails risks of abnormal offspring higher than those associated with natural human reproduction.

B.   In addition, if the research involves embryo transfer following human *in vitro* fertilization, embryo transfer will be attempted only with gametes obtained from lawfully married couples.

Discussion: This conclusion relates to the ethics of conducting research involving *in vitro* fertilization in general; it does not address the question of Departmental support of such research. The purpose of this more general conclusion is to provide guidance to Institutional Review Boards and other groups who are asked to review research that will not be supported by HEW. Whether or not the Department decides to provide funds for such research, the Board wishes to express its views regarding the conduct of human *in vitro* fertilization and embryo transfer, so that review groups may benefit from the deliberations of the Board as they conduct their own review of specific research proposals.

As emphasized above, the Board believes that much remains to be learned about the safety and effectiveness of these procedures before they can be considered standard, accepted medical practice. Research designed to provide reliable data regarding safety and efficacy is acceptable from an ethical standpoint if conducted within the constraints indicated above. In the case of research involving embryo transfer, the Board intends not only that the gametes be obtained from lawfully married couples but also that the embryo be transferred back to the wife whose ova were used for fertilization.

The Board also discussed research designed primarily to establish safety and efficacy but which may, in addition, obtain information of scientific importance unrelated to *in vitro* fertilization and embryo transfer. The Board believes that such research, if performed as a corollary to research designed primarily to establish safety and efficacy of *in vitro* fertilization and embryo transfer, would also be acceptable from an ethical standpoint.

Conclusion (3). —The Board finds it acceptable from an ethical standpoint for the department to support or conduct research involving human *in vitro* fertilization and embryo transfer, provided that the applicable conditions set forth in conclusion (2) are met. However, the Board has decided not to address the question of the level of funding, if any, which such research might be given.

. . .

2. *Research without embryo transfer.* As previously noted the risks of producing abnormal offspring are still undetermined; therefore, an important goal would be to gain as much information as possible from well-designed research on *in vitro* fertilization not involving embryo transfer in humans. The Department should conduct a careful scientific evaluation of the possibility, supported by some expert testimony before the Board, that animal research and studies involving human *in vitro* fertilization without embryo transfer, over a relatively short period, might substantially increase our knowledge concerning the possible risk of abnormal offspring as well as lead to the development of safe and more effective techniques.

3. *Research involving embryo transfer.* While initial research efforts designed to gain as much information as possible from animal studies and human research not involving embryo transfer may be desirable, the Board does not wish to discourage planning and preparation that may lead to clinical trials or other forms of research involving embryo transfer. The Department's participation in, or support of, clinical trials is often an effective method to evaluate the safety and efficacy of innovative medical procedures, particularly as the use of the procedures increases.

4. *Research for other purposes.* Potentially valuable information about reproductive biology, the etiology of birth defects, and other subjects may be revealed through research involving human *in vitro* fertilization without embryo transfer, and unrelated to the safety and efficacy of procedures for overcoming infertility. The Board makes no judgment at this time regarding the ethical acceptability of such research nor does it speculate about what research might be sufficiently compelling to justify the use of human embryos. Instead, it notes that applications for support of such research should be submitted to the Board for ethical review in accordance with 45 CFR 46.204(d).

5. *Pending Research Application.* Given the criteria specified in Conclusion (2) and incorporated in Conclusion (3) for evaluating research involving human *in vitro* fertilization, and the Board's views about Departmental support of such research, the Board recommends that the

Secretary refer the pending application of Vanderbilt University back to the National Institutes of Health for a determination as to whether the proposal meets those criteria and for further review in light of the considerations set forth in this report.

Conclusion (4). —The national institute of child health and human development (NICHD) and other appropriate agencies should work with professional societies, foreign governments and international organizations to collect, analyze and disseminate information derived from research (in both animals and humans) and clinical experience throughout the world involving *in vitro* fertilization and embryo transfer.

. . .

Conclusion (5). —The secretary should encourage the development of a uniform or model law to clarify the legal status of children born as a result of *in vitro* fertilization and embryo transfer. To the extent that funds may be necessary to develop such legislation, the department should consider providing appropriate support.

Discussion: The Board is concerned about the ambiguity regarding the legal status of children born following artificial insemination and a similar ambiguity that may surround the legal status of children born following *in vitro* fertilization and embryo transfer. The Board is also concerned about lack of clarity regarding the legal responsibilities of those who utilize, support, or permit use of such procedures. Because of the complexity of the legal problems involved in new techniques for human reproduction, the Board recommends that a model or uniform law be drafted that would establish with clarity the rights and responsibilities of donor and recipient "parents", of offspring and of those who participate in the process of reproduction through new technologies.

The Board urges that such a uniform or model law be drafted by the National Conference of Commissioners on Uniform State Laws, the American Law Institute, or some other qualified body. Because of the complex nature of the subject matter, however, the Board is aware that the task may be a major undertaking and suggest that the Department consider providing funds for drafting the legislation. Since the purpose is to safeguard the health and welfare of children and their families, it appears to be an appropriate project for Departmental support.

NOTES

1. A team of researchers at Harbor-UCLA Medical Center in Torrance, California have reported success with a new reproductive technique that involves a woman donating an ovum. This ovum, fertilized *in vivo* through artificial insemination, undergoes initial cleavage inside the donor. The physician then non-surgically, by gently washing out her uterus, removes the fertilized ovum from the donor and transfers it to the wife of the sperm donor, who then carries the child to term. "Prenatal adoption" and "adoptive pregnancy" are two common names given to this procedure.

The California team reported that in July 1983 it had successfully impregnated two of the five infertile women chosen to participate in the initial procedure. It emphasized that the procedure's initial success rate was greater than that for *in vitro* fertilization procedures and that it is available to women who cannot or choose not to undergo the laparoscopy necessary to get the ova to be fertilized *in vitro*. Furthermore, the researchers feel this procedure could benefit couples who must isolate the mother's genetic complement but who still want a child biologically related to one parent. See Non-Surgical Transfer of In Vivo Fertilized Donated Ova to Five Infertile Women: Report of Two Pregnancies, Lancet 223

(July 23, 1983); Lyons, Two Donated Human Embryos Said to Impregnate Two Women, New York Times, July 22, 1983, at Al, col. 5; Hilts, Two Embryos Transplanted in Humans, Washington Post, July 22, 1983 at Al, col. 2; Schmeck, "Pre-Natal Adoption" Is the Objective of New Technique, New York Times, June 14, 1983, at Cl, col. 4. The first birth of a baby to a woman who received an embryo transfer was announced on February 3, 1984. The birth had occurred two weeks previously. Richard G. Seed, the inventor of the transfer process, will try to patent the technique. The technique was developed without government support, and allegedly investors spent more than $3 million on its development. Washington Post, Feb. 4, 1984, at A14, col. 1.

Consider the legal and social implications of such a procedure. Whom should the state recognize as the child's mother for health regulation (e.g., birth certificate) purposes? What rights might the ovum donor assert to the child? What about compensation for the donor? Is this "babyselling"? Do you think that analogies to adoption or to artificial insemination will be helpful to courts and legal theorists in dealing with these problems? How would you as an attorney advise a client who came to you for legal advice before participating in this procedure?

2. Much current research would benefit from use of human embryos or fetal tissue. Medical scientists believe, for example, that some diseases of the brain and central nervous system might be treated by transplanting tissue from aborted human embryos. Schmeck, Fetal Research: New Field Offers Promise Amid Problems, New York Times, July 5, 1983, at Cl, col. 6. Legal and ethical questions arise concerning how such embryos or tissues are to be obtained, particularly where they are products of induced abortions. Existing regulations governing fetal research in the United States define the "fetus" as, "the product of conception from the time of implantation (as evidenced by any of the presumptive signs of pregnancy) . . . until a determination is made following expulsion or extraction of the fetus, that it is viable." 45 CFR § 46.203(c). They also make it difficult for researchers to obtain the products of induced abortions by providing:

(3) individuals engaged in the activity [fetal research] will have no part in: (i) any decisions as to the timing, method, and procedures used to terminate the pregnancy, and (ii) determining the viability of the fetus at the termination of the pregnancy; and

(4) no procedural changes which may cause greater than minimal risk to the fetus or the pregnant woman will be introduced into the procedure for terminating the pregnancy solely in the interest of the activity.

(b) no inducements, monetary or otherwise, may be offered to terminate pregnancy for purposes of the activity.

Id. at § 46.206.

It would be possible, therefore, under existing regulations to take ova from women with their consent, fertilize these ova with sperm randomly obtained from donors or sperm banks and develop the resultant embryos at least until the stage at which they were ready for implantation. See Soupart, Present and Possible Future Research in the Use of Human Embryos in Abortion and the Status of the Fetus, 67–104 (Bondeson, Engelhardt, Spicker and Winship, eds 1983). How might the government attempt to regulate these activities? Would government regulation be effective? If not, what would? Or is regulation unnecessary?

3. In late 1982 the Medical Research Council (MRC) in Great Britain published regulations for its members, allowing research that is "scientifically sound, clearly defined and directly relevant to clinical problems" on embryos developed no further than the implantation stage (no longer than 13–14 days). The regulations also restrict researchers' ability to store embryos, but they do allow for interspecies fertilization studies, at least through early cleavage development. In mid-1983 a government committee, known as the Warnock Committee, was established to study embryo experimentation. It is expected to submit its report in 1984. For general discussion of the debate on embryo experimentation in Great Britain, see New Embryo Furor in Britain, New York Times, Feb. 13, 1982, at A2,

col. 2; Research on Embryos: Ethics Under Fire, 95 New Scientist 891 (1982); Okay for Human Embryo Research, 285 The Economist 99 (1982); Embryology Needs Rules, Not Laws, 302 Nature 735 (1983); Societies Urge Softer Line, 302 Nature 739 (1983).

4. Suppose you were asked to serve on a committee similar to that established in Great Britain (supra note 3); what would be your principal concerns? How would you want the committee to resolve them? Would your concerns depend upon a particular definition of when life begins?

5. An extremely controversial technique in which researchers and physicians at work in fertility-related activities place great hope and which could prove extremely important in embryonic experimentation is embryo cryopreservation, the freezing of an embryo for defrosting and transferral to a female who will carry the embryo to term. One researcher active in this area has labeled cryopreservation the "state of the art" in embryo preservation and fertility research. Soupart, Present and Possible Future Research in the Use of Human Embryos in Abortion and the Status of the Fetus 67, 77 (Bondeson, Engelhardt, Spicker, Winship, eds. 1983).

The procedure, which has been successfully used to freeze embryos of mice, rats, rabbits, sheep, goats and cattle, involves slowly cooling the embryo down to -80 degrees centigrade in the presence of a protectant chemical solution, storing the frozen embryo in liquid nitrogen at -196 degrees centigrade, with the technician paying special attention not to allow ice to form inside the cells. Intracellular ice is a common cause of cell death during cryopreservation. The survival rate for nonhuman embryos stored in this manner, approximately 90 percent as evidenced by live births, is as great after 60 months in frozen storage as after 24 hours. Id. at 77–78.

When an embryo is to be transplanted, it is slowly defrosted. The cryoprotectant is diluted out at $0°$ degrees centigrade. Using a technique similar to that used in transplanting an embryo recently fertilized *in vitro*, the physician transfers the embryo into a female's uterus or oviduct, depending on the embryo's development. Embryos are frozen at the 8–16 cell stage of development. The female's reproductive cycle must be at the stage during which implantation will occur. Id. at 76–78.

Cryopreservation gained increased prominence in early 1983 when Australian researchers announced that they had impregnated a woman unable to conceive naturally with an embryo which had been cryopreserved for four months. The pregnancy eventually ended with a spontaneous abortion.

Medical, legal and ethical theorists were divided in their reactions to the developments. A leading Australian judge said that his nation's legal system was unprepared for the problems this new procedure would raise. Researchers cautioned that the quest for scientific information should never take precedence over the significance of human existence. See Schmeck, Fetal Research: New Field Offers Promise Amid Problems, New York Times, July 5, 1983, at C6, col. 6; 98 Doctors Split Over Freeze-Thaw Embryos, 98 New Scientist 525 (1983); Frozen Embryos Trigger Debate by Australians, Washington Post, May 17, 1983, at A1, col. 6.

What legal problems do you anticipate will result from preserving fertilized ova? Are these consequences significantly different from those produced by preserving ova or sperm?

6. For a discussion of embryo manipulation through genetic engineering, see Ch. 1, Sec. D.1., supra. For a comprehensive evaluation of the status of *in vitro* fertilization suggesting that storage of frozen embryos and embryo transfers with third party contributors go far beyond the original therapeutic justifications, see Grobstein, Flower and Mendeloff, External Human Fertilization: An Evaluation of Policy, 222 Science 127 (1983). See also C. Grobstein, From Chance to Purpose: An Appraisal of External Human Fertilization (1981).

d. Cloning

**JAMES D. WATSON,
MOVING TOWARD THE CLONAL MAN**

226 The Atlantic 50 (May 1971).

The notion that man might sometime soon be reproduced asexually upsets many people. The main public effect of the remarkable clonal frog produced some ten years ago in Oxford by the zoologist John Gurdon has not been awe of the elegant scientific implication of this frog's existence, but fear that a similar experiment might someday be done with human cells. Until recently, however, this foreboding has seemed more like a science fiction scenario than a real problem which the human race has to live with.

.   .   .

Today, however, we must face up to the fact that the unexpectedly rapid progress of R. G. Edwards and P. S. Steptoe in working out the conditions for routine test-tube conception of human eggs means that human embryological development need no longer be a process shrouded in secrecy. It can become instead an event wide-open to a variety of experimental manipulations.   .   .   .

.   .   .

[For human cloning] experiments to be successful, techniques would have to be developed which allow the insertion of adult diploid nuclei into human eggs which previously have had their maternal haploid nucleus removed.* At first sight, this task is a very tall order since human eggs are much smaller than those of frogs, the only vertebrates which have so far been cloned. Insertion by micropipettes, the device used in the case of the frog, is always likely to damage human eggs irreversibly. Recently, however, the development of simple techniques for fusing animal cells has raised the strong possibility that further refinements of the cell-fusion method will allow the routine introduction of human diploid nuclei into enucleated human eggs. Activation of such eggs to divide to become blastocysts, followed by implantation into suitable uteri, should lead to the development of healthy fetuses, and subsequent normal-appearing babies.

The growing up to adulthood of these first clonal humans could be a very startling event, a fact already appreciated by many magazine editors, one of whom commissioned a cover with multiple copies of Ringo Starr, another of whom gave us overblown multiple likenesses of the current sex goddess, Raquel Welch. It takes little imagination to perceive that different people will have highly different fantasies, some perhaps imagining the existence of countless people with the features of Picasso or Frank Sinatra or Walt Frazier or Doris Day. And would monarchs like the Shah of Iran, knowing they might never be able to have a normal male heir, consider the possibility of having a son whose genetic constitution would be identical to their own?

---

* The process would involve removing and discarding the 23 chromosome nucleus from an ovum and replacing it with the 46 chromosome nuclus from a somatic cell from the same or another individual. By 1984, Dr. Watson had concluded that the cloning of mammals from adult tissues is very unlikely ever to occur, and that even the cloning of mouse embryo cells is suspect (as reported in the Note on p. 1329, infra). [Eds.]

Clearly, even more bizarre possibilities can be thought of, and so we might have expected that many biologists, particularly those whose work impinges upon this possibility, would seriously ponder its implication, and begin a dialogue which would educate the world's citizens and offer suggestions which our legislative bodies might consider in framing national science policies. On the whole, however, this has not happened. Though a number of scientific papers devoted to the problem of genetic engineering have casually mentioned that clonal reproduction may someday be with us, the discussion to which I am party has been so vague and devoid of meaningful time estimates as to be virtually soporific.

Does this effective silence imply a conspiracy to keep the general public unaware of a potential threat to their basic ways of life? Could it be motivated by fear that the general reaction will be a further damning of all science, thereby decreasing even more the limited money available for pure research? Or does it merely tell us that most scientists do live such an ivory-tower existence that they are capable of thinking rationally only about pure science, dismissing more practical matters as subjects for the lawyers, students, clergy, and politicians to face up to?

One or both of these possibilities may explain why more scientists have not taken cloning before the public. The main reason, I suspect, is that the prospect to most biologists still looks too remote and chancy— not worthy of immediate attention when other matters, like nuclear-weapon overproliferation and pesticide and auto-exhaust pollution, present society with immediate threats to its orderly continuation. Though scientists as a group form the most future-oriented of all professions, there are few of us who concentrate on events unlikely to become reality within the next decade or two.

To almost all the intellectually most adventurous geneticists, the seemingly distant time when cloning might first occur is more to the point than its far-reaching implication, were it to be practiced seriously. . . .

This position, however, fails to allow for what I believe will be a frenetic rush to do experimental manipulation with human eggs once they have become a readily available commodity. . . . Most of these excess eggs would likely be used for a variety of valid experimental purposes . . . Others could be devoted to finding methods for curing certain genetic diseases, conceivably through use of cell-fusion methods which now seem to be the correct route to cloning. The temptation to try cloning itself thus will always be close at hand.

No reason, of course, dictates that such cloning experiments need occur. Most of the medical people capable of such experimentation would probably steer clear of any step which looked as though its real purpose were to clone. But it would be short-sighted to assume that everyone would instinctively recoil from such purposes. Some people may sincerely believe the world desperately needs many copies of really exceptional people if we are to fight our way out of the ever-increasing computer-mediated complexity that makes our individual brains so frequently inadequate.

Moreover, given the widespread development of the safe clinical procedures for handling human eggs, cloning experiments would not be prohibitively expensive. They need not be restricted to the super-powers. All smaller countries now possess the resources required for eventual success. Furthermore, there need not exist the coercion of a totalitarian state to provide the surrogate mothers. There already are such widespread divergences regarding the sacredness of the act of human reproduction that the boring meaninglessness of the lives of many women would be sufficient cause for their willingness to participate in such experimentation, be it legal or illegal. Thus, if the matter proceeds in its current nondirected fashion, a human being born of clonal reproduction most likely will appear on the earth within the next twenty to fifty years, and even sooner, if some nation should actively promote the venture.

The first reaction of most people to the arrival of these asexually produced children, I suspect, would be one of despair. The nature of the bond between parents and their children, not to mention everyone's values about the individual's uniqueness, could be changed beyond recognition, and by a science which they never understood but which until recently appeared to provide more good than harm. Certainly to many people, particularly those with strong religious backgrounds, our most sensible course of action would be to de-emphasize all those forms of research which would circumvent the normal sexual reproductive process. If this step were taken, experiments on cell fusion might no longer be supported by federal funds or tax-exempt organizations. Prohibition of such research would most certainly put off the day when diploid nuclei could satisfactorily be inserted into enucleated human eggs. Even more effective would be to take steps quickly to make illegal, or to reaffirm the illegality of, any experimental work with human embryos.

Neither of the prohibitions, however, is likely to take place. In the first place, the cell-fusion technique now offers one of the best avenues for understanding the genetic basis of cancer. Today, all over the world, cancer cells are being fused with normal cells to pinpoint those specific chromosomes responsible for given forms of cancer. In addition, fusion techniques are the basis of many genetic efforts to unravel the biochemistry of diseases like cystic fibrosis or multiple sclerosis. Any attempts now to stop such work using the argument that cloning represents a greater threat than a disease like cancer is likely to be considered irresponsible by virtually anyone able to understand the matter.

Though more people would initially go along with a prohibition of work on human embryos, many may have a change of heart when they ponder the mess which the population explosion poses. The current projections are so horrendous that responsible people are likely to consider the need for more basic embryological facts much more relevant to our self-interest than the not-very-immediate threat of a few clonal men existing some decades ahead. And the potentially militant lobby of infertile couples who see test-tube conception as their only route to the joys of raising children of their own making would carry even more weight. So, scientists like Edwards are likely to get a go-ahead signal even if, almost perversely, the immediate consequences of their "population-money"-supported research will be the production of still more babies.

Complicating any effort at effective legislative guidance is the multiplicity of places where work . . . could occur, thereby making unlikely the possibility that such manipulations would have the same legal (or illegal) status throughout the world. . . .

Thus, all nations formulating policies to handle the implications of *in vitro* human embryo experimentation must realize that the problem is essentially an international one. Even if one or more countries should stop such research, their action could effectively be neutralized by the response of a neighboring country. This most disconcerting impotence also holds for the United States. If our congressional representatives, upon learning where the matter now stands, should decide that they want none of it and pass very strict laws against human embryo experimentation, their action would not seriously set back the current scientific and medical momentum which brings us close to the possibility of surrogate mothers, if not human clonal reproduction. . . .

. . . Thus it appears to me most desirable that as many people as possible be informed about the new ways of human reproduction and their potential consequences, both good and bad.

This is a matter far too important to be left solely in the hands of the scientific and medical communities. The belief that surrogate mothers and clonal babies are inevitable because science always moves forward, an attitude expressed to me recently by a scientific colleague, represents a form of laissez-faire nonsense dismally reminiscent of the creed that American business, if left to itself, will solve everybody's problems. Just as the success of a corporate body in making money need not set the human condition ahead, neither does every scientific advance automatically make our lives more "meaningful." No doubt the person whose experimental skill will eventually bring forth a clonal baby will be given wide notoriety. But the child who grows up knowing that the world wants another Picasso may view his creator in a different light.

I would thus hope that over the next decade wide-reaching discussion would occur, at the informal as well as formal legislative level, about the manifold problems which are bound to arise if test-tube conception becomes a common occurrence. A blanket declaration of the worldwide illegality of human cloning might be one result of a serious effort to ask the world in which direction it wished to move. Admittedly the vast effort, required for even the most limited international arrangement, will turn off some people—those who believe the matter is of marginal importance now, and that it is a red herring designed to take our minds off our callous attitudes toward war, poverty, and racial prejudice. But if we do not think about it now, the possibility of our having a free choice will one day suddenly be gone.

NOTE

It should be noted that research on clonal reproduction is being conducted with animals. Researchers have been able to produce frog clones for several years. Researchers reported in 1981 that they had produced mouse "clones"— although the nuclei came from a seven-day-old mouse embryo rather than from cells of an adult animal. See Illmensee and Hoppe, 23 Cell 9 (1981); Hoppe and Illmensee, 79 Proc. Nat'l. Acad. Sci. U.S.A. 1912 (1982). More recently, in the June 17, 1983 issue of Science, Drs. James McGrath and Davor Solter reported successful experiments in transplanting body-cell nuclei from one mouse embryo to another enucleated mouse embryo. This procedure led to the birth of mice genetically related to the nuclei donor, not to the mother who carried the embryos to term.

Illmensee's research has been the subject of intense investigation recently. Some of his colleagues have accused him of scientific fraud, claiming that he falsified research data in a series of experiments following those reported here. See Illmensee Inquiry Finds Chaos—But No Fraud, New Scientist, Feb. 23, 1984, at 3; Illmensee Fraud Charges Intensify, New Scientist, Mar. 15, 1984, at 7; Illmensee Faces Funding Cutoff, 224 Science 265 (1984).

BROMHALL v. RORVIK

United States District Court for the Eastern District of Pennsylvania, 1979.
478 F.Supp. 361.

MEMORANDUM AND ORDER

FULLAM, DISTRICT JUDGE.

In January 1978, the defendant J. B. Lippincott Company ("Lippincott") published a book authored by the defendant Rorvik entitled *In His Image*, subtitled *The Cloning of a Man*. The book purports to be a factual account of a successful experiment, conducted in great secrecy, resulting in the creation of a human genetic "twin" by cloning.

Plaintiff is an eminent British scientist, a recognized authority in the field of experimental embryology. He asserts that the book is a hoax and has brought this action to recover damages for libel, malicious invasion of privacy, and infringement of common law copyright, and to obtain equitable relief. The defendant Rorvik has moved to dismiss for lack of personal jurisdiction, and the defendant Lippincott has filed a Motion to Dismiss which will be treated as a Motion for Summary Judgment.

. . .

[The court first determined that it had personal jurisdiction over Rorvik and that service of process was satisfactory.]

. . .

II. DEFENDANT LIPPINCOTT'S MOTION TO DISMISS

For purposes of disposing of the motion filed by defendant Lippincott, it must be assumed, as alleged by the plaintiff, that the book *In His Image, the Cloning of a Man* is an elaborate hoax, perpetrated by both defendants for pecuniary gain. The question remains, whether any actionable wrong has been done this plaintiff.

From plaintiff's standpoint, the facts may be summarized as follows: Plaintiff is, as mentioned above, a distinguished scientist who is a recognized authority in the field of experimental embryology. His (unpublished) doctoral thesis at Oxford University is entitled "An Investigation of Nuclear Transplantation in the Mammalian Egg," and is an account of his extensive original research and experimentation involving the use of "both micro-injection and virally-induced cell fusion to transfer body-cell nuclei into unfertilized rabbit eggs."

The defendant Rorvik is a free-lance reporter who has written extensively on medical and scientific subjects. In 1977, in the course of writing *In His Image*, Rorvik wrote to plaintiff, seeking information about the current status of plaintiff's work in the field. The ostensible purpose of the inquiry was to aid Rorvik in the preparation of a serious article or book surveying the current status of scientific research in the field of cell-transplantation. In response to this inquiry, plaintiff sent Rorvik, among other things, a nine-page, previously unpublished, summary of his doctoral thesis.

In his book, Rorvik describes the successful cloning as having occurred in 1976, by scientists whose identity must be kept secret, and who therefore are referred to in the book as "Paul" and "Darwin." At pages 179–180 of the book, the following appears:

"Darwin said that the makeup of the medium in which the nuclei were briefly deposited prior to swift fusion with egg cytoplasm was of utmost importance. Paul and he had made some discoveries related to some of the proteins and enzymes contained in eggs and embryos. These, too, had furthered the work and might prove very useful in work unrelated to cloning as well.

"Darwin, who by this time had enjoyed at least three glasses of wine, said that in his opinion no one would match his accomplishments for another 10 years, at least. Then, embarrassed a bit by his own immodesty, he added that this would be so partly because others would be afraid to try.

"As a matter of fact, however, before the year was out we would learn of the work of an Oxford scientist who had gone, if not 'straight for the throat,' then in at least an only slightly wavering line. This researcher reported in *Nature* that he had activated rabbit eggs with cold shock, used Sendai virus to fuse them with rabbit body cells, and had achieved, out of numerous efforts, four embryos that divided regularly at normal rates all the way to the morula stage, at which point they might conceivably have been successfully implanted, had the researcher been prepared to go that far."

At this point, a footnote (32) identifies plaintiff as the Oxford scientist referred to and sets forth at great length and in detail the techniques employed by plaintiff in his research, and the results of his experiments.

Also included in the book is a bibliography which lists some 18 "unsigned reports" and approximately 219 "signed reports and books" (including 17 by Rorvik himself). This bibliography lists plaintiff's doctoral thesis, a 1975 article by plaintiff in Nature magazine, and a "personal communication, July 18, 1977." Only two or three other "personal communications" are listed in the bibliography.

In support of his libel claims, plaintiff asserts that the book is false and defamatory in the following respects: (1) it conveys the impression that plaintiff's own research had as its ultimate goal the cloning of human beings, and (2) it conveys the impression that plaintiff believed in and supported the scientific authenticity of the secret cloning experiment described in the book.

The direct references to plaintiff in the book are plainly not false, nor are they alleged to be false. However, the basic premise of the book, namely, that a human being was successfully cloned, is (at least for present purposes) false. But accurate statements about the plaintiff do not become libelous merely because they are included in a book which is false in other respects.

[The court determined that Pennsylvania law would govern the case.]

. . .

In my judgment, the words used in the publication complained of are incapable of defamatory meaning; the innuendo ascribed to the words used is entirely unwarranted. Plaintiff simply does not have a claim for defamation.

. . .

[The court dismissed the plaintiff's copyright claims, finding that the 1976 Copyright Act effectively abolished common-law copyrights.]

. . .

The issues are not so clear, however, with respect to plaintiff's claims for invasion of privacy and for equitable relief. While the issues are not free from doubt, I believe summary disposition of these claims is not warranted.

A. *Claims for Equitable Relief*

The claim asserted in Count V of the Complaint is based upon the theory that, after fraudulently obtaining the nine-page abstract of plaintiff's doctoral thesis, as mentioned above, Rorvik appropriated plaintiff's creation, in that the experimental techniques described in the book as having been used successfully in cloning a human being "are identical to those techniques developed by plaintiff in his research and communicated to defendants by plaintiff." Plaintiff alleges that the defendants have received and will receive substantial sums of money from the book, that the unlawful and unauthorized use of plaintiff's experimental techniques has greatly enhanced the sales potential and credibility of the book; that defendants have geen unjustly enriched as a result of their improper actions; and that plaintiff is therefore entitled to an accounting and payment of some portion of the proceeds derived or to be derived from publication of the book and subsidiary publication rights.

Defendant Lippincott's Motion to Dismiss makes the following arguments: (1) the allegedly misappropriated material lacks sufficient originality or concreteness to warrant protection; (2) plaintiff was adequately advised by Rorvik of the use to which the material would be put; (3) plaintiff provided the material voluntarily, and therefore consented to its use; (4) the Complaint is not sufficiently specific to meet the requirements of F.R.Civ.P. 9(b) for claims based on fraud; and (5) all of plaintiff's Count V claims come within the scope of the Copyright Act of 1976, 17 U.S.C. §§ 101 *et seq.*, and are preempted by operation of that statute. None of these arguments justifies dismissal at this stage.

. . .

[The court then detailed its reasoning, finding that the record raised issues of fact that it could not decide on a motion to dismiss and that the plaintiff's claims in Count V related to an *idea*, which is not within the scope of the 1976 Copyright Act.]

. . .

B. *Invasion of Privacy*

Section 652A of the Restatement of Torts 2d establishes four categories of invasions of the right of privacy which are actionable: unreasonable intrusion upon the seclusion of another (§ 652B); appropriation of another's name or likeness (§ 652C); unreasonable publicity given to the other's private life (§ 652D); or publicity that unreasonably places another in a false light before the public (§ 652E). Comment c under § 652A includes the following:

"(c) Thus far, as indicated in the decisions of the courts, the four forms of invasion of the right of privacy stated in this Section are the ones that have clearly become crystallized and generally been held to be actionable as a matter of tort liability. Other forms may still appear, particularly since some courts and in particular the Supreme

Court of the United States, have spoken in very broad general terms of a somewhat undefined 'right of privacy' as a ground for various constitutional decisions involving indeterminate civil and personal rights . . . Nothing in this Chapter is intended to exclude the possibility of future developments in the tort law of privacy."

Plaintiff relies upon the fourth type of invasion of privacy, that covered by § 652E:

"Publicity Placing Person in False Light

"One who gives publicity to a matter concerning another that places the other before the public in a false light is subject to liability to the other for invasion of his privacy, if

"(a) the false light in which the other was placed would be highly offensive to a reasonable person, and

"(b) the actor had knowledge of or acted in reckless disregard as to the falsity of the publicized matter and the false light in which the other would be placed."

The cause of action contemplated by this language differs from a claim of defamation in at least two respects: publicity (i.e., widespread dissemination), rather than mere publication, is required; and the false statement or imputation need not be defamatory. But the imputation must still be false, and, as discussed above, the statements directly concerning plaintiff in the defendant's book cannot reasonably be interpreted as false. I therefore conclude that plaintiff's claims do not fit squarely within § 652E. The only arguably "false light" in which plaintiff may have been placed by the publication would be if the reference in the bibliography to a "personal communication" from the plaintiff could reasonably be interpreted as an assertion that the plaintiff supported Rorvik's efforts (an interpretation which I have ruled out, above), or as an assertion that plaintiff and Rorvik were friends or colleagues. The latter proposition seems equally dubious, and, in any event, a mere claim of friendship, however false, could scarcely be regarded as "highly offensive to a reasonable person."

Upon analysis, I believe plaintiff's claims for invasion of privacy do not fit within any of the categories listed in the Restatement but do share some of the attributes of the various kinds of claims there recognized. In a sense, defendants may have given unreasonable publicity to certain aspects of plaintiff's private life (§ 652D) in that they gave wide public dissemination to the relatively private information that plaintiff's research funds had been terminated.

To some extent, defendants can be said to have appropriated plaintiff's name for their own use and benefit (§ 652C), although not precisely in the absolute sense contemplated by that section. Plaintiff's claim can be viewed as an assertion that the defendants appropriated plaintiff's name and reputation to the extent of using them to lend a false air of scholarship to Rorvik's literary efforts. To the extent that they appropriated his original ideas and laboratory techniques, the claim falls within the equitable action discussed above. But to the extent that they appropriated his name and reputation, and thereby drew him against his will into the limelight of public controversy, it may be that they invaded privacy interests entitled to the law's protection.

In this developing area of the law, I am not prepared to rule at this stage that a Pennsylvania court would refuse to recognize a tortious injury in these circumstances. I believe the issues can be better examined after fuller development of the facts. Whether plaintiff's standing in the scientific community has been adversely affected, whether plaintiff's entry into the limelight of public controversy (there is a reference in the record to Congressional hearings on the underlying issues, as a result of defendants' book) was involuntary, or a self-inflicted wound; and the degree of malice or other culpability on the part of the defendants—all these issues may bear upon the ultimate determination, and should be more fully developed before a final decision is rendered. . . .

The Motion to Dismiss Count II of the Complaint will be denied.

NOTE

The *Bromhall* suit was settled by the author and publisher for an undisclosed sum. An apology from the publisher, however, was a part of the settlement. New York Times, Apr. 8, 1982, at C24, col. 5.

What do you think motivated the plaintiff in Bromhall v. Rorvik to bring suit? How might the decision affect the willingness of scientists to conduct and to disseminate the results of "sensitive" research? What problems might those scientists engaged in cloning research or research with human ova or embryos encounter after publication of a book such as In His Image? What are some of the possible roles lawyers might play in any controversy over the conduct of such research?

C. THE IMPACT OF GENETIC TECHNOLOGY: AIDING REPRODUCTION, PROVIDING THERAPY OR PERFECTING PERSONS?

The relatively recent and rapid advances in genetic screening techniques and increased awareness and availability of genetic counseling provide better opportunities for individuals to make informed health care and reproductive decisions. These changes also raise significant legal, ethical and social issues for patients, their families, health care providers and society in general.

Genetic screening, the testing of an asymptomatic population to identify people who may possess a specific genotype,[1] may be undertaken for several purposes. These purposes include, for example, screening to test worker susceptibility to disease from exposure to substances in the work place, and to assist in the achievement of research-related objectives.[2] This section will focus on the use of genetic screening to improve health care by preventive or remedial means and to provide relevant information for reproductive choices.

In studying the material, consider what role, if any, the government should play in genetic screening programs. If governmental participation in some form is warranted, should such participation be at the federal level, state level, or both? Should involvement of persons be mandatory as opposed to voluntary? Should the nature of the individual's involvement depend on the purpose of the specific genetic screening program? Alternatively consider to what extent parental prerogatives should be rec-

---

1. This is the definition of genetic screening used by the President's Commission, Screening and Counseling for Genetic Conditions at 2 (1983).

2. An example of such an activity would be screening a population to determine the frequency and distribution of a specified gene.

ognized and enforced. What information concerning genetic risks is a prospective parent(s) entitled to receive? From whom? How can a parent(s) be assured that persons conveying genetic information are qualified?

1. GENETIC SCREENING

PRESIDENT'S COMMISSION FOR THE STUDY OF ETHICAL PROBLEMS IN MEDICINE AND BIOMEDICAL AND BEHAVIORAL RESEARCH, SCREENING AND COUNSELING FOR GENETIC CONDITIONS

Appendix B (Basic Concepts) 109–115 (1983).

The Genetic Building Blocks

The molecular basis of inheritance in most organisms, plant and animal, is the chemical **deoxyribonucleic acid** (DNA). The molecules that make up DNA can be thought of as code letters, capable of combining into a great variety of "words." These "words" direct two major processes, **replication** and **protein synthesis.** Replication involves the production of identical DNA sequences so that when a cell divides, each daughter cell receives a complete copy of the original cell's genetic information. Protein synthesis involves the production of **proteins,** such as **enzymes,** each of which plays a very specific role in the structure and functioning of the organism. Through the process of evolution, each species has accumulated its own set of genetic information that both maintains the continuity of interspecies diversity and facilitates intraspecies diversity in sexually reproducing organisms. Thus, humans give birth only to other humans, although each individual has very different physical and functional characteristics.

A **gene** consists of a small segment of DNA that directs the synthesis of **amino acids,** which are the building blocks of proteins. Genes are packaged in units called **chromosomes** (which are actually visible under a light microscope during certain stages of cell division). Human beings normally have a set of 46 chromosomes, which contain all the genes. The term **genome** is used to describe this full complement of genes; each individual (with the exception of identical siblings) possesses a unique genome. The set consists of 23 pairs of chromosomes, with each pair containing one chromosome from the mother and one from the father. The 44 chromosomes in 22 of these pairs are called **autosomes;** the two chromosomes in the 23rd pair are **sex chromosomes.** In males, this is an X and a Y (XY); in females, two X chromosomes (XX). (Very occasionally, people have different combinations of X and Y chromosomes.)

The human body is made up of **somatic cells**—the cells composing parts of the body such as tissues and organs—and **germ cells**—eggs or sperm or their precursors. The chromosomes are contained within the **nucleus** of all these cells. During the formation of eggs or sperm the number of chromosomes is halved by a process called **meiosis.** Consequently, when an egg is fertilized, its 23 chromosomes (22 autosomes and one X chromosome) join with the sperm's 23 chromosomes (22 autosomes and either an X or a Y chromosome), resulting in the full set of 46 chromosomes. The fertilized egg then undergoes cell division (termed

mitosis), during which identical daughter cells are formed. The development of the organism occurs through a coordinated pattern involving both multiplication of cells and their differentiation into distinct parts of the body—bones, connective tissue, muscles, and so forth. Though all the cells in a developing organism normally contain identical genes, the genetic information is expressed differently from cell to cell early in gestation. Through the process of differentiation, most of the genes in each cell "switch off," that is, they stop synthesizing proteins. The specific proteins made by the small fraction of genes that remain active determine how the cell becomes differentiated—that is, how it functions in a limited capacity, as a blood cell or a brain cell or a kidney cell and so forth. The specialized gene products of each of these cells—the proteins—are the materials that form the structure of the organism and through which its functioning is coordinated.

Patterns of Inheritance

The genetic information in the nucleus of each cell interacts with the environment in which an organism lives. Factors in the environment thus affect the way genes are expressed. Many medical geneticists study the relative significance of the genetic and environmental components of a disease or disorder. Studies of twins, of families, and of the general population have helped provide a better understanding of the contributing factors in each particular case. As a result, many diseases have been classified as "genetic" according to specific inheritance patterns that enable an expert to estimate the risk of getting the disease.

The genes are arranged in very specific patterns along the chromosomes. A change in the number, arrangement, or molecular sequence of the genes as a result of gene-gene and/or gene-environment interactions is called a **mutation**. Mutations may either occur **de novo** or be inherited. They are the basis of natural evolution. Some mutations, however, have bad consequences for the organism—these are commonly labeled "genetic diseases." Every human being inherits about six or seven deleterious mutations that under certain circumstances can cause serious illness.

Genetic diseases or defects can often be categorized as **monogenic** (involving a mutation in a single gene), **multifactorial** (involving an interaction between the environment and more than one gene), or **chromosomal** (caused by an imbalance in genetic material). If a disease or birth defect falls into any of these categories, risk estimates can often be calculated.

Monogenic Disorders. People possess two copies of each gene, one from the mother and one from the father. The various forms of a gene at any particular location on a chromosome are known as **alleles.** In addition to a gene's normal form, variant alleles can occur through mutation; mutations that are not lethal are then passed on to future generations. When the two copies of a particular gene are the same, the individual is termed **homozygous** for that gene; when the alleles are different, the individual is **heterozygous.**

Autosomal Recessive. Sometimes the existence of a single variant gene does not cause any abnormality in an individual's functioning because the necessary "instructions" for the functioning of the cell are supplied by the other, normal gene. The presence of a variant gene leads to a disease only when it occurs on both autosomes in a pair; in other words, when both parents contribute genetic material containing the same variation, their child is homozygous for that variant form of the gene.[1] A genetic disorder that occurs in this fashion is termed **autosomal recessive.** Cystic fibrosis, phenylketonuria (PKU), Tay-Sachs disease, and sickle-cell anemia are examples of autosomal recessive conditions. Many other human characteristics besides those termed diseases are also inherited in a recessive fashion. For example, the ability to taste the organic compound phenylthio-urea is inherited in this way. The substance is intensely bitter to those who can detect it, but one individual in four is unable to taste it. In the case of a recessive **disease,** the variant allele is not expressed and the normal allele dominates.

A heterozygote for a particular variant gene is sometimes termed a "carrier" for the condition associated with that variant gene because he or she does not manifest the disease but is capable of passing the variant gene to offspring. If two carriers mate, each child they have has a 25% chance of having two abnormal genes (and, thus, of having the condition), a 50% chance of being an unaffected carrier, and a 25% chance of not having the abnormal gene in question.

Autosomal Dominant. Some variant genes are **dominant,** that is, their effects are expressed even if their allele on the paired chromosome is normal. Consequently, people manifest autosomal dominant disorders even if they have only one variant allele in the relevant pair. "Carriers"—who would typically be affected by the disorder themselves—can pass on an autosomal dominant disorder even if their mates do not carry the same variant gene. A couple in which one person is a carrier (a heterozygote with one variant dominant allele and one normal recessive allele) and the other person is a homozygote (with two recessive normal alleles) has a 50% chance with each pregnancy of having a child with an autosomal dominant disorder and a 50% chance of having an unaffected child. Huntington's disease, achondroplastic dwarfism, and polycystic kidney disease are examples of autosomal dominant disorders.

X–linked Recessive. An X-linked recessive disorder is caused by a variant recessive allele on the X chromosome. These disorders occur most frequently in males; because males have only one X chromosome, a variant gene on that chromosome cannot be "hidden" by a dominant normal gene on the other chromosome of the pair. Since females usually have two X chromosomes, they are unlikely to have X-linked recessive disorders; the normal gene on the second X chromosome dominates and supplies the genetic information necessary for normal functioning.[2] The sons of women who are carriers of a variant X-linked recessive allele have a 50% chance of having the disorder; the daughters of such women have a 50% chance of being unaffected carriers, like their mothers. Hemophilia is an example of an X-linked recessive disorder.

X-linked Dominant. In X-linked dominant conditions, the variant allele on the X chromosome is dominant over the normal allele. Therefore, a heterozygous woman with only one variant allele would be affected, as would all males who inherited the variant allele. X-linked dominant con-

---

1. Usually, both parents would be heterozygotes; if the disease is not a lethal one, a parent could be a homozygous him or herself. Alternatively, the parent may not have the abnormal gene in his or her own somatic cells, but it may have occurred in the germ cell as a new mutation.

2. A female will have an X-linked recessive disorder only when she receives one variant X from her mother (who is probably unaffected) and another from her father, either through a germinal mutation or because he was affected by the variant gene.

ditions are rare. Vitamin-D resistant rickets is an example of a disease with this inheritance pattern.

Multifactorial Disorders. "Multifactorial" disorders result from interactions among numerous genes and environmental factors. According to a widely accepted "threshold" theory, a certain number of causative alleles must be present to place an individual "at risk" for a multifactorial disorder; in the case of birth defects, an environmental interaction at a specific time in development is also required for the disorder to be expressed. Because family members share many of the same genes, relatives of an individual with a multifactorial disorder are at an increased risk for having the "threshold" number of causative alleles, and may be exposed to similar environmental influences. Thus, the risk for first-degree relatives is greater because they share more of the same alleles than second-degree relatives do, who in turn are at greater risk than third-degree relatives, and so on. Examples of multifactorial disorders with substantial genetic causation are neural tube defects, cleft lip with or without cleft palate, and club foot.

Chromosomal Defects. A deviation in the amount of chromosomal material typically leads to abnormalities. There are several types of deviations—termed **aneuploidies**—involving too many or too few chromosomes. They include **trisomies** (when there are three copies of a particular chromosome rather than two) and **monosomies** (when one chromosome in a pair is missing). Rearrangements of portions of chromosomes are termed **translocations, inversions, deletions,** and **additions.** An individual who carries a chromosomal rearrangement in which genetic material that is missing on one chromosome has been **balanced** by the translocation of the same material on another chromosome is usually clinically normal. Such a person, however, has a higher than normal risk of having miscarriages or of giving birth to a child with a variant chromosome pattern because during meiosis too much or too little chromosomal material may be passed on to any particular germ cell.

Down syndrome, the most common cause of mental retardation, is characterized by an extra number 21 chromosome. Thus, individuals with Down syndrome (also called trisomy–21) usually have cells containing 47 rather than 46 chromosomes. Most cases arise because of spontaneous mutations during the production of germ cells or early in the cellular development after fertilization, even though the parents have a normal chromosomal pattern. Couples with a child with Down syndrome of this type face a somewhat higher risk than the rest of the population of having a second child with the condition. Sometimes, however, one parent has a balanced translocation, and meiosis results in a germ cell containing extra chromosomal fragments. In this case, the parents clearly have a higher than average risk of recurrence of the disorder in future pregnancies.

Most chromosomal abnormalities of the autosomes cause serious and widespread defects that are clinically apparent in infancy. In contrast, abnormalities of the sex chromosomes tend to be much less obvious; in fact, they may go undiagnosed until adolescence or adulthood. An example of this condition is Klinefelter syndrome.

Genetic Heterogeneity. Some disorders or defects actually may stem from a variety of sources, genetic and nongenetic. For example, retinitis pigmentosa, a rare disorder affecting the eye, can be inherited as an autosomal recessive, an autosomal dominant, or an X-linked recessive disorder. Consequently, risk estimates for future pregnancies must always consider whether the disorder could be inherited in more than one way.

LINUS PAULING,
REFLECTIONS ON THE NEW BIOLOGY

15 U.C.L.A.L.Rev. 267, 268–272 (1968).

Molecular medicine may, in one sense, be said to have originated in 1949, when it was shown that patients with the disease sickle-cell anemia have in the red cells of their blood a form of hemoglobin differing in its molecular structure from that present in the red cells of other human beings. It was evident that the molecules of sickle-cell-anemia hemoglobin are manufactured under the guidance of a mutated gene, and that the difference in molecular structure of these molecules from those of normal hemoglobin, a very small difference, is responsible for the manifestations of the disease. Sickle-cell anemia is the first disease to have been called a molecular disease.

The nature of legal problems that arise as a consequence of the development of molecular biology and molecular medicine may be illustrated by reference to sickle-cell anemia. Patients with this disease are homozygotes, persons who possess two sickle-cell genes, one of which has been inherited from the father and one from the mother. They lead a life of suffering and die an early death, almost always without progeny. The parents are heterozygotes, each having one sickle-cell gene and one normal hemoglobin ß-chain gene . . .. The manifestations of the sickle-cell gene in heterozygotes are minor. But there is some evidence that possession of the gene provides protection against malaria, and the gene was valuable for this reason. At the present time in the United States, there are about two million sickle-cell-anemia heterozygotes, and it is estimated that there are about one hundred thousand married couples with both the husband and the wife sickle-cell heterozygotes. In such a marriage, the probability of each child born that the child would be a sickle-cell-anemia homozygote, doomed to a life of suffering and an early death, is twenty-five percent. Each year about twelve hundred babies with this disease are born in the United States.

. . .

If all pairs of sickle-cell-anemia heterozygotes were to refrain from having children, there would be no infants born with this disease. This suffering would then be eliminated.

Should not all young people be tested for heterozygosity in this gene, be given the information as to whether or not they possess the gene, and advised about the consequences of marriage of two possessors of the gene? The test for heterozygosity is an extremely simple one . . .. I have suggested that there should be tatooed on the forehead of every young person a symbol showing possession of the sickle-cell gene or whatever other similar gene, such as the gene for phenylketonuria, that he has been found to possess in single dose. If this were done, two young people carrying the same seriously defective gene in single dose would recognize this situation at first sight, and would refrain from falling in love with one another. It is my opinion that legislation along this line, compulsory testing for defective genes before marriage, and some form of public or semi-public display of this possession, should be adopted.

. . .

In forming the opinion presented above I have made application of what I consider to be a basic ethical principle, the principle of minimization of human suffering. I believe that we can take actions to decrease the amount of suffering in the world, and that it is our duty to take these actions. I believe that the principle of the minimization of human suffering is a fundamental principle, essentially contained in the teachings of all great religious leaders, but also the consequence of rational consideration of ethical problems. I believe that almost all ethical problems, and legal problems not satisfactorily covered by existing law, can be solved, although often not without effort and difficulty, by the application of this principle.

If all sickle-cell-anemia heterozygotes in the United States were to be identified by the simple blood test mentioned above, and all were to refrain from marrying other similar heterozygotes, but instead married individuals who were normal with respect to their hemoglobin, no babies with sickle-cell anemia would be born. If, however, the fertility of the marriages between heterozygotes and normals were the same as for other marriages the incidence of the sickle-cell gene in the following generation would be the same as in the present generation. . . .

Here the question of the possibility of legislation about marriages of heterozygotes and about limitation of the number of children arises. I feel that the identification of heterozygotes can be and should be made compulsory, but limiting the number of progeny should be carried out through a process of education and the provision of information. This process of provision of information should, of course, be made compulsory by law.

. . .

The foregoing discussion deals with negative eugenics, the science of taking action to prevent the birth of more or less grossly defective human beings and to decrease the incidence of the factors that produce defects. The problem of positive eugenics is a far more complicated one. The difficulty in deciding what characteristics are valuable and what steps should be taken to increase the fraction of human beings with these characteristics in following generations is so great that, except for one circumstance, we might feel justified in postponing its discussion for some years or decades until the time has come when it could be carried out with greater confidence. The circumstance that prevents this postponement is the widespread use of artificial insemination by donor. I have seen estimates as high as one million of the number of children who have been born in the United States as a consequence of use of this technique. Hermann Muller was, before his death, especially outspoken in advocating that the problem of the wise selection of donors of semen for artificial insemination should be discussed. He emphasized that the majority of donors are from a professional group that, on the average, may have some desirable qualities, but that it is not the professional group that leads in intelligence (average IQ), and that failure to discuss the question of selection of donors may well be causing us to be rejecting an opportunity to improve the human race in a small but nevertheless significant way. I do not have a solution to this problem; but I agree with Muller that it is an important problem. I think that it is, in fact, a problem about which there is need for legislation, legislation which would set certain minimum standards of health, desirable characteristics, and family history for donors.

NOTES

1. Do you agree with Pauling that carrier screening should be mandatory? Consider the conclusion of the President's Commission, Screening and Counseling for Genetic Conditions 6 (1983):

> Mandatory genetic screening programs are only justified when voluntary testing proves inadequate to prevent serious harm to the defenseless, such as children, that could be avoided were screening performed. The goals of "a healthy gene pool" or a reduction in health costs cannot justify compulsory genetic screening.

Suppose the condition screened for can be successfully treated. Would mandatory screening be warranted? Would it be constitutional? Does your answer depend on whether treatment is invariably successful? Successful less than 50 percent of the time? Does your answer depend upon whether the screened individual is a newborn or a fetus? Does it depend on the risk to the infant, fetus or mother (in the case of intrauterine therapy)? The degree of the procedure's intrusion into privacy?

Screening to detect phenylketonuria (PKU), a metabolic disorder that causes brain damage after birth, is the best known example of screening for therapeutic objectives. Brain damage can be prevented if the disease is discovered shortly after birth and the infant is placed on a diet that restricts the affected child's intake of food containing phenylalanine. A study of a voluntary Maryland program for PKU screening started in 1976 indicated that the rate of parental refusal is only .05 percent. President's Commission, Screening and Counseling for Genetic Conditions 51 (1983). If the Maryland program has such high "compliance," should there be a presumption in favor of voluntary screening programs?

Until quite recently, prenatal diagnostic techniques were used primarily to detect serious genetic and congenital abnormalities for which there was no prospect of treatment. Diagnosis of such conditions often led, therefore, to the abortion of the affected fetus. More recently, diagnosis of some fetal abnormalities has led to the possibility of effective *in utero* treatment. Our increasing ability to offer intrauterine treatment may not necessarily result, however, in increased options for parents. Treating the fetus as a patient may have the consequence of extending the scope of parental obligations owed children to include fetuses. Would such an extension be desirable? See the discussion at Sec. A.1., supra.

2. Carrier screening began in the United States in the 1970s with the initiation of programs to screen for carriers of sickle cell anemia and Tay-Sachs disease. In contrast to Pauling's views, most programs were voluntary, although a few states passed laws requiring screening of persons with sickle cell anemia and the sickle cell trait. In 1972 Congress enacted the National Sickle Cell Anemia Control Act, which provided funding for research and educational activities of voluntary programs; as a result, many states changed their mandatory laws.

a. Tay-Sachs disease is caused by improper production of the enzyme hexosaminidase A, which results in severe neurological problems and death, usually by age four. This autosomal recessive disease occurs rarely in all populations but at a relatively high frequency among Jews of eastern European descent. Researchers developed a fairly simple blood test fifteen years ago, thus allowing for mass screening of people in the high risk population. Researchers attribute the success of such programs to the test's ease and accuracy, the careful community-based planning behind the screening program, the affected population's education about the program and their socio-economic status, and the confidential treatment of test results. In addition, prenatal screening was available so that an "at-risk" couple could detect the occurrence of the disease in a fetus and abort the pregnancy, if they so chose.

b. By comparison, carrier screening programs for sickle cell anemia have generally been unsuccessful. Researchers suggest that poor planning, inadequate counseling and education of the affected population about screening, lack of confidential treatment of test results, and dispersion of the Black community all have

led to the screening programs' failure. Perhaps most important, no adequate prenatal test was available early in the screening programs' history, so "at-risk" couples either had to "take their chances" of conceiving children with sickle cell anemia or forego normal reproduction and turn instead to sterilization, adoption or
artificial insemination. Moreover, knowledge about sickle cell disease has increased since Professor Pauling wrote the preceding article; the condition has
been found to be less severe in many cases than was earlier believed, and better
treatment methods have been developed. See President's Commission, Screening
and Counseling for Genetic Conditions 18–23 (1983); National Academy of Sciences, Genetic Screening: Programs, Principles and Research (1975). See also
Powledge and Fletcher, Guidelines for the Ethical, Social, and Legal Issues in Prenatal Diagnosis, 300 New Eng.J.Med. 168 (1979); Lappe et al., Ethical and Social
Issues in Screening for Genetic Disease, 286 New Eng.J.Med. 1129 (1972).

3. In many PKU screening programs, the child is screened prior to discharge
from the hospital nursery, often without the informed consent of the parent(s).
Some doctors recommend a follow-up blood test several weeks after the first to
insure that the infant does not have PKU. One study demonstrated that the follow-up test detects only one case in 560,000. Should cost-benefit analysis be
used to determine whether a mandatory follow-up test should be required?

For further discussion of screening for metabolic disorders, see National Academy of Sciences, Genetic Screening: Programs, Principles and Research 23–93
(1975); Annas, Mandatory PKU Screening: The Other Side of the Looking Glass,
72 Am.J.Pub. Health 1401 (1982); P. Reilly, Genetics, Law and Social Policy
(1977); Levy and Mitchell, The Current Status of Newborn Screening, Hospital
Practice, July 1982, at 89; Sepe, Levy and Mount, An Evaluation of Routine Follow-up Blood Screening of Infants for Phenylketonuria, 300 New Eng.J.Med. 606
(1979); President's Commission, Screening and Counseling for Genetic Conditions 12–15 (1983).

4. Should individuals be permitted unrestricted access to genetic services?
The President's Commission concluded that prenatal diagnosis to determine the
sex of the fetus and selective abortion should be "discouraged" because it would
be Draconian (and probably impossible) to prohibit it. John Fletcher, an ethicist
who has written extensively on genetics, takes a different view.

Two types of parents request fetal sex identification by amniocentesis: the
first group risk transmitting a sex-linked hereditary disorder and the second
want to select the gender of their next child. Physicians generally encourage
the first type of parent but discourage the second.

Prenatal diagnosis for sex choice is controversial because of ethical objections to the use of abortion for such a reason and because of the question of
whether amniocentesis . . . can prudently be used for this purpose. The
issue is complex and involves many competing ethical claims.

I have re-evaluated my position on this issue . . . .

My earlier position was based on four main points. In the first place, I
argued that parents with this request ought to be discouraged because sex is
not a disease. I saw prenatal diagnosis as a tool that ethically could be used to
diagnose hereditary diseases or congenital defects in the fetus. Secondly, I
stressed that abortion for sex choice could contribute to social inequality between the sexes because of a preference for male offspring. Thirdly, I criticized sex choice as a "frivolous" reason for abortion that could not be successfully defended in the company of serious moral persons. My fourth point was
that amniocentesis was a scarce resource in the light of the total number of
pregnancies at risk. Requests for fetal sex identification could swamp an already overloaded system or delay laboratory work in cases of serious genetic
diseases.

. . .

My re-evaluation assumes that the basis for the policy of discouragement is
the belief of most physicians who perform prenatal diagnosis that abortion for
sex choice is morally unjustifiable. Those who reason as I did also use the

scarce-resource argument and are wary of the use of prenatal diagnosis for "social engineering" to plan the sex of children. In practice, however, discouragement based on opposition to abortion for sex choice is weightier than the other two reasons. Most of us have an uneasy conscience about the number of abortions performed in the United States and about the lack of moral seriousness with which abortion is sometimes requested and carried out. We have preferred to use prenatal diagnosis in the context of saving fetal lives. I personally believe that sex choice is not a compelling reason for abortion. The first moral response of most who think about the issue is close to queasiness. Yet, the issue does not turn on the validity of opposition to abortion for sex choice. The issue turns on the validity of the legal rules on abortion defined by the Supreme Court, which do not require that a woman state reasons in a public or medical forum for early to mid-trimester abortion. . . .

Is this the best rule to apply in abortion? Yes, if one holds, as I do, that the woman's right to decide is the overriding consideration in the abortion issue. The rationale for the legal rule omitting a test of reasons is that a woman has the right to control her reproduction and the risks involved in a pregnancy. To employ public or medical tests of reasons provides opportunities to obstruct and defeat society's obligation to grant women the freedom to determine their own reproductive futures. To prevent obstruction of self determination, it is better to have no public tests of reasons.

. . .

Given the ethical and legal posture discussed above, one must be willing to accept the fact that some abortions will be performed for trivial reasons. The existence of some trivial reasons should not deter us from the larger goal of protecting the right of women to make such decisions in the first place. That is what is at stake in the issue under discussion. My major argument is that it is inconsistent to support an abortion law that protects the absolute right of women to decide and, at the same time, to block access to information about the fetus because one thinks that an abortion may be foolishly sought on the basis of the information.

. . .

Fletcher, Ethics and Amniocentesis for Fetal Sex Identification, 301 New Eng.J. Med. 550 (1979). If we allow parents to determine the sex of their offspring will it upset the approximate balance of numbers between the sexes? Some research indicates a preference for males. See When Sex Choice is Cheap and Easy, Will the Boys Outnumber the Girls? 8 Hastings Ctr.Rep. 2 (1978).

5. Genetic diseases occur infrequently in the general population. Consequently, genetic screening has usually been restricted to "high-risk" groups because of the high number of false positives that are a likely result of broad-based screening and the expense that general screening would entail. The President's Commission concluded that "equity is best served" by such an approach. Genetic Screening and Counseling 84 (1983). It recommended the following:

Access to screening may take account of the incidence of genetic disease in various racial or ethnic groups within the population without violating principles of equity, justice and fairness.

Id. at 8. Do you agree? Is it likely that such a policy would have the effect of stigmatizing persons in "high-risk" groups? Is the burden of having a child with a genetic disease any less for a person who is not a member, or does not know that he or she is a member, of a "high-risk" group? If it is acceptable to take into account the incidence of genetic disease within racial and ethnic groups, should it also be permissible to take into account the incidence of disease in different age categories? If data shows increasing incidence of a disease with increasing age, can any cutoff point be justified? For many years only women age 35 or older have been counseled about amniocentesis in order to detect the presence of chromosomal defects (unless there were other risk factors present). With respect to that practice, the President's Commission recommended:

> First, as limitations on access move from the research context to implicit (or explicit) policies on the availability of a genetic service they should be subjected to review by a broadly based process that will be responsive to the full range of relevant considerations, to changes in the facts over time, and to the needs of the excluded group(s). Second in light of the facts concerning this particular policy the Commission believes the common medical practice of only informing women age 35 or older about amniocentesis should be reevaluated to determine whether fairness and equity would support a more flexible policy that made amniocentesis more generally available to younger women.

Id. at 81. Do you agree? Is it likely that a more flexible policy would overburden available resources?

6. The future of genetic screening lies with the development of a "map" of "gene markers," as described in Chapter 1, which make it possible to detect the existence of an abnormal gene without having to measure its metabolic or other effects. This capability has already proven itself in the prenatal diagnosis of hemoglobin disorders like sickle-cell anemia, and in the presymptomatic diagnosis of Huntington's Disease. Early diagnosis of this disease, a fatal neurological condition, is beneficial because it usually does not become manifest until an afflicted person is at least in his or her twenties or thirties and may already have children, each of whom has a 50 percent chance of affliction. The new techniques may make it possible to relieve a great deal of suffering; they also raise some possibilities that might prove less beneficial. Should parents and physicians "screen" embryos (*in utero* or *in vitro*) until they find one with the desired genes—or at least without undesired genes? Should health and life insurance companies be allowed to screen before issuing policies? If we permit such screening, what does that do to notions of "spreading the risk" or other aspects of fairness? Should these issues be addressed by the medical profession or by government? If by the government, at what level, state or federal?

Consider Maryland's approach to decisionmaking with respect to genetic screening. Should other states adopt this approach? Should the statute be modified? In what way(s)? Will Maryland's structure work equally well with future genetic screening issues?

COMMISSION ON HEREDITARY DISORDERS

43 Md. Code Ann. §§ 814–821.

§ 814. Legislative findings and declarations.

The General Assembly hereby finds and declares:

(a) That each person in the State of Maryland is entitled to the highest level of health care attainable, and to protection from inadequate health services not in the person's best interest;

(b) That hereditary disorders are often costly, tragic, and sometimes deadly burdens to the health and well-being of the citizens of Maryland;

(c) That detection through screening of hereditary disorders can lead to the alleviation of the disability of some hereditary disorders and contribute to the further understanding and accumulation of medical knowledge about other hereditary disorders which may lead to their eventual alleviation or cure;

(d) That there are different severities of hereditary disorders, that some hereditary disorders have little effect on the normal functioning of individuals, and that some hereditary disorders may be wholly or partially alleviated through medical intervention and treatment;

(e) That all or most persons are carriers of some disorders which may be transmitted through the hereditary process, and that carriers of hereditary disorders are substantially unaffected by that fact;

(f) That carriers of hereditary disorders should not be stigmatized, and should not be discriminated against by any person within the State of Maryland;

(g) That medical knowledge concerning the identification and diagnosis of different hereditary disorders, and the treatment and cure of different hereditary disorders, is rapidly expanding, and often at an uneven rate, resulting in the discovery and identification of hereditary disorders long before treatment or cure for such disorders can be found;

(h) That specific legislation designed to alleviate the problems associated with specific hereditary disorders may tend to be inflexible in the face of rapidly expanding medical knowledge;

(i) That State policy regarding hereditary disorders should be made with full public knowledge, in light of expert opinion, and should be constantly reviewed to consider changing medical knowledge and ensure full public protection;

(j) That participation of persons in hereditary disorder programs in the State of Maryland should be wholly voluntary, and that all information obtained from persons involved in hereditary disorder programs in the State should be held strictly confidential;

(k) That in order to ensure that State policies and programs for any hereditary disorder comply with the principles established herein, and that in order to preserve and protect the freedom, health, and well-being of the citizens of the State of Maryland from improper treatment or advice, discrimination, violation of privacy, or undue anxiety resultant from programs on hereditary disorders, the legislature finds it necessary to establish a Commission on Hereditary Disorders.

§ 815. Commission created; composition; appointment, terms, compensation and expenses of members; vacancies; meetings; chairman and vice-chairman.

(a) The Commission on Hereditary Disorders is hereby created.

(b) The Commission on Hereditary Disorders, hereinafter referred to as the Commission, shall be composed of eleven members. The members shall be appointed as provided below. . . .

(c) One member of the Commission shall be a member of the Senate of the State of Maryland and shall be appointed by the President of the Senate. One member of the Commission shall be a member of the House of Delegates of the State of Maryland and shall be appointed by the Speaker of the House of Delegates. Five members of the Commission shall be appointed by the Governor at his sole discretion, provided that these members are not health professionals nor involved in the administration or ownership of any health care institution or health insurance organization, nor the spouse of a health professional, administrator, or owner. Four of the members shall be licensed medical physicians knowledgeable in the diagnosis and treatment of hereditary disorders who shall be appointed as follows: one each from a list of three names submitted at least three months prior to the date for making appointments by each of the following bodies: the Monumental Medical Society of Baltimore; the Medical and Chirurgical Faculty of Maryland; the faculty of the

University of Maryland School of Medicine; and the faculty of the Johns Hopkins University medical institutions. If the list is not so submitted, the Governor shall appoint, at his sole discretion, a member who is a licensed medical physician knowledgeable in the diagnosis and treatment of hereditary disorders. Five representatives of the Department of Health and Mental Hygiene, one of whom shall represent the statewide comprehensive health planning agency, shall be appointed by the Secretary of the Department of Health and Mental Hygiene, to serve as ex officio, nonvoting members of the Commission.

. . .

(e) The full Commission shall meet at least twice each year. . . . The Governor shall appoint a chairman to serve for one year from the date of the first meeting of the Commission. Thereafter, the Commission shall choose from among its number a chairman and a vice-chairman by majority vote, who shall hold their respective offices for two years and until their successors are chosen. Such officers may succeed themselves.

. . .

§ 817. Powers of Commission; meaning of "hereditary disorder."

(a) In order to preserve and protect the health and welfare of the citizens of the State of Maryland, the Commission on Hereditary Disorders shall have the power to:

(1) Establish and promulgate rules, regulations, and standards for the detection and management of hereditary disorders in the State of Maryland;

(2) Gather and disseminate information to further the public's understanding of hereditary disorders;

(3) Establish systems for recording information obtained in programs regulated by the Commission;

(4) Reevaluate on a continuous basis the need for and efficacy of State programs on hereditary disorders;

(5) Investigate unjustified discrimination resulting from identification as a carrier of a hereditary disorder, and make recommendations as it deems necessary to end such unjustified discrimination. Such powers to investigate discrimination resulting from identification as a carrier of a hereditary disorder shall not preclude, or need to be antecedent to, any person or group of persons seeking redress through any other means.

(b) For the purposes of this subtitle, hereditary disorder means any disorder resultant from the genetic material DNA (Deoxyribonucleic acid) which is transmitted from a parent or parents to his or her child;

§ 818. Principles governing rules, regulations and standards promulgated by Commission.

The rules, regulations, and standards established and promulgated by the Commission shall be in accord with the principles established herein. The Commission may establish such other principles not contrary to those established hereunder as it deems necessary to promote and protect the public health and safety. Such principles shall include:

(a) That the public, especially communities and groups of persons particularly affected by programs on hereditary disorders, has been consulted before any rules, regulations, and standards are adopted by the Commission;

(b) That the incidence of each hereditary disorder and the cost of detection and management of each hereditary disorder be considered by the Commission; and that where appropriate, State and national experts in the medical, psychological, ethical, social, and economic effects of programs for the detection and management of hereditary disorders be consulted by the Commission.

(c) That information on the operation of all programs on hereditary disorders within the State, except for confidential information obtained from participants in such programs, be open and freely available to the public;

(d) That procedures established for use in programs, facilities, and projects be accurate, provide maximum information, and be subject to minimum misinterpretation, and that these procedures be regularly subjected to review;

(e) That no test or tests be performed on any individual over 18 years of age over the objection of any such individual or any individual under 18 or an incompetent over the objections of his parent or guardian and that no test or tests be performed unless such individual, parent or guardian is fully informed of the purpose or purposes of testing for hereditary disorders and the carrier state of hereditary disorders, and is given a reasonable opportunity to object to such testing;

(f) That no program require mandatory participation, restriction of childbearing, or be a prerequisite to eligibility for, or receipt of any other service or assistance from or to participation in any other program;

(g) That counseling services for hereditary disorders be available to all persons involved in screening programs, that such counseling be nondirective; and that such counseling emphasize informing the client and not require restriction of childbearing;

(h) That all participants in programs on hereditary disorders be protected from undue physical or mental harm, be informed of the nature of risks involved in participation in such a program or project, be informed of the nature and cost of available therapies or maintenance programs for those affected by hereditary disorders, and be informed of the possible benefits and risks of such therapies and programs;

(i) That all unambiguous diagnostic results be made available to the individual over 18 years of age or if the individual is under 18 or an incompetent to his parent or guardian, through a physician or other source of health care; and that all information obtained from any individual, or from specimens from any individual be held confidential and be considered a confidential medical record except for such information as the individual, parent or guardian consents to be released, provided that the individual is informed of the scope of the information requested to be released and the purpose or purposes for releasing such information; and except for statistical data compiled without reference to the identity of any individual;

(j) That all information gathered by the Commission, or by other agencies, entities and individuals conducting programs and projects on hereditary disorders, other than statistical information and information which the individual allows to be released through his informed consent, be kept in code; and that public and private access to individual patient data be limited to data compiled without the individual's name.

. . .

2. GENETIC COUNSELING

AUBREY MILUNSKY,
GENETIC COUNSELING: PRINCIPLES AND PRACTICE

in The Prevention of Genetic Disease and Mental Retardation
64–71 (A. Milunsky ed. 1975).

Genetic counseling is a communication process concerning the occurrence and the risks of recurrence of genetic disorders within a family. The aim of such counseling is to provide the consultand(s) * with the fullest comprehension of all the implications of the disease in question and all the possible available options. A further goal, and intrinsic to the expressed aims of counseling, is helping families through their problems, their decision-making, and their adjustments. While the primary strategy of counseling is to achieve understanding that leads to rational decisions, there is also the obvious hope that such decisions will indeed lead to a decrease in the incidence of serious genetic disease and will prevent the suffering of both patient and family. Most counselors would probably agree with the broad definition and goals of counseling as stated above. It has already become apparent, however, that opinions about how this information should be conveyed and whether or not it should be withheld vary among counselors.

. . .

GUIDING PRINCIPLES IN GENETIC COUNSELING

. . .

Accurate Diagnosis

Genetic counseling simply cannot begin without the establishment of an accurate diagnosis. It is a common experience for clinical geneticists to see patients referred for counseling for whom the alleged diagnosis is clearly incorrect. Great care and attention must be exercised either in confirming the diagnosis or in obtaining sufficient data to ensure the certainty of the diagnosis in question. Earlier photographs of a previously deceased offspring, autopsy reports, hospital records of other affected family members, results of carrier detection tests elsewhere, and other similar information may be crucial in the confirmation of the exact diagnosis. Failure to reach a proper diagnosis is not rare, however.

Data may be insufficient, tests may still be inconclusive, the syndrome may not have been described before, or other complicated considerations may induce hesitation in diagnosis. In such instances counseling could be very misleading. . . .

Noncoercive and Nondirective Counseling

The role of the counselor is to assist consultands in recognizing *their personal* major priorities crucial to their decision-making. The counselor's expertise is his or her special perspective which allows discernment of problems often not immediately obvious to the consultand(s). Hence,

_____
* The term "consultand" denotes the person or persons receiving counseling.

the previously unrecognized, highly developed distaste of one parent for living with a retarded child in the house may become apparent to the other spouse only during counseling. Their ackowledgment of this facet may have a compelling effect on their decision-making. Failure to consider the *short- and long-term effects* of a child with genetic disease on the siblings is common. Indeed, with their feelings and concerns about *themselves* often foremost in their minds, prospective parents often give little attention to the possible effects of the particular genetic disease on a *future child.* Hence, the counselor should *not* be seen in the role of advising or telling consultands what they ought to do, or how they should act, but in helping them recognize and anticipate issues and problems before they occur.

. . . In line with this thinking, the majority of counselors have indeed perceived themselves as being nondirective. [D]ata indicate that 54 per cent of counselors tend to leave all decisions to the parents, and only 7 per cent either always tell the parents what they would do in the same circumstance or give outright advice as to what parents "ought" to do. However, the data further suggest that 64 per cent of counselors report that it has always been appropriate to inform consultands in a way that would guide them toward an appropriate decision. This apparent contra-indication in the data highlights the difficult dilemma and possible paradox confronting counselors. In the main, counselors try to remain impartial and objective as they communicate all the information consultands require for rational decision-making. Paradox invariably arises when counselors recognize their parallel desire to decrease the frequency of serious genetic disease and to maintain their objectivity. . . .

. . . .

Parental Counseling

. . .

. . . [It] is a mandatory principle that genetic counseling be provided to *both* parents at the same time. The complex issues of guilt, culpability, family prejudices, serious differences of opinion between spouses, and ignorance and fear—to mention only a few—form the basis of this important principle. Too often the more concerned parent comes alone to counseling with resulting emotional chaos, incorrect interpretation to the spouse, or lack of appreciation of the true risk situation. No substitute—including letters—can take the place of face-to-face discussions, with opportunities for questions and interchange of unacknowledged ignorance or issues.

. . . .

NOTES

1. There has been much debate over whether counselors should be merely information givers or also advisors. This debate highlights the two most prevalent views of genetic counseling: genetic counseling as preventative medicine, in which the counselor focuses on the severity and recurrence of a disease; and genetic counseling as "counseling" in the traditional sense, in which the counselor focuses on the values and expectations of his or her clients. Should the counselor force prospective parents to realize the seriousness of a disease that their future children may have? For example, should the counselor take the parents to a hospital to see the crippling effects of a disease that their future children may bear? Or should the counselor merely explain the nature and potential severity of a

genetic disease and explore options with the prospective parents? Why is one approach or another preferable?

Most counselors agree that their primary job is to relay information to their clients in order to prevent disease, lessen counselee anxiety and advance understanding of genetics. In a recent survey of genetic counselors, many (those who focus on a client's expectations and values) felt that to achieve these goals, counselors should also discuss so-called "psychosocial issues" such as the client's religious beliefs, attitudes toward contraception, economic situation, family effects, social stigma, alternative forms of parenthood, extended family member concerns and sterilization. See Sorenson and Culbert, Professional Orientations to Contemporary Genetic Counseling in Genetic Counseling: Facts, Values, and Norms 85–102 (Capron et al. eds. 1979). Is it appropriate for an individual trained in health care to be playing the role of moral advisor? Should these roles be left to the clergy and/or psychotherapists?

Does Milunsky's view that the majority of genetic counselors prefer the nondirective approach indicate a practice different from physicians' usual practices? What do you think accounts for the difference?

2. Genetic screening for a specific genetic condition sometimes detects additional information that could be traumatic for the person screened or related individuals. Should genetic counselors always provide such information? Consider the recommendation of the President's Commission:

> Decisions regarding the release of incidental findings . . . or sensitive findings . . . should begin with a presumption in favor of disclosure, while still protecting a client's other interests, as determined on an individual basis. In the case of nonpaternity, accurate information about the risk of the mother and putative father bearing an affected child should be provided even when full disclosure is not made.

Screening and Counseling for Genetic Conditions 7 (1983).

Suppose, for example, in the course of testing for Down's Syndrome, the counselor discovered that the fetus is an XY-female. The XY-female will have undescended testes and no internal female reproductive organs. The testes pose a substantial threat of causing cancer unless they are surgically removed, and the lack of a uterus and ovaries leaves the XY-female sterile. Yet, the person in all other important aspects will be a female. The XY-female and her parents might suffer severe psychological trauma upon disclosure of the condition, yet the health risks and consequences the condition creates strongly compel prompt disclosure. Do you agree that the counselor should divulge the information to the prospective parents? What considerations control your determination? Would you apply these same factors to all situations concerning decisions whether or not to divulge additional genetic information?

Suppose genetic screening disclosed that a tested fetus or child has a genetic disease, such as sickle cell anemia or Tay-Sachs disease, but medical records of the putative father show that he is not a carrier of the disease. Should the nonpaternity be explicitly disclosed? Should the counselor disclose only the fact that the fetus is affected? Do you agree with Milunsky that both parents should be counseled at the same time? The President's Commission determined that no one strategy would be suitable for all situations. Do you agree? Would a better approach be to inform all couples before testing that nonpaternity might be discovered?

3. A related issue is whether to disclose genetic information to relatives who could benefit from the information. The President's Commission favors disclosure in some circumstances. It concluded:

> The requirements of confidentiality can be overridden and genetic information released to relatives (or their physicians) if and only if the following four conditions are met: (a) reasonable efforts to elicit voluntary consent to disclosure have failed; (b) there is a high probability both that harm will occur if the information is withheld and that the disclosed information will actually be used to avert harm; (c) the harm that identifiable individuals would suffer if the

information is not disclosed would be serious; and (d) appropriate precautions are taken to ensure that only the genetic information needed for diagnosis and/or treatment of the disease in question is disclosed.

> • When it is known in advance that the results of a proposed screening program could be uniquely helpful in preventing serious harm to the biological relatives of individuals screened, it may be justifiable to make access to that program conditional upon prior agreement to disclose the results of the screening.

Screening and Counseling for Genetic Conditions 6 (1983).

Has the Commission provided for an adequate balancing of a test subject's confidentiality privilege against any claims relatives might have on relevant genetic information? Why? How might this conflict arise in real-life situations? See discussion of access to genetic information in AID and surrogate relationships, Sec. 2.A., supra. For general discussion, see Reilly, Genetics, Law, and Social Policy (1977).

4. When genetic counseling began in the 1920's, "experts" in social reform did most of the work; biologists and medical researchers assumed the task in the late 1950's. In the past ten years, genetic counselors have been mostly pediatricians and Ph.D's in genetics or biology. Psychotherapists and members of the clergy have also played roles in counseling. The use of nurses, nurse practitioners, midwives, professional social workers, and physician's assistants in genetic counseling is becoming more common, especially in large clinical settings. The use of these professionals has been advocated for several reasons: it is much less expensive than employing doctors; these professionals have broader experience in interpersonal communication than do M.D.'s or researchers; busy doctors will have more time to deal with the more serious cases; these professionals are more likely to have socioeconomic, racial and educational backgrounds similar to those of their patients; and, finally, the general hierarchical structure in medicine will be softened.

The American Board of Medical Genetics has instituted a certification process involving examination of the several categories of genetic professionals. In December 1981 approximately five hundred professionals passed the first exam. President's Commission, Screening and Counseling for Genetic Conditions 36–37 (1983).

Should genetic counselors be licensed? Health care workers have criticized state licensing programs for their failure to control the quality of health care; economists have pointed to the increased medical costs consumers must bear as a result of limiting the entry of more individuals into a practice area. Is the field of genetics too controversial and important for the government to ignore? For an argument against state licensing, see Reilly, Professional Identification: Issues in Licensing and Certification in Genetic Counseling: Facts, Values, and Norms 291–305 (Capron et al. eds. 1979). For additional discussion of the role of licensure in controlling the quality of health services provided consumers, see Ch. 3, Sec. A.4., supra.

BERMAN v. ALLAN

Supreme Court of New Jersey, 1979.
80 N.J. 421, 404 A.2d 8.

PASHMAN, J. In Gleitman v. Cosgrove, 49 N.J. 22, 227 A.2d 689 (1967), decided 12 years ago, this Court refused to recognize as valid causes of action either a claim for "wrongful life" asserted on behalf of a physically deformed infant or a claim for "wrongful birth" put forth by the infant's parents. . . . In this case, we are called upon to assess the continued validity of both of our holdings in *Gleitman.*

On September 11, 1975, Paul and Shirley Berman, suing both in their own names and as Guardians *ad litem* for their infant daughter Sharon, instituted the present malpractice action against Ronald Allan and Michael Attardi, medical doctors licensed by the State of New Jersey. Two causes of action were alleged. The first, a claim for damages based upon "wrongful life," was asserted by Mr. Berman on behalf of the infant Sharon. The second, a claim denominated "wrongful birth," sought compensation for injuries suffered by the parents in their own right.

The factual allegations underlying each of these prayers for relief can be briefly summarized. From February 19 until November 3, 1974, Mrs. Berman, while pregnant with Sharon, was under the care and supervision of Drs. Allan and Attardi, both of whom are specialists in gynecology and obstetrics. At the time of her pregnancy, Mrs. Berman was 38 years of age. On November 3, Sharon was born afflicted with Down's Syndrome—a genetic defect commonly referred to as mongolism.

Plaintiffs allege that defendants deviated from accepted medical standards by failing to inform Mrs. Berman during her pregnancy of the existence of a procedure known as amniocentesis. This procedure involves the insertion of a long needle into a mother's uterus and the removal therefrom of a sample of amniotic fluid containing living fetal cells. Through "karyotype analysis"—a procedure in which the number and structure of the cells' chromosomes are examined—the sex of the fetus as well as the presence of gross chromosomal defects can be detected. . . . Prenatal diagnosis of genetic abnormalities is potentially available for approximately 60 to 90 metabolic defects, including Tay-Sachs Disease and Down's Syndrome. . . .

Due to Mrs. Berman's age at the time of her conception, plaintiffs contend that the risk that her child, if born, would be afflicted with Down's Syndrome was sufficiently great that sound medical practice at the time of pregnancy required defendants to inform her both of this risk and the availability of amniocentesis as a method of determining whether in her particular case that risk would come to fruition. Had defendants so informed Mrs. Berman, the complaint continues, she would have submitted to the amniocentesis procedure, discovered that the child, if born, would suffer from Down's Syndrome, and had the fetus aborted.

As a result of defendants' alleged negligence, the infant Sharon, through her Guardian *ad litem*, seeks compensation for the physical and emotional pain and suffering which she will endure throughout life because of her mongoloid condition. Mr. and Mrs. Berman, the child's parents, request damages in their own right both for the emotional anguish which they have experienced and will continue to experience on account of Sharon's birth defect, and the medical and other costs which they will incur in order to properly raise, educate and supervise the child.

On November 4, 1977, the trial judge granted summary judgment in favor of defendants on the ground that plaintiffs had failed to state any actionable claim for relief. . . . On December 22, 1977, plaintiffs filed a notice of appeal to the Appellate Division. While the matter was pending before the appellate judges, we directly certified the case to this Court on our own motion.

. . . .

II

The claim for damages asserted on behalf of the infant Sharon has aptly been labeled a cause of action grounded upon "wrongful life." Sharon does not contend that absent defendants' negligence she would have come into the world in a normal and healthy state. There is no suggestion in either the pleadings below or the medical literature which we have scrutinized that any therapy could have been prescribed which would have decreased the risk that, upon birth, Sharon would suffer from Down's Syndrome. Rather, the gist of the infant's complaint is that had defendants informed her mother of the availability of amniocentesis, Sharon would never have come into existence.

As such, this case presents issues different from those involved in malpractice actions where a plaintiff asserts that a defendant's deviation from sound medical practices *increased* the probability that an infant would be born with defects. Nor are we here confronted with a situation in which an individual's negligence while a child was in gestation caused what otherwise would have been a normal and healthy child to come into the world in an impaired condition. Here, defendants' alleged negligence neither caused the mongoloid condition nor increased the risk that such a condition would occur. In the words of the *Gleitman* majority, "the infant plaintiff [asserts] . . . not that [she] should have been born without defects but [rather] that [she] should not have been born at all. . . ." 49 N.J. at 28, 227 A.2d at 692. In essence, Sharon claims that her very life is "wrongful."

. . .

The primary purpose of tort law is that of compensating plaintiffs for the injuries they have suffered wrongfully at the hands of others. As such, damages are ordinarily computed by "comparing the condition plaintiff would have been in, had the defendants not been negligent, with plaintiff's impaired condition as a result of the negligence." Id. at 28, 227 A.2d at 692. In the case of a claim predicated upon wrongful life, such a computation would require the trier of fact to measure the difference in value between life in an impaired condition and the "utter void of nonexistence." *Gleitman,* supra, 49 N.J. at 28, 227 A.2d 689. Such an endeavor, however, is literally impossible. As Chief Justice Weintraub noted, man, "who knows nothing of death or nothingness," simply cannot affix a price tag to non-life. Id. at 63 (Weintraub, C.J., concurring & dissenting).

Nevertheless, although relevant to our determination, we would be extremely reluctant today to deny the validity of Sharon's complaint solely because damages are difficult to ascertain. The courts of this and other jurisdictions have long held that where a wrong itself is of such a nature as to preclude the computation of damages with precise exactitude, it would be a "perversion of fundamental principles of justice to deny all relief to the injured [party], and thereby relieve the wrongdoer from making any amend for his acts." To be sure, damages may not be determined by mere speculation or guess and, as defendants emphasize, placing a value upon non-life is not simply difficult—it is humanly impossible. Nonetheless, were the *measure* of damages our sole concern, it is possible that some judicial remedy could be fashioned which would redress plaintiff, if only in part, for injuries suffered. . . .

Difficulty in the *measure* of damages is not, however, our sole or even primary concern. Although we conclude, as did the *Gleitman* majority, that Sharon has failed to state an actionable claim for relief, we base our result upon a different premise—that Sharon has not suffered any damage cognizable at law by being brought into existence.

One of the most deeply held beliefs of our society is that life—whether experienced with or without a major physical handicap—is more precious than non-life. See In re Quinlan, 70 N.J. 10, 19 & n. 1, 355 A.2d 647 (1976). Concrete manifestations of this belief are not difficult to discover. The documents which set forth the principles upon which our society is founded are replete with references to the sanctity of life. The federal constitution characterizes life as one of three fundamental rights of which no man can be deprived without due process of law. U.S.Const., Amends. V and XIV. Our own state constitution proclaims that the "enjoying and defending [of] life" is a natural right. N.J.Const. (1947), Art. I, § 1. The Declaration of Independence states that the primacy of man's "unalienable" right to life is a "self-evident truth." Nowhere in these documents is there to be found an indication that the lives of persons suffering from physical handicaps are to be less cherished than those of non-handicapped human beings.

. . .

Finally, we would be remiss if we did not take judicial notice of the high esteem which our society accords to those involved in the medical profession. The reason for this is clear. Physicians are the preservers of life.

No man is perfect. Each of us suffers from some ailments or defects, whether major or minor, which make impossible participation in all the activities the world has to offer. But our lives are not thereby rendered less precious than those of others whose defects are less pervasive or less severe.

We recognize that as a mongoloid child, Sharon's abilities will be more circumscribed than those of normal, healthy children and that she, unlike them, will experience a great deal of physical and emotional pain and anguish. We sympathize with her plight. We cannot, however, say that she would have been better off had she never been brought into the world. Notwithstanding her affliction with Down's Syndrome, Sharon, by virtue of her birth, will be able to love and be loved and to experience happiness and pleasure—emotions which are truly the essence of life and which are far more valuable than the suffering she may endure. To rule otherwise would require us to disavow the basic assumption upon which our society is based. This we cannot do.

Accordingly, we hold that Sharon has failed to state a valid cause of action founded upon "wrongful life."

III

The validity of the parents' claim for relief calls into play considerations different from those involved in the infant's complaint. As in the case of the infant, Mr. and Mrs. Berman do not assert that defendants increased the risk that Sharon, if born, would be afflicted with Down's Syndrome. Rather, at bottom, they allege that they were tortiously injured because Mrs. Berman was deprived of the option of making a meaningful decision as to whether to abort the fetus, see *Gleitman*, supra, 49 N.J. at 63–65, 227 A.2d 689 (Weintraub, C.J., concurring & dissenting)—a decision which, at least during the first trimester of pregnancy, is not subject to state interference, see Roe v. Wade, 410 U.S. 113, 93 S.Ct. 705, 35 L.Ed.2d 147 (1973). They thus claim that Sharon's "birth"—as opposed to her "life"—was wrongful.

Two items of damage are requested in order to redress this allegedly tortious injury: (1) the medical and other costs that will be incurred in order to properly raise, supervise and educate the child; and (2) compensation for the emotional anguish that has been and will continue to be experienced on account of Sharon's condition.

. . .

. . . The Supreme Court's ruling in *Roe v. Wade,* supra, clearly establishes that a woman possesses a constitutional right to decide whether her fetus should be aborted, at least during the first trimester of pregnancy. Public policy now supports, rather than militates against, the proposition that she not be impermissibly denied a meaningful opportunity to make that decision.

As in all other cases of tortious injury, a physician whose negligence has deprived a mother of this opportunity should be required to make amends for the damage which he has proximately caused. Any other ruling would in effect immunize from liability those in the medical field providing inadequate guidance to persons who would choose to exercise their constitutional right to abort fetuses which, if born, would suffer from genetic defects. Accordingly, we hold that a cause of action founded upon wrongful birth is a legally cognizable claim.

Troublesome, however, is the measure of damages. As noted earlier, the first item sought to be recompensed is the medical and other expenses that will be incurred in order to properly raise, educate and supervise the child. Although these costs were "caused" by defendants' negligence in the sense that but for the failure to inform, the child would not have come into existence, we conclude that this item of damage should not be recoverable. In essence, Mr. and Mrs. Berman desire to retain all the benefits inhering in the birth of the child—i.e., the love and joy they will experience as parents—while saddling defendants with the enormous expenses attendant upon her rearing. Under the facts and circumstances here alleged, we find that such an award would be wholly disproportionate to the culpability involved, and that allowance of such a recovery would both constitute a windfall to the parents and place too unreasonable a financial burden upon physicians.

The parents' claim for emotional damages stands upon a different footing. In failing to inform Mrs. Berman of the availability of amniocentesis, defendants directly deprived her—and, derivatively, her husband—of the option to accept or reject a parental relationship with the child and thus caused them to experience mental and emotional anguish upon their realization that they had given birth to a child afflicted with Down's Syndrome. We feel that the monetary equivalent of this distress is an appropriate measure of the harm suffered by the parents deriving from Mrs. Berman's loss of her right to abort the fetus. See *Gleitman,* supra, 49 N.J. at 64–65, 227 A.2d 689 (Weintraub, C.J., concurring & dissenting).

Unlike the *Gleitman* majority, we do not feel that placing a monetary value upon the emotional suffering that Mr. and Mrs. Berman have and will continue to experience is an impossible task for the trier of fact. In the 12 years that have elapsed since *Gleitman* was decided, courts have come to recognize that mental and emotional distress is just as "real" as physical pain, and that its valuation is no more difficult. Consequently, damages for such distress have been ruled allowable in an increasing number of contexts. Moreover, . . . to deny Mr. and Mrs. Berman redress for their injuries merely because damages cannot be measured with precise exactitude would constitute a perversion of fundamental principles of justice. . . .

Consequently, we hold that Mr. and Mrs. Berman have stated actionable claims for relief. Should their allegations be proven at trial, they are entitled to be recompensed for the mental and emotional anguish they have suffered and will continue to suffer on account of Sharon's condition.

Accordingly, the judgment of the trial court is affirmed in part and reversed in part, and this case remanded for a plenary trial.

HANDLER, J., concurring in part and dissenting in part.

. . .

The Court now recognizes that the parents of the impaired child have a cause of action for the doctors' breach of duty to render competent medical advice and services and that they are entitled to compensation for their mental and emotional suffering over the birth of their damaged child. I agree with this. However, I hold to a somewhat broader view of mental and emotional injury in these circumstances and would also include as an element of these damages impaired parenthood or parental capacity.

The Court does not, in its opinion, recognize as sustainable a cause of action on behalf of the child. On this, I differ. The child, in my view, was owed directly during its gestation, a duty of reasonable care from the same physicians who undertook to care for its mother—then expectant—and that duty, to render complete and competent medical advice, was seriously breached. The child, concededly, did not become defective because of the physicians' dereliction; nevertheless, it suffered a form of injury or loss in having been born of parents whose parental capacity may have been substantially diminished by the negligence of their doctors. This is a loss to the child which should be recompensed. . . .

I

. . .

Because of the unique nature of the tort, involving as it does the denial of the opportunity to decide whether to become the parents of a handicapped child, the suffering of the parents assumes another, important dimension. There should be recognized in the stressful setting of this case the reality of moral injury. Such injury may be thought of as the deprivation of moral initiative and ethical choice. Cf. Gleitman v. Cosgrove, supra, 49 N.J. at 64–65, 227 A.2d 689 (Weintraub, C.J., concurring and dissenting). Persons, confronted with the awesome decision of whether or not to allow the birth of a defective child, face a moral dilemma of enormous consequence. They deal with a profound moral problem. To be denied the opportunity—indeed, the right—to apply one's own moral values in reaching that decision, is a serious, irreversible wrong. Cf. In re Quinlan, 70 N.J. 10, 355 A.2d 647 (1976). Shorn of ethical choice in bringing into the world a defective human being, some individuals will be torn by moral conflict. Moral suffering in this sense may be felt keenly by a person who, as matter of personal conscience, would choose not to allow the birth of such a child. The moral affront, however, is not diminished because the parents, if given the choice, would have permitted the birth of the child. The crucial moral decision, which was theirs to make, was denied them.

A full perception of the mental, emotional—and, I add, moral—suffering of parents in this situation reveals another aspect of their loss. Mental, emotional and moral suffering can involve diminished parental capacity. Such incapacity of the mother and father *qua* parents is brought about by the wrongful denial of a reasonable opportunity to learn of and anticipate the birth of a child with permanent defects, and to prepare for the heavy obligations entailed in rearing so unfortunate an individual. Such parents may experience great difficulty adjusting to their fate and accepting the child's impairment as nature's verdict. While some individuals confronted by tragedy respond magnificently and become exemplary parents, others do not. See e.g., Becker v. Schwartz, 46 N.Y.2d 401, 413 N.Y.S.2d 895, 386 N.E.2d 807 (Ct.App.1978) in which the parents subsequently put their mongoloid child up for adoption. N.Y. Times, Feb. 17, 1979, at 23, col. 1. Individuals suffering this form of parental incapacity or dysfunction are denied to a great extent the fuller joys, satisfaction and pride which comes with successful and effective parenting. This may endure for some time during the early developmental years of the child. Impaired parenthood, so understood, constitutes another dimension of the injury and loss suffered by plaintiffs in this case. In this sense, impaired parenthood, together with mental and emotional and moral suffering, should be recognized and compensated as elements of damages.

III

. . .

The Court proceeds on the notion that the claims of the infant plaintiff are based on her "wrongful life". . . . . It is acknowledged by the majority that this thesis—injury consisting of a wrongful life—poses insuperable analytical problems in admeasuring damages. . . . Nevertheless, the Court does not rest its rejection of the infant's claim upon the inordinate difficulty of measuring damages for her "wrongful life", as did the Court in *Gleitman*. Rather, the Court now says: "[As a matter of law,] Sharon has not suffered any damage cognizable [in] law by being brought into existence." Sharon, the Court states, has been given life and even with a handicap it "is more precious than non-life."

An adequate comprehension of the infant's claims under these circumstances starts with the realization that the infant has come into this world and is here, encumbered by an injury attributable to the malpractice of the doctors. That injury does not consist of the child's afflicted condition; her affliction was not the doctor's doing. Rather, the injury consists of a diminished childhood in being born of parents kept ignorant of her defective state while unborn and who, on that account, were less fit to accept and assume their parental responsibilities. The frightful weight of the child's natural handicap has been made more burdensome by defendants' negligence because her parents' capacity has been impaired; they are less able to cope with the extra-heavy parental obligations uniquely involved in providing a child so afflicted with the unfaltering love, constant devotion and extraordinary care such a child specially requires.

There has been some judicial appreciation of the notion that a diminished childhood may be the consequence of impaired parental capacity. In Berger v. Weber, 82 Mich.App. 199, 267 N.W.2d 124 (Ct.App.1978), the Court recognized a cause of action in a suit brought by a mentally retarded child to recover damages for the loss of society, companionship, love and affection of her mother as a result of injuries sustained by the mother in an auto accident. The mother had sustained both physical and psychological injuries and could no longer continue to administer to the peculiar needs of her retarded daughter. The Court upheld a cause of action for such losses when a parent is "severely" injured. It recognized that the loss of parental guidance and training can have a severe impact on a child's development and personality and found the reasons for denying a cause of action, such as lack of precedent, uncertainty of damages, possibility of double recovery and potential for a multiplicity of suits, unpersuasive. The Court also thought it anomalous to say that a child suffers a compensable loss in a wrongful death action when the parent is killed but not when a parent is injured so severely that he or she cannot perform the parental function. It concluded that the magnitude of the child's loss outweighs the factors which would militate against allowing recovery.

Plausibly, the child's injury and loss in the form of diminished childhood can be viewed as a derivative claim based solely on the parents' injury. . . .

Solution to this legal conundrum—whether and how to protect the infant's interests—should not turn on labels or definitions. It is to be emphasized in this case that the doctors' medical malpractice encompasses the child. Their negligence consists of the failure to render proper advice to Mrs. Berman as an *expectant* mother. Indisputably in this relationship the doctors were caring for the unborn child as well as the mother; the duty they owed Mrs. Berman enveloped a duty to the unborn child. The breach of that duty affects both. "The risk created by a negligent act of one who stands in a physician-patient relationship is of enormous consequence to mother and child." Friel v. Vineland Obst. and Gynecological Professional Assoc., supra, 166 N.J.Super. at 591, 400 A.2d at 153. Justice Jacobs offered a similar observation, dissenting in *Gleitman:* "While the wrong was done directly to Mrs. Gleitman, in truth and reality it vitally affected her entire immediate family." 49 N.J. at 50, 227 A.2d at 704.

No one is contending that any medical procedure consistent with sound medical practice would have served to avert or lessen the physicial defects of the infant, which she acquired congenitally, at the moment of conception. But the duty here owed was that of advising the parents fully as to the probability of the impaired physical condition of their unborn child and of the availability of a test which could have proved or disproved that medical prediction. The negligent breach of that duty carried with it the foreseeable consequence that the impaired infant would be born of parents whose parental fitness would be seriously undermined as a result of this professional mishandling, with the equally foreseeable result that the unborn child would be burdened with a diminished childhood.

    . . . [C]oncededly, the kind of injury suffered by the child in this context may not be readily divisible from that suffered by her wronged parents. There is nevertheless an intelligible distinction between a parent whose loss may involve the unhappiness, frustration and guilt which stem from inadequate parental performance, and the child whose loss is in lessened parental love, devotion and care. It would be unjust not to recognize the child's loss as compensable. As Justice Jacobs stressed in *Gleitman,* "such compensation as is received from the defendants . . . should be dedicated primarily to [the infant's] care and the lessening of [her] difficulties." 49 N.J. at 50, 227 A.2d at 704. To the extent the child's loss may mirror that of the parents, the court can avoid duplicating compensation by careful instructions to the jury, special interrogatories and by the molding of any award.

. . .

NOTE

Cf. Becker v. Schwartz, 46 N.Y.2d 401, 413 N.Y.S.2d 895, 386 N.E.2d 807 (1978) (parents of Down's Syndrome infant may recover damages for economic but not emotional injuries from physician who failed to inform thirty-seven year old mother of risks of pregnancy and availability of amniocentesis). The *Becker* litigation took an ironic twist with the revelation that another couple had adopted the child involved during the litigation. New York Times, Feb. 17, 1979, at 24, col. 1.

Although *Berman* confined recovery for negligent genetic counseling to the parents, a few courts have allowed the child to recover as well. The leading cases include Turpin v. Sortini, 31 Cal.3d 220, 182 Cal.Rptr. 337, 643 P.2d 954 (1982) (child born with hereditary deafness may recover special but not general damages for expenses she will incur when no longer supported by her parents and for special training and equipment from doctor who failed to inform parents that condition of first child was hereditary prior to conception of plaintiff) and Harbeson v. Parke-Davis, Inc., 98 Wn.2d 460, 656 P.2d 483 (1983) (under Federal Tort Claims Act, child can recover extraordinary expenses to be incurred during her lifetime as result of her congenital defects after Air Force doctors negligently failed to inform parents of danger of Dilantin, a nonconvulsant drug prescribed to ease mother's epileptic seizures).

Prior to *Turpin,* California allowed child recovery in Curlender v. Bio-Science Laboratories, 106 Cal.App.3d 811, 165 Cal.Rptr. 477 (1980), where the court held that a child born with Tay-Sachs disease had a cause of action against physicians who had failed to inform her parents that they were carriers of Tay-Sachs disease. *Curlender* left open the possibility that genetically deformed children could sue their parents for knowingly proceeding with the birth. Id., at 829, 165 Cal.Rptr., at 488. In response, the California legislature amended its civil code to provide:

(a) No cause of action arises against a parent of a child based upon the claim that the child should not have been conceived or, if conceived, should not have been allowed to have been born alive.

(b) The failure or refusal of a parent to prevent the live birth of his or her child shall not be a defense in any action against a third party, nor shall the failure or refusal be considered in awarding damages in any such action.

(c) As used in this section "conceived" means the fertilization of a human ovum by a human sperm.

Cal.Civ.Code § 43.6 (West 1981).

Can we fairly judge whether professionals have breached their obligations of care when diagnosis of genetic disease is in such a state of flux, when the professional group involved is relatively new and varied, and when what is at stake is nondisclosure where the "treatment" is to abort the affected fetus? As the cases indicate, courts have had difficulty in defining the wrong that might have been done. The issue has been hotly debated. See, e.g., Furrow, Diminished Lives and Malpractice: Courts Stalled in Transition, 10 Law Med. & Health Care 100 (1982); Taub, Wrongful Life—Its Problems Are Not Just Semantic: A Reply to Furrow, 10 Law Med. & Health Care 208 (1982).

For thoughtful discussion of these issues, see generally Capron, Tort Liability in Genetic Counseling, 79 Colum.L.Rev. 618 (1979); Note, Father and Mother Know Best: Defining Liability of Physicians for Inadequate Genetic Counseling, 87 Yale L.J. 1488 (1978).

Chapter Nine

EMERGING ENERGY SOURCES

A. SOLAR POWER

---

1. GOVERNMENT SUPPORT FOR SOLAR ENERGY

JIMMY CARTER, SOLAR ENERGY

President's Message to Congress, 15 Weekly Comp.Pres.Doc.
1097, 1099–1101 (1979).

On Sun Day, May 3, 1978 we began a national mobilization in our country toward the time when our major sources of energy will be derived from the sun. On that day, I committed our Nation and our Government to developing an aggressive policy to harness solar and renewable sources of energy. I ordered a major government-wide review to determine how best to marshal the tools of the government to hasten the day when solar and renewable sources of energy become our primary energy resources. As a result of that study, we are now able to set an ambitious goal for the use of solar energy and to make a long term commitment to a society based largely on renewable sources of energy. . . .

The government-wide survey I commissioned concluded that many solar technologies are available and economical today. These are here and now technologies ready for use in our homes, schools, factories, and farms. Solar hot water heating is competitive economically today against electric power in virtually every region of the country. Application of passive design principles that take into account energy efficiency and make maximum use of the direct power of the sun in the intrinsic design of the structure is both good economics and good common sense. Burning of wood, some uses of biomass for electricity generation, and low head hydropower have repeatedly been shown to be cost competitive.

Numerous other solar and renewable resources applications are close to economic competitiveness, among them solar space heating, solar industrial process heat, wind-generated electricity, many biomass conversion systems, and some photovoltaic applications.

We have a great potential and a great opportunity to expand dramatically the contribution of solar energy between now and the end of this century. I am today establishing for our country an ambitious and very important goal for solar and renewable sources of energy. It is a challenge to our country and to our ingenuity.

We should commit ourselves to a national goal of meeting one fifth—20 percent—of our energy needs with solar and renewable resources by the end of this century. This goal sets a high standard against which we

1361

can collectively measure our progress in reducing our dependence on oil imports and securing our country's energy future. It will require that all of us examine carefully the potential solar and renewable technologies hold for our country and invest in these systems wherever we can. . . .

The Department of Energy has a particularly significant responsibility in aiding the development and encouraging the use of solar energy technologies, in providing back-up information and training for users of solar, and, generally, in directing our government-funded research and development program to ensure that future solar and renewable technologies are given the resources and institutional support that they need.

As a governnment-wide study, the Domestic Policy Review of Solar Energy has provided a unique opportunity to draw together the disparate functions of government and determine how best to marshal all of the government's tools to accelerate the use of solar and renewable resources. As a result of that study, the set of programs and funding recommendations that I have already made and am adding to today will provide more than $1 billion for solar energy in fiscal year 1980, with a sustained Federal commitment to solar energy in the years beyond. The fiscal year 1980 budget will be the highest ever recommended by any President for solar energy. It is a significant milestone for our country.

This $1 billion of Federal expenditures—divided between incentives for current use of solar and renewable resources such as tax credits, loans and grants, support activities to develop standards, model building codes, and information programs, and longer term research and development—launches our Nation well on the way toward our solar goal. It is a commitment we will sustain in the years ahead. . . .

U.S. DEPARTMENT OF ENERGY, SOLAR ENERGY

Program Summary Document, III–I—III–4, VI–38—VI–39 (1980).

The DOE Solar Energy Program encompasses the development of energy supply systems which derive energy directly or indirectly from the sun. The Program comprises: Biomass Energy Systems, Photovoltaic Energy Systems, Wind Energy Conversion Systems, Solar Thermal Power Systems, Ocean Systems, Agricultural and Industrial Process Heat, Active Heating and Cooling Systems, and Passive and Hybrid Heating and Cooling Systems. A brief description of the eight major technology programs is provided below:

Biomass Energy Systems. Biomass is renewable organic material such as terrestrial or aquatic vegetation, or animal, agricultural and forestry residues. This material contains stored chemical energy produced by plants from solar energy. Biomass can be collected and burned directly, or converted to liquid fuels (fuel oils, alcohols), or gaseous fuels (medium-Btu gas, synthetic natural gas) or other energy-intensive products (hydrogen, ammonia, petrochemical substitutes) that can supplement or replace similar products made from conventional fossil fuels.

Photovoltaic Energy Systems. Sunlight is converted into electricity by "solar cells" which can be made from a number of different semiconductor materials. Intensive research is under way to create improved, high-efficiency, lower cost photovoltaic devices. In general, there are two generic types—"flat-plate arrays" that operate on direct sunlight at normal intensity and "concentrators" that increase the intensity of sunlight as much as two thousand times.

Wind Energy Conversion Systems. These systems employ a wind-driven machine to turn an electric generator or mechanical device. Wind derives its energy from the sun's heating of the earth's surface and atmosphere.

Solar Thermal Power Systems. The sun's heat is concentrated and used to heat water or some other fluid to provide industrial process heat or to drive a turbogenerator. The primary objective is to provide an alternative to fossil fuels for industrial and utility applications. Applications that provide both heat and electricity called "total energy systems" are also included in this area.

Ocean Systems. Ocean-stored solar energy has potential as a renewable source of baseload electricity and energy-intensive products. Systems currently being studied and developed include ocean thermal energy conversion, salinity gradients, ocean currents, and wave energy. These concepts, at various stages of development, use resources that are available in different geographic areas.

Agricultural/Industrial Process Heat. Agricultural and industrial process heat applications use a range of solar collection systems to produce hot air, hot water, and steam within three primary temperature ranges (low, less than 212°F; intermediate, 212° to 350°F; and high, greater than 350°F) to support farm and industrial operations. Depending on the system design and application, heat from these collection systems is injected into the process directly or through heat exchangers. The actual energy uses and range of temperatures are more diverse than in building space heating applications and require specific process designs.

Active Heating and Cooling. Active solar heating and cooling systems employ predominately flat plate collector technology. Modular or site built collection systems convert insolation into thermal energy by absorbing radiation. Mechanical subsystems transfer the heat into the building using air or liquids, where it goes directly to heat space, heat service water, or is stored for later use. Swimming pool heating, domestic water heating, and to some extent space heating, are the leading commercial applications. Solar cooling technology, which provides for more economic year-round employment of solar collection systems, has not yet been demonstrated to be cost-effective.

Passive and Hybrid Heating and Cooling. Passive and hybrid solar buildings employ designs that maximize the benefits of natural energy flows and minimize dependence on conventional energy resources and mechanical equipment. Passive solar heating systems use elements of the building to collect, store, and distribute energy. Passive cooling also uses elements of the building to store and distribute energy and, when prevailing conditions are favorable, to discharge heat to the cooler part of the environment (sky, atmosphere, ground). When other solar technologies (active systems or photovoltaics, for example) are integrated in the design, the result is considered a hybrid solar application. . . .

. . . .

Congress passed the National Energy Act in late 1978, in five acts: the Public Utility Regulatory Policies Act of 1978, the Energy Tax Act of 1978, the National Energy Conservation Policy Act, the Powerplant and

Industrial Fuel Use Act of 1978, and the Natural Gas Policy Act of 1978. There is no single, unified portion of the energy package dealing with solar energy. Instead, references are scattered through the legislation. The most important are found in the National Energy Tax Act and the National Energy Conservation Policy Act.

The Energy Tax Act provides tax credits for home installation of solar energy devices, including wind energy and geothermal equipment (30% of the first $2,000 and 20% of the next $8,000 spent) for a maximum credit of $2,200. For example, a homeowner installing $3,000 worth of solar collectors would be eligible for a tax credit of $800. This provision is retroactive to the date of the President's energy message, April 20, 1977, and extends through 1985. The Act provides for a 10% investment tax credit (in addition to the permanent investment credit) to businesses or industries which install solar, wind, or biomass conversion systems. The Act also eliminates Federal excise taxes on purchases of "gasohol," an automotive fuel consisting of a mix of gasoline and at least 10% alcohol.

Besides the National Energy Act, there were a number of other laws that were enacted during the 95th Congress (1977–78) which have an impact on solar energy. Two in particular deserve mention. The Photovoltaic RD&D Act (P.L. 95–570) proposed a 10-year, $1.5 billion research and development effort and 'sets goals of doubling the production of photovoltaic cells annually with a cumulative production total of 4 million kW by 1988. The Military Construction Authorization Act (P.L. 95–356) requires that all new family housing and 25% of all other military construction use solar equipment where cost-effective. The numerous other laws which were passed include: financial incentives for small businesses and farmers, establishment of the Energy Extension Service to disseminate information to the public, and several programs to encourage international application of solar energy.

The National Energy Conservation Policy Act could have a significant impact on the development of solar energy in the United States. The Act authorized a 2-year program to install $100 million of solar heating and cooling equipment on federal buildings and a 3-year program to purchase $98 million of photovoltaic cells for remote federal installations. It also authorizes the Federal National Mortgage Association to make loans at reduced rates to homeowners installing solar systems, federal home improvement loan insurance for solar systems, and 50–50 matching grants to help public and private nonprofit schools and hospitals (as well as local governments) implement energy conservation measures, including solar installation in their buildings.

The National Energy Conservation Policy Act requires that utility companies inform their customers about energy conservation measures, including solar systems, and arrange financing if asked to do so. An advance notice of final rules was recently published for the Residential Conservation Service. Other provisions touching utilities and solar energy are found in the Public Utility Regulatory Policies Act, which prohibits discriminatory standby (backup) rates and sellback rates for small power generators and cogenerators. In the long run, the federal action should increase the installation of photovoltaic, wind and low head hydro systems.

Two other parts of the energy package, the Powerplant and Industrial Fuel Use Act and the Natural Gas Policy Act, are expected to indirectly encourage the use of solar energy. The Fuel Use Act prohibits, with many exceptions, the use of natural gas and oil in new construction of electric power plants and large industrial boilers. While the major result will be an increase in the use of coal, solar systems may be more widely used for some applications. The Natural Gas Act may make solar energy more competitive by the phased lifting of the ceiling on natural gas prices. . . .

NOTE

One difficulty with long-term planning in research and development is the sensitivity of the budget to the changing political climate. President Carter's ambitious goals for solar energy in the year 2000 became more difficult to reach in light of federal funding cutbacks in the Reagan administration. The federal solar budget of about $400 million in 1980 was cut to roughly $200 million by 1983. Compare U.S. Dept. of Energy, Solar Energy: Program Summary Document III–4 (1980) with U.S. Office of Management and Budget, Budget of the United States Government, Fiscal Year 1984 App. I–J4 (1983).

The Reagan administration reduced spending for solar projects on the ground that, apart from basic research, the private sector should carry the burden of developing solar energy. U.S. Office of Management and Budget, Special Analysis, Budget of the United States Government, Fiscal Year 1984 K–4 (1983). As noted in Ch. 4, Sec. B.2., supra, the case for federal spending is generally regarded as stronger for basic research than for products ready to be sold commercially. Some believe, however, that energy, because of its importance to national security and because of its environmental impact, requires federal intervention beyond the basic research stage. Do you think the private marketplace will provide the appropriate level of solar energy development? Is your answer the same for nuclear energy? See Ch. 2, Sec. B.1, supra. Do the tax credits provided in the Energy Tax Act intrude on the market more or less than direct federal spending? Many states supplement the federal tax credits with various state tax incentives for solar devices. See S. Kraemer, Solar Law 271–290 (1978).

The very term "solar energy" may mislead federal policy makers. Whether or not biomass energy, which comes from burning vegetation, should technically be called "solar," should it compete, for budgetary purposes, with a relatively new, high-technology area like photovoltaics, which convert sunlight directly to electricity? This is a microcosm of the general problem involved in formulating federal science policy in the absence of a science budget—two items compete for funding because they are both viewed as "solar," even though in many other respects they have little in common. See Ch. 4, Sec. B.2., supra. For an analysis of the relationship between federal agency organization and the development of solar power, see Rhodes, Implementing Federal Solar Policy: Learning From the Nuclear Power Experience, 3 J. Energy L. & Pol'y. 189 (1983).

AMERICAN PAPER INSTITUTE, INC. v. AMERICAN ELECTRIC POWER SERVICE CORP.

Supreme Court of the United States, 1983.
461 U.S. —, 103 S.Ct. 1921, 76 L.Ed.2d 22.

JUSTICE MARSHALL delivered the opinion of the Court.

This case concerns two rules promulgated by the Federal Energy Regulatory Commission (FERC) pursuant to § 210 of the Public Utility Regulatory Policies Act of 1978 (PURPA), 16 U.S.C. § 824a–3 (Supp. V). The first rule requires electric utilities to purchase electric energy from cogenerators and small power producers at a rate equal to the purchasing utility's full avoided cost, i.e., the cost the utility would have incurred had it generated the electricity itself or purchased the electricity from another source. The second rule requires utilities to make such interconnections with cogenerators and small power producers as are necessary to effect purchases or sales of electricity authorized by PURPA. The Court of Appeals held that FERC had not adequately explained its adoption of the full-avoided-cost rule, and that it exceeded its statutory authority in promulgating the interconnection rule. 675 F.2d 1221 (CADC 1982). We reverse.

I

A

Section 210 of PURPA was designed to encourage the development of cogeneration and small power production facilities.[1] As we noted in FERC v. Mississippi, 456 U.S. 742, 750, 102 S.Ct. 2126, 2132, 72 L.Ed.2d 532 (1982) (footnote omitted), "Congress believed that increased use of these sources of energy would reduce the demand for traditional fossil fuels," and it recognized that electric utilities had traditionally been "reluctant to purchase power from, and to sell power to, the nontraditional facilities." Accordingly, Congress directed FERC to prescribe, within one year of the statute's enactment, rules requiring electric utilities to deal with qualifying cogeneration and small power production facilities. PURPA § 210(a), 16 U.S.C. § 824a–3(a) (Supp. V). With respect to the purchase of electricity from cogeneration and small power production facilities, Congress provided that the rate to be set by the Commission

"(1) shall be just and reasonable to the electric consumers of the electric utility and in the public interest, and

(2) shall not discriminate against qualifying cogenerators or qualifying small power producers.

No such rule prescribed under subsection (a) of this section shall provide for a rate which exceeds the incremental cost to the electric utility of alternative electric energy." PURPA § 210(b), 16 U.S.C. § 824a–3(b) (Supp. V).

Following rulemaking proceedings, FERC promulgated regulations governing transactions between utilities and those cogeneration and small power production facilities, designated as "qualifying facilities," 18 CFR 292.201–292.207, that may invoke the provisions of PURPA to sell electricity to and purchase electricity from utilities.

The first regulation at issue in this case, 18 CFR 292.304(b)(2) (1982), requires a utility to purchase electricity from a qualifying facility at a rate equal to the utility's full avoided cost. The utility's full avoided cost is "the cost to the electric utility of the electric energy which, but for the purchase from such cogenerator or small power producer, such utility would generate or purchase from another source." PURPA § 210(d), 16 U.S.C. § 824a–3(d) (Supp. V). See 18 CFR 292.101(b)(6) (1982) (the term full "avoided costs" used in the regulations is the equivalent of the term "incremental cost of alternative electric energy" used in § 210(d) of PURPA). In its order accompanying the promulgation of this rule, FERC explained its decision to set the rate at full avoided cost rather than at a

---

1. The statute defines a "cogeneration facility" as a facility that produces both electric energy and steam or some other form of useful energy, such as heat. 16 U.S.C. § 796(18)(A) (Supp. V). A "small power production" facility is a facility that has a production capacity of not more than 80 megawatts and produces electric power from biomass, waste, or renewable resources such as wind, water, or solar energy. 16 U.S.C. § 796(17)(A) (Supp. V).

level that would result in direct rate savings for utility customers by permitting a utility to obtain energy at a cost less than the cost to the utility of producing the energy itself or purchasing it from an alternative source. 45 Fed.Reg. 12214 (Feb. 15, 1980). The Commission emphasized the need to provide incentives for the development of cogeneration and small power production:

> "[I]n most instances, if part of the savings from cogeneration and small power production were allocated among the utilities' ratepayers, any rate reductions will be insignificant for any individual consumer. On the other hand, if these savings are allocated to the relatively small class of qualifying cogenerators and small power producers, they may provide a significant incentive for a higher growth rate of these technologies." Id., at 12222.

The Commission noted that "ratepayers and the nation as a whole will benefit from the decreased reliance on scarce fossil fuels, such as oil and gas, and the more efficient use of energy." Ibid.

FERC rejected proposals that it set the rate for the purchase of electricity from qualifying facilities at a fixed percentage of the purchasing utility's full avoided cost:

> "[I]n most situations, a qualifying cogenerator or small power producer will only produce energy if its marginal cost of production is less than the price he receives for its output. If some fixed percentage is used, a qualifying facility may cease to produce additional units of energy when its costs exceed the price to be paid by the utility. If this occurs, the utility will be forced to operate generating units which either are less efficient than those which would have been used by the qualifying facility, or which consume fossil fuel rather than the alternative fuel which would have been consumed by the qualifying facility had the price been set at full avoided cost." Id., at 12222–12223.

The second regulation at issue here, 18 CFR 292.303 (1982), provides that electric utilities shall purchase electricity made available by qualifying facilities, sell electricity to qualifying facilities upon request, and, most important for present purposes, "make such interconnections with any qualifying facility as may be necessary to accomplish purchases or sales under this subpart." 18 CFR 292.303(c)(1) (1982). An interconnection is a physical connection that allows electricity to flow from one entity to another.

In its order the Commission rejected the contention that § 210(e)(3) of PURPA requires it to afford an opportunity for an evidentiary hearing to any utility that is unwilling to make an interconnection with a qualifying facility that has invoked the provisions of PURPA to enter into a purchase or sale with the utility. Section 210(e)(3) provides in relevant part:

> "No qualifying small power production facility or qualifying cogeneration facility may be exempted under this subsection from—
>
> . . .
>
> (B) the provisions of section 210 . . . or 212 of the Federal Power Act or the necessary authorities for enforcement of any such provision under the Federal Power Act . . . ."

Sections 210 and 212 of the Federal Power Act (FPA), 16 U.S.C. §§ 824i and 824k (Supp. V), describe the procedure to be followed by FERC when an electric utility, Federal power marketing agency, cogenerator, or small power producer applies for an order requiring another such facility to make an interconnection. Section 210 provides that, upon receipt of an application for an order requiring an interconnection, the Commission shall issue notice to each affected State regulatory authority, utility, Federal power marketing agency, and owner or operator of a cogeneration facility or small power production facility, and to the public, § 210(b)(1), 16 U.S.C. § 824i(b)(1) (Supp. V), afford an opportunity for an evidentiary hearing, § 210(b)(2), 16 U.S.C. § 824i(b)(2) (Supp. V), and issue an order approving the application only if it determines that approval

"(1) is in the public interest,

(2) would—

(A) encourage overall conservation of energy or capital,

(B) optimize the efficiency of use of facilities and resources, or

(C) improve the reliability of any electric utility system or Federal power marketing agency to which the order applies, and

(3) meets the requirements of [§ 212 of the FPA]."

Section 212 of the FPA, 16 U.S.C. § 824k (Supp. V), provides that an order approving an interconnection under § 210 may be issued only if the Commission determines that the interconnection is not likely to result in a reasonably ascertainable uncompensated loss for any electric utility, cogenerator, or small power producer, impose an undue burden on any such facility, unreasonably impair the reliability of any electric utility, or impair the ability of any electric utility to supply adequate service to its customers.

In concluding that an evidentiary hearing under the FPA is not required prior to an interconnection necessary to complete a purchase or sale authorized by PURPA, the Commission reasoned that § 210(a) of PURPA "provides a general mandate for the Commission to prescribe rules necessary to encourage cogeneration and small power production." 45 Fed.Reg., at 12221. The Commission also emphasized that "a basic purpose of section 210 of PURPA is to provide a market for the electricity generated by small power producers and cogenerators," and that "to require facilities to go through the complex procedures set forth in section 210 of the Federal Power Act would, in most circumstances, significantly frustrate" the achievement of that purpose. Ibid.

. . .

II

The first question before us is whether FERC's action in promulgating the full-avoided-cost rule was "arbitrary, capricious, [or] an abuse of discretion." 5 U.S.C. § 706(2)(A). We cannot answer this question simply by noting that the full-avoided-cost rule is within the range of permissible rates that Congress established in § 210(b) of PURPA. The Commission plainly has the authority to adopt a full-avoided-cost rule, for PURPA sets full avoided cost as the maximum rate that the Commission may prescribe. Whether the Commission properly exercised that authority is a separate issue. To decide whether the Commission's action was "arbitrary, capricious, [or] an abuse of discretion," we must determine whether the agency adequately considered the factors relevant to choosing a rate that will best serve the purposes of the statute, and whether the agency committed "a clear error of judgment." Citizens to Preserve Overton Park v. Volpe, 401 U.S. 402, 416, 91 S.Ct. 814, 823, 28 L.Ed.2d 136 (1971).

FERC's explanation of its reasons for promulgating the full-avoided-cost rule must be examined in light of the criteria set forth in § 210(b) of PURPA, 16 U.S.C. § 824a–3(b) (Supp. V), which provides that the purchase rate established by the Commission must be "just and reasonable to the electric consumers of the electric utility and in the public interest" and must not discriminate against qualifying facilities. Since the full-avoided-cost rule plainly satisfies the nondiscrimination requirement, we need only consider whether FERC adequately explained why the rule is "just and reasonable to the electric consumers of the electric utility and in the public interest."

We cannot accept respondents' suggestion, Brief at 9 and n. 4, that the "just and reasonable" language in § 210(b) was intended to require that the purchase rate be set " 'at the lowest possible reasonable rate consistent with the maintenance of adequate service in the public interest.' " Atlantic Refining Co. v. Public Service Comm'n of New York, 360 U.S. 378, 388, 79 S.Ct. 1246, 1253, 3 L.Ed.2d 1312 (1959), quoting the original version of the Natural Gas Act. Simply on the basis of the statutory language, we would be reluctant to infer that Congress intended the terms "just and reasonable," which are frequently associated with cost-of-service utility rate-making, see, e.g., NAACP v. FPC, 425 U.S. 662, 666, 96 S.Ct. 1806, 1809, 48 L.Ed.2d 284 (1976), to adopt a cost-of-service approach in the very different context of cogeneration and small power production by nontraditional facilities. The legislative history confirms, moreover, that Congress did not intend to impose traditional ratemaking concepts on sales by qualifying facilities to utilities. The Conference Report states in pertinent part:

"It is not the intention of the conferees that cogenerators and small power producers become subject . . . to the type of examination which is traditionally given to electric utility rate applications to determine what is the just and reasonable rate that they should receive for their electric power. The conferees recognize that cogenerators and small power producers are different from electric utilities, not being guaranteed a rate of return on their activities generally or on the activities vis-a-vis the sale of power to the utility and whose risk in proceeding forward in the cogeneration or small power production enterprise is not guaranteed to be recoverable.

". . . [C]ogeneration is to be encouraged under this section and therefore the examination of the level of rates which should apply to the purchase by the utility of the cogenerator's or small power producer's power should not be burdened by the same examination as are utility rate applications, but rather in a less burdensome manner. The establishment of utility type regulation over them would act as a significant disincentive to firms interested in cogeneration and small power production." H.R.Conf.Rep. No. 95–1750, supra, at 97–98, U.S.Code Cong. & Admin.News 1978, pp. 7831–7832.

In contrast, a subsequent passage in the Conference Report explicitly states that the "just and reasonable" language of § 210(c), 16 U.S.C. § 824a–3(c), which concerns sales *by* utilities *to* qualifying facilities, "*is* intended to refer to traditional utility rate-making concepts." H.R.Conf. Rep. No. 95–1750, supra, at 98, U.S.Code Cong. & Admin.News 1978, p. 7832 (emphasis added).

The Commission did not ignore the interest of electric utility consumers "in receiving electric energy at equitable rates." H.R.Conf.Rep. No.

95–1750, supra, at 97, U.S.Code Cong. & Admin.News 1978, p. 7831.[9] The Commission recognized that the full-avoided-cost rule would not directly provide any rate savings to electric utility consumers, but deemed it more important that the rule could "provide a significant incentive for a higher growth rate" of co-generation and small power production, and that "these ratepayers and the nation as a whole will benefit from the decreased reliance on scarce fossil fuels, such as oil and gas, and the more efficient use of energy." 45 Fed.Reg., at 12222. As the Commission explained, a purchase rate established at a fixed percentage of avoided cost would discourage production of electric energy by qualifying facilities whose marginal costs exceeded the rate that a purchasing utility would be required to pay under this approach, whereas those same facilities would retain an incentive to produce energy under the full-avoided-cost rule so long as their marginal costs did not exceed the full avoided cost of the purchasing utility. Id., at 12222–12223.

The Commission would have encountered considerable difficulty had it attempted to determine an appropriate rate less than full avoided cost. A wide variety of technologies are used in cogeneration and small power production, including internal combustion engines, steam turbines, combustion turbines, windmills, solar cells, and hydro turbines. Facilities may vary greatly in capacity. It would have been extremely difficult, if not impossible, for the Commission to make any useful estimate of the amount of cogeneration and small power production that would be discouraged by setting the rate at a level lower than full avoided cost.

It bears emphasizing that the full-avoided-cost rule is not as inflexible as might appear at first glance. First, any state regulatory authority and any nonregulated utility may apply to the Commission for a waiver of the rule. A waiver may be granted if the applicant demonstrates that a full-avoided-cost rate is unnecessary to encourage cogeneration and small power production. 18 CFR 292.403 (1982). Second, a qualifying facility and a utility may negotiate a contract setting a price that is lower than a full-avoided-cost rate. 18 CFR 202.301(b)(1) (1982). Because the full-avoided-cost rule is subject to revision by the Commission as it obtains experience with the effects of the rule, it may often be in the interest of a qualifying facility to negotiate a long-term contract at a lower rate. The Commission's rule simply establishes the rate that applies in the absence of a waiver or a specific contractual agreement.

Under these circumstances it was not unreasonable for the Commission to prescribe the maximum rate authorized by PURPA. The Commission's order makes clear that the Commission considered the relevant factors and deemed it most important at this time to provide the maximum incentive for the development of cogeneration and small power production, in light of the Commission's judgment that the entire country will

---

9. We interpret the "just and reasonable" language of § 210(b) to require consideration of potential rate savings for electric utility consumers. Of course, even when utilities purchase electric energy from qualifying facilities at full avoided cost rather than at some lower rate, the rates the utilities charge their customers will not be increased, for by hypothesis the utilities would have incurred the same costs had they generated the energy themselves or purchased it from other sources. Moreover, a utility's existing rates will ordinarily have been determined to be "just and reasonable" by the appropriate state regulatory authority. But it does not follow that the full-avoided-cost rule is necessarily "just and reasonable to the electric consumers of the electric utilities" within the meaning of § 210(b) of PURPA. Unless the "just and reasonable" language is to be regarded as mere surplusage, it must be interpreted to mandate consideration of rate savings for consumers that could be produced by setting the rate at a level lower than the statutory ceiling.

ultimately benefit from the increased development of these technologies and the resulting decrease in the nation's dependence on fossil fuels. The Commission has a statutory mandate to set a rate that is "in the public interest," and as this Court stated in NAACP v. FPC, supra, 425 U.S., at 669, 96 S.Ct., at 1811, "the words 'public interest' in a regulatory statute . . . take meaning from the purposes of the regulatory legislation." The basic purpose of § 210 of PURPA was to increase the utilization of cogeneration and small power production facilities and to reduce reliance on fossil fuels. See FERC v. Mississippi, supra, 456 U.S. at 750, 102 S.Ct., at 2132. At this early stage in the implementation of PURPA, it was reasonable for the Commission to prescribe the maximum rate authorized by Congress and thereby provide the maximum incentive for the development of cogeneration and small power production.

III

Absent § 210(e)(3) of PURPA, there would be no doubt as to the validity of the Commission's interconnection rule. Section 210(a) of PURPA, 16 U.S.C. § 824a–3(a) (Supp. V), provides the Commission with general authority to promulgate

> "such rules as it determines necessary to encourage cogeneration and small power production which rules require electric utilities to offer to—
>
> (1) sell electric energy to qualifying cogeneration facilities and qualifying small power production facilities and
>
> (2) purchase electric energy from such facilities."

The authority to promulgate such rules as are necessary to require purchases and sales plainly encompasses the power to promulgate rules requiring utilities to make physical connections with qualifying facilities in order to consummate purchases and sales authorized by PURPA. No purchase or sale can be completed without an interconnection between the buyer and seller.

In the absence of a specific provision to the contrary, the Commission's power to promulgate rules under PURPA requiring interconnections would not be negated by the provisions of the FPA that give the Commission the authority to conduct adjudicatory proceedings and issue orders requiring interconnections. As a general matter, the existence of power to proceed by adjudication under one statute is in no way inconsistent with the existence of power to proceed by rulemaking under another statute. Moreover, there is nothing in the FPA to suggest that the Commission must proceed by adjudication in determining the obligations of facilities within its jurisdiction to make interconnections. On the contrary, Congress expressly provided in § 212(e) of the FPA, 16 U.S.C. § 824k(e) (Supp. V), that § 210 of the FPA shall not be construed "as requiring any person to utilize the authority of [§ 210] . . . in lieu of any other authority of law," or "as limiting, impairing, or otherwise affecting any authority of the Commission under any other provision of law."

The critical question, therefore, is whether § 210(e)(3) of PURPA deprives FERC of the power it would otherwise have under § 210(a) of PURPA to promulgate rules requiring utilities to make such interconnections with qualifying facilities as are necessary to effect purchases or sales authorized by the Act. In holding the interconnection rule invalid, the

Court of Appeals relied upon what it took to be "the literal meaning" of § 210(e)(3), 675 F.2d, at 1240, which states in pertinent part that

> "No qualifying small power production facility or qualifying cogeneration facility may be exempted under this subsection from—
>
> . . .
>
> (B) the provisions of section 210 . . . or 212 of the Federal Power Act or the necessary authorities for enforcement of any such provision under the Federal Power Act . . . ."

The Court of Appeals interpreted § 210(e)(3) of PURPA to mean that FERC may not promulgate a rule requiring utilities to interconnect with qualifying facilities in order to complete purchases and sales the utilities are required to enter into under PURPA, but must instead afford an opportunity for an evidentiary hearing under §§ 210 and 212 of the FPA in the case of each purchase and sale.

While the language of § 210(e)(3) of PURPA can be so interpreted, the purposes of PURPA strongly support the Commission's contrary reading of that provision. The purposes of the statute make it most unlikely that Congress could have intended that an evidentiary hearing be held for every interconnection necessary to consummate a purchase or sale of electricity authorized by the Act. Evidentiary hearings under § 210 of the FPA entail a determination of whether a proposed interconnection (1) is in the public interest, and (2) would encourage overall conservation of energy or capital, optimize the efficiency of use of facilities and resources, or improve the reliability of the affected utility systems. 16 U.S.C. § 824i(a)(1) (Supp. V). It is highly doubtful that Congress could have intended that the Commission make such a determination every time a qualifying facility seeks to hook up with a utility to complete a purchase or sale under PURPA, for Congress itself determined in enacting PURPA that these purchases and sales are in the public interest, and that the development of cogeneration and small power production will help to conserve energy and capital and ensure the more efficient use of the nation's resources.

Providing an opportunity for evidentiary hearings before the Commission for every interconnection necessary to complete a purchase or sale under PURPA would seriously impede the very development of cogeneration and small power production that Congress sought to facilitate. Many of the facilities in question are small operations. By definition a small power production facility has a production capacity of no more than 80 megawatts, 16 U.S.C. § 796(17)(A)(ii) (Supp. V), and cogeneration facilities may also be of modest size. Many owners of qualifying facilities would have little incentive to purchase or sell electric energy if they had to go through an evidentiary hearing before FERC in Washington, D.C., every time they needed to hook up with a utility to consummate a purchase or sale. The average cost to FERC of a contested interconnection proceeding is currently more than $57,000, see FERC Notice of Proposed Rulemaking, Docket RM 82–38–000, Fees Applicable to Electric Utilities, Cogenerators, and Small Power Producers, at 29–30 (Sept. 1, 1982), and the costs to private parties are doubtless also substantial. If we were to hold that utilities must be provided an opportunity for a hearing whenever a qualifying facility seeks an interconnection in order to effectuate a purchase or sale under PURPA, we would be "imput[ing] to Congress a purpose to paralyze with one hand what it sought to promote with the other." Clark v. Uebersee Finanz-Korporation, A.G., 332 U.S. 480, 489,

68 S.Ct. 174, 178, 92 L.Ed. 88 (1947). Cf. E.I. duPont deNemours & Co.
v. Train, 430 U.S. 112, 132–133, 97 S.Ct. 965, 977–978, 51 L.Ed.2d 204
(1977); Permian Basin Area Rate Cases, 390 U.S. 747, 777, 88 S.Ct.
1344, 1365, 20 L.Ed.2d 312 (1968).

We agree with the Commission that, in light of the entire statutory
scheme, § 210(e)(3) of PURPA may reasonably be interpreted to forbid
the Commission to exempt qualifying facilities from being the target of
applications under the FPA for orders "requiring . . . [a] physical
connection," FPA § 210(a)(1), but not to forbid the Commission to grant
qualifying facilities the right to obtain interconnections without applying
for an order under the FPA. The use of the word "exempted" in
§ 210(e)(3) is consistent with an intent to ensure only that qualifying facilities not be immunized from the requirements that the Commission
may impose under §§ 210 and 212 of the FPA. The term "exemption" is
ordinarily used to denote relief from a duty or service. See, e.g., Black's
Law Dictionary 513 (5th ed. 1979) (to "exempt" is "to relieve, excuse or
set free from a duty or service imposed upon the general class to which
the individual exempted belongs"). The only duty that §§ 210 and 212
of the FPA directly impose upon any facility is the duty to obey an order
"requiring . . . [a] physical connection." Section 212(e) of the FPA
expressly states that § 210 of the FPA shall *not* be construed "as requiring
any persons to utilize the authority of [§ 210] . . . in lieu of any other authority of law." Significantly, the Commission's interconnection rule
does not immunize qualifying facilities from the only requirement that
§§ 210 and 212 of the FPA do directly impose on them—the requirement
that they obey an interconnection order issued under those provisions.
Qualifying facilities remain subject to applications by other facilities for
orders requiring them to make interconnections. The Commission's rule
simply permits qualifying facilities to take certain steps to require *other
parties*, namely, electric utilities, to make interconnections.

The Commission's interconnection rule represents "a contemporaneous construction of a statute by the men charged with the responsibility of
setting its machinery in motion, of making the parts work efficiently and
smoothly while they are yet untried and new." Udall v. Tallman, 380
U.S. 1, 16, 85 S.Ct. 792, 801, 13 L.Ed.2d 616 (1965), quoting Power Reactor Development Co. v. International Union of Electrical, Radio & Machine Workers, 367 U.S. 396, 408, 81 S.Ct. 1529, 1535, 6 L.Ed.2d 924
(1961). To uphold it, "we need not find that [FERC's] construction is
the only reasonable one, or even that it is the result we would have
reached had the question arisen in the first instance in judicial proceedings." Unemployment Compensation Comm'n v. Aragon, 329 U.S. 143,
153, 67 S.Ct. 245, 250, 91 L.Ed. 136 (1946). See Mourning v. Family
Publications Service, 411 U.S. 356, 371–372, 93 S.Ct. 1652, 1661–1662,
36 L.Ed.2d 318 (1973). We need only conclude that it is a reasonable
interpretation of the relevant provisions. For the reasons stated above,
we do conclude that the Commission's interpretation is reasonable and
that the Court of Appeals erred in rejecting that interpretation.

NOTE

On both issues in *American Paper Institute* the Court gave considerable deference
to the Federal Energy Regulatory Commission. Should the Court have examined
the agency's assumptions more closely? Should Congress have provided the
agency with more specific guidance? Reconsider, in this light, the materials on

agency decisionmaking, congressional delegation, and judicial review in Ch. 4, supra.

Do you agree with the substance of the agency's judgments in *American Paper Institute?* How much more are you willing to pay for electricity this year so that "the entire country will ultimately benefit from the increased development of these [new] technologies . . . "? Is utility pricing policy a sensible way to encourage solar energy as compared with, for example, direct federal grants to those building solar power plants? Can state decisionmaking, as opposed to federal, play an integral role in utility rate issues even when federal energy policy is involved? Compare Pacific Gas & Electric Co. v. State Energy Resources Conservation and Development Commission, Ch. 4, Sec. C. 2., supra.

2. PRIVATE REGULATION OF SOLAR ENERGY

a. Zoning

Because solar devices are often located on individual homes and businesses, they are often subject to various zoning laws. Because zoning in the United States has long been left largely to local governments, see Euclid v. Ambler Co., 272 U.S. 365, 47 S.Ct. 114, 71 L.Ed. 303 (1926), this is an area in which new technology must contend with a variety of local restrictions, with, as the cases below demonstrate, a corresponding variety of results.

D'AURIO v. BOARD OF ZONING APPEALS

Supreme Court of New York, Albany County, 1978.
92 Misc.2d 898, 401 N.Y.S.2d 425.

ROGER J. MINER, JUSTICE.

Petitioners seek to annul the determination of respondent denying their application for an area zoning variance for the installation of a solar heating unit at their property in the Town of Colonie.

Desiring to install the solar heating unit, and being unable to comply with zoning ordinance requirements that each front yard have a minimum depth of 50 feet and be free of any structures, petitioners sought an area variance from the respondent Board of Zoning Appeals. The application was denied after public hearing, respondent having concluded that there are no unusual circumstances and conditions affecting petitioners' property ". . . that are peculiar to said property and do not apply generally to other property in the vicinity."

Petitioners occupy a corner lot. Although there appears to be sufficient space at the rear of the lot for the installation of a solar heating unit in compliance with the zoning ordinance, the unit apparently would not be most effective there. The unit was purchased for $4,000 and is designed as an auxiliary system connected to the oil-fuel furnace system of the residence. It is placed on skids and the solar heating panels are 8 feet in height. The unit is 8 feet wide at the base and is 20 feet 9 inches in length.

It is contended that the determination under attack denies petitioners the right to choose an energy source; that it denies them the right to make a normal improvement permitted under the use provisions of the zoning ordinance; that it is contrary to state and federal energy policy; that it represents the application of an incorrect test for variance; that it ignores the possibility of granting a variance upon a condition for landscaping; and that it ". . . represents an unconscionable, selfish and reactionary position against energy conservation."

The contention of petitioners must be rejected. A request for an area variance involves a determination as to whether practical difficulties will result from strict compliance with the zoning ordinance and the decision of the local zoning board in this regard should be sustained where there is a rational basis for its decision. (Matter of Cown v. Kern, 41 N.Y.2d 591, 394 N.Y.S.2d 579, 363 N.E.2d 305.) Moreover, the existence of a self-created hardship does not entitle the land owner to a variance. (Matter of National Merritt v. Weist, 41 N.Y.2d 438, 393 N.Y.S.2d 379, 361 N.E.2d 1028.) The petitioners here have not demonstrated practical difficulties or significant economic injury. (Matter of Fulling v. Palumbo, 21 N.Y.2d 30, 286 N.Y.S.2d 249, 233 N.E.2d 272.) At most, they have shown personal convenience. (Matter of Fuhst v. Foley, 57 A.D.2d 956, 395 N.Y.S.2d 74.) The court concludes that, with respect to petitioners' application for an area variance, the respondent did not act in a manner that was in any way arbitrary, unreasonable, irrational or indicative of bad faith. (See 2 Anderson, New York Zoning, Law and Prac. [2d ed.] §§ 18.31–18.45.)

Submit judgment for respondent.

KATZ v. BODKIN

Supreme Court of New York, 1979.
9 Envir.Rep. 20423.

WOOD, J.:

By notice of petition dated February 23, 1979, petitioners seek judgment, pursuant to Civ. Prac. Article 78, reversing respondents' determination which denied petitioners a variance from Article VIII, § 89–45A of the Zoning Ordinance of the Town of Mamaroneck which sought leave to erect solar panels on the roof of petitioners' house to aid in the use of a domestic hot water system. Petitioners seek an order of the court directing the granting of such variance or, alternatively, a judgment declaring said Zoning section unconstitutional.

By order to show cause dated March 19, 1979 (Ferraro, J.), Common Cause, a national organization, seeks an order, through its counsel, permitting it to file a memorandum of law as *Amicus Curiae.*

The foregoing applications are hereby consolidated for disposition.

The application by Common Cause for leave to submit a memorandum of law as *Amicus Curiae* is granted. Intervention, to the extent sought, will not in any way delay determination of this matter nor has any viable prejudice been shown. (3 Car., Wait 2d, § 19:142.)

On October 11, 1978 petitioner, Arthur A. Katz, formally applied to the Mamaroneck building department for a permit to construct a solar panel domestic hot water system. The panels were to be placed on the roof of the applicant's home. On October 24, 1978 the building inspector disapproved the application as not in compliance "with Article VIII Section 89–45A 'Height Exceptions' which restricts the total area of mechanical equipment to 10 percent of area of supporting roof. Proposed mechanical equipment will cover 20 percent of supporting roof." (Petitioners' Exhibit A.)

The pertinent section of the zoning ordinance is § 89–45 which states, in pertinent part:

A.   The height limitations of this ordinance shall not apply to . . . necessary mechanical or amateur electronic devices and appurtenances usually carried above the roof level. Such features, however, shall be erected only to such heights as are necessary to accomplish the purpose they are intended to serve, and the total area covered by such features shall not exceed ten percent (10%) of the area of the roof on which they are located.

By application dated October 11, 1978, petitioner appealed to the Town Zoning Board of Appeals (ZBA) for a modification of § 89–45A "to allow the installation of 75 sq. ft. of solar collectors at the rear of the dwelling covering 20 percent of the roof area to which they are attached." (Petitioners' Exhibit B.) In substantiation of the appeal, petitioners stated that through such solar collecting a saving of energy would be effected, would be ecologically sound and, in furtherance thereof, the United States Department of HUD had awarded petitioners a $400 grant toward the expense of the installation. . . .

The denial of the application was followed by the adoption of a resolution by the ZBA wherein it was resolved that the Board denied the application on the following grounds:

1.   Applicant failed to show that the solar collectors could not be located elsewhere on his dwelling where the same efficiency would be provided and be more aesthetically pleasing to the neighborhood.

2.   Applicant failed to show that energy could be conserved by other construction methods.

3.   Petitioners' land presented no special circumstances or conditions peculiar thereto.

4.   Facts and circumstances claimed by petitioner to entitle him to the variance [are] not such as would deprive him of the reasonable use of his land.

5.   The granting of the variance would not be in harmony with the general purposes and intent of the zoning ordinance and not aesthetically in keeping with the residential neighborhood.

Petitioners claim these assigned grounds for denial are arbitrary, capricious, and unsupported by the evidence adduced at the public hearing.

In answer to the grounds assigned for denial, petitioner alleges that, as to 1. above, his contractor, Mr. Flohr, testified that due to tree shading, only the higher part of petitioners' roof was adequate for the proper functioning of the solar panels and no contrary evidence on this point was adduced.

Further, as to 1. above, the ZBA stated a failure to show that another location of the solar panels would be more aesthetically pleasing and in 5. above, would not be aesthetically in keeping with the residential neighborhood. Petitioner maintains that at the public meeting not only did no neighbors speak in opposition to his application but several residents spoke in favor thereof.

As to 2. above, it was suggested by the ZBA, that better insulation of the house could better serve to conserve energy. Petitioner contends his house was adequately insulated and, in any event, the ZBA should have no concern with petitioners' method of seeking conservation of energy.

Additionally, as to 5. above, the finding by the ZBA that the granting of the variance would not be in harmony with the general purposes and intent of the zoning ordinance, petitioner contends that Town Law, § 263, in defining the purposes of zoning, states that such regulations:

. . . shall be made with reasonable consideration, among other things, as to the character of the district and its peculiar suitability for particular uses, and with a view to conserving the value of the buildings and encouraging the most appropriate use of land throughout such municipality. . . .

.   .   .

Petitioners state that the ZBA determination of January 30, 1979, based as it was on the hearing of November 22, 1978, must be amended and reversed for the following reasons:

1. The pertinent section of the zoning ordinance (Article VIII, § 89–45A) does not apply to the construction sought by petitioners and, thus, reliance thereon by the ZBA was misplaced.

2. Even if that section were applicable to petitioners' proposed construction, petitioners have adduced sufficient evidence to justify the granting thereof based on practical difficulties and the refusal of the ZBA to even consider the resubmission was arbitrary, capricious, and an abuse of discretion.

3. Even if that section were applicable the refusal of the ZBA to grant a variance amounts to a restriction of conversions to and utilization of energy saving devices and is, thus, against present public policy.

.   .   .

Concededly, § 89–45A of the Zoning Ordinance does not apply to petitioners' proposed installation insofar as the latter is not a spire, cupola dome, chimney, ventilator, skylight, water tank, or bulkhead. Nor does this court find that the proposed installation falls within the ordinance prohibition against "necessary mechanical or amateur electronic devices and appurtenances."

It must be remembered "that zoning ordinances, being in derogation of common-law property rights, are to be strictly construed against the municipality and in favor of the landowner (citing authorities)" Matter of Sibarco Stations, Inc. v. Town Board of Vestal, 29 A.D.2d 907(1), 908 (N.Y. App.Div.1968), reversed on other grounds, 24 N.Y.2d 900, and "unless the intent of the ordinance is clearly to be found in the language used, its provisions should not be extended by implication (citing cases)" Salem Trader Restaurants, Inc. v. Reitfort, 63 Misc.2d 753, 755 (N.Y.Sup. Ct.1970). No evidence was adduced before the ZBA to bring petitioners' proposed construction within the specific definitions enunciated in Zoning Ordinance, § 89–45A; rather, the only evidence on this point is the affidavit of March 27, 1979 of one Nicolaysen, a professional engineer and neighbor of petitioners, wherein he clearly gives his professional opinion that the proposed construction does not fall within the ordinance (Katz reply affidavit).

Petitioner contends, further, that the restriction that the "feature" placed on a roof shall not exceed 10 percent of the area of the roof on which located has been misapplied in this instance. Petitioners' roof is made up of eight separate and principle sections and the proposed solar panels are to be located on one of such sections. The ZBA has determined that the ordinance meaning restricts the feature to no more than 10 percent of the supporting roof—that roof physically supporting the panels. It is felt by this court and so held that such an interpretation by the ZBA is unrealistic and in violation of the specific words of the ordinance which refers merely to "the area of the roof on which . . . located" and not to the "supporting" roof.

Even if § 89–45A were applicable to petitioners' proposed construction, this court finds and so holds that petitioners have shown practical difficulty sufficient to justify an area variance (Matter of Wilcox v. ZBA of the City of Yonkers, 17 N.Y.2d 249, 254 (N.Y.Ct.App.1966)). Concededly, "practical difficulties are something less than unnecessary hardship." (2 Anderson, N.Y. Zoning 2d, § 18.33.) For consideration in the determination of practical difficulties are the following criteria, as enunciated in Wachsberger v. Michalis, 19 Misc.2d 909 (N.Y.Sup.Ct.1959):

    1.   How substantial the variance is in relation to the requirement;

    2.   The effect, if the variance is allowed, of the increased population density thus produced or available governmental facilities;

    3.   Whether a substantial change will be produced in the character of the neighborhood or a substantial detriment to adjoining properties created;

    4.   Whether the difficulty can be obviated by some feasible method other than a variance;

    5.   Whether in view of the manner in which the difficulty arose and in consideration of all the above factors the interests of justice will be served by allowing the variance. (See: 2 Anderson, N.Y. Zoning 2d, § 18.33.)

It is clear, at least to this court, that in the application of the above criteria, petitioners would be entitled to a variance if, indeed, such is necessary in view of the foregoing.

Of even greater import, in this day of what for better expression may be termed the energy crunch, the purposes of restrictive zoning must, to some extent, give way to declared policy of governments to conserve energy in all ways possible yet consistent with environmental standards.

Zoning regulations must be enacted by those to whom such responsibility is assigned in a manner consistent with the promotion of "health and general welfare" and with "reasonable consideration, among other things, as to the character of the district . . . and with a view to conserving the value of buildings and encouraging the most appropriate use of land throughout such municipality" (Town Law, § 263).

In the accomplishment of the above, it is incumbent upon the zoning agency to adopt an attitude other than an ostrich head-in-the-sand approach, especially when adoption to changing scientific advances follows and complies with national and state interests in energy conservation. It has been said that "our increasing dependence on foreign energy supplies presents, a serious threat to the national security of the United States and to the health, safety and welfare of its citizens" (Department of Energy Organization Act of 1977, 12 U.S.C. § 7111(2)) and that, further, "the mass production and use of equipment utilizing solar energy will . . . promote the national defense." (Solar Energy Research Development and Demonstration Act of 1974, 42 U.S.C. § 5511(a)(7) (1977).) See also: Solar Heating and Cooling Demonstration Act of 1974, 42 U.S.C. § 5501.

In keeping with and in furtherance of this declared public policy, the United States government in its Energy Tax Act of 1978 (§ 101, 92 Stat. 3174, et seq. 26 U.S.C. § 1) has provided a monetary incentive for domestic solar hot water systems for private dwellings which has been followed by similar state expression of public policy and monetary tax relief. (N.Y. State Energy Law, L.1976, ch. 819.) This latter law (§ 3–105(2)) imposes upon municipalities the duty to review their rules and regulations and to not only make them consistent with the state declared policy for energy conservation but, where inconsistent, to make necessary changes to comply with the Act's stated purposes.

.   .   .

In view of the foregoing, this court finds as a matter of law that the actions of the ZBA in refusing to grant the variance sought were arbitrary and capricious and in violation of law and accordingly, the said board is directed to forthwith issue the building permit sought, and petitioners' application therefore is granted, without costs, disbursements, or counsel fees.

Submit judgment on notice.

C. JENSON AND W. FANTLE, SOLDIERS GROVE: MOVING INTO THE SOLAR AGE

Alternative Sources of Energy, May/June 1980, at 7.

The shining promise of solar energy is fast becoming reality for one upper-Midwestern community. With construction already underway, Soldiers Grove, Wisconsin, will soon be a showcase for alternative energy planning and technologies.

Soldiers Grove is moving—moving their community and commercial center to a new location and moving from the fossil fuel age into the solar age. The village's recently passed architectural principles take maximum advantage of solar energy and specify that all relocation structures must be at least 50 percent solar heated.

For years, this small, rural southwestern Wisconsin community (pop. 524) has been locked in a struggle with nature. Built on the floodplain of the volatile Kickapoo River, the people of Soldiers Grove have frequently watched the river's waters spill over the banks and cover large portions of the downtown community. As the waters receded, the townspeople would clean up, repair the damage and return to their daily routines. .   .   . Even before the flood of 1978, the desperate village board had made the decision to relocate. They backed that decision with the $82,000 purchase of 190 acres of high ground about half a mile from the Kickapoo River. .   .   .

The villagers solicited architectural and planning services for the relocation project from 20 firms around the upper Midwest. The village people knew exactly what they wanted—a solar community. Local resident Eileen Schoville summed up village sentiments when she said that the community had to "learn to think in terms of 1980 or maybe the year 2000 priorities."

After hearing individual presentations from the architectural firms, the village hired the Chicago-based Hawkweed Group in August, 1979. Hawkweed has an extensive background in community assistance and specializes solely in passive and site-built solar designs. .   .   . At the heart of what is known as a Planned Unit Development (PUD), are specific architectural design standards. These are now law in Soldiers Grove. The PUD standards seek to establish a community identity and consistency by mandating certain building forms and materials while encouraging individual expression within the design standards. The PUD design standards contain a section entitled "Renewable Resources," which reads:

". . . all buildings must be at least 50 percent solar heated. Although both active and passive systems in suitable combinations will be allowed, the use of passive systems is encouraged. Active collection devices must be integrated with the surface to which they are affixed. In practice this means that they must be parallel with the wall or roof of which they are a part . . . ."

The PUD design standards, in keeping with local climatic conditions, do not permit flat roofs or mansard roofs, limit exterior siding material of each building to wood (a renewable resource abundant in the area), and prohibit any false fronts on buildings. . . . Under construction at the relocation site is a $250,000 branch bank. This particular building (not one of Hawkweed's) was to feature a site built active solar system that would provide over 70% of the building's heat. That would have the bank well within the 50% solar zoning ordinance, but when the bank management priced the system and found that it would add $27,200 to their construction bill, the system was quietly dropped.

It did not land quietly however. After seeing the south facing roof being shingled over, the villagers realized that the bank was not going to comply with the 50% solar heat zoning ordinance. Zoning Administrator Ron Swiggum issued a citation for non-compliance to the bank's owners upon confirming that they had dropped the solar feature. One has to wonder if Swiggum's name will finds its way into solar history books of the future as the first man to issue a citation to someone for trying to build a structure without solar heating!

The citation was appealed to the Village Board of Appeals, but before the hearing was held, a spontaneous petition against a zoning variance for the bank sprang up. Most villagers approached signed the petition. At the appeal hearing, the building's LaCrosse, Wisconsin architects pointed to energy saving features in their design and told the hearing board that the building was designed "in the spirit of the relocation project." The energy saving features included earth berming, heavy insulation and insulated interior walls for zoned heating. The Wisconsin Department of Local Affairs and Development was also present at the hearing and their representative offered a solar need analysis of the bank building. They concluded that with a few minor modifications, including passive solar skylights, no more than $4,000 would be required to bring the building into compliance with the solar zoning ordinance.

Given this information, the villagers' petition, and some other strongly worded opinions expressed at the hearing, the Appeals Board unanimously voted to deny the variance. The bank's vice-president has indicated, since then, a willingness to "live with this decision." The villagers' strong reaction against this first challenge to their solar zoning ordinance has served to both confirm and strengthen their commitment to go solar. Hawkweed's Rodney Wright called this the "first time in the history of the country that you HAD to go solar." . . .

NOTE

A traditional use of zoning is to prevent operation of businesses in residential areas. If an individual wants to operate an auto repair shop out of his or her garage and therefore seeks a zoning variance, should the court, following *Katz*, consider the strong national policy in favor of full employment? Is *Katz* consistent with an ordinance, like that in Soldiers Grove, that requires solar devices? Would you favor wider adoption of a San Diego County ordinance that requires solar water heaters in new homes built in certain locations? See A Cloudy Forecast for Solar Industry, Washington Post, Oct. 16, 1982, at E2, col. 3.

As the cases above indicate, zoning authorities wield a powerful tool for impeding or promoting solar energy. Is it an appropriate tool? If zoning is to play a role in energy policy should zoning ordinances be federal or state-wide as opposed to the present local approach?

Restrictive covenants in many residential communities that forbid, for aesthetic reasons, certain appliances and installations on roofs raise similar issues. See, e.g., Comment, Solar Energy and Restrictive Covenants: The Conflict Between Public Policy and Private Zoning, 67 Calif.L.Rev. 350 (1979). California has enacted a statute that renders void any covenant "which effectively prohibits or restricts the installation or use of a solar energy system . . . ." Cal.Civil Code § 714 (West 1978).

Local building codes may also present an obstacle to the installation of solar energy devices. Should such codes be weakened or changed to accommodate solar devices? See W. Thomas, A. Miller and R. Robbins, Overcoming Legal Uncertainties About Use of Solar Energy Systems, 16–17 (1978).

b. Access to Sunlight

**FONTAINEBLEAU HOTEL CORP. v. FORTY–FIVE
TWENTY–FIVE, INC.**

District Court of Appeals of Florida, Third District, 1959.
114 So.2d 357.

PER CURIAM.

This is an interlocutory appeal from an order temporarily enjoining the appellants from continuing with the construction of a fourteen-story addition to the Fontainebleau Hotel, owned and operated by the appellants. Appellee, plaintiff below, owns the Eden Roc Hotel, which was constructed in 1955, about a year after the Fontainebleau, and adjoins the Fontainebleau on the north. Both are luxury hotels, facing the Atlantic Ocean. The proposed addition to the Fontainebleau is being constructed twenty feet from its north property line, 130 feet from the mean high water mark of the Atlantic Ocean, and 76 feet 8 inches from the ocean bulkhead line. The 14-story tower will extend 160 feet above grade in height and is 416 feet long from east to west. During the winter months, from around two o'clock in the afternoon for the remainder of the day, the shadow of the addition will extend over the cabana, swimming pool, and sunbathing areas of the Eden Roc, which are located in the southern portion of its property.

In this action, plaintiff-appellee sought to enjoin the defendants-appellants from proceeding with the construction of the addition to the Fontainebleau (it appears to have been roughly eight stories high at the time suit was filed), alleging that the construction would interfere with the light and air on the beach in front of the Eden Roc and cast a shadow of such size as to render the beach wholly unfitted for the use and enjoyment of its guests, to the irreparable injury of the plaintiff; further, that the construction of such addition on the north side of defendants' property, rather than the south side, was actuated by malice and ill will on the part of the defendants' president toward the plaintiff's president; and that the construction was in violation of a building ordinance requiring a 100-foot setback from the ocean. It was also alleged that the construction would interfere with the easements of light and air enjoyed by plaintiff and its predecessors in title for more than twenty years and "impliedly granted by virtue of the acts of the plaintiff's predecessors in title, as well as under the common law and the express recognition of such rights by virtue of Chapter 9837, Laws of Florida 1923 . . . ." Some attempt was also made to allege an easement by implication in favor of the plaintiff's property, as the dominant, and against the defendants' property as the servient, tenement.

The defendants' answer denied the material allegations of the complaint, pleaded laches and estoppel by judgment.

The chancellor heard considerable testimony on the issues made by the complaint and the answer and, as noted, entered a temporary injunction restraining the defendants from continuing with the construction of the addition. His reason for so doing was stated by him, in a memorandum opinion, as follows:

> "In granting the temporary injunction in this case the Court wishes to make several things very clear. The ruling is not based on any alleged presumptive title nor prescriptive right of the plaintiff to light and air nor is it based on any deed restrictions nor recorded plats in the title of the plaintiff nor of the defendant nor of any plat of record. It is not based on any zoning ordinance nor on any provision of the building code of the City of Miami Beach nor on the decision of any court, nisi prius or appellate. It is based solely on the proposition that no one has a right to use his property to the injury of another. In this case it is clear from the evidence that the proposed use by the Fontainebleau will materially damage the Eden Roc. There is evidence indicating that the construction of the proposed annex by the Fontainebleau is malicious or deliberate for the purpose of injuring the Eden Roc, but it is scarcely sufficient, standing alone, to afford a basis for equitable relief."

This is indeed a novel application of the maxim *sic utere tuo ut alienum non laedas.* This maxim does not mean that one must never use his own property in such a way as to do any injury to his neighbor. Beckman v. Marshall, Fla.1956, 85 So.2d 552. It means only that one must use his property so as not to injure the lawful *rights* of another. Cason v. Florida Power Co., 74 Fla. 1, 76 So. 535, L.R.A.1918A, 1034. In Reaver v. Martin Theatres, Fla.1951, 52 So.2d 682, 683, 25 A.L.R.2d 1451, under this maxim, it was stated that "it is well settled that a property owner may put his own property to any reasonable and lawful use, so long as he does not thereby deprive the adjoining landowner of any right of enjoyment of his property *which is recognized and protected by law, and so long as his use is not such a one as the law will pronounce a nuisance.*" [Emphasis supplied.]

No American decision has been cited, and independent research has revealed none, in which it has been held that—in the absence of some contractual or statutory obligation—a landowner has a legal right to the free flow of light and air across the adjoining land of his neighbor. Even at common law, the landowner had no legal right, in the absence of an easement or uninterrupted use and enjoyment for a period of 20 years, to unobstructed light and air from the adjoining land. Blumberg v. Weiss, 1941, 129 N.J.Eq. 34, 17 A.2d 823; 1 Am.Jur., Adjoining Landowners, § 51. And the English doctrine of "ancient lights" has been unanimously repudiated in this country.   1 Am.Jur., Adjoining Landowners, § 49, p. 533; Lynch v. Hill, 1939, 24 Del.Ch. 86, 6 A.2d 614, overruling Clawson v. Primrose, 4 Del.Ch. 643.

There being, then, no legal right to the free flow of light and air from the adjoining land, it is universally held that where a structure serves a useful and beneficial purpose, it does not give rise to a cause of action, either for damages or for an injunction under the maxim *sic utere tuo ut alienum non laedas,* even though it causes injury to another by cutting off the light and air and interfering with the view that would otherwise be available over adjoining land in its natural state, regardless of the fact that the structure may have been erected partly for spite.   See the cases collected in the annotation in 133 A.L.R. at pp. 701 et seq.; 1 Am.Jur., Adjoining Landowners, § 54, p. 536; Taliaferro v. Salyer, 1958, 162 Cal. App.2d 685, 328 P.2d 799; Musumeci v. Leonardo, 1950, 77 R.I. 255, 75 A.2d 175; Harrison v. Langlinais, Tex.Civ.App.1958, 312 S.W.2d 286; Granberry v. Jones, 1949, 188 Tenn. 51, 216 S.W.2d 721; Letts v. Kessler, 1896, 54 Ohio St. 73, 42 N.E. 765; Kulbitsky v. Zimnoch, 1950, 196 Md. 504, 77 A.2d 14; Southern Advertising Co. v. Sherman, Tenn.App. 1957, 308 S.W.2d 491.

We see no reason for departing from this universal rule.   If, as contended on behalf of plaintiff, public policy demands that a landowner in the Miami Beach area refrain from constructing buildings on his premises that will cast a shadow on the adjoining premises, an amendment of its comprehensive planning and zoning ordinance, applicable to the public as a whole, is the means by which such purpose should be achieved.   (No opinion is expressed here as to the validity of such an ordinance, if one should be enacted pursuant to the requirements of law.   Cf. City of Miami Beach v. State ex rel. Fontainebleau Hotel Corp., Fla.App.1959, 108 So.2d 614, 619; certiorari denied, Fla.1959, 111 So.2d 437.)   But to change the universal rule—and the custom followed in this state since its inception—that adjoining landowners have an equal right under the law to build to the line of their respective tracts and to such a height as is desired by them (in the absence, of course, of building restrictions or regulations) amounts, in our opinion, to judicial legislation.   As stated in Musumeci v. Leonardo, supra [77 R.I. 255, 75 A.2d 177], "So use your own as not to injure another's property is, indeed, a sound and salutary principle for the promotion of justice, but it may not and should not be applied so as gratuitously to confer upon an adjacent property owner incorporeal rights incidental to his ownership of land which the law does not sanction."

. . .

Since it affirmatively appears that the plaintiff has not established a cause of action against the defendants by reason of the structure here in question, the order granting a temporary injunction should be and it is hereby reversed with directions to dismiss the complaint.

Reversed with directions.

HORTON, C.J., and CARROLL, CHAS., J., and CABOT, TED, ASSOCIATE JUDGE concur.

SANDY F. KRAEMER, SOLAR LAW

130–132 (1978).

These rulings [like Fontainebleau] find their genesis in the repudiation of the English doctrine of "ancient lights" under which a landowner acquired by uninterrupted use an easement over adjoining property for the passage of light and air. The doctrine of ancient lights has been disavowed repeatedly in the United States.

The doctrine of ancient lights provides that if a landowner has received light from across his neighbor's land for a certain time, he has the right to continue enjoying it. The length of time necessary to establish this right in England is now twenty-seven years. The British devised an ingenious aid for determining the light entitlement, called the "grumble line". The "grumble line" is the position in a room at which an ordinary person reading ordinary print grumbles and turns on the artificial light. The rule of thumb seems to be that if at least one-half of the room is between the "grumble line" and the window, there is a reasonable amount of light entering it. Engineers have developed an empirical standard for the position of the "grumble line" that is equivalent to one foot-candle on the top of a desk 33 inches (84 cm.) high. In conjunction with the 50–50 rule, if over one-half of the room at 33 inches above the floor receives one foot-candle, the room is considered to receive an adequate amount of light from the window to satisfy the doctrine of ancient light. A problem exists, of course, in that architectural styles change, as does the concept of reasonableness, causing all sorts of conflicts, not to mention that a solar collector requires a great deal more light than that required to make a man refrain from a "grumble." This treatment of solar energy rights has been associated by commentators with the claims that the sun is rarely seen in England.

The major reason [American] courts have rejected this doctrine is that it conflicts with the goal of full development of property. The classic American high-rise metropolitan core areas of our greatest cities could not have been built under the Ancient Lights Doctrine. While full development is being questioned today, it was a useful and important policy for a young nation with expanding frontiers. The doctrine of ancient lights, if accepted, would have restricted full development under some circumstances. Some courts apparently fear that recognition of a cause of action for creating a shadow will prevent any use of adjoining land. In residential areas normal use of the property should not cause shadows on a collector unless trees are planted too near to the lot line. In other areas, only those buildings tall enough and close enough to the collector will blot out the sun's rays.

NOTE

As Kraemer indicates, the American rejection of the doctrine of ancient lights poses a problem for residential solar energy. When, for example, a homeowner in Hawaii with solar collectors on her house sought to prevent construction of an adjoining building that would shade her collectors, the court granted summary judgment for the defendant. Siu v. McCully Citron Co., No. 56405 Civ. 105–106 (Hawaii, Jan. 9, 1979), reported in 1 Solar L.Rep. 542 (1979), discussed in Gergacz, Legal Aspects of Solar Energy: Statutory Approaches for Access to Sunlight, 10 B.C.Envt'l.Aff.L.Rev. 1, 2 (1982). Does the following case persuade you that American courts should support the ancient lights idea in cases involving solar energy?

PRAH v. MARETTI

Supreme Court of Wisconsin, 1982.
108 Wis.2d 223, 321 N.W.2d 182.

SHIRLEY S. ABRAHAMSON, J.   This appeal from a judgment of the circuit court for Waukesha county, Max Raskin, circuit judge, was certified to this court by the court of appeals, sec. (Rule) 809.61, Stats. 1979–80, as presenting an issue of first impression, namely, whether an owner of a solar-heated residence states a claim upon which relief can be granted when he asserts that his neighbor's proposed construction of a residence (which conforms to existing deed restrictions and local ordinances) interferes with his access to an unobstructed path for sunlight across the neighbor's property. This case thus involves a conflict between one landowner (Glenn Prah, the plaintiff) interested in unobstructed access to sunlight across adjoining property as a natural source of energy and an adjoining landowner (Richard D. Maretti, the defendant) interested in the development of his land.

The circuit court concluded that the plaintiff presented no claim upon which relief could be granted and granted summary judgment for the defendant. We reverse the judgment of the circuit court and remand the cause to the circuit court for further proceedings.

I.

According to the complaint, the plaintiff is the owner of a residence which was constructed during the years 1978–1979. The complaint alleges that the residence has a solar system which includes collectors on the roof to supply energy for heat and hot water and that after the plaintiff built his solar-heated house, the defendant purchased the lot adjacent to and immediately to the south of the plaintiff's lot and commenced planning construction of a home. The complaint further states that when the plaintiff learned of defendant's plans to build the house he advised the defendant that if the house were built at the proposed location, defendant's house would substantially and adversely affect the integrity of plaintiff's solar system and could cause plaintiff other damage. Nevertheless, the defendant began construction. The complaint further alleges that the plaintiff is entitled to "unrestricted use of the sun and its solar power" and demands judgment for injunctive relief and damages.

After filing his complaint, the plaintiff moved for a temporary injunction to restrain and enjoin construction by the defendant. In ruling on that motion the circuit court heard testimony, received affidavits and viewed the site.

The record made on the motion reveals the following additional facts: Plaintiff's home was the first residence built in the subdivision, and although plaintiff did not build his house in the center of the lot it was built in accordance with applicable restrictions. Plaintiff advised defendant that if the defendant's home were built at the proposed site it would cause a shadowing effect on the solar collectors which would reduce the efficiency of the system and possibly damage the system. To avoid these adverse effects, plaintiff requested defendant to locate his home an additional several feet away from the plaintiff's lot line, the exact number being disputed. Plaintiff and defendant failed to reach an agreement on the location of defendant's home before defendant started construction. The Architectural Control Committee and the Planning Commission of the

City of Muskego approved the defendant's plans for his home, including its location on the lot. After such approval, the defendant apparently changed the grade of the property without prior notice to the Architectural Control Committee. The problem with defendant's proposed construction, as far as the plaintiff's interests are concerned, arises from a combination of the grade and the distance of defendant's home from the defendant's lot line.

The circuit court denied plaintiff's motion for injunctive relief, declared it would entertain a motion for summary judgment and thereafter entered judgment in favor of the defendant.

. . . .

We consider first whether the complaint states a claim for relief based on common law private nuisance. This state has long recognized that an owner of land does not have an absolute or unlimited right to use the land in a way which injures the rights of others. The rights of neighboring landowners are relative; the uses by one must not unreasonably impair the uses or enjoyment of the other. VI-A *American Law of Property* sec. 28.22, pp. 64–65 (1954). When one landowner's use of his or her property unreasonably interferes with another's enjoyment of his or her property, that use is said to be a private nuisance. Hoene v. Milwaukee, 17 Wis.2d 209, 214, 116 N.W.2d 112 (1962); Metzger v. Hochrein, 107 Wis. 267, 269, 83 N.W. 308 (1900). See also Prosser, *Law of Torts* sec. 89, p. 591 (2d ed. 1971).

The private nuisance doctrine has traditionally been employed in this state to balance the rights of landowners, and this court has recently adopted the analysis of private nuisance set forth in the Restatement (Second) of Torts. CEW Mgmt. Corp. v. First Federal Savings & Loan Association, 88 Wis.2d 631, 633, 277 N.W.2d 766 (1979). The Restatement defines private nuisance as "a nontrespassory invasion of another's interest in the private use and enjoyment of land." Restatement (Second) of Torts, Sec. 821D (1977). The phrase "interest in the private use and enjoyment of land" as used in sec. 821D is broadly defined to include any disturbance of the enjoyment of property. The comment in the Restatement describes the landowner's interest protected by private nuisance law as follows:

"The phrase 'interest in the use and enjoyment of land' is used in this Restatement in a broad sense. It comprehends not only the interests that a person may have in the actual present use of land for residential, agricultural, commercial, industrial and other purposes, but also his interests in having the present use value of the land unimpaired by changes in its physical condition. Thus the destruction of trees on vacant land is as much an invasion of the owner's interest in its use and enjoyment as is the destruction of crops or flowers that he is growing on the land for his present use. 'Interest in use and enjoyment' also comprehends the pleasure, comfort and enjoyment that a person normally derives from the occupancy of land. Freedom from discomfort and annoyance while using land is often as important to a person as freedom from physical interruption with his use or freedom from detrimental change in the physical condition of the land itself." Restatement (Second) of Torts, Sec. 821D, Comment b, p. 101 (1977)

Although the defendant's obstruction of the plaintiff's access to sunlight appears to fall within the Restatement's broad concept of a private nuisance as a nontrespassory invasion of another's interest in the private use and enjoyment of land, the defendant asserts that he has a right to develop his property in compliance with statutes, ordinances and private covenants without regard to the effect of such development upon the plaintiff's access to sunlight. In essence, the defendant is asking this court to hold that the private nuisance doctrine is not applicable in the instant case and that his right to develop his land is a right which is *per se* superior to his neighbor's interest in access to sunlight. This position is expressed in the maxim "cujus est solum, ejus est usque ad coelum et ad infernos," that is, the owner of land owns up to the sky and down to the center of the earth. The rights of the surface owner are, however, not unlimited. U.S. v. Causby, 328 U.S. 256, 260–1, 66 S.Ct. 1062, 1065, 90 L.Ed. 1206 (1946). See also 114.03, Stats.1979–80.

The defendant is not completely correct in asserting that the common law did not protect a landowner's access to sunlight across adjoining property. At English common law a landowner could acquire a right to receive sunlight across adjoining land by both express agreement and under the judge-made doctrine of "ancient lights." Under the doctrine of ancient lights if the landowner had received sunlight across adjoining property for a specified period of time, the landowner was entitled to continue to receive unobstructed access to sunlight across the adjoining property. Under the doctrine the landowner acquired a negative prescriptive easement and could prevent the adjoining landowner from obstructing access to light.

Although American courts have not been as receptive to protecting a landowner's access to sunlight as the English courts, American courts have afforded some protection to a landowner's interest in access to sunlight. American courts honor express easements to sunlight. American courts initially enforced the English common law doctrine of ancient lights, but later every state which considered the doctrine repudiated it as inconsistent with the needs of a developing country. Indeed, for just that reason this court concluded that an easement to light and air over adjacent property could not be created or acquired by prescription and has been unwilling to recognize such an easement by implication. Depner v. United States National Bank, 202 Wis. 405, 408, 232 N.W. 851 (1930); Miller v. Hoeschler, 126 Wis. 263, 268–69, 105 N.W. 790 (1905).

Many jurisdictions in this country have protected a landowner from malicious obstruction of access to light (the spite fence cases) under the common law private nuisance doctrine. If an activity is motivated by malice it lacks utility and the harm it causes others outweighs any social values. VI–A Law of Property sec. 28.28, p. 79 (1954). This court was reluctant to protect a landowner's interest in sunlight even against a spite fence, only to be overruled by the legislature. Shortly after this court upheld a landowner's right to erect a useless and unsightly sixteen-foot spite fence four feet from his neighbor's windows, Metzger v. Hochrein, 107 N.W. 267, 83 N.W. 308 (1900), the legislature enacted a law specifically defining a spite fence as an actionable private nuisance. Thus a landowner's interest in sunlight has been protected in this country by common law private nuisance law at least in the narrow context of the modern American rule invalidating spite fences. See, e.g., Sundowner, Inc. v. King, 95 Idaho 367, 509 P.2d 785 (1973); Restatement (Second) of Torts, sec. 829 (1977).

This court's reluctance in the nineteenth and early part of the twentieth century to provide broader protection for a landowner's access to sunlight was premised on three policy considerations. First, the right of landowners to use their property as they wished, as long as they did not cause physical damage to a neighbor, was jealously guarded. Metzger v. Hochrein, 107 Wis. 267, 272, 83 N.W. 308 (1900).

Second, sunlight was valued only for aesthetic enjoyment or as illumination. Since artificial light could be used for illumination, loss of sunlight was at most a personal annoyance which was given little, if any, weight by society.

Third, society had a significant interest in not restricting or impeding land development. Dillman v. Hoffman, 38 Wis. 559, 574 (1875). This court repeatedly emphasized that in the growth period of the nineteenth and early twentieth centuries change is to be expected and is essential to property and that recognition of a right to sunlight would hinder property development. The court expressed this concept as follows:

> "As the city grows, large grounds appurtenant to residences must be cut up to supply more residences. . . . The cistern, the outhouse, the cesspool, and the private drain must disappear in deference to the public waterworks and sewer; the terrace and the garden, to the need for more complete occupancy. . . . Strict limitation [on the recognition of easements of light and air over adjacent premises is] in accord with the popular conception upon which real estate has been and is daily being conveyed in Wisconsin and to be essential to easy and rapid development at least of our municipalities." Miller v. Hoeschler, supra, 126 Wis. at 268, 270, 105 N.W. 790; quoted with approval in *Depner*, supra, 202 Wis. at 409, 232 N.W. 851.

Considering these three policies, this court concluded that in the absence of an express agreement granting access to sunlight, a landowner's obstruction of another's access to sunlight was not actionable. Miller v. Hoeschler, supra, 126 Wis. at 271, 105 N.W. 709; Depner v. United States National Bank, supra, 202 Wis. at 410, 232 N.W. 851. These three policies are no longer fully accepted or applicable. They reflect factual circumstances and social priorities that are now obsolete.

First, society has increasingly regulated the use of land by the landowner for the general welfare. Euclid v. Ambler Realty Co., 272 U.S. 365, 47 S.Ct. 114, 71 L.Ed. 303 (1926); Just v. Marinette, 56 Wis.2d 7, 201 N.W.2d 761 (1972).

Second, access to sunlight has taken on a new significance in recent years. In this case the plaintiff seeks to protect access to sunlight, not for aesthetic reasons or as a source of illumination but as a source of energy. Access to sunlight as an energy source is of significance both to the landowner who invests in solar collectors and to a society which has an interest in developing alternative sources of energy.

Third, the policy of favoring unhindered private development in an expanding economy is no longer in harmony with the realities of our society. State v. Deetz, 66 Wis.2d 1, 224 N.W.2d 407 (1974). The need for easy and rapid development is not as great today as it once was, while our perception of the value of sunlight as a source of energy has increased significantly.

Courts should not implement obsolete policies that have lost their vigor over the course of the years. The law of private nuisance is better suited to resolve landowners' disputes about property development in the 1980's than is a rigid rule which does not recognize a landowner's interest in access to sunlight. As we said in Ballstadt v. Pagel, 202 Wis. 484, 489, 232 N.W. 862 (1930), "What is regarded in law as constituting a nuisance in modern times would no doubt have been tolerated without question in former times." We read State v. Deetz, 66 Wis.2d 1, 224 N.W.2d 407 (1974), as an endorsement of the application of common law nuisance to situations involving the conflicting interests of landowners and as rejecting *per se* exclusions to the nuisance law reasonable use doctrine.

In *Deetz* the court abandoned the rigid common law common enemy rule with respect to surface water and adopted the private nuisance reasonable use rule, namely that the landowner is subject to liability if his or her interference with the flow of surface waters unreasonably invades a neighbor's interest in the use and enjoyment of land. Restatement (Second) of Torts, sec. 822, 826, 829 (1977). This court concluded that the common enemy rule which served society "well in the days of burgeoning national expansion of the mid-nineteenth and early-twentieth centuries" should be abandoned because it was no longer "in harmony with the realities of our society." *Deetz*, supra, 66 Wis.2d at 14–15. We recognized in *Deetz* that common law rules adapt to changing social values and conditions.

Yet the defendant would have us ignore the flexible private nuisance law as a means of resolving the dispute between the landowners in this case and would have us adopt an approach, already abandoned in *Deetz*, of favoring the unrestricted development of land and of applying a rigid and inflexible rule protecting his right to build on his land and disregarding any interest of the plaintiff in the use and enjoyment of his land. This we refuse to do.

Private nuisance law, the law traditionally used to adjudicate conflicts between private landowners, has the flexibility to protect both a landowner's right of access to sunlight and another landowner's right to develop land. Private nuisance law is better suited to regulate access to sunlight in modern society and is more in harmony with legislative policy and the prior decisions of this court than is an inflexible doctrine of non-recognition of any interest in access to sunlight across adjoining land.

We therefore hold that private nuisance law, that is, the reasonable use doctrine as set forth in the Restatement, is applicable to the instant case. Recognition of a nuisance claim for unreasonable obstruction of access to sunlight will not prevent land development or unduly hinder the use of adjoining land. It will promote the reasonable use and enjoyment of land in a manner suitable to the 1980's. That obstruction of access to light might be found to constitute a nuisance in certain circumstances does not mean that it will be or must be found to constitute a nuisance under all circumstances. The result in each case depends on whether the conduct complained of is unreasonable.

Accordingly we hold that the plaintiff in this case has stated a claim under which relief can be granted. Nonetheless we do not determine whether the plaintiff in this case is entitled to relief. In order to be entitled to relief the plaintiff must prove the elements required to establish actionable nuisance, and the conduct of the defendant herein must be judged by the reasonable use doctrine.

IV.

The defendant asserts that even if we hold that the private nuisance doctrine applies to obstruction of access to sunlight across adjoining land, the circuit court's granting of summary judgment should be affirmed.

Although the memorandum decision of the circuit court in the instant case is unclear, it appears that the circuit court recognized that the common law private nuisance doctrine was applicable but concluded that defendant's conduct was not unreasonable. The circuit court apparently attempted to balance the utility of the defendant's conduct with the gravity of the harm. Sec. 826, Restatement (Second) of Torts (1977). The defendant urges us to accept the circuit court's balance as adequate. We decline to do so.

The circuit court concluded that because the defendant's proposed house was in conformity with zoning regulations, building codes and deed restrictions, the defendant's use of the land was reasonable. This court has concluded that a landowner's compliance with zoning laws does not automatically bar a nuisance claim. Compliance with the law "is not the controlling factor, though it is, of course, entitled to some weight." Bie v. Ingersoll, 27 Wis.2d 490, 495, 135 N.W.2d 250 (1965). The circuit court also concluded that the plaintiff could have avoided any harm by locating his own house in a better place. Again, plaintiff's ability to avoid the harm is a relevant but not a conclusive factor. See secs. 826, 827, 828, Restatement (Second) of Torts (1977).

Furthermore, our examination of the record leads us to conclude that the record does not furnish an adequate basis for the circuit court to apply the proper legal principles on summary judgment. The application of the reasonable use standard in nuisance cases normally requires a full exposition of all underlying facts and circumstances. Too little is known in this case of such matters as the extent of the harm to the plaintiff, the suitability of solar heat in that neighborhood, the availability of remedies to the plaintiff, and the costs to the defendant of avoiding the harm. Summary judgment is not an appropriate procedural vehicle in this case when the circuit court must weigh evidence which has not been presented at trial. 6 (Pt. 2) Moore's Federal Practice, 56.15 [7], pp. 56–638 (1982); 10 Wright and Miller, Federal Practice and Procedure—Civil, secs. 2729, 2731 (1973).

Because the plaintiff has stated a claim of common law private nuisance upon which relief can be granted, the judgment of the circuit court must be reversed. We need not, and do not, reach the question of whether the complaint states a claim under sec. 844.01, Stats.1979–80, or under the doctrine of prior appropriation. Attoe v. Madison Professional Policemen's Assoc., 79 Wis.2d 199, 205, 255 N.W.2d 489 (1977).

For the reasons set forth, we reverse the judgment of the circuit court dismissing the complaint and remand the matter to circuit court for further proceedings not inconsistent with this opinion.

By the Court. The judgment of the circuit court is reversed and the cause remanded for proceedings not inconsistent with this opinion.

WILLIAM G. CALLOW, J. (dissenting). The majority has adopted the Restatement's reasonable use doctrine to grant an owner of a solar heated home a cause of action against his neighbor who, in acting entirely within the applicable ordinances and statutes, seeks to design and build his home in such a location that it may, at various times during the day, shade the plaintiff's solar collector, thereby impeding the efficiency of his heating system during several months of the year. Because I believe the facts of this case clearly reveal that a cause of action for private nuisance will not lie, I dissent.

I would submit that any policy decisions in this area are best left for the legislature. "What is 'desirable' or 'advisable' or 'ought to be' is a question of policy, not a question of fact. What is 'necessary' or what is 'in the best interest' is not a fact and its determination by the judiciary is an exercise of legislative power when each involves political considerations." In re City of Beloit, 37 Wis.2d 637, 644, 155 N.W.2d 633 (1968). See generally Holifield v. Setco Industries, Inc., 42 Wis.2d 750, 758, 160 N.W.2d 177 (1969); Comment, Solar Rights: Guaranteeing a Place in the Sun, 57 Or.L.Rev. 94, 126–27 (1977) (litigation is a slow, costly, and uncertain method of reform). I would concur with these observations of the trial judge: "While temptation lingers for the court to declare by judicial fiat what is right and what should be done, under the facts in this case, such action under our form of constitutional government where the three branches each have their defined jurisdiction and power, would be an intrusion of judicial egoism over legislative passivity."

The legislature has recently acted in this area. Chapter 354, Laws of 1981 (effective May 7, 1982 [after the dispute in this case arose]), was enacted to provide the underlying legislation enabling local governments to enact ordinances establishing procedures for guaranteeing access to sunlight. This court's intrusion into an area where legislative action is being taken is unwarranted, and it may undermine a legislative scheme for orderly development not yet fully operational.

Chapter 354, Laws of 1981, sec. 66.032, provides specific conditions for solar access permits. In part that section provides for impermissible interference with solar collectors within specific limitations:

"66.032 Solar access permits. (1) . . .

"(f) 'Impermissible interference' means the blockage of solar energy from a collector surface or proposed collector surface for which a permit has been granted under this section during a collector use period if such blockage is by any structure or vegetation on property, an owner of which was notified under sub. (3)(b). *'Impermissible interference' does not include*:

"1. Blockage by a narrow protrusion, including but not limited to a pole or wire, which does not substantially interfere with absorption of solar energy by a solar collector.

"2. *Blockage by any structure constructed, under construction or for which a building permit has been applied for before the date the last notice is mailed or delivered under sub. (3)(b).*

"3. Blockage by any vegetation planted before the date the last notice is mailed or delivered under sub. (3)(b) unless a municipality by ordinance under sub. (2) defines impermissible interference to include such vegetation." (Emphasis added.)

Sec. 66.032(3)(b) provides for notice:

"(3) Permit applications.

"(b) An agency shall determine if an application is satisfactorily completed and shall notify the applicant of its determination. If an applicant receives notice that an application has been satisfactorily completed, *the applicant shall deliver by certified mail or by hand a notice to the owner of any property which the applicant proposes to be restricted by the permit under* sub. (7). The applicant shall submit to the agency a copy of a signed receipt for every notice delivered under this paragraph. The agency shall supply the notice form. The information on the form may include, without limitation because of enumeration:

"1. The name and address of the applicant, and the address of the land upon which the solar collector is or will be located.

"2. That an application has been filed by the applicant.

"3. That the permit, if granted, may affect the rights of the notified owner to develop his or her property and to plant vegetation.

"4. The telephone number, address and office hours of the agency.

"5. That *any person may request a hearing* under sub. (4) within 30 days after receipt of the notice, and the address and procedure for filing the request." (Emphasis added.)

This legislative scheme would deal with the type of problem presented in the present case and precludes the need for judicial activism in this area. . . . . ..

NOTE

Many states have enacted statutes providing access to sunlight for solar energy devices under certain conditions. See, Gergacz, Legal Aspects of Solar Energy: Statutory Approaches for Access to Sunlight, 10 B.C. Envtl. Aff. L.Rev. 1 (1982). These statutes embody numerous choices and compromises; some, for example, distinguish between shading caused by vegetation as opposed to that caused by buildings; some distinguish between various types of solar devices. Id. Should the courts or the legislature make these kinds of choices? Do you agree with the assertion in *Prah* that development of an expanding economy is less significant today than it was earlier in American history and thus restrictions on development to provide access to sunlight make more sense today than in the past?

The evolution of legal rules that balance development and access to sunlight is similar to changes in other areas of the law. Many American jurisdictions, for example, enacted in the 19th century "fencing out" statutes that limited strict liability to cases in which a defendant's cattle broke through a plaintiff's fence and caused property damage; when the country became more settled, however, legislatures switched to "fencing in" statutes that imposed strict liability on owners of cattle unless they fenced in their livestock. W. Prosser, J. Wade and V. Schwartz, Torts (7th ed.) 706–07 (1982).

The practical impact of changing the legal rule for access to sunlight may be less obvious than first appears. Under the traditional rule, when you wished to put up a solar collector, you could buy from your neighbor an express easement to light. See, e.g., R. Powell, The Law of Real Property ¶ 414(8) (1949). When the traditional rule is changed—whether by a decision like *Prah* or by statute—the process is reversed: your neighbor who wishes to shade your house now has to buy from you your right to sunlight. It is possible, depending on such factors as the cost of bargaining, that two neighbors will, through bargaining with each other, reach the same outcome regardless of which rule governs. A considerable literature in law and economics has developed around problems of this type. Seminal pieces include Coase, The Problem of Social Cost, 3 J.Law & Econ. 1 (1960); Calabresi, Transaction Costs, Resource Allocation and Liability Rules—A Comment, 11 J.Law & Econ. 67 (1968).

3. PUBLIC REGULATION OF SOLAR ENERGY: THE ENVIRONMENTAL IMPACT ISSUES

JIMMY CARTER, SOLAR ENERGY

President's Message to Congress, 15 Weekly Comp. of Pres.Doc. 1098 (1979).

Energy from the sun is clean and safe. It will not pollute the air we breathe or the water we drink. It does not run the risk of an accident which may threaten the health or life of our citizens. There are no toxic wastes to cause disposal problems. . . .

OFFICE OF TECHNOLOGY ASSESSMENT, APPLICATION OF SOLAR ENERGY TO TODAY'S ENERGY NEEDS

395–397, 421–423 (1978).

All photovoltaic installations will consist of small, individual generating units—the photovoltaic cell. Individual cells will probably range in size from a few millimeters to a meter in linear dimension. A surprising variety of such cells is available or is in advanced development since it has only been in the past 5 years that serious attention has been given to designing cells for use in anything other than spacecraft. . . .

Silicon is a relatively poor absorber of light and, as a result, cells must be 50 to 200 microns thick to capture an acceptable fraction of the incident light. . . .

GaAs or CdS/Cu_2S are also much better absorbers of light than crystalline silicon, so cells made from these materials can be thinner and tolerate smaller crystal grains than was possible with the crystalline silicon. . . .

Enthusiasm about cells based on materials other than silicon must be tempered to some extent by uncertainties about the health hazards which they may present and about the limits imposed on their production by U.S. and world supplies of component materials. Both cadmium and arsenic, used in GaAs cells, are toxic and while it may be possible to reduce the hazards they present to manageable proportions and while both materials are already used extensively in commercial products and manufacturing, it clearly will be necessary to examine these hazards with some care before recommending an energy system which would significantly increase the use of these materials near populated areas. Domestic supplies of both cadmium and gallium will be sufficient to supply annual production rates in excess of several thousand megawatts a year but production beyond this level could tax domestic supplies and, in the case of cadmium, known world reserves limit the ultimate potential of CdS/Cu_2S devices to about the level of current U.S. energy consumption.

SILICON

Silicon is nontoxic and in plentiful supply (about one atom in five in the Earth's crust is a silicon atom), although current production rates of purified silicon are not adequate to support a large solar industry. The manufacture of silicon devices with present techniques involves the use of a number of hazardous chemicals (PH_3, BCl_3, H_2S_2, HCl, HCN). Existing State and Federal laws should be sufficient to ensure that releases of these materials into the air and water are kept to acceptable levels, although vigilance will be needed to ensure compliance with these regulations. Meeting the standards may add to the cost of the devices.

CADMIUM

Cadmium is a cumulative heavy-metal poison with a half-life in the human body of 10 to 25 years. Cadmium poisoning is believed to lead to accelerated aging, increased risk of cancer, heart disease, lung damage, birth defects, and other problems. Chronic exposure to airborne cadmium can lead to emphysema and other respiratory problems. Cadmium, however, is used in many commercial and industrial products; it is used for corrosion protection on bolts and screws, in paints, plastics, rubber tires, motor oil, fungicides, and some types of fertilizers. Increased use of cadmium resulting from large-scale manufacture of CdS/Cu_2S cells could result in increased release of cadmium from mining, refining, and manufacturing of the cell, and it would increase the amount of cadmium present in products located near populated areas, thereby increasing the risk of exposure in the event of fires, accidents, or the demolition of buildings.

More stringent standards may be needed both in manufacturing processes involving the material and in permitting usage of the material in commercial products. At present, cadmium is not subject to any environmental controls, but under both the Toxic Substance Control Act (P.L. 94–469) and the Resource Conservation and Recovery Act (P.L. 94–580), EPA has jurisdiction over its regulation which, if instituted, could include both solar and other household uses.

It is apparently possible to significantly reduce the cadmium released in the manufacturing process, and it appears that with proper encapsulation CdS cells can be used in residential areas with minimal hazard. Exposure to the material would only occur during fires, accidental breakage, or building demolition. The acceptability of such exposure can be judged better when meaningful standards have been developed.

U.S. production of cadmium in 1970 could support the annual manufacture of cell arrays with a peak output of 5,000 to 20,000 MWe (assuming cells are 10–percent efficient). World production is about five times greater than U.S. production. The higher figure applies to the spray process for manufacturing cells, which results in cells about 6 microns thick. Significant increases in cadmium production may be achievable, however, if demand increases. Identified U.S. reserves of cadmium are sufficient to produce cells with an annual output equal to the current U.S. consumption of electricity. Known world reserves are about five times greater than U.S. reserves.

GALLIUM ARSENIDE

Undisassociated GaAs is harmful but apparently not highly toxic. A lethal dose for an average adult is about one-third kg (0.7 lb). To ingest this much GaAs, a person would have to eat the amount of GaAs in about $20m^2$ (200 square feet) of flat-plate arrays or the amount of GaAs in a field of concentrating arrays covering about 3 acres, clearly a Herculean task. The coatings and protective encapsulation placed on cells should be able to reduce any hazards associated with normal operation of GaAs devices to acceptable levels.

The major danger arises when the material disassociates as a result of a fire or some other accident, since many arsenic compounds are highly

toxic and recognized carcinogens. The AS_2O_3 which would be released in a fire could contaminate land and water near the fire site. Since the cells would most probably be used in connection with high concentrations of sunlight, care must be taken to ensure that the materials do not vaporize and escape if a breakdown in the cell cooling system occurs. The amounts of arsenic used in a concentrating collector, however, would be extremely small. A device with a concentration ratio of 1,000 would, for example, use only about 0.16 gm per m^2 of collector area. This concentration is 250 to 1,500 times smaller than the concentration of As_2O_3 recommended by the U.S. Department of Agriculture for weed control.
. . .

TRACY KIDDER,
THE FUTURE OF THE PHOTOVOLTAIC CELL

245 Atlantic 68, 74 (June, 1980).

Two promising raw materials for solar cells incorporate cadmium, a deadly substance, and the famously lethal arsenic. Solar cells containing these substances and spread across the countryside could have unpleasant side effects. The prospect, albeit an unlikely one, of several million houses, each containing two dozen lead-calcium batteries in its basement to store the power from a photovaltaic roof, ought to worry environmentalists.

Today's techniques of purifying silicon and turning it into solar cells require both a great deal of energy and the use of several toxic chemicals. A boom in photovoltaics would put a burden on the nation's resources. Large amounts of metals, plastics, and glass would be consumed. And if cadmium should become the raw material of choice, there might not be enough of it to go around. The earth doesn't lack for silicon, but by late 1979 a shortage of adequately purified silicon loomed over the entire electronics industry, and the price was going up. .   .   .

NOTE

Compare President Carter's optimistic assessment of solar energy's environmental impact with President Eisenhower's statements about nuclear power in Ch. 2, Sec. B.1, supra. The latest scientific advances often look perfectly safe and utterly inexpensive at first. Analyze closely, for example, the Office of Technology Assessment's statement about silicon, supra. Is it not an understatement to say that meeting environmental standards for at least five hazardous chemicals "may add to the cost of the devices"?

Photovoltaics are not the only solar device that affects the environment. Ordinary solar collectors, for example, are often insulated with materials containing styrine, a suspected carcinogen, while the collector's working fluid often uses ethylene glycol, a toxic chemical, to retard corrosion. See 1 Office of Technology Assessment, Application of Solar Technology to Today's Energy Needs 284 (1978).

Advocates of solar energy may disserve their cause by arguing that solar is free of costs or risks. A clear focus today on the possible environmental impact of solar energy can lead to planning that will reduce environmental hazards in the future. The difficult problem is to assess adequately solar's environmental impact without unduly hampering scientific and technological research that may lead in unexpected and desirable directions. See Ch. 2, Sec. A.1, supra.

4. SOLAR ENERGY AND SOCIAL STRUCTURE: THE HARD PATH vs. SOFT PATH DEBATE

E.F. SCHUMACHER, SMALL IS BEAUTIFUL

147, 156–158 (1973).

Suddenly, if not altogether surprisingly, the modern world, shaped by modern technology, finds itself involved in three crises simultaneously. First, human nature revolts against inhuman technological, organisational, and political patterns, which it experiences as suffocating and debilitating; second, the living environment which supports human life aches and groans and gives signs of partial breakdown; and, third, it is clear to anyone fully knowledgeable in the subject matter that the inroads being made into the world's non-renewable resources, particularly those of fossil fuels, are such that serious bottlenecks and virtual exhaustion loom ahead in the quite foreseeable future. . . . Strange to say, the Sermon on the Mount gives pretty precise instructions on how to construct an outlook that could lead to an Economics of Survival.

— How blessed are those who know that they are poor:

the Kingdom of Heaven is theirs.

— How blessed are the sorrowful;

they shall find consolation.

— How blessed are those of a gentle spirit;

they shall have the earth for their possession.

— How blessed are those who hunger and thirst to see right prevail;

they shall be satisfied;

— How blessed are the peacemakers;

God shall call them his sons.

It may seem daring to connect these beatitudes with matters of technology and economics. But may it not be that we are in trouble precisely because we have failed for so long to make this connection? It is not difficult to discern what these beatitudes may mean for us today:

— We are poor, not demigods.

— We have plenty to be sorrowful about, and are not emerging into a golden age.

— We need a gentle approach, a non-violent spirit, and small is beautiful.

— We must concern ourselves with justice and see right prevail.

— And all this, only this, can enable us to become peacemakers.

The home-comers base themselves upon a different picture of man from that which motivates the people of the forward stampede. It would be very superficial to say that the latter believe in "growth" while the former do not. In a sense, everybody believes in growth, and rightly so, because growth is an essential feature of life. The whole point, however, is to give to the idea of growth a qualitative determination; for there are always many things that ought to be growing and many things that ought to be diminishing.

Equally, it would be very superficial to say that the home-comers do not believe in progress, which also can be said to be an essential feature of all life. The whole point is to determine what constitutes progress. And the home-comers believe that the direction which modern technology has taken and is continuing to pursue—towards ever-greater size, ever-higher speeds, and ever-increased violence, in defiance of all laws of natural harmony—is the opposite of progress. Hence the call for taking stock and finding a new orientation. The stocktaking indicates that we are destroying our very basis of existence, and the reorientation is based on remembering what human life is really about.

In one way or another everybody will have to take sides in this great conflict. To "leave it to the experts" means to side with the people of the forward stampede. It is widely accepted that politics is too important a matter to be left to experts. Today, the main content of politics is economics, and the main content of economics is technology. If politics cannot be left to the experts, neither can economics and technology. . . .

AMORY LOVINS,
ENERGY STRATEGY: THE ROAD NOT TAKEN?

55 Foreign Affairs 55, 77–81 (October, 1976).

There exists today a body of energy technologies that have certain specific features in common and that offer great technical, economic and political attractions, yet for which there is no generic term. For lack of a more satisfactory term, I shall call them "soft" technologies: a textural description, intended to mean not vague, mushy, speculative or ephemeral, but rather flexible, resilient, sustainable and benign. Energy paths dependent on soft technologies . . . will be called "soft" energy paths, as the "hard" technologies . . . constitute a "hard" path (in both senses). The distinction between hard and soft energy paths rests not on how much energy is used, but on the technical and sociopolitical *structure* of the energy system, thus focusing our attention on consequent and crucial political differences.

. . . [T]he social structure is significantly shaped by the rapid deployment of soft technologies. These are defined by five characteristics:

— They rely on renewable energy flows that are always there whether we use them or not, such as sun and wind and vegetation: on energy income, not on depletable energy capital.

— They are diverse, so that energy supply is an aggregate of very many individually modest contributions, each designed for maximum effectiveness in particular circumstances.

— They are flexible and relatively low-technology—which does not mean unsophisticated, but rather, easy to understand and use without esoteric skills, accessible rather than arcane.

— They are matched in *scale* and in geographic distribution to end-use needs, taking advantage of the free distribution of most natural energy flows.

— They are matched in *energy quality* to end-use needs: a key feature that deserves immediate explanation. . . .

A feature of soft technologies as essential as their fitting end-use needs (for a different reason) is their appropriate scale, which can achieve important types of economies not available to larger, more centralized systems. This is done in five ways, of which the first is reducing and sharing overheads. Roughly half your electricity bill is fixed distribution costs to pay the overheads of a sprawling energy system: transmission lines, transformers, cables, meters and people to read them, planners, headquarters, billing computers, interoffice memos, advertising agencies. For electrical and some fossil-fuel systems, distribution accounts for more than half of total capital cost, and administration for a significant fraction of total operating cost. Local or domestic energy systems can reduce or even eliminate these infrastructure costs. The resulting savings can far outweigh the extra costs of the dispersed maintenance infrastructure that the small systems require, particularly where that infrastructure already exists or can be shared (e.g., plumbers fixing solar heaters as well as sinks).

Small scale brings further savings by virtually eliminating distribution losses, which are cumulative and pervasive in centralized energy systems (particularly those using high-quality energy). Small systems also avoid direct diseconomies of scale, such as the frequent unreliability of large units and the related need to provide instant "spinning reserve" capacity on electrical grids to replace large stations that suddenly fail. Small systems with short lead times greatly reduce exposure to interest escalation and mistimed demand forecasts—major indirect diseconomies of large scale.

The fifth type of economy available to small systems arises from mass production. Consider, as Henrik Harboe suggests, the 100-odd million cars in this country. In round numbers, each car probably has an average cost of less than $4,000 and a shaft power over 100 kilowatts (134 horse-power). Presumably a good engineer could build a generator and up-grade an automobile engine to a reliable, 35-percent-efficient diesel at no greater total cost, yielding a mass-produced diesel generator unit costing less than $40 per kW. In contrast, the motive capacity in our central power stations—currently totaling about 1/40 as much as in our cars—costs perhaps ten times more per kW, partly because it is not mass-produced. It is not surprising that at least one foreign car maker hopes to go into the wind-machine and heat-pump business. Such a market can be entered incrementally, without the billions of dollars' investment required for, say, liquefying natural gas or gasifying coal. It may require a production philosophy oriented toward technical simplicity, low replacement cost, slow obsolescence, high reliability, high volume and low markup; but these are familiar concepts in mass production. Industrial resistance would presumably melt when—as with pollution-abatement equipment—the scope for profit was perceived.

This is not to say that all energy systems need be at domestic scale. For example, the medium scale of urban neighborhoods and rural villages offers fine prospects for solar collectors—especially for adding collectors to existing buildings of which some (perhaps with large flat roofs) can take excess collector area while others cannot take any. They could be joined via communal heat storage systems, saving on labor cost and on heat losses. The costly craftwork of remodeling existing systems—"backfitting" idiosyncratic houses with individual collectors—could there-by be greatly reduced. Despite these advantages, medium-scale solar technologies are currently receiving little attention apart from a condo-minium-village project in Vermont sponsored by the Department of Housing and Urban Development and the 100-dwelling-unit Mejannes-le-Clap project in France.

The schemes that dominate ERDA's solar research budget—such as making electricity from huge collectors in the desert, or from temperature differences in the oceans, or from Brooklyn Bridge-like satellites in outer space—do not satisfy our criteria, for they are ingenious high-technology ways to supply energy in a form and at a scale inappropriate to most end-use needs. Not all solar technologies are soft. Nor, for the same reason, is nuclear fusion a soft technology. But many genuine soft technologies are now available and are now economic. What are some of them?

Solar heating and, imminently, cooling head the list. They are incrementally cheaper than electric heating, and far more inflation-proof, practically anywhere in the world. In the United States (with fairly high average sunlight levels), they are cheaper than present electric heating virtually anywhere, cheaper than oil heat in many parts, and cheaper than gas and coal in some. Even in the least favorable parts of the continental United States, far more sunlight falls on a typical building than is required to heat and cool it without supplement; whether this is considered economic depends on how the accounts are done. The difference in solar input between the most and least favorable parts of the lower 49 states is generally less than two-fold, and in cold regions, the long heating season can improve solar economics.

Ingenious ways of backfitting existing urban and rural buildings (even large commercial ones) or their neighborhoods with efficient and exceedingly reliable solar collectors are being rapidly developed in both the private and public sectors. . . .

AMORY LOVINS, PREPARED TESTIMONY

in The Energy Controversy
28–31 (H. Nash, ed. 1979).

Hard and soft technologies have very different implications for technologists. Hard technologies are demanding and frustrating. They are not much fun to do and are therefore unlikely to be done well. While they strain technology to (and beyond) its limits, the scope they offer for innovation is of a rather narrow, routine sort, and is buried within huge, anonymous research teams. The systems are beyond the developmental reach of all but a few giant corporations, liberally aided by public subsidies, subventions, and bailouts. The disproportionate talent and money devoted to hard technologies gives their proponents disproportionate influence, reinforcing the trend and discouraging good technologists from devoting their careers to soft technologies—which then cannot absorb funds effectively for lack of good people. And once hard technologies are developed, the enormous investments required to tool up to make them effectively exclude small business from the market, thus sacrificing rapid and sustained returns in money, energy, and jobs for all but a small segment of society.

Soft technologies have a completely different character. They are best developed by innovative small businesses and even individuals, for they offer immense scope for basically new ideas. Their challenge lies not in complexity but in simplicity. They permit but do not require mass production, thus encouraging local manufacture, by capital-saving and labor-intensive methods, of equipment adapted to local needs, materials, and skills. Soft technologies are multi-purpose and can be integrated with buildings and with transport and food systems, saving on infrastructure. Their diversity matches our own pluralism: there is a soft energy system to match any settlement pattern. Soft technologies do not distort political structures or priorities; they improve the quality of work by emphasizing personal ingenuity, responsibility, and craftsmanship; they are inherently non-violent, and are therefore a livelihood that technologists can have good dreams about. . . .

The choice between the soft and hard paths is urgent. Though each path is only illustrative and embraces an infinite spectrum of variations on a theme, there is a deep structural and conceptual dichotomy between them. Soft and hard *technologies* are not *technically* incompatible: in principle, nuclear power stations and solar collectors can coexist. But soft and hard *paths* are *culturally* incompatible: each path entails a certain evolution of social values and perceptions that makes the other kind of world harder to imagine. The two paths are *institutionally* antagonistic: the policy actions, institutions, and political commitments required for each (especially for the hard path) would seriously inhibit the other. And they are *logistically* competitive: every dollar, every bit of sweat and technical talent, every barrel of irreplaceable oil, every year that we devote to the very demanding high technologies is a resource that we cannot use to pursue the elements of a soft path urgently enough to make them work together properly. In this sense, technologies like nuclear power are not only unnecessary but a positive encumbrance, for their resource commitments foreclose other and more attractive options, delaying soft technologies until the fossil-fuel bridge has been burned. Thus we must, with due deliberate speed, choose one path or the other, before one has foreclosed the other or before nuclear proliferation has foreclosed both. We should use fossil fuels—thriftily—to capitalize a transition as nearly as possible straight to our ultimate energy-income sources, because we won't have another chance to get there. . . .

ADEN B. MEINEL AND MARJORIE P. MEINEL, SOFT PATH LEADS TO A NEW DARK AGE

in The Energy Controversy
225, 226–228, 232–233 (H. Nash, ed. 1979).

When Lovins discusses solar and other exotic options, he is naive, accepting only what pleases him and ignoring very fundamental problems as though they did not exist. There are problems for both high technology and low technology solar options. We have traced the discouraging history of attempts to inject new low-level solar technology into developing countries and know that the facts of capital and economics are as inexorable in these societies as in advanced societies. To like only simple technology and eschew any technology that appears beyond the comprehension of the average individual is an illusion.

Our work has taken us to much of the world, and we have seen that Lovins' type of simple society does exist in some developing countries. His proposals greatly resemble Mahatma Gandhi's "cottage industries," held by many educated Indians to have been a diversion from the effort to improve the lot of the masses. One of the greatest improvements in the welfare of the village inhabitants in India has been, contrary to Lovins' hypothesis, the electrification of the villages. This step parallels the dramatic changes caused by the Rural Electrification Agency in the United States in the '30's, a period before the personal knowledge of most of the population today. His proposal also has echoes of Mao's "great leap forward," wherein technology was forced toward backyard industries, including even steel smelting! It, too, was a notable failure of an enticing dream. For the industrialized world to toy with such a set of ideas could be the beginning of a irreversible process leading downward, one from which recovery might be denied as problem piles upon problem and acrimony upon acrimony. . . . [T]he alternative which we prefer, and which Mr. Lovins would dismiss as a "hard" technology, is the production of electric power or hydrogen on large-scale solar farms located in the arid southwest on land not now in use.

Our advocacy of large-scale solar power farms is contrary to the stream of popular enthusiasm. Small-scale individual applications are the center of attention today. We feel this is contrary to the way society has gone for centuries, in fact, ever since the isolated castle of the Middle Ages gave way slowly before renewed commerce and order. There is no reason why each of us could not have our own gasoline, or diesel, powered generator and water well today—as Mr. Lovins advocates—except that it would be inconvenient, unreliable and costly. We have lived in a solar-heated house with a solar-heated swimming pool. We do not think many other persons, other than avid do-it-yourselfers, would enjoy it after the novelty wore off.

Solar energy may first come into use on people's rooftops, but we are certain that, as soon as possible, they will prefer to have it delivered as electrical energy and transportable fuels. People already use electrical energy for a vast array of needs and luxuries. Public and private utilities provide it for us and take care that the system supplies it with high reliability. American industry is geared to produce electricity-consuming devices. Solar electric power therefore meets the requirement of minimum perturbation of the socio-economic system we live in, a requirement that must be met for change to be socially acceptable.

We think that the utilities have a long future of delivering energy and water to consumers at the lowest possible cost and maximum convenience, whether the energy be fossil, nuclear, geothermal, wind or solar. For everyone to abandon the utility and get his own energy system seems like a step back toward the Dark Ages, or like a person abandoning the ship to cling to his personal life jacket. We have confidence in the viability of the ship. . . .

KARL MARX, THE GRUNDRISSE

152 (McClellan, ed. 1971).

No special sagacity is required in order to understand that, beginning with free labour or wage-labour for example, which arose after the abolition of slavery, machines can only develop in opposition to living labour, as a hostile power and alien property, i.e. they must, as capital, oppose the worker. But it is equally easy to see that machines do not cease to be agents of social production, once they become, for example, the property of associated workers. But in the first case, their means of distribution (the fact that they do not belong to the workers) is itself a condition of the means of production that is founded on wage-labour. In the second case, an altered means of distribution will derive from a new, altered basis of production emerging from the historical process. . . .

NOTE

Would Lovins or Schumacher accept "hard" technologies if those technologies were controlled by "the people"? Is that what Marx advocates? Would the Meinels accept "soft" technologies if they believed those technologies to be consistent with increasing wealth and economic growth?

Is the pocket calculator a "hard" or a "soft" technology? What difference does it make?

Lovins' views have sparked much debate, particularly on the issue of whether his approach could actually satisfy world energy needs at reasonable cost. See, e.g., Alternative Long Range Energy Strategies: Joint Hearing Before the House Select Committee on Small Business and the House Committee on Interior and Insular Affairs, 94th Congress, 2nd Sess. (1976).

As Lovins notes, not all solar devices are "soft." "Hard" solar technologies, such as central power stations fueled by heat from mirrors, would fit in with current utility systems. See *American Paper Institute*, Ch. 9, Sec. A.1., supra. "Soft," decentralized solar energy systems, such as rooftop collectors, may in part or in whole supplant those systems. Utility pricing structures could arguably encourage the use of collectors combined with traditional sources of electricity for those times when collectors are inadequate. See, e.g., Lawrence and Minan, Solar Energy and Public Utility Rate Regulation, 26 UCLA L.Rev. 550 (1979). If you had a choice, and costs were equal, would you prefer electricity from a central source or from a rooftop collector? Does it matter which system gives you more personal control and responsibility in areas such as system repair?

The hard vs. soft path debate indicates how scientific and technological developments can alter the very structure of a society. In deciding whether or not to encourage a particular area of science, does cost benefit analysis adequately consider this type of impact? See Ch. 10, Sec. B.2, infra. Compare also Tribe's analysis in Ch. 1, Sec. D.2, supra.

In the long run, can following the hard or soft path do any more than postpone the painful process of accommodating population growth to a world of finite resources? See Hardin, The Tragedy of the Commons, 162 Science 1243 (1968).

B. NUCLEAR FUSION

---

1. THE NATURE OF FUSION ENERGY

U.S. DEPARTMENT OF ENERGY, MAGNETIC FUSION

Program Summary Document 2–9 (1979).

Albert Einstein's special theory of relativity showed that mass can be converted to energy via his famous formula, $E = mc^2$, where m represents the change in mass from an initial state to the related final state and c represents the speed of light. The two practical methods for achieving this conversion involve the fission and fusion of atomic nuclei. In fission, heavy atoms, such as uranium, are split apart. The mass of the resulting material is less than that of the original atom, so there is a net release of energy corresponding to the change in total mass. The second method for transforming mass into energy is fusion, in which nuclei of light atoms, such as hydrogen, are joined together to form a larger nucleus. However, the mass of the resulting nucleus is less than the sum of the masses of the light nuclei, and energy corresponding once again to the reduction in total mass is released.

Of the various possible fusion reactions, the most likely near-term fusion reaction involves two isotopes of hydrogen (H): deuterium (D) and tritium (T). . . .

For sustained fusion reactions to take place, three conditions must be satisfied:

(1) The fusion fuel must be heated and maintained at a temperature near its ignition point (approximately 100,000,000 K for the D–T reaction). At this temperature, the fuel charge will exist entirely in the plasma state; that is, as a totally ionized gas.

(2) The energy in the plasma must be confined for a time, t, sufficient to ensure that, on the average, the energy (heat) from the burning fuel charge is greater than or equal to the energy supplied to heat and confine the plasma.

(3) The plasma must have a density, n, sufficiently high to ensure that the ions are close enough for reactions to occur. (The density is the number of ions per unit volume of plasma.) . . .

In a fusion plasma, positively charged particles repel each other; this repulsive force comes into play long before the nuclei are close enough for a reaction to occur (this is why fusion reactions are inherently more difficult to produce than fission reactions). Forcing the nuclei to come close enough for a reaction to occur requires extremely high temperatures (of the order of 100,000,000 K). At such high temperatures, nearly all the atoms will be stripped of their electrons. The material then consists of positively charged nuclei, called ions, and free negatively charged electrons. The positive electrical charges of the ions and the negative charges of the electrons balance exactly, so that the plasma as a whole is electrically neutral. It behaves in many respects like a gas, but because of the presence of electrically charged particles, it conducts electricity and is affected by magnetic fields.

A temperature of 100,000,000 K is difficult to relate to ordinary experience. For comparison, most heat-resistant materials used in industry, such as ceramics, melt at about 4000 K, and the interior of the sun is estimated to be about 15,000,000 K. Plasma heating to the extraordinary temperatures required is accomplished using several methods. A plasma can be heated to temperatures as high as a few million degrees by passing an electric current through it. This is called ohmic (or resistance) heating and depends on the electrical resistance of the plasma. As the temperature increases, the resistance of the plasma decreases and eventually becomes too low for resistance heating to be effective. Another procedure used to heat plasmas to higher temperatures is by neutral-beam injection into the plasma. The neutral beams are stripped of their electrons and collide with the plasma ions and electrons, thereby raising their temperatures. Because neutral-beam heating is more dependent upon mechanical resistance (i.e., ionizing collisions) than upon the electrical resistance of the plasma, it can be used as an effective supplementary technique to raise plasma temperatures higher than those achieved by ohmic heating alone. . . .

[T]wo fundamentally different approaches are being followed toward development of fusion energy: 1) magnetic confinement, and 2) inertial confinement. In magnetic confinement, the hot ionized gases (plasmas) which will undergo fusion reactions are contained in carefully shaped magnetic fields. A combination of resistive and supplemental (e.g., neutral-beam injection) heating is used to raise the plasma temperature to that required for substantial fusion reactions. In inertial confinement, the fuel which will undergo fusion reactions is contained within a small pellet. A large amount of energy is deposited into the pellet by an appropriate device, such as a laser beam, thus raising the pellet temperature high enough to cause the fusion reactions. Within each of these conceptual approaches there are many different schemes for achieving a controlled thermonuclear reaction.

Although scientists have been able to produce conditions in the laboratory approaching those necessary for the production of fusion energy, these experiments have not yet produced more energy than was invested. In other words, net energy gain from fusion plasma reactions has not yet been attained by either approach. However, researchers are confident that this demonstration will be made within the next 4–6 years. While the highest immediate priority is to demonstrate scientific feasibility, lesser priorities are simultaneously given to projects which aim beyond that demonstration (e.g., commercialization studies). . . .

NOTE

In 1983, the federal government, primarily through the Department of Energy, spent about $500 million on fusion research, the bulk of it for magnetic as opposed to inertial confinement. The private sector played a relatively small role—fusion requires costly basic research and returns an uncertain payoff. The major goal of the fusion program is to generate electricity through the same method used with nuclear fission, coal or oil: the heat generated in the reactor boils water, producing steam to turn turbines that generate electricity. The attraction of fusion is that the fuel, deuterium, is quite abundant.

The Department of Energy hopes that the Tokamak Fusion Test Reactor, a magnetic confinement device under construction in Princeton, New Jersey, will demonstrate the scientific feasibility of fusion in the mid-1980's by producing more energy from fusion reactions than is used in creating them. A demonstration of scientific feasibility for an inertial confinement device is predicted to come somewhat later. Demonstrating scientific feasibility will not, of course, prove that fusion reactors are economical or safe. The Department does not believe that fusion will make a substantial contribution to the nation's electricity requirements until well into the next century. See 217 Science 236 (1982).

2. PUBLIC FUNDING OF THE FUSION PROGRAM: THE SEARCH FOR A BREAKTHROUGH

BILL PETERSON,
U.S. MAKES MAJOR ADVANCE IN NUCLEAR FUSION

The Washington Post, Aug. 13, 1978 at A1, col. 1.

Princeton University scientists have made a major advance in the race to tame nuclear fusion—the hydrogen bomb process—which a top government energy expert said yesterday could lead to the production of the first practical working fusion reactors.

Using a small, donut-shaped test reactor, the scientists produced sunlike temperatures of more than 60 million degrees centigrade inside a kind of magnetic bottle.

"It is the first time we've produced the actual conditions of a fusion reactor in a scale-model device," said Dr. Stephen O. Dean, director of the Department of Energy's magnetic confinement systems division.

"This is the biggest thing that has ever happened in fusion research," he said.

"The question of whether fusion is feasible from a scientific point of view has now been answered," Dean added. "The practical questions of what price it will cost and when it will be duplicated commercially are now engineering and economic questions."

The potential payoff is unlimited electrical energy, one of the prerequisites for the long-term survival of advanced civilization. . . .

HEARING, SUBCOMMITTEE ON FOSSIL AND NUCLEAR ENERGY RESEARCH, DEVELOPMENT AND DEMONSTRATION OF THE HOUSE COMMITTEE ON SCIENCE AND TECHNOLOGY

95th Cong., 2d Sess. 1–67 (1978).

MR. FLOWERS. I would like to call this committee to order.

I thank the Chairman, Mr. Teague, for allowing me to chair this hearing because of my intense interest in the subject matter. It is under my subcommittee's jurisdiction.

I would like to welcome our distinguished friends from the Department of Energy. Of course, our hearing today is an occasion for oversight and, I trust, congratulations, although signals we have gotten are somewhat murky and cloudy. The other reason for this hearing, I think, is to clarify exactly what it is that we have heard about recently.

I know that on occasion I have to explain the fusion concept to the general public, and I know I am not the best qualified person to do that; I can do it in very simplistic terms, but when you get beyond that, most of us have trouble with it, and most of us would have trouble trying to understand exactly what this breakthrough amounts to.

We can understand the problems that we have encountered in developing and containing fusion energy, of course; but I think that this is a very apropos time for us to go into it and we deeply appreciate your presence, gentlemen, in aiding us in this quest.

The fusion program with its promise of almost limitless energy supplies has been a dream for a long time. It has been a dream of clean and abundant energy; it has been pursued by a group of dedicated scientists; it has crossed national boundaries and has persisted through 30 years or more of practice and theoretical obstacles. These recent results from your magnetic fusion program are indicating that the next step will work, and if so, the dream is surer to become reality than many skeptics thought, and probably is closer in a time frame than many people had thought, although I think that we must say, in a word of caution, that this does not mean fusion is just around the corner, and I don't think you gentlemen are here to tell us that this morning.

We have asked you to testify and describe the current status and future plans of the magnetic fusion program. It will be helpful, of course, for us on the committee to hear about the results at the Princeton Large Torus and put them into perspective for the rest of the program.

It is always a pleasure to recognize success and I certainly want to sincerely congratulate the Department of Energy and all of those highly skilled scientists and technicians who participated in this program.

In the nature of pure research, sometimes you don't have a chance to thank and express appreciation to those who have been involved, and it is noteworthy that in this case we can, and I certainly want to do that. I want to welcome you, Dr. Deutch and Dr. Gottlieb and Mr. Kintner, and thank you for being here. Let us proceed as you see fit, unless other members of the committee would like to comment at this time.

Mr. Chairman, would you like to have a word?

MR. FUQUA. I would just like to say that we are very pleased at the results that came from the recent Princeton research project, and I want to congratulate all of you. We have been working a long time in this area. I realize we have just scratched the surface. We have a long time to wait; but I think that this has been significant.

MR. FLOWERS. Mr. Roe, would you like to have a word?

MR. ROE. I would rather listen than speak, but I do think it is appropriate to comment and welcome the gentlemen here and the distinguished panel we have. I particularly give my regards to Dr. Gottlieb. It is always interesting to know that the great sovereign State of New Jersey is out in front and leading what is happening.

MR. FLOWERS. I was wondering if Princeton was in your district.

MR. ROE. Temporarily; it is a little south of my district.

MR. FLOWERS. There is a little fallover, carryover, of some sort.

MR. ROE. Like a great deal of feeling of warmth and affection for these great achievements.

MR. FLOWERS. Mr. Rudd?

MR. RUDD. Thank you, Mr. Chairman.

I am very pleased to be here to hear—

MR. FLOWERS. Princeton is not in Arizona, too?

MR. RUDD [continuing]. These very distinguished scientists. I would like to just ask for the benefit of those people who are in my position and nonscientists, if you would preface your remarks, if it is possible, and the chairman used the word, "simplistic," with some sort of an understandable overview of what we are going to get into, if that is possible.

MR. FLOWERS. Eldon, you have been on this committee for almost 2 years now, with me as chairman of the subcommittee, and that is a requirement. I think these people know that we are talking to people, and not to just scientist to scientist, and we certainly know that they are going to do that.

MR. RUDD. I would certainly appreciate that effort.

Thank you, Mr. Chairman. Thank you, gentlemen.

MR. FLOWERS. Would the gentleman from Tennessee like to make a comment, too?

MR. GORE. Certainly, Mr. Chairman.

I will try to hold them down a little bit, just to say that Princeton is not in my district or near my district, but neither is Princeton solely responsible for the magnificent achievements that we are here to listen to.

Tennessee has played quite a role in this breakthrough, if indeed it can be called a breakthrough, and we are all very excited about the progress being made here. There has been a change in attitude about the fusion program as a result of the recent achievements, and I think this is a most appropriate time to review the status of the program, and I am glad to participate in it.

MR. FLOWERS. Actually, I guess that I must make some additional comment before I yield to you gentlemen.

Obviously, had the program been at the University of Alabama in Tuscaloosa, we would have been having this meeting several years ago, congratulating you on this breakthrough; but please proceed. . . .

MR. KINTNER. I would like to talk to the significance of the Princeton results, from the point of view of the Program Director and to try to put these results in practical, everyday terms which you can understand. . . .

There is now experimental evidence that we can confine fusion plasma at conditions leading to net energy production on Earth in devices of reasonable size and reasonable magnetic field strength. We have not done that yet because we have not yet had available a device designed to do it, but the Princeton results allow us to predict the size and characteristics of such a device. In fact, because of bold decisions taken several years ago, we already have well underway a machine which turns out to be almost ideal from that point of view, the Tokamak fusion test reactor, which is being built at Princeton, the groundbreaking for which was last October.

More than half the hardware for that device is already on order. We now have every reason to believe that the scientific feasibility of fusion will be demonstrated in TFTR in 1983.

There are, of course, many complex questions, including those of impurities, magnetic field efficiency, pulse duration, and even more engineering and technology questions that remain before us; but they are more questions of goodness or economics than of physical feasibility. There is no remaining theoretical or experimental evidence indicating that man will not be able to create and control an energy producing fusion plasma. I think that is a profound conclusion, that it is something we should be proud of and should use to our overall advantage. . . .

I agree with John Deutch that much hard effort in both physics and engineering will be required before practical, economic fusion is a reality. We need a strong, steady commitment to fusion over a long time, but we in the program feel such a commitment is fully justified by the great implications of success and the excellent progress being made, of which the Princeton result is the latest and most significant example.

Thank you very much.

MR. FLOWERS. Mr. Kintner, let me ask you something, in very simplistic terms, for Mr. Rudd and myself. Maybe I am going to ask Dr. Gottlieb to give us his explanation of how fusion works, but we are into, I guess, what everybody realizes is the football season and the political season, too, but football is predominant where I come from.

Now in terms of what this breakthrough or near breakthrough amounts to, is it a first down, or 4-yard gain, or what does it amount to?

MR. KINTNER. I think we have returned the kickoff back to a very good field position.

MR. FLOWERS. Well, would you say we got it back to about the 40-yard line or something like that?

MR. KINTNER. I would say we are at least at midfield.

MR. FLOWERS. That is good. That is the way I like to hear you people talk now. There was a whole lot of stuff in there I didn't understand, but now you are getting down to the nub, I think. . . .

MR. GORE. Thank you, Mr. Chairman.

From what I have heard this morning, gentlemen, I would say that the use of the word "breakthrough" is appropriate. The results achieved in this most recent test have changed completely the attitude of the scientific community toward the feasibility of fusion, at least that is what I am hearing you say this morning.

I heard fusion described 1½ years ago when I came to the Congress as a technological shot that might very well never come to pass.

After the information that triggered this hearing, everyone now assumes that it can be done. Questions remain, but they are questions of much smaller magnitude. So I would say even though breakthrough metaphorically implies a sudden event, I think that we have seen what is essentially a breakthrough in this program.

I don't want to quarrel with words, but would you agree, Dr. Deutch?

DR. DEUTCH. No, Mr. Gore, I would not agree. I would not agree and I would not agree most emphatically. First of all let me tell you what I mean by breakthrough. A breakthrough is something which will substantially reduce either the time or the cost required to reach practical realization of the technology.

MR. GORE. If I could stop you there, that is not the way I am defining breakthrough.

DR. DEUTCH. Then we can reach agreement rapidly.

MR. GORE. Dealing on this subcommittee with numerous energy technologies, certainty of development is a factor that becomes critical for us as we evaluate the level of funding desired for a program. When we evaluate the feasibility of research and development programs compared to each other, the certainty of success is one of the critical factors that we look at. Indeed, this is also true as we map out an energy strategy for the next several decades.

If we increase the certainty that a new technology can come on line, it increases our flexibility to allocate those resources that limit our current energy technology. So, insofar as for me it increases the certainty dramatically I see it as a breakthrough.

DR. DEUTCH. You want me to be agreeable?

MR. GORE. No; I don't. I want to get a fix on this program.

DR. DEUTCH. My view of it is the following: It was the last and decisive scientific accomplishment that told us that the technology was going to be scientifically feasible, and it came in a welcome way, it came quicker, it came better than expected. As a scientific accomplishment, its importance cannot be overestimated. It was an extremely important scientific accomplishment, and it did nail down that last important parameter that leads us to the conviction that we will be able to demonstrate scientific feasibility. In that regard it certainly is essential.

But if our objective is, as it should be, to ultimately make this into a practical, economic, workable, power system, the number of hurdles that we have to overcome, the time, the expense, and technical ingenuity required, have not been circumvented by this event. . . .

MR. GORE. But would you no longer describe fusion as a technological long shot?

DR. DEUTCH. Sir, I did not do that before this experiment.

MR. GORE. Well, that was the administration's view of fusion 18 months ago. The view of a lot of people.

DR. DEUTCH. Eighteen months ago I was not there, as Professor Gottlieb would advise you.

MR. GORE. I don't want to belabor the point. I think it is relevant to the line of questioning pursued by my colleague from New York. If we have results like these, which tell us it can be done, then shouldn't we reevaluate the amount of attention that we pay to this program.

You say on page 2 of your complete statement, and I am quoting:

Before the middle of the next century, sometime between 2020 and 2050, by current estimate, diminishing reserves of oil, natural gas and fossil fuels will force us to place increasing reliance on inexhaustibles.

Now, I submit to you I believe my colleague from New Jersey is right, that we are facing problems relating to diminishing reserves of conventional fuels right now, not by 2050, and we need to place increasing reliance on energy sources such as fusion now, not somewhere between 2020 and 2050.

If we increase the certainty that positive results will come, I think we do need to reevaluate the attention paid to the program.

You say at another point in your testimony that the current level of funding was deemed to be appropriate, but decreases would, in fact, delay the day of commercial availability of fusion. You do not deal with the converse: Can increases in funding speed up the day at which fusion is commercially available?

DR. DEUTCH. First, let me say we have reevaluated the program; that was really the thrust of my entire testimony, Mr. Gore. We have looked at the program in excruciating detail, and with greater attention and greater technological precision than almost any other program we have.

MR. GORE. With OMB looking over your shoulder, you have the constraints that all of the administration witnesses who come up here have to make sure that the funding for none of these alternative energy technologies really moves too far out in front of any other, thereby holding them back on a kind of moderate course. But this sense of urgency I share; if we can get it a decade earlier or several years earlier by paying a lot more attention and by funding it at a higher level, then I think the argument in favor of doing so is very strong.

DR. DEUTCH. Can I continue?

MR. GORE. Yes, please do.

DR. DEUTCH. Let me continue for a moment; I wanted to address two other points that you made. OMB looking over our shoulder is not the stage we are talking about now. We are talking about the internal deliberations at our Department.

The second point I want to make is that perhaps the phrases in my testimony were not correctly chosen about ultimate renewable and the 2020 to 2050 time frame. What I was talking about then was long term in the sense Mr. Roe meant it. We have to start working on substituting energy fossil fuels now, which we are doing through the Department's program on coal conversion. I was looking one stage beyond that. I hope that that was not badly conveyed in the testimony.

Finally, let me talk about budget increases. It is absolutely correct that a lot of people will argue for larger budget increases here in the hopes that we can move that date significantly.

Between now and the time when we make a decision for an engineering test facility, the relationship between budget size and pace of progress is less than it is going to be after that point because we are still working on scientific basis of the technology. Of course, there is some flexibility there, I am not saying to you there is no sensitivity in terms of dates, but it is only—

MR. GORE. Now wait a minute. Let me stop you there.

In other words, we could move the date up if we increased funding. Is that the way I interpret that last sentence?

DR. DEUTCH. I am sure we could move the date up slightly with increased funding.

MR. GORE. What do you mean "slightly"? Instead of 2020, 2000?

DR. DEUTCH. No, no. Sir, I didn't make myself clear. I was talking about the time period between now and the mid-1980's when we will want to look at an engineering test facility for fusion. We can influence that date by one year, perhaps, maybe a bit more, with money. But the time when we can really influence the pace is after that when we have the proper scientific and engineering basis set and the choice will be the pace and the speed at which you want to build very expensive facilities.

So I am trying to argue that during this period now we are getting the basic scientific and engineering knowledge and the material science knowledge. Do not assume that you can cut a decade off this time schedule by doubling the budget.

If it proves out from the basic materials science, from the basic engineering and scientific phases, after you get the engineering test facility, we will be much more able to influence the pace of the program through budget changes. This would be comparable to the breeder program where we are really choosing time and dollars and the basic technology is set. We are not yet at that stage with the fusion program. . . .

WILLIAM D. METZ,
REPORT OF FUSION BREAKTHROUGH PROVES TO BE A MEDIA EVENT

201 Science 792–794 (1978).

On the weekend of 12 and 13 August, the unlikely subject of fusion suddenly became the leading news story in the country.

"Scientists at Princeton University have produced a controlled thermonuclear fusion reaction that experts are hailing as a major technical breakthrough," said the Knight-Ridder wire service in a story that was carried by 50 to 100 newspapers. "U.S. Makes Major Advance in Nuclear Fusion," was the banner headline of the Washington Post's leading front-page story on Sunday morning. Radio and TV stations throughout the weekend reported the story with all the urgency of an international crisis, and by the end of the 2-day media blitz, many citizens apparently got the impression that after years of waiting for proof, fusion had finally been achieved. The message was so strong and so positive that it seemed—for 48 hours at least—that the energy crisis was over, solar energy and nuclear power were no longer needed, and that the future would be assured through fusion.

The heady optimism did not last long. By Monday afternoon, the Department of Energy, which had sponsored the Princeton research, was saying that no breakthrough had occurred, and that the results, while "gratifying," would make no change in the timetable or the funding for government fusion research, which is expected to require at least 50 more years to bear fruition. John Deutch, of the Department of Energy, said that the Princeton result came "sooner and in stronger form than we anticipated," but he characterized it only as "an item that bears on the first step" of a lengthy, costly, technically demanding development process.

One of the principal reasons for confusion was that the reports of the weekend had seemed to indicate that fusion had reached the long-awaited goal of energy breakeven—the point where a reacting fusion plasma produces more energy than it consumes. But the head of the Princeton laboratory, Melvin Gottlieb, said that the experiment in question had not made breakeven. However, he told a Washington press conference on Monday afternoon, 14 August, that "we're on schedule and I'm confident we will achieve breakeven" with a larger experiment due to begin operation in the 1980's.

What actually happened at Princeton that garnered so much attention? It was the dramatic conclusion of a sometimes discouraging experiment with a 3-meter diameter doughnut-shaped device called a tokamak, which can serve as a type of "magnetic bottle" for containing fusion reactions. The device, named the Princeton Large Torus, ran into severe engineering difficulties soon after it was built in 1976, but by spring of this year it was working well and by summer it was producing the highest temperature ever recorded for a tokamak. That temperature, according to Harold Eubank who conducted the experiment along with Walter Stodiek, was 50 to 55 million degrees Celsius, about six times higher than the temperature in the fusion experiment that had come closest to breakeven, one carried out with the Alcator tokamak at MIT in 1976. In order to get such a high temperature, however, Eubank and Stodiek had to lower the density of the plasma in their experiment. Temperature, density, and the length of time the plasma is contained are all important in magnetic fusion experiments and must simultaneously meet certain criteria for a self-sustained reaction to be achieved. Although the temperature was six times higher than MIT's, the combined measure of density and confinement time (which was 15 thousandths of a second) gave a value, Eubank told Science, which was 30 times worse than that attained in the MIT experiment. These results were obtained in July.

The significance of the Princeton result was not that it came close to breakeven, because MIT had improved somewhat on its 1976 result and still held the nearness-to-breakeven record. Rather, it was that in reaching such a high temperatue the Princeton experiment had entered a plasma regime where wild fluctuations, called "trapped ion instabilities," were expected to degrade the confinement properties of a tokamak. These fluctuations had been earmarked by many in the fusion program as the biggest unresolved physics question that stood in the way of the development of tokamaks, which have been the leading candidates among various types of magnetic bottles since soon after they were invented in Russia in 1968. No evidence of the predicted fluctuations was found. Thus there was rejoicing at Princeton, and the news was quickly conveyed to Washington where the Department of Energy's fusion program has had to live with level or slightly decreasing budgets (in constant dollars) in the past 2 years.

The news spread quickly within the fusion community, but it took 2 weeks more to make national headlines. By 31 July, the nuclear trade press was reporting a big breakthrough at Princeton due to be announced in mid-August. The early part of August was also the time when the various program officials, in charge of solar, nuclear, fossil, and fusion research, were sending their fiscal 1980 budgets to the highest levels of the energy department for review.

By Friday 11 August, many science reporters knew something had happened at Princeton, but those who called the Department of Energy's press office were asked to wait through the weekend. That evening, a reporter for the Knight-Ridder newspapers heard of it, and put out the first story. The reporter, Dave Hess, says he could not confirm it until an unnamed official of the energy department's fusion office "very reluctantly" substantiated the reports. The Miami *Herald* published Hess's story on Saturday morning, and the Associated Press wire service, which had a considerably larger list of subscribers than Knight-Ridder, carried a bulletin based on the Miami *Herald* story.

A number of radio stations reported breakthroughs in fusion during the day Saturday, and by 3 p.m. a political reporter for the Washington *Post*, who happened to have weekend duty, found out about it. Bill Peterson says that the Department of Energy's Public Relations Office told him that industry sources had been trying to promote the story for weeks, and that scientists at Princeton said they were under embargo not to talk until the department okayed it. Peterson says that he was stuck until he thumbed through some literature that members of the Fusion Energy Foundation, an obscure and well-financed group that is allied with the U.S. Labor Party, had left behind after visiting him a couple of weeks earlier. In it, he found the name of Stephen O. Dean, the head of magnetic confinement systems and the architect of the fusion program's 20-year development plan. Dean, Peterson says, seemed angry with the embargo and "blew the story." Peterson quoted Dean extensively, and reported the achievement of the high temperatures for the first time.

Sunday morning, the story was on the front page, not only in Washington but also in Philadelphia and Detroit and other large cities. The whole weekend had been a slow one for national news, and fusion got full play. By nighttime, it was on the network TV news, where an unnamed Department of Energy spokesman was quoted as cautioning about big announcements at budget time. Early Monday morning, there was still so much unqualified optimism in the media that Department of Energy press spokesman, Jim Bishop, issued a bulletin cautioning that the Princeton work was only a "significant development." At the long-rumored press conference, finally scheduled on Monday afternoon, both Deutch, from the Department of Energy, and Gottlieb, from Princeton, said that some reports had been overblown.

NOTE

The 1978 incident discussed above was not the first time fusion received headline treatment. As long ago as the late 1950's, newspapers in England wrote about early fusion research with the implication that practical applications would soon arrive. Pease, Fusion Research 25 Years After Zeta, New Scientist, Jan. 20, 1983, at 166–67.

Scientific research is a difficult topic for the daily media to cover. In general, the news slights continuing processes, such as day-to-day research, in favor of dramatic events. See, e.g. B. Roshco, Newsmaking 16, 18–19 (1975). As Walter Lippman wrote, "the news does not tell you how the seed is germinating in the ground, but it may tell you when the first sprout breaks through the surface." W. Lippman, Public Opinion 341 (1950). This may result in undue emphasis on scientific events that appear to be breakthroughs at the expense of explaining the general course and content of important areas of basic research.

Members of Congress at times display a similar interest in dramatic results because such results are politically more attractive than long term research. See Ch. 4, Sec. B.2., supra. A funding program based solely on a desire for quick, visible results may lead to disappointment. Basic research is difficult to program; advances may come at unexpected times and places. See POLANYI, Ch. 2, Sec. A.1., supra.

The banter in the testimony above about whose district was responsible for the favorable fusion results should not be taken too lightly. Members of Congress have an understandable interest in winning federal investments for their districts. Major laboratories are at least as attractive in that respect as dams and military bases.

Is there any way to reduce the preoccupation with breakthroughs when public policy decisions about science are made? Would broad public education concerning the nature and goals of basic research make a difference? At what level of schooling should such education take place?

3. FUSION'S ENVIRONMENTAL IMPACT: WHEN AND HOW SHOULD IT BE ASSESSED?

U.S. ENERGY RESEARCH AND DEVELOPMENT ADMINISTRATION, FUSION POWER BY MAGNETIC CONFINEMENT

13–17 (1977) (ERDA 77 63).

QUESTIONS	ANSWERS
What are the environmental and safety advantages of fusion power?	1 The attractiveness of controlled nuclear fusion as a future major energy supply is due largely to two characteristics: a fuel supply that is accessible, abundant and cheap; and the potential for achieving a high degree of safety with a low level of social and environmental impact . . . . The other important long-term alternatives are solar energy and nuclear fission. Compared to solar, fusion offers the potential for a more compact, more flexible and less costly means to produce large scale commercial power. Compared to fission, fusion offers less long-lived radioactive waste, smaller potential hazard from accidents, and no weapons grade materials to divert. Fusion is not without its potential risks and environmental impacts . . . the point is that relative to other long-term sources of energy those potential risks and impacts are small.

QUESTIONS	ANSWERS

How abundant are fuel sources for fusion compared to alternate energy options?

2 Fusion reactors will initially use deuterium and tritium for fuel although advanced fusion power systems may be able to use deuterium alone. The supply of deuterium in the oceans is about 50 thousand billion tons, which would last millions of years at current energy consumption rates . . . . The annual deuterium fuel requirements in a fusion economy could be produced cheaply from seawater by a small separation plant. Tritium does not occur in nature and must be obtained by bombarding lithium with neutrons. Lithium is found in land-based deposits or can be extracted from seawater. Land based reserves should be ample for centuries (Ref. 3–1). The amount of lithium in seawater is virtually limitless. Table 3–1 summarizes the availability of fuels for fusion, fission and conventional fossil fuels.

TABLE 3–1
SOME FUEL RESOURCES AND
CONSUMPTION RATES
(Ref. 3–4)

	Energy "Q"[1]
Fuel	
World oil reserves, 1974	4
World ultimately recoverable gas, oil, coal	240
U.S. uranium to $250/kg, used in LMFBR	700
U.S. lithium reserves (13,000 to 25,000 k Wh/g)	250 to 500
Uranium in oceans, used in LMFBR	200,000
Lithium supply in oceans (25,000 k Wh/g)	22,000,000
Deuterium supply in oceans	16,000,000,000
Consumption rates	
World energy use in 1974	0.25
U.S. energy used for electricity in 1974	0.02
Total annual energy for 8 billion people at 6 k W/person[2]	1.5

1. $1 \text{"Q"} = 10^{18}$ BTU ≈ 1 trillion GJ.

2. Rate corresponds to Sweden in 1973.

Are there other materials needed for fusion power?

3 First generation conceptual designs of fusion reactors indicate that their construction may require use of some scarce materials such as chrome in stainless steel . . . . The size of this problem depends on the design of the particular reactor in question. Partly as a result of these potential scarcities and their associated costs, increased attention is being given to the more abundant materials and ways to decrease reactor material needs are being studied. For example, raising the plasma power density will reduce the reactor size for a given electrical output, and the successful incorporation of ceramic materials would replace scarce structural materials with highly abundant ones.

I understand that the fusion fuel, tritium, is radioactive. Can you explain the safety implications of this?

4 Tritium is indeed radioactive and must be handled carefully. However, tritium is a relatively low hazard radioactive material. It emits only very weak radiation; its maximum allowable concentration is among the highest for any radioactive material. It is excreted rapidly from the body and cannot be biologically concentrated in the environment, in foodchains or in man. It decays quickly (12.3 years) to harmless helium and thus poses no long term hazard. Although of less hazard than many other radioactive materials, tritium must nevertheless be handled carefully and releases to the environment must be strictly controlled.

Is it possible for large amounts of tritium to be released accidentally from a fusion reactor?

5   Substantial amounts of tritium (estimates range from one to tens of kilograms) will be present in large fusion reactors. It is difficult to conceive of any accident that would release all the tritium, though significant releases can certainly be postulated. An estimate of the potential hazard due to a very large tritium release under the worst climatic conditions has been made . . . . These estimates showed that even with very conservative "worst case" assumptions, it would be unlikely that any member of the public would be killed. The potential danger due to a tritium release from a fusion reactor is enormously less than the hazard potential of release of volatile fission products from a fission reactor. Thus, while injuries and some deaths could conceivably occur, large scale danger is very unlikely if not impossible. Further, any potential contamination would disperse rapidly, and decay quickly, eliminating risk of long term contamination.

Could we avoid tritium altogether by proceeding directly to the deuterium fuel cycle?

6   There are several cycles which use deuterium as the primary fuel and which do not require tritium production from lithium. There are also other fusion cycles using lithium, beryllium or boron fuels that are essentially free of neutrons and tritium. However, all these fuel cycles require much higher temperatures and better plasma confinement than the D–T cycle. While they hold promise for a fusion power system that has minimal environmental impact, present research is naturally aiming towards the more attainable D–T reaction. Additionally, the fusion power density of the D–T cycle is at least 100 times higher than that of the advanced cycles and thus should lead to a smaller, more economical system . . . .

Are there other radioactive materials involved in fusion power?

7   Yes. The D–T and D–D fusion fuel cycles produce neutrons as one of their reaction products. These can "activate" the materials in a fusion reactor, making them radioactive. However, these activation products are not inherent to the fusion process. That is, the magnitude and nature of the waste can be controlled by design since the activation is produced in the structural material and not in the fusion reaction itself. The activation products of structural materials are generally non-volatile, are bound up in the structural material and are extremely difficult to release to the environment even in accident situations. Further, use of low residual activation materials (aluminum, graphite, silicon carbide and some ceramics) may make it possible to essentially eliminate production of long lived activation products . . . .

If some of the advanced cycles mentioned in question 6 are ever realized very few neutrons will be emitted from the fusion plasma and much smaller quantities of radioactive products will be produced for any type of structural material.

QUESTIONS	ANSWERS

How much radioactivity might be produced in a fusion reactor?

8 Present conceptual designs estimate that the relative biological hazard potential of induced activities in fusion plants will be 10 to 1000 times less than in fission power plants . . . . Table 3–2 shows a comparison of the biological hazard potential for the long term radioactive wastes from different proposed structural materials in fusion reactors and from fuel in fission plants (Ref. 3–7).

TABLE 3–2
LONG–TERM RADIOACTIVE WASTES FROM FUSION AND FISSION SYSTEMS AFTER 100–YR DECAY
(From Ref. 3–9)

System	Biological Hazard Potential [*]
Fusion (Candidate materials)	
Type 316 stainless steel	0.0001
Niobium-zirconium alloy	0.8
Vanadium-titanium alloy	negligible
Aluminum	0.04
Fission	
Plutonium-239	1000.0
Strontium-90	1.3
Cesium-137	0.23

[*] $(km)^3$ of air required to dilute radioactive wastes to their maximum permissible concentration per megawatt thermal power.

Is it possible for the plasma to go unstable and cause a hot spot on the wall? Would this constitute a safety problem?

9 Our rapidly expanding knowledge of plasma stability indicates that plasma disruptions leading to hot spots should not occur in reactor-size plasmas, though this is not a certainty. If a severe disruption were to take place, the stored energy in the plasma could be dumped on a small area of the first wall. This would cause rapid overheating and possibly local melting of the vacuum vessel. Simultaneously, the electrical current in the plasma could be transferred to the surrounding structure, possibly causing large stresses.

If rupture of the vacuum vessel should occur, the tritium in the plasma might be released to the reactor hall. Since the amount of tritium would be very small (less than 1 gram) and the hall cleanup system would be designed to handle such a load, no danger to the public is likely. In addition, the plasma would be extinguished as soon as the disruption occurs because it would instantly cool below ignition temperature, and no additional fusion energy would be released. While there does not seem to be a significant safety problem, plant economics will dictate that disruptions be made extremely improbable (less than one event per plant lifetime) to avoid unnecessarily long shutdowns.

It has been stated that a runaway reactor or nuclear explosion is not possible. Can you explain why?

10 Nuclear runaway is not possible with fusion reactors. If too much fuel is added to the reactor plasma, confinement is lost, the fusion rate drops off, and the power level is reduced. The power level in a fusion reactor will be maintained by a balancing of the confining magnetic fields, the rate of plasma heating, and the rate of fueling. If any of these systems malfunctions, the power level will drop and, without corrective actions, the reactor would shut down. There is no mechanism by which there can be any kind of nuclear explosion

QUESTIONS	ANSWERS

. . . since fusion fuels do not undergo a nuclear "chain reaction."

Can the "loss of cooling accident" (LOCA) that is a concern in fission reactors be avoided with fusion reactors?

11 To a great extent, yes. Due to the decay heat from activated materials, a fusion reactor will probably have to continue to be cooled for a while after it is turned off. The decay heat power density in a fusion reactor will be about 10 times smaller than that in a light water fission reactor and about 60 times less than that in a fast breeder reactor . . . . Because of this low level of decay heat a fusion reactor could tolerate loss of cooling for some time before damage to the reactor would occur. Because of the relatively low biological hazard potential discussed previously, it is unlikely that loss of cooling would pose a significant hazard to the public.

Nuclear sabotage and terrorism have been of concern to fission reactors. Does fusion power avoid this problem?

12 Yes. Tritium cannot be stolen and used, in itself, to make a nuclear bomb. There is no known way to trigger a fusion bomb other than with a fission bomb using uranium-235 or plutonium-239. Having such a bomb, a well-organized, highly technical group conceivably could add tritium and other fusion materials to increase the power of the device. Such use of tritium to develop the hydrogen bomb required a massive national program in the U.S. and it is not considered plausible that a radical group could assemble the funds, the massive research, nor the technical expertise to use tritium for nuclear blackmail . . . . Moreover, there would be little incentive to go beyond a fission bomb since it is destructive enough. Any group or nation sophisticated enough to design and fabricate a workable fusion explosive, with or without a fission trigger, will be sophisticated enough to do so without having a fusion reactor. Thus, the existence of fusion reactors will not give access to tritium to groups that otherwise could not obtain it . . . .

Most magnetic confinement methods use large superconducting magnets. What would happen if these magnets fail?

13 Failure of a large confinement magnet will result in decay of the magnetic field and loss of the ability to confine the plasma. Under conceivable conditions, sudden release of the magnet's large quantities of stored energy could occur as a result of magnet transition from the superconducting to the normal state. This energy release could damage the magnet and require extensive repairs but no other plant damage should occur as a result.

Have extensive safety analyses been carried out on fusion reactors?

14 Substantial analyses have been performed. However, they have been limited somewhat by the lack of engineering design detail for commercial fusion power plants. Even now the amount of information available from reactor conceptual designs is barely adequate to allow in-depth calculations of the probability and effects of potential accidents. However, the need for early evaluation of possible safety hazards is recognized and studies are in progress at several national laboratories and universities.

NOTE

It is perhaps inevitable that the Energy Research and Development Administration, the predecessor to the Department of Energy, took an upbeat view of fusion in the layperson's guide excerpted above. First of all, the agency itself was doing the research it was describing. Secondly, fusion, like nuclear fission and solar energy, benefits from the initial assumption of safety that seems to accompany new technologies. See Ch. 2, Sec. B.1., and Ch. 9, Sec. A.3., supra. As with fission and solar, fusion may well raise serious safety and environmental issues. The ERDA document above described tritium, for example, as relatively benign, yet when a non-fusion plant in Arizona released tritium in 1979, the public outcry was substantial. See, e.g., Long and Kay, State Seized Tritium at Atomics, Arizona Daily Star, September 26, 1979, at A1, col. 1. From the perspective of public policy, does it matter whether the outcry reflected "perceived" as opposed to "actual" risks? See Ch. 2, Sec. B.1., supra.

Is it meaningful to analyze the environmental impacts of fusion now or should we wait until research progresses further? The following sections address that question in the context of the National Environmental Policy Act and of broader policy considerations.

The National Environmental Policy Act's requirement of an environmental impact statement for federal actions significantly affecting the quality of the human environment has injected environmental values into numerous science-related issues. One issue of particular importance to a program like fusion research is when an impact statement must be done on the broad consequences of the fusion program as a whole, rather than on individual test facilities. Judicial consideration of when NEPA requires such "programmatic" statements in the research and development field began with the following case, which involves the breeder, a type of fission reactor discussed in Ch. 2, Sec. B.2., supra.

SCIENTISTS' INSTITUTE FOR PUBLIC INFORMATION v. ATOMIC ENERGY COMMISSION

United States Court of Appeals of the District of Columbia Circuit, 1973.
481 F.2d 1079, 1082, 1093–1094.

J. SKELLY WRIGHT, CIRCUIT JUDGE.

Appellant claims that the Atomic Energy Commission's Liquid Metal Fast Breeder Reactor program involves a "recommendation or report on proposals for legislation and other major Federal actions significantly affecting the quality of the human environment . . ." under Section 102(C) of the National Environmental Policy Act (NEPA), 42 U.S.C. § 4332(C) (1970), and that the Commission is therefore required to issue a "detailed [environmental impact] statement" for the program. The District Court held that no statement was presently required since, in its view, the program was still in the research and development stage and no specific implementing action which would significantly affect the environment had yet been taken.

. . .

III. TIMING THE NEPA STATEMENT

Whether a statement on the overall LMFBR program should be issued now or at some uncertain date in the future is the most difficult question presented by this case. It was especially troubling to the District Court, as reflected in the following colloquy with counsel for appellant:

"I say this: I say there comes a time, we start out with E equals MC², we both agreed you don't have to have the impact statement then. Then there comes a time when there are a thousand of these breeder plants in existence all over the country.

"Sometime before that, surely as anything under the present law, there has to be an impact statement, and a long time before that, actually.

"But the question is, exactly where in this chain do we have to have an impact statement."

In our view, the timing question can best be answered by reference to the underlying policies of NEPA in favor of meaningful, timely information on the effects of agency action. In the early stages of research, when little is known about the technology and when future application of the technology is both doubtful and remote, it may well be impossible to draft a meaningful impact statement. Predictions as to the possible effects of application of the technology would tend toward uninformative generalities, arrived at by guesswork rather than analysis. NEPA requires predictions, but not prophecy, and impact statements ought not to be modeled upon the works of Jules Verne or H. G. Wells. At the other end of the spectrum, by the time commercial feasibility of the technology is conclusively demonstrated, and the effects of application of the technology certain, the purposes of NEPA will already have been thwarted. Substantial investments will have been made in development of the technology and options will have been precluded without consideration of environmental factors. Any statement prepared at such a late date will no doubt be thorough, detailed and accurate, but it will be of little help in ensuring that decisions reflect environmental concerns. Thus we are pulled in two directions. Statements must be written late enough in the development process to contain meaningful information, but they must be written early enough so that whatever information is contained can practically serve as an input into the decision making process.

Determining when to draft an impact statement for a technology development program obviously requires a reconciliation of these competing concerns. Some balance must be struck and several factors should be weighed in the balance. How likely is the technology to prove commercially feasible, and how soon will that occur? To what extent is meaningful information presently available on the effects of application of the technology and of alternatives and their effects? To what extent are irretrievable commitments being made and options precluded as the development program progresses? How severe will be the environmental effects if the technology does prove commercially feasible? . . .

[The D.C. Circuit applied the balancing test developed in *Scientists' Institute* a few years later in a case involving a Department of Interior coal leasing program in the Northern Great Plains. This time, unlike *Scientists' Institute*, the U.S. Supreme Court reviewed the D.C Circuit's decision, with the following result.]

KLEPPE v. SIERRA CLUB

Supreme Court of the United States, 1976.
427 U.S. 390, 96 S.Ct. 2718, 49 L.Ed.2d 576.

. . .

. . . The Court of Appeals accordingly devised its own four-part "balancing" test for determining when, during the contemplation of a plan or other type of federal action, an agency must begin a statement. The factors to be considered were identified as the likelihood and imminence of the program's coming to fruition, the extent to which information is available on the effects of implementing the expected program and on alternatives thereto, the extent to which irretrievable commitments are being made and options precluded "as refinement of the proposal progresses," and the severity of the environmental effects should the action be implemented. . . .

The Court's reasoning and action find no support in the language or legislative history of NEPA. The statute clearly states when an impact statement is required, and mentions nothing about a balancing of factors. Rather, as we noted last Term, under the first sentence of § 102(2)(C) the moment at which an agency must have a final statement ready "is the time at which it makes a recommendation or report on a *proposal* for federal action." Aberdeen & Rockfish R. Co. v. SCRAP, 422 U.S. 289, 320, 95 S.Ct. 2336, 2356, 45 L.Ed.2d 191 (1975) (*SCRAP II*) (emphasis in original). The procedural duty imposed upon agencies by this section is quite precise, and the role of the courts in enforcing that duty is similarly precise. A court has no authority to depart from the statutory language and, by a balancing of court-devised factors, determine a point during the germination process of a potential proposal at which an impact statement *should be prepared*. Such an assertion of judicial authority would leave the agencies uncertain as to their procedural duties under NEPA, would invite judicial involvement in the day-to-day decisionmaking process of the agencies, and would invite litigation. As the contemplation of a project and the accompanying study thereof do not necessarily result in a proposal for major federal action, it may be assumed that the balancing process devised by the Court of Appeals also would result in the preparation of a good many unnecessary impact statements.[15]

NOTE

Pursuant to *Kleppe*, an agency need not do a programmatic impact statement on fusion research—or any other area of research and development—until the agency formally "proposes" an overall program. Most commentary on *Kleppe* has contended that the decision weakens NEPA's effort to inform agency decisions with environmental values at an early point. See, e.g., Note, Program Environmental Impact Statement: Review and Remedies, 75 Mich.L.Rev. 107, 117 (1976); Note, The Scope of the Program EIS Requirement: The Need for a Coherent Judicial Approach, 30 Stan.L.Rev. 767, 791–792 (1978).

Even under *Kleppe* a court could conceivably find that an agency had made a "proposal" for a broad fusion program despite the agency's statement that it had not yet done so. The Council on Environmental Quality's regulations provide that a proposal:

> . . . exists at that stage in the development of an action when an agency subject to the Act has a goal and is actively preparing to make a decision on one or more alternative means of accomplishing that goal and the effects can be meaningfully evaluated . . . . A proposal may exist in fact as well as by agency declaration that one exists.

40 C.F.R. § 1508.23 (1981).

---

15. This is not to say that § 102(2)(C) imposes no duties upon an agency prior to its making a report or recommendation on a proposal for action. The section states that prior to preparing the impact statement the responsible official "shall consult with and obtain the comments of any Federal agency which has jurisdiction by law or special expertise with respect to any environmental impact involved." Thus, the section contemplates a consideration of environmental factors by agencies during the evolution of a report or recommendation on a proposal. But the time at which a court enters the process is when the report or recommendation on the proposal is made, and someone protests either the absence or the adequacy of the final impact statement. This is the point at which an agency's action has reached sufficient maturity to assure that judicial intervention will not hazard unnecessary disruption.

Kleppe does not remove the agency's obligation to do impact statements on individual fusion research facilities, and such statements have in fact been done. Those statements emphasize the siting and operation of the individual facility, not the overall implications of fusion energy. See, e.g., Energy Research and Development Administration, Final Environmental Impact Statement, Tokamak Fusion Test Reactor Facilities (1975) (ERDA 1544).

Is the balancing test devised by the court of appeals in *Scientists' Institute* and rejected in *Kleppe* sound as a matter of policy? Should Congress amend NEPA to require impact statements on scientific research programs when that balancing test indicates that such statements would be fruitful? The section that follows provides contrasting views on whether the fusion program today could be subjected to meaningful environmental analysis.

NATIONAL ACADEMY OF SCIENCES, ENERGY IN TRANSITION 1985–2010

47–48 (1979).

Four energy sources—nuclear fission with breeding, solar energy in various forms, controlled thermonuclear fusion, and geothermal energy—offer the potential for indefinitely sustainable energy supply. That is, each could supply up to 10 times our present energy requirements for thousands of years (or much more). They differ widely in their readiness for use, in their probable side effects, and in their economics. Present knowledge is insufficient for meaningful economic comparisons and permits only limited comparisons by other criteria, such as environmental and safety risks or the likelihood of successful technical development. The degree of risk associated with a technology often depends on details of engineering design and on compromises between safety and economics that cannot be foreseen until the technology has been translated into full-scale designs with considerable practical operating experience to back up assessments of component reliability and the like. A technology in the conceptual stage often appears less risky than it will after the practical engineering questions have been faced.

The government's program in long-term energy supply, to allow realistic choices of long-term options, should include sustained research and development of many of these technologies. Priorities at this stage should depend more on the likelihood of significant technical progress than on economic comparisons among existing versions. New technical developments and changes in resource economics are likely to alter comparative cost assessments radically. Furthermore, a combination of long-term sources is likely to offer more flexibility and overall reliability than dependence on a single system. The ultimate total cost of deploying a new energy technology on a broad scale is so much larger than the research and development costs that maintaining an array of options in the development stage is fully justified. A cost advantage of a few percent in a deployed system would easily pay for all the research and development that produced it.

STEVEN GOLDBERG,
CONTROLLING BASIC SCIENCE: THE CASE OF
NUCLEAR FUSION

68 Geo.L.J. 683, 694–696, 724 (1980).

Legal control of a new technology generally comes too late. Once a technology is ready for the marketplace banning or altering it can mean wasting millions of dollars and many years of research and development. Moreover, even when a technology proves dangerous enough to justify a sudden restriction, it may have built up enough political and economic momentum to steamroller efforts at control. . . .

Early research decisions may, whether deliberately or not, tilt the balance on later social issues. Accordingly, efforts to determine the social implications of research must be made early so that social values can play an appropriate role in research choices. Some scientists resist such a notion, but this calculus simply refines an initial decision to fund a particular line of research. If the government decides that fusion deserves over $500 million a year, it will surely not be indifferent to whether that money is being spent productively.

Of course, social control must be sensitive to the nature of basic science. Such developments as Einstein's expansion of Maxwell's equations or the laser's impact on fusion illustrate the need for the free play of apparently unrelated ideas. But this creative need does not mandate governmental neglect; occasions arise in which the social and scientific implications of a given line of research become sufficiently clear to justify making policy decisions. In the early 1970's, for example, the federal government ceased funding a major research project on nuclear engines for space rockets long before an operational system was built, primarily because the space shuttle, a competitor for funds, seemed a more promising venture. Research on nuclear engines for rockets might have led to unexpected breakthroughs beneficial to society, but that possibility does not require that the research, once begun, should enjoy freedom from scrutiny.

The need for social input is easier to state than to execute. When implementation of a technology is as distant as the commercialization of the fusion reactor, its effect on the economy, environment, or public safety is uncertain. We must nonetheless attempt to assess that impact and to determine what choices, both explicit or implicit, will be made as research continues.

The fusion reactor's primary role of generating electricity immediately raises the question of the reactor's size. Fusion reactors, like modern coal, oil, and nuclear plants, will serve as central generating stations providing electricity to a large population. Fusion plants, however, may be considerably larger than present power plants. A modern nuclear fission plant generates about 1,000 megawatts of electricity, enough to provide for the needs of a city of 600,000 people. Some estimates indicate that, to be efficient, commercial tokamak reactors would have to generate 5,000 megawatts of electricity. Because reactors of this type would further centralize generation of electricity, the already difficult issues of power plant siting, electricity transmission, and political control of power generation would become even more difficult in a fusion economy. It is not, however, inevitable that fusion reactors will further centralize the generation of electricity. Some believe that tokamaks could be roughly the size of modern power plants, while non-tokamak reactors, including laser systems, might be even smaller.

With plants of any size, predicting the economics of fusion power is difficult. The cost of its fuel will be competitive with coal or uranium, but fuel costs represent only a part of reactor costs. Demonstrating the scientific feasibility of fusion will not demonstrate its engineering or commercial feasibility; whether a practical, workable device can be built and operated at reasonable cost is a separate inquiry. The engineering and economic aspects of fusion raise a host of questions ranging from the availability of materials to the costs of operation. Tokamaks and other magnetic systems, for example, must demonstrate the feasibility of maintaining the large superconducting magnets necessary to confine plasma. Scientists must also confront the materials problems raised when particle bombardment erodes reactor components. Problems also confront the development of commercially feasible inertial confinement devices; lasers, for example, must be shown to be sufficiently durable and inexpensive to make the system workable.

As utilities using nuclear fission and coal have discovered, economic feasibility does not end the debate over electricity generation. Safety and environmental issues often dominate that debate; fusion reactors will not be exempt. The major issue is likely to be radioactivity, whether absorbed by reactor employees, released in small amounts in normal operation, or dispersed in large amounts in an accident. Radioactivity will be created by two sources in fusion reactors. First, neutrons produced in a fusion reaction will make reactor components radioactive. The extent of this problem will depend on the type of materials used in the components. Second, the radioactive tritium used as fuel diffuses through most metals at high temperatures. It is, however, less hazardous and has a shorter half-life than the radioactive materials used in fission reactors. On the whole, the radioactivity problems of fusion, including waste disposal, appear potentially less severe than those involved with fission. Such problems nonetheless require considerable study and testing before environmental and safety decisions can be made. These safety and environmental considerations vary with the type of fusion reactor. Inertial confinement systems, for example, may involve smaller inventories of tritium than tokamaks. . . . If present trends continue, [assessment of nuclear fusion] is likely to come too late. Consider a likely scenario for nuclear fusion. In the immediate future the magnetic confinement program, which includes the tokamak, receives increased support relative to inertial confinement because the former is nearer to scientific feasibility. After feasibility is demonstrated, the magnetic confinement approach becomes the subject of a crash program, with inertial confinement increasingly ignored. Department of Energy policymakers present only token resistance to enormous pressures from the science bureaucracy, while legislators support the magnetic confinement program because it promises quick results. Judicial challenges, if any, fall victim to a narrow reading of NEPA. When magnetic confinement reactors are built, however, public scrutiny, including that of legislators, begins to focus on radiation levels, reactor size, and related matters. Progress on magnetic confinement becomes mired in debate, while suggestions are heard to revive the long-forgotten inertial confinement approach. Nonetheless, magnetic confinement has built up enough momentum to survive this late-blooming technology assessment effort, and the reactors continue in use, although reduced to a limited and controversial role.

In short, the experiences of the breeder and light water reactors may be repeated with fusion. The scenario is oversimplified, lumping, for example, numerous approaches under the general headings of "magnetic" and "inertial" confinement. Moreover, it is not yet possible to say whether magnetic confinement or inertial confinement is superior from a social perspective. The danger is that one will soon be chosen over the other for scientific and bureaucratic reasons and that choice will be difficult or impossible to reverse. The remedy is vigorous social control of science now, long before reactors are built, so that necessary choices will be made in light of social considerations. . . .

NOTE

What do the above theses imply about the freedom of scientific research?

The conflict between the desire to keep options open on a variety of technologies and the pressure to support heavily the leading technology in the hope of producing more immediate results pulls the fusion program in two directions. At present, several possible fusion concepts are at various stages of development. See, e.g., Division of Policy Research and Analysis, National Science Foundation, Workshop on Alternate Fusion Concepts and Their Utilization Projections, No. 82045 (Jan.1980); Conn, The Engineering of Magnetic Fusion Reactors, 249 Scientific American 60 (Oct.1983). Recent research shows promising possibilities for new smaller-scale fusion devices. See Waldrop, Compact Fusion: Small is Beautiful, 219 Science 154 (1983). On the other hand, agency and legislative pressures continue to mount for choosing "a single course" for building a fusion reactor. See Experts Back All the Runners in the Fusion Race, New Scientist 675 (Sept. 9, 1982). At some point, given the level of public investment, choices will have to be made. What information would you want before deciding on the type of fusion research to be emphasized? How would you go about obtaining such information?

ELECTRIC POWER RESEARCH INSTITUTE, A FEASIBILITY STUDY FOR ENHANCING THE DEVELOPMENT OF FUSION ENERGY

124–128 (March, 1979).

The large [fusion] reactor (1000MWe) . . . increases the problem of financing and risk such that the only option, without significant government participation, is that of a joint venture consisting of several utilities. Preferably, in this case, a single utility would take the lead to provide focused management. Since the capital commitment is so large, the joint venture may not be viable and government participation would be required during the introductory phase. There are many options for government participation of which three are shown; (1) A government guarantee for the loan or a guaranteed cost of electricity from the plant; (2) Government ownership of the fusion unique portion of the plant or ownership of the total plant with a utility operating the plant (in either case); and (3) a Government owned and operated facility. . . .

It is not yet clear that fusion will scale down to a viable 200 MWe power reactor; therefore, it is prudent to conclude that significant government financial support will be required during the fusion introductory phase. The government support must be planned jointly with utilities and industry and structured to promote successful commercialization. The test of commercialization will be that the required private sector investment be a good business proposition. The challenge will be to structure the development and commercialization process such that concerns, some of which are shown in Figure 15, are alleviated. . . .

Figure 15 Government Participation Can Be Counter Productive in Promoting Commercialization

- Government may promote an approach that cannot survive in a free market

- Differing objectives, between government and industry, in executing the program.

- A concern that the government may prematurely drop its support of a program because of higher priority or shifting public opinion.

- Subsidy may discourage private investment because of proprietary rights.

- May encourage companies to get into the game for near term subsidized business but without long term commitment and financial resources to support commercialization. . . .

NOTE

Fusion is undeniably a "hard" technology; Lovins has described it as a "complex, costly, large-scale, centralized high-technology way to make electricity—all of which goes in the wrong direction." Lovins, Energy Strategy: The Road Not Taken, 55 Foreign Affairs 55, n. 20 (1976). It does not follow, however, that current utilities are enthusiastic about fusion. From their point of view, a technology can be so large as to invite excessive federal intrusion in a commercial setting. The electric utility industry, in part through the utility-sponsored Electric Power Research Institute, has become significantly involved in fusion issues. See, e.g., Division of Policy Research and Analysis, National Science Foundation, Workshop on Mobilization of the Private Sector in Effective Development of Fusion Energy, No. 81024 (Sept.1980). Should government fusion policy emphasize making the technology compatible with current utilities? Is your answer the same for solar energy?

As a "hard," centralized technology, fusion avoids the issues of zoning and access to sunlight that complicate many solar options, while retaining the issues involved with siting and politically controlling centralized plants. Should these factors be considered in deciding whether to emphasize research on fusion over solar?

Many believe that American society today cannot turn back from life-styles based on a centralized, high-technology approach to energy. Certain enclaves within America, however, have rejected the dominant approach. In upholding the right of the Amish to keep their children out of high school, the Supreme Court noted that "Amish society emphasizes informal learning-through-doing; a life of 'goodness,' rather than a life of intellect; wisdom, rather than technical knowledge; community welfare, rather than competition; and separation from, rather than integration with, contemporary worldly society." Wisconsin v. Yoder, 406 U.S. 205, 211, 92 S.Ct. 1526, 1531, 32 L.Ed.2d 15, 22 (1972). Are you attracted to these values? Are they consistent with advanced technology?

Even if America has chosen a certain level of technology, many other countries have not finally resolved the question of whether and how to introduce modern technology. In Tanzania, for example, President Nyerere's controversial ujamaa program has sought to bring tribal populations into villages to facilitate the introduction of modern science and medicine. See, e.g., Howe, Tanzanian Self-Help Villages Crowded, New York Times, Oct. 5, 1970, at 5, col. 3. Do you believe modern science and medicine will benefit tribal groups in Tanzania? If not, are you willing to give up modern conveniences yourself? Is there any basis for treating yourself differently in this respect from those in other cultures?

Chapter Ten

ADVANCED COMPUTER SYSTEMS

A. COMPUTERS, COMMUNICATION AND PRIVACY

Computers are, of course, an important part of American society today and their implications are frequently analyzed in terms of a variety of legal doctrines. Thus cases and commentaries abound on computer programs as intellectual property, on liability for defects in computer programs, on computer crimes, and on various aspects of computers and privacy. See, e.g., Tunick, Computer Law: An Overview, 13 Loy.L.A.L. Rev. 315 (1980). But computer technology continues to develop quickly and to create new challenges for settled legal doctrines in a variety of ways. The materials that follow concern communications and the privacy implications of central data banks—areas in which advances in computers will raise legal and social issues in the years to come.

1. BREAKING THE BARRIER BETWEEN DATA PROCESSING AND COMMUNICATIONS: THE FCC COMPUTER INQUIRY

HANAN SAMET, COMPUTERS AND COMMUNICATION: THE FCC DILEMMA IN DETERMINING WHAT TO REGULATE

28 DePaul L.Rev. 71, 72–73, 75–76, 80–83 (1978).

Traditionally, the FCC has regulated the communications carriage services, an industry which often exhibits natural monopoly characteristics. The Communications Act of 1934 was passed in recognition of this fact as well as to ensure the availability of efficient service at reasonable charges to the entire country. It was felt that only through such regulation could every citizen be protected against potential abuses of such monopolies. However, such regulation also has the effect of shielding the carriers from competition in activities which are incidental to carriage and are not in themselves natural monopolies. Increasingly, carriers are finding it beneficial to use computers to perform these "incidental" functions and it is in this region that the different market philosophies of the computer and communications sectors are on a collision course.

Computers and data processing services have traditionally been unregulated. This industry has thrived on competition and has been spurred by it. Currently, however, its members are finding themselves competing to some degree with the communications common carriers. In particular, the computer industry would like to have a share of the communications market which is incidental to carriage, thus the collision of the two sec-

tors. The problems of determining how to allocate the market in services, which are incidental to carriage, arise, in part, from the 1934 Communications Act which appears to subject such communications activities to regulation. The regulated carriers claim that such services are clearly within their domain, while the data processing industry claims that these services should be unregulated and unavailable to the regulated carriers.
. . . .

COMPUTER INQUIRY I

The first computer inquiry was prompted, in part, by a dispute between the Bunker Ramo Corporation and Western Union.[19] The conflict occurred when Western Union, pursuant to its tariff, refused to sell communications circuits to Bunker Ramo, contending that Bunker Ramo had engaged in the resale of communications services, a process forbidden to non-common carriers. Confronted with this controversy, the FCC characterized its Inquiry as involving two questions. The first was one of a policy nature: whether or not data processing was to be regulated. The second was concerned with the communications common carrier's role in providing data processing services. The second question was further complicated by the existence of services in which data processing and communications were so closely intertwined that a simple distinction would be difficult to make.

The Nonregulation of Data Processing

In dealing with the question of whether to regulate data processing, the FCC observed that since computers were not in existence at the time the Communications Act of 1934 was enacted, it could not turn to the Act for assistance in determining whether it had any authority for the regulation of data processing. Instead, it turned to *United States v. Southwestern Cable Co.* which affirmed a grant of expansive powers to the FCC. Therefore, the Commission concluded that it had authority to regulate "communications facilities and services not in existence, or even anticipated, at the time the Communications Act of 1934 was enacted."

Prior to any attempt to draw a line between communications and data processing, the FCC pointed to the record before it as demonstrating that pure data processing services were essentially a competitive business and,

---

19. Bunker Ramo had a stock price quotation system, Telequote III, which offered users up to date information on any stock traded on the exchange. This service used private line wires of Western Union. Subsequently, Bunker Ramo introduced a new service, Telequote IV, which enabled users to communicate with each other through the use of the Bunker Ramo computer as a store forward device. An order would be sent to the computer and stored there until polled by another computer which would forward it to the appropriate broker or trader. Although it had willingly provided carriage services for the Telequote III offering, Western Union balked at doing the same for the Telequote IV offering. In the Telequote III offering users had no choice as to what type of information was being communicated. Only recorded stock price quota-

tions were transmitted. This was not the case, however, in the Telequote IV offering.

Western Union's action was undoubtedly based on its fear that given this communication capability, there was nothing to prevent users, as well as Bunker Ramo, from using their facilities for all types of communications. Bunker Ramo subsequently withdrew the Telequote IV offering and thus the FCC never did have the opportunity to rule on the issue. See Comment, Federal Communications Commission Regulation of Domestic Computer Communications: A Competitive Reformation, 22 Buffalo L.Rev. 947, 961 (1973); Note, the FCC Computer Inquiry: Interfaces of Competitive and Regulated Markets, 71 Mich.L.Rev. 172, 192 (1972); Note, Computer Services and the Federal Regulation of Communications, 116 U.Pa.L.Rev. 328, 329 (1967).

therefore, in no need of regulation. Consequently, the Commission concluded that it saw "no need to assert regulatory authority over data processing services whether or not such services employ communications facilities in order to link the terminals of the subscribers to centralized computers." Nevertheless, it did reserve the option to re-examine its policies should there "develop significant changes in the structure of the data processing industry, or, if abuses emerge which require the exercise of corrective action by the Commission . . . ." . . . . Computer Inquiry I dealt with services in which communications and data processing services were intertwined—the so-called "hybrid services." In evaluating whether a hybrid service was to be regulated, the FCC decided it would determine the primary functions performed by the service. If it was primarily a data processing service, then the entity which offered the service would not be subject to common carrier regulation. If, however, the offering was designed primarily to meet the communications needs of the subscriber then it would be regulated subject to the Communications Act whether or not the offeror was a common carrier. . . .

COMPUTER INQUIRY II

Increasingly, as computing functions are being decentralized, there is a growing merger of data processing and communications activities in "intelligent" terminals. Such terminals are furnished to the user by both the regulated common carriers and members of the unregulated terminal equipment manufacturing sector. Nevertheless, the terminals are under the control of the user rather than the carrier or manufacturer. These advances raise the question of whether the "intelligence" is data processing or communications. The definitions promulgated in Computer Inquiry I are inadequate since they were directed at a computing environment in which data processing was performed by a central processor, and thus are of little help when new applications are being considered.

In order to cope with such issues, the FCC undertook to revise the rules set forth in Computer Inquiry I. . . .

FCC OPINION: SECOND COMPUTER INQUIRY

45 Fed.Reg. 31,319–31,321 (1980).

I. *Introduction*

1. Under consideration are issues addressed in the Notice of Inquiry and Proposed Rulemaking (Notice), 61 FCC 2d 103; Supplemental Notice of Inquiry and Enlargement of Proposed Rulemaking (Supplemental Notice), 64 FCC 2d 771; and Tentative Decision and Further Notice of Inquiry and Rulemaking (Tentative Decision), 72 FCC 2d 358 adopted in this proceeding. Commonly referred to as the "Second Computer Inquiry," this proceeding focuses on regulatory issues emanating from the greater utilization of computer processing technology and its varied market applications. The thrust of this proceeding is threefold: a) to determine whether enhanced services which are provided over common carrier telecommunication facilities should be subject to regulation and, if so, to what extent; b) to examine the competitive and technological evolution of customer premises equipment, with a view toward determining whether the continuation of traditional regulation of terminal equipment is in the public interest; and c) to determine, consistent with the statutory man-

date set forth in the Communications Act of 1934, as amended, 47 U.S.C. § 151, the role of communication common carriers in the provision of enhanced services and customer-premises equipment.

II. *Summary of Decision Network Services*

2. In addressing the regulatory problems raised by the confluence of communications and data processing, we concluded in the Tentative Decision that a revised definitional structure standing alone would not adequately resolve the issues before us. We thought it necessary to address the structure under which competitive computer processing services are provided. In so doing we distinguished three categories of service—voice, "basic non-voice" (BNV) and "enhanced non-voice" (ENV). We proposed a resale structure for the carrier provision of ENV services under which carriers owning transmission facilities would be required to provide ENV services through a separate corporate entity that would acquire the necessary transmission facilities pursuant to tariff. At the same time we proposed new definitions for distinguishing the communications or data processing nature of ENV services, and proposed to eliminate our "maximum separation" policy for resale carriers, thereby allowing them to offer both ENV communications and ENV data processing services through common computer facilities. It was thought that the need to artificially structure or limit services provided to consumers would be substantially reduced under this structure. Any ENV data processing service could be provided by a resale carrier on a non-tariffed basis.

3. In setting forth this resale structure, we also identified various regulatory implications that we perceived flowing from this structure and discussed alternative means of alleviating certain regulatory constraints. We set forth specific options for consideration in reaching a final decision, and sought comment on the public interest considerations relevant to adoption of the different options.

4. In response to the resale structure and the various options put forth for consideration, the comments focused on the appropriateness of establishing three categories of service (voice, BNV and ENV), the viability of the proposed definitional structure for distinguishing the communications or data processing nature of ENV services, and whether ENV services should be subject to regulation. Concerning carrier participation in the provision of ENV services, the comments addressed whether the resale structure is appropriate, whether it must necessarily be applied to all carriers owning transmission facilities, and the appropriate degree of corporate separation required for those carriers that must offer ENV services through a separate subsidiary.

5. Based on the voluminous record compiled in this proceeding, we adopt a regulatory scheme that distinguishes between the common carrier offering of basic transmission services and the offering of enhanced services. Although more simplified terminology is employed, this basic/enhanced dichotomy for network services is consistent with the approach taken in the Tentative Decision. We find that basic service is limited to the common carrier offering of transmission capacity for the movement of information, whereas enhanced service combines basic service with computer processing applications that act on the format, content, code, protocol or similar aspects of the subscriber's transmitted information, or provide the subscriber additional, different, or restructured information, or involve subscriber interaction with stored information.

6. As the Tentative Decision recognizes, it is in the provision of enhanced services that uncertainty as to the communications or data processing nature of a service is significant. In the course of this proceeding we have made several attempts to adopt a definitional scheme that would provide an adequate regulatory demarcation between regulated communications services and unregulated data processing services. We conclude that the record does not support adoption of the definitional scheme proposed in the Tentative Decision and that any attempt to so categorize enhanced services is unnecessary under our statutory mandate and would be contrary to the public interest. Such use of a definitional scheme to classify various types of enhanced services would not result in regulatory certainty in the marketplace and would most likely result in the direct or indirect expansion of unnecessary regulation over currently unregulated vendors of enhanced services and deprive consumers of increased opportunities to have these services tailored to their individual needs.

7. The decision sets forth the regulatory scheme for basic and enhanced services. The common carrier offering of basic transmission services are communications services and regulated as such under traditional Title II concepts. Consistent with the determinations made in the First Computer Inquiry, we find that regulation of enhanced services is not required in furtherance of some overall statutory objective. In fact, the absence of traditional public utility regulation of enhanced services offers the greatest potential for efficient utilization and full exploitation of the interstate telecommunications network. Significant public benefits accrue to the Commission's regulatory process, providers of basic and enhanced services, and consumers under this approach.

Customer-Premises Equipment

8. In the Tentative Decision we proposed a regulatory scheme for carrier-provided customer-premises equipment (CPE) based on whether the CPE performed more than a basic media conversion (BMC) function. We attempted to set forth a structure under which carriers could, separate from their basic transmission services, provide CPE that incorporated various computer processing applications. We sought comment, however, as to whether any regulatory distinction should be made between the various kinds of CPE offered by carriers, and whether all such equipment should be deregulated. We find that the public interest would not be served by classifying CPE based on whether or not more than a basic media conversion function is performed. We conclude that, in light of increasing sophistication of all types of CPE and the varied uses to which CPE can be put while under the user's control, it is likely that any given classification scheme would impose an artificial, uneconomic constraint on the design and use of CPE. In general, no regulatory distinction should be made between various types of carrier-provided CPE.

9. As to the appropriate regulatory scheme for CPE, we find that the tariffing of CPE in conjunction with regulated communications services has a direct effect on rates charged for interstate services. To the extent rates for interstate services bear costs attributable to carrier-provided CPE regulation serves to thwart the competitive provision of CPE. The continuation of tariff-type regulation over carrier-provided CPE neither recognizes the role of carriers as competitive providers of CPE, nor does it reflect the severability of CPE from transmission services. We conclude that CPE is a severable commodity from the provision of transmission ser-

vices and that regulation of CPE under Title II is not required and is no longer warranted.

10.   We appreciate that implementation of our decision to exclude carrier-provided CPE from regulation requires the eventual removal of CPE related costs from a carrier's rate base and its ultimate exclusion from the jurisdictional separations process. A transition period is established to allow for the orderly removal of CPE investment and other CPE related costs from the jurisdictional separations process. During this transition period, a Federal-State Joint Board will consider whether modifications to the separations process are warranted in light of the removal of CPE.

11.   We consider as well whether it is necessary to apply the resale structure set forth in the Tentative Decision to all carriers owning transmission facilities. We address whether certain carriers should be required to offer enhanced services on a resale basis through a separate corporate entity and whether CPE should likewise be marketed through an entity separate from that providing basic services.

12.   Weighing the public interest benefits of our objectives and the economic tradeoffs inherent in a separate subsidiary requirement, we have determined that limited imposition of the requirement will best serve the communications ratepayer and the public interest more generally. There is little need to subject carriers to the resale structure if such entities lack significant potential to cross-subsidize or to engage in other anticompetitive conduct. We find that only AT&T and GT&E present a sufficiently substantial threat such that they should be required to establish separate corporate entities for the provision of enhanced services and customer-premises equipment. We will not require any other underlying carrier to form separate entities for the provision of these services and CPE. Accordingly, we are removing the maximum separation requirements for all carriers except those under direct or common control of AT&T or GT&E. In reaching this conclusion we recognize that a reasonable balance can be struck only following a weighing of all appropriate circumstances bearing upon the risks that largely captive monopoly ratepayers will be burdened by anti-competitive conduct on the one hand and that opportunities for economic efficiencies redounding to their benefit may be lost on the other. The locus of the balance changes with circumstances. Because we have the flexibility under the Communications Act to adjust the balance as circumstances change or additional evidence is brought to light, we opt for a solution in which only AT&T and GT&E must form separate subsidiaries to offer ENHANCED service or CPE. Similarly, in establishing guidelines governing the relationship of the separated entities with their affiliates, we opt for a pragmatic approach which we can adjust when and if necessary.

13.   Finally, we believe that our action does not preclude AT&T from offering enhanced services and CPE under the provisions of the 1956 Western Electric consent decree. . . .

SEPARATE STATEMENT OF COMMISSIONER TYRONE BROWN

The decision and order we adopt today is probably the most important the Commission will issue during my time here. There have been days during the past 2½ years when I feared that this agency lacked the machinery to reach a final decision in this very complex proceeding. I compliment the staff of our Common Carrier Bureau and the other offices that participated for presenting The Commission with an approach and order that will, in my judgment, serve the long-term interests of the two "dominant" carriers, AT&T and GT&E, the interests of their competitors in the enhanced services and equipment markets, and the interests of the consuming public.

1. *What does today's decision accomplish?* First, it establishes a clear line of demarcation between "basic" communications (or pure transmission) services and enhanced "communications" services, permitting traditional common carriers and their competitors in new enhanced offerings to know beforehand whether their service will be regulated by the FCC. *Second*, our decision, after a transition period, provides for uniform deregulation of customer premises equipment—ranging from the "plain old telephone" to the smartest of the "smart terminals"—so that the marketplace rather than this agency will decide what equipment and which providers will attract the consumer's dollars. *Third*, the decision frees AT&T to compete, on a nontariff basis, with other regulated and unregulated firms in the rapidly growing enhanced services and equipment markets, so long as AT&T's offerings fall within the broad subject-matter jurisdiction of this agency. *Fourth*, the decision requires AT&T and GT&E each to establish a separate subsidiary for their enhanced services and equipment offerings, to assure customers of their monopoly services, and their competitors, that monopoly ratepayers will not fund their entry into the enhanced markets. . . .

SEPARATE STATEMENT OF CHAIRMAN CHARLES D. FERRIS

Today we have removed the barricades from the door to the information age. The supply of communications products and services will be limited only by the ingenuity of businessmen and scientists. Government will no longer be a barrier that prevents or delays the introduction of innovations in technology.

We have all read a great deal about the marvelous inventions that the convergence of computer and communications technology will make possible. Consumers and businessmen will have highly intelligent communications products and services in their homes and offices that will increase productivity, save energy and improve the quality of life.

As long as the development of new telecommunications products was subject to the whim of the regulatory process, however, the evolution of this industry was subject to uncertainty. Now communications business entrepreneurs can be sure that the marketplace and not the government will decide their fate. They will be willing to invest more money, and the communications market will develop more rapidly.

In a very real sense this proceeding began in 1966 with the initiation of the *First Computer Inquiry*. The rules developed there were intended for the world of the large capacity central processing unit, accessed by telephone lines from remote unintelligent terminals. In that world, a line between communications and data processing was defensible.

The advent of distributed data processing, however, made the *Computer I* rules obsolete. With the minicomputer it became possible to process data accessed from a central computer memory. The new "smart" terminals were both data processors and communications devices. Smart networks, such as Telenet's packet switched service, were next.

It became clear that the Commission would be called upon more and more to make arbitrary decisions. These decisions were made more difficult by the desire to allow AT&T to participate in the evolving communications/data processing markets in spite of the *1956 Consent Decree*. It became clear that there was a very real danger that in extending the grasp of regulation to allow AT&T to compete, its competitors would be ensnarled in needless regulation.

Moreover, AT&T was subjected to inevitable delays in introducing new products and services along the boundary line. Clearing the regulatory hurdle was only the first step. Appeals from competitors inevitably followed.

Thus, to deal with these problems, we have today's *Final Order* in the *Second Computer Inquiry*.

In brief, we have decided to free all of the new, enhanced services from Title II regulation. We accomplish this result by recognizing that the new products made possible by the convergence of computers and communications are outside the scope of Title II of the Communications Act. Indeed, the "rapid, efficient, nation-wide" communication service "at reasonable prices" called for in Section I of the Act is most likely to be fostered by limiting our traditional regulatory activities to the basic transmission and switching activities that are the building blocks upon which the new products and services will be erected.

Just as I am convinced that this result is in the public interest, I am convinced that the Commission's charter is flexible enough to allow it.
. . .

NOTE

The Federal Communications Commission's effort to grapple with computers illustrates the profound impact of technology on the legal system. Regulation of telephone communications was based on the existence of a market structure determined by the costs of duplicative telephone systems. The various changes wrought by technology on this market structure subjected legal principles to continuing pressure. Indeed, technology ultimately can change the very meaning of the concepts that a legal system employs—in the past, one used telephones to communicate and computers to calculate; in the future, integrated information management systems are likely to do both and even to blur the distinction between "communication" and "calculation."

The movement to deregulate computer services has continued even beyond the Second Computer Inquiry. The requirement in that decision that AT&T set up a separate subsidiary before beginning to compete in the provision of enhanced services and customer-premises equipment has come under scrutiny. With the structure of the telephone industry changed after settlement of an antitrust proceeding, the FCC may allow the twenty-two operating companies spun off from AT&T to market computer services and the like without setting up separate subsidiaries. See FCC Takes Action to Affect Competitive Posture of AT&T, Antitrust & Trade Reg.Rep. (BNA) No. 1103, at 390 (Feb. 24, 1983).

Developments such as the Second Computer Inquiry and the AT&T antitrust settlement have thrust the communications industry into an increasingly competitive environment. These events have called into question the FCC's traditional goal of providing telephone service to all Americans, even where provision of such service does not generate high profits. See, e.g., Federal Communications Commission, MTS and WATS Market Structure, 48 Fed.Reg. 10,319 (1983). If communications and computer services are becoming inextricably intertwined, should we adopt a national goal of providing computer services for all Americans? In his first speech as a Senator, Frank Lautenberg, former chairman of a data processing company, warned that unequal access by the poor to computer services and skills creates "the potential for new and distressing divisions in our society." 129 Cong.Rec. S7764–5 (daily ed. June 7, 1973) (statement of Sen. Lautenberg).

Is the case for universal access to computers stronger or weaker than the case for such access to medical services? See generally Ch. 5, Sec. B.1., supra.

Computers are not the only technology altering the communications industry, as the growth of cable television and other services demonstrates. Many of these developments have stretched the limits of traditional FCC doctrines. Consider, for example, direct broadcast satellites that can transmit programming directly to antennae located on individual homes. Programming from one such "station" may reach roughly one-tenth the area of the United States. Should the FCC apply its local service policy rules to such a station? See D. Rice, Regulation of Direct Broadcast Satellites: International Constraints and Domestic Options in Rice, Botein and Samuels, Development and Regulation of New Communications Technologies, 31, 65 (1980). On September 23, 1982, the FCC approved a construction permit for the first experimental direct broadcast satellite system for the general public, although Commissioner Quello noted in his concurrence "continuing concern about the potential adverse impact Direct Broadcast Satellite programming may have on local broadcast service." In re Application of Satellite Television Corp., 91 F.C.C.2d 953, 1000 (1982) (Quello, C., concurring).

RICHARD E. WILEY AND RICHARD M. NEUSTADT, "VIDEOTEX" CALLS FOR NEW LEGAL, REGULATORY THINKING

Legal Times of Washington 11 (July 6, 1981).

A lawyer settles down at his desk to read the morning news. He pushes a couple of buttons on his television set and a newspaper story about a client is immediately displayed on the screen. When he finishes the story, the attorney presses more buttons to see how the other papers have played the story. The news is good, so he decides to go to the theater after work. In an instant, he is able to review a list of all the plays in town. He pushes a few more buttons to reserve his seats, paying for them with an automatic deduction from his bank account.

The foregoing, however fanciful it may appear, is a familiar scenario for futurists. And in just the last few months, the concept of a multi-faceted electronic information service has become a practical concern for communications policy makers.

The new technology is called "videotex." It displays pages of text and graphics on a television set, home computer, or other video device. The pages are stored in a computer data base and may be transmitted into the home or office by broadcast signals, telephone wires, or cable television. "Teletex" systems operate one-way, transmitting a continuous cycle of pages so that the user's terminal can "grab" one and display it. Videotex also works as a two-way service—the user signals the computer to request a page, and the computer sends that page back down for display. (The Lexis legal research system is an example of the two-way approach.)

Videotex should be relatively inexpensive. If terminals are manufactured in bulk and built into TV receivers, they may add as little as $50 to the cost of the set. Some systems will charge a monthly fee, and others may be advertiser-supported and free to the subscriber.

This technology makes available diverse sources of information. Each television station can broadcast a teletext service of about 200 pages on a currently unused portion of the TV signal. A cable TV system can do the same or can dedicate a whole channel to teletext, with about 5,000 pages available. With a two-way system, the user can reach any number of data bases, each with hundreds of thousands, or even millions, of pages. In addition, the two-way systems allow shopping and banking from home as well as "electronic mail."

Videotex may become a key mass medium by the end of the decade, but first a number of important policy questions must be answered. These decisions will chart the future course of the new electronic information service. . . .

The Communications Act and FCC regulations impose extensive rules on broadcasting content—such as the equal time law governing coverage of political candidates and the fairness doctrine which requires balanced treatment of controversial issues. These content-oriented rules may be inappropriate for videotex. They have been criticized as unnecessary and even unconstitutional restraints on journalistic freedom.

The rules are premised on the concept of scarcity—that is, the limited availability of broadcast frequencies. Congress currently is considering abolishing some of these restrictions for radio because of the proliferation of stations. However, the rules remain for television and, indeed, apply even to most cable TV services despite cable's multiple channel capacity.

The new videotex services promise a so-called "economy of abundance" and, accordingly, it seems difficult to justify any regulation of the new medium based on a scarcity concept. Moreover, since equal time, fairness and other similar rules are wholly unknown in the print world, their application to electronic publishing raises a number of serious legal and constitutional questions. Congressional action is needed to ensure that electronic information services can develop without undue restrictions on content.

New technology is shaking up old definitions in areas like banking and consumer protection. Home banking terminals will undermine the long-standing restrictions on the geographical areas where a financial institution can operate. Disclosure and "cooling off" requirements for sales and extensions of credit were designed for written contracts and face-to-face sales. It is not clear how these rules will apply when transactions are made electronically, without use of paper.

Electronic publishing can flow easily across international boundaries. The technology lets a user in the country dial up a data base in another. System operators are already worrying about how to handle copyright protections, and some countries are considering restrictions on "trans-border data flow" for reasons of privacy, national security, or economic protectionism.

All of these questions arise because videotex cuts across established legal and regulatory pigeonholes. It is both communications and publishing. It may deliver identical services over TV frequencies, cable channels and telephone lines. And it promises diversity and abundance where, at least in broadcasting, there has been a scarcity of outlets in the past.

Videotex promises to deliver new and potentially valuable services to the American public. It also will pose some of the most intriguing questions which will arise in the communications law field during the next five years.

NOTE

Wiley and Neustadt suggest that application of the fairness doctrine may not be justified in the case of videotex. The fairness doctrine requires broadcasters to present public issues and to give fair coverage to each side of those issues. Red Lion Broadcasting Co. v. Federal Communications Commission, 395 U.S. 367, 89 S.Ct. 1794, 23 L.Ed.2d 371 (1969). Newspapers, on the other hand, cannot be subjected to requirements of this type because of the First Amendment. Miami Herald Publishing Co. v. Tornillo, 418 U.S. 241, 94 S.Ct. 2831, 41 L.Ed.2d 730 (1974). How would you decide whether videotex should be subjected to the fairness doctrine? Should it depend on whether using videotex is more like watching television or reading a newspaper? Or should the decision rest on scarcity, because the Court in *Red Lion* said, "the First Amendment confers no right on licensees . . . to an unconditional monopoly of a scarce resource which the Government has denied others the right to use."? 395 U.S., at 391, 89 S.Ct., at 1807. If a single videotex service garners 80 percent of the American market and 100 competitors split the remaining 20 percent, should the scarcity rationale for the fairness doctrine be triggered? If the experience with the regulation of cable television is any guide, the courts will find the constitutional status of videotex a thorny question. The courts of appeals have divided on whether cable is the equivalent of newspapers for first amendment purposes. Compare Federal Communications Commission v. Midwest Video Corp., 571 F.2d 1025 (8th Cir. 1978), affirmed on statutory grounds, 440 U.S. 689, 99 S.Ct. 1435, 59 L.Ed.2d 692 (1979), with Community Communications v. City of Boulder, 660 F.2d 1370 (10th Cir.1981).

The novel legal questions raised by videotex are likely to be addressed in the first instance in a highly traditional administrative law format: agency rulemaking or adjudication, followed in some cases by judicial review. This has been the pattern with FCC regulation of computer services, supra, with NRC regulation of nuclear energy, see Ch. 2, Sec. B.1, supra, and with a variety of other science policy issues, see Ch. 4, Sec. C.1., supra. What strengths and weaknesses does the FCC have in the area of new technologies compared with Congress or the courts? Is the FCC equally well-suited to decide all of the issues raised by these technologies?

2.　CENTRAL DATA BANKS, HOME COMPUTERS AND PRIVACY

SHIBLEY v. TIME, INC.

Court of Appeals of Ohio, Cuyahoga County, 1975.
45 Ohio App.2d 69, 341 N.E.2d 337.

JOHN V. CORRIGAN, JUDGE.

Plaintiff, Norman W. Shibley, and intervenor, Joseph Kalk, have both filed appeals from the trial court's granting of all defendants' motions to dismiss the complaint and crossclaim for failure to state a claim upon which relief can be granted. . . .

This action originated with the plaintiff's complaint against the publishers of Time Magazine, Esquire, Playboy, and Ladies Home Journal and against the issuer of American Express credit cards. The complaint alleged that the defendants' practice of selling subscription lists to direct mail advertising businesses without the prior consent of subscribers constituted an invasion of privacy and unjust enrichment. . . .

Appellants' argument on appeal is that defendants' practice of renting and selling subscription lists constitutes an invasion of privacy because it amounts to a sale of individual "personality profiles," which subjects the subscribers to solicitations from direct mail advertisers. The reasoning behind this position is the contention that the buyers of these lists are able to draw certain conclusions about the financial position, social habits, and general personality of the persons on the lists by virtue of the fact that they subscribe to certain publications and that this information is then used in determining the type of advertisement to be sent. This, appellants contend, is an invasion of privacy which was not consented to nor made a part of the original subscription contract. The argument then continues that defendants have therefore been unjustly enriched at the subscribers' expense.

We cannot agree with appellants that this practice constitutes an invasion of privacy and therefore find that the trial court correctly granted defendants' motions to dismiss. Invasion of privacy, as it is recognized in Ohio, is defined in the second syllabus of Housh v. Peth (1956), 165 Ohio St. 35, 133 N.E.2d 340, as follows:

> "An actionable invasion of the right of privacy is the unwarranted appropriation or exploitation of one's personality, the publicizing of one's private affairs with which the public has no legitimate concern, or the wrongful intrusion into one's private activities in such a manner as to outrage or cause mental suffering, shame or humiliation to a person of ordinary sensibilities."

Recognizing that their situation does not fall within any definition of invasion of privacy as yet propounded, appellants nevertheless attempt to bring themselves within *Housh v. Peth*, supra by arguing that defendants' activity constitutes an "appropriation of one's personality." It is clear from a reading of the authorities dealing with invasion of privacy that the "appropriation or exploitation of one's personality" referred to in *Housh* refers to those situations where the plaintiff's name or likeness is displayed to the public to indicate that the plaintiff indorses the defendant's product or business. See W. Prosser, Law of Torts § 117 (4th ed. 1971). The activity complained of here does not fall within that classification.

That defendants' activity does not constitute an invasion of privacy is indicated by the fact that the Ohio legislature has enacted R.C. 4503.26 permitting the sale of names and addresses of registrants of motor vehicles. The present state of the law as to the relation between the right of privacy and the practice of selling subscription lists to direct mail advertisers is summarized in a case challenging the constitutionality of a New York statute authorizing the Commissioner of Motor Vehicles to sell registration lists. Lamont v. Commissioner of Motor Vehicles (1967), D.C., 269 F.Supp. 880. In that case the court stated:

> ". . . The mail box, however noxious its advertising contents often seem to judges as well as other people, is hardly the kind of enclave that requires constitutional defense to protect 'the privacies of life.' The short, though regular, journey from mail box to trash can . . . is an acceptable burden, at least so far as the Constitution is concerned . . . ."

The right of privacy does not extend to the mailbox and therefore it is constitutionally permissible to sell subscription lists to direct mail advertisers. It necessarily follows that the practice complained of here does not constitute an invasion of privacy even if appellants' unsupported assertion that this amounts to the sale of "personality profiles" is taken as true because these profiles are only used to determine what type of advertisement is to be sent.

Appellants have requested that this court make new law by expanding the present concept of invasion of privacy to include the practice complained of here. It is not within our province to create a specific right which is not recognized at common law. The forum to which appellants should look is the legislature because the appropriate remedy in this situation is the creation of a statutory right. . . .

WHALEN v. ROE

Supreme Court of the United States, 1977.
429 U.S. 589, 97 S.Ct. 869, 51 L.Ed.2d 64.

MR. JUSTICE STEVENS delivered the opinion of the Court.

The constitutional question presented is whether the State of New York may record, in a centralized computer file, the names and addresses of all persons who have obtained, pursuant to a doctor's prescription, certain drugs for which there is both a lawful and an unlawful market.

The District Court enjoined enforcement of the portions of the New York State Controlled Substances Act of 1972 which require such recording on the ground that they violate appellees' constitutionally protected rights of privacy. We noted probable jurisdiction of the appeal by the Commissioner of Health, 424 U.S. 907, 96 S.Ct. 1100, 47 L.Ed.2d 310, and now reverse.

Many drugs have both legitimate and illegitimate uses. In response to a concern that such drugs were being diverted into unlawful channels, in 1970 the New York Legislature created a special commission to evaluate the State's drug-control laws. The commission found the existing laws deficient in several respects. There was no effective way to prevent the use of stolen or revised prescriptions, to prevent unscrupulous pharmacists from repeatedly refilling prescriptions, to prevent users from obtaining prescriptions from more than one doctor, or to prevent doctors from over-prescribing, either by authorizing an excessive amount in one prescription or by giving one patient multiple prescriptions. In drafting new legislation to correct such defects, the commission consulted with enforcement officials in California and Illinois where central reporting systems were being used effectively.

The new New York statute classified potentially harmful drugs in five schedules. Drugs, such as heroin, which are highly abused and have no recognized medical use, are in Schedule I; they cannot be prescribed. Schedules II through V include drugs which have a progressively lower potential for abuse but also have a recognized medical use. Our concern is limited to Schedule II, which includes the most dangerous of the legitimate drugs.

With an exception for emergencies, the Act requires that all prescriptions for Schedule II drugs be prepared by the physician in triplicate on an official form. The completed form identifies the prescribing physician; the dispensing pharmacy; the drug and dosage; and the name, address, and age of the patient. One copy of the form is retained by the physician, the second by the pharmacist, and the third is forwarded to the New York State Department of Health in Albany. A prescription made on an official form may not exceed a 30-day supply, and may not be refilled.

The District Court found that about 100,000 Schedule II prescription forms are delivered to a receiving room at the Department of Health in Albany each month. They are sorted, coded, and logged and then taken to another room where the data on the forms is recorded on magnetic tapes for processing by a computer. Thereafter, the forms are returned to the receiving room to be retained in a vault for a five-year period and then destroyed as required by the statute. The receiving room is surrounded by a locked wire fence and protected by an alarm system. The computer tapes containing the prescription data are kept in a locked cabinet. When the tapes are used, the computer is run "off-line," which means that no terminal outside of the computer room can read or record any information. Public disclosure of the identity of patients is expressly prohibited by the statute and by a Department of Health regulation. Willful violation of these prohibitions is a crime punishable by up to one year in prison and a $2,000 fine. At the time of trial there were 17 Department of Health employees with access to the files; in addition, there were 24 investigators with authority to investigate cases of overdispensing which might be identified by the computer. Twenty months after the effective date of the Act, the computerized data had only been used in two investigations involving alleged overuse by specific patients.

A few days before the Act became effective, this litigation was commenced by a group of patients regularly receiving prescriptions for Schedule II drugs, by doctors who prescribe such drugs, and by two associations of physicians. After various preliminary proceedings, a three-judge District Court conducted a one-day trial. Appellees offered evidence tending to prove that persons in need of treatment with Schedule II drugs will from time to time decline such treatment because of their fear that the misuse of the computerized data will cause them to be stigmatized as "drug addicts." . . .

Appellees contend that the statute invades a constitutionally protected "zone of privacy." The cases sometimes characterized as protecting "privacy" have in fact involved at least two different kinds of interests. One is the individual interest in avoiding disclosure of personal matters, and another is the interest in independence in making certain kinds of important decisions. Appellees argue that both of these interests are impaired by this statute. The mere existence in readily available form of the information about patients' use of Schedule II drugs creates a genuine concern that the information will become publicly known and that it will adversely affect their reputations. This concern makes some patients reluctant to use, and some doctors reluctant to prescribe, such drugs even when their use is medically indicated. It follows, they argue, that the making of decisions about matters vital to the care of their health is inevitably affected by the statute. Thus, the statute threatens to impair both their interest in the nondisclosure of private information and also their interest in making important decisions independently.

We are persuaded, however, that the New York program does not, on its face, pose a sufficiently grievous threat to either interest to establish a constitutional violation.

Public disclosure of patient information can come about in three ways. Health Department employees may violate the statute by failing, either deliberately or negligently, to maintain proper security. A patient or a doctor may be accused of a violation and the stored data may be offered in evidence in a judicial proceeding. Or, thirdly, a doctor, a pharmacist, or the patient may voluntarily reveal information on a prescription form.

The third possibility existed under the prior law and is entirely unrelated to the existence of the computerized data bank. Neither of the other two possibilities provides a proper ground for attacking the statute as invalid on its face. There is no support in the record, or in the experience of the two States that New York has emulated, for an assumption that the security provisions of the statute will be administered improperly. And the remote possibility that judicial supervision of the evidentiary use of particular items of stored information will provide inadequate protection against unwarranted disclosures is surely not a sufficient reason for invalidating the entire patient-identification program.

Even without public disclosure, it is, of course, true that private information must be disclosed to the authorized employees of the New York Department of Health. Such disclosures, however, are not significantly different from those that were required under the prior law. Nor are they meaningfully distinguishable from a host of other unpleasant invasions of privacy that are associated with many facets of health care. Unquestionably, some individuals' concern for their own privacy may lead them to avoid or to postpone needed medical attention. Nevertheless, disclosures of private medical information to doctors, to hospital personnel, to insurance companies, and to public health agencies are often an essential part of modern medical practice even when the disclosure may reflect unfavorably on the character of the patient. Requiring such disclosures to representatives of the State having responsibility for the health of the community, does not automatically amount to an impermissible invasion of privacy.

Appellees also argue, however, that even if unwarranted disclosures do not actually occur, the knowledge that the information is readily available in a computerized file creates a genuine concern that causes some persons to decline needed medication. The record supports the conclusion that some use of Schedule II drugs has been discouraged by that concern; it also is clear, however, that about 100,000 prescriptions for such drugs were being filled each month prior to the entry of the District Court's injunction. Clearly, therefore, the statute did not deprive the public of access to the drugs.

. . .

A final word about issues we have not decided. We are not unaware of the threat to privacy implicit in the accumulation of vast amounts of personal information in computerized data banks or other massive government files. The collection of taxes, the distribution of welfare and social security benefits, the supervision of public health, the direction of our Armed Forces, and the enforcement of the criminal laws all require the orderly preservation of great quantities of information, much of which is personal in character and potentially embarassing or harmful if disclosed. The right to collect and use such data for public purposes is typically accompanied by a concomitant statutory or regulatory duty to avoid unwarranted disclosures. Recognizing that in some circumstances that duty arguably has its roots in the Constitution, nevertheless New York's statutory scheme, and its implementing administrative procedures, evidence a proper concern with, and protection of, the individual's interest in privacy. We therefore need not, and do not, decide any question which might be presented by the unwarranted disclosure of accumulated private data—whether intentional or unintentional—or by a system that did not contain comparable security provisions. We simply hold that this record does not establish an invasion of any right or liberty protected by the Fourteenth Amendment.

Reversed.

MR. JUSTICE BRENNAN, concurring.

I write only to express my understanding of the opinion of the Court, which I join.

The New York statute under attack requires doctors to disclose to the State information about prescriptions for certain drugs with a high potential for abuse, and provides for the storage of that information in a central computer file. The Court recognizes that an individual's "interest in avoiding disclosure of personal matters" is an aspect of the right of privacy, ante, at 876–877, and nn. 24–25, but holds that in this case, any such interest has not been seriously enough invaded by the State to require a showing that its program was indispensable to the State's effort to control drug abuse.

The information disclosed by the physician under this program is made available only to a small number of public health officials with a legitimate interest in the information. As the record makes clear, New York has long required doctors to make this information available to its officials on request, and that practice is not challenged here. Such limited reporting requirements in the medical field are familiar, ante, at 878 n. 29, and are not generally regarded as an invasion of privacy. Broad dissemination by state officials of such information, however, would clearly implicate constitutionally protected privacy rights, and would presumably be justified only by compelling state interests. See, e.g., Roe v. Wade, 410 U.S. 113, 155–156, 93 S.Ct. 705, 728, 35 L.Ed.2d 147 (1973).

What is more troubling about this scheme, however, is the central computer storage of the data thus collected. Obviously, as the State argues, collection and storage of data by the State that is in itself legitimate is not rendered unconstitutional simply because new technology makes the State's operations more efficient. However, as the example of the Fourth Amendment shows, the Constitution puts limits not only on the type of information the State may gather, but also on the means it may use to gather it. The central storage and easy accessibility of computerized data vastly increase the potential for abuse of that information, and I am not prepared to say that future developments will not demonstrate the necessity of some curb on such technology.

In this case, as the Court's opinon makes clear, the State's carefully designed program includes numerous safeguards intended to forestall the danger of indiscriminate disclosure. Given this serious and, so far as the record shows, successful effort to prevent abuse and limit access to the personal information at issue, I cannot say that the statute's provisions for computer storage, on their face, amount to a deprivation of constitutionally protected privacy interests, any more than the more traditional reporting provisions.

In the absence of such a deprivation, the State was not required to prove that the challenged statute is absolutely necessary to its attempt to control drug abuse. Of course, a statute that did effect such a deprivation would only be consistent with the Constitution if it were necessary to promote a compelling state interest. Roe v. Wade, supra; Eisenstadt v. Baird, 405 U.S. 438, 464, 92 S.Ct. 1029, 1043–1044, 31 L.Ed.2d 349 (1972) (White, J., concurring in result).

MR. JUSTICE STEWART, concurring.

In Katz v. United States, 389 U.S. 347, 88 S.Ct. 507, 19 L.Ed.2d 576, the Court made clear that although the Constitution affords protection against certain kinds of government intrusions into personal and private matters, there is no "general constitutional 'right to privacy.' . . . [T]he protection of a person's *general* right to privacy—his right to be let alone by other people—is, like the protection of his property and of his very life, left largely to the law of the individual States." Id., at 350–351, 88 S.Ct., at 510 (footnote omitted).

Mr. Justice Brennan's concurring opinion states that "[b]road dissemination by state officials of [the information collected by New York State] . . . would clearly implicate constitutionally protected privacy rights . . . ." Ante, at 880. The only possible support in his opinion for this statement is its earlier reference to two footnotes in the Court's opinion, ibid., citing ante, at 876–877, and nn. 24–25 (majority opinion). The footnotes, however, cite to only two Court opinions, and those two cases do not support the proposition advanced by Mr. Justice Brennan.

The first case referred to, Griswold v. Connecticut, 381 U.S. 479, 85 S.Ct. 1678, 14 L.Ed.2d 510, held that a State cannot constitutionally prohibit a married couple from using contraceptives in the privacy of their home. Although the broad language of the opinion includes a discussion of privacy, see id., at 484–485, 85 S.Ct., at 1681–1682, the constitutional protection there discovered also related to (1) marriage, see id., at 485–486, 85 S.Ct., at 1682; id., at 495, 85 S.Ct., at 1687–1688 (Goldberg, J., concurring); id., at 500, 85 S.Ct., at 1690 (Harlan, J., concurring in judgment), citing Poe v. Ullman, 367 U.S. 497, 522, 81 S.Ct. 1752, 1766, 6 L.Ed.2d 989 (Harlan, J., dissenting); 381 U.S., at 502–503, 85 S.Ct., at 1691–1692 (White, J., concurring in judgment); (2) privacy *in the home,* see id., at 484–485, 85 S.Ct., at 1681–1682 (majority opinion); id., at 495, 85 S.Ct., at 1687 (Goldberg, J., concurring); id., at 500, 85 S.Ct, at 1690 (Harlan, J., concurring in judgment), citing *Poe v. Ullman,* supra, at 522, 81 S.Ct., at 1766 (Harlan, J., dissenting); and (3) the right to use contraceptives, see 381 U.S., at 503, 85 S.Ct., at 1691–1692 (White, J., concurring in judgment); see also Roe v. Wade, 410 U.S. 113, 169–170, 93 S.Ct. 705, 735, 35 L.Ed.2d 147 (Stewart, J., concurring). Whatever the *ratio decidendi* of *Griswold,* it does not recognize a general interest in freedom from disclosure of private information.

The other case referred to, Stanley v. Georgia, 394 U.S. 557, 89 S.Ct. 1243, 22 L.Ed.2d 542, held that an individual cannot constitutionally be prosecuted for possession of obscene materials in his home. Although *Stanley* makes some reference to privacy rights, id., at 564, 89 S.Ct., at 1247–1248, the holding there was simply that the *First* Amendment—as made applicable to the States by the Fourteenth—protects a person's right to read what he chooses in circumstances where that choice poses no threat to the sensibilities or welfare of others, id., at 565–568, 89 S.Ct., at 1248–1250.

Upon the understanding that nothing the Court says today is contrary to the above views, I join its opinion and judgment.

NOTE

The fundamental question for those who fear that centralized computer systems invade privacy is whether the computer itself is the problem. An enormous index card file can contain a good deal of information. It may well be that the computer's ability to cross-reference files quickly is more important than the simple storage of information. If you consent to provide your name and address to a magazine, as in *Shibley*, and you consent to provide medical information to a doctor, as in *Whalen*, are you consenting to the combining of that data? Does it matter who has access to the combined data or how they will use it? The courts have generally been reluctant to impose common law or constitutional restraints on computerized information systems. A number of state and federal statutes, however, attempt to limit the use of credit and other information stored on computer files. See Comment, The Use and Abuse of Computerized Information, 44 Alb.L. Rev. 589 (1980). Do people worry that credit information on computer files might be in error? Or are people actually more concerned with the possibility that computerized credit files might be unusually accurate?

As *Whalen* indicates, the constitutional concept of privacy has uncertain application to computers. Do you agree with Justice Brennan or Justice Stewart on this matter? What relevance, if any, do the views of the Framers of the Constitution have to an issue involving, in part, a technology they never imagined?

Certain constitutional privacy doctrines are said to turn on our expectations. Wiretapping a public telephone booth is a "search" under the fourth amendment and thus typically requires a warrant, Katz v. United States, 389 U.S. 347, 88 S.Ct. 507, 19 L.Ed.2d 576 (1967), while placing a concealed transmitter on an undercover agent does not give rise to Fourth Amendment protection because a wrongdoer has no justifiable expectation that the person he is talking to will not repeat the conversation elsewhere. United States v. White, 401 U.S. 745, 91 S.Ct. 1122, 28 L.Ed.2d 453 (1971). Should the Court require a warrant to wiretap a computerized bank terminal in order to get information on financial transactions? To the extent that the terminal is similar to a human teller, does that mean, under *White*, that no warrant is required? What ought our society's attitude be towards the confidentiality of communications with computers?

The *Katz-White* line of cases may also be implicated in another set of privacy issues involving modern technologies. The Supreme Court has upheld the warrantless monitoring of signals from a radio transmitter placed in a drum that ended up at a clandestine drug laboratory. United States v. Knotts, 460 U.S. ___, 103 S.Ct. 1081, 75 L.Ed.2d 55 (1983). Confronted with the contention that this sort of government practice would permit the " 'twenty-four hour surveillance of any citizen,' " the Court replied that "if such dragnet type of enforcement practices . . . occur, there will be time enough then to determine whether different constitutional principles may be applicable." Id., at ___, 103 S.Ct., at 1086, 75 L.Ed.2d, at 63. Eight days after the Court's decision, newspapers reported a New Mexico pilot program requiring probationary offenders who must go home after work to wear an electronic bracelet. The bracelet emits a code fed through the offender's telephone to a computer—if the offender removes the bracelet or goes more than 1000 feet from his telephone, a signal is sent to the computer. See Here's a New Kind of Slave Bracelet, Washington Post, March 10, 1983, at A8, col. 1. Are these the "dragnet type law enforcement practices" to which the Court alluded? Without the bracelet, the probationary offenders might have to go to jail during non-working hours. Does this new technology enhance or diminish an offender's freedom?

PAUL RUSSO, CHIH–CHUNG WANG, PHILIP BALTZER AND JOSEPH WEIZBECKER, MICROPROCESSORS IN CONSUMER PRODUCTS

in The Microelectronics Revolution
130, 134–135 (T. Forester ed. 1981).

During the late 1960s and early 1970s, cable TV manufacturers were gearing up for what was supposed to be a major increase in the use of two-way CATV [cable] systems. In the "wired-city" concepts espoused during that era, planned uses of two-way CATV were limited only by one's imagination. Unfortunately, two factors dominated in slowing down this potentially rapid growth—technical proplems in two-way transmission and the high costs of putting specialized control centres in consumer homes.

A two-way CATV system consists basically of head-end (headquarters) equipment, usually computer controlled, a cable network connecting all the users with the head-end, and control centres or terminals at each user installation. The frequency spectrum is typically divided into bands for forward (head-end to subscriber) and reverse (subscriber to head-end) transmission. The bulk of the frequency spectrum is assigned to the forward band, most of which is utilized for broadcast TV signals, with a small band reserved for data. In addition, a small part of the spectrum is used for data transmission from subscribers to the head-end. The types of two-way functions achievable cover such applications as home security, interactive shopping, weather information, remote electronic fund transfer including banking, and message services (electronic mail). Additional proposed functions include remote game playing, information retrieval and wake-up services.

The impact of LSI [large-scale integrated circuit microprocessors] in home terminal design and in computer-based head-end equipment needs no comment. The microprocessor, however, is only begining to impact the two-way CATV business. Under design are microprocessor-based pay-TV systems for hotels and motels, which can provide additional communication services, such as room and message status, room service requests, and security. It will not be long before microprocessors impact home two-way CATV terminals, since many new functions and expanded flexibility will be made possible at incremental cost. . . .

NOTE

If modern computer technology does indeed hasten the development of the "wired-city," what are the implications for privacy? If home computers are routinely linked with other computers, protection of personal information may require special safeguards. Issues may also arise concerning the wiretapping of computer systems. Do these dangers outweigh the conveniences of life in a computerized "wired-city"?

Extensive use of sophisticated home computers linked to other systems might impact broadly on the structure of society, but the nature of the impact is surprisingly hard to predict. Would people stay home more, interacting with their computers, or go out more because they have more leisure time? Would people talk with other people more or less? In your view is the home computer a decentralized "soft" technology or a dehumanizing "hard" technology? See Ch. 9, Sec. A.4., supra.

B. ARTIFICIAL INTELLIGENCE AND HUMAN VALUES

---

1. CAN COMPUTERS THINK?

BERTRAM RAPHAEL, THE THINKING COMPUTER

1–6, 159–164, 309–316 (1976).

In the mid-1940's the first experimental computers consisted of rooms full of equipment that cost millions of dollars, were available only to a few elite scientists, and constantly broke down. Today, in the mid-1970's, machines with similar computational speed and precision can be purchased in any department store for about $100, fit in the palm of your hand, and work reliably for years. Today's large computers are many millions of times more powerful than the legendary ENIAC, JOHNIAC, and WHIRLWIND machines of less than thirty years ago. Clearly computers are evolving at a rapid rate. They are becoming faster, more accurate, more reliable, physically smaller, and about twenty-five percent less expensive every year. But are they becoming any smarter? How does one go about trying to educate a computer, anyway? And why would anyone want a computer to be smart? This book will attempt to answer such questions.

By 1950 the feasibility of computers had been well established in the laboratory and the world's first commercially produced computer, UNIVAC I, was purchased by the Census Bureau of the United States government.[1] Even as the world was just beginning to discover the existence of computers, a few dreamers were thinking about the distant future of such devices. In a famous paper published in 1950,[2] A.M. Turing, a British mathematician, wrote.

> We may hope that machines will eventually compete with men in all purely intellectual fields. But which are the best ones to start with? Even this is a difficult decision. Many people think that a very abstract activity, like the playing of chess, would be best. It can also be maintained that it is best to provide the machine with the best sense organs that money can buy, and then teach it to understand and speak English. This process could follow the normal teaching of a child. Things would be pointed out and named, etc. Again I do not know what the right answer is, but I think both approaches should be tried.

Since that day, computers have permeated our society. No large bank, insurance company, research laboratory, or educational institution can survive today without using computers. More than 100,000 computers are now in use in the United States. Most of these computers are still being used in essentially the same way the UNIVAC I was used: to

---

1. Coincidentally, the first widely used punched card system, invented by Hollerith in the 1870's, was also developed for the United States Census Bureau.

2. A.M. Turing, "Computing machinery and intelligence," *Mind,* 59 (1950): 433–460. Reprinted in Feigenbaum and Feldman, *Computers and Thought,* McGraw-Hill, 1963.

mechanize the drudgery of routine arithmetic calculations. A small number of computers, however, serve as experimental systems in laboratories with extravagant-sounding names like "Artificial Intelligence Center," where scientists quietly pursue Turing's dream.[3]

During the past quarter century both approaches suggested by Turing—the application of machines to abstract, formal activities like playing chess, and the development of machines that can see, hear, and understand—have been tried. So have other approaches, such as the development of complete robot systems. Most of the scientists engaged in these studies today are motivated by much more immediate goals than Turing's academic interest in machines that "will eventually compete with men in all purely intellectual fields." Rather than machines competing with men, these researchers believe that machines can and should help men, in all fields; just as mechanical machines have helped men in their physical activities for over a hundred years, computing machines should help men in their intellectual activities—and perhaps combined sensory, computer, and mechanical machine systems should help men in many of their complex perceptual and problem-solving activities. Certainly with all the problems facing mankind today—energy, pollution, inflation, international tension, and so on—men need all the help they can get, from any likely source, and soon.

Progress toward making computers smarter has been slow, and some critics have urged that this research be abandoned—although whether these critics are motivated by a belief that the work is wasteful because it is doomed to failure, or by a fear that it will succeed and produce dangerous results, is not always clear. The goals of this book are to explain some of the obstacles to making machines smarter, and how these obstacles are being attacked; to describe some of the successes that have already been achieved, and some that lie in the near future; to show that smarter computers are already beginning to move from the laboratory to important posts in society; and, most important, to point out that smarter computers are not a dangerous threat, but rather a promising hope for the future of mankind. . . .

Misleading myths

Many people share the belief that computers are inherently stupid, and that even a suggestion that computers might be made smarter is ridiculous. This belief is so widespread that most people—scientists as well as laymen—never even consider the many ways in which smarter computers might help them. Misconceptions about a computer's limitations seem to be based upon two widely accepted but basically untrue premises. Let us examine these myths in turn. By pointing out some of their fallacies, perhaps I can open your mind to the fascinating prospects for smarter computers.

The Arithmetic Myth. *A computer is nothing but a big fast arithmetic machine.*

This myth seems to be based upon the following erroneous reasoning.

1. Computers were originally needed to do the kinds of large arithmetic calculations that arose in the tasks of aiming ballistic weapons and of producing approximate solutions to equations of nuclear physics. [True.]

---

3. The term Artificial Intelligence is widely used as the name of the branch of computer science that studies how to make computers smarter.

2.   Therefore, the designers of computers intended them to be only big, fast arithmetic calculating machines. [Doubtful. The basic design and operations of computers are much more general, as we shall see below.]

3.   Therefore, computers are nothing but big fast arithmetic machines. [False! Although the intentions of the original designers of computers are subject to wide interpretation,[4] when we study the capabilities of today's machines objectively we find much more powerful, more flexible systems.]

Computers are arithmetic machines, certainly; virtually every computer has wired into it the ability to add and subtract. But are they "nothing but" arithmetic machines? Certainly not. Take the reference manual for any computer, and scan through its "instruction set": the collection of basic operations it has been designed and wired to perform. You will see a few, perhaps as many as ten or twenty, operations that bear some close resemblance to arithmetic—e.g., ADD, DIVIDE, FLOATING SUBTRACT, MULTIPLY STEP, and so on—but you will also see many, perhaps one or two hundred, operations that have relatively little to do with arithmetic—e.g., STORE, LOAD, TEST, SHIFT, READ, WRITE, REWIND TAPE, SKIP, MOVE, MASK, MATCH, TRANSFER, and so on.

To see why computers must be able to perform so many nonarithmetic operations, consider as an example the simple task of preparing the pay checks for a business firm. This is a common job for a computer. But is it a job for a "big fast arithmetic machine"? If a human accountant did the job, he might sit down with the record books, time cards, check forms, and a small calculating machine. In a simple case, he would use the machine to multiply each employee's hourly salary by the number of hours the employee had worked and write the answer on a check.

Now suppose we want a computer to do a similar job. What *program*— sequence of elementary operations—must we give it? The program will have to do everything that both the accountant and his calculating machine did when the job was done by hand. True, the computer will have to do an occasional MULTIPLY operation, just as the calculator did; but it will also be very busy doing all the things the accountant did: looking up an employee's name, looking up his hourly salary, noting the salary in a convenient place, checking whether the employee was listed as away on vacation or sick leave and if he was not then looking for the record of his time card, finding where the total hours worked was noted, copying that total in a convenient place, supervising the MULTIPLY calculation, finding and positioning the next blank check (if the book of blank checks is empty then starting another book), copying the employee's name onto the check, dating the check, copying the calculated pay onto the check, imprinting a facsimile of a signature on the check, and moving the check to the "done" pile. Even in this trivial job a computer would have to spend almost all its effort doing what a man would do, and very little doing what a calculator would do.

Almost all the time that a computer works on the problem just described, and in fact much of the time that any computer works on any problem, the computer is positioning, comparing, moving, choosing,

---

4. I am reminded of the story of the little old lady who walked up to Wernher von Braun, the rocket expert, at the end of his lecture and asked, "Dr. von Braun, why do people want to fly to the moon? Why don't they sit home and watch television, like the good Lord intended?"

copying .   . ., but it is not doing arithmetic. Rather than calling a computer "nothing but a big fast arithmetic machine," it is much more accurate to say that a computer is *a big, fast, general-purpose symbol-manipulating machine*. With this definition as a foundation, we can progress in later chapters to an appreciation of how it is possible to develop flexible, decision-making, problem-solving, perceiving computers—in short, smart computers.

The Stupid Computer Myth. *A computer is an obedient intellectual slave that can do only what it is told to do.*

This second myth is even more persistent that the first one, and even more damaging in the way it tends to constrain our thinking. Suppose I gave you the pieces of a jigsaw puzzle and told you, "by the way, these pieces cannot be fit together." Would you try very hard to fit the pieces together? Why should anyone try to build a smart computer, if he is told over and over again that computers are inherently stupid?

The stupid-computer myth has been repeated and generally accepted for more than a hundred years. In 1842, after Professor Babbage of Cambridge designed his Analytical Engine, a large-scale mechanical digital computer (which unfortunately was never completed), his friend Lady Lovelace wrote, "The Analytical Engine has no pretensions to *originate* anything. It can do *whatever we know how to order* it to perform." There is no question that Lady Lovelace's argument, and all the subsequent versions of the stupid-computer myth, are true, in a certain literal sense: a computer must be given its program of instructions, and it will always do exactly what those instructions tell it to do (unless, of course, one of its circuits fails). And yet this basic truth is not a real restriction on the intelligence of computers at all.

A couple of examples will resolve this paradox. One of the first scientists to challenge the stupid-computer myth was A.L. Samuel of IBM. In 1961, he developed a program to make a computer play checkers. After practicing by playing against itself for a while on the new computers in the basement of an IBM manufacturing plant, the program could consistently beat Samuel, its creator. How was this possible? Samuel had figured out how to order the computer to learn to play a better game.
.   .   .

In 1969 "Shakey," a computer-controlled robot at Stanford Research Institute, could find its way from room to room, avoiding or rearranging obstacles according to general instructions such as "Block Door 3 with Box 5," even though its program had never before considered that particluar task or that particular arrangement of obstacles. How? Shakey's designers had figured out how to program a robot to find its own way around and to solve, for itself, a wide class of problems.

The claim that a computer "can only do what it is told to do" does not mean that computers must be stupid; rather, it clarifies the challenge of how to make computers smarter; we must figure out how to tell (i.e., program) a computer to be smarter. Can we tell a computer how to learn? To create? To invent? Why not? I'd bet even Lady Lovelace would have agreed that the task of figuring out "how to order" a computer "to originate" something would be a fascinating and meaningful research challenge.

.   .   .

Can a computer learn?

I am frequently asked this question, and it always makes me feel uncomfortable. The reason it makes me uncomfortable is that I know I cannot give a convincing answer, at least not in the 30 seconds typically available, because whoever asked the question almost always does not have any clear idea himself of what he means by "learn," and is already convinced that, whatever "learning" is, a computer cannot do it. Before reading on to the next paragraph, think about it yourself for a few moments. What do you think learning means? Do you think a computer can be made to do it?

A widely-used but rather superficial definition of learning is simply, "Improvement of performance as a result of experience." Therefore one is said to be able (or unable) to learn all of the following:

(a) the multiplication table;
Lincoln's Gettysburg Address;
the route home from school;

(b) to ride a bicycle;
to recognize colors;
to tune a piano;

(c) long division;
grammar;
how to tie a bow;

(d) to understand the meanings of new words;
to beat a master at chess;
to compose a symphony.

In each example, at some given time a person does not know (or is unable to do) something, but later, after a period of study and practice, he does know it (or is able to do it); therefore the same word, *learning*, is applied to all the situations. However, the natures of the activities are vastly different; we would not expect the same memory mechanisms to be at work when we remember that $8 \times 7 = 56$, when we recognize the color chartreuse, when we tie our shoes, and when we understand the word *omphaloskepsis*. Therefore we should not expect the mechanisms for acquiring all these different kinds of knowledge to be the same. Actually, psychologists, who are most concerned with studying and explaining the nature of "learning," tend to avoid using this word, much as biologists avoid the word "living" and some computer scientists avoid the word "algorithm." These words have such varied common interpretations that they can no longer be used in a precise technical sense. Since I am not a psychologist, however, I feel free to continue using (perhaps misusing) the word "learning," and shall attempt to describe some of the different kinds of learning that people, and perhaps computers, can do.

Learning processes can be divided into at least four categories, corresponding to the four groupings in the above list. Although most significant tasks certainly require a combination of elementary abilities, each of the above items resembles the other items in its group more than the items in the other groups. We shall call the four categories:

(a) *rote* learning;

(b) *parameter* learning;

(c) *method* learning;

(d) *concept* learning.

Category *a*, rote learning, consists simply of transferring raw data into memory in such a way that it can be retrieved upon demand when needed. The nature of the retrieval index varies with the nature of the data. The multiplication table must be highly indexed, so that I can get to any entry rapidly. If I had to figure out how much 8×7 is—e.g. by counting by eights—then I could not consider that the $8 \times 7 = 56$ entry in the table had been learned. Lincoln's Address, on the other hand, usually needs to be learned only straight through from the beginning. I am not expected to be able to answer quickly questions like, "What sentence comes just before the phrase, 'The world will little know nor long remember'?" Similarly, the route home from school can be considered adequately learned if I always turn left when I get to the fire station, even if I cannot describe the route to someone else.

Category *b*, parameter learning, consists of situations in which a basic framework of fundamental abilities exists before the learning begins; the principal knowledge acquired by learning consists of how to combine or relate already known abilities in order to produce new, more-effective results. Thus when a child learns to ride a bicycle he does not memorize and then recall any specific pieces of data. Instead, he develops coordination between certain leg and arm muscles, which he already knows how to use, and certain built-in balance sensors, that have always told him whether he was right-side up. Similarly, learning what color chartreuse is means building an association between the word "chartreuse," whose spelling and pronounciation is perhaps first learned by rote, and a certain portion of the range of wavelengths of light that the basic hardware of the eye (and brain) is capable of perceiving. A piano tuner learns to apply his inherent ability to recognize when the sound frequencies of two tones are related by certain small whole-number ratios. Tone-deaf people who cannot perceive such relationships can never learn to do this. The term *parameter*, applied to such learning situations, refers to the fact that the learning process can usually be described in terms of the assignment of numerical values to parameters. These parameters determine the relative importance or extent of the inherent capabilities whose specific applications are being learned. For example, in bicycle riding one parameter relates how far the bike must lean over to compensate for a given angular turn of the handlebars. In color perception, a parameter specifies the wavelength of the color boundary between chartreuse and, say, gold.

Method learning, category *c*, refers to the acquisition of *procedures* that can be used to solve whole classes of problems. Thus when one "learns" long division one really acquires, usually by rote learning, a method that can be used to solve an infinite number of specific arithmetic problems. Before the days of computers, some psychologists may have puzzled over how the solutions to an infinite number of problems could be represented compactly in human memory. Now, of course, just about every subroutine in every programming language is an example of how such procedures may be encoded. (Note that method learning does not imply method *discovery*. How many students invent the long-division procedure for themselves, when they "learn" long division?) Grammar is essentially procedural knowledge; the ability to recognize grammatical sentences and the ability to construct grammatical sentences are the basic demonstrations of understanding the grammar of any language. Grammar is in fact generally represented by both descriptive rules and procedures for using those rules (parsing) in sentence recognition and construction. Finally, certain physical abilities are also basically procedural in nature; in order to tie a bow, one must have two ends of string (or ribbon, or cloth) firmly under control, make a loop in one, wrap the other around it, and so on. This procedure, like the long-division procedure, is applicable to a huge family of specific problems and must be followed in a precise step-by-step fashion.

Our fourth category, concept learning (*d*), refers to the least-well understood and therefore most difficult forms of learning. Perhaps it is a catch-all category, containing anything anyone might like to consider to be learning that does not fit into categories *a*, *b*, or *c*. Still, it seems to have certain clear identifying characteristics. When someone "learns" to be a top-level chess player, musician, artist, or performer in almost any occupation, we can no longer identify specific facts, parametric relationships, or procedural methods that explain his outstanding performance. Somehow Mr. Fischer (Bobby, the chess champion, not Herman, the machinist) has learned to play chess better than anyone else in the world. But today nobody, including himself, can identify just what it is he has learned that gives him this championship ability: what facts, what parameters, what methods. If we could list the precise characteristics of championship knowledge, then we could give any number of people—and computers—the same knowledge, and all the resulting champions would be exactly equally matched (resulting in some rather dull tournaments).

Since we do not yet understand the detailed nature of skill at chess, or musical or artistic ability, and how it is acquired, we are free to believe in either of two alternatives.

Either

1. All knowledge and ability can be acquired by rote, parameter, or method learning. We merely have not yet discovered the right ways to express the significant facts and procedures of chess, music, and so on, to fit them into this framework.

Or

2. There exists at least one, and perhaps many, basic kinds of learning (and corresponding knowledge structures) in addition to rote, parameter, and method learning. We must discover and understand the nature of these additional learning mechanisms and knowledge representations before we can hope really to understand and imitate true chess (and musical and so on) expertise.

Which alternative do you believe? Most people probably pick 2, because the easiest way to interpret unexplainable performance is to attribute it to an unknown mechanism. However, this can be a cowardly way to avoid the real problem; if you believe that the magician's utterance "ABRACADABRA!" produced the rabbit out of thin air, then you do not have to look further for a different explanation. The more typical scientific approach is to choose an alternative like 1: i.e., assume that the known methods or theories can be applied to new problem situations; attempt to stretch the limits of these methods or theories in order to apply them; and, only when such an attempt fails, invent or discover a new method or theory to broaden the scope of the complete knowledge system. In this way, computer scientists began in the 1950's with rote learning, developed well-understood theories of parameter learning in the early 1960's, explored the limits of these theories in the mid 1960's and began to add method learning to their bag of tricks, and by the 1970's were considering what additional methods, if any, should be developed next to increase the intellectual power of automatic systems.

Learning the meaning of a new word is perhaps the simplest example of concept learning. The result of the learning process is a completely new structure of relationships. The meaning of a noun—e.g., *chair*—involves understanding that it is a piece of furniture, that it is used for sitting upon, that it is only big enough for one person at a time, that it may have arms, and so on. Concept learning might be viewed as a very general kind of parameter learning; all the elementary components must be present and the learning process consists of joining them together appropriately. However, the joining process creates new structures that could not have been formed merely by adjusting predefined parameters.

Finally, concept learning can include not only the creation of new structures, but also the creation of new procedures (and possibly the creation of procedures for creating procedures), so that perhaps it will be a basis for explaining creativity, ingenuity, the discovery of the long division algorithm (or the proof of a new theorem), the development of a new, perhaps subconscious, method for selecting a chess move, or the invention of a new musical theme. Thus I personally now lean toward alternative 2, but limit it to the following working hypothesis: There exists precisely one basic kind of learning, called *concept* learning, in addition to rote, parameter, and method learning. Concept learning is the mechanism for combining facts, parameters, and methods, in order to create more-complex structures representing new facts, parameters and methods.

Perhaps the next few years' research will determine whether this working hypothesis is correct, or whether concept learning can be reduced to a special case of parameter or method learning, or whether yet a fifth (and sixth, and so on) form of learning should be added to our basic collection. . . . Now let's look at just a few of the ways in which smarter computers are beginning to promote the advance of science.

Mathematics

Mathematics provides basic tools for much of science, as well as being a fascinating field for research in its own right. Arithmetic, an elementary branch of mathematics, has long been considered most natural for computers. However, since about 1960, several nonnumeric branches of mathematics have succumbed to computerization.

Next to arithmetic, algebra is probably the most widely used branch of mathematics. The automatic solution of symbolic algebraic equations was one of the first applications for symbol-manipulation programming techniques. Strategies were developed for simplifying, factoring, and otherwise rearranging algebraic expressions, and for solving sets of dozens or even hundreds of simultaneous algebraic equations. Today physicists and engineers have available special programming languages, subroutines, and interactive computer aids enabling them to perform high-speed, error-free, algebraic calculations far beyond their former manual abilities.

Integral calculus was once the first branch of higher mathematics faced by students that forced them to use their ingenuity, rather than cook-book solution algorithms. Since "stupid" computers solve problems only according to strictly algorithmic rules, they could not do integrals. Yet in 1962 James Slagle at MIT developed a program that did do integrals about as well as MIT freshmen; in fact it scored 88% on an MIT calculus final exam. This smarter computer worked largely by modeling the students' approach to solving calculus problems, much as Newell and Simon modelled other kinds of problem-solving behavior. The only reason Slagle's program did not score 100% was that it did not "know" the method of partial fractions, which was needed for some of the problems. The computer's memory was not large enough to hold programs for applying that method along with all its other programs.

Later, Joel Moses and other MIT computer scientists improved upon Slagle's program by replacing the techniques used by naive students with new methods developed by expert mathematicians. Now the calculus program has been combined with the algebra-manipulation system, equation solvers, and other mathematical aids, into a system called MACSYMA, a system for mathematics and symbolic algebra. This system is available as a working tool for thousands of scientists who have access to it at any time by means of a network of computers that extends from Hawaii across the United States to England and Norway.

Chapter 4 explained some of the basic ideas of mathematical logic, in particular the resolution approach to proving theorems in predicate calculus. At that time we were interested in how such formal deductive methods could be applied to automatic methods for solving a variety of different common-sense reasoning problems. Here, though, I want to point out the principal reason such methods were developed: to automate the use of mathematical logic itself. Mathematicians are continuing to improve predicate-calculus proof procedures and are begining to use them as working tools, just as they use calculus and algebra systems. Versions of automatic theorem-proving systems have been tailored for use in various specialized branches of mathematics such as set theory, and have already helped mathematicians develop new results.

Chemistry

Can smarter computers help with the intellectual work of professional scientists? One program has already achieved an impressive degree of competence on an important problem of analytic chemistry: the DENDRAL system, developed by Feigenbaum and Lederberg at Stanford University, is a computer program written to solve problems of inductive inference in organic chemistry. The system identifies the chemical composition and the organic structure of various chemical compounds, when given as data the results of certain standard tests such as the "mass spectrograph." For some families of molecules the program is an expert, even when compared with the best human scientists. It has solved problems that caused difficulty for professional chemists, and has even found errors in published chemical tables.

The DENDRAL system, which is the result of years of development effort by a joint team of computer scientists and chemists, has several key components.

1. Pattern classification ability, used for extracting key features from the experimental data.

2. An understanding of basic rules of chemistry, such as how chemical structures join together and what determines unstable compounds.

3. A model of the theory of operation of the mass spectrometer, so that trial answers may be tested by simulating the instrument and comparing its simulated results with the actual data.

4. Packages of special empirical rules, given to the system by human experts that apply only to limited classes of compounds.

The last of these components is the most important. DENDRAL generally performs extremely well when it has much specialized knowledge that is applicable to its current problem, and often performs rather poorly when it must fall back upon its knowledge of general principles. (Of course, the same can be said about almost any human problem solver.) Therefore the current continuing DENDRAL research program is studying how different types of expert knowledge may be acquired by a computer and combined, in a DENDRAL-like framework, into future automatic experts for other branches of science.

Computer Science

How can smarter computers be applied to the problems of computer science itself? An exciting new example of computer science helping itself is the research area called *automatic programming*.

Twenty years ago the major problem of computer science was to build a reliable computer. In comparison to the design, construction, and maintenance of the hardware, the problem of *programming*—the design, construction, and maintenance of the "software"—was considered to be so easy and unimportant that it received very little attention.

Today in most computer installations programming costs have caught up with the hardware costs . . . .. Although high-level languages and interactive systems have improved programming methodology considerably, the process of creating a large error-free program is still a slow, frustrating, largely trial-and-error activity. Most programs can never be thoroughly tested; they are designed to be able to work with literally millions of possible inputs, only a tiny fraction of which can ever be tried out. Generally the programmer chooses a few test cases that he hopes are typical, makes the program work properly on them, and then crosses his fingers and puts the program—e.g., an automatic billing system—into general use. Later, when errors turn up, and Mr. Raphael's credit-card bills continue to be sent to Vienna months after the billing system was notified that he had moved to San Francisco, the programmer must be called back for a job peculiarly called "maintaining" his program—and Mr. Raphael is tempted to swear at the "stupid computer."

Scientists are now developing methods to avoid such problems by using smarter computer programs to test and correct other programs. Instead of testing a program by trying some test cases, this new approach is to try to *prove* that a program will do what it is supposed to. If the proof fails, then the testing program can often figure out, from the way the proof failed, what's wrong with the program. These smarter program-proving programs may make use of a combination of formal logical proof methods, special-purpose knowledge about the particular task and programming language being tested, and perhaps even a model of the way a skilled programmer thinks.

Another approach to the automatic programming task is to develop a program that can actually create other programs. If such a program-writing program is good enough it will produce nothing but absolutely correct programs, and the problems of program testing and correction will just disappear.

Automatic program-testing and program-writing programs are still in their earliest developmental stages. It will be years before such systems can be put to practical use, but the work that has been done on them has given us confidence that such a day will come. Someday we shall be able to describe to a computer in English what task we want it to do, and a language-understanding system will call upon an automatic programming system to create a new program especially tailored for the desired task.

Other Areas

What else can smarter computers do for mankind? Think about the growing automatic capabilities discussed in this book—problem solving, perception, language understanding, representation of knowledge, expert performance in science and mathematics, and so on—and dream a little. Here are a few suggestions, to get you started.

Service Information. Our society seems to be desperately short of skilled technicians and repairmen. The cost of hiring a plumber, carpenter, auto mechanic, or electrician, has skyrocketed. We have been forced to become a nation of do-it-yourselfers. And yet, "doing it yourself" is often nearly impossible because of the absence of good information. Think of the last time you tried to fix a toaster, lawn mower, or faucet. Did you wonder which screw to take off first? Did you take apart more than you really needed to? Did you have parts left over when you were through? Direction sheets and how-to-do-it books are sometimes helpful, but even if you have exactly the right one for your job (which is rare) it is usually hard to figure out and doesn't answer your particular questions. Now suppose that a smart computer had all the information about the thing you wanted to fix, and all the knowledge needed about how to go about fixing it. All you would have to do is telephone the computer and ask for its advice.

Entertainment Center. Recreation is a rapidly growing industry. Although people have enjoyed the challenge of games of cards, darts, or backgammon for hundreds of years, it is not always possible to find an interested opponent at the appropriate level of skill, and many would occasionally like more varied, challenging games. Once again, think about calling up your friendly computer. It could certainly carry on an interesting game of chess or checkers. It might play scrabble, at whatever skill level you choose to specify, either two-handed or with as many simulated additional players as you wish. Plugged into your home TV system, the computer would be glad to play a simulated game of ping-pong, or imitate a pin-ball machine with as many bumpers and flippers as you care to specify.

Music and Art. Computers have long been used to compose musical pieces and to create novel drawings: usually to the ridicule of the critics. They have not yet been programmed to create works that appeal to the esthetic sensibilities of human connoisseurs. However, they certainly provide new tools, new media, for the human artist. A computer-controlled sound synthesizer can create any sound or combination of sounds the composer can imagine, including many that are not possible with any existing musical instrument. A computer-controlled plotter can draw geometric patterns with greater precision and patience than a human artist. As the computer becomes smarter, it can begin to collaborate with the composer or artist, instead of just following orders. It can fill in or modify passages according to general guidelines, combining its innovative abilities with those of the human, and produce compositions that neither the human nor the computer could have conceived of independently.

Actually, significant steps have already been taken toward using smarter computers in each of the above ways. But, even if they hadn't been yet, they soon would be. Thinking computers are here, waiting to be still further educated and then put to good use. All it takes is your ideas about where to use them. . . . Some of the readers of this book will be upset. They will think, "If this book is true, computers are going to replace teachers, doctors, laborers, mechanics, even computer programmers. We are going to be taught and guided by computers, diagnosed and treated by computers, play games with computers, and be subjected to computer-composed music and art. Society will be dehumanized! Computers will take over!"

I believe such forecasts of doom are incredibly misleading, even though they contain a kernel of truth. Listen to the same voices a hundred years ago: "Machines are going to replace ditch-diggers, lumberjacks, coachmen, hay-balers, even blacksmiths. Machines will take over!" Or, a hundred thousand years ago: "Fire will cook our food, heat our caves, even provide light at night. Fire will take over!" Each prediction true, but each truth turned into an essential benefit, rather than a threat, for mankind.

Yes, computers, if misused, can possibly "dehumanize" society; but they can, and I believe they will, have just the opposite effect. Computers in education can free human teachers of drudgery, and allow them to devote the bulk of their time to personal guidance of those students who most need it. Computers in medicine can raise the level of health care to a decent minimum for all, and allow doctors to concentrate on giving vital emotional support when needed, and dealing with novel problems at the forefront of their specialties. Computers in industry can free laborers from mindless jobs in unpleasant and dangerous environments, and can raise the average standard of living (and reduce inflation) by increasing productivity.

As computers become more intelligent, they will certainly cause some problems in society, and may force us to devise new ways to distribute our jobs, our wealth, and our time. Such problems and their possible solutions are well beyond the scope of this book. In the long run, however, I am confident that computers are here to stay, to the immense benefit of mankind. We must learn to understand them and to live with them. I hope this book has made some contribution toward that understanding.

JOSEPH WEIZENBAUM, COMPUTER POWER AND HUMAN REASON

207–210, 226–227 (1976).

The question I am trying to pursue here is, "What human objectives and purposes may not be appropriately delegated to computers?" We can design an automatic pilot, and delegate to it the task of keeping an airplane flying on a predetermined course. That seems an appropriate thing for machines to do. It is also technically feasible to build a computer system that will interview patients applying for help at a psychiatric out-patient clinic and produce their psychiatric profiles complete with charts, graphs, and natural-language commentary. The question is not whether such a thing *can* be done, but whether it is appropriate to delegate this hitherto human function to a machine.

The artificial intelligentsia argue, as we have seen, that there is no domain of human thought over which machines cannot range. They take for granted that machines can think the sorts of thoughts a psychiatrist thinks when engaged with his patient. They argue that efficiency and cost considerations dictate that machines ought to be delegated such responsibilities. As Professor John McCarthy once put it to me during a debate, "What do judges know that we cannot tell a computer?" His answer to the question—which is really just our question again, only in different form—is, of course, "Nothing." And it is, as he then argued, perfectly appropriate for artificial intelligence to strive to build machines for making judicial decisions.

The proposition that judges and psychiatrists know nothing that we cannot tell computers follows from the much more general proposition subscribed to by the artificial intelligentsia, namely, that there is nothing at all which humans know that cannot, at least in principle, be somehow made accessible to computers.

Not all computer scientists are still so naive as to believe, as they were once charged with believing, that knowledge consists of merely some organization of "facts." The various language-understanding and vision programs, for example store some of their knowledge in the form of assertions, i.e., axioms and theorems, and other of it in the form of processes. Indeed, in the course of planning and executing some of their complex procedures, these programs compose subprograms, that is, generate new processes, that were not explicitly supplied by human programmers. Some existing computer systems, particularly the so-called hand-eye machines, gain knowledge by directly sensing their environments. Such machines thus come to know things not only by being told them explicitly, but also by discovering them while interacting with the world. Finally, it is possible to instruct computers in certain skills, for example, how to balance a broomstick on one of its ends, by showing them how to do these things even when the instructor is himself quite incapable of verbalizing how he does the trick. The fact, then, and it *is* a fact, that humans know things which they cannot communicate in the form of spoken or written language is not by itself sufficient to establish that there is some knowledge computers cannot acquire at all.

But lest my "admission" that computers have the power to acquire knowledge in many diverse ways be taken to mean more than I intend it to mean, let me make my position very clear:

First (and least important), the ability of even the most advanced of currently existing computer systems to acquire information by means other than what Schank called "being spoon-fed" is still extremely limited. The power of existing heuristic methods for extracting knowledge even from natural-language texts directly "spoonfed" to computers rests precariously on, in Winograd's words, "the tiniest bit of relevant knowledge." It is simply absurd to believe that any currently existing computer system can come to know in any way whatever what, say, a two-year-old child knows about children's blocks.

Second, it is not obvious that all human knowledge is encodable in "information structures," however complex. A human may know, for example, just what kind of emotional impact touching another person's hand will have both on the other person and on himself. The acquisition of that knowledge is certainly not a function of the brain alone; it cannot be simply a process in which an information structure from some source in the world is transmitted to some destination in the brain. The knowledge involved is in part kinesthetic; its acquisition involves having a hand, to say the very least. There are, in other words, some things humans know by virtue of having a human body. No organism that does not have a human body can know these things in the same way humans know them. Every symbolic representation of them must lose some information that is essential for some human purposes.

Third, and the hand-touching example will do here too, there are some things people come to know only as a consequence of having been treated as human beings by other human beings. I shall say more about this in a moment.

Fourth, and finally, even the kinds of knowledge that appear superficially to be communicable from one human being to another in language alone are in fact not altogether so communicable. Claude Shannon showed that, even in abstract information theory, the "information content" of a message is not a function of the message alone but depends crucially on the state of knowledge, on the expectations, of the receiver. The message "Am arriving on 7 o'clock plane, love, Bill" has a different information content for Bill's wife, who knew he was coming home, but not on precisely what airplane, than for a girl who wasn't expecting Bill at all and who is surprised by his declaration of love.

Human language in actual use is infinitely more problematical than those aspects of it that are amenable to treatment by information theory, of course. But even the example I have cited illustrates that language involves the histories of those using it, hence the history of society, indeed, of all humanity generally. And language in human use is not merely functional in the way that computer languages are functional. It does not identify things and words only with immediate goals to be achieved or with objects to be transformed. The human use of language manifests human memory. And that is a quite different thing than the store of the computer, which has been anthropomorphized into "memory." The former gives rise to hopes and fears, for example. It is hard to see what it could mean to say that a computer hopes.

These considerations touch not only on certain technical limitations of computers, but also on the central question of what it means to be a human being and what it means to be a computer.

I accept the idea that a modern computer system is sufficiently complex and autonomous to warrant our talking about it as an organism. Given that it can both sense and affect its environment, I even grant that it can, in an extremely limited sense, be "socialized," that is, modified by its experiences with its world. I grant also that a suitably constructed robot can be made to develop a sense of itself, that it can, for example, learn to distinguish between parts of itself and objects outside of itself, that it can be made to assign a higher priority to guarding its own parts against physical damage than to similarly guarding objects external to itself, and that it can form a model of itself which could, in some sense, be considered a kind of self-consciousness. When I say therefore that I am willing to regard such a robot as an "organism," I declare my willingness to consider it a kind of animal. And I have already agreed that I see no way to put a bound on the degree of intelligence such an organism could, at least in principle, attain.

I make these stipulations, as the lawyers would call them, not because I believe that what any reasonable observer would call a socialized robot is going to be developed in the "visible future"—I do not believe that—but to avoid the unnecessary, interminable, and ultimately sterile exercise of making a catalogue of what computers will and will not be able to do, either here and now or ever. That exercise would deflect us from the primary question, namely, whether there are objectives that are not appropriately assignable to machines.

If both machines and humans are socializable, then we must ask in what way the socialization of the human must necessarily be different from that of the machine. The answer is, of course, so obvious that it makes the very asking of the question appear ludicrous, if indeed not obscene. It is a sign of the madness of our time that this issue has to be addressed at all.

Every organism is socialized by the process of dealing with problems that confront it. The very biological properties that differentiate one species from another also determine that each species will confront problems different from those faced by any other. Every species will, if only for that reason, be socialized differently. . . .

An American judge, therefore, no matter what his intelligence and fairmindedness, could not sit in a Japanese family court. His intelligence is simply alien to the problems that arise in Japanese culture. The United States Supreme Court actively recognized this while it still had jurisdiction over distant territories. For example, in the case of Diaz v. Gonzales, which was originally tried in Puerto Rico, the court refused to set aside the judgment of the court of original jurisdiction, that is, of the native court. Justice Oliver W. Holmes, writing the opinion of the Court, stated,

> "This Court has stated many times the deference due to understanding of the local courts upon matters of purely local concern. This is especially true when dealing with the decisions of a Court inheriting and brought up in a different system from that which prevails here. When we contemplate such a system from the outside it seems like a wall of stone, every part even with all the others, except so far as our own local education may lead us to see subordinations to which we are accustomed. But to one brought up within it, varying emphasis, tacit assumptions, unwritten practices, a thousand influences gained only from life, may give to the different parts wholly new values that logic and grammar never could have got from the books."

Every human intelligence is thus alien to a great many domains of thought and action. There are vast areas of authentically human concern in every culture in which no member of another culture can possibly make responsible decisions. It is not that the outsider is unable to decide at all—he can always flip coins, for example—it is rather that the *basis* on which he would have to decide must be inappropriate to the context in which the decision is to be made.

What could be more obvious than the fact that, whatever intelligence a computer can muster, however it may be acquired, it must always and necessarily be absolutely alien to any and all authentic human concerns? The very asking of the question, "What does a judge (or a psychiatrist) know that we cannot tell a computer?" is a monstrous obscenity. That it has to be put into print at all, even for the purpose of exposing its morbidity, is a sign of the madness of our times.

Computers can make judicial decisions, computers can make psychiatric judgments. They can flip coins in much more sophisticated ways than can the most patient human being. The point is that they *ought* not be given such tasks. They may even be able to arrive at "correct" decisions in some cases—but always and necessarily on bases no human being should be willing to accept.

There have been many debates on "Computers and Mind." What I conclude here is that the relevant issues are neither technological nor even mathematical; they are ethical. They cannot be settled by asking questions beginning with "can." The limits of the applicability of computers are ultimately statable only in terms of oughts. What emerges as the most elementary insight is that, since we do not now have any ways of making computers wise, we ought not now to give computers tasks that demand wisdom.

NOTE

Do you agree with Raphael's analysis of the nature of human learning? If not, how would you describe how a person learns?

Weizenbaum, in his discussion of Diaz v. Gonzales, seems to regard it as desirable that a judge from one culture not evaluate conduct in a different culture. Does this mean that a middle-class judge should not hear cases involving poor people? Would you favor "computerized justice," if it were possible, because it would stamp out racial and cultural bias?

The question of how one decides if a computer can think has excited considerable controversy. One famous approach, devised by Alan Turing, turns on whether a computer could convince a human expert, in a fair test, that it was answering questions just as a human would. Do you agree that if a computer could translate from English to Chinese, that means the computer was thinking in the same sense that a human translator thinks? See Searle, The Myth of the Computer, New York Review of Books, April 29, 1982, at 3.

ROBERT HELLAWELL,
CHOOSE: A COMPUTER PROGRAM FOR LEGAL
PLANNING AND ANALYSIS

19 Colum.J.Transnat'l.L. 339, 340–346, 356–357 (1981).

I. INTRODUCTION

This article describes a computer program called CHOOSE. It is designed to assist a lawyer in the work of legal planning and analysis.[1] The problem it addresses is highly specific: whether tax considerations favor a branch or a foreign subsidiary as a vehicle for a foreign mining investment. Although the problem is narrow, the programming method is general and can be used for a wide variety of legal problems. Essentially CHOOSE asks the user various questions and records the answers. When it has the necessary data, CHOOSE makes calculations and draws certain conclusions helpful to the user in working out the problems. CHOOSE makes its calculations and draws its conclusions by following

---

1. Although computers are widely used by lawyers for finding precedents, retrieval of data and other items, they have been largely neglected in the lawyer's central job of legal planning and analysis. Moreover, there has been surprisingly little study of the subject. See Hellawell, A Computer Program For Legal Planning and Analysis: Taxation of Stock Redemptions, 80 Colum.L. Rev. 1363 (1980).

very detailed instructions set out in the program which incorporates the complex legal provisions relevant to the problem.

The user need know nothing about computers to run CHOOSE. However, it is designed for lawyers knowledgeable in the legal area involved and, therefore, contains only a small amount of textual material explaining the law. The assumption is that a lawyer offering tax advice on the organization of a foreign mining venture would have substantial prior knowledge. Other programs, on other problems, might be designed on a very different assumption.[3]

CHOOSE serves its user in two main ways: it saves time and helps guard against error. . . .

II. THE LEGAL PROBLEM

Choosing between a foreign subsidiary and a branch for a foreign mining investment involves a trade-off between the advantage of percentage depletion available to a branch and the advantage of deferral available to a subsidiary. Deferral refers to the fact that the foreign source earnings of a corporation organized in a foreign country (with certain exceptions not relevant to this problem) are not taxable in the United States, even if the foreign corporation is a wholly-owned subsidiary of a domestic corporation. Of course, if and when the subsidiary pays any part of the earnings to its domestic parent, the parent is taxable by the United States on the dividend. Hence the word deferral: United States tax on the subsidiary's foreign earnings is deferred until the earnings are repatriated as dividends. This provides an obvious advantage over immediate United States taxation of the foreign earnings, at least where the United States tax is higher than the foreign tax.

On the other hand a foreign subsidiary is not able to use the often generous United States percentage depletion provisions. This is not because of any specific prohibition of such benefits to foreign corporations but rather because that result stems naturally from deferral itself: the foreign subsidiary is not subject to United States tax on its earnings and, therefore, it simply has no occasion to use deductions provided by United States law. The subsidiary's dividends, of course, are taxable to the parent, but dividends, whether domestic or foreign, are not the sort of income against which one may deduct percentage depletion.

Contrast the tax treatment of a branch with that of a subsidiary. A branch is not a separate legal entity: it is simply a part of the corporation that owns it and its income is simply the income of the corporation that owns it. Therefore, the income of a foreign branch of a domestic corporation is taxable by the United States because the United States taxes all income of its domestic corporations, whether that income is earned in the United States or elsewhere. This is a strict rule of United States tax jurisdiction. For example, a corporation organized in Delaware would be taxable by the United States on all of its income even though all its shareholders were German, all its officers were in Germany and it did business only in Germany.

3. In that case the program would provide textual material explaining the relevant law and analyzing the problems in its operation and citations to outside authority. The program could be designed so that any particular item of information would be presented to the user only when the particular facts of the user's case called for it. Where the user's facts led into an unclear legal situation, the user would be informed and perhaps given an opinion or other advice.

Depending on the facts of the particular situation the advantage of deferral may be greater or less than that of percentage depletion. It will turn on many things, including the foreign tax rates, the United States rates, the level of earnings and the amount of dividends throughout the life of the project. Accordingly, to judge whether to use a branch or a subsidiary one must:

1. Guess what the future earnings, dividends, tax rates and so forth will be.

2. On the basis of those guesses, estimate taxes for each year of the project for both a subsidiary and a branch.

However, since you cannot be sure of your guesses on tax rates, dividends and other factors, you must try to work out the general range of fact patterns which are both likely to occur and which will result in an appreciable advantage for either a branch or a subsidiary. Only when that is done can the planner make the best guess as to which form of investment will prove the better one. In most cases the patterns which favor one form or the other are difficult to determine without working through the tax rules and then the calculations for a number of different fact situations.

CHOOSE helps the lawyer in this process. It will apply the law and make the calculations for each new set of facts so rapidly (and accurately) that it will not only save the lawyer time but, as a practical matter, will allow him to test a larger variety of facts, and thus determine more clearly the range of fact patterns that will favor one or the other form of investment.

III. WHAT THE PROGRAM DOES

The work of determining the tax for both a branch and a subsidiary for any particular year can be separated into four parts. First, the total foreign taxes are determined. This requires information on gross income, deductions, the foreign corporate tax rates and the foreign withholding rates. Second, the United States tax before credit is determined. Usually much or all of the information used to determine the foreign tax can again be used here. But since the Treasury computes the United States tax (even on foreign income) under United States tax concepts of, for example, gross income and deductions, the program must check with the user to determine if new figures are needed. In the case of a branch the percentage depletion calculation is made at this point. This requires information about the percentage depletion rate, the "gross income from the property" as that term is used in the Internal Revenue Code and the mineral royalty paid, if any. The maximum percentage depletion deduction is one half the taxable income from the property, so this amount must be determined. Finally, the cost depletion figure is needed since it is used if it exceeds percentage depletion.

Computation of the foreign tax credit (which reduces the United States tax dollar for dollar) comes next. This is a complex operation, both arithmetically and legally. In the subsidiary case, the parent, because of deferral, has not paid any foreign tax on the profits of the subsidiary. That tax was paid by the subsidiary. However, the subsidiary pays no United States tax and, therefore, if the foreign tax is to be used as a credit it must be used by the parent. This is allowed, but it creates certain complications. Code Section 902(a) is the key provision. It "deems" a certain amount of the foreign tax to have been paid by the parent, as follows:

(a) Treatment of Taxes Paid by Foreign Corporation—For purposes of this subpart, a domestic corporation which owns at least 10 percent of the voting stock of a foreign corporation from which it receives dividends in any taxable year shall be deemed to have paid the same proportion of any income, war profits, or excess profits taxes paid or deemed to be paid by such foreign corporation to any foreign country or to any possession of the United States, on or with respect to the accumulated profits of such foreign corporation from which such dividends were paid, which the amount of such dividends (determined without regard to section 78) bears to the amount of such accumulated profits in excess of such income, war profits, and excess profits taxes (other than those deemed paid).

Without taking the space to completely describe the process, it will suffice to say that Code Section 78 directs taxpayer to "gross-up" the dividend from the subsidiary by the amount of the foreign corporate tax deemed paid (as calculated under Code Section 902(a) above). The dividend plus the gross-up becomes the gross income of the parent on which the United States tax before credit is calculated. The deemed-paid foreign tax is then taken as a credit against that tax.

The fourth and last step is working out two possible extras. The first of these is the excess credit. When the project generates more foreign tax credit in a particular year than can be used against that year's U.S. tax on project income, the overage is called "excess credit". The Code allows a taxpayer to use such excess credit in one of two ways. First, taxpayer may use the excess credit against the U.S. tax on other more lightly-taxed foreign income of that year, subject to the limitations of Section 904. Second, taxpayer may carry over and use the excess credit in other years (two back and five forward), again subject to the limitations of Section 904.

Code Section 901(e) limits the allowable excess credit. It is a tricky provision, reading in part:

(1) Reduction in Amount Allowed . . . .. the amount of any income, war profits, and excess profits taxes paid or accrued during the taxable year to any foreign country or possession of the United States with respect to foreign mineral income from sources within such country or possession which would (but for this paragraph) be allowed under such subsection shall be reduced by the amount (if any) by which—

(A) the amount of such taxes (or, if smaller, the amount of the tax which would be computed under this chapter with respect to such income determined without the deduction allowed under section 613), exceeds

(B) the amount of the tax computed under this chapter with respect to such income.

In effect, Code Section 901(e) wipes out an excess credit to the extent the excess results from the fact that the foreign tax on project income exceeds the United States tax by reason of United States percentage depletion. CHOOSE, using the rules of Code Section 901(e), works out how much the excess credit will be.

The second extra, available only in the case of a branch, is the possibility of a loss that may be used to offset non-project income or may be carried over to other years. When there is a branch loss, CHOOSE tells the user how much it is.

Having worked through the calculations for all years, CHOOSE will, on demand, display its results for any years requested or will summarize and present the totals for all years. This, of course, allows the user to compare the advantages of a subsidiary and a branch for the particular fact situation presented. The user may then change one or more facts (the foreign tax rate, for example) and CHOOSE will recalculate and, on request, display the new results. After considering the new results and comparing them to the results of previous fact situations, the user may continue, making as many changes and comparisons as he wishes.

IV. USING CHOOSE

CHOOSE is an interactive computer program with communication running between the user and the program throughout the session. The user regularly gives information and commands to the program, and the program regularly asks questions, makes comments, offers alternatives and gives results. The user of CHOOSE works at a typewriter-like keyboard with either a printer or a television-type screen (CRT). The printer permanently records both the user's and the program's typed statements while the CRT does not. But the CRT is likely to be much faster than the printer.

CHOOSE incorporates many aids for the user. First among these are devices to protect the user from his own errors. Unfortunately, experience demonstrates that human beings make errors in answering even the simplest questions. Mostly these are errors caused by striking the wrong typewriter key or by careless reading of the computer's questions. CHOOSE protects the user from a wide range of such errors. For example, the user is asked to type in the rate of the foreign corporation tax for a given year in the form of a decimal (e.g. .30 or .46). If the rate were 30% and the user typed in 30 (leaving out the decimal) the program would respond that the rate was more than 100% and ask the user to retype the answer. If the user is asked to type in a number and inadvertently types a letter in the process the program will signal the error and ask for the input to be repeated. This is a common and an understandable error of beginning users who are accustomed to using the typewriter letter "L" to signify the number 1. The computer insists on a numeral for numeric input. If the user attempts to input data for a year outside the span of years he earlier specified for the program, or attempts to input data that in various other ways falls outside specifications that the user has himself established, the program will notify him.

These and other very specific devices protect the user against many errors. But a more general device is probably the most useful. On request the program will print out all current data, exactly as it was input by the user, in easily-checked columnar form. Needless to say this service should be frequently used. The user may change the data many times during the program as he searches for turning points in the results. The display of current data lets the user know just where he is, in addition to helping him guard against error.

The program provides a projection of taxes for a period of up to 20 years and uses 15 items of data for each year. That could require the user to type in 300 different data items. However, the program deals with estimates of future items such as gross income, deductions and various tax rates. Inevitably many or all items will be the same for several if not all years of the projection. Accordingly, the program provides easy ways to make data items the same for multiple years.

More important, CHOOSE makes it very easy for the user to change one or more data items and get a new set of calculations. The user would, of course, change the data after a mistake in input, but the key use of this facility is to allow the user to quickly and easily compare the results for a variety of different situations: for example, change nothing but the foreign corporate tax rate and immediately new calculations and totals are available for all years. This facility will be illustrated in the sample run of the program.

On the user's request CHOOSE provides general instructions and a few explanations of the way the program handles the more complex legal provisions. But, for reasons noted earlier, the legal analysis, explanations and help provided by the program are kept to a minimum.[16] . . .

While it may take considerable time to develop a comprehensive library it seems inevitable that computer programs will some day be widely used in legal planning and analysis. CHOOSE is an example of a highly specific program, designed to assist a lawyer in an area in which the lawyer is expert. Other types of programs can be designed for very different circumstances. Perhaps a general practitioner might not choose to advise a mining company in making a foreign investment, but he might venture beyond the range of his everyday problems. Computer programs could help him. Like CHOOSE they could elicit the facts of his case by questioning and could work out the result by applying the law to the facts. Such programs, however, would contain a variety of explanatory material describing the law and the steps the program was taking. Among its other purposes, therefore, the program would serve as a text, but an especially useful and easy-to-use text. The user would not have to read the whole thing or determine, at his peril, the pertinent parts. Particular items of explanation would be displayed for the user when the facts stated by the user demonstrated their relevance. When the law applicable to a given set of facts was unclear the program would so inform the user, and would offer an explanation or an opinion on the outcome or refer the user to outside authorities.

With today's technology, a library of legal programs, if it existed, could be accessed in two main ways. First, a law firm might have its own small computer and purchase its own programs. Standard commercial programs would be satisfactory for most problems and for some special matters law firms might find it worthwhile to commission their own pro-

---

16. The current version of CHOOSE does not provide a facility to automatically discount future advantages and disadvantages by some user-specified interest rate. So long as the advantages of a branch or subsidiary are distributed more or less evenly throughout the life of a project, discounting would not be important. However, if the advantages of one form occur mainly in the early years of a project and the advantages of the other form occur mainly in the later years, discounting should be used to reduce all amounts to current value. Only then can the figures of various years be properly compared. With the current version of CHOOSE, the user would have to do this manually, but with a financial calculator it would be a simple job. An automatic discount facility, optional with the user and at a rate selected by the user, might usefully be added to later versions of CHOOSE.

Another possible addition would be an inflation adjuster which would automatically increase an item by a user-specified inflation rate when the same figure is input for a number of years.

grams. An intermediate approach would be to modify standard programs to fit the particular needs of the firm. CHOOSE, for example, could easily be modified to allow a projection of more than 20 years or to provide more detail on any item. The law firm could keep its programs on small disks which can be stored easily and quickly used. The user would simply select the program, insert it and turn on the terminal: almost immediately the beginning of the program would flash on the screen. All the hardware is currently available at prices that will fit the budget of a small law firm. The technology is developing rapidly and we can confidently expect even more convenient systems in the future. The second basic approach would be analogous to Lexis or Westlaw. A central computer would house the programs and multiple users would have access to them through remote terminals. Many firms might use both systems.

Computer programs for legal planning and analysis have substantial prospects. For the near term one can see certain of their uses clearly. For the far term one can only dimly sense their scope and importance.

MARGARET A. BODEN,
THE SOCIAL IMPLICATIONS OF INTELLIGENT MACHINES

in The Microelectronics Revolution
439, 440–441 (T. Forester ed. 1981).

[P]rofessionals participating in a multistage "Delphi" forecasting exercise [see Ch. 10, Sec. B.3., infra] have predicted that within the next thirty years (in many cases, within only ten or fifteen years), social applications of artificial intelligence will be widely, i.e. commercially, available. In general, the prototype is expected 5 ± 2 years ahead of the commercial version. The dates I shall mention are taken from this Delphi study (although my own view is that these predictions tend to underestimate the difficulties involved).

The applications forecasts run from robot housecleaners, chauffeurs and industrial workers, through programmed gameplayers and storytellers, to automatic teachers, physicians, legal justices, marriage counsellors and literary critics. In all these cases, the emphasis is on reasoned and flexible judgment on the program's part, as opposed to the storage and regurgitation of isolated facts, or the repetitive performance of a fixed sequence of discriminations and movements.

For example, the computer diagnosticians of the 1980s will not simply store lists of symptom-diagnosis pairs, or prescribe treatment in a blindly dogmatic (and apparently "objective") fashion. One current prototype is the MYCIN system, an interactive program that simulates a medical consultant specializing in infectious diseases. It engages in question-and-answer conversations (lasting twenty minutes on average) with doctors needing specialist help, and in seventy-five per cent of cases gives the same counsel as a human expert. The physician asks MYCIN for advice on the identification of micro-organisms and the prescription of antibiotics, and also for explanations of its advice expressed at the appropriate level of detail.

MYCIN's explanatory capacity enables physicians who disagree with specific aspects of the program's clinical rationale rationally to *reject* MYCIN's advice. It also helps nonspecialist doctors to learn more about the complexities of diagnosis and therapy in this class of diseases. And it allows human consultants to make general improvements in the program, by telling it about relevant knowledge that they realize in specific cases to be missing or inadequately stated.

A program like MYCIN involves artificial intelligence techniques. Quite apart from its (rather restricted) natural language understanding, its ability to explain itself on many different levels of detail implies a self-knowledge of its reasoning and goal-structure that are crucial to intelligent thinking. And its ability to learn by being told implies some mastery of the problem of making spontaneous inferences on the basis of input information, though admittedly only for a very limited area of discourse.

Many features of MYCIN would be embodied also in programmed legal arbiters (prototype predicted by 1988). These would not only search for relevant legal precedents in the judicial literature—a far from trivial task—but would also offer legal advice. Like MYCIN, legal arbiters will preferably be used to *augment* human judgement, rather than *replace* it. Accordingly, like MYCIN, they should when appropriate offer several (reasoned) alternative judgements, not just the one of which they are most confident. MYCIN's assessment of degrees of confidence is not a mere statistical probability measure. It takes into account psychological factors about the evidential relations of beliefs, factors that philosophers of science have considered in regard to "confirmation theory". Legal programs, too, would have to incorporate more subtle concepts of *confidence* and *evidence* than Bayesian [statistical] probability, in order to avoid judicial absurdities of various types. . . .

NOTE

What aspects of their work could legal practitioners computerize in the way Hellawell describes? Tax law may sound more "mechanical" than other areas of the law, but the skill of tax practitioners (and their salaries) might give you pause. If computers can play a major role in the future of law practice, should computer education play a major role in law schools today?

Do you agree with Boden's analogy between a computer that does medical consulting and one that serves as a "legal arbiter"? Are there fundamental differences in the reasoning methods of doctors and lawyers? What are they?

2. SHOULD COMPUTERS THINK?

BRUCE MAZLISH,
THE FOURTH DISCONTINUITY

Technology and Culture 1–8 (January 1967).

A famous cartoon in *The New Yorker* magazine shows a large computer with two scientists standing excitedly beside it. One of them holds in his hand the tape just produced by the machine, while the other gapes at the message printed on it. In clear letters, it says, "Cogito, ergo sum," the famous Cartesian phrase, "I think, therefore I am."

My next cartoon has not yet been drawn. It is a fantasy on my part. In it, a patient, wild of eye and hair on end, is lying on a couch in a psychiatrist's office talking to an analyst, who is obviously a machine. The analyst-machine is saying, "Of course I'm human—aren't you?" [1]

1. After finishing the early drafts of this article, I secured unexpected confirmation of my "fantasy" concerning an analyst-machine (which is not, in itself, critical to my thesis). A story in the *New York Times*, March 12, 1965, reports that "a computerized typewriter has been credited with remarkable success at a hospital here in radically improving the condition of several children suffering an extremely severe form

These two cartoons are a way of suggesting the threat which the increasingly perceived continuity between man and the machine poses to us today. It is with this topic that I wish to deal now, approaching it in terms of what I shall call the "fourth discontinuity." In order, however, to explain what I mean by the "fourth discontinuity," I must first place the term in a historical context.

In the eighteenth lecture of his *General Introduction to Psychoanalysis*, originally delivered at the University of Vienna between 1915 and 1917, Freud suggested his own place among the great thinkers of the past who had outraged man's naive self-love. First in the line was Copernicus, who taught that our earth "was not the center of the universe, but only a tiny speck in a world-system of a magnitude hardly conceivable." Second was Darwin, who "robbed man of his peculiar privilege of having been specially created, and relegated him to a descent from the animal world." Third, now, was Freud himself. On his own account, Freud admitted, or claimed, that psychoanalysis was "endeavoring to prove to the 'ego' of each one of us that he is not even master in his own house, but that he must remain content with the veriest scraps of information about what is going on unconsciously in his own mind."

A little later in 1917, Freud repeated his sketch concerning the three great shocks to man's ego. In his short essay, "A Difficulty in the Path of Psychoanalysis," he again discussed the cosmological, biological, and now psychological blows to human pride and, when challenged by his friend Karl Abraham, admitted, "You are right in saying that the enumeration of my last paper may give the impression of claiming a place beside Copernicus and Darwin."

There is some reason to believe that Freud may have derived his conviction from Ernst Haeckel, the German exponent of Darwinism, who in his book *Natürliche Schöpfungsgeschichte* (1889) compared Darwin's achievement with that of Copernicus and concluded that together they had helped remove the last traces of anthropomorphism from science. Whatever the origin of Freud's vision of himself as the last in the line of ego-shatterers, his assertion has been generally accepted by those, like Ernest Jones, who refer to him as the "Darwin of the Mind."

The most interesting extension of Freud's self-view, however, has come from the American psychologist, Jerome Bruner. Bruner's version of what Freud called his "transvaluation" is in terms of the elimination of discontinuities, where discontinuity means an emphasis on breaks or gaps in the phenomena of nature—for example, a stress on the sharp differences between physical bodies in the heavens or on earth or between one form of animal matter and another—instead of an emphasis on its continuity. Put the other way, the elimination of discontinuity, that is, the

of childhood schizophrenia. . . . What has particularly amazed a number of psychiatrists is that the children's improvement occurred without psychotherapy; only the machine was involved. It is almost as much human as it is machine. It talks, it listens, it responds to being touched, it makes pictures or charts, it comments and explains, it gives information and can be set up to do all this in any order. In short, the machine attempts to combine in a sort of science-fiction instrument all the best of two worlds—human and machine. It is called an Edison Responsive Environment Learning System. It is an extremely sophisticated 'talking' typewriter (a cross between an analogue and digital computer) that can teach children how to read and write. . . . Dr. Campbell Goodwin speculates that the machine was able to bring the autistic children to respond because it eliminated humans as communication factors. Once the children were able to communicate, something seemed to unlock in their minds, apparently enabling them to carry out further normal mental activities that had eluded them earlier."

establishment of a belief in a continuum of nature, can be seen as the creation of continuities, and this is the way Bruner phrases it. According to Bruner, the first continuity was established by the Greek physicist-philosophers of the sixth century, rather than by Copernicus. Thus, thinkers like Anaximander conceived of the phenomena of the physical world as "continuous and monistic, as governed by the common laws of matter." [5] The creating of the second continuity, that between man and the animal kingdom was, of course, Darwin's contribution, a necessary condition for Freud's work. With Freud, according to Bruner, the following continuities were established: the continuity of organic lawfulness, so that "accident in human affairs was no more to be brooked as 'explanation' than accident in nature"; the continuity of the primitive, infantile, and archaic as co-existing with the civilized and evolved; and the continuity between mental illness and mental health.

In this version of the three historic ego-smashings, man is placed on a continuous spectrum in relation to the universe, to the rest of the animal kingdom, and to himself. He is no longer discontinuous with the world around him. In an important sense, it can be contended, once man is able to accept this situation, he is in harmony with the rest of existence. Indeed, the longing of the early nineteenth-century romantics, and of all "alienated" beings since, for a sense of "connection" is fulfilled in an unexpected manner.

Yet, to use Bruner's phraseology, though not his idea, a fourth and major discontinuity, or dichotomy, still exists in our time. It is the discontinuity between man and machine. In fact, my thesis is that this fourth discontinuity must now be eliminated—indeed, we have started on the task—and that in the process man's ego will have to undergo another rude shock, similar to those administered by Copernicus (or Galileo), Darwin, and Freud. To put it bluntly, we are now coming to realize that man and the machines he creates are continuous and that the same conceptual schemes, for example, that help explain the workings of his brain also explain the workings of a "thinking machine." Man's pride and his refusal to acknowledge this continuity, is the substratum upon which the distrust of technology and an industrialized society has been reared. Ultimately, I believe, this last rests on man's refusal to understand and accept his own nature—as being continuous with the tools and machines he constructs. Let me now try to explain what is involved in this fourth discontinuity.

. . . .

The evidence seems strong today that man evolved from the other animals into humanity through a continuous interaction of tool, physical, and mental-emotional changes. The old view that early man arrived on the evolutionary scene, fully formed, and then proceeded to discover tools

---

5. For Bruner's views, see his "Freud and the Image of Man," Partisan Review, XXIII, No. 3 (Summer 1956), 340–47. In place of both Bruner's sixth-century Greek physicists and Freud's Copernicus, I would place Galileo as the breaker of the discontinuity that was thought to exist in the material world. It was Galileo, after all, who first demonstrated that the heavenly bodies are of the same substance as the "imperfect" earth and subject to the same mechanical laws. In his Dialogue on the Two Principal World Systems (1632), he not only supported the "world system" of Copernicus against Ptolemy but established that our "world," i.e., the earth, is a natural part of the other "world," i.e., the solar system. Hence, the universe at large is one "continuous" system, a view at best only implied in Copernicus. Whatever the correct attribution, Greek physicists, Copernicus, or Galileo, Freud's point is not in principle affected.

and the new ways of life which they made possible is no longer acceptable. As Sherwood L. Washburn, professor of anthropology at the University of California, puts it, "From the rapidly accumulating evidence it is now possible to speculate with some confidence on the manner in which the way of life made possible by tools changed the pressures of natural selection and so changed the structure of man." The details of Washburn's argument are fascinating, with its linking of tools with such physical traits as pelvic structure, bipedalism, brain structure, and so on, as well as with the organization of men in co-operative societies and the substitution of morality for hormonal control of sexual and other "social" activities. Washburn's conclusion is that "it was the success of the simplest tools that started the whole trend of human evolution and led to the civilizations of today."

Darwin, of course, had had a glimpse of the role of tools in man's evolution. It was Karl Marx, however, who first placed the subject in a new light. Accepting Benjamin Franklin's definition of man as a "tool-making animal," Marx suggested in Das Kapital that "the relics of the instruments of labor are of no less importance in the study of vanished socio-economic forms, than fossil bones are in the study of the organization of extinct species." As we know, Marx wished to dedicate his great work to Darwin—a dedication rejected by the cautious biologist—and we can see part of Marx's reason for this desire in the following revealing passage:

> Darwin has aroused our interest in the history of *natural technology*, that is to say in the origin of the organs of plants and animals as productive instruments utilised for the life purposes of those creatures. Does not the history of the origin of the productive organs of men in society, the organs which form the material basis of every kind of social organisation, deserve equal attention? Since, as Vico [in the New Science (1725)] says, the essence of the distinction between human history and natural history is that the former is the work of man and the latter is not, would not the history of *human technology* be easier to write than the history of natural technology? Technology reveals man's dealings with nature, discloses the direct productive activities of his life, thus throwing light upon social relations and the resultant mental conceptions.

Only a dogmatic anti-Marxist could deny that Marx's brilliant imagination had led him to perceive a part of the continuity between man and his tools. Drawn off the track, perhaps, by Vico's distinction between human and natural history as man-made and God-made, Marx might almost be given a place in the pantheon of Copernicus, Darwin, and Freud as a destroyer of man's discontinuities with the world about him. Before our present-day anthropologists, Marx had sensed the unbreakable connection between man's evolution as a social being and his development of tools. He did not sense, however, the second part of our subject, that man and his tools, especially in the form of modern, complicated machines, are part of a theoretical continuum.

. . .

The *locus classicus* of the modern insistence on the fourth discontinuity is, as is well known, the work of Descartes. In his *Discourse on Method*, for example, he sets up God and the soul on one side, as without spatial location or extension, and the material-mechanical world in all its aspects, on the other side. Insofar as man's mind or soul participates in reason—

which means God's reason—man knows this division or dualism of mind and matter, for, as Descartes points out, man could not know this fact from his mere understanding, which is based solely on his senses, "a location where it is clearly evident that the ideas of God and the soul have never been."

Once having established his God, and man's participation through reason in God, Descartes could advance daringly to the very precipice of a world without God. He conjures up a world in imaginary space and shows that it must run according to known natural laws. Similarly, he imagines that "God formed the body of a man just like our own, both in the external configuration of its members and in the internal configuration of its organs, without using in its composition any matter but that which I had described [i.e., physical matter]. I also assumed that God did not put into this body any rational soul [defined by Descartes as "that part of us distinct from the body whose essence . . . is only to think"]."

Analyzing this purely mechanical man, Descartes boasts of how he has shown "what changes must take place in the brain to cause wakefulness, sleep, and dreams; how light, sounds, odors, taste, heat, and all the other qualities of external objects can implant various ideas through the medium of the senses . . . I explained what must be understood by that animal sense which receives these ideas, by memory which retains them and by imagination which can change them in various ways and build new ones from them." In what way, then, does such a figure differ from real man? Descartes confronts his own created "man" forthrightly; it is worth quoting the whole of his statement:

> Here I paused to show that if there were any machines which had the organs and appearance of a monkey or of some other unreasoning animal, we would have no way of telling that it was not of the same nature as these animals. But if there were a machine which had such a resemblance to our bodies, and imitated our actions as far as possible, there would always be two absolutely certain methods of recognizing that it was still not truly a man. The first is that it could never use words or other signs for the purpose of communicating its thoughts to others, as we do. It indeed is conceivable that a machine could be so made that it would utter words, and even words appropriate to physical acts which cause some change in its organs; as, for example, if it was touched in some spot that it would ask what you wanted to say to it; if in another, that it would cry that it was hurt, and so on for similar things. But it could never modify its phrases to reply to the sense of whatever was said in its presence, as even the most stupid men can do. The second method of recognition is that although such machines could do many things as well as, or perhaps even better than, men, they would infallibly fail in certain others, by which we would discover that they did not act by understanding, but only by the disposition of their organs. For while reason is a universal instrument which can be used in all sorts of situations, the organs have to be arranged in a particular way for each particular action. From this it follows that it is morally impossible that there should be enough different devices in a machine to make it behave in all the occurrences of life as our reason makes us behave.

Put in its simplest terms, Descartes' two criteria for discriminating between man and the machine are that the latter has (1) no feedback mechanism ("it could never modify its phrases") and (2) no generalizing reason ("reason is a universal instrument which can be used in all sorts of situations"). But it is exactly in these points that, today, we are no longer able so surely to sustain the dichotomy. The work of Norbert Wiener and his followers, in cybernetics, indicates what can be done on the problem of feedback. Investigations into the way the brain itself forms concepts are basic to the attempt to build computers that can do the same, and the two efforts are going forward simultaneously, as in the work of Dr. W.K. Taylor of University College, London, and of others. As G. Rattray Taylor sums up the matter: "One can't therefore be quite as confident that computers will one day equal or surpass man in concept-forming ability as one can about memory, since the trick hasn't yet been done; but the possibilities point that way." In short, the gap between man's thinking and that of his thinking machines has been greatly narrowed by recent research.

Descartes, of course, would not have been happy to see such a development realized. To eliminate the dichotomy or discontinuity between man and machines would be, in effect, to banish God from the universe. The rational soul, Descartes insisted, "could not possibly be derived from the powers of matter . . . but must have been specially created." Special creation requires God, for Descartes' reasoning is circular. The shock to man's ego, of learning the Darwinian lesson that he was not "specially created," is, in this light, only an outlying tremor of the great earthquake that threatened man's view of God as well as of himself. The obstacles to removing not only the first three but also the fourth discontinuity are, clearly, deeply imbedded in man's pride of place.

How threatening these developments were can be seen in the case of Descartes' younger contemporary, Blaise Pascal. Aware that man is "a thinking reed," Pascal also realized that he was "engulfed in the infinite immensity of spaces whereof I know nothing, and which knows nothing of me." "I am terrified," he confessed. To escape his feeling of terror, Pascal fled from reason to faith, convinced that reason could not bring him to God. Was he haunted by his own construction, at age nineteen, of a calculating machine which, in principle, anticipated the modern digital computer? By his own remark that "the arithmetical machine produces effects which approach nearer to thought than all the actions of animals"? Ultimately, to escape the anxiety that filled his soul, Pascal commanded, "On thy knees, powerless reason."

Others, of course, walked where angels feared to tread. Thus, sensationalist psychologists and epistemologists, like Locke, Hume, or Condillac, without confronting the problem head on, treated the contents of man's reason as being formed by his sense impressions. Daring thinkers, like La Mettrie in his L'Homme Machine (1747) and Holbach, went all the way to a pure materialism. As La Mettrie put it in an anticipatory transcendence of the fourth discontinuity, "I believe thought to be so little incompatible with organized matter that it seems to be a property of it, like Electricity, Motive Force, Impenetrability, Extension, etc."

On the practical front, largely leaving aside the metaphysical aspects of the problem, Pascal's work on calculating machines was taken up by those like the eccentric nineteenth-century mathematician Charles Babbage, whose brilliant designs outran the technology available to him. Thus it remained for another century, the twentieth, to bring the matter to a head and to provide the combination of mathematics, experimental physics, and modern technology that created the machines that now confront us and reawaken the metaphysical question.

DOUGLAS R. HOFSTADTER,
GODEL, ESCHER, BACH

677–679 (1979).

Question: Will a thinking computer be able to add fast?

Speculation: Perhaps not. We ourselves are composed of hardware which does fancy calculations but that doesn't mean that our symbol level, where "we" are, knows how to carry out the same fancy calculations. Let me put it this way: there's no way that you can load numbers into your own neurons to add up your grocery bill. Luckily for you, your symbol level (i.e., *you*) can't gain access to the neurons which are doing your thinking—otherwise you'd get addle-brained. To paraphrase Descartes again:

"I think; therefore I have no access to the level where I sum."

Why should it not be the same for an intelligent program? It mustn't be allowed to gain access to the circuits which are doing its thinking—otherwise it'll get addle-CPU'd. Quite seriously, a machine that can pass the Turing test may well add as slowly as you or I do, and for similar reasons. It will represent the number 2 not just by the two bits "10", but as a full-fledged *concept* the way we do, replete with associations such as its homonyms "too" and "to", the words "couple" and "deuce", a host of mental images such as dots on dominoes, the shape of the numeral '2', the notions of alternations, evenness, oddness, and on and on . . . With all this "extra baggage" to carry around, an intelligent program will become quite slothful in its adding. Of course, we could give it a "pocket calculator", so to speak (or build one in). Then it could answer very fast, but its performance would be just like that of a person with a pocket calculator. There would be two separate parts to the machine: a reliable but mindless part and an intelligent but fallible part. You couldn't rely on the composite system to be reliable, any more than a composite of person and machine is necessarily reliable. So if it's right answers you're after, better stick to the pocket calculator alone—don't throw in the intelligence!

Question: Will there be chess programs that can beat anyone?

Speculation: No. There may be programs which can beat anyone at chess, but they will not be exclusively chess players. They will be programs of *general* intelligence, and they will be just as tempermental as people. "Do you want to play chess?" "No, I'm bored with chess. Let's talk about poetry." That may be the kind of dialogue you could have with a program that could beat everyone. That is because real intelligence inevitably depends on a total overview capacity—that is, a programmed ability to "jump out of the system", so to speak—at least roughly to the extent that we have that ability. Once that is present, you can't contain the program; it's gone beyond that certain critical point, and you just have to face the facts of what you've wrought.

. . .

NOTE

If a thinking machine, perhaps of the type described by Hofstadter, could be built, should it be built? Does ordinary cost-benefit analysis help in deciding that question, or would the existence of a thinking machine change the very meaning of "cost," "benefit" and "analysis"?　See Ch. 1, Sec. D.2., and Ch. 5, Sec. A., supra.

The "continuities" discussed by Mazlish—the discoveries of Copernicus, Darwin and Freud—have raised ethical and legal problems for centuries.　A thinking machine might raise similar issues.　Suppose, for example, a machine were designed that was totally capable of driving a car.　A high school textbook of the future might then state that, "the machines that drive our cars think and react just like the human drivers of the past."　Imagine a coalition of religious leaders convincing a state legislature to pass a statute banning such statements in textbooks. Is that statute constitutional?　See the discussion of Epperson v. Arkansas in Ch. 4, Sec. A.2., supra.　Apart from the issue of constitutionality, would you agree that machine drivers could someday "think and react" just like human drivers? Do you resist the notion of thinking machines because you believe it diminishes what it means to be human?　Is this simply another version of the evolution debate?

3.　PREDICTING THE FUTURE: SOCIAL CONTROL IN THE REALM OF UNCERTAINTY

Whether the issue is computers or other emerging areas in science and medicine, efforts to forecast the future often become central.　With even a little knowledge of what lies ahead, society's ability to promote or hinder an area of technology is greatly enhanced.　The excerpts that follow concern modern methods developed to predict uncertain events in a rapidly changing world.

NORMAN DALKEY AND OLAF HELMER, AN EXPERIMENTAL APPLICATION OF THE DELPHI METHOD TO THE USE OF EXPERTS

9 Management Science 458, 459–460 (1963).

"Project DELPHI" is the name for a study of the use of expert opinion that has been intermittently conducted at The RAND corporation.　The technique employed is called the DELPHI method.　Its object is to obtain the most reliable consensus of opinion of a group of experts.　It attempts to achieve this by a series of intensive questionnaires interspersed with controlled opinion feedback.

The present paper gives an account of an experiment conducted about ten years ago.　The content of the paper has, for security reasons, only now been released for open publication.

The experiment was designed to apply expert opinion to the selection, from the viewpoint of a Soviet strategic planner, of an optimal U.S. industrial target system and to the estimation of the number of A-bombs required to reduce the munitions output by a prescribed amount.

The technique employed involves the repeated individual questioning of the experts (by interview or questionnaire) and avoids direct confrontation of the experts with one another.

The questions, which are all centered around some central problem (in our present case, an estimate of bombing requirements), are designed to bring out the respondent's reasoning that went into his reply to the primary question, the factors he considers relevant to the problem, his own estimate of these factors, and information as to the kind of data that he feels would enable him to arrive at a better appraisal of these factors and, thereby, at a more confident answer to the primary question.　The information fed to the experts between rounds of questioning is generally of two kinds: It consists either of available data previously requested by some one of the experts (e.g., output statistics for steel mills), or of factors and considerations suggested as potentially relevant by one or another respondent (e.g., the extent to which power transmission facilities permit reallocation of electric power). With respect to the latter type of information, an attempt was made (not always successfully) to conceal the actual opinion of other respondents and merely to present the factor for consideration without introducing unnecessary bias.

This mode of controlled interaction among the respondents represents a deliberate attempt to avoid the disadvantages associated with more conventional uses of experts, such as round-table discussions or other milder forms of confrontation with opposing views. The method employed in the experiment appears to be more conducive to independent thought on the part of the experts and to aid them in the gradual formation of a considered opinion. Direct confrontation, on the other hand, all too often induces the hasty formulation of preconceived notions, an inclination to close one's mind to novel ideas, a tendency to defend a stand once taken or, alternatively and sometimes alternately, a predisposition to be swayed by persuasively stated opinions of others.

By systematically exploring the factors which influence the judgment of the individual expert, it becomes possible to correct any misconceptions that he may have harbored regarding empirical factors or theoretical assumptions underlying those factors, and to draw his attention to other factors which he may have overlooked in his first analysis of the situation. Needless to say, considerable discretion has to be exercised by the experimenters in any efforts designed to make an expert change his mind, in order to obtain results which are free of any bias on the experimenters' part. A device for helping to assure this is to feed in only such data as have been asked for by at least one respondent and are obtainable from reliable sources, and to suggest only such theoretical assumptions as seem to represent a consensus of a majority of respondents.

If the purpose of the experiment is the estimation of a numerical quantity (in our case the number of bombs required to do a certain job), it may be expected that, even if the views expressed initially are widely divergent, the individual estimates will show a tendency to converge as the experiment continues. This is almost inevitable in view of the progressively more penetrating analysis of the problem, achieved partly by means of the procedural feedback described above.

On the other hand, it cannot even ideally be expected that the final responses will coincide, since the uncertainties of the future call for intuitive probability estimates on the part of each respondent. To some extent this terminal disagreement can sometimes be decreased by applying justifiable corrections to the final answers. Such corrections are in fact an integral part of the procedure; they must, however, be based on a careful analysis of the responses, taking into account whatever can be learned regarding (i) a consensus as to basic assumptions, (ii) the sensitivity of the individuals' responses to changes in these basic assumptions, and (iii) their estimates of functional dependencies rather than mere point estimates. Essentially, the resulting corrections amount to a replacement of the individual expert's estimates concerning some of the components of the main problem by a consensus of estimates by all the experts. For example, in the experiment of this report, the problem of estimating the total number of bombs was factorable into that of determining, for each of several industries, what percentage of each industry must be destroyed and the average number of bombs per plant needed to do so. Each respondent made estimates of both these quantities. For the first, which involved the selection of the industries to be bombed, the choices made were too divergent to permit the taking of a consensus. The second estimate, however, was a perfect example of a case wherein a consensus would seem to yield more reliable results; accordingly we corrected the respondents' final answers by replacing their own numbers for bombs per plant by the median of all seven estimates. . . .

H. GERJUOY,
A NEW PERSPECTIVE ON FORECASTING METHODOLOGY

in The Study of the Future: An Agenda for Research.
14, 22–23 (W. Boucher, ed. 1977).

An algorithmic forecasting technique generates its forecast automatically, according to a set of operating rules—a program—that in principle can be followed by a computing machine, and often is. The operating rules constitute the forecasting algorithm. (As the term is used here, unlike some mathematical usage, an algorithm may include a random, not necessarily reproducible, step such as reference to a random number generating program or device.) By contrast, a judgmental forecasting technique depends on human input. For example, the forecast may be the average of estimates provided by a number of expert judges.

It should be noted that even algorithmic techniques ultimately descend from human judgments—about the particular algorithm to be used. Moreover, judgmental techniques usually rely on some computing algorithm (such as calculating an average) to generate useful forecasts from raw products of human judgment. This point is not trivial. It indicates that the distinction between algorithmic and judgmental forecasting has only the most remote bearing on choice between human and robot judgment; rather, the distinction pertains to what kinds of human judgments will be used, and at what points in the forecast-generating process they will enter. The forecasting process should be seen as one that requires certain tasks to be accomplished. At issue is which of these should be left to humans and which to machines.

One task is the consideration of available data. These may be data about the very variables whose values are to be forecasted, or they may be about other variables possibly related to them. All such data necessarily come from the past or present. Humans do better than machines when the quantity of data is either very small or very large. Machines can process and concurrently manipulate masses of information that overload humans, who must resort to what amounts to data sampling techniques. However, when the quantity of data exceeds machine storage capacity (presently large and rapidly growing larger), it is often difficult to program machines to select from among available data as adroitly as do expert humans. A comparable problem has been noted in connection with attempts to program chess-playing computers. The game is in principle subject to a closed, analytic solution, but the quantity of data that must be processed transcends the capacity of present machines. Therefore, machines, like humans, must "satisfice" rather than optimize when they select a chess move. However, to do so, the machines, like humans, must ignore some available information while considering other data, and here it has proven difficult to provide machines with the so-far unprogramable intuition that enables a chess master to select, before he has thought through to the end, which lines of play to analyze fully and which to ignore. See also "Considering Unprecedented Events or Not Considering Unprecedented Events" for possible research to determine the sources of expert judgment.

Another task is choice among alternative forecasts. Many, though by no means all, forecasting procedures involve, at least implicitly, alternative forecasts among which there must be a choice. When the alternatives stem from explicit differences in algorithm, it is generally possible to apply the alternative algorithms to the generation of retrospective "forecasts" about data already available. Then a basis for choice among alternatives may be the accuracy with which the alternative forecasting algorithms "predict" what is already known.

Here, too, when the quantity of information available exceeds the rather small amount that humans can handle, machines have a general advantage, unless the quantity of information becomes so large that they are overwhelmed, and then humans' superior ability to sample and select particularly relevant information once more gives them the advantage. However, a fundamental objection to evaluating a forecasting procedure in terms of its accuracy when used retrospectively is that this neglects the possibility that a poor fit may be due to the influence of unique events in the past that uniquely perturbed the trend.

The judgmental-algorithmic dichotomy can enter at a variety of levels in the consideration of the state-of-the-art in forecasting. A forecasting procedure may be algorithmic, for example, but the procedure for evaluating its accuracy may be judgmental. This is often the case when a time series is extrapolated using a "canned" extrapolation package. Such packages generally generate a variety of alternative extrapolations, depending on various algorithm options, such as the degree of polynomial to be used or whether mean error or mean squared error is to be minimized. Often the human users of such programs examine displays of alternative extrapolations and select the most "reasonable-looking." Clearly, this procedure is only marginally algorithmic or objective. The computer's function is essentially that of idea generator; it generates a variety of possible forecasts, and the human judges select from among them. Clearly, the greater the number of forecasts considered, the more the whole procedure is judgmental and the less it is algorithmic.

Unfortunately, when the "reasonableness" of forecasts is the basis for the selection or rejection of a forecasting procedure, the human judges who must decide whether particular forecasts are reasonable face a dilemma. On the one hand, an "unreasonable" forecast is necessarily a forecast that something will happen that the judges do not expect will happen. But if all forecasts are rejected that predict something unexpected, then the forecasting method used can never teach the judges anything new—and its chief use would seem to be to lend a coloration of science to their preconceptions.

On the other hand, a forecast can serve as a kind of stimulus to the imagination of human judges that prompts them to invent a scenario that makes the forecast probable. It thus can serve as a kind of psychological test of creativity that all too many "experts" pass with high marks. Research on the validity of the Delphi process, for example, has shown that expert judges, given "forecasts" that are falsely stated to be the consensus of other experts (but really are deliberately deflected off scale from the expert consensus), will sometimes abandon their previous estimates (which actually were close to the group consensus) in favor of the false "consensual" predictions. . . .

ALEXANDER MORGAN CAPRON, REFLECTIONS ON ISSUES POSED BY RECOMBINANT DNA MOLECULE TECHNOLOGY

265 Ann.N.Y.Acad.Sci. 71, 75–76 (1976).

If one were designing a body to appraise the potential implications of scientific developments as well as technological applications, the most difficult issue would probably be: How is the process to be triggered? If there is any distinction between science and technology, it might be that things we call "technological applications" are much easier to monitor because of the greater visibility that a development gains as someone, probably a commercial concern, gears up to manufacture it or otherwise to take advantage of its economic potential. Scientific developments, even ones that may have great impact, are initially known only in selected circles and are invisible outside brief discussions in esoteric journals. It takes a discerning observer first to spot and then to select out the really important developments.

The difficulty of the task is not, however, sufficient in my view to keep it from being done. For it to be done successfully, it cannot depend on an ad hoc body, such as the present National Commission, which, in its need to cut broadly across all areas, cannot hope to cut deeply enough into any of them to evaluate important but as yet inconspicuous developments. Thus, the best approach would seem to me to assign the task to a permanent organization, such as could be formed by broadening the mandate of the Office of Technology Assessment. I would also suggest that the OTA attempt the rather unusual step of developing ongoing and long-term relationships with appropriately trained scientists in university settings who would provide a sophisticated early warning system, by pointing to, and conducting initial evaluations of, significant new scientific discoveries. It will probably prove more realistic, more flexible, and much cheaper to rely on a network of such "science assessment groups" than to attempt to collect the necessary expertise in-house at OTA. Such arrangements seem possible to me under a liberal reading of Section 6(a) (1) of the Technology Assessment Act. . . .

NOTE

Would you label these methods of predicting the future as "science"? Even apart from the obvious difficulties in charting the unknown, there are problems of candor on the part of the predictor. It is a commonplace observation that people rewrite the history of the past to suit their present purposes. Is it not equally likely that people will write predictions of the future with the same ulterior motive?

Which of the approaches discussed in the materials above strikes you as most promising? Could predictors use computers, as discussed by Gerjuoy, in conjunction with the Delphi technique or with the approach suggested by Capron?

Each of the approaches outlined above relies, at least in part, on expert opinions about what will happen. What kind of expert would you consult to predict scientific advances? A top scientist in the field? A leading author? Consider the following excerpt written in 1950 by scientist and science fiction writer Isaac Asimov.

ISAAC ASIMOV, I, ROBOT

6–8 (1950).

I looked at my notes and I didn't like them. I'd spent three days at U.S. Robots and might as well have spent them at home with the Encyclopedia Tellurica.

Susan Calvin had been born in the year 1982, they said, which made her seventy-five now. Everyone knew that. Appropriately enough, U.S. Robots and Mechanical Men, Inc. was seventy-five also, since it had been in the year of Dr. Calvin's birth that Lawrence Robertson had first taken out incorporation papers for what eventually became the strangest industrial giant in man's history. Well, everyone knew that, too.

At the age of twenty, Susan Calvin had been part of the particular Psycho-Math seminar at which Dr. Alfred Lanning of U.S. Robots had demonstrated the first mobile robot to be equipped with a voice. It was a large, clumsy unbeautiful robot, smelling of machine-oil and destined for the projected mines on Mercury.—But, it could speak and make sense.

Susan said nothing at that seminar; took no part in the hectic discussion period that followed. She was a frosty girl, plain and colorless, who protected herself against a world she disliked by a mask-like expression and a hypertrophy of intellect. But as she watched and listened, she felt the stirrings of a cold enthusiasm.

She obtained her bachelor's degree at Columbia in 2003 and began graduate work in cybernetics.

All that had been done in the mid-twentieth century on "calculating machines" had been upset by Robertson and his positronic brain-paths. The miles of relays and photocells had given way to the spongy globe of plantinumiridium about the size of a human brain.

She learned to calculate the parameters necessary to fix the possible variables within the "positronic brain"; to construct "brains" on paper such that the responses to given stimuli could be accurately predicted.

In 2008, she obtained her Ph.D and joined United States Robots as a "Robopsychologist," becoming the first great practitioner of a new science. Lawrence Robertson was still president of the corporation; Alfred Lanning had become director of research.

For fifty years, she watched the direction of human progress change— and leap ahead.

Now she was retiring—as much as she ever could. At least, she was allowing someone else's name to be inset upon the door of her old office.

That, essentially, was what I had. I had a long list of her published papers, of the patents in her name; I had the chronological details of her promotions—In short I had her professional "vita" in full detail.

But that wasn't what I wanted.

I needed more than that for my feature articles for Interplanetary Press. Much more.

I told her so.

"Dr. Calvin," I said, as lushly as possible, "in the mind of the public you and U.S. Robots are identical. Your retirement will end an era and—"

"You want the human-interest angle?" She didn't smile at me. I don't think she ever smiles. But her eyes were sharp, though not angry. I felt her glance slide through me and out my occiput and knew that I was uncommonly transparent to her; that everybody was.

But I said, "That's right."

"Human interest out of robots? A contradiction."

"No, doctor. Out of you."

"Well, I've been called a robot myself. Surely, they've told you I'm not human."

They had, but there was no point in saying so.

She got up from her chair. She wasn't tall and she looked frail. I followed her to the window and we looked out.

The offices and factories of U.S. Robots were a small city; spaced and planned. It was flattened out like an aerial photograph.

"When I first came here," she said, "I had a little room in a building right about there where the fire-house is now." She pointed. "It was torn down before you were born. I shared the room with three others. I had half a desk. We built our robots all in one building. Output—three a week. Now look at us."

"Fifty years," I hackneyed, "is a long time."

"Not when you're looking back at them," she said. "You wondered how they vanished so quickly."

She went back to her desk and sat down. She didn't need expression on her face to look sad, somehow.

"How old are you?" she wanted to know.

"Thirty-two," I said.

"Then you don't remember a world without robots. There was a time when humanity faced the universe alone and without a friend. Now he has creatures to help him; stronger creatures than himself, more faithful, more useful, and absolutely devoted to him. Mankind is no longer alone. Have you ever thought of it that way?"

"I'm afraid I haven't. May I quote you?"

"You may. To you, a robot is a robot. Gears and metal; electricity and positrons.—Mind and iron! Human-made! if necessary, human-destroyed! But you haven't worked with them, so you don't know them. They're a cleaner better breed than we are."

I tried to nudge her gently with words, "We'd like to hear some of the things you could tell us; get your views on robots. The Interplanetary Press reaches the entire Solar System. Potential audience is three billion, Dr. Calvin. They ought to know what you could tell them on robots."

It wasn't necessary to nudge. She didn't hear me, but she was moving in the right direction.

"They might have known that from the start. We sold robots for Earth-use then—before my time it was, even. Of course, that was when robots could not talk. Afterward, they became more human and opposition began. The labor unions, of course, naturally opposed robot competition for human jobs, and various segments of religious opinion had their superstitious objections. It was all quite ridiculous and quite useless. And yet there it was." . . .

NOTE

Do you think Asimov's predictions concerning the future of computer technology will prove true? Considering that he wrote in 1950, one of his most striking predictions is that a woman will be the leading figure in the field. Is predicting social mores more or less difficult than predicting scientific developments?

Formal methodologies for predicting the future may have a way to go before they match the record of science fiction writers—some of whom have scientific training, but most of whom place greater stress on literary imagination. While science fiction writers are not always right, this may be another area in which technical data alone is insufficient. Can attorneys help develop mechanisms that combine technical information, social knowledge, and aesthetic imagination to predict and shape the future?

*

INDEX

†